THE
DICTIONARY
OF
CANADIAN
LAW

by
Daphne A. Dukelow, B.Sc., LL.B., LL.M.
Betsy Nuse, B.A. (Hon.)

A Carswell Publication

Canadian Cataloguing in Publication Data

Dukelow, Daphne A., 1948-
   The dictionary of Canadian law

ISBN 0-459-35671-2 (deluxe)
ISBN 0-459-35651-8 (bound) ISBN 0-459-35661-5 (pbk.)

1. Law — Canada — Dictionaries. I. Nuse, Betsy,
1947-   . II. Title.

KE183.D83 1991   349.71′03   C91-0941254

Typesetting: Video Text Inc., Barrie, Ontario, Canada

Preface

This first edition of The Dictionary of Canadian Law realizes the wish of publishing vice-president Gary Rodrigues, that Carswell undertake the monumental task of publishing a truly comprehensive, Canadian common law dictionary. We are grateful to Gary for the opportunity to work on this project, to Sharon Rodrigues, Lorie Acton, Diann Devins and Anne Walasek who collected statutory material over the years and to publisher Catherine McKeown for her understanding and support.

In compiling this work, we have attempted, as much as the constraints of time allowed, to honour the best current lexicographical principles. Thus this dictionary — both word list and definitions — was created largely from primary, Canadian sources: a term bank of definitions from federal and provincial statutes and regulations and a library of basic Canadian legal textbooks. The unique character of Canada is strongly reflected in the large number of terms which relate to the regulation of our country's natural resources, to agriculture and related industries. Where we needed to rely on another dictionary, our source has been the second edition Jowitt's Dictionary of English Law, published by Sweet and Maxwell of England. We are grateful to that company for the use of its material.

We wish to thank our good friends in Ontario and British Columbia who patiently listened to reports of our several trips through the alphabet and to bulletins regarding the most fascinating term of the day or week. To paraphrase Dr. Johnson, our work is ended, but not complete.

We known that this first effort will be improved upon. We believe that The Dictionary of Canadian Law underlines the importance of indigenous work to Canadian lexicography and will be useful to all people in the common law jurisdictions of Canada.

Daphne Dukelow
Betsy Nuse

Galiano, B.C.
December, 1990

How to Use This Dictionary

HEADWORD

ABBUTTALS. *n.* Limits or boundaries of land.

ABC. *abbr.* Advance booking charter. ———— abbreviation

FUNCTIONAL LABEL ———— **ABDICATE.** *v.* To refuse or renounce a thing.

ABSOLUTA SENTENTIA EXPOSITORE NON INDIGET. [L.] A clean statement requires no exposition. ———— ETYMOLOGY

DEFINITIONS ———— **ABUT.** *v.* 1. To border upon. 2. Includes having access thereto directly. *Community Planning Act.* S.N.B. 1976, c. 10, s. 1.

ACCEPTANCE. *n.* 1. Signification by an offeree of willingness to enter into a contract with an offeror on the offeror's terms. G.H.L. Fridman, *The Law of Contract in Canada*, 2d ed. (Toronto: Carswell, 1986) at 41. 2. Of a bill, the signification by the drawee of assent to the drawer's order to pay the bill. F.L.G. Tyler & N.E. Palmer, eds., *Grossley Vaines' Personal Property*, 5th ed. (London: Butterworths, 1973) at 235. 3. An acceptance completed by delivery or notification. *Bills of Exchange Act*, R.S.C. 1985, c. B-4, s. 2. 4. In sale of goods, involves taking possession of the goods by the buyer. See BLANK ~; CONDITIONAL ~; LOCAL ~; NON—~; PARTIAL ~; QUALIFIED ~.

CITATION OF AUTHORITY — text

statute

ACCIDENT. *n.* A wilful and intentional act, not being the act of the employee, and a fortuitous event occasioned by a physical or natural cause. *Workers Compensation acts.* See AIRCRAFT ~; ENVIRONMENTAL ~; FATAL ~; INDUSTRIAL ~; INEVITABLE ~; NON-INDUSTRIAL ~.

CROSS-REFERENCES

ACCIDENTAL DEATH INSURANCE. Insurance undertaken by an insurer as part of a contract of life insurance whereby the insurer undertakes to pay an additional amount of insurance money in the event of the death by accident of the person whose life is insured. *Insurance acts.*

CITATION OF AUTHORITY — general topical

ACCOMMODATION FACILITIES. See TRANSIENT ~.

HEADWORD USED FOR CROSS-REFERENCE ONLY

A4. Facsimile by amplitude modulation of the main carrier either directly or by frequency modulated sub-carrier. *General Radio Regulations, Part II*, C.R.C., c. 1372, s. 42.

TERM WITH A NUMERAL

AIR TIME. *var.* **AIR-TIME**. In respect of any aircraft, means the period of time commencing when the aircraft leaves the surface of the earth and terminating when the aircraft touches the surface of the earth at the next point of landing. See PRICE OF ~.

VARIANT SPELLING

ASSUMPSIT. [L. one promised] A form of action to recover damages for breach of a simple contract.

TRANSLATION INSIDE ETYMOLOGY BRACKET

BAIT. *v.* To set one animal against another which is tied or contained.

BAIT. *n.* Corn, wheat, oats or other cultivated grain or any product thereof or any manufactured product or material that may attract migratory game birds and includes plastic corn and any other imitation grain. *Migratory Birds Regulation*, C.R.C., c. 1035, s. 2.

HOMOGRAPH

CANADA. *n.* (a) The sea bed and subsoil of the submarine areas adjacent to the coasts of Canada in respect of which the Government of Canada or of a province grants a right, licence or privilege to explore for, drill for or take any minerals, petroleum, natural gas or any related hydrocarbons; and (b) the seas and airspace above the submarine areas referred to in paragraph (a) in respect of any activities carried on in connection with the exploration for or exploitation of the minerals, petroleum, natural gas or hydrocarbons referred to in that paragraph. *Income Tax Act*, R.S.C. 1952, c. 148 (as am. S.C. 1980-81-82-83, c. 48, s. 111), s. 255.

GEOGRAPHICAL CITATION

How to Use This Dictionary

Definitions in this dictionary are based largely on primary, Canadian sources: a term bank of definitions from the statutes of Canada, all provinces and the Northwest Territories and Ontario and federal regulations and a library of basic Canadian legal textbooks.

In general, material is presented not historically but by frequency of use in the sources considered. Some historical terms have been included, e.g. "capital murder", "non-capital murder" and any term which appeared in an earlier statute revision if this was the only definition available to us at the time.

Where definitions have been rewritten, we have attempted to remove sexual and racial bias, but material quoted verbatim has not been edited in this way.

Alphabetization

1. This dictionary is alphabetized absolutely by letter. Thus, the term "residential property" will be found after the term "resident" but before the term "resident owner".
2. Terms which include numerals are entered as though the numerals were spelled out. Thus, the term "A2" (= A two) will be found after the term "attrition" and before the term "au besoin".
3. Abbreviations are integrated into the main work in the alphabetical order described above, rather than listed separately.
4. Homographs are ordered by function: first verbs, then nouns, adjectives, adverbs, abbreviations. Thus, the entry for "charge" used as a verb precedes the entry for "charge" used as a noun.

Elements of Each Entry

1. HEADWORD/HEADWORDS
(a) The words or phrase is presently in boldface, upper case letters.
(b) Variant spellings follow the most common spelling, in order of the frequency of their use.

2. FUNCTIONAL LABEL
(a) This identifies the grammatical part of speech or function (e.g. use as an abbreviation) of the headword/headwords. See the Table of Abbreviations Used in This Dictionary (on the inside front cover) for the abbreviations used here.
(b) A headword entered for cross-reference purposes only is assigned a functional label only to distinguish it from any homograph.

3. ETYMOLOGY
(a) Presented in square brackets, these characters show the language of origin of a word or phrase which is or was originally in a language other than English. See the Table

of Abbreviations Used in This Dictionary (on the inside front cover) for the abbreviations used here.

(b) Where the word or phrase has adopted a more general meaning over time, a literal translation from the original language may be offered inside the brackets.

(c) A headword entered for cross-reference purposes only is assigned no etymological label.

4. DEFINITIONS

Multiple definitions are numbered. The most common or general definition is given first, less general or common definitions follow, ranked by frequency of use.

5. CITATION OF AUTHORITY

(a) Where no authority is cited, the definition is derived from multiple sources.

(b) Specific citations of legislation provide the chapter and section numbers. In most cases, legislation has been quoted verbatim, but occasionally minor editing has been done in the interest of clarity. Since this editing has been done and in some cases only the latest statute law revision has been used, those wishing to cite exactly are urged to refer to the original statutes.

(c) Specific citations of textual material provide exact page references. Since all textual material has been paraphrased or rewritten, those wishing to cite exactly are urged to refer to the original text.

(d) A general topical citation (italicized) limits a definition to a particular area of law.

(e) A general geographical citation (in ordinary type) limits a definition to a particular region or jurisdiction.

6. CROSS-REFERENCES

These refer the reader to more narrow or specific applications of the word or phrase or occasionally to related terms.

In the interest of saving space, the character "~" has been used to represent the headword/headwords in the cross-references which follow it.

A. *abbr.* 1. Anonymous. 2. Ampere. 3. Atto.

AB. *abbr.* Abridgment.

AB ABUSU AD USUM NON VALET CONSE-QUENTIA. [L.] One can draw no conclusion as to the legitimate use of a thing from its abuse.

ABANDON. *v.* Includes (a) a wilful omission to take charge of a child by a person who is under a legal duty to do so, and (b) dealing with a child in a manner that is likely to leave that child exposed to risk without protection. *Criminal Code*, R.S.C. 1985, c. C-46, s. 214.

ABANDONED GOODS. Goods left on residential premises by a tenant who has (a) abandoned the premises, or (b) vacated the premises on the expiration or termination of the residential tenancy agreement. *Landlord and Tenant Act*, R.S.A. 1980, c. L-6, s. 24.

ABANDONED MOTOR VEHICLE. A vehicle that has been left unattended without lawful authority and that appears to an officer, by reason of its age, appearance, mechanical condition or lack of number plates, to be abandoned. *Environmental Protection Act*, R.S.O. 1980, c. 141, s. 48.

ABANDONED MOTOR VEHICLE SITE. (i) A waste disposal site, A. that is classified by the regulations as a derelict motor vehicle site, B. that is not exempt under the regulations relating to Part V or Part VI, and C. for which a certificate of approval or a provisional certificate of approval has been issued pursuant to Part V, or (ii) any place that is approved in writing by the Director for the purpose of receiving and storing abandoned motor vehicles. *Environmental Protection Act*, R.S.O. 1980, c. 141, s. 48.

ABANDONED ORCHARD. An orchard, (i) the fruit of which has not been produced for sale for human consumption for two consecutive growing seasons, and (ii) that has been designated by a certificate of the Provincial Entomol-ogist as a neglected orchard. *Abandoned Orchards Act*, R.S.O. 1980, c. 1, s. 1.

ABANDONED VEHICLE. A vehicle, other than a derelict vehicle, that has been abandoned at an airport or otherwise remains unclaimed at an airport for a period of not less than 30 days. *Airport Personal Property Disposal Regulations*, C.R.C., c. 1563, s. 2.

ABANDONED WELL. A well that is not being used or maintained for future use as a well. *Ontario Water Resources Act*, R.R.O. 1980, Reg. 739, s. 1.

ABANDONEE. *n.* A person to whom rights to property are left.

ABANDONMENT. *n.* 1. Relinquishing, surrender, giving up property or rights. 2. Moving from one residence for purposes inconsistent with the retention of that residence as one's home with the intention of acquiring elsewhere a residence which is not merely of a temporary character. 3. An intention to abandon is required and not only non-use of a trade mark is sufficient to create abandonment. H.G. Fox, *The Canadian Law of Trade Marks and Unfair Competition*, 3d ed. (Toronto: Carswell, 1972) at 280. See NOTICE OF ~.

AB ANTIQUO. [L.] From ancient times.

AB ASSUETIC NON FIT INJURIA. [L.] From things to which one has become accustomed, no wrong can arise.

ABATE. *v.* To break down, destroy or remove; to lower the price.

ABATEMENT. *n.* Termination, reduction, destruction. See PLEA IN ~; TAX ~.

ABATEMENT OF NUISANCE. Removing or putting an end to nuisance.

ABATEMENT PROJECT. A project for the abatement of an undesirable environmental condition within the boundaries of a municipality and, without limiting the generality of the foregoing, includes (i) a plan designating the lands, works and buildings that are to be acquired and cleared; (ii) a description of the methods planned for the municipal direction and control of the use of land in the area, including zoning, building controls and standards of occupancy of buildings; (iii) a description of any changes in any planning scheme, building controls, or development plan affecting the municipality that are required in conjunction with carrying out the abatement project; (iv) the estimated costs of the abatement project; (v) a proposal for the planning and use of the lands that are to be acquired. *Clean Environment Act*, S.M. 1974, c. 41, s. 1.

ABATER. *n.* One who puts an end to a nuisance.

ABATOR. *n.* One who puts an end to a nuisance.

ABBATOIR. *n.* Premises where animals are slaughtered; premises where animals are slaughtered and meat is cut, wrapped, frozen, cured, smoked or aged.

ABBROACHMENT. *n.* Forestalling a market by buying up goods intended to be sold there.

ABBROCHEMENT. *n.* Forestalling a market by buying up goods intended to be sold there.

ABBUTTALS. *n.* Limits or boundaries of land.

ABC. *abbr.* Advance booking charter. See OPEN JAW ~.

ABC (DOMESTIC). *abbr.* Advance booking charter (domestic).

ABDICATE. *v.* To refuse or renounce a thing.

ABDICATION. *n.* Where a person in office voluntarily renounces it or gives it up.

ABDUCTION. *n.* 1. Take or cause to be taken away a person under 16 years of age from the possession of and against the will of the parent or guardian who has lawful charge of that person. *Criminal Code*, R.S.C. 1985, c. C-46, s. 280. 2. Unlawfully taking, enticing away, concealing, detaining, receiving or harbouring a person under 14 years of age with intent to deprive a parent or guardian of the possession of that person. *Criminal Code*, R.S.C. 1985, c. C-46, ss. 281-283. 3. Forcibly stealing or carrying away any person. See CHILD ~.

ABEARANCE. *n.* Behaviour.

ABET. *v.* To encourage; to maintain. See AID AND ABET.

ABEYANCE. *n.* 1. Lapse of an inheritance because it has no present owner. 2. In expectation.

ABILITY. *n.* Capacity to perform an act; skill. See NON-~.

AB INITIO. [L.] From the beginning.

AB INTESTATO. [L.] From an intestate.

AB IRATO. [L.] By a person in anger.

ABJURATION. *n.* Renunciation of an oath.

ABJURE. *v.* To renounce or abandon an oath.

ABODE. *n.* Place of residence. See PLACE OF ~; USUAL PLACE OF ~.

ABOLISH. *v.* To do away with.

ABOLITION. *n.* Doing away with something; destruction of thing.

ABORIGINAL LANGUAGE. An aboriginal language as defined in the Official Languages Act. *Elections Act*, S.N.W.T. 1986 (2d Sess.), c. 2, s. 204.

ABORIGINAL PERSON. An original, a native or an indigenous person. *Canadian Cultural Property Export Control List*, C.R.C., c. 448, s. 1.

ABORIGINE. *n.* The first, original or indigenous inhabitants of a country.

ABORTIFACIENT. *n.* Any instrument or substance used to cause an abortion. F.A. Jaffe, *A Guide to Pathological Evidence*, 2d ed. (Toronto: Carswell, 1983) at 167.

ABORTION. *n.* 1. Miscarriage or the premature expulsion of the fetus. 2. The interruption of a pregnancy. See THERAPEUTIC ~ COMMITTEE.

ABORTIONIST. *n.* One who carries out abortions.

ABOUT. *adv.* Approximately; nearly; around.

ABOUT TO BECOME UNEMPLOYED. In relation to a worker, means a worker who, though employed, has received written notice from his employer that he will become unemployed on a date specified in the notice. *Manpower Mobility Regulations*, C.R.C., c. 331, s. 2.

ABOVE PAR. At a premium, at a price above face or nominal value.

ABRADED MARGIN. An area of abrasion surrounding the wound where a bullet entered. F.A. Jaffe, *A Guide to Pathological Evidence*, 2d ed. (Toronto: Carswell, 1983) at 167.

ABR. *abbr.* Abridgment.

ABRASION. *n.* 1. Rubbing off; wearing. 2. Injury to the skin's surface. F.A. Jaffe, *A Guide to Pathological Evidence*, 2d ed. (Toronto: Carswell, 1983) at 9.

ABRIDGE. *v.* To shorten.

ABRIDGMENT. *n.* 1. Of law, a digest. 2. Of time, shortening. 3. *The Canadian Abridgment.*

ABROACHMENT. *n.* Forestalling a market by buying up goods intended to be sold there.

ABROAD. *adv.* 1. Outside the country. 2. At large, out of doors.

ABROGATE. *v.* To annul or cancel.

ABROGATION. *n.* Annulment; repeal of a law.

ABS. *abbr.* Automatic Block Signal System.

ABSCESS. *n.* A zone of destroyed tissue containing pus. F.A. Jaffe, *A Guide to Pathological Evidence*, 2d ed. (Toronto: Carswell, 1983) at 167.

ABSCOND. *v.* To flee in order to avoid legal responsibilities for debt or to escape arrest.

ABSCONDING DEBTOR. A debtor who hides to avoid arrest or service, or simply is not in the province. C.R.B. Dunlop, *Creditor—Debtor Law in Canada* (Toronto: Carswell, 1981) at 206.

ABSENCE. *n.* 1. Non-existence; want; lack. 2. Not being present. See LEAVE OF ~.

ABSENCE CUM DOLO ET CULPA. [L.] Wilful non-appearance to a writ or subpoena in order to avoid arrest or defeat or delay creditors.

ABSENCE WITHOUT LEAVE. A person absents himself without leave who (a) without authority leaves his place of duty; (b) without authority is absent from his place of duty; or (c) having been authorized to be absent from his place of duty, fails to return to his place of duty at the expiration of the period for which his absence was authorized. *National Defence Act*, R.S.C. 1970, c. N-4, s. 80.

ABSENT. *v.* To be away; to not be present.

ABSENT. *adj.* Away; not present.

ABSENTEE. *n.* Within the meaning of this Act means a person who, having had his usual place of residence or domicile in Ontario, has disappeared, whose whereabouts is unknown and as to whom there is no knowledge as to whether he is alive or dead. *Absentees Act*, R.S.O. 1980, c. 3, s. 1.

ABSENTEEISM. *n.* 1. Absence from work. 2. When employees absent themselves from work for insufficient reasons.

ABSENTE REO. [L.] The defendant being absent.

ABSOLUTA SENTENTIA EXPOSITORE NON INDIGET. [L.] A clear statement requires no exposition.

ABSOLUTE. *adj.* Unconditional; complete. See DECREE ~; ORDER ~; RULE ~.

ABSOLUTE ALCOHOL. Alcohol of a strength of 100 per cent. *Food and Drug Regulations*, C.R.C., c. 870, s. B.02.002.

ABSOLUTE ASSIGNMENT. Transfer of an entire thing.

ABSOLUTE CERTIFICATE OF TITLE. A certificate of title issued or heretofore issued on the registration of an absolute fee. *Land Title Act*, R.S.B.C. 1979, c. 219, s. 1.

ABSOLUTE DISCHARGE. A sentence by which accused is discharged although the charge is proven or a plea of guilty entered.

ABSOLUTE INTEREST. Complete and full ownership.

ABSOLUTE LIABILITY. 1. Liability regardless of intention or negligence. 2. An offence for which an accused is criminally liable even though the accused acted under a reasonable mistake of fact. P.K. McWilliams, *Canadian Criminal Evidence*, 3d ed. (Aurora: Canada Law Book, 1988) at 4-16.

ABSOLUTELY. *adv.* Unconditionally.

ABSOLUTE PRIVILEGE. Exemption from censure granted to (a) a defamatory statement made by a high executive officer acting in the course of duty, (b) matters relating to the affairs of state, (c) statements by members of Parliament during the course of its proceedings by it or any of its constituent bodies, or (d) any communication made in the course of, or incidental to, judicial and quasi-judicial proceedings. R.E. Brown, *The Law of Defamation in Canada* (Toronto: Carswell, 1987) at 11.

ABSOLUTE RESPONSIBILITY. Criminal liability regardless of fault. D. Stuart, *Canadian Criminal Law: a treatise*, 2d ed. (Toronto: Carswell, 1987) at 157.

ABSOLUTION. *n.* Acquittal; dispensation.

ABSOLVE. *v.* To pardon; to acquit of a crime.

ABSORPTION PLANT. Any plant for treating or processing gas by absorption or otherwise for the extraction from it of natural gasoline or other hydrocarbons. *Gas Utilities Act*, R.S.A. 1980, c. G-4, s. 1.

ABSQUE HOC. [L.] Without this.

ABSQUE IMPETITIONE VASTI. [L.] Without liability for waste.

ABSQUE TALI CAUSA. [L.] Without such cause.

ABSTENTION. *n.* Refusal to vote or debate.

ABSTRACT. *v.* To abridge; to remove.

ABSTRACT. *n.* Abridgment.

ABSTRACT. *adj.* Having no basis in fact. Robert J. Sharpe, ed., *Charter Litigation* (Toronto: Butterworths 1987) at 335.

ABSTRACT BOOK. Record in which each parcel of land is assigned a separate page on which details describing the document affecting title are inscribed. B.J. Reiter, R.C.B. Risk & B.N. McLellan, *Real Estate Law*, 3d ed. (Toronto: Emond Montgomery, 1986) at 457.

ABSTRACT INDEX. See REGISTER OF TITLE AND ~.

ABSTRACT OF TITLE. History of the title to land which shows any conveyance of the land or any interest in the land in chronological order.

ABUNDANS CAUTELA NON NOCET. [L.] Great caution causes no harm.

ABUSE. *v.* To make improper or excessive use of.

ABUSE. *n.* 1. Misuse; maltreatment. 2. Condition of (a) physical harm wherein a child suffers physical injury but does not include reasonable punishment administered by a parent or guardian; (b) malnutrition or mental ill-health of a degree that if not immediately remedied could seriously impair growth and development or result in permanent injury or death; or (c) sexual molestation. See ALCOHOL AND DRUG ~; CHILD ~; DRUG ~.

ABUSE OF DISTRESS. Use of chattels lawfully seized.

ABUSE OF PROCESS. Frivolous, vexatious or oppressive proceedings.

ABUT. *v.* 1. To border upon. 2. Includes having access thereto directly. *Community Planning Act*, S.N.B. 1976, c. 10, s. 1.

ABUTTALS. *n.* Limits or boundaries of land.

ABUTTING DIRECTLY. When used in reference to works of constructing, enlarging or extending a sewer or water main, shall apply to mains through private lands as well as to mains under streets. *Municipal Act*, R.S.B.C. 1979, c. 290, s. 649.

ABUTTING PARCEL. A lot or parcel or land abutting on that portion of the street wherein or whereon a work is or is to be made. *Municipalities Act*, R.S.N.B. 1973, c. M-22, s. 118.

A.C. *abbr.* Law Reports, Appeal Cases, 1891-.

A/C. *abbr.* Account.

ACADEMIC STAFF. Includes professors, asso-

ciate professors, assistant professors, lecturers, instructors.

ACADEMIC STAFF ASSOCIATION. The organization recognized by the college board as the official body representing the academic staff members of a public college. *College Act*, R.S.A. 1980, c. C-18, s. 1.

ACADEMIC YEAR. 1. The period of time from the first day of July in a calendar year to the last day of June in the calendar year then folowing, inclusive. 2. A period of studies, at a specified educational institution, that is recognized by that educational institution and the appropriate authority for a province as a distinct period for a course of studies at that institution and that is of not less than 26 weeks duration. *Canada Student Loans Act*, R.S.C. 1970, c. S-17, s. 2.

ACCEDAS AD CURIAM. [L.] That you go to the court.

ACCEDE. *v.* To consent; to agree.

ACCELERATED TRUST. A trust for a spouse created when it is an advantage for the taxpayer who created the estate that tax be levied when the trust comes into effect. D.M.W. Waters, *The Law of Trusts in Canada*, 2d ed. (Toronto: Carswell, 1984) at 30.

ACCELERATING PREMIUM. Bonus or incentive paid to employees and which increases as production increases.

ACCELERATION. *n.* Something which occurs when an interest in remainder falls into possession sooner than it might otherwise.

ACCELERATION CLAUSE. A clause in a contract which makes several periodic payments become due immediately upon default of the payor or permits a lender to call for payment of money due.

ACCELERATOR. See PARTICLE ~.

ACCELERATOR CONTROL SYSTEM. See DRIVER OPERATED.

ACCEPTABLE QUALITY. The characteristics and the quality of a consumer product that consumers can reasonably expect the product to have, having regard to all the relevant circumstances of the sale of the product, including the description of the product, its purchase price and the express warranties of the retail seller or manufacturer of the product.

ACCEPTANCE. *n.* 1. Signification by an offeree of willingness to enter into a contract with an offeror on the offeror's terms. G.H.L. Fridman, *The Law of Contract in Canada*, 2d ed. (Toronto: Carswell, 1986) at 41. 2. Of a bill, the signification by the drawee of assent to the drawer's order to pay the bill. E.L.G. Tyler & N.E. Palmer, eds., *Crossley Vaines' Personal Property*, 5th ed. (London: Butterworths, 1973) at 235. 3. An acceptance completed by delivery or notification. *Bills of Exchange Act*, R.S.C. 1985, c. B-4, s. 2. 4. In sale of goods, involves taking possession of the goods by the buyer. See BANKER'S ~; BLANK ~; CONDITIONAL ~; LOCAL ~; NON- ~; PARTIAL ~; QUALIFIED ~.

ACCEPTANCE LIMITS OF ERROR. The limits of error that apply to a device when the performance of the device is tested (a) at the time the class, type or design of that device is examined for approval, (b) at the time the device is inspected prior to its first use in trade, (c) at the time the measuring elements of the device are overhauled or repaired following the failure of the device on inspection to measure within the applicable limits of error, or (d) at any time within 30 days after the time referred to in paragraph (b) or (c). *Weights and Measures Regulations*, C.R.C., c. 1605, s. 2.

ACCEPTANCE OF BILL. The signification by the drawee of assent to the drawer's order to pay the bill. E.L.G. Tyler & N.E. Palmer, eds., *Crossley Vaines' Personal Property*, 5th ed. (London: Butterworths, 1973) at 235.

ACCEPTANCE OF SERVICE. To endorse on the back of a document or a copy of it acknowledgement that the document was duly served.

ACCEPTED ACREAGE. The acreage that, as provided in his contract, is to be sown by an insured person to the insurable crop to which his application for insurance relates, in a crop year stated in the contract. *Crop Insurance Act*, R.S.M. 1970, c. C310, s. 1.

ACCEPTED VALUE. The value that would be attributed by a municipal taxing authority to federal property, without regard to any ornamental, decorative or non-functional features thereof, as the base for computing the amount of real estate tax applicable to that property if it were taxable property.

ACCEPTOR. *n.* One who accepts a bill of exchange.

ACCESS. *n.* 1. Either the opportunity to examine an original record or the provision of a copy, at the option of the government. *Freedom of Information Act*, S.N.S. 1977, c. 10, s. 2. 2. Includes visitation. *Family Relations Act*, R.S.B.C. 1979, c. 121, s. 21. 3. An exit from or an entrance to a highway. *Highways Protection Act*, R.S.M. 1970, c. H50, s. 2. See LEVEL ~; NON-~; RIGHT OF ~.

ACCESSIBLE. *adj.* Approachable by person or tools as required, without undue hindrance or impediment. See READILY ~.

ACCESSIBLE LOCATION. Any point that can be reached by any part of the human body. *Radiation Emitting Devices Regulations*, C.R.C., c. 1370, s. 1.

ACCESSIO CEDIT PRINCIPALI. [L.] Any accessory thing, when incorporated in a principal thing, becomes part of that principal thing.

ACCESSION. *n.* Something belonging to one person which becomes the property of a second person because it was added to or incorporated with the second person's thing.

ACCESSION OF THE SOVEREIGN. The heir at once becomes the sovereign when a sovereign dies.

ACCESSIONS. *n.* Goods that are installed in or affixed to other goods.

ACCESSORIUM NON DUCIT, SED SEQUITUR SUUM PRINCIPALE. [L.] The incident passes with the grant of the principal, but the principal does not pass by the grant of the incident.

ACCESSORIUM NON TRAHIT PRINCIPALE. [L.] An accessory thing does not carry its principal with it.

ACCESSORIUM SEQUITUR PRINCIPALE. [L.] An accessory thing goes with its principal.

ACCESSORIUS SEQUITUR NATURAM SUI PRINCIPALIS. [L.] An accessory and the principal offender are of the same nature.

ACCESSORY. *n.* 1. Anything joined to another; thing incident to another. 2. When used to describe a building or structure, means a use, building or structure normally incidental or subordinate to the principal building or structure located on a lot. *Niagara Escarpment Planning and Development Act*, R.R.O. 1980, Reg. 685, s. 1. 3. One who is not the chief actor in an offence but who is in some way concerned in it either before the act was committed, or at its commission, or soon after the initial and main act has been committed. See PRINCIPAL AND ~.

ACCESSORY AFTER THE FACT. One who knowing that a person other than his or her spouse has been a party to an offence receives, comforts or assists that person for the purposes of enabling that person to escape. *Criminal Code*, R.S.C. 1985, c. C-46, s. 23.

ACCESSORY BEFORE THE FACT. One who counsels or procures another to commit an offence but who is not present when it is committed. D. Stuart, *Canadian Criminal Law:*

a treatise, 2d ed. (Toronto: Carswell, 1987) at 501.

ACCESSORY BUILDING. A subordinate building or portion of a main building that is not used for human habitation.

ACCESSORY WEIGHT. The total weight of the stock optional items with which the vehicle is capable of being equipped minus the total weight of the standard items that those optional items replace. *Motor Vehicle Safety Regulations*, C.R.C., c. 1038, s. 111.

ACCESS RIGHT. A right, granted in an order or agreement, of access to or visitation of a child. *Family Orders and Agreements Enforcement Assistance Act*, R.S.C. 1985 (2d Supp.), c. 4, s. 2.

ACCESS ROAD. 1. A road located on land not owned by a municipality and not dedicated and accepted as, or otherwise deemed at law to be, a public highway, that serves as a motor vehicle access route to one or more parcels of land. *Road Access Act*, R.S.O. 1980, c. 457, s. 1. 2. A road of a temporary nature used to reach sources of material or parts of a construction project, or for fire protection in timbered areas, and access to mining claims. 3. A road that leads from a public road to a waste disposal site. *Environmental Protection Act*, R.R.O. 1980, Reg. 309, s. 1.

ACCESS TO COMPANY PREMISES. A clause permitting union representatives entry to employer's premises even if they are not employees.

ACCESS TO EXIT. That part of a means of egress within a floor area that provides access to an exit serving the floor area. *Building Code Act*, R.R.O. 1980, Reg. 87, s. 1.

ACCESS-TO-PLANT CLAUSE. A clause which permits union representatives entry to employer's premises even if they are not employees.

ACCIDENT. *n.* A wilful and an intentional act, not being the act of the employee, and a fortuitous event occasioned by a physical or natural cause. *Workers Compensation acts.* See AIRCRAFT ~; ENVIRONMENTAL ~; FATAL ~; INDUSTRIAL ~; INEVITABLE ~; NON-INDUSTRIAL ~.

ACCIDENTAL. *adj.* Employed in contradistinction to wilful . . . produced by mere chance, or incapable of being traced to any cause: per Lord Denman in *Filliter v. Phipard* (1848), 11 Q.B. 347, 17 L.J.Q.B. 89, 116 E.R. 506 (U.K.).

ACCIDENTAL DEATH INSURANCE. Insurance undertaken by an insurer as part of a contract of life insurance whereby the insurer undertakes to pay an additional amount of insurance money in the event of the death by accident of the person whose life is insured. *Insurance acts.*

ACCIDENTAL MEANS. An effect which is not the natural or probable consequence of the means which produced it, an effect which does not ordinarily follow and cannot be reasonably anticipated from the use of those means, an effect which the actor did not intend to produce and which he cannot be charged with the design of producing. *Western Commercial Travelers' Assn. v. Smith* (1898), 40 L.R.A. 653.

ACCIDENT FUND. The fund provided for the payment of compensation, medical aid, outlays and expenses. *Workers Compensation acts.*

ACCIDENT INSURANCE. 1. Insurance by which the insurer undertakes, otherwise than incidentally to some other class of insurance defined by or under the Insurance Act, to pay insurance money in the event of accident to the person or persons insured, but does not include insurance by which the insurer undertakes to pay insurance money both in the event of death by accident and in the event of death from any other cause. *Insurance acts.* 2. Includes personal accident insurance, public liability insurance and employers' liability insurance. 3. The obligation of the insurer under this Act to pay benefits if loss from bodily injuries is sustained by an insured as the result of one of the perils mentioned in section 22. *The Automobile Accident Insurance Act*, R.S.S. 1978, c. A-35, s. 2. See GROUP ~.

ACCIDENT PREVENTION ASSOCIATION. A group formed by employers to provide education in accident prevention. D. Robertson, *Ontario Health and Safety Guide* (Toronto: Richard De Boo Ltd., 1988) at 5.13.

ACCIDENT PRONENESS. The tendency of a person to have accidents.

ACCOMMODATION. *n.* 1. Sleeping facilities provided on a commercial basis to the general public. *Air Carrier Regulations*, C.R.C., c. 3, s. 23. 2. The provision of lodging in hotels and motels. See HOSTEL ~; HOUSING ~; SANITARY ~; SEMI-PRIVATE ~; SERVICED HOUSING ~; SLEEPING ~; SLEEPING ~S; TOURIST ~; TRANSIENT ~.

ACCOMMODATION BILL. A bill accepted or endorsed without value to accommodate a party to the bill. The party who accommodates thus is in fact a surety for a principal debtor who may or may not be a party to the bill. I.F.G. Baxter, *The Law of Banking*, 3d ed. (Toronto: Carswell, 1981) at 116.

ACCOMMODATION CHARGE. The charge in

respect of nursing home care payable by a resident for accommodation and meals in a nursing home or an approved hospital. *Nursing Homes Act*, S.A. 1985, c. N-14.1, s. 1.

ACCOMMODATION FACILITIES. See TRANSIENT ~.

ACCOMMODATION PARTY. A party who signs a bill without receiving value, lending his or her name to another. I.F.G. Baxter, *The Law of Banking*, 3d ed. (Toronto: Carswell, 1981) at 116.

ACCOMMODATION SPACE. (a) Passenger spaces, (b) crew space, (c) offices, (d) pantries, and (e) space similar to any of the foregoing not being service spaces or open spaces on deck. *Hull Construction Regulations*, C.R.C., c. 1431, s. 2.

ACCOMMODATION UNIT. A room for the accommodation of the public that contains at least one bed.

ACCORD. *v.* To agree.

ACCORD. *n.* Agreement by which an obligation in contract or tort is satisfied.

ACCORD AND SATISFACTION. Agreement (accord) to release from an obligation purchased by means of any valuable consideration (satisfaction), which is not the actual performance of the obligation itself. C.R.B. Dunlop, *Creditor-Debtor Law in Canada* (Toronto: Carswell, 1981) at 29.

ACCOUNT. *n.* 1. Settlement of debits and credits between parties. 2. Any monetary obligation not evidenced by any chattel paper, instrument or securities. *Personal Property Security Act*, S.M. 1973, c. 5, s. 1. 3. An account with a bank. 4. Where a mortgagee did not take possession, ordinary items are the principal, the interest and the costs and items of expense which the mortgagee incurred and which are chargeable to the mortgagor by statute or under the terms of the mortgage or according to usual court practice. W.B. Rayner & R.H. McLaren, *Falconbridge on Mortgages*, 4th ed. (Toronto: Canada Law Book, 1977) at 639. 5. Any invoice, statement, claim, contract, journal voucher or other voucher or document claiming payment from a department on a single or recurring payment basis. *Account Verification and Payment Requisition Regulations*, C.R.C., c. 667, s. 2. See ~S; BANK ~; CAPITAL ~; CASH ~; CHARGE ~; DUTY TO ~; EXPENSE ~; HOLD BACK ~; MARGIN ~; MONEY OF ~; OMNIBUS ~; OPEN ~; PASS AN ~; ROYALTY DEDUCTION ~; STABILIZATION ~; STATEMENT OF ~.

ACCOUNTABLE. *adj.* Liable; responsible.

ACCOUNTABLE ADVANCE. (a) A sum of money advanced from and temporarily charged to an appropriation, and (b) a sum of money advanced from the sum of money described in paragraph (a), for which the person to whom the sum is advanced is required to make an accounting or a repayment in accordance with the Financial Administration Act and these Regulations. *Accountable Advances Regulations*, C.R.C., c. 668, s. 2.

ACCOUNTABLE RECEIPT. A written acknowledgement of receipt of a chattel or money, for which the person receiving it must account.

ACCOUNTANCY. See PUBLIC ~.

ACCOUNTANT. *n.* 1. A chartered accountant, a certified general accountant or a registered industrial accountant. 2. An accountant of the court. See FIRM OF ~S; PUBLIC ~.

ACCOUNT DEBTOR. A person who is obligated on chattel paper or on an intangible. *Personal Property Security Act*, R.S.O. 1980, c. 375, s. 1.

ACCOUNTING. *n.* See ACCRUAL METHOD OF ~; ACTION FOR ~; CURRENT VALUE ~; PRICE LEVEL ADJUSTED ~; PUBLIC ~ AND AUDITING.

ACCOUNTING PERIOD. Usually a year; fiscal year; period in respect of which financial statements are prepared.

ACCOUNT IS TO BE TAKEN. The account in credit and debit form, verified by affidavit, is brought into court.

ACCOUNTING PRINCIPLES. See GENERALLY ACCEPTED ~.

ACCOUNT PAYABLE. An amount which is owed to a regular trade creditor.

ACCOUNT RECEIVABLE. An amount which a regular trade debtor owes. See ACCOUNTS RECEIVABLE.

ACCOUNTS. *n.* The statement of profit and loss and the balance sheet. See ACCOUNT; BOOK ~; PUBLIC ~; TERRITORIAL ~.

ACCOUNTS RECEIVABLE. 1. The amounts which are owing by customers to a business for goods shipped to them. S.M. Beck *et al.*, *Cases and Materials on Partnerships and Canadian Business Corporations* (Toronto: The Carswell Company Limited, 1983) at 777. 2. Existing or future book debts, accounts, claims, moneys and choses in action or any class or part thereof and all contracts, securities, bills, notes, books, instruments and other documents securing, evidencing or in any way relating to the same or any of them, but shall not include uncalled share capital of the company or calls made but not paid. *Canada Corporations Act*, R.S.C. 1970, c. C-32, s. 3.

ACCOUNT STATED. Agreement on a sum of money which one person owes to another, from which agreement the law implies a promise to pay.

ACCOUNT SURPLUS. See BASIC ~.

ACCREDIT. *v.* To furnish a diplomat with sufficient credentials and authority to be duly received.

ACCREDITED EMPLOYERS' ORGANIZA-TION. An organization of employers that is accredited under this Act as the bargaining agent for a unit of employers. *Labour Relations Act*, R.S.O. 1980, c. 228, s. 1.

ACCREDITED HOSPITAL. A hospital accredited by the Canadian Council on Hospital Accreditation in which diagnostic services and medical, surgical and obstetrical treatment are provided. *Criminal Code*, R.S.C. 1985, c. C-46, s. 287(6).

ACCRETION. *n.* 1. Growth by accumulation to a thing, usually applied to the imperceptible and slow build-up of land from the sea, a river or lake. 2. Something which the mortgagor adds to property to improve its value for the mortgagee's benefit. W.B. Rayner & R.H. McLaren, *Falconbridge on Mortgages*, 4th ed. (Toronto: Canada Law Book, 1977) at 19.

ACCRUAL. *n.* Gradual vesting of a right in a person, without active intervention.

ACCRUAL METHOD OF ACCOUNTING. Report items of income when they are earned. Similarly, take a cost into account as an expense when it is incurred. W. Grover & F. Iacobucci, *Materials on Canadian Income Tax*, 4th ed. (Toronto: Richard De Boo Ltd., 1980) at 609.

ACCRUE. *v.* To increase; to arise.

ACCRUED. *adj.* Vested.

ACCRUED BENEFIT COST METHOD. A method of determining the annual cost of benefits under a pension plan whereby the cost of such benefits applicable to a particular plan year is taken as the actuarial value of the benefits that accrued in respect of service for that year. *Pension Benefits Standards Regulations*, C.R.C., c. 1252, s. 2.

ACCRUED DIVIDEND. A dividend declared but not yet paid.

ACCRUED TAX. Tax which has not yet become due and payable but which can be charged.

ACCRUED LIABILITY. The amount owing on a given day in respect of salaries, periodic payments, interest and similar items. S.M. Beck *et al.*, *Cases and Materials on Partnerships and Canadian Business Corporations* (Toronto: The Carswell Company Limited, 1983) at 779.

ACCRUING. See OWING OR ~.

ACCT. *abbr.* account.

ACCUMULATED DIVIDEND. A dividend due but not yet paid.

ACCUMULATED NET RETAIL EQUITY. The portion of the equity accumulated through debt retirement appropriations recorded for the Rural Power District relating to Ontario Hydro's rural retail system plus the portion of the balance recorded for rural retail customers in the Stabilization of Rates and Contingencies Account, in the books of Ontario Hydro. Ontario statutes.

ACCUMULATED PROFITS. Profits which have not been distributed.

ACCUMULATED WEALTH. See LOSS OF ~.

ACCUMULATION. *n.* 1. Adding of dividends, rents, and other incomes to capital. 2. Income from property is separated from the ownership of the property either to be an accretion to or to form the capital of any fund, or to be a restriction on and postponement of beneficial enjoyment of that property. In most jurisdictions, there is a statutory provision which limits provisions directing accumulation of income. T. Sheard, R. Hull & M.M.K. Fitzpatrick, *Canadian Forms of Wills*, 4th ed. (Toronto: Carswell, 1982) at 227-28.

ACCUMULATION TRUST. A trust requiring the trustee to accumulate specified income. D.M.W. Waters, *The Law of Trusts in Canada*, 2d ed. (Toronto: Carswell, 1984) at 491.

ACCUMULATIVE DIVIDEND. A dividend which accumulates from year to year if not paid.

ACCUSARE NEMO SE DEBET. [L.] One must not accuse oneself.

ACCUSARE NEMO SE DEBET NISI CORAM DEO. [L.] One is not bound to accuse oneself, except to God.

ACCUSATION. *n.* A charge that a person has committed a crime.

ACCUSATOR POST RATIONABILE TEMPUS NON EST AUDIENDUS, NISI SE BENE DE OMISSIONE EXCUSAVERIT. [L.] An accuser should not be heard after a reasonable time, unless the delay can be satisfactorily accounted for.

ACCUSE. *v.* To charge with a crime.

ACCUSED. *n.* 1. One charged with a crime. 2. Includes (a) a person to whom a peace officer has issued an appearance notice under s. 496, and (b) a person arrested for a criminal offence. *Criminal Code*, R.S.C. 1985, c. C-46, s. 493. 3. Includes a defendant. *Criminal Law Amendment Act*, R.S.C. 1985 (1st Supp.), c. 27, s. 154.

ACCUSED PERSON. "Conviction or convicted" does not include the case of a condemnation under foreign law by reason of contumacy, but "accused person" includes a person so condemned. *Extradition Act*, R.S.C. 1985, c. E-23, s. 2.

ACCUSTOMED. *adj.* Habitual; usual.

A.C.D.I. *abbr.* Annuaire canadien de droit international (Canadian Yearbook of International Law).

A.C.D.P. *abbr.* Annuaire canadien des droits de la personne (Canadian Human Rights Yearbook).

AC ETIAM. [L.] And also.

ACID. See MINERAL ~; ORGANIC ~; PHOSPHORIC ~.

ACID PHOSPHATASE. Enzymes found in significant concentration only in the secretion of the prostate gland. F.A. Jaffe, *A Guide to Pathological Evidence*, 2d ed. (Toronto: Carswell, 1983) at 167.

ACID TEST. To analyze balance sheets by calculating the ratio of liquid assets to current liabilities.

ACKNOWLEDGE. *v.* To admit; to accept responsibility.

ACKNOWLEDGEMENT. *n.* An admission that some claim or liability exists or that one owes a debt.

ACKNOWLEDGEMENT OF INSTRUMENT. A person certifies before someone in authority that the instrument is a free act.

A COELO USQUE AD CENTRUM. [L.] From the heavens down to the centre of the earth.

A COMMUNI OBSERVANTIA NON EST RECEDENDUM. [L.] There should not be a departure from common usage.

ACOUSTIC. See ELECTRO-MAGNETIC, ~, MECHANICAL OR OTHER DEVICE.

ACOUSTIC GAIN. At a specified frequency and under specified operating conditions, means the amount, in decibels, by which the sound pressure developed by the hearing aid earphone in the coupler exceeds the sound pressure level in the free field into which the hearing aid or its microphone, if separate, is introduced. *Medical Devices Regulations*, C.R.C., c. 871, s. 1.

ACQUIESCENCE. *n.* Occurs when a person knows his or her own rights and that they have been infringed, but, either at the time of infringement or after, by his or her conduct leads the person responsible for the infringement to believe that those rights were waived or abandoned.

ACQUIRE. *v.* 1. To obtain by any method and includes accept, receive, purchase, be vested with, lease, take possession, control or occupation of, and agree to do any of those things; but does not include expropriate. 2. Includes take, expropriate, and purchase, irrespective of whether the acquisition by the Commission be of its own volition, or pursuant to an obligation created or imposed upon it by, or under a statutory enactment or any contract. *Electric Power Act*, R.S.N.B. 1973, c. E-5, s. 1. See OFFER TO ~.

ACQUISITION. *n.* Includes every action or method by which land or a right, interest or estate in it may be obtained.

ACQUISITION COST AMOUNT. 1. For each eligible share of an eligible corporation that has been contributed to any stock savings plan, (i) if the share is contributed to a stock savings plan of an eligible investor immediately on its being withdrawn from another stock savings plan of the same eligible investor, an amount equal to the disposition cost amount of that share, and (ii) in any other case, an amount equal to the product obtained when the cost amount of the eligible share is multiplied by the eligible percentage applicable to the eligible share on the date it was acquired by the eligible investor. *Alberta Stock Savings Plan Act*, S.A. 1986, c. A-37.7, s. 28. 2. With respect to each eligible security that has been contributed to any stock savings plan: (i) if the security is contributed to a stock savings plan of an eligible investor immediately on its being withdrawn from another stock savings plan of the same eligible investor, an amount equal to the disposition cost amount of that security; and (ii) in any other case, an amount equal to 30% of the cost amount of the eligible security. *Stock Savings Tax Credit Act*, S.S. 1986, c. S-59.1, s. 2.

ACQUISITION COSTS. The consideration or compensation paid for acquisition of land, or on the expropriation of land, or the value thereof other than the value of any service or benefit that accrues to, passes to, or is provided to the persons from whom the land is acquired at the expense of the authority for which the land is required, or as a result of the use or development of the land by the authority, and includes the cost of any surveys or appraisals made in respect of the acquisition for or in respect of which a fee is paid, but does not include legal costs in respect of the acquisition or the expropriation. *Land Acquisition Act*, R.S.M. 1970, c. L40, s. 2.

ACQUISITIVE PRESCRIPTION. Prescription by which one acquires a right.

ACQUIT. *v.* 1. To find not guilty. 2. Originally, to free from pecuniary liability.

ACQUITTAL. *n.* A finding of "not guilty".

ACQUITTANCE. *n.* A written acknowledgement that a debt was paid.

ACQUITTED. *adj.* Absolved; found free from guilt.

ACRE. *n.* 1. A measure of land. 2. 4 840 square yards. *Weights and Measures Act*, S.C. 1970-71-72, c.36, schedule II. See QUOTA ~S.

ACREAGE. See ACCEPTED ~; INSURABLE ~.

ACROBATIC FLIGHT. Manoeuvres intentionally performed by an aircraft, involving an abrupt change in its attitude, an abnormal attitude or an abnormal variation in speed. *Air Regulations*, C.R.C., c. 2. s, 101.

ACROSS-THE-BOARD ADJUSTMENT. A change in pay rates for all employees of an employer or in one plant of the employer.

ACRYLONITRILE. *n.* A substance designated under the Ontario Occupational Health and Safety Act. D. Robertson, *Ontario Health and Safety Guide* (Toronto: Richard De Boo Ltd., 1988) at 5-17.

ACT. *v.* 1. To perform; to carry out functions. 2. To carry out a function or fill an office on a temporary basis. 3. Includes offering or undertaking to act and holding oneself out. *Insurance Act*, R.S.B.C. 1979, c. 200, s. 310.

ACT. *n.* 1. A statute. 2. Includes (a) an Act of Parliament, (b) an Act of the legislature of the former Province of Canada, (c) an Act of the legislature of a province, and (d) an Act or ordinance of the legislature of a province, territory or place in force at the time that province, territory or place became a province of Canada. *Criminal Code*, R.S.C. 1985, c. C-46, s. 2. 3. An Act of Parliament. *Interpretation Act*, R.S.C. 1985, c. I-21, s. 2. 4. As meaning an Act of a legislature, includes an ordinance of the Yukon Territory or of the Northwest Territories. *Interpretation Act*, R.S.C. 1985, c. I-21, s. 35. 5. An Act of the Legislature. 6. Includes enactment. *Interpretation Act*, R.S.O. 1980, c. 219, s. 30. 7. In relation to an offence or a civil wrong, includes (i) a series of acts, and (ii) an omission or series of omissions. *Interpretation Act*, P.E.I. 1981, c. 18, s. 26. 8. Includes a regulation, a decree, an ordinance or an order in council made under the authority of any act. *Charter of Human Rights and Freedoms*, R.S.Q. 1977, c. C-12, s. 56. 9. An act 1. of commission, or, 2. in certain particular cases, of omission, 3. by a human being, 4. that is voluntary, and, 5. has caused consequences, if consequences are included in the definition of the offence. D. Stuart, *Canadian Criminal Law: a treatise*, 2d ed. (Toronto: Carswell, 1987) at 66. See ADMINISTRATIVE ~; ADOPTIVE ~; ANTI-COMPETITIVE ~; ANTI-INFLATION ~ (CANADA); APPRENTICESHIP ~; ASSESSING ~; AUTHENTIC ~; AUTHORIZING ~; BRITISH NORTH AMERICA ~, 1867; BULK SALES ~; CANADA ~, 1982; CAMPBELL'S (LORD) ~; CARRIAGE BY AIR ~; COLONIAL LAWS VALIDITY ~, 1865; CONSOLIDATION ~; CONSTITUTION ~, 1867; CROW'S NEST PASS ~; DECEPTIVE ~S AND PRACTICES; DOWER ~S; EXTRA-PROVINCIAL ~; FEDERAL ~; FEDERAL OIL ~; FEDERAL OIL PRODUCTION ~; FINAL ~; FRAUDULENT ~; GOLD CLAUSES ~; HOUSING ~S; IMPERIAL ~S; INCOME TAX ~; JUDICIAL ~; LEGISLATIVE ~; LOCAL ~; LOCKE KING'S ~; LORD'S DAY ~; MARRIED WOMEN'S PROPERTY ~; MERCHANT SHIPPING ~S; MORTMAIN ~; NOTARIAL ~; OVERT ~; PERSONAL PROPERTY SECURITY ~; PIRATICAL ~S; PROHIBITED ~; PROVINCIAL ~; REGISTRY ~ SYSTEM; REVENUE ~; SALE OF GOODS ~; SPECIAL ~; WRONGFUL ~.

ACT. *abbr.* Acton, Privy Council.

ACTA CRIM. *abbr.* Acta Criminologica.

ACTA EXTERIORA INDICANT INTERIORA SECRETA. [L.] Exterior actions show interior secrets.

ACTA GESTIONIS. [L.] Private — commercial acts. J.G. McLeod, *The Conflict of Laws* (Calgary: Carswell, 1983) at 72.

ACTA IMPERII. [L.] Public acts. J.G. McLeod, *The Conflict of Laws* (Calgary: Carswell, 1983) at 72.

ACT FAIRLY. Duty to observe the first principles of natural justice for a limited purpose when exercising administrative functions. S.A. DeSmith, *Judicial Review of Administrative Action*, 4th ed. by J.M. Evans (London: Stevens, 1980) at 239. See FAIRNESS.

ACTING JOINTLY OR IN CONCERT. In this Part the following persons or companies are deemed to be acting jointly or in concert with an offeror in connection with an offer to acquire: (a) any person who or company that, as a result of any agreement, commitment or formal or informal understanding with the offeror or any joint actor: (i) acquires; or (ii) offers to acquire;

securities of the issuer of the same class as those subject to the offer to acquire or convertible securities whether or not any such person or company has an interest or potential interest in the outcome of the offer to acquire; (b) any person who or company that intends to exercise jointly or in concert with the offeror or any joint actor, any voting rights attaching to any securities of the offeree issuer beneficially owned or to be beneficially owned after the expiration of the offer to acquire. *Securities Act*, S.S. 1984-85-86, c. S-42.1, s. 96.

ACT IN PAIS. An act not contained in a deed or record.

ACT IN THE LAW. Any expression of the intention or will of the person concerned to create, transfer, or make extinct of a right, which is effective in law for that purpose.

ACTIO CONTRA DEFUNCTUM CAEPTA CONTINUITUR IN HAEREDES. [L.] Any action begun against a person who dies continues against that person's heirs.

ACTIO IN PERSONAM. [L.] A personal action.

ACTIO IN REM. [L.] An action in respect of a thing.

ACTION. *n.* 1. One party (the plaintiff) brings suit against another party (the defendant) for the protection or enforcement of a right, the prevention or redress of a wrong, or the punishment of an offence. 2. A civil proceeding in the court, commenced in such a manner as is prescribed in the rules, and without limiting the generality of the foregoing, includes set-off, counter-claim and garnishment, interpleader, and third party proceedings. 3. Includes counter-claim and set-off. *Bills of Exchange Act*, R.S.C. 1985, c. B-4, s. 2. 4. A civil proceeding, and includes a civil proceeding by or against the Crown. 5. Includes any proceeding in a court and any exercise of a self help remedy. *Limitation Act*, R.S.B.C. 1979, c. 236, s. 1. 6. Includes any civil proceeding, inquiry, arbitration, and a prosecution for an offence committed against a statute of the province or against a by-law or regulation made under the authority of any such statute, and any other prosecution or proceeding authorized or permitted to be tried, heard, had, or taken, by or before a court under the law of the province. 7. A civil proceeding that is not an application and includes a proceeding commenced in the Supreme Court or the District Court by, (i) statement of claim, (ii) notice of action, (iii) counterclaim, (iv) crossclaim, (v) third or subsequent party claim, or (vi) divorce petition or counterpetition, and a proceeding commenced in the Provincial Court (Civil Division) by claim. *Courts of Justice Act*, S.O. 1984, c. 11, s. 1. See

AFFIRMATIVE ~; CAUSE OF ~; CHOSE IN ~; CIRCUITY OF ~; CIVIL ~; CLASS ~; CONSOLIDATION OF ~S; CROSS-~; DERIVATIVE ~; DISCIPLINARY ~; DISCRIMINATORY ~; DOUBLE ~; ENEMY ~ OR COUNTERACTION AGAINST THE ENEMY; FAINT ~; FORMS OF ~; FROST ~; INDUSTRIAL ~; JOB ~; LIMITATION OF ~; MORAL ~; NOTICE OF ~; PERSONAL ~; PROBATE ~S; REAL ~; RELATOR ~; RELEVANT ~; RIGHT OF ~.

ACTIONABLE. *adj.* Capable of sustaining or giving rise to an action.

ACTION AREA PLAN. The statement of the city's policies and proposals for the comprehensive treatment during a period prescribed in it of an action area as a whole, by development, redevelopment or improvement of the whole or part of the area, or by the establishment and implementation of a social development program, or partly by one and partly by another method, and the identification of the types of treatments selected, and may be expressed in texts, maps or illustrations. *City of Winnipeg Act*, S.M. 1971, c. 105, s. 569.

ACTIONEM NON. [L.] A statement by a defendant in pleadings that a plaintiff should not have brought the action against the defendant.

ACTION EX DELICTO. An action to remedy a tort.

ACTION FOR ACCOUNTING. A cause of action which a debtor may have against a security holder who has seized and sold assets or a beneficiary may have against a trustee or other person acting in a fiduciary capacity to make known what has been done with property and to adjust and settle accounts between them.

ACTION FOR COLLISION. An action for damage caused by one or more ships to another ship or ships or to property or persons on board another ship or ships as a result of carrying out or omitting to carry out a manoeuvre, or as a result of non-compliance with law, even though there has been no actual collision. *Federal Court Act*, R.S.C. 1985, c. F-7, s. 2.

ACTION FOR DETINUE. A claim for damages caused by the improper withholding from the plaintiff of a chattel. D.M.W. Waters, *The Law of Trusts in Canada*, 2d ed. (Toronto: Carswell, 1984) at 1035.

ACTION FOR MONEY HAD AND RECEIVED. An action to recover money a defendant has received and which for reasons of equity the defendant should not retain.

ACTION FOR RECOVERY OF LAND. See EJECTMENT.

ACTION FOR REPLEVIN. An action in which a plaintiff seeks to recover possession of a chattel. D.M.W. Waters, *The Law of Trusts in Canada*, 2d ed. (Toronto: Carswell, 1984) at 1035-36.

ACTION FOR SALE. A mortgagee may choose to sue for an order requiring the sale of the property instead of foreclosure. W.B. Rayner & R.H. McLaren, *Falconbridge on Mortgages*, 4th ed. (Toronto: Canada Law Book, 1977) at 510.

ACTION IN PERSONAM. An action brought against a person for recovery of damages or other relief.

ACTION IN REM. A proceeding to determine the right to, or disposition of, a thing.

ACTION LEVEL. The level of a substance identified in a worker's body. D. Robertson, *Ontario Health and Safety Guide* (Toronto: Richard De Boo Ltd., 1988) at 5-18.

ACTION OF CONTRACT. An action arising on a breach of contract.

ACTION OF EJECTMENT. An action to recover possession of land. W.B. Rayner & R.H. McLaren, *Falconbridge on Mortgages*, 4th ed. (Toronto: Canada Law Book, 1977) at 411-412. See EJECTMENT.

ACTIO. NON. *abbr.* Actionem non.

ACTIO NON ACCREVIT INFRA SEX ANNOS. [L.] A plea in which the defendant alleges that the plaintiff's cause of action has not arisen within six years.

ACTIO NON DATUR NON DAMNIFICATO. [L.] No cause of action exists without the plaintiff having suffered damages.

ACTION ON THE CASE. An action brought to recover damages for injury or loss resulting indirectly or consequentially from the act complained of.

ACTION TO REDEEM. An action which may be brought by anyone with any interest in the equity of redemption, or who is liable for a mortgage debt and is sued for it. W.B. Rayner & R.H. McLaren, *Falconbridge on Mortgages*, 4th ed. (Toronto: Canada Law Book, 1977) at 554.

ACTIONUM GENERA MAXIME SUNT SERVANDA. [L.] The forms of action are to be preserved.

ACTIO PER QUOD CONSORTIUM AMISIT. [L.] The right of action of a husband against a defendant who has imprisoned, taken away or done physical harm to his wife so that and he is deprived of her services or society. K.D. Cooper-Stephenson & I.B. Saunders, *Personal*

Injury Damages in Canada (Toronto: Carswell, 1981) at 485.

ACTIO PER QUOD SERVITIUM AMISIT. [L.] A master's right of action against a defendant who has imprisoned, taken away or caused bodily harm to a servant so that the master is deprived of the servant's services. K.D. Cooper-Stephenson & I.B. Saunders, *Personal Injury Damages in Canada* (Toronto: Carswell, 1981) at 484.

ACTIO PERSONALIS MORITUR CUM PERSONA. [L.] A personal action and the person die together.

ACTIO QUAELIBET IN SUA VIA. [L.] Each action follows its own course.

ACTIVATION ANALYSIS. A method to detect trace elements in biological materials. F.A. Jaffe, *A Guide to Pathological Evidence*, 2d ed. (Toronto: Carswell, 1983) at 167.

ACTIVE. *adj.* Opposite of passive; engaged in activity.

ACTIVE ASSET. Money and the market value of assets readily convertible into money.

ACTIVE BUSINESS. In relation to any business carried on by a taxpayer resident in Canada, means any business carried on by the taxpayer other than a specified investment business or a personal services business. *Income Tax Act*, R.S.C. 1952, c. 148 (as am. S.C. 1984, c. 45, s. 92(1)), s. 248(1).

ACTIVE BUSINESS CARRIED ON BY A CORPORATION. Any business carried on by the corporation other than a specified investment business or a personal services business and includes an adventure or concern in the nature of trade. *Income Tax Act*, R.S.C. 1952, c. 148 (as am. S.C. 1984, c. 45, s. 40), s. 125(7)(a).

ACTIVE DEBT. A debt upon which one pays interest.

ACTIVE DOCUMENT. A document in current use for administrative or legal purposes. *Archives Act*, S.Q. 1983, c. 38, s. 2.

ACTIVE DUTY. Something which requires a trustee to carry out an activity such as making a maintenance payment, ensuring that an investment policy balances between income return and capital growth in the interest of both the one holding the remainder and the life tenant, keeping accurate accounts and retaining and instructing solicitors to the trust. D.M.W. Waters, *The Law of Trusts in Canada*, 2d ed. (Toronto: Carswell, 1984) at 28.

ACTIVE INGREDIENT. That ingredient of a control product to which the effects of the control product are attributed, including a synergist, but does not include a solvent, diluent, emulsifier or component that by itself is not primarily responsible for the control effect of the control product. *Pest Control Products Regulations*, C.R.C., c. 1253, s. 2.

ACTIVE LAYER. That region of soil located between the ground surface and the lower boundary of seasonal freezing and thawing. *Gas Pipeline Regulations*, C.R.C., c. 1052, s. 2.

ACTIVE MILITARY SERVICE. Full-time service in the armed forces of Canada or an ally at any time during World War II between September 10, 1939 and September 30, 1947, and at any time during the Korean Campaign between June 30, 1950 and January 1, 1954. *An Act to Amend the Members Superannuation Act*, S.N.B. 1986, c. 54, s. 1.

ACTIVE SERVICE. 1. Any service of a kind specified in the regulations to be active service, which service is deemed for the purposes of this Part to have terminated on discharge or, in the case of a person who underwent treatment in a veterans' hospital, as defined in the regulations, immediately following his discharge, on his release from that hospital. *Royal Canadian Mounted Police Act*, R.S.C. 1985, c. R-11, s. 3. 2. Full-time service as a member of (a) a component of the naval, army or air forces of Canada while that component was on active service having been placed on active service by the Governor in Council pursuant to the Militia Act, or (b) a component of the naval, army or air forces of Her Majesty other than the forces specified in paragraph (a) while members of that component were subject to service in a theatre of war. *Royal Canadian Mounted Police Superannuation Regulations*, C.R.C., c. 1393, s. 3.

ACTIVE SERVICE IN THE FORCES. 1. Any service in the forces of a kind designated in the regulations to be active service, which service is deemed for the purposes of this Part to have terminated on discharge or, in the case of a person who underwent treatment in a veterans' hospital, as defined in the regulations, immediately following his discharge, on that person's release from hospital. *Public Service Superannuation Act*, R.S.C. 1985, c. P-36, s. 3. 2. Full-time service as a member of (a) a component of the naval, army or air forces of Canada while that component was on active service having been placed on active service by the Governor in Council pursuant to the Militia Act, or (b) a component of the naval, army or air forces of Her Majesty other than the forces specified in paragraph (a), or any of the Allies of Her Majesty, while members of that component were subject to service in a theatre of war. *Public*

Service Superannuation Regulations, C.R.C., c. 1358, s. 3.

ACTIVE TRUST. A trust which requires a trustee to carry out duties connected with it. See ACTIVE DUTY.

ACTIVE TUBERCULOSIS. Includes (i) pulmonary tuberculosis that produces sputum containing tubercle bacilli; and (ii) tuberculosis other than the pulmonary form in which tubercle bacilli are found in the discharges from the diseased tissue; and (iii) a condition in which evidence by means of x-ray or other examination discloses that tuberculosis disease is active even though the affected person cannot or will not submit a specimen for examination. *Public Health Act*, R.S.N.S. 1967, c. 247, s. 75.

ACTIVITIES FOR THE DEVELOPMENT OF THE TERRITORY. Activities attached to the traditional culture and way of life of the Natives which are connected with the management of the environment and the development of the resources of the territory, and with the maintenance of optimum biological productivity, or with training programmes which fit with the activities contemplated in the programme. *An Act respecting income security for Cree hunters and trappers who are beneficiaries under the Agreement concerning James Bay and Northern Québec*, S.Q. 1979, c. 16, s. 1.

ACTIVITIES OF DAILY LIVING. Include personal hygiene, dressing, grooming, meal preparation and the taking of medication. *Homes for Special Care Act*, S.N.S. 1976, c. 12, s. 2.

ACTIVITY. See BUSINESS ~; CONCERTED ACTIVITIES; CONTINUOUS ~; COMMERCIAL ~; FIDUCIARY ACTIVITIES; FILM ~; MAJOR BUSINESS OR ~; MANUFACTURING OR PROCESSING ~; RECREATIONAL ACTIVITIES.

ACT OF ATTAINDER. An act attainting a person.

ACT OF BANKRUPTCY. An act which entitles another person to have a receiving order made against a debtor.

ACT OF GOD. 1. The operation of the forces of nature without the intervention of humans. John G. Fleming, *The Law of Torts*, 6th ed. (Sydney: The Law Book Company Limited, 1983) at 316. 2. An extraordinary circumstance which could not be foreseen and which could not be guarded against. *Pandorf & Co. v. Hamilton, Fraser & Co.* (1886), 17 Q.B.D. 670, 55 L.J.Q.B. 546 (U.K.).

ACT OF PARLIAMENT. A statute.

ACT OF THE LAW. The creation, transfer or extinction of a right by the operation of the law itself, in no way dependent on the consent of any concerned party.

ACT OF THE PARLIAMENT OF CANADA. An enactment. *Summary Proceedings Act,* S.P.E.I. 1977, c. 40, s. 4.

ACT OF THE PARTY. Any expression of the intention or will of the person concerned to create, transfer, or make extinct a right, which is effective in law for that purpose.

ACTOR. *n.* A doer; a person who acts. See JOINT ~.

ACTORE NON PROBANTE ABSOLVITUR REUS. [L.] When a plaintiff does not prove his or her case, judgment is for the defendant; when the prosecution fails to prove its case, the accused is acquitted.

ACTORI INCUMBIT ONUS PROBANDI. [L.] The plaintiff or prosecution carries the burden of proof.

ACT OR OMISSION. Includes, for greater certainty, attempting or conspiring to commit, counselling any person to commit, aiding or abetting any person in the commission of, or being an accessory after the fact in relation to, an act or omission. *Criminal Code,* R.S.C. 1985, c. C-46, s. 7(3.77) as added by R.S.C. 1985 (3d Supp.), c. 10, s. 1.

ACTOR SEQUITUR FORUM REI. [L.] A plaintiff must take the case to the defendant's jurisdiction.

ACT OR STATUTE. An Act or statute of the Legislature of Saskatchewan and includes an Ordinance of the North-West Territories in force in this province. *The Interpretation Act,* R.S.S. 1978, c. I-11, s. 21.

ACTS OF CIVIL STATUS. The entries made in the registers, kept according to law, for evidence of births, marriages and burials. *Interpretation Act,* R.S.Q. 1977, c. I-16, s. 61.

ACTS OF CRUELTY. Conduct creating a danger or an apprehension of danger to life, limb or health, or any course of conduct which in the opinion of the court is grossly insulting or intolerable or is of such a character, without proof of actual or apprehended personal violence or of actual or apprehended injury to health, that the wife, husband or children seeking maintenance could not reasonably be expected to be willing to live with the other spouse or the parent after such other spouse or such parent has been guilty of such conduct.

ACTUAL. *adj.* Real, in opposition to constructive, as in actual possession or actual occupation.

ACTUAL AUTHORITY. The relationship between agent and principal which the parties alone create by a consensual agreement. The expression includes express, implied and usual or customary authority. G.H.L. Fridman, *The Law of Agency,* 5th ed. (London: Butterworths, 1983) at 53.

ACTUAL BODILY HARM. Includes any injury or hurt.

ACTUAL CAUSATION. Causation in fact. K.D. Cooper-Stephenson & I.B. Saunders, *Personal Injury Damages in Canada* (Toronto: Carswell, 1981) at 637.

ACTUAL COST. The cost of a building project and includes, (i) fees payable for the services of an architect, professional engineer, or other consultant, (ii) the cost of purchasing and installing furnishings and equipment, (iii) the cost of land surveys, soil tests, permits, licences and legal fees, (iv) the cost of paving, sodding and landscaping, and (v) the cost of acquiring the land necessary for the building project. *Developmental Services Act,* R.R.O. 1980, Reg. 242, s. 4.

ACTUAL FRONTAGE. The distance which a parcel of land actually abuts on the work or highway. *Municipal Act,* R.S.B.C. 1979, c. 290, s. 480.

ACTUALITÉS. *n.* The periodical, Actualités.

ACTUALITÉS-JUSTICE. *n.* The periodical, Actualités-Justice.

ACTUAL LOSS. 1. In relation to any branch line means the excess of (a) the costs incurred by the company in any financial year thereof in the operation of the line and in the movement of traffic originating or terminating on the line over (b) the revenues of the company for that year from the operation of the line and from the movement of traffic originating or terminating on the line. *Railway Act,* R.S.C. 1985, c. R-3, s. 254. 2. In relation to a passenger-train service, (a) the excess, if any, of the costs incurred by the company in carrying passengers by the passenger-train service over (b) the revenues of the company attributable to the carrying of passengers by the passenger-train service. *Railway Act,* R.S.C. 1985, c. R-3, s. 264.

ACTUAL LOSS OR DAMAGE. Includes loss of income, including future income, and, with respect to any aboriginal peoples of Canada, includes loss of hunting, fishing and gathering opportunities. *Oil and Gas Production and Conservation Act,* R.S.C. 1985, c. O-7, s. 24.

ACTUALLY RECEIVED. The sum of money or benefit received by the borrower from the lender.

ACTUAL NOTICE. Knowledge shown to be actually brought to the attention of the party who is charged with it, either by the party's own admission or by the evidence of witnesses who can establish that the fact itself, not just something which would have led to the fact's discovery if an enquiry had been made, was brought to the party's knowledge. W.B. Rayner & R.H. McLaren, *Falconbridge on Mortgages*, 4th ed. (Toronto: Canada Law Book, 1977) at 133. See CONSTRUCTIVE NOTICE.

ACTUAL POSSESSION. Physical possession of goods or land.

ACTUAL PRODUCER. Producer actually engaged in the production of grain. *Canadian Wheat Board Act*, R.S.C. 1985, c. C-24, s. 2.

ACTUAL RESIDENCE. Physical presence. J.G. McLeod, *The Conflict of Laws* (Calgary: Carswell, 1983) at 181.

ACTUAL TOTAL LOSS. Either the insured item is destroyed or so damaged that it ceases to be what it was, or the assured is permanently deprived of the item.

ACTUAL VALUE. The value to the insured.

ACTUAL WORK. See DAY OF ~.

ACTUARIAL ASSUMPTIONS. The assumptions made in calculating the present value of benefits expected to be provided and the present value of contributions and special payments expected to be made under a pension plan concerning (a) the rates of investment income, and (b) the occurrence of events and existence of circumstances that govern the amount of benefits and contributions that are payable or may become payable and the time when they will be paid. *Pension Benefits Standards Regulations*, C.R.C., c. 1252, s. 2.

ACTUARIAL BASIS. The assumptions and methods generally accepted and used by a Fellow of the Canadian Institute of Actuaries to establish the costs of pension benefits, life insurance, disability insurance, health insurance or any other similar benefits including the actuarial equivalents of such benefits which costs depend upon the contingencies of human life, such as death, accident, sickness or disease. *Employment Standards Act*, R.R.O. 1980, Reg. 282, s. 1.

ACTUARIAL LIABILITIES. See GOING CONCERN.

ACTUARIALLY EQUIVALENT. Equivalent in accordance with the appropriate actuarial tables.

ACTUARIALLY SOUND. That on the basis of statistical data sufficient premiums will be credited to the fund continued under section 9 to pay the anticipated indemnities that will have to be met and provide a reasonable reserve against unforeseen losses. *The Saskatchewan Crop Insurance Act*, R.S.S. 1978, c. S-12, s. 2.

ACTUARIAL METHOD. See ARITHMETICAL OR ~.

ACTUARIAL TABLE. Statistical data organized to show average life expectancies of persons.

ACTUARY. *n.* A Fellow of the Canadian Institute of Actuaries.

ACTUS CURIAE NEMINEM GRAVABIT. [L.] The act of a court harms no one.

ACTUS DEI NEMINEM GRAVABIT. [L.] No one should be prejudiced by an act of God.

ACTUS DEI NEMINI FACIT INJURIAM. [L.] No person is responsible for the act of God.

ACTUS DEI MENIMI NOCET. [L.] No one should be prejudiced by an act of God.

ACTUS INCEPTUS CUJUS PERFECTIO PENDET EX VOLUNTATE PARTIUM REVOCARI POTEST; SI AUTEM PENDET EX VOLUNTATE TERTIAE PERSONAE VEL EX CONTINGENTI, REVOCARI NON POTEST; SI AUTEM PENDET EX VOLUNTATE TERTIAE PERSONAE VEL EX CONTINGENTI, REVOCARI NON POTEST. [L.] A transaction begun but not completed may be rescinded if its completion requires the parties' mutual consent; but it cannot be rescinded if its completion depends on a third party's consent or on a contingency.

ACTUS JUDICIARIUS CORAM NON JUDICE IRRITUS HABETUR; DE MINISTERIALI AUTEM A QUOCUNQUE PROVENIT RATUM ESTO. [L.] A judicial act done outside of or exceeding jurisdiction is invalid, but a ministerial act done outside of jurisdiction can be approved.

ACTUS LEGIS NEMINI EST DAMNOSUS. [L.] An act in the law should prejudice no one.

ACTUS LEGIS NEMINI FACIT INJURIAM. [L.] An act of the law can wrong no one.

ACTUS LEGITIMI NON RECIPIUNT MODUM. [L.] When the law sanctions doing something only in a particular manner, then it cannot be done differently.

ACTUS ME INVITO (FACTUS) NON EST MEUS ACTUS. [L.] When my will does not concur, what I do is not my act at all.

ACTUS NON FACIT REUM NISI MENS SIT REA. [L.] An act is only guilty when there is a guilty mind. D. Stuart, *Canadian Criminal Law: a treatise*, 2d ed. (Toronto: Carswell, 1987) at 1.

ACTUS REUS. [L.] A voluntary act of commission or of omission, in certain cases only, by a human being which caused consequences if consequences are part of the definition of the offence. D. Stuart, *Canadian Criminal Law: a treatise*, 2d ed. (Toronto: Carswell, 1987) at 66.

ACT WITHIN SCOPE OF EMPLOYMENT. To carry out assigned duties, functions or activities contemplated.

A.C.W.S. *abbr.* All Canada Weekly Summaries.

A.D. *abbr.* Anno Domini.

ADAPTER. *n.* Any means by which the coupling of one section or portion of standard hose of one thread may be connected to a hydrant, nozzle or another adapter or to the coupling of another section or portion of standard hose of a different thread. *Standard Hose Coupling Act*, R.S.N.S. 1967, c. 288, s. 1.

AD ARBITRIUM. [L.] At will.

AD AVIZANDUM. [L.] To be deliberated on.

AD DAMNUM. [L.] To the damage.

ADDENDUM. *n.* Something added.

ADDICT. *n.* 1. Any person addicted to the improper use of cocaine, opium, or their derivatives, or any other narcotic drug which for the time being is included in the schedule to the Opium and Narcotic Drug Act (Canada). 2. A person who is addicted to a substance other than alcohol. *Alcoholism and Drug Addiction Research Foundation Act*, R.S.O. 1980, c. 17, s. 1. See NARCOTIC ~.

ADDICTION. *n.* 1. The suffering from a disorder or disability of mind, as evidenced by a person being so given over to the use of alcohol or drugs that he is unable to control himself, or is incapable of managing his affairs, or places his family in danger or severe distress, or the use of drugs or intoxicating liquor to such an extent as to render the user dangerous to himself or others. *Mental Health Act*, R.S.M. 1970, c. M110, s. 2. 2. Addiction to a substance other than alcohol. *Alcoholism and Drug Addiction Research Foundation Act*, R.S.O. 1980, c. 17, s. 1.

AD DIEM. [L.] On the day appointed.

ADDITIONAL VOLUNTARY CONTRIBUTION. Under a pension plan means an optional contribution by a member that does not give rise to an obligation on the employer to make additional contributions.

ADDITIONAL WRITTEN WARRANTY. Any undertaking in writing by a warrantor that he will repair, replace, make a refund or take other remedial action with respect to a consumer product that breaks down, malfunctions or fails to meet the specifications set forth in the undertaking, and includes a service contract. *The Consumer Products Warranties Act*, R.S.S. 1978, c. C-30, s. 2.

ADDITIVE. See FOOD ~.

ADDRESS. *n.* 1. A petition. 2. A place of residence or business. 3. (i) Of the merchant means the place of that merchant's establishment or office indicated in the contract, or of a new establishment or office of which the merchant subsequently notifies the consumer, except a post office box; (ii) of the manufacturer means the place of one of that manufacturer's establishments in Canada, except a post office box; (iii) of the consumer means the place of that consumer's usual residence indicated in the contract, or of a new residence of which the consumer subsequently notifies the merchant. 4. In relation to the location of place of residence, office, polling station or other fixed location, includes the postal code assigned to the area in which the place of residence, office, polling station or other fixed location is located. See CLOSING ~; JOINT ~; RECORDED ~.

ADDRESS MAIL. Mail bearing the return address of the sender but not bearing a specific request that the mail be returned. *Undeliverable and Redirected Mail Regulations*, C.R.C., c. 1298, s. 2.

ADDUCE. *v.* To present; to lead, in connection with evidence; to bring forward.

AD EA QUAE FREQUENTIUS ACCIDUNT JURA ADAPTANTUR. [L.] The laws are fitted to more frequently occurring cases.

ADEMPTION. *n.* What occurs when a testator dies and the subject matter of a gift was converted into something else or destroyed by the testator's act or by duly appointed authority. T. Sheard, R. Hull & M.M.K. Fitzpatrick, *Canadian Forms of Wills*, 4th ed. (Toronto: Carswell, 1982) at 168.

ADEMPTION BY ADVANCEMENT. When a testator provides in a will for a child or another person to whom that testator stands *in loco parentis* and after that advances to that child or person a sum of money, it is presumed that the testator did not intend to provide a double portion to that child or person at the expense of other children. T. Sheard, R. Hull & M.M.K. Fitzpatrick, *Canadian Forms of Wills*, 4th ed. (Toronto: Carswell, 1982) at 170.

ADEQUATE. *adj.* Sufficient; suitable.

ADEQUATE CONSIDERATION. Sufficient consideration; reasonable value for what is received.

ADEQUATE NOTICE. Reasonably sufficient notice.

ADEQUATE VALUABLE CONSIDERATION. A consideration of fair and reasonable money value with relation to that of the property conveyed, assigned or transferred or a consideration of fair and reasonable money value with relation to the known or reasonably to be anticipated benefits of the contract, dealing or transaction. *Bankruptcy Act*, R.S.C. 1985, c. B-3, s. 97(2).

ADEQUATE VENTILATION. A supply of at least two hundred cubic feet of fresh air per minute for each person or animal employed in an underground mine and as much more as circumstances may require. *Coal Mines Regulation Act*, R.S.A. 1970, c. 52, s. 2.

AD FILUM AQUAE. [L.] To the centre line of a stream.

AD FILUM VIAE. [L.] To the centre of a road.

AD FINEM. [L.] Near or at the end.

ADFREEZING. *n.* The adhesion of wet soil to a foundation unit caused by freezing of the contact surface. *Building Code Act*, R.R.O. 1980, Reg. 87, s. 1.

AD HOC. [L.] 1. For a particular purpose. 2. Appointed specially for a specified short period of time or until the occurrence of a stated event. *Formal Documents Regulations*, C.R.C. c. 1331, s. 2.

AD HOC ARBITRATION. Arbitration of a particular dispute or group of related disputes.

AD IDEM. [L. at the same point] Said when parties agree.

AD INFINITUM. [L.] With no limit.

AD INQUIRENDUM. [L.] To make inquiry.

AD INTERIM. [L.] In the meantime.

ADIPOCERE. *n.* An easily crumbled, waxy substance derived from fatty tissues. F.A. Jaffe, *A Guide to Pathological Evidence*, 2d ed. (Toronto: Carswell, 1983) at 7.

ADIPOCIRE. *n.* An easily crumbled, waxy substance derived from fatty tissues. F.A. Jaffe, *A Guide to Pathological Evidence*, 2d ed. (Toronto: Carswell, 1983) at 167.

ADJACENT. *adj.* Neighbouring; near.

ADJACENT CLAIMS. Claims that are contiguous or are intended by the locator to be contiguous. *Canada Mining Regulations*, C.R.C., c. 1516, s. 2.

ADJACENT LAND. Land that is contiguous to the parcel that is the subject of the application for subdivision approval and includes land or a portion of land that would be contiguous if not for a public roadway, river or stream. *Planning Act*, R.S.A. 1980, c. P-9, s. 106.

ADJACENT SEAT. A designated seating position so located that a portion of its occupant space is, for a distance of 15 inches (38.1 cm) horizontal and parallel to an emergency exit and at a distance of not more than 10 inches (25.4 cm) therefrom. *Motor Vehicle Safety Regulations*, C.R.C., c. 1038, s. 2.

ADJECTIVE LAW. Law which relates to practice and procedure.

ADJOINING. *adj.* Touching; coterminous.

ADJOINING CLAIMS. Those mineral claims that come into contact one with the other at some point on the boundary lines or that share a common boundary.

ADJOINING LAND. 1. (i) Parcels of land that adjoin or corner, (ii) parcels of land separated by a road allowance or a surveyed highway or road that would adjoin or corner if they were not so separated. 2. Land immediately adjacent to the subject land.

ADJOURN. *v.* To postpone; to recess.

ADJOURNAMENTUM EST AD DIEM DICERE SEU DIEM DARE. [L.] Adjournment is appointing a day or giving a day.

ADJOURNMENT. *n.* 1. Postponement or putting off business to another time or place. 2. Of Parliament, an interruption during the course of one and the same session. A. Fraser, G.A. Birch & W.A. Dawson, eds., *Beauchesne's Rules and Forms of the House of Commons of Canada*, 5th ed. (Toronto: Carswell, 1978) at 54.

ADJUD. *abbr.* Adjudicator.

ADJUDICATE. *v.* To determine; to decide after a hearing.

ADJUDICATION. *n.* 1. The decision or judgment of a court. 2. Any decision, determination, refusal or award made under this Act pertaining to an allowance. *War Veterans Allowance Act*, R.S.C. 1985, c. W-3, s. 2. 3. A procedure to determine a rights dispute. *Civil Service Collective Bargaining Act*, S.N.S. 1978, c. 3, s. 2.

ADJUDICATOR. *n.* A person who hears and determines a reference to adjudication.

ADJUNCT. *adj.* Additional.

ADJUNCTUM ACCESSORIUM. [L.] An appurtenance; an accessory.

ADJURATION. *n.* Binding upon oath; swearing.

ADJUST. *v.* To determine amount to be paid by insurer to insured when loss occurs.

ADJUSTED COST BASE. To a taxpayer of any property at any time means, except as otherwise provided, (i) where the property is depreciable property of the taxpayer, the capital cost to him of the property as of that time, and, (ii) in any other case, the cost to the taxpayer of the property adjusted, as of that time, in accordance with section 53, except that (iii) for greater certainty, where any property of the taxpayer is property that was reacquired by him after having been previously disposed of by him, no adjustment to the cost to him of the property that was required to be made under section 53 before its reacquisition by him shall be made under that section to the cost to him of the property as reacquired property of the taxpayer, and (iv) in no case shall the adjusted cost base of any property at the time of its disposition by the taxpayer be less than nil. *Income Tax Act*, R.S.C. 1952, c. 148 (as am. S.C. 1970-71-72, c. 63), s. 54(a).

ADJUSTED EQUITY. An amount determined by correcting to their realizable value the book value of liabilities and assets on a balance sheet. A. Bissett-Johnson & W.M. Holland, eds., *Matrimonial Property Law in Canada* (Toronto: Carswell, 1980) at V.3.

ADJUSTED OPERATING PROFITS. Gross revenue from operations minus allowable costs. *Anti-Inflation Guidelines*.

ADJUSTER. *n.* A person who, for compensation, not being a barrister or solicitor acting in the usual course of his profession or a trustee or an agent of the property insured, directly or indirectly solicits the right to negotiate the settlement of a loss under a contract of insurance on behalf of the insured or the insurer, or claims to be an adjuster of losses under such contracts. See CLAIMS ~.

ADJUSTMENT. *n.* 1. Settlement and ascertainment of the amount of indemnity which an insured may receive under a policy. 2. A calculated procedure, force or thrust designed to move one structure in relation to another, particularly of the spinal column, to remove subluxations or fixations and to mobilize the affected structures for the purpose of restoring or maintaining health. *Chiropractic Profession Act*, R.S.A. 1980, c. C-9, s. 1. See ACROSS-THE-BOARD ~; CHIROPRACTIC ~; CN ~; COST-OF-LIVING ~; EQUALIZATION OR ~ LEVY; GENERAL ~; INTERIM ~; STATEMENT OF ~S; VALUATION ~.

ADJUSTMENT HARDWARE. Hardware designed for adjusting the size of a seat belt assembly to fit the user, including such hardware as may be integral with a buckle, a retractor or attachment hardware. *Motor Vehicle Safety Regulations*, C.R.C., c. 1038, s. 209.

ADJUSTMENT LEVY. In the context of product marketing schemes, a pooling of proceeds, so that producers' returns are equalized even if the product was actually sold at different prices in different markets. P.W. Hogg, *Constitutional Law of Canada*, 2d ed. (Toronto: Carswell, 1985) at 614.

ADJUSTMENT TIME. Of a taxpayer in respect of a business is (i) in the case of a corporation formed as a result of an amalgamation occurring after June 30, 1988, the time immediately before the amalgamation, (ii) in the case of any other corporation, the time immediately after the commencement of its first taxation year commencing after June 30, 1988, and (iii) for any other taxpayer, the time immediately after commencement of the taxpayer's first fiscal period commencing after 1987 in respect of the business. *Income Tax Act*, R.S.C. 1952, c. 148 (as am. S.C. 1988, c. 55, s. 7(4)), s. 14(5)(c).

AD LARGUM. [L.] At large.

AD LIB. *abbr.* Ad libitum.

AD LIBITUM. [L.] At pleasure.

AD LITEM. [L.] For a suit; for the purposes of a suit. See GUARDIAN ~.

AD LONGUM. [L.] At length.

ADM. CT. *abbr.* Admiralty Court.

ADMEASUREMENT. *n.* Ascertainment.

AD MEDIUM FILUM AQUAE. [L.] Up to the imaginary line down the centre of a river.

AD MEDIUM FILUM VIAE. [L.] Up to the imaginary line down the centre of a road.

ADMIN. *abbr.* Administrator.

ADMINISTER. *v.* 1. To manage; to control. 2. Includes prescribe, give, sell, furnish, distribute or deliver. *Food and Drug Regulations*, C.R.C., c. 870, c. G.04.001.

ADMINISTERED PRICE. (i) A price, user charge or fee charged by a public agency, and (ii) a price, user charge or fee required, permitted or authorized by a public regulatory agency to be charged by another person.

ADMINISTERING. *adj.* Acting as guardian or custodian or trustee or executor or administrator of the estate of a person or a deceased person. *Public Trustee Act*, S.N.S. 1973, c. 12, s. 2.

ADMINISTRATION. *n.* 1. Of an estate, means to assemble the deceased's assets, pay all legitimate debts and distribute the rest to those entitled. J.G. McLeod, *The Conflict of Laws* (Calgary: Carswell, 1983) at 406. 2. Letters of administration of the property of deceased persons, whether with or without the will annexed and whether granted for general, special or limited purposes. 3. In respect of a ship, the government of the country in which the ship is registered. See ANCILLARY ~; DEPOSIT ~ CONTRACT; GRANT OF ~; GRANT OF ~ WITH WILL ANNEXED; LETTERS OF ~; LIMITED ~; PRAIRIE FARM REHABILITATION ~.

ADMINISTRATION COST. The cost of (i) maintaining the premises and office equipment of the corporation, (ii) ordinary office expenses, (iii) production and distribution of informative material, including newsletters, notices of meetings and similar materials, (iv) secretarial services, and (v) advertising and publicity. *Ontario Heritage Act*, R.R.O. 1980, Reg. 712, s. 1.

ADMINISTRATION COSTS. Salaries and travelling expenses of members and employees of an authority, office rent, maintenance and purchase of office equipment, expenses connected with exhibits, visual equipment and printed matter for educational purposes, and all expenditures necessary for carrying out the objects of an authority other than capital expenses and maintenance costs of approved projects. *Conservation Authorities Act*, R.S.O. 1980, c. 85, s. 1.

ADMINISTRATION OF JUSTICE. 1. The provision, maintenance and operation of, (a) the courts of justice of the Province of Ontario, including small claims courts and provincial courts; (b) land registry offices; (c) jails; and (d) the offices of coroners, clerks of the peace and Crown attorneys, for the performance of their functions, including any functions delegated to such courts, institutions or offices or any official thereof by or under any Act. *Administration of Justice Act*, R.S.O. 1980, c. 6, s. 1. 2. (a) Provision, maintenance and operation of (i) courts of justice in the Province; (ii) court registry and land title offices; (iii) correctional centres as defined in the Correction Act, and prisons and lockups operated by police forces; (iv) the offices of coroner, Crown counsel, probation officers, court workers and sheriffs, and their officers; and (v) the police forces, for the purpose of their functions, including functions given to the courts or offices, or to any official of them under an Act or rule or regulation made under an Act; (b) prosecution of offences; and (c) provision of adequate legal services, including the operation of legal aid offices. *Justice Administration Act*, R.S.B.C. 1979, c. 211, s. 1.

ADMINISTRATIVE. *adj.* That which concerns ministerial or executive action.

ADMINISTRATIVE ACT. To adopt a policy, to make and issue a specific direction, and to apply a general rule to a particular case. S.A. DeSmith, *Judicial Review of Administrative Action*, 4th ed. by J.M. Evans (London: Stevens, 1980) at 71.

ADMINISTRATIVE AND TECHNICAL STAFF. People with communication, secretarial or clerical duties. J.G. McLeod, *The Conflict of Laws* (Calgary: Carswell, 1983) at 76.

ADMINISTRATIVE DISCRETION. In the work of an administrative agency, consideration not entirely susceptible of proof or disproof in relation to which the agency must make decisions.

ADMINISTRATIVE EXPENSES. 1. Include the salaries of the personnel, the cost of conveying pupils, the cost of text-books, tuition fees paid to other institutions, the cost of maintenance of schools and of repairs deemed tenant's repairs. *Education Act*, R.S.Q. 1977, c. I-14, s. 441. 2. Any expenses related to managing a business.

ADMINISTRATIVE LAW. 1. Law relating to public administration. 2. The law which relates to the organization, duties and quasi-judicial and judicial powers of the executive, to proceedings before tribunals and to the making of subordinate legislation.

ADMINISTRATIVE PURPOSE. In relation to the use of personal information about an individual, means the use of that information in a decision-making process that directly affects that individual. *Privacy Act*, R.S.C. 1985, c. P-21, s. 3.

ADMINISTRATIVE TRIBUNAL. A person or body before whom a matter is heard; contrasted with a court.

ADMINISTRATOR. *n.* 1. One who is appointed to administer the estate of a person who died without appointing an executor in a will or without leaving a will. 2. A person appointed to administer a plan, fund or organization. 3. The clerk, secretary treasurer or treasurer of an urban municipality. *Urban Municipal Administrators Act*, S.S. 1980-81, s. U-8.1, s. 2. 4. A person appointed by the Minister to administer the property of deceased Indians and includes a person who, by reason of his office, is instructed to initiate or conclude the administration of an estate. *Indian Estates Regulations*, C.R.C., c. 954, s. 2. See FUND ~; LITIGATION ~; URBAN MUNICIPAL ~.

ADMINISTRATOR AD LITEM. An administrator for the purposes of litigation. G.D. Watson & C. Perkins, eds., *Holmested & Watson: Ontario Civil Procedure* (Toronto: Carswell, 1984) at CJA-179.

ADMINISTRATOR DE SON TORT. A person who is neither an executor nor an administrator but is either involved with the deceased's property or does other things characteristic of an executor.

ADMINISTRATOR WITH WILL ANNEXED. An administrator appointed to administer a testator's estate where the executors named in the will refuse or are unable to act.

ADMINISTRATRIX. *n.* A woman appointed to administer the estate of a person who died without appointing an executor in a will or without leaving a will.

ADMIN. L.J. *abbr.* Administrative Law Journal.

ADMIN. L.R. *abbr.* Administrative Law Reports, 1983-.

ADMIRALTY COURT. The Federal Court. *Canada Shipping Act*, R.S.C. 1985, c. S-9, s. 2.

ADMIRALTY LAW. Maritime law.

ADMIRALTY PROCEEDING. The Federal Court Act sets out the maritime or Admiralty jurisdiction of the Federal Court. See CANADIAN MARITIME LAW.

ADMISSIBLE EVIDENCE. Relevant evidence not otherwise excluded.

ADMISSION. *n.* 1. Confession. 2. Facts admitted by the opposite party in civil proceeding or allegations made by the plaintiff and not disputed by the defendant. 3. Entry to any place of entertainment. 4. Entry or landing. *Immigration Act*, R.S.C. 1985, c. I-2, s. 2. 5. Call to the bar. 6. Official acceptance of a patient or resident into the hospital or facility. See FIRST ~; FORMAL ~; PRICE OF ~; SOLEMN ~; UNSOLEMN ~.

ADMISSION DIAGNOSIS. The diagnosis given to explain admission.

ADMISSION IN JUDICIUM. A solemn admission. P.K. McWilliams, *Canadian Criminal Evidence*, 3d ed. (Aurora: Canada Law Book, 1988) at 14-1.

ADMISSION OF SERVICE. Acknowledgement that a true copy of the document was received.

ADMISSION PRICE. Includes (i) the fee or charge paid by or collected from a person for entrance to a place of amusement, (ii) where entrance to a place of amusement is allowed on the basis of a season ticket or annual ticket, the fee or charge paid by or collected from the purchaser of the season ticket or annual ticket, (iii) the rental price for a toboggan on toboggan slides open to the public, (iv) the fee or charge paid or collected for a ride on a riding device or amusement ride, (v) the fee or charge paid or collected for participation in a game at a midway, carnival or circus, (vi) the fee or charge paid or collected as a rental price of skates at an ice rink or for roller skates at a roller skating facility open to the public, (vii) any fee or charge which, although not charged for entrance to a place of amusement, is charged for the right to sit or use any particular seat, or box or stand in the place of amusement or for any privilege or right to use or sit in any particular place of amusement not given to a person who does not pay the fee or charge, and (viii) where a person is allowed entrance by means of a complimentary pass or ticket to a place of amusement for the entrance to which a fee or charge is paid by or collected from other persons, the fee or charge paid by or collected from a person who had paid the fee or charge and has the same or similar rights and privileges in the place of amusement as the person allowed entrance by means of a complimentary pass or ticket. *Municipal Act*, S.M. 1974, c. 33, s. 20. See PRICE OF ADMISSION.

ADMITTING OFFICER. The physician responsible for approving the admission of patients. *Mental Health Act*, R.S.A. 1970, c. 231, s. 2.

AD OFFICUM JUSTICIARIORUM SPECTAT, UNICUIQUE CORAM EIS PLACITANTI JUSTITIAM EXHIBERE. [L.] It is the duty of judicial officers to administer justice to everyone who pleads before them.

ADOLESCENT. *n.* A person who has reached his sixteenth birthday but has not reached his eighteenth birthday. *Employment Standards Act*, R.S.M. 1970, c. E110, s. 2.

ADOPT. *v.* To accept a contract as binding; to select; to choose.

ADOPTED CHILD. A person who was adopted in Ontario. For all purposes of law, as of the date of the making of an adoption order, (a) the adopted child becomes the child of the adopting parent and the adopting parent becomes the parent of the adopted child; and (b) the adopted child ceases to be the child of the person who was his or her parent before the adoption order was made and that person ceases to be the parent of the adopted child, except where the person is the spouse of the adopting parent, as if the adopted child had been born to the adopting parent. *Child and Family Services Act*, S.O. 1984, c. 55, s. 152.

ADOPTION. *n.* An act which creates a familial relationship in which the adopted child is in law and fact, treated as the adoptive family's natural child. J.G. McLeod, *The Conflict of Laws* (Calgary: Carswell, 1983) at 310.

ADOPTION BY REFERENCE. Incorporation of a separate statement, statute, by-law, etc. into the original statement, statute, by-law, etc. by referring to it.

ADOPTION OF CONTRACT. Acceptance of a contract as binding.

ADOPTIVE ACT. An act must be adopted either by the vote of a public body or the vote of a particular number of persons.

AD PROXIMUM ANTECEDENS FIAT RELATIO, NISI IMPEDIATUR SENTENTIA. [L.] Unless the context requires otherwise, relative words refer to the last antecedent.

AD QUAESTIONEM (OR QUESTIONES) FACTI NON RESPONDENT JUDICES; AD QUAESTIONEM (OR QUESTIONES) JURIS NON RESPONDENT JURATORES. [L.] In cases tried by a judge and jury, the judge should not decide questions of fact and the jury should not decide questions of law.

AD QUAESTIONEM LEGIS RESPONDENT JUDICES. [L.] Judges decide points of law.

AD QUEM. [L.] To whom; to which.

AD QUOD DAMNUM. [L.] To what damage.

ADS. *abbr.* [L. ad sectam] At the suit of. Used when the defendant's name is put first in the title of a proceeding.

AD SECTAM. [L. at the suit of] Used in its abbreviated form ads. or ats. when the defendant's name is put first in the title of a proceeding.

A.D.T. *abbr.* Anti-Dumping Tribunal.

AD TUNC ET IBIDEM. [L.] Then and there.

ADULT. *n.* 1. One who is neither a young person nor a child. 2. A person who is no longer required by law in the province in which he resides to attend school. *National Training Act*, R.S.C. 1985, c. N-19, s. 2. 3. A person who is or is apparently sixteen years of age or older. 4. A person eighteen years of age or more. 5. A person who has reached the age of majority. 6. A person who has attained the age of 19 years. 7. An individual who is married or has attained the age of eighteen years. *Income Tax acts.* 8. A person whose age is at least one year greater than the regular school leaving age in the province in which he resides, including a person who is engaged in domestic service at home whether or not such person has at any time been a member of the labour force. *Adult Occupational Training Act*, S.C. 1972, c. 14, s. 3. See DEPENDANT ~; DEPENDENT ~; NEGLECTED ~.

ADULT EDUCATOR. A person employed full-time as an instructor or organizer of education programs for adults. *Education Act*, S.N.W.T. 1976 (3d Sess.), c. 2, s. 2.

ADULT ENTERTAINMENT PARLOUR. Any premises or part thereof in which is provided, in pursuance of a trade, calling, business or occupation, goods or services appealing to or designed to appeal to erotic or sexual appetites or inclinations. *Municipal Act*, R.S.O. 1980, c. 302, s. 222.

ADULTERATED. *adj.* Deteriorated by the addition of any substance to a maple product or the substitution for any maple product or for any part thereof of any colourable imitation. *Maple Products Industry Act*, R.S.C. 1970, c. M-2, s. 2.

ADULTERATION. *n.* Mixing into any substance intended for sale an ingredient which is either dangerous to health or which turns the substance into something other than what it is represented to be.

ADULTERINE. *n.* The child of an adulterous relationship.

ADULTERY. *n.* Voluntary sexual intercourse between a spouse and any person other than his wife or her husband while the marriage exists.

ADULT FILM. A film that produces or reproduces an adult motion picture. *Motion Picture Act*, S.B.C. 1986, c. 17, s. 1.

ADULT FILM DISTRIBUTOR. A person who distributes adult films to an adult film retailer or to another adult film distributor. *Motion Picture Act*, S.B.C. 1986, c. 17, s. 1.

ADULT FILM RETAILER. A person who distributes adult films to the public, but does not include an adult film distributor. *Motion Picture Act*, S.B.C. 1986, c. 17, s. 1.

ADULT IN NEED OF PROTECTION. An adult who, in the premises where he resides, (i) is a victim of physical abuse, sexual abuse, mental cruelty or a combination thereof, is incapable of protecting himself therefrom by reason of physical disability or mental infirmity, and refuses, delays or is unable to make provision for his protection therefrom, or (ii) is not receiving adequate care and attention, is incapable of caring adequately for himself by reason of physical disability or mental infirmity, and refuses, delays or is unable to make provision for his adequate care and attention. *Adult Protection Act*, S.N.S. 1985, c. 2, s. 3.

ADULT MOTION PICTURE. (a) A motion picture that was submitted for review under the former Act or under section 2(1) of this Act for the purpose of exhibition in a theatre and, following the review, (i) was not approved, (ii) was approved, but had a portion removed, or (iii) was approved, but with a condition that it may only be exhibited in theatres designated by the director, (b) a motion picture that has not been reviewed under section 5 that depicts (i) explicit sexual scenes, (ii) the coercing, through the use or threat of physical force or by other means, of a person to engage in a sexual act, where that sexual act is depicted in explicit sexual scenes or sexually suggestive scenes, (iii) incest or necrophilia, (iv) bondage in a sexual context, (v) persons who are or who appear to be under the age of 14 involved in sexually suggestive scenes, whether or not they appear nude or partially nude, (vi) persons who are or who appear to be under the age of 18 involved in explicit sexual scenes, (vii) explicit sexual scenes involving violence, (viii) scenes of brutality or torture to persons or animals, depicted in a realistic and explicit manner, or (ix) sexual conduct between a human being and an animal, or (c) a motion picture that contains scenes that depict conduct or an activity that is prescribed in a regulation made under section 14(d). *Motion Picture Act*, S.B.C. 1986, c. 17, s. 1.

ADULT PERSON. A person 18 years of age or more. *The Devolution of Real Property Act*, R.S.S. 1978, c. D-27, s. 2.

ADULT TEST GROUP. A group of adults consisting of at least 100 adults who (a) are healthy, normal and without an obvious physical or mental handicap, (b) are between 18 and 45 years of age, and (c) represent evenly, within plus or minus 10 per cent, each yearly age between 18 and 45 years calculated to the nearest year. *Hazardous Products (Hazardous Substances) Regulations*, C.R.C., c. 926, s. 1.

A. DU N. *abbr.* Annales du notariat et de l'enregistrement.

ADV. *abbr.* [L.] Adversus.

AD VALOREM. [L.] According to their value; used in reference to customs or duties.

ADVANCE. *v.* 1. To pay before due; to furnish money on credit; to loan. 2. Includes lend and give.

ADVANCE. *n.* 1. An advance payment to a producer in respect of a crop that the producer has actually produced. *Advance Payments for Crops Act*, R.S.C. 1985 (1st Supp.), c. 38, s. 2. 2. Payment made before due. See ACCOUNTABLE ~; HARVESTING ~S; PROGRESS ~S; STANDING ~; TEMPORARY ~.

ADVANCE BOOKING CHARTER. A round-trip international charter originating at one point in Canada, destined for one point in a foreign country and terminating at the originating point in Canada, and operated by one or two licensed air carriers under a contract with a charterer, or contracts with charterers, where (a) one charterer or all the charterers contract for the full capacity of the aircraft, and (b) each charterer contracts for at least 40 seats for hire to the public at a price per seat that is not less than the pro rata of the charter cost thereof to the charterer. *Air Carrier Regulations*, C.R.C., c. 3, s. 54.

ADVANCE BOOKING CHARTER (DOMESTIC). A round-trip domestic charter originating at one point in Canada, destined for one point in Canada and terminating at the originating point in Canada and operated by one or two licensed air carriers under a contract with a charterer, or contracts with charterers, where (a) one charterer or all the charterers contract for the full capacity of the aircraft, and (b) each charterer contracts for at least 40 seats for hire to the public at a price per seat that is not less than the pro rata of the charter cost thereof to the charterer. *Air Carrier Regulations*, C.R.C., c. 3, s. 83. See INTER-REGIONAL ~; REGIONAL ~.

ADVANCED LIFE SUPPORT SERVICE. A service established and maintained for the purpose of providing the persons, facilities and equipment necessary to administer medical treatment to any sick or injured person at any time prior to the admission of that person as a patient in a hospital as defined in the Public Hospitals Act where that person is in immediate need of such admission, and whose life would be endangered were it not for such treatment. *Advanced Life Support Services Act*, S.N.B. 1976, c. A-3.01, s. 1.

ADVANCED TREATMENT WORKS. Water pollution control works that are intended to provide treatment more extensive than that obtained with secondary treatment works, and includes chemical precipitation, coagulation, filtration, adsorption, ion exchange, effluent irrigation or such other methods as the minister may describe and approve. *The Water Pollution Control Assistance Act*, R.S.S. 1978, c. W-5, s. 2.

ADVANCEMENT. *n.* 1. Promotion. 2. A single outlay for a defined purpose. 3. Paying to a beneficiary part of the capital of a gift before the actual time when the capital falls into the beneficiary's hands. D.M.W. Waters, *The Law of Trusts in Canada*, 2d ed. (Toronto: Carswell, 1984) at 930. 4. An equitable doctrine in which, when a purchase or investment is made by a person in loco parentis in the name of a child or by a spouse in the name of a spouse, the presumption is that the purchase or investment was intended as an advancement for the benefit of the child or spouse. This rebuts the ordinary presumption of a resulting trust in favour of the person who paid the money. See ADEMPTION BY ~; PRESUMPTION OF ~.

ADVANCE PAYMENT. 1. A payment made by or on behalf of Her Majesty under the terms of a contract before the performance of that part of the contract in respect of which the payment in made. *Government Contracts Regulations*, C.R.C., c. 701, s. 2. 2. A payment for grain made to a producer under the authority of this Act. *Prairie Grain Advance Payments Act*, R.S.C. 1985, c. P-18, s. 2.

ADVANCE POLL. A poll taken in advance of polling day. *Election Act*, R.S.A. 1980, c. E-2, s. 1.

ADVANCE POLLING DAY. The day preceding ordinary polling day.

ADVANCE VOTE. A vote taken in advance of election day. *Local Authorities Election Act*, S.A. 1983, c. L-27.5, s. 1.

ADVANTAGE. See COLLATERAL ~.

ADVENTITIOUS. *adj.* Incidental; unexpected.

AD VENTREM INSPICIENDUM. [L.] To inspect the womb.

ADVENTURE. *n.* A hazardous enterprise. See JOINT ~; MARINE ~; MIS~.

ADVENTURE IN THE NATURE OF TRADE. An adventure is in the nature of trade when it has none of the essential characteristics of an investment, but is a mere speculation if the purpose is not to earn income, but to turn to profit on prompt realization. *M.N.R. v. Sissons*, [1969] S.C.R. 507; [1969] C.T.C. 184; 69 D.T.C. 5152.

ADVERSARIAL SYSTEM. A system by which disputes between opposing parties are resolved.

ADVERSARY. *n.* A party opposed to another in interest; a litigant.

ADVERSARY SYSTEM. See ADVERSARIAL SYSTEM.

ADVERSE. *adj.* Opposed in interest; unfavourable.

ADVERSE CLAIM. Includes a claim that a transfer was or would be wrongful or that a particular adverse person is the owner of or has an interest in the security. *Corporations acts.*

ADVERSE EFFECT. 1. An unwanted effect brought about by the normal dose of a drug. F.A. Jaffe, *A Guide to Pathological Evidence*, 2d ed. (Toronto: Carswell, 1983) at 61. 2. (i) Impairment of the quality of the natural environment for any use that can be made of it, (ii) injury or damage to property or to plant or animal life,

(iii) harm or material discomfort to any person, (iv) an adverse effect on the health of any person, (v) impairment of the safety of any person, (vi) rendering any property or plant or animal life unfit for use by people, (vii) loss of enjoyment of normal use of property, and (viii) interference with the normal conduct of business.

ADVERSE IN INTEREST. Parties not necessarily opposite, i.e., two defendants whose interests are opposed.

ADVERSE PARTY. The opposite party.

ADVERSE POSSESSION. Occupation of realty which conflicts with the true owner's right.

ADVERSE WITNESS. A witness who has a hostile mind to the party who is examining her or him.

ADVERSUS. [L.] Against, abbreviated v.

ADVERSUS EXTRANEOS VITIOSA POSSESSIO PRODESSE SOLET. [L.] Prior possession is good title unless anyone can show better.

ADVERTISE. *v.* To make any representation to the public by any means whatever for the purpose of promoting directly or indirectly the sale of a product.

ADVERTISE AND TO MAKE USE OF ADVERTISING. See TO ADVERTISE AND TO MAKE USE OF ADVERTISING.

ADVERTISEMENT. *n.* 1. Any representation by any means whatever for the purpose of promoting directly or indirectly the sale or disposal of any product. 2. Includes (i) an advertisement in a newspaper, magazine or other publication or circular; (ii) an advertisement shown on a billboard sign, handbill or similar item that is located elsewhere than on the business premises of the credit grantor on whose behalf the advertisement is being made; (iii) a message broadcast by television or radio. See POLITICAL ~; PUBLIC ~.

ADVERTISER. *n.* A person who prepares, publishes or broadcasts an advertisement or who causes an advertisement to be prepared, published or broadcast. *Consumer Protection Act*, S.Q. 1978, c. 9, s. 1.

ADVERTISING. *n.* Includes television and radio commercials, newspaper and magazine advertisments and all other sales material generally disseminated through the communications media. See POLITICAL ~.

ADVERTISING MATERIAL. 1. Includes commercial messages, but does not include (a) announcements promoting services that a licensee is licensed to provide, (b) public service announcements, (c) announcements promoting programs transmitted by Canadian stations, or (d) channel identification announcements. *Cable Television Regulations*, C.R.C., c. 374, s. 2. 2. Includes (a) commercial messages, (b) public service announcements, and (c) advertisements for stations, networks or programs, but does not include station and network identification or notices concerning future programs voiced over credits. *Television Broadcasting Regulations*, C.R.C., c. 381, s. 2. 3. Catalogues, price-lists and trade notices. *Advertising Material Remission Order*, C.R.C., c. 739, s. 2.

ADVERTISING MATTER. Information bulletins, booklets, programs and memoranda relating to a meeting or convention or to products displayed at a meeting or convention. *Foreign Organizations Remission Order*, C.R.C., c. 766, s. 2.

ADVICE. See APPROPRIATE ~.

ADVISEMENT. *n.* Deliberation.

ADVISER. *var* ADVISOR. *n.* A person or company engaging in or claiming to engage in the business of advising others as to the investing in or the buying or selling of securities. See COMMODITY CONTRACTS ~; LEGAL ~; SECURITIES ~.

ADVISORY COMMITTEE. A committee established under a statute to provide advice, usually to the government of the day.

ADVISORY COUNCIL. See ADVISORY COMMITTEE; CANADIAN ~ ON THE STATUS OF WOMEN.

ADVISORY OPINION. An answer to a hypothetical question put to a court.

ADVISORY SERVICES. The provision of one aeronautical radio station to another such station of flight safety information, including aeronautical weather information and serviceability reports in respect of aerodromes, air navigation aids and approach aids, but does not include the provision of IFR air traffic control clearances, instructions or procedures. *Aeronautical Communications Standards and Procedures Order*, C.R.C., c. 20, s. 2.

ADVOCACY. *n.* The act of pleading for, supporting a position or viewpoint.

ADVOCATE. *n.* 1. The supporter of a cause who assists a client with advice and pleads for the client. 2. A barrister and solicitor. 3. An advocate or a notary and, in another Canadian province, a barrister or a solicitor. *An Act to Amend the Taxation Act and Other Fiscal Legislation*, S.Q. 1985, c. 25, s. 17. 4. A person entered on the Roll. *Barreau du Québec Act*, R.S.Q. 1977, c. B-1, s. 1.

ADVOCATE. *n.* The periodical, Advocate.

ADVOCATES' Q. *abbr.* The Advocates' Quarterly.

ADVOCATES' SOC. J. *abbr.* The Advocates' Society Journal.

ADVOCATE (TOR.) *abbr.* The Advocate, published by the Student Law Society, Faculty of Law, University of Toronto.

ADVOCATE (VAN.) *abbr.* The Advocate, published by the Vancouver Bar Association.

ADVOW. *v.* To maintain or justify an act.

AECB. *abbr.* Atomic Energy Control Board.

AECL. *abbr.* Atomic Energy of Canada Limited.

AEDIFICARE IN TUO PROPRIO SOLO NON LICET QUOD ALTERI NOCEAT. [L.] One is permitted to build on one's own land any structure as long as it does not interfere with the rights of another.

AEDIFICATIO (OR AEDIFICATUM) SOLO, SOLO CEDIT. [L.] Whatever is built on land becomes part of the land.

AEQUITAS EST CORRECTIO JUSTAE LEGIS QUA PARTE DEFICIT QUOD GENERATIM LATA EST. [L.] Equity corrects a just law which is defective because of its universality.

AEQUITAS EST PERFECTA QUAEDAM RATIO QUAE JUS SCRIPTUM INTERPRETATUR ET EMENDAT; NULLA SCRIPTURA COMPREHENSA, SED SOLUM IN VERA RATIONE CONSISTENS. [L.] Equity is a complete system, which though unwritten and based on right reason alone, interprets and amends the law.

AEQUITAS EST QUASI EQUALITAS. [L.] Equity is, in a manner of speaking, equality.

AEQUITAS FACTUM HABET QUOD FIERI OPORTUIT. [L.] Equity regards that what ought to have been done was done.

AEQUITAS NUNQUAM CONTRAVENIT LEGIS. [L.] Equity never contravenes the common law.

AEQUITAS SEQUITUR LEGEM. [L.] Equity follows the law.

AEQUUM ET BONUM EST LEX LEGUM. [L.] What is equitable and good is the law of laws.

AERADIO STATION. An aeronautical service facility operated by the Minister of Transport that provides (a) flight advisory and flight planning services, and (b) air to ground communication services on radio frequencies specified in aeronautical charts and information publications issued from time to time by the Minister. *Flight Plans and Flight Notifications Order,* C.R.C., c. 45, s. 2.

AERIAL TRAMWAY. Any type of overhead transportation effected by the use of a cable or cables excepting a vertical elevator. *Railway Act,* R.S.B.C. 1979, c. 354, s. 1.

AERODROME. *n.* Any area of land, water (including the frozen surface thereof) or other supporting surface used, designed, prepared, equipped or set apart for use either in whole or in part for the arrival, departure, movement or servicing of aircraft and includes any buildings, installations and equipment situated thereon or associated therewith. *Aeronautics Act,* R.S.C. 1985 (1st Supp.), c. 33, s. 3. See DESIGNATED ~.

AERODROME TRAFFIC ZONE. An airspace extending upwards vertically from the surface of the earth and designated as an aerodrome traffic zone in the Designated Airspace Handbook issued under the authority of the Minister. *Air Regulations,* C.R.C., c. 2, s. 101.

AERONAUTICAL PRODUCT. Any aircraft, aircraft engine, aircraft propeller or aircraft appliance or part or the component parts of any of those things. *Aeronautics Act,* R.S.C. 1985 (1st Supp.), c. 33, s. 3.

AERONAUTICAL RADIO STATION. (a) An air station located in an aircraft capable of two-way voice communication with another such air station, an air traffic control unit and any aeradio ground station, (b) an air traffic control unit capable of two-way voice communication operated by the Department of Transport including (i) an area control centre established to provide air traffic control service to IFR flights, (ii) a terminal control unit, and (iii) a control tower or a temporary or mobile air traffic control unit established to provide for the control of air traffic, or (c) an aeradio ground station operated by the Department of Transport capable of two-way voice communication other than an air traffic control unit. *Aeronautical Communications Standards and Procedures Order,* C.R.C., c. 20, s. 2.

AERONAUTICS. *n.* Includes control over air navigation, regulation of airports, investigation of air accidents and claims for damage to cargo based on the Carriage by Air Act, but does not include claims against an air carrier for breach of a contract of carriage or negligence. D. Sgayias *et al., Federal Court Practice 1988* (Toronto: Carswell, 1987) at 147.

AEROPLANE. *n.* A power-driven heavier-than-air aircraft, deriving its lift in flight from aerodynamic reactions on surfaces that remain fixed under given conditions of flight. *Air Regulations,* C.R.C., c. 2, s. 101. See LARGE ~; SMALL ~.

AFFAIRS. *n.* 1. That which concerns a person in trade or property. 2. The relationships among a body corporate, its affiliates and the shareholders, directors and officers of those bodies corporate but does not include the business carried on by those bodies corporate. See CONSUMER AND CORPORATE ~ CANADA; EXTERNAL ~ CANADA; INDIAN AND NORTHERN ~ CANADA; INTERGOVERNMENTAL ~; VETERANS' ~.

AFFECT. *v.* To act upon; to influence.

AFFECTED LIVESTOCK. Livestock having a communicable disease. *Livestock Diseases Act,* R.S.A. 1980, c. L-22, s. 1.

AFFECTED SECURITY. A participating security of a corporation in which the interest of the holder would be terminated by reason of a going private transaction. *Business Corporations Act, 1982,* S.O. 1982, c. 4, s. 189.

AFFECTION. See NATURAL ~.

AFFECTUS PUNITUR LICET NON SEQUATUR EFFECTUS. [L.] A person is punished for an attempt, even though the person fails.

AFFIANCE. *n.* The promise between a man and woman to marry.

AFFIANT. *n.* A person who makes an affidavit.

AFFIDAVIT. *n.* 1. A written statement supported by the oath of the deponent or by a solemn affirmation, administered and attested by any person authorized by law to administer oaths. 2. Includes a statutory declaration. 3. An affirmation when made by a person entitled to affirm. 4. Includes a solemn declaration, or statutory declaration and an agreed statement of facts. *Judicature Act,* S.Nfld. 1986, c. 42, s. 2. See COMMISSIONER FOR TAKING ~S; CROSS-EXAMINATION ON ~; OATH OR ~.

AFFIDAVIT OF DOCUMENTS. A descriptive listing of the documents which a party to an action possesses, controls or has in their power.

AFFIDAVIT OF MANUFACTURER. An attestation submitted by a manufacturer on a form prescribed by or acceptable to the chief inspector that the boiler or pressure vessel described therein has been fabricated in accordance with an approved design which has been registered. *Boiler and Pressure Vessel Act,* R.S. Nfld. 1970, c. 24, s. 2.

AFFIDAVIT OF MERITS. An affidavit which

a defendant files and which responds to a specially endorsed writ.

AFFIDAVIT OF SERVICE. An affidavit certifying that a document has been served on a party to a proceeding.

AFFILIATE. *n.* 1. Where used to indicate a relationship between corporations, means any corporation where one is the subsidiary of the other, or both are subsidiaries of the same corporation, or (a) each of them is controlled by the same person or the same group of persons, or (b) one of them is controlled by one person and the other is controlled by an associate, as defined in paragraphs (e) or (f) of the definition of "associate", of that person. *Small Business Venture Capital Act*, S.B.C. 1985, c. 56, s. 1. 2. An affiliated body corporate. 2. An affiliated corporation. See FOREIGN ~; NON-BANK ~ OF A FOREIGN BANK.

AFFILIATED BARGAINING AGENT. A bargaining agent that, according to established trade union practice in the construction industry, represents employees who commonly bargain separately and apart from other employees and is subordinate or directly related to, or is, a provincial, national or international trade union and includes an employee bargaining agency. *Labour Relations Act*, R.S.O. 1980, c. 228, s. 137.

AFFILIATED COMPANY. One company is affiliated with another company if one of them is the subsidiary of the other or both are subsidiaries of the same company or each of them is controlled by the same person.

AFFILIATED POLITICAL ORGANIZATION. Any political organization that is affiliated with and endorsed by a political party or one or more constituency associations registered under this Act. *Election Finances Act*, S.O. 1986, c. 33, s. 27.

AFFILIATED UNION. A union which is a member of a federation, either directly or as a member of a federation which is a member thereof. *Savings and Credit Unions Act*, R.S.Q. 1977, c. C-4, s. 1.

AFFILIATION. *n.* 1. The establishment of a bond between two or more organizations. 2. A process through which a married woman living apart from her husband, a single woman or a widow obtains an order requiring the putative father of her child to pay for the child's education and maintenance. See POLITICAL ~.

AFFILIATION AGREEMENT. An agreement between any person and a station that includes a provision for reserved time. *Broadcasting regulations.*

AFFILIATION PROCEEDING. An application or action to determine paternity of a child.

AFFINITAS AFFINITATIS. [L.] A relationship which is not based on affinity or consanguinity, i.e. the relationship between one's brother and one's spouse's sister.

AFFINITY. *n.* Relationship through marriage.

AFFIRM. *v.* 1. To promise in solemn form to tell the truth while giving evidence or when making an affidavit. 2. To confirm a lower court's decision. 3. When a party who is entitled to void a contract but chooses not to avoid the contract, to carry it out or act as though bound by it, the party is said to affirm the contract.

AFFIRMANCE. *n.* Confirmation of something which could be voided.

AFFIRMANT. *n.* One who solemnly affirms.

AFFIRMANTI NON NEGANTI INCUMBIT PROBATIO. [L.] The burden of proof lies on the party who is affirming a fact not on the party trying to disprove it.

AFFIRMATION. *n.* A solemn declaration with no oath. A person who objects to taking an oath may affirm, and the affirmation has the same effect as an oath. See OATH OR ~ OF CITIZENSHIP.

AFFIRMATIVE. *adj.* Asserting positively.

AFFIRMATIVE ACTION. A program intended to assist disadvantaged groups.

AFFIRMATIVE PREGNANT. An assertion implying a negation in favour of the adverse party.

AFFIXED. *adj.* As applied to goods means erected upon or affixed or annexed to land in such manner and under such circumstances as to constitute them fixtures. *Conditional Sales acts.*

AFFOREST. *v.* To change land into forest.

AFFORESTATION. *n.* Changing land to forest.

AFFRANCHISE. *v.* To make free.

AFFRAY. *n.* Fighting; a skirmish.

AFFREIGHTMENT. *n.* A contract in which a shipowner agrees to carry goods in exchange for a reward.

A5. Television by amplitude modulation. *General Radio Regulations, Part II*, C.R.C., c. 1372, s. 42.

AFL. *abbr.* American Federation of Labour.

AFORESAID. *adj.* Mentioned previously.

AFORETHOUGHT. *adj.* Considered or thought of previously.

A FORTIORI. [L.] 1. By so much stronger reason. 2. Much more.

A4. Facsimile by amplitude modulation of the main carrier either directly or by frequency modulated sub-carrier. *General Radio Regulations, Part II,* C.R.C., c. 1372, s. 42.

AFTER-ACQUIRED CLAUSE. In a security instrument, a charge on the debtor's future or after-acquired property as well as any additions to the property which the debtor may acquire. F. Bennett, *Receiverships* (Toronto: Carswell, 1985) at 28.

AFTER-ACQUIRED PROPERTY. Property acquired after marriage. See AFTER-ACQUIRED CLAUSE.

AFTERBIRTH. *n.* A flat, round organ where the embryo is impanted which contains both fetal and maternal blood vessels and through which an embryo receives nourishment and oxygen. F.A. Jaffe, *A Guide to Pathological Evidence,* 2d ed. (Toronto: Carswell, 1983) at 181 and 182.

AFTERCARE. *n.* The assistance made available to persons discharged from imprisonment, parole or probation. *Corrections Act,* R.S.N.W.T. 1974, c. C-18, s. 2.

AFTER DATE. In a bill of exchange, a phrase fixing the date of payment, e.g., "two months after date, pay . . .".

AFTERGLOW. *n.* The glow remaining on the splint of a match after the flame has been extinguished. *Hazardous Products (Matches) Regulations,* C.R.C., c. 929, s. 2.

AFTER-MARKET. *n.* The market in a security once it has been sold initially by the issuer.

AFTER PERPENDICULAR. A perpendicular that coincides with the after end of the length (L) of a ship. *Load Line Regulations (Inland),* C.R.C., c. 1440, s. 1.

AFTER SIGHT. To specify time for payment of a bill of exchange the time must be specified and begins with the date of acceptance by the drawee.

AFT PERPENDICULAR. A perpendicular that coincides with the after side of the rudder post, or where no rudder post is fitted, with the centreline of the rudder stock. *Arctic Shipping Pollution Prevention Regulations,* C.R.C., c. 353, schedule VI, s. 1.

A(F) ULTIMATE AND A(F) AND A(M) ULTIMATE TABLES. The tables so entitled appearing in the "Mortality of Annuitants 1900-1920" published on behalf of the Institute of Actuaries and The Faculty of Actuaries in Scotland, 1924.

Public Service Superannuation Regulations, C.R.C., c. 1358, s. 2.

A(F) ULTIMATE TABLE. The table so entitled appearing in the "Mortality of Annuitants 1900-1920" published on behalf of the Institute of Actuaries and the Faculty of Actuaries in Scotland, 1924.

A.G. *abbr.* Attorney General.

AGAINST INTEREST. Used to describe a statement or admission which is adverse to the position or interest of the person making the statement or admission.

AGE. *n.* 1. An age of 45 years or more or less than 65 years. *Humans Rights acts.* 2. Any age of 18 years or more but less than 65 years. *Saskatchewan Human Rights Code,* S.S. 1979, c. S-24.1, s. 2. 3. Nineteen years of age and over. *Human Rights Code,* R.S.N.B. 1973, c. H-11, s. 2. 4. An age that is 18 years or more, except in subsection 4(1) where "age" means an age that is 18 years or more and less than 65 years. *Human Rights Code, 1981,* S.O. 1981, c. 53, s. 9. 5. The period during which an alcoholic beverage is kept under such conditions of storage as may be necessary to render it potable or to develop its characteristic flavour or bouquet. *Food and Drug Regulations,* C.R.C., c. 870, s. B.02.002. See CERTIFICATE OF ~; FULL ~; LEGAL ~; NON-~; PENSIONABLE ~; RETIREMENT ~.

AGE CERTIFICATE. Document issued in connection with statutory restrictions on child labour and authorizing employment of a minor.

AGENCY. *n.* A relationship existing between two persons. One, called the agent, is legally considered to represent the other, called the principal, in a way which affects the principal's legal position in relation to third parties. G.H.L. Fridman, *The Law of Agency,* 5th ed. (London: Butterworths, 1983) at 9. See APPROPRIATE ~; BURGLAR ALARM ~; BUSINESS ~; CANADIAN INTERNATIONAL DEVELOPMENT ~; CHIEF ~; CHIEF EXECUTIVE OFFICER OF AN ~; COLLECTION ~; CROWN ~; DESIGNATED ~; DETECTIVE ~; DOUBLE ~; EMPLOYMENT ~; EXPORT CREDITS ~; EXPRESS ~; EXTRA-PROVINCIAL ~; GOVERNMENT ~; GOVERNMENT RELATED ~; HEALTH ~; INDIAN ~; INSURANCE ~; LAW OF ~; MARKETING ~; MUNICIPAL ~; NON-PROFIT ~; OFFICIAL ~; PAY ~; PERSONAL REPORTING ~; PLACEMENT ~; PROVINCIALLY APPROVED ~; PUBLIC ~; PUBLIC HOUSING ~; REPORTING ~; SECURITY GUARD ~; SELLING ~; SETTLEMENT ~; TERRITORIAL ~; WELFARE ~.

AGENCY BY ESTOPPEL. A relationship legally treated as one of principal and agent, in which the parties' conduct seems to express consent that they are principal and agent. G.H.L. Fridman, *The Law of Agency*, 5th ed. (London: Butterworths, 1983) at 97.

AGENCY FROM COHABITATION. A rebuttable presumption of fact that one spouse actually still cohabiting with the other is the other's agent. G.H.L. Fridman, *The Law of Agency*, 5th ed. (London: Butterworths, 1983) at 127.

AGENCY OF A FOREIGN STATE. Any legal entity that is an organ of the foreign state but that is separate from the foreign state. *State Immunity Act*, R.S.C. 1985, c. S-18, s. 2.

AGENCY OF GOVERNMENT. Any board, commission, association, or other body, whether incorporated or unincorporated, that is established under an Act of the Legislature and all the members of which, or all the members of the board of management or board of directors of which, (i) are appointed by an Act of the Legislature or the Lieutenant Governor in Council, and (ii) in the discharge of their duties are public officers or servants of the Crown, or for the proper discharge of their duties are, directly or indirectly, responsible to the Crown.

AGENCY OF NECESSITY. A situation which comes into existence in an unforeseen situation or sudden danger when a person performs acts to another's property or similar interests. G.H.L. Fridman, *The Law of Agency*, 5th ed. (London: Butterworths, 1983) at 117-118.

AGENCY OF THE CROWN. (i) Any board, commission, association, or other body, whether incorporated or unincorporated, all the members of which, or all the members of the board of management or board of directors of which, (A) are appointed by an Act of the Legislature or by order of the Lieutenant Governor in Council; or (B) if not so appointed, in the discharge of their duties are public officers or servants of the Crown, or for the proper discharge of their duties are, directly or indirectly, responsible to the Crown; or (ii) any corporation the election of the board of directors of which is controlled by the Crown, directly or indirectly, through ownership of shares of the capital stock thereof by the Crown or by a board, commission, association, or other body to which sub-clause (i) applies.

AGENCY STORE. A liquor store operated by an agent.

AGENDA. *n.* A schedule or list of the business items to be considered at a meeting.

AGENT. *n.* 1. One who acts for another whether for any form of remuneration or not. 2. A person who, for another or others, for compensation, gain or reward, or hope or promise thereof, either alone or through one or more officials or salesmen, trades in real estate. 3. A person who for compensation solicits insurance on behalf of any insurer or transmits for another person, an application for or a policy of insurance to or from such insurer or offers to act or assumes to act in the negotiation of such insurance or in negotiating the continuance or renewal of insurance contracts. 4. In relation to Her Majesty in right of Canada or in right of a province, any agent of Her Majesty in either such right and includes a municipal or public body empowered to perform a function of government in Canada, any corporation empowered to perform a function or duty on behalf of Her Majesty in either such right or any body corporate controlled directly or indirectly by Her Majesty in either such right, but does not include an official or corporation performing a function or duty in connection with (A) the administration or management of an estate or property of an individual, or (B) the administration, management or investment of a fund established to provide compensation, hospitalization, medical care, annuity, pension or similar benefits to particular classes of individuals, or moneys derived from such a fund. 5. A person who has a mandate to represent a candidate in a polling-station. *Elections acts.* 6. In relation to the government of a foreign state or any political subdivision thereof, a person empowered to perform a function or duty on behalf of the government of the foreign state or political subdivision, other than a function or duty in connection with the administration or management of the estate or property of an individual. 7. A person appointed by the owner of a mine site, mine or coal processing plant to act as a representative of the owner. 8. Includes an employee. *Criminal Code*, R.S.C. 1985, c. C-46, s. 426(4). See AUTHORIZED ~; BARGAINING ~; BIOLOGICAL ~; BURGLAR ALARM ~; BUSINESS ~; CANDIDATE'S ~; CHIEF ~; CLEANING ~; COLLECTING ~; COLLECTION ~; COMMISSION ~; DEL CREDERE ~; ELECTORAL DISTRICT ~; EMPLOYER'S ~; EXCLUSIVE ~; FISCAL ~; FORWARDING ~; GELLING ~; GENERAL ~; INFECTIOUS ~; INSURANCE ~; INSURER'S ~; JELLING ~; LAND ~; LITERARY ~; MERCANTILE ~; NEWS-~; OFFICIAL ~; PARLIAMENTARY ~; PATENT ~; PRINCIPAL AND ~; RECORDED ~; REGISTERED ~; REGISTERING ~; REVISING ~; SANITIZING ~; SPECIAL ~; TRADE MARK ~; TRANSFER ~; TRAVEL ~.

AGENT CORPORATION. A Crown corporation that is expressly declared by or pursuant to any other Act of Parliament to be an agent of the Crown. *Financial Administration Act*, R.S.C, 1985, c. F-11, s. 83.

AGENTES ET CONSENTIENTES PARI POENA PLECTENTUR. [L.] Those who do something and those who consent to its being done are punished equally.

AGENT-GENERAL. *n.* The representative of a province in another country.

AGENT OF A CANDIDATE. A person authorized in writing by a candidate to represent that candidate at an election or at any proceeding of an election.

AGENT OF A PARTICIPANT. A person who by a record admitted in evidence under this section appears to be or is otherwise proven to be an officer, agent, servant, employee or representative of a participant. *Combines Investigation Act*, R.S.C. 1985 (2d Supp.), c. 19, s. 40.

AGENT OF NECESSITY. See AGENCY OF NECESSITY.

AGENT OF THE CROWN. See AGENT OF GOVERNMENT.

AGENT PROVOCATEUR. One who entices another to commit an offence which one would not otherwise have committed and then informs against the other person in respect of the offence.

AGENT'S LIEN. An agent may hold onto goods in possession until the principal has satisfied the agent's claims. G.H.L. Fridman, *The Law of Agency*, 5th ed. (London: Butterworths, 1983) at 178.

AGE OF CONSENT. The age at which a person may marry without parental approval.

AGE OF CRIMINAL RESPONSIBILITY. The age at which a child may be held responsible for a criminal act.

AGE OF MAJORITY. 18 or 19 years of age; traditionally was 21 years of age; the age at which a person has full rights and responsibilities in legal matters.

AGE OF RETIREMENT. Of a judge, means the age, fixed by law, at which the judge ceases to hold office. *Judges Act*, R.S.C. 1985, c. J-1, s. 2.

AGE STRIP STAMP. A stamp that indicates thereon the year of manufacture of the spirits contained in the bottle, flask or other package to which the stamp is affixed. *Distillery Regulations*, C.R.C., c. 569, s. 2.

AGGRAVATED ASSAULT. Wounding, maiming, disfiguring or endangering the life of the complainant. *Criminal Code*, R.S.C. 1985, c. C-46, s. 268.

AGGRAVATED DAMAGES. Non-pecuniary damages awarded to mitigate a plaintiff's feelings when the defendant's misbehaviour has been hurtful. K.D. Cooper-Stephenson & I.B. Saunders, *Personal Injury Damages in Canada* (Toronto: Carswell, 1981) at 55.

AGGRAVATED SEXUAL ASSAULT. Wounding, maiming, disfiguring or endangering the life of the complainant in committing a sexual assault. *Criminal Code*, R.S.C. 1985, c. C-46, s. 273.

AGGRAVATION. *n.* Increasing the enormity of a wrong.

AGGREGATE. *n.* Collection of people, parts or things in order to form a whole. See CORPORATION ~, INDUSTRIAL ~.

AGGREGATE LAND HOLDING. Of a person: includes all land holdings of that person and all land holdings of that person's spouse and dependent children.

AGGREGATE MATERIAL. Any material or materials, including, but not limited to, gravel, slag, limestone, crushed rock, sand, hydrated lime, cement, furnace ash, asbestos, glass or sulphur, or any two or more of them, used to produce asphalt paving when mixed with bituminous asphalt. *Environmental Protection Act*, R.R.O. 1980, Reg. 297, s. 1.

AGGREGATE TAXABLE VALUE. In relation to gifts made by a donor in a year, means the aggregate of the taxable value of each gift made by the donor in the year whether or not the donor was a resident at the time the gifts were made. *Gift Tax acts*.

AGGREGATE VALUE. The real value of the property at the time of the death, after deducting therefrom the debts and charges then existing and allowed. *Succession Duties Act*, R.S.Q. 1977, c. D-16, s. 15.

AGGREGATION. *n.* Adding together all property passing at death in a single estate to ascertain succession.

AGGRESSOR. *n.* One who begins a quarrel or dispute.

AGGRIEVED. *adj.* Injured; having suffered injury or loss. See PERSON ~.

AGISTER. *n.* A person other than a livery, boarding or sales stable keeper who, for a money consideration or its equivalent, feeds, grazes, stables, boards or cares for animals. *Agisters and Livery Stable Keepers Act*, R.S.N.W.T. 1974, c. A-2, s. 2.

AGISTMENT. *n.* A contract of bailment arising where one person (the agister) takes another person's horses, cattle, or other animals to graze on the agister's land for reward with the implication that the agister will redeliver them to the owner on demand.

AGNATE. *n.* A relative by the father's side.

AGNATION. *n.* Relatedness by the father's side.

AGOMEN. *n.* Nickname; a name which originates in a personal condition or attribute.

AGNOMINATION. *n.* A surname.

AGONAL. *adj.* Relating to the last moments of life. F.A. Jaffe, *A Guide to Pathological Evidence*, 2d ed. (Toronto: Carswell, 1983) at 167.

AGREE. *v.* To concur; to make an agreement.

AGREED. *adj.* Settled.

AGREED CHARGE. A charge agreed on between a carrier and a shipper as provided in this Act and includes the conditions attached thereto. *Transport Act*, R.S.C. 1985, c. T-17, s. 2.

AGREEING PROVINCE. A province that has entered into an agreement with the government of Canada under which the government of Canada will collect taxes payable under that province's income tax statute and will make payments to that province in respect of the taxes so collected. *Provincial Income Tax acts.*

AGREED STATEMENT OF FACTS. A statement of facts relating to evidence to which the parties agree and on which the case will be decided. P.K. McWilliams, *Canadian Criminal Evidence*, 3d ed. (Aurora: Canada Law Book, 1988) at 1-13.

AGREEMENT. *n.* 1. Two or more persons together express a common intention in order to alter their duties and rights. 2. A contract. 3. A collective agreement. See AFFILIATION ~; ALL-UNION ~; ARBITRATION ~; AREA ~; ASSOCIATION ~; ASSUMPTION ~; BACK-TO-WORK ~; BOUNDARY BY ~; COHABITATION ~; COLLECTIVE ~; COLLECTIVE BARGAINING ~; COMPANY-WIDE ~; CREDIT ~; CROP SHARE ~; CULTURAL PROPERTY ~; CUSTODY ~; DEALER ~; FOSTER PARENT ~; GUARDIANSHIP ~; HIRE-PURCHASE ~; INDUSTRY-WIDE ~; INTERGOVERNMENTAL ~; INTERIM ~; LISTING ~; LOAN ~; MANAGEMENT ~; MASTER ~; MEDICAL-SURGICAL SERVICES ~; MEMORANDUM OF ~; NATURAL RESOURCES ~; PAROL ~; PATERNITY ~; POOLING ~; PRELIMINARY ~; PRICE MAINTENANCE ~; PRODUCTIVITY ~; PROVINCIAL ~; PURCHASE ~; RECIPROCAL TAXATION ~; RECIPROCAL TRANSFER ~; RECOGNITION ~; RECREATIONAL ~; REINSURANCE ~; RESIDENTIAL TENANCY ~; SECURITY ~; SEPARATION ~; SOLUS ~; SPECIALIZATION ~; SPOUSAL ~; SUBDIVISION ~; TAX RENTAL ~; TENANCY ~; TIMBER ~; TIME-SHARING ~; TRADE ~; TIME SALE ~; UNANIMOUS SHAREHOLDER ~; UNDERWRITING ~; UNIT ~.

AGREEMENT FOR SALE. A contract for the sale of an interest in land under which the purchaser agrees to pay the purchase price over a period of time, in the manner stated in the contract, and on payment of which the vendor is obliged to convey the interest in land to the purchaser, but does not include a contract under which (a) the purchase price is payable in less than 6 months from the time the contract was entered into, and (b) the purchaser is not, during the 6 month period, entitled to possession of the land that is the subject-matter of the contract. *Law Reform Act*, S.B.C. 1985, c. 10, s. 16.1.

AGREEMENT OF TRANSFER. The agreement made on the twentieth day of March, 1930, between the Government of Canada and the Government of Saskatchewan for the transfer of the natural resources of the province, and set forth in the schedule to chapter 87 of the statutes of 1930, and includes all amendments pursuant thereto. *The Provincial Lands Act*, R.S.S. 1978, c. P-31, s. 2.

AGREEMENT TO SELL. 1. A contract of sale in writing under which (i) an interest in goods may be transferred to a purchaser (A) at a time in the future, or (B) subject to some condition to be fulfilled. 2. A written agreement for the sale of farm produce that is stored or to be stored made between a grain elevator operator and an owner of farm produce. *Grain Elevator Storage Act, 1983*, S.O. 1983, c. 40, s. 1.

AGRICULTURAL. *adj.* Pertaining to agriculture, farming.

AGRICULTURAL AND VOCATIONAL COLLEGE. A college established pursuant to this Act for the purpose of teaching practical and scientific farming, household economy, domestic science and such other subjects as the Board prescribes. *Agricultural and Vocational Colleges Act*, R.S.A. 1970, c. 9, s. 2.

AGRICULTURAL ASSOCIATION. See COOPERATIVE ~; SPECIALIZED ~.

AGRICULTURAL CHEMICAL. Any substance or mixture of substances intended or represented for use, or sold, as a fertilizer, pesticide, plant growth regulator or soil supplement, or any other substance or mixture of substances used to control plant or animal pests or to promote or control plant growth, except drugs and medicines intended for human or veterinary use.

AGRICULTURAL COMMODITY. Any natural or processed product of agriculture.

AGRICULTURAL CORPORATION. A corporation: (i) which is primarily engaged in the business of farming; (ii) of which not less than sixty per cent of all issued voting shares are legally and beneficially owned by farmers who are resident persons; and (iii) of which not less than sixty per cent of all issued shares are legally and beneficially owned by farmers who are resident persons. *The Saskatchewan Farm Ownership Act*, R.S.S. 1978, c. S-17, s. 2.

AGRICULTURAL CREDIT. Financial assistance given to a farm operator. *Agricultural Credit Act*, R.S.B.C. 1979, c. 8, s. 1.

AGRICULTURAL DEVELOPMENT. See SPECIAL ~.

AGRICULTURAL ENTERPRISE. An enterprise or undertaking engaged in production, processing or distribution of food or other agricultural products, or in providing services to the agricultural industry, whether a person, association, partnership, corporation, marketing board, marketing commission, institute or producer or consumer cooperative that (a) qualifies as an agricultural enterprise under this Act and regulations; and (b) is approved by the minister. *Farm Product Industry Act*, R.S.B.C. 1979, c. 124, s. 1.

AGRICULTURAL EQUIPMENT. Implements, apparatus, appliances and machinery, of any kind usually affixed to real property, for use on a farm, but does not include a farm electric system.

AGRICULTURAL EXPLOITATION. A farm, developed by the farmer personally or through employees. Quebec statutes.

AGRICULTURAL FAIR ASSOCIATION. An organization of district, county or provincial scope whose purpose is to hold exhibitions of livestock, poultry, agricultural produce and the products of kindred agricultural and homemaking arts. *Agricultural Associations Act*, R.S.N.B. 1973, s. A-5, s. 1.

AGRICULTURAL FEEDS. Includes all feed for livestock, all hay and straw and any drug or medicine fed to or injected into livestock or poultry. *Retail Sales Tax Act*, R.R.O. 1980, Reg. 904, s. 1.

AGRICULTURAL IMPLEMENT. A vehicle designed and adapted exclusively for agricultural, horticultural or livestock raising operations. *Highway Traffic Act*, S.S. 1986, c. H-3.1, s. 2.

AGRICULTURAL IMPLEMENTS. Tools, implements, apparatus, appliances and machines, of any kind not usually affixed to real property, for use on or in connection with a farm, and vehicles for use in the business of farming and, without restricting the generality of the foregoing, includes plows, harrows, drills, seeders, cultivators, mowing machines, reapers, binders, threshing machines, combines, leaf tobacco tying machines, tractors, movable granaries, trucks for carrying products of agriculture, equipment for bee-keeping, cream separators, churns, washing machines, spraying apparatus, portable irrigation apparatus, incubators, milking machines, refrigerators and heating and cooking appliances for farming operations or use in the farm home of a kind not usually affixed to real property. *Bank Act*, R.S.C. 1985, c. B-1, s. 2.

AGRICULTURAL INDUSTRY. Includes all aspects of the production, processing and distribution of agricultural products and related services. *Farm Product Industry Act*, R.S.B.C. 1979, c. 124, s. 1.

AGRICULTURAL LAND. Land that is zoned for agricultural use, or is assessed or is actually used as farm or agricultural land or as an orchard.

AGRICULTURAL LIMESTONE. Includes pulverized limestone and marl for use on lands. *Agriculture and Marketing Act*, R.S.N.S. 1967, c. 3, s. 101.

AGRICULTURAL OPERATION. The production or any step in the production of livestock, grain, forage crops, poultry, furs, honey or any other agricultural product. See SPECIALIZED ~.

AGRICULTURAL OPERATIONS COOPERATIVE. A cooperative whose main object and principal activity is the operation of an economic farm of which it is the owner or lessee, provided that all of its members are natural persons, that at least sixty per cent of the common shares are owned by farm operators and that the majority of its members are farm operators among whom the principal occupation of the majority is the operation of such farm. Quebec statutes.

AGRICULTURAL OPERATIONS CORPORATION. A corporation whose principal object and principal activity is the operation of an economic farm of which it is the owner or lessee, provided that all of its shareholders are physical persons and that not less than sixty per cent of the issued shares of each class are owned by farm operators among whom the principal occupation of the majority is the operation of such farm. Quebec statutes.

AGRICULTURAL OPERATIONS PARTNER-SHIP. (1) A partnership whose principal object is the joint operation of an economic farm of which it is the owner or lessee, composed of natural persons and in which at least sixty per cent of the interests are owned by one or several farm operators the principal occupation of whom or of the majority of whom is the operation of such farm; or (2) several natural persons who are the undivided owners of an economic farm when at least sixty per cent of the property rights in such farm are held by one or several farm operators the principal occupation of whom or of the majority of whom is the operation of such farm. Quebec statutes.

AGRICULTURAL ORGANIZATION. Includes an agricultural co-operative, agricultural association, agricultural society, agricultural club and any branch or any of them. *Agricultural Committees Act*, R.S.O. 1980, c. 9, s. 1.

AGRICULTURAL PRODUCT. Livestock (including fur—bearing animals raised in captivity), eggs, poultry, milk, vegetables, fruit, honey and maple syrup and products thereof, leaf tobacco, grass seed, legume seed, feed grains and oil seed, fleeces and skins of animals.

AGRICULTURAL SOCIETY. A community group of farmers organized for the general promotion of agriculture within that community. *Agricultural Associations Act*, R.S.N.B. 1973, c. A-5, s. 1.

AGRICULTURAL WASTE. Waste, other than sewage, resulting from farm operations, including animal husbandry and where a farm operation is carried on in respect of food packing, food preserving, animal slaughtering or meat packing, includes the waste from such operations. *Environmental Protection Act*, R.R.O. 1980, Reg. 309, s. 1.

AGRICULTURE. *n.* 1. The cultivation of the soil or the raising of livestock. 2. Includes tillage of the soil, livestock raising, beekeeping, poultry raising, dairying, fruit growing, woodlot management and fur farming. See BUSINESS OF ~; PRODUCTS OF ~.

AGRICULTURE CANADA. The federal government department responsible for programmes, policies and regulations which relate to agriculture and food.

AGRICULTURIST. *n.* A person who uses farm land for agricultural or forestry production. *Pesticides Act*, R.R.O. 1980, Reg. 751, s. 1.

AGROLOGIST. *n.* A person who is qualified to teach or to practise the science and art of agriculture or to conduct scientific experiments and research in relation thereto.

AGROLOGIST IN TRAINING. A person registered as an agrologist in training under an act.

AGROLOGY. *n.* The acquisition or application of scientific knowledge relating to agriculture. See PRACTISE ~.

AGT. *abbr.* The Alberta Government Telephones Commission. *Telecommunications Statutes Amendment Act*, S.A. 1985, c. 52, s. 4.

A.I.C. *abbr.* Affaires d'immigration en appel.

AID. See FIRST- ~; HEARING ~; LEGAL ~; MEDICAL ~; SHELTER ~; SUPPLEMENTARY ~.

AID AND ABET. 1. To be actually or constructively present when a crime is committed. D. Stuart, *Canadian Criminal Law: a treatise*, 2d ed. (Toronto: Carswell, 1987) at 501. 2. To do some act to help or to render aid in the actual perpetration of a crime.

AIDE. See NURSING ~; TEACHING ~.

AID TO NAVIGATION. A buoy, beacon, lighthouse, lightship or any other structure or device installed, built or maintained for the purpose of assisting the navigation of vessels. *Aids to Navigation Protection Regulations*, C.R.C., c. 1403, s. 2.

AIR. *n.* 1. The atmosphere, but does not include the atmosphere in a mine or man-made enclosure that is not open to the weather. 2. Open air not enclosed in a building, structure, machine, chimney, stack or flue. 3. Includes enclosed air. *Environmental Assessment Act*, R.S.O. 1980, c. 140, s. 1. See AMBIENT ~; CARRIAGE BY ~ ACT; COMPRESSED ~; OPEN ~.

AIR AMBULANCE. Ambulance service using aircraft.

AIR-BLAST MACHINE. A pesticide application device utilizing an independent mechanically produced stream of air to assist the carrying of the pesticide beyond the orifice of the device. *Pesticides Act*, R.R.O. 1980, Reg. 751, s. 1.

AIR BRAKE SYSTEM. A system that uses air as a medium for transmitting pressure or force from the driver control to the service brake, but does not include a system that uses compressed air or vacuum only to assist the driver in applying muscular force to hydraulic or mechanical components. *Motor Vehicle Safety Regulations*, C.R.C., c. 1038, s. 2.

AIR BREAK. The unobstructed vertical distance between the lowest point of an indirect drainage system and the flood level rim of the fixture into which it discharges. *Ontario Water Resources Act*, R.R.O. 1980, Reg. 736, s. 1.

AIR CARRIER. Any person who operates a commercial air service. See CANADIAN ~; CERTIFIED ~; FOREIGN ~; FOREIGN NON-SCHEDULED UNIT TOLL ~; FOREIGN SCHEDULED ~; INTERNATIONAL ~.

AIR CONDITIONING. See REFRIGERA-TION AND ~ MECHANIC.

AIR CONTAMINANT. Any solid, liquid, gas or odour or a combination of any of them that, if emitted into the ambient air, would create or contribute to the creation of air pollution.

AIRCRAFT. *n.* Any machine capable of deriving support in the atmosphere from reactions of the air, other than a machine designed to derive support in the atmosphere from reactions against the earth's surface of air expelled from the machine, and includes a rocket. See CANA-DIAN ~; COMMERCIAL ~; DANGEROUS OPERATION OF ~; ESSENTIAL ~ EQUIP-MENT; FALLING ~ INSURANCE; FOREIGN ~; HEAVIER-THAN-AIR ~; INTERNA-TIONAL ~; LIGHTER-THAN-AIR ~; MULTI-ENGINE ~; OVERTAKING ~; PRESSUR-IZED ~; PRIVATE ~; STATE ~; ULTRA-LIGHT ~.

AIRCRAFT ACCIDENT. An occurrence associated with the operation of an aircraft that takes place between the time that any person boards the aircraft with the intention of flight and the time that all such persons have disembarked therefrom, in which (a) any person suffers death or serious injury as a result of being in or upon the aircraft or by direct contact with the aircraft or anything attached thereto, or (b) the aircraft receives substantial damage or is destroyed. *Air Regulations,* C.R.C., c. 2, s, 101.

AIRCRAFT ACCIDENT SITE. The area of land or water where an aircraft accident has occurred and includes any area in which are located the aircraft, any contents from or parts of the aircraft and any cuts, impressions, slashes, tears or other marks in or upon the ground or on any structure, vegetation or other matter located thereon that are made by the aircraft or the contents or parts of the aircraft. *Air Regulations,* C.R.C., c. 2, s. 101.

AIRCRAFT ENGINE. See CANADIAN ~.

AIRCRAFT GASOLINE. Any fuel used for the operation of an aircraft or in the testing of the engine of an aircraft on the ground. *Gasoline Tax Act,* R.S.M. 1970, c. G40, s. 2.

AIRCRAFT INSURANCE. Insurance against loss of or damage to an aircraft and against liability for loss or damage to persons or property caused by an aircraft or by the operation thereof. *Insurance acts.*

AIRCRAFT MATERIAL. Engines, fittings, armament, ammunition, bombs, missiles, gear, instruments and apparatus, used or intended for use in connection with aircraft or the operation thereof, and components and accessories of aircraft and substances used to provide motive power or lubrication for or in connection with aircraft or the operation thereof. *National Defence Act,* R.S.C. 1985, c. N-5, s. 2.

AIR CUSHION VEHICLE. 1. A machine designed to derive support in the atmosphere primarily from reactions against the earth's surface of air expelled from the machine. 2. Hovercraft.

AIR EMBOLISM. Blockage of blood vessels by air bubbles. F.A. Jaffe, *A Guide to Pathological Evidence,* 2d ed. (Toronto: Carswell, 1983) at 175.

AIR GAP. When used with reference to a supply system, means the unobstructed vertical distance through the free atmosphere between (i) the lowest opening from any pipe or faucet supplying water to a tank or fixture, and (ii) the flood level rim of the tank or fixture. *Ontario Water Resources Act,* R.R.O. 1980, Reg. 736, s. 1.

AIR HANDLING SYSTEM. An assembly of connected ducts, plenums or other air passages with associated fittings through which air is conducted, but does not include a cooking exhaust system. *Hotel Fire Safety Act,* R.R.O. 1980, Reg. 505, s. 2.

AIR LETTER. See FORCES ~.

AIR LINE. See COMMERCIAL ~.

AIR LOCK. A chamber designed for the passage of persons or material or both persons and material from one place to another place having a different air pressure. *Occupational Health and Safety Act,* R.R.O. 1980, Reg. 691, s. 240.

AIR POLLUTION. A condition of the ambient air, arising wholly or partly from the presence therein of one or more air contaminants, that endangers the health, safety or welfare of persons, that interferes with normal enjoyment of life or property, that endangers the health of animal life or that causes damage to plant life or to property.

AIR POLLUTION EPISODE. An occasion when air contamination is at such a level and for such a period of time that the air contamination may become the cause of increased human sickness and mortality. *Environmental Protection Act,* R.R.O. 1980, Reg. 308, s. 1.

AIR POLLUTION INDEX. A series of numbers expressing the relative levels of air pollution and taking into consideration one or more air contaminants. *Environmental Protection Act*, R.R.O. 1980, Reg. 308, s. 1.

AIRPORT. *n.* An aerodrome in respect of which a Canadian aviation document is in force. *Aeronautics Act*, R.S.C. 1985 (1st Supp.), c. 33, s. 3. See ALTERNATE ~; CONTROLLED ~; FEDERAL ~; OPEN ~.

AIRPORT LOUNGE. A room in an airport restricted to passengers waiting to board a departing aircraft. *Liquor Licence Act*, R.R.O. 1980, Reg. 581, s. 1.

AIRPORT MANAGER. The Department of Transport official in charge of the airport or that person's duly authorized representative.

AIRPORT SITE. Any land, not being a part of an existing airport, (a) the title of which is vested in or that otherwise belongs to Her Majesty in right of Canada, or (b) in respect of which a notice of intention to expropriate under section 5 of the Expropriation Act has been registered and that is declared by order of the Governor in Council to be required for use as an airport. *Aeronautics Act*, R.S.C. 1985 (1st Supp.), c. 33, s. 5.4.

AIRPORT TRAFFIC. All traffic on the manoeuvring area of an airport or aerodrome and all aircraft flying in the vicinity of an airport or aerodrome.

AIR PRESSURE. See MAXIMUM ~.

AIR QUALITY. See NATIONAL AMBIENT ~ OBJECTIVE.

AIR RACE. See LOW-LEVEL ~.

AIR RAID PRECAUTIONS WORKER. A person registered as a volunteer worker in a designated area by an official body organized for air raid precautions purposes, a duly registered voluntary evacuation worker or a person designated as such by the Commission. *Civilian War Pensions and Allowances Act*, R.S.C. 1985, c. C-31, s. 30.

AIR RECEIVER. A pressure vessel that contains, distributes or otherwise handles air under pressure. *Boilers and Pressure Vessels Act*, R.R.O. 1980, Reg. 84, s. 1.

AIR SAMPLING. See ENVIRONMENTAL MONITORING.

AIR SERVICE. Any air service performed by aircraft for the public transport of passengers, mail or cargo. *An Act respecting the International Air Transport Association*, S.C. 1974-75-76, c. 111, s. 1(a). See COMMERCIAL ~.

AIRSHIP. *n.* A power-driven lighter-than-air aircraft. *Air Regulations*, C.R.C., c. 2, s. 101.

AIR SHOW. An aerial display or demonstration

before an assembly of persons by one or more aircraft. *Special Aviation Events Safety Order*, C.R.C., c. 66, s. 2.

AIRSPACE. *var.* **AIR SPACE.** See CONTROLLED ~; HIGH LEVEL ~; LOW LEVEL ~; MINIMUM ~.

AIR SPACE PARCEL. A volumetric parcel, whether or not occupied in whole or in part by a building or other structure, shown as such in an air space plan. *Land Title Act*, R.S.B.C. 1979, c. 219, s. 135.

AIR-SUPPORTED STRUCTURE. A structure consisting of a pliable membrane which achieves and maintains its shape and support by internal air pressure. *Building Code Act*, R.R.O. 1980, Reg. 87, s. 1.

AIR-TERMINAL. *n.* A pointed tube or rod extending upwards from a conductor. *Lightning Rods Act*, R.R.O. 1980, Reg. 577, s. 1.

AIR-TERMINAL SUPPORT. A device used for the purpose of holding an air-terminal firmly in position. *Lightning Rods Act*, R.R.O. 1980, Reg. 577, s. 1.

AIR TIME. *var.* **AIR-TIME.** In respect of any aircraft, means the period of time commencing when the aircraft leaves the surface of the earth and terminating when the aircraft touches the surface of the earth at the next point of landing. See PRICE OF ~.

AIR-TO-AIR GAIN. At a specified frequency and under specified operating conditions, means the amount, in decibels, by which the sound pressure developed by the hearing aid earphone in the coupler exceeds the sound pressure level in the free field into which the hearing aid or its microphone, if separate, is introduced. *Medical Devices Regulations*, C.R.C., c. 871, s. 1.

AIR TRAFFIC CONTROL CLEARANCE. Authorization by an air traffic control unit for an aircraft to proceed within controlled airspace under specified conditions. *Air Regulations*, C.R.C., c. 2, s. 101.

AIR TRAFFIC CONTROL INSTRUCTION. A directive issued by an air traffic control unit for air traffic control purposes. *Air Regulations*, C.R.C., c. 2, s. 101.

AIR TRAFFIC CONTROL RECORDING. The whole or any part of any recording, transcript or substantial summary of voice communications respecting matters of air traffic control or related matters that take place between any of the following persons, namely, air traffic controllers, aircraft crew members, vehicle operators, flight service station specialists and persons who relay air traffic control messages.

Canadian Aviation Safety Board Act, R.S.C. 1985, c. C-12, s. 36.

AIR TRAFFIC CONTROL SERVICE. A service as specified in Part VI, provided for the purposes of (a) preventing collisions (i) between aircraft, and (ii) on the manoeuvring area between aircraft and obstructions, and (b) expediting and maintaining an orderly flow of air traffic. *Air Regulations*, C.R.C., c. 2, s. 101.

AIR TRAFFIC CONTROL UNIT. (a) An area control centre established to provide air traffic control service to IFR flights, (b) a terminal control unit established to provide air traffic control service to IFR flights operating within a terminal control area, or (c) an airport control tower unit established to provide air traffic control service to airport traffic, as the circumstances require. *Air Regulations*, C.R.C., c. 2, s. 101.

AIR TRANSPORT. The carriage by aeroplanes or rotorcraft of persons or property or mail for hire or reward.

AIR TRANSPORTATION SERVICE. Includes air ambulance service and personnel transportation. *Department of Revenue, Supply and Services Amendment Act, 1982 (No. 2)*, S.S. 1982-83, c. 31, s. 3.

AIR TRANSPORT ENTERPRISE. Includes those persons, corporate bodies and unincorporated bodies, companies, firms, partnerships, societies and associations, now or hereafter operating an air service for public hire, under proper authority, in the transport of passengers, mail or cargo under the flag of a State eligible for membership in the International Civil Aviation Organization. *An Act respecting the International Air Transport Association*, S.C. 1974-75-76, c. 111, s. 1(b).

AIR VENT. An outlet at the upper end of the well casing that allows for equalization of air pressure between the inside of the well casing and the atmosphere, and for the release of gases from the well. *Ontario Water Resources Act*, R.R.O. 1980, Reg. 739, s. 1.

AIRWORTHINESS. See CERTIFICATE OF ~.

AIRWORTHY. *adj.* In respect of an aircraft or aircraft part, in a fit and safe state for flight and in conformity with the standards of airworthiness established by the Minister in respect of that aircraft or aircraft part. *Air Regulations*, C.R.C., c. 2, s. 101.

AISLE. See POURING ~.

ALARM. See SECURITY ~.

ALARM MONITOR. A security employee whose duties are, by his security employee licence, restricted to the monitoring of security alarms. *Miscellaneous Statutes Amendment Act (No. 2)*, S.B.C. 1986, c. 16, s. 37.

ALARM SERVICE. A person who (a) sells, supplies, installs or offers to install security alarms, or (b) repairs, maintains, monitors or responds to security alarms that are installed on the property of another, but no person is an alarm service or carries on an alarm service by reason only that (c) he sells, supplies or provides a security alarm, if he does not, as part of the transaction, visit or inspect the premises on which the security alarm is or has been or is to be installed, or (d) he monitors a security alarm installed on the property of another, if he (i) does so for no fee or other consideration, and (ii) is not otherwise required to be licensed under this Act. *Miscellaneous Statutes Amendment Act (No. 2)*, S.B.C. 1986, c. 16, s. 37.

ALARM SIGNAL. A signal indicating an emergency such as an alarm for fire from a manual box, a water flow alarm, an alarm from an automatic fire alarm system or other emergency signal. *Building Code Act*, R.R.O. 1980, Reg. 87, s. 1. See RADIOTELEGRAPH ~; RADIO-TELEPHONE ~.

ALBERTA. See GOVERNMENT OF ~; LAW OF ~; RESIDENT IN ~; RESIDENT OF ~.

ALBERTA BORDER PRICE. With respect to the term of a federal-provincial agreement or any period during that term, the amount determined as the Alberta border price for the term or that period, as the case may be, under the federal-provincial agreement. *Natural Gas Pricing Agreement Amendment Act, 1981*, S.A. 1981, c. 57, s. 2.

ALBERTA COMPANY. A body corporate incorporated and registered under the Companies Act or any of its predecessors. *Business Corporations Act*, S.A. 1981, c. B-15, s. 1.

ALBERTA CONTRACT. A subsisting contract of insurance that (i) has for its subject (A) property that at the time of the making of the contract is in Alberta or is in transit to or from Alberta, or (B) the life, safety, fidelity or insurable interest of a person who at the time of the making of the contract is resident in, or has its head office in, Alberta, or (ii) makes provision for payment thereunder primarily to a resident of Alberta or to an incorporated company that has its head office in Alberta. *Insurance Act*, R.S.A. 1980, c. I-5, s. 67.

ALBERTA CORPORATION. A corporation incorporated by or pursuant to an Act of the Legislature and which is controlled by residents of Alberta but does not include a non-profit religious corporation. *Nursing Homes Act*, R.S.A. 1980, c. N-14, s. 1.

ALBERTA LAND SURVEYOR. An individual who holds a certificate of registration and an annual certificate to engage in the practice of surveying under this Act. *Land Surveyors Act*, S.A. 1981, s. L-4.1, s. 1.

ALBERTAN. See RESIDENT ~.

ALBERTA RESOURCE PROPERTY. A property that is (i) a right, licence or privilege to explore for, drill for or take petroleum, natural gas or petroleum and natural gas in Alberta, (ii) a petroleum or natural gas well in Alberta, (iii) a rental or royalty computed by reference to the amount or value of production from a petroleum or natural gas well in Alberta, or (iv) a right or interest of any nature whatsoever or howsoever described in any property referred to in subclauses (i) to (iii), including a right to receive proceeds of disposition in respect of a disposition of that property. *Corporate Income Tax Act*, S.A. 1983, c. 2, s. 26.

ALCOHOL. *n.* 1. A product of fermentation or distillation of grains, fruits or other agricultural products rectified once or more than once whatever may be the origin thereof, and includes synthetic ethyl alcohol. 2. Any material or substance, whether in liquid or any other form, containing any proportion by mass or by volume of absolute ethyl alcohol (C_2H_5OH). *Excise Act*, R.S.C. 1985, c. E-14, s. 3. See ABSOLUTE ~; DENATURED ~; ETHYL ~; GRAIN ~; SPECIALLY DENATURED ~; WOOD ~.

ALCOHOL AND DRUG ABUSE. The use of any substance by a person in quantities that creates a condition in the person that is characterized by physical, psychological or social problems. *Alcoholism and Drug Abuse Amendment Act*, S.A. 1985, c. 6, s. 3.

ALCOHOLIC. *n.* A person who suffers from the illness of alcoholism.

ALCOHOLIC BEVERAGES. The five varieties of beverages defined in this section, namely: alcohol, spirits, wine, cider and beer, and every liquid or solid containing alcohol, spirits, wine, cider or beer and capable of being consumed by a human being. Any liquid or solid containing more than one of the five varieties above mentioned is considered as belonging to that variety which has the higher percentage of alcohol, in the following order: alcohol, spirits, wine, cider and beer. *An Act respecting the Commission de Contrôle des Permis D'alcool*, R.S.Q. 1977, c. C-33, s. 2.

ALCOHOLIC LIQUOR. Any alcoholic, spirituous, vinous, fermented or malt liquor, or combination of liquors, and all drinks or drinkable liquids and consumable solids, patented or not, containing three per cent and upwards of alcohol by volume. *Liquor Control Act*, R.S. Nfld. 1973, c. 103, s. 2.

ALCOHOLISM. *n.* 1. Any diseased condition produced by the action of alcohol upon the human system. 2. Any dependent condition produced by the action of alcohol on the human system.

ALDERMAN. *n.* A member of a council of a municipality other than the mayor.

ALEATORY CONTRACT. A contract which depends on an uncertain event or contingency. Raoul Colinvaux, *The Law of Insurance*, 5th ed. (London: Sweet & Maxwell, 1984) at 3.

ALGOR MORTIS. [L.] The cold state of the body after death. F.A. Jaffe, *A Guide to Pathological Evidence*, 2d ed. (Toronto: Carswell, 1983) at 168.

ALIA ENORMIA. [L.] Other wrongs.

ALIAS. *n.* A name by which a person is known.

ALIAS DICTUS. [L.] Otherwise called.

ALIAS WRIT. A replacement for an earlier writ which has been lost or has become ineffectual.

ALIBI. *n.* A denial that the accused committed the crime. P.K. McWilliams, *Canadian Criminal Evidence*, 3d ed. (Aurora: Canada Law Book, 1988) at 28-32.

ALIEN. *v.* To transfer; to convey.

ALIEN. *n.* 1. At common law, the subject of a foreign government who was not born within the allegiance of the Crown. 2. A person who is not a Canadian citizen, Commonwealth citizen, British subject or citizen of the Republic of Ireland. *Canadian Citizenship Act*, R.S.C. 1970, c. C-19, s. 2. See ENEMY ~; NON-RESIDENT ~.

ALIENABILITY. *n.* The quality of being transferable.

ALIENATE. *v.* 1. To transfer; to convey. 2. To transfer property.

ALIENATED. *adj.* Includes (a) alienated by disposition by a railway company whether by severance, sale, agreement for sale, deed, lease, licence, agreement to lease or license, or by any other form of agreement or method by which any part of the title or right of occupancy or use is transferred to a person or by which the right to use or sever timber is transferred to a person; and (b) used by the railway company for other than railroad purposes. *Esquimalt and Nanaimo Railway Belt Act*, R.S.B.C. 1979, c. 112, s. 1.

ALIENATIO LICET PROHIBEATUR, CON-SENSU TAMEN OMNIUM IN FAVOREM QUORUM PROHIBITA EST POTEST FIERI. [L.] Although alienation is prohibited, those in whose interests it is prohibited may consent to it.

ALIENATION. *n.* The transfer or conveyance of property to another. See RESTRAINT ON ~.

ALIENATION IN MORTMAIN. The transfer of tenements or lands to any corporation.

ALIENATIO REI PREFERTUR JURI ACCRESCENDI. [L.] The law prefers alienation to the accumulation of property.

ALIENEE. *n.* One to whom property is transferred.

ALIEN FRIEND. The subject of an enemy government who resides in Canada. J.G. McLeod, *The Conflict of Laws* (Calgary: Carswell, 1983) at 64.

ALIENI JURIS. [L.] Under the power of someone else, as opposed to sui juris.

ALIEN NEE. One who is born an alien.

ALIENOR. *n.* A person who transfers property.

ALIGNMENT AND BRAKES MECHANIC. A person engaged in the repair and maintenance of motor vehicles who, (i) tests for and corrects faulty alignment of wheels, axles, frames and steering mechanisms including wheel balancing, and (ii) adjusts, disassembles, repairs and reassembles foundation brake systems, and controls and components pertaining to them. *Apprenticeship and Tradesmen's Qualification Act*, R.R.O. 1980, Reg. 21, s. 1.

ALII PER ALIUM NON ACQUIRITUR OBLIGATIO. [L.] One person cannot incur a liability through another.

ALIMENTARY. *adj.* Protective.

ALIMONY. *n.* Includes a sum made payable for the maintenance of a wife, former wife, husband, former husband or a child pursuant to a judgment of divorce, nullity of marriage or judicial separation. *Maintenance Orders Enforcement acts.*

ALIO INTUITU. [L.] With another motive.

ALIQUID CONCEDITUR NE INJURIA REMANEAT IMPUNITA, QUOD ALIAS NON CONCEDITUR. [L.] Something is conceded, which would otherwise not be conceded, so that an injury will be punished.

ALIQUIS NON DEBET ESSE JUDEX IN PROPRIA CAUSA QUIA NON POTEST ESSE JUDEX ET PARS. [L.] No one man should judge their cause, because a person cannot be judge and a party at the same time.

ALITER. [L.] Otherwise.

ALIUD EST CELARE, ALIUD TACERE. [L.] Silence is one thing, concealment another.

ALIUD EST POSSIDERE, ALIUD ESSE IN POSSESSIONE. [L.] To possess is one thing, and to be in possession another.

ALIUNDE. [L.] From some other place or person.

ALIVE. *adj.* Electrically connected to a source of potential difference, or electrically charged so as to have a potential different from that of the earth. *Power Corporation Act*, R.R.O. 1980, Reg. 794, s. 0.

ALKALI. *n.* Includes sodium hydroxide, potassium hydroxide, ammonia and ammonium hydroxide and any combination thereof. *Hazardous Products (Hazardous Substances) Regulations*, C.R.C., c. 926, s. 2.

ALKALI METAL AMALGAM. A combination of sodium metal or potassium metal with mercury. *Chlor-Alkali Mercury National Emission Standards Regulations*, C.R.C., c. 406, s. 2.

ALLEGANS CONTRARIA NON EST AUDIENDUS. [L.] One who makes inconsistent statements should not be heard.

ALLEGANS SUAM TURPITUDINEM NON EST AUDIENDA. [L.] A person alleging personal infamy should not be heard.

ALLEGARI NON DEBUIT QUOD PROBATUM NON RELEVAT. [L.] Whatever would be irrelevant if proved should not be heard.

ALLEGATA ET PROBATA. [L.] Things alleged and proved.

ALLEGATIO CONTRA FACTUM NON EST ADMITTENDA. [L.] An allegation contrary to that which a person has made in a deed is not permitted.

ALLEGATION. *n.* Assertion.

ALLEGE. *v.* To state, assert. See MIS~.

ALLEGIANCE. *n.* Obedience owed to the sovereign or government. See OATH OF ~.

ALLEGIARE. To justify or defend by due course of law.

ALL E.R. *abbr.* All England Law Reports.

ALLER SANS JOUR. [Fr.] To go without day.

ALLEVIARE. To pay or levy an accustomed fine.

ALLEY. *n.* 1. A narrow highway intended chiefly to give access to the rear of buildings and parcels of land. *Highway Traffic Act*, R.S.A. 1980, c. H-7, s. 1. 2. A highway that is not more than 9 metres wide. *The Highway Traffic Act*, S.M. 1985-86, c. 3, s. 223(4).

ALL FOURS. A phrase to describe cases which agree in all their circumstances.

ALLIANCE. *n.* 1. A league. 2. Relation by marriage or any form of blood relationship.

ALLIED TRADES FEDERATION. An organization of unions or union locals in the same industry formed to co-ordinate the activities of members.

ALLISION. *n.* One vessel running against another.

ALLOCATED LAND. Public land allocated for occupation by a settlement association. *Metis Betterment Act*, R.S.A. 1980, c. M-14, s. 1.

ALLOCATED PRODUCTION. Oil or gas authorized by the minister to be produced. *The Oil and Gas Conservation Act*, R.S.S. 1978, c. O-2, s. 2.

ALLOCATED RETAINED EARNINGS. Earnings which have been retained by a credit union in any form wherein the extent of each member's interest in the retained earnings is or can be identified. *Credit Union Act*, S.S. 1984-85-86, c. C-45-1, s. 2.

ALLOCATION. *n.* Appropriation or assignment of funds to particular purposes or people.

ALLOCATION IN PROPORTION TO BORROWING. For a taxation year means an amount credited by a credit union to a person who was a member of the credit union in the year on terms that the member is entitled to or will receive payment thereof, computed at a rate in relation to (i) the amount of interest payable by the member on money borrowed from the credit union, or (ii) the amount of money borrowed by the member from the credit union, if the amount was credited at the same rate in relation to the amount of interest or money, as the case may be, as the rate at which amounts were similarly credited for the year to all other members of the credit union of the same class. *Income Tax Act*, R.S.C. 1952, c. 148 (as am. S.C. 1980-81-82-83, c. 48, s. 78 (3), (4)), s. 137(6)(a).

ALLOCATION IN PROPORTION TO PATRONAGE. For a taxation year means an amount credited by a taxpayer to a customer of that year on terms that the customer is entitled to or will receive payment thereof, computed at a rate in relation to the quantity, quality or value of the goods or products acquired, marketed, handled, dealt in or sold, or services rendered by the taxpayer from, on behalf of or to the customer, whether as principal or as agent of the customer or otherwise, with appropriate differences in the rate for different classes, grades or qualities therof, if (i) the amount was credited (A) within the year or within 12 months thereafter, and (B) at the same rate in relation to quantity, quality or value aforesaid as the rate at which amounts were similarly credited to all other customers of that year who were members or to all other customers of that year, as the case may be, with appropriate differences aforesaid for different classes, grades or qualities, and (ii) the prospect that amounts would be so credited was held forth by the taxpayer to his customers of that year who were members or non-member customers of that year, as the case may be. *Income Tax Act*, R.S.C. 1952, c. 148 (as am. S.C. 1970-71-72, c. 63), c. 135(4)(a).

ALLOCATUR. [L.] It is allowed.

ALLOCUTUS. *n.* The unsworn statement of an accused at trial.

ALLODARII. *n.* [L.] Tenants having as great an estate as subjects can enjoy; owners of allodial lands.

ALLODIAL LANDS. *var.* **ALODIAL LANDS.** Lands held absolutely and not the estate of any lord or superior.

ALLOGRAPH. *n.* A document not written by any of the parties to the document.

ALLONGE. *n.* A slip of paper annexed to a bill of exchange to accommodate endorsements.

ALLOT. *v.* 1. To indicate that something should belong solely to a specific person. 2. To appropriate shares to those who applied for them.

ALL OTHER PERILS. Includes only perils similar in kind to the perils specifically mentioned in the policy. *Marine Insurance Act*, R.S.N.B. 1973, s. M-1, s. 31.

ALLOTMENT. *n.* 1. Distribution of land. 2. The portion of land distributed. 3. A corporation's acceptance of an offer to purchase shares. S.M. Beck *et al.*, *Cases and Materials on Partnerships and Canadian Business Corporations*, (Toronto: The Carswell Company Limited, 1983) at 790. 4. The total number of dozens of eggs that a producer is entitled to market in intraprovincial, interprovincial and export trade pursuant to the Canadian Egg Marketing Agency Quota Regulations and the order made by the Commodity Board under the Plan. *Ontario Egg Marketing Levies Order*, C.R.C., c. 182, s. 1. 5. A basic allotment or a market allotment, or both. *Canadian Turkey Marketing Quota Regulations*, C.R.C., c. 661, s. 2. 6. An application for shares providing that the applicant takes a specified quantity of shares or a smaller amount if allotted or the board of director's acceptance, by resolution, of such an application of shares. H. Sutherland, D.B. Horsley & J.M. Edmiston, eds., *Fraser's Handbook on Canadian Company Law*, 7th ed. (Toronto: Carswell, 1985) at 108. See BASIC ~.

ALLOTMENT CERTIFICATE. (a) A document issued by the Agency to a producer certifying the allotment allotted to him, or (b) a list issued by the Agency containing the names of producers and certifying the allotment of each producer whose name is on the list. *Canadian Turkey Marketing Quota Regulations*, C.R.C., c. 661, s. 2.

ALLOW. *v.* To permit; to admit something is valid.

ALLOWABLE. *adj.* When the term is used in connection with a well, means the amount of oil or gas a well is permitted to produce after application of any applicable penalty factor. See BASE ~.

ALLOWABLE ANNUAL CUT. A rate of timber harvesting specified for an area of land. *Forest Act*, R.S.B.C. 1979, c. 140, s. 1. See ANNUAL ALLOWABLE CUT.

ALLOWABLE BEARING PRESSURE. The maximum pressure that may be safely applied to a soil or rock by the foundation unit considered in design under expected loading and subsurface conditions. *Building Code Act*, R.R.O. 1980, Reg. 87, s. 1.

ALLOWABLE BUSINESS INVESTMENT LOSS. Of a taxpayer for a taxation year from the disposition of any property is 3/4 of his business investment loss for the year from the disposition of that property. *Income Tax Act*, R.S.C. 1952, c. 148 (as am. S.C. 1988, c. 55, s. 19), s. 38(c).

ALLOWABLE CAPITAL LOSS. Of a taxpayer for a taxation year from the disposition of any property is 3/4 of his capital loss for the year from the disposition of that property. *Income Tax Act*, R.S.C. 1952, c. 148 (as am. S.C. 1988, c. 55, s. 19), s. 38(b).

ALLOWABLE CUT. See ALLOWABLE ANNUAL CUT; ANNUAL ~.

ALLOWABLE DISTRIBUTION SYSTEM PRESSURE. The maximum pressure at which rural gas distribution systems may be operated as prescribed by the appropriate licences under the Pipeline Act and by the regulations under the Gas Protection Act. *Rural Gas Act*, R.S.A. 1980, c. R-19, s. 1.

ALLOWABLE EXPENDITURES. Expenditures made in relation to an interest that are approved by the Minister. *Oil and Gas Act*, R.S.C. 1985, c. O-6, s. 2.

ALLOWABLE LOAD. The maximum load that may be safely applied to a foundation unit considered in design under expected loading and subsurface conditions. *Building Code Act*, R.R.O. 1980, Reg. 87, s. 1.

ALLOWABLE PRODUCTION. Oil or gas authorized by the minister to be produced. *The Oil and Gas Conservation Act*, R.S.S. 1978, c. O-2, s. 2.

ALLOWANCE. *n.* 1. A limited predetermined sum of money paid to enable the recipient to provide for certain kinds of expenses; its amount is determined in advance and, once paid, it is at the complete disposition of the recipient who is not required to account for it. *The Queen v. Pascoe*, [1975] C.T.C. 58, 75 D.T.C. 5427 (Fed. C.A.). 2. Any discount, rebate, price concession or other advantage that is or purports to be offered or granted for advertising or display purposes and is collateral to a sale or sales of products but is not applied directly to the selling price. *Combines Investigation Act*, R.S.C. 1985, c. C-34, s. 51. 3. Compensation payable (i) in respect of a position, or in respect of some of the positions in a class, by reason of duties of a special nature, or (ii) for duties that an employee is required to perform in addition to the duties of his position. *Public Service Act*, R.S.N.W.T. 1974, c. P-13, s. 2. See BASIC ~; DEPLETION ~; FAMILY ~; FLOATING ~; NET ~; RETIRING ~; ROAD ~; SOCIAL ~; SPECIAL ~; SPOUSE'S ~; SUBSISTENCE ~; SUPERANNUATION ~; TRADE-IN ~; TREATMENT ~; UNEARNED ~; VALUATION ~.

ALLOWANCE PRICE. The contract price per litre of heating oil sold for domestic purposes in Alberta less the domestic heating oil allowance. *Fuel Oil Administration Act*, R.S.A. 1980, c. F-21, s. 16.

ALLOWANCES FOR DOUBTFUL LOANS. The allowance that is made for the estimated loss that a credit union is likely to experience as a result of doubtful loans. *Credit Union Act*, S.S. 1984-85-86, c. C-45-1, s. 2.

ALLOWED TIME. The time allowed for faulty material, tool care, rest periods in connection with incentive wage plans.

ALLOY. *n.* When applied to steel, means steel that contains one or more of the following elements in the quantity, by weight, respectively indicated: (a) over 1.65 per cent of manganese; (b) over 0.25 per cent of phosphorus; (c) over 0.35 per cent of sulphur; (d) over 0.60 per cent of silicon; (e) over 0.60 per cent of copper; (f) over 0.30 per cent of aluminum; (g) over 0.20 per cent of chromium; (h) over 0.30 per cent of cobalt; (i) over 0.35 per cent of lead; (j) over

0.50 per cent of nickel; (k) over 0.30 per cent of tungsten; or (l) over 0.10 per cent of any other metallic element. *Customs Tariff*, R.S.C. 1985, c. C-54, s. 2. See LEAD ~; LIGHT METAL ~.

ALL PROPER COSTS AND EXPENSES. Costs limited to the tariff scale and to party-and-party costs. M.M. Orkin, *The Law of Costs*, 2d ed. (Aurora: Canada Law Book, 1987) at 1-13.

ALL-RISK INSURANCE. Insurance against loss in respect of an insured crop caused by drought, flood, hail, wind, frost, lightning, excessive rain, snow, hurricane, tornado, wild life, insect infestation, plant disease or any other peril designated by the board of regulation published in The Saskatchewan Gazette; and for the purpose of this clause "wild life" means ducks, geese, sandhill cranes, deer, elks, antelope or bears. *The Saskatchewan Crop Insurance Act*, R.S.S. 1978, c. S-12, s. 2.

ALL RISKS. In a contract of insurance, may be used to refer to the quantum of loss, covering the actual amount of the loss but not necessarily insuring against all casualties. Raoul Colinvaux, *The Law of Insurance*, 5th ed. (London: Sweet & Maxwell, 1984) at 68.

ALL-ROUND LIGHT. A light showing an unbroken light over an arc of the horizon of 360 degrees. *Collision Regulations*, C.R.C., c. 1416, Rule 3.

ALL TERRAIN VEHICLE. *var.* **ALL-TERRAIN VEHICLE.** 1. Any motor vehicle designed or adapted for off-road use. 2. A wheeled or tracked motor vehicle designed for travel primarily on unprepared surfaces such as open country and marshland. 3. Dirt bikes, dune buggies, motorized snow vehicles and amphibious machines. 4. A self-propelled vehicle designed to be driven, (i) exclusively on snow or ice, or both, or (ii) on land and water.

ALL-UNION AGREEMENT. Collective agreement under which employer agrees to a closed shop.

ALLUREMENT. *n.* An object which attracts. J.V. DiCastri, *Occupiers' Liability* (Vancouver: Burroughs/Carswell, 1980) at 111.

ALLUVION. *n.* An addition to existing land formed when sand and earth wash up from the sea or a river.

ALLY. *n.* 1. A nation which has entered into an alliance. 2. Includes a person who, in the board's opinion, in combination, in concert or in accordance with a common understanding with the employer assists him in a lockout or in resisting a lawful strike. *Labour Code*, R.S.B.C. 1979, c. 212, s. 85.

ALMS. *n.* Charitable donations.

ALMSHOUSE. *n.* A house where poor people may live free of charge.

ALODY. *n.* Land which may be inherited.

ALTA. *abbr.* Alberta.

ALTA. L. REV. *abbr.* Alberta Law Review.

ALTA. L.R. *abbr.* Alberta Law Reports, 1908-1932.

ALTA. L.R.B.R. *abbr.* Alberta Labour Relations Board Reports.

ALTA. L. REV. *abbr.* Alberta Law Review.

ALTA. L.R. (2d). *abbr.* Alberta Law Reports, Second Series, 1977-.

ALTA PRODITIO. [L.] High treason.

ALTA TENURA. [L.] Highest or free tenure.

ALTER. *v.* 1. To change in any manner. 2. To restore, renovate, repair or disturb. 3. To create, add to, vary and delete.

ALTERATION. *n.* 1. Replacement, removal or addition, a change. 2. Addition or erasure. 3. The structural alterations to the exterior or interior of any building or structure that are designed to improve, modernize or increase the usefulness of any building or structure and includes the (a) purchase of material for any such purpose, (b) relocation of any equipment, and (c) alteration of plumbing, heating, ventilating, water supply or air conditioning systems or parts thereof. See DETRIMENTAL VARIATION OR ~; MAJOR ~; STRUCTURAL ~; STRUCTURAL ~S OR STRUCTURALLY ALTERED; SUBSTANTIAL ~.

ALTERED. *adj.* Changed.

ALTER EGO. [L.] Second self.

ALTERIUS CIRCUMVENTIO ALII NON PRAEBET ACTIONEM. [L.] A fraud successful on one person does not allow another to bring an action.

ALTERNAT. *n.* A custom among diplomats by which the places and rank of different powers who have similar rights and claims to precedence are varied occasionally, either by lot or in a certain regular order. In some treaties and conventions, it is customary for the parties to change place in the preamble and the signatures, so that each power holds, in the copy which will be delivered to it, first place.

ALTERNATE AIRPORT. An aerodrome specified in a flight plan to which a flight may proceed when a landing at the intended destination becomes inadvisable. *Air Regulations*, C.R.C., c. 2, s. 101.

ALTERNATIVA PETITIO NON EST AUDIENDA. [L.] An alternate petition will not be heard.

ALTERNATIVE. *n.* One of several possibilities.

ALTERNATIVE DISPUTE RESOLUTION. A term for processes such as arbitration, conciliation, mediation and settlement, designed to settle disputes without formal trials.

ALTERNATIVE FUEL. Natural gas and any product obtained therefrom that is capable of being used as a fuel and coal and any product obtained therefrom that is capable of being so used. *Energy Supplies Emergency Act*, R.S.C. 1985, c. E-9, s. 22(3).

ALTERNATIVE MEASURES. Measures other than judicial proceedings under this Act used to deal with a young person alleged to have committed an offence. *Young Offenders Act*, R.S.C. 1985, c. Y-1, s. 2.

ALTIMETER SETTING REGION. A low level airspace designated and defined as such in the Designated Airspace Handbook. *Altimeter Setting Procedures Order*, C.R.C., c. 33, s. 2.

ALTITUDE. *n.* The altitude indicated on an altimeter set to the current altimeter setting in accordance with the requirements of the Altimeter Setting Procedures Order. *Cruising Altitudes Order*, C.R.C., c. 39, s. 2. See CRUISING ∼.

ALTO ET BASSO. [L.] High and low.

ALTUM MARE. [L.] The high sea.

ALUMINUM-SHEATHED CABLE. A cable consisting of one or more conductors of approved type assembled into a core and covered with a liquid-and-gas-tight sheath of aluminum or aluminum alloy. *Power Corporation Act*, R.R.O. 1980, Reg. 794, s. 0.

ALUMNI ASSOCIATION. An association of graduates of a university.

ALUMNUS. *n.* [L.] A person educated at a university or college.

A.M. *abbr.* 1. [L. ante meridiem] Before noon. 2. Amplitude modulation. *Radio Broadcasting regulations*.

AMALGAM. See ALKALI METAL ∼.

AMALGAMATED ASSOCIATION. An association formed by an amalgamation of cooperative associations that is confirmed by the issuance of a certificate of amalgamation. *Canada Cooperative Associations Act*, R.S.C. 1985, c. C-40, s. 129.

AMALGAMATED COMPANY. A company that results from an amalgamation.

AMALGAMATION. *n.* A term describing various ways the interests of two or more companies may unite. H. Sutherland, D.B. Horsley & J.M. Edmiston, eds., *Fraser's Handbook on Canadian Company Law*, 7th ed. (Toronto: Carswell, 1985) at 513. See STATUTORY ∼.

AMALGAMATION OR RECONSTRUCTION. An arrangement pursuant to which an association (in this subsection called "the transferor association") transfers or sells or proposes to transfer or sell to any other association (in this subsection called "the transferee association"), the whole or a subtantial part of the business and assets of the transferor association for a consideration consisting in whole or in part of shares, debentures or other securities of the transferee association and, either any part of such consideration is proposed to be distributed among members or shareholders of the transferor association of any class, or the transferor association proposes to cease carrying on the business or part of its business so sold or transferred or proposed to be sold or transferred. *Canada Cooperative Associations Act*, R.S.C. 1985, c. C-40, s. 125(6).

AMANUENSIS. *n.* A person who writes or copies on another's behalf.

AMATEUR. *n.* When used in respect of a natural person, means a person who has not at any time, (i) entered or competed in any athletic contest or exhibition for a staked bet, private or public money or gate receipts, or received any consideration for his services as an athlete except merchandise or an order for merchandise not exceeding $35 in value, or reasonable travelling and living expenses actually incurred while going to, remaining at, and returning from, the place of contest or exhibition, (ii) taught, pursued or assisted in the pursuit of any athletics as a means of livelihood, (iii) sold or pledged his prizes, or (iv) promoted or managed an athletic contest or exhibition for personal gain. *Athletics Control Act*, R.R.O. 1980, Reg. 76, s. 1.

AMATEUR. *adj.* When used in respect of an athletic association, club, corporation, league or unincorporated organization, means that the association, club, corporation, league or unincorporated organization is composed of amateurs or is ordinarily recognized as being composed of amateurs. *Athletics Control Act*, R.R.O. 1980, Reg. 76, s. 1.

AMATEUR ATHLETIC ASSOCIATION. See REGISTERED CANADIAN ∼.

AMATEUR SPORT. 1. Any athletic activity

that is engaged in solely for recreation, fitness or pleasure and not as a means of livelihood. 2. Sport in which the participants receive no remuneration for their services as participants. *Combines Investigation Act*, R.S.C. 1985, c. C-34, s. 6(2). See FITNESS AND ~ CANADA.

AMBASSADOR. *n.* A diplomatic agent representing a foreign government. J.G. McLeod, *The Conflict of Laws* (Calgary: Carswell, 1983) at 76.

AMBER. See FOSSIL ~.

AMBIDEXTER. *n.* One who takes bribes from both sides.

AMBIENT AIR. The atmosphere surrounding the earth but does not include the atmosphere within a structure or within any underground space. See NATIONAL ~ QUALITY OBJECTIVE.

AMBIGUA RESPONSIO CONTRA PROFERENTEM EST ACCIPIENDA. [L.] An ambiguous response is interpreted against the person who makes it.

AMBIGUIS CASIBUS SEMPER PRAESUMITUR PRO REGE. [L.] In doubtful cases, the presumption is always in favour of the Crown.

AMBIGUITAS VERBORUM LATENS VERIFICATIONE SUPPLETUR, NAM QUOD EX FACTO ORITUR AMBIGUUM VERIFICATIONE FACTI TOLLITUR. [L.] A latent ambiguity in wording may be explained by evidence; for whatever ambiguity arises on evidence extrinsic to an instrument may be removed by similar evidence.

AMBIGUITAS VERBORUM PATENS NULLA VERIFICATIONE EXCLUDITUR. [L.] A patent ambiguity in the wording of a written instrument may not be cleared up by extrinsic evidence.

AMBIGUITY. *n.* Doubtfulness; double meaning; obscurity. See PATENT ~.

AMBIGUUM PLACITUM INTERPRETARI DEBET CONTRA PROFERENTEM. [L.] An ambiguous pleading should be interpreted against the party who prepares it.

AMBIT. *n.* Limit; the bounds encompassing any thing.

AMBULANCE. *n.* A conveyance that is used, or intended to be used, for the purpose of transporting persons requiring medical attention or under medical care, and that is designed and constructed, or equipped, for that purpose. See AIR ~.

AMBULANCE ATTENDANT. A person who is employed or engaged, with or without remuneration, on a full-time or part-time basis, to attend and assist patients while they are receiving ambulance services.

AMBULANCE DRIVER. A person who is employed or engaged, with or without remuneration, on a full-time or part-time basis, to drive or pilot an ambulance vehicle while it is being used to provide ambulance services.

AMBULANCE SERVICE. The service of transporting a patient by means of an ambulance vehicle, and may include the service of carrying the patient into and out of the ambulance vehicle and the service of attending and assisting the patient while being so transported or carried.

AMBULANCE SERVICE INDUSTRY. Every establishment where ambulance services are carried out, and includes ambulance drivers, drivers' helpers and first-aid attendants employed in the operation of ambulance services. *Employment Standards Act*, R.R.O. 1980, Reg. 281, s. 1.

AMBULANCE SERVICES PROGRAM. A system for making ambulance services available to a community and includes the ambulance vehicles and other equipment necessary to the provision of the ambulance services. *The Ambulance Services Act*, S.M. 1985-86, c. 7, s. 1.

AMBULANCE VEHICLE. Any motor vehicle or aircraft that is used for the transportation of patients and that is specifically designed, constructed and equipped for that purpose. *The Ambulance Services Act*, S.M. 1985-86, c. 7, s. 1.

AMBULATORIA EST VOLUNTAS DEFUNCTI USQUE AD VITAE SUPREMUM EXITUM. [L.] The will of a deceased person is movable until the last moment of life.

AMBULATORY. *adj.* 1. The ability of a person to move about without the assistance of mechanical aids or devices and without assistance from another person. *Homes for Special Care Act*, S.N.S. 1976, c. 12, s. 2. 2. Able to be altered or revoked. See SEMI-~.

AMBULATORY BUSINESS. A business with no fixed head office.

AMELIORATING WASTE. Acts which improve an inheritance, even though they technically amount to waste.

AMENABLE. *adj.* Capable of being led; tractable; responsible or subject to.

AMEND. *v.* To modify, vary or discharge.

AMENDING CLAUSE. Amending procedures for the Constitution absent from the B.N.A. Act but supplied by the Constitution Act, 1982.

AMENDING FORMULA. See DOMESTIC ~.

AMENDMENT. *n.* 1. Alteration. 2. Deletion, addition or modification. See ARTICLES OF ~.

AMENDS. *n.* Satisfaction.

AMENITY. *n.* A feature adding to enjoyment of property. See LOSS OF AMENITIES.

A MENSA ET THORO. [L.] From board and bed.

AMENTIA. *n.* Insanity.

AMERCIAMENT. *var.* **AMERCEMENT.** *n.* Pecuniary penalty, at a court's discretion.

AMERICAN FEDERATION OF LABOUR. A federation of labour unions joined to the CIO.

AMERICAN PLAICE. A fish of the species Hippoglossoides platessoides (Fab.). *Northwest Atlantic Fisheries Regulations*, C.R.C., c. 860, s. 2.

AMI. *n.* [Fr.] Friend.

AMICUS CURIAE. [L.] Friend of the court.

AMIDSHIPS. *adv.* or *adj.* 1. At the middle of the length. 2. The mid-point of the length of a fishing vessel. *Small Fishing Vessel Inspection Regulations*, C.R.C., c. 1486, s. 2. 3. The middle of the length between the perpendiculars. *Hull Construction Regulations*, C.R.C., c. 1431, Schedule 1, s. 11. 4. The middle of the length of the summer load waterline as defined in subsection (2). *General Load Line Rules*, C.R.C., c. 1425, Schedule 1, s. 1.

AMITTERE CURIAM. [L. to lose court] To be forbidden to attend court.

AMITTERE LEGEM TERRAE. [L.] To lose the law of the land.

AMITTERE LIBERAM LEGEM. [L.] To lose the liberty of being sworn in court.

AMMONIA. See ANHYDROUS ~.

AMMONIA NITROGEN. The nitrogen in ammonia that results from the operation of a plant and that is contained in the effluent from that plant.

AMMONIUM NITRATE. The chemical compound NH_4NO_3 in granular, prilled, flake, crystalline or other solid form. *Ammonium Nitrate Storage Facilities Regulations*, C.R.C., c. 1145, s. 2.

AMMUNITION. *n.* An explosive of any class when enclosed in a case or contrivance or otherwise adapted or prepared so as to form a cartridge or charge for small arms, cannon, any other weapon or blasting, or so as to form any safety or other fuse for blasting or shells or so as to form any tube for firing explosives or so as to form a percussive cap, detonator, shell, torpedo, war rocket or other contrivance other than a firework. See CENTRE FIRE ~; SHIP'S ~; WADCUTTER ~.

AMNESTY. *n.* A government grant of general pardon for past offences.

AMNIOTIC FLUID. Liquid in which the fetus is suspended in the amniotic sac. F.A. Jaffe, *A Guide to Pathological Evidence*, 2d ed. (Toronto: Carswell, 1983) at 168.

AMNIOTIC FLUID EMBOLISM. An embolism formed from the solid elements of amniotic fluid. F.A. Jaffe, *A Guide to Pathological Evidence*, 2d ed. (Toronto: Carswell, 1983) at 175.

AMORTIZATION. *var.* **AMORTISATION.** *n.* 1. Reduction of the amount owing under a mortgage or debt by instalment payments. 2. Of a blended payment mortgage, the period of time needed to pay all the principal and interest, assuming fixed monthly payments. D.J. Donahue & P.D. Quinn, *Real Estate Practice in Ontario*, 4th ed. (Toronto: Butterworths, 1990) at 227.

AMORTIZED VALUE. When used in relation to the value of a redeemable security at any date after purchase, means a value so determined that, if the security were purchased at that date and at that value, the yield would be the same as the yield would be with reference to original purchase price.

AMOTION. *n.* Removal.

AMOUNT. *n.* 1. Money expressed in terms of the quantity of money. 2. Rights or things expressed in terms of the money value of the rights or things. 3. In respect of a contract, means the consideration to be given by the contracting authority under the terms of the contract, whether the consideration is fixed or estimated. *Government Contracts Regulations*, C.R.C., c. 701, s. 2. See ACQUISITION COST ~; COST ~; DEDUCTIBLE ~; DEFERRED ~; DEPOSITED ~; LOAN ~; MEDIAN ~; PER CAPITA ~; PRINCIPAL ~; REASONABLE ~ FOR A RESERVE.

AMOUNT CHARGED. In respect of a taxable service, means any amount paid or payable by a person for the taxable service, before any amount paid or payable in respect of any tax under this Part of imposed under an Act of the legislature of a province respecting retail sales tax is added thereto. *Excise Tax Act*, R.S.C. 1985 (1st Supp.), c. 15, s. 21.1.

AMOUNT CONTRIBUTED. A contribution by the taxpayer to a registered party or an officially nominated candidate in the form of cash or in the form of a negotiable instrument issued by the taxpayer, but does not include (a) a contribution made by an official agent of an officially nominated candidate or a registered agent of a registered party (in his capacity as such official agent or registered agent, as the case may be) to another such official agent or registered agent, as the case may be; or (b) a contribution in respect of which the taxpayer has received or is entitled to receive a financial benefit of any kind (other than a prescribed financial benefit or a deduction pursuant to subsection (3)) from a government, municipality or other public authority, whether as a grant, subsidy, forgivable loan or deduction from tax or an allowance or otherwise. *Income Tax Act*, R.S.C. 1952, c. 148 (as am. S.C. 1984, c. 1, s. 72(1)), s. 127(4.1).

AMOUNT DUE ON THE JUDGMENT. Includes the costs incurred subsequently to those forming part of the judgment, and which may be recovered by an execution issued upon the judgment. *Collection Act*, R.S.N.S. 1967, s. 39, s. 1.

AMOUNT PAID OUT. That portion of a pool determined by multiplying the pay-out price of each pari-mutuel ticket by the number of such tickets. *Race Track Supervision Regulations*, C.R.C., c. 441, s. 2.

AMOUNT PAYABLE. 1. Any or all of (a) an amount payable under this Act by the person; (b) an amount payable under the Unemployment Insurance Act, 1971 by the person; (c) an amount payable under the Canada Pension Plan by the person; and (d) an amount payable by the person under an Act of a province with which the Minister of Finance has entered into an agreement for the collection of taxes payable to the province under that Act. *Income Tax Act*, R.S.C. 1952, c. 148 (as am. S.C. 1988, c. 55, s. 168), s. 223(1). 2. In respect of a policy loan at a particular time, means the amount of the policy loan and the interest thereon that is outstanding at that time. *Income Tax Act*, R.S.C. 1952, c. 148 (as am. S.C. 1977-78, c. 1, s. 68(17)), s. 138(12)(b.1). 3. An amount shall be deemed not to have become payable to a beneficiary in a taxation year unless it was paid in the year to him or he was entitled in the year to enforce payment thereof. *Income Tax Act*, R.S.C. 1952, c. 148 (as am. S.C. 1988, c. 55, s. 71(15)), s. 104(24).

AMOUNT TAXABLE. Taxable paid up capital or taxable paid up capital employed in Canada.

AMOVE. *v.* To remove from a position or place.

AMPACITY. *n.* Current-carrying capacity expressed in amperes.

AMPERE. *n.* 1. The unit of measurement of electric current, being a constant current that, if maintained in two straight parallel conductors in infinite length, of negligible circular cross-section and placed one metre apart in vacuum, would produce between those conductors a force equal to 2 x 10^{-7} newton per metre of length. *Weights and Measures Act*, S.C. 1970-71-72, c. 36, schedule 1. 2. The current that, when constantly maintained in two straight parallel conductors of infinite length, of infinitesimal circular sections and placed one centimetre apart in a vacuum, will produce a force equal to two one-hundredths of a dyne per centimetre of length. *Electric and Photometric Units Act*, R.S.C. 1970, c. E-3, s. 2.

AMPHETAMINE. *n.* A drug which stimulates the central nervous system. F.A. Jaffe, *A Guide to Pathological Evidence*, 2d ed. (Toronto: Carswell, 1983) at 168.

AMPHIBIAN. *n.* A vertebrate of the class Amphibia and includes the eggs and other developmental life stages.

AMPHITHEATRE. *n.* An establishment comprising stepped rows of seats and an arena disposed so as to allow the presentation of a match or spectacle. *An Act respecting the Commission de Contrôle des Permis D'alcool*, R.S.Q. 1977, c. C-33, s. 2.

AMPLIATION. *n.* Deferral of judgment until the matter can be further examined.

AMPLITUDE. See PULSE ~.

A.M. STATION. See REGIONAL ~.

AMUSEMENT. *n.* Any contest, dance, entertainment, exhibition, game, performance, program, riding device or amusement ride, or show. See PLACE OF ~; TRAVELLING ~.

AMUSEMENT DEVICE. A machine, contrivance, structure or vehicle used in an amusement park to entertain members of the public by moving them or causing them to be moved.

AMUSEMENT MACHINE. A contrivance for providing amusement or a game of skill. *An Act respecting lotteries, racing, publicity contests and amusement machines*, S.Q. 1978, c. 36, s. 1.

AMUSEMENT OWNER. Includes every person who for gain conducts a place of amusement or operates an amusement device, or who for gain permits the public or some of them to participate or indulge in any amusement or recreation whatsoever, but does not include a theatre owner where only a performance is given in the theatre.

AMUSEMENT PARK. A facility, open to the public, used in connection with a carnival, fair, shopping centre, resort, park or place of entertainment where amusement devices are provided.

AMUSEMENT RIDE. A device or combination of devices designed to entertain or amuse people by physically moving them.

AMY. *n.* A friend.

AN. *abbr.* Anonymous.

ANAESTHETIC. *n.* A procedure that causes the loss of sensation of pain in the whole or any part of the body.

ANAGRAPH. *n.* A written record.

ANAL. DE POL. *abbr.* Analyse de Politiques.

ANALGESIC. *n.* A drug which relieves pain. F.A. Jaffe, *A Guide to Pathological Evidence*, 2d ed. (Toronto: Carswell, 1983) at 168.

ANALOGY. *n.* Similarity or identity of degree; one may reason by analogy to compare cases governed by the same general principle in a different subject-matter.

ANALYSIS. *n.* 1. Separation into component parts or elements. 2. Physical or bacteriological as well as chemical analysis. See ACTIVATION ~.

ANALYST. *n.* A person appointed or designated to carry out analysis under a statute. See DEPARTMENTAL ~; PROVINCIAL ~.

ANAPHYLAXIS. *n.* An acute reaction which occurs when an individual is exposed to an allergen to which that person is hypersensitive. F.A. Jaffe, *A Guide to Pathological Evidence*, 2d ed. (Toronto: Carswell, 1983) at 168.

ANARCHY. *n.* Non-existence of government.

ANATOCISM. *n.* Accepting compound interest on a loan.

ANCESTOR. *n.* One from whom a person is descended; progenitor. See DESCENDANTS OF ANY ~.

ANCESTRAL. *adj.* Relating to ancestors.

ANCHORAGE. *n.* 1. A toll to be paid by vessels anchoring in a port. 2. Any area in a harbour where a vessel is permitted to moor by means of its anchor. *National Harbours Board Operating By-law*, C.R.C., c. 1064, s. 2. 3. The provision for transferring seat belt assembly loads to the vehicle structure. *Motor Vehicle Safety Regulations*, C.R.C., c. 1038, s. 210.

ANCIENT. *adj.* Old.

ANCILLARY. *adj.* Aiding; assisting; auxiliary.

ANCILLARY ADMINISTRATION. Administration of a portion of an estate in a second jurisdiction where property of the deceased is located or where the deceased had a cause of action.

ANCILLARY JURISDICTION. Jurisdiction of a federal court over ancillary proceedings which it could not consider if they were independently presented. P.W. Hogg, *Constitutional Law of Canada*, 2d ed. (Toronto: Carswell, 1985) at 146-147.

ANCILLARY RELIEF. Auxiliary relief.

ANCIPITUS USUS. [L.] Of doubtful use.

ANDROLEPSY. *n.* One nation arrests the citizens or subjects of another to compel something of the latter.

A. NELS. *abbr.* Aven Nelson. *Weed Control Act*, R.R.O. 1980, Reg. 944, s. 1.

ANEMIA. *n.* The diminution of the number of red blood corpuscles and is distinguished by paleness of all tissues. *Meat Inspection Regulations*, C.R.C., c. 1032, s. 46.

ANENCEPHALY. *n.* Non-existence of the brain. F.A. Jaffe, *A Guide to Pathological Evidence*, 2d ed. (Toronto: Carswell, 1983) at 93.

ANEURYSM. *n.* A localized bulge in a chamber of the heart or blood vessel caused by weakness in its wall. F.A. Jaffe, *A Guide to Pathological Evidence*, 2d ed. (Toronto: Carswell, 1983) at 168. See ARTERIOR-VENOUS ~; BERRY ~; CONGENITAL ~; DISSECTING ~; FUSIFORM ~; MYCOTIC ~; SACCULAR ~; TRAUMATIC ~.

ANGLE. *v.* To take or attempt to take fish by means of hook and line and includes casting or trolling. *Saskatchewan Fishery Regulations*, C.R.C., c. 853, s. 2.

ANGLER. *n.* A person taking or attempting to take fish by means of a hook and line or a hook, line and rod when he is tending it and includes a person who is casting or trolling but does not include a person taking or attempting to take fish by means of a set line when he is not tending it. *Ontario Fishery Regulations*, C.R.C., c. 849, s. 2.

ANGLIAE JURA IN OMNI CASU LIBERTATIS DANT FAVOREM. [L.] The laws of England favour liberty in all cases.

ANGLING. *n.* Fishing or attempting to fish with a hook and line, or a hook, line and rod. See ICE ~.

ANGLING GUIDE. A person licensed as an angling guide under this Act. *Wildlife Act*, S.B.C. 1982, c. 57, s. 1.

ANHYDROUS AMMONIA. Dry ammonia gas in liquified form and is not to be confused with aqua ammonia which is a solution of ammonia gas in water. *Anhydrous Ammonia Bulk Storage Regulations*, C.R.C., c. 1146, s. 2.

ANIMAL. *n.* 1. Any living being of the animal kingdom other than a human being. Veterinary acts. 2. (i) Any animal other than man, (ii) includes mammals, birds, fish, amphibians, reptiles, invertebrates, insects and animals similar to insects, wild or domestic, living or dead. 3. All animals except humans and includes vertebrates, invertebrates and micro-organisms whether wild, domestic, living or dead. 4. A mammal, reptile, amphibian or bird. 5. Includes a bee, a fertilized egg or ovum, live poultry and a reptile. Animal Disease and Protection acts. 6. A domestic animal, the meat of which is red meat and is to be or intended to be used for human consumption and, without limiting the generality of the foregoing, does not include poultry or rabbits. *Meat Inspection (Nova Scotia) Act*, S.N.S. 1984, c. 7, s. 2. 7. A bull, cow, steer, heifer, calf, horse, sheep, swine, goat, domestic rabbit or poultry. Meat Inspection acts. See CLASS OF ~; DANGEROUS ~; DEAD ~; DOMESTIC ~; ENTIRE ~; EXOTIC ~; FALLEN ~; FOOD ~; FOREIGN ~S; FUR ~; FUR-BEARING ~; GAME ~; MEAT ~; MISCHIEVOUS ~; NUISANCE ~; PREDATORY ~; REGISTERED ~; STRAY ~.

ANIMAL BY-PRODUCT. Includes blood, bones, bristles, feathers, flesh, hair, hides, hoofs, horns, offal, serum, skins and wool, and fertilizers and feed stuffs containing any of the foregoing. *Animal Disease and Protection Act*, R.S.C. 1985, c. A-11, s. 2.

ANIMAL DEADYARD. A place where (a) disabled or diseased animals and the bodies of dead animals are brought and animal by-products removed therefrom; or (b) animal by-products are brought. *Animal Disease and Protection Act*, R.S.C. 1985, c. A-11, s. 2.

ANIMAL EMBRYO. The fertilized ovum of an animal. *Animal Disease and Protection Regulations*, C.R.C., c. 296, s. 2.

ANIMAL EMBRYO TRANSPLANT CENTRE. A place in which animal embryos are transplanted to other female animals. *Animal Disease and Protection Regulations*, C.R.C., c. 296, s. 2.

ANIMAL FOOD. Anything intended as nutriment for animals and includes any of the constituent elements of an animal ration. *Animal Disease and Protection Act*, R.S.C. 1985, c. A-11, s. 2.

ANIMAL FOOD PLANT. A place where animal food is prepared or manufactured. *Animal Disease and Protection Act*, S.C. 1974-75-76, c. 86, s. 3.

ANIMAL FOOD STORAGE PLANT. A business that provides facilities to store frozen food for animal consumption. *Frozen Food Act*, R.S.A. 1970, c. 150, s. 2.

ANIMAL HEALTH TECHNICIAN. A person: (i) who holds a certificate or document indicating completion of a course of formal study or training approved by the association; (ii) whose name has been entered by the registrar on the current register of animal health technicians; and (iii) who, under the direction or supervision of a member named by the association, is permitted to perform the technical procedures set out in the bylaws of the association. Veterinarians acts.

ANIMAL PRODUCT. 1. Includes cream, eggs, milk and semen. *Animal Disease and Protection Act*, R.S.C. 1985, c. A-11, s. 2. 2. Any product produced by or from an animal and includes any part of an animal, whether edible or non-edible, and any by-product of an animal or imitation animal product.

ANIMAL RUNNING AT LARGE. (i) An animal that is off the premises of its owner, and is not under the immediate, continuous and effective control of its owner, or (ii) an animal, whether under the control of its owner or not, grazing upon lands other than lands in respect of which the owner of the animal has the right of occupation, or upon a highway or road allowance.

ANIMALS DOMITAE NATURAE. [L.] Domestic animals.

ANIMALS FERAE NATURAE. [L.] Wild animals.

ANIMAL UNIT MONTH. The amount of forage required for one month by an average animal of the genus bos, aged 6 months or older. *Range Act*, R.S.B.C. 1979, c. 355, s. 1.

ANIMO. *adv.* [L.] With intention.

ANIMUS. *n.* [L.] Intent; intention.

ANIMUS AD SE OMNE DUCIT. [L.] Intention draws all law to itself.

ANIMUS CANCELLANDI. [L.] Intention to cancel or destroy.

ANIMUS CONTRAHENDI. [L.] Intention that the language or conduct of parties should result in a contract. G.H.L. Fridman, *The Law of Contract in Canada*, 2d ed. (Toronto: Carswell, 1986) at 25.

ANIMUS DEDICANDI. [L.] Intention to dedicate.

ANIMUS DOMINI. [L.] Intention to hold as owner.

ANIMUS ET FACTUM. [L.] Combination of an intention with an act.

ANIMUS FURANDI. [L.] The intention to steal.

ANIMUS HOMINIS EST ANIMA SCRIPTI. [L.] A person's intention is the soul of whatever is written.

ANIMUS MANENDI. [L.] Intention to remain.

ANIMUS NON REVERTENDI. [L.] Intention not to return.

ANIMUS POSSIDENDI. [L.] Intention to possess.

ANIMUS QUO. [L.] Intention with which.

ANIMUS RECIPIENDI. [L.] Intention to receive.

ANIMUS REVERTENDI. [L.] Intention to return.

ANIMUS REVOCANDI. [L.] Intention to revoke.

ANIMUS TESTANDI. [L.] Intention to make a will.

ANN. AIR & SPACE L. *abbr.* Annals of Air and Space Law (Annales de droit aérien et spatial).

ANN. AIR & SP. L. *abbr.* Annals of Air and Space Law.

ANN. CAN. D. DE LA PERSONNE *abbr.* Annuaire canadien des droits de la personne (Canadian Human Rights Yearbook).

ANN. CAN. D. INT. *abbr.* Annuaire canadien de droit international (Canadian Yearbook of International Law).

ANN. D. AÉRIEN & SPATIAL *abbr.* Annales de droit aérien et spatial (Annals of Air and Space Law).

ANNEX. *v.* To add to.

ANNEXATION. *n.* 1. Adding land to a municipality or nation. 2. Incorporation of a municipality into another municipality.

ANNI NUBILES. [L.] When one is old enough to marry.

ANNIVERSARY DATE. 1. The day and month on which the current registration or renewal of registration was granted. 2. In relation to a timber licence means the first day of April in each year regardless of the day and month when that licence is issued. *Crown Lands Act*, R.S.N.B. 1973, c. C-38, s. 1.

ANNIVERSARY MONTH. The month in each year that is the same as the month in which the original event occurred.

ANNO DOMINI. [L.] In the year of the Lord.

ANNO REGNI. [L.] In the year of the reign.

ANNOTATION. *n.* Description; explanation; comment.

ANNOUNCEMENT. See CLASSIFIED ~.

ANNOYANCE. *n.* Something distressing.

ANNUAL. *adj.* Calculated in any one year.

ANNUAL ALLOWABLE CUT. The total volume of timber that may be harvested in one year or the total amount of forested land on which the timber may be harvested in one year. *Forests Act*, R.S.A. 1980, c. F-16, s. 1.

ANNUAL ANNUITY AMOUNT. Of an individual in respect of an income-averaging annuity contract means the aggregate of the equal payments described in subparagraph (b)(iii) that, under the contract, are receivable by the individual in the 12-month period commencing on the day that the first such payment under the contract becomes receivable by him. *Income Tax Act*, R.S.C. 1952, c. 148 (as am. S.C. 1970-71-72, c. 63), s. 61(4)(a).

ANNUAL CUT. See ALLOWABLE ~; ANNUAL ALLOWABLE CUT.

ANNUAL DEBT CHARGES. The amount required in each year to meet the payments of principal and interest due on money borrowed, before or after the coming into force of this Act, for the purpose of constructing sewerage collection and disposal facilities, the repayment of which is amortized over a period of not less than 20 years and, for the purposes of this Act, includes that portion of the annual requisition of a regional district on a municipality attributable to the borrowing of money by the regional district for that purpose. *Sewerage Assistance Act*, R.S.B.C. 1979, c. 384, s. 1.

ANNUAL EMPLOYMENT PLAN. A system under which an employer provides a specified number of hours of work in a year.

ANNUAL GAINS LIMIT. Of an individual for a taxation year means the amount, if any, by which (a) the amount that would be determined in respect of the individual for the year under paragraph 3(b) in respect of capital gains and capital losses if the only properties referred to in that paragraph were properties disposed of by him after 1984 exceeds the aggregate of (b) the amount of his net capital losses for other taxation years deducted in computing his taxable income for the year under paragraph 111(1)(b), and (c) the aggregate of all his allowable business investment losses for the year. *Income Tax Act*, R.S.C. 1952, c. 148 (as am. S.C. 1988, c. 55, s. 81(1)), s. 110.6(1).

ANNUAL GENERAL MEETING. Includes the general meeting of shareholders at which the directors of a company are elected.

ANNUAL HOLIDAY PAY. In respect of any period of employment of an employee: (i) subject to subclause (ii), means, during each year of his employment or portion thereof with any one employer, three fifty-seconds of the employee's total wage for that year of employment or portion thereof during which the employee worked; (ii) means, during the year of his employment or portion thereof with any one employer in which he first becomes entitled or would have become entitled to four weeks' annual holiday under section 30 and during each year thereafter, four fifty-seconds of the employee's total wage for the year of employment or portion thereof during which the employee worked. *The Labour Standards Act*, R.S.S. 1978, c. L-1, s. 2.

ANNUAL INCOME. See NET ~.

ANNUALLY. *adv.* Yearly.

ANNUAL OUTLAY. All yearly maintenance, operation and depreciation costs, and necessary amortization costs other than instalments of the capital cost, incurred in respect of regulating or storage works together with interest on the capital cost. *Dominion Water Power Regulations*, C.R.C., c. 1603, s. 55.

ANNUAL PERCENTAGE RATE. In relation to a credit transaction, the percentage rate for each period of time that, when multiplied by the principal amount owing under the credit transaction that is outstanding at the end of each period, will produce an amount or amounts the total of which is equal to the credit charges in relation to the credit transaction, expressed as a rate per annum. *Consumer Credit Transactions Act*, S.A. 1985, c. 22.5, s. 1.

ANNUAL RECEIPTS. The income from the sale of each unit of a product, plus the compensation, subsidies or grants obtained during the year from government agencies. *Farm Income Stabilization Insurance Act*, R.S.Q. 1977, c. A-31, s. 1.

ANNUAL REGISTER. 1. The register of names of members who have paid their annual fees for the current year. *Nova Scotia Land Surveyors Act*, S.N.S. 1986, c. 59, s. 1. 2. The register of names of members who hold annual licences for the current year. *The Dental Profession Act*, R.S.S. 1978, c. D-5, s. 2.

ANNUAL RETURN. A yearly statement which companies are required to file under governing legislation and which sets out prescribed information. H. Sutherland, D.B. Horsley & J.M. Edmiston, eds., *Fraser's Handbook on Canadian Company Law*, 7th ed. (Toronto: Carswell, 1985) at 599.

ANNUAL SALARY RATE. An employee's basic hourly or daily or bi-weekly rate of pay, as the case may be, multiplied by the number of basic hours or days or bi-weekly periods in one year of continuous employment, but this amount shall not be less than the employee's salary during the immediately preceding 12 months of his employment. *Civil Service Superannuation Act*, S.M. 1974, c. 66, s. 1.

ANNUAL STATEMENT. A yearly statement which companies are required to file under governing legislation and which sets out prescribed information. H. Sutherland, D.B. Horsley & J.M. Edmiston, eds., *Fraser's Handbook on Canadian Company Law*, 7th ed. (Toronto: Carswell, 1985) at 599.

ANNUAL SUMMARY. A yearly statement which companies are required to file under governing legislation and which sets out prescribed information. H. Sutherland, D.B. Horsley & J.M. Edmiston, eds., *Fraser's Handbook on Canadian Company Law*, 7th ed. (Toronto: Carswell, 1985) at 599.

ANNUAL VALUE. The rental value of a property for a year. See FULL NET ~.

ANNUAL WEALTH TAX. This form of tax on wealth is a tax of a person's total assets minus the persons's liabilities. W. Grover & F. Iacobucci, *Materials on Canadian Income Tax*, 4th ed. (Toronto: Richard De Boo Ltd., 1980) at 36.

ANNUITANT. *n.* 1. A person in receipt of, or entitled to the receipt of, an annuity. 2. (i) Until such time after maturity of the plan as his spouse becomes entitled, as a consequence of his death, to receive benefits to be paid out of or under the plan, the individual referred to in subparagraph (j)(i) or (ii) for whom, under a retirement savings plan, a retirement income is to be provided, and (ii) thereafter, his spouse. *Income Tax Act*, R.S.C. 1952, c. 148 (as am. S.C. 1979, c. 5, s. 46), c. 146(1)(a). 3. Under a retirement income fund at any particular time means the individual to whom the carrier has undertaken to make the payments described in paragraph (f) out of or under the fund. *Income Tax Act*, R.S.C. 1952, c. 148 (as am. S.C. 1977-78, c. 32, s. 35), c. 146.3(1)(a).

ANNUITIES. *n.* Includes salaries and pensions. *Apportionment acts*.

ANNUITY. *n.* Includes an amount payable on a periodic basis, whether payable at intervals longer or shorter than a year and whether payable under a contract, will or trust or otherwise. See DEFERRED ~; IMMEDIATE ~; LIFE ~.

ANNUITY AMOUNT. See ANNUAL ~.

ANNUITY CONTRACT. A contract that provides for payment of an income for a specified period or for life and under which the sole benefit stated to be payable by reason of death does not exceed the sum of the amounts paid as consideration for the contract together with interest.

ANNUITY METHOD. A way in which a court calculates the cost of an annuity to provide income for a plaintiff over an estimated period without earnings or, in the case of permanent disability, a guaranteed life annuity for medical and other expenses. K.D. Cooper-Stephenson & I.B. Saunders, *Personal Injury Damages in Canada* (Toronto: Carswell, 1981) at 73.

ANNUL. *v.* To deprive of effectiveness or operation.

ANNULAR SPACE. Open space between the casing and the sides of a well. *Ontario Water Resources Act*, R.R.O. 1980, Reg. 739, s. 1.

ANNULMENT. *n.* Making void; depriving of effectiveness or operation.

ANON. *abbr.* Anonymous.

A NON POSSE AD NON ESSE SEQUITUR ARGUMENTUM NECESSARIE NEGATIVE, LICET NON AFFIRMATIVE. [L.] Because a thing cannot be done, you draw the conclusion that it was not done; but just because a thing has not been done, you should not conclude it is impossible.

ANONYMOUS. *n.* A nameless person.

ANONYMOUS. *adj.* Nameless.

ANOXIA. *n.* Total deficiency of oxygen. F.A. Jaffe, *A Guide to Pathological Evidence*, 2d ed. (Toronto: Carswell, 1983) at 168.

ANSI. *abbr.* American National Standards Institute.

ANSWER. *n.* What is delivered by a respondent who wishes to oppose the claim in a petition. G.D. Watson & C. Perkins, eds., *Holmested & Watson: Ontario Civil Procedure* (Toronto: Carswell, 1984) at 70-4.

ANTE. [L.] Before.

ANTECEDENT. *n.* Some time prior.

ANTECEDENT. *adj.* Prior in time.

ANTEDATE. *v.* To date a document before the day it is executed.

ANTE LITEM MOTAM. [L.] Before litigation was begun.

ANTE-NUPTIAL. *var.* **ANTENUPTIAL.** *adj.* Before marriage.

ANTERIOR. *adj.* Before, facing towards the front, in front of. F.A. Jaffe, *A Guide to Pathological Evidence*, 2d ed. (Toronto: Carswell, 1983) at 168.

ANTHROPOMETRY. *n.* Measurement of the human body.

ANTHROPOMORPHIC TEST DEVICE. A representation of a human being used in the measurement of the conditions that a human being would experience in a vehicle when the vehicle is subjected to approved test methods. *Motor Vehicle Safety Regulations*, C.R.C., c. 1038, s. 2.

ANTHROPOPHAGY. *n.* The act of animals eating a human body. F.A. Jaffe, *A Guide to Pathological Evidence*, 2d ed. (Toronto: Carswell, 1983) at 168.

ANTIBIOTIC. *n.* A drug or a veterinary biologic prepared from micro-organisms or made synthetically that inhibits the growth of micro-organisms.

ANTICIPATION. *n.* Taking or doing something before the chosen time.

ANTICIPATORY BREACH. Repudiation of contractual obligations before they fall due. G.H.L. Fridman, *The Law of Contract in Canada*, 2d ed. (Toronto: Carswell, 1986) at 558.

ANTICIPATORY CREDIT. Permitting an exporter to draw on credit prior to shipment by tender of particular documents. I.F.G. Baxter, *The Law of Banking*, 3d ed. (Toronto: Carswell, 1981) at 156.

ANTI-COMPETITIVE ACT. Without restricting the generality of the term, includes any of the following acts: (a) squeezing, by a vertically integrated supplier, of the margin available to an unintegrated customer who competes with the supplier, for the purpose of impeding or preventing the customer's entry into, or expansion in, a market; (b) acquisition by a supplier of a customer who would otherwise be available to a competitor of the supplier, or acquisition by a customer of a supplier who would otherwise be available to a competitor of the customer, for the purpose of impeding or preventing the competitor's entry into or eliminating the competitor from, a market; (c) freight equalization on the plant of a competitor for the purpose of impeding or preventing the competitor's entry into, or eliminating the competitor from, a market; (d) use of fighting brands introduced selectively on a temporary basis to discipline or eliminate a competitor; (e) pre-emption of scarce facilities or resources required by a competitor for the operation of business, with the object of withholding the facilities or resources from a market; (f) buying up of products to prevent the erosion of existing price levels; (g) adoption of product specifications that are incompatible with products produced by any other person and are designed to prevent his entry into, or to eliminate him from, a market; (h) requiring or inducing a supplier to sell only or primarily to certain customers, or to refrain from selling to a competitor, with the object of preventing a competitor's entry into, or expansion in, a market; and (i) selling articles at a price lower than the acquisition cost for the purpose of disciplining or eliminating a competitor. *Combines Investigation Act*, R.S.C. 1985 (2d Supp.), c. 19, s. 78.

ANTIGRAPHY. *n.* The counterpart or copy of a deed.

ANTI-INFLATION ACT (CANADA). An Act to provide for the restraint of profit margins, prices, dividends and compensation in Canada passed by the Parliament of Canada at the First Session of the Thirtieth Parliament. *Anti-Inflation (Nova Scotia) Act*, S.N.S. 1975, c. 54, s. 2.

ANTI-LOCK SYSTEM. A portion of a service brake system that automatically controls the degree of rotational wheel slip at one or more wheels of the vehicle during braking. *Motor Vehicle Safety Regulations*, C.R.C., c. 1038, s. 2.

ANTI-MANIFESTO. *var.* **ANTI MANIFESTO.** The reply to another belligerent's manifesto.

ANTIMONY. *n.* A poisonous metallic element used in making the core of jacketed bullets and soft bullets. F.A. Jaffe, *A Guide to Pathological Evidence*, 2d ed. (Toronto: Carswell, 1983) at 168-69.

ANTINOMY. *n.* A contradiction between two legal propositions; opposition to a particular law.

ANTIQUE. *n.* Curios, objects of art or of historical interest and home furnishing that through passage of time have increased in interest and value. *Salvage Dealers Licensing Act*, R.S.N.B. 1973, c. S-3, s. 1.

ANTIQUE FIREARM. Any firearm manufactured before 1898 that was not designed to use rim-fire or centre-fire ammunition and that has not been redesigned to use that ammunition or, if so designed or redesigned, is capable only of using rim-fire or centre-fire ammunition that is no longer commercially manufactured. *Criminal Code*, R.S.C. 1985, c. C-46, s. 84.

ANTIQUE MOTOR VEHICLE. A motor vehicle that is 25 years of age or older, is owned as a collector's item and is operated solely for use in exhibitions, club activities, parades and other similar functions and is not used for general transportation. *Highway Traffic Act*, R.S.A. 1980, c. H-7, s. 1.

ANTIQUE REPRODUCTION VEHICLE. A vehicle that is designed to be a scaled reproduction of an antique vehicle and (a) may contain contemporary design components; (b) has a motor that produces 8 kW (10.73 bhp) or less; (c) is intended for use exclusively in parades, exhibitions and demonstrations; and (d) bears a label, permanently affixed in a conspicuous position, stating that the vehicle is not to be used for public transportation, but is intended for use in parades, exhibitions and demonstrations.

ANTIQUE VEHICLE. 1. A vehicle more than 30 years old that, when restored to a condition comparable to that on the date of its manufacture, retains the original components or incorporates replacement components with original design characteristics. Canada regulations. 2. A motor vehicle that is at least 25 years old and has been restored to original condition. *Motor Vehicle Act*, S.N.B. 1977, c. 32, s. 1.

ANTIQUITY. *n.* Any antiquity (other than spirits or wines) produced more than 100 years prior to the date of importation. *Antiquities Import Regulations*, C.R.C., c. 511, s. 2.

ANTITRUST LAW. A law of a foreign jurisdiction of a kind commonly known as an antitrust law, and includes a law having directly or indirectly as a purpose the preservation or enhancement of competition between business enterprises or the prevention or repression of monopolies or restrictive practices in trade or commerce. *Foreign Extraterritorial Measures Act*, R.S.C. 1985, c. F-29, s. 2.

ANTON PILLER ORDER. An ex parte order for seizure, inspection or preservation of documents which is properly granted where a plaintiff has an extremely strong prima facie case, damage potential is serious and there is clear evidence that the defendant possesses incriminating documents or property and may dispose of it before motion on notice can be made.

A., N.W.T. & Y. TAX R. *abbr.* Alberta, N.W.T. & Yukon Tax Reports.

A1. Telegraphy by amplitude modulation without the use of modulating audio frequency (on-off keying). *General Radio Regulations, Part II*, C.R.C., c. 1372, s. 42.

AORTA. *n.* The main artery which emerges from the heart. F.A. Jaffe, *A Guide to Pathological Evidence*, 2d ed. (Toronto: Carswell, 1983) at 169.

APARTMENT. *n.* A self-contained residential

accommodation unit that (a) has cooking, sleeping, bathroom and living room facilities; and (b) is located in an apartment building. *Home Owner Grant Act*, S.B.C. 1980, c. 18, s. 1.

APARTMENT BLOCK. A house or building, portions of which are rented or leased as residents to five [or three] or more tenants or families living independently of each other but having common rights in the halls, stairways, yards or other conveniences. Saskatchewan statutes.

APARTMENT BUILDING. A building that is divided into multiple dwelling units or suites. See OWNER OCCUPIED ~.

APATISATIO. *n.* Compact; agreement.

APERTURE. See EFFECTIVE ~; EXIT ~.

APIARY. *n.* 1. A place where bees are kept. 2. A place where bees or beehive or beekeeping equipment are kept. *Bee Act*, R.S.B.C. 1979, c. 27, s. 1.

APICES JURIS NON SUNT JURA. [L.] Extremes in law make bad law.

APNOEA. *n.* Lack of breath.

A POSTERIORI. [L.] From what comes after.

APP. *abbr.* Appeal.

APPARATUS. *n.* 1. Includes any machine, instrument or device. *Electricity and Gas Inspection Act*, R.S.C. 1985, c. E-4, s. 2. 2. Any device, mechanism or instrument using gas to produce heat, light or power, including its connecting piping and its vent for carrying off the products of gas combustion. *Gas Distribution Act*, R.S.Q. 1977, c. D-10, s. 1. 3. System electrical equipment of which system conductors form part or are connected thereto and includes all electrical transmission circuits, electrical machines, switch-gear, fittings and accessories. *Coal Mines Regulation Act*, R.S.N.S. 1967, c. 36, s. 84. See BREATHING ~; RADIO ~; SCIENTIFIC ~.

APPARENT. *adj.* Readily perceived.

APPARENT AUTHORITY. Authority which an agent appears to have.

APP. CAS. *abbr.* Law Reports, Appeal Cases, 1875-1890.

APPEAL. *n.* 1. Examination by a higher court of the decision of an inferior court. 2. Proceeding to set aside or vary any judgment of the court appealed from. *Supreme Court Act*, R.S.C. 1985, c. S-26, s. 2. 3. Includes a judicial revision or review of a judgment, decision, order, direction, determination, finding or conviction, and a case stated or reserved, and a removal of proceedings by way of certiorari or otherwise. *Insurance acts.* 4. Includes any proceeding by way of discharg-

ing or setting aside a judgment or an application for a new trial or a stay of execution. *Reciprocal Enforcement of Judgments (U.K.) acts.* See COURT OF ~, CROSS-~; FEDERAL COURT OF ~; FEDERAL COURT—~ DIVISION; NOTICE OF ~; TRIBUNAL ~.

APPEAL BOARD. A board established under a statute to hear appeals from administrative decisions or from decisions of first level tribunals. See IMMIGRATION ~; PENSION ~.

APPEAL COURT. 1. (a) In the Provinces of Ontario, Nova Scotia, British Columbia and Newfoundland, the district or county court of the district or county where the adjudication was made; (b) in the Province of Quebec, the Superior Court; (c) in the Provinces of New Brunswick, Manitoba, Saskatchewan and Alberta, the Court of Queen's Bench; (d) in the province of Prince Edward Island, the Supreme Court; and (e) in the Yukon Territory and Northwest Territories, the Supreme Court. *Criminal Code*, R.S.C. 1985, c. C-46, s. 100(11). 2. For purposes of sections 813 to 828, means (a) in the Province of Ontario, the county court of the district or county or group of counties where the adjudication was made; (b) in the province of Quebec, the Superior Court; (c) in the Province of Nova Scotia, the county court of the district or county where the cause of the proceedings arose; (d) in the Provinces of New Brunswick, Manitoba, Saskatchewan and Alberta, the Court of Queen's Bench; (e) in the Province of British Columbia, the county court of the county where the adjudication was made; (f) in the Province of Prince Edward Island, the Supreme Court; (g) in the Province of Newfoundland, the district court of the judicial district where the cause of the proceedings arose; and (h) in the Yukon and Northwest Territories, a judge of the Supreme Court thereof. *Criminal Code*, R.S.C. 1985, c. C-46, s. 812. 3. For the purposes of sections 830 to 838, means, in any province, the superior court of criminal jurisdiction for the province. *Criminal Law Amendment Act*, R.S.C. 1985 (1st Supp.), c. 27, s. 829. 4. In this section, means (a) in relation to each of the Provinces of Ontario, Quebec, New Brunswick, British Columbia, Manitoba, Saskatchewan, Alberta and Newfoundland, the Court of Appeal of the Province; and (b) in relation to the Province of Nova Scotia, the Appeal Division of the Supreme Court. *Judges Act*, R.S.C. 1985, c. J-1, s. 24(6). See COURT MARTIAL ~.

APPEALS TRIBUNAL. See APPEAL BOARD.

APPEAL TRIBUNAL. See APPEAL BOARD.

APPEAR. See PROMISE TO ~.

APPEARANCE. *n.* A document filed in court which indicates that a person will participate in proceedings or will defend. See CONDI-TIONAL ~; NON-~.

APPEARANCE FORFEIT. The amount of money that a boxer, under a written contract to appear in a professional boxing contest or exhibition, agrees to pay in accordance with this Regulation upon his failure to so appear. *Athletics Control Act*, R.R.O. 1980, Reg. 76, s. 2.

APPEARANCE NOTICE. 1. A document which requires people to appear in court to answer charges against them. 2. A notice in Form 9 issued by a peace officer. *Criminal Code*, R.S.C. 1985, c. C-46, s. 493.

APPEARANCE OF THE INJURY OR DIS-EASE. Includes the recurrence of an injury or disease that has been so improved as to have removed the resultant disability. *Pension Act*, R.S.C. 1985, c. P-6, s. 2.

APPEARING CONSPICUOUSLY. Written in such a way that the person against whom words so noted or appearing are to operate ought reasonably to notice them. *Business Corporations Act, 1982*, S.O. 1982, c. 4, s. 53.

APPELLANT. *n.* The party bringing an appeal.

APPELLATE. *adj.* Appealed to.

APPELLATE COURT. In respect of an appeal from a court, means the court exercising appellate jurisdiction with respect to that appeal.

APPELLATE JURISDICTION. A superior court's power to review the decision of a lower court.

APPELLEE. *n.* One against whom the appeal is made.

APPELLOR. *n.* A criminal who accuses an accomplice; a person who challenges a jury.

APPENDANT. *adj.* Annexed to or belonging to another.

APPENDIX. *n.* In connection with an appeal, a volume referred to which contains the material documents or other evidence used in the lower court.

APPERTAIN. *v.* To belong to.

APPERTIZE. *v.* To heat food immediately after it is hermetically sealed in a container at a temperature and for a time (a) sufficient to destroy pathogenic and spoilage organisms; and (b) so that it will remain stable and safe under non-refrigerated conditions of storage and distribution. *Meat Inspection Regulations*, C.R.C., c. 1032, s. 2.

APPLE-GROWER. *n.* Every physical person who cultivates apple trees in Quebec. *An Act Respecting the Commission de Contrôle des Permis D'alcool*, R.S.Q. 1977, c. C-33, s. 2.

APPLE JUICE FROM CONCENTRATE. The product that is obtained by the addition of water to concentrated apple juice. *Processed Fruit and Vegetable Regulations*, C.R.C., c. 291, Schedule I, c. 5.

APPLES. *n.* All varieties of apples produced in Ontario but does not include crabapples. *Crop Insurance Act (Ontario)*, R.R.O. 1980, Reg. 198, s. 3.

APPLIANCE. *n.* 1. Any device which utilizes gas to produce light, heat or power or any combination of them. 2. A device designed for use in heating and cooling systems operated by fuel or electricity and includes all components, controls, wiring and piping required to be part of the device by the applicable standard referred to in this Regulation. *Building Code Act*, R.R.O. 1980, Reg. 87, s. 1. 3. A receptacle or equipment that receives or collects water, liquids or sewage and discharges water, liquids or sewage directly into an indirect waste pipe or a fixture. *Ontario Water Resources Act*, R.R.O. 1980, Reg. 736, s. 1. See DENTAL ~S; FUEL-FIRED ~; HOUSE-HOLD ~; OPHTHALMIC ~; OPTICAL ~; ORTHOPAEDIC ~S; PROSTHETIC ~; SPACE-HEATING ~.

APPLIANCES OR WORKS. Poles, wires, conduits, transformers, pipes, pipe lines or any other works, structures or appliances placed on or under a highway by an operating corporation. *Public Service Works on Highways Act*, R.S.O. 1980, c. 420, s. 1.

APPLICANT. *n.* 1. A person who applies or on whose behalf an application is made for assistance, a benefit, a loan or grant. 2. A person applying for a licence, registration, permit or passport. 3. One who brings an application or petition. See INDEPENDENT ~.

APPLICATIO EST VITA REGULAE. [L.] The application is the life of a rule.

APPLICATION. *n.* 1. A request. 2. A motion to a judge or court. 3. The commencement of proceedings before a court of tribunal. See DUE ~; EXTERNAL ~; INTERLOCUTORY ~; NOTICE OF ~; SUMMARY ~.

APPLICATION FOR CERTIFICATION. A request by a trade union to a labour relations board for designation as bargaining agent for a unit of employees.

APPLICATOR. See COMMERCIAL ~.

APPLIED SCIENCE. See SCHOOL OF ~.

APPLY. *v.* 1. To request; to make application; to bring a motion to a court. 2. In respect of a label, to attach to, imprint on, include in or cause to accompany in any other way a product. 3. In relation to a mark, includes any application or attachment thereof to, or any use thereof on, in connection with or in relation to (a) an article, (b) anything attached to an article, (c) anything to which an article is attached, (d) anything in or on which an article is, or (e) anything so used or placed as to lead to a reasonable belief that the mark thereon is meant to be taken as a mark on an article. See LIBERTY TO ~.

APPOINT. *v.* To select; to designate; to assign an office or duty.

APPOINTED DAY. A day designated for a particular purpose.

APPOINTEE. *n.* A person chosen for some purpose.

APPOINTMENT. *n.* 1. Designation of a person to fill an office. 2. An appointment made in the exercise of a power to appoint property among several objects. *Power of Appointment Act,* R.S.B.C. 1979, c. 333, s. 1. See NON-IMPERA-TIVE ~; POWER OF ~.

APPOINTOR. *n.* One given a power; a person who names someone else for an office.

APPORTIONMENT. *n.* A division of a whole into proportional parts according to the claimants' rights.

APPRAISAL. *n.* Valuation. See COLLECTIVE ~; INDIVIDUAL ~.

APPRAISAL REMEDY. A procedure which permits minority or dissenting shareholders to require the corporation to buy out their shares at an appraised price in prescribed situations.

APPRAISAL RIGHT. See APPRAISAL REMEDY.

APPRAISE. *v.* To estimate or set the value of a thing.

APPRAISEMENT. *n.* The act of valuing property. Appraisement of a ship may be ordered by Federal Court.

APPRAISER. *n.* 1. A person appointed to engage in valuations. 2. A property valuator. See DAMAGE ~; QUALIFIED ~.

APPRECIATION. *n.* 1. Growth in value. 2. An increase in an asset's value strictly due to inflation or market fluctuations. A. Bissett-Johnson & W.M. Holland, eds, *Matrimonial Property Law in Canada* (Toronto: Carswell, 1980) at M-6.

APPREHENSION. *n.* 1. Capturing a person on a criminal charge. 2. The act of taking a child into custody.

APPRENDRE. *n.* [Fr.] A profit or fee to be received or taken.

APPRENTICE. *n.* 1. A person who is at least sixteen years of age and who has entered into a contract under which he is to receive, from or through an employer, training and instruction in a trade. 2. A person who works as assistant to a journeyman with a view to qualify as a journeyman. 3. A person who has been duly registered with the association for training in pharmacy pursuant to the provisions of this Act and the bylaws, rules and regulations. *The Pharmacy Act,* R.S.S. 1978, c. P-9, s. 2. 4. An adult enrolled at a manpower centre of Quebec for the purpose of learning a trade or vocation. Quebec acts. 5. Includes a cadet and a midshipman. *Crew Accommodation Regulations,* C.R.C., c. 1418, s. 2. See PRE-~.

APPRENTICE PILOT. A person who is training to become a licensed pilot. *Pilotage Act,* R.S.C. 1985, c. P-14, s. 2.

APPRENTICESHIP. *n.* A method of vocational training the program of which is intended to qualify an apprentice and includes a period of practical training with an employer and, generally, courses in relevant technical and vocational subjects. *Manpower Vocational Training and Qualification Act,* R.S.Q. 1977, c. F-5, s. 1. See CONTRACT OF ~; INDENTURED ~; TERM OF ~.

APPRENTICESHIP ACT. Statute governing the terms of apprenticeships.

APPRO. *abbr.* Approval.

APPROACH SIGNAL. A fixed signal used in connection with one or more signals to govern the approach thereto. *Regulations No. O-8, Uniform Code of Operating Rules,* C.R.C., c. 1175, Part III, s. 2.

APPROACH SURFACE. 1. An imaginary inclined plane extending upward and outward from the end of each strip along and at right angles to the projected centre line thereof. *Airport Zoning Regulations,* Canada regulations. 2. An imaginary inclined plane the lower end of which is a horizontal line at right angles to the centre line of a strip and passing through a point at the strip end on the centre line of the strip. *Airport Zoning Regulations,* Canada regulations.

APPROACH WHARF. That section of a wharf or wall as defined by appropriate signs immediately above and below a lock. *Canal Regulations,* C.R.C., c. 1564, s. 2.

APPROPRIATE. *v.* 1. To make something some person's property. 2. To earmark for a purpose.

APPROPRIATE ADVICE. In relation to any

fact or circumstance means the advice of competent persons qualified, in their respective spheres, to advise on the professional or technical aspects of that fact or that circumstance, as the case may be. *Limitation of Actions Act*, S.M. 1980, c. 28, s. 3.

APPROPRIATE AGENCY. The agency for the province or territory in which the person by whom or on whose behalf a notice of intention is signed has his place of business or if that person has more than one place of business in Canada and the places of business are not in the same province or territory, the agency for the province or territory in which that person has his principal place of business or if that person has no place of business, then agency for the province or territory in which the person resides; and, in respect of any notice of intention registered before December 1, 1980, means the office in which registration was required to be made by the law in force at the time of such registration. *Bank Act*, R.S.C. 1985, c. B-1, s. 178(5).

APPROPRIATE AUTHORITY. The public body or agency designated as responsible for a particular subject matter.

APPROPRIATE CHIEF JUSTICE. For the purposes of this section, (a) in relation to the Province of Ontario, the Chief Justice of the High Court of Justice; (b) in relation to the Province of Quebec, the Chief Justice of the Superior Court; (c) in relation to the Provinces of Nova Scotia and Newfoundland, respectively, the Chief Justice of the Supreme Court, Trial Division; (d) in relation to the Provinces of New Brunswick, Manitoba, Saskatchewan and Alberta, respectively, the Chief Justice of the Court of Queen's Bench; (e) in relation to the Provinces of British Columbia and Prince Edward Island, respectively, the Chief Justice of the Supreme Court; and (f) in relation to the Yukon Territory and the Northwest Territories, respectively, the Chief Justice of the Court of Appeal thereof. *Criminal Code*, R.S.C. 1985, c. C-46, s. 745(6).

APPROPRIATE DEPUTY HEAD. In respect of a person employed in the public service of Canada, (a) if the person is employed in a position in or under a department named in Schedule I to the Financial Administration Act, the deputy minister thereof; and (b) if the person is employed in a position in any other portion of the public service of Canada, the chief executive officer thereof. *Canada Elections Act — Special Voting Rules*, R.S.C. 1985, c. E-2, s. 2.

APPROPRIATE FOR COLLECTIVE BARGAINING. With reference to a unit, means a unit that is appropriate for such purposes whether it is an employer unit, craft unit, technical unit, plant unit, or any other unit and whether or not the employees therein are employed by one or more employer.

APPROPRIATE MINISTER. 1. (a) With respect to a department mentioned in paragraph (a) of the definition "department", the Minister presiding over the department, (b) with respect to any other department, the Minister designated by the Governor in Council as the appropriate Minister, (c) with respect to the Senate and the House of Commons, the respective Speaker, and with respect to the Library of Parliament, the Speakers of the Senate and the House of Commons, and (d) with respect to a Crown corporation, the appropriate Minister as defined in subsection 83(1). *Financial Administration Act*, R.S.C. 1985, c. F-11, s. 2. 2. (a) In relation to a parent Crown corporation, (i) the Minister specified by or pursuant to any other Act of Parliament as the Minister in respect of that corporation, or (ii) if no Minister is specified as described in subparagraph (i), such member of the Queen's Privy Council for Canada as is designated by order of the Governor in Council as the appropriate Minister for the corporation, and (b) in relation to a wholly-owned subsidiary, the appropriate Minister, as defined in paragraph (a), for the parent Crown corporation that wholly owns the subsidiary. *Financial Administration Act*, R.S.C. 1985, c. F-11, s. 83. 3. In relation to a public servant, means the minister who under the Financial Administration Act is the appropriate minister with respect to the department in which the public servant is employed. *Public Servants Inventions Act*, R.S.C. 1985, c. P-32, s. 2.

APPROPRIATE PAYING OFFICER. In relation to a Crown debt, means the paying officer who makes the payments in respect of that debt. *Financial Administration Act*, R.S.C. 1985, c. F-11, s. 66.

APPROPRIATE PERSON. (a) The person specified by the security or by special endorsement to be entitled to the security; (b) if a person described in paragraph (a) is described as a fiduciary but is no longer serving in the described capacity, either that person or his successor; (c) if the security or endorsement mentioned in paragraph (a) specifies more than one person as fiduciaries and one or more are no longer serving in the described capacity, the remaining fiduciary or fiduciaries, whether or not a successor has been appointed or qualified; (d) if a person described in paragraph (a) is an individual and is without capacity to act by reason of death, incompetence, infancy, minority or otherwise, his fiduciary; (e) if the security or endorsement mentioned in paragraph (a) specifies more than one person with right of survivorship and by reason of death all cannot sign, the survivor or survivors; (f) a person having power to sign under applicable law or a power of attorney; or (g) to the extent that a person described in paragraphs (a) to (f) may act through an agent, his authorized agent. *Canada Business Corporations Act*, R.S.C. 1985, c. C-44, s. 65.

APPROPRIATE UNIT. A unit of employees appropriate for the purpose of bargaining collectively. *The Trade Union Act*, R.S.S. 1978, c. T-17, s. 2.

APPROPRIATION. *n.* 1. Means by which Parliament or a legislature regulates the expenditure of public money voted to be applied to particular purposes. 2. Any authority of Parliament to pay money out of the Consolidated Revenue Fund. *Financial Administration Act*, R.S.C. 1985, c. F-11, s. 2. 3. Any authority of a legislature to pay money out of the Consolidated Fund. 4. An authorization contained in any Ordinance to make a disbursement from the Revenue Fund and, unless the context requires otherwise, includes a statutory appropriation. *Financial Administration Act*, S.N.W.T. 1982, c. 2, s. 2. 5. Includes a revolving fund, working capital advance and special account. *Accountable Advances Regulations*, C.R.C., c. 668, s. 2. See MIS~; STATUTORY ~.

APPROPRIATION BILL. A bill ordered to be brought in by the House when it concurs with the Estimates. A. Fraser, G.A. Birch & W.A. Dawson, eds., *Beauchesne's Rules and Forms of the House of Commons of Canada*, 5th ed. (Toronto: Carswell, 1978) at 173.

APPROVAL. *n.* Confirmation; acceptance; ratification. See SALE ON ~.

APPROVE. *v.* To confirm, accept, ratify.

APPROVED. *adj.* Authorized, directed or ratified.

APPROVED COMPLEMENT. The number of bassinets, beds, and cribs for newborns which a provincial authority approves for a hospital.

APPROVED CONTAINER. 1. A container of a kind that is designed to receive a sample of the breath of a person for chemical analysis and that is approved as suitable for the purposes of this section by order of the Attorney General of Canada. *Criminal Code*, R.S.C. 1985, c. C-46, s. 255(6). 2. (a) In respect of breath samples a container of a kind that is designed to receive a sample of the breath of a person for analysis and is approved as suitable for the purposes of section 258 by order of the Attorney General of Canada; and (b) in respect of blood samples,

a container of a kind that is designed to receive a sample of the blood of a person for analysis and is approved as suitable for the purposes of section 258 by order of the Attorney General of Canada. *Criminal Law Amendment Act*, R.S.C. 1985 (1st Supp.), c. 27, s. 254.

APPROVED COURSE OF STUDY. A course or courses of study at an eligible institution of at least four weeks duration approved by the Minister leading to a certificate, diploma or degree. *Ministry of Colleges and Universities Act*, R.R.O. 1980, Reg. 644, s. 1.

APPROVED CREDIT AGENCY. A lending agency that may be approved by the Lieutenant Governor in Council for the purpose of making loans to the society or the company for the purposes of this Act. *The Co-operative Guarantee Act*, R.S.S. 1978, c. C-35, s. 2.

APPROVED DEVICE. A colostomy or ileostomy set that is prescribed by a physician and that is approved by the Director. Ontario regulations.

APPROVED DRUG AND PHARMACEUTICAL. (i) A drug prescribed by a physician or member of the Royal College of Dental Surgeons of Ontario and approved by the Minister of Health for Ontario, and (ii) a drug and medication listed in Schedules A and B established for the purposes of Part VI of the Health Disciplines Act or registered under the Proprietary or Patent Medicine Act (Canada), that is not prescribed by a physician or a member of the Royal College of Dental Surgeons of Ontario and that is approved by the Director. Ontario regulations.

APPROVED EMPLOYER. An employer for the benefit of whose employees there is an established superannuation or pension fund or plan approved by the Minister for the purposes of this Part, and includes the administrator of any such superannuation or pension fund or plan established for those employees. *Public Service Superannuation Act*, R.S.C. 1985, c. P-36, s. 40.

APPROVED FACILITY. Any institution, building or other premises or place, established for the diagnosis or treatment of persons afflicted with or suffering from sickness, disease or injury, or for the treatment of convalescent or chronically ill persons that is approved under this Act. *Hospitals Act*, R.S.P.E.I. 1974, c. H-11, s. 1.

APPROVED FIRE-DOOR. A fire-door including the hardware which has been approved and labelled by the Underwriters' Laboratories of Canada or Underwriters' Laboratories Incorporated, for the location in which it is used. *Power Corporation Act*, R.R.O. 1980, Reg. 794, s. 0.

APPROVED HATCHERY SUPPLY FLOCK.
A flock of poultry that is (a) a primary breeding flock or a flock descended from a primary breeding flock; and (b) designated as an approved hatchery supply flock in accordance with regulations in force in the province in which the flock is located. *Hatchery Regulations,* C.R.C., c. 1023, s. 2.

APPROVED HOME. A home certified in accordance with legislation in which patients may be placed from a psychiatric facility.

APPROVED HOSPITAL. A hospital in a province approved for the purposes of this section by the Minister of Health of that province. *Criminal Code,* R.S.C. 1985, c. C-46, s. 287(6).

APPROVED INSTALLMENT CREDIT AGENCY. A corporation, other than a bank, that is authorized to lend money to a purchaser of goods or to purchase obligations representing loans or advances to a purchaser of goods and is approved by the Governor in Council for the purpose of making loans under Part V. *National Housing Act,* R.S.C. 1985, c. N-11, s. 2.

APPROVED INSTRUMENT. 1. An instrument of a kind that is designed to receive and make a chemical analysis of a sample of the breath of a person in order to measure the proportion of alcohol in the blood of that person and that is approved as suitable for the purposes of this section by order of the Attorney General of Canada. *Criminal Code,* R.S.C. 1985, c. C-46, s. 255(6). 2. An instrument of a kind that is designed to receive and make an analysis of a sample of the breath of a person in order to measure the concentration of alcohol in the blood of that person and is approved as suitable for the purposes of section 258 by order of the Attorney General of Canada. *Criminal Law Amendment Act,* R.S.C. 1985 (1st Supp.), c. 27, s. 254.

APPROVED LENDER. A lender or lending institution approved for purposes of making loans under governing legislation.

APPROVED LOAN. 1. A loan in respect of which the Corporation has given an undertaking pursuant to subsection 5(2). *National Housing Act,* R.S.C, 1985, c. N-11, s. 2. 2. A loan in respect of which the Corporation has given an undertaking pursuant to section 32(1)(b). *Alberta Mortgage and Housing Corporation Act,* S.A. 1984, c. A-32.5, s. 1.

APPROVED PROGRAM OF STUDY. Courses leading to a certificate, diploma or degree. Ontario regulations.

APPROVED SCREENING DEVICE. A device of a kind that is designed to ascertain the presence of alcohol in the blood of a person and that is approved for the purposes of this section by order of the Attorney General of Canada. *Criminal Law Amendment Act,* R.S.C. 1985 (1st Supp.), c. 27, s. 254.

APPROVED SECURITIES. Securities of or guaranteed by Canada or by any province of Canada, securities of an incorporated municipality of Canada, and such other securities as are authorized for the investment of trust funds under the law of the province in which they are offered for deposit and approved by the superintendent of insurance of the provinces of Canada in which the insurer is carrying on business. *Insurance Act,* R.S.O. 1980, c. 218, s. 45.

APPROVED SHARE. A share of the capital stock of a prescribed labour-sponsored venture capital corporation acquired by an individual where he is the first person, other than a broker or dealer in securities, to be a registered holder thereof. *Income Tax Act,* R.S.C. 1952, c. 148 (as am. S.C. 1986, c. 6, s. 73), s. 127.4(1).

APPROVEMENT. *n.* Improvement.

APPROVING AUTHORITY. (a) Any officer not below the rank of brigadier-general; or (b) an officer not below the rank of colonel designated by the Minister as an approving authority for the purposes of this section. *National Defence Act,* R.S.C. 1985, c. N-5, s. 163(3).

APPROXIMATELY. *adv.* An interval or amount that does not vary from the average interval or amount by more than 10 per cent. *Consumer Protection Act,* R.R.O. 1980, Reg. 181, s. 18.

APPROXIMATE ODDS. The odds calculated in accordance with these Regulations before betting on a race has closed. *Race Track Supervision Regulations,* C.R.C., c. 441, s. 2.

APPROXIMATE ODDS CALCULATOR. A person who calculates the approximate odds. *Race Track Supervision Regulations,* C.R.C., c. 441, s. 2.

APPURTENANCE. *n.* One thing which belongs to another thing.

APPURTENANT. *adj.* Belonging or pertaining to.

A.P.R. *abbr.* Atlantic Provinces Reports, 1975-.

A PRIORI. [L.] From cause to effect.

APRON. *n.* That part of an aerodrome or airport, other than the manoeuvring area, intended to accommodate the loading and unloading of passengers and cargo, the refuelling, servicing, maintenance and parking of aircraft, and any movement of aircraft, vehicles and pedestrians necessary for such purposes. See CONTROLLED ~. Canada regulations.

APRON TRAFFIC. All aircraft, vehicles, pedestrians and equipment utilizing the apron area of the airport. *Airport Traffic Regulations*, C.R.C., c. 886, s. 2.

APRON TRAFFIC CONTROL CLEARANCE. Authorization by an apron traffic control unit for an aircraft to proceed on a controlled apron. *Airport Traffic Regulations*, C.R.C., c. 886, s. 64.

APRON TRAFFIC CONTROL INSTRUCTION. A directive issued by an apron traffic control unit for airport apron traffic and gate control purposes. *Airport Traffic Regulations*, C.R.C., c. 886, s. 64.

APRON TRAFFIC CONTROL UNIT. Staff of an airport that provides apron traffic control service at the airport and includes the staff of a mobile control vehicle. *Airport Traffic Regulations*, C.R.C., c. 886, s. 64.

APT. *abbr.* Apartment.

APT DESCRIPTIVE WORDS. Metes and bounds description and includes an abbreviated description. *Land Title Act*, R.S.B.C. 1979, c. 219, s. 1.

APTITUDE TEST. A test designed to measure abilities such as mechanical or clerical, or to determine ability to learn a second or subsequent language.

APT WORDS. Words which produce the intended legal effect.

AQUA CEDIT SOLO. [L.] The water goes with the soil.

AQUACULTURAL PLANT. A fish-breeding plant or an establishment in which aquatic plants are cultivated or harvested commercially. *Aquaculture Credit Act*, S.Q. 1984, c. 21, s. 1.

AQUACULTURAL PRODUCE. Aquatic flora and fauna raised or being raised as part of an aquacultural operation. *Aquacultural Act*, S.N.S. 1983, c. 2, s. 2.

AQUACULTURE. *n.* 1. (1) The commercial production or breeding of fish, amphibians, echinoderms, crustaceans or shellfish or their eggs, sexual products or larvae for consumption or stocking purposes; or (2) the commercial cultivation or harvesting of aquatic plants. 2. Any activity in which energy, materials and organisms are intentionally manipulated in aquatic or marine systems in order to increase the productivity of the desired organic products including edible products, industrial products and decorative materials.

AQUA CURRIT ET DEBET CURRERE. [L.] Water flows and should flow.

AQUAGE. *n.* Watercourse.

AQUAGIUM. *n.* Watercourse.

AQUATIC. *adj.* Refers to fresh, brackish or marine water. *Aquaculture Act*, S.N.S. 1983, c. 2, s. 2.

AQUATIC PLANT. Includes benthic and detached algae, marine flowering plants, brown algae, red algae, green algae and phytoplankton. *Fisheries Act*, R.S.B.C. 1979, c. 137, s. 12.

AQUATIC RIGHTS. Rights which persons have to running or still water.

AQUICULTURAL PLANT. See ECONOMIC ~.

AQUIFER. *n.* A water-bearing formation that transmits or is capable of transmitting water in sufficient quantities to serve as a source of water supply. *Ontario Water Resources Act*, R.R.O. 1980, Reg. 739, s. 1.

A.R. *abbr.* 1. Anno Regni. 2. Alberta Reports, 1977-.

ARABLE. *adj.* Suitable for purposes of cultivation.

ARABLE LAND. Land which is suitable for cultivation.

ARACHNOID MATER. The middle membrane which covers the brain and spinal cord. F.A. Jaffe, *A Guide to Pathological Evidence*, 2d ed. (Toronto: Carswell, 1983) at 169.

ARB. *abbr.* Arbitrator.

ARB. BD. *abbr.* Arbitration Board.

ARBITER. *n.* Referee; arbitrator.

ARBITRABILITY. *n.* The capability of matter to be determined by an arbitrator or referee.

ARBITRAGE. *n.* The act of purchasing in one place, where a thing is cheaper, and selling somewhere else simultaneously.

ARBITRAL AWARD. An award made by a board or an arbitrator appointed in respect of a dispute. See FOREIGN ~.

ARBITRAL TRIBUNAL. A sole arbitrator or a panel of arbitrators.

ARBITRAMENT. *n.* The award or decision of arbitrators upon a matter of dispute.

ARBITRAMENT AND AWARD. When parties had submitted a question to an arbitrator and received an award, they could successfully plead this in an action for damages as a good defence to the action.

ARBITRAMENTUM AEQUUM TRIBUIT CUIQUE SUUM. [L.] A just arbitrament awards right to each person.

ARBITRARILY. *adv.* Capriciously; without limits of power.

ARBITRARILY DETAINED. Detained without proper procedures having been followed.

ARBITRARILY IMPRISONED. Imprisoned without proper procedures having been followed.

ARBITRARY. *adj.* Capricious, unreasonable or unjustifiable.

ARBITRARY PUNISHMENT. Punishment ordered at a judge's discretion.

ARBITRATION. *n.* 1. The determination of a dispute by an arbitrator. 2. A procedure to determine an interest dispute. See AD HOC ~; COMMERCIAL ~; COMPULSORY ~; GRIEVANCE ~; INTEREST ~; LABOUR ~; STAY OF ~.

ARBITRATION AGREEMENT. An agreement by the parties to submit to arbitration all or certain disputes which have arisen or which may arise between them in respect of a defined legal relationship, whether contractual or not. An arbitration agreement may be in the form of an arbitration clause in a contract or in the form of a separate agreement. See INTERNATIONAL ~.

ARBITRATION BOARD. A board constituted by or pursuant to a collective agreement or by agreement between the parties of a collective agreement.

ARBITRATION CLAUSE. The clause in a contract providing for submission of disputes under contract to arbitration for resolution.

ARBITRATOR. *n.* 1. A person who decides disputes on the basis of evidence which the parties adduce. D.J.M. Brown and D.M. Beatty, *Canadian Labour Arbitration*, 2d ed. (Aurora: Canada Law Book, 1977) at 13. 2. Includes umpire and referee in the nature of an arbitrator. See BROADCASTING ~; PERMANENT ~; PROFESSIONAL ~.

ARBITRIUM EST JUDICIUM. [L.] The award of an arbitrator is the same as a judgment.

ARBOR DUM CRESCIT; LIGNUM CUM CRESCERE NESCIT. [L.] While growing a tree is called a tree, but it is called timber when it has reached its fullest growth.

ARCHAEOLOGICAL INVESTIGATION. Investigation by any person in or on lands in or of the province for the purpose of discovering in or forming part of the soil (including, without limitation of the generality of the word "soil", soil under any water, fresh or salt) within or of the province remains of ancient civilization or historic objects but does not include studies, surveys or examinations which do not involve interference with, or removal of, (i) the soil, or (ii) any historic objects in, or partly in, the soil.

ARCHAEOLOGICAL OBJECT. An object that is the product of human art, workmanship or use, including plant and animal remains that have been modified by or deposited due to human activities, and that is of value for its historic or archaeological significance.

ARCHAEOLOGICAL PROPERTY. Any moveable or immoveable property indicating prehistoric or historic human occupation. *Cultural Property Act*, R.S.Q. 1977, c. B-4, s. 1.

ARCHAEOLOGICAL RESOURCE. A work of man that (i) is primarily of value for its prehistoric, historic, cultural or scientific significance, and (ii) is or was buried or partially buried in land in Alberta or submerged beneath the surface of any watercourse or permanent body of water in Alberta, and includes those works of man or classes of works of man designated by the regulations as archaeological resources. *Historical Resources Act*, R.S.A. 1980, c. H-8, s. 1.

ARCHAEOLOGICAL SITE. 1. A place where archaeological property is found. *Cultural Property Act*, R.S.Q. 1977, c. B-4, s. 1. 2. A site or work of archaeological, ethnological or historical importance, interest or significance or where an archaeological specimen is found, and includes explorers' cairns. Canada regulations.

ARCHAEOLOGICAL SPECIMEN. An object or specimen of archaeological, ethnological or historical importance, interest or significance and includes explorers' documents. Canada regulations.

ARCHETYPE. *n.* The original from which copies are made.

ARCHITECT. *n.* 1. A person who is engaged for hire, gain or hope of reward in (i) the planning, designing or supervision of, or (ii) the supplying of plans, drawings or specifications for, the erection, construction, enlargement or alteration of buildings for other persons, but does not include a person employed by a registered architect as a draftsman, student clerk of works, superintendent or in any other similar capacity, nor a superintendent of buildings paid by the owner thereof and acting under the directions and control of a registered architect. 2. A person who is registered or licensed or who holds a certificate of practice or a temporary licence under the Architects Act or is registered as a member of the provincial association of architects.

ARCHITECT'S CERTIFICATE. A certificate of completion required by a building contract.

ARCHITECTS FIRM. A partnership or corporation (i) that (A) confines its practice to providing architectural consulting services, or (B) if it does not confine its practice to providing architectural consulting services, engages in a practice satisfactory to the Joint Board, and (ii) in which registered architects (A) hold a majority interest, and (B) control the partnership or corporation, and that is otherwise entitled to engage in the practice of architecture. Alberta statutes.

ARCHITECTURAL SERVICES. Services that are part of or are related to the practice of architecture. *Architects Act*, S.O. 1984, c. 12, s. 1.

ARCHITECTURAL WORK OF ART. Any building or structure having an artistic character or design, in respect of that character or design, or any model for the building or structure, but the protection afforded by this Act is confined to the artistic character and design, and does not extend to processes or methods of construction. *Copyright Act*, R.S.C. 1985, c. C-42, s. 2.

ARCHITECTURE. See PRACTICE OF ~.

ARCHIVES. *n.* 1. A place where old records are kept. 2. The body of documents of all kinds, regardless of date, created or received by a person or body in meeting requirements or carrying on activities, preserved for their general information value. *Archives Act*, S.Q. 1983, c. 38, s. 2. See PRIVATE ~; PUBLIC ~; PUBLIC ~ CANADA.

ARCHIVIST. *n.* One who maintains archives.

ARCTIC WATERS. The waters adjacent to the mainland and islands of the Canadian arctic within the area enclosed by the sixtieth parallel of north latitude, the one hundred and forty-first meridian of west longitude and a line measured seaward from the nearest Canadian land a distance of one hundred nautical miles, except that in the area between the islands of the Canadian arctic and Greenland, where the line of equidistance between the islands of the Canadian arctic and Greenland is less than one hundred nautical miles from the nearest Canadian land, that line shall be substituted for the line measured seaward one hundred nautical miles from the nearest Canadian land. *Arctic Waters Pollution Prevention Act*, R.S.C. 1985, c. A-12, s. 2.

AREA. *n.* 1. A district designated for a particular purpose. 2. A city, town, village, county, municipal district or improvement district. 3. A polling district or districts, or a part of a polling district or districts. See ATTENDANCE ~; BASIC ~; BUILDING ~; BUILT-UP ~; BURNING PERMIT ~; CLAIM ~; COMMON ~S; COMMUNITY IMPROVEMENT PROJECT ~; COMPULSORY PILOTAGE ~; CONTROL ~; CONVENTION ~; CROWN RESERVE ~; DANGER ~; DRAINAGE ~; FELLING ~; FIRE HAZARD ~; FLOOR ~; FLYING DISPLAY ~; FOREST ~; FOREST FIRE ~; FORWARD SORTATION ~; FRONT ~; GREENSPOND ~; GROSS ~; GROUP PICNIC ~; GULF ~; HEAD IMPACT ~; LABOUR MARKET ~; LAKE SHORE ~; LAND DEVELOPMENT ~; LANDING ~; LEASE ~; LICENCE ~; LIVESTOCK AUCTION SALE ~; LOADING ~; LOCAL OPTION ~; LOT ~; LURE CROP ~; MANOEUVRING ~; MARINE ~; MERGED ~; METROPOLITAN ~; MINING ~; MOVEMENT ~; NATURAL ~; NATURE CONSERVANCY ~; NEIGHBOURHOOD IMPROVEMENT ~; NO SHOOTING ~; OCCUPIED ~; OCEAN SHORE ~; OFFSHORE ~; OUTSIDE CUSTOMS ~; PELVIC IMPACT ~; PERMIT ~; PROTECTED ~; PUBLIC OYSTER FISHING ~; PUBLIC PARKING ~; PURE WATER ~S; QUARANTINE ~; RAMP ~; REDEVELOPMENT ~; RESTRICTED ~; RESTRICTED SPEED ~; RETENTION ~; RURAL ~; SERVICE ~; SHORE ~; SPACING ~; SPEED LIMIT ~; TAILINGS IMPOUNDMENT ~; TARGET ~; TAXATION ~; TUBERCULOSIS-ACCREDITED ~; UNIT ~; UPPER ISLAND COVE AND BRYANT'S COVE ~; URBAN ~; VACANT ~; WORKING ~.

AREA AGREEMENT. A collective agreement covering a geographical area.

AREA AUTHORITY. The governing body of an area. *Conservation and Development Amendment Act, 1979*, S.S. 1979, c. 11, s. 3.

AREA CONTROL LIST. A list of countries established under section 4. *Export and Import Permits Act*, R.S.C. 1985, c. E-19, s. 2.

AREA DRAIN. A drain installed to collect surface water from an open area. *Ontario Water Resources Act*, R.R.O. 1980, Reg. 736, s. 1.

AREA FRANCHISE. A contract, agreement or arrangement between a franchisor and a subfranchisor whereby the subfranchisor for a consideration given or agreed to be given in whole or in part for that purpose, is granted the right to trade in the franchise. *Franchises Act*, R.S.A. 1980, c. F-17, s. 1.

AREA PRACTICE. The custom prevailing in a geographical area concerning employees' rights and benefits.

AREA TAX. Any tax that is levied on the owners of real property and that is computed by applying a rate to all or part of the assessed dimension of real property and includes any tax levied on the owners of real property that is in the nature of a local improvement tax, a development tax or a redevelopment tax but does not include a tax in respect of mineral rights. *Municipal Grants Act*, R.S.C. 1985, c. M-13, s. 2.

AREA-WIDE BARGAINING. Negotiation of a collective agreement between a union and the employers in a geographical area.

AREA YIELD. The average yield of an insurable crop in an area greater than an insurance unit. *The Saskatchewan Crop Insurance Act*, R.S.S. 1978, c. S-12, s. 2.

ARENDRE. *var.* **A RENDRE.** *v.* [Fr.] To yield; to render.

ARENTARE. *v.* To rent.

A RESCRIPTIS VALET ARGUMENTUM. [L.] An argument based on ancient writs is sound.

ARGENTINE. *n.* A fish of the species Argentiva silvus. *Northwest Atlantic Fisheries Regulations*, C.R.C., c. 860, s. 2.

ARGUENDO. [L.] While arguing.

ARGUMENT. *n.* A method of establishing belief by using a course of reasoning. See CLOSING ~; ORAL ~.

ARGUMENT A CONTRARIO. A reason advanced to treat two compared propositions in contrary fashion.

ARGUMENTATIVE. *adj.* 1. In describing a pleading, containing not only allegations of fact but arguments as to how those facts bear on the disputed matter. 2. In the old common law pleading, described a pleading in which a material fact was stated by inference only.

ARGUMENTUM AB AUCTORITATE EST FORTISSIMUM IN LEGE. [L.] An argument based on authority is the most effective known to the law.

ARGUMENTUM AB AUCTORITATE PLURIMUM VALET IN LEGE. [L.] An argument based on authority has the greatest weight in the law.

ARGUMENTUM AB IMPOSSIBILI PLURIMUM VALET IN LEGE. [L.] An argument deduced from the fact that something is impossible has much weight in the law.

ARGUMENTUM AB INCONVENIENTI PLURIMUM VALET IN LEGE. [L.] An argument based on inconvenience has great weight in the law.

ARGUMENTUM A COMMUNITER ACCIDENTIBUS IN JURE FREQUENS EST. [L.] The argument that an event or thing commonly happens is often made in the law.

ARGUMENTUM A DIVISIONE EST FORTISSIMUM IN JURE. [L.] Argument by division is the most effective known to the law.

ARGUMENTUM A FORTIORI. [L.] Argument from the stronger to the weaker.

ARGUMENTUM A MAJORI AD MINUS NEGATIVE NON VALET; VALET E CONVERSO. [L.] Argument in the negative from the greater to the less is not useful; but argument in the negative from the less to the greater is.

ARGUMENTUM A SIMILI VALET IN LEGE. [L.] An argument from a similar case prevails in law.

ARITHMETICAL OR ACTUARIAL METHOD. The court first determines the appropriate discount rate to deal with projected interest and inflation rates when calculating a lump sum to produce an annual income of a certain amount which will exhaust itself after a certain period. K.D. Cooper-Stephenson & I.B. Saunders, *Personal Injury Damages in Canada* (Toronto: Carswell, 1981) at 74.

ARMA IN ARMATOS SUMERE JURA SINUNT. [L.] To use arms against persons who are armed is justifiable.

ARMED FORCES. 1. Includes army, naval and air forces or services, combatant or non-combatant, but does not include surgical, medical, nursing and other services that are engaged solely in humanitarian work and under the control or supervision of the Canadian Red Cross or other recognized Canadian humanitarian society. *Foreign Enlistment Act*, R.S.C. 1985, c. F-28, s. 2. 2. The Merchant Marine, Naval, Army and Air Forces of Canada or an ally. *An Act to Amend the Members Superannuation Act*, S.N.B. 1986, c. 54, s. 1.

ARMISTICE. *n.* Cessation of hostilities.

ARM OF THE SEA. A river, bay, port, cove, or creek where water, salt or fresh, ebbs and flows.

ARMOURED CABLE. A cable provided with a wrapping of steel wires forming an integral part of the assembly, primarily for the purpose of mechanical protection but which may also be used to provide continuity to ground. *Coal Mines Regulation Act*, R.S.N.S. 1967, c. 36, s. 84.

ARMOURED CAR SERVICE. A person who provides the service of transporting property in an armoured vehicle and who employs for that purpose a person who is in possession of a firearm for use in connection with his employment. *Private Investigators and Security Agencies Act*, S.B.C. 1980, c. 45, s. 1.

ARM'S LENGTH. *var.* **ARM'S-LENGTH.** (a) Related persons shall be deemed not to deal with each other at arm's length; and (b) it is a question of fact whether persons not related to each other were at a particular time dealing with each other at arm's length. *Income Tax Act*, R.S.C. 1952, c. 148 (as am. S.C. 1970-71-72, c. 63), s. 251(1). See AT ~.

ARM'S LENGTH SALE. 1. A sale of goods by a licensed manufacturer to a person with whom the licensed manufacturer is dealing at arm's length, within the meaning of section 251 of the Income Tax Act, at the time of the sale. *Excise Tax Act*, R.S.C. 1985 (2d Supp.), c. 7, s. 68.21. 2. The provision of a taxable service for an amount charged by a licensee to a person with whom the licensee is dealing at arm's length, within the meaning of section 251 of the Income Tax Act, at the time the service is provided. *Excise Tax Act*, R.S.C. 1985 (2d Supp.), c. 7, s. 68.15.

ARMY. *n.* The military force of a country intended to operate on land.

AROMA. See NORMAL FLAVOUR AND ~.

ARPENT. *n.* 1. As a measure of area 32 400 square feet (French measure), a unit of measurement to describe certain land in Quebec. *Weights and Measures Act*, S.C. 1970-71-72, c. 26, Schedule III. 2. As a measure of length 180 feet (French measure), a unit of measurement to describe certain land in Quebec. *Weights and Measures Act*, S.C. 1970-71-72, c.26, Schedule III.

ARRAIGN. *v.* To bring a prisoner to the bar of a court to answer a charge.

ARRAIGNMENT. *n.* Calling a prisoner by name, reading the indictment, demanding of the prisoner whether he or she is guilty or not guilty, and entering the prisoner's plea.

ARRANGEMENT. *n.* With respect to a corporation, includes, (a) a reorganization of the shares of any class or series of the corporation or of the stated capital of any such class or series; (b) the addition to or removal from the articles of the corporation of any provision or the change of any such provision; (c) an amalgamation of the corporation with another corporation; (d) an amalgamation of a body corporate with a corporation that results in an amalgamated corporation; (e) a transfer of all or substantially all the property of the corporation to another body corporate in exchange for securities, money or other property of the body corporate; (f) an exchange of securities of the corporation held by security holders for other securities, money or other property of the corporation or securities, money or other property of another body corporate that is not a take-over bid as defined in the Securities Act; (g) a liquidation or dissolution of the corporation; (h) any other reorganization or scheme involving the business or affairs of the corporation or of any or all of the holders of its securities or of any options or rights to acquire any of its securities that is, at law, an arrangement; and (i) any combination of the foregoing. See EXTRADITION ~; PREVENIENT ~; TRADE-IN ~.

ARREARAGE. *n.* An amount overdue and unpaid.

ARREARS. *n.* Amounts overdue and unpaid. See IN ~; TAX ~.

ARREARS OF TAX. Tax unpaid and outstanding after the expiry of the year in which they were imposed, and includes penalties for default in payment.

ARRENDARE. *v.* To lease land by the year.

ARREST. *n.* 1. Actual restraint on a person's liberty against that person's will imposed by applying force or by circumstances that threaten using force. 2. An admiralty action brought against a ship. J.G. McLeod, *The Conflict of Laws* (Calgary: Carswell, 1983) at 111. 3. Seizure of property under a warrant of the Federal Court. D. Sgayias *et al.*, *Federal Court Practice 1988* (Toronto: Carswell, 1987) at 535. See CARDIAC ~; FALSE ~.

ARRESTOR. See FLAME ~.

ARRESTS, ETC., OF KINGS, PRINCES, AND PEOPLE. Refers to political or executive acts, and does not include a loss caused by riot or by ordinary judicial process. *Insurance Act*, R.S.N.S. 1967, c. 148, s. 273.

ARROW. See FISH ~.

ARSENAL. *n.* Storage place for arms.

ARSENIC. *n.* A common, poisonous constituent of insecticides, weed killers, and rat killers which is a designated substance under the Ontario Occupational Health and Safety Act. D. Robertson, *Ontario Health and Safety Guide* (Toronto: Richard De Boo Ltd., 1988) at 5-26.

ARSON. *n.* (1) Wilfully setting fire to (a) a building or structure, whether completed or not; (b) a stack of vegetable produce or of mineral or vegetable fuel; (c) a mine; (d) a well of combustible substance; (e) a vessel or aircraft, whether completed or not; (f) timber or materials placed in a shipyard for building, repairing or fitting out a ship; (g) military or public stores or munitions of war; (h) a crop, whether standing or cut down; or (i) any wood, forest, or natural growth, or any lumber, timber, log, float, boom, dam or slide. (2) Wilfully and for a fraudulent purpose setting fire to property not mentioned in subsection (1). *Criminal Code*, R.S.C. 1985, c. C-46, s. 433.

ART. *n.* The mode, method or manner used to achieve a result. H.G. Fox, *The Canadian Law and Practice Relating to Letters Patent for Inventions*, 4th ed. (Toronto: Carswell, 1969) at 16. See WORDS OF ~; WORK OF ~.

ARTEFACT. *n.* An artificially produced, not a natural, change. F.A. Jaffe, *A Guide to Pathological Evidence*, 2d ed. (Toronto: Carswell, 1983) at 169. See IATROGENIC ~; POST MORTEM ~.

ARTERIAL HIGHWAY. A highway classified by the Minister as an arterial highway under the Highway Act. *All-Terrain Vehicle Act*, S.N.B. 1985, c. A-7.11, s. 1.

ARTERIOR-VENOUS ANEURYSM. An aneurysm including a direct connection between an artery and a vein. F.A. Jaffe, *A Guide to Pathological Evidence*, 2d ed. (Toronto: Carswell, 1983) at 168.

ARTERIOSCLEROSIS. *n.* Hardening, thickening and loss of elasticity of the walls of arteries, often accompanied by narrowing of their lumens. F.A. Jaffe, *A Guide to Pathological Evidence*, 2d ed. (Toronto: Carswell, 1983) at 169.

ARTERY. *n.* A vessel which carries blood from the heart to the body's tissues. F.A. Jaffe, *A Guide to Pathological Evidence*, 2d ed. (Toronto: Carswell, 1983) at 169. See CORONARY ~.

ARTICLE. *n.* 1. Real and personal property of every description including (a) money, (b) deeds and instruments relating to or evidencing the title or right to property or an interest, immediate, contingent or otherwise, in a corporation or in any assets of a corporation, (c) deeds and instruments giving a right to recover or receive property, (d) tickets or like evidence of right to be in attendance at a particular place at a particular time or times or of a right to transportation, and (e) energy, however generated. *Combines Investigation Act*, R.S.C. 1985, c. C-34, s. 2. 2. Includes each separate type, size, weight and quality in which an article, within the meaning assigned by section 2, is produced. *Combines Investigation Act*, R.S.C. 1985 (2d Supp.), c. 19, s. 85. 3. Any article of merchandise, and includes any portion of any article of merchandise, whether a distinct part thereof or not, other than an article or a part thereof designated by the regulations. *Precious Metals Marking Act*, R.S.C. 1985, c. P-19, s. 2. See

DANGEROUS ~; MULTI-SERVICE ~; PATENTED ~; PLATED ~; PRECIOUS METAL ~; SECOND-HAND ~; SINGLE-SERVICE ~.

ARTICLED CLERK. A student-at-law bound by contract in writing to service with a member of the Law Society, who has filed articles of clerkship in accordance with the governing legislation.

ARTICLED STUDENT. 1. Any person validly holding a certificate of admission to the training period prescribed by by-law of the General Council. *Barreau du Québec Act*, R.S.Q. 1977, c. B-1, s. 1. 2. A person enrolled in the Bar Admission Course during the time he is not in attendance at the teaching period thereof. *Legal Aid Act*, R.R.O. 1980, Reg. 575, s. 1. 3. A person over eighteen years of age who has been duly registered by the council as a student. *The Saskatchewan Embalmers Act*, R.S.S. 1978, c. S-15, s. 2.

ARTICLES. *n.* 1. Clauses contained in a document. 2. The document itself. 3. Includes watches, jewellery and all other articles that are usually mended or repaired by a jeweller. *Liens on Goods and Chattels Act*, R.S.N.B. 1973, c. L-6, s. 1. 4. An agreement respecting training and service between a member of the Association and a student. *Surveyors acts.* 5. The original or restated articles of incorporation, articles of amendment, articles of amalgamation, articles of continuance, articles of reorganization, articles of arrangement, articles of dissolution, articles of revival and includes any amendments thereto. *Corporation acts.*

ARTICLES OF AMENDMENT. A document which changes the capital structure or the constitution of a company and is ordinarily authorized by a special resolution of the shareholders. H. Sutherland, D.B. Horsley & J.M. Edmiston, eds., *Fraser's Handbook on Canadian Company Law*, 7th ed. (Toronto: Carswell, 1985) at 453.

ARTICLES OF ASSOCIATION. Contain the internal regulations of a corporation. One of the incorporating documents in some jurisdictions. S.M. Beck *et al.*, *Cases and Materials on Partnerships and Canadian Business Corporations* (Toronto: The Carswell Company Limited, 1983) at 159.

ARTICLES OF CONTINUANCE. A document which permits a body corporate incorporated in one jurisdiction to be reconstituted in another.

ARTICLES OF INCORPORATION. 1. Incorporation takes place when these articles are delivered to the appropriate Director and a certificate of incorporation is issued. H. Sutherland, D.B. Horsley & J.M. Edmiston, eds., *Fras-*

er's *Handbook on Canadian Company Law*, 7th ed. (Toronto: Carswell, 1985) at 3. 2. The original or restated articles of incorporation, articles of amalgamation, letters patent, supplementary letters patent, a special Act and any other instrument by which a corporation is incorporated, and includes any amendments thereto. 3. Correspond to memorandum of association in those jurisdictions using that method of incorporation. S.M. Beck *et al.*, *Cases and Materials on Partnerships and Canadian Business Corporations* (Toronto: The Carswell Company Limited, 1983) at 159.

ARTICLES OF WAR. A code of laws which regulates armed forces.

ARTICULATED VEHICLE. A vehicle which can be divided into more than one part.

ARTIFACT. *n.* 1. An object (i) that is the product of human art or workmanship or both; (ii) that is of value primarily for its historic or archaeological importance or interest; and (iii) that is or has been discovered beneath the surface of the earth or uncovered from beneath the surface of the earth, whether by human activity or by natural causes. *Historic Sites and Objects Act*, R.S.M. 1970, c. H70, s. 2. 2. Any object made or worked by man, associated with historic or prehistoric cultures. *Canadian Cultural Property Export Control List*, C.R.C., c. 448, s. 1.

ARTIFICE. *n.* Contrivance or device; used to refer to fraud or deceit.

ARTIFICER. *n.* A person who is employed largely in manual labour.

ARTIFICIAL BREEDING ASSOCIATION. Any organization or person carrying on the business of the artificial insemination of domestic animals. *The Artificial Insemination (Animals) Act*, R.S.S. 1978, c. A-27, s. 2.

ARTIFICIAL BREEDING SERVICE CENTRE. An establishment where semen is collected, processed or stored and supplied to an artificial breeding association. *The Artificial Insemination (Animals) Act*, R.S.S. 1978, c. A-27, s. 2.

ARTIFICIAL FLY. 1. A single or double hook dressed with silk, tinsel, wool, fur, feathers or any combination of these or other materials commonly used in making artificial flies, but does not include a fly that has a spinning device or a weight to cause the fly to sink. 2. A wet or dry fishing fly (a) the body of which is made of plastic, cork or rubber, (b) that has not more than two hooks on a common shank, and (c) to which is attached no biological material, paste, eggs or worms other than feathers, fur, hair or fibre. *Alberta Fishery Regulations*, C.R.C., c. 838, s. 2.

ARTIFICIAL INSEMINATION. Depositing semen in the genital tract of a female domestic animal by other than the natural method.

ARTIFICIAL INSEMINATION BUSINESS. The business of collecting, acquiring, processing, storing, distributing or inseminating semen, as the case may be. *Artificial Insemination of Domestic Animals Amendment Act, 1981*, S.A. 1981, c. 6, s. 2.

ARTIFICIAL INSEMINATION CENTRE. An establishment where semen is collected, stored or distributed for purposes of artificial insemination.

ARTIFICIAL PERSON. A body corporate or other body given the status of a person by law.

ARTISTIC CHARACTERISTICS. See TRADITIONAL OR ~.

ARTISTIC ENDEAVOUR. Of an individual means the business of creating paintings, prints, etchings, drawings, sculptures or similar works of art, where such works of art are created by the individual, but does not include a business of reproducing works of art. *Income Tax Act*, R.S.C. 1952, c. 148 (as am. S.C. 1986, c. 6, s. 5), s. 10(8).

ARTISTIC WORK. Includes works of painting, drawing, sculpture and artistic craftsmanship, and architectural works of art and engravings and photographs. *Copyright Act*, R.S.C. 1985, c. C-42, s. 2. See EVERY ORIGINAL LITERARY, DRAMATIC, MUSICAL AND ~.

ARTS. *n.* The arts of the theatre, literature, music, painting, sculpture, architecture or the graphic arts, and includes any other similar creative or interpretive activity. See NATIONAL ~ CENTRE; PERFORMING ~.

A RUBRO AD NIGRUM. [L. from the red to the black] To deduce the meaning of a statute (formerly printed in black) from its title (formerly printed in red).

AS AGAINST. To contrast the positions of two people by referring to a different relationship between one of them and a third person.

ASBESTOS. *n.* 1. Naturally occurring, highly fibrous, heat insulating and chemically inert silicate minerals belonging to either serpentine or amphibole groups and include chrysolite, crocidolite, amosite, anthophyllite, tremolite and actinolite and any other mineral commonly known as asbestos. *(Foreign Judgments) Miscellaneous Statutes Amendment Act*, S.B.C. 1984, c. 26, s. 41.1. 2. A substance designated under the Ontario Occupational Health and Safety Act. D. Robertson, *Ontario Health and Safety Guide* (Toronto: Richard De Boo Ltd., 1988) at 5-28.

ASBESTOS FIBRE. A fibre of asbestos with a length of more than 5 microns and a ratio of length to breadth of three to one or more. *Asbestos Mining and Milling National Emission Standards Regulations*, C.R.C., c. 405, s. 2.

ASBESTOSIS. *n.* An industrial disease of the lungs.

AS BETWEEN. To contrast the positions of two people by referring to a different relationship between one of them and a third person.

ASCAP. *abbr.* American Society of Composers, Authors and Publishers.

ASCENDANT. *n.* The ancestor of a family.

ASCENDING REGISTER. A mechanical device in a postage meter that records the total value of impressions made by an impression die or the total dollar value of postage used. *Postage Meters Regulations*, C.R.C., c. 1287, s. 2.

ASCERTAINABLE POINT. A point found or reestablished in its original position on a line or boundary established during the original survey or on a line or boundary established during the survey of a plan of subdivision registered under the Land Titles Act or the Registry Act. *Surveys Act*, R.S.O. 1980, c. 493, s. 1.

ASCERTAINED GOODS. More particularly identified goods. G.H.L. Fridman, *Sale of Goods in Canada*, 3d ed. (Toronto: Carswell, 1986) at 56.

ASH. See INCINERATOR ~.

ASPHALT PAVING PLANT. Equipment designed to dry aggregate material and to mix the aggregate material with bituminous asphalt. *Environmental Protection Act*, R.R.O. 1980, Reg. 297, s. 1.

ASPHYXIA. *n.* Deprivation of oxygen when there is an inadequate oxygen supply or the tissues cannot use oxygen. F.A. Jaffe, *A Guide to Pathological Evidence*, 2d ed. (Toronto: Carswell, 1983) at 103. See TRAUMATIC ~.

ASPIRING FARMER. Any natural person not less than eighteen nor more than forty years of age who, being the owner or lessee of a farm, practises farming without making it his principal occupation and undertakes to make it his principal occupation within the delays and according to the conditions fixed by regulation. Quebec statutes.

ASPORTATION. *n.* Carrying away.

ASPORTAVIT. [L.] One carried away.

ASSASSINATION. *n.* Murder of a public figure for political motives.

ASSAULT. *n.* 1. Applying force intentionally to another person, directly or indirectly, without their consent; attempting or threatening, by an act or gesture, to apply force to another person if he has or causes the other person to believe upon reasonable grounds that he has, present ability to effect his purpose; or accosting or impeding another person or begging while openly wearing or carrying a weapon or imitation thereof. *Criminal Code*, R.S.C. 1985, c. C-46, s. 265(1). 2. In tort law, intentionally causing another person to fear imminent contact of a harmful or offensive nature. John G. Fleming, *The Law of Torts*, 6th ed. (Sydney: The Law Book Company Limited, 1983) at 24. See AGGRAVATED ~; COMMON ~.

ASSAULT AND BATTERY. The actual carrying out of the threatened harmful or offensive contact. John G. Fleming, *The Law of Torts*, 6th ed. (Sydney: The Law Book Company Limited, 1983) at 24.

ASSAY. *n.* 1. The quantitative determination by a recognized method for a metal or other constituent of a mine sample. *Canada Mining Regulations*, C.R.C., c. 1516, s. 2. 2. The quantification of an element in sample of rock, mineral, ore or metallurgical product. *Ministry of Energy, Mines and Petroleum Resources*, R.S.B.C. 1979, c. 270, s. 13.

ASSAYER. *n.* A person who performs an assay. *Ministry of Energy, Mines and Petroleum Resources*, R.S.B.C. 1979, c. 270, s. 13.

ASSEMBLÉE NATIONALE. See PRESIDENT OF ~.

ASSEMBLER. n. A manufacturer engaged in the business of altering vehicles that bear the national safety mark. *Motor Vehicle Safety Regulations*, C.R.C., c. 1038, s. 2.

ASSEMBLY. *n.* 1. A meeting of persons. 2. The Legislative Assembly of a province. 3. The House of Assembly of a province. See AXLE ~; FIFTH WHEEL ~; GENERAL ~; LAND ~; LEGISLATIVE ~; MULTI-OUTLET ~; OCCUPANT RESTRAINT ~; PARCEL COMPARTMENT ~; PLACE OF ~; PRODUCT RESTRAINT ~; UNLAWFUL ~.

ASSEMBLY BUILDING. A building or portions of buildings used for the congregating of persons for civic, political, social, travel, educational, recreational, or like purposes or for the consumption of food or drink. *Fire Prevention Act*, S.N.S. 1976, c. 9, s. 2.

ASSEMBLY-LINE WORK. The item being manufactured is moved along a conveyor system in order that employees may perform specific tasks on the item.

ASSEMBLY OCCUPANCY. Occupancy for gatherings of persons for civic, educational, political, recreational, religious, social, travel or other similar purpose, or for the consumption of food or drink.

ASSEMBLY YARD. Premises to which producers may deliver their hogs. Canada regulations.

ASSEMBLY YARD OPERATOR. The owner or operator of an assembly yard. Canada regulations.

ASSENSIO MENTIUM. [L.] Mutual consent needed to validate a contract.

ASSENT. *n.* See MUTUALITY OF ~; ROYAL ~.

ASSENT. *v.* To agree to, concur in or recognize a matter.

ASSESS. *v.* 1. To ascertain. 2. To value property for tax purposes.

ASSESS. *abbr.* Assessment.

ASSESSABLE PROPERTY. 1. The property shown on the assessment roll of a municipality and in respect of which (i) taxes for school purposes are required to be paid, or (ii) grants in lieu of taxes for school purposes are paid under an Act of the Legislature or an Act of Parliament. Manitoba statutes. 2. (i) Land and land covered by water; (ii) trees, bushes, shrubs and things growing upon land; (iii) mines, excavations, underground improvements and quarries; (iv) minerals, gas, oil, gems, salt, gypsum, commercially extractable stone or rock, precious or rare earth, moss or fossils in or under land; (v) buildings and structures erected or placed upon, in, over, under or affixed to land; (vi) machinery, equipment, appliances, storage and working tanks, and other things, including the supporting foundations and footings, that form an integral part of an operational unit designed for or used in processing or manufacturing except that where different lines of production equipment are used in a food processing operation for processing perishable crops at different times in the year, then only the machinery, equipment, appliances, storage and working tanks, and other things used in the line or lines that are in use for the greatest part of the production; (vii) mobile homes used for residential or commercial purposes; and (viii) rafts, floats, houseboats, and any other devices of a like nature or kind that are anchored or secured to property and used for residential or commercial purposes, whether or not they are owned by the owner of the property to which they are secured; but does not include (ix) land used as public streets, roads and highways; (x) growing or unharvested agricultural crops in or on land. *Assessment Act*, S.N.S. 1977, c. 22, s. 1.

ASSESSED. See SPECIALLY ~.

ASSESSED COSTS. Costs which have been assessed by an assessment officer; taxed costs.

ASSESSED DIMENSION. The frontage, area, other dimension or other attribute of real property established by an assessment authority for the purpose of computing a frontage or area tax. *Municipal Grants Act*, R.S.C. 1985, c. M-13, s. 2.

ASSESSED OWNER. The person appearing by the records kept by the Collector of Taxes to be the owner of any parcel of real property, unless it appears by such records that the parcel is held by an owner under agreement, in which case "assessed owner" means such owner under agreement. In the case of a parcel of Crown lands it shall mean the occupier of the said parcel. *Vancouver Charter*, R.S.B.C. 1979, c. 55, s. 498.

ASSESSED VALUE. The value established for any real property by an assessment authority for the purpose of computing a real property tax. *Municipal Grants Act*, R.S.C. 1985, c. M-13, s. 2.

ASSESSING ACT. Any Act pursuant to which an assessing authority is empowered to assess and levy rates, charges or taxes on land or in respect of the ownership of land, and includes any bylaws or regulations made under the authority of any such Act.

ASSESSING AUTHORITY. A local authority, school board or other authority having power to assess and levy rates, charges or taxes on land or in respect of the ownership of land.

ASSESSMENT. *n.* 1. Valuation of property for taxation purposes. 2. The determination of an amount payable. 3. The work to be done or the payment to be made each year to entitle the owner of a mineral claim to a certificate of work. *Yukon Quartz Mining Act*, R.S.C. 1985, c. Y-4, s. 2. See CERTIFICATE OF ~; COMMERCIAL ~; CORPORATION ~; ENVIRONMENTAL ~; ENVIRONMENTAL IMPACT ~; EQUALIZED ~; LEVEL OF ~; MUNICIPAL ~ PER CAPITA; MUNICIPAL ~ PER ROAD KILOMETRE; MUNICIPAL ~ PER ROAD MILE; NET ~; NIL ~; OTHER ~; OVERALL ~ PER CAPITA; OVERALL ~ PER ROAD KILOMETRE; REGIONAL ~ OFFICE; SCHOOL ~; SECURITY ~; SPECIAL ~; STANDARDIZED ~; UNIT OF ~.

ASSESSMENT AND TAX ROLL. The roll listing all persons in whose name real property is assessed and containing such information as is prescribed by regulation. *An Act to Amend the Assessment Act*, N.B. 1983, c. 12, s. 1.

ASSESSMENT AUTHORITY. An authority that has power by or under an Act of Parliament or the legislature of a province to establish the assessed dimension or assessed value of real property. *Municipal Grants Act*, R.S.C. 1985, c. M-13, s. 2.

ASSESSMENT BASE. See MUNICIPAL ~.

ASSESSMENT LIST. A copy of the assessment and tax roll for a municipality or other taxing authority. *An Act to Amend the Assessment Act*, N.B. 1983, c. 12, s. 1.

ASSESSMENT OF COSTS. Calculation of the procedural costs to which a party is entitled, formerly taxation of costs.

ASSESSMENT OFFICER. Taxing officer; officer of the court who carries out assessments of costs.

ASSESSMENT ROLL. An assessment roll prepared in accordance with a municipal act. See REVISED ~.

ASSESSMENT WORK. The prescribed work required to be carried out under a licence. *Mineral Act*, S. Nfld. 1975-76, c. 44, s. 2.

ASSESS O. *abbr.* Assessment Officer.

ASSESSOR. *n.* 1. The official who evaluates property for tax purposes. 2. A specialist who assists the court in determining a matter. D. Sgayias *et al.*, *Federal Court Practice 1988* (Toronto: Carswell, 1987) at 494.

ASSET. *n.* Any real or personal property or legal or equitable interest therein including money, accounts receivable or inventory. See ACTIVE ~; BALANCE SHEET ~S; BUSINESS ~; CAPITAL ~S; COMMERCIAL ~; CONTINGENT ~S; CURRENT ~S; DEPRECIATING ~S; ELIGIBLE ~ COST; FAMILY ~; FARMING ~S; FISHING ~S; FIXED ~; GOING CONCERN ~S; LENDING ~; LIQUID ~S; MATRIMONIAL ~S; PROCESSING ~S; QUALIFIED ~S; REDUNDANT ~; SOCIAL ~; SURPLUS ~S; SURPLUS CROWN ~S; TOTAL ~S; WASTING ~.

ASSETS IN CANADA. 1. All deposits that a British company has made with the Receiver General and all assets that have been vested in trust for the British company under, and for the purposes of, this Act. *Canadian and British Insurance Companies Act*, R.S.C. 1985, c. I-12, s. 193. 2. All deposits that a company has made with the Receiver General and all assets that have been vested in trust for the company under and for the purposes of this Act. *Foreign Insurance Companies Act*, R.S.C. 1985, c. I-13, s. 2.

ASSEVERATION. *n.* Positive assertion, affirmation.

ASSIGN. *v.* 1. To transfer property. 2. For a person to execute and perform every necessary or suitable deed or act for assigning, surrendering or otherwise transferring land of which that person is possessed, either for the whole estate or for any less estate. *Trustee acts.*

ASSIGN. *n.* A person to whom something is transferred or given.

ASSIGNATUS UTITUR JURE AUCTORIS. [L.] An assignee enjoys the authority of the principal.

ASSIGNED RISK PLAN. A plan operated by insurers licensed to issue motor vehicle liability policies.

ASSIGNEE. *n.* 1. The person to whom something is transferred. 2. Includes any person in whom the right or benefit concerned has become vested, as a result of any assignment or series of assignments. *Consumer Protection acts.* 3. Any person to whom an assignment of book debts is made. *Assignment of Book Debts acts.*

ASSIGNMENT. *n.* 1. Act of assigning, or the document by which a thing is assigned. 2. A transfer by a tenant of the full term remaining under the tenant's lease. W.B. Rayner & R.H. McLaren, *Falconbridge on Mortgages*, 4th ed. (Toronto: Canada Law Book, 1977) at 100. 3. Includes every legal and equitable assignment, whether absolute or by way of security, and every mortgage or other charge upon book debts. *Assignment of Book Debts acts.* 4. An assignment filed with the official receiver. *Bankruptcy Act*, R.S.C. 1985, c. B-3, s. 2. See ABSOLUTE ~.

ASSIGNMENT OF BOOK ACCOUNTS. Includes a transfer, declaration of trust without transfer, power of attorney, authority or licence to seize or acquire book accounts, or any other agreement to dispose of book accounts or an interest in them, but does not include (a) an assignment of a debt due at the date of assignment from a specified debtor; (b) an assignment of a debt growing due or to grow due under a specified contract; (c) an assignment of book accounts included in an authorized assignment under the Bankruptcy Act (Canada); (d) a marriage settlement; (e) a bill of exchange, promissory note, cheque, bill of lading or warehouse receipt; or (f) a corporation's mortgage or charge, specific or floating, of its book accounts, and contained in (i) a trust deed or similar document to secure its bonds, debentures or debenture stock; or (ii) its bonds, debentures, debenture stock, secured or not secured. *Book Accounts Assignment Act*, R.S.B.C. 1979, c. 32, s. 1.

ASSIGNMENT OF BOOK DEBTS. Includes

every legal or equitable assignment by way of security of book debts and every mortgage or other charge upon book debts. *Corporation Securities Registration acts.*

ASSIGNMENT OF SECURITY INTEREST. A notice of the assignment of a security interest or any part thereof in respect of which a security notice has been registered under this Part. *Canada Petroleum Resources,* R.S.C. 1985 (2d Supp.), c. 36, s. 84.

ASSIGNOR. *n.* 1. One who makes a transfer. 2. A corporation making an assignment of book debts. *Corporation Securities Registration acts.* 3. Any person making an assignment of book debts. *Assignment of Book Debts acts.*

ASSISE. *var.* **ASSIZE.** *n.* The trial of a civil action before a travelling judge.

ASSISTANCE. *n.* 1. Any amount, other than a prescribed amount, received or receivable at any time from a person or government, municipality or other public authority whether such amount is by way of a grant, subsidy, rebate, forgivable loan, deduction from royalty or tax, rebate of royalty or tax, investment allowance or any other form of assistance or benefit. *Income Tax Act,* R.S.C. 1952, c. 148 (as am. S.C. 1986, c. 55, s. 11(6)), s. 66(15)(a.1). 2. Aid in any form to or in respect of persons in need for the purpose of providing or providing for all or any of the following: (a) food, shelter, clothing, fuel, utilities, household supplies and personal requirements (hereinafter referred to as "basic requirements"); (b) prescribed items incidental to carrying on a trade or other employment and other prescribed special needs of any kind; (c) care in a home for special care; (d) travel and transportation; (e) funerals and burials; (f) health care services; (g) prescribed welfare services purchased by or at the request of a provincially approved agency; and (h) comfort allowances and other prescribed needs of residents or patients in hospitals or other prescribed institutions. *Canada Assistance Plan,* R.S.C. 1985, c. C-1, s. 2. 3. Old age assistance provided under provincial law to the persons and under the conditions specified in this Act and the regulations. *Old Age Assistance Act,* R.S.C. 1970, c. O-5, s. 2. See CANADA ~ PLAN; FINANCIAL ~; GOVERNMENT ~; INCOME ~; MUNICIPAL ~; SOCIAL ~; STUDENT FINANCIAL ~; WRIT OF ~.

ASSISTANT. *n.* Any person employed in or about a shop and wholly or mainly employed in serving customers, receiving orders or despatching goods, or in any office connected with a shop. *Hours of Work Act,* R.S.Nfld. 1970, c. 158, s. 2. See CLERK ~; DENTAL ~; ELEC-TION ~; LAY ~; NURSING ~; OPTOMETRIC ~.

ASSIZE. See ASSISE.

ASSN. *abbr.* Association.

ASSN. CAN. REL. IND. *abbr.* Association canadienne des relations industrielles. Congrès. Travaux. (Canadian Industrial Relations Association. Annual Meeting. Proceedings).

ASSOCIATE. *n.* 1. Where used to indicate a relationship with any person or company means, (i) any company of which such person or company beneficially owns, directly or indirectly, voting securities carrying more than 10 per cent of the voting rights attached to all voting securities of the company for the time being outstanding, (ii) any partner of that person or company, (iii) any trust or estate in which such person or company has a substantial beneficial interest or as to which such person or company serves as trustee or in a similar capacity, (iv) the spouse or any parent, son or daughter, brother or sister of that person, or (v) any relative of such person or of that person's spouse who has the same home as such person. 2. (a) Where a broker is a partnership, any partner; (b) where a broker is a corporation, any director or officer of the corporation, or a person who has a material interest in the corporation; (c) any manager or salesman of a broker; (d) any spouse of a broker or of an individual mentioned in clauses (a) to (c); or (e) any corporation, firm, partnership, association, syndicate or other unincorporated organization in which a broker or any person mentioned in clauses (a) to (d) has a material interest. *The Real Estate Brokers Act, 1987,* S.S. 1986-87-88, c. R-2.1, s. 54. 3. A person, whether directly or indirectly through one or more intermediaries, (i) who has the power to direct or to cause to be directed the management and policies of any gas transmitter, distributor or storage company, (ii) whose management and policies any gas transmitter, distributor or storage company has the power to direct or to cause to be directed, (iii) whose management and policies any other person has the power to direct or to cause to be directed, provided that such other person has such power to direct or to cause to be directed the management and policies of any gas transmitter, distributor or storage company. *Ontario Energy Board Act,* R.S.O. 1980, c. 332, s. 1.

ASSOCIATE CHIEF JUDGE. The Associate Chief Judge of the Court. *Tax Court of Canada Act,* R.S.C. 1985, c. T-2, s. 2.

ASSOCIATE CHIEF JUSTICE. The Associate Chief Justice of the Court. *Federal Court Act,* R.S.C. 1985, c. F-7, s. 2.

ASSOCIATED. *adj.* In relation to objects, objects forming a collection assembled by a person, objects that originate from a common source or objects devoted to a single theme, person, place, event or thing. *Canadian Cultural Property Export Control List*, C.R.C., c. 448, s. 1.

ASSOCIATED CORPORATION. 1. One corporation is associated with another in a taxation year if at any time in the year, (a) one of the corporations controlled, directly or indirectly in any manner whatever, the other; (b) both of the corporations were controlled directly or indirectly in any manner whatever, by the same person or group of persons; (c) each of the corporations was controlled, directly or indirectly in any manner whatever, by a person and the person who so controlled one of the corporations was related to the person who so controlled the other, and either of those persons owned, in respect of each corporation, not less than 25% of the issued shares of any class, other than a specified class, of the capital stock thereof; (d) one of the corporations was controlled, directly or indirectly in any manner whatever, by a person and that person was related to each member of a group of persons that so controlled the other corporation, and that person owned, in respect of the other corporation, not less than 25% of the issued shares of any class, other than a specified class, of the capital stock thereof; or (e) each of the corporations was controlled, directly or indirectly in any manner whatever, by a related group and each of the members of one of the related groups was related to all of the members of the other related group, and one or more persons who were members of both related groups, either alone or together, owned, in respect of each corporation, not less than 25% of the issued shares of any class, other than a specified class of the capital stock thereof. *Income Tax Act*, R.S.C. 1952, c. 148 (as am. S.C. 1988, c. 55, s. 192(1)), s. 256(1). 2. A corporation other than a central credit union that is controlled by (a) two or more credit unions, or (b) two or more credit unions and one or more other corporations each of which is controlled by a credit union. *Credit Union Amendment Act*, S.B.C. 1980, c. 8, s. 1.

ASSOCIATED GOVERNMENT. Her Majesty's Government in the United Kingdom, any other government of the Commonwealth, the government of a country that is a member of the North Atlantic Treaty Organization or the government of any other country designated by the Governor in Council as being a country the defence of which is vital to the defence of Canada. *Defence Production Act*, R.S.C. 1985, c. D-1, s. 2.

ASSOCIATED PERSONS. Persons associated with each other, namely, (a) persons related to each other; or (b) persons not related to each other, but not dealing with each other at arm's length. *Special Imports Measures Act*, R.S.C. 1985, c. S-15, s. 2.

ASSOCIATED PRODUCT. Any product of petroleum other than gasoline, wax and asphalt. *Gasoline Handling Act*, R.S.O. 1980, c. 185, s. 1.

ASSOCIATED TRADE MARKS. Confusing trade marks which the applicant owns. H.G. Fox, *The Canadian Law of Trade Marks and Unfair Competition*, 3d ed. (Toronto: Carswell, 1972) at 210.

ASSOCIATES OF THE NON-RESIDENT. With reference to any particular day, (a) any shareholders associated with the non-resident on that day; and (b) any persons who would be deemed to be shareholders associated with the non-resident on that day if both the non-resident and such persons were shareholders. Canada statutes.

ASSOCIATES OF THE RESIDENT. With reference to any particular day, (a) any shareholders associated with the resident on that day; and (b) any persons who would, under subsection 109(2), be deemed to be shareholders associated with the resident on that day if both he and such persons were shareholders. *Bank Act*, R.S.C. 1985, c. B-1, s. 113.

ASSOCIATION. *n.* 1. An employers' organization, a trade union, a professional association or a business or trade association. 2. Any association of persons formed in any foreign country on the plan known as Lloyd's, whereby each member of the association that participates in a policy becomes liable for a stated, limited or proportionate part of the whole amount payable under the policy. *Foreign Insurance Companies Act*, R.S.C. 1985, c. I-13, s. 2. 3. An association incorporated by or pursuant to an Act of Parliament or of the legislature of a province that owns or leases a race-course and conducts horse-races in the ordinary course of its business and, to the extent that the applicable legislation requires that the purposes of the association be expressly stated in its constituting instrument, having as one of its purposes the conduct of horse-races. *Criminal Code*, R.S.C. 1985 (1st Supp.), c. 47, s. 1(12). 4. A cooperative credit society incorporated by special Act or by letters patent issued under this Act. *Cooperative Credit Association Act*, R.S.C. 1985, c. C-41, s. 2. 5. Any cooperative association, federation or corporation to which this Act applies. *Canada Cooperative Associations Act*, R.S.C. 1985, c. C-40, s. 3. See ACADEMIC STAFF ~; ACCI-

DENT PREVENTION ~; AGRICULTURAL FAIR ~; ALUMNI ~; AMALGAMATED ~; ARTICLES OF ~; ARTIFICIAL BREEDING ~; BODY OF ~; BOND OF ~; BUSINESS OR ~; BUSINESS OR TRADE ~; BUSINESS, PROFESSIONAL OR TRADE ~; CANADIAN PAYMENTS ~; CANADIAN STANDARDS ~; CERTIFIED ~; COMPENSATION ~; CONSTITUENCY ~; CONSUMERS' ~; COOPERATIVE ~; DENTISTS IN ~; DISTRICT ~; EMPLOYERS' ~; FACILITY ~; FARM ~; FEEDER ~; GRAZING AND FODDER ~; HOUSING ~; INSTRUCTORS ~; LABOUR ~; LAKE, FOREST AND FUR ~; LAND IMPROVEMENT ~; LIVESTOCK ~; LLOYD'S ~; MACHINERY ~; MANUFACTURING ~; MEMORANDUM OF ~; MUTUAL ~; NATIONAL FIRE PREVENTION ~; OCCUPATIONAL ~; PENSION FUND ~; POLICE ~; PRODUCTION SERVICE ~; PROFESSIONAL ~; RIGHT OF ~; TERRITORIAL ~; TRAVEL ~; UNION ~.

ASSOCIATION AGREEMENT. Collective bargaining agreement made with an employers' association.

ASSOCIATION OF EMPLOYEES. 1. A group of employees constituted as a professional syndicate, union, brotherhood or otherwise, having as its objects the study, safeguarding and development of the economic, social and educational interests of its members and particularly the negotiation and application of collective agreements. *Labour Code*, R.S.Q. 1977, c. C-27, s. 1. 2. A group of employees (i) organized for the purpose of improving their economic conditions, and (ii) free from undue influence, domination, restraint or interference by employers or associations of employers. *Alberta Labour Act*, R.S.A. 1970, c. 196, s. 43.

ASSOCIATION OF PRODUCERS. A farmers' cooperative syndicate, a farmers' cooperative association, a cooperative agricultural association, a farmers' association or professional syndicate, a union, a federation or confederation of such bodies or a professional or cooperative group of producers. Quebec statutes.

ASSOCIATION STEWARD. A person appointed by an association to act as its representative. *Race Track Supervision Regulations*, C.R.C., c. 441, s. 2.

ASSUETUDE. *n.* Custom.

ASSUME. *v.* To take on a debt or obligation.

ASSUMPSIT. [L. one promised] A form of action to recover damages for breach of a simple contract.

ASSUMPTION AGREEMENT. An arrangement by which a purchaser in a new subdivision

contracts directly with a mortgagee to make mortgage payments so that the developer in released from the covenant with the mortgage lender. D.J. Donahue & P.D. Quinn, *Real Estate Practice in Ontario*, 4th ed. (Toronto: Butterworths, 1990) at 231.

ASSUMPTION OF RISK. See VOLUNTARY ~.

ASSUMPTIONS. See ACTUARIAL ~.

ASSURANCE. *n.* 1. A transfer, deed or instrument, other than a will, by which land may be conveyed or transferred. *Limitation of Actions acts*. 2. Includes a gift, conveyance, appointment, lease, transfer, settlement, mortgage, charge, encumbrance, devise, bequest and every other assurance by deed, will or other instrument. *Mortmain and Charitable Uses Act*, R.S.O. 1980, c. 297, s. 1. 3. Insurance. See FINANCIAL ~; RE~.

ASSURANCE FUND. A fund established under a statute to indemnify certain persons against loss. See LAND TITLES ~; PRE-NEED ~.

ASSURANCES. *n.* The periodical, Assurances.

ASSURE. *v.* To make certain; to insure.

ASSURED. *n.* One who is indemnified against particular events.

ASSURER. *n.* Indemnifier; insurer.

ASTIPULATION. *n.* Mutual agreement.

ASTM. *abbr.* The American Society for Testing and Materials.

ASYLUM. *n.* A sanctuary; a place for the treatment of the mentally ill. See LOCAL ~ FOR HARMLESS INSANE.

ASYPHYXIA. *n.* Death due to lack of oxygen or inability of tissues to use oxygen. F.A. Jaffe, *A Guide to Pathological Evidence*, 2d ed. (Toronto: Carswell, 1983) at 169. See TRAUMATIC ~.

AT AN ELECTION. 1. In respect of an election in any electoral district, means the period commencing with the issue of the writ for that election and terminating on polling day or, where the writ is withdrawn or deemed to be withdrawn, terminating on the day that the writ is withdrawn or deemed to be withdrawn. 2. Includes the period between the dissolution of the House of Assembly, or the occurrence of a vacancy in consequence of which a writ for an election is eventually issued, and when a candidate is declared elected. *Elections Act*, R.S.N.S. 1967, c. 83, s. 2.

AT ARM'S LENGTH. Parties are said to be at arm's length when they are not under the control or influence of each other.

ATAXIA. *n.* A condition in which it is difficult to perform voluntary movements. F.A. Jaffe, *A Guide to Pathological Evidence*, 2d ed. (Toronto: Carswell, 1983) at 78.

ATC. *abbr.* An air traffic control unit. *Flight Plans and Flight Notifications Order*, C.R.C., c. 45, s. 2.

A TEMPORE CUJUS CONTRARII MEMORIA NON EXISTET. [L.] From a time of which no memory to the contrary exists.

ATHEROMA. *n.* A form of arteriosclerosis in which fibrous tissue locally proliferates and fat deposits narrow the lumen. F.A. Jaffe, *A Guide to Pathological Evidence*, 2d ed. (Toronto: Carswell, 1983) at 169.

A3. Telephony by amplitude modulation. *General Radio Regulations, Part II*, C.R.C., c. 1372, s. 42.

ATLANTIC ACCORD. The Memorandum of Agreement between the Government of Canada and the Government of the province on offshore oil and gas resource management and revenue sharing dated February 11, 1985, and includes any amendments thereto. *Canada-Newfoundland Atlantic Accord Implementation (Newfoundland) Act*, S. Nfld. 1986, c. 37, s. 2.

ATLANTIC FISHERIES. All the activities relating to the harvesting, processing and marketing of fish in the Provinces of Quebec, Nova Scotia, New Brunswick, Prince Edward Island and Newfoundland and in the fishing zones of Canada, as defined pursuant to subsection 4(1) of the Territorial Sea and Fishing Zones Act, on the Atlantic coast of Canada. *Atlantic Fisheries Restructuring Act*, R.S.C. 1985, c. A-14, s. 2.

ATLANTIC FLIGHT. Any flight to or from Canada, St. Pierre and Miquelon or the United States that crosses a part of the Atlantic Ocean except a flight between Canada and a place other than Canada in North, Central or South America or the West Indies. *National Defence Aerodrome Fees Regulations*, C.R.C., c. 714, s. 2.

ATLANTIC PROVINCES. The Provinces of Nova Scotia, New Brunswick, Prince Edward Island and Newfoundland. *Handicapped Persons' Education Act*, S.N.S. 1973-74, c. 5, s. 3.

ATLANTIC REGION. The region comprising the Provinces of New Brunswick, Nova Scotia, Prince Edward Island and Newfoundland. *Department of Regional Economic Expansion Act*, R.S.C. 1970, c. R-4, s. 2.

ATLANTIC SALMON. Includes "ouananiche". *Ontario Fishery Regulations*, C.R.C., c. 849, s. 2.

AT LARGE. 1. Off the premises of the owner and not muzzled or under the control of any person. *The Sheep Protection and Dog Licensing Act*, R.S.S. 1978, c. S-49, s. 2. 2. Not under control. *Dog Act*, S.P.E.I. 1974, c. 10, s. 1. See DANGEROUS TO BE ~; RUN ~; RUNNING ~.

ATLAS. See PRINTED ~ OR CARTOGRAPHIC BOOK.

ATMOSPHERE. *n.* The ambient air surrounding the earth, excluding the air within any structure or underground space. *Environment Quality Act*, R.S.Q. 1977, c. Q-2, s. 1.

ATOMIC ENERGY. All energy of whatever type derived from or created by the transmutation of atoms. *Atomic Energy Control Act*, R.S.C. 1985, c. A-16, s. 2.

ATOMIC ENERGY CONTROL BOARD. The federal body which enforces and administers the Atomic Energy Control Act and its regulations.

ATOMIC ENERGY OF CANADA LIMITED. A federal corporation with mandate to research and develop peaceful uses for atomic energy, including developing nuclear power systems and applications for radioisotopes and radiation in industry and medicine.

AT PAR. Of stocks or bonds, sold or issued at face value.

ATS. *abbr.* At the suit of. Used when the defendant's name is put first in the title of a proceeding.

AT SIGHT. In reference to bills of exchange, payable on demand.

ATTACH. *v.* To take or apprehend; to take goods as well as persons. See ATTACHMENT.

ATTACHE. *n.* [Fr.] A person associated with an embassy.

ATTACHED. *adj.* Fastened so that each layer of material adheres at every point of contact with the next underlying layer. *Motor Vehicle Safety Regulations*, C.R.C., c. 1038, s. 302.

ATTACHMENT. *n.* Arresting a person under an order of committal; seizing of or placing property under the control of a court. See REATTACHMENT; WRIT OF ~.

ATTACHMENT HARDWARE. Hardware designed for securing a seat belt assembly to a vehicle. *Motor Vehicle Safety Regulations*, C.R.C., c. 1038, s. 209.

ATTACHMENT OF DEBTS. Where judgment for the payment of money is obtained against a person to whom another person owes money, an order is made that all debts owing or accruing from that person (called the garnishee) to the judgment debtor be applied to the judgment debt.

ATTAINDER. *n.* Formerly, when judgment of outlawry or death was made against a person convicted of felony or treason, the principal consequences were the forfeiture and escheat of the convict's lands and the corruption of the convict's blood so that the convict was not able to hold or inherit land or transmit a title by descent to any other person. See ACT OF ~.

ATTAINT. *adj.* Describing a person under attainder.

ATTAINTURE. *n.* Censure under law.

ATTEMPT. *n.* Having an intent to commit an offence, and doing or omitting to do anything for the purpose of carrying out the intention whether or not it was possible under the circumstances to commit the offence. *Criminal Code*, R.S.C. 1985, c. C-46, s. 24(1).

ATTENDANCE. See AVERAGE ~.

ATTENDANCE AREA. A portion of a school division containing one or more operating schools. *The Education Act*, R.S.S. 1978, c. E-0.1, s. 2.

ATTENDANCE BONUS. A bonus paid for an especially good attendance record.

ATTENDANCE MONEY. 1. Conduct money. 2. Reimbursement paid to a witness for reasonable expenses incurred while going to, staying at and returning from the place where a discovery or trial is held.

ATTENDANT. *n.* 1. A person who, as the whole or a part of his normal duties, (i) operates an elevating device that is equipped with operating devices that are automatically rendered inoperative should an unsafe condition for operation of the elevating device arise, or (ii) actively engages in or supervises the loading, passage or unloading of persons or freight on an elevating device. *Elevating Devices Act*, R.S.O. 1980, c. 135, s. 1. 2. A person who owes duty or service to another person. See AMBULANCE ~; CABIN ~; DRIVER ~; FIRST-AID ~; SERVICE STATION ~.

ATTENDANT. *adj.* Accompanying.

ATTENDING DENTIST. A member of the dental staff who attends a patient in the hospital. *Public Hospitals Act*, R.R.O. 1980, Reg. 865, s. 1.

ATTENDING PHYSICIAN. The physician to whom responsibility for the observation, care and treatment of a patient has been assigned.

ATTENDING PSYCHIATRIST. The psychiatrist to whom responsibility for the observation,

care and treatment of a patient has been assigned.

ATTENUATION. *n.* The decrease in radiation intensity caused by absorption and scattering in a medium.

ATTEST. *v.* To witness an event or act.

ATTESTATION. *n.* Witnessing a written instrument and signing it as a witness.

ATTESTATION CLAUSE. The witness to the execution of a written instrument signs this sentence, stating that he or she has witnessed it.

ATTESTING WITNESS. A person who has seen someone else sign a written document or execute a deed.

ATTIC. *n.* The space between the roof and the ceiling of the top storey or between a dwarf wall and a sloping roof. *Building Code Act*, R.R.O. 1980, Reg. 87, s. 1.

ATTINCTUS. *adj.* [L.] Under attaint.

ATTO. *pref.* 10^{-18}, prefix for multiples and submultiples of Basic, Supplementary and Derived Units of Measurement. *Weights and Measures Act*, S.C. 1970-71-72, c. 36, schedule 1, part V.

ATTORN. *v.* To turn over; to agree to recognize a new owner as landlord.

ATTORNARE REM. [L.] To appropriate or assign goods or money to a particular service or use.

ATTORNEY. *n.* 1. A person appointed to act in place of or to represent another. 2. Lawyer. 3. Patent agent. 4. A person who is, by virtue of section 11 of the Act, an officer of the Court. *Federal Court Rules*, C.R.C., c. 663, s. 2. See CROWN ~; POWER OF ~.

ATTORNEY GENERAL. 1. The principal law officer of the Crown, a Minister of the Crown. 2. (a) The Attorney General or Solicitor General of the province in which proceedings to which this Act applies are taken and includes his lawful deputy; and (b) with respect to (i) the Yukon Territory and the Northwest Territories, and (ii) proceedings commenced at the instance of the Government of Canada and conducted by or on behalf of that Government in respect of a contravention of or conspiracy to contravene any Act of Parliament other than this Act or a regulation made thereunder means the Attorney General of Canada and includes his lawful deputy. *Criminal Code*, R.S.C. 1985, c. C-46, s. 2.

ATTORNEY GENERAL OF THE PROVINCE. The minister of the Crown of the province who is responsible for judicial affairs. *Judges Act*, R.S.C. 1985, c. J-1, s. 2.

ATTORNMENT. *n.* Agreement to become a new owner's tenant or a mortgagee's tenant. See BAILMENT BY ~.

ATTRIBUTE. *n.* With reference to a person, means the race, creed, colour, nationality, ancestry, place of origin, sex or geographical location of the person, and includes the race, creed, colour, nationality, ancestry, place of origin, sex or geographical location of a person connected with the person or of nationals of a country with the government of which the person conducts, has conducted or may conduct business. *Discriminatory Business Practices Act*, R.S.O. 1980, c. 119, s. 4. See OTHER ~.

ATTRIBUTION. *n.* To assign income or property to another person for certain purposes.

ATTRITION. *n.* Reduction of number of members of the work force by death, retirement or resignation.

A2. Telegraphy by amplitude modulation using the keying of a modulating audio frequency or the keying of the modulated emission; including in special cases, an unkeyed modulated emission. *General Radio Regulations, Part II*, C.R.C., c. 1372, s. 42.

AU BESOIN. [Fr.] In the event of need.

AUCTION. *n.* Public sale of property to the highest bidder. See DUTCH ~; TOBACCO ~ EXCHANGE.

AUCTIONEER. *n.* 1. Agent whose usual business is to sell by public auction goods or other property. G.H.L. Fridman, *The Law of Agency*, 5th ed. (London: Butterworths, 1983) at 40. 2. An individual who conducts the bidding at a sale by auction of any property.

AUCTION MARKET. See LIVESTOCK ~.

AUCTOR. *n.* [L.] Vendor; seller.

AUCTOR IN REM SUAM. [L.] Agent for personal advantage.

AUCTOR REGIT ACTUM. [L.] It is the law of the country that bestows on someone the power to perform an act which determines the validity of any act committed in that capacity. J.G. McLeod, *The Conflict of Laws* (Calgary: Carswell, 1983) at 779.

AUCUPIA VERBORUM SUNT JUDICE INDIGNA. [L.] Quibbles are beneath a judge's dignity.

AUDI ALTERAM PARTEM. [L. hear the other side] Both sides must be heard.

AUDIENCE. *n.* Interview; hearing. See PREAUDIENCE.

AUDIENCE ROOM. Any room or apartment that, in any public building, is intended to accommodate or to be used for any public meeting or assemblage of persons. *Public Buildings Act*, R.S.M. 1970, c. P200, s. 2.

AUDIOLOGIST. *n.* A person whose name is entered in the register as an audiologist. *Speech-Language Pathology and Audiology Act*, S.N.B. 1987, c. 71, s. 2.

AUDIOLOGY. *n.* The provision or conduct of non-medical assessment and interpretation, evaluation, habilitative, rehabilitative, counselling, guidance and research services relating to auditory function including the planning, direction and conduct of remedial programs designed to restore and improve auditory function and speech reading, the giving of directions for the supply of hearing aids, and the sale of hearing aids. *Speech-Language Pathology and Audiology Act*, S.N.B. 1987, c. 71, s. 2.

AUDIT. *n.* Examination of accounts.

AUDIT COMMITTEE. A committee of the board of directors of a corporation who nominate auditors and work with them.

AUDITING. See PUBLIC ACCOUNTING AND ~.

AUDITING STANDARDS. See GENERALLY ACCEPTED ~.

AUDITOR. *n.* 1. One who reviews and verifies accounts. 2. A person who is a member in good standing of any corporation, association or institute of professional accountants, and includes a firm every partner of which is such a person. See BROKERS' ~; INDEPENDENT ~; PROVINCIAL ~; QUALIFIED ~.

AUDITOR GENERAL. 1. The Auditor General of Canada appointed pursuant to subsection 3(1). *Auditor General Act*, R.S.C. 1985, c. A-17, s. 2. 2. A person appointed under a provincial Act.

AUDITOR GENERAL OF CANADA. 1. The officer appointed pursuant to subsection 3(1) of the Auditor General Act. *Financial Administration Act*, R.S.C. 1985, c. F-11, s. 2. 2. The federal official who examines Canada's public accounts, including those relating to public property, Crown corporations and the Consolidated Revenue Fund.

AUGMENTED CHANNEL SERVICE. The service provided by a licensee on channels other than those on which its basic service is provided. *Cable Television Regulations*, C.R.C., c. 374, s. 2.

AUGMENTING SERVICE. Any period, subsequent to the grant of a pension, of continuous full-time paid service of one year or more (a) in the forces; (b) in the naval, army or air forces of Canada or the Canadian Forces, other than the forces, if during such period the officer or man receives the pay of his rank as though he were in the forces; and (c) in the public service, in respect of which he is not entitled to an annuity. *Defence Services Pension Continuation Regulations*, C.R.C., c. 554, s. 2.

AUGUSTA LEGIBUS SOLUTA NON EST. [L.] The spouse of a ruler is not above the law.

AUNT. *n.* In relation to any person, means a sister of the mother or father of that person. *Immigration Regulations*, C.R.C., c. 940, s. 2.

AUTHENTIC. *adj.* Original; genuine.

AUTHENTIC ACT. Something executed before a notary or another duly authorized public official.

AUTHENTICATION. *n.* An attestation made by an officer certifying that a record is in proper form and that the officer is the proper person to so certify.

AUTHENTICITY. *n.* 1. Proven of an original when it was written, printed, executed or signed as it claims to have been. G.D. Watson & C. Perkins, eds., *Holmested & Watson: Ontario Civil Procedure* (Toronto: Carswell, 1984) at 51-3. 2. Proven of a copy when it is a true copy of the original. G.D. Watson & C. Perkins, eds., *Holmested & Watson: Ontario Civil Procedure* (Toronto: Carswell, 1984) at 51-3. 3. Proven of the copy of a letter, telecommunication or telegram when the original was sent as claimed and received by the addressee. G.D. Watson & C. Perkins, eds., *Holmested & Watson: Ontario Civil Procedure* (Toronto: Carswell, 1984) at 51-3.

AUTHOR. *n.* 1. The person who actually composes, draws or writes. H.G. Fox, *The Canadian Law of Copyright and Industrial Designs*, 2d ed. (Toronto: Carswell, 1967) at 238. 2. Includes the legal representatives of a deceased author. *Copyright Act*, R.S.C. 1985, c. C-42, s. 60(3). See CANADIAN ~; WORK OF JOINT ~SHIP.

AUTHORITY. *n.* 1. A statute, case or text cited in support of a legal opinion or argument. 2. A legal power given by one person to another to do some act. 3. A person authorized to exercise a statutory power. *Administrative Procedures Act*, R.S.A. 1980, c. A-2, s. 1. 4. Body given powers by statute to oversee or carry out a government function. See ACTUAL ~; APPARENT ~; APPROPRIATE ~; APPROVING ~; AREA ~; ASSESSING ~; ASSESSMENT ~; BINDING ~; BUILDING ~; CITATION OF AUTHORITIES; COMPETENT ~; DETAINING ~; EDUCATION ~; ELECTED ~; EXPROPRIATING ~; ELECTRICAL ~; EXPROPRIATION ~; FIRE CONTROL ~; HIGHWAY ~; IMPLIED ~; LICENSING ~; LOCAL ~; MUNICIPAL ~; OPERATING ~; OSTENSIBLE ~; PARTY ~; PERSUASIVE ~; PROPER ~; PUBLIC ~; REGULATION-MAKING ~; REPORTING ~; REQUISITIONING ~; ROAD ~; ST. LAWRENCE SEAWAY ~; SPEED ~; STATUTORY ~; SUPPLY ~; TAXING ~; USUAL OR CUSTOMARY ~.

AUTHORIZATION. *n.* 1. Licence; certificate; registration. 2. An authorization to intercept a private communication given under section 186 or subsection 188(2). *Criminal Code*, R.S.C. 1985, c. C-46, s. 183. See SPECIAL ~.

AUTHORIZE. *v.* To empower.

AUTHORIZED. *adj.* Properly empowered to perform any specified duty or to do any specified act.

AUTHORIZED AGENT. Any person authorized by the Minister to accept subscriptions for or make sales of securities. *Financial Administration Act*, R.S.C. 1985, c. F-11, s. 2.

AUTHORIZED CAPITAL. The total amount of capital which, by its incorporating documents, a company is authorized to issue.

AUTHORIZED CHARGE. A charge made directly to a patient for insured services. Hospitals or Health Insurance acts.

AUTHORIZED EMERGENCY VEHICLE. (a) A motor vehicle operated by a peace officer in the course of duty or employment, (b) a fire department or fire fighting vehicle, and (c) an ambulance.

AUTHORIZED ENTITY. 1. A political party, party authority or independent candidate holding an authorization under this title. *Election Act*, S.Q. 1984, c. 51, s. 316. 2. A registered optometrist, a professional corporation and a member of a class or category of practising members established under the regulations. *Optometry Profession Act*, S.A. 1983, c. O-10, s. 1. 3. A certified general accountant, a professional corporation and a student member. *Certified General Accountants Act*, S.A. 1984, c. C-3.5, s. 1.

AUTHORIZED EXPLOSIVE. Any explosive that is declared to be an authorized explosive in accordance with the regulations. *Explosives Act*, R.S.C. 1985, c. E-17, s. 2.

AUTHORIZED INSURER. An insurance company lawfully authorized or permitted to carry on business in a province.

AUTHORIZED INVESTMENT. A security in which a trust permits its trustee to invest funds.

AUTHORIZED LIMIT. The maximum amount by which the assets exceed the liabilities in a revolving fund. *Revolving Funds Act*, S.N.W.T. 1986 (1st Sess.), c. 16, s. 2.

AUTHORIZED OFFICIAL. A person who is authorized to act as the representative of a collection agent or broker and is named in the licence of the collection agent or broker.

AUTHORIZED PARTY. See CANDIDATE OF AN ~.

AUTHORIZED PERSON. 1. A person authorized by legislation to perform a specified function under it. 2. An owner or occupier of premises, forest land or land used for agricultural purposes and an agent of an owner or occupier thereof. *Trespass Act*, S.N.B. 1983, c. T-11.2, s. 1.

AUTHORIZING ACT. 1. An Act designated as an authorizing Act in the regulations. *Chattel Security Registries Act*, S.A. 1983, c. C-7.1, s. 1. 2. The Act of the Legislature other than this Act under which an authority is granted power to acquire land by expropriation. *Expropriation Act*, S.M. 1970, c. 78, s. 1.

AUTHORIZING INSTRUMENT. 1. (a) In relation to the special welfare program, the Acts mentioned in the definition "special welfare program" in this section and includes any agreements entered into under those Acts; and (b) in relation to the established programs, Part V of this Act and the Canada Health Act. *Federal-Provincial Fiscal Arrangements Act*, R.S.C. 1985, c. F-8, s. 26. 2. (i) A law, contract or instrument that requires, provides for or permits service by mail, and (ii) if the common law requires or permits service by mail, the common law. *Judicature Act*, R.S.A. 1980, c. J-1, s. 33.

AUTHORSHIP. See JOINT ~.

AUTO. *abbr.* Automobile.

AUTO BODY REPAIRER. A person engaged in the repair of motor vehicles who, (i) hammers out dents in body panels, fenders and skirting, (ii) files, grinds, sands, fills and finishes ready for priming, any dented, welded or pierced area, (iii) by heat treatment, shrinks or stretches metal panels, (iv) welds breaks in body areas, (v) tests for and corrects faulty alignment of frames, (vi) paints and glazes, and (vii) removes and installs body parts. *Apprenticeship and Tradesmen's Qualification Act*, R.R.O. 1980, Reg. 22, s. 1.

AUTOBUS. *n.* A vehicle equipped for the transportation of persons, at least eight at a time, and effects such transportation for a pecuniary consideration. *Highway Code*, R.S.Q. 1977, c. C-24, s. 1.

AUTOCRACY. *n.* Unlimited monarchy.

AUTOGRAPH. *n.* 1. The handwriting of a person. 2. The signature of a person.

AUTOLYSIS. *n.* Enzymes normally present in cells and tissues dissolving them. F.A. Jaffe, *A Guide to Pathological Evidence*, 2d ed. (Toronto: Carswell, 1983) at 169.

AUTOMATED TELLER. A machine normally unattended by an employee of a credit union; that (a) receives cash from; (b) disburses cash to; or (c) provides services of the credit union to a member on receiving an instruction from the member. *Credit Union Amendment Act*, S.B.C. 1980, c. 8, s. 1.

AUTOMATIC. *adj.* Refers to machinery not requiring the assistance of a human operator to complete its function or functions during each complete cycle of operations. *Export Control List*, C.R.C., c. 601, s. 3358. See SEMI- ~.

AUTOMATIC BLOCK SIGNAL SYSTEM. A series of consecutive blocks governed by block signals, cab signals, or both, actuated by a train or engine, or by certain conditions affecting the use of a block. *Regulations No. 0-8, Uniform Code of Operating Rules*, C.R.C., c. 1175, Part III, s. 2.

AUTOMATIC CHECK-OFF. The deduction of union dues from wages by an employer.

AUTOMATIC DISTRIBUTOR. Any machine and any apparatus, with or without mechanism, automatic or otherwise, and any other article or collection of articles, in whatever form or under whatever name it is commonly known, which serves or is intended to serve, or the make or the arrangement of which indicates that it is intended for the sale or delivery of merchandise, or services or of any purpose whatsoever, whatever its mode of operation may be. *Licenses Act*, S.Q. 1978, c. 36, s. 134.

AUTOMATIC ENFORCEMENT. After someone assigns the order for payment to an enforcement office, all of the debtor's payments are made to the office instead of to the creditor so that the office may monitor compliance with the order. C.R.B. Dunlop, *Creditor-Debtor Law in Canada*, Second Cumulative Supplement (Toronto: Carswell, 1986) at 222.

AUTOMATIC FIREARM. A firearm that is capable of firing bullets in rapid succession during one pressure of the trigger. *Fish and Wildlife Act*, S.N.B. 1980, c. F-14.1, s. 1.

AUTOMATIC HOIST. A mine hoist that can be operated by controls situated at shaft stations or on the shaft conveyance. *Occupational Health and Safety Act*, R.R.O. 1980, Reg. 694, s. 1.

AUTOMATIC-LOCKING RETRACTOR. A retractor incorporating adjustment hardware that has a positive self-locking mechanism that is capable when locked of withstanding restraint forces. *Motor Vehicle Safety Regulations*, C.R.C., c. 1038, s. 209.

AUTOMATIC RENEWAL. Extension of an agreement from year to year or period of time to period of time when no notice of termination is given by either party.

AUTOMATIC SWITCH. An electro-mechanical device designed to open, under both overload and short-circuit conditions, a current-carrying circuit without injury to the device, and includes only the type designed to trip on a pre-determined over-current. *Coal Mines Regulation Act*, R.S.N.S. 1967, c. 36, s. 84.

AUTOMATIC TABULATING EQUIPMENT. Apparatus that automatically examines and totals votes recorded on ballot cards and tabulates the results. *Municipal Elections Act*, R.R.O. 1980, Reg. 692, s. 1.

AUTOMATIC WAGE ADJUSTMENT. A wage increase which occurs upon the happening of a specified event.

AUTOMATIC WAGE PROGRESSION. A system of wage increases based upon length of service.

AUTOMATIC WEAPON. Any firearm that is capable of firing bullets in rapid succession during one pressure of the trigger. *An Act respecting hunting and fishing rights in the James Bay and New Québec territories*, S.Q. 1978, c. 92, s. 18.

AUTOMATISM. *n.* Involuntary personal action.

AUTOMOBILE. *n.* 1. Any vehicle propelled by any power other than muscular force and adapted for transportation on the public highways but not on rails. 2. Includes all self-propelled vehicles, their trailers, accessories and equipment, but not railway rolling stock, watercraft or aircraft of any kind. 3. Includes a trolley bus and a self-propelled vehicle, and the trailers, accessories and equipment of automobiles, but does not include railway rolling stock that runs on rails, watercraft or aircraft. 4. A motor vehicle. 5. Every vehicle propelled by any power other than muscular force, and which is adapted for transportation on the public highways, but not on rails, and comprise, as private vehicles, the pleasure vehicle, the farm vehicle and the service vehicle and the commercial vehicle, and, as public vehicles, the autobus, the taxi and the delivery car. *Highway Code*, R.S.Q. 1977, c. C-

24, s. 1. See DAMAGE CAUSED BY AN ~; SCRAP ~; UNIDENTIFIED ~; UNINSURED ~; USED ~.

AUTOMOBILE COMPONENTS. See CANADIAN ~.

AUTOMOBILE DEALER. A person who carries on the business of buying and selling (or both buying and selling) new or used automobiles (or both new and used automobiles) whether for his own account or the account of any other person, or who holds himself out as carrying on the business of such buying and selling, or both such buying and selling. *Automobile Dealers Act*, S. Nfld. 1973, c. 15, s. 2.

AUTOMOBILE INSURANCE. Insurance (a) against liability arising out of, (i) bodily injury to or the death of a person, or (ii) loss of or damage to property, caused by an automobile or the use or operation thereof; or (b) against loss of or damage to an automobile and the loss of use thereof, and includes insurance otherwise coming within the class of accident insurance where the accident is caused by an automobile or the use or operation thereof, whether liability exists or not, if the contract also includes insurance described in clause (a). *Insurance acts.*

AUTOMOBILE JUNK YARD. Premises where three or more unserviceable, discarded or junked motor vehicles, bodies, engines or other component parts thereof are gathered, located or placed.

AUTOMOBILE MASTER KEY. Includes a key, pick, rocker key or other instrument designed or adapted to operate the ignition or other switches or locks of a series of motor vehicles. *Criminal Code*, R.S.C. 1985, c. C-46, s. 353(5).

AUTOMOBILE SERVICE STATION. A place for supplying fuel, oil and minor accessories for motor vehicles at retail prices directly to the user and for making minor servicing or running repairs essential to the operation of motor vehicles. Canada regulations.

AUTOMOTIVE MACHINIST. A person who reconditions and rebuilds internal combustion engines and associated components, power trains, brake system components and suspension system components. *Apprenticeship and Tradesmen's Qualification Act*, R.R.O. 1980, Reg. 23, s. 1.

AUTOMOTIVE PAINTER. A person engaged in the refinishing of motor vehicle bodies who, (i) sands, spot fills, primes and paints, (ii) dries or bakes newly painted surfaces, (iii) masks and tapes for multi-tone paint work and protective requirements, (iv) applies decals, transfers, stencils and other types of identification to finished paint work, (v) mixes paint and components and matches colours, and (vi) refinishes galvanized outer panels and anodized aluminum moulding. *Apprenticeship and Tradesmen's Qualification Act*, R.R.O. 1980, Reg. 24, s. 1.

AUTOMOTIVE PROGRAM. The Canada-United States Agreement on Automotive Products, Order in Council 1965-99, and the Letters of Commitment addressed to the Minister of Industry from the several automotive products manufacturers, taken together. *Automotive Manufacturing Assistance Regulations*, C.R.C., c. 966, s. 2.

AUTONOMY. *n.* National political independence. See LOCAL ~.

AUTOPSY. *n.* 1. Necropsy; postmortem. F.A. Jaffe, *A Guide to Pathological Evidence*, 2d ed. (Toronto: Carswell, 1983) at 1. 2. The dissection of a body for the purpose of examining organs and tissues to determine the cause of death or manner of death or the identity of the deceased and may include chemical, histological, microbiological or serological tests and other laboratory investigations. *Fatality Inquiries Act*, R.S.A. 1980, c. F-6, s. 1.

AUTOROUTE. *n.* 1. A toll-charge, limited access, rapid-transit highway. *Autoroutes Act*, R.S.Q. 1977, c. A-34, s. 1. 2. A public highway defined as an autoroute by the Minister and specially identified as such by an official traffic sign. Such word does not include an autoroute within the meaning of the Autoroutes Act (chapter A-34). *Highway Code*, R.S.Q. 1977, c. C-24, s. 56.

AUTO TRANSPORTER. A truck and a trailer designed for use in combination to transport motor vehicles where the truck is designed to carry cargo other than at the fifth wheel and that cargo is to be loaded only be means of the trailer. *Motor Vehicle Safety Regulations*, C.R.C., c. 1038, s. 2.

AUTRE. *adj.* [Fr.] Another.

AUTRE DROIT. [Fr.] In another's right.

AUTREFOIS ACQUIT. [Fr. formerly acquitted] An accused may not be prosecuted when he or she has been tried for and acquitted of the same offence before a court of competent jurisdiction.

AUTREFOIS CONVICT. [Fr. formerly convicted] An accused may not be prosecuted when he or she claims to have been tried and convicted for the same offence before a court of competent jurisidiction.

AUTRE VIE. [Fr.] The life of another (period of time). See POUR ~.

AUXILIARY. *n.* See DENTAL ~; RELIGIOUS ~.

AUXILIARY. *adj.* Assisting.

AUXILIARY FAN. A fan temporarily required within a mine for the more effective ventilation of any working place in the mine during the development of such working place. *Coal Mines Regulation Act*, R.S.N.S. 1967, c. 36, s. 3.

AUXILIARY GROUNDING. An additional grounding connected to a main grounding. *Lightning Rods Act*, R.R.O. 1980, Reg. 577, s. 1.

AUXILIARY GUTTER. A raceway consisting of a sheet metal enclosure used to supplement the wiring space of electrical equipment and to enclose interconnecting conductors. *Power Corporation Act*, R.R.O. 1980, Reg. 794, s. 0.

AUXILIARY HOSPITAL. A hospital for the treatment of long term or chronic illnesses, diseases or infirmities or severe mental disorder. *Hospitals Act*, R.S.A. 1980, c. H-11, s. 1.

AUXILIARY LAMP. Denotes any combination of reflector, lens and lamp bulb designed to illuminate the roadway close to and forward or forward and to the sides of the motor vehicle and otherwise meeting the requirements of this section. *Highway Traffic Act*, R.S.A. 1980, c. H-7, s. 40.

AUXILIARY LIGHT. Denotes any combination of reflector, lens and light bulb that meets the requirements of this section and is designed to illuminate the roadway close to and forward or forward and to the sides of a motor vehicle. *Vehicles Act*, R.S.N.W.T. 1974, c. V-2, s. 70.

AUXILIARY VESSEL. A vessel used in conjunction with a registered commercial fishing vessel or registered fixed commercial fishing unit in setting or recovering fishing gear. *Atlantic Fishing Registration and Licensing Regulations*, C.R.C., s. 808, s. 2.

AUXILIUM. *n.* [L.] Aid.

AUXILIUM CURIAE. [L.] The suit or request of one party that a court cite and convene another party to warrant something.

AUXILIUM FACERE ALICUI IN CURIA REGIS. [L.] To become the friend and solicitor of another in the sovereign's courts.

AUXILIUM REGIS. [L. the king's aid] Money levied for royal and public service use such as taxes which Parliament grants.

AVAIL. *n.* Profit from land.

AVAILABLE MARKET. A particular situation of trade, area and goods in which there is enough demand that, if a purchaser defaults, the goods in question can readily be sold. G.H.L. Fridman, *Sale of Goods in Canada*, 3d ed. (Toronto: Carswell, 1986) at 359.

AVAILS. *n.* Proceeds; profits.

AVAL. *n.* [Fr.] Surety.

AVER. *v.* To allege.

AVERAGE. *n.* 1. A medium. 2. Loss or damage to goods on board a ship. See RACE ~.

AVERAGE ATTENDANCE. The attendance of pupils for any school term ascertained by dividing the aggregate days attendances of all pupils enrolled during such term by the total number of teaching days school was actually in operation during the term. *The Secondary Education Act*, R.S.S. 1978, c. S-41, s. 2.

AVERAGE BASIC COST OF BENEFIT. In relation to any year, means the average of the yearly basic cost of benefit for the three year period that ends concurrently with the second year preceding the year in respect of which the average is computed. *Unemployment Insurance Act*, R.S.C. 1985, c. U-1, s. 49.

AVERAGE NATIONAL RATE OF UNEMPLOYMENT. The monthly national rates of unemployment in a year averaged for the year. *Unemployment Insurance Act*, R.S.C. 1985, c. U-1, s. 2.

AVERAGE WEEKLY INSURABLE EARNINGS. In respect of an employee, means the average of his weekly insurable earnings, as determined pursuant to the Unemployment Insurance Act, from employment at a Canadian establishment for the twenty weeks of employment immediately preceding his effective date of lay-off. *Labour Adjustments Benefits Act*, R.S.C. 1985, c. L-1, s. 2.

AVERAGE YIELD. The average total orchard production of the insured person over the preceding six years allowing for, (i) age of trees, (ii) biennial bearing, (iii) tree removal, and (iv) change in acreage. Ontario regulations. See LONG TERM ~.

A VERBIS LEGIS NON EST RECEDENDUM. [L.] The words of a statute must not be departed from.

AVERMENT. *n.* 1. Allegation. 2. In a pleading, affirmation of any matter. See IMMATERIAL ~; PREFATORY ~;

AVIATION. See CANADIAN ~ SAFETY BOARD; SPECIAL ~ EVENT.

AVIATION FUEL. Any gas or liquid that is sold to be used or is used to create power to propel an aircraft.

AVIATION OCCURRENCE. (a) Any accident or incident associated with the operation of aircraft; and (b) any situation or condition that the Board has reasonable grounds to believe could, if left unattended, induce an accident or incident described in paragraph (a). *Canadian Aviation Safety Board Act*, R.S.C. 1985, c. C-12, s. 2.

A VINCULO MATRIMONII. [L.] From the ties of wedlock.

AVOCAT. *n.* [Fr.] Barrister, advocate.

AVOID. *v.* To make a transaction void.

AVOIDABLE HAZARD. A threat of injury to the health of the user of a cosmetic that can be (a) predicted from the composition of the cosmetic, the toxicology of the ingredients and the site of application thereof; (b) reasonably anticipated during normal use; and (c) eliminated by specified limitations on the usage of the cosmetic. *Cosmetic Regulations*, C.R.C., c. 869, s. 24.

AVOIDANCE. *n.* Avoiding, setting aside or vacating. See CONFESSION AND ~; TAX ~.

AVOIRDUPOIS. *n.* [Fr.] The method of measuring and weighing in which 16 ounces equals a pound.

AVOUCH. *v.* To maintain or justify an act.

AVOUCHER. *n.* Requesting that an undertaking be fulfilled by the warrantor.

AVOW. *v.* To maintain or justify an act.

AVULSION. *n.* 1. Land which current or flood tears off from property to which it originally belonged and adds to the property of another or land joined to another's property when a river changes its course. 2. Tearing away a tissue or part. F.A. Jaffe, *A Guide to Pathological Evidence*, 2d ed. (Toronto: Carswell, 1983) at 9.

AWARD. *n.* 1. Judgment. 2. Instrument which embodies an arbitrator's decision. 3. A pension, allowance, bonus or grant payable under this Act. *Pension Act*, R.S.C. 1985, c. P-6, s. 2. 4. Includes umpirage and a certificate in the nature of an award. *Arbitration acts*. See ARBITRAL ~; ARBITRAMENT AND ~.

AWG. The American (or Brown and Sharpe) wire gauge as applied to non-ferrous conductors and non-ferrous sheet metal. *Power Corporation Act*, R.R.O. 1980, Reg. 794, s. 0.

A.W.L.D. *abbr.* Alberta Weekly Law Digest.

AWNING. *n.* A roof-like covering of canvas or similar fabric material or metal that projects outwards above a window or doorway of any building. *National Parks Signs Regulations*, C.R.C., c. 1130, s. 2.

AXIOM. *n.* A truth which is indisputable.

AXLE. *n.* 1. A straight line, real or imaginary, extending the width of the vehicle at right angles to the centre line thereof, on which the wheels revolve. *Roads Act*, R.S.P.E.I. 1974, c. R-15, s. 1. 2. A single axle which transfers the load carried by it approximately equally to the wheel or wheels attached to each end of the axle. *Highway Traffic Act*, R.S. Nfld. 1970, c. 152, s. 2. 3. (i) One or more shafts on which or with which two or more wheels revolve, and (ii) the wheels on each shaft. 4. An assembly of two or more wheels whose centres are in one transverse vertical plane and which are transmitting weight to the highway. *Highway Traffic Act*, R.S.O. 1980, c. 198, s. 97. See CONVERSION ~; DUAL ~; FLOATING ~; NUMBER OF ~S; PONY ~; SINGLE ~; TANDEM ~; TRIPLE ~.

AXLE ASSEMBLY. All the wheels of a vehicle, the centres of which may be included between two vertical parallel transverse planes one metre apart, extending across the full width of the vehicle. *The Highway Traffic Act*, S.M. 1985-86, c. 3, s. 1. See GROSS WEIGHT OF ANY ~.

AXLE GROUP. 1. Two or more axle assemblies the centres of which are not less than one metre and not more than 1.8 metres apart and which are either articulated from a common attachment to the vehicle or are separately attached to the vehicle and have a common connecting mechanism that equalizes the load carried by each axle assembly. *The Highway Traffic Act*, S.M. 1985-86, c. 3, s. 1. 2. Two or more axles on a vehicle or combination of vehicles and situated as specified in the regulations. *Motor Transport Act*, R.S.A. 1980, c. M-20, s. 1. See FOUR ~; THREE ~; TWO ~.

AXLE GROUP WEIGHT. That part of the gross vehicle weight in kilograms transmitted to the highway by a two axle group, three axle group or four axle group. *Highway Traffic Act*, R.S.O. 1980, c. 198, s. 97.

AXLE LOAD. The mass measured under the wheels of an axle or of the axles included in one category established by regulation, resulting from the distribution on such wheels of the mass of a road vehicle or combination of road vehicles, including accessories, equipment and load. *Highway Safety Code*, S.Q. 1986, c. 91, s. 462.

AXLE UNIT. Any single, dual axle or triple axle. *Highway Traffic Act*, R.S.O. 1980, c. 198, s. 97.

AXLE UNIT WEIGHT. That part of the gross vehicle weight in kilograms transmitted to the highway by an axle unit. *Highway Traffic Act*, R.S.O. 1980, c. 198, s. 97.

AXLE WEIGHT. The combined weight which all the wheels on any one axle impose on the road. See TANDEM ~.

A0. An emission unkeyed or unmodulated. *General Radio Regulations*, Part II, C.R.C., c. 1372, s. 42.

AZOOSPERMIA. *n.* Total absence of sperm cells in semen. F.A. Jaffe, *A Guide to Pathological Evidence*, 2d ed. (Toronto: Carswell, 1983) at 169.

B. *abbr.* 1. Baron. 2. The breadth of the super-structure at the middle of its length. *Load Line Regulations (Sea)*, C.R.C., c. 1441, s. 35. 3. The basic royalty oil in barrels computed under subsection (1). *Indian Oil and Gas Regulations*, C.R.C., c. 963, s. 1. 4. Of a ship, breadth.

BABCOCK TEST BOTTLE OR BABCOCK PIPETTE. Respectively, a glass bottle or a glass pipette that is suitable for use as a measure in the determination of the percentage of fat in milk and milk products by the Babcock method. *Babcock Test Bottles and Pipettes Regulations*, C.R.C., c. 1135, s. 2.

BACHELOR. *n.* 1. The first degree in a university. 2. A never married man.

BACHELOR DWELLING UNIT. A dwelling unit for 1 or 2 adults with or without 1 bedroom. *Building Code Act*, R.R.O. 1980, Reg. 87, s. 1.

BACK. *v.* To countersign; to endorse.

BACKADATION. *n.* The percentage which a seller of shares, deliverable on a certain date, pays for the privilege of delaying delivery until another date.

BACK A WARRANT. For one justice to endorse a warrant issued by the justice of another district or jurisdiction permitting it be executed in the first justice's jurisdiction.

BACK-BOND. *var.* **BACKBOND.** *n.* A bond of indemnity which one gives to a surety.

BACK FLOW. Such flow of (i) water from any place, or (ii) any solid, liquid or gaseous substance or any combination thereof, into a distributing pipe for potable water as may make the water in that pipe non-potable. *Ontario Water Resources Act*, R.R.O. 1980, Reg. 736, s. 1.

BACKFLOW PREVENTER. A device used in a water supply pipe which, (i) incorporates two or more check valves to prohibit the reverse flow of the water, irrespective of pressure differentials, where the maximum working pressure is not exceeded, and (ii) contains integral safeguards to make it fail-safe in the event of a malfunction of one or more of the check valves. *Ontario Water Resources Act*, R.R.O. 1980, Reg. 736, s. 1.

BACKING. *n.* The structural base to which the pile, face or outer surface is woven, tufted, hooked, knitted or otherwise attached in a pile fabric or floor covering. *Textile Labelling and Advertising Regulations*, C.R.C., c. 1551, s. 25.

BACK LANE. A highway situated wholly within the limits of any city, town or village or restricted speed area or reduced restricted speed area which has been designed, constructed and intended to provide access to and service at the rear of places of residence or business and includes alleys having a width of not more than 9 metres. *The Highway Traffic Act*, S.M. 1985-86, c. 3, s. 1.

BACK PAY. Wages due for services performed in the past.

BACKSHEET. *n.* A page attached to the back and facing in the opposite direction to other pages of a document filed in a court proceeding; gives the title of the proceeding and other information.

BACK-TO-BACK CREDIT. Secondary credit which an exporter requests the confirming bank to extend to a supplier of goods. It covers the same goods which are the subject of the confirmed credit to the exporter. I.F.G. Baxter, *The Law of Banking*, 3d ed. (Toronto: Carswell, 1981) at 156.

BACK-TO-BACK FLIGHTS. A series of operationally inter-related return charters where traffic carried outbound is returned on an inbound flight of a subsequent return operation the outbound flight of which was used to transport other outbound return traffic in that series and includes the last return operation in the series transporting only inbound traffic previously carried outbound on a flight in the series. *Air Carrier Regulations*, C.R.C., c. 3, s. 23.

BACK-TO-WORK AGREEMENT. Terms under which employees will return to work following settlement of a strike.

BACK-TO-WORK MOVEMENT. An effort to persuade employees to end a strike.

BACKTRACK. *v.* To displace junior employees when the seniority rights of other workers are exercised.

BACK VENT. A pipe installed to vent a trap or waste pipe and connected to the vent system at a point above the fixture served by the trap or waste pipe. *Ontario Water Resources Act*, R.R.O. 1980, Reg. 736, s. 1.

BACKWARDATION. *n.* The percentage which a seller of shares, deliverable on a certain date, pays for the privilege of delaying delivery until another date.

BACKWATER VALVE. A valve installed in a building drain or building sewer to prevent sewage from flowing back into the building. *Ontario Water Resources Act*, R.R.O. 1980, Reg. 736, s. 1.

BACTERIAL CULTURE. The coagulum made by growth of harmless acid-producing bacteria in milk, reconstituted milk powder or reconstituted skim milk powder.

BAD. *adj.* In pleadings, unsound.

BAD DEBT. A debt which is irrecoverable.

BAD FAITH. Concerning the exercise of statutory powers, dishonesty and malice. S.A. DeSmith, *Judicial Review of Administrative Action*, 4th ed. by J.M. Evans (London: Stevens, 1980) at 335.

BADGES OF FRAUD. The six signs and marks of fraud. C.R.B. Dunlop, *Creditor-Debtor Law in Canada* (Toronto: Carswell, 1981) at 526.

BAD TITLE. Unmarketable title; one which conveys no or a very limited interest to the purchaser and a purchaser cannot be forced to accept.

BAFFLE. *n.* A non-liquid-tight transverse partition in a cargo tank. *Gasoline Handling Act*, R.R.O. 1980, Reg. 439, s. 1.

BAG. *n.* 1. Something containing drugs. F.A. Jaffe, *A Guide to Pathological Evidence*, 2d ed. (Toronto: Carswell, 1983) at 169. 2. 50 pounds. *Crop Insurance Act (Ontario)*, R.R.O. 1980, Reg. 213, s. 3. See COLLECTOR ~; DIRECT ~; MAIL ~.

BAGGAGE. *n.* Such articles, effects and other personal property of a passenger as are necessary or appropriate for wear, use, comfort or convenience in connection with his trip. *Air Carrier Regulations*.

BAG NET. 1. A net (a) that is attached to stakes, (b) the bag of which floats with the tide or current, and (c) that is capable of catching fish without enmeshing them. *Canada Regulations*. 2. Fishing gear that (a) consists of wings or leaders, (b) terminates in a bag-shaped net, (c) is attached to a stake, (d) floats with the tide, and (e) catches fish without enmeshing them. *Quebec Fishery Regulations*, C.R.C., c. 852, s. 2.

BAG SERVICE. A service whereby a post office assigns a number to bags provided by an applicant for the service and delivers mail addressed to that person or firm to those bags. *Mail Receptacles Regulations*, C.R.C., c. 1282, s. 21.

BAIL. *v.* To free a person arrested or imprisoned after a particular day and place to appear are set and security is taken.

BAIL. *n.* 1. Security given by the persons into whose hands an accused is delivered. They bind themselves or become bail for the person's due appearance when required and, if they fear the person's escape, they have the legal power to deliver that person to prison. 2. In any Admiralty proceeding, that which may be taken to answer any judgment so that the Court may release property under arrest. D. Sgayias *et al.*, *Federal Court Practice 1988* (Toronto: Carswell, 1987) at 539. See JUSTIFYING ~.

BAILABLE. *adj.* Possible to give bail.

BAIL-BOND. *n.* An instrument executed by sureties.

BAILEE. *n.* A person to whom goods are entrusted for a specific purpose with no intention of transferring the ownership.

BAILER. *n.* A container that can be held in the hand and used for clearing a boat of water. *Small Vessel Regulations*, C.R.C., c. 1487, s. 2.

BAILIFF. *n.* 1. A sheriff's officer or person employed by a sheriff to make arrests and executions and serve writs. 2. A person who, for remuneration, acts or assists a person to act, or represents to a person that he is acting or is available to act, on behalf of another person in repossessing, seizing or distraining any chattel, or in evicting a person from property. 3. An officer of justice empowered to serve written proceedings issuing out of any court, carry our judicial decisions that are executory and perform any other duty that devolves upon a bailiff by law. *Bailiffs Act*, R.S.Q. 1977, c. H-4, s. 1. 4. Includes a constable who under the Small Claims Courts Act may execute an attachment or perform other service. *Woodmen's Lien for Wages Act*, R.S.O. 1980, c. 537, s. 1.

BAILING. See PACKING AND ~.

BAILIWICK. *n.* Geographic jurisdiction of a sheriff or bailiff.

BAILMENT. *n.* A variety of relationships in law which have in common that one person possesses another's chattel. E.L.G. Tyler & N.E. Palmer, eds., *Crossley Vaines' Personal Property*, 5th ed. (London: Butterworths, 1973) at 70. See GRATUITOUS ~.

BAILMENT BY ATTORNMENT. Occurs when, with the bailor's consent, a bailee delivers the goods to another person to hold, making that person bailee of the bailor. E.L.G. Tyler & N.E. Palmer, eds., *Crossley Vaines' Personal Property*, 5th ed. (London: Butterworths, 1973) at 84.

BAILOR. *n.* A person who entrusts something to another person for a specific purpose.

BAIT. *v.* To set one animal against another which is tied or contained.

BAIT. *n.* Corn, wheat, oats or other cultivated grain or any product thereof or any manufactured product or material that may attract migratory game birds and includes plastic corn and any other imitation grain. *Migratory Birds Regulation*, C.R.C., c. 1035, s. 2.

BAIT AND SWITCH. To attract customers by advertising goods at a low price in hopes of selling them goods at a higher price.

BAIT FISH. 1. Fish of the families (a) Catostomidae, commonly known as suckers, (b) Cyprinidae, commonly known as minnows, except Cyprinus carpio, commonly known as carp, and Carassius auratus, commonly known as gold fish, and (c) Gasterosteidae, commonly known as sticklebacks. *Alberta Fishery Regulations*, C.R.C., c. 838, s. 2. 2. Any member of the minnow family Cyprinidae except carp, Cyprinus carpio Linnaeus and gold-fish, Carrassius auratus Linnaeus, the mudminnow family Umbridae, the sucker family Catostomidae, the stickleback family Gasterosteidae, the trout-perch family Percopsidae, the sculpin family Cottidae, the genus Leuchcithys of the whitefish family Coregonidae, and the darter subfamily Etheostomatinae. *Ontario Fishery Regulations*, C.R.C., c. 849, s. 2.

BAIT STATION AREA. An area established pursuant to an agreement between the Government of Canada and the government of a province where bait is deposited for the purpose of luring migratory birds from unharvested crops. *Migratory Birds Regulations*, C.R.C., c. 1035, s. 2.

BAIT TRAP. A small hoop net, without wings or leaders, that is used to catch fish or bait. *Quebec Fishery Regulations*, C.R.C., c. 852, s. 2.

BAKERY PRODUCT. Includes every kind and description of cakes, pastries, pies and other products ordinarily made in a bake shop. *Bread Act*, R.S.A. 1970, c. 34, s. 2.

BAKESHOP. *n.* 1. A building, premises, workshop, room or place in which bread is made for sale or sold. 2. A building or part of a building or any premises, workshop, room or place principally used for the preparation, making and baking of bread or a bakery product for sale but does not include the bake rooms of hotels or restaurants in so far as the bread or a bakery product made there is sold only for consumption on the premises or otherwise than in loaves. *Bread Act*, R.S.A. 1970, c. 34, s. 2.

BALANCE. *n.* The difference between the total debit entries and total credit entries in an account; the remainder. See OPERATING ~.

BALANCE OF PROBABILITIES. Greater likelihood. K.D. Cooper-Stephenson & I.B. Saunders, *Personal Injury Damages in Canada* (Toronto: Carswell, 1981) at 102.

BALANCE OF TRADE. The difference between the value of the imports into and exports from a country.

BALANCE-SHEET. *n.* A statement showing the assets and liabilities of a business.

BALANCE SHEET ASSETS. The assets of a pension plan consisting of cash, invested assets, due and accrued income, the present value of the balance of special payments required to be made as the result of previous actuarial reviews and, except where the annual cost of benefits is determined on the accrued benefit cost method, the present value of future normal costs. *Pension Benefits Standards Regulations*, C.R.C., c. 1252, s. 2.

BALANCED FEED. See COMPLETE FEED OR ~.

BALE. *n.* Goods wrapped in cloth and bound with cord.

BALEEN WHALE. Any whale other than a toothed whale. *Whaling Convention Act*, R.S.C. 1970, c. W-8, Schedule, s. 18.

BALLAST. *n.* Anything within a vessel which keeps it in proper trim and prevents capsizing.

BALLASTAGE. *n.* A toll paid when ballast is taken from the bottom of a harbour or port.

BALLAST WATER. Water, carried in a vessel for stability and seaworthiness, that is discharged from the vessel to a refinery prior to loading the vessel and includes water used for cargo or ballast tank cleaning. *Petroleum Refinery Liquid Effluent Regulations*, C.R.C., c. 828, s. 2.

BALLISTICS. *n.* The science of the behaviour of projectiles. F.A. Jaffe, *A Guide to Pathological Evidence*, 2d ed. (Toronto: Carswell, 1983) at 169. See EXTERNAL ~; INTERNAL ~; TERMINAL ~; WOUND ~.

BALLOON. *n.* A motorless lighter-than-air aircraft. *Air Regulations*, C.R.C., c. 2, s. 101.

BALLOON PAYMENT. A large, final payment of principal due because a mortgage loan is for a short term and is not fully amortized. D.J. Donahue & P.D. Quinn, *Real Estate Practice in Ontario*, 4th ed. (Toronto: Butterworths, 1990) at 227.

BALLOT. *n.* 1. The paper by which a voter casts his vote at an election. *Elections Act*, S.M. 1980, c. 67, s. 1. 2. The portion of a ballot paper which has been marked by an elector, detached from the counterfoil, and deposited in the ballot box. See SPOILED ~.

BALLOT CARD. A pre-scored data processing card upon which all votes may be recorded. *Municipal Elections Act*, R.R.O. 1980, Reg. 682, s. 1.

BALLOT LABEL. The pages specially prepared for use with the voting recorder, printed with the names of candidates for all offices to be elected and any questions or by-laws submitted to the electors for opinion or assent used in conjunction with ballot cards. *Municipal Elections Act*, R.R.O. 1980, Reg. 682, s. 1.

BALLOT PAPERS. The paper by which a voter casts his vote at an election. *Elections Act*, S.M. 1980, c. 67, s. 1. See REJECTED ~; SPOILED ~.

BAN. *v.* To exclude; to expel; to prevent.

BAN. *n.* A proclamation or public notice which publicizes an intended marriage.

BANC. *n.* A bench or seat of justice.

BANCO. *n.* A bench or seat of justice.

BAND. *n.* 1. A body of Indians (a) for whose use and benefit in common, lands, the legal title of which is vested in Her Majesty, have been set apart before, on or after September 4, 1951, (b) for whose use and benefit in common, moneys are held by Her Majesty, or (c) declared by the Governor in Council to be a band for the purposes of this Act. *Indian Act*, R.S.C. 1985, c. I-5, s. 2. 2. With reference to a reserve or surrendered lands, means the band for whose use and benefit the reserve or the surrendered lands were set apart. *Indian Act*, R.S.C. 1985,

c. I-5, s. 2. See COUNCIL OF THE ~; INDIAN ~; MEMBER OF A ~.

BAND COUNCIL. The council of the band as defined in the *Indian Act* (Canada).

BAND COUNCILLOR. A councillor of a band within the meaning of the *Indian Act* (Canada).

BANDIT. *n.* An outlaw; a person who is put under the ban by law.

BAND LIST. A list of persons that is maintained under section 8 by a band or in the Department. *Indian Act*, R.S.C. 1985 (1st Supp.), c. 32, s. 1.

BANG'S DISEASE. 1. Brucellosis in cattle. *Animal Husbandry Act*, R.S.M. 1970, c. A90, s. 109. 2. An infectious and contagious disease of cattle caused by the brucella abortus. *Bang's Disease Eradication Act*, R.S.P.E.I. 1974, c. B-2, s. 1.

BANISHMENT. *n.* Expulsion from a nation; loss of nationality.

BANK. *n.* 1. A bank to which the Bank Act applies. *Interpretation Act*, R.S.C. 1985, c. I-21, s. 35. 2. An incorporated bank or savings bank carrying on business in Canada. 3. A bank to which the Bank Act or the Quebec Savings Banks Act applies. 4. (a) A bank, (b) a credit union, caisse populaire or other cooperative credit society that is designated by the Minister on the application of that society as a bank for the purposes of this Act, (c) a corporation that carries on the business of a trust company within the meaning of the Trust Companies Act, the business of a loan company within the meaning of the Loan Companies Act, or the business of insurance within the meaning of the Canadian and British Insurance Companies Act, and that is designated by the Minister on the application of that corporation as a bank for the purposes of this Act, and (d) a Province of Alberta Treasury Branch established pursuant to The Treasury Branches Act as enacted by the Legislature of the Province of Alberta. *Canadian Wheat Board Act*, R.S.C. 1985, c. C-24, s. 2. 5. Includes every member of the Canadian Payments Association established under the Canadian Payments Association Act and every local cooperative credit society, as defined in that Act, that is a member of a central, as defined in that Act, that is a member of the Canadian Payments Association. *Bills of Exchange Act*, R.S.C. 1985, c. B-4, s. 164. 6. The Bank of Canada. *Bank of Canada Act*, R.S.C. 1985, c. B-2, s. 2. 7. An establishment or corporation in any country authorized to receive deposits and to pay out money on a customer's order, and includes its agencies and successors. *Military Rules of Evidence*, C.R.C., c. 1049, s. 107. See CHARTERED ~; CONFIRMING ~; DATA ~;

DISTRIBUTING ~; FEDERAL BUSINESS DEVELOPMENT ~; FOREIGN ~; ISSUING ~; ~; OFFICER OF A ~; ORGAN AND TISSUE ~; PERSONAL INFORMATION ~; RECEIVING ~; RESPONSIBLE OFFICER OF THE ~; SAVINGS ~; SEMEN ~.

BANK ACCOUNT. A chequing account, savings accounts, certificate of deposit or transfer account and includes any other type of account authorized to be established by a bank. *Financial Administration Act*, R.S.N.W.T. 1974, c. F-4, s. 2. See DEPARTMENTAL ~; JOINT ~.

BANK-BOOK. See BANK PASS BOOK.

BANK DEBENTURES. Instruments evidencing unsecured indebtedness of a bank issued in accordance with section 132. *Bank Act*, R.S.C. 1985, c. B-1, s. 2.

BANK DEPOSIT. Money which a depositor loans to the bank and which the bank must repay according to the contract. I.F.G. Baxter, *The Law of Banking*, 3d ed. (Toronto: Carswell, 1981) at 2.

BANKER. *n.* 1. A person who receives money from customers and pays it out again in an agreed on manner. 2. Any person, persons, partnership or company carrying on the business of bankers, or any bank, or the liquidators, receivers or trustees of any bank that is being wound up, and any savings bank. *Bankers (Books) Act*, R.S. Nfld. 1970, c. 19, s. 2. 3. A chartered bank, provincial savings office or registered trust company. *Law Society Act*, R.R.O. 1980, Reg. 574, s. 1.

BANKER'S ACCEPTANCE. A draft drawn on and accepted by a bank used to pay for goods sold in import-export transactions and as a source of financing in trade.

BANKER'S BOOKS. Includes ledgers, day books, cash books, account books, and all other books used in the ordinary business of the bank. *Bankers (Books) Act*, R.S. Nfld. 1970, c. 19, s. 2.

BANKING. *n.* Taking money on deposit from the public, issuing, paying and collecting cheques and related activities. I.F.G. Baxter, *The Law of Banking*, 3d ed. (Toronto: Carswell, 1981) at 197.

BANKING INSTRUMENT. A cheque, draft, telegraphic or electronic transfer or other similar instrument. *Financial Administration Act*, S.B.C. 1981, c. 15, s. 1.

BANK-NOTE. *n.* Includes any negotiable instrument (a) issued by or on behalf of a person carrying on the business of banking in or out of Canada, and (b) issued under the authority of Parliament or under the lawful authority of the government of a state other than Canada, intended to be used as money or as the equivalent of money, immediately on issue or at some time subsequent thereto, and includes bank bills and bank post bills. *Criminal Code*, R.S.C. 1985, c. C-46, s. 2.

BANK OF CANADA. The federal body which devises and carries out monetary policy and is the fiscal agent of the government of Canada. By the Bank of Canada Act, this is the only body authorized to issue notes for circulation in Canada.

BANK OF CANADA RATE. The rate of interest set by the Bank of Canada for loans by the Bank of Canada to the chartered banks, as published by the Bank of Canada. *Teachers' Superannuation Act, 1983*, S.O. 1983, c. 84, s. 1.

BANK PASS BOOK. A record of the credits and debits in a customer's account. I.F.G. Baxter, *The Law of Banking*, 3d ed. (Toronto: Carswell, 1981) at 37.

BANK RATE. The bank rate established by the Bank of Canada as the minimum rate at which the Bank of Canada makes short-term advances to the chartered banks. *Courts of Justice Act*, S.O. 1984, c. 11, s. 137.

BANKRUPT. *n.* A person who has made an assignment or against whom a receiving order has been made. *Bankruptcy Act*, R.S.C. 1985, c. B-3, s. 2.

BANKRUPT. *adj.* The legal status of a person who has made an assignment or against whom a receiving order has been made. *Bankruptcy Act*, R.S.C. 1985, c. B-3, s. 2.

BANKRUPTCY. *n.* 1. The state of being bankrupt or the fact of becoming bankrupt. *Bankruptcy Act*, R.S.C. 1985, c. B-3, s. 2. 2. A legal means for a debtor to get out of debt. J.G. McLeod, *The Conflict of Laws* (Calgary: Carswell, 1983) at 433. 3. The condition of a trader who has discontinued his payments. *Interpretation Act*, R.S.Q. 1977, c. I-16, s. 61. See ACT OF ~; CLAIM PROVABLE IN ~; TRUSTEE IN ~.

BANK SERVICE CORPORATION. In relation to a particular bank, means a Canadian corporation that is (a) a subsidiary of that bank or of another bank service corporation that is wholly-owned by that bank that (i) owns no shares in any other corporation except another wholly-owned bank service corporation of that bank, and (ii) engages solely in the acquisition, holding, maintenance, improvement, development, repair, servicing, leasing, disposition or other dealing with real property of a nature that, and for the purposes and for the duration for which, the bank is permitted to acquire, lease or hold pursuant to sections 184, 185 and 199, (b) any other corporation more than ten per cent of the voting shares of which are held by the bank and in respect of which the Minister has advised the bank in writing that subject to such conditions or restrictions as he deems appropriate, the corporation is deemed to be a bank service corporation of that bank for the purposes of this Act, if (i) the corporation owns no shares in any other corporation, other than one that is its wholly-owned subsidiary engaged solely in the activities described in this subparagraph, and the corporation is engaged solely in the acquisition, holding, maintenance, improvement, development, repair, servicing, leasing, disposition or other dealing with real property of a nature that, and for the purposes and for the duration for which, the bank is permitted to acquire, lease or hold pursuant to sections 184, 185 and 199, or (ii) the bank owns more than ten per cent of the voting shares of the corporation on December 1, 1980 and the corporation conforms substantially to the description in subparagraph (i), or (c) a wholly-owned subsidiary of that bank or of another bank service corporation of that bank or a corporation that is wholly-owned jointly by that bank and one or more other banks that (i) owns no shares in any other corporation except another bank service corporation, and (ii) is engaged solely in the provision of a service to that bank or the banks by which it is jointly owned. *Bank Act,* R.S.C. 1985, c. B-1, s. 193.

BANKSMAN. *n.* A person appointed by the owner, agent or manager of an underground mine to have charge of the machinery located at the pit head or surface entrance of the mine. *Coal Mines Regulation Act,* R.S.A. 1970, c. 52, s. 2.

BANNS. *n.* (pl.) A proclamation or public notice which publicizes an intended marriage.

BANNER. *v.* To carry picket signs on the picket line.

BANNS OF MARRIAGE. The proclamation of an intended marriage in a church.

BANQUIER. *n.* The periodical, Le Banquier.

BAR. *n.* 1. A barrier which separates the judge's bench and the front row of counsel's seats from the rest of the court; Queen's counsel are the only counsel allowed within the bar. 2. Obstacle; barrier. 3. The Corporation professionelle des avocats du Québec constituted by section 3. *Barreau du Québec Act,* R.S.Q. 1977, c. B-1, s. 1. See CALL TO THE ~; IRON ~; OUTER ~; ROCK ~.

BAR ADMISSION EXAMINATION. An examination in general subjects related to the practice of law, including practice, procedure, ethics and statutes of a province or Canada or both.

BARBER. *n.* Any person who, for hire, gain, or hope of reward, performs any one, or any combination, of the following services for other persons: (i) cuts or trims hair, (ii) tints, bleaches or dyes hair, (iii) shampoos hair and scalp, (iv) gives hair or scalp treatments or facial massages, (v) curls or waves hair by any means, (vi) performs any other operation with respect to dressing hair to obtain an intended effect or according to a particular style. *Barbers Act,* S.M. 1972, c. 65, s. 1.

BARBERING. *n.* Engaging in the shaving of the face or cutting or trimming or singeing of the hair or beard for hire, gain or hope of reward or in connection with any of the foregoing the shampooing or massaging or the treating of the head or face, or in respect of any of them the charging for any material used in connection with them. *Barbers Act,* R.S.B.C. 1979, c. 25, s. 1.

BARBER SHOP. *var.* **BARBERSHOP.** *n.* A place, room, premises, building or part of them where the occupation of barbering is carried on.

BARBITURATE. *n.* A general term for derivatives of barbituric acid which depress of the nervous system and are used as anaesthetics, anticonvulsants, hypnotics or sedatives and include pentobarbital, phenobarbital and thiopental. F.A. Jaffe, *A Guide to Pathological Evidence,* 2d ed. (Toronto: Carswell, 1983) at 76, 169 and 170.

BARE LICENSEE. A mere licensee; a person permitted by the occupier of property to be or go on the property.

BARE TRUST. Arises when a person who holds property in trust at the absolute disposal and for the absolute benefit of other people. The bare trustee has no personal interest in the property, and the sole duty to convey or transfer it to the beneficiary on demand. This is also known as a simple trust or naked trust.

BARGAIN. *v.* To contract; to enter into an agreement; to negotiate an agreement.

BARGAIN. *n.* Contract; agreement. See CATCHING ~; PLEA ~.

BARGAIN AND SALE. A contract for the sale of chattels, of an estate or of any interest in land followed by payment of the price agreed.

BARGAIN AND SELL. Convey for a consideration. *Conveyancing Act,* R.S.N.S. 1967, c. 56, s. 6.

BARGAIN COLLECTIVELY. To negotiate in

good faith with a view to entering into, renewing or revising a collective agreement.

BARGAINEE. *n.* The person to whom the subject matter of a bargain and sale passes.

BARGAINER. *n.* The person who transfers the subject matter of a bargain and sale.

BARGAINING. See AREA-WIDE ~; BLUE-SKY ~; COLLECTIVE ~; COMPANY-WIDE ~; INDIVIDUAL ~; INDUSTRY-WIDE ~; MULTI-EMPLOYER ~; MULTI-PLANT ~; MULTI-UNION ~; PACKAGE ~; PATTERN ~; SINGLE-PLANT ~.

BARGAINING AGENCY. See EMPLOYEE ~; EMPLOYER ~.

BARGAINING AGENT. 1. A trade union employee organization or other organization that acts on behalf of employees or other groups of workers in collective bargaining. 2. An employee organization. See AFFILIATED ~; CERTIFIED ~.

BARGAINING COLLECTIVELY. 1. Negotiating in good faith with a view to the conclusion of a collective bargaining agreement, or a renewal or revision or a bargaining agreement, the embodiment in writing or writings of the terms of agreement arrived at in negotiations or required to be inserted in a collective bargaining agreement by this Act, the execution by or on behalf of the parties of such agreement, and the negotiating from time to time for the settlement of disputes and grievances of employees covered by the agreement or represented by a trade union representing the majority of employees in an appropriate unit. *The Trade Union Act*, R.S.S. 1978, c. T-17, s. 2. 2. Negotiating in good faith with a view to the conclusion of a collective bargaining agreement or a renewal or revision or a collective bargaining agreement and the embodiment in writing of the terms of agreement arrived at in negotiations or required to be inserted in a collective bargaining agreement by statute. Saskatchewan statutes.

BARGAINING COUNCIL. The council of trade unions certified under section 57 of the Labour Code as bargaining agent for employees of the employer. *B.C. Railway Dispute Settlement Act*, S.B.C. 1985, c. 21, s. 1.

BARGAINING HISTORY. The relationships which have existed between the parties.

BARGAINING RIGHT. See EXCLUSIVE ~.

BARGAINING UNIT. 1. A unit of employees appropriate for collective bargaining. 2. A group of employees usually designated by class of employee, geographical location, work performed, or by a combination of these concepts.

D.J.M. Brown and D.M. Beatty, *Canadian Labour Arbitration*, 2d ed. (Aurora: Canada Law Book, 1977) at 208.

BARGAINING UNIT WORK. Tasks usually performed by a member of a bargaining unit. D.J.M. Brown and D.M. Beatty, *Canadian Labour Arbitration*, 2d ed. (Aurora: Canada Law Book, 1977) at 214. See UNIT OR ~.

BARGAINOR. *n.* The person who transfers the subject matter of a bargain and sale.

BARGAIN PRICE. (a) A price that is represented in an advertisement to be a bargain price by reference to an ordinary price or otherwise; or (b) a price that a person who reads, hears or sees the advertisement would reasonably understand to be a bargain price by reason of the prices at which the product advertised or like products are ordinarily sold. *Combines Investigation Act*, R.S.C. 1985, c. C-34, s. 57.

BARGE. *n.* A non-self-propelled barge, scow, dredge, pile-driver, hopper, pontoon or houseboat. *Collision Regulations*, C.R.C., c. 1416, s. 2.

BARLEYCORN. *n.* A nominal rent.

BARLEY PRODUCT. Any substance produced by processing or manufacturing barley, alone or together with any other material or substance, designated by the Governor in Council by regulation as a barley product for the purposes of this Part. *Canadian Wheat Board Act*, R.S.C. 1970, c. C-12, s. 2.

BAR OF DOWER. Giving up of dower.

BARON. *n.* The former title of judges of certain courts. See COVERT-~.

BARR. *abbr.* The Barrister (Can.).

BARRATOR. *n.* A person who routinely brings, stirs up or maintains quarrels or suits.

BARRATRY. *n.* 1. Includes every wrongful act wilfully committed by the master or crew to the prejudice of the owner, or, as the case may be, the charterer. *Insurance acts.* 2. An offence committed by a barrator.

BARRED. See STATUTE ~.

BARREL. *n.* 1. 34.9722 standard gallons within the meaning of subsection 13(1) of the Weights and Measures Act, being chapter W-7 of the Revised Statutes of Canada, 1970. *Petroleum Administration Act*, S.C. 1974-75-76, c. 47, s. 4. 2. 35 standard Canadian gallons as defined by the Weights and Measures Act (Canada). *Environmental Protection Act*, R.R.O. 1980, Reg. 303, s. 1. 3. The portion of a firearm in the shape of a tube through which a projectile passes. F.A. Jaffe, *A Guide to Pathological Evidence*, 2d ed. (Toronto: Carswell, 1983) at 170.

BARREN BOTTOM. Includes those parts of the beds and bottoms of any bays, rivers, harbors or creeks where no natural or live oyster beds are found to exist at the time of the application for and granting of any lease under an Act. Oyster Fisheries acts.

BARRETOR. *n.* A person who routinely brings, stirs up or maintains quarrels or suits.

BARRIER. See FIXED COLLISION ~.

BARRISTER. *n.* 1. Usually refers to a lawyer who appears as an advocate in court. 2. Includes solicitor. *Barristers and Solicitors Act*, R.S.N.S. 1967, c. 18, s. 1.

BARRISTER. *abbr.* Barrister (1894-1897).

BARRISTER AND SOLICITOR. A member of the Law Society other than an honorary member or a student member thereof. *Legal Aid Act*, R.S.O. 1980, c. 234, s. 1.

BAR SEINE. Netting that is floated at the top, weighted at the bottom and used to impound fish along the shore. *Atlantic Coast Herring Regulations*, C.R.C., c. 804, s. 2.

BAR SINK. A receptacle for the disposal of liquid wastes only. *Ontario Water Resources Act*, R.R.O. 1980, Reg. 736, s. 1.

BARTER. *v.* To exchange goods for goods.

BASAL FEED. A mixed feed, other than a chop feed, that contains ingredients added only to supply carbohydrates. *Feeds Regulations*, C.R.C., c. 665, s. 2.

BASE. *n.* 1. Bottom; foundation. 2. In respect of a commercial air service, means the city, town or place specified in a licence from which an air carrier is authorized to provide service and that is identified where necessary by reference to latitude and longitude. *Air Carrier Regulations*, C.R.C., c. 3, s. 2. See CAPITAL ~; COST ~; EARNINGS ~; INITIAL ~; OPERATING ~; RATE ~; REVENUE ~.

BASE. *adj.* Inferior; impure.

BASE ALLOWABLE. The amount of production which according to a Board order could be taken if no penalty factor, whether its purpose be for proration, for avoidance of waste or for protection of the rights of others, were to be applied. *Oil and Gas Conservation Act*, R.S.A. 1980, c. O-5, s. 1.

BASE CALENDAR YEAR. The calendar year ending immediately before the current fiscal year.

BASE INCOME. See MONTHLY ~.

BASE LENGTH. The distance measured between the centres of the first axle of the front axle of a vehicle or combination of vehicles and the last axle of a vehicle or combination of vehicles. *Highway Traffic Act*, R.R.O. 1980, Reg. 470, s. 1.

BASE LINE. Of a creek or river means a traverse line following the general direction of the centre bottom lands of the valley of the creek or river, surveyed and established under the direction and with the approval of the Commissioner. *Yukon Placer Mining Act*, R.S.C. 1985, c. Y-3, s. 2.

BASE LOAN. (a) A loan, to an applicant for protection, and (b) in relation to any assignment of a contract or its ceasing to be in force in accordance with section 68, means a loan, to the applicant for protection under the contract, of money borrowed for a term referred to in subsection 65(1), other than a term referred to in subparagraph 65(1)(b)(iii), by the applicant. *National Housing Act*, R.S.C. 1985, c. N-11, s. 64.

BASEMENT. *n.* 1. Any storey below the first storey measured from the top of each floor to the top of the floor next below. *Building Code Act*, R.R.O. 1980, Reg. 87, s. 1. 2. That portion of a hotel between two floor levels that is situated below the first storey. *Hotel Fire Safety Act*, R.R.O. 1980, Reg. 505, s. 2.

BASE OF OPERATIONS. A licensed tourist establishment or an air carrier licensed by the Canadian Transport Commission and Transport Canada located in Ontario at or from which a tourist outfitter maintains facilities for communication, transportation and the complete maintenance of office records. *Tourism Act*, R.R.O. 1980, Reg. 936, s. 1.

BASE PRESSURE INDEX. A device which, when connected to a positive displacement gas meter, automatically multiplies the volume passed by the meter by the ratio of absolute line pressure at the meter to the base pressure, thus registering the volume on the index in terms of base pressure. *Gas and Gas Meters Regulations*, C.R.C., c. 876, s. 23.

BASE PRICE. In relation to an agricultural commodity, means the base price as established under section 9. *Agricultural Stabilization Act*, R.S.C. 1985, c. A-8, s. 2. See OLD OIL ~.

BASE RATE. The rate of pay for work excluding bonuses and overtime.

BASE RATE SCALE. The scale set out in Schedule II indicating an amount per tonne for the movement of grain over each range of distance set out in the scale. *Western Grain Transportation Act*, R.S.C. 1985, c. W-8, s. 34.

BASE VOLUME INDEX. A device that, when

used in conjunction with a positive displacement gas meter, automatically multiplies the volume passed by the meter by two factors: (a) the ratio of absolute line pressure at the meter to base pressure, and (b) the ratio of the absolute base temperature to the absolute flowing temperature of the gas, thus causing the index to register the volume in terms of base pressure and base temperature. *Gas and Gas Meters Regulations*, C.R.C., c. 876, s. 24.

BASIC ACCOUNT DEFICIT. The amount, if any, by which the total sums credited as at any time to the Unemployment Insurance Account under paragraph 114(a) are less than the total sums charged as at that time to the Unemployment Insurance Account under section 117 to pay the basic cost of benefit. *Unemployment Insurance Act*, R.S.C. 1985, c. U-1, s. 49.

BASIC ACCOUNT SURPLUS. The amount, if any, by which the total sums credited as at any time to the Unemployment Insurance Account under paragraph 114(a) exceed the total sums charged as at that time to the Unemployment Insurance Account under section 117 to pay the basic cost of benefit. *Unemployment Insurance Act*, R.S.C. 1985, c. U-1, s. 49.

BASIC ALLOTMENT. A base measurement in quantity of turkey meat from which the market allotment of a producer is established. *Canadian Turkey Marketing Quota Regulations*, C.R.C., c. 661, s. 2.

BASIC ALLOWANCE. 1. (a) In the case of a former member, the annual allowance he was receiving under this Part at the time of his death, and (b) in the case of a member, the annual allowance he would have been eligible to receive under this Part if he had ceased to be a member immediately before his death. *Members of Parliament Retiring Allowances Act*, R.S.C. 1985, c. M-5, s. 31(6). 2. (i) In the case of a member, the annual allowance he would have been eligible to receive under this Ordinance, except for an annual allowance payable pursuant to paragraph 13(b), if he had ceased to be a member on the day immediately before his death, and (ii) in the case of a former member who is in receipt of an annual allowance, the annual allowance he was receiving pursuant to this Ordinance at the time of his death except for an annual allowance payable pursuant to paragraph 13(b). *Council Retiring Allowances Act*, S.N.W.T. 1981 (3d Sess.), c. 3, s. 2.

BASIC AREA. The horizontal projected area inside the perimeter of the exterior or boundary walls. *Hotel Fire Safety Act*, R.R.O. 1980, Reg. 505, s. 2.

BASIC BENEFIT. 1. With respect to a participant, means the salary of the participant if it is a multiple of two hundred and fifty dollars or the nearest multiple of two hundred and fifty dollars above the salary of the participant if it is not a multiple of two hundred and fifty dollars, subject to a reduction, to be made as of such time as the regulations prescribe, of one-tenth of that amount for every year of age in excess of sixty attained by the participant, except that (a) in the case of a participant who is employed in the Public Service, the basic benefit shall be not less than (i) one-sixth of his salary if that one-sixth is a multiple of two hundred and fifty dollars, or the nearest multiple of two hundred and fifty dollars above one-sixth of his salary if that one-sixth is not a multiple of two hundred and fifty dollars, or (ii) five hundred dollars, whichever is the greater, and (b) in the case of an elective participant who, on ceasing to be employed in the Public Service or to be a member of the regular force, was entitled under Part I to an immediate annuity, the basic benefit shall be not less than five hundred dollars. *Public Service Superannuation Act*, R.S.C. 1985, c. P-36, s. 47. 2. With respect to a participant, means that salary of the participant if it is a multiple of two hundred and fifty dollars or the nearest multiple of two hundred and fifty dollars above the salary of the participant if it is not a multiple of two hundred and fifty dollars, subject to a reduction, to be made as of such time as the regulations prescribe, of one-tenth of that amount for every year of age in excess of sixty attained by the participant, except that in the case of an elective participant who, on ceasing to be a member of the regular force or on ceasing to be employed in the Public Service, was entitled under Part I or under the Defence Services Pension Continuation Act, chapter D-3 of the Revised Statutes of Canada, 1970, to an immediate annuity or pension the basic benefit shall not be less than five hundred dollars. *Canadian Forces Superannuation Act*, R.S.C. 1985, c. C-17, s. 60.

BASIC CARE. The types and levels of basic services prescribed in the regulations to be provided to residents. *Nursing Homes Act*, S.A. 1985, c. N-14.1, s. 1.

BASIC CARE EXPENDITURES. Those expenditures incurred with respect to the day to day operation of the residence including expenditures for shelter, salaries and benefits, food, clothing, transportation, administration, recreation and incidentals. *Children's Residential Services Act*, R.R.O. 1980, Reg. 101, s. 23.

BASIC COST OF BENEFIT. In relation to any year, means the amount paid out of the Consolidated Revenue Fund pursuant to section 117 to pay (a) initial benefits in respect of that year, (b) benefits under subsection 19(2), (c) the costs

BASIC EARNINGS PER SHARE

of administration of this Act, as determined in the manner prescribed, and (d) benefits under sections 21 and 24. *Unemployment Insurance Act*, R.S.C. 1985, c. U-1, s. 49. See AVERAGE ~.

BASIC EARNINGS PER SHARE. The amount of income attributable to each outstanding share that carries as an incident of ownership the right to participate in earnings to an unlimited degree.

BASIC EQUIPMENT. All equipment approved by the Minister as necessary and reasonable to enable a facility to commence its function as determined at the time of its completion or renovation, provided that such equipment is installed and ready for use not later than twelve months after the date of completion of the construction project or renovation program. Ontario regulations.

BASIC FREQUENCY RESPONSE. One of the family of frequency responses that is chosen as a reference condition for purposes of description. *Medical Devices Regulations*, C.R.C., c. 871, s. 1.

BASIC HEALTH SERVICES. (i) Insured services, (ii) those services that are rendered by a dental surgeon in the field of oral surgery and are specified in the regulations but are not within the definition of insured service, (iii) optometric services, (iv) chiropractic services, (v) services and appliances provided by a podiatrist, and (vi) services provided by an osteopath. *Alberta Health Care Insurance Act*, R.S.A. 1970, c. 166, s. 2.

BASIC HERD LIVESTOCK. Female cattle, sheep or swine of a breeding age with or without an appropriate complement of male stock and may include (a) in the case of cattle, up to a normal two-year progeny, and (b) in the case of sheep, up to a normal one-year progeny. *Veterans' Land Regulations*, C.R.C., c. 1594, s. 2.

BASIC NECESSITIES. Things, goods and services that are essential to a person's health and well—being, including food, clothing, shelter, household and personal requirements, medical, hospital, optical, dental and other remedial treatment, care and attention, and an adequate funeral on death.

BASIC NUMBER OF CONTRIBUTORY MONTHS. In the case of any contributor, means one hundred and twenty minus the number of months for which a disability pension was payable to him under this Act or under a provincial pension plan. *Canada Pension Plan*, R.S.C. 1985, c. C-8, s. 42.

BASIC PREMIUM. That portion of the premium that is based upon criteria established under the regulations but does not include any additional premium or any surcharge. *Insurance acts.*

BASIC PULSE INTERVAL. The rate of an implantable pulse generator free of modifying cardiac or other electromagnetic influences. *Medical Devices Regulations*, C.R.C., c. 871, s. 1.

BASIC RATE. A rate determined in the manner prescribed by any order made from time to time by the Governor in Council for the purposes of this section, being not less than the average yield, determined in the manner prescribed by that order, from Government of Canada treasury bills. *Expropriation Act*, R.S.C. 1985, c. E-21, s. 36.

BASIC RATE OF WAGES. The basic hourly wage rate of an employee excluding any premium or bonus rates paid under any specific conditions of his employment. *Canada Labour Standards Regulations*, C.R.C., c. 986, s. 19.

BASIC SERVICE. The service provided by a licensee on channels that a conventional 12 channel VHF television receiver is capable of receiving without the use of any device to increase its capacity to receive channels. *Cable Television Regulations*, C.R.C., c. 374, s. 2.

BASIC TAX RATE. See FEDERAL ~.

BASIC UNIT RENT. The amount of rent charged for a rental unit exclusive of any separate charges. *Residential Rent Regulation Act*, S.O. 1986, c. 63, s. 97.

BASIC WAGE. Minimum wage.

BASIC WELL-HEAD PRICE. The price at the well-head of a barrel of oil produced in Saskatchewan set out in schedule I of this Act. *The Oil and Gas Conservation, Stabilization and Development Act*, R.S.S. 1978, c. O-3, s. 2.

BASIN. *n.* Any navigable area, whether or not it includes a part of the normal canal prism provided for the loading, unloading, turning or passing of vessels. *Canal Regulations*, C.R.C., c. 1564, s. 2.

BASIS. See ACTUARIAL ~; CASH ~; COOPERATIVE ~; FULL-TIME ~; PART-TIME ~.

BASKET CLAUSE. Clause intended to ensure that the document covers a larger number of persons or instances than are actually specified in the document.

BASKET DRAG RAKE. A drag rake with a device attached to the rear and forward portions so as to form an enclosure. *Atlantic Coast Marine Plant Regulations*, C.R.C., c. 805, s. 2.

BASTARD. *n.* A person born to unmarried parents.

BASTARDIZE. *v.* To declare someone a bastard; to give evidence to prove that someone is a bastard.

BASTARDY ORDER. Affiliation order.

BASTARDY PROCEEDING. Affiliation proceeding.

BASTART. *n.* Bastard.

BATHER. *n.* A person dressed for bathing. *Public Health Act*, R.R.O. 1980, Reg. 849, s. 1.

BATHROOM. A room containing a bathtub or a shower. *Power Corporation Act*, R.R.O. 1980, Reg. 794, s. 0.

BATTERY. *n.* 1. Bringing about, intentionally, an offensive or harmful contact with another person. John G. Fleming, *The Law of Torts*, 6th ed., (Sydney: The Law Book Company Limited, 1983) at 23. 2. A system or arrangement of tanks or other surface equipment receiving the effluents of one or more wells prior to delivery to market or other disposition, and may include equipment or devices for separating the effluents into oil, gas, crude bitumen or water and for measurement. Oil and Gas acts. See ASSAULT AND ~; STORAGE ~.

BATTERY SERVICE STATION. A building or part of a building within which or in connection with which, any service is rendered in the ordinary course of business upon a storage battery by recharging it or by the making of repairs thereto or the supplying of parts therefor. *Garage Keepers Act*, R.S.M. 1970, c. G10, s. 14.

BATTERY SITE. That portion of the surface of land, other than a well site or roadway, required for access to and to accommodate separators, treaters, dehydrators, storage tanks, surface reservoirs, pumps and other equipment, including above ground pressure maintenance facilities, that are necessary to measure, separate or store prior to shipping to market or disposal, or necessary to produce, the fluids, minerals, and water, or any of them, from wells. *The Surface Rights Acquisition and Compensation Act*, R.S.S. 1978, c. S-65, s. 2.

BAWDY HOUSE. *n.* A brothel. See COMMON ~.

B.C. *abbr.* British Columbia.

B.C.A.A. *abbr.* B.C. Assessment Authority.

B.C.B.C. *abbr.* B.C. Buildings Corporation.

B.C. BR. LECT. *abbr.* Canadian Bar Association, British Columbia Branch Lectures.

B.C. CORPS. L.G. *abbr.* British Columbia Corporations Law Guide.

B.C.E.C. *abbr.* B.C. Enterprise Corporation.

B.C.F.C. *abbr.* B.C. Ferry Corporation.

B.C.F.R. *abbr.* B.C. Forest Resources Commission.

B.C.H.P. *abbr.* B.C. Hydro and Power Authority.

B.C.L.C. *abbr.* B.C. Lottery Corporation.

B.C.L.N. *abbr.* British Columbia Law Notes.

B.C.L.R. *abbr.* British Columbia Law Reports, 1977-1988.

B.C.L.R.B. DEC. *abbr.* British Columbia Labour Relations Board Decisions.

B.C.L.R. (2D). *abbr.* British Columbia Law Reports (Second Series) 1988.

B.C.P.C. *abbr.* B.C. Pavilion Corporation.

B.C.P.E. *abbr.* B.C. Petroleum Corporation.

B.C.R. *abbr.* 1. British Columbia Reports, 1867-1947. 2. B.C. Rail Ltd.

B.C.S.C. *abbr.* B.C. Systems Corporation.

B.C.S.T. *abbr.* B.C. Stena Lines Ltd.

B.C.T. *abbr.* B.C. Transit.

B.C.T.C. *abbr.* B.C. Trade Development Corporation.

B.C.T.R. *abbr.* British Columbia Tax Reports.

B.C.U.C. *abbr.* B.C. Utilities Commission.

B.C.W.L.D. *abbr.* British Columbia Weekly Law Digest.

BD. *abbr.* Board.

BEACH. *n.* 1. Land lying within 300 metres (984 feet) landward from the ordinary low water mark of any body of tidal water but only until the elevation of that land first reaches a height of 15 metres (49 feet) above such low water mark. *Quarry Materials Act*, S. Nfld. 1975-76, c. 45, s. 2. 2. That area of land on the coastline lying to the seaward of the mean high watermark and that area of land to landward immediately adjacent thereto to the distance determined by the Governor in Council, and includes any lakeshore area declared by the Governor in Council to be a beach. *Beaches Preservation and Protection Act*, S.N.S. 1975, c. 6, s. 3.

BEACH SEINE. Netting that is floated at the top, weighted at the bottom and used to impound fish along the shore. *Atlantic Coast Herring Regulations*, C.R.C., c. 804, s. 2.

BEACON. *n.* Lighthouse. See DEWIZ ~.

BEAD. *n.* That part of the tire made of steel wires wrapped or reinforced by ply cords, that is shaped to fit the rim.

BEAD SEPARATION. A breakdown of bond between components in the bead area of a tire.

BEAM. *n.* 1. The light projected from a pair of lighted headlamps. *Highway Traffic Act*, R.R.O. 1980, Reg. 469, s. 19. 2. A collection of rays that may be parallel, convergent or divergent. *Radiation Emitting Devices Regulations*, C.R.C., c. 1370, s. 1. See USEFUL ~.

BEAN. *n.* Black beans or black turtle soup beans of any variety, class or grade grown or harvested within Manitoba that are used or intended to be used mainly for human consumption. *Manitoba Bean Order*, C.R.C., c. 151, s. 2.

BEANS. *n.* White pea beans and yellow-eye beans produced in Ontario. Canada Regulations. See CANNED ~; CANNED ~ WITH SEASONING.

BEAR. *n.* One who expects a fall in the price of shares.

BEARER. *n.* 1. The person in possession of a bill or note that is payable to bearer. *Bills of Exchange Act*, R.S.C. 1985, c. B-4, s. 2. 2. The person in possession of a security payable to bearer or endorsed in blank. See FUR-BEARER.

BEARER FORM. When applied to a security means a security that is payable to bearer according to its terms and not by reason of any endorsement. *Business Corporations Act, 1982*, S.O. 1982, c. 4, s. 53.

BEARING SUPPORT. A structural member or system of structural members supporting masonry and resisting all applied loads. *Building Code Act*, R.R.O. 1980, Reg. 87, s. 1.

BEARING SURFACE. The contact surface between a foundation unit and the soil or rock upon which it bears. *Building Code Act*, R.R.O. 1980, Reg. 87, s. 1.

BECAUSE OF HANDICAP. For the reason that the person has or has had, or is believed to have or have had, (i) any degree of physical disability, infirmity, malformation or disfigurement that is caused by bodily injury, birth defect or illness and, without limiting the generality of the foregoing, including diabetes mellitus, epilepsy, any degree of paralysis, amputation, lack of physical co-ordination, blindness or visual impediment, deafness or hearing impediment, muteness or speech impediment, or physical reliance on a dog guide or on a wheelchair or other remedial appliance or device, (ii) a condition of mental retardation or impairment, (iii) a learning disability, or a dysfunction in one or more of the processes involved in understanding or using symbols or spoken language, or (iv) a mental disorder. *Human Rights Code, 1981*, S.O. 1981, c. 53, s. 9.

BED. See RIVER ~.

BEDDING. *n.* Any mattress, mattress type pad, boxspring, quilt, comforter, sleeping bag, mattress protector pad, pillow or quilted bedspread, that contains stuffing concealed by fabric or other flexible material or any such article that can be used for sleeping or reclining purposes, but does not include decorator cushions. *Upholstered and Stuffed Articles Act*, R.R.O. 1980, Reg. 940, s. 1.

BEDROCK. *n.* The solid rock underlying unconsolidated material such as sand, gravel and clay. *Ontario Water Resources Act*, R.R.O. 1980, Reg. 739, s. 1.

BEDROOM. *n.* A room specially arranged to accommodate one or more travellers and provided with at least one window, its door opening into a closed or open passage used to connect the rooms with each other and with the remainder of the establishment. *An Act Respecting the Commission de Contrôle des Permis D'alcool*, R.S.Q. 1977, c. C-33, s. 2.

BEE. *n.* The insect (i) Apis mellifera, or (ii) Megachile rotundata. See PACKAGE ~S.

BEEF. *n.* Live cattle for slaughter or the whole or any part of a cattle carcass of any variety, grade or class. See STRIPPED ~.

BEEHIVE EQUIPMENT. Hives, supers, hive covers, hive floors, queen excluders, frames, combs, and includes the honey, brood and pollen in the combs. *Bee Act*, R.S.B.C. 1979, c. 27, s. 1.

BEEKEEPER. *var.* **BEE-KEEPER.** *n.* 1. A person who owns, or partnership that owns or possesses any bees or any honeycombs or brood combs suited to the maintenance and keeping of bees. 2. A person who owns or controls bees or beehives or beekeeping equipment.

BEEKEEPING EQUIPMENT. 1. Hives, parts of hives, and utensils used in the maintenance and keeping of bees and includes, when kept in conjunction with hives, parts of hives and utensils used in the maintenance and keeping of bees, honey, wax, pollen and royal jelly. 2. Equipment used in the rearing or keeping of bees that is capable of transmitting disease among bees. *The Apiaries Act*, R.S.S. 1978, c. A-22, s. 2.

BEER. *n.* 1. The beverage obtained by the alcoholic fermentation in drinking water of an infusion or decoction of barley, malt, hops or any other similar product. 2. All fermented liquor brewed in whole or in part from malt, grain or any saccharine matter without any process of distillation. *Excise Act*, R.S.C. 1985, c. E-14, s. 4. 3. As applied to distilleries, means all liquor made in whole or in part from grain, malt or other saccharine matter, whether or not the liquor is fermented or unfermented. *Excise Act*, R.S.C. 1985, c. E-14, s. 4. See LIGHT ~; NEAR ~.

BEER LICENCE. A beer parlour licence, a beer vendor's licence, a brewer's retail licence, or a club beer licence. *Liquor Control Act*, R.S.M. 1970, c. L160, s. 2.

BEE-WAX REFUSE. Damaged honeycombs, honeycomb cappings or the material remaining after the first rendering of used honeycombs or honeycomb cappings. *Bees Act*, R.S.O. 1980, c. 42, s. 1.

BEGGAR. *n.* A person who begs or gathers alms.

BEGIN. See RIGHT TO ~.

BEGINNER. See LICENSED ~.

BEING. See IN ~.

BELGIUM. *n.* Used in a geographical sense means the territory of the Kingdom of Belgium, including any area beyond the territorial waters of Belgium which is an area within which Belgium may exercise rights with respect to the sea-bed and sub-soil and their natural resources. *Canada-Belgium Income Tax Convention Act*, S.C. 1974-75-76, c. 104, Schedule II, Article III, s. 1.

BELLIGERENT. *n.* A country or group of people waging war as determined by the law of nations.

BELLO PARTA CEDUNT RESPUBLICAE. [L.] The spoils of war belong to the Crown.

BELL TRAP. A trap where the pipe conveying water from the trap is covered by a bell so that the water flowing through the trap passes under the rim of the bell and over the end of the pipe. *Ontario Water Resources Act*, R.R.O. 1980, Reg. 736, s. 85.

BELLUM JUSTUM. [L.] Just war.

BELONG. *v.* To be the property of, to be owned.

BELOW PAR. At a price lower than face or nominal value; at a discount.

BELT. See SAFETY ~; SEAT ~; SHELTER ~.

BELT ASSEMBLY. See SEAT ~.

BELT INJURY. See SEAT ~.

BELUGA. *n.* A cetacean (Delphinapterus leucas) of the dolphin family, also known as the white whale. *Beluga Protection Regulations*, C.R.C., c. 809, s. 2.

BENCH. *n.* 1. The judge's seat in a court. 2. A single judge. 3. Judges collectively. See QUEEN'S ~.

BENCHER. *n.* An elected governing official of a provincial law society.

BENCH WARRANT. A court-issued warrant to arrest a person.

BENDS. See DECOMPRESSION SICKNESS.

BENEDICTA EST EXPOSITIO QUANDO RES REDIMITUR A DESTRUCTIONE. [L.] Well-spoken is the statement which saves anything from destruction.

BENEFICIAL INTEREST. 1. The interest of a beneficiary or beneficial owner. 2. An interest arising out of the beneficial ownership of securities. 3. Includes ownership through a trustee, legal representative, agent or other intermediary.

BENEFICIAL OWNER. 1. (i) A person who has the right to drill into a unit of minerals and produce therefrom oil and gas or potash and to appropriate the oil and gas or potash he produced either to himself or others or to deliver up the oil and gas or potash to others, or (ii) where the owner exercises his rights to drill into a unit of minerals and produces therefrom, that owner. *Mineral Taxation Act*, S.M. 1974, c. 60, s. 1. 2. Of oil and gas rights means a person beneficially entitled thereto, whether or not he is also the registered owner thereof, and the area beneficially owned by him refers to his net interest therein expressed as a unit of area. Saskatchewan statutes.

BENEFICIAL OWNERSHIP. Includes ownership through a trustee, legal representative, agent or other intermediary.

BENEFICIAL USE. A use of water, including the method of diversion, storage, transportation, and application, that is reasonable and consistent with the public interest in the proper utilization of water resources, including but not being limited to domestic, agricultural, industrial, power, municipal, navigational, fish and wildlife, and recreational uses.

BENEFICIARY. *n.* 1. A person designated or appointed as one to whom or for whose benefit insurance money is to be payable. 2. A person entitled to benefit from a trust or will. 3. A person entitled to receive benefits under a statutory scheme. 4. In respect of an education savings plan, means a person, designated by a subscriber, to whom or on whose behalf an educational assistance payment under the plan is agreed to be paid if he qualifies under the plan. *Income Tax Act*, R.S.C. 1952, c. 148 (as am. S.C. 1974-75-76, c. 26, s. 100), s. 146.1(1)(a). See CONTRACT ~; FOREIGN ~; OTHER ~; PREFERRED ~.

BENEFICIARY COUNTRY. A country to which the benefits of the General Preferential Tariff have been extended pursuant to subsection 3.2(1) of the Customs Tariff. *General Preferential Tariff Rules of Origin Regulations*, C.R.C., c. 528, s. 2.

BENEFIT. *n.* 1. A pension; a monetary amount paid under a pension or other plan. 2. A drug or other good or service that is supplied to an eligible person. 3. Compensation or an indemnity paid in money, financial assistance or services. 4. The advantages to any lands, roads, buildings or other structures from the construction, improvement, repair or maintenance of a drainage works such as will result in a higher market value or increased crop production or improved appearance or better control of surface or subsurface water, or any other advantages relating to the betterment of lands, roads, buildings or other structures. *Drainage Act*, R.S.O. 1980, c. 126, s. 1. 5. Includes any amount received out of or under a retirement savings plan other than (i) the portion thereof received by a person other than the annuitant that can reasonably be regarded as part of the amount included in computing the income of an annuitant by virtue of subsections (8.8) and (8.9), (ii) an amount received by the person with whom the annuitant has the contract or arrangement described in paragraph (j) as a premium under the plan, and (iii) an amount, or part thereof, received in respect of the income of the trust under the plan for a taxation year for which the trust was not exempt from tax by virtue of paragraph (4)(c) and without restricting the generality of the foregoing includes any amount paid to an annuitant under the plan (iv) in accordance with the terms of the plan, (v) resulting from an amendment to or modification of the plan, or (vi) resulting from the termination of the plan. *Income Tax Act*, R.S.C. 1952, c. 148 (as am. S.C. 1979, c. 5, s. 46), s. 146(1)(b). See BASIC ~; BRIDGING ~; COLLATERAL ~; CONDITIONAL ~; DEATH ~; DEFERRED ~; DEFINED ~; DEFINED CONTRIBUTION ~; FEDERAL ~S; FRINGE ~; IMMEDIATE ~; LABOUR ADJUSTMENT ~S; MUTUAL ~S; PENSION ~; SICK AND FUNERAL ~S; SPECIAL ~; STRIKE ~; SUPPLEMENTARY ~; TAX ~.

BENEFIT COST STATEMENT. A statement relating the anticipated benefits expressed in dollars to the total estimated cost of the drainage works. *Drainage Act*, R.S.O. 1980, c. 126, s. 1.

BENEFIT PERIOD. The period of time during which an insured person is entitled to insured services. *Health Insurance Act*, R.R.O. 1980, Reg. 452, s. 1.

BENEFIT PLAN. See DEFINED ~; DISABILITY INCOME INSURANCE OR ~; EMPLOYEE ~; HEALTH INSURANCE OR ~.

BENEFITS PLAN. A plan for the employment of Canadians and for providing Canadian manufacturers, consultants, contractors and service companies with a full and fair opportunity to participate on a competitive basis in the supply of goods and services used in any proposed work or activity referred to in the benefits plan. *Petroleum Resources Act*, R.S.C. 1985 (2d Supp.), c. 36, s. 52. See CANADA-NEWFOUNDLAND ~.

BENEFIT PROVISION. See DEFINED ~.

BENEFIT SOCIETY. See FRATERNAL ~; TRADE UNION ~.

BENEVOLENCE. See CONTRACT OF ~.

BENEVOLENT. *adj.* Charitable; conferring benefits; philanthropic.

BENEVOLENTIA REGIS HABENDA. [L.] Having the sovereign's good will; having the sovereign's pardon.

BENEVOLENT PURPOSE. A charitable, educational, religious, or welfare purpose or other purpose to the public advantage or benefit.

BENIGNAE FACIENDAE SUNT INTERPRETATIONES ET VERBA INTENTIONI DEBENT INSERVIRE. [L.] Liberal interpretation ought to be the rule, and words ought to serve intention.

BENIGNAE SUNT FACIENDAE INTERPRETATIONES CARTARUM PROPTER SIMPLICITATEM LAICORUM UT RES MAGIS VALEAT QUAM PEREAT. [L.] Because of the simplicity of laypeople, charters should be interpreted liberally so that the intention prevails rather than goes to waste.

BENIGNIOR SENTENTIA IN VERBIS GENERALIBUS SEU DUBIIS, EST PRAEFERENDA. [L.] A more favourable construction should be placed on general or doubtful terms.

BENZEDRINE. *n.* The Smith, Kline and French Laboratories brand of amphetamine sulphate. F.A. Jaffe, *A Guide to Pathological Evidence*, 2d ed. (Toronto: Carswell, 1983) at 170.

BENZENE. *n.* A substance designated under the Ontario Occupational Health and Safety Act. D. Robertson, *Ontario Health and Safety Guide* (Toronto: Richard De Boo Ltd., 1988) at 5-28C.

BEQUEATH. *v.* To leave through a will.

BEQUEST. *n.* Personal property given by will. See RESIDUARY ~; SPECIFIC ~.

BEREAVEMENT LEAVE. Time off without loss of pay to gather together with relatives at a time of personal tragedy for mutual comfort, to assist in making arrangements for the funeral of the deceased and for the immediate and after care of the deceased's survivors, and to enable the employee to bear his grief privately without immediate exposure to the comparative harshness of his working environment. *Re Dominion Glass Co. Ltd.* (1973), 4 L.A.C. (2d) 345 (Johnston) at 353.

BERNE CONVENTION. The international convention drawn up at Berne in 1886 which created an international union for the protection of artistic and literary copyright.

BERRIES. *n.* Strawberries and raspberries produced in Ontario that are used by a processor for processing. *Ontario Berry-for-Processing Order,* C.R.C., c. 178, s. 2. See CANNED ~; UNDEVELOPED ~.

BERRY ANEURYSM. The rupture of this aneurysm involving an artery at the base of the brain commonly causes sudden death in young or middle aged adults. F.A. Jaffe, *A Guide to Pathological Evidence,* 2d ed. (Toronto: Carswell, 1983) at 168.

BERTH. *n.* 1. A location at any wharf, pier, quay or similar facility at which a vessel may be secured. *National Harbours Board Operating By-law,* C.R.C., c. 1064, s. 2. 2. Includes a wharf, pier, anchorage or mooring buoy. Canada regulations. See FOREST MANAGEMENT ~; PULPWOOD ~; SLEEPER ~; TIMBER ~.

BERTHAGE. *n.* 1. A charge on a vessel (a) while occupying a berth or while fast to or tied up alongside any other vessel occupying a berth at any wharf, pier, jetty, bulkhead or other similar facility under the administration, management and control of or under lease from the Commissioners within the harbour, and (b) while not moored at but loading or unloading by lighter from or to any facilities referred to in paragraph (a). Canada regulations. 2. A charge levied on a vessel in respect of the period of time that the vessel is (a) moored to a wharf, (b) occupying a berth or any space at or near a wharf, or (c) secured in any manner whatever to a vessel that is subject to berthage. Canada regulations.

BESET. See WATCH AND ~.

BESTES KE GAIGNENT SA TERRE. [Fr.] Beasts of the plough.

BEST EVIDENCE RULE. Wherever possible, the original of a document must be produced. P.K. McWilliams, *Canadian Criminal Evidence,*

3d ed. (Aurora: Canada Law Book, 1988) at 6-1.

BESTIALITY. *n.* The act of a human being having sexual intercourse with an animal.

BEST INTERESTS OF THE CHILD. The best interests of the child in the circumstances having regard, in addition to all other relevant considerations to (i) the mental, emotional and physical needs of the child and the appropriate care or treatment, or both, to meet such need, (ii) the child's opportunity to have a parent-child relationship as a wanted and needed member within a family structure, (iii) the child's mental, emotional and physical stages of development, (iv) the effect upon the child of any disruption of the child's sense of continuity and need for permanency, (v) the merits and the risk of any plan proposed by the agency that would be caring for the child compared with the merits and the risk of the child returning to or remaining with his or her parents, (vi) the views and preferences of the child where such views and preferences are appropriate and can reasonably be ascertained, and (vii) the effect upon the child of any delay in the final disposition in the proceedings.

BET. *n.* 1. A bet that is placed on any contingency or event that is to take place in or out of Canada, and without restricting the generality of the foregoing, includes a bet that is placed on any contingency relating to a horse-race, fight, match or sporting event that is to take place in or out of Canada. *Criminal Code,* R.S.C. 1985, c. C-46, s. 197. 2. A bet placed under the system known as pari mutuel wagering. *Pari Mutuel Tax Act,* S.A. 1985, c. P-1.1, s. 1.

BETTER BUSINESS BUREAU. An organization which provides information to consumers regarding local businesses.

BETTER EQUITY. When one claimant should have priority over the others because of notice, priority in time or some other reason.

BETTERMENT. *n.* Increasing property value.

BETTING. *n.* A wagering contract under which financial consideration is made payable as the result of a contingency.

BETTING HOUSE. See COMMON ~.

BETTOR. *n.* A person who bets through the agency of a pari-mutuel system. *Pari-Mutuel Tax Act,* S.M. 1974, c. 64, s. 1.

BEVERAGE. *n.* Beer, carbonated soft drinks and any other liquor intended for human consumption by drinking. See ALCOHOLIC ~S.

BEVERAGE ROOM. The premises specified in a beverage room licence and used for the sale of beer under that licence. *Liquor Licensing Act*, R.S.A. 1970, c. 212, s. 2.

BEYOND A REASONABLE DOUBT. The standard of proof required in criminal cases.

BEYOND SEAS. Does not include any part of Canada, or of the British dominions in North America, or of the United States of America in North America. *Limitation of Actions Act*, R.S.N.B. 1973, c. L-8, s. 1.

BEYOND THE SEAS. In this Act, shall be meant any place beyond the limits of the Government of Newfoundland. *Limitation of Actions (Personal) and Guarantees Act*, R.S. Nfld. 1970, c. 206, s. 7.

B.F.L.R. *abbr.* Banking & Finance Law Review.

BIAS. *n.* 1. Prejudice. 2. Anything which tends or is seen as tending to cause someone acting in a judicial capacity to decide a case on another basis than the evidence.

BIAS PLY TIRE. A pneumatic tire in which the ply cords that extend to the beads are laid at alternate angles substantially less than 90 degrees to the centreline of the tread. Canada Regulations.

BI-CAMERAL. *adj.* Having two chambers: in Canada, refers to the two houses of Parliament, the House of Commons and the Senate.

BICYCLE. *n.* 1. Every device propelled by human power upon which a person may ride, having two tandem wheels. 2. Any cycle propelled by human power on which a person may ride, regardless of the number of wheels it has. *Highway Traffic Act*, R.S.A. 1980, c. H-7, s. 143. See MOTOR ASSISTED ~; POWER ~.

BID. *v.* 1. To make an offer at an auction.

BID. *n.* A take over bid or an issuer bid. *Securities acts.* See EXPIRATION OF ~; FORMAL ~; ISSUER ~; QUALIFIED ~; TAKE OVER ~.

BID BOND. 1. A bond given to guarantee entry into a contract. *Government Contracts Regulations*, C.R.C., c. 701, s. 2. 2. A bond that is conditioned upon the bidder on a contract entering into the contract, if the contract is awarded to him, and furnishing any required payment bond and performance bond. *Business Loans, Guarantees and Indemnities Act*, S.N.W.T. 1983 (1st Sess.), c. 1, s. 3.

BID CIRCULAR. A take over bid circular or an issuer bid circular, as the case may be. *Securities Act*, S.B.C. 1985, c. 83, s. 74.

BIDDER. *n.* At an auction, a person who makes an offer.

BIDDING. *n.* Quoting cost or price for a contract in response to a request or call for bids or tenders.

BID-RIGGING. *n.* (a) An agreement or arrangement between or among two or more persons whereby one or more of those persons agrees or undertakes not to submit a bid in response to a call or request for bids or tenders, or (b) the submission, in response to a call or request for bids or tenders, of bids or tenders that are arrived at by agreement or arrangement between or among two or more bidders or tenderers, where the agreement or arrangement is not made known to the person calling for or requesting the bids or tenders at or before the time when any bid or tender is made by any person who is a party to the agreement or arrangement. *Combines Investigation Act*, R.S.C. 1985, c. C-34, s. 47.

BIENS. *n.* [Fr.] Property.

BIGAMOUS. *adj.* Said of marriage entered into by a party already married.

BIGAMUS. *n.* A bigamous person.

BIGAMY. *n.* Every one commits bigamy who (a) in Canada, (i) being married, goes through a form of marriage with another person, (ii) knowing that another person is married, goes through a form of marriage with that person, or (iii) on the same day or simultaneously, goes through a form of marriage with more than one person; or (b) being a Canadian citizen resident in Canada leaves Canada with intent to do anything mentioned in subparagraphs (a)(i) to (iii) and, pursuant thereto, does outside Canada anything mentioned in those subparagraphs in circumstances mentioned therein. *Criminal Code*, R.S.C. 1985, c. C-46, s. 290(1).

BIG GAME. Bison, pronghorn antelope, mountain sheep or mountain goat, any of the deer family whether known as elk, wapiti, caribou, moose, deer or otherwise, bear, cougar and musk-ox.

BIG GAME FARM. A place on which big game animals are kept for the purposes of propagation or for sale, gain, profit or pleasure. *Wildlife Act*, R.S.A. 1970, c. 391, s. 2.

BILAGINE. *n.* By-law.

BILATERAL. *adj.* Involving two agreeing parties.

BILATERAL CONTRACT. A contract in which each of the two parties is bound to fulfil obligations towards the other.

BILGE BOUNDARY LINE. A line that in elevation is parallel to the line of the keel and coincident amidships with the boundary between the side of the hull and the upper turn of bilge. *Arctic Shipping Pollution Prevention Regulations*, C.R.C., c. 353, Schedule VI, s. 1.

BILINGUAL DISTRICT. A federal bilingual district established by the Governor in Council under section 13. *Official Languages Act*, R.S.C. 1985, c. O-3, s. 2.

BILINGUAL POSITION. A position identified by the deputy head as having duties that require a knowledge and use of both official languages. *Official Languages Exclusion Approval Order*, C.R.C., c. 1349, s. 2.

BILL. *n.* 1. Writing; a letter. 2. An account. 3. In parliamentary practice, the first stage in the enactment of a statute. 4. An order. 5. A bill of exchange. *Bills of Exchange Act*, R.S.C. 1985, c. B-4, s. 2. See ACCEPTANCE OF ~; ACCOMMODATION ~; APPROPRIATION ~; EXCHEQUER ~; FOREIGN ~; GOVERNMENT ~; INLAND ~; MONEY ~; PRIVATE ~; PRIVATE MEMBER'S ~; PUBLIC ~; SKELETON ~; SHIPPING ~; TREASURY ~; TRUE ~; WAY- ~.

BILLA VERA. [L.] True bill.

BILLBOARD. *n.* An announcement at the commencement or end of any program naming the sponsor, if any. Broadcasting Regulations.

BILLET. *v.* 1. To offer accommodation to soldiers and their horses.

BILLET. *n.* A dwelling in which soldiers stay.

BILLFISH. *n.* A fish of the species Scomberesox saurus. *Northwest Atlantic Fisheries Regulations*, C.R.C., c. 860, s. 2.

BILLIARD-RICOCHET EFFECT. Deflection of succeeding shot gun pellets by the pellets which had already penetrated the tissue and been slowed. F.A. Jaffe, *A Guide to Pathological Evidence*, 2d ed. (Toronto: Carswell, 1983) at 170.

BILLIARD ROOM. A room or rooms in a building, house, shed, tent or other place in which a billiard table is set up for hire or gain, and includes an annex, addition, or extension thereto of which the proprietor of a billiard room is the owner, lessee, tenant, or occupant, or over which he has control. *Billiard Rooms Act*, R.S.A. 1970, c. 28, s. 2.

BILLIARDS. *n.* Includes pool, bagatelle or any other similar game. *Billiard Rooms Act*, R.S.A. 1970, c. 28, s. 2.

BILLIARD TABLE. In addition to its proper meaning, also means boards used for the games of pigeon-hole, Mississippi, pool, bagatelle or other like games. *Licences Act*, R.S.Q 1977, c. L-3, s. 80.

BILLING. See EXTRA ~.

BILLING DEMAND. The greater of (a) the peak power demand in kilowatts established during the current billing period, or (b) 75 per cent of the peak power demand in kilowatts recorded during the 11 months immediately preceding the current billing period. *Quebec Electricity Service By-law*, C.R.C., c. 1086, s. 2.

BILLING PERIOD. The time between two consecutive meter readings taken at approximately the same date each month. *Quebec Electricity Service By-law*, C.R.C., c. 1086, s. 2.

BILL OF COSTS. A document setting out the claim for legal fees and disbursements in a proceeding.

BILL OF EXCHANGE. An unconditional order in writing, addressed by one person to another, signed by the person giving it, requiring the person to whom it is addressed to pay, on demand or at a fixed or determinable future time, a sum certain in money to or to the order of a specified person or to bearer. *Bills of Exchange Act*, R.S.C. 1985, c. B-4, s. 16(1).

BILL OF INDICTMENT. The printed or written accusation of crime made against one or more people. S. Mitchell, P.J. Richardson & D.A. Thomas, eds., *Archibold Pleading, Evidence and Practice in Criminal Cases*, 43d ed. (London: Sweet & Maxwell, 1988) at 2.

BILL OF LADING. Includes all receipts for goods, wares and merchandise accompanied by an undertaking (a) to move the goods, wares and merchandise from the place where they were received to some other place, by any means whatever, or (b) to deliver at a place other than the place where the goods, wares and merchandise were received a like quantity of goods, wares and merchandise of the same or a similar grade or kind. *Bank Act*, R.S.C. 1985, c. B-1, s. 2.

BILL OF RIGHTS. 1. The Canadian Bill of Rights. 2. The English Statute 1688, 1 Will. & Mary, sess. 2, c. 2. 3. The first 10 amendments to the U.S. Constitution. See CANADIAN ~.

BILL OF SALE. A document in writing in conformity with this Act evidencing a sale or mortgage of chattels but does not include a bill of lading, a warehouse receipt, a warrant or order for the delivery of goods, or any other document used in the ordinary course of business as proof of the possession or control of goods or authorizing or purporting to authorize the possessor of the document to transfer either by endorsement or delivery or to receive goods thereby represented. Bills of Sale acts.

BIND. *v.* To obligate; to secure payment.

BINDER. *n.* A written memorandum providing temporary insurance coverage until a policy is issued. See MEAT ~.

BINDING AUTHORITY. Compelling authority; a decision of a higher court which a lower court must follow.

BIND OVER. To enter into a bond before the court to keep the peace and be of good behaviour.

BINNING. See SPECIAL ~.

BIOCHEMICAL OXYGEN DEMAND. The quantity of oxygen utilized in the biochemical oxidation of organic matter during a 5-day period.

BIOCHEMICAL OXYGEN DEMANDING MATTER. The substance contained in the effluent from a plant that results from the operation of a plant and that will exert a biochemical oxygen demand. Canada regulations.

BIOLOGICAL AGENT. Includes sera, immune globulins, vaccines and toxoids. *Public Health Act*, S.A. 1984, c. P-27.1, s. 1.

BIOLOGICAL FATHER. The man (i) who is married to the biological mother at the time of the birth of the child, (ii) acknowledged by the biological mother as the biological father of the child, (iii) declared by a court to be the biological father of the child, or (iv) who satisfies the Minister that he is the biological father of the child. *Child Welfare Act*, S.A. 1984, c. 8.1, s. 1.

BIOLOGICAL MOTHER. The woman who gave birth to the child. *Child Welfare Act*, S.A. 1984, c. 8.1, s. 1.

BIOLOGICS. See VETERINARY ~.

BIPARTITE. *adj.* Having two parts.

BIRD. *n.* An animal of the class Aves, and its eggs. *Wildlife Act*, S.B.C. 1982, c. 57, s. 1. See GALLINACEOUS ~; GAME ~; MIGRATORY ~S; SONG ~.

BIRD OF PREY. Any hawk, falcon, eagle, owl, osprey, vulture or any other species of the families Falconidae, Cathartidae, Accipitridae, Pandionidae, or Strigidae, the eggs of those birds and any part of those birds or eggs. *Wildlife Act*, R.S.A. 1980, c. W-9, s. 1.

BIRD OF THE PARROT FAMILY. Parrot, Amazon, Mexican double head, African grey, cockatoo, macaw, love-bird, lorie, lorikeet, and any other member of the species psittacidae. *Animal Disease and Protection Regulations*, C.R.C., c. 296, s. 2.

BIRRETUM. *n.* [L.] A thin cap fitted close to the shape of the head; cap worn by judges; black cap.

BIRRETUS. *n.* [L.] A thin cap fitted close to the shape of the head; cap worn by judges; black cap.

BIRTH. *n.* The complete expulsion or extraction from its mother, irrespective of the duration of pregnancy, of a product of conception in which, after such expulsion or extraction, there is breathing, beating of the heart, pulsation of the umbilical cord, or unmistakable movement of voluntary muscle, whether or not the umbilical cord has been cut or the placenta is attached. *Vital Statistics acts.*

BIRTH INJURY. An injury like brain damage or a fracture to the skull sustained during the birth of an infant. F.A. Jaffe, *A Guide to Pathological Evidence*, 2d ed. (Toronto: Carswell, 1983) at 170.

BIRTH PARENT. When used in reference to a child, means a person who is the child's parent at the time of the child's birth. *Child and Family Services Act*, S.O. 1984, c. 55, s. 130.

BISHOP. *n.* The cleric appointed to administer a diocese; this term includes an archbishop, a bishop, an eparch, a vicar apostolic, a prefect apostolic, a prelate nullius, an abbot nullius, an apostolic administrator, a vicar capitular, a vicar general, a pro-vicar in a vicariate apostolic, a pro-prefect in a prefecture apostolic, a vicar deputed to a vicariate apostolic or to a prefecture apostolic, and a cleric specially deputed for such purpose by a bishop. *An Act Respecting Fabriques*, R.S.Q. 1977, c. F-1, s. 1.

BISSEXTILE. *n.* The extra day added in leap years.

BITUMEN. See CRUDE ~.

BITUMINOUS SANDS. The oil sands being within townships 84 to 104 inclusive in ranges 4 to 18 inclusive, west of the 4th meridian and occurring in the McMurray formation. *Mines and Minerals Act*, R.S.A. 1980, c. M-15, s. 121.

BITUMINOUS SHALE. Bituminous shale, oil shale, albertite, kerogen and includes all other such substances intimately associated therewith.

BITUMINOUS SHALE BY-PRODUCTS. All minerals intimately associated with bituminous shale and which because of this intimate association are produced with or recovered from bituminous shale and bituminous shale products during bituminous shale production operations. *Bituminous Shale Act*, S.N.B. 1976, c. B-4.1, s. 1.

BITUMINOUS SHALE EVALUATION WELL. A hole made or being made by drilling, boring, or in any other manner, for the purpose of ascertaining the existence of bituminous shale in the subsurface, or from which bituminous shale products are to be obtained. *Bituminous Shale Act*, S.N.B. 1976, c. B-4.1, s. 1.

BITUMINOUS SHALE PRODUCTION OPERATIONS. Any operation or process for the recovery of bituminous shale products, including open pit mining, underground mining or any in situ process which reduces organic matter, or hydrocarbons not otherwise recoverable by conventional oil and natural gas production techniques, contained in the bituminous shale, to bituminous shale products. *Bituminous Shale Act*, S.N.B. 1976, c. B-4.1, s. 1.

BLACK CAP. The cap worn by judges when pronouncing sentence of death.

BLACKCOD POT. A metal framed enclosure that is covered with netting or expanded metal and has one or more openings through which the fish enter the enclosure. *Foreign Vessel Fishing Regulations*, C.R.C., c. 815, s. 2.

BLACKCOD TRAP. See BLACKCOD POT.

BLACK LIST. A list of persons with whom those compiling the list advise that no one should have dealings of a certain type.

BLACKMAIL. *n.* Menacing and making unwarranted demands. See EXTORTION.

BLACK MARKETING. Unauthorized dealing in or offering rationed, prohibited or restricted goods or services.

BLACK ROT. A condition in which the interior of an egg appears partially or wholly black in colour. *Live Stock and Live Stock Products Act*, R.R.O. 1980, Reg. 582, s. 1.

BLACK SMOKE. Smoke that appears black or approximately black. *Air Pollution Regulations*, C.R.C., c. 1404, s. 2.

BLACK STEEL. Steel that is not coated with any metallic substance. *Ontario Water Resources Act*, R.R.O. 1980, Reg. 736, s. 1.

BLACK WROUGHT IRON. Wrought iron that is not coated with any metallic substance. *Ontario Water Resources Act*, R.R.O. 1980, Reg. 736, s. 1.

BLANK ACCEPTANCE. An acceptance written across a bill before it is filled out.

BLANK ENDORSEMENT. An endorsement written on the back of a bill of exchange before the bill is filled out.

BLANKET INSURANCE. That class of group insurance which covers loss arising from specific hazards incident to or defined by reference to a particular activity or activities. *Insurance acts.*

BLANKET MORTGAGE. A second mortgage, granted when the first mortgage is small and

at a low interest rate, whose principal includes the whole principal of the first mortgage even though the whole amount is not immediately advanced. The second mortgagee must make payments under the first mortgage as long as the second mortgage is valid. If the first mortgage matures, the mortgagee must pay it off and obtain a discharge so that the second mortgage becomes a first mortgage. D.J. Donahue & P.D. Quinn, *Real Estate Practice in Ontario*, 4th ed. (Toronto: Butterworths, 1990) at 226.

BLANKING OFF. Preventing the flow of any substance to or from a confined space by means of a solid plate that completely blocks the flow of such material and that is not dependent for its effectiveness on a valve or similar device. *Canada Confined Spaces Regulations*, C.R.C., c. 996, s. 2.

BLASPHEMY. *n.* Speech against God purposefully to incite contempt and hatred.

BLAST. See PROLONGED ~; SHORT ~.

BLASTER. *n.* A person who has charge of explosives and their use in a surface mine.

BLDG. *abbr.* Building.

BLEND. *v.* Of payment of principal and interest, to mix so that they are indistinguishable and inseparable. W.B. Rayner & R.H. McLaren, *Falconbridge on Mortgages*, 4th ed. (Toronto: Canada Law Book, 1977) at 665.

BLENDED. *adj.* 1. Describes a combined payment of principal money with interest. W.B. Rayner & R.H. McLaren, *Falconbridge on Mortgages*, 4th ed. (Toronto: Canada Law Book, 1977) at 662. 2. As applied to any fur, means that the surface of the fur has been treated by brushing with reagents to change its colour. *Fur Garments Labelling Regulations*, C.R.C., c. 1138, s. 2.

BLENDED FUEL. Fuel oil coloured or identified by a substance prescribed pursuant to section 15(j) when that substance is in a concentration that differs from the concentration prescribed by regulation in respect of marked fuel. *Fuel Oil Administration Act*, R.S.A. 1980, c. F-21, s. 1.

BLENDED FUND. A mixed fund obtained from different sources.

BLENDED PAYMENT. A periodic payment on a loan, a definite amount of which is applied first towards interest and the rest of which is applied to reducing the principal.

BLIND. *adj.* 1. If the visual acuity in both eyes with proper refractive lenses is 20/200 (6/60) or less with Snellen Chart or equivalent, or if the greatest diameter of the field of vision in both eyes is less than 20 degrees. *Blind Persons Regulations*, C.R.C., c. 371, s. 2. 2. A person is deemed to be blind if his vision renders him incapable of doing work for which sight is essential. *Workmen's Compensation Act*, R.S.Q. 1977, c. A-3, s. 121.

BLIND PERSON. 1. A person who is registered as blind with the Canadian National Institute for the Blind, or who, on account of blindness, receives a pension, or who is certified by a qualified eye specialist as not having more than 6/60 vision according to Snellen's Chart after correction with glasses. 2. A person who is apparently blind and dependent on a guide dog or white cane.

BLIND TRUST. A trust in which an office holder transfers all personal wealth to a trustee to invest, reinvest and manage in a normal way according to the powers given to the trustee by an instrument. At no time may the trustee give any account to the settlor or office holder of the actual assets held. D.M.W. Waters, *The Law of Trusts in Canada*, 2d ed. (Toronto: Carswell, 1984) at 438.

BLIND WORKER. A worker as defined by the Workers' Compensation Act, and possessing a central visual acuity of his better eye reading 6-60 or 20-200 or less, either with or without glasses. *Blind Workers' Compensation Act*, R.S.A. 1980, c. B-7, s. 1.

BLIND WORKMAN. A worker or a workman possessing a central visual acuity in his better eye reading 6-60 or 20-200 (Snellen) or less. *Blind Workmen's Compensation acts.*

BLISTER. *n.* Fluid which collects underneath the surface layer of the skin. F.A. Jaffe, *A Guide to Pathological Evidence*, 2d ed. (Toronto: Carswell, 1983) at 9.

BLOATER FILLETS. Fillets of salted, smoked, round herring. *Fish Inspection Regulations*, C.R.C., c. 802, s. 2.

BLOATERS. *n.* Salted, smoked, round herring. *Fish Inspection Regulations*, C.R.C., c. 802, s. 2.

BLOCK. *n.* 1. A piece of land in a registered subdivision that is not itself subdivided, and includes part of a block. *The Tax Enforcement Act*, R.S.S. 1978, c. T-2, s. 2. 2. An area or part of a pool consisting of production spacing units grouped for the purpose of obtaining a common, aggregate production allowable. *Oil and Gas Conservation Act*, R.S.A. 1980, c. O-5, s. 1. 3. An area bounded by 5 minutes of latitude and 7 minutes 30 seconds of longitude. *Petroleum or Natural Gas Act*, R.S.B.C. 1979, c. 323, s. 1. 4. A length of track of defined limits, the use of which by trains or engines is governed by block signals, cab signals, or both. *Regulations*

No. 0-8, Uniform Code of Operating Rules, C.R.C., c. 1175, Part III, s. 2. See APARTMENT ~; QUARTER HOUR ~; STEREOTYPE ~.

BLOCKADE. *n.* Cutting off all of an enemy's external communication. See PACIFIC ~; PAPER ~.

BLOCK INDICATOR. A device located at hand operated or spring switches to indicate track occupancy in the block or blocks to which it refers. *Regulations No. 0-8, Uniform Code of Operating Rules*, C.R.C., c. 1175, Part III, s. 2.

BLOCK OF SHARES. With respect to any class of the capital stock of a corporation, (a) 100 shares, if the fair market value of one share of the class is less than $25, (b) 25 shares, if the fair market value of one share of the class is $25 or more but less than $100, and (c) 10 shares, if the fair market value of one share of the class is $100 or more. *Income Tax Regulations*, C.R.C., c. 945, s. 4802.

BLOCK OF UNITS. With respect to any class of units of a trust, (a) 100 units, if the fair market value of one unit of the class is less than $25, (b) 25 units, if the fair market value of one unit of the class is $25 or more but less than $100, and (c) 10 units, if the fair market value of one unit of the class is $100 or more. *Income Tax Regulations*, C.R.C., c. 945, s. 4802.

BLOCK OUTLINE SURVEY. A survey in which special survey monuments are established at suitable points at or near certain or all street intersections or angles in street lines, or in cases where no streets exist, then at other suitable points.

BLOCK SIGNAL. A fixed signal at the entrance of a block to govern trains and engines entering and using that block. *Regulations No. 0-8, Uniform Code of Operating Rules*, C.R.C., c. 1175, Part III, s. 2.

BLOOD. *n.* Cells suspended in fluid plasma. F.A. Jaffe, *A Guide to Pathological Evidence*, 2d ed. (Toronto: Carswell, 1983) at 155. See CORRUPTION OF ~; PULLORUM TEST OR ~ TEST.

BLOOD CLOT. A streak or clot of blood on the yolk or in the white. *Live Stock and Live Stock Products Act*, R.R.O. 1980, Reg. 582, s. 1.

BLOOD GROUPS. Classification of blood types based on the two red cell antigens, A and B. F.A. Jaffe, *A Guide to Pathological Evidence*, 2d ed. (Toronto: Carswell, 1983) at 170.

BLOOD MEAL. Dried blood of an animal. *Animal Disease and Protection Regulations*, C.R.C., c. 296, s. 2.

BLOOD RING. A ring of blood on the yolk.

Live Stock and Live Stock Products Act, R.R.O. 1980, Reg. 582, s. 1.

BLOOD SPOT. A small particle of blood on the yolk or in the albumen of an egg.

BLOODY EGG. An egg through which blood is diffused. *Live Stock and Live Stock Products Act*, R.R.O. 1980, Reg. 582, s. 1.

BLOWGUN. See YAQUA ~.

BLOWOUT. *n.* The unintentional and uncontrolled escape of oil or gas, as from a drilling well when high formation pressure is encountered. *Canada Oil and Gas Drilling and Production Regulations*, C.R.C., c. 1517, s. 2.

BLOWOUT PREVENTER. A casing-head control fitted with special gates or rams that can be closed around the drill pipe and completely close the top of the casing if the pipe is withdrawn. *Canada Oil and Gas Drilling and Production Regulations*, C.R.C., c. 1517, s. 2.

B.L.R. *abbr.* Business Law Reports, 1977-.

BLUE CHIP. Highest quality securities.

BLUE COLLAR WORKER. An employee engaged in maintenance or production as opposed to one employed in an office or professionally.

BLUEFIN. *n.* Any fish of the species Thunnus thynnus. *Bluefin Sport Fishery Regulations*, C.R.C., c. 810, s. 2.

BLUE LIGHT. Includes a blue reflector or other device that gives or is capable of giving the effect of a blue light. *Motor Vehicle Act*, R.S.N.S. 1967, c. 191, s. 162.

BLUENOSE. *n.* Includes the Bluenose II and any successor vessels. *Schooner Bluenose Foundation Act*, S.N.S. 1983, c. 12, s. 2.

BLUE-SKY BARGAINING. Proposals by negotiators which are so unreasonable that there is no chance of their acceptance.

BLUE-SKY LAW. A law to protect investors from fraud in connection with sales of securities.

BLUE VELVET. Blue-coloured tablets of the antihistamine tripelennamine. F.A. Jaffe, *A Guide to Pathological Evidence*, 2d ed. (Toronto: Carswell, 1983) at 170.

BLUE WHALE. Any whale known by the name of blue whale, Sibbald's rorqual, or sulphur bottom. *Whaling Convention Act*, R.S.C. 1970, c. W-8, Schedule, s. 18.

B.N.A. ACT(S). *abbr.* British North America Act(s).

BOARD. *n.* 1. A body of persons to which certain powers are delegated or assigned or who are elected for certain purposes. 2. The governing body of an institution. 3. The board of directors of a corporation. 4. The board of governors, management or directors, or the trustees, commission or other person or group of persons having the control and management of an accredited or approved hospital. *Criminal Code*, R.S.C. 1985, c. C-46, s. 287(6). See APPEAL ~; ARBITRATION ~; ATOMIC ENERGY CONTROL ~; CANADA LABOUR RELATIONS ~; CANADIAN AVIATION SAFETY ~; CANADIAN WHEAT ~; CHECK-IN ~; CONCILIATION ~; DIVING ~; EXAMINING ~; EXPROPRIATION ~; FEDERAL ~ COMMISSION OR OTHER TRIBUNAL; HOSPITAL ~; JOINT PRACTICE ~; LIBRARY ~; LOCAL ~; NATIONAL ENERGY ~; NATIONAL FILM ~; PANEL-BOARD; PENSION APPEALS ~; PRODUCERS' ~; PUBLIC SERVICE STAFF RELATIONS ~; REVIEW ~; SELECTION ~; TARIFF ~; TREASURY ~ OF CANADA; TRIPARTITE ~.

BOARDING CHARGE. A charge for placing cargo on customer pallets. *Pacific Terminal Tariff By-law*, C.R.C., c. 1083, s. 41.

BOARDING HOME. A building, part of a building, group of buildings or other place in which, for a fee, gain or reward, food and lodging together with care or attention are furnished or are available to four or more persons who because of age, infirmity, physical or mental defect, or other disability, require care and attention, but does not include, (i) a place maintained by a person to whom the inmates are related by blood or marriage; (ii) a public hospital, mental hospital, tuberculosis hospital, maternity hospital or sanatorium, a municipal home, a jail, prison or reformatory; (iii) a maternity home that is licensed under the Child Welfare Act; (iv) a nursing home to which the Nursing Homes Act applies; or (v) a hotel that is licensed under the Hotel Regulations Act. *Boarding Homes Act*, R.S.N.S. 1967, c. 25, s. 1. See CHILDREN'S ~; MATERNITY ~.

BOARDING HOUSE. A building or structure or part of a building or structure kept, used or advertised as or held out to be a place where sleeping accommodation is furnished to the public as regular roomers. See MATERNITY ~.

BOARDING STABLE KEEPER. A person who, for a money consideration or its equivalent, stables, boards or cares for animals.

BOARDING STATION. See PILOT ~.

BOARD LOT. A unit in which shares are traded on a stock exchange.

BOARD MEMBER. A member of a board.

Local Government Election Act, S.S. 1982-83, c. L-30.1, s. 2.

BOARD OF DIRECTORS. The board of directors of a corporation.

BOARD OF GOVERNORS. 1. The board of directors, board of management or other head of a hospital legally authorized to manage the affairs of the hospital. *The Hospital Standards Act*, R.S.S. 1978, c. H-10, s. 23. 2. The board of governors of a university.

BOARD OF HEALTH. The board of health of a city, town, village or rural municipality.

BOARD OF REFEREES. Those to whom one refers a dispute for decision.

BOARD OF TRADE. Includes chamber of commerce, and, for the purposes of the appointment of weighers of grain under this Act, means any board of trade or chamber of commerce, incorporated under any Act of Parliament, of the legislature of the former Province of Canada or of the legislature of any province. *Boards of Trade Act*, R.S.C. 1985, c. B-6, s. 2. 2. A corporation incorporated or continued under this Act as a membership corporation to carry on the activities of promoting and improving trade and commerce and thereby promoting and improving the economic, civic and social welfare of a district. *Non-Profit Corporations Act*, S.S. 1979, c. N-41, s. 176. 3. The board of trade or chamber of commerce for any city, town or place in Canada that is nearest to any harbour or anchorage of ships. *Canada Shipping Act*, R.S.C. 1985, c. S-9, s. 2.

BOARD OF TRUSTEES. The board of trustees of a school district. *The Larger School Units Act*, R.S.S. 1978, c. L-7, s. 2.

BOARDS. Includes lives, abides, dwells and lodges. *School Act*, R.S.B.C. 1979, c. 375, s. 154.

BOAT. *n.* 1. Includes any vessel used or designed to be used in navigation. Saskatchewan statutes. 2. Every type of ship, boat or vessel not required to be registered under the provisions of the Canada Shipping Act. *Assessment Act*, R.S.N.S. 1967, c. 14, s. 1. 3. A watercraft or other artificial contrivance used or capable of being used as a means of transportation on water other than an all terrain vehicle. *Provincial Parks Act*, R.R.O. 1980, Reg. 822, s. 1. See EXCURSION ~; HOUSE- ~; MOTOR ~; PLEASURE ~; POWER ~; SUITABLE ~; WORKING ~.

BOAT SEINE. Fishing gear that is attached to the bow of a fishing vessel and pushed through the water so that fish may be caught when the gear is lifted out of the water. *Manitoba Fishery Regulations*, C.R.C., c. 843, s. 2.

BOAT TRAILER. A trailer that is designed to transport a boat and has cradle-type mountings that permit the launching of the boat from the rear of the trailer. *Motor Vehicle Safety Regulations*, C.R.C., c. 1038, s. 100.

B.O.D. *abbr.* Biochemical oxygen demand.

BODILY HARM. Any hurt or injury to the complainant that interferes with the health or comfort of the complainant and that is more than merely transient or trifling in nature. *Criminal Code*, R.S.C. 1985, c. C-46, s. 267(2). See ACTUAL ~.

BODILY INJURY. 1. Physical, psychological or mental injury including death as well as damage to the clothing worn by the victim at the time of the accident. *An Act to Amend the Insurance Act*, S.N.S. 1982, c. 31, s. 33. 2. Physical, psychological or mental injury, including death, and any damage caused to a victim in an accident, except property damage as defined in paragraph 12. *Automobile Insurance Act*, R.S.Q. 1977, c. A-25, s. 1.

BODILY INJURY LIABILITY INSURANCE. The obligation of the insurer under this Act to pay insurance money in the event of the death of or bodily injury to any person as the result of one of the perils mentioned in section 42. *The Automobile Accident Insurance Act*, R.S.S. 1978, c. A-35, s. 2.

BODY. *n.* 1. The main section of any document or instrument. 2. In writs, a person. 3. A dead human body or the remains of a dead human body. *Fatality Inquiries Act*, R.S.A. 1980, c. F-6, s. 1. See CAROTID ~; COOPERATIVE ~; DEAD ~; GOVERNMENT ~; PAROCHIAL ~; PERSON LAWFULLY IN POSSESSION OF THE ~; PUBLIC ~; RELIGIOUS ~; SELF-REGULATING ~; WATER ~.

BODY CORPORATE. 1. A company or other body corporate wherever or however incorporated. 2. Any incorporated corporation, incorporated association, incorporated syndicate or other incorporated organization wheresoever incorporated. 3. A bank or a financial institution. *Bank Act*, R.S.C. 1985, c. B-1, s. 254.

BODY-GRIPPING TRAP. A trap designed to capture an animal by seizing and holding the animal by any part of its body but does not include a trap designed to capture a mouse or a rat. *Game and Fish Act*, R.S.O. 1980, c. 182, s. 1.

BODY OF ASSOCIATION. The characteristic common to all of the members which leads them to join together in a credit union. *Credit Union Act*, S.S. 1984-85-86, c. C-45.1, s. 2.

BODY OF WATER. 1. Includes any body of flowing or standing water whether naturally or artificially created. 2. Any surface or subterranean source of fresh or salt water within the province, whether such source usually contains water or not, and includes coastal water within the province, any river, stream, brook, creek, water course, lake, pond, spring, lagoon, ravine, gulch, canal and any other flowing or standing water and the land usually or at any time occupied by any such body of water. *Department of Provincial Affairs and Environment Act*, S. Nfld. 1973, c. 39, s. 2. See OPEN ~; STANDING ~.

BODY POLITIC. A nation; a corporation.

BODY-RUB. *n.* Includes the kneading, manipulating, rubbing, massaging, touching, or stimulating, by any means, of a person's body or part thereof but does not include medical or therapeutic treatment given by a person otherwise duly qualified, licensed or registered so to do under the laws of the province of Ontario. *Municipal Act*, R.S.O. 1980, c. 302, s. 221.

BODY-RUB PARLOUR. Includes any premises or part thereof where a body-rub is performed, offered or solicited in pursuance of a trade, calling, business or occupation, but does not include any premises or part thereof where the body-rubs performed are for the purpose of medical or therapeutic treatment and are performed or offered by persons otherwise duly qualified, licensed or registered so to do under the laws of the Province of Ontario. *Municipal Act*, R.S.O. 1980, c. 302, s. 221.

BOILER. *n.* A vessel in which steam or other vapour can be generated under pressure or in which a liquid can be put under pressure by the direct application of a heat source. See CHEMICAL RECOVERY ~; COILED TUBE ~; DUAL CONTROL ~; ELECTRIC ~; FIRED STEAM ~; HIGH PRESSURE ~; HOT WATER ~; LOCOMOTIVE ~; LOW PRESSURE ~; MINIATURE ~; POWER ~; STEAM ~; THERMAL LIQUID ~; USED ~, PRESSURE VESSEL OR PLANT.

BOILER AND MACHINERY INSURANCE. 1. Insurance against loss or damage to property and against liability for loss or damage to persons or property through the explosion, collapse, rupture or breakdown of, or accident to, boilers or machinery of any kind. *Insurance acts*. 2. Insurance coming within the class of boiler insurance or machinery insurance. *Classes of Insurance Regulations*, C.R.C., c. 977, s. 6.

BOILER HORSE POWER. *var.* **BOILER HORSEPOWER.** The rating of a boiler determined by allowing one boiler horse power for each unit in the greatest of the following numbers: (i) the number that is the quotient obtained by dividing by ten the number of the square feet in the area of the heating surface of the boiler; or (ii) the number that is the quotient obtained by dividing by $34^1/_2$ the number of pounds of water, from and at a temperature of two hundred and twelve degrees Fahrenheit or one hundred degrees centigrade, that the boiler is capable of evaporating in an hour; or (iii) the number that is the quotient obtained by dividing the maximum firing rate, calculated in British Thermal Units per hour, by thirty-three thousand, five hundred; or (iv) where electric power is used as a heat source, the number that is the quotient obtained by dividing the maximum aggregate kilowatt capacity of the heating elements by ten.

BOILER INSURANCE. 1. Insurance against (a) liability arising out of (i) bodily injury to, or the death of, a person, or (ii) the loss of, or damage to, property, or (b) the loss of, or damage to, property, caused by the explosion or rupture of, or accident to, pressure vessels of any kind and pipes, engines and machinery connected therewith or operated thereby. *Classes of Insurance Regulations*, C.R.C., c. 977, s. 5. 2. Includes (a) "boiler insurance", which means insurance against liability for loss or damage to persons or property and against damage to property or loss caused by explosion of, rupture of or accident to steam boilers and pipes, engines and machinery connected with them or operated by them; and (b) "machinery insurance", which means insurance against liability for loss or damage to persons or property and against damage to property or loss caused by breakdown of machinery. *Insurance Act*, R.S.B.C. 1979, c. 200, s. 1. See STEAM ~.

BOILER PLANT. Any plant which consists of one or more vessels or structures in which by the application of heat, steam may be generated or water put under pressure at a temperature in excess of two hundred fifty degrees Fahrenheit, and of a capacity prescribed by the regulations, together with any pipe, fitting or equipment attached thereto or used in connection therewith and includes a steam turbine. *Stationary Engineers Act*, S.N.S. 1979-80, c. 18, s. 2.

BOILERPLATE. *n.* Standard clauses used in legal documents of a particular kind.

BOILER RATING. The rating for measuring the capacity of a boiler in kilowatts as determined in the regulations. *Boilers and Pressure Vessels acts*.

BOIL-OVER. *n.* A term used to describe the action that occurs when a hot layer of crude petroleum or similar liquid comes into contact with an underlying layer of a more volatile liquid and causes that liquid to flash into vapour; the expansion produced by the conversion of the entrapped liquid vapour results in a violent surface action. *Flammable Liquids Bulk Storage Regulations*, C.R.C., c. 1148, s. 2.

BOLUS. *n.* A round, moist mass of food for swallowing. F.A. Jaffe, *A Guide to Pathological Evidence*, 2d ed. (Toronto: Carswell, 1983) at 170.

BOMB. See TEAR ~S.

BONA. *n.* [L.] Goods; property.

BONA. *adj.* [L.] Good.

BONA FIDE. *adj.* [L. in good faith] Honest.

BONA FIDE DEALER. A person who deals generally with the sale of supplies of the type being purchased and who trades generally through normal trade channels.

BONA FIDE FARMER. A person who (i) owns or leases land and operates a farm, or (ii) owns shares in a farm corporation that operates a farm, and who (iii) spends more than 50% of his working time on the farm, and (iv) receives annually more gross cash income from the sale of farm products than from wages for work performed off the farm. *Prince Edward Island Lands Protection Act*, S.P.E.I. 1982, c. 16, s. 1.

BONAE FIDEI POSSESSOR IN ID TANTUM QUOD AD SE PERVENERIT, TENETUR. [L.] One who possesses in good faith is liable only for what has come to her or him.

BONA FIDE NEWS REPORTING. Includes interviews, commentaries or other works prepared for and published by any newspaper, magazine or other periodical publication or broadcast on the facilities of any broadcasting undertaking without charge to any political party, constituency association or candidate registered under this Act. *Election Finances Act*, S.O. 1986, c. 33, s. 1.

BONA FIDE PENSION PLAN. Any pension plan established for employees to which contributions were made, on a regular basis, by the employees and the employer principally for the purpose of providing a pension to the employees upon retirement. *Public Service Superannuation Act*, R.S.N.B. 1973, c. P-26, s. 26.

BONA FIDE PURCHASER. 1. A purchaser for value in good faith and without notice of any adverse claim who takes delivery of a security in bearer form or of a security in registered form issued to her or him, endorsed to her or him or endorsed in blank. 2. A purchaser for value, in good faith and without notice of any adverse claim, (i) who takes delivery of a security certificate in bearer form or order form or of a security certificate in registered form issued

to him or endorsed to him or endorsed in blank, (ii) in whose name an uncertificated security is registered or recorded in records maintained by or on behalf of the issuer as a result of the issue or transfer of the security to him, or (iii) who is a transferee or pledgee as provided in section 85. *Business Corporations Amendment Act*, S.O. 1986, c. 57, s. 7.

BONA FIDE RESIDENT OF NEWFOUND-LAND. A person with Canadian citizenship who has resided in the province for a continuous period of not less than one year. *Fishing Ships (Bounties) Act*, R.S. Nfld. 1970, c. 137, s. 2.

BONA FIDES. [L.] Good faith.

BONA FIDES NON PATITUR UT BIS IDEM EXIGATUR. [L.] Good faith does not permit the same thing to be demanded twice.

BONA FIDE SUPPLIER. A person who deals generally with the sale of supplies of the type being purchased and who trades generally through normal trade channels.

BONA FORISFACTA. [L.] Forfeited goods.

BONA GESTURA. [L.] Good behaviour.

BONA MOBILIA. [L.] Movable goods and effects.

BONA VACANTIA. [L.] Things found which have no apparent owner and which belong to the Crown. W.B. Rayner & R.H. McLaren, *Falconbridge on Mortgages*, 4th ed. (Toronto: Canada Law Book, 1977) at 337.

BONA WAVIATA. [L.] Goods thrown away or waived.

BOND. *n.* 1. A contract under seal to pay an amount of money or a sealed writing which acknowledges a debt. 2. Government obligations which are ordinarily unsecured and obligations of large public corporations. H. Sutherland, D.B. Horsley & J.M. Edmiston, eds., *Fraser's Handbook on Canadian Company Law*, 7th ed. (Toronto: Carswell, 1985) at 310. 3. An agreement in writing signed by the guarantor under which the guarantor undertakes, upon the default of another person named in the agreement in paying a debt or a debt of a class of debts specified in the agreement (i) to pay a sum of money; or (ii) to pay the debt. *Guarantors' Liability Act*, R.S.M. 1970, c. G120, s. 2. 4. Includes a debenture, debenture stock or other evidences of indebtedness. *Companies Creditors Arrangement Act*, R.S.C. 1985, c. C-36, s. 2. 5. Includes a contract of insurance. *Protection of Securities Regulations*, Canada regulations. See BACK-~; BAIL-~; D BID ~; BONDS; BOTTOMRY ~; COUPON ~; FIDELITY ~; GOVERNMENT GUARANTEED ~; GUARANTEE ~; IN ~; JOINT INSURED ~;

BONI JUDICIS EST LITES DIRIMERE

MORTGAGE ~; PAYMENT ~; PEACE ~; PERFORMANCE ~; SINGLE INSURED ~; SURETY ~.

BONDAGE. *n.* Enslavement.

BONDED. *adj.* In permanent and tight mechanical and electrical contact. *Lightning Rods Act*, R.R.O. 1980, Reg. 577, s. 1.

BONDED CARRIER. Any person who has been authorized under the Act to transport goods in bond. *Customs Sufferance Warehouses Regulations*, C.R.C., c. 461, s. 2.

BONDED GOODS. Dutiable goods for which a bond was given for payment of the duty.

BONDED MANUFACTURER. A person who carries on under bond and subject to departmental regulations the manufacture of articles in the production of which goods subject to excise are used in combination with other materials. *Excise Act*, R.S.C. 1985, c. E-14, s. 5.

BONDED MANUFACTORY. Any place or premises licensed to use spirits or other goods subject to excise in the manufacture of articles under formula approved by the Minister, and every place or premises where any of those articles are warehoused, stored or kept shall be held to form a part of the bonded manufactory to which it is attached or appurtenant. *Excise Act*, R.S.C. 1985, c. E-14, s. 5.

BONDED WAREHOUSE. A place licensed as a bonded warehouse by the Minister under section 24. *Customs Act*, R.S.C. 1985 (2d Supp.), c. 1, s. 2.

BONDEE. *n.* A person named in a bond upon whose default in paying a debt or a debt of a class of debts specified in the bond the guarantor undertakes to pay a sum of money or to pay the debt. *Guarantors' Liability Act*, R.S.M. 1970, c. G120, s. 2.

BONDHOLDER'S TRUST. Assets pledged by a company which is borrowing from a bondholder are vested in a trustee as legal owner. The trustee's duties and powers arise traditionally only when the issuer or guarantor of the bonds defaults. D.M.W. Waters, *The Law of Trusts in Canada*, 2d ed. (Toronto: Carswell, 1984) at 449.

BONDING. *n.* Includes the provision of security. *Bonding Act*, R.S.B.C. 1979, c. 31, s. 1.

BONDING LINE. A commitment by the Commissioner to a surety which allows the surety to issue, upon prescribed terms and conditions, bid bonds, payment bonds and performance bonds to a business enterprise specified by the Commissioner, and to be indemnified by the Commissioner in respect of such bonds issued.

Business Loans, Guarantees and Indemnities Act, S.N.W.T. 1983 (1st Sess.), c. 1, s. 3.

BONDING WAREHOUSE. Any warehouse in which goods subject to excise may be stored or deposited without payment of the duty imposed by this Act. *Excise Act*, R.S.C. 1985, c. E-14, s. 2.

BOND OF ASSOCIATION. Includes groups having a common bond of occupation or association, the residents within a well defined neighbourhood, community or rural or urban district, including a rural trading area, employees of a common employer or members of a bona fide fraternal, religious, co-operative, labour, rural, educational and similar organizations, and members of the immediate family of such persons. *Credit Unions and Caisses Populaires Act*, S.M. 1977, c. 51, s. 1.

BONDS. *n.* 1. Includes debentures. 2. All securities issued or guaranteed by any government, including treasury bonds, short-term notes and deposit certificates, whether negotiable or not, shall be regarded as bonds. *Caisse de Dépôt et Placement du Québec Act*, R.S.Q. 1977, c. C-2, s. 24. See BOND; LONG-TERM ~ OF CANADA.

BONDSMAN. *n.* A surety.

BONE MARROW EMBOLISM. An embolism in a blood vessel caused by bone marrow fragments. F.A. Jaffe, *A Guide to Pathological Evidence*, 2d ed. (Toronto: Carswell, 1983) at 175.

BONE MEAL. Ground animal bones, hoofs or horns that have been heated under a minimum of 138 kilopascals (20 pounds) steam pressure for at least 1 hour at not less than 118°C (250°F). *Animal Disease and Protection Regulations*, C.R.C., c. 296, s. 2.

BONI JUDICIS EST AMPLIARE JURISDICTIONEM. [L.] It is the duty of a good judge to extend her or his jurisdiction. Quoted this way, this maxim is incorrect. See BONI JUDICIS EST AMPLIARE JUSTITIAM.

BONI JUDICIS EST AMPLIARE JUSTITIAM. [L.] It is the duty of a good judge to amplify the remedies.

BONI JUDICIS EST JUDICIUM SINE DILATIONE MANDARE EXECUTIONI. [L.] It is the duty of a good judge to order that judgment be executed without delay.

BONI JUDICIS EST LITES DIRIMERE, NE LIS EX LITE ORITUR, ET INTEREST REIPUBLICAE UT SINT FINES LITIUM. [L.] A good judge disposes of cases so that one lawsuit does not lead to another; and it is in the public interest that there should be limits on litigation.

BONUS. *n.* 1. Gratuity; premium. 2. Discount, premium, dues, commission, brokerage fee, finders fee or other payment made by a borrower to a mortgage lender or mortgage broker. *Mortgage Brokers Act*, S. Nfld. 1975-76, c. 49, s. 2. 3. The amount by which the amount secured under a mortgage exceeds the amount actually advanced. *Expropriations Act*, R.S.O. 1980, c. 148, s. 17. 4. Money paid or a financial benefit or benefits provided in lieu of money. *School Act*, R.S.B.C. 1979, c. 375, s. 131. See ATTENDANCE ~; GROUP ~.

BONUS INTEREST PAYMENT. For a taxation year means an amount credited by a credit union to a person who was a member of the credit union in the year on terms that the member is entitled to or will receive payment thereof, computed at a rate in relation to (i) the amount of interest payable in respect of the year by the credit union to the member on money standing to his credit from time to time in the records or books of account of the credit union, or (ii) the amount of money standing to the member's credit from time to time in the year in the records or books of account of the credit union, if the amount was credited at the same rate in relation to the amount of interest or money, as the case may be, as the rate at which amounts were similarly credited in the year to all other members of the credit union of the same class. *Income Tax Act*, R.S.C. 1952, c. 148 (as am. S.C. 1980-81-82-83, c. 48, s. 78(3), (4)), s. 137(6)(a.1).

BONUS JUDEX SECUNDUM AEQUUM ET BONUS JUDICAT, ET AEQUITATEM STRICTO JURI PRAEFERT. [L.] A good judge decides using fairness and good, and prefers equity to legal strictness.

BOOK. *n.* 1. Includes every volume, part or division of a volume, pamphlet, sheet of letterpress, sheet of music, map, chart or plan separately published. *Copyright Act*, R.S.C. 1985, c. C-42, s. 2. 2. Library matter of every kind, nature and description and includes any document, paper, record, tape or other thing published by a publisher, on or in which information is written, recorded, stored or reproduced. *National Library Act*, R.S.C. 1985, c. N-12, s. 2. 3. Includes a loose-leaf book or binder. *Interpretation Act*, R.S.M. 1970, c. I80, s. 23. 4. Includes a file, index and an electronic data bank. 5. (a) A non-periodical printed publication containing not less than 48 pages of text or illustrations or both, not including the cover pages, regardless of how it is assembled; (b) a non-periodical printed publication which is a collection of poems, containing not less than 32 pages of text or illustrations or both, not including the cover pages; (c) a non-periodical printed publication

intended for children, containing not less than 16 pages of text or illustrations or both, or in the form of cartoons with or without text, bound in paper or hardback; (d) a non-periodical printed publication, presented in the form of cartoons for adults, containing not less than 16 pages, with text, bound in paper or hardback; (e) a non-periodical printed publication dealing solely with music, bound in paper or hardback, or an instrument method or music score, regardless of the number of pages; (f) a serial publication, whether of material described in subparagraphs (a) to (e), in several parts, or of volumes published successively under a common title over an undefined period but not necessarily at regular intervals; but excluding school manuals. *An Act respecting the development of Quebec firms in the book industry*, S.Q. 1979, c. 68, s. 1. See ABSTRACT ~; BOOKS; CASH ~; DAY-~; HORN~; INCLUDIBLE ~; PERMIT ~; POLL ~; PRINTED ~ OF PHOTOGRAPHS; PRINTED ~OF PICTURES OR DESIGNS; PRINTED ~ OR PAMPHLET.

BOOK ACCOUNTS. All the accounts and debts current and future as in the ordinary course of business would be entered in the books, whether entered or not, and includes all books, documents and papers relating to the accounts and debts. *Book Accounts Assignment Act*, R.S.B.C. 1979, c. 32, s. 1. See ASSIGNMENT OF ~.

BOOK DEBTS. All existing or future debts that in the ordinary course of business would be entered in books, whether actually entered or not, and includes any part or class thereof. *Assignment of Book Debts acts*. See ASSIGNMENT OF ~.

BOOK DEPOSIT. Two copies of a book published in Canada which its publisher must deliver to the National Librarian. H.G. Fox, *The Canadian Law of Copyright and Industrial Designs*, 2d ed. (Toronto: Carswell, 1967) at 536.

BOOKMAKER. *n.* A person who takes bets as a business.

BOOKS. *n.* Includes loose-leaf books where reasonable precautions are taken against the misuse of them. *Corporations Act*, R.S.O. 1980, c. 95, s. 1. See BANKER'S ~; BOOK.

BOOKS AND PAPERS. Includes accounts, deeds, writings and documents.

BOOKSELLER. *n.* Any person whose main or secondary activity is the sale of books to the public in Quebec. *An Act respecting the development of Quebec firms in the book industry*, S.Q. 1979, c. 68, s. 1.

BOOKS OR PAPERS. Includes accounts, deeds, writings and documents.

BOOK VALUE. The amount at which an asset or liability is recorded in the financial statement of a business. See NET ~.

BOOM. *n.* The projecting part of a back-hoe, shovel, crane or similar lifting device from which a load is likely to be supported. Ontario regulations.

BOOM CHAIN. A chain with toggles attached for use in the booming of logs. *Boom Chain Brand Act,* R.S.B.C. 1979, c. 33, s. 1.

BOOSTER FAN. A fan operated within a mine in conjunction with the main fan to assist in the ventilation of the mine. *Coal Mines Regulation Act,* R.S.N.S. 1967, c. 36, s. 3.

BOOTH. See POLLING ~.

BORE. *v.* To bore, drill or dig into the ground. *Ground Water Control Act,* R.S.A. 1970, c. 162, s. 2.

BORE. *n.* The interior of a firearm barrel. F.A. Jaffe, *A Guide to Pathological Evidence,* 2d ed. (Toronto: Carswell, 1983) at 170.

BORE DIAMETER. Caliber. F.A. Jaffe, *A Guide to Pathological Evidence,* 2d ed. (Toronto: Carswell, 1983) at 170.

BORING CLAIM. A tract of land, containing minerals that have been reserved to the Crown, acquired for the purpose of boring for coal, oil shale, or salt. *Mines Act,* R.S.M. 1970, c. M160, s. 1.

BORN OUT OF WEDLOCK. Born to a woman who, at the date of the conception of the child (i) was unmarried, or (ii) was a married woman who, for a period of at least two months immediately prior to that date had been living separate and apart from her husband, and who has continued to be unmarried or to live separate and apart from her husband up to the date of the birth of the child. *Child Welfare Act,* R.S.N.W.T. 1974, c. C-3, s. 2.

BOROUGH. *n.* A town.

BORROWED MONEY. Includes the proceeds to a taxpayer from the sale of a post-dated bill drawn by the taxpayer on a bank to which the Bank Act (Statutes of Canada) or the Quebec Savings Banks Act (Statutes of Canada) applies.

BORROWER. *n.* 1. A person to whom a loan has been made. 2. A person who receives credit. 3. A person borrowing money or obtaining credit and includes a buyer of goods or services on credit and a hirer of goods on hire-purchase. *Consumer Protection Act,* R.S.M. 1970, c. C200, s. 1. See JOINT ~S.

BORROWER'S CHARGES. Charges, prescribed by the Governor in Council, advanced by an approved lender in accordance with normal mortgage practices to safeguard the interests of the mortgagee and the Corporation. *National Housing Act,* R.S.C. 1985, c. N-11, s. 2.

BORROWING. *n.* A loan obtained including a line of credit. See ALLOCATION IN PROPORTION TO ~; COST OF ~.

BOSS. *n.* 1. Employer, supervisor. 2. A protuberance or knob that is on the outside of a pipe and that causes the pipe wall to be thicker at that point than the rest of the pipe wall. *Ontario Water Resources Act,* R.R.O. 1980, Reg. 736, s. 1.

BOTTLE TRAP. A trap that retains liquids in a closed chamber and the water seal of which is made by submerging the inlet or outlet pipe in the liquids or by a partition submerged in the liquids. *Ontario Water Resources Act,* R.R.O. 1980, Reg. 736, s. 85.

BOTTOM. See BARREN ~.

BOTTOMRY BOND. 1. The hypothecation or mortgage of a ship in which her bottom or keel is pledged. 2. An agreement entered into by a ship's owner in which the borrower undertakes to repay money advanced for the use of the ship with interest if the ship ends her voyage successfully.

BOULDERS. *n.* Rock fragments whose greatest dimensions exceed 8 in. *Building Code Act,* R.R.O. 1980, Reg. 87, s. 4.2.1.4.

BOULEVARD. *n.* 1. In an urban area, that part of a highway that (i) is not roadway, and (ii) is that part of the sidewalk that is not especially adapted to the use of or ordinarily used by pedestrians. *Highway Traffic Act,* R.S.A. 1980, c. H-7, s. 1. 2. The area between the curb lines, the lateral lines or the shoulder of a roadway and the adjacent property line. *Motor Vehicle Act,* R.S.B.C. 1979, c. 288, s. 115. 3. That portion of a highway, on either side or in the centre thereof, that is adjacent to the travelled portion thereof and is levelled and maintained, for the purpose of improving the appearance of the highway, (i) by the planting thereon of grass, flowers, trees, or shrubs, or all or any of those things; or (ii) by paving or otherwise surfacing it as provided in subsection (2) of section 239; or (iii) by treating part thereof as stated in sub-clause (i), and part thereof as stated in sub-clause (ii) and by regularly cutting the grass thereon, if any, and trimming, pruning, or otherwise caring for the trees, shrubs, and flowers. *Municipal Act,* S.M. 1970, c. M-100, s. 2.

BOUNDARIES. *n.* Includes corporate limits. *Town Act,* R.S.P.E.I. 1974, c. T-4, s. 1.

BOUNDARY. *n.* 1. Limit of territory; an imaginary line which divides two pieces of land. 2. The international boundary between Canada and the United States as determined and marked by the Commission. *International Boundary Commission Act*, R.S.C. 1985, c. I-16, s. 2. 3. A location's surface boundary and its vertical extension. *Geothermal Resources Act*, S.B.C. 1982, c. 14, s. 1. See CONVENTIONAL ~; FISHING ~ SIGN; NATURAL ~; OBLITERATED ~; SEAWARD ~.

BOUNDARY BY AGREEMENT. A conventional boundary located by agreement between the Crown and the adjoining owner. *Land Act*, R.S.B.C. 1979, c. 214, s. 1.

BOUNDARY LINE. *var.* **BOUNDARY-LINE.** The vertical plane or line in which the surface boundary of the tract or parcel lies. *Mines and Minerals Act*, R.S.A. 1970, c. 238, s. 80. See CONVENTIONAL ~; SINUOUS ~.

BOUNDARY MONUMENT. A buoy, post, tablet, cairn or other object or structure placed, erected or maintained by the Commission to mark the boundary and includes a reference monument, triangulation station or other marker or structure placed, erected or maintained by the Commission to assist in determining the boundary. *International Boundary Commission Act*, R.S.C. 1985, c. I-16, s. 2.

BOUNDARY SURVEY. A survey to determine the boundaries of the land covered by a mineral claim or a mining lease. *Mining Act*, S.N.B. 1985, c. M-14.1, s. 1.

BOUNDARY WATERS. The waters from main shore to main shore of the lakes and rivers and connecting waterways, or the portions thereof, along which the international boundary between the United States and Canada passes, including all bays, arms, and inlets thereof, but not including tributary waters which in their natural channels would flow into such lakes, rivers and waterways, or waters flowing from such lakes, rivers, and waterways, or the waters of rivers flowing across the boundary. *Canada Water Act*, R.S.C. 1985, c. C-11, s. 2.

BOUND OVER. See BIND OVER.

BOUNDS. See METES AND ~.

BOUNTY. *n.* 1. Money or premium paid for the fulfilment of a particular service. 2. A bounty payable in accordance with this Act on the rebuilding or repairing of a vessel. *Fishing and Coasting Vessels Rebuilding and Repairs (Bounties) Act*, R.S. Nfld. 1970, c. 136, s. 2. 3. A bounty payable by a municipality under this Act for killing a predator or a nuisance animal. *Predator Control Act*, R.S.M. 1970, c. P110, s. 2.

BOUT. *n.* A contest or exhibition between two contestants. *Athletics Control Act*, R.R.O. 1980, Reg. 76, s. 2.

BOW. *n.* A longbow or crossbow. *Wildlife Act*, S.B.C. 1982, c. 57, s. 1. See CROSS~; LONG~.

BOW FISHING. Fishing with a bow and arrow. *Manitoba Fishery Regulations*, C.R.C., c. 843, s. 2.

BOW SECTION. The foremost (a) one-third length of a ship, in the case of a ship 50 feet in length or under, (b) 17 feet of a ship, in the case of a ship over 50 feet but under 70 feet in length, and (c) one-quarter length of a ship, in the case of a ship 70 feet in length or over. *Hull Construction Regulations*, C.R.C., c. 1431, s. 100.

BOX. *n.* 1. Any crate, carton, or other outer covering or wrapper in which containers are packed. *Farm Products Grades and Sales Act*, R.R.O. 1980, Reg. 337, s. 1. 2. A container made to contain fifteen dozen eggs in individual compartments designed to prevent the eggs being damaged in handling. 3. A rigid rectangular receptacle capable of holding a maximum of 100 pounds of fresh fish packed in ice with a maximum depth of 12 inches of fish and ice, and constructed with rigid sides so as to be capable of supporting other boxes with no crushing effect on the contents. *Alberta Fishery Regulations*, C.R.C., c. 838, s. 2. See CUT OUT ~; END ~; LOCK ~; MAIL ~; SERVICE ~.

BOXER. *n.* A person who engages in boxing for monetary reward.

BOXHOLDER. *n.* A person or firm to whom a lock box or bag service is provided. *Mail Receptacles Regulations*, C.R.C., c. 1282, s. 21.

BOXING. *n.* Professional boxing contests or exhibitions and does not include amateur boxing unless the context so requires. *Boxing Authority Act*, S.N.S. 1973, s. 3, s. 2.

BOX NET. A net that (a) is made and set in the form of a box, (b) has a trap into which fish are guided by a leader, and (c) is capable of catching fish without enmeshing them.

BOY. *n.* Any male person under the age of 18 years. Nova Scotia statutes.

BOYCOTT. *v.* To take part in a boycott.

BOYCOTT. *n.* An organized refusal to deal with a particular person or business. See CONSUMER ~; PRODUCTION ~; SECONDARY ~.

BOYS' LONGS. Pants of not more than 32 inches waist measurement manufactured for wear by boys. *Industrial Standards Act*, R.R.O. 1980, Reg. 522, s. 1.

B.R. *abbr.* 1. Cour du Banc de la Reine/du Roi. 2. Recueils de jurisprudence de la Cour de banc de la Reine (du Roi) de Québec. 3. Rapports judiciaires du Québec, Cour du Banc de la Reine (ou du Roi) (Quebec Official Reports, Queen's (or King's) Bench, 1892-1941).

[ ] B.R. *abbr.* 1. Rapports judiciaires du Québec, Cour du Banc de la Reine (ou du Roi), 1942-1966. 2. Recueils de jurisprudence du Québec, Cour du Banc de la Reine, 1967-1969.

BRACING CHARGE. A charge for furnishing labour or materials for bracing or securing goods on railway cars or other vehicles, but does not include the cost of covering goods. *Pacific Terminal Tariff By-law*, C.R.C., c. 1083, s. 41.

BRACKISH WATER. Water situated in tidal areas where fresh water mixes with marine water. *Aquaculture Act*, S.N.S. 1983, c. 2, s. 2.

BRAIN INFARCT. Blockage of an artery in the brain. F.A. Jaffe, *A Guide to Pathological Evidence*, 2d ed. (Toronto: Carswell, 1983) at 46.

BRAKE. See AIR ~ SYSTEM; EMERGENCY ~; PARKING ~; SERVICE ~.

BRAKE FLUID. Brake fluid for use in hydraulic brake systems, except hydraulic system mineral oil. *Motor Vehicle Safety Regulations*, C.R.C., c. 1038, s. 2.

BRAKE HORSE POWER. *var.* **BRAKE HORSEPOWER.** 1. The aggregate horse power on a shaft from all elements driving it. *Operating Engineers and Firemen Act*, R.S.M. 1970, c. O50, s. 2. 2. The effective or useful horsepower developed by a prime mover as measured by a weigh scale and a brake applied to its driving shaft or by other means approved by the chief officer, and one brake horsepower is equivalent to 2,544 British thermal units per hour or to 0.02544 Therm-hours. *Operating Engineers Act*, R.S.O. 1980, c. 363, s. 1. 3. As applied to motor-driven ships, means the continuous brake horsepower as rated by the manufacturer of the engine. *Marine Engineers Examination Regulations*, C.R.C., c. 1443, s. 2.

BRANCH. *n.* 1. An agency, the head office and any other office of a bank. *Bank Act*, R.S.C. 1985, c. B-1, s. 2. 2. An office or place of business separate and apart from the head office, providing services similar to those available at the head office. See FACTORY ~; HORIZONTAL ~.

BRANCH CIRCUIT. That part of a circuit extending beyond the final overcurrent devices in the circuit. See MULTI-WIRE ~.

BRANCH-CONDUCTOR. *n.* A conductor that branches off at an angle from a continuous run

of conductor. *Lightning Rods Act*, R.R.O. 1980, Reg. 577, s. 1.

BRANCH LINE. A line of railway in Canada of a railway company that is subject to the jurisdiction of Parliament that, relative to a main line within the company's railway system in Canada of which it forms a part, is a subsidiary, secondary, local or feeder line of railway, and includes a part of any subsidiary, secondary, local or feeder line of railway. *Railway Act*, R.S.C. 1985, c. R-3, s. 254.

BRANCH OFFICE. 1. Any location, other than the head office, at which business is carried on. *Produce Licensing Regulations*, C.R.C., c. 292, s. 2. 2. A place at which the public is invited to deal in the conduct of the business of an itinerant seller. *Consumer Protection Act*, R.R.O. 1980, Reg. 181, s. 1.

BRANCH SCHOOL. Includes a franchise or franchised school. *Private Vocational Schools Act*, R.R.O. 1980, Reg. 801, s. 1.

BRANCH VENT. A vent pipe connecting one or more individual vent pipes to a vent stack or a stack vent. *Ontario Water Resources Act*, R.R.O. 1980, Reg. 736, s. 1.

BRAND. *n.* 1. A character or combination of characters impressed or intended to be impressed on the skin or hide of stock to show ownership of the stock. 2. Any mark, stencil, stamp, label or writing placed on any milk product or package containing a milk product. *Farm Products Grades and Sales Act*, R.R.O. 1980, Reg. 327, s. 1. 3. A character or mark which may be impressed on a boom chain for purposes of identification. *Boom Chain Brand Act*, R.S.B.C. 1979, c. 33, s. 1. 4. Any distinctive mark or trade name, other than a name or grade required by these Regulations, applied by the manufacturer, registrant or vendor to a feed, fertilizer or supplement to distinguish it from any other feed, fertilizer or supplement. Canada regulations. See IDENTIFICATION ~; SINGLE CHARACTER ~.

BRANDEIS BRIEF. A social science brief in which empirical data is appended to or included in a factum. P.W. Hogg, *Constitutional Law of Canada*, 2d ed. (Toronto: Carswell, 1985) at 182.

BRANDHEMATOM. *n.* Blood clots collected extradurally in a body which has been exposed to intense heat. F.A. Jaffe, *A Guide to Pathological Evidence*, 2d ed. (Toronto: Carswell, 1983) at 170.

BRAND READER. A person appointed by a municipality to give an accurate description of an estray. *Domestic Animals (Municipalities) Act*, R.S.A. 1970, c. 112, s. 2.

BRANDY. See CANADIAN ~.

BRAWL. *v.* To create a disturbance.

BREACH. *n.* 1. Encroachment of a right. 2. Disregard of a duty. 3. Non-execution of a contract. G.H.L. Fridman, *The Law of Contract in Canada*, 2d ed. (Toronto: Carswell, 1986) at 523. See ANTICIPATORY ~; FUNDAMENTAL ~; POUND-~; PRISON ~; SUBSTANTIAL ~.

BREACH OF A SUBSTANTIAL CHARACTER. (i) That a consumer product, or the level of performance of the retail seller or manufacturer of a consumer product, departs substantially from what consumers can reasonably expect, having regard to all the relevant circumstances of the sale of the product, including the description of the product, its purchase price, the statutory warranties and express warranties of the retail seller or the manufacturer of the product; or (ii) that a consumer product is totally or substantially unfit for all the usual purposes of such product or for any particular purpose for which, to the knowledge of the retail seller, the product is being bought. *The Consumer Products Warranties Act*, R.S.S. 1978, c. C-30, s. 2.

BREACH OF CLOSE. Unjustified entry on another person's land.

BREACH OF CONTRACT. See INTENTIONAL INDUCEMENT OF ~.

BREACH OF PRISON. Escape from a prison.

BREACH OF PRIVILEGE. Contempt of Parliament.

BREACH OF PROMISE TO MARRY. Conduct which formerly permitted a common law action for damages.

BREACH OF THE PEACE. The violation of the peace, quiet, and security to which one is legally entitled.

BREACH OF TRUST. The violation of duty by an executor, public officer, trustee or other person who acts in a fiduciary capacity.

BREAD. *n.* 1. All products of flour or meal in which yeast, or any other ingredient for raising flour is used, irrespective of variety, colour, form or name. *Bread Act*, R.S.A. 1970, c. 34, s. 2. 2. Bread commonly known as white bread however baked and without regard to the ingredients thereof. *Merchandise Inspection Act*, R.S.N.S. 1967, c. 182, s. 1. See FANCY ~; FRUIT ~; SMALL ~; STALE ~; STANDARD ~.

BREADED FISH. Fish or fish flesh that is coated with batter and breading.

BREADTH. *n.* The maximum breadth of a ship, measured amidships, (a) in the case of a ship with a metal shell, to the moulded line of the frame, and (b) in the case of a ship with a shell of a material other than metal, to the outer surface of the hull. Canada regulations.

BREAK. *v.* (a) To break any part, internal or external, or (b) to open any thing that is used or intended to be used to close or to cover an internal or external opening. *Criminal Code*, R.S.C. 1985, c. C-46, s. 321.

BREAK. *n.* (a) With respect to the calculation of a pool, the sum total of (i) any cents remaining from a division of a net pool, to create a calculating pool, plus (ii) any odd cents over any multiple of $0.05 in the amount calculated in accordance with these Regulations to be payable in respect of each dollar bet, and (b) with respect to a horse, the running of the horse at other than its designated gait. *Race Track Supervision Regulations*, C.R.C., s. 441, s. 2. See AIR ~; PAID ~.

BREAK AND ENTER. Obtain entrance by a threat or artifice or by collusion with a person within, or enter without lawful justification or excuse by a permanent or temporary opening. *Criminal Code*, R.S.C. 1985, c. C-46, s. 350(b). See ENTER.

BREAKER. See CIRCUIT-~; VACUUM ~

BREAKING. See NEW ~.

BREAKING AND ENTERING. See BREAK AND ENTER.

BREAKING STRENGTH. With respect to a rope, the breaking strength as shown in a test certificate provided by the Nova Scotia Government Testing Laboratory or by a testing laboratory approved by the Chief Inspector. *Coal Mines (CBDC) Safety Regulations*, C.R.C., c. 1011, s. 2.

BREAST PACK. A manner of packing in which the poultry is packed in a single layer and is in a flat position with the entire breast visible. *Dressed and Eviscerated Poultry Regulations*, C.R.C., s. 283, s. 2.

BREATHALYZER. *n.* An instrument to measure alcohol content in the blood by analysis of a breath sample. See APPROVED INSTRUMENT.

BREATHING APPARATUS. An approved apparatus that, in an oxygen deficient atmosphere or an atmosphere contaminated by a toxic or dangerous substance, will provide oxygen or an adequate supply of air that is safe to breathe to a person engulfed in that atmosphere, and includes breathing apparatus approved by the United States Bureau of Mines. *Canada Confined Spaces Regulations*, C.R.C., c. 996, s. 2.

BREECHING. *n.* A flue pipe or chamber for receiving flue gases from one or more flue connections and for discharging these gases through a single flue connection. *Building Code Act*, R.R.O. 1980, Reg. 87, s. 1.

BREEDER TURKEY. 1. A turkey that is 30 weeks old or more at the time of delivery for slaughtering. *Canadian Turkey Marketing Quota Regulations*, C.R.C., c. 661, s. 2. (Part III) 2. A turkey that is 182 days old or more. *Canadian Turkey Marketing Quota Regulations*, C.R.C., c. 661, s. 2. (Part VIII).

BREEDING POND. A body of water used for breeding fish for non-commercial purposes with a view to restocking. *An Act Respecting the Conservation and Development of Wildlife*, S.Q. 1983, c. 39, s. 1.

B.R.E.F. *abbr.* 1. Bureau de révision de l'évaluation foncière. 2. Décisions du Bureau de révision de l'évaluation foncière du Québec.

BREVE. *n.* [L.] A writ to summon a person or which commands something to be done.

BREVE ITA DICITUR, QUIA REM DE QUA AGITUR, ET INTENTIONEM PETENTIS, PAUCIS VERBIS BREVITER ENARRAT. [L.] A writ is so named because it states briefly in few words the matter in dispute, and the intention of the party who seeks relief.

BREVE JUDICALE NON CADIT PRO DEFECTU FORMAE. [L.] A judicial writ does not fail through a formal defect.

BREVET RANK. The authority of the rank immediately above that held by an officer.

BREVIATE. *n.* Explanatory memorandum accompanying a bill in the legislature.

BREVI MANU. [L.] By direct action.

BREWER. *n.* 1. A manufacturer of beer for commercial purposes. 2. Any person who conducts, works, occupies or carries on any brewery, either personally or by an agent. *Excise Act*, R.S.C. 1985, c. E-14, s. 4. 3. (a) The Société des alcools du Québec; (b) every person being the holder of a brewer's permit issued under the Quebec Liquor Corporation Act (1971, chapter 20); (c) every person operating an interprovincial or international passenger transport undertaking (i) on land; or (ii) on water and operating as a carrier between various ports of the province. *Licenses Act*, S.Q. 1978, c. 34, s. 9.

BREWERY. *n.* Any place or premises where any beer is manufactured, and all offices, granaries, mash-rooms, cooling-rooms, vaults, yards, cellars and store-rooms connected therewith or in which any material to be used in the manufacture of beer is kept or stored, where any process of manufacture is carried on, where any apparatus connected with that manufacture is kept or used or where any of the products of brewing or fermentation are kept or stored, shall be held to be included in and to form part of the brewery to which they are attached or appurtenant. *Excise Act*, R.S.C. 1985, c. E-14, s. 4.

BRIBE. *n.* A gift to any person holding a position of trust or in public or judicial office intended to induce that person to betray trust or disregard official duty for the giver's benefit.

BRIBERY OF JUDICIAL OFFICER. Occurs when the holder of a judicial office, or a member of Parliament or a legislature corruptly accepts or obtains, agrees to accept or attempts to obtain any money, valuable consideration, office, place or employment for himself or another person in respect of anything done or omitted or to be done or omitted by him in his official capacity or, when another person gives or offers corruptly to a person who holds a judicial office or is a member of Parliament or a legislature any money, valuable consideration, office, place or employment in respect of anything done or omitted or to be done or omitted by him in his official capacity for himself or another person. *Criminal Code*, R.S.C. 1985, c. C-46, s. 119.

BRIBERY OF OFFICERS. Occurs when (a) a justice, police commissioner, peace officer, public officer, or officer of a juvenile court, or being employed in the administration of criminal law, corruptly (i) accepts or obtains, (ii) agrees to accept, or (iii) attempts to obtain, for himself or any other person any money, valuable consideration, office, place or employment with intent (iv) to interfere with the administration of justice, (v) to procure or facilitate the commission of an offence, or (vi) to protect from detection or punishment a person who has committed or who intends to commit an offence, or (b) anyone gives or offers, corruptly, to a person mentioned in paragraph (a) any money, valuable consideration, office, place or employment with intent that the person should do anything mentioned in subparagraph (a)(iv), (v) or (vi). *Criminal Code*, R.S.C. 1985, c. C-46, s. 120.

BRICK AND STONE MASON. A person who (i) constructs, erects, installs and repairs with brick, concrete block, insulation and other masonry units, walls, arches, paving, floors, fireplaces, chimneys, smoke-stacks and other structures, (ii) cuts and trims all brick, concrete block and other masonry units by hand tools and power activated equipment, (iii) lays firebrick and other refractory materials to walls, arches and floors in the construction of furnaces or to lining furnaces and retorts or to enclosing boilers, tanks and heat treating furnaces, (iv) has a comprehensive knowledge of tools to perform in the trade, (v) reads and understands blueprints, sketches, specifications, codes and manufacturers' literature used in the layout and erection of a structure. *Apprenticeship and Tradesmen's Qualification Act*, R.R.O. 1980, Reg. 26, s. 1.

BRIDE'S TROUSSEAU. Goods acquired for use in the household of a newly married couple, but does not include goods acquired for commercial purposes, vehicles, boats or aircraft. *Returning Residents Special Exemption Regulations*, C.R.C., c. 545, s. 2.

BRIDGE. *n.* 1. Any structure used or intended to be used for the purpose of carrying traffic on a highway over or across a river, stream, ravine, railway or other highway. 2. Includes a viaduct, culvert, subway and embankment, and a pavement on a bridge. See COUNTY ~; INTERNATIONAL ~; OVERHEAD ~.

BRIDGE FINANCING. Construction of a building using a borrower's own funds or interim loans. D.J. Donahue & P.D. Quinn, *Real Estate Practice in Ontario*, 4th ed. (Toronto: Butterworths, 1990) at 225.

BRIDGEMASTER. *n.* A person actually on duty in charge of a bridge. *Canal Regulations*, C.R.C., c. 1564, s. 2.

BRIDGE POLICE. Any National Harbours Board constable in charge of traffic on the bridge. Canada regulations.

BRIDGE TOLL. A charge on every vehicle, including the driver and passengers, entering upon or using the Bridge for (a) a one-way passage between the Island of Montreal and the south shore of the St. Lawrence River, (b) a one-way passage between St. Paul Island and the south shore of the St. Lawrence River, or (c) a round-trip between the Island of Montreal and St. Paul Island. *Champlain Bridge Tariff By-law*, C.R.C., c. 1074, s. 2.

BRIDGING BENEFIT. A periodical payment provided under a pension plan to a member of the pension plan for a temporary period of time after retirement for the purpose of supplementing the member's pension benefit until the member is eligible to receive benefits under the Old Age Security Act or commences to receive retirement benefits under the Canada Pension Plan or the Quebec Pension Plan. *Pension Benefits Act*, S.N.B. 1987, c. P-5.1, s. 1.

BRIDGING SUPPLEMENT. A periodical payment made to a member of a plan on his retirement, that, (a) will supplement the income of the member between the date of his retirement and the commencement of payment of benefits to the member under the terms of the Old Age Security Act (Canada), the Canada Pension Plan, and The Quebec Pension Plan, as the case may be; and (b) will terminate in whole or in part upon the commencement of payment of benefits to the member under the plans referred to in clause (a). *Pension Benefits Act*, R.R.O. 1980, Reg. 746, s. 16.

BRIEF. *n.* A file of all pleadings, documents and memoranda which serves as the basis for argument by the lawyer in the matter in court. See BRANDEIS ~; SOCIAL SCIENCE ~.

BRINE. *n.* 1. An aqueous solution of mineral salts occurring in a natural state and containing more than one per cent of mineral salts in solution. *Yukon Quartz Mining Act*, R.S.C. 1985, c. Y-4, s. 2. 2. A solution of common salt (sodium chloride) and fresh water, or sea water with or without the addition of salt. *Fish Inspection Regulations*, C.R.C., c. 802, s. 2. 3. A solution of sodium chloride or potassium chloride in water. *Chlor-Alkali Mercury National Emission Standards Regulations*, C.R.C., c. 406, s. 2. 4. Any natural aqueous solution containing more than 4% by weight of dissolved solids. *Mining Act*, R.S.Q. 1977, c. M-13, s. 1. See EXPLORATION LICENCE FOR ~; OIL FIELD ~.

BRINE CURING PLANT. See SALMON ~.

BRINE PACK. A pack in which a water and salt solution is used as the packing media with or without the addition of sugar. *Processed Fruit and Vegetable Regulations*, C.R.C., c. 291, s. 2.

BRINE WELL. A hole or opening in the ground for use in brining. *Mining Act*, R.S.O. 1980, c. 268, s. 162.

BRINING. *n.* The extraction of salt in solution by any method. *Mining Act*, R.S.O. 1980, c. 268, s. 162.

BRISTLES. See RAW WOOL, HAIR OR ~.

BRITISH COLUMBIA. The Province of British Columbia other than (a) the part known as the Peace River District, and (b) except for the purpose of making payments related to the cost of feed grain transported into the Creston-Wynndel Areas, the part known as the Creston-Wynndel Areas. *Livestock Feed Assistance Act*, R.S.C. 1985, c. L-10, s. 2. See LEGISLATIVE LIBRARY OF ~; PORT IN ~.

BRITISH COLUMBIA CONTRACT. A subsisting contract of insurance that (a) has for its subject (i) property that, at the time of the making of the contract, is in the Province or is in transit to or from the Province; or (ii) the life, safety, fidelity or insurable interest of a person who, at the time of the making of the contract, is resident in, or has its head office in, the Province; or (b) makes provision for payment under it primarily to a resident of the Province or to an incorporated company that has its head office in the Province. *Insurance Act*, R.S.B.C. 1979, c. 200, s. 54.

BRITISH COMMONWEALTH. Has the same meaning as Commonwealth. *Interpretation Act*, R.S.C. 1985, c. I-21, s. 35.

BRITISH COMMONWEALTH OF NATIONS. Has the same meaning as Commonwealth. *Interpretation Act*, R.S.C. 1985, c. I-21, s. 35.

BRITISH COMPANY. Any corporation incorporated under the laws of the United Kingdom or of any other Commonwealth country, or any political subdivision or dependent territory thereof other than Canada or a province, for the purpose of carrying on the business of insurance, and includes any association of persons formed in any such country, political subdivision or dependent territory on the plan known as Lloyd's, whereby each member of the association that participates in a policy becomes liable for a stated, limited or proportionate part of the whole amount payable under the policy. *Canadian and British Insurance Companies Act*, R.S.C. 1985, c. I-12, s. 2.

BRITISH NORTH AMERICA ACT, 1867. Renamed the Constitution Act, 1867 in 1982, this Act gave effect to the confederation scheme by uniting the provinces of Canada, Nova Scotia and New Brunswick. P.W. Hogg, *Constitutional Law of Canada*, 2d ed. (Toronto: Carswell, 1985) at 2, 29 and 30.

BRITISH POSSESSION. 1. Any dominion of Her Majesty exclusive of the United Kingdom of Great Britain and Northern Ireland, and Canada. *Evidence acts.* 2. Any part of the British Commonwealth exclusive of the United Kingdom. *Probate Recognition Act*, R.S.B.C. 1979, c. 339, s. 1.

BRITISH SHIP. Includes a Canadian ship. *Canada Shipping Act*, R.S.C. 1985, c. S-9, s. 2.

BRITISH SUBJECT. 1. A person who by virtue of the Citizenship Act (Canada) has in Canada the status of a British subject. *Barristers and Solicitors Act*, R.S.B.C. 1979, c. 26, s. 1. 2. Is deemed to include a citizen of the Republic of Ireland. *Election Act*, R.S. Nfld. 1970, c. 106, s. 2. 3. Includes Canadian citizen. *Interpretation Act*, R.S.N.B. 1973, c. I-13, s. 38. 4. Includes any person who, under the law of any country in the Commonwealth, is a citizen of that country. *Interpretation Act*, R.S.M. 1970, c. I80, s. 23.

BRITISH THERMAL UNIT. The amount of heat required to raise the temperature of one pound of water by one degree Fahrenheit.

BROADCASTER. *n.* A person licensed by the Commission to carry on a broadcasting transmitting undertaking. *Broadcasting Act*, R.S.C. 1985, c. B-9, s. 2.

BROADCASTING. *n.* 1. Any radiocommunication in which the transmissions are intended for direct reception by the general public. 2. The dissemination of writing, signs, signals, pictures and sounds of all kinds, intended to be received by the public either directly or through the medium of relay stations, by means of (i) any form of wireless radioelectric communication utilizing Hertzian waves, including radiotelegraph and radiotelephone, or (ii) cables, wires, fibre-optic linkages or laser beams. See CANADIAN ~ CORPORATION.

BROADCASTING ARBITRATOR. The person appointed Broadcasting Arbitrator by the Chief Electoral Officer pursuant to this Act. *Canada Elections Act*, R.S.C. 1985, c. E-2, s. 2.

BROADCASTING FIRM. A person who operates an audio or an audio and video broadcasting station the programmes of which are intended to be received directly by the general public, and any network of such stations. *An Act respecting educational programming*, S.Q. 1979, c. 52, s. 1.

BROADCASTING LICENCE. A licence to carry on a broadcasting undertaking issued under this Act. *Broadcasting Act*, R.S.C. 1985, c. B-9, s. 2.

BROADCASTING UNDERTAKING. Includes a broadcasting transmitting undertaking, a broadcasting receiving undertaking and a network operation, located in whole or in part within Canada or on a ship or aircraft registered in Canada. See FOREIGN ~.

BROADCAST TIME. The total hours of broadcasting by any station in a 24—hour period. Broadcasting regulations.

BROCAGE. *n.* The commission which one pays to a broker.

BROILER. *n.* Any class of chicken under six months of age, not raised or used for egg production. Canada regulations.

BROILER CHICKEN. A chicken or any class or part thereof produced from the egg of a domestic hen where the live chicken weighs five and one-half pounds or less.

BROILER TURKEY. A turkey that is less than 17 weeks old at the time of delivery for slaughtering. *Canadian Turkey Marketing Quota Regulations*, C.R.C., c. 661, s. 2.

BROKEN CONCESSION. A concession any boundary of which is broken in whole or in part by a lake or river. *Surveys Act*, R.S.O. 1980, c. 493, s. 1.

BROKEN FRONTS. In Ontario surveys, the base line followed the inner ends of inlets and consequently an irregularly shaped area, known as broken fronts, frequently appeared in front of the line. B.J. Reiter, R.C.B. Risk & B.N. McLellan, *Real Estate Law*, 3d ed. (Toronto: Emond-Montgomery, 1986) at 628 and 629.

BROKEN LOT. An irregular lot or a regular lot whose area is diminished or increased by a natural or artificial feature shown on the original plan. *Surveys Act*, R.S.O. 1980, c. 493, s. 1.

BROKEN PEA. One which while having little or none of its interior substance separated from it, is crushed or broken from the natural shape but does not include skins and cracked peas which do not materially affect the shape of the pea. *Processed Fruit and Vegetable Regulations*, C.R.C., c. 291, Schedule I, s. 39.

BROKEN SEAL. A seal that has been rendered ineffective. *Electricity Inspection Act*, R.S.C. 1970, c. E-4, s. 2.

BROKEN STOWAGE. In a ship, space which is not occupied by cargo.

BROKER. *n.* 1. One who negotiates or makes contracts for the sale of property. 2. A person who is engaged for full or part time in the business of buying and selling securities and who, in the transaction concerned, acts for, or buys a security from, or sells a security to a customer. 3. A person who, for another or others, for compensation, gain or reward or hope or promise thereof, either alone or through one or more officials or salesmen, trades in real estate, or a person who claims to be such a person. 4. A person who, for compensation, acts or aids in any manner in negotiating contracts of insurance or placing risks or effecting insurance, or in negotiating the continuance or renewal of insurance contracts for another person. *Insurance acts.* 5. A person licensed to transact business as a custom-house broker. *Custom-House Brokers Licensing Regulations*, C.R.C., c. 456, s. 2. See CUSTOMS ~; INSURANCE ~; MINERAL INTEREST ~; MINERAL LEASE ~; MONEY ~; SPECIAL ~; SUBMORTGAGE ~; TAXI-CAB ~; VESSEL ~.

BROKERAGE. *n.* The commission which one pays to a broker.

BROKER-DEALER. *var.* **BROKER DEALER.** Any person or company that is recognized as a broker-dealer that engaged either for full or part time in the business of trading in securities in the capacity of an agent or principal.

BROKER-DRIVER. *n.* A person who has

entered into an agreement in writing pursuant to which he has undertaken to drive a motor vehicle on behalf of the operator of such motor vehicle who is a registrant and to be responsible for the purchase of the fuel he uses to generate power in such motor vehicle. *Motor Vehicle Fuel Tax Act*, R.R.O. 1980, Reg. 667, s. 1.

BROKERS' AUDITOR. An accountant or firm of accountants charged with auditing the books and accounts of members of a stock exchange within the meaning of this section and whose name is on the panel of brokers' auditors drawn up by the executive committee. *Securities Act*, R.S.Q. 1977, c. V-1, s. 81.

BROOD COMB. A structure of cells in which bees lay their eggs or in which immature bees are being reared or have been reared. *The Apiaries Act*, R.S.S. 1978, c. A-22, s. 2.

BROS. *abbr.* Brothers.

BROTHEL. *n.* A place where people are allowed to resort for illicit intercourse.

BROTHER. *n.* 1. Includes half-brother. *Criminal Code*, R.S.C. 1985, c. C-46, s. 155(4). 2. Includes brother-in-law. See HALF ~.

BRUCELLOSIS. *n.* An infectious disease of cattle caused by the organism brucella abortus.

BRUISE. *n.* A hemorrhage into the tissue under the skin. F.A. Jaffe, *A Guide to Pathological Evidence*, 2d ed. (Toronto: Carswell, 1983) at 10.

BRUTUM FULMEN. [L. an empty noise] An empty threat.

BS. *abbr.* The breadth of the ship at the middle of the length of the superstructure. *Load Line Regulations (Sea)*, C.R.C., c. 1441, s. 35.

B-S GAUGE. The Brown and Sharp wire gauge which applies to nonferrous conductors. *Coal Mines Regulation Act*, R.S.N.S. 1967, c. 36, s. 84.

B.T.U. *abbr.* British Thermal Unit.

BUCKET SHOP. A securities broker who does not belong to a recognized stock exchange.

BUCKING. *n.* The act of sawing a log or a tree that has been felled into smaller pieces. *Occupational Health and Safety Act*, R.R.O. 1980, Reg. 692, s. 107.

BUCKLE. *n.* A quick release connector that secures a person in a seat belt assembly. *Motor Vehicle Safety Regulations*, C.R.C., c. 1038, s. 209.

BUCK SHOT. Shotgun pellets. F.A. Jaffe, *A Guide to Pathological Evidence*, 2d ed. (Toronto: Carswell, 1983) at 170.

BUDGET. *n.* A statement of the amounts of

estimated revenues and expenditures. See CASH ~.

BUDGETARY REQUIREMENTS. The basic requirements of a person and his dependants, if any, and any other of the items and services described in paragraphs (b) to (h) of the definition "assistance" in section 2 of the Act that, in the opinion of the provincial authority, are essential to the health or well-being of that person and his dependants, if any. *Canada Assistance Plan Regulations*, C.R.C., c. 382, s. 2.

BUDGETING. See PARTNERSHIP ~.

BUDGET SPEECH. The speech made when the Minister of Finance completes estimates for a financial year. A. Fraser, G.A. Birch & W.A. Dawson, eds., *Beauchesne's Rules and Forms of the House of Commons of Canada*, 5th ed. (Toronto: Carswell, 1978) at 174.

BUGGERY. *n.* Sodomy, anal intercourse.

BUILD. See RE~.

BUILDER. *n.* A person who builds houses for sale or for rent. *National Housing Act*, R.S.C. 1985, c. N-11, s. 2. See OWNER-~.

BUILDER AND CONTRACTOR. A person, company or corporation contracting with, or employed directly by, the proprietor for the doing of work or the placing or furnishing of machinery or materials on, in, or about, any building or erection, or in connection with any building or erection, or for the performance of any kind of work or labour whatever in which more than two persons are employed. *Builders and Workmen Act*, R.S.M. 1970, c. B90, s. 2.

BUILDER'S CERTIFICATE. A certificate which the builder of a ship signs which contains (a) an accurate account of the tonnage and denomination of the ship, as the builder estimates, (b) the place where and the time when it was built, (c) the name of any people on whose account the ship was built, and (d) if there was any sale of the ship or a share of it, the bill of sale under which the ship was vested in the applicant for registry. R.M. Fernandes & C. Burke, *The Annotated Canada Shipping Act* (Toronto: Butterworths, 1988) at 42.

BUILDER'S MORTGAGE. A mortgage of a recorded vessel. *Canada Shipping Act*, R.S.C. 1985, c. S-9, s. 2.

BUILDING. *n.* 1. A structure consisting of foundations, walls or roof, with or without other parts. 2. A structure that is used or intended to be used for the purpose of supporting or sheltering persons or animals or storing property. 3. Includes a structure, erection, mine or work built, erected or constructed on or in land. 4. Includes a trailer, mobile home or portable

shack. 5. Every structure, erection, excavation, alteration or improvement whatsoever placed on, over or under land, or attached, anchored or moored to land, and includes mobile structures, vehicles and marine vessels adapted or constructed for residential, commercial, industrial and other like uses, and any part of a building as so defined and any fixtures that form part of a building. *Urban and Rural Planning Amendment Act*, S. Nfld. 1982, c. 26, s. 1. 6. Includes any structure or enclosure occupied by employees. Canada regulations. 7. In respect of a ship, includes the conversion of a ship. *Shipbuilding Industry Assistance Regulations*, C.R.C., c. 348, s. 2. See ACCESSORY ~; APARTMENT ~; ASSEMBLY ~; BUILDINGS; CHURCH ~; DILAPIDATED ~; INSTITUTIONAL ~; MERCANTILE ~; NON-COMBUSTIBLE ~; NON-CONFORMING ~; OFFICE ~; ON-SITE ~ OR STRUCTURE; POST-DISASTER ~; PRECINCTS OF THE ~; PUBLIC ~; RESIDENTIAL ~; ROAD ~; SUBORDINATE ~.

BUILDING AREA. The greatest horizontal area of a building within the outside surface of exterior walls or, where a firewall is to be constructed, within the outside surface of exterior walls and the centre line of firewalls.

BUILDING AUTHORITY. The provincial or municipal authority that administers the law in respect of the structural safety of buildings in the area in which a building is located. *Canada Building Safety Regulations*, C.R.C., c. 995, s. 2.

BUILDING CODE. Detailed specifications for the design and construction of buildings which ensure structural safety, fire safety and the occupants' health. D. Robertson, *Ontario Health and Safety Guide* (Toronto: Richard De Boo Ltd., 1988) at 5-35. See NATIONAL ~ OF CANADA.

BUILDING CONSTRUCTION CODE. A code of building construction standards.

BUILDING CONSTRUCTION STANDARD. A standard for (i) construction materials, or plumbing or electrical materials or installations, or equipment or appliances, or any combination thereof, to be used or installed in any building or part of a building, or (ii) the method to be used in the construction or demolition of any building or part of a building. *Buildings and Mobile Homes Act*, S.M. 1974, c. 54, s. 1.

BUILDING CONTRACT. A contract to build anything.

BUILDING CONTRACTOR. Includes a subcontractor and any subcontractor of a subcontractor and means any person undertaking in the province any contract to construct, install, build, alter, reconstruct, remodel, repair or demolish buildings, plants, wharves, bridges, canals, locks, elevators, docks, harbours, tunnels, waterways, highways, roads, railways, ships or other similar works, and includes the preparation for and the laying of the foundation of any such work as well as the installation of machinery, equipment or appurtenances. *Building Contractors (Licensing) Act*, R.S. Nfld. 1970, c. 26, s. 2.

BUILDING DEVELOPMENT. A project or undertaking designed to provide, or to facilitate in any way the provision, repair, rehabilitation or improvement of, housing accommodation with or without public buildings, recreational facilities, industrial and commercial buildings or space appropriate therefor. *Housing Development Act*, R.S.O. 1980, c. 209, s. 1.

BUILDING DEVELOPMENT CORPORA-TION. A corporation authorized to undertake a building development that is approved by the Lieutenant Governor in Council, and includes any authority established by a municipality to undertake a building development. *Housing Development Act*, R.S.O. 1980, c. 209, s. 1.

BUILDING DRAIN. The horizontal piping of drainage piping in or adjacent to a building or other structure that receives the discharge from drainage piping and conveys it to the building sewer, and includes offsets. *Ontario Water Resources Act*, R.R.O. 1980, Reg. 736, s. 1.

BUILDING FACING. See EXPOSING ~.

BUILDING HEIGHT. The number of storeys contained between the roof and the floor of the first storey. *Building Code Act*, R.R.O. 1980, Reg. 87, s. 1.

BUILDING INSPECTOR. An inspector appointed by a municipality to administer and enforce the building code.

BUILDING LEASE. 1. A lease of a vacant piece of land on which the lessee covenants to erect a building or to pull down an old building and erect a new one on the site. 2. The lease of land for a rent called ground rent.

BUILDING LINE. The line to which the front of all buildings shall be set back from the road improvement line or road line. *Local Government Act*, S. Nfld. 1972, c. 32, s. 2.

BUILDING MATERIALS. Includes goods that become so incorporated or built into a building that their removal therefrom would necessarily involve the removal or destruction of some other part of the building and thereby cause substantial damage to the building apart from the value of the goods removed; but does not include goods that are severable from the land merely by unscrewing, unbolting, unclamping, uncou-

pling, or by some other method of disconnection; and does not include machinery installed in a building for use in the carrying on of an industry, where the only substantial damage, apart from the value of the machinery removed, that would necessarily be caused to the building in removing the machinery therefrom, is that arising from the removal or destruction of the bed or casing on or in which the machinery is set and the making or enlargement of an opening in the walls of the building sufficient for the removal of the machinery. *Conditional Sales acts.*

BUILDING PERMIT. A permit, issued under a building bylaw of a municipality, authorizing the construction of all or part of any structure.

BUILDING PROJECT. A project composed of one or more of the following elements: (i) the purchase or other acquisition of all or any part of an existing building or buildings including the land contiguous thereto, (ii) any renovations or alterations to an existing building or buildings, (iii) additions to an existing building or buildings, (iv) the purchase or other acquisition of vacant land for the purpose of constructing a building or buildings thereon, (v) the erection of a new building, or any part thereof, (vi) the demolition of a building, and (vii) the installation of public utilities, sewers and items or services necessary for access to the land or building or buildings.

BUILDING RAISING. The raising of a building or structure required by reason of damage or potential damage to the building or structure. *Shoreline Property Assistance Amendment Act*, S.O. 1986, c. 22, s. 1.

BUILDING RELOCATION. The relocation of a building or structure by reason of damage or potential damage to the building or structure. *Shoreline Property Assistance Amendment Act*, S.O. 1986, c. 22, s. 1.

BUILDING REPAIRS. Repairs to a building or structure required by reason of damage to the building or structure. *Shoreline Property Assistance Amendment Act*, S.O. 1986, c. 22, s. 1.

BUILDINGS. *n.* Any structure that is assessable as part of assessable property but does not include the earth or soil upon which it rests. Manitoba statutes. See BUILDING; FACTORY BUILT ~; FARM ~; PARLIAMENT ~.

BUILDING SCHEME. A scheme of development which comes into existence where defined land is laid out in parcels and intended to be sold to different purchasers or leased or subleased to different lessees, each of whom enters into a restrictive covenant with the common vendor or lessor agreeing that his particular parcel shall be subject to certain restrictions as to use; the restrictive covenants constituting a special local law applicable to the defined land and the benefit and burden of the covenants passing to, as the case may be, the purchaser, lessee or sublessee of the parcel and his successors in title. *Land Title Act*, R.S.B.C. 1979, c. 219, s. 1.

BUILDING SEWER. That part of a drainage piping outside a building or other structure, that connects a building drain to the main sewer or, where the place of disposal of the sewage is on the property, to the place of disposal on the property and that commences at a point three feet from the outer face of the wall of the building or other structure and terminates at the property line or place of disposal on the property. *Ontario Water Resources Act*, R.R.O. 1980, Reg. 736, s. 1.

BUILDING SITE. The location on which construction of a structure is about to commence or is in progress, and may be all or part of a subdivided parcel of land.

BUILDING STORM DRAIN. The horizontal piping of storm drainage piping in or adjacent to a building that receives the discharge from storm drainage piping and conveys it to the building storm sewer, and includes offsets. *Ontario Water Resources Act*, R.R.O. 1980, Reg. 736, s. 1.

BUILDING STORM SEWER. That part of storm drainage piping outside a building or other structure that connects the building storm drain to the main storm sewer or, where the place of disposal is on the property, to the place of disposal on the property, and that commences at a point three feet from the outer face of the wall of the building or other structure and terminates at the property line or place of disposal on the property. *Ontario Water Resources Act*, R.R.O. 1980, Reg. 736, s. 1.

BUILDING TRADES COUNCIL. Association of craft unions in the construction and building industry.

BUILDING TRAP. A running hand hole trap installed in a building drain to prevent circulation of air between the building drain and the building sewer. *Ontario Water Resources Act*, R.R.O. 1980, Reg. 736, s. 1.

BUILDING UNIT. See MODULAR ~.

BUILDING USED FOR SLEEPING ACCOMMODATIONS. Includes, (a) a hotel, (b) a building in which lodgings are let, (c) a building in which an educational institution lodges its students, (d) a hospital, sanatorium or infirmary, (e) a convent, and (f) a building in which inmates of an orphanage, children's home, home for aged persons or almshouse are lodged.

BUILT-UP AREA. An area of land where (i) not less than 50 per cent of the frontage upon one side of a road for a distance of not less than 200 metres is occupied by dwellings, buildings used for business purposes, schools or churches, or (ii) not less than 50 per cent of the frontage upon both sides of a road for a distance of not less than 100 metres is occupied by dwellings, buildings used for business purposes, schools or churches, or (iii) not more than 200 metres of a road separates any land described in subparagraph (i) or (ii) from any other land described in subparagraph i or ii, or (iv) a plan of subdivision has been registered.

BUILT-UP DISTRICT. The territory contiguous to a highway not within a municipality or other inhabited area where (i) not less than fifty per centum of the frontage upon one side of the highway for a distance of not less than six hundred feet is occupied by dwellings, buildings used for business purposes, schools or churches, (ii) not less than fifty per centum of the frontage upon both sides of the highway for a distance of not less than three hundred feet is occupied by dwellings, buildings used for business purposes, schools or churches, or (iii) not more than six hundred feet of highway separates any territory described in subparagraph (i) or (ii) from any other territory described in subparagraph (i) or (ii), and signs are displayed in accordance with the regulations, if any. *Highway Traffic Act*, R.S. Nfld. 1970, c. 152, s. 2.

BULK. See GOODS IN ~; IN ~; STOCK IN ~.

BULK CARGO. Such goods as are loose or in mass and generally must be shovelled, pumped, blown, scooped or forked in the handling and, without limiting the generality of the foregoing, shall be deemed to include (a) barley, buckwheat, corn, dried beans, dried peas, flaxseed, rapeseed and other oil seeds, flour, grain screenings, mill feed containing not more than 35 per cent of ingredients other than grain or grain products, oats, rye and wheat, loose or in sacks, (b) cement, loose or in sacks, (c) coke and petroleum coke, loose or in sacks, (d) domestic package freight, (e) liquids carried in ships' tanks, (f) ores and minerals (crude, screened, sized or concentrated, but not otherwise processed) loose or in sacks, including alumina, bauxite, coal, gravel, phosphate rock, sand, stone and sulphur, (g) pig iron, scrap iron and scrap steel, (h) pulpwood, poles and logs, loose or bundled, (i) raw sugar, loose or in sacks, and (j) woodpulp, loose or in bales. *St. Lawrence Seaway Wharfage and Storage Charges Tariff*, C.R.C., c. 1396, s. 2.

BULK CONTAINER. A container that has a

weight capacity of more than 8 pounds. *Honey Regulations*, C.R.C., c. 287, s. 2.

BULK GOODS. Carloads of coal, coal products, wood, sand, gravel, brick, scrap metal, and of such other goods as may be approved by the Commission. *Railway Act*, R.S.C. 1985, c. R-3, s. 311(3).

BULKHEAD. *n.* A structure built for impounding water or confining air under pressure in a crosscut, drift or other mine opening and constructed in a manner to close off completely the crosscut, drift or other mine opening.

BULKHEAD DECK. The uppermost deck up to which transverse watertight bulkheads are carried. *Hull Construction Regulations*, C.R.C., c. 1431, s. 2.

BULK MILK COOLER. A stationary farm storage tank maintained in a milkhouse and used for cooling and storing milk for sale and includes fixtures and equipment incidental to the use thereof. *Dairy Act*, S.M. 1980, c. 44, s. 1.

BULK MILK TRANSFER STATION. Any location where bulk milk or cream is transferred from one tank-truck to another. *Milk Act*, R.R.O. 1980, Reg. 629, s. 1.

BULK MOTIVE FUEL. Motive fuel stored in tanks or other containers that are not part of the regular fuel storage supply system of a motor vehicle, engine, machine or equipment. *Motive Fuel Tax Act*, S.M. 1980, c. 69, s. 34.

BULK PLANT. One or more storage tanks, including the appurtenances thereof, where gasoline or an associated product is received by pipe line, tank vessel, tank car or tank vehicle and is stored in bulk for subsequent transmission by pipe line or transportation or distribution by tank vessel, tank car or tank vehicle.

BULK SALE. Sale of stock or part of stock which is out of the vendor's usual course of business or trade. G.H.L. Fridman, *Sale of Goods in Canada*, 3d ed. (Toronto: Carswell, 1986) at 489. See SALE IN BULK.

BULK SALES ACT. An act to protect creditors of a vendor who (a) sells stock, or a part of it, out of the usual course of business or trade or (b) sells what is substantially the vendor's stock or interest in the business. G.H.L. Fridman, *Sale of Goods in Canada*, 3d ed. (Toronto: Carswell, 1986) at 489.

BULK STORAGE CONTAINER. A bin; a hopper; a silo. D. Robertson, *Ontario Health and Safety Guide* (Toronto: Richard De Boo Ltd., 1988) at 5-39.

BULK STORAGE TANK. Includes any static storage tank in which gasoline or an associated product is contained, but does not include a supply tank that is connected to the heating appliance that it serves.

BULK TANK. See FARM ~.

BULK TRANSPORT FACILITIES. Includes any property, real or personal, designed or suited, or capable of being used, for the transportation of goods in bulk either by means of ships or by a company to which the Railway Act applies including any facilities for loading, unloading and storing goods in bulk and any facilities owned or controlled by or in possession of any person operating transport facilities. *Transport Control Regulations*, C.R.C., c. 1566, s. 2.

BULL. *n.* One who buys shares expecting prices on the stock exchange to rise. See PURE-BRED ~; SCRUB ~.

BULL. ACBD. *abbr.* Bulletin ACBD (CALL Newsletter).

BULL. AVOCATS. *abbr.* Le Bulletin des avocats (Solicitor's Journal).

BULL. CCDJ. *abbr.* Bulletin d'information juridique du CCDJ (CLIC's Legal Materials Letter).

BULLET. *n.* A projectile which a rifled weapon fires. F.A. Jaffe, *A Guide to Pathological Evidence*, 2d ed. (Toronto: Carswell, 1983) at 170. See TANDEM ~.

BULLET EMBOLISM. An embolism caused by a bullet or bullet fragments. F.A. Jaffe, *A Guide to Pathological Evidence*, 2d ed. (Toronto: Carswell, 1983) at 175.

BULLETIN. See INFORMATION ~.

BULLION. *n.* 1. Uncoined silver and gold. 2. A precious metal alloy product of processing in the form of bars, plates, lumps or other masses and includes crude bullion and refined bullion. *Mining Tax Act*, R.R.O. 1980, Reg. 639, s. 1.

"BULLOCK" ORDER. As long as it was reasonable for the plaintiff to join the other defendants, an order obtained by a plaintiff that unsuccessful defendants pay the costs of the successful defendant. M.M. Orkin, *The Law of Costs*, 2d ed. (Aurora: Canada Law Book, 1987) at 2-25.

BUMPER. *n.* A device designed to be affixed to the front and rear of a motor vehicle of the passenger car type and capable of preventing or minimizing the damage to other parts of the motor vehicle. *The Highway Traffic Act*, S.M. 1985-86, c. 3, s. 49(4).

BUMPER FRACTURE. A below-the-knee leg fracture caused by the bumper of a motor vehicle. F.A. Jaffe, *A Guide to Pathological*

Evidence, 2d ed. (Toronto: Carswell, 1983) at 176 and 177.

BUMPING. *n.* When a lay-off occurs, an employee with greater seniority displaces, or bumps, a more junior employee from a job. D.J.M. Brown and D.M. Beatty, *Canadian Labour Arbitration*, 2d ed. (Aurora: Canada Law Book, 1977) at 285. See CLOCK- ~.

BUNCHING. *n.* When gains which have accrued over several years are, for tax purposes, realized and recognized in a single year. W. Grover & F. Iacobucci, *Materials on Canadian Income Tax*, 4th ed. (Toronto: Richard De Boo Ltd., 1980) at 157.

BUNKER FUEL. A residual fuel oil which when used for heating requires or would ordinarily require preheating. *Motive Fuel Tax Act*, S.M. 1980, c. 69, s. 34. See MARINE ~; MARKED ~.

BUOY. *n.* 1. Any type of buoy or float anchored in position either permanently or temporarily and maintained as a signal or aid to navigation. *Private Buoy Regulations*, C.R.C., c. 1460, s. 2. 2. A mooring buoy. See FAIRWAY ~; GOVERNMENT ~; PORT HAND ~; PRIVATE ~; STARBOARD HAND ~.

BUOYAGE. *n.* A charge on a vessel for the use of a buoy, dolphin or similar facility that is under the administration, management and control of or under lease from the Board at a harbour and not used in conjunction with a facility for which berthage is assessable. *Berthage, Buoyage and Anchorage Charges Tariff By-law*, C.R.C., c. 1061, s. 2.

BURDEN. *n.* The duty to perform an obligation. See EVIDENTIARY ~; LEGAL ~ OF PROOF.

BURDEN OF PERSUASION. The burden of convincing the court of the existence or non-existence, or probable existence or non-existence, of any fact. *Military Rules of Evidence*, C.R.C., c. 1049, s. 2.

BURDEN OF PROOF. Party who asserts the affirmative must adduce evidence to prove it.

BUREAU. *n.* 1. An office. 2. A name applied to certain public bodies. See BETTER BUSINESS ~; CREDIT ~; RATING ~.

BUREAUCRACY. *n.* An organization with a hierarchical structure, inflexible rules and procedures.

BURGESS. *n.* 1. A person who is entitled to vote as a burgess in a municipality. 2. A person who: (i) is at least eighteen years of age; and (ii) is a Canadian citizen or other British subject; and (A) is the registered owner of taxable real property in the municipality; provided that where property is owned under bona fide agreement for sale burgess shall mean the puchaser; or (B) is assessed as an occupant in the municipality; or (C) is assessed for a business in the municipality; or (D) is a shareholder of a duly incorporated co-operative association located in the municipality and established to provide housing for its members residing therein; or (E) where such person is not in his own right qualified under paragraph (A), (B), (C) or (D), he is the spouse of a person mentioned in paragraph (A), (B), (C) or (D) and resides with that person in the municipality; except where the municipality is a summer resort village, in which case the spouse resides with that person in the province. *The Urban Municipal Elections Act*, R.S.S. 1978, c. U-9, s. 2. See RESIDENT ~.

BURGLAR ALARM AGENCY. The business of selling, providing, installing or servicing burglar alarm systems or of monitoring a signal from premises protected by a burglar alarm system or of providing the services of a burglar alarm agent. *Private Investigators and Security Guards Act*, S.N.B. 1980, c. 41, s. 2.

BURGLAR ALARM AGENT. A person who sells, installs, services, tests or patrols a burglar alarm system or acts as an operator to receive signals or respond in person to alarm warnings of a burglar alarm system. *Private Investigators and Security Guards Act*, S.N.B. 1980, c. 41, s. 2.

BURGLAR ALARM SYSTEM. A system consisting of a device or devices to provide warnings against intrusion, including burglary, robbery, theft or vandalism. *Private Investigators and Security Guards Act*, S.N.B. 1980, c. 41, s. 2.

BURGLARY. *n.* The common law offence of breaking and entering a dwelling-house at night with intent to commit a crime there.

BURGLARY INSURANCE. Insurance against loss or damage by burglary, house-breaking, robbery or theft.

BURIAL. *n.* 1. The burial of human remains and includes the permanent placement of human remains in a building or structure. *Cemetery and Funeral Services Act*, S.N.S. 1983, c. 4, s. 2. 2. Includes cremation. 3. (i) The provision of a grave for burial where a grave is not provided free of charge under section 53 of the Cemeteries Act, (ii) the opening and closing of a grave, (iii) the perpetual care of a grave, (iv) where required, a grave marker, and (v) such other services and items in addition to those set out in subclauses (i) to (iv), both inclusive, as approved by the Director. *Homes for Special Care Act*, R.R.O. 1980, Reg. 501, s. 1.

BURIAL PERMIT. A permit to bury, cremate, remove or otherwise dispose of a dead body. *Vital Statistics acts.*

BURIED FACILITIES. Telecommunication facilities buried below ground surface and which are not encased in cement, wood or some other enclosure. *Alberta Government Telephones Act,* R.S.A. 1980, c. A-23, s. 27.

BURKING. *n.* An assailant sits on the victim's chest causing traumatic asyphyxia. F.A. Jaffe, *A Guide to Pathological Evidence,* 2d ed. (Toronto: Carswell, 1983) at 170 and 171.

BURKISM. *n.* The practice of killing persons for the purpose of selling their bodies for dissection.

BURN. *n.* An injury effected by dry heat. F.A. Jaffe, *A Guide to Pathological Evidence,* 2d ed. (Toronto: Carswell, 1983) at 171.

BURNING PERMIT AREA. A provincial forest and every quarter section of land lying wholly or partly within 4.5 kilometres of the boundaries of a provincial forest, and includes any other area that may be designated as a burning permit area by the minister. *Prairie and Forest Fires Act,* S.S. 1982-83, c. P-22.1, s. 2.

BURSAR. *n.* 1. The business administrator of a School. *Education Act,* R.R.O. 1980, Reg. 268, s. 1. 2. A college treasurer.

BURSARY. *n.* 1. A sum of money granted without having special regard to the quality of the academic work of the person to whom it is granted but having regard to an expressed willingness of that person to provide insured services in Saskatchewan at some future time. *The Medical Scholarships and Bursaries Act,* R.S.S. 1978, c. M-11, s. 2. 2. A loan for educational and training purposes in respect of health to assist in the financing of studies at a school or at an institution other than a degree-granting college or university, repayable by the performance of agreed upon services to the public. *Ministry of Culture and Recreation Act,* R.R.O. 1980, Reg. 654, s. 1.

BURSTING PRESSURE. Of a condom, means the air pressure in the condom at the time it bursts when tested according to the method specified in Part II. *Medical Devices Regulations,* C.R.C., c. 871, s. 1.

BURSTING VOLUME. Of a condom, means the volume of air contained in the condom at bursting pressure. *Medical Devices Regulations,* C.R.C., c. 871, s. 1.

BUS. *n.* 1. Any vehicle adapted to carry more than six to twelve adult passengers in addition to the driver. 2. A conductor which serves as a common connection for the corresponding conductors of two or more circuits. *Power Corporation Act,* R.R.O. 1980, Reg. 794, s. 0. See AUTO~; PUBLIC MOTOR ~; SCHOOL ~; TROLLEY ~.

BUS. & L. *abbr.* Business & the Law.

BUSHEL. *n.* 1. 8 gallons. *Weights and Measures Act,* S.C. 1970-71-72, c. 36, Schedule II. 2. 56 pounds of shelled corn or seed corn the kernal moisture content of which does not exceed 15.5 per cent. *Crop Insurance Act (Ontario),* R.R.O. 1980, Reg. 205, s. 3. 3. In this Act, unless a bushel by measure is expressly referred to, and in any contract respecting grain, unless the parties otherwise expressly agree, the word "bushel", when used with respect to oats, means a quantity weighing 34 pounds, when used with respect to barley or buckwheat, means a quantity weighing 48 pounds, when used with respect to Indian corn, flaxseed or rye, means a quantity weighing 56 pounds, or when used with respect to peas or wheat, means a quantity weighing 60 pounds. *Canada Grain Act,* R.S.C. 1970, c. G-16, s. 165.

BUSINESS. *n.* 1. Includes a profession, calling, trade, manufacture or undertaking of any kind whatsoever and includes an adventure or concern in the nature of trade but does not include an office or employment. 2. An undertaking carried on for the purpose of gain or profit, and includes an interest in any such undertaking. *Real Estate and Business Brokers acts.* 3. Any business, profession, trade, calling, manufacture or undertaking of any kind carried on in Canada or elsewhere whether for profit or otherwise, including any activity or operation carried on or performed in Canada or elsewhere by any government, by any department, branch, board, commission or agency of any government, by any court or other tribunal or by any other body or authority performing a function of government. *Canada Evidence Act,* R.S.C. 1985, c. C-5, s. 30(12). 4. The business of (a) manufacturing, producing, transporting, acquiring, supplying, storing and otherwise dealing in articles, and (b) acquiring, supplying and otherwise dealing in services. *Combines Investigation Act,* R.S.C. 1985, c. C-34, s. 2. 5. Those lawful objects and purposes for which a company is established. 6. The land and buildings used for a commercial enterprise. See ACTIVE ~; AMBULATORY ~; ARTIFICIAL INSEMINATION ~; CANADIAN ~; CARRY ON ~; CARRYING ON ~; COMMON FORM ~; CONTENTIOUS ~; COURSE OF ~; DOING ~; EMBRYO TRANSFER ~; ENGAGING IN ~; FAMILY ~ CORPORATION; FEDERAL ~ DEVELOPMENT BANK; FEDERAL WORK, UNDERTAKING OR ~; FISH ~ OR ENTERPRISE; INCOME FROM A ~ (OR PROPERTY); INSEMINATING ~; LIFE INSURANCE ~; MAJOR ~ OR ACTIVITY; MANUFACTURING ~; NON-CONTEN-

TIOUS ~; NON-QUALIFYING ~; NON-RES-
IDENT ~; OPERATING ~; PRINCIPAL
PLACE OF ~; PURPOSES RELATING TO
THE ~ OF A DEALER; RELATED ~; RES-
IDENT ~; RETAIL ~; SECURITY ~.

BUSINESS ACTIVITY. Includes any profession, activity or enterprise which may lawfully
be carried on. *The Northern Saskatchewan Economic Development Act*, R.S.S. 1978, c. N-7, s.
3.

BUSINESS AGENCY. A corporation, a trust or
any other person under the effective management or control of a congregation. *Taxation Act*,
S.Q. 1978, c. 26, s. 166.

BUSINESS AGENT. Executive officer of a local
union who administers the union's affairs.

BUSINESS ASSET. Property owned by one
spouse and used principally in the course of a
business carried on by that spouse, either alone
or jointly with others, and includes shares that
the spouse owns in a corporation through which
he or she carries on a business.

BUSINESS COMBINATION. An acquisition of
all or substantially all of the property of one
body corporate by another or an amalgamation
of two or more bodies corporate.

BUSINESS DAY. 1. A day other than Saturday
or a holiday. 2. In respect of any investments
of a company listed or dealt in on a stock
exchange, a day on which the principal stock
exchange is open for trading in stocks and
securities. 3. A day other than a Saturday,
Sunday or holiday. *An Act to Revise the Securities
Act*, S.N.S. 1984, c. 11, s. 75.

BUSINESS DISTRICT. 1. The territory contiguous to a portion of a highway having a length
of 200 m along which there are buildings used
for business, industrial or public purposes occupying (a) at least 100 m of frontage on one side
of that portion; or (b) at least 100 m collectively
on both sides of that portion; and includes that
portion of the highway. *Motor Vehicle Act*,
R.S.B.C. 1979, c. 288, s. 115. 2. A territory
contiguous to a highway upon which fifty per
cent or more of the frontage for a distance of
not less than three hundred feet is occupied by
business premises and includes a section of a
highway so designated by the traffic authority
by the erection of appropriate signs.

BUSINESS ENTERPRISE. 1. An enterprise
carried on or about to be carried on in Canada
for gain or profit where the principal business
carried on or about to be carried on therein
comes within any of the following classes of
businesses, namely, (a) manufacturing, (b)
wholesale trade, (c) retail trade, (d) service
businesses, (e) construction, (f) transportation,

or (g) communications, but does not include the
business of a profession recognized as such by
a law of Canada or a province or a business
having as its object the furtherance of a charitable or religious purpose. *Small Business Loans
Act*, R.S.C. 1985, c. S-11, s. 2. 2. An industry,
trade, service or tourist business or commercial
business undertaking. See SMALL ~.

BUSINESS IMPROVEMENT LOAN. A loan
made by a lender to a proprietor of a small
business enterprise for the purpose of financing
(a) the purchase, installation, renovation,
improvement or modernization of equipment of
a kind usually affixed to real property, (b) the
purchase, renovation, improvement or modernization of equipment of a kind not usually
affixed to real property, (c) the renovation,
improvement or modernization of premises or
the purchase, construction, alteration or extension of premises, or (d) the purchase of land
necessary for the operation of a business enterprise. *Small Business Loans Act*, R.S.C. 1985, c.
S-11, s. 2.

BUSINESS INVESTMENT LOSS. See
ALLOWABLE ~.

BUSINESS NAME. The name under which a
business is carried on or is to be carried on and
includes a firm name.

BUSINESS OCCUPANCY. Occupancy for the
transaction of business.

BUSINESS OCCUPANCY TAX. A tax levied
on occupants in respect of their use or occupation of real property for the purpose of or in
connection with a business. *Municipal Grants
Act*, R.S.C. 1985, c. M-13, s. 2.

BUSINESS OF AGRICULTURE. Includes (i)
the cultivation, production, improvement, use or
protection of agricultural plants, (ii) the raising,
feeding, improvement, protection or use of farm
animals, poultry or bees, (iii) the production,
processing, marketing, financing or protection
of agricultural products and supplies, (iv) the
classification, cultivation, use, fertilization, conservation or improvement of soils for agricultural or related purposes, (v) the on-farm
management of waste products, (vi) the making
of economic, statistical or sociological studies
of any aspect of the agricultural industry, (vii)
the utilization or control of energy or water for
agricultural purposes, (viii) the agricultural use
of building, structures, machinery or equipment,
(ix) the identification or control of weeds and
the pests of agricultural plants or animals, (x)
any other agricultural pursuits that may be
deemed by the council advisable for inclusion.
An Act to Amend the Agrologists Act, P.E.I. 1981,
c. 2, s. 1.

BUSINESS OF A PRIVATE INVESTIGATOR. Includes the business of (a) obtaining or furnishing information on (i) the personal character or actions of a person; or (ii) the character of the business or occupation of a person; (b) watching, guarding or patrolling for the protection of persons or property; and (c) doing other work, either in whole or in part, ordinarily done by investigators. *Private Investigators Act*, R.S.B.C. 1979, c. 337, s. 10.

BUSINESS OF FIRE INSURANCE IN THE PROVINCE. All contracts of fire insurance including fire insurance on automobiles on which premiums are receivable from or in respect of persons whose property insured thereunder was situated in the province at the time their premiums became payable. *Fire Prevention Act*, S.P.E.I. 1983, c. 16, s. 1.

BUSINESS OF INSURANCE. The making of any contract of insurance, and includes any act or acts of inducement to enter into a contract of insurance, and any act or acts relating to the performance thereof or the rendering of any service in connection therewith.

BUSINESS OF INVESTMENT. With respect to a corporation, means the borrowing of money by the corporation on the security of its bonds, debentures, notes or other evidences of indebtedness and the use of some or all of the proceeds of such borrowing for (a) the making of loans, whether secured or unsecured, (b) the purchase of (i) bonds, debentures, notes or other evidences of indebtedness of individuals or corporations, (ii) shares of corporations, (iii) bonds, debentures, notes or other evidences of indebtedness of or guaranteed by a government or a municipality, or (iv) conditional sales contracts, accounts receivable, bills of sale, chattel mortgages, bills of exchange or other obligations representing part or all of the sale price of merchandise or services, (c) the purchase or improvement of real property other than real property reasonably required for occupation or anticipated occupation by the corporation, or any corporation referred to in subsection (4), in the transaction of its business, or (d) the replacement or retiring of earlier borrowings some or all of the proceeds of which have been used for the purposes set out in paragraphs (a) to (c). *Investment Companies Act*, R.S.C. 1985, c. I-22, s. 2.

BUSINESS OF SUPPLY. Considering estimates for interim supply, passing all stages of any bill based on them, and considering opposition motions. A. Fraser, G.A. Birch & W.A. Dawson, eds., *Beauchesne's Rules and Forms of the House of Commons of Canada*, 5th ed. (Toronto: Carswell, 1978) at 167.

BUSINESS OR ASSOCIATION. An individual, an association, or a partnership carrying on business.

BUSINESS OR TRADE ASSOCIATION. An organization of persons that by an enactment, agreement or custom has power to admit, suspend, expel or direct persons in relation to any business or trade. *Human Rights codes.*

BUSINESS PREMISES. 1. A site where dealer carries on business. *Vehicle Dealers and Salesmen Act*, S.P.E.I. 1975, c. 33, s. 1. 2. Does not include a dwelling.

BUSINESS, PROFESSIONAL OR TRADE ASSOCIATION. Includes an organization of persons which by an enactment, agreement or custom has power to admit, suspend, expel or direct persons in relation to any business or trade or in the practice of any occupation or calling. *Human Rights Act*, S.P.E.I. 1975, c. 72, s. 1.

BUSINESS PROPERTY. Real property used for or occupied by any industry, trade, business, profession or vocation, but does not include (a) farm real property and without limiting the generality thereof, poultry farms and hog farms; (b) nursery gardens and market gardens; (c) timberlands; (d) apartment buildings, rooming houses, bunkhouses, trailers used as bunkhouses; (e) buildings owned, occupied or used by a farmer and operated primarily to store or package products raised on his own farm or on land occupied or used by him for farming purposes; (f) lots occupied by mobile homes used as residences. *Assessment Act*, R.S.N.B. 1973, c. A-14, s. 5. See FORMER ~.

BUSINESS PURPOSES. See COMMERCIAL OR ~.

BUSINESS TRANSACTED IN THE PROVINCE. (a) In the case of property insurance, all contracts on which premiums are receivable from, or in respect of, persons whose property was situated in the province at the time their premiums became payable; and (b) in the case of other insurance, all contracts on which premiums are receivable from, or in respect of persons who were resident in the province at the time their premiums became payable.

BUS. Q. *abbr.* Business Quarterly.

BUS SERVICE. A service for the transportation of passengers by bus for reward between points within the limits of the City. *City of St John's Act*, R.S. Nfld. 1970, c. 40, s. 228. See CHARTERED ~.

BUS TRAILER. A vehicle having a designated seating capacity of more than 10 and designed primarily to be drawn behind another vehicle.

Motor Vehicle Safety Regulations, C.R.C., c. 1038, s. 2.

BUSWAY. *n.* A raceway consisting of a system of metal troughing, including its elbows, tees, crosses and straight runs, containing conductors supported on insulators. *Power Corporation Act*, R.R.O. 980, Reg. 794, s. 0.

BUTANES. *n.* In addition to its normal scientific meaning, a mixture mainly of butanes which ordinarily may contain some propane or pentanes plus. *Oil and Gas Conservation Act*, R.S.A. 1980, c. O-5, s. 1.

BUTCHER. *n.* 1. A person who is engaged in the business of dealing in and selling to the public by retail the flesh of meat animals. 2. A person engaged in the business of slaughtering meat animals, but does not include the operator of an abbatoir where livestock is inspected by an inspector prior to slaughter. *Livestock Brand Inspection Act*, R.S.A. 1980, c. L-21, s. 1.

BUTTER. *n.* The food prepared by gathering the milk-fat of milk or cream into a mass that may also contain a portion of the other milk constituents not separated in good manufacturing practice, with or without salt or food colour, and that contains, (i) not less than 80 per cent milk-fat, (ii) no fat or oil other than milk-fat, and (iii) not more than 16 per cent water. *Farm Products Grades and Sales Act*, R.R.O. 1980, Reg. 327, s. 1. See CREAMERY ~; DAIRY ~; PROCESS ~; RENOVATED ~; REWORKED ~; WHEY ~.

BUTTERFAT DIFFERENTIAL. The value in cents of each 1/10th of a kilogram of butterfat above or below 3.6 kilograms per hectolitre of milk. *Milk Prices Review Act*, S.M. 1980, c. 63, s. 1.

BUTTERMILK. *n.* Grade A milk from which a portion of the milk-fat is removed and that (i) is prepared by adding a bacterial culture to milk, partly-skimmed milk or skim-milk, (ii) exhibits a developed acidity in excess of that found in the milk product to which the bacterial culture has been added, (iii) may contain added salt and stabilizers, and (iv) contains not more than 3.25 per cent milk-fat. *Milk Act*, R.R.O. 1980, Reg. 622, s. 3.

BUTTERMILK POWDER. Dried buttermilk that contains not more than 5 per cent by weight of water and no fat or oil other than milk-fat. *Farm Products Grades and Sales Act*, R.R.O. 1980, Reg. 327, s. 1.

BUTTON MUSHROOMS. Mushrooms with veils completely closed and stems removed immediately below the veil. *Processed Fruit and Vegetable Regulations*, C.R.C., c. 291, Schedule I, s. 35.

BUY. *v.* 1. To purchase; to acquire by payment of money or equivalent. 2. Includes acquiring by exchange or trade. *Automobile Dealers Act*, S. Nfld. 1973, c. 15, s. 2.

BUY-DOWN. See INTEREST ~.

BUYER. *n.* 1. A purchaser. 2. A person who buys or agrees to buy goods. 3. A person who buys or hires goods by a conditional sale. 4. A person who acquires stock in bulk. *Bulk Sales acts.* 5. A person who purchases goods or services on credit and includes that person's agent. 6. An individual who leases or purchases goods or services under an executory contract, and includes his agent. *Consumer Protection Act*, R.S.B.C. 1979, c. 65, s. 1. 7. Includes a person who hires or leases goods for consumption where, (i) he has an option to purchase the goods, or (ii) upon compliance with agreed terms, he will become the owner of the goods or will be entitled to keep them without further payment. *Consumer Protection Act*, R.S.O. 1980, c. 87, s. 37. See CONTRACT ~; GRAIN ~; HOME ~; SECOND ~.

BUYER'S PREMISES. The place specified in the sales contract as the buyer's address, or, if the address shown does not specifically identify that place by a municipal address, land description or other description sufficient to distinguish that place from any other, the place where the buyer actually resided at the time the sales contract was made. *Direct Sales Cancellation Act*, R.S.A. 1980, c. D-35, s. 8.

BUY IN. For the original owner or person with interest in a property to purchase it at a mortgage, tax or other forced sale.

BUY ON MARGIN. To purchase securities partly on credit extended by a broker.

BY-ELECTION. *n.* 1. An election other than a general election. 2. An election held in a constituency on a date on which there is no general election. 3. An election held to fill a vacancy in the office of mayor, councillor or trustee at a time other than a general election.

BY-LAW. *var.* **BYLAW.** *n.* 1. A rule or resolution adopted by a corporation to regulate its operations. 2. A law which a municipality makes. 3. Includes a resolution on which the opinion of the electors is to be obtained. *Municipal Election acts.* See CHARTER ~; LOCAL OPTION ~; MONEY ~; ORDINARY ~; PROPOSED ~; REFERRED ~; SPECIAL ~; ZONING ~.

BY-PRODUCT. See ANIMAL ~; MEAT ~; PRODUCTS OR ~S.

BY-PRODUCTS OF FISH CURING. Such by-products produced in a participating province. *Saltfish Act*, R.S.C. 1985, c. S-4, s. 19.

BY THE PIECE. By the piece, cord, thousand superficial feet, or other measurement whereby the quantity of logs or timber or lumber is measured. *Woodmen's Lien Act*, R.S.N.B. 1973, c. W-12, s. 1.

C. *abbr.* 1. Court. 2. Chapter. 3. Chancellor. 4. Centi. 5. Coulomb.

C.A. *abbr.* 1. Court of Appeal. 2. Cour d'appel. 3. Recueils de jurisprudence de la Cour d'appel de Québec (Quebec Court of Appeals Reports).

[ ] C.A. *abbr.* Recueils de jurisprudence du Québec, Cour d'appel, 1970-.

CAB. See TAXI ~.

CABAL. *n.* 1. A small association formed for the purpose of intrigue. 2. An intrigue.

CABARET. *n.* A room in which musical entertainment occurs in association with a restaurant.

CAB CARD. See CAVR ~.

CABIN. *n.* A one-room structure equipped for sleeping. *Tourism Act,* R.R.O. 1980, Reg. 936, s. 1. See PORTABLE ~.

CABIN ATTENDANT. A crew member, other than a flight crew member, assigned to duty in a passenger-carrying aeroplane or rotorcraft during flight time. Canada regulations.

CABIN ESTABLISHMENT. A tourist establishment comprised of four or more cabins arranged singly or in pairs. *Tourism Act,* R.R.O. 1980, Reg. 936, s. 1.

CABINET. *n.* 1. A body composed of the Prime Minister or Premier and Ministers of the Crown or a committee of Privy council (federal) or Executive Council (provincial) which determines the direction of and makes policy decisions for the government. It is usually composed of members of the Prime Minister's or Premier's political party who have been elected as members of the House of Commons or the Legislature and is often referred to as "the government". 2. An enclosure of adequate mechanical strength, composed entirely of fire- and absorption-resistant material, designed either for surface or flush mounting and provided with a frame, matt, or trim, in which swinging doors are hung. *Power Corporation Act,*

R.R.O. 1980, Reg. 794, s. 0. 3. Of a device means a structure that encloses and confines the X-ray source of the device and the material to be irradiated in the device. *Radiation Emitting Devices Regulations,* C.R.C., c. 1370, s. 1.

CABINET GOVERNMENT. Government in which Prime Minister or Premier selects members of her or his own party elected to Parliament and perhaps others to be Ministers of the Crown. This group collectively form the Cabinet, the policy-making arm of government. The Ministers and Cabinet are responsible to Parliament for the conduct of the government. The government remains in power so long as it has the confidence of a majority of the House of Commons or the Legislature. In theory, the Privy Council or Executive Council advises the formal head of state (the Governor General or Lieutenant Governor) though, in fact, the Committee of Council, known as the Cabinet, carries out this function in most situations.

CABINET MINISTER. A member of Cabinet who is responsible for a portfolio, usually a ministry or department of government. This person acts as political head of the ministry or department and is responsible to Parliament for the affairs of that ministry or department or the conduct of that portfolio.

CABIN PRESSURE ALTITUDE. The pressure altitude in the cabin of an aircraft. *Oxygen Equipment Order,* C.R.C., c. 52, s. 2.

CABIN TENT. A structure of wood, wood products, metal or canvas or a combination of these materials not exceeding 15 feet in width and 15 feet in length so designed and constructed that it is collapsible or may be removed in sections. *National Parks Camping Regulations,* C.R.C., c. 1116, s. 2.

CABIN TRAILER. A structure of wood or of wood products, metal or canvas, or a combination of these materials, erected on a wood or steel chassis with wheels attached, designed for use as living quarters, capable of being transported behind a motor vehicle and licensed under the laws of a province or state. *National Parks Camping Regulations*, C.R.C., c. 1116, s. 2.

CABLE. *n.* 1. The rope to which the anchor of a ship is fastened. 2. A number of wires twisted or braided to form a conductor. *Lightning Rods Act*, R.R.O. 1980, Reg. 577, s. 1. 3. One or more stranded conductors insulated from one another and further insulated from the mass of the earth. See ALUMINUM-SHEATHED ~; ARMORED ~; FERRY ~; FLEXIBLE SCREENED TRAILING ~; MINERAL-INSULATED ~; PLIABLE ARMORED ~; RAISED ~.

CABLECASTER. See COMMERCIAL ~; COMMUNITY ~.

CABLECASTING FIRM. A person who operates a cable or wire network or system that distributes one or more audio or audio and video programmings intended to entertain, inform or instruct the audience linked with it. *An Act respecting educational programming*, S.Q. 1979, c. 52, s. 1.

CABLECAST PROGRAMMING. The orderly presentation of messages by a cablecaster. *The Community Cablecasters Act*, R.S.S. 1978, c. C-17, s. 2.

CABLECAST SERVICE. The arrangement whereby cablecast programming is originated from tapes, films, cassettes or discs, or as live productions, from one or more locations within the province and is received by persons at one or more other locations within the province and is rendered intelligible by one or more electronic terminal devices: (i) for educational, entertainment, cultural or information purposes; (ii) for a toll; and (iii) by means of a cable system; but does not include any transmission, emission, reception or distribution of signs, signals, writing, images, sounds or intelligence of any nature by means of electromagnetic waves propagated in space without artificial guide. *The Community Cablecasters Act*, R.S.S. 1978, c. C-17, s. 2.

CABLE REEL TRAILER. A vehicle designed to be drawn behind another vehicle for the exclusive purpose of carrying a drum or reel of cable. *Motor Vehicle Safety Regulations*, C.R.C., c. 1038, s. 2.

CABLE SYSTEM. Any poles, wires, cables, amplifiers, anchors, pipes or conduits, or any combination thereof connecting one or more locations within the province from which messages occupying a band width of twenty kilohertz or more are presented with one or more other locations within the province at which such messages are received.

CABLETROUGH. *n.* A raceway consisting of metal troughing and fittings constructed that insulated conductors and cables may be readily installed or removed without injury either to conductors or their covering. See NON-VENTILATED ~; VENTILATED ~.

CABLEWAY. See VENTILATED FLEXIBLE ~.

CAB SIGNAL. A signal located in engineman's compartment or cab, indicating a condition affecting the movement of a train or engine and used in conjunction with interlocking or block signals, or in lieu of block signals. *Regulations No. 0-8, Uniform Code of Operating Rules*, C.R.C., Part III, s. 2.

C.A.C.F.P. *abbr.* Comité d'appel de la commission de la Fonction publique.

CACHEXIA. *n.* The advanced state of constitutional disorders, wasting, anemia, hydremia or weakness. *Meat Inspection Regulations*, C.R.C., c. 1032, s. 46.

CADASTRAL OPERATION. A division, a subdivision, a new subdivision, a redivision, a cancellation, a correction, an addition or a replacement of lot numbers effected under the Cadastre Act. *An Act to Amend Various Legislative Provisions Respecting Municipalities*, S.Q. 1982, c. 2, s. 53.

CADAVER. *n.* A dead body, a corpse.

CADAVERIC. *adj.* Related to a dead body. F.A. Jaffe, *A Guide to Pathological Evidence*, 2d ed. (Toronto: Carswell, 1983) at 171.

CADAVERIC RIGIDITY. See RIGOR MORTIS.

CADAVERIC SPASM. See RIGOR MORTIS.

CADIT QUAESTIO. [L.] The matter allows no further argument.

CAESAREAN OPERATION. Delivery of a fetus through an abdominal incision.

CAETERIS PARIBUS. [L.] Other things being equal.

CAFE CORONARY. Asphyxia caused by a bolus of food impacting the windpipe or larynx. F.A. Jaffe, *A Guide to Pathological Evidence*, 2d ed. (Toronto: Carswell, 1983) at 171.

CAGETENDER. *n.* A person designated to give mine shaft signals, to supervise a shaft conveyance, to maintain discipline, to enforce load limits and to notify the hoist operator of heavy or irregular loads. D. Robertson, *Ontario Health and Safety Guide* (Toronto: Richard De Boo Ltd., 1988) at 5-41.

CAHIERS PROP. INTEL. *abbr.* Les Cahiers de propriété intellectuelle.

C.A.I. *abbr.* 1. Commission d'appel de l'immigration. 2. Décisions de la Commission d'accès à l'information.

CAISSON. *n.* 1. A casing sunk or constructed below ground or water level whether or not it is designed to contain air above atmospheric pressure and includes an excavation drilled by an auger into which a worker enters or is required to enter to work. 2. A deep foundation unit, made of materials such as wood, steel or concrete or combination thereof, which is either premanufactured and placed by driving, jacking, jetting or screwing, or cast-in-place in a hole formed by driving, excavating or boring. *Building Code Act*, R.R.O. 1980, Reg. 87, s. 1.

CALCULATED. *adj.* Intended to produce a certain result, effect.

CALCULATED TO DECEIVE. Describes a trade mark meant to so nearly resemble another that it is likely to deceive or cause confusion about the origin of goods or services or to suggest that the goods or services associated with both trade marks are from the same source. H.G. Fox, *The Canadian Law of Trade Marks and Unfair Competition*, 3d ed. (Toronto: Carswell, 1972) at 672.

CALCULATING POOL. That portion of the total pool remaining after deduction of (a) legal percentages, and (b) where required by these Regulations, monies bet on winning horses. *Race Track Supervision Regulations*, C.R.C., c. 441, s. 2.

CALCULATOR. *n.* A person who calculates the pay-out prices in any pool. *Race Track Supervision Regulations*, C.R.C., c. 441, s. 2. See APPROXIMATE ODDS ~.

CALENDAR. *n.* The order of the division of time into years, months, weeks, days.

CALENDAR MONTH. A period of time of thirty days in April, June, September and November, of thirty-one days in the remainder of the months, except February, which has twenty-eight days, except in a leap-year, when it has twenty-nine days. See MONTH.

CALENDAR QUARTER. A period of three consecutive months ending on the last day of March, June, September or December. *Television Broadcasting Regulations*, C.R.C., c. 381, s. 2.

CALENDAR YEAR. 1. The period from the first day of January to the last day of December then following, inclusive. 2. A period of one year, commencing on any day in the year. See BASE ~; YEAR.

CALF. *n.* 1. A head of cattle under the age of one year. 2. A bovine apparently under six months of age. *Animal Disease and Protection Regulations*, C.R.C., c. 296, s. 2. 3. An immature narwhal that is light in appearance and less than 6 feet in length, measured from the point of the upper jaw to the notch between the tail flukes. *Narwhal Protection Regulations*, C.R.C., c. 820, s. 2.

CALIBRE. *n.* Of a firearm's barrel, the inside diameter. In a rifled barrel, the distance from land to land. F.A. Jaffe, *A Guide to Pathological Evidence*, 2d ed. (Toronto: Carswell, 1983) at 171.

CALL. *v.* 1. To make a request or demand. 2. To demand shareholders pay amount remaining on unpaid shares.

CALL. *n.* 1. Includes instalment, assessment and any other amount paid, payable or agreed to be paid in respect of a share. H. Sutherland, D.B. Horsley & J.M. Edmiston, eds., *Fraser's Handbook on Canadian Company Law*, 7th ed. (Toronto: Carswell, 1985) at 136. 2. An option to demand delivery of a specified number of shares at a fixed price within a specified time but does not include an option or a right to acquire shares of the corporation that granted the option or right to acquire. 3. A request or command to come or assemble. 4. A demand for payment.

CALLABLE. *adj.* Describes an option to pay on call before maturity.

CALL-BACK CLAUSE. A provision that an employee required to report for work receives guaranteed minimum compensation whether or not work is performed. D.J.M. Brown and D.M. Beatty, *Canadian Labour Arbitration*, 2d ed. (Aurora: Canada Law Book, 1977) at 614.

CALL-BACK PAY. A minimum number of hours' pay guaranteed to an employee who is called back to work at a time outside the employee's scheduled hours of work.

CALLING. *n.* A business; occupation; profession; trade; vocation.

CALL-IN CLAUSE. A provision that an employee required to report for work receives guaranteed minimum compensation whether or not work is performed. D.J.M. Brown and D.M. Beatty, *Canadian Labour Arbitration*, 2d ed. (Aurora: Canada Law Book, 1977) at 614.

CALL-IN PAY OR PREMIUM. A minimum number of hours' pay paid to an employee required to report to work outside the employee's scheduled work time.

CALLIPHORA VOMITORIA. The larvae of this common fly hatch in recently dead bodies and help the tissues disintegrate. F.A. Jaffe, *A Guide to Pathological Evidence*, 2d ed. (Toronto: Carswell, 1983) at 171.

CALL NEWSL. *abbr.* CALL Newsletter (Bulletin ACBD).

CALL TO THE BAR. 1. Admission to the Law Society of a province or to membership in the legal profession of a province. 2. The conferral on students of the degree of barrister-at-law.

CALLUS. *n.* Tissue which grows to connect fragments of a broken bone. F.A. Jaffe, *A Guide to Pathological Evidence*, 2d ed. (Toronto: Carswell, 1983) at 171.

CALUMNIATOR. *n.* One who accuses falsely.

CAM. *abbr.* Cameron's Privy Council Decisions, 1832-1929.

CA MAG. *abbr.* CA Magazine.

CAMBIST. *n.* One who deals in bills of exchange and promissory notes.

CAM. DIG. *abbr.* Cameron's Digest.

CAMERA. *n.* 1. A judge's chambers. 2. A room. See IN ~.

CAMERALISTICS. *n.* The study of public finance.

CAMP. *n.* A person's temporary place to live while away from the usual place of residence. See CORRECTIONAL ~; DAY ~; DEFENCE ~; LOGGING ~; OUTPOST ~; RECREATIONAL ~; STANDARD ~; TOURIST ~; TRAILER ~; VACATION ~.

CAMPAIGN EXPENSE. Any expense incurred in relation to an election by or on behalf of a political party, constituency association or candidate during the period commencing with the issue of a writ for an election and terminating on polling day.

CAMPAIGN PERIOD. The period commencing with the issue of the writ for an election and terminating on polling day or at a later date specified by statute.

CAMPBELL'S (LORD) ACT. The vernacular name of the Fatal Accidents Act, 1846, U.K.

CAMPER. *n.* A person in attendance at a camp. See MOBILE ~S.

CAMPGROUND. See PUBLIC ~.

CAMPING. See NON-PROFIT PROGRAM OF ~.

CAMPING ESTABLISHMENT. Premises operated for the accommodation of the travelling or vacationing public comprising land used or maintained as grounds for camping or for parking recreational vehicles.

CAM. S.C. *abbr.* Reports Hitherto Unpublished, Supreme Court of Canada, Cameron, 1880-1900.

CAN. *n.* Includes any hermetically sealed glass bottle, package or container.

CAN. *abbr.* Canada.

CANADA. *n.* (a) The sea bed and subsoil of the submarine areas adjacent to the coasts of Canada in respect of which the Government of Canada or of a province grants a right, licence or privilege to explore for, drill for or take any minerals, petroleum, natural gas or any related hydrocarbons; and (b) the seas and airspace above the submarine areas referred to in paragraph (a) in respect of any activities carried on in connection with the exploration for or exploitation of the minerals, petroleum, natural gas or hydrocarbons referred to in that paragraph. *Income Tax Act*, R.S.C. 1952, c. 148 (as am. S.C. 1980-81-82-83, c. 48, s. 111), s. 255. See ASSETS IN ~; AUDITOR GENERAL OF ~; BANK OF ~; COASTAL WATERS OF ~; COASTING TRADE OF ~; COAST OF ~; CONSTITUTION OF ~; CONSUMERS' ASSOCIATION OF ~; CORPORATION INCORPORATED IN ~; COURT OF ~; DEFENCE OF ~; EASTERN ~; ECONOMIC COUNCIL OF ~; GOVERNMENT OF ~; GOVERNOR OF ~; INFORMATION COMMISSIONER OF ~; INLAND WATERS OF ~; LAW OF ~; LAW REFORM COMMISSION OF ~; LAWS OF ~; LIFE INSURANCE POLICY IN ~; LONG-TERM BONDS OF ~; LOWER ~; MEDICAL RESEARCH COUNCIL OF ~; MINOR WATERS OF ~; MONEY PAID TO ~ FOR A SPECIAL PURPOSE; NATIONAL BUILDING CODE OF ~; NATIONAL LIBRARY OF ~; NATIONAL MUSEUMS OF ~; NATIONAL RESEARCH COUNCIL OF ~; NATURAL RESERVOIR IN ~; NATURAL SCIENCES AND ENGINEERING RESEARCH COUNCIL OF ~; PAID-UP CAPITAL EMPLOYED IN ~; PARLIAMENT OF ~; POLICYHOLDER IN ~; POLICY IN ~; PRIVACY COMMISSIONER OF ~; PUBLISHED IN ~; QUEEN'S PRIVY COUNCIL FOR ~; RESIDENT OF ~; SCIENCE COUNCIL OF ~; SOCIAL SCIENCES AND HUMANITIES RESEARCH COUNCIL OF ~; STANDARDS COUNCIL OF ~; SUPREME COURT OF ~; TREASURY BOARD OF ~; WESTERN ~; WITHIN ~; WORKS FOR THE GENERAL ADVANTAGE OF ~.

CANADA ACT, 1982. The statute of the Parliament of the United Kingdom which gave effect to the Constitution Act, 1982 proclaimed in force April 17, 1982. This statute patriated the Constitution and terminated the power of the U.K. Parliament to legislate for Canada.

CANADA ASSISTANCE PLAN. A group of income-support programmes and social services which began in the 1940s and 1950s. P.W. Hogg, *Constitutional Law of Canada*, 2d ed. (Toronto: Carswell, 1985) at 120.

CANADA CORPORATION. A body corporate incorporated by or under an Act of the Parliament of Canada.

CANADA COUNCIL. A federal body which offers services and grants to arts organizations and professional artists in music, dance, theatre, visual and media arts, writing and publishing.

CANADA DEPOSIT INSURANCE CORPORATION. A federal body with power to insure qualified Canadian currency deposits which member institutions hold and which makes loans to those institutions and to co-operative credit societies, finance corporations and other related organizations.

CANADA FOUNDATION SUBSTANDARD. Shall have on its tag, label or exterior surface a statement, in respect of the seed contained therein, as to the percentage of germination of a representative sample of the seed and the date on which the germination test was completed. *Seeds Regulations*, C.R.C., c. 1400, s. 13.

CANADA LABOUR RELATIONS BOARD. An administrative tribunal whose functions and powers are established by the Canada Labour Code.

CANADA LANDS. 1. Any lands belonging to Her Majesty in right of Canada or of which the Government of Canada has power to dispose that are situated in the Yukon Territory, the Northwest Territories or in any National Park of Canada and any lands under water belonging to Her Majesty in right of Canada or in respect of any rights in which the Government of Canada has power to dispose. 2. Lands that belong to Her Majesty in right of Canada, or in respect of which Her Majesty in right of Canada has the right to dispose of or to exploit the natural resources, and that are situated in (a) the Yukon Territory, the Northwest Territories or Sable Island, or (b) those submarine areas, not within a province, adjacent to the coast of Canada and extending throughout the natural prolongation of the land territory of Canada to the outer edge of the continental margin or to a distance of two hundred nautical miles from the baselines from which the breadth of the territorial sea of Canada is measured, whichever is the greater.

CANADA LANDS SURVEYOR. A person who holds a commission. *Canada Lands Surveys Act*, R.S.C. 1985, c. L-6, s. 2.

CANADA MORTGAGE AND HOUSING CORPORATION. The federal corporation which administers the National Housing Act, insures the mortgage loans which approved lenders make for new and existing homeowner and rental housing or for dwellings which non-profit and co-operative associations build.

CANADA-NEWFOUNDLAND BENEFITS PLAN. A plan for the employment of Canadians and, in particular, members of the labour force of the province and, subject to paragraph (d) of subsection (3), for providing manufacturers, consultants, contractors and service companies in the province and other parts of Canada with a full and fair opportunity to participate on a competitive basis in the supply of goods and services used in any proposed work or activity referred to in the benefits plan. *Canada-Newfoundland Atlantic Accord Implementation (Newfoundland) Act*, S. Nfld. 1986, c. 37, s. 45.

CANADA PEDIGREED GRADE. A grade that contains one of the words "foundation", "registered" or "certified" as part of the grade name. *Seeds Regulations*, C.R.C., c. 1400, s. 2.

CANADA PENSION PLAN. A contributory federal social insurance program which provides income protection, disability and survivor benefits at retirement. K.D. Cooper-Stephenson & I.B. Saunders, *Personal Injury Damages in Canada* (Toronto: Carswell, 1981) at 2.

CANADA POST CORPORATION. The body which gathers, sorts and delivers mail in Canada.

CANADA POST OFFICE. The activities [formerly] conducted under the direction and control of the Postmaster General. *Post Office Act*, R.S.C. 1970, c. P-14, s. 2.

CANADA REGISTERED SUBSTANDARD. Shall have on its tag, label or exterior surface a statement, in respect of the seed contained therein, as to the percentage of germination of a representative sample of the seed and the date on which the germination test was completed. *Seeds Regulations*, C.R.C., c. 1400, s. 13.

CANADA SECURITY. In respect of a life insurer that carried on a business in Canada in a taxation year, means a bond, debenture, mortgage, hypothec, agreement of sale or any other indebtedness that was property used by it in the year in, or held by it in the year in the course of, carrying on its life insurance business in Canada, other than property included in a segregated fund. *Income Tax Act*, R.S.C. 1952, c. 148 (as am. S.C. 1980-81-82-83, c. 140, s. 96(8)), s. 138(12)(c).

CANADA SUPPORTED PUPIL. A pupil who resides on land owned or administered by the

Government of Canada, who attends a school in a division, and for the education of whom the Government of Canada makes contributions to the division. *An Act to Amend the Education Administration Act and the Public Schools Act,* S.M. 1980-81, c. 34, s. 171(1).

CANADA TWIST. The unstemmed, unflavoured and unpressed leaf of tobacco grown in Canada, twisted and made into coils by a manufacturer of tobacco. *Excise Act,* R.S.C. 1985, c. E-14, s. 6.

CANADIAN. *n.* 1. A Canadian citizen. 2. A Canadian government, whether federal, provincial or local, or an agency thereof. 3. An entity that is Canadian-controlled. 4. (a) A resident Canadian, (b) a partnership of which a majority of the members are resident Canadians and in which interests representing in value more than 50 per cent of the total value of the partnership property are owned by resident Canadians, (c) a trust established by a resident Canadian (i) a majority of the trustees of which are resident Canadians, or (ii) in which beneficial interests representing in value more than 50 per cent of the total value of the trust property are owned by resident Canadians, (d) Her Majesty in right of Canada or of a province or territory of Canada or a municipal corporation or public board or commission in Canada, or (e) a body corporate (i) incorporated under the laws of Canada or a province, (ii) of which a majority of the directors are Canadian, and (iii) of which more than 50 per cent of the voting shares are beneficially owned or over which control or direction is exercised by Canadians. *Canada Business Corporations Regulations,* C.R.C., c. 426, s. 51. See NON-~; NON-RESIDENT ~; RESIDENT ~.

CANADIAN ADVISORY COUNCIL ON THE STATUS OF WOMEN. A body established to offer the federal government advice concerning issues which affect women and to increase public awareness of those issues.

CANADIAN AIR CARRIER. Any air carrier that carries on business principally in Canada and (a) is incorporated or registered in Canada, or (b) has its head office in Canada. *Air Carrier Regulations,* C.R.C., c. 3, s. 2.

CANADIAN AIRCRAFT. An aircraft registered in Canada.

CANADIAN AIRCRAFT ENGINE. An aircraft engine (a) that was manufactured in Canada; or (b) on which duty and taxes were paid under the Customs Tariff and the Excise Tax Act. Canada regulations.

CANADIAN AUTHOR. A writer or translator who is a Canadian citizen or who has been

lawfully admitted to Canada for permanent residence.

CANADIAN AUTOMOBILE COMPONENTS. Parts and accessories or parts thereof that are manufactured in Canada and exported out of Canada for use in the manufacture of automobiles in a foreign country. *Automobile Components Remission Order,* C.R.C., c. 742, s. 2.

CANADIAN AVIATION SAFETY BOARD. An independent body with mandate to advance aviation safety. It investigates aviation occurrences, makes public reports of its findings and recommends measures to reduce or eliminate safety problems.

CANADIAN BILL OF RIGHTS. This bill, enacted by 8-9 Elizabeth II, c. 44 (R.S.C. 1985, Appendix III), was the first attempt in Canada to give statutory recognition and protection to certain human rights, fundamental freedoms of religion, speech, assembly and association and the press and procedural rights. See BILL OF RIGHTS.

CANADIAN BRANDY. Spirits distilled exclusively from the juices of native fruits, without the addition of sugar or other saccharine matter. *Excise Act,* R.S.C. 1985, c. E-14, s. 3.

CANADIAN BROADCASTING CORPORATION. The publicly owned corporation with mandate to provide Canada's national broadcasting service.

CANADIAN BUSINESS. Business carried on in Canada that has (a) a place of business in Canada, (b) an individual or individuals in Canada who are employed or self-employed in connection with the business, and (c) assets in Canada used in carrying on the business. *Investment Canada Act,* R.S.C. 1985 (1st Supp.), c. 28, s. 3. See NEW ~.

CANADIAN CHARTER OF RIGHTS AND FREEDOMS. Part I of the Constitution Act, 1982 which guarantees rights and freedoms. See CHARTER.

CANADIAN CITIZEN. A citizen within the meaning of the Citizenship Act. *Immigration Act,* R.S.C. 1985, c. I-2, s. 2.

CANADIAN COAST GUARD SHIP. A government ship entrusted for management or operation to the Marine Operations Branch of the Department of Transport. *Registration of Government Ships Regulations,* C.R.C., c. 1463, s. 2.

CANADIAN COMMODITY FUTURES EXAMINATION. An examination relating to the Canadian commodity futures industry that has been prepared and is administered by the Canadian Securities Institute.

CANADIAN COMPANY. A company formed or incorporated by or under any Act of Parliament of Canada or of the Legislature of any province.

CANADIAN CONTENT. (a) Any materials or supplies, (b) any services of a professional or non-professional or other nature, or (c) the financial arrangements which are or may be purchased, used, required, created, obtained, manufactured, produced, refined, assembled, loaned, secured, assured or hypothecated, as the case may be, in Canada, by or from (d) an individual who is a Canadian citizen or a person ordinarily resident in Canada, (e) a corporation incorporated in Canada that maintains one or more establishments in Canada to which employees of the corporation employed in connection with the business ordinarily report for work, and (f) any number of individuals described in paragraph (d) or corporations described in paragraph (e) or combination of those individuals or corporations, if any one or more of those comprising that number or combination are either individuals who, either alone or jointly, or in concert with one or more other individuals or corporations, control or are in a position to control the conduct of business. *National Energy Board Rules of Practice and Procedure*, C.R.C., c. 1057, s. 2.

CANADIAN-CONTROLLED PRIVATE CORPORATION. A private corporation that is a Canadian corporation other than a corporation controlled, directly or indirectly in any manner whatever, by one or more non-resident persons, by one or more public corporations (other than a prescribed venture capital corporation) or by any combination thereof. *Income Tax Act*, R.S.C. 1952, c. 148 (as am. S.C. 1984, c. 45, s. 40), s. 125(7)(b).

CANADIAN CORPORATION. 1. At any time means a corporation that was resident in Canada at that time and was (i) incorporated in Canada, or (ii) resident in Canada throughout the period commencing June 18, 1971 and ending at that time. *Income Tax Act*, R.S.C. 1952, c. 148 (as am. S.C. 1977-78, c. 1, s. 44(1)), s. 89(1)(a). 2. A corporation incorporated by or under a law of Canada or a province. *Bank Act*, R.S.C. 1985, c. B-1, s. 193.

CANADIAN CUSTOMS WATERS. The waters forming that part of the sea that is adjacent to and extends nine marine miles beyond Canadian waters.

CANADIAN DOMESTIC AIRSPACE. All navigable airspace of Canada designated and defined as such in the Designated Airspace Handbook. Canada regulations.

CANADIAN ELECTRICAL CODE. The code of electrical facility standards published by the Canadian Standards Association as amended from time to time. *Canada Electrical Safety Regulations*, C.R.C., c. 998, s. 2.

CANADIAN EQUIPMENT. Equipment manufactured in Canada or entered for consumption into Canada in accordance with the Customs Tariff and Excise Tax Act. *Exposed and Processed Film and Recorded Video Tape Remission Order*, C.R.C., c. 763, s. 2.

CANADIAN EQUIVALENT RATE. The interest rate that the issuer of the foreign debt would have been required to undertake to pay if the debt had been issued in Canada.

CANADIAN FABRIC. A fabric that has been woven in Canada, whether or not it contains imported materials. *Customs Drawback Shirting Fabrics Regulations*, C.R.C., c. 487, s. 2.

CANADIAN FEATURE FILM. A feature film or feature film production which will have a significant Canadian creative, artistic and technical content, and that arrangements have been made to ensure that the copyright in the completed film will be beneficially owned by an individual resident in Canada, by a corporation incorporated under the laws of Canada or a province or by any combination of such persons; or that provision has been made for the production of the film under a co-production agreement entered into between Canada and another country.

CANADIAN FILM. Film manufactured in Canada or entered for consumption into Canada in accordance with the Customs Tariff and Excise Tax Act. *Exposed and Processed Film and Recorded Video Tape Remission Order*, C.R.C., c. 763, s. 2.

CANADIAN FISHERIES WATERS. All waters in the fishing zones of Canada, all waters in the territorial sea of Canada and all internal waters of Canada.

CANADIAN FISHING VESSEL. A fishing vessel that is registered or licensed in Canada under the Canada Shipping Act and is owned by one or more persons each of whom is a Canadian citizen, a person resident and domiciled in Canada or a corporation incorporated under the laws of Canada or of a province, having its principal place of business in Canada, or that is not required to be registered or licensed in Canada but is owned as described.

CANADIAN FORCES. The armed forces of Her Majesty raised by Canada. See OVERSEAS ~ SCHOOL STAFF.

CANADIAN FORCES ELECTOR. A member of the Canadian Forces who is qualified and entitled to vote under Special Voting Rules. *Special Voting Rules*, R.S.C. 1985, c. E-2, Schedule II, s. 2.

CANADIAN FORCES POST OFFICE. A military post office operated outside Canada by the Canadian Forces Postal Services to provide postal facilities for a Canadian formation outside Canada and for Canadian naval ships on cruise to a place that is not in Canada, the United States or any possession of the United States. Canada regulations.

CANADIAN GOODS. Goods that are the growth, produce or manufacture of Canada. *Canadian Goods Abroad Remission Order*, C.R.C., c. 747, s. 2.

CANADIAN GOVERNMENT RAILWAYS. (a) The lines of railway or parts thereof, (b) the property, works or interests, and (c) the powers, rights or privileges the management and operation of which are entrusted to the National Company by any order in council.

CANADIAN HUMAN RIGHTS COMMISSION. The federal commission which administers the Canadian Human Rights Act.

CANADIAN IMPORT TRIBUNAL. The federal tribunal which determines if subsidized, dumped or low-cost imports threaten or cause material injury to production of like goods in Canada.

CANADIAN INTERNATIONAL DEVELOPMENT AGENCY. The federal body which controls and supervises the official international development assistance program of Canada.

CANADIAN INVESTMENT FINANCE COURSE. A course prepared and conducted by the Canadian Securities Institute.

CANADIAN INVESTMENT FUNDS COURSE. A course prepared and conducted by the Educational Division of the Investment Funds Institute of Canada.

CANADIAN ISSUE. (i) In relation to a newspaper, an issue, including a special issue, (A) the type of which, other than the type for advertisements or features, is set in Canada, (B) the whole of which, exclusive of any comics supplement, is printed in Canada, (C) that is edited in Canada by individuals resident in Canada, (D) that is published in Canada, and (ii) in relation to a periodical, an issue, including a special issue, (A) the type of which, other than the type for advertisements, is set in Canada, (B) that is printed in Canada, (C) that is edited in Canada by individuals resident in Canada, (D) that is published in Canada, but does not include an issue of periodical (E) that is produced or published under a licence granted by a person who produces or publishes issues of a periodical that are printed, edited or published outside Canada, or (F) the contents of which, excluding advertisements, are substantially the same as the contents of an issue of a periodical, or the contents of one or more issues of one or more periodicals, that was or were printed, edited or published outside Canada. *Income Tax Act*, R.S.C. 1952, c. 148 (as added by S.C. 1965, c. 18, s. 4), c. 19(5)(a).

CANADIAN JUDICIAL COUNCIL. A body constituted to encourage better, uniform, and efficient judicial service in county and superior courts.

CANADIAN LABOUR CONGRESS. See CENTRAL LABOUR CONGRESS.

CANADIAN MARITIME LAW. Administered by the Exchequer Court of Canada on its Admiralty side by virtue of the Admiralty Act, chapter A-1 of the Revised Statutes of Canada, 1970, or any other statute, or that would have been so administered if that Court had had, on its Admiralty side, unlimited jurisdiction in relation to maritime and admiralty matters, as that law has been altered by this Act or any other Act of Parliament. *Federal Court Act*, R.S.C. 1985, c. F-7, s. 2.

CANADIAN NATIONAL. Canadian national as defined in the Canadian Nationals Act, chapter 21 of the Revised Statutes of Canada, 1927. *Civilian War Pensions and Allowances Act*, R.S.C. 1985, c. C-31, s. 6.

CANADIAN NATIONAL RAILWAY COMPANY. A national communications and transportation company.

CANADIAN NATIONAL RAILWAYS. (a) The National Company, (b) all the companies in Canada mentioned or referred to in the schedule and any company formed by any consolidation or amalgamation of any two or more of those companies, and (c) all companies in Canada controlled directly or indirectly by the National Company and declared by the Governor in Council to be comprised in Canadian National Railways. *Canadian National Railways Act*, R.S.C. 1985, c. C-19, s. 2.

CANADIAN NEWSPAPER. See DAILY ~; WEEKLY ~.

CANADIAN NEWSPAPER OR PERIODICAL. A newspaper or periodical the exclusive right to produce and publish issues of which is held by one or more of the following: (i) a Canadian citizen, (ii) a partnership of which at least 3/4 of the members are Canadian citizens and in which interests representing in value at least 3/4 of the total value of the partnership property are beneficially owned by Canadian citizens, (iii) an association or society of which at least 3/4 of the members are Canadian citizens, (iv) Her Majesty in right of Canada or a province, or a municipality in Canada, or (v) a corporation (A) that is incorporated under the laws of Canada or a province, (B) of which the chairman or other presiding officer and at least 3/4 of the directors or other similar officers are Canadian citizens, and (C) of which, if it is a corporation having share capital, at least 3/4 of the shares having full voting rights under all circumstances, and shares representing in the aggregate at least 3/4 of the paid-up capital, are beneficially owned by Canadian citizens or by corporations other than corporations controlled by citizens or subjects of a country other than Canada. *Income Tax Act*, R.S.C. 1952, c. 148 (as. am. S.C. 1988, c. 55, s. 11), s. 19(5)(b).

CANADIAN NON-RESIDENT. Any person who is not a resident but who is domiciled in Canada. *Wild-life Conservation Act*, S.Q. 1978, c. 65, s. 1.

CANADIAN OFFENDER. A Canadian citizen, within the meaning of the Citizenship Act, irrespective of age, who has been found guilty of an offence and is subject to supervision either in confinement or at large by reason of parole, probation or any other form of supervision without confinement, in a foreign state. *Transfer of Offenders Act*, R.S.C. 1985, c. T-15, s. 2.

CANADIAN-OWNED. *adj.* Wholly owned by any of the following individuals, corporations or groups carrying on business in Canada: (a) an individual who is a resident of Canada within the meaning of section 250 of the Income Tax Act, (b) a corporation incorporated in Canada under federal or provincial law, or (c) a group comprised of individuals or corporations or both at least one of the members of which is a person referred to in paragraph (a) or (b). *Customs and Excise Offshore Application Act*, R.S.C. 1985, c. C-53, s. 2.

CANADIAN OWNERSHIP RATE. The level of Canadian ownership as determined under this Act or any other Act of Parliament providing for the determination of Canadian ownership rates. *Oil and Gas Act*, R.S.C. 1985, c. O-6, s. 2.

CANADIAN PARTNERSHIP. (a) A partnership all of the members of which were, at any time in respect of which the expression is relevant, resident in Canada, and (b) a reference to a person or a taxpayer who is a member of a particular partnership shall include a reference to another partnership that is a member of the particular partnership. *Income Tax Act*, R.S.C. 1952, c. 148 (as am. S.C. 1986, c. 55, s. 27(1)), s. 102.

CANADIAN PAYMENTS ASSOCIATION. A corporation whose members are: (a) The Bank of Canada; (b) any bank under the Bank Act, and any savings bank under the Quebec Savings Bank Act; (c) any trust company, loan company, central cooperative credit society, some credit unions, and any other party who "accepts deposits transferable by order to a third party", if that party meets certain requirements. I.F.G. Baxter, *The Law of Banking*, 3d ed. (Toronto: Carswell, 1981) at 174.

CANADIAN PRINCIPAL EQUIVALENT. The amount in Canadian dollars that, on the basis of the rate of exchange that applies to the foreign debt, equals the face value in the currency or unit of monetary value of the foreign debt. *Energy Rate Stabilization Act*, S.M. 1979, c. 42, s. 1.

CANADIAN PRODUCER. A person who produces in Canada any textile and clothing goods. *Textile and Clothing Board Act*, R.S.C. 1985, c. T-9, s. 2.

CANADIAN PROPERTY. (a) Property of a corporation that would be taxable Canadian property if at no time in the year the corporation had been resident in Canada, and (ii) any other property not being foreign property within the meaning assigned by section 206. *Income Tax Act*, R.S.C. 1952, c. 148 (as am. S.C. 1974-75-76, c. 26, s. 90(1)), s. 133(8)(b).

CANADIAN RADIO-TELEVISION AND TELECOMMUNICATIONS COMMISSION. The federal body which supervises and regulates every aspect of Canadian broadcasting (television, radio, cable and pay television and specialty services) and regulates federal telecommunications carriers.

CANADIAN REFERENCE STANDARD. When used with reference to a sex hormone product the standard established by the Director from whom portions thereof for the comparative testing may be obtained. *Food and Drug Regulations*, C.R.C., c. 870, s. C.02.001.

CANADIAN REGISTERED COMPANY. An insurer that is registered under the Canadian and British Insurance Companies Act (Canada), or under the Foreign Insurance Companies Act (Canada), and in either case has obtained its certificate of registry from the Minister of Finance of Canada. *Insurance Act*, R.S.A. 1980, c. I-5, s. 1.

CANADIAN RESOURCE PROPERTY. Of a taxpayer means any property of the taxpayer that is (i) any right, licence or privilege to explore for, drill for or take petroleum, natural gas or related hydrocarbons in Canada, (ii) any right, licence or privilege to (A) store underground petroleum, natural gas or related hydrocarbons in Canada, or (B) prospect, explore, drill or mine for minerals in a minerals resource in Canada, (iii) any oil or gas well in Canada or any real property in Canada the principal value of which depends upon its petroleum or natural gas content (but not including any depreciable property used or to be used in connection with the extraction or removal of petroleum or natural gas therefrom), (iv) any rental or royalty computed by reference to the amount or value of production from an oil or gas well in Canada or from a natural accumulation of petroleum or natural gas in Canada, (v) any rental or royalty computed by reference to the amount or value of production from a mineral resource in Canada, (vi) any real property in Canada the principal value of which depends upon its mineral resource content (but not including any depreciable property used or to be used in connection with the extraction or removal of minerals therefrom), or (vii) any right to or interest in any property described in any of subparagraphs (i) to (vi), other than such a right or interest that the taxpayer has by virtue of being a beneficiary of a trust. *Income Tax Act*, R.S.C. 1952, c. 148 (as am. S.C. 1986, c. 6, s. 31(2)), c. 66(15)(c).

CANADIAN SALT WATER FISHERMAN. A British subject who served on a ship engaged in the fishing industry of Canada in Canadian tidal waters. *Civilian War Pensions and Allowances Act*, R.S.C. 1985, c. C-31, s. 6.

CANADIAN SECURITIES COURSE. A course prepared and conducted by the Canadian Securities Institute and so designated.

CANADIAN SECURITIES DEALER. A person who holds, under a law of a province relating to trading in securities, a subsisting and unsuspended licence or registration that entitles him to trade in the shares of companies. *Northern Mineral Exploration Assistance Regulations*, C.R.C., c. 332, s. 2.

CANADIAN SECURITY. A security (other than a prescribed security) that is a share of the capital stock of a corporation resident in Canada, a unit of a mutual fund trust or a bond, debenture, bill, note, mortgage, hypothec or similar obligation issued by a person resident in Canada. *Income Tax Act*, R.S.C. 1952, c. 148 (as am. S.C. 1986, c. 6, s. 17(5)), s. 39(6).

CANADIAN SERVICE. Any period of service, other than Newfoundland service, that may be counted as pensionable service for the purposes of the Act. *Public Service Superannuation Regulations*, C.R.C., c. 1358, s. 42.

CANADIAN SHIP. A ship registered in Canada either under this Act or under the Merchant Shipping Acts before August 1, 1936. *Canada*

Shipping Act, R.S.C. 1985, c. S-9, s. 2. See HER MAJESTY'S ~.

CANADIAN STANDARDS ASSOCIATION. A national standard-setting organization which certifies products covered by its standards. D. Robertson, *Ontario Health and Safety Guide* (Toronto: Richard De Boo Ltd., 1988) at 5-42.

CANADIAN TRANSPORT COMMISSION. The federal body which regulates transportation which is under federal jurisdiction in Canada (i.e. by air, water, rail and commodity pipeline) and certain kinds of interprovincial commercial motor transport.

CANADIAN VEHICLE. A vehicle that (a) was manufactured in Canada, or (b) was entered into Canada for consumption pursuant to the Customs Tariff and the Excise Tax Act. *Canadian Goods Abroad Remission Order*, C.R.C., c. 747, s. 2.

CANADIAN VESSEL. A vessel that (a) was manufactured in Canada, or (b) was entered into Canada for consumption pursuant to the Customs Tariff and the Excise Tax Act. *Canadian Goods Abroad Remission Order*, C.R.C., c. 747, s. 2.

CANADIAN VIDEO TAPE. Video tape manufactured in Canada or entered for consumption into Canada in accordance with the Customs Tariff and Excise Tax Act. *Exposed and Processed Film and Recorded Video Tape Remission Order*, C.R.C., c. 763, s. 2.

CANADIAN WARSHIP. A ship of war, a military transport or a military supply ship owned, operated or controlled by the Government of Canada. Canada regulations.

CANADIAN WATERS. The territorial sea of Canada and all internal waters of Canada.

CANADIAN WHEAT BOARD. The federal body, established under the Canadian Wheat Board Act, which supervises export sales of barley, oats and wheat produced in Western Canada and domestic sales of these grains intended for human consumption. It controls the delivery of all major grains, coordinating grain movement to terminal elevators.

CANAL. *n.* A canal, lock or navigable channel and all works and property appertaining or incidental to the canal, lock or channel. See OWNERS OF A DOCK OR ~.

CAN-AM L.J. *abbr.* Canadian-American Law Journal.

CAN. BANKER. *abbr.* Canadian Banker.

CAN. BAR J. *abbr.* Canadian Bar Journal.

CAN. BAR REV. *abbr.* The Canadian Bar Review (La Revue du Barreau canadien).

CAN. BUS. L.J. *abbr.* Canadian Business Law Journal (Revue canadienne du droit de commerce).

CANCEL. *v.* In the case of an instrument, to draw lines across it intending to indicate it is no longer in force.

CANCELLATION. See PURCHASE FOR ~.

CANCELLATION CLAUSE. A clause in an agreement that permits the parties to cancel and terminate their agreement.

CANCELLED CHEQUE. A cheque which bears the indication that it has been honoured by the bank upon which it was drawn.

CANCELLI. *n.* [L. lattice] 1. The rails enclosing the bar of a court. 2. The lines drawn on the face of a document indicating the document is revoked or annulled.

CANCER. *n.* Includes all forms and types of malignant and premalignant conditions.

CAN. C.L.G. *abbr.* Canadian Commercial Law Guide.

CAN. COMMUNIC. L. REV. *abbr.* Canadian Communications Law Review.

CAN. COMMUNITY L.J. *abbr.* Canadian Community Law Journal (Revue canadienne de droit communautaire).

CAN. COMPET. POLICY REC. *abbr.* Canadian Competition Policy Record.

CAN. COMP. POL. REC. *abbr.* Canadian Competition Policy Record.

CAN. COMPUTER L.R. *abbr.* Canadian Computer Law Reporter

CAN. COM. R. *abbr.* Canadian Commercial Reports, 1901-1905.

CAN. COUNCIL INT. L. *abbr.* Canadian Council on International Law. Conference. Proceedings. (Conseil canadien de droit international. Congrès. Travaux).

CAN. COUNCIL INT'L L. PROC. *abbr.* Canadian Council on International Law, Proceedings.

CAN. CRIM. FORUM. *abbr.* Canadian Criminology Forum (Le Forum canadien de criminologie).

CAN. CURR. TAX. *abbr.* Canadian Current Tax.

CAN. CURRENT TAX. *abbr.* Canadian Current Tax.

CANDELA. *n.* The unit for the measurement of luminous intensity, being the luminous inten-

sity, in the perpendicular direction, of a surface of 1/600 000 square metre of a full radiator at the temperature of freezing platinum under a pressure of 101 325 newtons per square metre.

C. & F. *abbr.* Cost and freight. In a sales contract, means that the price includes cost and freight and the buyer must arrange insurance.

CANDIDATE. *n.* 1. Any person elected to serve as a member, and any person who has been nominated as a candidate at an election. 2. An applicant for a commission. *Canada Lands Surveys Act*, R.S.C. 1985, c. L-6, s. 2. See AGENT OF A ~; ELECTION EXPENSES OF A ~; INDEPENDENT ~; OFFICIAL ~.

CANDIDATE AT AN ELECTION. A person elected to serve in a legislature and a person who is nominated as a candidate at an election who declares or is declared by others to be a candidate on or after the date of the issue of the writ or after the dissolution or vacancy in consequence of which the writ has been issued.

CANDIDATE OF AN AUTHORIZED PARTY. A person designated by an authorized party to be the candidate of this party for office as member of the council, whose nomination-paper has been accepted by the returning-officer. *An Act respecting the 1978 elections in certain municipalities and amending the Cities and Towns Act*, S.Q. 1978, c. 63, s. 2.

CANDIDATE'S AGENT. A person authorized in writing by a candidate to represent that candidate at an election or at any proceeding of an election.

CANDLING. *n.* Examination of the internal condition of an egg by rotating it in front of or over a source of light that illuminates the contents.

C & S. *abbr.* Clarke & Scully's Drainage Cases (Ont.), 1898-1903.

CANDY. *n.* Cocaine.

CANDY MAN. A seller of cocaine.

CANE. See WHITE ~.

CAN. ENV. L.N. *abbr.* Canadian Environmental Law News.

CAN. F.L.G. *abbr.* Canadian Family Law Guide.

CAN. H.R. ADVOC. *abbr.* Canadian Human Rights Advocate.

CAN. HUM. RTS. Y.B. *abbr.* Canadian Human Rights Yearbook (Annuaire canadien des droits de le personne).

CAN. IND. REL. ASSOC. *abbr.* Canadian Industrial Relations Association. Annual Meeting. Proceedings (Association canadienne des relations industrielles. Congrès. Travaux).

CAN. INTELL. PROP. REV. *abbr.* Canadian Intellectual Property Review.

CAN. I.T.G.R. *abbr.* Canada Income Tax Guide Report.

CAN. J. CRIM. *abbr.* Canadian Journal of Criminology (Revue canadienne de criminologie).

CAN. J. CRIM. & CORR. *abbr.* Canadian Journal of Criminology and Corrections.

CAN. J. FAM. L. *abbr.* Canadian Journal of Family Law (Revue canadienne de droit familial).

CAN. J. INS. L. *abbr.* Canadian Journal of Insurance Law.

CAN. J.L. & JURIS. *abbr.* The Canadian Journal of Law and Jurisprudence.

CAN. J.L. & SOCIETY. *abbr.* Canadian Journal of Law and Society (Revue canadienne de droit et société).

CAN. J. WOMEN & LAW. *abbr.* Canadian Journal of Women and the Law (Revue juridique "La femme et le droit").

CAN. LAW. *abbr.* Canadian Lawyer.

CAN. LAWYER. *abbr.* Canadian Lawyer.

CAN. LEGAL STUD. *abbr.* Canadian Legal Studies.

CAN. L.J. *abbr.* Canada Law Journal.

CAN. L.R.B.R. *abbr.* Canadian Labour Relations Board Reports, 1974-.

[ ] CAN. L.R.B.R. *abbr.* Canadian Labour Relations Board Reports.

CAN. L. REV. *abbr.* Canadian Law Review (1901-1907).

CAN. L.T. (1881-1922). *abbr.* Canadian Law Times.

CAN. MUN. J. *abbr.* Canadian Municipal Journal.

CANNED BEANS. Canned green or wax beans packed in any style set out in this section. *Processed Fruit and Vegetable Regulations*, C.R.C., c. 291, Schedule I, s. 10(1).

CANNED BEANS WITH SEASONING. Canned green or wax beans packed in any style outlined in this section with the addition of not more than 15 per cent by weight of the product of any or all of the following ingredients: dill seeds, dill flavourings, vinegar, pieces of green peppers, pieces of red peppers, tomatoes, onions, garlic and any other natural flavouring ingre-

dient. *Processed Fruit and Vegetable Regulations*, C.R.C., c. 291, Schedule I, s. 10(1).

CANNED BERRIES. Includes such small fruits as raspberries, blackberries, boysenberries, currants, gooseberries, loganberries, lawtonberries and thimbleberries. *Processed Fruit and Vegetable Regulations*, C.R.C., c. 291, Schedule I, s. 17(1).

CANNED FISH. Includes any fish packed in a hermetically sealed container and treated with heat to prevent spoilage and to destroy pathogenic organisms.

CANNED FOODS. Includes foods except fish and shellfish that have been pre-heated, cooked, preserved, condensed, evaporated, dehydrated, dried, or otherwise processed or prepared for food, and are placed in any closed can, bottle, package, or container. *Meat and Canned Foods Act*, R.S.C. 1970, c. M-6, s. 2.

CANNED FRUITS AND FRUIT PRODUCTS. (a) Shall be the product prepared by heat processing properly prepared fresh fruit, with or without sugar, invert sugar, dextrose or glucose, in dry or liquid form, (b) shall be packed in hermetically sealed containers, and (c) may contain, in the case of a particular fruit or fruit product, any other substance the addition of which to that fruit or fruit product is authorized in this Table. *Processed Fruit and Vegetable Regulations*, C.R.C., c. 291, Schedule I, s. 1.

CANNED MUSHROOMS. The product prepared from clean, sound, fresh mushrooms of the cultivated type packed with or without salt, ascorbic acid, citric acid or any combination thereof. *Processed Fruit and Vegetable Regulations*, C.R.C., c. 291, Schedule I, s. 35.

CANNED PEACHES. Peaches packed "whole", "halved", "sliced", "diced" or "quartered". *Processed Fruit and Vegetable Regulations*, C.R.C., c. 291, Schedule I, s. 36.

CANNED PEARS. Pears packed "whole", "halved", "sliced", "diced" or "quartered". *Processed Fruit and Vegetable Regulations*, C.R.C., c. 291, Schedule I, s. 37.

CANNED POTATO PRODUCTS PLANT. Includes any plant where raw potatoes are peeled and shaped for distribution in a canned and preserved condition. *Potato Processing Plant Liquid Effluent Regulations*, C.R.C., c. 829, s. 2.

CANNED SWEET POTATOES. Sweet potatoes packed in a liquid packing medium consisting of water or a syrup or else "vacuum packed" without any packing media. *Processed Fruit and Vegetable Regulations*, C.R.C., c. 291, Schedule I, s. 45.

CANNED VEGETABLES. (a) Shall be the

product prepared by heat processing properly prepared fresh vegetables, with or without (i) sugar, invert sugar, dextrose or glucose in dry or liquid form, (ii) salt, and (iii) a firming agent, (b) shall be packed in hermetically sealed containers, and (c) may contain, in the case of a particular vegetable, any other substance, the addition of which to that vegetable is authorized in this Table. *Processed Fruit and Vegetable Regulations*, C.R.C., c. 291, Schedule I, s. 1.

CANNERY. *n.* The buildings, structures, machinery, appurtenances, appliances, apparatus and chemicals occupied or used in the business of canning or bottling fish or shellfish. See HERRING ~; SALMON ~; SHELLFISH ~; TUNA FISH ~.

CANON. *n.* 1. A rule of law. 2. A church dignitary.

CANONIST. *n.* A professor of church law.

CANON LAW. A body of Roman church law, compiled from the opinions of the fathers of the church, the decrees of general councils and the Vatican.

CANOPY. *n.* Any roof-like structure projecting more than twelve inches from the wall of a building.

CAN. PETRO. TAX J. *abbr.* Canadian Petroleum Tax Journal.

CAN. PUB. POL. *abbr.* Canadian Public Policy.

CAN. S.L.R. *abbr.* Canadian Securities Law Reports.

CAN. S.T.R. *abbr.* Canadian Sales Tax Reports.

CAN. TAX FOUND. *abbr.* Canadian Tax Foundation (Conference Report).

CAN. TAX J. *abbr.* Canadian Tax Journal (Revue fiscale canadienne).

CAN. TAX N. *abbr.* Canadian Tax News.

CAN. TAX'N: J. TAX POL'Y. *abbr.* Canadian Taxation: A Journal of Tax Policy.

CANTEEN. *n.* A wardroom, mess, cafeteria, dining area, common room, or other room to which the public is not ordinarily admitted situated in or on a base, station, camp, campus, institution or other facility. See FORCES ~; MILITARY ~.

CAN.-U.S. L.J. *abbr.* Canada-United States Law Journal.

CANVASS. *v.* To personally solicit votes or donations.

CANVASSER. *n.* Any person who approaches electors to obtain their votes in favour of a candidate. *Election Act*, R.S.Q. 1977, c. E-3, s. 2.

CAN. Y.B. INT. L. *abbr.* Canadian Year Book of International Law (Annuaire canadien de droit international).

CAN. Y.B. INT'L. L. *abbr.* Canadian Year Book of International Law.

CAP. *n.* A capsule; a quantity of a drug like cocaine. F.A. Jaffe, *A Guide to Pathological Evidence*, 2d ed. (Toronto: Carswell, 1983) at 171. See BLACK ~.

CAP. *abbr.* Chapter.

C.A.P.A.C. *abbr.* Composers, Authors and Publishers Association of Canada Limited.

CAPACITY. *n.* The capacity to understand and appreciate the nature of a consent or agreement and the consequences of giving, withholding, or revoking the consent or making, not making or terminating the agreement. *Child and Family Services Act*, S.O. 1984, c. 55, s. 4. See CARRYING ~; CONTRACTUAL ~; DESIGN ~; FISCAL ~; FULL-LOAD ~; MAXIMUM ~; RATED BED ~; RATED ~; RATED GENERATOR ~; REPRESENTATIVE ~; TESTAMENTARY ~; TRUST ~.

CAPAX DOLI. [L.] Capable of committing crime.

CAPELIN. *n.* A fish of the species Mallotus villosus. *Northwest Atlantic Fisheries Regulations*, C.R.C., c. 860, s. 2.

CAPIAS. [L. that you take] The name of writs which direct the sheriff to arrest the person named in the writs.

CAPIAS AD AUDIENDUM JUDICIUM. [L. that you take to hear judgment] A writ of capias issued in order to bring a criminal to receive judgment.

CAPIAS AD RESPONDENDUM. [L. that you take to answer] A writ issued for the arrest of a person.

CAPIAS AD SATISFACIENDUM. [L. that you take to satisfy] A writ for the arrest of the judgment debtor in a civil action when the judgment had not been satisfied.

CAPIAS EXTENDI FACIAS. [L. that you take and cause to be extended] A writ of execution issued against a debtor of the Crown, commanding the sheriff to arrest the debtor and "cause to be extended" the debtor's lands and goods.

CAPIAS IN WITHERNAM. [L. and AS. that you take by way of reprisals] A writ directing the sheriff to take other goods of the defendant when the goods ordered to be replevied were concealed so that the sheriff could not replevy them.

CAPIAS PRO FINE. [L. that you take for the fine] A writ issued for the arrest of a person who was fined for an offence.

CAPITAL. *n.* 1. The means with which a business is carried on. 2. In estates, used in contradistinction to income. 3. Money raised through issuing shares, certificates, bonds, debentures, long-term notes or any other long-term obligation, contributed or earned surplus and reserves. See AUTHORIZED ~; CIRCULATING ~; EQUITY ~; FIXED ~; FLOATING ~; ISSUED ~; LIQUID ~; LOAN ~; NATIONAL ~ COMMISSION; NATIONAL ~ REGION; NOMINAL ~; PAID-UP ~; SHARE ~; STATED ~; SUBSCRIBED ~; UNCALLED ~; WORKING ~.

CAPITAL ACCOUNT. The amount by which the assets of a person employed in the business exceed the liabilities arising from the business and all money advanced or loaned to the person for capital account.

CAPITAL ASSETS. Things used in a business to earn the income — land, buildings, plant, machinery, motor vehicles, ships. *Canada Steamship Lines Ltd. v. M.N.R.*, [1966] C.T.C. 255; 66 D.T.C. 5305 (Exch. Ct.).

CAPITAL BASE. The shareholders' equity of a company.

CAPITAL COST. The cost involved in acquiring, constructing, designing, equipping, adding to, replacing or altering a capital work. See ORIGINAL ~.

CAPITAL EXPENDITURE. An outlay or the incurrence of a liability for the construction or acquisition or, for the addition to, a tangible asset.

CAPITAL FUND. The Alberta Capital Fund. *Financial Administration Amendment Act*, S.A. 1986, c. 16, s. 1(1).

CAPITAL GAIN. The profit earned when property is sold for more than was paid for it. See TAXABLE ~.

CAPITAL GAIN OR LOSS. The difference between the proceeds of disposition and the combination of the adjusted cost base and any expenses incurred when making the disposition. W. Grover & F. Iacobucci, *Materials of Canadian Income Tax*, 4th ed. (Toronto: Richard De Boo Ltd., 1980) at 485.

CAPITAL IMPROVEMENT. An addition to or an extension, enlargement, alteration, replacement or other improvement of a work of such nature or character that it is usually and properly

accounted for as a capital asset. *Municipal Act*, R.S.O. 1980, c. 302, s. 218.

CAPITAL INTEREST. Of a taxpayer in a trust means (i) in the case of a personal trust or prescribed trust, a right (whether immediate or future and whether absolute or contingent) of the taxpayer as a beneficiary under the trust to, or to receive, all or any part of the capital of the trust, and (ii) in any other case, a right of the taxpayer as a beneficiary under the trust. *Income Tax Act*, R.S.C. 1952, c. 148 (as am. S.C. 1988, c. 55, s. 75(2)), s. 108(1)(c).

CAPITALISATION. *var.* **CAPITALIZATION.** *n.* 1. The total amount of shares and other securities issued by a corporation. 2. An estimate of yearly revenue in terms of the amount of capital which it is necessary to invest at a given rate of interest in order to receive that revenue. See NET ~.

CAPITAL LOSS. See ALLOWABLE ~; CAPITAL GAIN OR LOSS; CARRY-OVER OF ~ES.

CAPITAL MAINTENANCE. Replacement of the capital resources of a firm before profit is calculated. W. Grover & F. Iacobucci, *Materials on Canadian Income Tax*, 4th ed. (Toronto: Richard De Boo Ltd., 1980) at 601.

CAPITAL MURDER. A classification formerly used under the Criminal Code where a person personally caused or assisted in causing the death of (a) a police officer, police constable, constable, sheriff, deputy sheriff, sheriff's officer or other person employed for the preservation and maintenance of the public peace, acting in the course of that officer's duties, or (b) the warden, deputy warden, instructor, keeper, gaoler, guard or other officer or permanent employee of a prison, acting in the course of that officer's duties, or counselled or procured another person to do any act causing or assisting in causing the death.

CAPITAL PROPERTY. (i) Any depreciable property of the taxpayer, and (ii) any property (other than depreciable property), any gain or loss from the disposition of which would, if the property were disposed of, be a capital gain or a capital loss, as the case may be, of the taxpayer. *Income Tax Act*, R.S.C. 1952, c. 148 (as am. S.C. 1970-71-72, c. 63), s. 54(b).

CAPITAL PUNISHMENT. Punishment by death.

CAPITAL RECEIPTS. All principal money received by a province from the sale of Crown lands, or other assets of a province and all principal repayments of capital advances and principal money received through the sale, pledge or other disposition of securities of a province for capital purposes.

CAPITAL SECURITY. Any share of any class of shares of a company or any bond, debenture, note or other obligation of a company, whether secured or unsecured.

CAPITAL STOCK. See PAID IN ~.

CAPITAL TRANSACTION. The general concept is that a transaction whereby an enduring asset or advantage is acquired for the business is a capital transaction. *Associated Investors v. M.N.R.*, [1967] C.T.C. 138, 67 D.T.C. 5096.

CAPITAL WORKS. Any building or other structure built on or into the land, and machinery, equipment, and apparatus that are affixed to or incorporated into such building or structure for the purpose of improving the serviceability or utility of the building.

CAPITATION. *n.* A person-by-person tax.

CAPITULARY. *n.* A legal code.

CAPITULATION. *n.* The act of surrendering upon negotiated terms.

CAPON. See CHICKEN ~.

CAPPED FUSE. A safety fuse to which a detonator has been attached by crimping.

CAPPINGS. *n.* The covering and adhering honey over comb cells, pollen or brood, that is removed before the honey extracting process. *Bee Act*, R.S.B.C. 1979, c. 27, s. 1.

CAP STEMS. Small stems by which the berries are attached to the branches. *Processed Fruit and Vegetable Regulations*, C.R.C., c. 291, Schedule I, s. 18.

CAPTAIN. See MINE RESCUE TEAM ~.

CAPTATOR. *n.* A person who receives a gift or legacy by means of artifice.

CAPTION. *n.* The formal heading of an affidavit, deposition, indictment, information or recognisance which states before whom it was taken, found or made.

CAPTIVE UNION. A union formed or controlled by the employer.

CAPTURE. See FREE OF ~ AND SEIZURE.

CAPTURE. *v.* To take; arrest; seize.

CAPUT ANNI. [L.] New Year's Day.

CAPUT MORTUUM. [L.] Obsolete; dead.

CAR. See COMPETITION ~; CONSIGNED ~; DELIVERY ~; PASSENGER ~; RAILWAY ~; STREET ~; TANK ~; TOW ~.

CARAT. *n.* 200 milligrams. *Weights and Measures Act*, S.C. 1970-71-72, c. 36, Schedule II.

CARBON FIBRES AND FILAMENTS. Includes admixtures, in tow, tape or sheet form, of carbon fibres or filaments with up to 45 per cent, by weight, of resins. *Carbon Fibres and Filaments Remission Order*, C.R.C., c. 748, s. 2.

CARBON MONOXIDE. A toxic gas, an important part of motor exhaust gas and coal gas, which can combine with hemoglobin and produce asphyxia. F.A. Jaffe, *A Guide to Pathological Evidence*, 2d ed. (Toronto: Carswell, 1983) at 171.

CARBOXYHEMOGLOBIN. *n.* A product of hemoglobin and carbon monoxide. F.A. Jaffe, *A Guide to Pathological Evidence*, 2d ed. (Toronto: Carswell, 1983) at 74.

CARCASS. *n.* 1. The carcass of an animal. Canada regulations. 2. The tire structure except tread and sidewall rubber. Canada regulations. See DRESSED ~; LAMB ~; MUTTON ~.

CARCER AD HOMINES CUSTODIENDOS, NON AD PUNIENDOS, DARI DEBET. [L.] A prison should be used for the custody not the punishment of persons.

CARCINOGEN. *n.* An agent or substance which can induce cancer. D. Robertson, *Ontario Health and Safety Guide* (Toronto: Richard De Boo Ltd., 1988) at 5-42A.

CAR COAT. See STATION WAGON OR ~.

CARD. See BALLOT ~; CREDIT ~; RACING ~; REGISTRATION ~; SHOP ~.

CARDIAC ARREST. The state in which no effective heart beat occurs when the heart stops totally or the heart muscle quivers ineffectually. F.A. Jaffe, *A Guide to Pathological Evidence*, 2d ed. (Toronto: Carswell, 1983) at 171.

CARDIAC PACEMAKER. An implantable device that consists of a pulse generator and one or more leads and is designed to deliver electrical impulses to stimulate the heart. *Medical Devices Regulations*, C.R.C., c. 871, Schedule III, s. 1.

CARDIAC TAMPONADE. Compression of the heart when fluid accumulates rapidly in the pericardial sac, caused by bleeding into the pericardial cavity when the heart is ruptured or is wounded by penetration. F.A. Jaffe, *A Guide to Pathological Evidence*, 2d ed. (Toronto: Carswell, 1983) at 171.

CARE. *n.* 1. Safekeeping. 2. Includes such nursing, personal or supervisory care as is normally provided by or under the supervision of skilled nursing personnel. *Nursing Home Care Benefits Regulations*, C.R.C., c. 334, s. 2. See

AFTER~; BASIC ~; CHILD IN ~; COMMU-NITY ~ FACILITY; CUSTODIAL ~; DAY ~; ENDOWMENT ~; EXTENDED ~; FOSTER ~; HABILITATION AND ~; HEALTH ~; MEDICAL ~; NON-WARD ~; NURSING ~; NURSING HOME ~; PERPETUAL ~; PERSONAL ~; PROTECTIVE ~; RESIDENTIAL ~; SKILLED NURSING ~; SPECIAL ~; SUPERVISORY ~; SURGICAL ~.

CARE AND CUSTODY. All parental rights, duties and responsibilities toward a child.

CAREER. See OF ~.

CARE FACILITY. A hospital or a similar institution that provides care and treatment for chronic diseases. See SOCIAL ~.

CARE FUND. An irrevocable trust fund required to be established by an operator for the specified care and maintenance of graves in a cemetery.

CARELESSLY. See DRIVE ~; OPERATE ~.

CARE SERVICES. Services consisting of provision of continual residential accommodations with meals and housekeeping, supervisory services, personal services.

CARETAKER'S PREMISES. Residential premises used for residential purposes by a person employed as a caretaker, janitor, manager, watchman, security guard, or superintendent in respect of the building in which the residential premises are situated.

CARETAKER'S UNIT. A rental unit used by a person employed as a caretaker, janitor, manager, watchman, security guard or superintendent in respect of the residential complex in which the rental unit is situated. *Residential Tenancies Act*, R.S.O. 1980, c. 452, s. 1.

CAREY. *abbr.* Manitoba Reports, temp. Wood, 1875.

CARGO. *n.* 1. The load of a ship or other carrier. 2. Goods that are imported into or conveyed through Canada in bond or are intended to be so imported or conveyed. *Customs Cargo Control Regulations*, C.R.C., c. 459, s. 2. See BULK ~; FIXED ~GEAR; GENERAL ~; GRAIN ~; HOT ~; TIMBER DECK ~.

CARGO CONTAINER. A container or chassis that is rigid, reusable, capable of being mounted or dismounted and handled by standard container lifting equipment and that is used by ocean carriers for transportation of goods on board vessels and includes any container that is insulated, refrigerated or dry cargo, or described as flat rack, vehicle rack, liquid tank or open top. Canada regulations.

CARGO SHIP. A ship that is not a fishing vessel, a passenger ship or a pleasure yacht. *Canada Shipping Act*, R.S.C. 1985, c. S-9, s. 2.

CARGO TANK UNIT. A mobile unit consisting of a tank mounted on a truck, trailer or semi-trailer chassis and of a type that is commonly employed for the road transportation of liquids and gases, but does not include B.T.C. or I.C.C. compressed gas cylinders mounted in racks attached to a truck, trailer or semi-trailer chassis. *Piggyback Cargo Tanks Regulations*, C.R.C., c. 1163, s. 2.

CARGO-TYPE DOOR. A door designed primarily to accommodate cargo loading and includes a two-part door that latches to itself. *Motor Vehicle Safety Regulations*, C.R.C., c. 1038, s. 206.

CARNAL KNOWLEDGE. Coitus, copulation, sexual intercourse.

CARNET. *n.* An A.T.A. (Admission Temporaire-Temporary Admission) Carnet referred to in the Customs Convention on the A.T.A. Carnet for the Temporary Admission of Goods. Canada regulations.

CARNIVORE. See FUR-BEARING ~.

CAROTID BODY. An organ located in the side of the neck and concerned with blood pressure regulation. F.A. Jaffe, *A Guide to Pathological Evidence*, 2d ed. (Toronto: Carswell, 1983) at 171.

CARPORT. *n.* An open-sided roofed automobile shelter. *Jasper Townsite Zoning Regulations*, C.R.C., c. 1111, s. 2.

CARRIAGE BY AIR ACT. This act gives binding force in Canada to the Warsaw convention. J.G. McLeod, *The Conflict of Laws* (Calgary: Carswell, 1983) at 106.

CARRIER. *n.* 1. Any person engaged for hire or reward in transport of persons or commodities by railway, water, aircraft, motor vehicle undertaking or commodity pipeline. 2. An insurer. 3. A person who, without apparent symptoms of a communicable disease, harbours and may disseminate an infectious agent. *Public Health Act*, S.A. 1984, c. P-27.1, s. 1. See AIR ~; CHEMICAL ~; COMBINATION ~; COMMON ~; CRANE ~; ELIGIBLE ~; FEDERAL ~; INTERJURISDICTIONAL ~; LOCAL ~; MOTOR ~; OCEAN ~; PAPER ~; PUBLIC ~; SEA ~.

CARROT. See PEAS AND ~S.

CARRY. *v.* 1. Includes to store or have in possession. 2. In connection with insurance, to possess or hold.

CARRY COSTS. A verdict carries costs when the party for whom the verdict is given becomes entitled to costs as an incident of the verdict.

CARRYING CAPACITY. In respect of a vehicle, means the gross vehicle weight rating (manufacturer's rating) of the vehicle less the aggregate of the weight of the unloaded vehicle and the weight of all necessary equipment, fuel and tires. *Explosives Regulations*, C.R.C., c. 599, s. 48.

CARRYING CHARGE. A charge made by creditor in addition to interest.

CARRYING COSTS. A verdict carries costs when the party for whom the verdict is given becomes entitled to costs as an incident of the verdict.

CARRYING ON BUSINESS. The transaction of any of the ordinary business of a corporation or person, including franchises, whether or not by means of an employee or an agent and whether or not the corporation or person has a resident agent or representative or a warehouse, office or place of business in the province. *Licensing Act*, S.P.E.I. 1976, c. 18, s. 2.

CARRY ON. To carry on, perform, operate, keep, hold, occupy, deal in or use, for gain, whether as principal or as agent.

CARRY ON BUSINESS. 1. Any action for the promotion or execution of any purpose of business. 2. Transaction of business.

CARRY ON BUSINESS AS A MORTGAGE BROKER. (i) Solicit a person to borrow or lend money to be secured by a mortgage, (ii) negotiate a mortgage transaction, (iii) collect mortgage payments and otherwise administer mortgages, or (iv) buy, sell or exchange mortgages or offer to do so, on behalf of another person and for money or other consideration.

CARRY-OVER OF CAPITAL LOSSES. Capital losses may be deducted from capital gains or income of other years. W. Grover & F. Iacobucci, *Materials on Canadian Income Tax*, 4th ed. (Toronto: Richard De Boo Ltd., 1980) at 525.

CARTA DE NON ENTE NON VALET. [L.] A charter concerning something which does not exist is of no worth.

CARTA DE UNA PARTE. A one-sided charter; a deed poll.

CARTAE LIBERTATUM. [L.] The British charters of liberties, the Carta de Foresta and Magna Carta.

CARTA NON EST NISI VERTIGIUM DONATIONIS. [L.] The deed is nothing but the

covering of the grant; the grant is what is really important.

CARTARUM SUPER FIDEM, MORTUIS TESTIBUS, AD PATRIAM, DE NECESSITUDINE, RECURRENDUM EST. [L.] When the witnesses are dead the validity of charters must be decided by a jury.

CART. B.N.A. *abbr.* Cartwright's Constitutional Cases (Can.), 1868-1896.

CARTE BLANCHE. [Fr. white card] 1. Unlimited authority. 2. A blank card signed at the bottom which gives another person power to write anything above the signature.

CARTEL. *n.* 1. An agreement between producers of raw materials or goods. 2. A wartime agreement regarding the treatment or liberation of prisoners, the treatment of messengers between the conflicting sides or maintenance of postal and telegraphic communication.

CARTEL-SHIP. *n.* A vessel commissioned in wartime which sails under safe conduct to exchange prisoners or to carry a particular proposal from one side to another.

CARTILAGE. See THYROID ~.

CARTOGRAPHIC BOOK. See PRINTED ATLAS OR ~.

CARTOGRAPHIC RECORD OR DOCUMENT. (a) A collection of cartographic representations composed of manuscript or printed material that is bound, stitched or fastened together to form a unit that has no established dates of printing for the unit as a whole, (b) a single sheet containing thereon cartographic representations irrespective of folding, or (c) cartographic material (i) unattached and issued in a combination other than a printed book, such as boxed maps, irrespective of their dates of printing, or (ii) in a loose format that clearly forms a single unit of visual information. *Canadian Cultural Property Export Control List*, C.R.C., c. 448, s. 1.

CARTON. *n.* A container made to contain 6, 12, 18, 24 or 30 eggs, with a separate compartment for each egg. *Egg Regulations*, C.R.C., c. 284, s. 2.

CARTRIDGE. *n.* 1. A unit of ammunition composed of projectile, cartridge case, primer and propellant, or, in the case of shotgun ammunition, shell, pellets and wads. F.A. Jaffe, *A Guide to Pathological Evidence*, 2d ed. (Toronto: Carswell, 1983) at 171. 2. A stick of explosives enclosed in a wrapping of waterproof paper. See PRIMER ~; RIM-FIRE SHELL OR ~; SAFETY ~.

CARTRIDGE CASE. A metal or plastic cylinder of firearm ammunition containing propellant; primer and projectile are inserted into it. F.A. Jaffe, *A Guide to Pathological Evidence*, 2d ed. (Toronto: Carswell, 1983) at 171.

C.A.S. *abbr.* 1. Children's Aid Societ(y)(ies). 2. Décisions de la Commission des affaires sociales.

CA. SA. *abbr.* Capias ad satisfaciendum.

CASE. *v.* 1. For a potential thief or burglar to inspect a premises. 2. The operation of adding to raw leaf tobacco any flavouring materials. *Excise Act*, R.S.C. 1985, c. E-14, s. 6.

CASE. *n.* 1. An action; a trial; a decision which involves some point of law important enough that it is published in a law report. 2. A sealed package, carton or container. 3. Any envelope or container specially designed, by its form and arrangement, to receive a firearm. *Wild-life Conservation Act*, S.Q. 1978, c. 65, s. 1. 4. A container made to contain 30 dozen eggs. *Egg Regulations*, C.R.C., c. 284, s. 2. See ACTION ON THE ~; CARTRIDGE ~; HALLMARK ~; LEADING ~; MCNAGHTEN'S ~; MOOT ~; SPECIAL ~; STATED ~; TEST ~.

CASE LAW. The decisions of judges relating to particular matters in contrast to statute law; case law is a source of law and forms legal precedents.

CASE READY FOR JUDGMENT. A case in which the trial has been completed and which has been taken under advisement. *Code of Civil Procedure*, R.S.Q. 1977, c. C-25, s. 4.

CASE STATED. A written statement requesting an opinion on a question of law.

CASH. *v.* To convert a negotiable instrument to money.

CASH. *n.* 1. Money. 2. Bank notes and coins. *Accountable Advances Regulations*, C.R.C., c. 668, s. 2. 2. Includes cheques, bills of exchange, money orders and sums credited to an account. See PETTY ~ EXPENDITURE.

CASH ACCOUNT. 1. In bookkeeping, a record of cash transactions. 2. A brokerage firm account which is settled on a cash basis. See MARGIN ACCOUNT.

CASH AGAINST DOCUMENTS. An invoiced amount due when a bill of lading is presented.

CASH BASIS. An accounting method which recognizes income when actually received and expenses when actually paid out. See ACCRUAL METHOD OF ACCOUNTING.

CASH BOOK. An accounting record that combines cash receipts and disbursements.

CASH BUDGET. The estimated cash receipts and disbursements for a future period.

CASH DIVIDEND. The portion of profits and surplus paid to shareholders by a corporation in cash, in contrast with a stock dividend.

CASH GRAIN. Grain that is in a position to be sold for cash on delivery of documents of title representing grain of the specified grade or grades pursuant to contracts for immediate or deferred delivery. *Grain Futures Act*, R.S.C. 1985, c. G-11, s. 2.

CASHIER. *v.* To dismiss from command or a position of authority.

CASHIER. *n.* 1. A person who collects and records payments at a business. 2. A person who cashes winning pari-mutuel tickets. *Race Track Supervision Regulations*, C.R.C., c. 441, s. 2.

CASH METHOD. An accounting method which recognizes income when actually received and expenses when actually paid out. See ACCRUAL METHOD OF ACCOUNTING.

CASH-MUTUAL CORPORATION. A corporation without share capital that is empowered to undertake insurance on both the cash plan and the mutual plan.

CASH-MUTUAL INSURANCE COMPANY. A company without share capital or with guarantee capital stock subject to repayment by the company, in respect of which the dividend rate is limited by its act or instrument of incorporation, which is empowered to undertake insurance on both the cash plan and the mutual plan.

CASH ON DELIVERY. A sale of goods on condition that cash be paid on delivery.

CASH PRICE. The price that would be charged by the seller for the goods or services to a buyer who paid cash for them at the time of purchase or hiring.

CASH PURCHASE TICKET. A document issued in respect of grain delivered to a primary elevator as evidence of the purchase of the grain by the operator of the elevator and entitling the holder of the document to payment by the operator for the grain of the purchase price stated in the document. *Canada Grain Act*, R.S.C. 1985, c. G-10, s. 2.

CASH SURRENDER VALUE. 1. The amount an insurer will return to a policyholder upon cancellation of the policy. 2. At a particular time of a life insurance policy means its cash surrender value at that time computed without regard to any policy loans made under the policy, any policy dividends (other than paid-up additions) payable under the policy or any interest payable on such dividends. *Income Tax Act*, R.S.C. 1952, c. 148 (as added by S.C. 1968-69, c. 44, s. 20), s. 148(9)(b).

CASING. *n.* 1. Pipe or tubing installed in a well to support the sides of the well. *Ontario Water Resources Act*, R.R.O. 1980, Reg. 739, s. 1. 2. A skinlike case for processed meat. *Meat Inspection Regulations*, C.R.C., c. 1032, s. 2. 3. The operation of adding to raw leaf tobacco any flavouring materials. *Excise Act*, R.S.C. 1985, c. E-14, s. 6.

CASPAR'S RULE. At roughly similar temperature a body after lying in the open air putrifies in one week the same amount as a body lying in water putrifies in two weeks or a body lying in earth in the usual manner putrifies in eight weeks. F.A. Jaffe, *A Guide to Pathological Evidence*, 2d ed. (Toronto: Carswell, 1983) at 171 and 172.

CASSETUR BILLA. [L.] Let the bill be quashed.

CASSETUR BREVE. [L.] Let the writ be quashed.

CASS. PRAC. CAS. *abbr.* Cassels' Practice Cases (Can.).

CASS. S.C. *abbr.* Cassels' Supreme Court Decisions.

CAST. *v.* To deposit formally, as to cast a ballot.

CASTING VOTE. The deciding vote to break equality of votes, cast by the chair or presiding officer. Whether the chair has a casting vote depends on provisions of the relevant statute, by-laws, standing orders, regulations or articles.

CASUAL EMPLOYEE. A person engaged to perform work of a casual nature or in an emergency.

CASUAL IMPORTER. A person who is not normally engaged in the importation of goods into Canada. *Casual Importer Regulations*, C.R.C., c. 453, s. 2.

CASUALTY. See SHIPPING ~.

CASUAL WORKER. A person who works occasionally.

CASUS BELLI. [L.] An incident which causes or justifies war.

CASUS FOEDERIS. [L.] An event which, through the terms of a treaty, entitles one allied nation to help from another or others.

CASUS FORTUITUS NON EST SPERANDUS; ET NEMO TENETUR DIVINARE. [L.] No reliance should be placed on an event which may or may not happen; and, if it does happen, no one can foresee that it will happen.

CASUS NON PRAESTATUR. [L.] An accident for which one did not take responsibility.

CASUS OMISSUS. [L.] Something which should have been, but was not, provided for.

CASUS OMISSUS ET OBLIVIONI DATUS DISPOSITIONI COMMUNIS JURIS RELINQUITUR. [L.] A point not treated by statute law must be decided according to common law.

CATALOGUE. *n.* A bound, stitched, sewed or stapled book or pamphlet containing a list and description of goods, wares, merchandise or services, with specific information, with or without price.

CATALYTIC CONVERTER. A device through which exhaust from a motor is passed in order to prevent or lessen the emission of a contaminant and which device would be impaired in its functioning by the use of leaded gasoline as a fuel for operation of the motor.

CATCH. *n.* Any unprocessed product or natural by-product of the sea or of any other body of water caught or taken by a crew and includes Irish moss, kelp and whales but does not include fish scales, and (a) where only a portion of a catch is delivered to a buyer, means the portion delivered, and (b) where more than one catch or portion thereof is delivered to a buyer at one time, means the catches or portions thereof so delivered. *Unemployment Insurance Regulations*, C.R.C., c. 1576, s. 74. See FRESH ~; INCIDENTAL ~.

CATCHING BARGAIN. An agreement to loan or pay money made on unfavourable terms to a person having property in reversion or expectancy.

CATCHPOLE. *n.* A bailiff or sheriff's officer.

CATCH-WEIGHT. *n.* A meat product that because of its nature cannot ordinarily be portioned to a predetermined quantity and is, as a result, usually sold in packages of varying quantity. *Meat Inspection Regulations*, C.R.C., c. 1032, s. 2.

CATCHWEIGHT PACKAGE. Any transparent package sold on a weight basis in which the produce is readily visible and which contains not more than three pounds net weight. *Farm Products Grades and Sales Act*, R.R.O. 1980, Reg. 332, s. 1.

CATCH WEIGHT PRODUCT. A product that because of its nature cannot normally be portioned to a predetermined quantity and is, as a result, usually sold in packages of varying quantity. Canada regulations.

CATCH-WEIGHTS. *n.* When used in a professional boxing contract means the actual weights of the contestants where no mention of specific weights is made in the contract. *Athletics Control Act*, R.R.O. 1980, Reg. 76, s. 2.

CATEGORY. See OCCUPATIONAL ~.

C.A.T. (QUÉ.). *abbr.* Commission des accidents du travail (Québec).

CAT ROAD. An unsurfaced road of a temporary nature over which logs or materials are dragged by any means. *Highway (Industrial) Act*, R.S.B.S. 1979, c. 168, s. 1.

CATTLE. *n.* 1. Neat cattle or an animal of the bovine species by whatever technical or familiar name it is known, and includes any horse, mule, ass, pig, sheep or goat. *Criminal Code*, R.S.C. 1985, c. C-46, s. 2. 2. A bull, cow, ox, heifer, steer or calf. See OWNER OF ~; PEDIGREED ~; PURE BRED ~; REACTING ~.

CATTLE PEST. The insect known as hypoderma bovis or hypoderma lineatum and commonly known as the warble fly. *Cattle Pest Control Act*, S.N.S. 1970, c. 2, s. 1.

CATTLE WITH HORNS. Cattle that are not polled or have not been dehorned.

CATV. *abbr.* Community Antenna Television, a system by which television signals are received from distant stations on large antennae and transmitted by cable to individual consumers.

CAUCUS. *n.* A group of members who are elected to the Assembly and who belong to the same political party. See OPPOSITION ~; THIRD PARTY ~.

CAUSA CAUSANS. [L.] The immediate cause; the last of a chain of causes.

CAUSAE DOTIS, VITAE, LIBERTATIS, FISCI, SUNT INTER FAVORABILIA, IN LEGE. [L.] Causes of dower, life, liberty, revenue are among the things favoured in law.

CAUSA MORTIS. [L.] Because of death; in case of death.

CAUSA PROXIMA. [L.] The immediate cause.

CAUSA PROXIMA NON REMOTA SPECTATUR. [L.] The immediate, not the remote, cause should be considered.

CAUSA SINE QUA NON. [L.] The cause without which the event would not have occurred.

CAUSATION. See ACTUAL ~; FACTUAL ~; LEGAL ~.

CAUSATION IN FACT. Factual causation. K.D. Cooper-Stephenson & I.B. Saunders, *Personal Injury Damages in Canada* (Toronto: Carswell, 1981) at 637.

CAUSE. *v.* To produce an effect.

CAUSE. *n.* 1. A suit or action. 2. That which produces an effect and includes any action, suit or other original proceeding between a plaintiff and a defendant and any criminal proceeding by the Crown. 3. In negligence cases, the defendant's fault is a cause of the damage if the damage would not have occurred but for the defendant's fault and the fault is not a cause if the damage would have happened with or without the defendant's fault. John G. Fleming, *The Law of Torts*, 6th ed. (Sydney: The Law Book Company Limited, 1983) at 171. See CHALLENGE FOR ~; COSTS IN THE ~; MATRIMONIAL ~; NECESSARY ~; PROBABLE ~; REASONABLE AND PROBABLE ~; TESTAMENTARY MATTERS AND ~S.

CAUSE CÉLÈBRE. [Fr.] A matter of great interest or importance.

CAUSE OF ACTION. 1. The factual circumstances which give rise to a right to sue. 2. The right to institute a civil proceeding.

CAUSE OF DEATH. 1. Whatever violence or wound disrupts the vital processes and brings about death. F.A. Jaffe, *A Guide to Pathological Evidence*, 2d ed. (Toronto: Carswell, 1983) at 10. 2. The medical cause of death according to the International Statistical Classification of Diseases, Injuries and Causes of Death as last revised by the International Conference assembled for that purpose and published by the World Health Organization. *Fatality Inquiries Act*, R.S.A. 1980, c. F-6, s. 1.

CAUTION. *n.* 1. A warning. 2. A warning given to an accused concerning possibly incriminating statements.

CAUTIO PRO EXPENSIS. [L.] Security for costs.

CAUTIOUS. *adj.* Careful.

C.A.V. *abbr.* Curia advisari vult.

CAVEAT. *n.* [L. let one take heed] 1. A document filed by an inventor before filing an application. H.G. Fox, *The Canadian Law and Practice Relating to Letters Patent for Inventions*, 4th ed. (Toronto: Carswell, 1969) at 242. 2. An entry made in a registry office so that previous notice is given to the person entering the caveat before a certain step is taken.

CAVEAT ACTOR. [L.] Let the doer beware.

CAVEAT EMPTOR. [L.] Let the buyer beware.

CAVEAT EMPTOR; QUI IGNORARE NON DEBUIT QUOD JUS ALIENUM EMIT. [L.] A purchaser must be on guard; for the purchaser has no right to ignore the fact that what was bought belongs to someone else besides the vendor.

CAVEATOR. *n.* The person who gives, files or registers a caveat.

CAVEAT PAYMENT. A person who wants to prevent paying money out of court may file a notice and the Registry must enter a caveat in its caveat payment book. D. Sgayias *et al.*, *Federal Court Practice 1988* (Toronto: Carswell, 1987) at 546.

CAVEAT RELEASE. A person who wants to prevent releasing property under arrest may file a notice, and the Registry must enter a caveat in its caveat release book. D. Sgayias *et al.*, *Federal Court Practice 1988* (Toronto: Carswell, 1987) at 546.

CAVEAT VENDITOR. [L.] Let the seller beware.

CAVEAT VIATOR. [L.] Let the traveller beware.

CAVEAT WARRANT. To give bail to an action or counter-claim that may be or may have been brought against property so that the Registry enters a caveat in its caveat warrant book. D. Sgayias *et al.*, *Federal Court Practice 1988* (Toronto: Carswell, 1987) at 545.

CAVITY. *n.* A structure that encloses and confines a microwave field. *Radiation Emitting Devices Regulations*, C.R.C., c. 1379, s. 1. See PERMANENT ~; TEMPORARY ~.

CAVITY WALL. A construction of masonry laid up with a cavity between the wythes tied together with metal ties or bonding units, the cavity of which may or may not contain insulation.

CAVR CAB CARD. A permit issued pursuant to the Canadian Agreement on Vehicle Registration.

C.B.A. PAPERS. *abbr.* Canadian Bar Association Papers.

C.B.A. Y.B. *abbr.* Canadian Bar Year Book.

CBC. *abbr.* Canadian Broadcasting Corporation.

C.B.E.S. *abbr.* Cour du Bien-être social.

C.B.R. *abbr.* Canadian Bankruptcy Reports, 1920-1960.

C.B.R. (N.S.). *abbr.* Canadian Bankruptcy Reports, New Series, 1960-.

CC. *abbr.* Cubic centimetre.

C.C.A.S. *abbr.* Catholic Children's Aid Societ(y)(ies).

C.C.C. *abbr.* Canadian Criminal Cases, 1893-1962.

[ ] C.C.C. *abbr.* Canadian Criminal Cases, 1963-1970.

C.C.C. (2D). *abbr.* Canadian Criminal Cases (Second Series), 1971-1983.

C.C.C. (3D). *abbr.* Canadian Criminal Cases (Third Series), 1983-.

C.C.D.P. *abbr.* Commission canadienne des droits de la personne.

C.C.E.A. *abbr.* Commission de contrôle de l'énergie atomique.

C.C.E.L. *abbr.* Canadian Cases on Employment Law, 1983-.

C. CIRC. *abbr.* Cour de circuit.

CCL. *abbr.* Canadian Congress of Labour, which is now part of the Canadian Labour Congress.

[ ] C.C.L. *abbr.* Canadian Current Law.

C.C.L.I. *abbr.* Canadian Cases on the Law of Insurance, 1983-.

C.C.L.R. *abbr.* Canada Corporations Law Reports.

C.C.L.T. *abbr.* Canadian Cases of the Law of Torts, 1976-.

C.C.P. *abbr.* Commission canadienne des pensions.

C.C.R.T. *abbr.* Conseil canadien des relations de travail.

CD. *abbr.* Candela.

C. DE D. *abbr.* Les Cahiers de droit.

C. DE L'É. *abbr.* Cour de l'Échiquier.

C. DE L'I.Q.A.J. *abbr.* Cahiers de l'institut québécois d'administration judiciaire.

CDIC. *abbr.* Canada Deposit Insurance Corporation.

C. DIST. *abbr.* Cour de district.

C. DIV. *abbr.* Cour divisionnaire.

CDN. *abbr.* Canadian.

CEASE. *v.* To stop; to suspend activity.

C.E.B. & P.G.R. *abbr.* Canadian Employment Benefits and Pension Guide Reports.

C.E.C.M. *abbr.* Commission des écoles catholiques de Montréal.

CEDE. *v.* 1. To give up or yield. 2. To transfer. 3. To surrender.

C.E.G.S.B. *abbr.* Crown Employees Grievance Settlement Board.

CEILING. *n.* 1. An upper limit on wages or

hours. 2. The lowest height at which a broken or overcast condition exists, or the vertical visibility when an obscured condition such as snow, smoke or fog exists, whichever is the lower. *Air Regulations*, C.R.C., c. 2, s. 101.

CELEBRATION OF MARRIAGE. The formal act by which two persons become husband and wife.

CELIBACY. *n.* The state or condition of remaining single or unmarried, usually used in connection with one who has vowed to remain single or unmarried.

CELL. *n.* 1. In respect of a landfilling site, means a deposit of waste that has been sealed by cover material so that no waste deposited in the cell is exposed to the atmosphere. *Environmental Protection Act*, R.R.O. 1980, Reg. 309, s. 1. 2. One of the hollow spaces, suitable for use as a raceway, of a cellular metal or cellular concrete floor, the axis of the cell being parallel to the longitudinal axis of the floor members. *Power Corporation Act*, R.R.O. 1980, Reg. 794, s. 0. See MERCURY ~.

CELLAR. *n.* 1. An underground room; a basement. 2. A basement that is more than 50 per cent below grade.

CELL ROOM. In respect of (a) a structure housing one or more mercury cells, means the structure, and (b) mercury cells not housed in a structure, means the mercury cells. *Chlor-Alkali Mercury National Emission Standards Regulations*, C.R.C., c. 406, s. 2.

CELLULAR DEATH. The death of cells or even whole organs which follows death by several hours. F.A. Jaffe, *A Guide to Pathological Evidence*, 2d ed. (Toronto: Carswell, 1983) at 2 and 3.

CELLULAR FLOOR. An assembly of metal or concrete floor members containing cells. *Power Corporation Act*, R.R.O. 1980, Reg. 794, s. 0.

C.E.L.R. *abbr.* Canadian Environmental Law Reports.

C.E.L.R. (N.S.). *abbr.* Canadian Environmental Law Reports (New Series).

CEMENTED SAND AND GRAVEL. A mixture of sand and gravel or boulders thoroughly cemented together as a hard layer which will not soften in its natural bed when wet. *Building Code Act*, R.R.O. 1980, Reg. 87, s. 4.2.1.9.

CEMENT MASON. A person who does concrete finishing by hand or with mechanical equipment, does all phases of waterproofing and restoration of concrete, does rubbing-up and repairing of hardened concrete surfaces, places and finishes epoxy, plastic and other composi-tion materials, and finishes and exposes aggregate in pre-cast and architectural concrete.

CEMETERY. *n.* Land that is set apart or used as a place for the interment of the dead or in which human bodies have been buried. See FAMILY ~; PREARRANGED ~ CONTRACT; PRENEED ~ PLAN.

CEMETERY COMPANY. A corporation that is the owner of a cemetery.

CEMETERY GOODS OR SERVICES. The goods supplied by the cemetery or crematorium in conjunction with the burial or cremation of human remains or the services performed by the cemetery or crematorium relative to the installation or provision of any of the goods.

CEMETERY OR PERPETUAL CARE TRUST. A trust, usually created by will, to keep up and maintain one or more designated graves or other burial places within a burial site or cemetery. D.M.W. Waters, *The Law of Trusts in Canada*, 2d ed. (Toronto: Carswell, 1984) at 436.

CEMETERY SERVICES. The opening and closing of graves, compartments, crypts or other spaces and services related thereto.

CEMETERY SUPPLIES. Burial vaults, grave stones, grave markers, monuments or bases for use in a cemetery.

CENSOR. *n.* A person who regulates or prohibits distribution, production or exhibition of films or publication of books, plays, etc.

CENSORSHIP. *n.* The prohibition or regulation of publication, distribution or production of books, plays, films.

CENSURE. *n.* An official reprimand; condemnation.

CENSUS. *n.* A count or enumeration of the people. See GENERAL ~; PENULTIMATE DECENNIAL ~.

CENSUS REGALIS. [L.] The annual income or revenue of the Crown.

CENT. *n.* 1. A coin. 2. One hundredth part of a dollar.

CENTAL. *n.* 100 pounds. *Weights and Measures Act*, S.C. 1970-71-72, c. 36, schedule II.

CENTI. *pref.* 10^{-2}. A prefix for multiples and submultiples of basic, supplementary and derived units of measurement. *Weights and Measures Act*, S.C. 1970-71-72, c. 36, Schedule 1.

CENTIMETRE. See CUBIC ~.

CENTIN. *n.* Used in the French version of the laws of Quebec, means the coin called "cent" in the laws of Canada and in the English version of the laws of Quebec. *Interpretation Act*, R.S.Q. 1977, c. I-16, s. 61.

CENTRAL COOPERATIVE CREDIT SOCIETY. A cooperative organization incorporated or organized by or pursuant to an Act of Parliament or of the legislature of a province, the membership or shareholders of which consist wholly or substantially of local cooperative credit societies and the principal purpose of which is to provide services to its members. *Bank Act*, R.S.C. 1985, c. B-1, s. 2.

CENTRAL CREDIT UNION. An organization of credit unions.

CENTRAL HIRING HALL. A central location where unionized workers are referred to seasonal or casual jobs.

CENTRALIST. *adj.* Describes a form of federal government in which greater power is given to the central or federal government.

CENTRALIZED TRAFFIC CONTROL. A system in ABS territory under which train or engine movements are authorized by block signals whose indications supersede the superiority of trains for both opposing and following movements on the same track. *Regulations No. 0-8, Uniform Code of Operating Rules*, C.R.C., c. 1175, Part III, s. 2.

CENTRAL LABOUR CONGRESS. An affiliation of unions, directly chartered locals, provincial labour federations and local labour councils organized to co-ordinate activities at the national level.

CENTRAL POLITICAL PARTY ORGANIZATION. The permanent and continuing office and staff of a recognized political party. *Election Act*, R.S.M. 1970, c. E30, s. 2.

CENTRAL STANDARD TIME. The mean time of the ninetieth degree of longitude west from Greenwich which is six hours behind Greenwich time.

CENTRE. See ANIMAL EMBRYO TRANSPLANT ~; CLASSIFICATION ~; COMMUNITY ~; CORRECTIONAL ~; DAY CARE ~; DISPATCH ~; DRYING ~; GERIATRIC ~; HOSPITAL ~; INFORMATION ~; JUDICIAL ~; MENTAL HEALTH ~; NATIONAL ARTS ~; OBSERVATION ~; RECREATION ~; REGIONAL ~; REMAND ~; SHOPPING ~; SOCIAL SERVICE ~; SPECIMEN COLLECTION ~; STOP-OVER ~; SUPERVISION ~; TREATMENT ~.

CENTRE FIRE AMMUNITION. Firearm ammunition in which the primer is located in the centre of the base of the cartridge case in a well. F.A. Jaffe, *A Guide to Pathological Evidence*, 2d ed. (Toronto: Carswell, 1983) at 172.

CENTRE LINE. Either (a) the centre of a roadway measured from the curbs or, in the absence of curbs, from the edges of the roadway, or (b) where on a laned roadway there are more lanes available for traffic in one direction than the other direction the line dividing the lanes for traffic in different directions except, in both cases, on a one-way roadway.

CENTRE OF OSSIFICATION. A point where bone forms. F.A. Jaffe, *A Guide to Pathological Evidence*, 2d ed. (Toronto: Carswell, 1983) at 181.

CENTRE POINT OF AN INTERSECTION. The point where the centre line of the through part of a highway meets the centre line of, or the centre line of the prolongation of, another highway that intersects or meets the highway.

CENTRE TANK. Any tank inboard a longitudinal bulkhead. *Oil Pollution Prevention Regulations*, C.R.C., c. 1454, s. 33.

CENTURY. *n.* 1. One hundred. 2. One hundred years.

C.E.P.A.R. *abbr.* Canadian Estate Planning and Administration Reporter.

CEPI CORPUS ET PARATUM HABEO. [L. I have taken the body and have it ready] The return to a writ of capias or attachment by a sheriff to indicate that the defendant is in custody.

CEPIT. [L.] Did carry away.

CEPIT IN ALIO LOCO. [L.] A plea in replevin, stating that the defendant has taken the goods in a different place than the one mentioned in the declaration.

C.E.P.R. *abbr.* Canadian Estate Planning and Administration Reporter.

C.E.R. *abbr.* Canadian Customs and Excise reports, 1980-.

CEREBRAL EDEMA. A swelling of brain tissue. F.A. Jaffe, *A Guide to Pathological Evidence*, 2d ed. (Toronto: Carswell, 1983) at 120.

CEREBROSPINAL FLUID. A clear fluid which circulates in the cavities of the brain and the space surrounding the spinal cord and brain. F.A. Jaffe, *A Guide to Pathological Evidence*, 2d ed. (Toronto: Carswell, 1983) at 172.

CEREMONY. See CIVIL ~.

CERTA DEBET ESSE INTENTIO, ET NARRATIO, ET CERTUM FUNDAMENTUM, ET CERTA RES QUAE DEDUCITUR IN JUDICIUM. [L.] In a pleading, the intention, the declaration and the cause of action should be clear, and so should the point which the court is asked to decide.

CERTAIN. *adj.* 1. Definitive. 2. Free from doubt.

CERTAINTY. *n.* 1. Accuracy; absence of doubt. 2. Precision. See THREE CERTAINTIES.

CERTIFICATE. *n.* 1. An official assurance or representation concerning a matter within the knowledge or authority of the person making the certificate. 2. A medical certificate recommending the care, supervision and control of a mentally disordered person in a hospital. *Mental Health Act*, R.S.A. 1970, c. 231, s. 2. 3. A document issued to identify those who have passed the required examinations or are members of a professional organization. 4. A document issued granting authority to operate a public service or commercial vehicle. *Public Service Vehicles Act*, R.S.A. 1970, c. 300, s. 2. See AGE ~; ALLOTMENT ~; ARCHITECT'S ~; BUILDER'S ~; DRIVER'S ~; DUPLICATE ~; ELIGIBILITY ~; EMPLOYMENT ~; FIRE-ARMS ACQUISITION ~; FIRST AID ~; GUARANTEED INVESTMENT ~; HEALTH ~; HUNTER'S ~; INVESTMENT ~; LOAD LINE CONVENTION ~; MEDICAL ~; NOISE ~; NOTARIAL ~; OPERATOR'S ~; OWNER'S ~; PILOTAGE ~; QUOTA ~; REGISTRATION ~; RENEWAL ~; SECURITY ~; SECURITY OR SECURITY ~; SHARE ~; TONNAGE MEASUREMENT ~.

CERTIFICATE OF AGE. A document issued in connection with statutory restrictions on child labour and authorizing employment of a minor. See AGE CERTIFICATE.

CERTIFICATE OF AIRWORTHINESS. A conditional certificate of fitness for flight issued in respect of a particular aircraft under Part II of these Regulations or under the laws of the state in which the aircraft is registered. *Air Regulations*, C.R.C., c. 2, s. 101.

CERTIFICATE OF ASSESSMENT. A document given by an assessment officer to signify the completion of an assessment of party-and-party costs. M.M. Orkin, *The Law of Costs*, 2d ed. (Aurora: Canada Law Book, 1987) at 6-23.

CERTIFICATE OF CITIZENSHIP. A certificate of citizenship issued or granted under an act.

CERTIFICATE OF COMPLETION. A certificate given by an architect under whose supervision a building contract has been carried out; contractor is generally not entitled to payment until the certificate is given.

CERTIFICATE OF CONTINUANCE. A certificate which permits a body corporate incorporated in one province or federally to be continued in a second jurisdiction if such continuance is authorized by the laws of the jurisdiction where it is incorporated. H. Sutherland, D.B. Horsley & J.M. Edmiston, eds., *Fraser's Handbook on Canadian Company Law*, 7th ed. (Toronto: Carswell, 1985) at 481.

CERTIFICATE OF CONVICTION. A certificate stating that an accused was convicted of an indictable offence, drawn up by a judge or magistrate when requested to do so by the prosecutor, the accused or a peace officer.

CERTIFICATE OF INCORPORATION. Documentary evidence, including letters patent, a special act or any other instrument, by which a corporation is incorporated stating that a corporation exists and was duly incorporated under the appropriate statute.

CERTIFICATE OF LIS PENDENS. A former term for a certificate of pending litigation. G.D. Watson & C. Perkins, eds., *Holmested & Watson: Ontario Civil Procedure* (Toronto: Carswell, 1984) at CJA-179. See CERTIFICATE OF PENDING LITIGATION.

CERTIFICATE OF NATURALIZATION. A certificate of naturalization granted under any act that was in force in Canada at any time before January 1, 1947.

CERTIFICATE OF PENDING LITIGATION. A notice, registered in the proper land registry office, of the commencement of a proceeding in which an interest in land is at issue. G.D. Watson & C. Perkins, eds., *Holmested & Watson: Ontario Civil Procedure* (Toronto: Carswell, 1984) at CJA-132.

CERTIFICATE OF READINESS. A former term for the document which a party in an action filed to indicate that the party is ready for trial. See now NOTICE OF READINESS FOR TRIAL.

CERTIFICATE OF REGISTRATION. A certificate issued by an association setting out the name, registration number, date of birth, sex, identification, sire and dam of an animal registered in the records of the association, the name of the owner of the animal. *Livestock Pedigree Act*, R.S.C. 1985, c. L-11, s. 2.

CERTIFICATE OF RENUNCIATION. A certificate of renunciation issued under section 9. *Citizenship Act*, R.S.C. 1985, c. C-29, s. 2.

CERTIFICATE OF TAXATION. A certificate signed and inscribed by a taxing officer when a bill of costs has been taxed. M.M. Orkin, *The Law of Costs*, 2d ed. (Aurora: Canada Law Book, 1987) at 12-9. See also CERTIFICATE OF ASSESSMENT.

CERTIFICATE OF TEST OF MATERIAL. (a) A certificate issued by a classification society, an approved test laboratory or an approved manufacturer that describes a quantity of material and the marks by which it may be identified, and specifies the physical tests to which the material has been subjected and the numerical results of those tests, or (b) a certificate by a classification society that describes a quantity of material and the marks by which it may be identified, and specifies the general class into which the material falls according to the rules of that classification society. *Steamship Machinery Construction Regulations*, C.R.C., c. 1491, s. 2.

CERTIFICATE OF TITLE. A certificate of title granted pursuant to a Land Titles Act. See ABSOLUTE ~; DUPLICATE ~.

CERTIFICATION. *n.* 1. A written attestation of a training organization as to the level of achievement attained by a student in an occupational training program. 2. The entry of the name of a person in the register. See APPLICATION FOR ~.

CERTIFICATION MARK. A mark that is used for the purpose of distinguishing or so as to distinguish wares or services that are of a defined standard with respect to (a) the character or quality of the wares or services, (b) the working conditions under which the wares have been produced or the services performed, (c) the class of persons by whom the wares have been produced or the services performed, or (d) the area within which the wares have been produced or the services performed, from wares or services that are not of that defined standard. *Trade-marks Act*, R.S.C. 1985, c. T-13, s. 2.

CERTIFICATION OF LABOUR UNION. Official recognition by a labour relations board of a union as bargaining representative for employees in a particular bargaining unit.

CERTIFIED AIR CARRIER. (a) An air carrier that, pursuant to the Air Carrier Regulations made under the Aeronautics Act, is authorized by the Canadian Transport Commission to operate as an air carrier or as a commercial air service, (b) a foreign air carrier that is authorized by the Canadian Transport Commission to operate international charter flights from and to Canada, and (c) an air carrier, other than an air carrier described in paragraph (a) or (b), that itself or by its agent sells in Canada transportation of a person by air that is to be provided in whole or in part by an air carrier described in paragraph (a) or (b). *Excise Tax Act*, R.S.C. 1985, c. E-15, s. 8.

CERTIFIED ASSOCIATION. The association recognized by decision of the investigator, the investigation commissioner or the Court as the representative of all or some of the employees of an employer. *Labour Code*, R.S.Q. 1977, c. C-27, s. 1.

CERTIFIED BARGAINING AGENT. A bargaining agent that has been certified under this Act and the certification of which has not been revoked. *Trade Union Act*, R.S.N.S. 1967, c. 311, s. 1.

CERTIFIED CHEQUE. When a cheque is certified at the holder's request, this amounts to payment in due course and discharge of the cheque according to the Bills of Exchange Act. But a cheque certified at the drawer's request clearly does not discharge the instrument. I.F.G. Baxter, *The Law of Banking*, 3d ed. (Toronto: Carswell, 1981) at 6-7.

CERTIFIED COPY. 1. A copy certified to be a true copy. 2. i. In relation to a document of a corporation, a copy of the document certified to be a true copy by an officer thereof, ii. in relation to a document issued by a court, a copy of the document certified to be a true copy under the seal of the court and signed by the registrar or clerk thereof, iii. in relation to a document in the custody of the Director, a copy of the document certified to be a true copy by the Director and signed by the Director or by such officer of the Ministry as is designated by the regulations. *Business Corporations Act, 1982*, S.O. 1982, c. 4, s. 1.

CERTIFIED COUNCIL OF TRADE UNIONS. A council of trade unions that is certified under this Act as the bargaining agent for a bargaining unit of employees of an employer. *Labour Relations Act*, R.S.O. 1980, c. 228, s. 1.

CERTIFIED GENERAL ACCOUNTANT. See PRACTICE OF ~.

CERTIFIED INSTITUTION. An institution that by a certificate issued by the Minister of National Health and Welfare is certified to be (a) a bona fide public institution whose principal purpose is to provide care for children or aged, infirm or incapacitated persons and (b) in receipt annually of aid from the Government of Canada or the government of a province for the care of persons described in paragraph (a). *Excise Tax Act*, R.S.C. 1985 (2d Supp.), c. 7, s. 68.24.

CERTIFIED MAIL. Mail for which (a) a signature is obtained on delivery, (b) proof of delivery is returned to the sender, and (c) a record of delivery is retained by the Post Office Department. *Special Services and Fees Regulations*, C.R.C., c. 1296, s. 39.

CERTIFIED NON-CANADIAN SHIP. A ship other than a Canadian ship, when employed on a voyage that the Director of Marine Services of the Department of Transport certifies was essential to the prosecution of the War on behalf of His Majesty or His Majesty's allies. *Civilian War Pensions and Allowances Act*, R.S.C. 1985, c. C-31, s. 6.

CERTIFIED RECORD. A plan or field notes prepared in a manner satisfactory to the registrar-general, and certified to as accurate by a surveyor, showing the particulars of a survey made by the surveyor.

CERTIFIED STATUS. With respect to seed, means that (a) the crop from which the seed is derived meets the standards established by the Association and a crop certificate designated "certified" has been issued for that crop by the Association, or (b) if of foreign origin, the seed is certified as being of certified status by an approved certifying agency. *Seeds Regulations*, C.R.C., c. 1400, s. 2.

CERTIFIED UNION. A union recognized by a labour relations board as bargaining agent of a group of workers.

CERTIFIER. See PAYMENT ~.

CERTIFY. *v.* To attest to the truth of a state of affairs.

CERTIORARI. *n.* An order to "bring up" to a court on the basis of lack of jurisdiction the record of a statutory tribunal or lower court to be quashed. S.A. DeSmith, *Judicial Review of Administrative Action*, 4th ed. by J.M. Evans (London: Stevens, 1980) at 25.

CERTIORARI IN AID. An application for certiorari made in connection with another application, usually "in aid" of habeas corpus.

CERTUM EST QUOD CERTUM REDDI POTEST. [L.] What is capable of being made certain is to be treated as certain.

CERVIX. *n.* The neck of the uterus which connects the vagina with the uterine cavity. F.A. Jaffe, *A Guide to Pathological Evidence*, 2d ed. (Toronto: Carswell, 1983) at 172.

C.E.S.H.G. *abbr.* Canadian Employment, Safety and Health Guide.

CESSANTE CAUSA, CESSAT EFFECTUS. [L.] When the cause ceases, the effect ceases.

CESSANTE RATIONE LEGIS, CESSAT IPSA LEX. [L.] When the reason of the law ceases, the law itself ceases.

CESSANTE STATU PRIMITIVO, CESSAT DERIVATIVUS. [L.] When the original estate determines, the derivative estate ceases.

CESSAT EXECUTIO. [L.] Suspension or stopping of execution.

CESSATION. *n.* Termination of membership of a member in the society and the striking of his name from the roll of notaries public. *Notaries Act*, R.S.B.C. 1979, c. 299, s. 1.

CESSATION OF CHARGE. An instrument which acknowledges that the claim against real property contained in a charge has been discharged.

CESSER. *n.* Occurs when a term annuity determines or comes to an end.

CESSET PROCESSUS. [L.] A stay of proceedings which is entered on a record.

CESSION. *n.* Ceding, yielding, giving up.

CESSURE. *n.* Ceding, giving over; departing from.

CESTUI QUE TRUST. *pl.* **CESTUIS QUE TRUST.** A beneficiary; beneficial owner of trust property.

CESTUI QUE USE. One for whose use (or benefit) someone else held land or other hereditaments.

CESTUI QUE VIE. One for whose life someone else holds an estate or interest in property. See TENANT POUR AUTRE VIE.

CETERIS PARIBUS. [L.] Other things being equal.

CF. *abbr.* Compare.

C.F. *abbr.* 1. Cour fédérale. 2. In sales contract, means price included cost and freight. 2. Recueils de jurisprudence de la Cour fédérale du Canada.

C.F. & I. See C.I.F.

C.F. (APPEL). *abbr.* Cour fédérale du Canada—Cour d'appel.

C.F.I. See C.I.F.

C.F.L.Q. *abbr.* Canadian Family Law Quarterly.

CFPO. *abbr.* Canadian Forces Post Office.

C.F. (1RE E INST.). *abbr.* Cour fédérale du Canada—Division de première instance.

C.F.S. COMM. *abbr.* Corporate and Financial Services Commission.

CGSB. *abbr.* The Canadian Government Specifications Board. Canada regulations.

CH. *abbr.* 1. Chapter. 2. Chancery.

[ ] CH. *abbr.* Law Reports, Chancery, 1891-.

CHAIN. *n.* 1. 22 yards. *Weights and Measures Act*, S.C. 1970-71-72, c. 36, Schedule II. 2. An old surveyors' measure equal to 100 links or 66 feet. See BOOM ~.

CHAIN OF TITLE. Tracking successive transfers or other conveyances of a particular parcel of land.

CHAIN PICKETING. Patrolling a place of business by a single file of closely ranked persons to form a human chain barring the entrance.

CHAIN STORE. Any branch retail store operated or controlled directly or controlled indirectly by any person, firm or corporation, who or which either within or outside the province operates or controls four or more retail stores, either directly or indirectly and/or through parent, subsidiary or affiliated persons, firms or corporations. *Licensing Act*, R.S.P.E.I. 1974, c. L-15, s. 1.

CHAIN THEATRE. Any branch theatre house operated or controlled directly or indirectly by any person, firm or corporation, who or which either within or outside the province operates or controls four or more branch theatre houses, either directly or indirectly and/or through parent, subsidiary, or affiliated persons, firms or corporations. *Licensing Act*, R.S.P.E.I. 1974, c. L-15, s. 1.

CHAIN WHOLESALE STORE. Any branch wholesale store operated or controlled directly or controlled indirectly by any person, firm or corporation, who or which either within or outside the province operates or controls four or more wholesale stores, either directly or indirectly and/or through parent, subsidiary or affiliated persons, firms or corporations. *Licensing Act*, R.S.P.E.I. 1974, c. L-15, s. 1.

CHAIRMAN. *n.* 1. A person who presides at meetings of the board of directors of a corporation. 2. A person occupying the position of chairman, by whatever name called, of the board of directors of a corporation. *Financial Administration Act*, R.S.C. 1985, c. F-11, s. 83. 3. A person appointed or elected head of a board, committee, commission or foundation. 4. The person specifically appointed by the bishop to call and preside over, in a parish or chapelry, the fabrique meeting or the meeting of the parishioners or, failing such an appointment, the pastor or ministering cleric. *An Act to Amend the Summary Convictions Act, the Code of Civil Procedure and Other Legislation*, S.Q. 1982, c. 32, s. 88. See IMPARTIAL ~; SHOP ~.

CHALLENGE. *v.* 1. To object. 2. To take exception against a juror. See PEREMPTORY ~.

CHALLENGE FOR CAUSE. The suitability of a juror is objected to on basis of knowledge of the case or lack of qualifications or impartiality.

CHAMBER. *n.* The place where legislative assemblies are held; the assemblies themselves. See FIRING ~; WORKING ~.

CHAMBERLAIN. *n.* The keeper, manager or director of a chamber or chambers.

CHAMBER OF COMMERCE. 1. A corporation incorporated or continued under this Act as a membership corporation to carry on the activities of promoting and improving trade and commerce and thereby promoting and improving the economic, civic and social welfare of a district. *Non-profit Corporations Act*, S.S. 1979, c. N-41, s. 176. 2. The board of trade or chamber of commerce for any city, town or place in Canada that is nearest to any harbour or anchorage of ships. *Canada Shipping Act*, R.S.C. 1985, c. S-9, s. 2.

CHAMBERS. *n.* Judge's office; a room in which motions or applications or other business not required to be carried out in court is transacted.

CHAMOIS. *n.* Leather produced from (a) the skin of the mountain antelope or chamois, or (b) sheep or lamb skin from which the grain has been removed prior to tanning, where the tanning process is restricted to the oxidation of fish or marine animal oils and where a suede finish has been applied to one or both sides of the leather. *Chamois Labelling Regulations*, C.R.C., c. 1137, s. 2.

CHAMPAGNE. *n.* Wine produced in the district of France called Champagne.

CHAMPERTOR. *n.* A person who brings suits in order to have part of the gain or proceeds.

CHAMPERTY. *n.* An agreement under which a third person is to share in the proceeds of a litigated claim; a form of maintenance. See MAINTENANCE AND ~.

CHANCE. *n.* An accident; absence of explainable causation; risk. See SALE OF A ~.

CHANCELLOR. *n.* 1. The highest official of a university. 2. The presiding judge of a court of chancery. 3. The cleric entrusted with the keeping of the archives of a diocese. *An Act Respecting Fabriques*, R.S.Q. 1977, c. F-1, s. 1. See VICE-~.

CHANCE-MEDLEY. *n.* A sudden or casual affray.

CHANCERY. *n.* Originally an office where writs were issued. See COURT OF ~.

CHANGE. *v.* To alter; substitute; modify; exchange.

CHANGE. *n.* 1. Alteration, substitution, modification. 2. Exchange of money for money of another denomination. See MATERIAL ~; POST MORTEM ~; RATE OF COST ~; SIG-

NIFICANT ~; STRUCTURAL ~; TECHNO-LOGICAL ~.

CHANGE OF NAME. Any change in the name of a physical person by alteration, substitution, addition or abandonment. *Change of Name Act*, R.S.Q. 1977, c. C-10, s. 1.

CHANGE OF PARTIES. Occurs where parties to litigation are added or substituted.

CHANGE OF POSSESSION. Such change of possession as is open and reasonably sufficient to afford public notice thereof. *Bills of Sale Acts.*

CHANGE OF SOLICITOR. The change of lawyer representing a client in an action effected by filing notice in court.

CHANGE ROOM. A room that is used by employees as a room within which to change from their street clothes to their work clothes before starting work, and from their work clothes to their street clothes after finishing work, and includes a locker room. *Canada Sanitation Regulations*, C.R.C., c. 1009, s. 2.

CHANNEL. *n.* 1. The bed in which a river flows; watercourse; the course followed in navigating a river or other body of water. 2. Includes a space between a transmitter and receiver of telecommunications and any other channel of transmission of telecommunications. *The Education and Health Tax Act*, R.S.S. 1978, c. E-3, s. 3. See AUGMENTED ~ SERVICE; COMMUNITY ~; RESTRICTED ~.

CHAPEL. *n.* A place of worship.

CHAPELRY. *n.* A territory canonically erected as a chapelry for the purposes of the Roman Catholic religion and the benefit of the faithful of such religion. *An Act Respecting Fabriques*, R.S.Q. 1977, c. F-1, s. 1.

CHAPLAIN. *n.* The member of the clergy attached to a unit of the armed forces or an institution such as a hospital, university or prison.

CHAR. *n.* Arctic char Salvelinus alpinus and includes sea-run speckled trout Salvelinus Fontinalis. *Newfoundland Fishery Regulations*, C.R.C., c. 846, s. 347.

CHARACTER. *n.* 1. A device, name, signature, word, letter or numeral. *Livestock Brand Act*, R.S.B.C. 1979, c. 241, s. 1. 2. The inclination of a person to act in a particular way relating to integrity, peaceableness, lawfulness, honesty and ultimately veracity. P.K. McWilliams, *Canadian Criminal Evidence*, 3d ed. (Aurora: Canada Law Book, 1988) at 39-1.

CHARACTERISTICS. See PHYSICAL ~; TRADITIONAL OR ARTISTIC ~.

CHARACTERIZATION. *n.* A matter of classifying, categorizing or assimilating elements of a concept into the overall concept. J.G. McLeod, *The Conflict of Laws* (Calgary: Carswell, 1983) at 26.

CHARGE. *v.* 1. With respect to tolls, includes power to a company to quote, demand, levy, take and receive and sue for and recover, in any court of competent jurisdiction. *Railway Act*, R.S.B.C. 1979, c. 354, s. 1. 2. To give instructions to a jury. 3. To take proceedings or lay an information against a person believed to have committed an offence. 4. To lay a duty upon a person. 5. To impose a tax. 6. To purchase on credit.

CHARGE. *n.* 1. A registered interest less than fee simple and a registered encumbrance on land. *Condominium Act*, R.S.B.C. 1979, c. 61, s. 1. 2. An instrument creating security against property for payment of a debt or obligation. 3. The amount required, as the price of a thing or service sold or supplied. 4. A judge's instruction to a jury. 5. A price or rate. 6. Includes every encumbrance on land. *Court Order Enforcement Act*, R.S.B.C. 1979, c. 75, s. 42. 7. As related to taxation or other financial encumbrance or burden imposed on or in respect of land, personal property, or persons, (A) the imposition of that taxation, encumbrance, or burden; or (B) that tax, encumbrance, or burden itself. 8. A charge on land given for the purpose of securing the payment of a debt or the performance of an obligation. 9. An explosive and a detonator, or an explosive, a detonator and primer that is exploded as a single unit. *Occupational Health and Safety Act*, R.R.O. 1980, Reg. 694, s. 1. See ACCOMMODATION ~; AGREED ~; AUTHORIZED ~; BOARDING ~; BRACING ~; CARRYING ~; CESSATION OF ~; CHARGES; CONTAINER HANDLING ~; CONTAINER REHANDLING ~; CRANE HIRE ~; CRANE MOVING ~; DEBT ~; DELIVERING ~; DIRECT ~ CO-OPERATIVE; DISTRIBUTION ~; EQUITABLE ~; FIXED ~; FLOATING ~; HANDLING ~; HAVE ~ OF; HAVING ~ OF; HEAVY-LIFT ~; INSURANCE ~; LIFT ~; LIGHTER ~; LOADING ~; OFFICER IN ~; OVERDRAFT ~; OVERTIME ~; PASSENGER ~; PROPRIETARY ~; RECEIVING ~; REDOCUMENTATION ~; REGULATORY ~; RENT ~; SALVAGE ~; SPECIFIC ~; STORAGE ~; SUB-ORDER DELIVERY ~; SWITCHING ~; TERMINAL ~; THROUGHOUT ~; TIME ~; TOLL OR ~; UNLOADING ~; USER ~; WINTERING ~.

CHARGEABLE. *adj.* Capable of or subject to being charged with a duty or obligation.

CHARGE ACCOUNT. An arrangement with a store or financial institution permitting purchase of goods and services on credit under which purchaser agrees to pay within specified time or periodically.

CHARGED. *adj.* Accused of an offence. See AMOUNT ~.

CHARGE D'AFFAIRES. [Fr.] A diplomatic agent.

CHARGEE. *n.* A person in whose favour a charge is given. *Land Registration Reform Act*, S.O. 1984, c. 32, s. 1.

CHARGES. *n.* Expenses; costs. See BORROWER'S ~; CHARGE; CREDIT ~; CROWN ~; DEBT ~; SEPARATE ~; SIDE WHARFAGE ~; TERMINAL ~.

CHARGE-SHEET. *n.* A paper kept at a police station to record the names of the persons brought into custody, the accusation, and the accuser's name in each case.

CHARGE THE JURY. A judge gives instructions to a jury before it deliberates with regard to the law as it applies to the case heard by them.

CHARGE TO THE JURY. See CHARGE THE JURY.

CHARGING ORDER. 1. A creditor can apply to a judge to order that shares of or in any public company stand charged with the payment of the judgment debt. 2. An order made for the benefit of a solicitor against funds in court or property realized through the endeavours of the solicitor.

CHARGOR. *n.* A person who gives a charge. *Land Registration Reform Act*, S.O. 1984, c. 32, s. 1.

CHARITABLE. *adj.* Having purposes of a charity.

CHARITABLE CORPORATION. A body constituted exclusively for charitable purposes no part of the income of which is payable to, or is otherwise available for the personal benefit of, any proprietor, member or shareholder thereof.

CHARITABLE FOUNDATION. 1. A corporation or trust, other than a charitable organization, constituted and operated exclusively for charitable purposes. 2. A corporation or trust constituted and operated exclusively for charitable purposes, no part of the income of which is payable to, or is otherwise available for, the personal benefit of any proprietor, member, shareholder, trustee or settlor thereof and that is not a charitable organization. *Income Tax Act*, R.S.C. 1952, c. 148 (as added by S.C. 1976-77, c. 4, s. 60(1)), s. 149.1(a).

CHARITABLE INSTITUTION. All or any part of a building or buildings maintained and oper-

ated by an approved corporation for persons requiring residential, sheltered, specialized or group care.

CHARITABLE ORGANIZATION. An organization, whether or not incorporated, (i) all the resources of which are devoted to charitable activities carried on by the organization itself, (ii) no part of the income of which is payable to, or is otherwise available for, the personal benefit of any proprietor, member, shareholder, trustee or settlor thereof, (iii) more than 50% of the directors, trustees, officers or like officials of which deal with each other and with each of the other directors, trustees, officers or officials at arm's length, and (iv) where it has been designated as a private foundation or public foundation pursuant to subsection (6.3) or 110(8.1) or (8.2) or has applied after February 15, 1984 for registration under paragraph 110(8)(c) or under the definition "registered charity" in subsection 248(1) not more than 50% of the capital of which has been contributed or otherwise paid into the organization by one person or members of a group of persons who do not deal with each other at arm's length and, for the purpose of this subparagraph, a reference to any person or to members of a group does not include a reference to Her Majesty in right of Canada or a province, a municipality, another registered charity that is not a private foundation, or any club, society or association described in paragraph 149(1)(l). *Income Tax Act*, R.S.C. 1952, c. 148 (as added by S.C. 1976-77, c. 4, s. 60(1)), s. 149.1(b).

CHARITABLE PURPOSE. 1. The relief of poverty, education, the advancement of religion. 2. Includes other purposes beneficial to the community and includes the advancement of (a) recreation; (b) sports or athletics; (c) aid to the disabled and handicapped; (d) culture; and (e) youth or senior citizens.

CHARITABLE PURPOSES. Includes the disbursement of funds to qualified donees. *Income Tax Act*, R.S.C. 1952, c. 148 (as added by S.C. 1976-77, c. 4, s. 60(1)), s. 149.1(c).

CHARITABLE TRUSTS. (a) Trusts for the relief of poverty, (b) trusts for the advancement of education, (c) trusts for the advancement of religion, (d) trusts for other purposes beneficial to the community not falling under any of the preceding heads. *Commrs. of Income Tax v. Pemsel*, [1891] A.C. 531 at 583 per Lord Macnaghten.

CHARITY. *n.* 1. A charitable organization or charitable foundation. *Income Tax Act*, R.S.C. 1952, c. 148 (as added by S.C. 1976-77, c. 4, s. 60(1)), s. 149.1(d). 2. Any person, association, institute or organization under whose auspices funds for benevolent, educational, cultural, charitable or religious purposes are to be raised. *Charities Act*, R.S.P.E.I. 1974, c. C-4, s. 2. See EMPLOYEES' ~ TRUST; REGISTERED ~.

CHARTER. *n.* 1. The Canadian Charter of Rights and Freedoms, Part I of the Constitution Act, 1982. 2. Includes any act, statute, or ordinance by or under which a corporation has been incorporated and any letters patent, supplementary letters patent, certificate of incorporation, memorandum of association, and any other document evidencing corporate existence. 3. An agreement to supply a vessel or aircraft for a voyage or a period of time. See ADVANCE BOOKING ~; ENTITY ~; INCLUSIVE TOUR ~; TERM ~; TIME ~.

CHARTER AIR CARRIER. See FOREIGN ~.

CHARTER AND REGULATIONS. The charter of a corporation and its articles, bylaws, rules and regulations.

CHARTER BY-LAW. By-law of an association that is subject to the approval of the Minister. *Canada Cooperative Associations Act*, R.S.C. 1985, c. C-40, s. 3.

CHARTERED ACCOUNTANT. See PRACTICE OF A ~.

CHARTERED BANK. A bank to which the *Bank Act* (Canada) applies, and includes a branch, agency, and office of a bank.

CHARTERED BUS SERVICE. Service by means of a bus that is engaged solely to transport the persons engaging it on one occasion or for one trip to a stated destination and, if so required, return therefrom to the point of origin. *City of Winnipeg Act*, S.M. 1971, c. 105, s. 565.

CHARTERED COMPANY. A company incorporated by Royal Charter such as the Hudson's Bay Company.

CHARTERED SHIP. A ship hired; a ship subject to charter party.

CHARTERED TRIP. One specific trip for which a public vehicle is engaged, hired or chartered for the transportation exclusively of a group of persons and for which one fare or charge only is collected. *Public Vehicles Act*, R.R.O. 1980, Reg. 888, s. 1.

CHARTERER. *n.* One who hires a ship or aircraft for a certain period or for a voyage.

CHARTER PARTY. *vars.* **CHARTERPARTY**, **CHARTER-PARTY.** An agreement to use or hire a ship or to convey goods for a specified period or on a specified voyage.

CHASE. *v.* To pursue rapidly with intent to overtake or send away.

CHASSIS-CAB. *n.* A vehicle consisting of a chassis that is capable of being driven, drawn or self-propelled, upon which may be mounted a cab, and that is designed to receive (a) a passenger-carrying body including a body that incorporates a prime mover, or (b) a work performing structure other than a fifth-wheel coupling. Canada regulations.

CHASTE. *adj.* Applied to unmarried woman who has not had sexual intercourse.

CHASTITY. *n.* Purity; the state of being chaste.

CHATTEL. *n.* Colloquially used to refer to chattel mortgage. See CHATTELS; INCORPOREAL ~.

CHATTEL MORTGAGE. A loan transaction in which goods are used as security. G.H.L. Fridman, *Sale of Goods in Canada*, 3d ed. (Toronto: Carswell, 1986) at 265.

CHATTEL PAPER. One or more than one writing that expresses both a monetary obligation and a security interest in specific goods.

CHATTELS. *n.* Goods and chattels capable of complete transfer by delivery, and includes, when separately assigned or charged, fixtures and growing crops, but does not include chattel interests in real property or fixtures when assigned together with a freehold or leasehold interest in any land or building to which they are affixed, or growing crops when assigned together with any interest in the land on which they grow, or a ship or vessel registered under the Canada Shipping Act or the Merchant Shipping Act, 1894 (Imperial), or a share in such a ship or vessel, or an interest in the stock, funds or securities of a government or in the capital of a corporation, or a book debt or other chose in action. (*Bills of Sale Acts*). See GOODS AND ~; PERSONAL ~.

CHATTELS PERSONAL. "Pure personalty", either in action or in possession. E.L.G. Tyler & N.E. Palmer, eds., *Crossley Vaines' Personal Property*, 5th ed. (London: Butterworths, 1973) at 11.

CHATTELS REAL. Leaseholds.

CHAUD-MEDLEY. See CHANCE-MEDLEY.

CHAUFFEUR. *n.* A person who drives motor vehicles as a means of livelihood.

CHAUFFEUR'S LICENCE. See RESTRICTED ~.

CH. D. *abbr.* Law Reports, Chancery Division, 1875-1890.

CHEAP. *adj.* With low price.

CHEAT. *v.* To obtain another's property fraudulently.

CHECKERBOARD. *v.* To divide land in the manner of a checkerboard so that one person owns the "red squares" and another owns the "black squares". The owners on title may be nominees or trustees for the actual landowner, or the actual landowner might retain "one set of squares" and transfer the "other set" to a nominee. B.J. Reiter, R.C.B. Risk & B.N. McLellan, *Real Estate Law*, 3d ed. (Toronto: Emond Montgomery, 1986) at 397.

CHECK-IN BOARD. A board on which employees hang brass checks to show attendance.

CHECK-OFF. *n.* A system which requires the employer to deduct from wages and remit to the union the dues stipulated, with respect to the persons covered by the collective agreement. See AUTOMATIC ~.

CHEDDAR CHEESE. 1. Cheese made (i) from the matted and milled curd of milk by the cheddar process, or (ii) from milk by another procedure that produces a finished cheese having the same physical and chemical properties as the cheese produced by the cheddar process, and (b) may contain (i) a colouring matter approved under the Food and Drug Regulations, or (ii) bacterial culture. *Canada Dairy Products Regulations*, C.R.C., c. 553, s. 2. 2. Cheese made by the cheddar process from matted and milled curd obtained from milk, to which no skim milk has been added or from which no milk-fat has been removed, by the action of rennet or other coagulating agent, with or without the addition of not more than 2 per cent bacterial culture, and that contains on the dry basis not less than 48 per cent milk-fat and no fat or oil other than milk-fat. *Farm Products Grades and Sales Act*, R.R.O. 1980, Reg. 327, s. 1.

CHEESE. *n.* Cheese made by coagulating the casein of milk, skim milk, evaporated milk, evaporated skim milk, cream, milk powder or skim milk powder, or a mixture thereof, with or without the addition of cream, milk powder, skim milk powder or small amounts of other ingredients such as ripening ferments, harmless acid-producing bacterial cultures, special mould cultures, salt, seasoning, special flavouring materials, food colour or permitted preservatives. *Farm Products Grades and Sales Act*, R.R.O. 1980, Reg. 327, s. 1. See CHEDDAR ~; PACKAGE ~; PROCESS ~; WHOLE ~.

CHEESE FACTORY. A place where milk from cows or goats is manufactured into cheese.

CHEMICAL. See AGRICULTURAL ~; CORROSIVE ~; HAZARDOUS ~; NEW ~.

CHEMICAL CARRIER. A ship that is specially constructed or adapted for the carriage of dangerous chemicals and is engaged in the carriage of such chemicals. *Navigating Appliances Regulations*, C.R.C., c. 1449, s. 2.

CHEMICAL RECOVERY BOILER. A boiler that is capable of being fuelled by the black liquor that results from the Kraft sulphate pulp manufacturing process. *Power Engineers and Boiler and Pressure Vessel Safety Act*, S.B.C. 1981, c. 25, s. 1.

CHEMICAL STILL. Any distilling apparatus that is kept and used by any person for the sole purpose of distilling water or reclaiming alcohol previously used in or for the preparation or manufacture of chemical, medicinal or pharmaceutical preparations, or that is used for scientific or industrial purposes, and not used for the manufacture or distillation of spirits. *Excise Act*, R.S.C. 1985, c. E-14, s. 3.

CHEMIST. See MARINE ~; PHARMACEUTICAL ~.

CHEMISTRY. See PRACTICE OF PROFESSIONAL ~.

CHEQUE. *n.* Includes a bill of exchange drawn on any institution that makes it a business practice to honour bills of exchange or any particular kind thereof drawn on it by depositors. *Criminal Code*, R.S.C. 1985, c. C-46, s. 362(5) and 364(3). See CANCELLED ~; CERTIFIED ~; CROSSED ~; STALE ~.

CHEQUE REQUISITION. A requisition issued by the appropriate Minister and addressed to the Receiver General for a payment to be made by means of a cheque. *Account Verification and Payment Requisition Regulations*, C.R.C., c. 667, s. 2.

CHEST. See FLOATING ~.

CHEVISANCE. *n.* An unlawful contract or bargain.

C.H.F.L.G. *abbr.* Canadian Health Facilities Law Guide.

CHICANE. *v.* To use trickery.

CHICK. *n.* In relation to any species, an avian up to 72 hours of age that has not been fed or watered. *Animal Disease and Protection Regulations*, C.R.C., c. 296, s. 2.

CHICKEN. *n.* 1. Young birds of either sex that have flexible cartilage at the posterior end of the breast or keel bone and tender meat and soft skin of smooth texture. *Dressed and Eviscerated Poultry Regulations*, C.R.C., c. 283, s. 53. 2. Squab, broilers, fryers, roasters, poulards, capons and stags. *Meat Inspection Regulations*, C.R.C., c. 1032, s. 135. See BROILER ~; ROASTER ~.

CHICKEN CAPON. Male chicken that has undergone a process resulting in a complete removal or inactivation of the sex organs, and that has flexible cartilage at the posterior end of the breast or keel bone, tender meat and soft skin of smooth texture. *Dressed and Eviscerated Poultry Regulations*, C.R.C., c. 283, s. 53.

CHICKEN FAT CLOT. Mainly of white blood cells, bright yellow in colour, forming the top layer of a clot. It is used to determine the position of a body after death. F.A. Jaffe, *A Guide to Pathological Evidence*, 2d ed. (Toronto: Carswell, 1983) at 172.

CHICKEN HADDIE. Canned haddock, cod, cusk or hake, or any combination thereof, that has not been ground, but does not include dark or sow hake. *Fish Inspection Regulations*, C.R.C., c. 802, s. 2.

CHICKS. *n.* Poultry under one month old.

CHICKS-FOR-PLACEMENT. Female chickens twenty weeks of age or less.

CHICOT. *n.* A dead tree or a dead limb of a tree. *Occupational Health and Safety Act*, R.R.O. 1980, Reg. 692, s. 107.

CHIEF. See DEPUTY ~; FIRE ~; IN ~.

CHIEF AGENCY. The principal office or place of business.

CHIEF AGENT. 1. In respect of any registered party, means the registered agent of that party who is recorded in the registry of agents of registered parties maintained by the Chief Electoral Officer. *Canada Elections Act*, R.S.C. 1985, c. E-2, s. 2. 2. The chief agent of a company in Canada, named as such in a power of attorney.

CHIEF ELECTORAL OFFICER. The Chief Electoral Officer appointed under The Elections Act.

CHIEF ENGINEER. The person who is responsible for the operation of a boiler or steam plant.

CHIEF EXECUTIVE OFFICER. 1. The person appointed by the board of governors of a hospital to be responsible to the board for the day by day administration of the hospital. 2. (i) The Deputy Minister in any Department of the Government of the province, (ii) the Auditor General, (iii) the Clerk of the Executive Council, and (iv) any other official head of any agency designated by the Lieutenant Governor in Council to function as a Deputy Minister for the purposes of this Act. *Newfoundland Public Service Commission Act*, S. Nfld. 1973, c. 116, s. 2.

CHIEF EXECUTIVE OFFICER OF AN AGENCY. The person entrusted by law, with regard to his staff or the staff of an agency, with the powers of the chief executive officer of an agency, or, if such is not the case, the person exercising the highest authority in the agency. *Civil Service Act*, S.Q. 1978, c. 15, s. 1.

CHIEF GAME OFFICER. Of a province means a person appointed as chief or director of a provincial agency concerned with the administration of a provincial wildlife act. *Migratory Birds Regulations*, C.R.C., c. 1035, s. 2.

CHIEF GOVERNMENT WHIP. See CHIEF WHIP.

CHIEF INSPECTOR. The officer employed as chief inspector for the purpose of an act.

CHIEF JUDGE. 1. The person having authority to assign duties to the judge. *Courts of Justice Act*, S.O. 1984, c. 11, s. 133. 2. The chief justice, chief judge or other person recognized by law as having rank or status senior to all other members of, or having the supervision of, that court, but where that court is a superior court constituted with divisions, then the person having such rank or status in relation to all other members of the division of which the particular judge is a member. *Judges Act*, R.S.C. 1985, c. J-1, s. 41(4).

CHIEF JUSTICE. The chief justice, chief judge or other person recognized by law as having rank or status senior to all other members of, or having the supervision of, that court, but where that court is a superior court constituted with divisions, then the person having such rank or status in relation to all other members of the division of which the particular judge is a member. *Judges Act*, R.S.C. 1985, c. J-1, s. 41(4). See APPROPRIATE ~; ASSOCIATE ~.

CHIEF LIBRARIAN. The functionary appointed under this act to manage and control the National Library. *An Act Respecting the Bibliothèque Nationale du Québec*, R.S.Q. 1977, c. B-2, s. 1.

CHIEF OFFICE. The principal office or place of business of any licensed insurer.

CHIEF OFFICER. 1. Includes the mayor of a city, town or village or the chairman of a county or the reeve of a municipal district and in the case of an improvement district, the Minister. *Tax Recovery Act*, R.S.A. 1980, c. T-1, s. 1. 2. The chief of police of any police force and includes an officer acting as such chief of police. *Police Act*, S.N.S. 1985, c. 33, s. 1.

CHIEF OFFICER OF CUSTOMS. Collector or other chief or only officer of customs at any port. *Canada Shipping Act*, R.S.C. 1985, c. S-9, s. 2.

CHIEF OPERATING ENGINEER. An operating engineer who at all times has charge of and the responsibility for the safe operation of a plant.

CHIEF OPERATOR. An operator or an operating engineer who at all times has charge of and the responsibility for the safe operation of a compressor plant or a refrigeration plant.

CHIEF OPPOSITION WHIP. See CHIEF WHIP.

CHIEF PENSIONS ADVOCATE. The Chief Pensions Advocate referred to in section 18. *Pensions Act*, R.S.C. 1985, c. P-6, s. 2.

CHIEF PROVINCIAL FIREARMS OFFICER. A person who has been designated in writing by the Attorney General of a province as the chief provincial firearms officer for that province. *Criminal Code*, R.S.C. 1985, c. C-46, s. 84(1).

CHIEF REPRESENTATIVE. A person who is recognized by the Government of Canada as the chief representative in Canada of a country in respect of which this Act applies, whether such person is known by the title of High Commissioner for that country or by another title. *Diplomatic Immunities (Commonwealth Countries) Act*, R.S.C. 1970, c. D-4, s. 2.

CHIEF STATIONARY ENGINEER. A stationary engineer who is designated by a mine manager to supervise the operation, maintenance and repair of all machinery, boilers and pressure vessels used in the operation of a coal mine. *Coal Mines (CBDC) Safety Regulations*, C.R.C., c. 1011, s. 2.

CHIEF STATISTICIAN. Chief Statistician of Canada appointed under subsection 4(1) of the Statistics Act. *Statistics Act*, R.S.C. 1985, c. S-19, s. 2.

CHIEF SURVEYOR. The Chief Surveyor of Land Titles Offices. *The Lands Surveys Act*, R.S.S. 1978, c. L-4, s. 2.

CHIEF WHIP. Each party in Parliament has a person who keeps members of that party informed about the business of the House, ensures these members attend, determines pairing arrangements so that the votes of members who cannot attend divisions will be neutralized and not lost, and supplies lists of members to serve on the various House committees. A. Fraser, G.A. Birch & W.A. Dawson, eds., *Beauchesne's Rules and Forms of the House of Commons of Canada*, 5th ed. (Toronto: Carswell, 1978) at 50.

CHILD. *n.* 1. A person who has not attained the age of majority. 2. A person who (i) has not reached the age of majority, (ii) has not been married, and (iii) is not a parent with legal custody of his or her child. 3. An unmarried person under the age of majority. 4. Includes, where the context requires, a child en ventre sa mere. 5. Includes son, daughter, grand-son, grand-daughter, step-son, and step-daughter. 6. Includes a child lawfully adopted. 7. Any other child to whom another person stood in loco parentis. 8. An individual of compulsory school age. 9. Includes an adopted child and an illegitimate child. *Criminal Code*, R.S.C. 1985, c. C-46, s. 214. 10. A person who is or, in the absence of evidence to the contrary, appears to be under the age of twelve years. *Young Offenders Act*, R.S.C. 1985, c. Y-1, s. 2. 11. (a) A person of whom the taxpayer is the natural parent whether the person was born within or outside marriage; (b) a person who is wholly dependent on the taxpayer for support and of whom the taxpayer has, or immediately before the person attained the age of 19 years had, in law or in fact, the custody and control; (c) a child of the taxpayer's spouse; (d) an adopted child of the taxpayer; and (e) a spouse of a child of the taxpayer. *Income Tax Act*, R.S.C. 1952, c. 148 (as am. S.C. 1988, c. 55, s. 191(1)), s. 252(1). 12. For the purposes of this section and sections 40, 44, 73 and 146, child of a taxpayer includes (i) a child of his child, (ii) a child of his child's child, and (iii) a person who, at any time before he attained the age of 19 years, was wholly dependent on the taxpayer for support and of whom the taxpayer had, at that time, in law or in fact, the custody and control. *Income Tax Act*, R.S.C. 1952, c. 148 (as am. S.C. 1988, c. 55, s. 49(4)), s. 70(10)(a). 13. A person under the age of 13, 14, 15, 16, 17, 18, 19, or 21 years of age. 14. A person who is between the ages of 6-12, or 5-13 years inclusive. See ADOPTED ~; BEST INTERESTS OF THE ~; DEPENDANT ~; DEPENDENT ~; DESERTED ~; DISABLED CONTRIBUTOR'S ~; DOMICILE OF THE ~; FATHER OF A ~; FOSTER ~; HANDICAPPED ~REN; ILLEGITIMATE ~; IMMIGRANT ~; INFANT ~; INVALID ~; MENTALLY RETARDED ~; MINOR ~; MODERATELY RETARDED ~; NATURAL ~; NEGLECTED ~; NEWLY-BORN ~; POSTHUMOUS ~; RETARDED ~.

CHILD ABDUCTION. The kidnapping of a child by the parent not awarded custody.

CHILD ABUSE. Physical, mental, sexual, emotional mistreatment of a child.

CHILD CARE EXPENSE. An expense incurred in a taxation year for the purpose of providing in Canada, for an eligible child of a taxpayer, child care services including baby sitting services, day nursery services or services provided at a boarding school or camp if the services were provided (i) to enable the taxpayer, or the supporting person of the child for the year, who resided with the child at the time the expense was incurred, (A) to perform the duties of an office or employment, (B) to carry on a business either alone or as a partner actively engaged in the business, (C) to undertake an occupational training course in respect of which he received a training allowance paid to him under the National Training Act, or (D) to carry on research or any similar work in respect of which he received a grant, and (ii) by a resident of Canada other than a person (A) who is the father or the mother of the child, (B) who is a supporting person of the child or was under 21 years of age and connected with the taxpayer or his spouse by blood relationship, marriage, or adoption, or (C) in respect of whom an amount is deducted under section 118 in computing the tax payable under this Part for the year by the taxpayer or by a supporting person of the child. *Income Tax Act*, R.S.C. 1952, c. 148 (as am. S.C. 1988, c. 55, s. 39(4) to (6)), s. 63(3)(a) in part.

CHILD CARE FACILITY. A building, structure or enclosure in which day care is provided to more than five children with or without charge, for more than two hours and less than twelve hours per day, but does not include a building, structure or enclosure in which day care in provided solely on Sundays. *Child Care Facilities Act*, R.S.P.E.I. 1974, c. C-5, s. 2.

CHILD CARE RESOURCE. A child's own home, a foster home, group living home, community sponsored home, diagnostic centre, attendance centre, any other facility established for the care, treatment, training and rehabilitation of children.

CHILD CARE SERVICES. Assessment, counselling, referral, child protection and child placement services, voluntary care, homemaker, day care, consulting services, research and evaluation services with respect to child care services and similar services.

CHILD CARE WORKER. A person qualified by education, formal training or experience to work with children in a children's institution and whose duties are limited to the direct relationship with and supervision of the residents. *Children's Institutions Act*, R.R.O. 1980, Reg. 98, s. 8.

CHILD CARING FACILITY. A foster home, a licensed boarding home for a child under sixteen years, a group home, a place of safety, a residential centre, a receiving home, a training centre, a training school or such other facility as the Minister may approve or license as a child caring facility. *Children's Services Act*, S.N.S. 1976, c. 8. s. 2.

CHILD CARING INSTITUTION. A building, part of a building, group of buildings or other place of accommodation, other than the private dwelling of a family, wherein care, food and lodging are furnished, with or without charge, for two or more children living apart from their parents or guardians, or any place of accommodation designated as a child caring institution by the Minister. *Child Welfare Act*, R.S.N.S. 1967, c. 231, s. 56.

CHILD DEVELOPMENT SERVICE. A service for a child with a developmental or physical handicap, for the family of a child with a developmental or physical handicap, or for the child and the family. *Child and Family Services Act*, S.C. 1984, c. 55, s. 3.

CHILD IN CARE. 1. A child who is in the care, or the care and custody of an agency. *Children's Services Act*, S.N.S. 1976, c. 8, s. 2. 2. A child who is receiving residential services from a service provider and includes (a) a child who is in the care of a foster parent; and (b) a child who is detained in a place of temporary detention, committed to secure or open custody under the Young Offenders Act (Canada), or held in a place of open custody under section 91 of Part IV (Young Offenders). *Child and Family Services Act*, S.O. 1984, c. 55, s. 95.

CHILD IN NEED OF PROTECTION. A child (a) who is not receiving proper care, education, supervision, guidance or control; (b) who is in the custody of a person who is unable or unwilling to care for the child, or whose behaviour or way of life creates a danger for the child; (c) who has been physically abused, neglected or sexually exploited or is in danger of consistently threatening behaviour; (d) who is forced or induced to do work disproportionate to his strength or to perform for the public in a manner that is unacceptable for his age; (e) whose behaviour, condition, environment or associations is injurious or threatens to be injurious to himself or others; (f) for whom the parent or person is whose custody he is neglects or refuses to provide or obtain proper medical or surgical care or treatment necessary for his health and well-being where it is recommended by a duly qualified medical practitioner; (g) whose emotional or mental health and development is endangered or is likely to be endangered by the lack of affection, guidance and discipline or continuity of care in the child's life; (h) for whom the parent or person is whose custody he is neglects, refuses or is unable to provide the services and assistance needed by the child because of the child's physical, mental, or emotional handicap or disability; (i) who is living in a situation where there is severe domestic violence; (j) who is beyond the control of the person caring for him; (k) who is living apart from his parents without their consent; or (l) who is pregnant and refuses or is unable to provide properly and adequately for the health and welfare needs of herself and her child both before and after the birth of her child. *Family and Child Services Act*, S.P.E.I. 1981, c. 12, s. 2.

CHILD LABOUR. Work prohibited by statute by minors when minor is under age specified by statute.

CHILD OF THE MARRIAGE. A child of two spouses or former spouses who, at the material time, (a) is under the age of sixteen years, or (b) is sixteen years of age or over and under their charge but unable, by reason of illness, disability or other cause, to withdraw from their charge or to obtain the necessaries of life. *Divorce Act*, R.S.C. 1985 (2d Supp.), c. 3, s. 2.

CHILDREN'S AID SOCIETY. An organized or incorporated society having among its objects the promotion of family and child welfare.

CHILDREN'S BOARDING HOME. A home other than the home of the parents or relatives by blood or marriage in which children are placed for more than a month by a parent or guardian privately for care and supervision and from whom payment is received by the owners or operators of the boarding home. *Child Welfare Act*, S.M. 1974, c. 30, s. 1.

CHILDREN'S CLOTHING. (a) Children's dresses, suits, coats, blouses, sweaters, undershirts, pyjamas, combinations, snow-suits, overalls and such other children's garments that fit the upper half of or the whole body, up to and including girl's commercial trade size 14X or boy's commercial trade size 18 or girl's "Canada Standard size" 14X or boy's "Canada Standard size" 18 or sweaters designated for girls or boys and sized small, medium and large, (b) children's trousers, slacks, jeans, slims, undershorts, briefs, outer shorts and other children's garments that fit at or below the waist, up to and including girl's commercial trade size 14X and boy's commercial trade size 18 or girl's "Canada Standard Size" 14X or boy's "Canada Standard Size" 18, depending upon the size designation applicable, (c) boy's dress and sport shirts as designated for boys, up to and including commercial trade size designation 14 1/2 or "Canada Standard Size" 14 neck, depending upon the size designation applicable, (d) children's hose, up to and including girl's commercial trade size designation 10 and boy's commercial trade size designation 10 1/2 or stretchy socks designated for children, (e) children's hats in styles designated for children, up to and including girl's commercial trade size designation 22 and boy's commercial trade size designation 7 1/8, and (f) children's gloves in styles designed for chil-

dren, up to and including girl's and boy's commercial trade size designation 7. *Retail Sales Tax Act*, R.R.O. 1980, Reg. 904, s. 1.

CHILDREN'S GUARDIAN. The person appointed by the Minister as the Children's Guardian for the purposes of this Act. *Child Welfare Act*, S.A. 1984, c. 8.1, s. 1.

CHILDREN'S INSTITUTION. All or any part of a building or buildings maintained and operated for children and other persons requiring sheltered, specialized or group care.

CHILDREN'S MENTAL HEALTH CENTRE. All or any part of a building or buildings maintained and operated to provide services for children suffering from mental, emotional or psychiatric disorders or any combination thereof. *Children's Mental Health Services Act*, R.S.O. 1980, c. 69, s. 1.

CHILDREN'S RESIDENCE. A parent model residence where five or more children not of common parentage, or a staff model residence where three or more children not of common parentage, live and receive residential care, and includes a foster home or other home or institution that is supervised or operated by a children's aid society.

CHILD-RESISTANT CONTAINER. A container that, when tested in accordance with the procedure prescribed in Schedule IV, (a) cannot be opened, prior to the demonstration described in subitem 7(1) of that Schedule, by at least 85 per cent of the children in the child test group and by at least 80 per cent of the children in the child test group after the demonstration, and (b) within three minutes, can be opened and, if it is a container designed to be closed securely after having been opened, closed securely by at least 90 per cent of the persons in the adult test group. *Hazardous Products (Hazardous Substances) Regulations*, C.R.C., c. 926, s. 2.

CHILD TEST GROUP. A group of children consisting of at least 200 children who (a) are healthy, normal and without an obvious physical or mental handicap, (b) are between 42 and 51 months of age, and (c) represent evenly, within plus or minus 10 per cent, each monthly age between 42 and 51 months calculated to the nearest month. *Hazardous Products (Hazardous Substances) Regulations*, C.R.C., c. 926, s. 1.

CHILD TREATMENT SERVICE. A service for a child with a mental or psychiatric disorder, for the family of a child with a mental or psychiatric disorder, or for the child and the family. *Child and Family Services Act*, S.O. 1984, c. 55, s. 3.

CHILD WELFARE AGENCY. An agency that has been approved by the Lieutenant Governor in Council and having among its objects the protection of children from cruelty, the amelioration of family conditions that lead to neglect of children, or the care and control of children in need of protection. *Children's Protection Act*, R.S.P.E.I. 1974, c. C-7, s. 1.

CHILD WELFARE AUTHORITY. Any provincially approved agency that has been designated by or under the provincial law or by the provincial authority for the purpose of administering or assisting in the administration of any law of the province relating to the protection and care of children. *Canada Assistance Plan*, R.S.C. 1985, c. C-1, s. 2.

CHILD WELFARE SERVICE. A residential or non-residential service, child protection service, adoption service, individual or family counselling.

CHILLED SHOT. Shot pellets which are especially hardened. F.A. Jaffe, *A Guide to Pathological Evidence*, 2d ed. (Toronto: Carswell, 1983) at 183.

CHILLERS. *n.* Those heat recovery units or heat recovery chillers that are installed in a central air-conditioning system specifically designed to incorporate such units or chillers for the purpose of recovery of heat from the system and its subsequent utilization, and does not include pipes, ducts or other related parts of the system of which the heat recovery unit or chiller is a part. *Retail Sales Tax Act*, R.R.O. 1980, Reg. 903, s. 1.

CHIMNEY. *n.* A primarily vertical shaft enclosing at least one flue for conducting flue gases to the outdoors. *Building Code Act*, R.R.O. 1980, Reg. 87, s. 1. See FACTORY-BUILT ~; METAL ~.

CHIMNEY LINER. A conduit containing a chimney flue used as a lining of a masonry or concrete chimney. *Building Code Act*, R.R.O. 1980, Reg. 87, s. 1.

CHINESE WALLS. A method in which a law firm may represent more than one client in the same transaction by having the lawyer who represents one side keep everything confidential from the lawyer who represents the other.

CHIPPING. *n.* A condition in which small pieces are missing from the outer surface of a brake cup. *Motor Vehicle Safety Regulations*, C.R.C., c. 1038, s. 2.

CHIROGRAPH. *n.* A deed or other public instrument in writing, which was attested by the subscription of witnesses.

CHIROGRAPHUM APUD DEBITOREM REPERTUM PRAESUMITUR SOLUTUM. [L.] When a person possesses a document requiring payment of money, this gives rise to a presumption that the money was paid.

CHIROPODIST. *n.* A person, other than a legally qualified medical practitioner, who practises or advertises or holds himself out in any way as practising the treatment of any ailment, disease, defect or disability of the human foot. *Chiropody Act*, R.S.O. 1980, c. 72, s. 1.

CHIROPODY. *n.* The study and treatment of ailments of the human foot. See PRACTICE OF THE PROFESSION OF ~.

CHIROPRACTIC. *n.* The branch of the healing arts that is concerned with the restoration and maintenance of health by the adjustment by hand only of the articulations of the human body and that is involved primarily with the relationship of the spinal column to the nervous system. *Chiropractors (Amendment) Act*, S.B.C. 1983, c. 20, s. 5.

CHIROPRACTIC ADJUSTMENT. A calculated procedure, force or thrust designed to affect the nervous system, primarily by movement of one structure in relation to another within the spinal column and other articulations. *Chiropractic Profession Act*, S.A. 1984, c. C-9.1, s. 1.

CHIROPRACTOR. *n.* A person whose method of treatment of the human body for disease and the causes of disease is confined solely to chiropractic. *Chiropractors Act*, R.S.B.C. 1979, c. 50, s. 1.

CHIRURGEON. *n.* A surgeon.

CHITTY'S L.J. *abbr.* Chitty's Law Journal, 1953-.

CHLORATE MIXTURE. Any explosive containing a chlorate. Canada regulations.

CHLORINE. *n.* The chemical element Cl_2 in liquid or gaseous form and containing not more than 150 parts per million of water. *Chlorine Tank Car Unloading Facilities Regulations*, C.R.C., c. 1147, s. 2. See RESIDUAL ~ CONTENT.

CHLOROBIPHENYLS. *n.* Those chlorobiphenyls that have the molecular formula $C^{12}H^{10-n}Cl^n$ in which "n" is greater than 2. *Chlorobyiphenyl Regulations No. 1*, C.R.C., c. 564, s. 2.

CHOICE OF LAW. In conflict of laws, the determination of what law should govern a matter.

CHOKE. *n.* Narrowing of the muzzle end of a shotgun barrel so that the area of scatter of shotgun pellets is smaller. F.A. Jaffe, *A Guide to Pathological Evidence*, 2d ed. (Toronto: Carswell, 1983) at 172.

CHOKING. *n.* Suffocation caused by obstructing the upper air passages. F.A. Jaffe, *A Guide to Pathological Evidence*, 2d ed. (Toronto: Carswell, 1983) at 172.

CHOP FEED. The feed obtained by grinding, chopping or crushing (a) wheat, rye, barley, oats (Avena sativa), Indian corn, buckwheat (Fagopyrum esculentum), flax, field peas, field beans or soy beans, either alone or in combination with one another, or (b) Mixed Feed Oats as set out in the Canada Grain Act, No. 1 Feed Screenings as described in Schedule III, or No. 2 Feed Screenings as described in Schedule III. *Feeds Regulations*, C.R.C., c. 665, s. 2.

CHOSE. *n.* [Fr.] A chattel personal, either in action or in possession. See CHATTEL.

CHOSE IN ACTION. 1. An intangible. 2. All incorporeal things and rights, not including choses in possession or chattels real which constitute personality. E.L.G. Tyler & N.E. Palmer, eds., *Crossley Vaines' Personal Property*, 5th ed. (London: Butterworths, 1973) at 11. 3. Personal property rights which may not be claimed by taking physical possession but only enforced or claimed by action. G.H.L. Fridman, *The Law of Contract in Canada*, 2d ed. (Toronto: Carswell, 1986) at 619.

CHOSE IN POSSESSION. 1. A tangible. E.L.G. Tyler & N.E. Palmer, eds., *Crossley Vaines' Personal Property*, 5th ed. (London: Butterworths, 1973) at 14. 2. A corporeal thing, movable, tangible and visible, always in someone's possession. E.L.G. Tyler & N.E. Palmer, eds., *Crossley Vaines' Personal Property*, 5th ed. (London: Butterworths, 1973) at 11.

CH. R. *abbr.* Upper Canada Chambers Reports, 1857-1872.

C.H.R.C. *abbr.* Canadian Human Rights Commission.

CHRISTIAN NAME. The name given at baptism; first name. See SURNAME AND ~S.

CHRISTMAS DAY. December 25.

CHRISTMAS PERIOD. The period which includes the twelve clear working days immediately preceding Christmas Day.

CHRISTMAS TREE. A tree, whether sheared or unsheared, that is, (i) sold, offered for sale or intended to be sold severed from its root system and with its bark, branches and foliage mainly intact, and (ii) of the coniferous species, including but not limited to, (A) Douglas fir (Pseudotsuga Menziesii), (B) Balsam fir (Abies balsomea), (C) Black spruce (Picea mariana), (D) White spruce (Picea glauca), (E) Scotch pine (Pinus sylvestis), (F) Norway spruce (Picea excelsa), (G) Red Pine (Pinus resinosa), and (H) Red spruce (Picea rubens). *Farm Products Grades and Sales Act*, R.R.O. 1980, Reg. 331, s. 1.

CHRISTMAS TREE PLANTATION. A group of coniferous trees that are planted or growing on land for the production of Christmas trees. *Forestry Act*, R.R.O. 1980, Reg. 397, s. 1.

CHRISTMAS VACATION. The period which begins December 21 and ends January 7, including both days. D. Sgayias *et al.*, *Federal Court Practice 1988* (Toronto: Carswell, 1987) at 253.

CHROMATIN. *n.* The carrier of genetic information in the nuclei of cells which can be stained with basic dyes. F.A. Jaffe, *A Guide to Pathological Evidence*, 2d ed. (Toronto: Carswell, 1983) at 172. See SEX ~.

CHRONIC. *adj.* Used in connection with diseases, of long duration or with slowly progressive symptoms; distinguished from acute.

CHRONICALLY DEPRESSED RENT. The gross potential rent for a residential complex where (a) the rent is more than 20 per cent below the gross potential rent for residential complexes that are comparable to the residential complex, in terms of number and type of rental units, quality and location; and (b) the rate of return on the landlord's equity in respect of the residential complex is less than 10 per cent. *Residential Rent Regulation Act*, S.O. 1986, c. 63, s. 91.

CHRONICALLY ILL PERSON. A person afflicted with or suffering from any chronic illness, sickness, injury or other condition of a long-term nature requiring treatment.

C.H.R.R. *abbr.* Canadian Human Rights Reporter, 1980-.

C.H.S. CHART. *abbr.* Canadian Hydrographic Service Chart.

CHUNKING. *n.* The breaking away of pieces of the tread or sidewall of a tire. *Motor Vehicle Tire Safety Regulations*, C.R.C., c. 1039, s. 2.

CHURCH. *n.* 1. Any church, chapel, or other building or place used for public worship. *Freedom of Worship Act*, R.S.Q. 1977, c. L-2, s. 3. 2. A group of persons who form a religious body. *Religious Corporations Act*, R.S.Q. 1977, c. C-71, s. 1.

CHURCH BUILDING. A church, chapel or meeting house or a residence for the minister.

CHURCHWARDEN. *n.* 1. The guardian or keeper of the church. 2. The representative of the parish. 3. An officer of a church or congregation.

CHURNING. *n.* Excessive trading of a client's account by a stockbroker.

CHUTE. See LETTER ~.

CHY. CHRS. *abbr.* Upper Canada Chancery Chambers Reports.

C.I.B.C. *abbr.* Canadian Imperial Bank of Commerce.

CIDA. *abbr.* Canadian International Development Agency.

CIDER. *n.* 1. The beverage obtained by the alcoholic fermentation of fruit juice. 2. Cider that is considered to be an alcoholic beverage by the law of the province relating to the advertising of cider. *Broadcasting regulations* (Canada). See STRONG ~; WEAK ~.

CIE. *abbr.* [Fr. compagnie] Company.

C.I.F. *abbr.* Cost insurance and freight.

C.I.F. CONTRACT. A contract in which price includes cost of the goods, insurance while in transit and freight charges incurred. G.H.L. Fridman, *Sale of Goods in Canada*, 3d ed. (Toronto: Carswell, 1986) at 480.

CIGAR. *n.* Every description of cigar, cigarillo and cheroot and any roll or tubular construction intended for smoking that consists of a filler composed of pieces of natural or reconstituted leaf tobacco, a binder of natural or reconstituted leaf tobacco in which the filler is wrapped and a wrapper of natural or reconstituted leaf tobacco. *Excise Act*, R.S.C. 1985, c. E-14, s. 6.

CIGARETTE. *n.* 1. Every description of cigarette and any roll or tubular construction intended for smoking that is not a cigar, and where any cigarette exceeds one hundred and two millimetres (102 mm) in length, each seventy-six millimetres (76 mm) or fraction thereof shall be deemed to be a separate cigarette. *Excise Act*, R.S.C. 1985, c. E-14, s. 6. 2. Includes any small cigar made of tobacco rolled up in paper, tobacco leaf or any other material. *Tobacco Restraint Act*, R.S.C. 1970, c. T-9, s. 7.

CIGAR MANUFACTORY. Any place or premises where raw leaf tobacco is worked up into a cigar, and every workshop, office, storeroom, shed, yard or other place where any of the raw material is or is to be stored, where any process connected with the manufacture or preparation of cigars is or is intended to be carried on or where any of the products of the manufacture are or are intended to be stored. *Excise Act*, R.S.C. 1985, c. E-14, s. 6.

CIGAR MANUFACTURER. Any person who either personally or by an agent, carries on the manufacture of cigars, and the casing, packing, cutting, pressing, grinding, rolling, drying, crushing or stemming of any raw leaf tobacco for manufacture into cigars. *Excise Act*, R.S.C. 1985, c. E-14, s. 6.

CIGAR STAMP. Any stamp affixed to any package of cigars. *Excise Act*, R.S.C. 1985, c. E-14, s. 6.

C.I.L.R. *abbr.* 1. Canadian Insurance Law Reports. 2. Canadian Insurance Law Review.

CINEMATOGRAPH. *n.* 1. A moving picture machine or other similar apparatus. 2. Includes any work produced by any process analogous to cinematography. *Copyright Act*, R.S.C. 1985, c. C-42, s. 2.

CINEMATOGRAPHIC FILM. Positive or negative film containing continuous images designed to create the illusion of motion and includes film issued in any form in a set under a single title. *Canadian Cultural Property Export Control List*, C.R.C., c. 448, s. 1.

CIO. *abbr.* Congress of Industrial Organizations, a federation of national and international industrial unions.

C.I.P.R. *abbr.* Canadian Intellectual Property Reports, 1984-.

CIRCA. [L.] About; around.

CIRC. CT. *abbr.* Circuit Court.

CIRCUIT. *n.* 1. Any complete conductor, loop, path or unit current-carrying part of the system conductors and that portion of a system controlled by a switch or protected by a cut-out. *Coal Mines Regulation Act*, R.S.N.S. 1967, c. 36, s. 84. 2. A single telecommunication channel of intelligence by signals, sounds, pictures or writings of all kinds for any one of the services mentioned in paragraph 4(a). *External Submarine Cable Regulations*, C.R.C., c. 1515, s. 2. 3. One or more race courses on which successive days of racing or race meetings are held. *Race Track Supervision Regulations*, C.R.C., c. 441, s. 2. See BRANCH ~; CONTROL ~; NON-INCENDIVE ~; REMOTE CONTROL ~; SIGNAL ~; VOLTAGE OF A ~.

CIRCUIT-BREAKER. *n.* An electro-mechanical device designed to automatically open a current-carrying circuit on a pre-determined over-current, under both overload and short-circuit conditions without injury to the device. *Power Corporation Act*, R.R.O. 1980, Reg. 794, s. 0.

CIRCUIT INTERRUPTER. See GROUND FAULT ~.

CIRCUITUS EST EVITANDUS. [L.] Circuity should be avoided.

CIRCUIT VENT. A vent that functions for two

or more traps and extends to a vent stack from a point on a horizontal branch in front of the last connected fixture. *Ontario Water Resources Act*, R.R.O. 1980, Reg. 736, s. 1.

CIRCUITY OF ACTION. A more complex course of proceeding than is necessary; a multiplicity of actions.

CIRCULAR. *n.* A take-over bid circular; an issuer bid circular; an amendment to a take-over bid circular or issuer bid circular; a notice of change; and a notice of variation. *Securities Act*, S.S. 1984-85-86, C.S. 42.1, s. 96. See BID ~; INFORMATION ~.

CIRCULAR NOTE. A bank's request in writing that one of its correspondents abroad pay a certain sum to a certain person.

CIRCULATING CAPITAL. A part of the subscribed capital of a company intended to be temporarily circulated in business in the form of goods, money or other assets, which capital, or its proceeds, is intended to return to the company increased so that it can be used repeatedly, always to return with some increase. W. Grover & F. Iacobucci, *Materials on Canadian Income Tax*, 4th ed. (Toronto: Richard De Boo Ltd., 1980) at 298.

CIRCULATION. *n.* 1. Transmission from person to person or place to place. 2. Of a newspaper or periodical, the number of readers or number of copies printed.

CIRCUMSTANCE. *n.* 1. An attendant or auxiliary fact. 2. Includes any communication made to or information received by the assured. Insurance Acts.

CIRCUMSTANTIAL EVIDENCE. 1. Any fact which another fact relevant to an issue or another fact in issue may infer. P.K. McWilliams, *Canadian Criminal Evidence*, 3d ed. (Aurora: Canada Law Book, 1988) at 5-1. 2. Evidence tending to establish the existence or non-existence of a fact that is not one of the elements of the offence charged, where the existence or non-existence of that fact reasonably leads to an inference concerning the existence or non-existence of a fact that is one of the elements of the offence charged. *Military Rules of Evidence*, C.R.C., c. 1049, s. 2.

CIT. *abbr.* 1. Citizen. 2. Citizenship.

C.I.T. *abbr.* Canadian Import Tribunal.

CITATIO AD REASSUMENDAM CAUSAM. [L.] A citation to revive a cause which issues against the heir of the party who died pending the original suit.

CITATION. *n.* 1. Calling on a person who is not a party to a proceeding or an action to appear in court. 2. In probate matters, notice of proceedings given to anyone whose interests are or may be affected.

CITATION OF AUTHORITIES. A reference to case or statute law to establish or support propositions of law advanced.

CITATOR. *n.* A set of books which provides historical information regarding statutes, cumulates amendments to statutes since the last revision or consolidation of the statutes and traces judicial consideration of sections of statutes.

CITE. *v.* 1. To refer to legal authorities. 2. To name in citation.

CITIZEN. *n.* A Canadian citizen. *Citizenship Act*, R.S.C. 1985, c. C-29, s. 2. See CANADIAN ~; SENIOR ~.

CITIZENSHIP. *n.* Canadian citizenship. *Citizenship Act*, R.S.C. 1985, c. C-29, s. 2. See CERTIFICATE OF ~; OATH OR AFFIRMATION OF ~.

CITIZENSHIP COURT. An office of the Department of the Secretary of State or other place where a citizenship judge performs his duties under the Act. *Citizenship Regulations*, C.R.C., c. 400, s. 2.

CITIZENSHIP JUDGE. A citizenship judge appointed under the Citizenship Act. *Citizenship Act*, R.S.C. 1985, c. C-29, s. 2.

CITY. *n.* A municipal corporation incorporated as a city.

CITY CENTRAL. A council created to correlate activities of union locals within a community.

CITY COMMISSIONERS. The commissioners of a city. *The Urban Municipality Act*, R.S.S. 1978, c. U-10, s. 2.

CITY GATE. The plant or premises where gas received from a pipeline is metered, reduced in pressure and prepared for distribution to individual users of the gas. *Gas Act*, R.S.B.C. 1979, c. 149, s. 1.

CITY INDUSTRIAL UNION COUNCIL. A body composed of CIO locals from a city.

CITY MANAGER. The manager of a city. *The Urban Municipality Act*, R.S.S. 1978, c. U-10, s. 2.

CITY MOTOR VEHICLE OPERATOR. A motor vehicle operator who operates exclusively within a 10-mile radius of his home terminal and is not a bus operator and includes any motor vehicle operator who is classified as a city motor vehicle operator in a collective agreement entered into between his employer and a trade union acting on his behalf or who is not classified in any such agreement but is considered to be a city motor vehicle operator according to the prevailing industry practice in the geographical area where he is employed. *Motor Vehicle Operators Hours of Work Regulations*, C.R.C., c. 990, s. 2.

CIVIC HOLIDAY. The first Monday in August. *Public Service Act*, R.R.O. 1980, Reg. 881, s. 62.

CIVIL. *adj.* Of legal matters, private as opposed to criminal.

CIVIL ACTION. Any type of action except criminal proceedings.

CIVIL AIRCRAFT. 1. Any aircraft other than a military aircraft. *Air Regulations*, C.R.C., c. 2, s. 101. 2. All aircraft other than aircraft operated by the Canadian Forces, a police force in Canada or persons engaged in the administration or enforcement of the Customs Act, or the Excise Act. *Criminal Code*, R.S.C. 1985, c. C-46, s. 78(2).

CIVIL AVIATION INSPECTOR. (a) An employee who is required to conduct flight tests to determine the competency of flight crew personnel and to inspect commercial air operations, or (b) an employee who is required to monitor in-flight cabin procedures in use in commercial air operations. *Flying Accidents Compensation Regulations*, C.R.C., c. 10, s. 2.

CIVIL CEREMONY. A marriage performed by a judge or justice of the peace, distinguished from a religious ceremony.

CIVIL CODE. The Civil Code of Lower Canada. *Interpretation Act*, R.S.Q. 1977, c. I-16, s. 61.

CIVIL COMMOTION INSURANCE. Insurance against loss of or damage to the property insured caused by bombardment, invasion, insurrection, mutiny, civil war or commotion, riot, act of foreign enemy, hostilities or warlike operations, whether war is declared or not, revolution, rebellion, conspiracy, usurped power or military, naval or air force operations, vandalism or malicious mischief.

CIVIL COURT. A court of ordinary criminal jurisdiction in Canada and includes a court of summary jurisdiction. *National Defence Act*, R.S.C. 1985, c. N-5, s. 2.

CIVIL CUSTODY. The holding under arrest or in confinement of a person by the police or other competent civil authority, and includes confinement in a penitentiary or civil prison. *National Defence Act*, R.S.C. 1985, c. N-5, s. 2.

CIVIL DEFENCE. Planning, organization, establishing and operating salvage, precaution-

ary and safety measures, controls, facilities and services of all kinds vital and necessary for the public welfare for meeting, preventing, reducing and overcoming the effects of enemy action or civil disaster. *Emergency Program Act*, R.S.B.C. 1979, c. 106, s. 1.

CIVIL DISASTER. A disaster occurring within the province from fire, flood, earthquake, tempest, or other cause, not attributable to enemy attack, sabotage, or other hostile action, whereby injury or loss is or may be caused to some or all of the citizens of the province or to their property, or both. *Emergency Measures Act*, R.S.M. 1970, c. E80, s. 2.

CIVILIAN. *n.* 1. A private citizen, not a member of the armed forces. 2. A person knowledgeable in civil law.

CIVILIAN MEMBER OF OVERSEAS AIR CREW. A person, other than a member of the forces, who was employed by the Air Ministry of the United Kingdom to make trans-Atlantic flights ferrying aircraft from Canada, and who, at the commencement of that employment, was domiciled in Canada. *Civilian War Pensions and Allowances Act*, R.S.C. 1985, c. C-31, s. 52.

CIVILISATION. *n.* A law, act of judgment or justice which makes a criminal matter civil.

CIVILITER MORTUUS. [L. civilly defunct] Dead in law.

CIVIL LAW. The legal system of Quebec based on the Civil Code and ultimately Roman law.

CIVIL LIBERTIES. 1. A range of values that contribute to the freedom and dignity of the individual which are recognized by Canadian law in various ways. P.W. Hogg, *Constitutional Law of Canada*, 2d ed. (Toronto: Carswell, 1985) at 627. 2. Rights protected by the Charter of Rights and Freedoms: freedom of assembly, association, religion and expression (s. 2), voting rights (s. 3), mobility rights (s. 6), procedural and legal rights (ss. 7-14), the right to equal protection under the law (ss. 15, 28) and language rights (ss. 16-23). P.W. Hogg, *Constitutional Law of Canada*, 2d ed. (Toronto: Carswell, 1985) at 259.

CIVIL MARRIAGE CEREMONY. A marriage performed by a judge or justice of the peace, distinguished from a religious ceremony.

CIVIL MATTER. A cause, issue or matter, other than a criminal matter, that involves or might involve a jury and includes an assessment of damages. *Juries Act*, S.N.S. 1969, c. 12, s. 1.

CIVIL PRISON. Any prison, jail or other place in Canada in which offenders sentenced by a civil court in Canada to imprisonment for less than two years can be confined, and, if sentenced outside Canada, any prison, jail or other place in which a person, sentenced to that term of imprisonment by a civil court having jurisdiction in the place where the sentence was passed, can for the time being be confined. *National Defence Act*, R.S.C. 1985, c. N-5, s. 2.

CIVIL PROCEDURE. The law governing the process and practice of civil litigation. See RULES OF ~.

CIVIL RIGHTS. 1. Those rights referred to in the list of provincial powers in the Constitution Act, 1867 are primarily proprietary, contractual or tortious rights. P.W. Hogg, *Constitutional Law of Canada*, 2d ed. (Toronto: Carswell, 1985) at 455. 2. Procedural rights of an individual. See CIVIL LIBERTIES; PROPERTY AND ~.

CIVIL RIGHTS IN THE PROVINCE. Proprietary, contractual or tortious rights referred to in the Constitution Act, 1867. P.W. Hogg, *Constitutional Law of Canada*, 2d ed. (Toronto: Carswell, 1985) at 455.

CIVIL SERVANT. 1. A person appointed to the service of the Crown. 2. A member of the civil service. 3. A member of the staff of a department or Ministry of Government.

CIVIL SERVICE. 1. The employees of the government. 2. The positions in the public service of the Province to which appointments may be made by the Civil Service Commission and such other positions as may be designated as positions in the Civil Service by the Governor in Council. *Civil Service Act*, R.S.N.S. 1967, c. 34, s. 1.

CIVIL STATUS. See ACTS OF ~; OFFICERS OF ~.

CIVIL SUIT. See CIVIL ACTION.

C.J. *abbr.* Chief Justice.

C.J.A.L.P. *abbr.* Canadian Journal of Administrative Law & Practice.

C.J.W.L. *abbr.* Canadian Journal of Women and the Law (Revue juridique "La femme et le droit").

CLADDING. See EXTERIOR ~.

CLAIM. *n.* 1. The demand or the subject matter for which any action, suit, or proceeding is brought. 2. A right, title, interest, encumbrance or demand of any kind affecting land. 3. A parcel of land marked out on the ground under a prospector's licence in conformity with the Mining Act. *Mining Act*, R.S.Q. 1977, c. M-13, s. 1. 4. Any parcel of land located or granted for placer mining. *Yukon Placer Mining Act*, R.S.C. 1985, c. Y-3, s. 2. 5. Indebtedness, liability or obligation of any kind that, if unsecured, would be a debt provable in bankruptcy within the

meaning of the Bankruptcy Act. *Companies Creditors Arrangement Act*, R.S.C. 1985, c. C-36, s. 12. 6. The amount of claim in respect of jurisdiction in matters of salvage, means the amount claimed in the proceeding or suit before the receiver of wrecks, or in the court in which the suit or proceeding is taken. *Canada Shipping Act*, R.S.C. 1985, c. S-9, s. 2. 7. Includes the probable costs in a proceeding. *Rules of the Supreme Court*, S.Nfld. 1986, r. 28.01. See ADJACENT ~S; ADJOINING ~; ADVERSE ~; BORING ~; COUNTER~; CROSS~; DORMANT ~; FULL ~; MINERAL ~; MINING ~; NOTICE OF ~; PROFESSIONAL LIABILITY ~; PROVABLE ~; QUARRYING ~; QUIT ~; STATEMENT OF ~; THIRD PARTY ~; TWO POST ~; UNPATENTED MINING ~.

CLAIMANT. *n.* 1. One who makes a claim. 2. A person who has or is alleged to have a right to maintenance. 3. Any person who claims or asserts or seeks to realize a lien. 4. A person who applies or has applied for benefit or compensation. 5. A person other than an insured to whom monies may be payable under a contract. *Insurance Adjusters, Agents and Brokers Act*, S.Nfld. 1986, c. 36, s. 2. See LIEN ~; MAJOR ATTACHMENT ~; MINOR ATTACHMENT ~; ORIGINAL ~; PREFERRED ~.

CLAIM AREA. The land covered by a mineral claim. *Mining Act*, S.N.B. 1985, c. M-14.1, s. 1.

CLAIM FOR BENEFIT. See INITIAL ~.

CLAIM PROVABLE. Any claim or liability provable in proceedings under this Act by a creditor. *Bankruptcy Act*, R.S.C. 1985, c. B-3, s. 2.

CLAIM PROVABLE IN BANKRUPTCY. Any claim or liability provable in proceedings under this Act by a creditor. *Bankruptcy Act*, R.S.C. 1985, c. B-3, s. 2.

CLAIMS ADJUSTER. Every person who, in insurance matters, on behalf of another and for remuneration or on behalf of an employer, investigates a loss, assesses damage arising from it or negotiates settlement of the claim.

CLAIMS RATIO. With respect to any particular period for policies issued by a company with respect to a particular class of insurance, the ratio of the claims incurred during that period under those policies, including applicable adjustment expenses, to the premiums earned during that period in respect of those policies. See EXPECTED ~.

CLAM. *n.* Includes a soft shell, long neck or squirt clam, bar clam and quahaug. Canada regulations.

CLAM DELINQUENTES MAGIS PUNIUN-TUR QUAM PALAM. [L.] Those who sin secretly are punished more severely than those who sin openly.

CLAM, VI, AUT PRECARIO. [L.] Secretly, violently or suppliantly.

CLARIFIED. See CLEAR OR ~.

CLASS. *n.* 1. A group of persons or things having common attributes. 2. Includes, in relation to securities, a series of a class of securities. See COMMERCIAL ~; CONSTRAINED-~; FEMALE-DOMINATED ~; GOODS OF THE SAME ~ OR KIND; INADMISSIBLE ~; MALE-DOMINATED ~; SPECIFIED ~; TRAIN OF SUPERIOR ~.

CLASS ACTION. 1. A representative proceeding. 2. One or more of a group of people who have the same interest may, or may be authorized by a court to, bring or defend an action for the benefit or on behalf of all. G.D. Watson & C. Perkins, eds., *Holmested & Watson: Ontario Civil Procedure* (Toronto: Carswell, 1984) at 12-2. 3. The procedure which enables one member to sue without a mandate on behalf of all the members. *Code of Civil Procedure*, S.Q. 1978, c. 8, s. 3.

CLASS A GEAR. Gear made from wrought iron, or from mild steel that contains less than 0.20 per cent carbon. *Tackle Regulations*, C.R.C., c. 1494, s. 2.

CLASS B GEAR. Gear made from mild steel that contains not less than 0.20 per cent carbon, or from alloy steel. *Tackle Regulations*, C.R.C., c. 1494, s. 2.

CLASSED SHIP. A ship that is classed with a classification society.

CLASS GIFT. A gift to a number of persons who are united or connected by some common tie . . . the testator was looking to the body as a whole rather than to the members constituting the body as individuals . . . if one or more of that body died in his lifetime the survivors should take the gift between them. *Kingsbury v. Walter*, [1901] A.C. 187 at 191, per Lord Macnaghten.

CLASSIFICATION. See COLOUR ~; FIRE HAZARD ~; JOB ~; OCCUPATIONAL ~.

CLASSIFICATION CENTRE. An institution for the study and diagnosis of persons under sentence to determine the type of institution and type of treatment most suitable to effect the rehabilitation of those persons. *Corrections Act*, R.S.N.B. 1973, c. C-26, s. 1.

CLASSIFICATION OFFICER. A person responsible for classifying a prisoner as maximum, medium or minimum for security purposes.

CLASSIFICATION OF MURDER. Murder is first degree murder or second degree murder. *Criminal Code*, R.S.C. 1985, c. C-46, s. 231(1).

CLASSIFICATION SOCIETY. 1. A society or association for the classification and registry of shipping approved by the Minister of Transport under the Canada Shipping Act. Canada regulations. 2. Lloyd's Register of Shipping, Bureau Veritas, American Bureau of Shipping, Det norske Veritas, Germanischer Lloyd, and Registro Italiano Navale. *Steamship Machinery Construction Regulations*, C.R.C., c. 1491, Schedule 1, s. 2.

CLASSIFICATION SURVEY. A survey of a steamship made by a surveyor to a classification society. *Inspection of Classed Ships Regulations*, C.R.C., c. 1434, s. 2.

CLASSIFIED ANNOUNCEMENT. An announcement respecting goods or services offered or sought by persons not normally engaged in the business of dealing in those goods or services. *Television Broadcasting Regulations*, C.R.C., c. 381, s. 2.

CLASSIFY. *v.* In relation to a position means to assign a class and grade to a position. *Public Service Act*, R.S.N.W.T. 1974, c. P-13, s. 2.

CLASS MEETING. A meeting of members who hold shares of a particular class. *Company Act*, R.S.B.C. 1979, c. 59, s. 1.

CLASS OF ANIMAL. A group of animals of a particular species segregated on the basis of age, breed or other recognized division, as determined by the taxpayer at the time of election under this section. *Income Tax Regulations*, C.R.C., c. 945, s. 1802.

CLASS OF OCCUPANCY. The use or intended use of a building, as defined in the Building Code. *Building Code Act*, S.N.S. 1986, c. 3, s. 2.

CLASS OF PERSONS. Class of persons designated or described by the Attorney General having reference to age, sex, nature of offence, locality of conviction, length of sentence or other factor whatsoever, or any combination of factors, as the Attorney General in his absolute discretion sees fit. *Court and Penal Institutions Act*, R.S.N.S. 1967, c. 67, s. 31.

CLASS OF POSITIONS. A group of positions involving duties and responsibilities so similar that the same or like qualifications may reasonably be required for, and the same schedule or grade of pay can be reasonably applied to, all positions in the group. *The Pay Equity Act*, S.M. 1985-86, c. 21, s. 1.

CLASS OF SECURITIES. Includes a series of a class of securities.

CLASS OF SUBSTANCES. 1. Any two or more substances that (i) contain the same chemical moiety, or (ii) have similar chemical properties and the same type of chemical structure. 2. Class of substances whose members have similar physio-chemical or toxicological properties. *Environmental Contaminants Act*, R.S.C. 1985, c. E-12, s. 7(1).

CLAUSE. *n.* 1. A paragraph or division of a contract. 2. A sentence or part of a sentence. 3. A numbered portion of a bill called a section once the bill becomes law. A. Fraser, G.A. Birch & W.A. Dawson, eds., *Beauchesne's Rules and Forms of the House of Commons of Canada*, 5th ed. (Toronto: Carswell, 1978) at 219. See ACCELERATION ~; ACCESS-TO-PLANT ~; AFTER-ACQUIRED ~; AMENDING ~; ARBITRATION ~; ATTESTATION ~; BASKET ~; CALL-BACK ~; CALL-IN ~; CANCELLATION ~; COLA ~; DEFEASANCE ~; DISCIPLINE ~; DISCLAIMER ~; ENACTING ~; ENTRENCHMENT ~; ESCALATION ~; EXCEPTIONS ~; EXCLUSION ~; EXCLUSIVE JURISDICTION ~; EXEMPTION ~; FINALITY ~; GRANDFATHER ~; GREEN ~; INCHMAREE ~; INTERPRETATION ~; MOST-FAVOURED NATION ~; NO-CERTIORARI ~; PRIVATIVE ~; RECOGNITION ~; RED ~; REMEDY ~; REOPENING ~; RESCISSION ~; REVERSE ONUS ~.

CLAUSULAE INCONSUETAE SEMPER INDUCUNT SUSPICIONEM. [L.] Unusual clauses in a document always create suspicion.

CLAUSULA GENERALIS DE RESIDUO NON EA COMPLECTITUR, QUAE NON EJUSDEM SINT GENERIS CUM IIS QUAE SPECIATIM DICTA FUERINT. [L.] A general remainder clause does not include things which are not of the same kind with those which have been named specially.

CLAUSULA GENERALIS NON REFERTUR AD EXPRESSA. [L.] A general clause does not refer to matters expressly provided.

CLAUSULA REBUS SIC STANTIBUS. [L.] Agreement is intended by the parties to be binding only until there is a vital change in the circumstances.

CLAUSULA VEL DISPOSITIO INUTILIS PER PRESUMPTIONEM VEL CAUSAM REMOTAM EX POST FACTO NON FULCITUR. [L.] An unnecessary clause or disposition is not supported by a remote presumption or a cause arising after the event.

CLAY. *n.* A soil (i) the particles of which are not visible to the naked eye, (ii) dry lumps of which are not easily powdered by the fingers, (iii) that, after shaking a small saturated pat vigorously in the hand, does not exhibit a wet shiny surface, and (iv) that shines when moist and stroked with a knife. *Building Code Act*, R.R.O. 1980, Reg. 87, s. 4.2.1.6.

CLAY-SHALE. *n.* Fine-grained, finely laminated, will swell on wetting, and will disintegrate on its first drying and wetting cycle. *Building Code Act*, R.R.O. 1980, Reg. 87, c. 4.2.1.9.

CLC. *abbr.* Canadian Labour Congress.

CLEAN. *adj.* Of fruit, the appearance is not affected by dirt, dust, spray residue or other foreign material.

CLEANER. See DRY ~.

CLEAN HANDS DOCTRINE. An equitable doctrine which requires that the plaintiff or applicant come to a court of equity free from taint of fraud or the like in connection with the claim.

CLEANING AGENT. Any laundry detergent, dishwashing compound, household cleaner, metal cleaner, degreasing compound, commercial cleaner, industrial cleaner, phosphate compound or other substance intended to be used for cleaning purposes. *Canada Water Act*, R.S.C. 1985, c. C-11, s. 19.

CLEAN-OUT. *n.* A device that has a removable cap or plug securely attached to it and is so constructed that it can be installed in a pipe so that the cap or plug can be removed to permit pipe cleaning apparatus to be inserted into the pipe. *Ontario Water Resources Act*, R.R.O. 1980, Reg. 736, s. 1.

CLEANSING. *n.* The process by which shellfish are assisted to rid themselves of sewage and other bacteria either by artificial sterilization of water or by re-laying them for a specified time in pure water areas approved by the Minister. *Fishery Regulations*, Canada regulations.

CLEAR. *adj.* 1. Free from doubt. 2. Free from encumbrance, lien or charge. 3. Free from deductions.

CLEARANCE. *n.* 1. A certificate issued to indicate compliance with law or regulations. 2. The distance from an object to the nearest point of roof, sides or floor. *Coal Mines Regulation Act*, R.S.N.S. 1967, c. 36, s. 3. 3. An authorization by a marine traffic regulator for a vessel, a seaplane or an air cushion vehicle to proceed or manoeuvre as authorized. Canada regulations. See AIR TRAFFIC CONTROL ~; APRON TRAFFIC CONTROL ~.

CLEAR DAYS. Complete days in counting time

for items such as notice; both first and last days are omitted.

CLEAR FUEL. Fuel which contains no dye or less dye than the minimum quantity of dye prescribed. *Fuel Tax Act*, S.O. 1981, c. 59, s. 1.

CLEARING. *n.* 1. In banking, making exchanges and settling balances among banks. 2. In transport, departing having complied with customs regulations.

CLEARING HOUSE. 1. An association or organization, whether incorporated or unincorporated, or part of a commodity futures exchange, through which trades in commodity contracts entered into on that exchange are cleared. 2. The following clearing house associations referred to in Order in Council P.C. 1976-590: Winnipeg Commodity Clearing Ltd., British Columbia Grain Shippers' Clearance Association and Lake Shippers' Clearance Association. *Grain Futures Regulations*, C.R.C., c. 892, s. 2.

CLEARING MEMBER. A person registered as a member of a clearing house recognized by the Montreal Exchange. *An Act to Amend Taxation Act and Other Fiscal Legislation*, S.Q. 1985, c. 25, s. 143.

CLEARING SYSTEM. A mechanism by which debit and credit positions between banks are ascertained and cheques are sorted. The balances are settled by making transfers in the Chartered Banks' accounts with the Bank of Canada. I.F.G. Baxter, *The Law of Banking*, 3d ed. (Toronto: Carswell, 1981) at 173.

CLEAR OPENING. An opening of any shape through which the largest sphere that may be passed is one of a diameter equal to the dimension specified for the opening. *Hull Construction Regulations*, C.R.C., c. 1431, s. 100.

CLEAR OR CLARIFIED. The style typical of apple juice that has been completely clarified and that ranges in colour from a light to medium amber shade. *Processed Fruit and Vegetable Regulations*, C.R.C., c. 291, Schedule I, s. 3.

CLEAR TITLE. Good title; title free from encumbrances.

CLEAT. *n.* A member of shoring and timbering that directly resists the downward movement of a wale or strut. *Occupational Health and Safety Act*, R.R.O. 1980, Reg. 691, s. 167.

CLERGY. *n.* 1. A minister of a religious denomination. 2. Collectively: ministers, priests, rabbis.

CLERGYMAN. *n.* 1. A minister, priest, commissioner and staff officer of the Salvation Army and rabbi. 2. A person duly ordained, appointed or commissioned by a religious body. 3. Includes

any priest, rabbi, elder, evangelist, missionary or commissioned officer ordained or appointed by the religious body to which he belongs. *Marriage Act*, R.S.B.C. 1979, c. 251, s. 1. See REGISTERED ~.

CLERIC. *n.* A person who is charged with the solemnization of the ceremony of marriage by a religious denomination. See MINISTERING ~.

CLERICAL. *adj.* 1. Pertaining to clergy. 2. Relating to the office of clerk.

CLERICAL ERROR. An error in a document which was a slip or mistake of the person preparing or copying it.

CLERK. *n.* 1. The officer of a court who accepts filings, issues process, keeps records. 2. An officer of a municipality. 3. An officer of the Legislative Assembly or House of Commons. 4. The clerk of the Crown, chief clerk, registrar or prothonotary of the court, or, in Ontario, the senior registrar of the Supreme Court of Ontario, or any other officer of the court prescribed for the purpose in question. *Dominion Controverted Elections Act*, R.S.C. 1985, c. C-39, c. 2. 5. A research assistant to a judge or judges. See ARTICLED ~; COURT ~; LAW ~ AND PARLIAMENTARY COUNSEL; MUNICIPAL ~.

CLERK ASSISTANT. A person appointed by the Speaker of the House of Commons to discharge any duties assigned by the Clerk of the House. A. Fraser, G.A. Birch & W.A. Dawson, eds., *Beauchesne's Rules and Forms of the House of Commons of Canada*, 5th ed. (Toronto: Carswell, 1978) at 44.

CLERK-AT-THE-TABLE. A person appointed by the Speaker of the House of Commons to discharge any duties assigned by the Clerk of the House. A. Fraser, G.A. Birch & W.A. Dawson, eds., *Beauchesne's Rules and Forms of the House of Commons of Canada*, 5th ed. (Toronto: Carswell, 1978) at 44.

CLERK OF THE COURT. The officer of a court who accepts filings, issues process, keeps records.

CLERK OF THE HOUSE OF COMMONS. The chief advisor to the Speaker and to the House of Commons on matters of procedure who supervises all officers and clerks working in the House. A. Fraser, G.A. Birch & W.A. Dawson, eds., *Beauchesne's Rules and Forms of the House of Commons of Canada*, 5th ed. (Toronto: Carswell, 1978) at 43.

CLERK OF THE PEACE. The person who assists justices of the peace to draw indictments, enter judgments, issue process and administer the courts.

CLERK OF THE QUEEN'S PRIVY COUNCIL. Clerk of the Privy Council and Secretary to the Cabinet. *Interpretation Act*, R.S.C. 1985, c. I-21, s. 35.

CLERKSHIP. *n.* The training given in a pharmacy by a pharmacist to a student or graduate. *Pharmacists Act*, R.S.B.C. 1979, c. 326, s. 1.

CLIC LETTER. *abbr.* CLIC's Legal Materials Letter (Bulletin d'information juridique du CCDJ).

CLIENT. *n.* 1. A person who receives services. 2. A person or body of persons on whose behalf a lawyer receives money for services. 3. A person or body of persons on whose behalf an agent receives money in connection with his business. *Real Estate Act*, R.S.B.C. 1979, c. 356, s. 1.

CLINIC. *n.* A medical facility. See FORENSIC ~; MENTAL HEALTH ~; SEXUALLY TRANSMITTED DISEASES ~.

CLINICAL EXAMINATION. An examination for venereal disease consisting of a physical examination, the taking of samples or specimens from the body on the same occasion as the physical examination and the testing of the samples or specimens at the place where the samples or specimens were taken. *Venereal Diseases Prevention Act*, R.S.A. 1980, c. V-2, s. 1. See PSYCHIATRIC ~.

CLINICAL STAFF. Every person, including a physician or dentist, is considered to be a member of the clinical staff of an establishment who, being the holder of a college or university diploma, occupies a position with the establishment in the field of such diploma and directly connected with health services, social services, research or teaching, as are those persons who carry on the professional activities of nursing assistants for the establishment. *Health Services and Social Services Act*, R.S.Q. 1977, s. S-5, s. 1.

CLIP. *n.* The removable magazine of a firearm which contains unfired cartridges. F.A. Jaffe, *A Guide to Pathological Evidence*, 2d ed. (Toronto: Carswell, 1983) at 172.

CLIPPING. *n.* Impairing, diminishing or lightening a current gold or silver coin with intent that it should pass for a current gold or silver coin. *Criminal Code*, R.S.C. 1985, c. C-46, s. 413.

C.L.L.C. *abbr.* Canadian Labour Law Cases.

C.L.L.R. *abbr.* Canadian Labour Law Reports, 1973-.

CLOCK-BUMPING. *n.* Receiving credit on a

time card, as a worker, for more hours than were actually worked.

CLOCK HOUR. A period of 60 minutes commencing on each hour and terminating immediately prior to the hour. *Television Broadcasting Regulations*, C.R.C., c. 381, s. 2.

CLOCK OVERTIME. A premium for work after specified regular working hours.

CLOG ON EQUITY OF REDEMPTION. 1. A provision, repugnant to either a contractual or an equitable right to redeem, which is void. W.B. Rayner & R.H. McLaren, *Falconbridge on Mortgages*, 4th ed. (Toronto: Canada Law Book, 1977) at 54. 2. A device which prevents a mortgagor from getting property back after the obligations under the mortgage are discharged. D.J. Donahue & P.D. Quinn, *Real Estate Practice in Ontario*, 4th ed. (Toronto: Butterworths, 1990) at 232-233.

CLOSE. *n.* Conclusion. See BREACH OF ~.

CLOSE COMPANY. A company in which shares are held by one shareholder or a very small number of shareholders.

CLOSE CORPORATION. A corporation in which shares are held by one shareholder or a very small number of shareholders.

CLOSED. *adj.* Not open for the serving of customers or the receiving of orders from customers. See EFFECTIVELY ~.

CLOSED-CIRCUIT TELEVISION COMPANY. Includes a person operating for a fee or charge a television-signal receiving antenna or similar device, or equipment for the transmission of television signals to television receivers or subscribers, or any or all of such devices and equipment. *Vancouver Charter*, R.S.B.C. 1979, c. 55, s. 398.

CLOSED CIRCUIT TELEVISED CONTEST. A contest or exhibition televised through the means of closed circuit television, film projection or any other electronic projection device. *Boxing Authority Act*, S.N.S. 1981, c. 55, s. 1.

CLOSED CIRCUIT TELEVISED EXHIBITION. A contest or exhibition televised through the means of closed circuit television, film projection or any other electronic projection device. *Boxing Authority Act*, S.N.S. 1981, c. 55, s. 1.

CLOSED CIRCUIT TELEVISION CORPORATION. Includes a person operating for a fee or charge a television signal receiving antenna or similar device, or equipment for the transmission of television signals to television receivers of subscribers, or any or all of those devices and equipment. *Assessment Act*, R.S.B.C. 1979, c. 21, s. 1.

CLOSED COMPANY. A company whose constituting documents provide for restrictions on the free transfer of shares, prohibit any distribution of securities to the public and limit the number of its shareholders to 50, exclusive of present or former employees of the company or of a subsidiary.

CLOSED COMPETITION. A competition that is open only to employees.

CLOSED CONSTRUCTION. With respect to a fishing vessel, means a fishing vessel of which more than 50 per cent of the length is covered full width, at or above the gunwale level, by decks or permanent enclosures. *Small Fishing Vessel Inspection Regulations*, C.R.C., c. 1486, s. 2.

CLOSED PACKAGE. Any package the contents of which cannot be satisfactorily inspected without removing the cover, lid or other closing device.

CLOSED SEASON. A specified period during which a species of wildlife or fish shall not be hunted, taken or fished.

CLOSED SHOP. A place of employment in which the employer has agreed to employ only union members.

CLOSED SHOP CONTRACT. An agreement requiring the employer to employ only union members.

CLOSED SPIRIT-RECEIVER. The vessel or vessels into which the spirit is conveyed for measurement. *Excise Act*, R.S.C. 1985, c. E-14, s. 3.

CLOSED TIME. A specified period during which fish, to which the expression applies, may not be fished. Fishery regulations.

CLOSED-TYPE HOT-WATER HEATING SYSTEM. A system in which water is heated and circulated and which is not vented to the atmosphere. *Boiler and Pressure Vessel Act*, R.S. Nfld. 1970, c. 24, s. 2.

CLOSED TYPE HOT WATER SYSTEM. A system in which water is heated and circulated and which is not vented to atmosphere. *Boiler and Pressure Vessel Act*, R.S.B.C. 1979, c. 30, s. 1.

CLOSED UNION. A union in which membership is restricted.

CLOSELY HELD CORPORATION. A private corporation the shares of which are not listed on a stock exchange.

CLOSE OF PLEADINGS. When either the plaintiff delivers a reply to every defence in the action or the time to deliver a reply has expired; and it has been noted that every defendant who is in default in delivering a defence in the action is in default. G.D. Watson & C. Perkins, eds., *Holmested & Watson: Ontario Civil Procedure* (Toronto: Carswell, 1984) at 25-4.

CLOSE SEASON. A period during which the hunting or fishing for migratory birds, fur animals, game or fish is prohibited.

CLOSE THE DEAL. To complete a transaction by exchanging documents and funds.

CLOSE TIME. A specified period during which fish to which it applies may not be fished. *Fisheries Act*, R.S.C. 1985, c. F-14, s. 2.

CLOSING ADDRESS. A statement made by counsel at conclusion of a trial before a jury.

CLOSING APPLIANCE. See TYPE 'A' ~; TYPE 'B' ~.

CLOSING ARGUMENT. A statement made by counsel at conclusion of a trial before a judge.

CLOSING A TRANSACTION. A meeting between the lawyers or agents representing the parties to complete the transaction by exchanging documents and funds.

CLOSING DAY. See UNIFORM ~.

CLOSING-OUT SALE. Any sale or intended sale at retail of goods, wares or merchandise: (i) that is in any way represented, held out, advertised or described by any of the terms "bankrupt", "insolvent", "assignee's", "adjuster's", "trustee's", "executor's", "administrator's", "receiver's", "liquidation", "wholesaler's", "jobber's", "manufacturer's", "moving out", "selling out", "closing-out", "closing stock", "fire", "smoke", "water damage", "landlord's", "lease expired", "creditor's" or "forced", or by any similar words or expressions; or (ii) wherein it is in any way represented, held out or advertised that the goods, wares or merchandise are the property of or have been acquired or purchased from or are being sold by or on behalf of any bankrupt, insolvent person, assignee, adjuster, trustee, executor, administrator, receiver, wholesaler, jobber, or manufacturer, or are the property of or have been acquired or purchased from or are being sold by or on behalf of any other retailer; or (iii) wherein it is in any way represented, held out or advertised that the goods, wares or merchandise have been damaged by fire, smoke, water or any other injurious agent, or are offered or will be offered for sale by reason of any action on the part of a landlord or creditor, or because of the expiry of a lease, or because the vendor thereof or any agent or principal of the vendor is either discontinuing business or changing his place of business, or has done so, or intends to do so, or because the vendor or any agent or principal of the vendor is in any way forced to offer the goods, wares or merchandise for sale. *The Closing-out Sales Act*, R.S.S. 1978, c. C-13, s. 2.

CLOSURE. *n.* 1. A procedure to conclude debate to force the House of Commons to decide a subject. A. Fraser, G.A. Birch & W.A. Dawson, eds., *Beauchesne's Rules and Forms of the House of Commons of Canada*, 5th ed. (Toronto: Carswell, 1978) at 117. 2. A device for shutting off an opening through a construction assembly, such as a door or a shutter, and includes all components such as hardware, frames and anchors. *Building Code Act*, R.R.O. 1980, Reg. 87, s. 1.

CLOT. *n.* A semi-solid, soft coagulated mass formed in stagnant blood. F.A. Jaffe, *A Guide to Pathological Evidence*, 2d ed. (Toronto: Carswell, 1983) at 172. See BLOOD ~; CHICKEN FAT ~; CURRANT JELLY ~; POST MORTEM ~.

CLOTHING. See CHILDREN'S ~; TEXTILE AND ~ GOODS.

CLOTHING LENGTH. Any wool used in woolen manufacture that is too short in fibre to be combed. *Wool Grading Regulations*, C.R.C., c. 294, s. 2.

CLOTTING. See COAGULATION.

CLOVER. *n.* Red clover, alsike clover or white clover or a mixture thereof. *Hay and Straw Inspection Regulations*, C.R.C., c. 920, s. 1.

C.L.R. *abbr.* Construction Law Reports, 1983-.

C.L.R.B. *abbr.* Canada Labour Relations Board.

C.L.R.B.R. (N.S.). *abbr.* Canadian Labour Relations Board Reports (New Series).

C.L.S. *abbr.* Canada Labour Service.

C.L.T. *abbr.* Canadian Law Times, 1881-1922.

C.L.T. (OCC. N.). *abbr.* Canadian Law Times, Occasional Notes.

CLUB. *n.* 1. An association of individuals for purposes of mutual entertainment and convenience. 2. A social, sporting, community, benevolent or fraternal order or society, or any branch thereof. See FLYING ~; FRATERNAL ~; LABOUR ~; MEMBER OF A ~; VETERANS' ~.

CLUB MEMBER. A person who, whether as a charter member or admitted in accordance with the by-laws or rules of a club, has become a member thereof, who maintains membership by the payment of regular periodic dues in the manner provided by the rules or by-laws, and whose name and address are entered on the list of members.

CLUSTER. *n.* Three or more cap stems with or without berries attached. *Processed Fruit and Vegetables Regulations*, C.R.C., c. 291, Schedule I, s. 18.

C. MAG. *abbr.* Cour de magistrat.

C.M.A.R. *abbr.* Canadian Court Martial Appeal Reports, 1957-.

CMHC. *abbr.* 1. Canada Mortgage and Housing Corporation. 2. Central Mortgage and Housing Corporation.

C.M.M. *abbr.* Cour municipale de Montréal.

CMND. *abbr.* Command papers.

C.M.P.R. *abbr.* Canadian Mortgage Practice Reports.

C.M.Q. *abbr.* Cour municipale de Québec.

C. MUN. *abbr.* Cour municipale.

CMVSS. *abbr.* Canada Motor Vehicle Safety Standard.

CN. *abbr.* 1. Canadian National. 2. Canadian National Railway Company.

CN ADJUSTMENT. In respect of any crop year, means the amount paid to the Canadian National Railway Company in respect of that crop year pursuant to section 57. *Western Grain Transportation Act*, R.S.C. 1985, c. W-8, s. 55.

C.N.L.C. *abbr.* Commission nationale de libérations conditionnelles.

C.N.L.R. *abbr.* Canadian Native Law Reporter.

C.N.R. *abbr.* Canadian National Railway Company.

CO. *abbr.* Company.

C/O. *symbol* Care of.

COACH. See TRAILER ~; TROLLEY ~.

COADJUTOR. *n.* A helper, assistant or ally.

COAGULATION. *n.* 1. Transformation of a liquid to a semi-solid or solid mass. 2. In blood, formation of fibrin which creates a thrombus or clot. F.A. Jaffe, *A Guide to Pathological Evidence*, 2d ed. (Toronto: Carswell, 1983) at 172.

COAL. *n.* 1. Includes coke, briquettes, fabricoal and other coal products suitable for fuel. 2. Anthracite coal and bituminous coal.

COAL GAS. Methane occurring naturally in coal seams and associated strata and includes methane obtainable by methane extraction.

Petroleum Resources Act, S.N.S. 1979-80, c. 12, s. 2.

COAL LAND. Land in which the coal or the right to explore for, develop and produce coal, is vested in or reserved to the Crown. *Coal Act*, R.S.B.C. 1979, c. 51, s. 1.

COAL MINE. Any opening or excavation in or working of ground for the purpose of prospecting, exploring, mining, opening up, developing or proving any coal or coal bearing deposit, and includes (a) any place where coal mining is or may be carried on, and (b) all works, machinery, plant, buildings and premises below or above ground belonging to or used in connection with a coal mine. *Mines Act*, S.B.C. 1980, c. 28, s. 1.

COAL MINER. A person employed underground in any coal mine to cut, shear, break or loosen coal from the solid, whether by hand or machinery, and possessed of a certificate of competency as such. *Coal Mines Regulation Act*, R.S.N.S. 1967, c. 36, s. 3.

COAL MINERS' PNEUMONOCONIOSIS. A fibrotic condition occasioning loss of lung function caused by inhaled coal dust combined with tuberculosis of the lung. *Workmen's Compensation Act*, R.S.N.S. 1967, c. 343, s. 147.

COAL PROCESSING PLANT. An installation for upgrading the quality of coal or for producing a marketable solid fuel, and includes any coal storage facility directly associated with it. *Coal Conservation Act*, R.S.A. 1980, c. C-14, s. 1.

COARSE FISH. 1. (a) Any member of the gar family Lepisosteidae, (b) bowfin or dogfish, Amia calva Linnaeus, (c) bullhead, catfish or any member of the family Ictaluridae, (d) burbot or ling, Lota lota (Linnaeus), (e) carp, Cyprinus carpio Linnaeus or any member of the family Cyprinidae, (f) eel, Anguilla rostrata (LeSueur), (g) freshwater drum or sheepshead, Aplodinotus grunniens Rafinesque, (h) smelt, Osmerus mordax (Mitchill), and (i) sucker, mullet, red horse or any member of the family Catostomidae. *Ontario Fishery Regulations*, C.R.C., c. 849, s. 2. Any fish other than sport fish but does not include Atlantic salmon. *New Brunswick Fishery Regulations*, C.R.C., c. 844, s. 2.

COARSE GRAIN. Oats, barley, and any oat product or barley product. *Coarse Grain Marketing Control Act*, R.S.M. 1970, c. C140, c. 2.

COAST. *n.* The edge of land bordered by a sea.

COASTAL CADIZ. *abbr.* Coastal Canadian Air Defence Identification Zone.

COASTAL CANADIAN AIR DEFENCE IDENTIFICATION ZONE. The airspace extending upward from the surface of the earth in those areas off the coasts of Canada described in Schedule I. *Security Control of Air Traffic Order*, C.R.C., c. 63, s. 2.

COASTAL TRADE. The regular employment and operation of ships in the waters of the region, the waters of Puget Sound, the Strait of Juan de Fuca and the coastal waters of the State of Alaska not west of Cook Inlet. *Pacific Pilotage Regulations*, C.R.C., c. 1270, s. 2.

COASTAL WATERS. Includes waters in the fishing zones of Canada adjacent to British Columbia, all waters in the territorial sea of Canada adjacent to British Columbia, and all internal waters of British Columbia. *Fisheries Act*, R.S.B.C. 1979, c. 137, s. 12.

COASTAL WATERS OF CANADA. 1. Includes all of Queen Charlotte Sound, all the Strait of Georgia and the Canadian waters of the Strait of Juan de Fuca. *Criminal Code*, R.S.C. 1985, c. C-46, s. 339(6). 2. All Canadian fisheries waters not within the geographical limits of any province. *Fisheries Act*, R.S.C. 1985, c. F-14, s. 47.

COAST GUARD SHIP. See CANADIAN ~.

COASTING. *n.* The carrying by water transportation of goods and materials of every description to or from ports in Newfoundland. *Fishing and Coasting Vessels Rebuilding and Repairs (Bounties) Act*, R.S.Nfld. 1970, c. 136, s. 2.

COASTING TRADE. 1. The employment of ships in the transportation of goods for hire or reward by water or land and water from one port or place in Canada to another port or place in Canada either directly or by way of a foreign port or in the transportation of passengers from one port or place in Canada to another port or place in Canada either directly or by way of a foreign port. *Coastwise and Foreign Shipping (Customs) Regulations*, C.R.C., c. 454, s. 2. 2. The carrying of goods but not passengers from one port to another in Newfoundland or from ports outside Newfoundland to ports in Newfoundland or to ports outside Newfoundland from ports in Newfoundland. *Coasting Vessels (Bounties) Act*, R.S. Nfld. 1970, c. 46, s. 2.

COASTING TRADE OF CANADA. The carriage by water of goods or passengers from one port or place in Canada to another port or place in Canada. *Canada Shipping Act*, R.S.C. 1985, c. S-9, s. 2.

COAST OF CANADA. The sea-coast of Canada and the salt water bays, gulfs and harbours on the sea-coast of Canada. *Canada Shipping Act*, R.S.C. 1985, c. S-9, s. 2.

COAST STATION. A station operated in a terrestrial service and located on land or on board a ship that is permanently moored and is used for communication with ships at sea. *General Radio Regulations, Part II,* C.R.C., c. 1372, s. 2.

COAT. See STATION WAGON OR CAR ~.

COAT-TAIL RIDER. 1. A unionized employee who has not paid dues. 2. An employee who is not a union member but benefits from the advantages won by a union.

COCAINE. *n.* An alkaloid made from the leaves of Erythroxylon trees, a cerebral stimulant systemically, a local anaesthetic topically. F.A. Jaffe, *A Guide to Pathological Evidence,* 2d ed. (Toronto: Carswell, 1983) at 172.

COCK PIT. Keeping a cock pit is illegal. *Criminal Code,* R.S.C. 1985, c. C-46, s. 447.

COCKPIT VOICE RECORDER. A system of cockpit voice recording equipment that has been approved by the Minister. Canada regulations.

COCKTAIL. See LOBSTER ~.

COCKTAIL MIXING UNIT. A combination food holding tray and sink forming part of the bar facilities where alcoholic beverages are dispensed. *Ontario Water Resources Act,* R.R.O. 1980, Reg. 736. s. 1.

CO. CT. *abbr.* County Court.

COD. *n.* A fish of the species Gadus morhua. *Northwest Atlantic Fisheries Regulations,* C.R.C., c. 860, s. 2. See LING ~.

C.O.D. *abbr.* See CASH ON DELIVERY.

CODE. *n.* 1. A collection or system of laws, i.e. Code Napoléon or Civil Code. 2. A consolidation of existing statute and common law, i.e. Criminal Code. 3. Guidelines for a process or use of equipment to ensure safety, efficiency, or a level of quality established and published by a competent authority, i.e. building code, safety code. 4. A group of letters or symbols identifying pari-mutuel tickets with a particular race or racing card. *Race Track Supervision Regulations,* C.R.C., c. 441, s. 2. 5. The code used by the Department to identify carriers. *Customs Cargo Control Regulations,* C.R.C., c. 459, s. 2. See BUILDING ~; BUILDING CONSTRUCTION ~; CIVIL ~; CRIMINAL ~; CSA ELEVATOR ~; FIRE ~; FORWARD SORTATION AREA ~; I.M.C.O. ~; LABOUR ~; POSTAL ~; RECOGNIZED ~; UNIFORM ~.

CODE CIVIL. The civil law of Quebec.

CODE MARK. A combination of letters, symbols and numbers that identifies an inspector.

CODE NAPOLÉON. A collection of civil law prepared by Napoléon Bonaparte.

COD-END. *n.* A bag-like extension attached to the after end of the belly of a trawl net and used to retain the catch. Canada regulations.

CODE NUMBER. In relation to a carrier, means the code number assigned by the Department to the carrier. *Customs Cargo Control Regulations,* C.R.C., c. 459, s. 2.

CODE OF CONDUCT. The regulations made pursuant to section 38. *Royal Canadian Mounted Police Act,* R.S.C. 1985 (2d Supp.), c. 8, s. 2.

CODE OF SERVICE DISCIPLINE. The provisions of Parts IV to IX. *National Defence Act,* R.S.C. 1985, c. N-5, s. 2.

CODE OF SIGNALS. See STANDARD ~.

CODICIL. *n.* An addition or change made to a will by a testator.

CODIFICATION. *n.* The collection of all the principles of any system or subject of law into one body of statutes or single statute.

CODIFYING STATUTE. A single statute which aims to state all the law on a particular subject by combining pre-existing statutory provisions with common law rules relating to the subject. P. St. J. Langan, ed., *Maxwell on The Interpretation of Statutes,* 12th ed. (Bombay: N.M. Tripathi, 1976) at 25.

COD NET. A gill net that is used for taking cod. *Newfoundland Fishery Regulations,* C.R.C., c. 846, s. 2.

COD TRAP. A trap net not less than 30 fathoms in circumference and not less than 6 fathoms deep that is used for taking cod and includes the leader thereof, but the leader shall be not less than 30 fathoms in length and not less than 6 fathoms deep at the point where it joins the doorway. *Newfoundland Fishery Regulations,* C.R.C., c. 846, s. 2.

COD TRAP OPERATOR. A person who ordinarily prosecutes the codfishery as captain of a cod trap crew and operates a boat and cod trap. *Newfoundland Fishery Regulations,* C.R.C., c. 846, s. 2.

CO-EMPT. *v.* To purchase all of any commodity.

COERCION. *n.* 1. Compulsion. 2. Compelling by force or threats.

COFFERDAM. *n.* A structure constructed all or in part below water level or below the level of the water table in the ground and intended to provide a place in which to work that is free of water. *Occupational Health and Safety Act,* R.R.O. 1980, Reg. 691, s. 1.

COGITATIONIS POENAM NEMO MERETUR. [L.] No one deserves punishment for a thought.

COGNISANCE. *n.* 1. Knowledge. 2. To take cognisance means to take judicial notice.

COGNIZOR. *n.* Shall include any number of cognizors in the same recognizance, whether as principals or sureties, unless such interpretation be inconsistent with the context. *Criminal Cases Recognizance Act*, R.S.Q. 1977, c. C-7, s. 1.

COGNOVIT. [L.] He or she has confessed.

COHABIT. *v.* 1. To live together in a conjugal relationship, whether within or outside marriage. 2. To live together in a family relationship. *Child and Family Services and Family Relations Act*, S.N.B. 1980, c. C-2.1, s. 1.

COHABITATION. See AGENCY FROM ~; PERIOD OF ~.

COHABITATION AGREEMENT. (1) A man and a woman who are cohabiting and not married to one another may enter into an agreement in which they agree on their respective rights and obligations during cohabitation, or upon ceasing to cohabit or death, including, (a) ownership in or division of property; (b) support obligations; (c) the right to direct the education and moral training of their children, but not the right to custody of or access to their children; and (d) any other matter in the settlement of their affairs. *Family Law Reform Act*, R.S.O. 1980, c. 152, s. 50.

COHAEREDES SUNT QUASI UNUM CORPUS, PROPTER UNITATEM JURIS QUOD HABENT. [L.] Co-heirs are considered one person because of the unity of title which they possess.

CO-HEIR. *n.* One of several people among whom an inheritance is divided.

CO-HEIRESS. *n.* A woman who shared an inheritance equally with another woman.

CO-HOLDER. *n.* A person in whose name a claim is recorded under these Regulations either jointly or in common with another person. *Canada Mining Regulations*, C.R.C., c. 1516, s. 2.

COILED TUBE BOILER. A boiler with one or more coiled tubes having attached thereto a forced circulation water pump, a pressure limiting device and a prepurge flame failure device. *Operating Engineers Act*, R.R.O. 1980, Reg. 740, s. 1.

COIN. *v.* To stamp pieces of metal into a set shape and size and place marks on them under the aegis of a government.

COIN. *n.* A piece of metal stamped with certain marks and put into circulation as money of a certain value by a government. See SUBSIDIARY ~.

COITUS INTERRUPTUS. [L.] Interrupted sexual intercourse.

COKE OVEN EMISSIONS. Condensed vapours and benzene soluble particulates emitted into the atmosphere from a metallurgical coke oven, a substance designated under the Ontario Occupational Health and Safety Act. D. Robertson, *Ontario Health and Safety Guide* (Toronto: Richard De Boo Ltd., 1988) at 5-52.

COLA. *abbr.* Cost-of-living adjustment.

COLA CLAUSE. An agreement to provide employees with an increase in wages tied to an index such as the Consumer Price Index prepared by Statistics Canada.

COLD-ROLLED. See HOT-ROLLED OR ~.

COLD STORAGE. The storage of articles of food at or below a temperature of forty-five degrees Fahrenheit, such temperatures being artificially reproduced. *Food and Drug Act*, R.S.Nfld. 1970, c. 139, s. 2.

COLD STORAGE PLANT. Buildings, structures, machinery, appurtenances, appliances and apparatus occupied or used in the business of freezing and storing any article for human consumption. *Cold Storage Plants Loan Act*, R.S.N.S. 1967, s. 37, s. 1. See FISH ~.

COLD STORE. An establishment employing refrigerating machinery or ice or any other artificial cooling method for the storage of foods at or below a temperature of forty-five degrees Fahrenheit. *Food and Drug Act*, R.S.Nfld. 1970, c. 139, s. 2.

COLD STORED EGGS. Eggs held in a cold storage room at temperatures between 2 degrees Celsius and -2 degrees Celsius. *Live Stock and Live Stock Products Act*, R.R.O. 1980, Reg. 582, s. 1.

COLD TURKEY. To stop taking drugs suddenly. F.A. Jaffe, *A Guide to Pathological Evidence*, 2d ed. (Toronto: Carswell, 1983) at 172.

COLLATERAL. *n.* Property used to secure the payment of a debt or performance of an obligation.

COLLATERAL. *adj.* 1. By the side of. 2. In addition to.

COLLATERAL ADVANTAGE. Something which makes a mortgagee's remuneration for a loan exceed the proper interest rate. W.B. Rayner & R.H. McLaren, *Falconbridge on Mort-*

gages, 4th ed. (Toronto: Canada Law Book, 1977) at 50.

COLLATERAL BENEFIT. In a tort claim, a third party's contribution to the plaintiff's physical or financial well-being. K.D. Cooper-Stephenson & I.B. Saunders, *Personal Injury Damages in Canada* (Toronto: Carswell, 1981) at 467.

COLLATERAL CONTRACT. A statement, on the strength of which a person enters into a contract, may give rise to an entirely separate contract "collateral" to the main contract made between the maker of the statement and the person to whom the statement was made.

COLLATERAL QUESTION. A question connected to the merits or the heart of an inquiry but which is not the major question to be decided. S.A. DeSmith, *Judicial Review of Administrative Action*, 4th ed. by J.M. Evans (London: Stevens, 1980) at 114.

COLLATERAL RELATIVE. A person whose relationship to a second person is not in the direct line of descent from the second person, i.e. a brother's child.

COLLATERAL SECURITY. Security for payment of a debt or obligation given in addition to the principal security.

COLLATERAL SUCCESSOR. Where used with reference to a deceased means a successor to property of the deceased who is (i) the spouse of a brother or sister of the deceased, or (ii) the child of a brother or sister of the deceased, or (iii) the brother or sister of a parent of the deceased, or (iv) the child of a brother or sister of the parent of the deceased, or (v) the spouse of any person described in sub-clause (ii), (iii) or (iv), and in this clause "brother" includes a half-brother and "sister" includes a half-sister. *Statute Amendments (Taxation) Act*, S.M. 1977, c. 58, s. 15.

COLLATERAL TERM. Outside or distinct from the terms of the main contract.

COLLATIO BONORUM. [L.] A contribution of goods.

COLLATION. *n.* Comparing a copy with its original to ensure its accuracy and completeness.

COLLECTING AGENT. A person whose business is the collecting, either by himself or through a representative, of debts owing to other persons. *Collecting Agents Act*, R.S.Q. 1977, c. A-9, s. 1.

COLLECTION. *n.* A bank's handling of commercial and financial documents according to instructions received. I.F.G. Baxter, *The Law of Banking*, 3d ed. (Toronto: Carswell, 1981) at 141. See PARTICULATE ~ EFFICIENCY.

COLLECTION AGENCY. A person, other than a collector, who carries on the business (i) of collecting or attempting to collect debts for other persons, (ii) of collecting or attempting to collect debts under any name which differs from that of the creditor to whom the debt is owed, (iii) of offering or undertaking to act for a debtor in arrangements or negotiations with creditors or receiving money from a debtor for distribution to creditors in consideration of a fee, commission or other remuneration that is payable by the debtor, (iv) of offering or undertaking to act for a creditor in realizing on any security given to the creditor for a debt, (v) of selling or offering to sell any collection system, device or scheme intended or calculated to be used to collect debts, or (vi) of receiving money periodically from persons for distribution to creditors of those persons.

COLLECTION AGENT. A person other than a collector who: (i) collects debts for others; (ii) offers or undertakes to collect debts for others; (iii) solicits accounts for collection; (iv) collects debts owed to him under a name which differs from that under which he is the creditor; (v) mails to debtors or offers or undertakes to mail to debtors, on behalf of a creditor collection letters; (vi) for a fee or other consideration or hope or promise thereof, enters into an arrangement under the terms of which he agrees or undertakes to pay to a vendor any amount in respect of goods or services sold or supplied by the vendor to a person other than the collection agent; (vii) offers or undertakes to act for a debtor in arrangements or negotiations with his creditors; or (viii) receives money periodically from a debtor for distribution to his creditors; and includes a person who takes an assignment of a debt or debts due at the date of assignment from a specified debtor or debtors. *The Collection Agents Act*, R.S.S. 1978, c. C-15, s. 2.

COLLECTION AGREEMENT. See TAX ~.

COLLECTION SYSTEM. See INDIVIDUAL ~.

COLLECTIVE AGREEMENT. An agreement in writing between an employer or an employer's organization acting on behalf of employers, and a bargaining agent of employees acting on behalf of a unit of employees containing provisions respecting terms and conditions of employment and related matters.

COLLECTIVE APPRAISAL. A sampling taken on various cultivated farms in the same zone to determine the actual yield of the insured crops in the zone. *Crop Insurance Act*, R.S.Q. 1977, c. A-30, s. 1.

COLLECTIVE BARGAINING. Negotiating with a view to the conclusion of a collective agreement or the renewal or revision thereof. See APPROPRIATE FOR ~.

COLLECTIVE BARGAINING AGREEMENT. An agreement in writing between an employer or an employer's organization acting on behalf of an employer, on the one hand, and a bargaining agent of employees acting on behalf of the employees, on the other hand, containing terms or conditions of employment of employees.

COLLECTIVE WORK. (a) An encyclopedia, dictionary, year book or similar work, (b) a newspaper, review, magazine or similar periodical, and (c) any work written in distinct parts by different authors, or in which works or parts of works of different authors are incorporated. *Copyright Act*, R.S.C. 1985, c. C-42, s. 2.

COLLECTOR. *n.* 1. A person authorized or required by or pursuant to a revenue act or by agreement to collect a tax. 2. Every officer of customs and excise who is appointed to collect the duties imposed by this Act in any defined district or excise division. *Excise Act*, R.S.C. 1985, c. E-14, s. 2. 3. A person employed, appointed or authorized by a collection agency to solicit business or collect debts for the agency or to deal with or trace debtors for the agency. 4. A person engaged in the business of collecting dead animals. *Dead Animal Disposal Act*, R.S.O. 1980, c. 112, s. 1. See DISTRICT ~.

COLLECTOR BAG. A receptacle into which dried egg is discharged from an egg dryer in operation. *Processed Egg Regulations*, C.R.C., c. 290, s. 2.

COLLEGATARY. *n.* One of a group of people who shares a common legacy.

COLLEGE. *n.* 1. A corporation, company, or society having certain privileges, i.e., College of Physicians and Surgeons. 2. A community college. 3. A regional college. 4. A college of applied arts and technology. See AGRICULTURAL AND VOCATIONAL ~; HERALDS' ~; PRIVATE ~.

COLLEGE OF PHYSICIANS AND SURGEONS. The licensing and governing body of the medical profession in a province.

COLLIERY. *n.* A mine.

COLLIMATOR. *n.* A device or mechanism that limits the shape and size of the useful beam. *Radiation Emitting Devices Regulations*, C.R.C., c. 1370, s. 1.

COLLISION. *n.* The striking by a vessel of another vessel or a ship. *Fishing Vessel Insurance Regulations*, C.R.C., c. 325, s. 2. See ACTION FOR ~; FIXED ~ BARRIER.

COLLISION REGULATIONS. 1. International Regulations for preventing collision at sea and the Rules of the Road for navigating the Great Lakes, their connecting and tributary waters and the St. Lawrence River as far east as the lower exit of the Lachine Canal and the Victoria Bridge at Montreal. *Canada Shipping Act*, R.S.C. 1985, c. S-9, s. 2. 2. (a) In relation to vessels in the St. Peters, Canso, St. Ours and Chambly Canals, the Regulations for Preventing Collisions at Sea established under the Canada Shipping Act, and (b) in relation to vessels in the Ste. Anne, Carillon, Grenville, Rideau, Trent and Murray Canals, the Rules of the Road for the Great Lakes established under the Canada Shipping Act. *Canal Regulations*, C.R.C., c. 1564, s. 2.

COLLOQUIUM. *n.* In pleading in a libel or slander action, the plaintiff must show that the statement complained of was "published of and concerning the plaintiff." R.E. Brown, *The Law of Defamation in Canada* (Toronto: Carswell, 1987) at 218.

COLLUSION. *n.* 1. Coming together to commit fraud or to deceive. 2. An agreement or conspiracy to which an applicant for a divorce is either directly or indirectly a party for the purpose of subverting the administration of justice, and includes any agreement, understanding or arrangement to fabricate or suppress evidence or to deceive the court, but does not include an agreement to the extent that it provides for separation between the parties, financial support, division of property or the custody of any child of the marriage. *Divorce Act*, R.S.C. 1985 (2d Supp.), c. 3, s. 11(4).

COLONIAL LAW. In a colony discovered and occupied, the laws of England; in a conquered colony or one ceded to England, its own laws until England changed them.

COLONIAL LAWS VALIDITY ACT, 1865. The British Act confirming the capacity of legislatures in the colonies to enact laws inconsistent with English laws. P.W. Hogg, *Constitutional Law of Canada*, 2d ed. (Toronto: Carswell, 1985) at 39.

COLONY. *n.* 1. A place settled by people from an older city or country. 2. A number of persons who hold land or any interest therein as communal property, whether as owners, lessees or otherwise, and whether in the name of trustees or as a corporation or otherwise, and includes a number of persons who propose to acquire land to be held in such manner. 3. Queen, brood and accompanying bees. *Bee Act*, R.S.B.C. 1979, s. 27, s. 1. 4. Unless the context otherwise requires, the Province of Newfoundland. *Interpretation Act*, R.S.Nfld. 1970, c. 182, s. 26.

COLORE OFFICI. [L.] Colour of office. See DURESS ~.

COLOUR. *v.* In respect of fuel means the addition to fuel of dye in the proportion prescribed by a person so authorized by the Minister. *Fuel Tax Act, 1981*, S.O. 1981, c. 59, s. 1.

COLOUR. *n.* Appearance, pretext or pretence, apparent or prima facie. See FOOD ~; SYNTHETIC ~.

COLOURABILITY. *n.* A doctrine invoked when a statute is addressed to a matter outside jurisdiction though it bears the formal trappings of a matter within the jurisdiction of the enacting legislature. P.W. Hogg, *Constitutional Law of Canada*, 2d ed. (Toronto: Carswell, 1985) at 322.

COLOURABLE. *adj.* In appearance but not in substance what it claims to be.

COLOURABLE IMITATION. 1. A trademark with such similar appearance as a registered trade mark that confusion is likely, though not a deliberate imitation intended to deceive. H.G. Fox, *The Canadian Law of Trade Marks and Unfair Competition*, 3d ed. (Toronto: Carswell, 1972) at 379. 2. Cane sugar or brown sugar of glucose or any other similar substance or any combination of them to which artificial maple flavour has been added. *Maple Products Industry Act*, R.S.C. 1970, c. M-2, s. 2.

COLOUR CLASSIFICATION. In respect of honey, means its hue or shade of colour as set out in Tables I and II of Schedule I as determined by use of a honey classifier approved by the Minister or by use of a Phund honey grader. *Honey Regulations*, C.R.C., c. 287, s. 2.

COLOURED FUEL. Fuel which contains dye.

COLOURED FUEL OIL. Any fuel oil that has been coloured.

COLOURING. *n.* The adding to fuel oil of any quantity of natural or chemical products furnished by the Minister for the purpose of identifying fuel oil. *Fuel Tax Act*, R.S.Q. 1977, c. T-1, s. 1.

COLOURING PERMIT. A permit issued by the Minister that authorizes a person to colour tax-exempt gasoline. *Gasoline Tax Act*, S.Nfld. 1977, c. 76, s. 1.

COLOUR OF OFFICE. Pretense of authority to carry out an act for which the actor has no authority.

COLOUR OF RIGHT. An honest belief in a state of facts which, if it did exist, would excuse or justify the act done.

COLUMBARIUM. *n.* A structure designed to store the ashes of cremated human remains.

COLUMN. See STEERING ~.

COMA. *n.* A profoundly unconscious state. F.A. Jaffe, *A Guide to Pathological Evidence*, 2d ed. (Toronto: Carswell, 1983) at 172.

COMB. *n.* A structure of cells composed of beeswax. *Bee Act*, R.S.B.C. 1979, s. 27, s. 1. See BROOD ~.

COMB HONEY. Honey that is in the honeycomb. *Farm Products Grades and Sales Act*, R.R.O. 1980, Reg. 337, s. 1.

COMBINATION. *n.* An association of persons for a particular purpose. See BUSINESS ~; TRACTOR-FLOAT ~; TRACTOR-TRAILER ~; TRADE ~.

COMBINATION CARRIER. A tanker designed to carry, in bulk, oil or solid cargoes. *Fire Detection and Extinguishing Equipment Regulations*, C.R.C., c. 1422, s. 2.

COMBINATION OF ROAD VEHICLES. A combination of vehicles consisting of a motor vehicle drawing a trailer, a semi-trailer or a detachable axle. *Highway Safety Code*, S.Q. 1986, c. 91, s. 4.

COMBINATION OF VEHICLES. Every combination of truck, truck trailer, semi-trailer and trailer.

COMBINED PIPELINE. A commodity pipeline through which oil or gas, or both, can be moved.

COMBUSTIBLE CONSTRUCTION. As applied to a building means that type of construction in which the structural elements are constructed wholly or partly of wood members which do not meet the requirements for heavy timber (mill type) construction and may include noncombustible as well as combustible elements. *Power Corporation Act*, R.R.O. 1980, Reg. 794, s. 0.

COMBUSTIBLE DUST. Any dust that will burn or explode in the air when exposed to a flame or any other ignition source. *Canada Dangerous Substances Regulations*, C.R.C., c. 997, s. 2.

COMBUSTIBLE MATERIAL. Material other than incombustible material. *Hull Construction Regulations*, C.R.C., c. 1431, s. 2.

COMFORT STATION. A building containing flush water closets, electrical lighting and running water.

COMIC. See CRIME ~.

COMITATU COMMISSO. [L.] A commission or writ to act as sheriff.

COMITATUS. *n.* [L.] A county.

COMITY. See INTERNATIONAL ~.

COMITY OF NATIONS. A code of behaviour towards one another which nations observe from mutual convenience or courtesy.

COMM. *abbr.* Commission.

COMMAND. See SECOND-IN- ~; VESSEL NOT UNDER ~.

COMMANDEER. *v.* To seize a thing or require a thing to be used for military purposes.

COMMAND PAPERS. In Britain, papers presented to Parliament at the Crown's command.

COMMENCEMENT. *n.* When used with reference to an enactment, means the time at which the enactment comes into force.

COMMERCE. *n.* Trade; exchange of goods or property. See CHAMBER OF ~; TRADE AND ~.

COMMERCIA BELLI. [L.] Agreements between warring states, such as a capitulation or truce.

COMMERCIAL. *adj.* 1. Connected with trade and commerce in general. 2. Of real property, principally used for the sale of goods or services.

COMMERCIAL ACTIVITY. The conduct of any activity and the provision of any service, accommodation, material or supply that is necessary to promote and develop tourism in the province and includes: (i) an activity or service, accommodation, material or supply that is for the general use of or for the entertainment, sporting or aesthetic enjoyment of the public; (ii) the provision of maps, stationery, printing, books, pamphlets, postcards, souvenirs and other forms of promotion, sports equipment, supplies and labour; (iii) the maintenance of buildings and other structures; and (iv) the maintenance and replacement of equipment. *Department of Tourism and Renewable Resources Amendment Act*, S.S. 1982-83, c. 32, s. 3.

COMMERCIAL AIRCRAFT. An aircraft operated or available for operation for hire or reward. Canada regulations.

COMMERCIAL AIRLINE. A person who operates a commercial air service.

COMMERCIAL AIR SERVICE. Any use of aircraft for hire or reward. *Aeronautics Act*, R.S.C. 1985 (1st Supp.), c. 33, s. 3.

COMMERCIAL APPLICATOR. A person who performs or enters into a contract to control or exterminate pests for hire or reward. *Pest Control Products (Nova Scotia) Act*, S.N.S. 1986, c. 16, s. 3.

COMMERCIAL ARBITRATION. An adjudicative process, either voluntary or ad hoc, involving the application and interpretation of agreements. D.J.M. Brown and D.M. Beatty, *Canadian Labour Arbitration*, 2d ed. (Aurora: Canada Law Book, 1977) at 2 and 3.

COMMERCIAL ASSESSMENT. (i) The assessment of real property that is used as the basis for computing business assessment including the assessment for real property that is rented and occupied or used by the Crown in right of Canada or any province or any board, commission, corporation or other agency thereof, or by any municipal corporation or local board thereof, and (ii) business assessment, and (iii) the assessment for mineral lands, railway lands, other than railway lands actually in use for residential and farming purposes, and pipe lines, according to the last revised assessment roll. *Municipal Act*, R.S.O. 1980, c. 302, s. 365. See EQUALIZED ~.

COMMERCIAL ASSET. An asset that is not a family asset, including rights under a life insurance policy, life or fixed term annuity policy, accident and sickness insurance policy, pension scheme or plan, superannuation scheme or plan, and any investment including deposits with a bank, trust company, credit union or other financial institution other than in a savings account, chequing account or current account ordinarily used for shelter or transportation or for household, educational, recreational, social or aesthetic purposes but not including savings bonds or deposit receipts intended to be used for shelter or transportation or for household, educational, recreational, social or aesthetic purposes. *Marital Property Act*, S.M. 1978, c. 24, s. 1.

COMMERCIAL CABLECASTER. Any cablecaster other than a community cablecaster. *The Community Cablecasters Act*, R.S.S. 1978, c. C-17, s. 2.

COMMERCIAL CLASS. A class of pest control product designated as such by the Federal Regulatory Authority. *Pest Control Products (Nova Scotia) Act*, S.N.S. 1986, c. 16, s. 3.

COMMERCIAL CROP. Plants grown on a cultivated farm and intended mainly for sale, including grain-corn and alfalfa grown for commercial purposes. *Crop Insurance Act*, R.S.Q. 1977, c. A-30, s. 1.

COMMERCIAL DISCOVERY. A discovery of oil, gas or petroleum that has been demonstrated to contain reserves that justify the investment of capital and effort to bring the discovery to production.

COMMERCIAL ENTERPRISE. A sole proprietorship, partnership, co-operative or corporation having for its object the acquisition of gain.

COMMERCIAL ESTABLISHMENT. Any establishment or other place where commodities are, or merchandise is, sold or offered for sale at retail.

COMMERCIAL FACILITY. 1. The structures, machinery and equipment that constitute the necessary components of a commercial operation. *Regional Development Incentives Act*, S.C. 1970-71-72, c. 10, s. 1. 2. A commercial cold storage or a commercial bait freezing facility equipped with mechanical refrigeration. *Fishery Products Storage Regulations*, C.R.C., c. 862, s. 2.

COMMERCIAL FISH. Fish other than game fish. *Ontario Fishery Regulations*, C.R.C., c. 849, s. 2.

COMMERCIAL FISHERMAN. The master and crew of a fishing vessel, the master and crew of a fish packing vessel and any other person who contributes in any manner to the catching or landing of fish for sale or commercial use. *Workers' Compensation Act*, R.S.B.C. 1979, c. 437, s. 4.

COMMERCIAL FISHING. 1. Fishing for sale or barter. Canada regulations. 2. The taking for sale of fish, other than game fish, by means of any hook line, trolling line, spear, minnow trap, dip net, hoop net, pound net, seine net, trammel net or trawl net. *Ontario Fishery Regulations*, C.R.C., c. 849, s. 2. 3. Fishing for or catching fish or harvesting marine plants, all or any portion of which are sold, offered for sale, traded or bartered. *Atlantic Fishing Registration and Licensing Regulations*, C.R.C., c. 808, s. 2. See FIXED ~ UNIT.

COMMERCIAL FISHING VESSEL. 1. Any fishing vessel (a) the catch or any portion of the catch of which is sold, offered for sale, traded or bartered, (b) that is used in processing fish, or (c) that is used in transporting unprocessed fish. *Atlantic Fishing Registration and Licensing Regulations*, C.R.C., c. 808, s. 2. 2. A fishing vessel that is used in commercial fishing. *Pacific Fishery Regulations and Licensing Regulations*, C.R.C., c. 824, s. 2.

COMMERCIAL FISH POND. An artificially constructed pond that is used by the owner to sell angling rights to the general public. *Fish and Wildlife Act*, S.N.B. 1980, c. F-14.1, s. 1.

COMMERCIAL FLYING SCHOOL. A flying school licensed by the Canadian Transport Commission. *Air Services Fees Regulations*, C.R.C., c. 5, s. 2.

COMMERCIAL FOREST OPERATION. An operation involving the cutting or felling of trees for sale.

COMMERCIAL GAS WELL. A well that is on production from a gas bearing zone or a well in which casing is run and that will be placed on production under reasonably foreseeable circumstances. *Petroleum and Natural Gas Act*, R.S.B.C. 1979, c. 323, s. 1.

COMMERCIAL LAW. The law of contracts, bankruptcy, intellectual property, corporations and partnerships and any other subjects dealing with rights and relations of persons engaged in commerce or trade.

COMMERCIAL LETTER OF CREDIT. 1. An irrevocable document issued by a buyer's bank in favour of a seller. The issuing bank will accept drafts drawn upon it for the price of the goods when the seller tenders shipping documents. G.H.L. Fridman, *Sale of Goods in Canada*, 3d ed. (Toronto: Carswell, 1986) at 260. 2. A document issued by a bank on an importer's application in which the bank undertakes to pay an exporter when the exporter complies with certain terms. I.F.G. Baxter, *The Law of Banking*, 3d ed. (Toronto: Carswell, 1981) at 141.

COMMERCIAL LICENCE. See ZONE ~.

COMMERCIAL MARINA. A place located on or adjacent to a body of water or a watercourse where overnight moorings, moorings for a fee, storage, repairs, or marine fuel are ordinarily provided for or supplied to pleasure boats in which toilets are installed and includes a place operated by a boat or yacht club. *Environmental Protection Act*, R.R.O. 1980, Reg. 310, s. 1.

COMMERCIAL MESSAGE. Any commercial announcement and includes any announcement that mentions an advertiser, any product or service of an advertiser or any activity being promoted by an advertiser, including any such mention in a list of prizes, but does not include any classified announcement or any announcement made on behalf of a station or a network that does not contain the name of any other advertiser or his products. *Television Broadcasting Regulations*, C.R.C., c. 381, s. 2.

COMMERCIAL MOTOR VEHICLE. 1. A motor vehicle having attached thereto a truck or delivery body and includes an ambulance, hearse, casket wagon, fire apparatus, police patrol, motor bus, and other motor vehicles used for the transportation of goods. 2. Any automobile, truck, tractor or other motor vehicle or machine used alone or in combination with a trailer or semi-trailer in the commercial carriage of passengers or goods and driven, propelled, drawn or carried by mechanical power. *Com-*

mercial Motor Vehicle (Customs) Regulations, C.R.C., c. 455, s. 2.

COMMERCIAL OPERATION. See INDUSTRIAL OR ~.

COMMERCIAL OR BUSINESS PURPOSES. Any activity conducted by a person for the purpose of earning income from an office, employment, business or property to the extent that the cost of the gasoline used directly in that activity is deductible in computing that person's income for a taxation year pursuant to the provisions of Part I of the Income Tax Act. *Gasoline Excise Tax Regulations,* C.R.C., c. 592, s. 4.

COMMERCIAL PAPER. A bill of exchange, cheque, promissory note, negotiable instrument, conditional sale agreement, lien note, hire purchase agreement, chattel mortgage, bill of lading, bill of sale, warehouse receipt, guarantee, instrument of assignment, things in action and, in addition, any document of title that passes ownership or possession and on which credit can be raised. *Interpretation Act,* R.S.B.C. 1979, c. 206, s. 29.

COMMERCIAL PASSENGER VEHICLE. Any taxi, bus or other vehicle used or intended for use in the transportation of persons for compensation. *Airport Traffic Regulations,* C.R.C., c. 886, s. 2.

COMMERCIAL PETROLEUM WELL. A well that is on production from an oil bearing zone or a well in which casing is run and that will be placed on production under reasonably foreseeable circumstances. *Petroleum and Natural Gas Act,* R.S.B.C. 1979, c. 323, s. 1.

COMMERCIAL PRODUCTION. Output from a well of such quantity of crude oil, liquid hydrocarbons, natural gas and natural gas liquids as, having regard to the cost of drilling and production and the price, kind and quality of such production, would justify from a commercial and economic standpoint the drilling of a similar well in the immediate surroundings.

COMMERCIAL PROPERTY. All property except residential property and resource property.

COMMERCIAL QUANTITY. Applied to a discovery of petroleum or natural gas, means a quantity obtained or anticipated which justifies the drilling of new wells in the vicinity of the discovery, taking into account the quality of the product, possible markets and other economic factors.

COMMERCIAL REALTY. Real property owned by the Crown or any person, used for or occupied by any industry, trade, business, profession, vocation or government business.

COMMERCIAL SAMPLE. (a) Any goods that are representative of a particular category of goods produced outside Canada and that are imported solely for the purpose of being exhibited or demonstrated to solicit orders for similar goods to be supplied from outside Canada, and (b) any films, charts, projectors and scale models, and similar items, imported solely for the purpose of illustrating a particular category of goods produced outside Canada to solicit orders for similar goods to be supplied from outside Canada. *Commercial Samples Remission Order,* C.R.C., c. 251, s. 2.

COMMERCIAL SCALE. See WORK ON A ~.

COMMERCIAL SEED. Seed that is not derived from an inspected seed crop for which a crop registration certificate or a seed crop certificate as defined in the Seeds Act (Canada) has been issued. *Community Seed Cleaning Plant Loans Act,* R.S.M. 1970, c. S70, s. 2.

COMMERCIAL SPEECH. Labelling; advertising. P.W. Hogg, *Constitutional Law of Canada,* 2d ed. (Toronto: Carswell, 1985) at 719.

COMMERCIAL STRUCTURE. See MOBILE INDUSTRIAL OR ~.

COMMERCIAL TENANT. A tenant of a commercial property. *Assessment Act,* S. Nfld. 1986, c. 43, s. 2.

COMMERCIAL TIME. Any period of two minutes or less during which a broadcaster normally presents commercial messages, public service announcements or station or network identification. *Canada Elections Act,* R.S.C. 1985, c. E-2, s. 2.

COMMERCIAL TREATY. An international treaty concerning financial or economic relations.

COMMERCIAL UNIT. In human rights legislation, any building or other structure or part thereof that is used or occupied or is intended, arranged or designed to be used or occupied for the manufacture, sale, resale, processing, reprocessing, displaying, storing, handling, garaging or distribution of personal property, or any space that is used or occupied or is intended, arranged or designed to be used or occupied as a separate business or professional unit or office in any building or other structure or a part thereof.

COMMERCIAL USE. 1. A use in connection with a trade, business, profession, manufacture or other venture for profit. 2. Any use other than for residential or agricultural purposes.

COMMERCIAL VALUE. In respect of any

goods or services donated or provided at less than their true value: (i) where the person by whom the goods or services are donated or provided is in the business of supplying such goods or services, the lowest amount charged by him for an equivalent amount of the same goods or services at or about the time they are donated or provided; (ii) where the person by whom the goods or services are donated or provided is not in the business of supplying such goods or services, the lowest amount charged for an equivalent amount of the same goods or services at or about the time that the goods or services are donated or provided on a commercial basis in the market area in which the goods or services are donated or provided; but where the amount determined to be the commercial value of any goods or services in accordance with subclause (i) or (ii) is $25 or less, 'commercial value' means a nil amount. *The Election Amendment Act*, R.S.S. 1978 (Supp.), c. 23, s. 3.

COMMERCIAL VEHICLE. 1. A motor vehicle designed or adapted for the carrying of freight, goods, wares or merchandise. 2. A motor vehicle or trailer operated on a highway for the transportation of livestock or livestock products for gain or compensation, or by or on behalf of a person dealing in livestock or livestock products. See PUBLIC ~.

COMMERCIUM JURE GENTIUM COMMUNE ESSE DEBET, ET NON IN MONOPOLIUM ET PRIVATUM PAUCORUM QUAESTUM CONVERTENDUM. [L.] Trade, by law, ought to be free to all, and not monopolized into private gain for a few.

COMMINGLE. *v.* 1. To mass together. 2. Of funds, to mix into one larger fund.

COMMINUTED FISH. Fish flesh that has been ground to a fine, uniform consistency. *Fish Inspection Regulations*, C.R.C., c. 802, s. 2.

COMMINUTED FRACTURE. A fracture with several fragments because the bone splintered. F.A. Jaffe, *A Guide to Pathological Evidence*, 2d ed. (Toronto: Carswell, 1983) at 176 and 177.

COMMISSARY. *n.* 1. A person who is sent or delegated to execute some function as the representative of a superior. 2. In the military, an officer who is responsible for furnishing provisions, clothing, etc.

COMMISSION. *n.* 1. The authority or order to act. 2. Remuneration paid to an agent or employee based on price. 3. An authority given to a person or persons to administer a program or statute, manage a fund or a public utility, investigate a matter or perform some other public function. 4. The name of a body which carries out the functions listed in definition #3. See CANADIAN HUMAN RIGHTS ~; CANADIAN RADIO-TELEVISION AND TELECOMMUNICATIONS ~; CANADIAN TRANSPORT ~; DEL CREDERE ~; EUROPEAN ~ OF HUMAN RIGHTS; EXTRA-PROVINCIAL ~; FEDERAL BOARD, ~ OR OTHER TRIBUNAL; INTERNATIONAL JOINT ~; LAW REFORM ~ OF CANADA; MUNICIPAL ~; NATIONAL CAPITAL ~; PROPRIETOR ~; PUBLIC SERVICE ~; RESTRICTIVE TRADE PRACTICES ~; ROYAL ~; SERVICE ~.

COMMISSION AGENT. 1. A person who receives goods for a principal and is employed to sell them for remuneration or commission. 2. Any person who receives and handles produce on commission. *Fruit, Vegetables and Honey Act*, R.S.C. 1970, c. F-31, s. 2.

COMMISSION COUNSEL. A counsel employed by the Minister to assist the court holding an investigation. *Shipping Inquiries and Investigations Rules*, C.R.C., c. 1479, s. 2.

COMMISSIONER. *n.* 1. A person authorised by letters patent, statute or other lawful warrant to examine any matters or execute a public office. 2. A member of a commission. 3. A person authorized to take the evidence of another person. 4. The Commissioner of the Royal Canadian Mounted Police. *Criminal Code*, R.S.C. 1985, c. C-46, s. 84. 5. The Commissioner of the Northwest Territories. *Northwest Territories Act*, R.S.C. 1985, c. N-27, s. 2. 6. The Commissioner of the Yukon Territory. *Yukon Act*, R.S.C. 1985, c. Y-2, s. 2. See CITY ~S; CONCILIATION ~; DOMINION FIRE ~; FAMILY LAW ~; INFORMATION ~; FIRE ~; INFORMATION ~ OF CANADA; MARRIAGE ~; PRIVACY ~; PRIVACY ~ OF CANADA.

COMMISSIONER FOR TAKING AFFIDAVITS. One authorized to administer affirmations or oaths.

COMMISSIONER IN COUNCIL. The Commissioner of the Northwest Territories or Yukon acting by and with the advice and consent of the Council.

COMMISSIONER MERCHANT. 1. Any person, partnership or corporation that is engaged in the business of negotiating, for a commission, purchases or sales of livestock at a stockyard or arriving at or for delivery to a packer's yard and that expends or receives moneys on behalf of a purchaser or vendor. *Livestock and Livestock Products Act*, R.S.C. 1985, c. L-9, s. 10. 2. Any person or partnership engaged in the business of buying or selling livestock or livestock products for a commission. *Livestock and Livestock Products Act*, R.S.C. 1985, c. L-9, s. 31.

COMMISSIONER OF OFFICIAL LAN-GUAGES. The federal official empowered to see that both Canada's official languages, French and English, have equal status, rights and privileges in federal institutions.

COMMISSIONERS OF INTERNAL ECON-OMY. The Speaker and four members of the House of Commons who are members of the Queen's Privy Council for Canada appointed by the Governor in Council. A. Fraser, G.A. Birch & W.A. Dawson, eds., *Beauchesne's Rules and Forms of the House of Commons of Canada*, 5th ed. (Toronto: Carswell, 1978) at 251.

COMMISSION EVIDENCE. A way to preserve or secure evidence when a witness is, because of (i) physical disability caused by illness, or (ii) any other good and sufficient reason, not able to attend a trial at the time it is held. P.K. McWilliams, *Canadian Criminal Evidence*, 3d ed. (Aurora: Canada Law Book, 1988) at 8-82.

COMMISSION FIRM. A person who buys or sells cattle for another on commission. *Cattle Horn Act*, R.S.B.C. 1979, c. 44, s. 1.

COMMISSION OF THE PEACE. A commission by which a number of persons are appointed as justices of the peace.

COMMISSION ROGATORY. A means of collecting evidence for courts of one country through the courts of another country.

COMMISSION STEWARD. A person appointed by a Commission to represent that Commission. *Race Track Supervision Regulations*, C.R.C., c. 441, s. 2.

COMMIT. *v.* 1. To send to prison by reason of lawful authority. 2. To send to trial, i.e. a provincial court judge commits a person to trial before another court. 3. To refer a bill to a committee in which the bill is considered and reported. A. Fraser, G.A. Birch & W.A. Dawson, eds., *Beauchesne's Rules and Forms of the House of Commons of Canada*, 5th ed. (Toronto: Carswell, 1978) at 228. 4. To direct that a person be confined in a psychiatric facility. See RE ~.

COMMITMENT. *n.* 1. An agreement or promise to do something. 2. Sending a person to prison. 3. Directing that a person be confined in a psychiatric facility. See GOVERNMENT ~; LOAN ~; MORTGAGE ~.

COMMITMENT LETTER. A letter prepared by a lender, setting out the conditions and terms upon which the lender is willing to advance money to a borrower. B.J. Reiter, R.C.B. Risk

& B.N. McLellan, *Real Estate Law*, 3d ed. (Toronto: Emond Montgomery, 1986) at 976.

COMMITTAL ORDER. A court order for the committal of a person to a correctional facility or a federal penitentiary.

COMMITTEE. *n.* 1. A group of persons elected or appointed to whom any matter is referred by a legislative body, corporation or other institution. 2. A person appointed by the court to look after a person or the affairs of a person or a mentally incompetent person. See ADVISORY ~; AUDIT ~; DISCIPLINE ~; FINANCE ~; GRAIN STANDARDS ~; HOSPITAL MEDI-CAL STAFF REVIEW ~; JOINT ~; JOINT PRACTICE ~; JOINT TRAINING ~; JUDI-CIAL ~; MEDICAL STAFF ~; PARLIAMEN-TARY ~; PROVINCIAL ~; REVIEW ~; SAFETY AND HEALTH ~; SELECT ~; SPE-CIAL ~; STANDING ~; STEERING ~; STRIKING ~; TERRITORIAL ~; WAYS AND MEANS ~.

COMMITTEEMAN. See UNION ~.

COMMITTEE OF THE WHOLE HOUSE. 1. The membership of the House when a chairman instead of the Speaker presides. This committee must consider all matters concerning taxation and any other matters which, in the opinion of the House, it may more fitly discuss. A. Fraser, G.A. Birch & W.A. Dawson, eds., *Beauchesne's Rules and Forms of the House of Commons of Canada*, 5th ed. (Toronto: Carswell, 1978) at 161.

COMMODATUM. *n.* [L.] An agreement to loan useful goods or chattels free of charge, to be used and later restored in specie. E.L.G. Tyler & N.E. Palmer, eds., *Crossley Vaines' Personal Property*, 5th ed. (London: Butterworths, 1973) at 85. See CONTRACT OF ~.

COMMODITY. *n.* 1. Tangible personal property of every kind. *Ministry of Government Services Act*, R.S.O. 1980, c. 279, s. 1. 2. The various kinds of freight, merchandise and goods carried on a public motor truck. *Motor Carrier Act*, R.S.N.B. 1973, c. M-16, s. 1. 3. Any agricultural product, forest product, product of the sea, mineral, metal, hydrocarbon fuel, currency or precious stone or other gem in the original or a processed state. See AGRICULTURAL ~; DANGEROUS ~; ENERGY ~; INDIVIDU-ALLY MEASURED ~; NAMED ~.

COMMODITY CONTRACT. A commodity futures contract or commodity futures option. *Commodity Contract Act*, R.S.B.C. 1979, c. 56, s. 1. See OPEN ~.

COMMODITY CONTRACTS ADVISER. A person who (a) carries on the business of or holds himself out as carrying on the business of (i)

advising others concerning trading in commodity contracts; or (ii) distributing or publishing analyses or reports respecting commodities; or (b) is employed either generally or in a particular case by a commodity contracts adviser to do one or more of the tasks referred to in subparagraph (i) or (ii). *Commodity Contract Act*, R.S.B.C. 1979, c. 56, s. 1.

COMMODITY CONTRACTS DEALER. A person who carries on the business of trading in commodity contracts in the capacity of principal or agent. *Commodity Contract Act*, R.S.B.C. 1979, c. 56, s. 1.

COMMODITY CONTRACTS SALESMAN. A person who is employed by a commodity contracts dealer to make trades in commodity contracts on behalf of the commodity contracts dealer. *Commodity Contract Act*, R.S.B.C. 1979, c. 56, s. 1.

COMMODITY EXCHANGE. An association or organization, whether incorporated or unincorporated, operated to provide the facilities necessary for the trading of commodity contracts by open auction. *Commodity Contract Amendment Act*, S.B.C. 1985, c. 2, s. 1.

COMMODITY FUTURES CONTRACT. A contract to make or take delivery of a specified cash equivalent to the full value of the contract, or the specified quantity or quality, grade or size of a commodity during a designated future month at a price agreed on. See OPEN ~.

COMMODITY FUTURES EXAMINATION. See CANADIAN ~; NATIONAL ~.

COMMODITY FUTURES EXCHANGE. An association or organization, whether incorporated or unincorporated, operated for the purpose of providing the physical facilities necessary for the trading of contracts by open auction.

COMMODITY FUTURES OPTION. A right, acquired for a consideration, to assume a long or short position in relation to a commodity futures contract at a specified price and within a specified period of time and any other option of which the subject is a commodity futures contract.

COMMODITY OPTION. A right, acquired for a consideration, to assume a long or short position in relation to a commodity at a specified price and within a specified period of time and any other option of which the subject is a commodity. *Commodity Contract Amendment Act*, S.B.C. 1985, c. 2, s. 1.

COMMODITY PIPELINE. A pipeline for the transmission of commodities and includes all branches, extensions, pumps, racks, compres-sors, loading facilities, storage facilities, reservoirs, tanks, interstation systems of communication by telephone, telegraph or radio and real or personal property and works connected therewith, but does not include a pipeline for the transmission solely of oil or gas, or both. *National Transportation Act*, R.S.C. 1985, c. N-20, s. 2.

COMMODITY PIPELINE COMPANY. A person named in an Act of Parliament and having authority under that Act to construct or operate a commodity pipeline, or a person authorized by an Act of Parliament to construct or operate a commodity pipeline with respect to which that Act has special reference.

COMMODITY RATE. A toll applicable to specifically named commodities. *Air Carrier Regulations*, C.R.C., c. 3, s. 2.

COMMODITY SUPERVISORS' EXAMINATION. An examination relating to the supervision of a dealer's business that has been prepared by and is administered by the Canadian Securities Institute and is so designated by that Institute. *Commodity Futures Act*, R.R.O. 1980, Reg. 114, s. 7.

COMMODITY VALUE OF GAS. The aggregate of (i) the thermal value of gas determined by reference to the volume-weight average prices of substitutable energy sources competing with gas for the various end uses of gas in the consuming markets served, directly or through exchange, by the buyer of gas under a gas purchase contract, and (ii) the premium value of gas determined by reference to its inherent special qualities when compared with competing energy sources. *Arbitration Act*, R.S.A. 1980, c. A-43, s. 17.

COMMODUM EX INJURIA NON ORITUR. [L.] No legal advantage can arise out of a wrong.

COMMON. *n.* An interest one person can enjoy in the land of another, i.e. common of pasture is the right to pasture cattle on another person's land. See TENANCY IN ~.

COMMON. *adj.* Usual, ordinary; shared.

COMMONABLE. *adj.* Used of something by, over or in respect of which one may exercise a right of common.

COMMONALTY. *n.* The people.

COMMON AREAS. Areas controlled by a landlord and used for access to residential premises or for the service or enjoyment of a tenant.

COMMON ASSAULT. An assault which does not amount to an aggravated assault.

COMMON BAWDY-HOUSE. A place that is (a)

kept or occupied, or (b) resorted to by one or more persons for the purpose of prostitution or the practice of acts of indecency. *Criminal Code*, R.S.C. 1985, c. C-46, c. 197.

COMMON BETTING HOUSE. A place that is opened, kept or used for the purpose of (a) enabling, encouraging or assisting persons who resort thereto to bet between themselves or with the keeper, or (b) enabling any person to receive, record, register, transmit or pay bets or to announce the results of betting. *Criminal Code*, R.S.C. 1985, c. C-46, s. 197.

COMMON CARRIER. A person who undertakes, for hire, to transport the hirer's goods. E.L.G. Tyler & N.E. Palmer, eds., *Crossley Vaines' Personal Property*, 5th ed. (London: Butterworths, 1973) at 119.

COMMON ELEMENTS. All property, except the condominium units, owned in common by all of the owners of units. B.J. Reiter, R.C.B. Risk & B.N. McLellan, *Real Estate Law*, 3d ed. (Toronto: Emond Montgomery, 1986) at 660.

COMMON EMPLOYMENT. The general rule that a master is liable for damage caused by the negligence of a servant in the course of employment used to be subject to an exception: that where the person injured was the fellow-servant of and engaged in common employment with the person whose negligence caused the injury, the master was not liable in an action at common law. *Priestley v. Fowler* (1837) 3 M. & W. 1.

COMMON EXPENSES. The expenses of the performance of the objects and duties of a condominium corporation and any expenses specified as common expenses in a declaration.

COMMON FACILITY. An improvement in the common property that is available for the use of all the owners of a condominium.

COMMON FORM BUSINESS. The business of obtaining probate or administration where there is no contention as to the right thereto, including the passing of probates and administration through court when the contest is terminated, and all business of a non-contentious nature to be taken in a surrogate court in matters of testacy and intestacy not being proceedings in a suit, and also the business of lodging caveats against the grant of probate or administration.

COMMON GAMING HOUSE. A place that is (a) kept for gain to which persons resort for the purpose of playing games, or (b) kept or used for the purpose of playing games (i) in which a bank is kept by one or more but not all of the players, (ii) in which all or any portion of the bets on or proceeds from a game is paid, directly or indirectly, to the keeper of the place, (iii) in which, directly or indirectly, a fee is charged to or paid by the players for the privilege of playing or participating in a game or using gaming equipment, or (iv) in which the chances of winning are not equally favourable to all persons who play the game, including the person, if any, who conducts the game. *Criminal Code*, R.S.C. 1985, c. C-46, s. 197.

COMMON INTEREST. 1. In condominium law, the interest in the common elements appurtenant to a unit. 2. In occupier's liability, a mutuality of interest or advantage to invitor and invitee. J.V. DiCastri, *Occupiers' Liability* (Vancouver: Burroughs/Carswell, 1980) at 35.

COMMON JAIL. Any place other than a penitentiary in which persons charged with offences are usually kept and detained in custody.

COMMON LAW. 1. In contrast to statute law, law which relies for its authority on the decisions of the courts and is recorded in the law reports as decisions of judges along with the reasons for their decisions. 2. In contrast to canon (or ecclesiastical) and the civil (or Roman) law, the system of law in provinces other than Quebec.

COMMON LAW MARRIAGE. *var.* **COMMON-LAW MARRIAGE.** A relationship in which two persons live together as husband and wife without being married in a church or by a judge.

COMMON-LAW RELATIONSHIP. The relationship between a man and a woman who are common-law spouses. *The Teachers' Pensions Amendment Act*, S.M. 1985-86, c. 31, s. 1.

COMMON LAW SPOUSE. *var.* **COMMON-LAW SPOUSE.** Includes any man or woman who although not legally married to a person lives and cohabits with that person as the spouse of that person and is known as such in the community in which they have lived.

COMMON LAW UNION. Cohabitation by a man and a woman who publicly present themselves as spouses.

COMMON-LAW WIFE. A woman who, although not legally married to a man, cohabits with him and is recognized as his wife in the community in which they live.

COMMON MARKET. The popular name for the European Economic Community.

COMMON MISTAKE. See MISTAKE.

COMMON NUISANCE. The offence of committing a common nuisance consists of doing an unlawful act or failing to discharge a legal duty and thereby (a) endangering the lives, safety, health, property or comfort or the public, or (b) obstructing the public in the exercise or enjoyment or any right that is common to all the subjects of Her Majesty in Canada. *Criminal Code*, R.S.C. 1985, c. C-46, s. 180(2).

COMMON PARENTAGE. Having one common parent.

COMMON PLEAS. The British court which was a superior court of record.

COMMON PROPERTY. The part of the land included in a condominium plan that is not included in any unit shown in the condominium plan.

COMMON PURPOSE CHARTER. A return passenger charter originating in Canada where one or more charterers contract for the entire capacity of an aircraft in order to provide air transportation at a price per seat (a) to and from a CPC event, or (b) in connection with a CPC educational program. *Air Carrier Regulations*, C.R.C., c. 3, s. 23.

COMMON ROAD. An access road on which public money has been expended for its repair or maintenance. *Road Access Act*, R.S.O. 1980, c. 457, s. 1.

COMMONS. See HOUSE OF ~.

COMMON SHARE. 1. A share to which no special rights or privileges attach. 2. A share the holder of which is not precluded upon the reduction or redemption of the capital stock from participating in the assets of the corporation beyond the amount paid up thereon plus a fixed premium and a defined rate of dividend. *Income Tax Act*, R.S.C. 1952, c. 148 (as am. S.C. 1970-71-72, c. 63), s. 248(1).

COMMON SURPLUS. The excess of all receipts of the corporation over the expenses. *Condominium Act*, R.S.O. 1980, c. 84, s. 1.

COMMON TRUST FUND. A fund maintained by a trust company in which money belonging to various estates and trusts in its care are combined to facilitate investment.

COMMON USE. Used by more than one person.

COMMONWEALTH. *n.* 1. The social state of a country. 2. A republic. 3. The Australian federation called the Commonwealth of Australia. 4. The British government from 1649 to 1660. 5. The association of countries named in the schedule. *Interpretation Act*, R.S.C. 1985, c. I-21, s. 35. See BRITISH ~.

COMMONWEALTH AND DEPENDENT TERRITORIES. The several Commonwealth countries and their colonies, possessions, dependencies, protectorates, protected states, condominiums and trust territories. *Interpretation Act*, R.S.C. 1985, c. I-21, s. 35.

COMMONWEALTH COUNTRY. 1. A country (a) whose government was a party to the British Commonwealth Merchant Shipping Agreement signed at London on December 10, 1931, or (b) that was included within the ambit of that Agreement in 1931 and the government of which, as a government of a separate entity within the association of the Commonwealth of Nations, continues to participate in that Agreement, and includes the colonies, possessions, dependencies, protectorates, protected states, condominiums and trust territories of any such country. *Canada Shipping Act*, R.S.C. 1985, c. S-9, s. 2. 2. A country that is a member of the association of such countries.

COMMONWEALTH OF NATIONS. See BRITISH ~.

COMMORIENTES. *n.* [L.] People who die in the same accident or on the same occasion.

COMMR. *abbr.* Commissioner.

COMMUNAL PROPERTY. (i) Land held by a colony in such a manner that no member of the colony has any individual or personal ownership or right of ownership in the land, and each member shares in the distribution of profits or benefits according to his needs or in equal measure with his fellow members, and (ii) land held by a member of the colony by personal ownership or right of ownership or under a lease, if the land is used in conjunction with and as part of other land held in the manner described in subclause (i). *Communal Property Act*, R.S.A. 1970, c. 59, s. 2.

COMMUNE. *n.* A small community of people who share common interests and who own property together.

COMMUNE CONCILIUM REGNI. [L.] The common council of the monarch and parliament.

COMMUNICABLE DISEASE. a. An illness due to an infectious agent or its toxic products which is transmitted directly or indirectly to a well person from an infected person or animal, or through the agency of an intermediate animal host, of a vector, or of the inanimate environment. 2. An infectious or contagious disease. *Animal Disease and Protection Regulations*, C.R.C., c. 296, s. 2.

COMMUNICATING. *n.* Includes communicating by telephone, broadcasting or other audible or visible means. *Criminal Code*, R.S.C. 1985, c. C-46, s. 319(7).

COMMUNICATION LINE. A line for telegraphic, telephonic, signalling or other intelligence purposes. *Wire Crossings and Proximities Regulations*, C.R.C., c. 1195, s. 2.

COMMUNICATIONS. *n.* 1. A method, manner or means by which information is transmitted, imparted or exchanged and includes the transmission and reception of sound, pictures, signs, signals, data or messages by means of wire, cable, waves or an electrical, electronic, magnetic, electromagnetic or optical means. 2. The business of radio and television broadcasting and the furnishing of community antenna services, telephone services and other electrical or electronic communication services. *Small Business Loans Regulations*, C.R.C., c. 1501, s. 3. See CONFIDENTIAL ~; DEPARTMENT OF ~; DISTRESS COMMUNICATION ~; PENITENTIAL COMMUNICATION ~; PRIVATE COMMUNICATION; PRIVILEGED COMMUNICATION; PUBLIC ~; RADIOCOMMUNICATION.

COMMUNICATION SYSTEM. An electrical system whereby intelligence or signals may be transmitted to or through a central station, including telephone, telegraph, district messenger, fire and burglar alarm, watchman or sprinkler supervisory system, and other central station systems of a similar nature, which commonly receive the power supply necessary for their operation from central office or local power sources.

COMMUNIS ERROR FACIT JUS. [L.] A common error may make law.

COMMUNITY. *n.* 1. A city, town or village. *The Community Planning Profession Act*, R.S.S. 1978, c. C-21, c. 2. 2. A geographic unit or group of persons sharing common interests within a geographic unit who provide or receive services on a collective basis. 3. A group of persons living together and observing common rules under the direction of a superior. 4. The Communauté urbaine de Montréal, the Communauté urbaine de Québec or the Communauté régionale de l'Outaouais. 5. Any area which is not a municipality. See CREE ~; FULL ~; NATIVE ~; REMOTE ~; SEPARATED ~; VACATED ~.

COMMUNITY ANTENNA TELEVISION. A system by which television signals are received from distant stations on large antennae and transmitted by cable to individual consumers.

COMMUNITY-BASED RESIDENTIAL FACILITY. A place offering accommodation or treatment (a) to paroled inmates and other persons, or (b) exclusively to paroled inmates and inmates who are subject to mandatory supervision, and includes a psychiatric hospital or facility and a penitentiary. *Parole and Penitentiary Act*, R.S.C. 1985 (2d Supp.), c. 34, s. 21.2.

COMMUNITY CABLECASTER. A provider of cablecast service and cablecast programming.

COMMUNITY CARE FACILITY. A facility that provides personal care, supervision, social or educational training, physical or mental rehabilitative therapy, with or without charge to persons not related by blood or marriage to an operator of the facility.

COMMUNITY CENTRE. Any public land improved, or buildings erected and equipped to provide recreational, sporting, cultural, or adult educational facilities for the public use of the community.

COMMUNITY CHANNEL. In relation to a licensee, the television channel provided by the licensee on its undertaking for the distribution of community programming. *Cable Television Regulations*, C.R.C., c. 374, s. 2.

COMMUNITY CREDIT UNION. A credit union whose membership is open to all persons residing or working within a defined geographical area. *Credit Unions and Caisses Populaires Act*, R.R.O. 1980, Reg. 196, c. 1.

COMMUNITY DEVELOPMENT SERVICES. Services designed to encourage and assist residents of a community to participate in or continue to participate in improving the social and economic conditions of the community for the purpose of preventing, lessening or removing the causes and effects of poverty, child neglect or dependence on public assistance in the community.

COMMUNITY HALL. Includes the building, lands or other property used or intended to be used or capable of being used for social, educational, recreational or community purposes, public meetings, public library or for entertainment or amusement, and includes all lands and buildings used or intended to be used or capable of being used for athletic purposes. *Community Act*, R.S.N.S. 1967, c. 41, s. 1.

COMMUNITY HOUSING PROJECT. A project, together with the land on which it is situated, consisting of detached, semidetached or row housing, hostel or dormitory housing units, apartments or any combination or form therof undertaken to provide decent, safe and sanitary housing accommodation in compliance with standards approved by the Government for lease or sale to families of low income. *Alberta Mortgage and Housing Corporation Act*, S.A. 1984, c. A-32.5, s. 1.

COMMUNITY IMPROVEMENT. The planning or replanning, design or redesign, resubdivision, clearance, development or redevelopment, reconstruction and rehabilitation, or any of them, of a community improvement project area, and the provision of such residential, commercial, industrial, public, recreational, institutional, religious, charitable or other uses, buildings, works, improvements or facilities, or spaces therefor, as may be appropriate or necessary. *Planning Act, 1983*, S.O. 1983, c. 1, s. 28.

COMMUNITY IMPROVEMENT PLAN. A plan approved by the Minister for the community improvement of a community improvement project area. *Planning Act, 1983*, S.O. 1983, c. 1, s. 28.

COMMUNITY IMPROVEMENT PROJECT AREA. An area within a municipality, the community improvement of which in the opinion of the council is desirable because of age, dilapidation, overcrowding, faulty arrangement, unsuitability of buildings or for any other reason. *Planning Act, 1983*, S.O. 1983, c. 1, s. 28.

COMMUNITY OF PROPERTY. See COMMUNITY PROPERTY REGIME; DEFERRED ~.

COMMUNITY ORGANIZATION. See LOCAL ~.

COMMUNITY PASTURE. (i) A community grazing reserve, or (ii) public land subject to a grazing lease or permit between the Government and a grazing association or a group of individuals. *Livestock Identification and Brand Inspection Act*, S.A. 1985, c. L-22.5, s. 1.

COMMUNITY PLAN. See OFFICIAL ~.

COMMUNITY PLANNING. See PRACTICE OF PROFESSIONAL ~.

COMMUNITY PLANNING OFFICE. An office, whether of a department or agency of a government or of a person or persons engaged in private business, in which the principal work is the preparation of comprehensive plans of development and in which is employed on a full-time basis, in a senior position, a person who has a degree or diploma in community planning from a recognized university or an institution of learning of equivalent status. *The Community Planning Profession Act*, R.S.S. 1978, c. C-21, s. 2.

COMMUNITY PROGRAMMING. 1. Programming that is distributed by a licensee on its community channel and is produced (a) by the licensee, (b) with or without the assistance of the licensee, by members of the community or communities served by the licensee, (c) by another licensee or by members of the community or communities served by another licensee if such programming is integrated into programming produced by the licensee or by members of the community or communities served by it,

or (d) by a network operator licensed by the Commission to provide community programming to the licensee, and includes announcements promoting services that the licensee is licensed to provide, public service announcements, announcements promoting programs transmitted by Canadian stations and channel identification announcements. *Cable Television Regulations*, C.R.C., c. 374, s. 2. 2. The presentation by a cablecaster to its subscribers of messages based on the resources of a municipality served in whole or in part by the cablecaster and directed toward the well-being of the residents of such municipality. *The Community Cablecasters Act*, R.S.S. 1978, c. C-17, s. 2.

COMMUNITY PROPERTY. Real and personal property held for or owned by the community. *Community Act*, R.S.N.S. 1967, c. 41, s. 1.

COMMUNITY PROPERTY REGIME. An arrangement whereby spouses share all property which one or both may own. A. Bissett-Johnson & W.M. Holland, eds, *Matrimonial Property Law in Canada* (Toronto: Carswell, 1980) at A-5.

COMMUNITY RECREATION CENTRE. Land or all or any part of a building or buildings or structure established in accordance with this Act that is maintained and operated for community recreation activity. *Community Recreation Centres Act*, R.S.O. 1980, c. 80, s. 1.

COMMUNITY SALE. A sale or offering for sale of livestock at an established and recognized place of business where livestock is assembled for that purpose, or, at a railway depot, siding or car or at dock side or from a vessel thereat.

COMMUNITY SERVICE CENTRE. See LOCAL ~.

COMMUNITY SERVICE ORDER. An order requiring an offender to perform unpaid work in the community under supervision.

COMMUNITY SOCIAL SERVICES. Services that are protective, preventive, developmental or rehabilitative in nature and which (a) facilitate access to the necessities of life; (b) assist disabled or disadvantaged persons to live as normally and independently as possible or support them in doing so; (c) prevent the need for institutional care as well as provide alternatives to it; (d) support or assist the aged, children or families; (e) facilitate or support the involvement and participation of people in their communities; (f) enhance or maintain employment skills and capabilities of persons; (g) provide protection to children and adults; (h) provide information and refer people to available services.

COMMUNITY WELFARE. Includes the establishment, maintenance and operation of any one or more of the following: a public or community hall, a club room, a rest room, a library, a recreational ground, a theatre, an ice rink, or any other facilities operated solely for social welfare, health, civic improvement, public entertainment or recreation, no part of the income of which is payable to or otherwise available for the personal benefit of any member or patron. *The Co-operative Associations Act*, R.S.S. 1978, c. C-34, s. 82.

COMMUTATION. *n.* 1. Conversion. 2. Reduction of a punishment or penalty. 3. Change to the right to receive a gross or fixed payment from the right to receive a periodic or variable payment.

COMMUTED. *adj.* Of a sentence or penalty, changed from greater to lesser.

COMMUTED PENSION. A final payment in lieu of annual pension.

COMMUTED VALUE. In relation to benefits that a person has a present or future entitlement to receive, the actuarial present value of those benefits determined, as of the time in question, on the basis of actuarial assumptions and methods that are adequate and appropriate and in accordance with generally accepted actuarial principles.

COMPACT TIP HEADS. That the head structure is practically compact and that head and bracts may be somewhat elongated but not so developed as to be open to the extent of exposing curd-like leaf buds. *Processed Fruit and Vegetable Regulations*, C.R.C., c. 291, Schedule I, s. 8.

COMPANION. *n.* The title granted certain members of honorary orders. See CONSTANT ~.

COMPANY. *n.* 1. An association of people formed to carry on some business or undertaking in the association's name. 2. Any body corporate. 3. A body corporate with share capital. 4. May include unincorporated association, co-operative association, partnership, single proprietor or person. 5. An entity distinct and separate in law from its individual shareholders or members. H. Sutherland, D.B. Horsley & J.M. Edmiston, eds., *Fraser's Handbook on Canadian Company Law*, 7th ed. (Toronto: Carswell, 1985) at 1. See AFFILIATED ~; ALBERTA ~; AMALGAMATED ~; BRITISH ~; CANADIAN ~; CANADIAN NATIONAL RAILWAY ~; CEMETERY ~; CHARTERED ~; CLOSE ~; CLOSED ~; COMMODITY PIPELINE ~; CONSTRAINED-SHARE ~; CONTROLLED ~; DEBTOR ~; DEFUNCT ~; DISTRIBUTION ~; DOMESTIC ~; DOMICILED ~; DOMINION ~; ELEVATOR ~; EXTRA-PROVINCIAL ~; EXTRA-TERRITORIAL ~; FEDERAL ~; FINANCE ~; FOREIGN ~; GAS ~; GAS EXPORT ~; GUARANTEE ~; HOLDING ~; HOUSING ~; HUDSON'S BAY ~; INCORPORATED ~; INDUSTRIAL ~; INSURANCE ~; INVESTMENT ~; JOINT STOCK ~; LIFE ~; LIMITED ~; LOAN ~; MANAGEMENT ~; MINING ~; MUTUAL ~; MUTUAL INSURANCE ~; NATIONAL ~; NON-RESIDENT ~; NOT-FOR-PROFIT ~; OFFEREE ~; PARENT ~; PIPE LINE ~; PRIVATE ~; PROSPECTING ~; PROVINCIAL ~; PUBLIC ~; RAILWAY ~; RELATED COMPANIES; RELATED PERSON OR ~; REPORTING ~; REVIVED ~; SHIPPING ~; SMALL LOANS ~; SPECIALLY LIMITED ~; STORAGE ~; SUBSIDIARY ~; SURETY ~; TELEGRAPH ~; TELEPHONE ~; TRADING ~; TRANSPORTATION ~; UTILITY ~.

COMPANY DOMINATED ORGANIZATION. A labour organization, the formation or administration of which an employer or employer's agent has dominated or interfered with or to which an employer or employer's agent has contributed financial or other support. *The Trade Union Act*, R.S.S. 1978, c. T-17, s. 2.

COMPANY-DOMINATED UNION. A union created with employer support or controlled by the employer.

COMPANY LIMITED BY GUARANTEE. A company having the liability of its members limited by the memorandum to the amount that the members may respectively thereby undertake to contribute to the assets of the company in the event of its being wound up. *Companies Act*, R.S.A. 1980, c. C-20, s. 1.

COMPANY LIMITED BY SHARES. A company having the liability of its members limited to the amount, if any, unpaid on the shares respectively held by them. *Companies Act*, R.S.A. 1980, c. C-20, s. 1.

COMPANY MAN. An employee who is extremely loyal to the employer.

COMPANY PIPELINE. A pipeline to transport oil, gas, solids or water that a company under this Act is authorized to construct or operate, and includes all branches, extensions, tanks, reservoirs, pumps, racks and loading facilities; interstation systems of communication by telephone, telegraph or radio; property and works connected with it. *Pipeline Act*, R.S.B.C. 1979, c. 328, s. 1.

COMPANY STORE. A store maintained by an employer.

COMPANY TOWN. A community owned by an employer.

COMPANY UNION. 1. A union the membership of which is limited to one company. 2. A union dominated by an employer.

COMPANY-WIDE AGREEMENT. An agreement between an employer and a union affecting all plants belonging to the employer.

COMPANY-WIDE BARGAINING. Negotiation of an agreement between an employer operating more than one plant and the union representing workers in all the plants.

COMPARISON METHOD. A method of measurement of the response of a hearing aid, alternative to the substitution method, sometimes employed for reasons of practical convenience, in which the hearing aid and the microphone employed to measure the free-field sound pressure are placed simultaneously at two different points in the sound field, which points are such that the results obtained agree within specified limits of accuracy with the corresponding results obtained by the substitution method. *Medical Devices Regulations*, C.R.C., c. 871, s. 1.

COMPARTMENT. *n.* A lower hold, or a cargo space bounded by permanent bulkheads at each end, and having decks with closed hatchways above and below; an insulated chamber, even though situated in a compartment as defined above, may be considered to be a separate compartment, provided that each chamber is surrounded by a steel bulkhead; a deckhouse or a masthouse can be considered to be a separate compartment. *Dangerous Goods Shipping Regulations*, C.R.C., c. 1419, s. 16. See FILLED ~; FIRE ~; PARCEL ~ ASSEMBLY; PARCEL ~ UNIT; WATERTIGHT ~.

COMPARTMENT DOOR. See INTERIOR ~.

COMPASSING. *n.* Contriving; imagining.

COMPELLABILITY. *n.* Any person can be called upon and must give evidence unless an exception can be shown. P.K. McWilliams, *Canadian Criminal Evidence*, 3d ed. (Aurora: Canada Law Book, 1988) at 34-22.

COMPELLABLE. *adj.* Required by law to give evidence. S. Mitchell, P.J. Richardson & D.A. Thomas, eds., *Archbold Pleading, Evidence and Practice in Criminal Cases*, 43d ed. (London: Sweet & Maxwell, 1988) at 461.

COMPELLATIVUS. *n.* [L.] An accuser; an adversary.

COMPELLING PRESUMPTION. Facts sufficient to require that a given conclusion be drawn from them. John G. Fleming, *The Law of Torts*, 6th ed. (Sydney: The Law Book Company Limited, 1983) at 296.

COMPENDIA SUNT DISPENDIA. [L.] Summaries are not reliable.

COMPENSABLE INJURY. A personal injury a worker suffers during employment which prevents the worker from earning the usual, full wages. D. Robertson, *Ontario Health and Safety Guide* (Toronto: Richard De Boo Ltd., 1988) at 5-58.

COMPENSATION. *n.* 1. An action to make things equivalent; satisfy or make amends. 2. A rate, remuneration, reimbursement or consideration of any kind paid, payable or received, directly or indirectly. 3. The total amount of money or value that is required to be paid in respect of land expropriated. 4. Gain or reward. See CRIMINAL INJURIES ~; IMPORT ~; TOLL, GAIN OR ~; WORKERS' ~.

COMPENSATION ASSOCIATION. A body corporate or unincorporated association the purpose of which is to provide compensation to claimants and policyholders of insolvent insurers.

COMPENSATION OF VICTIMS OF CRIME. Benefits provided by the government to victims of crime in the form of ex gratia payments. John G. Fleming, *The Law of Torts*, 6th ed. (Sydney: The Law Book Company Limited, 1983) at 33.

COMPENSATION ORDER. A court by which a person is convicted or discharged may make an order requiring that person to pay compensation for any loss or damage to property resulting from the offence.

COMPENSATION PLAN. The provisions, however established, for the determination and administration of compensation, and includes such provisions contained in a collective agreement or established bilaterally between an employer and an employee, unilaterally by an employer of an employee, or by or pursuant to an enactment. See DEFERRED ~; GROUP ~.

COMPENSATION RATES. Single rates of remuneration or ranges of rates of remuneration, including cost-of-living adjustments, or, where no such rates or ranges exist, any fixed or ascertainable amounts of remuneration.

COMPENSATORY TIME OFF. 1. Time off in lieu of overtime pay. 2. Extra time off allowed when an employee's regular day off falls on a holiday.

COMPETENCY. *n.* Ability to understand the nature of an oath is the basic test of a person's competency to testify. P.K. McWilliams, *Canadian Criminal Evidence*, 3d ed. (Aurora: Canada Law Book, 1988) at 34-15.

COMPETENT. *adj.* 1. Legally allowed to give

evidence during a trial. 2. Having adequate skill and knowledge. See MENTALLY ~.

COMPETENT AUTHORITY. A person or body authorized by statute to perform an act or carry out a function.

COMPETENT COURT. 1. The Federal Court or any superior, county or district court, except where the context otherwise requires. *Commercial Arbitration Act*, R.S.C. 1985 (2d Supp.), c. 17, s. 6. 2. For the purposes of the International Law, a reference to "court" or "competent court", where in the context it means a court in New Brunswick, means The Court of Queen's Bench of New Brunswick except where the context otherwise requires. *International Commercial Arbitration Act*, S.N.B. 1987, c. I-12.2, s. 9.

COMPETENT PERSON. A person who, i. is qualified because of his knowledge, training and experience to organize the work and its performance, ii. is familiar with the provisions of this Act and the regulations that apply to the work, and iii. has knowledge of any potential or actual danger to health or safety in the work place. *Occupational Health and Safety Act*, R.S.O. 1980, c. 321, s. 1.

COMPETITION. *n.* 1. A situation when two or more businesses seek customers in the same marketplace. 2. A contest in which more than two boxers take part. *Athletics Control Act*, R.R.O. 1980, Reg. 76, s. 8. See CLOSED ~; OPEN ~.

COMPETITION CAR. A four-wheeled vehicle designed for use exclusively on racing circuits. Canada regulations.

COMPETITION MOTORCYCLE. A vehicle having steering handlebars completely constrained from rotating in relation to the axle of one wheel in contact with the ground and designed for travel on not more than three wheels in contact with the ground and for use exclusively in competition circuits. Canada regulations.

COMPETITION SNOWMOBILE. A vehicle of not more than 1,000 pounds weight designed primarily for travel on snow, having one or more steering skis and driven by means of an endless belt or belts in contact with the ground, and designed for use exclusively on competition circuits. *Motor Vehicle Safety Regulations*, C.R.C., c. 1038, s. 2.

COMPLAINANT. *n.* 1. The victim of an alleged offence. *Criminal Code*, R.S.C. 1985, c. C-46, s. 2. 2. A person who lodges or files a formal complaint.

COMPLAINT. *n.* 1. An allegation or allega-tions, made orally or in writing by a member of the public, concerning misconduct of a public officer or of a contravention or violation of a statute. 2. An extra-judicial statement concerning an offence made after the alleged commission of that offence to a person other than the accused by the person in respect of whom it is alleged to have been committed. *Military Rules of Evidence*, C.R.C., c. 1049, s. 31.

COMPLEMENT. *n.* 1. The number of persons comprising the master and crew of a ship. Canada regulations. 2. The number of persons a ship is allowed to carry by the certificate issued in respect of the ship. *Life Saving Equipment Regulations*, C.R.C., c. 1436, s. 2. See APPROVED ~.

COMPLETE. *v.* To finish.

COMPLETE. *adj.* Finished; entire.

COMPLETED. *adj.* 1. Whenever used with reference to a contract for an improvement, means substantial performance, not necessarily total performance. *Builders Lien Act*, R.S.B.C. 1979, c. 40, s. 1. 2. In relation to an eligible ship, means that (a) a certificate of registry has been issued for the ship pursuant to the Canada Shipping Act, (b) where required by the Canada Shipping Act, a steamship inspection certificate has been issued for the ship pursuant to that Act, and (c) where the eligible ship is a fishing vessel, any fishing trials of the ship deemed necessary by the Minister of Fisheries for Canada have been carried out to the satisfaction of that Minister. *Ship Construction Subsidy Regulations*, C.R.C., c. 347, s. 2.

COMPLETED CONTRACT METHOD. In the completed contract method you accumulate your costs of the contract over the entire life of the contract and take nothing into income. At the time when the contract is completed you take your total receipts or billings on the contract, deduct from them the total cost over the years of that contract and that item comes into profit and loss. That is taken on only the last year of the contract . . . *Wilson and Wilson Ltd. v. M.N.R.*, [1960] C.T.C. 1, 60 D.T.C. 1018 (Exch. Ct.).

COMPLETE FEED OR BALANCED FEED. For the purposes of registration and guaranteed analysis, a mixed feed that, when used for the kind of livestock and for the purpose stated on the label, will provide all of the nutritional requirements necessary for maintenance of normal health or for promoting production except (a) water, in the case of monogastric animals other than horses, and (b) water or roughage or both in the case of ruminant animals and horses. *Feeds Regulations*, C.R.C., c. 665, s. 2.

COMPLETE SURVEY. A survey which, in addition to the requirements for a block outline survey, defines on the ground every angle of every parcel.

COMPLETION. *n.* Performance of a contract. See CERTIFICATE OF ~; DATE OF ~.

COMPLETION BOND. See PERFORMANCE BOND.

COMPLETION DATE. The date on which the total depth of a well is reached. *Petroleum Resources Act*, R.R.O. 1980, Reg. 752, s. 1.

COMPLETION LOAN. The advance of the whole amount, minus costs, of a mortgage loan by a lender to a borrower when construction of the borrower's new building is completed, the lender has inspected the building and is satisfied. D.J. Donahue & P.D. Quinn, *Real Estate Practice in Ontario*, 4th ed. (Toronto: Butterworths, 1990) at 224.

COMPLETION OF THE CONTRACT. Substantial performance, not necessarily total performance, of the contract. *Mechanics' Lien acts.*

COMPLEX. See HOUSING ~; OFFICE ~; RESIDENTIAL ~.

COMPLIANCE ORDER. Either an order, like a quia timet order or order for specific performance, that someone take positive action, or an order, like an injunction, that certain conduct be stopped. D.J.M. Brown and D.M. Beatty, *Canadian Labour Arbitration*, 2d ed. (Aurora: Canada Law Book, 1977) at 76.

COMPLICE. *n.* An accomplice, an associate.

COMPLICITY. *n.* Being an accomplice; being involved in crime or conspiracy.

COMPLY. *v.* To conform; yield; accept.

COMPONENT. *n.* An individual unit of food that is combined as an individual unit of food with one or more other individual units of food to form an ingredient. Canada regulations. See PRESSURE ~; PRICE ~; VEHICLE ~.

COMPONENT PROCESS CATEGORY. A basic unit of processing in the operations of a mill. *Pulp and Paper Effluent Regulations*, C.R.C., c. 830, s. 2.

COMPOSITE. See INDUSTRIAL ~.

COMPOSITE PILE. A pile consisting of sections of dissimilar materials of varying lengths. *Building Code Act*, R.R.O. 1980, Reg. 87, s. 1.

COMPOSITE SAMPLE. 1. (a) A quantity of undiluted effluent consisting of a minimum of three equal volumes of effluent or three volumes proportionate to flow that have been collected at approximately equal time intervals over a sampling period of not less than 7 hours and not more than 24 hours, or (b) a quantity of undiluted effluent collected continually at an equal rate or at a rate proportionate to flow over a sampling period of not less than 7 hours and not more than 24 hours. *Metal Mining Liquid Effluent Regulations*, C.R.C., c. 819, s. 2. 2. The contents of a receptacle into which samples of effluent from a mill have been delivered by a sampling device. *Pulp and Paper Effluent Regulations*, C.R.C., c. 830, s. 2.

COMPOSITE UNIT. A pushing vessel rigidly connected to the vessel being pushed. *Collision Regulations*, C.R.C., c. 1416, s. 2.

COMPOSITION. *n.* 1. An arrangement for the payment of debts. 2. Refers to the total number of judges of a court and number of judges who must be drawn from each different region. P.W. Hogg, *Constitutional Law of Canada*, 2d ed. (Toronto: Carswell, 1985) at 65. See FIREWORKS ~.

COMPOS MENTIS. [L.] Sound mind.

COMPOSTING. *n.* The treatment of waste by aerobic decomposition of organic matter by bacterial action for the production of stabilized humus. *Environmental Protection Act*, R.R.O. 1980, Reg. 309, s. 1.

COMPOUND. *n.* See IGNITION ~.

COMPOUND. *v.* 1. To compromise; to effect a composition with a creditor. 2. To combine; to unite.

COMPOUND FRACTURE. A fracture which communicates through a wound to the outside. F.A. Jaffe, *A Guide to Pathological Evidence*, 2d ed. (Toronto: Carswell, 1983) at 176 and 177.

COMPOUND INTEREST. Interest charged on interest.

COMPREHENSIVE FREQUENCY RESPONSE. A family of frequency responses (frequency-response curves) that cover essentially the full range of operation of the hearing aid. *Medical Devices Regulations*, C.R.C., c. 871, s. 1.

COMPREHENSIVE INSURANCE. 1. The obligation of the insurer to pay insurance money to an insured in the event of loss of or damage to a vehicle. 2. Insurance against a loss in production of apples in which a reduction in grade or quality caused by an insured peril may be deemed to decrease the actual yield harvested. *Crop Insurance Act (Ontario)*, R.R.O. 1980, Reg. 198, s. 3.

COMPREHENSIVE PLAN OF DEVELOPMENT. A study of the development characteristics of a community or region, made for the purpose of formulating plans, reports or legal instruments to guide, control or otherwise influence the physical development of the community or region or any part thereof, where such plans, reports or legal instruments are an integral part of and are contained in and expressed by the study and include an examination of at least the population, land use, economic base and transportation characteristics of the community or region in terms of their existing conditions, trends and probable future conditions, together with a formulation of development proposals relating to those aspects of the community or region or any part thereof; provided that the information contained in the study is in sufficient detail to permit the evaluation of the implications that the characteristics examined may have for any plans, reports or legal instruments designed to influence the physical development of the community or region or any part thereof.

COMPREHENSIVE ZONE SYSTEM. Regulations containing text and zoning maps designed to regulate the development or redevelopment of land. *Planning Act*, R.S.P.E.I. 1974, c. P-6, s. 1.

COMPRESSED AIR. Air mechanically raised to a pressure higher than atmospheric pressure. *Occupational Health and Safety Act*, R.R.O. 1980, Reg. 691, s. 240.

COMPRESSED-AIR PLANT. A plant in which pressure vessels contain, distribute or otherwise handle air under pressure of more than fifteen pounds.

COMPRESSED GAS. A gas or a combination of gases that is contained under pressure whether or not the gases are liquefied, vapourized, dissolved or in any combination of these states.

COMPRESSED GAS PLANT. *var.* **COMPRESSED-GAS PLANT.** A plant used for producing, manufacturing, transferring, storing, distributing or otherwise handling compressed gas.

COMPRESSED GAS SYSTEM. The complete installation of pressure vessels, piping, fittings, compressors, machinery and other equipment used for producing, manufacturing, transferring, storing, distributing or otherwise handling compressed gas. *Boiler and Pressure Vessel Act*, R.S. Nfld. 1970, c. 24, s. 2.

COMPRESSED INFLAMMABLE GAS. Any material with a gauge pressure exceeding 25 pounds per square inch at 70°F, or any liquid inflammable material having a Reid vapour pressure exceeding 40 pounds per square inch

at 100°F. *Electric Sparks Prevention Regulations*, C.R.C., c. 1181, s. 3.

COMPRESSED WORK WEEK. Longer hours worked each of a smaller number of days than is usual.

COMPRESSION INJURY. An injury caused when a force acts perpendicularly to the surface of a tissue or organ. F.A. Jaffe, *A Guide to Pathological Evidence*, 2d ed. (Toronto: Carswell, 1983) at 178.

COMPRESSOR PLANT. Includes the machinery and equipment used for compressing or storing air or other gas under pressure.

COMPROMISE. *n.* 1. A prospective litigant refrains from taking an action in return for the intended defendant's promise; or an action already commenced that is settled by such an agreement. G.H.L. Fridman, *The Law of Contract in Canada*, 2d ed. (Toronto: Carswell, 1986) at 85. 2. An arrangement between a company and its members or creditors with any class of shareholders affecting their rights. H. Sutherland, D.B. Horsley & J.M. Edmiston, eds., *Fraser's Handbook on Canadian Company Law*, 7th ed. (Toronto: Carswell, 1985) at 497. 3. An adjustment or settlement of taxes, due and unpaid, whereby the taxpayer is authorized to pay, and the local authority to accept, a lesser amount thereof than is shown in the books of the local authority in respect of lands purchased by it at its own tax sale. *Municipal Board Act*, R.S.M. 1970, c. M240, s. 90.

COMPROMISSARII SUNT JUDICES. [L.] Those who arbitrate are judges.

COMP. TRIB. *abbr.* Competition Tribunal.

COMPTROLLER. *n.* One who examines the accounts of collectors of public money. See CONTROLLER.

COMPULSION. *n.* Duress; force. See PRACTICAL ~.

COMPULSORY. *adj.* Forced; coerced.

COMPULSORY ARBITRATION. Arbitration that is required by law.

COMPULSORY LICENCE. Of patents in general, a licence ordered if there has been an abuse of exclusive rights; also a licence ordered for patents used for the production or preparation of medicine or food. H.G. Fox, *The Canadian Law and Practice Relating to Letters Patent for Inventions*, 4th ed. (Toronto: Carswell, 1969) at 304.

COMPULSORY PILOTAGE. In respect of a ship, the requirement that the ship be under the conduct of a licensed pilot or the holder of a pilotage certificate.

COMPULSORY PILOTAGE AREA. An area of water in which ships are subject to compulsory pilotage.

COMPULSORY POWER. Includes the taking, entering upon, flooding, or overflowing of land without the consent of the owner thereof. *Electric Power Act*, R.S.N.B. 1973, c. E-5, c. 1.

COMPULSORY PURCHASE. To acquire land for public purposes.

COMPULSORY RETIREMENT AGE. 65 years of age. *Teachers Pension Plan Act*, R.S.Q. 1977, c. R-11, s. 1.

COMPULSORY SCHOOL AGE. Over the age of 7 years and under the age of 16 years.

COMPULSORY SCHOOL ATTENDANCE. The attendance of a child at school that is required by statute.

COMPULSORY SCHOOL LAW. A statute requiring children to attend school.

COMPULSORY TRUCE. A cooling-off period imposed by statute during which a labour dispute is investigated by an official agency, and strikes and lock-outs are prohibited.

COMPULSORY UNIONISM. Employment conditional on union membership.

COMPURGATION. *n.* In criminal matters, a method by which the oaths of a number of people concerning the character of an accused were accepted as proof of innocence; or in civil matters, where such oaths proved that the claim made against the defendant was not well founded.

COMPURGATOR. *n.* A person who swore that she or he believed the accused in a criminal matter or the defendant in a civil matter.

COMPUTER. See DUAL ~.

COMPUTER L. *abbr.* Computer Law.

COMPUTER PROGRAM. Data representing instructions or statements that, when executed in a computer system, causes the computer system to perform a function. *Criminal Code*, R.S.C. 1985, c. C-46, s. 342.1(2), as added by *Criminal Law Amendment Act*, R.S.C. 1985 (1st Supp.), c. 27, s. 45.

COMPUTER SERVICE. Includes data processing and the storage or retrieval of data. *Criminal Code*, R.S.C. 1985, c. C-46, s. 342.1(2) as added by *Criminal Law Amendment Act*, R.S.C. 1985 (1st Supp.), c. 27, s. 45.

COMPUTER SOFTWARE. Packaged or prewritten computer software programs that are designed for general application, or the right to use those programs, and includes modifications to those programs.

COMPUTER SYSTEM. A device that, or a group of interconnected or related devices one or more of which, (a) contains computer programs or other data, and (b) pursuant to computer programs, (i) performs logic and control, and (ii) may perform any other function. *Criminal Code*, R.S.C. 1985, c. C-46, s. 342.1(2) as added by *Criminal Law Amendment Act*, R.S.C. 1985 (1st Supp.), c. 27, s. 45.

CON. *adj.* Short form for confidence, as a "con game".

CON. *prep.* [L.] With.

CON. *pref.* Together.

CONCEAL. *v.* To hide, cover, keep from view; to prevent discovery.

CONCEALED. *adj.* Rendered permanently inaccessible by the structure or finish of a building. *Power Corporation Act*, R.R.O. 1980, Reg. 794, s. 0.

CONCEALED DANGER. A deceptively safe appearance which hides a potential cause of injury. J.V. DiCastri, *Occupiers' Liability* (Vancouver: Burroughs/Carswell, 1980) at 97.

CONCEALING BODY OF CHILD. It is an offence to dispose of the dead body of a child with intent to conceal the fact that its mother has been delivered of it whether it died before, during or after birth. *Criminal Code*, R.S.C. 1985, c. C-46, s. 243.

CONCEALMENT. *n.* Failure to disclose a fact. See HEADLAMP ~ DEVICE.

CONCEALMENT OF BIRTH. See CONCEALING BODY OF CHILD.

CONCENTRATE. *v.* To separate and accumulate valuable minerals from gangue in one or more stages by removing the valuable minerals from it to form a concentrate without changing the chemical identity of these minerals.

CONCENTRATE. *n.* See APPLE JUICE FROM ~.

CONCENTRATED APPLE JUICE. The product that is prepared from unfermented single strength apple juice that is concentrated to not less than 68 per cent soluble solids. *Processed Fruit and Vegetable Regulations*, C.R.C., c. 291, Schedule I, s. 4.

CONCENTRATED MILK PLANT. 1. A place at which milk is condensed, evaporated, powdered or converted into casein. *Milk Act*, R.S.P.E.I. 1974, c. M-10, s. 1. 2. A plant in which milk or cream is processed into a milk product other than butter or cheese or a fluid milk product. *Milk Act*, R.S.O. 1980, c. 266, s. 1.

CONCENTRATION. *n.* Any treatment of ore, reject or tailing to separate a mineral substance from its gangue and obtain a concentrate. *Mining Duties Act*, R.S.Q. 1977, c. D-15, s. 20.

CONCEPTION. *n.* The beginning of pregnancy; fertilization of the ovum by spermatozoon.

CONCERN. *v.* To relate, be of interest or importance to. See PERSON ~ ED.

CONCERNING. *adj.* Relating to; affecting.

CONCERT. *n.* To act in concert is to act together to bring about a planned result.

CONCERTED ACTIVITIES. Employees acting together to achieve improvements in conditions of work.

CONCESSI. [L.] I granted.

CONCESSIMUS. [L.] We granted.

CONCESSION. *n.* 1. A tier of township lots. *Surveys Act*, R.S.O. 1980, c. 493, s. 1. 2. A public authority grants land to a private person to establish something, i.e. an industry, a railway. 3. A grant by an owner of a place of amusement or business to a person permitting them to perform a service or sell articles on the premises. See BROKEN ~; FOREST ~; MINING ~; TAX ~; UNDERGROUND MINING ~.

CONCESSION OPERATOR. A person holding a concession, right or privilege to perform any service or sell any articles at a race track. *Harness Racing Commission Act*, R.S.N.S. 1967, c. 124, s. 1.

CONCESSIO VERSUS CONCEDENTEM LATAM INTERPRETATIONEM HABERE DEBET. [L.] A grant should be given a wide interpretation, that is to be strictly construed, against the grantor.

CONCESSIT SOLVERE. [L.] One granted and one agreed to pay.

CONCESSOR. *n.* One who grants.

CONCILIATION. *n.* The process by which a third party attempts to assist an employer and a trade union to achieve a collective agreement.

CONCILIATION BOARD. A board established under labour legislation for the investigation and conciliation of a dispute.

CONCILIATION COMMISSIONER. A person appointed by the Minister of Labour under the Labour Code. *Labour Code*, R.S.C. 1985, c. L-2, s. 3.

CONCILIATION OFFICER. A person whose duties include the conciliation of disputes and who is under the control and direction of the Minister of Labour.

CONCILIATOR. *n.* A person appointed to assist the parties to collective bargaining in reaching agreement.

CONCILIUM. *n.* [L.] A court; the time and place set for a meeting.

CONCLUDE. *v.* To finish; to bar or estop.

CONCLUSION. *n.* 1. The finish, end, summation. 2. A rule of law or an irrefutable presumption.

CONCLUSION OF FACT. An inference or result drawn from evidence.

CONCLUSION OF LAW. A finding of law; a statement of law applicable to a matter.

CONCLUSIVE. *adj.* Final, decisive, clear.

CONCORD. *n.* An agreement to settle or refrain from bringing an action.

CONCORDAT. *n.* 1. An agreement between two or more governments. 2. A treaty or agreement between the Pope and a head of state.

CONCUBINAGE. *n.* Living together, co-habiting as if married.

CONCUBINE. *n.* A mistress.

CONCUR. *v.* To agree, consent.

CONCURRENCE. *n.* Agreement, consent.

CONCURRENT. *adj.* Contemporaneous.

CONCURRENT JURISDICTION. Two or more courts or tribunals having authority to try or hear the same subject matter.

CONCURRENTLY. *adv.* At the same time, contemporaneously.

CONCURRENT SENTENCE. Two or more terms of imprisonment served simultaneously.

CONCURRENT WRIT. A duplicate of an original writ. See ALIAS WRIT.

CONCURRING OPINION. The decision of a judge agreeing in the decision though not necessarily the reasons of other judge(s).

CONCUSSION. *n.* A violent impact causing diffuse injury to an organ. F.A. Jaffe, *A Guide to Pathological Evidence*, 2d ed. (Toronto: Carswell, 1983) at 173.

CONDEMN. *v.* 1. To find guilty. 2. To sentence. 3. In admiralty law, to find that a vessel is a prize. 4. To expropriate. 5. To declare a building unfit for use or occupation. 6. In relation to a food animal or a meat product, means to determine that the food animal or meat product is unfit for human or animal food. *Meat Inspection Regulations*, C.R.C., c. 1032, s. 2.

CONDEMNATION. *n.* 1. An order that a building is unfit for use or occupation. 2. Expropriation. 3. A judgment that a prize or captured vessel has been lawfully captured.

CONDENSATE. *n.* A liquid hydrocarbon product that existed in the reservoir in a gaseous phase at original conditions and that is recovered from a gas stream when pressure and temperatures are reduced to not lower than those at atmospheric conditions.

CONDENSED MILK. Milk from which water has been evaporated and to which sugar or dextrose, or both, with or without added vitamin D, have been added.

CONDENSED MILK FACTORY. A place where milk or cream is manufactured into condensed or evaporated milk products. *Agriculture and Marketing Act*, R.S.N.S. 1967, c. 3, s. 174.

CONDENSERY. See MILK ~.

CONDITIO BENEFICIALIS QUAESTATUM CONSTRUIT, BENIGNE, SECUNDUM VERBORUM INTENTIONEM, EST INTERPRETANDA; ODIOSA, AUTEM, QUAE STATUM DESTRUIT, STRICTE, SECUNDUM VERBORUM PROPRIETATEM, ACCIPIENDA. [L.] A beneficial condition which creates an estate should be interpreted generously, according to the intention behind the words; but a condition which destroys an estate is undesirable and should be interpreted strictly.

CONDITIO DICITUR CUM QUID IN CASUM INCERTUM QUI POTEST TENDERE AD ESSE AUT NON ESSE CONFERTUR. [L.] When something is given on an uncertain event which may or may not come into existence, it is called a condition.

CONDITION. *n.* 1. A provision or declaration in which an event must happen before a right may exist. 2. A term in a valid contract which is so essential or fundamental that a buyer may consider that the contract is repudiated if the term is broken. G.H.L. Fridman, *Sale of Goods in Canada*, 3d ed. (Toronto: Carswell, 1986) at 158. 3. Includes a warranty, representation or proviso. *An Act to Amend the Standard Forms of Conveyances Act*, N.B. 1984, c. 63, s. 2. 4. An observable medical symptom, sign or condition, or combination of related medical symptoms, signs or conditions. 5. Refers to the wholeness of the blueberries. *Processed Fruit and Vegetable Regulations*, C.R.C., c. 291, Schedule I, s. 18. See DEPENDENT ~; EXPRESS ~; IMPLIED ~; INSANITARY ~; LOADED ~; PERMISSIBLE ~; PRECEDENT ~; PRE-

EXISTING OR UNDERLYING ~; RESOLUTIVE ~; RESOLUTORY ~; SANITARY ~; TURNING ~ OUT ~.

CONDITIONAL. *adj.* Dependent upon, subject to.

CONDITIONAL ACCEPTANCE. The acceptor pays only when a condition stated in the bill is fulfilled. E.L.G. Tyler & N.E. Palmer, eds., *Crossley Vaines' Personal Property*, 5th ed. (London: Butterworths, 1973) at 236.

CONDITIONAL APPEARANCE. A motion filed by a defendant, with leave of the Court, to object to an irregularity in the commencement of the proceeding or the court's jurisdiction. D. Sgayias *et al.*, *Federal Court Practice 1988* (Toronto: Carswell, 1987) at 372.

CONDITIONAL BENEFIT. A benefit which may be received only if the potential recipient is not awarded damages for the same loss which the benefit is supposed to compensate. K.D. Cooper-Stephenson & I.B. Saunders, *Personal Injury Damages in Canada* (Toronto: Carswell, 1981) at 488.

CONDITIONAL DISCHARGE. Disposition of a criminal matter by which a person is deemed not to be convicted after serving a period of probation.

CONDITIONAL LIBERATION. The release of an inmate during a term of imprisonment. *An Act to promote the parole of inmates and to amend the Probation and Houses of Detention Act*, S.Q. 1978, c. 22, s. 1.

CONDITIONAL LICENCE. A licence authorizing an activity prior to the issue of a final licence.

CONDITIONAL OFFER. 1. An offer which is not final until a condition is fulfilled. 2. A proposal to settle a strike with reservations.

CONDITIONAL PARTICIPANT. A participant who is not a full participant. *Western Grain Stabilization Act*, R.S.C. 1985, c. W-7, s. 2.

CONDITIONAL SALE. 1. A contract for the sale of goods under which possession is to be delivered to a buyer and the property in the goods is to vest in him at a subsequent time on payment of the whole or part of the price or on the performance of any other condition. 2. A contract for the hiring of goods under which it is agreed that the hirer will become or have the option of becoming the owner of the goods on compliance with the terms of the contract.

CONDITIONAL WILL. A will which takes effect only in the event of the testator's death in a certain way, such as by accident, or during a certain period, such as on a trip; the will does

CONDITION DEFECT

not take effect unless the specified condition is met. T. Sheard, R. Hull & M.M.K. Fitzpatrick, *Canadian Forms of Wills*, 4th ed. (Toronto: Carswell, 1982) at 139.

CONDITION DEFECT. Any defect that may develop in an agricultural product during storage or transit.

CONDITIONER. *n* A mineral feed that is represented for the treatment of a specified disease or to aid recovery from a specific disease or delility and is for use only while the disease or debility persists. *Feeds Regulations*, C.R.C., c. 665, s. 2. See WATER ~.

CONDITIONES QUAELIBET ODIOSAE; MAXIME AUTEM CONTRA MATRIMONIUM ET COMMERCIUM. [L.] All conditions are objectionable, but especially those which are in restraint of marriage and trade.

CONDITION OF EMPLOYMENT. 1. A qualification or circumstance required for employment. 2. All matters and circumstances in any way affecting employers and employees in respect of the employment relationship. *Employment Standards Act*, S.B.C. 1980, c. 10, s. 1.

CONDITION OF SALE. A term upon which an interest is to be sold by auction or tender.

CONDITION PRECEDENT. A term of an agreement requiring an event to take place before the agreement becomes binding. See TRUE ~.

CONDITION SUBSEQUENT. A term of an agreement requiring that the agreement be valid and binding unless and until a specified event or occurrence happens. G.H.L. Fridman, *Sale of Goods in Canada*, 3d ed. (Toronto: Carswell, 1986) at 28.

CONDITIO PRAECEDENS ADIMPLERI DEBET PRIUSQUAM SEQUATUR EFFECTUS. [L.] The condition precedent must be fulfilled before any effect can follow.

CONDO. *abbr.* Condominium.

CONDOM. *n.* A sheath or covering intended to be worn on the penis during coitus for the purpose of preventing conception or reducing the risk of transmission of disease and includes any substance or mixture of substances applied to the finished condom before it is packaged. *Medical Devices Regulations*, C.R.C., c. 871, s. 1.

CONDOMINIUM. *n.* 1. A system of property ownership of multi-unit housing or commercial projects in which each unit owner is a tenant-in-common of the common elements and each unit is owned separately in fee simple. B.J. Reiter, R.C.B. Risk & B.N. McLellan, *Real Estate Law*,

3d ed. (Toronto: Emond Montgomery, 1986) at 660. 2. Two or more subjects of international law jointly exercise sovereignty over one territory. See TIME-SHARING ~.

CONDOMINIUM PLAN. A plan that (i) is described in the heading thereto as a condominium plan; (ii) shows the whole or any part of the building included therein as being divided into two or more units; and (iii) complies with the requirements of the legislation.

CONDOMINIUM PROJECT. The lands and interests appurtenant thereto that are described or proposed to be described in any description required by the Condominium Act and which include or are proposed to include units to be used as homes. *Ontario New Home Warranties Plan Act*, R.R.O. 1980, Reg. 726, s. 1.

CONDOMINIUM UNIT. A bounded space in a building designated or described as a separate unit on a registered condominium or strata lot plan or description, or a similar plan or description registered pursuant to the laws of a province, and intended for human habitation and includes any interest in land appertaining to ownership of the unit. *National Housing Act*, R.S.C. 1985, c. N-11, s. 2.

CONDONATION. *n.* 1. Acquiescence, forgiveness. 2. Forgiveness of a breach of marital duty; reinstatement of the spouse who has committed the wrong.

CONDUCT. *v.* To manage; to lead.

CONDUCT. *n.* 1. Any act or omission. 2. Personal behaviour. See CODE OF ~; EXCUSABLE ~; IMPROPER ~; MIS~; SAFE-~; UNPROFESSIONAL ~.

CONDUCTIO. See CONTRACT OF LOCATIO ET ~.

CONDUCT MONEY. 1. Fees payable to witnesses to defray expenses of coming to testify. 2. Attendance money.

CONDUCTOR. *n.* 1. A wire, cable or other form of metal installed for the purpose of conveying electric current from one piece of electrical equipment to another or to ground. 2. A person in charge or having the chief direction of any railway train. See BRANCH-~; DEAD-END ~; DOWN-~; GROUNDING ~; NEUTRAL ~.

CONDUCT UNBECOMING. Any act or conduct, whether or not disgraceful or dishonourable, which (i) is inimical to the best interests of the public or the members of the society; or (ii) tends to harm the standing of the legal profession generally. *Legal Profession Amendment Act, 1981*, S.S. 1980-81, c. 64, s. 3.

CONDUCT UNBECOMING A MEMBER OF THE SOCIETY. Includes any matter, conduct or thing that is deemed in the judgment of the benchers to be contrary to the best interest of the public or of the legal profession, or that tends to harm the standing of the legal profession. *Barristers and Solicitors Act*, R.S.B.C. 1979, s. 26, s. 1.

CONDUIT. *n.* 1. i. A sewer, ii. a water main, iii. a duct or cable for a telegraphic, telephonic, television or electrical service, iv. a pipe or duct for the transportation of any solid, liquid or gas. 2. A raceway of circular cross-section into which it is intended that conductors be drawn.

C1. Volume in cubic metres of a centre tank breached by the assumed damage calculated in accordance with section 2, except that a value equal to zero may be given for a clean ballast tank. *Oil Pollution Prevention Regulations*, C.R.C., c. 1454, Schedule III, s. 1.

CONF. COMMEM. MEREDITH. *abbr.* Conférences commémoratives Meredith (Meredith Memorial Lectures).

CONFECTIONER. *n.* A person, firm, or corporation, who sells by retail only all or any of the following: biscuits, plain or fancy, bon-bons, cakes, candied gums, candies, chewing gum, chocolate bars, chocolates, ice-cream, ice-cream cones, pastries, popcorn, confectionery, bread, milk, butter, or soft drinks. *Shops Regulation Act*, R.S.M. 1970, c. S110, s. 3.

CONFECTIONS. *n.* Includes chocolate coated nuts and preparations of fruits, nuts or popcorn in combination with chocolate, sugar or honey. *Retail Sales Tax Act*, R.R.O. 1980, Reg. 904, s. 1.

CONFEDERACY. *n.* In international law, two or more states joined for their mutual welfare.

CONFEDERATION. *n.* 1. A loose association of states in which the state governments take precedence over the central government. P.W. Hogg, *Constitutional Law of Canada*, 2d ed. (Toronto: Carswell, 1985) at 82. 2. A league of nations or states. 3. A compact for mutual support.

CONFERENCE. *n.* 1. A meeting of persons for consideration of matters, exchange of opinions. 2. The representative assembly of a church. 3. An association of athletic teams. See FIRST MINISTERS' ~; PRE-TRIAL ~; SHIPPING ~.

CONFESS. *v.* To admit; to concede.

CONFESSIO FACTA IN JUDICIO OMNI PROBATIONE MAJOR EST. [L.] An admission made during judicial proceedings has greater weight than any proof.

CONFESSION. *n.* 1. An admission of guilt. 2. In civil procedure, a formal admission. 3. Formerly, a plea of guilty. F. Kaufman, *The Admissibility of Confessions*, 3d ed. (Toronto: Carswell, 1980) at 1. 4. A statement made by an accused person, whether before or after he is accused of an offence, that is completely or partially self-incriminating with respect to the offence of which he is accused. *Military Rules of Evidence*, C.R.C., c. 1049, s. 2. See EXCULPATORY ~; INCULPATORY ~.

CONFESSION AND AVOIDANCE. A pleading in which, though the defendant admits the plaintiff's allegation, the defendant then sets out other facts which deprive the allegation of the legal consequences for which the plaintiff argued. G.D. Watson & C. Perkins, eds., *Holmested & Watson: Ontario Civil Procedure* (Toronto: Carswell, 1984) at 25-19.

CONFESSUS IN JUDICIO PRO JUDICATO HABETUR, ET QUODAMMODO SUA SENTENTIA DAMNATUR. [L.] Those who make confessions are held to have decided their own cases against themselves.

CONFIDENCE. *n.* 1. Trust, reliance. 2. A communication made in reliance on another's discretion.

CONFIDENCE GAME. Obtaining money or property by a trick or device.

CONFIDENCE OF THE QUEEN'S PRIVY COUNCIL FOR CANADA. Includes, without restricting the generality thereof, information contained in (a) a memorandum the purpose of which is to present proposals or recommendations to Council; (b) a discussion paper the purpose of which is to present background explanations, analyses of problems or policy options to Council for consideration by Council in making decisions; (c) an agendum of Council or a record recording deliberations or decisions of Council; (d) a record used for or reflecting communications or discussion between ministers of the Crown on matters relating to the making of government decisions or the formulation of government policy; (e) a record the purpose of which is to brief Ministers of the Crown in relation to matters that are brought before, or are proposed to be brought before, Council or that are the subject of communications or discussion referred to in paragraph (d); and (f) draft legislation. *Canada Evidence Act*, R.S.C. 1985, c. C-5, c. 39(2).

CONFIDENTIAL. *adj.* Intended to be kept secret.

CONFIDENTIAL CAPACITY. See PERSON EMPLOYED IN A MANAGERIAL OR ~.

CONFIDENTIAL COMMUNICATION. Privileged communication; a statement made in circumstances which indicate an intention that it be kept in confidence.

CONFIDENTIALITY. *n.* The state of being confidential.

CONFIDENTIAL RELATION. A relation of trust which gives rise to an expectation that communications will be held in confidence; fiduciary relation.

CONFIGURATION. See FORWARD CONTROL ~.

CONFINED SPACE. A space in which, because of its construction, location, contents or work activity therein, the accumulation of a hazardous gas, vapour, dust or fume or the creation of an oxygen-deficient atmosphere may occur. *Occupational Health and Safety Act*, R.R.O. 1980, Reg. 692, s. 1.

CONFINEMENT. *n.* The state of being shut in; restraint; imprisonment. See SOLITARY ~. See HAZARDOUS ~.

CONFIRM. *v.* To ratify; to make firm or certain; to give approval.

CONFIRMARE EST ID QUOD PRIUS INFIRMUM FUIT FIRMARE. [L.] To confirm is to strengthen that which was weak before.

CONFIRMARE NEMO POTEST PRIUSQUAM JUS EI ACCIDERIT. [L.] No one can confirm a right before the right accrues.

CONFIRMATIO EST NULLA UBI DONUM PRAECEDENS EST INVALIDUM. [L.] Confirmation is void where the preceding gift was void.

CONFIRMATION. *n.* Formal approval; ratification; a document which validates an agreement.

CONFIRMATION ORDER. 1. A confirmation order made under the Reciprocal Enforcement of Maintenance Orders Act or under the corresponding enactment of a reciprocating state. 2. An order of a court confirming the order of another court.

CONFIRMATIO OMNES SUPPLET DEFECTUS, LICET ID QUOD ACTUM EST AB INITIO NON VALUIT. [L.] Confirmation makes up for any defects, even though what had been done was not valid at the beginning.

CONFIRMED CREDIT. A credit in which another bank adds its confirmation.

CONFIRMING BANK. A bank that agrees to honour the credit issued by another bank.

CONFISCATE. *v.* To seize property; to forfeit property.

CONFISCATION. *n.* Seizure or forfeiture of property.

CONFITENS REUS. [L.] An accused who admits guilt.

CONFLICT. See FALSE ~.

CONFLICT OF INTEREST. Occurs when a person in a position to effect an official decision has a personal or financial interest in the outcome of the decision.

CONFLICT OF LAWS. Private international law, the branch of law concerned with private relations which contain a foreign element.

CONFORMATION. *n.* The general outline of the muscle formation of a carcass. *Veal Carcass Grading Regulations*, C.R.C., c. 293, s. 2.

CONFORMING USE. In zoning or planning, use of property which complies with restrictions of use in effect in respect of the property.

CONFORMITY. *n.* Correspondence in some respect; agreement.

CONFUSING. *adj.* 1. When applied as an adjective to a trade-mark or trade-name, means a trade-mark or trade-name the use of which would cause confusion in the manner and circumstances described in the Trade-Marks Act. *Trade-Marks Act*, R.S.C. 1985, c. T-13, s. 2. 2. In relation to a corporate name, means a corporate name the use of which causes confusion with a trade mark or trade name in the manner described in section 13. *Canada Business Corporations Regulations*, C.R.C., c. 426, s. 12.

CONFUSION. *n.* Where more than one person's goods are so mixed together that the individual possessions can no longer be identified.

CON GAME. See CONFIDENCE GAME.

CONGENITAL. *adj.* Present at birth.

CONGENITAL ANEURYSM. The rupture of this aneurysm involving an artery at the base of the brain commonly causes sudden death in young or middle aged adults. F.A. Jaffe, *A Guide to Pathological Evidence*, 2d ed. (Toronto: Carswell, 1983) at 168.

CONGESTION LIVIDITY. Lividity caused when the blood distends the skin capillaries. F.A. Jaffe, *A Guide to Pathological Evidence*, 2d ed. (Toronto: Carswell, 1983) at 179. See HYPOSTATIC OR CONGESTION ~.

CONGREGATION. *n.* A body of individuals, whether or not incorporated, that adheres to the practices and beliefs of the religious organization of which it is a constituent part. See MEMBER OF A ~.

CONGRESS. *n.* An assembly of persons who

meet to consider measures related to their common concerns.

CONGRESS OF INDUSTRIAL ORGANIZATIONS. A federation of national and international industrial unions.

CONJOINTS. *n.* People married to one another.

CONJUGAL. *adj.* Related to the married state.

CONJUGAL RIGHTS. Each spouse's right to the society, comfort and affection of the other spouse.

CONJUNCTIVE. *adj.* Joining two concepts.

CONJURATIO. *n.* [L.] An oath.

CONMINGLE. *v.* With reference to gas, means the mixing together or blending of gases for transmission through pipelines and other facilities.

CONNECTED. See PERSON ~.

CONNECTING FACTOR. Part of the choice of law rule: an element which connects a system of law with the facts of a particular case. J.G. McLeod, *The Conflict of Laws* (Calgary: Carswell, 1983) at 137.

CONNECTOR. *n.* A device used to make a connection between two conductors or between a conductor and another part of a system or between a conductor and a metallic object. *Lightning Rods Act*, R.R.O. 1980, Reg. 577, s. 1. See VENT ~.

CONNIVANCE. *n.* Culpable agreement to doing wrong.

CONQUEST. *n.* In international law, the occupation of enemy territory by force.

CONSANGUINITY. *n.* Relationship by descent: either collaterally, i.e. from a common ancestor or lineally, i.e. mother and daughter. See LINEAL ~.

CONSCIENCE. *n.* Moral sense.

CONSCIENTIOUS OBJECTOR. A person who, on moral or religious grounds, thinks it wrong to resist force with force and to kill.

CONSCRIPTION. *n.* Compulsory enrolment in the military service.

CONSECUTIVE. *adj.* One after the other; following.

CONSECUTIVE DAYS. All the days in a period of days beginning at 12.01 a.m. on one day and following in consecutive order. *Canada Motor Vehicle Operators Hours of Service Regulations*, C.R.C., c. 1005, s. 2.

CONSECUTIVELY. *adv.* Successively; following one after the other.

CONSECUTIVE SENTENCES. One sentence follows another in time.

CONSEIL CAN. D. INT. *abbr.* Conseil canadien de droit international. Congrès. Travaux (Canadian Council of International Law. Conference. Proceedings).

CONSENSUS AD IDEM. [L. agreement to the same thing] The consent required for a contract to be binding.

CONSENSUS FACIT LEGEM. [L.] Consent makes the law.

CONSENSUS NON CONCUBITUS FACIT MATRIMONIUM; ET CONSENTIRE NON POSSUNT ANTE ANNOS NUBILES. [L.] Consent, not coitus, constitutes marriage; and the parties cannot consent before reaching marriageable years.

CONSENSUS TOLLIT ERROREM. [L.] Consent removes error.

CONSENT. *n.* Freely given agreement. See AGE OF ~; INFORMED ~; ROYAL ~.

CONSENTIENTIS ET AGENTIS PARI POENA PLECTANTUR. [L.] Those consenting to and those perpetrating a crime are punished equally.

CONSENT JUDGMENT. A judgment the terms of which are agreed to by the parties.

CONSEQUENCE. See TAX ~ S.

CONSEQUENTIAL DAMAGES. The loss which occurs indirectly from the act complained of.

CONSERVATION. *n.* 1. Includes the prevention of waste, improvident or uneconomic production or disposition of natural resources. 2. Rehabilitation or development. See MANAGEMENT AND ~ ZONE.

CONSERVATION PARK. A park primarily intended to ensure the permanent protection of territory representative of the natural regions of Quebec, or of natural sites presenting exceptional features, while rendering them accessible to the public for the purposes of education and cross-country recreation. *Parks Act*, R.S.Q. 1977, c. P-9, s. 1.

CONSERVATION PURPOSE. The use and storage of water or the construction of works in and about streams for the purpose of conserving fish or wildlife. *Water Act*, R.S.B.C. 1979, c. 429, s. 1.

CONSERVATOR. *n.* One who protects, preserves, or maintains.

CONSERVE. *v.* To keep; to save.

CONSIDER. *v.* To examine, inspect; to turn one's mind to.

CONSIDERATIO CURIAE. [L.] The judgment of the court.

CONSIDERATION. *n.* 1. In a contract, an interest, right, profit or benefit accrues to the one party while some detriment, forebearance, loss or responsibility is suffered or undertaken by the other party. G.H.L. Fridman, *The Law of Contract in Canada*, 2d ed. (Toronto: Carswell, 1986) at 75. 2. In a contract for the sale of goods, it is called the price and must be in money. G.H.L. Fridman, *Sale of Goods in Canada*, 3d ed. (Toronto: Carswell, 1986) at 42. See ADEQUATE ~; EXCLUDED ~; EXECUTED ~; EXECUTORY ~; FUTURE ~; GOOD ~; MERITORIOUS ~; PAST ~; PRESENT ~; VALUABLE ~.

CONSIDERATUM EST PER CURIAM. [L.] The court has considered.

CONSIDERED. *adj.* Determined; regarded.

CONSIGNED. *adj.* Shipped, consigned or entrusted to a mercantile agent for sale, reconsignment or other disposition. *The Sales on Consignment Act*, R.S.S. 1978, c. S-4, s. 2.

CONSIGNED CAR. A carlot of grain consigned to an operator under a delivery and settlement agreement between the operator and the owner of the grain. *Canada Grain Regulations*, C.R.C., c. 889, s. 2.

CONSIGNEE. *n.* A person to whom the goods are sent.

CONSIGNMENT. *n.* 1. Sending goods to another to sell or purchase. 2. The goods themselves.

CONSIGNOR. *n.* 1. A person who consigns goods. 2. (i) A person other than a person who, (A) arranges, sells or offers for sale, or (B) negotiates for, or (C) holds himself out as one who sells, or (D) furnishes or provides, transportation services where the transportation service offered is to be or has been in part furnished by a carrier other than that person, or (E) is a forwarding agent, a transportation broker, a cartage agent or any person engaged in a similar operation or anyone who enters into a pooling of freight arrangement, or (ii) a common carrier by rail, a common carrier by air or a common carrier by water, where the transportation of goods is incidental to an immediate prior or subsequent transportation of goods by a common carrier by rail, a common carrier by air or a common carrier by water. *Public Commercial Vehicles Act*, R.R.O. 1980, Reg. 832, s. 1.

CONSIST. *v.* To be made up of.

CONSISTENT. *adj.* Harmonious; in agreement with.

CONSOL. *abbr.* Consolidated.

CONSOLATION DOUBLE. The pay-out price of a daily double ticket on a horse that was declared the official winner of the first half of the daily double coupled with a horse, entry or mutuel field in the second half of the daily double that did not start in the race. *Race Track Supervision Regulations*, C.R.C., c. 441, s. 2.

CONSOLIDATE. *v.* To combine, unite.

CONSOLIDATED FUND. The aggregate of all public money that is on hand and on deposit to the credit of a province.

CONSOLIDATED LOAN. A loan acquired for the purpose of consolidating liabilities.

CONSOLIDATED REVENUE FUND. 1. Aggregate of all public moneys that are on deposit at the credit of the Receiver General. *Financial Administration Act*, R.S.C. 1985, c. F-11, s. 2. 2. The aggregate of all public moneys that are on deposit at the credit of the Treasurer or in the name of any agency of the Crown approved by the Lieutenant Governor in Council. *Ministry of Treasury and Economics Act*, R.S.O. 1980, c. 291, s. 1.

CONSOLIDATED TAXES. Arrears of taxes less the amount of any discount by which the arrears may be reduced. *Local Tax Arrears Consolidation Act*, R.S.A. 1980, c. L-29, s. 1.

CONSOLIDATING STATUTE. A statute which draws together, with only minor amendments and improvements, all statutory provisions related to a particular topic into a single act. P.St.J. Langan, ed., *Maxwell on The Interpretation of Statutes*, 12th ed. (Bombay: N.M. Tripathi, 1976) at 20 and 21.

CONSOLIDATION. *n.* 1. In statute law, the uniting of many acts of Parliament into one. 2. The healing or stabilization of an employment injury following which no improvement of the state of health of the injured worker is foreseeable. *An Act Respecting Industrial Accidents and Occupational Diseases*, S.Q. 1985, c. 6, s. 2. See POSTAL ~ POINT.

CONSOLIDATION ACT. An act, usually with amendments, which repeals a number of earlier acts and includes, sometimes, some rules of the common law.

CONSOLIDATION OF ACTIONS. The combination of proceedings involving the same parties or issues.

CONSORT. *n.* Either of a man and a woman who (a) are married and cohabiting or (b) are living together as husband and wife and who

(i) have been residing together for three years, or for one year if a child has been born of their union and (ii) are publicly represented as consorts. *An Act respecting Labour standards*, S.Q. 1979, c. 45, s. 1. 2. A man and a woman who are married and cohabit, or who live together as husband and wife. See QUEEN ~.

CONSORTIUM. *n.* One spouse's right to the assistance, company and cooperation of the other.

CONSPICUOUSLY. See APPEARING ~; NOTED ~.

CONSPIRACY. *n.* Both the intention and the agreement of two or more persons to do a lawful act by unlawful means or to do an unlawful act. Conspiracy is committed once the parties have agreed to do things; they need not perform any acts. P.K. McWilliams, *Canadian Criminal Evidence*, 3d ed. (Aurora: Canada Law Book, 1988) at 22-1. 2. In tort law a combination the main motive of which is injury to the plaintiff or the promotion of an "unjustifiable" end. See CRIMINAL ~; SEDITIOUS ~.

CONSPIRACY DOCTRINE. An early labour law theory which considered self-organization of employees as equivalent to a conspiracy at common law.

CONSPIRATOR. *n.* A person who takes part in a conspiracy.

CONSTABLE. *n.* 1. Any member of the Royal Canadian Mounted Police other than a commissioned officer. 2. A member of the Newfoundland Constabulary Force or a member of the Royal Canadian Mounted Police stationed in Newfoundland. Newfoundland statutes. 3. Includes any sheriff, deputy sheriff, police officer, constable, bailiff, keeper of a jail or prison, or other person employed or deputized for the preservation of the public peace. 4. A constable, police or other officer, and any person acting to aid such an officer. See PRIVATE ~; SPECIAL ~.

CONSTANT COMPANION. Being a belt containing a concealed stainless steel knife; and (b) any other weapon similar to the weapon described in paragraph (a). *Prohibited Weapons Order, No. 4*, C.R.C., c. 436, s. 2.

CONSTANT WAGE PLAN. A method of paying steady amount of wages during fluctuating work weeks without incurring charges for overtime.

CONSTAT. [L.] It appears.

CONSTATING INSTRUMENT. Includes any statute, letters patent, memorandum of association, articles of association, certificate of incorporation, certificate of continuance, by-laws, regulations or other instrument by which a body corporate is incorporated or continued or that governs or regulates the affairs of a body corporate. Newfoundland statutes.

CONSTITUENCY. *n.* A place or territorial area entitled to return a member to serve in a legislative assembly or in Parliament. See URBAN ~.

CONSTITUENCY ASSOCIATION. In an electoral district, means the association or organization endorsed by a registered party as the official association of that party in the electoral district.

CONSTITUENCY WORK. Any work directly connected with a member's responsibilities as a member. *Legislative Assembly and Executive Council Act*, S.N.W.T. 1985 (2d Sess.), c. 4, s. 2.

CONSTITUENT. *n.* 1. One entitled to vote in a constituency. 2. Includes sulphur extracted from natural gas. *Natural Gas Price Act*, S.B.C. 1985, c. 53, s. 1.

CONSTITUENT PART. (a) Any of the following parts of a consumer textile article: (i) a section or backing described in section 34 or 35, or (ii) a lining, interlining, padding or filling described in section 37 or 38 or any trimming or findings, or (b) a consumer textile article exclusive of any part that (i) is described in subparagraph (a)(ii), and (ii) the article contains. *Textile Labelling and Advertising Regulations*, C.R.C., c. 1551, s. 25.

CONSTITUTION. *n.* 1. The body of law which establishes the framework of government for a nation or an organization. 2. The supreme law of Canada. *Constitution Act, 1982*, s. 52(1), being Schedule B of the *Canada Act, 1982* (U.K.), 1982, c. 11.

CONSTITUTION ACT, 1867. The act originally called the British North America Act (BNA Act).

CONSTITUTIONAL LAW. The body of law which deals with the distribution or exercise of the powers of government.

CONSTITUTIONAL REMEDY. A remedy under section 24(1) of the Canadian Charter of Rights and Freedoms other than a remedy consisting of the exclusion of evidence or consequential on such exclusion. *Constitutional Question Act*, S.B.C. 1982, c. 5, s. 1.

CONSTITUTIONES TEMPORE POSTERIORES POTIORES SUNT HIS QUAE IPSAS PRAECESSERUNT. [L.] More recent laws prevail over those which preceded them.

CONSTITUTION OF CANADA. Includes (a)

The Canada Act 1982, including this Act; (b) the Acts and orders referred to in the schedule; and (c) any amendment to any Act or order referred to in paragraph (a) or (b). *Constitution Act, 1982*, s. 52(2), being Schedule B of the *Canada Act, 1982* (U.K.), 1982, c. 11.

CONSTRAINED-CLASS. *n.* The class of persons specified in the articles of a constrained share corporation as being ineligible to hold, as a class, more than the maximum aggregate holdings. *Canada Business Corporations Regulations*, C.R.C., c. 426, s. 51.

CONSTRAINED-SHARE COMPANY. A category of company permitted to restrict the transfer of its shares in order to comply with requirements contained in legislation regarding Canadian ownership or control. S.M. Beck *et al.*, *Cases and Materials on Partnerships and Canadian Business Corporations* (Toronto: The Carswell Co., 1983) at 157.

CONSTRAINED SHARE CORPORATION. A corporation that has amended its articles under section 168 of the Act to constrain the issue or transfer of its voting shares. *Canada Business Corporations Regulations*, C.R.C., c. 426, s. 51.

CONSTRUCT. *v.* 1. To do anything in the erection, installation, extension, material alteration or repair of a building. 2. When used with respect to a well, means bore, dig, drill or otherwise make, extend or alter. *Ontario Water Resources Amendment Act, 1981*, S.O. 1981, c. 50, s. 1. 3. Includes to reconstruct, wholly or in part, when the lifetime of the work has expired.

CONSTRUCTIO LEGIS NON FACIT INJURIAM. [L.] The law is construed so as not to create injury.

CONSTRUCTION. *n.* 1. The way to ascertain the meaning of a written document. 2. Building, erection, alteration, repair, dismantling, demolition, structural maintenance, painting, moving, land clearing, earth moving, grading, excavating, street and highway building, concreting, equipment installation and alteration and the structural installation of construction components and materials. 3. In respect of a ship, includes the conversion of a ship. *Shipbuilding Industry Assistance Regulations*, C.R.C., c. 348, s. 2. See CLOSED ~; COMBUSTIBLE ~; COST OF ~; DENTURE ~; FIRE RESISTIVE ~; HEAVY TIMBER ~; LANDSCAPE ~; MILL ~; NONCOMBUSTIBLE ~; OPEN ~.

CONSTRUCTION CONTRACT. 1. A contract for erecting, remodelling or repairing a building or other structure on land and includes lump-sum, cost-plus and time and material contracts. 2. An agreement entered into for the construc-

tion, repair, renovation or restoration of any work except a vessel and includes (a) an agreement for the supply and erection of a prefabricated structure, (b) an agreement relating to dredging, (c) an agreement relating to demolition, and (d) an agreement for the hire of equipment to be used in or incidentally to the execution of a work. *Government Contracts Regulations*, C.R.C., c. 701, s. 2.

CONSTRUCTION CONTRACTOR. A person who undertakes a construction project, whether for his own benefit or for the benefit of another, or who enters into a contract, agreement or other arrangement whereby he agrees to undertake a construction project. *Construction Projects Labour-Management Relations Act*, S.N.S. 1971-72, c. 1, s. 2.

CONSTRUCTION HOIST. A mechanism used in connection with the construction, alteration, maintenance or demolition of a building, structure or other work, including its hoistway enclosure, affixed to a building or structure and equipped with a car, bucket or platform that (a) moves in guides, or is otherwise guided, at an angle exceeding 70 degrees from the horizontal, and (b) is used for raising or lowering workers, materials or both, in connection with the construction, alteration, maintenance or demolition of a building, structure or other work.

CONSTRUCTION INDUSTRY. The businesses that are engaged in constructing, altering, decorating, repairing or demolishing buildings, structures, roads, sewers, water or gas mains, pipe lines, tunnels, bridges, canals or other works at the site thereof.

CONSTRUCTION LIEN. A claim secured against real property made to ensure payment for materials furnished or work performed for construction.

CONSTRUCTION LOAN. Financing construction of a new building through progressive advances or draws. D.J. Donahue & P.D. Quinn, *Real Estate Practice in Ontario*, 4th ed. (Toronto: Butterworths, 1990) at 225.

CONSTRUCTION PROJECT. Construction work that is carried out as a separate and distinct undertaking. See NEW ~.

CONSTRUCTION SITE. A place where foundation, erection, maintenance, renovation, repair, alteration or demolition work is carried out in respect of a building or of civil engineering works, on and at the site itself, including the preparatory work of land clearing or earth moving and the lodging, eating or recreational facilities put at the disposal of the construction workers by the employer.

CONSTRUCTION SUB-CONTRACTOR. A person who enters a contract, agreement or other arrangement with a construction contractor or with a person who has a contract, agreement or other arrangement with a construction contractor for the performance of any construction work on a construction project. *Construction Projects Labour-Management Relations Act,* S.N.S. 1970-71, c. 1, s. 2.

CONSTRUCTION TRADE NEWSPAPER. A newspaper having circulation generally throughout Ontario, that is published no less frequently than on all days except Saturdays and holidays, and in which calls for tender on construction contracts are customarily published, and that is primarily devoted to the publication of matters of concern to the construction industry. *Construction Lien Act, 1983,* S.O. 1983, c. 6, s. 1.

CONSTRUCTION WORK. Foundation, erection, maintenance, renovation, repair, alteration and demolition work on buildings and on civil engineering works carried out on the job site itself and in the vicinity thereof, including the preparatory work on the site.

CONSTRUCTIVE. *adj.* Arising out of law without reference to any party's intention.

CONSTRUCTIVE DESERTION. One spouse by misconduct forces the other spouse to leave the home.

CONSTRUCTIVE DISCHARGE. Actions by the employer which cause an employee to resign.

CONSTRUCTIVE DISCRIMINATION. The imposition of requirements that are designed to assist a particular group.

CONSTRUCTIVE EVICTION. Acts by the landlord which deprive a tenant of enjoyment of the property so that it is untenantable.

CONSTRUCTIVE NOTICE. Knowledge attributed to someone who fails to make proper inquiries into the title of property purchased, who fails to investigate a fact, brought to notice, which suggests that a claim exists, or who deliberately does not inquire in order to avoid notice. See EQUITABLE DOCTRINE OF ~.

CONSTRUCTIVE POSSESSION. Presumptive possession or attributed possession knowingly. P.K. McWilliams, *Canadian Criminal Evidence,* 3d ed. (Aurora: Canada Law Book, 1988) at 19-3.

CONSTRUCTIVE TOTAL LOSS. A loss where (a) an insured property is abandoned because it appears to the Minister, on reasonable grounds, that the total loss of the property is unavoidable, or (b) the expenditure necessary to avoid the total loss of the insured property and to repair such property would exceed the insured value for total loss thereof. *Fishing Vessel Insurance Regulations,* C.R.C., c. 325, s. 2.

CONSTRUCTIVE TRUST. A trust arising by operation of law from unjust enrichment which obliges the constructive trustee to hold property partially or wholly for the person to whom the trustee owes an obligation.

CONSTRUCTOR. *n.* 1. A person who contracts with any person to undertake all or part of the work on a construction site. 2. An owner who contracts with more than one person for the work or part of the work at a construction site, or undertakes all or part of the work at a construction site.

CONSTRUE. *v.* To interpret; to ascertain the meaning of.

CONSUETUDINARY LAW. Customary law.

CONSUETUDO. *n.* [L.] Custom.

CONSUETUDO DEBET ESSE CERTA; NAM INCERTA PRO NULLIS HABENTUR. [L.] A custom ought to be certain because uncertain things are considered worthless.

CONSUETUDO EST ALTERA LEX. [L.] Custom is another law.

CONSUETUDO EST OPTIMUS INTERPRES LEGUM. [L.] The best interpreter of law is custom.

CONSUETUDO ET COMMUNIS ASSUETUDO VINCIT LEGEM NON SCRIPTAM, SI SIT SPECIALIS; ET INTERPRETATUR LEGEM SCRIPTAM, SI LEX SIT GENERALIS. [L.] Custom and common sense override unwritten law, if it is special; and interpret the written law if it is general.

CONSUETUDO EX CERTA CAUSA RATIONABILI USITATA PRIVAT COMMUNEM LEGEM. [L.] The common law is superceded by a custom grounded in a particular cause and reasonably applied.

CONSUETUDO, LICET SIT MAGNAE AUCTORITATIS, NUNQUAM TAMEN PRAEJUDICAT MANIFESTAE VERITATI. [L.] A custom, though it be of great authority, should never prejudice manifest truth.

CONSUETUDO LOCI OBSERVANDA EST. [L.] One should observe the custom of a place.

CONSUETUDO NEQUE INJURIA ORIRI NEQUE TOLLI POTEST. [L.] An unlawful act can neither establish nor abrogate a custom.

CONSUETUDO REGNI ANGLIAE EST LEX ANGLIAE. [L.] England's custom is England's law.

CONSUETUDO SEMEL REPROBATA NON POTEST AMPLIUS INDUCI. [L.] Once a custom has been disallowed it cannot be relied upon again.

CONSUETUDO VINCIT COMMUNEM LEGEM. [L.] Custom overrides the common law.

CONSUL. *n.* The agent of a foreign state who assists nationals of the state and protects the state's commercial interests. J.G. McLeod, *The Conflict of Laws* (Calgary: Carswell, 1983) at 77. See VICE-~.

CONSULAR OFFICER. A consular officer of Canada or any person for the time being discharging the duties of a consular officer of Canada, and, in the absence of a consular officer of Canada or such other person, means a consul-general, consul or vice-consul of the United Kingdom or any person for the time being discharging the duties of consul-general, consul or vice-consul of the United Kingdom, and, when used in relation to a country other than Canada, means the officer recognized by Her Majesty as a consular officer of that country. *Canada Shipping Act*, R.S.C. 1985, c. S-9. s. 2. See DIPLOMATIC OR ~.

CONSULAR PROPERTY. (a) Real property in Canada owned by a foreign or Commonwealth government and used as an official residence of the head of a consular post or trade commission, and (b) the chancery or office in Canada of a consular post or trade commission of a foreign or Commonwealth government. *Consular Property Grants Order*, C.R.C., c. 321, s. 2.

CONSULATE. *n.* The residence or office of a consul.

CONSULTANT. *n.* A person appointed under a security instrument to review the value of any property which may be realized subject to the security instrument and a debtor's financial viability. F. Bennett, *Receiverships* (Toronto: Carswell, 1985) at 3. See MEDICAL ~; SECURITY ~.

CONSULTARY RESPONSE. The court's opinion in a special case.

CONSULTATION. *n.* 1. Conferring, meeting to discuss with patient or client. 2. Discussion with a view to mutual agreement or understanding, but does not include conciliation, arbitration or any other form of process or authority binding on the parties thereto. *Hospitals Act*, R.S.P.E.I. 1974, c. H-11, s. 42.

CONSUMABLE STORES. Includes fuel oils, lubricants, provisions and supplies required for a voyage or flight and medical and surgical supplies. *Export of Consumable Stores Supplied to Vessels and Aircraft Permit*, C.R.C., c. 609, s. 2.

CONSUME. *v.* With respect to liquor, includes putting liquor to any use, by drinking or otherwise. *Liquor Control and Licensing Act*, R.S.B.C. 1979, c. 237, s. 1.

CONSUMER. *n.* 1. A natural person. 2. An individual. 3. A person who (a) utilizes or intends to utilize within a province goods for personal consumption, or for the consumption of any other person at personal expense, or (b) utilizes or intends to utilize within a province goods on behalf of or as the agent for a principal, who desired or desires to so utilize such goods for consumption by the principal or by any other person at the expense of the principal. 4. Any person who applies or intends to apply tangible personal property in the province (i) to personal consumption or use or to the consumption or use of another person at the expense of the first-mentioned person, or (ii) on behalf of, or as agent for, a principal, to the consumption or use of the principal or of any other person at the expense of that principal. 5. (i) A person who purchases goods or services under a time sale agreement or a continuous deferred payment plan, (ii) a borrower of funds under a loan agreement, or (iii) a person who purchases goods or services or obtains money by the use of a credit card, and includes a person not referred to in subclauses (i) to (iii) who enters into a credit agreement with a credit grantor. 6. A person who uses marketable pipeline gas (a) as a fuel or an energy source, (b) in the manufacture of products of trade and commerce, or (c) for any other purpose, other than resale. *Excise Tax Act*, R.S.C. 1985, c. E-15, s. 29. 7. Any person, firm or corporation having his domicile or its place of business, as the case may be, in Quebec and there publishing or printing, or there causing to be published or printed, a newspaper. *Forest Resources Utilization Act*, R.S.Q. 1977, c. U-2, s. 1. 8. When used to refer to a consumer of water, means the person actually drinking or otherwise using the water whether or not he is the owner of the premises at which the water is received or whether or not he has the purchase contract with a public utilities commission or other water supplier. *Ontario Water Resources Act*, R.R.O. 1980, Reg. 726, s. 23. 9. Any corporation, commission, company, person, association of persons, whatsoever, their lessees, trustees, liquidators or receivers utilizing electrical power or energy directly for heat, light or power purposes. See REGISTERED ~.

CONSUMER AND CORPORATE AFFAIRS CANADA. The federal ministry responsible for efficient conduct of the marketplace, satisfactory to both business and consumers, and for promoting confidence in private enterprise.

CONSUMER BOYCOTT. General refusal to buy an employer's products.

CONSUMER CONTAINER. A container that has a weight capacity of 8 pounds of less. *Honey Regulations*, C.R.C., c. 287, s. 2.

CONSUMER CREDIT. Loans to individuals to facilitate purchase of goods or services.

CONSUMER DEBT. Debt incurred by an individual for personal or household goods and services.

CONSUMER GOODS. Goods that are used or acquired for use primarily for personal, family or household purposes.

CONSUMER GOODS OR SERVICES. Goods or services the cost of which was not deductible by the taxpayer in computing the income from a business or property. *Income Tax Act*, R.S.C. 1952, c. 148 (as am. S.C. 1970-71-72, c. 63), s. 135(4).

CONSUMER OF TOBACCO. A person who, within a province, purchases from a vendor tobacco at a retail sale in the province for personal consumption or for the consumption of other persons at personal expense or who, within the province, purchases from a vendor tobacco at a retail sale in the province on behalf of or as agent for a principal who desires to acquire such tobacco for consumption by such principal or other persons at the expense of such principal.

CONSUMER ORGANIZATION. Any corporation that has as one of its objects the protection or advancement of the interests of consumers and is not incorporated for the purpose of acquiring gain for its members. *Unfair Trade Practices Act*, R.S.A. 1980, c. U-3, s. 1.

CONSUMER OUTLET. Any premises at which gasoline or an associated product of the operator of the outlet is put into the fuel tanks of motor vehicles used by the operator of the outlet or into portable containers used by the operator of the outlet. *Gasoline Handling Act*, R.S.O. 1980, c. 185, c. 1.

CONSUMER PRICE INDEX. The consumer price index for Canada as published by Statistics Canada under the authority of the Statistics Act (Canada). See EARLIER ~.

CONSUMER PRODUCT. (i) Any goods ordinarily used for personal, family or household purposes and, without restricting the generality of the foregoing, includes any goods ordinarily used for personal, family or household purposes that are designed to be attached to or installed in any real or personal property, whether or not they are so attached or installed; and (ii) includes any goods bought for agricultural or fishing purposes by an individual or by a family farming corporation.

CONSUMER PROTECTION LEGISLATION. Legislation regulating business practices of those dealing with consumers.

CONSUMER PUMP. A tank or receptacle of more than two hundred and fifty gallon or one thousand one hundred and thirty-six litre capacity used or intended to be used for the storage of taxable gasoline or taxable motive fuel for consumption and not for resale, and equipped with a pump for dispensing such gasoline or motive fuel. *Gasoline and Motive Fuel Tax Act*, S.N.B. 1976, c. 26, s. 1.

CONSUMER PURCHASE. A purchase, other than a cash purchase, of goods or services or an agreement to purchase goods or services (i) by an individual other than for resale or for use in the course of a business, profession or calling, and (ii) from a person who is engaged in the business of selling or providing those goods or services.

CONSUMER REPORT. A written, oral or other communication by a consumer reporting agency of credit information or personal information, or both, pertaining to a consumer.

CONSUMER REPORTING AGENCY. A person who, for gain or profit, or on a regular cooperative non-profit basis, furnishes consumer reports.

CONSUMER REPRESENTATION. A representation, statement, offer, request or proposal, (i) made respecting or with a view to the supplying of goods or services, or both, to a consumer, or (ii) made for the purpose of or with a view to receiving consideration for goods or services, or both, supplied or purporting to have been supplied to a consumer.

CONSUMER SALE. A contract of sale of goods or services including an agreement of sale as well as a sale and a conditional sale of goods made in the ordinary course of business to a purchaser for personal consumption or use but does not include a sale, (a) to a purchaser for resale; (b) to a purchaser whose purchase is in the course of carrying on business; (c) to an association of individuals, a partnership or a corporation; or (d) by a trustee in bankruptcy, a receiver, a liquidator or a person acting under the order of a court.

CONSUMERS' ASSOCIATION. An association incorporated or registered under this Act for the main purpose of purchasing, procuring, processing, manufacturing, exchanging, hiring and dealing in goods, wares and merchandise, including farm supplies, for sale at retail to its members and patrons. *The Co-operative Associations Act*, R.S.S. 1978, c. C-34, s. 70.

CONSUMERS' ASSOCIATION OF CANADA. A national, non-profit organization that represents and educates consumers.

CONSUMER'S COOPERATIVE. A cooperative which purchases consumer goods for resale to its members.

CONSUMER'S SERVICE. All that portion of the consumer's installation from the service box or its equivalent up to and including the point at which the supply authority makes connection. *Power Corporation Act*, R.R.O. 1980, Reg. 794, s. 0.

CONSUMER TEXTILE ARTICLE. (a) Any textile fibre, yarn or fabric, or (b) any product made in whole or in part from a textile fibre, yarn or fabric that is in the form in which it is or is to be sold to any person for consumption or use, other than consumption or use in the manufacturing, processing or finishing of any product for sale. *Textile Labelling Act*, R.S.C. 1985, c. T-10, s. 2.

CONSUMER TRANSACTION. (i) A sale or lease of goods or any other disposition of goods for a consideration, whether or not the sale, lease or disposition includes any agreement or arrangement under which services are provided, (ii) an agreement or arrangement under which services are provided for a consideration, or (iii) an award by chance of goods or services or both.

CONSUMER UNIT. A quantity of a regulated product that does not exceed in the aggregate 800 pounds and does not include more than 400 pounds of cherries or 600 pounds of other stone tree fruits. *British Columbia Tree Fruit Export Regulations*, C.R.C., c. 146, s. 2.

CONSUMMATE. *v.* To finish; to complete a marriage by engaging in sexual intercourse.

CONSUMMATE. *adj.* Completed; possessing extra skill or ability; excellent.

CONSUMMATION. *n.* Completion; act of sexual intercourse after marriage which completes the marriage.

CONSUMPTION. *n.* 1. Includes (i) use, (ii) the incorporation into any structure, building or fixture, of goods including those manufactured by the consumer or further processed or otherwise improved personally, (iii) the provision of goods by way of promotional distribution. 2. In relation to crude oil or gas, the action of using one of them as a fuel or energy source or consuming it in the manufacture of products of

trade and commerce. *Energy Administration Act*, R.S.C. 1985, c. E-6, s. 20. See FUEL ~.

CONTACT. *n.* Any person or animal suspected to have been in association with an infected person or animal or a contaminated environment to a sufficient degree to have had the opportunity to become infected with a disease. See PERSONAL ~.

CONTACT FLATTENING. The shaping of muscles caused by contact with any hard surface during rigor mortis. F.A. Jaffe, *A Guide to Pathological Evidence*, 2d ed. (Toronto: Carswell, 1983) at 173.

CONTACT RING. See GREY RING.

CONTAGIOUS. *adj.* Communicable by close contact or inoculation.

CONTAGIOUS DISEASE. A disease which may be transmitted by one animal or person to another by direct contact or otherwise. See INFECTIOUS DISEASE.

CONTAINER. *n.* 1. The articles and devices used to package tangible personal property for shipment or delivery, such as bags, cans, barrels, boxes, bottles, drums, carboys, cartons, sacks, pallets and cores. 2. A receptacle, package, wrapper or confining band in which a product is offered for sale but does not include package liners or shipping containers or any outer wrapping or box that is not customarily displayed to the consumer. *Consumer Packaging and Labelling Act*, R.S.C. 1985, c. C-38, s. 2. 3. An article of transport equipment, including one that is carried on a chassis, that is strong enough to be suitable for repeated use and is designed to facilitate the transportation of goods by one or more means of transport without intermediate reloading, but does not include a vehicle. *Transportation of Dangerous Goods Act*, R.S.C. 1985, c. T-19, s. 2. See APPROVED ~; BULK ~; BULK STORAGE ~; CARGO ~; CHILD-RESISTANT ~; CONSUMER ~; DISPOSABLE ~; MASTER ~; NON-REFILLABLE ~; NON-RETURNABLE ~; ORNAMENTAL ~; PORTABLE ~; REFILLABLE ~; RETURNABLE ~; SHIPPING ~.

CONTAINER FREIGHT STATION. A location on a container terminal used for receiving and delivering goods and stuffing and destuffing containers. *Pacific Terminal Tariff By-law*, C.R.C., c. 1083, s. 32.

CONTAINER HANDLING CHARGE. A charge for moving containers that are loaded on or unloaded from vessels that are not specially designed for carrying containers when the containers are being moved between a place of rest and the ship's tackle. *Pacific Terminal Tariff By-law*, C.R.C., c. 1083, s. 32.

CONTAINERIZED GOODS. Goods that are received in a container for movement intact between vessels and inland carriers. *Pacific Terminal Tariff By-law*, C.R.C., c. 1083, s. 2.

CONTAINER OPERATOR. A person who employs cargo containers in the international carriage of goods. *Cargo Container (Customs) Regulations*, C.R.C., c. 452, s. 2.

CONTAINER REHANDLING CHARGE. A charge for handling containers within the terminal area, which charge is in addition to the container handling charge and the through-put charge. *Pacific Terminal Tariff By-law*, C.R.C., c. 1083, s. 32.

CONTAINER STORAGE AREA. An area of open or ground space or a similar area provided by the Board for storing inbound or outbound empty containers where arrangements for storage are made prior to the expiration of free time. *Pacific Terminal Tariff By-law*, C.R.C., c. 1083, s. 32.

CONTAINER THROUGHPUT. Includes the following services: (a) sorting containers once in the container yard in accordance with instructions from the vessel, (b) preparing an outbound dangerous cargo list, a reefer container list, an exceptions list, an inbound outturn report and a rehandling report, (c) visually inspecting empty and loaded containers and reporting any damage or defect to the vessel, (d) planning the layout of containers in the container yards, (e) plugging and unplugging reefer containers in the container yard and periodic checking of container temperature, (f) weighing containers once, if required, on scales at the container yard and recording weights, (g) ordering railway cars and providing liaison with railways, inland carriers and trucking companies, (h) berthing and spotting vessels, (i) ordinary receiving and delivery documentation, including equipment interchange receipts and a daily report of container yard damage to containers and any containers that were received in a damaged state, (j) moving empty containers from the container freight station to the container storage area after the containers are destuffed, and (k) planning stowage of containers on board cellular container vessels including stability calculations, but does not include (l) handling lines or pilotage; or (m) loading or unloading containers on or from a truck, chassis or railway car. *Pacific Terminal Tariff By-law*, C.R.C., c. 1083, s. 32.

CONTAINER YARD. A designated area within a terminal area where containers in transit between vessels and inland carriers are temporarily held or assembled. *Pacific Terminal Tariff By-law*, C.R.C., c. 1083, s. 32.

CONTAMINANT. *n.* Any solid, liquid, gas, waste, odour, heat, sound, vibration, radiation, or a combination of any of them that (i) is foreign to or in excess of the natural constituents of the environment; or (ii) affects the natural, physical, chemical, or biological quality of the environment; or (iii) is or is likely to be injurious to the health or safety of a person; or (iv) is or is likely to be injurious or damaging to property; or (v) is or is likely to be injurious or damaging to plant or animal life; or (vi) interferes or is likely to interfere with visibility; or (vii) interferes or is likely to interfere with the normal conduct of business, or (viii) interferes or is likely to interfere with the comfort, well-being or enjoyment of a person. See AIR ~; SOURCE OF ~; WATER ~.

CONTAMINATED. *adj.* In respect of grain, containing any substance in sufficient quantity that the grain is unfit for consumption by persons and animals. *Canada Grain Act*, R.S.C. 1985, c. G-10, s. 2.

CONTAMINATED MILK. Milk or milk product that contains a material, substance or organism that will render it less valuable or unfit for human consumption. *Dairy Act*, S.M. 1980, c. 44, s. 1.

CONTAMINATION. *n.* 1. (i) Deterioration of the environment which the Minister believes on reasonable and probable grounds is or may be sufficient to render it unfit or undesirable for normal use, or (ii) the presence of a hazard, other than to the target organism, which the Minister believes on reasonable and probable grounds is or may be detrimental to the normal physiological functions of human, animal or plant life. *Pest Control Products (Nova Scotia) Act*, S.N.S. 1986, c. 16, s. 3. 2. The presence of an infectious agent on a body surface, or on or in an inanimate article or substance including food. *Public Health Act*, S.A. 1984, c. P-27.1, s. 1. See SOURCE OF ~.

CONTANGO. *n.* A charge paid by a buyer of stock for being allowed to delay taking delivery until a date later than that originally agreed.

CONTEMNOR. *n.* One who commits contempt of court.

CONTEMPLATE. *v.* To view, consider, study, ponder.

CONTEMPLATION. *n.* Consideration of a matter.

CONTEMPORANEA EXPOSITIO EST FORTISSIMA IN LEGE. [L.] The meaning openly given by current or long professional use should be taken as the true one. P.St.J. Langan, ed., *Maxwell on The Interpretation of Statutes*, 12th ed. (Bombay: N.M. Tripathi, 1976) at 264.

CONTEMPORANEA EXPOSITIO EST OPTIMA ET FORTISSIMA IN LEGE. [L.] The current meaning is the best and most compelling in law.

CONTEMPT. *n.* 1. A person who was required by law to attend or remain in attendance for the purpose of giving evidence, who fails, without lawful excuse, to attend or remain in attendance, is guilty of contempt of court. *Criminal Code*, R.S.C. 1985, c. C-46, s. 708(1). 2. An order is made against a person and the person fails to comply, or a person makes an undertaking and fails to comply with it. 3. An act which shows disrespect for a court's authority or tends to hinder the course of justice.

CONTEMPT OF PARLIAMENT. To obstruct the due course of proceedings in either House of Parliament.

CONTEMPTUOUS DAMAGES. Small damages awarded to a plaintiff who sustained no loss, but whose legal rights were technically infringed though in the court's opinion the action should not have been brought. K.D. Cooper-Stephenson & I.B. Saunders, *Personal Injury Damages in Canada* (Toronto: Carswell, 1981) at 69.

CONTENT. See CANADIAN ~; JOB ~; PROVINCIAL ~; RESIDUAL CHLORINE ~.

CONTENTIOUS. *adj.* Contested.

CONTENTIOUS BUSINESS. (i) The proving of a will in solemn form, (ii) proceedings in which the right to obtain or retain a grant is in dispute, and (iii) proceedings to discharge a caveat. *Administration of Estates Act*, R.S.A. 1980, c. A-1, s. 1.

CONTENTIOUS JURISDICTION. Authority to hear and determine matters which parties dispute.

CONTEST. *v.* To oppose, resist, dispute.

CONTEST. *n.* A boxing match in which the contestants compete for monetary reward and includes a closed circuit televised contest. *Boxing Authority Act*, S.N.S. 1981, c. 55, s. 1. See LEADERSHIP ~ PERIOD; PHYSICAL ~; PROFESSIONAL ~ OR EXHIBITION; PUBLICITY ~.

CONTESTANT. See LEADERSHIP ~.

CONTESTATIO LITIS EGET TERMINOS CONTRADICTARIOS. [L.] The joinder of issue requires contradictory terms.

CONTESTATION. *n.* A controversy; a disputed issue.

CONTESTED DIVORCE. A divorce action in which a respondent delivers an answer.

CONTEXT. *n.* Parts of text surrounding the portion under consideration.

CONTIGUITY. *n.* In international law, proximity to neighbouring territory.

CONTIGUOUS. *adj.* Having at least one common boundary between adjoining claims. *Mines Act*, R.S.N.S. 1967, c. 185, s. 52.

CONTIGUOUS LAND. One or more parcels or lots of lands the aggregate area of which is continuous and unbroken, so that, in the case of there being more than one parcel or lot, each parcel or lot thereof touches or adjoins one or more of the other parcels or lots.

CONTINENTAL SHELF. 1. The shallow area of the ocean which adjoins each continent. P.W. Hogg, *Constitutional Law of Canada*, 2d ed. (Toronto: Carswell, 1985) at 586. 2. The seabed and subsoil of those submarine areas that extend beyond the territorial sea throughout the natural prolongation of the land territory of Canada to the outer edge of the continental margin or to a distance of two hundred nautical miles from the inner limits of the territorial sea, whichever is the greater, or that extend to such other limits as are prescribed. *Customs and Excise Offshore Application Act*, R.S.C. 1985, c. C-53, s. 2.

CONTINGENCY. *n.* 1. Accident, sickness, strikes and unemployment. K.D. Cooper-Stephenson & I.B. Saunders, *Personal Injury Damages in Canada Supplement to June 30, 1987* (Toronto: Carswell, 1987) at 244. 2. An uncertain event on which an estate, interest, liability, right or obligation depends for its existence. See MITIGATION ~.

CONTINGENCY CONTRACT. A contract made by a solicitor or barrister practising in the province, with a person (herein referred to as "the client"), as to the remuneration to be paid to, or retained by, the solicitor or barrister for services rendered or to be rendered to the client whereby, for those services, the solicitor or barrister is to receive or retain, in lieu of, or in addition to, any remuneration to which he might otherwise be entitled, (a) a portion of the proceeds of the subject matter of the action or proceedings in which the solicitor or barrister is or is to be employed; or (b) a portion of the money or property in respect of which the solicitor or barrister is or may be retained or employed, whether or not an action or proceeding therefor has been commenced or is contemplated; or (c) a commission or a percentage of the amount recovered or defended or of the value of the property about which any transaction, action or proceeding, is concerned. *Law Society Act*, R.S.M. 1970, c. L100, s. 49.

CONTINGENCY INSURANCE. An agreement by an insurer to pay when an event occurs regardless of the loss suffered. Examples are life or accident insurance. Raoul Colinvaux, *The Law of Insurance*, 5th ed. (London: Sweet & Maxwell, 1984) at 9.

CONTINGENCY LEVY. An assessment or levy made on members of a society, order, association, or corporation on the occasion of the happening to any member thereof of any one or more of certain contingencies upon the happening of which that member or the member's beneficiaries become entitled to receive the proceeds of that assessment or levy.

CONTINGENCY RESERVE FUND. A fund for the expenditures, other than annual, of the strata corporation for repair, maintenance and replacement of the common property, common facilities and other assets of the strata corporation, including where applicable, without limiting the generality of the foregoing, the roof, exterior of the buildings, roads, sidewalks, sewers, heating, electrical and plumbing systems, elevators, laundry and recreational facilities. *Condominium Act*, R.S.B.C. 1979, c. 61, s. 1.

CONTINGENCY WITH A DOUBLE ASPECT. An interest that will vest only if the next preceding interest never vests in any way.

CONTINGENT. *adj.* Conditional upon the occurrence of some future uncertain event.

CONTINGENT ASSETS. Assets without known value to the company until fulfilment of conditions regarded as uncertain. Canada regulations.

CONTINGENT LEGACY. A legacy bequeathed payable on happening of a contingency.

CONTINGENT LIABILITIES. Liabilities that may, under certain conditions, become obligations of the company but are not direct or assumed obligations on the date of the balance sheet. Canada regulations.

CONTINGENT LIABILITY. A liability which will become fixed upon the occurrence of a future, uncertain event.

CONTINGENT REMAINDER. A remainder which depends on an uncertain condition or event that may never be performed or happen, or which may not be performed or happen until after a preceding estate is determined.

CONTINGENT RIGHT. Includes a contingent or executory interest, a possibility coupled with an interest, whether the object of the gift or limitation of the interest or possibility is or is not ascertained, also a right of entry, whether immediate or future, and whether vested or contingent.

CONTINUANCE. See CERTIFICATE OF ~.

CONTINUATION. *n.* Statutes governing corporations may permit a corporation to continue its corporate existence under the law of another jurisdiction. S.M. Beck *et al.*, *Cases and Materials on Partnerships and Canadian Business Corporations*, (Toronto: The Carswell Company Limited, 1983) at 153.

CONTINUATION SCHOOL. A room or department maintained exclusively for grade eight and one or more high school grades and includes any school or department of a school that is organized so as to provide for the intermediate section and that provides instruction for grades seven, eight and nine. *The School Act*, R.S.S. 1978, c. S-36, s. 2.

CONTINUE. See ORDER TO ~.

CONTINUED. *adj.* A company incorporated under one act may in certain circumstances be "continued" under the laws of some other jurisdiction so that its existence is maintained subject to the laws of the second jurisdiction.

CONTINUING. *adj.* Ongoing; enduring.

CONTINUING EDUCATION. Includes education or training offered by an institution to adult persons on a part time or short term basis. *College and Institute Act*, R.S.B.C. 1979, c. 53, s. 1.

CONTINUING GARNISHMENT. Capturing all present and future income payments above those exempted by statute until a debt is paid. C.R.B. Dunlop, *Creditor-Debtor Law in Canada* (Toronto: Carswell, 1981) at 262.

CONTINUOUS. *adj.* 1. Uninterrupted. 2. In relation to membership in a pension plan or to employment, means without regard to periods of temporary interruption of the membership or employment. *Pension Benefits Standards Act*, R.S.C. 1985 (2d Supp.), c. 32, s. 2.

CONTINUOUS ACTIVITY. Work requiring an employee be constantly available.

CONTINUOUS DEFERRED PAYMENT PLAN. A sale or an agreement to sell under which (i) purchases on credit can be made from time to time by a purchaser, and (ii) the credit charges, if any, are computed from time to time in relation to the unpaid balance on all the purchases.

CONTINUOUS DISCLOSURE. An obligation imposed on a company with publicly traded securities to make public statements concerning any material changes in its affairs in order that there is a continuous flow of information to the securities market. S.M. Beck *et al.*, *Cases and Materials on Partnerships and Canadian Business*

Corporations, (Toronto: The Carswell Company Limited, 1983) at 494.

CONTINUOUS DUTY. A requirement of service that demands operation at a substantially constant load for an indefinitely long time. *Power Corporation Act,* R.R.O. 1980, Reg. 794. s. 0.

CONTINUOUS INDUSTRY. A manufacturing process carried on without interruption.

CONTINUOUSLY. *adv.* Without ceasing; without break.

CONTINUOUSLY-OPERATING PLANT. *var.* **CONTINUOUSLY OPERATING PLANT.** (i) An industrial plant; or (ii) an establishment, factory, works, or undertaking, in or about any industry, in which, in each seven-day period, operations once commenced normally continue day and night without cessation until the completion of the regularly scheduled operations for that period.

CONTINUOUS OPERATION. That part of an establishment, industry or service in which in each seven day period operations once commenced normally continue day and night without cessation until the completion of the regularly scheduled operations for that period. *Employment Standards Act,* R.S.O. 1980, c. 137, s. 26. See EMPLOYED IN A ~.

CONTINUOUS PERIOD. A period of service or membership in a pension plan calculated without regard to temporary interruptions in that service or membership. *Pension Benefits Standards Act,* R.S.C. 1985, c. P-7, s. 2. See SERVICE FOR A ~.

CONTINUOUS RATING. The brake horsepower and speed stated by the manufacturer to be the highest at which an engine will give satisfactory service when operating continuously for not less than 24 hours. *Large Fishing Vessel Inspection Regulations,* C.R.C., c. 1435, s. 2.

CONTINUOUS SERVICE. Uninterrupted service of a person as an employee.

CONTINUOUS TRIP. A trip without cessation or stopover from the place of commencement to the destination of the shipment other than a cessation or stopover made: (i) to refuel the vehicle, (ii) to effect any required repairs or to perform any other required maintenance with respect to the vehicle, (iii) to provide a reasonable rest period for the driver of the vehicle, (iv) in the case of emergency, (v) to effect the pickup or delivery of goods, or (vi) to effect the transfer of goods or interchange of trailers by a person who is the holder of a Class C operating licence or who is the holder of an operating licence that includes the terms of a Class C operating licence if the goods transferred or the trailers interchanged are transported within the Class C authority of the person to whom the goods are transferred or the trailer interchanged. *Public Commercial Vehicles Act,* R.R.O. 1980, Reg. 832, s. 1.

CONTINUOUS WASTE AND VENT. A vent pipe that is a vertical extension of a vertical waste pipe and includes the vertical waste pipe. *Ontario Water Resources Act,* R.R.O. 1980, Reg. 736, s. 1.

CONTOUR. See OFFICIAL ~.

CONTRA. [L.] Against.

CONTRABAND. *n.* 1. Goods not permitted to be exported or imported, bought or sold. 2. Anything that is in a prisoner's possession in circumstances in which possession thereof is forbidden by any act or regulation, or by an order of general or specific application within the prison or penitentiary in which the prisoner is confined.

CONTRA BONOS MORES. [L.] Contrary to good morals.

CONTRACAUSATOR. *n.* A criminal; a person prosecuted for a crime.

CONTRACEPTIVE. *n.* A device for preventing conception.

CONTRACEPTIVE. *adj.* Preventing conception.

CONTRACEPTIVE DEVICE. Any instrument, apparatus, contrivance or substance other than a drug, that is manufactured, sold or represented for use in the prevention of conception. *Food and Drugs Act,* R.S.C. 1985, c. F-27, s. 2.

CONTRACT. *n.* 1. An agreement between two or more persons, recognized by law, which gives rise to obligations that the courts may enforce. G.H.L. Fridman, *The Law of Contract in Canada,* 2d ed. (Toronto: Carswell, 1986) at 3. 2. A promise, or set of promises, which one person gives in exchange for the promise, or set of promises, of another person. G.H.L. Fridman, *The Law of Contract in Canada,* 2d ed. (Toronto: Carswell, 1986) at 1. See ACTION OF ~; ADOPTION OF ~; ALBERTA ~; ALEATORY ~; ANNUITY ~; BILATERAL ~; BRITISH COLUMBIA ~; BUILDING ~; C.I.F. ~; CLOSED SHOP ~; COLLATERAL ~; COMMODITY ~; COMMODITY FUTURES ~; COMPLETED ~ METHOD; COMPLETION OF THE ~; CONSTRUCTION ~; CONTINGENCY ~; COST-PLUS ~; DEFENCE ~; DEPOSIT ADMINISTRATION ~; DIRECT SALES ~; DISTRIBUTION ~; DOMESTIC ~; ESSENCE OF THE ~; EXECUTED ~; EXEC-

UTORY ~; FIRM PRICE ~; FIXED PRICE ~; FOOD PLAN ~; F.O.R. ~; FORMAL ~; FREEDOM OF ~; GAS ~; GAS PURCHASE ~; GOODS ~; GOVERNMENT ~; GROUP ~; HONEYMOON ~; ILLEGAL ~; IMMORAL ~; IMPLIED ~; INCOME-AVERAGING ANNUITY ~; INDUSTRIAL ~; INFORMAL ~; INSULATION ~; INVESTMENT ~; LAW OF ~; MANAGEMENT ~; MANITOBA ~; MARRIAGE ~; MATERIAL ~; MEDICAL ~; MULTI-YEAR ~; NAKED ~; NEWFOUND-LAND ~; ONTARIO ~; ORAL ~; PAROL ~; PATRONAGE ~; PREARRANGED CEMETERY ~; PRE-EXISTING ~; PRE-INCORPO-RATION ~; PROBATIONARY ~; PRODUCER-SHIPPER ~; QUASI-~; REGULAR PAYMENT ~; SALES ~; SASKATCHEWAN ~; SERVICE ~; SIMPLE ~; SPECIALTY ~; TERM ~; TRAINING ~; UNILATERAL ~; UNION ~; VALUE OF THE ~; WAGERING ~.

CONTRACT AIR CARRIER. See FOREIGN.

CONTRACT BENEFICIARY. Any person who (i) is named in a prepaid funeral contract; and (ii) on whose death funeral services are to be performed or funeral goods are to be provided or delivered pursuant to a prepaid funeral contract. *Prepaid Funeral Services Act*, S.S. 1986, c. P-22.3, s. 2.

CONTRACT BUYER. Any person, whether or not a contract beneficiary, who purchases funeral goods or funeral services pursuant to a prepaid funeral contract. *Prepaid Funeral Services Act*, S.S. 1986, c. P-22.3, s. 2.

CONTRACT COMPLETE BUYER. Person who has purchased the minimum quantity of goods required by the terms of the negative option scheme. *Consumer Protection Act*, R.S.B.C. 1979, c. 65, s. 39.

CONTRACT DATE. The date on which a contract is signed by both parties.

CONTRACT DELIVERY POINT. (i) With reference to a gas sales contract, the point at which delivery is taken by the original buyer under the gas sales contract, or (ii) with reference to a resale contract, the point at which delivery is taken by the second buyer under the resale contract.

CONTRACT EMPLOYEE. An employee engaged by means of a contract for temporary employment for a fixed term.

CONTRACT FIELD PRICE. With reference to a gas sales contract or a resale contract, the price of gas under the contract, whether the price is specified in the contract or is redetermined pursuant to the contract by agreement or by arbitration. *Natural Gas Pricing Agreement Act*, R.S.A. 1980, c. N-4, s. 1.

CONTRACT FOR FUTURE SERVICES. An executory contract that includes a provision for services of a prescribed type or class to be rendered in the future on a continuing basis.

CONTRACT FOR SALE. A sale in which the thing sold is exchanged for a consideration in money or money's worth.

CONTRACT HOLDER. A person, other than a corporation, who has entered into an income-averaging annuity contract with a trustee. *The Queen's Bench Amendment Act*, R.S.S. 1978 (Supp.), c. 57, s. 2.

CONTRACT HOSPITAL. 1. A private or industrial hospital with which a province has contracted for the provision of insured services to insured persons. *Hospital Insurance Regulations*, C.R.C., c. 936, s. 2. 2. A hospital with which the Department has entered into an agreement for the priority use of beds or out-patient facilities for the treatment of patients under these Regulations. *Veterans Treatment Regulations*, C.R.C., c. 1585, s. 2.

CONTRACTING ELECTRICIAN. A person who, for another, carries out, or causes to be carried out, electrical installation work, or renovation, alteration or repair work on electrical installations for purposes of electric lighting, heating or power.

CONTRACTING PARTY. 1. Any person who is about to enter into, or has already entered into, a marriage. *Marriage Settlement Act*, R.S.M. 1970, c. M60, s. 2. 2. (i) A producer of farm products who has entered into a contract with a licensee, or (ii) a licensee who has entered into a contract with a producer of farm products, respecting the marketing of any farm product. *Farm Products Grades and Sales Act*, R.S.O. 1980, c. 157, s. 1.

CONTRACTING STATE. Any state that has ratified or adhered to a convention and whose denunciation thereof has not become effective. See COURT OF A ~; RESIDENT OF A ~.

CONTRACT LAW. The branch of private law dealing with drafting, interpretation and enforcement of contracts between persons.

CONTRACT OF APPRENTICESHIP. A written agreement entered into in accordance with this Act and the regulations, if any, between a person who is sixteen years of age or older and an employer, under which the person agrees with the employer to learn a trade requiring a minimum of four thousand hours of reasonably continuous employment and which provides for a course of related technical instruction for the person. *Apprenticeship Act*, R.S. Nfld. 1970, c. 12, s. 2.

CONTRACT OF BENEVOLENCE. A contract made which benefits only one contracting party, as a mandate or deposit.

CONTRACT OF COMMODATUM. A contract concerning a loan of useful goods. D.M.W. Waters, *The Law of Trusts in Canada*, 2d ed. (Toronto: Carswell, 1984) at 63.

CONTRACT OF DEPOSITUM. A contract of deposit. D.M.W. Waters, *The Law of Trusts in Canada*, 2d ed. (Toronto: Carswell, 1984) at 63.

CONTRACT OF EMPLOYMENT. A contract by which an employee agrees to provide services to an employer.

CONTRACT OF INDEMNITY. A contract designed to compensate for loss, i.e. an insurance contract. I.F.G. Baxter, *The Law of Banking*, 3d ed. (Toronto: Carswell, 1981) at 223.

CONTRACT OF INSURANCE. 1. An agreement by which an insurer, for a premium, agrees to indemnify the insured against loss. 2. A policy, certificate, interim receipt, renewal receipt, or writing evidencing the contract, whether sealed or not, and a binding oral agreement.

CONTRACT OF LIFE INSURANCE. See REPLACEMENT OF A ~.

CONTRACT OF LOCATIO ET CONDUCTIO. A contract about hiring. D.M.W. Waters, *The Law of Trusts in Canada*, 2d ed. (Toronto: Carswell, 1984) at 63.

CONTRACT OF MARINE INSURANCE. A contract whereby the insurer undertakes to indemnify the assured, in manner and to the extent thereby agreed, against marine losses, that is to say, the losses incident to marine adventure. Raoul Colinvaux, *The Law of Insurance*, 5th ed. (London: Sweet & Maxwell, 1984) at 8.

CONTRACT OF PIGNUS. A contract relating to a pledge. D.M.W. Waters, *The Law of Trusts in Canada*, 2d ed. (Toronto: Carswell, 1984) at 63.

CONTRACT OF SALE. Includes an agreement to sell as well as sale. *Sale of Goods acts*.

CONTRACT OF SERVICE. A contract, whether or not in writing, in which an employer, either expressly or by implication, in return for the payment of a wage to an employee, reserves the right of control and direction of the manner and method by which the employee carries out the duties to be performed under the contract, but does not include a contract entered into by an employee qualified in or training for qualification in and working for an employer in the

practice of (i) accountancy, architecture, law, medicine, pharmacy, professional engineering, surveying, teaching, veterinary science, and (ii) such other professions and occupations as may be prescribed. *Labour Standards Act*, S. Nfld. 1977, c. 52, s. 2.

CONTRACTOR. *n.* 1. Any person who, for another, carries out construction work or causes it to be carried out or makes or submits tenders, personally or through another person, to carry out such work for personal profit. 2. A person who enters into a pre-incorporation contract in the name of or on behalf of a corporation before its incorporation. 3. Any person or body that has undertaken to supply electricity or gas to any purchaser. See BUILDER AND ~; BUILDING ~; CONSTRUCTION ~; DEPENDENT ~; ELECTRICAL ~; FARM LABOUR ~; GENERAL ~; INDEPENDENT ~; MAIL ~; NON-RESIDENT ~; PERSONAL SERVICE ~; PLUMBING ~; PRIME ~; PRINCIPAL ~; SERVICE ~.

CONTRACT OUT. 1. To make a contract or agreement in accordance with which a significant part of the work regularly done by the employees of an employer is to be done by some other person or persons. *Trade Union Act*, S.N.S. 1972, c. 19, s. 1. 2. To agree with others for whose benefit a statute has been passed to deprive oneself of the benefit of the statute.

CONTRACT PHYSICIAN. A legally qualified medical practitioner who has entered into a medical contract with an employer. *Public Health Act*, R.R.O. 1980, Reg. 834, s. 36.

CONTRACT PRICE. The price to be paid under a contract or sub-contract for performance of the contract or sub-contract. *The Builders' Liens Act*, S.M. 1980-81, c. 7, s. 1. See TOTAL ~.

CONTRACT RATE. Rate to be charged for the transportation of goods shipped by a shipper who has entered into a patronage contract. *Shipping Conference Exemption Act*, R.S.C. 1985, c. S-10, s. 5(2).

CONTRACT SELLER. A person who, as seller or provider of or the person undertaking to provide counselling, advice, funeral services or funeral goods, enters into, proposes to enter into or solicits another person to enter into a prepaid funeral contract. *Prepaid Funeral Services Act*, S.S. 1986, c. P-22.3, s. 2.

CONTRACTUAL CAPACITY. Persons under the age of majority or with disordered minds lack the power to give consent and therefore cannot contract. G.H.L. Fridman, *The Law of Contract in Canada*, 2d ed. (Toronto: Carswell, 1986) at 126.

CONTRACTUAL PLAN. Any contract or other arrangement for the purchase of shares or units of a mutual fund by payments over a specified period or by a specified number of payments where the amount deducted from any one of the payments as sales charges is larger than the amount that would have been deducted from such payment for sales charges if deductions had been made from each payment at a constant rate for the duration of the plan. *Securities acts.*

CONTRACTUAL PROMISE. An assurance made for, or supported by a consideration. G.H.L. Fridman, *The Law of Contract in Canada*, 2d ed. (Toronto: Carswell, 1986) at 9.

CONTRACT UNDER SEAL. A contract in writing which is signed and sealed by the parties; a specialty contract.

CONTRACTUS EX TURPI CAUSA VEL CONTRA BONOS MORES, NULLUS EST. [L.] A contract based on a base consideration or against morality is null.

CONTRADICT. *v.* To disprove; to prove a fact conflicting with other evidence.

CONTRADICTION IN TERMS. A group of words the parts of which are expressly inconsistent.

CONTRADICTORY EVIDENCE. Evidence disproving earlier evidence.

CONTRAFACTION. *n.* Counterfeiting.

CONTRA FORMAM STATUTI. [L.] Against the form of the statute: the concluding words of an indictment.

CONTRA NEGANTEM PRINCIPIA NON EST DISPUTANDUM. [L.] There is no arguing with a person who refuses to admit first principles.

CONTRA NON VALENTEM AGERE NULLA CURRIT PRAESCRIPTIO. [L.] No time limitation runs against a person unable to bring an action.

CONTRA PACEM. [L.] Against the peace.

CONTRA PROFERENTEM. [L. against the party putting forward] In case of ambiguity, a document is interpreted to the detriment of the party who drafted it.

CONTRARY. *adj.* Against; opposed to.

CONTRATENERE. [L.] To withhold.

CONTRAVENTION. *n.* 1. Failure to comply. 2. Non-compliance.

CONTRE COUP FRACTURE. Stress at a point of impact causes this fracture, usually of bones in the skull. F.A. Jaffe, *A Guide to Pathological Evidence*, 2d ed. (Toronto: Carswell, 1983) at 176 and 177.

CONTRECOUP INJURY. *var.* **CONTRE COUP INJURY.** Injury to an organ which occurs on the side opposite to the one which suffered impact. F.A. Jaffe, *A Guide to Pathological Evidence*, 2d ed. (Toronto: Carswell, 1983) at 173.

CONTRECTATIO REI ALIENAE, ANIMO FURANDI, EST FURTUM. [L.] To appropriate property not one's own, with the intention of stealing, is theft.

CONTRIBUTE. See AMOUNT ~D.

CONTRIBUTION. *n.* 1. Includes a loan, advance, deposit and gift. *Canada Elections Act*, R.S.C. 1985, c. E-2, s. 229(3). 2. Indemnity. 3. The performance by all parties jointly liable, by contract or otherwise, of their shares of the liability. 4. Because the parties are equally liable for a debt and no one can be found primarily liable, the plaintiff obtains only partial reimbursement or recoupment. G.H.L. Fridman & J.G. McLeod, *Restitution* (Toronto: Carswell, 1982) at 347. 5. An amount payable or sum paid under an agreement, usually a pension plan or agreement between governments. 6. Any money or real or personal property that is provided (i) to a political party, constituency association or candidate, or (ii) for the benefit of a political party, constitutency association or candidate with its or the candidate's consent, without compensation from that political party, constituency association or candidate. See ADDITIONAL VOLUNTARY ~; DEFINED ~ BENEFIT; EMPLOYEE ~S; EMPLOYER'S ~; MERITORIOUS ~; RATES OF ~; RETURN OF ~S; VOLUNTARY ADDITIONAL ~; VOLUNTARY ~S.

CONTRIBUTION WEEK. A week for which contributions in respect of the earnings of an insured person during that week are payable and have been paid. *Unemployment Insurance Act*, R.S.C. 1970, c. U-2, s. 2.

CONTRIBUTOR. *n.* 1. An employee required to make contributions to a pension plan. 2. A person who ships stock to a livestock auction sale area, slaughterhouse, feed lot or stockdealer. See DISABLED ~'S CHILD.

CONTRIBUTORY. *n.* A person liable to contribute to the assets of a company that is being wound up.

CONTRIBUTORY. *adj.* Joining in the promotion of a purpose.

CONTRIBUTORY MONTHS. See BASIC NUMBER OF ~.

CONTRIBUTORY NEGLIGENCE. A plaintiff

who fails to take reasonable care contributes to the personal injury complained of. J.V. DiCastri, *Occupiers' Liability* (Vancouver: Burroughs/Carswell, 1980) at 258.

CONTRIBUTORY PENSION BENEFIT. A pension benefit or part of a pension benefit to which a member is required to make contributions under the terms of a pension plan. *Pension Benefits Act*, S.N.B. 1987, c. P-5.1, s. 1.

CONTRIBUTORY PENSION PLAN. A plan for pension of employees to which employees themselves contribute as well as employer.

CONTRIBUTORY SERVICE. Service for which an employee receives remuneration from an employer and makes the required contributions as specified by this Act. *The Municipal Employees' Superannuation Act*, R.S.S. 1978, c. M-26, s. 2.

CONTROL. *v.* With reference to a noxious or nuisance weed, to (i) carry out measures designed to inhibit propagation of the weed, (ii) destroy the weed, or (iii) carry out measures prescribed by an inspector for the control of the weed. *Weed Control Act*, R.S.A. 1980, c. W-6, s. 1.

CONTROL. *n.* 1. Power to direct. 2. In respect of a body corporate, means (a) control in any manner that results in control in fact, whether directly through the ownership of shares, stocks, equities or securities or indirectly through a trust, a contract, the ownership of shares, stocks, equities or securities of another body corporate or otherwise, or (b) the ability to appoint, elect or cause the appointment or election of a majority of the directors of the body corporate, whether or not that ability is exercised. See EFFECTIVE ~; EXPORT ~ LIST; FIRE ~ AUTHORITY; GAS HAZARD ~ STANDARDS; MEDICAL ~; OPERATIONAL ~; SERVICE ~; SURVEY ~; UNDER ~; USER ~.

CONTROL AREA. A controlled airspace extending upwards vertically from a specified height above the surface of the earth and designated as a control area in the Designated Airspace Handbook issued under the authority of the Minister. *Air Regulations*, C.R.C., c. 2, s. 101.

CONTROL CIRCUIT. The circuit that carries the electric signals directing the performance of a control device, but does not carry the power which the device controls. *Power Corporation Act*, R.R.O. 1980, Reg. 794, s. 0.

CONTROL DEVICE. 1. As the context may require, a parking control device or traffic control device. *Department of Public Works Act*, S.M. 1974, c. 45, s. 2. 2. A device that will safely

disconnect an electrical facility from its source of energy. *Canada Electrical Safety Regulations*, C.R.C., c. 998, s. 2.

CONTROL SYSTEM. See DRIVER-OPERATOR ACCELERATOR ~.

CONTROL ZONE. See TEMPORARY ~.

CONTROLLED-ACCESS HIGHWAY. *var.* **CONTROLLED ACCESS HIGHWAY.** 1. A highway (a) on to which persons have a right to enter from abutting land, and (b) from which persons have a right to enter on to abutting land, only at fixed locations. 2. The highway or portions designated or designed for through traffic. *Highway Act*, R.S.B.C. 1979, c. 167, s. 55. 3. A provincial highway.

CONTROLLED AIRPORT. An airport at which an air traffic control unit is provided. *Air Regulations*, C.R.C., c. 2, s. 101.

CONTROLLED AIRSPACE. An airspace of defined dimensions within which air traffic control service is provided. *Air Regulations*, C.R.C., c. 2, s. 101.

CONTROLLED APRON. An apron at an airport where apron traffic control service is provided. *Airport Traffic Regulations*, C.R.C., c. 886, s. 64.

CONTROLLED COMPANY. A company is controlled by another company or person or by two or more companies if, but only if, (a) shares of the first-mentioned company carrying more than fifty per cent of the votes for the election of directors are held, otherwise than by way of security only, by or for the benefit of that other company or person or by or for the benefit of those other companies; and (b) the votes carried by such shares are sufficient, if exercised, to elect a majority of the board of directors of the first-mentioned company. *Companies Act*, R.S.M. 1970, c. C160, s. 117.

CONTROLLED CORPORATION. See SUBSIDIARY ~.

CONTROLLED DRUG. Any drug or other substance included in Schedule G. *Food and Drug Act*, R.S.C. 1985, c. F-27, s. 38.

CONTROLLED FINANCIAL CORPORATION. See SUBSIDIARY ~.

CONTROLLED FOREIGN AFFILIATE. At any time, of a taxpayer resident in Canada means a foreign affiliate of the taxpayer that was, at that time, controlled, directly or indirectly in any manner whatever, by (i) the taxpayer, (ii) the taxpayer and not more than four other persons resident in Canada, or (iii) a related group of which the taxpayer was a member. *Income Tax Act*, R.S.C. 1952, c. 148 (as am. S.C. 1974-75-76, c. 26, s. 59), s. 95.

CONTROLLED OPERATION. See SUBSIDIARY ~.

CONTROLLED PRODUCT. Hazardous material which is regulated under a workplace hazardous materials information system. D. Robertson, *Ontario Health and Safety Guide* (Toronto: Richard De Boo Ltd., 1988) at 5-86.

CONTROLLER. *n.* 1. An official who examines and verifies the accounts of other officials. 2. A device or a group of devices for controlling in some predetermined manner the electic power delivered to the apparatus to which it is connected. *Power Corporation Act*, R.R.O. 1980, Reg. 794, s. 0. See COMPTROLLER.

CONTROLLING INTEREST. The interest that a person has in a corporation when that person beneficially owns, directly or indirectly, or exercises control or direction over, equity shares of the corporation carrying more than 10 per cent (or in some statutes, 25 per cent) of the voting rights attached to all equity shares of the corporation for the time being outstanding.

CONTROL LIST. The Canadian Cultural Property Export Control List established under the Act. *Cultural Property Export and Import Act*, R.S.C. 1985, c. C-51, s. 2. See AREA ~, IMPORT ~.

CONTROL OF CORPORATION. Beneficial ownership of more than 50% of its issued capital, having full voting rights in all circumstances, by (a) one person; or (b) a group of persons not dealing with each other at arm's length. *Forest Act*, R.S.B.C. 1979, c. 140, s. 1.

CONTROL ORDER. Order the person to whom it is directed to do any one or more of the following, namely, (a) to limit or control the rate of addition, emission or discharge of the contaminant into the natural environment in accordance with the directions set out in the order; (b) to stop the addition, emission or discharge of the contaminant into the natural environment, (i) permanently, (ii) for a specified period, or (iii) in the circumstances set out in the order; (c) to comply with any directions set out in the order relating to the manner in which the contaminant may be added, emitted or discharged into the natural environment; (d) to comply with any directions set out in the order relating to the procedures to be followed in the control or elimination of the addition, emission or discharge of the contaminant into the natural environment; and (e) to install, replace or alter any equipment or thing designed to control or eliminate the addition, emission or discharge of the contaminant into the natural environment.

Environmental Protection Act, R.S.O. 1980, c. 141, s. 113.

CONTROL PANEL. The portion of the external surface of a microwave oven on which the user controls are mounted. *Radiation Emitting Devices Regulations*, C.R.C., c. 1370, s. 1.

CONTROL PERSON. Any person or company or any combination of persons and companies holding (i) a sufficient number of any of the securities of an issuer so as to affect materially the control of that issuer; or (ii) more than 20% of the voting rights attached to all voting securities of the issuer for the time being outstanding, except where there is evidence showing that the holding of those voting rights does not affect materially the control of that issuer. *Securities acts.*

CONTROL PROJECT. See WATER ~.

CONTROL PRODUCT. Any product, device, organism, substance or thing that is manufactured, represented, sold or used as a means for directly or indirectly controlling, preventing, destroying, mitigating, attracting or repelling any pest, and includes (a) any compound or substance that enhances or modifies or is intended to enhance or modify the physical or chemical characteristics of a control product to which it is added, and (b) any active ingredient used for the manufacture of a control product. *Pest Control Products Act*, R.S.C. 1985, c. P-9, s. 2.

CONTROL STATION. Includes (a) a radiotelegraph room, and (b) any other enclosed space that houses (i) a compass, a direction-finder, radar equipment, a steering wheel or other similar equipment used in navigation, (ii) a central indicator connected with a system for the detection of fire or smoke, or (iii) an emergency generator. *Hull Construction Regulations*, C.R.C., c. 1431, s. 2.

CONTROL STATUS. With respect to a person, whether or not the person is Canadian controlled as determined under this Act and the regulations. *Canadian Ownership and Control Determination Act*, R.S.C. 1985, c. C-20, s. 2.

CONTROL WORKS. See WATER ~; WATER POLLUTION ~.

CONTROL VALVE. See ELECTRICALLY SUPERVISED ~.

CONTROL ZONE. A controlled airspace extending upwards vertically from the surface of the earth and designated as a control zone in the Designated Airspace Handbook issued under the authority of the Minister. *Air Regulations*, C.R.C., c. 2, s. 101.

CONTUMACY. *n.* Failure or refusal to obey an order or to attend court as required.

CONTUSION. *n.* Injury to a tissue with no surface disruption. F.A. Jaffe, *A Guide to Pathological Evidence*, 2d ed. (Toronto: Carswell, 1983) at 10.

CONVALESCENT PERSON. A person whose condition, in the opinion of a medical practitioner, has passed the acute or emergency state and is improving or can be improved by continued medical and skilled nursing care in a convalescent unit or a hospital for convalescent patients. *Public Hospitals Act*, R.R.O. 1980, Reg. 865, s. 1.

CONVENIENCE. See FLAG OF ~.

CONVENTIO. *n.* [L.] A covenant; an agreement.

CONVENTION. *n.* 1. An agreement between states which is intended to be binding in international law. P.W. Hogg, *Constitutional Law of Canada*, 2d ed. (Toronto: Carswell, 1985) at 241. 2. A rule of the Constitution which prescribes the way legal powers should be exercised but are not enforced by the courts. P.W. Hogg, *Constitutional Law of Canada*, 2d ed. (Toronto: Carswell, 1985) at 12. 3. A meeting, assembly. See BERNE ~; EUROPEAN ~ ON HUMAN RIGHTS; GENEVA ~S; HAGUE ~S; LOAD LINE ~; 1968 ~; SAFETY ~; SEAMEN'S ARTICLES ~; SEAMEN'S REPATRIATION ~; SUB-JUDICE ~; UNIVERSAL COPYRIGHT ~; UNIVERSAL POSTAL ~.

CONVENTIONAL. *adj.* Not found in the usual legal sources, i.e. statutes or decided cases. P.W. Hogg, *Constitutional Law of Canada*, 2d ed. (Toronto: Carswell, 1985) at 191.

CONVENTIONAL BOUNDARY. A boundary consisting of a straight line or a series of straight lines of fixed direction and length conforming as nearly as possible to the natural boundary, but eliminating minor sinuosities. *Land Act*, R.S.B.C. 1979, s. 214, s. 1.

CONVENTIONAL BOUNDARY-LINE. *var.* **CONVENTIONAL BOUNDARY LINE.** Those portions of the boundary marked on the ground by survey monuments and shown on the map-sheets by a series of straight lines connecting the survey monuments.

CONVENTIONAL INTERNATIONAL LAW. (a) Any convention, treaty or other international agreement that is in force and to which Canada is a party, or (b) any convention, treaty or other international agreement that is in force and the provisions of which Canada has agreed to accept and apply in an armed conflict in which it is involved. *Criminal Code*, R.S.C. 1985, c. C-46,

s. 7(3.76) as added by R.S.C. 1985 (3d Supp.), c. 30, s. 1.

CONVENTION AREA. All waters, other than territorial waters, of the North Pacific Ocean including the adjacent seas. *North Pacific Fisheries Convention Act*, R.S.C. 1985, c. F-18, s. 2.

CONVENTION MATERIALS. (a) Banners, flags, papers, shields, stand decorations, backdrops or other decorations, (b) stationery, paper clips, pens, pencils and similar items but does not include office machines, and (c) identification badges. *Foreign Organizations Remission Order*, C.R.C., c. 766, s. 2.

CONVENTION REFUGEE. A person who, by reason of well-founded fear of persecution for reasons of race, religion, nationality, membership in a particular social group or political opinion, (a) is outside the country of his nationality and is unable or, by reason of such fear, is unwilling to avail himself of the protection of that country, or (b) not having a country of nationality, is outside the country of his former habitual residence and is unable or, by reason of such fear, is unwilling to return to that country. *Immigration Act*, R.S.C. 1985, c. I-2, s. 2.

CONVENTION WATERS. 1. The territorial waters and the high seas off the western coasts of Canada and the United States and the southern and western coasts of Alaska. *Northern Pacific Halibut Fisheries Convention Act*, R.S.C. 1985, c. F-19, s. 2. 2. The waters of the Pacific Ocean north of the thirtieth parallel of north latitude, and includes the Bering Sea, the Okhotsk Sea and the Sea of Japan. *Pacific Fur Seals Convention Act*, R.S.C. 1985, c. F-33, s. 2. 3. Waters defined in Article 1 of the Convention. *Pacific Salmon Fisheries Convention Act*, R.S.C. 1985, c. F-20, s. 2.

CONVENTIO PRIVATORUM NON POTEST PUBLICO JURI DEROGARE. [L.] No private agreement can derogate from the rights of the public.

CONVENTIO VINCIT LEGEM. [L.] An express agreement prevails against the law.

CONVERTER. See CATALYTIC ~.

CONVERSATION. *n.* Behaviour, conduct. See CRIMINAL ~.

CONVERSE. *n.* The subject and predicate in a proposition are transposed, i.e. the converse of "X is Y" is "Y is X".

CONVERSION. *n.* 1. A wrong committed when one person converts to personal use, or wrongfully deprives a second person of the use and possession of that second person's goods. E.L.G. Tyler & N.E. Palmer, eds., *Crossley Vaines' Personal Property*, 5th ed. (London: Butterworths, 1973) at 19. 2. Includes intentionally changing the identity of a chattel by destruction, consumption or other physical alteration. John G. Fleming, *The Law of Torts*, 6th ed. (Sydney: The Law Book Company Limited, 1983) at 56. 3. In respect of a vessel, means a conversion or major alteration in Canada by a taxpayer in accordance with plans approved in writing by the Minister of Regional Industrial Expansion for the purposes of this Act. *Income Tax Act*, R.S.C. 1952, c. 148 (as am. S.C. 1968-69, c. 28, s. 105), s. 13(21)(a). See COST OF ~; RE~; SNOWMOBILE ~ VEHICLE.

CONVERSION AXLE. A mechanical device consisting of a single axle designed to convert a two-axle power unit into a three-axle power unit. *The Vehicles Act*, R.S.S. 1978, c. V-3, s. 2.

CONVERSION UNIT. A mechanical device consisting of a single axle designed to convert a two-axle vehicle into a three-axle vehicle. *Highway Traffic Act*, R.S.O. 1980, c. 198, s. 1.

CONVERT. *v.* To change shares into shares of another class, in the manner specified in the share provisions. H. Sutherland, D.B. Horsley & J.M. Edmiston, eds., *Fraser's Handbook on Canadian Company Law*, 7th ed. (Toronto: Carswell, 1985) at 76.

CONVERTIBLE. *n.* A passenger car having a top or roof that can be installed, erected, folded, retracted, dismantled or removed at the convenience of the user, but excludes an open-body type vehicle. *Motor Vehicle Safety Regulations*, C.R.C., c. 1038, s. 210.

CONVERTIBLE MORTGAGE. A mortgage in which the lender has the option to purchase the property at a certain price, usually the market value of the property when the term of the mortgage began. D.J. Donahue & P.D. Quinn, *Real Estate Practice in Ontario*, 4th ed. (Toronto: Butterworths, 1990) at 232.

CONVERTIBLE SECURITY. 1. A security that is convertible into or exchangeable for a security of another class or that carries the right or obligation to acquire a security of another class, whether or not (a) the right to convert or exchange or the right or obligation to acquire is conditional, or (b) the same issuer has issued both classes of securities, and, for purposes of this definition, a security that is convertible into a security of another class shall be deemed to be convertible into a security of each class into which the latter security may be converted, directly or indirectly, through securities of one or more classes of securities that are themselves convertible. *Securities Act*, S.B.C. 1985, c. 83, s. 74. 2. In relation to a security of a particular class: (i) a security convertible into or exchangeable for a security of that class prior to the

expiration of the bid; (ii) a security carrying a warrant or right to acquire or to convert into or exchange for a security of that class that is exercisable prior to expiration of the bid; or (iii) an option, warrant, right or subscription privilege to acquire or to convert into or exchange for a security of that class or a security mentioned in subclause (i) or (ii) that is exercisable prior to expiration of the bid.

CONVEY. *v.* 1. To create a property right or change it between persons. 2. Applied to any person, means the execution by that person of every necessary or suitable assurance for conveying or disposing to another land of or in which the first person is seised or entitled to a contingent right, either for the first person's whole estate or for any less estate, together with the performance of all formalities required by law to validate the conveyance. *Trustee acts*. 3. Includes the granting, assigning, releasing, surrendering, leasing or disposing of land in Ontario, agreeing to sell land in Ontario, or the giving of an option upon or with respect to any land in Ontario, whether the effect of any of the foregoing is to bring into existence an interest of any kind in land or is only for the purpose of giving effect to or formal recognition to any interest of whatsoever kind that theretofore existed in land, but "convey" does not include any transfer of land for the purpose only of securing a debt or loan, or any transfer by a creditor for the purpose only of returning land that had been used as security for a debt or loan. *Land Transfer Tax Act*, R.S.O. 1980, s. 231, s. 1.

CONVEYANCE. *n.* 1. Any instrument by which a freehold or leasehold estate, or other interest in real estate, may be transferred or affected. 2. Includes transfer, assignment, delivery over, payment, gift, grant, alienation, bargain, charge, incumbrance, limitation of use or uses of, in, to or out of real property or personal property by writing or otherwise. 3. Includes ships, vessels, aircraft, trains, and motor and other vehicles. See DOCUMENT OF ~; FIXED ~; FRAUDULENT ~; MAIL ~; RE~; SHAFT ~; TOWED ~; VOLUNTARY ~.

CONVEYANCE OF LAND. Unless an exception is specially made therein, includes all houses, outhouses, edifices, barns, stables, yards, gardens, orchards, commons, trees, woods, underwoods, mounds, fences, hedges, ditches, ways, waters, watercourses, lights, liberties, privileges, easements, profits, commodities, emoluments, hereditaments and appurtenances whatsoever to such land belonging or in anywise appertaining, or with such land demised, held, used, occupied and enjoyed or taken or known as part or parcel thereof, and, if the conveyance purports to convey an estate in fee simple, also the reversion and reversions, remainder and remainders, yearly and other rents, issues and profits of the same land and of every part and parcel thereof, and all the estate, right, title, interest, inheritance, use, trust, property, profit, possession, claim and demand whatsoever of the grantor into, out of or upon the same land, and every part and parcel thereof, with their and every of their appurtenances. *Conveyancing and Law of Property Act*, R.S.O. 1980, c. 90, s. 15.

CONVEYANCE ORDER. An order for the conveyance of distressed seamen issued to the master of a British ship. *Distressed Seamen Regulations*, C.R.C., c. 1420, s. 2.

CONVEYANCER. *n.* A paralegal or lawyer whose chief practice is conveyancing.

CONVEYANCE SYSTEM. The whole of the pipes used for the conveyance of gas to the point of junction with a distribution network, including the equipment, machines, structures, gasometers, meters and other devices and accessories connected therewith. *Gas Distribution Act*, R.S.Q. 1977, c. D-10, s. 1.

CONVEYANCING. *n.* Part of a lawyer's business which concerns alienating and transmitting property and other rights from one person to another.

CONVEYING PURPOSE. The carriage of water for licensees. *Water Act*, R.S.B.C. 1979, c. 429, s. 1.

CONVEYOR. *n.* A device that transports material into or within a cavity. *Radiation Emitting Devices Regulations*, C.R.C., c. 1370, s. 1.

CONVICT. *v.* To find guilty of offence.

CONVICT. *n.* A person against whom judgment of imprisonment has been pronounced or recorded by a court. See SERVICE ~.

CONVICTED. *adj.* 1. Includes an adjudgment of delinquency under the Juvenile Delinquents Act (Canada) for contravening a provision or enactment referred to in this section and the granting of an absolute or conditional discharge. *Wildlife Act*, S.B.C. 1982, c. 57, s. 25. 2. Does not include the case of a condemnation under foreign law by reason of contumacy. *Extradition Act*, R.S.C. 1985, c. E-23, s. 2.

CONVICTION. *n.* 1. Finding of guilt for, or a plea of guilty to, an offence in respect of which a conditional discharge is granted. 2. Does not include the case of a condemnation under foreign law by reason of contumacy. *Extradition Act*, R.S.C. 1985, c. E-23, s. 2. See CERTIFICATE OF ~; DATE OF ~; FIRST ~; SECOND ~; SUBSEQUENT ~; THIRD ~.

CONVOCATION. *n.* A regular or special meeting of the benchers convened for the purpose of transacting business of the Society. *Law Society Act*, R.S.O. 1980, c. 233, s. 1.

CONVOY. *n.* Ships of war sent by a country in wartime to escort and protect merchant ships which belong to that country.

COOK. See SHIP'S ~.

COOK ADM. *abbr.* Cook, Admiralty (Que.), 1873-1884.

COOKING UNIT. See SEPARATE BUILT-IN ~.

COOLER. See BULK MILK ~; WATER ~.

COOLING-OFF PERIOD. *var.* **COOLING OFF PERIOD.** 1. An opportunity to resile from a contract and cancel it within a specified time period. G.H.L. Fridman, *Sale of Goods in Canada*, 3d ed. (Toronto: Carswell, 1986) at 492. 2. The time before which a strike or lock-out may begin.

COOLING TIME. See VIRTUAL ~.

COOLING WATER. Water, from an air-conditioning apparatus or from a cooling or refrigeration process, which causes only thermal pollution. *An Act to Amend the Act Respecting the Communauté Urbaine de Montréal and Other Legislation*, S.Q. 1985, c. 31, s. 11.

CO-OP. *abbr.* Cooperative.

COOPERANT. *n.* Any expert, adviser, teacher, tradesman or other person engaged for service under the Canadian Development Cooperation Program. *Technical and Educational Assistance Regulations*, C.R.C., c. 351, s. 2.

COOPERATIVE. *var.* **CO-OPERATIVE.** *n.* 1. Corporation in which persons having economic and social needs in common unite for the prosecution of an enterprise according to the rules of cooperative action to meet those needs. *Cooperatives Act*, S.Q. 1982, c. 26, s. 3. 2. A rental residential property other than a condominium, that is (a) owned or leased or otherwise held by or on behalf of more than one person, where any owner or lessee has the right to present or future exclusive possession of a unit in the rental residential property, or (b) owned or leased or otherwise held by a corporation having more than one shareholder or member where any one of the shareholders or members, by reason of owning shares in or being a member of the corporation, has the right to present or future exclusive possession of a unit in the rental residential property. See AGRICULTURAL OPERATIONS ~; CONSUMER'S ~; DIRECT CHARGE ~; INSIDER OF A ~; INVESTMENT ~; LAND ~.

COOPERATIVE AGRICULTURAL ASSOCIATION. An agricultural cooperative governed by the Cooperatives Act. *Cooperatives Act*, S.Q. 1982, c. 26, s. 314.

COOPERATIVE ASSOCIATION. *var.* **CO-OPERATIVE ASSOCIATION.** 1. Any cooperative association or federation incorporated by or pursuant to an Act of Parliament or of the legislature of a province. *Canada Cooperative Associations Act*, R.S.C. 1985, c. C-40, s. 3. 2. A co-operative corporation of producers of farm products to which the Co-operative Corporations Act applies and which was incorporated for the purpose of grading, cleaning, packing, storing, drying, processing or marketing farm products. See FEDERAL ~; PROVINCIAL ~; RURAL GAS ~.

COOPERATIVE BASIS. *var.* **CO-OPERATIVE BASIS.** The carrying on of an enterprise organized, operated and administered in accordance with the following principles and methods: (a) except in the case of an association the charter by-laws of which provide otherwise, each member or delegate has only one vote, (b) no member or delegate may vote by proxy except that a member of an association may vote by proxy for the election of directors if the charter by-laws of the association so provide, (c) interest or dividends on share or loan capital is limited to the percentage fixed in the articles of incorporation or application for continuation, or by-laws of the organization, (d) the enterprise is operated as nearly as possible at cost after providing for reasonable reserves and the payment or crediting of interest or dividends on share or loan capital, and (e) any surplus funds arising from the business of the organization, after providing for such reasonable reserves and interest or dividends, unless used to maintain or improve services of the organization for its members or donated for community welfare or the propagation of cooperative principles, are distributed in whole or in part among the members or the members and patrons of the organization in proportion to the volume of business they have done with or through the organization.

COOPERATIVE BODY. A federation of savings and credit unions, a cooperative association or a regional or provincial cooperative agricultural association, a federation of cooperative associations or of cooperative agricultural associations, a mutual association, or a federation of such associations, and an association or corporation incorporated in Canada the majority of the common shares of which are held, directly or indirectly, by cooperative institutions. *An Act respecting the Fédération de Québec des Unions régionales des Caisses Populaires Desjardin*, S.Q. 1979, c. 46, s. 2.

COOPERATIVE CORPORATION. 1. A corporation that was incorporated by or under a law of Canada or a province providing for the establishment of the corporation or respecting the establishment of cooperative corporations for the purpose of marketing (including processing incident to or connected therewith) natural products belonging to or acquired from its members or customers, of purchasing supplies, equipment or household necessaries for or to be sold to its members or customers or of performing services for its members or customers, if (a) the statute by or under which it was incorporated, its charter, articles of association or by-laws or its contracts with its members or its members and customers held forth the prospect that payments would be made to them in proportion to patronage, (b) none of its members (except other cooperative corporations) have more than one vote in the conduct of the affairs of the corporation, and (c) at least 90 per cent of its members are individuals, other cooperative corporations or corporations or partnerships that carry on the business of farming and at least 90 per cent of its shares, if any, are held by such persons or partnerships. *Income Tax Act*, R.S.C. 1952, c. 148 (as am. S.C. 1970-71-72, c. 63), s. 136. 2. Includes a corporation as defined in the Company Act that is the owner of land, where a majority of the persons entitled to occupy all or a portion of that land, or the buildings on it, is, or is intended or entitled to become, the shareholders or owners, directly or indirectly, of that corporation. *Real Estate Act*, R.S.B.C. 1979, c. 356, s. 1.

COOPERATIVE CREDIT SOCIETY. A cooperative organization the objects of which include the making of loans to, and the receiving of deposits from, its members. *Cooperative Credit Associations Act*, R.S.C. 1985, c. C-41, s. 2. See CENTRAL ~; FEDERATION OF COOPERATIVE CREDIT SOCIETIES; LOCAL ~.

COOPERATIVE FARM ASSOCIATION. A cooperative association incorporated under the legislation of any province, having not less than three members engaged in farming and having a majority of members principally occupied in farming, the principal object and business of the association being (a) farming on a cooperative basis, or (b) purchasing or using farm machinery, buildings or land or making improvements to land primarily for the benefit of its members as farmers. *Farm Syndicates Credit Regulations*, C.R.C., c. 662, s. 2.

COOPERATIVE FEDERALISM. Relationships between the executives of the national and provincial governments to develop mechanisms to continuously redistribute powers and resources without resorting to the courts or the constitutional amending process. P.W. Hogg, *Constitutional Law of Canada*, 2d ed. (Toronto: Carswell, 1985) at 106 and 107.

COOPERATIVE HOUSING ASSOCIATION. A cooperative association incorporated under the laws of Canada or any province, having as its principal aim or object the construction, on a cooperative basis, of single-family dwellings. *Veterans' Land Act*, R.S.C. 1970, c. V-4, s. 65.

CO-OPERATIVE HOUSING CORPORA-TION. An association, incorporated subject to the terms and conditions of the legislation governing such incorporation, and formed and operated for the purpose of providing its members with the right to inhabit, by reason of ownership of shares therein, a housing unit owned by the corporation. To qualify as a principal residence, a share in such a corporation must have been acquired by a taxpayer solely to acquire the right to inhabit a housing unit owned by the corporation. *Interpretation Bulletin IT-120R, December 6, 1976.* See NON-PROFIT ~.

COOPERATIVE HOUSING PROJECT. A housing project built or acquired by a cooperative association incorporated under the laws of Canada or of any province. *National Housing Act*, R.S.C. 1985, c. N-11, s. 2.

CO-OPERATIVE INSURANCE COMPANY. An insurer incorporated or registered under The Co-operative Associations Act or any former Co-operative Associations Act. *The Saskatchewan Insurance Act*, R.S.S. 1978, c. S-26, s. 2.

CO-OPERATIVE LISTING. An exclusive listing which permits one agent to use the facilities of sub-agents appointed in one or more ways. B.J. Reiter, R.C.B. Risk & B.N. McLellan, *Real Estate Law*, 3d ed. (Toronto: Emond Montgomery, 1986) at 75.

COOPERATIVE MARKETING CONTRACT. A contract entered into by a person with an association to deliver to or sell through the association any thing caught, grown, made or produced by him, or on his behalf, or in which he has an interest, that person being one of a number of persons with whom the association has entered into contracts of a similar nature. *Cooperative Association Act*, R.S.B.C. 1979, c. 66, s. 1.

COOPERATIVE PLAN. An agreement or arrangement for the marketing of agricultural products that provides for (a) equal returns for primary producers for agricultural products of the like grade and quality, (b) the return to primary producers of the proceeds of the sale of all agricultural products delivered under the agreement or arrangement and produced during the year, after deduction of processing, carrying and selling costs and reserves, if any, and (c) an initial payment to primary producers of the agricultural product to which the agreement relates of an amount fixed by regulations made by the Governor in Council on the recommendation of the Minister with respect to a reasonable amount that does not exceed the amount estimated by the Minister to be the amount by which the average wholesale price according to grade and quality of the agricultural product for the year in respect of which the initial payment will be made will exceed the processing, carrying and selling costs thereof for that year. *Agricultural Products Cooperative Marketing Act*, R.S.C. 1985, c. A-5, s. 2.

CO-OPERATIVE PRINCIPLES. (i) Open membership subject to such natural limitations as may be prescribed by the constitution of the society; (ii) one member–one vote, with no proxy voting; (iii) low interest on capital; and (iv) the return or credit to members, in proportion to patronage, of the net surplus of the society remaining after provision is made for expenses of operation, bonuses, interest on capital, if any, and reserves, or the collective use of any net surplus for the social or economic benefit of members or the disposal of it for any of those objects. *Co-operative Societies (Amendment) Act*, S. Nfld. 1975-76, c. 71, s. 1.

COOPERATIVE RESIDENCE. A self contained dwelling unit, in a housing project consisting of self-contained dwelling units, and owned by a cooperative association incorporated under the Cooperative Association Act. *Home Purchase Assistance Act*, R.S.B.C. 1979, c. 172, s. 1.

COOPERATIVE UNDERTAKING. A cooperative governed by the Cooperatives Act (1982, chapter 26), a cooperative syndicate incorporated under the Cooperative Syndicates Act (R.S.Q., chapter S-38) for economic purposes other than credit and providence and a federation of cooperatives or a confederation of federations of those cooperatives. *Cooperatives Act*, S.Q. 1982, c. 26, s. 321.

COOPERATIVE UNIT. The interest of a person in a cooperative corporation that includes (a) a right to use or occupy a part of the land that the cooperative corporation owns or has an interest in; or (b) a present or future right of ownership of one or more shares of, or other evidence of ownership of, an interest in the cooperative corporation. *Real Estate Act*, R.S.B.C. 1979, c. 356, s. 1.

COOPERATOR. See SUBSCRIBING ~.

CO-OP SHARE. A share in the capital stock of an association to which no special preferences, rights, conditions, restrictions, limitations or prohibitions are attached either by the articles of association or application for continuation or amalgamation of the association or by the charter by-laws thereof.

CO-ORDINATE. *adj.* Describing clauses in a statute governed equally by another clause.

CO-ORDINATE MONUMENT. A bronze cap suitably inscribed and (a) imbedded in a reinforced concrete post set in a concrete base, or (b) placed as prescribed by regulations under surveys legislation.

CO-ORDINATE SURVEY. A survey made for the purpose of establishing the location of points on the surface of the earth by geographic or grid co-ordinates. *Surveys Act*, R.R.O. 1980, Reg. 929, s. 1.

CO-ORDINATE SURVEY SYSTEM. A system of plane rectangular co-ordinates for locating points on the earth's surface.

CO-OWNER. *n.* The person who owns property in common or jointly with one or more other persons. See JOINT TENANT; TENANCY IN COMMON.

COPARCENER. *n.* A person to whom an estate in common with one or more other persons has descended.

COPIED. *adj.* Includes reproduced by a photographic process. *Registry Act*, R.S.N.S. 1967, c. 265, s. 1.

CO-PILOT. *n.* A licensed pilot assigned to duty as a pilot in an aircraft during flight time, other than as (a) a pilot-in-command, or (b) a pilot receiving flying instruction. See FIRST ~; SECOND ~.

COPULATIO VERBORUM INDICAT ACCEPTATIONEM IN EODEM SENSU. [L.] The joining of words shows that their meaning is to be understood in the same sense.

COPY. *n.* 1. A document written or taken from another document. 2. A reproduction of the original. 3. In relation to any record, includes a print, whether enlarged or not, from a photographic film of the record. *Canada Evidence Act*, R.S.C. 1985, c. C-5, s. 30(12). See CERTIFIED ~; EXAMINED ~; TRUE ~.

COPYRIGHT. *n.* 1. The sole right to produce or reproduce the work or any substantial part thereof in any material form whatever, to perform, or in the case of a lecture to deliver, the work or any substantial part thereof in public or, if the work is unpublished, to publish the work or any substantial part thereof, and includes the

sole right (a) to produce, reproduce, perform or publish any translation of the work, (b) in the case of a dramatic work, to convert it into a novel or other non-dramatic work, (c) in the case of a novel or other non-dramatic work, or of an artistic work, to convert it into a dramatic work, by way of performance in public or otherwise, (d) in the case of a literary, dramatic or musical work, to make any record, perforated roll, cinematograph film or other contrivance by means of which the work may be mechanically performed or delivered, (e) subject to subsection (2), in the case of any literary, dramatic, musical or artistic work, to reproduce, adapt and publicly present the work by cinematograph, if the author has given the work an original character, and (f) in the case of any literary, dramatic, musical or artistic work, to communicate the work by radio communication, and to authorize any such acts. *Copyright Act*, R.S.C. 1985, c. C-42, s. 3. 2. In the case of a work that according to the law in force immediately before January 1, 1924 has not been published before that date and statutory copyright wherein depends on publication, includes the right at common law, if any, to restrain publication or other dealing with the work. *Copyright Act*, R.S.C. 1985, c. C-42, s. 71. 3. An intangible incorporeal right, like a privilege or franchise, which has no material substance. H.G. Fox, *The Canadian Law of Copyright and Industrial Designs*, 2d ed. (Toronto: Carswell, 1967) at 286. See OWNER OF A ~; UNIVERSAL ~ CONVENTION.

COR. *abbr.* [L. coram] In the presence of.

CORAM JUDICE. [L.] In the presence of a judge; before an appropriate or properly constituted court.

CORAM NON JUDICE. [L.] Before a person who is not a judge.

CORAM PARIBUS. [L.] Before one's peers.

CORD. *n.* 1. 128 cubic feet. *Weights and Measures Act*, S.C. 1970-71-72, vol. 1, c. 36, schedule II. 2. The strands forming the plies of a tire. See DETONATING ~; POWER SUPPLY ~; UMBILICAL ~.

CORD SEPARATION. The parting of cords from adjacent rubber compounds. Canada regulations.

CORD SET. A length of flexible cord or power supply cable with an attachment plug connected to one end of it and a cord connector connected to its other end. *Power Corporation Act*, R.R.O. 1980, Reg. 794, s. 0.

CO-RESPONDENT. *n.* A person identified in a divorce pleading as the party involved in a matrimonial offence with a spouse.

COR. JUD. *abbr.* Correspondances Judiciaires (Que.).

CORN. See GRAIN ~; SEED ~.

CORNER. *n.* A point in an intersection of boundaries of land. Surveys Acts. See LOST ~; UNDISPUTED ~.

CORNER LOT. A lot situated at a junction or intersection of two streets.

CORNER POST. See LEGAL ~.

COROLLARY. *n.* A collateral or secondary consequence.

COROLLARY RELIEF. 1. Relief collateral to or secondary to the main relief granted in an action. 2. In divorce, custody or maintenance.

COROLLARY RELIEF PROCEEDING. A proceeding in a court in which either or both former spouses seek a support order or a custody order or both such orders. *Divorce Act*, R.S.C. 1985 (2d Supp.), c. 3, s. 2.

CORONARY. See CAFE~.

CORONARY ARTERY. The artery which arises from the aorta and supplies the heart. F.A. Jaffe, *A Guide to Pathological Evidence*, 2d ed. (Toronto: Carswell, 1983) at 169.

CORONARY THROMBOSIS. Obstruction of a coronary artery by a thrombus. F.A. Jaffe, *A Guide to Pathological Evidence*, 2d ed. (Toronto: Carswell, 1983) at 173.

CORONER. *n.* The official who investigates the death of any person who was killed or died in suspicious circumstances.

CORP. *abbr.* Corporation.

CORP. MGMT. TAX CONF. *abbr.* Canadian Tax Foundation. Corporate Management Tax Conference. Proceedings.

CORPORAL. *n.* In the army, a non-commissioned rank.

CORPORAL. *adj.* Bodily; relating to the body.

CORPORAL OATH. Touching the Bible or other holy book with the hand while taking an oath.

CORPORATE NAME. A name given to a corporation.

CORPORATE PURPOSES. Any effort to influence the voting of members or debenture holders of a corporation at any meeting, to acquire or sell shares or debentures of the corporation, or to effect an amalgamation or reorganization of the corporation. *Company Act*, R.S.B.C. 1979, c. 59, s. 1. See PAID-UP CAPITAL FOR ~.

CORPORATE SEAL. The impression of the company's name on important documents such as share certificates, bonds and debentures. H. Sutherland, D.B. Horsley & J.M. Edmiston, eds., *Fraser's Handbook on Canadian Company Law*, 7th ed. (Toronto: Carswell, 1985) at 339.

CORPORATE SECURITY. Every security interest in personal property or fixtures created by a corporation and contained (i) in a trust deed or other writing to secure bonds, debentures or debenture stock of the corporation or of any other corporation; or (ii) in any bonds, debentures or debenture stock of the corporation as well as in the trust deed or other writing securing the same, or in a trust deed or other writing securing the bonds, debentures or debenture stock of any other corporation; or (iii) in any bonds, debentures or debenture stock or any series of bonds or debentures of the corporation not secured by a separate writing. *Personal Property Security Act*, S.M. 1973, s. 5, s. 1.

CORPORATE VEIL. See PIERCE ~.

CORPORATION. *n.* 1. A legal entity distinct from its shareholders or members with liability separate from its shareholders or members vested with the capacity of continuous succession. 2. A body corporate with or without share capital. See ACTIVE BUSINESS CARRIED ON BY A ~; AGENT ~; AGRICULTURAL ~; AGRICULTURAL OPERATIONS ~; ALBERTA ~; ASSOCIATED ~; BANK SERVICE ~; BUILDING DEVELOPMENT ~; CANADA ~; CANADA DEPOSIT INSURANCE ~; CANADA MORTGAGE AND HOUSING ~; CANADA POST ~; CANADIAN BROADCASTING ~; CANADIAN ~; CASH-MUTUAL ~; CHARITABLE ~; CLOSELY HELD ~; CONSTRAINED SHARE ~; CONTROL OF ~; COOPERATIVE ~; COUNTY ~; CROWN CONTROLLED ~; CROWN ~; CROWN OWNED ~; DEPARTMENTAL ~; DEPOSIT INSURANCE ~; DISTRIBUTING ~; DOMESTIC ~; DOMINION ~; ELEEMOSYNARY ~; EXCLUDED ~; EXECUTIVE OFFICER OF A ~; EXHIBITION ~; EXPORT DEVELOPMENT ~; EXTRA-PROVINCIAL ~; FACTORING ~; FAMILY BUSINESS ~; FAMILY ~; FAMILY FARM ~; FAMILY FARMING ~; FAMILY FISHING ~; FARM CREDIT ~ CANADA; FARM ~; FINANCIAL ~; FINANCIAL INTERMEDIARY ~; FIRE AND CASUALTY ~; FOREIGN CONTROLLED ~; FOREIGN ~; FORMER ~; GOVERNMENT ~; HOLDING ~; INDEPENDENT ~; INSURANCE ~; INVESTMENT ~; LAY ~; LEASING ~; LOAN ~; LOCAL PORT ~; MEMBERSHIP ~; MUNICIPAL ~; MUTUAL ~; MUTUAL FUND ~; MUTUAL INSURANCE ~; NON-PROFIT ~; NON-RESIDENT ~; NORTHERN VILLAGE ~; OFFE-

REE ~; OFFERING ~; OPERATING ~; PARENT ~; PIPE LINE ~; PRINCIPAL-BUSINESS ~; PRIVATE ~; PROFESSIONAL ~; PROVINCIAL ~; PUBLIC ~; PUBLIC SERVICE ~; QUALIFYING ~; REAL ESTATE ~; RESIDENCE OF A ~; SCHOOL ~; SERVICE ~; SMALL BUSINESS ~; SUBSIDIARY CONTROLLED ~; SUBSIDIARY CONTROLLED FINANCIAL ~; SUBSIDIARY ~; SUBSIDIARY WHOLLY OWNED ~; TERRITORIAL ~; TRUST ~; TRUST OR LOAN ~; VENTURE CAPITAL ~; WATER SUPPLY ~.

CORPORATION AGGREGATE. A corporation with several members, created by the Crown through Royal Prerogative or by statute. G.H.L. Fridman, *The Law of Contract in Canada*, 2d ed. (Toronto: Carswell, 1986) at 151.

CORPORATION ASSESSMENT. The assessment of land liable to taxation, of which a corporation is the owner or tenant, and business assessment of a corporation, but does not include the assessment of land that is assessed to a person other than a corporation as a tenant. *Assessment Act*, R.S.O. 1980, c. 31, s. 1.

CORPORATION CONTROLLED BY AN INDIVIDUAL. A corporation that, at the time in respect of which the expression is being applied, was controlled, whether directly or indirectly and whether through holding a majority of the shares of the corporation or of any other corporation or in any other manner whatever, by the individual or by any other person on behalf of the individual. Gift Tax acts.

CORPORATION CONTROLLED BY ANOTHER. A corporation is controlled by another if more than 50 per cent of its issued share capital having full voting rights under all circumstances belongs to the other corporation, to persons with whom the other corporation does not deal at arm's length, or to the other corporation and persons with whom the other corporation does not deal at arm's length. *Taxation Act*, R.S.Q. 1977, c. I-3, s. 739.

CORPORATION CONTROLLED BY THE DECEASED. A corporation that, at the time in respect of which the expression is being applied, was controlled, whether directly or indirectly and whether through holding a majority of the shares of the corporation or of any other corporation or in any other manner whatever, by the deceased or by any other person on behalf of the deceased. Succession Duty or Estate Tax acts.

CORPORATION INCORPORATED IN CANADA. Includes a corporation incorporated in any part of Canada before or after it became part of Canada.

CORPORATION NOT RESIDENT IN CANADA. Any corporation validly incorporated, whatever be the nature and place of its incorporation, (a) of which more than 50 per cent of the shares of its capital stock to which are attached full voting rights are owned by one or more persons not resident in Canada; (b) more than one-half of the directors of which are physical persons who are persons not resident in Canada; (c) more than one-half of the members of which, in the case of a corporation without capital stock, are persons not resident in Canada; or (d) which is controlled directly or indirectly in any manner whatever by one or more persons not resident in Canada. *Land Transfer Duties Act*, R.S.Q. 1977, c. D-17, s. 1.

CORPORATION NUMBER. The number assigned by the Director to a corporation in accordance with the Business Corporations Act. *Business Corporations Act, 1982*, S.O. 1982, c. 4, s. 1.

CORPORATION SOLE. The corporate status granted an individual natural person by the law, which is distinct from that individual's natural personality. The main example is the Crown. G.H.L. Fridman, *The Law of Contract in Canada*, 2d ed. (Toronto: Carswell, 1986) at 151.

CORPOREAL. *adj.* Having an objective, material existence.

CORPOREAL HEREDITAMENT. Tangible property capable of being inherited.

CORPOREAL PROPERTY. Property having a physical existence.

CORPORE ET ANIMO, NEQUE PER SE CORPORE, NEQUE PER SE ANIMO. [L.] Once a domicile is established, it can only be changed by residing in another country together with intending to remain there indefinitely. J.G. McLeod, *The Conflict of Laws* (Calgary: Carswell, 1983) at 779.

CORPS. See MINE RESCUE ~.

CORPS DIPLOMATIQUE. [Fr.] Ambassadors and diplomatic persons at a particular capital.

CORPSE. *n.* The dead body of a person.

CORPUS. *n.* [L.] The capital of a fund in contrast to income.

CORPUS DELICTI. [L. body of the offence] The ingredients of an offence: commonly, the dead body.

CORPUS HUMANUM NON RECIPIT AESTIMATIONEM. [L.] A human body cannot be valued.

CORPUS POSSESSIONIS. [L.] Actual power to direct or retain a thing.

CORRECTION. *n.* In respect of a device that has been sold, means any action taken in respect of the device by the manufacturer or importer thereof after becoming aware that the device (a) is or may be hazardous to health; (b) fails or may fail to conform with any claims made by the manufacturer or importer relating to the effectiveness, benefits, performance characteristics or safety of the device; or (c) does not comply with the Act or these Regulations, to recall or correct the device or to notify the owner or user of the device of the defectiveness thereof. *Medical Devices Regulations*, C.R.C., c. 871, s. 2.

CORRECTIONAL CAMP. Any minimum security facility designated by the minister for the purpose of training or employing persons committed thereto under an order of committal or as a condition of a probation order. *The Corrections Act*, R.S.S. 1978, c. C-40, s. 2.

CORRECTIONAL CENTRE. A lawful place of confinement, jail, prison, lockup, place of imprisonment, camp, correctional institution.

CORRECTIONAL EXTENSION PROGRAM. A correctional program that is operated either wholly or partly outside of a correctional centre to facilitate the rehabilitation of inmates and their return to the community. *Corrections Act*, R.S.N.W.T. 1974, c. C-18, s. 2.

CORRECTIONAL FACILITY. A jail, prison, correctional centre for the custody of offenders.

CORRECTIONAL INSTITUTION. Any building, correctional camp, rehabilitation camp, reformatory, forensic clinic, work site, gaol or place for the reception and lawful custody of inmates.

CORRECTIONAL SERVICE CANADA. The federal body which supervises federal penal institutions, administers court-imposed sentences of two years and greater, preparing offenders for return to society.

CORRESPONDENCE. See PUBLIC ~.

CORRIDOR. See PEDESTRIAN ~; PUBLIC ~.

CORR. JUD. *abbr.* Correspondances judiciaires (1906).

CORROBORATE. *v.* In reference to evidence, to add weight to or strengthen.

CORROBORATION. *n.* Confirmation of a witness's evidence by independent testimony.

CORROSION-RESISTANT MATERIAL. Any material that maintains its original surface characteristics after, (i) repeated exposure to food, soil, moisture or heat, or (ii) exposure to any substance used in cleansing and disinfecting. *Public Health Act*, R.R.O. 1980, Reg. 840, s. 1.

CORROSIVE CHEMICAL. Includes hydrochloric acid, sulphuric acid, sodium hydrogen sulphate, nitric acid, phosphoric acid, acetic acid, trichloracetic acid, formic acid, lactic acid, oxalic acid and salts thereof, sodium hydroxide, potassium hydroxide, ammonia and ammonium hydroxide, phenol, o-cresol, m-cresol and p-cresol, silver nitrate, zinc chloride and iodine. *Hazardous Products (Hazardous Substances) Regulations*, C.R.C., c. 926, s. 2.

CORROSIVE PRODUCT. Any product that contains a corrosive chemical that has a pH of 2.5 or less or 11.5 or more when prepared for use according to the directions on the label of the product or in the manner that is customary or usual. *Hazardous Products (Hazardous Substances) Regulations*, C.R.C., c. 926, s. 2.

CORRUPT. *v.* To alter morals and behaviour from good to bad.

CORRUPT. *adj.* Spoiled; debased; depraved.

CORRUPTING MORALS. (1) The offence of (a) making, printing, publishing, distributing, circulating, or having in his possession for the purpose of publication, distribution or circulation any obscene written matter, picture, model, phonograph record or other thing whatever, or (b) making, printing, publishing, distributing, selling or having in his possession for the purpose of publication, distribution or circulation, a crime comic. (2) The offence of knowingly, without lawful justification or excuse, (a) selling, exposing to public view or having in his possession for such a purpose any obscene written matter, picture, model, phonograph record or other thing whatever, (b) publicly exhibiting a disgusting object or an indecent show, (c) offering to sell, advertising, or publishing an advertisement of, or having for sale or disposal, any means, instructions, medicine, drug or article intended or represented as a method of causing abortion or miscarriage, or (d) advertising or publishing an advertisement of any means, instructions, medicine, drug or article intended or represented as a method for restoring sexual virility or curing venereal diseases or diseases of the generative organs. *Criminal Code*, R.S.C. 1985, c. C-46, s. 163.

CORRUPTION. *n.* Granting of favours inconsistent with official duties.

CORRUPTION OF BLOOD. An effect of attainder, when a person attainted was considered corrupted by the crime, so that the person could no longer hold land, inherit it or leave it to any heirs.

CORRUPT PRACTICE. 1. Bribery, treating,

illegal payment and undue influence. 2. Corrupt practice recognized as such by the law and custom of Parliament.

COSEN. *v.* To cheat; to defraud.

COSENAGE. *n.* The condition of being kin, consanguinity.

CO-SIGNER. *n.* A person who agrees to sign a promissory note, or other agreement, together with the maker and be responsible if the maker should default.

COSMETIC. *n.* Any substance or mixture of substances manufactured, sold or represented for use in cleansing, improving or altering the complexion, skin, hair or teeth, and includes deodorants and perfumes. *Food and Drugs Act,* R.S.C. 1985, c. F-27, s. 2.

COSMETICS. *n.* Goods, whether possessing therapeutic or prophylactic properties or not, commonly or commercially known as toilet articles, preparations or cosmetics, that are intended for use or application for toilet purposes, of for use in connection with the care of the human body, including the hair, nails, eyes, teeth, or any other part or parts thereof, whether for cleansing, deodorizing, beautifying, preserving or restoring, and includes toilet soaps, shaving soaps and shaving creams, skin creams and lotions, shampoos, mouth washes, oral rinses, toothpastes, tooth powders, denture creams and adhesives, antiseptics, bleaches, depilatories, perfumes, scents and similar preparations. *Excise Tax Act,* R.S.C. 1985, c. E-15, s. 2.

COST. *n.* 1. Price; expense. 2. To an insurer of acquiring a mortgage or hypothec includes any amount advanced by the insurer to the borrower by way of loan under the terms of the mortgage or hypothec. *Income Tax Act,* R.S.C. 1952, c. 148 (as am. S.C. 1980-81-82-83, c. 140, s. 96(7)), s. 138(12)(d). 3. Of a loan means the whole of the cost of the loan to the borrower whether the cost is called interest or is claimed as discount, deduction from an advance, commission, brokerage, chattel mortgage and recording fees, fines, penalties or charges for inquiries, defaults or renewals or otherwise, and whether paid to or charged by the lender or paid to or charged by any other person, and whether fixed and determined by the loan contract itself, or in whole or in part by any other collateral contract or document by which the charges, if any, imposed under the loan contract or the terms of the repayment of the loan are effectively varied. *Small Loans Act,* R.S.C. 1970, c. S-11, s. 2. See ACTUAL ~; ADMINISTRATION ~; BENEFIT ~ STATEMENT; CAPITAL ~; ~S; ELIGIBLE ASSET ~; ELIGIBLE ~ OR EXPENSE; ESTIMATED ~; F.O.B. ~; FUTURE ~ OF INSURED SERVICES; OPPORTUNITY ~; ORIGINAL ~ OF THE LAND; OWNER'S PORTION OF THE ~; OWNER'S SHARE OF THE ~; PAST ~ OF INSURED SERVICES; PUBLICATION ~; PURCHASER'S ~ OF A SHARE; RATE OF ~ CHANGE.

COST AMOUNT. 1. To a taxpayer of any property at any time means, except as expressly otherwise provided in this Act, (a) where the property was depreciable property of the taxpayer of a prescribed class, that proportion of the undepreciated capital cost to him of property of that class at that time that the capital cost to him of the property is of the capital cost to him of all property of that class, (b) where the property was capital property (other than depreciable property) of the taxpayer, its adjusted cost base to him at that time, (c) where the property was property described in an inventory of the taxpayer, its value at that time as determined for the purpose of computing his income, (d) where the property was eligible capital property of the taxpayer in respect of a business, the cumulative eligible capital of the taxpayer in respect of the business at that time, (e) where the property was a debt owing to the taxpayer (other than the amount in respect of such property that was deducted under paragraph 20(1)(p) in computing the taxpayer's income for a taxation year ending before that time) or any other right of the taxpayer to receive an amount, the amortized cost of the property to the taxpayer at that time or, where the property does not have an amortized cost to the taxpayer, the amount of the debt or other right that was outstanding at that time (e.1) where the property was a policy loan (within the meaning assigned by paragraph 138(12)(k.1) of an insurer, nil, and (f) in any other case, the cost to the taxpayer of the property as determined for the purpose of computing his income, except to the extent that such cost has been deducted in computing his income for any taxation year ending before that time. *Income Tax Act,* R.S.C. 1952, c. 148 (as am. S.C. 1988, c. 55, s. 188(2)), s. 248(1). 2. (i) In any case where any money or property of the trust has been distributed by the trust to the taxpayer in full satisfaction of the whole of his capital interest or part thereof, as the case may be, (whether on the winding-up of the trust or otherwise), the aggregate of the money so distributed and all amounts each of which is the cost amount to the trust, immediately before the distribution, of each such property so distributed to the taxpayer, and (ii) in any other case, that proportion of the amount, if any, by which the aggregate of all money of the trust on hand immediately before that time and all amounts each of which is the cost amount to the trust, immediately before that time, of each property of the trust exceeds the aggregate of all amounts each of which is the amount of any debt owing by the trust, or of any other obligation of the trust to pay any amount, that was outstanding immediately before that time, that (A) the fair market value at that time of the capital interest or part thereof, as the case may be, in the trust, is of (B) the fair market value at that time of all capital interests in the trust. *Income Tax Act*, R.S.C. 1952, c. 148 (as am. S.C. 1988, c. 55, s. 75), s. 108(1)(d). 3. With respect to an eligible security issued pursuant to a certificate of eligibility: (i) if the eligible security is issued for consideration consisting only of money, the amount of money paid by the eligible investor for the eligible security, including any applicable underwriters' fees paid by the eligible investor for the eligible security but not including: (A) any brokerage or custody fee or similar charge; or (B) any amount paid to acquire a warrant that evidenced the right to acquire the eligible security; or (ii) if the eligible security is issued for consideration consisting only of property or past service or partly of money and partly of property or past service, an amount not exceeding the amount, if any, by which the aggregate of: (A) the amount, if any, of money paid by the eligible investor for the eligible security, as determined in accordance with subclause (i); and (B) the fair market value of the property or past service in consideration for which the eligible security was issued; exceeds the fair market value of any consideration issued or granted by the eligible issuer other than an eligible security or a warrant that evidences the right to acquire an eligible security. *Stock Savings Tax Credit Act*, S.S. 1986, c. S-59.1, s. 2. See DISPOSITION ~.

COST BASE. See ADJUSTED ~; ADJUSTED ~ OF CAPITAL PROPERTY; ADJUSTED ~ OF DEPRECIABLE PROPERTY.

COST OF BENEFIT. See ACCRUED BENEFIT COST METHOD; BASIC ~.

COST OF BORROWING. 1. In relation to any loan or advance, (a) the interest or discount thereon, and (b) such charges in connection therewith as are payable by the borrower to a bank or to any person from whom a bank receives any charges directly or indirectly and as are prescribed to be included in the cost of borrowing. *Bank Act*, R.S.C. 1985, c. B-1, s. 202(2). 2. (a) When used in relation to variable credit, the charges that a borrower or buyer is required to pay on the unpaid balance from time to time; or (b) when used in relation to a form of credit other than variable credit, the amount by which the total sum that borrower is required to pay, if the payments required are made as they become due, exceeds the principal sum.

Consumer Protection Act, R.S.B.C. 1979, s. 65, s. 1.

COST OF COMPENSATION. See FULL ~.

COST OF CONSTRUCTION. The aggregate of (a) the cost or appraised value of the land, whichever is the lesser, or, in the case of land acquired by gift or devise, the appraised value of the land, (b) actual expenditure for building, (c) the architectural, legal and other expenses and carrying charges necessary to complete the house or housing project, (d) where work is done by the owner, such amount as the Corporation may fix as the value of the work, and (e) land development costs and carrying charges. *National Housing Act*, R.S.C. 1985, c. N-11, s. 2.

COST OF CONSTRUCTION OF A FAMILY UNIT. The portion of the total cost of construction of a housing project that is attributable to the particular unit, the total cost being apportioned among the various family housing units on the basis of the relative housing accommodation provided by each unit. *National Housing Act*, R.S.C. 1985, c. N-11, s. 2.

COST OF CONVERSION. The aggregate of (a) the cost of acquiring the land and building or the appraised value thereof, whichever is the lesser, (b) the actual expenditure for converting the building into a housing project, and (c) the architectural, legal and other expenses necessary to complete the project. *National Housing Act*, R.S.C. 1985, c. N-11, s. 2.

COST OF FUTURE CARE. Especially medical and hospitalization expenses which a plaintiff incurs but which would not have been incurred except for the injury. K.D. Cooper-Stephenson & I.B. Saunders, *Personal Injury Damages in Canada* (Toronto: Carswell, 1981) at 52.

COST OF GOODS SOLD. The remainder obtained when the value of the closing inventory is subtracted from the value of the opening inventory plus the laid down cost of the product purchased. *Anti-Inflation Guidelines*, C.R.C., c. 302, s. 2.

COST OF INSURED SERVICES. The difference between the amount that the person, as a beneficiary, is liable to pay to the hospital and the amount for which he would have been liable to the hospital if he were not a beneficiary. *Hospitals Act*, R.S.A. 1980, c. H-11, s. 58.

COST OF LABOUR. (i) The actual wages paid to all workmen up to and including the foremen for their time actually spent on the work and in travelling to and from the work, and the cost of food, lodging and transportation for such workmen where necessary for the proper carrying out of the work, (ii) the cost to the operating corporation of contributions related to such wages in respect of workmen's compensation, vacation pay, unemployment insurance, pension or insurance benefits and other similar benefits, (iii) the cost of using mechanical labour-saving equipment in the work, (iv) necessary transportation charges for equipment used in the work, and (v) the cost of explosives. *Public Service Works on Highways Act*, R.S.O. 1980, c. 420, s. 1.

COST OF LIVING. The relationship between the cost of goods to the consumer and buying power of wages.

COST-OF-LIVING ADJUSTMENT. A change in wages or pension payments designed to offset changes in cost of living.

COST OF LOAN. The whole cost to the debtor of money lent, and includes interest, discount, subscription, premium, dues, bonus, commission, brokerage fees and charges, but does not include registration or filing fees prescribed by or pursuant to any statute. Unconscionable Transactions Act, R.S.A. 1980, c. U-2, s. 1.

COST OF PREPARING THE REPLOTTING SCHEME. The following costs payable with respect to a replotting scheme: (i) appraisal costs, (ii) survey costs, (iii) costs paid to prepare a plan of subdivision, (iv) subdivision approving authority costs, and (v) land title costs. *Planning Act*, R.S.A. 1980, c. P-9, s. 123.

COST OF PRODUCTION. An amount that in accordance with good business principles and practices fairly reflects the manufacturing or production costs of the goods at the time of shipment to Canada. *Customs Act*, R.S.C. 1970, c. C-40, s. 35.

COST OF THE LOAN. The whole cost to the debtor of money lent and includes interest, discount, subscription, premium, dues, bonus, commission, brokerage fees and charges, but not actual lawful and necessary disbursements made to a registrar of deeds, a prothonotary, a clerk of a county or municipal court, a sheriff or a treasurer of a city, town or municipality. *Unconscionable Transactions Relief acts.*

COST OF WORK. (i) The total cost to the client including any taxes which may be recoverable by the client and the contractor's overhead and profit, necessary to complete the work for which the architect has prepared drawings and specifications or for which he is responsible, but (ii) does not include the architect's fees, fees of other special consultants, or the salary or wages of a clerk of works or other person performing a similar function. *Architects Act*, R.S.A. 1970, c. 22, s. 2.

COST-PLUS CONTRACT. A contract to sell a product or perform work for the selling price or contractor's costs plus a percentage or plus a fixed fee.

COSTS. *n.* 1. Charges payable for legal services. 2. Money expended to prosecute or defend a suit which a party is entitled to recover. 3. The costs and charges after they have been ascertained, of committing and conveying to prison the person against whom costs have been awarded. *Criminal Code*, R.S.C. 1985, c. C-46, s. 809(5). See ACQUISITION ~; ADMINISTRATION ~; ALL PROPER ~ AND EXPENSES; ASSESSED ~; ASSESSMENT OF ~; BILL OF ~; CARRY ~; CARRYING ~; COST; EXTRA-JUDICIAL ~; FIXED ~; FULL ~; JUDICIAL ~; MAINTENANCE ~; NO ORDER AS TO ~; NORMAL ~; OPERATING ~; PARTY-AND-PARTY ~; SALVAGE ~; SECURITY FOR ~; SOLICITOR-AND-CLIENT ~; TANKER FREIGHT ~; TAXATION OF ~; TAXED ~; WITH ~.

COSTS IF DEMANDED. An expression inserted in a judgment when either the successful party is a body like the Crown or the unsuccessful party faces financial ruin. M.M. Orkin, *The Law of Costs*, 2d ed. (Aurora: Canada Law Book, 1987) at 1-12.

COSTS, INSURANCE AND FREIGHT. See C.I.F., C.I.F. CONTRACT.

COSTS IN THE ACTION. See COSTS IN THE CAUSE.

COSTS IN THE CAUSE. An expression meaning that the costs of the proceeding will be awarded to whichever party is successful at trial. M.M. Orkin, *The Law of Costs*, 2d ed. (Aurora: Canada Law Book, 1987) at 1-10.

COSTS OF AND INCIDENTAL TO. Party-and-party costs. M.M. Orkin, *The Law of Costs*, 2d ed. (Aurora: Canada Law Book, 1987) at 1-13.

COSTS OF THE DAY. Costs awarded when adjournment of the trial was caused by one party's default. M.M. Orkin, *The Law of Costs*, 2d ed. (Aurora: Canada Law Book, 1987) at 2-73.

COSTS OF THE WORK. See VALUE OF THE WORK AND ~.

COSTS OF THIS HEARING. Costs which include both preparation for the hearing and the hearing itself. M.M. Orkin, *The Law of Costs*, 2d ed. (Aurora: Canada Law Book, 1987) at 1-12.

COSTS OF THIS PROCEEDING. Costs for all interlocutory motions and services, not only costs at trial. M.M. Orkin, *The Law of Costs*,

2d ed. (Aurora: Canada Law Book, 1987) at 1-12.

COSTS REASONABLY INCURRED. Party-and-party costs. M.M. Orkin, *The Law of Costs*, 2d ed. (Aurora: Canada Law Book, 1987) at 1-13.

COSTS TO THE SUCCESSFUL PARTY IN THE CAUSE. See COSTS IN THE CAUSE.

CO-SURETY. *n.* One who shares a surety's obligations.

COT DEATH. See CRIB DEATH.

COTENANCY. *n.* Includes tenancy in common and joint tenancy.

COTTAGE. *n.* 1. A small house. 2. A building to accommodate one or more guests, (i) that contains at least two rooms, and (ii) that may or may not contain facilities for guests to prepare and cook food. *Tourism Act*, R.R.O. 1980, Reg. 936, s. 1. 3. A building in which facilities are provided for cooking and for shelter for one or more persons living therein, as a single and non-profit housekeeping unit. *Public Lands Act*, R.R.O. 1980, Reg. 879, s. 1. See PRIVATE ~.

COTTAGE ESTABLISHMENT. A tourist establishment comprising four or more cottages owned and operated by the same person. *Tourism Act*, R.R.O. 1980, Reg. 936, s. 1.

COUCHANT. [Fr.] Lying down.

COULOMB. *n.* The quantity of electricity transported in one second by a current of one ampere. *Weights and Measures Act*, S.C. 1970-71-72, c. 36, schedule 1.

COUNCIL. *n.* 1. An assembly of people for governmental or municipal purposes. 2. The governing body of a city, village, summer village, municipal district, county or other municipality. 3. The Queen's Privy Council for Canada, committees of the Queen's Privy Council for Canada, Cabinet and committees of Cabinet. *Canada Evidence Act*, R.S.C. 1985, c. C-5, s. 39(3). 4. An advisory body to government. 5. Used to describe the governing body of an association, i.e. professional organizations. 6. Used in the title of administrative agencies. 7. An association of unions within an area. See BAND ~; BARGAINING ~; BUILDING TRADES ~; CANADA ~; COMMISSIONER IN ~; COUNTY ~; DISTRICT ~; ECONOMIC ~ OF CANADA; EXECUTIVE ~; GOVERNOR GENERAL IN ~; GOVERNOR IN ~; HEAD OF ~; HEAD OF THE ~; JUDICIAL ~; LEGISLATIVE ~; LIEUTENANT GOVERNOR IN ~; LOCAL ~; MEDICAL RESEARCH ~ OF CANADA; MEMBER OF ~; MEMBER OF THE ~; MUNICIPAL ~; NATIONAL RESEARCH ~; NATIONAL RESEARCH ~ OF CANADA; NATURAL SCIENCES AND ENGINEERING RESEARCH ~ OF CANADA; ORDER IN ~; PRIVY ~; SCIENCE ~ OF CANADA; SETTLEMENT ~; SOCIAL SCIENCES AND HUMANITIES RESEARCH ~ OF CANADA; STANDARDS ~ OF CANADA; STUDENTS ~.

COUNCILLOR. *n.* A member of or a person serving on a council. See BAND ~.

COUNCIL OF THE BAND. (a) In the case of a band to which section 74 applies, the council established pursuant to that section, (b) in the case of a band to which section 74 does not apply, the council chosen according to the custom of the band, or, where there is no council, the chief of the band chosen according to the custom of the band. *Indian Act*, R.S.C. 1985, c. I-5, s. 2.

COUNCIL OF TRADE UNIONS. 1. Two or more trade unions that have formed a council of trade unions, one of the purposes of which is the regulation of relations between employers and employees. *Canada Labour Relations Board Regulations*, C.R.C., c. 1014, s. 2. 2. A council that is formed for the purpose of representing or that according to established bargaining practice represents trade unions. *Industrial Relations Act*, R.S.N.B. 1973, c. I-4, s. 38. 3. Includes an allied council, a trades council, a joint board or another association of trade unions. See CERTIFIED ~.

COUNSEL. *v.* 1. To procure, solicit or incite. *Criminal Law Amendment Act*, R.S.C. 1985 (1st Supp.), c. 27, s. 7(3). 2. To advise or recommend.

COUNSEL. *n.* 1. A barrister or solicitor, in respect of the matters or things that barristers and solicitors, respectively, are authorized by law of a province to do or perform in relation to legal proceedings. *Criminal Code*, R.S.C. 1985, c. C-46, s. 2. 2. When used in respect of proceedings in a provincial court (criminal division) includes an agent. *Provincial Offenses Act*, R.S.O. 1980, c. 400, s. 92. 3. Any person authorized by an interested party to represent that party before a tribunal. See COMMISSION ~; CROWN ~; DUTY ~; HOUSE ~; INVESTMENT ~; QUEEN'S ~; RIGHT TO ~.

COUNSELLING. See INVESTMENT ~.

COUNT. *n.* A charge in an information or indictment. *Criminal Code*, R.S.C. 1985, c. C-46, s. 2. See RE~.

COUNTENANCE. *v.* To encourage; to aid and abet.

COUNTERCLAIM. *n.* A defendant's assertion in the main action of a right or claim against the plaintiff.

COUNTERFEASANCE. *n.* Forging.

COUNTERFEIT. *n.* An unauthorized imitation intended to be used to defraud by passing off.

COUNTERFEIT COIN. See COUNTERFEIT MONEY.

COUNTERFEIT MONEY. Includes (a) a false coin or false paper money that resembles or is apparently intended to resemble or pass for a current coin or current paper money, (b) a forged bank-note or forged blank bank-note, whether complete or incomplete, (c) a genuine coin or genuine paper money that is prepared or altered to resemble or pass for a current coin or current paper money of a higher denomination, (d) a current coin from which the milling is removed by filing or cutting the edges and on which new milling is made to restore its appearance, (e) a coin cased with gold, silver or nickel, as the case may be, that is intended to resemble or pass for a current gold, silver or nickel coin, and (f) a coin or a piece of metal or mixed metals that is washed or coloured by any means with a wash or material capable of producing the appearance of gold, silver or nickel and that is intended to resemble or pass for a current gold, silver or nickel coin. *Criminal Code*, R.S.C. 1985, c. C-46, s. 448.

COUNTERFEIT TOKEN OF VALUE. A counterfeit excise stamp, postage stamp or other evidence of value, by whatever technical, trivial or deceptive designation it may be described, and includes genuine coin or paper money that has no value as money. *Criminal Code*, R.S.C. 1985, c. C-46, s. 448.

COUNTERFOIL. *n.* The complementary part of a cheque or receipt used to preserve a record of the contents.

COUNTERMAND. *v.* To revoke; to recall.

COUNTER OFFER. *var.* **COUNTER-OFFER.** A statement by the offeree rejecting the offer and creating a new offer.

COUNTERPART. *n.* A part which corresponds; a duplicate.

COUNTERPETITION. *n.* A claim for relief against the petitioner by respondent in a divorce proceeding.

COUNTER-PROPOSAL. *n.* An opposing offer made in collective bargaining following an offer or proposal by the other party.

COUNTER-SIGN. *var.* **COUNTERSIGN.** *v.* For a subordinate to sign to vouch for the authenticity of any writing by the superior.

COUNTER-SIGNATURE. *var.* **COUNTER-SIGNATURE.** *n.* The endorsement on a royal instrument or on a document under the sign-manual of the signature of Her Majesty's responsible Canadian minister. *Seals Act*, R.S.C. 1985, c. S-6, s. 2.

COUNTERVAIL. *v.* To compensate; to balance.

COUNTERVAILING DUTIES AGREEMENT. See SUBSIDIES AND ~.

COUNTRY. *n.* The total territory which is subject under a single sovereign to a single body of law. J.G. McLeod, *The Conflict of Laws* (Calgary: Carswell, 1983) at 5. See BENEFICIARY ~; COMMONWEALTH ~; FOREIGN ~.

COUNTRY OF EXPORT. 1. In respect of goods, the country from which the goods are shipped directly to Canada. *Customs Act*, R.S.C. 1985 (2d Supp.), c. 1, s. 45. 2. In the case of dumped goods, the country from which the goods were shipped directly to Canada or, if the goods have not been shipped directly to Canada, the country from which the goods would be shipped directly to Canada under normal conditions of trade and, in the case of subsidized goods, the country in which the subsidy originated. *Special Imports Measures Act*, R.S.C. 1985, c. S-15, s. 2.

COUNTRY OF ORIGIN. 1. (a) The country of the Union in which the applicant for registration of a trade-mark had at the date of the application a real and effective industrial or commercial establishment, or (b) if the applicant for registration of a trade-mark did not at the date of the application have in a country of the Union an establishment as described in paragraph (a), the country of the Union where he on that date had his domicile, or (c) if the applicant for registration of a trade-mark did not at the date of the application have in a country of the Union an establishment as described in paragraph (a) or a domicile as described in paragraph (b), the country of the Union of which he was on that date a citizen or national. *Trade-marks Act*, R.S.C. 1985, c. T-13, s. 2. 2. The country in which (a) a textile fibre was grown or made, or (b) any textile fibre product not included in paragraph (a) was substantially made. *Textile Labelling and Advertising Regulations*, C.R.C., c. 1551, s. 2. 3. (a) With respect to an animal, the country from which an animal was imported into Canada, where the animal has lived for 60 days in that country in association with other animals of its own species and in any other case means the country in which the animal was born, and (b) with respect to an animal by-product, the country in which the animal by-product was taken from an animal. *Animal Disease and Protection Regulations*, C.R.C., c. 296, s. 2.

COUNTRY OF THE BRITISH COMMONWEALTH. For the purposes of this Act a country listed in Schedule I or a country declared for the purposes of this Act to be a country of the British Commonwealth of Nations by proclamation issued under this Act, and includes, in the case of any such country, all colonies, dependencies or territories thereof. *Canadian Citizenship Act*, R.S.C. 1970, c. C-19, s. 2.

COUNTRY OF THE UNION. Any country that is a member of the Union for the Protection of Industrial Property constituted under the Convention. *Trade-marks Act*, R.S.C. 1985, c. T-13, s. 2.

COUNTRY SALE. A public sale of livestock at any place other than a market.

COUNTY. *n.* A territorial division for electoral, judicial or local government purposes. See ~ MUNICIPALITY; DISTRICT OR ~.

COUNTY BRIDGE. A bridge under the exclusive jurisdiction of the council of a county. *Municipal Act*, R.S.O. 1980, c. 302, s. 254.

COUNTY CORPORATION. The corporation or its territory, according to the context. *An Act to Amend Various Legislative Provisions Respecting Municipalities*, S.Q. 1982, c. 2, s. 136.

COUNTY COUNCIL. The municipal council of a county.

COUNTY COURT. 1. A court with jurisdiction limited to a county by territory and limited by subject matter. P.W. Hogg, *Constitutional Law of Canada*, 2d ed. (Toronto: Carswell, 1985) at 134. 2. In its application to the Province of Ontario includes, and in its application to the Province of Newfoundland means, "district court". *Interpretation Act*, R.S.C. 1985, c. I-21, s. 35.

COUNTY COURT JUDGE. See SENIOR ~.

COUNTY LEVY. See NET ~.

COUNTY MUNICIPALITY. A municipality, other than a city, that forms part of a county or regional municipality that is not in the territorial districts. *Education Act*, R.S.O. 1980, c. 129, s. 1.

COUPLER. *n.* A device, having a cavity of predetermined shape and volume, that is used for the loading of earphones in conjunction with a calibrated microphone adapted to measure the sound pressure developed in the cavity. *Medical Devices Regulations*, C.R.C., c. 871, s. 1.

COUPON. *n.* Part of a commercial instrument designed to be cut off, which evidences something connected with the contract the instrument represents, usually interest.

COUPON BOND. A bond registrable as to principal only; interest is paid through coupons, payable to bearer, attached to the instrument. H. Sutherland, D.B. Horsley & J.M. Edmiston, eds., *Fraser's Handbook on Canadian Company Law*, 7th ed. (Toronto: Carswell, 1985) at 311.

COUPON DEBENTURE. A debenture registrable as to principal only; interest is paid through coupons, payable to bearer, attached to the instrument. H. Sutherland, D.B. Horsley & J.M. Edmiston, eds., *Fraser's Handbook on Canadian Company Law*, 7th ed. (Toronto: Carswell, 1985) at 311.

COURIER. *n.* An individual who, on personal account or as an employee of another person, provides to members of the public the service of carrying items of value in personal custody.

COURSE. *n.* A specific unit of study. *Public Schools Act*, S.M. 1980, c. 33, s. 1. See CANADIAN SECURITIES ~; DENOMINATIONAL THEOLOGICAL ~; HOME STUDY ~; ORDER OF ~; SECONDARY ~; TRAINING ~; UNIVERSITY ~; UPDATING ~; WATER ~.

COURSE LOAD. See NORMAL FULL-TIME ~.

COURSE OF BUSINESS. The normal activities of business.

COURSE OF EMPLOYMENT. 1. The normal activities of an employee while serving the employer. 2. Includes unauthorized acts of an employee which are wrongful and unauthorized modes of performing the work which is authorized. John G. Fleming, *The Law of Torts*, 6th ed. (Sydney: The Law Book Company Limited, 1983) at 349.

COURSE OF STUDY. See APPROVED ~.

COURT. *n.* 1. A place where justice is administered; a body or part of the judicial system. 2. A place where a sovereign resides. 3. The court or a judge of the court. 4. Includes a judge, arbitrator, umpire, commissioner, provincial judge, justice of the peace or other office or person having by law or by the consent of the parties authority to hear, receive and examine evidence. *Evidence acts.* 5. A court having jurisdiction in an action for the recovery of a debt or money demand to the amount claimed by a creditor in respect of money lent. *Unconscionable Transactions Relief Acts.* 6. An authority having jurisdiction to make an order. *Maintenance Orders Enforcement acts.* 7. The Federal Court or any superior, county or district court, except where the context otherwise requires. *Commercial Arbitration Act*, R.S.C. 1985 (2d Supp.), c. 17, s. 6. 8. Includes a person or statutory body having, by law or consent of parties, authority to hear, receive and examine evidence. *Land Title Act*, R.S.B.C. 1979, c. 219,

s. 23. See ADMIRALTY ~; APPEAL ~; APPELLATE ~; CITIZENSHIP ~; CIVIL ~; COMPETENT ~; COUNTY ~; DISTRICT ~; DIVIDED ~; DIVISIONAL ~; ECCLESIAS-TICAL ~; ELECTION ~; ENCLOSED ~; EUROPEAN ~; EUROPEAN ~ OF HUMAN RIGHTS; EXCHEQUER ~; FEDERAL ~; FRIEND OF THE ~; FULL ~; INFERIOR ~; INTERNATIONAL ~ OF JUSTICE; NAVAL ~; NIGHT ~; OFFICE OF THE ~; OPEN ~; ORDINARY ~; ORIGINAL ~; PAYMENT INTO ~; POLICE ~; PRIZE ~; PROVINCIAL ~; REGISTERING ~; REGISTRATION ~; RULES OF ~; SERVICE ~; SMALL CLAIMS ~; STATUTORY ~; SUMMARY CONVIC-TION ~; SUMMARY TRIAL ~; SUPERIOR ~; SUPREME ~; SUPREME ~ OF CANADA; SUPREME ~ OF ONTARIO; TERRITORIAL ~; TRAILER ~; TRIAL ~; YOUTH ~.

COURT APPEALED FROM. The court from which the appeal is brought directly to the Supreme Court, whether that court is one of original jurisdiction or a court of appeal. *Supreme Court Act*, R.S.C. 1985, c. S-26, s. 2.

COURT-APPOINTED RECEIVER. A receiver which a court appoints when it judges that it is "just or convenient" to do so. F. Bennett, *Receiverships* (Toronto: Carswell, 1985) at 2.

COURT CLERK. The chief administrator of a court who issues process, enters orders and performs other duties.

COURTESY VEHICLE. A motor vehicle operated by a commercial enterprise for the purpose of transporting customers of that enterprise between an airport and the place of business of that enterprise. *Government Airport Concession Operations Regulations*, C.R.C., c. 1565, s. 2.

COURT IN ALBERTA. Includes board, commission, tribunal or other body in Alberta. *Interprovincial Subpoena Act*, S.A. 1981, s. I-8.1, s. 1.

COURT MARTIAL. 1. A court which tries offences against naval, military or air force discipline, or offences committed by a member of the armed forces against the ordinary law. 2. Includes a General Court Martial, a Special General Court Martial, a Disciplinary Court Martial and a Standing Court Martial. *National Defence Act*, R.S.C. 1985, c. N-5, s. 2. 3. For the purposes of this section and section 250, "court martial", in addition to the tribunals referred to in the definition "court martial" in section 2, includes a commissioner taking evidence under this Act. *National Defence Act*, R.S.C. 1985, c. N-5, s. 249.

COURT MARTIAL APPEAL COURT. The Court Martial Appeal Court of Canada estab-lished by section 234. *National Defence Act*, R.S.C. 1985, c. N-5, s. 2.

COURT OF A CONTRACTING STATE. (i) In relation to the United Kingdom, any court of the United Kingdom or of any territory to which this Convention extends pursuant to Article XIII; (ii) in relation to Canada, the Federal Court of Canada or any court of a province or territory to which this Convention extends pursuant to Article XII. *Civil and Commercial Judgments Convention*, R.S.C. 1985, c. C-30, s. 1.

COURT OF APPEAL. 1. (a) In the Province of Ontario, the Court of Appeal, (b) in the Province of Quebec, the Court of Appeal, (c) in the Province of Nova Scotia, the Appeal Division of the Supreme Court, (d) in the Province of New Brunswick, the Court of Appeal, (e) in the Province of British Columbia, the Court of Appeal, (f) in the Province of Prince Edward Island, the Appeal Division of the Supreme Court, (g) in the Province of Manitoba, the Court of Appeal, (h) in the Province of Saskatchewan, the Court of Appeal, (i) in the Province of Alberta, the Court of Appeal, (j) in the Province of Newfoundland, the Court of Appeal, (k) in the Yukon Territory, the Court of Appeal, and (l) in the Northwest Territories, the Court of Appeal. *Criminal Code*, R.S.C. 1985, c. C-46, s. 2. 2. The court of appeal, as defined by the definition "court of appeal" in section 2, for the province or territory in which the trial of a person by indictment is held. *Criminal Code*, R.S.C. 1985, c. C-46, s. 673. 3. The court to which an appeal lies from an order of a court. *Canada Business Corporations Act*, R.S.C. 1985, c. C-44, s. 2.

COURT OF CANADA. The Federal Court of Canada or any court of a province or territory to which this Convention extends pursuant to Article XII. *Civil and Commercial Judgments Convention*, R.S.C. 1985, c. C-30, s. 1.

COURT OF CHANCERY. The main English court in which the part of law known as equity was enforced. The Lord Chancellor presided, assisted by the Master of the Rolls and judges called Vice-Chancellors.

COURT OF CRIMINAL JURISDICTION. (a) A court of general or quarter sessions of the peace, when presided over by a superior court judge or a county or district court judge, or in the cities of Montreal and Quebec, by a munic-ipal judge of the city, as the case may be, or a judge of the sessions of the peace, and (b) a magistrate or judge acting under Part XIX. *Criminal Code*, R.S.C. 1985, c. C-46, s. 2.

COURT OF FIRST INSTANCE. A court before which an action is first brought for trial.

COURT OF LAST RESORT. The court from which there is no further appeal.

COURT OF PROBATE. 1. Any court having jurisdiction in matters of probate. *Probate Recognition Act*, R.S.B.C. 1979, c. 339, s. 1. 2. (i) The court of probate for the district which has jurisdiction in respect to the administration of the estate in which the minor is a participant; (ii) if there is no such estate, or if it has been administered, the court of probate for the district in which the estate of the infant is in whole or in part situated; or (iii) if the infant has no such estate, the court of probate for the district in which the infant resides. *Guardianship Act*, R.S.N.S. 1967, c. 121, s. 1.

COURT OF QUEEN'S BENCH. Her Majesty's Court of Queen's Bench for Saskatchewan. *Securities Act*, S.S. 1984-85-86, c. S-42.1, s. 2.

COURT OF RECORD. Any court which keeps a record of its judicial acts and proceedings.

COURT OF THE UNITED KINGDOM. Any court of the United Kingdom or of any territory to which this Convention extends pursuant to Article XIII. *Civil and Commercial Judgments Convention*, R.S.C. 1985, c. C-30, s. 1.

COURT RECORD. The records of the office of any court and documents filed therein.

COURT REPORTER. A person who records proceedings of a court and the evidence given in court.

COUSIN. *n.* A collateral relation, not including sisters and brothers and their descendants, or the sisters and brothers of an ancestor.

COUSIN-GERMAN. *n.* The child of a brother or sister.

COUT. DIG. *abbr.* Coutlee's Digest.

COUT. S.C. *abbr.* Notes of Unreported Cases, Supreme Court of Canada (Coutlee), 1875-1907.

COVE. See UPPER ISLAND ~ AND BRYANT'S ~ AREA.

COVENANT. *n.* 1. An agreement in writing signed and delivered and in the past under seal. 2. Includes a warranty, representation or proviso. *An Act to Amend the Standard Forms of Conveyances Act*, S.N.B. 1984, c. 63, s. 2. See DEED OF ~; RESTRICTIVE ~; SEVERAL ~; USUAL ~.

COVENANT FOR FURTHER ASSURANCE. A standard covenant which a vendor undertakes to protect the purchaser's interest in something purchased; the vendor agrees, at the purchaser's request and cost, to execute a further convey-ance or other document to more perfectly assure the subject-matter conveyed.

COVENANT FOR PAYMENT. An agreement that the mortgagor will pay the mortgage money and interest.

COVER. *v.* 1. To insure. 2. To buy back securities sold short.

COVERAGE. *n.* 1. The right conferred upon a person to be indemnified against liability for, or to be compensated for, death, injury, loss, or damage. 2. The percentage, as determined by the regulations, of the long-term average yield in any area for any insurable crop that is to be the basis for determining whether an insured person has suffered a loss against which he is insured under a contract. *The Saskatchewan Crop Insurance Act*, R.S.S. 1978, c. S-12, s. 2. See EXTENDED ~; INSURANCE ~.

COVERING. See METALLIC ~.

COVER NOTE. A document given to an insured to indicate insurance is in effect.

COVERT. *adj.* 1. Hidden. 2. Of a woman, under the protection of her husband. See FEMME ~.

COVERT-BARON. *adj.* Under the protection of a husband.

COVERTURE. *n.* A woman's condition during marriage; the fact that she is married.

COVIN. *n.* Conspiracy to defraud.

COVINOUS. *adj.* Fraudulent.

COYOTE. *n.* The prairie wolf and includes the immature young of such animal. *The Wolf and Coyote Bounty Act*, R.S.S. 1978, c. W-15, s. 2.

C.P. *abbr.* 1. Canadian Pacific. 2. Common Pleas. 3. Cour provinciale. 4. Recueils de jurisprudence, Cour provinciale.

CP. *abbr.* Compare.

CPC. *abbr.* Common purpose charter.

C.P.C. *abbr.* 1. Carswell's Practice Cases, 1976-1985. 2. Canadian Pension Commission.

CPC EDUCATIONAL PROGRAM. A program for educational purposes organized with the written concurrence of the appropriate school authorities for the exclusive benefit of full time elementary or secondary school students or both of the schools participating, who are accompanied by educational staff of those schools or parents of participating students as leaders or chaperones, in the proportion of one leader or chaperone for not more than 20 and not less than 10 such students. *Air Carrier Regulations*, C.R.C., c. 3, s. 23.

CPC EVENT. A presentation, performance,

exhibition, competition, gathering or activity that (a) is of apparent and considerable significance unrelated to the general interest inherent in travel, and (b) is not being created or organized for the primary purpose of generating charter air traffic. *Air Carrier Regulations*, C.R.C., c. 3, s. 23.

C.P.C. (2D). *abbr.* Carswell's Practice Cases (Second Series) 1985-.

C.P.D. *abbr.* Law Reports, Common Pleas Division.

C.P. DIV. CIV. *abbr.* Cour provinciale, Division civile.

C.P. DIV. CRIM. *abbr.* Cour provinciale, Division criminelle.

C.P. DIV. FAM. *abbr.* Cour provinciale, Division de la famille.

C.P. DU N. *abbr.* Cours de perfectionnement du Notariat.

C.P.R. *abbr.* 1. Canadian Patent Reporter, 1942-1971. 2. Canadian Pacific Railway Company.

C. PROV. *abbr.* Cour provinciale.

C.P.R. (N.S.). *abbr.* Canadian Patent Reporter (New [Third] Series).

C.P.R. (2D). *abbr.* Canadian Patent Reporter (Second Series), 1971-1984.

C.P.R. (3D). *abbr.* Canadian Patent Reporter (Third Series), 1985-.

C.R. *abbr.* Criminal Reports (Canada), 1946-1967.

CRAB. See SNOW ~; SOFT-SHELLED ~.

CRAB TRAP. (a) A metal or wood framed enclosure covered with netting or wire mesh and having one or more openings, or (b) a similar enclosure constructed from synthetic materials. *Pacific Shellfish Regulations*, C.R.C., c. 826, s. 2.

C.R.A.C. *abbr.* Canadian Reports, Appeal Cases, 1828-1913.

CRACKING. *n.* Any parting within the tread, sidewall or innerliner of a tire extending to the cord. *Motor Vehicle Tire Safety Regulations*, C.R.C., c. 1039, s. 2.

CRAFT. *n.* 1. A skilled trade. 2. A small boat. 3. A guild. See PLEASURE ~; WATER-EXCURSION ~.

CRAFT UNION. A union, membership in which is restricted to workers having a particular skill.

CRAFT UNIT. A collective bargaining unit consisting of employees having a particular skill.

CRANE. *n.* 1. A crane used in handling containers at a container terminal. *Pacific Terminal Tariff By-law*, C.R.C., c. 1083, s. 32. 2. A cargo crane or a Colby crane. *Vancouver Crane Tariff By-law*, C.R.C., c. 1099, s. 2. See PRODUCTION ~; SERVICE ~.

CRANE CARRIER. A self-propelled wheeled vehicle that is constructed for the purpose of having a crane unit mounted thereon. *Crane Carrier and Specified Commercial Vehicles Remission Order*, C.R.C., c. 753, s. 2.

CRANE HIRE CHARGE. A charge for the use of the crane, consisting of a time charge and a lift charge. *Montreal Floating Crane No. 1 Heavy-Lift Tariff By-law*, C.R.C., c. 1077, s. 2.

CRANE MOVING CHARGE. A charge for moving the crane, whether carrying a lift or not, to or from any job. *Montreal Floating Crane No. 1 Heavy-Lift Tariff By-law*, C.R.C., c. 1077, s. 2.

CRANE SERVICE. 1. A service provided by the Board to a hirer involving the use of the crane in lifting goods without lightering but does not include slinging the goods into or unslinging them from the crane. *Sept-Iles Crane Tariff By-law*, C.R.C., c. 1094, s. 2. 2. (a) Moving the crane at the request of a hirer from its berth or anchorage at the Port of Montreal to a job, and (b) lifting any article by means of the crane. *St. Lawrence Seaway Heavy-Lift Tariff By-law*, C.R.C., c. 1395, s. 2.

CRANIAL SUTURES. Fibrous bands where the bones of the vault of the skull unite. F.A. Jaffe, *A Guide to Pathological Evidence*, 2d ed. (Toronto: Carswell, 1983) at 173.

CRANIUM. *n.* The portion of the skull which surrounds the brain. F.A. Jaffe, *A Guide to Pathological Evidence*, 2d ed. (Toronto: Carswell, 1983) at 173.

CRANKCASE EMISSIONS. Air pollutant emitted into the atmosphere through any opening in the crankcase. *Motor Vehicle Safety Regulations*, C.R.C., c. 1038, s. 1100.

CRAPPIE. *n.* Includes black crappie, calico bass or speckled bass Pomoxis nigromaculatus (LeSueur), and white crappie Promoxis annularis Rafinesque. *Ontario Fishery Regulations*, C.R.C., c. 849, s. 2.

CRASSA NEGLIGENTIA. [L.] Gross negligence.

CRAVE. *v.* To ask in a formal manner.

C.R.C. *abbr.* Canadian Railway Cases.

CREAM. *n.* 1. The portion of milk that rises to the surface on standing or is separated by centrifugal force. 2. The fatty liquid obtained by separating the constituents of milk. See MILK AND ~; STERILIZED CANNED ~; WHIPPING ~.

CREAMERY. *n.* The premises in which milk or cream is processed into creamery butter.

CREAMERY BUTTER. 1. Butter manufactured in a creamery from pasteurized milk fat and containing no substance other than water, milk solids, bacterial culture, common salt and colouring matter. *Canada Dairy Products Regulations*, C.R.C., c. 553, s. 2. 2. Butter manufactured in a creamery exclusively from milk, or from cream separated from milk, or from both, and with or without added water, food colour or common salt. *Farm Products Grades and Sales Act*, R.R.O. 1980, Reg. 327, s. 1.

CREAMERY OPERATOR. A person engaged in the manufacture of creamery butter at a plant. *Milk Act*, R.R.O. 1980, Reg. 618, s. 1.

CREAM RECEIVING STATION. A place where milk or cream is received and purchased for the purpose of being forwarded to a dairy manufacturing plant for processing or manufacturing.

CREAM STATION. Any building operated as a branch of a creamery where cream is received from individual patrons by an agent of the creamery and where that agent weighs, samples, grades, tests or stores the cream before it is transported or forwarded to that creamery in the individual patrons' cans or transferred to shipping cans for the purpose of being transported or forwarded.

CREAM TRANSFER STATION. Premises at which cream is received for the purpose of being transported to a plant for processing. *Milk Amendment Act*, S.O. 1984, c. 25, s. 1.

CREATION OF CURRENCY. To finance government expenditure by printing money. W. Grover & F. Iacobucci, *Materials on Canadian Income Tax*, 4th ed. (Toronto: Richard DeBoo Ltd., 1980) at 15.

CREATION OF LIEN. Mechanics', construction or builder's liens are created when work or services are performed or materials are placed or furnished. D.N. Macklem & D.I. Bristow, *Construction and Mechanics' Liens in Canada*, 5th ed. (Toronto: Carswell, 1985) at 10.

CREDIBILITY. *n.* 1. Worthiness of belief. 2. The degree of credit the court should give to the testimony of a witness. *Military Rules of Evidence*, C.R.C., c. 1049, s. 2.

CREDIBLE. *adj.* Believable; worthy of belief.

CREDIT. *n.* 1. Belief in a person's trustworthiness. 2. An arrangement for obtaining loans or advances. *Bank Act*, R.S.C. 1985, c. B-1, s. 202(2). 3. The advancing of money, goods or services to or on behalf of another for repayment at a later time, whether or not there is cost of borrowing, and includes variable credit. *Consumer Protections acts*. 4. Credit for which a borrower is required to pay and that is (i) given under an agreement between a seller and a buyer to purchase goods or services by which all or part of the purchase price is payable after the agreement is entered into; or (ii) given by the advancement of money. *The Cost of Credit Disclosure Act*, R.S.S. 1978, c. C-41, s. 2. 5. Recognition granted to a pupil by a principal as prima facie evidence that the pupil has successfully completed a quantity of work. See AGRICULTURAL ~; ANTICIPATORY ~; BACK-TO-BACK ~; CONFIRMED ~; CONSUMER ~; CUMULATIVE ~; DOCUMENTARY ~; EXPORT ~S AGENCY; FARM ~ CORPORATION CANADA; IRREVOCABLE ~; LETTER OF ~; PAST SERVICE ~; PENSION BENEFIT ~; PENSION ~; REVOLVING ~; SALE ON ~; SECONDARY ~; SERVICE ~; TAX ~; UNIVERSITY ~; VARIABLE ~.

CREDIT ADVANCED. The aggregate of the money and the monetary value of any goods, services or benefits actually advanced or to be advanced under an agreement or arrangement minus the aggregate of any required deposit balance and any fee, fine, penalty, commission and other similar charge or expense directly or indirectly incurred under the original or any collateral agreement or arrangement. *Criminal Code*, R.S.C. 1985, c. C-46, s. 347(2).

CREDIT AGENCY. See APPROVED ~.

CREDIT AGREEMENT. An agreement entered into by a person under which that person may enter into a credit transaction with the credit grantor. *Consumer Credit Transactions Act*, S.A. 1985, c. C-22.5, s. 1.

CREDIT BALANCES. See FREE ~.

CREDIT BUREAU. An organization which collects information relating to the credit, responsibility and character of individuals and businesses for the purpose of providing the information to its members.

CREDIT CARD. Any card, plate, coupon book or other device issued or otherwise distributed for the purpose of being used (a) on presentation to obtain, on credit, money, goods, services or any other thing of value, or (b) in an automated teller machine, a remote service unit or a similar automated banking device to obtain any of the services offered through the machine, unit or device. *Criminal Law Amendment Act*, R.S.C. 1985 (1st Supp.), c. 27, s. 42. See UNSOLICITED ~.

CREDIT CARD CUSTOMER. The person (i) to whom a credit card is issued, and (ii) who is liable to the credit grantor who issued the credit card for the indebtedness incurred with the credit card. *Consumer Credit Transactions Act*, S.A. 1985, c. C-22.5, s. 28.

CREDIT CHARGES. 1. The amount the consumer must pay under the contract in addition to (a) the net capital in the case of a contract for the loan of money or a contract extending variable credit; (b) the net capital and the down payment in the case of a contract involving credit. *Consumer Protection Act*, S.Q. 1978, c. 9, s. 69. 2. (i) When used in relation to a time sale agreement, the difference between (A) the total amount that the buyer has to pay in the transaction (if the payments are made as they become due), and (B) the sum of the cash selling price, the official fee, if any, and the insurance charges, if any, actually paid by the credit grantor to an insurance company on behalf of the buyer on his request, (ii) when used in relation to a loan agreement, the difference between (A) the total amount that the borrower has to pay in the transaction (if the payments are made as they become due), and (B) the sum of the amount the borrower actually receives from the credit grantor, the official fee, if any, and the insurance charges, if any, actually paid by the credit grantor to an insurance company on behalf of the borrower on his request, and (iii) when used in relation to a continuous deferred payment plan or a revolving loan agreement, the charges that the buyer or borrower is required to pay periodically on the unpaid balance from time to time for the privilege of purchasing or borrowing on the plan. *Credit and Loan Agreement Act*, R.S.A. 1980, c. C-30, s. 1.

CREDITED SERVICE. In connection with pension plans, period of service with an employer or in an office to which holders are entitled to pensions.

CREDIT GRANTOR. A person who in the course of carrying on his business (i) enters into a credit agreement with a consumer, (ii) is the seller under a time sale agreement, (iii) is the seller under a continuous deferred payment plan, (iv) is the lender under a loan agreement, (v) is the issuer of a credit card, (vi) is the lender under a mortgage, (vii) is the broker under a mortgage where the money is being lent by a person other than a lender referred to in subclause (vi), or (viii) is the lessor under a lease, and includes an assignee of that person where the person assigns his interest, other than as security, under a credit agreement or credit transaction. *Consumer Credit Transactions Act*, S.A. 1985, c. C-22.5, s. 1.

CREDIT INFORMATION. Information about a consumer as to name, age, occupation, place of residence, previous places of residence, marital status, spouse's name and age, number of dependants, particulars of education or professional qualifications, places of employment, previous places of employment, estimated income, paying habits, outstanding debt obligations, cost of living obligations and assets. *Consumer Reporting acts.*

CREDIT INSTITUTION. A bank, treasury branch, credit union or a trust company.

CREDIT INSURANCE. Insurance against loss to the insured through insolvency or default of a person to whom credit is given in respect of goods, wares or merchandise. *Insurance acts.*

CREDIT LINE. The amount of money a lender agrees to supply to a person.

CREDIT NOTE. A note issued by a business indicating that a customer is entitled to be credited by the issuer with a certain amount.

CREDITOR. *n.* 1. A person to whom another person owes a debt. 2. A person having a claim, preferred, secured or unsecured, provable as a claim under this Act. *Bankruptcy Act*, R.S.C. 1985, c. B-3, s. 2. 3. A person to whose credit a deposited amount stands or who is otherwise legally entitled to claim a deposited amount. *Canada Post Corporation Act*, R.S.C. 1985, c. C-10, s. 39. 4. (i) A vendor under a conditional sales agreement or the vendor's assignee; (ii) a mortgagee under a chattel mortgage agreement or the mortgagee's assignee. 5. (i) In relation to a writ of execution, any person entitled to enforce by execution the payment of any money payable pursuant to any judgment or order that is enforceable by execution, and (ii) in relation to a distress, the person who has the power of distress. 6. The person or corporation entitled to receive the amount due on a judgment. 7. Includes the person advancing money lent and the assignee of any claim arising or security given in respect of money lent. *Unconscionable Transactions acts.* 8. A person who supplies labour, materials or services used or reasonably required to be used in the performance of a contract with the Crown for the construction, alteration, demolition, repair, or maintenance of a public work. *Public Works Creditors' Payment Acts.* See EXECUTION ~; JUDGMENT ~; PETITIONING ~; PREFERRED ~; REGISTERED ~; SECURED ~; SECURED TRADE ~; UNSECURED ~; UNSECURED TRADE ~.

CREDITOR'S GROUP ACCIDENT INSURANCE. Accident insurance effected by a creditor whereby the lives or well-being or the lives and well-being of a number of that creditor's debtors are insured severally under a single contract. *Insurance acts.*

CREDITOR'S GROUP INSURANCE. 1. Insurance effected by a creditor in respect of the lives of that creditor's debtors whereby the lives of the debtors are insured severally under a single contract. *Insurance acts.* 2. Insurance effected by a creditor whereby the lives or well-being, or the lives and well-being, of a number of that creditor's debtors are insured severally under a single contract. *Insurance acts.*

CREDITOR'S GROUP SICKNESS INSURANCE. Sickness insurance effected by a creditor whereby the lives or well-being or the lives and well-being of a number of that creditor's debtors are insured severally under a single contract. *Insurance acts.*

CREDITORS' MEETING. The first meeting of creditors of a bankrupt.

CREDITORS' RELIEF STATUTE. A statute which forces a judgment creditor to share pari passu any proceeds of execution with other unsecured creditors who filed writs of execution or certificates with the sheriff. C.R.B. Dunlop, *Creditor-Debtor Law in Canada* (Toronto: Carswell, 1981) at 416.

CREDIT RATE. The actual annual percentage of a credit charge.

CREDIT RATING. Evaluation of the credit worthiness of a business or individual based on ability to pay and past performance in paying debt.

CREDIT REPORT. A report of credit information or of a credit rating based on credit information, supplied by a credit reporting agency.

CREDIT REPORTING AGENCY. A person who is engaged in providing credit reports to any other person, whether for remuneration or otherwise.

CREDIT SOCIETY. See COOPERATIVE ~.

CREDIT TRANSACTION. (i) A purchase of goods or services under a continuous deferred payment plan or a time sale agreement, (ii) a loan, or (iii) a purchase of goods or services or the obtaining of money by the use of a credit card. *Consumer Credit Transactions Act*, S.A. 1985, c. C-22.5, s. 1.

CREDIT UNION. 1. A co-operative society, including caisses populaires, that provides its members with financial and other services. 2. A corporation, association or federation incorporated or organized as a credit union or cooperative credit society if (i) it derived all or substantially all of its revenues from (A) loans made to, or cashing cheques for, members, (B) debt obligations or securities of, or guaranteed by, the Government of Canada or a province, a Canadian municipality, or an agency thereof, or debt obligations or securities of a municipal or public body performing a function of government in Canada or an agency thereof, (C) debt obligations of or deposits with, or guaranteed by, a corporation, commission or association not less than 90% of the shares or capital of which was owned by the Government of Canada or a province or by a municipality in Canada, (D) debt obligations or of deposits with, or guaranteed by, a bank to which the Bank Act or the Quebec Savings Banks Act applies, or debt obligations of or deposits with a corporation licensed or otherwise authorized under a law of Canada or a province to carry on in Canada the business of offering to the public its services as trustee, (E) charges, fees and dues levied against members or members of members, (F) loans made to or deposits with a credit union or cooperative credit society of which it is a member, (G) a prescribed revenue source, (ii) all or substantially all the members thereof having full voting rights therein were corporations, associations or federations (A) incorporated as credit unions or cooperative credit societies, all of which derived all or substantially all of their revenues from the sources described in subparagraph (i), or all or substantially all of the members of which were credit unions, cooperatives or a combination thereof, (B) incorporated, organized or registered under, or governed by a law of Canada or a province with respect to cooperatives, or (C) incorporated or organized for charitable purposes, or were corporations, associations or federations no part of the income of which was payable to, or otherwise available for the personal benefit of, any shareholder or member thereof, or (iii) the corporation, association or federation would be a credit union by virtue of subparagraph (ii) if all the members (other than individuals) having full voting rights in each member thereof that is a credit union were members having full voting rights in the corporation, association or federation. *Income Tax Act*, R.S.C. 1952, c. 148 (as am. S.C. 1970-71-72, c. 63), s. 137(6)(b). 3. A co-operative, non-profit credit society, incorporated as a limited company under this Act for the purpose of providing a source of credit for provident and productive purposes at fair and reasonable rates of interest, of encouraging and promoting habits of thrift among its members, of affording its members an opportunity to accumulate their savings; and of giving its members the use and control of their money for their mutual benefits. *Credit Union Act*, R.S.P.E.I. 1974, c. C-28, s. 1. See CENTRAL ~; COMMUNITY ~.

CREE COMMUNITY. A collectivity composed of all the Crees enrolled or entitled to be enrolled on a community list in accordance with the Act respecting Cree and Inuit Native persons (1978, chapter 97). *Cree Villages Act*, S.Q. 1978, c. 88, s. 1.

CREE TALLYMAN. A Cree person recognized by a Cree community as responsible for the supervision of the activities related to the exercising of the right to harvest on a Cree trapline. *An Act respecting hunting and fishing rights in the James Bay and New Quebec territories*, S.Q. 1978, c. 92, s. 1.

CREE TRAPLINE. An area where the activities related to the exercise of the right to harvest are by tradition carried on under the supervision of a Cree tallyman. *An Act respecting hunting and fishing rights in the James Bay and New Quebec territories*, S.Q. 1978, c. 92, s. 1.

CREED. *n.* A system of religious belief.

CREEK. *n.* All natural watercourses, whether usually containing water or not, and that portion of any stream below the point where it enters the valley of the parent stream, but does not include streams that have an average width of one hundred and fifty feet. *Yukon Placer Mining Act*, R.S.C. 1985, c. Y-3, s. 2.

CREMATION. *n.* Disposal of a dead body by incineration.

CREMATORIUM. *n.* A building fitted with the proper appliances for the purpose of the incineration and cremation of human remains.

CREMATORY. *n.* A building fitted with proper appliances for the purpose of incinerating or cremating dead human bodies.

CREPUSCULUM. *n.* [L.] Twilight.

CRESCENTE MALITIA CRESCERE DEBET ET POENA. [L.] Where malice increases, punishment should also increase.

CREST. *n.* The heraldic device over a coat of arms.

C. RÉV. *abbr.* Cour de révision.

CREW. *n.* 1. Persons responsible for navigating a ship or aircraft. 2. The officers, seamen and apprentices of a ship. *Crew Accommodation Regulations*, C.R.C., c. 1418, s. 2. 3. Any group of fishermen who generally engage in making a catch together or who have actually engaged in making a catch together, and in the case of a single fisherman, "crew" or "member of a crew" as the case may be, means that single fisherman. *Unemployment Insurance Regulations*, C.R.C., c. 1576, s. 74. See MEMBER OF A ~.

CREW LIST. A list of members of the crew of a ship or aircraft.

CREW MEMBER. A person assigned to duty in an aircraft during flight time. Canada regulations. See FLIGHT ~.

CRIB DEATH. Sudden infant death syndrome: the sudden death of an apparently well infant, who is usually between three and twelve months old. F.A. Jaffe, *A Guide to Pathological Evidence*, 2d ed. (Toronto: Carswell, 1983) at 173.

CRICOID CARTILAGE. The cartilage which is lowermost in the larynx. F.A. Jaffe, *A Guide to Pathological Evidence*, 2d ed. (Toronto: Carswell, 1983) at 173.

CRI DE PAIS. [Fr.] A hue and cry.

CRIER. *n.* An officer of the court who made proclamations.

CRIME. *n.* 1. Conduct which society's laws prohibit. S.A. Cohen, *Due Process of Law* (Toronto: Carswell, 1977) at 1. 2. An offence against the State, as the public's representative, for which the offender will be punished. John G. Fleming, *The Law of Torts*, 6th ed. (Sydney: The Law Book Company Limited, 1983) at 1. 3. (a) An indictable offence under an Act of Canada, and (b) an offence, under an Act of Canada or of a province, that is punishable only on summary conviction. See EXTRADITION ~; GRAVE ~; WAR ~.

CRIME AGAINST HUMANITY. Murder, extermination, enslavement, deportation, persecution or any other inhumane act or omission that is committed against any civilian population or any identifiable group of persons, whether or not it constitutes a contravention of the law in force at the time and in the place of its commission, and that, at that time and in that place, constitutes a contravention of customary international law or conventional international law or is criminal according to the general principles of law recognized by the community of nations. *Criminal Code*, R.S.C. 1985, c. C-46, s. 7(3.76) as added by R.S.C. 1985 (3d Supp.), c. 30, s. 1.

CRIME COMIC. A magazine, periodical or book that exclusively or substantially comprises matter depicting pictorially (a) the commission of crimes, real or fictitious; or (b) events connected with the commission of crimes, real or fictitious, whether occurring before or after the commission of the crime. *Criminal Code*, R.S.C. 1985, c. C-46, s. 163(7).

CRIMEN FALSI. [L.] Forgery; perjury; suppression of evidence.

CRIMEN FURTI. [L.] Theft.

CRIMEN INCENDII. [L.] Arson.

CRIMEN LAESAE MAJESTATIS OMNIA ALIA CRIMINA EXCEDIT QUOAD POENAM. [L.] Treason is punished most severely of all crimes.

CRIMEN RAPTUS. [L.] Rape.

CRIMEN ROBERIAE. [L.] Robbery.

CRIME VICTIM. Any person killed or injured in Quebec: (a) by reason of the act or omission of any other person occurring in or resulting directly from the commission of an offence the description of which corresponds to the criminal offences mentioned in the schedule of this act; (b) while lawfully arresting or attempting to arrest an offender or suspected offender or assisting a peace officer making an arrest; (c) while lawfully preventing or attempting to prevent the commission of an offence or suspected offence, or assisting a peace officer preventing or attempting to prevent the commission of an offence or suspected offence. *Crime Victims Compensation Act*, R.S.Q. 1977, c. I-6, s. 3. See COMPENSATION FOR VICTIMS OF CRIME.

CRIMINAL. *n.* A person found guilty of an offence. See FUGITIVE ~; HABITUAL ~.

CRIMINAL. *adj.* Relating to crimes or to the administration of the law in respect of crimes.

CRIMINAL CODE. The Criminal Code, R.S.C. 1985, c. C-46 as amended from time to time.

CRIMINAL CONSPIRACY. An agreement by two or more people to do something together prohibited by statute. D. Stuart, *Canadian Criminal Law: a treatise*, 2d ed. (Toronto: Carswell, 1987) at 568.

CRIMINAL CONVERSATION. A husband's claim for damages for adultery.

CRIMINAL INJURIES COMPENSATION. A statutory plan to compensate victims of specified crimes, or anyone injured while attempting to arrest a person, assist a peace officer or preserve the peace. K.D. Cooper-Stephenson & I.B. Saunders, *Personal Injury Damages in Canada* (Toronto: Carswell, 1981) at 3.

CRIMINALIZATION. *n.* Rendering an act criminal and therefore punishable.

CRIMINAL JURISDICTION. See SUPERIOR COURT OF ~.

CRIMINAL JUSTICE SYSTEM. The sum of criminal law processes intended ultimately to control crime. S.A. Cohen, *Due Process of Law* (Toronto: Carswell, 1977) at 1.

CRIMINAL LAW. A law which declares acts to be crimes and prescribes punishment for those crimes.

CRIMINAL MATTER. A prosecution or trial for an offence triable by a judge or jury in accordance with the Criminal Code of Canada.

CRIMINAL NEGLIGENCE. Every one is criminally negligent who (a) in doing anything, or (b) in omitting to do anything that it is his duty to do shows wanton or reckless disregard for the lives or safety of other persons. *Criminal Code*, R.S.C. 1985, c. C-46, s. 219.

CRIMINAL OFFENCE. 1. An offence against an Act of Parliament. *Transfer of Offenders Act*, R.S.C. 1985, c. T-15, s. 2. 2. An indictable offence under an Act of the Parliament of Canada. See QUASI-~; SERIOUS ~.

CRIMINAL PROCEDURE. The law relating to the process followed by the criminal justice system.

CRIMINAL PROCEEDING. Includes any prosecution for an offence under any statute of the Province. *Evidence Act*, R.S.N.S. 1967, c. 94, s. 1.

CRIMINAL RATE. An effective annual rate of interest calculated in accordance with generally accepted actuarial practices and principles that exceeds sixty per cent on the credit advanced under an agreement or arrangement. *Criminal Code*, R.S.C. 1985, c. C-46, s. 347(2).

CRIMINAL RESPONSIBILITY. See AGE OF ~.

CRIMINAL SANCTIONS. Fines, imprisonment and probation.

CRIMINATE. *v.* To implicate.

CRIMINATION. See SELF-INCRIMINATION.

CRIMINOLOGIE. *abbr.* Journal published by Presses de l'Université de Montréal.

CRIMINOLOGY. *n.* The study of the nature, causes, treatment or punishment of criminal behaviour. D. Stuart, *Canadian Criminal Law: a Treatise*, 2d ed. (Toronto: Carswell, 1987) at 47.

CRIM. L.Q. *abbr.* Criminal Law Quarterly.

CRINKLE CUT. Potatoes cut into strips with corrugated surfaces of cross-sectional dimensions varying from approximately 3/8 by 3/8 inch to approximately 1/2 by 1/2 inch. *Processed Fruit and Vegetable Regulations*, C.R.C., c. 291, schedule I, s. 44.

CRITERIA. See EXPOSURE ~.

CRITICAL ENGINE. The engine the failure of which gives the most adverse effect on the aircraft characteristics relative to the aircraft under consideration. *Air Regulations*, C.R.C., c. 2, s. 101.

CRITICAL INDUSTRY. An industry designated under section 4 as a critical industry or the part or class of an industry that is so designated. *Critical Industries Act*, S.B.C. 1985, c. 47, s. 1.

CRITICAL INJURY. A serious injury which results in life being placed in jeopardy, substantial loss of blood, unconsciousness, burns to major part of the body, fracture of a leg or arm, or loss of sight in an eye. D. Robertson, *Ontario Health and Safety Guide* (Toronto: Richard De Boo Ltd., 1988) at 5-92.

CRITICAL PERIOD. The period concomitant with or consecutive to a natural disaster which creates an emergency situation for a certain number of producers or the period during which an unforeseen and uncontrollable collapse in the selling prices of a designated production seriously affects a large number of producers and that the Gouvernement acknowledges as such for the time that it indicates; the orders in council indicating the beginning and end of a period must be published in the Gazette officielle du Québec. *An Act to Promote Special Credit to Agricultural Producers During Critical Periods*, R.S.Q. 1977, c. C-79, s. 1.

CRITICAL WILDLIFE AREA. Land in a wildlife management area which is designated as a critical wildlife area. *Wildlife Act*, S.B.C. 1982, c. 57, s. 1.

CRITICISM. *n.* The opinion of any person about a book, play or visual image.

C.R.N.S. *abbr.* Criminal Reports, New Series, 1967-1978.

C.R.O. *abbr.* Commission des relations ouvrières.

CROOK. *n.* A criminal; swindler.

CROOKED. *adj.* Dishonest, not trustworthy.

CROP. *n.* 1. (a) Such field crops, either cultivated or uncultivated, as are designated by the Minister, and (b) maple syrup and honey. *Advance Payments for Crops Act*, R.S.C. 1985 (1st Supp.), c. 38, s. 2. 2. An unharvested agricultural crop, whether standing or cut, but does not include stubble fields or other fields from which the crop has been removed. *Migratory Birds Regulations*, C.R.C., c. 1035, s. 2. See COMMERCIAL ~; ~S; GROWING ~; INDUSTRIAL ~; INSURABLE ~; INSURED ~; MIXED FARMING ~; VINE ~.

CROP FAILURE. Failure of grain crops grown in any year on mortgaged land or on land sold under agreement for sale, due to causes beyond the control of the mortgagor or purchaser, to the extent that the sum realizable from the said crops is less than a sum equal to six dollars per acre sown to grain in that year on the land. *The Farm Security Act*, R.S.S. 1978, c. F-9, s. 6.

CROP INSURANCE. 1. Insurance against loss of or damage to growing crops from risks or perils to which such crops may be exposed. *The Saskatchewan Insurance Act*, R.S.S. 1978, c. S-26, s. 2. 2. Insurance against loss in respect of an insured crop caused by drought, flood, hail, wind, frost, lightning, excessive rain, snow, hurricane, tornado, wild life, insect infestation, plant disease or any other peril designated by the board of regulation published in The Saskatchewan Gazette. *The Saskatchewan Crop Insurance Act*, R.S.S. 1978, c. S-12, s. 2.

CROPS. *n.* 1. The products of the soil, and without limiting the generality of the foregoing, includes all sorts of grain, grass, hay, hops, fruit, pulse, potatoes, beets, turnips and other products of the soil. *Landlord and Tenant Act*, R.S.N.B. 1973, c. L-1. s. 1. 2. (i) Crops of grain whether growing or severed, and (ii) includes all grain obtained therefrom. *Agricultural Relief Advances Act*, R.S.A. 1980, c. A-10, s. 1. 3. (i) Crops of wheat, oats, barley, flax, rye, speltz and safflower; (ii) crops of field peas, fava beans, buckwheat, rape, mustard, grass and clover grown for seed; and (iii) crops of field corn and sunflowers grown for seed or fodder. *The Municipal Hail Insurance Act*, R.S.S. 1978, c. M-29, s. 2. See CROP; GRAIN OR ~; HARVESTING OF ~; ROOT ~; STANDING ~.

CROP SHARE AGREEMENT. (i) An agreement entered into by the board of directors of an irrigation district, the Irrigation Land Manager or by the Crown in right of Canada, (A) for the sale of land that is irrigated in whole or in part, (B) extinguishing any water right payments for the irrigation of land, or (C) providing for payment as, for or on account of water right payments with respect to land, under which the purchase or other money payable is payable by the delivery of a share of the crop on the land to which the agreement relates, and (ii) includes a crop lease entered into by a body or person mentioned in subclause (i) under which the rent payable is a share of the crop grown on the leased land and the lessee is or may become entitled to purchase the land. *Crop Payments (Irrigated Land Sales) Act*, R.S.A. 1980, c. C-36, s. 1.

CROP SHARE CULTIVATION LEASE. A cultivation lease granted under the Public Lands Act for which the rent or other consideration consists of a share of the crop grown on the land cultivated. *Crown Cultivation Leases Act*, R.S.A. 1980, c. C-37, s. 1.

CROP SHARE HOMESTEAD LEASE. (i) A homestead lease, (ii) an accrued area lease, or (iii) a cultivation permit, granted under the Public Lands Act and for which the rent or other consideration consists of a share of the crop grown on the land cultivated. *Crown Cultivation Leases Act*, R.S.A. 1980, c. C-37, s. 1.

CROP YEAR. 1. The period commencing on August 1 in any year and terminating on July 31 in the year next following. 2. The period from the first day of April to the 31st day of March in the next succeeding year. 3. A period from the 1st day of September in one year to the 31st day of August in the next year. 4. The calendar year in which the crop is normally harvested.

CROSS. *n.* The Memorial Cross, which shall be a cross patonce in silver, suspended by a purple ribbon; at the end of the upright a crown; at the foot, and at the end of each arm, a maple leaf; in the centre, within a wreath of laurel, the Royal Cypher of the reigning monarch; engraved with the number, rank and name of the sailor, soldier, airman, merchant seaman or fire fighter commemorated. *Memorial Cross Order (World War II)*, C.R.C., c. 1623, s. 2. See VARIETAL.

CROSS-ACTION. *n.* An action brought by a defendant against the plaintiff in the original action.

CROSS-APPEAL. *var.* **CROSS APPEAL.** An appeal by the respondent to an appeal.

CROSSBOW. *n.* A bow fixed across a stock with a groove for the arrow or bolt and a mechanism for holding and releasing the string.

CROSSCLAIM. *n.* A claim by one defendant against a co-defendant.

CROSS-COUNTRY RECREATION. A type of recreation characterized by the use of little frequented territory and the use of relatively simple equipment. *Parks Act*, R.S.Q. 1977, c. P-9, s. 1.

CROSSED CHEQUE. Two parallel lines drawn across the cheque to indicate it cannot be endorsed.

CROSS-EXAMINATION. *n.* The opposite side's examination of a witness which usually follows examination in chief. It is used to weaken the effect of the witness's testimony, to discredit the witness and to elicit evidence in favour of the cross-examining party. P.K. McWilliams, *Canadian Criminal Evidence*, 3d ed. (Aurora: Canada Law Book, 1988) at 37-3 and 37-4.

CROSS-EXAMINATION ON AFFIDAVIT. The opposite party's examination of an affiant on the contents of the affiant's affidavit.

CROSSING. *n.* 1. A place where pedestrians may cross a street, highway or railway. 2. A railway crossing of a highway or highway crossing of a railway. See RAILWAY ~.

CROSSING GUARD. See SCHOOL ~.

CROSSOVER. See PEDESTRIAN ~.

CROSS PICKETING. Picketing by two groups having different objectives.

CROSS WALK. *var.* **CROSSWALK.** (i) A clearly marked pedestrian crossing; or (ii) if there is no clearly marked pedestrian crossing, the prolongation through the intersection of the lateral boundary lines of the adjacent or intersecting sidewalks at the end of a block.

CROWN. *n.* 1. In Canada, the federal government and each of the provincial governments. 2. Depending on the context, Her Majesty the Queen in right of a Province, Canada or both a province and Canada. 3. Used when speaking of the rights, duties or prerogatives of the sovereign. 4. Any of the Commonwealth governments which represent the head, which is Her Majesty. 5. The Sovereign of the United Kingdom, Canada and Her other Realms and Territories, and Head of the Commonwealth. See AGENCY OF THE ~; DEMISE OF THE ~; EMPLOYED BY OR UNDER THE ~; FEDERAL ~; LAW OFFICER OF THE ~; MINISTER OF THE ~; PLEA OF THE ~; PREROGATIVE RIGHTS OF THE ~; PROCEEDING AGAINST THE ~.

CROWN AGENCY. 1. Any board, commission, association, or other body, whether incorporated or unincorporated, all the members of which, or of the board of management or board of directors of which, (i) are appointed by an Act of the Legislature or by order of the Lieutenant Governor in Council, or (ii) if not so appointed, in the discharge of their duties are public officers or servants of the Crown, or for the proper discharge of their duties are directly or indirectly responsible to the Crown, or any corporation the election of the board of directors of which is controlled by the Crown, directly or indirectly, through ownership of the shares of the capital stock thereof by the Crown or by a board, commission, association, or other body which is a Crown agency within the meaning of this definition. *An Act to Amend the Legislative Assembly Act*, S.M. 1980-81, c. 2, s. 2. 2. A board, commission, railway, public utility, university, manufactory, company or agency, owned, controlled or operated by Her Majesty in right of Ontario, or by the Government of Ontario, or under the authority of the Legislature or the Lieutenant Governor in Council. *Crown Agency Act*, R.S.O. 1980, c. 106, s. 1.

CROWN ASSETS. See SURPLUS ~.

CROWN ATTORNEY. 1. An agent of the Attorney General; prosecutor in criminal matters on behalf of the Crown. 2. A lawyer who advises concerning police activity. S.A. Cohen, *Due Process of Law* (Toronto: Carswell, 1977) at 48-49.

CROWN CHARGES. All charges, fees, assessment levies and dues in respect of Crown timber, costs, expenses and penalties imposed under this Act or the regulations or payable to the Crown by virtue of any contract.

CROWN CONTROLLED CORPORATION. 1. A corporation that is not an agency of the Crown and having 50 per cent or more of its issued and outstanding shares vested in Her Majesty in right of Ontario or having the appointment of a majority of its board of directors made or approved by the Lieutenant Governor in Council. *Audit Act*, R.S.O. 1980, c. 35, s. 1. 2. Any corporation or entity in which the government owns more than 50 per cent of the issued and outstanding voting shares. *Audit Act*, S.P.E.I. 1980, c. 10, s. 1.

CROWN-CONTROLLED ORGANIZATION. (i) A corporation that is incorporated by or under an Act of the Legislature, other than a local or private act, one or more but less than a majority of whose members or directors are appointed or designated, either by their personal names or by their names of office, by an Act of the Legislature or regulations under an Act of the Legislature, by an order of the Lieutenant Governor in Council or of a Minister of the Crown or by any combination thereof, or (ii) an unincorporated board, commission, council or other body that is not a department or part of a department, one or more but less than a majority of whose members are appointed or designated, either by their personal names or by their names of office, by an Act of the Legislature or regulations under an Act of the Legislature, by an order of the Lieutenant Governor in Council or of a Minister of the Crown or by any combination thereof, that is responsible for the administration of public money or assets owned by the Crown, and includes a corporation, more than 50 per cent but less than 100 per cent of whose issued voting shares are owned by the Crown or held in trust for the Crown or are partly owned by the Crown and partly held in trust for the Crown. *Auditor General Act*, R.S.A. 1980, c. A-49, s. 1.

CROWN CORPORATION. 1. A corporation that is accountable, through a Minister, to the Legislative Assembly or Parliament for the conduct of its affairs. 2. A corporation of which not less than 90 per cent of the shares ordinarily entitled to vote in an election for directors are owned by the government of the Province or of Canada. 3. A corporation of which all the directors or members of the governing body are appointed by the Lieutenant Governor in Council or the Governor General in Council. 4. A corporation which under any Act of the Province or of Canada is designated as such. See PARENT ~.

CROWN COUN. REV. *abbr.* Crown Counsel's Review.

CROWN COUNSEL. (i) A barrister and solicitor or a student-at-law employed by the Department of the Attorney General, or (ii) an agent of the Attorney General. *Summary Convictions Act*, R.S.A. 1980, c. S-26.1, s. 1.

CROWN DEBT. Any existing or future debt due or becoming due by the Crown, and any other chose in action in respect of which there is a right of recovery enforceable by action against the Crown. *Financial Administration Act*, R.S.C. 1985, c. F-11, s. 66.

CROWN DISPOSITION. The rights granted by the Crown under a Crown lease or any other instrument issued under this Act, or under any predecessor statute, by which the Crown has granted to any person any right or privilege to explore or prospect for any Crown mineral, or any other right to or interest in any Crown mineral or any Crown mineral lands. *Crown Minerals Act*, S.S. 1984-85-86, c. C-50.2, s. 2.

CROWN EMPLOYEE. A person employed in the service of the Crown or any agency of the Crown, but does not include an employee of Ontario Hydro or the Ontario Northland Transportation Commission. *Public Service Act*, R.S.O. 1980, c. 418, s. 1.

CROWN ENTITY. For the purposes of this Act, any board, commission, association or other body corporate, all the members of which, or all the members of the board of management or board of directors of which, (i) are appointed by an Act of the Legislature or by the Lieutenant Governor in Council, or (ii) are elected, directly or indirectly by the government in its capacity as shareholder, or by a corporation which is owned or controlled by the government, or (iii) if not so appointed or elected, are, in the discharge of their duties, public officers or servants of the Crown, or, for the purpose of the discharge of their duties are, directly or indirectly, responsible to the Crown, but does not include any board, commission, association or other body, the employees of which are subject to The Civil Service Act. *The Pay Equity Act*, S.M. 1985-86, c. 21, s. 1.

CROWN GRANT. 1. A transfer of Crown lands to a private person. 2. An instrument in writing conveying Crown land in fee simple. *Land Act*,

R.S.B.C. 1979, c. 214, s. 1. 3. (a) Any grant, lease, or licence of occupation, absolute, limited or conditional, of or relating to any of the Crown or public lands of the province; and (b) any licence, lease or grant of any mining or other rights or interest of or in any lands in the province granted by or issuing from Her Majesty or from the Government of the province, or any department of the Government of the province. *Judicature Act*, S.Nfld 1986, c. 42, s. 136.

CROWN IMMUNITY. 1. The common law rule that the Crown is not bound by a statute, unless by express words or necessary implication. 2. Statutory provisions in the various Interpretation Acts to the effect that the Crown is not bound unless by express words.

CROWN LAND. 1. Land, whether or not it is covered by water, or an interest in land, vested in the Crown. British Columbia statutes. 2. Land vested in Her Majesty in right of Canada but does not include Commissioner's Land. *Home Owners' Property Tax Rebate Act*, S.N.W.T. 1981 (2d Sess.), c. 4, s. 2. See VACANT ∼.

CROWN LANDS. 1. Such Crown or public lands or Crown domain as are within the Province and belong to Her Majesty in right of the Province, and whether or not any water flow over or cover the same. 2. All lands within the province except (A) such as may be in the use or occupation of any department of the Government of the province or of any officer or servant thereof as such, (B) such lands as may, before the enactment of this Act, have been lawfully set apart or appropriated for any public purposes, and (C) lands lawfully alienated from the Crown, and (ii) lands deemed to be Crown lands pursuant to section 133.2. *Crown Lands (Amendment) Act*, S.Nfld. 1983, c. 80, s. 1. 3. All Crown lands, lands transferred to Québec, clergy lands or lands of the Jesuits' estates, Crown domain of seigniory of Lauzon, which have not been alienated by the Crown. *Mining Act*, R.S.Q. 1977, c. M-13, s. 1.

CROWN LEASE. A lease issued under this Act, or under any predecessor statute, by which the Crown has granted to any person the right to extract, recover or produce any Crown mineral. *Crown Minerals Act*, S.S. 1984-85-86, c. C-50.2, s. 2.

CROWN MINERAL. Any mineral that may be found on, in or under any Crown mineral lands. *Crown Minerals Act*, S.S. 1984-85-86, c. C-50.2, s. 2.

CROWN MINERAL LANDS. The mineral interest of the Crown in any lands in Saskatchewan whether or not the surface rights in any of those lands are also the property of the Crown. Saskatchewan statutes.

CROWN OIL. All oil: (i) produced from Crown lands; (ii) allocated to the Crown or to Crown lands under a voluntary pooling arrangement, a pooling order, an agreement for unit operation or a unit operation order made pursuant to The Oil and Gas Conservation Act and the regulations thereunder; or (iii) produced from or allocated to any other lands as may be prescribed from time to time by the regulations. *Oil Well Income Tax Amendment Act, 1980*, S.S. 1980-81, s. 16, c. 3.

CROWN OWNED CORPORATION. Any corporation or entity in which the government owns more than 50 per cent of the issued and outstanding voting shares. *Audit Act*, S.P.E.I. 1980, c. 10, s. 1.

CROWN PETROLEUM. Petroleum which is vested in Her Majesty in right of the province by virtue of this Act. *Petroleum and Natural Gas Act*, R.S.Nfld. 1970, c. 294, s. 2.

CROWN PRIVILEGE. The rule of evidence which states that relevant evidence which is otherwise admissible must not be admitted if to do so would injure the public interest. P.W. Hogg, *Constitutional Law of Canada*, 2d ed. (Toronto: Carswell, 1985) at 223 and 224.

CROWN PROPERTY. 1. Real property of the Crown in right of Alberta, other than mines and minerals and the property mentioned in section 6. *Crown Property Municipal Grants Act*, R.S.A. 1980, c. C-38, s. 1. 2. As the context may require but subject to the Highway Traffic Act, any land, lot, grounds, roadway, passageway, driveway, building or structure, or an area of any of the foregoing, or any thing, owned or controlled by the Crown in right of the province and under the control of the minister under this Act. *Department of Public Works Act*, S.M. 1974, c. 45, s. 2.

CROWN RANGE. Crown land included within the boundaries of a range district, but does not include Crown land that is subject to a lease issued under the Land Act. *Range Act*, R.S.B.C. 1979, c. 355, s. 1.

CROWN RESERVE. Land which vests in the Crown which is not dedicated to the public. Manitoba statutes.

CROWN RESERVE AREA. Portions of the offshore area in respect of which no interest is in force. *Canada-Newfoundland Atlantic Accord Implementation (Newfoundland) Act*, S. Nfld. 1986, c. 37, s. 47.

CROWN RESERVE LANDS. 1. Canada lands in respect of which no interest is in force. *Oil and Gas Act*, R.S.C. 1985, c. O-6, s. 2. 2. Frontier lands in respect of which no interest is in force. *Canada Petroleum Resources Act*, R.S.C. 1985

(2d Supp.), c. 36, s. 2. 3. Nova Scotia lands in respect of which no interest is in force. *Offshore Oil and Gas Act*, S.N.S. 1984, c. 8, s. 2.

CROWN ROYALTY. Of a person for a taxation year in respect of the production in the year of petroleum or gas from a well or bituminous sands, oil sands or oil shale deposit or the ownership of a natural reservoir of gas or petroleum in Canada or a bituminous sands, oil sands or oil shale deposit in Canada means the amount, if any, by which the aggregate of the amounts, (a) paid, payable or receivable as prescribed in respect of that production or ownership, (b) included in computing his income for the year by virtue of paragraph 12(1)(o) of the Income Tax Act in respect of that production or ownership, (c) that were not deductible in computing his income for the year by virtue of paragraph 18(1)(m) of the Income Tax Act in respect of that production or ownership, (d) by which, in respect of the disposition by him of that production, his proceeds of disposition were increased by virtue of subsection 69(6) of the Income Tax Act, and (e) by which, in respect of the acquisition by him of that production, his cost was reduced by virtue of subsection 69(7) of the Income Tax Act exceeds the aggregate of all reimbursements referred to in section 80.2 of the Income Tax Act received or receivable by him for the year in respect of that production or ownership. *Petroleum and Gas Revenue Tax Act*, R.S.C. 1985, c. P-12, s. 2. See INCREMENTAL ~.

CROWN SHARE. 1. The share reserved to Her Majesty in right of Canada under this Act. *Oil and Gas Act*, R.S.C. 1985, c. O-6, s. 28. 2. The share reserved to Her Majesty in right of the Province pursuant to this Act. *Offshore Oil and Gas Act*, S.N.S. 1984, c. 8, s. 2.

CROWN SHIP. A ship, as defined in the Canada Shipping Act, that is owned by or is in the exclusive possession of the Crown. *Crown Liability Act*, R.S.C. 1985, c. C-50, s. 2.

CROWN'S NEWSL. *abbr.* Crown's Newsletter.

CROWN TIMBER. 1. Includes any trees, timber and products of the forest in respect whereof the Crown is enabled to demand and receive any stumpage, royalty, revenue or money. 2. Timber on Crown land, or timber reserved to the Crown. *Forest Act*, R.S.B.C. 1979, c. 140, s. 1. 3. Timber on public lands or timber that is the property of the Crown under the management of the Minister on lands other than public lands. *Crown Timber Act*, R.S.O. 1980, c. 109, s. 1.

CROWN WARDSHIP ORDER. An order of a court making the Crown the legal guardian of a child in need of protection.

CROW'S NEST PASS ACT. An Act to authorize a Subsidy for a Railway through the Crow's Nest Pass, chapter 5 of the Statutes of Canada, 1897, and includes any Act, regulation or order that amends that Act. *Western Grain Transportation Act*, R.S.C. 1985, c. W-8, s. 2.

C.R.P. *abbr.* Conseil de révision des pensions.

C.R.R. *abbr.* Canadian Rights Reporter.

C.R.T.C. *abbr.* 1. Canadian Railway and Transport Cases, 1902-1966. 2. Canadian Radio-television and Telecommunications Commission (Conseil de la radio-diffusion et des télécommunications canadiennes).

C.R.T.F.P. *abbr.* Commission des relations de travail dans la Fonction publique.

C.R. (3d). *abbr.* Criminal Reports (Third Series), 1978-.

C.R.T.Q. *abbr.* Commission des relations du travail (Québec).

CRUDE BITUMEN. A naturally occurring viscous mixture, mainly of hydrocarbons heavier than pentane, that may contain sulphur compounds and that, in its naturally occurring viscous state, will not flow to a well.

CRUDE OIL. A mixture mainly of pentanes and heavier hydrocarbons, which may be contaminated with sulphur compounds, that is recovered or is recoverable at a well from an underground reservoir and that is liquid at the conditions under which its volume is measured or estimated, and includes all other hydrocarbon mixtures so recovered or recoverable except raw gas or condensate. See HEAVY ~; SYNTHETIC ~.

CRUDE PETROLEUM. A flammable liquid with a flash point below 150°F and consisting of an unrefined mixture of natural liquid hydrocarbons as obtained from the earth. *Flammable Liquids Bulk Storage Regulations*, C.R.C., c. 1148, s. 2.

CRUDE WHALE OIL. Rendered fat from a whale. *Meat Inspection Regulations*, C.R.C., c. 1032, s. 169.

CRUELTY. *n.* Conduct that creates a danger to life, limb or health, and includes any course of conduct that in the opinion of the Court is grossly insulting and intolerable, or is of such a character that the person seeking a separation could not reasonably be expected to be willing to live with the other after he or she has been guilty of such conduct. *Domestic Relations acts.* See ACTS OF ~.

CRUISING ALTITUDE. An altitude, as shown by a constant altimeter indication in relation to a fixed and defined datum, maintained during a flight or portion thereof. *Air Regulations*, C.R.C., c. 2, s. 101.

CRUSH. See INITIAL ~ RESISTANCE; INTERMEDIATE ~ RESISTANCE; PEAK ~ RESISTANCE.

CRUSHED. *adj.* The style typical of apple juice that has not been clarified and that contains suspended visible particles of apple pulp. *Processed Fruit and Vegetable Regulations*, C.R.C., c. 291, schedule I, s. 3.

CRUSH SYNDROME. 1. Kidney failure brought about by a serious crushing injury, usually to a limb. 2. Kidney failure following transfusion of incompatible blood. F.A. Jaffe, *A Guide to Pathological Evidence*, 2d ed. (Toronto: Carswell, 1983) at 184 and 185.

CRY DE PAIS. See CRI DE PAIS.

CRYER. *n.* A court officer who makes proclamations.

CRYPT. *n.* An underground chamber located under the main floor of a church or other building. *An Act to Amend the Cemetery Companies Act*, S.N.B. 1984, c. 18, s. 1.

CRYSTALLIZATION. *n.* When a debtor under a security instrument defaults and the security under the instrument becomes enforceable against that debtor any floating charges attach to the property of the debtor at that moment. F. Bennett, *Receiverships* (Toronto: Carswell, 1985) at 41 and 42.

CRYSTALLIZE. *v.* To convert a floating charge into a fixed charge. F. Bennett, *Receiverships* (Toronto: Carswell, 1985) at 33. See DE-~.

C.S. *abbr.* 1. Cour supérieure. 2. Cour suprême (provinciale). 3. Recueils de jurisprudence de la Cour supérieure de Québec (Quebec Superior Court Reports). 4. Rapports judiciaires du Québec, Cour supérieure, 1892-1941 (Official Reports, Superior Court).

[ ] C.S. *abbr.* 1. Rapports judiciaires du Québec, Cour supérieure, 1942-1966. 2. Recueils de jurisprudence du Québec, Cour Supérieure, 1967-.

C.S.A. *abbr.* Canadian Standards Association.

CSA ELEVATOR CODE. The Safety Code for Elevators, Dumbwaiters and Escalators of the Canadian Standards Association, CSA Standard B44-1966, as amended from time to time. Canada regulations.

CSA INDUSTRIAL LIGHTING STANDARD. The Canadian Standards Association Standard C92.1-1967, as amended from time to time. *Canada Safe Illumination Regulations*, C.R.C., c. 1008, s. 2.

CSA STANDARD. A standard published by the Canadian Standards Association. *Occupational Health and Safety Act*, R.R.O. 1980, Reg. 694, s. 1.

C.S.C. *abbr.* Cour suprême du Canada.

C.S. CAN. *abbr.* Cour Suprême du Canada.

C.S.P. *abbr.* 1. Cour des Sessions de la paix. 2. Recueils de jurisprudence, Cour des Sessions de la Paix.

C.S.P. QUÉ. *abbr.* Cour des sessions de la paix (Québec) (Court of Sessions of the Peace (Quebec)).

C.S. QUÉ. *abbr.* Cour supérieure (Québec).

C.S.R. *abbr.* Commission scolaire régionale.

CT. *abbr.* Court.

C.T. *abbr.* Commission du tarif.

C.T.C. *abbr.* 1. Canadian Transport Cases, 1966-. 2. Canadian Transport Commission (Commission canadienne des transports). 3. Centralized Traffic Control.

[ ] C.T.C. *abbr.* Canada Tax Cases, 1917-1971.

CTC(A). The Air Transport Committee of the Canadian Transport Commission. Canada regulations.

[ ] C.T.C. (N.S.). *abbr.* Canada Tax Cases, 1971-.

C.T.C. REGULATIONS. Regulations for the Transportation of Dangerous Commodities by Rail. Canada regulations.

CT. CRIM. APP. *abbr.* Court of Criminal Appeals.

C.T.C.U.M. *abbr.* Commission de transport de la communauté urbaine de Montréal.

CTEE. *abbr.* Committee.

C.T.M. *abbr.* Canada Tax Manual.

CT. MARTIAL APP. CT. *abbr.* Court Martial Appeal Court.

C.T.Q. *abbr.* Commission des transports du Québec.

C. TRANS. C. *abbr.* Canadian Transport Cases.

CT. REV. *abbr.* Court of Review.

CT. SESS. P. *abbr.* Court of Sessions of the Peace.

C.T./T.T. *abbr.* Décisions du Commissaire du travail et du Tribunal du travail.

CUBIC CENTIMETRE. 1. Interchangeable with the term "millilitre". *Food and Drug Regulations*, C.R.C., c. 870, c. A.01.010. 2. In relation to gases, means the quantity of the gases that occupies a volume of 1 cubic centimetre at 25 degrees Celsius and at a pressure of 760 millimetres of mercury (being the equivalent of a pressure of 100.9 kPa). *Asbestos Mining and Milling National Emission Standards Regulations,* C.R.C., c. 405, s. 2.

CUBIC FOOT. 1/27 cubic yard. *Weights and Measures Act,* S.C. 1970-71-72, c. 36, schedule II. See STANDARD ~.

CUBIC INCH. 1/1 728 cubic foot. *Weights and Measures Act,* S.C. 1970-71-72, c. 36, schedule II.

CUBIC METRE. For a volume of (a) natural gas, that volume measured at 101.325 kPa and 15°C; and (b) petroleum, that volume measured at 15°C. *Petroleum or Natural Gas Act,* R.S.B.C. 1979, c. 323, s. 1. See NORMAL ~.

CUBIC YARD. A volume equal to that of a cube each side of which measures one yard. *Weights and Measures Act,* S.C. 1970-71-72, c. 36, schedule II.

CUCUMBER. See FIELD ~ S; GREEN-HOUSE ~S.

CUI BONO. [L.] To whose good.

CUICUNQUE ALIQUID QUID CONCEDIT CONCEDERE VIDETUR ET ID SINE QUO RES IPSA ESSE NON POTUIT. [L.] A grantor must grant that thing without which the first thing granted would be useless.

CUILIBET IN SUA ARTE PERITO EST CREDENDUM. [L.] A person who is skilled in a profession should be believed.

CUILIBET LICET RENUNTIARE JURI PRO SE INTRODUCTO. [L.] Anyone can waive the advantage of a law made solely for the protection and benefit of the individual in a private capacity as long as this does not infringe any public policy or right. P.St.J. Langan, ed., *Maxwell on The Interpretation of Statutes,* 12th ed. (Bombay: N.M. Tripathi, 1976) at 328.

CUI LICET QUOD MAJUS NON DEBET QUOD MINUS EST NON LICERE. [L.] The one who has authority to do a greater thing should not be prevented from doing a lesser thing.

CUJUS EST DARE EJUS EST DISPONERE. [L.] The one who gives something can also control its disposition.

CUJUS EST INSTITUERE EJUS EST ABRO-GARE. [L.] The one who initiates may also abrogate.

CUJUS EST SOLUM EJUS EST USQUE AD COELUM. [L. one who owns the soil owns up to the sky] The owner of land owns whatever is above it.

CUL DE SAC. *var.* **CUL-DE-SAC.** A street or road open only at one end.

CULL. *n.* A defective log as defined by the manual of scaling instructions. *Crown Timber Act,* R.S.O. 1980, c. 109, s. 1.

CULLER. *n.* Any person employed or engaged in measuring logs for building or other purposes cut upon Crown Lands or subject to any dues for the purposes of administration or revenue. *Cullers Act,* R.S.Q. 1977, c. M-12, s. 2.

CULPA. *n.* [L.] Fault; neglect.

CULPABILITY. *n.* Blame.

CULPABLE. *adj.* That which is to be blamed.

CULPABLE HOMICIDE. 1. Murder or man-slaughter or infanticide. *Criminal Code,* R.S.C. 1985, c. C-46, s. 222(4). 2. A person commits culpable homicide when he causes the death of a human being, (a) by means of an unlawful act, (b) by criminal negligence, (c) by causing that human being, by threats or fear of violence or by deception, to do anything that causes his death, or (d) by wilfully frightening that human being, in the case of a child or sick person. *Criminal Code,* R.S.C. 1985, c. C-46, s. 222(5).

CULPA CARET QUI SCIT SED PROHIBERE NON POTEST. [L.] Anyone who knows but cannot prevent is free from blame.

CULPA EST IMMISCERE SE REI AD SE NON PERTINENTI. [L.] It is wrong for someone to interfere in a matter not related to oneself.

CULPA LATA DOLO AEQUIPARATUR. [L.] Gross negligence is equivalent to purposeful wrong.

CULPRIT. *n.* A person accused of an offence; a person found guilty of an offence.

CULTIVATED LAND. 1. (a) Pasture fields seeded with cultivated grass, (b) land on which planted crops are growing, (c) land which is or which is usually prepared for the growing of planted crops, (d) Christmas tree plantations, (e) forest experimental lots, (f) managed sugar bush stands, and (g) orchards. 2. Land that in the year of award was seeded to crop or was in summer-fallow and includes (a) land that was seeded to grass in any year if the productivity thereof was maintained in the year of award, and (b) land of a farmer that in three out of five years inmmediately preceding the year of award had been seeded or summer-fallowed, but owing to natural causes beyond his control could not be seeded or summer-fallowed in the year of award. *Prairie Farm Assistance Act,* R.S.C. 1970, c. P-

16, s. 2. 3. Land that is used for farming purposes. *Division Fence Act*, S.P.E.I. 1975, c. 43, s. 1.

CULTIVATION LEASE. See CROP SHARE ∼.

CULTURAL PROPERTY. Property belonging to any one or more of the following categories: (a) collections and specimens of fauna, flora, minerals and objects of palaeontological interest; (b) property relating to history, including the history of science and technology and military and social history, to national leaders, academics and scientists and to events of national importance; (c) products of archaeological excavations or of archaeological discoveries; (d) elements of artistic or historical monuments or archaeological sites that have been dismantled or dismembered; (e) antiquities, including inscriptions, coins and engraved seals; (f) objects of ethnological interest; (g) property of artistic interest, including (i) pictures, paintings and drawings produced entirely by hand on any support and in any material; (ii) works of statuary art and sculpture in any material; (iii) engravings, prints and lithographs; (iv) artistic assemblages and montages in any material; (h) manuscripts, books, documents and publications of special interest; (i) postage, revenue and similar stamps; (j) archives, including sound, photographic and cinematographic archives; (k) articles of furniture and musical instruments. *Foreign Cultural Property Immunity Act*, S.A. 1985, c. F-12.5, s. 1. See FOREIGN ∼.

CULTURAL PROPERTY AGREEMENT. In relation to a foreign State, means an agreement between Canada and the foreign State or an international agreement to which Canada and the foreign State are both parties, relating to the prevention of illicit international traffic in cultural property. *Cultural Property Export and Import Act*, R.S.C. 1985, c. C-51, s. 37.

CULTURE. See BACTERIAL ∼.

C.U.M. *abbr.* Communauté urbaine de Montréal.

CUM DIV. *abbr.* Cum dividend.

CUM DIVIDEND. With dividend; when a share is sold cum div. the purchaser receives any declared and not yet paid dividend.

CUM DUO INTER SE PUGNANTIA REPERIUNTUR IN TESTAMENTO ULTIMUM RATUM EST. [L.] Where two clauses in a will are inconsistent, the one appearing later in the will should be considered valid.

CUM GRANO SALIS. [L.] With a grain of salt.

CUM IN TESTAMENTO AMBIGUE AUT ETIAM PERPERAM SCRIPTUM EST, BENIGNE INTERPRETARI DEBET ET SECUNDUM ID QUOD CREDIBILE EST

COGITATUM CREDENDUM EST. [L.] Where an ambiguous, or even incorrect, expression occurs in a will, it should be interpreted liberally and in accordance with what it is thought the testator intended.

CUM PAR DELICTUM EST DUORUM SEMPER ONERATUR PETITOR ET MELIOR HABETUR POSSESSORIS CAUSA. [L.] When both parties are at fault it is the plaintiff who must fail, and the person in possession has the stronger case.

CUM RIGHTS. A purchaser of shares cum rights has the right to claim the rights to new shares or warrants which are about to be issued.

CUM TESTAMENTO ANNEXO. [L. with the will annexed] Administration with the will annexed is granted when a testator has not named an executor or the executor named is not willing to act.

CUMULATIVE. *adj.* Additional, to be added together, to be taken in succession.

CUMULATIVE CREDIT. The amount of credit available for each period is spelled out, and any balance unspent in one period may be carried over into the next. I.F.G. Baxter, *The Law of Banking*, 3d ed. (Toronto: Carswell, 1981) at 156.

CUMULATIVE GAINS LIMIT. Of an individual at the end of a taxation year means the amount, if any, by which (a) the aggregate of all amounts each of which is the amount determined in respect of the individual for the year or a preceding taxation year ending after 1984 under paragraph (a) of the definition "annual gains limit" exceeds the aggregate of (b) the aggregate of all amounts each of which is the amount determined in respect of the individual for the year or a preceding taxation year ending after 1984 under paragraph (b) or (c) of the definition "annual gains limit" or an amount deducted by the individual under paragraph 3(e) for his 1985 taxation year, (c) the aggregate of all amounts each of which is an amount deducted by the individual under this section in computing his taxable income for a preceding taxation year, and (d) his cumulative net investment loss at the end of the year. *Income Tax Act*, R.S.C. 1952, c. 148 (as am. S.C. 1988, c. 55, s. 81(2)), s. 110.6(1).

CUMULATIVE LEGACY. A legacy given in addition to a prior legacy in the same will.

CUMULATIVE NET INVESTMENT LOSS. Of an individual at the end of a taxation year means the amount, if any, by which (a) the aggregate of all amounts each of which is the investment expense of the individual for the year or a preceding taxation year ending after 1987 exceeds (b) the aggregate of all amounts each of which is the investment income of the individual for the year or a preceding taxation year ending after 1987. *Income Tax Act*, R.S.C. 1952, c. 148 (as am. S.C. 1988, c. 55, s. 81(4)), s. 110.6(1).

CUMULATIVE PREFERENCE SHARE. A share the dividend of which cumulates from year to year.

CUMULATIVE REMEDY. A mode of procedure available in addition to another possible remedy; opposite to alternative remedy.

CUMULATIVE TALLY ADJUSTMENT. In respect of any crop year, means an amount equal to the aggregate of (a) the annual tally adjustment for that crop year, and (b) the cumulative tally adjustment for the preceding crop year. *Western Grain Transportation Act*, R.S.C. 1985 (1st Supp.), c. 43, s. 12.

CUMULATIVE VOTING. A voting method which permits all votes attached to all a shareholder's shares to be cast for one candidate for board of directors of a corporation.

C.U.Q. *abbr.* Communauté urbaine de Québec.

CURATIVE. *adj.* Intended to remedy.

CURATIVE SECTION. A provision that one will substantially comply with provisions, such as registration of the claim for lien, so that no lien is invalidated because one failed to comply with the requirements of such a section unless the Court judges that some person was prejudiced thereby (and then the award is only to the extent of that prejudice). D.N. Macklem & D.I. Bristow, *Construction and Mechanics' Liens in Canada*, 5th ed. (Toronto: Carswell, 1985) at 9.

CURATIVE STATUTE. A statute designed to operate on past events, acts or transactions so that irregularities and errors are corrected and acts which would otherwise be ineffective for the intended purpose are rendered valid. B.J. Reiter, R.C.B. Risk & B.N. McLellan, *Real Estate Law*, 3d ed. (Toronto: Emond Montgomery, 1986) at 527.

CURATOR. *n.* A protector of property.

CURBING. *n.* Includes a curbing of any material in or along a street, whether constructed in connection with or apart from the laying down of a pavement or sidewalk, or with or without a projection for the purpose of a gutter.

CURB WEIGHT. 1. The weight of a vehicle with standard equipment and carrying its maximum capacity of fuel, oil and coolant and includes the weight of any air-conditioning equipment on the vehicle and the amount by which the weight of any optional engine with which the vehicle is equipped exceeds the weight of the standard engine. *Motor Vehicle Safety Regulations*, C.R.C., c. 1038, s. 2. 2. The actual weight of a motor vehicle when unladen but including the body, batteries, loose tools, spare wheels and other usual equipment and a full supply of water and fuel used for the purposes of propulsion. *Highway Traffic Act*, R.S. Nfld. 1970, c. 152, s. 2.

CURE. *v.* To add a substance to a meat product for the purpose of preventing or delaying undesirable or unwholesome changes as well as to enhance colour, flavour and texture. *Meat Inspection Regulations*, C.R.C., c. 1032, s. 2.

CURED FISH. Fish that has received curing. *Saltfish Act*, R.S.C. 1985, c. S-4, s. 2.

CURE TITLE. To remove encumbrances or claims in order to create good or clear title.

CURFEW. *n.* A law requiring persons to remove themselves from the streets at a certain time of night.

CURIA. *n.* [L.] A court of justice.

CURIA ADVISARI VULT. [L.] The court will consider the matter.

CURIA PARLIAMENTI SUIS PROPRIIS LEGIBUS SUBSISTIT. [L.] The court of Parliament functions under its own peculiar laws.

CURIA REGIS. [L.] The monarch's court.

CURING. *n.* Processing with salt or with salt and drying. *Saltfish Act*, R.S.C. 1985, c. S-4, s. 2.

CURING PLANT. See SALMON BRINE ~.

CURRANT JELLY CLOT. Mainly red blood cells, dark red in colour, forming the lower part of a clot. F.A. Jaffe, *A Guide to Pathological Evidence*, 2d ed. (Toronto: Carswell, 1983) at 172.

CURRENCY. *n.* 1. A period during which something is in force. 2. The medium of exchange which circulates in a country. 3. Money. See CREATION OF ~; EURO-~ MARKET.

CURRENT. *n.* See OVER ~ DEVICE.

CURRENT. *adj.* Lawfully current in Canada or elsewhere by virtue of law, proclamation or regulation in force in Canada or elsewhere as the case may be. *Criminal Code*, R.S.C. 1985, c. C-46, s. 448.

CURRENT ASSETS. Cash, accounts receivable, inventory and assets which could be converted to cash in the near future.

CURRENT DEPOSIT. A deposit out of which money may be withdrawn on presentation of a bill of exchange. *Credit Union Act*, R.S.A. 1980, c. C-31, s. 1.

CURRENT EXPENDITURE. An expenditure for operating purposes or a permanent improvement from funds other than those arising from the sale of a debenture, from a capital loan or from a loan pending the sale of a debenture. *Education Act*, R.S.O. 1980, c. 129, s. 1.

CURRENT LIABILITY. A debt due within a short period of time.

CURRENT LOAN. Any loan which is not a funded obligation. *Provincial Finance Act*, S.N.S. 1973, c. 49, s. 4.

CURRENT NET PRICE. The price payable for the unused part by the dealer as shown in the vendor's current price list and without taking into account any allowance granted by the vendor. *Farm Machinery and Equipment Act*, S.M. 1971, s. 83, s. 32.

CURRENT OF TRAFFIC. The movement of trains on a main track in one direction specified by the rules. *Regulations No. O-8, Uniform Code of Operating Rules*, C.R.C., c. 1175, Part III, s. 2.

CURRENT REVENUE. All amounts earned and the amounts to which one may become entitled, other than by borrowing, that may be used to meet expenditures.

CURRENT SERVICE COST. The amount of money that the employer of employees, who are members of a pension plan, is required by the plan, this Act and the regulations to pay into the plan in a fiscal year of the plan to cover the cost of benefits accrued during the fiscal year. *Pension Benefits Amendment Act, 1983*, S.O. 1983, c. 1, s. 1.

CURRENT VALUE ACCOUNTING. One approximates changes in the value of tangible assets by estimating the values of specific items. W. Grover & F. Iacobucci, *Materials on Canadian Income Tax*, 4th ed. (Toronto: Richard De Boo Ltd., 1980) at 602.

CURRENT YEAR TAXES. Unpaid real property taxes levied for the current year but does not include arrears, penalties, delinquent taxes or interest. *Home Owner Grant Act*, S.B.C. 1980, c. 18, s. 1.

CURRICULUM. *n.* Studies set out for a particular period.

CURR. LEGAL PROBS. *abbr.* Current Legal Problems.

CURSE. *v.* To swear.

CURSUS CURIAE EST LEX CURIAE. [L.] The practice of the court is the law of the court.

CURTESY. *n.* The interest in a wife's fee simple which a husband will have after her death until his own.

CURTILAGE. *n.* A courtyard, field or land including any buildings on it lying near and belonging to a dwelling. C.R.B. Dunlop, *Creditor-Debtor Law in Canada* (Toronto: Carswell, 1981) at 390.

CUSHION TANK. A pressure vessel designed for installation in a closed hot water heating system to provide an air cushion for the expansion of water. *Boilers and Pressure Vessels Act*, R.R.O. 1980, Reg. 84, s. 1.

CUSTANTIA. *n.* [L.] Costs.

CUSTODIAL CARE. The personal care, assistance and protection required by a person who has reached the apparent limit of recovery and whose condition is such that such care is necessary or who has such a degree of senile deterioration that such care is necessary but who does not require continued medical and skilled nursing care in a hospital.

CUSTODIA LEGIS. [L.] The custody of the law.

CUSTODIAL EMPLOYEE. A guard; an after hours security guard

CUSTODIAL FACILITY. See YOUTH ~.

CUSTODIAL PERSON. A person who, in the opinion of a medical practitioner, requires custodial care. *Public Hospitals Act*, R.R.O. 1980, Reg. 865, s. 1.

CUSTODIAN. *n.* 1. A person in whose custody a package is placed. 2. A person acting as a custodian for a clearing agency. *Business Corporations Amendment Act*, S.O. 1986, c. 57, s. 7. 3. A person designated by an order to have custody of the property of a member. *Law Society Act*, R.S.M. 1970, c. L100, s. 51. 4. A custodian of securities issued by a mutual fund held for the benefit of plan holders under a custodial agreement or other arrangement. *Securities Act, 1980*, S.M. 1980, c. 50, s. 48.

CUSTODY. *n.* 1. Detention, physical care or control pursuant to a committal order or an arrest. *Corrections Act*, S.N.S. 1986, c. 6, s. 3. 2. Includes care, upbringing and any other incident of custody. *Divorce Act*, R.S.C. 1985 (2d Supp.), c. 3, s. 2. 3. The authority and responsibility for possessing the child physically and providing for the daily requirements related to life and development of the child. *Family and Child Services Act*, P.E.I. 1981, c. 12, s. 1. 4. Physical control. See CARE AND ~; CIVIL ~; JOINT ~; LEGAL ~; OPEN ~; PLACE OF ~; PLACE OF SECURE ~; PROTECTIVE ~;

RIGHT OF ~; SECURE ~; SERVICE ~; SOLE ~.

CUSTODY AGREEMENT. Any agreement with respect to the custody, care or control of a child.

CUSTODY ORDER. 1. The order of any court with respect to the custody, care or control of a child. 2. An order, or that part of an order, of an extra-provincial tribunal that grants custody of a child to any person and includes provisions, if any, granting another person a right of access or visitation to the child. *Extra-provincial Custody Orders Enforcement acts.* 3. An order made under subsection 16(1). *Divorce Act*, R.S.C. 1985 (2d Supp.), c. 3, s. 2.

CUSTODY PROVISION. A provision of an order or agreement awarding custody of a child. *Family Orders and Agreements Enforcement Assistance Act*, R.S.C. 1985 (2d supp.), c. 4, s. 2.

CUSTOM. *n.* An unwritten law or right, established through long use.

CUSTOMARY. *adj.* According to custom; usual.

CUSTOMARY AUTHORITY. See USUAL OR ~.

CUSTOMARY INTERNATIONAL LAW. A national practice accepted as international law.

CUSTOM DUTY. The fee payable when importing goods.

CUSTOMER. *n.* 1. A customer of a taxpayer and includes a person who sells or delivers goods or products to the taxpayer, or for whom the taxpayer renders services. *Income Tax Act*, R.S.C. 1952, c. 148 (as am. S.C. 1970-71-72, c. 63), s. 135(4)(c). 2. Any person, excepting an employee, agent or mandatary of the owner of a commercial establishment, present in the establishment or on the premises thereof in such a manner that he may purchase products sold by the establishment. *An Act to Amend the Act Respecting Commercial Establishments Business Hours*, S.Q. 1984, c. 17, s. 1. See CREDIT CARD ~; FOREIGN ~; INDUSTRIAL ~; NON-MEMBER ~; SEASONAL ~; WHOLESALE ~; YEARLY ~.

CUSTOMER-FORMULA FEED. (a) Feed prepared in accordance with a formula supplied and signed by the person on whose behalf the feed is to be prepared, or (b) feed mixed with any other substance as a service for a purchaser upon his signed request, and that is not intended for resale by that person or purchaser. *Feeds Regulations*, C.R.C., c. 665, s. 2.

CUSTOMER-FORMULA FERTILIZER. A fertilizer prepared in accordance with a written formula that sets forth the name, amount and analysis of each ingredient, the fertilizer grade of the total mixture and the signature of the person for whose use for fertilizing purposes it has been prepared. *Fertilizers Regulations*, C.R.C., c. 666, s. 2.

CUSTOM-HOUSE. *n.* The office where any duty payable or receivable upon import or export is paid or received.

CUSTOM OF THE TRADE. Any practice usually observed by people dealing in a particular product.

CUSTOM OPERATOR. A person who purchases a new farm implement and uses or permits the use of that farm implement for hire or for service to others for valuable consideration to the extent of at least 50 per cent of the annual use of that farm implement.

CUSTOMS. *n.* Duties charged when goods are imported into, or exported out of, a country. See CANADIAN ~ WATERS; CHIEF OFFICER OF ~; OUTSIDE ~ AREA; REVENUE CANADA, ~ AND EXCISE.

CUSTOMS BROKER. A person who acts as agent to clear goods through customs.

CUSTOMS CONTROL. See POST AUDIT ~ SYSTEM.

CUSTOMS DUTY. The tax when goods are imported.

CUSTOMS DUTY STAMPS. Stamps issued by the Deputy Minister indicating the prepayment of customs duty on any goods specified in the tariff item. *Printed Matter Prepayment Regulations*, C.R.C., c. 541, s. 2.

CUSTOMS EXPRESS BRANCH WAREHOUSE. A warehouse for the safekeeping, examination and appraisal by customs of imported goods carried by means of air or rail express. *Customs Warehousing Regulations*, C.R.C., c. 462, s. 2.

CUSTOMS LAWS. See FEDERAL ~.

CUSTOMS OFFICE. A place designated as a customs office by the Minister. *Customs Act*, R.S.C. 1985 (2d Supp.), c. 1, s. 2.

CUSTOMS OFFICER. The collector or chief officer of customs at a port.

CUSTOMS PORT. A seaport appointed as a port or place of entry pursuant to section 282 of the Customs Act. *Transitional United States Fishing Vessel Licence Exemption Regulations*, C.R.C., c. 415, s. 2.

CUSTOMS UNION. An agreement between

countries for the unification of territories for purposes of customs.

CUSTOMS WAREHOUSE. Includes sufferance warehouse, bonding warehouse and examining warehouse. *Customs Act*, R.S.C. 1970, c. C-40, s. 2.

CUSTOM WORK. Work done or a service provided by the department with respect to public improvements on a fee for service basis. *Highways Amendment Act*, S.S. 1982-83, c. 36, s. 3.

CUSTOS STATUM HAEREDIS IN CUSTODIA EXISTENTIS MELIOREM, NON DETERIOREM, FACERE POTEST. [L.] A person can only improve, not worsen, the estate of an heir for whom the person is a guardian.

CUT. *v.* Of drugs, to dilute. F.A. Jaffe, *A Guide to Pathological Evidence*, 2d ed. (Toronto: Carswell, 1983) at 173.

CUT. *n.* 1. The incised wound which a sharp object caused. F.A. Jaffe, *A Guide to Pathological Evidence*, 2d ed. (Toronto: Carswell, 1983) at 173. 2. Canned beans consisting of pods cut transversely into pieces not more than 2 inches in length and not less than 3/4 inch in length, and may contain shorter end pieces that result from cutting. *Processed Fruit and Vegetable Regulations*, C.R.C., c. 291, schedule I, s. 10(1). 3. Canned sweet potatoes that consist of cut units and include some pieces or broken units. *Processed Fruit and Vegetable Regulations*, C.R.C., c. 291, schedule I, s. 45. See PRIMAL ~.

CUTBACK. *n.* A reduction in production of a manufacturer possibly requiring layoffs of employees.

CUTIS ANSERINA. [L.] Goose flesh, goose pimples.

CUT-OFF LANDS. Lands that had before 1916 been appropriated by the Province for the use and benefit of Indians but that, pursuant to the Indian Affairs Settlement Act, S.B.C. 1919, c. 32, the British Columbia Indian Affairs Settlement Act, S.C. 1920, c. 51, and the report of the Royal Commission on Indian Affairs in the Province of British Columbia of June 30, 1916, as approved by Dominion Privy Council Order 1265 of July 19, 1924 and British Columbia Order in Council 911 of July 26, 1923, ceased to be so appropriated, but "cut-off lands" does not include any lands in the Railway Belt or Peace River Block. *Indian Cut-Off Lands Dispute Act*, S.B.C. 1982, c. 50, s. 1.

CUT-OUT. *var.* **CUT OUT.** A device installed to isolate manually a circuit from its source of supply. *Coal Mines Regulation Act*, R.S.N.S. 1967, c. 36, s. 84. See THERMAL ~.

CUT OUT BOX. An enclosure of adequate mechanical strength, composed entirely of fire-resistant and absorption-resistant material, designed for surface mounting and having swinging doors or covers secured directly to, and telescoping with, the walls of the box proper. *Power Corporation Act*, R.R.O. 1980, Reg. 794, s. 0.

CUTS. *n.* Canned beans consisting of pods cut transversely into pieces not more than 2 inches in length and not less than 3/4 inch in length, and may contain shorter end pieces that result from cutting. *Processed Fruit and Vegetable Regulations*, C.R.C., c. 291, schedule I, s. 10(1).

CUTTER. See SNOWMOBILE ~.

CWT. *abbr.* 1. One hundred pounds. 2. 112 lb. *Dangerous Goods Shipping Regulations*, C.R.C., c. 1419, s. 2.

CYANIDE. *n.* A poisonous chemical constituent of insecticide. F.A. Jaffe, *A Guide to Pathological Evidence*, 2d ed. (Toronto: Carswell, 1983) at 173.

CYANOSIS. *n.* Blue or grey discolouration of the mucous membranes and skin where insufficiently oxygenated blood has circulated. F.A. Jaffe, *A Guide to Pathological Evidence*, 2d ed. (Toronto: Carswell, 1983) at 173.

CYCLE. *n.* 1. A prescribed amount of time. 2. A bicycle, a motor cycle or a moped. 3. A device having any number of wheels that is propelled by human power and on which a person may ride. *Motor Vehicle Act*, R.S.B.C. 1979, c. 288, s. 115. See MOTOR~; MOTOR DRIVEN ~.

CYLINDER. *n.* Of a revolver, the circular magazine. F.A. Jaffe, *A Guide to Pathological Evidence*, 2d ed. (Toronto: Carswell, 1983) at 173. See PORTABLE ~S.

CYLINDRICAL GRADUATED STANDARD. A local standard of volume or capacity that is made of glass or metal, has a cylindrical shape and, if made entirely of glass, shows graduations on the glass and, if made of metal, shows graduations that are adjacent to a glass window in the metal. *Weights and Measures Regulations*, C.R.C., c. 1605, s. 53.

CY-PRÈS. [Fr. near to it] The doctrine of construction applied so that a testator's intentions are followed as nearly as possible in a case where a gift would otherwise fail.

CYST. See POTATO ~ NEMATODE.

D

D. *abbr.* 1. Day. 2. Deci. 3. Depth for freeboard. 4. Draught.

DA. *abbr.* Deca.

DACTYLOGRAPHY. *n.* The study of fingerprints as means of identifying persons.

DAILY. *adj.* Every day.

DAILY CANADIAN NEWSPAPER. A Canadian newspaper that is ordinarily published more frequently than once a week. *Post Office Act*, R.S.C. 1970, c. P-14, s. 11.

DAILY DOUBLE. A betting transaction in which a purchaser of a ticket undertakes to select the winner of each of the two races on which that feature is operated. *Race Track Supervision Regulations*, C.R.C., c. 441, s. 2.

DAILY RATE. Compensation for a day's work.

DAILY WAGE. The wage to which an employee would be entitled if the employee worked on a normal working day of the employer that is not a general holiday. *Employment Standards Act*, R.S.A. 1980, c. E-10.1, s. 41.

DAIRY. *n.* 1. Premises in which milk is processed into fluid milk products. 2. Includes, (a) creamery; and (b) pasteurization plant. 3. A place at which milk or cream is purchased or received for the purpose of being pasteurized, standardized or otherwise processed and resold to the wholesale or retail trade or to the wholesale and retail trade. 4. A place where one or more cows or goats are kept, a part of all of the milk or cream from which is sold, offered for sale or delivered for human consumption, and includes all buildings, yards and premises occupied or used in connection with the production of milk. *The Public Health Act*, R.S.S. 1978, c. P-37, s. 2.

DAIRY BUTTER. Butter, other than creamery butter and whey butter.

DAIRY DRINK. Milk to which there has been added chocolate or other flavouring. *Public Health Act*, R.S.N.S. 1967, c. 247, s. 1.

DAIRY FARM. 1. A place where cattle are kept for milking. *Milk Industry Act*, R.S.B.C. 1979, c. 258, s. 1. 2. Any place where one or more cows or goats are kept, and part or all of the milk produced by those cows or goats is sold, offered for sale or held in possession for sale for human consumption, and includes all buildings, premises and equipment occupied or used in connection with the production of milk. *Dairy Act*, S.M. 1980, c. 44, s. 3.

DAIRY FARMER. The owner or occupier of a dairy farm, and includes the manager or other person in charge of a dairy farm. *Milk Industry Act*, R.S.B.C. 1979, c. 258, s. 1.

DAIRY MANUFACTURING PLANT. 1. An establishment in which dairy product is processed, manufactured, reprocessed, packed or repacked. 2. A dairy, a cheese factory, a creamery, a cream receiving station, a concentrated milk plant, milk receiving station, a milk condensery, an ice cream plant, a process cheese plant, or a skimming station, or a combination of any two or more of them.

DAIRY PLANT. A cheese factory, a creamery, a cream receiving station, a milk condensery, an ice cream plant, a cheese processing plant, a plant where milk or cream is received for the purpose of being pasteurized, homogenized, standardized or otherwise processed for sale to the wholesale or retail trade, or a combination of any two or more of them.

DAIRY PLANT PERSONNEL. Persons engaged in specific duties in relation to dairy products for the performance of which the licences are required under standards and qualifications established by regulation. *Milk Industry Act*, R.S.B.C. 1979, c. 258, s. 1.

DAIRY PRODUCER. A person, partnership, or company who, in Prince Edward Island, produces milk or cream for sale. *Dairy Producers Act,* S.P.E.I. 1976, c. 37, s. 2.

DAIRY PRODUCT. Milk, cream, butter, cheese, condensed milk, evaporated milk, milk powder, dry milk, ice cream, malted milk, sherbet, dried whey, condensed whey, casein, sodium caseinate, yogurt or any other product manufactured wholly or mainly from milk. See IMITATION ~.

DAIRY PRODUCTS TRADE. The undertaking for commercial purposes of producing, handling, processing, pasteurizing, homogenizing, bottling, transporting, delivering or selling milk or cream for human consumption, or any one or more of such undertakings. *Dairy Products Act,* R.S.N.B. 1973, c. D-2, s. 1.

DAIRYWORKER. *n.* A buttermaker or a cheesemaker who is the holder of a dairyworker's certificate with a buttermaker's or a cheesemaker's option, as the case may be. *Milk Act,* R.R.O. 1980, Reg. 629, s. 1.

DALHOUSIE L.J. *abbr.* Dalhousie Law Journal.

DAM. *n.* 1. Any structure built for the purpose of impounding water in any drift, crosscut or other mine opening and constructed in such a manner as to permit an unobstructed overflow of the water. 2. Includes a channel, diversion, dock, groyne, light, pier, slide, warning device, wharf or work for the control and regulation of water and any building, road, structure, service or temporary installation necessary or incidental thereto.

DAMAGE. *n.* 1. Harm; loss. 2. In relation to any damage to property within the meaning of section 3, means any loss or damage to property, whether real or personal, and, for the purposes of any other provision of this Act, includes any damage arising out of or attributable to any loss of or damage to that property. *Nuclear Liability Act,* R.S.C. 1985, c. N-28, s. 2. 3. Damage caused by high water levels of or the impact of ice on a lake, river or other body of water or by damage to or erosion of the shore of a lake, river or body of water caused by the elements. *Shoreline Property Assistance Amendment Act,* S.O. 1986, c. 22, s. 1. See ACTUAL LOSS OR ~; ~S; NEGATIVE ~; PERSONAL ~; POSITIVE ~; PROPERTY ~; SPECIAL ~; STIPULATED ~; SUBSTANTIAL ~.

DAMAGE APPRAISER. A person who, for compensation or for promise or expectation of compensation, engages in the business of establishing the amount of loss resulting from any damage to the real or personal property of another person. *Insurance Act,* S.N.B. 1976, c. 34, s. 1.

DAMAGE CAUSED BY AN AUTOMOBILE. Any damage caused by or by the use of an automobile or by the load of an automobile, including damage caused by a trailer used with an automobile, but excluding damage caused by the autonomous act of an animal that is part of the load. *An Act to Amend the Automobile Insurance Act and Other Legislation,* S.Q. 1982, c. 59, s. 1.

DAMAGE FAISANT. Doing damage.

DAMAGE FEASANT. Doing damage.

DAMAGES. *n.* 1. Pecuniary compensation for a wrong, either a breach of contract or a tort. K.D. Cooper-Stephenson & I.B. Saunders, *Personal Injury Damages in Canada* (Toronto: Carswell, 1981) at 4. 2. Pecuniary and non-pecuniary damages and, without restricting the generality of this definition, includes (a) out-of-pocket expenses reasonably incurred for the benefit of the deceased; (b) a reasonable allowance for travel expenses incurred in visiting the deceased between the time of the injury and the death; (c) where, as a result of the injury, a person for whose benefit the action is brought provided nursing, housekeeping or other services for the deceased between the time of the injury and the death, a reasonable allowance for loss of income or the value of the services; (d) an amount to compensate for the loss of guidance, care and companionship that a person for whose benefit the action is brought might reasonably have expected to receive from the deceased if the death had not occurred. *Fatal Injuries Act,* S.N.S. 1986, c. 30, s. 1. See AGGRAVATED ~; CONSEQUENTIAL ~; CONTEMPTUOUS ~; DAMAGE; DERISORY ~; EXEMPLARY ~; FUTURE ~; GENERAL ~; LIQUIDATED ~; MEASURE OF ~; MITIGATION OF ~; NOMINAL ~; PUNITIVE ~; UNLIQUIDATED ~; VINDICTIVE ~.

DAMKEEPER. *n.* A person actually on duty in charge of a dam. *Canal Regulations,* C.R.C., c. 1564, s. 2.

DAMNA. *n.* [L.] Damages.

DAMNIFICATION. *n.* Whatever causes loss or damage.

DAMNIFY. *v.* To injure; to cause personal loss.

DAMNUM. *n.* [L.] 1. Damage. 2. Harm. 3. Loss.

DAMNUM ABSQUE INJURIA. [L.] Loss without an injury.

DAMNUM SENTIRE NON VIDETUR QUI SIBI DAMNUM DEDIT. [L.] A person is seen not to have suffered damage where that person caused it.

DAMNUM SENTIT DOMINUS. [L.] The owner suffers the damage.

DAMNUM SINE INJURIS ESSE POTEST. [L.] There may be damage inflicted without any thing being done which the law considers an injury.

DAMP GRAIN. Any grain within the meaning of this Act that has a moisture content that classifies it as damp grain in the Canada Grain Regulations made pursuant to the Canada Grain Act. *Prairie Grain Advance Payment Act*, R.S.C. 1985, c. P-18, s. 9(5).

DAMP LOCATION. A location which is normally or periodically subject to condensation of moisture in, on or adjacent to electrical equipment. *Power Corporation Act*, R.R.O. 1980, Reg. 794, s. 0.

DANCE HALL. Any hall, pavilion, place, premises, room, tent or structure of any kind kept or used for public dancing, and includes a cafe, hotel, or restaurant where facilities are supplied and used for public dancing.

DANGER. *n.* Any hazard or condition that could reasonably be expected to cause injury or illness to a person exposed thereto before the hazard or condition can be corrected. *Canada Labour Code*, R.S.C. 1985 (1st Supp.), c. 9, s. 122. See CONCEALED ~; UNUSUAL ~.

DANGER AREA. Any area within which (a) a crane, hoist, shovel or other materials handling equipment that is readily mobile, or (b) equipment with wide swinging booms or other similar parts is operating and might injure any person. *Canada Materials Handling Regulations*, C.R.C., c. 1004, s. 60.

DANGER OF POLLUTION. Any accumulation of material at a particular location, any artificial disturbance of land, any material storage or disposal facility, any transfer operation, any transport facility, any pipeline, tank, drum, excavation, depression, pond or impoundment situated in or on the ground or in buildings, whether natural or artificial and whether lined or unlined, for either storage or transport, as the case may be, of useful or waste materials that could through use or misuse, seepage, leaching, accidents, leaks, breaks, negligence, acts of animals or persons or acts of God, release contaminants directly or indirectly into or upon the waters of the Province and any application or disposal of materials or chemicals into or upon the environment unless such material or chemical is a pesticide controlled by or under the Pesticides Control Act. *Clean Environment Act*, S.N.B. 1976, c. 19, s. 1.

DANGEROUS. *adj.* With reference to any person, means dangerous to himself or any other person. *Health and Public Welfare Act*, R.S. Nfld. 1970, c. 151, s. 97. See GOODS OF ~ NATURE.

DANGEROUS ANIMAL. Animals ferae naturae which are normally dangerous and animals mansuetae naturae which are normally harmless but individuals may be dangerous. John G. Fleming, *The Law of Torts*, 6th ed. (Sydney: The Law Book Company Limited, 1983) at 329.

DANGEROUS ARTICLE. Includes inflammable or corrosive liquids and liquified petroleum gas. *Motor Vehicle Act*, R.S.B.C. 1979, c. 288, s. 1.

DANGEROUS COMMODITY. Any substance subject to the Regulations for the Transportation of Dangerous Commodities by Rail or subject to any other regulation or order issued by the Commission to control its hazard. Canada regulations.

DANGEROUS DISEASE. Any disease, other than a disease included in the schedule, the introduction of which into Canada would, in the opinion of the quarantine officer concerned, constitute a grave danger to public health in Canada. *Quarantine Act*, R.S.C. 1985, c. Q-1, s. 2.

DANGEROUS DRIVING. See DANGEROUS OPERATION OF MOTOR VEHICLES.

DANGEROUS GOODS. 1. Any product, substance or organism included by its nature or by the regulations in any of the classes listed in the schedule. *Transportation of Dangerous Goods acts*. 2. Goods that by reason of their nature, quantity or mode of stowage are either singly or collectively liable to endanger the lives of the passengers or imperil the ship, and includes all substances determined by the Governor in Council, in regulations made by him, to be dangerous goods. *Canada Shipping Act*, R.S.C. 1985, c. S-9, s. 2.

DANGEROUS OPERATION OF AIRCRAFT. Operating an aircraft in a manner that is dangerous to the public, having regard to all the circumstances, including the nature and condition of that aircraft or the place or air space in or through which the aircraft is operated. *Criminal Code*, R.S.C. 1985, c. C-46, s. 249(1)(c).

DANGEROUS OPERATION OF MOTOR VEHICLES. Operating a motor vehicle on a street, road, highway or other public place in a manner that is dangerous to the public, having regard to all the circumstances, including the nature, condition and use of such place and the amount of traffic that at the time is or might reasonably be expected to be on that place. *Criminal Code*, R.S.C. 1985, c. C-46, s. 249(1)(a).

DANGEROUS OPERATION OF VESSELS. Operating a vessel or any water skis, surf board, water sled or other towed object on or over any of the internal waters of Canada or the territorial sea of Canada, in a manner that is dangerous to the public, having regard to all the circumstances, including the nature and condition of such waters or sea and the use that at the time is or might reasonably be expected to be made of such waters or sea. *Criminal Code*, R.S.C. 1985, c. C-46, s. 249(1)(b).

DANGEROUS SEXUAL OFFENDER. A person who, by his conduct in any sexual matter, has shown a failure to control his sexual impulses, and who is likely to cause injury, pain or other evil to any person, through failure in the future to control his sexual impulses. *Criminal Code*, R.S.C. 1970, c. C-34, s. 687.

DANGEROUS SUBSTANCE. Any substance that, because of a property it possesses, is dangerous to the safety or health of any person who is exposed to it.

DANGEROUS TO BE AT LARGE. With reference to any person, means dangerous to himself or any other person. *Health and Public Welfare Act*, R.S. Nfld. 1970, c. 151, s. 97.

DANGER ZONE. An area or space upon a highway which is so marked or indicated under the provisions of this Act by the proper signs plainly visible. *Motor Vehicle Act*, R.S.N.S. 1967, c. 191, s. 1.

DANS LOCUM CONTRACTUI. [L.] Which gives rise to the contract.

DARE. *v.* [L.] To hand over property.

DARE AD REMANENTIAM. [L.] To give away for ever or in fee.

DARKNESS. *n.* The period from 1/2 hour after sunset to 1/2 hour before sunrise and any other occasion when there is not sufficient light to render clearly discernible a substantial object on the highway at a distance of 60 m. *Motor Vehicle Act*, R.S.B.C. 1979, c. 288, s. 209.

DARRAIGN. *v.* 1. To answer an accusation; to settle a controversy. 2. Of a legal account, to clear.

DARREIN. *n.* [Fr.] The last.

DASH. *n.* A race decided in one trial. *Race Track Supervision Regulations*, C.R.C., c. 441, s. 2.

DATA. *n.* 1. Facts. 2. Representations of information or of concepts that are being prepared or have been prepared in a form suitable for use in a computer system. *Criminal Code*, R.S.C. 1985, c. C-46 (as am. by *Criminal Law Amendment Act*, R.S.C. 1985 (1st Supp.), c. 27), s. 342.1(2).

DATA BANK. A tape or disc in which the names of electors may be stored in a sequence for later use. *Election Act*, R.S.P.E.I. 1974, c. E-1, s. 1.

DATA PROCESSING SERVICES. All activities, procedures and methods relating to or facilitating the storing, retrieving, sorting, merging, calculating and transforming of information and data whether manually or with the assistance or by means of the use of machines.

DATE. *n.* The year and the day of the month. See AFTER ~; ANNIVERSARY ~; COMPLETION ~; CONTRACT ~; DECLARATION ~; DUE ~; DURABLE LIFE ~; EFFECTIVE ~; ENUMERATION ~; EXPIRATION ~; FIXED ~; INITIAL APPEARANCE ~; LAPSE ~; MATURITY ~; PROCLAMATION ~; REDEMPTION ~; VALUATION ~.

DATE OF COMPLETION. 1. The date that is certified by the Minister as being the date on which the project is completed to the extent necessary to enable the Minister to supply water or to receive, treat and dispose of sewage, as the case may be. *Ontario Water Resources Act*, R.S.O. 1980, c. 361, s. 1. 2. The date on which the well-construction equipment is removed from the site of a well. *Ontario Water Resources Act*, R.R.O. 1980, Reg. 739, s. 1.

DATE OF CONVICTION. The day on which a conviction for a summary offence was first entered by a court. *Summary Offences Relief Act*, S.N.S. 1970, c. 18, s. 1.

DATE OF DELIVERY. The date when the pregnancy of an employee terminates with the birth of a child or the pregnancy otherwise terminates. *Employment Standards Act*, R.S.A. 1980, c. E-10.1, s. 58.

DATE OF DEPOSIT. With respect to any moneys constituting a deposit, the day on which credit for the moneys is given to the account of the depositor or the day on which an instrument is issued for such moneys by the member institution, as the case may be. *Canada Deposit Insurance Corporation Act*, R.S.C. 1985, c. C-3, s. 52(1).

DATE OF LEAVING. The day on which a patient leaves.

DATE OF LEGITIMATION. The date of the marriage leading to the legitimation or, when the marriage occurred before the commencement of this Act, the commencement of this Act. *Legitimacy Act*, R.S. Nfld. 1970, c. 203, s. 2.

DATE OF LOADING. The date the product was cleared for export by the host government at the port of loading. Canada regulations.

DATE OF MANUFACTURE. (a) In the case of a product for which a standard of potency exists, the date it satisfactorily passes a potency test, (b) in the case of an animal product for which no standard of potency exists, the date of its removal from the animal, and (c) in the case of a product other than an animal product for which no standard of potency exists, the date of cessation of growth. *Food and Drug Regulations*, C.R.C., c. 870, c. C.04.001.

DATE OF MATURITY. The date, excluding days of grace, on which the debt will be fully paid if every payment is made according to the original terms of the security agreement. *Personal Property Security Act*, R.R.O. 1980, Reg. 749, s. 1.

DATE OF POSSESSION. 1. The day upon which the expropriating authority became entitled to take physical possession or make use of the land to which a notice of confirmation relates. 2. The date on which the home is completed for possession by an owner as specified in the applicable certificate of completion and possession. *Ontario New Home Warranties Plan Act*, R R.O. 1980, Reg. 726, s. 1.

DATE OF RETIREMENT. See NORMAL ~.

DATE OF THE OFFER. The day on which an offer was accepted. *Expropriation acts.*

DATE OF THE ORDER. The date the order is made, notwithstanding that the order is not entered or enforceable on that date, or that the order is varied on appeal, and in the case of an order directing a reference, the date the report on the reference is confirmed. *Courts of Justice Act*, S.O. 1984, c. 11, s. 137.

DATIF. *n.* That which may be disposed of or given at pleasure or will; officially appointed.

DATIVE. *n.* That which may be disposed of or given at pleasure or will; officially appointed.

DATUM. *n.* [L. a thing given] The primary principle.

DAUGHTER. See SON AND ~.

DAUHVAL. *n.* Any unclaimed dead whale found free floating.

DAY. *n.* 1. 86 400 seconds. *Weights and Measures Act*, S.C. 1970-71-72, c. 36, schedule 1. 2. A calendar day. 3. The period between 6 o'clock in the forenoon and 9 o'clock in the afternoon of the same day. *Criminal Code*, R.S.C. 1985, c. C-46, s. 2. 4. Any period of 24 consecutive hours. 5. A clear day and a period of days shall be deemed to commence on the day following the event which began the period and shall be deemed to terminate on midnight of the last day of the period except that if the last day of the period falls on Saturday, Sunday or a holiday the period shall terminate on midnight of the

day next following that is a business day. Securities acts. See APPOINTED ~; BUSINESS ~; CHRISTMAS ~; CLEAR ~S; CONSECUTIVE ~S; COSTS OF THE ~; ELECTION ~; FERIAL ~; FRACTION OF A ~; GALE-~; HOURS OF THE ~; INSTRUCTIONAL ~; JURIDICAL ~; LAST ~ OF THE TAXATION YEAR; LAY- ~; LORD'S ~; MAN-~; NOMINATION ~; NON-BUSINESS ~S; NON-INSTRUCTIONAL ~; ONE ~; ORDER OF THE ~; PATIENT-~; PAY ~; POLLING ~; PRODUCTION ~; REMEMBRANCE ~; RESERVABLE ~; SITTING ~ OF PARLIAMENT; SPECIFIED ~; TEACHING ~; VALUATION ~; WITHOUT ~; WORK ~; WORKING ~.

DAY-BOOK. *n.* A journal in which the transactions of the day are recorded.

DAY CAMP. A camp or resort that admits persons for temporary custody for a continuous period not exceeding twenty-four hours. *Public Health Act*, R.R.O. 1980, Reg. 849, s. 1.

DAY CARE. A service that provides daytime care of children outside their own homes by an authorized person, with or without charge. See HOME ~; PRIVATE-HOME ~; SCHOOL ~.

DAY CARE AGENCY. See HOME ~; PRIVATE-HOME ~.

DAY CARE CENTRE. *var.* **DAY CARE CENTER.** Any place in which day care services are offered.

DAY CARE FACILITY. A place, exclusive of a nursery school, in which a number of children exceeding the number specified in the regulations for the purpose of this definition receive care apart from their parents or guardians for a period not exceeding eighteen consecutive hours. *Child Welfare Act*, S.M. 1973, c. 26, s. 1.

DAY CARE HOME. Premises in which day care either alone or in combination with parental care is provided or offered at any time and which is the home of the person providing the day care. *Community Child Day Care Standards Amendment Act*, S.M. 1985-86, c. 9, s. 1.

DAY CARE SERVICES. The providing of care to children under the age of twelve years, for a period of less than twenty-four hours, apart from their parents or guardian. *Day Care Act*, R.S.N.B. 1973, c. D-4.1, s. 1.

DAY LABOURER. An unskilled worker hired by the day.

DAYLIGHT. *n.* 1. One-half hour before sunrise to one-half hour after sunset on the same day. 2. In respect of any place in Canada, the period of time in any day when the centre of the sun's disc is less that 6° below the horizon, and in any place where the sun rises and sets daily, may be considered to be the period of time commencing 1/2 hour before sunrise and ending 1/2 hour after sunset. *Air Regulations*, C.R.C., c. 2, s. 101.

DAYLIGHT SAVING TIME. The time one hour in advance of (later than) Standard Time.

DAY NURSERY. A building, part of a building or other place, whether known as a day nursery, nursery school, kindergarten, play school or by any other name, which for compensation or otherwise receives, for temporary care or custody on a daily or hourly basis, children.

DAY OF ACTUAL WORK. A period of work recognized by the employer as the daily working shift of the employee. *Employment Standards Act*, R.S.B.C. 1979, c. 107, s. 1.

DAY OF NOMINATION. The day upon which nominations close. *Elections Act*, R.S.N.B. 1973, c. E-3, s. 2.

DAY OF POLLING. The day fixed for holding the poll at an election.

DAY OF REST. See PRESCRIBED ~; WEEKLY ~.

DAY PAROLE. Parole the terms and conditions of which require the inmate to whom it is granted to return to prison from time to time during the duration of the parole or to return to prison after a specified period. *Parole Act*, R.S.C. 1985, c. P-2, s. 2.

DAY-PATIENT. *n.* A patient in an in-patient facility who is given sustenance and other services provided to in-patients except that he does not occupy a bed in the facility overnight. *The Mental Health Act*, R.S.S. 1978, c. M-13, s. 2.

DAY SHIP. A ship on which the crew is not required to sleep on board. *Towboat Crew Accommodation Regulations*, C.R.C., c. 1498, s. 2.

DAYS OF GRACE. Time allowed to make a payment or do some other act when the time originally allowed has expired.

DAYS STAY. The number of days during which a patient is hospitalized.

DAY'S TREATMENT. Necessary medical or surgical treatment in a hospital of a patient for a complete period of 24 hours commencing and ending at midnight, but the hours of necessary treatment in a hospital of a patient during the day of his admission and the day of his discharge shall be counted together as one day's treatment. *Hospital Act*, R.S.B.C. 1979, c. 176, s. 1.

DAY'S WORK. Eight hours work, but in a case

of drilling or surveying or geological or geophysical or other special work, the Minister may allow another unit as a day's work. Mining acts.

DAY TIME. *var.* **DAYTIME.** One-half hour before sunrise to one-half hour after sunset on the same day.

DAY VFR. In respect of the flight of any aircraft in Canada, a flight conducted in accordance with VFR during the hours of daylight. *Air Regulations*, C.R.C., c. 2, s. 101.

DBH. The diameter of the stem of a tree measured at a point that is four and one-half feet above ground. *Trees Act*, R.S.O. 1980, c. 510, s. 1.

D.C.A. *abbr.* Dorion, Décisions de la Cour d'Appel (Queen's Bench Reports).

D.D.C.P. *abbr.* Décisions disciplinaires concernant les Corporations professionnelles.

DE. *prep.* [L.] Of; from; concerning.

DEAD. *adj.* When applied to electrical equipment means that the current-carrying electrical equipment is free from any electrical connection to a source of potential difference and from electrical charge or has not a potential different from that of earth. *Power Corporation Act*, R.R.O. 1980, Reg. 794, s. 0.

DEAD ANIMAL. The carcass, or any part thereof, of a horse, goat, sheep, swine or head of cattle that has died from any cause other than slaughter.

DEAD BODY. A corpse.

DEAD END. A branch leading from drainage piping or a vent pipe that ends in a cap, plug or other closed fitting. *Ontario Water Resources Act*, R.R.O. 1980, Reg. 736, s. 1.

DEAD-END CONDUCTOR. A conductor having no grounding other than through the conductor from which it branches. *Lightning Rods Act*, R.R.O. 1980, Reg. 577, s. 1.

DEAD FREIGHT. The amount a charterer pays for part of the carrying capacity of a ship which the charterer contracted but did not in fact use.

DEAD FRONT. When applied to electrical equipment means that the electrical equipment is so constructed that all live parts, except the wells for plug fuses in panelboards and in enclosed branch-circuit cut-outs, are enclosed in such manner as to be inaccessible. *Power Corporation Act*, R.R.O. 1980, Reg. 794, s. 0.

DEADHEAD. *v.* To transport railway equipment or employees, not in service, from one terminal to another.

DEAD HEAT. The official result of a race in

which more than one horse finished in first, second, third or fourth place, as the case may be. *Race Track Supervision Regulations*, C.R.C., c. 441, s. 2.

DEAD LOAD. The weight of all permanent structural and nonstructural components of a building. *Building Code Act*, R.R.O. 1980, Reg. 87, s. 1.

DEAD PLEDGE. A mortgage.

DEAD RENT. A fixed rent payable whether a mine is productive or not.

DEAD SHIP. A ship normally self-propelled that is without the use of its propelling power, but does not include a ship warped from one berth to another solely by means of mooring lines attached to a wharf, to the shore or to a mooring buoy. Canada regulations.

DEAD TIME. Time lost by an employee because of equipment breakdown, lack of materials or other causes beyond the employee's control.

DEAD USE. Future use.

DEADWEIGHT. *n.* The difference in tonnes between the weight of water of a specific gravity of 1.025 displaced by a ship loaded to the load water line corresponding to the assigned summer freeboard and the weight of such water displaced by the ship without cargo, fuel, lubricating oil, ballast water, fresh water or feedwater in tanks, consumable stores, passengers, crew and their effects. *Fire Detection and Extinguishing Equipment Regulations*, C.R.C., c. 1422, s. 2.

DEAD WHALE. A dead whale that was not killed for the purpose of food in accordance with the commonly accepted practice of killing whales for that purpose, and includes a dauhval. *Meat Inspection Regulations*, C.R.C., c. 1032, s. 169.

DEADYARD. See ANIMAL ~.

DEAF PERSON. A person whose hearing is impaired to a degree that he would benefit from a hearing dog and who is certified as a deaf person for the purposes of this Act by the authority nominated for the purpose by the regulations. *Blind Persons' Rights Amendment Act, 1983*, S.A. 1983, c. 19, s. 2.

DEALER. *n.* 1. Person whose business is to buy items and sell them to other persons. 2. A person who trades in securities as principal or agent. Securities acts. See AUTOMOBILE ~; BONA FIDE ~; BROKER-~; CANADIAN SECURITIES ~; COMMODITY CONTRACTS ~; FIRST ~; FISH ~; FUR ~; GRAIN ~; HEARING AID ~; INDEPENDENT ~; INVESTMENT ~; LICENSED ~; LIVESTOCK ~; MILK ~; MOBILE HOME ~; MONEY MARKET ~S; MORTGAGE ~; MOTOR ~; MOTOR VEHICLE ~; NON-RESIDENT CONTROLLED ~; OIL AND GAS ~; PURPOSES RELATING TO THE BUSINESS OF A ~; QUALIFIED ~; RETAIL ~; SALVAGE ~; SECOND-HAND ~; SEED ~; SUB-BROKER ~; WHOLESALE ~.

DEALER AGREEMENT. The agreement or contract between a manufacturer, distributor, and a new motor vehicle dealer, which purports to establish the legal rights and obligations of the parties to the agreement or contract with regard to the purchase and sale of new motor vehicles and accessories for motor vehicles. *Motor Vehicle Franchise Act*, S.N.B. 1987, c. 70, s. 1.

DEALER PRINCIPAL. The person or persons exercising controlling ownership and/or management control of the new motor vehicle dealership. Such persons shall be as indicated in the dealer agreement signed by the new motor vehicle dealer. *Motor Vehicle Franchise Act*, S.N.B. 1987, c. 70, s. 1.

DEALER-SHIPPER. *n.* Any person who sells or offers to sell, buys, receives, assembles, packs, ships or transports fresh fruit or grapes but does not include (a) a servant employed by and driving a vehicle owned by a producer, shipper or dealer-shipper, (b) a railway company, or (c) a person who transports fresh fruit or grapes by motor vehicle as the agent of the producer. Canada regulations.

DEALER'S PLATE. A plate issued to a dealer to be attached by him to a vehicle which he is using for demonstration purposes with a view to the sale of the vehicle. *Highway Traffic Act*, R.S.Nfld. 1970, c. 152, s. 2.

DEALING. See EXCLUSIVE ~.

DEALING IN OR WITH. Includes buying, selling, owning, leasing, hiring, lending, borrowing, exchanging, acquiring, importing, storing, supplying, chartering, operating, delivering, transporting, distributing, dispensing, shipping, conveying, installing or using. *Transport Control Regulations*, C.R.C., c. 1566, s. 2.

DE AMBITU. [L.] Concerning bribery.

DEATH. *n.* 1. The loss of signs of life such as movement, growth, reproduction and metabolism. F.A. Jaffe, *A Guide to Pathological Evidence*, 2d ed. (Toronto: Carswell, 1983) at 2. 2. The permanent end of all vital functions. F.A. Jaffe, *A Guide to Pathological Evidence*, 2d ed. (Toronto: Carswell, 1983) at 173 and 174. 3. The death of a natural person and includes a stillbirth as defined in the Vital Statistics Act. *Coroners Act*, S.N.W.T. 1985 (3d Sess.), c. 2, s. 2. 4.

Includes death presumed for official purposes. *Pensioners Act*, R.S.C. 1985, c. P-6, s. 2. See CAUSE OF ~; CELLULAR ~; COT ~; CRIB ~; MANNER OF ~; MOLECULAR ~; NEONATAL ~; PROPERTY PASSING ON THE ~; REPORTABLE ~; SOMATIC ~; SUDDEN INFANT ~ SYNDROME.

DEATH BENEFIT. The amount received by a survivor or the deceased's estate upon or after the death of an employee in recognition of the employee's service in office or employment.

DEATHSMAN. *n.* Hangman; executioner.

DE AUDITU. [L.] Hearsay.

DEBATES. See OFFICIAL REPORT OF ~.

DEBASEMENT. *n.* A reduction of standard of fineness of coinage.

DE BENE ESSE. [L.] To consider something well done for the moment, but when it is examined or tried more fully, it must stand or fall on its own merit.

DEBENTURE. *n.* 1. Any corporate obligation unsecured or frequently secured by a floating charge. H. Sutherland, D.B. Horsley & J.M. Edmiston, eds., *Fraser's Handbook on Canadian Company Law*, 7th ed. (Toronto: Carswell, 1985) at 310. 2. An instrument acknowledging or creating a corporation's debt. F. Bennett, *Receiverships* (Toronto: Carswell, 1985) at 58. 3. Includes debenture stock, bonds and any other securities of a company constituting a charge on the assets of the company. 4. Includes debenture stock and bonds and any other securities of a company whether constituting a charge on the assets of the company or not; but does not include shares in the capital stock of a company, or bills of exchange, promissory notes, cheques or other like negotiable documents. *Companies Act*, R.S.N.S. 1967, c. 42, s. 1. 5. A debenture of a municipality. See BANK ~S; COUPON ~.

DEBENTURE RATE. In relation to a fiscal year, means the weighted average of the rate of interest of the Province of Ontario debentures issued in the fiscal year under section 72. *Teachers' Superannuation Act, 1983*, S.O. 1983, c. 84, s. 1.

DEBENTURE STOCK. A fund or stock which represents money borrowed by a company or public body charged on its property. The title of each original holder is entered in a register.

DEBENTURE TRUST DEED. A deed which vests a security in trustees in order to give greater security to the debenture holders.

DEBET ET DETINET. [L.] One owes and detains.

DEBET ET SOLET. [L.] One owes and is accustomed.

DEBILE FUNDAMENTUM FALLIT OPUS. [L.] A weak foundation destroys the work.

DEBIT. *n.* A sum due or owing.

DEBITA SEQUUNTUR PERSONAM DEBITORIS. [L.] Debts follow the debtor's person.

DEBIT NOTE. A note which states that the account of the person to whom it is sent will be debited.

DEBITOR. *n.* A debtor; the person against whom another has a personal right.

DEBITOR NON PRAESUMITUR DONARE. [L.] It is not presumed a debtor will give.

DEBOTORUM PACTIONIBUS CREDITORUM PETITIO NEC TOLLI NEC MINUI POTEST. [L.] Creditors' rights can neither be removed nor diminished by agreements among the debtors.

DEBITUM CONNEXIUM. [L.] A debt which gives rise to a lien.

DEBITUM ET CONTRACTUS SUNT NULLIUS LOCI. [L.] Debt and contract have no place.

DEBITUM IN PRAESENTI, SOLVENDUM IN FUTURO. [L.] Owed currently though payable in the future.

DE BONIS ASPORTATIS. [L.] For goods taken away. See TRESPASS ~.

DE BONIS NON. *abbr.* [L.] De bonis non administratis.

DE BONIS NON ADMINISTRATIS. [L.] A grant made when an administrator dies without having fully administered an estate or an executor dies intestate.

DE BONIS PROPRIIS. [L.] Of a person's own goods.

DE BONIS TESTATORIS. [L.] Of a testator's goods.

DEBRIS. *n.* 1. Any installation or structure on the seabed of those submarine areas described in paragraph 3(b) that was put in place in the course of any work or activity authorized pursuant to paragraph 5(1)(b) and that has been abandoned without such authorization as may be required by or pursuant to this Act or any material that has broken away or has been jettisoned, or that has been displaced from the seabed, in the course of any such work or activity. *Petroleum Resources Act*, R.S.C. 1985 (2d Supp.), c. 36, s. 123. 2. All inflammable waste material. *Forest Fires Act*, R.S.N.B. 1973, c. F-20, s. 1.

DEBT. *n.* 1. An amount of money due one person from another. 2. Includes any item or part of the debt forming the subject of the judgment and includes alimony and maintenance. 3. Includes any obligation for the payment of money. *Municipal acts, Ontario.* 4. A debt of any kind whatever, whether secured or unsecured and whether under seal or otherwise, and includes a bill of exchange or promissory note, whether negotiable or otherwise. *Estate Tax acts.* See ACTIVE ~; ATTACHMENT OF ~S; BAD ~; BOOK ~S; CONSUMER ~; CROWN ~; FOREIGN ~; FUNDED ~; INSURANCE OF ~S; JUDGMENT ~; LONG-TERM ~; MARITAL ~S; NATIONAL ~; PAST ~; PUBLIC ~; SPECIALITY ~; TERRITORIAL ~.

DEBT CHARGE. The amount of money necessary annually, i. to pay the principal due on long-term debt not payable from a sinking fund, ii. to provide a fund for the redemption of debentures payable from a sinking fund, and iii. to pay the interest due on all debt referred to in subparagraphs i and ii. *Education Act*, R.S.O. 1980, c. 129, s. 1.

DEBT CHARGES. The amount required annually to pay the interest on and repay the principal of a debenture issue as they fall due. *Municipal Services Act*, R.S.N.S. 1967, c. 203, s. 1. See ANNUAL ~.

DEBTEE. *n.* A creditor.

DEBT OBLIGATION. A mortgage, bond, debenture, note or other similar obligation of a corporation, whether secured or unsecured.

DEBT SERVICE. See GROSS ~ RATIO.

DEBTOR. *n.* 1. One who owes a debt. 2. A person to whom or on whose account money lent is advanced and includes every surety and endorser or other person liable for the repayment of money lent or upon agreement or collateral or other security given in respect thereof. *Unconscionable Transactions Relief acts.* 3. An insolvent person and any person who, at the time an act of bankruptcy was committed by him, resided or carried on business in Canada and, where the context requires, includes a bankrupt. *Bankruptcy Act*, R.S.C. 1985, c. B-3, s. 2. 4. (i) In relation to a writ of execution, any person liable for the payment of any money under a writ of execution, and (ii) in relation to a distress, the person who is liable for the payment of any money or the delivery up of any goods or chattels, which payment or delivery up is enforceable by distress or by proceedings in the nature of distress. See ABSCONDING ~; ACCOUNT ~; JUDGMENT ~; LOCALITY OF ~; MAINTENANCE ~; PRINCIPAL ~; TAX ~.

DEBTOR COMPANY. Any company that (a) is bankrupt or insolvent, (b) has committed an act of bankruptcy within the meaning of the Bankruptcy Act or is deemed insolvent within the meaning of the Winding-up Act, whether or not proceedings in respect of the company have been taken under either of those Acts, (c) has made an authorized assignment or against which a receiving order has been made under the Bankruptcy Act, or (d) is in the course of being wound up under the Winding-up Act because the company is insolvent. *Companies Creditors Arrangement Act*, R.S.C. 1985, c. C-36, s. 2.

DEBT POOLING SYSTEM. An arrangement or procedure whereby a debtor pays to one person money to be distributed or paid, according to a system, by that person to more than 2 creditors of the debtor. *Debt Collection Act*, R.S.B.C. 1979, c. 88, s. 1.

DEBT SECURITY. Any bond, debenture, note or similar instrument representing indebtedness, whether secured or unsecured. *Securities Act*, R.R.O. 1980, Reg. 910, s. 1.

DECA. *pref.* 10^1. Prefix for multiples and submultiples of basic, supplementary and derived units of measurement. *Weights and Measures Act*, S.C. 1970-71-72, c. 36, schedule 1.

DE CAETERO. [L.] From now on.

DECAY. *n.* Soft, mushy or leaking breakdown of the tissue, from whatever cause, and commonly known as "soft rot". *Fresh Fruit and Vegetable Regulations*, C.R.C., c. 285, s. 1.

DÉC. B.-C. *abbr.* Décisions des Tribunaux du Bas-Canada (1851-1867).

DECEASED. *n.* 1. A dead person. 2. A testator or a person dying intestate. Dependants Relief acts. 3. Includes any deceased person whether or not any tax is payable under this Act in respect of the death of that person. *Estate Tax acts.* See CORPORATION CONTROLLED BY THE ~; PROPERTY OF THE ~.

DECEASED INMATE. See ESTATE OF A ~.

DECEASED MEMBER. Includes any member who has been officially reported as dead or presumed dead in accordance with the appropriate service regulations from time to time in force. *Estates Regulations*, C.R.C., c. 1048, s. 2.

DECEASED PERSON. The body of a deceased person or of a stillborn child or a foetus. *Public Health Protection Act*, R.S.Q. 1977, c. P-35, s. 1.

DECEIT. *n.* Fraud; a false statement made knowing that it was false or without any belief in its truth or recklessly, without caring whether it was true or not (and therefore without any genuine belief in it), and intending that the plaintiff should rely upon it and that the statement was relied upon by the plaintiff and caused damage. *Derry v. Peek* (1889) 14 App. Cas. 337.

DECEIVE. *v.* To induce a person to believe that something which is false is true. See CALCULATED TO ~.

DECEPTIVE ACT OR PRACTICE. False, misleading or deceptive consumer representation. See UNFAIR OR ~ IN THE BUSINESS OF INSURANCE.

DECERTIFICATION. *n.* Removal of a union's right to represent a group of employees for collective bargaining purposes.

DECHARACTERIZE. *v.* To change the natural appearance of a meat product by mixing it with an innocuous substance. *Meat Inspection Regulations,* C.R.C., c. 1032, s. 2.

DECI. *pref.* 10^{-1}. Prefix for multiples and submultiples of basic, supplementary and derived units of measurement. *Weights and Measures Act,* S.C. 1970-71-72, c. 36, schedule 1.

DECIDUOUS TEETH. A child's first teeth. F.A. Jaffe, *A Guide to Pathological Evidence,* 2d ed. (Toronto: Carswell, 1983) at 174.

DECISION. *n.* 1. A judgment, ruling, order, finding, or determination of a court. 2. An order, a determination and a declaration. *Canada Labour Code,* R.S.C. 1985, c. L-2, s. 20(3). 3. A direction, decision, order, ruling or requirement made under a power or right conferred by this Act or the regulations. *Securities acts.* 4. The reasons given by the Court for its judgment or other order. *Judicature Act,* S. Nfld. 1986, c. 42, s. 2. See STATUTORY POWER OF ~.

DECK. *n.* 1. The area immediately surrounding a pool. *Public Health Act,* R.R.O. 1980, Reg. 849, s. 1. 2. A series of pre-printed pari-mutuel tickets that are consecutively numbered from zero. *Race Track Supervision Regulations,* C.R.C., c. 441, s. 2. See BULKHEAD ~; FREEBOARD ~; MAIN ~; ON ~; PEDESTRIAN ~; SHELTER ~ SPACE; STRENGTH ~; SUPERSTRUCTURE ~; UNDER ~.

DECK COVERING. See PERMANENT ~.

DECK LINE. The line indicating the uppermost complete deck of a ship as defined by the Load Line Rules. *Canada Shipping Act,* R.S.C. 1985, c. S-9, s. 2.

DECK OFFICER. See SENIOR WATCH KEEPING ~.

DECK WATCH. That part of the complement that is required for the purpose of attending to the navigation or security of a ship. Canada regulations. See PERSON IN CHARGE OF THE ~.

DECK WATCH OFFICER. A person who has the immediate charge of the navigation and safety of a ship, but does not include a pilot. Canada regulations.

DECLARANT. *n.* 1. One who makes a declaration. 2. The owner or owners in fee simple of the land described in the description at the time of registration of a declaration and description of the land, and includes any successor or assignee or such owner or owners but does not include a bona fide purchaser of a unit who actually pays fair market value or any successor or assignee of such purchaser. *Condominium acts.* 3. The person who originally makes a hearsay statement. *Military Rules of Evidence,* C.R.C., c. 1049, s. 2.

DECLARATION. *n.* 1. A formal statement of the opinion or decision of a court on the rights of interested parties or the construction of a will, deed or other written instrument. 2. A method to determine a dispute when the applicant's legal rights are unclear. 3. An instrument signed by the insured (i) with respect to which an endorsement is made on the policy; or (ii) that identifies the contract; or (iii) that describes the insurance or insurance fund or a part thereof, in which the applicant designates, or alters or revokes the designation of, a personal representative or a beneficiary as one to whom or for whose benefit insurance money is to be payable. *Insurance acts.* 4. A solemn declaration in the form and manner from time to time provided by the provincial evidence acts or by the Canada Evidence Act. 5. Includes any document by which an action is originated in the Trial Division. *Federal Court Rules,* C.R.C., c. 663, s. 2. See DYING ~; SOLEMN ~; STATUTORY ~.

DECLARATION DATE. Where used in relation to a commodity futures option, means that date on which the option expires. *Commodity Contract acts.*

DECLARATION OF SHARES. A statement in writing by applicants for a license or lease or by lessees or licensees declaring as between themselves the interest of each in such license or lease. *Mines Act,* R.S.N.S. 1967, c. 185, s. 1.

DECLARATION OF SYDNEY. A statement made in 1968 by the 22nd World Medical Assembly in Sydney, Australia that determination of death should be the responsibility of a physician and should be based on ordinary clinical criteria supplemented by an electroencephalograph. In a case in which a patient is considered to be a possible organ donor, two physicians should ascertain the point of death and they should have no concern with the subsequent transplant. F.A. Jaffe, *A Guide to*

Pathological Evidence, 2d ed. (Toronto: Carswell, 1983) at 184.

DECLARATION OF TRUST. Creation of a trust when the trust property is already held by the intended trustee by execution of a deed declaring that the trustee holds the property in trust for the executor of the deed.

DECLARATION OF WAR. The formal announcement that one nation intends to treat another nation as an enemy.

DECLARATION POLICY. A policy of insurance which covers goods which are declared from time to time. Raoul Colinvaux, *The Law of Insurance*, 5th ed. (London: Sweet & Maxwell, 1984) at 309.

DECLARATORY JUDGMENT. Declaring the parties' rights or expressing the court's opinion on a question of law, without ordering that anything be done.

DECLARATORY POWER. The power of the federal Parliament under s. 92(10)(C) of the Constitution Act, 1867 to bring a local work into federal jurisdiction by declaring that it is "for the general advantage of Canada". P.W. Hogg, *Constitutional Law of Canada*, 2d ed. (Toronto: Carswell, 1985) at 92.

DECLARATORY RELIEF. Relief sought from the court by the applicant is a declaration.

DECLARATORY STATUTE. A declaration or formal statement of existing law.

DECLARE. *v.* To assert, proclaim, state formally.

DECOMPOSED. *adj.* Having an offensive or objectionable odour, flavour, colour or textural defect associated with spoilage. *Fish Inspection acts.*

DECOMPRESSION SICKNESS. A condition of bodily malfunction caused by a change from a higher air pressure to a lower air pressure and includes the condition commonly known as the bends. *Occupational Health and Safety Act,* R.R.O. 1980, Reg. 691, s. 240.

DECONTAMINATION. See TERMINAL ~.

DE CORPORE COMITATUS. [L.] From the body of the county.

DECOY. *n.* Enticement, lure.

DECREE. *n.* 1. Judgment. 2. An order-in-council making obligatory, amending, extending or repealing any collective agreement. *Collective Agreement Decrees Act,* R.S.Q. 1977, c. D-2, s. 1.

DECREE ABSOLUTE. 1. A final decree. 2. The final court order in a divorce action.

DECREE NISI. 1. A provisional decree which will become final or absolute unless there is reason shown not to do so. 2. A provisional court order which terminates marriage.

DECREE OF FORECLOSURE. This document states that a mortgagor will be finally foreclosed or deprived of the equitable right to redeem, unless, within a specified time, that mortgagor does redeem. W.B. Rayner & R.H. McLaren, *Falconbridge on Mortgages*, 4th ed. (Toronto: Canada Law Book, 1977) at 447.

DECRIMINALIZATION. *n.* The removal of a matter from the Criminal Code; changing the law so that an act is no longer a crime.

DR-CRYSTALLIZE. *v.* To discharge the receiver and manager shortly after appointment under a floating charge. F. Bennett, *Receiverships* (Toronto: Carswell, 1985) at 10. See CRYSTALLIZATION.

DEDICATE. *v.* To make public a private road.

DEDICATION. *n.* The express or tacit opening of a road for public use.

DE DIE IN DIEM. [L.] From day to day.

DEDI ET CONCESSI. [L.] I gave and granted.

DEDITION. *n.* Surrender; yielding up.

DE DONIS. [L.] Concerning gifts.

DEDUCT. *v.* Includes withhold. *Canada Pension Plan,* R.S.C. 1985, c. C-8, s. 2.

DEDUCTIBLE AMOUNT. (i) With reference to the Fund, the amount, if any, prescribed by the by-laws as the amount to be deducted from any claim paid from the Fund, and (ii) with reference to a group contract, the amount, if any, specified in the contract as the amount that the insurer is entitled to deduct from the amount of any claim for which the insurer is liable under the contract. *Statutes governing professions.*

DEDUCTION. *n.* 1. An amount deducted, taken away. 2. An amount withheld by an employer from an employee's wages for union dues, taxes, pension, insurance. 3. An amount permitted by tax laws to be subtracted from income before computing tax. See ROYALTY ~ ACCOUNT.

DEDUCTION AT SOURCE. A withholding, made by an employer from the remuneration of an employee with respect to the employee's contribution. *Québec Pension Plan Act,* R.S.Q. 1977, c. R-9, s. 1.

DEDUCTIVE VALUE. In respect of goods, the value of the goods determined in accordance with subsection 51(2). *Customs Act,* R.S.C. 1985 (2d Supp.), c. 1, s. 45.

DEED. *n.* 1. A document signed, sealed and

delivered, through which an interest, property or right passes. 2. Any instrument whereby real property is conveyed, transferred, assigned to or vested in any person. *Real Property Transfer Tax Act*, S.N.B. 1983, c. R-2.1, s. 1. 3. Every deed or writing of whatsoever nature or kind relating to or affecting any interest in or title to land in the province, except a mortgage. Prince Edward Island statutes. 4. Any instrument or writing not testamentary in character, whereby property is conveyed, transferred, assigned or vested in any person, but does not include a mortgage or an agreement of sale or a lease for a term less than twenty-five years, or a deed given by a clerk of a municipal unit in pursuance of a sale for rates and taxes. *Municipal Land Transfer Tax Act*, S.N.S. 1967-68, c. 10, s. 1. See DISENTAILING ~; EXECUTION OF ~S; QUIT-CLAIM ~; REGISTRAR OF ~S; REGISTRY OF ~S; SUPPLEMENTAL ~; TAX ~; TRUST ~.

DEED OF COVENANT. A deed in which one party formally agrees to do certain things with another.

DEED OF GIFT. A deed which transfers property as a gift.

DEED OF GRANT. A deed which grants property.

DEED OF LOAN. A deed of hypothecary loan or of loan on pledged property. *An Act to promote long term farm credit by private institutions*, S.Q. 1978, c. 50, s. 1.

DEED-POLL. *n.* A declaration of the act and intention of a grantor of property, so named because it was formerly polled (shaved even) at the top, whereas an indenture was indented (cut in acute angles).

DEED TO USES. A deed purporting to grant or convey land to such uses as the grantee may appoint, regardless of the method of appointment specified in the deed, and, until appointment or in default of appointment, purporting to grant or convey the land in the use of the grantee absolutely, and includes every such deed containing words of like import, but does not include a mortgage. *Registry Act*, R.S.O. 1980, c. 445, s. 59.

DEEM. *v.* To treat as if; to hold; to consider.

DEEMED TRUST. A trust created by statute which is designed to protect certain classes of creditors or to insure the recovery of certain taxes. F. Bennett, *Receiverships* (Toronto: Carswell, 1985) at 242.

DEEPENED WELL. An oil or gas well that, after (a) being capable of producing petroleum or gas from an accumulation of petroleum or gas, or (b) being drilled for the purpose of producing petroleum or gas from an accumulation of petroleum or gas and having been abandoned, is deepened by further drilling commenced after March 31, 1985 for the purpose of producing petroleum or gas from a different accumulation of petroleum or gas. *Petroleum and Gas Revenue Tax Act*, R.S.C. 1985 (2d Supp.), c. 2, s. 2.

DEEPEST SUBDIVISION LOADLINE. The water line that corresponds to the greatest draught. *Hull Construction Regulations*, C.R.C., c. 1431, s. 2.

DEEP FOUNDATION. A foundation unit that provides support for a building by transferring loads either by end-bearing to a soil or rock at considerable depth below the building, or by adhesion or friction, or both, in the soil or rock in which it is placed. *Building Code Act*, R.R.O. 1980, Reg. 87, s. 1.

DEEP PRODUCTION. See NEW ~.

DEEP WATERWAY. Adequate provision for navigation requiring a controlling channel depth of twenty-seven feet with a depth of thirty feet over lock sills in general in accordance with paragraph (j) of the preliminary article of the Agreement between Canada and the United States providing for the Development of Navigation and Power in the Great Lakes-St. Lawrence Basin dated March 19, 1941. *St. Lawrence Seaway Authority Act*, R.S.C. 1985, c. S-2, s. 2.

DEEP WELL DISPOSAL. The discharge of liquid waste into a geological formation by means of a well. *Environmental Protection Act*, R.R.O. 1980, Reg. 303, s. 1.

DEER. *n.* An animal of the species known as Coast or Columbian, mule, red, white tailed or fallow deer. *Wildlife Act*, R.S.B.C. 1979, c. 433, s. 1.

DEER FAMILY. The family Cervidae. *Wildlife Act*, R.S.B.C. 1979, c. 433, s. 1.

DE FACTO. [L.] In fact.

DE FACTO POSSESSION. Physical control.

DEFALCATION. *n.* Includes any fraudulent act or omission of a public officer that occasions loss in money or property to (a) Her Majesty, or (b) persons other than Her Majesty, when such money or property was in the custody of the public officer in the course of his official duties, whether such loss is recovered or not. *Public Officers Guarantee Regulations*, C.R.C., c. 723, s. 2.

DEFAMATION. *n.* Libel or slander. *Defamation acts.*

DEFAMATORY. *adj.* Tending to lower the reputation of someone in the opinion of right thinking members of society. R.E. Brown, *The Law of Defamation in Canada* (Toronto: Carswell, 1987) at 9.

DEFAMATORY LIBEL. Matter published without lawful justification or excuse, that is likely to injure the reputation of any person by exposing him to hatred, contempt or ridicule, or that is designed to insult the person of or concerning whom it is published. A defamatory libel may be expressed directly or by insinuation or irony (a) in words legibly marked upon any substance, or (b) by any object signifying a defamatory libel otherwise than by words. *Criminal Code*, R.S.C. 1985, c. C-46, s. 298.

DEFAULT. *n.* 1. The failure to pay or otherwise perform the obligation secured when due or the occurrence of any event whereupon under the terms of the security agreement the security becomes enforceable. *Personal Property Security acts.* 2. The omission of something one should do; neglect. 3. Non-attendance in court. See EVENT OF ~; SAVER ~.

DEFAULTER. *n.* One who fails, usually in paying.

DEFAULT JUDGMENT. The final judgment awarded to the plaintiff when the defendant fails to file an appearance or statment of defence.

DEFEASANCE. *n.* 1. A condition appended to an estate which defeats the estat when performed or a deed which defeats an estate. 2. A condition on an obligation which defeats it when performed.

DEFEASANCE CLAUSE. A proviso that a mortgage will become void on payment of the mortgage money. Thus, if one pays strictly according to the proviso, the estate without release or reconveyance becomes revested in the mortgagor or becomes vested in any other person entitled to it by subsequent mortgage or assignment from the mortgagor. W.B. Rayner & R.H. McLaren, *Falconbridge on Mortgages*, 4th ed. (Toronto: Canada Law Book, 1977) at 366.

DEFEASIBLE. *adj.* Able to be abrogated or annulled.

DEFEAT. *v.* To frustrate, prevent.

DEFECT. *n.* Absence of an essential. See CONDITION ~; INHERENT ~; LATENT ~; PATENT ~; PHYSICAL ~.

DEFECT IN A DOCUMENT. Includes any error, omission or want or particularity in a document, any failure of a document to comply with the requirements of this Act, any discrepancy between the contents of a document and the evidence that is given at trial, and every defect that but for this section, might make a document invalid. *Provincial Offences Procedure Act*, S.N.B. 1987, c. P-22.1, s. 105.

DEFECT IN THE PROCEEDINGS. Includes any failure of a judge to exercise jurisdiction or to appear at the time and place to which proceedings are adjourned and every other defect of procedure that, but for this section, might deprive the judge of jurisdiction. *Provincial Offences Procedure Act*, S.N.B. 1987, c. P-22.1, s. 105.

DEFECTIVE. *n.* Any person, not an infant, who, not having been declared, under The Mental Health Act, to be a mentally disordered person, is incapable, from infirmity of mind, of managing his own affairs. *Trustee Act*, R.S.M. 1970, c. T160, s. 2. See MENTAL ~.

DEFECTIVE UNITS. Units damaged by internal or external discolouration, poor peeling, blemishes and insect or mechanical injury. *Processed Fruit and Vegetable Regulations*, C.R.C., c. 291.

DEFECTUM SANGUINIS. [L.] Failure of bloodline.

DEFENCE. *n.* 1. A defendant's denial of a plaintiff's complaint. 2. A guard; a justification; a protection. 3. Includes counter-claim. *Bills of Exchange Act*, R.S.C. 1985, c. B-4, s. 2. See CIVIL ~; DEPARTMENT OF NATIONAL ~; EXTRANEOUS ~; INHERENT ~; STATEMENT OF ~.

DEFENCE CAMP. A camp or barracks of the Canadian Forces within a municipality established by the Minister of National Defence. *Municipal Act*, S.M. 1970, c. 100, s. 442.

DEFENCE CONTRACT. (a) A contract with Her Majesty or an agent of Her Majesty, or with an associated government, that in any way relates to defence supplies or to defence projects or to the designing, manufacturing, producing, constructing, finishing, assembling, transporting, repairing, maintaining, servicing or storing of, or dealing in, defence supplies or defence projects, and (b) a defence subcontract. *Defence Production Act*, R.S.C. 1985, c. D-1, s. 2.

DEFENCE ESTABLISHMENT. Any area or structure under the control of the Minister of National Defence, and the materiel and other things situated in or on any such area or structure.

DEFENCE FLIGHT NOTIFICATION. A flight notification that (a) contains the information required to be contained in a flight notification by the Flight Plans and Flight Notifications Order, and (b) states the flight level or altitude above sea level and the true airspeed to be flown.

Security Control of Air Traffic Order, C.R.C., c. 63, s. 2.

DEFENCE OF CANADA OR ANY STATE ALLIED OR ASSOCIATED WITH CANADA. The efforts of Canada and of foreign states toward the detection, prevention or suppression of activities of any foreign state directed toward actual or potential attack or other acts of aggression against Canada or any state allied or associated with Canada. *Access to Information Act*, R.S.C. 1985, c. A-1, s. 15(2).

DEFENCE PROJECTS. Buildings, aerodromes, airports, dockyards, roads, defence fortifications or other military works, or works required for the protection, maintenance or storage of defence supplies. *Defence Production Act*, R.S.C. 1985, c. D-1, s. 2.

DEFENCE SUBCONTRACT. A contract or arrangement between any persons whomever, (a) to perform all or any part of the work or service or make or furnish any article or material for the purpose of any other defence contract, (b) under which any amount payable is contingent on the entry into of any other defence contract or determined with reference to any amount payable under or otherwise by reference to any other defence contract, or (c) under which any part of the services performed or to be performed consists of soliciting, attempting to negotiate or negotiating any other defence contract or soliciting or negotiating for the purchase or sale of any articles, materials or services required to fulfil any other defence contract, and, for greater certainty but not so as to limit the foregoing, for the purposes of this definition the expression "other defence contract" includes a defence subcontract. *Defence Production Act*, R.S.C. 1985, c. D-1, s. 2.

DEFENCE SUPPLIES. (a) Arms, ammunition, implements of war, vehicles, mechanical and other equipment, watercraft, amphibious craft, aircraft, animals, articles, materials, substances and things required or used for the purposes of the defence of Canada or for cooperative efforts for defence being carried on by Canada and an associated government, (b) ships of all kinds, and (c) articles, materials, substances and things of all kinds used for the production or supply of anything mentioned in paragraph (a) or (b) or for the construction of defence projects. *Defence Production Act*, R.S.C. 1985, c. D-1, s. 2.

DEFENCE WOUND. A wound, sustained by the victim of an attack, while trying to grab or fend off the attacker's sharp weapon. F.A. Jaffe, *A Guide to Pathological Evidence*, 2d ed. (Toronto: Carswell, 1983) at 187.

DEFEND. *v.* To deny. See NOTICE OF INTENT TO ~.

DEFENDANT. *n.* 1. Includes every person served with any writ of summons or process, or served with notice of, or entitled to attend, any proceedings. 2. A person against whom an action is commenced. 3. A person to whom a summons is issued. 4. Includes a plaintiff against whom a counterclaim is brought.

DEFENDEMUS. [L.] We will defend.

DEFENDERE SE PER CORPUS SUUM. [L.] To defend oneself with one's own body.

DEFENDERE UNICA MANU. [L. to defend oneself with the mere hand] A denial of an accusation under oath.

DEFENERATION. *n.* Lending money on usury.

DEFERRED AMOUNT. At the end of a taxation year under a salary deferral arrangement in respect of a taxpayer means (a) in the case of a trust governed by the arrangement, any amount that a person has a right under the arrangement at the end of the year to receive after the end of the year where the amount has been received, is receivable or may at any time become receivable by the trust as, on account or in lieu of salary or wages of the taxpayer for services rendered in the year or a preceding taxation year, and (b) in any other case, any amount that a person has a right under the arrangement at the end of the year to receive after the end of the year, and for the purposes of this definition a right under the arrangement shall include a right that is subject to one or more conditions unless there is a substantial risk that any one of those conditions will not be satisfied. *Income Tax Act*, R.S.C. 1952, c. 148 (as added by S.C. 1986, c. 55), s. 248(1).

DEFERRED ANNUITY. An annuity that becomes payable to the contributor at the time he reaches sixty years of age or another age specified by the governing statute.

DEFERRED BENEFIT. The benefit that accrues upon completion of the works but which is not derived or derivable therefrom until a sewer or water main upon which the land will abut is constructed as part of the works. *Municipal Act*, R.S.O. 1980, c. 302, s. 218.

DEFERRED COMMUNITY OF PROPERTY. Each spouse retains separate property during marriage, but when the marriage dissolves, each spouse is entitled to one-half of all property which forms the community. J.G. McLeod, *The Conflict of Laws* (Calgary: Carswell, 1983) at 372.

DEFERRED COMPENSATION PLAN. The

employer pays an amount equal to a percent of the salary into the plan, and the plan pays the employee the accumulated credits thirty days after the employee completes the employment. A. Bissett-Johnson & W.M. Holland, eds, *Matrimonial Property Law in Canada* (Toronto: Carswell, 1980) at BC-18.

DEFERRED LIFE ANNUITY. A life annuity that commences at retirement date.

DEFERRED PAYMENT PLAN. See CONTINUOUS ~.

DEFERRED PENSION. A pension benefit, payment of which is deferred until the person entitled to the pension benefit reaches the normal retirement date under the pension plan.

DEFERRED PENSION BENEFIT. A pension benefit other than an immediate pension benefit. *Pension Benefits Standards Act*, R.S.C. 1985 (2d Supp.), c. 32, s. 2.

DEFERRED PROFIT SHARING PLAN. A plan which allows an employer to share company profits with employees. W. Grover and F. Iacobucci, *Materials on Canadian Income Tax*, 4th ed. (Toronto: Richard De Boo Ltd., 1980) at 444.

DEFERRED SHARING SCHEME. The sharing of matrimonial property is deferred until the happening of an event such as marriage breakdown. A. Bissett-Johnson & W.M. Holland, eds., *Matrimonial Property Law in Canada* (Toronto: Carswell, 1980) at A-5.

DEFERRED STOCK. A stock entitling holders to all the remaining net earnings after dividends have been paid to the preferred stock and ordinary stockholders.

DEFERRED TRUST. Tax is deferred on the spouse's interest under the trust until that spouse's interest ends on his or her death. D.M.W. Waters, *The Law of Trusts in Canada*, 2d ed. (Toronto: Carswell, 1984) at 30.

DEFICIENCY. See EXPERIENCE ~; MARGIN ~; MENTAL ~; OXYGEN ~.

DEFICIENTE UNO (SANGUINE) NON POTEST ESSE HAERES. [L.] A person lacking one bloodline cannot be heir.

DEFICIT. *n.* Loss; an amount by which expenditures exceed revenue. See BASIC ACCOUNT ~.

DE FIDE ET OFFICIO JUDICIS NON RECIPITUR QUAESTIO; SED DE SCIENTIA SIVE SIT ERROR JURIS SIVE FACTI. [L.] No question can be entertained regarding the good faith and integrity of a judge.

DEFILEMENT. *n.* Corruption; debasing.

DEFINE. *v.* To explain the meaning; to limit; to clarify.

DEFINED BENEFIT. A pension benefit other than a defined contribution benefit. *Pension Benefits Act*, S.N.B. 1987, c. P-5.1, s. 1.

DEFINED BENEFIT PLAN. A pension plan where the pension benefits under the plan are determined in accordance with a formula set forth in the plan and where the employer contributions under the plan are not so determined. *Pension Benefits Standards Regulations*, C.R.C., c. 1252, s. 2.

DEFINED BENEFIT PROVISION. A provision of a pension plan under which pension benefits for a member are determined in any way other than that described in the definition "defined contribution provision". *Pension Benefit Standards Act*, R.S.C. 1985 (2d Supp.), c. 32, s. 2.

DEFINED CONTRIBUTION BENEFIT. A pension benefit that is determined with reference to and provided by contributions, and the interest on the contributions, paid by or for the credit of a member of a pension plan and determined on an individual account basis. *Pension Benefits Act*, S.N.B. 1987, c. P-5.1, s. 1.

DEFINED CONTRIBUTION PLAN. A pension plan that consists of defined contribution provisions and does not contain defined benefit provisions, other than (a) a defined benefit provision relating to pension benefits accrued in respect of employment before the effective date of the pension plan, or (b) a defined benefit provision that provides for a minimum pension benefit whose additional value is not significant in the Superintendent's opinion. *Pension Benefit Standards Act*, R.S.C. 1985 (2d Supp.), c. 32, s. 2.

DEFINED CONTRIBUTION PROVISION. A provision of a pension plan under which pension benefits for a member are determined solely as a function of the amount of pension benefit that can be provided by (a) contributions made by and on behalf of that member, and (b) interest earnings and other gains and losses allocated to that member. *Pension Benefit Standards Act*, R.S.C. 1985 (2d Supp.), c. 32, s. 2.

DEFINITION SECTION. A statutory provision which states that particular words and phrases, when used in the statute, will bear certain meanings. P.St.J. Langan, ed., *Maxwell on The Interpretation of Statutes*, 12th ed. (Bombay: N.M. Tripathi, 1976) at 270.

DEFOG. *v.* To remove moisture from the inside surface of the glass. *Motor Vehicle Safety Regulations*, C.R.C., c. 1038, s. 103.

DEFORCEMENT. *n.* Holding lands to which someone else is entitled.

DEFRAUD. *v.* To deprive of property by means of fraud; to practise fraud.

DEFROST. *v.* To melt frost or ice on the inside or outside surface of the glass. *Motor Vehicle Safety Regulations*, C.R.C., c. 1038, s. 103.

DEFUNCT. *adj.* No longer in operation; no longer carrying on business.

DEFUNCT COMPANY. A company which is no longer carrying on business.

DEGRADATION. *n.* A loss of dignity.

DEGREE. *n.* 1. A difference in relative importance between members of the same species. 2. One step in the line of consanguinity or descent. 3. Any recognition in writing of academic achievement which is called a degree; and includes the degrees of bachelor, master and doctor.

DEGREE OF ARC. P/180 radian. *Weights and Measures Act*, S.C. 1970-71-72, c. 36, schedule I.

DEHORS. [Fr.] Outside.

DEHYDRATED. *adj.* May only be prefixed to the name of a ground hay product when the hay from which the product was ground was dried rapidly by artificial heat. *Feeds Regulations*, C.R.C., c. 665, s. 8.

DEHYDRATED POTATO PRODUCTS PLANT. Includes any plant where raw potatoes are processed to remove moisture by heat, vacuum or air drying, with the finished product distributed as granules, flakes or slices. *Potato Processing Plant Liquid Effluent Regulations*, C.R.C., c. 829, s. 2.

DEHYDRATOR. *n.* An apparatus designed and used to remove water from raw gas. *Oil and Gas Conservation Act*, R.S.A. 1980, c. O-5, s. 1.

DE INCREMENTO. [L.] Of increase.

DE INJURIA SUA PROPRIA ABSQUE TALI CAUSA. [L.] Of a personal wrong and not for the cause alleged.

DEJURATION. *n.* Swearing a solemn oath.

DE JURE. [L.] By right; lawful.

DE JURE JUDICES DE FACTO JURATORES RESPONDENT. [L.] Judges answer to the law, a jury to fact.

DELATOR. *n.* [L.] An accuser; an informer.

DELAWARE MERGER. A subsidiary company with minority shareholders is merged with a shell subsidiary in exchange for a cash or share option in the parent company. W. Grover and F. Iacobucci, *Materials on Canadian Income Tax*, 4th ed. (Toronto: Richard De Boo Ltd., 1980) at 1057.

DELAY. *v.* To postpone, to put off.

DELAY. *n.* See DISMISSAL FOR ~; PRESCRIBED ~.

DELAYED RETIREMENT. Withdrawal from the workforce after the normal retirement date.

DEL CREDERE. Guarantee; warranty.

DEL CREDERE AGENT. A mercantile agent who will indemnify the principal if the third party fails to pay as contracted in respect of goods. G.H.L. Fridman, *The Law of Agency*, 5th ed. (London: Butterworths, 1983) at 38.

DEL CREDERE COMMISSION. An extra commission paid to a del credere agent. G.H.L. Fridman, *The Law of Agency*, 5th ed. (London: Butterworths, 1983) at 38.

DELECTUS PERSONAE. [L.] The selection of a person.

DELEGATA POTESTAS NON POTEST DELEGARI. [L.] A power already delegated cannot be delegated again.

DELEGATE. *n.* An individual elected to represent a division of the members at meetings of a credit union. *Credit Unions and Caisses Populaires Act*, S.M. 1977, c. 51, s. 1.

DELEGATED LEGISLATION. 1. Subordinate legislation made by authorities other than Parliament or a legislature. P.W. Hogg, *Constitutional Law of Canada*, 2d ed. (Toronto: Carswell, 1985) at 284. 2. A statutory instrument. S.A. DeSmith, *Judicial Review of Administrative Action*, 4th ed. by J.M. Evans (London: Stevens, 1980) at 147.

DELEGATION. *n.* 1. Entrusting someone else to act in one's place. 2. The assignment of a debt to someone else.

DELEGATUS NON POTEST DELEGARE. [L.] One who already is a delegate cannot delegate.

DELERIUM. *n.* Disorientation of the mind. F.A. Jaffe, *A Guide to Pathological Evidence*, 2d ed. (Toronto: Carswell, 1983) at 174.

DELETERIOUS. *adj.* Harmful.

DELETERIOUS SUBSTANCE. (a) Any substance that, if added to any water, would degrade or alter or form part of a process of degradation or alteration of the quality of that water so that it is rendered or is likely to be rendered deleterious to fish or fish habitat or to the use by man of fish that frequent that water, or (b) any water that contains a substance in such quantity or concentration, or that has been so treated, processed or changed, by heat or other means, from a natural state that it would, if added to any other water, degrade or alter or form part of a process of degradation or alteration of the quality of that water so that it is rendered or is likely to be rendered deleterious to fish or fish habitat or to the use by man of fish that frequent that water, and without limiting the generality of the foregoing includes (c) any substance or class of substances prescribed pursuant to paragraph (2)(a), (d) any water that contains any substance or class of substances in a quantity or concentration that is equal to or in excess of a quantity or concentration prescribed in respect of that substance or class of substances pursuant to paragraph (2)(b), and (e) any water that has been subjected to a treatment, process or change prescribed pursuant to paragraph (2)(c). *Fisheries Act*, R.S.C. 1985, c. F-14, s. 34.

DELIBERANDUM EST DIU QUOD STATUENDUM EST SEMEL. [L.] One should long deliberate on anything which is to be decided once and for all.

DELIBERATE. *v.* To consider.

DELIBERATE. *adj.* Carefully considered; wilful.

DELICATUS DEBITOR EST ODIOSUS IN LEGE. [L.] A luxurious debtor is repugnant in law.

DELICT. *n.* A tort; a crime.

DELICTUM. *n.* [L.] A tort.

DELINEATION WELL. A well that is so located in relation to another well penetrating an accumulation of petroleum, oil or gas that there is a reasonable expectation that another portion of that accumulation will be penetrated by the first-mentioned well and that the drilling is necessary in order to determine the commercial value of the accumulation.

DELINQUENCY. *n.* Failure; omission.

DELINQUENT. See JUVENILE ~.

DELIST. *v.* To remove a security from its trading on the stock exchange.

DELIVER. *v.* 1. With reference to a notice or other document, includes mail to or leave with a person, or deposit in a person's mail box or receptacle at the person's residence or place of business. 2. To place by means of a hose or other article capable of transmitting liquids.

DELIVERABLE STATE. Goods in such a state that the buyer would, under contract, be bound to take delivery of them. Sale of Goods acts.

DELIVERED PRICING. The practice of refusing a customer, or person seeking to become a customer, delivery of an article at any place in which the supplier engages in a practice of making delivery of the article to any other of the supplier's customers on the same trade terms that would be available to the first-mentioned customer if his place of business were located in that place. *Combines Investigation Act*, R.S.C. 1985 (2d Supp.), c. 19, s. 80.

DELIVERING CHARGE. A charge for moving goods from an ordinary place of rest to railway flat cars or the tailgate or bed of motor transport vehicles when goods are handled by fork lift equipment only, but does not include the cost of labour or materials for bracing or otherwise securing the goods. *Pacific Terminal Tariff By-law*, C.R.C., c. 1083, s. 28.

DELIVERY. *n.* 1. The voluntary transfer of possession from one person to another. *Sale of Goods acts.* 2. Transfer of possession, actual or constructive, from one person to another. 3. In relation to a lecture, includes delivery by means of any mechanical instrument. *Copyright Act*, R.S.C. 1985, c. C-42, s. 2. 4. As applied to mail, means delivery to the addressee thereof, and, for the purposes of this Act, (a) leaving mail at the residence or place of business of the addressee, (b) depositing mail in a post office box or rural mail box or any other receptacle provided for the receipt of mail, or (c) leaving mail with the addressee or his servant or agent or with any other person considered to be authorized to receive mail, according to the usual manner of delivering that addressee's mail, is deemed to be delivery to the addressee. *Post Office Act*, R.S.C. 1970, c. P-14, s. 2. 5. The natural or the lawfully, medically induced end of a pregnancy by child-birth, whether or not the child is viable. *An Act respecting Labour Standards*, S.Q. 1979, c. 45, s. 1. 6. Transfer from one premises to another for any purpose. *Live Stock and Live Stock Products Act*, R.R.O. 1980, Reg. 582, s. 1. See CASH ON ~; DATE OF ~; GAOL ~; NON-~; RE~; WRIT OF ~.

DELIVERY CAR. 1. Is equipped for the transportation of merchandise, and effects such transportation for a pecuniary consideration; it includes the vehicle which is equipped for the transportation of persons and merchandise but which does not come within the conditions required to be considered as a farm vehicle. *Highway Code*, R.S.Q. 1977, c. C-24, s. 1. 2. A passenger motor vehicle or a sedan delivery used, in either case, for delivery purposes, but does not include a public service vehicle or a taxicab. *The Highway Traffic Act*, S.M. 1985-86, c. 3, s. 1.

DELIVERY CHARGE. See SUB-ORDER ~.

DELUSION. *n.* False belief.

DEM. *abbr.* On the demise of. In a British action of ejectment before 1852, the plaintiff in the action would be styled "Doe dem. Smith."

DEMAIN. See DEMESNE.

DEMAINE. See DEMESNE.

DEMAND. *n.* 1. A claim that a person offer something due. 2. A request that a person do something which she or he is legally bound to do once the request is made. See BILLING ~; BIOCHEMICAL OXYGEN ~; LIQUIDATED ~; MARKET ~; STALE ~; THIRD PARTY ~.

DEMANDANT. *n.* The plaintiff in a real action.

DEMAND LETTER. A letter requesting immediate payment of debt.

DEMAND LIABILITY. The total of the amount of deposits and investment money of the company withdrawable or repayable or maturing in less than 100 days. *Trust Companies Act*, R.S.A. 1980, c. T-9, s. 111.

DEMAND NOTE. A promissory note payable on demand.

DEMEASE. *n.* Death.

DEMENTIA. *n.* Unalterable mental deterioration. F.A. Jaffe, *A Guide to Pathological Evidence*, 2d ed. (Toronto: Carswell, 1983) at 174.

DEMERIT POINT. A demerit point assessed against a person under the regulations made under The Manitoba Public Insurance Corporation Act or a demerit point assessed against a driver by the registrar on the basis of an accident in which the driver was involved and for which the registrar, in his absolute discretion, feels the driver was wholly or partly responsible. *The Highway Traffic Act*, S.M. 1985-86, c. 3, s. 334(8).

DEMESNE. *n.* The private property of a lord which was not granted out in tenancy.

DEMESNIAL. *adj.* Relating to a demesne.

DEMIDIETAS. *n.* A half; moiety.

DE MINIMIS NON CURAT LEX. [L.] The law does not bother itself about trifles.

DEMISE. *n.* Includes any and every agreement or transaction whether in writing or by deed or parol whereby one person may become the tenant of another. See RE~.

DEMISE OF THE CROWN. The death, deposition or abdication of the sovereign.

DEMOLISH. *v.* To destroy.

DEMOLITION. *n.* The doing of anything in the removal of a building or any material part thereof.

DEMOLITION ORDER. If a building is unfit for occupation and cannot be repaired at reasonable cost it may be ordered demolished.

DEMONETISATION. *n.* A declaration that certain coins are no longer legal tender.

DEMONSTRATION. *n.* The act of showing, displaying or exhibiting an aircraft in Canada for the purpose of explaining or proving its qualities and capabilities to prospective customers. *Imported Demonstration Aircraft Remission Order*, C.R.C., c. 771, s. 2.

DEMONSTRATION OR RESEARCH PROJECT. (i) A project that is designed to test, in a specified situation, the applicability of new or modified methods of providing welfare services as a means of improving such services, or (ii) a project that is intended to make a contribution to knowledge by systematically collecting, organizing and evaluating data relating to welfare problems or matters by experimentally testing an hypothesis relating to such problems or matters, where the project is to be completed within a specified time and has been approved as a demonstration project or as a research project pursuant to the rules made by the Governor in Council for the purposes of the National Welfare Grants program. *Canada Assistance Plan Regulations*, C.R.C., c. 382, s. 3.

DEMONSTRATIVE EVIDENCE. Real things as opposed to testimony, i.e., weapons, models, maps, photographs.

DEMONSTRATIVE LEGACY. A legacy, general in nature, which is supposed to be satisfied out of part of a testator's property or a specified fund. T. Sheard, R. Hull & M.M.K. Fitzpatrick, *Canadian Forms of Wills*, 4th ed. (Toronto: Carswell, 1982) at 158.

DEMORATUR. [L.] One demurs.

DE MORTE HOMINIS NULLA EST CUNCTATIO LONGA. [L.] There is no long delay concerning a person's death.

DEMOTE. *v.* To reduce the salary of an employee by transferring him to a position with a lower maximum salary or by reducing the salary of his present position. *Civil Service Act*, S.P.E.I. 1983, c. 4, s. 1.

DEMOTION. *n.* A change of employment from one class to another having a lower maximum salary. *Civil Service acts*.

DEMOUNTABLE RIM. A supporting member for a tire or tire and tube assembly, that does not have a permanently attached centre component. *Motor Vehicle Safety Regulations*, C.R.C., c. 1038, s. 2.

DEMUR. *v.* To object by demurrer.

DEMURRABLE. *adj.* Said of pleading which does not state facts to support the claim.

DEMURRAGE. *n.* 1. A charge payable on goods in transit remaining on Board property after the expiration of free time. *Wharfage Charges By-law*, C.R.C., c. 1066, s. 2. 2. An allowance made to a shipowner for detaining a ship in port after the agreed-on sailing time.

DEMURRER. *n.* A pleading by which one party admitted the facts as stated in the opponent's pleading and waited for the court to decide if that party was bound to answer.

DENARII. [L.] Available money.

DENATURE. *v.* To make a meat product repulsive in appearance or odour by adding a substance to it. *Meat Inspection Regulations*, C.R.C., c. 1032, s. 2.

DENATURED ALCOHOL. 1. Alcohol in suitable admixture with such denaturants as to render it in the judgment of the Minister nonpotable and to prevent recovery of the ethyl alcohol. *Excise Act*, R.S.C. 1985, c. E-14, s. 243. 2. A mixture of (i) alcohol derived from biomass materials, and (ii) soluble by-products of fermentation, containing not more than 1 per cent of water. *Gasoline Tax Act*, S.M. 1980, c. 69, s. 5.

DENATURED SPIRITS. Spirits in suitable admixture with such denaturants as to render them in the opinion of the Minister non-potable and to prevent recovery of the ethyl alcohol. *Excise Act*, R.S.C. 1985, c. E-14, s. 243.

DENIAL. *n.* 1. Disputing the allegations of the opposite party. G.D. Watson & C. Perkins, eds., *Holmested & Watson: Ontario Civil Procedure* (Toronto: Carswell, 1984) at 25-19. 2. The refusal by a department to provide access to information, to correct a record or to make a notation on a record upon a request being made pursuant to this Act. *Freedom of Information Act*, S.N.S. 1977, c. 10, s. 2.

DENIZATION. *n.* Enfranchising, making free.

DENIZEN. *n.* A native-born citizen of a country.

DENOMINATION. *n.* 1. A value or size of currency. 2. A religious organization and members bearing a particular name. 3. The act of naming. See RECOGNIZED ~; RELIGIOUS ~.

DENOMINATIONAL THEOLOGICAL COURSE. Any course or subject offered by a university or college, for which credits are given

only for a degree or diploma in theology, and for which credits are not given by all other universities or colleges granting degrees or diplomas in theology. *Universities Grants Commission Act*, R.S.M. 1970, c. U50, s. 1.

DE NON APPARENTIBUS, ET NON EXISTENTIBUS, EADEM EST RATIO. [L.] The rule is the same concerning things which do not appear and things which do not exist.

DE NOVO. [L.] Fresh; new. See TRIAL ~.

DE NOVO HEARING. A rehearing.

DENSE. *adj.* 1. If it is not possible for a man of average weight to push a wooden picket more than 1 1/2 in. into the soil. *Building Code Act*, R.R.O. 1980, Reg. 87, s. 4.2.1.5. 2. When it requires 30 or more blows per foot in a penetration test. *Building Code Act*, R.R.O. 1980, Reg. 87, s. 4.2.1.5.

DENSITY. *n.* 1. The total number of residential properties in an area municipality divided by the hectares in the area municipality correct to three places of decimals. *Ontario Unconditional Grants Act*, R.S.O. 1980, c. 359, s. 1. 2. The shade of smoke at the point of emission to the outdoor atmosphere. *Air Pollution and Smoke Control Regulations*, C.R.C., c. 1143, s. 2. See FILLING ~.

DENTAL APPLIANCES. (a) Gold, amalgam, porcelain or any other kind of dental filling and cotton used in preparing the patient's teeth for filling and other supplies likewise used, (b) materials to be processed, fabricated into, attached to or incorporated into a denture or dental appliance, or (c) impression materials for use in dentistry, if used by a dentist or denture therapist.

DENTAL ASSISTANT. A dental assistant employed by a dentist or a professional corporation to perform such duties, tasks and functions and subject to such conditions, limitations and restrictions as are prescribed. *New Brunswick Dental Act, 1985*, S.N.B. 1985, c. 73, s. 2.

DENTAL AUXILIARY. A person other than a dentist who is qualified to perform dental services specified.

DENTAL EDUCATION PROGRAMS. Dental education programs approved by the Board and includes such education programs as may be required as qualifications for the practice of dentistry or the specialties thereof or for registration under this Act. *New Brunswick Dental Act, 1985*, S.N.B. 1985, c. 73, s. 2.

DENTAL HYGIENE. The performance of dental services of a preventive and educational nature and includes the performance of dental prophylaxes, the application on teeth of topical fluorides or other anticariogenic agents, the rendering of first aid and the taking and developing of x-rays. *Dental Profession Act*, R.S.N.W.T. 1974, c. D-3, s. 2.

DENTAL HYGIENIST. A person whose name is entered in the prescribed dental hygienists register and is entitled to perform the duties, tasks and functions which are prescribed, subject to such conditions, limitations and restrictions as are prescribed. *New Brunswick Dental Act, 1985*, S.N.B. 1985, c. 73, s. 2.

DENTAL LABORATORY. Any place where the art or business of dental technology is practised or carried on. *Dental Technicians Act*, R.S.N.S. 1967, c. 76, s. 1.

DENTAL MECHANIC. A person who makes, produces, reproduces, contracts, furnishes, supplies, alters or repairs (i) an upper prosthetic denture or upper dental plate for another person who has no live teeth in his upper jaw, or (ii) a lower prosthetic denture or lower dental plate for another person who has no live teeth in his lower jaw, or (iii) complete prosthetic dentures or complete dental plates for another person who has no live teeth in his mouth, and who, for any of those purposes, takes necessary impressions of the inside of the mouth of that other person. *Dental Mechanics Act*, S.M. 1970, c. 103, s. 1.

DENTAL NURSE. A person who is trained to provide dental nursing services. *The Saskatchewan Dental Nurses Act*, R.S.S. 1978, c. S-13, s. 2.

DENTAL PROSTHETIC SERVICE. (i) The making, fitting, constructing, altering, reproducing or repairing of a complete upper or lower removable prosthetic denture, the furnishing or supplying of such a denture directly to a person or advising the use of any such denture; (ii) the taking or making, or the giving of advice, assistance or facilities respecting the taking or making, of any impression, bite, cast or design preparatory to, or for the purpose of, making, constructing, fitting, furnishing, supplying, altering, repairing or reproducing any such complete upper or lower removable prosthetic denture but does not include the insertion or fitting of an immediate denture in the mouth of the intended wearer or the adjustment of an immediate denture and does not include a technique or procedure that alters any oral tissue. *The Denturists Act*, R.S.S. 1978, c. D-7, s. 2.

DENTAL SERVICES. See SURGICAL-~.

DENTAL STAFF. The dentist or dentists to whom the board has granted the privilege of attending patients in the hospital in co-operation with a member of the medical staff. *Public Hospitals Act*, R.R.O. 1980, Reg. 865, s. 1.

DENTAL SURGERY. Any professional service usually performed by a dentist or dental surgeon and includes (a) the diagnosis or treatment of, and the prescribing, treating and operating for the prevention, alleviation or correction of any injury, disease, pain, deficiency, deformity, defect, lesion, disorder or physical condition of, to, in, or from any human tooth, mandible or maxilla or associated structures or tissues, including the prescribing, treating and administering of x-rays, anaesthetics, drugs and medicines in connection therewith; (b) the making, producing, reproducing, constructing, fitting, furnishing, supplying, altering, or repairing, prescribing or advising the use of any prosthetic denture, bridge, appliance or thing for any of the purposes indicated in paragraph (a) or to replace, improve or supplement any human tooth, or to prevent, alleviate, correct or improve any condition in the human oral cavity, or to be used in, upon or in connection with any human tooth, jaw or associated structure or tissue, or in the treatment of any condition thereof; (c) the taking or making, or the giving of advice or assistance or the providing of facilities for the taking or making of any impression, bite or cast and design preparatory to, or for the purpose of, or with a view to making, producing, reproducing, constructing, fitting, furnishing, supplying, altering or repairing any such prosthetic denture, bridge, appliance or thing; (d) any specialty of dentistry; (e) the dental procedures performed by a dental hygienist or dental assistant.

DENTAL TECHNICIAN. 1. A person who on the prescriptions or orders of dentists or physicians makes, produces, reproduces, constructs, furnishes, supplies, alters or repairs any prosthetic denture, bridge, appliance or thing to be used in, on or in connection with a human tooth or associated structure or tissue, or in the treatment of any condition thereof. 2. A person who practises the art or business of dental technology.

DENTAL TECHNOLOGY. The art or business of manufacturing or repairing any prosthetic denture, bridge, appliance or device to be used in, upon or in connection with any human tooth, jaw or associated structure or tissue, or in the treatment of any condition thereof. *Dental Technicians Act*, R.S.N.S. 1967, c. 76, s. 1.

DENTAL THERAPIST. A person who is trained to provide dental therapy services. *Dental Therapists Act*, S.S. 1980-81, c. D-6.1, s. 2.

DENTAL THERAPY. The performance of dental services under the direction and control of a dentist and includes (i) the performance of uncomplicated dental restorations, (ii) the uncomplicated removal of teeth, (iii) the performance of dental prophylaxes, (iv) the application on teeth of topical fluorides or other anticariogenic agents, and (v) the taking and developing of x-rays of teeth. *Dental Profession Act*, R.S.N.W.T. 1974, c. D-3, s. 2.

DENTIST. *n.* A person lawfully entitled to practise dentistry in the place in which the practice is carried on by that person. See ATTENDING ~.

DENTISTRY. *n.* Any professional service usually performed by a dentist and includes (i) the diagnosis or treatment of and the prescribing, treating or operating for the prevention, alleviation or correction of any injury, disease, pain, deficiency, deformity, defect, lesion, disorder or physical condition of, to, in or from any human tooth or jaw or associated structure or tissue; (ii) the making, producing, reproducing, constructing, fitting, furnishing, supplying, altering or repairing or prescribing or advising the use of any prosthetic denture, bridge, appliance or thing for any of the purposes indicated in subclause (i) or the replacement, improvement or supplementing of a human tooth or jaw or associated structure or tissue or the prevention, alleviation, correction or improvement of a condition on or in connection with a human tooth or jaw or associated structure or tissue, or in connection with the treatment of any condition thereof; (iii) the taking or making, or the giving of advice or assistance or providing of facilities for the taking or making, of an impression, bite, cast or design preparatory to, for the purpose of or with a view to the making, producing, reproducing, constructing, fitting, furnishing, supplying, altering or repairing of any prosthetic denture, bridge, appliance or thing; (iv) the evaluation, approval or disapproval, with or without conditions, of a dental treatment plan submitted by a licensed member, registered practitioner or professional corporation for approval in accordance with an agreement under which proposed dental treatment must be approved by or on behalf of an insurer before the patient will be entitled to reimbursement under the plan. See PRACTICE OF ~.

DENTISTS IN ASSOCIATION. Dentists practising together in the same suite of offices in the same building and sharing the expenses of their practices. *Dental Technicians Act*, R.S.N.S. 1967, c. 76, s. 8.

DENTURE CONSTRUCTION. (i) The making and repairing of any complete upper or complete lower denture, or (ii) taking of impressions, bite registrations, try-ins and insertions for the making, producing, constructing and furnishing of any complete upper or lower denture for the intended wearer thereof.

DENTURE THERAPIST. A person licensed under the Denture Therapists Act to engage in the practice of denture therapy or the practice of supervised denture therapy. *Retail Sales Tax Act*, R.R.O. 1980, Reg. 904, s. 1.

DENTURIST. *n.* 1. A person who provides a dental prosthetic service. *Denturist acts.* 2. A person licensed to engage in the practice of denturology. *Denturists' Act*, S.N.B. 1986, c. 90, s. 2. 3. A person licensed in the practice of denture technology. *Denturist Act*, S.N.S. 1973, c. 5, s. 2.

DENTURE TECHNOLOGY. See PRACTICE OF ~.

DENTURE THERAPY. See PRACTICE OF ~.

DENTUROLOGY. See PRACTICE OF ~.

DENUDER. *n.* A horizontal or vertical container that is part of a chlor-alkali mercury cell and in which water and alkali metal amalgam are converted to alkali metal hydroxide, metallic mercury and hydrogen gas in a short-circuited electrolytic reaction. *Chlor-Alkali Mercury National Emission Standards Regulations*, C.R.C., c. 406, s. 2.

DEP. *abbr.* Deputy.

DEPARTMENT. *n.* 1. A department, secretariat, ministry, office or other similar agency of the executive government. 2. (a) Any of the departments named in Schedule I, (b) any other division or branch of the public service of Canada, including a commission appointed under the Inquiries Act, designated by the Governor in Council as a department for the purposes of this Act, (c) the staffs of the Senate, the House of Commons and the Library of Parliament, and (d) any department corporations. *Financial Administration Act*, R.S.C. 1985, c. F-11, s. 2. 3. An academic unit administered by a head. 4. A branch of the civil service over which a minister presides. See FIRE ~; GOVERNMENT ~; HEAD OF A ~; HEAD OF THE ~; MEDICAL ~; PARI-MUTUEL ~; PUBLIC ~.

DEPARTMENTAL ANALYST. A person employed as a chemical analyst in any department or agency of the government of Canada or of any province. *Excise Act*, R.S.C. 1985, c. E-14, s. 2.

DEPARTMENTAL BANK ACCOUNT. A bank account authorized by the Receiver General to be established by the appropriate Minister in a bank designated by the Minister of Finance, or in any branch of such a bank, in the name of the department of the appropriate Minister, or in the name of a branch or division thereof, for the purpose of operating an accountable advance from the Consolidated Revenue Fund. *Accountable Advances Regulations*, C.R.C., c. 668, s. 2.

DEPARTMENTAL CORPORATION. A corporation named in Schedule II. *Financial Administration Act*, R.S.C. 1985, c. F-11, s. 2.

DEPARTMENTAL HOSPITAL. A hospital or other institution or a clinic for the examination, treatment or care of patients and that is wholly operated by the Department. *Veterans Treatment Regulations*, C.R.C., c. 1585, s. 2.

DEPARTMENTAL ROAD. (i) A provincial trunk highway; (ii) a provincial road; (iii) any highway in unorganized territory; but does not include parking lots, or roads or driveways, on grounds appurtenant to a public work as defined in The Department of Public Works Act, any highway the cost of construction or maintenance of which is paid from and out of the Consolidated Fund with moneys authorized to be expended for the purposes of any other Act of the Legislature, any highway built and maintained at the expense of the Government of Canada, or any highway built and maintained on private land by the owner of the land. *Highways Department Act*, R.S.M. 1970, c. H40, s. 2.

DEPARTMENTAL SENIORITY. Seniority which is lost if an employee moves to another department of the employer's business.

DEPARTMENT HEAD. 1. A member of the Executive Council charged with the administration of a department or agency. 2. The non-elected head of a department.

DEPARTMENT OF COMMUNICATIONS. The federal ministry responsible for any facility, system or undertaking related to communications and telecommunications.

DEPARTMENT OF FINANCE CANADA. The federal ministry which is the government's chief advisor on financial and economic affairs and which provides information on federal budgets.

DEPARTMENT OF INSURANCE CANADA. The federal body which supervises all federally licensed or registered financial institutions except chartered banks.

DEPARTMENT OF JUSTICE CANADA. The federal ministry which oversees every legal matter under federal jurisdiction, advises on legislative acts and provides legal advice to the Governor General.

DEPARTMENT OF NATIONAL DEFENCE. The federal ministry which manages and controls the Armed Forces of Canada and everything related to national defence including civil defence.

DEPARTMENT OF REGIONAL INDUSTRIAL EXPANSION. The federal ministry empowered to promote productive investment in industrial renewal and development in every region of Canada, particularly economically underprivileged areas.

DEPARTMENT OF TRANSPORT REGULATIONS. The Dangerous Goods Shipping Regulations. *National Harbours Board Operating By-law*, C.R.C., c. 1064, s. 106.

DEPARTURE NOTICE. A notice issued pursuant to subsection 32(7). *Immigration Act*, R.S.C. 1985, c. I-2, s. 2.

DEPARTURE TAX. A capital gains tax imposed on taxpayers who cease to be residents of Canada. W. Grover and F. Iacobucci, *Materials on Canadian Income Tax*, 4th ed. (Toronto: Richard De Boo, Ltd.) at 115.

DEPENDANT. *n.* 1. A person who depends upon another for maintenance. 2. A person to whom another has an obligation to provide support. See DEPENDENT; PRIMARY ∼; SECONDARY ∼.

DEPENDANT ADULT. An adult who, (i) lives with a head of a family or a parent or person in loco parentis, (ii) is a member of the family with which he lives, and (iii) is wholly dependent upon the head of the family or a parent or person in loco parentis for support and maintenance, and includes the female spouse living with the male spouse and a person who although not legally married to the head of the family lives with him as if they were husband and wife. *General Welfare Assistance Act*, R.R.O. 1980, Reg. 441, s. 1.

DEPENDANT CHILD. A person who (i) is dependent for support upon his or her mother or father, or (ii) is dependent for support upon a person who stands in loco parentis to him or her, and (ii) meets the age requirements and the other particulars as defined in legislation.

DEPENDANT ELECTOR. Except where otherwise specified, a dependant of a Canadian Forces elector or Public Service elector who is qualified and entitled, under section 22 or 35, to vote under these Rules. *Special Voting Rules*, R.S.C. 1985, c. E-2, Schedule II, s. 2.

DEPENDENCY. *n.* In relation to a narcotic, a state of psychological or physical dependence, or both, on a narcotic following its use on a periodic or continuous basis. *Heroin Treatment Act*, R.S.B.C. 1979, c. 166, s. 1. See DOMICILE OF ∼; DRUG ∼; LOSS OF ∼ ON INCOME.

DEPENDENT. *n.* 1. The father, mother, grandfather, grandmother, brother, sister, uncle, aunt, niece or nephew, or child or grandchild of any age, who at the date of the death of the employee or pensioner is, by reason of mental or physical infirmity, dependent upon that person for support. 2. A child or other relative of a deceased victim who was, in whole or in part, dependent upon the income of the victim at the time of the victim's death. 3. A child under the age of eighteen years, an unmarried child under the age of twenty-one years who is attending an approved educational institution on a fulltime basis and the surviving spouse of an employee. See DEPENDENTS.

DEPENDENT ADULT. A person in respect of whom (i) a guardianship order is in effect, (ii) a trusteeship order is in effect, or (iii) both a guardianship order and a trusteeship order are in effect. *Dependent Adults Act*, R.S.A. 1980, c. D-32, s. 1.

DEPENDENT CHILD. 1. A dependent child who is under the age of 18 years. 2. Of a contributor, means a child of the contributor who has never been married and who (a) is less than eighteen years of age, (b) is eighteen or more years of age but less than twenty-five years of age and is in full-time attendance at a school or university as defined by regulation, having been in such attendance substantially without interruption as defined by regulation since he reached eighteen years of age or the contributor died, whichever occurred later, or (c) is a child other than a child described in paragraph (b), is eighteen or more years of age and is disabled, having been disabled without interruption since the time he reached eighteen years of age or the contributor died, whichever occurred later. *Canada Pension Plan*, R.S.C. 1985, c. C-8,. s. 42. See SURVIVING SPOUSE WITH DEPENDENT CHILDREN.

DEPENDENT CONDITION. With respect to a person, means the condition of being without sufficient income or assets, other than the premises in which the person resides, to maintain that person. *Pension Act*, R.S.C. 1985, c. P-6, s. 2.

DEPENDENT CONTRACTOR. 1. Person, whether or not employed under a contract of employment and whether or not furnishing her or his own tools, vehicles, equipment, machinery, material or any other thing, who performs work or services for another person on such terms and conditions to be in a position of economic dependence upon that person, is under an obligation to perform duties mainly for that person and is in a relationship with that person more closely resembling that of an employee than an independent contractor. 2. (a) The owner, purchaser or lessee of a vehicle used for hauling, other than on rails or tracks, livestock, liquids, goods, merchandise or other materials, who is a party to a contract, oral or in writing,

under the terms of which he is (i) required to provide the vehicle by means of which he performs the contract and to operate the vehicle in accordance with the contract, and (ii) is entitled to retain for his own use from time to time any sum of money that remains after the cost of his performance of the contract is deducted from the amount he is paid, in accordance with the contract, for that performance, (b) a fisherman who, pursuant to an arrangement to which he is a party, is entitled to a percentage or other part of the proceeds of a joint fishing venture in which he participates with other persons, and (c) any other person who, whether or not employed under a contract of employment, performs work or services for another person on such terms and conditions that he is, in relation to that other person, in a position of economic dependence on, and under an obligation to perform duties for, that other person. *Canada Labour Code*, R.S.C. 1985, c. L-2, s. 3.

DEPENDENT FATHER. A father who is permanently unemployable by reason of physical or mental disability, and includes a father who is blind or otherwise disabled as defined by the legislation.

DEPENDENT HUSBAND. A husband who by reason of physical or mental infirmity is unable to provide himself with the necessaries of life without the assistance of an insured. *The Automobile Accident Insurance Act*, R.S.S. 1978, c. A-35, s. 2.

DEPENDENT PARENT. A parent who by reason of age, disease or infirmity is unable to maintain himself or herself.

DEPENDENT RELATIVE REVOCATION. Where a will is revoked by a codicil it is a question whether it was the intention of the testator that the provisions of the will are to be effective if those contained in the codicil are declared to be invalid. *Murray v. Murray*, [1956] 1 W.L.R. 605.

DEPENDENT RIGHT. Any right, encumbrance or other consideration in, relating to, dependent on or calculated by reference to the share or production in respect of or imputable to the share of an interest holder, but does not include any debt or other obligation secured by an encumbrance. *Oil and Gas acts.*

DEPENDENTS. *n.* 1. Those members of the victim's family and any stranger who stood in loco parentis to the victim, or to whom the victim stood in loco parentis, and who were wholly or partly dependent upon the victim's income or work for support at the time of death. *Crime Victims Compensation acts.* 2. The members of the family of a worker who were wholly or partly dependent upon that person's earnings at the time of the worker's death. *Workers' Compensation acts*. 3. Such person as a person, against whom a maintenance order is made, is liable to maintain according to the law in force in the place where the maintenance order is made. *Maintenance Orders Enforcement acts*. See DEPENDANT; DEPENDENT.

DEPENDENT TERRITORIES. See COMMONWEALTH AND ~.

DEPENDENT WIDOW. The woman who was the legal wife and a dependant of an employee immediately before his death. *Workmen's Compensation Act*, R.S.O. 1980, c. 539, s. 1.

DEPENDENT WIDOWER. 1. The man who was the legal husband and a dependant of an employee immediately before her death. *Workmen's Compensation Act*, R.S.O. 1980, c. 539, s. 1. 2. A person wholly dependent upon his spouse. *Legislative Assembly Retirement Allowances Act*, R.S.P.E.I. 1974, c. L-12, s. 1.

DEPENDENT YOUTH. A person resident in Canada who has attained the age of sixteen years and has not attained the age of eighteen years and (a) is in full-time attendance at a school or university, or (b) is, by reason of any mental or physical infirmity, precluded from attending or attending on a full-time basis at a school or university. *Youth Allowances Act*, R.S.C. 1970, c. Y-1, s. 2.

DEPLANE. *v.* To disembark from an aircraft for the purpose of terminating a flight. *Air Transportation Tax Regulations*, C.R.C., c. 583, s. 2.

DEPLETION ALLOWANCE. An extra deduction, after the taxpayer amortizes or deducts any actual exploration and development expenses. W. Grover and F. Iacobucci, *Materials on Canadian Income Tax*, 4th ed. (Toronto: Richard De Boo Ltd., 1980) at 1214.

DEP. M.N.R. (CUSTOMS & EXCISE). *abbr.* Deputy Minister of National Revenue for Customs and Excise.

DEPONENT. *n.* 1. A person who testifies that certain facts are true. 2. One who makes an affidavit.

DEPORTATION. *n.* The removal under this Act of a person from any place in Canada to the place whence he came to Canada or to the country of his nationality or citizenship or to the country of his birth or to such country as may be approved by the Minister under this Act, as the case may be. *Immigration Act*, R.S.C. 1970, c. I-2, s. 2.

DEPORTATION ORDER. A deportation order made under subsection 32(2), (5) or (6), 37(5) or (6), 73(2) or 74(1) or (3) and includes a deportation order made under the authority of (a) subsection 40(10) of the Immigration Act, 1976, chapter 52 of the Statutes of Canada, 1976-77, as it read immediately prior to July 16, 1984, or (b) any immigration laws that were in force in Canada prior to April 10, 1978. *Immigration Act*, R.S.C. 1985, c. I-2, s. 2.

DEPOSE. *v.* 1. To remove from high office or a throne. 2. To affirm by making a deposition.

DEPOSIT. *n.* 1. The unpaid balance of the aggregate of moneys received or held by a federal or provincial institution, from or on behalf of a person in the usual course of business, for which the institution (a) has given or is obligated to give credit to that person's account or has issued or is obligated to issue a receipt, certificate, debenture (other than a debenture issued by a bank to which the Bank Act applies), transferable instrument, draft, certified draft or cheque, traveller's cheque, prepaid letter of credit, money order or other instrument in respect of which the institution is primarily liable, and (b) is obligated to repay the moneys on a fixed day, on demand by that person or within a specified period of time following demand by that person, including any interest accrued or payable to that person. *Canada Deposit Insurance Corporation Act*, R.S.C. 1985, c. C-3, s. 2. 2. Money paid as an earnest or security for a person to perform a contract. 3. A loan of money at interest or at a discount or repayable at a premium in money or otherwise but does not include a loan of money to a corporation in connection with the issue and sale of its bonds, debentures, notes or other written evidences of indebtedness. *Deposit Regulation Act*, R.S.A. 1980, c. D-33, s. 1. 4. Any discharging, spraying, releasing, spilling, leaking, seeping, pouring, emitting, emptying, throwing, dumping or placing. *Fisheries Act*, R.S.C. 1985, c. F-14, s. 34. See BANK ~; BOOK ~; CURRENT ~; DATE OF ~; NON-CHEQUABLE ~S; OIL SANDS ~; SECURITY ~; SOLICITATION OF ~S.

DEPOSIT ADMINISTRATION CONTRACT. A contract with an insurance company where moneys paid under the contract for the purposes of a pension plan are credited to an account but not allocated to individual members of the plan prior to their retirement. *Pension Benefits Standards Regulations*, C.R.C., c. 1252, s. 2.

DEPOSITARY. *n.* A specified government or international organization where instruments of ratification of a multilateral treaty are to be deposited. P.W. Hogg, *Constitutional Law of Canada*, 2d ed. (Toronto: Carswell, 1985) at 244.

DEPOSIT AT A POST OFFICE. To leave in a post office or with a person authorized by the

Postmaster General to receive mailable matter. *Post Office Act*, R.S.C. 1970, c. P-14, s. 2.

DEPOSIT BALANCE. See REQUIRED ~.

DEPOSITED. *adj.* Includes filed, registered, recorded and kept. *Document Disposal Act*, R.S.B.C. 1979, c. 95, s. 1.

DEPOSITED AMOUNT. An amount that, after the coming into force of this section, is put on deposit with the Corporation or left with the Corporation for transmission by post, but does not include an amount paid to the Corporation on account of services or products to be provided at a future date. *Canada Post Corporation Act*, R.S.C. 1985, c. C-10, s. 39.

DEPOSIT INSTITUTION. (i) A bank to which the Bank Act (Canada) applies, (ii) a loan corporation or trust company registered under the Loan and Trust Corporations Act, (iii) a credit union or credit union league incorporated under the provisions of the Credit Unions and Caisses Populaires Act, and (iv) a member commercial bank of the Federal Reserve System of the United States of America. *Commodity Futures Act*, R.R.O. 1980, Reg. 114, s. 7.

DEPOSIT INSURANCE. The insurance referred to in paragraph (7)(a). *Canada Deposit Insurance Corporation Act*, R.S.C. 1985, c. C-3, s. 2. See CANADA ~ CORPORATION; POLICY OF ~.

DEPOSIT INSURANCE CORPORATION. (a) A corporation that was incorporated by or under a law of Canada or a province respecting the establishment of a stabilization fund or board if (A) it was incorporated primarily (I) to provide or administer a stabilization, liquidity or mutual aid fund for credit unions, and (II) to assist in the payment of any losses suffered by members of credit unions in liquidation, and (B) throughout any taxation year in respect of which the expression is being applied, (I) it was a Canadian corporation, and (II) the cost amount to the corporation of its investment property was at least 50 per cent of the cost amount to it of all its property (other than a debt obligation of, or a share of the capital stock of, a member institution issued by the member institution at a time when it was in financial difficulty), or (ii) a corporation incorporated by the Canada Deposit Insurance Corporation Act. *Income Tax Act*, R.S.C. 1952, c. 148 (as am. S.C. 1987, c. 46, s. 49(2.1)), s. 137.1(5)(a).

DEPOSITION. *n.* Every affidavit, affirmation or statement made under oath.

DEPOSIT OF RECORDS. The handing over of a notary's record to the prothonotary of a judicial district for preservation in the archives of such district. *Notarial Act*, R.S.Q. 1977, c. N-2, s. 1.

DEPOSITOR. *n.* 1. A person whose account has been or is to be credited in respect of moneys constituting a deposit or part of a deposit or a person to whom a member institution is liable in respect of an instrument issued for moneys constituting a deposit or part of a deposit. *Canada Deposit Insurance Corporation Act*, R.S.C. 1985, c. C-3, s. 52(1). 2. A person who has entered into a contract with the minister providing for the making of deposits in a branch. *Treasury Branches acts.*

DEPOSITORY. *n.* A bank, trust company or person holding by way of deposit or otherwise money, trust funds or assets of any kind relating to the business of a member as a barrister or solicitor.

DEPOSIT RECEIPT. 1. A receipt executed by the vendor and the Corporation, confirming to the purchaser the benefits of the Plan in respect of the purchase agreement. *Ontario New Home Warranties Plan Act*, R.R.O. 1980, Reg. 726, s. 1. 2. When an insured pays all or part of the premium, the combination of a receipt for the premium with a cover note. Raoul Colinvaux, *The Law of Insurance*, 5th ed. (London: Sweet & Maxwell, 1984) at 19.

DEPOSITUM. *n.* A simple bailment of goods. E.L.G. Tyler & N.E. Palmer, eds., *Crossley Vaines' Personal Property*, 5th ed. (London: Butterworths, 1973) at 85. See CONTRACT OF ~.

DEPOT. *n.* A place established or operated as a business by any person for the collection and disposal of empty containers. *Beverage Container Act*, R.S.A. 1980, c. B-4, s. 1. See FILM ~.

DEPRECIABLE ASSETS. The assets resulting from (a) the preproduction development costs in respect of a mine, (b) the aggregate expenditures for the purchase and installation of mining, milling, smelting, refining and power plant and equipment in the Province essential to the production of the output of a mine in the Province, (c) those expenditures prescribed by regulation, and (d) any other expenditures that, in the opinion of the mine assessor, are fair and reasonable expenditures that are related to the production of the output of a mine in the Province and that are not deducted under paragraph 2.1(6)(b), but does not include expenditures made for the purchase of, or in acquiring an option to purchase, mining properties. *An Act to Amend the Metallic Minerals Tax Act*, S.N.B. 1987, c. 35, s. 1.

DEPRECIABLE PROCESSING ASSETS. Machinery, equipment, plant, buildings, works and improvements used in the processing of minerals or mineral products, but excludes them when they are no longer used for that purpose. *Mineral Resource Tax Amendment Act*, S.B.C. 1980, c. 27, s. 4.

DEPRECIABLE PROPERTY. Of a taxpayer as of any time in a taxation year means property acquired by the taxpayer in respect of which he has been allowed, or, if he owned the property at the end of the year, would be entitled to, a deduction under regulations made under paragraph 20(1)(a) in computing income for that year or a previous taxation year. *Income Tax Act*, R.S.C. 1952, c. 148 (as am. S.C. 1980-81-82-83, c. 48, s. 5(5)), s. 13(21)(b).

DEPRECIATION. *n.* A loss in value of an asset attributable to any cause. See STRAIGHT-LINE ~.

DEPRESSED FRACTURE. A fracture, often in the vault of the skull, in which fragments are depressed towards the brain. F.A. Jaffe, *A Guide to Pathological Evidence*, 2d ed. (Toronto: Carswell, 1983) at 176 and 177.

DEPRIVATION. *n.* 1. Removal of an offender's rights in property. S. Mitchell, P.J. Richardson & D.A. Thomas, eds., *Archbold Pleading, Evidence and Practice in Criminal Cases*, 43d ed. (London: Sweet & Maxwell, 1988) at 813. 2. Deprived of the necessities for proper sustenance of life. *Animal Diseases Act*, S.M. 1974, c. 52, s. 1.

DEPT. *abbr.* Department.

DEPTH. *n.* 1. The vertical dimension from the highest point of an excavation to a point level with the lowest point of the excavation. *Occupational Health and Safety Act*, R.R.O. 1980, Reg. 691, s. 1. 2. In respect of a ship, the vertical distance in metres at amidships from the top of the keel plate to the uppermost continuous deck, fore and aft, that extends to the side of the ship and, for the purpose of this definition, the continuity of a deck is deemed not to be affected by the existence of tonnage openings, engine spaces or a step in the deck. *Great Lakes Pilotage Tariff Regulations*, C.R.C., c. 1267, s. 2. See LOT ~; MOULDED ~; REAR YARD ~; TRENCH ~.

DEPTH FOR FREEBOARD. 1. The distance measured from the same point as moulded depth, and to the upper surface of the freeboard deck or stringer plate, with no allowance for sheathing, and in the case of a ship having a rounded gunwale with a radius greater than four per cent of the breadth (B) or having topsides of unusual form, means the depth for freeboard

of a ship having a midship section with vertical topsides and with the same round of beam and area of topside section equal to that provided by the actual midship section. *Load Line Regulations (Inland)*, C.R.C., c. 1440, s. 1. 2. (a) The moulded depth amidships, plus the thickness of the freeboard deck stringer plate, where fitted, plus T (L minus S) if the exposed freeboard deck is sheathed, where T is the mean thickness of the exposed sheathing clear of deck openings, and S of the total length of superstructures as defined in paragraph (9)(d). (b) The depth for freeboard (D) in a ship having a rounded gunwale with a radius greater than four per cent of the breadth (B) or having topsides of unusual form is the depth for freeboard of a ship having a midship section with vertical topsides and with the same round of beam and area of topside section equal to that provided by the actual midship section. *Load Line Regulations (Sea)*, C.R.C., c. 1441, s. 3.

DEPURATION. *n.* The process of removing micro-organisms that may be dangerous to humans from live shellfish in a controlled environment. *Sanitary Control of Shellfish Fisheries Regulations*, C.R.C., c. 832, s. 2.

DEPUTY. *n.* One who acts instead of another, or who exercises an office in another person's name.

DEPUTY CHIEF. The one person who has been appointed by the council of the municipality to act in the place of the chief of the fire department in his absence or in the case of a vacancy in the office. *Fire Departments Act*, R.S.O. 1980, c. 164, s. 1.

DEPUTY HEAD. *var.* **DEPUTY-HEAD.** 1. The deputy of the member of the Executive Council presiding over a department and all others whom the Governor in Council designates as having the status of deputy. 2. The deputy minister of a department or the chief executive officer of an agency. See APPROPRIATE ~.

DEPUTY MARSHAL. In the Federal Court, each deputy sheriff is ex officio a deputy marshal. D. Sgayias *et al.*, *Federal Court Practice 1988* (Toronto: Carswell, 1987) at 56.

DEPUTY MINISTER. 1. The senior civil servant in a department who advises the minister and is the senior administrator of that department. P.W. Hogg, *Constitutional Law of Canada*, 2d ed. (Toronto: Carswell, 1985) at 197. 2. (a) The deputy of a minister, (b) an officer who, by an Act, is declared to have the status of a deputy minister, or (c) a person designated as a deputy minister.

DEPUTY SPEAKER. 1. A member elected by the House of Commons to be a Chairman of

Committees. A. Fraser, G.A. Birch & W.A. Dawson, eds., *Beauchesne's Rules and Forms of the House of Commons of Canada*, 5th ed. (Toronto: Carswell, 1978) at 41. 2. The Deputy Speaker and Chairman of Committees of a legislative assembly. 3. The Deputy Speaker and chairperson of the Committee of the Whole.

DERAIGN. *v.* To displace; to prove.

DERELICT. *adj.* Abandoned.

DERELICTION. *n.* Abandoning something.

DERELICT MOTOR VEHICLE. A motor vehicle that, i. is inoperable, and ii. has no market value as a means of transportation, or, has a market value as a means of transportation that is less than the cost of repairs required to put it into operable condition. *Environmental Protection Act*, R.R.O. 1980, Reg. 309, s. 1.

DERELICT VEHICLE. 1. An object shall be conclusively deemed to be a derelict vehicle if it is not a new and unused vehicle, and if (a) it is not in operating condition; (b) it does not have attached thereto, and exposed thereon, one or more number plates issued under The Highway Traffic Act for the current registration year under that Act; (c) it is kept in the open; and (d) the owner thereof either (i) has abandoned it; or (ii) is keeping it primarily for the purposes of salvaging or selling parts therefrom, or for the eventual sale thereof as scrap metal; and a derelict vehicle also includes the body or chassis of a used motor vehicle all or some of the parts of which have been removed, and to which clauses (b), (c), and (d) apply. *Municipal Act*, S.M. 1970, c. 100, s. 294. 2. A vehicle, other than an abandoned vehicle, that (a) has been abandoned at an airport or otherwise remains unclaimed at an airport for a period of not less than 14 days, and (b) has a market value less than $200. *Airport Personal Property Disposal Regulations*, C.R.C., c. 1563, s. 2.

DERISORY DAMAGES. Small damages awarded to a plaintiff who sustained no loss, but whose legal rights were technically infringed though in the court's opinion the action should not have been brought. K.D. Cooper-Stephenson & I.B. Saunders, *Personal Injury Damages in Canada* (Toronto: Carswell, 1981) at 69.

DERIVATIVA POTESTAS NON POTEST ESSE MAJOR PRIMITIVA. [L.] A derivative power cannot be greater than the power from which it was derived.

DERIVATIVE ACTION. A suit by a shareholder to enforce a corporation's rights.

DERIVATIVE EVIDENCE. Evidence obtained directly or indirectly a private communication was intercepted.

DERIVATIVE MORTGAGE. A mortgage of a mortgage or a sub-mortgage. W.B. Rayner & R.H. McLaren, *Falconbridge on Mortgages*, 4th ed. (Toronto: Canada Law Book, 1977) at 251.

DERMAL NITRATE TEST. See PARAFFIN TEST.

DEROGATE. *v.* To destroy; to evade; to prejudice.

DEROGATION. *n.* Evading an act passed or a rule made in the interest of the public, not for the actors' benefit.

DESCENDANT. *n.* Lineal progeny; child; grandchild. See DIRECT ~.

DESCENDANTS OF ANY ANCESTOR. Extends to all persons who must trace their descent through such ancestor. *Probate Act*, R.S.P.E.I. 1974, c. P-19, s. 1.

DESCENDING REGISTER. A mechanical device in a postage meter that records the balance of prepaid postage remaining unused. *Postage Meters Regulations*, C.R.C., c. 1287, s. 2.

DESCENT. *n.* The title to inherit real property by reason of consanguinity, as well when the heir is an ancestor or collateral relation as where he is a child or other issue. *Probate Act*, R.S.P.E.I. 1974, c. P-19, s. 1. See LINEAL ~; ROOT OF ~.

DESCRIBED MINERAL SPECIMEN. A mineral specimen for which scientific data, illustrations or descriptions appear in a professional publication. *Canadian Cultural Property Export Control List*, C.R.C., c. 448, s. 1.

DESCRIPTION. *n.* Identification of goods or other attributes which apply to identified, defined goods. G.H.L. Fridman, *Sale of Goods in Canada*, 3d ed. (Toronto: Carswell, 1986) at 175. See LEGAL ~; MIS~.

DESCRIPTIVE LABEL. Anything that purports to designate or describe any fur in any garment including label, display card, ticket or tag, whether attached to such garment or not, invoice, receipt, bill of sale or other trade documents, and advertisement or poster. *Fur Garments Labelling Regulations*, C.R.C., c. 1138, s. 2.

DESECRATE. *v.* To profane, violate sanctity.

DESERTED CHILD. A child (A) whose parent, without reasonable excuse, fails to provide reasonable maintenance, or (B) who has left or has been removed from the home of the parent because of neglect by or misconduct or acts of cruelty of the parent.

DESERTED HUSBAND. Includes a husband

who either is living apart from his wife or, even though living under the same roof with her, has forsaken all or the greater part of the normal incidents, generally implied by the term "cohabitation", of the matrimonial relationship, because of his wife's (i) assaults or other acts of cruelty towards him or their children, (ii) adultery which has not been condoned, (iii) refusal or neglect, if in receipt of an income, without reasonable excuse to supply her husband and their children, if any, with adequate food, clothing or other necessaries, or (iv) being a person who by reason of frequent drinking of intoxicating liquor or addiction to drugs is incapable of managing herself or her affairs and is an unfit and improper person to have the custody and control of her children, and this paragraph applies to a wife living apart from her husband under a separation agreement whether or not the agreement contains express provisions excluding the operation of this Act, if the wife is in default under the agreement. *Maintenance Act*, S. Nfld. 1973, c. 119, s. 3.

DESERTED WIFE. 1. Wife whose husband without sufficient cause fails to provide her with reasonable maintenance. 2. Includes a wife who either is living apart from her husband or, even though living under the same roof with him, has forsaken all or the greater part of the normal incidents, generally implied by the term "cohabitation", of the matrimonial relationship, because of her husband's (i) assaults or other acts of cruelty towards her or their children, (ii) adultery which has not been condoned, (iii) refusal or neglect without reasonable excuse to supply his wife and their children, if any, with adequate food, clothing or other necessaries, or (iv) being a person who by reason of frequent drinking of intoxicating liquor or addiction to drugs is incapable of managing himself or his affairs and is an unfit and improper person to have the custody and control of his children, and this paragraph applies to a husband living apart from his wife under a separation agreement whether or not the agreement contains express provisions excluding the operation of this Act, if the husband is in default under the agreement. *Maintenance Act*, S. Nfld. 1973, c. 119, s. 3.

DESERTING SPOUSE. A person is deemed to have been deserted: (i) when the person's spouse has, without sufficient cause, refused or neglected to supply food or other necessaries; (ii) when the person's spouse is guilty of adultery which has not been condoned; or (iii) when the person is living apart from the spouse because of the spouse's acts of cruelty; (b) a child is deemed to have been deserted by his parent: (i) when the parent has, without sufficient cause, refused or neglected to supply food or other necessaries; or (ii) when the child has left or has

been removed from the home of the parent because of neglect by or misconduct or acts of cruelty of the parent; (c) the man and woman described in subclause (1)(b)(ii) or (iii) are deemed to be the parents of a child mentioned in subclause (1)(b)(ii) or (iii), as the case may be. *Canadian Charter of Rights and Freedoms Consequential Act*, S.S. 1984-85-86, c. 38, s. 4.

DESERTION. *n.* 1. Separation of one spouse from the other, with a deliberate intention and, without reasonable cause and the other spouse's consent, to end cohabitation permanently. 2. A person deserts who, (a) being on or having been warned for active service, duty during an emergency or other important service, is absent without authority with the intention of avoiding that service; (b) having been warned that his vessel is under sailing orders, is absent without authority with the intention of missing that vessel; (c) absents himself without authority from his place of duty with the intention of remaining absent from his place of duty; (d) is absent without authority from his place of duty and at any time during such absence forms the intention of remaining absent from his place of duty; or (e) while absent with authority from his place of duty, with the intention of remaining absent from his place of duty, does any act or omits to do anything the natural and probable consequence of which act or omission is to preclude his being at his place of duty at the time required. *National Defence Act*, R.S.C. 1970, c. N-4, s. 78. See CONSTRUCTIVE ~.

DESIGN. *n.* 1. A plan, sketch, drawing, graphic representation or specification intended to govern the construction, enlargement or alteration of a building or part of a building and related site development. 2. With reference to a boiler, pressure vessel or plant or an elevating device, means its plan or pattern, and includes drawings, specifications, and where required, the calculations and a model. 3. A representation or pattern which is visibly applied to a manufactured article. H.G. Fox, *The Canadian Law of Copyright and Industrial Designs*, 2d ed. (Toronto: Carswell, 1967) at 652. See INDUSTRIAL ~; INTERIOR ~; PRINTED BOOK OF PICTURES AND ~S.

DESIGNATE. *n.* A person appointed.

DESIGNATED AERODROME. A Canadian aerodrome designated by the Minister as a regular aerodrome, refuelling aerodrome or alternate aerodrome. *Air Carrier Regulations*, C.R.C., c. 3, s. 15.

DESIGNATED AGENCY. A person designated by a marketing commission or producer board as the agency by or though which a regulated product is or is not to be marketed.

DESIGNATED DRUG. Any of the following controlled drugs: (a) amphetamine and its salts, (b) benzphetamine and its salts, (c) methamphetamine and its salts, (d) phenmetrazine and its salts, or (e) phendimetrazine and its salts. *Food and Drug Regulations*, C.R.C., c. 870, c. G.04.001.

DESIGNATED EDUCATIONAL INSTITUTION. (a) An educational institution in Canada that is (i) a university, college or other educational institution designated by the Lieutenant Governor in Council of a province as a specified educational institution under the Canada Student Loans Act or recognized by the Minister of Education of the Province of Quebec for the purposes of the Student Loans and Scholarships Act of the Province of Quebec, or (ii) certified by the Minister of Employment and Immigration to be an educational institution providing courses, other than courses designed for university credit, that furnish a person with skills for, or improve a person's skills in, an occupation, (b) a university outside Canada at which the individual referred to in subsection (2) was enrolled in a course, of not less than 13 consecutive weeks duration, leading to a degree, or (c) if the individual referred to in subsection (2) resided, throughout the year referred to therein, in Canada near the boundary between Canada and the United States, an educational institution in the United States to which he commuted that is a university, college or other educational institution providing courses at a post-secondary school level. *Income Tax Act*, R.S.C. 1952, c. 148 (as added by S.C. 1988, c. 55, s. 92), c. 118.6(1).

DESIGNATED GROUP. Women, aboriginal peoples, persons with disabilities and persons who are, because of their race or colour, in a visible minority in Canada. *Employment Equity Act*, R.S.C. 1985 (2d Supp.), c. 23, s. 3.

DESIGNATED IMPORTER. A person who imports automobiles into Canada that are manufactured in a foreign country and who has been designated by the manufacturer of the automobiles to be that manufacturer's representative in Canada. *Automobile Components Remission Order*, C.R.C., c. 742, s. 2.

DESIGNATED INFORMATION. Information as to the race, creed, colour, nationality, ancestry, place of origin, sex or geographical location of a person. *Discriminatory Business Practices Act*, R.S.O. 1980, c. 119, s. 1.

DESIGNATED PERILS. Hail, drought, excessive rainfall, excessive moisture, flood, frost, wind including tornado, disease, including rust, and pests. *Crop Insurance Act*, R.S.M. 1970, c. C310, s. 1.

DESIGNATED PROVINCE. A province or territory of Canada that is designated by regulation as a province or territory in which there is in force legislation substantially similar to this Act. *Pension Benefits acts.*

DESIGNATED SEATING CAPACITY. With reference to a vehicle, the number of designated seating positions provided in that vehicle. *Motor Vehicle Safety Regulations*, C.R.C., c. 1038, s. 2. See OUTBOARD ~.

DESIGNATED SEATING POSITION. Any plan view position intended by the manufacturer to provide seating accommodation while the vehicle is in motion for a person at least as large as a 5th percentile adult female, as defined in section 100 of Schedule IV, but does not include any plan view position of temporary or folding jump seats or other auxiliary seating accommodation. *Motor Vehicle Safety Regulations*, C.R.C., c. 1038, s. 2.

DESIGNATED SUBSTANCE. A biological, chemical or physical agent or combination thereof prescribed as a designated substance to which the exposure of a worker is prohibited, regulated, restricted, limited or controlled. *Occupational Health and Safety Act*, R.S.O. 1980, c. 321, s. 1.

DESIGNATIO JUSTICIARIORUM EST A REGE; JURISDICTIO VERO ORDINARIA A LEGE. [L.] The sovereign appoints justices, but the law gives them their ordinary jurisdiction.

DESIGNATION. *n.* The instrument designating a person or purpose; specifying which person is to receive a benefit or perform a function or other purpose. See MODEL ~; SIZE ~.

DESIGNATIO PERSONAE. [L.] The description of a party or person to a contract or deed.

DESIGNATIO UNIUS EST EXCLUSIO ALTERIUS, ET EXPRESSUM FACIT CESSARE TACITUM. [L.] Mentioning one thing excludes another; when you mention one thing expressly, anything you did not mention ceases.

DESIGN BEARING PRESSURE. The pressure applied by a foundation unit to soil or rock and which is not greater than the allowable bearing pressure. *Building Code Act*, R.R.O. 1980, Reg. 87, s. 1.

DESIGN CAPACITY. The load that a foundation is designed to transfer to the supporting soil or rock. *Building Code Act*, R.R.O. 1980, Reg. 87, s. 1.

DESIGNED PRESSURE. The pressure that a boiler, pressure vessel or pressure plant is designed to withstand. *Boiler and Pressure Vessel Act*, R.S.Nfld. 1970, c. 24, s. 2.

DESIGNER. *n.* The person responsible for the

design. *Building Code Act*, R.R.O. 1980, Reg. 87, s. 1.

DESIGN LOAD. The load applied to a foundation unit and which is not greater than the allowable load. *Building Code Act*, R.R.O. 1980, Reg. 87, s. 1.

DESIGN PRESSURE. 1. The maximum pressure that a boiler, pressure vessel or plant is designed to withstand safely when operating normally. *Boiler and Pressure Vessels acts.* 2. Synonymous with "maximum allowable working pressure" as used in the A.S.M.E. Boiler and Pressure Vessel Code. Canada regulations.

DESIGN PROPERTY. A property of the soil or rock used in proportioning and determining the design capacity of a foundation.

DESIGN SUBMISSION. Drawings, specifications, calculation sheets, work test certificates and any other information prescribed by regulation for an elevating device or part thereof submitted to the Ministry for the purpose of registration. *Elevating Devices Act*, R.S.O. 1980, c. 135, s. 1.

DE SIMILIBUS IDEM EST JUDICIUM. [L.] In similar cases the judgment is the same.

DESIRABLE QUALIFICATIONS. In relation to a position or class of positions, means the factors or circumstances that are desirable, having regard to the nature of the duties to be performed, and that are to be taken into account, in addition to the essential qualifications for the position or class of positions, when assessing candidates for the position or class of positions. *Public Service Employment Regulations*, C.R.C., c. 1337, s. 2.

DE SON TORT. See EXECUTOR ~; TRUSTEE ~.

DE SON TORT DEMESNE. Of one's own wrong.

DESPATCH. *v.* To send off quickly.

DESPATCH. *n.* A letter, message or order concerning affairs of state sent with speed.

DESPATCHER. *n.* A person actually on duty operating a marine radiotelephone station for controlling ship traffic entering or within a canal. *Canal Regulations*, C.R.C., c. 1564, s. 2.

DESPITUS. *n.* One who is contemptible.

DESPONSATION. *n.* Betrothal of people to each other.

DESPOT. *n.* A person governing with unlimited authority.

DESPOTISM. *n.* Absolute governing power.

DESTINATION. *n.* The point to which the passengers or goods to be transported on a charter flight are bound. *Air Carrier Regulations*, C.R.C., c. 3, s. 23. See IMMOVEABLE BY ~; PLACE OF ~.

DESTITUTE WIFE. A wife who is in necessitous circumstances because of her husband's refusal or neglect, without sufficient cause, to supply her and their infant children, (if any) with food, clothing and other necessaries. *Children's Act*, R.S.P.E.I. 1974, c. C-6, s. 58.

DESTROY. *v.* 1. Includes slaughter and other means of disposal. *Animal Disease and Protection Act*, R.S.C. 1985, c. A-11, s. 2. 2. With reference to a restricted weed, to (i) kill all growing parts of the weed, or (ii) render the reproductive mechanisms of the weed non-viable. *Weed Control acts.*

DESTRUCTIO. *n.* [L.] Waste.

DESTRUCTION SCHEDULES. See RETENTION AND ~.

DESTRUCTIVE TEST. A test on a sample of shaft rope wherein the shaft rope is broken during the test by a tensile testing machine. *Occupational Health and Safety Act*, R.R.O. 1980, Reg. 694, s. 1.

DESUETUDE. *n.* Disuse.

DETACHED STORE. (a) A building well and substantially constructed of brick, stone, concrete, or other fire-resistant substance or of wood covered or treated with fire-resistant material, and (b) a bin well and substantially constructed of wood covered or treated with fire-resistant material, which building, or bin is (c) detached from any dwelling house and situated at a safe distance from any highway, street, public thoroughfare, or public place; (d) made and closed so as to prevent unauthorized persons having access thereto, and to secure it from danger from without; and (e) exclusively used for the keeping of explosives. *Explosives Regulations*, C.R.C., c. 599, s. 134.

DETACHIARE. *v.* To seize another's goods or person.

DETAINED. See ARBITRARILY ~.

DETAINEE. See SERVICE ~.

DETAINER. *n.* Wrongful retention. See FORCIBLE ~.

DETAINING AUTHORITY. An immigration officer, constable or peace officer, who holds a person in custody under the authority of the Act or the Immigration Act. *Immigration Appeal Board Rules*, C.R.C., c. 943, s. 2.

DETECTIVE AGENCY. Any person who, for remuneration, acts as a detective, investigates offences, gathers or supplies information on the character or behaviour of others, or provides the services of guards or watchmen. *An Act Respecting Detective or Security Agencies*, R.S.Q. 1977, c. A-8, s. 1.

DETECTOR. *n.* The image receptor or other device that interacts with the X-rays to produce a signal corresponding to the intensity of the X-rays incident on it. *Radiation Emitting Devices Regulations*, C.R.C., c. 1370, s. 1. See HEAT ~; PRODUCTS OF COMBUSTION ~; SMOKE ~.

DETENTION. *n.* 1. Mandatory restraint. P.W. Hogg, *Constitutional Law of Canada*, 2d ed. (Toronto: Carswell, 1985) at 757. 2. Deprivation of liberty using physical constraint. P.K. McWilliams, *Canadian Criminal Evidence*, 3d ed. (Aurora: Canada Law Book, 1988) at 4-55. See HOUSE OF ~; PLACE OF ~; PLACE OF SECURE TEMPORARY ~; PLACE OF TEMPORARY ~; PREVENTIVE ~.

DETENTION HOME. Any place including a reception centre, group foster home, foster home and institution for the reception and temporary detention of a child.

DETENTION ORDER. An order that the accused be denied bail until trial.

DETER. *v.* To discourage; to prevent.

DETERIORATION. *n.* The destructive effect which wear and tear causes to property.

DETERMINABLE. *adj.* Coming to an end.

DETERMINATE SENTENCE. A sentence of imprisonment for a limited period of time.

DETERMINE. *v.* To come to an end.

DETERMINED. *adj.* Decided; fixed; delimited.

DETERMINED LIFE. (i) In the case of wooden ships, up to ten years, (ii) in the case of fibreglass or aluminum ships, up to fifteen years, and (iii) in the case of steel ships, up to twenty years from the date of issue by the director of the certificate referred to in section 11. *Fishing Ships (Bounties) Act*, S. Nfld. 1980, c. 31, s. 1.

DETERRENCE. *n.* Tendency to prevent.

DETERRENT. *n.* A penalty imposed with view to preventing others from committing same act.

DETERRENT. *adj.* Preventative.

DETINET. [L.] One detains.

DETINUE. *n.* An action for the unlawful detention of a chattel after its return has been demanded. E.L.G. Tyler & N.E. Palmer, eds., *Crossley Vaines' Personal Property*, 5th ed. (London: Butterworths, 1973) at 7. See ACTION FOR ~.

DETINUIT. [L.] One detained.

DETONATING CORD. An explosive core contained in a waterproof covering that for detonation requires an ordinary detonator and fuse attached. *Mining Regulation Act*, R.S.B.C. 1979, c. 265, s. 41.

DETONATING FUSE. An explosive core contained within a waterproof textile covering which for detonation requires an ordinary detonator and fuse attached thereto. *Metalliferous Mines Act*, R.S.N.S. 1967, c. 183, s. 14.

DETONATOR. *n.* 1. A device used in firing charges of explosives in the form of cartridges and includes a blasting cap, electric blasting cap and delay electric blasting cap. 2. A capsule or case that is of such strength and construction, and contains an explosive of the fulminate class in such quantity that the explosion of one capsule or case will communicate the explosion to other like capsules or cases. Canada regulations.

DETRIMENTAL VARIATION OR ALTERATION. A change (i) that causes or is likely to cause (A) impairment of the quality of the environment for any use that can be made of it, or (B) physical injury or serious discomfort to any person, or (C) injury or damage to property or plant or animal life or which renders any property or plant or animal life unfit for the use to which it is normally put, or significantly disturbs the natural ecological balance, or (ii) contrary to the permissible level established by the Minister by regulation. *Environmental Protection Act*, S.N.S. 1973, c. 6, s. 2.

DETROIT RIVER GROUP. The geological formations generally known as the Detroit River Group of formations of Devonian age. *Environmental Protection Act*, R.R.O. 1980, Reg. 303, s. 1.

DEUTEROGAMY. *n.* A second marriage.

DEV. *abbr.* Development.

DEVALUATION. *n.* An official reduction in the amount of gold relating to the paper value of currency.

DEVASTAVIT. [L.] One has wasted.

DEVELOPED LAND. Land that has been subdivided for the uses and purposes specified in an approved plan of subdivision and includes land that has been improved with the provision of sewer or water services. *Northern Administration Amendment Act, 1979*, S.S. 1979, c. 44, s. 8.

DEVELOPED LENGTH. When used with reference to a pipe, means its length along the centre line of the pipe. *Ontario Water Resources Act*, R.R.O. 1980, Reg. 736, s. 1.

DEVELOPED UNIT. A drainage unit that has a well completed therein that is capable of producing oil or gas in paying quantities. *The Oil and Gas Conservation Act*, R.S.S. 1978, c. O-2, s. 2.

DEVELOPED WELL. A well that obtains oil from a producing area and that is not a new well. *Mineral Taxation Act*, S.M. 1974, c. 60, s. 2.

DEVELOPER. *n.* 1. The owner of lands on which development is proposed. 2. A person who, on the date that a condominium plan is presented for registration, is the registered owner of the land included in the plan. 3. A person who applies for a building permit in respect of a major retail development. 4. A person who, alone or in conjunction with other persons, sells or offers for sale to the public (i) residential units, or (ii) proposed residential units, that have not previously been sold to the public. See OWNER ~.

DEVELOPMENT. *n.* 1. (a) The carrying out of any construction or excavation or other operations in, on, over or under land, or (b) the making of a change in the use or the intensity of use of land, buildings or premises. 2. Any act or deed which prevents beneficiaries from exercising their hunting, fishing and trapping activities, except for "pre-development". *An Act respecting the land regime in the James Bay and New Quebec territories*, S.Q. 1979, c. 25, s. 50. 3. A major retail development. See ACTIVITIES FOR THE ~ OF THE TERRITORY; BUILDING ~; CANADIAN INTERNATIONAL ~ AGENCY; CHILD ~ SERVICE; COMMUNITY ~ SERVICES; EXPLORATION AND ~; EXPORT ~ CORPORATION; FEDERAL BUSINESS ~ BANK; HYDRO ~; INITIAL ~; LAND ~ AREA; PLANNED UNIT ~; POWER ~; PRE-~; RE~; RESOURCE PROTECTION AND ~ SERVICE; SPECIAL AGRICULTURAL ~; STORAGE ~.

DEVELOPMENTAL HANDICAP. A condition of mental impairment present or occurring in a person's formative years that is associated with limitations in adaptive behaviour.

DEVELOPMENT COSTS. See PREPRODUCTION ~; PRODUCTION ~.

DEVELOPMENT EXPENDITURE. See PROVINCIAL ~.

DEVELOPMENT EXPENSE. See ELIGIBLE ~.

DEVELOPMENT INCENTIVE. A primary development inventive, a secondary development incentive or a special development incentive described in section 4. *An Act to amend the Regional Development Incentives Act*, R.S.C. 1970 (2d Supp.), c. 25, s. 1.

DEVELOPMENT INDEX. The index that may be established pursuant to regulations made under paragraph 15(a). *Industrial and Regional Development Act*, R.S.C. 1985, c. I-8, s. 2.

DEVELOPMENT LICENCE. *var.* **DEVELOPMENT LICENSE.** A licence by which the holder thereof is granted the right to hold a mineral deposit on a designated area for a period of one year. *Mineral Resources acts.*

DEVELOPMENT PERMIT. A permit, issued by a council of a municipality, that authorizes development, but does not include a building permit. *The Planning and Development Act*, R.S.S. 1978, c. P-13, s. 2.

DEVELOPMENT PLAN. 1. A plan, policy and program, or any part thereof, approved by the Lieutenant Governor in Council, covering a development planning area or a portion thereof, as defined therein, designed to promote the optimum economic, social, environmental and physical condition of the area, and consisting of the texts and maps describing the program and policy. *Ontario Planning and Development Act*, R.S.O. 1980, c. 354, s. 1. 2. A plan submitted pursuant to subsection (2) of section 134 for the purpose of obtaining approval of the general approach of developing a pool or field as proposed in the plan. *Canada-Newfoundland Atlantic Accord Implementation (Newfoundland) Act*, S. Nfld. 1986, c. 37, s. 2. 3. A plan for the drilling of such number of wells as are, in the opinion of the minister, sufficient to enable production of a geothermal resource underlying a lease to begin, including the provision of piping, equipment, reinjection wells and controls required to produce the geothermal resource, but does not include plans for the commercial utilization of the geothermal resource or for converting it into any other form of energy. *Geothermal Resources Act*, S.B.C. 1982, c. 14, s. 1. See URBAN ~.

DEVELOPMENT TAX. A compulsory levy imposed by a municipality on real property situated within a defined area that is (a) payable by a taxable owner of real property by virtue of his ownership of such property or of specified actions undertaken by him to develop such property, (b) calculated by reference to all or part of the frontage, area or other attribute of land or buildings of the owner, (c) assessed at a uniform rate upon owners of real property liable to pay the tax, and (d) levied for the purpose of financing all or part of the capital cost of the construction or reconstruction of a trunk or arterial road or any other capital service that has been, is being or will be carried out within the defined area, but does not include a levy in respect of which payments by way of a grant may be made under section 4 or 6 of the Municipal Grants Act or a levy on real property paid to a municipality in the form of a land transfer or of cash in lieu thereof. *Development Tax and Redevelopment Tax Grant Regulations*, C.R.C., c. 322, s. 2.

DEVELOPMENT WELL. A well that, at the time of application for drilling authority, is so located in relation to another well or wells penetrating an accumulation of oil or gas that it is considered to be a well or part of a well drilled for the purpose of production or observation or for the injection or disposal of fluid into or from the accumulation. Oil and Gas acts.

DEVIATION. *n.* A major change in the method of performance agreed on in a contract. E.L.G. Tyler & N.E. Palmer, eds., *Crossley Vaines' Personal Property*, 5th ed. (London: Butterworths, 1973) at 103.

DEVICE. *n.* 1. Any article, instrument, apparatus or contrivance, including any component, part or accessory thereof, manufactured, sold or represented for use in (a) the diagnosis, treatment, mitigation or prevention of a disease, disorder or abnormal physical state, or the symptoms thereof, in man or animal, (b) restoring, correcting or modifying a body function or the body structure of man or animal, (c) the diagnosis of pregnancy in humans or animals, or (d) the care of humans or animals during pregnancy and at and after birth of the offspring, including care of the offspring, and includes a contraceptive device but does not include a drug. *Food and Drugs Act*, R.S.C. 1985, c. F-27, s. 2. 2. Any weight, weighing machine, static measure or measuring machine and includes any equipment and accessories attached to or used in conjunction with the device that have or can have an effect on the accuracy of the device. *Weights and Measures Act*, R.S.C. 1985, c. W-6, s. 2. 3. Any article, instrument, apparatus, contrivance or gadget that, by itself or in conjunction with a control product, is used as a means to control pests directly or indirectly. *Pest Control Products Regulations*, C.R.C., c. 1253, s. 2. 4. A demonstration-type gas discharge device. *Radiation Emitting Devices Regulations*, C.R.C., c. 1370, s. 1. See AMUSEMENT ~; ANTHRO-POMORPHIC TEST ~; APPROVED ~; CONTRACEPTIVE ~; CONTROL ~; ELECTROMAGNETIC, ACOUSTIC, MECHANICAL OR OTHER ~; ELECTROMAGNETIC ~; ELEVATING ~; FIXED ~S; FLUORINATION

~; FUEL METERING ~; HEADLAMP CONCEALMENT ~; HEAT RECOVERY UNITS OR ~; HOLD-OPEN ~; HYDRAULIC ~; LIFTING ~; NEW ~; OVER CURRENT ~; OVERLOAD ~; PACKING ~; PARKING CONTROL ~; RADAR WARNING ~; RADIATION EMITTING ~; REMOVEABLE ~S; SAFETY ~; SUBLIMINAL ~; TEST ~A; TEST ~B; TRAFFIC CONTROL ~.

DEVISE. *n.* A disposition or gift by will. See EXECUTORY ~; SPECIFIC ~.

DEVISED. *adj.* Left in a will. E.L.G. Tyler & N.E. Palmer, eds., *Crossley Vaines' Personal Property*, 5th ed. (London: Butterworths, 1973) at 7.

DEVISEE. *n.* Includes the heir of a devisee and the devisee of an heir, and any person who claims right by devolution of title of a similar description. *Trustees acts.* See RESIDUARY ~.

DEVISER. *n.* A testator.

DEVISOR. *n.* A testator.

DEVOLUTION. *n.* The transfer of an interest in property from one person to another through the operation of law, e.g., on bankruptcy or death.

DEWIZ. *abbr.* Distant Early Warning Identification Zone.

DEWIZ BEACON. A non-directional radio navigation aid beacon lying within the DEWIZ and described in Schedule IV. *Security Control of Air Traffic Order*, C.R.C., c. 63, s. 2.

DIAGNOSIS. *n.* The process of ascertaining a disease or ailment by its general symptoms. *Podiatrists Act*, R.S.B.C. 1979, c. 330, s. 1. See ADMISSION ~; SECONDARY ~.

DIAGNOSTIC LABORATORY. Subject to subsection (6), a place where (a) the diagnostic examination or treatment of patients, by means of radiation emitting or non-radiation emitting medical imaging devices, is performed, or (b) operations and procedures for the examination and analysis of specimens taken from the human body are performed to obtain information for diagnosis, prophylaxis or treatment, but does not include (a) the office of a medical practitioner, wherein diagnostic laboratory procedures are performed solely for the diagnosis of patients of the medical practitioner, and where the procedures are confined to such procedures as may be listed from time to time in the "Short List" of laboratory procedures set out in the laboratory section of the Physicians' Manual published by the commission; or (b) the office of a dentist, as defined in The Dental Association Act, wherein diagnostic laboratory procedures are performed solely for the diagnosis of patients of the dentist; or (c) the office of a chiropractor, as defined in The Chiropractic Act, wherein diagnostic laboratory procedures are performed solely for diagnostic purposes. *The Health Insurance Act*, S.M. 1985-86, c. 39, s. 140(3.5 and 3.6).

DIAGNOSTIC X-RAY EQUIPMENT. X-ray equipment used in a medical, dental, chiropractic or other health occupation for the purpose of making a diagnosis, but does not include x-ray equipment used exclusively for radiation therapy or for producing industrial or veterinary radiographs. *Radiation Protection Act*, S.A. 1985, c. R-2.1, s. 14.

DIALECTICS. *n.* An area of logic dealing with the modes and rules of reasoning.

DIAMETER. *n.* 1. When applied to pipes and tubes, means the actual inside diameter. *Customs Tariff*, R.S.C. 1985, c. C-54, s. 2. 2. The greatest diameter at right angles to the longitudinal axis. *Farm Products Grades and Sales Act*, R.R.O. 1980, Reg. 332, s. 1. 3. With respect to a laser beam, means the minimum diameter of a circular aperture that, when placed to intercept the beam with the plane of the circular aperture perpendicular to the direction of propagation of the beam, will permit 0.865 of the total beam power to be transmitted. *Radiation Emitting Devices Regulations*, C.R.C., c. 1370, s. 1. See BORE ~.

DIARIUM. *n.* Daily food.

DIATOM. *n.* A single-celled microscopic alga. F.A. Jaffe, *A Guide to Pathological Evidence*, 2d ed. (Toronto: Carswell, 1983) at 174.

DICED. *adj.* Peeled and cut into approximate cubes. *Processed Fruit and Vegetable Regulations*, C.R.C., c. 291.

DICTA. *n.* Plural of DICTUM.

DICTUM. *n.* A judge's observation on a legal question suggested by the case under consideration when no decision is required.

DIE. See POSTAGE INDICIA IMPRESSION ~; POSTMARK IMPRESSION ~; PRINTING ~; TOOL AND ~ MAKER.

DIES. *n.* Solid or hollow forms used for shaping goods in process by stamping, pressing, extruding, drawing, or threading, and includes taps. *Retail Sales Tax Act*, R.R.O. 1980, Reg. 903, s. 1.

DIES AD QUEM. [L.] A day until which interest is payable.

DIES AMORIS. [L.] A day of favour.

DIES A QUO. [L.] The day from which.

DIES CEDIT. [L.] The day commences.

DIES DATUS. [L.] A given day.

DIES DOMINICUS NON EST JURIDICUS. [L.] The Lord's Day is not a day for legal business.

DIESEL FUEL. 1. Includes any fuel oil that is suitable for use in internal combustion engines of the compression-ignition type, other than any such fuel oil that is intended for use and is actually used as heating oil. *Excise Tax Act*, R.S.C. 1985, c. E-15, s. 2. 2. Any fuel petroleum product other than gasoline. *The Fuel Petroleum Products Act*, R.S.S. 1978, c. F-23, s. 2. See MARINE ~.

DIESEL OIL. 1. The products distilled from petroleum which are capable of developing the power required for operating internal combustion engines and which are commonly known as diesel oil, semi-diesel oil or fuel oil and includes any other products determined by the Minister to be diesel oil. *Gasoline and Diesel Oil Tax acts*. 2. Includes the refined petroleum products commercially known as diesel fuel and engine distillates and any other refined petroleum product declared by the Lieutenant-Governor in Council to be diesel oil within the meaning of this Act. *Gasoline, Diesel Oil and Home Heating Oil Pricing Act*, S.N.B. 1987, c. G-3.1, s. 1. See HEAVY ~.

DIES GRATIAE. [L.] A day of grace.

DIES INCEPTUS PRO COMPLETO HABETUR. [L.] A day begun is considered to be complete.

DIES JURIDICUS. [L.] A court-day.

DIES NON. *abbr.* Dies non juridicus.

DIES NON JURIDICUS. [L.] A day on which legal business cannot be transacted.

DIET. *n.* An assembly gathered to consider matters.

DIETETICS. *n.* The science and art dealing with the application of the principles of nutrition in the feeding of individuals or groups under different economic or health conditions. *Registered Dietitians Association Act*, R.S.A. 1980, c. R-10, s. 1. See PRACTICE OF ~.

DIETITIAN. See REGISTERED ~.

DIET OLEOMARGARINE. Oleomargarine containing forty per cent or less of fat. *Oleomargarine Act*, R.S.N.B. 1973, c. O-4, s. 1.

DIE WITHOUT ISSUE. A want or failure of issue in the lifetime or at the time of the death of that person and not an indefinite failure of issue, subject to any contrary intention appearing by the will or to any requirements as to age or otherwise therein contained for obtaining a vested estate. *Wills acts.*

DIE WITHOUT LEAVING ISSUE. A want or failure of issue in the lifetime or at the time of death of that person, and do not mean an indefinite failure of issue unless a contrary intention appears by the will. *Wills acts.*

DIFFACERE. [L.] To destroy.

DIFFERENCE. *n.* A difference arising (i) as to the interpretation, application or operation of a collective agreement, (ii) with respect to a contravention or alleged contravention of a collective agreement, or (iii) as to whether a difference referred to in subclauses (i) and (ii) can be the subject of adjudication. *Public Service Employee Relations Act*, R.S.A. 1980, c. P-33, s. 1.

DIFFERENTIAL. See RURAL RATE ~; SEX ~; SHIFT ~; WAGE ~.

DIFFERENTIAL PIECE RATE. A system of wages in which two or more piece rates are used.

DIFFERENT SYSTEMS. Systems which derive their energy from different transformers or from different banks of transformers or from different generators or other sources. *Power Corporation Act*, R.R.O. 1980, Reg. 794, s. 0.

DIFFUSION LIVIDITY. Spreading of hemoglobin into the tissues and dependent parts of the skin after approximately 8 hours. F.A. Jaffe, *A Guide to Pathological Evidence*, 2d ed. (Toronto: Carswell, 1983) at 5 and 179.

DIGAMIA. *n.* A second marriage entered into after the first marriage ends.

DIGAMY. *n.* A second marriage entered into after the first marriage ends.

DIGEST. *n.* 1. A gathering of rules of law based on particular cases, in contrast to a code. 2. An arrangement of the summarized decisions of courts made either alphabetically or systematically. 3. A private author's collection of abstract rules or principles of law.

DIGNITY. *n.* The privilege of bearing a title of honour or nobility.

DIJUDICATION. *n.* Judicial decision.

DILAPIDATED BUILDING. Includes a building which is structurally sound but by virtue of broken windows, torn roofing or other defects is in a condition of substantial disrepair. *Unsightly Property Act*, S.P.E.I. 1977, c. 43, s. 1.

DILAPIDATION. *n.* Disrepair; decay.

DILATORY. *adj.* Tending to cause delay in decision making.

DILATORY MOTION. A proposal that the original question be disposed of either permanently or for the time being. A. Fraser, G.A. Birch & W.A. Dawson, eds., *Beauchesne's Rules and Forms of the House of Commons of Canada*, 5th ed. (Toronto: Carswell, 1978) at 151.

DILIGENCE. *n.* Care.

DILIGENTIA. [L.] Care, diligence.

DILUENT. *n.* Any substance other than a synthetic colour present in a colour mixture or preparation. *Food and Drug Regulations*, C.R.C., c. 870, s. B.06.001.

DIMENSION. See ASSESSED ~; PROPERTY ~; SHOULDER ROOM ~.

DIMINUTION. *n.* Decrease.

DINARCHY. *n.* Government by two people.

DINING ROOM. 1. A place established and operated as a business which provides, for a consideration, meals and attendant services for the public. *The Liquor Licensing Act*, R.S.S. 1978, c. L-21, s. 2. 2. (i) A part of a hotel, inn, restaurant or railway car provided with special accommodation, facilities and equipment as may be prescribed for the serving of regular meals in consideration of payment therefor, as well as the sale of cigars, cigarettes, tobacco, and other articles incidental to the sale of regular meals, and (ii) such other parts of a hotel, inn, restaurant or railway car as are deemed by the Board to be suitable for occasional use as an additional dining area. *Liquor Licensing Act*, R.S.A. 1970, c. 212, s. 2.

DIOCESAN. *adj.* Relating to a diocese.

DIOCESE. *n.* 1. A territory under the jurisdiction of a Roman Catholic bishop and situated wholly or in part within the limits of Québec; this term includes an archdiocese, a diocese, an eparchy, a vicariate apostolic, a prefecture apostolic, a prelacy nullius and an abbacy nullius. *An Act Respecting Fabriques*, R.S.Q. 1977, c. F-1, s. 1. 2. Any territorial division, present or future, subject to the jurisdiction of a bishop and situated in whole or in part within the limits of Québec; such term includes specifically archdiocese, diocese, exarchate, abbey nullius, apostolic vicariate and apostolic prefecture. *Roman Catholic Bishops Act*, R.S.Q. 1977, c. E-17, s. 1. 3. Area of bishop's jurisdiction.

DIPHENYLAMINE TEST. See PARAFFIN TEST.

DIPLOMA. *n.* A certificate, less than a degree, awarded by a college.

DIPLOMACY. *n.* Conduct of negotiations between countries.

DIPLOMATIC OR CONSULAR OFFICER. Includes an ambassador, envoy, minister, chargé d'affaires, counsellor, secretary, attaché, consul-general, consul, vice-consul, pro-consul, consular agent, acting consul-general, acting consul, acting vice-consul, acting consular agent, high commissioner, permanent delegate, adviser, acting high commissioner, and acting permanent delegate. *Interpretation Act*, R.S.C. 1985, c. I-21, s. 35.

DIPLOMATIC PRIVILEGE. Not an absolute privilege; it is displaced when a member of the diplomatic corps has contravened the law with the intention of imperilling the safety of the State. P.K. McWilliams, *Canadian Criminal Evidence*, 3d ed. (Aurora: Canada Law Book, 1988) at 35-74.

DIPLOMATIC PROTECTION. Assistance which nations grant to their citizens against other nations.

DIPLOMATICS. *n.* The art of evaluating ancient charters, diplomas or public documents and judging them true and false.

DIP NET. 1. A net the bottom of which is closed to form a bag and that is hung on a ring or frame attached to a pole or handle. Canada regulations. 2. A small net that is fixed to a frame that is usually square, is suspended on a rope and is used to catch fish. *Quebec Fishery Regulations*, C.R.C., c. 852, s. 2.

DIPTERA. *n.* The order of insects composed of true flies which includes the species Calliphora vomitoria. F.A. Jaffe, *A Guide to Pathological Evidence*, 2d ed. (Toronto: Carswell, 1983) at 174.

DIR. *abbr.* Director.

DIRECT. *v.* To order; to instruct to lead.

DIRECT. *adj.* Immediate; by the shortest route.

DIRECT BAG. A bag weighing 60 pounds or less that contains printed papers intended for one addressee at one address outside Canada. *Third Class Mail Regulations*, C.R.C., c. 1297, s. 2.

DIRECT CHARGE CO-OPERATIVE. A co-operative that deals with its members and prospective members only in products or services on a cost basis and that directly charges its members a fee to cover the operating expenses of the co-operative. *Co-operative Corporations Act*, R.S.O. 1980, c. 91, s. 1.

DIRECT DESCENDANT. The son, daughter, stepson, stepdaughter, grandson, granddaughter, grand-stepson, grand-stepdaughter, great-grandson, great-granddaughter, great-great-stepson or great-great stepdaughter of an individual, or the spouse of any of them. *Land Bank Amendment Act, 1979*, S.S. 1979, c. 34, s. 3.

DIRECTED VERDICT. See MOTION FOR ~.

DIRECT EQUITY PERCENTAGE. With respect to formal equity owned by a person in any particular person, (a) where the particular person does not have more than one class of formal equity within the meaning of the regulations, the percentage of the formal equity of the particular person that is owned by the person, and (b) where the particular person has more than one class of formal equity within the meaning of the regulations, subject to the regulations, the aggregate fair market value of the formal equity of the particular person that is owned by the person, expressed as a percentage of the aggregate fair market value of all the formal equity of the particular person. *Canadian Ownership and Control Determination Act*, R.S.C. 1985, c. C-20, s. 2.

DIRECT EVIDENCE. 1. A witness' testimony as to what was observed through the senses. P.K. McWilliams, *Canadian Criminal Evidence*, 3d ed. (Aurora: Canada Law Book, 1988) at 1-11. 2. Evidence which is adduced to prove a fact. P.K. McWilliams, *Canadian Criminal Evidence*, 3d ed. (Aurora: Canada Law Book, 1988) at 1-12. 3. Evidence tending directly to establish the existence or non-existence of an element of the offence charged. *Military Rules of Evidence*, C.R.C., c. 1049, s. 2.

DIRECT EXAMINATION. Questioning of a witness by the party which called that witness.

DIRECT EXPANSION COILS. The piping in which liquid refrigerant is vaporized to produce ice in a rink for hockey, skating or curling. *Boilers and Pressure Vessels Act*, R.R.O. 1980, Reg. 84, s. 1.

DIRECTION. *n.* The judge's instructions to the jury as to what the law is. See FACING ~; MIS~; NON-~; OPPOSING ~; SIDEWARD ~; TRAIN OF SUPERIOR ~.

DIRECTIONAL DIVIDING LINE. A line marked or placed on a roadway as provided in section 108, not necessarily at the centre thereof, to indicate to the drivers of vehicles the portions of the roadway that may be used for traffic proceeding in each direction and, in the case of a roadway on which no such line is marked or placed, means the centre line. *The Highway Traffic Act*, S.M. 1985-86, c. 3, s. 1.

DIRECTION OF TRAFFIC FLOW. The direction for traffic in a route that is indicated by arrows on a reference chart. *Collision Regulations*, C.R.C., c. 1416, s. 2.

DIRECTIONS FOR USE. Full information as

to the procedures recommended for achieving optimum performance of a device, and includes cautions, warnings, contra-indications and possible adverse effects. *Medical Devices Regulations*, C.R.C., c. 871, s. 2.

DIRECTIVE. *n.* An order.

DIRECTLY CHARTERED LOCAL. A union local which receives its charter from a central labour congress and is not part of an international or national union.

DIRECTOR. *n.* 1. A person who manages the affairs and business of the company. H. Sutherland, D.B. Horsley & J.M. Edmiston, eds., *Fraser's Handbook on Canadian Company Law*, 7th ed. (Toronto: Carswell, 1985) at 201. 2. Where used in relation to a person, includes a person acting in a capacity similar to that of a director of a company. *Securities acts.* 3. Includes a trustee, officer, member of an executive committee and any person occupying a similar position. *Societies acts.* 4. Includes commissioners, governors and other officials of any body corporate with comparable responsibilities, whether or not they are called directors. 5. The title of the head or administrator of a government program or office. See BOARD OF ~S; FUNERAL ~; INFORMATION BANK ~; LABORATORY ~; MANAGING ~; MEDICAL ~; MEETING OF ~S; OFFICER-~; PARTNERS', ~S' AND SENIOR OFFICERS' QUALIFYING EXAMINATION; PROVINCIAL ~.

DIRECTORY. *n.* A provision which is simply a direction or instruction with no obligatory force; no invalidating consequence will follow if it is disregarded, unlike an imperative provision, which must be followed.

DIRECT SALE. 1. A sale which involves a consumer and takes place at the buyer's dwelling. G.H.L. Fridman, *Sale of Goods in Canada*, 3d ed. (Toronto: Carswell, 1986) at 492. 2. A sale by a direct seller acting in the course of business as such. Direct Sellers acts.

DIRECT SALES CONTRACT. A written or oral agreement for the direct sale of goods or services. *Direct Sellers acts.*

DIRECT SELLER. A person who: (i) goes from house to house selling or offering for sale, or soliciting orders for the future delivery of goods or services; or (ii) by telephone offers for sale or solicits orders for the future delivery of goods or services.

DIRECT SELLING. Selling, offering for sale or soliciting of orders for the sale of goods or services by (i) going from house to house, (ii) telephone communication, or (iii) mail.

DIRECT TAX. Described by John Stuart Mill in 1848 : "A direct tax is one which is demanded from the very person who it is intended or desired should pay it." P.W. Hogg, *Constitutional Law of Canada*, 2d ed. (Toronto: Carswell, 1985) at 605.

DIRECT TRANSFER CHARGE. A charge on goods that are (a) moved directly between a vessel and open railway cars or open motor vehicles, or (b) moved directly between a vessel and barges or scows that are alongside it. *Pacific Terminal Tariff By-law*, C.R.C., c. 1083, s. 41.

DIRIMENT IMPEDIMENT. A bar to a marriage which invalidates it ipso jure.

DIRT. *n.* Any egg yolk, manure, soil or foreign matter that can be readily removed from the shell of an egg. *Egg Regulations*, C.R.C., c. 284, s. 2.

DISABILITY. *n.* 1. The absence of legal ability to do certain acts or enjoy certain benefits. 2. The incapacity of a minor or of a person who is mentally incompetent. 3. Any previous or existing mental or physical disability and includes disfigurement and previous or existing dependence on alcohol or a drug. *Canadian Human Rights Act*, R.S.C. 1985, c. H-6, s. 25. 4. The loss or lessening of the power to will and to do any normal mental or physical act. *Pension Act*, R.S.C. 1985, c. P-6, s. 2. See MENTAL ~; PARTY UNDER ~; PERSON UNDER ~; PHYSICAL ~; SERIOUS OR PROLONGED ~; TOTAL AND PERMANENT ~; TOTAL ~.

DISABILITY INCOME INSURANCE OR BENEFIT PLAN. Includes a plan, fund or arrangement provided, furnished or offered by an employer to an employee that provides benefits to an employee for loss of income because of sickness, accident or disability and includes, (i) a short-term disability income insurance or benefit plan, fund or arrangement that is other than a long-term disability income plan, and (ii) a long-term disability income insurance or benefit plan, fund or arrangement under which the payments or benefits to an employee are payable for a period of not less than fifty-two weeks or until recovery, retirement or death, whichever is the lesser. *Employment Standards Act*, R.R.O. 1980, Reg. 282, s. 1.

DISABILITY INSURANCE. Insurance undertaken by an insurer as part of a contract of life insurance whereby the insurer undertakes to pay insurance money or to provide other benefits in the event that the person whose life is insured becomes disabled as a result of bodily injury or disease.

DISABILITY PLAN. A long term disability income continuance plan, under which an employee who, as a result of illness or other disability rendering him unable to perform his regular duties, is entitled to be paid a percentage of his salary in accordance with that plan. Alberta statutes.

DISABLE. *v.* To bring about a disability.

DISABLED. *adj.* Incapable of pursuing regularly any substantially gainful occupation.

DISABLED CONTRIBUTOR'S CHILD. A dependent child of a contributor who is disabled.

DISABLED PERSON. 1. A person who because of physical or mental impairment is incapable of pursuing regularly any substantially gainful occupation. 2. A person who has an employment handicap or a person who is eligible for rehabilitation services. *The Rehabilitation Act*, R.S.S. 1978, c. R-17, s. 2. 3. (i) A person who has a physical, mental, psychological, emotional or other impairment that impedes him from participating to the best of his ability in social and economic activities, (ii) a person who is eligible for rehabilitation services under the terms of an agreement entered into pursuant to section 7, or (iii) a person whose participation in social and economic activities in relation to his ability, is impeded by familial, social or other extrinsic factors. *Rehabilitation of Disabled Persons Act*, R.S.P.E.I. 1974, c. R-12, s. 2. 4. One who, because of physical or mental impairment, including congenital or genetic abnormality, suffers absence or reduction of functional competence which substantially limits his ability to carry out normal daily activities. *Child and Family Services and Family Relations Act*, S.N.B. 1980, c. C-2.1, s. 1.

DISABLING INJURY. 1. An injury during employment which prevents a worker from earning full wages in the work at which the worker was employed before the injury. D. Robertson, *Ontario Health and Safety Guide* (Toronto: Richard De Boo Ltd., 1988) at 5-104. 2. Any work injury that (a) prevents an employee from reporting for work or effectively performing all of the duties connected with his regular work on any day subsequent to the day on which the injury occurred, whether or not that day was a holiday or other non-working day, or (b) results in the loss by an employee of a body member or part thereof or in a complete loss of its usefulness or in the permanent impairment of a body function whether or not the employee is prevented from reporting for work or effectively performing his regular work as described in paragraph (a). *Canada Accident Investigation and Reporting Regulations*, C.R.C., c. 993, s. 2.

DISABLING INJURY FREQUENCY RATE. The number of disabling injuries per million man hours worked. *Canada Accident Investigation and Reporting Regulations*, C.R.C., c. 993, s. 2.

DISADVANTAGED PERSON. A person (a) who, as a result of age, infirmity or other disability, has needs that, in the opinion of the Corporation, are not adequately met by housing accommodation ordinarily available on the current housing market in the area in which the person lives, or (b) to whom, in accordance with the regulations, household income is attributable in an amount that is, in the opinion of the Corporation, insufficient to permit the person to acquire housing accommodation adequate for the person's household needs on the current housing market in the area in which the person lives. *National Housing Act*, R.S.C. 1985, c. N-11, s. 54.

DISAFFECTION. *n.* Disloyalty to established authority.

DISAFFIRM. *v.* To repudiate; to deny.

DISAGREEMENT. *n.* A grantee's or lessee's refusal to accept an estate or lease.

DISALLOWANCE. *n.* 1. The Queen's power to annul any statute enacted by the Parliament of Canada. P.W. Hogg, *Constitutional Law of Canada*, 2d ed. (Toronto: Carswell, 1985) at 192. 2. The federal power vested in the Governor General in Council to annul provincial statutes. P.W. Hogg, *Constitutional Law of Canada*, 2d ed. (Toronto: Carswell, 1985) at 192.

DISASTER. *n.* 1. A calamity caused by accident, by an act of war or insurrection or by the forces of nature, that has resulted or may result in serious harm to the safety, health or welfare of people, or in widespread damage to property. 2. An emergency in any community caused by fire, flood, tempest or other calamity not resulting from enemy attack, sabotage or other hostile action. See CIVIL ~; NATURAL ~; PEACE-TIME ~; POST-~ BUILDING.

DISBAR. *v.* To expel a lawyer from membership in a law society.

DISBARMENT. *n.* Cessation of membership in the society, and in the case of a barrister means the striking of his name from the barristers' roll, and in the case of a solicitor, means the striking of his name from the solicitors' roll. *Barristers and Solicitors Act*, R.S.B.C. 1979, c. 26, s. 1.

DISBURSEMENT. *n.* 1. An expenditure or any other payment or transfer of public money. 2. Money expended or paid out on behalf of the client, such as a fee paid to a court officer or court reporter or witness fees, for which a lawyer is entitled to a credit when an account is submitted.

DISCARD. *n.* Presently unusable solid or liquid

materials removed or rejected during mining or processing operations.

DISCARD SITE. An area within which discard is stored, either temporarily or permanently.

DISCHARGE. *v.* 1. To release a person from an obligation. 2. To deprive a right or obligation of its binding force. 3. Section 662.1 of the Code gives judges discretion to release an accused after guilt is determined absolutely or on conditions a probation order prescribes. D. Stuart, *Canadian Criminal Law: a Treatise*, 2d ed. (Toronto: Carswell, 1987) at 494.

DISCHARGE. *n.* 1. Release of the patient. 2. An instrument by which one terminates an obligation under contract. 3. Includes, but not so as to limit its meaning, any spilling, leaking, pumping, pouring, emitting, emptying, throwing or dumping. 4. Termination of employment by an employer other than a lay-off. 5. Honourable termination of service in or with the regular forces. See ABSOLUTE ~; CONDITIONAL ~; CONSTRUCTIVE ~.

DISCHARGE AND PARTIAL DISCHARGE. Include any tax sale or other proceeding whereby title to the lands or part of the lands included in a mortgage or encumbrance is issued clear of, and unaffected by, the mortgage or encumbrance. *Real Property Act*, R.S.M. 1970, c. R30, s. 101.

DISCHARGED. *adj.* 1. Relieved from further performance of the contract. *Frustrated Contracts acts.* 2. Of a payment, made or paid.

DISCHARGED INMATE. An inmate who has been released as a result of the expiration of his sentence or the operation of remission or who has been released on parole other than day parole. *Penitentiary Act*, R.S.C. 1985, c. P-5, s. 34(2).

DISCHARGE FROM SERVICE. Includes any termination of service. *Veterans Insurance Act*, R.S.C. 1970, c. V-3, s. 2.

DISCHARGE POINT. See FINAL ~.

DISCHARGE TUBE. See GAS ~.

DISCIPLINARY ACTION. An action that adversely affects a worker with respect to terms or conditions of employment. *Occupational Health and Safety Amendment Act, 1983*, S.A. 1983, c. 39, s. 2.

DISCIPLINARY COMMITTEE. See DISCIPLINE COMMITTEE.

DISCIPLINARY MATTER. Any matter involving an allegation of professional misconduct or fitness to practise on the part of a member, student or professional corporation.

DISCIPLINE. *n.* Correction; punishment. See PROGRESSIVE ~.

DISCIPLINE CLAUSE. A clause in a collective agreement permitting an employer to punish employees for disobedience.

DISCIPLINE COMMITTEE. A committee established under a statute regulating one of the self-governing professions.

DISCLAIM. *v.* To repudiate; to refuse to recognize.

DISCLAIMER. *n.* 1. The act of renouncing generally substantiated by a deed. 2. A disclaimer made under the laws of a province other than the Province of Québec and includes a renunciation of a succession made under the laws of Québec unless it is made in favour of a person. *An Act to Amend the Taxation Act and Other Fiscal Legislation*, S.Q. 1986, c. 19, s. 3. 3. Allows a trademark registration to contain something which, if it stood alone, would be non-distinctive, but which constitutes one element of a distinctive totality. H.G. Fox, *The Canadian Law of Trade Marks and Unfair Competition*, 3d ed. (Toronto: Carswell, 1972) at 238.

DISCLAIMER CLAUSE. A clause in a contract denying that guarantees or other representations have been made.

DISCLAIMER OF REPRESENTATIVE STATUS. A union's statement that it no longer represents certain workers.

DISCLOSED PRINCIPAL. A person whose existence the agent has revealed to the third party, but whose exact identity is still unknown. G.H.L. Fridman, *The Law of Agency*, 5th ed. (London: Butterworths, 1983) at 187.

DISCLOSURE. *n.* 1. A revelation. 2. The part of the specification other than the claims. *Patent Rules*, C.R.C., c. 1250, s. 2. See CONTINUOUS ~; FULL ~; TIMELY ~.

DISCLOSURE LABEL. A representation label that complies with the Act and these Regulations as to its form and as to (a) the information that it shows with respect to the consumer textile to which it is applied, and (b) the manner in which such information is shown, and where the information required by section 11 is shown in two labels pursuant to subsection 14(3) or 14(4), means both labels. *Textile Labelling and Advertising Regulations*, C.R.C., c. 1551, s. 3.

DISCONNECTING MEANS. A device, group of devices, or other means whereby the conductors of a circuit can be disconnected from their source of supply. *Power Corporation Act*, R.R.O. 1980, Reg. 794, s. 0.

DISCONTINUANCE. *n.* 1. Breaking off; interruption. 2. In procedure, the plaintiff voluntarily putting an end to an action.

DISCOUNT. *n.* 1. Lessening, diminishing. 2. The excess of the par or stated value of any security issued or resold over the value of the consideration received for the security. Canada regulations.

DISCOUNTER. *n.* A person who acquires, for a consideration, a right to a refund of tax from the person entitled to it.

DISCOUNT RATE. The rate, expressed as a percentage, used in calculating the present value of future damages. *Attorney General Statutes Amendment Act*, S.B.C. 1981, c. 10, s. 51.

DISCOVERT. *n.* A spinster; a widow.

DISCOVERY. *n.* Disclosure by the parties before trial of information and documents. See COMMERCIAL ~; EXAMINATION FOR ~; SIGNIFICANT ~.

DISCREDIT. *v.* To throw doubt on the testimony of a witness.

DISCRETIO EST DISCERNERE PER LEGEM QUID SIT JUSTUM. [L.] Discretion is to distinguish through law what is just.

DISCRETION. *n.* 1. Freedom to choose among possible courses of action. S.A. Cohen, *Due Process of Law* (Toronto: Carswell, 1977) at 197. 2. A person's own judgment of what is best in a given situation. See ADMINISTRATIVE ~; JUDICIAL ~.

DISCRETIONARY. *adj.* At the discretion of someone; not available as of right.

DISCRETIONARY DUTY. Something required of a trustee, such as allocating trust property, choosing how much a beneficiary should have, or choosing who should have a benefit from among a class of beneficiaries, and then how much that particular beneficiary should have. D.M.W. Waters, *The Law of Trusts in Canada*, 2d ed. (Toronto: Carswell, 1984) at 28-29.

DISCRETIONARY REMEDY. Given at a court's discretion, not available as of right.

DISCRETIONARY TRUST. A trust in which trustees are given absolute discretion concerning the allocation of the capital and income of the trust fund to beneficiaries.

DISCRIMINATION. *n.* Treating one person differently than another without proper justification. See CONSTRUCTIVE ~.

DISCRIMINATORY ACTION. Any action by an employer which adversely affects a worker with respect to any terms or conditions of employment or opportunity for promotion, and

includes the action of dismissal, layoff, suspension, demotion, transfer of job or location, reduction in wages, change in hours of work or reprimand. *Occupational Health and Safety acts*.

DISC WHEEL. A supporting member for a tire or tire and tube assembly, comprising a rim with a dish shaped component that is permanently attached to the inner circumference of the rim. *Motor Vehicle Safety Regulations*, C.R.C., c. 1038, s. 2.

DISEASE. *n.* 1. Any condition that adversely affects the health of an animal. 2. A condition that exists in a plant or seed as the result of the action of virus, fungus, bacterium, or any other similar or allied organism and that injures or may injure the plant or any part thereof. See APPEARANCE OF THE INJURY OR ~; BANG'S ~; COMMUNICABLE ~; CONTAGIOUS ~; DANGEROUS ~; DUTCH ELM ~; ENDEMIC ~; EPIDEMIC ~; FRUIT TREE ~; INDUSTRIAL ~; INFECTIOUS ~; NOTIFIABLE ~; OCCUPATIONAL ~; PLANT ~; REPORTABLE ~; SEXUALLY TRANSMITTED ~; VENEREAL ~; VIRULENT ~.

DISEASED. *adj.* 1. Infected with an infectious or contagious disease. 2. Affected by disease.

DISENTAILING DEED. An assurance through which a tenant in tail blocks the entail in order to convert it into a fee simple.

DISENTITLED. *adj.* Not entitled.

DISFIGUREMENT. *n.* An external injury which detracts from personal appearance.

DISFRANCHISEMENT. *n.* Depriving of a franchise, privilege or immunity.

DISHONOUR. *v.* To neglect or refuse to accept or pay a bill of exchange when it is duly presented for payment. See NOTICE OF ~.

DISINCARCERATE. *v.* To free from prison; to set at liberty.

DISINFECTION. *n.* 1. The destruction of infectious agents outside the body by any means. *Public Health Act*, S.A. 1984, c. P-27.1, s. 1. 2. The application by inspectors or other persons authorized by the Minister, of chemical materials on infected surfaces, areas or objects for the purpose of killing insects, viruses, fungus, bacteria or other organisms that are designated plant diseases by the regulations. *Plant Disease Eradication Act*, R.S.P.E.I. 1974, c. P-7, s. 1. See TERMINAL ~.

DISINFESTATION. *n.* The destruction or removal, by any physical or chemical process, of animal forms present on domestic animals or humans or in the environment. *Public Health Act*, S.A. 1984, c. P-27.1, s. 1.

DISINTERMENT. *n.* Exhumation.

DISJUNCTIVE TERM. Usually expressed by the word "or" which indicates alternative conditions or matters.

DISMISS. *v.* 1. In employment, to fire, let go, terminate. 2. In proceedings, to refuse the remedy requested.

DISMISSAL. See WRONGFUL ~.

DISMISSAL FOR DELAY. Dismissal of the plaintiff's action when that plaintiff has not taken any of certain steps specified. G.D. Watson & C. Perkins, eds., *Holmested & Watson: Ontario Civil Procedure* (Toronto: Carswell, 1984) at 24-5.

DISMISSAL FOR WANT OF PROSECUTION. See DISMISSAL FOR DELAY.

DISMISSAL PAY. Severance pay.

DISMISSAL WITHOUT PREJUDICE. One action is dismissed, but another action for the same relief may be commenced.

DISMORTGAGE. *v.* To deliver from mortgage.

DISORDER. See MENTAL ~; PSYCHIATRIC ~; PSYCHOPATHIC ~.

DISORDERLY HOUSE. 1. A common bawdy-house, a common betting house or a common gaming house. *Criminal Code*, R.S.C. 1985, c. C-46, s. 197. 2. House situated in Québec, used for any of the purposes whatsoever which constitute a disorderly house within the meaning of Part V of the Criminal Code of Canada, or used for trading, transportation, keeping or delivery of alcoholic beverages, contrary to the provisions of the Act respecting the Commission de contrôle des permis d'alcool (chapter C-33) or of the Act respecting the Société des alcools du Québec (chapter S-13), or of any other law respecting the above objects. *Disorderly Houses Act*, R.S.Q. 1977, c. M-2, s. 13.

DISPARAGEMENT. *n.* A statement which casts doubt on ownership of property or on quality of goods.

DISPARITY. See WAGE ~.

DISPATCH. *v.* To send off quickly.

DISPATCH. *n.* A letter, message or order concerning affairs of state sent with speed.

DISPATCH CENTRE. A radio station, within the meaning of the Radio Act (Canada), that is equipped to receive calls for ambulance service and to dispatch ambulances by radio or telephone and that is used for such purpose. *Ambulance Act*, R.R.O. 1980, Reg. 14, s. 1.

DISPATCHER. *n.* A person who operates radio or telephone equipment at a dispatch centre for the purpose of receiving calls for ambulance service and dispatching ambulances. *Ambulance Act*, R.R.O. 1980, Reg. 14, s. 1.

DISPENSARY. *n.* A place where prescriptions, drugs, chemicals and poisons are (i) sold by retail, or (ii) compounded, or (iii) dispensed, or (iv) supplied or distributed.

DISPENSATION. *n.* Freedom from a legal obligation; liberty to do a forbidden thing.

DISPENSE. *v.* Includes the preparation and release of a drug prescribed in a prescription and the taking of steps to ensure the pharmaceutical and therapeutic suitability of a drug for its intended use.

DISPENSER. *n.* A person who dispenses a drug pursuant to a prescription. See LAY ~; OPHTHALMIC ~.

DISPENSING. *n.* Includes the responsibility for taking all reasonable steps to ensure pharmaceutical and therapeutic appropriateness as well as the preparing and releasing of the prescribed medication. *Pharmacy Act*, S.N.S. 1981, c. 39, s. 1. See OPHTHALMIC ~; OPTICAL ~.

DISPENSING OPTICIAN. A person who (a) supplies, prepares and dispenses optical appliances, (b) interprets complete prescriptions of duly qualified medical practitioners and Optometrists, and (c) fits, adjusts, and adapts optical appliances to the human face and eyes in accordance with the complete prescriptions of duly qualified medical practitioners and Optometrists. *New Brunswick Guild of Dispensing Opticians Incorporation Act*, S.N.B. 1976, c. 68, s. 2.

DISPLAY. See FLYING ~ AREA.

DISPLAY GOODS. Goods imported for the purpose of display at a convention or public exhibition pursuant to tariff item 70000-1 of Schedule A to the Customs Tariff. *Display Goods Temporary Importation Regulations*, C.R.C., c. 524, s. 2.

DISPLAY PANEL. Part of a label applied on or affixed to the package for a control product but does not include a leaflet or brochure unless it is part of the label. *Pest Control Products Regulations*, C.R.C., c. 1253, s. 2. See PRINCIPAL ~.

DISPOSABLE CONTAINER. A container, (a) that is used to contain a product or products sold or intended for sale and that will not be accepted for reuse as a container and refilled with the same product or products by the manufacturer, processor, distributor or retail vendor of the product or products; or (b) for which no deposit is or will be charged at the time of sale of the product or products at retail and for which, as a used container, no money or money's worth will be paid or given by a manufacturer, processor, distributor or retail vendor of the product or products sold or intended for sale in the container. *Environmental Protection Act*, R.R.O. 1980, Reg. 306, s. 1.

DISPOSAL. *n.* The transfer or sale of the right, title or interest in assets in the form of output product, plant, equipment, buildings, or related property to the control and possession of another person. *Mining Tax Act*, R.R.O. 1980, Reg. 639, s. 1. See DEEP WELL ~; WASTE ~ SITE.

DISPOSE. *v.* To transfer by any method and includes assign, give, sell, grant, charge, convey, bequeath, devise, lease, divest, release and agree to do any of those things. *Interpretation Act*, R.S.B.C. 1979, c. 206, s. 29.

DISPOSING. *n.* Includes discharging, dumping, throwing, dropping, discarding, abandoning, spilling, leaking, pumping, pouring, emitting or emptying, or any 2 or more of them, whether intentional or accidental. *Litter Act*, R.S.A. 1980, c. L-19, s. 1.

DISPOSITION. *n.* 1. Final settlement or sentencing of a criminal case. 2. Of any property, except as expressly otherwise provided, includes (i) any transaction or event entitling a taxpayer to proceeds of disposition of property, (ii) any transaction or event by which (A) any property of a taxpayer that is a share, bond, debenture, note, certificate, mortgage, hypothec, agreement of sale or similar property, or an interest therein, is redeemed in whole or in part or is cancelled, (B) any debt owing to a taxpayer or any other right of taxpayer to receive an amount is settled or cancelled, (C) any share owned by a taxpayer is converted by virtue of an amalgamation or merger, or (D) any option held by a taxpayer to acquire or dispose of property expires, and (ii) any transfer of property to a trust, or any transfer of property of a trust to any beneficiary under the trust, except as provided in subparagraph (v), but for greater certainty, does not include (iv) any transfer of property for the purpose only of securing a debt or a loan, or any transfer by a creditor for the purpose only of returning property that had been used as security for a debt or a loan, (v) any transfer of property by virtue of which there is a change in the legal ownership of the property without any change in the beneficial ownership thereof, other than a transfer by a trust resident in Canada to a trust not resident in Canada or a transfer to a trust governed by (A) a registered retirement savings plan, (B) a deferred profit sharing plan, (C) an employees profit sharing plan, or (D) a registered retirement income fund by a person who is, immediately after the transfer, a beneficiary under the plan or fund, or a transfer by any such trust governed by a plan or fund to a beneficiary thereunder, (vi) any issue by a corporation of a bond, debenture, note, certificate, mortgage or hypothec of the corporation, or (vii) any issue by a corporation of a share of its capital stock, or any other transaction that, but for this subparagraph, would be a disposition by a corporation of a share of its capital stock. *Income Tax Act*, R.S.C. 1952, c. 148 (as am. S.C. 1986, c. 6, s. 27(1)), s. 54(c). 3. The act of disposal or an instrument by which that act is affected or evidenced, and includes a Crown grant, order in council, transfer, assurance, lease, licence, permit, contract or agreement and every other instrument whereby lands or any right, interest or estate in land may be transferred, disposed of or affected, or by which the Crown divests itself of or creates any right, interest or estate in land. 4. Any disposition that may be made of a body under the Cemeteries Act. *Anatomy Act*, R.S.O. 1980, c. 21, s. 1. 5. Includes any arrangement or ordering in the nature of a disposition, whether by one transaction or a number of transactions effected for the purpose or in any other manner whatever. *Estate Tax acts.* 6. In relation to an interest in a life insurance policy, includes (i) a surrender thereof, (ii) a policy loan made after March 31, 1978, (iii) the dissolution of that interest by virtue of the maturity of the policy, (iv) a disposition of that interest by operation of law only, and (iv.1) the payment by an insurer of an amount (other than an annuity payment, a policy loan or a policy dividend) in respect of a policy (other than a policy described in paragraph (1)(a), (b), (c), (d) or (e)) that is a life annuity contract, as defined by regulation, entered into after November 16, 1978, and before November 13, 1981, but does not include (v) an assignment of all or any part of an interest in the policy for the purpose of securing a debt or a loan other than a policy loan, (vi) a lapse of the policy in consequence of the premiums under the policy remaining unpaid, if the policy was reinstated not later than 60 days after the end of the calender year in which the lapse occurred, (vii) a payment under a policy as a disability benefit or an accidental death benefit, (viii) an annuity payment, (ix) a payment under a life insurance policy (other than an annuity contract) that (A) was last acquired before December 2, 1982, or (B) is an exempt policy in consequence of the death of any person whose life was insured under the policy, or (x) any transaction or event by which an individual becomes entitled to receive, under the terms of an exempt policy, all of the proceeds (including or excluding policy dividends) payable under the policy in the form of an annuity contract or annuity payments, if, at the time of that transaction or event, the individual whose life is insured under the policy was totally and permanently disabled. *Income Tax Act*, R.S.C. 1952, c. 148 (as am. S.C. 1970-71-72, c. 63), s. 148(9)(c). See CROWN ~; PRE-~ REPORT; PROCEEDS OF ~; TIMBER ~.

DISPOSITION COST AMOUNT. (i) For each eligible share of the same type and class of an eligible corporation that (A) has a different acquisition cost amount from other eligible shares of the same type and class of the eligible corporation, and (B) is contributed to a stock savings plan, the amount determined in accordance with a reasonable method adopted by the eligible investor and applied consistently to all eligible shares of that type and class disposed of from that stock savings plan, and (ii) for each other eligible share contributed to a stock savings plan, its acquisition cost amount. *Stock Savings Plan acts.*

DISPOSITIVE POWER. 1. The authority to distribute trust property, either capital or income or both, to a beneficiary or among several beneficiaries. D.M.W. Waters, *The Law of Trusts in Canada*, 2d ed. (Toronto: Carswell, 1984) at 691. 2. The authority of a trustee to draw on capital or income to maintain a beneficiary during infancy, or to give capital to a widow who takes an income interest under a testamentary trust when her husband dies. D.M.W. Waters, *The Law of Trusts in Canada*, 2d ed. (Toronto: Carswell, 1984) at 72.

DISPOSITIVE POWER OR DISCRETION. Authorization given to a trustee to allocate or distribute trust property to a beneficiary of the trust. D.M.W. Waters, *The Law of Trusts in Canada*, 2d ed. (Toronto: Carswell, 1984) at 911.

DISPOSSESSION. *n.* Ouster; removal from possession.

DISPROOF. *n.* Proof that not the accused but a third party committed the crime. P.K. McWilliams, *Canadian Criminal Evidence*, 3d ed. (Aurora: Canada Law Book, 1988) at 18-27.

DISPROVE. *v.* To refute; to prove to be false.

DISPUTE. *n.* 1. A difference or apprehended difference arising in connection with the entering into, renewing or revision of a collective agreement. 2. Any dispute or difference or apprehended dispute or difference between an employer and one or more employees or a bargaining agent acting on behalf of the employees, as to matters or things affecting or relating to terms or conditions of employment or work done or to be done by the employee or employees or as to privileges, rights and duties of the employer or the employee or employees. See ALTERNATIVE ~ RESOLUTION; INDUSTRIAL ~; INTEREST ~; INTER-

UNION ~; JURISDICTIONAL ~; LABOUR ~; LABOUR-MANAGEMENT ~; NOTICE OF ~; PROCESS FOR RESOLUTION OF A ~; WORK-ASSIGNMENT ~.

DISQUALIFIED. *adj.* 1. Not eligible. 2. In which some condition precedent was not fulfilled.

DISS. *abbr.* Dissentiente.

DISSECTION. *n.* Anatomical examination of a corpse.

DISSEISE. *v.* To deprive; to dispossess.

DISSEISIN. *n.* Wrongful deprivation of the seisin of land. See NOVEL ~; RE~.

DISSEISINAM SATIS FACIT, QUI UTI NON PERMITTIT POSSESSOREM, VEL MINUS COMMODE, LICET OMNINO NON EXPELLAT. [L.] Not permitting the possessor to enjoy or making the enjoyment less beneficial, although not total expulsion, amounts to disseisin.

DISSEISOR. *n.* A person who unlawfully expels another from land.

DISSEISSE. *n.* One turned out of possession.

DISSENT. *n.* Disagreement; the decision of a judge who does not agree with the majority of the members of the court.

DISSENTIENTE. *adj.* Used in reports of judgments where one or more judges do not agree with the majority of the members of the court.

DISSENTING OFFEREE. 1. An offeree who does not accept a take-over bid. 2. A person who acquires from an offeree a share for which a take-over bid is made.

DISSENTING OPINION. The individual opinion of a judge who does not agree with the majority of the members of the court.

DISSENTING SHAREHOLDER. Includes a shareholder who has not accepted the offer or assented to the plan or arrangement and any shareholder who has failed or refused to transfer his shares to the transferee company in accordance with the contract.

DISSIGNARE. *v.* [L.] To break or open a seal.

DISSIPATE. *v.* To jeopardize the financial security of a household by the squandering of property. *Matrimonial Property Act*, S.S. 1979, c. M-6.1, s. 2.

DISSIPATING ASSETS. Jeopardizing the financial security of a household by grossly and irresponsibly squandering assets. *Marital Property Act*, S.M. 1977, c. 48, s. 1.

DISSIPATION. *n.* The jeopardizing of the financial security of a household by the gross and irresponsible squandering of an asset. *Marital Property Act*, S.M. 1978, c. 24, s. 1.

DISSOCIATION. *n.* In prison, solitary confinement.

DISSOLUTION. *n.* 1. Putting an end to a legal entity or relation. 2. Of marriage, divorce. A. Bissett-Johnson & W.M. Holland, eds, *Matrimonial Property Law in Canada* (Toronto: Carswell, 1980) at BC-7. 3. Of Parliament, dissolution either by the expiration of five years or by proclamation. A. Fraser, G.A. Birch & W.A. Dawson, eds., *Beauchesne's Rules and Forms of the House of Commons of Canada*, 5th ed. (Toronto: Carswell, 1978) at 54. 4. Of a corporation, ending of corporate existence with the termination of operations and with no assets.

DISSOLUTION OF MARRIAGE. See ANNULMENT OF MARRIAGE.

DISSOLVE. *v.* To annul; to cancel; to put an end to.

DIST. *abbr.* District.

DISTAL. *adj.* More distant from the origin or from the trunk of the body. F.A. Jaffe, *A Guide to Pathological Evidence*, 2d ed. (Toronto: Carswell, 1983) at 174.

DISTANCE. See LIMITING ~; TRAVEL ~.

DISTANT EARLY WARNING IDENTIFICATION ZONE. The airspace extending upward from the surface of the earth in that area of Canada described in Schedule III. *Security Control of Air Traffic Order*, C.R.C., c. 63, s. 2.

DIST. CT. *abbr.* District Court.

DISTILLER. *n.* Any person who conducts, works, occupies or carries on any distillery, who rectifies any spirits by any process whatever, either by himself or his agent, or who has in his possession, complete or partially completed, or who imports, makes or manufactures, in whole or in part, any still, worm, rectifying or other apparatus suitable for the manufacture of spirits, and everyone who makes or keeps beer or wash prepared, in preparation or fit for distilling, or low wines or faints, or who has in his possession or use a still or rectifying apparatus, shall be deemed to be a distiller. *Excise Act*, R.S.C. 1985, c. E-14, s. 3.

DISTILLERY. *n.* Any plant or premises where (a) any process of fermentation for the production of wash is carried on, (b) any wash is kept or produced for the purpose of distillation, (c) any mash-tub, fermenting-tub, worm or still for the distillation of spirits is set up or used, (d) any process of distillation whatever of spirits is carried on, (e) any process of rectification of spirits, either by re-distillation or filtration, or other process is carried on, (f) any spirits are manufactured or produced from any substance whatever, by any process whatever, or (g) any still, rectifier or other apparatus, suitable for the manufacture of spirits, is in whole or in part manufactured, made or kept, and every office, workshop, warehouse, granary, fermenting-room, mash-house, still-room, rectifying-house, vault, cellar, shed, yard or other place owned or occupied by or on behalf of, or for the use of, any distiller, or in which any part of his business as such is transacted, where any grain, matter, material or apparatus suitable for or adapted to the production of spirits, or that is or is to be used in the production or rectification of spirits, is kept or stored, where any other products of the distillery are kept or stored or where any process of manufacture is carried on, shall be held to be included in and to form part of the distillery to which it is attached or appurtenant. *Excise Act*, R.S.C. 1985, c. E-14, s. 3.

DISTINCTIVE. *adj.* 1. In relation to a trade-mark, means a trade-mark that actually distinguishes the wares or services in association with which it is used by its owner from the wares or services of others or is adapted so to distinguish them. *Trade-Marks Act*, R.S.C. 1985, c. T-13, s. 2. 2. In relation to a trade name, means a trade name that actually distinguishes the business in association with which it is used by its owner from the business of others or that is adapted so as to distinguish them. *Corporations Regulations*, Canada regulations.

DISTINGUENDA SUNT TEMPORA. [L.] The context of the times must be considered.

DISTINGUISH. *v.* To clarify an essential difference.

DISTINGUISHING GUISE. (a) A shaping of wares or their containers, or (b) a mode of wrapping or packaging wares the appearance of which is used by a person for the purpose of distinguishing or so as to distinguish wares or services manufactured, sold, leased, hired or performed by him from those manufactured, sold, leased, hired or performed by others. *Trade-Marks Act*, R.S.C. 1985, c. T-13, s. 2.

DISTINGUISHING MARK. A distinguishing mark that is appropriated for use on public stores pursuant to Section 416. *Criminal Code*, R.S.C. 1985, c. C-46, s. 417.

DISTRAIN. *v.* To seize goods using distress.

DISTRAINER. *n.* One who seizes a distress.

DISTRAINOR. *n.* One who seizes a distress.

DISTRAINT. *n.* 1. Seizing. 2. Satisfying the wrong committed by taking a personal chattel from the wrongdoer and delivering to the party injured. E.L.G. Tyler & N.E. Palmer, eds., *Crossley Vaines' Personal Property*, 5th ed. (London: Butterworths, 1973) at 493.

DISTRESS. *n.* 1. A seizure, without legal process, of a personal chattel from a wrongdoer's possession and delivery of it into the injured party's hands. 2. Property which was distrained. 3. The state of being in need of proper care, food or shelter or by being injured, sick, abused, in pain or suffering or being subject to undue or unnecessary hardship, privation or neglect. *Animal Protection acts.* See ABUSE OF ~; GRAND ~; POWER OF ~.

DISTRESS COMMUNICATION. A radiocommunication transmitted for the purpose of requesting immediate assistance in a case of grave and imminent danger, preceded, in the case of aeronautical and maritime mobile services, by the signal "SOS" when sent by radiotelegraphy and by the spoken word "MAYDAY" when sent by radiotelephony. *General Radio Regulations, Part II*, C.R.C., c. 1372, s. 2.

DISTRESSED SEAMAN. A person who is in distress in a place outside Canada, having been shipwrecked, discharged or left behind from a ship on which he was engaged. *Distressed Seamen Regulations*, C.R.C., c. 1420, s. 2.

DISTRESS FUND. A public fund established after a disaster. K.D. Cooper-Stephenson & I.B. Saunders, *Personal Injury Damages in Canada* (Toronto: Carswell, 1981) at 498.

DISTRIBUTE. *v.* 1. To deliver, handle, keep for sale or sell. 2. Includes rent, lease, sell or supply, or to make an offer to do any of those things. *Motion Picture Act*, S.B.C. 1986, c. 17, s. 1. 3. To calculate a pool in accordance with these Regulations. *Race Track Supervision Regulations*, C.R.C., c. 441, s. 2.

DISTRIBUTING BANK. A bank, any of the issued securities of which are or were part of a distribution to the public and remain outstanding and are held by more than one person. *Bank Act*, R.S.C. 1985, c. B-1, s. 168.

DISTRIBUTING CORPORATION. 1. A corporation, any of the issued securities of which are or were part of a distribution to the public and remain outstanding and are held by more than one person. 2. A corporation (i) any of whose issued shares, or securities which may or might be exchanged for or converted into shares, were part of a distribution to the public, and (ii) which has more than 15 shareholders. *Business Corporations Act*, S.A. 1981, s. B-15, s. 1.

DISTRIBUTING PIPE. A pipe to convey water from a service pipe to a fixture or to an outlet and includes the control valves and fittings connected to it, but does not include a meter or control valve or other device owned and controlled by the supplier of the water. *Ontario Water Resources Act*, R.R.O. 1980, Reg. 736, s. 1.

DISTRIBUTION. *n.* 1. Where used in relation to trading in securities, (a) a trade in a security of an issuer that has not been previously issued, (b) a trade by or on behalf of an issuer in a previously issued security of that issuer that has been redeemed or purchased by or donated to that issuer, (c) a trade in a previously issued security of an issuer from the holdings of a control person, (d) a trade by or on behalf of an underwriter in a security which was acquired by that underwriter, acting as underwriter, before the coming into force of this section, if that security continues, on the day this section comes into force, to be owned by or on behalf of that underwriter so acting, (e) a transaction or series of transactions involving further purchases and sales in the course of or incidental to a distribution. *Securities acts.* 2. (a) A trade by or on behalf of a bank in securities of the bank that have not previously been issued, (b) a trade by or on behalf of a bank in previously issued securities of the bank that have been redeemed or purchased by the bank, or (c) a trade in previously issued securities of a bank from the holdings of any person or group of persons who act in concert and who hold in excess of ten per cent of the shares of any class of voting shares of the bank. *Bank Act*, R.S.C. 1985, c. B-1, s. 145. 3. Division of property of an estate after debts and expenses of administration are paid. See OCCUPANT ~; PRIMARY ~ TO THE PUBLIC; PROMOTIONAL ~; RETAIL ~; SAMPLES FOR MASS ~; SAMPLES FOR SELECTIVE ~; WHOLESALE ~.

DISTRIBUTION AND SALE TO THE PUBLIC. Distribution and sale (a) to a person or persons with whom the vendor deals at arm's length, or (b) to a person or persons with whom the vendor does not deal at arm's length for resale directly or indirectly to persons with whom the vendor does deal at arm's length. *Public Utilities Income Tax Transfer Act*, R.S.C. 1985, c. P-37, s. 2.

DISTRIBUTION CHARGE. A charge on inbound goods in respect of (a) sorting the goods within the main mark or other than within the main mark, or (b) breaking down piles of goods to reach certain marks or specifically numbered packages. *Pacific Terminal Tariff By-law*, C.R.C., c. 1083, s. 41.

DISTRIBUTION COMPANY. A person or company distributing securities under a distribution contract. *Securities acts.*

DISTRIBUTION CONTRACT. A contract between a mutual fund or its trustees or other legal representative and a person or company under which that person or company is granted the right to purchase the shares or units of the mutual fund for distribution or to distribute the shares or units of the mutual fund on behalf of the mutual fund. *Securities acts.*

DISTRIBUTION EQUIPMENT. Posts, pipes, wires, transmission mains, distribution mains and other apparatus of a public utility used to supply service to the utility customers. *Utilities Commission Act*, S.B.C. 1980, c. 60, s. 1.

DISTRIBUTION LINE. 1. A pipe used for transmitting gas for domestic, commercial or industrial purposes and includes the installations in connection with that pipe. *Pipeline Amendment Act, 1984*, S.A. 1984, c. 32, s. 2. 2. A pipe used for transmitting gas for domestic, commercial or industrial purposes from a gas line, secondary line or a well and includes the installations in connection therewith, but does not include any pipe or installation on, within or under a building. *Pipe Line Act*, S.N.B. 1976, c. P-8.1, s. 1.

DISTRIBUTION MAIN. Pipe used for the transmission and distribution of gas at a pressure not exceeding 700 kPa (gauge), for any distance between a city gate and a service pipe. *Gas Act*, R.S.B.C. 1979, c. 149, s. 1.

DISTRIBUTION NETWORK. The whole of the pipes, except those mentioned in paragraph k, and of the equipment, machines, structures, gasometers, meters and other devices and accessories installed in a given territory and used for the distribution of gas to consumers in such territory. *Gas Distribution Act*, R.S.Q. 1977, c. D-10, s. 1.

DISTRIBUTION OF POWERS. The division of legislative powers between regional authorities (provincial legislatures) and a central authority (the federal Parliament) which is the essence of a federal constitution, binds the regional and central authorities, and cannot be altered by the unilateral action of any one of them. P.W. Hogg, *Constitutional Law of Canada*, 2d ed. (Toronto: Carswell, 1985) at 309 and 310.

DISTRIBUTION PIPELINE. See LOW PRESSURE ~.

DISTRIBUTION SYSTEM. 1. A system for the supply of electric energy to premises in a city, town, village or hamlet or on a farm, from an electrical generating plant or main substation existing for the purpose of supplying such premises. 2. A system for the supply of gas to consumers' premises from collection or transmission systems. 3. A cable network that carries a signal from the head end into the dwellings of subscribers who pay the cable company rent for the service. P.W. Hogg, *Constitutional Law of Canada*, 2d ed. (Toronto: Carswell, 1985) at 504. See ALLOWABLE ~ PRESSURE; ELECTRIC ~; GAS ~; RURAL ~.

DISTRIBUTION TO THE PUBLIC. 1. Where used in relation to trading in securities, means a distribution that is made for the purpose of distributing to the public securities issued by an issuer, where such trades are made directly or indirectly to the public through an underwriter or otherwise. 2. (a) A transaction or series of transactions entered into for the purpose of distributing to the public securities issued by a corporation (i) that have not previously been distributed to the public, or (ii) that have previously been distributed to the public but have subsequently been redeemed or purchased by the issuer, or (b) a transaction or series of transactions in previously distributed securities of a corporation entered into for the purpose of distributing such securities to the public where the securities form all or part of or are derived from the holdings of any person or group of persons who act in concert and who hold a sufficient number of any of the securities of the corporation to materially affect the control of the corporation, whether such transactions are made directly with members of the public or indirectly through an underwriter or otherwise, and includes any transaction or series of transactions involving a purchase and sale or a repurchase and resale in the course of or that are incidental to the distribution. *Bank Act*, R.S.C. 1985, c. B-1, s. 190. See GENERATION AND SALE FOR ~.

DISTRIBUTOR. *n.* 1. A person engaged in the business of selling to other persons, for the purpose of resale. 2. A person engaged in selling or distributing a product directly or indirectly to consumers. See AUTOMATIC ~; ELECTRICITY ~; MOTION PICTURE ~; MUTUAL FUND ~; PROMOTIONAL ~; PYRAMID ~; RETAIL ~; VIDEO ~; WHOLESALE ~.

DISTRICT. *n.* 1. A regional administrative unit. 2. A judicial district. 3. A local improvement district. 4. A school district. See BILINGUAL ~; BUILT-UP ~; BUSINESS ~; ELECTORAL ~; HISTORIC ~; INDIAN ~; JUDICIAL ~; LAND USE ~; LOCAL IMPROVEMENT ~; MULTI-MEMBER ~; NATURAL ~; POLLING ~; RESIDENCE ~; RURAL ~; SINGLE MEMBER ~; TOWN ~; UNORGANIZED ~; URBAN ~; VILLAGE ~.

DISTRICT ASSOCIATION. An association of persons supporting an authorized political party in an electoral district.

DISTRICT COLLECTOR. A collector having jurisdiction over the ports within a customs district. Canada regulations.

DISTRICT COUNCIL. An organization of union locals in a particular geographical area.

DISTRICT COURT. 1. A court limited in territorial jurisdiction and by subject matter. P.W. Hogg, *Constitutional Law of Canada*, 2d ed. (Toronto: Carswell, 1985) at 134. 2. District Court sitting in the county or district in which the land is located. *Municipal Tax Sales Act*, S.O. 1984, c. 48, s. 1.

DISTRICT COURT OF ONTARIO. An amalgamation of the county and district courts, the courts of general sessions of the peace and the county and district court judges' criminal courts into a single court of record. G.D. Watson & C. Perkins, eds., *Holmested & Watson: Ontario Civil Procedure* (Toronto: Carswell, 1984) at CJA-42 and 43.

DISTRICT INSPECTOR. The principal inspector for a district. *Canada Grain Regulations*, C.R.C., c. 889, s. 2.

DISTRICTIS. *n.* Distraint; distress.

DISTRICT MUNICIPALITY. A municipality, except a city, in a territorial district. *Education Act*, R.S.O. 1980, c. 129, s. 1.

DISTRICT OR COUNTY. Includes any territorial or judicial division or place in and for which there is such judge, justice, justice's court, officer, or prison, as is mentioned in the context.

DISTRICT OR ELECTORAL DISTRICT. Includes any territorial or judicial division or place in and for which there is such justice of the peace, officer or house of detention as is mentioned in the context. *Summary Convictions Act*, R.S.Q. 1977, c. P-15, s. 1.

DISTRICT OR SPLIT. A part of an underground mine having an independent intake airway commencing from a main intake airway, and an independent return airway terminating at a main return airway. *Coal Mines Regulation Act*, R.S.A. 1970, c. 52, s. 2.

DISTRICT PLAN. A plan for a district within the city or the additional zone which consists of text and maps or illustrations formulating in such detail as the council thinks appropriate, proposals for the development and use of land in the district, and a description of the measures which the council considers should be undertaken for the improvement of the physical, social and economic environment and transportation within the district. *City of Winnipeg Act*, S.M. 1971, c. 105, s. 569.

DISTRINGAS. [L. that you distrain]. A writ directing a sheriff to distrain on a certain person for a particular purpose.

DISTURBANCE. *n.* 1. Infringement of an easement, franchise, profit à prendre or similar right. 2. A disturbance of the peace and quiet of the occupants of an inn by fighting, screaming, shouting, singing or otherwise causing loud noise. *Innkeepers Act*, R.S.A. 1980, c. I-4, s. 9. 3. Causing a tenant to leave through force, menace, persuasion or otherwise. See GROUND ~; SURFACE ~.

DITCH. *n.* 1. A drain open or covered wholly or in part whether in the channel or a natural stream, creek or watercourse or not, and includes the work and material necessary for bridges, culverts, catch basins and guards. 2. Includes a flume, pipe, race or other artificial means for conducting water by its own weight, to be used for mining purposes. 3. A ditch open or covered wholly or in part, whether in the channel of a natural stream, creek or watercourse or not, heretofore or hereafter constructed, repaired, maintained or improved, and all the work and materials necessary for any bridge, culvert, catch basin or guards connected therewith. See DRAINAGE ~.

DIV. *abbr.* Divisional.

DIV. & MATR. CAUSES CT. *abbr.* Divorce and Matrimonial Causes Court.

DIV. CT. *abbr.* Divisional Court.

DIVERGENCE. *n.* With respect to a laser beam, means the full angle of spread of the beam. *Radiation Emitting Devices Regulations*, C.R.C., c. 1370, s. 1.

DIVERS. *adj.* [Fr.] Various, sundry.

DIVERSION. *n.* The taking or removing of water from any river, stream, lake or body of water that is the property of the Province, by means of any mechanical contrivance of works, and includes the impounding of water. *Water Resources Act*, R.S.A. 1970, c. 388, s. 2.

DIVERSITY. *n.* A prisoner's plea to bar execution, alleging that it was another who was attainted.

DIVERT. *v.* 1. Or a word of similar import, means to take water from a stream, and includes to cause water to leave the channel of a stream and make a change in or about the channel that permits water to leave it. 2. Includes take, remove, and impound. See TEMPORARY ~ ED.

DIVEST. *v.* 1. To take away; to deprive. 2. To remove an estate or interest which was already vested in a person.

DIVIDED COURT. Applied to a court consisting of more than one judge when the decision or opinion of the court is not unanimous.

DIVIDEND. *n.* 1. The division of profits of a corporation or trust. 2. A distribution by a corporation of its profits and surplus funds to its shareholders in accordance with their interests. S.M. Beck *et al*, *Cases and Materials on Partnerships and Canadian Business Corporations,* (Toronto: The Carswell Company Limited, 1983) at 814. 3. Includes bonus or any distribution to shareholders as such. 4. Without restricting the ordinary meaning thereof, includes an amount payable, or subject to be credited, by an insurer to its insured and that is composed in whole or in part of a portion of the amount previously paid by the insured as a premium or as a deposit or payment under a reciprocal contract of indemnity or inter-insurance. *The Insurance Premiums Tax Act*, R.S.S. 1978, c. I-10, s. 2. 5. Includes a stock dividend and any other form of corporate distribution otherwise than upon the winding-up of a corporation or the discontinuance of its business. *Anti-Inflation Act*, S.C. 1974-75-76, c. 75, s. 2. See ACCRUED ~; ACCUMULATED ~; ACCUMULATIVE ~; CASH ~; CUM ~; ~S; EXCLUDED ~; INTERIM ~; NONCUMULATIVE ~; SCRIP ~; STOCK ~; TAXABLE ~.

DIVIDENDA. *n.* [L.] One section of an indenture.

DIVIDEND RIGHT. See UNLIMITED ~.

DIVIDENDS. *n.* Includes all payments made by the name of dividend, bonus or otherwise out of revenues of trading or other public companies divisible between all or any of the members, whether such payments are usually made or declared at any fixed times or otherwise, but does not include payments in the nature of a return or reimbursement of capital. Apportionment acts. See DIVIDEND.

DIVIDING LINE. See DIRECTIONAL ~.

DIVINATIO, NON INTERPRETATIO EST, QUAE OMNINO RECEDIT A LITERA. [L.] An interpretation which departs totally from the original is a guess, not an interpretation.

DIVING BOARD. A flexible board. *Public Health Act*, R.R.O. 1980, Reg. 849, s. 1.

DIVING PLATFORM. A rigid platform. *Public Health Act*, R.R.O. 1980, Reg. 849, s. 1.

DIVISA. *n.* [L.] 1. An award, device or decree. 2. A devise. 3. Limits or bounds of a farm or parish. 4. A court held on a boundary in order to settle tenants' disputes.

DIVISION. *n.* 1. A Parliamentary roll call necessary if the Speaker cannot decide from the members' voices if the motion was carried or lost. A. Fraser, G.A. Birch & W.A. Dawson, eds., *Beauchesne's Rules and Forms of the House of Commons of Canada*, 5th ed. (Toronto: Carswell, 1978) at 75. 2. A group of grades taught in a school and into which the school grades are divided. 3. The territory in and for which a small claims court is prescribed. *Small Claims Court Act*, R.S.O. 1980, c. 476, s. 1. 4. An administrative unit. 5. That portion of a railway assigned to the supervision of a Superintendent or other designated officer. *Regulations No. O-8, Uniform Code of Operating Rules*, C.R.C., c. 1175, Part III, c. 2. See EASTERN ~; ELECTORAL ~; ESTATES ~; EXCISE ~; INTERMEDIATE ~; JUNIOR ~; POLLING ~; PRIMARY ~; SENIOR ~; TERRITORIAL ~; TRADE ~; TRIAL ~; WESTERN ~.

DIVISIONAL COURT. A division of the High Court of Ontario.

DIVORCE. *n.* 1. The termination of a marriage by law. 2. Dissolution and annulment of marriage and includes nullity of marriage. *Vital Statistics Act*, R.S.O. 1980, c. 524, s. 1. See CONTESTED ~; NO-FAULT ~; UNCONTESTED ~.

DIVORCE PROCEEDING. A proceeding in a court in which either or both spouses seek a divorce alone or together with a support order or a custody order or both such orders. *Divorce Act*, R.S.C. 1985 (2d Supp.), c. 3, s. 2.

D.L.Q. *abbr.* Droits et libertés au Québec.

D.L.R. *abbr.* Dominion Law Reports, 1912-1922.

[ ] D.L.R. *abbr.* Dominion Law Reports, 1923-1955.

D.L.R. (4TH). *abbr.* Dominion Law Reports (Fourth Series), 1984-.

D.L.R. (2D). *abbr.* Dominion Law Reports (Second Series), 1956-1968.

D.L.R. (3D). *abbr.* Dominion Law Reports (Third Series), 1969-1984.

DND. *abbr.* Department of National Defence.

D.O.A. *abbr.* Dead on arrival.

DOC. *abbr.* Department of Communications.

DOCK. *n.* 1. The physical location in which a prisoner is placed during trial in a criminal court. 2. Includes wet docks and basins, tidal-docks and basins, locks, cuts, entrances, dry docks, graving docks, gridirons, slips, quays, wharfs, piers, stages, landing places and jetties. *Canada Shipping Act*, R.S.C. 1985, c. S-9, s. 578(4). 3. Includes a groyne, wharf, jetty, gabion, and any like structure that is affixed to, floating on or suspended over public lands. *Provincial Parks Act*, R.R.O. 1980, Reg. 822, s. 1. 4. Includes floating dry docks. *Dry Dock Subsidies Act*, R.S.C. 1985, c. D-4, s. 2. See DRY ~; OWNERS OF A ~ OR CANAL.

DOCKAGE. *n.* 1. Any material intermixed with a parcel of grain, other than kernels of grain of a standard or quality fixed by or under this Act for a grade of that grain, that must and can be separated from the parcel of grain before that grade can be assigned to the grain. *Canada Grain Act*, R.S.C. 1985, c. G-10, s. 2. 2. The charge on a vessel while occupying a berth or while fast to or tied up alongside any other vessel occupying a berth at the wharf. Canada regulations.

DOCKET. *v.* To make a list of entries; to keep track of time spent on matters.

DOCKET. *n.* 1. A record of the time and disbursements a lawyer spent on a particular matter. 2. A list of cases to be heard.

DOCKING. *n.* 1. Deduction from wages as a penalty. 2. The manoeuvring of a ship to a berth. See UN ~.

DOCK WARRANT. A document resembling a bill of lading and issued by a dock owner or dock company authorizing delivery of certain goods to a named person or to that person's assigns by endorsement.

DOCTOR. *n.* Medical practitioner; physician; surgeon.

DOCTRINE. See CLEAN HANDS ~; EQUITABLE ~ OF CONSTRUCTIVE NOTICE.

DOCTRINE OF SHELTERING. Anyone who buys with notice from another person who bought without notice can be sheltered under the first buyer. W.B. Rayner & R.H. McLaren, *Falconbridge on Mortgages*, 4th ed. (Toronto: Canada Law Book, 1977) at 149.

DOCTRINE OF SUBROGATION. If a mortgagee or unpaid vendor insures an interest in property and receives insurance money when a loss occurs, and if that mortgagee or vendor afterwards receives the mortgage money or the purchase price with no deduction on account of the insurance, that mortgagee or vendor is liable to the insurer for a sum equal to the insurance money received, because one is not entitled to more than full indemnification. W.B. Rayner & R.H. McLaren, *Falconbridge on Mortgages*, 4th ed. (Toronto: Canada Law Book, 1977) at 792.

DOCTRINE OF THE TABULA IN NAUFRAGIO. An equitable mortgagee who takes with no notice of an earlier equitable mortgage may get in the legal estate and in some cases obtain priority over the earlier mortgagee. W.B. Rayner & R.H. McLaren, *Falconbridge on Mortgages*, 4th ed. (Toronto: Canada Law Book, 1977) at 126.

DOCUMENT. *n.* 1. Any paper, parchment or other material on which is recorded or marked anything that is capable of being read or understood by a person, computer system or other device, and includes a credit card, but does not include trade-marks on articles of commerce or inscriptions on stone or metal or other like material. *Criminal Law Amendment Act*, R.S.C. 1985 (1st Supp.), c. 27, s. 42. 2. Includes a plan of survey and any certificate, affidavit, statutory declaration or other proof as to the birth, baptism, marriage, divorce, death, burial, descendants or pedigree of any person, or as to the existence or non-existence, happening or non-happening of any fact, event or occurrence upon which the title to land may depend, a notice of sale, or other notice necessary to the exercise of any power of sale or appointment or other power relating to land, and a receipt for payment of money under a registered instrument. *Registry Act*, R.S.O. 1980, c. 445, s. 98. 3. Includes an assignment, a renewal statement, an affidavit and a certificate of discharge. *Assignment of Book Debts acts*. 4. Includes books, maps, plans, drawings, and photographs. 5. Includes summons, notice, order, certificate, register and legal process. *Companies acts*. 6. In addition to its usual meaning, includes an entry in a book or a register. 7. An order, regulation, bylaw, rule, schedule, contract, report, return or statement, or a copy thereof, or an amendment thereto or a copy of an amendment thereto, or any other document, that is required by any Act to be laid before or submitted to the Legislative Assembly at any session. *The Tabling of Documents Act*, R.S.S. 1978, c. T-1, s. 2. 8. Includes a sound recording, videotape, film, photograph, chart, graph, map, plan, survey, book of account and information recorded or stored by means of any device. *Environment Enforcement Statute Law Amendment Act*, S.O. 1986, c. 68, s. 1. See ACTIVE ~; CARTOGRAPHIC RECORD OR ~; DEFECT IN A ~; ~S; ELECTION ~; FALSE ~; FOREIGN-BASED INFORMATION OR ~; IDENTIFICATION ~; INACTIVE ~; MANUSCRIPT, RECORD, OR ~; OFFICIAL ~; ORIGINATING ~; PHOTOGRAPHIC RECORD OR ~; PICTORIAL RECORD OR ~; PUBLIC ~; REGISTERED ~; RESPONDING ~; SECURITY ~; SEMI-ACTIVE ~; SHIPPING ~; STATE ~.

DOCUMENTARY CREDIT. A conditional letter of credit providing that any draft drawn under it may be negotiated only if bills of lading, invoices and insurance policies valued at least equally to the draft accompany the draft.

DOCUMENTARY EVIDENCE. A document or paper adduced to prove its contents. P.K. McWilliams, *Canadian Criminal Evidence*, 3d ed. (Aurora: Canada Law Book, 1988) at 1-12.

DOCUMENTED. See PROPERLY ~.

DOCUMENT OF CONVEYANCE. Any instrument by which a land holding is or may be acquired and includes a trust document but does not include a will or testamentary document. *Land Holdings Disclosure Act*, S.N.S. 1969, c. 13, s. 1.

DOCUMENT OF RECORDED SOUND. (a) An object that consists of one or more recorded sequences enregistered at one time or sequentially over a period of time on or in a single object, (b) objects of recorded sound issued in a set under a single title irrespective of the date or dates of recording of the individual units in the set, or (c) a collection of physically separated objects of recorded sound where the collection clearly forms a single unit. *Canadian Cultural Property Export Control List*, C.R.C., c. 448, s. 1.

DOCUMENT OF TITLE. 1. Includes any bill of lading, dock warrant, warehousekeeper's certificate and warrant or order for the delivery of goods and any other document used in the ordinary course of business as proof of the possession or control of goods, or authorizing or purporting to authorize, either by endorsement or by delivery, the possessor of the document to transfer or receive goods thereby represented. 2. Any writing that purports to be issued by or addressed to a bailee and purports to cover such goods in the bailee's possession as are identified or fungible portions of an identified mass, and that in the ordinary course of business is treated as establishing that the person in possession of it is entitled to receive, hold and dispose of the document and the goods it covers. *Personal Property Security acts*.

DOCUMENT OF TITLE TO GOODS. 1. Includes a bought and sold note, bill of lading, warrant, certificate or order for the delivery or transfer of goods or any other valuable thing, and any other document used in the ordinary course of business as evidence of the possession or control of goods, authorizing or purporting to authorize, by endorsement or by delivery, the person in possession of the document to transfer or receive any goods thereby represented or therein mentioned or referred to. *Criminal Code*, R.S.C. 1985, c. C-46, s. 2. 2. Any bill of lading, dock warrant, warehouse keeper's certificate, and warrant or order for the delivery of goods, and any other document used in the ordinary course of business as proof of the possession or control of goods, or authorizing or purporting to authorize, either by endorsement or by delivery, the possessor of the document to transfer or receive goods thereby represented. *Sale of Goods acts*.

DOCUMENT OF TITLE TO LANDS. Includes any writing that is or contains evidence of the title, or any part of the title, to real property, and any notarial or registrar's copy thereof and any duplicate instrument, memorial, certificate or document authorized or required by any law in force in any part of Canada with respect to registration of titles that relates to title to real property or to any interest in real property.

DOCUMENT OF TRANSMISSION. (a) A document to be granted or issued by any court or competent authority in Canada or elsewhere and being (i) letters probate of the will of the deceased person, (ii) letters of administration of the estate of the deceased person, or (iii) any other judicial or official instrument under which the title, whether beneficial or as trustee, or the administration or control of the personal estate of the deceased person is claimed to vest or to be confirmed; (b) a copy of any document described in paragraph (a), or an extract therefrom, purporting to be authenticated under the seal of the court or competent authority; or (c) a notarial copy of the will of the deceased person, if the will is in notarial or authentic form according to the law of the Province of Quebec. *Loan Companies Act*, R.S.C. 1985, c. L-12, s. 42.

DOCUMENTS. *n.* Includes any of the following, whether computerized or not: books, records, writings, vouchers, invoices, accounts and statements, financial or otherwise. See AFFIDAVIT OF ~; CASH AGAINST ~; DOCUMENT; ELECTION ~.

DOCUMENT UNDER THE SIGN-MANUAL. An instrument, in respect of Canada, that, under the present practice, is issued in the name and under the signature of Her Majesty the Queen without any seal. *Seals Act*, R.S.C. 1985, c. S-6, s. 2.

DOG. *n.* 1. A dog, male or female, and includes an animal that is a cross between a dog and a wolf. 2. Any of the species Canis familiaris Linnaeus. See GUARD ~; GUIDE ~; HEARING ~; HUSKY ~; OWNER OF A ~; SLEIGH ~.

DOGFISH. *n.* A fish of the species the family name of which is (Squalidae). *Northwest Atlantic Fisheries Regulations*, C.R.C., c. 860, s. 2.

DOGFISH REDUCTION PLANT. A building, structure, machinery, appurtenances, appliances and apparatus occupied and used in the business of producing oil, fish meal, fish scrap, chicken feed or fertilizer from dogfish. *Fisheries Act*, R.S.B.C. 1979, c. 137, s. 12.

DOG GUIDE. A dog trained to guide a visually handicapped person.

DOGWOOD. *n.* The shrub or tree, Cornus nuttallii, commonly known as western flowering dogwood. *Dogwood, Rhododendron and Trillium Protection Act*, R.S.B.C. 1979, c. 96, s. 1.

DOING BUSINESS. The transaction of any of the ordinary business of a corporation or person, including franchises, whether or not by means of an employee or an agent and whether or not the corporation or person has a resident agent or representative or a warehouse, office or place of business in the province. *Licensing Act*, S.P.E.I. 1976, c. 18, s. 2.

DOLE. *n.* 1. The act of distributing. 2. An allotment. 3. Unemployment benefits or welfare assistance.

DOLI CAPAX. [L.] Capable of a criminal act.

DOLI INCAPAX. [L.] Not capable of a criminal act.

DOLLAR. *n.* A money unit equivalent to one hundred cents. See EURO-~.

DOLLY. See TRAILER CONVERTER ~.

DOLO MALO PACTUM SE NON SERVATURUM. [L.] A contract arising through fraudulent deceit will not be upheld.

DOLOSUS VERSATUR IN GENERALIBUS. [L.] A person intending to deceive uses general terms.

DOLUS. *n.* [L.] Fraud; guilt; wilful injury.

DOLUS CIRCUITU NON PURGATUR. [L.] Fraud is not excused by going a roundabout way.

DOLUS DANS LOCUM CONTRACTUI. [L.] Fraud or deceit which gives rise to a contract.

DOM. *abbr.* Dominion.

DOMESTIC. *n.* 1. A natural person engaged by an individual for remuneration, whose main duty is, in the dwelling of the individual, (1) to do housework, or (2) to care for a child or a sick, handicapped or aged person and who lives in the dwelling. *An Act Respecting Industrial Accidents and Occupational Diseases*, S.Q. 1985, c. 6, s. 2. 2. An employee in the employ of a natural person whose main function is the performance of domestic duties in the dwelling of that person; this word does not, however, include an employee whose main duty is the care of a child, or of a disabled, handicapped or aged person. *An Act respecting labour standards*, S.Q. 1979, c. 45, s. 1.

DOMESTIC AIRSPACE. See CANADIAN ~.

DOMESTIC AMENDING FORMULA. A procedure to amend the Constitution in Canada without the need to involve the British Parliament.

DOMESTIC ANIMAL. 1. A horse, a dog or any other animal that is kept under human control or by habit or training lives in association with man. 2. Cattle, horses, swine, sheep, goats and poultry.

DOMESTIC CADIZ. *abbr.* Domestic Canadian Air Defence Identification Zone.

DOMESTIC CANADIAN AIR DEFENCE IDENTIFICATION ZONE. The airspace extending upward from the surface of the earth in that area of Canada described in Schedule II. *Security Control of Air Traffic Order*, C.R.C., c. 63, s. 2.

DOMESTIC COMPANY. Any body corporate that (i) is incorporated by or under any Act of Newfoundland or Province of Newfoundland, as the case may be, other than the former Act or this Act, and (ii) is not an agent of Her Majesty in right of the Province. *Corporations Act*, S. Nfld. 1986, c. 12, s. 429.

DOMESTIC CONTRACT. A cohabitation agreement, marriage contract, separation agreement or agreement between a deceased spouse's administrator or executor and the surviving spouse. A. Bissett-Johnson & W.M. Holland, eds, *Matrimonial Property Law in Canada* (Toronto: Carswell, 1980) at N-93.

DOMESTIC CORPORATION. A body corporate that is incorporated by or under the authority of an Act of the Legislature of Nova Scotia, and has gain for its purpose or object. *Corporations Registration Act*, R.S.N.S. 1967, c. 59, s. 28.

DOMESTIC ESTABLISHMENT. See SELF-CONTAINED ~.

DOMESTIC FISHING. Fishing for personal use but not for sale or barter. *Northwest Territories Fishery Regulations*, C.R.C., c. 847, s. 2.

DOMESTIC FISHING LICENCE. A licence authorizing a person to engage in domestic fishing. *Northwest Territories Fishery Regulations*, C.R.C., c. 847, s. 2.

DOMESTIC FLIGHT. A flight between points in Canada. *Air Services Fees Regulations*, C.R.C., c. 5, s. 2.

DOMESTIC FOURTH CLASS MAIL. All mailable matter, weighing more than 1 pound and not requiring payment at the first class mail rate or acceptable at second or third class mail rates, that is posted in Canada in accordance with these Regulations for delivery in Canada.

Fourth Class Mail Regulations, C.R.C., c. 1279, s. 2.

DOMESTIC HEN. The hen of the domestic chicken of the species Gallus domesticus.

DOMESTIC JURISDICTION. The sphere in which sovereign nations may act freely.

DOMESTIC PETROLEUM. Petroleum from a natural reservoir in Canada and petroleum produced, extracted, recovered or manufactured in Canada otherwise than from a natural reservoir. *Energy Administration Act*, R.S.C. 1985, c. E-6, s. 56.

DOMESTIC PURCHASER. A purchaser of bunker fuel, crude oil, propane or marked or coloured motive fuel who uses it solely to heat a dwelling unit in which he resides. *Motive Fuel Tax Act*, R.S.M. 1970, c. M220, s. 2.

DOMESTIC PURPOSE. 1. The use of water for household requirements, sanitation and fire prevention, the watering of domestic animals and poultry and the irrigation of a garden. 2. The use of water for normal household requirements, including sanitation, human consumption and food preparation. *Health Act*, R.S.B.C. 1979, c. 161, s. 21. 3. Household and sanitary purposes, and all purposes connected with the watering of stock and the working of agricultural machinery by steam, but does not include the sale or barter of water for such purposes. *Water Rights acts*. 4. With reference to heating oil, means the use of heating oil in domestic appliances or for heating or lighting premises used as a private dwelling. *Fuel Oil Administration Act*, R.S.A. 1980, c. F-21, s. 16.

DOMESTIC SERVANT. A person who is employed by a householder, (i) as a sitter to attend primarily to the needs of a child who is a member of the household, (ii) as a companion to attend to the needs of an aged, infirm or ill member of the household, or (iii) as a domestic to perform services in the household who works twenty-four hours a week or less. *Employment Standards Act*, R.R.O. 1980, Reg. 285, s. 1.

DOMESTIC THIRD CLASS MAIL. Mailable matter that consists of books and weighs 35 pounds or less and all other mailable matter that (a) weighs 1 pound or less, (b) does not require payment at the first class mail rate, (c) is not acceptable at second class mail rates, and (d) is posted in Canada in accordance with these Regulations for delivery in Canada. *Third Class Mail Regulations*, C.R.C., c. 1297, s. 2.

DOMESTIC USE. The use of waters for household requirements, sanitation and fire prevention, for the watering of domestic animals and poultry and for irrigation of a garden adjoining a dwelling-house that is not ordinarily used in the growth of produce for a market, but does not include the sale or barter of waters for any such use. *Northern Inland Waters Act*, R.S.C. 1985, c. N-25, s. 2.

DOMESTIC WASTE. Any waste other than industrial waste. *Arctic Waters Pollution Prevention Regulations*, C.R.C., c. 354, s. 3.

DOMESTIC WASTE WATER. Waste water from the plumbing system of a building and not mixed with underground, surface, rain or cooling water nor with industrial waste water. *An Act to Amend the Act Respecting the Communauté Urbaine de Montréal and Other Legislation*, S.Q. 1985, c. 31, s. 11.

DOMESTIC WINE. Wine fermented in Canada. *Manufacturers in Bond Regulations*, C.R.C., c. 575, s. 2.

DOMESTIC WORKSHOP. Every establishment in which only the members of the family are employed, either under the authority of the father or mother, or of the tutor or guardian, provided such establishment be not classed as dangerous, unhealthy, or incommodious, or that the work be not done by means of steam boilers or other motors. *Industrial and Commercial Establishments Act*, R.S.Q. 1977, c. E-15, s. 2.

DOMICILE. *n.* A person's permanent home or principal establishment to which that person intends to return after every absence. See ELECTION OF ~; PLACE OF ~.

DOMICILE BY REVERTER. The domicile of a person who loses a domicile and does not immediately acquire another. J.G. McLeod, *The Conflict of Laws* (Calgary: Carswell, 1983) at 143.

DOMICILED COMPANY. Any company, corporation or body politic, wherever and however incorporated or constituted (i) whose head office, principal place of business or statutory domicile is declared to be located or situated within the province by its memorandum of association, letters patent of incorporation, charter, articles of association, bylaws, or otherwise, or which keeps or causes to be kept within the province a principal or branch transfer agency or register or other transfer agency or register of issued securities, (ii) that maintains, keeps or locates or causes to be maintained, kept or located in an office within the province of a trust company incorporated under the laws of the province or licensed to carry on business in the province, such head office or principal place of business or statutory domicile or any such transfer agency or register, and (iii) whose business and assets are not situated or carried on in the province save as hereinafter provided, and of which ninety-five per cent in number and value of the issued securities are owned by non-resident persons or by a domiciled company or are owned and held by trusts or trustees for the benefit of non-resident persons, or non-resident persons and persons not yet born. *Domiciled Companies Act*, R.S.P.E.I. 1974, c. D-16, s. 1.

DOMICILE OF CHOICE. The domicile of one presently intending to reside indefinitely or permanently in the country. J.G. McLeod, *The Conflict of Laws* (Calgary: Carswell, 1983) at 159.

DOMICILE OF DEPENDENCY. A person's domicile, after domicile of origin, which the law still regards that the person could not select himself or herself. J.G. McLeod, *The Conflict of Laws* (Calgary: Carswell, 1983) at 143.

DOMICILE OF ORIGIN. A person's first domicile, determined by birth. J.G. McLeod, *The Conflict of Laws* (Calgary: Carswell, 1983) at 143.

DOMICILE OF THE CHILD. The last place of residence of his father and mother, tutor or guardian, during twelve consecutive months. *Youth Protection Act*, R.S.Q. 1977, c. P-34, s. 1.

DOMINA. *n.* [L.] The former title of a woman who was a peeress in her own right; a dame.

DOMINANT POSITION. A person is said to have a dominant position when he holds more than 20% of the voting securities of the offeree issuer. The securities owned by a person's associate must be included in computing the percentage of the person's holdings. *Securities Act*, S.Q. 1982, s. 48, s. 110.

DOMINANT TENEMENT. A subject or tenement to the benefit of which an easement or servitude is constituted.

DOMINICAL. *adj.* Belonging to the Lord's Day, or Sunday.

DOMINICUM. *n.* [L.] Demesne.

DOMINION. *n.* 1. Any of the following Dominions, that is to say, the Dominion of Canada, the Commonwealth of Australia, the Dominion of New Zealand, the Union of South Africa, the Irish Free State and Newfoundland. *Statute of Westminster, 1931*, (U.K.), 22 Geo. 5, c. 4, s. 1, reprinted in R.S.C. 1985, App. Doc. No. 27. 2. Dominion of Canada. *Interpretation Act*, R.S.Q. 1977, c. I-16, s. 61. 3. Includes kingdom, empire, republic, commonwealth, state, province, territory, colony, possession, and protectorate heretofore or now existing or hereafter constituted; and, where parts of a dominion are under both a central and a local legislature, includes both all parts under the central legislature and each part under a local legislature. *Evidence Act*, R.S.N.B. 1973, c. E-11, s. 71. See HER MAJESTY'S ~.

DOMINION COMPANY. A company incorporated by or under an Act of the Parliament of Canada.

DOMINION CORPORATION. A body corporate that is incorporated by or under the authority of an Act of the Parliament of Canada, and has gain for its purpose or object. *Corporations Registration Act*, R.S.N.S. 1967, c. 59, s. 28.

DOMINION FIRE COMMISSIONER. The officer designated by the Minister of Public Works to administer the Government Property Fire Prevention Regulations. Canada regulations.

DOMINION GEODESIST. The Dominion Geodesist and Director of the Geodetic Survey, in the Department of Energy, Mines and Resources. *Territorial Land Use Regulations*, C.R.C., c. 1524, s. 2.

DOMINION TIMBER BERTH. Any area for which a licence or permit was granted by the Dominion of Canada prior to the fifteenth day of July, 1930, for the cutting of timber. *Forest Act*, R.S.M. 1970, c. F150, s. 2.

DOMINION WATER-POWERS. Any waterpowers on public lands, or any other waterpowers that are the property of Canada and have been or may be placed under the control and management of the Minister. *Dominion Water Powers Act*, R.S.C. 1985, c. W-4, s. 2.

DOMINIUM. *n.* [L.] Absolute ownership.

DOMINIUM NON POTEST ESSE IN PENDENTI. [L.] Ownership cannot be held in suspense.

DOMINUS LITIS. [L. master of the suit] One who has control over a judicial proceeding or an action.

DOMINUS NAVIS. [L.] A ship's absolute owner.

DOM. PROC. *abbr.* Domus Procerum.

DOMUS PROCERUM. [L.] The British House of Lords.

DOMUS SUA CUIQUE EST TUTISSIMUM REFUGIUM. [L.] To every person, one's house is one's surest refuge.

DONA CLANDESTINA SUNT SEMPER SUSPICIOSA. [L.] Clandestine gifts are always suspicious.

DONARI VIDETUR, QUOD NULLO JURE COGENTE CONCEDITUR. [L.] A thing is considered to be given when it is transferred any way except by virtue of a right.

DONATIO. *n.* [L.] Gift.

DONATIO INTER VIVOS. [L.] A gift between persons still living.

DONATIO MORTIS CAUSA. [L.] A gift made in contemplation of the death of the donor, to take effect only upon the death of the donor.

DONATION. *n.* Includes any gift, testamentary disposition, deed, trust or other form of contribution.

DONATIONES SUNT STRICTI JURIS, NE QUIS PLUS DONASSE PRAESUMATUR, QUAM IN DONATIONE EXPRESSIT. [L.] Gifts are to be strictly examined to prevent a person being presumed to have given more than is expressed in the grant.

DONATION IN KIND. Any property other than money given or provided to or for the benefit of a recognized party or a candidate without compensation from the recognized party or candidate, and includes services of an employee of the taxpayer provided to a recognized party or a candidate without compensation from the recognized party or candidate.

DONATIO NON PRAESUMITUR. [L.] A gift is not enjoyed beforehand.

DONATIO PERFICITUR POSSESSIONE ACCIPIENTIS. [L.] A gift is perfected when the donee possesses the subject-matter.

DONATIO PROPTER NUPTIAM. [L.] A gift on account of marriage.

DONATIVE PROMISE. A promise to confer a benefit by gift. G.H.L. Fridman, *The Law of Contract in Canada*, 2d ed. (Toronto: Carswell, 1986) at 73.

DONATOR NUNQUAM DESINIT POSSIDERE ANTEQUAM DONATARIUS INCIPIAT POSSIDERE. [L.] The donor never ceases to have possession until the receiver begins to possess.

DONEE. *n.* 1. Any person who receives or has received the benefit of a gift, including a gift deemed, for the purposes of this Act, to have been made. *Gift Tax acts.* 2. One to whom a gift is made. 3. A person to whom a power of appointment is given is sometimes called the donee of the power.

DONOR. *n.* 1. One who gives. 2. Any individual who makes or has made a gift, including a gift deemed, for the purposes of this Act, to have been made. *Gift Tax acts.* 3. A person who, (i) in writing at any time, or (ii) orally in the presence of at least two witnesses during his last illness, has requested that his body or a specified part or parts thereof be used after his death for therapeutic purposes or for the purposes of

medical education or research. *Human Tissue acts.*

DOOR. *n.* With respect to a cavity, means a movable or removable structure that in the closed position is designed to prevent access to the cavity. *Radiation Emitting Devices Regulations*, C.R.C., c. 1370, s. 1. See CARGO-TYPE ~; EXIT ~S; FIRE ~; OUTER ~S.

D.O.R. *abbr.* Desires an opportunity to redeem. A notice filed by a defendant in an action for foreclosure or sale when the defendant wishes to have a chance to redeem the property.

DORMANT CLAIM. A suspended claim.

DORMIT ALIQUANDO LEX, MORITUR NUNQUAM. [L.] A law occasionally sleeps, but it never dies.

DORMIUNT ALIQUANDO LEGES, NUNQUAM MORIUNTUR. [L.] The laws occasionally sleep, but they never die.

DORSAL. *adj.* Posterior.

DOS. *n.* Dower.

DOSAGE FORM. The form in which a prescription drug is manufactured in order to be suitable for administration irrespective of the size or type of container in which it is packaged. *Pharmaceutical Industry Development Assistance Regulations*, C.R.C., c. 337, s. 2.

DOSE. *n.* The quantity of energy absorbed per unit of mass by any material from X-rays, or from secondary particles generated by X-rays, falling upon or penetrating the material. *Public Health Act*, R.R.O. 1980, Reg. 855, s. 1.

DOSEMETER. *n.* Any device that, in the opinion of the Minister, may be reliably used for measuring or estimating dose or dose-rate. *Public Health Act*, R.R.O. 1980, Reg. 855, s. 1.

DOSE-RATE. *n.* Dose per unit of time. *Public Health Act*, R.R.O. 1980, Reg. 855, s. 1.

DOTAL. *adj.* Relating to the dos or dower.

DOTATION. *n.* 1. Giving a portion or dowry. 2. In general, endowment.

DOT SPECS. See US ~.

DOUBLE. See CONSOLATION ~; DAILY ~.

DOUBLE ACTION. As applied to handguns, cocking of the hammer when the trigger is pulled. F.A. Jaffe, *A Guide to Pathological Evidence*, 2d ed. (Toronto: Carswell, 1983) at 174.

DOUBLE AGENCY. A situation occurring when a security holder appoints a receiver/manager to take possession of a debtor's business and realize on it, and at the same time that receiver/manager is considered the debtor's agent in order to manage the business and contract with third parties. F. Bennett, *Receiverships* (Toronto: Carswell, 1985) at 7.

DOUBLE ENTRY. Describing books of account kept by posting each entry as a debit and credit.

DOUBLE FRONT TOWNSHIP. A township where the usual practice in the original survey was to survey the township boundaries, the proof lines and base lines, if any, and the concession lines forming the front boundaries of the half lots and to establish the front corners of the half lots and divide the concessions in lots having regular dimensions of 30 chains in width and 66.67 chains in depth and make a road allowance 1 chain wide between every fifth lot and between each concession. *Surveys Act*, R.R.O. 1980, Reg. 928, Meth. 42.

DOUBLE HOOP NET. A hoop net having two pots joined by one lead. *Ontario Fishery Regulations*, C.R.C., c. 849, s. 47.

DOUBLE INDEMNITY INSURANCE. Insurance undertaken by an insurer as part of a life insurance contract whereby the terms of the policy provide for the duration of the insurance for more than one year and for payment only in the event of the death of the insured by accident of an additional amount of insurance money not exceeding the amount payable in the event of death from other causes.

DOUBLE INSURANCE. Two or more insurances on the same interest, the same risk and the same subject.

DOUBLE JEOPARDY. A second prosecution for the same offence. See RULE AGAINST ~.

DOUBLE RECOVERY. An injured plaintiff or dependant in a fatal accident action may both keep a benefit and recover full damages as if no benefit was received. K.D. Cooper-Stephenson & I.B. Saunders, *Personal Injury Damages in Canada* (Toronto: Carswell, 1981) at 469.

DOUBLE RENT. A penalty on a tenant who holds over after notice to quit expires.

DOUBLE TICKETING. The practice of charging the higher of two prices marked on an item.

DOUBLE TIME. Twice the worker's usual rate of pay.

DOUBLE VALUE. A penalty on an overholding tenant of double the yearly value of the land or double rent.

DOUBLE WASTE. Committed by a tenant who allows a house needing repair to be wasted and then illegally fells timber to repair it.

DOUBTFUL LOAN. Any loan in connection with which the board, manager or credit committee of a credit union or an officer of the credit union who has examined the circumstances related to the loan believes there is doubt about the credit union's ability to collect the full amount of the principal and interest owing. *Credit Union Act*, S.S. 1984-85-86, c. C-45.1, s. 2. See ALLOWANCES FOR ~S.

DOUKHOBER. *n.* A person exempted or entitled to claim exemption, or who, on production of a certificate, might have become or would now be entitled to claim exemption, from military service by reason of the order of the Governor in Council of December 6, 1898, and every descendant of any such person, whether born in the Province or elsewhere. *Marriage Act*, R.S.B.C. 1979, c. 251, s. 1.

DO UT DES. [L.] I give so you may give.

DO UT FACIAS. [L.] I give so you may perform.

DOW. *v.* To endow; to give.

DOWABLE. *adj.* With claim to dower.

DOWAGER. *n.* An endowed widow; the widow of nobility. See QUEEN ~.

DOWER. *n.* A life interest in one-third of any freehold estate of inheritance of which the husband died solely seised in possession either through a tenant or by himself and which he either brought with him into the marriage or acquired afterwards. A. Bissett-Johnson & W.M. Holland, eds., *Matrimonial Property Law in Canada* (Toronto: Carswell, 1980) at I-10. See BAR OF ~.

DOWER ACTS. Provincial acts which increased the scope of common law dower by affording the wife right to her husband's equivalent equitable interests in land. A. Bissett-Johnson & W.M. Holland, eds., *Matrimonial Property Law in Canada* (Toronto: Carswell, 1980) at I-10.

DOWER RIGHTS. All rights given by this Act to the spouse of a married person in respect of the homestead and property of the married person, and without restricting the generality of the foregoing, includes (i) the right to prevent disposition of the homestead by withholding consent, (ii) the right of action for damages against the married person if a disposition of the homestead that results in the registration of the title in the name of any other person is made without consent, (iii) the right to obtain payment from the Assurance Fund of an unsatisfied judgment against the married person in respect of a disposition of the homestead that is made without consent and that results in the registration of the title in the name of any other person, (iv) the right of the surviving spouse to a life estate in the homestead of the deceased married person, and (v) the right of the surviving spouse to a life estate in the personal property of the deceased married person that is exempt from seizure under execution. *Dower Act*, R.S.A. 1980, c. D-38, s. 1.

DOWN. *adj.* As applied to a cable, means that the cable is resting on the river bed. *Ferry Cable Regulations*, C.R.C., c. 1230, s. 2.

DOWN-CONDUCTOR. *n.* The vertical portion of a conductor that ends at a ground connection. *Lightning Rods Act*, R.R.O. 1980, Reg. 577, s. 1.

DOWN GRADING. Demotion to a job with a lower rate of pay.

DOWN PAYMENT. A sum of money, the value of a negotiable instrument payable on demand, or the agreed value of goods, given on account at the time of the contract. *Consumer Protection acts.*

DOWN PERIOD. A period when a plant is closed for repairs to machinery, other maintenance or alterations.

DOWNSTREAM INVESTMENT. Where a person or a group of persons owns beneficially, directly or indirectly, or is deemed to own beneficially, equity shares of a corporation, that person or group of persons shall be deemed to own beneficially a proportion of the equity shares of any other corporation that are owned beneficially, directly or indirectly, by the first mentioned corporation, which proportion shall equal the proportion of the equity shares of the first mentioned corporation that are owned beneficially, directly or indirectly, or that pursuant to this subsection are deemed to be owned beneficially, by that person or group of persons.

DOWNTIME. *n.* A brief period of time during which no work is possible because of machinery breakdown, adjustment or the like.

DOWRESS. *n.* A widow with claim to dower.

DOWRY. *n.* Marriage goods which a wife brings to the marriage.

D.P. *abbr.* Domus Procerum.

D.P.P. *abbr.* Director of Public Prosecutions.

DRACHM. *n.* 1. One eighth of an ounce apothecaries. 2. One eighth of a fluid ounce.

DRAFT. *n.* 1. An order drawn by one person on another for the payment of money, i.e. a bill of exchange or cheque. 2. An order for the payment of money drawn by one banker on another. See RE-~.

DRAFTSMAN. *n.* Any person who drafts a legal document.

DRAGGER. *n.* A vessel (a) of an overall length that does not exceed 100 feet, and (b) that is equipped with an otter trawl or other trawl of a similar type for catching fish. *Otter Trawl Fishing Regulations*, C.R.C., c. 821, s. 2.

DRAG RAKE. Any gear that is towed over the ocean floor by a vessel for the purpose of collecting marine plants. *Atlantic Coast Marine Plant Regulations*, C.R.C., c. 805, s. 2. See BASKET ~.

DRAG SEINE. A net weighted at the bottom, floated at the top and cast from a boat so as to enclose an area of water between it and the shore, and then drawn ashore. Canada regulations.

DRAIN. *n.* 1. Any drain used for the drainage of one building or premises only for the purpose of communicating therefrom with a sewer, septic-tank, cesspool or other like receptacle, into which the drainage of two or more houses or premises occupied by different persons is conveyed. *City of St. John's Act*, R.S. Nfld. 1970, c. 40, s. 2. 2. A drain open or covered wholly or in part, whether in the channel of a natural stream, creek or watercourse or not, heretofore or hereafter constructed, repaired, maintained or improved, and all the work and materials necessary for any bridge, culvert, catch basin or guards connected therewith. See AREA ~; BUILDING ~; FLOOD ~; FOUNDATION ~; HOUSE-~; LATERAL ~; SUB-SURFACE ~.

DRAINAGE. *n.* Any surface or underground conduits used chiefly for agricultural hydraulics for the supplying, irrigation and draining of farm land and includes natural and artificial watercourses used for those purposes. *An Act Respecting the Ministère de l'Agriculture*, R.S.Q. 1977, c. M-14, s. 22. See LAND ~.

DRAINAGE AREA. For a point, the area which contributes runoff to that point.

DRAINAGE DITCH. A man-made water course, added to the natural land drainage system, primarily to collect and convey water and that, for some period each year, does not contain flowing water. *Pesticides Act*, R.R.O. 1980, Reg. 751, s. 1.

DRAINAGE PIPING. All the connected piping that conveys sewage to a place of disposal, including the building drain, building sewer, soil pipe, soil stack, waste stack and waste pipe but does not include, i. a main sewer, and ii. piping used for sewage in a sewage plant. *Ontario Water Resources Act*, R.R.O. 1980, Reg. 736, s. 1. See STORM ~.

DRAINAGE SYSTEM. See SANITARY ~.

DRAINAGE UNIT. The area allocated to a well

for the purpose of drilling for and producing oil or gas, and includes all subsurface areas bounded by the vertical planes in which the surface boundaries lie. *Oil and Natural Gas acts.*

DRAINAGE WORK. 1. A drainage system constructed of tile, pipe or tubing of any material beneath the surface of agricultural land, including integral inlets and outlets, for the purpose of improving the productivity of the land drained. 2. The construction of a drain, and includes the deepening, straightening, widening of, the clearing of obstructions from, or otherwise improving a stream, creek, or watercourse, the lowering of the waters of a lake or pond and the construction of necessary guards in connection therewith.

DRAINAGE WORKS. 1. Includes a drain constructed by any means, including the improving of a natural watercourse, and includes works necessary to regulate the water table or water level within or on any lands or to regulate the level of the waters of a drain, reservoir, lake or pond, and includes a dam, embankment, wall, protective works or any combination thereof. *Drainage Act,* R.S.O. 1980, c. 126, s. 1. 2. Includes, in addition to the actions necessary to prepare and draft plans and specifications, all work required for drainage, in particular, the levelling of excavated material, the removal of obstacles, the arranging, improvement, maintenance and, if applicable, the operation of a land irrigation or drainage system or any other hydraulic works necessary for the drainage or irrigation of land. *An Act Respecting the Ministère de l'agriculture,* R.S.Q. 1977, c. M-14, s. 22. See DRAIN OR ~.

DRAINED WEIGHT. The weight of the edible contents of a container of fish after the liquid has been drained by a method approved by the Minister. *Fish Inspection Regulations,* C.R.C., c. 802, s. 2.

DRAIN OR DRAINAGE WORKS. Includes a floodway or a dike. *Expropriation Act,* R.S.M. 1970, c. E190, s. 26.

DRAM. *n.* 1/16 ounce. *Weights and Measures Act,* S.C. 1970-71-72, c. 36, schedule II. See FLUID ~.

DRAMATIC WORK. Includes any piece of recitation, choreographic work or entertainment in dumb show, the scenic arrangement or acting form of which is fixed in writing or otherwise, and any cinematograph production where the arrangement or acting form or the combination of incidents represented give the work an original character. *Copyright Act,* R.S.C. 1985, c. C-42, s. 2. See EVERY ORIGINAL LITERARY, DRAMATIC, MUSICAL AND ARTISTIC WORK.

DRAPER. *abbr.* Draper (Ont.), 1828-1831.

DRAUGHT. *n.* 1. An order drawn by one person on another for the payment of money, i.e. a bill of exchange or cheque. 2. An order for the payment of money drawn by one banker on another. 3. The vertical distance from the moulded base line amidships to a subdivision load water line (section 2). *Hull Construction Regulations,* C.R.C., c. 1431. 4. The deepest draught of a ship at the time pilotage services are performed. Canada regulations. See SUMMER ~; VESSEL CONSTRAINED BY HER ~.

DRAW. *v.* To write a bill of exchange and sign it.

DRAWBACK. *n.* The remitting or paying back of duties previously paid on a commodity when it is exported.

DRAWEE. *n.* The person to whom a bill of exchange is addressed.

DRAWER. *n.* The person who signs or makes a bill of exchange.

DRAWING. *n.* A unique artistic representation or work including calligraphy, usually on paper, parchment or vellum, executed in media such as pen and ink, ink wash, black or colour chalk, pastels, charcoal, graphite, watercolour, gouache or metal-point. *Canadian Cultural Property Export Control List,* C.R.C., c. 448, s. 1. See MOTOR ~; STEAM ~.

DRESS. *n.* An object that is armour, headdress, pantaloons, a tunic with trappings, accoutrements or such other associated articles that form a part of military apparel. *Canadian Cultural Property Export Control List,* C.R.C., c. 448, s. 1.

DRESSED CARCASS. The edible parts of a carcass but does not include the edible organs.

DRESSED POULTRY. Poultry, other than eviscerated poultry, from which the blood and feathers or blood, feathers and wing tips have been removed. *Dressed and Eviscerated Poultry Regulations,* C.R.C., c. 283, s. 2.

DRESSED STURGEON. A sturgeon from which the head, tail and entrails have been removed. *Ontario Fishery Regulations,* C.R.C., c. 849, s. 2.

DRESSED WEIGHT. The weight of the fish after the gills and entrails have been removed. Fishery regulations. See HEADLESS ~.

DRIE. *abbr.* Department of Regional Industrial Expansion.

DRIED. See KILN ~.

DRIED EGG. Whole egg, egg yolk or albumen

in dried form. *Processed Egg Regulations*, C.R.C., c. 290, s. 2.

DRIED GRAIN. Damp or tough grain that has been dried by a grain drier. *Prairie Grain Advance Payment Act*, R.S.C. 1985, c. P-18, s. 9(5).

DRIED WHOLE EGG MIX. Dried whole egg containing added ingredients not exceeding 32 per cent by weight. *Processed Egg Regulations*, C.R.C., c. 290, s. 2.

DRIED YOLK MIX. Dried yolk containing added ingredients not exceeding 22 per cent by weight. *Processed Egg Regulations*, C.R.C., c. 290, s. 2.

DRIER. See GRAIN ~.

DRIFT. See TAX ~.

DRIFT NET. 1. A floating gill net that is neither anchored or staked but floats freely with the tide or current. 2. A net that is used to catch fish by enmeshing them and that does not enclose an area of water. *Atlantic Coast Herring Regulations*, C.R.C., c. 804, s. 2. 3. Has the same meaning as "gill net". *Fishery regulations.*

DRILL. *v.* To construct a well by drilling, boring, digging, washing, coring or by any other method by which a well can be constructed. *Well Drilling Act*, R.S.N.S. 1967, c. 337, s. 1.

DRILLER. *n.* (i) A person who is engaged or authorized by the licensee to undertake, or (ii) a licensee who personally undertakes, a drilling operation at a well or an operation preparatory or incidental to the drilling of a well or the reconditioning or abandonment of a well. *Ground Water Control Act*, R.S.A. 1980, c. G-11, s. 1. See WELL ~.

DRILLING. *n.* The drilling, boring, driving, jetting or reconditioning of a well.

DRILLING MACHINE. A machine, together with attachments, that is designed to be used or is used to drill a well.

DRILLING OR EXPLORATION EXPENSE. Incurred on or in respect of exploring or drilling for petroleum or natural gas includes any expense incurred on or in respect of (i) drilling or converting a well for the disposal of waste liquids from a petroleum or natural gas well, (ii) drilling for water or gas for injection into a petroleum or natural gas formation, or (iii) drilling or converting a well for the injection of water or gas to assist in the recovery of petroleum or natural gas from another well. *Income Tax Act*, R.S.C. 1952, c. 148 (as am. S.C. 1974-75-76, c. 26, s. 35(22)), s. 66(15)(d).

DRILLING RESERVATION. See HOLDER OF A ~.

DRINK. See DAIRY ~; SOFT ~.

DRIVE-AWAY UNIT. (a) A motor vehicle that is towing another motor vehicle or trailer together with that other motor vehicle or trailer, all the wheels of which are on the highway; or (b) subject to subsection 67(9), any combination of motor vehicles (i) one of which is entirely carried on the motor vehicle, (ii) one of which moves under its own motive power, and (iii) others which are partly towed and partly carried so that only the rear wheels of the other motor vehicles are in contact with the roadway. *The Highway Traffic Act*, S.M. 1985-86, c. 3, s. 8(1).

DRIVE CARELESSLY. To drive a vehicle on a highway without due care and attention or without reasonable consideration for other persons using the highway. *The Highway Traffic Act*, S.M. 1985-86, c. 3, s. 188(1).

DRIVER. *n.* 1. A person who drives or is in actual physical control of a vehicle or who is exercising control over or steering a vehicle being towed or pushed by another vehicle. 2. Includes a person who has the care or control of a motor vehicle whether it is in motion or not. 3. Includes street car operator. *Highway Traffic Amendment Act*, S.O. 1984, c. 21, s. 10. 4. Includes the rider of a bicycle. *Motor Vehicle Act*, R.S.N.S. 1967, c. 191, s. 125. 5. Includes the owner of the vehicle. *Highway Traffic Act*, R.S. Nfld. 1970, c. 152, s. 190. 6. The occupant of a vehicle seated immediately behind the steering control system. *Motor Vehicle Safety Regulations*, C.R.C., c. 1038, s. 2. See AMBULANCE ~, BROKER-~; TAXI ~.

DRIVER ATTENDANT. A person who, in the course of providing ambulance service to a patient in Ontario, (i) operates, drives or otherwise has the actual care or control of an ambulance, or (ii) attends, assists or renders first aid or emergency medical care, but does not include a physician, intern, nurse, nursing assistant, respiratory technologist or other skilled and duly qualified medical technician who attends on a call for ambulance service with at least two driver attendants for the purpose of rendering specialized health care services to a specific patient. *Ambulance Act*, R.R.O. 1980, Reg. 14, s. 1.

DRIVER IMPROVEMENT PROGRAM. A course of study or instruction for the improvement of the knowledge, attitudes and skills of persons in the operation of motor vehicles.

DRIVER INSTRUCTOR. A person who holds a driver instructor's certificate issued by the Department of Education and who is engaged in the business of giving instruction for hire, fee or tuition in the driving of motor vehicles or the preparation of an applicant for an examination for a licence. *The Vehicles Act*, R.S.S. 1978, c. V-3, s. 2.

DRIVER-OPERATED ACCELERATOR CONTROL SYSTEM. All components of a vehicle, except the fuel metering device, that regulate engine speed in direct response to movement of the driver-operated control and that return the throttle to the idle position upon release of the driver-operated control. *Motor Vehicle Safety Regulations*, C.R.C., c. 1038, s. 2.

DRIVER OR OPERATOR. A person who drives or is in actual physical control of a vehicle. *Highway Traffic Act*, R.S.A. 1980, c. H-7, s. 1.

DRIVER SALESMAN. Person who works an assigned route, delivering goods and collecting payments as well as selling goods.

DRIVER'S CERTIFICATE. A certificate issued under this Act or the regulations to a person who, under the Motor Vehicle Act, may obtain a driver's licence, and may be part of the driver's licence or a separate document. *Insurance (Motor Vehicle) Act*, R.S.B.C. 1979, c. 204, s. 1.

DRIVER'S LICENCE. 1. A licence which has been issued authorizing the person to whom it is issued to drive a motor vehicle and which has not expired, been suspended or cancelled. 2. A licence or a permit to drive a motor vehicle on a public highway. 3. Includes a motorized snow vehicle operator's licence. *Highway Traffic Amendment Act*, S.O. 1984, c. 21, s. 5.

DRIVER'S LICENSE. A chauffeur's license, an operator's license or a beginner's license. *Motor Vehicle Act*, R.S.N.S. 1967, c. 191, s. 1.

DRIVER'S POLICY. A motor vehicle liability policy insuring a person named therein in respect of the operation or use by him of any automobile other than an automobile owned by him or registered in his name. *Insurance acts.*

DRIVER TRAINING SCHOOL. A person, firm or association that is engaged in the business of giving instructions for hire, fee or tuition on the driving of motor vehicles or in the preparation for an examination for a driver's licence. *Vehicle Administration Act*, S.S. 1986, c. V-2.1, s. 2.

DRIVEWAY. *n.* A clearly defined private road, way, drive, path or passage or a like opening or space which is wide enough, but not wider than is necessary, for the passage of a motor vehicle, whereby the owner, occupier or user of property has vehicular access from a roadway to a point within the property. *Highway Traffic Act*, R.S. Nfld. 1970, c. 152, s. 2. See PRIVATE ~.

DRIVE-YOURSELF MOTOR VEHICLE. A motor vehicle kept for hire that may be hired or rented by the hour, day, week, or longer, without a driver. *Taxicab Act*, R.S.M. 1970, c. T10, s. 2.

DRIVING CARELESSLY. See DRIVE CARE-LESSLY.

DRIVING INSTRUCTOR. A person who teaches other persons to operate motor vehicles and receives compensation therefor, but does not include a licensed teacher under contract in a recognized educational institution who instructs in the operation of a motor vehicle in a private driver education training course carried on in the institution. *Motor Vehicle Act*, R.S.N.B. 1973, c. M-17, s. 90.

DRIVING PRIVILEGE. (a) The privilege of applying for, obtaining or holding a licence to operate a motor vehicle in the Province, and (b) the privilege of operating a motor vehicle in the province under section 78 or 80. *Motor Vehicle Act*, R.S.N.B. 1973, c. M-17, s. 294.

DRIVING TIME. The period of time that a motor vehicle operator is at the controls of a motor vehicle and the engine is in operation. *Canada Motor Vehicle Operators Hours of Service Regulations*, C.R.C., c. 1005, s. 2.

DROIT. *n.* [Fr.] Equity; justice; right.

DROITURAL. *adj.* Relating to right.

DROP SHIPMENT. Shipment of goods directly from manufacturer to dealer or consumer, not through a wholesaler.

DROVER. *n.* Any person or partnership engaged in the business of selling his livestock at a stockyard on his own account. *Livestock and Livestock Products Act*, R.S.C. 1985, c. L-9, s. 10.

DROWNING. *n.* Death caused by immersing the nose and mouth in fluid. F.A. Jaffe, *A Guide to Pathological Evidence*, 2d ed. (Toronto: Carswell, 1983) at 174. See DRY ~; SECONDARY ~; WET ~.

D.R.S. *abbr.* Dominion Report Service.

DRUG. *n.* 1. Any substance or mixture of substances manufactured, sold or represented for use in (a) the diagnosis, treatment, mitigation or prevention of a disease, disorder, abnormal physical state, or the symptoms thereof, in man or animal, (b) restoring, correcting or modifying organic functions in man or animal, or (c) disinfection in premises in which food is manufactured, prepared or kept. 2. Does not include a drug or other substance defined as a controlled drug by Part III or as a restricted drug by Part IV. *Food and Drugs Act*, R.S.C. 1985, c. F-27, s. 37(2). 3. Any substance that is capable of producing a state of euphoria, depression, hallucination or intoxication in a human being. 4. (i) Any substance that is named in the latest edition from time to time of the British Pharmacopoeia, the British Pharmaceutical Codex, the Pharmacopoeia of the United States of America, the National Formulary, the New and Nonofficial remedies, the Canadian Formulary, the Codex Français or the Pharmacopoea Internationalis, or (ii) any preparation containing any substance mentioned in subclause (i), or (iii) any substance or mixture of substances manufactured, sold or represented for use in (A) the diagnosis, treatment, mitigation or prevention of a disease, disorder, abnormal physical state or the symptoms thereof, in man or animal; (B) restoring, correcting or modifying organic functions in man or animal; or (C) disinfection in premises in which food is manufactured, prepared or kept, or for the control of vermin in such premises. 5. A substance, whether in crude form, refined form, prepared dosage form or any other form whatever, intended or capable of being used for medicine or for the preparation or production of medicine. *Patent Rules*, C.R.C., c. 1250, s. 117. See APPROVED ~ AND PHARMACEUTICAL; CONTROLLED ~; DESIGNATED ~; HALLUCINOGENIC ~; INTERCHANGEABLE ~; NEW ~; OFFICIAL ~; PRESCRIPTION ~; RESTRICTED ~; SPECIFIED ~; VETERINARY ~.

DRUG ABUSE. (a) Addiction to a substance other than alcohol; or (b) the use, whether habitual or not, of a substance other than alcohol that is capable of inducing euphoria, hallucinations or intoxication in a person.

DRUG ABUSER. A person who abuses or is addicted to a drug.

DRUG DEPENDENCY. 1. A state of psychological or physical reliance or both on one or more chemical substances that alter mood, perception, consciousness or behaviour to the apparent detriment of the person or society or both as a result of the periodic or continuous use or administration of one or more chemical substances and includes the use of nicotine or alcohol or both. *Drug Dependency Act*, S.N.S. 1971-72, c. 3, s. 2. 2. A state of psychological or physical reliance, or both, on a chemical substance other than alcohol that alters mood, perception, consciousness or behaviour to the apparent detriment of the person using the substance or society, or both, resulting from the continuous use of the substance other than under the supervision of a physician. *Alcoholism and Drug Dependency Commission of New Brunswick Act*, R.S.N.B. 1973, c. A-7.1, s. 1.

DRUGGIST. *n.* A pharmaceutical chemist registered and entitled to practise.

DRUG INTERACTION. Reinforcement or cancellation of each other's effects when two drugs are present in a person's body at the same time. F.A. Jaffe, *A Guide to Pathological Evidence*, 2d ed. (Toronto: Carswell, 1983) at 61.

DRUGLESS PRACTITIONER. A person who practises or advertises or holds himself out in any way as practising the treatment of any ailment, disease, defect or disability of the human body by manipulation, adjustment, manual or electro-therapy or by any similar method. *Drugless Practitioners Act*, R.S.O. 1980, c. 127, s. 1.

DRUGLESS THERAPIST. Any person who practises or advertises or holds himself out in any way as practising the treatment by diagnosis, including all diagnostic methods, direction, advice, written or otherwise, of any ailment, disease, defect or disability of the human body by methods taught in colleges of drugless therapy or naturopathy and approved by the Board. *Drugless Practitioners Act*, R.R.O. 1980, Reg. 250, s. 1.

DRUG PRODUCT. See LISTED ~.

DRUGS AND MEDICINES. Includes, (a) X-ray pictures, (b) any substance, mixture of substances or any article that may be used for the diagnosis, treatment, mitigation or prevention of disease in man or animal, and (c) any substance or mixture of substances that may be used in restoring, correcting or modifying organic functions, but does not include weight reducing dietary supplements as defined by the Minister, disinfectants such as creoline, rodent exterminators, cosmetics of all kinds, medicated or otherwise, including hair tonics, shampoos, toothpastes, shaving creams, beauty aids and toiletries, depilatories and perfumes. *Retail Sales Tax Act*, R.R.O. 1980, Reg. 904, s. 1.

DRUG STORE. A place where prescriptions, medicines, drugs, chemicals and poisons are compounded or prepared or sold by retail.

DRUG USER. A person who (i) is addicted to the use of a substance other than alcohol, or (ii) uses, whether habitually or not, a substance other than alcohol for the purpose of inducing euphoria, hallucinations or intoxication.

DRUM HOIST. The type of hoisting engine where the rope is anchored to and spooled on to a drum.

DRUM TRAP. A trap where the inlet and outlet are in the sides of the cylinder of the trap. *Ontario Water Resources Act*, R.R.O. 1980, Reg. 736, s. 85.

DRUNKARD. See HABITUAL ~.

DRUNKENNESS. *n.* Intoxication.

DRY. *adj.* A condition that does not include uncombined water. *National Emission Standards Regulations*, Canada regulations.

DRY CLEANER. A person who understands and is capable of carrying out the process of, (i) cleaning garments in either manual or automatic equipment by immersion and·agitation or by immersion only in volatile solvents, including but not being restricted to solvents of the petroleum distillate type, the coal tar distillate type, the chlorinated hydrocarbon type and including any or all of the processes incidental to cleaning garments by immersion in volatile solvents, (ii) wet cleaning of garments by immersion in water or by the application, manually or by any mechanical device, of water or any detergent and water, or by spraying or brushing the garments with water and any detergent or with water vapour or with chemicals and water or steam, (iii) pressing or finishing, or both, being the process of restoring garments to their original shape, dimensions or contour or to the condition in which the garments were received from the customer or as directed by the customer, and including the removal of wrinkles, stresses, bulges and impressions, imprint marks and shine from garments by the application, either manually or mechanically and with or without dry or wet cleaning, of pressure, heat, moisture, water vapour or steam, (iv) removing spots or stains or localized areas of soil from garments before or after the garments are dry or wet cleaned or by manual or mechanical means, other than dry or wet cleaning, such as by brushing or spraying with water detergents and volatile or imflammable solvents or with chemicals or both, (v) repairing, being the process of making alterations as required by the customer to garments, such as by minor repairs and alterations, by reaffixing, replacing or restoring buttons or other fastening devices and decorative materials to the garments either before or after one of the processes referred to in this clause, (vi) identification of fabrics, fabric construction, designs and finishes, (vii) cleaning shirts by immersion in water, including the use of washing formulae and chemicals, and of special finishes and a knowledge of the control of water and temperature, the operation of necessary equipment and the control of quality in the proper processing and finishing of shirt laundry, and (viii) basic management, production, quality control, garment identification, pricing, packaging and servicing to the customer. *Apprenticeship and Tradesmen's Qualification Act*, R.R.O. 1980, Reg. 31, s. 1.

DRY DOCK. Includes floating dry docks. *Dry Dock Subsidies Act*, R.S.C. 1985, c. D-4, s. 2.

DRY DROWNING. Suffocation caused by a spasm in the larynx when small quantities of fluid are inhaled. F.A. Jaffe, *A Guide to Pathological Evidence*, 2d ed. (Toronto: Carswell, 1983) at 174.

DRYER. See EGG ~.

DRY EXCHANGE. An old term for covering and disguising usury: though something was supposed to pass on both sides, it passed on one side only.

DRYING CENTRE. An establishment, other than a regional centre, where services are offered for the handling, drying, screening and grading of grain in conformity with the grading system established by regulation. *Grain Act*, S.Q. 1979, c. 84, s. 1.

DRY LEASE. A lease of an aircraft under the terms of which the lessor does not provide, directly or indirectly, the aircrew to operate the aircraft. *Air Carrier Regulations*, C.R.C., c. 3, s. 2.

DRY MEAT. The meat of shellfish contained in a can that has been processed and allowed to cool thoroughly and is opened and upturned for not less than one minute and not more than one and one-half minutes so as to permit free drainage of the liquor therefrom. *Meat and Canned Foods Act*, R.S.C. 1970, c. M-6, s. 2.

DRY-RENT. *n.* Rent-seck; rent reserved with no distress clause.

DRY SALTERY. See HERRING ~; SALMON ~.

DRY SKIMMED MILK. Dry skimmed milk, powdered skimmed milk or skimmed milk powder intended for human consumption. *Canada Dairy Products Regulations*, C.R.C., c. 553, s. 32.

DRY VENT. A vent pipe that is not a wet vent. *Ontario Water Resources Act*, R.R.O. 1980, Reg. 736, s. 1.

D.T.C. *abbr.* Dominion Tax Cases.

DUAL AXLE. Any two consecutive axles whose centres are more than forty inches or one metre apart and (i) are articulated from a common attachment to the vehicle, or (ii) designed to equalize the load between the two axles.

DUAL COMPUTER. A unit comprised of two separate approved computers that is capable of computing pay-out prices from data received directly from the totalizator system. *Race Track Supervision Regulations*, C.R.C., c. 441, s. 2.

DUAL CONTROL BOILER. A boiler or boilers having attached thereto a low-pressure control device and a pressure-recording device. *Oper-*

ating Engineers Act, R.R.O. 1980, Reg. 740, s. 1.

DUAL CONTROL SWITCH. A power operated switch also equipped for hand operation. *Regulations No. O-8, Uniform Code of Operating Rules*, C.R.C., c. 1175, Part III, c. 2.

DUAL-CONTROL TRAINING VEHICLE. A motor vehicle equipped with at least two brake pedals and two steering wheels and so designed that the vehicle can be operated from either the right or left hand position. *Highway Traffic Act*, R.S. Nfld. 1970, c. 152, s. 2.

DUAL KNOB. Two concentric or two separate knobs, one of which controls the VHF channel selector or tuning mechanism and the other controls the UHF channel selector or tuning mechanism. *General Radio Regulations, Part II*, C.R.C., c. 1372, s. 131.

DUAL NATIONALITY. Citizenship in two countries.

DUAL-PURPOSE VEHICLE. A motor vehicle, other than one commonly known as a passenger car, designed by the manufacturer for the transportation of persons and goods. *Public Commercial Vehicles Act*, R.S.O. 1980, c. 407, s. 1.

DUAL RATE SYSTEM. An arrangement of the rates to be charged for the transportation of goods into contract rates and non-contract rates, and in which the contract rate for the transportation of specific goods described therein is lower than the non-contract rate for those goods. *Shipping Conference Exemption Act*, R.S.C. 1985, c. S-10, s. 5(2).

DUAL VALUATION. A method of valuation of a fishing vessel for insurance purposes establishing one insured value for total loss and a second insured value for partial loss. *Fishing Vessel Insurance Regulations*, C.R.C., c. 325, s. 2.

DUAL VENT. A vent pipe connecting at a junction of waste pipes serving two fixtures and serving as a common vent pipe for both fixtures. *Ontario Water Resources Act*, R.R.O. 1980, Reg. 736, s. 1.

DUARCHY. *n.* Government in which two govern jointly.

DUBITANTE. *adj.* [L. doubting] Used in a law report to describe a judge's doubt that a proposition is correct without a decision that it is wrong.

DUCK. See MATURE ~S; YOUNG ~S.

DUCT. See EXHAUST ~; RETURN ~; SUPPLY ~.

DUCTILE FLEXURAL WALL. A ductile flexural member cantilevering from the foundation consisting of a ductile reinforced concrete wall designed and detailed according to CSA A23.3-1974 "Code for the Design of Concrete Structures for Buildings," Special Provisions for Seismic Design, as revised to 1 May, 1975. *Building Code Act*, R.R.O. 1980, Reg. 87, s. 1.

DUCTILE MOMENT-RESISTING SPACE FRAME. A space frame that is designed to resist the specifed seismic forces and in addition has adequate ductility or energy-absorptive capacity. *Building Code Act*, R.R.O. 1980, Reg. 87, s. 1.

DUE. *adj.* Payable; owing.

DUE APPLICATION. Includes such information, evidence and material as an official requires to be furnished; and also the payment of the fees prescribed in respect of any application, certificate or document required or issued by virtue of an act.

DUE COURSE. See HOLDER IN ~.

DUE DATE. (a) In relation to the payment of a royalty on a mineral, the last day of the month following the month of production or the last day of the month in which the proceeds of sale of the mineral are received, whichever is later, and (b) in relation to the payment of a sum of money due and payable under an agreement other than a royalty on a mineral, the date specified in the agreement for the payment of that sum of money. *Mine and Minerals Act*, R.S.A. 1980, c. M-15, s. 38.

DUELLING. *n.* Challenging or attempting by any means to provoke another person to fight a duel, attempting to provoke a person to challenge another person to fight a duel, or accepting a challenge to fight a duel is an offence. *Criminal Code*, R.S.C. 1985, c. C-46, s. 71.

DUE PROCESS. Administration of law through the courts following rules and principles established by our system of jurisprudence to enforce and protect private rights; notice and the opportunity to be heard and to defend are its essential elements.

DUES. *n.* Fees, rates, charges or other moneys payable by any person to the Crown under and by virtue of a lease, licence or permit. See HARBOUR ~; PILOTAGE ~; UNION ~.

DULOCRACY. *n.* A government in which servants and slaves dominate.

DULY. *adv.* In the proper manner; regularly.

DULY QUALIFIED. Used in connection with a tradesman or a trade, the expression includes a tradesman in that trade who holds a valid subsisting certificate of proficiency in that trade. *Apprenticeship and Tradesmen's Qualification Act*, R.S.P.E.I. 1974, c. A-13, s. 1.

DULY QUALIFIED MEDICAL PRACTITIONER. Person registered and holding a current licence from the college authorizing the person to practise medicine.

DUM BENE SE GESSERIT. [L.] During good conduct.

DUMBWAITER. *var.* **DUMB-WAITER.** *n.* A mechanism affixed to a building or structure, equipped with a car or platform that moves in guides in a substantially vertical direction, the total compartment height of which does not exceed four feet, that is loaded or unloaded and controlled manually, that is used exclusively for lifting or lowering freight.

DUM CASTA VIXERIT. [L.] As long as she lives chastely.

DUMP. *n.* A place where scrapped objects are deposited, whether or not such objects are intended to be sold or recycled; it includes in particular an old car dump. See RURAL ~.

DUMPED. *adj.* In relation to any goods, means that the normal value of the goods exceeds the export price thereof. *Special Imports Measures Act*, R.S.C. 1985, c. S-15, s. 2.

DUMPING. *n.* Any deliberate disposal, from ships, aircraft, platforms or other man-made structures at sea, of any substance but does not include (a) any disposal that is incidental to or derived from the normal operations of a ship or aircraft or of any equipment thereof, other than the disposal of substances from a ship or aircraft operated for the purpose of disposing of the substances at sea, and (b) any discharge that is incidental to or derived from the exploration for, exploitation of and associated off-shore processing of sea bed mineral resources. *Ocean Dumping Control*, R.S.C. 1985, c. O-2, s. 2. See MARGIN OF ~.

DUMP VEHICLE. A commercial motor vehicle used for the transportation and dumping or spreading of sand, gravel, earth, crushed or uncut rock, slag, rubble, salt, calcium chloride, snow, ice or any mixture thereof, asphalt mixes or scrap metal. *Highway Traffic Act*, R.R.O. 1980, Reg. 483, s. 1.

DUM SOLA. [L.] As long as she remains single or unmarried.

DUM SOLA ET CASTA. [L.] As long as she remains unmarried and lives chastely.

DUM VIDUA. [L.] As long as she remains a widow.

DUNE. See SAND ~.

DUNGEON. *n.* A secure prison.

DUNNAGE. *n.* Wood or other material laid against the bottom and sides of a vessel's hold.

DUODECIMA MANU. [L.] Twelve witnesses to wipe out a criminal's offence.

DUODENA. *n.* [L.] A jury of 12.

DUODENA MANU. [L.] Twelve witnesses to wipe out a criminal's offence.

DUO NON POSSUNT IN SOLIDO UNAM REM POSSIDERE. [L.] Two people cannot possess one thing in entirety.

DUO SUNT INSTRUMENTA AD OMNES RES AUT CONFIRMANDAS AUT IMPUGNANDAS, RATIO ET AUCTORITAS. [L.] There are two ways to either confirm or impugn things: reason and authority.

DUPLEX. *n.* A unit within a separate and detaching building permanently erected on land within Nova Scotia which building consists of two self-contained units within the confines of the building, each of which provides housing accommodation for a single family within the confines of the unit. *Homeowner's Incentive Act*, S.N.S. 1970-71, c. 1, s. 2. See HOME-OWNER ~; RENTAL ~.

DUPLEX RECEPTACLE. Two contact devices, on the same yoke, installed at an outlet for the connection of two attachment plugs. *Power Corporation Act*, R.R.O. 1980, Reg. 794, s. 0.

DUPLICATE. *v.* To copy.

DUPLICATE. *n.* 1. A copy. 2. The duplicate, delivered or issued to the person entitled thereto, of the certificate of title in the register. *Land Titles acts.*

DUPLICATE CERTIFICATE. The duplicate, delivered or issued to the person entitled thereto, of the certificate of title in the register. *Land Titles acts.*

DUPLICATE CERTIFICATE OF TITLE. An exact copy of the certificate in the register; when an entry is made on the certificate in the register, the same entry must be made on the duplicate certificate. W.B. Rayner & R.H. McLaren, *Falconbridge on Mortgages*, 4th ed. (Toronto: Canada Law Book, 1977) at 213.

DUPLICATE ORIGINAL. The first copy of a document which was executed as though it were also an original.

DUPLICATE PLAN. A true copy of the plan.

DUPLICATE WILL. One copy of a will kept by the executor, the other deposited with someone else.

DUPLICITY. *n.* One count of an indictment

may not charge a defendant with committing two or more distinct offences.

DURABLE LIFE. The period, commencing on the day on which a prepackaged product is packaged for retail sale, during which the product, when it is stored under conditions appropriate to that product, will retain, without any appreciable deterioration, its normal wholesomeness, palatability, nutritional value and any other qualities claimed for it by the manufacturer. *Food and Drug Regulations*, C.R.C., c. 870, s. B.01.001.

DURABLE LIFE DATE. 1. A date on packaged goods indicating by when the contents should be consumed; best before date. 2. The date on which the durable life of a prepackaged product ends. *Food and Drug Regulations*, C.R.C., c. 870, s. B.01.001.

DURA MATER. [L.] A sturdy fibrous membrane attached to the inside of the skull. F.A. Jaffe, *A Guide to Pathological Evidence*, 2d ed. (Toronto: Carswell, 1983) at 117.

DURANTE. [L.] During.

DURANTE ABSENTIA. [L.] During absence.

DURANTE BENE PLACITO. [L.] 1. During pleasure. 2. During the Crown's pleasure.

DURANTE MINORE AETATE. [L.] During the state of minority.

DURANTE VIDUIDATE. [L.] During the widowed state.

DURANTE VITA. [L.] During life.

DURATION. See PULSE ~.

DURESS. *n.* 1. In defence to a criminal charge, the Criminal Code requires that a threat be "of immediate death or bodily harm from a person who is present when the offence is committed". D. Stuart, *Canadian Criminal Law: a Treatise*, 2d ed. (Toronto: Carswell, 1987) at 397. 2. Threats to another's property, threats of physical violence or economic duress which induces a contract. G.H.L. Fridman, *The Law of Contract in Canada*, 2d ed. (Toronto: Carswell, 1986) at 294 and 295. See ECONOMIC ~.

DURESS COLORE OFFICII. [L.] Abuse of an official or governmental position in which the offical requires a person to pay in order to obtain some authority, licence, permission or power to act or proceed in a particular way. G.H.L. Fridman & J.G. McLeod, *Restitution* (Toronto: Carswell, 1982) at 195.

DURESS OF PROPERTY. Wrongful seizure or detention of a plaintiff's goods. G.H.L. Fridman & J.G. McLeod, *Restitution* (Toronto: Carswell, 1982) at 191.

DURESS OF THE PERSON. Actual or threatened physical violence to a person, or violence or threatened violence to the physical safety of others, such as members of a payer's family. G.H.L. Fridman & J.G. McLeod, *Restitution* (Toronto: Carswell, 1982) at 185-186.

DURHAM REPORT. The 1839 report which recommended that the two Canadas unite. P.W. Hogg, *Constitutional Law of Canada*, 2d ed. (Toronto: Carswell, 1985) at 28.

DURING AN ELECTION. 1. In respect of an election in any electoral district, means the period commencing with the issue of the writ for that election and terminating on polling day or, where the writ is withdrawn or deemed to be withdrawn, terminating on the day that the writ is withdrawn or deemed to be withdrawn. 2. The period from issue of a writ of election to the close of the polls on the day on which polling takes place; or, in the case of an election in which no poll is granted, the period from the issue of the writ of election to the close of the nominations on the day of nomination. *Election Act*, R.S.M. 1970, c. E-30, s. 2. 3. Includes the period between the dissolution of the House of Assembly, or the occurrence of a vacancy in consequence of which a writ for an election is eventually issued, and when a candidate is declared elected. *Elections Act*, R.S.N.S. 1967, c. 83, s. 2. 4. Includes the period from the issue of the writ of election until the elected candidate is returned as elected.

DURING THE COURSE OF SHIPMENT. Loading and unloading and any acts preparatory to loading, shipping or unloading. *Canada Agricultural Products Standards Act*, R.S.C. 1985, c. A-7, s. 19(2).

DURING THE ELECTION. The period from issue of a writ of election to the close of the polls on the day on which polling takes place; or, in the case of an election in which no poll is granted, the period from the issue of the writ of election to the close of the nominations on the day of nomination. *Election Act*, R.S.M. 1970, c. E-30, s. 2.

DUST. See COMBUSTIBLE ~; SILICEOUS ~.

DUST EXPOSURE OCCUPATION. (i) Any employment underground in a mine; (ii) any employment at the surface of a mine in ore or rock crushing operations in which the ore or rock being crushed is not constantly kept in a moistened or wet condition by the use of water or chemical solutions; (iii) any employment at the surface of a mine that is designated by an inspector as a dust exposure occupation; or (iv) any employment in assay grinding rooms or in wet concentrating plants not isolated from dry crushing plants.

DUTCH AUCTION. Offering property for sale at auction at high value and gradually lowering the price until it is sold.

DUTCH ELM DISEASE. The disease caused by the fungus Ceratocystis Ulmi. *Dutch Elm Disease Act*, S.M. 1980, c. 65, s. 1.

DUTIES. *n.* 1. Any duties or taxes levied on imported goods under the Customs Tariff, the Excise Tax Act, the Excise Act, the Special Import Measures Act or any other law relating to customs. 2. In addition to its ordinary meaning, the fees, price or cost of licences or permits, taxes and other imposts and contributions provided for by a fiscal law. *Ministère du Revenu Act*, R.S.Q. 1977, c. M-31, s. 1. See PILOTAGE ~.

DUTY. *n.* 1. A requirement which the law recognizes to avoid conduct characterized by unreasonable risk of danger to other persons. John G. Fleming, *The Law of Torts*, 6th ed. (Sydney: The Law Book Company Limited, 1983) at 129. 2. A duty imposed by law. *Criminal Code*, R.S.C. 1985, c. C-46, s. 219(2). 3. A requirement of service that specifies the degree of regularity of the load. *Power Corporation Act*, R.R.O. 1980, Reg. 794, s. 0. See ACTIVE ~; CONTINUOUS ~; CUSTOM ~; CUSTOMS ~; DISCRETIONARY ~; ESTATE ~; EXCISE ~; INTERMITTENT ~; MINISTERIAL ~; PERIODIC ~; PROBATE ~; SHORT TIME ~; STAMP ~; SUCCESSION ~; VALUE FOR ~; VARYING ~.

DUTY COUNSEL. A lawyer appointed to assist any person appearing in court without having retained a lawyer.

DUTY OF A MEMBER OF THE LEGISLATIVE ASSEMBLY. Includes (i) travelling to and from sessions of the Legislative Assembly, (ii) travelling to and from a committee of the Legislative Assembly, (iii) travelling inside and outside Alberta on the business of the Legislative Assembly or of a committee of it or on the business of the Government of Alberta, and (iv) in the case of a member of the Executive Council, all his duties as a member of the Executive Council. *M.L.A. Compensation Act*, R.S.A. 1980, c. M-17, s. 1.

DUTY OF CARE. See NEIGHBOUR TEST.

DUTY PAID VALUE. The value of the article as it would be determined for the purpose of calculating an ad valorem duty on the importation of that article into Canada under the laws relating to the customs and the Customs Tariff whether that article is in fact subject to ad valorem or other duty or not, plus the amount of the customs duties, if any, payable thereon. *Excise Tax Act*, R.S.C. 1985, c. E-15.

DUTY TO ACCOUNT. The duty of a trustee to have his accounts always ready, to afford all reasonable facilities for inspection and examination, and to give full information whenever required. *Sandford v. Porter* (1889), 16 O.A.R. 565 at 571.

DUTY TO MITIGATE. The requirement that the plaintiff take all reasonable steps to minimize a loss which follows a breach of contract or injury.

DVFR FLIGHT PLAN. A flight plan that (a) includes the information required in a VFR flight plan as set out in the Flight Plans and Flight Notifications Order, and (b) states the flight level or altitude above sea level to be flown. *Security Control of Air Traffic Order*, C.R.C., c. 63, s. 2.

DWARF SIGNAL. A low signal used as a block or interlocking signal. *Regulations No. O-8, Uniform Code of Operating Rules*, C.R.C., c. 1175, Part III, s. 2.

DWELLING. *n.* A premises or any part thereof occupied as living accommodation. See MULTIPLE ~; MULTIPLE-FAMILY ~; MULTIPLE UNIT ~; NEW ~; ONE-FAMILY ~; RAILWAY STATION- ~; SEMI-DETACHED ~; SINGLE-FAMILY ~; TWO-FAMILY ~.

DWELLING-HOUSE. *var.* **DWELLING HOUSE.** The whole or any part of a building or structure that is kept or occupied as a permanent or temporary residence, and includes (a) a building within the curtilage of a dwelling-house that is connected to it by a doorway or by a covered and enclosed passage-way, and (b) a unit that is designed to be mobile and to be used as a permanent or temporary residence and that is being used as such a residence.

DWELLING UNIT. A room or suite of rooms used or intended to be used as a domicile by one or more persons and usually containing cooking, eating, living, sleeping and sanitary facilities. See BACHELOR ~; RESIDENTIAL ~; SELF-CONTAINED ~.

D.W.I. *abbr.* Died without issue.

DYE. *n.* 1. Chemical substances prescribed for the purpose of blending with fuel to make coloured fuel. *Fuel Tax Act, 1981*, S.O. 1981, c. 59, s. 1. 2. The principal dye and associated subsidiary and isomeric dyes contained in a synthetic colour. *Food and Drug Regulations*, C.R.C., c. 870, c. B.06.001.

DYE-POINT. *n.* A terminal designated by the Minister for the purpose of colouring fuel. *Fuel Tax Act, 1981*, S.O. 1981, c. 59, s. 1.

DYING DECLARATION. A statement made in extremity, when the party is about to die. P.K.

McWilliams, *Canadian Criminal Evidence*, 3d ed. (Aurora: Canada Law Book, 1988) at 8-25.

DYING WITHOUT ISSUE. Dying without any child being born before or after death.

DYKE. *n.* An embankment, wall, fill, piling, pump, gate, floodbox, pipe, sluice, culvert, canal, ditch, drain or any other thing that is constructed, assembled or installed to prevent the flooding of land. *Dyke Maintenance Act*, R.S.B.C. 1979, c. 99, s. 1. See PRIVATE ~.

DYNE. *n.* That force which, acting on one gramme for one second, generates a velocity of one centimetre per second. *Electric and Photometric Units Act*, R.S.C. 1970, c. E-3, s. 2.

DYSNOMY. *n.* Making unsatisfactory laws.

E

E. *abbr.* Effective length of superstructure or trunk.

EADEM MENS PRAESUMITUR REGIS QUAE EST JURIS, ET QUAE ESSE DEBET, PRAESERTIM IN DUBIIS. [L.] It is presumed that the mind of the sovereign conforms with the law, and what should be, particularly in doubtful cases.

E. & A. *abbr.* Error and Appeal Reports (Grant) (Ont.), 1846-1866.

E. & O.E. *abbr.* Errors and omissions excepted.

EARLIER CONSUMER PRICE INDEX. The Consumer Price Index for the twelve-month period immediately before the twelve-month period of the later Consumer Price Index. *Family Allowances Act*, R.S.C. 1985, c. F-1, s. 13(7).

EARLY RETIREMENT. Withdrawal of an employee from the workforce before the normal date for retirement.

EARMARK. *n.* A mark of ownership or identity.

EARNED INCOME. 1. The aggregate of (i) salary or wages, superannuation or pension benefits, retiring allowances, death benefits, royalties in respect of a work or invention of which the taxpayer was the author or inventor, amounts included in computing the income of the taxpayer by virtue of paragraph 56(1)(b) or (c), amounts received by the taxpayer from a trustee under a supplementary unemployment benefit plan, amounts included in computing the income of the taxpayer by virtue of this section and amounts included in computing the income of the taxpayer by virtue of subsections 146.2(6) and 147(10) and (15), (ii) income from the carrying on of a business either alone or as a partner actively engaged in the business, (iii) rental income from real property, and (iv) amounts deductible under paragraph 8(1)(m) in computing the income of the taxpayer, minus (v) losses from the carrying on of a business either alone or as a partner actively engaged

in the business, (vi) losses from the rental of real property, and (vii) amounts deductible under paragraph 60(j), (j.1), (l) or (m) or under subsection (6) or (7) in computing the income of the taxpayer. *Income Tax Act*, R.S.C. 1952, c. 148 (as am. S.C. 1988, c. 55, s. 130(1)), s. 146(1)(c). 2. Of a taxpayer means the aggregate of (i) all salaries, wages and other remuneration, including gratuities, received by him in respect of, in the course of, or by virtue of offices and employments, and all amounts included in computing his income by virtue of sections 6 and 7, (ii) amounts included in computing his income by virtue of paragraph 56(1)(m), (n) or (o), and (iii) his incomes from all businesses carried on either alone or as a partner actively engaged in the business. *Income Tax Act*, R.S.C. 1952, c. 148 (as am. S.C. 1970-71-72, c. 63), s. 63(3)(b).

EARNED INCOME IN KIND. An individual's net accretion of economic power whose talents or energy produce beneficial goods or services. W. Grover and F. Iacobucci, *Materials on Canadian Income Tax*, 4th ed. (Toronto: Richard De Boo Ltd., 1980) at 157.

EARNED REMISSION. Shortening of a sentence in respect of time during which a prisoner applies himself or herself industriously.

EARNEST. *n.* Something given by the buyer and accepted by the seller at the time of the contract which indicates the contract is completed. G.H.L. Fridman, *Sale of Goods in Canada*, 3d ed. (Toronto: Carswell, 1986) at 45.

EARNINGS. *n.* The pay received or receivable by an employee for work done for an employer. See ALLOCATED RETAINED ~; INSURABLE ~; INTERUPTION OF ~; MAINTAINABLE ~; NET ~; PENSIONABLE ~; PROSPECTIVE LOSS OF ~ OR PROFITS; RECORD OF ~; RETAINED ~.

EARNINGS AND WAGES. Include any remuneration capable of being estimated in terms of money. *Workmen's Compensation Act*, R.S.O. 1980, c. 539, s. 1.

EARNINGS BASE. The maximum valuation of physical assets fixed by the commission upon which a public utility may earn a percentage of profit established by the commission; or such other method of computing a maximum profit as may be determined by the commission. *Electric Power and Telephone Act*, R.S.P.E.I. 1974, c. E-3, s. 1.

EARNINGS PER SHARE. See BASIC ∼; FULLY DILUTED ∼.

EARTHQUAKE INSURANCE. Insurance against loss of or damage to property caused by an earthquake.

EARTH STATION. A station operated in a space service and located on the earth's surface, including a station on board a ship or aircraft. *General Radio Regulations, Part II*, C.R.C. 1372, c. 2. See SATELLITE TELECOMMUNICATION SYSTEM.

EARTHWORK. *n.* 1. Any dump or heap of earth, sand, or gravel or any place from which earth, sand, or gravel has been removed. *Noxious Weeds acts.* 2. Construction composed of clay, shale or heavy loam and containing more more than 10 per cent by volume of sand, gravel or stone. *Gasoline Handling Act*, R.R.O. 1980, Reg. 439, s. 1.

EARWITNESS. *n.* One who can bear witness to something heard personally.

EASEMENT. *n.* 1. A landowner's right to use another's land for a special purpose. 2. An easement, right of way, right or licence in the nature of an easement, profit a prendre or other incorporeal hereditament, but does not include such an easement arising by operation of law. *Condominium Act*, R.R.O. 1980, Reg. 121, s. 13. 3. See REGISTERED ∼.

EASEMENT IN GROSS. An easement created by private grant or statute, e.g. a power line or pipeline. J.V. DiCastri, *Occupiers' Liability* (Vancouver: Burroughs/Carswell, 1980) at 212.

EAST COAST PORT. All ports, from and including the Port of Montreal along the St. Lawrence River to the East Coast of Canada, along the East Coast of Canada and in the Province of Newfoundland. *East Coast Shipping Employees Hours of Work Regulations, 1975*, C.R.C., c. 987, s. 2.

EASTERN CANADA. All that part of Canada lying east of the eighty-ninth meridian of west longitude and such other areas in Ontario as the Governor in Council may designate. *Livestock Feed Assistance Act*, R.S.C. 1985, c. L-10, s. 2.

EASTERN DIVISION. That part of Canada not included in the Western Division. *Canada Grain Act*, R.S.C. 1985, c. G-10, s. 2.

EASTERN GRAIN. Grain grown in the Eastern Division. *Canada Grain Act*, R.S.C. 1985, c. G-10, s. 2.

EASTERN LINES. The lines of railway now operated as part of the Canadian National Railways and situated within the Provinces of New Brunswick, Nova Scotia, and Prince Edward Island, and the lines of railway, similarly operated, in the Province of Quebec extending from the southern provincial boundary near Matapédpia and near Courchesne to Diamond Junction and Lévis. *Maritime Freight Rates Act*, R.S.C. 1985, c. M-1, s. 2.

EASTERNMOST. *adj.* The half compass circle from but not including true north through east to and including true south. *Fishing Gear Marking Regulations*, C.R.C., c. 813, s. 2.

EASTERN PORT. The ports of Halifax, Saint John, West Saint John and Montreal and any of the ports of the St. Lawrence River to the east of Montreal. *Railway Act*, R.S.C. 1985, c. R-3, s. 281.

EASTERN RATES. (a) In relation to grain, the freight rates applying on November 30, 1960 to the movement of grain in bulk for export from any inland point to an Eastern port, and (b) in relation to flour, the freight rates applying on September 30, 1966 to the movement of flour for export from any inland point to an Eastern port. *Railway Act*, R.S.C. 1985, c. R-3, s. 281.

EASTERN TOWNSHIPS. The territory comprising the electoral districts of Sherbrooke, Stanstead, Compton, Wolfe, Richmond, Shefford, Brome, Missisquoi and the parishes of Lake Megantic, Ste-Cécile, St-Hubert, St-Jean, Vianney, Woburn, Marsboro, Piopolis, Val Racine, Notre-Dame des Bois, Milan, Nantes, St-Romain and Stornoway in the electoral district of Frontenac. *Eastern Townships Wood Order*, C.R.C., c. 261, s. 2.

EAT INDE SINE DIE. [L. that one may go from there without a day] Attendance had been fully satisfied, and the defendant is free to go.

EATING ESTABLISHMENT. See PUBLIC ∼.

EATING PLACE. See PUBLIC ∼.

EAVES. *n.* The roof's edge, built to extend beyond the walls of a building.

E.C.B. *abbr.* Expropriations Compensation Board.

ECCHYMOSIS. *n.* Bleeding into skin, mucous or serous membrane. F.A. Jaffe, *A Guide to*

Pathological Evidence, 2d ed. (Toronto: Carswell, 1983) at 174.

ECCLESIASTIC. *adj.* Set apart for or belonging to the church.

ECCLESIASTICAL. *adj.* Set apart for or belonging to the church.

ECCLESIASTICAL COURT. A court with jurisdiction in ecclesiastical matters only.

ECCLESIASTICAL LAW. Law which relates to the government, obligations and rights of a church.

ECE. *abbr.* The United Nations Economic Commission for Europe, Inland Transport Committee. *Motor Vehicle Safety Regulations*, C.R.C., c. 1038, s. 2.

ECOLOGICAL RESERVE. Any territory reserved by the Gouvernement composed of public lands if it considers that measure necessary: (a) to preserve such territory in its natural state; (b) to reserve such territory for scientific research and, if need be, for education; or (c) to safeguard animal and plant species threatened with disappearance or extinction. *Ecological Reserves Act*, R.S.Q. 1977, c. R-26, s. 1 & 2. See MANAGED ~; WHOLLY-PROTECTED ~.

ECOLOGY. *n.* The study of the inter-relationship of living things, including humans and plants, with their respective environments.

ECONOMICALLY UNDERPRIVILEGED PERSON. Any person to whom legal aid may be granted as a special need under the Social Aid Act (R.S.Q., chapter A-16) or, if he is not eligible thereunder, any person who in the opinion of the Commission or, as the case may be, of a legal aid corporation, lacks sufficient financial means to assert a right, obtain legal counsel or retain the services of an advocate or notary without depriving himself of necessary means of subsistence, according to the criteria established by regulation under subparagraph a of section 80. *An Act to Amend the Legal Aid Act*, S.Q. 1982, c. 36. s, 2.

ECONOMIC AQUICULTURAL PLANT. An aquicultural plant which, taking into account all of its resources, is capable of producing a revenue enabling its operator to pay the operating costs thereof, including maintenance and depreciation, to fulfill his obligations and to support his family adequately. *Aquaculture Credit Act*, S.Q. 1984, c. 21, s. 1.

ECONOMIC COUNCIL OF CANADA. An independent federal body which publishes a yearly review of Canada's economic problems and prospects for the medium term and may conduct economic studies at the government's request or on its own.

ECONOMIC DURESS. Excess charges for some service, i.e. to provide an arbitral award, to fulfill a contract by which a party demanding further payment is already bound, or to require additional payment to free goods from distraint. G.H.L. Fridman & J.G. McLeod, *Restitution* (Toronto: Carswell, 1982) at 213.

ECONOMIC ENTERPRISE. An enterprise in which is carried on any industry, trade, business or other undertaking of any kind whatsoever. *Communities Economic Development Fund Act*, S.M. 1971, c. 84, s. 1.

ECONOMIC FARM. Any farm which, taking into account all of its resources, is capable of producing a revenue which enables the operator thereof to pay the operating costs thereof, including maintenance and depreciation, to fulfill his obligations and to support his family adequately. Quebec statutes.

ECONOMIC FARM UNIT. A farm capable of producing income sufficent to support the operator of the farm and the operator's family, if any, and to repay moneys borrowed to establish the unit.

ECONOMIC LOSS. The loss experienced by a landlord whose rate of return on the landlord's invested equity and capitalized losses in respect of a residential complex is less than the rate of return made applicable to that residential complex by subsection 80 (1), but does not include a financial loss. *Residential Rent Regulation Act*, S.O. 1986, c. 63, s. 1.

ECONOMIC PLAN. A scheme approved by the commissioner that includes an authorization for a business enterprise and a public body to enter into an agreement that an impost payable by the business enterprise to the public body shall be paid at a rate, or in an amount, or determined or calculated in a manner different from that required or authorized under an Act listed in the Schedule. *Critical Industries Act*, S.B.C. 1985, c. 47, s. 1.

ECONOMIC SANCTION. The enforcement of international duties or responsibilities by asserting financial and economic pressure.

ECONOMIC STRIKE. A strike to force increases in wages or improvement of other working conditions.

ECONOMY. *n.* The acquisition, at the lowest cost and at the appropriate time, of financial, human and physical resources in appropriate quantity and quality. *Auditor General Act*, S.Q. 1985, c. 38, s. 21.

E CONVERSO. [L.] Conversely.

ECOSYSTEM. *n.* A complete system composed of people, animals, and plants in a defined area, together with the soil, atmosphere and climate comprising their habitat in that area.

ECUMENICAL. *adj.* Universal, general.

EDEMA. *n.* Presence of excess amounts of fluid in tissue. F.A. Jaffe, *A Guide to Pathological Evidence,* 2d ed. (Toronto: Carswell, 1983) at 174. See CEREBRAL ~; PULMONARY ~.

EDIBLE. *adj.* Fit for food. *Meat Inspection Act (Ontario),* R.R.O. 1980, Reg. 607, s. 1.

EDIBLE OIL PRODUCT. A food substance, other than a dairy product, of whatever origin, source or composition that is manufactured for human consumption wholly or in part from a fat or oil other than that of milk. *Edible Oil Products Act,* R.S.O. 1980, c. 128, s. 1.

EDIBLE SECTION. As applied to a registered establishment, means the part of the establishment in which any meat product is prepared or kept. *Meat Inspection Regulations,* C.R.C., c. 1032, s. 2.

EDICT. *n.* A command, proclamation.

EDITION. *n.* The number of copies of a work printed at one time or from the same typesetting.

EDUC. & L.J. *abbr.* Education and Law Journal.

EDUCATION. See CONTINUING ~; ENGLISH LANGUAGE ~; FRENCH LANGUAGE ~; GENERAL ~; OFFICERS OF ~; POST-SECONDARY ~; SECONDARY ~; SELF-IMPROVEMENT ~; VOCATIONAL ~.

EDUCATIONAL ASSISTANCE PAYMENT. Any amount, other than a refund of payments, paid or payable under an education savings plan to or for a beneficiary to assist him to further his education at the post-secondary school level. *Income Tax Act,* R.S.C. 1952, c. 148 (as am. S.C. 1974-75-76, c. 26, s. 100), s. 146.1(1)(b).

EDUCATIONAL ESTABLISHMENT. (a) A university established by special charter, the University of Québec, as well as a constituent university or superior school within the meaning of the University of Québec Act (chapter U-1); (b) a general and vocational college within the meaning of the General and Vocational Colleges Act (chapter C-29); (c) any other establishment designated by the Gouvernement which provides instruction at the college or university level. *An Act to Enable Municipalities to Tax Certain Educational Establishments,* R.S.Q. 1977, c. M-40, s. 1.

EDUCATIONAL INSTITUTION. 1. An institution of learning that offers courses at a post-secondary level. 2. A technical or vocational school, a university, college or other school of higher education. See DESIGNATED ~; SPECIFIED ~.

EDUCATIONAL INCREMENT. Salary recognition or wage increment offered to employees with certain educational qualifications. D.J.M. Brown and D.M. Beatty, *Canadian Labour Arbitration,* 2d ed. (Aurora: Canada Law Book, 1977) at 563.

EDUCATIONAL PROGRAM. See CPC ~; DENTAL ~S; QUALIFYING ~.

EDUCATIONAL PROGRAMMING. The presentation by a cablecaster of messages (i) designed to be presented in such a context as to provide a continuity of learning opportunity aimed at the acquisition or improvement of knowledge or the enlargement of understanding of members of the audience to whom such programming is directed; (ii) intended to provide information on the availability of courses of instruction; or (iii) intended to publicize special education events within the educational system. *The Community Cablecasters Act,* R.S.S. 1978, c. C-17, s. 2.

EDUCATIONAL PROJECT. A procedure by which a school defines its specific objectives, drafts and carries out a plan of action and revises the plan periodically with the participation of the pupils, the parents, and the staff of the school and of the school board. *Education Act,* S.Q. 1979, c. 80, s. 1.

EDUCATIONAL REGISTER. The register on which associate members who are students in clinical training who have not qualified are registered. *The Medical Act,* S.M. 1980-81, c. 11, s. 1.

EDUCATION AUTHORITY. A corporation that is incorporated by two or more bands or councils of bands for the purpose of providing for the educational needs of the members of such bands. *Education Amendment Act, 1982,* S.O. 1982, c. 32, s. 1. See LOCAL ~.

EDUCATION PROGRAM. See NURSING ~; SPECIAL ~.

EDUCATION SAVINGS PLAN. A contract entered into at any time between an individual (in this section referred to as a "subscriber") and a person or organization (in this section referred to as a "promoter") under which in consideration of payment by the subscriber of any periodic or other amount as consideration under the contract, the promoter agrees to pay or to cause to be paid to or for a beneficiary education assistance payments. *Income Tax Act,* R.S.C. 1952, c. 148 (as am. S.C. 1974-75-76, c. 26, s. 100), s. 146.1(1)(c). See REGISTERED ~.

EDUCATION SERVICES. See SPECIAL ~.

EDUCATOR. See ADULT ~.

EFFECT. See ADVERSE ~; ~S; PARADOX-ICAL ~; RETROACTIVE ~; RETROSPEC-TIVE ~; SIDE ~.

EFFECTIVE. *adj.* In relation to absorbent material, means material of a nature capable of minimizing the hazard of the liquid conveyed, and so disposed as to prevent movement and to ensure that the inner container or containers remain completely surrounded under all ordinary conditions of transport and, where reasonably possible, of sufficient quantity to be capable of absorbing the liquid completely in the event of breakage of the container. *Dangerous Goods Shipping Regulations*, C.R.C., c. 1419, s. 2.

EFFECTIVE APERTURE. With respect to a radiation detecting element at a given frequency, means the quotient obtained by dividing P by I, where (a) P equals the power extracted from a plane wave field at the given frequency by the radiation detecting element, and (b) I equals the power per unit area on the wave front of the plane wave field. *Radiation Emitting Devices Regulations*, C.R.C., c. 1370, s. 1.

EFFECTIVE CONTROL. Includes any control over any right, title or interest in or to agricultural lands or over a corporation that a person or corporation exercises directly or indirectly (i) through direct or indirect ownership of the right, title or interest, or of the shares or securities of the corporation, or (ii) through direct or indirect control over a corporation, syndicate or other body which has direct or indirect ownership of the right, title or interest or of the shares or securities of the corporation. *An Act to Amend the Agricultural Lands Protection Act*, S.M. 1980-81, c. 36, s. 2.

EFFECTIVE DATE. 1. As applicable to an annuity contract, unless otherwise defined therein, means the date on which the first premium payment is made. *Government Annuities Regulations*, C.R.C., c. 879, s. 2. 2. In relation to a pension plan or an amendment thereto, the date on which the plan or the amendment, as the case may be, comes into effect. *Pension Benefits Standards Regulations*, C.R.C., c. 1252, s. 2.

EFFECTIVE DATE OF LAY-OFF. The date of lay-off of an employee that occurs within a lay-off period.

EFFECTIVE FOCAL SPOT. The projection of the focal spot on the plane that is perpendicular to the X-ray beam axis and that passes through the centre of the focal spot. *Radiation Emitting Devices Regulations*, C.R.C., c. 1370, s. 1.

EFFECTIVE LENGTH OF SUPERSTRUC-TURE OR TRUNK. In metres, (a) S, in the case of an enclosed superstructure, other than a raised quarter deck, with a height equal to or great that Hs, (b) S × (height/Hs), in the case of an enclosed superstructure, other than a raised quarter deck, with a height less than Hs, (c) S or 0.6 L, whichever is lesser, in the case of an enclosed superstructure that is a raised quarter deck with a height equal to or greater than 2/3 Hs and having an intact front bulkhead, (d) S × (height/Hs), in the case of an enclosed superstructure that is a raised quarter deck with a height less than 2/3 Hs or does not have an intact front bulkhead, (e) length × (mean breadth/B), in the case of a trunk with a height equal to or greater than Hs, and (f) length × (mean breadth/B)(Height/Hs) in the case of a trunk with a height less than Hs. *Load Line Regulations (Inland)*, C.R.C., c. 1440, s. 16.

EFFECTIVELY CLOSED. That a container may be regarded as effectvely closed if it is so constructed and secured that it is for practical purposes watertight and will maintain its water-tightness under all usual conditions. *Dangerous Goods Shipping Regulations*, C.R.C., c. 1419, s. 2.

EFFECTIVENESS. *n.* The achievement, to the best degree, of the objectives or other intended effects of a program, an organization or an activity. *Auditor General Act*, S.Q. 1985, c. 38, s. 321.

EFFECTIVE OPENING. The cross-sectional area of a faucet, fitting or pipe at the point of discharge. *Ontario Water Resources Act*, R.R.O. 1980, Reg. 736, s. 1.

EFFECTIVE RATE. The rate of real property tax or of frontage or area tax that, in the opinion of the Minister, would be applicable to any federal property if that property were taxable property. *Municipal Grants Act*, R.S.C. 1985, c. M-13, s. 2.

EFFECTS. *n.* 1. Chattels, goods and property. 2. Includes the proceeds of any sale of the effects if those effects are sold under this section. *Shipping Act*, R.S.C. 1985, c. S-9, s. 279(8). See EFFECT; SETTLER'S ~.

EFFICIENCY. *n.* The conversion, in the best ratio, of resources into goods and services. *Auditor General Act*, S.Q. 1985, c. 38, s. 21. See PARTICULATE COLLECTION ~.

EFFICIENT TRUNK. A trunk or similar structure that does not extend to the sides of the ship and that meets the following requirements: (a) the trunk is at least as strong as the superstructure, (b) no hatchways are in the freeboard deck in way of the trunk, however, small access openings with watertight covers are permitted in the freeboard deck, (c) the trunk deck stringer provides a satisfactory gangway and sufficient lateral stiffness, (d) a permanent working platform fore and aft fitted with guard-rails is provided by the trunk deck, or by detached trunks connected to superstructures by efficient permanent gangways, (e) open-rails are fitted for at least half the length of the parts of the freeboard deck in way of the trunk that are in exposed positions, (f) ventilators on the freeboard deck adjacent to the trunk are capable of being closed watertight and the means of closing are permanently attached to the ventilators, (g) the machinery casings are protected by the trunk, by an enclosed superstructure of at least standard height or by a deckhouse of the same height as and of strength and weathertightness equivalent to such a superstructure, (h) the breadth of the trunk is at least 60 per cent of the breadth of the ship, and (i) where there is no superstructure, the length of the trunk is at last 0.6 L. *Load Line Regulations (Inland)*, C.R.C., c. 1440, s. 1.

EFFIGY. *n.* The representation of a person.

EFFLUENT. *n.* 1. A deleterious material flowing in or out of a drain, sewer, outfall, sewage disposal system or works. *Pollution Control Act*, R.S.B.C. 1979, c. 332, s. 1. 2. The liquid discharge from water pollution control works. *The Water Pollution Control Assistance Act*, R.S.S. 1978, c. W-5, s. 2. 3. All wastewaters deposited by a plant and includes process water, cooling water, tank drainage, storm water, wastes from water and wastewater treatment facilities and run-off from lands used for the storage or treatment of wastewater and sludges associated with the operation of a plant. 4. Includes mine water effluent, mill process effluent, tailings impoundment area effluent, treatment pond or treatment facility effluent, seepage and surface drainage. *Metal Mining Liquid Effluent Regulations*, C.R.C., c. 819, s. 2. See MILL PROCESS ~; MINE WATER ~.

EFFLUENT GAS STREAM. The combination of gases and solids being emitted from a process or operation. *Environmental Protection Act*, R.R.O. 1980, Reg. 295, s. 1.

EFFLUENT IRRIGATION. The application of effluent to land for the purposes of effluent disposal and growing vegetation. *The Water Pollution Control Assistance Act*, R.S.S. 1978, c. W-5, s. 2.

E.G. *abbr.* [L. exempli gratia] For instance.

EGALITY. *n.* Equality.

EGG. *n.* 1. An egg of a domestic hen in the shell. 2. An egg, i. of the domestic chicken of the species Gallis Domesticus, or ii. of the domestic turkey of the species Meleagris Gal-

lopavo, but does not include a partly formed egg that has been removed from a slaughtered domestic hen or domestic turkey. 3. Egg of a domestic hen other than hatching eggs. 4. The egg of a migratory bird and includes parts of such eggs. See BLOODY ~; COLD STORED ~S; DRIED ~; DRIED WHOLE ~ MIX; FROZEN ~; HATCHING ~S; INEDIBLE ~; PROCESSED ~; WHOLE ~; YOLK-REPLACED ~.

EGG DRYER. Equipment used for converting liquid egg to dried egg by the extraction of moisture. *Processed Egg Regulations*, C.R.C., c. 290, s. 2.

EGG-GRADING STATION. Premises for the grading, packing and marking of eggs. *Live Stock and Live Stock Products Act*, R.R.O. 1980, Reg. 582, s. 1.

EGGSHELL FRACTURE. The fracture of a flat bone which shows a quantity of intercommunicating fracture lines, whether or not fragments are displaced. F.A. Jaffe, *A Guide to Pathological Evidence*, 2d ed. (Toronto: Carswell, 1983) at 176 and 177.

EGG SOLID. 1. Egg yolk or albumen, or a combination thereof, that contains no shell or water. *Live Stock and Live Stock Products Act*, R.R.O. 1980, Reg. 583, s. 1. 2. Egg yolk or albumen that contains, or egg yolk and albumen that contain, no shell or water. *Processed Egg Regulations*, C.R.C., c. 290, s. 2.

EGG STATION. Premises for the grading, packing and marking of eggs.

EGISTMENT. See AGISTMENT.

EGRESS. See MEANS OF ~.

EI INCUMBIT PROBATIO, QUI DICIT, NON QUI NEGAT: CUM RERUM NATURAM FACTUM NEGANTIS PROBATIO NULLA SIT. [L.] The proof lies upon the one who affirms, not the one who denies; since, by the nature of things, one who denies a fact cannot prove it.

EI QUI AFFIRMAT, NON EI QUI NEGAT, INCUMBIT PROBATIO. [L.] The burden of proof lies on the one who affirms a fact, not on the one who denies it.

EJECIT INFRA TERMINUM. [L.] Ejected before the end of the term.

EJECTMENT. *n.* The action to recover the possession of land by persons not in possession but with an immediate right to possession. John G. Fleming, *The Law of Torts*, 6th ed. (Sydney: The Law Book Company Limited, 1983) at 44.

EJECTOR. *n.* A mechanism to expel an empty cartridge from a firearm after the extractor withdraws it from the firing chamber. F.A. Jaffe,

A Guide to Pathological Evidence, 2d ed. (Toronto: Carswell, 1983) at 174.

EJURATION. *n.* Resigning or renouncing one's place.

EJUSDEM GENERIS. [L. of the same kind] A general word which follows particular and specific words of a similar nature, takes its meaning from them and is considered to be limited to the same genus as those words. P. St. J. Langan, ed., *Maxwell on The Interpretation of Statutes*, 12th ed. (Bombay: N.M. Tripathi, 1976) at 297.

EJUS EST INTERPRETARI CUJUS EST CONDERE. [L.] The one who establishes the law also interprets it.

EJUS NULLA CULPA EST CUI PARERE NECESSE SIT. [L.] The one who is bound to obey is not at fault.

ELDERLY PERSON. 1. One who has reached the age of 65 years, and, in the absence of positive evidence of age, means a person who apparently has reached that age. *Child and Family Services and Family Relations Act*, S.N.B. 1980, c. C-2.1, s. 1. 2. A person of advanced years who is not suffering from any chronic disease that incapacitates him. *Homes for the Aged Act*, R.S.A. 1970, c. 170, s. 2.

ELDERLY PERSONS. (i) An unmarried person of sixty-five or more years of age whose annual income, including assistance under The Old Age Assistance Act, or the Old Age Assistance Act (Canada), or the Old Age Security Act (Canada), does not exceed an amount equal to five times the annual rental for the accommodation that he occupies in an elderly persons' housing unit or a hostel, or (ii) a married person of sixty-five or more years of age whose annual income together with that of his spouse, including assistance under The Old Age Assistance Act, or the Old Age Assistance Act (Canada), or the Old Age Security Act (Canada), does not exceed an amount equal to five times the annual rental for the accommodation that he and his spouse occupy in an elderly persons' housing unit or a hostel, or (iii) a married person who is the spouse of a person to whom sub-clause (ii) refers. *Elderly and Infirm Persons' Housing Act*, R.S.M. 1970, c. E20, s. 2.

ELDERLY PERSONS' HOUSING UNIT. Housing accommodation that has separate kitchen and bathroom facilities for either one or two elderly persons who are capable of living independently. *Elderly and Infirm Persons' Housing Act*, R.S.M. 1970, c. E20, s. 2.

ELECTED AUTHORITY. (i) A council under the Municipal Government Act, (ii) a council under the County Act, or (iii) a board of trustees

under the School Act. *Local Authorities Election Act*, S.A. 1983, c. L-27.5, s. 1.

ELECTION. *n.* 1. Making a choice. 2. Deciding on a representative. See AT AN ~; BY-~; CANDIDATE AT AN ~; DURING AN ~; DURING THE ~; FIRST ~; GENERAL ~; NEW ~; REGULAR ~; THROUGH AN ~; THROUGHOUT AN ~.

ELECTION ASSISTANT. A person appointed by the clerk to assist in the conduct of an election. *Municipal Elections Act*, R.S.O. 1980, c. 308, s. 1.

ELECTION COURT. A court constituted under The Controverted Elections Act for the trial of a petition. *The Election Act*, R.S.S. 1978, c. E-6, s. 2.

ELECTION DAY. The day fixed for voting at an election. *Local Authorities Election Act*, S.A. 1983, c. L-27.5, s. 1.

ELECTION DOCUMENT. Any document or writing issued under the authority of an Act of Parliament or the legislature of a province with respect to an election held pursuant to the authority of that Act. *Criminal Code*, R.S.C. 1985, c. C-46, s. 377(2).

ELECTION DOCUMENTS. The papers directed in this Act to be transmitted to the Chief Electoral Officer, after an election, by the returning officer, namely, (a) the writ with the return of the election endorsed thereon, (b) the nomination papers filed by the candidates, (c) the reserve supply of undistributed blank ballot papers, (d) the enumerators' record books used in urban polling divisions, (e) the index books prepared by enumerators in rural polling divisions, (f) the revising officers' record sheets and other papers relating to the revision of the list of electors in urban polling divisions, (g) the statements of the polls from which the official addition of the votes was made, (h) the other returns from the various polling stations enclosed in sealed envelopes, as prescribed in sections 160 to 167, and containing (i) the poll book used at the poll, (ii) a packet of stubs and unused ballot papers, (iii) packets of ballots papers cast for the various candidates, (iv) a packet of spoiled ballot papers, (v) a packet of rejected ballot papers, and (vi) a packet containing the official list of electors used at the poll, the written appointments of candidates' agents and the used transfer certificates, if any, and proxy certificates, if any, (i) the used and unused outer envelopes referred to in paragraph 293(1)(b), and (j) the Record of Voting in the Office of the Returning Officer kept pursuant to sections 292 and 293. *Canada Elections Act*, R.S.C. 1985, c. E-2, s. 2.

ELECTION EXPENSES. (a) Amounts paid, (b) liabilities incurred, (c) the commercial value of goods and services donated or provided, other than volunteer labour, and (d) amounts that represent the differences between amounts paid and liabilities incurred for goods and services, other than volunteer labour, and the commercial value thereof where they are provided at less than their commercial value, (all of which are in this definition referred to as "the cost") for the purpose of promoting or opposing, directly and during an election, a particular registered party, or the election of a particular candidate, and without limiting the generality of the foregoing, includes (e) the cost of acquiring the right to the use of time on the facilities of any broadcasting undertaking, or of acquiring the right to the publication of an advertisement in any periodical publication, (f) the cost of acquiring the services of any person, including remuneration and expenses paid to the person or on behalf of the person, as an official agent or registered agent or otherwise, except where the services are donated or provided at materially less than their commercial value, (g) the cost of acquiring meeting space, of provision of light refreshment and of acquiring and distributing mailing objects, material or devices of a promotional nature, and (h) the cost of goods or services provided by a government, crown corporation or any other public agency, when those costs are incurred for a purpose set out in this definition.

ELECTION EXPENSES OF A CANDIDATE. Election expenses incurred or authorized, or deemed to have been incurred or authorized, by the official agent of that candidate.

ELECTION EXPENSES OF A REGISTERED POLITICAL PARTY. Election expenses incurred or authorized, or deemed to have been incurred or authorized, by the chief agent of that party.

ELECTION LIST. The list of petitions presented under this Act required by this Act to be made out by the clerk of the court. *Dominion Controverted Elections Act*, R.S.C. 1985, c. C-39, s. 2.

ELECTION MATERIAL. 1. Includes instructions, forms, record books, index books, ballot papers, poll books and copies of Acts, regulations or rules and portions thereof, and any other supplies. *Canada Elections Act*, R.S.C. 1970 (1st Supp.), c. 14, s. 115. 2. Any poster, leaflet, pamphlet or advertisement whether printed or broadcast by radio or television, the purpose of which is to persuade voters to vote for a particular candidate or the candidates of a particular party. *Elections Act*, S.M. 1980, c. 67, s. 177.

ELECTION OF DOMICILE. The indication by a notary of the place where he intends to practise his profession. *Notarial Act*, R.S.Q. 1977, c. N-2, s. 1.

ELECTION OFFICER. The Chief Electoral Officer, the Assistant Chief Electoral Officer and every returning officer, assistant returning officer, deputy returning officer, poll clerk, enumerator, revising officer and revising agent and includes any person having any duty to perform pursuant to this Act, to the faithful performance of which duty he may be sworn. *Elections acts*.

ELECTION OFFICIAL. Includes a returning officer, deputy returning officer, poll clerk, revising officer, nomination officer, enumerators and any other supervisory officers and assistants appointed pursuant to section 29 or 30. *Local Government Election Act*, S.S. 1982-83, c. L-30.1, s. 2.

ELECTION PAPERS. 1. The papers directed in this Act to be transmitted to the Chief Electoral Officer, after an election, by the returning officer, namely, (a) the writ with the return of the election endorsed thereon, (b) the nomination papers filed by the candidates, (c) the reserve supply of undistributed blank ballot papers, (d) the enumerators' record books used in urban polling divisions, (e) the index books prepared by enumerators in rural polling divisions, (f) the revising officers' record sheets and other papers relating to the revision of the list of electors in urban polling divisions, (g) the statements of the polls from which the official addition of the votes was made, (h) the other returns from the various polling stations enclosed in sealed envelopes, as prescribed in sections 160 to 167, and containing (i) the poll book used at the poll, (ii) a packet of stubs and unused ballot papers, (iii) packets of ballot papers cast for the various candidates, (iv) a packet of spoiled ballot papers, (v) a packet of rejected ballot papers, and (vi) a packet containing the official list of electors used at the poll, the written appointments of candidates' agents and the used transfer certificates, if any, and proxy certificates, if any, (i) the used and unused outer envelopes referred to in paragraph 293(1)(b), and (j) the Record of Voting in the Office of the Returning Officer kept pursuant to sections 292 and 293. *Canada Elections Act*, R.S.C. 1985, c. E-2, s. 2. 2. The papers required under this Act to be transmitted by the returning officer to the Chief Electoral Officer after an election, and, without limiting the generality of the foregoing, include (i) writs of elections with the returns of the elections endorsed thereon, (ii) nomination papers filed by candidates, (iii) enumerators' record books, (iv) statements of polls after the count by the deputy returning officers, (v) poll books used at polls, (vi) ballot papers, (vii) certified lists of electors used at polls, including any lists of additions thereto, and (viii) any written oath required under this Act. *Elections acts.*

ELECTION PERIOD. The period commencing on the day of issue of the writ instituting the holding of an election and ending on polling day.

ELECTION PETITION. 1. A petition presented in pursuance of the Controverted Elections Act. 2. A petition complaining of an undue return or undue election of a member, or of no return, or of a double return, or of any unlawful act by any candidate not returned by which he is alleged to have become disqualified to sit in the assembly, or of the conduct of any returning or deputy returning officer. *Controverted Elections Act*, R.S.M. 1970, c. C210, s. 2. 3. A petition complaining of an undue return or undue election of a member, of no return or a double return, of matters contained in a special return made or of any unlawful act by any candidate not returned by which he is alleged to have become disqualified to sit in the House of Commons or legislative assembly.

ELECTIONS CANADA. The federal body which supervises the administrative conduct of Canadian federal elections.

ELECTIO SEMEL FACTA ET PLACITUM TESTATUM NON PATITUR REGRESSUM. QUOD SEMEL PLACUIT IN ELECTIONIBUS AMPLIUS DISPLICERE NON POTEST. [L.] Once an election is made and a plea witnessed there is no recall. In elections whatever once pleased a person cannot displease after further consideration.

ELECTIVE INSURED HEALTH SERVICES. Insured health services other than services that are provided in an emergency or in any other circumstance in which medical care is required without delay. *Canada Health Act*, R.S.C. 1985, c. C-6, s. 2.

ELECTOR. *n.* 1. Person eligible to vote at an election. 2. A person entitled to vote at an election. 3. A person qualified to vote at an election. 4. Any person who is or who claims to be registered as an elector in the list of voters for any electoral district; or who is, or claims to be, entitled to vote in any election. See CANADIAN FORCES ~; DEPENDANT ~; LIST OF ~S; MUNICIPAL ~S; PROPRIETARY ~; PUBLIC SCHOOL ~S; PUBLIC SERVICE ~; QUALIFIED ~; RESIDENT ~; SEPARATE SCHOOL ~; VETERAN ~.

ELECTORAL DISTRICT. 1. An area entitled to elect a member to serve in a legislature. 2.

The area from which a school board member is to be elected. See DISTRICT OR ~.

ELECTORAL DISTRICT AGENT. In relation to a registered party, means a person whose name is recorded in the registry of agents of registered parties maintained by the Chief Electoral Officer pursuant to subsection 33(1) and who is designated as such by the chief agent of the party. *Canada Elections Act*, R.S.C. 1985, c. E-2, s. 2.

ELECTORAL DIVISION. Any territorial division or district entitled to return a member. See URBAN ~.

ELECTORAL OFFICER. See CHIEF ~.

ELECTORAL PRECINCT. A territorial division effected in view of the election of a member to the Assemblée nationale du Québec in accordance with the Act respecting electoral representation (1979, c. 57). *Election Act*, S.Q. 1979, c. 56, s. 1.

ELECTORAL QUOTIENT. In respect of a province, the quotient obtained by dividing its population, determined according to the results of the then most recent decennial census, by the number of members to be assigned to it under any of Rules 1 to 5(3) in the readjustment following the completion of that census. *Constitution Act, 1974*, S.C. 1974-75-76, c. 13, s. 6, reprinted in R.S.C. 1985, App. Doc. No. 40.

ELECTRICAL AUTHORITY. A person, board, commission or corporation that the federal government or a provincial or municipal government has authorized to approve electrical facilities for safety purposes in the area in which the lighting system referred to therein is located. *Canada Safe Illumination Regulations*, C.R.C., c. 1008, s. 5.

ELECTRICAL CODE. See CANADIAN ~.

ELECTRICAL CONTRACTOR. Includes a person who installs electrical equipment for another person, and includes a utility corporation that installs electrical equipment for another person.

ELECTRICAL EQUIPMENT. Any apparatus, appliance, device, instrument, fitting, fixture, machinery, material or thing used, or capable of being used, in or for: (i) the generation, transformation, transmission, distribution, supply or utilization of electric power or energy; or (ii) the protection of buildings or premises from damage by lightning; and includes any assemblage or combination of materials or things used, or capable of being used or adapted, to serve or perform any purpose or function when connected to an electrical installation, notwithstanding that any of the materials or things may be mechanical, metallic or non-electric in origin.

ELECTRICAL FACILITY. Any equipment, device, apparatus, wiring, conductor, assembly or part thereof that is employed for the generation, transformation, transmission, distribution, storage, control, measurement or utilization of electricial energy and that has an ampacity and voltage that is dangerous to employees. *Canada Electrical Safety Regulations*, C.R.C., c. 998, s. 2.

ELECTRICAL INSTALLATION. 1. The wires, machinery, apparatus, appliances, devices, material and equipment used in, on or about a building, structure or premises by a supply authority or a consumer for the generation, receipt, distribution or use of electrical power or energy. 2. The wires, machinery, apparatus, appliances, devices, material and equipment used in, on or about a building, structure or premises by a consumer for the use of electrical power or energy, but does not include the wires, machinery, apparatus, appliances, devices, material and equipment used in the carrying out of any of the following work or services: (a) motor rewinding, (b) repairing radios and other electronic equipment, (c) installing or maintaining electrical conductors or equipment in aircrafts, ships, rolling stock or railways or automotive equipment, (d) generating or distributing electrical energy by a corporation or person as a principal business, (e) constructing or maintaining telephone, telegraph or other systems of communication, (f) installing a boiler that is within the scope of the Boiler and Pressure Vessel Act, or (g) installing an elevating device that is within the scope of the Elevators and Lifts Act. *Electrical Installation and Inspection Act*, S.N.B. 1976, c. E-4.1, s. 1. See WORK OF ~.

ELECTRICALLY SUPERVISED CONTROL VALVE. A valve permanently fitted with a mechanical device to actuate electrical contacts upon initiation of valve actuation. *Building Code Act*, R.R.O. 1980, Reg. 87, s. 1.

ELECTRICAL METALLIC TUBING. A metal raceway into which it is intended that conductors shall be drawn, and which has a circular cross-section, a wall thinner than that of rigid metal conduit and an outside diameter sufficiently different from that of rigid conduit to render it impracticable for threading it with standard pipe-thread. *Power Corporation Act*, R.R.O. 1980, Reg. 794, s. 0.

ELECTRICAL MOBILE EQUIPMENT. Equipment which during its operating cycle is required to move along the ground while energized and which receives its current through a trailing cable. *Occupational Health and Safety Act*, R.R.O. 1980, Reg. 694, s. 1.

ELECTRICAL ROOM. A room that is intended for the exclusive installation of electrical equipment. *Power Corporation Act*, R.R.O. 1980, Reg. 794, s. 0.

ELECTRICAL SAFETY CODE. An Ontario regulation made under the Power Corporation Act and based on CSA Standard C22.1-1982, Canadian Electrical Code. D. Robertson, *Ontario Health and Safety Guide* (Toronto: Richard De Boo Ltd., 1988) at 5-141.

ELECTRICAL SUPPLY STATION. Any building, room or enclosure within which is situated electrical supply apparatus and which is accessible only to authorized persons, and includes generating stations, substations, transformer compartments or enclosures, storage battery charging rooms, and other such stations or enclosures. *Coal Mines Regulation Act*, R.S.N.S. 1967, c. 36, s. 84.

ELECTRICAL TREATMENT. The administration of electricity to the foot or leg by means of electrodes, rays and the like, other than Xray unless used for diagnostic purposes. *Podiatrists Act*, R.S.B.C. 1979, c. 330, s. 1.

ELECTRICAL UTILITY. A person or organization that, as its prime purpose, performs one or more of the functions of generating, transmitting or distributing electric energy, otherwise than for consumption by such person or organization. *National Energy Board Part VI Regulations*, C.R.C., c. 1056, s. 2.

ELECTRICAL WORK. 1. The actual installation, repair and maintenance of cables, conduits, wiring, switchgear, transmission lines, transformers, motors and generators used for the production, transmission and utilization of electrical energy for light and power purposes. 2. Includes the installation of lightning rods. *Electrical Installation and Inspection Act*, S.N.B. 1976, c. E-4.1, s. 1.

ELECTRICAL WORKER. See QUALIFIED ~.

ELECTRIC BOILER. A boiler heated by electricity. *Power Engineers and Boilers and Pressure Vessel Safety Act*, S.B.C. 1981, c. 25, s. 1.

ELECTRIC DISTRIBUTION SYSTEM. Any system, works, plant, equipment or service, for the delivery, distribution or furnishing of electric energy directly to the consumer, but does not include a power plant or transmission line.

ELECTRIC ELEVATOR. An elevator in which the motion of the car or platform is obtained through an electric motor applied directly to the elevator machinery. *Power Corporation Act*, R.R.O. 1980, Reg. 794, s. 0.

ELECTRIC ENERGY. 1. Includes electric power that is produced, transmitted, distributed or furnished by a public utility. *Electric Power and Telephone Act*, S.P.E.I. 1984, c. 20, s. 1. 2. In addition to its ordinary meaning includes (i) energy associated with an electromotive force, and (ii) power and reactive power and other electromagnetic effects associated with electric energy. *Hydro and Electric Energy Act*, R.S.A. 1980, c. H-13, s. 1.

ELECTRICIAN. *n.* A person who, (i) lays out, assembles, installs, repairs, maintains, connects or tests electrical fixtures, apparatus, control equipment and wiring for systems of alarm, communication, light, heat or power in buildings or other structures, (ii) plans proposed installations from blueprints, sketches or specifications and installs panel boards, switch boxes, pull boxes and other related electrical devices, (iii) measures, cuts, threads, bends, assembles and installs conduits and other types of electrical conductor enclosures that connect panels, boxes, outlets and other related electrical devices, (iv) installs brackets, hangers or equipment for supporting electrical equipment, (v) installs in or draws electrical conductors through conductor enclosures, (vi) prepares conductors for splicing or electrical connections, secures conductor connections by soldering or other mechanical means and reinsulates and protects conductor connections, or (vii) tests electrical equipment for proper function, but does not include a person who is permanently employed on an industrial plant at a limited purpose occupation in the electrical trade. *Apprenticeship and Tradesmen's Qualification Act*, R.R.O. 1980, Reg. 32, s. 1. See CONTRACTING ~; JOURNEYMAN ~; MASTER ~.

ELECTRICITY. *n.* Electric power, energy or current. See SURPLUS ~.

ELECTRICITY DISTRIBUTOR. 1. Designates any person, partnership or corporation operating an undertaking for the production, sale or distribution of electric power. *Master Electricians Act*, R.S.Q. 1977, c. M-3, s. 1. 2. When such word designates an electricity distributor: any person, firm or corporation carrying on an electricty undertaking; such terms also include their lessees, trustees, liquidators or assignees, but do not include municipal corporations, Hydro-Québec or any cooperative contemplated in the Rural Electrification Act (1945, c. 48). *Régie de l'électricité et du gaz Act*, R.S.Q. 1977, c. R-6, s. 1.

ELECTRICITY SYSTEM. A system of lighting, heating or energy or power production by means of electricity. *Electricity Municipalization Act*, R.S.Q. 1977, c. M-38, s. 2.

ELECTRICITY UNDERTAKING. Any undertaking for the production, sale or distribution of electricity. *Régie de l'électricité et du gaz Act*, R.S.Q. 1977, c. R-6, s. 1.

ELECTRIC POWER. The rate of transferring electric energy, expressed in units of kilowatts or megawatts. *National Energy Board Part VI Regulations*, C.R.C., c. 1056, s. 2.

ELECTRIC SWITCH LOCK. An electric lock connected with a hand operated switch to prevent its operation until the lock is released. *Regulations No. O-8, Uniform Code of Operating Rules*, C.R.C., c. 1175, Part III, c. 2.

ELECTRIC SYSTEM. See FARM ~; FUEL AND ~S MECHANIC.

ELECTRIC TRAMWAY. A railroad, railway or tramway for the conveyance of passengers or goods, or either of them, operated by electric motive power. *Corporations Tax Act*, R.S.N.S. 1967, c. 61, s. 1.

ELECTRIC UTILITY. A person who owns or operates equipment or facilities in the province for the production, generation, transmission, sale, delivery or furnishing of electrical power for compensation to two or more premises, and includes a lessee, trustee, receiver or liquidator of that person. *Electrical Inspection and Licensing Act, 1981*, S.S. 1980-81, c. E-7.1, s. 2.

ELECTROCUTION. *n.* Death caused when an electric current passes through the body. F.A. Jaffe, *A Guide to Pathological Evidence*, 2d ed. (Toronto: Carswell, 1983) at 174.

ELECTRODE. *n.* An electrically conductive element that interfaces with body tissue. *Medical Devices Regulations*, C.R.C., c. 871, s. 1. See GROUND ~.

ELECTRO-MAGNETIC, ACOUSTIC, MECHANICAL OR OTHER DEVICE. 1. Any device or apparatus that is used or is capable of being used to intercept a private communication, but does not include a hearing aid used to correct subnormal hearing of the user to not better than normal hearing. 2. Any device or apparatus that is used or capable of being used to intercept any function of a computer system, but does not include a hearing aid used to correct subnormal hearing of the user to not better than normal hearing. *Criminal Code*, R.S.C. 1985, c. C-46, s. 342.1(2) as added by *Criminal Law Amendment Act*, R.S.C. 1985 (1st Supp.), c. 27, s. 45.

ELECTROMAGNETIC DEVICE. A device using an electromagnetic system for examining a shaft rope. *Occupational Health and Safety Act*, R.R.O. 1980, Reg. 694, s. 1.

ELECTRONIC EQUIPMENT. Any electronic equipment proved to be of significant benefit in the navigation of a ship or in the catching of fish by a ship. *Fishing Ships (Bounties) Act*, R.S.Nfld. 1970, c. 137, s. 2.

ELECTROPHORESIS. *n.* A technique to separate various proteins using an electric current. F.A. Jaffe, *A Guide to Pathological Evidence*, 2d ed. (Toronto: Carswell, 1983) at 174 and 175.

ELEEMOSYNA. *n.* Alms.

ELEEMOSYNARY CORPORATION. A body corporate established to perpetually distribute free alms or its founder's gift.

ELEGIT. *n.* [L. one has chosen]. A writ of execution by which a judgment creditor is awarded the debtor's land to hold until the debt is satisfied. See WRIT OF ~.

ELEMENTARY PUPIL. A person enrolled in one of the grades from Grade 1 to Grade 7 in a public school and a person enrolled in a kindergarten class established in a public school under this Act. *School Act*, R.S.B.C. 1979, c. 375, s. 1.

ELEMENTARY SCHOOL. 1. A public school in which accommodation and tuition are provided exclusively or mainly for elementary pupils. *School Act*, R.S.B.C. 1979, c. 375, s. 1. 2. An independent school in which tuition or tuition and accommodation are provided primarily for persons who, if they were attending a public school would be enrolled in one of the grades from Grade 1 to Grade 7 or in a kindergarten class. *School Support (Independent) Act*, R.S.B.C. 1979, c. 378, s. 1. 3. A public school, Roman Catholic separate school, or Protestant separate school. *Education Act*, R.S.O. 1980, c. 129, s. 1.

ELEMENTS. See COMMON ~.

ELEVATING DEVICE. A non-portable device for hoisting and lowering or moving persons or freight, and includes an elevator, dumbwaiter, escalator, moving walk, manlift, passenger ropeway, incline lift, construction hoist, stage lift, platform lift and stairway lift.

ELEVATION. See GEODETIC ~.

ELEVATOR. *n.* 1. Any mechanism equipped with a car or platform that moves in guides and that is used to transport persons or things from one level to another level and includes an escalator, a dumb-waiter, a hoist, a ski lift, a ski tow, and any other hoisting apparatus or appliance together with the mechanisms, equipment, controls, gates, loading and unloading

thresholds, signals, and appurtenances of or to any of those things. 2. A grain elevator, warehouse or mill that has been declared by Parliament to be a work for the general advantage of Canada. *Canadian Wheat Board Act*, R.S.C. 1985, c. C-24, s. 2. 3. Any premises constructed for the purpose of handling and storing grain received directly from producers, otherwise than as a part of the farming operation of a particular producer, and into which grain may be received, at which grain may be weighed, cleaned, dried, elevated and stored and out of which grain may be discharged. *New Brunswick Grain Act*, S.N.B. 1980, c. N-5.1, s. 1. 4. (a) Any premises in the Western Division (i) into which grain may be received or out of which grain may be discharged directly from or to railway cars or ships, (ii) constructed for the purpose of handling and storing grain received directly from producers, otherwise than as a part of the farming operation of a particular producer, and into which grain may be received, at which grain may be weighed, elevated and stored and out of which grain may be discharged, or (iii) constructed for the purpose of handling and storing grain as part of the operation of a flour mill, feed mill, seed cleaning plant, malt house, distillery, grain oil extraction plant or other grain processing plant, and into which grain may be received, at which grain may be weighed, elevated and stored and out of which grain may be discharged for processing or otherwise, (b) any premises in the Eastern Division, situated along Lake Superior, Lake Huron, Lake St. Clair, Lake Erie, Lake Ontario or the canals or other navigable waters connecting those Lakes or the St. Lawrence River or any tidal waters, and into which grain may be received directly from railway cars or ships and out of which grain may be discharged directly to ships, (c) the portion of any premises in the Eastern Division named in Schedule II that is used for the purpose of storing grain, (d) any premises in the Eastern Division constructed for the purpose of handling and storing grain received directly from producers, otherwise than as a part of the farming operation of a particular producer, and into which grain may be received, at which grain may be weighed, elevated and stored and out of which grain may be discharged, and (e) any premises in the Eastern Division constructed for the purpose of handling and storing grain as a part of the operation of a flour mill, feed mill, seed cleaning plant, malt house, distillery, grain oil extraction plant or other grain processing plant, and into which grain may be received, at which grain may be weighed, elevated and stored and out of which grain may be discharged for processing or otherwise, including any such premises owned and operated by Her Majesty in right of Canada or a province or any agent thereof. *Canada Grain Act*, R.S.C. 1985, c. G-10, s. 2. See CSA ~ CODE; ELECTRIC ~; GRAIN ~; MILL ~; PRIMARY ~; PROCESS ~; TERMINAL ~; TRANSFER ~.

ELEVATOR COMPANY. An incorporated company or association of incorporated companies that operates or controls one hundred or more county elevators in the Provinces of Manitoba, Saskatchewan, Alberta or British Columbia. *Wheat Cooperative Marketing Act*, R.S.C. 1970, c. W-9, s. 2.

ELEVATOR MACHINERY. The machinery and its equipment used in raising and lowering the elevator car or platform. *Power Corporation Act*, R.R.O. 1980, Reg. 794, s. 0.

ELEVATOR RECEIPT. A document in prescribed form issued in respect of grain delivered to an elevator acknowledging receipt of the grain and, subject to any conditions contained therein or in this Act, entitling the holder of the document (a) to the delivery of grain of the same kind, grade and quantity as the grain referred to in the document, or (b) in the case of a document issued for specially binned grain, to delivery of the identical grain. *Canada Grain Act*, R.S.C. 1985, c. G-10, s. 2.

ELIGIBILITY. *n.* Qualification.

ELIGIBLE ASSET COST. A prescribed outlay or expense in respect of a prescribed asset used in the petroleum industry. *Petroleum Incentives Program*, R.S.C. 1985, c. P-13, s. 2.

ELIGIBLE CARRIER. A common air carrier licensed by the Canadian Transport Commission to provide commercial air service. *Temporary Export of Aircraft Remission Order*, C.R.C., c. 799, s. 2.

ELIGIBLE COST OR EXPENSE. An eligible asset cost, eligible development expense or eligible exploration expense. *Petroleum Incentives Program*, R.S.C. 1985, c. P-13, s. 2.

ELIGIBLE COSTS. See ESTIMATED ~.

ELIGIBLE DEVELOPMENT EXPENSE. A prescribed outlay or expense in respect of the development of lands for the purpose of producing oil or gas or both. *Petroleum Incentives Program*, R.S.C. 1985, c. P-13, s. 2.

ELIGIBLE EXPLORATION EXPENDITURES. Expenditures on actual exploration for new mineral ore in the Province for work, as defined by regulation. *An Act to Amend the Metallic Minerals Tax Act*, S.N.B. 1987, c. 35, s. 1.

ELIGIBLE EXPLORATION EXPENSE. A prescribed outlay or expense in respect of the exploration for oil or gas or both. *Petroleum Incentives Program*, R.S.C. 1985, c. P-13, s. 2.

ELIGIBLE LIST. A register, maintained by the Secretary, listing foreign air carriers that may apply to the Committee to operate international charter flights. *Air Carrier Regulations*, C.R.C., c. 3, s. 23.

ELIGIBILITY CERTIFICATE. A certificate completed as prescribed by a Commission outlining such particulars of a horse and its past performances as the Commission may require. *Race Track Supervision Regulations*, C.R.C., c. 441, s. 2.

ELISOR. *n.* Elector.

E.L.J. *abbr.* Education & Law Journal.

ELM TREE. A tree of the ulmus species. *Dutch Elm Disease Act*, S.M. 1980, c. 65, s. 1.

ELOIGNE. *v.* To distance; to go far away.

ELOIGNMENT. *n.* Removal; sending far away.

ELOINE. *v.* To distance; to go far away.

ELONGATA. *n.* A return made by a sheriff who found that goods had been eloigned.

ELONGATUS. *n.* A return to a writ stating that the person was out of the sheriff's jurisdiction.

E.L.R. *abbr.* Eastern Law Reporter, 1906-1914.

EMANATION. *n.* That which issues or proceeds from some source.

EMBALMER. *n.* Any person who preserves a dead human body, entire or in part.

EMBALMING. *n.* The preservation of the dead human body, entire or in part, by the use of chemical substances, fluids or gases, either by outward application of such chemical substances, fluids or gases on the body or by the vascular introduction of the same into the body by vascular or hypodermic injection, or by direct application into the organs and cavities.

EMBARASSING. *adj.* When describing pleading means ambiguous, unintelligible, stating immaterial matters which raise irrelevant issues that may cause delay and expense or containing unnecessary or irrelevant allegations. Also used to describe a claim or defence which a party is not entitled to use. I.H. Jacob, ed., *Bullen and Leake and Jacob's Precedents of Pleadings*, 12th ed. (London: Sweet and Maxwell, 1975) at 147.

EMBARGO. *n.* Forbidding passage; an arrest, detention or stopping of a ship.

EMBASSAGE. *n.* 1. An ambassador's establishment. 2. The commission given by a nation to an ambassador, to deal with another nation.

EMBASSY. *n.* 1. An ambassador's establishment. 2. The commission given by a nation to an ambassador, to deal with another nation.

EMBEZZLEMENT. *n.* Conversion to personal use of any chattel, money or valuable security received or taken into possession by an employee for, in the name or on account of the employer.

EMBLEM. See FLORAL ~ OF ONTARIO; OFFICIAL ~.

EMBLEMENTS. *n.* Annual crops produced by agricultural labour.

EMBOLISM. *n.* Clogging of a blood vessel by an embolus. F.A. Jaffe, *A Guide to Pathological Evidence*, 2d ed. (Toronto: Carswell, 1983) at 175. See AIR ~; AMNIOTIC FLUID ~; BONE MARROW ~; BULLET ~; FAT ~; PULMO-NARY ~; TALCUM ~.

EMBOLUS. *n.* A mass of undissolved matter which plugs a vessel that is too narrow to permit it to pass. F.A. Jaffe, *A Guide to Pathological Evidence*, 2d ed. (Toronto: Carswell, 1983) at 175.

EMBRACEOR. *n.* A person who tries to influence a jury.

EMBRACERY. *n.* A common law offence of attempting to instruct or influence any jury member or giving a reward to a jury member for something done by that member.

EMBRYO. *n.* The child developing in the uterus during the first three months of pregnancy. F.A. Jaffe, *A Guide to Pathological Evidence*, 2d ed. (Toronto: Carswell, 1983) at 175. See ANIMAL ~.

EMBRYO TRANSFER BUSINESS. The business of collecting, acquiring, processing, storing, distributing or implanting embryos, as the case may be. *Artificial Insemination of Domestic Animals Amendment Act, 1981*, S.A. 1981, c. 6, s. 2.

EMENDARE. *v.* [L.] To give compensation for some crime or trespass which has been committed.

EMENDATIO. *n.* [L.] The power to amend and correct abuses, following specified measures and rules.

EMERGENCY. *n.* 1. A present or imminent event that is or could affect the health, safety or welfare of people or could cause damage to property. 2. War, invasion, riot or insurrection, real or apprehended. *National Defence Act*, R.S.C. 1985, c. N-5, s. 2. 3. Any flood, tempest, hurricane, act of war by Her Majesty's enemies, insurrection, rebellion and any other occurrence which, in the opinion of the Minister, is or constitutes an emergency. 4. A situation where

delay in responding to a call for ambulance service could endanger the life, limb or a vital organ of a patient. *Ambulance Act*, R.R.O. 1980, Reg. 14, s. 1. See ENVIRONMENTAL ~; WAR ~.

EMERGENCY BRAKE. A mechanism designed to stop a vehicle after a failure of the service brake system. *Motor Vehicle Safety Regulations*, C.R.C., c. 1038, s. 2.

EMERGENCY HEALTH SERVICE. The provision of first aid or medical services in emergency situations. *Health Emergency Act*, R.S.B.C. 1979, c. 162, s. 1.

EMERGENCY LIGHTING SYSTEM. A lighting system that will, in the event of the failure of the regular lighting system on any premises, provide dependable illumination to enable the carrying out of all emergency measures including the evacuation of all employees from those premises. *Canada Safe Illumination Regulations*, C.R.C., c. 1008, s. 2.

EMERGENCY LIGHTS. All lights required by law for the purpose of facilitating safe exit in case of fire or other emergency. *Power Corporation Act*, R.R.O. 1980, Reg. 794, s. 0.

EMERGENCY-LOCKING RETRACTOR. A retractor incorporating adjustment hardware that has a locking mechanism that is activated by vehicle acceleration, webbing movement in relation to the vehicle, or other automatic action during an emergency and is capable when locked of withstanding restraint forces. *Motor Vehicle Safety Regulations*, C.R.C., c. 1038, s. 209.

EMERGENCY MEASURES. 1. Courses of action to be taken in the event of a disaster to save lives, to come to the assistance of persons in distress, to safeguard property, or to abate the effects of the disaster. 2. The planning, organization, establishment and operation of defensive, precautionary and safety measures, controls, facilities and services of all kinds, other than those for which the military forces or other agencies of the Government of Canada are primarily responsible, necessary or desirable in the public interest for meeting, reducing, preventing and overcoming the effects of civil disaster or a war emergency and, without limiting the generality of the foregoing, includes (i) the preparation and carrying out of all plans and measures necessary to ensure the survival and continuity of civil government in the province in times of civil disaster or war emergency, (ii) the preservation of law and order, (iii) the control of traffic, including the movement of persons and property and the maintenance, clearance and repair of roads, (iv) the establishment of areas in the province, and the provision of appropriate services in those areas, for the reception, accommodation and feeding of persons evacuated from other areas which have been or are likely to be subject to civil disaster, hostile action or enemy attack, (v) the organization of emergency medical services and public health and welfare measures, (vi) the organization of fire-fighting, rescue and salvage services and radio-active fall-out detection services, (vii) the maintenance and repair of public utilities, (viii) assistance to municipalities in the development of emergency measures within their jurisdictions, (ix) liaison with the Government of Canada, other provinces of Canada and municipalities of Newfoundland in all matters relating to emergency planning, and (x) the institution of training and public information programmes to ensure the existence of adequately trained and equipped forces to meet the emergency requirements of the province and to keep the civilian population fully informed of the measures which have been adopted and the action which they should take for their safety, welfare and well-being in times of civil disaster or war emergency. *Emergency Measures Act*, R.S.Nfld. 1970, c. 108, s. 2.

EMERGENCY PLANNING CANADA. The federal body which plans federal response to peacetime emergencies and the continuation of the government in case of nuclear attack.

EMERGENCY VEHICLE. 1. A vehicle used (i) for police duty, or (ii) by a fire department, or (iii) as an ambulance, or (iv) for purposes related to maintenance of a public utility and designated as an emergency vehicle by a traffic authority, or (v) under the authority of a municipality, as a fire-pumper, or (vi) by a volunteer fire-fighter responding to a fire or other emergency. 2. A cardiac arrest emergency vehicle operated by or under the authority of a hospital. See AUTHORIZED ~.

EMIGRATION. *n.* The act of moving from one country to another with no intention of returning.

EMINENCE. *n.* The honorary title of a cardinal.

EMINENT DOMAIN. A government's right to take private property for public purposes, a doctrine which is American in origin. See EXPROPRIATION.

EMISSARY. *n.* One person sent on a mission as agent of another person.

EMISSION. See COKE OVEN ~S; CRANKCASE ~S; EVAPORATIVE ~S; EXHAUST ~S; FUGITIVE ~; POINT OF ~; VISIBLE ~.

EMOLUMENTS. *n.* Includes fees, percentages and other payments made or consideration given, directly or indirectly, to a director as such,

and the money value of any allowances or perquisites belonging to his office. *Companies Act*, R.S.N.S. 1967, c. 42, s. 112.

EMPANEL. *v.* For a sheriff to write or enter on a roll the names of a jury the sheriff summoned.

EMPARLANCE. See IMPARLANCE.

EMPEROR. *n.* A sovereign, superior to a queen or king, who rules a large domain or territory.

EMPHYTEUSIS. *n.* The right to enjoy all the fruits, and dispose at pleasure of another's property on condition a yearly rent is paid.

EMPIRE. *n.* An emperor's jurisdiction or dominion.

EMPIRIC. *n.* An experienced medical or surgical practitioner without legal or scientific qualification; a quack.

EMPIRICAL. *adj.* That which is based on experience, experiment or observation.

EMPLANE. *v.* To board an aircraft for a flight. *Air Transportation Tax Regulations*, C.R.C., c. 583, s. 2.

EMPLEAD. *v.* To accuse; to indict; to bring a charge against.

EMPLOYED. *adj.* Performing the duties of an office or employment. See FULLY ~; REGULARLY ~.

EMPLOYED BY OR UNDER THE CROWN. Includes employed by or under any board, commission or other body established, organized or functioning as an administrative unit of the Province. *Industrial Standards Act*, R.S.N.B. 1973, c. I-6, s. 1.

EMPLOYED IN A CONTINUOUS OPERATION. Employment in (a) any industrial establishment in which, in each seven day period, operations once begun normally continue without cessation until the completion of the regularly scheduled operations for that period; (b) any operations or services concerned with the running of trains, planes, ships, trucks and other vehicles, whether in scheduled or non-scheduled operations; (c) any telephone, radio, television, telegraph or other communication or broadcasting operations or services; or (d) any operation or service normally carried on without regard to Sundays or public holidays. *Canada Labour Code*, R.S.C. 1985, c. L-2, s. 191.

EMPLOYEE. *n.* 1. Any person employed by an employer and includes a dependent contractor and a private constable, but does not include a person who performs management functions or is employed in a confidential capacity in matters relating to industrial relations. *Canada Labour*

Code, R.S.C. 1985, c. L-2, s. 3. 2. Includes an officer. 3. Any person who is in receipt of or entitled to any compensation for labour or services performed for another. 4. Any person who performs duties and functions that entitle that person to compensation on a regular basis. 5. A person who is in receipt of or entitled to wages. 6. Includes an officer or director of a corporation or of an unincorporated organization and an agent acting for a principal on a substantially full-time basis. 7. Includes a dependent contractor. *Labour Relations Act*, R.S.O. 1980, c. 228, s. 1. 8. A natural person who is employed by an employer. See ASSOCIATION OF ~S; CASUAL ~; CONTRACT ~; CROWN ~; CUSTODIAL ~; FEMALE ~; FULL-TIME ~; HEAVY CONSTRUCTION ~S; LINE ~; MUNICIPAL ~; NON-OPERATING ~; PART-TIME ~; PERMANENT ~; PLANT PROTECTION ~; PROBATIONARY ~; PROFESSIONAL ~; PUBLIC ~; PUBLIC SECTOR ~; QUALIFIED ~; REDUNDANT ~; REGULAR ~; RELIEF ~; RETIRED ~; SEASONAL ~; SECURITY ~; SESSIONAL ~; STUDENT ~; TEMPORARY ~; TERM ~; UNIONIZED ~; WAGE ~.

EMPLOYEE-ASSOCIATIONS GROUP. Any union, federation, corporation or other organization which an association of employees representing persons contemplated by this act joins, or to which it belongs or is affiliated. *An Act respecting the organization of the management and union parties in view of collective bargaining in the sectors of education, social affairs and government agencies*, S.Q. 1978, c. 14, s. 1.

EMPLOYEE BARGAINING AGENCY. An organization of affiliated bargaining agents that are subordinate or directly related to the same provincial, national or international trade union, and that may include the parent or related provincial, national or international trade union, formed for purposes that include the representation of affiliated bargaining agents in bargaining and which may be a single provincial, national or international trade union. *Labour Relations Act*, R.S.O. 1980, c. 228, s. 137.

EMPLOYEE BENEFIT PLAN. A system to provide increased security to workers through schemes such as group insurance and cash benefits.

EMPLOYEE CONTRIBUTIONS. (i) Current service contributions, (ii) any contributions for prior service made by a participant, (iii) any part of a sum transferred into the Plan under a reciprocal agreement that is recognized by the Minister as employee contributions. *Pensions Plan acts*, Alberta.

EMPLOYEE HANDBOOK. Book issued to employees to familiarize them with their work, the employer's business, and company rules and policies.

EMPLOYEE ORGANIZATION. 1. Any organization of employees the purposes of which include the regulation of relations between the employer and its employees and includes, unless the context otherwise requires, a council of employee organizations. 2. A local or provincial organization or association of employees, or a local or provincial branch of a national or international organization or association of employees within the province and that has as one of its purposes the regulation in the province of relations between employers and employees through collective bargaining. 3. Any organization other than a trade union that bargains collectively for any employees in Alberta and for the purposes of this Act all branches in Alberta of an employee organization are deemed to be one organization. *Election Finances and Contributions Disclosure Act*, R.S.A. 1980, c. E-3, s. 1.

EMPLOYEE REPRESENTATIVE. 1. A person elected in accordance with the regulations by persons who are employed by a Crown entity or external agency, and who are employees within the meaning of The Labour Relations Act but who have no bargaining agent. *The Pay Equity Act*, S.M. 1985-86, c. 21, s. 1. 2. A person who is nominated by a person who has a grievance to act on his behalf in respect of the grievance. *Public Service Act*, R.R.O. 1980, Reg. 881, s. 36.

EMPLOYEES' CHARITY TRUST. A registered charity that is organized for the purpose of remitting, to other registered charities, donations that are collected from employees by an employer by means of payroll deductions. *Income Tax Regulations*, C.R.C., c. 945, s. 3500.

EMPLOYEES' MUTUAL BENEFIT SOCIETY. *var.* **EMPLOYEES MUTUAL BENEFIT SOCIETY.** A society incorporated by the officers or officers and employees of a corporation for the purpose of providing support and pensions to such of the officers or employees as become incapacitated or as cease to be employed by the corporation or for the purpose of paying pensions, annuities or gratuities to or for dependants of such officers or employees or funeral benefits upon the death of such officers or employees. *Insurance acts*.

EMPLOYEES' ORGANIZATION. Includes an organization of employees formed for purposes that include the regulation of relations between employees and employers.

EMPLOYEE'S PREMIUM. The percentage of his insurable earnings that a person employed in insurable employment is required to pay under section 51. *Unemployment Insurance Act*, R.S.C. 1985, c. U-1, s. 2.

EMPLOYEES PROFIT SHARING PLAN. An arrangement under which payments computed by reference to his profits from his business or by reference to his profits from his business and the profits, if any, from the business of a corporation with whom he does not deal at arm's length are made by an employer to a trustee in trust for the benefit of officers or employees of the employer or of a corporation with whom the employer does not deal at arm's length (whether or not payments are also made to the trustee by the officers or employees), and under which the trustee has, since the commencement of the plan or the end of 1949, whichever is the later, each year allocated either contingently or absolutely to individual officers or employees, (a) all amounts received by him from the employer or from the corporation with whom the employer does not deal at arm's length, (b) all profits from the trust property (computed without regard to any capital gain made by the trust or capital loss sustained by it at any time since the end of 1955), (c) all capital gains and capital losses of the trust for taxation years ending after 1971, and (d) all amounts in respect of which employees who have, after 1971, ceased to be beneficiaries under the arrangement are deemed by subsection (9) to have made a payment on account of tax under this Part, in such manner that the aggregate of all such amounts, profits, gains and losses, minus such portion thereof as has been paid to beneficiaries under the trust, is allocated either contingently or absolutely to officers or employees who are beneficiaries thereunder. *Income Tax Act*, R.S.C. 1952, c. 148 (as am. S.C. 1970-71-72, c. 63), s. 144(1).

EMPLOYEES' REPRESENTATIVE. A person appointed as a member of a board who, in the opinion of the minister, represents the employees in respect of whom the board may or is required to make recommendations. *Construction Industry Wages Act*, R.S.M. 1970, c. C190, s. 2.

EMPLOYEE TRUST. An arrangement (other than an employees profit sharing plan, a deferred profit sharing plan or a plan referred to in subsection 147(15) as a "revoked plan") established after 1979 (a) under which payments are made by one or more employers to a trustee in trust solely to provide to employees or former employees of (i) the employer, or (ii) a person with whom the employer does not deal at arm's length, benefits the right to which vests at the time of each such payment and the amount of which does not depend on the individual's position, performance or compensation as an employee, (b) under which the trustee has, since

the commencement of the arrangement, each year allocated to individuals who are beneficiaries thereunder, in such manner as is reasonable, the amount, if any, by which the aggregate of all amounts each of which is (i) an amount received under the arrangement by the trustee in the year from an employer or from a person with whom the employer does not deal at arm's length, (ii) the amount that would, if this Act were read without reference to subsection 104(6), be the income of the trust for the year (other than a taxable capital gain from the disposition of property) from a property or other source other than a business, or (iii) a capital gain of the trust for the year from the disposition of property exceeds the aggregate of all amounts each of which is (iv) the loss of the trust for the year (other than an allowable capital loss from the disposition of property) from a property or other source other than a business, or (v) a capital loss of the trust for the year from the disposition of property, and (c) the trustee of which has elected to qualify the arrangement as an employee trust in its return of income filed within 90 days from the end of its first taxation year. *Income Tax Act*, R.S.C. 1952, c. 148 (as am. S.C. 1980-81-82-83, c. 48, s. 108(4)), s. 248(1).

EMPLOYER. *n.* 1. Any person who employs one or more employees. 2. In relation to an officer, means the person from whom the officer receives remuneration. 3. Includes every person responsible for the payment of the wages of an employee under any act or law. 4. (a) Any person who employs one or more employees, and (b) in respect of a dependent contractor, such person as, in the opinion of the Board, has a relationship with the dependent contractor to such extent that the arrangement that governs the performance of services by the dependent contractor for that person can be the subject of collective bargaining. *Canada Labour Code*, R.S.C. 1985, c. L-2, s. 3. 5. Includes every person, firm, corporation, agent, manager, representative, contractor or subcontractor having control or direction of, or responsible, directly or indirectly, for the employment of any employee. 6. Includes every person having in service under a contract of hiring or apprenticeship, written or oral, express or implied, a person engaged in work in or about an industry, establishment, factory, office, shop, undertaking, work, trade or business. 7. Includes any person, partnership or corporation who has charge of all or part of an industrial or commercial establishment on his own account or on account of another person, partnership or corporation, as a contractor, subcontractor, manager, supervisor, foreman or agent, or otherwise. *Industrial and Commercial Establishments Act*, R.S.Q. 1977, c. E-15, s. 2. See APPROVED ~;

PARTICIPATING ~; PROFESSIONAL ~; PUBLIC SECTOR ~; PUBLIC SERVICE ~; RECIPROCATING ~; RECIPROCATING MANITOBA ~; SEPARATE ~; SUCCESSOR ~; UNIONIZED ~.

EMPLOYER BARGAINING AGENCY. An employers' organization or group of employers' organizations formed for purposes that include the representation of employers in bargaining. *Labour Relations Act*, R.S.O. 1980, c. 228, s. 137.

EMPLOYER ORGANIZATION. Any organization of employers formed for purposes including the regulating of relations between employees and employers. *Anti-Inflation Act*, S.C. 1974-75-76, c. 98, s. 1.

EMPLOYER RIGHTS. Rights, such as hiring and price fixing, which management generally argues are not proper subjects of collective bargaining.

EMPLOYER'S AGENT. (i) A person or association acting on behalf of an employer; (ii) any officer, official, foreman or other representative or employee of an employer acting in any way on behalf of an employer with respect to the hiring or discharging or any of the terms or conditions of employment of the employees of the employer. *The Trade Union Act*, R.S.S. 1978, c. T-17, s. 2.

EMPLOYERS' ASSOCIATION. A group organization of employers having as its objects the study and safeguarding of the economic interests of its members, and particularly assistance in the negotiation and application of collective agreements. *Labour Code*, R.S.Q. 1977, c. C-27, s. 1.

EMPLOYER'S CONTRIBUTION. The amount paid by the taxpayer in the year or within 120 days from the end of the year to or under a registered pension fund or plan in respect of services rendered by employees of the taxpayer in the year. *Income Tax Regulations*, C.R.C., c. 945, s. 2700.

EMPLOYERS' LIABILITY INSURANCE. *var.* **EMPLOYER'S LIABILITY INSURANCE.** 1. Insurance, not being insurance incidental to some other class of insurance defined by or under this Act, against loss to an employer through liability for accidental injury to or death of an employee arising out of or in the course of his employment, but does not include worker's compensation insurance. *Insurance acts*. 2. Insurance against liability for loss or damage to employees caused by bodily injury, disability or death arising out or of in the course of employment. *Insurance Act*, R.S.B.C. 1979, c. 200, s. 1.

EMPLOYERS' ORGANIZATION. Organization of employers formed for purposes that include the regulation of relations between employers and employees. See ACCREDITED ~; REPRESENTATIVE ~.

EMPLOYER'S PREMIUM. The amount that an employer of an insured person is required to pay under section 51 in respect of that insured person. *Unemployment Insurance Act*, R.S.C. 1985, c. U-1, s. 2.

EMPLOYMENT. *n.* 1. The performance of services under an express or implied contract of service or apprenticeship, and includes the tenure of an office. 2. Any activity for which a person receives or might reasonably be expected to receive valuable consideration. 3. The position of an individual in the service of some other person, including Her Majesty or a foreign state or sovereign. 4. The act of employing or the state of being employed. See ACT WITHIN SCOPE OF ~; COMMON ~; CONDITION OF ~; CONTRACT OF ~; COURSE OF ~; EQUIVALENT ~; EXCEPTED ~; FAIR ~ PRACTICE; FULL ~; FULL TIME ~; INCLUDED ~; INSURABLE ~; LONGSHORING ~; MULTI-EMPLOYER ~; PENSIONABLE ~; PERIOD OF ~; PLACE OF ~; PROVINCIAL ~; RE-~ LIST; SEASONAL ~; SELF-~; SUITABLE ~; TERMINATION OF ~; TERMS OF ~; WORK SHARING ~; YEAR OF ~.

EMPLOYMENT AGENCY. 1. Includes a person who undertakes, with or without compensation, to procure employees for employers and a person who undertakes, with or without compensation, to procure employment for persons. *Human Rights codes*. 2. The business of procuring for a fee, reward or other remuneration, (i) persons for employment, or (ii) employment for persons, and includes the business of counselling or testing persons for a fee, reward or other remuneration to assist them in securing employment. *Employment Agencies Act*, R.S.O. 1980, c. 136, s. 1.

EMPLOYMENT AND IMMIGRATION CANADA. The federal ministry with mandate to develop and utilize human resources.

EMPLOYMENT CERTIFICATE. Permit issued by a school authority to allow work by children.

EMPLOYMENT EXAMINATION. An examination conducted by the commission for positions in a particular class, admission to which is not limited to persons employed in the public service. *Public or Civil Service acts*.

EMPLOYMENT HANDICAP. A physical or mental condition that constitutes, contributes to or if not corrected will probably result in an obstruction of occupational performance. *The Rehabilitation Act*, R.S.S. 1978, c. R-17, s. 2.

EMPLOYMENT INJURY. Personal injury, including disablement, caused by an industrial accident, occupational disease or employment hazard. *Canada Labour Code*, R.S.C. 1985, c. L-2, s. 122.

EMPLOYMENT LIST. A list of persons who have passed an employment examination. *Civil Service acts.*

EMPLOYMENT PLAN. See ANNUAL ~.

EMPLOYMENT PREMISES. Residential premises provided by an employer to an employee to occupy during his employment. *Residential Tenancy Act*, S.B.C. 1984, c. 15, s. 1.

EMPLOYMENT PURPOSES. The purposes of taking into employment, granting promotion, reassigning employment duties or retaining as an employee. *Consumer Reporting acts.*

EMPLOYMENT RECORD. Any document or record that is necessary in order to determine whether an employee is entitled to wages, overtime pay, entitlements or maternity benefits.

EMPLOYMENT STANDARD. A requirement imposed upon an employer in favour of an employee by this Act or the regulations. *Employment Standards Act*, R.S.O. 1980, c. 137, s. 1.

EMPLOYMENT VISA. A prescribed form authorizing the person named therein to engage in employment in Canada. *Immigration Regulations*, C.R.C., c. 940, s. 5.

EMPORIUM. *n.* A place where trading takes place.

EMPTIO REI SPERATAE. [L.] A conditional contract which binds the parties only if something comes into existence. G.H.L. Fridman, *Sale of Goods in Canada*, 3d ed. (Toronto: Carswell, 1986) at 55.

EMPTIO SPEI. [L.] The sale of a chance. G.H.L. Fridman, *Sale of Goods in Canada*, 3d ed. (Toronto: Carswell, 1986) at 55.

EMPTOR. *n.* A buyer.

EMPTY. *adj.* When used with reference to a container or tank for gasoline or an associated product, means voided of its contents as far as is practicable by suction or pouring. *Gasoline Handling Act*, R.R.O. 1980, Reg. 439, s. 1.

ENABLING STATUTE. A statute which gives power or authority.

ENACT. *v.* 1. To decree; to establish by law. 2. Includes to issue, make, establish or prescribe.

ENACTING CLAUSE. In federal statutes, "Her Majesty, by and with the advice and consent of the Senate and House of Commons of Canada, enacts as follows:" A. Fraser, G.A. Birch & W.A. Dawson, eds., *Beauchesne's Rules and Forms of the House of Commons of Canada*, 5th ed. (Toronto: Carswell, 1978) at 219.

ENACTMENT. *n.* 1. An act or a regulation or any portion of an act or regulation, and as applied to a territory of Canada, includes an ordinance of the territory. 2. An act of the legislature of a province or a regulation, bylaw or other instrument having the force of law made under the authority of an act.

EN AUTRE DROIT. [Fr.] In another's right.

EN BLOC VALUE. The aggregate value of an entire business. A. Bissett-Johnson & W.M. Holland, eds, *Matrimonial Property Law in Canada* (Toronto: Carswell, 1980) at V-8.

ENCLOSED. See WHOLLY ~.

ENCLOSED COURT. A covered space enclosed by walls or buildings open to a roof having a horizontal dimension such that a cylinder at least 30 ft in diameter can be contained within the full height of the space, and the space is visually open in whole or in part to 3 or more storeys above the floor of the space. *Building Code Act*, R.R.O. 1980, Reg. 87, s. 1.

ENCLOSED LAND. 1. Land that is surrounded by a natural or man made barrier sufficient to exclude or contain livestock. *Livestock Act*, S.B.C. 1980, c. 24, s. 1. 2. Includes land in a rural area that is (a) surrounded by a lawful fence defined by or under this Act; (b) surrounded by a lawful fence and a natural boundary or by a natural boundary alone; or (c) being used for agricultural, pastoral or horticultural purposes, and at the corners, gates and points of access of which are posted notices prohibiting trespass. *Trespass Act*, R.S.B.C. 1979, c. 41, s. 1. 3. Land that is used for farming purposes. *Division Fence Act*, S.P.E.I. 1975, c. 43, s. 1.

ENCLOSED PANELBOARD. An assembly of buses and connections, over-current devices and control apparatus with or without switches, or other equipment, installed in a cabinet. *Power Corporation Act*, R.R.O. 1980, Reg. 794, s. 0.

ENCLOSED SUPERSTRUCTURE. A superstructure with (a) enclosing bulkheads complying with the requirements of section 3 of this Schedule, (b) access openings, if any, in the bulkheads fitted with doors that comply with section 4 of this Schedule, (c) all other openings in the sides or ends of the superstructure fitted with efficient weathertight means of closing, (d) discharges that comply with section 14 of this Schedule, (e) side scuttles that comply with section 11 of this Schedule, and (f) in the case of a bridge, poop or raised quarter-deck, such access that the crew can reach accommodations, machinery or other working spaces inside the superstructure by alternative means that are available at all times when bulkhead openings are closed. *Load Line Regulations (Inland)*, C.R.C., c. 1440, s. 1.

ENCLOSED WALKWAY. A walkway that has 50 per cent or less of its perimeter open to the outdoors. *Building Code Act*, R.R.O. 1980, Reg. 87, s. 1.

ENCLOSURE. *n.* Fencing in property in order to cultivate it. See HOISTWAY ~; PROTEC-TIVE ~.

ENCROACHMENT. *n.* An attempt to extend a right a person already possesses.

ENCUMBRANCE. *n.* Any charge on land, created or effected for any purpose whatever, including mortgages, mechanics' liens when authorized by statute or ordinance, and executions against lands, unless expressly distinguished.

ENCUMBRANCEE. *n.* The owner of an encumbrance.

ENCUMBRANCER. *n.* The owner of any land or of any estate or interest in land subject to any encumbrance. See SUBSEQUENT ~.

ENCYCLOPEDIA. *n.* A collective work containing a series of articles by many contributors.

ENDANGERED SPECIES. Any species or subspecies of fauna or flora threatened with extinction by reason of (a) the destruction of its habitat or a drastic modification or severe curtailment thereof, (b) disease, (c) over-exploitation, (d) predation, (e) the use of chemicals, or (f) any combination of the foregoing factors, and declared by regulation to be endangered.

END BOX. A container located on an end of a mercury cell that functions as a collection point for mercury, alkali metal amalgam and brine. *Chlor-Alkali Mercury National Emission Standards Regulations*, C.R.C., c. 406, s. 2.

ENDEAVOUR. See ARTISTIC ~.

ENDEMIC DISEASE. A disease which routinely occurs in a certain place and is due to lasting local causes.

ENDORSE. *v.* Includes imprinting a stamp on the face of articles or other documents sent to the Director. *Business Corporations Act, 1982*, S.O. 1982, c. 4, s. 1.

ENDORSED. *adj.* Written on any instrument or on any paper attached thereto by the registrar.

ENDORSEMENT. *n.* 1. Anything written by the registrar upon an instrument or upon a paper attached thereto. 2. An endorsement completed by delivery. *Bills of Exchange Act*, R.S.C. 1985, c. B-4, s. 2. 3. Includes entry, memorandum and notation. 4. An ordinary signature. I.F.G. Baxter, *The Law of Banking*, 3d ed. (Toronto: Carswell, 1981) at 96. 5. The inscribing of additional qualifications on a certificate. *Masters and Mates Examination Regulations*, C.R.C., c. 1444, s. 2. See BLANK ~.

ENDOW. *v.* To entitle to dower.

ENDOWMENT. *n.* 1. Assigning or giving dower. 2. Any kind of property belonging permanently to a charity.

ENDOWMENT CARE. The preservation, improvement, embellishment and maintenance, in perpetuity and in a proper manner, of grave stones, grave markers, monuments, lots, plots, compartments, crypts or other space, in a cemetery, or of compartments in a columbarium or mausoleum. *Cemeteries Act*, R.S.A. 1980, c. C-2, s. 1.

ENDOWMENT CARE FUNDS. Funds and property received by an owner for the purpose of providing endowment care generally of a cemetery, columbarium or mausoleum, or of any particular part thereof, whether received (i) under this Act or otherwise, or (ii) under the terms of a contract, trust or gift or otherwise, and includes money deducted and set aside under section 38 and the deposits made by an owner and referred to in section 39. *Cemeteries Act*, R.S.A. 1980, c. C-2, s. 1.

ENDOWMENT INSURANCE. An undertaking to pay an ascertained or ascertainable sum at a fixed future date, if the person whose life is insured is then alive, or at his death, if he dies before such date. *Insurance acts*.

END USER. The buyer of gas under a gas contract who purchases the gas for the purpose of using or consuming it. *Arbitration Amendment Act*, S.A. 1986, c. 10, s. 17(1).

ENEMY. *n.* Includes armed mutineers, armed rebels, armed rioters and pirates. *National Defence Act*, R.S.C. 1985, c. N-5, s. 2.

ENEMY ACTION OR COUNTERACTION AGAINST THE ENEMY. 1. Includes extraordinary marine hazards occasioned by the War and encountered by a Canadian ship or by a certified non-Canadian ship when employed on a voyage that in the opinion of the Commission was essential to the prosecution of the War on behalf of His Majesty or His Majesty's allies. *Civilian War Pensions and Allowances Act*, R.S.C. 1985, c. C-31, s. 6. 2. Includes extraordinary hazards occasioned by the War. *Civilian War Pensions and Allowances Act*, R.S.C. 1985, c. C-

31, s. 48. 3. Includes extraordinary aerial or other hazards occasioned by the War. *Civilian War Pensions and Allowances Act*, R.S.C. 1985, c. C-31, s. 52.

ENEMY ALIEN. Any person, without regard to nationality, who willingly resides or carries on business within an area which is occupied by or belongs to a country with whom that person's nation is at war. J.G. McLeod, *The Conflict of Laws* (Calgary: Carswell, 1983) at 64.

ENERGY. *n.* 1. Electric power and energy. 2. As the context may require, (i) energy in any form and howsoever produced, generated or collected, but not including energy in the form of animal or human muscular power, or (ii) the sources, fuels or processes, or any of them, that are or may be used to produce, generate or collect energy as defined in sub-clause (i), or (iii) both energy as defined in sub-clause (i) and the sources, fuels and processes, or any of them, as defined in sub-clause (ii). *Manitoba Energy Council Act*, S.M. 1980, c. 79, s. 1. 3. (a) Electricity, (b) heat which is supplied through a district heating system by hot water, hot air or steam, (c) manufactured gas, liquified petroleum gas, natural gas, oil or any other combustible material which is supplied through a pipeline or any other distribution system directly to a customer. *Northwest Territories Energy Corporation Act*, S.N.W.T. 1986 (1st Sess.), c. 10, s. 2. 4. Electricity, gas, steam and any other form of energy, hydraulic, thermic or other. See ATOMIC ~; ATOMIC ~ CONTROL BOARD; ATOMIC ~ OF CANADA LIMITED; ELECTRIC ~; FIRM ~; HEAT ~; HYDRO ~; INTERRUPTIBLE ~; NATIONAL ~ BOARD.

ENERGY COMMODITY. Oil and gas and any prescribed product resulting from the processing or refining of oil or gas and, where there is a designation in respect of coal, thorium and uranium, or any of those substances, under section 10, includes all those substances, or the designated substance, as the case may be, and any prescribed product resulting from the processing or refining of the designated substance or substances. *Energy Monitoring Act*, R.S.C. 1985, c. E-8, s. 2.

ENERGY ENTERPRISE. Any individual, corporation, partnership, trust or organization engaged in the exploration for, or the development, production, processing or refining of, any energy commodity in Canada. *Energy Monitoring Act*, R.S.C. 1985, c. E-8, s. 2.

ENERGY, MINES AND RESOURCES CANADA. The federal ministry with mandate to discover, develop and intelligently use Canada's energy and mineral resources and to foster greater knowledge of the country's landmass.

ENERGY RESOURCE. 1. Any natural resource that can be used as a source of any form of energy. 2. Includes natural gas and oil, and all other natural forms of petroleum and hydrocarbon, both gaseous and in liquid form, coal and all other natural bituminous fuels, electrical power and all means of generation of electrical power, and all means by which energy is, or may be, generated.

ENERGY STORAGE FACILITY. A place where an energy resource is accumulated or stored in bulk as part of the process of being transported or distributed. *Utilities Commission Act*, S.B.C. 1980, c. 60, s. 16.

ENERGY TRANSFER. Electric energy transmitted through an inter-utility transfer point. *National Energy Board Regulations, Part VI*, C.R.C., c. 1056, s. 2.

ENERGY TRANSHIPMENT TERMINAL. A place where an energy resource is accumulated or stored in bulk as part of the process of being transported or distributed. *Utilities Commission Act*, S.B.C. 1980, c. 60, s. 16.

ENERGY USE PROJECT. A mill, factory, plant, smelter, oil refinery, metal refinery or other undertaking or facility designed to use, convert or process an energy resource or coal, or any combination of them, at the rate of 3 PJ or more a year, and for the purpose of this definition an energy resource other than electricity is used, converted or processed at that rate where it is of a quantity capable of yielding that amount of energy by combustion. *Utilities Commission Act*, S.B.C. 1980, c. 60, s. 16.

ENERGY UTILITY. A person, including his lessee, trustee, receiver or liquidator, who owns or operates in the Province equipment or facilities for the production, generation, storage, transmission, sale, delivery or furnishing of gas, electricity, steam or any other agency for the production of light, heat, cold or power to or for the public or any corporation for compensation. *Energy Act*, R.S.B.C. 1979, c. 108, s. 1.

ENERGY VECTOR. Any source, material or electromagnetic wave, field, plasma, pressure and any direct or indirect cause of transfer, storage or liberation of energy. *Environment Quality Act*, R.S.Q. 1977, c. Q-2, s. 1.

ENFEOFF. *v.* To give possession of lands or tenements.

ENFEOFFMENT. *n.* 1. Investing with a dignity or possession. 2. The deed or instrument by which one invests another with possessions.

ENFORCEMENT. See AUTOMATIC ~.

ENFORCEMENT OFFICER. A member of the Royal Canadian Mounted Police, a municipal police officer, a wildlife officer, a fishery officer, a forest officer, a parks officer, a patrol officer, a conservation officer or a peace officer.

ENFORCEMENT SERVICE. See PROVINCIAL ~.

ENFRANCHISE. *v.* 1. To bestow a liberty; to make free. 2. To give someone the liberty to vote at an election.

ENGAGEMENT. *n.* Any promise or undertaking. See INTERMEDIATE ~; SHORT ~.

ENGAGING IN BUSINESS. Includes selling goods or services to or buying goods or services. *Discriminatory Business Practices Act*, R.S.O. 1980, c. 119, s. 4.

ENGINE. *n.* 1. A steam or an internal combustion engine and includes the clutch, reduction gears, shaft, propeller, control and such accessories as properly form part of a mechanism for the propulsion of a fishing vessel. *Fisheries Improvement Loans Act*, R.S.C. 1985, c. F-22, s. 2. 2. Any steam locomotive, traction engine, logging, stationary or portable engine or other power producing plant or similar device. *Forest Protection Act*, R.S.N.W.T. 1974, c. F-8, s. 2. 3. A unit propelled by any form of energy, or a combination of such units operated from a single control, used in train or yard service. *Regulations No. O-8, Uniform Code of Operating Rules*, C.R.C., c. 1175, Part III, s. 2. 4. Includes a turbine. *Operating Engineers Act*, R.R.O. 1980, Reg. 740, s. 1. See CRITICAL ~; INTERNAL COMBUSTION ~; MODEL ROCKET ~; PROPULSION ~; STATIONARY ~; TRACTION ~; VEHICLE ~; YARD ~.

ENGINEER. *n.* 1. A person who through specialized education, training and experience is skilled in the principles and practice of engineering. 2. A person qualified to make repairs to any totalizator or electrical equipment used in connection with a pari-mutuel department. *Race Track Supervision Regulations*, C.R.C., c. 441, s. 2. See CHIEF ~; FOREST ~; INSPECTING ~; MINE SAFETY ~; MUNICIPAL ~; PROFESSIONAL ~; SHIFT ~.

ENGINEERING. *n.* 1. The application of scientific principles and knowledge to practical ends such as the investigation, design, construction, or operation of works and systems for the benefit of man. *Engineering Profession Act*, S.N.B. 1986, c. 88, s. 2. 2. The science and art of designing, investigating, supervising the construction, maintenance or operation of, making specifications, inventories or appraisals of, and consultations or reports on: machinery, structures, works, plants, mines, mineral deposits, processes, transportation systems, transmission systems and communication systems or any other part thereof. See NATURAL SCIENCES AND ~ RESEARCH COUNCIL OF CANADA; PRACTICE OF ~; PRACTICE OF PROFESSIONAL ~.

ENGINEERING RESEARCH OR FEASIBILITY STUDY. Includes work undertaken to facilitate the design or to analyse the viability of engineering technology, systems or schemes to be used in the exploration for or the development, production or transportation of petroleum.

ENGINEERING TECHNOLOGY. The application of technical knowledge and skill by certified engineering technicians and certified engineering technologists. *Engineering Technology Act*, S.N.B. 1986, c. 92, s. 2.

ENGINEERING WORK. Any work of construction or alteration or repair of a railway, harbour, dock, canal, sewer or system of waterworks; and outside electrical construction of all kinds, including the alteration and repair of outside wires, cables, apparatus and appliances; and includes any other work for the construction, alteration or repair of which machinery driven by steam, water or other mechanical power is used. *The Workmen's Compensation Act*, R.S.S. 1978, c. W-18, s. 3.

ENGINEER-IN-TRAINING. *n.* A person who has fulfilled the academic requirements for registration and has enrolled with an association, but because of age or insufficient experience is not eligible for registration.

ENGINEER ON THE WATCH. (a) The senior engineer in charge of the entire watch, or (b) where there are two or more engineers on each regular watch, an assistant engineer on such watch. *Marine Engineer Examination Regulations*, C.R.C., c. 1443, s. 2.

ENGINEERS FIRM. A partnership or corporation (i) that (A) confines its practice to providing engineering consulting services, or (B) if it does not confine its practice to providing engineering consulting services, engages in a practice satisfactory to the Joint Board, and (ii) in which professional engineers (A) hold a majority interest, and (B) control the partnership or corporation, and that is otherwise entitled to engage in the practice of engineering under this Act. Alberta statutes.

ENGINEMAN. *n.* The employee in charge of and responsible for the operation of an engine. *Regulations No. O-8, Uniform Code of Operating Rules*, C.R.C., c. 1175, Part III, s. 2. See STATIONARY ~.

ENGINE ROOM. All the main propelling

machinery space of the ship. *Hull Construction Regulations*, C.R.C., c. 1431, s. 100.

ENGLISH LANGUAGE EDUCATION. A school program using English as the language of instruction. *An Act to Amend the School Act*, S.P.E.I. 1980, c. 48, s. 9.

ENGLISH REPORTS. The reprinted reports of English cases from 1220 to 1865.

ENGRAVINGS. *n.* Includes etchings, lithographs, woodcuts, prints and other similar works, not being photographs. *Copyright Act*, R.S.C. 1985, c. C-42, s. 2.

ENGROSS. *v.* 1. To type or write an agreement, deed or like document from a draft with all amounts, dates and words set out at length, and with the formal attestation and testatum clauses, so that the document is ready to be executed. 2. Formerly, to write in a particular script derived from the courthand in which records were written in ancient times.

ENHANCED RECOVERY. The increased recovery from a pool achieved by artificial means or by the application of energy extrinsic to the pool, which artificial means or application includes pressuring, cycling, pressure maintenance or injection to the pool of a substance or form of energy but does not include the injection in a well of a substance or form of energy for the sole purpose of (i) aiding in the lifting of fluids in the well, or (ii) stimulation of the reservoir at or near the well by mechanical, chemical, thermal or explosive means.

ENJOIN. *v.* To prohibit by court order, the effect of an injunction.

ENJOYMENT. *n.* The use or application of a right. See QUIET ~.

ENLARGE. *v.* To lengthen time.

ENLISTMENT. See RECORDED ON MEDICAL EXAMINATION PRIOR TO ~.

EN OWEL MAIN. [Fr.] In equal hand.

ENQUIRY. See INQUIRY.

ENRG. *abbr.* Enregistré.

ENRICHMENT. See UNJUST ~.

ENROL. *v.* 1. To cause any person to become a member of the Canadian Forces. *National Defence Act*, R.S.C. 1985, c. N-5, s. 2. 2. To enter or copy a document into an official record.

ENSEINT. [Fr.] Pregnancy.

ENSIENT. [Fr.] Pregnancy.

ENS LEGIS. [L.] A legal entity.

ENTAIL. *n.* Limitation of land to a person and that person's heirs.

ENTER. *v.* 1. When any part of his body or any part of an instrument that he uses is within anything that is being entered. *Criminal Code*, R.S.C. 1985, c. C-46, s. 350(a). 2. To come onto land. 3. To note, in a record or book, a transcript of a document or a transaction. See BREAK AND ~.

ENTER AND USE. The act of a permittee, or lessee, his or their servants, agents and contractors of entering into and upon and using any portion of the lands of any person within the province for the purpose of exploring and of making surveys and examinations, using water and of opening, boring, drilling, excavating, laying, erecting or building derricks, wells, slush pits, pumps, powers, surface rods, pipe lines, tanks, roads, works, drains, and other related installations and of doing all the acts or things authorized. *Oil, Natural Gas and Minerals Act*, R.S.P.E.I. 1974, c. O-3, s. 2.

ENTER JUDGMENT. To deliver to the Registrar an order embodying a judgment or to cause the Registrar to make a formal record of a judgment. *Rules of the Supreme Court*, S.Nfld. 1986, r. 1, s. 1.03.

ENTERPRISE. See AGRICULTURAL ~; AIR TRANSPORT ~; BUSINESS ~; COMMERCIAL ~; ECONOMIC ~; ENERGY ~; FISH BUSINESS OR ~; FISHERY ~; INDUSTRIAL ~; MUNICIPAL ~; SMALL BUSINESS ~.

ENTERTAINMENT. *n.* 1. Any contest, game, race, dance, apparatus, amusement, display, device, exhibition, attraction, performance, presentation, program, show or motion picture, operated either indoors or out of doors, in order to obtain money, or its equivalent, from the people who attend. *Entertainments Act*, R.S.P.E.I. 1974, c. E-7, s. 1. 2. Includes a circus, contest, dance, exhibition, fair, game, movie-picture or stage performance. Newfoundland statutes. See PLACE OF ~.

ENTERTAINMENT HALL. (i) A hall, pavilion, place, premises, room, tent or structure of any kind kept or used for public concerts, carnival shows, dances or other social gatherings, and (ii) includes a cafe, hotel or restaurant where facilities are supplied and used for public dancing. *Amusements Act*, R.S.A. 1970, c. 18, s. 2.

ENTERTAINMENT PARLOUR. See ADULT ~.

ENTICEMENT. *n.* The deliberate inducement of a wife to leave her husband. The inducement must be made with knowledge of her marital status and with intent to interfere with the wife's duty to give consortium to her husband. John G. Fleming, *The Law of Torts*, 6th ed. (Sydney: The Law Book Company Limited, 1983) at 614.

ENTICING. *adj.* Soliciting, alluring.

ENTIRE ANIMAL. (i) A stallion over the age of 15 months, or (ii) a bull or jack over the age of nine months, or (iii) a ram, he-goat or boar over the age of five months. *Domestic Animals (Municipalities) Act*, R.S.A. 1970, c. 112, s. 2.

ENTIRE TENANCY. Sole possession in one person.

ENTIRETY. See TENANCY BY THE ~.

ENTITLE. *v.* To bestow a right.

ENTITLEMENT. *n.* A decision by the Commission or the Pension Review Board that a pension is payable for a disability or would be so payable if the disability were of a degree sufficient to warrant payment of a pension. *Veterans Treatment Regulations*, C.R.C., c. 1585, s. 2.

ENTITY. *n.* A corporation, partnership, trust or joint venture. *Investment Canada Act*, R.S.C. 1985 (1st Supp.), c. 28, s. 3. See AUTHORIZED ~; CROWN ~; FOREIGN ~; GOVERNMENT ENTITIES; NON-RESIDENT ~.

ENTITY CHARTER. A charter in which (a) the cost of transportation of passengers or goods is paid by one person, company or organization without any contribution, direct or indirect, from any other person, and (b) no charge or other financial obligation is imposed on any passenger as a condition of carriage or otherwise in connection with the trip. *Air Carrier Regulations*, C.R.C., c. 3, s. 23.

ENTOMOLOGY. *n.* The study of insects.

EN TOUTE JUSTICE. A journal published by Association canadienne d'assistance jurisique, d'information et de recherche des handicapés.

ENTRANCE. See MINE ~.

ENTRANCE FEE. Includes every charge made for seating accommodation, whether or not payment is required before entrance.

ENTRANCE RATE. The rate of pay an employee receives when first hired.

ENTRANT AS OF RIGHT. A person who is empowered or permitted by law to enter premises without the permission of the occupier of those premises. *Occupiers' Liability Act*, R.S.A. 1980, c. O-3, s. 1.

ENTRAPMENT. *n.* Inducement by an agent provocateur or by police conduct to commit a crime.

ENTRENCHED. *adj.* Able to be altered solely through a constitutional amendment. P.W. Hogg, *Constitutional Law of Canada*, 2d ed. (Toronto: Carswell, 1985) at 4 and 5.

ENTRENCHMENT CLAUSE. Section 52(3) of the Constitution Act, 1982: "Amendments to the Constitution of Canada shall be made only in accordance with the authority contained in the Constitution of Canada."

ENTREPOT. *n.* [Fr.] A warehouse where goods already bought await resale.

ENTREPRENEUR. *n.* [Fr.] An individual who undertakes a business which employs others.

ENTRY. *n.* 1. Going onto land. 2. Setting down a record in a book. 3. Lawful permission to come into Canada as a visitor. *Immigration Act*, R.S.C. 1985, c. I-2, s. 2. 4. Not only the record of a claim in the books of the mining recorder, but also the grant which may be issued for the claim. 5. Includes recording by photographic plate, microphotographic film or photocopy negative. *Judicature Act and Matrimonial Causes Act*, R.R.O. 1980, Reg. 540, s. 2. 6. (a) In respect of the calculation of a pool, two or more horses that are entered or run in a race and that for the purpose of pari-mutuel betting are considered as one horse except as provided for exactor and quinella betting, and (b) in respect of the entry of a horse in a race, the completion of an entry form by the owner or trainer of a horse, for such horse to compete in a specific race. *Race Track Supervision Regulations*, C.R.C., c. 441, s. 2. See DOUBLE ~; FORCIBLE ~; PORT OF ~; RE-~; RIGHT OF ~; SINGLE ~.

ENUMERATION. *n.* A general residence to residence visitation to obtain applications for registration for the purpose of compiling new lists of voters. *Election Act*, S.B.C. 1982, c. 48, s. 1. See GENERAL ~; SPECIAL ~.

ENUMERATION DATE. 1. In respect of an election in an electoral district, the date for the commencement of the preparation of the preliminary lists of electors for that election. 2. The thirty-third day before polling day. *Elections Act*, S.N.W.T. 1986 (2d Sess.), c. 2, s. 2.

ENUMERATION YEAR. A calendar year in which a general enumeration takes place. *Election Act*, R.S.A. 1980, c. E-2, s. 1.

ENUMERATOR. *n.* 1. A person appointed to compile or revise a list of electors. 2. A person who takes a census.

ENURE. *v.* To take effect; to operate.

ENVELOPE. See INNER ~; OUTER ~.

EN VENTRE SA MÈRE. [Fr. in the mother's womb] Describes an unborn child.

ENVIRONMENT. *n.* 1. The air, water, ice, snow and land and all animal and plant life therein. 2. Includes (i) air, land or water, (ii) plant and animal life, including human life, (iii) the social, economic, recreational, cultural and aesthetic conditions and factors that influence the life of humans or a community, (iv) any building, structure, machine or other device or thing made by humans, (v) any solid, liquid, gas, odour, heat, sound, vibration or radiation resulting directly or indirectly from the activities of humans, or (vi) any part or combination of the foregoing and the interrelationships between any two or more of them. 3. The total of all the conditions and elements that make up the surroundings of an individual animal. See NATURAL ~.

ENVIRONMENTAL ACCIDENT. The release of a contaminant into the environment, otherwise than in accordance with the regulations or an order of the commission, which, having regard to the environment in which the release takes place and to the nature of the contaminant released, creates or may create a hazard to human life or health, to other living organisms, or to the physical environment. *Clean Environment Act*, S.M. 1980, c. 59, s. 2.

ENVIRONMENTAL ASSESSMENT. A process by which the environmental impact of an undertaking is predicted and evaluated before the undertaking has begun or occurred. *Environmental Assessment Act*, S.Nfld. 1980, c. 3, s. 2.

ENVIRONMENTAL EMERGENCY. An occurrence or natural disaster that affects the environment and includes (a) a flood, (b) a landslide, and (c) a spill or leakage of oil or of a poisonous or dangerous substance. *Environment Management Act*, S.B.C. 1981, c. 14, s. 1.

ENVIRONMENTAL IMPACT. Any change in the present or future environment that would result from an undertaking. *Environmental Assessment Act*, S.Nfld. 1980, c. 3, s. 2.

ENVIRONMENTAL IMPACT ASSESSMENT. A process by which the environmental impact caused by or resulting from an undertaking is predicted and evaluated. *An Act to Amend the Clean Environment Act*, S.N.B. 1983, c. 17, s. 6.

ENVIRONMENTAL IMPACT STATEMENT. A report that presents the results of a complete environmental assessment. *Environmental Assessment Act*, S.Nfld. 1980, c. 3, s. 2.

ENVIRONMENTAL MONITORING. Analysis and sampling of the environment so that the concentration of a potentially hazardous substance and the degree of workers' exposure to it may be determined. D. Robertson, *Ontario Health and Safety Guide* (Toronto: Richard De Boo Ltd., 1988) at 5-152.

ENVIRONMENTAL PREVIEW REPORT. A report that presents the results of a preliminary environmental assessment based only on readily available information, and in which certain essential subjects may be incompletely treated due to a lack of data. *Environmental Assessment Act*, S.Nfld. 1980, c. 3, s. 2.

ENVIRONMENTAL STUDY. Work pertaining to the measurement or statistical evaluation of the physical, chemical and biological elements of the lands, oceans or coastal zones, including winds, waves, tides, currents, precipitation, ice cover and movement, icebergs, pollution effects, flora and fauna both onshore and offshore, human activity and habitation and any related matters.

ENVIRONMENT CANADA. The federal ministry responsible for managing and protecting migratory birds, providing information on climate, weather, sea and ice conditions and air quality, protecting and enhancing the natural environment (i.e. soil, water and air) and conserving renewable land, water and wildlife resources.

ENVOY. *n.* 1. A diplomatic agent sent to one nation from another. 2. The envoy of a foreign sovereign power accredited to Her Majesty in right of Canada. *Diplomatic Immunities (Commonwealth Countries) Act*, R.S.C. 1970, c. D-4, s. 2.

ENZYME. *n.* A protein which acts as a catalyst in a chemical reaction. F.A. Jaffe, *A Guide to Pathological Evidence*, 2d ed. (Toronto: Carswell, 1983) at 175.

EODEM LIGAMINE QUO LIGATUM EST DISSOLVITUR. [L.] An obligation is ended the same way in which it was imposed.

EODEM MODO QUO QUID CONSTITUITUR, EODEM MODO DESTRUITUR. [L.] A thing is destroyed in the same way it was made.

E.O.E. *abbr.* Errors and omissions excepted.

EO INSTANTI. [L. at that moment] At the same moment; immediately.

EO NOMINE. [L.] By that name.

EPIDEMIC. *n.* The occurrence in a community of a number of cases of a communicable disease in excess of normal expectations. *Public Health Act*, S.A. 1984, c. P-27.1, s. 1.

EPIDEMIC DISEASE. A disease generally occurring in a community or among a people at a particular time, and produced by peculiar causes not usually found in that locality.

EPIDERMIS. *n.* Skin. F.A. Jaffe, *A Guide to Pathological Evidence*, 2d ed. (Toronto: Carswell, 1983) at 29.

EPIDURAL HEMORRHAGE. A venous or

arterial hemorrhage between the dura mater and the skull. F.A. Jaffe, *A Guide to Pathological Evidence*, 2d ed. (Toronto: Carswell, 1983) at 118.

EPIGLOTTIS. *n.* A structure at the base of the tongue which protects the opening of the larynx while one swallows. F.A. Jaffe, *A Guide to Pathological Evidence*, 2d ed. (Toronto: Carswell, 1983) at 175.

EPIGLOTTITIS. *n.* Inflammation of the epiglottis. F.A. Jaffe, *A Guide to Pathological Evidence*, 2d ed. (Toronto: Carswell, 1983) at 175.

EPILEPSY. *n.* A group of disorders characterized by episodic impairment or frequent convulsions and loss of consciousness. F.A. Jaffe, *A Guide to Pathological Evidence*, 2d ed. (Toronto: Carswell, 1983) at 175.

EPIPHYSEAL INJURY. Dislocation of a bone's epiphysis, often caused when an extremity is pulled too forcefully. F.A. Jaffe, *A Guide to Pathological Evidence*, 2d ed. (Toronto: Carswell, 1983) at 175.

EPIPHYSIS. *n.* The part of a bone which a layer of cartilage separates from the main part during childhood but which unites with the main part during adolescence or early adult life. F.A. Jaffe, *A Guide to Pathological Evidence*, 2d ed. (Toronto: Carswell, 1983) at 175 and 176.

EPISCOPATE. *n.* A bishop's jurisdiction.

EPISODE. See AIR POLLUTION ~.

EPOCH. *n.* The beginning of a new computation of time. See GREGORIAN ~.

EPOCHA. *n.* The beginning of a new computation of time.

EQUAL. *adj.* Subject to all requirements, qualifications and considerations that are not a prohibited ground of discrimination. *Human Rights Code, 1981*, S.O. 1981, s. 53, s. 9.

EQUALITY. See PROCEDURAL ~.

EQUALITY BEFORE THE LAW. The principle by which the law must be applied to everyone equally and every member of society must be treated the same way before the law.

EQUALIZATION LEVY. In the context of product marketing schemes, a pooling of proceeds, so that producers' returns are equalized even if the product was actually sold at different prices in different markets. P.W. Hogg, *Constitutional Law of Canada*, 2d ed. (Toronto: Carswell, 1985) at 614.

EQUALIZATION PAYMENT. Payment to a province to bring its share of tax rental payments up to the same per capita amount as the average per capita yield in the two provinces with the highest yield. P.W. Hogg, *Constitutional Law of Canada*, 2d ed. (Toronto: Carswell, 1985) at 114.

EQUALIZED ASSESSMENT. The assessment upon which taxes are levied in the municipality or locality.

EQUALIZED COMMERCIAL ASSESSMENT. The total of commercial assessment as equalized by the application of the equalization factor or factors applicable to the assessment or assessments. *Municipal Act*, R.S.O. 1980, c. 302, s. 365.

EQUALIZED RESIDENTIAL AND FARM ASSESSMENT. The total of residential and farm assessment as equalized by the application of the equalization factor or factors applicable to the assessment or assessments. *Municipal Act*, R.S.O. 1980, c. 302, s. 365.

EQUAL PAY FOR EQUAL WORK. The same wage rate applied to jobs with no consideration of sex, race or other factors not related to ability to perform the work.

EQUINE. *n.* A horse, ass, mule or zebra. *Animal Disease and Protection Regulations*, C.R.C., c. 296, s. 2.

EQUIP. *v.* In relation to a ship, includes the furnishing of anything that is used for the purpose of fitting or adapting the ship for the seas or for naval service. *Foreign Enlistment Act*, R.S.C. 1985, c. F-28, s. 2.

EQUIPMENT. *n.* 1. Apparatus, device, mechanism, structure, machine, machinery, tool, device, contrivance or vehicle. 2. Goods that are not inventory or consumer goods. *Personal Property Security acts.* 3. Includes life-boats, life-saving equipment, apparatus for the detection and extinguishing of fire, fire-control plans, line-throwing apparatus, anchors, cables, pilot ladders, means of making sound signals and distress signals, compasses, lights, signals, navigating appliances and all other apparatus or equipment designed or required for the safety of the ship or the protection of the passengers and crew, but does not include radio apparatus other than radio apparatus for survival craft. *Canada Shipping Act*, R.S.C. 1985, c. S-9, s. 2. See AGRICULTURAL ~; AUTOMATIC TABULATING ~; BASIC ~; BEEHIVE ~; BEEKEEPING ~; CANADIAN ~; DISTRIBUTION ~; ELECTRICAL ~; ELECTRONIC ~; ESSENTIAL AIRCRAFT ~; FARM ~; FIRE DEPARTMENT ~; FIRE-EXTINGUISHING ~; FISHING ~; FISHING ~ AND SUPPLIES; FOOD PREPARATION ~; FORESTRY ~; FUEL-BURNING ~; GAMING ~; GAS ~; GAS OR OIL WELL ~; GEOPHYSICAL ~; GROUNDING ~; HEAVY DUTY ~; IONIZING RADIATION ~; LUMBERING ~; MATE-

RIALS HANDLING ~; MILKING ~; MINING ~; MOBILE ~; NON-IONIZING RADIATION ~; OIL, NATURAL GAS, OR SALT PRODUCTION ~; PERMISSIBLE ~; PLUMBING ~; PORTABLE ~; PROTECTIVE BREATHING ~; PROTECTIVE ~; RADIATION ~; RECORDING ~; SELF-PROPELLED ~; SHELTER ~; SPECIAL MOBILE ~; STORAGE ~; TRANSMISSION ~; TRANSPORTABLE ~; UTILIZATION ~; VENTILATION ~; WELDING ~; X-RAY ~.

EQUIPMENT TRUST. A means for a company to raise funds on the security of equipment, established by setting up a certificate or indenture. D.M.W. Waters, *The Law of Trusts in Canada*, 2d ed. (Toronto: Carswell, 1984) at 452.

EQUITABLE. *adj.* Fair; according to the rules of equity.

EQUITABLE CHARGE. A security for a debt which does not provide the lender with a legal estate in the charged property.

EQUITABLE DOCTRINE OF CONSTRUCTIVE NOTICE. Any equitable claim is good against a mortgagee who should have known of it by acting prudently, i.e., if the mortgagee had made the usual title search. Mortgagees are obliged to be both honest and diligent. W.B. Rayner & R.H. McLaren, *Falconbridge on Mortgages*, 4th ed. (Toronto: Canada Law Book, 1977) at 115.

EQUITABLE ESTATE. A right relating to property which another person or the equitable owner in another capacity legally owns.

EQUITABLE ESTOPPEL. Once one party makes a representation about a present or past fact and the other party relies on it detrimentally, the representor cannot repudiate the representation and put forward the true facts. G.H.L. Fridman, *The Law of Contract in Canada*, 2d ed. (Toronto: Carswell, 1986) at 110.

EQUITABLE EXECUTION. Where a judgment creditor may not take in execution interests in property under processes at law, the creditor may have a receiver appointed.

EQUITABLE INTEREST. A right relating to property which another person or the equitable owner in another capacity legally owns.

EQUITABLE LEASEHOLD MORTGAGE. A mortgage created when one agrees to make a lease or sub-lease, to assign a lease, to deposit title deeds or to do any other thing which creates an equitable charge of freehold. W.B. Rayner & R.H. McLaren, *Falconbridge on Mortgages*, 4th ed. (Toronto: Canada Law Book, 1977) at 97.

EQUITABLE LIEN. 1. A lien not tied to possession. 2. An equitable right, such as an unpaid

vendor's lien or a purchaser's lien, which the law confers on one person in the form of a charge on the real property of another person until particular claims are satisfied. W.B. Rayner & R.H. McLaren, *Falconbridge on Mortgages*, 4th ed. (Toronto: Canada Law Book, 1977) at 9-10.

EQUITABLE MORTGAGE. 1. Commonly, a charge or mortgage other than a statutory or registered mortgage. W.B. Rayner & R.H. McLaren, *Falconbridge on Mortgages*, 4th ed. (Toronto: Canada Law Book, 1977) at 236. 2. A mortgage may be equitable either (1) because the interest mortgaged is future or equitable, or (2) because the mortgagor did not execute an instrument adequate to transfer the legal estate, e.g. a mortgage of the equity of redemption. Such a mortgage may also be created by depositing title deeds. W.B. Rayner & R.H. McLaren, *Falconbridge on Mortgages*, 4th ed. (Toronto: Canada Law Book, 1977) at 81.

EQUITABLE SHARE. See JUST AND ~.

EQUITY. *n.* 1. Fairness. 2. That part of the general law which provides remedies not available at common law in many cases. 3. Equity of redemption. 4. In business, the excess of assets over liabilities. 5. The aggregate of (a) the share capital, (b) earned surplus, (c) contributed surplus, (d) other surplus or deficit accounts, (e) shareholders' loans that are subordinated to all other liabilities, and (f) the proprietor's or partner capital accounts, less such accounts as unreasonably inflate the net worth of the applicant. Canada regulations. See ACCUMULATED NET RETAIL ~; ADJUSTED ~; BETTER ~; DIRECT ~ PERCENTAGE; FORMAL ~; INFORMAL ~; MAXIMS OF ~; PAY ~; SHAREHOLDERS' ~; TAX ~ OF A PARTNERSHIP.

EQUITY ACCOUNT. See VOLUNTARY ~.

EQUITY CAPITAL. Of a corporation, the amount of consideration paid in money for which the outstanding equity shares of the corporation have been issued.

EQUITY OF A STATUTE. When a fact situation falls within a statute's spirit and intent, though apparently not its letter, it is within the equity of that statute.

EQUITY OF REDEMPTION. 1. A mortgagor's right to redeem a mortgage. 2. The interest remaining in a mortgagor after the execution of one or more mortgages upon any lands. 3. The amount by which a property's value exceeds the total charges, liens or mortgages against it. See CLOG ON ~.

EQUITY SECURITIES. Shares of any class of

a corporation and any rights in connection therewith. *Bank Act*, R.S.C. 1985, c. B-1, s. 190.

EQUITY SHARE. 1. A share of a class of shares of a corporation carrying voting rights under all circumstances and a share of a class of shares carrying voting rights by reason of the occurrence of a contingency that has occurred and is continuing. 2. A voting security and any security of an issuer that carries the residual right to participate in earnings of the issuer and in its assets on liquidation or winding up. 3. Any security other than a debt obligation of a corporation. *Business Corporations Act, 1982*, S.O. 1982, c. 4, s. 186. 4. (i) A share, other than an excluded share or a non-participating share, the owner of which has, as owner thereof, a right (A) to a dividend, and (B) to a part of the surplus of the corporation after repayment of capital and payment of dividend arrears on the redemption of the share, a reduction of the capital of the corporation or the winding-up of the corporation, at least as great, in any event, as the right of the owner of any other share, other than a non-participating share, of the corporation, when the magnitude of the right in each case is expressed as a rate based on the paid-up capital value of the share to which the right relates, or (ii) a share, other than an excluded share or a non-participating share, the owner of which has, as owner thereof, a right (A) to a dividend, after a dividend at a rate not in excess of 12% per annum of the paid-up capital value of each share has been paid to the owners of shares of a class other than the class to which that share belongs, and (B) part of the surplus of the corporation after repayment of capital and payment of dividend arrears on the redemption of the share, a reduction of the capital of the corporation or the winding-up of the corporation, after a payment of a part of the surplus at a rate not in excess of 10% of the paid-up capital value of each share has been made to the owners of shares of a class other than the class to which that share belongs, at least as great, in any event, as the right of the owner of any other share, other than a non-participating share, of the corporation, when the magnitude of the right in each case is expressed as a rate based on the paid-up capital value of the share to which the right relates. *Income Tax Act*, R.S.C. 1952, c. 148 (as am. S.C. 1980-81-82-83, c. 140, c. 113), s. 204(a).

EQUITY SHARES. Shares of any class, whether or not preferred as to dividends or assets, which have unlimited dividend rights. *Loan and Trust Companies Act*, S.N.B. 1987, c. L-11.2, s. 74.

EQUIVALENCY. *n.* A principle which permits deviation from regulated requirements and specifications as long as the alternative designs, sizes, compositions or arrangements provide better or equal strength as well as health and safety protection. D. Robertson, *Ontario Health and Safety Guide* (Toronto: Richard De Boo Ltd., 1988) at 5-153.

EQUIVALENT. See ACTUARIALLY ~; PENSION ~; WATER ~.

EQUIVALENT EMPLOYMENT. Employment of a similar nature to the employment held by the worker when he suffered the employment injury, from the standpoint of vocational qualifications required, wages, social benefits, duration and working conditions. *An Act Respecting Industrial Accidents and Occupational Diseases*, S.Q. 1985, c. 6, s. 2.

EQUIVALENT RATE. See CANADIAN ~.

ERBP. See WET ~.

EROTIC. See SERVICES DESIGNED TO APPEAL TO ~ OR SEXUAL APPETITES OR INCLINATIONS.

ERRANT. *adj.* Wandering.

ERRATA. *n.* [L.] Errors.

ERRATUM. *n.* [L.] Error.

ERROR. *n.* 1. Incorrect information, and includes omission of information. *Vital Statistics acts.* 2. In old common law practice, a mistake in the proceeding which either the court in which it occurred or a superior court must correct. 3. In any certificate or field note is in reality a percentage correction factor, which shall be calculated in accordance with the following formula:

$$\text{The field note "error"} = \frac{R - T}{R} \times 100$$

Gas and Gas Meters Regulations, C.R.C., c. 876, s. 20. See ACCEPTANCE LIMITS OF ~; CLERICAL ~; IN-SERVICE LIMITS OF ~; WRIT OF ~.

ERRORES AD SUA PRINCIPIA REFERRE, EST REFELLERE. [L.] To refute errors, go back to their origin.

ERROR FRUTATUS NUDA VERITATE IN MULTIS EST PROBABILIOR; ET SAEPE-NUMERO RATIONIBUS VINCIT VERITA-TEM ERROR. [L.] A well-dressed error often seems more probable than naked truth; it repeatedly conquers truth by reasoning.

ERROR NOMINIS. [L.] A mistake as to a person's name.

ERROR OF LAW. When a court or tribunal errs in applying the law to a case on trial.

ERROR OF REGISTRATION. The difference between the "registered amount" and the "true amount"; that is, R - T = e where R is the registered amount, T is the true amount, e is the error of registration. *Gas and Gas Meters Regulations*, C.R.C., c. 876, s. 20.

ERROR PERSONAE. [L.] Mistaken identity.

ERROR QUI NON RESTITUR, APPRO-BATUR. [L.] The one who is able to rectify a mistake but does not is deemed to have approved.

ERRORS EXCEPTED. A phrase intended to excuse a small mistake or oversight in a stated account.

ESCALATION CLAUSE. 1. Clause in lease providing for increases in rent based on some factor such as tax increases. 2. Clause in wage contract or collective agreement providing for a raise in rate of pay based on a factor such as the Consumer Price Index.

ESCALATOR. *n.* 1. A moving, inclined, continuous stairway or runway used for raising or lowering passengers. 2. A power-driven, inclined, continuous stairway or runway affixed to a building or structure that is used for lifting or lowering persons and that serves two or more floors or permanent levels of the building or structure, and includes its hoistway enclosure. *Elevators and Lifts Act*, R.S.N.S. 1967, c. 85, s. 1.

ESCALATOR CLAUSE. See ESCALATION CLAUSE.

ESCAPE. *v.* Breaking prison, escaping from lawful custody or, without lawful excuse, being at large before the expiration of a term of imprisonment to which a person has been sentenced. *Criminal Code*, R.S.C. 1985, c. C-46, s. 149(3).

ESCAPE INTERVAL. The time between the sensing of a spontaneous beat and the succeeding output pulse of a triggered pulse generator. *Medical Devices Regulations*, C.R.C., c. 871, s. 1.

ESCHEAT. *n.* The reversion of land or other property to the Crown when a company is dissolved or a person dies intestate without heirs.

ESCROW. *n.* Holding something in trust until a contingency happens or a condition is performed. See STOCK ~ TRUST.

ESPIONAGE. *n.* Spying.

ESQ. *abbr.* Esquire.

ESQUIRE. *n.* A title which confers dignity.

ESSENCE OF THE CONTRACT. Describes a provision in a contract which both parties agreed at the time they entered into the contract was so important that performance of the contract without strict compliance with that provision would be pointless.

ESSENTIAL AIRCRAFT EQUIPMENT. An item, component or system installed in an aircraft, that (a) has a primary role of providing information or performing a function required by regulation or order, or (b) is directly related to the airworthiness of the aircraft. *Aircraft Minimum Equipment List Order*, C.R.C., c. 25, s. 2.

ESSENTIAL PARTS. All integral and body parts of a vehicle of a type required to be registered hereunder, the removal, alteration or substitution of which would tend to conceal the identity of the vehicle or substantially alter its appearance, model, type or mode of operation.

ESSENTIAL POWERS. See STATUS AND ~.

ESSENTIAL QUALIFICATIONS. In relation to a position or class of positions, means the minimum factors or circumstances that are necessary having regard to the nature of the duties of the position or class of positions. *Public Service Employment Regulations*, C.R.C., c. 1337, s. 2.

ESSENTIAL SERVICES. A class of services designated to be maintained during strikes; employees employed in such jobs have limited or no right to strike.

ESTABLISHED PLACE OF BUSINESS. A place actually occupied whether continuously or at regular periods by a dealer or manufacturer where books and records are kept and a large share of the business is transacted.

ESTABLISHMENT. *n.* 1. A place of business or the place where an undertaking or a part thereof is carried on. 2. The positions in a department to which appointments may be made by the Minister. *Public Service (Amendment) Act*, S.N.W.T. 1986 (1st Sess.), c. 14, s. 4. 3. Any place where fish are processed for sale or stored for sale. 4. The act of a natural person or of a group operation of taking up an activity as their principal occupation or principal activity. 5. Any place in which animals are slaughtered or meat products are prepared, packaged, labelled or stored. 6. (a) Any establishment provided with special accommodation so that, for payment, lodging or food are habitually available there, excluding an establishment where, for payment by the week or by the month, lodging or food and lodging is or are habitually available, and excluding an educational, charitable, hospitalizing or sheltering institution or other similar institution; (b) premises where alcoholic beverages are sold for consumption there; (c) an autobus, a railway train or a ship, in Québec, on which meals or alcoholic beverages are served; (d) an enterprise which sells, delivers or serves meals for consumption elsewhere; or (e) a tavern within the meaning of section 27 of the Act respecting liquor permits (R.S.Q., chapter P-9.1). *An Act to Amend Various Fiscal Laws*, S.Q. 1982, c. 38, s. 31. 7. A lounge, restaurant, tavern, club, hotel, motel, tourist home, or military mess. *Liquor Control Act*, S.Nfld. 1977, c. 111, s. 1. 8. A local community service centre, a hospital centre, a functional rehabilitation centre, a social service centre or a reception centre. *Health Services and Social Services Act*, R.S.Q. 1977, c. S-5, s. 1. 9. Any premises where a permit is in use or where alcoholic beverages are manufactured under any act of the Parliament of Canada. *An Act Respecting the Commission de Contrôle des Permis D'alcool*, R.S.Q. 1977, c. C-33, s. 2. See CABIN ~; CAMPING ~; COMMERCIAL ~; COTTAGE ~; DEFENCE ~; EDUCATIONAL ~; FUNERAL SERVICES ~; HATCHERY ~; HEAD OF ~; INDUSTRIAL ~; OUTPOST ~; PERMANENT ~; RETAIL BUSINESS ~; RETAIL ~; RIDING HORSE ~; SELF-CONTAINED DOMESTIC ~; SEMI-PRESERVING ~; TOURIST ~.

EST. & TR. J. *abbr.* Estates & Trusts Journal.

EST. & TR. Q. *abbr.* Estates & Trusts Quarterly.

ESTATE. *n.* 1. An interest in land. 2. All the property of which a testator or an intestate had power to dispose by will, otherwise than by virtue of a special power of appointment, less the amount of funeral, testamentary and administration expenses, debts and liabilities, and succession duties payable out of the estate on death. 3. Includes both real and personal property. *Intestate Succession acts.* See EQUITABLE ~; EXECUTORY ~; EXPECTANT ~; FREEHOLD ~; FUTURE ~; HEIRS, NEXT OF KIN OR ~; INSOLVENT ~; LEASEHOLD ~; LIFE ~; PARTICULAR ~; PERSONAL ~; QUALITY OF ~; QUANTITY OF ~; REAL ~; SERVICE ~.

ESTATE AD REMANENTIAM. [L.] Property held in fee simple.

ESTATE AND PROPERTY. All the real and personal, tangible and intangible property of a collector or vendor, whether subject to liens, charges or encumbrances or whether free and clear of liens, charges or encumbrances. *Retail Sales Tax acts.*

ESTATE DUTY. A tax generally imposed on "property passing" when someone dies; its rate is based on the size of the estate. D.M.W. Waters, *The Law of Trusts in Canada*, 2d ed. (Toronto: Carswell, 1984) at 477.

ESTATE FREEZE. A transaction which replaces growth assets, i.e. common shares of an operating business corporation, with assets of limited growth potential, i.e. preferred shares, so that a ceiling approximately equal to the value at the date of the freeze is placed on the value of those assets for capital gain and succession duty purposes. Thus any future growth in the value of the assets usually benefits subsequent generations, who become common shareholders. W. Grover & F. Iacobucci, *Materials on Canadian Income Tax*, 4th ed. (Toronto: Richard De Boo Ltd., 1980) at 793.

ESTATE IN A MINERAL. An estate in fee simple in a mineral or an estate for a life or lives in being in a mineral. *Mines and Minerals Amendment Act, 1983*, S.A. 1983, c. 36, s. 2.

ESTATE OF A DECEASED INMATE. The following parts of the estate of an inmate who dies while serving a term of imprisonment in a penitentiary: (a) any pay that, under the regulations, was due or otherwise payable to the inmate at the time of the inmate's death; (b) any moneys standing to the inmate's credit at that time in any fund maintained or controlled by the Service; and (c) any personal belongings, including cash, found on the inmate or in the possession of the inmate at the time of death or that are in the care or custody of the Service at that time. *Penitentiary Act*, R.S.C. 1985, c. P-5. s. 36(2).

ESTATE IN LAND. Includes a statutory right given or reserved to the Crown to enter any lands or premises for the purpose of doing any work, construction, repair or maintenance in, upon, through, over or under any such lands or premises.

ESTATE OR PROPERTY. 1. All the assets of the vendor, real and personal, tangible and intangible, whether subject to liens, charges or encumbrances or whether free and clear of such claims, and without limiting the generality of the foregoing, includes lands, accounts receivable, claims, demands, inventory, chattels, equipment, mortgages, leases and generally all the vendor's undertaking, property and assets. *Retail Sales Tax Act*, S.M. 1980, c. 69, s. 61. 2. Real and personal estate.

ESTATE PLANNING. Arranging business and property interests to pass to heirs and successors in such a way as to receive maximum benefit of laws relating to wills, income tax, estate tax, succession duty, property, insurance, securities, and so on.

ESTATE PUR AUTRE VIE. [Fr.] A grant to one person for the life of another. E.L.G. Tyler & N.E. Palmer, eds., *Crossley Vaines' Personal*

Property, 5th ed. (London: Butterworths, 1973) at 5.

ESTATES DIVISION. The Supreme Court of Prince Edward Island (Estates Division) or any judge thereof.

ESTATE TAX. A tax levied on all a deceased person's property, irrespective of its location or who may inherit it. P.W. Hogg, *Constitutional Law of Canada*, 2d ed. (Toronto: Carswell, 1985) at 610.

ESTIMATE. *n.* A representation as to the future price of a consumer transaction. *Trade Practice Act*, R.S.B.C. 1979, c. 406, s. 1. See ~S; FINAL ~.

ESTIMATED COST. The most current estimate prepared by an engineer, architect, official, planner or construction contractor of the cost of an underaking which estimate has been submitted to the council or other governing body of a municipality or a committee thereof and has been accepted by it as the basis upon which the undertaking is to be proceeded with, but does not include any costs for, (i) the acquisition of land, (ii) feasibility studies and design carried out for the undertaking, or (iii) the operation of the undertaking, and where an undertaking is being constructed in phases includes the costs of all phases. *Environmental Assessment Act*, R.R.O. 1980, Reg. 293, s. 5.

ESTIMATED ELIGIBLE COSTS. In respect of any crop year, means an amount equal to the aggregate of (a) the volume-related variable costs of the railway companies for the movement of grain and their line-related variable costs for grain dependent branch lines, as estimated by the Commission pursuant to section 40, and (b) the contribution to the constant costs of the railway companies, being, in respect of the 1986-87 and subsequent crop years, twenty per cent of the volume-related variable costs. *Western Grain Transportation Act*, R.S.C. 1985, c. W-8, s. 34.

ESTIMATES. *n.* Spending estimates of the Crown transmitted to the legislature and divided into classes, each one corresponding to a separate programme and each class divided into votes, on which the House committees may make separate decisions. A. Fraser, G.A. Birch & W.A. Dawson, eds., *Beauchesne's Rules and Forms of the House of Commons of Canada*, 5th ed. (Toronto: Carswell, 1978) at 169. See ESTIMATE.

ESTOPPEL. *n.* 1. One who has allowed another to believe in the existence of a particular state of affairs, and the other has relied on the belief, cannot argue later that the true state of affairs was different, if to do so would be detrimental to the other. G.H.L. Fridman, *The Law of Agency*, 5th ed. (London: Butterworths, 1983) at 97. 2. A rule of evidence under which a party may not deny the existence of some state of facts which that party asserted previously. See AGENCY BY ~; EQUITABLE ~; PROMISSORY ~; PROPRIETARY ~; QUASI-~.

ESTOVER. *n.* Alimony.

ESTRAY. *n.* 1. An animal that is running at large. 2. An animal found on the premises of a person other than its owner.

ESTREAT. *n.* 1. Now used only in connection with forfeitures, fines and recognizances; if the condition of a recognizance is broken, the recognizance is forfeited, and, when it is estreated, the cognisors become the Crown's debtors. 2. Formerly, a copy of a court record of a court. A recognizance was estreated or extracted when a copy was made from the original and sent for the proper authority to enforce.

ESTREPEMENT. *n.* 1. Spoil or waste which prejudices a tenant for life in reversion made by that tenant on any land. 2. Formerly, the power to cut down trees without it being considered waste.

ET ADJORNATUR. [L.] And it is adjourned.

ET AL. *abbr.* 1. Et alii. 2. Et alius.

ET ALII. [L.] And others.

ET ALIUS. [L.] And another.

ETHANE. *n.* In addition to its normal scientific meaning, a mixture mainly of ethane, which may ordinarily contain some methane or propane. Alberta statutes.

ETHNOGRAPHIC ART. See OBJECT OF ~.

ETHYL ALCOHOL. Any material or substance, whether in liquid or any other form, containing any proportion by mass or by volume of absolute ethyl alcohol (C^2H^5OH). *Excise Act*, R.S.C. 1985, c. E-14, s. 3. See VOLUME OF ABSOLUTE ~.

ETHYLENE OXIDE. A substance designated under the Ontario Occupational Health and Safety Act. D. Robertson, *Ontario Health and Safety Guide* (Toronto: Richard De Boo Ltd., 1988) at 5-154.

E.T.R. *abbr.* Estates & Trusts Reports, 1977-.

ET SEQ. *abbr.* 1. Et sequentes. 2. Et sequentia.

ET SEQUENTES. [L.] And those following.

ET SEQUENTIA. [L.] And the following.

ET UX. *abbr.* Et uxor.

ET UXOR. [L.] And wife.

EUNDO, MORANDO, ET REDEUNDO. [L.] By going, remaining and returning.

EUNOMY. *n.* A constitution of good, well-administered laws.

EURO-CURRENCY MARKET. A market in which transactions are denominated in a currency other than the currency of the nation where the business is conducted. I.F.G. Baxter, *The Law of Banking*, 3d ed. (Toronto: Carswell, 1981) at 161.

EURO-DOLLAR. *n.* A United States dollar entry in the account of a bank or bank branch located outside the United States. I.F.G. Baxter, *The Law of Banking*, 3d ed. (Toronto: Carswell, 1981) at 163.

EUROPEAN COMMISSION OF HUMAN RIGHTS. A body which individuals in member states may petition to claim a violation of the European Convention on Human Rights. P.W. Hogg, *Constitutional Law of Canada*, 2d ed. (Toronto: Carswell, 1985) at 663.

EUROPEAN CONVENTION ON HUMAN RIGHTS. A convention which came into force in 1953 and has been observed by the United Kingdom and other European countries and which guarantees many of the same civil liberties as the Canadian Charter or Rights and Freedoms. P.W. Hogg, *Constitutional Law of Canada*, 2d ed. (Toronto: Carswell, 1985) at 663.

EUROPEAN COURT. The Court of Justice of the European Community.

EUROPEAN COURT OF HUMAN RIGHTS. The court to which the European Commission on Human Rights refers some petitions for decision. P.W. Hogg, *Constitutional Law of Canada*, 2d ed. (Toronto: Carswell, 1985) at 663 and 664.

EUTHANASIA. *n.* The deliberate infliction of an intended death upon an animal other than death that arises directly as an immediate result of an experimental or testing procedure. *Animals for Research Act*, R.R.O. 1980, Reg. 18, s. 1.

EVADER. *n.* A person who (a) during World War I or World War II (i) served in the naval, army or air forces of Canada or Newfoundland, (ii) served in the naval, army or air forces of His Majesty or any of the countries allied with His Majesty during World War I or World War II and was domiciled in Canada or Newfoundland at the time of his enlistment, or (iii) was a person referred to in any of paragraphs (a) to (e) of the definition "civilian prisoner of war" who was a civilian, (b) landed in or entered enemy or enemy occupied territory, (c) became separated from his unit, other than a person who became separated while performing duties as a special agent, and (d) evaded capture during World War I or World War II or subsequent thereto. *Compensation for Former Prisoners of War Act*, R.S.C. 1985, c. F-31, s. 2.

EVALUATION WELL. A well which when being drilled is expected by the Board to penetrate a pool or oil sands deposit and which is drilled for the sole purpose of evaluation. *Oil and Gas Conservation Act*, R.S.A. 1980, c. O-5, s. 1. See BITUMINOUS SHALE ~.

EVAPORATED MILK. Milk from which water has been evaporated, with or without, i. added vitamin D, or ii. disodium phosphate or sodium citrate, or both, added in a total quantity of not more than 0.1 per cent of the finished product, and that contains not less than, iii. 25.5 per cent milk solids, and iv. 7.8 per cent milk-fat. *Farm Products Grades and Sales Act*, R.R.O. 1980, Reg. 327, s. 1.

EVAPORATED PARTLY SKIMMED MILK. Evaporated skim milk from which only part of the milk-fat has been removed. *Farm Products Grades and Sales Act*, R.R.O. 1980, Reg. 327, s. 1.

EVAPORATED SKIM MILK. Milk that has been concentrated to at least one-half of its original volume by the removal of water, and from which any of the milk-fat has been removed, with or without added vitamin D. *Farm Products Grades and Sales Act*, R.R.O. 1980, Reg. 327, s. 1.

EVAPORATIVE EMISSIONS. Any hydrocarbon component of motor gasoline emitted into the atmosphere from the fuel tank or carburetor of a vehicle. *Motor Vehicle Safety Regulations*, C.R.C., c. 1038, s. 1100.

EVASION. *n.* The act of escaping by the use of artifice. See TAX ~.

EVASIVE. *adj.* Describes a pleading which answers the other party's pleading by a half-denial or a half-admission or fails to answer a substantial point.

EVENT. *n.* An activity at which more than one thousand persons attend or are expected to attend on any single day. *Municipal Act*, S.M. 1971, c. 27, s. 46. See CPC ~; OUTDOOR ~; SPECIAL AVIATION ~.

EVENT OF DEFAULT. An event specified in a trust indenture on the occurrence of which (i) a security interest constituted by the trust indenture becomes enforceable, or (ii) the principal, interest or other money payable under the trust indenture become or may be declared to be payable before maturity, but the event is not an event of default until all conditions prescribed by the trust indenture in connection with that event for the giving of notice or the lapse of time or otherwise have been satisfied.

EVENTUS VARIOS RES NOVA SEMPER HABET. [L.] An innovation always produces varying results.

EVERY ONE. Includes Her Majesty and public bodies, bodies corporate, societies, companies and inhabitants of counties, parishes, municipalities or other districts in relation to the acts and things that they are capable of doing and owning respectively. *Criminal Code*, R.S.C. 1985, c. C-46, s. 2.

EVERY ORIGINAL LITERARY, DRAMATIC, MUSICAL AND ARTISTIC WORK. Includes every original production in the literary, scientific or artistic domain, whatever may be the mode or form of its expression, such as books, pamphlets and other writings, lectures, dramatic or dramatico-musical works, musical works or compositions with or without words, illustrations, sketches and plastic works relative to geography, topography, architecture or science. *Copyright Act*, R.S.C. 1985, c. C-42, s. 2.

EVICTION. *n.* The act of dispossessing; recovering land through legal action. See CONSTRUCTIVE ~.

EVIDENCE. *n.* 1. Every means by which an alleged fact is either proved or disproved. F.A. Jaffe, *A Guide to Pathological Evidence*, 2d ed. (Toronto: Carswell, 1983) at 176. 2. An assertion of fact, opinion, belief or knowledge, whether material or not and whether admissible or not. *Criminal Code*, R.S.C. 1985, c. C-46, s. 118 as am. by *Criminal Law Amendment Act*, R.S.C. 1985 (1st Supp.), c. 27, s. 15. 3. For the purposes of this section, does not include evidence that is not material. *Criminal Code*, R.S.C. 1985, c. C-46, s. 136(2). 4. Includes judgments, decisions, opinions, speeches, reports and all other matters done or said by or before a court, including matters relating to procedure. 5. Includes the opinion, decision and judgment of the judge of the court in a proceeding, the opening and closing address of counsel in the trial of criminal offences and the oral instructions given to the jury by the presiding judge. *Recording of Evidence by Sound Recording Machine Act*, R.S.N.B. 1973, c. R-5, s. 1. 6. Anything that has a significant rational tendency to make something manifest. *Military Rules of Evidence*, C.R.C., c. 1049, s. 2. See ADMISSIBLE ~; CIRCUMSTANTIAL ~; COMMISSION ~; CONTRADICTORY ~; DEMONSTRATIVE ~; DERIVATIVE ~; DIRECT ~; DOCUMENTARY ~; EXPERT ~; EXTRINSIC ~; HEARSAY ~; INDIRECT ~; ITEM OF ~; MATERIAL ~; MINUTES OF PROCEEDINGS AND ~; ORIGINAL ~; PAROL ~; POSITIVE ~; PRESUMPTIVE ~; PRIMA FACIE ~; PRIMARY ~; REAL ~; REBUTTAL ~; RELEVANT ~; SECONDARY ~; SIMILAR-FACT ~; TESTIMONIAL ~; TRACE ~; WEIGHT OF ~.

EVIDENTIARY BURDEN. Used, in contrast to persuasive burden, to describe the effect of a statutory presumption which relieves the prosecution from leading evidence to prove a material fact and used to describe the burden imposed on the defence by a mandatory rebuttable presumption that they lead evidence to avoid certain conviction. P.K. McWilliams, *Canadian Criminal Evidence*, 3d ed. (Aurora: Canada Law Book, 1988) at 25-2 and 25-3.

EVISCERATED DOMESTIC RABBIT. A rabbit that has been slaughtered for food and from which the head, blood, skin, feet, and respiratory, digestve, urinary and genital organs have been removed and is ready to cook without the need of further processing of any cut-up or disjointed portion of such domestic rabbit. *Meat Inspection Regulations*, C.R.C., c. 1032, s. 162.

EVISCERATED POULTRY. Slaughtered poultry from which the blood, feathers, head, legs at the hock joints, oil sac, and viscera, including the respiratory, digestive, reproductive and urinary systems have been removed.

EVISCERATING STATION. A place where dressed poultry is eviscerated and graded. *Dressed and Eviscerated Poultry Regulations*, C.R.C., c. 283, s. 2.

EVOCATION. *n.* Withdrawal of a case from an inferior court's cognizance.

EX ABUNDANTI CAUTELA. [L.] Out of abundant caution.

EXACTION. *n.* A form of extortion in which an officer of the law takes a fee or reward where none was due, takes more than was due or takes the fee or reward before it was due.

EXACTOR. *n.* A betting transaction in which a purchaser of a ticket undertakes to select the correct order of finish of the first two horses to finish the race on which that feature is operated. *Race Track Supervision Regulations*, C.R.C., c. 441, s. 2.

EXACTOR REGIS. [L.] The sovereign's tax collector.

EX AEQUO ET BONO. [L. out of what is equal and good] In equity and good conscience.

EXAMINATION. *n.* 1. The questioning of a person under oath. 2. An interview, conducted by an immigration officer, of a person seeking to come into Canada at a port of entry. *Immi-*

gration Act, R.S.C. 1985, c. I-2, s. 2. 3. The examination of a candidate. *Canada Lands Surveys Act*, R.S.C. 1985, c. L-6, s. 2. 4. The examination of an unclothed body with or without the removal of body tissue or fluids for the purpose of toxicological examinations. *Fatality Inquiries Act*, R.S.A. 1980, c. F-6, s. 1. See BAR ADMISSION ~; CLINICAL ~; COMMODITY SUPERVISORS' ~; CROSS-~; DIRECT ~; EMPLOYMENT ~; MEDICAL ~; NATIONAL COMMODITY FUTURES ~; PRELIMINARY ~; PROMOTIONAL ~; PROMOTION ~; RE-~; REGISTERED REPRESENTATIVE ~; SPECIAL ~.

EXAMINATION FOR DISCOVERY. One party questioning another party or person under affirmation or oath as a method of pre-trial discovery.

EXAMINATION IN AID OF EXECUTION. A creditor examining the judgment debtor or other people to determine the debtor's ability to settle the judgment. C.R.B. Dunlop, *Creditor—Debtor Law in Canada* (Toronto: Carswell, 1981) at 109.

EXAMINATION-IN-CHIEF. *n.* Questioning of a witness by the counsel for the party who called that witness to adduce evidence which supports the case of that party.

EXAMINED COPY. A copy proved to have been compared with the original and to correspond to it. *Military Rules of Evidence*, C.R.C., c. 1049, s. 2.

EXAMINER. *n.* 1. A person whom a court appoints to examine witnesses in an action. 2. A person appointed to examine into and pass upon the qualifications of a person applying for a driver's licence. 3. A functionary having jurisdiction to enforce and conduct an examination, or make an order, or issue a warrant under this Act. *Collection Act*, R.S.N.S. 1967, c. 39, s. 1. 4. An examiner of master and mates appointed pursuant to section 126 of the Act. *Certification of Able Seamen Regulations*, C.R.C., c. 1411, s. 2. 5. A person whose qualifications to make examinations have been certified by an oculist or optometrist designated by the railway company after being instructed by an oculist or optometrist on the use of the instruments required for such examination, and who is selected by such company to make such examinations. *Railway Vision and Hearing Examinations Regulations*, C.R.C., c. 1173, s. 2. See FINGERPRINT ~; MINE ~; OFFICIAL ~; SPECIAL ~.

EXAMINER. *abbr.* Examiner (L'Observateur) (Que.).

EXAMINER (L'OBSERVATEUR). *abbr.* Examiner (L'Observateur) (1861).

EXAMINING BOARD. A body established under this act for the purpose of assessing the vocational qualifications of adults in a trade or vocation. *Manpower Vocational Training and Qualification Act*, R.S.Q. 1977, c. F-5, s. 1.

EXAMINING STAFF. The Commissioner, Assistant Commissioner and examiners. *Patent Rules*, C.R.C., c. 1250, s. 2.

EXAMINING WAREHOUSE. A warehouse for the safekeeping, examination and appraisal by customs of goods. *Customs Warehousing Regulations*, C.R.C., c. 462, s. 2. See HIGHWAY FRONTIER ~.

EX ANTECEDENTIBUS ET CONSEQUENTIBUS FIT OPTIMA INTERPRETATIO. [L.] The best interpretation is made by referring to what goes before and to what comes after.

EX ASSENSU PATRIS. [L.] With the father's assent.

EXCAMBIATOR. *n.* A broker; one who exchanges lands.

EXCAMBIUM. *n.* An exchange; a place where traders meet to do business.

EX CATHEDRA. [L.] With the weight of authority.

EXCAVATION. *n.* 1. The space created by the removal of soil, rock or fill for the purposes of construction. *Building Code Act*, R.R.O. 1980, Reg. 87, s. 1. 2. A trench in the ground at a depth of more than four feet. *The Building Trades Protection Act*, R.S.S. 1978, c. B-8, s. 2.

EXCELLENCY. *n.* The title of the Governor General.

EXCEPTED EMPLOYMENT. (a) Employment by Her Majesty in right of Canada; and (b) any employment that is excepted from included employment by any regulation made under subsection (6). *Pension Benefits Standards Act*, R.S.C. 1985 (2d Supp.), c. 32, s. 4(5).

EXCEPTIONAL PUPIL. A pupil whose behavioural, communicational, intellectual, physical or multiple exceptionalities are such that he is considered to need placement in a special education program by a committee, established under subparagraph iii of paragraph 5 of subsection 10 (1), of the board, i. of which he is a resident pupil, ii. that admits or enrols the pupil other than pursuant to an agreement with another board for the provision of education, or iii. to which the cost of education in respect of the pupil is payable by the Minister. *Education Act*, R.S.O. 1980, c. 129, s. 1.

EXCEPTIONS CLAUSE. A clause in a contract which excludes liability.

EXCEPTIO PROBAT REGULAM DE REBUS NON EXCEPTIS. [L.] An exception proves the rule concerning the unexceptional things.

EXCEPTIO SEMPER ULTIMA PONENDA EST. [L.] An exception should always be put last.

EXCEPTIS EXCIPIENDIS. [L.] Including all exceptions.

EXCERPTA. *n.* [L.] Extracts.

EXCERPT. *n.* An extract.

EXCESS PAYMENT. The amount of any advance or assistance or welfare payment that was paid by an authority to a person for a month or any portion thereof and that would not have been paid if the benefit that was subsequently payable under the Act to that person in respect of that period had in fact been paid during that period. *Canada Pension Plan Regulations*, C.R.C., c. 385, s. 76.

EXCESS PROPORTION OF FAT. A degree of fatness necessitating an extensive trimming to achieve consumer acceptance. *Beef Carcass Grading Regulations*, C.R.C., c. 282, s. 2.

EXCHANGE. *n.* 1. When the consideration is giving other goods, it is a contract of barter or exchange. G.H.L. Fridman, *Sale of Goods in Canada*, 3d ed. (Toronto: Carswell, 1986) at 22. 2. A group of persons formed for the purpose of exchanging reciprocal contracts of indemnity or inter-insurance with each other through the same attorney. 3. A centralized market facility, operated by the Corporation for placing of insurance risks, including reinsurance, with syndicates, either alone, with other syndicates or other insurers, to share the risks for a price negotiated within the facility. *Canadian Insurance Exchange Act*, S.O. 1986, c. 70, s. 1. 4. A building or location where agents, merchants, brokers, bankers and others meet at certain times to trade. 5. The value of one country's currency expressed in the terms of another. 6. With reference to gas, means the exchange of gas received by the corporation into its gas pipeline for delivery to a point in the corporation's system to which physical transmission of that gas is not practical, for other gas in the corporation's system which can practically be delivered to that point. *Nova, An Alberta Corporation Act*, R.S.A. 1980, c. N-12, s. 1. 7. A group of subscribers exchanging reciprocal contracts of indemnity or inter-insurance with each other through the same attorney. 8. The following exchanges referred to in Order in Council P.C. 1976-590: Winnipeg Commodity Exchange and Vancouver Grain Exchange. *Grain Futures Regulations*, C.R.C., c. 892, s. 2. See BILL OF ~; COMMODITY ~; COMMOD-

ITY FUTURES ~; DRY ~; FILM ~; INTER-INSURANCE ~; LIVESTOCK ~; RATE OF ~; RECIPROCAL ~; RECIPROCAL OR INTER-INSURANCE ~; TOBACCO AUCTION ~; VIDEO ~; WINNIPEG GRAIN AND PRODUCE ~ CLEARING ASSOCIATION LIMITED; WINNIPEG GRAIN ~.

EXCHANGE SYSTEM. A system in which separate pre-printed pari-mutuel tickets are used for each half of the daily double feature and the winning tickets on the first half of the daily double feature are exchanged for a ticket on the second half of the daily double feature. *Race Track Supervision Regulations*, C.R.C., c. 441, s. 2.

EXCHANGE VALUE. Rental value. *An Act respecting municipal taxation and providing amendments to certain legislation*, S.Q. 1979, c. 72, s. 191.

EXCHEAT. See ESCHEAT.

EXCHEQUER BILL. A bank-note, bond, note, debenture or security that is issued or guaranteed by Her Majesty under the authority of Parliament or the legislature of a province. *Criminal Code*, R.S.C. 1985, c. C-46, s. 321.

EXCHEQUER BILL PAPER. Paper that is used to manufacture exchequer bills. *Criminal Code*, R.S.C. 1985, c. C-46, s. 321.

EXCHEQUER COURT. The Exchequer Court of Canada, replaced by The Federal Court in 1971. See JUDGE OF THE ~; PRESIDENT OF THE ~.

EXCISE. See REVENUE CANADA, CUSTOMS AND ~; SUBJECT TO ~.

EXCISE DIVISION. The district or territory under the survey of the collector. *Excise Act*, R.S.C. 1985, c. E-14, s. 3.

EXCISE DUTY. A tax on the distribution or manufacture of goods. P.W. Hogg, *Constitutional Law of Canada*, 2d ed. (Toronto: Carswell, 1985) at 606.

EXCISE STAMP. A stamp prepared for the purposes of this Act pursuant to a direction of the Minister under section 60. *Excise Tax Act*, R.S.C. 1985, c. E-15, s. 2.

EXCISE TAXES. 1. The taxes imposed under the Excise Tax Act. *Duties Relief Act*, R.S.C. 1985 (2d Supp.), c. 21, s. 2. 2. Taxes on the quantity of goods manufactured. W. Grover & F. Iacobucci, *Materials of Canadian Income Tax*, 4th ed. (Toronto: Richard De Boo Ltd., 1980) at 25.

EXCLAMATION. See SPONTANEOUS ~.

EXCLUDED CONSIDERATION. Consideration received by an individual that is (a) indebtedness; (b) a share of the capital stock of a corporation; or (c) a right to receive indebtedness or a share of the capital stock of a corporation. *Income Tax Act*, R.S.C. 1952, c. 148 (as am. S.C. 1986, c. 55, s. 19(2)), s. 74.4(1).

EXCLUDED CORPORATION. For a taxation year means a corporation that is, at any time in the year, (a) controlled directly or indirectly, in any manner whatever, by (i) one or more persons exempt from tax under this Part by virtue of section 149, (ii) Her Majesty in right of a province, a Canadian municipality or any other public authority, or (iii) any combination of persons each of which is a person referred to in subparagraph (i) or (ii), or (b) related to any person referred to in paragraph (a). *Income Tax Act*, R.S.C. 1952, c. 148 (as am. S.C. 1986, c. 6, s. 72), s. 127.1(2).

EXCLUDED DIVIDEND. A dividend (a) paid by a corporation to a shareholder that had a substantial interest in the corporation at the time the dividend was paid, (b) paid by a corporation that was a financial intermediary corporation or a private holding corporation at the time the dividend was paid, (c) paid by a particular corporation that would, but for paragraphs (h) and (i) of the definition "financial intermediary corporation", have been a financial intermediary corporation at the time the dividend was paid, except where the dividend was paid to a controlling corporation in respect of the particular corporation or to a specified person (within the meaning assigned by paragraph (h) of the definition "taxable preferred share" in subsection 248(1)) in relation to such a controlling corporation, (d) paid by a mortgage investment corporation, or (e) that is a capital gains dividend within the meaning assigned by subsection 131(1). *Income Tax Act*, R.S.C. 1952, c. 148 (as am. S.C. 1988, c. 55, s. 159(1)), s. 191(1).

EXCLUDED OBLIGATION. Any bond, debenture, bill, note, mortgage, hypothec or similar obligation, (i) referred to in subparagraph 212(1)(b)(ii) or (iii), (ii) if, under the terms of the obligation or any agreement relating thereto, the issuer thereof is not obliged to pay more than 25% of the principal amount thereof within 5 years of the date of its issue except in the event of a failure or default under the said terms or agreement, (iii) that is prescribed to be a public issue security, or (iv) that was issued for an amount not less than 97% of the principal amount thereof, and the yield from which, expressed in terms of an annual rate on the amount for which the obligation was issued, (which annual rate shall, if the terms of the obligation or any agreement relating thereto conferred upon the holder thereof a right to demand payment of the principal amount of the obligation or the amount outstanding as or on account of the principal amount thereof, as the case may be, before the maturity of the obligation, be calculated on the basis of the yield that produces the highest annual rate obtainable either on the maturity of the obligation or conditional upon the exercise of any such right) does not exceed 4/3 of the interest stipulated to be payable on the obligation, expressed in terms of an annual rate on (A) the principal amount thereof, if no amount is payable on account the principal amount before the maturity of the obligation, or (B) the amount outstanding from time to time as or on account of the principal amount thereof, in any other case. *Income Tax Act*, R.S.C. 1952, c. 148 (as am. S.C. 1970-71-72, c. 63), s. 214(8)(a).

EXCLUDED SHARE. Each share of the capital stock of a private corporation where (i) the paid-up capital of the corporation that is represented by all its issued and outstanding shares that would, but for this paragraph, be equity shares is less than 50% of the paid-up capital of the corporation that is represented by all its issued and outstanding shares other than non-participating shares, or (ii) a non-participating share of the corporation is issued and outstanding and the owner of which has, as owner thereof, a right to a dividend (A) at a fixed annual rate in excess of 12%, or (B) at an annual rate not in excess of a fixed maximum annual rate, if the fixed maximum annual rate is in excess of 12%, when the right to the dividend is expressed as a rate based on the paid-up capital value of the share to which the right relates. *Income Tax Act*, R.S.C. 1952, c. 148 (as am. S.C. 1980-81-82-83, c. 140, s. 113), s. 204(a.1).

EXCLUSION. *n.* Of a witness is at the discretion of the trial judge who may, at any party's request, order that the witness stay out of the courtroom until called to give evidence. G.D. Watson & C. Perkins, eds., *Holmested & Watson: Ontario Civil Procedure* (Toronto: Carswell, 1984) at 52-4.

EXCLUSION CLAUSE. A clause that removes certain obligations from consideration or limits a party's liabilities for not performing or mis-performing the contract. G.H.L. Fridman, *Sale of Goods in Canada*, 3d ed. (Toronto: Carswell, 1986) at 282.

EXCLUSION ORDER. An exclusion order made under any of subsections 32(5), 37(5), 73(2) or 74(1) or (3). *Immigration Act*, R.S.C. 1985, c. I-2, s. 2.

EXCLUSIVE AGENT. An agent with the sole right to act on the principal's behalf in regard of a particular transaction, type of transaction or property.

EXCLUSIVE BARGAINING RIGHT. The right of the union, which is designated as bargaining representative, to bargain collectively for all employees in the unit which it represents.

EXCLUSIVE DEALING. (a) Any practice whereby a supplier of a product, as a condition of supplying that product to a customer, requires that customer to (i) deal only or primarily in products supplied by or designated by the supplier or his nominee, or (ii) refrain from dealing in a specified class or kind of product except as supplied by the supplier or his nominee, and (b) any practice whereby a supplier of a product induces a customer to meet a condition set out in subparagraph (a)(i) or (ii) by offering to supply the product to him on more favourable terms or conditions if the customer agrees to meet the condition set out in either of those subparagraphs. *Combines Investigation Act,* R.S.C. 1985, c. C-34, s. 39.

EXCLUSIVE JURISDICTION CLAUSE. A clause which states that a tribunal has exclusive and unreviewable jurisdiction to decide issues before it. P.W. Hogg, *Constitutional Law of Canada,* 2d ed. (Toronto: Carswell, 1985) at 162.

EXCLUSIVE LISTING. When a vendor names one broker to act as agent in the sale of property, that agent has the sole, exclusive and irrevocable right to sell that property during a defined time period. B.J. Reiter, R.C.B. Risk & B.N. McLellan, *Real Estate Law,* 3d ed. (Toronto: Emond Montgomery, 1986) at 75.

EXCLUSIVE NURSING PRACTICE. The application of professional nursing knowledge for compensation for the purpose of (i) caring for physically or mentally ill persons, or (ii) caring for and assessing the health of well persons, and includes the administration of any drug or medicine, as defined in the Pharmaceutical Association Act, that is permitted by law to be prescribed and administered to a person. *Nursing Profession Act,* S.A. 1983, c. N-14.5, s. 1.

EXCLUSIVE POSSESSION. The right to occupy premises without any interference by another person.

EXCLUSIVE RIGHT OF WAY. When used in connection with a bus service means a roadway, including entrances and exits, constructed for use by buses and upon which the public is not permitted to drive motor vehicles but not including accesses to stations and stops, or turning, storage and service facilities not otherwise associated with such a right of way, nor a reserved bus lane on an existing road. *Environmental Assessment Act,* R.R.O. 1980, Reg. 293, s. 5.

EXCLUSIVE USE PORTION. A part of the common elements that is to be used by the owners of one or more designated units and not by all the owners. *Condominium Act,* R.R.O. 1980, Reg. 122, s. 1.

EXCOMMUNICATION. *n.* An ecclesiastical punishment in which a person is expelled from membership in the church.

EX CONCESSIS. [L. from what was conceded] Admittedly.

EX CONTRACTU. [L.] From contract.

EX. C.R. *abbr.* 1. Exchequer Court of Canada Reports. 2. Exchequer Court Reports of Canada, 1875-1922.

Ç Ç EX. C.R. *abbr.* Canada Law Reports Exchequer Court, 1923-1971.

EX. CT. *abbr.* Exchequer Court.

EXCULPATORY CONFESSION. A statement which relieves the person giving it of guilt or responsibility.

EX CURIA. [L.] Out of court.

EXCURSION BOAT. A boat which is used to transport the public on pleasure excursions. *An Act to Amend the Liquor Control Act,* S.N.B. 1985, c. 57, s. 1.

EXCURSION CRAFT. See WATER-~.

EXCUSABLE CONDUCT. Conduct which is acceptable, carries no legal consequences.

EXCUSAT AUT EXTENUAT DELICTUM IN CAPITALIBUS QUOD NON OPERATOR IDEM IN CIVILIBUS. [L.] In capital cases, a wrong is excused or diminished which would not be treated the same way in civil cases.

EXCUSE. See LAWFUL ~.

EXCUSS. *n.* Distress.

EXCUSSION. *n.* Legal seizure.

EX. D. *abbr.* Law Reports, Exchequer Division, 1875-1890.

EX DEBITO JUSTITIAE. [L.] The remedy to which an applicant is rightfully entitled.

EX DELICTO. [L.] From wrong or tort. See ACTION ~.

EX DIUTURNITATE TEMPORIS OMNIS PRAESUNUNITUR ESSE RITE ET SOLEMNITUR ACTA. [L.] After the passage of time, all things are presumed to have been done correctly and customarily.

EX DIV. *abbr.* Ex dividend.

EX DIVIDEND. [L. without dividend] When selling stocks and shares on which a dividend was declared or is anticipated ex div., the buyer may not claim the dividend.

EX DOLO MALO NON ORITUR ACTIO. [L.] An action does not arise from a fraud.

EXEAT. [L.] Let the person go.

EXECUTE. *v.* 1. To carry into effect; to complete. 2. Of a deed, to sign, seal and deliver it. 3. Of a judgment or court order, to enforce it or carry it into effect. 4. Of a writ, to obey the instructions within it.

EXECUTED. *adj.* Completed, done.

EXECUTED CONSIDERATION. Something done in exchange for a promise.

EXECUTED CONTRACT. When nothing remains for either party to do, and the transaction is complete.

EXECUTED TRUST. A trust after the estate is conveyed to trustees for particular beneficiaries.

EXECUTIO EST EXECUTIO JURIS SECUNDUM JUDICIUM. [L.] Execution is the functioning of the law according to the judgment.

EXECUTIO EST FINIS ET FRUCTUS LEGIS. [L.] Execution is the object and fruit of the law.

EXECUTIO JURIS NON HABET INJURIAM. [L.] The execution of a legal process does no harm.

EXECUTION. *n.* 1. The process of enforcing or carrying out a judgment. 2. An execution issued out of the Supreme Court or a county court against goods and chattels, lands and tenements of a judgment debtor. *Memorials and Executions Act*, R.S.N.B. 1973, c. M-9, s. 1. 3. A writ of fieri facias, and every subsequent writ for giving effect to a writ of fieri facias. See EQUITABLE ~; EXAMINATION IN AID OF ~; LEGAL ~; SUBSISTING ~; WRIT OF ~.

EXECUTION CREDITOR. Includes a person in whose name or on whose behalf a writ of execution is issued on a judgment.

EXECUTION OF DEEDS. The signing, sealing, and delivery of documents.

EXECUTIVE. *n.* The Crown in its administrative role; the government. This includes government officials and departments directed by ministers of the Crown and the principal executive body, the Cabinet, headed by the Prime Minister. See CHIEF ~ OFFICER; SENIOR ~.

EXECUTIVE AUTHORITY. See GOVERNING ~.

EXECUTIVE COUNCIL. 1. The premier and members of cabinet of a province. 2. The Executive Council of the Government of the Northwest Territories composed of the Commissioner and the Executive Members. *Interpretation Act*, S.N.W.T. 1983 (2d Sess.), c. 4, s. 1.

EXECUTIVE GOVERNMENT. The Lieutenant-Governor and the Conseil exécutif du Québec. *Interpretation Act*, R.S.Q. 1977, c. I-16, s. 61.

EXECUTIVE MEMBER. A member of the Council who is assigned by the Commissioner the responsibility for aspects of government administration which include that enactment or its subject matter or the department to which its context refers. *Interpretation Act*, S.N.W.T. 1983 (2d Sess.), c. 4, s. 2.

EXECUTIVE OFFICER. 1. Person who is employed by a corporation and who has power to guide or control the policies or purposes of the corporation. *Workers' Compensation Act*, R.S.N.W.T. 1974, c. W-4, s. 9. 2. The president, vice-president, secretary and treasurer of a credit union. *Credit Union Act*, R.S.P.E.I. 1974, c. C-28, s. 1.

EXECUTIVE OFFICER OF A CORPORATION. The president of the corporation, the chairman of the board of directors of the corporation, a vice-president of the corporation, the secretary of the corporation, an assistant secretary of the corporation, the treasurer of the corporation, an assistant treasurer of the corporation, or a director of the corporation. *Workmen's Compensation Act*, S.M. 1972, c. 46, s. 1.

EXECUTOR. *n.* 1. A person appointed in a testator's will to carry out directions and requests set out there and to distribute property according to the will's provisions. 2. Where used in referring to the executor of a deceased includes an executor of the will of the deceased, an administrator of the estate of the deceased, and an executor de son tort of any property of the deceased. *Succession Duty Tax acts.* See ~ OF AN ~; LIMITED ~; SUBSTITUTED ~.

EXECUTOR DE SON TORT. A stranger who acts as executor or administrator without just authority.

EXECUTOR LUCRATUS. [L.] An executor who has assets in hand.

EXECUTOR OF AN EXECUTOR. When an executor dies, any interest in a testator's estate and any effects vested in that executor devolve upon the executor's executor.

EXECUTORY. *adj.* Still to be effected, in contrast to executed.

EXECUTORY CONSIDERATION. A promise, which amounts to consideration, to do, give or pay something in the future. G.H.L. Fridman, *The Law of Contract in Canada*, 2d ed. (Toronto: Carswell, 1986) at 96.

EXECUTORY CONTRACT. A contract between a buyer and a seller for the purchase and sale of goods or services in respect of which delivery of the goods or performance of the services or payment in full of the consideration is not made at the time the contract is entered into.

EXECUTORY DEVISE. Legal limitation of a future interest in lands by a will.

EXECUTORY ESTATE. An interest dependant on some subsequent contingency or event for its enjoyment.

EXECUTORY INTEREST. A legal interest in the future. E.L.G. Tyler & N.E. Palmer, eds., *Crossley Vaines' Personal Property*, 5th ed. (London: Butterworths, 1973) at 42.

EXECUTORY LIMITATION. A limitation, by will or deed, of a future interest.

EXECUTORY TRUST. An imperfect trust which requires some act to perfect it.

EXECUTRIX. *n.* A woman appointed by a testator to carry out the instructions in the will.

EXEMPLARY DAMAGES. Damages designed to deter and punish. K.D. Cooper-Stephenson & I.B. Saunders, *Personal Injury Damages in Canada* (Toronto: Carswell, 1981) at 56.

EXEMPLIFICATION. *n.* The official copy of a document made under a court's or public functionary's seal.

EXEMPLI GRATIA. [L. for example] For instance.

EXEMPT INCOME. Money or property received or acquired by a person in such circumstances that it is, by reason of any provision of Part I, not included in computing his income, but for greater certainty does not include a dividend on a share. *Income Tax Act*, R.S.C. 1952, c. 148 (as am. S.C. 1988, c. 55, s. 188(1)), s. 248(1).

EXEMPTION. *n.* Immunity; being free from duty or tax.

EXEMPTION CLAUSE. A clause in a contract which frees a party from liability.

EXEMPT OFFER. 1. (i) An offer to purchase shares by way of private agreement with fewer than 15 shareholders and not made to shareholders generally, (ii) an offer to purchase shares to be effected through the facilities of a stock exchange or in the over-the-counter market, (iii) an offer to purchase shares in a private company, (iv) an offer exempted by order of the Com-

mission or the Court. *Securities acts.* 2. An offer (a) to fewer than fifteen shareholders to purchase shares by way of separate agreements, (b) to purchase shares through a stock exchange or in the over-the-counter market in such circumstances as may be prescribed, (c) to purchase shares of a corporation that has fewer than fifteen shareholders, two or more joint holders being counted as one shareholder, (d) exempted under section 204, or (e) by a corporation to repurchase its own shares to be held under section 32. *Canada Business Corporations Act*, R.S.C. 1985, c. C-44, s. 194.

EXEQUATOR. *n.* [L.] A permission given by the government of one country to the commercial agent or consul of another country to discharge his or her functions in the first-mentioned country.

EXERCISE. *v.* To use.

EXERCITORIAL POWER. The trust given to the master of a ship.

EXERCITOR NAVIS. [L.] The temporary charterer or owner of a ship.

EX FACTO ILLICITIO NON ORITUR ACTIO. [L.] See EX TURPI CAUSA NON ORITUR ACTIO.

EX FACTO JUS ORITUR. [L.] Law is grounded in fact.

EXFREDIARE. *v.* To breach the peace.

EX GRATIA. [L.] Voluntary. K.D. Cooper-Stephenson & I.B. Saunders, *Personal Injury Damages in Canada* (Toronto: Carswell, 1981) at 501.

EXHAUST DUCT. A duct through which air is conveyed from a room or space to the outdoors. *Building Code Act*, R.R.O. 1980, Reg. 87, s. 1.

EXHAUST EMISSIONS. Air pollutant emitted into the atmosphere from any opening downstream from the exhaust port of a vehicle engine. *Motor Vehicle Safety Regulations*, C.R.C., c. 1038, s. 1100.

EXHIBIT. *v.* When used in respect of film or moving pictures, means to show film for viewing for direct or indirect gain or for viewing by the public. *Theatres Act*, R.S.O. 1980, c. 498, s. 1.

EXHIBIT. *n.* A document or object admitted as evidence in court. F.A. Jaffe, *A Guide to Pathological Evidence*, 2d ed. (Toronto: Carswell, 1983) at 176.

EXHIBITANT. *n.* One who exhibits something.

EXHIBITION. *n.* 1. Showing, projecting or otherwise displaying of film in a theatre to the public. *Film and Video Classification Act*, S.S.

1984-85-86, c. F-13.2, s. 2. 2. A boxing match in which the contestants do not compete for monetary reward other than the receipt of proper and reasonable expenses incurred through their participation in such exhibition and includes a closed circuit televised exhibition. *Boxing Authority Act*, S.N.S. 1981, s. 55, s. 1. See FAIR OR ~; PROFESSIONAL CONTEST OR ~; PUBLIC ~; TRAVELLING ~.

EXHIBITION CORPORATION. A corporation empowered pursuant to provincial law to hold an agricultural exhibition. *Agricultural Exhibition Loans Order*, C.R.C., c. 318, s. 2.

EXHIBITION FACILITIES. A building or a building complex or part of a building complex intended for use for agricultural exhibitions and other purposes that, in the opinion of the Minister, would be of benefit to the citizens of surrounding commmunities. *Agricultural Exhibition Loans Order*, C.R.C., c. 318, s. 2.

EXHIBITOR. *n.* A person who engages in exhibition of films on a continual and successive basis. *Film and Video Classification Act*, S.S. 1984-85-86, c. F-13.2, s. 2. See ITINERANT ~.

EXHUMATION. *n.* Disinterring a body from a grave in a burial ground or cemetery. F.A. Jaffe, *A Guide to Pathological Evidence*, 2d ed. (Toronto: Carswell, 1983) at 23.

EXIGENCE. *n.* Need; want; demand.

EXIGENCY. *n.* Need; want; demand.

EXIGIBLE. *adj.* 1. Subject to execution. 2. Able to be demanded or required.

EXIGI FACIAS. [L.] That you cause to be demanded.

EXILE. *n.* Banishment; the banished person.

EX IMPROVISO. [L.] Spontaneously. S.A. Cohen, *Due Process of Law* (Toronto: Carswell, 1977) at 315.

EX-INMATE. *n.* A person who was an inmate of a penitentiary and who has completed his sentence and has been legally discharged. *Penitentiary Inmates Accident Compensation Order*, C.R.C., c. 326, s. 2.

EXISTING SHIP. A ship that is not a new ship. Canada regulations.

EXISTING USE. The use to which land has already been put.

EXIT. *n.* 1. That part of a means of egress that leads from the floor area it serves, including any doorway heading directly from a floor area, to a public thoroughfare or to an open space. 2. i. Includes aisles, doorways, corridors, hallways, passageways, stairways, ramps, lobbies, foyers,

vestibules, but ii. does not include, A. escalators, elevators, slide escapes, turnstiles, revolving doors, overhead doors, sliding doors, folding doors, and doorways to enclosed courts, B. ladders, hatches or windows, except where approved as an alternate means of egress from boiler, furnace, mechanical service, electrical service, or other service rooms, C. ramps with a gradient in excess of one in eight, and D. doorways and passageways leading the public through boiler rooms, furnace rooms, kitchens or other service rooms. *Hotel Fire Safety Act*, R.R.O. 1980, Reg. 505, s. 2. See ACCESS TO ~; HORIZONTAL ~; MEANS OF ~.

EXIT APERTURE. An opening or window in the protective enclosure of a laser scanner that is designed to allow laser radiation to be transmitted to the outside. *Radiation Emitting Devices Regulations*, C.R.C., c. 1370, s. 1.

EXIT DOORS. The doors by which persons can obtain egress directly and immediately from and beyond an audience room. *Public Buildings Act*, R.S.M. 1970, c. P200, s. 2.

EXIT INTERVIEW. A discussion between employer and employee when the employee is about to leave employment.

EXIT LEVEL. The lowest level in an exclosed exit stairway from which an exterior door provides access to a public thoroughfare or to an open space with access to a public thoroughfare at approximately the same level either directly or through a vestibule or exit corridor. *Building Code Act*, R.R.O. 1980, Reg. 87, s. 1.

EXIT LIGHTS. All lights required by law for the purpose of facilitating safe exit in case of fire or other emergency. *Power Corporation Act*, R.R.O. 1980, Reg. 794, s. 0.

EXIT STOREY. A storey from which an exterior door provides direct access at approximately the same level to a public thoroughfare or to an open space with access to a public thoroughfare. *Building Code Act*, R.R.O. 1980, Reg. 87, s. 1.

EXITUS. *n.* [L. issue or offspring] 1. Annual rents and profits from lands and tenements. 2. A close of pleadings; a joinder of issue.

EXLEGALITICUS. *n.* [L.] One prosecuted as an outlaw.

EX LEX. *n.* An outlaw.

EX MALEFICIO NON ORITUR CONTRACTUS. [L.] A contract cannot arise from an illegal act.

EX MERO MOTU. [L.] Of one's own accord.

EX MULTITUDINE SIGNORUM COLLIGITUR IDENTITAS VERA. [L.] True identity is pieced together from many representations.

EX NECESSITATE LEGIS. [L.] From the necessity of law.

EX NECESSITATE REI. [L.] Out of the necessity of the thing or case.

EX NEW. Without the right to the new shares which will be issued.

EX NIHILO NIHIL FIT. [L.] Nothing comes out of nothing. S.A. DeSmith, *Judicial Review of Administrative Action*, 4th ed. by J.M. Evans (London: Stevens, 1980) at 152.

EX NON SCRIPTO JUS VENIT QUOD USUS COMPROBAVIT. [L.] A body of law which custom has validated comes into existence without anything being written.

EX NUDO PACTO NON ORITUR ACTIO. [L.] An action does not arise from an agreement with no consideration.

EX OFFICIO. [L.] By virtue of one's office.

EXONERATION. *n.* Relief from liability when that liability is thrown on another person.

EXONERETUR. [L.] Let the person be discharged.

EXOR. *abbr.* Executor.

EXORDIUM. *n.* [L.] The beginning part or introduction of a speech.

EXOTIC ANIMAL. An animal of a species or type that is not indigenous to a province and that in its natural habitat is usually found wild in nature.

EXOTIC FISH. Those species of fish which are not indigenous to the Province. *Fish and Wildlife Act*, S.N.B. 1980, c. F-14.1, s. 1.

EXOTIC WILDLIFE. All birds, mammals and other vertebrates that are not indigenous to a province and that in their natural habitat are usually wild by nature, and includes any part of such birds, mammals or other vertebrates.

EX PACTO ILLICITO NON ORITUR ACTIO. [L.] No action can arise out of an illegal contract.

EXPANSIBLE FLUID. (i) Any vapour or gaseous substance, or (ii) any liquid under a pressure and at a temperature that is such that the liquid will change to a gas or vapour when the pressure is reduced to atmospheric pressure.

EXPANSION COILS. See DIRECT ~.

EXPANSION LINE. The addition to any part of a rural gas utility of a pipline to provide gas service to a location that could have been but was not supplied with gas service from that part of the rural gas utility at the time that part was constructed. *Rural Gas Act*, R.S.A. 1980, c. R-19, s. 1.

EX PARTE. [L. on behalf of] Describes an application made by one party to a proceeding when the other party is absent.

EX PARTE MATERNA. [L.] Claiming through the mother's line.

EX PARTE PATERNA. [L.] Claiming through the father's line.

EXPATRIATION. *n.* Renouncing allegiance to one's native country when one becomes the citizen of a foreign country.

EXPECTANCY. See IN ~.

EXPECTANT. *adj.* Relating to; depending on.

EXPECTANT ESTATE. An interest one will possess and enjoy at some future time, i.e. a reversion or remainder.

EXPECTANT HEIR. One who has a hope of succession or reversionary right to property but little or no property currently available.

EXPECTATION OF LIFE. The number of years which someone of a certain age may, given equal chances, expect to live. See LOSS OF ~.

EXPECTED CLAIMS RATIO. The claims ratio that the company expects to experience under policies issued by it with respect to a particular class of insurance during the unexpired terms of the policies. *Insurance acts*.

EXPEDIMENT. *n.* The total amount of a person's goods and chattels.

EXPEDITION. See SCIENTIFIC OR EXPLORATORY ~.

EXPEDIT REIPUBLICAE NE SUA RE QUIS MALE UTATUR. [L.] It is in the public interest that one should not use one's own property badly.

EXPEDIT REIPUBLICAE UT FINIS SIT LITIUM. [L.] It is in the public interest that litigation end.

EXPENDITURE. *n.* 1. (i) Payment authorized by a supply vote, (ii) a reimbursement under the authority of one supply vote, of a payment charged against another supply vote, (iii) a payment authorized by a statutory appropriation, other than a statutory appropriation authorizing a payment to a revolving fund, or (iv) a payment from a revolving fund. 2. Any expense made for political purposes by a political party, an association or a candidate. See ALLOWABLE ~S; BASIC CARE ~S; CAPITAL ~; CURRENT ~; ELIGIBLE EXPLORATION ~S; PETTY CASH ~; TAX ~; WORKING ~.

EXPENSAE LITIS. [L. expenses of the cause] Costs.

EXPENSE. *n.* 1. Money laid out for the purposes of trade, profession or vocation. 2. Includes, in relation to the conducting of a trial with a jury, (i) the costs of summoning a jury panel and any costs incidental to the summoning, (ii) the fees and allowances paid to jurors, (iii) costs arising from the order of a judge to view evidence . . . (iv) costs for food, refreshments, accommodation and other requirements for a jury. *Jury Act*, S.A. 1982, c. J-2.1, s. 1. See ADMINISTRATIVE ~S; CAMPAIGN ~; CHILD CARE ~; COMMON ~S; DRILLING OR EXPLORATION ~; ELECTION ~S; ELIGIBLE COST OR ~; ELIGIBLE EXPLORATION ~; FUNERAL ~S; GENERAL ~S; LABOUR ~; LIVING ~; LIVING ~S; ONTARIO EXPLORATION AND DEVELOPMENT ~S; OPERATING ~; PERSONAL ~S; PREPAID ~; REGULATED ~S; TRAVELLING ~S; WORKING ~S.

EXPENSE ACCOUNT. A list of obligations incurred while working on behalf of one's employer.

EXPENSES LEVY. Defrayal of expenses of administering a product marketing scheme. P.W. Hogg, *Constitutional Law of Canada*, 2d ed. (Toronto: Carswell, 1985) at 614.

EXPERIENCE DEFICIENCY. When applied to a pension plan, means any deficit, determined at the time of a review of the plan, that is attributable to factors other than, (i) the existence of an initial unfunded liability, or (ii) the failure of the employer to make any payment as required by the terms of the plan or by the Act or this Regulation. *Pension Benefits Act*, R.R.O. 1980, Reg. 746, s. 1.

EXPERIENCE RATING. In insurance, a means of determining rates by using the experience of losses by the insured over a period of time.

EXPERIENTIAL INCREMENT. Salary recognition or wage increment offered to employees with certain experiential qualifications. D.J.M. Brown and D.M. Beatty, *Canadian Labour Arbitration*, 2d ed. (Aurora: Canada Law Book, 1977) at 563.

EXPERIMENTAL PROJECT. Work or activity involving the utilization of methods or equipment that are untried or unproven.

EXPERIMENTAL SCHEME. A scheme or operation (i) for the recovery of oil sands or crude bitumen, or (ii) for the processing of crude bitumen, derivatives of crude bitumen or declared oil sands not designed for commercial purposes, utilizing methods that may be untried or unproven in a particular application and includes, but is not limited to, test and pilot schemes. *Oil Sands Conservation Act*, S.A. 1983, c. O-5.5, s. 1.

EXPERIMENTAL TREATMENT. Any treatment that poses a significant risk of harm to the patient, other than one that is: (i) commonly accepted for treatment of the mental disorder involved or supported by widely accepted scientific studies; and (ii) provided by a qualified health professional. *Mental Health Services Act*, S.S. 1984-85-86, c. M-13.1, s. 2.

EXPERIMENTAL WELL. A well drilled or being drilled or operated pursuant to an experimental scheme approved by the Board under this Act, the Oil and Gas Conservation Act, The Oil and Gas Wells Act, The Oil and Gas Resources Conservation Act, The Oil and Gas Conservation Act, chapter 63 of the Statutes of Alberta, 1957 or The Oil and Gas Conservation Act, 1969. *Oil Sands Conservation Act*, S.A. 1983, c. O-5.5, s. 1.

EXPERIMENT INFORMATION. Any information that (i) relates to a participant, (ii) is gathered for the purposes of an experiment, and (iii) is of such a nature that the participant to whom it relates is identifiable therefrom, or a record of that information or any of it, or any return, document or other paper writing containing that information or any of it, or a record or copy of that return, document or writing. *Social Services Administration Act*, S.M. 1974, c. 34, s. 17.

EXPERT. *n.* Includes engineer, valuer, accountant, and any other person whose profession gives authority to a statement made by that person. *Companies acts*.

EXPERT EVIDENCE. The admissible opinion of someone whose competency to form an opinion on some subject before the court was acquired by a special course of study or experience, e.g., in engineering, foreign law or medicine.

EXPIRATION DATE. 1. Any date prescribed by these Regulations as the expiration date and after which a drug is not recommended for use. *Food and Drug Regulations*, C.R.C., c. 870, s. C.01.001. 2. Of a device means the date after which the device is not recommended by the manufacturer for use. *Medical Devices Regulations*, C.R.C., c. 871, s. 2. 3. A date designating the end of the period during which a veterinary biologic, when properly stored and handled, may be expected to be effective. *Animal Disease and Protection Regulations*, C.R.C., c. 296, s. 2. 4. The date (a) after which the manufacturer does not recommend that an infant formula be consumed, and (b) before which an infant formula complies with the requirements of this Division. *Food and Drug Regulations*, C.R.C., c. 870, s. B.25.001.

EXPIRATION OF BID. The later of: (i) the expiration of the period, including any extensions, during which securities may be deposited under a bid; and (ii) the time at which the offeror becomes obligated by the terms of the bid to take up or reject securities deposited under the bid. *Securities acts.*

EXPLANATORY NOTE. Technically not part of a bill and printed on the page across from the relevant clause. A. Fraser, G.A. Birch & W.A. Dawson, eds., *Beauchesne's Rules and Forms of the House of Commons of Canada*, 5th ed. (Toronto: Carswell, 1978) at 220.

EXPLANATORY PLAN. A plan that (a) is not based on a survey but on existing descriptions, plans or records of the land title office; and (b) is certified correct in accordance with the records of the land title office by a British Columbia land surveyor. *Land Title Act*, R.S.B.C. 1979, c. 219, s. 1.

EXPLOITATION. See AGRICULTURAL ~.

EXPLORATION. *n.* Any operations on or over land or water to determine geologic or other conditions underlying the surface of land or water, but does not include any kind of operation exempted from this Part by the regulations. *Mines and Minerals Act*, R.S.A. 1980, c. M-15, s. 150. See GEOPHYSICAL ~; GEOTHERMAL ~; MINERAL ~.

EXPLORATION AND DEVELOPMENT. Prospecting, exploring, surveying, drilling or other activities as may be prescribed. *Mineral Act*, R.S.B.C. 1979, c. 259, s. 1.

EXPLORATION AND DEVELOPMENT EXPENSE TAX CREDIT. The amount, if any, by which (a) the aggregate of all amounts each of which is an amount that the taxpayer (i) would have been eligible to receive in respect of outlays or expenses made or incurred by him before the end of the taxation year under a prescribed program of the Government of Canada or of a province providing incentives for the exploration for and development of petroleum and gas in Canada, and (ii) has waived his entitlement to receive, in accordance with the applicable provisions of that program, on or before the date he is required to file a return of production revenue pursuant to section 11 for the taxation year exceeds (b) the aggregate of all amounts, if any, each of which was an amount deducted under subsection (5) from the tax payable under this Part by the taxpayer for any preceding taxation year. *Petroleum and Gas Revenue Tax Act*, R.S.C. 1985, c. P-12, s. 9(6).

EXPLORATION EXPENSE. See DRILLING AND ~.

EXPLORATION LICENCE. *var.* **EXPLORATION LICENSE.** 1. A licence to explore lands for the purpose of finding petroleum and natural gas there. *Mining Act*, R.S.Q. 1977, c. M-13, s. 1. 2. A license by which the holder thereof is granted the right to search and prospect for minerals on a designated area for a period of one year.

EXPLORATION LICENCE FOR BRINE. The authorization to explore land to find brine there. *Mining Act*, R.S.Q. 1977, c. M-13, s. 1.

EXPLORATION OPERATIONS. Any work or acts done in connection with or incidental to exploration. *Land Surface Conservation and Reclamation Act*, R.S.A. 1980, c. L-3, s. 1.

EXPLORATORY EXPEDITION. See SCIENTIFIC OR ~.

EXPLORATORY PROGRAM. A geological or geophysical study, investigation, reconnaissance or survey undertaken to establish the geological or physical settings of coal in a given area, or to ascertain the nature, quality or extent of coal occurrences in a given area. *Coal Conservation Act*, R.S.A. 1980, c. C-14, s. 1.

EXPLORATORY WELL. 1. A well other than a development well or delineation well. 2. A well drilled on a geological feature on which a significant discovery has not been made. 3. A well that is bored, drilled or deepened for the purpose of discovering a pool of oil or gas. *Petroleum Resources Act*, R.R.O. 1980, Reg. 752, s. 1.

EXPLORATORY WORK. Work in connection with or incidental to searching, drilling or testing for oil or gas and includes geological, geochemical or geophysical examinations.

EXPLORE. See TO PROSPECT AND TO ~.

EXPLOSION-HAZARD LOCATION. Any location where gasoline or an associated product that can produce a dangerous atmosphere is stored, or where leakage or spillage of the gasoline or associated products could occur and includes service stations, bulk plants, tank truck or tank car filling facilities, storage areas for packaged Class I or Class II gasoline or associated products, or empty containers and pump houses. *Gasoline Handling Act*, R.R.O. 1980, Reg. 439, s. 1.

EXPLOSION INSURANCE. 1. Insurance against loss of or damage to property of any kind caused by explosion, bombardment, invasion, insurrection, riot, civil war or commotion or military or usurped power. *Insurance Act*, R.S.A. 1980, c. I-5, s. 1. 2. Insurance against loss of or damage to the property insured caused by explosion of steam boilers and pipes and engines and machinery connected therewith. *Insurance Act*, R.S.B.C. 1979, c. 200, s. 1. 3. Insurance against the loss of, or damage to, property caused by explosion and includes insurance coming within the class of civil commotion insurance. *Classes of Insurance Regulations*, C.R.C., c. 977, s. 11. See LIMITED OR INHERENT ~.

EXPLOSION-PROOF. *adj.* Enclosed in a case which is capable of withstanding without damage an explosion which may occur within it of a specified gas or vapour and which is also capable of preventing the ignition of a specified gas or vapour surrounding the enclosure from sparks, flashes or explosion of the specified gas or vapour within the enclosure.

EXPLOSIVE. *n.* 1. Any substance that is made, manufactured or used to produce an explosion or detonation or a pyrotechnic effect, and includes gunpowder, propellant powders, blasting agents, dynamite, detonating cord, lead azide, detonators, ammunition of all descriptions, rockets, fireworks, fireworks compositions, safety flares and other signals. *Explosives Act*, R.S.C. 1985, c. E-17, s. 2. 2. Gunpowder, blasting powder, nitroglycerine, gun-cotton, dynamite, blasting gelatine, gelignite, fulminates of mercury or of other metals and every other substance made, manufactured or used with a view to producing a violent effect by explosion. *Explosives Use Act*, R.S.N.W.T. 1974, c. E-6, s. 2. 3. A substance that is made, manufactured or used to produce an explosion or detonation and includes gunpowder, propellant powder, dynamite, detonating cord, blasting agent, slurry, water gel and detonator. *Occupational Health and Safety Act*, R.R.O. 1980, Reg. 694, s. 1. 4. Includes blasting agents, blasting supplies, and accessories such as blasting caps, boosters, plastic cap holders, electric starters, squibs, shunt connectors, safety fuse assemblies, igniter cord connectors, hot wire lighters, and primacord connectors and closing tubes. *Retail Sales Tax Act*, R.R.O. 1980, Reg. 903, s. 1. 5. A substance or device that, when detonated or fired, creates a violent shock wave in water. *Northwest Territories Fishery Regulations*, C.R.C., c. 847, s. 2. See AUTHORIZED ~.

EXPLOSIVE ACTUATED TOOL. A tool that is designed to be held in the hand and that is actuated by an explosive charge. *Canada Hand Tools Regulations*, C.R.C., c. 1002, s. 2.

EXPLOSIVE SUBSTANCE. Includes (a) anything intended to be used to make an explosive substance, (b) anything, or any part thereof, used or intended to be used, or adapted to cause, or to aid in causing an explosion in or with an explosive substance, (c) an incendiary grenade, fire bomb, molotov cocktail or other similar incendiary substance or device and a delaying mechanism or other thing intended for use in connection with such a substance or device. *Criminal Code*, R.S.C. 1985, c. C-46, s. 2 as am. by *Criminal Law Amendment Act*, R.S.C. 1985 (1st Supp.), c. 27, s. 2.

EXPORT. *v.* 1. Ship from Canada to any other country or from any province to any other province. 2. (a) Subject to paragraph (b), where oil is transported by pipeline, to deliver it at its point of delivery outside Canada, (b) where oil is transported by pipeline from the offshore area as defined in section 20, to deliver it at its point of delivery outside that area and Canada, and (c) where oil is transported by any other means, to send it (i) from Canada other than to export it within the meaning of subsection 16(1), or (ii) to a place outside Canada from the offshore area as defined in section 20. *Energy Administration Act*, R.S.C. 1985, c. E-6, s. 4. 3. In respect of transportation fuel, means (a) the delivery by an exporter of that fuel to a person other than an exporter in order that the person may take it from Canada by means of an aircraft or vessel for immediate use by that aircraft or vessel, or (b) the taking by an exporter of that fuel from Canada by means of an aircraft or vessel for use by that aircraft or vessel. *Energy Administration Act*, R.S.C. 1985, c. E-6, s. 16. 4. With reference to (a) power, to send from Canada by a line of wire or other conductor power produced in Canada, (b) oil, (i) to export within the meaning of any provision of the Energy Administration Act that defines export for the purposes of any charge imposed under that Act in relation to fuel for use by an aircraft or a vessel, or (ii) to send or take by any means (A) from Canada, or (B) to a place outside Canada from any area of land not within a province that belongs to Her Majesty in right of Canada or in respect of which Her Majesty in right of Canada has the right to dispose of or exploit the natural resources and that is situated in those submarine areas adjacent to the coast of Canada and extending throughout the natural prolongation of the land territory of Canada to the outer edge of the continental margin or to a distance of two hundred nautical miles from the baselines from which the breadth of the territorial sea of Canada is measured, whichever is greater, or (c) gas, to effect any one of the operations referred to in subparagraph (b)(ii). *National Energy Board Act*, R.S.C. 1985, c. N-7, s. 2. 5. In respect of grain, means shipment by vessel within the meaning of the Canada Shipping Act to any destination outside Canada and shipment by any other mode of transport to the United States for use of the grain in that country and not for shipment out of that country. *Western Grain Transportation Act*, R.S.C. 1985, c. W-8, s. 2. 6. Export from Canada. *Customs Act*, R.S.C. 1985 (2d Supp.), c. 1, s. 2.

EXPORT. *n.* See COUNTRY OF ~.

EXPORT CONTROL LIST. A list of goods established under section 3. *Export and Import Permits Act*, R.S.C. 1985, c. E-19, s. 2.

EXPORT CREDITS AGENCY. Any corporation, commission, board, agency of a government or body incorporated or established in a country other than Canada and having purposes similar to those of the Corporation. *Export Development Act*, R.S.C. 1985, c. E-20, s. 23.

EXPORT DEVELOPMENT CORPORATION. A federal corporation which offers bank guarantee and insurance services to Canadian exporters and encourages export trade by arranging credit for foreign buyers.

EXPORT MARK. A trade mark used exclusively on goods which will be exported. H.G. Fox, *The Canadian Law of Trade Marks and Unfair Competition*, 3d ed. (Toronto: Carswell, 1972) at 64.

EXPORT MARKET. Any country to which goods of any kind are ordinarily exported from Canada. *Industrial Research and Development Incentives Regulations*, C.R.C., c. 965, s. 4.

EXPORT PERMIT. 1. A permit to export issued by a permit officer under this Act. *Cultural Property Export and Import Act*, R.S.C. 1985, c. C-51, s. 2. 2. Includes any authorization in writing to remove game from a province issued by an authority thereto competent within that province. *Game Export Act*, R.S.C. 1985, c. G-1, s. 2.

EXPORT POWER GRID. A power grid in Canada from which electric energy may be exported. *National Energy Board Part VI Regulations*, C.R.C., c. 1056, s. 2.

EXPORT STANDARD SAMPLE. In respect of a grade of grain, a sample of grain of that grade designated by the Commission. *Canada Grain Act*, R.S.C. 1985, c. G-10, s. 2.

EXPORT TAX. A tax on goods to be exported. P.W. Hogg, *Constitutional Law of Canada*, 2d ed. (Toronto: Carswell, 1985) at 607.

EXPORT TRANSACTION. A transaction involving (a) the export of goods out of Canada, (b) the manufacture, treatment or servicing of goods for, or the sale or leasing of goods to, a foreign customer, (c) the sale or licensing of any right in a patent, trade-mark or copyright to a foreign customer, (d) the rendering to a foreign customer of any managerial, construction, tech-nological, marketing or other services, or (e) the purchase in Canada by a person carrying on business or other activities in Canada of goods that that person will use outside Canada or will lease to another person or a foreign government for use outside Canada. *Export Development Act*, R.S.C. 1985, c. E-20, s. 23.

EXPOSE. *v.* Includes (a) a wilful omission to take charge of a child by a person who is under a legal duty to do so, and (b) dealing with a child in a manner that is likely to leave that child exposed to risk without protection. *Criminal Code*, R.S.C. 1985, c. C-46, s. 214.

EXPOSED. *adj.* 1. As applied to wiring methods means not concealed. *Power Corporation Act*, R.R.O. 1980, Reg. 794, s. 0. 2. As applied to live parts means that a live part can be inadvertently touched or approached more closely than is safe by any person and the term is applied to parts not suitably guarded, isolated or insulated. *Power Corporation Act*, R.R.O. 1980, Reg. 794, s. 0.

EXPOSED POSITION. A position that is (a) exposed to weather and sea, or (b) within a structure, so exposed, other than an enclosed superstructure. *Load Line Regulations (Inland)*, C.R.C., c. 1440, s. 1.

EXPOSING BUILDING FACING. That part of the exterior wall of a building which faces one direction and is located between ground level and the ceiling of its top storey, or where a building is divided into fire compartments, the exterior wall of a fire compartment which faces one direction. *Building Code Act*, R.R.O. 1980, Reg. 87, s. 1.

EXPOSITIO. *n.* [L.] A statement which explains.

EX POST FACTO. [L. by something done after] Describes a statute which, after the fact, either makes an act punishable which was not punishable when it was done, or which imposes punishment for an act which is different from what would have been inflicted when the act was done.

EXPOSURE CRITERIA. The concentration of any potentially harmful substance in the air above which a worker may or should not be exposed. D. Robertson, *Ontario Health and Safety Guide* (Toronto: Richard De Boo Ltd., 1988) at 5-162.

EXPOSURE RECORD. In Ontario, the control program specified by a designated substance regulation requires that a record be kept for each worker affected. D. Robertson, *Ontario Health and Safety Guide* (Toronto: Richard De Boo Ltd., 1988) at 5-162A.

EX PRAECEDENTIBUS ET CONSEQUEN-TIBUS EST OPTIMA INTERPRETATIO. [L.] The best interpretation comes from what precedes and follows.

EXPRESS. *adj.* Of some act showing intention, means done to communicate the intention directly, as opposed to by implication.

EXPRESS AGENCY. Agency deliberately created and limited by the agreement or contract terms. G.H.L. Fridman, *The Law of Agency*, 5th ed. (London: Butterworths, 1983) at 53.

EXPRESSA NON PROSUNT QUAE NON EXPRESSA PRODERUNT. [L.] If a benefit is produced without using certain words, then nothing is gained by using those words.

EXPRESS CONDITION. A term specified in the agreement.

EXPRESS FREIGHT. Freight carried faster than ordinary freight. *Public Service Vehicles Act*, R.S.A. 1970, c. 300, s. 2.

EXPRESSIO EORUM QUAE TACITE INSUNT NIHIL OPERATUR. [L.] The expression of things which are tacitly implied accomplishes nothing.

EXPRESSIO UNIUS EST EXCLUSIO ALTE-RIUS. [L.] To express one thing is to exclude another.

EXPRESS TERM. A term particularly mentioned, agreed on by the parties, and its character, content and form expressed in any exchange between them when the contract was made. G.H.L. Fridman, *The Law of Contract in Canada*, 2d ed. (Toronto: Carswell, 1986) at 427.

EXPRESS TOLL. Any toll, rate or charge to be charged by any company, or any person or corporation other than the company, to any persons, for hire or otherwise, for or in connection with the collecting, receiving, caring for or handling of any goods for the purpose of sending, carrying or transporting them by express, or for or in connection with the sending, carrying, transporting or delivery by express of any goods, or for any service incidental thereto, or for or in connection with any or either of those objects, where the whole or any portion of the carriage or transportation of such goods is by rail on the railway of the company. *Railway Act*, R.S.C. 1985, c. R-3, s. 2.

EXPRESS TRUST. A trust which comes into existence because the settlor has expressed the intention to accomplish that effect. D.M.W. Waters, *The Law of Trusts in Canada*, 2d ed. (Toronto: Carswell, 1984) at 299.

EXPRESSUM FACIT CESSARE TACITUM. [L.] When certain things are mentioned expressly, then what is not mentioned is excluded.

EXPRESSWAY. *n.* A divided arterial highway that is accessible only from intersecting arterial streets at intersections at grade that have been approved by the Minister, and, where required by the volume of traffic, at grade separated interchanges that have been approved by the Minister. *Public Transportation and Highway Improvement Act*, R.S.O. 1980, c. 421, s. 99.

EXPROPRIATE. *v.* 1. For an expropriating authority to take land without the consent of the owner in the exercise of its statutory powers. 2. To take land without the consent of the owner and, subject to the Water Act and the Clean Environment Act, includes diverting or authorizing the diversion of a watercourse where such diversion affects land of an owner other than the person diverting or seeking the authorization to divert the watercourse but does not include the cancellation or suspension of any lease, licence or permit under the Crown Lands Act or regulations thereto, or the withdrawal or removal, in accordance with that Act and regulations thereto, of any land from a licence made thereunder. *Expropriation Act*, R.S.N.B. 1973, c. E-14, s. 1.

EXPROPRIATED. *adj.* 1. Taken by the Crown under Part I. *Expropriation Act*, R.S.C. 1985, c. E-21, s. 2. 2. Said of minority shareholders when their right to cause a corporation to buy back their shares arises. A. Bissett-Johnson & W.M. Holland, eds, *Matrimonial Property Law in Canada* (Toronto: Carswell, 1980) at V-19.

EXPROPRIATED INTEREST. Any right, estate or interest that has been lost, in whole or in part, by the registration of a notice of confirmation under Part I. *Expropriation Act*, R.S.C. 1985, c. E-21, s. 2.

EXPROPRIATING AUTHORITY. The Crown or an association or person empowered to acquire land by expropriation.

EXPROPRIATION. *n.* 1. The acquisition of title to land without the consent of the owner. 2. Taking without the consent of the owner.

EXPROPRIATION AUTHORITY. The Crown, a Minister of the Crown or any person or body that under or by virtue of an enactment has an expropriation power. *Expropriation Procedure Act*, S.N.S. 1969, c. 9, s. 1.

EXPROPRIATION BOARD. The board, person or other body having the power to order termination of a right of entry order as to the whole or part of any land affected by the order. *Land Surface Conservation and Reclamation Act*, R.S.A. 1980, c. L-3, s. 34.

EXPROPRIATION POWER. The power or authority granted by an enactment to enter upon, take and expropriate land without the consent of the owner of the land. *Expropriation Procedure Act*, S.N.S. 1969, c. 9, s. 1.

EX PROPRIO MOTU. [L.] Of one's own accord.

EX PROVISIONE MARITI. [L.] From the husband's provision.

EXPUNGE. *v.* To strike out all or part of a document or pleading. G.D. Watson & C. Perkins, eds., *Holmested & Watson: Ontario Civil Procedure* (Toronto: Carswell, 1984) at 25-7.

EXPUNGEMENT. *n.* The jurisdiction to amend or strike out any entry in the register because at the application date the entry as it appears on the register does not correctly define or express the existing rights of the person who appears to be the registered owner of the mark. H.G. Fox, *The Canadian Law of Trade Marks and Unfair Competition*, 3d ed. (Toronto: Carswell, 1972) at 301.

EXPURGATION. *n.* Cleansing; purging.

EXQ. *abbr.* Ex quay.

EX QUAY. *var.* **EX-QUAY.** Describes the contract in which a seller must make goods available to the buyer at the quay at a certain destination. I.F.G. Baxter, *The Law of Banking*, 3d ed. (Toronto: Carswell, 1981) at 136.

EX REL. *abbr.* Ex relatione.

EX RELATIONE. [L. from information or a narrative] On the information a citizen called the relator.

EX RIGHTS. Without any right to the new issue of shares which will be made to shareholders.

EXS. *abbr.* Ex ship.

EXSANGUINATION. *n.* Death due to blood leaving the circulatory system. F.A. Jaffe, *A Guide to Pathological Evidence*, 2d ed. (Toronto: Carswell, 1983) at 176.

EX SHIP. Describes the contract in which a seller must make goods available to the buyer on the ship at a certain destination. I.F.G. Baxter, *The Law of Banking*, 3d ed. (Toronto: Carswell, 1981) at 136.

EX-STORE. *adj.* Describes the contract in which the buyer must collect the goods from the store or works. G.H.L. Fridman, *Sale of Goods in Canada*, 3d ed. (Toronto: Carswell, 1986) at 485.

EXTANT. *adj.* Existing.

EXTENDED. See FULLY ~.

EXTENDED CARE. 1. Skilled nursing and personal care given by or under the supervision of a registered nurse or registered nursing assistant under the direction of a physician to a resident for a minimum of one and one-half hours per day. *Homes for Special Care Act*, R.R.O. 1980, Reg. 501, s. 1. 2. On-going treatment of a patient with little chance of recovery or a long-term illness.

EXTENDED CARE FACILITY. Includes a nursing home, home for the aged or other extended care facility. *Pharmacy Act*, S.N.S. 1981, c. 39, s. 1.

EXTENDED CARE UNIT. A part of a nursing home in which residents in need of extended care are lodged. *Nursing Homes Act*, R.R.O. 1980, Reg. 690, s. 1.

EXTENDED COVERAGE. Insurance against (a) loss arising from the destruction in whole or in part of stands of fruit trees or perennial plants other than trees; or (b) loss arising when the seeding or planting of a crop is prevented by excess ground moisture, weather or other agricultural hazards. *Crop Insurance Act*, R.S.C. 1985, c. C-48, s. 9.

EXTENDED FAMILY. 1. When used in reference to a child, means the persons to whom the child is related by blood, marriage or adoption. *Child and Family Services Act*, S.O. 1984, c. 55, s. 37. 2. Includes in addition to the persons in the definition of "family" in section 1, any unmarried adult cohabiting with any of those persons of the opposite sex who is an unmarried adult in a relationship of some permanence. *The Child and Family Services Act*, S.M. 1985-86, c. 8, s. 55.

EXTENDED HEALTH CARE SERVICES. The following services, as more particularly defined in the regulations, provided for residents of a province, namely, (a) nursing home intermediate care service, (b) adult residential care service, (c) home care service, and (d) ambulatory health care service. *Canada Health Act*, R.S.C. 1985, c. C-6, s. 2.

EXTENDED MEAT PRODUCT. A meat product to which a meat product extender has been added. Canada regulations.

EXTENDED POULTRY PRODUCT. A poultry product to which a poultry product extender has been added. *Food and Drug Regulations*, C.R.C., c. 870, s. B.01.001.

EXTENDER. See MEAT PRODUCT ~; POULTRY PRODUCT ~.

EXTENDI FACIAS. [L. you cause to be extended] A writ of extent.

EXTENSION. *n.* 1. Includes any reasonable

extension of the service and facilities of every public utility. 2. An indulgence by giving time to pay a debt or perform an obligation.

EXTENSION INSURANCE. Automobile insurance that is in excess of the limits, or reduces the deductible amount or otherwise supplements one or more of the coverages, in a universal compulsory automobile insurance plan.

EXTENSION MEASURE. The distance between the extreme angles of a single mesh measured inside and between the knots after the twine has been saturated in water and extended until taut but without straining or breaking the twine or slipping a knot. *Fishery regulations.*

EXTENSION TRESTLE LADDER. A combination of a trestle ladder and a vertically-adjustable single ladder with suitable means for securely locking the ladders together. *Occupational Health and Safety Act*, R.R.O. 1980, Reg. 691, s. 1.

EXTENSIVE INTERPRETATION. Interpretation which is liberal.

EXTENT. *n.* The special writ to recover debts owed to the Crown which at one time differed from an ordinary writ of execution because a debtor's land and goods could be taken all at once in order to force payment of the debt. See RE-~; WRIT OF ~.

EXTERIOR. *adj.* In direct contact with the weather. *Hull Construction Regulations*, C.R.C., c. 1431, s. 100.

EXTERIOR CLADDING. Those components of a building which are exposed to the outdoor environment and are intended to provide protection against wind, water or vapour. *Building Code Act*, R.R.O. 1980, Reg. 87, s. 1.

EXTERMINATION. *n.* The destruction, prevention or control of a pest by means of a pesticide. *Agricultural Chemicals Act*, R.S.A. 1980, c. A-6, s. 1. See LAND ~; STRUCTURAL ~; WATER ~.

EXTERNAL AFFAIRS CANADA. The federal ministry which executes the government's foreign policy by supervising relations between Canada and other countries, represents Canada at international conferences and in foreign countries, develops and promotes international trade and assists Canadians travelling abroad.

EXTERNAL APPLICATION. Application to the outer surface of the body. *Health Disciplines Act*, R.R.O. 1980, Reg. 451, s. 1.

EXTERNAL BALLISTICS. Studying the behaviour of projectiles in flight. F.A. Jaffe, *A*

Guide to Pathological Evidence, 2d ed. (Toronto: Carswell, 1983) at 169.

EXTERNALLY FINANCED TRANSACTION. Occurs when money to acquire a business interest comes from outside the business. A. Bissett-Johnson & W.M. Holland, eds., *Matrimonial Property Law in Canada* (Toronto: Carswell, 1980) at V-12.

EXTERNAL SUBMARINE CABLE. A telecommunication service by submarine cable between any place in Canada and any place outside Canada or between places outside Canada through Canada, but does not include any service by a submarine cable wholly under fresh water. *Telegraph Act*, R.S.C. 1985, c. T-5, s. 40.

EXTERNAL SURFACE. With respect to a microwave oven, means the outside surface of the cabinet or other enclosure of the oven and includes the plane of any exit or entry port for conveyorized ovens. *Radiation Emitting Devices Regulations*, C.R.C., c. 1370, s. 1.

EXTERNAL TELECOMMUNICATION SERVICES. The telecommunication services between Canada and any place outside Canada. *Teleglobe Canada Act*, R.S.C. 1985, c. T-4, s. 2.

EXTINCTIVE PRESCRIPTION. Limitation of an action because time has passed.

EXTINGUISHED. *adj.* Of a right or obligation, no longer existing.

EXTORTIO EST CRIMEN QUANDO QUIS COLORE OFFICII EXTORQUET QUOD NON EST DEBITUM, VEL SUPRA DEBITUM, VEL ANTE TEMPUS QUOD EST DEBITUM. [L.] Extortion is a crime committed when someone, through colour of office, demands something which is not due, something more than what is due or something before the time that it is due.

EXTORTION. *n.* Every one commits extortion who, without reasonable justification or excuse and with intent to obtain anything, by threats, accusation, menaces or violence induces or attempts to induce any person, whether or not he is the person threatened, accused or menaced or to whom violence is shown, to do anything or cause anything to be done. *Criminal Code*, R.S.C. 1985, c. C-46, s. 346(1).

EXTRA BILLING. The billing for an insured health service rendered to an insured person by a medical practitioner or a dentist in an amount in addition to any amount paid or to be paid for that service by the health care insurance plan of a province. *Canada Health Act*, R.S.C. 1985, c. C-6, s. 2.

EXTRACRANIAL. *adj.* Not in the skull. F.A.

Jaffe, *A Guide to Pathological Evidence*, 2d ed. (Toronto: Carswell, 1983) at 117.

EXTRACT. See HOUSEHOLD ~S.

EXTRACTION. See METHANE ~.

EXTRACTION PLANT. Any plant or equipment, other than a well, used for the extraction of oil or other substances produced in association with oil from surface or subsurface deposits of oil sand, bitumen, bituminous sand, oil shale or other deposits from which oil may be extracted. *Canada Oil and Gas Land Regulations*, C.R.C., c. 1518, s. 2.

EXTRACTOR. *n.* A device which removes a fired cartridge from a firing chamber. F.A. Jaffe, *A Guide to Pathological Evidence*, 2d ed. (Toronto: Carswell, 1983) at 176.

EXTRADITION. *n.* One state's surrender of someone accused or convicted of a crime to the officials of another state where the crime was committed.

EXTRADITION ARRANGEMENT. A treaty, convention or arrangement that extends to Canada made by Her Majesty with a foreign state for the surrender of fugitive criminals. *Extradition Act*, R.S.C. 1985, c. E-23, s. 2.

EXTRADITION CRIME. (a) Any crime that, if committed in Canada, or within Canadian jurisdiction, would be one of the crimes described in Schedule I, and (b) in the application of this Act to the case of an extradition arrangement, any crime described in the arrangement, whether or not it is included in that Schedule. *Extradition Act*, R.S.C. 1985, c. E-23, s. 2.

EXTRADURAL HEMORRHAGE. A venous or arterial hemorrhage located between the dura mater and the skull. F.A. Jaffe, *A Guide to Pathological Evidence*, 2d ed. (Toronto: Carswell, 1983) at 118.

EXTRAJUDICIAL. *var.* **EXTRA-JUDICIAL.** *adj.* Out of the usual conduct of legal procedure.

EXTRAJUDICIAL COSTS. Fees or costs, whether provided for in the tariff or not, which an advocate may charge for professional services or in addition to judicial costs, and which arise from the practice of the profession of advocate. *Barreau du Québec Act*, R.S.Q. 1977, c. B-1, s. 1.

EXTRA-JUDICIAL SERVICE. A judge of the Supreme or District Court acts as an arbitrator, conciliator or referee or sits on a commission of inquiry authorized by an act of the legislature or an agreement made under an act. G.D. Watson & C. Perkins, eds., *Holmested & Watson:*

Ontario Civil Procedure (Toronto: Carswell, 1984) at CJA-119.

EXTRA-JUDICIAL STATEMENT. In any proceedings of a court martial a hearsay statement that has been made by a declarant, other than in the course of those proceedings or in the course of taking evidence taken on commission for that court martial, and includes (a) words, oral or written, used by him, (b) the adoption, in some way, in whole or in part, of meaningful words uttered by another person as an accurate expression of the declarant's own observations or experience, and (c) the expression, in an intelligible manner, of the declarant's observation or experience. *Military Rules of Evidence*, C.R.C., c. 1049, s. 2.

EXTRA LEGEM POSITUS EST CIVILITER MORTUUS. [L.] One placed outside the law is dead civilly.

EXTRA-LOW VOLTAGE. Any voltage up to and including 30 volts. *Power Corporation Act*, R.R.O. 1980, Reg. 794, s. 0.

EXTRA-LOW-VOLTAGE POWER CIRCUIT. A circuit, such as valve operator and similar circuits, which is neither a remote control circuit nor a signal circuit, but which operates at not more than 30 volts and which is supplied from a transformer or other device restricted in its rated output to 1,000 volt-amperes and approved for the purpose, but in which the current is not limited in accordance with the requirements for a Class 2 circuit. *Power Corporation Act*, R.R.O. 1980, Reg. 794, s. 0.

EXTRANEOUS DEFENCE. One which raises a new issue which oversteps the Crown's case. P.K. McWilliams, *Canadian Criminal Evidence*, 3d ed. (Aurora: Canada Law Book, 1988) at 25-8.

EXTRAORDINARY REMEDY. A writ of mandamus, quo warranto or habeas corpus.

EXTRAORDINARY RESOLUTION. 1. A resolution passed by a majority of not less than three-fourths of the members of the company for the time being entitled to vote present in person or by proxy (in cases where by the act, charter, or instrument of incorporation, or the regulations of the company, proxies are allowed) at any general meeting of which notice specifying the intention to propose such resolution has been duly given. 2. A resolution passed by 2/3 of the members entitled to vote who are present in person at a general meeting of which notice specifying the intention to propose the resolution as an extraordinary resolution has been given.

EXTRAORDINARY TRAFFIC. Includes carriage of goods or persons over a highway whether in vehicles drawn by animal power or propelled by other means, that in conjunction with the nature of existing condition of the highway is so extraordinary or improper in the quality or quantity of the goods or the number of persons carried, or in the mode or time of use of the highway, or in the speed at which the vehicles are driven or operated, as, in the opinion of minister, substantially alters or increases the burden imposed on the highway through its proper use by ordinary traffic, and causes damage and expense to the highway beyond what is reasonable or ordinary. *Highway Act*, R.S.B.C. 1979, c. 167, s. 26.

EXTRA-PROVINCIAL ACT. An Act of the Parliament of Canada, or an Act of a Legislature of another province, with objects similar to those of this Act. *Natural Products Marketing acts.*

EXTRA-PROVINCIAL AGENCY. A board, commission or other body constituted under an extra-provincial Act with objects similar to this Act. *The Natural Products Marketing Act*, R.S.S. 1978, c. N-3, s. 2.

EXTRA-PROVINCIAL COMMISSION. A board, commission or other agency established by another jurisdiction that performs a similar function in that jurisdiction that the Alberta Securities Commission performs in Alberta. *Securities Act*, S.A. 1981, c. S-6.1, s. 1.

EXTRA-PROVINCIAL COMPANY. *var.* **EXTRAPROVINCIAL COMPANY.** A company incorporated outside the province to which reference is made.

EXTRA-PROVINCIAL CORPORATION. 1. A body corporate incorporated otherwise than by or under the act of a legislature. 2. A company or certain class of companies incorporated in another jurisdiction which must become licensed or registered if they carry on business in a province. H. Sutherland, D.B. Horsley & J.M. Edmiston, eds., *Fraser's Handbook on Canadian Company Law*, 7th ed. (Toronto: Carswell, 1985) at 573.

EXTRA-PROVINCIAL LIMITED PARTNER-SHIP. A limited partnership organized under the laws of a jurisdiction outside a province.

EXTRA-PROVINCIAL ORDER. *var.* **EXTRA-PROVINCIAL ORDER.** An order, or that part of an order, of an extraprovincial tribunal that grants to a person custody of or access to a child.

EXTRAPROVINCIAL SOCIETY. A society or association, incorporated or otherwise, formed outside the Province, and includes a branch of that society or association, but does not include a society or association, incorporated or otherwise, formed to acquire profit or gain or that

has a capital dividend into shares. *Society Act*, R.S.B.C. 1979, c. 390, s. 1.

EXTRA-PROVINCIAL TRANSPORT. The transport of passengers or goods by means of an extra-provincial undertaking. *Motor Vehicle Transport Act*, R.S.C. 1985, c. M-12, s. 2.

EXTRA-PROVINCIAL TRIBUNAL. *var.* **EXTRAPROVINCIAL TRIBUNAL.** A court or tribunal outside the province that has jurisdiction to grant to a person custody of or access to a child.

EXTRA PROVINCIAL UNDERTAKING. *var.* **EXTRA-PROVINCIAL UNDERTAKING.** A work or an undertaking for the transport of passengers or goods by motor vehicle, connecting a province with any of the other provinces or extending beyond the limits of a province. *Motor Vehicles Transport acts.*

EXTRA-REGIONAL TELEVISION STATION. In relation to a licensee, means any television broadcasting station licensed by the Commission whose Grade A or Grade B official contour does not enclose any part of the licensed area but whose Grade B official contour's closest point is located 20 miles or less from the local head end of the licensee's undertaking. *Cable Television Regulations*, C.R.C., c. 374, s. 2.

EXTRA-TERRITORIAL. *adj.* Outside the territory of the jurisdiction which enacted the law in question.

EXTRA-TERRITORIAL COMPANY. A company (i) incorporated otherwise than by or under an Ordinance, or (ii) incorporated by or under an Ordinance and not subject to the legislative authority of the Territories, and includes a company incorporated by or under an Act of the Parliament of Canada. *Companies Act*, R.S.N.W.T. 1974, c. C-7, s. 2.

EXTRA-TERRITORIAL TRIBUNAL. A court or tribunal outside the Territories with authority to grant custody of a child. *Extra-Territorial Custody Orders Enforcement Act*, S.N.W.T. 1981 (2d Sess.), c. 2, s. 2.

EXTRA TERRITORIUM JUS DICENTI IMPUNE NON PARETUR. [L.] The sentence of a judge acting outside proper jurisdiction can be safely disobeyed.

EXTRA TRAIN. A train not authorized by a time table schedule. *Regulations No. O-8, Uniform Code of Operating Rules*, C.R.C., c. 1175, Part III, s. 2.

EXTRA VIAM. [L.] Out of the way.

EXTRA VIRES. [L.] Beyond powers. See ULTRA VIRES.

EXTRINSIC EVIDENCE. Evidence which comes from outside a contract but is used to interpret the contract.

EX TURPI CAUSA NON ORITUR ACTIO. [L.] A claim cannot arise from a base cause like the breach of a statute or a contract which is contrary to public policy. G.H.L. Fridman, *The Law of Contract in Canada*, 2d ed. (Toronto: Carswell, 1986) at 396.

EXUERE PATRIAM. [L.] To cast off one's citizenship; to expatriate oneself.

EX VI TERMINI. [L.] From the force of a term.

EX WAREHOUSE. A seller must pay all charges through discharge from a warehouse.

EX WHARF. A seller must pay all charges through delivery from a wharf.

EX WORKS. A seller has goods available at its factory or works so a buyer's responsibility begins there. I.F.G. Baxter, *The Law of Banking*, 3d ed. (Toronto: Carswell, 1981) at 136.

EYE-WITNESS. *n.* One who testifies about facts she or he has seen.

F

F. *abbr.* 1. Farad. 2. Femto. 3. Freeboard.

F.A.A. *abbr.* Free from all average. Used in marine insurance to mean an underwriter is not liable unless there is total loss of the insured property.

FABRIC. *n.* Any material woven, knitted, crocheted, knotted, braided, felted, bonded, laminated or otherwise produced from, or in combination with, a textile fibre. *Textile Labelling Act,* R.S.C. 1985, c. T-10, s. 2. See CANADIAN ~; IMPORTED ~; NARROW ~.

FABRICS. *n.* Fabrics, whether woven, nonwoven, knitted or tufted. *Textile and Clothing Board Act,* R.S.C. 1985, c. T-9, s. 2.

FABRIQUE. *n.* A corporation constituted under this Act and consisting of the pastor of a parish or the ministering cleric of a chapelry and the churchwardens of such parish or chapelry. *An Act Respecting Fabriques,* R.S.Q. 1977, c. F-1, s. 1.

FACE. See WORKING ~.

FACE VALUE. The nominal value printed or written on the face of a bond, debenture, note, share certificate or other document indicating its par value.

FACIAS. [L. that you cause] See FIERI FACIAS.

FACILITY. *n.* 1. Includes an installation, plant, factory or place where goods are or may be handled. *Transport of Dangerous Goods Act,* S.B.C. 1985, c. 17, s. 1. 2. Any place where a person can receive treatment for communicable diseases. *Public Health Act,* S.A. 1984, c. P-27.1, s. 1. 3. The buildings, structures, machinery, equipment and apparatus that constitute the necessary components of a new or established manufacturing facility. 4. An institution, psychiatric centre, psychiatric ward, mental health clinic or any other building or portion thereof set aside for the care, treatment or training of mentally disordered persons. 5. Any place designated by the regulations in which assistance

and services or either of them are provided for persons with a developmental handicap. *Developmental Services Act,* R.S.O. 1980, c. 118, s. 1. 6. A place, other than a pharmacy, from which Schedule A drugs are distributed. *Pharmacists Act,* R.S.B.C. 1979, c. 326, s. 1. 7. A day care centre or a day care home. 8. A building or part of a building, other than a private dwelling or a correctional institution, used for the care, custody or treatment of children. *Family and Child Services Act,* S.P.E.I. 1981, c. 12, s. 1. 9. A place that is operated by or receives its current operating funds or part of them directly or indirectly from the Government of Alberta and that is (i) a place of care for persons who are aged or infirm or who require special care, (ii) an institution or shelter as defined in Part 2 of the Child Welfare Act, or (iii) a hostel or other establishment operated to provide accommodation and maintenance for not less than 4 unemployed or indigent persons, other than one that is defined as a hospital under the Health Facilities Review Committee Act or a correctional institution under the Corrections Act. *Social Care Facilities Review Committee Act,* R.S.A. 1980, c. S-15, s. 1. 10. A commercial ice-making or ice-storing facility and includes that part of a vessel that can be suitably fitted with equipment for refrigerating sea water or preserving ice so that unfrozen fish on the vessel can be chilled to the temperature of melting ice (32° Fahrenheit). *Fish-Chilling Assistance Regulations,* C.R.C., c. 861, s. 2. See APPROVED ~; BURIED FACILITIES; CARE ~; CHILD CARE ~; CHILD CARING ~; COMMERCIAL ~; COMMON ~; COMMUNITY CARE ~; CORRECTIONAL ~; DAY CARE ~; ELECTRICAL ~: EXHIBITION FACILITIES; EXTENDED CARE ~; HAZARDOUS WASTE MANAGEMENT ~; HEALTH ~; HOSPITAL FACILITIES; HYGIENE FACILITIES; IN-PATIENT ~; LOCK-UP ~; NUCLEAR ~; OPTOMETRIC ~; OUTDOOR ADVERTISING FACILITIES; PORT ~; PRE-SCHOOL ~; PRODUCTION FACILITIES;

PSYCHIATRIC ~; PUMP-OUT ~; RADIA-TION ~; RECREATION ~; RESEARCH FACILITIES; RESIDENTIAL CARE ~; RETAIL DISTRIBUTION FACILITIES; SAN-ITARY ~; SERVICE FACILITIES; SERVICES AND FACILITIES; SEWAGE ~; SEWAGE TREATMENT ~; SOCIAL CARE ~; SUPPLY ~; SURFACE FACILITIES; TIMBER PRO-CESSING ~; TRANSPORTATION ~; UNLOADING ~; WASTE WATER TREAT-MENT ~; WOOD PROCESSING ~.

FACILITY ASSOCIATION. The unincorporated non-profit association of insurers known as a facility association, established for the purpose of allocating automobile insurance risks to ensure the availability of insurance to owners of automobiles.

FACING DIRECTION. The direction toward which an occupant is faced or to be faced in an installed product. *Children's Car Seats and Harnesses Regulations*, C.R.C., c. 921, s. 2.

FACIO UT DES. [L.] I do that you may give.

FACIO UT FACIAS. [L.] I do that you may do.

FACSIMILE. *n.* An accurate reproduction of a book, instrument, document or record and includes a print from microfilm and a printed copy generated by or produced from a computer record. *Land Registration Reform Act*, S.O. 1984, c. 32.

FACT. *n.* An event, circumstance, thing done. See ACCESSORY AFTER THE ~; ACCESSORY BEFORE THE ~; CAUSATION IN ~; CONCLUSION OF ~; MATERIAL ~; MISTAKE OF ~; MIXED QUESTION OF LAW AND ~; PRESUMPTIONS OF ~.

FACTA PROBANDA. [L.] Facts which must be proved; facts in issue.

FACTA PROBANTIA. [L.] Facts given in evidence to prove facta probanda; evidentiary facts.

FACTO. [L.] In fact.

FACTOR. *n.* 1. One who loans money on security of accounts receivable or merchandise and inventory or both, but who is in no way connected with selling them. I.F.G. Baxter, *The Law of Banking*, 3d ed. (Toronto: Carswell, 1981) at 190. 2. An agent who disposes of or sells products in the agent's control or possession. G.H.L. Fridman, *Sale of Goods in Canada*, 3d ed. (Toronto: Carswell, 1986) at 493. See CONNECTING ~; PROVINCIAL CONTENT ~; RHESUS ~; SIZE ~; TIME ~.

FACTORAGE. *n.* The commission which a factor receives.

FACTORIES AND INDUSTRIAL BUILD-INGS. Those buildings used for processing, assembling, mixing, storing, packaging, finishing or decorating, repairing or similar operations. *Fire Prevention Act*, S.N.S. 1976, c. 9, s. 2.

FACTORING CORPORATION. A corporation (a) that is incorporated or continued under an Act of Parliament, and (b) the activities of which are confined to acting as a factor in relation to accounts receivable including the activities referred to in subsection 173(3), the lending of money and the raising of money for the purpose of financing such activities. *Bank Act*, R.S.C. 1985, c. B-1, s. 193.

FACTORING OF RECEIVABLES. Purchasing discounting short-term business accounts receivable. I.F.G. Baxter, *The Law of Banking*, 3d ed. (Toronto: Carswell, 1981) at 191.

FACTOR OF SAFETY. The number of times the breaking strength of a shaft rope exceeds the weight it supports at a specified location on the rope. *Occupational Health and Safety Act*, R.R.O. 1980, Reg. 694, s. 1.

FACTORY. *n.* 1. A building, premises, workshop, structure, room or place where (a) any manufacturing process or assembling in connection with the manufacturing of products is carried on, (b) thermal, hydraulic, electrical or other form of energy or power is used to move or work any machinery or device in the preparing, inspecting, manufacturing or finishing, or in a process incidental to the preparing, inspecting, manufacturing or finishing, of a product or is used to aid the manufacturing carried on there, or (c) manual labour is performed by way of trade or for purposes of gain in or incidental to the making of a product, or the altering, repairing, ornamenting, finishing, storing, cleaning, washing or adapting for sale of a product, and includes a facility used for the maintenance of aircraft, locomotives and motor vehicles. 2. Any building, structure, premises or land in or on which the manufacture or any part of the process of manufacture of an explosive is carried on, the site on which the building, structure or premises are situated, and all other buildings, structures or premises within such a site. *Explosives Act*, R.S.C. 1985, c. E-17, s. 2. See CHEESE ~; CONDENSED MILK ~; ICE CREAM ~.

FACTORY BRANCH. An office maintained by a manufacturer or distributor for the purpose of selling or offering for sale, vehicles to a distributor, wholesaler or new motor vehicle dealer, or for directing or supervising in whole or in part factory or distributor representatives. The term includes any sales promotion organization maintained by a manufacturer or distributor which is engaged in promoting the sale of a

F

particular make of new motor vehicle in this Province to a new motor vehicle dealer. *Motor Vehicle Franchise Act*, S.N.B. 1987, c. 70, s. 1.

FACTORY BUILT BUILDINGS. Buildings which are manufactured either wholly or in part, at an off-site location. *Buildings and Mobile Homes Act*, S.M. 1977, c. 29, s. 1.

FACTORY-BUILT CHIMNEY. A chimney consisting entirely of factory-made parts, each designed to be assembled with the other without requiring fabrication on site. *Building Code Act*, R.R.O. 1980, Reg. 87, s. 1.

FACTORY-BUILT HOME. A manufactured home or a mobile home. *An Act to Amend the Mobile Homes Act*, S.N.B. 1987, c. 37, s. 2.

FACTORY BUILT HOUSING. Housing that is partly or totally built in a factory and then transported in sections or as a complete unit to a site where it is erected or stationed and provided with the necessary services to make it a habitable unit that, when occupied, is void of transport features such as wheels, tires, axles, brakes or lamps. *Ontario Water Resources Act*, R.R.O. 1980, Reg. 736, s. 1.

FACTORY REPRESENTATIVE. An agent or employee of a manufacturer, distributor, or factory branch retained or employed for the purpose of making or promoting the sale of new motor vehicles or for supervising or contracting with new motor vehicle dealers or proposed motor vehicle dealers. *Motor Vehicle Franchise Act*, S.N.B. 1987, c. 70, s. 1.

FACTORY SHIP. A ship in or on which whales are treated whether wholly or in part. *Whaling Convention Act*, R.S.C. 1970, c. W-8, s. 2.

FACTUAL CAUSATION. A causal link between any facts which constitute the breach of contract or tortious conduct and the loss or injury for which the plaintiff claims compensation. K.D. Cooper-Stephenson & I.B. Saunders, *Personal Injury Damages in Canada* (Toronto: Carswell, 1981) at 637.

FACTUAL INFORMATION. Information on a subject as to name, age, place of residence, previous places of residence, marital status, spouse's name and age, number of dependents, particulars of education or professional qualifications, places of employment, previous places of employment, estimated income, paying habits, outstanding credit obligations, cost of living obligations, matters of public record and any information voluntarily supplied by the subject of a personal investigation. *Personal Investigations Act*, S.M. 1971, s. 23, s. 1.

FACTUM. *n.* [L.] 1. A deed; an act. 2. A statement of facts and law which each party files in an application, appeal or motion.

FACTUM A JUDICE QUOD AD EJUS OFFICIUM NON SPECTAT NON RATUM EST. [L.] Anything which a judge does outside a judge's function is not valid just because that person is a judge.

FACULTAS PROBATIONUM NON EST ANGUSTANDA. [L.] The opportunity to prove should not be limited.

FACULTY. *n.* 1. An ability, a capacity. 2. In a university, an administrative unit headed by a dean. 3. A faculty of a university and includes professors, associate professors, assistant professors, lecturers, instructors and all other persons engaged in the work of teaching or giving instruction at a university.

FACULTY MEMBER. A person employed by a university on a full time basis who serves as an instructor, lecturer, assistant professor, associate professor, professor, or in an equivalent designated position.

FAILURE. See CROP ~.

FAILURE OF ISSUE. Death without issue.

FAINT ACTION. An action which was feigned.

FAINT PLEADER. A collusive, false or fraudulent method of pleading.

FAIR COMMENT. A defence to an action for libel if the statement is made in good faith and honestly, not maliciously and is a fair and sincere expression of opinion on true facts known to the people to whom the comment was addressed. R.E. Brown, *The Law of Defamation in Canada* (Toronto: Carswell, 1987) at 13.

FAIR EMPLOYMENT PRACTICE. Practice of offering equal employment opportunities to persons regardless of race, national origin, colour, religion, age, sex, marital status, physical handicap or conviction for which a pardon has been granted.

FAIR HEARING. The opportunity to fully answer and defend, adequately to state one's case. P.K. McWilliams, *Canadian Criminal Evidence*, 3d ed. (Aurora: Canada Law Book, 1988) at 4-17.

FAIRLY. See ACT ~.

FAIR MARKET VALUE. 1. The price which would be expected to be received by a willing seller from a willing buyer on the open market. 2. Of a security, means (i) in the case of a security listed or traded on a stock exchange in Canada, the quoted price at that time determined, (ii) in the case of a security that is a share of the capital stock of a mutual fund corporation, a unit of a mutual fund trust or an interest in a related segregated fund trust, the amount that would be received in respect of that share, unit or interest if it were redeemed or disposed of at that time.

FAIRNESS. *n.* The duty of an administrator to act fairly regarding procedure. Any administrator must, minimally, let the party affected by her or his decision understand the case against that party and provide the party with a fair chance to answer it or to be heard.

FAIR OPPORTUNITY. The chance for accused persons to present their cases and to know the relevant evidence.

FAIR OR EXHIBITION. An event where agricultural or fishing products are presented or where activities relating to agriculture or fishing take place. *Criminal Code*, R.S.C. 1985, c. C-46, s. 206(3.1) as added by R.S.C. 1985 (1st Supp.), c. 52, s. 2.

FAIR START POLE. In a harness horse race, means a yellow pole or marker that is erected off the racing strip adjacent to the hub rail protruding not less than 2 feet above the height of the hub rail, located 10 feet nearer the starting point than the 1/16 mile pole or such other distance as may be approved. *Race Track Supervision Regulations*, C.R.C., c. 441, s. 2.

FAIR VALUE. 1. Value which is equitable and just in the circumstances; fair market value, intrinsic value or value to owner. A. Bissett-Johnson & W.M. Holland, eds., *Matrimonial Property Law in Canada* (Toronto: Carswell, 1980) at V-2. 2. Includes (a) the price for which the goods were purchased including the value in terms of Canadian money of services rendered and things exchanged and other considerations accepted by the vendor or person from whom the property passed, as the price or on account of the price of the goods purchased, (b) the cost of or charges for customs, excise and transportation, whether or not such are shown separately in the vendor's books or on any invoice, (c) the cost of installation where the contract under which the goods were acquired provides for the acquisition of goods and their installation for one consideration, and (d) the cost, including materials, labour, and manufacturing overhead of goods produced by the vendor or person for their own consumption or use. *Sales Tax acts*.

FAIR WAGES. Such wages as are generally accepted as current for competent workers in the district in which the work is being performed for the character or class of work in which those workers are respectively engaged, but shall in all cases be such wages as are fair and reasonable.

FAIRWAY BUOY. A buoy marking the fairway. *Private Buoy Regulations*, C.R.C., c. 1460, Schedule.

FAIT. *n.* [Fr.] Writing; a deed.

FAIT ENROLLE. [Fr.] A deed enrolled.

FALLEN ANIMAL. A horse, goat, sheep, swine or head of cattle that has been disabled by disease, emaciation or other condition that is likely to cause death. *Dead Animal Disposal Act*, R.S.O. 1980, c. 112, s. 1.

FALLING AIRCRAFT INSURANCE. Insurance against loss of or damage to the property insured caused by aircraft or objects falling from aircraft.

FALLOW. See SUMMER ~.

FALLOW-LAND. *n.* Land ploughed but not planted and, after a succession of crops, left uncultivated for a while.

FALL SESSION. A session of the Legislature that commences after the month of September in any year. *The Tabling of Documents Act*, R.S.S. 1978, c. T-1, s. 2.

FALSA DEMONSTRATIONE LEGATUM NON PERIMITUR. [L.] A legacy should not fail because of an incorrect description.

FALSA DEMONSTRATIO NON NOCET. [L.] A false description does make void.

FALSA ORTHOGRAPHIA NON VITIAT CONCESSIONEM; FALSA GRAMMATICA NON VITIAT CONCESSIONEM. [L.] Bad spelling or bad grammar do not invalidate a grant.

FALSE ARREST. Unlawful arrest; arrest without lawful authority.

FALSE CONFLICT. In a conflict of laws case, it may not matter which system of law one applies because the relevant laws of all countries, including the forum, lead to identical conclusions or are the same in substance. J.G. McLeod, *The Conflict of Laws* (Calgary: Carswell, 1983) at 31.

FALSE DOCUMENT. A document (a) the whole or a material part of which purports to be made by or on behalf of a person (i) who did not make it or authorize it to be made, or (ii) who did not in fact exist, (b) that is made by or on behalf of the person who purports to make it but is false in some material particular, (c) that is made in the name of an existing person, by him or under his authority, with a fraudulent intention that it should pass as being made by a person, real or fictitious, other than the person who makes it or under whose authority it is made. *Criminal Code*, R.S.C. 1985, c. C-46, s. 321.

FALSEHOOD. See INJURIOUS ~.

FALSE IMPRISONMENT. Intentional restraint of a person's liberty without lawful authority by preventing the person from leaving a place or actively confining them. John G. Fleming, *The Law of Torts*, 6th ed. (Sydney: The Law Book Company Limited, 1983) at 26.

FALSE NEWS. See SPREADING ~.

FALSE OR MISLEADING REPRESENTATION. 1. Includes (a) any representation in which expressions, words, figures, depictions or symbols are used, arranged or shown in a manner that may reasonably be regarded as qualifying the declared net quantity of a pre-packaged product or as likely to deceive a consumer with respect to the net quantity of a prepackaged product; (b) any expression, word, figure, depiction or symbol that implies or may reasonably be regarded as implying that a prepackaged product contains any matter not contained in it or does not contain any matter in fact contained in it; and (c) any description or illustration of the type, quality, performance, function, origin or method of manufacture or production of a prepackaged product that may reasonably be regarded as likely to deceive a consumer with respect to the matter so described or illustrated. *Consumer Packaging and Labelling Act*, R.S.C. 1985, c. C-38, s. 7(2). 2. Includes (a) any representation in which expressions, words, figures, depictions or symbols are arranged or shown in a manner that may reasonably be regarded as likely to deceive any person with respect to textile fibre content; (b) any expression, word, figure, depiction or symbol that implies or may reasonably be regarded as implying that a textile fibre product contains any fibre, fur or hair not contained in the product; and (c) any description of the type, quality, performance, origin or method of manufacture or production of a textile fibre product that may reasonably be regarded as likely to deceive any person with respect to the matter so described. *Textile Labelling Act*, R.S.C. 1985, c. T-10, s. 5(3).

FALSE INNUENDO. A meaning which is attributed to the natural and ordinary meaning of a word but which arises only by implication or inference. R.E. Brown, *The Law of Defamation in Canada* (Toronto: Carswell, 1987) at 158.

FALSE PRETENCE. A representation of a matter of fact either present or past, made by words or otherwise, that is known by the person who makes it to be false and that is made with a fraudulent intent to induce the person to whom

it is made to act upon it. *Criminal Code*, R.S.C. 1985, c. C-46, s. 361.

FALSE REPRESENTATION. See DECEIT; FALSE PRETENCE; MISREPRESENTATION; REPRESENTATION.

FALSEWORK. *n.* The structural supports and bracing for forms. *Occupational Health and Safety Act*, R.R.O. 1980, Reg. 691, s. 1.

FALSI CRIMEN. [L.] Fraudulently concealing or suborning in order to hide the truth, committed in words when a witness swears falsely; in writing when someone antedates a contract; or in doing something when a person sells using false weights and measures.

FALSUS IN UNO, FALSUS IN OMNIBUS. [L.] False in one, false in everything.

[ ] FAM. *abbr.* Law Reports, Family Division, 1972-.

FAM. CT. *abbr.* 1. Family Court. 2. Provincial Court (Family Division).

FAMILIA. *n.* [L. family] The servants of a certain master; land adequate to maintain a family.

FAMILY. *n.* 1. The husband, wife, child, step-child, parent, step-parent, brother, sister, half-brother, half-sister, step-brother, step-sister, in each case whether legitimate or illegitimate, of a person. 2. Includes a man and woman living together as husband and wife, whether or not married in a permanent relationship, or the survivor of either, and includes the children of both or either, natural or adopted or to whom either stands in loco parentis, and any person lawfully related to any of the aforementioned persons. 3. The parents and any children wholly or substantially maintained by those parents. *Family Allowance Act*, R.S.C. 1985, c. F-1, s. 2. 4. (i) In the case of an unmarried adult, that person and his unmarried children who are not adults, and (ii) in the case of a married adult, that person and his spouse and the unmarried children of either or both of them who are not adults but does not include an individual who is included in any other family or who is not a member of the congregation in which the family is included. *Income Tax Act*, R.S.C. 1952, c. 148 (as am. S.C. 1977-78, c. 1, s. 71), s. 143(5)(c). 5. A child's parent, step-parent, siblings, grandparent, aunt, uncle, cousin, guardian, person in loco parentis to a child and a spouse of any of those persons. *The Child and Family Services Act*, S.M. 1985-86, c. 8, s. 1. 6. Used in a broad sense and means persons allied or related by blood, or by legal or customary marriage or adoption. *An Act respecting hunting and fishing rights in the James Bay and New Québec territories*, S.Q. 1978, c. 92, s. 19. See

DEER ~; EXTENDED ~; FOSTER ~; HEAD OF A ~; HEAD OF ~; IMMEDIATE ~; MEMBER OF A ~; MEMBER OF ~.

FAMILY ALLOWANCE. An amount payable in respect of a child pursuant to subsection 3(1) or (2), whichever is applicable. *Family Allowance Act*, R.S.C. 1985, c. F-1, s. 2.

FAMILY ALLOWANCE RECIPIENT. A person who received or is in receipt of an allowance or a family allowance pursuant to the Family Allowances Act, chapter F-1 of the Revised Statutes of Canada, 1970, as it read immediately before being repealed or the Family Allowances Act, for that period prior to a child reaching seven years of age, and such other persons as may be prescribed by regulation. *Canada Pension Plan*, R.S.C. 1985, c. C-8, s. 42.

FAMILY ASSET. A matrimonial home and property owned by one spouse or both spouses and ordinarily used or enjoyed by both spouses or one or more of their children while the spouses are residing together for shelter or transportation or for household, educational, recreational, social or aesthetic purposes, and includes, (i) money in an account with a chartered bank, savings office, credit union or trust company where the account is ordinarily used for shelter or transportation or for household, educational, recreational, social or aesthetic purposes, (ii) where property owned by a corporation, partnership or trustee would, if it were owned by a spouse, be a family asset, shares in the corporation or an interest in the partnership or trust owned by the spouse having a market value equal to the value of the benefit the spouse has in respect of the property, (iii) property over which a spouse has, either alone or in conjunction with another person, a power of appointment exercisable in favour of himself or herself, if the property would be a family asset if it were owned by the spouse, and (iv) property disposed of by a spouse but over which the spouse has, either alone or in conjunction with another person, a power to revoke the disposition or a power to consume, invoke or dispose of the property, if the property would be a family asset if it were owned by the spouse, but does not include property that the spouses have agreed by a domestic contract is not to be included in the family assets.

FAMILY BUSINESS CORPORATION. A corporation in which, at the date of registration of any conveyance with respect to which the expression is being applied, all of the issued shares except for directors' qualifying shares are owned by a person or persons, each of whom is not a non-resident person and each of whom is a member of the family of each transferor of the land being conveyed, and where any of

such persons is a corporation the provisions of clauses 3(1)(c) and (d) are applicable to such corporation. *Land Transfer Tax Act*, R.R.O. 1980, Reg. 563, s. 1.

FAMILY CEMETERY. A cemetery used for the burial of the remains of persons related by blood, marriage, or adoption to the person responsible for the cemetery. *An Act to Amend the Cemetery Companies Act*, S.N.B. 1984, c. 18, s. 1.

FAMILY CORPORATION. A corporation in which all the voting shares are owned by (a) one natural person, or (b) one natural person plus one or any number of his father, mother, brother, sister, child, spouse or his spouse's mother, father or child. *Residential Tenancy Act*, S.B.C. 1984, c. 15, s. 1.

FAMILY FARM. 1. A farming enterprise managed by a farmer in respect of which the necessary labour is performed primarily by him and his family, if any. *The Family Farm Credit Act*, R.S.S. 1978, c. F-5, s. 2. 2. A farm operated by a junior farmer and one or more of a spouse of the junior farmer and any persons related to the junior farmer through blood relationship or adoption. *Equality Rights Statute Law Amendment Act*, S.O. 1986, c. 64, s. 20. 3. Land that (a) is classified as a farm under the Assessment Act, and (b) is operated by (i) an individual, or (ii) a corporation whose sole activity is the operation of the land as a farm and at least 75% of whose issued capital is beneficially owned by an individual actively engaged in operating the land as a farm. *Motor Fuel Tax Act*, S.B.C. 1985, c. 76, s. 1. See INTEREST IN A ~ PARTNERSHIP.

FAMILY FARM CORPORATION. A corporation that is throughout the taxation year a corporation, (i) all shares of the capital stock of which that confer on the holder thereof the right to vote were owned by one individual ordinarily resident in Canada or by that individual and a member or members of his family ordinarily resident in Canada or by another family farm corporation, (ii) 75 per cent of the assets of which were farming assets, and (iii) which carried on the business of farming in Ontario through the employment of a shareholder or a member of his family actually engaged in the operation of the farm. *Corporations Tax Amendment Act, 1981*, S.O. 1981, c. 37, s. 1.

FAMILY FARMING CORPORATION. A corporation the principal object and business of which is farming or fishing and with respect to which at least ninety-five per cent of the shares are owned wholly by persons related to one another by blood, marriage or adoption and with respect to which at least fifty-one per cent of the shares are owned by a shareholder or shareholders principally occupied in the farming or fishing operations of the corporation. *The Consumer Products Warranties Act*, R.S.S. 1978, c. 30, s. 3.

FAMILY FARM TRUCK. A farm vehicle, as defined in the Commercial Transport Regulations, that is used in the operation of a family farm. *Motor Fuel Tax Act*, S.B.C. 1985, c. 76, s. 1.

FAMILY FISHING CORPORATION. A corporation that is throughout the taxation year a corporation, (i) all shares of the capital stock of which that confer on the holder thereof the right to vote were owned by one individual ordinarily resident in Canada or by that individual and a member or members of his family ordinarily resident in Canada or by another family fishing corporation, (ii) 75 per cent of the assets of which were fishing assets, and (iii) which carried on the business of fishing in Ontario through the employment of a shareholder or a member of his family actually engaged in the operation of the business. *Corporations Tax Amendment Act, 1981*, S.O. 1981, c. 37, s. 1.

FAMILY HOME. The home which is the home of the owner held by him in fee simple or to which he holds the equity of redemption and is used by him for his family residence together with the land immediately appurtenant thereto not exceeding one and one-half acres and any immediately appurtenant outbuildings. *Expropriation Act*, S.N.S. 1973, c. 7, s. 3.

FAMILY HOUSING UNIT. A unit providing therein living, sleeping, eating, food preparation and sanitary facilities for one family, with or without other essential facilities shared with other family housing units.

FAMILY INCOME. See MONTHLY ~; RESIDUAL ~.

FAMILY IN NEED. A family whose monetary requirements for regularly recurring needs determined under the regulations exceed its income as determined under the regulations. *Family Benefits Act*, S.N.B. 1977, c. 8, s. 4.

FAMILY INSURANCE. 1. Insurance whereby the lives of the insured and one or more persons related to that person by blood, marriage or adoption are insured under a single contract between an insurer and the insured. 2. Insurance whereby the lives or well-being, or the lives and well-being, of the insured and one or more persons related to that person by blood, marriage or adoption are insured under a single contract between the insurer and the insured.

FAMILY LAW COMMISSIONER. One whom a judge directs to investigate and report on an issue relating to access, custody or maintenance.

FAMILY MATTER. A cause of action in respect of (a) the custody of, maintenance for, or access to a child by a parent or guardian; (b) the maintenance of a person by a spouse; or (c) the division or redistribution of real or personal property between members of a family, that is, under any Act, instituted or capable of being instituted in a court. *Evidence Act*, R.S.B.C. 1979, c. 116, s. 78.

FAMILY NAME. 1. A surname that does not contain more than one word which may occur alone as a surname. 2. A family name which is a single unhyphenated word.

FAMILY OF LOW INCOME. A family that receives a total family income that, in the opinion of the housing authority, is insufficient to permit it to rent housing accommodation adequate for its needs at the current rental market in the area in which the family lives.

FAMILY ORDER. A custody and access order; a money order for support; a property order. C.R.B. Dunlop, *Creditor-Debtor Law in Canada*, Second Cumulative Supplement (Toronto: Carswell, 1986) at 208.

FAMILY PROPERTY. The assets which, immediately before death of a deceased, were owned, either jointly or severally, by the deceased and the spouse of the deceased and which were acquired by them while married and co-habiting but excluding (a) the homestead (as defined in The Dower Act) of the deceased; (b) articles of personal apparel; (c) any gift, inheritance or trust benefit conferred upon the deceased, or the spouse of the deceased, with the express or implied intention of benefiting the deceased or the spouse of the deceased, as the case may be, exclusively; (d) any income that was derived from any asset described in clause (c), where the asset is conferred with the express or implied intention that the income should benefit the recipient exclusively; (e) any amount received as a damage award or settlement in tort in favour of the deceased or the spouse of the deceased, except to the extent that the award or settlement is compensation for loss to both; (f) the proceeds of any insurance claim of the deceased or the spouse of the deceased for damages, except to the extent that the proceeds are compensation for loss to both; (g) the cash surrender value of any insurance policy, the premiums of which were paid by some person other than the deceased or the spouse of the deceased as a gift in favour of the deceased or the spouse of the deceased, as the case may be, with the express or implied intention of benefiting the deceased or the spouse of the deceased, as the case may be, exclusively; (h) any asset that prior to the death of the deceased had been shared by the deceased and the spouse of the deceased in equal, or approximately equal, shares. *Statute Amendments (Taxation) Act*, S.M. 1977, c. 58, s. 18. See NET ~.

FAMILY PROVISION. A support provision, a custody provision or an access right. *Family Orders and Agreements Enforcement Assistance Act*, R.S.C. 1985 (2d Supp.), c. 4, s. 2.

FAMILY STATUS. The status of being in a parent and child relationship. *Human Rights Code, 1981*, S.O. 1981, c. 53, s. 9.

FAMILY UNIT. 1. The husband and wife. Saskatchewan statutes. 2. (i) An individual and his spouse, or (ii) any individuals occupying the same principal residence, whether or not they are related to each other. *Ontario Pensioners Property Tax Assistance Act*, R.S.O. 1980, c. 352, s. 1. 3. Includes a husband, wife, and any relative of the husband or wife residing in one dwelling. *Juries Act*, S.N.S. 1969, c. 12, s. 4. See COST OF CONSTRUCTION OF A ~.

FAM. L. REV. *abbr.* Family Law Review, 1978-.

FAN. *n.* Any mechanical device used to circulate air through mine workings. See AUXILIARY ~; BOOSTER ~.

FANCY BREAD. All crimp, French, rye, 100 per cent whole wheat, Vienna, twist or cottage bread or any other style of bread not made by the ordinary process and generally known to the trade and to the public as fancy bread. *Bread Act*, R.S.A. 1970, c. 34, s. 2.

FAN OPERATOR. A person who holds a certificate as a stationary engineer or a permit as a fan operator that is issued by the Board and who is designated by a mine manager to operate and control a fan. *Coal Mines (CBDC) Safety Regulations*, C.R.C., c. 1011, s. 2.

FARAD. *n.* The capacitance of a capacitor between the equipotential surfaces of which there appears a difference of potential of one volt when the capacitor is charged by a quantity of electricity equal to one coulomb. *Weights and Measures Act*, S.C. 1970-71-72, c. 36, schedule 1.

FARE. *n.* Money paid for conveyance by any means.

FARM. *n.* 1. Land in Canada used for the purpose of farming, which term includes livestock raising, dairying, bee-keeping, fruit growing, the growing of trees and all tillage of the soil. 2. An area of land that is suitable for purposes of agricultural production, including a greenhouse, fur or tree farming operation. 3. An immoveable (1) that is exploited for purposes of agriculture or horticulture, in a hot house or in the open, aviculture, bee-keeping or the raising of livestock, or as an orchard, sugar bush or farm woodlot, if that exploitation is real and continuous, and (2) that is not used mainly for residential purposes or for purposes of pleasure, recreation or sport, or intended to be so used. *An Act respecting municipal taxation and providing amendments to certain legislation*, S.Q. 1979, c. 72, s. 1. 4. Premises the whole or part of which are used for agricultural purposes and, without limiting the generality of the foregoing, includes premises used for, (i) the production of plants for the purpose of the sale of such plants, or any part thereof, and (ii) the production, including breeding, rearing or fattening of animals for the purpose of the sale of such animals, or any part thereof, or for the purpose of racing or exhibiting such animals. *Workmen's Compensation Act*, R.R.O. 1980, Reg. 951, s. 1. See BIG GAME ~; DAIRY ~; ECONOMIC ~; FAMILY ~; FUR ~; GAME BIRD ~; LIVESTOCK ~; PRAIRIE ~ REHABILITATION ADMINISTRATION; TOBACCO ~; WILD ANIMAL ~; WILDLIFE ~.

FARM AND RESIDENTIAL PROPERTY. (i) Land, including buildings, used solely for the production of primary agricultural and horticultural products, including flowers, shrubs, trees, honey and furs and including fallow land and pasture land, or that part thereof that is used solely for those purposes, (ii) land, including buildings, used solely for residential occupation, or that part thereof that is used solely for that purpose, but not including hotels, motels, tourist camps and other similar types of transient accommodation, (iii) undeveloped, unimproved, vacant or abandoned land that is not under a planning scheme or a zoning by-law; (iv) undeveloped, unimproved, vacant or abandoned land that is under a planning scheme or a zoning by-law but that, under that planning scheme or zoning by-law, is usable only for residential or agricultural purposes or both, (v) buildings that are classified as personal property and are used solely for residential occupation, or that part thereof that is used solely for that purpose, but not including hotels, motels, tourist camps and other similar types of transient accommodation. *An Act to Amend the Education Administration Act and the Public Schools Act*, S.M. 1980-81, c. 34, s. 171(1).

FARM APPLICANT. A person who, having established a residence upon farm land as owner, tenant or lessee or as purchaser under an agreement for sale for the purpose of conducting farming operations thereon, has applied to a company for telephone service thereon in accordance with this Act and the regulations, whether or not that residence is his chief place of residence. *The Rural Telephone Act*, R.S.S. 1978, c. R-27, s. 2.

FARM ASSESSMENT. See EQUALIZED RESIDENTIAL AND ~.

FARM ASSOCIATION. Includes an association having as its principal objects or any of them the purchasing, leasing or otherwise acquiring, developing, maintaining and operating land as a farming enterprise on behalf of its members or rendering to the members as producers services ancillary to such principal objects or any of them. *The Co-operative Production Associations Act*, R.S.S. 1978, c. C-37, s. 55. See COOPERATIVE ~.

FARM BUILDINGS. 1. Buildings situated on a parcel of land improved and used exclusively for the purpose of growing grain or forage crops, raising or keeping farm stock, growing horticultural crops including edible mushrooms, and the owner, tenant, lessee or occupant of the land derives his income from the sale or disposal of the grain or forage, farm stock, horticultural crops or edible mushrooms raised, kept or grown on the land, and include farm residences on the land. *Revenue Act*, S.M. 1980, c. 69, s. 66. 2. The improvements, other than a farm residence, used for farming operations and situated on farm land outside a city, town, new town, village or summer village. *Municipal Taxation Act*, R.S.A. 1980, c. M-31, s. 1.

FARM BULK TANK. A stationary storage tank used only for the holding and cooling of milk on the premises of a producer and includes fixtures thereto and the equipment required for the use of the tank. *Milk Act*, R.R.O. 1980, Reg. 629, s. 1.

FARM CREDIT CORPORATION CANADA. The federal body which helps farmers and people who want to become farmers to buy, develop and maintain viable farm businesses.

FARM CORPORATION. A corporation (i) which is primarily engaged in the business of agriculture, and (ii) of which not less than 75% of all issued and voting shares are beneficially owned by bona fide farmers who are resident persons. *Prince Edward Island Lands Protection Act*, S.P.E.I. 1982, s. 16, s. 1.

FARM ELECTRIC SYSTEM. All machinery, apparatus and appliances for the generation or distribution of electricity on a farm whether or not affixed to real property.

FARM EQUIPMENT. (a) Machinery, (b) mechanical milk coolers, and (c) equipment and tools normally used in the operation of a farm that are not affixed to the land and includes trucks and mobile homes. *Farm Credit Regulations*, C.R.C., c. 644, s. 1. See UNUSED FARM MACHINERY AND EQUIPMENT; USED FARM MACHINERY AND EQUIPMENT.

FARM EQUIPMENT MECHANIC. A person who, (i) inspects, disassembles, adjusts, repairs, overhauls, assembles or reassembles and tests farm equipment, (ii) inspects, tests, adjusts, and replaces components of self-contained coolers used on the farm exclusively for farm produce, and (iii) installs, inspects, maintains and removes automotive-type air-conditioning and heating systems for operator cabs on farm equipment. *Apprenticeship and Tradesmen's Qualification Act*, R.R.O. 1980, Reg. 33, s. 1.

FARMER. *n.* 1. (a) An individual whose principal occupation is farming, (b) a farming corporation as defined by regulation, (c) an individual who is the owner of farm land that is being farmed by a farming corporation where that individual is a shareholder of the corporation and is principally occupied in the farming operations of that corporation, (d) a cooperative farm association as defined by regulation, and (e) an individual who is the owner of farm land that is being farmed by a cooperative farm association where that individual is a member of the association and is principally occupied in the farming operations of that association. *Farm Credit Act*, R.S.C. 1985, c. F-2, s. 2. 2. A person who is in possession of a farm and whose principal occupation consists of farming that farm. 3. A producer of primary agricultural products for sale. See ASPIRING ~; BONA FIDE ~; DAIRY ~; FULL-TIME ~; FUR ~; INSOLVENT ~; NECESSITOUS ~.

FARMERS ASSOCIATION. See PROVINCIAL ~.

FARM IMPLEMENT. Includes any implement, equipment, engine, motor, machine, combine, tractor or attachment used or intended for use in farming operations. See UNUSED ~; USED ~.

FARM IMPROVEMENT LOAN. A loan made by a lender to a farmer for the purpose of financing (a) the purchase of, major repair to or major overhaul of agricultural implements or equipment for bee-keeping, (b) the purchase of livestock or bee-stock, (c) the purchase or installation of, major repair to or major overhaul of agricultural equipment or a farm electric system, (d) the alteration or improvement of a farm electric system, (e) the erection or construction of fencing or works of drainage on a farm, (f) the construction, repair or alteration of, or making additions to, any building or structure on a farm, (g) the purchase, by the owner of a farm, of additional land for the purpose of farming, or (h) any work for the improvement or development of a farm designated in the regulations. *Farm Improvement Loans Act*, R.S.C. 1985, c. F-3, s. 2.

FARM INCOME ASSURANCE PLAN. Any program, arrangement, or plan that provides in any way for the paying of moneys to, or guaranteeing or assuring of income for, such farmers or classes of farmers in the province as the Lieutenant Governor in Council may designate; and includes the Manitoba Beef Producers Income Assurance Plan. *Farm Income Assurance Plans Act*, S.M. 1977, c. 17, s. 1.

FARM INCOME PLAN. Any programme, arrangement, proposal, plan, scheme, or similar measure, howsoever described, that provides in any way for the paying of moneys to, or guaranteeing or assuring of income for, such farmers or classes of farmers as the Lieutenant-Governor in Council designates. *Farm Income Assurance Act*, S.N.B. 1975, c. F-5.1, s. 1.

FARMING. *n.* 1. Includes livestock raising, beekeeping, dairying, fruit growing, tillage of the soil and any other husbandry activity that the Corporation prescribes in writing as farming for the purposes of this definition. *Farm Credit Act*, R.S.C. 1985, c. F-2, s. 2. 2. The production of field-grown crops, cultivated and uncultivated, and horticultural crops, the raising of livestock, poultry and fur-bearing animals, the production of eggs, milk, honey, maple syrup, tobacco, wood from woodlots, fibre and fodder crops and the production or raising of any other prescribed thing or animal. *Farm Debt Act*, R.S.C. 1985 (2d Supp.), c. 25, s. 2. 3. Includes tillage of the soil, livestock raising or exhibiting, maintaining of horses for racing, raising of poultry, fur farming, dairy farming, fruit growing and the keeping of bees, but does not include an office or employment under a person engaged in the business of farming. *Income Tax Act*, R.S.C. 1952, c. 148 (as am. S.C. 1970-71-72, c. 63), s. 248(1).

FARMING ASSETS. (i) Cash, trade accounts receivable, supplies and inventory of commodities or things produced, raised or grown through farming, (ii) land, buildings, equipment, machinery, and live stock that are used chiefly in the operation of the farm by the corporation, (iii) any right or licence granted or issued under any Act of the Legislature that permits or regulates the production or sale of any commodity or thing produced, raised or grown through farming, (iv) the building in which a shareholder or member or members of his family reside who are engaged in the operation of the farm if that building is on land that is used or is contiguous to land used by that shareholder or member or members of his family in the operation of the farm, (v) shares in another family farm corporation. *Corporations Tax Act*, R.S.O. 1980, c. 97, s. 1.

FARMING OPERATIONS. 1. (i) The planting, growing and sale of trees, shrubs or sod, (ii) the raising or production of crops, livestock, fish, pheasants or poultry, (iii) fur production, or (iv) beekeeping. *Real Property Statutes Amendment Act, 1983 (No. 2)*, S.A. 1983, c. 97, s. 2. 2. The production, or any step in the production, of livestock, grain, forage crops, poultry, furs, honey or any other agricultural product and, without limiting the generality of the foregoing, includes (i) the personal use of a farm truck owned or operated by a farmer, (ii) the heating of buildings located on a farm and used in connection with the production, or any step in the production, of livestock, grain, forage crops, poultry, furs, honey or any other agricultural product, and the heating of dwellings on that farm, (iii) the transportation of livestock, grain, forage crops, poultry, furs, honey or any other agricultural product by the farmer who produced them, and (iv) any operation designated by the regulations as a farming operation for the purposes of this clause, but does not include (v) any other type of business operation carried on by a farmer, or (vi) the transportation of livestock, grain, forage crops, poultry, furs, honey or any other agricultural product by a processor or by any person other than the farmer who produced them, if the transportation is for hire or gain. *Fuel Oil Administration Act*, R.S.A. 1980, c. F-21, s. 1.

FARMING PURPOSES. Agricultural production and the pasturage and production of livestock. *Division Fence Act*, S.P.E.I. 1975, c. 43, s. 1.

FARM JOURNAL. A newspaper or periodical having broad distribution in the farm community. *Farm Products Marketing Act*, R.S.Q. 1977, c. M-35, s. 1.

FARM LABOUR CONTRACTOR. An employer whose employees do work in connection with the planting, cultivating or harvesting of any horticultural or agricultural product, for or under the direction of another person. *Employment Standards Act*, S.B.C. 1980, c. 10, s. 60.

FARM LABOURER. A person who is employed by a farmer to work on a farm and whose chief occupation is farming. *An Act to Amend the Fish and Game Protection Act*, S.P.E.I. 1983, c. 17, s. 1.

FARM LAND. *var.* **FARMLAND.** Land that is being farmed or is shortly to be farmed and includes buildings and other improvements thereon. See TREE ~.

FARM MACHINERY. (i) A tractor, (ii) a farm implement powered by an internal combustion engine, whether it is self-propelled or not, (iii) a stationary engine located on a farm, or (iv) any vehicle, implement, machine or equipment designated as farm machinery. See UNUSED ~ AND EQUIPMENT; USED ~ AND EQUIPMENT.

FARM OPERATOR. Any physical person whose principal occupation is agriculture. Quebec statutes.

FARMOUT. *n.* A common agreement in the oil and gas industry under which one party does something on another party's land, for example drill a well, to earn an interest in that land. W. Grover & F. Iacobucci, *Materials on Canadian Income Tax*, 4th ed. (Toronto: Richard De Boo Ltd., 1980) at 1202.

FARM PRODUCE. Beans, corn, grain, grass seeds and oil seeds and all kinds thereof produced in Ontario. *Grain Elevator Storage Act, 1983*, S.O. 1983, c. 40, s. 1.

FARM PRODUCT. 1. Those plants and animals useful to mankind and includes, but is not limited to, (i) forages and sod crops, grains and field crops, (ii) poultry and poultry products, (iii) livestock and livestock products, and (iv) fruits, vegetables, mushrooms, tobacco, nuts, flower and floral products, nursery products, apiaries and fur-bearing animal products. 2. Any agricultural, horticultural, avicultural or forest product, in its raw state or partly or wholly processed by the producer, including, among other things, farm and farm-yard animals, live or slaughtered, the flesh of such animals, poultry, eggs, wool, dairy products, grain, fruits, vegetables, maple products, honey, tobacco, wood, beverages or foodstuffs derived from agricultural products and any other agricultural product or commodity designated by the Government. *An Act to Amend the Farm Producers Act*, S.Q. 1982, s. 60, s. 2. 3. Animals, meats, eggs, poultry, wool, dairy products, grains, seeds, fruit, fruit products, vegetables, vegetable products, maple products, honey, tobacco, wood, or any class or part of any such product, and such articles of food or drink manufactured or derived in whole or in part from any such product, and such other natural products of agriculture as are designated in the regulations, and, for the purposes of this Act, fish shall be deemed to be a farm product. *Farm Products Marketing Act*, R.S.O. 1980, c. 158, s. 1.

FARM PROPERTY. 1. The land and complementary buildings used for agricultural purposes but does not include any residential property in connection therewith. *Assessment Act*, S.N.S. 1975, c. 57, s. 1. 2. The piece or parcel of land upon which is situate the residence of the farmer regardless of the size of the parcel of land as long as it is one assessment. *Residential Property Tax Act*, S.N.S. 1973-74, c. 10, s. 3. 3. Includes farm implements, livestock and whatever is necessary to operate a farm. *Taxation Act*, R.S.Q. 1977, c. I-3, s. 1212. 4. Arable land and complementary buildings, operated as a farm enterprise by a bona fide farmer and farm property includes land leased from the Crown and operated as part of a farm enterprise, but excludes land leased or rented from owners who are not bona fide farmers. *Real Property Assessment Act*, R.S.P.E.I. 1974, c. R-5, s. 4.

FARM RESIDENCE. The improvement used as a residence by a person who carries on farming operations and situated on farm land outside a city, town, new town, village or summer village. *Municipal Taxation Act*, R.S.A. 1980, c. M-31, s. 1.

FARM STATION. An experimental farm station established under this Act. *Experimental Farm Stations Act*, R.S.C. 1985, c. E-16, s. 2.

FARMSTEAD. *n.* The land on which farm buildings are situated and all adjacent land used or that may be used for shelterbelts, gardens, lawns, storage, shelter, traffic, water supply, water transmission, water storage, services and other facilities contributing to the beneficial use of farm buildings, and includes the buildings, vegetation and other developments or improvements pertaining to the land. *The Family Farm Improvement Act*, R.S.S. 1978, c. F-6, s. 2.

FARM STOCK. (i) Cattle, (ii) sheep, (iii) goats, (iv) swine, (v) poultry, (vi) fur-bearing animals kept in captivity for the production of fur, (vii) bees, or (viii) horses, other than horses boarded for another person or kept or raised for showing, riding, racing or amusement. Manitoba statutes.

FARM STRUCTURE. A structure used for agricultural or forestry production but does not include a structure used primarily for storage or human habitation. *Pesticides Act*, R.R.O. 1980, Reg. 751, s. 1.

FARM SUBSCRIBER. A person engaged in farming operations and receiving from a company, in his name, telephone service upon farm land. *The Rural Telephone Act*, R.S.S. 1978, c. R-27, s. 2.

FARM SYNDICATE. (a) A cooperative farm association, (b) a farming corporation in which three or more shareholders are engaged in farming, the principal occupation of a majority of whom is farming, or (c) an association formed by an agreement in writing, approved by the Corporation, between individuals, farming corporations or any combination thereof where any three or more of those individuals or the shareholders of any of those farming corporations are engaged in farming and the principal occupation of a majority of them is farming. *Farm Syndicates Credit Act*, R.S.C. 1985, c. F-5, s. 2.

FARM TRACTOR. A motor vehicle designed and used primarily as an implement of husbandry for drawing agricultural equipment.

FARM TRAILER. A trailer owned by an actual farmer and operated in the marketing of the produce, including livestock, of his own farm, or in the conveyance of property for use thereon. *The Highway Traffic Act*, S.M. 1985-86, c. 3, s. 1.

FARM TRUCK. 1. A truck owned by a farmer. Manitoba statutes. 2. A motor vehicle classified by and registered with the board as a farm truck. *The Vehicles Act*, R.S.S. 1978, c. V-3, s. 2.

FARM USE. An occupation or use of land for farm purposes, including husbandry of land, plants and animals and any other similar activity designated as farm use by regulation. *Agricultural Land Commission Act*, R.S.B.C. 1979, c. 9, s. 1.

FARM VEHICLE. A farm machine or other machine or equipment (i) that is identifiable by manufacturer's serial number cut, embossed or otherwise permanently marked or attached on it, (ii) that is used, or intended for use, in any type of farming operations, and (iii) that is not a motor vehicle. *Garagemen's Lien Act*, R.S.A. 1980, c. G-1, s. 1. See OVER-DIMENSIONAL ~.

FARM WASTE. Includes unconsumed mink or fox food, mink or fox manure, carcasses of fur animals or any kind or species thereof or any kind of disposable material from a fur farm or from any animal, matter or thing used in connection with or as part of a fur farm. *Fur Farms Act*, R.S. Nfld. 1970, c. 146, s. 2.

F.A.S. *abbr.* Free alongside ship. A seller undertakes to deliver goods alongside a ship at the seller's own expense. G.H.L. Fridman, *Sale of Goods in Canada*, 3d ed. (Toronto: Carswell, 1986) at 484-485.

FASTENER. *n.* A device used to hold a conductor in place. *Lightning Rods Act*, R.R.O. 1980, Reg. 577, s. 1.

FAT. *n.* Any fat or oil, whether of animal, vegetable, marine or mineral origin. See EXCESS PROPORTION OF ~; MILK ~.

FATAL ACCIDENT. An accident causing the death of a worker under circumstances that entitle that worker's dependents, if any, to compensation under this Act. *Workers' Compensation acts.*

FAT EMBOLISM. Obstruction by fat droplets of capillary blood vessels. F.A. Jaffe, *A Guide to Pathological Evidence*, 2d ed. (Toronto: Carswell, 1983) at 175.

FATETUR FACINUS QUI JUDICIUM FUGIT. [L.] One who flees judgment admits guilt.

FATHER. *n.* 1. Includes grandfather. *Maintenance Order acts.* 2. The person named as the cause of the pregnancy. *Children of Unmarried Parents Act*, R.S.N.B. 1973, c. C-3, s. 1. 3. A person who takes care of a child of whom he is the legitimate, natural or adoptive father, or the stepfather. *Family Allowances Act*, R.S.Q., 1977, c. A-17, s. 1. 4. Of a taxpayer includes a father-in-law. *Taxation Act*, R.S.Q. 1977, c. I-3, s. 1. 5. Includes one of two or more persons who may be the possible father. *The Children of Unmarried Parents Act*, R.S.S. 1978, c. C-8, s. 2. 6. Includes the husband of the mother of a mentally disordered person born in wedlock. *Mental Health Act*, R.S.B.C. 1979, c. 256, s. 1. See BIOLOGICAL ~; DEPENDENT ~; POSSIBLE ~; PUTATIVE ~.

FATHER OF A CHILD. In any one of the following circumstances: 1. The person is married to the mother of the child at the time of the birth of the child. 2. The person was married to the mother of the child by a marriage that was terminated by death or judgment of nullity within 300 days before the birth of the child or by divorce where the decree nisi was granted within 300 days before the birth of the child. 3. The person marries the mother of the child after the birth of the child and acknowledges that he is the natural father. 4. The person was cohabiting with the mother of the child in a relationship of some permanence at the time of the birth of the child or the child was born within 300 days after they ceased to cohabit. 5. The person and the mother of the child have filed a statutory declaration under subsection 6(8) of the Vital Statistics Act or a request under subsection 6(5) of that Act, or either under a similar provision under the corresponding Act in another jurisdiction in Canada. 6. The person has been found or recognized in his lifetime by a court of competent jurisdiction in Canada to be the father of the child. *Children's Law Reform Act*, R.S.O. 1980, c. 68, s. 8.

FAUCES TERRAE. [L.] A gulf; a narrow inlet of a body of water.

FAUCET. *n.* A water tap.

FAULT. *n.* Wrongful act or default. Sales of goods acts.

FAVORABILIA IN LEGE SUNT FISCUS, DOS, VITA, LIBERTAS. [L.] See CAUSAE DOTIS, VITAE, LIBERTATIS, FISCI, SUNT INTER FAVORABILIA, IN LEGE.

FAVORABILIORES REI POTIUS QUAM ACTORES HABENTUR. [L.] The law is on the defendant's side rather than the plaintiff's.

FAVORABILIORES SUNT EXECUTIONES ALIIS PROCESSIBUS QUIBUSCUNQUE. [L.] Executions are preferred more than all other process.

FBDB. *abbr.* Federal Business Development Bank.

F.C. *abbr.* 1. Federal Court. 2. Federal Court of Canada Reports.

[ ] F.C. *abbr.* Canada Federal Court Reports, 1971- (Recueil des arrêts de la Cour fédérale du Canada).

F.C.A.D. *abbr.* Federal Court Appellate Division.

F.C.S. *abbr.* Free of capture and seizure. In marine insurance policies, indicates that the underwriter is not liable for capture or seizure of either the cargo or the ship.

F.C.T.D. *abbr.* Federal Court Trial Division.

FEALTY. *n.* 1. A mutual bond of obligation or special oath of fidelity between a lord and a tenant. 2. The general oath of allegiance of a subject to a sovereign.

FEASANCE. *n.* Executing or doing something. See MIS~; NON~.

FEASIBILITY STUDY. See ENGINEERING RESEARCH OR ~; RESEARCH OR ~.

FEATHERBEDDING. *n.* When payment is sought for work not done, work done with more workers than necessary or excess work.

FEATURE. *n.* The daily double, quinella, exactor, triactor, quadactor or such other pool as may be authorized pursuant to paragraph 126(4)(b). *Race Track Supervision Regulations*, C.R.C., c. 441, s. 2. See SPECIAL ~; TOUR ~S.

FEATURE FILM. See CANADIAN ~.

FEATURE MOTION PICTURE. A motion picture film in excess of 60 minutes duration that has been produced for exhibition in a commercial motion picture theatre. *Cable Television Regulations*, C.R.C., c. 374, s. 2.

FEATURE POOL. The monies bet on a feature. *Race Track Supervision Regulations*, C.R.C., c. 441, s. 2.

FED. *abbr.* Federal.

FED. C.A. *abbr.* Federal Court of Canada—Appeal Division.

FEDERAL. *adj.* As applied to state documents, means of or pertaining to Canada. Evidence acts.

FEDERAL ACT. A law passed by the Parliament of Canada.

FEDERAL AIRPORT. Includes a military aerodrome. *Aeronautics Act*, R.S.C. 1985 (1st Supp.), c. 33, s. 5.4(1).

FEDERAL BASIC TAX RATE. Of a taxpayer for a taxation year means the proportion that his tax payable under the federal Act for the year is of his taxable income for the year, expressed as a percentage. *Alberta Income Tax Act*, R.S.A. 1980, c. A-31, s. 11.

FEDERAL BENEFITS. Benefits payable under the Canada Pension Plan and to which any dependants are entitled as a result of the death, together with any benefits to which the dependent spouse is or becomes entitled under the Canada Pension Plan as a result of having retired or reached retirement age. *Workers Compensation Act*, R.S.B.C. 1979, c. 437, s. 17.

FEDERAL BOARD, COMMISSION OR OTHER TRIBUNAL. 1. Any body or any person or persons having, exercising or purporting to exercise jurisdiction or powers conferred by or under an Act of Parliament, other than any such body constituted or established by or under a law of a province or any such person or persons appointed under or in accordance with a law of a province or under section 96 of the Constitution Act, 1867. *Federal Court Act*, R.S.C. 1985, c. F-7, s. 2. 2. Any board, commission, tribunal or person who is expressly charged by or pursuant to an enactment of Parliament with the responsibility of making decisions or recommendations related directly or indirectly to the production, supply, acquisition or distribution of a product and includes an ad hoc commission of inquiry charged with any such responsibility but does not include a court. *Combines Investigation Act*, R.S.C. 1985, c. C-34, s. 30(2).

FEDERAL BUSINESS DEVELOPMENT BANK. The bank, incorporated under the Federal Business Development Bank Act (Canada), which offers financial and management services to help businesses establish and develop themselves in Canada.

FEDERAL CARRIER. A person who operates an extraprovincial undertaking. *Motor Vehicle Transport Act*, R.S.C. 1985, c. M-12, s. 2.

FEDERAL COMPANY. 1. A corporation incorporated or continued by or under an Act of Canada and not discontinued by or under an Act of Canada and includes the Governor and Company of Adventurers of England trading into Hudson's Bay. *Company Act*, R.S.B.C. 1979, c. 59, s. 1. 2. A trust company incorporated by or pursuant to an Act of the Parliament of

Canada. *Trust Companies Act*, R.S.A. 1980, c. T-9, s. 1. 3. An extra-provincial company that is incorporated by or under an Act of the Parliament of Canada. *Corporations Act*, S. Nfld. 1986, c. 12, s. 429.

FEDERAL COOPERATIVE ASSOCIATION. A cooperative association, federation or corporation to which this Act applies and any corporation that is authorized to apply under subsection 7(1) for a certificate of continuation. *Canada Cooperative Association Act*, R.S.C. 1985, c. C-40, s. 129.

FEDERAL COURT. 1. The Federal Court of Canada. *Interpretation Act*, R.S.C. 1985, c. I-21, s. 35. 2. The Federal Court—Trial Division. *Petroleum and Gas Revenue Tax Act*, R.S.C. 1985, c. P-12, s. 2.

FEDERAL COURT—APPEAL DIVISION. That division of the Federal Court of Canada called the Federal Court—Appeal Division or referred to as the Court of Appeal or Federal Court of Appeal by the Federal Court Act. *Interpretation Act*, R.S.C. 1985, c. I-21, s. 35.

FEDERAL COURT OF APPEAL. That division of the Federal Court of Canada called the Federal Court—Appeal Division or referred to as the Court of Appeal or Federal Court of Appeal by the Federal Court Act. *Interpretation Act*, R.S.C. 1985, c. I-21, s. 35.

FEDERAL COURT—TRIAL DIVISION. That division of the Federal Court of Canada so named by the Federal Court Act. *Interpretation Act*, R.S.C. 1985, c. I-21, s. 35.

FEDERAL CROWN. Her Majesty in right of Canada.

FEDERAL CUSTOMS LAWS. Includes (a) Acts of Parliament, (b) regulations within the meaning of the Statutory Instruments Act, and (c) rules of law applicable in connection with those Acts or regulations, that relate to customs or excise, whether those Acts, regulations or rules come into force before or after June 30, 1983 and, for greater certainty but without restricting the generality of the foregoing, includes the following Acts, namely, the Anti-dumping Act, chapter A-15 of the Revised Statutes of Canada, 1970, Customs Act, chapter C-40 of the Revised Statutes of Canada, 1970, Customs Tariff, Excise Act, Excise Tax Act, Export and Import Permits Act and Importation of Intoxicating Liquors Act. *Customs and Excise Offshore Application*, R.S.C. 1985, c. C-53, s. 2.

FEDERAL GOVERNMENT. 1. A person or body which exercises power delegated to it by two or more independent states which have mutually agreed not to exercise certain sovereign powers but to delegate the exercise of those powers to the person or body they have chosen jointly. 2. The Governor General in Council.

FEDERAL HOSPITAL. A hospital that is owned or operated by Canada. *Hospital Insurance Regulations*, C.R.C., c. 936, s. 2.

FEDERAL INSTITUTION. A bank or company referred to in section 8. *Canada Deposit Insurance Corporation Act*, R.S.C. 1985, c. C-3, s. 2.

FEDERALISM. See COOPERATIVE ~.

FEDERAL JURISDICTION. The legislative jurisdiction of the Parliament of Canada.

FEDERAL OFFENCE. An offence as defined by the Young Offenders Act (Canada).

FEDERAL OIL ACT. The Canada Oil and Gas Act. *Canada-Nova Scotia Oil and Gas Agreement (Nova Scotia) Act*, S.N.S. 1984, c. 2, s. 2.

FEDERAL OIL PRODUCTION ACT. The Oil and Gas Production and Conservation Act (Canada). *Canada-Nova Scotia Oil and Gas Agreement (Nova Scotia) Act*, S.N.S. 1984, c. 2, s. 2.

FEDERAL PARAMOUNTCY. The rule that the federal law prevails, which applies when there is a provincial law and a federal law which are each valid but inconsistent or conflicting. P.W. Hogg, *Constitutional Law of Canada*, 2d ed. (Toronto: Carswell, 1985) at 354.

FEDERAL PARLIAMENT. The parliament of Canada.

FEDERAL PRINCIPLE. The division of powers so that those of the central and those of the regional governments are each, within their sphere, co-ordinate and independent. P.W. Hogg, *Constitutional Law of Canada*, 2d ed. (Toronto: Carswell, 1985) at 81.

FEDERAL PROPERTY. (a) Real property owned by Her Majesty in right of Canada that is under the management, charge and direction of a minister of the Crown, (b) real property owned by Her Majesty in right of Canada that is, by virtue of a lease to a corporation included in Schedule III or IV, under the management, charge and direction of that corporation, (c) real property subject to an emphyteutic lease to Her Majesty in right of Canada that is under the management, charge and direction of a minister of the Crown, (d) a building owned by Her Majesty in right of Canada that is under the management, charge and direction of a minister of the Crown and that is situated on tax exempt land owned by a person other than Her Majesty in right of Canada or administered and controlled by Her Majesty in right of a province, and (e) such real property occupied or used by a minister of the Crown and administered and controlled by Her Majesty in right of a province as is prescribed. *Municipal Grants Act*, R.S.C. 1985, c. M-13, s. 2. See PROVINCIALLY OCCUPIED ~.

FEDERAL REFERENCE. A function of the Supreme Court, imposed by the Supreme Court Act, to give advisory opinions on questions which the federal government refers to the Court. P.W. Hogg, *Constitutional Law of Canada*, 2d ed. (Toronto: Carswell, 1985) at 177.

FEDERAL REGULATION. A regulation, as amended from time to time, made under the federal Act. Income Tax acts.

FEDERAL RESEARCH PERMIT. A permit issued by the Federal Regulatory Authority to conduct research in the area of pest control products. *Pest Control Products (Nova Scotia) Act*, S.N.S. 1986, c. 16, s. 3.

FEDERAL STATE. Distribution of government power between one central, federal or national authority and several regional, state or provincial authorities with the result that every individual is subject to the laws of two authorities. P.W. Hogg, *Constitutional Law of Canada*, 2d ed. (Toronto: Carswell, 1985) at 80.

FEDERAL STATUTE. A law passed by the Parliament of Canada.

FEDERAL TERRITORY. An area under the authority of the federal Parliament. P.W. Hogg, *Constitutional Law of Canada*, 2d ed. (Toronto: Carswell, 1985) at 31.

FEDERAL WATERS. Waters under the exclusive legislative jurisdiction of Parliament. *Canada Water Act*, R.S.C. 1985, c. C-11, s. 2.

FEDERAL WORK, UNDERTAKING OR BUSINESS. Any work, undertaking or business that is within the legislative authority of Parliament, including, without restricting the generality of the foregoing, (a) a work, undertaking or business operated or carried on for or in connection with navigation and shipping, whether inland or maritime, including the operation of ships and transportation by ship anywhere in Canada, (b) a railway, canal, telegraph or other work or undertaking connecting any province with any other province, or extending beyond the limits of a province, (c) a line of ships connecting a province with any other province, or extending beyond the limits of a province, (d) a ferry between any province and any other province or between any province and any country other than Canada, (e) aerodromes, aircraft or a line of air transportation, (f) a radio broadcasting station, (g) a bank, (h) a work or undertaking that, although wholly situated within a province, is before or after its execution declared by Parliament to be for the general advantage of Canada and for the advantage of two or more of the provinces, and (i) a work, undertaking or business outside the exclusive legislative authority of the legislatures of the provinces. *Canada Labour Code*, R.S.C. 1985, c. L-2, s. 2.

FEDERATION. *n.* A composite state whose constitution distributes certain functions to a central authority and others to member states. See ALLIED TRADES ~; FOUNDER ~; PROVINCIAL ~; SPECIALIZED ~.

FEDERATION OF COOPERATIVE CREDIT SOCIETIES. A federation, league or corporation incorporated or organized by or pursuant to an Act of Parliament or of the legislature of a province, the membership or the shareholders of which include two or more central cooperative credit societies.

FED. T.D. *abbr.* Federal Court of Canada—Trial Division.

FEE. *n.* 1. Property which could descend to the heirs of the owner for the time being if the owner did not dispose of it while alive or by will. 2. Recompense or reward for services. 3. An amount to be paid when filing documents. See ENTRANCE ~; FRANCHISE ~; INITIATION ~; LICENSE ~; MANAGEMENT ~S; MONTHLY ~S; OFFICIAL ~; OVERTIME ~S; PROVINCIAL TAX OR ~.

FEEBLE-MINDED PERSON. A person in whom there exists, and has existed from birth or from an early age, mental defectiveness not amounting to imbecility, but so pronounced that the person requires care, supervision and control for his protection or for the protection of others. *Criminal Code*, R.S.C. 1985, c. C-46, s. 2.

FEED. *v.* To offer additional support; to strengthen after the fact, i.e. a subsequently acquired interest feeds an estoppel.

FEED. *n.* Any substance or mixture of substances containing amino acids, anti-oxidants, carbohydrates, condiments, enzymes, fats, minerals, non-protein nitrogen products, proteins or vitamins, or pelletizing, colouring, foaming or flavouring agents and any other substance manufactured, sold or represented for use (a) for consumption by livestock, (b) for providing the nutritional requirements of livestock, or (c) for the purpose of preventing or correcting nutritional disorders of livestock, or any substance for use in any such substance or mixture of substances. *Feeds Act*, R.S.C. 1985, c. F-9, s. 2. See AGRICULTURAL ~S; BASAL ~; CHOP ~; CUSTOMER-FORMULA ~;

MEDICATED ~; MINERAL ~; TRACE-MINERAL-SALT ~.

FEEDER. *n.* A conductor or group of conductors which transmits electrical energy from a service supply, transformer, switchboard, distribution centre, generator, or other source of supply to the branch-circuit over-current devices. *Power Corporation Act*, R.R.O. 1980, Reg. 794, s. 0. See LIVESTOCK ~.

FEEDER ASSOCIATION. An association incorporated under an Act of the Legislature and having for its object the assisting of its members to acquire livestock for growing and finishing. *Feeder Associations Guarantee Act*, R.S.A. 1980, c. F-8, s. 1.

FEED GRAIN. 1. Wheat, other than grades of wheat grown in the designated area and designated by regulation not to be feed grain for the purposes of this Act, oats and barley and such other grains and grain products as may be designated by regulation as feed grain for the purposes of this Act. *Livestock Feed Assistance Act*, R.S.C. 1985, c. L-10, s. 2. 2. Grain that is used or intended to be used for human or animal consumption. *New Brunswick Grain Act*, S.N.B. 1980, c. N-5.1, s. 1. 3. (a) In respect of wheat, wheat of the grade No. 3 Canada Western Red Spring or wheat of any equivalent or lower level of excellence, (b) in respect of oats, oats of the grade No. 1 Feed or oats of any lower level of excellence, and (c) in respect of barley, barley of the grade No. 1 Feed or barley of any lower level of excellence. Canada regulations.

FEED LOT. *var.* **FEEDLOT.** Land enclosed by a fence or other means on which stock is fed, or intended to be fed, in confinement.

FEED MILL OPERATOR. A person who purchases grain from producers and processes the grain into feed, for sale. *Western Grain Stabilization Regulations*, C.R.C., c. 1607, s. 2.

FEED STOCK. Includes any form of flora or fauna given or intended to be given as food to aquacultural produce. *Aquaculture Act*, S.N.S. 1983, c. 2, s. 2.

FEE GENERATING SERVICES. Those services which a solicitor would ordinarily render in civil matters on the understanding that he would receive no remuneration from the client except out of the proceeds generated through pursuing the matter. *The Community Legal Services (Saskatchewan) Act*, R.S.S. 1978, c. C-20, s. 2.

FEE INDEMNITY INSURANCE. Insurance whereby an insurer undertakes to pay on behalf of a person, or to indemnify a person, for the payment of professional or other fees incurred by that person for services rendered but does not include insurance coming within the class of accident and sickness insurance. *Classes of Insurance Regulations*, C.R.C., c. 977, s. 13.

FEE REVENUE. In respect of a broadcasting undertaking, means the total revenue derived from the licensed activity of the broadcasting undertaking whether received by the licensee of the broadcasting undertaking or by an associated corporation and, without limiting the generality of the foregoing, includes (a) revenue that is derived from the sale of air time of the broadcasting undertaking by the Canadian Broadcasting Corporation and paid by the Corporation to the licensee, and (b) where the broadcasting undertaking consists of an originating broadcasting transmitting station and one or more rebroadcasting transmitting stations, any revenue received in respect of such rebroadcasting transmitting stations. *Broadcasting Licence Fee Regulations*, C.R.C., c. 373, s. 2.

FEE SIMPLE. The most extensive form of freehold estate possible which arises from a grant to a person and any of the person's heirs. E.L.G. Tyler & N.E. Palmer, eds., *Crossley Vaines' Personal Property*, 5th ed. (London: Butterworths, 1973) at 4. See REGISTERED OWNER IN ~.

FEE TAIL. A lesser freehold estate which arises from a grant to a person and heirs, limited to the grantee's own issue. E.L.G. Tyler & N.E. Palmer, eds., *Crossley Vaines' Personal Property*, 5th ed. (London: Butterworths, 1973) at 5.

FELLING AREA. An area where trees are being felled and into which they might fall. *Occupational Health and Safety Act*, R.R.O. 1980, Reg. 692, s. 107.

FELLOWSHIP. *n.* A loan for educational and training purposes in respect of health to assist in the financing of a program of advanced study or research at a university or health institution approved by the Minister repayable by the performance of agreed upon services to the public. *Ministry of Health Act*, R.R.O. 1980, Reg. 654, s. 1.

FELO DE SE. [L. a felon with respect to oneself] A person who commits suicide.

FELON. *n.* A person who was convicted of felony.

FELONIAE CEPIT ET ASPORTAVIT. [L.] One feloniously took and carried off.

FELONIA IMPLICATUR IN QUALIBET PRODITIONE. [L.] Felony is involved in every treason.

FELONY. *n.* Originally the condition of having forfeited goods and lands to the Crown when convicted of a certain offence; later the offence which caused such forfeiture, distinguished from misdemeanour, after conviction for which forfeiture did not follow. See MISPRISION OF ~.

FEMALE-DOMINATED CLASS. (i) A class in which there are 10 or more incumbents, as of the date any public sector employer is required to commence action to implement pay equity, of whom 70% or more are women, (ii) in the case of a public sector employer which employs 500 or more employees as of the date referred to in sub-clause (i), such other classes, irrespective of the number of incumbents and gender distribution, as the employer, bargaining agents and employee representatives affected may agree should be considered female-dominated, and (iii) in the case of a public sector employer which employs less than 500 employees as of the date referred to in sub-clause (i), such other classes as may be further defined in the regulations. *The Pay Equity Act*, S.M. 1985-86, c. 21, s. 1.

FEMALE EMPLOYEE. Does not include a female employee who is employed as a domestic servant in any premises where board or lodging for less than three persons is provided for remuneration. *Labour Standards Act*, S. Nfld. 1977, c. 52, s. 38.

FEME. *n.* A woman; a wife.

FEME COVERT. A woman who is married.

FEME SOLE. A woman who is unmarried: spinster, widow or divorced.

FEMININE. *adj.* Relating to females.

FEMTO. *pref.* 10^{-15}. Prefix for multiples and submultiples of Basic, Supplementary and Derived Units of Measurement. *Weights and Measures Act*, S.C. 1970-71-72, c. 36, schedule 1, part V.

FENCE. See LAWFUL ~; RAILWAY ~.

FENERATION. *n.* 1. Usury. 2. Interest on loaned money.

FEOD. See FEUD.

FEODAL. *adj.* Belonging to or of a feod.

FEODALITY. See FEALTY.

FEODAL SYSTEM. See FEUDAL SYSTEM.

FEODATORY. *n.* The tenant who holds an estate through feudal service.

FEOFFEE. *n.* One who is put in possession.

FEOFFMENT. *n.* Formerly, the transfer of freehold land by livery of seisin and word of mouth; now, giving the transferee corporal possession of a land or tenement.

FEOFFOR. *n.* A person who makes a feoffment.

FERAE NATURAE. [L.] Having a wild nature.

FERIAE. *n.* [L.] Holidays.

FERIAL DAY. A holiday; feast.

FERRET. *n.* Any of the domesticated forms of the old world polecat (Putorius putorius) used for hunting. *Game and Fish Act*, R.S.O. 1980, c. 182, s. 1.

FERRIAGE. *n.* A ferry fare.

FERROUS FOUNDRY. The part of a building, or premises, or the workshop, structure, room or place in which iron or any of its alloys is cast in moulds or where core-making, shake-out or cleaning of any casting or other dust-causing or odour-causing operation ancillary to the casting process is carried on. *Environmental Protection Act*, R.R.O. 1980, Reg. 295, s. 1.

FERRY. *n.* 1. A scow, barge or boat used for the purpose of carrying passengers, freight, vehicles or animals across a river, stream or other body of water and includes any cable and appliances connected therewith. *The Highway Act*, R.S.S. 1978, c. H-3, s. 2. 2. Any and all methods and means of water transport including, but not limited to, ships, boats, vessels, barges, hydrofoils and hovercraft. *Ferry Corporation Act*, R.S.B.C. 1979, c. 128, s. 1.

FERRY CABLE. Any ferry cable, rod, chain or other device put across, over, in or under any navigable water for working a ferry. *Navigable Waters Protection Act*, R.S.C. 1985, c. N-22, s. 29.

FERRY VESSEL. Any vessel, having provision only for deck passengers and for vehicles, that is operated on a short run on a schedule between two points over the most direct water route and offers a public service of a type normally attributed to a bridge or tunnel. *Hull Construction Regulations*, C.R.C., c. 1431, s. 2.

FERTILIZER. *n.* 1. Any substance or mixture of substances, containing nitrogen, phosphorus, potassium or other plant food, manufactured, sold or represented for use as a plant nutrient. 2. Includes agricultural lime, peat moss and similar soil conditioners. *Retail Sales Tax Act*, R.R.O. 1980, Reg. 904, s. 1. See CUSTOMER-FORMULA ~; MIXED ~; SPECIALTY ~.

FERTILIZER-PESTICIDE. *n.* Any fertilizer that contains a pesticide. *Fertilizers Regulations*, C.R.C., c. 666, s. 2.

FESANCE. *n.* An act.

FESTINATIO JUSTITIAE NOVERCA. [L.] The stepmother of justice is haste.

FESTINUM REMEDIUM. [L.] A prompt remedy.

FESTUM. *n.* [L.] A feast.

FETTLER. *n.* An employee who makes minor repairs and puts things in order.

FETUS. *n.* A child developing in the uterus during the last two thirds of pregnancy. F.A. Jaffe, *A Guide to Pathological Evidence*, 2d ed. (Toronto: Carswell, 1983) at 176. See FOETUS.

FEUD. *n.* A grant of land made by a feudal lord or superior which is held by the grantee in return for services rendered.

FEUDAL SYSTEM. A peculiar system in which absolute or nominal ownership of land was in one feudal superior or lord while the occupation, use and benefit was in the feudal inferior or tenant who rendered the lord certain services.

FEUDATORY. *n.* The tenant who holds an estate through feudal service.

F4. Facsimile by direct frequency modulation of the carrier frequency. *General Radio Regulations*, Part II, C.R.C., c. 1372, s. 42.

F.G.A. *abbr.* Free from general average. In marine insurance policies, means that the underwriters are not liable for general average losses.

FIAT. *n.* [L. let it be done] A decree; order or warrant made by a judge or public officer to allow certain processes.

FIAT JUSTITIA. [L.] Let justice be done.

FIAT JUSTITIA, RUAT COELUM. [L.] Let justice be done, even though the heavens fall.

FIAT QUOD PRIUS FIERI CONSUEVIT. [L.] Let what was usually done before be done.

FIAUNT. *n.* [L.] Warrant.

FIBRE. See ASBESTOS ~; CARBON ~S AND FILAMENTS; FLAX ~; MAN-MADE ~; TEXTILE ~; WOOD ~.

FIBREBOARD. *n.* Includes plywood. *Dangerous Goods Shipping Regulations*, C.R.C., c. 1419, s. 2.

FIBRILLATION. See VENTRICULAR ~.

FIBROUS AND FILAMENTARY MATERIALS. Includes (a) continuous monofilament; (b) continuous yarns and rovings; (c) tapes, woven fabrics and random mats; (d) chopped fibres, staple fibres and coherent fibre blankets; (e) whiskers, either monocrystalline or polycrystalline, of any length. *Export Control List*, C.R.C., c. 601, s. 6763.

FICTIO LEGIS NON OPERATUR DAMNUM VEL INJURIAM. [L.] A legal fiction does not operate to cause loss or injustice.

FICTION. *n.* A rule of law which assumes something which is false is true, and will not allow it to be disproved.

FICTITIOUS IDENTIFICATION PLATE OR MARKER. An identification plate, sticker or marker which has not been issued under this Act or which has not been issued for the registration year in which it is used or which is attached to a vehicle other than that for which it was issued but does not include an identification plate, sticker or marker on a foreign vehicle lawfully operated in the province. *Highway Traffic Act*, R.S. Nfld. 1970, c. 152, s. 2.

FICTITIOUS MARKER. A registration marker which has not been furnished and delivered by the Bureau, or which has not been furnished and delivered for the current registration year, or which is placed on another vehicle than that for which it has been delivered by the Bureau. *Highway Code*, R.S.Q. 1977, c. C-24, s. 1.

FICTITIOUS NUMBER PLATE. A number plate or sticker that has not been issued under the Highway Traffic Act or that has not been issued for the registration year in which it is used or that is attached to a vehicle other than that for which it was issued, but does not include number plates or stickers on foreign vehicles lawfully operated in the province.

FICTITIOUS PAYEE. A person who is to receive money, but who does not exist.

FICTITIOUS REGISTRATION PLATE. A registration plate not furnished and issued by the division or not furnished and issued for the current registration year, or that is attached to a vehicle other than that for which it was issued by the division but does not include registration plates on foreign vehicles lawfully operated in New Brunswick. *Motor Vehicle Act*, R.S.N.B. 1973, c. M-17, s. 1.

FIDEI-COMMISSUM. *n.* [L.] A disposition by will in which the testator obliges the receiver to transfer the object to a third person.

FIDE-JUSSOR. *n.* [L] A surety.

FIDELITY BOND. (i) A promise to make good financial loss resulting from the dishonesty of employees, or (ii) a financial guarantee of the performance of an implied obligation. *Insurance Adjusters Act*, R.S. Nfld. 1970, c. 175, s. 2.

FIDELITY INSURANCE. (a) Insurance against loss caused by the unfaithful performance of duties by a person in a position of trust; or (b) insurance whereby an insurer undertakes to guarantee the proper fulfilment of the duties of an office. *Classes of Insurance Regulations*, C.R.C., c. 977, s. 14.

FIDUCIARY. *n.* 1. A person who holds something in trust. 2. Any trustee, guardian, committee, curator, tutor, executor, administrator or representative of a deceased person, or any other person acting in a fiduciary capacity.

FIDUCIARY ACTIVITIES. (a) Those activities enumerated in paragraphs 71(b), (c), and (d) of the Trust Companies Act, (b) the activities of an agent or attorney in winding-up an estate, (c) activities generally associated with the conduct of any matter in the nature of a trust, and (d) the activities involved in acting as managing agent of an estate or a property for or on behalf of any person. *Bank Act*, R.S.C. 1985, c. B-1, s. 174.

FIEF. *n.* A fee; a manor.

FIELD. *n.* (a) The surface area underlaid or appearing to be underlaid by one or more pools; and (b) the subsurface regions vertically beneath that surface area. See MUTUEL ~.

FIELD CUCUMBERS. Cucumbers that are not greenhouse cucumbers. *Fresh Fruit and Vegetable Regulations*, C.R.C., c. 285, s. 1.

FIELD OF VIEW. The space forward of a transverse vertical plane tangent to the rearmost boundary of the SAE 99th percentile eye range countour of SAE Recommended Practice J941a Passenger Car Driver's Eye Range, (August 1967). *Motor Vehicle Safety Regulations*, C.R.C., c. 1038, s. 107.

FIELD PRICE. See CONTRACT ~; REGULATED ~.

FIELD RHUBARB. Rhubarb that has not been grown in artificial conditions under glass or other protective covering. *Fresh Fruit and Vegetable Regulations*, C.R.C., c. 285, s. 1.

FIELD TOMATOES. Tomatoes that are not greenhouse tomatoes. *Fresh Fruit and Vegetable Regulations*, C.R.C., c. 285, s. 1.

FIELD VALUE. The commodity value of gas less just and reasonable costs, charges and deductions that are or may be fixed, determined or allowed for the transportation and distribution of that gas from the point of sale under the gas purchase contract to the point of end use. *Arbitration Act*, R.S.A. 1980, c. A-43, s. 17.

FIELD WORK. The work performed in the search for occurrences of placer or lode mineral deposits. *Prospectors' Assistance Regulations*, C.R.C., c. 338, s. 2.

FIERI FACIAS. [L. that you cause to be made] A writ of execution used to levy a judgment debt. See WRIT OF ~.

FIERI FECI. [L. I have caused to be made] A return made by the sheriff who executed a writ of execution.

FIERI NON DEBUIT, SED FACTUM VALET. [L.] It should not have been done, but once done is binding.

FI. FA. *abbr.* Fieri facias.

FIFO. *abbr.* First in, first out.

FIFO METHOD OF INVENTORY VALUATION. By assuming that the first items purchased were disposed of first, the cost of the inventory on hand at the end of a period is calculated using the cost of the most recently acquired items. W. Grover & F. Iacobucci, *Materials on Canadian Income Tax*, 4th ed. (Toronto: Richard De Boo Ltd., 1980) at 643.

FIFTH FREEDOM. The privilege of a foreign air carrier operating a charter to take on or put down in Canada persons or goods destined to, or coming from, the territory of a country other than that of the foreign air carrier. *Air Carrier Regulations*, C.R.C., c. 3, s. 23.

FIFTH WHEEL ASSEMBLY. A coupling device having its lower-half mounted on the rear portion of a vehicle frame or the frame of a trailer converter dolly and its upper-half fastened to the underside of the forward portion of a semi-trailer for the purpose of supporting and towing the semi-trailer. *Highway Traffic Act*, R.R.O. 1980, Reg. 489, s. 1.

FIGHT. See PRIZE ~.

FIGURE. *n.* A numerical character.

FILAMENTARY MATERIALS. See FIBROUS AND ~.

FILAMENT. See MONO ~.

FILAMENTS. See CARBON FIBRES AND ~.

FILE. *v.* To leave with the appropriate office for keeping.

FILE. *n.* All the information about a consumer recorded or retained by a credit reporting agency regardless of how the information is stored. See PERSONAL ~.

FILED SUBDIVISION PLAN. A plan of subdivision (a) approved by a development officer under this Act, or by the Provincial Planning Board or a commission under a previous Act, and filed in the registry office, or (b) filed in the registry office when there was no subdivision by-law or regulation under this or a previous Act applicable to the land comprised in the plan. *Community Planning Act*, R.S.N.B. 1973, c. C-12, s. 47.

FILIAFAMILIAS. *n.* [L.] A daughter.

FILIATION. *n.* The relationship of a son to his father.

FILIATIO NON POTEST PROBARI. [L.] Filiation cannot be proved.

FILIBUSTER. *n.* A tactic used to delay legislative action.

FILING. *n.* The entering in the daybook of any instrument. *Land Titles acts.*

FILIUSFAMILIAS. *n.* [L.] A son.

FILIUS MULIERATUS. [L.] The oldest legitimate son of a woman who was unlawfully connected with the father before marriage.

FILIUS NULLIUS. [L. son of no one] A bastard.

FILIUS POPULI. [L. son of the people] A bastard.

FILL. *n.* Earth, gravel, sand, rubbish, garbage or any other material, whether similar to or different from any of the aforementioned materials and whether originating on the site or elsewhere, used or capable of being used to raise or in any way affect the contours of the ground. See INERT ~.

FILL-AND-DRAW POOL. A pool so operated that the water is completely drained to waste intermittently and replaced by make-up water. *Public Health Act*, R.R.O. 1980, Reg. 849, s. 1.

FILL-AND-DRAW SWIMMING POOL. A swimming pool so operated that the water is completely drained to waste intermittently and replaced by make-up water. *Public Health Act*, R.R.O. 1980, Reg. 849, s. 1.

FILLED COMPARTMENT. A compartment in which, after loading with bulk grain and trimming as required by section 5, the grain is at its highest possible level. *Grain Cargo Regulations*, C.R.C., c. 1427, s. 2.

FILLER. *n.* 1. (a) Flour or meal prepared from grain or potato, but not from a legume, (b) processed wheat flour containing not less than the equivalent of 80 per cent dextrose as determined by the official method, (b) bread, biscuit or bakery products, but not those containing or made with a legume, (d) milk powder, skim milk powder, buttermilk powder or whey powder, and (e) starch. *Food and Drug Regulations*, C.R.C., c. 870. 2. (a) Flour or meal prepared from grain or potatoes, (b) processed wheat flour containing not less than the equivalent of 80 per cent dextrose, as determined by a method approved by the Minister, (c) bread, biscuit or bakery products, except those containing or made with a legume, or (d) milk powder, skim milk powder, buttermilk powder or whey powder. *Fish Inspection Regulations*, C.R.C., c. 802, s. 2. 3. A food added to a meat product to increase its bulk.

Meat Inspection Regulations, C.R.C., c. 1032, s. 2.

FILLETS. *n.* (a) Slices of fish flesh of irregular size and shape that have been removed from the carcass of a fish by cuts made parallel to the backbone, or (b) slices of fish flesh described in paragraph (a) that have been cut into sections and from which all internal organs, head, fins, bones, except intramuscular or lateral bones, and all discoloured flesh have been removed. Canada regulations.

FILLING DENSITY. The percentage figure obtained when the maximum weight of anhydrous ammonia or of liquefied petroleum gas that may be in a container is divided by the water weight capacity of the tank and the result is multiplied by 100; all capacities shall be measured at a liquid temperature of 60°F. *Bulk Storage Regulations*, Canada regulations.

FILLING STATION. Any pump, tank, store, vehicle, place or premises, where or from which gasoline is sold at retail.

FILM. *n.* 1. Photographic film, pre-recorded video tapes, pre-recorded video discs and includes any other object or device on or within which there is recorded, by photographic, electronic or other means, the contents of a motion picture, and from which, by the use of a projector, machine or other appropriate technology, the motion picture may be viewed, exhibited or projected. 2. Motion pictures, still photographs, photographic displays, filmstrips and such other forms of visual presentation as consist primarily of photographs or photographic reproductions. *National Film Act*, R.S.C. 1985, c. N-8, s. 2. 3. A work produced by a technical means that results in a cinematographic effect, regardless of the medium employed. *Cinema Act*, S.Q. 1983, c. 37, s. 1. See ADULT ~; CANADIAN ~; CINEMATOGRAPHIC ~; MINIATURE ~; NATIONAL ~ BOARD; PHOTOGRAPHIC ~; SAFETY ~; SILENT ~ SUBJECT; SOUND ~ SUBJECT; STANDARD ~; TELE~ CANADA; VIDEO~.

FILM ACTIVITY. Any activity relating to the production, distribution, projection or exhibition of films.

FILM DEPOT. Any building or premises in which film is assembled for shipment. *Theatres Act*, R.S.O. 1980, c. 498, s. 1.

FILM DISTRIBUTOR. See ADULT ~.

FILM EXCHANGE. 1. The business of distributing film. 2. A place where film is stored, rented, sold, leased or supplied. See THEATRE ~.

FILM-MAKER. *n.* A person creatively engaged

in film production. *Canadian Film Development Corporation Act*, R.S.C. 1985, c. C-16, s. 2.

FILM PRODUCTION. The creative, artistic and technical process of producing a film. *Canadian Film Development Corporation Act*, R.S.C. 1985, c. C-16, s. 2.

FILM RETAILER. See ADULT ~.

FILM SOCIETY. A nonprofit cultural organization, membership of which is by annual subscription and limited to persons who are not less than 18 years of age and the objects of which are to encourage the appreciation of motion pictures as an art and a medium of information and education by exhibiting motion pictures to members only, and to discuss films exhibited and to provide its members with information respecting motion pictures.

FILM TECHNICIAN. A person engaged in the technical or administrative aspects of film production. *Canadian Film Development Corporation Act*, R.S.C. 1985, c. C-16, s. 2.

FILTER. *n.* Material placed in the useful beam to attenuate preferentially the lower energy radiations. *Radiation Emitting Devices Regulations*, C.R.C., c. 1370, s. 1.

FILUM AQUAE. See AD MEDIUM FILUM AQUAE.

FILUM VIAE. See AD MEDIUM FILUM VIAE.

FINAL. *adj.* Last; conclusive; terminated.

FINAL ACT. A document which summarizes the work of, and any agreements reached at, an international conference.

FINAL DISCHARGE POINT. The point beyond which the operator of a mine exercises no further control over an effluent. *Metal Mining Liquid Effluent Regulations*, C.R.C., c. 819, s. 2.

FINAL ESTIMATE. The estimate of the cost of the work made by the architect and submitted to the client the nearest in time to the calling of tenders. *Architects Act*, R.S.A. 1970, c. 32, s. 2.

FINALITY CLAUSE. A statement in a statute that decisions of a tribunal shall not be subject to review. P.W. Hogg, *Constitutional Law of Canada*, 2d ed. (Toronto: Carswell, 1985) at 162.

FINAL JUDGMENT. Any judgment, rule, order or decision that determines in whole or in part any substantive right of any of the parties in controversy in any judicial proceeding.

FINAL LICENCE. A licence authorizing the diversion, use or storage of water for power purposes, or the transmission and distribution of water-power. *Dominion Water Power Regulations*, C.R.C., c. 1603, s. 2.

FINAL ODDS. The odds calculated after the close of betting on a race. *Race Track Supervision Regulations*, C.R.C., c. 441, s. 2.

FINAL ORDER. 1. An order made when a court has personal jurisdiction over all parties. It is not final in a juridical sense because the original court may vary it. It is called final to contrast it to a provisional order. C.R.B. Dunlop, *Creditor—Debtor Law in Canada*, Second Cumulative Supplement (Toronto: Carswell, 1986) at 226. 2. An order made in a proceeding of which the claimant and respondent had proper notice and in which they had an opportunity to be present or represented and includes (a) the maintenance provisions in a written agreement between a claimant and a respondent where those provisions are enforceable in the state in which the agreement was made as if contained in an order of a court of that state, and (b) a confirmation order made in a reciprocating state. *Reciprocal Enforcement of Maintenance Orders acts*.

FINANCE. See DEPARTMENT OF ~ CANADA.

FINANCE COMMITTEE. The officials who control and manage money held in the Supreme Court of Ontario. G.D. Watson & C. Perkins, eds., *Holmested & Watson: Ontario Civil Procedure* (Toronto: Carswell, 1984) at CJA-41.

FINANCE COMPANY. Includes a corporation whose main or chief business is buying or selling and dealing in mortgages, conditional sales agreements, lien notes, bills or other similar obligations or property, or advancing or lending money and taking as security for the repayment thereof a mortgage of chattels. See SALES ~.

FINANCIAL ASSISTANCE. Includes assistance by way of grant, loan, loan guarantee, the purchase or guarantee of bonds, debentures, notes or other debt obligations, and the purchase or other acquisition of any common or preferred shares or other equity securities. See STUDENT ~.

FINANCIAL ASSURANCE. One or more of (a) cash, in the amount specified in the approval or order, (b) a letter of credit from a bank, in the amount and terms specified in the approval or order, (c) negotiable securities issued or guaranteed by the Government of Ontario or the Government of Canada in the amount specified in the approval or order, (d) a personal bond accompanied by collateral security, each in the form, terms and amount specified in the approval or order, (e) a bond or guarantee company approved under the Guarantee Companies Securities Act, in the form, terms and amount specified in the approval or order, (f) a bond of a guarantor, other than a guarantee company, accompanied by collateral security each in the form, terms and amount specified in the approval or order, (g) an agreement, in the form and terms specified in the approval or order, and (h) an agreement, in the forms and terms prescribed by the regulations. *Environment Enforcement Statute Law Amendment Act*, S.O. 1986, c. 68, s. 7.

FINANCIAL CENTRE. See INTERNATIONAL ~.

FINANCIAL CORPORATION. 1. A corporation that is (a) a loan company within the meaning of the Loan Companies Act, (b) an investment company within the meaning of the Investment Companies Act, or (c) an insurance company within the meaning of the Canadian and British Insurance Companies Act, and that is a resident and does not accept deposits from the public. *Bank Act*, R.S.C. 1985, c. B-1, s. 109. 2. A Canadian corporation, other than a corporation carrying on an insurance business, eighty per cent or more of the assets of which are made up of debt securities and loans receivable. *Bank Act*, R.S.C. 1985, c. B-1, s. 193. See SUBSIDIARY CONTROLLED ~.

FINANCIAL INSTITUTION. 1. The Bank of Canada, the Federal Business Development Bank and any institution incorporated in Canada that accepts deposits of money from its members or the public, and includes a branch, agency or office of any such bank or institution. 2. A corporation that (a) is a bank, (b) is authorized under the laws of Canada or a province to carry on the business of offering its services as a trustee to the public, or (c) is authorized under the laws of Canada or a province to accept deposits from the public and carries on the business of lending money on the security of real estate or investing money in mortgages or hypothecs on real estate. *Income Tax Act*, R.S.C. 1952, c. 148 (as am. S.C. 1986, c. 6, s. 100), s. 190(1). See REGULATED ~; RESTRICTED ~; SPECIFIED ~.

FINANCIAL INTEREST. Includes any interest, direct, indirect or contingent, (i) whether as owner, part owner or owner of an interest, beneficial owner, owner of stock, owner through trusteeship, investment or otherwise, (ii) in management, whether by management agreement, partnership agreement or other agreement of any kind, or (iii) by reason of having loaned or advanced or caused to be loaned or advanced money, money's worth or any thing of value with or without security, but does not include any direct, indirect or contingent interest in the Alberta Brewers' Agents Limited, or any direct,

indirect or contingent interest in the equipment used by a licensee in the business of selling beverages, other than liquor, or any direct, indirect or contingent interest in the supplying of services in connection with that equipment, or any interest in a company incorporated under Part 9 of the Companies Act or in a railway company not operating solely within Alberta. *Liquor Control Act*, R.S.A. 1980, c. L-17, s. 68.

FINANCIAL INTERMEDIARY. Includes a bank, trust company, loan company, insurance company, investment company and a body corporate carrying on business as a securities broker, dealer or underwriter. *Canada Business Corporations Regulations*, C.R.C., c. 426, s. 57.

FINANCIAL INTERMEDIARY CORPORATION. A corporation that is (a) a corporation described in clause 146(1)(j)(ii)(B), (b) an investment corporation, (c) a mortgage investment corporation, (d) a mutual fund corporation, (e) a prescribed venture capital corporation, or (f) a prescribed labour-sponsored venture capital corporation, but does not include (g) a prescribed corporation, (h) a corporation that is controlled by or for the benefit of one or more corporations (each of which is referred to in this subsection as a "controlling corporation") other than financial intermediary corporations or private holding corporations unless the controlling corporations and specified persons (within the meaning assigned by paragraph (h) of the definition "taxable preferred share" in subsection 248(1)) in relation to the controlling corporations do not own in aggregate shares of the capital stock of the corporation having a fair market value of more than 10% of the fair market value of all of the issued and outstanding shares of the capital stock of the corporation (such fair market values being determined without regard to any voting rights attaching to such shares), or (i) any particular corporation in which another corporation (other than a financial intermediary corporation or a private holding corporation) has a substantial interest unless the other corporation and specified persons (within the meaning assigned by paragraph (h) of the definition "taxable preferred share" in subsection 248(1)) in relation to the other corporation do not own in aggregate shares of the capital stock of the particular corporation having a fair market value of more than 10% of the fair market value of all of the issued and outstanding shares of the capital stock of the particular corporation (such fair market values being determined without regard to any voting rights attaching to such shares). *Income Tax Act*, R.S.C. 1952, c. 148 (as am. S.C. 1988, c. 55, c. 159(1)), s. 191(1).

FINANCIAL LEASE. A credit device which

permits the lessee to have rights and obligations of ownership, while the lessor continues to be the technical owner. I.F.G. Baxter, *The Law of Banking*, 3d ed. (Toronto: Carswell, 1981) at 187.

FINANCIAL LOSS. The loss experienced by a landlord whose total costs that have been or will be experienced and that are allowed in an application made under this Act in respect of a residential complex for an annual accounting period exceed the revenue for the same period. *Residential Rent Regulation Act*, S.O. 1986, c. 63, s. 1.

FINANCIAL RESOURCES. With the exception of the exemptions specified in the regulations, any one or more of the following things: (i) All the real and personal property of an applicant, a recipient or a dependant of the applicant or recipient, including the net income from any such property, (ii) allowances, pensions, insurance benefits, and income from business farming or any other source received by an applicant, recipient or a dependant of the applicant or recipient, (iii) gifts and gratuities whether in cash or in kind received by an applicant, recipient or a dependent of the applicant or recipient on a one time basis or otherwise, (iv) the value attributed by the director to free shelter, free board and free lodging, received by an applicant, recipient or a dependant of the applicant or recipient. *Social Allowances Act*, S.M. 1980, c. 37, s. 1.

FINANCIAL RESPONSIBILITY. See PROOF OF ~.

FINANCIAL STATEMENT. A summary of financial condition of a business or organization, usually a balance sheet and statement of profit and loss.

FINANCIAL SUPPORT ORDER. An order or judgment for maintenance, alimony or support, including an order or judgment for arrears of payments, made pursuant to the Divorce Act, or pursuant to the law of a province relating to family financial support.

FINANCIAL YEAR. The year in respect of which the accounts of the company or of the business are made up.

FINANCING. See BRIDGE ~; PERMANENT ~.

FINDER. *n.* A person who restrains a stray. *The Stray Animals Act*, R.S.S. 1978, c. S-60, s. 2.

FINDING. *n.* The conclusion drawn after an inquiry of fact.

FINDING OF GUILT. The plea of guilty by a defendant to an offence or the finding that a defendant is guilty of an offence made before or by a court that makes an order directing that the defendant be discharged for the offence either absolutely or on the conditions prescribed in a probation order, where (a) the order directing the discharge is not subject to further appeal; or (b) no appeal is taken in respect of the order directing the discharge. *Evidence acts.*

FINDINGS. *n.* Any textile fibre products that (a) have been added to a consumer textile article for a functional purpose other than filling, stuffing or providing warmth, whether or not they also serve a decorative purpose, (b) differ in textile fibre content from the article to which they have been added, and (c) do not constitute a part of the outer surface of the article to which they have been added unless they are incorporated at or along an edge thereof, and without limiting the generality of the foregoing, includes (d) belting, binding, tape, stiffening, facing, interfacing, thread, buttons, slide fasteners, hook and loop pile fasteners, garters, gussets, leg and wrist bands, waist bands and concealed pockets, (e) any lining (other than a laminated or bonded lining), interlining or padding incorporated primarily for structural purposes and not for warmth, and (f) any padding affixed to the underside of floor coverings. *Textile Labelling and Advertising Regulations*, C.R.C., c. 1551, s. 25.

FINE. *n.* 1. A pecuniary penalty or other sum of money. *Criminal Code*. 2. A sum of money ordered to be paid to the Crown by an offender, as a punishment for the offence.

FINE. *adj.* Of very smooth texture and generally inconspicuous. *Fresh Fruit and Vegetable Regulations*, C.R.C., c. 285, s. 13.

FINE FORCE. One does something de fine force when one is compelled and it is absolutely necessary.

FINE MATERIAL. That portion of aggregate material that will pass through a number 200 sieve as designated in the American Society of Testing Materials publication number ASTM-E-11-61. *Environmental Protection Act*, R.R.O. 1980, Reg. 297, s. 1.

FINENESS. *n.* In respect of any substance, means the percentage of that substance passing through a sieve containing 10,000 openings of equal size to the square inch, the openings of which are square and are each 149 microns in width. *Fertilizers Regulations*, C.R.C., c. 666, s. 2.

FINE SAND. A soil consisting of particles passing a No. 40 sieve but retained on a No. 200 sieve. *Building Code Act*, R.R.O. 1980, Reg. 87, s. 4.2.1.4.

FINFISH. *n.* Any of several species of fish having fins. *Fishery regulations.*

FINGERPRINT. *n.* The pattern in the skin on the finger tips, used to identify people.

FINGERPRINT EXAMINER. A person designated as such for the purposes of this section by the Solicitor General of Canada. *Criminal Code*, R.S.C. 1985, c. C-46, s. 667(5).

FINIS FINEM LITIBUS IMPONIT. [L.] A fine puts an end to an action.

FINISHED PRODUCT. The net quantity of saleable material produced by a plant. *Meat and Poultry Products Plant Liquid Effluent Regulations*, C.R.C., c. 818, s. 2.

FINIS REI ATTENDENDUS EST. [L.] One must bear in mind the awaited outcome.

FINIS UNIUS DIEI EST PRINCIPIUM ALTERIUS. [L.] The end of one day is the start of another.

FINITIO. *n.* [L.] Death.

FIN WHALE. Any whale known by the name of common finback, common rorqual, finback, finner, fin whale, herring whale, razorback, or true fin whale. *Whaling Convention Act*, R.S.C. 1970, c. W-8, Schedule, s. 18.

FIRE. See FOREST ~ AREA; STANDARD ~ TEST.

FIRE ALARM SIGNAL. An audible alarm or sound which is capable of notifying the occupants of the hotel. *Hotel Fire Safety Act*, R.R.O. 1980, Reg. 505, s. 2.

FIRE ALARM SIGNALLING DEVICE. A sounding device that emits the fire alarm signal. *Hotel Fire Safety Act*, R.R.O. 1980, Reg. 505, s. 2.

FIRE AND CASUALTY CORPORATION. A corporation incorporated under the laws of Canada or any province of Canada to undertake contracts of insurance other than contracts of life insurance.

FIREARM. *var.* FIRE-ARM. *n.* 1. Any barrelled weapon from which any shot, bullet or other missile can be discharged and that is capable of causing serious bodily injury or death to a person, and includes any frame or receiver of such a barrelled weapon and anything that can be adapted for use as a firearm. *Criminal Code*, R.S.C. 1985, c. C-46, s. 84. 2. Includes a device that propels a projectile by means of an explosion, compressed gas or spring and includes a rifle, shotgun, handgun or spring gun. 3. Crossbow or longbow. See ANTIQUE ~; AUTOMATIC ~; LOADED ~; LOCAL REGISTRAR OF ~S; SEALED ~.

FIREARMS ACQUISITION CERTIFICATE. A firearms acquisition certificate issued by a firearms officer under section 106 or a hunting licence, certificate, permit or other document issued under the authority of a law of a province that, by virtue of an order issued under section 107, is deemed to be a firearms acquisition certificate. *Criminal Code*, R.S.C. 1985, c. C-46, s. 84.

FIREARMS OFFICER. Any person who has been designated in writing as a firearms officer by the Commissioner or the Attorney General of a province or who is a member of a class of persons that has been so designated. *Criminal Code*, R.S.C. 1985, c. C-46, s. 84.

FIRE CHIEF. The person in charge of a fire department or fire brigade.

FIRE CODE. Safety standards for buildings and premises designed to prevent the outbreak of fire and to insure that emergency facilities and procedures to deal promptly with fires are available. D. Robertson, *Ontario Health and Safety Guide* (Toronto: Richard De Boo Ltd., 1988) at 5-165.

FIRE COMMISSIONER. A person appointed as a Fire Commissioner pursuant to a provincial statute. *Canada Fire Safety Regulations*, C.R.C., c. 1000, s. 2. See DOMINION ~.

FIRE COMPARTMENT. An enclosed space in a building that is separated from all parts of the building by enclosing construction providing a fire separation having a required fire-resistance rating. *Building Code Act*, R.R.O. 1980, Reg. 87, s. 1.

FIRE CONTROL AUTHORITY. An official of a government forestry service or other fire control agency responsible for the fire protection of persons and property including Crown lands. *Forest Fire Control Operations Order*, C.R.C., c. 13, s. 2.

FIRE DAMPER. 1. A closure which consists of a normally held open damper installed in an air distribution system or in a wall or floor assembly, and designed to close automatically in the event of fire in order to maintain the integrity of the fire separation. *Building Code Act*, R.R.O. 1980, Reg. 87, s. 1. 2. A blade or damper arranged to interrupt air flow through part of an air handling system, so as to restrict the passage of heat and smoke. *Hotel Fire Safety Act*, R.R.O. 1980, Reg. 505, s. 2.

FIRE DEPARTMENT. 1. Includes fire brigade. *Fire Services Act*, R.S.B.C. 1979, c. 133, s. 1. 2. A fire department organized under the Municipal Act and equipped with one or more motorized fire pumpers meeting the prescribed standards. *Fire Departments Act*, R.S.O. 1980, s. 164, s. 1. See PAID ~.

FIRE DEPARTMENT EQUIPMENT. Includes all fire hydrants, nozzles, hose, adapters, couplings, attachments and appliances ordinarily used by a fire department. *Standard Hose Coupling Act*, R.S.N.S. 1967, c. 288, s. 1.

FIRE DEPARTMENT VEHICLE. Includes an emergency crash extrication vehicle owned and operated by a rescue organization approved by the Minister in writing for the purposes of this Part. *Highway Traffic Act*, R.S.O. 1980, c. 198, s. 43.

FIRE DOOR. *var.* **FIRE-DOOR.** A solid steel or hollow-steel or steel-clad door and frame or combination thereof or other approved door and frame that is self-closing and in which wired glass panels are permitted, and i. a door in which the area of any individual panel of wired glass does not exceed 1,296 square inches and has a 3/4-hour fire resistance rating, and ii. a door in which the total area of any wired glass does not exceed 100 square inches and has a 1 1/2-hour fire resistance rating. *Hotel Fire Safety Act*, R.R.O. 1980, Reg. 505, s. 2. See APPROVED ~.

FIRED STEAM BOILER. A pressure vessel in which steam is generated by the application of heat resulting from the combustion of fuel in a solid, liquid or gaseous form. *Boilers and Pressure Vessels acts*.

FIRED VESSEL. A vessel that is directly heated by (a) a flame or the hot gases of combustion, (b) electricity, (c) rays from a radioactive source, or (d) molecular agitation arising from the process of fission. *Boilers and Pressure Vessels Act*, R.S.O. 1980, c. 46, s. 1.

FIRE EXTINGUISHER. An appliance, container or apparatus containing any liquid, powder or gas, whether under pressure or not and designed, or purporting to be designed, for the purpose of extinguishing fire in its incipient stage.

FIRE EXTINGUISHER RATING. The rating of an extinguisher for extinguishing capacity and class of fire.

FIRE-EXTINGUISHING EQUIPMENT. A fire hose, an extinguisher or other similar equipment used to fight a fire. *Occupational Health and Safety Act*, R.R.O. 1980, Reg. 694, s. 1.

FIRE FIGHTER. Any person who served during World War II as a member of the Corps of (Civilian) Canadian Fire Fighters for Service in the United Kingdom, who was on service while in receipt of pay and allowances as a fire fighter outside the continents of North and South America, the islands adjacent thereto and the territorial waters thereof, including service in Greenland, Iceland or the Aleutian Islands but not including service in Newfoundland, Bermuda or the West Indies. *Memorial Cross Order (World War II)*, C.R.C., c. 1623, s. 2. See FULL-TIME ~; VOLUNTEER ~.

FIREFIGHTERS. *var.* **FIRE FIGHTERS.** 1. A trade union certified for a unit in which the majority of employees has as its principal duties the fighting of fires and the carrying out of rescue operations. *Essential Service Disputes Act*, R.S.B.C. 1979, c. 113, s. 1. 2. The persons, including officers and technicians, employed by a municipality and assigned exclusively to fire protection and fire prevention duties (which may include the performance of ambulance or rescue services). *Firefighters and Policemen Labour Relations Act*, R.S.A. 1980, c. F-11, s. 1.

FIRE FIGHTING. Includes controlling and extinguishing a fire. *Prairie and Forest Fires Act*, S.S. 1982-83, c. P-22.1, s. 2.

FIRE GUARDIAN. Includes (i) the provincial forester, fire control officers, foresters, regional directors, regional supervisors, and all conservation officers, engineering aids and technicians employed in the department; (ii) all regional park supervisors and conservation officers employed in the Parks Branch of The Department of Tourism and Recreation; (iii) persons appointed or designated under section 13 as temporary fire wardens, fire guardians or honorary fire guardians; and (iv) officers and constables of the Royal Canadian Mounted Police. *Fires Prevention Act*, R.S.M. 1970, c. F80, s. 2.

FIRE HAZARD. A condition that will cause a fire to start or a condition that will increase the extent or severity of the fire. *Fire Prevention Act*, S.N.S. 1976, c. 9, s. 2.

FIRE HAZARD AREA. i. An area where a fire hazard may be created by smoking, matches or other means of producing heat or fire and which has been designated as such by the supervisor in charge of the mine, or ii. a storage area where oil, grease or flammable liquids are stored in excess of 500 litres. *Occupational Health and Safety Act*, R.R.O. 1980, Reg. 694, s. 1.

FIRE HAZARD CLASSIFICATION. The flame spread, fuel contributed and smoke developed rating assigned to a material from an approved test of a representative specimen conducted by, i. The National Research Council of Canada, ii. Underwriters' Laboratories of Canada, or iii. any other approved testing laboratory. *Hotel Fire Safety Act*, R.R.O. 1980, Reg. 505, s. 2.

FIRE INSURANCE. 1. Insurance, not being insurance incidental to some other class of insurance defined by or under this Act, against loss of or damage to property through fire, lightning or explosion due to ignition. *Insurance acts.* 2. Insurance against the loss of, or damage to, property caused by fire, lighting, explosion due to ignition, smoke, and the breakage of or the leakage from a sprinkler or other fire protection equipment or system. *Classes of Insurance Regulations*, C.R.C., c. 977, s. 15. See BUSINESS OF ~ IN THE PROVINCE.

FIRE LOAD. The combustible contents of a room or floor area expressed in terms of the average weight of combustible materials per square foot, and includes the furnishings, finished floor, wall and ceiling finishes, trim and temporary and movable partitions. *Building Code Act*, R.R.O. 1980, Reg. 87, s. 1.

FIRE MARSHAL. A person appointed as Fire Marshal pursuant to a provincial statute. *Canada Fire Safety Regulations*, C.R.C., c. 1000, s. 2.

FIRE PREVENTION. Includes fire inspections, determination of the cause of fire, measures for prevention of the spread of fire, fire protection and alarm systems, watchman's fire prevention services, minimization of damage subsequent to fire and protection of life. *Government Property Fire Prevention Regulations*, C.R.C., c. 704, s. 2. See NATIONAL ~ ASSOCIATION.

FIRE PREVENTION SERVICE. Includes the provision of a fire prevention, detection, control or suppression service that may be required by a department or agency of the government of Saskatchewan, or another province or of Canada. *Department of Revenue, Supply and Services Amendment Act, 1982 (No. 2)*, S.S. 1982-83, c. 31, s. 3.

FIREPROOF. *adj.* Composed, constructed or made of fire resistant or incombustible materials. *Petroleum Products Act*, R.S.N.W.T. 1974, c. P-5, s. 2.

FIRE PROTECTION. 1. Activities concerned with the prevention, detection and extinguishment, of fires in portions of the province that are not in an urban area; and includes the prevention of fire occurrence and of the spread of fire on lands not in an urban area where human life, property, protective vegetation, forage, or wild life, is endangered by the fire. *Fires Prevention Act*, R.S.M. 1970, c. F-80, s. 2. 2. All aspects of fire safety including fire prevention, suppression, investigation, public education and information and training and advising. *Fire Prevention Act*, S.A. 1982, c. F-10.1, s. 1.

FIRE PROTECTION INSTALLER. See SPRINKLER AND ~.

FIRE-PROTECTION RATING. The time in hours or fraction thereof that a closure, window assembly or glass block assembly will withstand the passage of flame when exposed to fire under specified conditions of test and performance criteria or as otherwise prescribed in this Regulation. *Building Code Act*, R.R.O. 1980, Reg. 87, s. 1.

FIRE RESISTANCE. The property of a material or assembly to withstand fire or give protection from it and when it is applied to elements or buildings, it is characterized by the ability to confine a fire or to continue to perform a given structural function, or both.

FIRE RESISTANCE RATING. *var.* **FIRE-RESISTANCE RATING.** 1. The rating assigned after a testing of the time of fire resistance of a representative specimen conducted by The National Research Council of Canada, Underwriters' Laboratories of Canada or any other approved testing laboratory. 2. The rating in hours or fraction thereof that a material or assembly of materials will withstand the passage of flame and the transmission of heat when exposed to fire.

FIRE RESISTING. As applied to buildings means constructed of masonry, reinforced concrete, or equivalent materials in accordance with the requirements of the fire underwriters. *Power Corporation Act*, R.R.O. 1980, Reg. 794, s. 0.

FIRE RESISTIVE CONSTRUCTION. Having structural parts, in so far as walls, floors and partitions are concerned, constructed wholly of non-flammable materials, but structural parts do not include (a) any roof structure not forming in whole or in part the walls or ceiling of any room or rooms, (b) finished floors, (c) doors, door-frames and trim, (d) windows, window-frames and trim, or (e) base, handrails, mouldings, grounds and the like. *Hotels Act*, R.S.N.B. 1973, c. H-10, s. 1.

FIRE-RETARDANT TREATED WOOD. Wood or a wood product that has its surface-burning characteristics such as flame spread, rate of fuel contribution and density of smoke developed, reduced by impregnation with fire-retardant chemicals. *Building Code Act*, R.R.O. 1980, Reg. 87, s. 1.

FIRE SEASON. The period in each year when a permit to burn is required before a fire may be set.

FIRE SEPARATION. 1. A barrier against the spread of fire and smoke. 2. A construction assembly that acts as a barrier against the spread of fire and that may or may not have a fire-resistance rating or a fire-protection rating.

FIRE SERVICES PERSONNEL. Persons regularly employed by a municipal fire department, appointed as auxiliary members of a fire department, or acting voluntarily as fire fighters. *Fire Services Act*, R.S.B.C. 1979, c. 133, s. 1.

FIRE STOP. A draft-tight barrier within or between construction assemblies that acts to retard the passage of smoke and flame. *Building Code Act*, R.R.O. 1980, Reg. 87, s. 1.

FIRE STOP FLAP. A device intended for use in horizontal assemblies required to have a fire-resistance rating and incorporating protective ceiling membranes, which operates to close off a duct opening through the membrane in the event of a fire. *Building Code Act*, R.R.O. 1980, Reg. 87, s. 1.

FIRE SUPPRESSION SYSTEM. An installation for the specific purpose of controlling a fire in a particular place. *Occupational Health and Safety Act*, R.R.O. 1980, Reg. 694, s. 1.

FIREWALL. *var.* **FIRE WALL.** A type of fire separation of non-combustible construction that subdivides a building or separates adjoining buildings to resist the spread of fire and that has a fire-resistance rating prescribed in the Building Code and has structural stability to remain intact under fire conditions for the fire-resistance time for which it is rated. Ontario statutes.

FIRE WARDEN. A person who is an employee of a provincial government and whose duties include preventing and extinguishing forest fires. *National Parks Fire Protection Regulations*, C.R.C., c. 1119, s. 2.

FIREWORKS. *n.* 1. Include cannon crackers, fireballs, fire crackers, mines, Roman candles, sky rockets, squibs, torpedoes and any other explosive designated as a firework by regulation. 2. Includes fireworks composition and manufactured fireworks. *Explosives Regulations*, C.R.C., c. 599, s. 2. See HIGH HAZARD ~; LOW HAZARD ~; MANUFACTURED ~.

FIREWORKS COMPOSITION. Any chemical compound or mechanically mixed preparation of an explosive or inflammable nature that is used for the purpose of making any manufactured fireworks and is not included in any other class of explosives, and includes any star or coloured fire composition that is not manufactured fireworks. *Explosives Regulations*, C.R.C., c. 599, s. 2.

FIRING CHAMBER. The part of a firearm in which a cartridge rests in the position from which it can be fired. F.A. Jaffe, *A Guide to Pathological Evidence*, 2d ed. (Toronto: Carswell, 1983) at 176.

FIRING PIN. A device to strike and thus ignite the primer in a cartridge. F.A. Jaffe, *A Guide to Pathological Evidence*, 2d ed. (Toronto: Carswell, 1983) at 176.

FIRM. *n.* 1. (i) A person who is sole proprietor of a business carried on under a registered business name, or (ii) the persons who are associated as partners in a business carried on by the partnership under a registered business name. 2. A sole practitioner or proprietorship, a partnership or a corporation. *Certified General Accountants Act*, S.N.B. 1986, c. 86, s. 2. See ARCHITECTS ~; BROADCASTING ~; CABLECASTING ~; COMMISSION ~; ENGINEERS ~; JOINT ~; SUPPLY ~.

FIRM. *adj.* 1. Not soft, puffy, shrivelled or water soaked. 2. Not soft, flabby or shrivelled.

FIRMA. *n.* [L.] Provisions; rent.

FIRM ENERGY. Electric energy intended to be available at all times during a period covered by an agreement respecting the sale thereof. *National Energy Board Part VI Regulations*, C.R.C., c. 1056, s. 2.

FIRMIOR ET POTENTIOR EST OPERATIO LEGIS QUAM DISPOSITIO HOMINIS. [L.] The operation of law is stronger and more powerful than a human arrangement.

FIRM NAME. The name under which a business is carried on.

FIRM OF ACCOUNTANTS. A partnership, the members of which are accountants engaged in the practice of accounting, or a corporation incorporated under the laws of a province that is engaged in the practice of accounting. *Bank Act*, R.S.C. 1985, c. B-1, s. 236.

FIRM POWER. Electric power or power-production capacity intended to be available at all times during a period covered by an agreement respecting the sale thereof. *National Energy Board Part VI Regulations*, C.R.C., c. 1056, s. 2.

FIRM PRICE CONTRACT. A contract that sets the total amount payable thereunder or pursuant to which the total amount payable is the product obtained by multiplying the number of identical units of work performed or identical items delivered by a predetermined fixed price for each unit or item. *Government Contracts Regulations*, C.R.C., c. 701, s. 2.

FIRM RIPE. That stage of the ripening process of an apple when the flesh is crisp and does not yield to slight pressure. *Fresh Fruit and Vegetable Regulations*, C.R.C., c. 285, s. 1.

FIRM-RIPE. *adj.* That (a) the field tomato shows from 75 per cent to 100 per cent pink or red colour, and (b) not more than 10 per cent of the field tomatoes by count are semi-ripe. *Fresh Fruit and Vegetable Regulations*, C.R.C., c. 285, s. 1.

FIRST. *adj.* When used with reference to the connection of a fixture to a horizontal branch, means nearest to the waste stack or soil stack. *Ontario Water Resources Act*, R.R.O. 1980, Reg. 736, s. 1.

FIRST ADMISSION. Acceptance of a person who has no record of previous such care into a psychiatric inpatient facility.

FIRST-AID. *n.* Emergency or other treatment or care that conforms with the recommended practice of the St. John Ambulance Association and is provided by an employer for any injury or illness of an employee arising from his work. Canada regulations.

FIRST-AID ATTENDANT. A qualified person appointed by an employer to administer first-aid. *Canada First-Aid Regulations*, C.R.C., c. 1001, s. 2.

FIRST AID CERTIFICATE. A certificate of proficiency in first aid issued by the St. John's Ambulance Brigade, the Red Cross Society, the Knights of Malta or any other approved body. *Certification of Lifeboat Men Regulations*, C.R.C., c. 1412, s. 2.

FIRST-AID ROOM. A room provided by an employer to be used exclusively for first-aid or medical purposes. *Canada First-Aid Regulations*, C.R.C., c. 1001, s. 2.

FIRST-AID STATION. A place other than a first-aid room where first-aid supplies, instruments or equipment are stored for use. *Canada First-Aid Regulations*, C.R.C., c. 1001, s. 2.

FIRST CLASS MAIL. 1. Mail, any item of which is not greater than 66 pounds in weight, that is (a) a letter, postcard or similar communication wholly or partly typewritten or handwritten, (b) a receipt, an invoice or a similar statement relating to a specified sum of money and sent by post to a specified person, or (c) mail sent by post at the discretion of the sender at a rate of postage set out in these Regulations. *Domestic First Class Mail Regulations*, C.R.C., c. 1278, s. 2. 2. (a) Letters, postcards, aerogrammes and other similar communications wholly or partly in handwriting or typewriting, (b) receipts, invoices, and other similar statements relating to specified sums of money and directed to specified persons, or (c) any other items of mail that are, by choice of the sender, prepaid at the rate of postage set out in these Regulations. *International First Class Mail Regulations*, C.R.C., c. 1280, s. 2.

FIRST CONVICTION. The earliest conviction within a period of five years preceding the date of the latest conviction. *Vehicles Amendment Act, 1981*, S.S. 1980-81, s. 94, s. 7.

FIRST CO-PILOT. A co-pilot assigned to duty as second-in-command of an aircraft during flight time. *Pilot Licence Privileges Order*, C.R.C., c. 54, s. 2.

FIRST DEALER. A person who sells under his own name or labels meat products prepared by some other person. Canada regulations.

FIRST DEGREE MURDER. 1. Murder when it is planned and deliberate. *Criminal Code*, R.S.C. 1985, c. C-46, s. 231. 2. Irrespective of whether it is planned and deliberate (a) when the victim is a police officer or one of other named officials. *Criminal Code*, R.S.C. 1985, c. C-46, s. 231. 3. When death is caused while committing or attempting to commit hijacking an aircraft, sexual assault, sexual assault with a weapon, threats to a third party or causing bodily harm, aggravated sexual assault, kidnapping and forcible confinement, or hostage taking. *Criminal Code*, R.S.C. 1985, c. C-46, s. 231.

FIRST ELECTION. 1. An election held under this Act for the purpose of taking a vote as to the formation of an irrigation district and, when necessary, electing the first board. *The Irrigation Districts Act*, R.S.S. 1978, c. I-15, s. 2. 2. An election held for the purpose of taking a vote on the formation of a district. *Drainage Districts Act*, R.S.A. 1980, c. D-39, s. 1.

FIRST FLOOR. The first floor above the basement and where no basement exists means the lowest floor of the building. *Hotels Act*, R.S.N.B. 1973, c. H-10, s. 1.

FIRST FRUITS. A term from feudal times for one year's profits of land after a tenant's death, which profits belonged to the monarch.

FIRST IMPRESSION. Describes a case which presents a new question of law for which there is no precedent.

FIRST IN, FIRST OUT. See FIFO.

FIRST INSPECTION. Inspection of a ship during construction and includes the initial inspection of a ship transferred from registry elsewhere than in Canada to Canadian registry. *Hull Inspection Regulations*, C.R.C., c. 1431, s. 2.

FIRST INSTANCE. See COURT OF ~.

FIRST ISSUE OF STOCK. All stock subscribed for and allotted prior to the first meeting of shareholders of the company for organization and election of directors, and upon which at least ten per cent has been paid. *Railway Act*, R.S.Q. 1977, c. C-14, s. 6.

FIRST MINISTERS' CONFERENCE. A federal-provincial conference of the federal Prime Minister and the provincial Premiers. P.W. Hogg, *Constitutional Law of Canada*, 2d ed. (Toronto: Carswell, 1985) at 107.

FIRST MORTGAGE. A mortgage which has priority over all other similar mortgages against the same land.

FIRST MORTGAGE BOND. A corporate obligation secured by a first mortgage on real estate. H. Sutherland, D.B. Horsley & J.M. Edmiston, eds., *Fraser's Handbook on Canadian Company Law*, 7th ed. (Toronto: Carswell, 1985) at 310.

FIRST OFFENDER. One who was convicted for the first time.

FIRST OPEN WATER. Describes water immediately after ice breaks up so that navigation is possible.

FIRST-PARTY INSURANCE. Insurance which indemnifies the insured without reference to fault. John G. Fleming, *The Law of Torts*, 6th ed. (Sydney: The Law Book Company Limited, 1983) at 365.

FIRST PROCESSING. The first change in the form of materials such as agricultural products.

FIRST READING. A purely formal stage of parliamentary deliberation decided without amendment or debate, coupled with an order to print the bill. A. Fraser, G.A. Birch & W.A. Dawson, eds., *Beauchesne's Rules and Forms of the House of Commons of Canada*, 5th ed. (Toronto: Carswell, 1978) at 220.

FIRST STOREY. The storey with its floor closest to grade and having its ceiling more than 6 ft. above grade. *Building Code Act*, R.R.O. 1980, Reg. 87, s. 1.

FIRST TITLE. The title of a volume of natural gas that arises by reason of the fact that the natural gas becomes a chattel. *Natural Gas Price Act*, S.B.C. 1985, c. 53, s. 1.

FISCAL. *adj.* Relating to revenue.

FISCAL AGENT. A fiscal agent appointed under Part IV and includes the Bank of Canada. *Financial Administration Act*, R.S.C. 1985, c. F-11, s. 2.

FISCAL CAPACITY. The capacity of a province to raise taxes. P.W. Hogg, *Constitutional Law of Canada*, 2d ed. (Toronto: Carswell, 1985) at 118.

FISCAL LAW. This act, the Act to promote industrial development by means of fiscal advantages (chapter D-9), the Act respecting the payment of allowances to certain self-employed workers (chapter P-1), or any act imposing duties, the administration of which is entrusted to the Minister. *Ministère du Revenu Act*, R.S.Q. 1977, c. M-31, s. 1.

FISCAL PERIOD. The period for which the accounts of the business of the taxpayer have been ordinarily made up and accepted for purposes of assessment under the Income Tax Act.

FISCAL YEAR. 1. When used to mean the fiscal year of the government means the period from April 1 in one year to March 31 in the next year. 2. The period for which the business accounts of a corporation or a business of a taxpayer are made up and accepted for the purposes of the Income Tax Act. See PREVIOUS ~.

FISH. *v.* 1. To catch or take or attempt to catch or take fish by any method. 2. To angle.

FISH. *n.* 1. (a) Portions of fish, (b) shellfish, crustaceans, marine animals, marine plants and portions thereof, (c) the eggs, spawn, larvae, spat and juvenile stages of fish, shellfish, crustaceans and marine animals, and (d) such fish products and by-products as are prescribed pursuant to section 43. *Fisheries Act*, R.S.C. 1985 (1st Supp.), c. 35, s. 1. 2. Fish of the cod family (Gadidae). *Saltfish Act*, R.S.C. 1985, c. S-4, s. 2. See BAIT ~; BREADED ~; CANNED ~; COARSE ~; COMMERCIAL ~; COMMINUTED ~; CURED ~; DOG~; EXOTIC ~; FIN~; GROUND~; PROCESSING OF ~; SPORT ~; UNCLEAN ~; WATER FREQUENTED BY ~; WILD ~.

FISH ARROW. An arrow with retractable or detachable barbs. *Manitoba Fishery Regulations*, C.R.C., c. 843, s. 2.

FISH-BREEDING PLANT. An establishment in which the commercial production or breeding of fish, amphibians, echinoderms, crustaceans or shellfish or their eggs, sexual products or larvae is carried on for consumption or stocking purposes. *Aquaculture Credit Act*, S.Q. 1984, c. 21, s. 1.

FISH BUSINESS OR ENTERPRISE. Any business or enterprise that includes in its operations (a) the catching, producing, processing, buying, selling, exporting or marketing of fish or fish products; or (b) the manufacture, importation, distribution, purchase or sale of gear, engines, equipment or supplies of any kind used in fishing or in equipping a boat or vessel for fishing activity. *Fishing Industry Advisory Board Act*, S.Nfld. 1977, c. 30, s. 1.

FISH BUYING STATION. (a) A building, structure, machinery, appurtenances, appliances and apparatus; (b) a vehicle; and (c) a vessel, scow, barge or float, within the Province or its coastal waters, with or without installed propulsion machinery, used in the business of buying, collecting, assembling, eviscerating, transporting, conveying, packing or carrying fish direct from a fisherman. *Fisheries Act*, R.S.B.C. 1979, c. 137, s. 12.

FISH COLD STORAGE PLANT. A building, structure, machinery, appurtenances, appliances and apparatus occupied and used in the business of freezing fish or storing frozen fish, either alone or in conjunction with any other business, but excludes (a) a fish buying station as defined in this section; (b) a licensed fishing vessel engaged in fishing, eviscerating and freezing on board the product of its catch, or while delivering that catch; or (c) a building, equipment or plant occupied or used by a person for storing fish for the purpose only of resale by him at retail in the Province. *Fisheries Act*, R.S.B.C. 1979, c. 137, s. 12.

FISH CURING. See BY-PRODUCTS OF ~.

FISH DEALER. A person who, not being the holder of a subsisting commercial fisherman's licence issued pursuant to the Fishery Regulations for the Province of Saskatchewan under the Fisheries Act (Canada), sells or barters fish or offers fish for sale or barter or has in his possession fish for sale or barter, and includes a person who goes from house to house selling or bartering fish or offering fish for sale or barter or soliciting orders for fish for future delivery, but does not include a person who sells or barters fish or offers fish for sale or barter or has in his possession fish for sale or barter by retail sale only. *The Fisheries Act*, R.S.S. 1978, c. F-16, s. 2.

FISHERIES. *n.* 1. The business of catching, harvesting, raising, cultivating and handling of fish directly or indirectly by a fisherman. 2. Any fishery, including the sealfishery, which fishermen regularly carry on as a means of making a livelihood and includes the catching of fish and every other phase of fishery production. See ATLANTIC ~; CANADIAN ~ WATERS; FISHERY.

FISHERIES AND OCEANS. The federal ministry which oversees coastal and inland fisheries, hydrography, marine sciences and small craft harbours.

FISHERIES OF NEWFOUNDLAND. Any fishery, including the sealfishery, which fishermen residing in the province and discharging their fish in ports in the province regularly carry on as a means of making a livelihood and includes the catching of fish and every other phase of fishery production but not the collection of fish or fish products. *Fishing Ships (Bounties) Act*, R.S.Nfld. 1970, c. 137, s. 2.

FISHERIES PRODUCT. Any natural product of the commercial fisheries of Canada designated by the Governor in Council and includes any product derived therefrom, if so designated. *Fisheries Prices Support Act*, R.S.C. 1985, c. F-23, s. 2.

FISHERMAN. *n.* 1. Every person who takes, attempts to take, or assists in taking fish or shellfish from the sea. 2. A person whose business consists in whole or in part of fishing. *Bank Act*, R.S.C. 1985, c. B-1, s. 2. 3. (a) A person who has or intends to acquire a prescribed interest in a fishing vessel or a proprietary share in a fishing vessel, or (b) a person who has a prescribed interest in a weir, or similar fish catching or trapping device, that is affixed to the ground, or a proprietary share in such a weir or similar fish catching or trapping device, and whose principal occupation is participation in a primary fishing enterprise. *Fisheries Improvement Loans Act*, R.S.C. 1985, c. F-22, s. 2. 4. (a) The holder of a commercial fishing licence, (b) a hired hand who derives all or a substantial portion of his income from employment as such on a fishing vessel, (c) a fishing vessel owner who derives all or a substantial portion of his income from the rental of fishing vessels to holders of commercial fishing licences, and (d) a person who derives all or a substantial portion of his income from the handling of fish on shore directly after the landing thereof from fishing vessels, but does not include a person engaged in the processing of fish. *Canada Shipping Act*, R.S.C. 1985, c. S-9, s. 654. See COMMERCIAL ~; YEAR-ROUND ~.

FISHERMAN'S LICENCE. See ZONE ~.

FISHERY. *n.* 1. Includes (a) the places in Canadian fisheries waters where, and the times when, fishing and related activities occur, including such packing, transporting and processing operations as are within the jurisdiction of Parliament, and (b) the person engaged and the fishing vessels, fishing gear and other equipment used in the activities referred to in paragraph (a). *Fisheries Act*, R.S.C. 1985 (1st Supp.), c. 35, s. 1. 2. Includes the area, locality, place or station in or on which a pound, seine, net, weir or other fishing appliance is used, set, placed or located, and the area, tract or stretch of water in or from which fish may be taken by the said pound, seine, net, weir or other fishing appliance, and also the pound, seine, net, weir, or other fishing appliance used in connection therewith. *Fisheries Act*, R.S.C. 1985 (1st Supp.), c. 35, s. 5. See FISHERIES.

FISHERY ENTERPRISE. Any person that is engaged directly or indirectly in, or controls or is controlled by a person that is engaged directly or indirectly in, the Atlantic Fisheries. *Atlantic Fisheries Restructuring Act*, R.S.C. 1985, c. A-14, s. 2.

FISHERY GUARDIAN. A person appointed as a fishery guardian pursuant to subsection 5(3). *Fisheries Act*, R.S.C. 1985, c. F-14, s. 2.

FISHERY LEASE. A lease conferring for a term therein mentioned, upon the lessee therein named, the right to take and keep, for the purpose of fishing, under and subject to the provisions of this Act and of all regulations made hereunder, the exclusive or other possession of any Crown lands therein described, with the exclusive or other right to fish in any waters flowing over or covering the same, at such time, and in such manner, and with such restrictions, and subject to such regulations as may be permitted, regulated or prescribed by any lawful authority in that behalf. *Fisheries Act*, R.S.N.B. 1973, c. F-15, s. 1.

FISHERY OFFICER. A person appointed as a fishery officer pursuant to subsection 5(1) or designated as a fishery officer pursuant to subsection 5(5). *Fisheries Act*, R.S.C. 1985, c. F-14, s. 2.

FISHERY PRODUCTS. Includes any fishery resources and any products derived from fishery resources. *Fisheries Development Act*, R.S.C. 1985, c. F-21, s. 2.

FISHERY RESOURCES. 1. Includes fish, molluscs, crustaceans, marine mammals and marine plants. *Fisheries Development Act*, R.S.C. 1985, c. F-21, s. 2. 2. Includes all vertebrate and invertebrate animals and all plants which spend all or part of their life in the aquatic and marine environment. *Fisheries Act*, S.N.S. 1977, c. 9, s. 2.

FISH HABITAT. Spawning grounds and nursery, rearing, food supply and migration areas on which fish depend directly or indirectly in order to carry out their life processes. *Fisheries Act*, R.S.C. 1985, c. F-14, s. 34.

FISHING. *n.* 1. Fishing for, catching or attempting to catch fish by any method. *Fisheries Act*, R.S.C. 1985, c. F-14, s. 2. 2. Includes fishing for or catching shellfish, crustaceans and marine animals but does not include an office or employment under a person engaged in the business of fishing. *Income Tax Act*, R.S.C. 1952, c. 148 (as am. S.C. 1970-71-72, c. 63), c. 248(1). See BOW ~; COMMERCIAL ~; DOMESTIC ~; FAMILY ~ CORPORATION; FLY ~; FOOD ~; ICE ~; LAWFULLY ~; RECREATIONAL ~; SKIN-DIVING ~; SPORT ~; VESSEL ENGAGED IN ~; WINTER ~.

FISHING ASSETS. (i) Cash, trade acounts receivable, supplies and inventory used in the fishing business, (ii) land, buildings, boats, ships, equipment, machinery and nets that are used chiefly in the operation of the fishing business by the corporation, (iii) any right or licence granted or issued under any Act of the Legislature that permits or regulates the catching or sale of fish, and (iv) shares in another family fishing corporation. *Corporations Tax Act*, R.S.O. 1980, c. 97, s. 1.

FISHING BOUNDARY SIGN. (a) In respect of tidal waters, a triangular sign or marker the sides of which are approximately equal and at least 5 feet in length and approximately 5 inches in width, erected by a fishery officer or fishery guardian to designate a fishing limit or other point, and (b) in respect of non-tidal waters, a triangular sign or marker the sides of which are approximately equal and at least 20 inches in length, erected by a conservation officer, fishery officer or fishery guardian to designate a fishing limit or other point. Canada regulations.

FISHING ENTERPRISE. See PRIMARY ~.

FISHING EQUIPMENT. Equipment of a prescribed class or kind used in connection with a primary fishing enterprise but does not include a shore installation. *Fisheries Improvement Loans Act*, R.S.C. 1985, c. F-22, s. 2. See MECHANIZED ~.

FISHING EQUIPMENT AND SUPPLIES. Equipment, apparatus, appliances and supplies for use in the operation of a fishing vessel and not forming part thereof, or for use in fishing, and, without restricting the generality of the foregoing, includes detachable engines and machinery, lines, hooks, trawls, nets, anchors, traps, bait, salt, fuel and stores. *Bank Act*, R.S.C. 1985, c. B-1, s. 2.

FISHING GEAR. Any net, line or other gear used for catching fish. *Fishing Gear Marking Regulations*, C.R.C., c. 813, s. 2.

FISHING INDUSTRY. Includes the catching, harvesting, raising, handling, processing, marketing and distributing of fisheries resources and products and includes aquaculture. *Fisheries Development Act*, S.N.S. 1978, c. 7, s. 2.

FISHING LICENCE. A licence granting for the time therein mentioned to the licensee therein named, upon payment of the licence fee therein stipulated for, the right to fish in any waters flowing over or covering Crown lands therein described or other lands, or in respect of which the Legislature has authority to legislate for the purposes of this Act, at such time and in such manner, and with such restrictions, and subject to such regulations as may be permitted, regulated or prescribed by any lawful authority in that behalf; but no fishing licence shall be deemed to be or be construed to operate as or in the nature of a lease or demise. *Fisheries Act*, R.S.N.B. 1973, s. F-15, s. 1. See DOMESTIC ~; PERSONAL COMMERCIAL ~.

FISHING LODGE. See HUNTING OR ~.

FISHING OPERATION. An operation in which

a vessel is used for (a) the capture of fish or the harvesting of a marine resource for profit, (b) the treatment of fish or a marine resource, (c) the transporting of fish or a marine resource from any fishing apparatus, vessel or collection centre of fish, or (d) the enforcement of any regulation made under the Fisheries Act. *Fishing Vessel Insurance Regulations*, C.R.C., c. 325, s. 2.

FISHING OR RECREATIONAL HARBOUR. (a) Any harbour, wharf, pier, breakwater, slipway, marina or part thereof, together with machinery, works, land and structures related or attached thereto, and (b) any other facility, installation, works or part thereof located on or adjacent to water where accommodation or services are provided principally for fishing or recreational vessels or the occupants thereof. *Fishing and Recreational Harbours Act*, R.S.C. 1985, c. F-24, s. 2.

FISHING POND. A body of water having an area of not more than 10 hectares containing exclusively breeding fish, closed on all sides to hold the fish captive, situated on private property and used for angling. *An Act Respecting the Conservation and Development of Wildlife*, S.Q. 1983, c. 39, s. 1.

FISHING PORTS. Harbours, ports, coves, heads, points, bays, inlets and communities which are used by fishing vessels or in which fishery products are off-loaded or processed and, so as not to limit the generality of the foregoing, as the regulations may prescribe. *Fisheries Act*, S.N.S. 1977, c. 9, s. 2.

FISHING PRESERVE. An artificial or man-made body of water lying wholly within the boundaries of privately-owned land, containing water from surface run-off, natural springs, ground water or water diverted or pumped from a stream or lake but not being composed of natural streams, ponds or lakes or water impounded by the damming of natural streams and in which fish propagated under a licence or fish taken under a commercial fishing licence are released for angling purposes. *Game and Fish Act*, R.S.O. 1980, c. 182, s. 1. See PRIVATE ~; PUBLIC ~.

FISHING SHIP. A ship engaged in deep-sea fishing, sealing or whaling. Canada regulations.

FISHING STATION. A building or place where fish are collected from commercial fishermen. *Manitoba Fishery Regulations*, C.R.C., c. 843, s. 2.

FISHING VESSEL. 1. Includes any ship or boat or any other description of vessel used in or equipped for (a) fishing or processing or transporting fish from fishing grounds, (b) taking,

processing or transporting marine plants, or (c) provisioning, servicing, repairing or maintaining any vessels of a foreign fishing fleet while at sea. 2. A ship that is employed in catching fish, whales, seals, walrus or other living resources of the sea, and that does not carry passengers or cargo. *Canada Shipping Act*, R.S.C. 1985, c. S-9, s. 2. See CANADIAN ~; COMMERCIAL ~; FOREIGN ~; FRENCH ~; HERRING ~; UNITED STATES ~.

FISHING ZONES. The fishing zones of Canada prescribed pursuant to the Territorial Sea and Fishing Zones Act. Canada regulations.

FISH LIVER REDUCTION PLANT. A building, structure, machinery, appurtenances, appliances and apparatus occupied and used in the business of producing fish oil from fish livers. *Fisheries Act*, R.S.B.C. 1979, c. 137, s. 12.

FISH OFFAL REDUCTION PLANT. A building, structure, machinery, appurtenances, appliances and apparatus occupied and used in the business of producing oil, fish meal, fish scrap, chicken feed or fertilizer from fish offal. *Fisheries Act*, R.S.B.C. 1979, c. 137, s. 12.

FISH PLANT. Buildings, structures, machinery, appurtenances, appliances, apparatus and chemicals occupied or used: (i) to prepare, cut or otherwise process any type of salt fish or fishery product for sale whether or not further treated by smoking, cutting or drying and whether or not in barrels, butts, tubs, or other containers and whether or not sold in such containers; (ii) to prepare fish or shellfish for sale by icing, cutting, shucking or any other method or combination of methods and whether or not smoked or otherwise processed; (iii) to freeze fish or shellfish for sale; (iv) to store or handle fish or shellfish or to store or handle fish or shellfish on behalf of any other person; (v) to prepare fertilizer, animal or poultry food, meal, vitamin concentrates or glue by the drying, cooking or other treatment of fish or shellfish; (vi) to prepare fish oils whether such oils are refined or not; but does not include buildings, structures, machinery, appurtenances, appliances, apparatus and chemicals occupied or used by (vii) a fisherman who prepares, stores or handles fish or shellfish caught only by himself; (viii) a person who prepares, stores or handles fish or shellfish for the purpose only of resale by him at retail or for his personal and occasional use. *Fisheries Act*, R.S.N.S. 1967, c. 109, s. 1.

FISH POND. See COMMERCIAL ~; PRIVATE ~; RAINBOW TROUT ~.

FISH PROCESSING PLANT. (a) A building, structure, machinery, appurtenances, appliances and apparatus; and (b) a vessel, scow, barge or float, within coastal waters, with or without installed propulsion machinery, either ashore or afloat, occupied and used in the business of processing fish. *Fisheries Act*, R.S.B.C. 1979, c. 137, s. 12.

FISHWHEEL. *n.* An implement set in a river or stream to catch fish by utilizing the water flow. *Pacific Commercial Salmon Fishery Regulations*, C.R.C., c. 823, s. 2.

FISSIONABLE SUBSTANCE. Any prescribed substance that is, or from which can be obtained, a substance capable of releasing atomic energy by nuclear fission. *Atomic Energy Control Regulations*, C.R.C., c. 365, s. 2.

FITNESS. *n.* The physical and mental condition of an individual that enables that person to function at their best in society.

FITNESS AND AMATEUR SPORT CANADA. The federal ministry with mandate to encourage Canadians to be fit and to participate and excel in amateur sport.

FITTER. *n.* A person who (i) reads and interprets drawings, specifications and bills of material, reference charts and tables, (ii) selects mechanical measuring, checking, layout tools and devices, (iii) assembles metal plates and metal sections to form a complete unit, to the limits of accuracy shown in the shop drawings, connecting components by tack welding or bolting, (iv) performs measuring, checking, layout operations and selects work piece materials and is familiar with the operation of straightening machines and equipment, and (v) safely turns and handles individual pieces or complete assemblies using cranes or other lifting equipment, but does not include a person or class of persons in a limited purpose occupation that, in the opinion of the Director, does not equate with the definition of fitter (structural steel/platework). *Apprenticeship and Tradesmen's Qualification Act*, R.R.O. 1980, Reg. 34, s. 1. See GAS ~.

FITTING. *n.* A safety valve, stop valve, automatic stop-and-check valve, a blow-down valve, reducing valve, water gauge, gauge cock, pressure gauge, injector, test cock, fusible plug, regulating or controlling device, and pipe fittings, attached to or used in connection with a boiler, pressure vessel or plant. See GAS-~.

FITTING-OUT. *n.* The time served on work suitable for the training of an engineer or electrician while preparing the machinery of a ship for operation. *Marine Engineer Examination Regulations*, C.R.C., c. 1443, s. 2.

FIX. *n.* A usually intravenous injection of a narcotic. F.A. Jaffe, *A Guide to Pathological Evidence*, 2d ed. (Toronto: Carswell, 1983) at 176.

FIXED ASSET. Property used in a business which will not be used or converted into cash during the current fiscal year. See NET ~.

FIXED CAPITAL. That which a company retains, in the shape of assets upon which the subscribed capital has been expended, and which assets either themselves produce income, independent of any further action of the company, or being retained by the company are made use of to produce income or gain profits. *Ammonia Soda Company, Ltd. v. Chamberlain*, [1918] 1 Ch. 266.

FIXED CAPITAL REQUIREMENTS. Includes requirements in respect of capital assets such as land, buildings and equipment that may be expected to serve the company, co-operative association or credit union for a period of years. *The Co-operative Guarantee Act*, R.S.S. 1978, c. C-35, s. 2.

FIXED CARGO GEAR. Ships' cranes, winches and other hoisting appliances, derrick booms, derricks and mast bands, goose-necks, eyebolts and all other permanent attachments to any part of a ship used in connection with the processes, also shore cranes and other shore based appliances employed in loading or unloading a ship. *Tackle Regulations*, C.R.C., c. 1494, s. 2.

FIXED CHARGE. A security interest similar to the charge which a typical real property mortgage creates. It is a charge on specific property, contrasted to a floating charge.

FIXED COLLISION BARRIER. A device that (a) consists of (i) a structure with a flat, vertical, unyielding impact surface that is of a size sufficient to ensure that no portion of a vehicle striking the surface projects or passes beyond the surface, and (ii) a horizontal approach surface that does not impede vehicle motion during impact and that is of a size sufficient to ensure that a vehicle will be able to attain a stable attitude during its approach to the impact surface, and (b) does not absorb any significant portion of the kinetic energy of a vehicle striking the impact surface. *Motor Vehicle Safety Regulations*, C.R.C., c. 1038, s. 100.

FIXED COMMERCIAL FISHING UNIT. A salmon trap net, mackerel trap net, sea fish trap net or herring weir that is fixed and is used in commercial fishing. *Atlantic Fishing Registration and Licensing Regulations*, C.R.C., c. 808, s. 2.

FIXED CONVEYANCE. A fixed system or device for conveyance to which this Act applies. *Elevator and Fixed Conveyances Act*, R.S.A. 1980, c. E-7, s. 1.

FIXED COSTS. Costs set as a lump sum without being constrained by tariffs. M.M.

Orkin, *The Law of Costs*, 2d ed. (Aurora: Canada Law Book, 1987) at 2-5.

FIXED DATE. Includes any numbered day, or any Monday, Tuesday, or as the case may be, numbered, alternate or recurring, of a stated month or months. *Insurance acts.*

FIXED DEVICES. Fixed prostheses added to or set in natural teeth. *Dental Act*, R.S.Q. 1977, c. D-3, s. 27.

FIXED PRICE CONTRACT. Contract in which the price is preset regardless of actual cost.

FIXED-SHIFT. *n.* The same working hours set for a period of time.

FIXED SIGNAL. A signal of fixed location indicating a condition affecting the movement of a train or engine. *Regulations No. O-8, Uniform Code of Operating Rules*, C.R.C., c. 1175, Part III, s. 2.

FIXED TERM. See DEFINITE SENTENCE.

FIXED TERM TENANCY AGREEMENT. A tenancy agreement with a predetermined expiry date. *Residential Tenancy Act*, S.B.C. 1984, c. 15, s. 1.

FIXTURE. *n.* 1. Includes machinery, equipment or apparatus that is (a) installed in or attached to a building, structure or land, and (b) used directly in the manufacture, production, processing, storage, handling, packaging, display, transportation, transmission or distribution of tangible personal property or in the provision of a service but does not include machinery, equipment or apparatus installed for the purpose of heating, air conditioning, lifting of passengers or freight, lighting or sewage disposal in a building or structure. *Social Service Tax Amendment Act*, S.B.C. 1981, c. 8, s. 1. 2. A receptacle or equipment that receives water, liquids or sewage and discharges water, liquids or sewage directly into drainage piping. *Ontario Water Resources Act*, R.R.O. 1980, Reg. 736, s. 1.

FIXTURES. *n.* 1. Personal chattels connected with or fastened to land. 2. All appurtenances, furniture, furnishing, equipment, fixtures, services and facilities supplied or to be supplied by a landlord to a tenant under a tenancy agreement. *The Residential Tenancies Act*, R.S.S. 1978, c. R-22, s. 2. 3. Goods that are installed in or affixed to a mobile home. *Mobile Home Act*, R.S.B.C. 1979, c. 281, s. 1. See PRODUCT HOLDING ~; TRADE ~.

FIXTURE TRAP. A trap integral with or serving a fixture and includes an interceptor serving as a trap for a fixture. *Ontario Water Resources Act*, R.R.O. 1980, Reg. 736, s. 1.

FIXTURE UNIT. The unit in which the hydraulic load produced by fixtures is expressed and determined under section 80. *Ontario Water Resources Act*, R.R.O. 1980, Reg. 736, s. 1.

FLAG. *n.* A banner; ensign; standard. See LAW OF ~; PILOT ~.

FLAGMAN. *n.* 1. A person employed by a traffic authority, or a contractor doing work on behalf of a traffic authority, for the purpose of directing the movement of traffic on any portion of a highway under construction, or where repair work or other work is being carried on. *The Highway Traffic Act*, S.M. 1985-86, c. 3, s. 77(10). 2. Includes a brakeman or other trainman on a train of a railway who, in connection with the operation of the train, is warning people on a highway. *The Highway Traffic Act*, S.M. 1985-86, c. 3, s. 134(2).

FLAG OF CONVENIENCE. Refers to practice of registering ships in countries with favourable laws.

FLAGRANTE DELICTO. [L. while the crime is glaring] While committing the offence charged.

FLAG STATE. Of a foreign fishing vessel means the state in which the vessel is registered or, where the vessel is not registered, the state whose flag the vessel is entitled to fly. Canada regulations.

FLAME ARRESTOR. A device consisting of a group of parallel metal plates, tubes, fins or screens or a similar device with a large surface area for heat dissipation, which is designed to prevent the entrance of flame into a storage tank through a vent or similar opening. *Flammable Liquids Bulk Storage Regulations*, C.R.C., c. 1148, s. 2.

FLAME-RETARDANT. *adj.* When applied to a material means that the material will not burn for more than a specified period of time and will not permit flame to travel or extend beyond a specified distance. *Power Corporation Act*, R.R.O. 1980, Reg. 794, s. 0.

FLAME-SPREAD RATING. *var.* **FLAME SPREAD RATING.** 1. An index or classification indicating the extent of spread-of-flame on the surface of a material or an assembly of materials as determined in a standard fire test as prescribed in this Regulation. *Building Code Act*, R.R.O. 1980, Reg. 87, s. 1. 2. The rating applied to a surface that has been tested in accordance with the American Society for Testing and Materials Test No. E84-61 Standard Method of Test for Surface Burning Characteristics for Building Materials (Tunnel Test). *Towboat Crew Accommodation Regulations*, C.R.C., c. 1498, s. 2.

FLAMMABLE. *adj.* Capable of being easily set on fire. *Power Corporation Act*, R.R.O. 1980, Reg. 794, s. 0.

FLAMMABLE LIQUID. 1. Any liquid that has a flash point of twenty-one degrees Celsius or less as determined by a Tagliabue or equivalent closed-cup device. *Metric Conversion Act*, S.N.B. 1977, c. M-11.1, s. 13. 2. A liquid having a flash point below 37.8° Celsius, and a vapour pressure below 275 kilopascals absolute at 37.8° Celsius. *Occupational Health and Safety Act*, R.R.O. 1980, Reg. 692, s. 1. 3. (i) Gasoline, naphtha, or distillate, or any other petroleum product, having a flash point at or below 80 degrees Fahrenheit according to the Tagliabue Open Tester; or (ii) kerosene, fuel oil or distillate, or any other petroleum products, having a flash point above 80 degrees Fahrenheit and below 175 degrees Fahrenheit according to the Tagliabue Open Tester. *The Fire Prevention Act*, R.S.S. 1978, c. F-15, s. 2. 4. Any liquid with a flash point below 175°F, as determined by Tagliabue's Open Cup Tester, and having a Reid vapour pressure not exceeding 40 psi absolute at 100°F or any liquid with a flash point of 175°F or above when it is heated by artificial means to a temperature not less than its flash point temperature. *Flammable Liquids Bulk Storage Regulations*, C.R.C., c. 1148, s. 2. 5. Any liquid having a flash point, as determined by a method recommended by the National Fire Protection Association, below 140 degrees Fahrenheit and having a vapor pressure not exceeding 40 pounds per square inch absolute at 100 degrees Fahrenheit. *Canada Dangerous Substances Regulations*, C.R.C., c. 997, s. 2.

FLANGE TAPS. Small diameter pipes tapped into the flanges between which the orifice plate is fitted, so as to permit the measurement of the gas pressure on the up-stream and down-stream sides of the orifice. *Gas and Gas Meters Regulations*, C.R.C., c. 876, s. 25.

FLANK. *n.* The longer side of a regularly-shaped corner lot except where the lot is square, in which case it means the side designated by the assessor as the flank. *The Local Improvements Act*, R.S.S. 1978, c. L-33, s. 2.

FLASHING LIGHT. A light flashing at regular intervals at a frequency of 120 flashes or more per minute. *Collision Regulations*, C.R.C., c. 1416, Rule 3.

FLASH POINT. *var.* **FLASHPOINT.** 1. The lowest temperature, determined by using a Tagliabue closed-cup tester, at which the vapour of a product of petroleum forms a flammable mixture in air. *Gasoline Handling Act*, R.S.O. 1980, c. 185, s. 1. 2. The flash point of fuel as determined by the Pensky Marten closed cup test. *Steamship Machinery Construction Regulations*, C.R.C., c. 1491, s. 2. 3. The lowest temperature at which the application of a test method, as determined by the Tagliabue open-cup test method, causes the vapour at the surface of a liquid to ignite but not to continue to burn. *Hazardous Products (Hazardous Substances) Regulations*, C.R.C., c. 926, s. 2.

FLAT. *n.* A self-contained separate residence.

FLAT-RATE PENSION PLAN. Provides a fixed amount of pension regardless of wages or years of service.

FLAT ROOF. A roof that is horizontal or has a vertical rise of not more than one foor for each six feet measured horizontally. *Lightning Rods Act*, R.R.O. 1980, Reg. 577, s. 1.

FLAVOUR. See NORMAL ~ AND AROMA; NORMAL ~ AND ODOUR.

FLAVOURED MILK. Grade A milk that contains not less than 3 per cent milk-fat and to which flavouring, salt, stabilizing agents and sweetening agents may be added. *Milk Act*, R.R.O. 1980, Reg. 622, s. 3.

FLAVOURED PARTLY-SKIMMED MILK. Grade A milk that contains not less than 1.8 per cent nor more than 2.2 per cent milk-fat and to which flavouring, salt, stabilizing agents and sweetening agents may be added. *Milk Act*, R.R.O. 1980, Reg. 622, s. 3.

FLAVOURED SKIM-MILK. Grade A milk that contains not more than .3 per cent milk-fat and not less than 8 per cent milk solids other than milk-fat and to which flavouring, salt, stabilizing agents and sweetening agents may be added. *Milk Act*, R.R.O. 1980, Reg. 622, s. 3.

FLAX FIBRE. The scutched product of retted flax straw that may be used in spinning. *Inspection and Sale Act*, R.S.C. 1970, c. I-14, s. 13.

FLEA MARKET. A place where five or more persons or one or more organizations, or a combination thereof, sell goods for a non-profit purpose, seventy-five per cent or more of which goods are second hand or used. *Lord's Day (Nova Scotia) Act*, S.N.S. 1974, c. 40, s. 1.

FLEET MAIL OFFICE. A military post office operated by the Canadian Forces Postal Services to provide postal facilities for Canadian naval ships on cruise to a place in Canada, the United States, any possession of the United States or any other foreign country. Canada regulations.

FLEXIBLE SCHEDULE. Work hours and period are not fixed but vary with product requirements.

FLEXIBLE SCREENED TRAILING CABLE. A cable similar in construction to a flexible trailing cable but the power conductors of which are sheathed either individually or collectively by a fine screening of braided copper wires and further covered with a tough insulation to afford mechanical protection. *Coal Mines Regulation Act*, R.S.N.S. 1967, c. 36, s. 84.

FLEXIBLE TRAILING CABLE. A cable the conductors of which, including a ground conductor, are finely stranded for flexibility and protected by natural or synthetic rubber insulation with an over-all covering of tough insulation to afford mechanical protection. *Coal Mines Regulation Act*, R.S.N.S. 1967, c. 36, s. 84.

FLEXIBLE TUBING. Flexible non-metallic tubing commonly known as loom for the mechanical protection of insulated wires. *Power Corporation Act*, R.R.O. 1980, Reg. 794, s. 0.

FLEX TIME. Work hours per work period are fixed but the number of hours worked per day may be varied.

FLIGHT. *n.* 1. The act of flying or moving through the air. *Criminal Code*, R.S.C. 1985, c. C-46, s. 7(8). 2. The movement of an aircraft from the point of take-off to the first point of landing. Canada regulations. 3. Air transportation between two or more airports. *Air Transportation Tax Regulations*, C.R.C., c. 583, s. 2. See ACROBATIC ~; ATLANTIC ~; BACK-TO-BACK ~S; DOMESTIC ~; IFR ~; IN ~; INTERNATIONAL ~; NON-SCHEDULED ~; POLAR ~; POSITIONING ~; SCHEDULED ~; SONIC ~; SUPERSONIC ~; TRANS-OCEANIC ~; VFR ~.

FLIGHT CREW MEMBER. A pilot, flight engineer or flight navigator assigned to duty in an aeroplane during flight time. Canada regulations.

FLIGHT INFORMATION REGION. An airspace of defined dimension extending upwards from the surface of the earth within which flight information service and alerting service is provided. *Air Regulations*, C.R.C., c. 2, s. 101.

FLIGHT LEVEL. The altitude, expressed in hundreds of feet, indicated on an altimeter set to 29.92 inches of mercury or 1 013.2 millibars. Canada regulations.

FLIGHT LINE. A predetermined directional line of flight within a flying display area. *Special Aviation Events Safety Order*, C.R.C., c. 66, s. 2.

FLIGHT NOTIFICATION. See DEFENCE ~.

FLIGHT PLAN. See DVFR ~; OPERATIONAL ~.

FLIGHT TIME. The total time from the moment the aircraft first moves under its own power for the purpose of taking off until the

moment it comes to rest at the end of the flight. *Air Regulations*, C.R.C., c. 2, s. 101.

FLIGHT VISIBILITY. The average range of visibility at any given time forward from the cockpit of an aircraft in flight. *Air Regulations*, C.R.C., c. 2, s. 101.

FLIGHT WATCH SYSTEM. A system described in the operations manual for the monitoring of an aeroplane during flight time. Canada regulations.

FLIPPER. *n.* 1. A can of fish, one end of which can bulges, with or without jarring, after it has been processed and cooled. *Fish Inspection Act*, R.S.Nfld. 1970, c. 132, s. 12. 2. A can with one end bulging as the result of over-filling or failing to exhaust the can properly at the time of packing, and when pressure is exerted on that end of the can the opposite end is readily flipped out. *Processed Fruit and Vegetable Regulations*, C.R.C., c. 291, s. 2.

FLOAT. *n.* 1. A floating structure designed for the mooring or berthing of vessels and includes a floating wharf. *Government Wharves Regulations*, C.R.C., c. 881, s. 2. 2. A non-self-propelled vehicle of a semi-trailer type designed for the purpose of being towed and of carrying construction equipment or other heavy equipment or material. See TRACTOR- ~; COMBINATION.

FLOATER. *n.* A body decomposing in water. F.A. Jaffe, *A Guide to Pathological Evidence*, 2d ed. (Toronto: Carswell, 1983) at 176.

FLOATING ALLOWANCE. A payment in addition to regular wages to compensate for increases in cost of living.

FLOATING AXLE. One which is designed to carry load only under certain conditions. *Roads Act*, R.S.P.E.I. 1974, c. R-15, s. 1.

FLOATING CAPITAL. Capital available to meet current expenditure.

FLOATING CHARGE. A security which is for the time being an equitable charge on the assets of a going concern. It permits the business to carry on and the property comprised in it to be dealt with until the charge crystallizes.

FLOATING CHEST. A chest unstable because of multiple rib fractures in which loose rib fragments inhibit inhalation. F.A. Jaffe, *A Guide to Pathological Evidence*, 2d ed. (Toronto: Carswell, 1983) at 176.

FLOATING POLICY. A policy of insurance which covers all goods ascertainable at the time of loss, up to a certain amount. Raoul Colinvaux, *The Law of Insurance*, 5th ed. (London: Sweet & Maxwell, 1984) at 309.

FLOCK. See APPROVED HATCHERY SUPPLY ~; MULTIPLIER BREEDING ~; PRIMARY BREEDING ~.

FLOCK OF ORIGIN. The flock or herd of which an animal was a member, where the animal was a member of that flock or herd for not less than 60 days immediately preceding its importation into Canada and in any other case means the flock or herd in which it was born. *Animal Disease and Protection Regulations*, C.R.C., c. 296, s. 2.

FLOOD. *v.* See RIGHT TO ~.

FLOOD. *n.* The temporary covering by water of land or all or a portion of buildings or structures, caused by the overflow of a watercourse or standing body of water. *The Water Resources Management Act*, R.S.S. 1978, c. W-7, s. 2.

FLOODABLE LENGTH. In relation to any portion of a ship at any draught, means the maximum length of that portion having its centre at a given point in the ship that, at that draught and under such of the assumptions of permeability set forth in Schedule I as are applicable in the circumstances, can be flooded without submerging any part of the ship's margin line when the ship has no list. *Hull Construction Regulations*, C.R.C., c. 1431, s. 2.

FLOOD CONTROL WORKS. Water control works used for the purpose of preventing or controlling floods. *The Water Resources Management Act*, R.S.S. 1978, c. W-7, s. 2.

FLOOD DRAIN. A drain to receive water from a floor of a building and in its simplest form shall consist of a strainer or grate set flush with the upper surface of a floor so that water passing down through the strainer or grate enters a connected drainage pipe and without limiting the generality of the foregoing shall include, when located between the strainer and the connected pipe or nipple, any ancillary part such as a floor drain body, water stop, trap, backwater valve or primer connection. *Ontario Water Resources Act*, R.R.O. 1980, Reg. 736, s. 1.

FLOOD HAZARD AREA. See SPECIAL ~.

FLOOD LEVEL. The level at which water begins to overflow the top or rim of a fixture. *Ontario Water Resources Act*, R.R.O. 1980, Reg. 736, s. 1.

FLOOD LEVEL RIM. The top edge of a receptacle from which water overflows. *Ontario Water Resources Act*, R.R.O. 1980, Reg. 736, s. 1.

FLOOD PROOFING. The use of devices, equipment, construction, materials, measures or practices to protect buildings, structures or land from damage due to flooding. *The Water Resources Management Act*, R.S.S. 1978, c. W-7, s. 2.

FLOOR. *n.* A lower limit, as on rates of pay. See CELLULAR ~; FIRST ~; GROUND ~.

FLOOR AREA. 1. The space on any storey of a building between exterior walls and required firewalls, including the space occupied by interior walls and partitions, but not including exits and vertical spaces that pierce the storey. *Building Code Act*, R.R.O. 1980, Reg. 87, s. 1. 2. The area of any room, floor, or part of a floor of a hotel, measured from the inside surface of the walls which form its boundaries. *Hotel Fire Safety Act*, R.R.O. 1980, Reg. 505, s. 2. See TOTAL ~.

FLOOR SPACE. The superficial area of every floor in the building in which business is carried on, and includes the superficial area of any land not forming the site of a building but occupied or used for the purpose of or incidental to the exercise or carrying on of a business.

FLOOR TRADER. A person who is employed by a commodity contracts dealer to enter into contracts on the floor of a commodity exchange on behalf of the commodity contracts dealer.

FLORAL EMBLEM OF ONTARIO. The flower known botanically as the trillium grandiflorum and popularly known as the white trillium. *Floral Emblem Act*, R.S.O. 1980, c. 170, s. 1.

FLOTSAM. *n.* Goods afloat on the surface of the sea.

FLOUNDER. See WINTER ~; WITCH ~; YELLOWTAIL ~.

FLOUR. *n.* Flour milled from grain. *Railway Act*, R.S.C. 1985, c. R-3, s. 281.

FLOW. See BACK ~.

FLOWING WELL. A well that has a static water level above the surface of the ground. *Ontario Water Resources Act*, R.R.O. 1980, Reg. 739, s. 1.

FLOW LINE. 1. A pipe for (i) the transmission of fluids from an oil well or wells to a tank, battery or common pipeline manifold, or (ii) the transmission of water obtained from oil or gas for disposal to other than an underground formation. 2. A pipeline serving to interconnect wellheads with separators, treaters, dehydrators, field storage tanks or field storage batteries.

FLOW RATE. See MAXIMUM ~.

FLOW-THROUGH SHARE. A share (other than a prescribed share) of the capital stock of a principal-business corporation that is issued to a person pursuant to an agreement in writing entered into between the person and the corporation after February 1986, under which the corporation agrees (i) to incur, during the period commencing on the day the agreement was entered into and ending 24 months after the end of the month that includes that day, Canadian exploration expenses, Canadian development expenses or Canadian oil and gas property expenses in an amount not less than the consideration for which the share is to be issued, and (ii) to renounce, within that period or within 30 days thereafter, in prescribed form to the person in respect of the share, an amount in respect of the Canadian exploration expenses, Canadian development expenses or Canadian oil and gas property expenses so incurred by it not exceeding the consideration received by the corporation for the share, and includes a right of a person to have such a share issued to him and any interest acquired in such a share by a person pursuant to such an agreement. *Income Tax Act*, R.S.C. 1952, c. 148 (as am. S.C. 1986, c. 55, s. 11(7)), s. 66(15)(d.1).

FLOW-THROUGH SWIMMING POOL. A swimming pool in which during any time when the pool is in use the water is undergoing continuous displacement to waste by make-up water only. *Public Health Act*, R.R.O. 1980, Reg. 849, s. 1.

F.L.R.A.C. *abbr.* Family Law Reform Act Cases, 1980-.

FLUCTUATING WORKWEEK. Employee's hours of work vary from week to week.

FLUE. *n.* An enclosed passageway for conveying flue gases. *Building Code Act*, R.R.O. 1980, Reg. 87, s. 1.

FLUE COLLAR. The portion of a fuel-fired appliance designed for the attachment of the flue pipe or breeching. *Building Code Act*, R.R.O. 1980, Reg. 87, s. 1.

FLUE PIPE. The pipe connecting the flue collar of an appliance to a chimney. *Building Code Act*, R.R.O. 1980, Reg. 87, s. 1.

FLUFF. *n.* The chick down and dust remaining in a hatching machine following completion of a hatch of poultry. *Hatchery Regulations*, C.R.C., c. 1023, s. 2.

FLUID. See AMNIOTIC ~; BRAKE ~; CEREBROSPINAL ~; EXPANSIBLE ~.

FLUID DRAM. 1/8 fluid ounce. *Weights and Measures Act*, S.C. 1970-71-72, c. 36, schedule II.

FLUID MILK. 1. Raw, pasteurized milk or sterilized whole milk for sale to consumers. *Milk Act*, R.S.P.E.I. 1974, c. M-10, s. 1. 2. Milk,

including milk lawfully reconstituted, wholly or in part from milk powder, with a butterfat content not exceeding 8% of the weight thereof, whether or not it is processed by the addition thereto or the subtraction therefrom of any substance, and sold by a distributor or a producer to a consumer for consumption as milk. *Milk Prices Review Act*, S.M. 1980, c. 63, s. 1.

FLUID OUNCE. 1/160 gallon. *Weights and Measures Act*, S.C. 1970-71-72, c. 36, schedule II.

FLUIDS LINE. A pipe for the transmission of fluids other than (i) oil, (ii) gas, (iii) carbon monoxide produced from coal, (iv) water for a waterworks system that is a public utility, (v) sewage, or (vi) water where the pipe forms part of a works or undertaking constructed under the authority of an interim licence or licence issued pursuant to the Water Resources Act, and includes installations in connection with that pipe but does not include a flow line or secondary line. *Pipeline Act*, R.S.A. 1980, c. P-8, s. 1.

FLUMINA ET PORTUS PUBLICA SUNT, IDEOQUE JUS PISCANDI OMNIBUS COMMUNE EST. [L.] Navigable rivers and ports are public; therefore all have a common right to fish there.

FLUORIDATION SYSTEM. A system comprising equipment and materials for the addition of a chemical compound to release fluoride ions into a public water supply.

FLUORINATION DEVICE. A system which may be installed in a filtration plant, permitting the control of fluorine concentration in the water treated by such plant. *Public Health Protection Act*, R.S.Q. 1977, c. P-35, s. 1.

FLUSH DECK SHIP. A ship with no superstructure on the freeboard deck. Canada regulations.

FLUSH VALVE. A valve for flushing a sanitary unit. *Ontario Water Resources Act*, R.R.O. 1980, Reg. 736, s. 1.

FLY. See ARTIFICIAL ~; WEIGHTED ~.

FLY-ASH. *n.* Particulate matter removed from combustion flue gases. *Environmental Protection Act*, R.R.O. 1980, Reg. 309, s. 1.

FLYER. *n.* An item of householder mail not exceeding 4 ounces in weight that (a) is not in card or envelope form, and (b) is not enclosed in an envelope. *Third Class Mail Regulations*, C.R.C., c. 1297, s. 2.

FLY FISHING. 1. To cast upon water and retrieve in the usual and ordinary manner an unbaited, unweighted artificial fly attached to a line to which no extra weight has been added, but does not include trolling. 2. Angling by the use of an artificial fly or flies that are attached to a line or to a leader that is attached to a line. *Fishery regulations*, Canada regulations.

FLY-IN. *n.* A prearranged meeting of a number of aircraft at a specified aerodrome (a) for the purpose of competitive flying, or (b) to which the public is invited. *Special Aviation Events Safety Order*, C.R.C., c. 66, s. 2.

FLYING CLUB. A flying club that is a member of the Royal Canadian Flying Clubs Association. *Air Services Fees Regulations*, C.R.C., c. 5, s. 2.

FLYING DISPLAY AREA. That airspace at an aerodrome where an aircraft participating in an air show may perform. *Special Aviation Events Safety Order*, C.R.C., c. 66, s. 2.

FLYING REVENUES. All revenues derived from flying activities in the performance of the commercial air services authorized by the Committee to be performed. *Air Carrier Regulations*, C.R.C., c. 3, s. 145.

FLYING SCHOOL. See COMMERCIAL ~.

F.M. *abbr.* Frequency modulation.

F.M. STATION. See LOCAL ~; REGIONAL ~.

FMO. *abbr.* Fleet Mail Office.

FOAL. *n.* A young horse. *Riding Horse Establishments Act*, R.S.O. 1980, c. 455, s. 1.

F.O.B. *abbr.* Free on board. Describing a seller's responsibility to have goods placed on board a particular ship. I.F.G. Baxter, *The Law of Banking*, 3d ed. (Toronto: Carswell, 1981) at 136.

F.O.B. COST. (a) In relation to a quantity of crude oil, the free on board cost at the port of loading in the country in which the petroleum was produced, extracted, recovered or derived, and (b) in relation to a quantity of petroleum product, the free on board cost at the port from which the petroleum product is transported to Canada. *Oil Import Compensation Regulations No. 1, 1975*, C.R.C., c. 335, s. 2.

FOCAL SPOT. The section at which the anode of an X-ray tube intercepts the electron beam. *Radiation Emitting Devices Regulations*, C.R.C., c. 1370, s. 1. See EFFECTIVE ~.

FODDER. *n.* Hay or other material ordinarily used for animal food. See GRAZING AND ~ ASSOCIATION.

FOENERATION. *n.* Making money available for usury.

FOETUS. *n.* [L.] An unborn product of conception after the embryo stage. See FETUS.

FOG. See DE~.

FOG LAMP. Denotes any combination of reflector, lens and lamp bulb designed to illuminate the roadway close to and forward or forward and to the sides of the motor vehicle and otherwise meeting the requirements of this section. *Highway Traffic Act*, R.S.A. 1980, c. H-7, s. 40.

FOG LIGHT. Denotes any combination of reflector, lens and light bulb that meets the requirements of this section and is designed to illuminate the roadway close to and forward or forward and to the sides of a motor vehicle. *Vehicles Act*, R.S.N.W.T. 1974, c. V-2, s. 70.

FOLIO. *n.* 1. One hundred words. 2. Ninety words. *Interpretation Act*, R.S.N.S. 1967, c. 151, s. 6.

F1. Telegraphy by frequency modulation without the use of modulating audio frequency (frequency shift keying) including frequency shift teletype. *General Radio Regulations*, Part II, C.R.C., c. 1372, s. 42.

FONTANELLE. *n.* A soft spot between the skull bones of an infant or fetus. F.A. Jaffe, *A Guide to Pathological Evidence*, 2d ed. (Toronto: Carswell, 1983) at 176.

FOOD. *n.* 1. Any article manufactured, sold or represented for use as food or drink for man, chewing gum, and any ingredient that may be mixed with food for any purpose whatever. *Food and Drugs Act*, R.S.C. 1985, c. F-27, s. 2. 2. Every article that (i) is used by human or animal for food, drink, confectionery or condiment, or (ii) enters into the composition of the same, whether simple, blended, mixed or compound. See ANIMAL ~; CANNED ~S; HAZARDOUS ~; INFANT ~; JUNIOR ~; LOCAL ~; MEDICINAL ~; PRE-PACKAGED ~; SPECIALTY ~; STRAINED ~; TEST MARKET ~; UNFIT FOR ~; UNSTANDARDIZED ~.

FOOD ADDITIVE. 1. Any substance, including any source of radiation, the use of which results, or may reasonably be expected to result in it or its by-products becoming part of or affecting the characteristics of a food, but does not include (a) any nutritive material that is used, recognized or commonly sold as an article or ingredient of food; (b) vitamins, mineral nutrients and amino acids; (c) spices, seasonings, flavouring preparations, essential oils, oleoresins and natural extractives; (d) agricultural chemicals; (e) food packaging materials and components thereof; and (f) drugs recommended for administration to animals that may be consumed as food. *Food and Drug Regulations*, C.R.C., c. 870, s. B.01.001. 2. Any substance listed in Column III of Schedule X and any other substance used in or on a meat product that (a) does not have nutritive value, or (b) is a vitamin, an amino acid, a seasoning or a flavouring. *Meat Inspection Regulations*, C.R.C., c. 1032, s. 2.

FOOD ANIMAL. Bovine animals, swine, horses, sheep, goats, whales, bison, domestic rabbit, deer, elk, moose or birds. *Meat Inspection Regulations*, C.R.C., c. 1032, s. 2.

FOOD COLOUR. 1. Those colours permitted for use in or upon food by Division 6. *Food and Drug Regulations*, C.R.C., c. 870, c. B.01.001. 2. Beta-carotene.

FOOD CONTACT SURFACE. Any surface with which food comes in contact during its preparation, processing, packaging, service or storage. *Public Health Act*, R.R.O. 1980, Reg. 840, s. 1.

FOOD FISHING. Catching fish for personal consumption but not for sale or barter. *Newfoundland Fishery Regulations*, C.R.C., c. 846, s. 347.

FOOD PLAN CONTRACT. A contract between a buyer and a seller for the purchase and sale of food in amounts in excess of 25 kg. in respect of which delivery of the food is not made at the time the contract is made and includes a membership scheme or plan or other service or matter arising from or related to the purchase and sale of food. *Consumer Protection Act*, R.S.B.C. 1979, c. 65, s. 38.

FOOD PREMISE. A premises where food or milk is manufactured, processed, prepared, stored, handled, displayed, distributed, transported, sold or offered for sale, but does not include a private residence. *Health Protection and Promotion Act, 1983*, S.O. 1983, c. 10, s. 1.

FOOD PREPARATION EQUIPMENT. The following classes of tangible personal property: blenders and mixers, bowls, pots, pans and tins for cooking and baking, broilers and grills, ovens, kitchen ranges and food warming equipment, coffee makers, dishwashers, flatware, dishes, glasses, serving trays and kitchen utensils, food choppers, slicers and grinders, freestanding kitchen refrigerators, toasters, but does not include food wrapping and storage equipment, mobile buffets and mobile cooking units, refrigerated displays, table linens, waste disposal equipment and compactors, fixtures or drink or ice cream dispensers or parts for the maintenance and repair of tangible personal property described in this paragraph. *Retail Sales Tax Act*, R.R.O. 1980, Reg. 903, s. 1.

FOOD PRODUCT. Any article of food prepared wholly or in part from fruit or vegetable. *Processed Fruit and Vegetable Regulations*, C.R.C., c. 291, s. 2.

FOOD PRODUCTS. Includes insulin, vitamins, saccharin, sucaryl and any dietary supplement or adjunct that is not a drug or medicine, and meals packaged or wrapped for consumption off the premises where sold, but does not include liquor, beer, wine, prepared meals, soft drinks, chewing gum, lozenges, candies, confections, dog, cat, bird and other animal foods, root beer and root beer extracts, malt and malt extracts. *Retail Sales Tax Act*, R.R.O. 1980, Reg. 904, s. 1.

FOOD SERVICE PREMISES. Any food premises where meals or meal portions are prepared for immediate consumption or sold or served in a form which will permit immediate consumption on the premises or elsewhere, but does not include retail or wholesale grocery premises where facilities are not provided for eating on the premises. *Public Health Act*, R.R.O. 1980, Reg. 840, s. 1.

FOODSTUFFS. *n.* All food used for human consumption. *Public Health Act*, R.S.N.S. 1967, c. 247, s. 1.

FOOT. *n.* 1. 1/3 yard. *Weights and Measures Act*, S.C. 1970-71-72, c. 36, schedule II. 2. 12.789 inches. Unit of measurement to describe certain land in Quebec. *Weights and Measures Act*, S.C. 1970-71-72, c. 36, schedule III. See CUBIC ~; RATE PER ~; SQUARE ~.

FOOT FRONTAGE. The lineal measurement in feet of a frontage. *Municipalities Act*, R.S.N.B. 1973, c. M-22, s. 118.

FOOTWEAR. *n.* Any form of footwear other than footwear the main component of which is canvas. Canada regulations.

F.O.R. *abbr.* Free on rail.

FORAGE. See PERENNIAL ~.

FORCE. *n.* 1. Violence. 2. The Royal Canadian Mounted Police. 3. The officers, non-commissioned officers and men of the permanent militia corps, and includes the permanent staff of the militia. *Defence Services Pension Continuation Act*, R.S.C. 1970, c. D-3, s. 2. 4. The Permanent Active Air Force and any other component of the Royal Canadian Air Force the members of which are enlisted or appointed for continuing full-time service. *Defence Services Pension Continuation Act*, R.S.C. 1970, c. D-3, s. 41. 5. When used in reference to police, the necessary personnel, equipment, furnishings, vehicles and facilities and includes a police department. Nova Scotia statutes. See FINE ~; LABOUR ~; MEMBER OF A ~; MEMBER OF THE ~;

405

POLICE ~; REGULAR ~; RESERVE ~; SERVICE IN THE ~; SPECIAL ~; VISITING ~.

FORCED-AIR FURNACE. A furnace equipped with a fan that provides the primary means for circulation of air. *Building Code Act*, R.R.O. 1980, Reg. 87, s. 1.

FORCED VENTILATION. Oxygen for which standards are prescribed in any pharmacopeia mentioned in Schedule B to the Act. *Medical Devices Regulations*, C.R.C., c. 871, s. 1.

FORCE MAJEURE. [Fr.] Irresistible urge.

FORCES. *n.* 1. Except in the definition of "regular force", means the naval, army or air forces of His Majesty or of any of the Allies of His Majesty during World War I or World War II. *Public Service Superannuation Act*, R.S.C. 1985, c. P-36, s. 3. 2. In the case of World War II, any of His Majesty's naval, army or air forces, the Royal Canadian Mounted Police, the Corps of (Civilian) Canadian Fire Fighters for Service in the United Kingdom, the armed forces of the United States, the Fighting French forces and any other force designated by the Governor in Council for the purposes of this Part. *Public Service Superannuation Act*, R.S.C. 1985, c. P-36, s. 6(2). See ARMED ~; CANADIAN ~; HER MAJESTY'S ~; MEMBER OF THE ~.

FORCES AIR LETTER. An item of stationery, authorized by the Postmaster General, for use by (a) any member of the Canadian Forces who is served through a Canadian Forces Post Office or Fleet Mail Office address in writing to persons in Canada, and (b) any person in Canada in writing to any such member of the Canadian Forces. *Armed Forces Postal Regulations*, C.R.C., c. 1274, s. 2.

FORCES CANTEEN. A mess or canteen operated in connection with a component unit of the Canadian Forces, both regular and reserve, or the Royal Canadian Mounted Police Force, in a camp, armoury, barracks, base, or station, of any one or more of these units or establishments in New Brunswick. *Liquor Control Act*, R.S.N.B. 1973, c. L-10, s. 1.

FORCIBLE DETAINER. 1. Refusal to restore goods to another though sufficient means were tendered. 2. Detaining any lands or tenements with threats or violence after entering them peaceably.

FORCIBLE ENTRY. Violently entering any land or tenement in order to take possession.

F.O.R. CONTRACT. A seller undertakes to deliver goods into railway cars at the station at personal expense. G.H.L. Fridman, *Sale of Goods in Canada*, 3d ed. (Toronto: Carswell, 1986) at 485.

FORE. *n.* The direction in which the occupant of a seat faces when seated normally in such seat. *Motor Vehicle Safety Regulations*, C.R.C., c. 1038, s. 210.

FORECASTLE. *n.* A continuous superstructure extending aft from the bow. *Hull Construction Regulations*, C.R.C., c. 1431, s. 100.

FORECLOSURE. *n.* 1. An action brought by a mortgagee when a mortgagor is in default asking that a day be fixed on which the mortgagor is to pay off the debt, and that in default of payment the mortgagor may be foreclosed of, that is deprived of his right to redeem, the equity of redemption. 2. A proceeding, commenced by a vendor under an agreement for sale, in which the relief claimed is an order for one or more of the following: (a) specific performance of the agreement, (b) cancellation of the agreement, or (c) determination of the agreement. *Law Reform Act*, S.B.C. 1985, c. 10, s. 16.1. See DECREE OF ~.

FOREGOER. *n.* A royal purveyor.

FOREGROUND FORMAT. As applied to any time segment and subject to subsections (2) and (3), means a format of presentation, other than gramophone format or rolling format, in which (a) the intrinsic intellectual content of the matter being broadcast is entirely related to a particular theme or subject, (b) the duration of the presentation, including interruptions, is at least 15 minutes, and (c) the presentation is broadcast without interruption or accompanying broadcast matter other than matter within content category number 8 or 9. *Radio (F.M.) Broadcasting Regulations*, C.R.C., c. 380, s. 14.

FOREIGN. *adj.* 1. Out of a certain nation's jurisdiction. 2. Not included in the British Commonwealth. *Law Society Act*, R.S.M. 1970, c. L100, s. 2.

FOREIGN AFFILIATE. 1. At any time, of a taxpayer (other than a non-resident-owned investment corporation) resident in Canada means a corporation (other than a corporation resident in Canada), in which, at that time, the taxpayer's equity percentage was not less than 10%. *Income Tax Act*, R.S.C. 1952, c. 148 (as am. S.C. 1974-75-76, c. 26, s. 59), s. 95(1)(d). 2. In relation to an insured, a corporation carrying on business outside Canada that, directly or indirectly, (a) is controlled by the insured; (b) controls the insured; or (c) is controlled by a person who directly or indirectly controls the insured. *Export Development Act*, R.S.C. 1985, c. E-20, s. 25. See CONTROLLED ~.

FOREIGN AIR CARRIER. Any air carrier that

is not a Canadian air carrier. *Air Carrier Regulations*, C.R.C., c. 3, s. 2.

FOREIGN AIRCRAFT. An aeroplane registered outside Canada of more than 12,500 pounds maximum certificated take-off weight that is used in a domestic or international scheduled or charter commercial air service. Canada regulations.

FOREIGN ANIMALS. Animals not already introduced into Canadian territory, outside of quarantine stations. *Animal Disease and Protection Act*, R.S.C. 1985, c. A-11, s. 2.

FOREIGN ARBITRAL AWARD. An arbitral award made pursuant to an arbitration agreement and made outside Canada. *Foreign Arbitral Awards Act*, S.O. 1986, c. 25, s. 1.

FOREIGN BANK. A corporation, association, partnership or other institution incorporated or established by, pursuant to or in accordance with the laws of a country other than Canada, or a department or agency of the government of a country other than Canada or a political subdivision of such a country, that (a) is a bank according to the laws of any country other than Canada where it carries on business, (b) carries on a business in a country other than Canada that, if carried on in Canada, would be wholly or to a significant extent, the business of banking, (c) acquires, adopts or retains a name that, in any language, includes the word "bank", "banks" or "banking", either alone or in combination with other words, or any word or words of import equivalent thereto to indicate or describe its business, (d) engages in the business of lending money and accepting deposit liabilities transferable by cheque or other instrument, (e) is an affiliate of a corporation that is a foreign bank within the meaning of this definition, or (f) controls a corporation that is a foreign bank within the meaning of this definition, but does not include (g) an affiliate of a Schedule I bank, (h) a corporation, association, partnership or other institution, or department or agency of a government, that is a foreign bank within the meaning of this definition by reason only of paragraph (c) or (e) and that is not in the business of engaging in financial activities, or (i) a corporation, association, partnership or other institution, or department or agency of a government, that is exempted from being a foreign bank by order of the Minister made pursuant to subsection (3), which order has not expired as provided in that subsection. *Bank Act*, R.S.C. 1985, c. B-1, s. 2. See NON-BANK AFFILIATE OF A ~.

FOREIGN BANK SUBSIDIARY. A bank that is a Schedule II bank as a result of the holding of its shares by one or more foreign banks. *Bank Act*, R.S.C. 1985, c. B-1, s. 2.

FOREIGN-BASED INFORMATION OR DOCUMENT. Any information or document which is available or located outside Canada and which may be relevant to the administration or enforcement of this Act. *Income Tax Act*, R.S.C. 1952, c. 148 (as am. S.C. 1988, c. 55, s. 175), s. 231.6(1).

FOREIGN BENEFICIARY. A beneficiary who is resident in a country designated by regulation made under this section. *Estates Administration Amendment Act, 1983*, S.O. 1983, c. 23, s. 1.

FOREIGN BILL. A bill that is neither drawn in Canada upon a person resident in Canada nor drawn and payable in Canada. I.F.G. Baxter, *The Law of Banking*, 3d ed. (Toronto: Carswell, 1981) at 117.

FOREIGN BROADCASTING UNDERTAKING. A network operation or a broadcasting transmitting undertaking located outside Canada or on a ship or aircraft not registered in Canada. *Income Tax Act*, R.S.C. 1952, c. 148 (as am. S.C. 1974-75-76, c. 106, s. 3), s. 19.1(4).

FOREIGN CHARTER AIR CARRIER. A foreign international air carrier classified as Class 9-4 or a foreign international air carrier operating charter flights in or out of Canada under a permit issued by the Committee. *Air Carrier Regulations*, C.R.C., c. 3, s. 145.

FOREIGN COMPANY. 1. A company formed or incorporated by or under the laws of any country other than Canada. 2. A company incorporated otherwise than by or under the act of a legislature and includes a dominion company.

FOREIGN CONTRACT AIR CARRIER. A foreign international air carrier classified as Class 9-5. *Air Carrier Regulations*, C.R.C., c. 3, s. 145.

FOREIGN CONTROLLED CORPORATION. A corporation that is effectively controlled directly or indirectly by a person who is not a resident of Canada. *An Act to Amend the Agricultural Lands Protection Act*, S.M. 1980-81, c. 36, s. 2.

FOREIGN CORPORATION. 1. A corporation incorporated otherwise than under a law of Canada or a province. 2. A company or corporation that (a) is organized and exists under the laws of any jurisdiction other than New Brunswick, and (b) has determined to protect its interests in time of war or other emergency by transferring its registered office to New Brunswick. *Foreign Resident Corporations Act*, S.N.B. 1984, c. F-19.1, s. 1.

FOREIGN COUNTRY. Any country other than the designated province, whether a kingdom, empire, republic, commonwealth, state, dominion, province, territory, colony, possession or protectorate, or a part thereof. *Foreign Judgments acts.* See INVESTMENT IN A ~.

FOREIGN CULTURAL PROPERTY. In relation to a reciprocating State, means any object that is specifically designated by that State as being of importance for archaeology, prehistory, history, literature, art or science. *Cultural Property Export and Import Act,* R.S.C. 1985, c. C-51, s. 37.

FOREIGN CUSTOMER. (a) In respect of export credits insurance and guarantees, a person carrying on business or other activities outside Canada and includes a foreign government, (b) in respect of export loans and guarantees, a person, including a foreign government, carrying on business or other activities outside Canada with whom the Corporation or another person carrying on business or other activities in Canada has dealings, and (c) in respect of an export transaction described in paragraph (e) of the definition of that term in this subsection, the person referred to in that paragraph as purchasing goods in Canada. *Export Development Act,* R.S.C. 1985, c. E-20, s. 23.

FOREIGN DEBT. The bonds, debentures, notes and loans repayable in a foreign currency or a foreign unit of monetary value that were issued and sold or arranged (i) by Manitoba Hydro, or (ii) by the government for the purposes of making or funding advances to Manitoba Hydro, and includes any bond, debenture, note or loan repayable in a foreign currency or foreign unit of monetary value issued and sold or arranged by Manitoba Hydro or the government for the purpose of payment, refunding, refinancing or renewal in whole or in part of any bond, debenture, note or loan issued and sold or arranged by Manitoba Hydro, or by the government for the purpose of making or funding advances to Manitoba Hydro, and, where the context requires, means the amount in Canadian dollars of the debt due or accruing due under such bonds, debentures, notes and loans. *Energy Rate Stabilization Act,* S.M. 1979, c. 42, s. 1.

FOREIGN ENTITY. A corporation that is not resident in Canada, a partnership, organization, fund or entity that is not resident in or is situated in Canada or a trust contemplated in section 596. *An Act to Amend Various Fiscal Laws and Other Legislation,* S.Q. 1986, c. 15, s. 90.

FOREIGN FISHING VESSEL. A fishing vessel that is not a Canadian fishing vessel. *Coastal Fisheries Protection Act,* R.S.C. 1985, c. C-33, s. 2.

FOREIGN-GOING. *adj.* When used with reference to a ship, means employed on foreign voyages. *Canada Shipping Act,* R.S.C. 1985, c. S-9, s. 2.

FOREIGN GOVERNMENT. The government or any agency thereof of a foreign country or the government or any agency thereof of any political subdivision of a foreign country. *Export Development Act,* R.S.C. 1985, c. E-20, s. 23.

FOREIGN GRAIN. Any grain grown outside Canada and includes screenings from such a grain and every grain product manufactured or processed from such a grain. *Canada Grain Act,* R.S.C. 1985, c. G-10, s. 2.

FOREIGN GRANT. A grant of probate or administration or other document purporting to be of the same nature granted by a court in (i) a province or territory of Canada, (ii) the United Kingdom or any British possession, colony or dependency, or (iii) a member nation of the British Commonwealth.

FOREIGN INCOME. Of an individual for a taxation year means the aggregate of (a) his incomes for the year from businesses carried on by him in countries other than Canada, and (b) his incomes for the year from sources in countries other than Canada in respect of which he had paid non-business-income taxes, within the meaning assigned by paragraph 126(7)(c), to governments of countries other than Canada. *Income Tax Act,* R.S.C. 1952, c. 148 (as am. S.C. 1986, c. 55, s. 50), s. 127.54(1).

FOREIGN JUDGMENT. A judgment or order of a court of a foreign country, whether heretofore or hereafter obtained, whereby a sum of money is with or without costs made payable or whereby costs only are made payable. *Foreign Judgments acts.*

FOREIGN JURISDICTION. A province, state, country or other jurisdiction outside the province enacting the legislation.

FOREIGN LIFE CORPORATION. A corporation incorporated outside Canada to undertake contracts of life insurance.

FOREIGN LOAN CORPORATION. 1. Any corporation incorporated outside Canada to exercise the powers that a loan corporation incorporated in Ontario possesses. *Loan and Trust Corporations Act,* R.R.O. 1980, Reg. 593, s. 1. 2. A corporation incorporated outside Canada to exercise the powers set forth in section 60 of the Act. *Loan Companies Investment (Special Shares) Regulations,* C.R.C., c. 1029, s. 2.

FOREIGN MATERIAL. 1. Any material intermixed with a parcel of grain, other than kernels of grain of a standard of quality fixed by or under this Act for a grade of that grain, that is of such a character and in such limited quantity that it need not be separated from the parcel of grain before that grade can be assigned to the grain. *Canada Grain Act*, R.S.C. 1985, c. G-10, s. 2. 2. (a) Mature chess (Bromus secalinus), mature green or yellow foxtail (Seteria viridis and S. lutescens), spear grass (Stipa spp.), wire grass (Aristida Spp.), wild barley (Hordeum jubatum, H. murinum, H. pusillum) and other weeds, (b) such sedges, rushes and other plants that are coarse and woody or otherwise unsuitable for feed, and (c) ripe grain hay, grain straw, grain or grass stubble, chaff, corn stalks and other objectionable matter which may be present naturally in hay. *Hay and Straw Inspection Regulations*, C.R.C., c. 920, s. 1. See INJURIOUS ~.

FOREIGN MERGER. A merger or combination of two or more corporations each of which was, immediately before the merger or combination, resident in a country other than Canada (each of which is in this section and section 95 referred to as a "predecessor foreign corporation") to form one corporate entity resident in the country in which all the predecessor foreign corporations were resident (in this section and section 95 referred to as the "new foreign corporation") in such manner that (a) all or substantially all of the property (except amounts receivable from any predecessor foreign corporation or shares of the capital stock of any predecessor foreign corporation) of the predecessor foreign corporations immediately before the merger or combination becomes property of the new foreign corporation by virtue of the merger or combination, (b) all or substantially all of the liabilities (except amounts payable to any predecessor foreign corporation) of the predecessor foreign corporations immediately before the merger or combination become liabilities of the new foreign corporation by virtue of the merger or combination, and (c) all or substantially all of the shares of the capital stock of the predecessor foreign corporations (except any such shares owned by any predecessor foreign corporation) are exchanged for or become shares of the capital stock of the new foreign corporation by virtue of the merger or combination, otherwise than as a result of the distribution of property to one corporation upon the winding-up of another corporation. *Income Tax Act*, R.S.C. 1952, c. 148 (as am. S.C. 1980-81-82-83, c. 140, s. 52(8)), s. 87(8.1).

FOREIGN NON-RESIDENT. Any person who is not a resident and is domiciled outside Canada. *Wild-life Conservation Act*, S.Q. 1978, c. 65, s. 1.

FOREIGN NON-SCHEDULED UNIT TOLL AIR CARRIER. A foreign international air carrier classified as Class 9-2 or Class 9-3. *Air Carrier Regulations*, C.R.C., c. 3, s. 145.

FOREIGN OFFENDER. A citizen or a national of a foreign state, irrespective of age, who has been found guilty of a criminal offence and is subject to supervision either in confinement or at large by reason of parole, probation or any other form of supervision without confinement, in Canada. *Transfer of Offenders Act*, R.S.C. 1985, c. T-15, s. 2.

FOREIGN ORGANIZATION. A corporation whose head office is outside Canada or an association that is not incorporated and has members who are not residents of Canada but does not include a Canadian branch of any such association. *Foreign Organizations Remission Order*, C.R.C., c. 766, s. 2.

FOREIGN PETROLEUM. Petroleum other than domestic petroleum. *Energy Administration Act*, R.S.C. 1985, c. E-6, s. 56.

FOREIGN PROPERTY. (a) Tangible property situated outside Canada except automotive equipment registered in Canada, (b) automotive equipment not registered in Canada pursuant to the laws of Canada or a province, (c) intangible property (other than any property described in paragraphs (d) to (g)) situated outside Canada including, without restricting the generality of the foregoing, any patent under the laws of a country other than Canada and any licence in respect thereof, (d) any share of the capital stock of a corporation other than a Canadian corporation, (d.1) any share of the capital stock of or any debt obligation issued by a Canadian corporation, if shares of the corporation may reasonably be considered to derive their value, directly or indirectly, primarily from portfolio investments in property that is foreign property, but not including a share of a corporation listed on a prescribed stock exchange in Canada that is of a class of the capital stock of the corporation no share of which has been issued after December 4, 1985 (otherwise than pursuant to an agreement in writing entered into before 5:00 p.m. Eastern Standard Time on December 4, 1985), (e) any share of the capital stock of a mutual fund corporation that is neither an investment corporation nor a registered investment except as prescribed by regulation, (f) any property that, under the terms or conditions thereof or any agreement relating thereto, is convertible into, is exchangeable for or confers a right to acquire, property that is foreign property, but not including property that is (i) a share of the capital stock of a Canadian corporation listed on a prescribed stock exchange in Canada, or (ii) a right issued before 1984 and listed on a prescribed stock exchange in Canada to acquire a share of the capital stock of a Canadian corporation, (g) any bond, debenture, mortgage, hypothec, note or similar obligation of, or issued by, a person not resident in Canada, except any such bond, debenture, mortgage, hypothec, note or similar obligation issued or guaranteed by (i) the International Bank for Reconstruction and Development, (ii) The Inter-American Development Bank, (iii) the Asian Development Bank, (iv) the Caribbean Development Bank, or (v) a prescribed person, (h) any interest in or right to any property that is foreign property by virtue of paragraphs (a) to (g), and (i) except as prescribed by regulation, any interest in, or right to acquire an interest in, a trust (other than a registered investment) or a partnership. *Income Tax Act*, R.S.C. 1952, c. 148 (as am. S.C. 1986, c. 6, s. 110), s. 206(1).

FOREIGN RESOURCE PROPERTY. Any property that would be a Canadian resource property of the taxpayer if paragraph (c) were read as if the references therein to "in Canada" were read as references to "outside Canada". *Income Tax Act*, R.S.C. 1952, c. 148 (as am. S.C. 1970-71-72, c. 63), s. 66(15)(f).

FOREIGN SCHEDULED AIR CARRIER. A foreign international air carrier classified as Class 8. *Air Carrier Regulations*, C.R.C., c. 3, s. 145.

FOREIGN SERVICE OFFICER. A Canadian diplomatic or consular officer, including a trade commissioner or immigration officer, accredited to or carrying out official duties in the country in which a person making an application or a registration or giving a notice pursuant to the Act resides or, if there is no such officer in that country, such an officer accredited to or carrying out official duties in a nearby country. *Citizenship Regulations*, C.R.C., c. 400, s. 2.

FOREIGN SHIP. A ship other than a British ship. *Canada Shipping Act*, R.S.C. 1985, c. S-9, s. 2.

FOREIGN STATE. 1. Includes every dominion other than the United Kingdom of Great Britain and Northern Ireland, Canada or a British possession. *Evidence acts.* 2. Any state other than Canada. 3. Includes every colony, dependency and constituent part of the foreign state, and every vessel of a foreign state is deemed to be within the jurisdiction of and to be part of the state. *Extradition Act*, R.S.C. 1985, c. E-23, s. 2. 4. Includes any foreign prince, colony, province or part of any province or people, or any person or persons exercising or assuming to

exercise the powers of government in or over any foreign country, colony, province or part of any province or people. *Foreign Enlistment Act*, R.S.C. 1985, c. F-28, s. 2. 5. Includes (a) any sovereign or other head of the foreign state or of any political subdivision of the foreign state while acting as such in a public capacity, (b) any government of the foreign state or of any political subdivision of the foreign state, including any of its departments, and any agency of the foreign state, and (c) any political subdivision of the foreign state. 6. A state, the name of which is set out in the schedule, with which Canada has entered into a treaty on the transfer of offenders. *Transfer of Offenders Act*, R.S.C. 1985, c. T-15, s. 2. See AGENCY OF A ~.

FOREIGN SUBSTANCE. 1. In respect of a milk product means any substance that is incorporated into or placed in the milk product, other than substances normal for the composition of the milk product. *Farm Products Grades and Sales Act*, R.R.O. 1980, Reg. 327, s. 1. 2. Any substance whatever that is not a natural component of the blood, saliva, urine or other bodily substance of a horse. *Race Track Supervision Regulations*, C.R.C., c. 441, s. 2.

FOREIGN TAXES. Of an individual for a taxation year means the aggregate of the business-income taxes, within the meaning assigned by paragraph 126(7)(a), paid by him for the year in respect of businesses carried on by him in countries other than Canada and 2/3 of the non-business-income taxes, within the meaning assigned by paragraph 126(7)(c), paid by him for the year to the governments of countries other than Canada. *Income Tax Act*, R.S.C. 1952, c. 148 (as am. S.C. 1986, c. 55, s. 50), s. 127.54(1).

FOREIGN TRIBUNAL. A tribunal of a foreign state or of an organization of states. *Foreign Extraterritorial Measures Act*, R.S.C. 1985, c. F-29, s. 2.

FOREIGN TRUST. A trust that is not resident in Canada in a taxation year and of which a beneficiary, at any time in the year, is a person resident in Canada, a corporation or trust with which such a person is not dealing at arm's length or a controlled foreign affiliate of such a person. *An Act to Amend the Taxation Act and the Act Respecting the Application of the Taxation Act*, S.Q. 1984, c. 15, s. 130.

FOREIGN TRUST CORPORATION. A corporation incorporated outside Canada to exercise the powers set forth in section 63 of the Act. *Trust Companies Investment (Special Shares) Regulations*, C.R.C., c. 1570, s. 2.

FOREIGN VEHICLE. A motor vehicle, trailer or semi-trailer which is brought into a province otherwise than in the ordinary course of business by or through a manufacturer or dealer and which has not been registered in that province.

FOREIGN VOYAGE. A voyage extending beyond the area of a home-trade voyage and not being an inland or minor waters voyage. *Canada Shipping Act*, R.S.C. 1985, c. S-9, s. 2.

FOREIGN WARSHIP. A ship of war, a military transport or military supply ship owned, operated or controlled by the government of any country other than Canada. Canada regulations.

FOREIGN YACHT. A ship registered in a country other than Canada and used exclusively for pleasure purposes. Canada regulations.

FOREJUDGER. *n.* A judgment which deprives someone of something in question.

FOREMAN. *n.* 1. The member of a jury who speaks for that body. 2. A supervisory employee. 3. A person who (i) in an underground mine, aside from other duties he might have, inspects all roadways, working places and other accessible parts of a mine, and determines that roadways, approaches and working places are safe before a shift is allowed to enter, or (ii) in a surface mine, is next in authority to the manager or assistant manager. *Coal Mines Safety Act*, R.S.A. 1980, c. C-15, s. 1. See SENIOR ~.

FORENSIC. *adj.* Applied to the law; belonging to law courts.

FORENSIC CLINIC. Any place or facility for the reception, diagnosis, classification and treatment of persons charged with an offence or sentenced to imprisonment, in order to determine, recommend and provide the best course of treatment for the antisocial behaviour of such persons. *Corrections Act*, R.S.M. 1970, c. C230, s. 32.

FORENSIC MEDICINE. 1. Legal medicine. 2. Medical skills and knowledge which may be used to solve legal problems. F.A. Jaffe, *A Guide to Pathological Evidence*, 2d ed. (Toronto: Carswell, 1983) at 1. 3. Jurisprudence of medicine.

FORENSIC ODONTOLOGY. The study of the teeth of an unidentified body during autopsy. F.A. Jaffe, *A Guide to Pathological Evidence*, 2d ed. (Toronto: Carswell, 1983) at 30.

FORENSIC PSYCHIATRY. Includes psychiatric consultation, assessment, therapy or treatment services provided to the courts or to other components of the administration of justice. *Forensic Psychiatry Act*, R.S.B.C. 1979, c. 139, s. 1.

FORESCHOKE. *adj.* Abandoned; disclaimed.

FORESEEABLE. *adj.* A risk is foreseeable when a reasonable person would consider it real and not fanciful or far-fetched. John G. Fleming, *The Law of Torts*, 6th ed. (Sydney: The Law Book Company Limited, 1983) at 109.

FORESEEABILITY. *n.* A reasonable person's ability to anticipate the consequences of his or her action.

FORESHORE. *n.* The land between the low water mark and the highest high water mark. *Sea Plants Act*, R.S.P.E.I. 1974, c. S-3, s. 2.

FOREST. *n.* 1. Land in Canada covered with timber stands or that, formerly so covered, is not put to any use inconsistent with forestry, and includes a sugar bush. 2. The plant cover on any forest land whether standing, dead trees or scrub plants or grass. 3. A plant association consisting predominantly of trees. *Forests Act*, S.N.S. 1986, c. 10, s. 3. 4. Includes wood, barren or tract covered by underwood or any dry vegetable matter. *Fire Prevention Act*, S.P.E.I. 1983, c. 16, s. 1. 5. Land containing timber, shrubs, slash or peat. *Forest Act*, R.S.B.C. 1979, c. 140, s. 108. See LAKE, ~ AND FUR ASSOCIATION; PRODUCTS OF THE ~; PROTECTION ~; PROVINCIAL ~; PUBLIC ~.

FORESTALL. *v.* To forcibly obstruct the way.

FOREST AREA. Any uncultivated land that, by reason of the existence of trees, grass or other vegetation thereon, possesses timber, forage, recreational, wildlife or other value. *Forest Protection Act*, R.S.N.W.T. 1974, c. F-8, s. 2.

FOREST CONCESSION. Any licence, lease, contract of lease and hire or of farming-out, or agreement of any kind granting to any person, firm or corporation, under any law, the right to cut wood on any land or lands of the public domain of Québec. *Forest Resources Utilization Act*, R.S.Q. 1977, c. U-2, s. 1.

FOREST ENGINEER. Any person practising the profession of engineer and qualified to give advice upon or supervise, execute, or direct the execution of the following works: the inventory, classification and valuation of the soil and crops of forest, the preparation of maps and topographical plans of forests; the management, maintenance, conservation, lumbering, reforestation and protection of woods and forests, sylviculture; forest photogrammetry; logging and transportation of woods, the exploitation of forests and other forest resources; the application of forest engineering sciences to economical wood utilization; the preparation of maps, estimates and specifications, working plans and reports concerning forest management and any engineering work relating to the execution of the above-mentioned purposes and the preparation of plans in connection with such works. *Forest Engineers Act*, R.S.Q. 1977, c. I-10, s. 2.

FOREST FIRE AREA. An area on the surface of the earth described by a Notice to Airmen (NOTAM) and upon which standing timber, grass or any other vegetation or buildings are smouldering or burning. *Forest Fire Control Operations Order*, C.R.C., c. 13, s. 2.

FOREST INDUSTRIES. All persons or corporations engaged in the manufacturing, or processing of primary forest products. *Forest Products Act*, R.S.N.B. 1973, c. F-21, s. 1.

FOREST INDUSTRY. All operations in or incidental to the production or manufacture of articles produced from wood. *Labour Standards Code Act*, S.N.S. 1971-72, c. 10, s. 1.

FOREST INDUSTRY OPERATION. The harvesting and transporting of trees, including Christmas trees, and the processing of trees into logs or lumber and includes employment incidental to the above operations or immediately connected therewith. *Industrial Safety Act*, S.N.S. 1981, c. 29, s. 1.

FOREST LAND. 1. Any uncultivated land in a province on which trees or shrubs are growing or standing; any barren, dry marsh, or bog, whether the land is owned by the Crown or by private persons, or held under lease from the Crown. 2. Land bearing forest growth or land from which the forest has been removed but which shows surface evidence of past forest occupancy and is not now in other use. *Forests Act*, S.N.S. 1986, c. 10, s. 3. 3. Any land lying outside the boundaries of a city or town and not cultivated for agricultural purposes, on which trees, shrubs, plants or grass are growing, together with roads thereon, other than public highways. New Brunswick statutes. 4. A wooded area, forest stand, tract covered by underbrush, barren ground, marsh or bog, but does not include (a) an area which is apparently a tree plantation area or a Christmas Tree management area; (b) a special forestry study area; (c) the immediate area where any activity is apparently being carried out on woodlands for the purpose of harvesting a forest product; (d) a commercial berry growing area. *Trespass to Property Act*, S.P.E.I. 1984, c. 37, s. 13. 5. Land included in a timber lease or timber licence issued under an enactment of the Legislature or of Canada (a) for which a stumpage, as defined in the Forest Act, has not been reserved or not made payable to the Crown in right of the Province; (b) which is held for the specific purpose of cutting and removing timber, and for no other purpose while so held; and (c) which has been classified as forest land for taxation

purposes under the Taxation (Rural Area) Act. *Assessment Act*, R.S.B.C. 1979, c. 21, s. 1.

FOREST LOAN. A loan granted under the Forestry Credit Act (R.S.Q., chapter C-78) or the Act to promote forest credit by private institutions (1983, chapter 16). *An Act to Promote Forest Credit by Private Institutions*, S.Q. 1983, c. 16, s. 66.

FOREST MANAGEMENT. The practical application of scientific, economic and social principles to the administration of forest land for specified objectives. *Forests Act*, S.N.S. 1986, c. 10, s. 3.

FOREST MANAGEMENT BERTH. Any area for which a forest management licence is granted under this Act for the purpose of providing timber in a sustained yield basis to a wood-using industry. *Forest Act*, R.S.M. 1970, c. F150, s. 2.

FOREST MANAGEMENT PLAN. A master plan prepared for the proper management of an area of forest land for the continuous production of timber therefrom. *The Forest Act*, R.S.S. 1978, c. F-19, s. 2.

FOREST MANAGEMENT PROGRAM. A program designed to provide for more effective management of Crown lands and to encourage and assist private landowners to manage their land more effectively by providing professional and technical advice and assistance, training programs and suitable financial incentives. Nova Scotia statutes.

FOREST MANAGEMENT UNIT. An area which may be subject to a separate management plan, and from which sustained yield is sought as the object of management. *Forest Act*, R.S.M. 1970, c. F150, s. 2.

FOREST OPERATION. See COMMERCIAL ~.

FOREST OWNER. A physical person having full ownership of his forest except one engaged in wood processing otherwise than on a small scale industrial basis, as defined by regulation. *Forestry Credit Act*, R.S.Q. 1977, c. C-78, s. 1.

FOREST PLANTATION. A young artificially forested area established by planting or by direct seeding. *Snow Vehicles Act*, S.N.S. 1981, c. 51, s. 1.

FOREST PRODUCT. Wood in its raw state or transformed into pulp or wood-pulp by mechanical, chemical or other processes. *Forest Resources Utilization Act*, R.S.Q. 1977, c. U-2, s. 1. See PRIMARY ~; SECONDARY ~.

FOREST PRODUCTS. 1. Includes logs, bolts and billets of wood for the manufacture of lumber, pulp, etc., and also pit props, hewn ties, poles, piling, posts, fuelwood, and any other such products of trees in the form in which they are to be used. *Scalers Act*, R.S.N.B. 1973, c. S-4, s. 1. 2. Includes pulp, pulpwood, paper, veneer, plywood, lumber, timber, poles, posts, chips and other products accruing from a forest harvesting operation. *Prairie and Forest Fires Act*, S.S. 1982-83, c. P-22.1, s. 2. 3. Logs, even if they are flatted, wood chips, railway ties and spoolwood. *Taxation Act*, R.S.Q. 1977, c. I-3, s. 1176. See SPECIAL ~.

FOREST PROPERTY. Any lot of land, excluding any buildings or structures thereon, not used for agricultural purposes that is not used or intended to be used for residential or commercial or industrial purposes or any combination of such purposes.

FOREST ROAD. 1. A road on Crown Lands to the fullest extent of the right-of-way of such road and includes the bridges thereon but does not include a highway as defined in the Highway Act, or a logging road. *Crown Lands and Forests Act*, S.N.B. 1980, c. C-38.1, s. 1. 2. A road or part of a road on a public land under the jurisdiction of the Minister of Lands and Forests. *Lands and Forests Act*, R.S.Q. 1977, c. T-9, s. 98.

FOREST TREE PEST. Any vertebrate or invertebrate animal or any virus, fungus, or bacterium or other organism that is injurious to trees commonly found growing in a forest or windbreak or the products from such trees and that is designated as a forest tree pest in the regulations. *Forest Tree Pest Control Act*, R.S.O. 1980, c. 174, s. 1.

FORESTRY. *n.* The conservation, cultivation, improvement, harvesting and rational utilization of timber stands and the resources contained therein and obtainable therefrom, and includes the operation of a sugar bush. See PRACTICE OF PROFESSIONAL ~.

FORESTRY EQUIPMENT. Implements, apparatus, appliances and machinery, of any kind usually affixed to real property, for use in a forest. *Bank Act*, R.S.C. 1985, c. B-1, s. 2.

FORESTRY IMPLEMENTS. Tools, implements, apparatus, appliances and machines, of any kind not usually affixed to real property, for use in forestry, and includes vehicles for use in forestry. *Bank Act*, R.S.C. 1985, c. B-1, s. 2.

FORESTRY OPERATION. Any work within or upon forest land for the purpose of forest management. *Forests Act*, S.N.S. 1986, c. 10, s. 3.

FORESTRY PRODUCER. A person whose business consists in whole or in part of forestry and includes a producer of maple products. *Bank Act*, R.S.C. 1985, c. B-1, s. 2.

FORESTRY PURPOSES. Includes the production of wood and wood products, provision of proper environmental conditions for wild life, protection against floods and erosion, recreation, and protection and production of water supplies. Ontario statutes.

FORESTRY ROAD. Includes all bridges, culverts, ditches and other structures made in connection with a road. *Forests Act*, R.S.A. 1970, c. 147, s. 44.

FORFEIT. *v.* To forfeit to Her Majesty in right of Canada. *Customs Act*, R.S.C. 1985 (2d Supp.), c. 1, s. 2.

FORFEIT. *adj.* See APPEARANCE ~.

FORFEITURE. *n.* The surrender of goods or chattels to punish someone for a crime, for failure to comply with terms of a recognizance or pay duty or fulfil some obligation and to compensate the person to whom they were forfeited for any injury. See RELIEF AGAINST ~.

FORGED PASSPORT. See UTTERING ~.

FORGERY. *n.* Making a false document, knowing it to be false, with intent (a) that it should in any way be used or acted upon as genuine, to the prejudice of any one whether within Canada or not, or (b) that some person should be induced, by the belief that it is genuine, to do or to refrain from doing anything, whether within Canada or not. *Criminal Code*, R.S.C. 1985, c. C-46, s. 366.

FORGERY INSURANCE. Insurance against loss sustained by reason of forgery.

FORGERY OF PASSPORT. Everyone who, while in or out of Canada, (a) forges a passport, or (b) knowing that a passport is forged (i) uses, deals with or acts upon it, or (ii) causes or attempts to cause any person to use, deal with, or act upon it, as if the passport were genuine, is guilty of an offence. *Criminal Code*, R.S.C. 1985, c. C-46, s. 57.

FORGE WELD. Is applicable to joints made between plates which are welded together by means of hammering or rolling, and in which no added metal is included. *Steamship Machinery Construction Regulations*, C.R.C., c. 1491, Schedule IV, s. 1.

FORJUDGE. *v.* To deprive someone of some thing or right by judgment.

FORM. *n.* The contents or structure of a document distinguished from its substance. See BEARER ~; COMMON ~ BUSINESS; DOS-

AGE ~; FULLY REGISTERED ~; ORDER ~; PROPER ~; REGISTERED ~.

FORMAL BID. (i) A bid that is not an exempt take-over bid; or (ii) a bid that is an exempt bid and with respect to which the offeror has communicated to offerees a disclosure document.

FORMAL CONTRACT. A deed; a contract under seal. G.H.L. Fridman, *The Law of Contract in Canada*, 2d ed. (Toronto: Carswell, 1986) at 10.

FORMA LEGALIS FORMA ESSENTIALIS. [L.] Legal form is the essential form.

FORMAL EQUITY. (a) With respect to a corporation, any share of the corporation, other than a share excluded by the regulations, that is, or is deemed under the regulations to be, issued and outstanding, (b) with respect to a partnership, any interest or right in the capital or income, or both, of the partnership, (c) with respect to a trust, any beneficial interest in the property of the trust, and (d) with respect to any other person, such interest or right in respect of that person as is prescribed. *Canadian Ownership and Control Determination*, R.S.C. 1985, c. C-20, s. 2.

FORMAL PATIENT. A person admitted to and detained in a facility pursuant to admission certificates or detained in a facility pursuant to renewal certificates. *Medical Health Act*, R.S.A. 1980, c. M-13, s. 1.

FORMA PAUPERIS. See IN ~.

FORMAT. See FOREGROUND ~; GRAMOPHONE ~; MOSAIC ~; ROLLING ~.

FORMER BUSINESS PROPERTY. Of a taxpayer means a capital property that was used by him primarily for the purpose of gaining or producing income from a business, and that was real property or an interest therein of the taxpayer, but does not include, (a) a rental property of the taxpayer, (b) land subjacent to a rental property of the taxpayer, (c) land contiguous to land referred to in paragraph (b) that is a parking area, driveway, yard or garden or that is otherwise necessary for the use of the rental property referred to therein, or (d) a leasehold interest in any property described in paragraphs (a) to (c), and, for the purposes of this definition, "rental property" of a taxpayer means real property owned by the taxpayer, whether jointly with another person or otherwise, if the property was used by the taxpayer in the taxation year in respect of which the expression is being applied principally for the purpose of gaining or producing gross revenue that is rent, but, for the greater certainty, does not include a property leased by the taxpayer to a lessee, in the ordinary course of the taxpayer's business of selling goods or rendering services, under an agreement by which the lessee undertakes to use the property to carry on the business of selling or promoting the sale of the taxpayer's goods or services. *Income Tax Act*, R.S.C. 1952, c. 148 (as am. S.C. 1977-78, c. 1, s. 98(3)), s. 248(1).

FORMER CORPORATION. In respect of (a) an amalgamation of corporations, a "predecessor corporation" described in subsection 87(1) of the Income Tax Act, or (b) a winding-up of a corporation, a "subsidiary" described in subsection 88(1) of the Income Tax Act. *Petroleum and Gas Revenue Tax Act*, R.S.C. 1985, c. P-12, s. 6(5).

FORMER MEMBER. In relation to a pension plan, an employee or former employee who has terminated membership or commenced a pension or whose plan has been terminated, and who retains a present or future entitlement to receive a benefit under the plan.

FORMER PARCEL. A parcel existing prior to the completion of the replotting scheme, and includes any portion of land formerly a portion of a highway, park or public square, or of land indicated as such on a plan of subdivision deposited in the land title office. *Municipal Act*, R.S.B.C. 1979, c. 290, s. 886.

FORMER RESIDENT. A non-resident who has resided in the province for a continuous period of not less than five years after his twelfth birthday. *Fish and Wildlife Act*, S.N.B. 1980, c. F-14.1, s. 1.

FORMER SPOUSE. Includes a party to a voidable or void marriage, as the case may be. *Income Tax Act*, R.S.C. 1952, c. 148 (as am. S.C. 1988, c. 55, s. 191(2)), s. 252(3).

FORM OF MARRIAGE. Includes a ceremony of marriage that is recognized as valid (a) by the law of the place where it was celebrated, or (b) by the law of the place where an accused is tried, notwithstanding that it is not recognized as valid by the law of the place where it was celebrated. *Criminal Code*, R.S.C. 1985, c. C-46, s. 214.

FORM OF PROXY. A written or printed form that, upon completion and execution by or on behalf of a shareholder, security holder or member becomes a proxy.

FORMS OF ACTION. The common law procedural devices compliance with which was necessary to seek a remedy before the courts, ex. assumpsit, trespass on the case.

FORMULA. See FULTON-FAVREAU ~; INFANT ~; NETBACK PRICING ~; RAND ~; VANCOUVER ~.

FORMULARY. *n.* 1. A precedent; a form. 2. The formulary established pursuant to section 4. *The Prescription Drugs Act*, R.S.S. 1978, c. P-23, s. 2.

FORMULATION. *n.* In relation to a meat product, means a statement of (a) its ingredients and components, (b) the proportions of its ingredients, (c) the method of its manufacture, and (d) the name of the meat product to be used on labels. *Meat Inspection Regulations*, C.R.C., c. 1032, s. 2.

FORNICATION. *n.* Voluntary sexual intercourse between two people not married to each other.

FOR REMUNERATION. In addition to its usual meaning, in consideration of any direct or indirect commission or benefit, promise of remuneration or intention to obtain remuneration. *Insurance Act*, R.S.Q. 1977, c. A-32, s. 1.

FORSPEAKER. *n.* In a proceeding, an advocate or attorney.

FORTHWITH. *adv.* Within a reasonable time, considering the circumstances and the object.

FORTIFIED WINE. Any alcoholic beverage obtained by the fermentation of the natural sugar content of fruits or of other agricultural products containing sugar, including honey and milk, and that contains more than fourteen per centum of alcohol by volume. *Liquor Control Act*, R.S.M. 1970, c. L160, s. 2.

FORTIOR EST CUSTODIA LEGIS QUAM HOMINIS. [L.] Legal custody is stronger than personal.

FORTIOR ET POTENTIOR EST DISPOSITIO LEGIS QUAM HOMINIS. [L.] A legal arrangement is stronger and more powerful than a personal one.

FORTUNE-TELLING. *n.* Fraudulently undertaking, for a consideration, to tell fortunes is an offence. *Criminal Code*, R.S.C. 1985, c. C-46, s. 365.

FORTY-HOUR WEEK. Overtime must be paid for longer work hours; an historic goal of the labour movement.

FORUM. *n.* [L. a place] The place where legal remedies can be sought, a court.

FORUM CAN. CRIM. *abbr.* Le Forum canadien de criminologie (Canadian Criminology Forum).

FORUM CONVENIENS. [L.] The place where a trial may be held most conveniently.

FORUM NON CONVENIENS. [L.] Refers to a court's discretionary power to decline jurisdiction over a proceeding which may be more properly tried elsewhere. J.G. McLeod, *The Conflict of Laws* (Calgary: Carswell, 1983) at 779.

FORUM ORIGINIS. [L.] The court of the place of a person's domicile by birth.

FORUM REI. [L.] The court of the place where the subject thing or person is situated.

FORWARD CONTROL CONFIGURATION. A configuration in which more than half of the engine length is rearward of the foremost point of the windshield base and the steering wheel hub is in the forward quarter of the vehicle. *Motor Vehicle Safety Regulations*, C.R.C., c. 1038, s. 203.

FORWARDER. See FREIGHT ~.

FORWARDING AGENT. One who accepts and forwards goods, paying the cost of transportation and receiving in return compensation from the owners. The agent has no concern in the vehicles or vessels by which the goods are transported and no interest in the freight itself.

FORWARD PERPENDICULAR. A vertical line intersecting the point where the foreside of the stem of a ship crosses the waterline on which the length is measured. Canada regulations.

FORWARD SORTATION AREA. A specific geographical area identified by an FSA code. *Mail Preparation Regulations*, C.R.C., c. 1281, s. 2.

FORWARD SORTATION AREA CODE. The first three characters of a postal code. *Mail Preparation Regulations*, C.R.C., c. 1281, s. 2.

FOSSIL. *n.* The preserved remains or traces of animals or plants that lived in the geological past but does not include (a) fossil fuels or fossiliferous rock intended for industrial use, or (b) a carving or a sculpture made by man from fossiliferous or fossilized matter. *Canadian Cultural Property Export Control List*, C.R.C., c. 448, s. 1. See INVERTEBRATE ~; PLANT ~; VERTEBRATE ~; VERTEBRATE TRACE ~.

FOSSIL AMBER. Fossil resin with or without inclusions. *Canadian Cultural Property Export Control List*, C.R.C., c. 448, s. 1.

FOSSIL SPECIMEN. See TYPE ~.

FOSTER CARE. The provision of residential care to a child, by and in the home of a person who, i. receives compensation for caring for the child, except under the Family Benefits Act, the General Welfare Assistance Act, or the regulations made under either of them, and ii. is not the child's parent or a person with whom the child has been placed for adoption under Part VII. *Child and Family Services Act*, S.O. 1984, c. 55, s. 3.

FOSTER CHILD. A child whose parents are unable, in the opinion of the provincial authority, to support him and who is cared for (by a person or persons standing in loco parentis to him) in a private home approved as a suitable place of care by a child welfare authority or by a person designated for that purpose by the provincial authority. *Canada Assistance Plan Regulations*, C.R.C., c. 382, s. 2.

FOSTER FAMILY. A family which takes charge of one or several adults or children, to a maximum number of nine, who are entrusted to it through a social service centre. *Health Services and Special Services Act*, R.S.Q. 1977, c. S-5, s. 1.

FOSTER HOME. 1. A home, other than the home of the child's parent, in which a child is placed for care and supervision but not for the purposes of adoption. 2. With respect to a child who lacks normal parental relations, means a home other than that of parents or relatives, in which such child may be placed to be treated as a member of the family. See GROUP ~.

FOSTER PARENT. 1. An adult who as part of his family, cares for a child on behalf of the Minister. *Child and Family Services and Family Relations Act*, S.N.B. 1980, c. C-2.1, s. 1. 2. Any person who conducts, maintains, operates, or manages a foster home.

FOSTER PARENT AGREEMENT. An agreement entered into between a foster parent and the Minister transferring all or part of the care, custody and control of the child from the Minister to the foster parent. *Child and Family Services and Family Relations Act*, S.N.B. 1980, c. C-2.1, s. 43.

F.O.T. *abbr.* Free on truck. Describing a seller's responsibility to have the goods placed on a truck. I.F.G. Baxter, *The Law of Banking*, 3d ed. (Toronto: Carswell, 1981) at 136.

FOUL HOOKING. Fishing with a hook or hooks attached to a line manipulated in such a manner as to pierce a fish in any part of its body other than its mouth. *National Parks Fishing Regulations*, C.R.C., c. 1120, s. 2.

FOULING. *n.* Placement of powder and lubricant residue on the inside of a firearm barrel or on skin surrounding the entrance wound of a bullet. F.A. Jaffe, *A Guide to Pathological Evidence*, 2d ed. (Toronto: Carswell, 1983) at 176.

FOUNDATION. *n.* 1. A corporation established to receive, hold, administer and apply any property or the income from it for purposes or objects in connection with a hospital, other public or charitable purpose. 2. A system or arrangement of foundation units through which

the loads from a building are transferred to supporting soil or rock. *Building Code Act*, R.R.O. 1980, Reg. 87, s. 1. See CHARITABLE ~; DEEP ~; SHALLOW ~.

FOUNDATION DRAIN. A drain installed below the surface of the ground to collect and convey water from the foundation of a building or other structure. *Ontario Water Resources Act*, R.R.O. 1980, Reg. 736, s. 1.

FOUNDATION LOCAL GOVERNMENT DISTRICT. A local government district or a part of a local government district that is not within a school district. *Public Schools Act*, S.M. 1980, c. 33, s. 171.

FOUNDATION MUNICIPALITY. A municipality or a part of a municipality that is not within a school district. *Public Schools Act*, S.M. 1980, c. 33, s. 171.

FOUNDATION STATUS. With respect to seed, means that (a) the crop from which the seed is derived meets the standards established by the Association and a crop certificate designated "foundation" has been issued for that crop by the Association, or (b) if of foreign origin, the seed is certified as being of foundation status by an approved certifying agency. *Seeds Regulations*, C.R.C., c. 1400, s. 2.

FOUNDATION UNIT. One of the structural members of the foundation of a building such as a footing, raft or pile. *Building Code Act*, R.R.O. 1980, Reg. 87, s. 1.

FOUNDER. *n.* 1. A person who has signed the memorandum of association or who has been admitted as a member at the time of the organization meeting. *Cooperative Associations Act*, R.S.Q. 1977, c. A-24, s. 1. 2. A person who has signed the founding memorandum of a union or was admitted as a member at the organization meeting. *Savings and Credit Unions Act*, R.S.Q. 1977, c. C-4, s. 1.

FOUNDER FEDERATION. The federation upon whose application the security fund corporation has been incorporated. *An Act respecting security fund corporations*, S.Q. 1979, c. 53, s. 1.

FOUNDRY. *n.* The part of a building or premises or the workshop, structure, room or place in which base metals or their alloys are cast in moulds, other than permanent moulds, or where core-making, shakeout or cleaning or any casting or other dust-causing operation ancillary to the casting process is carried on. *Occupational Health and Safety Act*, R.R.O. 1980, Reg. 692, s. 1. See FERROUS ~.

FOUR AXLE GROUP. Four consecutive axles, not including the front axle of a motor vehicle,

(i) that are entirely within either a motor vehicle or trailer or semi-trailer, and (ii) in which the spacings between the consecutive axles do not exceed 2.5 metres. *Highway Traffic Act*, R.S.O. 1980, c. 198, s. 97.

4-H PROGRAM. A program designed for the education and training of farm boys and girls through local 4-H clubs. *The Saskatchewan 4-H Foundation Act*, R.S.S. 1978, c. S-18, s. 2.

FOURTH CLASS MAIL. See DOMESTIC ~.

FOURTH FREEDOM. The privilege of a foreign air carrier operating a charter to take on in Canada persons or goods destined to the territory of the country of the foreign air carrier and includes the privilege to put down such persons in Canada upon return from that country. *Air Carrier Regulations*, C.R.C., c. 2, s. 23.

F.O.W. *abbr.* First open water. Describes water immediately after ice breaks up so that navigation is possible.

FOWL. *n.* 1. A domestic hen more than twenty weeks of age. 2. Domesticated fowl. 3. Mature birds of either sex with rigid cartilage at the posterior end of the breast or keel bone; male birds may have lengthy hard spur development. *Dressed and Eviscerated Poultry Regulations*, C.R.C., c. 283, s. 53.

FOX PAT. C. *abbr.* Fox's Patent, Trade Mark, Design and Copyright Cases, 1940-1971.

F.P.A. *abbr.* Free from particular average. In marine insurance, means an underwriter is liable only for total loss, either actual or constructive.

F.P.R. *abbr.* Fisheries Pollution Reports.

FRACTIONEM DIEI NON RECIPIT LEX. [L.] The law does not recognize a fraction of a day.

FRACTION OF A DAY. The portion of a day recognized only in cases of necessity and for judicial purposes.

FRACTURE. *n.* The break in a bone. F.A. Jaffe, *A Guide to Pathological Evidence*, 2d ed. (Toronto: Carswell, 1983) at 176 and 177. See BUMPER ~; COMMINUTED ~; COMPOUND ~; CONTRE COUP ~; DEPRESSED ~; EGGSHELL ~; GREENSTICK ~; HAIRLINE ~; RADIATING ~.

FRAME. *v.* To fabricate false evidence so it appears someone else committed an offence.

FRAME. *n.* See SPACE ~.

FRANC. See GOLD ~.

FRANCHISE. *n.* 1. At common law, a royal privilege. 2. An agreement whereby the right to supply electricity, natural gas or natural gas liquids to the residents of a defined area is given. 3. A contract, agreement or arrangement, either expressed or implied, whether oral or written, between 2 or more persons by which a franchisee is required to pay directly or indirectly a franchise fee in consideration for any of the following: (i) the right to engage in the business of offering, selling or distributing the goods manufactured, processed or distributed or the services organized and directed by the franchisor, (ii) the right to engage in the business of offering, selling or distributing any goods or services under a marketing plan or system prescribed or controlled by the franchisor, (iii) the right to engage in a business which is associated with the franchisor's trademark, service mark, trade name, logotype, advertising or any business symbol designating the franchisor or its associate, (iv) the right to engage in a business in which the franchisee is reliant on the franchisor for the continued supply of goods or services, or (v) the right to recruit additional franchisees or subfranchisors, but excluding contracts, agreements or arrangements between manufacturers or if the franchisor is the Crown, a Crown agency or a municipal corporation. See AREA ~; PYRAMID ~; PYRAMID SALES ~; SPECIAL ~.

FRANCHISEE. *n.* A person to whom a franchise is granted.

FRANCHISE FEE. Any consideration exchanged or agreed to be exchanged for the granting of the franchise agreement and, without limiting the generality of the foregoing, the consideration may include (i) any fee or charge that a franchisee or subfranchisor is required to pay or agrees to pay, (ii) any payment for goods or services, (iii) any service which the franchisee or subfranchisor is required to perform or agrees to perform, or (iv) any loan, guarantee or other commercial consideration exigible from the franchisee or subfranchisor at the discretion of the franchisor or subfranchisor for the right to engage in business under a franchise agreement, but the following are not franchise fees: (v) the purchase of or agreement to purchase goods in a reasonable amount at the current wholesale market rate; (vi) the purchase of or the agreement to purchase services in a reasonable amount at the current market rate; (vii) the payment of a reasonable service charge to the issuer of a credit card by an establishment accepting or honouring the credit card. *Franchises Act*, R.S.A. 1980, c. F-17, s. 1.

FRANCHISOR. *n.* A person who grants a franchise.

FRANGIBLE. *adj.* Brittle, easily broken. F.A. Jaffe, *A Guide to Pathological Evidence*, 2d ed. (Toronto: Carswell, 1983) at 177.

FRATER CONSANGUINEUS. [L.] A brother by the father's side.

FRATER FRATRI UTERINO NON SUCCEDET IN HAEREDITATE PATERNA. [L.] A brother may not succeed a brother by the mother's side in a paternal inheritance.

FRATERNAL BENEFIT SOCIETY. A corporation having a representative form of government and incorporated for fraternal, benevolent or religious purposes among which purposes is the insuring of the members, or the spouses or children of the members thereof, exclusively, against accident, sickness, disability or death, and includes a corporation incorporated for those purposes on the mutual plan for the purpose of so insuring the members, or the spouses or children of the members, thereof, exclusively.

FRATERNAL CLUB. A chartered branch of an established fraternal organization in Canada with not fewer than fifty members. *Liquor Licence Act*, R.R.O. 1980, Reg. 581, s. 1.

FRATERNAL SOCIETY. A society, order or association incorporated for the purpose of making with its members only, and not for profit, contracts of life, accident or sickness insurance in accordance with its constitution, by-laws and rules and the governing statute.

FRATERNIA. *n.* [L.] A brotherhood, fraternity.

FRATER NUTRICIUS. [L.] A bastard brother.

FRATER UTERINUS. [L.] A brother by the mother's side.

FRATRES CONJURATI. [L.] Sworn brothers.

FRATRICIDE. *n.* The murder of a sibling.

FRAUD. *n.* 1. (1) Every one who, by deceit, falsehood or other fraudulent means, whether or not it is a false pretence within the meaning of this Act defrauds the public or any person whether ascertained or not, of any property, money or valuable security, is guilty of an offence. (2) Every one who, by deceit, falsehood or other fraudulent means, whether or not it is a false pretence within the meaning of this Act, with intent to defraud, affects the public market price of stocks, shares, merchandise or anything that is offered for sale to the public, is guilty of an offence. *Criminal Code*, R.S.C. 1985, c. C-46, s. 380 in part. See BADGES OF ~; STATUTE OF ~S.

FRAUDULENT ACT. 1. In connection with a trade in real estate: (i) any intentional misrepresentation by word, conduct or manner of a material fact, present or past, and an intentional omission to disclose such a material fact; (ii) a promise or representation as to the future that is beyond reasonable expectation and that is not made in good faith; (iii) the failure, within a reasonable time, properly to account for or pay over to the person entitled thereto any moneys received; (iv) the failure on the part of a broker or salesman to disclose to all parties concerned whether he or she is acting as a principal or as an agent in the trade; (v) any course of conduct or business calculated or put forward with intent to deceive the public or the purchaser or the vendor as to the value of any real estate; (vi) the failure on the part of a broker or salesman to disclose to a vendor of any real estate for whom he or she acts directly or indirectly any offer to purchase same, received by the broker or salesman; (vii) the gaining of, or attempt to gain, a commission, fee or gross profit so large and so exorbitant as to be unconscionable and unreasonable; (viii) generally, any artifice, agreement, device, scheme, course of conduct or business, to obtain money, profit or property by any of the means hereinbefore set forth or otherwise contrary to law, or by wrongful or dishonest dealing, and anything specifically defined in the regulations as coming within the meaning of this definition. 2. (i) Any fictitious or pretended trade in any security; (ii) the gaining or attempt to gain, directly or indirectly, through a trade in any security, a commission, fee or gross profit so large and exorbitant as to be unconscionable and unreasonable; (iii) any course of conduct or business which is calculated or put forward with intent to deceive the public or the purchaser or the vendor of any security as to the nature of any transaction or as to the value of such security. 3. (i) The making of any material false statement in any application, registration statement, prospectus, information, material or evidence submitted, or given to the Minister, the Minister's representative, or to the Registrar under this Act, or the regulations; (ii) the violation of any provision relating to trading securities; (iii) the failure on the part of a broker, manager or salesman to disclose to all parties concerned whether he or she is acting as a principal or as an agent in the trade.

FRAUDULENT CONVEYANCE. A conveyance which defrauds, delays or hinders creditors and others. A. Bissett-Johnson & W.M. Holland, eds., *Matrimonial Property Law in Canada* (Toronto: Carswell, 1980) at I-33.

FRAUDULENT MISREPRESENTATION. A statement known to be false by the party who made it. G.H.L. Fridman, *Sale of Goods in Canada*, 3d ed. (Toronto: Carswell, 1986) at 152.

FRAUDULENT PREFERENCE. An act by the debtor in regard to property which benefits one creditor over others.

FRAUS EST CELARE FRAUDEM. [L.] To conceal fraud is fraud.

FRAUS EST ODIOSA ET NON PRAESU-MENDA. [L.] Fraud is hateful and not to be undertaken.

FRAUS ET DOLUS NEMINI PATROCINARI DEBENT. [L.] Fraud and deceit ought not to provide a defence to anyone.

FRAUS ET JUS NUNQUAM COHABITANT. [L.] Fraud and justice never dwell together.

FRAUS LEGIS. [L. fraud of the law] The use of legal proceedings with fraudulent intent.

FRAY. See AFFRAY.

FREE. *adj.* When applied to any goods described in Schedule II, means that the goods may be imported and taken out of the warehouse for consumption in Canada, without duty. *Customs Tariff*, R.S.C. 1985, c. C-54, s. 2.

FREE ALONGSIDE SHIP. A seller undertakes to deliver goods alongside a ship at the seller's own expense. G.H.L. Fridman, *Sale of Goods in Canada*, 3d ed. (Toronto: Carswell, 1986) at 484-485.

FREEBOARD. *n.* 1. The vertical distance amidships from the subdivision load water line to the margin line. *Hull Construction Regulations*, C.R.C., c. 1431, Schedule 1, s. 11. 2. A distance that is calculated in respect of a ship in accordance with these Regulations and measured vertically downwards from a position coinciding with the midpoint of the upper edge of the deck line. *Load Line Regulations*, Canada regulations. See DEPTH FOR ~.

FREEBOARD DECK. The uppermost complete deck having permanent means of closing all openings in weather portions of the deck in accordance with sections 3 to 10, and in flush deck ships and ships with detached superstructures means the upper deck; in ships having discontinuous freeboard decks within superstructures that are not intact, or that are not fitted with Class 1 closing appliances as defined in subsection (12), the lowest line of the deck below the superstructure deck shall be deemed to be the freeboard deck. *General Load Line Rules*, C.R.C., c. 1425, Schedule 1, s. 1.

FREEBOARD RATIO. $\dfrac{f}{d}$

is the ratio between the freeboard (f) and the draught (d). *Hull Construction Regulations*, C.R.C., c. 1431, Schedule 1, s. 11.

FREE CAPITAL. See NET ~.

FREE CREDIT BALANCES. Includes moneys received from, or held for the account of, clients by a registrant, i. for investment pending the investment and payment for securities purchased by the clients from or through the registrant where the registrant does not own such securities at the time of purchase or has not purchased them on behalf of the client, pending the purchase thereof by the registrant, and ii. as proceeds of securities purchased from clients or sold by the registrant for the account of clients where securities have been delivered to the registrant but payment has not been made pending payment of such proceeds to the clients. *Securities Act*, R.R.O. 1980, Reg. 910, s. 84.

FREEDOM. See FIFTH ~; FOURTH ~; THIRD ~.

FREEDOM OF CONTRACT. The parties to a contract are left by the court to use their own discretion and to make their own agreement. G.H.L. Fridman, *The Law of Contract in Canada*, 2d ed. (Toronto: Carswell, 1986) at 82.

FREEDOM OF SPEECH. A privilege and fundamental right of any member of Parliament on the House floor and in committee. A. Fraser, G.A. Birch & W.A. Dawson, eds., *Beauchesne's Rules and Forms of the House of Commons of Canada*, 5th ed. (Toronto: Carswell, 1978) at 20.

FREE FROM GENERAL AVERAGE. In marine insurance policies, means that the underwriters are not liable for general average losses.

FREE FROM PARTICULAR AVERAGE. In marine insurance policies, means that an underwriter is liable only for total loss, either actual or constructive.

FREEHOLD. *n.* Has not only its usual signification, but extends to all lands and hereditaments for the conveyance of which a bargain and sale, or lease for a year, as well as a release, would formerly have been used. *Real Property Act*, R.S.P.E.I. 1974, c. R-4, s. 1.

FREEHOLDER. *n.* One who possesses a freehold estate.

FREEHOLD ESTATE. An interest in land by which the freeholder is entitled to hold the land for an unfixed and uncertain period of time.

FREEHOLD GAS. All gas (i) produced from freehold lands; or (ii) allocated to freehold lands, or to the holder of any right thereto or interest therein, under a voluntary pooling arrangement, a pooling order, an agreement for unit operation or a unit operation order made pursuant to The Oil and Gas Conservation Act and the regulations thereunder. *Freehold Oil and Gas Production Tax Act*, S.S. 1982-83, c. F-22.1, s. 2.

FREEHOLD LANDS. 1. All lands in a province, and all rights thereto and interests therein, that are not Crown lands, and, for greater certainty,

FREEHOLD MINERAL INTEREST

includes all Crown-acquired lands. 2. Lands other than Crown Lands and other lands vested in Her Majesty. *Crown Lands and Forests Act,* S.N.B. 1980, c. C-38.1, s. 1.

FREEHOLD MINERAL INTEREST. The estate or interest of a person, other than the Province, in a mineral on or below the surface of mineral land whether or not that estate or interest is registered as a charge against the title of that land. *Mineral Land Tax Amendment Act,* S.B.C. 1981, c. 19, s. 1.

FREEHOLD OIL. 1. All oil other than Crown oil. *Oil Well Income Tax Amendment Act, 1980,* S.S. 1980-81, c. 16, s. 3. 2. All oil (i) produced from freehold lands; or (ii) allocated to freehold lands, or to the holder of any right thereto or interest therein, under a voluntary pooling arrangement, a pooling order, an agreement for unit operation or a unit operation order made pursuant to The Oil and Gas Conservation Act and the regulations thereunder. *Freehold Oil and Gas Production Tax Act,* S.S. 1982-83, c. F-22.1, s. 2.

FREEHOLD WELL. In relation to the continuation of a lease, means a well that, in the opinion of the Minister, is capable of producing (i) petroleum in paying quantity from the same zone as that in which petroleum rights are granted under the lease, or (ii) natural gas in paying quantity from the same zone as that in which natural gas rights are granted under the lease, if the title to all the petroleum or natural gas, as the case may be, in the spacing unit for the well is not owned by the Crown in right of Alberta. *Mines and Minerals Amendment Act,* S.A. 1985, c. 39, s. 6.

FREE OF CAPTURE AND SEIZURE. In marine insurance policies, indicates that the underwriter is not liable for capture or seizure of either the cargo or the ship.

FREE ON BOARD. Describing a seller's responsibility to have goods placed on board a particular ship. I.F.G. Baxter, *The Law of Banking,* 3d ed. (Toronto: Carswell, 1981) at 136.

FREE ON TRUCK. Describing a seller's responsibility to have the goods placed on a truck. I.F.G. Baxter, *The Law of Banking,* 3d ed. (Toronto: Carswell, 1981) at 136.

FREE RIDER. A non-union worker who benefits from the gains made by union activities.

FREE TIME. In respect of goods, means a period of time during which goods may be kept on a wharf without the payment of storage charges thereon. Canada regulations.

FREE VOTE. A parliamentary division on a question for which party lines are ignored. A.

Fraser, G.A. Birch & W.A. Dawson, eds., *Beauchesne's Rules and Forms of the House of Commons of Canada,* 5th ed. (Toronto: Carswell, 1978) at 75.

FREEWAY. *n.* A divided arterial highway that is accessible only from intersecting arterial streets at grade separated interchanges that have been approved by the Minister. *Public Transportation and Highway Improvement Act,* R.S.O. 1980, c. 421, s. 99.

FREEZE. See ESTATE ~; QUICK ~.

FREIGHT. *n.* 1. Includes the profit derivable by ship owners from the employment of their ships to carry their own goods or movables, as well as freight payable by a third party, but does not include passage-money. *Insurance acts.* 2. Any substance, article or thing. *Elevators and Lifts acts.* 3. Includes personal property of every description that may be conveyed on a motor vehicle or trailer, except a passenger's personal baggage. *Motor Carrier acts.* See DEAD ~; EXPRESS ~; PACKAGE ~.

FREIGHT CAPACITY. See GROSS ~.

FREIGHT FORWARDER. Any person not the holder of an operating licence who transports or offers to transport or provides the transportation or offers to provide the transportation of goods on a highway for compensation and who, (i) assembles and consolidates or provides for assembling and consolidating shipments of such goods, and performs or provides for distributing operations with respect to such consolidated shipments, and (ii) assumes responsibility for the transportation of such property from point of receipt to point of destination, and (iii) utilizes a commercial motor vehicle or trailer as defined in the Highway Traffic Act, or a dual-purpose vehicle for the whole or any part of the transportation of such goods beyond an urban zone. *Public Commercial Vehicles Act,* R.S.O. 1980, c. 407, s. 1.

FREIGHT TO PRICE RATIO. In respect of any calendar year, means an amount equal to the quotient, expressed as a percentage, obtained by dividing the average cost to the shipper of moving one tonne of grain in that calendar year by the weighted average price for that calendar year. *Western Grain Transportation Act,* R.S.C. 1985, c. W-8, s. 61.

FREIGHT VEHICLE. A vehicle operated by or on behalf of any person carrying on upon any highway the business of a carrier of freight for gain. *Motor Carrier Act,* R.S.N.S. 1967, c. 190, s. 1. See LIMITED ~; PRIVATE ~; PUBLIC ~.

FRIEND. See ALIEN ~.

FRENCH FISHING VESSEL. A fishing vessel that is registered in France or, in the case of a vessel that is not registered, a fishing vessel that is entitled to fly the flag of France. *Transitional French Fishing Vessel Licence Exemption Regulations*, C.R.C., c. 414, s. 2.

FRENCH LANGUAGE EDUCATION. A school program using French as the language of instruction. *An Act to Amend the School Act*, S.P.E.I. 1985, c. 39, s. 1.

FRENCH-LANGUAGE INSTRUCTIONAL UNIT. A class, group of classes or school in which French is the language of instruction. Ontario statutes.

FRENCH-SPEAKING PERSON. A child of a person who has the right under subsection 23 (1) or (2), without regard to subsection 23 (3), of the Canadian Charter of Rights and Freedoms to have his or her children receive their primary and secondary school instruction in the French language in Ontario. *Education Amendment Act (No. 2)*, S.O. 1986, c. 29, s. 1.

FRENCH-SPEAKING RATEPAYER. A person who is entitled to vote at an election of members of the board and who has the right under subsection 23 (1) or (2), without regard to subsection 23 (3), of the Canadian Charter of Rights and Freedoms to have his or her children receive their primary and secondary school instruction in the French language in Ontario. *Education Amendment Act (No. 2)*, S.O. 1986, c. 29, s. 1.

FREQUENCY RATE. See DISABLING INJURY ~.

FREQUENCY RESPONSE. The air-to-air gain of the hearing aid expressed as a function of the frequency under specified test conditions. *Medical Devices Regulations*, C.R.C., c. 871, s. 1. See BASIC ~; COMPREHENSIVE ~.

FREQUENTIA ACTUS MULTUM OPERATUR. [L.] The frequency of an act is of great effect.

FRESH. *adj.* In relation to (a) a meat product other than sausages, means untreated except by refrigeration, and (b) sausages, means prepared from meat that is untreated except by refrigeration. *Meat Inspection Regulations*, C.R.C., c. 1032, s. 2.

FRESH CATCH. A catch that is not cured or processed. *Unemployment Insurance Regulations*, C.R.C., c. 1576, s. 74.

FRESH FRUIT. Peaches, pears, plums and prunes produced in Ontario, other than peaches, pears, plums and prunes that are used for processing. Canada regulations.

FRESH GRAPES. Grapes produced in Ontario other than grapes that are used by a processor for processing. Canada regulations.

FRESHWATER MARSH. An inland area, lying between dry land and a lake, pond, river or stream, where the water table is ordinarily near or above the surface of the land and which is characterized by aquatic and grass-like vegetation. *An Act to Amend the Trespass Act*, S.N.B. 1985, c. 70, s. 1.

FRESH WATER PRODUCT. Any fish, shellfish or crustacean unable to live in a marine environment and any batrachian, including parts of such animals and the products or by-products derived therefrom. *An Act to Amend the Agricultural Products, Marine Products and Food Act*, S.Q, 1983, c. 53, s. 1.

FRICTION HOIST. The type of hoist where the rope passes over or around a driving pulley, and where the rope is driven by the friction between it and the pulley tread material.

FRIEND. See NEXT ~.

FRIENDLY SOCIETY. A society, order, association or company formed or incorporated and operated for the purpose of making with its members only, and not for profit, contracts under which (i) sickness, accident and disability benefits, or any one or more of them, not exceeding five dollars per week, or (ii) funeral benefits not exceeding one hundred and fifty dollars, or all of those benefits may be paid only to its members or their beneficiaries in accordance with its charter and this Act. *Insurance acts*.

FRIENDLY SUIT. A suit brought which parties mutually arrange to bring to obtain a decision on a point which interests both.

FRIEND OF THE COURT. Any person who, with leave of a judge or at the invitation of a presiding judge or master, and without becoming a party to the proceeding, intervenes to render assistance to the court by way of argument. G.D. Watson & C. Perkins, eds., *Holmested & Watson: Ontario Civil Procedure* (Toronto: Carswell, 1984) at 13-2.

FRINGE BENEFIT. With respect to an employee, means the value per hour, based on regular hours of work of the employee, of any amount paid either directly or indirectly and either immediately or at some future time, by the employer to or in respect of the employee or his dependants over and above regular wage rates for or in respect of each hour or regular hours of work worked by the employee and, without limiting the generality of the foregoing, includes the value per hour of regular hours of work of an employee of any contribution by the employer (i) in respect of any pension or superannuation plan other than the Canada Pension Plan, (ii) in respect of any insurance, mutual benefit, sick benefit or death benefit plan other than the Canada Pension Plan or the plan administered under The Workers Compensation Act, and (iii) in respect of any plan to pay benefits during periods of unemployment other than the plan administered under the Unemployment Insurance Act (Canada), and also includes general holiday pay and vacation pay or the value per hour of regular hours of any period of vacation to which the employee may become entitled and shift premiums, cost of living bonuses, production bonuses and any other premiums or bonuses which are paid to the employee in respect of work done. *Employment Standards Act*, S.M. 1977, c. 50, s. 1.

FRINGE GROUP. Employees whose activities are on the borderline so far as application of a statute is concerned or who perform tasks connected with but not identical to work performed by bargaining unit members.

FRINGE TIME. Time spent in preparatory or winding-up activities.

FRIVOLOUS OR VEXATIOUS ACTION. See VEXATIOUS ACTION.

FROM. *conj.* Ordinarily excludes the day from which time is to be measured.

FRONTAGE. *n.* 1. When used in reference to a lot abutting directly on a work, means that side or limit of the lot that abuts directly on the work. 2. Any limit or limits of a summer resort location contiguous to or adjacent to a lake, river or road but, where a summer resort location has limits contiguous to or adjacent to a lake or river and a road, "frontage" means the limit or limits contiguous to or adjacent to the lake or river. *Public Lands Act*, R.R.O. 1980, Reg. 879, s. 1. See ACTUAL ~; FOOT ~; TAXABLE ~; TOTAL ACTUAL ~; TOTAL TAXABLE ~.

FRONTAGE TAX. Any tax that is levied on the owners of real property and that is computed by applying a rate to all or part of the assessed dimension of real property and includes any tax levied on the owners of real property that is in the nature of a local improvement tax, a development tax or a redevelopment tax but does not include a tax in respect of mineral rights. *Municipal Grants Act*, R.S.C. 1985, c. M-13, s. 2.

FRONT AND REAR TOWNSHIP. 1. One where the usual practice in the original survey was to survey the boundaries, base lines, if any, and the side lines of the lots and establish the corners of the lots and make road allowances between each concession and along the side lines between each second lot. *Surveys Act*,

R.R.O. 1980, Reg. 928, Meth. 1. 2. A lot with an area of 100 acres and dimensions of 50 chains by 20 chains. B.J. Reiter, R.C.B. Risk & B.N. McLellan, *Real Estate Law*, 3d ed. (Toronto: Emond Montgomery, 1986) at 627.

FRONT AREA. All Canadian waters and territories and waters of the Atlantic Ocean bounded on the north by Latitude 60° north and on the south by a straight line drawn due east from Cape Race, Newfoundland and on the west by the coast of Newfoundland and including all the waters of the Strait of Belle Isle southwest to a straight line drawn from the lighthouse at Amour Point to the lighthouse on Flowers Island in Flowers Cove, Newfoundland. *Seal Protection Regulations*, C.R.C., c. 833, s. 2.

FRONT AXLE WEIGHT. (i) For a single front axle, that part of the gross vehicle weight transmitted to the highway by the front axle, (ii) for a dual front axle, one-half of that part of the gross vehicle weight transmitted to the highway by the front axle, and (iii) for a triple front axle, one-third of that part of the gross vehicle weight transmitted to the highway by the front axle. *Highway Traffic Act*, R.R.O. 1980, Reg. 470, s. 1.

FRONTIER. See HIGHWAY ~ EXAMINING WAREHOUSE.

FRONTIER LANDS. Lands that belong to Her Majesty in right of Canada, or in respect of which Her Majesty in right of Canada has the right to dispose of or exploit the natural resources, and that are situated in (a) the Yukon Territory, the Northwest Territories or Sable Island, or (b) those submarine areas, not within a province, adjacent to the coast of Canada and extending throughout the natural prolongation of the land territory of Canada to the outer edge of the continental margin or to a distance of two hundred nautical miles from the baselines from which the breadth of the territorial sea of Canada is measured, whichever is the greater. *Petroleum Resources Act*, R.S.C. 1985 (2d supp.), c. 36, s. 2.

FRONTIER PORT. The first port at which the vehicle carrying the goods to be entered arrives by land in Canada after crossing the frontier, and the sea, lake or river port at which the vessel in which the goods are carried arrives direct from a port or place out of Canada. *Customs Act*, R.S.C. 1970, c. C-40, s. 2.

FRONTING. *adj.* Includes abutting. *City of Winnipeg Act*, S.M. 1971, c. 105, s. 351.

FRONTS. See BROKEN ~.

FRONT YARD. A yard extending across the full width of a lot on which a building or structure is situate, and extending from the front lot line to the part of the building or structure that is nearest to the front lot line. *Niagara Escarpment Planning and Development Act*, R.R.O. 1980, Reg. 685, s. 1.

FROST. See DE~.

FROST ACTION. The phenomenon that occurs when water in soil is subjected to freezing which, because of the water ice phase change or ice lens growth, results in a total volume increase or the build-up of expansive forces under confined conditions or both, and the subsequent thawing that leads to loss of soil strength and increased compressibility. *Building Code Act*, R.R.O. 1980, Reg. 87, s. 1.

FROZEN. *adj.* 1. Refers to a trust in which the trustee is required only to hold the original assets and return them to the settlor when the trust ends. D.M.W. Waters, *The Law of Trusts in Canada*, 2d ed. (Toronto: Carswell, 1984) at 438. 2. Preserved by freezing temperature and does not include any surface freezing that may occur during holding and transportation. *Food and Drug Regulations*, C.R.C., c. 870, c. B.01.080.

FROZEN EGG. Whole egg, egg yolk or albumen in frozen form. *Processed Egg Regulations*, C.R.C., c. 290, s. 2.

FROZEN EGG MIX. Frozen egg containing added ingredients not exceeding 12 per cent by weight. *Processed Egg Regulations*, C.R.C., c. 290, s. 2.

FROZEN FOOD LOCKER PLANT. A business that provides individual lockers to store frozen food for human consumption.

FROZEN POTATO PRODUCTS PLANT. Includes any plant where raw potatoes are processed and the final potato product is distributed in a frozen condition. *Potato Processing Plant Liquid Effluent Regulations*, C.R.C., c. 829, s. 2.

FROZEN SENIORITY. Seniority protected but not allowed to increase during a period of layoff.

FROZEN TRUST. A trust for an office holder in which the trustee retains original assets and simply transfers them back to the settlor when the trust ends. D.M.W. Waters, *The Law of Trusts in Canada*, 2d ed. (Toronto: Carswell, 1984) at 438.

FRUCTUS AUGENT HAEREDITATEM. [L.] A yearly increase enriches an inheritance.

FRUCTUS INDUSTRIALES. [L.] Crops like wheat, barley and potatoes, which includes both emblements (crops produced annually by agriculture) and industrial growing crops (products of the soil which are not annual or permanent,

like artificial grass and clover). G.H.L. Fridman, *Sale of Goods in Canada*, 3d ed. (Toronto: Carswell, 1986) at 17-18.

FRUCTUS NATURALES. [L.] Natural product of land.

FRUIT. *n.* Fruit known botanically as such of any kind grown in Canada, but does not include any species of wild fruit in respect of which no grade is established. *Fruit, Vegetables and Honey Act*, R.S.C. 1970, c. F-31, s. 2. See CANNED ~S AND ~ PRODUCTS; FRESH ~; STEMLESS ~; TENDER ~.

FRUIT AND PRODUCE. Includes dairy products, eggs, fish, honey, maple products, poultry and vegetables. *Ontario Food Terminal Act*, R.S.O. 1980, c. 334, s. 1.

FRUIT BREAD. All bread containing a preponderance of such ingredients as currants, raisins, nuts, shortening and sugar and generally known to the trade and to the public as fruit bread and nut bread respectively. *Bread Act*, R.S.A. 1970, c. 34, s. 2.

FRUITERER. *n.* A person, firm or corporation, who sells by retail only all or any of the following: fresh fruits, fresh vegetables, nuts, table figs, table raisins, dates, and fresh oysters. *Shops Regulation Act*, R.S.M. 1970, c. S110, s. 3.

FRUIT JUICE. The unfermented liquid expressed from sound ripe fresh fruit, and includes any such liquid that is heat treated and chilled. *Food and Drug Regulations*, C.R.C., c. 870, c. B.11.001.

FRUIT TREE DISEASE. Any disease or injury of a fruit tree that is caused by an insect, virus, fungus, bacterium or other organism. *Abandoned Orchards Act*, R.S.O. 1980, c. 1, s. 1.

FRUIT TREES. (i) Apple trees, (ii) cherry trees, (iii) grape vines, (iv) peach trees, (v) pear trees, (vi) plum trees, and (vii) such other fruit-producing trees, shrubs or vines as are designated in the regulations. *Abandoned Orchards Act*, R.S.O. 1980, c. 1, s. 1.

FRUSCA TERRAE. [L.] Wasteland; desert land.

FRUSTRA FIT PER PLURA, QUOD FIERI POTEST PER PAUCIORA. [L.] It is useless to employ many agents when fewer will suffice.

FRUSTRA LEGIS AUXILIUM QUAERIT QUI IN LEGEM COMMITTIT. [L.] It is vain for one who commits an offence against the law to seek the help of the law.

FRUSTRA PROBATUR QUOD PROBATUM NON RELEVAT. [L.] To prove anything which does not improve your case is useless.

FRUSTRATION

FRUSTRATION. *n.* Of a contract, when a change of circumstances makes it legally or physically impossible to perform or when a change of circumstances makes the contract a different commercial venture from the one the parties originally undertook. G.H.L. Fridman, *Sale of Goods in Canada*, 3d ed. (Toronto: Carswell, 1986) at 299-300.

FRUSTRUM TERRAE. [L.] A parcel or piece of land.

FSA. *abbr.* Forward sortation area.

FSA CODE. See RURAL ~; URBAN ~.

F3. Telephony by frequency modulation. *General Radio Regulations*, Part II, C.R.C., c. 1372, s. 42.

F.T.R. *abbr.* Federal Trial Reports.

F2. Telegraphy by frequency modulation using the keying of a modulating audio frequency or audio frequencies or the keying of the modulated emission; including in special cases, an unkeyed emission modulated by audio frequencies. *General Radio Regulations, Part II*, C.R.C., c. 1372, s. 42.

FUEL. *n.* Any form of matter that, in it primary use, is combusted or oxidized for the generation of energy. See ALTERNATIVE ~; AVIATION ~; BLENDED ~; BUNKER ~; CLEAR ~; COLOURED ~; DIESEL ~; LOCOMOTIVE ~; MARKED ~; MOTIVE ~; TAXABLE ~; TRANSPORTATION ~.

FUEL AND ELECTRIC SYSTEMS MECHANIC. A person engaged in the repair and maintenance of motor vehicles who, (i) repairs and adjusts fuel systems, (ii) installs, repairs and removes ignition systems, generators, alternators, starters, coils, panel instruments, wiring and other electrical systems and equipment, (iii) performs a complete tune-up of an engine, and (iv) installs, inspects, maintains and removes motor vehicle air-conditioning systems. *Apprenticeship and Tradesmen's Qualification Act*, R.R.O. 1980, Reg. 35, s. 1.

FUEL-BURNING EQUIPMENT. *var.* FUEL BURNING EQUIPMENT. 1. Any equipment, apparatus, device, mechanism or structure that burns solid, liquid or gaseous fuel for the purpose of vehicle transportation, heating, drying, generating power, processing steam or any combination thereof. 2. Includes equipment designed to burn fuel, but does not include an internal combustion engine. *Environmental Protection Act*, R.R.O. 1980, Reg. 308, s. 1.

FUEL CONSUMPTION. The quantity of fuel used by a motor vehicle when driven a given distance. *Motor Vehicle Fuel Consumption Standards Act*, R.S.C. 1985, c. M-9, s. 2.

FUEL CONSUMPTION NUMBER. A number that represents the fuel consumption of a motor vehicle under controlled test conditions. *Motor Vehicle Fuel Consumption Standards Act*, R.S.C. 1985, c. M-9, s. 2.

FUEL CONSUMPTION STANDARD. A standard prescribed pursuant to section 3. *Motor Vehicle Fuel Consumption Standards Act*, R.S.C. 1985, c. M-9, s. 2.

FUEL-FIRED APPLIANCE. A device designed for use in heating and cooling systems operated on fuel and includes all components, controls, wiring and piping required to be part of the device. *Children's Residential Services Act*, R.R.O. 1980, Reg. 101, s. 23.

FUEL METERING DEVICE. The carburetor, fuel injector, fuel distributor or fuel injection pump. *Motor Vehicle Safety Regulations*, C.R.C., c. 1038, s. 2.

FUEL OIL. 1. The liquid derived from petroleum or natural gas, and any other liquid, by whatever name known or sold, containing any derivative of coal, petroleum or natural gas used to produce a flame for heating, cooking or raising steam, but does not include gasoline. 2. Furnace oil, stove oil, bunker fuel oil and diesel fuel oil. 3. A liquid that is capable of being used for the generation of power in an internal combustion engine, including liquified petroleum gas and, without derogating from the generality of the foregoing, includes (i) all liquid products obtained, whether by distillation or condensation or absorption or any other process, from petroleum, natural gas, casing head or natural gasoline, benzol, benzine, naphtha, coal, coal tar, bituminous sands, oil shales, kerosene, gas oil and any combination of any of those products, and prepared, advertised, offered for sale, sold for use as or used for or capable of being used for the generation of power in an internal combustion engine, and (ii) a product obtained by blending any of those liquid products with another product if the resultant product so obtained is capable of use for the generation of power in an internal combustion engine. *Fuel Oil Licensing Act*, R.S.A. 1980, c. F-22, s. 1. See COLOURED ~.

FUEL PETROLEUM PRODUCT. (i) Any liquid product that is obtained or recovered from petroleum, natural gas or coal, whether by distillation, condensation, absorption or otherwise; (ii) any combination of liquid products that are so obtained or recovered; or (iii) any natural gas or manufactured gas; that, by combustion, develops the power required for the purpose of operating internal combustion engines, and includes crude oil and every other liquid product and combination of liquid products, whether or not obtained or recovered from petroleum, that is capable of fulfilling the same purpose by means of combustion; but does not include such gas or liquid product as may be declared by the Lieutenant Governor in Council not to be a fuel petroleum product for the purpose of this Act. *The Fuel Petroleum Products Act*, R.S.S. 1978, c. F-23, s. 2.

FUEL SPILLAGE. The fall, flow or run of fuel from a vehicle but does not include wetness resulting from capillary action. *Motor Vehicle Safety Regulations*, C.R.C., c. 1038, s. 2.

FUEL SYSTEM. With reference to anything powered by an internal combustion engine, includes a fuel tank, carburetor, fuel pump, fuel filter, fuel injection system, pipes or any other thing in physical association with the engine that contains fuel oil or through which fuel oil passes during the operation of the engine. *Fuel Oil Administration Act*, R.S.A. 1980, c. F-21, s. 1.

FUEL TANK. A tank or container that is (i) originally provided by the manufacturer of a motor vehicle to carry the fuel required to propel it, or (ii) carried in or upon a motor vehicle and capable of being easily connected to its fuel system. See VEHICLE ~.

FUGAM FECIT. [L.] One fled.

FUGITIVE. *n.* 1. A person accused of having committed an offence to which this Act applies in any part of Her Majesty's Realms and Territories, except Canada, and who has left that part. *Fugitive Offenders Act*, R.S.C. 1985, c. F-32, s. 2. 2. A person being or suspected of being in Canada, who is accused or convicted of an extradition crime committed within the jurisdiction of a foreign state. *Extradition Act*, R.S.C. 1985, c. E-23, s. 2.

FUGITIVE CRIMINAL. A person being or suspected of being in Canada, who is accused or convicted of an extradition crime committed within the jurisdiction of a foreign state. *Extradition Act*, R.S.C. 1985, c. E-23, s. 2.

FUGITIVE EMISSION. A dust, fog, fume, gas, liquid, mist, solid or vapour which escapes from emission control equipment, process equipment or from a product. D. Robertson, *Ontario Health and Safety Guide* (Toronto: Richard De Boo Ltd., 1988) at 5-194.

FUGITIVE'S GOODS. The goods of a person which were forfeited because the person fled.

FULL AGE. Age of majority.

FULL AND VALUABLE CONSIDERATION. Includes such a consideration either actually paid upon or before the making of the assurance, or reserved or made payable to the vendor or any other person by way of rent, rent charge, or other annual payment, in perpetuity, or for any term of years, or other period, with or without a right of re-entry for non-payment thereof, or partly paid and partly reserved, as aforesaid. *Mortmain and Charitable Uses Act*, R.S.O. 1980, c. 297, s. 1.

FULL CLAIM. Any mineral claim of the full size. *Yukon Quartz Mining Act*, R.S.C. 1985, c. Y-4, s. 2.

FULL COMMUNITY. All immovables and movables acquired during marriage over which the husband has wide powers of administration. J.G. McLeod, *The Conflict of Laws* (Calgary: Carswell, 1983) at 371.

FULL COST OF COMPENSATION. Includes (i) compensation, burial expenses, the cost of furnishing medical aid and all other amounts payable under or by virtue of the Workers' Compensation Act, by reason of an accident to a blind worker for which the worker is entitled to compensation under that Act, and (ii) the capitalized sum or present value of the sum required as determined by the Board to provide for future payments of compensation to the worker or the worker's dependants. *Blind Workers' Compensation acts.*

FULL COSTS. Party-and-party costs, except in expropriation proceedings where the term means costs as between client and solicitor. M.M. Orkin, *The Law of Costs*, 2d ed. (Aurora: Canada Law Book, 1987) at 1-13.

FULL COURT. A court with all judges present.

FULL DISCLOSURE. The provision of the cost of borrowing in terms of annual rate of interest and in dollar terms.

FULL EMPLOYMENT. Work available to all persons willing and able to work.

FULL-LOAD CAPACITY. The maximum weight of commodity per unit time that a conveyor scale can discharge as set out in the notice of approval. *Weights and Measures Regulations*, C.R.C., c. 1605, s. 57.

FULL NET ANNUAL VALUE. The rent at which the property might reasonably be expected to be let from year to year. *City of St. John's Act*, R.S. Nfld. 1970, c. 40, s. 2.

FULL-TIME BASIS. In relation to an employee of a particular class, means engaged to work, throughout the year, all or substantially all of the normally scheduled hours of work established for persons in that class of employees. *Pension Benefits Standards Act*, R.S.C. 1985 (2d Supp.), c. 32, s. 2.

FULL-TIME EMPLOYEE. An employee whose regular work week exceeds thirty hours.

Inflation Restraint Act, 1982, S.O. 1982, c. 55, s. 4.

FULL TIME EMPLOYMENT. *var.* **FULL-TIME EMPLOYMENT.** 1. Employment requiring continuous service in an office or position, where the employee is normally required to work the minimum number of hours prescribed by the person having authority to establish the hours of such employment. 2. Employment in the Public Service requiring continuous service in an office or position, where the employee is required to work at least twenty-nine hours per week. *Public Service Superannuation Act*, S.N.B. 1977, c. 43, s. 1.

FULL-TIME FARMER. During the calendar year means an individual who, in that year, i. owns a share of the capital stock of a family farm corporation of that individual, ii. leases land to a full-time farmer who is his spouse or his child, a corporation, any share of the capital stock of which is a share of the capital stock of a family farm corporation of his spouse or any of his children, or a partnership, an interest in which is an interest in a family farm partnership of his spouse or any of his children, where the land is used in the year in the business of farming in Canada by his spouse, any of his children, the corporation or the partnership, or iii. is actively engaged in the business of farming in Canada other than an individual who in the year has or would have, if he sustained sufficient losses from the business of farming, a restricted farm loss for the year. *An Act to Amend Various Fiscal Laws and Other Legislation*, S.Q. 1986, c. 15, s. 132.

FULL-TIME FIRE FIGHTER. *var.* **FULL-TIME FIRE-FIGHTER.** 1. A person regularly employed in the fire department on a full-time salaried basis and assigned exclusively to fire protection or fire prevention duties, and includes officers and technicians. 2. A person regularly employed in the fire department on a full-time salaried basis and assigned exclusively to fire protection or fire prevention duties but does not include the fire chief or a deputy fire chief or any other person having authority to employ or discharge a full-time fire-fighter or regularly acting in a confidential capacity on behalf of the fire chief or the city or any board, commission or other body established to manage, control and operate the fire department.

FULL-TIME INSTRUCTION. When used with reference to an occupational training course means 24 hours a week or more of instruction. *Adult Occupational Training Regulations*, C.R.C., c. 1, s. 2.

FULL-TIME SEASONAL EMPLOYMENT. In reference to a person, that the person normally

is (a) employed in employment for which he receives a salary or wages, or (b) self-employed for at least 35 hours per week during a period that occurs each year during the open season for the district in which that person resides. *Lobster Fishery Regulations*, C.R.C., c. 817, s. 2.

FULL TIME TEACHER. A teacher who is engaged to teach and who teaches for a full teaching day as that day is from time to time prescribed under the Education Act or by the board by whom the teacher is engaged. *Teachers' Pension Act*, R.S.N.S. 1967, c. 301, s. 1.

FULL TRAILER. A vehicle that is towed by another vehicle and is so designed and used that the whole of its weight and load is carried on its own axles and includes a combination consisting of a semi-trailer and a trailer converter dolly. *Highway Traffic Act*, R.R.O. 1980, Reg. 489, s. 1.

FULLY DILUTED EARNINGS PER SHARE. The amount of income attributable to each share that would, if all potential conversions, exercises and contingent issuances had occurred during the period, be outstanding and have as an incident of ownership the right to participate in earnings to an unlimited degree, calculated in the manner prescribed in the regulations.

FULLY EMPLOYED. In reference to a person, that the person normally is (a) employed in employment for which he receives a salary or wages, or (b) self-employed for 12 months each year. *Lobster Fishery Regulations*, C.R.C., c. 817, s. 2.

FULLY EXTENDED. With respect to the mesh of a net, means that the sides of the mesh are stretched diagonally so as to form two parallel straight lines. *Quebec Fishery Regulations*, C.R.C., c. 852, s. 2.

FULLY FUNDED. When applied to a pension plan, means a pension plan that at any particular time has assets that will provide for the payment of all pension and other benefits required to be paid under the terms of the plan in respect of service rendered by employees and former employees prior to that time, and has no unpaid initial unfunded liabilities or experience deficiencies. *Pension Benefits Act*, R.R.O. 1980, Reg. 746, s. 1.

FULLY OPENED. The position of the headlamp concealment device in which the headlamp is in the design open operation position. *Motor Vehicle Safety Regulations*, C.R.C., c. 1038, s. 114.

FULLY PAID. With reference to any share, means a share on which there remains no liability, actual or contingent, to the issuing corporation. *Trust Companies Act*, R.S.A. 1980, c. T-9, s. 1.

FULLY REGISTERED FORM. Of bonds or debentures with both principal and interest payable to the registered holders. H. Sutherland, D.B. Horsley & J.M. Edmiston, eds., *Fraser's Handbook on Canadian Company Law*, 7th ed. (Toronto: Carswell, 1985) at 311.

FULLY-SECRET TRUST. During the deceased's lifetime, both that the person who receives the property on the deceased's death should act as a trustee and what the objects of the trust are must have been communicated. D.M.W. Waters, *The Law of Trusts in Canada*, 2d ed. (Toronto: Carswell, 1984) at 223.

FULLY SERVICED UNIT. A family housing unit supplied with heating, hot and cold water, stove, refrigerator and full janitor service. *National Housing Loan Regulations*, C.R.C., c. 1108, s. 2.

FULMINATE. *n.* Any chemical compound or mechanical mixture, whether included in the foregoing classes or not, that by reason of its great susceptibility to detonation is suitable for employment in percussion caps or any other appliances for developing detonation, or that by reason of its extreme sensibility to explosion and its great instability (that is to say readiness to undergo decomposition from very slight exciting causes) is essentially dangerous. Canada regulations.

FULTON-FAVREAU FORMULA. A constitutional amending procedure which required the unanimous consent of all provincial Legislatures and the federal Parliament for significant amendments. P.W. Hogg, *Constitutional Law of Canada*, 2d ed. (Toronto: Carswell, 1985) at 54.

FUMIGANT. *n.* A chemical or thing that, for uses regulated by the Federal Regulatory Authority, emits fumes, smoke or gas used to destroy or control pests. *Pest Control Products (Nova Scotia) Act*, S.N.S. 1986, c. 16, s. 3.

FUMIGATION. *n.* Treatment of any plant or other matter that is infested, or likely to be infested, with a pesticide in such a concentration, at such a temperature and for such a period of time as is necessary to ensure that the plant or other matter is no longer infested. *Plant Quarantine Regulations*, C.R.C., c. 1273, c. 2.

FUNCTION. *n.* 1. An object, power or duty or group of them. 2. Includes logic, control, arithmetic, deletion, storage and retrieval and communication or telecommunication to, from or within a computer system. *Criminal Code*, R.S.C. 1985, c. C-46, s. 342.1(2) as added by *Criminal Law Amendment Act*, R.S.C. 1985 (1st Supp.), c. 27, s. 45. 3. The purpose for which one uses

a trade mark. 4. Employment; carrying out an office. See FUND-RAISING ~.

FUNCTIONAL REHABILITATION CENTRE. Facilities to which persons are admitted whose physical independence is reduced to the point that they require intensive rehabilitation services for a certain time. *Health Services and Social Services Act*, R.S.Q. 1977, c. S-5, s. 1.

FUNCTIONARY. *n.* Any employee of the civil service other than a deputy-head or a workman. *Civil Service Act*, R.S.Q. 1977, c. F-3, s. 1.

FUNCTUS OFFICIO. [L. having discharged one's duty] Describes an arbitrator or judge who has made an award or order or given a decision which exhausts the authority of that office.

FUND. *n.* 1, A sum of money available to pay or discharge liabilities. 2. Capital, as opposed to income or interest. See ACCIDENT ~; ASSURANCE ~; BLENDED ~; CAPITAL ~; CARE ~; CONSOLIDATED ~; DISTRESS ~; ~S; GUARANTEED ~; INJURY ~; INSURANCE ~; LIEN ~; MAJOR LIEN ~; MUTUAL ~; NO-LOAD ~; PENSION ~; POOLED ~; REGULATED ~; RENT REDUCTION ~; RESERVE ~; RETIREMENT INCOME ~; REVENUE ~; REVOLVING ~; SEGREGATED ~; SINKING ~; SPECIAL ~; SPECIAL PURPOSE ~; STRIKE ~; SUPERANNUATION ~; TRUST ~.

FUND ADMINISTRATOR. A person or group of persons charged with the receipt, custody or handling of money in, or payments from, a regulated fund. *Financial Administration Act*, R.S.A. 1980, c. F-9, s. 1.

FUNDAMENTAL BREACH. Breach of a fundamental term which is not covered by an exclusion clause, contrasting to "ordinary" breach, i.e., breach of a warranty or condition. G.H.L. Fridman, *Sale of Goods in Canada*, 3d ed. (Toronto: Carswell, 1986) at 285.

FUNDAMENTAL JUSTICE. 1. A broader term than natural justice. P.K. McWilliams, *Canadian Criminal Evidence*, 3d ed. (Aurora: Canada Law Book, 1988) at 4-16. 2. Requires that one fully informs the accused of the offence supposedly committed, that one gives the accused fair opportunity to present a case and to know any relevant evidence and that one arrives at a decision judicially, using material properly before the court.

FUNDAMENTAL TERM. Something which must be performed, regardless of any clause in the contract which relieves a party from performing other terms or from being liable for breaching those terms. G.H.L. Fridman, *Sale of Goods in Canada*, 3d ed. (Toronto: Carswell, 1986) at 284-285.

FUNDED. See FULLY ~; PROVISIONALLY ~.

FUNDED DEBT. Securities issued by the Province of New Brunswick having a term to maturity of more than one year from their date of issue and that are not subject to serial repayment. *Provincial Loans Act*, R.S.N.B. 1973, c. P-22, s. 1.

FUNDED OBLIGATION. Any money indebtedness the principal amount of which, by its terms, is not payable on demand and the maturity date of which is more than twelve months after such indebtedness was incurred or, if renewed, last renewed. *Provincial Finance Act*, S.N.S. 1973, c. 49, s. 4.

FUNDED RATIO. In subparagraph (1)(b)(iii), means the ratio of the assets of a pension plan to the liabilities of the pension plan on a going-concern basis, as reported in the latest actuarial report respecting the pension plan filed with the Superintendent. *Pension Benefits Standards Act*, R.S.C. 1985 (2d Supp.), c. 32, s. 28(2).

FUNDI PATRIMONIALES. [L.] Lands belonging to an inheritance.

FUND-RAISING FUNCTION. *var.* **FUND RAISING FUNCTION.** Includes events or activities held for the purpose of raising funds for the political party, constituency association, candidate or leadership contestant by whom or on whose behalf the function is held. *Election Finances acts.*

FUNDS. *n.* All moneys or any other consideration received pursuant to the sale of a prepaid funeral contract, including all interest accrued or earned on those moneys or that other consideration. *Prepaid Funeral Services Act*, S.S. 1986, c. P-22.3, s. 2. See ENDOWMENT CARE ~; FUND; PERPETUAL CARE ~; PUBLIC ~; TRUST ~.

FUND UNION. A local or joint board with which an employer has contracted to contribute to the employees' pension fund.

FUNDUS. [L.] *n.* The bottom; the foundation.

FUNERAL. *n.* (i) The provision of a casket, embalming, graveside services and related services, (ii) the use of the facilities of a funeral home by friends and relatives of a deceased person for twenty-four hours and for religious services and transportation for a casket and clergy to a place of interment, (iii) the provision of a wooden outer case for a casket where required, (iv) the religious services at a burial, and (v) such other services and items in addition to those set out in subclauses (i) to (iv), as approved by the Director. *Homes for Special Care Act*, R.R.O. 1980, Reg. 501, s. 1. See PRE-ARRANGED ~ PLAN; PREPAID ~ CONTRACT.

FUNERAL BENEFITS. See SICK AND ~.

FUNERAL DIRECTOR. Any person who takes charge of a dead body for the purpose of burial, cremation, removal or other disposition. See INCAPACITATED ~.

FUNERAL EXPENSES. Expenses permitted before all other debts and charges against an estate.

FUNERAL GOODS. Those items of merchandise sold or offered for sale directly to the public which will be used in connection with a funeral or an alternative or final disposition of human remains. *Prepaid Funeral Services Act*, S.S. 1986, c. P-22.3, s. 2.

FUNERAL HOME. A facility or establishment, by whatever name called, offering or providing funeral merchandise or services to the public.

FUNERAL MERCHANDISE OR SERVICES. (i) The services offered or performed by a funeral director or embalmer incidental to the arrangements, care and preparation of human remains for burial, cremation or other disposition, or (ii) the merchandise, articles or supplies used, offered for sale or sold directly to the public by the funeral director, in conjunction with the related services, but does not include the sale of lots or any interest therein. *Cemetery and Funeral Services Act*, S.N.S. 1983, c. 4, s. 2.

FUNERAL SERVICES. Any services and commodities usual in the preparation for burial and the burial of the dead other than the supplying of lots, burial vaults, grave markers, vases and services rendered or to be rendered at the cemetery.

FUNERAL SERVICES ESTABLISHMENT. A premises established or maintained for the purpose of providing funeral services or funeral supplies to the public. *Funeral Services Act*, R.S.O. 1980, c. 180, s. 1.

FUNGIBLE. *n.* In relation to securities, securities of which any unit is, by nature or usage of trade, the equivalent of any other like unit.

FUNGIBLE GOODS. Goods of which any unit is, from its nature or by mercantile custom, treated as the equivalent of any other unit.

FUR. *n.* 1. The pelt or skin, or any part thereof, of any fur-bearing animal caught in the Territories, whether such pelt or skin or part thereof is in a raw state or is tanned or dressed. *Fur Export Act*, R.S.N.W.T. 1974, c. F-11, s. 2. 2. The skin of any animal, whether fur-bearing, hair-bearing or wool-bearing, that is not in the unhaired condition. *Fur Garments Labelling Reg-*

ulations, C.R.C., c. 1138, s. 2. See LAKE, FOREST AND ~ ASSOCIATION.

FURANDI ANIMUS. [L.] The intention to steal.

FUR ANIMAL. 1. Includes all animals wild by nature whose skins or pelts are commonly used for the manufacture of clothing or rugs, and are of marketable value, and also includes the parts of such animals, but does not include those animals kept upon a private fur farm or the parts of those animals. *The Fur Act,* R.S.S. 1978, c. F-24, s. 2. 2. Mink and foxes. *Fur Farms Act,* R.S. Nfld. 1970, c. 146, s. 2.

FUR-BEARER. *n.* Includes beaver, muskrat, mink, otter, lynx, wildcat, fox, wolf, raccoon, weasel, fisher, marten, squirrel, skunk and any other animal valuable for its fur. *Lands and Forests Act,* R.S.N.S. 1967, c. 163, s. 84.

FUR-BEARING ANIMAL. *var.* **FUR BEARING ANIMAL.** 1. Any animal that is wild by nature and whose pelt or skin is commonly used for commercial purposes. 2. Beaver, bobcat, badger, fisher, fox, hare, lynx, marten, mink, muskrat, otter, rabbit, raccoon, skunk, squirrel or weasel or ermine, wildcat, bear, wolverine, wolf, coyote and chinchilla.

FUR-BEARING ANIMAL RANCH. An area where fur bearing animals are raised and kept in their natural habitat and under the direct supervision of any person. *Wildlife Act,* R.S.M. 1970, c. W140, s. 2.

FUR-BEARING CARNIVORE. A wolverine, coyote or wolf and any other species declared to be fur-bearing carnivores by the regulations, or any part of those animals. *Wildlife Act,* R.S.A. 1980, c. W-9, s. 1.

FUR DEALER. A person who carries on or who is engaged in any manner in trafficking in the skins or pelts, or parts thereof, of fur-bearing animals or fur-bearing carnivores.

FUR FARM. *var.* **FUR-FARM.** 1. Any place where fur bearing animals are kept in captivity for the purpose of propagation or for sale, gain or profit. 2. A place where fur-bearing animals are kept in captivity.

FUR FARMER. A person whose occupation is operating a premises on which fur-bearing animals are kept in captivity for sale or for the purpose of selling their pelts. *Fisheries Act,* R.S.M. 1970, c. F90, s. 1.

FUR GARMENT. Any coat, jacket, cape, detached cuff, detached collar, scarf, cap, hat, glove or muff, the whole or part of the outer surface of which is trimmed with fur or consists of fur. *Fur Garments Labelling Regulations,* C.R.C., c. 1138, s. 2.

FURIOSI NULLA VOLUNTAS EST. [L.] Mad people have no free will.

FURIOSUS SOLO FURORE PUNITUR. [L.] A mad person is punished only by the madness.

FURIOSUS STIPULARE NON POTEST, NEC ALIQUID NEGOTIUM AGERE, QUIA NON INTELLIGIT QUOD AGIT. [L.] An insane person cannot enter into a contract or transact business because mad people do not know what they are doing.

FURLONG. *n.* 220 yards. *Weights and Measures Act,* S.C. 1970-71-72, c. 36, schedule II.

FURLOUGH. *n.* Temporary halt of employment.

FURNACE. *n.* A space-heating appliance using warm air as the heating medium and usually having provision for the attachment of ducts. *Building Code Act,* R.R.O. 1980, Reg. 87, s. 1. See FORCED-AIR ~; REVERBERATORY ~.

FURNITURE. See UPHOLSTERED ~.

FURNITURE AND HOUSEHOLD EFFECTS. Removable furniture and effects that are commonly found in the home but does not include construction material, electrical fixtures, windows, doors, screens, sinks or bathtubs or any other article capable of permanent fixture to a building. *Seasonal Residents' Remission Order,* C.R.C., c. 788, s. 2.

FUR RANCH. Premises on which fur bearing animals are kept, raised, bred or propagated, or any combination thereof, in captivity for sale of for the purpose of selling their pelts, but does not include a muskrat ranch. *Wildlife Act,* R.S.M. 1970, c. W140, s. 2.

FURRIER. *n.* A person who buys or otherwise acquires the raw skins or pelts, or parts thereof, of fur-bearing animals or fur-bearing carnivores for the purpose of manufacture. *Wildlife Act,* R.S.A. 1980, c. W-9, s. 1.

FURTHER ASSURANCE. See COVENANT FOR ~.

FUR TRADER. A person who is engaged in the business of buying, selling or trading in pelts or skins of fur bearing animals or other wildlife prescribed for the purpose of this definition, whether as principal, agent or employee, and whether the pelts or skins were obtained, taken or trapped by the fur trader or another person. *Wildlife Act,* S.B.C. 1982, c. 57, s. 1.

FURTUM. [L.] *n.* Theft, robbery.

FURTUM EST CONTRECTATIO REI ALIENAE FRAUDULENTA, CUM ANIMO FURANDI, INVITO ILLO DOMINO CUJUS RES ILLA FUERAT. [L.] Theft is wrongfully appropriating another person's property, without consent, and with the intent to steal it.

FURTUM NON EST UBI ITITIUM HABET DETENTIONIS PER DOMINUM REI. [L.] There is no theft where one has possession of the goods with the consent of the owner.

FUSE. *n.* 1. A device capable of automatically opening a circuit under predetermined overload conditions by the fusing of metal. *Coal Mines Regulation Act*, R.S.N.S. 1967, c. 36, s. 84. 2. Any safety fuse. See CAPPED ~; DETONATING ~; SAFETY ~.

FUSION WELD. Applicable to all welded joints made by the oxy-acetylene or the oxy-hydrogen process, the metal arc process with covered electrodes, or other electric arc process in which the arc stream and the deposited weld metal are shielded from atmospheric contamination. *Steamship Machinery Construction Regulations*, C.R.C., c. 1491, Schedule IV, s. 1.

FUTURE CARE. See COST OF ~.

FUTURE CONSIDERATION. A promise to something later.

FUTURE COST OF INSURED SERVICES. The estimated total cost of the future insured services made necessary as the result of an injury that will probably be required by a patient after the date of settlement or, where there is no settlement, the first day of trial. *Health Insurance Act*, R.S.O. 1980, c. 197, s. 1.

FUTURE DAMAGES. Damages to compensate for pecuniary losses to be incurred, or expenditures to be made, after the date of the trial judgment in a proceeding. *Law and Equity Act*, R.S.B.C. 1979, c. 224, s. 51 as added by *Attorney General Statutes Amendment Act*, S.B.C. 1981, c. 10, s. 30.

FUTURE ESTATE. An expectancy; a reversion; a remainder.

FUTURE GOODS. Goods to be manufactured or acquired by the seller, after the making of the contract of sale. *Sale of Goods acts.*

FUTURE INTEREST. See FUTURE ESTATE.

FUTURES. See COMMODITY ~ CONTRACT; GRAIN ~.

FUTURE SERVICES. See CONTRACT FOR ~.

FUTURES MEMBER. A member of the Corporation who conducts the business of trading commodities, options on commodities, commodity futures contracts and commodity futures options and who is admitted to membership in accordance with the by-laws. *Toronto Futures Exchange Act, 1983*, S.O. 1983, c. 19, s. 1.

FUTURE USE. See CONTINGENT USE.

G

G. *abbr.* Giga.

GAAP. *abbr.* Generally accepted accounting principles.

GAAR. *abbr.* General anti-avoidance rule.

GAAS. *abbr.* Generally accepted auditing standards.

GABEL. *n.* Excise, a tax on movables; a custom, rent or service. See LAND ~.

GABULUS DENARIORUM. [L.] Rent paid with money.

GAGE. *n.* [Fr.] Pledge or pawn; anything given as security.

GAGER DE DELIVERANCE. [Fr.] Pledge that a person, being sued, would deliver cattle he or she had distrained.

GAGER DEL LEY. [Fr.] Wager of law.

GAIN. *n.* Profits. See ACOUSTIC ~; AIR-TO-AIR ~; ANNUAL ~S LIMIT; CAPITAL ~; MAXIMUM ACOUSTIC ~; MAXIMUM AIR-TO-AIR ~; TOLL, ~ OR COMPENSATION.

GAINAGE. *n.* The profit raised by cultivating planted or tilled land.

GAIN OR REWARD. Any payment, consideration, compensation or gratuity, directly or indirectly charged, demanded, received or collected for the use of a vehicle by a person who, as owner, lessee, hirer, chauffeur, driver or otherwise, has possession of or control over the vehicle or has directed the movement of the vehicle. *Highway Traffic acts.*

GALE. *n.* A periodic rent payment.

GALE-DAY. *n.* Rent-day.

GALLERY. *n.* Of the parliamentary chamber, consists of a press gallery, visitors galleries called the public gallery, galleries for the diplomatic corps and departmental officials and private galleries. A. Fraser, G.A. Birch & W.A. Dawson, eds., *Beauchesne's Rules and Forms of the House of Commons of Canada*, 5th ed. (Toronto: Carswell, 1978) at 36.

GALLINACEOUS BIRD. Includes all species of grouse, partridge, pheasant, quail, ptarmigan, wild turkey and the eggs of all such species. *Fish and Wildlife Act*, S.N.B. 1980, c. F-14.1, s. 1.

GALLON. *n.* 1. 454 609/100 000 000 cubic metre. *Weights and Measures Act*, S.C. 1970-71-72, c. 36, schedule II. 2. A Canadian gallon, which for the purpose of this Regulation may be considered equivalent to an Imperial gallon. *Gasoline Handling Act*, R.R.O. 1980, Reg. 439, s. 1. 3. An imperial gallon. *City of St. John's Act*, R.S. Nfld. 1970, c. 40, s. 283. 4. For gasoline, (a) in liquid form, one imperial gallon; (b) in the form of natural gas, the number of cubic feet at atmospheric pressure the Lieutenant Governor in Council prescribes; and (c) in the form of liquified petroleum gas, the number of pounds the Lieutenant Governor in Council prescribes. *Gasoline Tax Act*, R.S.B.C. 1979, c. 153, s. 1. 5. When it applies to propane gas, butane gas or liquified petroleum gas, its equivalent to five and one-tenth pounds. *Fuel Tax Act*, R.S.Q. 1977, c. T-1, s. 1.

GALLOWS. *n.* A beam laid over a post or posts from which prisoners were hanged.

GALVANIZED. *adj.* Protected with a coating of zinc capable of withstanding four one-minute immersions in a saturated copper sulphate solution without showing a fixed deposit of copper. *Lightning Rods Act*, R.R.O. 1980, Reg. 577, s. 1.

GAMBLING. See GAMING.

GAME. *n.* 1. A game of chance or mixed chance and skill. *Criminal Code*, R.S.C. 1985, c. C-46, s. 197. 2. The carcass or any part of the carcass, including the skin, of any wild animal, domestically raised fur-bearing animal, wild fowl or wild bird. *Game Export Act*, R.S.C. 1985, c. G-1, s. 2. 3. Fur bearing animals, game animals and game birds, and also includes all species

G

431

of animals and birds that are wild by nature. 4. A game animal, game bird or fur-bearing animal, and includes any part of such animal. 5. Moose, caribou, deer, beaver, hares, wild rabbits, mink, otters, martens, muskrats, raccoons, bears, Canada lynx, wildcats, foxes and the following birds: the Anatidae, commonly known as swans; geese, excepting domestic geese, brant and river and sea ducks; the Rallidae, commonly know as rails and coots; the Limicolae, commonly known as shore birds; plovers, snipe, woodcock, sandpipers, tattlers and curlews; and the Gallinae, commonly known as grouse; pheasants, partridges and quails. *Lands and Forests Act*, R.S.N.S. 1967, c. 163, s. 84. 6. All wild animals, amphibians, reptiles and wild birds within any park, and the heads, skins and any or every part of such mammals, amphibians, reptiles and wild birds. *National Parks Game Regulations*, C.R.C., c. 1122, s. 2. See BIG ~; CONFIDENCE ~; SMALL ~.

GAME ANIMAL. 1. Moose, deer and rabbit or varying hare. *Game Act*, R.S.N.B. 1973, c. G-1, s. 1. 2. Any animal, except a fur-bearing animal, protected by this Act, and includes any part of such animal. *Game and Fish Act*, R.S.O. 1980, c. 182, s. 1.

GAME BIRD. 1. An upland game bird or a migratory game bird. 2. Includes (i) ducks, geese, swans and all other species of the order called Anseriformes; (ii) grouse, ptarmigan and all other species of the family called Tetraonidae; (iii) pheasants, Hungarian or European grey partridge, Chukar partridge and all other species of the family called Phasianidae; (iv) wild turkeys and all other species of the family called Meleagrididae; (v) cranes and all other species of the family called Gruidae; (vi) rails, coots and all other species of the family called Rallidae; (vii) plovers, turnstones and all other species of the family called Charadriidae; (viii) Wilson's snipes, curlews, sandpipers, greater and lesser yellowlegs, godwits and other snipelike birds and all other species of the family called Scolopacidae; (ix) Columbidae, including mourning doves and other families of the order Columbiformes; (x) the eggs of those birds and any part of those birds or eggs. *Wildlife Act*, R.S.A. 1980, c. W-9, s. 1. 3. Any bird protected by this Act or the Migratory Birds Convention Act, (Canada), and includes any part of such bird. *Game and Fish Act*, R.S.O. 1980, c. 182, s. 1. 4. Spruce partridge, birch partridge (ruffed grouse), Hungarian partridge (European gray partridge), pheasant and all birds protected under the Migratory Birds Convention Act, chapter M-12 of the Revised Statutes of Canada, 1970. *Game Act*, R.S.N.B. 1973, c. G-1, s. 1. See MIGRATORY ~S; UPLAND ~.

GAME BIRD FARM. A place on which game birds are kept for the purposes of propagation, or for sale, gain, profit or pleasure. *Wildlife Act*, R.S.A. 1970, c. 391, s. 2.

GAME BIRD HUNTING PRESERVE. Any area in which pheasants or other game birds propagated under a licence are released for hunting purposes. *Game and Fish Act*, R.S.O. 1980, c. 182, s. 1.

GAME FARM. See PROVINCIAL ~.

GAME OFFICER. A person declared by subsection 5(1) to be a game officer. *Game Export Act*, R.S.C. 1985, c. G-1, s. 2. See CHIEF ~.

GAME RANCHING. Raising big game for the purpose of selling its meat for human consumption. *Wildlife Act*, S.A. 1984, c. W-9.1, s. 1.

GAME SANCTUARY. A game sanctuary established pursuant to this Section and any part of the Province heretofore designated by the Governor in Council in which it shall be unlawful to hunt, take or kill or attempt to take or kill any game. *Lands and Forests Act*, R.S.N.S. 1967, c. 163, s. 161.

GAMING. *n.* Playing for money or money's worth at a lawful or unlawful game.

GAMING EQUIPMENT. Anything that is or may be used for the purpose of playing games or for betting. *Criminal Code*, R.S.C. 1985, c. C-46, s. 197.

GAMING HOUSE. See COMMON ~.

GANGRENE. *n.* The death of a portion of an organ or limb in a living body. F.A. Jaffe, *A Guide to Pathological Evidence*, 2d ed. (Toronto: Carswell, 1983) at 177.

GANG-HOOK. *n.* A combination of two or more hooks used as a unit. *National Parks Fishing Regulations*, C.R.C., c. 1120, s. 2.

GANG TRAPPED. That the waste piping from a group of two or more fixtures or other drainage openings is so arranged that all the fixtures or other drainage openings drain to a common trap, but the term shall not apply when the trap is a secondary trap such as a building trap or the trap of a fixture that receives waste from one or more indirect waste pipes. *Ontario Water Resources Act*, R.R.O. 1980, Reg. 736, s. 1.

GANGWAY. *n.* A defined passageway between a metal melting unit and a metal pouring area. *Occupational Health and Safety Act*, R.R.O. 1980, Reg. 692, s. 1.

GAOL. *n.* 1. Prison; place to confine offenders. 2. A provincial institution where lesser offences are punished.

GAOL DELIVERY. The commission of general

gaol delivery given to judges or commissioners of assize authorizing them to try, and to discharge from custody if acquitted, every prisoner in gaol for an alleged crime when they arrived at the circuit town.

GAOLER. *n.* One who keeps a prison.

GAP. See AIR ~.

GARAGE. *n.* A place or premises where motor vehicles are received for housing, storage or repairs for compensation. See PRIVATE ~; PUBLIC ~; REPAIR ~; REPAIRMAN'S ~; STORAGE ~.

GARAGE KEEPER. 1. A person, firm, or corporation, who or which renders service upon a motor vehicle in a garage for or at a charge, price, or consideration, in the ordinary course of business and as the principal employment or one of the principal employments of that person, firm, or corporation. 2. Any person who keeps a place of business for the sale of motor accessories or for the storage or repair of motor vehicles, aircraft, boats or outboard motors. *Repairers Lien Act*, R.S.B.C. 1979, c. 363, s. 1.

GARAGEMAN. *n.* A person who keeps a place of business for the housing, storage or repair of a motor vehicle and who receives compensation for such housing, storage or repair.

GARAGE OPERATOR. The person who operates an establishment where road vehicles are maintained or repaired, and receives payment therefor. *Highway Safety Code*, S.Q. 1986, c. 91, s. 661.

GARAGIST. *n.* The holder of a garage licence within the meaning of the Highway Code, as well as a person who operates an establishment where repairs are made to the body of the vehicle only, without any alteration being made therein, and where automobiles are not stored at the same time. *Automobile Insurance Act*, R.S.Q. 1977, c. A-25, s. 1.

GARBAGE. *n.* 1. Meat, scraps, offal, kitchen waste and fruit and vegetable refuse. *Animal Disease and Protection Regulations*, C.R.C., c. 296, s. 113. 2. Solid galley waste, food waste, paper, rags, plastics, glass, metal, bottles, crockery, junk or similar refuse. *Garbage Pollution Prevention Regulations*, C.R.C., c. 1424, s. 2. 3. Kitchen and household refuse, stove and furnace ashes and other waste matter, but does not include miscellaneous waste or trade waste. *National Parks Garbage Regulations*, C.R.C., c. 1123, s. 2.

GARBAGE GRINDER. See ON-SITE ~.

GARD. *n.* [Fr.] Care, custody, wardship.

GARDENING. See MARKET ~.

GARMENT. *n.* Any article of wearing apparel. *National Trade Mark Garment Sizing Regulations*, C.R.C., c. 1139, s. 2. See FUR ~.

GARNISH. *v.* 1. To attach a debt. 2. To warn.

GARNISHABLE MONEYS. Moneys authorized to be paid by Her Majesty by or under such Acts of Parliament or provisions thereof or programs thereunder as are designated by the regulations. *Family Orders and Agreements Enforcement Assistance Act*, R.S.C. 1985, c. 4, s. 23.

GARNISHEE. *n.* The person who owes a judgment debtor money and against whom the court issues garnishment process.

GARNISHEE SUMMONS. 1. First step in a garnishment proceding. C.R.B. Dunlop, *Creditor-Debtor Law in Canada* (Toronto: Carswell, 1981) at 268. 2. Includes any document or court order of like import.

GARNISHMENT. *n.* 1. A way to enforce a judgment by which money owed by the garnishee to the judgment debtor is attached to pay off the judgment debtor's debt to a judgment creditor. 2. Includes attachment. See CONTINUING ~; PROVINCIAL ~ LAW.

GARNISTURE. *n.* Furnishing; providing.

GARRANTY. See GUARANTEE.

GARROTTING. *n.* Asphyxia caused when a ligature is twisted around the neck. F.A. Jaffe, *A Guide to Pathological Evidence*, 2d ed. (Toronto: Carswell, 1983) at 177.

GAS. *n.* 1. Any hydrocarbon or mixture of hydrocarbons that, at a temperature of 15°C and a pressure of 101.325 kPa, is in a gaseous state. Canada statutes. 2. Natural gas or any fluid hydrocarbon, other than a hydrocarbon that is a liquid in its naturally occurring state, recovered from a natural reservoir in Canada. Canada statutes. 3. Natural gas whether or not produced in association with oil, and includes all liquid hydrocarbons resulting from the condensation of natural gas. 4. Raw gas or marketable gas or any constituent of raw gas, condensate or crude oil that is recovered in processing and that is gaseous at the conditions under which its volume is measured or estimated. 5. Natural gas, manufactured gas, liquified petroleum gas or any mixtures of such gases. 6. A gaseous mixture consisting primarily of methane. 7. Natural gas, manufactured gas, any variety or any mixture of either, liquified petroleum gas or any mixture of liquified petroleum gas and air, conveyed or distributed by tubing. Quebec statutes. 8. All natural gas, both before and after it has been subjected to absorption, purification, scrubbing or other treatment or process, and includes all fluid hydrocarbons not herein defined as oil or condensate. 9. Any gas, including casing-head gas, and any hydrocarbon other than oil. 10. Natural or manufactured or mixed gas, but does not include undiluted liquified petroleum gas. *Gas Act*, R.S.B.C. 1979, c. 149, s. 1. 11. Natural gas, inflammable manufactured gas, any type or blend of such gases, liquid petroleum gas or any blend of such gas and air (gaz). *Building Act*, S.O. 1985, c. 34, s. 7. 12. Natural gas, manufactured gas or propane or any mixture of any of them. *Provincial Land Tax Amendment Act, 1982*, S.O. 1982, s. 18, s. 6. See COAL ~; COMMODITY VALUE OF ~; COMPRESSED ~; COMPRESSED INFLAMMABLE ~; FREEHOLD ~; ILLEGAL ~; LEVIABLE ~; LIQUEFIED PETROLEUM ~; MANUFACTURED ~; MARKETABLE ~; NATURAL ~; NETBACK ~; OIL AND ~; OIL OR ~; PINTSCH ~; PRODUCTION OF OIL [OR] ~; PUTREFACTIVE ~ES; RAW ~; RURAL ~ CO-OPERATIVE ASSOCIATION; WARNING ~.

GAS COMPANY. A person engaged in the sale or distribution of gas in the Province. *Gas Act*, R.S.B.C. 1979, c. 149, s. 1.

GAS CONTRACT. A contract under which gas is sold and delivered by a seller to a buyer, and includes an agreement that varies or amends that contract and an arbitration award that relates to that contract. Alberta statutes.

GAS DISCHARGE TUBE. An electronic tube in which glow discharges or X-rays or both may be produced by the acceleration of electrons or ions. *Radiation Emitting Devices Regulations*, C.R.C., c. 1370, s. 1.

GAS DISTRIBUTION SYSTEM. A system (i) that includes the works, structures, erections, equipment, pipes, machinery, tools, appliances, compression stations, gate valves, check valves, gasometers, regulator stations, terminal facilities, appurtenances and other things that are used on or in connection with the system; and (ii) that is used for the distribution, delivery, furnishing, or sale of natural or manufactured gas directly to consumer inhabitants of a municipal corporation; but does not include (iii) a pipeline; or (iv) a building, plant, warehouse, or storage yard used for the purpose of obtaining and producing natural gas underlying the surface of the land or (v) a building, plant, warehouse, or storage yard used for the manufacture, refining or marketing of gas; or (vi) similar equipment, machinery, pipes, tools or appliances stored in such a building, plant, warehouse or storage yard. Manitoba statutes.

GAS EQUIPMENT. Includes machinery, equipment, appliances and devices of every kind

and description used or intended to be used in the transmission, distribution, supply or use of gas.

GAS EXPORT COMPANY. Any company that holds a government permit for the removal of gas from Alberta. *Nova, An Alberta Corporation Act*, R.S.A. 1980, c. N-12, s. 1.

GAS FITTER. *var.* **GAS-FITTER.** A person who installs, repairs or alters any gas installation or gas equipment.

GAS-FITTING. *n.* The installing, removing, altering or repairing of all gas piping from the gas meter to the point of consumption of the gas, of appliances, and of any device that is attached to or forms a part of any gas piping or gas venting system, including electrical apparatus and wiring, where work on combination gas and electrical fixtures or appliances is involved. *National Parks Natural Gas Regulations*, C.R.C., c. 1129, s. 2.

GAS HAZARD CONTROL STANDARDS. The standards published in 1964 by the Queen's Printer for the Marine Regulations Branch of the Department of Transport (Queen's Printer Catalogue No. T31-2464). *Esquimalt Graving Dock Regulations*, C.R.C., c. 1362, s. 2.

GAS INSTALLATION. 1. That portion of a distribution system within the corporate boundaries of a city, town or village and gas piping and equipment in or on any land or premises of the ultimate consumer, or mobile or fixed buildings or any vehicles, for utilization of gas as a fuel for heating, power or lighting, otherwise than in an industrial or manufacturing process, and (i) includes the connection of any such gas piping with any gas consuming equipment and any part of the gas system, and maintenance, alteration, extension and repair of any such gas piping, but (ii) does not include an electrical installation. 2. A facility or system, including fittings, that is owned or operated by a gas company and that is used for storing, conveying, measuring or regulating gas. *Gas Amendment Act*, S.B.C. 1981, c. 16, s. 2.

GASKET. *n.* A gasket made of butyl rubber or neoprene and containing no adulterants or reclaimed material and having a compression set after twenty-four hours at 158° Fahrenheit of not more than 15 per cent. *Ontario Water Resources Act*, R.R.O. 1980, Reg. 736, s. 72.

GAS LINE. 1. A pipe for the transmission of gas from a secondary line or storage facility to a distribution centre or storage facility and includes installations in connection with that pipe, but does not include a multiphase line, secondary line, flow line or distribution line. *Pipeline Act*, R.S.A. 1980, c. P-8, s. 1. 2. A pipe for the transmission of gas and any accompanying liquids and includes installations in connection therewith but does not include a secondary line, flow line, distribution line or private line. *Pipe Line Act*, S.N.B. 1976, c. P-8.1, s. 1.

GAS METER. See ORIFICE ~; POSITIVE DISPLACEMENT ~.

GASOHOL. *n.* A mixture of denatured alcohol manufactured in Canada and gasoline, in which the denatured alcohol content is not less than 10% of the total volume of the mixture. *Gasoline Tax Act*, S.M. 1980, c. 69, s. 6.

GAS OIL RATIO. *var.* **GAS-OIL RATIO.** 1. The ratio of cubic metres of natural gas produced to cubic metres of oil produced. 2. The number of cubic feet of gas produced per barrel of oil. *Canada Oil and Gas Drilling and Production Regulations*, C.R.C., c. 1517, s. 2.

GASOLINE. *n.* 1. Natural gas and any derivative of petroleum, natural gas or coal having a specific gravity of 0.801 7 or less at a temperature of 15.556 degrees Celsius or that is declared by regulation to be gasoline. 2. Natural gas and any derivative of petroleum, natural gas or coal having a specific gravity of .8017 or less at a temperature of 60 degrees Fahrenheit or that is declared by regulation to be gasoline. 3. The product distilled or recovered from petroleum which, by combustion, develops the power required for operating internal combustion engines and also means every other liquid product whether or not distilled or recovered from petroleum which fulfils the same purpose, by the same means and for the same end. 4. Gasoline type fuels for use in internal combustion engines other than aircraft engines. *Excise Tax Act*, R.S.C. 1985, c. E-15, s. 2. 5. Fuel that is not coloured fuel, aviation fuel, locomotive fuel, marine bunker fuel, marine diesel fuel or motive fuel. *Motor Fuel Tax Act*, S.B.C. 1985, c. 76, s. 1. 6. A product of petroleum that has a flash point below 100°F, and that is designed for use in an internal combustion engine. *Gasoline Handling Act*, R.S.O. 1980, c. 185, s. 1. See AIRCRAFT ~; LEADED ~; UNLEADED ~.

GASOLINE PUMP. A tank or receptacle of not less than fifty gallon or two hundred and twenty-seven litre capacity used or intended to be used for the storage of gasoline or motive fuel and equipped with a pump for dispensing such gasoline or motive fuel. *Gasoline and Motive Fuel Tax Act*, S.N.B. 1976, c. 26, s. 1.

GASOLINE SERVICE STATION. Any building, portion of a building, booth, stall, gasoline pump, or place, where, or by means of which, gasoline is offered for sale by retail for use in internal combustion engines or dispensed in sale by retail for such use, and the premises occupied or used in connection therewith, or any part of such premises that may be specified in a municipal by-law. *Shops Regulation Act*, R.S.M. 1970, c. S110, s. 2.

GAS OR OIL LEASE. Includes any agreement, whether by way of option, lease, grant or otherwise, granting the right to operate lands for the production and removal of natural gas or oil, or both, except a grant to so operate where the amount or payment of the consideration therefor is not dependent upon the operation of such lands or upon the production of gas or oil or upon the amount of gas or oil produced. *Gas and Oil Leases Act*, R.S.O. 1980, c. 184, s. 1.

GAS OR OIL WELL EQUIPMENT. Includes (a) equipment, structures and pipelines, other than a well casing, acquired to be used in a gas or oil field in the production therefrom of natural gas or crude oil, and (b) a pipeline acquired to be used solely for transmitting gas to a natural gas processing plant, but does not include (c) equipment or structures acquired for the refining of oil or the processing of natural gas including the separation therefrom of liquid hydrocarbons, sulphur or other joint products or by-products, or (d) a pipeline for removal of or collection for immediate removal of natural gas or crude oil from a gas or oil field except a pipeline referred to in paragraph (b). *Income Tax Regulations*, C.R.C., c. 945, s. 1104(2).

GASPÉ PENINSULA. That portion of the Gaspé region of the Province of Quebec that extends to the western border of Kamouraska County and includes the Magdalen Islands. *Income Tax Act*, R.S.C. 1952, c. 148 (as am. S.C. 1985, c. 45, s. 72(5)), s. 127(9).

GASPESIA REGION. That part of the Province of Quebec consisting of the following parishes: St-Fidèle de Restigouche, St-Conrad, Ste-Anne de Restigouche, Pointe à la Garde, Escuminac, St-Jean l'Évangéliste, St-Jean de Brébeuf, St-Louis de Gonzague, Carleton, Maria, New Richmond, St-Edgar, Paspébiac, St-Godefroi, Port Daniel, Gascons, Newport, Pellegrin, Chandler, Ste-Adélaïde de Pabos, Grande Rivière, Ste-Thérèse, St-Gabriel de Rameau, Caplan, St-Alphonse, St-Siméon, Bonaventure, St-Elzéar, New Carlisle, St-Jogues, Cap d'Espoir, Val d'Espoir, Percé, Barachois, St-Georges de Malbaie, Douglastown, Canne des Roches. *Gaspesia Pulpwood Order*, C.R.C., c. 250, s. 2.

GAS PIPE. Any tubing or pipe used or intended for the conveyance or distribution of gas, except the connecting piping of an apparatus.

GAS PIPELINE. *var.* **GAS PIPE LINE.** 1. A pipe line for the transportation, transmission, conduct, delivery, or furnishing of gas, directly or indirectly, to the public. Manitoba statutes. 2. A pipe or any system or arrangement of pipes wholly within Alberta whereby gas is conveyed from a well-head or other place where it is stored, processed or treated to any other place, (i) includes all property of any kind used for the purpose of, or in connection with, or incidental to the operation of a gas pipeline in the gathering, transporting, handling and delivery of gas, and (ii) without restricting the generality of the foregoing, includes tanks, surface reservoirs, pumps, racks, storage and loading facilities, compressors, compressor stations, pressure measuring and controlling equipment and fixtures, flow controlling and measuring equipment and fixtures, metering equipment and fixtures and heating, cooling and dehydrating equipment and fixtures, but (iv) does not include any pipe or any system or arrangement of pipes that constitutes a distribution system for the distribution of gas to ultimate consumers. *Gas Utilities Act*, R.S.A. 1980, c. G-4, s. 1.

GAS PLANT. See COMPRESSED ~.

GAS PROCESSING PLANT. An installation in Canada at which natural gas liquids or other components are removed from gas by means of field scrubbers, field separators or other field extraction facilities or at which natural gas liquids are removed from oil by those means. *Excise Tax Act*, R.S.C. 1985, c. E-15, s. 29.

GAS PRODUCER. A person who has the right to take or remove gas from a natural reservoir in Canada and includes an operator. *Excise Tax Act*, R.S.C. 1985, c. E-15, s. 29.

GAS-PROOF ROOM. A room so constructed and maintained that combustible gases or fumes cannot enter the room. *Gasoline Handling Act*, R.R.O. 1980, Reg. 439, s. 1.

GAS PURCHASE CONTRACT. A contract for the sale and purchase of gas produced in Alberta but does not include a contract for the sale of gas by the owner of a gas utility (as defined in the Gas Utilities Act) to a purchaser for consumption by that purchaser. *Arbitration Act*, R.S.A. 1980, c. A-43, s. 17.

GAS REPROCESSING PLANT. An installation in Canada at which natural gas liquids are removed from marketable pipeline gas and at which those liquids and the remaining marketable pipeline gas are not further processed. *Excise Tax Act*, R.S.C. 1985, c. E-15, s. 29.

GAS SALES CONTRACT. 1. A contract for the sale and delivery of gas in Alberta under which the producer of the gas is the seller. Alberta statutes. 2. A contract for the sale and delivery of natural gas under which a person agrees to sell natural gas to the corporation at the reg-

ulated selling price. *Natural Gas Price Act*, S.B.C. 1985, c. 53, s. 1.

GAS SOURCE. A point at which gas is supplied to a rural gas utility or an individual tap. *Rural Gas Act*, R.S.A. 1980, c. R-19, s. 1.

GAS TRANSMISSION LINE. A gas pipe line that is used and operated for the transportation, transmission, or conduct of gas to a distribution system and that has been so designated by the board under section 13. *Gas Pipe Line Act*, R.S.M. 1970, c. G50, s. 2.

GAS UNDERTAKING. Any undertaking for the sale, storage, conveyance or distribution of gas in Québec. *Régie de l'électricité et du gaz Act*, R.S.Q. 1977, c. R-6, s. 1.

GAS UTILITY. 1. A municipal corporation or a Crown corporation owning or operating pipe lines, pumping stations, regulator stations or other apparatus and equipment for the transmission, distribution, sale and supply to the public of natural gas. *The Gas and Electrical Rates (Public Corporations) Act*, R.S.S. 1978, c. G-3, s. 2. 2. A corporation which owns or operates in the Province equipment or facilities for the production, generation, storage, transmission, sale, delivery or furnishing of gas for the production of light, heat, cold or power to or for the public or any corporation for compensation, but does not include a company within the meaning of that word as defined in the National Energy Board Act (Canada). *Gas Utility Act*, R.S.B.C. 1979, c. 150, s. 1. 3. (i) Any gas pipeline, (ii) any system, works, plant, pipes, equipment or service for the production, gathering, conveying, transmission, transporting, delivery, furnishing or supplying of gas by retail or wholesale, either directly or indirectly, to or for the public or any member of the public, whether an individual or a corporation, other than the transportation, delivery, furnishing or supplying by retail or wholesale, either directly or indirectly, of liquified petroleum gas (except propane and butanes) by means of tank car, tank wagon, cylinder or vessel, (iii) any absorption plant or scrubbing plant, and (iv) any system, well, works, plant, equipment or service for the production of gas or capable of producing gas which may be declared by the Energy Resources Conservation Board to be a gas utility. *Gas Utilities Act*, R.S.A. 1980, c. G-4, s. 1. 4. Any pipeline, plant, system or equipment for the transmission, delivery or furnishing of gas to or for ultimate consumers, including (i) any system, well, works, plant, equipment or service for the production of gas or capable of producing gas which may be declared by the Energy Board to be a gas utility, but not including (ii) the transportation, delivery, furnishing or supplying by retail or wholesale, either directly or indirectly, of liquified petroleum gas including propane and butanes, by means of tank car, tank wagon, cylinder or vessel, unless it is a system of tanks, tank trucks or vessels for the storage and delivery to the public of propane or butane operated in conjunction with or ancillary to a gas utility. *An Act to Amend the Gas Utilities Act,* S.N.S. 1984, c. 61, s. 1. See OWNER OF A ~; RURAL ~.

GAS VENT. That portion of a venting system designed to convey vent gases vertically to the outside air from the vent connector of a gas-fired appliance, or directly from the appliance when a vent connector is not used, and includes any offsets. *Building Code Act,* R.R.O. 1980, Reg. 87, s. 1.

GAS WELL. 1. A well in which casing is run and that, in the opinion of the minister, is producing or is capable of producing from a natural gas bearing zone. *Petroleum and Natural Gas Amendment Act,* S.B.C. 1981, c. 24, s. 1. 2. A well (a) that produces natural gas not associated or blended with oil at the time of production, (b) that produces more than 30,000 cubic feet of natural gas to each barrel of oil from the same producing horizon, (c) wherein the gas producing stratum has been successfully segregated from the oil and the gas is produced separately, or (d) that is classified as a gas well by the Minister for any reason. *Canada Oil and Gas Drilling and Production Regulations,* C.R.C., c. 1517, s. 2. See COMMERCIAL ~.

GATE. See CITY ~; GROUND ~S.

GATE RECEIPTS. See GROSS ~.

GATHERING LINE. A pipe line used for the collection of oil or gas within a field. *The Pipe Lines Act,* R.S.S. 1978, c. P-12, s. 2.

GATINEAU VALLEY REGION. That part of the Province of Quebec consisting of the parishes of Grand Remous, Bois-Franc, Montcerf, Ste-Famille d'Aumond, Ste-Thérèse de Gatineau, Lac Ste-Marie, Maniwaki, Messines, Bouchette, Blue Sea Lake and Gracefield. *Gatineau Wood Order,* C.R.C., c. 262, s. 2.

GATING. *n.* Practice of arresting a person as soon as that person is released from prison under mandatory supervision.

GATT. *abbr.* General Agreement on Tariffs and Trade, a multi-lateral international agreement regarding tariffs.

GAUGE. *n.* 1. A measure of the diameter of wire or the thickness of sheet metal in accordance with the American Wire Gauge or Brown and Sharpe Gauge Standards. *Lightning Rods Act,* R.R.O. 1980, Reg. 577, s. 1. 2. A measure of shotgun bore diameter equal to the quantity of

solid lead balls of the bore diameter which weigh one pound. F.A. Jaffe, *A Guide to Pathological Evidence,* 2d ed. (Toronto: Carswell, 1983) at 177. 3. Of railways, the measure of their width. See B-S ~; NOMINAL ~; STANDARD ~; VOLUME-PRESSURE ~.

GAVEL. *n.* Rent, tribute, payment to someone higher in rank.

GAWR. *abbr.* Gross axle weight rating.

GAZETTE. *n.* 1. A government's official newspaper. 2. Journal published by the Law Society of Upper Canada. See OFFICIAL ~.

GEAR. See CLASS A ~; CLASS B ~; FISHING ~; FIXED CARGO ~.

GEESE. *n.* Goslings and old geese. *Meat Inspection Regulations,* C.R.C., c. 1032, s. 135. See MATURE ~; YOUNG ~.

GELD. *n.* A compensation, mulct, payment, price, tax, tribute, value.

GELDABLE. *adj.* Taxable.

GELLING AGENT. Gelatin, agar and carrageenan. *Food and Drug Regulations,* C.R.C., c. 870, s. B.01.001.

GEN. *abbr.* General.

GENEALOGY. *n.* A family history; specification of descendants in order of succession; pedigree.

GENEARCH. *n.* The chief person in a family.

GENERAL ACREAGE QUOTA. Any permission given by the Board to deliver grain, either under a permit book or otherwise. *Prairie Grain Advance Payment Act,* R.S.C. 1985, c. P-18, s. 2.

GENERAL ADJUSTMENT. A wage increase given to all employees.

GENERAL ADVANTAGE OF CANADA. See WORKS FOR ~.

GENERAL AGENT. 1. One who has authority to do something on behalf of a principal, or to act for a principal in any matter or in every matter regarding a particular business or trade or of a certain nature. G.H.L. Fridman, *The Law of Agency,* 5th ed. (London: Butterworths, 1983) at 33. 2. A person acting under authority from an insurer to supervise and appoint agents, inspect risks and otherwise transact business for, or as a representative of, such insurer. *The Saskatchewan Insurance Act,* R.S.S. 1978, c. S-26, s. 2.

GENERAL ASSEMBLY. All the sessions of the Legislative Assembly held subsequent to a general provincial election until the dissolution of the Legislature by the Lieutenant Governor.

Legislative Assembly Retirement Allowances Act, R.S.P.E.I. 1974, c. L-12, s. 1.

GENERAL AVERAGE. See FREE FROM ~.

GENERAL CARGO. All cargo not carried in bulk, that is, all cargo not carried loose or in mass.

GENERAL CENSUS. The census taken by the Government of Canada. *Election Act,* R.S.Q. 1977, c. E-3, s. 2.

GENERAL CONTRACTOR. A contractor whose principal activity consists of organizing or coordinating construction work entrusted to persons under his orders or to contractors to execute. *Building Contractors Vocational Qualifications Act,* R.S.Q. 1977, c. Q-1, s. 53.

GENERAL DAMAGES. 1. Damages which flow naturally from a wrongful act and thus the defendant knows will be claimed. K.D. Cooper-Stephenson & I.B. Saunders, *Personal Injury Damages in Canada* (Toronto: Carswell, 1981) at 42. 2. Any non-pecuniary loss and future pecuniary loss. K.D. Cooper-Stephenson & I.B. Saunders, *Personal Injury Damages in Canada* (Toronto: Carswell, 1981) at 43.

GENERALE DICTUM GENERALITER EST INTELLIGENDUM. [L.] A general dictum should be comprehended in a general sense.

GENERAL EDUCATION. Education at the pre-elementary or elementary level within the meaning of the regulations contemplated in section 30 of the Act respecting the Conseil supérieur de l'éducation (chapter C-60), and all education at the secondary or college level, within the meaning of the said regulations, of which the immediate object is not preparation for the practice of a vocation or trade and which enables the pupils to pursue studies at a higher level. *Private Education Act,* R.S.Q. 1977, c. E-9, s. 1.

GENERAL ELECTION. 1. An election in respect of which election writs are issued for all electoral districts. 2. An election that is held in respect of each constituency on the same day. 3. An election held for all the members of an elected authority to fill vacancies caused by the effluxion of time.

GENERALE NIHIL CERTI IMPLICAT. [L.] A general statement implies nothing definite.

GENERALE NIHIL PONIT. [L.] A general statement says nothing.

GENERAL ENUMERATION. An enumeration of electors in all electoral divisions. *Election Act,* R.S.A. 1980, c. E-2, s. 1.

GENERALE TANTUM VALET IN GENERALIBUS QUANTUM SINGULARE IN SINGU-

LIS. [L.] General words should be taken in a general sense, just as particular words refer only to particular things.

GENERAL EXPENSES. The direct and indirect costs, charges and expenses of producing and selling goods for export, other than the costs, charges and expenses referred to in paragraph (2)(a) and subsection (3). *Customs Act,* R.S.C. 1985 (2d Supp.), c. 1, s. 52(4).

GENERAL HOLIDAY. 1. New Year's Day, Good Friday, Victoria Day, Canada Day, Labour Day, Thanksgiving Day, Remembrance Day, Christmas Day and Boxing Day and includes any day substituted for any such holiday pursuant to section 195. *Canada Labour Code,* R.S.C. 1985, c. L-2, s. 166. 2. New Year's Day, Good Friday, Victoria Day, Dominion Day, Labour Day, Thanksgiving Day, or Christmas Day. *Employment Standards Act,* R.S.M. 1970, c. E110, s. 2. 3. New Year's Day, Good Friday, Victoria Day, Dominion Day, British Columbia Day, Labour Day, Thanksgiving Day, Remembrance Day and Christmas Day. *Employment Standards Act,* S.B.C. 1980, c. 10, s. 1. 4. New Year's Day, Good Friday, Dominion Day, the first Monday in August, Labour Day, Thanksgiving Day, Remembrance Day, Christmas Day, and the day fixed by the Governor-General for observation of the birthday of the reigning sovereign, and includes any day substituted for any such holiday pursuant to section 26. *Labour Standards Act,* S.N.W.T. 1976, c. 3, s. 1. 5. (i) New Year's Day, (ii) Good Friday, (iii) Victoria Day, (iv) Dominion Day, (v) Labour Day, (vi) Thanksgiving Day, (vii) Remembrance Day, (viii) Christmas Day, and (ix) any other day designated as a general holiday by the Lieutenant Governor in Council under an act.

GENERAL HOSPITAL. 1. A hospital in which diagnostic services and medical, surgical and obstetrical treatment are provided to persons having various illness, disabilities, injuries or other conditions. *The Hospital Standards Act,* R.S.S. 1978, c. H-10, s. 2. 2. A hospital providing diagnostic services and facilities for medical or surgical treatment in the acute phase for adults and children and obstetrical care, or any of them. *Hospitals Act,* R.S.A. 1980, c. H-11, s. 1.

GENERALIA SPECIALIBUS NON DEROGANT. [L.] 1. The general does not detract from the specific. 2. General words in a later act capable of sensible and reasonable application without extending them to any subject specially dealt with by earlier legislation should not be interpreted as indirectly repealing, altering, or derogating from earlier special legislation unless there is an indication that the later general words were intended. P.St.J. Langan, ed., *Maxwell on*

The Interpretation of Statutes, 12th ed. (Bombay: N.M. Tripathi, 1976) at 196.

GENERALIA VERBA SUNT GENERAL-ITER INTELLIGENDA. [L.] General words should be comprehended generally.

GENERALIBUS SPECIALIA DEROGANT. [L.] The special derogates from the general.

GENERAL INTENT. The intent to perform a wrongful act.

GENERALIS CLAUSULA NON PORRI-GITUR AD EA QUAE ANTEA SPECIAL-ITER SUNT COMPREHENSA. [L.] A general clause does not extend to things which were included in prior special words.

GENERALIS REGULA GENERALITER EST INTELLIGENDA. [L.] A general rule should be comprehended generally.

GENERAL JURISDICTION. Unrestricted and unlimited authority in any matter of substantive law, criminal or civil. S.A. Cohen, *Due Process of Law* (Toronto: Carswell, 1977) at 344.

GENERAL LIEN. A lien on personal property for an account due or general debt to the one who claims it, which operates as a form of floating charge on any of the debtor's personal property in the lien claimant's hands. D.N. Macklem & D.I. Bristow, *Construction and Mechanics' Liens in Canada*, 5th ed. (Toronto: Carswell, 1985) at 579.

GENERALLY ACCEPTED ACCOUNTING PRINCIPLES. Conventions, rules and procedures that set out accepted accounting practice, usually the principles established by the Canadian Institute of Chartered Accountants.

GENERALLY ACCEPTED AUDITING STANDARDS. Standards concerning an auditor's conduct in carrying out examinations.

GENERAL MACHINIST. A person who (i) sets up and operates to prescribed tolerances engine lathes and milling, grinding, drilling, sawing and boring machines, (ii) reads and interprets blueprints, operation and product-related reference charts and tables and selects mechanical measuring and checking and layout tools and devices, and (iii) performs measuring, checking and layout operations and selects work piece materials and the required cutting tools and abrasives for metal removal operations, but does not include a person or class of persons in a limited purpose occupation that, in the opinion of the Director, does not equate with the definition of general machinist. *Apprenticeship and Tradesmen's Qualification Act*, R.R.O. 1980, Reg. 38, s. 1.

GENERAL MANAGER. The chief executive officer of a corporation who has supervision over and directs the work of the staff of the corporation.

GENERAL MEASUREMENT POINT. In respect of any accommodation space, means (a) a point midway between two adjacent lamps; (b) a point midway between a lamp and any position on the boundary of the space; and (c) the central point of part of a space that is available for free movement where that part is shaded from the direct rays of a lamp by a re-entrant angle formed in the boundary of the space. *Towboat Crew Accommodation Regulations*, C.R.C., c. 1498, Schedule IV, s. 1.

GENERAL MEETING. Any annual, regular, special or class meeting of the members and, in the case of credit unions having a delegate structure, includes delegate meetings. *Credit Union Act*, S.S. 1984-85-86, c. C-45.1, s. 2. See ANNUAL ~.

GENERAL ORDER NO. 448. General Order No. 448 of the Board of Railway Commissioners for Canada dated Friday the 26th day of August 1927. *Western Grain Transportation Act*, R.S.C. 1985, c. W-8, s. 2.

GENERAL ORDERS. Includes Rules of Court. *Partition of Property Act*, R.S.B.C. 1979, c. 311, s. 1.

GENERAL PARTNER. Person associated with one or more other persons in an enterprise and assuming personal liability. See LIMITED PARTNERSHIP.

GENERAL PERMIT. A permit to export issued by the Minister under section 17. *Cultural Property Export and Import Act*, R.S.C. 1985, c. C-51, s. 2.

GENERAL POWER. 1. Includes any power or authority enabling the donee or other holder thereof either alone or jointly with or, with the consent, of any other person to appoint, appropriate or dispose of property as he sees fit, whether exercisable by instrument inter vivos or by will, or both, but does not include (i) any power exercisable in a fiduciary capacity under a disposition not made by the donee except to the extent that having regard to the fiduciary restrictions imposed upon the donee under the disposition it is reasonable to regard the donee or holder of the power as capable of conferring the property or any part thereof upon herself or himself for her or his own benefit, or (ii) any power exercisable as a mortgagee, or (iii) any power exercisable jointly with, or with the consent of, any other person (A) who has a substantial interest in the property to which the power relates, and (B) whose interest in that property would be adversely affected by the exercise of the power in favour of the donee or holder. 2. The power of a donee to appoint property to anyone, including her or himself. D.M.W. Waters, *The Law of Trusts in Canada*, 2d ed. (Toronto: Carswell, 1984) at 72.

GENERAL PRACTITIONER. Excepting an intern, a resident within the scope of his attributions or a physician who is a member of the civil service, means a physician holding a certificate in general medicine, family medicine or the equivalent or a physician who does not hold a specialist's certificate from the Corporation professionnelle des médecins du Québec. *An Act Respecting Resumption of the Dispensation of Medical Care in Québec*, S.Q. 1982, c. 20, s. 1.

GENERAL PROPERTY TAX. (i) A tax that is levied on the assessment, as shown on the assessment roll of the municipality, for municipal, school or hospital purposes; (ii) where levied, a local improvement tax under The Local Improvements Act shown on the tax notice; and (iii) where levied, a conservation and development tax under The Conservation and Development Act, shown on the tax notice. Saskatchewan statutes.

GENERAL REGISTER. An index of documents that do not affect any particular piece of land such as wills and powers of attorney which, when registered, are allotted a number and stored. B.J. Reiter, R.C.B. Risk & B.N. McLellan, *Real Estate Law*, 3d ed. (Toronto: Emond Montgomery, 1986) at 457.

GENERAL REVIEW. In relation to the construction, enlargement or alteration of a building, means an examination of the building to determine whether the construction, enlargement or alteration is in general conformity with the design governing the construction, enlargement or alteration, and reporting thereon.

GENERAL STRIKE. Cessation of work by all union members in a geographical area.

GENERAL TAX. A tax levied upon the taxable assessments in a municipality or local improvement district. *The Health Services Act*, R.S.S. 1978, c. H-1, s. 2.

GENERAL USE SWITCH. A switch intended for use in general distribution and branch-circuits and which is rated in amperes and capable of interrupting its rated current at rated voltage. *Power Corporation Act*, R.R.O. 1980, Reg. 794, s. 0.

GENERAL VERDICT. A jury's decision for either the defendant or the plaintiff generally.

GENERAL WORDS. In a conveyance, mortgage or assurance of corporeal hereditament, words which describe every kind of appurte-nance, easement or privilege, portions of the soil, fixtures or produce of the land and were added to the parcel or description of the property.

GENERATING CAPABILITY. See NET ~.

GENERATION. *n.* Production of hydraulic, electrical, pneumatic, steam, internal combustion engine, gas, oil, atomic or any other process.

GENERATION AND SALE FOR DISTRIBUTION TO THE PUBLIC. Generation and sale (a) to a person or persons with whom the vendor deals at arm's length, or (b) to a person or persons with whom the vendor does not deal at arm's length for resale directly or indirectly to persons with whom the vendor does deal at arm's length. *Public Utilities Income Tax Transfer Act*, R.S.C. 1985, c. P-37, s. 2.

GENERATOR. See PULSE ~; RADIONU-CLIDE ~; X-RAY ~.

GENERIC. *adj.* Relating to a group or class; chemical name of a drug.

GENETIC MARKER. An inherited characteristic used in a forensic investigation or paternity study. F.A. Jaffe, *A Guide to Pathological Evidence*, 2d ed. (Toronto: Carswell, 1983) at 177.

GENEVA CONVENTIONS. Agreements to ameliorate the condition of wounded and sick members of the armed forces in the field, to ameliorate the condition of sick, wounded and ship-wrecked members of the armed forces at sea, to treat prisoners of war and civilian persons in time of war in particular ways.

GENOCIDE. *n.* Any of the following acts committed with intent to destroy in whole or in part any identifiable group, namely, (a) killing members of the group, or (b) deliberately inflicting on the group conditions of life calculated to bring about its physical destruction. *Criminal Code*, R.S.C. 1985, c. C-46, s. 318(2).

GENS. *n.* [L.] Great family; nation; race.

GENUINE. *adj.* Free of forgery or counterfeiting.

GENUINE TRADE MARK. A trade mark that is true, real, authentic, not counterfeit or not spurious. H.G. Fox, *The Canadian Law of Trade Marks and Unfair Competition*, 3d ed. (Toronto: Carswell, 1972) at 671.

GENUS. *n.* [L.] A universal idea or quality common to a whole class, which differentiates every member of that class from all other classes.

GEODESIST. See DOMINION ~.

GEODETIC ELEVATION. An elevation designated by a regulation of the Surveyor General based on the Canadian Geodetic Datum, authorized by O/C 630 of the Privy Council of

Canada, dated March 11, 1935, and derived from a numbered precise bench mark established from it, and appearing in an official publication of the Geodetic Survey of Canada. *Land Title Act*, R.S.B.C. 1979, c. 219, s. 135.

GEOGRAPHIC WAGE DIFFERENTIAL. Difference in wages dependent on location of work.

GEOLOGIST. See PROFESSIONAL ~.

GEOLOGICAL WORK. Work involving direct collection, examination, processing or other analysis, in the field or laboratory, of lithological, paleontological or geochemical materials recovered from surface outcrops or the sea-floor or subsurface and includes the analysis and interpretation of mechanical well logs.

GEOLOGY. See PRACTICE OF ~; PROFESSIONAL ~.

GEOPHYSICAL EQUIPMENT. Equipment used for or in connection with or preparatory to geophysical exploration. *Oil, Natural Gas and Minerals Act*, R.S.P.E.I. 1974, c. O-3, s. 2.

GEOPHYSICAL EXPLORATION. Any investigation of the subsurface of the land and includes (a) seismic operations, (b) gravimetric operations, (c) magnetic operations, (d) electrical operations, (e) geochemical operations, (f) test drilling, and (g) any other operation employed to determine geologic or other subsurface conditions.

GEOPHYSICAL OPERATION. Any work or acts done in connection with or incidental to geophysical exploration. *Mines and Minerals Act*, R.S.A. 1970, c. 238, s. 187.

GEOPHYSICAL SURVEY. Any investigation carried out on the surface of the ground to determine the nature and structure of the subsurface. *Territorial Land Use Regulations*, C.R.C., c. 1524, s. 2.

GEOPHYSICAL WORK. Work involving the indirect measurement of the physical properties of rocks in order to determine the depth, thickness, structural configuration or history of deposition thereof and includes the processing, analysis and interpretation of material or data obtained from that work.

GEOPHYSICIST. See PROFESSIONAL ~.

GEOPHYSICS. See PRACTICE OF ~; PROFESSIONAL ~.

GEORGIAN BAY AND ST. LAWRENCE PORTS. The ports of Midland, Port McNicoll, Collingwood, Owen Sound, Goderich, Sarnia, Windsor, Port Colborne, Toronto, Kingston, Prescott, Montreal, Sorel, Trois-Rivières and Quebec City. *Feed Grain Reserve Stock Regulations*, C.R.C., c. 324, s. 2.

GEOTECHNICAL WORK. Work, in the field or laboratory, undertaken to determine the physical properties of materials recovered from the surface or subsurface or the seabed or its subsoil of any frontier lands. *Petroleum Resources Act*, R.S.C. 1985 (2d Supp.), c. 36, s. 101.

GEOTHERMAL EXPLORATION. Investigation of the subsurface of land for the presence of a geothermal resource by means of (a) seismic, gravimetric, magnetic, radiometric, electric, geological or geochemical operations, (b) well drilling or test hole drilling, or (c) any other method approved by the division head. *Geothermal Resources Act*, S.B.C. 1982, s. 14, s. 1.

GEOTHERMAL RESOURCE. The natural heat of the earth and all substances that derive an added value from it, including steam, water and water vapour heated by the natural heat of the earth and all substances dissolved in the steam, water or water vapour obtained from a well, but does not include (a) water that has a temperature less than 80°C at the point where it reaches the surface, or (b) hydrocarbons. *Geothermal Resources Act*, S.B.C. 1982, s. 14, s. 1.

GEOTHERMAL WELL. A well in which casing is run and that the minister considers is producing or capable of producing a geothermal resource from a geothermal resource bearing zone. *Geothermal Resources Act*, S.B.C. 1982, s. 14, s. 1.

GERIATRIC CENTRE. Includes a nursing home, supervisory care home, sheltered care home or other institution used primarily for the purpose of providing supervisory care, personal care and nursing care for persons who by reason of need, age, infirmity or blindness are unable to care for themselves. *The Election Act*, R.S.S. 1978, c. E-6, s. 2.

GERMAN. *n.* A brother; one related as closely as a brother. See COUSIN-GERMAN.

GESTATION. *n.* The period of development in the womb. F.A. Jaffe, *A Guide to Pathological Evidence*, 2d ed. (Toronto: Carswell, 1983) at 177.

GET. *n.* A bill of divorce under Hebraic law.

GETTLER-YAMAKAMI TEST. A test for blood chloride levels. F.A. Jaffe, *A Guide to Pathological Evidence*, 2d ed. (Toronto: Carswell, 1983) at 84.

GHOST WRITER. A writer who writes a story based on material supplied by a well-known person. H.G. Fox, *The Canadian Law of Copyright and Industrial Designs*, 2d ed. (Toronto: Carswell, 1967) at 246-247.

GIBBET. *n.* A beam laid over a post or posts from which prisoners were hanged.

GIBLETS. *n.* The liver from which the bile sac has been removed, the heart from which the pericardial sac has been removed and the gizzard from which the contents and lining have been removed. *Dressed and Eviscerated Poultry Regulations*, C.R.C., c. 283, s. 2.

GIFT. *n.* Gratuitous transfer of property ownership. E.L.G. Tyler & N.E. Palmer, eds., *Crossley Vaines' Personal Property*, 5th ed. (London: Butterworths, 1973) at 299. See CLASS ~; DEED OF ~; INTER VIVOS ~.

GIFT INTER VIVOS. A gift made by a living person to another living person.

GIFT TAX. Tax imposed on the transfer of property by gift.

GIGA. *pref.* 10^9. Prefix for multiples and submultiples of basic, supplementary and derived units of measurement. *Weights and Measures Act*, S.C. 1970-71-72, c. 36, schedule I.

GILD. *n.* 1. A tax; tribute. 2. A society formed for mutual benefit and protection.

GILDABLE. *adj.* Legally bound to pay gild.

GILDA MERCATORIA. [L.] A guild merchant; an assembly or meeting of merchants.

GILL. *n.* 1/32 gallon. *Weights and Measures Act*, S.C. 1970-71-72, c. 36, schedule II.

GILL NET. 1. A net that is used to catch fish by enmeshing them and that does not enclose an area of water. *Fishery Regulations*, Canada regulations. 2. A floating gill net that is neither anchored nor staked but floats freely with the tide or current. *Pacific Commercial Salmon Fishery Regulations*, C.R.C., c. 823, s. 2.

GILT-EDGED SECURITY. 1. A security contemplated in paragraph d, h or i or article 981o of the Civil Code. *Securities Act*, S.Q. 1982, c. 48, s. 5. 2. An investment of the highest class.

GIRL. See YOUNG ~.

GISTMENT. *n.* Agistment.

GIVE. *v.* To transfer property without compensation.

GIVEN NAME. 1. Includes a given name, Christian name or baptismal name. 2. Includes an initial.

GIVEN NAMES. Of the officiating or assisting notary, of the parties to deeds, of witnesses or of any other person, it means the given name or names by which such notary, parties, witnesses or other persons are usually described, and not necessarily all the given names entered in the act of birth. *Notarial Act*, R.S.Q. 1977, c. N-2, s. 47.

GIVE TIME. For a creditor to enter into a binding contract which permits a debtor to defer the payment of money or to do something after the time it was originally agreed the act should be done.

GIVE-WAY VESSEL. A vessel that is required by these Regulations to keep out of the way of another vessel. *Collision Regulations*, C.R.C., c. 1416, s. 2.

GLASS. *n.* Refers to glass in the doors, windows, side wings, or windshield, of a motor vehicle, but does not refer to the glass in frost shields or in storm windows installed on the outside of a bus. *The Highway Traffic Act*, S.M. 1985-86, c. 3, s. 52(1). See LAMINATED ~; PLATE ~ INSURANCE; SAFETY ~; TEMPERED ~; WIRED ~.

GLASS SCREEN. See WIRED ~.

GLAZIER AND METAL MECHANIC. Person who (i) performs layout, fabrication, assembly and installation of extruded frames, hardware, store fronts, wall facings, manual sliding doors, window sashes, manual door closers, automatic door operators and curtain walls, (ii) performs layout, fabrication, assembly and installation of suspended glass fronts, stuck glass fronts, auto glass, art glass, aquariums and similar special products, (iii) cuts, fits and installs glass in wood and metal frames for windows, skylights, store fronts and display cases, or on building fronts, interior walls, ceilings, tables and similar surfaces by means of mastic, screws or decorative moldings, and (iv) reads and understands design drawings, manufacturers' literature and installation diagrams. *Apprenticeship and Tradesmen's Qualification Act*, R.R.O. 1980, Reg. 39, s. 1.

GLEBE. *n.* The land held as part of an ecclesiastical benefice.

GLIDER. *n.* A motorless heavier-than-air aircraft, deriving its lift in flight from aerodynamic reactions on surfaces that remain fixed under given conditions of flight. *Air Regulations*, C.R.C., c. 2, s. 101.

GLOBAL SUM. An award in which no specific amount is allocated under separate heads of damage. K.D. Cooper-Stephenson & I.B. Saunders, *Personal Injury Damages in Canada* (Toronto: Carswell, 1981) at 47.

GLOSS. *n.* Interpretation consisting of an annotation, explanation or comment on any passage in a text. See SPECULAR ~.

GLOTTIS. *n.* The vocal cords including the space between. F.A. Jaffe, *A Guide to Patholog-*

ical Evidence, 2d ed. (Toronto: Carswell, 1983) at 177.

GLOW. See AFTER~.

GLUESTOCK. *n.* The hair, bones, hoofs, horns, fleshings, hide cuttings or parings of an animal or any other part of an animal that may be used in the manufacture of glue. *Animal Disease and Protection Regulations*, C.R.C., c. 296, s. 2.

G.M.A.C. *abbr.* General Motors Acceptance Corporation.

GNP. *abbr.* Gross national product.

GOB. *n.* The space in a mine from which coal has been mined and that has been allowed to subside or fall in. *Coal Mines (CBDC) Safety Regulations*, C.R.C., c. 1011, s. 2.

GODSON. *abbr.* Godson, Mining Commissioner's Cases (Ont.), 1911-1917.

GOING CONCERN ACTUARIAL LIABILITIES. The value of the liabilities of a pension plan determined on the basis of a going concern valuation of the plan. *Pension Benefits Standards Regulations*, C.R.C., c. 1252, s. 2.

GOING CONCERN ASSETS. The assets of a pension plan consisting of cash, invested assets, due and accrued income and, except where the annual cost of benefits is determined on the accrued benefit cost method, the present value of future normal costs. *Pension Benefits Standards Regulations*, C.R.C., c. 1252, s. 2.

GOING CONCERN UNFUNDED ACTUARIAL LIABILITY. The excess of going concern actuarial liabilities over going concern assets. *Pension Benefits Standards Regulations*, C.R.C., c. 1252, s. 2.

GOING CONCERN VALUATION. A valuation of assets and liabilities of a pension plan using methods and actuarial assumptions considered by the actuary who reviewed the plan to be in accordance with sound actuarial principles and practices for the valuation of a pension plan that is not expected to be terminated or wound-up for an indefinite period of time. *Pension Benefits Standards Regulations*, C.R.C., c. 1252, s. 2.

GOING-CONCERN VALUE. The nature of an established business or plant with its earning power already entirely or partly matured. A. Bissett-Johnson & W.M. Holland, eds., *Matrimonial Property Law in Canada* (Toronto: Carswell, 1980) at V-10.

GOING PRIVATE TRANSACTION. 1. Reorganization of a corporation in such a way as to eliminate its minority shareholders and convert to private company status. S.M. Beck *et al*, *Cases and Materials on Partnerships and Canadian Business Corporations*, (Toronto: The Carswell Company Limited, 1983) at 855. 2. An amalgamation, arrangement, consolidation or other transaction carried out under this Act by a corporation that would cause the interest of a holder of a participating security of the corporation to be terminated without the consent of the holder and without the substitution therefor of an interest of equivalent value in a participating security that, (i) is issued by the corporation, an affiliate of the corporation or a successor body corporate, and (ii) is not limited in the extent of its participation in earnings to any greater extent than the participating security for which it is substituted, but does not include, (iii) an acquisition under section 187, (iv) a redemption of, or other compulsory termination of the interest of the holder in, a security if the security is redeemed or otherwise acquired in accordance with the terms and conditions attaching thereto or under a requirement of the articles relating to the class of securities or of this Act, or (v) a proceeding under Part XVI. *Business Corporations Act, 1982*, S.O. 1982, c. 4, s. 189.

GOING RATE. The prevailing rate of wages.

GOLD BEARING QUARTZ. All gold bearing rock in situ. *Mines Act*, R.S.N.S. 1967, c. 185, s. 1.

GOLD CLAUSE OBLIGATION. Any obligation incurred before, on or after the 3rd day of June, 1939 (including any such obligation that has, at any time before, on or after that date, matured or been repudiated) that purports to give to the creditor a right to require payment in gold or in gold coin or in an amount of money measured thereby, and includes any such obligation of the Government of Canada or of any province. *Gold Clauses Act*, R.S.C. 1970, c. G-4, s. 2.

GOLD CLAUSES ACT. An act which declares any gold clause obligation, wherever payable, contrary to public policy. J.G. McLeod, *The Conflict of Laws* (Calgary: Carswell, 1983) at 516.

GOLDEN HANDSHAKE. A termination payment provided to a senior executive or manager.

GOLDEN PARACHUTE. When a change in control of a business occurs, a provision in the employment contract of senior officers guaranteeing several years salary if they lose or choose to leave their jobs as a result of the change. S.M. Beck *et al.*, *Cases and Materials on Partnerships and Canadian Business Corporations* (Toronto: The Carswell Company Limited, 1983) at 416.

GOLDEN RULE. When construing a statute, the ordinary meaning of the words and the ordinary rules of grammatical construction should be used unless that produces a result contrary to the intent of the legislators or leading to obvious repugnance or absurdity. P.St.J. Langan, ed., *Maxwell on The Interpretation of Statutes*, 12th ed. (Bombay: N.M. Tripathi, 1976) at 43.

GOLD FRANC. A unit consisting of sixty-five and one-half milligrams of gold of millesimal fineness nine hundred. *Canada Shipping Act*, R.S.C. 1985, c. S-9, s. 584.

GOLD MINE. 1. (a) Any work or undertaking in which ore containing gold is mined and the gold separated therefrom and refined, or (b) any work or undertaking in which ore containing gold is mined although the gold is separated therefrom or refined, or both separated therefrom and refined by a person other than the person operating the work or undertaking, under a contract with him pursuant to which the gold produced remains his property. *Emergency Gold Mining Assistance Act*, R.S.C. 1970, c. E-5, s. 2. 2. A mine where the gold produced from the mine is recovered in the operation area by the process of cyanidation and accounts for more than 50 per cent of the value of the output of the mine. *Metal Mining Liquid Effluent Regulations*, C.R.C., c. 819, s. 2.

GONZALES TEST. See PARAFFIN TEST.

GOOD. *adj.* When describing pleading, sound or valid.

GOOD CONSIDERATION. Consideration based on natural love and affection.

GOOD FAITH. 1. Honesty in fact in the conduct of the transaction concerned. 2. A thing is deemed to be done in good faith within the meaning of an act when it is in fact done honestly, whether it is done negligently or not. 3. Honesty in fact and the observation of reasonable commercial standards of fair dealing in the trade as defined in the common law. *Motor Vehicle Franchise Act*, S.N.B. 1987, c. 70, s. 1. See IN ~.

GOODS. *n.* 1. Chattels personal other than things in action or money, and includes emblements, industrial growing crops and things attached to or forming part of the land that are agreed to be severed before sale or under the contract of sale. 2. Includes tokens, coupons or other documents or things issued or sold by a seller to a buyer that are exchangeable or redeemable for goods or services. *Consumer Protection acts*. 3. Anything that is the subject of trade or commerce. *Criminal Code*, R.S.C. 1985, c. C-46, s. 379. 4. Any article that is or may be the subject of trade or commerce, but does not include land or any interest therein. *Bills of Exchange Act*, R.S.C. 1985, c. B-4, s. 188. 5.

Includes all personal property other than vessels. 6. For greater certainty, includes conveyances and animals. *Customs Act*, R.S.C. 1985 (2d Supp.), c. 1, s. 2. 7. Includes wares and merchandise. 8. Personal property. See ABANDONED ~; ASCERTAINED ~; BONDED ~; BULK ~; CANADIAN ~; CONSUMER ~; CONTAINERIZED ~; DANGEROUS ~; DISPLAY ~; DOCUMENT OF TITLE TO ~; FUGITIVE'S ~; FUNERAL ~; FUNGIBLE ~; FUTURE ~; HEALTH ~; HOT ~; HOUSEHOLD ~; IDENTICAL ~; INCINERATOR ~; LIKE ~; OBSOLETE OR SURPLUS ~; PREPACKAGED ~; QUALITY OF ~; SALE OF ~; SECOND-HAND ~; SHOP ~; SIMILAR ~; SPECIFIC ~; SUBSIDIZED ~; SYSTEM ~; TRESPASS TO ~; UNASCERTAINED ~; UNITIZED ~; UNSOLD ~; UNSOLICITED ~.

GOODS AND CHATTELS. 1. Things personal. 2. In addition to the things usually understood thereby, any movable property of any kind whatsoever which may be left with a keeper of a storage warehouse for storage. *Storage Warehouse Keepers Act*, R.S.N.S. 1967, c. 293, s. 1. 3. Includes shares and dividends of a stockholder in any incorporated company in New Brunswick having transferable joint stock. *Memorials and Executions Act*, R.S.N.B. 1973, c. M-9, s. 23.

GOODS CONTRACT. An agreement for the purchase of articles, commodities, equipment, goods, materials or supplies and includes (a) an agreement for printing or the reproduction of printed matter, and (b) an agreement for the construction or repair of a vessel. *Government Contracts Regulations*, C.R.C., c. 701, s. 2.

GOODS IN BULK. The following goods laden or freighted in ships and, except as otherwise provided in this definition, not bundled or enclosed in bags, bales, boxes, cases, casks, crates or any other container: (a) grain and grain products, including flour and mill feeds in bulk or in sacks, (b) ores and minerals (crude, screened, sized, refined or concentrated, but not otherwise processed), including ore concentrates in sacks, sand, stone and gravel, coal and coke, and liquids, (c) pulpwood, woodpulp, poles and logs, including pulpwood and woodpulp in bales, and (d) waste paper loaded as full ship's cargo, iron and steel scrap and pig iron. *Transport Act*, R.S.C. 1985, c. T-17, s. 2.

GOODS OF A DANGEROUS NATURE. Goods that by reason of their nature, quantity or mode of stowage are either singly or collectively liable to endanger the lives of the passengers or imperil the ship, and includes all substances determined by the Governor in Council, in regulations made by him, to be dangerous goods. *Canada Shipping Act*, R.S.C. 1985, c. S-9, s. 2.

GOODS OF THE SAME CLASS OR KIND. In relation to goods being appraised, means imported goods that (a) are within a group or range of imported goods produced by a particular industry or industry sector that includes identical goods and similar goods in relation to the goods being appraised, and (b) for the purposes of (i) section 51, were produced in any country and exported from any country, and (ii) section 52, were produced in and exported from the same country as the country in and from which the goods being appraised were produced and exported. *Customs Act*, R.S.C. 1985 (2d Supp.), c. 1, s. 45.

GOODS OR SERVICES. See CEMETERY ~; CONSUMER ~.

GOOD STANDING. See MEMBER IN ~.

GOODS, WARES AND MERCHANDISE. Includes products of agriculture, products of the forest, products of the quarry and mine, products of the sea, lakes and rivers, and all other articles of commerce. *Bank Act*, R.S.C. 1985, c. B-1, s. 2.

GOODWILL. *n.* Refers to the probability that customers will continue to patronize a business; the advantage of the reputation of a firm built up over time by providing good service or doing honest work.

GOOF BALL. See BARBITURATE.

GOON. *n.* A person who engages in violence during a strike.

GOOSE FLESH. See CUTIS ANSERINA.

GO PUBLIC. To issue shares of a corporation to the general public for the first time.

GORE. *n.* A parcel of land in the shape of a wedge.

GOUVERNEMENT. *n.* The Lieutenant-Governor and the Conseil exécutif du Québec. *Interpretation Act*, R.S.Q. 1977, I-16, s. 61.

GOVERNING AUTHORITY. See LOCAL ~.

GOVERNING EXECUTIVE AUTHORITY. The executive committee, executive board, management committee, grand executive committee, or such other board, committee or body as is charged under the constitution, bylaws and rules of a fraternal society with its general management between general meetings. *Insurance acts.*

GOVERNMENT. *n.* 1. The government of Canada or of any province and includes any department, commission, board or branch of any such government. *Canada Evidence Act*, R.S.C. 1985, c. C-5, s. 31. 2. (a) The Government of Canada, (b) the government of a province, or (c) Her Majesty in right of Canada or a province. *Criminal Code*, R.S.C. 1985, c. C-46, s. 118. 3. (i) Her Majesty in right of Canada or of a province, or (ii) the government of a foreign state or of a political subdivision of a foreign state. See AGENCY OF ~; ASSOCIATED ~; CABINET ~; CHIEF ~ WHIP; EXECUTIVE ~; FEDERAL ~; FOREIGN ~; HOST ~; LOCAL ~; MUNICIPAL ~; PARLIAMENTARY ~; RESPONSIBLE ~; SOVEREIGN ~.

GOVERNMENT AGENCY. 1. (a) A department of the government, (b) a corporation that is an agent of the Crown in right of a province, or (c) any corporation, commission, board or other body empowered to exercise quasi-judicial or governmental functions and whose members are appointed by an act of a legislature, a Lieutenant Governor in Council or a member of any executive council or any combination thereof. 2. Any board, commission or body, whether incorporated or not, all the members of which or all the members of the governing board of which (a) are appointed by an Act of a legislature or by a Lieutenant Governor in Council, or (b) if not so appointed are, in the discharge of their duties, public officers or servants of the Crown or, for the proper discharge of their duties, are directly or indirectly responsible to the Crown.

GOVERNMENTAL ORGANIZATION. A Ministry, commission, board or other administrative unit of the Government of Ontario, and includes any agency thereof. *Ombudsman Act*, R.S.O. 1980, c. 325, s. 1.

GOVERNMENT ASSISTANCE. Assistance from a government, municipality or other public authority whether as a grant, subsidy, forgivable loan, deduction from tax, investment allowance or as any other form of assistance other than as a deduction under subsection (5) or (6). *Income Tax Act*, R.S.C. 1952, c. 148 (as am. S.C. 1985, c. 45, s. 72(5)), s. 127(9).

GOVERNMENT BILL. A bill approved by cabinet and introduced into a legislature by a minister. P.W. Hogg, *Constitutional Law of Canada*, 2d ed. (Toronto: Carswell, 1985) at 203.

GOVERNMENT BODY. The Legislative Assembly, or a department or division of the Government of the Northwest Territories and includes the office of any commission, board, bureau or other branch of the public service of the Northwest Territories. *Archives Act*, S.N.W.T. 1981 (3d Sess.), c. 2, s. 2.

GOVERNMENT BUOY. A buoy maintained by Her Majesty in right of Canada or in right of any province or any agent thereof, or by a municipal corporation or by a corporation that is owned or controlled by Her Majesty in right of Canada. *Private Buoy Regulations*, C.R.C., c. 1460, s. 2.

GOVERNMENT COMMITMENT. In respect of any crop year, means an amount equal to the aggregate of (a) the Crow Benefit, and (b) the cumulative government share of the cost change in respect of that crop year, but shall not exceed the difference between the eligible costs and the base year revenues within the meaning of subsection 36(2) for the most recent base year within the meaning of subsection 40(1), as adjusted to take into account the tonnage of grain actually moved in that crop year. *Western Grain Transportation Act*, R.S.C. 1985, c. W-8, s. 55.

GOVERNMENT CONTRACT. Includes any contract entered into with the Crown: (i) for the supply to or by the Crown of any goods or services; (ii) for the disposition, by sale, lease or otherwise, of any land to or by the Crown; (iii) for the construction of any public work for the Crown; (iv) for the determination of compensation with respect to any land taken, purchased or damaged by the Crown; (v) for the determination of compensation to be paid by the Crown in cases not provided for in subclause (iv); (vi) for the lending of money to or by the Crown. *Members of the Legislative Assembly Conflict of Interests Act*, S.S. 1979, c. M-11.2, s. 2-(1).

GOVERNMENT CORPORATION. A corporation (a) that is, under an Act, an agent of the Crown, (b) of which the government owns, directly or indirectly, more than 50% of the issued voting shares, or (c) that is controlled by the government, and for the purpose of this definition a corporation is controlled by the government when a majority of the members of the corporation or of its board of directors or board of management consists of either or both of the following: (i) persons appointed as members by the Lieutenant Governor in Council, by a minister or by an Act; (ii) public officers acting as such. *Financial Administration Act*, S.B.C. 1981, c. 15, s. 1.

GOVERNMENT DEPARTMENT. A department of the Government of Canada or a board, commission, corporation or other body that is an agent of Her Majesty in right of Canada, but does not include the National Railways, as defined in the Canadian National-Canadian Pacific Act, chapter 39 of the Revised Statutes of Canada, 1952, the Canadian Broadcasting Corporation, the Bank of Canada, the Federal Business Development Bank, Air Canada or any corporation incorporated under the Air Canada Act, 1977, chapter 5 of the Statutes of Canada, 1977-78, or the Canada Ports Corporation.

Surplus Crown Assets Act, R.S.C. 1985, c. S-27, s. 2.

GOVERNMENT DISTRICT. See LOCAL ~.

GOVERNMENT ENTITIES. Includes (a) ministries of the Crown in right of the Province and their departments, branches, divisions and sections; and (b) boards, commissions, associations, colleges, hospitals and boards of school trustees, established under an Act, as designated by the board. *System Act*, R.S.B.C. 1979, c. 399, s. 1.

GOVERNMENT GUARANTEED BOND. A bond of the Government of Canada or a bond unconditionally guaranteed as to principal and interest by the Government of Canada that is (a) payable to bearer, (b) hypothecated to the Receiver General in accordance with the Domestic Bonds of Canada Regulations, or (c) registered in the name of the Receiver General. *Government Contracts Regulations*, C.R.C., c. 701, s. 2.

GOVERNMENT HOSPITAL FACILITY. Any land owned by the Crown in right of Alberta and under the administration of the Minister, including buildings and improvements thereon, that is used or is suitable for use in providing diagnostic services, treatment or care for ill or injured persons. *Department of Health Act*, R.S.A. 1970, c. 97, s. 11.

GOVERNMENT HOUSE. The building at 12845-102 Avenue in the City of Edmonton commonly known as "Government House". *Government House Act*, R.S.A. 1980, c. G-7, s. 1.

GOVERNMENT HOUSE LEADER. The member of the government, responsible to the Prime Minister, who arranges government business in the House of Commons. A. Fraser, G.A. Birch & W.A. Dawson, eds., *Beauchesne's Rules and Forms of the House of Commons of Canada*, 5th ed. (Toronto: Carswell, 1978) at 49.

GOVERNMENT INCENTIVE SECURITY. A security designed to enable the holder thereof to receive a grant or other monetary benefit, such as a right to a credit against taxes or a deduction in the determination of income for tax purposes, pursuant to provisions of a statute or a regulation of Canada or a province of Canada.

GOVERNMENT INSTITUTION. Any department or ministry of state of the Government of Canada listed in the schedule or any body or office listed in the schedule. *Privacy Act*, R.S.C. 1985, c. P-21, s. 3.

GOVERNMENT ISSUE. Machinery, machine tools, equipment or defence supplies furnished by the Minister or by an agent of Her Majesty on behalf of Her Majesty or on behalf of an associated government or acquired or purchased on behalf of Her Majesty or on behalf of an associated government with funds provided by the Minister or by an agent of Her Majesty or by an associated government. *Defence Production Act*, R.S.C. 1985, c. D-1, s. 2.

GOVERNMENT NEGOTIATOR. The President of the Treasury Board, established in accordance with any Act of the province governing financial administration, or such other person authorized by him to bargain collectively under his control and supervision on behalf of the employer.

GOVERNMENT OF ALBERTA. Her Majesty in right of Alberta.

GOVERNMENT OF CANADA. 1. Her Majesty in right of Canada. 2. The Crown in right of Canada, every corporation and agency thereof and the Governor General in Council.

GOVERNMENT OF MANITOBA. Her Majesty the Queen, acting for the Province of Manitoba. *Interpretation Act*, R.S.M. 1970, c. I80, s. 23.

GOVERNMENT OF ONTARIO. Includes every ministry thereof and every commission or board created by any Act of the Legislature. *Government Contracts Hours and Wages Act*, R.S.O. 1980, c. 190, s. 1.

GOVERNMENT OF PRINCE EDWARD ISLAND. Her Majesty in right of the province. *Interpretation Act*, S.P.E.I. 1981, c. 18, s. 26.

GOVERNMENT OF SASKATCHEWAN. The Crown in right of Saskatchewan, every corporation and agency thereof and the Lieutenant Governor in Council. Saskatchewan statutes.

GOVERNMENT OR HER MAJESTY. Her Majesty in right of the Province. *Stephenville Linerboard Mill (Agreement) Act*, S. Nfld. 1972, c. 38, s. 2.

GOVERNMENT PLAN. A plan of a government, other than the Government of Canada, that provides insurance for surgical and medical expenses and in which participation is compulsory. *Public Service Health Insurance Regulations*, C.R.C., c. 339, s. 2.

GOVERNMENT PROPERTY. Property owned or occupied by Her Majesty in right of Canada. *Government Property Traffic Regulations*, C.R.C., c. 887, s. 2.

GOVERNMENT PUBLICATION. Any document prepared by or for a department and reproduced for distribution or sale outside the government. *Legislative Library Act*, S.N.B. 1976, c. L-3.1, s. 1.

GOVERNMENT RELATED AGENCY. Includes Ontario Hydro, the Ontario Transportation Development Board, any public institution that is assisted by money appropriated by the Legislature and a corporation with or without share capital, the controlling interest of which is owned by the Crown in right of Ontario or whose bonds or debentures are guaranteed by the Crown in right of Ontario. *Ministry of Government Services Act*, R.S.O. 1980, c. 279, s. 1.

GOVERNMENT SECURITIES. 1. Bonds, debentures, notes or other evidences of indebtedness of, or guaranteed by, the Government of Canada or the government of any province. *Cooperative Credit Associations Act*, R.S.C. 1985, c. C-41, s. 49. 2. Notes, bonds, debentures or interest bearing or non-interest bearing treasury bills issued by the Crown or other securities under which the Crown is the debtor, but does not include an instrument given by the Crown as security for the repayment of an overdraft. *Financial Administration Act*, R.S.A. 1980, c. F-9, s. 60.

GOVERNMENT SHIP. A ship or vessel that is owned by and is in the service of Her Majesty in right of Canada or of any province or is, while so employed, wholly employed in the service of Her Majesty in that right. *Canada Shipping Act*, R.S.C. 1985, c. S-9, s. 2.

GOVERNMENT SUPPORTED INSTITUTION. A municipality, the board of a school district or a school division, the resident administrator of a local government district, the owner or operator of a hospital or personal care home who or which receives revenue from the Manitoba Health Services Commission, the board of health and social services district, the board of a water district, or the board of a housing authority. *Manitoba Data Services Act*, S.M. 1979, c. 36, s. 1.

GOVERNMENT TRUCK. (a) A commercial vehicle as defined in The Public Service Vehicles Act and owned and operated by the Government of Canada, the Government of Alberta, the council of a municipality or the board of a school district or division, but (b) does not include a school van used solely for the purpose of conveying school children to and from school. *Stock Inspection Act*, R.S.A. 1970, c. 352, s. 2.

GOVERNMENT VESSEL. Any vessel that belongs to or is in the service of Her Majesty in right of Canada. *Coastal Fisheries Protection Act*, R.S.C. 1985, c. C-33, s. 2.

GOVERNOR. *n.* 1. The Governor of the Bank or the person acting for the Governor pursuant to this Act. *Bank of Canada Act*, R.S.C. 1985, c. B-2, s. 2. 2. A member of a board. 3. The

Lieutenant Governor of the Province or the chief executive officer or administrator carrying on the Government of the Province on behalf and in the name of the Sovereign by whatever title he is designated. *Interpretation Act*, R.S.N.S. 1967, c. 151, s. 6. See BOARD OF ~S; LIEUTENANT ~.

GOVERNOR GENERAL. *var.* **GOVERNOR-GENERAL.** The Governor General of Canada or other chief executive officer or administrator carrying on the government of Canada on behalf and in the name of the Sovereign, by whatever title that person is designated.

GOVERNOR GENERAL IN COUNCIL. *var.* **GOVERNOR-GENERAL IN COUNCIL.** The Governor General or person administrating the government of Canada, acting by and with the advice or, or by and with the advice and consent of, or in conjunction with the Queen's Privy Council for Canada.

GOVERNOR IN COUNCIL. 1. The Governor General of Canada acting by and with the advice of, or by and with the advice and consent of, or in conjunction with the Queen's Privy Council for Canada. 2. The Lieutenant Governor acting by and with the advice of the Executive Council of the Province. *Interpretation Act*, R.S.N.S. 1967, c. 151, s. 6. See LIEUTENANT ~.

GOVERNOR OF CANADA. The Governor General of Canada or other chief executive officer or administrator carrying on the Government of Canada on behalf of and in the name of the Sovereign, by whatever title that officer is designated. *Interpretation Act*, R.S.C. 1985, c. I-21, s. 35.

GOVT. *abbr.* Government.

GO WITHOUT DAY. Formerly when a proceeding was dismissed, the plaintiff was said to go without day, i.e., the case was not adjourned to a day in the future.

GOWN. See SILK ~; STUFF ~.

GR. *abbr.* Upper Canada Chancery (Grant), 1849-1922.

GRAB SAMPLE. A quantity of undiluted effluent collected at any given time. *Metal Mining Liquid Effluent Regulations*, C.R.C., c. 819, s. 2.

GRACE. *n.* Dispensation; licence. See DAYS OF ~.

GRADE. *n.* 1. The lowest of the average levels of finished ground adjoining each exterior wall of a building, but does not include localized depressions such as for vehicle or pedestrian entrances. 2. The classification of any livestock or livestock product, fruit, vegetable or other product according to prescribed standards. 3.

Includes standard. 4. The percentage content of total nitrogen, available phosphoric acid and soluble potash stated in that sequence. *Fertilizers Regulations*, C.R.C., c. 666, s. 2. See CANADA PEDIGREED ~; PAY ~; SECONDARY SCHOOL ~.

GRADED. *adj.* When used with reference to a pipe, means its slope with reference to the true horizontal. *Ontario Water Resources Act*, R.R.O. 1980, Reg. 736, s. 1.

GRADE NAME. 1. Any mark, description or designation of a grade. 2. The name, or name and number, assigned to any grade of grain established by or under this Act and includes any abbreviation prescribed for that grade name. *Canada Grain Act*, R.S.C. 1985, c. G-10, s. 2. 3. (i) The name, or name and number, assigned to a grade of grain established by or pursuant to the Canada Grain Act, and (ii) a name, or name and number, so nearly resembling any such name, or name and number, as to be calculated or likely to cause confusion. *Grain Buyers Licensing Act*, R.S.A. 1980, c. G-9, s. 1.

GRADE OF PAY. A series of rates of remuneration for a class that provides for a minimum rate, a maximum rate, and such intermediate rates as may be considered necessary to permit periodic increases in remuneration. *Civil Service Act*, R.S.M. 1970, c. C110, s. 2.

GRADER. *n.* A person appointed or designated as a grader pursuant to legislation.

GRADE SEPARATION. A subway or an overhead bridge. *Railway Grade Separations Regulations*, C.R.C., c. 1191, s. 2.

GRADE SIGNAL. A stop and proceed signal equipped with a marker displaying the letter "G". *Regulations No. O-8, Uniform Code of Operating Rules*, C.R.C., c. 1175, Part III, s. 2.

GRADIENT. *n.* The deviation between the inclination of a road or railway and a level surface.

GRADING. See OFFICIAL ~.

GRADING STATION. A place, other than the premises of a producer grader, where dressed or eviscerated poultry or both dressed and eviscerated poultry is graded and packed. *Dressed and Eviscerated Poultry Regulations*, C.R.C., c. 283, s. 2.

GRADING STATION OPERATOR. A person who operates a station at which eggs are graded. *Canadian Egg Licensing Regulations*, C.R.C., c. 655, s. 2.

GRADUATE. *n.* A scholar who takes a university degree.

GRADUATED PAYMENT MORTGAGE. In

relation to an insured loan, a mortgage whereby the loan is to be repaid by instalments that increase in amount from time to time and for such period as may be agreed on between the approved lender and borrower and approved by the Corporation, according to a formula incorporated in the mortgage and calculated to take into account the fact that the initial instalment payments would, if maintained over the amortization period, be insufficient in amount to amortize the loan. *National Housing Act*, R.S.C. 1985, c. N-11, s. 14(3).

GRADUS. *n.* [L.] Degree; step.

GRADUS PARENTELAE. [L.] A pedigree; a family tree.

GRAFFER. *n.* A scrivener; a notary.

GRAFFIUM. *n.* A register; a writing-book.

GRAIN. *n.* 1. Includes wheat, oats, barley, rye, corn, buckwheat, flax, beans, peas and all kinds of seeds. 2. 1/7 000 pound. *Weights and Measures Act*, S.C. 1970-71-72, c. 36, schedule II. 3. Includes the seed of any cereal, legume, grass or fibre. *Seed Grain Purchase Act*, R.S.A. 1980, c. S-10, s. 1. 4. Wheat, barley, oats, corn, rye, Faba beans, soybeans, field peas or colza, or any other substance designated as grain by regulation. *Grain Act*, S.Q. 1979, c. 84, s. 1. See CASH ~; COARSE ~; DAMP ~; DRIED ~; EASTERN ~; FEED ~; FOREIGN ~; MIXED ~; SEED ~; SIX ~S; SPRING ~; TOUGH ~; WESTERN ~.

GRAIN ALCOHOL. Alcohol manufactured from grain.

GRAIN AND PRODUCE EXCHANGE. See WINNIPEG ~ CLEARING ASSOCIATION LIMITED.

GRAIN BUYER. A person who carries on or transacts the business of buying grain, either as principal or agent, and either for cash or under any form of contract with respect to delivery or payment, but does not include (i) a person who buys grain for seed, feed or otherwise for his own personal use, (ii) a person who is the holder of licence for flour milling or feed milling issued under the Licensing of Trades and Businesses Act and who buys grain that is to be milled, or used for manufacturing purposes, in the mill or mills of the licensee within Alberta, or (iii) the employee of either of those persons. *Grain Buyers Licensing Act*, R.S.A. 1980, c. G-9, s. 1.

GRAIN CARGO. A cargo of which the portion consisting of grain is more than one-quarter of the dead weight carrying capacity of the ship carrying it. *Canada Shipping Act*, R.S.C. 1985, c. S-9, s. 2.

GRAIN CORN. Shelled corn or ear corn. *Crop Insurance Act*, R.R.O. 1980, Reg. 205, s. 3.

GRAIN DEALER. A person who, for self or on behalf of another person, receives grain to store, sell, resell, manufacture or process it.

GRAIN DRIER. Any producer or other person who dries grain by artificial means.

GRAIN ELEVATOR. Any building, container, structure or receptacle in which farm produce is received for storage, but does not include, (i) premises where a producer receives or stores farm produce as farm feed for his own live stock or poultry, (ii) premises where a producer stores and sells farm produce actually produced by that producer, or (iii) premises where a terminal, transfer or processor grain elevator is licensed under any Act of the Parliament of Canada. *Grain Elevator Storage Act, 1983*, S.O. 1983, c. 40, s. 1.

GRAIN EXCHANGE. See WINNIPEG ~.

GRAIN FUTURES. Contracts negotiated by members of The Winnipeg Grain Exchange under the conditions and terms set forth in its by-laws or rules, as principals or agents, for the purchase or sale of grain to be accepted or delivered during future months in respect of which facilities for trading in grain futures have been provided by The Winnipeg Grain Exchange, but does not include contracts for the purchase or sale of cash grain. *Grain Futures Act*, R.S.C. 1985, c. G-11, s. 2.

GRAIN OR CROPS. Wheat, oats, barley, flax, rye, corn, peas, seed of alfalfa, seed of crested wheat grass, seed of brome grass, seed of clover, seed of sunflowers, seed of rape and seed of all commercial grasses. *The Local Improvement Districts Act*, R.S.S. 1978, c. L-31, s. 2.

GRAIN PRODUCT. Any product that is produced by processing or manufacturing any grain alone or with any other grain or substance and that may be presented for storage or handling at an elevator.

GRAIN SALE PROCEEDS. The amount of the purchase price of grain produced on land described in a permit book and sold under the permit book to or through a licensee or designated purchaser after the deduction from the purchase price of the grain of the charges that are applicable to the grain on its sale and includes the proceeds and amounts deemed by sections 19, 20 and 21 to be grain sale proceeds. *Western Grain Stabilization Act*, R.S.C. c. W-7, s. 2.

GRAIN SPIRIT. An alcoholic distillate, obtained from a mash of cereal grain or cereal grain products saccharified by the diastase of malt or by other natural enzyme and fermented by the action of yeast, and from which all or nearly all of the naturally occurring substances other than alcohol and water have been removed. *Food and Drug Regulations*, C.R.C., c. 870, c. B.02.002.

GRAIN STANDARDS COMMITTEE. (a) In the case of western grain, means the Western Grain Standards Committee; and (b) in the case of eastern grain, means the Eastern Grain Standards Committee. *Canada Grain Act*, R.S.C. 1985, c. G-10, s. 24(3).

GRAIN STORAGE RECEIPT. A receipt as prescribed by the regulations that is to be issued by a grain elevator operator or authorized representative to the owner of farm produce.

GRAMMATICA FALSA NON VITIAT CHARTAM. [L.] Bad grammar does not invalidate a deed.

GRAMOPHONE FORMAT. As applied to any time segment, means a format of presentation of broadcast matter in which one or more musical compositions are broadcast without interruption or accompanying broadcast matter other than (a) matter within content subcategory number 01, 09, 11, 12, 13, 14, 15, 16, 37 or 41, where the interruption for the presentation of such matter occurs not more than once, and (b) matter within content category number 8 or 9. *Radio (F.M.) Broadcasting Regulations*, C.R.C., c. 380, s. 14.

GRANDCHILD. *n.* 1. The child of a child. *Succession Law Reform Act*, R.S.O. 1980, c. 488, s. 1. 2. Includes the child of an adopted child. *Insurance acts.* 3. Includes any child or other lineal descendant of a child of the deceased. *Fatal Accidents Act*, S.P.E.I. 1978, c. 7, s. 1.

GRAND DISTRESS. Distress which extends to all the goods and chattels which the distrained party has within the county.

GRANDFATHER. *n.* Includes the grandfather of the spouse. *Taxation Act*, R.S.Q. 1977, c. I-3, s. 1.

GRANDFATHER CLAUSE. A provision allowing a period of time to comply with requirements of a statute or other requirements or permitting persons or situations to continue under new legislation although not technically qualified.

GRAND JURY. An inquisition which sits, receives indictments and hears evidence from the prosecution; any finding is only an accusation, to be tried afterwards.

GRANDMOTHER. *n.* Includes the grandmother of the spouse. *Taxation Act*, R.S.Q. 1977, c. I-3, s. 1.

GRANT. *n.* 1. Any grant of Crown land, whether by letters patent under the Great Seal, a notification or any other instrument whether in fee or for years, and whether direct from Her Majesty or by or pursuant to any statute. 2. A right created or transferred by the Crown, for example the grant of a charter, franchise, patent or pension. 3. Public money devoted to a special purpose. 4. (i) A grant of probate, (ii) a resealed grant of probate or administration, (iii) a grant of administration, or (iv) a grant of letters of guardianship of the person or estate, or both, of a minor. See CROWN ~; DEED OF ~; FOREIGN ~; LEGISLATIVE ~; PROPERTY IMPROVEMENT ~; RE-~.

GRANTEE. *n.* 1. A person to whom one makes a grant. 2. The person to whom real property is transferred by deed for value or otherwise. 3. Includes the bargainee, assignee, transferee, mortgagee or other person to whom a bill of sale is made.

GRANT OF ADMINISTRATION. The grant made when the proper court issues administration.

GRANT OF ADMINISTRATION WITH WILL ANNEXED. The grant made if the deceased leaves a will naming no executor or if the named executor declines to act. J.G. McLeod, *The Conflict of Laws* (Calgary: Carswell, 1983) at 400.

GRANT OF PROBATE. The grant made when the proper court issues probate.

GRANTOR. *n.* 1. A person who makes a grant. 2. Includes the bargainor, assignor, transferor, mortgagor, or other person by whom a bill of sale is made. *Bills of Sale acts.* See CREDIT ~.

GRAPES. See FRESH ~.

GRAPHIC MATERIAL. Books, manuscripts, records, documents, photographic positives or negatives, cinematographic film, maps or any designs or material whose primary object is the communication of information in a visual form other than written or printed language. *Canadian Cultural Property Export Control List*, C.R.C., c. 448, s. 1.

GRAPHIC MEDIUM. A model, map, diagram, photograph or other pictorial or graphic mode of description and includes a record of data, experience, communications or events made by accurate, mechanical, electrical or other scientific methods. *Military Rules of Evidence*, C.R.C., c. 1049, s. 82.

GRAPHIC REPRESENTATION. A representation produced by electrical, electronic, photographic, hand-drawn, or printing methods, and includes a representation produced on a video display terminal.

GRASS. See LAWN ~ MIXTURE; TURF ~ MIXTURE.

GRATIS. *adj.* [L.] Without reward or recompense.

GRATIS DICTUM. [L.] A mere assertion; a voluntary statement.

GRATUITOUS. *adj.* Without reward or recompense.

GRATUITOUS BAILMENT. Bailee takes charge of bailor's property without remuneration.

GRATUITOUS PROMISE. 1. Promise made without consideration. 2. A promise to confer a benefit as a gift. G.H.L. Fridman, *The Law of Contract in Canada*, 2d ed. (Toronto: Carswell, 1986) at 73.

GRATUITY. *n.* A tip; a reward for services rendered.

GRAVAMEN. *n.* The essence of the complaint or grievance.

GRAVE. *n.* Includes a place within a building or structure for the permanent placement of human remains. *Cemetery and Funeral Services Act,* S.N.S. 1983, c. 4, s. 2.

GRAVE CRIME. Any offence created by an Act of Parliament for which an offender may be sentenced to imprisonment for five years or more. *Diplomatic and Consular Privileges and Immunities Act,* R.S.C. 1985, c. P-22, s. 4.

GRAVE MARKER. A granite upright headstone, or a granite or bronze marker, which is of the standard established by the Department. *Veterans Burial Regulations,* C.R.C., c. 1583, s. 2.

GRAVEL. *n.* A soil consisting of particles smaller than 3 in. (76 mm), but retained on a No. 4 sieve. *Building Code Act,* R.R.O. 1980, Reg. 87, s. 4.2.1.4.

GRAY WHALE. Any whale known by the name of gray whale, California gray, devil fish, hard head, mussel digger, gray back, rip sack. *Whaling Convention Act,* R.S.C. 1970, c. W-8, Schedule, s. 18.

GRAZE. *n.* Abrasion caused when skin contacts a rough surface. F.A. Jaffe, *A Guide to Pathological Evidence,* 2d ed. (Toronto: Carswell, 1983) at 177.

GRAZING AND FODDER ASSOCIATION. Includes an association incorporated or registered under this Act having as its principal objects, or any of them, the operation and maintenance of land for the grazing of livestock or the production of feed and fodder for livestock required by members and patrons in livestock production or rendering to members and patrons as producers services ancillary to such principal objects or any of them. *The Co-operative Production Associations Act,* R.S.S. 1978, c. C-37, s. 59.

GRAZING SEASON. A period during which livestock may graze on Crown land under a grazing licence or grazing permit. *Range Act,* R.S.B.C. 1979, c. 355, s. 1.

GREAT LAKES. 1. Lakes Ontario, Erie, Huron (including Georgian Bay), Michigan and Superior, and their connecting waters. *Canada Shipping Act,* R.S.C. 1985, c. S-9, s. 2. 2. Lakes Ontario, Erie, Huron, including Georgian Bay, and Superior and their connecting waters and includes the St. Lawrence River and its tributaries as far seaward as the west end of the Island of Orleans. *Transport Act,* R.S.C. 1985, c. T-17, s. 2. See NORTH AMERICAN ~ ZONE.

GREAT LAKES BASIN. The Canadian waters of the Great Lakes, their connecting and tributary waters, and the St. Lawrence River as far east as St. Regis in the Province of Quebec. *Canada Shipping Act,* R.S.C. 1970, c. S-9, s. 362.

GREAT LAKES PORT. Any port on the Great Lakes or their connecting waters west of the Port of Cornwall. Canada regulations.

GREAT LAKES SHIP. A ship of not less than 50 tons register tonnage (a) engaged in trade on the Great Lakes and traversing foreign waters, or (b) proceeding directly from a Great Lakes port to any port in Canada east of and including the Port of Cornwall, Ontario, or vice versa. Canada regulations.

GREAT SEAL. 1. The Great Seal of Canada. *Interpretation Act,* R.S.C. 1985, c. I-21, s. 35. 2. The Great Seal of a province.

GREAT SEAL OF THE REALM. The Great Seal of the United Kingdom of Great Britain and Northern Ireland for which provision was made in Article XXIV of An Act for an Union of the two Kingdoms of England and Scotland, 5 Anne, 1706, chapter VIII [Statutes at Large, Volume IV], and includes the wafer seal. *Seals Act,* R.S.C. 1985, c. S-6, s. 2.

GREENBELT LAND. Land that is (a) considered by the minister to be suitable for preservation as greenbelt land under this Act; and (b) reserved or acquired for the purpose under section 2. *Greenbelt Act,* R.S.B.C. 1979, c. 157, s. 1.

GREEN CLAUSE. A clause endorsed on a commercial letter of credit in coloured ink which authorizes a bank to pay or accept drafts in return for an undertaking that a bill of lading and other documents will be provided when the goods are shipped. I.F.G. Baxter, *The Law of Banking*, 3d ed. (Toronto: Carswell, 1981) at 156.

GREEN HEAD. Any fresh untanned head of deer or moose. *Fish and Wildlife Act*, S.N.B. 1980, c. F-14.1, s. 1.

GREEN HIDE. Any fresh untanned hide of deer or moose. *Fish and Wildlife Act*, S.N.B. 1980, c. F-14.1, s. 1.

GREENHOUSE CUCUMBERS. Cucumbers that have been grown in artificial conditions under glass or other protective covering. *Fresh Fruit and Vegetable Regulations*, C.R.C., c. 285, s. 1.

GREENHOUSE TOMATOES. Tomatoes that have been grown in artificial conditions under glass or other protective covering. *Fresh Fruit and Vegetable Regulations*, C.R.C., c. 285, s. 1.

GREENHOUSE VEGETABLES. Tomatoes, cucumbers and lettuce produced in the Province of Ontario in a greenhouse or any other enclosure under glass, plastic or other material used for the purpose of controlling temperature and providing protection for growing plants. Canada regulations.

GREENLAND HALIBUT. A fish of the species Reinhardtius hippoglossus (Walb.). *Northwest Atlantic Fisheries Regulations*, C.R.C., c. 860, s. 2.

GREENSPOND AREA. The waters of Newfoundland adjacent to that part of the coast in the vicinity of Greenspond between a line drawn due east in the district of Bonavista North from the northern point of Loo Cove on the north and a line drawn due east from the southern point of Shoe Cove Point on the south. *Newfoundland Fishery Regulations*, C.R.C., c. 846, s. 344.

GREENSTICK FRACTURE. A fracture seen in children in which a long bone is partly broken and partly bent. F.A. Jaffe, *A Guide to Pathological Evidence*, 2d ed. (Toronto: Carswell, 1983) at 176 and 177.

GREGORIAN EPOCH. The Gregorian calendar reckoning which commenced in 1582.

GRENADIER. See ROUNDNOSE ~.

GREVE. *n.* A word of authority or power.

GREY RING. A grey discolouration around an entrance wound caused by bullet lubricant or by the metal of the bullet. F.A. Jaffe, *A Guide to Pathological Evidence*, 2d ed. (Toronto: Carswell, 1983) at 177.

GRID. See POWER ~.

GRID ROAD. A road or any portion thereof in: (a) a municipality; or (b) a local improvement district; that is designated as a grid road under section 5. *The Municipal Road Assistance Authority Act*, R.S.S. 1978, c. M-33, s. 2.

GRIEVANCE. *n.* 1. Includes any disagreement between the parties to a collective bargaining agreement with respect to the meaning or application of a collective agreement or any violation of a collective bargaining agreement. 2. A complaint made in writing setting forth the reasons for the complaint in respect of dismissal, working conditions, or terms of employment. *Public Service Act*, R.R.O. 1980, Reg. 881, s. 36. 3. A complaint in writing presented in accordance with the governing act by an employee personally or on behalf of the employee and one or more other employees, except that (a) for the purposes of any of the provisions of the governing act respecting grievances, a reference to an "employee" includes a person who would be a employee but for the fact that the person is employed in a managerial or confidential capacity, and (b) for the purposes of any of the provisions of the governing act respecting grievances with respect to disciplinary action resulting in discharge or suspension, a reference to an "employee" includes a former employee or a person who would be a former employee but for the fact that at the time of the discharge or suspension of that person the person was employed in a managerial or confidential capacity. See GROUP ~; POLICY ~.

GRIEVANCE ARBITRATION. An adjudicative process by which disputes over the application or operation of a collective agreement are resolved. D.J.M. Brown and D.M. Beatty, *Canadian Labour Arbitration*, 2d ed. (Aurora: Canada Law Book, 1977) at 1.

GRIEVANCE SETTLEMENT PROVISION. A provision for final settlement without stoppage of work, by arbitration or otherwise, of all differences between the parties to or persons bound by a collective agreement or on whose behalf it was entered into, concerning its meaning or violation. *Canada Labour Code Act*, R.S.C. 1970, c. L-1, s. 25.

GRIEVOR. *n.* A person who has a grievance. *Public Service Act*, R.R.O. 1980, Reg. 881, s. 36.

GRILSE. *n.* 1. A young salmon. *Fisheries Act*, R.S.N.B. 1973, c. F-15, s. 1. 2. Salmon of 3 pounds in weight or less undressed. *British Columbia Fishery (General) Regulations*, C.R.C., c. 840, s. 2.

GRINDING. *n.* The treatment of waste by uniformly reducing the waste to particles of controlled maximum size. *Environmental Protection Act*, R.R.O. 1980, Reg. 309, s. 1.

GROCERY. *n.* An establishment the main object of which is to sell foodstuffs. *An Act Respecting the Commission de Contrôle des Permis d'Alcool*, R.S.Q. 1977, c. C-33, s. 20.

GROOVE. *n.* The space between two adjacent tread ribs of a tire. Canada regulations.

GROOVES. See RIFLING.

GROSS. *n.* See IN ~.

GROSS. *adj.* Entire; absolute.

GROSS AREA. The total area of all floors above grade measured between the outside surfaces of exterior walls or, where no access or building service penetrates a firewall, between the outside surfaces of exterior walls and the centre line of firewalls but in a residential occupancy where access or a building service penetrates a firewall, the measurement may be taken to the centre line of the firewall. Ontario statutes.

GROSS AXLE WEIGHT RATING. The value specified by the vehicle manufacturer as the load-carrying capacity of a single axle system, as measured at the tire-ground interfaces. *Motor Vehicle Safety Regulations*, C.R.C., c. 1038, s. 2.

GROSS DEBT SERVICE RATIO. (a) In the case of a loan on a one-family dwelling, the ratio of the annual mortgage charges for principal, interest and taxes to the estimated gross annual income of the home owner or home purchaser, and (b) in the case of a loan on a home-owner duplex or a home-owner semi-detached house, the ratio of the annual mortgage charges for principal, interest and taxes to the estimated gross annual income of the home owner or home purchaser excluding rental derived from the housing unit not occupied by the home owner. *National Housing Loan Regulations*, C.R.C., c. 1108, s. 2.

GROSS FREIGHT CAPACITY. The aggregate obtained by multiplying the weight or mass of freight carried by the corporation by the distance the freight is carried. *Corporations Tax Act*, R.R.O. 1980, Reg. 191, s. 306.

GROSS GATE RECEIPTS. All money collected in respect of a boxing match including all television and film royalties or money collected to obtain the rights to represent the boxing match or exhibition in any form. *Boxing Authority Act*, S.N.S. 1981, c. 55, s. 1.

GROSS INCOME. 1. (a) The amount received or receivable in the taxation year for the sale or exchange of the output of a mine, and (b) the amount received or receivable in the taxation year from hedging, less (c) the actual and proper costs incurred as a result of hedging, and (d) any smelter charges for mineral ore (i) processed outside the province, by persons other than the operator, (ii) processed outside the province by the operator or by persons who, in the opinion of the minister, are associates of the operator if, in the opinion of the minister, the smelter charges are fair and reasonable, or (iii) processed within the province by persons other than (A) the operator, (B) a subsidiary of the operator, or (C) persons who, in the opinion of the minister, are associated with the operator. 2. Income from interest on loans to members and from interest and dividends on other investments less any rebates of interest paid to borrowers. *Credit Union Act*, S.N.S. 1969, c. 36, s. 8.

GROSS NATIONAL PRODUCT. See PER CAPITA ~.

GROSS NEGLIGENCE. Any act or omission in the carrying out of work of a professional engineer that shows a reckless or deliberate disregard of or indifference to the rights or safety of others. *Professional Engineers Act*, R.R.O. 1980, Reg. 804, s. 9.

GROSS OPERATING REVENUE. The revenue received from the operation of vehicles used in a public transit system including fares and rentals of chartered buses, but not including any revenue received from the sale of advertising space on or in the vehicles, or rental of garage or parking space, or from other activities not related to the carriage of passengers on the vehicles, or interest on investments or reserves. *Transit Grants Act*, R.S.M. 1970, c. T150, s. 1.

GROSS PROCEEDS. The actual price obtained at a sale where all charges on sale are paid by the sellers. *Maritime Insurance acts.*

GROSS REGISTERED TONS. The gross tonnage stated in the certificate of registry of a ship or, where the ship has more than one gross registered tonnage, means the largest gross registered tonnage of that ship. Canada regulations.

GROSS REVENUE. 1. Of a taxpayer for a taxation year, means the aggregate of (a) all amounts received in the year or receivable in the year (depending on the method regularly followed by the taxpayer in computing his income) otherwise than as or on account of capital, and (b) all amounts (other than amounts referred to in paragraph (a)) included in computing the taxpayer's income from a business or property for the year by virtue of paragraph 12(1)(o) or subsection 12(3), (4) or (8) or section 12.2. *Income Tax Act*, R.S.C. 1952, c. 148 (as am. S.C. 1980-81-82-83, c. 140, s. 128(2)), s. 248(1). 2. As applied to a fiscal period of a business enterprise, means the aggregate of all amounts received in the period or receivable in the period, depending on the method regularly followed in computing the profit from the enterprise, otherwise than as or on account of capital. *Small Business Loans Act*, R.S.C. 1985, c. S-11, s. 2. See GROSS SALES OR ~.

GROSS ROYALTY TRUST. A trust under the terms of which the trustee receives a percentage of gross proceeds, less taxes, from the producer. D.M.W. Waters, *The Law of Trusts in Canada*, 2d ed. (Toronto: Carswell, 1984) at 448.

GROSS SALES. The total dollar volume of gross sales during the preceding 12 months or, if the store has been in operation for less than 12 months, during those months that it has been in operation. *Urban Municipality Amendment Act*, S.S. 1986, c. 38, s. 4.

GROSS SALES OR GROSS REVENUE. Includes the actual gross sales, gross revenue, gross income or gross earnings, without any deductions whatsoever, earned, derived, accrued or received for the use of any company from any source whatsoever, the product of capital, labor, industry or skill of each and every company or corporation in this Province, which may arise from business transacted in the Province. *Corporations Tax Act*, R.S.N.S. 1967, c. 61, s. 1.

GROSS TONNAGE. The gross tonnage stated in the certificate of registry of a ship, or, where a ship is not registered, the figure found in accordance with the rules for the time being in force for the measurement of ships in respect of tonnage. *Canada Shipping Act*, R.S.C. 1985, c. S-9, s. 2. See REGISTERED ~.

GROSS VALUE. The wholesale price or, if there is no wholesale price, the estimated value, with, in either case, freight, landing charges and duty paid beforehand, except that in the case of goods or merchandise customarily sold in bond, the bonded price is deemed to be the gross value. *Marine Insurance acts.*

GROSS VEHICLE WEIGHT. 1. The manufacturer's gross weight rating for a vehicle. 2. The combined weight of the commercial vehicle and its load. *Commercial Transport Act*, R.S.B.C. 1979, c. 55, s. 1. 3. The total weight in kilograms transmitted to the highway by a vehicle, or combination of vehicles, and load. *Highway Traffic Act*, R.S.O. 1980, c. 198, s. 97.

GROSS VEHICLE WEIGHT RATING. The value specified by the vehicle manufacturer as the loaded weight of a single vehicle. Canada regulations.

GROSS WEIGHT. 1. The combined weight of vehicle and load. 2. With respect to any equipment, means the total weight of the equipment as specified by its manufacturer. *Airport Traffic Regulations*, C.R.C., c. 886, s. 52. See MAXIMUM ~; REGISTERED ~.

GROSS WEIGHT OF ANY AXLE ASSEMBLY. Includes the weight of the load on the axle assembly together with the weight of the axle assembly itself and the weight of the wheels connected with the axle assembly. *The Highway Traffic Act*, S.M. 1985-86, c. 3, s. 68(1).

GROUND. *n.* 1. Connection to earth. *Coal Mines Regulation Act*, R.S.N.S. 1967, c. 36, s. 84. 2. A connection to earth of electrical equipment by means of a ground electrode. *Power Corporation Act*, R.R.O. 1980, Reg. 794, s. 0. See PHEASANT SHOOTING ~; SAFETY ~; VOLTAGE TO ~.

GROUND DISTURBANCE. Any work, operation or activity that results in a disturbance of the earth including, without limitation, excavating, digging, trenching, plowing, drilling, tunneling, augering, backfilling, blasting, topsoil stripping, land levelling, peat removing, quarrying, clearing and grading, but does not include, (i) except as otherwise provided in subclause (ii), a disturbance of the earth to a depth of less than 30 centimetres that does not result in a reduction of the earth cover over the pipeline to a depth that is less than the cover provided when the pipeline was installed, (ii) cultivation to a depth of less than 45 centimetres below the surface of the ground, or (iii) any work, operation or activity that is specified in the regulations not to be a ground disturbance. *Pipeline Amendment Act, 1981*, S.A. 1981, c. 30, s. 2.

GROUNDED. *adj.* 1. Connected to the mass of the earth through a conductor and earth contact of adequately low resistance for the desired purpose. *Coal Mines Regulation Act*, R.S.N.S. 1967, c. 36, s. 84. 2. Connected effectually with the general mass of the earth through a grounding path of sufficiently low impedance and having current-carrying capacity sufficient at all times, under the most severe conditions which are likely to arise in practice, to prevent any current in the grounding conductor from causing a harmful voltage to exist; (a) between the grounding conductors and neighboring exposed conducting surfaces which are in good contact with the earth; or (b) between the grounding conductors and neighboring surfaces of the earth itself. *Power Corporation Act*, R.R.O. 1980, Reg. 794, s. 0.

GROUND ELECTRODE. A metallic water-piping system, or a metallic object or device buried in, or driven into, the earth so as to make intimate contact therewith, to which a grounding conductor is electrically and mechanically connected. *Power Corporation Act*, R.R.O. 1980, Reg. 794, s. 0.

GROUND FAULT CIRCUIT INTERRUPTER. A device which will interrupt, within a predetermined time, the electrical circuit to the load when a current to ground exceeds some predetermined value that is less than that required to operate the overcurrent protection device of the supply circuit. *Power Corporation Act*, R.R.O. 1980, Reg. 794, s. 0. See PORTABLE ~.

GROUNDFISH. *n.* 1. Demersal species of fish and includes flatfish, grey cod, ling cod, rockfish, black cod, hake, sea perch, pollock, skate and ratfish. *Pacific Fishery Registration and Licensing Regulations*, C.R.C., c. 824, s. 2. 2. Cod, haddock, hake, pollock, plaice, flounder or halibut. *Quebec Fishery Regulations*, C.R.C., c. 852, s. 2.

GROUNDFISH NET. A gill net used for the purpose of catching demersal species of fish. *Fishery regulations*, Canada regulations.

GROUND FLOOR. The lowest floor divided into self-contained units providing living accommodations. *Fire Prevention Act*, R.S.N.B. 1973, c. F-13, s. 1.

GROUND GATES. Any arrangement of horizontal bars placed in a gateway upon the ground. *Livestock Act*, R.S.Nfld. 1970, c. 210, s. 2.

GROUNDING. *n.* The portion of a conductor underground that makes electrical contact with the earth. *Lightning Rods Act*, R.R.O. 1980, Reg. 577, s. 1. See AUXILIARY ~; INDEPENDENT ~; MAIN ~; SAFETY ~.

GROUNDING CONDUCTOR. A path of copper or other suitable metal specially arranged as a means whereby electrical equipment is electrically connected to a ground electrode. *Power Corporation Act*, R.R.O. 1980, Reg. 794, s. 0.

GROUNDING EQUIPMENT. A permanent connection to ground of non-current carrying parts of apparatus which are insulated from the system. *Coal Mines Regulation Act*, R.S.N.S. 1967, c. 36, s. 84.

GROUNDING NETWORK. A grounded system of conductors to facilitate effective grounding. *Coal Mines Regulation Act*, R.S.N.S. 1967, c. 36, s. 84.

GROUNDING SYSTEM. All those cables and other conductors, clamps, ground clips and ground plates or rods by means of which the electrical installation is grounded.

GROUND LANDLORD. The owner of the freehold of any land, whether built upon or not, or who receives rent for land exclusive of the buildings which may be erected upon it. *City of St. John's Act*, R.S. Nfld. 1970, c. 40, s. 2.

GROUND LEASE. 1. Lease of bare land or land exclusive of any building on it. 2. A lease of land made for the purpose of this Part by the Crown, the federal Crown, a municipality, regional district or other public authority and registered in the books of the land title office. *Condominium Act*, R.S.B.C. 1979, c. 61, s. 92.

GROUND-RENT. *n.* Rent, usually for many years, generally rent payable for land on which the lessee erects buildings under a building lease.

GROUND-ROD. *n.* A solid rod of copper, copper-clad steel or galvanized steel that is used as a grounding. *Lightning Rods Act*, R.R.O. 1980, Reg. 577, s. 1.

GROUNDS. *n.* Reasons.

GROUND VISIBILITY. The visibility at an airport, as reported by an observer accredited by the Minister for the purpose. *Air Regulations*, C.R.C., c. 2, s. 101.

GROUND WATER. *var.* **GROUNDWATER.** 1. Water beneath the surface of the land. 2. A free standing body of water in the ground. *Building Code Act*, R.R.O. 1980, Reg. 87, s. 1. 3. All water in a zone of saturation beneath the land surface regardless of its origin and quality. *Northern Inland Waters Regulations*, C.R.C., c. 1234, s. 2. See PERCHED ~.

GROUNDWATER LEVEL. The top surface of a free standing body of water in the ground. *Building Code Act*, R.R.O. 1980, Reg. 87, s. 1.

GROUP. *n.* A number of persons travelling together as an entirety pursuant to a contract. *Air Carrier Regulations*, C.R.C., c. 3, s. 83. See ADULT TEST ~; BLOOD ~S; DESIGNATED ~; DETROIT RIVER ~; EMPLOYEE-ASSOCIATIONS ~; FRINGE ~; IDENTIFIABLE ~; INCLUSIVE TOUR ~; RELATED ~; RESEARCH ~; SEALING ~; SELLING ~; SHIPPER ~; UNRELATED ~; VOTING ~; YOUTH ~.

GROUP ACCIDENT INSURANCE. Accident insurance, other than creditor's group accident insurance, whereby the lives or well-being or the lives and well-being of a number of persons are insured severally under a single contract between an insurer and an employer or other person contracting with the insurer. *Insurance acts*. See CREDITOR'S ~.

GROUP BONUS. Wage incentive paid to some

workers who are jointly responsible for maintaining an aspect of output.

GROUP COMPENSATION PLAN. The scheme, arrangement or plan for regulating the terms and conditions that determine the nature and amount of compensation for any particular compensation group. *Public Sector Prices and Compensation Review Act, 1983*, S.O. 1983, c. 70, s. 1.

GROUP CONTRACT. A contract of insurance whereby two or more persons other than members of the same family are insured severally under a single contract of insurance. *Hospital Insurance acts.*

GROUP FOSTER HOME. A home where not less than four or more than eight children are placed by a child caring agency for full time care and supervision in a family setting. *Child Welfare Act*, S.M. 1974, c. 30, s. 1.

GROUP GRIEVANCE. A grievance in which several individual grievances are combined into a single complaint. D.J.M. Brown and D.M. Beatty, *Canadian Labour Arbitration*, 2d ed. (Aurora: Canada Law Book, 1977) at 94.

GROUP HOME. 1. A residence that is licensed or funded under an Act of the Parliament of Canada or the Province of Ontario for the accommodation of three to ten persons, exclusive of staff, living under supervision in a single housekeeping unit and who, by reason of their emotional, mental, social or physical condition or legal status, require a group living arrangement for their well being. *Municipal Act*, R.S.O. 1980, c. 302, s. 236. 2. A non-parental home providing care for not more than ten children in a family-type setting where the emphasis is on meeting the specialized needs of children but does not include a foster home, day care centre or an institution. *The Family Services Act*, R.S.S. 1978, c. F-7, s. 2.

GROUP INSURANCE. 1. Insurance other than creditor's group insurance and family insurance, whereby the lives or well-being, or the lives and well-being, of a number of persons are insured severally under a single contract between an insurer and an employer or other person. *Insurance acts.* 2. Insurance, other than creditor's group insurance and family insurance, whereby the lives of a number of persons are insured severally under a single contract between an insurer and an employer or other person. *Insurance acts.* See CREDITOR'S ~.

GROUP LIFE INSURED. A person whose life is insured by a contract of group insurance but does not include a person whose life is insured under the contract as a person dependent upon, or related to, the insured. *Insurance acts.*

GROUP MAIL BOX SYSTEM. A privately owned group of lock boxes in an apartment building or office complex designed for the receipt of the mail of all occupants of the building or complex and so constructed that each owner or tenant has an individual compartment that may be kept locked. *Mail Receptacles Regulations*, C.R.C., c. 1282, s. 2.

GROUP MANAGEMENT VENTURE. A co-operative or company formed for the purpose of implementing forest management activities on land of any members of the co-operative or company. *Forests Act*, S.N.S. 1986, c. 10, s. 3.

GROUP OPERATION. An agricultural operations corporation, an agricultural operations cooperative, an agricultural operations partnership or joint operators. *An Act to Promote the Establishment of Young Farmers*, S.Q. 1982, c. 29, s. 1.

GROUP PERSON INSURED. A person who is insured under a contract of group insurance and upon whom a right is conferred by the contract, but does not include a person who is insured thereunder as a person dependent upon or related to the insured. *Insurance acts.*

GROUP PICNIC AREA. An area designated by the Superintendent for use by groups of the public for barbecue parties, clambakes or other picnic purposes. *National Parks General Regulations*, C.R.C., c. 1124, s. 2.

GROUP SICKNESS INSURANCE. Sickness insurance, other than creditor's group sickness insurance, whereby the lives or well-being or the lives and well-being of a number of persons are insured severally under a single contract between an insurer and an employer or other person contracting with the insurer. *Insurance acts.* See CREDITOR'S ~.

GROUP SYSTEM. A system by which a weighted average rate of depreciation is calculated for a particular group of plant accounts, a plant account, or a group of assets within a plant account, and established in recognition of the fact that some part of the investment in a group of assets may be recovered through salvage realization and that there will be variations in the service lives of the assets constituting the group, even among assets of the same class. *Oil Pipeline Uniform Accounting Regulations*, Canada regulations.

GROUP TERM LIFE INSURANCE POLICY. With respect to a taxpayer, means a group life insurance policy under which no amount is payable to a person other than the group policyholder as a result of contributions made to or under the policy by the employer of the taxpayer before the death or disability of the taxpayer.

Income Tax Act, R.S.C. 1952, c. 148 (as am. S.C. 1970-71-72, c. 63), s. 248(1).

GROUP VENTURE. A co-operative or company formed for the purpose of implementing forest management activities on land of any members of the co-operative or company. *Pulpwood Marketing Act*, S.N.S. 1986, c. 52, s. 4.

GROWER. *n.* Any person owning, leasing or otherwise occupying land who farms that land. See APPLE-~.

GROWING CROP. Any plant growth, other than weeds, having a commercial value. *Weed Control Act*, R.S.A. 1980, c. W-6, s. 1.

GROWTH REGULATOR. See PLANT ~.

G.R.P. *abbr.* Glass reinforced plastic. *Life Saving Equipment Regulations*, C.R.C., c. 1436, s. 74.

G.S.P. *abbr.* General Sessions of the Peace.

G.T.P. *abbr.* Grand Trunk Pacific.

G.T.R. *abbr.* Grand Trunk Railway.

GUARANTEE. *n.* 1. A promise to answer for another's obligation. 2. A deed or written agreement whereby a person, not being a corporation, enters into an obligation to answer for an act or default or omission of another but does not include (i) a bill of exchange, cheque or promissory note, (ii) a partnership agreement, (iii) a bond or recognizance given to the Crown or to a court or pursuant to a statute, or (iv) a guarantee given on the sale of an interest in land or an interest in goods or chattels. *Guarantees Acknowledgement Act*, R.S.A. 1980, c. G-12, s. 1. See INCREMENTAL LOAN ~; PERFORMANCE ~; WAGE ~.

GUARANTEE BOND. A promise to perform an agreement or contract or to discharge a trust, duty or obligation upon default of a person liable for that performance or discharge or to pay money upon that default or in lieu of that performance or discharge or where there is loss or damage through that default. *Insurance Adjusters Act*, R.S.Nfld. 1970, c. 175, s. 2.

GUARANTEE COMPANY. An incorporated company empowered to grant guarantees, bonds, policies or contracts for the integrity and fidelity of employed persons, or in respect of any legal proceedings, or for other like purposes.

GUARANTEED. See GOVERNMENT ~ BOND.

GUARANTEED FUND. (i) With reference to a provincial company, the assets earmarked and definitely set aside by it pursuant to section 109, or (ii) with reference to an extra-provincial company, the assets earmarked and definitely set aside by it for the purpose of ensuring repayment of its deposits and investment money. *Trust Companies Act*, R.S.A. 1980, c. T-9, s. 1.

GUARANTEED INCOME SUPPLEMENT. The guaranteed income supplement payable pursuant to the Old Age Security Act. Canada regulations.

GUARANTEED INSTRUMENT. An instrument, the payment of which is guaranteed by the Corporation under this Act or the former Act. *Export Development Act*, R.S.C. 1985, c. E-20, s. 23.

GUARANTEED INVESTMENT CERTIFICATE. A certificate issued by a trust company in evidence of the deposit of guaranteed trust money and the guarantee thereof by the company. *Trust Companies Act*, R.S.C. 1985, c. T-20, s. 2.

GUARANTEED LOAN. A loan to a borrower made and guaranteed by a financial institution.

GUARANTEED PORTION. The portion of a guaranteed loan repayment of which is guaranteed by the province pursuant to this Act. *The Co-operative Guarantee Act*, R.S.S. 1978, c. C-35, s. 2.

GUARANTEED RATE. The amount a worker will receive regardless of achieving or exceeding a standard or quota.

GUARANTEED TRUST MONEY. Money received by a trust company in trust for investment subject to a guarantee by the company in respect of the payment of interest or the repayment of principal.

GUARANTEE INSURANCE. 1. The undertaking to perform an agreement or contract or to discharge a trust, duty or obligation upon default of the person liable for such performance or discharge or to pay money upon such default or in lieu of such performance or discharge, or where there is loss or damage through such default, but does not include credit insurance. *Insurance acts.* 2. The undertaking to perform an agreement or contract or to discharge a trust, duty or obligation upon default of the person liable for such performance or discharge or to pay money upon such default or in lieu of such performance or discharge or where there is loss or damage through such default, and includes insurance against loss or liability for loss due to the invalidity of the title to any property or of any instrument or to any defect in such title or instrument, but does not include credit insurance. *Insurance acts.* 3. Includes (a) "fidelity insurance", which means insurance against loss caused by the unfaithful performance of duties by a person in a position of trust or the guaranteeing of the proper fulfilment of the duties of any office; and (b) "surety insurance", which means the guaranteeing of the due performance of any contract or undertaking, or the payment of a penalty or indemnity for any default, but does not include insurance falling within the class of mortgage insurance. *Insurance Act,* R.S.B.C. 1979, c. 200, s. 1.

GUARANTEE OF ISOLATION. In respect of an electrical facility, a guarantee by the person in control of the facility that it is isolated. *Canada Electrical Safety Regulations,* C.R.C., c. 998, s. 2.

GUARANTEE OF SIGNATURE. A guarantee signed by or on behalf of a person reasonably believed by the issuer to be responsible.

GUARANTOR. *n.* 1. A surety, a person who is bound by a guarantee. 2. A person who undertakes under a bond, upon the default of the bondee in paying a debt or a debt of a class of debts specified in the bond, to pay a sum of money or to pay the debt. *Guarantors' Liability Act,* R.S.M. 1970, c. G120, s. 2.

GUARANTY. *n.* A promise to pay another's debt or to perform another's obligation.

GUARD. *n.* A protective barrier around openings in floors or at the open sides of stairs, landings, balconies, mezzanines, galleries, raised walkways or other locations to prevent accidental falls from one level to another and such barrier may or may not have openings through it. *Building Code Act,* R.R.O. 1980, Reg. 87, s. 1. See MACHINE ~; PRIVATE ~; SECURITY ~.

GUARD AGENCY. See SECURITY ~.

GUARDAGE. *n.* Keeping; wardship.

GUARD DOG. A dog used for the purpose of protecting persons or property. *Private Investigators and Security Guards Act,* S.N.B. 1976, c. 46, s. 1.

GUARDED. *adj.* 1. Protected in a manner designed to prevent a person (a) from falling through an opening or from one level to another, or (b) from making contact with a dangerous machine or other object. *Canada Building Safety Regulations,* C.R.C., c. 995, s. 2. 2. In respect of an electrical facility, that the facility is covered, shielded, fenced, enclosed or inaccessible by location or otherwise protected in a manner that will prevent or reduce, to the extent that is reasonably practicable, danger to any person who might touch or go near that facility. *Canada Electrical Safety Regulations,* C.R.C., c.

998, s. 2. 3. When applied to electrical equipment means that the electrical equipment is so covered, shielded, fenced, enclosed, or otherwise protected by means of suitable covers, casings, barriers, rails, screens, mats or platforms as to remove the likelihood of dangerous contact or approach by persons or objects. *Power Corporation Act,* R.R.O. 1980, Reg. 794, s. 0. 4. (i) In relation to a plant that every boiler, compressor or engine in the plant is guarded, and (ii) in relation to a boiler, compressor or engine, as the case may be, that the boiler, compressor or engine is provided with such devices in good operating condition as will ensure that the boiler, compressor or engine may be operated safely, notwithstanding that the operating engineer or operator in charge of the plant may be absent from the boiler room, compressor room or engine room, as the case may be or, where the boiler, compressor or engine is not enclosed in a room, from the immediate vicinity. *Operating Engineers Act,* R.R.O. 1980, Reg. 740, s. 1.

GUARDED PLANT. A plant that is equipped with fail-safe controls and audio and visual alarm systems and that is approved by the chief inspector. *The Boiler and Pressure Vessel Act,* R.S.S. 1978, c. B-5, s. 2.

GUARDIAN. *n.* 1. Includes any person who has in law or in fact the custody or control of another person. *Criminal Code,* R.S.C. 1985, c. C-46, s. 150. 2. Includes a person who has in law or in fact custody or control of a child. *Criminal Code,* R.S.C. 1985, c. C-46, s. 214. 3. In respect of a child, any person, other than a parent of the child, who is under a legal duty to provide for the child or who has, in law or in fact, the custody or control of the child. *Royal Canadian Mounted Police Act,* R.S.C. 1985 (2d Supp.), c. 8, s. 2. 4. A parent or other person who is under a legal duty to provide for a child. *Children's Residential Services Act,* R.R.O. 1980, Reg. 101, s. 1. 5. Includes a person acting in loco parentis to a child. See CHILDREN'S ~; FIRE ~; FISHERY ~; LEGAL ~; LITIGATION ~; OFFICIAL ~.

GUARDIAN AD LITEM. A litigation guardian. G.D. Watson & C. Perkins, eds., *Holmested & Watson: Ontario Civil Procedure* (Toronto: Carswell, 1984) at CJA-179.

GUARDIANSHIP. *n.* Granting full parental authority over a child which may be ordered for a particular reason, for example, to protect property. J.G. McLeod, *The Conflict of Laws* (Calgary: Carswell, 1983) at 296.

GUARDIANSHIP AGREEMENT. An agreement entered into under paragraph 44(1)(b) between the parent and the Minister permanently transferring from the parent to the Minister the guardianship of the child, including the custody, care and control of, and all parental rights and responsibilities with respect to, the child. *Child and Family Services and Family Relations Act*, S.N.B. 1980, c. C-2.1, s. 43.

GUARDIANSHIP ORDER. 1. An order which transfers the guardianship of the child, including the custody, care and control of, and all parental rights and responsibilities with respect to, the child. 2. Any order of a court appointing a person as a guardian.

GUEST. *n.* 1. A person who takes a room, whether for the day or for the night, but not a person who enters to obtain food, refreshment or entertainment only. *Innkeepers Act*, S. Nfld. 1982, c. 67, s. 2. 2. A person who contracts for sleeping accommodation in a hotel and includes each member of that person's party. 3. Any person, not otherwise prohibited by this Act from purchasing liquor, who enters club premises accompanied by a member of that club and who departs from the premises with, or prior to, that member. *Liquor Control Act*, R.S.N.B. 1973, c. L-10, s. 1.

GUEST STATUTE. A statute which imposes liability in respect of any gratuitous passenger on the driver of a car solely in a case of misconduct or gross negligence which is wanton, wilful or reckless. John G. Fleming, *The Law of Torts*, 6th ed. (Sydney: The Law Book Company Limited, 1983) at 116.

GUIDE. *n.* 1. A person who, for compensation or reward received or promised, accompanies and assists another person to hunt wildlife or angle for fish. 2. A person who for gain or reward accompanies or assists another person in any outdoor recreational activity. See ANGLING ~; DOG ~.

GUIDE DOG. A dog that is trained as a guide for a blind person by a recognized school.

GUIDE POST. See WOODEN ~.

GUILD. *n.* A company, corporation or fraternity formed for a commercial purpose.

GUILT. See FINDING OF ~.

GUILTY. *adj.* Having committed a tort or crime; used by a prisoner entering a plea and by a convicting jury. See NOT ~.

GUINEAS. *n.* Guinea chickens and guinea fowl. *Meat Inspection Regulations*, C.R.C., c. 1032, s. 135.

GUISE. See DISTINGUISHING ~.

GULF AREA. All the waters of the St. Lawrence River, Chaleur Bay, Northumberland Strait, and the Gulf of St. Lawrnece bounded on the north by a straight line drawn from the lighthouse at Amour Point to the lighthouse on Flowers Island in Flowers Cove, Newfoundland, and all the waters of Cabot Strait and of the Atlantic Ocean seaward thereof and seaward of the east coast of Nova Scotia and bounded on the north by a straight line drawn due east from Cape Race, Newfoundland. *Seal Protection Regulations*, C.R.C., c. 833, s. 2.

GULF OF ST. LAWRENCE. 1. The area bounded on the east by the west coast of the Island of Newfoundland, on the north by a line joining Flowers Island and Point Amour, Newfoundland, and on the southeast by a line joining Port aux Basques, Newfoundland, and Sydney, Nova Scotia. *Life Saving Equipment Regulations*, C.R.C., c. 1436, s. 2. 2. That area of the sea adjacent to the coast of Canada described as Zone 1 in the schedule to the Fishing Zones of Canada (Zones 1, 2 and 3) Order. *Atlantic Fishery Regulations*, C.R.C., c. 807, s. 2.

GUM SPIRITS OF TURPENTINE. A liquid obtained by steam-distillation of the gum of coniferous trees. *Turpentine Labelling Regulations*, C.R.C., c. 1140, s. 2.

GUN. *n.* 1. A firearm. F.A. Jaffe, *A Guide to Pathological Evidence*, 2d ed. (Toronto: Carswell, 1983) at 177. 2. A syringe. F.A. Jaffe, *A Guide to Pathological Evidence*, 2d ed. (Toronto: Carswell, 1983) at 177. 3. Any barrelled weapon from which any shot, bullet or other missile can be discharged and that is capable of causing serious injury or death to game, and includes anything that can be readily adapted for use as a gun or firearm. *Game Act*, R.S.N.B. 1973, c. G-1, s. 1. See STUD ~.

GUTTER. See AUXILIARY ~.

GVWR. *abbr.* Gross vehicle weight rating.

GYNAECOCRACY. *n.* Government by women.

GYNARCY. *n.* Government by women.

GYPSUM. *n.* Includes any gypsum bearing substance removed from a mine. *Gypsum Mining Income Tax Act*, R.S.N.S. 1967, c. 122, s. 1.

GYROPLANE. *n.* A heavier-than-air aircraft supported in flight by the reactions of the air on one or more rotors that rotate freely on substantially vertical axes. *Air Regulations*, C.R.C., c. 2, s. 101.

H. *abbr.* 1. Hour. 2. Henry. 3. Hecto.

HABEAS CORPUS. [L. that you have the body] See HABEAS CORPUS AD SUBJICIEN-DUM.

HABEAS CORPUS AD SUBJICIENDUM. [L.] An order that a person arrested be brought into a court or before a judge to determine if the imprisonment is lawful.

HABEMUS OPTIMUM TESTEM CONFIT-ENTEM REUM. [L.] We hold that an accused who pleads guilty is the best possible witness.

HABENDUM. *n.* [L. having] 1. The first word of a clause which follows a legal description of land which is being granted. 2. The section of a conveyance which sets out the amount of interest conveyed.

HABERE FACIAS POSSESSIONEM. [L. that you cause to have possession] A writ awarded to a plaintiff successful in an ejectment action.

HABILITATION AND CARE. The maintenance, training and other necessary care of a patient. *Hospital Schools Act*, R.S.N.B. 1973, c. H-8, s. 1.

HABITAT. *n.* 1. That kind of place or situation in which a human being, animal or plant lives. 2. Includes the soil, air, water, food and shelter components of the environment that are necessary to sustain wildlife. See FISH ~; WILD-LIFE ~.

HABITUAL CRIMINAL. According to provisions of the Criminal Code repealed in 1977, an offender who was "leading persistently a criminal life" and convicted of an indictable offence at least three times could be sentenced to preventative detention. P.W. Hogg, *Constitutional Law of Canada*, 2d ed. (Toronto: Carswell, 1985) at 780.

HABITUAL DRUNKARD. 1. A person who by reason of frequent drinking of intoxicating liquor is incapable at times of managing himself and his affairs, or is an unfit and improper person to have the custody and control of his infant children. *Wives' and Children's Maintenance Act*, R.S.M. 1970, c. W170, s. 2. 2. Any person who in the neighbourhood in which he resides has the reputation of being a drunkard. *Inebriates Guardianship Act*, R.S.N.S. 1967, c. 144, s. 1.

HABITUAL RESIDENCE. A regular, lasting physical presence. A. Bissett-Johnson & W.M. Holland, eds., *Matrimonial Property Law in Canada* (Toronto: Carswell, 1980) at A-9.

HABITUÉ. *n.* [Fr.] An alcoholic or drug habitue. *Private Sanitaria Act*, R.S.O. 1980, c. 391, s. 1.

HACK. *n.* A horse drawn vehicle used to transport passengers for compensation. *Motor Vehicle Act*, R.S.N.S. 1967, c. 191, s. 1.

HAD AND RECEIVED. See MONEY ~.

HADDIE. See CHICKEN ~.

HADDOCK. *n.* A fish of the species Melanogrammus aeglefinus (L.) *Northwest Atlantic Fisheries Regulations*, C.R.C., c. 860, s. 2.

HAEREDES PROXIMI. [L.] Offspring, children.

HAEREDES REMOTIORES. [L.] Heirs which were not offspring.

HAEREDIPETA. *n.* The next heir to property.

HAEREDITAS, ALIA CORPORALIS, ALIA INCORPORALIS; CORPORALIS EST, QUAE TANGI POTEST ET VIDERI; INCORPORALIS QUAE TANGI NON POTEST NEC VIDERI. [L.] Sometimes an inheritance is corporeal, sometimes incorporeal; a corporeal inheritance is visible and tangible; an incorporeal inheritance is invisible and intangible.

HAEREDITAS NIHIL ALIUD EST QUAM SUCCESSIO IN UNIVERSUM JUS QUOD DEFUNCTUS HABUERIT. [L.] Heirship is nothing but succession to everything a deceased possessed.

HAEREDITAS NUNQUAM ASCENDIT. [L.] Inheritance never ascends.

HAEREDUM APPELLATIONE VENIUNT HAEREDES HAEREDUM IN INFINITUM. [L.] Under the title of "heirs" come the heirs of heirs for ever.

HAERES. *n.* [L.] An heir.

HAERES EST AUT JURE PROPRIETATIS, AUT JURE REPRAESENTATIONIS. [L.] One is an heir by right of property, or by right of representation.

HAERES EST NOMEN JURIS, FILIUS EST NOMEN NATURAE. [L.] Heir is a label of law, child is a label of nature.

HAERES FACTUS. [L.] A chosen heir.

HAERES LEGITIMUS EST QUEM NUP-TIAE DEMONSTRANT. [L.] The lawful heir is one whom wedlock shows so to be.

HAERES NATUS. [L.] A born heir.

HAGUE CONVENTIONS. Agreements on rules of international law relating to matters such as the peaceful settlement of international disputes and the conduct of war.

HAIL INSURANCE. 1. Insurance against loss of or damage to crops caused by hail. 2. Insurance against loss of or damage to growing crops caused by hail. 3. Insurance against loss of or damage to crops in the field, whether growing or cut, caused by hail. *Insurance Act*, R.S.O. 1980, c. 218, s. 1. 4. Insurance against loss of or damage to property caused by hail. *Insurance Act*, R.S.B.C. 1979, c. 200, s. 1. See LIMITED ~.

HAIR. See LANUGO ~S; RAW WOOL, ~ OR BRISTLES.

HAIRDRESSER. *n.* A person who, (a) by hand or by the use of a mechanical application or appliance engages in the occupation of dressing, curling, waving, permanently waving, cleansing, bleaching or similar work on the hair of a person, including cutting the hair of female persons and of boys under 7 years of age; (b) by hand or by the use of a mechanical application or appliance, or by the use of cosmetic preparations, antiseptics, tonics, lotions, creams or similar preparations or compounds, engages in any one or more or any combination of manicuring the nails or massaging, cleansing or beautifying the scalp, face, neck, arms or bust of a person.

HAIRLINE FRACTURE. A barely visible linear bone fracture in which no bone fragments are displaced. F.A. Jaffe, *A Guide to Pathological Evidence*, 2d ed. (Toronto: Carswell, 1983) at 176 and 177.

HAKAPIK. *n.* An implement made of iron having a slightly bent spike of not more than 5 1/2 inches in length on one side of a ferrule and a blunt projection not more than 1/2 inch in length on the opposite side of the ferrule, the whole to weigh not less than 3/4 of a pound and having a head securely attached to a wooden handle not less than 42 inches or more than 60 inches in length and with a diameter of not less than 1 1/4 inches or more than 2 inches. *Seal Protection Regulations*, C.R.C., c. 833, s. 2.

HAKE. See RED ~; SILVER ~; WHITE ~.

HALF-BLOOD. *n.* One related through one parent only.

HALF BROTHER. A brother by only one parent's side.

HALF-SECRET TRUST. The deceased's will on its face makes the devisee or legatee a trustee, but does not state the objects of the trust. D.M.W. Waters, *The Law of Trusts in Canada*, 2d ed. (Toronto: Carswell, 1984) at 223.

HALF SISTER. A sister by only one parent's side.

HALF STOREY. A storey under a roof, the wall plates of which on at least two exterior walls are not more than 2 feet above the floor thereof. Canada regulations.

HALF-TIME PUPIL. A pupil who is enrolled in junior kindergarten or kindergarten and who, in respect of a cycle, is registered for an average of at least 150 minutes per school day. *Education Act*, R.R.O. 1980, Reg. 256, s. 1.

HALFWAY HOUSE. A dwelling, furnished, staffed and equipped for the purpose of providing accommodation to patients and where more care and supervision would be given to the patients being accommodated therein than if they had been placed in an approved home. *The Mental Health Act*, R.S.S. 1978, c. M-13, s. 2.

HALIBUT. *n.* The species of fish known as hippoglossus. *Northern Pacific Halibut Fisheries Convention Act*, R.S.C. 1985, c. F-19, s. 2. See GREENLAND ~.

HALIFAX. See PORT OF ~.

HALL. See DANCE ~; ENTERTAINMENT ~; HIRING ~; PUBLIC ~.

HALLMARK. *n.* A stamp affixed to articles of gold or silver as evidence of genuineness.

HALLMARK CASE. Another crime allegedly committed by the accused which is admissible because it bears a hallmark or characteristic in common with the crime for which the accused is being tried. P.K. McWilliams, *Canadian Crim-*

inal Evidence, 3d ed. (Aurora: Canada Law Book, 1988) at 11-15.

HALLUCINATION. *n.* An illusory sensory perception. F.A. Jaffe, *A Guide to Pathological Evidence*, 2d ed. (Toronto: Carswell, 1983) at 177.

HALLUCINOGENIC DRUG. A drug producing hallucination such as lysergic acid diethylamide (L.S.D.) or mescaline.

HAM. *n.* Meat from the hind leg of a pig. *Meat Inspection Regulations*, C.R.C., c. 1032, s. 2.

HAMLET. *n.* 1. (i) An unincorporated community consisting of a group of 5 or more occupied dwellings, a majority of which are on parcels of less than 1850 square metres, with a defined boundary, a distinct name and the existence of or provision for non-residential uses, that is designated as a hamlet by the council for the municipal district in which the community is located or by the Minister, or (ii) any area declared to be a hamlet by the Minister before July 1, 1986 unless the declaration is revoked by the Minister. *Municipal Government Amendment Act*, S.A. 1985, c. 43, s. 2. 2. A group of houses in a rural area the inhabitants of which have not been incorporated into a municipality. *Public Schools Act*, R.S.M. 1970, c. P250, s. 2. 3. Any area of land that has been subdivided into lots, blocks, or parcels, or as a townsite, and a plan or description of which has been registered in the land titles office of the land registration district in which it is situated, or that is used by some person for trade or business purposes other than farm purposes, but which has not been established as a village, and any area declared by an order of the minister to be a hamlet. *The Northern Administration Act*, R.S.S. 1978, c. N-5, s. 2.

HAMPERED SHIP. A ship that, to the knowledge of and so declared by the Authority, is unable to be navigated in a normal fashion because of excessive list, excessive trim by the head or stern, shifted deckloads, damage, faulty steering, faulty engines, lack of normal navigational aid equipment, faulty navigational aid equipment or other unseaworthy conditions. Canada regulations.

HANDBOOK. See EMPLOYEE ~.

HAND CARRIED WEAPON OR PIECE OF ORDNANCE. Includes (a) a small arm, staff-weapon or an edged weapon, and (b) a cannon or artillery piece that is muzzle loaded or breech loaded whether originally mounted or unmounted, that was used or designed to be used for a warlike purpose. *Canadian Cultural Property Export Control List*, C.R.C., c. 448, s. 1.

HANDICAP. See BECAUSE OF ~; DEVEL-OPMENTAL ~; EMPLOYMENT ~; PHYSI-CAL ~; PHYSICAL OR MENTAL ~.

HANDICAPPED CHILDREN. Children who have a physical or mental impairment that is likely to continue for a prolonged period of time and who as a result thereof are limited in activities pertaining to normal living as verified by objective psychological or medical findings and includes children with a developmental handicap. *Day Nurseries Act*, R.R.O. 1980, Reg. 235, s. 1.

HANDICAPPED PERSON. 1. A person limited in the performance of normal activities who is suffering, significantly and permanently, from a physical or mental deficiency, or who regularly uses a prosthesis or an orthopedic device or any other means of palliating the handicap. 2. A person who (a) is permanently dependent on a wheelchair, (b) has suffered loss of a limb, (c) has suffered the complete and permanent functional loss of the lower limbs. 3. A person who is handicapped visually or aurally. See PHYS-ICALLY ~; VISUALLY ~.

HANDLE. *v.* Includes use, store, treat, manufacture, generate, process, reprocess, sell, offer for sale and dispose. *Dangerous Goods and Hazardous Wastes Management Act*, S.N.S. 1986, c. 7, s. 2.

HANDLING. *n.* Loading, packing or placing, unloading, unpacking or removing or reloading, repacking or replacing dangerous goods in or from any container, packaging or means of transport or at any facility for the purposes of, in the course of or following transportation and includes storing dangerous goods in the course of transportation.

HANDLING CHARGE. 1. A charge on goods for their receipt at and stowage in the warehouse and delivery to the warehouse handling floor. *Montreal Cold Storage Warehouse Tariff By-law*, C.R.C., c. 1076, s. 2. 2. A charge for moving goods between ordinary places of rest and vessel slings. Canada regulations. See CONTAINER ~.

HANDLING RATES. Rates imposed for moving freight to or from ships' slings and includes rates imposed for ordinary sorting, piling and trucking in a shed. *Port Alberni Assembly Wharves By-law*, C.R.C., c. 913, s. 2.

HAND PICKED. That the fruit shows no evidence of rough handling or of having been on the ground. *Fresh Fruit and Vegetable Regulations*, C.R.C., c. 285, s. 1.

HAND TOOL. A tool that is designed to be held in the hand and that is operated by manual power. *Canada Hand Tools Regulations*, C.R.C., c. 1002, s. 2.

HANDWRITING. *n.* The form of writing peculiar to a person.

HANG. *v.* To suspend an animal by one or more legs. *Humane Slaughter Regulations*, C.R.C., c. 937, s. 2.

HANGING. *n.* Ligature strangulation caused by gravity. F.A. Jaffe, *A Guide to Pathological Evidence*, 2d ed. (Toronto: Carswell, 1983) at 177.

HANG UP. A tree that has not fallen to the ground after being, (i) partly or wholly separated from its stump, or (ii) displaced from its natural position. *Occupational Health and Safety Act*, R.R.O. 1980, Reg. 692, s. 107.

HANSARD. *n.* The official report of debates in Parliament.

HAPTOGLOBIN. *n.* A protein in blood plasma. F.A. Jaffe, *A Guide to Pathological Evidence*, 2d ed. (Toronto: Carswell, 1983) at 177.

HARASS. *v.* 1. Includes worry, exhaust, fatigue, annoy, plague, pester, tease or torment, but does not include the lawful hunting, trapping or capturing of wildlife. *Wildlife Act*, S.B.C. 1982, c. 57, s. 1. 2. To engage in a course of vexatious comment or conduct that is known or ought reasonably to be known to be unwelcome. *An Act to Amend the Newfoundland Human Rights Code*, S. Nfld. 1983, c. 62, s. 1. See SEXUALLY ~.

HARASSMENT. *n.* Engaging in a course of vexatious comment or conduct that is known or ought reasonably to be known to be unwelcome. *Human Rights Code, 1981*, S.O. 1981, c. 53, s. 9. See SEXUAL ~.

HARBOUR. *v.* To give refuge to, to shelter.

HARBOUR. *n.* Harbours and places properly so called whether proclaimed public harbours or not, and whether natural or artificial, to which ships may resort for shelter or to ship or unship goods or passengers. *Canada Shipping Act*, R.S.C. 1985, c. S-9, s. 2. See PUBLIC ~; SCHEDULED ~.

HARBOUR DUES. 1. A charge on a vessel entering the harbour. Canada regulations. 2. The rates payable in respect of a vessel using the harbour. Canada regulations.

HARBOUR TOLL. Every rate, toll and charge established or proposed to be established by any Act of Parliament or by, or with the approval of, the Governor in Council in respect of ships entering, using or leaving any harbour in Canada, the passengers thereof or goods loaded, unloaded, shipped, transhipped, moved in transit or stored in any harbour in Canada or on or in any wharf, dock, pier, warehouse or other facility within the limits of any such harbour or situated on lands appurtenant thereto. *Transport Act*, R.S.C. 1985, c. T-17, s. 2.

HARD. *adj.* Rock comparable to concrete with a compressive strength greater than 6,000 psi. *Building Code Act*, R.R.O. 1980, Reg. 87, s. 4.2.1.10. See MEDIUM ~.

HARD SWELL. A can with both ends bulging as a result of spoilage from gas-producing organisms. *Processed Fruit and Vegetable Regulations*, C.R.C., c. 291, s. 2.

HARD TO SERVE PUPIL. A pupil who, under this section, is determined to be unable to profit by instruction offered by a board due to a mental handicap or a mental and one or more additional handicaps. *Education Act*, R.S.O. 1980, c. 129, s. 34.

HARDWARE. *n.* 1. Any metal or rigid plastic part designed to secure a person in a vehicle in conjunction with straps or webbing. *Motor Vehicle Safety Regulations*, C.R.C., c. 1038, s. 209. 2. Any metal or rigid plastic part of an occupant restraint assembly or product restraint assembly. *Children's Car Seats and Harnesses Regulations*, C.R.C., c. 921, s. 2. See ADJUSTMENT ~; ATTACHMENT ~; PANIC ~.

HARDWOOD. *n.* Non-coniferous. *Crown Timber Act*, R.R.O. 1980, Reg. 234, s. 1.

HARM. See BODILY ~; SERIOUS ~.

HARMONY PLEDGE. Clause in which employer and union agree to co-operate on a particular subject.

HARNESS. See SAFETY ~.

HARNESS RACING. Horse racing in which the horses participating are harnessed to a sulky, carriage or similar vehicle. *Harness Racing Commission Act*, R.S.N.S. 1967, c. 124, s. 1.

HARPOON. *n.* An apparatus equipped with one or more points that is capable of catching fish by piercing or impaling them. *Quebec Fishery Regulations*, C.R.C., c. 852, s. 2.

HARR. & HODG. *abbr.* Harrison & Hodgins' Municipal Reports (Ont.), 1845-1851.

HARVEST. *v.* Cut, take, dredge, rake or otherwise obtain. *Fisheries Act*, R.S.C. 1985, c. F-14, s. 47. See RIGHT TO ~.

HARVESTER. *n.* A person in possession of or in charge of a harvesting machine. *Noxious Weeds Act*, R.S.M. 1970, c. N110, s. 1.

HARVESTING. *n.* 1. Includes gathering, raking, dragging, cutting, pumping, transporting, or by any other means acquiring sea plants or sea plant products whether on the foreshore or in the water, or whether attached to the solum or loose-lying, whether biologically living or not living. 2. Includes pasturing. *Crop Insurance Act (Ontario)*, R.R.O. 1980, Reg. 211, s. 3.

HARVESTING ADVANCES. The necessary goods supplied or services rendered to a farmer in connection with the cutting, harvesting or threshing of his crop by reason of which any of the following claims arise: (a) the claim of an employee for wages for work done in connection with the cutting or harvesting of any crop, including work done on or about any threshing machine; (b) then claim of the vendor of binder twine or fuel oil for the amount remaining unpaid of the purchase price of the binder twine or fuel oil in connection with the cutting, harvesting or threshing of any crop; (c) the claim of a person for the amount remaining unpaid for repairs carried out in connection with the cutting, harvesting or threshing of any crop; (d) the claim of the owner, operator or person for the time being entitled to the possession of any machinery for the amount owing for the rent of the machinery provided in connection with the cutting, harvesting or threshing of any crop; and includes all money advanced to the farmer to enable him to discharge any of the claims set out in clauses (a) to (d). *Harvesting Liens Act*, R.S.A. 1980, c. H-2, s. 1.

HARVESTING MACHINE. A machine that while moving or stationary harvests, threshes, or processes any forage or cereal crop, root crop, or the residue thereof. *Noxious Weeds Act*, R.S.M. 1970, c. N110, s. 1.

HARVESTING OF CROPS. Includes the cutting, swathing, combining, threshing, division into their respective shares as between landlord and tenant, and the removal, delivery and sale of such crops. *The Agricultural Leaseholds Act*, R.S.S. 1978, c. A-12, s. 2.

HASH. *n.* Hashish.

HASHISH. *n.* A resinous juice found in the upper leaves and the flowering tops of the plant Cannabis sativa. F.A. Jaffe, *A Guide to Pathological Evidence*, 2d ed. (Toronto: Carswell, 1983) at 177.

HATCH. *n.* An opening in a deck used for the purpose of the processes or for trimming or ventilation. *Tackle Regulations*, C.R.C., c. 1494, s. 2.

HATCHERY. *n.* Any place, buildings or premises equipped with an incubator capacity of one thousand or more eggs and used for incubation purposes. See APPROVED ~ SUPPLY FLOCK.

HATCHERY ESTABLISHMENT. Any establishment in which the rearing of fish takes place. *Quebec Fishery Regulations*, C.R.C., c. 852, s. 2.

HATCHERYMAN. *n.* Any person who operates a hatchery. *Livestock and Livestock Products Act*, R.S.C. 1985, c. L-9, s. 42.

HATCHING EGGS. 1. Eggs of a domestic hen produced for the purpose of hatching into chicks. 2. The fertilized eggs of poultry. *Animal Disease and Protection Regulations*, C.R.C., c. 296, s. 2.

HATCHWAY. *n.* The whole space within the square of the hatches, from the top deck to the bottom of the hold. *Tackle Regulations*, C.R.C., c. 1494, s. 2.

HATE PROPAGANDA. Any writing, sign or visible representation that advocates or promotes genocide or the communication of which by any person would constitute an offence under section 319. *Criminal Code*, R.S.C. 1985, c. C-46, s. 320(8) as am.

HAULED LIQUID INDUSTRIAL WASTE. Liquid waste, other than hauled sewage, that results from industrial processes or manufacturing or commercial operations and that is transported in a tank or other container for treatment or disposal, and includes sewage residue from sewage works that are subject to the provisions of the Ontario Water Resources Act. *Environmental Protection Act*, R.R.O. 1980, Reg. 309, s. 1.

HAULED SEWAGE. Waste removed from, (i) a cesspool, (ii) a septic tank system, (iii) a privy vault or privy pit, (iv) a chemical toilet, (v) a portable toilet, or (vi) a sewage holding tank. *Environmental Protection Act*, R.R.O. 1980, Reg. 309, s. 1.

HAUL ROAD. A road, other than a highway as defined in the Highway Traffic Act, on which vehicles used to haul logs are operated. *Occupational Health and Safety Act*, R.R.O. 1980, Reg. 692, s. 107.

HAVE. See TO ~ AND TO HOLD.

HAVE AND TO HOLD. See TO HAVE AND TO HOLD.

HAVE CHARGE OF. In relation to a plant, to have at all times while the plant is in operation general supervision of the operation and maintenance of the plant and of the power engineers operating the plant. See HAVING CHARGE OF.

HAVEN. *n.* A harbour or port; any place which contains or holds ships.

HAVE NO ISSUE. A want or failure of issue in the lifetime or at the time of death of that person, and not an indefinite failure of issue unless a contrary intention appears by the will. *Wills acts.*

HAVE-NOT PROVINCE. A province entitled

to an equalization grant. P.W. Hogg, *Constitutional Law of Canada*, 2d ed. (Toronto: Carswell, 1985) at 118.

HAVING CHARGE OF. When used in relation to a heating plant or a power plant, means to have at all times while the heating plant or power plant is in operation the duties of general supervision over the operation and maintenance of such heating plant or power plant and over stationary engineers engaged in the operation of such heating plant or power plant. *Boiler and Pressure Vessel Act*, R.S.N.B. 1973, c. B-7, s. 1. See HAVE CHARGE OF.

HAWKER. *n.* Any person who, whether as principal or agent, (i) goes from house to house selling or offering for sale any merchandise or services, or both, to any person, and who is not a wholesale or retail dealer in such merchandise or services, and not having a permanent place of business in the municipality, or (ii) offers or exposes for sale to any person by means of samples, patterns, cuts or blueprints, merchandise or services, or both, to be afterwards delivered in and shipped into the municipality, or (iii) sells merchandise or services, or both, on the streets or roads or elsewhere than at a building that is his permanent place of business, but does not include any person selling, (A) meat, fruit or other farm produce that has been produced, raised or grown by himself, or (B) fish of his own catching. *Municipal Government Act*, R.S.A. 1980, c. M-26, s. 1.

HAWKER AND PEDDLER. Any person who goes from place to place or to homes of other persons on foot or with any animal, vehicle, boat or other craft, carrying to sell or exposing for sale goods, wares or merchandise, or displaying samples or patterns of any such goods, wares or merchandise to be afterwards delivered, but does not include any person selling goods, wares or merchandise to or seeking orders therefor from persons, partnerships, associations or companies who are dealers therein and who buy to sell again, or any person selling or exposing for sale goods, wares or merchandise the growth, produce or manufacture of the province who is the manufacturer or producer thereof or who is the bona fide servant or employee and acting under the written authority of any such manufacturer or producer. Newfoundland statutes.

HAY. *n.* 1. The harvested, cured, unthreshed herbage of those kinds of forage plants that have recognized feeding value and are acceptable to Plant Products Division, and that (a) meet the class, mixture, grade, colour and other requirements as prescribed in the tables to this Schedule, (b) contains not more than 35 per cent of foreign material, and (c) is not coarse or woody. *Hay and Straw Inspection Regulations*, C.R.C.,

c. 920, s. 1. 2. Feed for live stock produced from grasses or legumes. *Crop Insurance Act (Ontario)*, R.R.O. 1980, Reg. 211, s. 3.

HAY AND PASTURE. Feed for live stock produced from grasses or legumes and, (i) fed as pasture, or (ii) cut and stored as hay or hay silage. *Crop Insurance Act (Ontario)*, R.R.O. 1980, Reg. 210, s. 3.

HAZARD. See AVOIDABLE ~; FIRE ~; HEALTH ~; NUCLEAR ENERGY ~.

HAZARDOUS CHEMICAL. Any substance, class of substances or mixture of substances that is entering or is likely to enter the environment in a quantity or concentration or under conditions that may constitute a danger to (i) the natural environment, (ii) plant or animal life, or (iii) human health. *Hazardous Chemicals Act*, R.S.A. 1980, c. H-3, s. 1.

HAZARDOUS CONFINED SPACE. A tank, silo, storage bin, process vessel or other enclosure, not designed or intended for human occupancy, in respect of which, when an employee is required to enter therein, special precautions are necessary to (a) protect the employee from a dangerous atmosphere therein, (b) prevent the employee from becoming entrapped in a material stored therein, or (c) otherwise ensure the employee's safety therein. *Canada Confined Spaces Regulations*, C.R.C., c. 996, s. 2.

HAZARDOUS FOOD. Any food consisting in whole or in part of milk, milk products, eggs, egg products, meat, poultry, fish, shellfish or any other food capable of supporting the growth of pathogenic organisms or the production of the toxins of such organisms. *Public Health Act*, R.R.O. 1980, Reg. 840, s. 1.

HAZARDOUS LOCATION. Premises, buildings, or parts thereof in which there exists the hazard of fire or explosion because, (i) highly flammable gases, flammable volatile liquids, mixtures or other highly flammable substances are manufactured or used or are stored in other than original containers, (ii) combustible dust or flyings are likely to be present in quantities sufficient to produce an explosive or combustible mixture, or where it is impracticable to prevent such dust or flyings from being deposited upon incandescent lamps or from collecting in or upon motors or other electrical equipment in such quantities as to produce overheating by reason of the prevention of normal radiation, (ii) easily ignitible fibres or materials producing combustible flyings are manufactured, handled or used in a free open state, or (iv) easily ignitible fibres or materials producing combustible flyings are stored in bales or containers but are not manufactured, handled or used in a free open state. *Power Corporation Act*, R.R.O. 1980, Reg. 794, s. 0.

HAZARDOUS OCCUPATION. A job classified as dangerous.

HAZARDOUS PRODUCT. Any product or substance included in Part I or II of the schedule. *Hazardous Products Act*, R.S.C. 1985, c. H-3, s. 2.

HAZARDOUS ROOM. A room in a factory or similar place where something is present which may ignite easily or explode, causing a fire or an imminently hazardous atmosphere. D. Robertson, *Ontario Health and Safety Guide* (Toronto: Richard De Boo Ltd., 1988) at 5-200.

HAZARDOUS WASTE. 1. Waste that requires special precautions in its storage, collection, transportation, treatment or disposal, to prevent damage to persons or property and includes explosive, flammable, volatile, radioactive, toxic and pathological waste. *Environmental Protection Act*, R.R.O. 1980, Reg. 309, s. 1. 2. A hazardous chemical disposed of or to be disposed of as waste. *Hazardous Chemicals Amendment Act, 1982*, S.A. 1982, c. 20, s. 2.

HAZARDOUS WASTE MANAGEMENT FACILITY. A facility for the reception, collection, movement, examination, storage, treatment or disposal of hazardous waste.

H.C. *abbr.* 1. High Court of Justice. 2. Haute Cour.

HEAD. *n.* 1. In respect of a government institution, means (a) in the case of a department or ministry of state, the member of the Queen's Privy Council for Canada presiding over that institution, or (b) in any other case, the person designated by order in council to be the head of that institution. Canada statutes. 2. The Minister of the Crown who has charge of a department, and the President of the Assemblée nationale. *Civil Service Act*, R.S.Q. 1977, c. F-3, s. 1. 3. (i) When used in respect of a fire-tube boiler, the plate into which the ends of the tubes are fitted, (ii) when used in respect of a water-tube boiler, the plate closing the ends of the drum, and (iii) when used in respect of a pressure vessel, the plate closing the part in which the gas, vapour or liquid is under pressure. *Boilers and Pressure Vessels Act*, R.R.O. 1980, Reg. 84, s. 1. See DEPARTMENT ~; DEPUTY ~; GREEN ~; PERMANENT ~; PIT ~.

HEAD END. An antenna positioned to receive signals from satellites or from television-broadcasting stations in the area. P.W. Hogg, *Constitutional Law of Canada*, 2d ed. (Toronto: Carswell, 1985) at 504. See LOCAL ~.

HEADER. *n.* 1. A pipe installed to provide an interconnection between two or more pipes all of which perform a similar or identical function. *Ontario Water Resources Act*, R.R.O. 1980, Reg. 736, s. 1. 2. A transverse raceway for electrical conductors, providing access to predetermined cells of a cellular metal or concrete floor permitting the installation of conductors from a distribution centre to the cells. *Power Corporation Act*, R.R.O. 1980, Reg. 794, s. 0.

HEAD IMPACT AREA. The non-glazed surfaces of the interior of the vehicle that are statically contractible by the head form of a measuring device in accordance with the following procedure or its graphic equivalent: (a) at each designated seating position, by placing the pivot point of the measuring device, (i) for seats that are adjustable fore and aft at (A) the seating reference point, and (B) a point 5 inches horizontally forward of the seating reference point displaced vertically 0.75 inch or a distance equal to the rise that results from a 5-inch forward adjustment of the seat, and (ii) for seats that are not adjustable fore and aft, at the seating reference point; (b) with the pivot point to top-of-head dimension at each value allowed by the device and the interior dimensions of the vehicle, by determining all contact points above the lower windshield glass line and forward of the seating reference point, and (c) beginning with head form at each contact point referred to in paragraph (b), and with the device in a vertical position if no contact point exists for a particular adjusted length, by pivoting the measuring device forward and downward through all arcs in vertical planes to 90 degree each side of the vertical longitudinal plane through the seating reference point until the head form contacts an interior surface or until it is tangent to a horizontal plant 1 inch above the seating reference point, whichever occurs first. *Motor Vehicle Safety Regulations*, C.R.C., c. 1038, s. 200.

HEADING. *n.* 1. A text prefixed to a section or group of sections in a modern statute. P.St.J. Langan, ed., *Maxwell on The Interpretation of Statutes*, 12th ed. (Bombay: N.M. Tripathi, 1976) at 11. 2. The direction in which the longitudinal axis of an aircraft is pointed, usually expressed in degrees from North (true, magnetic, compass or grid). *Air Regulations*, C.R.C., c. 2, s. 101.

HEADLAMP CONCEALMENT DEVICE. A device, including the operating system and components thereof, that provides concealment of one or more headlamps when it is not in use and includes a movable headlamp cover and a headlamp that is displaced for concealment purposes. *Motor Vehicle Safety Regulations*, C.R.C., c. 1038, s. 114.

HEAD LEASE. A contract under which (a) Her Majesty in right of Canada or a province grants, or (b) an owner in fee simple, other than Her Majesty in right of Canada or a province, grants for a period of not less than 10 years, any right, licence or privilege to explore for, drill for or take petroleum, natural gas or related hydrocarbons in Canada or to prospect, explore, drill or mine for minerals in a mineral resource in Canada. *Income Tax Act*, R.S.C. 1952, c. 148 (as am. S.C. 1986, c. 55, s. 73), s. 209(1).

HEADLESS DRAWN WEIGHT. The weight of a fish after the head, gills and entrails have been removed without cutting the belly. *Manitoba Fishery Regulations*, C.R.C., c. 843, s. 2.

HEADLESS DRESSED WEIGHT. The weight of the fish after the head, gills and entrails have been removed and the belly has been cut. *Manitoba Fishery Regulations*, C.R.C., c. 843, s. 2.

HEAD MONEY. Poll tax.

HEADNOTE. *n.* The summary of a reported case preceding the full report of the case.

HEAD OF A DEPARTMENT. (i) In the case of an unincorporated Crown agency, the minister charged with the administration of the Act under which the agency is established; (ii) in the case of an incorporated Crown agency, the chief executive officer of the agency, and (iii) in all other cases, the minister charged with the administration of the department. *The Freedom of Information Act*, S.M. 1985-86, c. 6, s. 1.

HEAD OF A FAMILY. 1. A person who has charge of a household and who has one or more dependants therein. 2. The member of a family who habitually is the chief provider for the needs of such family. *Social Aid Act*, R.S.Q. 1977, c. A-16, s. 1. See HEAD OF FAMILY.

HEAD OF COUNCIL. Includes a chairman of the board of an improvement district. *Emergency Plans Act, 1983*, S.O. 1983, c. 30, s. 1. See HEAD OF THE COUNCIL.

HEAD OF ESTABLISHMENT. Includes any person, partnership or corporation who has charge of all or part of an industrial or commercial establishment on his own account or on account of another person, partnership or corporation, as a contractor, subcontractor, manager, supervisor, foreman or agent, or otherwise. *Industrial and Commercial Establishments Act*, R.S.Q. 1977, c. E-15, s. 2.

HEAD OF FAMILY. The person in the family upon whom the other members are mainly dependent for support. *Immigration Act*, R.S.C. 1970, c. I-2, s. 2. See HEAD OF A FAMILY.

HEAD OFFICE. 1. The principal office or place of business of a corporation. 2. The place where the chief executive officer of an insurer carries on business. Insurance acts. 3. The place where the chief executive officers of the corporation transact its business. Trust Corporations acts.

HEAD OF MISSION. (a) An ambassador, high commissioner or consul-general of Canada; or (b) any other person appointed to represent Canada in another country or a portion of another country or at an international organization or diplomatic conference and designated head of mission by the Governor in Council. *Department of External Affairs Act*, R.S.C. 1985, c. E-22, s. 13.

HEAD OF POST. The person at a post who is in charge of the post and responsible for its operation. *Special Voting Rules*, R.S.C. 1985, c. E-2, Schedule II, s. 2.

HEAD OF THE COUNCIL. The mayor of a city or town, the overseer of a village or the reeve of a rural municipality. *The Tax Enforcement Act*, R.S.S. 1978, c. T-2, s. 2. See HEAD OF COUNCIL.

HEAD OF THE DEPARTMENT. The member of the Executive Council presiding over a department. *Civil Service Act*, R.S.N.S. 1967, c. 34, s. 1.

HEAD RESTRAINT. A device that limits rearward angular displacement of the occupant's head relative to his torso. Canada regulations.

HEAD SPACE. That space between the top edge or rim of the container and the upper level of the contents. *Processed Fruit and Vegetable Regulations*, C.R.C., c. 291, s. 2.

HEALTH. See BOARD OF ~; MEDICAL OFFICER OF ~; MINISTER OF ~; OCCUPATIONAL ~; RADIATION ~; SAFETY AND ~ COMMITTEE; SAFETY AND ~ REPRESENTATIVE.

HEALTH AGENCY. The regional board of a health region established pursuant to The Health Services Act or a non-profit association, corporation or other organization whose sole purpose and object is the payment for medical services and related services to and for its members or subscribers. *The Saskatchewan Medical Care Insurance Act*, R.S.S. 1978, c. S-29, s. 2.

HEALTH AND SAFETY REPRESENTATIVE. A health and safety representative elected by the employees at a place of employment. Occupational Health and Safety acts.

HEALTH AND WELFARE CANADA. The federal ministry with mandate to promote and preserve Canadians' health, social welfare and social security.

HEALTH CARE. 1. Includes (i) any examination, diagnosis, procedure or treatment undertaken to prevent any disease or ailment, (ii) any procedure undertaken for the purpose of preventing pregnancy, (iii) any procedure undertaken for the purpose of an examination or a diagnosis, (iv) any medical, surgical, obstetrical or dental treatment, and (v) anything done that is ancillary to any procedure, treatment, examination or diagnosis. *Dependent Adults Act*, R.S.A. 1980, c. D-32, s. 1. 2. Medical, surgical, obstetrical, optical, dental and nursing services, and includes drugs, dressings, prosthetic appliances and any other items or health services necessary to or commonly associated with the provision of any such specified services, but does not include any part of such items and health services payable under the Ontario Health Insurance Plan under the Health Insurance Act. *Developmental Services Act*, R.R.O. 1980, Reg. 242, s. 1.

HEALTH CARE INSURANCE PLAN. In relation to a province, a plan or plans established by the law of the province to provide for insured health services. *Canada Health Act*, R.S.C. 1985, c. C-6, s. 2.

HEALTH CARE PRACTITIONER. A person lawfully entitled under the law of a province to provide health services in the place in which the services are provided by that person. *Canada Health Act*, R.S.C. 1985, c. C-6, s. 2.

HEALTH CARE PROFESSIONAL. (a) A medical practitioner, (b) a person qualified and permitted under the Dentists Act to practise dentistry or dental surgery, (c) a registered nurse as defined in the Nurses (Registered) Act, (d) a person registered under the Nurses (Registered Psychiatric) Act as a member of the Registered Psychiatric Nurses Association of British Columbia, (e) a person licensed as a practical nurse under the Nurses (Licensed Practical) Act, (f) a massage practitioner, medical physical therapist, chartered physiotherapist or registered therapist as defined in the Physiotherapists Act, or (g) a pharmacist as defined in the Pharmacists Act. *Attorney General Statutes Amendment Act*, S.B.C. 1985, c. 65, s. 5.

HEALTH CARE SERVICES. Medical, surgical, obstetrical, optical, dental and nursing services, and includes drugs, dressings, prosthetic appliances and any other items or health services necessary to or commonly associated with the provision of any such specified services. See EXTENDED ~.

HEALTH CARE UNIONS. A trade union certified for a unit in which the majority of employees has as its principal duties the health care of patients or operation and maintenance of a hospital. *Essential Service Disputes Act*, R.S.B.C. 1979, c. 113, s. 1.

HEALTH CERTIFICATE. In respect of any plant or other matter means a certificate signed by an official of the country of origin of the plant or other matter who has been authorized by the government of that country to sign certificates as to the health of plants or other matter. *Plant Quarantine Regulations*, C.R.C., c. 1273, s. 5.

HEALTH FACILITY. 1. An ambulance service, a nursing home, a private hospital, a laboratory, a specimen collection centre, a hospital, health centre or other health program or service.

HEALTH GOODS. Any material, substance, mixture, compound or preparation, of whatever composition or in whatever form, sold or represented for use in the diagnosis, treatment, mitigation or prevention of a disease, a disorder, an abnormal physical state or the symptoms thereof in human beings or animals or for use in restoring, correcting or modifying organic functions in human beings or animals. *Excise Tax Act*, R.S.C. 1985 (2d Supp.), c. 7, s. 1(4).

HEALTH HAZARD. (i) A condition of a premises, (ii) a substance, thing, plant or animal other than man, or (iii) a solid, liquid, gas or combination of any of them, that has or that is likely to have an adverse effect on the health of any person. *Health Protection and Promotion Act, 1983*, S.O. 1983, c. 10, s. 1.

HEALTH INSURANCE OR BENEFIT PLAN. Includes a plan, fund or arrangement provided, furnished or offered by an employer to an employee that provides benefits to an employee, a spouse or dependant of an employee or deceased employee for medical, hospital, nursing, drug or dental expenses or other similar expenses. *Employment Standards Act*, R.R.O. 1980, Reg. 282, s. 1.

HEALTH L. CAN. *abbr.* Health Law in Canada.

HEALTH OFFICER. A medical health officer appointed for the enforcement of this Act or of any other Act of the Province relating to public health. *Health Act*, R.S.B.C. 1979, c. 161, s. 1.

HEALTH PRACTITIONER. Any person who provides health care or treatment to any person. *Public Health Act*, S.A. 1984, c. P-27.1, s. 1.

HEALTH PROTECTION. See RADIOLOGICAL ~.

HEALTH RESOURCES. (i) Community health facilities including health practitioners and personnel through which health services can be provided to persons in a community, and (ii) the operation of a mobile vision van by a non-profit organization to provide eye care in underserviced areas in Ontario. *Ministry of Health Act*, R.R.O. 1980, Reg. 658, s. 1.

HEALTH SERVICES. 1. Services provided by

a hospital or services provided by a licensed medical practitioner or dentist, a registered nurse or any other qualified person, and includes drugs, appliances and treatment prescribed by such medical practitioner or dentist or other qualified person. *The Health Services Act*, R.S.S. 1978, c. H-1, s. 2. 2. Basic health services, optional health services and extended health services. *Alberta Health Care Insurance Act*, R.S.A. 1980, c. A-24, s. 1. See BASIC ~; EMERGENCY HEALTH SERVICE; INSURED ~; LIVESTOCK ~; PRIVATE ~ PLAN; PUBLIC ~.

HEALTH TRAINING FACILITY. A school, hospital or other institution, or any portion thereof, (a) for the training of persons in the health professions or in occupations associated with the health professions, or (b) for the conducting of research in the health fields, but does not include residential accommodation. *Health Resources Fund Act*, R.S.C. 1970, c. H-4, s. 2.

HEALTHY. *adj.* Fresh and natural in appearance. *Farm Products Grades and Sales Act*, R.R.O. 1980, Reg. 331, s. 1.

HEARING. *n.* 1. Investigating a controversy. 2. Includes a trial. 3. In a broad sense includes making written representations. S.A. DeSmith, *Judicial Review of Administrative Action*, 4th ed. by J.M. Evans (London: Stevens, 1980) at 201. See COSTS OF THIS ~; DE NOVO ~; FAIR ~; PRELIMINARY ~; PUBLIC ~; RE-~; STATUS ~.

HEARING AID. A wearable instrument or device designed for or offered for aiding or compensating for impaired human hearing and parts or accessories for the instrument, including an earmould, but not including batteries and cords.

HEARING AID DEALER. Any person engaged in (i) testing or measuring human hearing by audiometer or any other means for the purpose of selecting, adapting, recommending or selling hearing aids; or (ii) selling or offering for sale hearing aids; or (iii) making impressions for earmoulds to be used in connection with hearing aids. *Hearing Aid Act*, S.M. 1971, c. 22, s. 1. See PRACTICE OF A ~ AND CONSULTANT.

HEARING DOG. A dog trained as a guide for a deaf person and having the qualifications prescribed by the regulations. *Blind Persons' Rights Amendment Act, 1983*, S.A. 1983, c. 19, s. 3.

HEARSAY EVIDENCE. Something which a witness heard another person say. P.K. McWilliams, *Canadian Criminal Evidence*, 3d ed. (Aurora: Canada Law Book, 1988) at 1-11.

HEART INFARCT. Occurs when a part of the heart muscle suffers local cellular breakdown as a result of inadequate blood supply. F.A. Jaffe, *A Guide to Pathological Evidence*, 2d ed. (Toronto: Carswell, 1983) at 46.

HEAT. See DEAD ~.

HEAT DETECTOR. A device for sensing an abnormally high air temperature or an abnormal rate of heat rise and automatically initiating a signal indicating this condition. *Building Code Act*, R.R.O. 1980, Reg. 87, s. 1.

HEAT ENERGY. Energy that is conveyed in the medium of steam, hot water, or hot air and that is produced for sale. *Power Corporation Amendment Act, 1981*, S.O. 1981, c. 16, s. 1.

HEATER. See SERVICE WATER ~; SPACE ~; STORAGE-TYPE WATER ~; UNIT ~.

HEAT EXHAUSTION. A state of collapse caused by loss of electrolytes and body fluids after exposure to high temperature. F.A. Jaffe, *A Guide to Pathological Evidence*, 2d ed. (Toronto: Carswell, 1983) at 177 and 178.

HEAT EXCHANGER. A pressure vessel under pressure of more than fifteen pounds used exclusively for transferring heat from one substance to another. *Boilers and Pressure Vessels Act*, R.R.O. 1980, Reg. 84, s. 1.

HEATING PLANT. 1. A steam plant used to generate steam for heating purposes. *Operating Engineers and Firemen Act*, R.S.M. 1970, c. O50, s. 2. 2. (i) Any one or more boilers in which steam or other vapour may be generated at a pressure not exceeding 103 (or 100) kilopascals and a temperature not exceeding 121 degrees Celsius, or (ii) any one or more boilers in which water or other liquid may be heated to a pressure not exceeding 1100 kilopascals and a temperature not exceeding 121 degrees Celsius at or near the outlet of the boiler, or (iii) any system or arrangement of boilers referred to in sub-clause (i) or (ii), and the engines, turbines, pressure vessels, pressure piping system, machinery or ancillary equipment of any kind used in connection therewith. See HIGH PRESSURE ~; LOW PRESSURE ~; TEMPORARY ~.

HEATING SURFACE. 1. The area of a boiler or pressure vessel that transfers heat. 2. Any part of the surface of a fired pressure vessel that is in contact with the fluid under pressure on one side and the products of combustion on the other side. *Boilers and Pressure Vessels acts*.

HEAT PUMP. A machine whose principal use is extracting heat from an area outside the building to heat that building.

HEAT RECOVERY UNIT OR DEVICE. A machine which extracts heat from water, air or gases that are not intended to be reused or recycled in any manufacturing or production process, or otherwise.

HEAT SOURCE. The flame or gases produced during the combustion process of any liquid, solid or gaseous fuel, but does not include the heat source of an electric boiler, which is the electrical energy consumed by the heating elements. *Power Engineers Act*, S.P.E.I. 1977, c. 29, s. 1.

HEAT TREATMENT. Either annealing or normalizing as described in Schedule II. *Tackle Regulations*, C.R.C., c. 1494, s. 2.

HEAVIER-THAN-AIR AIRCRAFT. Any aircraft deriving its lift from aerodynamic forces. *Air Regulations*, C.R.C., c. 2, s. 101.

HEAVY CONSTRUCTION EMPLOYEES. (i) Employees employed in the construction industry as operators of heavy construction equipment, and (ii) employees employed in the construction industry to do work that is necessarily incidental to work done by heavy construction equipment and who are not within the building construction trades. *Construction Industry Wages Act*, R.S.M. 1970, c. C190, s. 2.

HEAVY CRUDE OIL. A naturally occurring viscous mixture that consists mainly of hydrocarbons heavier than pentane, that may contain sulphur compounds and that in its naturally occurring state has a density of more than 900 kilograms per cubic metre. Alberta statutes.

HEAVY DIESEL OIL. Diesel oil, other than those distillates of which more than 50 per cent by volume distills at a temperature not exceeding 340°C when tested by the American Society for Testing and Materials, Standard Method D.86/59. *Oil Pollution Prevention Regulations*, C.R.C., c. 1454, s. 2.

HEAVY DUTY EQUIPMENT. Any mobile equipment and attachments thereto, used for building construction, engineering construction, logging, mining and farming operations. *Apprenticeship and Tradesmen's Qualification Act*, R.R.O. 1980, Reg. 42, s. 1.

HEAVY DUTY VEHICLE. (a) A bus, (b) a chassis-cab, (c) a multipurpose passenger vehicle, or (d) a truck having a gross vehicle weight rating of more than 6,000 pounds (2 721.6 kg) but does not include a passenger car. *Motor Vehicle Safety Regulations*, C.R.C., c. 1038, s. 2.

HEAVY HAULER TRAILER. A trailer that has (a) brake lines designed to adapt to separation or extension of the vehicle frame, or (b) a body that consists of only a platform the primary cargo-carrying surface of which is not more than 101.6 cm (40 inches) above the ground in an unloaded condition, but may include sides that are designed for easy removal and a permanent front end structure. *Motor Vehicle Safety Regulations*, C.R.C., c. 1038, s. 2.

HEAVY-LIFT CHARGE. A charge on goods for crane service consisting of a single, direct vertical lift. Canada regulations.

HEAVY PACK. A pack in which a minimum amount of water required for proper processing is used as the packing media. *Processed Fruit and Vegetable Regulations*, C.R.C., c. 291, s. 2.

HEAVY TIMBER CONSTRUCTION. 1. That type of combustible construction in which a degree of fire safety is attained by placing limitations on the sizes of wood structural members and on thickness and composition of wood floors and roofs, by avoidance of concealed spaces under floors and roofs and by use of required fastenings, construction details and adhesives for structural members. *Building Code Act*, R.R.O. 1980, Reg. 87, s. 1. 2. An approved type of wood construction in which a degree of fire endurance is attained by placing limitations on the minimum sizes of wood structural assemblies. *Hotel Fire Safety Act*, R.R.O. 1980, Reg. 505, s. 2.

HEAVY TURKEY. A turkey that is more than 103 days old and less than 161 days old. *Canadian Turkey Marketing Quota Regulations*, C.R.C., c. 661, s. 2.

HEAVY VEHICLE. A vehicle that has a gross weight exceeding 5000 kilograms, or a vehicle or combination of vehicles that transmits to the highway a weight in excess of 5000 kilograms. *St. Lawrence Parks Commission Act*, R.R.O. 1980, Reg. 909, s. 11.

HECTARAGE. See TOBACCO ~.

HECTARE. *n.* A metric measure of area equivalent to 100 ares or 10,000 square metres (approximately equal to 2.471 acres).

HECTO. *pref.* 10^2. Prefix for multiples and submultiples of basic, supplementary and derived units of measurement. *Weights and Measures Act*, S.C. 1970-71-72, c. 36, schedule I.

HEDGER. *n.* A person who carries on agricultural, mining, forestry, processing, manufacturing or other commercial activities and, as a necessary part of those activities, becomes exposed to a risk attendant on fluctuations in the price of a commodity and offsets that risk through trading in commodity contracts for the commodity or related commodities whether or not a particular trade is effected for that purpose, but the person is a hedger only with respect to these trades.

HEDGING. *n.* The fixing of a price for a mineral

commodity before delivery by means of a forward sale or a futures contract on a recognized commodity exchange, or the purchase or sale forward of a foreign currency related directly to the proceeds of the sale of the processed product of the mineral output, but does not include speculative currency hedging except to the extent that any one of these transactions determine the final price and proceeds for the product.

HEIGHT. *n.* 1. With reference to a building, the vertical distance of a building measured from the average level of the grade along the front of the building to (a) the parapet, in the case of a flat roof, (b) the deck line, in the case of a mansard roof, or (c) the mean height level between eaves and ridge, in the case of a gable, hip or gambrel roof. Canada regulations. 2. Of a letter, means the height of an upper case letter where words appear in upper case and the height of the lower case letter "o" when words appear in lower case or in a mixture of upper and lower case. Canada regulations. See BUILDING ~; STUMP ~.

HEIGHT ABOVE THE HULL. Height above the uppermost continuous deck. *Collision Regulations*, C.R.C., c. 1416, Annex I, s. 1.

HEIGHT OF SUPERSTRUCTURE. The least vertical height measured at the side from the top of the superstructure deck beams to the top of the freeboard deck beams. *Load Line Regulations (Inland)*, C.R.C., c. 1440, s. 1.

HEIR. *n.* Includes a person beneficially entitled to property of an intestate. See EXPECTANT ~; JOINT ~; LAST ~; PRESUMPTIVE ~; ULTIMATE ~.

HEIR APPARENT. One whose right of inheritance is indisputable provided the ancestor dies first; the eldest son of the sovereign.

HEIRDOM. *n.* Succession through inheritance.

HEIRESS. *n.* A female heir.

HEIRLOOM. *n.* Originally personal chattels like evidences of title, deeds and charters which went to an heir along with the inheritance.

HEIR PRESUMPTIVE. A person likely to be heir if the ancestor dies immediately but who could be displaced if a nearer heir is born.

HEIRSHIP. *n.* The condition or quality of being an heir; the relation between an heir and an ancestor.

HEIRS, NEXT OF KIN OR ESTATE. *var.* **HEIRS, NEXT-OF-KIN OR ESTATE.** Or the use of words of like import in a designation, shall be deemed to be a designation of a personal representative. Insurance acts.

HELD. *adj.* Decided.

HELICOPTER. *n.* A heavier-than-air aircraft supported in flight by the reactions of the air on one or more power-driven rotors on substantially vertical axes. *Air Regulations*, C.R.C., c. 2, s. 101.

HELIUM. *n.* In addition to its normal scientific meaning, a mixture mainly of helium which ordinarily may contain some nitrogen and methane.

HELPER. *n.* 1. A person, other than an apprentice, who is employed to assist the holder of a licence to do electrical work, but does not include a person who does unskilled labouring work only. *Electricians' Licence Act*, R.S.M. 1970, c. E50, s. 2. 2. A person who was employed and paid by Canadian Legion War Services Inc., The National Council of the Young Men's Christian Association of Canada, Knights of Columbus Canadian Army Huts or Salvation Army Canadian War Services to assist supervisors and who proceeded from Canada for attachment to (a) the Canadian naval forces under the authority of the Chief of Naval Personnel, (b) active units and formations of the Canadian army forces under the authority of the Adjutant-General, or (c) active units and formations of the Canadian air forces under the authority of the Air Member for Personnel. *Civilian War Pensions and Allowances Act*, R.S.C. 1985, c. C-31, s. 16. See MINER'S ~.

HEMATOCRIT. *n.* The volume of blood cells. F.A. Jaffe, *A Guide to Pathological Evidence*, 2d ed. (Toronto: Carswell, 1983) at 84.

HEMISPHERE. See WESTERN ~.

HEMOCONCENTRATION. *n.* The concentration of blood. F.A. Jaffe, *A Guide to Pathological Evidence*, 2d ed. (Toronto: Carswell, 1983) at 80 and 81.

HEMODILUTION. *n.* Blood thinning. F.A. Jaffe, *A Guide to Pathological Evidence*, 2d ed. (Toronto: Carswell, 1983) at 80.

HEMOLYSIS. *n.* Red blood cell breakdown. F.A. Jaffe, *A Guide to Pathological Evidence*, 2d ed. (Toronto: Carswell, 1983) at 80.

HEMOPERITONEUM. *n.* Free blood being present in the abdominal cavity. F.A. Jaffe, *A Guide to Pathological Evidence*, 2d ed. (Toronto: Carswell, 1983) at 178.

HEMORRHAGE. *n.* Blood escaping from a blood vessel. F.A. Jaffe, *A Guide to Pathological Evidence*, 2d ed. (Toronto: Carswell, 1983) at 178. See EPIDURAL ~; EXTRADURAL ~; INTRACEREBRAL ~; PETECHIAL ~; SUBARACHNOID ~; SUBDURAL ~.

HEMOSIDERIN. *n.* Healing; a reaction of white blood cells. F.A. Jaffe, *A Guide to Pathological Evidence,* 2d ed. (Toronto: Carswell, 1983) at 40.

HEMOTHORAX. *n.* Free blood being present in the chest cavity. F.A. Jaffe, *A Guide to Pathological Evidence,* 2d ed. (Toronto: Carswell, 1983) at 178.

HEN. *n.* The hen of any class of the domestic chicken belonging to the species Gallus Domesticus. Canada regulations. See DOMESTIC ~.

HENCHMAN. *n.* Originally an attendant, a page.

HENRY. *n.* The inductance of a closed circuit in which an electromotive force of one volt is produced when the electric current in the circuit varies uniformly at a rate of one ampere per second. *Weights and Measures Act,* S.C. 1970-71-72, c. 36, schedule I.

H.E.P.C. *abbr.* Hydro-Electric Power Commission.

HERALD. *n.* An English official who registers genealogies or adjusts coats of arms.

HERALDRY. *n.* The knowledge or field of study of a herald.

HERALDS' COLLEGE. The British College of Arms which grants coats of arms.

HERBICIDE. *n.* Any substance or mixture of substances used for the destruction or control of vegetation. See HORMONE TYPE ~; SELECTIVE ~.

HERO. See TUBERCULOSIS-ACCREDITED ~.

HERD OF ORIGIN. The flock or herd of which an animal was a member, where the animal was a member of that flock or herd for not less than 60 days immediately preceding its importation into Canada and in any other case means the flock or herd in which it was born. *Animal Disease and Protection Regulations,* C.R.C., c. 296, s. 2.

HEREAFTER. *adv.* Referring to the time after the commencement of the enactment containing that word. *Interpretation Act,* S.P.E.I. 1981, c. 18, s. 26. See NOW, NEXT, HERETOFORE AND ~.

HEREDITAMENT. *n.* Any kind of property which may be inherited. See CORPOREAL ~; INCORPOREAL ~; LANDS, TENEMENTS AND ~S.

HEREIN. *adv.* 1. Used in any section shall be understood to relate to the whole enactment, and not to that section only. *Interpretation Act,* R.S.C. 1985, c. I-21, s. 35. 2. Used in a section or part of an enactment, shall be construed as referring to the whole enactment and not to that section, provision or part only.

HEREOF. *adv.* Used in any section shall relate to the whole enactment and not only that section. *Interpretation Act,* R.S.N.B. 1973, c. I-13, s. 38.

HERETOFORE. See NOW, NEXT, ~ AND HEREAFTER.

HERITAGE. *adj.* Of historic, architectural, archaeological, palaeontological or scenic significance to the Province or a municipality, as the case may be. *Heritage Conservation Act,* R.S.B.C. 1979, c. 165, s. 1.

HERITAGE OBJECT. 1. An archaeological object, a palaeontological object, a natural heritage object, and an object designated as a heritage object. 2. Personal property of heritage significance. See NATURAL ~.

HERITAGE PROPERTY. Property, whether a work of nature or of man, that is primarily of interest for its archaeological, historical, cultural, scientific or aesthetic value, and includes, but is not limited to, a site where archaeological, historical, cultural or scientific property is found. *The Saskatchewan Heritage Act,* R.S.S. 1978, c. S-22, s. 2. See MUNICIPAL ~; PROVINCIAL ~.

HERITAGE RESOURCE. Includes (i) a heritage site, (ii) a heritage object, and (iii) any work or assembly of works of nature or of human endeavour that is of value for its archaeological, palaeontological, pre-historic, historic, cultural, natural, scientific or aesthetic features, and may be in the form of sites or objects or a combination thereof. *The Heritage Resources Act,* S.M. 1985-86, c. 10, s. 1.

HERITAGE RESOURCE IMPACT ASSESSMENT. A written assessment showing the impact that proposed work, activity or development or a proposed project, as described in section 12, is likely to have upon heritage resources or human remains. *The Heritage Resources Act,* S.M. 1985-86, c. 10, s. 1.

HERITAGE SITE. 1. Whether designated or not, land, including land covered by water, of heritage significance. *Heritage Conservation Act,* R.S.B.C. 1979, c. 165, s. 1. 2. A site designated as a heritage site.

HER MAJESTY. 1. Her Majesty in right of Canada or of a province. 2. The Sovereign of the United Kingdom, Canada and Her other Realms and Territories, and Head of the Commonwealth. See GOVERNMENT OR ~; OFFICE UNDER ~; SHIPS BELONGING TO ~; SUBJECT OF ~.

HER MAJESTY'S CANADIAN SHIP. Any

vessel of the Canadian Forces commissioned as a vessel of war. *National Defence Act*, R.S.C. 1985, c. N-5, s. 2.

HER MAJESTY'S DOMINIONS. The Commonwealth. *Interpretation Act*, R.S.M. 1970, c. I80, s. 23.

HER MAJESTY'S FORCES. The naval, army and air forces of Her Majesty wherever raised, and includes the Canadian Forces.

HER MAJESTY'S REALMS AND TERRITORIES. 1. All realms and territories under the sovereignty of Her Majesty. *Interpretation Act*, R.S.C. 1985, c. I-21, s. 35. 2. Any territories under Her Majesty's protection to which an order in council made under section 28 of the Copyright Act, 1911, passed by the Parliament of the United Kingdom, relates. *Copyright Act*, R.S.C. 1985, c. C-42, s. 2.

HERMENEUTICS. *n.* The art of construction and interpretation.

HERMETICALLY SEALED. In respect of a container, that it is so constructed and secured that it is for practical purposes airtight and will maintain its airtightness under all usual conditions. *Dangerous Goods Shipping Regulations*, C.R.C., c. 1419, s. 2.

HEROIN. *n.* Diacetyl morphine, a partly-synthetic narcotic illegally sold as a white powder, usually injected intravenously or subcutaneously but may be snuffed or smoked. F.A. Jaffe, *A Guide to Pathological Evidence*, 2d ed. (Toronto: Carswell, 1983) at 178.

HERRING. *n.* Fish of the species Clupea harengus or Clupea pallasii.

HERRING CANNERY. A building, structure, machinery, appurtenances, appliances and apparatus occupied and used in the business of herring canning, or of converting the natural herring into canned herring. *Fisheries Act*, R.S.B.C. 1979, c. 137, s. 12.

HERRING DRY SALTERY. A building, structure, machinery, appurtenances, appliances and apparatus occupied and used in the business of dry salting herring, or of converting the natural herring into dry salted herring, where the herring are not kept or shipped in a brine solution after being processed. *Fisheries Act*, R.S.B.C. 1979, c. 137, s. 12.

HERRING FISHING VESSEL. Any ship or other description of vessel used in or equipped for the commercial fishing, transporting or processing of herring and includes pumpers and carriers. *Atlantic Coast Herring Regulations*, C.R.C., c. 804, s. 2.

HERRING REDUCTION PLANT. A building,

structure, machinery, appurtenances, appliances and apparatus occupied and used in the business of producing oil, fish meal, fish scrap, chicken feed or fertilizer from herring. *Fisheries Act*, R.S.B.C. 1979, c. 137, s. 12.

HERRING WEIR. A fixed trap net consisting of one or more compartments each of which is constructed of stakes attached to the soil, held together with one or more sets of ribbands and surrounded by brush, twine or wire netting, into which fish are guided by one or more fixed leaders. Canada regulations.

HERTZ. *n.* The frequency of a periodic phenomenon of which the periodic time is one second. *Weights and Measures Act*, S.C. 1970-71-72, c. 36, schedule I.

HESITATION WOUND. Stabs or cuts which are tentative and made by a suicide before inflicting the deadly wound on himself or herself. F.A. Jaffe, *A Guide to Pathological Evidence*, 2d ed. (Toronto: Carswell, 1983) at 187.

HIDE. *n.* The untanned skin of livestock. *Livestock Brand Act*, S.B.C. 1980, c. 25, s. 1. See GREEN ~; RAW ~.

HIERARCHY. *n.* A body of persons organized according to authority, position or rank.

HIGH HAZARD FIREWORKS. Those Division 2 fireworks that, in the opinion of the Chief Inspector, present a special hazard to persons. *Explosives Regulations*, C.R.C., c. 599, s. 14.

HIGH LEVEL AIRSPACE. All airspace that is within the Canadian domestic airspace at or above 18,000 feet above mean sea level. *Radar Transponder Order*, C.R.C., c. 60, s. 2.

HIGHNESS. *n.* A title authorized by British letters patent of December 11, 1917 to apply to the children of any sovereign, the children of the sovereign's sons, and the eldest living son of the eldest son of any Prince of Wales. The Duke of Edinburgh may also be called Royal Highness.

HIGH OCCUPANT LOAD. An occupant load where the number of persons in a room or floor area is such that the area of floor per person is not more than 12 sq. ft. *Building Code Act*, R.R.O. 1980, Reg. 87, s. 1.

HIGH PRESSURE BOILER. 1. A boiler designed to carry and to operate at a working pressure of more than fifteen pounds. 2. A boiler designed to carry a working pressure of more than one hundred kilopascals but does not include such boiler if it is equipped with a safety valve that is set to relieve at not more than one hundred kilopascals. *The Boiler and Pressure Vessel Act*, R.S.S. 1978, c. B-5, s. 2.

HIGH PRESSURE HEATING PLANT. A boiler or two or more boilers on the same premises having a safety valve setting of more than fifteen pounds per square inch (one hundred and three kilopascals) when the boiler is used for producing steam, or a safety valve setting of more than one hundred and sixty pounds per square inch (one thousand one hundred kilopascals) when the boiler is used for producing hot water or when the temperature of the hot water produced is in excess of two hundred and fifty degrees Fahrenheit (one hundred and twenty degrees Celsius).

HIGH-RISE HOTEL. A hotel six or more storeys in height. *Hotel Fire Safety Act*, R.R.O. 1980, Reg. 505, s. 2.

HIGH SCHOOL. 1. One or more rooms or departments maintained exclusively for pupils above grade eight. *The School Act*, R.S.S. 1978, c. S-36, s. 2. 2. Includes collegiate institute. *The Secondary Education Act*, R.S.S. 1978, c. S-41, s. 2.

HIGH SEAS. The area of the ocean beyond territorial waters.

HIGH TREASON. Anyone commits high treason in Canada who kills or attempts to kill Her Majesty, or does her any bodily harm tending to death or destruction, maims or wounds her or imprisons or restrains her; levies war against Canada or does any act preparatory thereto; or assists an enemy at war with Canada, or any armed forces against whom Canadian Forces are engaged in hostilities whether or not a state of war exists between Canada and the country whose forces they are, and a Canadian citizen or person who owes allegiance to Her Majesty in right of Canada commits high treason who does any of these acts while in or out of Canada. *Criminal Code*, R.S.C. 1985, c. C-46, s. 46(1) and 3.

HIGH VOLTAGE. A voltage of 751 volts or more between any two conductors or between any conductor and ground. *Canada Electrical Safety Regulations*, C.R.C., c. 998, s. 2.

HIGH WATER MARK. See NORMAL ~.

HIGHWAY. *n.* 1. A public road, street, lane or other public way or communication. 2. A road to which the public has the right of access, and includes bridges over which or tunnels through which a road passes. *Criminal Code*, R.S.C. 1985, c. C-46, s. 2. 3. Includes a common and public highway, street, avenue, parkway, driveway, square, place, bridge, viaduct or trestle, any part of which is intended for or used by the general public for the passage of vehicles and includes the area between the lateral property lines thereof. 4. Any thoroughfare, street, road, trail, avenue, parkway, driveway, viaduct, lane, alley, square, bridge, causeway, trestleway or other place, whether publicly or privately owned, any part of which the public is ordinarily entitled or permitted to use for the passage or parking of vehicles, and includes a sidewalk (including the boulevard portion of the sidewalk), if a ditch lies adjacent to and parallel with the roadway, the ditch, and if a highway right of way is contained between fences or between a fence and one side of the roadway, all the land between the fences, or all the land between the fence and the edge of the roadway, as the case may be. 5. The entire width between the boundary lines of every street, road, lane, alley, park, parking lot, drive-in theatre, school yard, picnic site, beach, winter road across ice or place when any part thereof is ordinarily used by the general public for the passage or parking of motor vehicles primarily designed for use on a roadway, and includes the bridges thereon. *All-Terrain Vehicle Act*, S.N.B. 1985, c. A-7.11, s. 1. See ARTERIAL ~; CONTROLLED-ACCESS ~; ~S; LANED ~; LIMITED ACCESS ~; ONE-WAY ~; PROVINCIAL ~; PUBLIC ~; THROUGH ~.

HIGHWAY AND ROAD. A common and public highway or any part thereof, and includes a street, bridge, and any other structure incidental thereto or any part thereof. Ontario statutes.

HIGHWAY AUTHORITY. 1. The public authority having legal jurisdiction to open and maintain for the public highways in the area under its jurisdiction. *Highway and Railway Crossing at Grade Regulations*, C.R.C., c. 1184, s. 2. 2. (i) The council of a municipality as to public highways subject to its control and management, (ii) the Minister of Transportation as to public highways subject to his direction, control and management, or (iii) the Minister of Municipal Affairs, as to public highways in a special area that are subject to his direction, control and management. *Hydro and Electric Energy Act*, R.S.A. 1980, c. H-13, s. 1.

HIGHWAY FRONTIER EXAMINING WAREHOUSE. A warehouse for the safekeeping, examination and appraisal by customs of goods carried by commercial motor vehicle for clearance at a frontier port adjacent to the Canada-United States international boundary. *Customs Warehousing Regulations*, C.R.C., c. 462, s. 2.

HIGHWAY MOTOR VEHICLE OPERATOR. A motor vehicle operator who is not a bus operator or a city motor vehicle operator. *Motor Vehicle Operators Hours of Work Regulations*, C.R.C., c. 990, s. 2.

HIGHWAY OR ROAD. 1. (i) Means land used or surveyed for use as a public highway or road, and (ii) includes a bridge forming part of a public highway or road and any structure incidental to the public highway or road or bridge. 2. Includes any highway, road, road allowance, street, lane, or thoroughfare, dedicated to the public use as a highway or opened or made as a highway under this or any other Act of the Legislature, and any bridge, floodway, pier, ferry, square or public place, dedicated to the public use as a highway and any highway improvements or works thereon or appurtenant thereto. *Highway Department Act*, R.S.M. 1970, c. H40, s. 2.

HIGHWAY PROJECT AREA. (a) An area under construction as a highway, or (b) a highway under reconstruction or repair by any government. *Motor Fuel Tax Act*, S.B.C. 1985, c. 76, s. 1.

HIGHWAYS. *n.* Highways, docks, ferries, wharfs, parking lots in connection therewith, land held to provide clear view at road junctions and railroad crossings, and land acquired and held for future highways. *Municipal Tax Assistance Act*, R.S.O. 1980, c. 311, s. 1. See HIGHWAY.

HIJACKING. *n.* Unlawfully, by force or threat thereof, or by any form of intimidation, seizing or exercising control of an aircraft with intent (a) to cause any person on board the aircraft to be confined or imprisoned against his will, (b) to cause any person on board the aircraft to be transported against his will to any place other than the next scheduled place of landing of the aircraft, (c) to hold any person on board the aircraft for ransom or to service against his will, or (d) to cause the aircraft to deviate in a material respect from its flight plan. *Criminal Code*, R.S.C. 1985, c. C-46, s. 76.

HIRE. *n.* 1. A bailment for compensation or a reward; hiring something to use; labour and work, services and care to be bestowed or performed on the thing delivered, or the carriage of goods from one place to another. 2. The fare, toll, gain, fee or rate charged, collected, or intended to be charged or collected, from any person, for the carriage of a person or persons or property by or in a taxicab, and includes remuneration of any kind, paid, promised, or demanded, direct or indirect, as well as personal services or the sharing of any expenses of the operation of, or of work done by or upon, a taxicab. *Taxicab Act*, R.S.M. 1970, c. T10, s. 2. See CRANE ~ CHARGE.

HIRE OR REWARD. Any payment, consideration, gratuity or benefit, directly or indirectly charged, demanded, received or collected by any person for the use of an aircraft. *Aeronautics Act*, R.S.C. 1985 (1st Supp.), c. 33, s. 3.

HIRE-PURCHASE AGREEMENT. An agreement by which the hirer of goods may either terminate the agreement or purchase the goods. I.H. Jacob, ed., *Bullen and Leake and Jacob's Precedents of Pleadings*, 12th ed. (London: Sweet and Maxwell, 1975) at 480. See RETAIL HIRE-PURCHASE.

HIRER. *n.* 1. The person who requests the services of the crane. Canada regulations. 2. Any person receiving a tug service and includes an owner. *Churchill Tug Tariff By-law*, C.R.C., c. 1069, s. 2. 3. The person who requests the services of the derrick. *Hamilton Harbour Floating Derrick Tariff By-law*, C.R.C., c. 896, s. 2.

HIRING. See PREFERENTIAL ~; REFERRAL ~ SYSTEM.

HIRING HALL. An office operated by a union to fill requests for employees. See CENTRAL ~; JOINT ~.

HIS MAJESTY. The Sovereign of the United Kingdom, Canada and His other Realms and Territories, and Head of the Commonwealth.

HIS TESTIBUS. [L. these being witnesses] A phrase which used to be added to deeds.

HISTORICAL OBJECT. An object or specimen of historic significance includes an archaeological object and a palaeontological object. *Historical Objects Protection Act*, S.N.S. 1970, c. 8, s. 1.

HISTORIC DISTRICT. 1. A group or collection of buildings and their environs, in urban or rural areas, that are considered by the Minister to be of historic or architectural significance and designated to be an historic district by the Minister. *Historic Sites Protection Act*, S.N.B. 1976, c. 30, s. 1. 2. A territory, a municipality or part of a municipality designated as such by the Gouvernement because of the concentration of historic monuments or sites found there. *Cultural Property Act*, R.S.Q. 1977, c. B-4, s. 1.

HISTORIC MONUMENT. An immoveable which has historic interest because of its use or architecture. *Cultural Property Act*, R.S.Q. 1977, c. B-4, s. 1.

HISTORIC OBJECT. Any object of historical significance to or connected with archaeology.

HISTORIC PLACE. A site, building or other place of national historic interest or significance, and includes buildings or structures that are of national interest by reason of age or architectural design. *Historic Sites and Monuments Act*, R.S.C. 1985, c. H-4, s. 2.

HISTORIC PROPERTY. 1. Any manuscript, printed item, audio-visual document or man-made object whose conservation is of historic interest, excluding an immoveable. *Cultural Property Act*, R.S.Q. 1977, c. B-4, s. 1. 2. Any real property or structure which has historic or architectural interest because of its use and architecture and includes a place where events have occurred marking the history of the Province. *Historic Property Designation Act*, S.N.S. 1976, c. 11, s. 2.

HISTORIC RESOURCE. Any work of nature or of man that is primarily of value for its palaeontological, archaeological, prehistoric, historic, cultural, natural, scientific or aesthetic interest including, but not limited to, a palaeontological, archaeological, prehistoric, historic or natural site, structure or object. *Historical Resources Act*, R.S.A. 1980, c. H-8, s. 1.

HISTORIC SITE. Any building, structure, object or area that is significant in the history or culture of a province.

HISTORIC VEHICLE. A motor vehicle, (i) that is at least thirty years old, (ii) that is operated on a highway for the purpose of exhibition, tours or similar functions organized by a properly constituted automobile club, or for purposes of parades, repair, testing or demonstrations for sale, and (iii) that is substantially unchanged or unmodified from the original manufacturer's product. Ontario regulations.

HISTORY. See LEGISLATIVE ~.

HITCH. See TRAILER ~.

HIT AND RUN. Failing to remain at the scene of a motor vehicle accident.

HIVE. *n.* 1. Any cavity in which bees have constructed honeycomb. *Apiaries Amendment Act, 1979*, S.S. 1979, c. 1, s. 3. 2. Beehive equipment inhabited by live bees. *Bee Act*, R.S.B.C. 1979, c. 27, s. 1.

H.L. *abbr.* House of Lords.

H.O. *abbr.* Hearing Officer, Trade Marks.

HOARD. *v.* To acquire and keep goods not reasonably necessary to the person.

HOARDING. *n.* Fence set up around construction site.

HODG. *abbr.* Hodgins, Elections (Ont.), 1871-1879.

HODGES'S CASE. See RULE IN ~.

HOG. *n.* Any member of the species Sus Scrofa L. (domestic pig). Canada regulations. See OWNER OF ~S; SHIPPER OF ~S; SLAUGHTER ~.

HOIST. *n.* A drum or friction hoist used for transporting persons or materials in an underground mine. See AUTOMATIC ~; CON-STRUCTION ~; DRUM ~; FRICTION ~; SIX MONTHS' ~.

HOISTING PLANT. A hoist equipped with, (i) a drum and a hoisting rope or chain, or (ii) a hydraulic pump, that is driven by a prime mover or movers other than steam and that is used for raising, lowering or swinging material. See MINE ~; STEAM ~.

HOISTING ROPE. A steel wire rope manufactured in accordance with the most recent standard of the Canadian Standards Association for steel wire rope for mine hoisting and haulage purposes or any equivalent standard acceptable to the chief inspector. *Mining Regulation Act*, R.S.B.C. 1979, c. 265, s. 140.

HOIST OPERATOR. A stationary engineer who is designated by a mine manager to operate a hoist for the raising or lowering of persons or material in a mine. *Coal Mines (CBDC) Safety Regulations*, C.R.C., c. 1011, s. 2.

HOISTWAY. *n.* A shaftway, hatchway, well hole, or other vertical opening or space in which an elevator, escalator or dumb-waiter operates or is intended to operate.

HOISTWAY ENCLOSURE. Any structure which separates the hoistway, either wholly or in part, from the floors or landings through which the hoistway extends.

HOLD. *v.* Of a judge, to pronounce a legal opinion. See TO HAVE AND TO ~.

HOLD. *n.* 1. Any space within the main hull of a ship that is not part of the machinery space or a peak compartment. *Steamship Machinery Construction Regulations*, C.R.C., c. 1491, Schedule IX, s. 1. 2. A space contained between two permanent bulkheads. *Dangerous Goods Shipping Regulations*, C.R.C., c. 1419, s. 16. 3. A compartment below the deck of a ship suitable for the stowage of cargo. *Destructive Pests Inspection Fees Regulations*, C.R.C., c. 696, s. 2.

HOLDBACK. *var.* **HOLD BACK.** Amount required under a builders or construction lien act to be deducted from payments made under a contract or a sub-contract and retained for a period prescribed.

HOLD BACK ACCOUNT. An interest bearing account in a bank, trust company or credit union in the joint names of the owner and the contractor. *The Builders' Liens Act*, S.M. 1980-81, c. 7, s. 1.

HOLDBACK PAY. Wages withheld by the employer; the amount earned between the end of a pay period and pay day.

HOLDER. *n.* 1. A person in possession of a security issued or endorsed to that person, to bearer or in blank. 2. The payee or endorsee of a bill or note who is in possession of it, or the bearer thereof. *Bills of Exchange Act*, R.S.C. 1985, c. B-4, s. 2. 3. As applied to a negotiable receipt, means a person who has possession of the receipt and a right of property therein, and, as applied to a non-negotiable receipt, means a person named therein as the person to whom the goods are to be delivered or that person's transferee. *Warehouse Receipts acts*. 4. When used in relation to a permit, means the person in whose name the plate portion of a permit is issued. *Highway Traffic acts*. 5. A person or corporation deriving title from a mineral claim. 6. In relation to any document that entitles the person to whom it is delivered to the payment of money or the delivery of grain, means the person who, from time to time, is so entitled by virtue of (a) the issue or endorsement to him of the document, or (b) the delivery to him of the document after it has been endorsed in blank. *Canada Grain Act*, R.S.C. 1985, c. G-10, s. 2. 7. The person to whom a credit card is issued. *Consumer Protection acts*. 8. In respect of an interest or a share therein, the person indicated, in the register maintained pursuant to Part VIII, as the holder of the interest or the share. *Canada Petroleum Resources Act*, R.S.C. 1985 (2d Supp.), c. 36, s. 2. 9. In relation to any Canada lands, the registered holder of an interest or share in an interest in respect of those Canada lands including, where applicable, Her Majesty in right of Canada holding through the appropriate Minister or a designated Crown corporation. *Oil and Gas Act*, R.S.C. 1985, c. O-6, s. 2. 10. In relation to any Nova Scotia Lands, the registered holder of an interest or share in an interest in respect of those Nova Scotia Lands including, where applicable, Her Majesty holding through the appropriate minister or a designated Crown corporation. *Offshore Oil and Gas Act*, S.N.S. 1984, c. 8, s. 2. See CO-~; CONTRACT ~; INTEREST ~; LAMP ~; LAND~; LIEN~; LIMIT ~; PERMIT ~; PLAN ~; QUOTA ~; SECURITY ~; SURFACE ~.

HOLDER FOR VALUE. Someone who gives valuable consideration for a bill, who has a lien on it, or who claims through another holder for value. E.L.G. Tyler & N.E. Palmer, eds., *Crossley Vaines' Personal Property*, 5th ed. (London: Butterworths, 1973) at 232.

HOLDER IN DUE COURSE. A holder who takes a bill of exchange seemingly complete and regular, on condition (a) that the transfer is made before the bill is overdue, and without notice that it had been dishonoured previously if it was, and (b) that the bill, cheque or note is accepted for value and in good faith, and that at the time of the arrangement no notice of any defect in the title of the person giving the bill is offered.

HOLDER IN THE PROVINCE. In respect of an issuer, a holder of securities of the issuer whose last address as shown in the books of the issuer is in the province.

HOLDER OF A DRILLING RESERVATION. A person in whose name a drilling reservation is recorded in the records of the branch. *Petroleum or Natural Gas Act*, R.S.B.C. 1979, c. 323, s. 1.

HOLDER OF A LOCATION. A permittee, licensee, lessee or holder of a drilling reservation.

HOLDFAST. *n.* That portion of a marine plant by which it is attached to the ocean floor. *Atlantic Coast Marine Plant Regulations*, C.R.C., c. 805, s. 2.

HOLD HARMLESS. To assume liability in a situation and relieve the other party of responsibility.

HOLDING. *n.* Land rented to a tenant. See LAND ~; MAXIMUM AGGREGATE ~S; MAXIMUM INDIVIDUAL ~S.

HOLDING COMPANY. 1. A company the primary purpose of which is owning shares of one or more other companies. 2. A company is the holding company of another if, but only if, the other is its subsidiary. *Companies acts*. See INVESTMENT ~.

HOLDING CORPORATION. Includes any corporation as hereinbefore defined which is formed for the purpose of acquiring and holding all the shares or a controlling interest therein of other companies, and which actually does acquire or hold all such shares or a controlling interest therein, and which does not otherwise engage in any trade or business. *Corporations Registration Act*, R.S.N.S. 1967, c. 59, s. 28. See PRIVATE.

HOLDING TANK. A tank used for the collection and storage of sewage for eventual disposal. *Great Lakes Sewage Pollution Prevention Regulations*, C.R.C., c. 1429, s. 2.

HOLDING TRUST. The trustee retains assets until required under an independent agreement to transfer the assets to specific persons. D.M.W. Waters, *The Law of Trusts in Canada*, 2d ed. (Toronto: Carswell, 1984) at p. 101.

HOLD-OPEN DEVICE. An electrically actuated hold-open device listed by Underwriters' Laboratories of Canada or some other approved testing laboratory, that automatically closes a fire-door or smoke-door on activation of the fire-alarm signal or on power failure. *Hotel Fire Safety Act*, R.R.O. 1980, Reg. 505, s. 2.

HOLD OVER. For a lessee to keep possession of land after the lease has expired.

HOLE. See SHOT ~; TEST ~.

HOLIDAY. *n.* Any of the following days, namely, Sunday; New Year's Day; Good Friday, Easter Monday; Christmas Day; the birthday or the day fixed by proclamation for the celebration of the birthday of the reigning Sovereign; Victoria Day; Canada Day; the first Monday in September, designated Labour Day; Remembrance Day; any day appointed by proclamation to be observed as a day of general prayer or mourning or day of public rejoicing or thanksgiving; and any of the following additional days, namely, (a) in any province, any day appointed by proclamation of the lieutenant governor of the province to be observed as a public holiday or as a day of general prayer or mourning or day of public rejoicing or thanksgiving within the province, and any day that is a non-juridical day by virtue of an Act of the legislature of the province, and (b) in any city, town, municipality or other organized district, any day appointed to be observed as a civic holiday by resolution of the council or other authority charged with the administration of the civic or municipal affairs of the city, town, municipality or district. *Interpretation Act*, R.S.C. 1985, c. I-21, s. 35. See CIVIC ~; GENERAL ~; PUBLIC ~; SPECIAL ~.

HOLOGRAPH. *n.* A deed or writing written completely by the grantor.

HOLOGRAPH WILL. A will written entirely in the testator's own hand.

HOME. *n.* 1. A private dwelling occupied by persons who live as a household. 2. A home for the use of senior citizens. 3. (i) A self-contained one-family dwelling, detached or attached to one or more others by a common wall, (ii) a building composed of two self-contained, one-family dwellings under one ownership, or (iii) a condominium one-family dwelling unit, including the common interests appurtenant thereto. 4. A farm, ranch or other land on which a dwelling house is situated. *Names of Homes acts.* 5. A house, multiple-family dwelling or housing project or a building consisting of business premises and family housing units, where the repairs, alterations and additions may be fairly considered to be primarily for the benefit of the housing units, but does not include a building used as a hotel or summer residence or a building used for seasonal occupancy. *National Housing Loan Regulations*, C.R.C., c. 1108, s. 78. See APPROVED ~; BOARDING ~; DAY CARE ~; DETENTION ~; FACTORY-BUILT ~; FAMILY ~; FOSTER ~; FUNERAL ~; GROUP ~; JOINT ~; MANUFACTURED ~; MARITAL ~; MATERNITY ~; MATRIMONIAL ~; MOBILE ~; MODULAR ~; MOTOR ~; NURSING ~; OWNER-OCCUPIED ~; PERSONAL CARE ~; PERSON AT ~; PRIVATE-SERVICE ~; RECEIVING ~; SPECIAL CARE ~; TEMPORARY ~.

HOME BUYER. A person who buys the interest of an owner in a premises that is a home, whether built or not at the time of the agreement of purchase and sale in respect thereof is entered into, provided, (i) not more than 30 per cent of the purchase price, excluding money held in trust under section 53 of the Condominium Act, is paid prior to the conveyance, and (ii) the home is not conveyed until it is ready for occupancy, evidenced in the case of a new home by the issuance of a municipal permit authorizing occupancy or the issuance under the Ontario New Home Warranties Plan Act of a certificate of completion and possession. *Construction Lien Act, 1983*, S.O. 1983, c. 77, s. 1.

HOME CARE SERVICES. Services provided to any person who, because of illness or disability, requires care and support while living in the community and, without limiting the generality of the foregoing, includes: (i) assessment services and care co-ordination services; (ii) nursing services; (iii) home-making services; (iv) meal services; (v) home maintenance services.

HOME DAY CARE. Day care provided on a regular basis, for a consideration, by a natural person to up to four children, including that person's children, in a private residence, or, if he is assisted by an adult, to up to nine children, including the children of these two persons, in that private residence for periods which may exceed 24 consecutive hours. *An Act respecting child day care*, S.Q. 1979, c. 85, s. 1.

HOME DAY CARE AGENCY. A body authorized to coordinate all the home day care provided by persons it has recognized as persons responsible for home day care. *An Act respecting child day care*, S.Q. 1979, c. 85, s. 1.

HOME EXTENSION LOAN. A loan or a purchase of obligations representing loans or advances of money made before July 1, 1956 by a bank or approved instalment credit agency for the purpose of financing the alteration of, or the making of additions to, an existing home to add one or more family housing units thereto, but does not include a farm improvement loan as defined in the Farm Improvement Loans Act. *National Housing Act*, R.S.C. 1985, c. N-11, s. 45(2).

HOME FOR SPECIAL CARE. 1. A residential welfare institution that is of a kind prescribed for the purposes of this Act as a home for special care and that is listed in a schedule to an agreement under section 4, but does not include a hospital, correctional institution or institution whose primary purpose is education, other than that part of a hospital that is used as a residential welfare institution and that is listed in a schedule to an agreement under section 4. *Canada Assistance Plan*, R.S.C. 1985, c. C-1, s. 2. 2. A home for the care of persons requiring nursing, residential or sheltered care. *Homes for Special Care Act*, R.S.O. 1980, c. 202, s. 1.

HOME HEATING OIL. Includes the refined petroleum products commercially known as kerosene, stove oil, furnace oil, gas oil, distillate heating oil and number one, two and three fuel oils, and any other refined petroleum product declared by the Lieutenant-Governor in Council to be home heating within the meaning of this Act. *Gasoline, Diesel Oil and Home Heating Oil Pricing Act*, S.N.B. 1987, c. G-3.1, s. 1.

HOME IMPROVEMENT LOAN. A loan or a purchase of obligations representing loans or advances of money made by a bank or an approved instalment credit agency for the purpose of financing repairs, alterations and additions to a home but does not include a farm improvement loan as defined in the Farm Improvement Loans Act or a home extension loan as defined in subsection 45(2). *National Housing Act*, R.S.C. 1985, c. N-11, s. 2.

HOME IMPROVEMENTS. Improvements to the home of a farmer situated on a farm and includes (i) water systems, sewage systems, central heating systems, insulation, concrete basements, new floors, new roofs, new siding, painting, interior decorating and remodelling, and (ii) additions to the home when the addition is a bathroom or provides for a bathroom, but does not include household furnishings, electrical appliances or other things not affixed to the home. *Farm Home Improvements Act*, R.S.A. 1980, c. F-3, s. 1.

HOMEMAKER. *n.* 1. A person who performs housekeeping services, including cleaning, other than as a sitter only. *Employment Agencies Act*, R.R.O. 1980, Reg. 280, s. 1. 2. A person who provides homemaker services. *Family and Child Services acts.* 3. A person managing, maintaining and controlling an independent, domestic establishment and who neither: (i) engages in a definite regular occupation for wages or for profit; nor (ii) reports regularly to a place of employment apart from his residence. *Automobile Accident Insurance Amendment Act, 1981*, S.S. 1980-81, c. 34, s. 3. 4. A person approved by the local director or a Director and who remains or is placed on a premises for the purpose of caring for a child. *Child Welfare Act*, R.S.O. 1980, c. 66, s. 23.

HOMEMAKER SERVICES. 1. The tasks normally performed by a mother which have been assumed by a visiting homemaker within a family. *Family and Child Services Act*, S.P.E.I. 1981, c. 12, s. 1. 2. Includes (i) the care of a child or adult, (ii) the purchase and preparation of meals and special diets, (iii) housekeeping duties, exclusive of heavy or seasonal cleaning, (iv) laundry and mending of clothing, (v) simple bedside care under the direction of a physician or visiting nurse, and (vi) training recipients in housekeeping and homemaking skills. *Day Care and Homemaker Services Act*, S. Nfld. 1975, c. 67, s. 2.

HOMEMAKING SERVICES. Housekeeping services including, (i) the care of a child or children, (ii) meal planning, marketing and the preparation of nourishing meals, and the preparation of special diets where required, (iii) light housekeeping duties, exclusive of heavy or seasonal cleaning, (iv) light laundry, ironing and essential mending of clothing, (v) personal care, including assistance in walking, climbing or descending stairs, getting into or out of bed, eating, dressing, bathing and other matters of personal hygiene, (vi) simple bedside care, where required, under the direction of a physician or nurse, but not including nursing services, and (vii) training and instruction in household management and the care of children, provided in accordance with section 6 of the Act by a homemaker qualified under this Regulation. *Homemakers and Nurses Services Act*, R.R.O. 1980, Reg. 499, s. 1.

HOME NE SERRA PUNY PUR SUER DES BRIEFES EN COURT LE ROY, SOIT IL A DROIT OU A TORT. [Fr.] A person should not be punished for commencing an action in a sovereign's court, whether or not that person has a cause of action.

HOME OCCUPATION. An occupation conducted for gain or reward within a dwelling as a secondary use of that dwelling. Canada regulations.

HOME OWNER. The owner of a principal residence that is subject to a mortgage and includes that person's heirs, successors or assigns. Saskatchewan statutes.

HOME-OWNER DUPLEX. A house containing two family housing units (one of which is to be occupied by the owner) built one above the other, with separate entrances. *National Housing Loan Regulations*, C.R.C., c, 1108, s. 2.

HOME-OWNER SEMI-DETACHED HOUSE. A house containing two family housing units (one of which is to be occupied by the owner) built side by side, with separate entrances.

National Housing Loan Regulations, C.R.C., c. 1108, s. 2.

HOME OWNERSHIP SAVINGS PLAN. An arrangement under which payment is made by an individual in trust to a corporation resident in Canada and licensed or otherwise authorized under the laws of Canada or a province to carry on in Canada the business of offering to the public its services as trustee, of any periodic or other amount as a payment under the trust to be used, invested or otherwise applied by the corporation for the purpose of providing to that individual as the beneficiary under the arrangement an amount to be used for the purchase by him of his owner-occupied home. *Income Tax Act*, S.C. 1974-75-76, c. 26, s. 99. See REGISTERED ~.

HOME PURCHASE LOAN. That portion of any loan received or debt otherwise incurred by an individual in the circumstances described in subsection (1) that is used to acquire, or to repay a loan or debt that had been received or incurred to acquire, a dwelling for the habitation of (i) the individual by virtue of whose office or employment the loan is received or the debt is incurred, (ii) a specified shareholder of the corporation by virtue of whose services the loan is received or the debt is incurred, or (iii) a person related to a person described in subparagraph (i) or (ii), or that is used to repay a home purchase loan. *Income Tax Act*, R.S.C. 1952, c. 148 (as am. S.C. 1984, c. 45, s. 25(3)), s. 80.4(7)(a).

HOME RELOCATION LOAN. A loan received by an individual or his spouse in circumstances where he had commenced employment at a location in Canada (in this definition referred to as his "new work location") and by reason thereof has moved from the residence in Canada at which, before the move, he ordinarily resided (in this definition referred to as his "old residence") to a residence in Canada at which, after the move, he ordinarily resided (in this definition referred to as his "new residence") if (a) the distance between his old residence and his new work location is at least 40 kilometres greater than the distance between his new residence and his new work location, (b) the loan is used to acquire a dwelling for the habitation of the individual that is his new residence, (c) the loan is received in the circumstances described in subsection 80.4(1), and (d) the loan is designated by the individual to be a home relocation loan, but in no case shall more than one loan in respect of a particular move, or more than one loan at any particular time, be designated as a home relocation loan by the individual. *Income Tax Act*, R.S.C. 1952, c. 148 (as am. S.C. 1986, c. 6, s. 126(4)), s. 248(1).

HOMES FOR SPECIAL CARE. Nursing homes, hostels for indigent transients, homes for the aged, poor houses, alms houses, and hostel facilities provided for the aged within housing projects constructed under the National Housing Act. *Unemployment Assistance Act*, R.S.C. 1970, c. U-1, s. 4.

HOMESTEAD. *n.* 1. A dwelling occupied by an owner and the owner's spouse. A. Bissett-Johnson & W.M. Holland, eds., *Matrimonial Property Law in Canada* (Toronto: Carswell, 1980) at M-73 and M-74. 2. A parcel of land (i) on which the dwelling house occupied by the owner of the parcel as his residence is situated, and (ii) that consists of (A) not more than 4 adjoining lots in one block in a city, town or village as shown on a plan registered in the proper land titles office, or (B) not more than one quarter section of land other than land in a city, town or village. *Dower Act*, R.S.A. 1980, c. D-38, s. 1. 3. Land, whether leasehold or freehold, together with erections or buildings, with their rights, members and appurtenances, registered as a homestead; and an erection or building on a homestead, whether or not affixed to the soil, shall be taken to be land and part of the homestead. *Homestead Act*, R.S.B.C. 1979, c. 173, s. 1.

HOMESTEAD LAW. Legislation to protect a home against execution creditors. A. Bissett-Johnson & W.M. Holland, eds., *Matrimonial Property Law in Canada* (Toronto: Carswell, 1980) at I-47.

HOMESTEAD LEASE. See CROP SHARE ~.

HOME STUDY COURSE. Any course, text or matter for study offered by any person, whereby such person teaches or undertakes or proposes to teach or prepare students to study a trade or subjects through the use of the mail, express or other common carrier or by private carriers or by any other means of communication. *Trade Schools Regulation Act*, R.S.N.S. 1967, c. 310, s. 1.

HOME TERMINAL. Of a motor vehicle operator means the place of business of a motor carrier to which the operator normally reports for work. *Canada Motor Vehicle Operators Hours of Service Regulations*, C.R.C., c. 1005, s. 2.

HOME-TRADE SHIPS. Ships engaged in home-trade voyages. *Canada Shipping Act*, R.S.C. 1985, c. S-9, s. 2.

HOME-TRADE VOYAGE. A voyage, not being an inland or minor waters voyage, between places within the area following, namely, Canada, the United States other than Hawaii, St. Pierre and Miquelon, the West Indies, Mexico, Central America and the northeast coast of

South America, in the course of which a ship does not go south of the sixth parallel of north latitude. *Canada Shipping Act*, R.S.C. 1985, c. S-9, s. 2.

HOMEWORK. *n.* The doing of any work in the manufacture, preparation, improvement, repair, alteration, assembly or completion of any article or thing or any part thereof in premises occupied primarily as living accommodation.

HOMEWORKER. *n.* 1. A person who for wages, in his home or elsewhere in premises not occupied by his employer, engages in employment in respect of personal or household articles. *Factory Act*, R.S.B.C. 1979, c. 118, s. 32. 2. A person who for wages in the performance of work in his residence provides labour only. *Workplace Act*, S.B.C. 1985, c. 34, s. 5.

HOMICIDE. *n.* Directly or indirectly, by any means, causing the death of a human being. *Criminal Code*, R.S.C. 1985, c. C-46, s. 222(1). See CULPABLE ~; JUSTIFIABLE ~; NON CULPABLE ~.

HOMOGENIZED. *adj.* It has been treated in such a manner as to break up the fat globules to such an extent that after forty-eight hours of storage no visible cream separation occurs in the milk and the fat percentage of the top one hundred millilitres of milk in a quart bottle, or of proportionate volumes in containers of other sizes, does not differ by more than five per cent from the fat percentage of the remaining milk as determined after thorough mixing. *Public Health Act*, R.S.N.S. 1967, c. 247, s. 122.

HOMO POTEST ESSE HABILIS ET INHABILIS DIVERSIS TEMPORIBUS. [L.] A person may be capable and incapable at differing times.

HONEY. See COMB ~.

HONEYCOMB. *n.* A structure of cells used for, or capable of being used by bees for, the storage of honey. *Apiaries Amendment Act, 1979*, S.S. 1979, c. 1, s. 3.

HONEYMOON CONTRACT. An initial contract between an employer and union when the union accepts most or all of the employer's terms.

HONEY SUBSTITUTE. A product other than pure honey manufactured or derived in whole or in part from a farm product and prepared for the same uses as honey and resembling honey in appearance. *Farm Products Grades and Sales Act*, R.R.O. 1980, Reg. 337, s. 1.

HONORARIUM. *n.* A reward for service rendered; a non-compulsory fee.

HONOUR. *v.* 1. For a drawee to accept a bill of exchange. 2. For the maker of a note or the acceptor of a bill to pay it.

HONOUR. *n.* A title applied to judges and other officials.

HONOURABLE. *adj.* A title applied to judges and ministers of the Crown.

HOOD. *n.* Any exterior movable body panel forward of the windshield that is used to cover an engine, luggage, storage or battery compartment. *Motor Vehicle Safety Regulations*, C.R.C., c. 1038, s. 115.

HOOK. *n.* 1. In respect of angling, a single, double or treble pointed hook on a common shank or shaft. *Fishery regulations.* 2. (a) A single, double or multiple pointed hook on a common shaft, or (b) an artificial pad or lure having one or more hooks attached as part of it. *Alberta Fishery Regulations*, C.R.C., c. 838, s. 2. 3. When used with reference to angling, means (a) a single, double or multiple hook on a common shaft, or (b) an artificial bait or lure that is not spring loaded and that has one or more hooks attached as a part of it. *Manitoba Fishery Regulations*, C.R.C., c. 843, s. 2.

HOOKED. *adj.* Addicted.

HOOKING. See FOUL ~.

HOOP NET. 1. A box-shaped or funnel-shaped device that is made of netting or wire mesh fastened to hoops or frames and that is used to catch fish without enmeshing them. *Fishery regulations*, Canada regulations. 2. A net that (a) is stretched over frames, (b) has one or more pots, and (c) is secured in place by posts or other means. *Manitoba Fishery Regulations*, C.R.C., c. 843, s. 2. See DOUBLE ~; SINGLE ~.

HORIZONTAL BRANCH. That part of a waste pipe that is horizontal and installed to convey the discharge from more than one fixture. *Ontario Water Resources Act*, R.R.O. 1980, Reg. 736, s. 1.

HORIZONTAL CONTROL SYSTEM. A survey method based on a network of monuments, among which the angles and distances are measured with great accuracy. To locate any point in or near the network, one specifies coordinates derived from distances among the monuments and a co-ordinate axis. B.J. Reiter, R.C.B. Risk & B.N. McLellan, *Real Estate Law*, 3d ed. (Toronto: Emond Montgomery, 1986) at 641.

HORIZONTAL EXIT. That type of exit connecting 2 floor areas at substantially the same level by means of a doorway, vestibule, bridge or balcony, such floor areas being located either in different buildings or located in the same building and fully separated from each other by a firewall. *Building Code Act*, R.R.O. 1980, Reg. 87, s. 1.

HORIZONTAL SERVICE SPACE. A space such as an attic, duct, ceiling, roof or crawl space oriented essentially in a horizontal plane, concealed and generally inaccessible through which building service facilities such as pipes, ducts and wiring may pass. *Building Code Act*, R.R.O. 1980, Reg. 87, s. 1.

HORIZONTAL SURFACE. 1. An imaginary horizontal plane located 150 feet above the assigned elevation of the airport reference point. *Airport Zoning regulations.* 2. An imaginary horizontal plane located 150 feet above the assigned elevation of the airport reference point or an imaginary plane located 30 feet above the surface of the ground at any given point, whichever is the higher at that given point. Airport Zoning regulations.

HORIZONTAL UNION. Union the members of which belong to different crafts or work for different employers.

HORMONE. See SEX ~.

HORMONE TYPE HERBICIDE. Any pesticide containing, (i) 2,4-D, (ii) 2,4-DB, (iii) 2,4,5,-T, (iv) mecoprop, (v) fenoprop, (vi) MCPA, (vii) MCPB, (viii) dichlorprop, (ix) dicamba, (x) TBA, (xi) fenac, or (xii) picloram. *Pesticides Act*, R.R.O. 1980, Reg. 751, s. 1.

HORNBOOK. *n.* A primer.

HORS DE LA LOI. [Fr.] Outlawed.

HORS DE SON FEE. [Fr. out of one's fee] Describing land beyond the compass of a person's fee.

HORSE. *n.* 1. A stallion, mare, gelding, filly, colt, ass or mule. 2. Any animal of the equine species. *Riding Horse Establishment Act*, R.S.O. 1980, c. 455, s. 1. See RIDING ~ ESTABLISHMENT; SADDLE ~.

HORSEPOWER. *var.* **HORSE POWER.** 1. The capacity of any engine or plant or the standard by which that capacity is measured under the regulations. *Engine Operators Act*, R.S.N.S. 1967, c. 89, s. 1. 2. (a) With respect to boilers, 10 square feet of heating surface, (b) with respect to engines driven by steam or compressed air, the development of 33,000 foot-pounds of energy as measured by the volumetric displacement of the piston per minute under the mean effective pressure applied, and (c) with respect to engines driven by electricity, the consumption of 746 watts of electric energy. *Coal Mines (CBDC) Safety Regulations*, C.R.C., c. 1011, s. 2. See BOILER ~; BRAKE ~; NOMINAL ~.

HORSE RACING. Any race in which horses participate.

HORSE STABLE. A building, the whole or any part of which is used for the accommodation of horses in a riding horse establishment. *Riding Horse Establishments Act*, R.R.O. 1980, Reg. 905, s. 1.

HORSETAIL. *n.* A red marine plant of the species Furcellaria fastigiata. *Atlantic Coast Marine Plant Regulations*, C.R.C., c. 805, s. 2.

HORTICULTURAL OPERATION. See SPECIALIZED ~.

HORTICULTURE. *n.* (a) The operations relating to the propagating, producing, raising or harvesting of (i) legumes, flowers, shrubs or ornamental grasses, and (ii) seeds, seedlings, grafts and cuttings of legumes, flowers, shrubs or ornamental grasses, and (b) the operations relating to landscape gardening where the landscape gardening is incident to the carrying on of (i) any of the operations described in paragraph (a), or (ii) agriculture, and includes all the services incident to the carrying on of any of the operations described in paragraph (a) if those services are performed at the place where the operations are carried on. Canada regulations.

HOSE. See STANDARD ~.

HOSE SYSTEM. See STANDPIPE AND ~.

HOSPITAL. *n.* 1. Any hospital, sanitarium, sanatorium, nursing home or other institution operated for the observation, care or treatment of persons afflicted with or suffering from any physical or mental illness, disease or injury or for the observation, care or treatment of convalescent or chronically ill persons. 2. Includes hospitals, health centres, community health and social centres, nursing homes, a residence for a physician who is a member of the medical staff of the hospital, a residence for an employee of the hospital and other facilities related to a hospital. 3. Any establishment that admits or treats persons or animals for disease, infirmity or injury. 4. A hospital in which diagnostic services and medical, surgical and obstetrical treatment are provided to persons having various illnesses, disabilities, injuries or other conditions. 5. Any facility or portion thereof that provides hospital care, including acute, rehabilitative or chronic care, but does not include (a) a hospital or institution primarily for the mentally disordered, or (b) a facility or portion thereof that provides nursing home intermediate care service or adult residential care service, or comparable services for children. *Canada Health Act*, R.S.C. 1985, c. C-6, s. 2. See ACCREDITED ~; APPROVED ~; AUXILIARY ~; CONTRACT

~; DEPARTMENTAL ~; FEDERAL ~; GENERAL ~; MATERNITY ~; NON-DISTRICT ~; PRIVATE ~; PSYCHIATRIC ~; PUBLIC ~; TEACHING ~.

HOSPITAL BOARD. (i) The board of a general hospital district or auxiliary hospital district incorporated under The Alberta Hospitals Act; (ii) the owner of a non-district hospital within the meaning of The Alberta Hospitals Act; (iii) the owner of a contract nursing home within the meaning of The Nursing Homes Act; (iv) the board of directors of a Provincial General Hospital under The Provincial General Hospitals Act; (v) the Provincial Cancer Hospitals Board. *Department of Health Act*, R.S.A. 1970, c. 97, s. 11.

HOSPITAL CENTRE. Facilities to which persons are admitted for preventive purposes, medical diagnosis, medical treatment, physical or mental rehabilitation.

HOSPITAL FACILITIES. Includes laboratories, laundries and things, services and premises used or supplied in conjunction with a hospital or hospitals. *Hospital District Act*, R.S.B.C. 1979, c. 178, s. 1. See GOVERNMENT HOSPITAL FACILITY.

HOSPITALITY INDUSTRY. Every corporation, partnership, organization or individual providing accommodation, camping, food, beverage, information, entertainment, recreation and related services and facilities to persons travelling.

HOSPITALIZATION. See STANDARD WARD ~.

HOSPITAL MEDICAL STAFF REVIEW COMMITTEE. Any committee appointed by the board of an approved hospital or by the medical staff (a) to evaluate and control clinical practice in the hospital on a continuing basis for the purpose of maintaining and improving the safety and quality of patient care, or (b) to perform any functions in relation to the appraisal and control of the quality of patient care in the hospital. *Hospitals Act*, R.S.A. 1980, c. H-11, s. 31.

HOSPITAL PROJECT. Includes the establishment, acquisition, reconstruction, enlargement, operation and maintenance of a hospital or hospital facilities. *Hospital District Act*, R.S.B.C. 1979, c. 178, s. 1.

HOSPITAL PROPRIETOR. A person in whom the title to a hospital is vested and includes a person who holds possession of a hospital under a lease or sublease. *Hospitals Act*, S. Nfld. 1971, c. 81, s. 2.

HOSPITAL SCHOOL. A facility or portion thereof for the habilitation and care of persons presenting evidence of general retardation, specific learning disabilities, or any other related condition for which admission to a hospital school will be beneficial. *Hospital Schools Act*, R.S.N.B. 1973, c. H-8, s. 1.

HOSPITAL SERVICES. Any of the following services provided to in-patients or out-patients at a hospital, if the services are medically necessary for the purpose of maintaining health, preventing disease or diagnosing or treating an injury, illness or disability, namely, (a) accommodation and meals at the standard or public ward level and preferred accommodation if medically required, (b) nursing service, (c) laboratory, radiological and other diagnostic procedures, together with the necessary interpretations, (d) drugs, biologicals, and related preparations when administered in the hospital, (e) use of operating room, case room and anaesthetic facilities, including necessary equipment and supplies, (f) medical and surgical equipment and supplies, (g) use of radiotherapy facilities, (h) use of physiotherapy facilities, and (i) services provided by persons who receive remuneration therefor from the hospital, but does not include services that are excluded by the regulations. *Canada Health Act*, R.S.C. 1985, c. C-6, s. 2.

HOSPITIUM. *n.* [L. hospitality] The shelter provided by an inn.

HOST. See PLANT INDICATOR ~.

HOSTAGE. *n.* A person held in exchange for certain behaviour.

HOSTEL. *n.* 1. An institution for the temporary care of transient or homeless persons. 2. A building used for housing accommodation for three or more elderly persons who require minimal assistance or supervision around activities of daily living in which the kitchen and bathroom facilities, or bathroom facilities only, are used by three or more elderly persons. *Elderly and Infirm Persons' Housing Act*, R.S.M. 1970, c. E20, s. 2. 3. A building intended for use or used as a temporary place of lodging for individuals and containing communal cooking facilities or provision for cooking in any individual room or apartment, but does not include a hotel or motel. Canada regulations.

HOSTEL ACCOMMODATION. A hostel or dormitory type dwelling having shared food preparation or bathroom facilities. *Home Insulation Regulations*, C.R.C., c. 326, s. 2.

HOSTELER. *n.* An innkeeper.

HOSTEL UNIT. A unit of housing accommodations of which the occupant shares one or more of the facilities of sleeping, eating, food preparation or sanitary facilities, such facility being necessarily provided exclusively within the housing unit, and may include personal service or light nursing care. *Housing Corporation Act*, S.P.E.I. 1975, c. 14, s. 1.

HOSTES SUNT QUI NOBIS VEL QUIBUS NOS BELLUM DECERNIMUS; CAETERI PRODITORES VEL PRAEDONES SUNT. [L.] An enemy is one with whom we are at war; others are either traitors or robbers.

HOST GOVERNMENT. In relation to any quantity of petroleum, the government of the country in which that petroleum was produced, extracted, recovered or derived but does not include the government of a state, province or other political subdivision of that country. *Oil Import Compensation Regulations No. 1, 1975*, C.R.C., c. 335, s. 2.

HOSTILE ACTIVITIES. See SUBVERSIVE OR ~.

HOSTILE POSSESSION. See ADVERSE POSSESSION.

HOSTILE WITNESS. A witness whose demeanour, general attitude and evidence are such while under examination that the side which called that witness may, with the judge's leave, cross-examine.

HOT CARGO. Material shipped from a business the employees of which are on strike.

HOTCHPOT. *n.* A blend or mix of chattels and lands.

HOTEL. *n.* Any place where the public may, for a consideration, obtain sleeping accommodation, with or without meals. See HIGH-RISE ~; MOTOR ~; PUBLIC ~.

HOTELKEEPER. *n.* The person who has the management and control of a hotel. *Hotel Fire Safety Act*, R.S.O. 1980, Reg. 207, s. 1.

HOTEL SHIP. A ship designed to carry passengers in which berthed accommodation is available to persons for other than the purpose of a voyage. *Hull Construction Regulations*, C.R.C., c. 1431, s. 2.

HOT GOODS. Goods which workers refuse to handle because the producer of the goods is engaged in a labour dispute with other workers.

HOT PRODUCT. A product which workers refuse to handle because the producer of the product is engaged in a labour dispute with other workers.

HOT PURSUIT. A coastal state may pursue a foreign merchant ship which committed an offence against its local law within that state's territorial or national waters into the high seas.

HOT-ROLLED OR COLD-ROLLED. When applied to shapes, sections, bars, rods, plates, sheets or strips of iron or steel, includes shapes, sections, bars, rods, plates, sheets or strips that have been annealed, tempered, pickled, limed or polished. *Customs Tariff*, R.S.C. 1985, c. C-54, s. 2.

HOT SHOT. 1. Of a narcotic, an accidental fatal overdose. F.A. Jaffe, *A Guide to Pathological Evidence*, 2d ed. (Toronto: Carswell, 1983) at 178. 2. A narcotic to which poison was added. F.A. Jaffe, *A Guide to Pathological Evidence*, 2d ed. (Toronto: Carswell, 1983) at 178.

HOT TUB. See PUBLIC ~.

HOT WATER BOILER. A boiler connected in a closed type hot water heating system. *Boiler and Pressure Vessel Act*, R.S.B.C. 1979, c. 30, s. 1.

HOT-WATER HEATING SYSTEM. See OPEN-TYPE ~.

HOT WATER PLANT. See LOW PRESSURE ~.

HOT WATER STORAGE TANK. A pressure vessel used for the storage of hot water.

HOT WATER SYSTEM. See CLOSED TYPE ~.

HOT-WATER HEATING SYSTEM. See CLOSED-TYPE ~.

HOT WORK. Welding, burning, rivetting, drilling, grinding, chipping or any other work where flame is used or sparks are produced. *Safe Working Practices Regulations*, C.R.C., c. 1467, s. 2.

HOUR. *n.* 3 600 seconds. *Weights and Measures Act*, S.C. 1970-71-72, c. 36, schedule I. See CLOCK ~; KILOWATT-~; MAN-~; MAXIMUM ~S; PROHIBITED ~S; QUARTER ~ BLOCK; REGULAR ~S; SCHEDULE OF ~S OF LABOR; THERM ~; WORKING ~S.

HOURS OF THE DAY. This and all other references to time relate to local time.

HOURS OF WORK. The period of time during which an employee works for an employer.

HOUSE. *n.* 1. A building, together with the land on which it is situated, intended for human habitation comprising not more than two family housing units. 2. Includes school, church, hall, railway passenger station, factory, and any other building, hut or tent used for human habitation or work whether it is permanent or temporary and whether stationary or movable, and includes the curtilage thereof. 3. The portion, situated within the territory of Québec, of any building, construction, shelter, penthouse, shed or other erection, under whatever name known or designated, attached to the ground or portable, built, erected or placed on the surface or above or underground, permanently or temporarily, partly on the territory of Québec and partly on that of one of the United States of America or of another province of Canada. *Disorderly Houses Act*, R.S.Q. 1977, c. M-2, s. 13. 4. The House of Assembly. Nova Scotia statutes. 5. The Legislative Assembly. *Crown Corporation Reporting Act*, R.S.B.C. 1979, c. 84, s. 1. 6. The House of Commons. See ALMS~; BAWDY ~; BOARDING ~; CLEARING ~; CUSTOM-~; DISORDERLY ~; DWELLING-~; GOVERNMENT ~; HALFWAY ~; LODGING ~; MOBILE ~; PUBLIC ~; REFRESHMENT ~; ROOMING ~; ROW ~; SUPPLY ~; TENT ~; VICTUALLING ~.

HOUSE-BOAT. *n.* A boat designed, fitted or employed as a dwelling whether temporary or permanent. *Provincial Parks Act*, R.R.O. 1980, Reg. 822, s. 1.

HOUSEBREAKING. See BREAK AND ENTER.

HOUSEBREAKING INSTRUMENT. An instrument used to break in.

HOUSE COUNSEL. A lawyer employed by and acting as lawyer for a corporation or public entity.

HOUSE-DRAIN. *n.* A drain used for the drainage of a house or premises and made merely for the purpose of communicating therefrom with a private sewage disposal system or other like receptacle for sewage, or with a sewer in a street. *Public Health Act*, R.S.A. 1970, c. 294, s. 2.

HOUSEHOLD. *n.* A parcel of land separately assessed under paragraph 2 of subsection 13 (2) of the Assessment Act according to the last returned assessment roll that is used or intended to be used as a residence, except that in respect of a Canadian Forces Base, "household" means a self-contained living unit consisting of two or more rooms in which the occupants usually sleep and prepare and serve meals. *Ontario Unconditional Grants Amendment Act*, S.O. 1984, c. 23, s. 1. See HOUSE OR ~.

HOUSEHOLD APPLIANCE. A kitchen range, a refrigerator, a freezer, a dishwasher, a clothes washer, a clothes dryer or a television set. *Consumer Protection Act*, S.Q. 1978, c. 9, s. 182.

HOUSEHOLD ARTICLE. See PERSONAL OR ~.

HOUSEHOLD EFFECTS. See FURNITURE AND ~.

HOUSEHOLDER. *n.* The person in charge of any premises whether as owner, tenant, agent or otherwise. *Public Health acts.*

HOUSEHOLDER MAIL. Printed matter or samples that are unaddressed or addressed to "Householder", "Boxholder", "Occupant" or "Resident" without any further address. *Third Class Mail Regulations*, C.R.C., c. 1297, s. 2.

HOUSEHOLD EXTRACTS. Flavouring preparations manufactured for sale to the general public for use as a flavouring extract. *Manufacturers in Bond Regulations*, C.R.C., c. 575, s. 2.

HOUSEHOLD GOODS. 1. Personal property (i) that is owned by one or both spouses, and (ii) that was ordinarily used or enjoyed by one or both spouses or one or more of the children residing in the matrimonial home, for transportation, household, educational, recreational, social or aesthetic purposes. 2. Furniture, equipment, appliances and effects owned by one spouse or both spouses and ordinarily used or enjoyed by both spouses or by one or more of their children within or about a marital home while the spouses are or were cohabiting. New Brunswick statutes.

HOUSEKEEPER. *n.* Of the House of Commons, the Sergeant-at-Arms who is responsible for committee rooms, buildings, restaurants and all moveable property. A. Fraser, G.A. Birch & W.A. Dawson, eds., *Beauchesne's Rules and Forms of the House of Commons of Canada*, 5th ed. (Toronto: Carswell, 1978) at 45.

HOUSEKEEPING UNIT. One or more habitable rooms for use as a unit for dwelling purposes by one family and containing separate facilities for the preparation of food. Canada regulations.

HOUSE LEADER. See GOVERNMENT ~; OPPOSITION ~.

HOUSE OF COMMONS. The support of the majority of members of this body, elected by universal adult suffrage, is required for a Prime Minister and cabinet to govern. P.W. Hogg, *Constitutional Law of Canada*, 2d ed. (Toronto: Carswell, 1985) at 199. See CLERK OF THE ~.

HOUSE OF DETENTION. For the purposes of this act, means any place, other than a penitentiary, in which persons charged with offences are usually kept and detained in custody. *Summary Convictions Act*, R.S.Q. 1977, c. P-15, s. 1.

HOUSE OF LORDS. The body of lords spiritual and temporal who constitute the second branch of the British Parliament and act as a supreme court of appeal from the British Court of Appeal.

HOUSE ORGAN. A company publication.

HOUSE OR HOUSEHOLD. Includes a dwelling house, lodging house and hotel, and also includes a students' residence, fraternity house or other building in which any person in attendance as a student, pupil or teacher or employed in any capacity in or about a university, college, school or other institution of learning resides or is lodged. *Public Health Act*, R.S.O. 1980, c. 409, s. 1.

HOUSE PIPING. The gas piping in any premises beyond the outlet of the meter and the gas piping in any premises ahead of the meter which is not installed by or on behalf of the gas company. *Gas Act*, R.S.B.C. 1979, c. 149, s. 1.

HOUSE TRAILER. 1. A vehicle capable of being attached to and drawn by a motor vehicle and designed, constructed or equipped as a dwelling place, living abode or sleeping place. *Highway Traffic acts*. 2. A vehicle used or intended to be used as living quarters. *The Conditional Sales Act*, R.S.S. 1978, c. C-25, s. 2.

HOUSEWIFE. *n.* A woman managing, maintaining and controlling an independent domestic establishment, who does not either: (i) engage in a definite regular occupation for wages or for profit; or (ii) report regularly to a place of employment apart from her residence. *The Automobile Accident Insurance Act*, R.S.S. 1978, c. A-35, s. 2.

HOUSING. *n.* 1. Any buildings or structures suitable for human habitation and which are primarily used for that purpose. 2. Any unit, building or mobile home that provides in it living, sleeping, eating, food preparation and sanitary facilities for one or more persons, with or without essential facilities shared with other units, buildings or mobile homes. See CANADA MORTGAGE AND ~ CORPORATION; FACTORY BUILT ~; LOW INCOME ~; PROTECTIVE ~; PUBLIC ~; STUDENT ~; SUBSIDIZED PUBLIC ~.

HOUSING ACCOMMODATION. 1. Any place of dwelling and includes any place where other services are provided in addition to accommodation, but does not include a place of dwelling that is part of a building in which the owner or his family resides and where the occupant of the place of dwelling is required to share a bathroom or kitchen facility with the owner or his family. *Humans Rights Code acts*. 2. Any place of dwelling, except a place of dwelling that is part of a building in which the owner or his family or both, reside where the occupants of the place of dwelling are required to share (i) a bathroom or kitchen facility, or (ii) a common entrance, except in a duplex, apartment building or condominium, with the owner

of the dwelling or his family or both. *Human Rights Act*, S.M. 1978, c. 43, s. 1. See SERVICED ~.

HOUSING ACTS. The National Housing Act, the National Housing Act, chapter N-10 of the Revised Statutes of Canada, 1970, the National Housing Act, 1954, and the National Housing Act, chapter 188 of the Revised Statutes of Canada, 1952. *Canada Mortgage and Housing Corporation Act*, R.S.C. 1985, c. C-7, s. 2.

HOUSING ASSOCIATION. 1. (i) An association that builds or otherwise acquires housing accommodation and leases it to its members; (ii) an association that builds or otherwise acquires housing accommodation and sells it to its members for their individual ownership and use; (iii) an association that provides services to achieve or maintain the objectives described in subclause (i) or (ii); (iv) an association of corporate bodies of which at least eighty per cent of the members are housing associations and co-operative associations incorporated or registered under this Act and which has as its objectives any or all of those described in subclause (i), (ii) or (iii). *The Co-operative Associations Act*, R.S.S. 1978, c. C-34, s. 86. 2. Any society, body of trustees or company established for the purpose of, or amongst whose objects or powers are included those of constructing, improving or managing or facilitating or encouraging the construction or improvement of houses. *Housing Association (Loans) Act*, R.S. Nfld. 1970, c. 161, s. 2. See COOPERATIVE ~.

HOUSING COMPANY. A limited-dividend housing company (within the meaning of that expression as defined in section 2 of the National Housing Act), all or substantially all of the business of which is the construction, holding or management of low-rental housing projects. *Income Tax Act*, R.S.C. 1952, c. 148 (as am. S.C. 1979, c. 5, s. 51), s. 149(1)(n).

HOUSING COMPLEX. Several immoveables situated near one another and comprising together more than twelve dwellings, if such immoveables are administered jointly by the same person or by related persons within the meaning of the Taxation Act (R.S.Q., c. I-3), and if some of them have an accessory, a dependency or part of the structure, except a common wall, in common. *An Act to establish the Régie du logement*, S.Q. 1979, c. 48, s. 45.

HOUSING CORPORATION. See CO-OPERATIVE ~.

HOUSING PROJECT. A project consisting of one or more houses, one or more multiple-family dwellings, housing accommodation of the hostel or dormitory type, one or more condominium units or any combination thereof, together with any public space, recreational facilities, commercial space and other buildings appropriate to the project, but does not include a hotel. See COMMUNITY ~; COOPERATIVE ~; LOW-RENTAL ~; RENTAL ~; STUDENT ~.

HOUSING UNIT. 1. A unit that provides therein living, sleeping, eating, food preparation and sanitary facilities for one or more persons, with or without essential facilities shared with other housing units. 2. Includes (i) subject to subclauses (ii) and (iii), any premises that an individual ordinarily occupies and inhabits as his residence in the taxation year but does not include, (ii) premises that are part of a chronic care facility or other similar institution that is prescribed, or that are part of any charitable institution, home for special care, home for the aged, public nursing home or private nursing home, or (iii) premises, except any students' residence that is prescribed, during such time in a taxation year as, (A) such premises are exempt from the payment of taxes levied under the Provincial Land Tax Act, the Local Roads Boards Act or taxes for municipal and school purposes levied in respect of real property in Ontario that is assessed as residential or farm property, or (B) the owner does not pay a grant equal to the full amount of the taxes described in sub-clause (A) that would, if such premises were not exempt, be payable or a grant equal to an amount prescribed by the Minister in respect of such premises or class of premises, except when such excluded premises are occupied and inhabited by an individual of a class prescribed for the purpose of this clause. Ontario statutes. See ELDERLY PERSONS' ~; FAMILY ~.

H-POINT. *n.* The mechanically hinged tip point of a manikin that simulates the actual pivot centre of the human torso and thigh, described in SAE Recommended Practice J826 Manikins for Use In Defining Vehicle Seating Accommodation (November 1962). *Motor Vehicle Safety Regulations*, C.R.C., c. 1038, s. 100.

HUB. *n.* A rotating member that provides for mounting of disc wheels. *Motor Vehicle Safety Regulations*, C.R.C., c. 1038, s. 2.

HUDSON'S BAY COMPANY. The company incorporated by British royal charter in 1670 as "The Governor and Company of Adventurers of England trading into Hudson's Bay".

HUE AND CRY. In the old common law, pursuing felons and those who had wounded another with horn and voice.

HULL. *n.* The body of a vessel including the masts and rigging and all parts of its structure.

Canada Shipping Act, R.S.C. 1985, c. S-9, s. 2. See HEIGHT ABOVE THE ~.

HUMAN CONSUMPTION. See PRODUCT FOR ~.

HUMANITY. See CRIME AGAINST ~.

HUMANITIES. See SOCIAL SCIENCES AND ~ RESEARCH COUNCIL OF CANADA.

HUMAN REMAINS. 1. Remains of human bodies that in the opinion of the minister have heritage significance and that are situated or discovered outside a recognized cemetery or burial ground in respect of which there is some manner of identifying the persons buried therein. *The Heritage Resources Act*, S.M. 1985-86, c. 10, s. 43(1). 2. Includes cremated human remains. *Cemetery and Funeral Services Act*, S.N.S. 1983, c. 4, s. 2.

HUMAN RIGHTS. See CANADIAN ~ COMMISSION; EUROPEAN COMMISSION OF ~; EUROPEAN CONVENTION ON ~; EUROPEAN COURT OF ~.

HUMPBACK WHALE. Any whale known by the name of bunch, humpback, humpback whale, humpbacked whale, hump whale, or hunchbacked whale. *Whaling Convention Act*, R.S.C. 1970, c. W-8, Schedule, s. 18.

HUNDREDWEIGHT. *n.* 100 pounds. *Weights and Measures Act*, S.C. 1970-71-72, c. 36, schedule II.

HUNG JURY. A jury unable to reach a unanimous decision in a criminal case.

HUNT. *v.* 1. With reference to a wildlife or exotic animal, (i) shoot at, harass or worry, (ii) chase, pursue, follow after or on the trail of, search for, flush, stalk or lie in wait for, (iii) capture or wilfully injure or kill, or attempt to do so, or (iv) assist another person to hunt in a manner specified in subclause (i), (ii) or (iii) while that other person is so hunting. *Wildlife Act*, S.A. 1984, c. W-9.1, s. 1. 2. Includes shooting at, attracting, searching for, chasing, pursuing, following after or on the trail of, stalking or lying in wait for wildlife, or attempting to do any of those things, whether or not the wildlife is then or subsequently wounded, killed or captured, (a) with intention to capture the wildlife, or (b) while in possession of a firearm or other weapon. *Wildlife Act*, S.B.C. 1982, c. 57, s. 1.

HUNT. *abbr.* Hunter's Torrens Cases (Can.).

HUNTER'S CERTIFICATE. The document issued by the Minister, establishing that a person is recognized competent in the handling of firearms for hunting purposes. *Wild-life Conservation Act*, S.Q. 1978, c. 65, s. 1.

HUNTING. *n.* Includes taking, wounding, killing, chasing, pursuing, worrying, capturing, following after or on the trail of, searching for, shooting at, trapping, setting snares for, stalking or lying in wait for any wildlife, whether or not the wildlife is subsequently captured, wounded or killed. See SPORT ~.

HUNTING OR FISHING LODGE. An establishment erected in a hunting or fishing territory and equipped for lodging and meals.

HUNTING PRESERVE. See GAME BIRD ~; PHEASANT ~.

HUSBAND. *n.* A man who has entered into a marriage. See DEPENDENT ~; DESERTED ~.

HUSBAND OR WIFE. The legal spouse of an insured or, if the insured did not have a legal spouse at the time of his death who had an enforceable claim for benefits under this Act, the person who, at the time of the death of an insured and during the two years immediately preceding the accident out of which the claim arose, lived and manifested an intention of continuing to live together permanently with the insured as husband and wife even though they were not married. *The Automobile Accident Insurance Act*, R.S.S. 1978, c. A-35, s. 2.

HUSBANDRY. *n.* Farming. See IMPLEMENT OF ~.

HUSH-MONEY. *n.* A bribe to keep someone silent.

HUSKY DOG. Includes any dog of the breed or type to which that name is commonly applied, and in particular includes an Eskimo dog, an Alaskan Malamute, and a Siberian Husky (also known as a Samoyede), and also includes a dog that is partly of one of those breeds or strains, and the young of any such dog. *Animal Husbandry Act*, R.S.M. 1970, c. A90, s. 29.

HUSTINGS. *n.* A temporary wooden platform from which parliamentary candidates formerly addressed electors.

HUTESIUM ET CLAMOR. [L.] Hue and cry.

HYBRID. *n.* Being corn the first generation of a cross between two or more inbred lines or their combinations including single crosses, double crosses and three way crosses. *Seeds Regulations*, C.R.C., c. 1400, s. 19.

HYBRID OFFENCE. A crime which the Crown may choose to prosecute summarily or by indictment.

HYDRAULIC DEVICE. A fishing device used for the harvesting of shellfish by which the shellfish are lifted from the bottom of the water by the use of water under pressure. *Fishery regulations*.

HYDRAULICKING PURPOSE. The use of the water under head to move earth, sand, gravel or rock, except when the moving is done or proposed to be done in order to get mineral from it. *Water Act*, R.S.B.C. 1979, c. 429, s. 1.

HYDRAULIC SYSTEM MINERAL OIL. A mineral-oil-based fluid designed for use in motor vehicle brake systems in which none of the components contacting the fluid are SBR, EPDM, neoprene or natural rubber. *Motor Vehicle Safety Regulations*, C.R.C., c. 1038, s. 2.

HYDREMIA. *n.* The increase of water content of the blood and is distinguished by a watery and edematous condition of the subcutaneous tissues and body cavities. *Meat Inspection Regulations*, C.R.C., c. 1032, s. 46.

HYDROCARBON. *n.* 1. A chemical compound of hydrogen and carbon used as a fuel, either liquid or gaseous. *Energy Act*, R.S.O. 1980, c. 139, s. 1. 2. Does not include coal. Canada statutes.

HYDROCARBONS. *n.* Solid, liquid and gaseous hydrocarbons and any natural gas whether consisting of a single element or of two or more elements in chemical combination or uncombined and, without restricting the generality of the foregoing, includes oil-bearing shale, tar sands, crude oil, petroleum, helium and hydrogen sulphide. *Bank Act*, R.S.C. 1985, c. B-1, s. 2.

HYDRO DEVELOPMENT. (i) Means a project for the furnishing of hydro energy to a power plant, and (ii) includes dams, diversion works, water conduits and all structures, machinery, appliances, fixtures and equipment, and all appurtenances and lands and rights of way required in connection with that project. *Hydro and Electric Energy Act*, R.S.A. 1980, c. H-13, s. 1.

HYDROELECTRIC POWER PLANT. A facility for the generation of electricity, from the motion of water, or the position or potential motion of water, and includes associated dams, diversion works, water conduits and all structures, machinery, appliances, fixtures and equipment. *Utilities Commission Act*, S.B.C. 1980, c. 60, s. 16.

HYDRO ENERGY. Energy associated with the motion or the position and potential motion of water. *Hydro and Electric Energy Act*, R.S.A. 1980, c. H-13, s. 1.

HYDROGEN SWELL. A can with one or both ends bulging as a result of hydrogen gas produced inside the can from the reaction of the product on the metal of the container. *Processed Fruit and Vegetable Regulations*, C.R.C., c. 291, s. 2.

HYDROSTATIC TEST. A flotation test in which the buoyancy of lung tissue on water is observed to recognize live birth. F.A. Jaffe, *A Guide to Pathological Evidence*, 2d ed. (Toronto: Carswell, 1983) at 178.

HYGIENIST. See DENTAL ~.

HYGIENE. See DENTAL ~.

HYGIENE FACILITIES. Facilities for cleaning, washing and eating. D. Robertson, *Ontario Health and Safety Guide* (Toronto: Richard De Boo Ltd., 1988) at 5-214.

HYMEN. *n.* A roughly circular, thick membrane around the vaginal opening. F.A. Jaffe, *A Guide to Pathological Evidence*, 2d ed. (Toronto: Carswell, 1983) at 127.

HYOID BONE. A U-shaped bone above the larynx in the neck. F.A. Jaffe, *A Guide to Pathological Evidence*, 2d ed. (Toronto: Carswell, 1983) at 178.

HYPERKALEMIA. *n.* A marked increase in blood potassium. F.A. Jaffe, *A Guide to Pathological Evidence*, 2d ed. (Toronto: Carswell, 1983) at 80.

HYPERSENSITIVITY REACTION. A side effect or adverse reaction with an allergic or immunological basis. F.A. Jaffe, *A Guide to Pathological Evidence*, 2d ed. (Toronto: Carswell, 1983) at 61.

HYPERTHERMIA. *n.* Heat stroke. F.A. Jaffe, *A Guide to Pathological Evidence*, 2d ed. (Toronto: Carswell, 1983) at 42.

HYPERVOLEMIA. *n.* Greater blood volume. F.A. Jaffe, *A Guide to Pathological Evidence*, 2d ed. (Toronto: Carswell, 1983) at 80.

HYPNOTIC. *n.* A drug which brings on sleep. F.A. Jaffe, *A Guide to Pathological Evidence*, 2d ed. (Toronto: Carswell, 1983) at 178.

HYPNOTISM. *n.* A process or act intended to put any person into induced sleep or trance in order to make that person's mind more susceptible to direction or suggestion.

HYPOPHARYNX. *n.* The part of the pharynx below the palate. F.A. Jaffe, *A Guide to Pathological Evidence*, 2d ed. (Toronto: Carswell, 1983) at 181.

HYPOSTASIS. *n.* Blood settling into dependent parts of the body after death. F.A. Jaffe, *A Guide to Pathological Evidence*, 2d ed. (Toronto: Carswell, 1983) at 178.

HYPOSTATIC OR CONGESTION LIVIDITY. Lividity of the skin appearing a half hour after death when blood distends the capillary blood vessels. F.A. Jaffe, *A Guide to Pathological Evidence*, 2d ed. (Toronto: Carswell, 1983) at 5.

HYPOTHECATION. *n.* Pledging something as security for a demand or debt without giving up that thing.

HYPOTHERMIA. *n.* A condition of unusually low body temperature. F.A. Jaffe, *A Guide to Pathological Evidence*, 2d ed. (Toronto: Carswell, 1983) at 178.

HYPOTHETICAL. *adj.* Depending on an assumption of fact which may or may not be provable or true. Robert J. Sharpe, ed., *Charter Litigation* (Toronto: Butterworths 1987) at 335.

HYPOTHETICAL OR NOTIONAL MARKET. The valuation mechanism when there is no contemplated or actual open market transaction on the valuation date(s). A. Bissett-Johnson & W.M. Holland, eds., *Matrimonial Property Law in Canada* (Toronto: Carswell, 1980) at V-7.

HYPOVOLEMIA. *n.* Decreased blood volume. F.A. Jaffe, *A Guide to Pathological Evidence*, 2d ed. (Toronto: Carswell, 1983) at 81.

HYPOXIA. *n.* Being without enough oxygen. F.A. Jaffe, *A Guide to Pathological Evidence*, 2d ed. (Toronto: Carswell, 1983) at 178.

HZ. *abbr.* Hertz.

I.A.B. *abbr.* Immigration Appeal Board.

I.A.C. *abbr.* Immigration Appeal Cases, 1970-1976.

IATROGENIC. *adj.* Describes an injury or illness caused by a physician or unwise therapy. F.A. Jaffe, *A Guide to Pathological Evidence*, 2d ed. (Toronto: Carswell, 1983) at 178.

IATROGENIC ARTEFACT. A foreign object left accidentally after surgical or medical treatment. F.A. Jaffe, *A Guide to Pathological Evidence*, 2d ed. (Toronto: Carswell, 1983) at 13.

IBID. *abbr.* Ibidem.

IBIDEM. *adv.* [L.] In the same place.

I.B.M. *abbr.* International Business Machines.

I.C.B.C. *abbr.* Insurance Corporation of British Columbia.

ICE. *n.* The ice used for the preparation or preservation of food. *An Act to Amend the Agricultural Products, Marine Products and Food Act*, S.Q. 1983, c. 53, s. 1.

ICE ANGLING. Angling in ice-covered waters. *Manitoba Fishery Regulations*, C.R.C., c. 843, s. 2.

ICE BREAKER. *var.* **ICE-BREAKER.** *var.* **ICEBREAKER.** A ship designed and constructed for the purpose of assisting the passage of other ships through ice. *Arctic Waters Pollution Prevention Act*, R.S.C. 1985, c. A-12, s. 2.

ICE CREAM. The frozen food that is made from ice cream mix by freezing, with or without the addition of cocoa or chocolate syrup, fruit, nuts or confections, and that contains not less than (i) 36 per cent food solids, (ii) 10 per cent milk-fat, and (iii) 1.8 pounds of food solids per gallon, of which amount not less that 0.50 pound is milk-fat, and that does not contain more than, (iv) 0.5 per cent stabilizer, or (v) 100,000 bacteria per gram. *Farm Products Grades and Sales Act*, R.R.O. 1980, Reg. 327, s. 1.

ICE CREAM FACTORY. Any building where the milk or cream of cows is manufactured into ice cream or where any stage in the manufacture thereof is carried on.

ICE CREAM MIX. 1. The unfrozen pasteurized mixture from which ice cream is made. *Canada Dairy Products Regulations*, C.R.C., c. 553, s. 2. 2. The unfrozen pasteurized combination of cream, milk or other milk products sweetened with sugar, invert sugar, honey, dextrose, glucose, corn syrup or corn syrup solids, with or without, (i) egg, (ii) flavouring preparation, (iii) cocoa or chocolate syrup, (iv) food colour, (v) acid-reducing salts, or (vi) a stabilizer that is not more than 0.5 per cent of the finished product, and that contains not less than, (vii) 36 per cent food solids, and (viii) 10 per cent milk-fat. *Farm Products Grades and Sales Act*, R.R.O. 1980, Reg. 327, s. 1.

ICE CREAM PLANT. A place where ice cream, ice cream mix, milk shake mix, sherbet or any frozen dessert made wholly or mainly from milk is prepared, processed or manufactured for the purpose of sale to retail distributors.

ICE FISHING. Fishing or attempting to fish through the ice in inland waters. *Newfoundland Fishery Regulations*, C.R.C., c. 846, s. 2.

ICE MAKES. Formed ice of sufficient thickness to permit safe fishing operations to be carried on through the ice. *Manitoba Fishery Regulations*, C.R.C., c. 843, s. 2.

ICE PACKED POULTRY. Poultry that has been chilled and packed in chipped or crushed ice. *Dressed and Eviscerated Poultry Regulations*, C.R.C., c. 283, s. 2.

ICE SHELTER. Any structure that is located on or over ice over any water for more than one day and that is or may be used for shelter, privacy or the storage or sale of any thing. *Environmental Protection Act*, R.S.O. 1980, c. 141, s. 23.

ID. *abbr.* Idem.

ID CERTUM EST QUOD CERTUM REDDI POTEST. [L.] What is certain is what can be made certain.

IDEM. [L.] The same.

IDEM AGENS ET PATIENS ESSE NOT POTEST. [L.] It is impossible to do better than to suffer the same thing.

IDEM EST FACERE ET NON PROHIBERE CUM POSSIS; ET QUI NON PROHIBET CUM PROHIBERE POSSIT IN CULPA EST. [L.] It is the same thing to do an act as not to prevent it when prevention is possible; whoever has the power but does not prevent the commission of an offence is at fault.

IDEM EST NIHIL DICERE ET INSUFFI-CIENTER DICERE. [L.] It is the same to say nothing as to say what is insufficient.

IDEM EST NON ESSE ET NON APPARERE. [L.] In law, not to exist and not to appear to exist are the same.

IDEM PER IDEM. [L. the same for the same] Describes an illustration which adds nothing new to the question being considered.

IDEM SEMPER ANTECEDENTI PROXIMO REFERTUR. [L.] The word "idem" always refers to the closest antecedent.

IDEM SONANS. [L. sounding alike] Similar in sound. H.G. Fox, *The Canadian Law of Trade Marks and Unfair Competition*, 3d ed. (Toronto: Carswell, 1972) at 160.

IDENTICAL GOODS. In relation to goods being appraised, means imported goods that (a) are the same in all respects, including physical characteristics, quality and reputation, as the goods being appraised, except for minor differences in appearance that do not affect the value of the goods, (b) were produced in the same country as the country in which the goods being appraised were produced, and (c) were produced by or on behalf of the person by or on behalf of whom the goods being appraised were produced, but does not include imported goods where engineering, development work, art work, design work, plans or sketches undertaken in Canada were supplied, directly or indirectly, by the purchaser of those imported goods free of charge or at a reduced cost for use in connection with the production and sale for export of those imported goods. *Customs Act*, R.S.C. 1985 (2d Supp.), c. 1, s. 45.

IDENTICAL PROPERTY. A property which is the same in all material respects, so that a potential buyer would not prefer one as opposed to another. Income Tax Interpretation Bulletin IT-357, "Meaning of Identical Properties", paragraph 1.

IDENTICAL SIGNALS. Signals in which not less than 95 per cent of the program matter is the same. *Cable Television Regulations*, C.R.C., c. 374, s. 2.

IDENTIFIABLE GROUP. Any section of the public distinguished by colour, race, religion or ethnic origin. *Criminal Code*, R.S.C. 1985, c. C-46, s. 318(4).

IDENTIFICATION. *n.* Showing that some person or thing is the person or thing in question. See VALID ~.

IDENTIFICATION BRAND. A character or combination of characters impressed or intended to be impressed on the skin or hide of stock for a purpose other than showing the ownership of the stock. *Livestock Brand Act*, R.S.B.C. 1979, c. 241, s. 1.

IDENTIFICATION DOCUMENT. A passport, a certificate of citizenship, a birth or baptismal certificate or social insurance card capable of identifying the holder. *Air Carrier Regulations*, C.R.C., c. 3, s. 54.

IDENTIFICATION NUMBER. See VEHICLE ~.

IDENTIFICATION NUMBER PLATE. The number plate, issued by the board for a snowmobile registered under this Act, on which there is an imprint or to which there is attached a validation sticker or stickers showing the year and month in which the licence period expires. *The Snowmobile Act*, R.S.S. 1978, c. S-52, s. 2.

IDENTIFICATION PLATE OR MARKER. See FICTITIOUS ~.

IDENTIFICATION TAG. A tag used to mark a corner of a claim and made of a substance and of a size approved by the Minister and issued as one of a set of four by the Mining Recorder. *Canada Mining Regulations*, C.R.C., c. 1516, s. 2.

IDENTIFIED. *adj.* When applied to a conductor means that the conductor has a white or natural gray covering or has, where approved, a raised longitudinal ridge or ridges on the surface of the extruded covering indicating that the conductor is a grounded conductor, and when applied to other electrical equipment means that the terminals to which grounded conductors are to be connected have been distinguished for identifcation by being tinned, nickel-plated or otherwise suitably marked. *Power Corporation Act*, R.R.O. 1980, Reg. 794, s. 0.

IDENTIFY. *v.* To use one's trade mark in order to or intending to distinguish one's wares or services from those of others. H.G. Fox, *The Canadian Law of Trade Marks and Unfair Competition*, 3d ed. (Toronto: Carswell, 1972) at 18.

I

IDENTITAS VERA COLLIGITUR EX MULTITUDINE SIGNORUM. [L.] True identity is derived from many signs.

IDENTITY. *n.* Demonstration that a certain person or thing is the person or thing in question.

ID EST. [L. that is] That is to say.

IDIOSYNCRACY. *n.* An individual or unusual reaction, usually to drugs. F.A. Jaffe, *A Guide to Pathological Evidence*, 2d ed. (Toronto: Carswell, 1983) at 178.

IDLE POSITION. The position of the throttle at which it first comes in contact with an engine idle speed control appropriate for existing conditions according to the manufacturers' recommendations respecting engine speed adjustments for a cold engine, air conditioning, emission control and throttle setting devices. *Motor Vehicle Safety Regulations*, C.R.C., c. 1038, s. 2.

IDLE TIME. Non-productive time caused by waiting for work or repairs to equipment.

IDONEUM SE FACERE, IDONEARE SE. [L.] To atone oneself by oath for a crime of which one was accused.

IDONEUS HOMO. [L.] A proper person.

ID POSSUMUS QUOD DE JURE POSSUMUS. [L.] We can do what law permits us to do.

ID QUOD COMMUNE EST, NOSTRUM ESSE DICITUR. [L.] Whatever is common is said to be ours.

ID QUOD NOSTRUM EST SINE FACTO NOSTRO AD ALIUM TRANSFERRI NON POTEST. [L.] Whatever is ours may not be transferred to another except by our own action.

I.E. *abbr.* Id est.

IFR. *abbr.* The instrument flight rules. *Air Regulations*, C.R.C., c. 2, s. 101.

IFR FLIGHT. A flight conducted in accordance with the instrument flight rules. *Air Regulations*, C.R.C., c. 2, s. 101.

IGNETEGIUM. *n.* [L.] A curfew.

IGNITEGIUM. *n.* [L.] A curfew.

IGNITION COMPOUND. The chemical compound used to make the striking tip of a match. *Hazardous Products (Matches) Regulations*, C.R.C., c. 929, s. 2.

IGNORAMUS. [L.] We are ignorant.

IGNORANTIA EORUM QUAE QUIS SCIRE TENETUR NON EXCUSAT. [L.] Ignorance of things which everyone should know is no excuse.

IGNORANTIA FACTI EXCUSAT; IGNORANTIA JURIS NON EXCUSAT. [L.] Ignorance of fact is excusable; ignorance of the law is no excuse.

IGNORANTIA JUDICIS FORET CALAMITAS INNOCENTIS. [L.] A judge's ignorance would mean calamity for the innocent.

IGNORANTIA JURIS QUOD QUISQUE SCIRE TENETUR NON EXCUSAT. [L.] Ignorance of a law which everyone should know offers no excuse.

IGNORANTIA LEGIS NEMINEM EXCUSAT. [L.] Ignorance of law offers no one an excuse.

IJC. *abbr.* International Joint Commission.

ILL. See CHRONICALLY ~ PERSON.

ILLEGAL. *adj.* Opposed to law. G.H.L. Fridman, *The Law of Contract in Canada*, 2d ed. (Toronto: Carswell, 1986) at 100.

ILLEGAL CONTRACT. An agreement to do anything forbidden either by statute or by the common law.

ILLEGAL GAS. Gas produced from any well in the province in violation of this Act or any regulation or order made under the authority thereof. *The Oil and Gas Conservation Act*, R.S.S. 1978, c. O-2, s. 2.

ILLEGALLY ENLISTED PERSON. A person who has accepted or agreed to accept, or is about to leave Canada with intent to accept, any commission or engagement, or who has been induced to go on board a conveyance under a misapprehension or false representation of the service in which the person is to be engaged with the intention or in order that the person may accept or agree to accept any commission or engagement contrary to this Act. *Foreign Enlistment Act*, R.S.C. 1985, c. F-28, s. 2.

ILLEGAL OIL. Oil produced from any well in the province in violation of this Act or any regulation or order made under the authority thereof. *The Oil and Gas Conservation Act*, R.S.S. 1978, c. O-2, s. 2.

ILLEGAL PRACTICES. Acts in relation to elections that are declared to be illegal practices by the Canada Elections Act. *Dominion Controverted Elections Act*, R.S.C. 1985, c. C-39, s. 2.

ILLEGAL PRODUCT. A product derived in whole or in part from illegal oil or illegal gas. *The Oil and Gas Conservation Act*, R.S.S. 1978, c. O-2, s. 2.

ILLEGAL STRIKE. Strike called in violation of the law.

ILLEGAL WILDLIFE. Any wildlife or part thereof that has been hunted, trapped, taken or held in possession contrary to this Act or the regulations. *Wildlife Act*, R.S.A. 1980, c. W-9, s. 1.

ILLEGITIMATE CHILD. In respect of the estate of his father, an illegitimate child who was born out of wedlock and has not been legitimized by operation of law, and who was under the care, control, maintenance or protection, either physically or financially, of his father for a period of not less than one year immediately preceding his father's death. *Estate Administration Act*, R.S.B.C. 1979, c. 114, s. 85.

ILLEVIABLE. *adj.* Describes a duty or debt which ought or cannot be levied.

ILL HEALTH. See NOTIFIABLE CONDITION OF ~.

ILLICIT. *adj.* Not lawful.

ILLICITUM COLLEGIUM. [L.] An unlawful corporation.

ILLNESS. See MENTAL ~; OCCUPATIONAL ~.

ILLOCABLE. *adj.* Incapable of being hired or rented.

ILLUMINATION. See LEVEL OF ~.

ILLUS QUOD ALIAS LICITUM NON EST NECESSITAS FACIT LICITUM; ET NECESSITAS INDUCIT PRIVILEGIUM QUOD JURE PRIVATUR. [L.] Necessity permits what otherwise is not permitted; and necessity establishes a privilege which is justly removed.

I.L.O. *abbr.* International Labour Organization.

I.L.R. *abbr.* 1. Canadian Insurance Law Reports. 2. Insurance Law Reporter (Can.).

I.M.C.O. CODE. The International Maritime Dangerous Goods Code published by the Inter-Governmental Maritime Consultative Organization. *National Harbours Board Operating By-law*, C.R.C., c. 1064, s. 106.

IMITATION. See COLOURABLE ~.

IMITATION DAIRY PRODUCT. Any food substance other than a dairy product, of whatever origin, source or composition, that is manufactured (i) wholly or in part from a fat or oil, other than that of milk, (ii) for human consumption, and (iii) for the same or similar use as, and in semblance of, a dairy product, but does not include margarine as defined in the Margarine Act or any product intended for use as a dessert topping or as a coffee whitener. *Dairy Industry Act*, S.A. 1981, c. D-1.1, s. 1.

IMITATION MILK PRODUCT. Any food sub-stance other than milk or a manufactured milk product, of whatever origin, source or composition, that is manufactured for human consumption and for the same use as or in semblance of milk or a manufactured milk product, and that is manufactured wholly or in part from any fat or oil other than that of milk. *Milk Industry Act*, R.S.B.C. 1979, c. 258, s. 1.

IMMATERIAL AVERMENT. A statement which is not necessary.

IMMATERIAL ISSUE. An issue on some point which will not decide the outcome of an action.

IMMATURE. *adj.* (a) In relation to salmon, salmon in the parr or smolt stages or of less than 12 inches in length measured from the tip of the nose to the fork or cleft in the tail, and (b) in relation to ouananiche and rainbow trout, fish of less than 8 inches in length measured from the tip of the nose to the fork or cleft in the tail. *Newfoundland Fishery Regulations*, C.R.C., c, 846, s. 2.

IMMEDIATE ANNUITY. An annuity that becomes payable to the contributor immediately when the contributor becomes entitled. *Superannuation acts*.

IMMEDIATE BENEFIT. The benefit that accrues and is derived or derivable immediately upon completion of the works. *Municipal Act*, R.S.O. 1980, c. 302, s. 218.

IMMEDIATE FAMILY. 1. When used to indicate a relationship with any person, means (i) any spouse, son or daughter of that person who has the same home as that person, or (ii) any other relative of that person or of that person's spouse who has the same home as that person. 2. The husband, wife, son, daughter, brother, sister, mother, father or grandparent of an individual. *Credit Unions and Caisses Populaires Act*, S.M. 1977, c. 51, s. 1. 3. When used in reference to any person, includes (a) a parent or grandparent of the person; (b) a brother or sister of the person; (c) a brother or sister of the person's mother or father; (d) the spouse of any of the above, while the spouses are cohabiting; (e) the spouse of the parent, while the spouses are cohabiting. *Child and Family Services and Family Relations Act*, S.N.B. 1980, c. C-2.1, s. 1.

IMMEDIATELY. *adv.* Within reasonable time.

IMMEDIATE PENSION. A pension that becomes payable to a person immediately on his becoming entitled thereto. *Lieutenant Governors Superannuation Act*, R.S.C. 1985, c. L-8, s. 2.

IMMEDIATE PENSION BENEFIT. A pension benefit that is to commence within one year after the member becomes entitled to it. *Pension*

Benefits Standards Act, R.S.C. 1985 (2d Supp.), c. 32, s. 2.

IMMEMORIAL. *adj.* Beyond the memory of the law.

IMMEMORIAL USAGE. A very long-held practice; a custom.

IMMIGRANT. *n.* A person who seeks landing. *Immigration Act*, R.S.C. 1985, c. I-2, s. 2.

IMMIGRANT CHILD. A child who has been brought into a province for the purpose of settlement in a province, and who does not reside in the home of a parent within a province.

IMMIGRANT STATION. Any place designated by the Minister for the examination, treatment or detention of persons for any purpose under this Act. *Immigration Act*, R.S.C. 1985, c. I-2, s. 2.

IMMIGRATION. *n.* Entering a country for the purpose of establishing permanent residence in it. See EMPLOYMENT AND ~ CANADA.

IMMIGRATION APPEAL BOARD. A federal body which acts as an independent court to hear appeals of people ordered deported from Canada, whose relatives have been refused admission into Canada or those with refugee claims. The appeals may be on discretionary as well as legal grounds.

IMMIGRATION OFFICER. A person appointed or designated as an immigration officer pursuant to section 109. *Immigration Act*, R.S.C. 1985, c. I-2, s. 2.

IMM. L.R. (2d). *abbr.* Immigration Law Reporter (Second Series) 1987.

IMMORAL CONTRACT. A contract based on consideration contra bonos mores and considered void.

IMMOVABLE. *n.* Includes all interests in land and land. J.G. McLeod, *The Conflict of Laws* (Calgary: Carswell, 1983) at 317.

IMMOVABLE PROPERTY. Includes real property and any leasehold or other interest in land. *Wills Act*, R.S.N.W.T. 1974, c. W-3, s. 2.

IMMOVABLE PROPERTY AND REAL PROPERTY. With respect to property in Canada, are hereby declared to include (a) any right to explore for or exploit mineral deposits and sources in Canada and other natural resources in Canada, and (b) any right to an amount computed by reference to the production, including profit, from, or to the value of production from, mineral deposits and sources in Canada and other natural resources in Canada. *Income Tax Conventions Interpretation Act*, R.S.C. 1985, c. I-4, s. 5.

IMMOVEABLE. *n.* 1. An immoveable by nature within the meaning of the Civil Code or a moveable object placed by anyone for a permanency in or on an immoveable by nature. *An Act respecting municipal taxation and providing amendments to certain legislation*, S.Q. 1979, c. 72, s. 1. 2. Includes any land or premises that may be occupied separately. *Real Estate Assessment Act*, R.S.Q. 1977, c. E-16, s. 29. 3. Includes any edifice, building, house, premises, enclosed or unenclosed ground, in Québec, or any part of such edifice, building, house, premises or ground. *Physical Contests Act*, R.S.Q. 1977, c. C-52, s. 2.

IMMOVEABLE BY DESTINATION. Any moveable thing placed for a permanency by any person on or in an immoveable by nature. *Real Estate Assessment Act*, R.S.Q. 1977, c. E-16, s. 1.

IMMUNITY. *n.* The state of being free or exempt. See CROWN ~; PUBLIC INTEREST ~; SOVEREIGN ~.

IMMUNIZATION. *n.* The administration of a biological agent to a person to increase that person's resistance to the effect of an infectious agent or its toxic products. *Public Health Act*, S.A. 1984, c. P-27.1, s. 1.

IMMUNIZATION RECORD. A record of immunization maintained by a medical officer of health under this Act. *Immunization of School Pupils Act, 1982*, S.O. 1982, c. 41, s. 1.

IMPACT. See ENVIRONMENTAL ~; HEAD ~ AREA; PELVIC ~ AREA.

IMPACT ASSESSMENT. See HERITAGE RESOURCE ~.

IMPACT BY VEHICLES INSURANCE. Insurance against loss of or damage to the property insured caused by vehicles or objects falling from them.

IMPACT SIMULATION. A test to simulate a motor vehicle impact, carried out in accordance with the procedure described in Schedule III using (a) a test device B, or (b) where a product is designed for a child whose maximum weight is not more than 40 pounds, test device A. *Children's Car Seats and Harnesses Regulations*, C.R.C., c. 921, s. 2.

IMPACT SIMULATOR. See VEHICLE ~.

IMPACT STATEMENT. A statement which (i) specifies in detail the expected effect of a proposed major retail development on every community and shopping district within the forecast market areas, (ii) projects the effects on business within existing shopping areas in terms of retail space vacancies and retail sales volumes, (iii) considers a range of alternative projections for population growth and changes in the real disposable income of consumers, (iv) offers realistic predictions about the likelihood of the alternatives mentioned in subclause (iii), and (v) addresses any other issues specifically requested by the council. *An Act to Amend the Planning Act*, S.P.E.I. 1981, c. 28, s. 1.

IMPANEL. *v.* For a sheriff to write and enter a jury's names.

IMPARTIAL CHAIRMAN. The third, neutral member of a tripartite labour arbitration panel.

IMPARTIALITY. *n.* Lack of bias.

IMPASSE. *n.* A breakdown in collective bargaining when neither side will change its position.

IMPEACHMENT. *n.* Attack on a patent by striking at its validity. H.G. Fox, *The Canadian Law and Practice Relating to Letters Patent for Inventions*, 4th ed. (Toronto: Carswell, 1969) at 515.

IMPEDIMENT. See DIRIMENT ~.

IMPEDIMENT TO MARRIAGE. Marriage is not possible if (a) a prior marriage continues, (b) the parties are related in a prohibited degree, (c) if the marriage is arranged by error, force or fraud, (d) if either party is not old enough or is mentally or physically disabled.

IMPERFECT OBLIGATION. A moral duty which the law cannot enforce.

IMPERFECT TRUST. An executory trust which is not sufficiently constituted or declared.

IMPERIAL. *adj.* As applied to state documents, means of or pertaining to the United Kingdom of Great Britain and Northern Ireland and includes any kingdom that included England, whether known as the United Kingdom of Great Britain and Ireland or otherwise. *Evidence acts.*

IMPERIAL ACTS. The laws passed by the Imperial Parliament. *Interpretation Act*, R.S.Q. 1977, c. I-16, s. 61.

IMPERIALISM. *n.* Domination of one nation by another, whether direct or indirect.

IMPERIAL PARLIAMENT. The parliament of the United Kingdom of Great Britain and Northern Ireland, as at present constituted, or any former kingdom that included England, whether known as the United Kingdom of Great Britain and Ireland or otherwise. Evidence acts.

IMPERIAL STATUTES. The laws passed by the Imperial Parliament. *Interpretation Act*, R.S.Q. 1977, c. I-16, s. 61.

IMPERIAL UNITS. Units of measurement in feet and decimals of a foot. *Registry Act*, R.R.O. 1980, Reg. 898, s. 1.

IMPERITIA CULPAE ADNUMERATUR. [L.] Lack of skill is counted as a fault.

IMPERIUM. *n.* [L.] Entitlement to command, attributed to executive power.

IMPERSONATION. *n.* The act of representing that one is someone else, whether dead or living, fictitious or real.

IMPERTINENCE. *n.* Irrelevance.

IMPLEAD. *v.* To institute legal proceedings against a person.

IMPLEMENT. *n.* Any implement, equipment or machine that is used or intended for use on a farm. See AGRICULTURAL ~(S); FARM ~; FORESTRY ~S; UNUSED FARM ~; USED ~.

IMPLEMENT OF HUSBANDRY. A vehicle designed and adapted primarily for agricultural, horticultural or livestock raising operations. See SELF-PROPELLED ~.

IMPLICATION. *n.* An inference which is necessary or may be presumed and arises out of words or acts in evidence.

IMPLIED AUTHORITY. A certain authority which may be read into an agent's express authority. G.H.L. Fridman, *The Law of Agency*, 5th ed. (London: Butterworths, 1983) at 58.

IMPLIED CONDITION. In some circumstances a court has a right to conclude that everything the parties agreed is not contained in their oral statements or in the written documents which appear to constitute the contract. The additional term is said to exist in the agreement though unspecified; a statute may imply it. G.H.L. Fridman, *The Law of Contract in Canada*, 2d ed. (Toronto: Carswell, 1986) at 448.

IMPLIED CONTRACT. A contract which law concludes does exist from an act, circumstance or relationship.

IMPLIED MALICE. One presumes that the malice needed to support a cause of action exists when someone publishes a defamatory remark. R.E. Brown, *The Law of Defamation in Canada* (Toronto: Carswell, 1987) at 730.

IMPLIED TERM. A term which a contract must suggest, even if it does not express it, so that the parties' intention is not defeated.

IMPLIED TRUST. A trust which comes about when an equitable interpretation is put on the conduct situation of the parties, for example where one person voluntarily transfers property to another person or pays for property and has that property put into another person's name.

IMPLIED WARRANTY. See IMPLIED CONDITION.

IMPORT. v. 1. Import into Canada. *Customs Act*, R.S.C. 1985 (2d Supp.), c. 1, s. 2. 2. With reference to gas or oil, to bring into Canada through pipelines, by railway tank car, by tank truck or by tanker. *National Energy Board Act*, R.S.C. 1985, c. N-7, s. 2. 3. To bring into any province of Canada from any other country or any other province of Canada. Canada regulations. See CANADIAN ~ TRIBUNAL.

IMPORTATION. n. Bringing goods and merchandise into a country from overseas. See PORT OF ~; TIME OF ~.

IMPORT COMPENSATION. The amount that may be paid pursuant to these Regulations to an eligible importer in respect of a quantity of petroleum imported into Canada and includes any special payment made under section 11. *Oil Import Compensation Regulations No. 1, 1975*, C.R.C., c. 335, s. 2.

IMPORT CONTROL LIST. A list of goods established under section 5. *Export and Import Permits Act*, R.S.C. 1985, c. E-19, s. 2.

IMPORTED FABRIC. A fabric that has been woven in any country other than Canada, whether or not it contains Canadian materials, but does not include (a) a fabric imported free of duty, or (b) a fabric that would qualify for a drawback under any other regulations. *Customs Drawback Shirting Fabrics Regulations*, C.R.C., c. 487, s. 2.

IMPORTER. n. A person engaged in the business of importing goods into Canada. See CASUAL ~; DESIGNATED ~.

IMPORTS. n. Produce or goods brought from abroad into a country.

IMPOSITION. n. Contribution; tax.

IMPOSSIBILITY. n. Something either physical, legal or logical: physical when it is unnatural, legal when a rule of law makes it not possible to do and logical when it goes against the essential qualities of the transaction.

IMPOSSIBILIUM NULLA OBLIGATIO EST. [L.] There is no obligation to do the impossible.

IMPOST. n. A rate, charge, fee, tariff, rent, royalty, levy, tax, or any other payment payable under, regulated under or subject to control or approval under an act.

IMPOTENCE. n. Physical inability of any person to perform sexual intercourse.

IMPOTENTIA EXCUSAT LEGEM. [L.] When one is unable to do something one may plead the law as an excuse.

IMPOUND. v. To place in legal custody.

IMPOUNDMENT. n. The confining or holding of a stray by a poundkeeper for a period of time as prescribed in this Act. *The Stray Animals Act*, R.S.S. 1978, c. S-60, s. 2. See TAILINGS ~ AREA.

IMPRESCRIPTABLE RIGHT. A right which people may or may not use as they please, since it cannot be taken away by anyone else whose claim is founded on prescription.

IMPRIMATUR. [L.] Let it be printed.

IMPRISONED. See ARBITRARILY ~.

IMPRISONMENT. n. 1. An arrest which continues. S.A. Cohen, *Due Process of Law* (Toronto: Carswell, 1977) at 96. 2. Includes imprisonment in default of payment of a fine or penalty in money. See FALSE ~; TERM OF ~.

IMPROPER CONDUCT. 1. Includes wilful disobedience of orders, wilful self-inflicted wounding and vicious or criminal conduct. *Pension Act*, R.S.C. 1985, c. P-6, s. 2. 2. A member is guilty of improper conduct who (a) abandons a patient in danger without first ensuring that he has obtained alternative medical or nursing services; (b) in the course of her duties knowingly provides a false or misleading oral or written statement respecting birth, death, notice of disease, state of health, vaccination, course of treatment, or any other matter relating to life or health; (c) impersonates another member; (d) permits her name or picture to be used in connection with the advertisement of any product; (e) irresponsibly divulges professional confidences; (f) engages in discriminatory practices that affect services to patients; (g) acts fraudulently for the purpose of procuring registration; or (h) is convicted of a criminal offence the nature of which could affect the practice of nursing. *Nursing Profession Act*, S.N.W.T. 1975, c. 6, s. 23.

IMPROVE A ROAD. To gravel, stone or macadamize a road, or to cover the surface thereof with a layer of materials welded by means of cement, bitumen or mechanical pressure; or to harden the surface thereof with a mixture of sand and clay, following a process approved by the Minister of Transport. *Roads Act*, R.S.Q. 1977, c. V-8, s. 23.

IMPROVED LAND. 1. A parcel of land separately assessed that has a building thereon, and includes any land in actual use for agricultural purposes, although there is no building thereon. Ontario statutes. 2. Includes enclosed pasture lands.

IMPROVED REAL ESTATE. Real estate (i) on which there exists a building used or capable of being used for residential, commercial, industrial, educational, religious, charitable or recreational purposes, (ii) on which such a building is being constructed, (iii) which is provided with the utilities necessary to serve such a building with electric power, water and sewers but only when the land is being mortgaged for the purpose of financing the construction of such a building, (iv) on which actual farming or ranching operations are being conducted, or (v) that is restricted by law in its use to commercial, industrial or residential purposes by zoning or otherwise.

IMPROVED SIRE. Any stallion, bull, ram or boar, the pedigree of which is recorded in any of the Canadian National Livestock Records or any records recognized by the Canadian National Livestock Records Committee and that has been approved by the minister or an inspector appointed by him. *Animal Husbandry Act*, R.S.M. 1970, c. A90, s. 73.

IMPROVEMENT. *n.* 1. Anything constructed, erected, built, placed, dug or drilled, or intended to be constructed, erected, built, placed, dug or drilled, on or in land except a thing that is neither affixed to the land nor intended to be or become part of the land. 2. (i) A building or structure erected or placed on, in, over or under land, whether or not it is so affixed as to become transferred without special mention by a transfer of the land, (ii) any thing affixed to or integrated in a building or structure affixed to the land that would without special mention be transferred by a transfer of the land, (iii) machinery, equipment, appliances, working tanks and other things including the supporting foundations and footings, but excluding buildings and excluding tanks used exclusively for storage purposes, that form an integral part of an operational unit designed for or used in (A) processing or manufacturing, or (B) the production of natural resources or the transmission of natural resources, or products or by-products thereof, by pipeline, whether or not the machinery, equipment, appliances, working tanks or other things are so affixed as to become transferred without special mention by a transfer of the land, (iv) a mobile unit when located on land owned or being purchased by the owner or purchaser of the unit, other than (A) a mobile unit occupied by a bona fide tourist, or (B) a mobile unit intended for vacation use while not occupied for any purpose, and (v) machinery, equipment and appliances that form an integral part of an operational unit designed for or used in transmitting or receiving communication signals for public resale, whether or not the machinery, equipment or appliances are affixed so as to become transferred without special mention by a transfer of the land. *Municipal Taxation Act*,

R.S.A. 1980, c. M-31, s. 1. 3. Any modification of or addition to a drainage works intended to increase the effectiveness of the system. *Drainage Act*, R.S.O. 1980, c. 126, s. 1. See CAPITAL ~; COMMUNITY ~; DRIVER ~ PROGRAM; HOME ~S; INTERNATIONAL RIVER ~; LAND ~ ASSOCIATION; LAND ~ PURPOSE; LOCAL ~; LOCAL ~S; PERMANENT ~; PROPERTY ~ GRANT; PUBLIC ~; RIVER ~ PURPOSE; ROAD ~ LINE; ROADSIDE ~.

IMPROVEMENT PLAN. See COMMUNITY ~.

IMPROVEMENT PROJECT. See COMMUNITY ~ AREA.

IMPROVER. *n.* 1. A person who has been employed in a designated trade for a length of time not less than the term of apprenticeship specified in the appropriate apprenticeship standards, and, except for seasonal employment, is regularly employed in that trade and who is eligible for training to qualify as a journeyman in that trade. 2. A person selected for training in a designated occupation either to improve that person's capability in any area of the designated occupation or in preparation for qualification under this Act. *An Act to Amend the Industrial Training and Certification Act*, S.N.B. 1987, c. 27, s. 2.

IMPROVING LAND. The doing of any work which improves the character of the land and without limiting the generality of the foregoing includes (i) clearing the land of timber or scrub, (ii) landscaping the land, (iii) fencing the land, and (iv) demolishing structures on the land, but does not include tilling, seeding, cultivating or mowing the land for agricultural or forest production or the harvesting of a crop from the land or the cutting of timber from the land for sale. *The Builders' Lien Act*, S.M. 1980-81, c. 7, s. 1.

IMPUNITAS SEMPER AD DETERIORA INVITAT. [L.] Leaving a crime unpunished always invites worse crimes to be committed.

IMPUTED INCOME. Income with two salient qualities: (1) it is income in kind or non-cash income and (2) it originates outside of the market place. A.F. Sheppard, "The Taxation of Imputed Income and the Rule in *Sharkey v. Wernher*" (1973) Can. Bar Rev. 617 at 617-618.

IMPUTED INCOME FROM PROPERTY. The increase to a person's economic power if the person owns property which produces goods or services that the person or the person's family may enjoy. W. Grover & F. Iacobucci, *Materials on Canadian Income Tax*, 4th ed. (Toronto: Richard De Boo Ltd., 1980) at 157.

INACCESSIBLE. *adj.* When applied to a room or compartment means that the room or compartment is sufficiently remote from access or so placed or guarded that unauthorized persons cannot inadvertently enter the room or compartment, and when applied to electrical equipment means that the electrical equipment is covered by the structure or finish of the building in which it is installed or maintained or is sufficiently remote from access or so placed or guarded that unauthorized persons cannot inadvertently touch or interfere with the equipment. *Power Corporation Act*, R.R.O. 1980, Reg. 794, s. 0.

INACTIVE DOCUMENT. A document no longer used for administrative or legal purposes. *Archives Act*, S.Q. 1983, c. 38, s. 1.

INACTIVE MEMBER. A member or former member of the Society (i) who has no law partners and who has been disbarred or has otherwise ceased to be a member, or has been suspended, or is, by reason of physical or mental illness or for any other reason, unable to practise law; (ii) who has died and who, at the time of his death, had no law partners; (iii) who has absconded or is otherwise improperly absent from his place of practice or whose practice has been neglected for an unduly extended period; (iv) who, there are are reasonable grounds for believing, does not hold sufficient trust moneys to meet his trust liabilities; or (v) in respect of whom sufficient grounds for making an order under section 62 otherwise exist. *Law Society Act*, S.Nfld. 1977, c. 77, s. 61.

INADMISSIBLE CLASS. Any of the classes of persons described in section 19. *Immigration Act*, R.S.C. 1985, c. I-2, s. 2.

IN AEQUALI JURE MELIOR EST CONDITIO POSSIDENTIS. [L.] Where all parties' rights are equal, the actual possessor's claim is stronger.

INALIENABLE. *adj.* Not able to be transferred.

IN ALIENO SOLO. [L.] On another person's land.

IN ALIO LOCO. [L.] In some other place.

IN ALTA PRODITIONE NULLUS POTEST ESSE ACCESSORIUS SED PRINCIPALIS SOLUMMODO. [L.] In high treason no one can be an accessory but certainly one can be a principal.

IN AMBIGUA VOCE LEGIS EA POTIUS ACCIPIENDA EST SIGNIFICATIO QUAE VITIO CARET, PRAESERTIM CUM ETIAM VOLUNTAS LEGIS EX HOC COLLIGI POSSIT. [L.] Where the words of a statute are ambiguous, it is better to accept an interpretation which lacks defects, especially if one may see the intention of the act within it.

IN AMBIGUIS ORATIONIBUS MAXIME

SENTENTIA SPECTANDA EST EJUS QUI EAS PROTULISSET. [L.] When dealing with ambiguous words one should especially regard the intention of the one who used them.

IN ANGLIA NON EST INTERREGNUM. [L.] There is no interregnum in England.

IN ARBITRIO JUDICIS. [L.] At the judge's discretion.

IN ARREARS. Payment is overdue.

IN ARTICULO MORTIS. [L.] At the moment of death.

IN ATROCIORIBUS DELICTIS, PUNITUR AFFECTUS LICET NON SEQUATUR EFFECTUS. [L.] In the case of more horrible crimes, one punishes the intent even though there may be no effect.

INAUGURATION. *n.* Solemn induction into office.

IN AUTER DROIT. [Fr.] In the right of another.

IN AUTRE DROIT. [Fr.] In the right of another.

IN BANC. See BANC.

IN BANCO. See BANCO.

IN BANK. See BANC or BANCO.

IN BEING. 1. Living or en ventre sa mere. *Perpetuities acts.* 2. Living or conceived but unborn. *Perpetuities Act*, R.S.A. 1980, c. P-4, s. 1.

IN BONAM PARTEM. [L.] A word should prima facie be taken in its lawful and rightful sense. P. St. J. Langan, ed., *Maxwell on The Interpretation of Statutes*, 12th ed. (Bombay: N.M. Tripathi, 1976) at 274.

IN BOND. Subject to customs control. Canada regulations.

INBRED LINE. Being a relatively homozygous line produced by inbreeding and selection. *Seeds Regulations*, C.R.C., c. 1400, s. 19.

IN BULK. 1. In respect of a sale of gasoline or diesel fuel, means (a) in a quantity of five hundred litres or more, where the gasoline or diesel fuel is delivered to the purchaser at a retail outlet of the vendor, and (b) in any quantity, in any other case. *Excise Tax Act*, R.S.C. 1985 (2d Supp.), c. 7, s. 69. 2. For the purposes of subsection (5), means confined by the permanent structures of a ship or vessel, without intermediate containment or packaging. *Transportation of Dangerous Goods Act*, R.S.C. 1985, c. T-19, s. 3(6). 3. In relation to any pollutant carried on board a ship whether as cargo or otherwise, means in a quantity that exceeds a quantity prescribed by the Governor in Council with respect to that pollutant by any regulation made pursuant to paragraph 657(1)(p). *Canada Shipping Act*, R.S.C. 1985, c. S-9, s. 654. 4. In relation to oil carried on board a ship, whether as a cargo or otherwise, means in a quantity that exceeds 1,000 tons. *Maritime Pollution Claims Fund Regulations*, C.R.C., c. 1444, s. 2.

INC. *abbr.* 1. Incorporated. 2. Incorporé.

IN CAMERA. [L.] Describes a hearing which takes place either in a judge's private room or in a court with closed doors from which everyone except people involved in the case are excluded.

INCAPABLE. *adj.* Unable because of death, illness, absence from the province or otherwise. *Vital Statistics acts*.

INCAPACITATED. *adj.* In a condition of physical or mental illness or disability of such a nature as to render a person incapable of maintaining himself or his family. *Social Assistance Act*, S.Nfld. 1977, c. 102, s. 2.

INCAPACITATED FUNERAL DIRECTOR. A funeral director suffering from a physical or mental condition or disorder of a nature and extent making it desirable in the interests of the public or the funeral director that he no longer be permitted to engage in the practice of a funeral director or that his practice be restricted. *Funeral Services Act*, R.S.O. 1980, c. 180, s. 14.

INCAPACITATED LICENSEE. A licensee suffering from a physical or mental condition or disorder of a nature and extent making it desirable in the interests of the public or the licensee that he no longer be permitted to practise or that his practice be restricted. *Denture Therapists Act*, R.S.O. 1980, c. 115, s. 12.

INCAPACITATED MEMBER. 1. A member of a professional body suffering from a physical or mental condition or disorder of a nature and extent making it desirable in the interests of the public or the member that the member no longer be permitted to practise or that that practice be restricted. 2. A member suffering from a physical or mental condition, emotional disturbance or excessive use of alcohol or drugs, of a nature and extent making it desirable in the interests of the public or the member that he not be permitted to remain a member of the Institute, or that restrictions be imposed upon his membership. *Chartered Accountants' Act, 1986*, S.N.B. 1986, c. 87, s. 2.

INCAPACITY. *n.* 1. In criminal law, a quality attributed to people with severe mental disorders and young children and, not as widely, to those who are intoxicated. D. Stuart, *Canadian Criminal Law: a treatise*, 2d ed. (Toronto: Carswell, 1987) at 311. 2. A physical or mental condition or disorder suffered by a member of a professional body of such nature and extent that it is desirable in the interests of the public or the member that the member no longer be permitted to practice. See LEGAL ~.

INCARCERATE. *v.* To imprison.

INCARCERATION. *n.* Imprisonment.

IN CASU EXTREMAE NECESSITATIS OMNIA SUNT COMMUNIA. [L.] In the case of extreme necessity, all things are common.

INCAUTE FACTUM PRO NON FACTO HABETUR. [L.] Something done per incuriam is considered to have not been done at all.

INCENDIARISM. See ARSON.

INCENTIVE. See DEVELOPMENT ~; INDIRECT ~ PLAN.

INCENTIVE WAGE PLAN. A wage payment plan under which extra pay is provided for extra work, perfect attendance or the like.

INCERTA PRO NULLIS HABENTUR. [L.] Uncertain things are treated as nullities.

INCERTA QUANTITAS VITIAT ACTUM. [L.] Uncertainty about quantity makes a deed invalid.

INCEST. *n.* Knowing that another person is by blood relationship his or her parent, child, brother, sister, grandparent or grandchild, as the case may be, having sexual intercourse with that person. *Criminal Code*, R.S.C. 1985, c. C-46, s. 155.

INCH. *n.* 1/36 yard. *Weights and Measures Act*, S.C. 1970-71-72, c. 36, schedule II. See CUBIC ~; SQUARE ~.

INCHARTARE. To transfer using a written deed.

IN CHIEF. Describes the examination of a witness by the person who called that witness.

INCHMAREE CLAUSE. A widely-used clause in marine insurance policies which covers losses to a vessel's machinery or hull caused by negligence of any of the crew.

INCHOATE. *adj.* Commenced but not finished.

INCIDENT. *n.* Something which follows or appertains to another thing. See NUCLEAR ~.

INCIDENTAL CATCH. A catch of fish of a species other than a species toward which the fishing effort of a vessel is primarily directed. Canada regulations.

INCIDENTAL MOTION. A motion which is connected with and arises out of other motions. A. Fraser, G.A. Birch & W.A. Dawson, eds., *Beauchesne's Rules and Forms of the House of*

INCIDENTAL QUESTION

Commons of Canada, 5th ed. (Toronto: Carswell, 1978) at 151 and 152.

INCIDENTAL QUESTION. An issue which presents itself while the main question before the court is being decided and which must be solved before the main question can be answered. J.G. McLeod, *The Conflict of Laws* (Calgary: Carswell, 1983) at 50-51.

INCIDENTAL TRAFFIC. Passengers, baggage and goods other than those of a character for which no arrangement has been made prior to the commencement of a charter flight. *Air Carrier Regulations*, C.R.C., c. 3, schedule XIII, s. 37.

INCINERATION. *n.* The treatment of waste by controlled burning, including measures for limiting air pollution, to reduce the volume of the waste and to leave it in a more stable form for disposal. *Environmental Protection Act*, R.R.O. 1980, Reg. 309, s. 1.

INCINERATOR. *n.* Any equipment, apparatus, device or mechanism that is used for the burning of garbage, wood waste, refuse or other waste materials. See ON-SITE ~.

INCINERATOR ASH. The ash residue, other than fly-ash, resulting from incineration where the waste is reduced to ashes containing by weight less than 10 per cent of combustible materials. *Environmental Protection Act*, R.R.O. 1980, Reg. 309, s. 1.

INCINERATOR GOODS. (a) Materials for use exclusively in the construction of, or (b) machinery or apparatus, including equipment to be installed in a chimney or smoke stack, and repair and replacement parts therefor, for use directly and exclusively in the operation of an incinerator owned or to be owned by a municipality and used or to be used primarily for the incineration of waste for the municipality, but does not include motor vehicles, attachments therefor or office equipment. *Excise Tax Act*, R.S.C. 1985 (2d Supp.), c. 7, s. 68.27.

INCINERATOR WASTE. The residue from incineration, other than incinerator ash and fly-ash. *Environmental Protection Act*, R.R.O. 1980, Reg. 309, s. 1.

INCIPITUR. [L.] It begins.

INCITE. *v.* To arouse, provoke, encourage.

INCIVILE EST NISI TOTA SENTENTIA PERSPECTA DE ALIQUA PARTE JUDICARE. [L.] It is unreasonable to judge some part of a decision unless one considers the entire decision.

INCIVISM. *n.* Hostility to a country or government by one of its citizens.

INCLINE. *n.* An excavation that is driven in the earth or strata of an underground mine at an angle with the plane of the horizon and that is or may be used, (i) for ventilation or drainage, or (ii) for the ingress or egress of men, animals or material to or from the mine or part thereof. *Coal Mines Regulation Act*, R.S.A. 1970, c. 52, s. 2.

INCLINED PLANE. Includes slope. *Coal Mines Regulation Act*, R.S.N.S. 1967, c. 36, s. 3.

INCLINE LIFT. A mechanism having a power driven rope, belt or chain, with or without handholds or seats, for lifting or lowering persons or freight on an incline, and includes a ski lift and ski tow. *Elevators and Lifts acts*.

INCLOSED PROPERTY. Any land or water, a description of which is filed with the department, and advertised as "inclosed property" by the owner or lessee thereof over his signature by advertisement in a newspaper published in the province and by posting and maintaining in at least four prominent places at or near the boundaries of the property notices supplied by the department. *Fish and Game Protection Act*, R.S.P.E.I. 1974, c. F-8, s. 1.

INCLOSURE. *n.* Fencing in property in order to cultivate it.

INCLUDE. *v.* Used to enlarge the meaning of a phrase or word in a statute so that the phrase or word is interpreted according to its ordinary sense and is also interpreted as the interpretation clause specifies. P. St. J. Langan, ed., *Maxwell on The Interpretation of Statutes*, 12th ed. (Bombay: N.M. Tripathi, 1976) at 270.

INCLUDED EMPLOYMENT. Employment, other than excepted employment, on or in connection with the operation of any work, undertaking or business that is within the legislative authority of the Parliament of Canada, including, without restricting the generality of the foregoing, (a) any work, undertaking or business operated or carried on or in connection with navigation and shipping, whether inland or maritime, including the operation of a ship and transportation by ship anywhere in Canada; (b) any railway, canal, telegraph or other work or undertaking connecting a province with another province or extending beyond the limits of a province; (c) any line of steam or other ships connecting a province with another province or extending beyond the limits of a province; (d) any ferry between a province and another province or between a province and a country other than Canada; (e) any aerodrome, aircraft or line of air transportation; (f) any radio broadcasting station; (g) any bank; (h) any work, undertaking or business that, although wholly situated within a province, is before of after its execution

500

declared by the Parliament of Canada to be for the general advantage of Canada or for the advantage of two or more provinces; and (i) any work, undertaking or business outside the exclusive legislative authority of provincial legislatures, and any work, undertaking or business of a local or private nature in the Yukon Territory or the Northwest Territories. *Pension Benefits Standards Act*, R.S.C. 1985 (2d Supp.), c. 32, s. 4(4).

INCLUDED OFFENCE. An offence which has the same basic elements as the principal offence with which a person is charged.

INCLUDED PROVINCE. A province other than the Yukon Territory or the Northwest Territories, except a province providing a comprehensive pension plan unless at the time in respect of which the description is relevant there is in force an agreement entered into under subsection 4(3) with the government of that province. *Canada Pension Plan*, R.S.C. 1985, c. C-8, s. 114.

INCLUDIBLE BOOK. In the case of a publisher, a book published by him which is not a book published at the author's expense and, in the case of an accredited bookseller, a new book owned by him. *An Act Respecting the Guarantee of Certain Loans to Publishers and Booksellers*, R.S.Q. 1977, c. G-1, s. 1.

INCLUSIO UNIUS EST EXCLUSIO ALTERIUS. [L.] To include one is to exclude another.

INCLUSIVE TOUR. A round or circle trip performed in whole or in part by air for an inclusive tour price for the period the participants are away from the starting point of the journey. *Air Carrier Regulations*, C.R.C., c. 3. s. 23.

INCLUSIVE TOUR CHARTER. A charter under which an air carrier contracts with one or more tour operators to charter the entire capacity of an aircraft, for resale by the tour operator or operators at a per seat inclusive tour price. *Air Carrier Regulations*, C.R.C., c. 3, s. 23.

INCLUSIVE TOUR GROUP. A group of persons assembled at a point by a tour operator for the purpose of participating as a unit in an inclusive tour. *Air Carrier Regulations*, C.R.C., c. 3, s. 23.

INCLUSIVE TOUR PRICE. 1. Includes, for an inclusive tour group, the cost of (a) transportation, (b) accommodation, and (c) all other services and facilities in the tour program. *Air Carrier Regulations*, C.R.C., c. 3, s. 23. 2. For a participant in an inclusive tour group, the cost of (a) transportation, (b) accommodation, and (c) where applicable, tour features. *Air Carrier Regulations*, C.R.C., c. 3, s. 49.

INCOMBUSTIBLE MATERIAL. Material that, when heated to a temperature of 1,382°F (750°C), neither burns nor gives off flammable vapours in sufficient quantity to ignite at a pilot-flame. *Hull Construction Regulations*, C.R.C., c. 1431, s. 2.

INCOME. *n.* 1. The net receipts over disbursements in the taxation year in the totality of the taxpayer's business as an ongoing concern other than capital expenditures, gifts and the like. *Premium Iron Ores Ltd. v. M.N.R.*, [1966] S.C.R. 685; [1966] C.T.C. 311; 66 D.T.C. 5280 (S.C.C.). 2. Includes (i) the gross amount received or receivable as the product of capital, labour, industry, or skill, (ii) all moneys earned and all gratuities and annuities; (iii) all income, fees, revenue, rent, interest, dividends, or profits arising from any source, including the Dominion, provincial, and municipal governments. *Mining Tax acts*. 3. Includes wages, salaries, emoluments, gratuities and honoraria arising from employment; the fees, earnings and profits from any profession, trade, business or calling, after deducting the expenses of earning the same; interest and dividends received directly or indirectly from shares, stocks, bonds, debentures, deposits, mortgages, agreements for sale, estates, loans and other investments; pensions, annuities, retiring allowances, compensation and similar income from any person, business, estate, insurance or other company, government or government agency; whether or not the income arises or is earned in Nova Scotia or elsewhere. *Assessment Act*, R.S.N.S. 1967, c. 14, s. 1. 4. As used in reference to mining operations, means the net profit derived, or deemed by the mine assessor to have been derived, from mining operations by a person engaged therein without an allowance in respect of depletion, and if such a person receives a net profit by reason of the carrying on by him of the processing of minerals extracted by him, the total net profit to be deemed to have been derived by him from mining operations is that part of the total net profit received by him from the carrying on of mining and processing, remaining after deducting an amount computed as provided in subsection (2). *Mining Royalty and Tax Act*, R.S.M. 1970, c. M180, s. 2. See EARNED ~; EXEMPT ~; FOREIGN ~; GROSS ~; IMPUTED ~; LOW ~; MAXIMUM BENEFIT ~; MONTHLY ~; NET ~; NET ~ OR REVENUE; ORDINARY ~; PERSONAL ~; RESIDUAL ~ OF THE SURVIVING SPOUSE; RESIDUAL ~ OF THE WIDOW; RESOURCE ~; RETIREMENT ~; RETURN OF ~; TAXABLE ~; TAXABLE ~ EARNED IN CANADA.

INCOME ASSISTANCE. (a) Financial assistance; (b) assistance in kind; (c) aid in money or in kind to municipalities, boards, commissions, organizations or persons providing aid, care or health services to indigent, sick, elderly or infirm individuals and in reimbursing expenditures made by them; (d) money for funerals, burials or cremation; (e) health care services; or (f) generally any other form of aid that is necessary for the purpose of relieving poverty, neglect or suffering. *Guaranteed Available Income for Need Act*, R.S.B.C. 1979, c. 158, s. 1.

INCOME-AVERAGING ANNUITY CONTRACT. 1. Of an individual means a contract between the individual and a person licensed or otherwise authorized under the laws of Canada or a province to carry on in Canada an annuities business or a corporation licensed or otherwise authorized under the laws of Canada or a province to carry on in Canada the business of offering to the public its services as trustee, under which (i) in consideration of a qualifying payment as consideration under the contract, that person agrees to pay to the individual, commencing at a time not later than 10 months after the individual has made the qualifying payment, (A) an annuity to the individual for his life, with or without a guaranteed term not exceeding the number of years that is the lesser of (I) 15, and (II) 85 minus the age of the individual at the time the annuity payments commence, or (B) an annuity to the individual for a guaranteed term described in clause (A), or (ii) in consideration of a single payment in respect of his 1981 taxation year, other than a qualifying payment, made by the individual as consideration under the contract, that person makes all payments provided for under the contract to the individual before 1983 and under which no payments are provided except the single payment by the individual and, (iii) in respect of a contract referred to in subparagraph (i), equal annuity payments that are to be made annually or at more frequent periodic intervals, or (iv) in respect of a contract referred to in subparagraph (ii), payments described therein to the individual. *Income Tax Act*, R.S.C. 1952, c. 148 (as am. S.C. 1980-81-82-83, c. 140, s. 30(1)), s. 61(4)(b). 2. Of an individual means, except for the purposes of section 61, a contract (a) that is an income-averaging annuity contract within the meaning assigned by subsection 61(4), and (b) in respect of which the individual has made a deduction under section 61 in computing his income for a taxation year. *Income Tax Act*, R.S.C. 1952, c. 148 (as am. S.C. 1973-74, c. 14, s. 69(3)), s. 248(1).

INCOME ASSURANCE PLAN. See FARM ~.

INCOME FROM A BUSINESS (OR PROPERTY). A taxpayer's income from a business (or property) is his profit therefrom for the taxation year. *Income Tax Act*, R.S.C. 1952, c. 148 as amended by S.C. 1970-71-72, c. 63, subsection 9(1).

INCOME FROM PROPERTY. The profit therefrom for the year. *Income Tax Act*, R.S.C. 1952, c. 148 as amended by S.C. 1970-71-72, c. 63, section 9.

INCOME INSURANCE. See DISABILITY ~ OR BENEFIT PLAN.

INCOME INTEREST. Of a taxpayer in a trust means a right (whether immediate or future and whether absolute or contingent) of the taxpayer as a beneficiary under a personal trust to, or to receive, all or any part of the income of the trust. *Income Tax Act*, R.S.C. 1952, c. 148 (as am. S.C. 1988, c. 55, s. 75(5)), s. 108(1)(e).

INCOME SUPPLEMENT. See GUARANTEED ~.

INCOME TAX. Tax on net income, i.e., income after deducting expenses incurred in order to earn the income. P.W. Hogg, *Constitutional Law of Canada*, 2d ed. (Toronto: Carswell, 1985) at 607. See PROVINCIAL ~; TERRITORIAL ~.

INCOME TAX ACT. The Income Tax Act, chapter 148 of the Revised Statutes of Canada, 1952.

INCOME TAX REFUND. The amount payable to a person in respect of (i) an overpayment of tax paid under the Income Tax Act (Canada) or collected pursuant to an agreement entered into under section 7 of the Federal-Provincial Fiscal Arrangements and Established Programs Financing Act, 1977 (Canada), (ii) an agreement referred to in subclause (i) that is other than a refund of an overpayment of tax paid or collected, (iii) an overpayment of unemployment insurance premiums paid under the Unemployment Insurance Act, 1971 (Canada), or (iv) an overpayment of contributions paid under the Canada Pension Plan (Canada), including any interest payable on that overpayment or payment. *Consumer Credit Transactions Act*, S.A. 1985, c. 22.5, s. 1.

INCOME TAX STATUTE. With reference to an agreeing province, the law of that province that imposes a tax similar to the tax imposed under the federal Income Tax Act. *Income Tax acts*.

IMCOMMODUM NON SOLVIT ARGUMENDUM. [L.] Inconvenience does not spoil an argument.

INCOMPETENCE. *n.* Acts or omissions of the part of a member of a professional body, in that member's occupation, that demonstrate a lack of knowledge, skill or judgment, or disregard for the interests of the recipient of the services of such a nature and to such an extent as to render that member unfit to carry on the occupation.

INCOMPETENCY. See MENTAL ~.

INCOMPETENT. See MENTAL ~.

IN CONCERT. See ACTING JOINTLY OR ~.

IN CONJUNCTIVIS OPORTET UTRUMQUE, IN DISJUNCTIVIS SUFFICIT ALTERAM PARTEM ESSE VERAM. [L.] In conjunctives both should be true; in disjunctives it is enough that one is true.

IN CONSIMILI CASU, CONSIMILE DEBET ESSE REMEDIUM. [L.] In a similar case the remedy should be similar.

INCONSISTENT. *adj.* Repugnant; contradictory.

IN CONSUETUDINIBUS NON DIUTURNITAS TEMPORIS SED SOLIDITAS RATIONIS EST CONSIDERANDA. [L.] In the case of customs, one should consider not the length of time but the entirety of the reason.

INCONTESTABILITY. *n.* The quality of registration of a trade mark which may be attacked only upon the ground of prior use. H.G. Fox, *The Canadian Law of Trade Marks and Unfair Competition*, 3d ed. (Toronto: Carswell, 1972) at 252.

IN CONTRACTIS, BENIGNA; IN TESTAMENTIS, BENIGNIOR; IN RESTITUTIONIBUS, BENIGNISSIMA INTERPRETATIO FACIENDA EST. [L.] The interpretation of contracts should be liberal, of wills more liberal, and of restitutions most liberal.

IN CONTRACTIS TACITE INSUNT QUAE SUNT MORIS ET CONSUETUDINIS. [L.] In contracts, clauses in accord with custom and usage are implied.

IN CONVENTIONIBUS CONTRAHENTIUM VOLUNTAS POTIUS QUAM VERBA SPECTARI PLACUIT. [L.] In construing agreements, one should consider the parties' intention instead of the words actually used.

INCORPORATED. *adj.* One of the words which must be used as part of the name of a corporation. See CORPORATION ~ IN CANADA.

INCORPORATED COMPANY. Include any incorporated bank, and any corporation or body corporate established for any purpose of trade or profit, or for any purpose whatsoever from which revenue is intended to be derived. *Memorials and Executions Act*, R.S.N.B. 1973, c. M-9, s. 23.

INCORPORATION. *n.* Merger of one thing with another so that the two constitute one whole; the formation of a group of people into a corporation or body politic. See ARTICLES OF ~; CERTIFICATE OF ~; INSTRUMENT OF ~; PRE-~ CONTRACT.

INCORPORATOR. *n.* A person who signs articles of incorporation.

INCORPOREAL CHATTEL. An incorporeal right attached to chattels.

INCORPOREAL HEREDITAMENT. Property which is not tangible but can be inherited.

INCORPORÉE. *adj.* One of the words which must be used as part of the name of a corporation.

INCOTERMS. *n.* Rules for the interpretation of major terms used in international trade contracts published by the International Chamber of Commerce. I.F.G. Baxter, *The Law of Banking*, 3d ed. (Toronto: Carswell, 1981) at 135 and 136.

INCREASE. See INCREMENT ~; LENGTH-OF-SERVICE ~; MERIT ~; STATUTORY ~; SUBSEQUENT ~.

INCREMENT. *n.* 1. The monthly guaranteed annual income increment authorized to be paid under this Act, and is an amount equal to the amount by which one-twelfth of the guaranteed income limit applicable to a beneficiary exceeds the beneficiary's basic monthly income for the month for which the payment authorized under this Act is being made. *Ontario Guaranteed Annual Income Act*, R.S.O. 1980, c. 336, s. 1. 2. In respect of a job or position, means the difference between the compensation payable for a rate in the scale or rates applicable to the job or position and the next higher rate in that scale. *Anti-Inflation Guidelines*, C.R.C., c, 302, s. 51. See EXPERIENTIAL ~.

INCREMENTAL CROWN ROYALTY. Of a person for a taxation year means the aggregate of all amounts, each of which is (a) that proportion of his Crown royalty, if any, for the year in respect of a production royalty for the year that the portion of that production royalty that is an incremental production royalty for the year is of that production royalty for the year, or (b) the amount, if any, by which his Crown royalty for the year in respect of his production of old oil in the year from a well or mineral resource exceeds that proportion of that Crown royalty that the amount that would have been his gross revenue for the year from the disposition of old oil from the well or resource, if that old oil has been disposed of at its old oil base price, is of his gross revenue for the year from the disposition of that old oil. *Petroleum and Gas Revenue Tax Act*, R.S.C. 1985, c. P-12, s. 2.

INCREMENTAL LOAN GUARANTEE. A guarantee under which, after default by the borrower, the lender is entitled to apply any proceeds obtained from the realization of the security firstly in satisfaction of that portion of the unpaid balance of the loan that is not guaranteed by Her Majesty. *Regional Development Incentives Regulations*, C.R.C., c. 1386, s. 2.

INCREMENTAL OIL REVENUE. Of a person for a taxation year means the aggregate of amounts received or receivable by him as incremental production royalties for the year and the amount, if any, by which (a) his gross revenue for the year from the disposition of old oil exceeds (b) the amount that would have been his gross revenue for the year from the disposition of old oil if the oil had been disposed of at its old oil base price. *Petroleum and Gas Revenue Tax Act*, R.S.C. 1985, c. P-12, s. 2.

INCREMENTAL PRODUCTION ROYALTY. The amount, if any, by which a production royalty in respect of the production of old oil exceeds the amount that would be the production royalty in respect thereof if the old oil were valued at its old oil base price.

INCREMENTAL RESOURCE ROYALTY. The amount, if any, by which a resource royalty in respect of the production of old oil exceeds the amount that would be the resource royalty in respect thereof if the old oil were valued at its old oil base price.

INCREMENTAL TAX. Additional tax in recognition of the enhanced value of parcels of land or units of minerals due to the enhanced value of oil in, on or under the parcels of land or in the units of minerals. *Mineral Taxation Act*, S.M. 1974, c. 60, s. 3.

INCREMENT INCREASE. An increase in the pay of an employee of one step in pay range approved by the commission for the class of position held by the employee. *Civil Service Act*, R.S.P.E.I. 1974, c. C-9, s. 2.

INCREMENTUM. *n.* [L.] Improvement; increase.

IN CRIMINALIBUS PROBATIONES DEBENT ESSE LUCE CLARIORES. [L.] In criminal cases, proof ought to be more clear than light.

IN CRIMINALIBUS SUFFICIT GENERALIS MALITIA INTENTIONIS CUM FACTO PARIS GRADUS. [L.] When it is accompanied by the right act, what may be generally described as malice may be sufficient to constitute a crime.

INCROACHMENT. See ENCROACHMENT.

INCULPATORY CONFESSION. A statement which incriminates the maker.

INCUMBENT MINISTER. A minister in charge of a department, a minister of state, a minister-delegate and the President of the Assemblée nationale. *Civil Service Act*, S.Q. 1978, c. 15, s. 1.

INCUMBRANCE. *n.* Includes a mortgage and a trust for securing money and a lien and a charge of a portion, annuity or other capital or annual sum. *Conveyancing Act*, R.S.Nfld. 1970, c. 63, s. 2.

INCUMBRANCER. *n.* Includes every person entitled to the benefit of an incumbrance, or to require payment or discharge thereof. *Conveyancing Act*, R.S.Nfld. 1970, c. 63, s. 2.

IN CURIA. [L.] In an open court.

IN CUSTODIA LEGIS. [L.] In legal custody.

INDEBITATUS ASSUMPSIT. [L. the indebted undertook] A kind of action of assumpsit.

INDEFEASIBLE. *adj.* Not able to be voided.

INDEFEASIBLE TITLE. (a) A certificate of indefeasible title issued by the registrar under this Act or a former Act, at any time before this definition came into force, and (b) that part of the information stored in the register respecting one title number, that is required under section 173 (2) to be contained in a duplicate indefeasible title. *Land Title Act*, S.B.C. 1982, c. 60, s. 1.

INDEFENSUS. *n.* [L.] A person who was impleaded and refused to answer.

INDEFINITUM AEQUIPOLLET UNIVERSALI. [L.] What is indefinite is equivalent to universal.

INDEMNIFICATION. *n.* Making good.

INDEMNIFY. *v.* To make good the loss which someone suffered through another's act or default; to grant an indemnity; to agree to indemnify.

INDEMNITY. *n.* 1. An undertaking given by the government or a government corporation (a) to perform an obligation of a person under an agreement on the default of that person, or (b) to hold harmless a party to an agreement from a loss suffered as a result of the default of another party to the agreement, or as a result of a provision of the agreement, but does not include a guarantee. 2. The sessional pay authorized by a legislature to be paid to members. See CONTRACT OF ~; DOUBLE ~ INSURANCE; MONTH OF ~; REPLACEMENT ~; SESSIONAL ~.

INDEMNITY INSURANCE. The insurer agrees to make good a loss specified in the agreement. John G. Fleming, *The Law of Torts*,

6th ed. (Sydney: The Law Book Company Limited, 1983) at 365. See FEE ~.

INDENT. *v.* To cut the top of the first sheet or page of a document in a wavy or toothed line.

INDENTURE. *n.* A deed which two or more parties made. See NON-TRUST ~; TRUST ~.

INDENTURED APPRENTICESHIP. A long term apprenticeship agreement.

INDEPENDENT APPLICANT. A person 18 years of age or over who applies on his own behalf for admission to Canada for permanent residence. *Immigration Regulations*, C.R.C., c. 940, s. 2.

INDEPENDENT AUDITOR. An auditor who is a member in good standing of an institution or association of accountants incorporated by or under the authority of the legislature of a province but who is not, except as otherwise provided by the regulations, the same person or a member of the same firm or office of auditors as, or employed by the same employer as, the provincial auditor. *Federal-Provincial Fiscal Arrangements Act*, S.C. 1972, c. 8, s. 27.

INDEPENDENT CANDIDATE. A person, other than a candidate of an authorized party, whose nomination paper has been received by a returning officer.

INDEPENDENT CONTRACTOR. A person who undertakes with another person to produce a given result but so that, in the actual execution of the work, he is not under the orders or control of the person for whom he does it, and may use his own discretion in things not specified beforehand. *Employment Standards Act*, R.S.M. 1970, c. E110, s. 2.

INDEPENDENT CORPORATION. A corporation that the Canadian Radio-television and Telecommunications Commission is satisfied is not directly controlled by Her Majesty in right of a province or by a municipal government and that is designated by statute or by the lieutenant governor in council of a province for the purpose of broadcasting the following types of programming, namely, (a) programming designed to be presented in such a context as to provide a continuity of learning opportunity aimed at the acquisition or improvement of knowledge or the enlargement of understanding of members of the audience to whom such programming is directed and under circumstances such that the acquisition or improvement of such knowledge or the enlargement of such understanding is subject to supervision or assessment by a provincial authority by any appropriate means, and (b) programming providing information on the available courses of instruction or involving the broadcasting of special education events within

the educational system, which programming, taken as a whole, shall be designed to furnish educational opportunities and shall be distinctly different from general broadcasting available on the national broadcasting service or on privately owned broadcasting undertakings. *Direction to the CRTC (Ineligibility to Hold Broadcasting Licences)*, C.R.C., c. 377, s. 4.

INDEPENDENT DEALER. A bulk dealer who sells fuel oil but does not do so on consignment for an agent-dealer. *Fuel Oil Administration Amendment Act, 1984*, S.A. 1984, c. 19, s. 2.

INDEPENDENT GROUNDING. A grounding that is connected to some metallic object but not to the main system. *Lightning Rods Act*, R.R.O. 1980, Reg. 577, s. 1.

INDEPENDENT MEMBER. A member of a legislature who does not belong to a caucus.

INDEPENDENT OPERATOR. A natural person who carries on work for her or his own account, alone or in partnership, and does not employ any worker.

INDEPENDENT QUALIFIED APPRAISER. A qualified appraiser who is not in full-time employment of the insurer whose fund is being valued, or any associate or affiliated companies of the insurer. *Insurance Act*, R.R.O. 1980, Reg. 536, s. 1.

INDEPENDENT SCHOOL. A school that (a) is not a public school; (b) is maintained and operated in the Province by an authority; and (c) functions as an elementary school, secondary school or both. *School Support (Independent) Act*, R.S.B.C. 1979, c. 378, s. 1.

INDEPENDENT TORTFEASORS. See SEVERAL TORTFEASORS.

INDEPENDENT UNION LOCAL. A union not affiliated with any other labour organization.

INDEPENDENT WORKS. All works and plants outside of the power system that may be classed as tributary to independent undertakings of the licensee and not to the undertaking authorized. *Dominion Water Power Regulations*, C.R.C., c. 1603, s. 2.

INDETERMINATE SENTENCE. Imprisonment of undetermined length. P.W. Hogg, *Constitutional Law of Canada*, 2d ed. (Toronto: Carswell, 1985) at 780.

INDEX. *n.* [L.] An alphabetical list of separate subjects or items contained in a book, writing or similar thing. See AIR POLLUTION ~; BASE PRESSURE ~; BASE VOLUME ~; CONSUMER PRICE ~; DEVELOPMENT ~; PENSION ~.

INDEX ANIMI SERMO EST. [L.] Words are indicators of intent.

INDEXED SECURITY. A qualified security beneficially owned by a taxpayer under a Plan and, where the Plan is administered by a trader or dealer in securities, held in the care and custody of a trader or dealer in securities and registered in the name of a trader or dealer in securities or person who is a nominee for a trader or dealer in securities. *An Act to Amend Taxation Act and Other Fiscal Legislation*, S.Q. 1985, c. 25, s. 54.

INDEXED SECURITY INVESTMENT PLAN. A plan of investment in securities that are qualified securities in relation to the plan and that is evidenced by a written contract entered into between a person described in section 307.2 and a person resident in Canada or licensed to carry on business in Canada who is a trader or dealer in securities, a mutual fund corporation, a mutual fund trust or an insurer in respect of a related segregated fund trust, under which the latter person agrees to compute, for the purposes of the Income Tax Act (Statutes of Canada), any taxable capital gain or allowable capital loss of the person referred to in section 307.2 from the plan for each taxation year of such person in which the contract is in force. *An Act to Amend Taxation Act and Other Fiscal Legislation*, S.Q. 1985, c. 25, s. 54.

INDEXING. *n.* The process by which section 117 rate brackets and, formerly, individual deductions permitted by section 109 of the Income Tax Act are adjusted to reflect any increase in the cost of living index. W. Grover & F. Iacobucci, *Materials on Canadian Income Tax*, 4th ed. (Toronto: Richard De Boo Ltd., 1980) at 451.

INDIAN. *n.* 1. A person who pursuant to this Act is registered as an Indian or is entitled to be registered as an Indian. *Indian Act*, R.S.C. 1985, c. I-5, s. 2. 2. An Indian within the meaning of the Indian Act (Canada) but does not include an enfranchised Indian. *Vital Statistics acts*. 3. An individual who resides on a reserve and is registered as an Indian under the Indian Act (Canada). *Revenue Tax Act*, S.M. 1974, c. 57, s. 2. 4. A person of the North American Indian race, resident in the Province. *Indian Advisory Act*, R.S.B.C. 1979, c. 191, s. 1. See MENTALLY INCOMPETENT ~; STATUS ~.

INDIAN AGENCY. The reserves over which an Indian superintendent has jurisdiction. *The Vital Statistics Act*, R.S.S. 1978, c. V-7, s. 2.

INDIAN AND NORTHERN AFFAIRS CANADA. The federal ministry responsible for the Indian and Inuit people of Canada and for managing natural resources in the Northwest Territories and Yukon Territory.

INDIAN BAND. (a) Council of the band, as defined in the Indian Act, (b) band or council, as defined in the Cree-Naskapi (of Quebec) Act, chapter 18 of the Statutes of Canada, 1984, or (c) the Band or the Council, as defined in the Sechelt Indian Band Self-Government Act, chapter 27 of the Statutes of Canada, 1986. *National Housing Act*, R.S.C. 1985 (2d Supp.), c. 20, s. 7. See BAND.

INDIAN DISTRICT. The reserves over which an Indian superintendent has jurisdiction. *Vital Statistics Act*, R.S.B.C. 1979, c. 425, s. 1.

INDIAN LANDS. Lands reserved for the Indians, including any interests therein, surrendered in accordance with the Indian Act and includes any lands or interests in lands described in any grant, lease, permit, licence or other disposition referred to in section 5. *Indian Oil and Gas Act*, R.S.C. 1985, c. I-7, s. 2.

INDIAN MONEYS. All moneys collected, received or held by Her Majesty for the use and benefit of Indians or bands. *Indian Act*, R.S.C. 1985, c. I-5, s. 2.

INDIAN REGISTER. The register of persons that is maintained under section 5. *Indian Act*, R.S.C. 1985 (1st Supp.), c. 32, s. 1.

INDIAN RESERVE. (a) A reserve, as defined in the Indian Act; or (b) Category IA land or Category IA-N land, as defined in the Cree-Naskapi (of Quebec) Act, chapter 18 of the Statutes of Canada, 1984. *National Energy Board Act*, R.S.C. 1985, c. N-7, s. 78(3). See RESERVE.

INDIAN SETTLEMENT. Any group of Indians living in a district that is not an Indian reserve. *Quebec Fishery Regulations*, C.R.C., c. 852, s. 2.

INDIAN SUPERINTENDENT. A superintendent within the meaning of the Indian Act (Canada). *The Vital Statistics Act*, R.S.S. 1978, c. V-7, s. 2.

INDICATING SWITCH. A switch designed or marked to show readily whether the switch is in an "On" or "Off" position. *Power Corporation Act*, R.R.O. 1980, Reg. 794, s. 0.

INDICATION. *n.* A signal lens display that is activated by internal illumination. *Highway Traffic Amendment Act*, S.O. 1984, c. 21, s. 9. See SIGNAL ~.

INDICATOR. See PLANT ~ HOST.

INDICIA. *n.* [L.] 1. Marks; signs. 2. Facts which cause inferences to be made.

INDICTABLE OFFENCE. A criminal offence which is triable by way of indictment.

INDICTABLE ONLY OFFENCE. A criminal offence which can only be tried by way of indictment.

INDICTED. *adj.* Charged with a criminal offence in an indictment.

INDICTEE. *n.* The person who is presented with an indictment.

INDICTIO. *n.* [L.] An indictment.

INDICTMENT. *n.* 1. Includes (a) information or a count therein, (b) a plea, replication or other pleading, and (c) any record. *Criminal Code*, R.S.C. 1985, c. C-46, s. 2. 2. Includes an information or charge in respect of which a person has been tried for an indictable offence under Part XIX. *Criminal Code*, R.S.C. 1985, c. C-46, s. 673. See BILL OF ~.

INDICTOR. *n.* The one who indicts another person for an offence.

INDIFFERENT. *adj.* Not having any interest which may prevent impartial judgment.

INDIGENT. *n.* A patient whose account is not fully paid, or who, on the expiration of thirty days after he is discharged from the hospital or discontinues his attendance thereat, has not made arrangements satisfactory to the operator of the hospital for payment of his account. *Hospitals Act*, R.S.M. 1970, c. H120, s. 2.

INDIGENT PERSON. A person who is actually destitute of means from personal resources of obtaining food, clothing, shelter, medical advice, or attention and hospital care necessary for the immediate personal wants or those of any dependants.

INDIRECT EVIDENCE. Proof of related circumstances from which a controversial fact, not directly proved by documents or witnesses, may be inferred. See CIRCUMSTANTIAL EVIDENCE.

INDIRECT INCENTIVE PLAN. A plan under which the compensation of an employee under the plan (a) is determined by reference to the performance or profitability of the employer, (b) is determined by reference to the performance of, or the job or position held by, an employee, or (c) is, in whole or in part, in the form of shares or of an option or a right to acquire shares, and includes a profit sharing plan, bonus plan, performance award plan, employer-assisted stock purchase plan, stock option plan, phantom stock plan, stock appreciation plan, and an arrangement under which payments are contingent on the achievement of predetermined objectives, but does not include a deferred profit sharing plan as defined in subsection 147(1) of the Income Tax Act. *Anti-Inflation Guidelines*, C.R.C., c. 302, s. 59.

INDIRECT SERVICE WATER HEATER. A service water heater that derives its heat from a heating medium such as warm air, steam or hot water. *Building Code Act*, R.R.O. 1980, Reg. 87, s. 1.

INDIRECT TAX. A tax demanded from one person who expects and intends to be indemnified at another's expense; examples are customs or excise tax. W. Grover & F. Iacobucci, *Materials on Canadian Income Tax*, 4th ed. (Toronto: Richard De Boo Ltd., 1980) at 64.

INDIRECT WASTE. Waste that is not discharged directly into drainage piping. *Ontario Water Resources Act*, R.R.O. 1980, Reg. 736, s. 1.

INDIRECT WASTE PIPE. A waste pipe that does not connect directly with drainage piping, but discharges into it through a trapped fixture. *Ontario Water Resources Act*, R.R.O. 1980, Reg. 736, s. 1.

INDIVIDUAL. *n.* 1. A natural person. 2. A natural person, but does not include a partnership, unincorporated association, unincorporated syndicate, unincorporated organization, trust, or a natural person in the capacity of trustee, executor, administrator or other legal representative. 3. A person who is not a corporation. 4. Any person who is not a member of a family. *Social Aid Act*, R.S.Q. 1977, c. A-16, s. 1. 5. Shall not include close personal friends or business associates of the broker or salesman, or customers with whom he habitually trades. *Securities Act*, R.S.Q. 1977, c. V-1, s. 79. See CORPORATION CONTROLLED BY AN ~.

INDIVIDUAL APPRAISAL. A verification made on one producer's farm to determine the actual yield of his insured crop. *Crop Insurance Act*, R.S.Q. 1977, c. A-30, s. 1.

INDIVIDUAL BARGAINING. The right of an individual to present grievances not contrary to an existing union contract with the unit to which that individual belongs.

INDIVIDUAL COLLECTION SYSTEM. The collection of his own domestic wastes by a householder and the transportation of such wastes to a waste disposal site by the householder. *Environmental Protection Act*, R.R.O. 1980, Reg. 309, s. 1.

INDIVIDUALLY MEASURED COMMODITY. A commodity that is measured by a device that (a) records the measurement, or (b) is operated by a person who observes or records the measurement of each quantity of commodity measured by the device. *Weights and Measures Regulations*, C.R.C., c. 1605, s. 45.

INDIVIDUAL RATE. The actual rate of pay received by a person; a rate of pay based on each employee's qualifications.

INDIVIDUAL TAP. A connection made into a pipeline transmitting gas in order to provide gas service to a rural consumer outside the service area of a rural gas utility. *Rural Gas Act*, R.S.A. 1980, c. R-19, s. 1.

INDOCTRINATION. See LINE ~.

INDOOR POOL. A swimming pool where the pool and deck are totally or partially enclosed within a building or structure covered by a roof. *Public Health Act*, R.R.O. 1980, Reg. 849, s. 1.

INDORSEE. *n.* The individual to whom a bill of exchange, bill of lading or promissory note, for example, is assigned by indorsing it.

INDORSEMENT. *n.* Anything printed or written on the back of a document or deed. See QUALIFIED ~; RESTRICTIVE ~.

INDORSER. *n.* The person who indorses the holder or payee by writing her or his name on the back of a bill of exchange.

INDOWMENT. *n.* 1. Assigning or giving dower. 2. Any kind of property belonging permanently to a charity.

IN DUBIO HAEC LEGIS CONSTRUCTIO QUAM VERBA OSTENDUNT. [L.] In a doubtful situation, the construction which the words indicate is the legal construction.

INDUCEMENT. *n.* The assertion of motive; incitement to do something.

INDUCTIVE METHOD. Deduction of a general rule from a particular instance.

INDUST. L.J. *abbr.* Industrial Law Journal.

INDUSTRIAL ACCIDENT. A sudden and unforeseen event, attributable to any cause, which happens to a person, arising out of or in the course of his work and resulting in an employment injury to him. *An Act Respecting Industrial Accidents and Occupational Diseases*, S.Q. 1985, c. 6, s. 2.

INDUSTRIAL ACTION. (a) A strike, (b) picketing. *Labour Code Amendment Act*, S.B.C. 1984, c. 24, s. 3. See UNLAWFUL ~.

INDUSTRIAL AGGREGATE. In relation to an adjustment year is the average weekly earnings for all employees in Prince Edward Island for that year as published by Statistics Canada under the authority of the Statistics Act (Can) R.S.C. 1970, Chap. S-16. *An Act to Amend the Legislative Assembly Act*, S.P.E.I. 1986, c. 2, s. 1.

INDUSTRIAL AND INTELLECTUAL PROPERTY. The law which relates to industrial designs, patents and trade marks. H.G. Fox, *The Canadian Law of Copyright and Industrial Designs*, 2d ed. (Toronto: Carswell, 1967) at 3.

INDUSTRIAL BUILDINGS. See FACTORIES AND ~.

INDUSTRIAL COMPANY. A company other than a company recognized by the Board as a mining company or investment company. *Security Frauds Prevention Act*, R.S.N.B. 1973, c. S-6, s. 1.

INDUSTRIAL COMPOSITE. For an adjustment year means the average weekly wages and salaries of the Industrial Composite in Canada as published by Statistics Canada under the authority of the Statistics Act (Canada), as amended from time to time.

INDUSTRIAL CONTRACT. A contract of life insurance for an amount not exceeding $2000, exclusive of any benefit, surplus, profit, dividend or bonus also payable under the contract, and that provides for payment of premiums at fortnightly or shorter intervals, or, if the premiums are usually collected at the home of the insured, at monthly intervals. *Insurance acts.*

INDUSTRIAL CROP. A crop produced by human industry.

INDUSTRIAL CUSTOMER. A person purchasing electricity for the operation of a manufacturing, mining or processing plant or operation that is served with electricity at 60kV or higher. *Industrial Electricity Rate Discount Act*, S.B.C. 1985, c. 49, s. 1.

INDUSTRIAL DESIGN. A monopoly given to an original and new idea of configuration or shape relating to an article of commerce and visually appealing. H.G. Fox, *The Canadian Law of Copyright and Industrial Designs*, 2d ed. (Toronto: Carswell, 1967) at 5.

INDUSTRIAL DISEASE. 1. Includes, (i) a disease resulting from exposure to a substance relating to a particular process, a trade or occupation in an industry, (ii) a disease peculiar to or characteristic of a particular industrial process, trade or occupation, (iii) a medical condition that in the opinion of the Board requires a worker to be removed either temporarily or permanently from exposure to a substance because the condition may be a precursor to an industrial disease, or (iv) any of the diseases mentioned in Schedule 3 or 4. *Workers' Compensation Amendment Act, 1984 (No. 2)*, S.O. 1984, c. 58, s. 1. 2. Any disease in respect of which compensation is payable under the law of the province where the employee is usually employed respecting compensation for workmen and the dependants of deceased workmen. *Government Employees Compensation Act*,

R.S.C. 1985, c. G-5, s. 2. 3. Silicosis and any other disease that the Lieutenant Governor in Council may by Order declare to be an industrial disease. *Industrial Safety Act*, R.S.N.B. 1973, c. I-5, s. 1.

INDUSTRIAL DISPUTE. Any dispute or difference or apprehended dispute or difference between an employer and one or more employees or a bargaining agent acting on behalf of the employees, as to matters or things affecting or relating to terms or conditions of employment or work done or to be done by the employee or employees or as to privileges, rights and duties of the employer, the employee or employees.

INDUSTRIAL ENTERPRISE. An enterprise or undertaking, including a cooperative enterprise or undertaking, engaging in or carrying on, or proposing to engage in or carry on, in the Province, an industry, trade, business or other enterprise or undertaking of any kind, including, without limiting the generality of the foregoing, (a) a form of agriculture; (b) the processing of agricultural products; and (c) a form of the tourist industry. *Development Corporation Act*, R.S.B.C. 1979, c. 93, s. 1.

INDUSTRIAL ESTABLISHMENT. 1. A building or part of a building in which any manufacturing process, assembling or handling of materials in connection with the manfacturing, preparing, treating or finishing of any goods or products, is carried on. 2. An office building, factory, arena, shop or office, and any land, buildings and structures appertaining thereto. 3. Any federal work, undertaking or business and includes such branch, section or other division of a federal work, undertaking or business as is designated as an industrial establishment by regulations made under paragraph 264(b). *Canada Labour Code*, R.S.C. 1985, c. L-2, s. 166.

INDUSTRIAL MILK PLANT. A cheese factory, concentrated milk plant, creamery or milk receiving station.

INDUSTRIAL OCCUPANCY. Occupancy for assembling, fabricating, manufacturing, processing, repairing or storing of goods or materials or for producing, converting, processing or storing of energy, waste or natural resources.

INDUSTRIAL OPERATION. Any work within or upon forest land in which more than two people are engaged. *Forest Fires Act*, R.S.N.B. 1973, c. F-20, s. 1.

INDUSTRIAL OR COMMERCIAL OPERATION. An activity related to timber, forest, mining, drilling and construction activities, and includes any other activities that may be spec-

ified in the regulations. *Prairie and Forest Fires Act*, S.S. 1982-83, c. P-22.1, s. 2.

INDUSTRIAL OVEN. An oven used to bake and dry materials. D. Robertson, *Ontario Health and Safety Guide* (Toronto: Richard De Boo Ltd., 1988) at 5-214B.

INDUSTRIAL PLANT. Includes any factory or industry, and all works, plants and processes incidental to it. *Industrial Operation Compensation Act*, R.S.B.C. 1979, c. 195, s. 1.

INDUSTRIAL PROPERTY. 1. Copyright, industrial design, patent and trade mark matters. D. Sgayias *et al.*, *Federal Court Practice 1988* (Toronto: Carswell, 1987) at 516. 2. All patents of invention, copyrights, industrial designs, and any other intellectual or industrial property rights in every country where the same exist from time to time, all applications therefor arising from or acquired in connection therewith and all right to make such applications. *IDEA Corporation Act, 1981*, S.O. 1981, c. 34, s. 1.

INDUSTRIAL PURPOSES. The operation of railways, factories, stores or warehouses but does not include the sale or barter of water for any of those purposes. *Water Resources acts*.

INDUSTRIAL RADIOGRAPHY. Radiography for industrial purposes involving the use of radioactive prescribed substances or particle accelerators. *Atomic Energy Control Regulations*, C.R.C., c. 365, s. 18.

INDUSTRIAL RADIOLOGICAL TECHNICIAN. A person who operates an x-ray machine or uses radioactive isotopes for the examination or treatment of things other than living persons. *Radiological Technicians Act*, R.S.A. 1980, c. R-3, s. 1.

INDUSTRIAL RAILWAY. Any railway operated by or for an industry served thereby. *Montreal Harbour Railway Tariff By-law*, C.R.C., c. 1079, s. 2.

INDUSTRIAL RELATIONS. The interactions among unions, management, government, employees, and employers.

INDUSTRIAL RESTRUCTURING. Includes technological change. *Labour Adjustment Benefits Act*, R.S.C. 1985, c. L-1, s. 2.

INDUSTRIAL ROAD. 1. A road constructed or existing for transportation of natural resources, raw or manufactured, or transportation of machinery, materials or personnel by motor vehicle, and includes all bridges, wharves, log dumps and works forming a part of it, but does not include a public road, street, lane or other public communication; a privately owned road used by a farmer or resident for his own purposes; a road used exclusively for the construction and maintenance of electric power lines, telephone lines or pipe lines; roads and yards within manufacturing plants, industrial sites, storage yards, airports and construction sites; tote roads, cat roads and access roads. *Highway (Industrial) Act*, R.S.B.C. 1979, c. 168, s. 1. 2. Any road or highway or any portion thereof declared under The Highways Department Act to be an industrial road by the Lieutenant Governor in Council. *The Highway Traffic Act*, S.M. 1985-86, c. 3, s. 1.

INDUSTRIAL SCHOOL. Any industrial school or juvenile reformatory or other reformative institution or refuge for children duly approved by provincial statute or by the lieutenant governor in council in any province, and includes such an institution in a province other than that in which the committal is made, when such institution is otherwise available. *Juvenile Delinquents Act*, R.S.C. 1970, c. J-3, s. 2.

INDUSTRIAL SOURCE. Any facility, equipment, action, operation or treatment, that may be a source of an air contaminant, involving or relating to physical, chemical, industrial or manufacturing processes but does not include fuel-burning equipment or incinerators.

INDUSTRIAL STANDARDS SCHEDULE. A document which fixes the hours and wages for employees in various industries in a province.

INDUSTRIAL STRUCTURE. See MOBILE INDUSTRIAL OR COMMERCIAL STRUCTURE.

INDUSTRIAL SYSTEM. The whole or any part of an electric system primarily intended to serve one or more industrial operations of which the system forms a part and designated by the Board as an industrial system. *Hydro and Electric Energy Act*, R.S.A. 1980, c. H-13, s. 1.

INDUSTRIAL UNDERTAKING. 1. Any establishment, work, or undertaking in or about any industry, business, trade, or occupation. *Payment of Wages Act*, S.M. 1970, c. 44, s. 1. 2. Includes (i) mines, quarries, and other works for the extraction of minerals from the earth, (ii) industries in which articles are manufactured, altered, cleaned, repaired, ornamented, finished, adapted for sale, broken up or demolished, or in which minerals are transformed, including shipbuilding, and the generation, transformation, and transmission of electricity and motive power of any kind, (iii) construction, reconstruction, maintenance, repair, alteration or demolition of any building, railway, tramway, harbour, dock, pier, canal, inland waterway, road, tunnel, bridge, viaduct, sewer, drain, well, telegraphic or telephonic installation, electrical undertaking, gas work, waterwork, or other work of construction, as well as the preparation

for or laying the foundation of any such work or structure, and (iv) transport of passengers or goods by road or rail or inland waterways, including the handling of goods at docks, quays, wharves, and warehouses, but excluding transport by hand.

INDUSTRIAL UNION. A group whose members includes employees in a particular industry regardless of the actual nature of their work.

INDUSTRIAL UNION COUNCIL. See CITY ~.

INDUSTRIAL UNIT. A bargaining group made up of production and maintenance employees.

INDUSTRIAL WASTE. Any liquid, solid or other waste, or any combination thereof, resulting from any process of industry or manufacture or the exploration for, or development of, a natural resource and includes (a) storm water that has been contaminated through contact with useful or waste materials as a result of human activity, and (b) useful or waste material from a danger of pollution that becomes a contaminant. *Clean Environment Act*, S.N.B. 1975, c. 12, s. 1. See LIQUID ~.

INDUSTRIAL WASTE WATER. Waste water carrying solid, liquid or gaseous residue from (a) an industrial, manufacturing, commercial or institutional process or establishment, or any other process or establishment of the same nature; or (b) the development, recovery or processing of raw material.

INDUSTRY. *n.* 1. An establishment, undertaking, trade or business, whether it is carried on in conjunction with other occupations or separately. 2. Includes any business, calling, trade, profession, work or occupation. See AGRICULTURAL ~; AMBULANCE SERVICE ~; CONSTRUCTION ~; CONTINUOUS ~; CRITICAL ~; FISHING ~; FOREST ~; FOREST INDUSTRIES; HOSPITALITY ~; INTEGRATED ~; LOGGING ~; METALLIFEROUS MINING ~; PETROLEUM ~; RESOURCE-BASED ~; RETAIL GASOLINE SERVICE ~; SEASONAL ~; TRADE, ~ OR PROFESSION.

INDUSTRY-WIDE AGREEMENT. A collective agreement affecting all employees of an industry in a geographic area.

INDUSTRY-WIDE BARGAINING. Bargaining in respect of all employers and employees of an industry in a geographic area.

INEBRIATE. *n.* An intoxicated person.

INEDIBLE. *adj.* 1. Unfit for food. 2. In relation to a meat product, means a meat product (a) that has been condemned or denatured, (b) that by its nature is not edible, or (c) that is not customarily eaten by humans in Canada. *Meat Inspection Regulations*, C.R.C., c. 1032, s. 2.

INEDIBLE EGG. An egg that is not suitable for human consumption and includes an egg that, (i) is contaminated with an odour foreign to that of a normal egg, (ii) is musty or mouldy, (iii) has been in an incubator, or (iv) has any internal defect other than a meat spot or blood spot less than 1/8 inch diameter.

INEDIBLE PROCESSED EGG. Processed egg that contains any inedible egg or that is otherwise not suitable for human consumption.

IN EO QUOD PLUS SIT, SEMPER INEST ET MINUS. [L.] The less is always part of the greater.

INEQUITY. See INTER-PLANT ~.

INERT. *adj.* In relation to atmosphere or gas, means that the atmosphere or gas is so deficient in oxygen as to be incapable of propagating flame. *Fire Detection and Extinguishing Equipment Regulations*, C.R.C., c. 1422, s. 10.

INERT FILL. Earth or rock fill that contains no putrescible materials or soluble or decomposable chemical substances. *Environmental Protection Act*, R.R.O. 1980, Reg. 309, s. 1.

INERT MATTER. Includes straws, stems, awns, leaf, chaff and dirt. *Seeds Regulations*, C.R.C., c. 1400, s. 2.

IN ESSE. [L.] Which actually exists.

INEVITABLE ACCIDENT. An accident which cannot be avoided by exercising ordinary caution, care and skill.

IN EXPECTANCY. Executory, relating to some future thing. See INTEREST ~.

IN EXTENSO. [L.] From start to finish; omitting nothing.

IN EXTREMIS. [L.] At the very last.

IN FACIENDO. [L.] In feasance; in doing.

INFAMY. *n.* Disgrace in public; complete loss of character.

INFANT. *n.* 1. A person under the age of eighteen years. 2. Any person under the age of 19 years. *Public Trustee Act*, R.S.B.C. 1979, c. 348, s. 1. 3. Person who is unmarried and under the age of twenty-one years, and includes a child who is unborn at the death of its father. *Guardianship Act*, R.S.N.S. 1967, c. 121, s. 1. 4. A person who is under the age of one year. *Food and Drug Regulations*, C.R.C., c. 870, c. B.25.001. 5. A person under 3 years of age. *Aircraft Seats, Safety Belts and Safety Harnesses*

Order, C.R.C., c. 28, s. 2. See SUDDEN ~ DEATH SYNDROME.

INFANT CHILD. A child who has not attained the age of majority. *Change of Name Act*, S.N.S. 1977, c. 6, s. 2.

INFANT FOOD. A food that is sold or is labelled or advertised for consumption by infants. *Food and Drug Regulations*, C.R.C., c. 870, c. B.25.001.

INFANT FORMULA. A food that is sold or is labelled or advertised as a substitute for human milk in meeting the nutritional requirements of (a) infants with normal dietary needs, or (b) infants with special dietary needs, and that is of such consistency that when ready to serve, it passes freely through a nursing bottle nipple. *Food and Drug Regulations*, C.R.C., c. 870, c. B.25.001.

INFANTICIDE. *n.* 1. The murder of a child by its mother. F.A. Jaffe, *A Guide to Pathological Evidence*, 2d ed. (Toronto: Carswell, 1983) at 178. 2. A female person commits infanticide when by a wilful act or omission she causes the death of her newly-born child, if at the time of the act or omission she is not fully recovered from the effects of giving birth to the child and by reason thereof or of the effect of lactation consequent on the birth of the child her mind is then disturbed. *Criminal Code*, R.S.C. 1985, c. C-46, s. 233.

INFANT OR MINOR. A person under eighteen years of age. Saskatchewan statutes.

INFARCT. *n.* The death of part of an organ in a living body because its blood supply is suddenly obstructed. F.A. Jaffe, *A Guide to Pathological Evidence*, 2d ed. (Toronto: Carswell, 1983) at 178. See BRAIN ~.

IN FAVOREM VITAE, LIBERTATIS ET INNOCENTIAE OMNIA PRAESUMUNTUR. [L.] In partiality to life, liberty and innocence all things are presumed.

INFECTED. *adj.* 1. Infected with the causal organisms of a disease. *Bees Act*, R.S.O. 1980, c. 42, s. 1. 2. Having a venereal disease in a communicable stage. *Venereal Diseases Prevention Act*, R.S.A. 1980, c. V-2, s. 1.

INFECTED PERSON. See VENEREALLY ~.

INFECTION. *n.* The entry and multiplication of an infectious agent in the body of a person or animal. *Public Health Act*, S.A. 1984, c. P-27.1, s. 1.

INFECTIOUS. *adj.* Communicable in any manner, even at a distance.

INFECTIOUS AGENT. An organism or microorganism that is capable of producing a communicable disease. *Public Health Act*, S.A. 1984, c. P-27.1, s. 1.

INFECTIOUS DISEASE. 1. Tuberculosis, brucellosis, swine plague, caseous lymphadenitis, equine encephalomyelitis, foot rot in sheep, distemper in fur bearers and any disease or endo- or ecto-parasite of livestock that the Lieutenant Governor in Council declares to be an infectious or contagious disease for the purpose of this Act. *Livestock Disease Control Act*, R.S.B.C. 1979, c. 242, s. 1. 2. Includes a reportable disease. 3. Any disease included in the schedule. *Quarantine Act*, R.S.C. 1985, c. Q-1, s. 2.

INFERENCE. *n.* Facts sufficient that a particular conclusion may be drawn from them. John G. Fleming, *The Law of Torts*, 6th ed. (Sydney: The Law Book Company Limited, 1983) at 296.

INFERIOR COURT. 1. A court which is subject to the control of a higher court. 2. A court staffed by justices of the peace or magistrates which has jurisdiction over minor criminal offences and small civil claims. P.W. Hogg, *Constitutional Law of Canada*, 2d ed. (Toronto: Carswell, 1985) at 134.

INFESTED. *adj.* 1. Containing any injurious, noxious or troublesome insect or animal pest. 2. Contaminated with a pest or so exposed to a pest that contamination can reasonably be expected to exist. *Plant Quarantine Act*, R.S.C. 1985, c. P-15, s. 2.

IN FICTIONE JURIS SEMPER AEQUITAS EXISTIT. [L.] Equity is always manifested in legal fiction.

INFIELD. *n.* The area of a race course surrounded by the racing strip. *Race Track Supervision Regulations*, C.R.C., c. 441, s. 2.

IN FIERI. [L.] While something was being accomplished.

INFIRM. *adj.* As applied to any person, has reference to any mental or physical infirmity rendering that person incapable ordinarily of pursuing any substantially gainful occupation. *Estate Tax Act*, R.S.C. 1970, c. E-9, s. 62.

INFIRM PERSON. 1. A person who because of mental or physical disability is certified by a duly qualified medical practitioner as a person unable to provide or care for herself or himself and needs to be under the care or supervision of another person. 2. An institutionalized person whose age or health is such that they require institutional care or treatment.

IN FLAGRANTE DELICTO. [L.] In the actual act.

INFLAMMABLE. *adj.* And flammable are deemed to be synonymous. *Dangerous Goods Shipping Regulations*, C.R.C., c. 1419, s. 2.

INFLAMMABLE LIQUID. Any liquid that gives off inflammable vapours (as determined by the flash point from Tagliabue's open cup tester, as used for test of burning oils) at or below a temperature of 80°F. *Electric Sparks Prevention Regulations*, C.R.C., c. 1181, s. 3.

INFLAMMABLE MATERIAL. Trees, timber, brush, slash, grass, debris or other vegetation or things of a similar nature. *Forest Protection Act*, R.S.N.W.T. 1974, c. F-8, s. 2.

INFLAMMABLE PETROLEUM PRODUCTS. Any products obtained or recovered from petroleum, whether by distillation, condensation, absorption, or otherwise, that have a flash point below one hundred and seventy-five degrees Fahrenheit according to the Tagliabue Closed Cup Tester, and include any combination of such products. *Petroleum Products Act*, R.S.N.W.T. 1974, c. P-5, s. 2.

INFLATION. *n.* That the value of a single dollar in one year is greater than the value of a single dollar in the next year or any subsequent year in an inflationary spiral. W. Grover & F. Iacobucci, *Materials on Canadian Income Tax*, 4th ed. (Toronto: Richard De Boo Ltd., 1980) at 1017. See ANTI-~ ACT (CANADA).

INFLATION PRESSURE. See MAXIMUM PERMISSIBLE.

IN FLIGHT. From the time when all external doors are closed following embarkation until the later of (a) the time at which any such door is opened for the purpose of disembarkation, and (b) where the aircraft makes a forced landing in circumstances in which the owner or operator thereof or a person acting on behalf of either of them is not in control of the aircraft, the time at which control of the aircraft is restored to the owner or operator thereof or a person acting on behalf of either of them. *Criminal Code*, R.S.C. 1985, c. C-46, s. 7(8).

INFLUENCE. See UNDUE ~.

INFORMAL. *adj.* Lacking proper legal form.

INFORMAL CONTRACT. A parol or simple contract. G.H.L. Fridman, *The Law of Contract in Canada*, 2d ed. (Toronto: Carswell, 1986) at 10.

INFORMAL EQUITY. Subject to the regulations, any interest or right to participate in or benefit from, either currently or in the future, other than by way of formal equity, the assets, revenues or business activities of another person. *Canadian Ownership and Control Determination Act*, R.S.C. 1985, c. C-20, s. 2.

INFORMALITY. *n.* Lack of legal form.

INFORMANT. *n.* A person who lays an information. *Criminal Code*, R.S.C. 1985, c. C-46, s. 785.

IN FORMA PAUPERIS. [L. in the form of a poor person] A litigant allowed to proceed in this way is not liable to pay court costs.

INFORMATION. *n.* 1. Includes (a) a count in an information, and (b) a complaint in respect of which a justice is authorized by an Act of Parliament or an enactment made thereunder to make an order. *Criminal Code*, R.S.C. 1985, c. C-46, s. 785. 2. Information respecting a consumer's identity, residence, dependents, marital status, employment, borrowing and repayment history, income, assets and liabilities, credit worthiness, education, character, reputation, health, physical or personal characteristics or mode of living. *Consumer Reporting Act*, S.N.S. 1973, c. 4, s. 2. 3. Information in any form including information that is written, photographed, recorded or stored in any manner whatsoever and on file or in the possession or under the control of a department and includes personal information. *Freedom of Information Act*, S.N.S. 1977, c. 10, s. 2. See CREDIT ~; DESIGNATED ~; EXPERIMENT ~; FACTUAL ~; FLIGHT ~ REGION; FOREIGN-BASED ~ OR DOCUMENT; INVESTIGATIVE ~; MEDICAL ~; PERSONAL ~; PRIVILEGED ~; STATISTICAL ~; SUFFICIENT ~.

INFORMATION BANK. See PROVINCIAL ~.

INFORMATION BANK DIRECTOR. (a) With respect to any of the information banks controlled by the Department of National Health and Welfare that may be searched under this Part, the Minister of National Health and Welfare, and (b) with respect to any of the information banks controlled by the Canada Employment and Immigration Commission that may be searched under this Part, the Chairman of the Canada Employment and Immigration Commission. *Family Orders and Agreements Enforcement Assistance Act*, R.S.C. 1985 (2d Supp.), c. 4, s. 2.

INFORMATION BULLETIN. In respect of an area to be navigated by a ship, means the chart catalogue for that area published by the Canadian Hydrographic Service. *Charts and Publications Regulations*, C.R.C., c. 1415, s. 2.

INFORMATION BUREAU. See TOURIST ~.

INFORMATION CENTRE. A place that is held out to the public as being available for or engaged in furnishing travel information to the public, whether for hire or reward or otherwise. *Tourism Act*, R.S.O. 1980, c. 507, s. 1. See TOURIST ~.

INFORMATION CIRCULAR. An information circular prepared in accordance with the regulations. Securities acts.

INFORMATION COMMISSIONER. The Commissioner appointed under section 54. *Access to Information Act*, R.S.C. 1985, c. A-1, s. 3.

INFORMATION COMMISSIONER OF CANADA. A federal official appointed to hear complaints of government failure to comply with the rights provided by the Access to Information Act.

INFORMATUS NON SUM. [L. I am not informed] I have been given no instructions.

INFORMED CONSENT. An agreement a medical patient gives to a procedure after the risks involved are disclosed.

INFORMER. *n.* The one who commences an action or takes some other steps to recover a penalty.

INFORMER PRIVILEGE. The privilege attached to the identity of a person who provided information to police leading to an investigation.

INFRA. [L. under, underneath, below] In a document, reference to a later part or page of the document.

INFRA ANNUM LUCTUS. [L.] Within the mourning period.

INFRACTION. See PARKING ~.

INFRINGEMENT. *n.* 1. A complaint that the defendant has directly used and taken the plaintiff's trade mark totally, a colourable imitation or a substantial part of it. H.G. Fox, *The Canadian Law of Trade Marks and Unfair Competition*, 3d ed. (Toronto: Carswell, 1972) at 323. 2. Something which, if done by the actual copyright owner, would exercise the statutory right conferred on the owner. H.G. Fox, *The Canadian Law of Copyright and Industrial Designs*, 2d ed. (Toronto: Carswell, 1967) at 326. 3. Any act which interferes with full enjoyment of the patentee's monopoly by making, using or putting into practice the invention or any aspect of it that is included in the claims. H.G. Fox, *The Canadian Law and Practice Relating to Letters Patent for Inventions*, 4th ed. (Toronto: Carswell, 1969) at 349-350.

INFRINGING. *adj.* When applied to a copy of a work in which copyright subsists, means any copy, including any colourable imitation, made, or imported in contravention of this Act. *Copyright Act*, R.S.C. 1985, c. C-42, s. 2.

IN FUTURO. [L.] In future.

IN GENERALIBUS LATET ERROR. [L.] In generalities error lurks.

IN GOOD FAITH. A thing is deemed to be done "in good faith" when it is in fact done honestly, whether it be done negligently or not. *Sale of Goods acts.*

INGREDIENT. *n.* An individual unit of food that is combined as an individual unit of food with one or more other individual units of food to form an integral unit of food. Canada regulations. See ACTIVE ~; MEDICATING ~; SWEETENING ~.

INGRESS. *n.* Entry.

IN GROSS. Not appendant, appurtenant, or otherwise annexed to land. See EASEMENT ~.

INGROSS. *v.* To write a fair copy of an instrument or deed so that parties may formally execute it.

INHABITANT. *n.* 1. A permanent resident or a temporary resident having a permanent dwelling within the locality. *Municipal Act*, R.S.O. 1980, c. 302, s. 10. 2. Except for the purposes of sections 3 and 31, means a permanent resident of a Board area or an owner of property situate in a Board area, who is a Canadian citizen and who has attained the full age of eighteen years. *Local Services Boards Act*, R.S.O. 1980, c. 252, s. 1.

IN HAEC VERBA. [L.] In these actual words.

INHERENT DEFECT. An intrinsic fault or problem.

INHERENT DEFENCE. A defence such as lawful purpose, innocent intent or mistake of fact which simply denies the mens rea which must be proved by the prosecution. P.K. McWilliams, *Canadian Criminal Evidence*, 3d ed. (Aurora: Canada Law Book, 1988) at 25-8.

INHERENT JURISDICTION. In the administration of justice, this part of procedural law is exercisable in relation to the litigation process and may be invoked in relation to any person and respecting matters which were not issues between the parties in the litigation. S.A. Cohen, *Due Process of Law* (Toronto: Carswell, 1977) at 345.

INHERENT POWER. A power vested in a court that is not derived from statutory authority.

INHERITABLE. *adj.* Able to inherit.

INHERITANCE. *n.* What descended to the heir of the owner who died intestate, formerly a hereditament. See SEVERAL ~.

INHERITANCE TAX. Succession duty calculated upon the inheritance received by any beneficiary. P.W. Hogg, *Constitutional Law of Canada*, 2d ed. (Toronto: Carswell, 1985) at 610.

INHIBITOR. *n.* Any antibiotic, medicine or chemical preparation that can be detected in milk. *Milk Act*, R.R.O. 1980, Reg. 629, s. 1.

IN HIS QUAE DE JURE COMMUNI OMNIBUS CONCEDUNTUR, CONSUETUDO ALICUJUS PATRIAE VEL LOCI NON EST ALLEGANDA. [L.] In those things which common right concedes to all, the custom of a particular country or place should not be brought forward.

IN HIS QUAE SUNT FAVORABILIA ANIMAE, QUAMVIS SUNT DAMNOSA REBUS, FIAT ALIQUANDO EXTENSIO STATUTI. [L.] In things favourable to the spirit, though they may be injurious to things, the extension of a statute is sometimes made.

IN-HOME SERVICES. Services provided for a child, (i) in the child's own home, or (ii) in a place other than the child's own home where the child is receiving residential care. *Day Nurseries Act*, R.S.O. 1980, c. 111, s. 1.

IN INVIDIAM. [L.] In order to stir up prejudice.

IN INVITUM. [L.] Against one who is unwilling.

INIQUUM EST ALIQUEM REI SUAE ESSE JUDICEM. IN PROPRIA CAUSA NEMO JUDEX SIT. [L.] It is wrong for a person to judge his or her own cause. In certain cases no one can be a judge.

INITIAL. *n.* The first letter of a name.

INITIAL APPEARANCE DATE. The first date on which a defendant to whom a summons is issued is required to appear before a justice. *Summary Convictions Act*, R.S.A. 1980, c. S-26.1, s. 1.

INITIAL BASE. Of a trust means the aggregate of the values of all initial non-qualified investments held by the trust on December 21, 1966 when each such investment is valued at the lower of (i) its cost to the trust, and (ii) its fair market value on December 21, 1966. *Income Tax Act*, R.S.C. 1952, c. 148 (as am. S.C. 1970-71-72, c. 63), s. 204(b).

INITIAL CLAIM FOR BENEFIT. A claim made for the purpose of establishing a claimant's benefit period. *Unemployment Insurance Act*, R.S.C. 1985, c. U-1, s. 5.

INITIAL CRUSH RESISTANCE. The average force required to deform the door measured over the initial 152.4 mm (6 inches) of crush. *Motor Vehicle Safety Regulations*, C.R.C., c. 1038, s. 214.

INITIAL DEVELOPMENT. Such portion of the power or storage development as is specified in the interim licence as being required to be constructed before a final licence may be issued.

Dominion Water Power Regulations, C.R.C., c. 1603, s. 2.

INITIAL NON-QUALIFIED INVESTMENT. Of a trust means an investment held by the trust on December 21, 1966 that was, on that date, a non-qualified investment but does not include (i) any interest in a life insurance policy, or (ii) an equity share that would be a qualified investment if the date of acquisition of the share were December 21, 1966. *Income Tax Act*, R.S.C. 1952, c. 148 (as am. S.C. 1970-71-72, c. 63), s. 204(c).

INITIAL PAYMENT. 1. The sum paid or credited for merchandise delivered or money advanced to primary producers of an agricultural product to be marketed under only one cooperative plan. *Agricultural Products Co-operative Marketing Act*, R.S.C. 1985, c. A-5, s. 2. 2. (a) With respect to grain sold and delivered to The Canadian Wheat Board, the sum certain per bushel payable therefor under the Canadian Wheat Board Act, and (b) with respect to grain sold and delivered to any other person, the price paid therefor by the purchaser thereof. *Crop Insurance Act*, R.S.C. 1985, c. C-48, s. 13. 3. The sum certain per tonne basis in storage Thunder Bay or Vancouver payable pursuant to a marketing plan, at the time of delivery or at any time thereafter as may be agreed on, by the administrator of the plan to a producer participating in the plan for grain sold and delivered by him to the administrator. *Canadian Wheat Board Act*, R.S.C. 1985, c. C-24, s. 48. 4. (a) In respect of wheat, oats and barley, the sum certain basis in storage Thunder Bay or Vancouver payable pursuant to subsection 32(1) for the wheat, oats or barley to which the offence was committed; (b) in respect of rye, flaxseed and rapeseed, the price basis in storage Thunder Bay or Vancouver paid for the rye, flaxseed or rapeseed in relation to which the offence was committed; and (c) notwithstanding paragraphs (a) and (b), in respect of any grain the marketing of which is subject to a marketing plan established under Part VI, the sum certain basis in storage Thunder Bay or Vancouver payable pursuant to the marketing plan, at the time of delivery or at any time thereafter as may be agreed on, by the administrator of the plan to a producer participating in the plan for the grain in relation to which the offence was committed. *Canadian Wheat Board Act*, R.S.C. 1985, c. C-24, s. 68.

INITIAL PROCESSING OPERATION. An operation the product of which is a fuel or a material mainly used for further processing or manufacturing.

INITIAL STATION. The station at which a schedule is first timed on any subdivision is the initial station for that schedule, and for an extra train it is the station at which such train is created. *Regulations No. O-8, Uniform Code of Operating Rules*, C.R.C., c. 1175, Part III, s. 2.

INITIAL TRANSPORTATION CHARGES. In respect of an automobile means the costs incurred by a dealer in automobiles for transporting the automobile (before it has been used for any purpose whatever) from, (a) in the case of an automobile manufactured in Canada, the manufacturer's plant, and (b) in any other case, to the place in Canada, if any, at which the automobile was received or stored by a wholesale distributor, to the dealer's place of business. *Income Tax Regulations*, C.R.C., c. 945, s. 1102.

INITIAL UNFUNDED LIABILITY. 1. In respect of a pension plan, means (a) the going concern unfunded actuarial liability, (i) on the qualification date, in the case of a plan established before the qualification date, or (ii) on the effective date of the plan, in the case of a plan established on or after the qualification date, or (b) the amount by which the liabilities of the plan are increased (i) as a result of an amendment to the plan, on the effective date of the amendment, or (ii) as a result of a change in methods or bases of valuation, on the review date of the actuarial review for which the change is made. *Pension Benefits Standards Regulations*, C.R.C., c. 1252, s. 2. 2. The amount by which, on the 1st day of January, 1965, or the date on which a pension plan qualifies for registration, or subsequently as a result of an amendment or as a result of a change in actuarial assumptions, the assets are required to be augmented to ensure that the plan is fully funded. *Pension Benefits Act*, R.R.O. 1980, Reg. 746, s. 1.

INITIATION FEE. A sum charged when one becomes a member of a union or society.

IN JEOPARDY. At risk of being convicted of a criminal offence.

IN JUDICIIS MINORI AETATE SUCCURRITUR. [L.] In the courts' decisions, a minor is aided.

IN JUDICIO NON CREDITUR NISI JURATIS. [L.] In a trial no one's evidence is accepted unless that person has been sworn.

INJUNCTION. *n.* An equitable remedy by which one party must perform some act or refrain from some action harmful to the party who seeks relief. G.H.L. Fridman, *Sale of Goods in Canada*, 3d ed. (Toronto: Carswell, 1986) at 427. See INTERIM ~; INTERLOCUTORY ~; MANDATORY ~; MAREVA ~; PERMANENT ~; PERPETUAL ~; PROHIBITORY ~.

INJUNCTION QUIA TIMET. The injunction which a court awards to prevent an act which is threatened or feared. S.A. DeSmith, *Judicial Review of Administrative Action*, 4th ed. by J.M. Evans (London: Stevens, 1980) at 435.

INJURE. *v.* Includes to injure by wounding, worrying, terrifying or pursuing.

INJURED. *adj.* 1. Bodily harm, and includes mental or nervous shock and pregnancy. *Criminal Injury Compensation acts.* 2. In respect of live stock or poultry means injured by wounding, worrying or pursuing.

IN JURE, NON REMOTA CAUSA SED PROXIMA SPECTATUR. [L.] In law one regards the proximate, not the remote, cause.

IN JURE OMNIS DEFINITIO PERICULOSA EST. [L.] In law, all definition is hazardous.

INJURIA. *n.* [L.] An act which encroaches on some right.

INJURIA NON EXCUSAT INJURIUM. [L.] Wrong does not justify wrong.

INJURIA NON PRAESUMITUR. [L.] One should not presume wrongdoing.

INJURING LIABILITY. The part of the cost of the construction, improvement, maintenance or repair of a drainage works required to relieve the owners of any land or road from liability for injury caused by water artificially made to flow from such land or road upon any other land or road. *Drainage Act*, R.S.O. 1980, c. 126, s. 1.

INJURIOUS AFFECTION. (i) Where a statutory authority acquires part of the land of an owner, (A) the reduction in market value thereby caused to the remaining land of the owner by the acquisition or by the construction of the works thereon or by the use of the works thereon or any combination of them, and (B) such personal and business damages, resulting from the construction or use, or both, of the works as the statutory authority would be liable for if the construction or use were not under the authority of a statute, (ii) where the statutory authority does not acquire part of the land of an owner, (A) such reduction in the market value of the land of the owner, and (B) such personal and business damages, resulting from the construction and not the use of the works by the statutory authority, as the statutory authority would be liable for if the construction were not under the authority of a statute. *Expropriation acts.*

INJURIOUS FALSEHOOD. If an oral or written falsehood, neither defamatory nor actionable per se, is maliciously published and is calculated in the ordinary course of things to produce and does produce actual damage, it is possible to bring an action. I.H. Jacob, ed., *Bullen and Leake and Jacob's Precedents of Pleadings*, 12th ed. (London: Sweet and Maxwell, 1975) at 544.

INJURIOUS FOREIGN MATERIAL. Includes sand burrs, poisonous plants, harsh awned grasses such as mature wild barley and spear grass and other material which may be injurious when fed to livestock. *Hay and Straw Inspection Regulations*, C.R.C., c. 920, s. 1.

INJURIS ILLATA JUDICI, SEU LOCUM TENENTI REGIS, VIDETUR IPSI REGI ILLATA, MAXIME SI FIAT IN EXERCENTE OFFICIUM. [L.] An injury to a judge, that is, a person representing the monarch, is considered an injury to the very monarch, especially if it is done in the exercise of an office.

INJURY. *n.* 1. Any infringement of another's rights relating to person, property or reputation for which an action may be brought at law. 2. Actual bodily harm and includes pregnancy and mental or nervous shock. *Criminal Injuries Compensation acts.* 3. Disrupting tissue by violence. F.A. Jaffe, *A Guide to Pathological Evidence*, 2d ed. (Toronto: Carswell, 1983) at 178. 4. (i) An injury as a result of a chance event occasioned by a physical or natural cause, (ii) an injury as a result of a wilful and intentional act, not being the act of the worker, (iii) disablement, (iv) industrial disease, or (v) death as a result of an injury arising out of and in the course of employment and includes a recurrence of an injury and an aggravation of a pre-existing condition. *Workers' Compensation (Amendment) Act, 1986*, S.Nfld. 1986, c. 33, s. 1. See APPEARANCE OF THE ~ OF DISEASE; BIRTH ~; BODILY ~; COMPENSABLE ~; COMPRESSION ~; CONTRECOUP ~; CRITICAL ~; DISABLING ~; EMPLOYMENT ~; EPIPHYSEAL ~; MATERIAL ~; MINOR ~; PERSONAL ~; SEAT BELT ~; SERIOUS ~; SHEARING ~; STEERING WHEEL ~; WAR SERVICE ~; WHIPLASH ~; WORK ~.

INJURY FUND. The fund providing for the payment of compensation, medical aid, outlay and expenses under this Act. *Workers' Compensation Act, 1983*, S. Nfld. 1983, c. 48, s. 2.

INJUSTUM EST NISI TOTA LEGE INSPECTA UNA ALIQUA PARTICULA PROPOSITA JUDICARE VEL RESPONDERE. [L.] Unless the entire statute has been inspected, it is unreasonable to judge or respond to any particular thing set out in it.

IN JUS VOCARE. [L.] To take legal proceedings against someone.

INLAND BILL. A bill that is, or on the face of it purports to be, (a) both drawn and payable within Canada; or (b) drawn within Canada upon some person resident therein. *Bills of Exchange Act*, R.S.C. 1970, c. B-5, s. 25.

INLAND MARINE INSURANCE. Marine insurance in respect of subjects of insurance at risk above the harbour of Montreal. *Insurance Act*, R.S.A. 1980, c. I-5, s. 1.

INLAND NOTE. A note that is, or on the face of it purports to be, both made and payable within Canada. *Bills of Exchange Act*, R.S.C. 1970, c. B-5, s. 177.

INLAND POINT. (a) In relation to grain, any of the railway points along Georgian Bay, along Lake Huron or along any waterways directly or indirectly connecting with Lake Huron and not being farther east than Prescott, but including Prescott, and (b) in relation to flour, any point in Canada east of the 90th degree of west longitude. *Railway Act*, R.S.C. 1985, c. R-3, s. 281.

INLAND TRANSPORTATION INSURANCE. 1. Insurance, other than marine insurance, against loss of or damage to property: (i) while in transit or during delay incidental to transit; or (ii) where, in the opinion of the superintendent, the risk is substantially a transit risk. *Insurance acts.* 2. Insurance, other than marine insurance, against loss of or damage to property while in transit or during delay incidental to transit. *Insurance Act*, R.S.B.C. 1979, c. 200, s. 1.

INLAND VOYAGE. A voyage, not being a minor waters voyage, on the inland waters of Canada together with such part of any lake or river forming part of the inland waters of Canada as lies within the United States or on Lake Michigan. *Canada Shipping Act*, R.S.C. 1985, c. S-9, s. 2.

INLAND WATERS. 1. All the rivers, lakes and other fresh waters in Canada and includes the St. Lawrence River as far seaward as the straight lines drawn (a) from Cape-des-Rosiers to the western-most point of Anticosti Island, and (b) from Anticosti Island to the north shore of the St. Lawrence River along the meridian of longitude sixty-three degrees west. 2. Any of the waters within Newfoundland that are above low water spring tide or that are inland of a line between points marked by caution notices posted under authority of the Regional Director at or in the vicinity of the mouth of a river or stream flowing into the sea. *Newfoundland Fishery Regulations*, C.R.C., c. 846, s. 2.

INLAND WATERS OF CANADA. All the rivers, lakes and other navigable fresh waters within Canada, and includes the St. Lawrence River as far seaward as the straight line drawn (a) from Cape-des-Rosiers to the West Point Anticosti Island, and (b) from Anticosti Island to the north shore of the St. Lawrence River along the meridian of longitude sixty-three degrees west.

INLAND WATERS SHIP. A ship employed on an inland voyage. *Canada Shipping Act*, R.S.C. 1985, c. S-9, s. 2.

IN LIEU OF. Instead of.

IN LIMINE. [L.] At the beginning; preliminary.

IN LOCO PARENTIS. [L.] In the place of the parent.

IN MAJORE SUMMA CONTINETUR MINOR. [L.] The small sum is contained in the greater.

IN MALAM PARTEM. [L.] In a bad aspect.

IN MALEFICIIS VOLUNTAS, NON EXITUS, SPECTATUR. [L.] In the case of criminal acts one must regard the intention, not the result.

INMATE. *n.* 1. A person who, having been sentenced or committed to penitentiary, has been received and accepted at a penitentiary pursuant to the sentence or committal and has not been lawfully discharged therefrom or from any other place pursuant to section 23.1. *Penitentiary Act*, R.S.C. 1985 (2d Supp.), c. 35, s. 15. 2. A person admitted to a correctional facility pursuant to a committal order. 3. A person sentenced to a term of imprisonment in or detained in a correctional institution. See DISCHARGED ~; EX-~; PAROLED ~.

IN MEDIAS RES. [L. in the heart of the subject] Without any introduction or preface.

IN MERCY. At the direction of.

IN MORTUO. [L.] In a dead body. F.A. Jaffe, *A Guide to Pathological Evidence*, 2d ed. (Toronto: Carswell, 1983) at 178.

INN. *n.* 1. Includes hotel, inn, tavern, public house or other place of refreshment, the keeper of which is by law responsible for the goods and property of the guests. 2. (a) An inn as defined in the Hotel Keepers Act, or (b) a boarding house, rooming house or apartment hotel containing premises that are occupied under conditions that, at common law, would be considered a licence to occupy the premises. *Residential Tenancy Act*, S.B.C. 1980, c. 48, s. 1. 3. A building or structure in which accommodation or lodging, with or without food is furnished for a price to travelers and includes a cabin, a cottage, a housekeeping unit, a hotel, a lodge, a motel, a motor hotel, and a tourist home.

IN NEED OF PROTECTION. In relation to a

child, that he is (a) abused or neglected so that his safety or well being is endangered, (b) abandoned, (c) deprived of necessary care through the death, absence or disability of his parent, (d) deprived of necessary medical attention, or (e) absent from his home in circumstances that endanger his safety or well being. *Family and Child Service Act*, S.B.C. 1980, c. 11, s. 1. See ADULT ~; CHILD ~.

INNER ENVELOPE. The plain envelope supplied by the Chief Electoral Officer in which a ballot paper is to be enclosed after the ballot paper has been marked by an elector and before the ballot paper is transmitted to a special returning officer in an outer envelope. *Special Voting Rules*, R.S.C. 1985, c. E-2, Schedule II, s. 2.

INNER LABEL. 1. A label on or affixed to the immediate container of a cosmetic. *Cosmetic Regulations*, C.R.C., c. 869, s. 2. 2. The label on or affixed to an immediate container of a food or drug. *Food and Drug Regulations*, C.R.C., c. 870, c. A.01.010. 3. A label on, affixed to or impressed upon the outer surface of a device. *Medical Devices Regulations*, C.R.C., c. 871, s. 2.

INNERLINER. *n.* The layers forming the inside surface of a tubeless tire that contains the inflating medium within the tire. *Motor Vehicle Tire Safety Regulations*, C.R.C., c. 1039, s. 2.

INNERLINER SEPARATION. The parting of the innerliner from the cord. *Motor Vehicle Tire Safety Regulations*, C.R.C., c. 1039, s. 2.

INNER PACKAGE. A substantial case, bag, canister, covering, or other suitable container, made and closed so as to prevent any explosive from escaping.

INNKEEPER. *n.* 1. The keeper of an inn. 2. A person who is by law responsible for the property of guests and includes a keeper of a hotel, motel, auto court, cabin or other place or house who holds out that to the extent of the available accommodation the keeper will provide lodging to any person who comes as a guest, who appears able and willing to pay a reasonable sum for the services and facilities offered and who is in a fit state to be received.

INNOCENCE. See PRESUMPTION OF ~.

INNOCENT. *adj.* Negligently or in a circumstance which does not justify negligence being alleged. G.H.L. Fridman, *The Law of Contract in Canada*, 2d ed. (Toronto: Carswell, 1986) at 283 and 284.

INNOCENT MISREPRESENTATION. A misstatement which the party making it did not know was such. G.H.L. Fridman, *Sale of Goods in Canada*, 3d ed. (Toronto: Carswell, 1986) at 153.

INNOCENT PASSAGE. The right of a foreign ship to cross territorial waters.

IN NOVO CASU, NOVUM REMEDIUM APPONENDUM EST. [L.] In a new case a new remedy ought to be applied.

INNUENDO. *n.* Words not defamatory in their ordinary and plain meaning, but by virtue of circumstances or facts related to their publication. R.E. Brown, *The Law of Defamation in Canada* (Toronto: Carswell, 1987) at 154. See FALSE ~; LEGAL ~; POPULAR ~; TRUE ~.

IN ODIUM SPOLIATORIS OMNIA PRAESUMUNTUR. [L.] Everything possible should be presumed against a wrongdoer.

IN OMNIBUS QUIDEM, MAXIME TAMEN IN JURE, AEQUITAS SPECTANDA SIT. [L.] In all things, but particularly in law, equity should be regarded.

INOPERATIVE. *adj.* In relation to an item, component or system, that the item, component or system malfunctions to the extent that it does not accomplish its intended purpose or is not consistently functioning within its designed operating limits or tolerances. *Aircraft Minimum Equipment List Order*, C.R.C., c. 25, s. 2.

IN PACATO SOLO. [L.] In a place which is at peace.

IN PAIS. Describes a legal transaction which took place without legal proceedings.

IN PARI CAUSA POSSESSOR POTIOR HABERI DEBET. [L.] When two persons each having equally strong claims to property, the one in possession of the property should be preferred.

IN PARI DELICTO, POTIOR EST CONDITIO DEFENDENTIS. [L.] Where each party is equally at fault the defendant's position is superior. G.H.L. Fridman, *The Law of Contract in Canada*, 2d ed. (Toronto: Carswell, 1986) at 396.

IN PARI DELICTO, POTIOR EST CONDITIO POSSIDENTIS. [L.] Unless the parties are unequal, the one in possession has the advantage. G.H.L. Fridman & J.G. McLeod, *Restitution* (Toronto: Carswell, 1982) at 299.

IN PARI MATERIA. [L.] 1. In an analogous situation. 2. Describes statutes which deal with the same class, person or thing. P. St. J. Langan, ed., *Maxwell on The Interpretation of Statutes*, 12th ed. (Bombay: N.M. Tripathi, 1976) at 66.

IN-PATIENT. *var.* **INPATIENT.** *n.* A person admitted to a hospital for care and treatment and to whom the hospital has assigned a bed for overnight stay.

IN-PATIENT FACILITY. A facility with provision for continuous care of patients.

IN-PATIENT SERVICES. All of the following services to in-patients, namely, (a) accomodation and meals at the standard or public ward level, (b) necessary nursing service, (c) laboratory, radiological and other diagnostic procedures together with the necessary interpretations for the purpose of maintaining health, preventing disease and assisting in the diagnosis and treatment of any injury, illness or disability, (d) drugs, biologicals and related preparations as provided in an agreement when administered in the hospital, (e) use of operating room, case room and anaesthetic facilities, including necessary equipment and supplies, (f) routine surgical supplies, (g) use of radiotherapy facilities where available, (h) use of physiotherapy facilities where available, (i) services rendered by persons who receive remuneration therefor from the hospital.

IN PERPETUITY. Forever.

IN PERPETUUM. [L.] Forever.

IN PERSONAM. [L. in person] Describes an action the only purpose of which is to affect the rights of any parties to that action inter se. J.G. McLeod, *The Conflict of Laws* (Calgary: Carswell, 1983) at 60. See ACTION ~; JURA ~; JUS ~.

IN PLACE. Where used in reference to mineral means in the place or position where originally formed in the solid rock as distinguished from being in loose, fragmentary or broken rock, boulders, float, beds or deposits of gold or platinum bearing sand, earth, clay or gravel, or placer.

IN PLENO LUMINE. [L.] In daylight; in common knowledge; in public.

IN POENALIBUS CAUSIS BENIGNIUS INTERPRETANDUM EST. [L.] In relation to penalties, interpretation should be more lenient.

IN POSSE. Describes something which does not actually exist, but which may come to exist.

IN PRAESENTI. [L.] For the present time.

IN PROMPTU. [L.] At hand; in readiness.

IN PROPRIA PERSONA. [L.] In one's own proper person.

INQUEST. *n.* A judicial inquiry; an inquiry held before a coroner by a jury regarding the death of a person who was killed or died under suspicious circumstances or suddenly.

INQUIRY. *n.* An investigation; a hearing. See PUBLIC ~.

INQUISATORIAL SYSTEM. Proceedings in which the judge, not the parties, adduces evidence in contrast to the adversarial system.

IN QUO QUIS DELINQUIT, IN EO DE JURE EST PUNIENDUS. [L.] In that in which one offends, in that one should be punished according to law.

IN RE. [L.] In the matter of, regarding.

IN RE DUBIA MAGIS INFICIATIO QUAM AFFIRMATIO INTELLIGENDA. [L.] In a questionable case, the negative should be understood more than the affirmative.

IN REM. [L.] 1. Something done or directed with reference to no person in particular, and therefore with reference to or against anyone it might concern or the whole world. 2. Describes an action to determine the rights or interests of everyone with respect to a particular res, even though the action may involve only two people. J.G. McLeod, *The Conflict of Laws* (Calgary: Carswell, 1983) at 60. See ACTION ~; JURA ~; QUASI ~.

IN REPUBLICA MAXIME CONSERVANDA SUNT JURA BELLI. [L.] Rights recognised in war should be preserved to the fullest in the state.

IN RESTITUTIONEM, NON IN POENAM HAERES SUCCEDIT. [L.] An heir succeeds to a restitution, not to a penalty.

INS. *abbr.* Insurance.

INSANE. See LOCAL ASYLUM FOR HARMLESS ~.

INSANE PERSON. Includes a person, not an infant, who is incapable from infirmity of mind of managing his own affairs. *Incompetent Persons Act*, R.S.N.S. 1967, c. 135, s. 1.

INSANITARY CONDITION. A condition or circumstance (i) that is offensive; or (ii) that is, or may be, or might become injurious to health; or (iii) that prevents or hinders the suppression of disease; or (iv) that contaminates or pollutes, or may contaminate or pollute food, air, or water; or (v) that might render food, air, or water injurious to the health of any person; and includes a nuisance and any circumstances or condition declared to be an insanitary condition under the regulations. *Public Health Act*, R.S.M. 1970, c. P210, s. 2.

INSANITY. *n.* A state of mind which prevents a person from knowing the nature and quality of the act done, or, if that person did know it, from knowing that wrong was done. This constitutes a defence to a criminal charge.

INSCRIBE. *v.* To enter; to record.

INSECTIVOROUS BIRDS. See MIGRATORY ~.

INSEMINATING BUSINESS. A person who provides an artificial insemination service for domestic animals.

INSEMINATION. See ARTIFICIAL ~.

INSEMINATOR. *n.* A person who engages in the process of artificial insemination. *Artificial Insemination of Live Stock Act*, R.S.O. 1980, c. 29, s. 1.

INSERT. *n.* A label of a transparent material that contains the markings required by these Regulations and is inserted in a transparent bag containing poultry. *Dressed and Eviscerated Poultry Regulations*, C.R.C., c. 283, s. 2.

IN SERVICE. For the purpose of this section and section 77, an aircraft shall be deemed to be in service from the time when pre-flight preparation of the aircraft by ground personnel or the crew thereof begins for a specific flight until (a) the flight is cancelled before the aircraft is in flight, (b) twenty-four hours after the aircraft, having commenced the flight, lands, or (c) the aircraft, having commenced the flight, ceases to be in flight, whichever is the latest. *Criminal Code*, R.S.C. 1985, c. C-46, s. 7(9).

IN-SERVICE LIMITS OF ERROR. The limits of error that apply to a device when the performance of the device is tested at any time other than a time referred to in the definition of "acceptance limits of error". *Weights and Measures Regulations*, C.R.C., c. 1605, s. 2.

INSHORE TRAFFIC ZONE. A routing measure that is a designated area between the landward boundary of a traffic separation scheme and the adjacent coast that is intended for local traffic. *Collision Regulations*, C.R.C., c. 1416, s. 2.

INSIDER. *n.* With respect to a corporation, (i) the corporation, (ii) an affiliate of the corporation, (iii) a director or officer of the corporation, (iv) a person who beneficially owns, directly or indirectly, more than 10 per cent of the voting securities of the corporation or who exercises control or direction over more than 10 per cent of the votes attached to the voting securities of the corporation, (v) a person employed or retained by the corporation, or (vi) a person who receives specific confidential information from a person described in this clause or elsewhere, including a person described in this subclause, and who has knowledge that the person giving the information is a person described in this clause or elsewhere, including a person described in this subclause, (vii) every director

or senior officer of a company that is itself an insider or subsidiary of an issuer, (viii) an issuer where it has purchased, redeemed or otherwise acquired any of its securities, for so long as it holds any of its securities.

INSIDER INTEREST. The direct or indirect beneficial ownership of or control or direction over capital securities of a corporation. *Securities Act*, R.S.Q. 1977, c. V-1, s. 157.

INSIDER OF A CO-OPERATIVE. Any director or senior officer of a co-operative. *Co-operative Corporations Act*, R.S.O. 1980, c. 91, s. 111.

INSIDER TRADING. The purchasing or selling of securities by persons who have access to information which has not been made public and which may affect the market in the securities. S.M. Beck *et al.*, *Cases and Materials on Partnerships and Canadian Business Corporations*, (Toronto: The Carswell Company Limited, 1983) at 477.

INSIGNIA. *n.* [L.] Arms, ensigns.

IN SIMILI MATERIA. [L.] Dealing with similar or related subject-matter.

INSINUATION. *n.* Of a will, lodging it with a registrar to obtain probate.

IN SITU. [L.] In place; in the position originally held.

IN SITU OPERATION. (i) A scheme or operation ordinarily involving the use of well production operations for the recovery of crude bitumen from oil sands, or (ii) a scheme or operation designated by the Board as an in situ operation but does not include a mining operation. *Oil Sands Conservation Act*, S.A. 1983, c. O-5.5, s. 1.

IN SITU OPERATION SITE. An area within which an in situ operation is being conducted or that is the subject of an approval under this Act for an in situ operation, and includes a discard site and any area within which any facilities or equipment used in connection with the in situ operation are located. *Oil Sands Conservation Act*, S.A. 1983, c. O-5.5, s. 1.

IN SOLIDO. [L.] Completely.

IN SOLIDUM. [L.] For the entire sum.

INSOLVENCY. *n.* The state of a person who cannot pay his or her debts as they come due or who does not have enough property to enable payment of all those debts.

INSOLVENT. *adj.* 1. Unable to meet obligations as they come due in the ordinary course of business. 2. Either ceasing to pay one's debts in the ordinary course of business or unable to pay one's debts as they become due. 3. As applied to a corporation, means a corporation (i) that is, for any reason, unable to meet its liabilities to its creditors, as they generally become due, or (ii) the aggregate of the value of the assets of which is not, at a fair valuation, sufficient to enable it to meet all its liabilities to its creditors due or accruing due. *Companies Act*, R.S.M. 1970, c. C160, s. 2.

INSOLVENT ESTATE. The real and personal estate of a deceased person which is not sufficient for the payment in full of the debts and liabilities of the deceased person. *Estate Administration Act*, R.S.B.C. 1979, c. 114, s. 113.

INSOLVENT FARMER. A farmer (a) who is for any reason unable to meet his obligations as they generally become due, (b) who has ceased paying his current obligations in the ordinary course of business as they generally become due, or (c) the aggregate of whose property is not, at a fair valuation, sufficient, or if disposed of at a fairly conducted sale under legal process would not be sufficient, to enable payment of his obligations, due and accruing due. *Farm Debt Act*, R.S.C. 1985 (2d Supp.), c. 25, s. 2.

INSOLVENT PERSON. 1. A person who is not bankrupt and who resides or carries on business in Canada, whose liabilities to creditors provable as claims under this Act amount to one thousand dollars, and (a) who is for any reason unable to meet his obligations as they generally become due, (b) who has ceased paying his current obligations in the ordinary course of business as they generally become due, or (c) the aggregate of whose property is not, at a fair valuation, sufficient, or, if disposed of at a fairly conducted sale under legal process, would not be sufficient to enable payment of all his obligations, due and accruing due. *Bankruptcy Act*, R.S.C. 1985, c. B-3, s. 2. 2. Any person who is in insolvent circumstances, or is unable to pay his debts in full, or knows himself to be about to become insolvent. *Assignments and Preferences Act*, R.S.N.S. 1967, c. 16, s. 1.

IN SPECIE. [L. in its own form] In money or coin.

INSPECT. *v.* Includes test, survey, photograph, measure and record.

INSPECTING ENGINEER. An engineer who is directed to examine any railway or works, and includes two or more engineers, when two or more are so directed.

INSPECTION. *n.* The act of examining. See FIRST ~: OFFICIAL ~; SHOP ~.

INSPECTION MARK. A mark that is made by an inspector after an inspection of a device

and that consists of a symbol for the time being is used by inspectors and the date of the inspection. *Weights and Measures Regulations*, C.R.C., c. 1605, s. 2.

INSPECTION POINT. 1. Any place at which the Commission has made provision for the inspection of grain. *Canada Grain Act*, R.S.C. 1985, c. G-10, s. 2. 2. Any point or area at which an inspector attends. *Farm Products Grades and Sales Act*, R.R.O. 1980, Reg. 332, s. 1.

INSPECTION RECORD. See VEHICLE ~.

INSPECTION SIGN. See VEHICLE ~.

INSPECTION STATION. See OFFICIAL ~; VEHICLE ~.

INSPECTION STICKER. See VEHICLE ~.

INSPECTOR. *n.* 1. One who examines and reports. 2. A person appointed or designated under an act to carry out inspections or other duties prescribed. 3. The Inspector General of Banks appointed under subsection 245(1) of the Bank Act. See BUILDING ~; CHIEF ~; CIVIL AVIATION ~; DISTRICT ~.

INSPECTOR GENERAL. The Inspector General appointed pursuant to subsection 30(1). *Canadian Security Intelligence Service*, R.S.C. 1985, c. C-23, s. 2.

INSPEXIMUS. [L.] We have inspected.

INSTALL. *v.* Includes placing an appliance in position for temporary use, venting an appliance and connecting piping to an appliance. *Energy Act*, R.S.O. 1980, c. 139, s. 1.

INSTALLATION. *n.* 1. (i) Any equipment, apparatus, mechanism, machinery or instrument incidental to the operation of a pipeline, and (ii) any building or structure that houses or protects anything referred to in subclause (i), but does not include a refinery, processing plant, marketing plant or manufacturing plant. 2. The ceremony in which a person is inducted or invested with a charge, rank or office. See ELECTRICAL ~; GAS ~; IONIZING RADIATION ~; NON-IONIZING RADIATION ~; NUCLEAR INTALLATION; PIPING ~; POSTAL ~; PUBLIC UTILITY ~; RADIATION ~; SHORE ~.

INSTALLER. *n.* A person who places or installs a boiler or pressure vessel in position for operation and use, or connects a boiler or pressure vessel with other machinery or equipment for operation and use. *Steam and Pressure Plants Act*, R.S.M. 1970, c. S210, s. 2. See INSULATION ~; SPRINKLER AND FIRE PROTECTION ~.

INSTALMENT. *n.* One part of a debt.

INSTALMENT METHOD. The instalment system takes into income for the year only the gross profit content of the instalments actually received in the year, that is to say, the full amount of such payments less the cost of the merchandise content proportionate to them. *Publishers Guild of Canada v. M.N.R.*, [1957] C.T.C. 1; 57 D.T.C. 1017 (Exch. Ct.).

INSTANS EST FINIS UNIUS TEMPORIS ET PRINCIPIUM ALTERIUS. [L.] An instant ends one period of time and begins another.

INSTANTER. *adv.* [L.] At once, immediately.

INSTAR. *n.* A stage through which insect larvae develop. F.A. Jaffe, *A Guide to Pathological Evidence*, 2d ed. (Toronto: Carswell, 1983) at 178.

IN STATU QUO. [L.] In its former condition.

IN STIPULATIONIBUS CUM QUAERITUR QUID ACTUM SIT VERBA CONTRA STIPULATOREM INTERPRETANDA SUNT. [L.] When questioning what is done in agreements, words should be interpreted against the person who uses them.

INSTITUTE. *v.* To commence.

INSTITUTE. *n.* 1. An organization, body. 2. A treatise; a commentary. See RESEARCH ~.

INSTITUTION. *n.* 1. A bank, credit union, trust company, treasury branch or other similar person, a public school, college, hospital, gaol, penitentiary, correctional institution. 2. A society which promotes any public object, e.g. a charity. 3. A law, rite or ceremony imposed by authority, as a permanent rule of government or conduct. 4. An institution that is publicly owned and is operated solely for the benefit of the public, that is established for educational or cultural purposes and that conserves objects and exhibits them or otherwise makes them available to the public. *Cultural Property Export and Import Act*, R.S.C. 1985, c. C-51, s. 2. See CERTIFIED ~; CHARITABLE ~; CHILD CARING ~; CHILDREN'S ~; CORRECTIONAL ~; CREDIT ~; DEPOSIT ~; EDUCATIONAL ~; FEDERAL ~; FINANCIAL ~; GOVERNMENT ~; GOVERNMENT SUPPORTED ~; ~S; LENDING ~; MEMBER ~; PENAL ~; POST SECONDARY ~; PRIVATE TRAINING ~; PROVINCIALLY ADMINISTERED ~; PROVINCIALLY-OWNED ~; PUBLIC ~; REFORMATORY ~; RESIDENTIAL ~; UNIVERSITARIAN ~.

INSTITUTIONAL BUILDING. A building used for purposes such as medical or care of persons suffering from physical or mental illness, disease or infirmity, for the care of infants, convalescents or aged persons, orphanages, and for penal or corrective purposes which provide sleeping facilities for the occupants. *Fire Prevention Act*, S.N.S. 1976, c. 9, s. 2.

INSTITUTIONAL LANDS. Lands owned by the Crown, or by a university, (i) that are used as the site of an educational institution; and (ii) that are exempt from municipal taxation; and includes also (iii) any lands to which sub-clauses (i) and (ii) apply that are leased by the Crown or a university, to any college or other educational institution; (iv) such lands as are appurtenant to lands hereinbefore in this clause described and are necessarily or reasonably used for the purposes of a university, college, or other educational institution, including use as a campus or for recreational purposes; and (v) lands owned by a university that are used or occupied by any person under lease or permit for grazing or hay making purposes, or under a general permit for use or occupancy; and includes any building on any land hereinbefore in this clause described. *Municipal Act*, S.M. 1970, c. 100, s. 795.

INSTITUTIONAL OCCUPANCY. Occupancy for the harbouring, housing or detention of persons who require special care or treatment on account of their age or mental or physical limitations or who are involuntarily detained.

INSTITUTIONS. *n.* A person who (i) grants degrees, (ii) provides a program of post-secondary study leading to a degree, or (iii) sells, offers for sale or provides by agreement for a fee, reward or other remuneration, a degree, and includes a natural person, an association of natural persons, a partnership or a corporation that carries on any activity referred to in sub-clauses (i) to (iii). *Degree Granting Act*, S.N.S. 1983, c. 5, s. 2. See INSTITUTION.

INSTRUCT. *v.* 1. For a client to convey information to a solicitor. 2. For a client to authorize a solicitor to appear on their behalf.

INSTRUCTION. *n.* A motion which gives a committee power to do something otherwise impossible, or to direct it to so something otherwise impossible. A. Fraser, G.A. Birch & W.A. Dawson, eds., *Beauchesne's Rules and Forms of the House of Commons of Canada*, 5th ed. (Toronto: Carswell, 1978) at 229. See AIR TRAFFIC CONTROL ~; APRON TRAFFIC CONTROL ~; FULL-TIME ~; MARINE TRAFFIC ~; PART-TIME ~; PROGRAM OF ~; TECHNICAL ~.

INSTRUCTIONAL DAY. A school day that is designated as an instructional day on a school calendar and upon which day an instructional program that may include examinations is provided for each pupil whose program is governed by such calendar. *Education Act*, R.R.O. 1980, Reg. 273, s. 1.

INSTRUCTIONAL UNIT. See FRENCH-LANGUAGE ~.

INSTRUCTOR. *n.* A person who operates a motor vehicle for the purpose of instructing another person with regards to the skill and knowledge necessary for the safe operation of a motor vehicle. See DRIVER ~; DRIVING ~.

INSTRUCTORS ASSOCIATION. An organization recognized by the department and a college board concerned as the official body representing the instructional staff of a college. *The Community Colleges Act*, R.S.S. 1978, c. C-19, s. 2.

INSTRUMENT. *n.* 1. A formal legal document. 2. Any grant, certificate of title, conveyance, assurance, deed, map, plan, will, probate or exemplification of probate of will, letters of administration or an exemplification thereof, mortgage or encumbrance, or any other document in writing relating to or affecting the transfer of or other dealing with land or evidencing title thereto. *Land Titles Act*, R.S.C. 1985, c. L-5, s. 2. 3. A promissory note, bill of exchange or other negotiable instrument payable by a foreign customer or a bond, debenture or other evidence of indebtedness issued or given by a foreign customer and includes an agreement to pay. *Export Development Act*, R.S.C. 1985, c. E-20, s. 23. 4. Any instrument for measuring a line or angle. *Provincial Land Surveyors Act*, R.S.N.S. 1967, c. 243, s. 1. 5. Includes a statute. *Trustee Act*, R.S.N.S. 1967, c. 317, s. 1. See ACKNOWLEDGEMENT OF ~; APPROVED ~; AUTHORIZING ~; BANKING ~; CONSTATING ~; GUARANTEED ~; HOUSEBREAKING ~; NEGOTIABLE ~; PRIMARY ~ OF INDEBTEDNESS; PRIORITY PAYMENT ~; ROYAL ~; SCIENTIFIC ~; SECURITY ~; SELLING ~; STATUTORY ~; TESTAMENTARY ~.

INSTRUMENTA. *n.* [L.] Documents not under seal.

INSTRUMENT FLIGHT RULES. The rules set forth in Division IV or Part V of these Regulations and in the orders and directions made by the Minister thereunder. *Air Regulations*, C.R.C., c. 2, s. 101.

INSTRUMENT OF INCORPORATION. Original or restated letters patent of incorporation, letters patent of amalgamation, letters patent of continuance and any supplementary letters patent issued and any special act or charter incorporating a body corporate and any amendments to the special act or charter.

INSTRUMENT RECORD. A book, file, micrograph, electronic or other storage means for recording the receipt of instruments at a land

titles office. *Land Titles Act*, S.N.S. 1978, c. 8, s. 4.

INSTRUMENT REQUIRING TO BE STAMPED. Includes all matters, proceedings, memoranda, deeds, instruments, documents and papers, subject to the control of the Legislature and which, under this act, or any order-in-council, require to have any stamp attached thereto or impressed thereon, and also all letters patent, commissions, licenses, permits, certificates and instruments, whether originals, exemplifications or copies, which, under this act or any other act of the Legislature, or under any order-in-council founded on or recognized by any such act, require to have any stamp attached thereto or impressed theron. *Stamp Act*, R.S.Q. 1977, c. T-10, s. 4.

IN SUBSIDIUM. [L.] Supporting.

INSUFFICIENT. *adj.* To describe an answer or affidavit not complying with formal requirements.

INSULATED. *adj.* 1. Covered with insulating materials or insulated from ground and from other live parts of a system in a manner adequate and consistent with safe and reliable performance under the conditions of operation. *Coal Mines Regulation Act*, R.S.N.S. 1967, c. 36, s. 84. 2. Separated from other conducting surfaces by a dielectric material or air space having a degree of resistance to the passage of current and to disruptive discharge sufficiently high for the condition of use. *Power Corporation Act*, R.R.O. 1980, Reg. 794, s. 0.

INSULATING. *adj.* As applied to non-conducting substances means that they are capable of bringing about the condition defined as insulated. *Power Corporation Act*, R.R.O. 1980, Reg. 794, s. 0.

INSULATION. *n.* Material the chief purpose of which is to prevent heat from escaping from a building and which is not essential for the support or enclosure of the building, or for the finishing of the interior of the building. *Homeowners Tax and Insulation Assistance Act*, S.M. 1977, c. 60, s. 1.

INSULATION CONTRACT. A contract, whether verbal or written, between an owner and an insulation installer providing for the installation of insulation, or insulation and energy conserving material, in an eligible residence. *The Home Energy Loan Act*, R.S.S. 1978, c. H-4.1, s. 2.

INSULATION INSTALLER. An individual, firm or corporation that installs insulation for others.

INSULATION MATERIALS. See THERMAL ~.

INSULIN. *n.* The active principle of the pancreas that affects the metabolism of carbohydrates in the animal body and that is of value in the treatment of diabetes mellitus. *Food and Drug Regulations*, C.R.C., c. 870, c. C.03.050.

INSURABLE ACREAGE. The acreage seeded or to be seeded for harvest to any insurable crop with respect to each insurance unit, as reported by the insured person or as determined by the board in accordance with the regulations. *The Saskatchewan Crop Insurance Act*, R.S.S. 1978, c. S-12, s. 2.

INSURABLE CROP. 1. Wheat, oats, barley or any other agricultural crop declared by the regulations to be an insurable crop for the purposes of this act. *Crop Insurance acts.* 2. (i) Any one or more of the crops hereinafter named; or (ii) any one of such combination or groups of any two or more of the crops hereinafter named; that may be designated in the regulations from time to time as an insurable crop for the purposes of this Act in respect of such crop years as are designated in the regulations, namely, wheat, oats, barley, flax, sugar beets, rapeseed, mustard, peas, fall rye, potatoes, sunflowers and grain corn. *Crop Insurance Act*, R.S.M. 1970, c. C310, s. 1.

INSURABLE EARNINGS. In relation to any period, the total amount of the earnings from insurable employment for that period of an insured person or the maximum insurable earnings for that period as prescribed by or under this Act, whichever is the lesser. *Unemployment Insurance Act*, R.S.C. 1985, c. U-1, s. 2. See MAXIMUM ~.

INSURABLE EMPLOYMENT. Employment that is not included in excepted employment and is (a) employment in Canada by one or more employers, under any express or implied contract of service or apprenticeship, written or oral, whether the earnings of the employed person are received from the employer or some other person and whether the earnings are calculated by time or by the piece, or partly by time and partly by the piece, or otherwise; (b) employment in Canada as described in paragraph (a) under Her Majesty in right of Canada; (c) service in the Canadian Forces or in any police force; (d) employment included in insurable employment by regulation under section 4; and (e) employment in Canada of an individual as sponsor of a project under programs designed primarily to create employment and conducted by the Government of Canada pursuant to any Act of Parliament. *Unemployment Insurance Act*, R.S.C. 1985, c. U-1, s. 3.

INSURABLE INTEREST. 1. An enforceable proprietary or contractual interest in property or a person's life which would result in loss for the insured if the property was damaged or lost or if the life were lost. 2. A person has an insurable interest in his own life and well-being and in the life and well-being of, (a) his child or grandchild; (b) his spouse; (c) any person upon whom he is wholly or in part dependent for, or from whom he is receiving, support or education; (d) his officer or employee; and (e) any person in whom he has a pecuniary interest. Insurance acts.

INSURABLE LOAN. A loan by an approved lender for one or more of the purposes indicated in section 28 that qualifies to be insured under the regulations. *Alberta Mortgage and Housing Corporation Act*, S.A. 1984, c. A-32.5, s. 1.

INSURABLE PERSON. An operator of a farm who has an insurable interest in an insurable crop seeded or to be seeded thereon.

INSURABLE STATUS. The status by which a premium rate is determined for an insured person. *Health Insurance Act*, R.R.O. 1980, Reg. 452, s. 1.

INSURANCE. *n.* 1. The undertaking by one person to indemnify another person against loss or liability for loss in respect of a certain risk or peril to which the object of the insurance may be exposed, or to pay a sum of money or other thing of value upon the happening of a certain event. *Insurance acts.* 2. Insurance on the life or health of a borrower or buyer, or on property charged to secure payment of the indebtedness of a borrower or buyer to a lender or seller. *Consumer Protection acts.* 3. Accident insurance, sickness insurance, or accident and sickness insurance. *Insurance acts.* 4. Life insurance. *Insurance acts.* See ACCIDENTAL DEATH ~; ACCIDENT ~; AIRCRAFT ~; ALL-RISK ~; AUTOMOBILE ~; BLANKET ~; BOILER AND MACHINERY ~; BOILER ~; BURGLARY ~; BUSINESS OF ~; CIVIL COMMOTION ~; C O M P R E H E N S I V E ~; CONTINGENCY ~; CONTRACT OF ~; CONTRACT OF MARINE ~; CREDIT ~; CROP ~; DEPARTMENT OF ~ CANADA; DEPOSIT ~; DISABILITY ~; DOUBLE INDEMNITY ~; DOUBLE ~; EARTHQUAKE ~; ENDOWMENT ~; EXPLOSION ~; EXTENSION ~; FALLING AIRCRAFT ~; FAMILY ~; FIDELITY ~; FIRST-PARTY ~; FIRE ~; FORGERY ~; GROUP ~; GROUP ACCIDENT ~; GUARANTEE ~; HAIL ~; IMPACT BY VEHICLES ~; INDEMNITY ~; INLAND TRANSPORTATION ~; KEY MAN ~; LEGAL EXPENSE ~; LIABILITY ~; LIFE ~; LIMITED ~; LIVESTOCK ~; LOSS ~; MACHINERY ~; MARINE ~; MARITIME ~;

MORTGAGE ~; MOTOR VEHICLE ~; MUTUAL ~; NO-FAULT AUTO-ACCIDENT ~; OVER- ~; PERSONAL ACCIDENT ~; PERSONAL PROPERTY ~; PLATE GLASS ~; PLEASURE CRAFT ~; POLICY OF ~; PROPERTY DAMAGE ~; PROPERTY ~; PUBLIC LIABILITY ~; REAL PROPERTY ~; RE~; SICKNESS ~; SPRINKLER LEAKAGE ~; STEAM BOILER ~; SUM ~; SUPERINTENDENT OF ~; SURETY ~; THEFT ~; THIRD PARTY LIABILITY ~; TITLE ~; UNEMPLOYMENT ~; WATER DAMAGE ~; WEATHER ~; WINDSTORM ~; WORKERS' COMPENSATION ~; WORKMEN'S COMPENSATION ~.

INSURANCE AGENCY. A company which for compensation solicits on behalf of an insurer or transmits for a person other than itself an application for or a policy of insurance to or from the insurer or offers or acts or assumes to act in the solicitation for and negotiation of the insurance or in negotiating its continuance or renewal. *Companies Act*, R.S.Nfld. 1970, c. 54, s. 292.

INSURANCE AGENT. 1. Every person who, on behalf of another and for remuneration or on behalf of his employer but not on behalf of a person who, in the field of insurance, offers or enters into only contracts of additional warranty contemplated in paragraph a, transacts the business of insurance by negotiating for or placing risks, soliciting or obtaining applications for insurance, issuing policies or collecting premiums, including a special broker contemplated in section 346 and an insurance broker within the meaning of the Insurance Brokers Act (R.S.Q., chapter C-74). *An Act to Amend Various Legislation*, S.Q. 1984, c. 47, s. 22. 2. A person who solicits, obtains or takes an application for insurance, or negotiates for or procures insurance, or signs or delivers a policy, or collects or receives a premium. *Insurance Act*, R.S.B.C. 1979, c. 200, s. 310. 3. A person who: (i) solicits, negotiates or effects for or on behalf of any insurer a contract of insurance; (ii) for compensation, acts in the solicitation or negotiation of insurance; (iii) transmits, for compensation, for a person other than himself, an application for or a policy of insurance to or from an insurer; or (iv) retains as compensation any portion of a premium received by him; and includes a general agent but does not include an officer or salaried employee of an insurer. *The Saskatchewan Insurance Act*, R.S.S. 1978, c. S-26, s. 2.

INSURANCE BROKER. 1. An agent within the meaning of subsection i of section 1 of the Act respecting insurance (chapter A-32), who does not deal exclusively in insurance of the person and who, with respect to other categories of insurance, does not deal with only one insurer or only one group of insurers under joint management, whether or not he has an agency contract with such insurer or groups of insurers. *Insurance Brokers Act*, R.S.Q. 1977, c. C-74, s. 1. 2. Any person who for any compensation, commission or other thing of value, with respect to persons or property in Ontario, deals directly with the public and, (i) acts or aids in any manner in soliciting, negotiating or procuring the making of any contract of insurance or reinsurance, whether or not he has agreements with insurers allowing him to bind coverage and countersign insurance documents on behalf of insurers, or (ii) provides risk management services including claims assistance where required, or (iii) provides consulting or advisory services with respect to insurance or reinsurance, or (iv) holds himself out as an insurance consultant or examines, appraises, reviews or evaluates any insurance policy, plan or program or makes recommendations or gives advice with regard to any of the above. *Registered Insurance Brokers Act*, R.S.O. 1980, c. 444, s. 1.

INSURANCE CHARGE. The cost of insuring the risk assumed by the person who advances or is to advance credit under an agreement or arrangement, where the face amount of the insurance does not exceed the credit advanced. *Criminal Code*, R.S.C. 1985, c. C-46, s. 347(2).

INSURANCE COMPANY. 1. (a) An insurer, and (b) a Lloyd's association but does not include a fraternal society. *Insurance Amendment Act, 1984*, S.A. 1984, c. 23, s. 3. 2. A company transacting the business of insurance and includes any unincorporated association or reciprocal exchange transacting that business. *Winding-up Act*, R.S.C. 1985, c. W-11, s. 2. 3. A person or corporation carrying on in the Province the business of insurance, as defined in the Insurance Act, and includes a reciprocal or inter-insurance exchange and underwriters and syndicates of underwriters operating on the plan known as "Lloyds", but does not include (i) a fraternal society as defined in the Insurance Act, or (ii) a mutual insurance corporation in respect of any taxation year in which the net premium income in the Province of the corporation is to the extent of not less than fifty per cent thereof derived from the insurance of farm property or wholly derived from the insurance of churches, schools or other religious, educational or charitable institutions. *Insurance Premiums Tax Act*, R.S.N.S. 1967, c. 149, s. 1. 4. A joint stock company incorporated to transact insurance business and a mutual insurance company. See CASH-MUTUAL ~; CO-OPERATIVE ~; PROVINCIAL ~; PUBLIC ~.

INSURANCE CONTRACT. See VARIABLE ~.

INSURANCE CORPORATION. A corporation that carries on an insurance business. *Income Tax Act*, R.S.C. 1952, c. 148 (as am. S.C. 1970-71-72, c. 63), s. 248(1).

INSURANCE COVERAGE. Includes life insurance, medical insurance, dental plans, accident and sickness insurance, long-term disability insurance and liability insurance where provided by the relevant collective agreement or employment contract or by a union. *Corrections Act*, S.N.S. 1986, c. 6, s. 6.

INSURANCE FUND. As applied to a fraternal society or as applied to any corporation not incorporated exclusively for the transaction of insurance, includes all money, securities for money and assets appropriated by the rules of the society or corporation to the payment of insurance liabilities or appropriated for the management of the insurance branch or department or division of the society, or otherwise legally available for insurance liabilities, but does not include funds of a trade union appropriated to or applicable for the voluntary assistance of wage earners unemployed or upon strike. *Insurance acts.*

INSURANCE MONEY. The amount payable by an insurer under a contract, and includes all benefits, surplus, profits, dividends, bonuses and annuities payable under the contract. *Insurance acts.*

INSURANCE OF DEBTS. A creditor may insure the payment of an existing or contemplated debt. Raoul Colinvaux, *The Law of Insurance*, 5th ed. (London: Sweet & Maxwell, 1984) at 463.

INSURANCE ON THE CASH PLAN. Any insurance that is not mutual insurance.

INSURANCE PLAN. See HEALTH CARE ~; SELF-~.

INSURANCE PRACTICE. See UNFAIR ~.

INSURANCE SALESMAN. A person who is employed by an insurance agent to solicit, obtain or take an application for insurance other than life insurance, or to negotiate for or procure insurance other than life insurance, or to collect or receive a premium. *Insurance Act*, R.S.B.C. 1979, c. 200, s. 310.

INSURANCE SCHEME. A scheme of crop insurance established by provincial law. *Crop Insurance Act*, R.S.C. 1985, c. C-48, s. 2.

INSURANCE UNIT. All or any part of the insurable acreage in respect of which an insured person has an interest in the crop seeded or to be seeded theron. *The Saskatchewan Crop Insurance Act*, R.S.S. 1978, c. S-12, s. 2.

INSURED. *n.* 1. (a) In the case of group insurance means, in the provision of this Part relating to the designation of beneficiaries or of personal representatives as recipients of insurance money and their rights and status, the group person insured, and (b) in all other cases means the person who makes a contract with an insurer. *Insurance acts.* 2. A person insured by a contract whether named or not. *Insurance acts.* 3. A person who makes a contract with an insurer. *Insurance acts.* 4. Includes (i) a person to or in resepct of whom or to whose dependants benefits are payable if bodily injuries are sustained by him as a result of one of the perils mentioned in section 22 whether he is named in a certificate or not; (ii) a person to whom insurance money is payable if loss of or damage to a vehicle results from one of the perils mentioned in section 38; and (iii) a person to whom or on whose behalf insurance money is payable if bodily injury to or the death of others, or loss of or damage to the property of others, for which he is legally liable results from one of the perils mentioned in section 42 whether he is named in an owner's certificate or not. *The Automobile Accident Insurance Act*, R.S.S. 1978, c. A-35, s. 2. See NAMED ~.

INSURED. *adj.* See PERSON ~; SUM ~.

INSURED CROP. A crop insured under provincial law. *Crop Insurance Act*, R.S.C. 1985, c. C-48, s. 2.

INSURED HEALTH SERVICES. Hospital services, physician services and surgical-dental services provided to insured persons, but does not include any health services that a person is entitled to and eligible for under any other Act of Parliament or under any Act of the legislature of a province that relates to workers' or workmen's compensation. *Canada Health Act*, R.S.C. 1985, c. C-6, s. 2. See ELECTIVE ~.

INSURED LOAN. A loan in respect of which an insurance policy has been issued under this Act and is in force. *National Housing Act*, R.S.C. 1985, c. N-11, s. 2.

INSURED MEDICAL CARE SERVICES. All services rendered by medical practitioners that are medically required, but does not include services that a person is entitled to or eligible for under the Territorial Hospital Insurance Services Ordinance, the Workmen's Compensation Ordinance, any Act of the Parliament of Canada, except the Medical Care Act (Canada) or any Act of a province relating to workmen's compensation. *Medical Care Act*, R.S.N.W.T. 1974, c. M-9, s. 2.

INSURED MOTOR VEHICLE. 1. A motor vehicle the owner of which (i) is insured pursuant to Part 7 of the Insurance Act in respect of public liability, property damage and accident benefits, (ii) has deposited proof of financial repsonsibility in a form and in an amount satisfactory to the Minister under Part 4, or (iii) is a corporation that has complied with section 67, in respect of that motor vehicle. *Motor Vehicle Administration Act*, R.S.A. 1980, c. M-22, s. 1. 2. A motor vehicle, (i) that is insured under a motor vehicle liability policy in accordance with the Insurance Act, or (ii) in respect of which there is on deposit with the Registrar money, securities or a bond in an amount equal to the minimum limit of liability prescribed under section 219 of the Insurance Act, or (iii) in respect of which the owner is exempt from the payment of registration fees under the regulations made under the Highway Traffic Act, or (iv) that is registered under the Highway Traffic Act in the name of a municipality. *Motor Vehicle Accident Claims Act*, R.S.O. 1980, c. 298, s. 1.

INSURED OFF-HIGHWAY VEHICLE. An off-highway vehicle the owner of which is insured by a policy of insurance approved under Part 7 of the Insurance Act and containing the coverage and limits fixed by that Part for automobiles in relation to public liability, property damage and accident benefits in respect of that off-highway vehicle. *Off-Highway Vehicle Act*, R.S.A. 1980, c. O-4, s. 1.

INSURED PENSION PLAN. A pension plan that provides for the periodic payment of the contributions under the plan to a person authorized to carry on the business of insurance in Canada in accordance with the terms of a contract under which that person is obligated to pay the pension and other benefits set forth in the plan. *Pension Benefits Standards Regulations*, C.R.C., c. 1252, s. 2.

INSURED PERSON. 1. A person who enters into a subsisting contract of insurance with an insurer and includes (a) a person insured by a contract whether named or not; and (b) a person to whom or for whose benefit all or part of the proceeds of a contract of insurance is payable; and (c) a person entitled to have insurance money applied toward satisfaction of his judgment in accordance with the Insurance Act. *Insurance acts*. 2. A person who has entered into a contract. *Crop Insurance acts*. 3. In relation to a province, a resident of the province other than (a) a member of the Canadian Forces, (b) a member of the Royal Canadian Mounted Police who is appointed to a rank therein, (c) a person serving a term of imprisonment in a penitentiary as defined in the Penitentiary Act,

or (d) a resident of the province who has not completed such minimum period of residence or waiting period, not exceeding three months, as may be required by the province for eligibility for or entitlement to insured health services. *Canada Health Act*, R.S.C. 1985, c. C-6, s. 2. 4. A person who is or has been employed in insurable employment. *Unemployment Insurance Act*, R.S.C. 1985, c. U-1, s. 2. 5. A person who is entitled to insured services under the Health Insurance Act and the regulations made under it. *Health Care Accessibility Act*, S.O. 1986, c. 20, s. 1.

INSURED PLAN. A supplemental plan the pensions and other benefits of which are fully insured or guaranteed either by the government of Canada or that of any province, or by an insurance company or association registered in Québec. *Supplemental Pension Plans Act*, R.S.Q. 1977, c. R-17, s. 1.

INSURED SERVICES. 1. All services rendered by medical practitioners that are medically required, except any services that a person is eligible for and entitled to under any other Act of the Parliament of Canada or under any law of a province relating to workmen's compensation. *Medical Care Act*, R.S.C. 1970, c. M-8, s. 2. 2. The in-patient services and out-patient services to which residents of a province are entitled under provincial law without charge except a general charge by way of premium or other amount not related to a specific service and except authorized charges, but does not include services any person is entitled to and eligible for under any Act of the Parliament of Canada or a provincial legislature specified in an agreement. *Hospital Insurance and Diagnostic Services Act*, R.S.C. 1970, c. H-8, s. 2. See COST OF ~; FUTURE COST OF ~; PAST COST OF ~.

INSURED WORK. A work accepted by the Minister for the purposes of publishers loss insurance and for which the premium has been duly paid. *Publishers Loss Insurance Act*, R.S.Q. 1977, c. A-27, s. 1.

INSURER. *n.* 1. The person, corporation, underwriter, partnership, fraternal or other society, association, or syndicate who undertakes or agrees or offers to undertake a contract. *Insurance acts*. 2. Any corporation incorporated for the purpose of carrying on the business of insurance, any association of persons formed on the plan known as Lloyds whereby each associate underwriter becomes liable for a stated, limited or proportionate part of the whole amount insured under a contract of insurance, and any exchange. *Excise Tax Act*, R.S.C. 1985, c. E-15, s. 3. See AUTHORIZED ~; LIABILITY ~; LIFE ~; PROVINCIAL ~; RE~; SELF ~.

INSURER'S AGENT. Includes an insurer who maintains a place of business in the province and a representative of an insurer in the province. *Insurance Premiums Tax Act*, R.S.Nfld. 1970, c. 179, s. 2.

INSURGENT. *n.* Someone acting just short of belligerently, often a revolutionary.

INT. *abbr.* International.

INTACT. *adj.* In respect of a front bulkhead, without openings. *Load Line Regulations (Inland)*, C.R.C., c. 1440, s. 1.

INTANGIBLE. *n.* All personal property, including choses in action, that is not goods, chattel paper, documents of title, instruments or securities. *Personal Property Security acts.*

INTEGRATED INDUSTRY. An industry in which a manufacturer controls production from beginning to end.

INTEGRATED IRRADIANCE. The radiant energy incident per unit area of surface expressed as joules per square centimetre (J cm-2). *Radiation Emitting Devices Regulations*, C.R.C., c. 1370, s. 1.

INTEGRITY. *n.* In respect of any device or equipment, the ability of the device or equipment to retain all of the qualities essential to its safe, reliable and adequate performance. *Canada Protective Clothing and Equipment Regulations*, C.R.C., c. 1007, s. 2.

INTELLECTUAL PROPERTY. See INDUSTRIAL AND ~.

INTENSIVE LIVE STOCK OPERATION. The rearing, confinement or feeding of poultry, hogs, sheep or cattle in such number as may be prescribed by the regulations. *The Pollution (By Live Stock) Control Act*, R.S.S. 1978, c. P-16, s. 2.

INTENT. *n.* Aim, actual desire, design, end, objective or purpose. D. Stuart, *Canadian Criminal Law: a treatise*, 2d ed. (Toronto: Carswell, 1987) at 128. See GENERAL ~; SPECIFIC ~.

INTENTIO CAECA MALA. [L.] A secret intention is bad.

INTENTIO INSERVIRE DEBET LEGIBUS, NOT LEGES INTENTIONI. [L.] Intention ought to serve the laws, not the laws intention.

INTENTIONAL INFLICTION OF NERVOUS SHOCK. Conduct, including words, which causes severe emotional distress. John G. Fleming, *The Law of Torts*, 6th ed. (Sydney: The Law Book Company Limited, 1983) at 30.

INTENTIONAL INDUCEMENT OF BREACH OF CONTRACT. Liability arises where, knowing of the contract and with intent to prevent or hinder its performance, the defendant induces one party not to perform his part of the contract or the defendant commits a wrongful act to prevent the performance of the contract. John G. Fleming, *The Law of Torts*, 6th ed. (Sydney: The Law Book Company Limited, 1983) at 651.

INTENTIONAL TORT. A tort in which the wrongdoer either wishes to accomplish the result or believes the result will follow from his act and the result is an injury to the plaintiff. John G. Fleming, *The Law of Torts*, 6th ed. (Sydney: The Law Book Company Limited, 1983) at 71.

INTENT TO DEFEND. See NOTICE OF ~.

INTER-AGENCY CERTIFICATION TAG. A tag issued by the Plant Products Division of the Department in respect of seed certified by an approved certifying agency. *Seeds Regulations*, C.R.C., c. 1400, s. 2.

INTER ALIA. [L.] Among other things.

INTER ARMA LEGES SILENT. [L.] In war, laws stay silent.

INTERCEPT. *v.* 1. Includes listen to, record or acquire a communication or acquire the substance, meaning or purport thereof. 2. Includes listen to or record a function of a computer system, or acquire the substance, meaning or purport thereof. *Criminal Code*, R.S.C. 1985, c. C-46, s. 342.1(2) as added by *Criminal Law Amendment Act*, R.S.C. 1985 (2d Supp.), c. 27, s. 45.

INTERCEPTOR. *n.* A receptacle to prevent oil, grease, sand or other materials from passing into drainage piping. *Ontario Water Resources Act*, R.R.O. 1980, Reg. 736, s. 1.

INTERCHANGEABLE DRUG. A drug of equal quality that contains, in the same dosage form, the same amount of the same active ingredients as the drug prescribed. *Pharmacists Act*, R.S.B.C. 1979, c. 326, s. 1.

INTERCHANGEABLE PHARMACEUTICAL PRODUCT. A product containing a drug or drugs in the same amount, of the same active ingredients and in the same dosage form as that directed by a prescription.

INTERCHANGEABLE PRODUCT. A drug or combination of drugs identified by a specific product name or manufacturer and designated as interchangeable with one or more other such products. *Prescription Drug Cost Regulation Act*, S.O. 1986, c. 28, s. 1.

INTERCONNECTED SYSTEMS. The power system and all plants and works connected therewith, related thereto, interdependent upon it and similarly used in the generation, transmission and distribution of electrical energy. *Dominion Water Power Regulations*, C.R.C., c. 1603, s. 2.

INTER-DELEGATION. *n.* The delegation of provincial power to the federal level or of federal power to the provinces. P.W. Hogg, *Constitutional Law of Canada*, 2d ed. (Toronto: Carswell, 1985) at 295.

INTERDEPENDENT MANUFACTURING LOCATION. A manufacturing location of an employer in the Province, the continued operation of which is primarily dependent on the continued normal operation of another manufacturing location or manufacturing locations of the employer in the Province. *Trade Union Act*, S.N.S. 1979-80, c. 78, s. 1.

INTERDICTED PERSON. 1. Person to whom the sale of liquor is prohibited by order under this act. *Liquor Control acts.* 2. A person who is prohibited from having or consuming liquor by an order under this act. *Liquor acts.*

INTERDICTION. *n.* The declaration of any person incapable by reason of habitual drunkenness of the management of his or her own business or affairs. *Inebriates Guardianship Act*, R.S.N.S. 1967, c. 144, s. 1.

INTERESSE TERMINI. [L.] An executory interest which is a right of entry that a lessee acquires in land through a demise.

INTEREST. *n.* 1. Something which a person has in a thing when that person has advantages, duties, liabilities, losses or rights connected with it, whether ascertained or potential, present or future. 2. In the law of insurance, something which a person has in the life of a person or in property when the death of the person or destruction or damage to the property would expose that person to pecuniary liability or loss. 3. A sum owing in consideration for using another sum of money. 4. The aggregate of all charges and expenses, whether in the form of a fee, fine, penalty, commission or other similar charge or expense or in any other form, paid or payable for the advancing of credit under an agreement or arrangment, by or on behalf of the person to whom the credit is or is to be advanced, irrespective of the person to whom any such charges and expenses are or are to be paid or payable, but does not include any repayment of credit advanced or any insurance charge, official fee, overdraft charge, required deposit balance or, in the case of a mortgage transaction, any amount required to be paid on account of property taxes. *Criminal Code*, R.S.C. 1985, c. C-46, s. 347(2). 5. Any former exploration agreement, former lease, former permit, former special renewal permit, exploration

licence, production licence, or significant discovery licence. *Canada Petroleum Resources Act*, R.S.C. 1985 (2d Supp.), c. 36, s. 2. 6. Any former exploration agreement, former lease, former permit, former special renewal permit, exploration agreement, production licence or provisional lease. *Oil and Gas Act*, R.S.C. 1985, c. O-6, s. 2. 7. Includes a share, whether publicly traded or not, in a corporation or partnership that holds an interest in a mineral claim, a mining lease or a mine. *Mining Act*, S.N.B. 1985, c. M-14.1, s. 19. 8. The interest of a member or shareholder in a credit union and includes shares and obligations of any kind that: (i) arise by virtue of the bylaws of the credit union; and (ii) are owed by the credit union to the member or shareholder. *Credit Union Act*, S.S. 1984-85-86, c. C-45.1, s. 158. 9. In relation to a policy loan, means the amount in respect of the policy loan that is required to be paid under the terms and conditions of the policy in order to maintain the policyholder's interest in the policy. *Income Tax Act*, R.S.C. 1952, c. 148 (as am. S.C. 1977-78, c. 1, s. 68(18)), s. 138(12)(e.1). See ABSOLUTE ~; ADVERSE IN ~; AGAINST ~; BENEFICIAL ~; BEST ~S OF THE CHILD; CAPITAL ~; COMMON ~; COMPOUND ~; CONFLICT OF ~; CONTROLLING ~; EQUITABLE ~; EXECUTORY ~; EXPROPRIATED ~; FINANCIAL ~; INCOME ~; INSIDER ~; INSURABLE ~; LICENSEE WITH AN ~; LIFE ~; LOGGING ~; MATERIAL ~; MEMBERSHIP ~; MINERAL ~; OPEN ~; OWNERSHIP ~; PECUNIARY ~; POST-JUDGMENT ~; PRE-JUDGMENT ~; REVERSIONARY ~; ROYALTY ~; SECURITY ~; SIGNIFICANT ~; SUBSTANTIAL ~; TIME SHARE ~; UNDIVIDED ~; UNENCUMBERED ~; VOTING ~; WORKING ~.

INTEREST ARBITRATION. A type of dispute resolution by which an arbitrator determines the conditions, terms and rules which govern an employer-union-employee relationship. D.J.M. Brown and D.M. Beatty, *Canadian Labour Arbitration*, 2d ed. (Aurora: Canada Law Book, 1977) at 1.

INTEREST BUY-DOWN. A way a vendor arranges mortgage financing at less than the current market rate when interest rates are high through prepayment of part of the interest that the mortgagee requests so that the annual rate during the term is reduced. D.J. Donahue & P.D. Quinn, *Real Estate Practice in Ontario*, 4th ed. (Toronto: Butterworths, 1990) at 227.

INTEREST DISPUTE. A dispute to which Sections 13 to 33 inclusive of this Act apply and is a dispute arising between the employer and the employee as to the content of a collective agreement. *Civil Service Collective Bargaining Act*, S.N.S. 1978, c. 3, s. 2.

INTERESTED PARTY. 1. In subsection (1), "interested party", in respect of an inquiry, includes (a) the complainant who filed the notice of complaint, if any, giving rise to the inquiry; (b) a Canadian producer; (c) an importer, user or consumer of the textile and clothing goods that are the subject-matter of the inquiry; (d) any person or association representing any producer, importer, user or consumer of such goods; and (e) a labour union or unit thereof, or any other representative group of workers, representing any workers employed in the production of textile and clothing goods in Canada. *Textile and Clothing Board Act*, R.S.C. 1985 c. T-9, s. 14(2). 2. Includes (a) savings institutions, (b) trade unions, (c) employee associations, and (d) any other person, whether or not similar to the foregoing, whose cooperation may be conducive to the effective operation of a business enterprise. *Critical Industries Act*, S.B.C. 1985, c. 47, s. 1.

INTERESTED PERSON. 1. Includes (a) an offeree whether or not he deposits shares pursuant to a take-over bid; (b) an offeree corporation; (c) an offeror; and (d) a rival offeror. *Canada Business Corporations Act*, R.S.C. 1985, c. C-44, s. 205(4). 2. (a) A director of the Corporation or a member of a Council, (b) the spouse or a child, brother, sister or parent of a director or a member of a Council, or (c) the spouse of a child, brother, sister or parent of a director or a member of a Council. *Federal Business Development Bank Act*, R.S.C. 1985, c. F-6, s. 36. 3. Any person who is or would be affected by an order made under this act and includes (a) the next of kin of the person in respect of whom an order is made or for whom an order is applied; and (b) a person who holds property of the person in respect of whom an order is made or for whom an order is applied. *Presumption of Death acts.* 4. (i) The Public Trustee, (ii) the Public Guardian, or (iii) any other adult person who is concerned for the welfare of the person in respect of whom a guardianship order or trusteeship order is sought or has been obtained. *Dependent Adults Act*, R.S.A. 1980, c. D-32, s. 1. See PERSON INTERESTED.

INTEREST HOLDER. 1. In respect of an interest or a share therein, the person indicated, in the register maintained pursuant to Part VIII, as the holder of the interest or the share. *Canada Petroleum Resources Act*, R.S.C. 1985 (2d Supp.), c. 36, s. 2. 2. In relation to any Canada lands, the registered holder of an interest or share in an interest in respect of those Canada lands including, where applicable, Her Majesty in right of Canada holding through the appropriate Minister or a designated Crown corporation. *Oil and Gas Act*, R.S.C. 1985, c. O-6, s. 2. 3. In relation to any Nova Scotia Lands, the registered holder of an interest or share in an interest in respect of those Nova Scotia Lands including, where applicable, Her Majesty holding through the appropriate minister or a designated Crown corporation. *Offshore Oil and Gas Act*, S.N.S. 1984, c. 8, s. 2.

INTEREST IN A FAMILY FARM PARTNERSHIP. 1. Of a person at a particular time means an interest in a partnership that, at that time, carried on the business of farming in Canada in which it used all or substantially all of its property and in which that person, his spouse or his child was actively engaged. *Income Tax Act*, R.S.C. 1952, c. 148 (as am. S.C. 1977-78, c. 32, s. 14), s. 70(10)(c). 2. Of an individual (other than a trust that is not a personal trust) at any time means an interest owned by the individual at that time in a partnership all of substantially all of the property of which was, at that time, property used by (a) the partnership, (b) the individual, (c) where the individual is a personal trust, a beneficiary of the trust, (d) a spouse, child or parent of a person referred to in paragraph (b) or (c), or (e) a corporation, a share of the capital stock of which was a share of the capital stock of a family farm corporation of an individual referred to in parargraph (b), (c) or (d) throughout a period of at least 24 months before that time in the course of carrying on the business of farming in Canada in which any individual referred to in paragraph (b), (c) or (d) was actively engaged on a regular and continuous basis. *Income Tax Act*, R.S.C. 1952, c. 148 (as am. S.C. 1988, c. 55, s. 81(4)), s. 110.6(1).

INTEREST IN EXPECTANCY. Includes an estate or interest in remainder or reversion and any other future interest whether vested or contingent, but does not include a reversion expectant on the determination of a lease.

INTEREST IN LAND. 1. (i) Any estate in land less than an estate in fee simple; and (ii) any interest, right, easement, or right-of-way, in, to, or over, land other than the interest of the owner of an estate in fee simple. *Land Acquisition Act*, R.S.M. 1970, c. L40, s. 2. 2. Does not include an interest in mines, minerals, oil, gas, coal or bituminous shale. *Pipe Line Act*, S.N.B. 1976, c. P-8.1, s. 36. 3. In relation to land in the Province of Quebec, includes the interest of a lessee therein. *Expropriation Act*, R.S.C. 1985, c. E-21, s. 2. 4. Includes a statutory right given or reserved to the Crown to enter any lands or premises for the purpose of doing any work, construction, repair or maintenance in, upon, through, over or under any such lands or premises.

INTEREST IN THE PREMISES. An estate or interest of any nature, and includes a statutory right given or reserved to the Crown to enter any lands or premises belonging to any person or public authority for the purpose of doing any work, construction, repair or maintenance in, upon, through, over or under any lands or premises. *Construction Lien Act, 1983*, S.O. 1983, c. 6, s. 1.

INTEREST OF A MEMBER. Includes his shares in the association, if any; loan capital due to him and any other amount held to his credit by the association. *The Co-operative Production Associations Act*, R.S.S. 1978, c. C-37, s. 2.

INTEREST OWNER. The interest holder who holds an interest or the group of interest holders who hold all of the shares in an interest. See WORKING ~.

INTEREST PAYMENT. See BONUS ~.

INTEREST RATE. See POSTJUDGEMENT ~; PREJUDGEMENT ~; SPECIFIED ~.

INTEREST REIPUBLICAE NE MALEFICIA REMANEANT IMPUNITA. [L.] It is a concern of the state that wrongdoings do not go unpunished.

INTEREST REIPUBLICAE NE SUA QUIS MALE UTATUR. [L.] It is a concern of the state that people not wrongfully use their own property.

INTEREST REIPUBLICAE QUOD HOMINES CONSERVENTUR. [L.] It is a concern of the state that people are kept safe.

INTEREST REIPUBLICAE RES JUDICATAS NON RESCINDI. [L.] It is a concern of the state that judgments are not rescinded.

INTEREST REIPUBLICAE SUPREME HOMINUM TESTAMENTA RATA HABERI. [L.] It is a concern of the state that a person's last will be considered valid.

INTEREST REIPUBLICAE UT SIT FINIS LITIUM. [L.] It is a concern of the state that lawsuits be concluded.

INTEREST UPON INTEREST. Compound interest.

INTERFACE. See POOLING ~.

INTERGOVERNMENTAL AGREEMENT. An agreement between Her Majesty in right of a province and one or more of Her Majesty in right of Canada, Her Majesty in right of any other province and any other sovereign government.

INTERGOVERNMENTAL AFFAIRS. Any relationship between the Government of Ontario and the Government of Canada or a minister, agency or official thereof, the government of another province or territory of Canada or any minister, agency or official thereof, or the government of a foreign country or state or any agency thereof, of any municipality. *Ministry of Intergovernmental Affairs Act*, R.S.O. 1980, c. 283, s. 1.

INTERIM ADJUSTMENT. In respect of any crop year, means the amount by which, in the opinion of the Commission based on the revised grain tonnage forecast provided by the Administrator, the payments made or to be made to the railway companies in respect of that crop year pursuant to sections 56 and 57, without taking into account any reduction in a government payment to a railway company referred to in section 21 or any amount that has been withheld under section 56, will differ from the amount calculated under the definition "government committment". *Western Grain Transportation Act*, R.S.C. 1985, c. W-8, s. 55.

INTERIM AGREEMENT. A collective bargaining agreement which covers a period between the lapse of one contract and the completion of negotiations on another.

INTERIM DIVIDEND. A dividend paid during a company's financial year.

INTERIM INJUNCTION. 1. A species of interlocutory injunction granted for a very brief period until application for an interlocutory injunction is made. G.H.L. Fridman, *The Law of Contract in Canada*, 2d ed. (Toronto: Carswell, 1986) at 727. 2. Includes an interlocutory injunction. *Trade Practice Act*, R.S.B.C. 1979, c. 406, s. 1.

INTERIM LICENCE. A licence authorizing the preparation of general construction plans and the construction of works in pursuance of such plans. *Dominion Water Power Regulations*, C.R.C., c. 1603, s. 2.

INTERIM ORDER. An order which refers to time in between.

INTERIM RECEIVER. A person appointed under The Bankruptcy Act between filing a petition and making an order judging that the debtor is bankrupt. F. Bennett, *Receiverships* (Toronto: Carswell, 1985) at 3.

INTERIM RELEASE. See JUDICIAL ~.

INTERIM RELIEF. Interim custody; interim support. G.D. Watson & C. Perkins, eds., *Holmested & Watson: Ontario Civil Procedure* (Toronto: Carswell, 1984) at 70-38.

INTERIM SUPPLY. A measure to provide a

government with money to meet any obligations before its main estimates are approved. A. Fraser, G.A. Birch & W.A. Dawson, eds., *Beauchesne's Rules and Forms of the House of Commons of Canada*, 5th ed. (Toronto: Carswell, 1978) at 170.

INTERIM TERM INSURANCE. Insurance subject to the terms and conditions of the policy for which application is made, in respect of a period of less than one month commencing at such time as the first monthly premium is paid and terminating upon the due date of such premium. *Veterans Insurance Regulations*, C.R.C., c. 1587, s. 6.

INTER-INSURANCE EXCHANGE. A group of subscribers exchanging reciprocal contracts of indemnity or inter-insurance with each other through the same attorney. See RECIPROCAL OR ~.

INTERIOR. *adj.* Not in direct contact with the weather. *Hull Construction Regulations*, C.R.C., c. 1431, s. 100.

INTERIOR COMPARTMENT DOOR. Any door in the interior of a vehicle installed by the manufacturer as a cover for storage space normally used for personal effects. *Motor Vehicle Safety Regulations*, C.R.C., c. 1038, s. 201.

INTERIOR DESIGN. Representing oneself as a professional interior designer while carrying out the practice of those functions which have as their object the design of interior space. *Professional Interior Designers Institute of Manitoba Act*, S.M. 1980-81, c. 28, s. 1(1).

INTERIOR DESIGNER. See PROFESSIONAL ~.

INTERIOR LOT. A lot other than a corner lot. Canada regulations.

INTERJURISDICTIONAL CARRIER. A person who engages in the commercial transportation of goods or passengers and who operates for such purpose, (i) one or more motor vehicles licensed or required to be licensed under the Highway Traffic Act and operating inside and outside Ontario, (ii) one or more motor vessels operating under the Canada Shipping Act, or (iii) railway equipment operated on rails in connection with and as part of a public transportation system. *Fuel Tax Act, 1981*, S.O. 1981, c. 59, s. 1.

INTER-JURISDICTIONAL WATERS. Any waters, whether international, boundary or otherwise, that, whether wholly situated in a province or not, significantly affect the quantity or quality of waters outside the province. *Canada Water Act*, R.S.C. 1985, c. C-11, s. 2.

INTERLINEATION. *n.* Inserting anything into a document after it has been executed.

INTERLOCK. *n.* A component or set of components that prevents the generation of microwave power when access to a cavity is possible. *Radiation Emitting Devices Regulations*, C.R.C., c. 1370, s. 1. See SAFETY ~.

INTERLOCKING. *n.* An arrangement of signals and signal appliances so interconnected that their movements must succeed each other in proper sequence and for which interlocking rules are in effect. It may be operated manually or automatically. *Regulations No. O-8, Uniform Code of Operating Rules*, C.R.C., c. 1175, Part III, s. 2.

INTERLOCKING LIMITS. The tracks between the extreme or outer opposing interlocking signals of an interlocking. *Regulations No. O-8, Uniform Code of Operating Rules*, C.R.C., c. 1175, Part III, s. 2.

INTERLOCKING SIGNAL. A fixed signal at the entrance to or within interlocking limits to govern the use of the routes. *Regulations No. O-8, Uniform Code of Operating Rules*, C.R.C., c. 1175, Part III, s. 2.

INTERLOCKING STATION. A place from which an interlocking is operated. *Regulations No. O-8, Uniform Code of Operating Rules*, C.R.C., c. 1175, Part III, s. 2.

INTERLOCUTORY. *adj.* 1. Incidental to the major intent of an action. 2. Temporary, provisional, not final.

INTERLOCUTORY APPLICATION. An application in a pending proceeding. *Rules of the Supreme Court*, S.Nfld. 1986, r. 1, s. 1.03.

INTERLOCUTORY INJUNCTION. A measure intended to ensure that certain specified acts do not take place until the rights of the parties are finally determined by the court. G.H.L. Fridman, *The Law of Contract in Canada*, 2d ed. (Toronto: Carswell, 1986) at 727.

INTERLOPER. *n.* Someone who intercepts another persons's trade.

INTERMEDDLE. *v.* To interfere wrongly without any justification.

INTERMEDIARY. See FINANCIAL ~.

INTERMEDIATE CRUSH RESISTANCE. The average force required to deform the door measured over the initial 304.8 mm (12 inches) of crush. *Motor Vehicle Safety Regulations*, C.R.C., c. 1038, s. 214.

INTERMEDIATE DIVISION. The division of the organization of a school comprising the first four years of the program of studies immediately following the junior division. *Education Act*, R.S.O. 1980, c. 129, s. 1.

INTERMEDIATE ENGAGEMENT. A fixed period of service of a member of the regular force of such duration as is prescribed by regulation. *Canadian Forces Superannuation Act*, R.S.C. 1985, c. C-17, s. 2.

INTERMEDIATE NURSING CARE. Nursing and personal care given by or under the supervision of a registered nurse or registered nursing assistant under the direction of a physician to a resident for less than one and one-half hours per day. Ontario regulations.

INTERMEDIATE PORT. A place en route from the place where a seaman is first found in distress to the proper return port. *Distressed Seamen Regulations*, C.R.C., c, 1420, s. 2.

INTERMEDIATE PROVINCE. A province (other than Quebec) having a population greater than its population determined according to the results of the penultimate decennial census but not more than two and a half million and not less than one and a half million. *Constitution Act, 1974*, S.C. 1974-75-76, c. 13 reprinted as R.S.C. 1985, App. Document No. 40.

INTERMEDIATE PURCHASER. (i) With reference to marketable gas, a person who purchases marketable gas from a vendor or any other person except a supplier and who either (A) resells that marketable gas to another purchaser or to an eligible consumer, (B) delivers that gas to eligible consumers as a provider of gas service, or (C) consumes that marketable gas for the purpose of generating electric energy, (ii) with reference to a substance other than marketable gas, a person who is an intermediate purchaser as defined in the regulations. *Natural Gas Rebates Act*, R.S.A. 1980, c. N-5, s. 1.

INTERMENT. *n.* 1. Burial. 2. Includes cremation.

INTERMITTENT DUTY. A requirement of service that demands operation for definitely specified alternate intervals of, (i) load and no load, (ii) load and rest, or (iii) load, no load and rest. *Power Corporation Act*, R.R.O. 1980, Reg. 794, s. 0.

INTERN. *n.* A person who holds a degree in medicine granted by a university in Canada authorized to grant degrees in medicine, or a person holding qualifications approved as equivalent thereto by the Minister or by an official of the Ministry who is authorized by the Minister to grant such approval. *Ambulance Act*, R.R.O. 1980, Reg. 14, s. 1.

INTERNAL BALLISTICS. The behaviour of a projectile inside the weapon from which it was fired. F.A. Jaffe, *A Guide to Pathological Evidence*, 2d ed. (Toronto: Carswell, 1983) at 137.

INTERNAL COMBUSTION ENGINE. Includes a turbine engine that generates power by the use of fuel.

INTERNAL ECONOMY. See COMMISSIONERS OF ~.

INTERNAL LAW. In relation to any place excludes the choice of law rules of that place. *Succession Law Reform Act*, R.S.O. 1980, c. 488, s. 34.

INTERNALLY FINANCED TRANSACTION. A buyer purchases assets or shares of a business (a business interest) using that interest or assets to generate enough money to fund a major part or all of the purchase price. A. Bissett-Johnson & W.M. Holland, eds, *Matrimonial Property Law in Canada* (Toronto: Carswell, 1980) at V-12.

INTERNAL REGULATIONS. Includes by-laws, articles of association, rules or regulations relating to the management of the business and affairs of an extra-provincial corporation, by whatever name they are called, if they are made by the members or a class of members of, or the board of directors, board of management or other governing body of, the extra-provincial corporation. *Business Corporations Act*, S.A. 1981, c. B-15, s. 263.

INTERNAL USE. 1. Ingestion by mouth or application for systemic effect to any part of the body in which the drug comes into contact with mucous membrane. *Food and Drug Regulations*, C.R.C., c. 870, c. C.01.001. 2. Local or systemic absorption upon introduction into the body or by parenteral route or through a body orifice. *Health Disciplines Act*, R.R.O. 1980, Reg. 451, s. 1.

INTERNAL WATERS. Includes (a) any areas of the sea that are on the landward side of the baselines of the territorial sea and any areas of the sea, other than the territorial sea, in respect of which Canada has a historic or other title of sovereignty, and (b) the inland waters. *Customs Act*, R.S.C. 1985 (2d Supp.), c. 1, s. 2.

INTERNATIONAL AIR CARRIER. (a) A Canadian air carrier authorized to operate a commercial air service between Canada and any other country, or (b) a foreign air carrier licensed by its country of origin and licensed or authorized by the Committee to operate a commercial air service between Canada and any other country. *Air Carrier Regulations*, C.R.C., c. 3, s. 2.

INTERNATIONAL AIRCRAFT. An aircraft operating internationally in the transportation of passengers or goods for reward. Canada regulations.

INTERNATIONAL ARBITRATION AGREEMENT. An arbitration agreement in respect of a legal relationship, (a) that involves property that is outside Canada, (b) that envisages substantial performance or enforcement outside Canada, or (c) at least one party to which is domiciled or ordinarily resident outside Canada. *Foreign Arbitral Awards Act*, S.O. 1986, c. 25, s. 1.

INTERNATIONAL ARBITRATION LAW. The Model Law on International Commercial Arbitration, adopted by the United Nations Commission of International Trade Law on June 21, 1985, as set out in Schedule B. *International Commercial Arbitration Act*, S.N.W.T. 1986 (1st Sess.), c. 6, s. 2.

INTERNATIONAL BORDER PRICE. Of any gas means the price of that gas at the point it crosses the international boundary of Canada as specified in the licence of the National Energy Board authorizing the removal of that gas from Canada or as otherwise prescribed by the Government of Canada. *Natural Gas Price Administration Act*, R.S.A. 1980, c. N-3, s. 13.

INTERNATIONAL BRIDGE. A bridge or tunnel, including the approaches or facilities connected therewith, over or under any waterway being or running along or across the boundary between Canada and any foreign country. *Railway Act*, R.S.C. 1985, c. R-3, s. 9(3).

INTERNATIONAL COMITY. Rules of conduct which are observed in relations between states on account of courtesy.

INTERNATIONAL COURT OF JUSTICE. A judicial body created by the Charter of the United Nations.

INTERNATIONAL FINANCIAL CENTRE. Any business or part of a business (a) that is operated by a corporation; (b) all the activities of which are related to prescribed international transactions; (c) wherein the management of activities leading to such transactions is entirely carried on at Montréal; (d) the activities of which are grouped together in a place separate from that where the other activities of the corporation are conducted, where such is the case; (e) in respect of which the corporation keeps a separate accounting of its operations attributable thereto; (f) in respect of which the corporation holds a certificate in force, issued by a prescribed authority; and (g) that fulfils any other prescribed requirement. *An Act to Amend Various Fiscal Laws and Other Legislation*, S.Q. 1986, c. 15, s. 112.

INTERNATIONAL FLIGHT. A flight between Canada and a place outside of Canada. Canada regulations.

INTERNATIONAL JOINT COMMISSION. A body established by the 1909 Boundary Waters Treaty to prevent and solve disputes along the Canada-United States border. It also conducts investigations of issues relating to the 1978 Great Lakes Water Quality Agreement.

INTERNATIONAL LABOUR ORGANIZATION. A United Nations agency dealing with labour conditions and related matters.

INTERNATIONAL LAW. 1. Of two kinds: public international law, a code of rules which controls the conduct of independent nations in their relations with one another and private international law, a branch of municipal law which determines before what nation's courts a certain action or suit ought to be brought and by what nation's law it should be settled. 2. The Model Law on International Commercial Arbitration adopted by the United Nations Commission on International Trade Law on June 21, 1985. *International Commercial Arbitration acts*. See CONVENTIONAL ~; CUSTOMARY ~; PRIVATE ~.

INTERNATIONALLY PROTECTED PERSON. (a) A head of state, including any member of a collegial body that performs the functions of a head of state under the constitution of the state concerned, a head of a government or a minister of foreign affairs, whenever that person is in a state other than the state in which he holds that position or office, (b) a member of the family of a person described in paragraph (a) who accompanies that person in a state other than the state in which that person holds that position or office, (c) a representative or an official of a state or an official or agent of an international organization of an intergovernmental character who, at the time when and at the place where an offence referred to in subsection 7(3) is committed against his person or any property referred to in section 431 that is used by him, is entitled, pursuant to international law, to special protection from any attack on his person, freedom or dignity, or (d) a member of the family of a representative, official or agent described in paragraph (c) who forms part of his household, if the representative, official or agent, at the time when and at the place where any offence referred to in subsection 7(3) is committed against the member of his family or any property referred to in section 431 that is used by that member, is entitled, pursuant to international law, to special protection from any attack on his person, freedom or dignity. *Criminal Code*, R.S.C. 1985, c. C-46, s. 2.

INTERNATIONAL MORALITY. A code of

conduct which nations may be bound ethically, but not legally, to observe.

INTERNATIONAL ORGANIZATION. (a) Any specialized agency of which Canada is a member that is brought into relationship with the United Nations in accordance with Article 63 of the Charter of the United Nations, and (b) any international organization of which Canada is a member, the primary purpose of which is the maintenance of international peace or the economic or social well-being of a community of nations. Canada regulations.

INTERNATIONAL PERSONALITY. The status of a person or thing which has duties and rights under international law.

INTERNATIONAL POWER LINE. Facilities constructed or operated for the purpose of transmitting power from or to a place in Canada to or from a place outside Canada. *National Energy Board Act*, R.S.C. 1985, c. N-7, s. 2.

INTERNATIONAL PUBLIC POLICY. A doctrine which states that basic rules of international law override any treaty which is incompatible with them.

INTERNATIONAL RADIO REGULATIONS. The Radio Regulations and additional Radio Regulations annexed to the International Telecommunication Convention for the time being in effect. *Ship Station Radio Regulations, Part II*, C.R.C., c. 1474, s. 2.

INTERNATIONAL RIVER. Water flowing from any place in Canada to any place outside Canada. *International River Improvement Act*, R.S.C. 1985, c. I-20, s. 2.

INTERNATIONAL RIVER IMPROVEMENT. A dam, obstruction, canal, reservoir or other work the purpose or effect of which is (a) to increase, decrease or alter the natural flow of an international river, or (b) to interfere with, alter or affect the actual or potential use of the international river outside Canada. *International River Improvement Act*, R.S.C. 1985, c. I-20, s. 2.

INTERNATIONAL SERVICE. The use while loaded or empty of railway rolling stock dispatched on a direct route from a place in Canada to a place in the United States or from a place in the United States to a place in Canada and includes loading and unloading in Canada while on the direct route. Canada regulations.

INTERNATIONAL STANDARD CLASSIFICATION OF OCCUPATIONS. The booklet entitled "International Standard Classification of Occupations" that is published and revised from time to time by the International Labour Organization. *The Occupational Health and Safety Act*, R.S.S. 1978, c. O-1, s. 2.

INTERNATIONAL TRAFFIC. In respect of a non-resident person carrying on the business of transporting passengers or goods, any voyage made in the course of that business where the principal purpose of the voyage is to transport passengers or goods (a) from Canada to a place outside Canada, (b) from a place outside Canada to Canada, or (c) from a place outside Canada to another place outside Canada. *Income Tax Act*, R.S.C. 1952, c. 148 (as am. S.C. 1974-75-76, c. 26, s. 135(3)), s. 248(1).

INTERNATIONAL UNION. A union with locals in both the United States and Canada.

INTERNATIONAL VOYAGE. (a) When used with reference to Load Line Convention ships, means a voyage, not being an inland voyage, from a port in one country to a port in another country, either of those countries being a country to which the Load Line Convention applies, and (b) when used with reference to Safety Convention ships, means a voyage, not being an inland voyage, from a port in one country to a port in another country, either of those countries being a country to which the Safety Convention applies, and, for the purposes of this definition, every territory for the international relations of which a country to which the appropriate Convention applies is responsible or for which the United Nations is the administering authority shall be deemed to be a separate country. *Canada Shipping Act*, R.S.C. 1985, c. S-9, s. 2. See SHORT ~.

INTERNATIONAL WATERS. Waters of rivers that flow across the international boundary between the United States and Canada. *Canada Water Act*, R.S.C. 1985, c. C-11, s. 2.

INTERNATIONAL WILL. A will that has been made in accordance with the rules regarding an international will set out in the annex to the convention regarding international wills.

INTERNEE. See PROTECTED ~.

INTERNUNCIO. *n.* [L.] One who carries a message from one party to another; a representative of the Pope in another country.

INTERNUNCIUS. *n.* [L.] One who carries a message from one party to another; a representative of the Pope in another country.

INTER-PLANT INEQUITY. An inequality in pay rates between two plants where the same work is done.

INTERPLEADER. *n.* The process by which a person who expects to be or is sued by two or more parties with adverse claims to goods or a debt in the first person's hands, but in which the first person has no interest, obtains relief by arranging that the other parties try their rights between themselves. See STAKEHOLDER.

INTERPOLATE. *v.* To insert words in a finished document.

INTERPOLATION. *n.* The act of interpolating; the words which are inserted.

INTERPRETARE ET CONCORDARE LEGES LEGIBUS EST OPTIMUS INTER-PRETANDI MODUS. [L.] To interpret and to reconcile laws with other laws is the best method of interpretation.

INTERPRETATIO CHARTARUM BENIGNE FACIENDA EST UT RES MAGIS VALEAT QUAM PEREAT. [L.] The construction of deeds should be made liberally so that the thing fares well instead of coming to nothing.

INTERPRETATIO FIENDA EST UT RES MAGIS VALEAT QUAM PEREAT. [L.] Interpretation should be made so that the thing fares well instead of coming to nothing.

INTERPRETATION. *n.* 1. Construction of a document or statute. 2. Oral translation. See EXTENSIVE ~; RESTRICTIVE ~.

INTERPRETATION CLAUSE. A clause which sets out the meanings of particular words used in that statute.

INTERPRETATION SECTION. A section which sets out the meanings of particular words used in that statute.

INTERPRETER. *n.* At a trial, someone sworn to interpret the evidence of someone else who speaks a language which is not that of the proceedings, a mute or a hearing impaired person.

INTERPROVINCIAL. *adj.* Between provinces.

INTER-REGIONAL ABC (DOMESTIC). *abbr.* Inter-regional advance booking charter (domestic).

INTER-REGIONAL ADVANCE BOOKING CHARTER (DOMESTIC). An advance booking charter (domestic) or ABC (domestic) operated between two or more regional air carriers' operating territories. *Air Carrier Regulations*, C.R.C., c. 3, s. 83.

INTER-REGIONAL TRANSIT SYSTEM. A transit system that is principally operated, (i) in more than one regional area, and (ii) within the area of jurisdiction of the Authority. *Toronto Area Transit Operating Authority Act*, R.S.O. 1980, c. 505, s. 1.

INTERREGNUM. *n.* [L.] A time when a throne is vacant.

INTERROGATION. *n.* The conduct of an inquiry; the asking of questions. S.A. Cohen, *Due Process of Law* (Toronto: Carswell, 1977) at 71. See MODE A ~.

INTERROGATORY. *n.* A written question addressed to one party on behalf of the other party to a cause.

IN TERROREM. [L.] Terrifying.

INTERRUPTIBLE ENERGY. Electric energy made available under an agreement that permits curtailment or cessation of delivery at the option of the supplier. *National Energy Board Part VI Regulations*, C.R.C., c. 1056, s. 2.

INTERRUPTIBLE POWER. Electric power made available under an agreement that permits curtailment or cessation of availability at the option of the supplier. *National Energy Board Part VI Regulations*, C.R.C., c. 1056, s. 2.

INTERRUPTIO MULTIPLEX NON TOLLIT PRAESCRIPTIONEM SEMEL OBTENTAM. [L.] Frequent interruption does not remove a prescription which was already obtained.

INTERRUPTION. *n.* Breaking the continued enjoyment of a right. See POSTAL ~.

INTERRUPTION OF EARNINGS. That interruption that occurs in the earnings of an insured person when after a period of employment with an employer the insured person has a lay-off or separation from that employment or a reduction in his hours of work for that employer resulting in a prescribed reduction in earnings. *Unemployment Insurance Act*, R.S.C. 1985, c. U-1, s. 2.

INTER SE. [L.] Between themselves.

INTERSECTION. *n.* 1. The area embraced within the prolongation or connection of the lateral curb lines or, if none, then of the lateral boundary lines of two or more highways which join one another at an angle, whether or not one highway crosses the other. 2. Includes any portion of a highway indicated by markings on the surface of the roadway as a crossing place for pedestrians. *Highway Traffic Amendment Act*, S.O. 1984, c. 21, s. 16. See CENTRE POINT OF AN ~; POINT OF ~.

INTER-UNION DISPUTE. A conflict between unions with regard to which one should represent a group of employees or as to which one's members should perform work of a certain kind.

INTER-UTILITY TRANSFER. A transfer of any of the following classes, namely, (a) a sale transfer, being a transfer of electric power and energy under a contract of sale, (b) an equichange transfer, being an interchange of equal quantities of electric power or energy within a stated period, (c) a storage transfer, being an electric energy transfer "banked" for the time being in the form of water in reservoir space of another electrical utility, in the expectation that equivalent electric energy will be returned at a later time, (d) an adjustment transfer, being an electric power or energy transfer for purposes such as to adjust electric energy account balances, to compensate for services rendered, to deliver output entitlements, or to deliver upstream or downstream benefits, or (e) a carrier transfer, being a transfer of electric power or energy wheeled from one electrical utility through circuits of another electrical utility that acts as a carrier for delivery to a third party or to the originating utility. *National Energy Board Part VI Regulations*, C.R.C., c. 1056, s. 2.

INTER-UTILITY TRANSFER POINT. A stated point at which electric power and energy pass from the circuits of one electrical utility into the circuits of another electrical utility. *National Energy Board Part VI Regulations*, C.R.C., c. 1056, s. 2.

INTERVAL. See ESCAPE ~; LUCID ~; PULSE ~.

INTER-VEHICLE-UNIT DISTANCE. For a combination of vehicles means, (i) the distance measured between the centres of the last axle of the tractor and the first axle of the first trailer or semi-trailer, or (ii) the distance measured between the centres of the last axle of the first trailer or semi-trailer and the first axle of the second trailer or semi-trailer, whichever is smaller. *Highway Traffic Act*, R.R.O. 1980, Reg. 470, s. 1.

INTERVENANT. *n.* Someone who intervenes in a suit in which he or she was not originally involved.

INTERVENE. *v.* To move for leave to become an added party when one is not a party to a proceeding but claims, (a) to be interested in the subject matter of the proceeding; (b) that they may be adversely affected by the judgment in that proceeding; or (c) that there exists between them and any of the parties to the proceeding some question of fact or law like the questions at issue in the proceeding. G.D. Watson & C. Perkins, eds., *Holmested & Watson: Ontario Civil Procedure* (Toronto: Carswell, 1984) at 13-2.

INTERVENER. *n.* A person who files an intervention or who intervenes. See INTERVENOR; LOCAL ~.

INTERVENING PARCEL. (a) Any land in an existing district which lies between the point of diversion of water on an irrigation works of the board of that district and an irrigable parcel, and in respect of which the board does not have and did not at any time prior to May 2, 1968 acquire, any legal estate or interest or right permitting it to use that land for the purpose of delivering water from the point of diversion of water on the irrigation works of the board to the irrigable parcel, or (ii) any land, inside or outside the district, on or within which there exists any irrigation works or natural channels or features that from time to time during the 10-year period immediately preceding May 2, 1968 were used by the board of the district for the purpose of carrying water from any irrigation works of the board to any other place, whether or not the board had any legal estate or interest or right permitting it to do so. *Irrigation Act*, R.S.A. 1980, c. I-11, s. 191.

INTERVENOR. *n.* 1. Someone who, with leave of the court, voluntarily interposes in a proceeding. 2. A newsletter of the Canadian Environmental Law Association. See INTERVENER.

INTERVIEW. See EXIT ~.

INTER VIVOS. [L.] Between living people. See GIFT ~.

INTER VIVOS GIFT. A gift made while the donor is living.

INTER VIVOS TRUST. 1. A trust other than a testamentary trust. *Income Tax Act*, R.S.C. 1952, c. 148 (as am. S.C. 1970-71-72, c. 63), s. 108(1)(f). 2. Created by writing, a deed or oral declaration, a trust which is to take effect during the lifetime of the trust's creator. D.M.W. Waters, *The Law of Trusts in Canada*, 2d ed. (Toronto: Carswell, 1984) at 29.

INTESTACY. *n.* The condition or state of dying without a valid will.

IN TESTAMENTIS PLENIUS TESTATORIS INTENTIONEM SCRUTAMUR. [L.] In the case of wills, we examine the testator's intention even more fully.

INTESTATE. *n.* A person owning property who dies without a will.

INTESTATE. *adj.* See PERSON DYING ~.

INTIMIDATION. *n.* A tort in which one person, by threatening to do something unlawful, compels someone else not to do something that person wants to do or to do something which that person does not want to do so that the threatened party agrees to avoid the threat being executed, with the result that some person, whether it is the threatened person or a third party, is likely to be or is condemned by agreeing to act. I.H. Jacob, ed., *Bullen and Leake and Jacob's Precedents of Pleadings*, 12th ed. (London: Sweet and Maxwell, 1975) at 581.

INTOL AND UTTOL. A custom or toll paid for something exported or imported.

IN TOTIDEM VERBIS. [L.] In so many words.

IN TOTO. [L.] Completely, entirely, wholly.

IN TOTO ET PARS CONTINETUR. [L.] A part is contained within the whole.

INTOXICANT. *n.* Includes alcohol, alcoholic, spirituous, vinous, fermently malt or other intoxicating liquor or combination of liquors and mixed liquor a part of which is spiritous, vinous, fermented or otherwise intoxicating and all drinks, drinkable liquids, preparations or mixtures capable of human consumption that are intoxicating.

INTOXICATED. *adj.* Under the influence of alcohol to the extent that a person's physical and mental functioning is substantially impaired. *Treatment of Intoxicated Persons Act*, R.S.N.B. 1973, c. T-11.1, s. 1.

INTOXICATING LIQUOR. 1. Includes every spirituous or malt liquor, and every wine, and any and every combination of liquors or drinks that is intoxicating, and any mixed liquor capable of being used as a beverage, and part of which is spirituous or otherwise intoxicating. *Export Act*, R.S.C. 1985, c. E-18, s. 6(2). 2. Any liquor that is, by the law of the province for the time being in force, deemed to be intoxicating liquor and that it is unlawful to sell or have in possession without a permit or other authority of the government of the province or any board, commission, officer or other governmental agency authorized to issue the permit or grant the authority. *Importation of Intoxicating Liquors Act*, R.S.C. 1985, c. I-3, s. 2. 3. Any fermented, spirituous, beer or malt liquor or combination of such liquors that contain more than 2 1/2 per cent proof spirits. *Air Regulations*, C.R.C., c. 2, s. 823.

INTOXICATING VAPOUR. Any gas, vapour, fume or liquid that is emitted, given off or produced from a regulated matter.

INTOXICATION. See INVOLUNTARY ~.

INTRACARDIAL. *adj.* Delivered into the heart. *Animals for Research Act*, R.R.O. 1980, Reg. 18, s. 1.

INTRACEREBRAL HEMORRHAGE. Bleeding into the tissue of the brain. F.A. Jaffe, *A Guide to Pathological Evidence*, 2d ed. (Toronto: Carswell, 1983) at 46.

INTRACRANIAL. *adj.* Within the skull. F.A. Jaffe, *A Guide to Pathological Evidence*, 2d ed. (Toronto: Carswell, 1983) at 117.

IN TRADITIONIBUS SCRIPTORUM, NON QUOD DICTUM EST SED QUOD GESTUM EST INSPICITUR. [L.] In the delivery of deeds, what is regarded is not what was said but what was done.

IN TRANSIT. Under way, moored to a buoy, secured in a lock or at anchor. Canada regulations.

IN TRANSITU. [L.] During a passage.

INTRAPERITONEAL. *adj.* Delivered into the abdominal cavity. *Animals for Research Act*, R.R.O. 1980, Reg. 18, s. 1.

INTRATHORACIC. *adj.* Delivered into the thoracic cavity. *Animals for Research Act*, R.R.O. 1980, Reg. 18, s. 1.

INTRA-VEHICLE-UNIT DISTANCE. For a five or six axle vehicle without trailer or semi-trailer means, (i) the distance measured between the centres of the second and the third axles from the front of the vehicle, or (ii) the distance measured between the centres of the third and the fourth axles from the front of the vehicle, whichever is greater. *Highway Traffic Act*, R.R.O. 1980, Reg. 470, s. 1.

INTRAVENOUS. *adj.* Delivered into a vein.

INTRA VIRES. [L.] 1. Within the range of authority or power. 2. A law found to be valid because it was enacted under powers allocated to the legislative body which enacted it by the Constitution. P.W. Hogg, *Constitutional Law of Canada*, 2d ed. (Toronto: Carswell, 1985) at 310.

INTRINSICALLY SAFE. As applied to electrical equipment or electrical installation means that any sparking that may occur either in the normal use of the electrical equipment or installation or the use of the same under any condition of fault likely to occur therein in practice, is safe, such as to be incapable of causing an ignition of flammable gas, vapour or dust. *Power Corporation Act*, R.R.O. 1980, Reg. 794, s. 0.

INTRINSIC VALUE. When one cannot infer market value from current price quotations, the amount that, in an appraiser's judgment, property would sell for if (1) the market consisted of intelligent individuals; and (2) those individuals were interested in buying and selling the property solely with reference to its merit as an investment. A. Bissett-Johnson & W.M. Holland, eds, *Matrimonial Property Law in Canada* (Toronto: Carswell, 1980) at V-12.

INTRUSIVE PROCEDURE. (i) A mechanical means of controlling behaviour, (ii) an aversive stimulation technique, or (iii) any other procedure, that is prescribed as an intrusive procedure. *Child and Family Services Act*, S.O. 1874, c. 55, s. 108.

INUK. *n.* A person who is a direct descendant

of a person who is or was of the race of aborigines commonly referred to as Eskimos and possesses at least one-quarter of Inuk blood. Canada regulations.

INURE. *v.* To take effect.

INUTILIS LABOR ET SINE FRUCTUS NON EST EFFECTUS LEGIS. [L.] Law does nothing useless and fruitless.

IN VACUO. [L.] Without aim or goal.

INVADIARE. To mortgage or pledge land.

INVADIATUS. *n.* A person who gave surety to appear to answer a charge awaiting settlement.

IN VADIO. [L.] In pledge; in gage.

INVALID. *adj.* 1. Void, having no effect. 2. Physically or mentally incapable of earning financial remuneration.

INVALID CHILD. 1. Includes a child who, though not an invalid at the date of death of the worker, becomes an invalid before otherwise ceasing to be entitled to compensation. *Workers Compensation Act*, R.S.B.C. 1979, c. 437, s. 1. 2. Includes a child who, though not an invalid at the date of death of the victim, becomes an invalid before otherwise ceasing to be entitled to compensation. *Criminal Injury Compensation Act*, R.S.B.C. 1979, c. 83, s. 1.

INVECTA ET ILLATA. [L.] Ordinary equipment on the premises such as stock-in-trade and furniture which are covered by a landlord's hypothec.

INVENTION. *n.* Any new and useful art, process, machine, manufacture or composition of matter, or any new and useful improvement in any art, process, machine, manufacture or composition of matter.

INVENTIONES. *n.* [L.] A treasure-trove.

INVENTOR. *n.* The person who applies for a patent and had to invent the thing alone, not because another suggested it or because the person read about it. H.G. Fox, *The Canadian Law and Practice Relating to Letters Patent for Inventions*, 4th ed. (Toronto: Carswell, 1969) at 225.

INVENTORY. *n.* 1. A description of property the cost or value of which is relevant in computing a taxpayer's income from a business for a taxation year. *Income Tax Act*, R.S.C. 1952, c. 148 (as am. S.C. 1970-71-72, c. 63), s. 248(1). 2. A stock taking of forest-stand characteristics and volumes by means of aerial mapping and sampling on the ground to arrive at estimates of volume, growth and drain by selected categories. *Forests Act*, S.N.S. 1986, c. 10, s. 3. 3. Goods that are held by a person for sale or lease,

or that are to be furnished or have been furnished under a contract of service, or that are raw materials, work in process or materials used or consumed in a business or profession. *Personal Property Security acts.* 4. A schedule or list which accurately describes goods and chattels.

INVENTORYING. *n.* Includes the preparation of retention and destruction schedules of public documents. *Archives Act*, S.P.E.I. 1975, c. 64, s. 1.

INVENTORY VALUATION. See FIFO METHOD OF ~.

IN VENTRE SA MÈRE. [Fr.] In one's mother's womb. See EN VENTRE SA MÈRE.

IN VERBIS NON VERBA SED RES ET RATIO QUAERENDA EST. [L.] In interpreting words, one should look not at their literal meaning but at the intention and the reason of the user.

INVERTEBRATE FOSSIL. The fossilized remains of an animal that did not possess a backbone. *Canadian Cultural Property Export Control List*, C.R.C., c. 448, s. 1.

INVEST. *v.* To transfer possession; to contribute money.

INVESTIGATED PERSON. A person, corporation or other entity with respect to whose conduct a hearing by a review panel is being held or may be held.

INVESTIGATION. *n.* An investigation that (a) pertains to the administration or enforcement of an Act of Parliament; (b) is authorized by or pursuant to an Act of Parliament; or (c) is within a class of investigations specified in the regulations. *Access to Information Act*, R.S.C. 1985, c. A-1, s. 16(4). See ARCHAEOLOGICAL ~; PERSONAL ~; SUBSURFACE ~.

INVESTIGATIVE INFORMATION. Information respecting a consumer's character, general reputation, personal characteristics or mode of living that is obtained through personal interviews with neighbors, friends or associates of the consumer or with others to whom the consumer is known. *The Credit Reporting Agencies Act*, R.S.S. 1978, c. C-44, s. 2.

INVESTIGATOR. *n.* The person appointed to conduct an investigation. See PERSONAL INFORMATION ~; PRIVATE ~.

INVESTITURE. *n.* 1. The free transfer of possession or seisin. 2. The formal bestowal of office or honour.

INVESTMENT. *n.* 1. A purchase of a security of an issuer or a loan or advance to a person, but does not include a loan or advance, whether secured or unsecured, that is (a) made by mutual fund, its mutual fund manager or its mutual fund distributor, and (b) merely ancillary to the main business of the mutual fund, its manager or its distributor. 2. (a) An investment in a corporation by way of purchase of bonds, debentures, notes or other evidences of indebtedness thereof or shares thereof, or (b) a loan to a person or persons. 3. Includes the purchase price of the land, moneys expended on the installation of services, the laying out and construction of streets, sidewalks, lanes and the development of park areas, public space and facilities appropriate to a residential housing development, and such carrying charges and other expenses incurred by the company in respect of the land as may be approved by the Corporation, including taxes, insurance, repairs, and maintenance. *National Housing Act*, R.S.C. 1970, c. N-10, s. 20. 4. Any capital expenditure or expenditure for equipment, including the purchase price of furniture, fittings and tools or a library collection. *University Investments Act*, R.S.Q. 1977, c. I-17, s. 1. See AUTHORIZED ~; BUSINESS OF ~; DOWNSTREAM ~; NON-QUALIFIED ~; POOLED ~ TRUST; QUALIFIED ~; REGISTERED ~; TRUSTEE ~S; UNAUTHORIZED ~ OR LOAN.

INVESTMENT CANADA. A federal agency which offers investment services and information in order to encourage investment in Canada by both non-Canadians and Canadians.

INVESTMENT CERTIFICATE. (i) With reference to a provincial company, an agreement made between the company and another person pursuant to section 105 of this Act or section 68 of The Trust Companies Act, 1960, or (ii) with reference to an extra-provincial company, an agreement made between the company and another person before or after the commencement of this Act of similar purport to an agreement mentioned in section 105, and includes an instrument commonly known as a guaranteed investment certificate, guaranteed trust certificate or savings certificate. *Trust Companies Act*, R.S.A. 1980, c. T-9, s. 1.

INVESTMENT COMPANY. 1. A company (a) incorporated after January 1, 1972 primarily for the purpose of carrying on the business of investment, or (b) that carries on the business of investment, but does not include a company to which the Bank Act, the Quebec Savings Banks Act, chapter B-4 of the Revised Statutes of Canada, 1970, the Canadian and British Insurance Companies Act or the Cooperative Credit Associations Act applies or a loan company within the meaning of the Loan Companies Act. *Investment Companies Act*, R.S.C. 1985, c. I-22, s. 2. 2. A company the principal business of which is or will be the acquisition of or

investment in securities, and includes a company that issues any of the following that are not investment contracts within the meaning of the Investment Contract Act, that is to say, (a) investment certificates; (b) savings certificates; (c) savings contracts; (d) investment contracts; or (e) securities of a like nature. *Securities Act*, R.S.B.C. 1979, c. 380, s. 1. See MORTGAGE ~.

INVESTMENT CONTRACT. 1. A contract, agreement, certificate, instrument or writing containing an undertaking by an issuer to pay the holder thereof, or the holder's assignee or personal representative or other person, a stated or determinable maturity value in cash or its equivalent on a fixed or determinable date and containing optional settlement, cash surrender or loan values prior to or after maturity, the consideration for which consists of payments made or to be made to the issuer in instalments or periodically, or of a single sum, according to a plan fixed by the contract, whether or not the holder is or may be entitled to share in the profits or earnings of, or to receive additional credits or sums from, the issuer, but does not include a contract within the meaning of the Insurance Act. 2. Any debt obligation (other than a salary deferral arrangement, an income bond, an income debenture, a small business development bond, a small business bond or a prescribed contract). *Income Tax Act*, R.S.C. 1952, c. 148 (as am. S.C. 1986, c. 55, s. 3(3)0, s. 12(11)(a).

INVESTMENT CO-OPERATIVE. A co-operative: (i) that is incorporated pursuant to The Co-operatives Act; (ii) that has as one of its principal objects, as stated in its articles of incorporation, the investment of its equity capital in accordance with this Act; and (iii) all of whose members are employees of the same employer. *Labour-Sponsored Venture Capital Corporation Act*, S.S. 1986, c. L-0.2, s. 2.

INVESTMENT CORPORATION. A corporation that is approved by the Governor in Council for the purposes of section 146 of the Income Tax Act (Canada) and that issues investment contracts as described in that section.

INVESTMENT COUNSEL. Any person or company that engages in or holds herself, himself or itself out as engaging in the business of advising others as to the advisability of investing in or purchasing or selling specific securities and that is primarily engaged in giving continual advice as to the investment of funds on the basis of the individual needs of each client.

INVESTMENT COUNSELLING. The offering of advice to, or advising of, other persons on the advisability of investing in, purchasing or selling securities whether or not such other persons are ascertained but does not include the giving of such advice on a casual basis for no monetary consideration. *Bank Act*, R.S.C. 1985, c. B-1, s. 174.

INVESTMENT DEALER. 1. Any person or company that is a member, branch office, or associate member of the Investment Dealers Association of Canada or any person or company recognized by a commission as an investment dealer that engages either for the whole or part of her, his or its time in the business of trading in securities in the capacity of an agent or principal. 2. A person or company who or that (a) is a member or associate member of the British Columbia Bond Dealers' Association; (b) is a member or associate member of the Pacific District of the Investment Dealers' Association of Canada; or (c) is recognized by the superintendent as an investment dealer, and who or that engages either for the whole or part of his or its time in the business of trading in securities in the capacity of an agent or principal. *Securities Act*, R.S.B.C. 1979, c. 380, s. 1.

INVESTMENT FINANCE COURSE. See CANADIAN ~.

INVESTMENT FUNDS COURSE. See CANADIAN ~.

INVESTMENT HOLDING COMPANY. A company incorporated under the Companies Act whose objects as set forth in its memorandum of association are solely as follows: (a) to hold by way of investment any real or personal property whatsoever; (i) for purposes incidental to such holding to purchase or otherwise acquire and to sell or otherwise dispose of any such real or personal property; (c) for purposes incidental to such holding or purchase or sale, to draw, make, accept, endorse, discount, execute and issue promissory notes, bills of exchange, bills of lading, warrants and other negotiable or transferable instruments; (d) with the sanction of a special resolution, to guarantee the obligations of any shareholder and, as security for such guarantee, to mortgage, pledge, hypothecate or otherwise charge the whole or any part of its property; (e) to do all such other acts or things as are incidental or conducive to or consequential upon the attainment of the above objects. *Private Investment Holding Companies Act*, R.S.N.S. 1967, c. 236, s. 1.

INVESTMENT IN A FOREIGN COUNTRY. (a) The acquisition of shares, stock or any other interest in a corporation incorporated and carrying on, or proposing to carry on, business in a foreign country, (b) the acquisition of a right to share in the assets of a business carried on, or proposed to be carried on, in a foreign country,

whether as a corporation or otherwise, (c) the lending of money or extension of credit, by any means, to a person in a foreign country for use by him in or in connection with a business carried on, or proposed to be carried on, by him in that country, (d) the transferring of money, or the shipment of goods or equipment, to a foreign country for use in or in connection with a business carried on, or proposed to be carried on, in that country, (e) the acquisition, pursuant to a written agreement, of a right in respect of a business carried on, or proposed to be carried on, in a foreign country (i) to manage the business, (ii) to furnish administrative, financial, technical or general advisory services to the business, (iii) to participate in the profits of the business, or (iv) to receive a payment from the business, the amount of which is related to or determined by the use by the business of property of the recipient of the payment, the volume of the production or sales of the business or the value of the production or sales of the business, (f) the issuing by a person to another person of a guarantee of payment of an amount payable as a result of an investment described in any of paragraphs (a) to (e) that is made by that other person in a business carried on, or proposed to be carried on, in a foreign country, or (g) where there is a series of two or more guarantees each of which, except the first, is given in respect of a preceding guarantee in the series, the giving of any guarantee in the series if the first such guarantee is an investment in a foreign country by reason of paragraph (f). *Export Development Act*, R.S.C. 1985, c. E-20, s. 23.

INVESTMENT PLAN. See INDEXED SECURITY ~.

INVESTMENT PROPERTY. (i) Bonds, debentures, mortgages, hypothecs, notes or other similar obligations (A) of or guaranteed by the Government of Canada, (B) of the government of a province or an agent thereof, (C) of a municipality in Canada or a municipal or public body performing a function of government in Canada, (D) or a corporation, commission or association not less than 90% of the shares or capital of which is owned by Her Majesty in right of a province or by a Canadian municipality, or of a subsidiary wholly-owned corporation that is subsidiary to such a corporation, commission or association or (E) of an educational institution or a hospital if repayment of the principal amount thereof and payment of the interest thereon is to be made, or is guaranteed, assured or otherwise specifically provided for or secured by the government of a province, (ii) any deposits, deposit certifictes or guaranteed investment certificates with (A) a bank to which the Bank Act or the Quebec Savings Banks Act applies, (B) a corporation licensed or otherwise authorized under the laws of Canada or a province to carry on in Canada the business of offering to the public its services as trustee, or (C) a credit union or central that is a member of the Canadian Payments Association or a credit union that is a shareholder or member of a central that is a member of the Canadian Payments Association; (iii) any money of the corporation; and (iv) in relation to a particular deposit insurance corporation, debt obligations of, and shares of the capital stock of, a subsidiary wholly-owned corporation of the particular corporation where the subsidiary is deemed by subsection (5.1) to be a deposit insurance corporation. *Income Tax Act*, R.S.C. 1952, c. 148 (as am. S.C. 1988, c. 55, s. 124(4)), s. 137.1(5)(c).

INVESTMENT TRUST. A trust which collects, retains and invests funds for multiple purposes. D.M.W. Waters, *The Law of Trusts in Canada*, 2d ed. (Toronto: Carswell, 1984) at 101. See REAL ESTATE ~.

INVESTOR. *n.* 1. With respect to an applicant for a certificate, a person who has a total equity percentage in the applicant that is greater than zero. *Canadian Ownership and Control Determination Act*, R.S.C. 1985, c. C-20, s. 2. 2. A person carrying on business or other activities in Canada who is planning an investment in a foreign country. *Export Development Act*, R.S.C. 1985, c. E-20, s. 23. See RESIDENT ~.

IN VIRIDI OBSERVANTIA. [L.] Present to people's minds, and fully in force and operation.

INVITATION TO TREAT. A statement which indicates general commercial intent, the wish of that party to contract with another party if they can make suitable arrangements. G.H.L. Fridman, *The Law of Contract in Canada*, 2d ed. (Toronto: Carswell, 1986) at 30.

INVITEE. *n.* One who, is either impliedly or expressly invited to an occupier's premises for some purpose connected indirectly or directly with the occupier's business. In law, a guest is a licensee, not an invitee. J.V. DiCastri, *Occupiers' Liability* (Vancouver: Burroughs/Carswell, 1980) at 33.

INVITO BENEFICIUM NON DATUR. [L.] A benefit is not given to anyone who did not ask for it.

INVITOR. *n.* A person who invites another to her or his premises for business purposes.

IN VITRO. [L. in glass] In a test tube. F.A. Jaffe, *A Guide to Pathological Evidence*, 2d ed. (Toronto: Carswell, 1983) at 178.

IN VIVO. [L.] In a living body. F.A. Jaffe, *A Guide to Pathological Evidence*, 2d ed. (Toronto: Carswell, 1983) at 178.

INVOICE. *n.* A written account of the particulars of goods shipped or sent to a purchaser.

INVOICE PRICE. The price payable for unused farm machinery and equipment by the dealer as shown on the invoice prepared by the vendor less the amount of any unearned allowance granted by the vendor in respect of that unused farm machinery and equipment. *Farm Machinery and Equipment Act*, S.M. 1971, c. 83, s. 32.

INVOLUNTARY INTOXICATION. Intoxication which is not self-induced. D. Stuart, *Canadian Criminal Law: a treatise*, 2d ed. (Toronto: Carswell, 1987) at 364.

INVOLUNTARY PATIENT. A person who is detained in a psychiatric facility.

INVOLUNTARY PAYMENT. A payment which is not, in law or in fact, due to the one who is paid from the one paying. G.H.L. Fridman & J.G. McLeod, *Restitution* (Toronto: Carswell, 1982) at 62.

INWARD MOVEMENT. (a) Moving containers from the dock face to the container yard, sorting them once in accordance with instructions from the owner of the vessel, stacking them in the container yard and then moving them to an adjacent container freight station, and (b) moving empty containers from the container freight station to the container storage area after destuffing. *Pacific Terminal Tariff By-law*, C.R.C., c. 1083, s. 32.

IN WRITING. Printing, lithography and other modes of reprinting or reproducing words in visible form. *Industrial Enterprises Incorporated Act*, R.S.P.E.I. 1974, c. I-2, s. 2.

IONIZING RADIATION. Any atomic or subatomic particle or electromagnetic wave emitted or produced directly or indirectly by a machine or radioactive isotope and having sufficient kinetic or quantum energy to produce ionization.

IONIZING RADIATION EQUIPMENT. A device capable of emitting ionizing radiation, but does not include: (i) equipment operated at less than 15 kilovolts and not designed principally to produce useful radiation; (ii) equipment that is in storage, in transit or not being used or equipment operated in such a manner that it cannot produce radiation; (iii) any radioactive substance; or (iv) any other equipment or class of equipment specified in the regulations. *Radiation Health and Safety Act*, S.S. 1984-85-86, c. R-1.1, s. 2.

IONIZING RADIATION INSTALLATION. The whole or any part of a building or other place in which ionizing radiation equipment is manufactured, used or placed or installed for use, and includes that ionizing radiation equipment. *Radiation Health and Safety Act*, S.S. 1984-85-86, c. R-1.1, s. 2.

IOTA. *n.* The smallest possible quantity.

IOU. *abbr.* I owe you. The written admission or expression of a debt.

I.P.J. *abbr.* Intellectual Property Journal.

IPSE DIXIT. [L. one said it oneself] A simple assertion.

IPSISSIMA VERBA. [L.] The very same words.

IPSO FACTO. [L.] By the very same act.

IPSO JURE. [L.] By the very law.

I.R.B. *abbr.* Industrial Relations Board.

IRE AD LARGUM. [L. to go at large] To be set free; to escape.

IRHD. *abbr.* International Rubber Hardness Degrees as referred to in ASTM D1415-1968, Standard Test Method of International Hardness of Vulcanized Natural and Synthetic Rubbers. *Motor Vehicle Safety Regulations*, C.R.C., c. 1038, s. 2.

IRISH MOSS. The red seaweeds Chondrus, Gigartina and Furcellaria.

IRON BAR. An iron or steel bar five-eighths of an inch square and two feet long pointed at one end and planted in the ground so that the top of the bar is flush with the ground level. *Surveys Act*, R.R.O. 1980, Reg. 927, s. 1. See SHORT STANDARD ~; STANDARD ~.

IRON POST. 1. (i) A pointed iron tube at least thirty-six inches long and three-quarters of an inch in diameter, having the top four inches plugged and squared and weighing at least two and one-half pounds, termed a standard iron post; (ii) solid iron, round or square, at least thirty inches long and three-quarters of an inch in diameter; provided that in solid rock the length may be reduced to six inches. *The Land Surveys Act*, R.S.S. 1978, c. L-4, s. 2. 2. An iron or steel tube one and one-quarter inches inside diameter and thirty inches long filled with concrete, fitted with an iron or steel foot plate and a bronze identification cap on the top and planted so that the identification cap is flush with the ground level. *Surveys Act*, R.R.O. 1980, Reg. 927, s. 1.

IRONWORKER. *n.* A person who, (i) in the field, fabricates, assembles, installs, hoists, erects, dismantles, reconditions, adjusts, alters, repairs or services all structural ironwork, pre-cast or prestressed concrete, concrete reinforcing materials, ferrous and non-ferrous materials in curtain wall, ornamental and miscellaneous metal work and all other materials used in lieu thereof and applies sealants where applicable thereto, and moves and places machinery and heavy equipment, and (ii) reads and understands all shop and field drawings, including those taken from original architectural and engineering drawings, that are related to the work operations contained in subclause (i), but does not include a person employed as a shop-man on the fabrication and assembly of materials in an industrial manufacturing plant. *Apprenticeship and Tradesmen's Qualification Act*, R.R.O. 1980, Reg. 44, s. 1.

IRRADIANCE. *n.* Radiant power incident per unit area expressed as watts per square centimetre (W cm^{-2}). *Radiation Emitting Devices Regulations*, C.R.C., c. 1370, s. 1. See INTEGRATED ~.

IRREBUTTABLE. *adj.* Not rebuttable; not capable of disproof.

IRREGULARITY. *n.* A condition resulting when a judicial or extra-judicial proceeding is done wrongly or without proper formalities.

IRREGULAR LOT. A township lot whose boundaries according to the original plan do not conform within one degree to the bearings shown for the corresponding boundaries of the majority of the lots in the tier in which the lot occurs. *Surveys Act*, R.S.O. 1980, c. 493, s. 1.

IRREGULARLY-SHAPED LOT. A lot that is not rectangular. *The Local Improvements Act*, R.S.S. 1978, c. L-33, s. 2.

IRRELEVANT. *adj.* Not relevant.

IRREPLEVIABLE. *adj.* Unable to be replevied.

IRREPLEVISABLE. *adj.* Unable to be replevied.

IRREVOCABLE. *adj.* Not able to be revoked.

IRREVOCABLE CREDIT. The credit which an issuing bank agrees to consider irrevocable. I.F.G. Baxter, *The Law of Banking*, 3d ed. (Toronto: Carswell, 1981) at 149.

IRRIGABLE UNIT. Land in a district having the same owner and consisting of (a) a quarter-section, a part of a quarter-section described in a certificate of title or a surveyed lot, or (b) lands designated as an irrigable unit by the board pursuant to subsection (2). *Irrigation Act*, R.S.A. 1980, c. I-11, s. 58.

IRRIGATION. See EFFLUENT ~.

IRRIGATION PURPOSE. The beneficial use of water on cultivated land and hay meadows to nourish crops. *Water Act*, R.S.B.C. 1979, c. 429, s. 1.

IRRIGATION RATES. (i) The amount determined by multiplying the number of acres classified in the assessment roll of a district as "to be irrigated" by the annual rate, or (ii) with reference to a particular parcel, the amount determined by multiplying the number of acres in the parcel classified in the assessment roll as "to be irrigated" by the annual rate. *Irrigation Act*, R.S.A. 1980, c. I-11, s. 131.

IRRIGATION WORKS. Any structure, device, contrivance or thing, or any artificial body of water, used or to be used by a board in exercise or performance of its powers or duties with respect to supplying, carrying or delivering water or obtaining a supply of water or any other purpose in connection therewith or incidental thereto, and without derogating from the generality of the foregoing, includes any dike, dam, weir, breakwater, drainage works, ditch, basin, reservoir, artificial lake or other artificial watercourse or body of water, canal, tunnel, bridge, culvert, crib, embankment, headwork, flume, aqueduct, pipe, pump, measuring weir, floodgate, meter, and any contrivance for carrying or conducting water or used to deliver water or for measuring water, or any building, telephone line or other work in any way used in or in relation to the carrying out by a board of its obligations or responsibilities to supply water. *Irrigation Act*, R.S.A. 1980, c. I-11, s. 1.

ISCHEMIA. *n.* The condition of insufficient blood supply to tissue or an organ. F.A. Jaffe, *A Guide to Pathological Evidence*, 2d ed. (Toronto: Carswell, 1983) at 178.

ISLAND. *n.* 1. All land comprising an island, and includes surrounding land attached to and extending from an island, whether or not water flows over or under it. *Islands Trust Act*, R.S.B.C. 1979, c. 208, s. 1. 2. Unless the context otherwise requires, the Province of Newfoundland. *Interpretation Act*, R.S.Nfld. 1970, c. 182, s. 26. See PUMP ~.

ISLAND OF NEWFOUNDLAND. Includes all of the islands forming part of the province that are located either wholly or partly south of Cape Bauld. *Dog Act*, S.Nfld. 1975-76, c. 13, s. 2.

I.S.M. RADIO FREQUENCY GENERATOR. Any device, apparatus, equipment or other thing that (a) is operated for industrial, scientific, medical or similar purposes, (b) produces and utilizes radio frequency energy in its operations, and (c) is not used for radiocommunication. *Radio Interference Regulations*, C.R.C., c. 1374, s. 2.

ISOCYANATE. *n.* A substance designated under the Ontario Occupational Health and Safety Act. D. Robertson, *Ontario Health and Safety Guide* (Toronto: Richard De Boo Ltd., 1988) at 5-223.

ISOLATED. *adj.* In respect of an electrical facility, that the facility is separated or disconnected from every source of electrical, hydraulic, pneumatic or other kind of energy that is capable of making the facility dangerous. *Canada Electrical Safety Regulations*, C.R.C., c. 998, s. 2.

ISOLATED WORK PLACE. Any work place that, under normal travel conditions and using the fastest means of transportation that is readily available for emergency use, is more than 2 hours travel time from a physician or hospital. *Canada First-Aid Regulations*, C.R.C., c. 1001, s. 2.

ISOLATING SWITCH. A switch intended for isolating a circuit or electrical equipment from the source of supply of electrical power or energy, but does not include a switch intended for establishing or interrupting the flow of current in a circuit. *Power Corporation Act*, R.R.O. 1980, Reg. 794, s. 0.

ISOLATION. *n.* The separation of a person or animal infected with a communicable disease from other persons or animals for the period of infectivity in a place and under conditions that will prevent the direct or indirect conveyance of the infectious agent from the infected person or animal to a susceptible person or animal. See GUARANTEE OF ~.

ISOLATION ROOM. See SECURE ~.

ISOPHANE RATIO. The minimum number of milligrams of protamine required to precipitate 100 Internatinal Units of insulin and shall be determined by an acceptable method. *Food and Drug Regulations*, C.R.C., c. 870, c. C.03.084.

ISSUE. *v.* 1. In respect of an award, means make and publish to the parties to the arbitration. *Labour Code*, R.S.B.C. 1979, c. 212, s. 92. 2. With reference to a disposition that is required to be executed by the holder, means to mail or deliver 2 or more copies of the disposition to the intended holder for execution by him. *Public Lands Act*, R.S.A. 1980, c. P-30, s. 1. 3. Includes to renew. *Highway Traffic Act*, R.S.Nfld. 1970, c. 152, s. 2.

ISSUE. *n.* 1. A matter in dispute. 2. The first delivery of a bill or note, complete in form, to a person who takes it as a holder. *Bills of Exchange Act*, R.S.C. 1985, c. B-4, s. 2. 3. Includes all lawful lineal descendants of an ancestor. 4. Includes a descendant conceived before and born alive after the person's death. *Succession Law Reform Amendment Act*, S.O. 1986, c. 53, s. 1. 5. The number of copies of a work comprised in the first printing and intended for sale. See CANADIAN ~; DIE WITHOUT ~; DIE WITHOUT LEAVING ~; DYING WITHOUT ~; FAILURE OF ~; FIRST

~ OF STOCK; GOVERNMENT ~; HAVE NO ~; IMMATERIAL ~; JOINDER OF ~; MALE ~; OVER~; TENDER OF ~.

ISSUED. *adj.* Describes an originating process which a registrar dates, signs, seals with the seal of the court and to which a court file number is assigned. G.D. Watson & C. Perkins, eds., *Holmested & Watson: Ontario Civil Procedure* (Toronto: Carswell, 1984) at 14-5.

ISSUED CAPITAL. The quantity of shares allotted and issued. H. Sutherland, D.B. Horsley & J.M. Edmiston, eds., *Fraser's Handbook on Canadian Company Law*, 7th ed. (Toronto: Carswell, 1985) at 41.

ISSUED CAPITAL STOCK. As applied to a provincial company having common shares without par value, means the number of the issued common shares of the company. *Trust Companies Act*, R.S.A. 1980, c. T-9, s. 1. See SUBSCRIBED AND ~ OF THE COMPANY.

ISSUED SECURITIES. Includes any shares, stock, share warrants, share or stock purchase warrants, bonds, debentures, debenture stock, notes, bill of exchange, deposit certificates or receipts, participation certificates, open accounts or other evidences of indebtedness or rights issued by or on behalf of any domiciled company or under or for which any domiciled company is obligated or liable. *Domiciled Companies Act*, R.S.P.E.I. 1974, c. D-16, s. 1.

ISSUED SHARES. Of a corporation includes unissued shares, the issuing of which has been authorized by a properly passed resolution of the corporation as consideration for the conveyance to it of land in respect of which exemption from tax is claimed under this Regulation. *Land Transfer Tax Act*, R.R.O. 1980, Reg. 563, s. 1.

ISSUED TO THE PUBLIC. Merely by placing them on sale, inviting the public to acquire copies; it is unnecessary to advertise or inform the public that publication was made. H.G. Fox, *The Canadian Law of Copyright and Industrial Designs*, 2d ed. (Toronto: Carswell, 1967) at 70.

ISSUE MALE. Words which restrict gifts to descendants in the male line. T. Sheard, R. Hull & M.M.K. Fitzpatrick, *Canadian Forms of Wills*, 4th ed. (Toronto: Carswell, 1982) at 191.

ISSUE OF OUR MARRIAGE. Words which restrict gifts to the first generation only. T. Sheard, R. Hull & M.M.K. Fitzpatrick, *Canadian Forms of Wills*, 4th ed. (Toronto: Carswell, 1982) at 191.

ISSUER. *n.* 1. A person or company who has outstanding, issues or proposes to issue, a security or a body corporate, (i) that is required to maintain a securities register, (ii) that directly or indirectly creates fractional interests in its rights or property and issues security certificates or uncertified securities as evidence of the fractional interests, (iii) that places or authorizes the placing of its name on a security certificate, otherwise than as an authenticating trustee, registrar or transfer agent, or that otherwise authorizes the issue of a security certificate or an uncertificated security evidencing a share, participation or other interest in its property or in an enterprise or evidencing its duty to perform an obligation, or (iv) that becomes responsible for or in place of any other person described as an issuer. 2. The person who issues a credit card. 3. An issuer of marriage licences. See OFFEREE ~; PRIVATE ~; REPORTING ~; SECURITY ~.

ISSUER BID. An offer to acquire or an offer to redeem securities of an issuer, other than debt securities that are not convertible into equity securities, made by the issuer.

ISSUER OF MARRIAGE LICENCES. An issuer of marriage licences appointed under this Act, or a marriage commissioner acting by virtue of his office as an issuer of marriage licences. *Marriage Act*, R.S.B.C. 1979, c. 251, s. 1.

ISSUING BANK. That portion of a money room designated for issuing money to sellers and cashiers. *Race Track Supervision Regulations*, C.R.C., c. 441, s. 2.

ITA UTERE TUO UT ALIENUM NON LAEDAS. [L.] Use your own property so that you do not injure your neighbours'.

ITC. *abbr.* Inclusive tour charter.

ITEM. *n.* That portion of a vote used for a specific program purpose. *Financial Administration acts.* See LETTER-POST ~S; OPTIONAL ~S; PAYMENT ~.

ITEM OF EVIDENCE. Anything that a peace officer believes, on reasonable and probable grounds, may provide evidence of the commission of an offence. *Provincial Offences Procedure Act*, S.N.B. 1987, c. P-22.1, s. 1.

ITINERANT. *adj.* Travelling, on circuit.

ITINERANT EXHIBITOR. A person travelling from one place to another with a moving picture or cinematograph machine or similar apparatus, for the purpose of giving moving picture or cinematograph exhibitions. *The Theatres and Cinematographs Act*, R.S.S. 1978, c. T-11, s. 2.

ITINERANT MACHINE. A motor vehicle, aircraft, trailer or oil well drilling equipment. Alberta statutes.

ITINERANT MERCHANT. A merchant who,

personally or through a representative, elsewhere than at his address, (a) solicits a particular consumer for the purpose of making a contract; or (b) makes a contract with a consumer. *Consumer Protection Act*, S.Q. 1978, c. 9, s. 55.

ITINERANT SALESMAN. (i) A person who as vendor or agent for the vendor, such vendor not having his principal place of business in the city, goes about from place to place within the city selling goods or offering the same for sale directly to the consumer, or soliciting orders from the consumer for goods, or (ii) a person who goes about from place to place within the city taking orders for goods to be made, grown or completed, in whole or in part, outside the city by any person not having his principal place of business in the city. *City of Winnipeg Act*, S.M. 1971, c. 105, s. 521.

ITINERANT SELLER. A seller whose business includes the sale or offering for sale of goods or soliciting of orders for goods at a place other than the seller's permanent place of business, whether personally or by the seller's agent or employee.

ITINERANT VENDOR. Any vendor who, elsewhere than at his address, solicits the signing of a contract of sale from a specified consumer or makes a similar contract with a consumer. *Consumer Protection Act*, R.S.Q. 1977, c. P-40, s. 1.

ITINERANT WEATHER MINIMA. The minimum weather conditions specified in the Canada Air Pilot for use by aircraft. *Air Carriers Using Large Aeroplanes Order*, C.R.C., c. 21, s. 2.

J. *abbr.* 1. Justice. 2. Joule.

J.A. *abbr.* Justice of appeal.

JACKET. *n.* The partial or complete shell of hard metal which surrounds a bullet's soft metal core. F.A. Jaffe, *A Guide to Pathological Evidence,* 2d ed. (Toronto: Carswell, 1983) at 178 and 179. See LIFE~.

JACTITATION. *n.* A false pretension to marry.

JACTIVUS. *adj.* [L.] Lost by default; tossed away.

JACTUS. *n.* [L.] Throwing goods away.

JAIL. *n.* 1. A prison or gaol. 2. Includes a common jail and also includes a jail farm or correctional institution for the province established under this Act, but does not include a lockup or municipal jail. *Jails Act,* R.S.P.E.I. 1974, c. J-1, s. 2. See COMMON ~; GAOL; MUNICIPAL ~.

JAIL DELIVERY. See GAOL DELIVERY.

JAILER. See GAOLER.

JAIL PHYSICIAN. A physician in attendance in his professional capacity at a correctional institution, lock-up, reformatory or similar place. *Venereal Diseases Prevention Act,* R.S.A. 1980, c. V-2, s. 1.

J. BUS. L. *abbr.* Journal of Business Law.

J. CAN. STUDIES. *abbr.* Journal of Canadian Studies (Revue d'études canadiennes).

J.E. *abbr.* Jurisprudence Express.

JELLING AGENT. Gelatin, agar or carrageein. *Meat Inspection Regulations,* C.R.C., c. 1032, s. 2.

JEOPARDY. See DOUBLE ~; IN ~.

JETSAM. *n.* Goods thrown into the sea which sink and stay under water.

JETTISON. *v.* To throw goods overboard to lighten a vessel during a storm, to prevent capture or for any other good reason.

JEWEL. *n.* In respect of a designated article, a part formed of polished natural corundum or synthetic corundum that is incorporated in the mechanism of the article to bear the friction of a moving part or to transmit motion impulses between parts. *Watch Jewels Marking Regulations,* C.R.C., c. 1141, s. 2.

JEWELLER. *n.* Includes watchmaker. *Liens on Goods and Chattels Act,* R.S.N.B. 1973, c. L-6. s. 1.

J.I.B.C. *abbr.* Justice Institute of British Columbia.

JIGGING. *n.* Fishing for, catching or killing fish with a hook or hooks manipulated so as to pierce and hook a fish in any part of the body other than the mouth.

JIGS. *n.* Devices used in the accurate machining of goods in process which hold the goods firmly and guide the working tools. *Retail Sales Tax Act,* R.R.O. 1980, Reg. 903, s. 1.

J. JUGES PROV. *abbr.* Journal des juges provinciaux (Provincial Judges Journal).

J.L. & SOCIAL POL'Y. *abbr.* Journal of Law and Social Policy (Revue des lois et des politiques sociales).

J.M.V.L. *abbr.* Journal of Motor Vehicle Law.

JOB. *n.* A specific assignment of work; a full-time work position.

JOB ACTION. Action taken to enforce a union contract.

JOBBER. *n.* 1. Someone who buys and sells goods wholesale and handles goods on commission. G.H.L. Fridman, *Sale of Goods in Canada,* 3d ed. (Toronto: Carswell, 1986) at 493. 2. Any person who regularly distributes milk, and who obtains milk packaged, ready for distribution, from any vendor, but does not include any person who sells milk at retail in any store. *Milk Industry Act*, R.S.B.C. 1979, c. 258, s. 1.

JOB CLASSIFICATION. The rating of jobs based on skills and other requirements.

JOB CONTENT. The actual duties and functions which make up a job.

JOB CREATION PROJECT. A project that is approved by the Commission for the purposes of this section under a program designed primarily to create employment and conducted by the Government of Canada pursuant to any Act of Parliament. *Unemployment Insurance Act*, R.S.C. 1985, c. U-1, s. 25.

JOB RATE. The rate of pay for a job.

JOB-SITE STEWARD. A union member representing workers in settlement of disputes arising on job-sites in the construction industry.

JOB TRAINING PROGRAM. A job training program established or operated by the Minister of Manpower and prescribed in the regulations. *Student and Temporary Employment Act*, S.A. 1985, c. S-23.5, s. 1.

JOHN DOE. A made-up name used in legal proceedings for an imagined or unnamed plaintiff.

JOINDER. *n.* Coupling of matters, proceeding together. See MIS~; NON-~.

JOINDER OF CAUSES OF ACTION. The coupling of several matters in one proceeding or suit.

JOINDER OF ISSUE. Occurs when, at their time to plead, a party denies one particular part or every part of the previous pleading and does not allege any new facts to support their case so that the pleadings end completely or to some extent.

JOINDER OF PARTIES. The coupling of people as plaintiffs or defendants.

JOINDER SIMPLICITER. A charge, in the same indictment, of conspiracy to commit an offence and the commission of that offence. M.R. Goode, *Criminal Conspiracy in Canada* (Toronto: Carswell, 1975) at 170.

JOINT. *adj.* Combined; shared between many; possessed by the same party.

JOINT ACTOR. In relation to a person, an associate or affiliate of that person or a person acting jointly or in concert with that person.

JOINT ADDRESS. A House of Commons and Senate resolution which was passed by both Houses of Parliament. P.W. Hogg, *Constitutional Law of Canada*, 2d ed. (Toronto: Carswell, 1985) at 52.

JOINT ADVENTURE. An organization established for one special piece of business.

JOINT AND SEVERAL. Describes the obligation of two or more persons when all are liable jointly and each is liable severally.

JOINT AND SURVIVOR PENSION. A pension payable to the person entitled to the pension until that person or the person's spouse dies and after that in whole or in part for life to the survivor of the person and the person's spouse. *Pension Benefits Act*, S.N.B. 1987, c. P-5.1, s. 1.

JOINT AND SURVIVOR PENSION BENEFIT. An immediate pension benefit that continues at least until the death of the member or former member or the death of the spouse of the member or former member, whichever occurs later. *Pension Benefits Standards Act*, R.S.C. 1985 (2d Supp.), c. 32, s. 2.

JOINT AUTHORSHIP. A collaborative work of two or more authors in which one author's contribution is indistinct from the contribution of any other. H.G. Fox, *The Canadian Law of Copyright and Industrial Designs*, 2d ed. (Toronto: Carswell, 1967) at 244. See WORK OF ~.

JOINT BANK ACCOUNT. A common account in which associated people have funds and which all or some may draw upon on occasion. I.F.G. Baxter, *The Law of Banking*, 3d ed. (Toronto: Carswell, 1981) at 43.

JOINT BORROWERS. Several physical persons to whom a loan is granted jointly, who jointly operate an economic farm constituted of the aggregate of the farms of which they are the owners or lessees while sharing, according to the proportions determined among them, the income from the aggregate of such farms, provided that not less than sixty per cent of the aggregate of the interests in such farm are owned by one or several farmers. Quebec statutes.

JOINT COMMISSION. See INTERNATIONAL ~.

JOINT COMMITTEE. 1. A group consisting of members of both houses of Parliament, usually with an investigative or administrative purpose. A. Fraser, G.A. Birch & W.A. Dawson, eds., *Beauchesne's Rules and Forms of the House of Commons of Canada*, 5th ed. (Toronto: Carswell, 1978) at 189. 2. A committee appointed by the minister consisting of employers or their representatives and employees or their bargaining agents engaged in the trade in question. *The Apprenticeship and Tradesmen's Qualification Act*, R.S.S. 1978, c. A-23, s. 2.

JOINT CONTRIBUTORY PERIOD. The

period commencing on January 1, 1966 or with the month in which the elder of the two spouses reached eighteen years of age, whichever is later, and ending, (a) where both spouses are contributors, with the month in which the later of their respective contributory periods ends, or (b) where only one spouse is a contributor, with the later of (i) the month in which the contributor's contributory period ends, and (ii) the earlier of the month in which the non-contributor reaches seventy years of age and the month in which an application for an assignment of a retirement pension is approved, but excluding, where subsection (6) applies, any month that is excluded from the contributory period of both spouses pursuant to paragraph 49(c) or (d). *Canada Pension Plan*, R.S.C. 1985 (2d Supp.), c. 30, s. 65.1(8).

JOINT CUSTODY. Custody of children shared by both divorced or separated parents under an order or agreement.

JOINT DEPOSIT. See JOINT BANK ACCOUNT.

JOINT EARNINGS PLAN. Profits are divided between employees and shareholders.

JOINT FIRM. A firm of engineers and architects to which a certificate of authorization has been issued. *Engineering and Related Professions Act*, S.A. 1980 (Supp.), c. 8 s. 2.

JOINT HEIR. A co-heir.

JOINT HIRING HALL. A place or service sponsored by employers and union for purposes of filling requests for workers.

JOINT HOME. A home of two or more municipalities or councils of bands, as the case may be. *Homes for the Aged and Rest Homes Act*, R.S.O. 1980, c. 203, s. 1.

JOINT INSURED BOND. A bond under which a company is insured jointly with one or more corporations affiliated with the company. Canada regulations.

JOINT LINE MOVEMENT. Any rail traffic that passes over any continuous route in Canada operated by two or more railway companies. *Western Grain Transportation Act*, R.S.C. 1985, c. W-8, c. 49(2).

JOINTLY. See ACTING ~ OR IN CONCERT.

JOINTLY AND SEVERALLY. Describes parties who are liable separately or all together.

JOINT OPERATORS. Several natural persons who jointly operate an economic farm constituted of the aggregate of the farms of which they are the owners or lessees while sharing, according to the proportions determined among them, the income from the aggregate of such farms, provided that not less than sixty per cent of the aggregate of the interests in such farm are owned by one or several farmers. Quebec statutes.

JOINT PRACTICE BOARD. Joint Practice Board established under the Architects Act, 1984. *Professional Engineers Act*, S.O. 1984, c. 13, s. 1.

JOINT PRACTICE COMMITTEE. The Architect-Engineer Joint Practice Committee established pursuant to section 39 of this Act. *Architects Act*, S.N.B. 1987, c. 66, s. 2.

JOINT STOCK COMPANY. In English law, an unincorporated company or large partnership with transferable shares formed in the nineteenth century.

JOINT TARIFF. A tariff that applies to through service by two or more air carriers. *Air Carrier Regulations*, C.R.C., c. 3, s. 2.

JOINT TENANCY. Describes ownership when the four unities of possession, time, interest and title are present and there are no words of severance. A. Bissett-Johnson & W.M. Holland, eds, *Matrimonial Property Law in Canada* (Toronto: Carswell, 1980) at I-11.

JOINT TENANT. One who holds an undivided equal interest in the entire property; after death, the survivor acquires the deceased's interest.

JOINT TOLL. A toll that applies to through service by two or more air carriers. *Air Carrier Regulations*, C.R.C., c. 3, s. 2.

JOINT TORTFEASORS. Persons who have acted in common and whose action is the cause of the tort and who as a consequence are responsible for the same tort. John G. Fleming, *The Law of Torts*, 6th ed. (Sydney: The Law Book Company Limited, 1983) at 228.

JOINT TRAINING COMMITTEE. A committee formed for the purpose of training apprentices in a designated trade that: (i) consists of employers in the designated trade or their representatives and employees in the designated trade or their bargaining agents; and (ii) is recognized by the minister pursuant to section 24. *Apprenticeship and Trade Certification Act*, S.S. 1984-85-86, c. A-22.1, s. 2.

JOINTURE. *n.* A provision a husband makes to support his wife after he dies.

JOINT VENTURE. An association of two or more person or entities, where the relationship among those associated persons or entities does not, under the laws in force in Canada, constitute a corporation, a partnership or a trust and where, in the case of an investment to which this Act applies, all the undivided ownership interests in the assets of the Canadian business or in the voting interests of the entity that is the subject of the investment are or will be owned by all the persons or entities that are so associated. *Investment Canada Act*, R.S.C. 1985 (1st Supp.), c. 28, s. 3.

JOINT WILL. See MUTUAL WILL.

JOIST. See ROOF ~.

JOULE. *n.* The work done when the point of application of a force of one newton is displaced a distance of one metre in the direction of the force. *Weights and Measures Act*, S.C. 1970-71-72, c. 36, schedule I.

JOURNAL. *n.* A diary or day-book of transactions. See FARM ~.

JOURNALS. *n.* The official and permanent record of proceedings in the House of Commons. A. Fraser, G.A. Birch & W.A. Dawson, eds., *Beauchesne's Rules and Forms of the House of Commons of Canada*, 5th ed. (Toronto: Carswell, 1978) at 46.

JOURNEYMAN. *n.* A tradesman who holds a journeyman's certificate.

JOURNEYMAN ELECTRICIAN. A person who has completed his apprenticeship, holds a certificate of qualification issued under the Act respecting manpower vocational training and qualification (R.S.Q., c. F-5) and, as such, leases his services to perform work for the installation, renewal, altering or repairing of electrical installations, for purposes of electric lighting, heating or power. *Electricians and Electrical Installations Act*, S.Q. 1979, c. 75, s. 39.

JOYRIDE. *v.* To take away any conveyance without the owner's consent or unlawfully; to drive or allow oneself to be driven in a conveyance knowing it was taken unlawfully.

J.P. *abbr.* Justice of the peace.

J. PLAN. & ENV. L. *abbr.* Journal of Planning and Environmental Law.

J. SOCIAL WELFARE L. *abbr.* Journal of Social Welfare Law.

JUDEX AD QUEM. [L.] A judge to whom one makes an appeal.

JUDEX AEQUITATEM SEMPER SPECTARE DEBET. [L.] A judge should always bear equity in mind.

JUDEX A QUO. [L.] A judge from whom one makes an appeal.

JUDEX EST LEX LOQUENS. [L.] A judge is the law speaking.

JUDEX NON REDDIT PLUS QUAM QUOD PETENS IPSE REQUIRIT. [L.] A judge does not give more than what the very plaintiff requests.

JUDGE. *n.* 1. The person authorized to determine any question or cause in a court. 2. Includes any person lawfully presiding in a court. See ASSOCIATE CHIEF ~; CHIEF ~; CITIZENSHIP ~; PRESIDING ~; PROVINCIAL COURT ~; RACING ~; SENIOR COUNTY COURT ~; SENIOR ~; STARTING ~; TERRITORIAL ~; TRIAL ~S; YOUTH COURT ~.

JUDGE OF THE EXCHEQUER COURT. The President or a puisne judge of that Court. *Admiralty Act*, R.S.C. 1970, c. A-1, s. 2.

JUDGE'S NOTES. Notes usually taken by a judge when evidence is given viva voce.

JUDGES' RULES. Procedures devised in England which govern the taking of statements by police.

JUDGMENT. *n.* 1. A judicial decision; the determination of a court; a court's sentence or decision on the major question in a proceeding. 2. The reasons a court gives for a decision. 3. A judgment or an order of a court in any civil proceedings whereby any sum of money is payable, and includes an award in proceedings on an arbitration if the award has, in pursuance of the law in force in the province or territory where it was made, become enforceable in the same manner as a judgment given by a court therein. 4. Any decision, however described (judgment, order and the like), given by a court in a civil or commercial matter, and includes an award in proceedings on an arbitration if the award has become enforceable in the territory of origin in the same manner as a judgment given by a court in that territory. *Reciprocal Enforcement of Judgment (U.K.) acts.* 5. When used with reference to the court appealed from, includes any judgment, rule, order, decision, decree, decretal order or sentence thereof, and when used with reference to the Supreme Court, includes any judgment or order of that Court. *Supreme Court Act*, R.S.C. 1985, c. S-26, s. 2. See AMOUNT DUE ON THE ~; CONSENT ~; DECLARATORY ~; DEFAULT ~; ENTER ~; FINAL ~; FOREIGN ~; MERGER INTO ~; MOTION FOR ~; SUMMARY ~.

JUDGMENT CREDITOR. 1. The person by whom the judgment was obtained, and includes the executors, administrators, successors and assigns of that person. 2. The person in whose favour the judgment was given, and includes that person's executors, administrators, successors and assigns. 3. A person in whose favour an order for maintenance has been made.

JUDGMENT DEBT. A sum of money or any

costs, charges or expenses made payable by or under a judgment in a civil proceeding.

JUDGMENT DEBTOR. 1. Includes a party required to make a payment of money and costs, or either, under an order, and any executor, administrator or assignee of a judgment debtor. 2. The person against whom the judgment was given and includes any person against whom the judgment is enforceable under the law of the territory of origin. 3. The person liable for the payment of money payable under a judgment or order. 4. A person against whom a maintenance order has been given. 5. A person named in a garnishee summons in respect of whom garnishable moneys are sought to be garnisheed under this Part. *Family Orders and Agreements Enforcement Assistance Act*, R.S.C. 1985, c. 4, s. 23.

JUDGMENT FIRST GIVEN. (a) Shall, in a case where a judgment is reversed on appeal, be construed as a reference to the judgment first given that is not so reversed, and (b) shall, in a case where a judgment is varied on appeal, be construed as a reference to that judgment as so varied. *Tort-Feasors acts.*

JUDGMENT ORDER. Includes any sum of money or any costs, charges or expenses made payable by or under any judgment of a court in any civil proceeding. *Judgment Interest Act*, S.Nfld. 1983, c. 81, s. 2.

JUDGMENT SUMMONS. A summons which requires a judgment debtor to appear so that a court officer or judge may examine the debtor's income and assets. C.R.B. Dunlop, *Creditor-Debtor Law in Canada* (Toronto: Carswell, 1981) at 105.

JUDICES NON TENENTUR EXPRIMERE CAUSAM SENTENTIAE SUAE. [L.] Judges are not required to explain the reason for their decisions.

JUDICIA IN CURIA REGIS REDDITA NON ADNIHILENTUR, SED STENT IN SUO ROBORE, QUOUSQUE PER ERROR AUT ATTINCTAM ADNULLENTUR. [L.] Judgments given in the monarch's court should not be thought of as nothing, but should stand in full force until they are reversed through error or attaint.

JUDICIA IN DELIBERATIONIBUS CREBRO MATURESCUNT, IN ACCELERATO PROCESSU NUNQUAM. [L.] Judgments often ripen through deliberation, never in a hurried process.

JUDICIAL. *adj.* Observing those basic procedural requirements, the rules of natural justice. S.A. DeSmith, *Judicial Review of Administrative Action*, 4th ed. by J.M. Evans (London: Stevens, 1980) at 77.

JUDICIAL ACT. An act, performed by a competent authority after consideration of relevant facts and circumstances, which imposes liability or affects rights.

JUDICIAL CENTRE. A judicial centre of the Trial Division established pursuant to this Act. *Judicature Act*, S.Nfld. 1986, c. 42, s. 2.

JUDICIAL COMMITTEE. A committee of the Privy Council made up of Privy Councillors who are judges. They advise the Queen how to dispose of each appeal, and their advice is considered to be a binding judgment. P.W. Hogg, *Constitutional Law of Canada*, 2d ed. (Toronto: Carswell, 1985) at 16.

JUDICIAL COMMITTEE OF THE PRIVY COUNCIL. In the days of the British empire, the final appeal court from every colonial court. It continues as a Commonwealth court for Commonwealth nations which haved retained that appeal. P.W. Hogg, *Constitutional Law of Canada*, 2d ed. (Toronto: Carswell, 1985) at 166.

JUDICIAL COSTS. Costs provided for in the tariff, and taxable by the competent officer of a court. *Barreau du Québec Act*, R.S.Q. 1977, c. B-1, s. 1.

JUDICIAL COUNCIL. In Ontario, a body of provincial court judges which considers each proposed appointment of a provincial judge, reports to the Attorney General and receives and investigates any complaint against a provincial judge. G.D. Watson & C. Perkins, eds., *Holmested & Watson: Ontario Civil Procedure* (Toronto: Carswell, 1984) at CJA-86. See CANADIAN ~.

JUDICIAL DISCRETION. During a trial, the freedom of a judge to summarily decide certain matters which cannot afterwards be questioned.

JUDICIAL DISTRICT. A territory, county or district in respect of which a judge has been appointed to exercise judicial functions. *Canada Elections Act*, R.S.C. 1985, c. E-2, s. 2.

JUDICIAL INTERIM RELEASE. The judge's setting free the accused between committal for trial and the trial's completion.

JUDICIAL LEGISLATION. Growth or advancement of law through a judicial decision.

JUDICIAL NOTICE. 1. The acceptance, by a judicial body, of the truth of some state of affairs or fact that is so generally or commonly known that no proof is needed. P.K. McWilliams, *Canadian Criminal Evidence*, 3d ed. (Aurora: Canada Law Book, 1988) at 24-1. 2. Acceptance by a court of the truth of a fact or matter without requiring the introduction of evidence to prove its truth. *Military Rules of Evidence*, C.R.C., c. 1049, s. 2.

JUDICIAL OFFICE. The office of a judge of a superior or county court or of the Tax Court of Canada. *Judges Act*, R.S.C. 1985, c. J-1, s. 42(4).

JUDICIAL OFFICER. See BRIBERY OF ~.

JUDICIAL PROCEEDING. 1. A proceeding (a) in or under the authority of a court of justice, (b) before the Senate or House of Commons or a committee of the Senate or House of Commons, or before a legislative council, legislative assembly or house of assembly or a committee thereof that is authorized by law to administer an oath, (c) before a court, judge, justice, provincial court judge or coroner, (d) before an arbitrator or umpire, or a person or body of persons authorized by law to make an inquiry and take evidence therein under oath, or (e) before a tribunal by which a legal right or legal liability may be established, whether or not the proceeding is invalid for want of jurisdiction or for any other reason. *Criminal Code*, R.S.C. 1985, c. C-46, s. 118 as am. by R.S.C. 1985 (1st Supp.), c. 27, s. 15. 2. Includes any action, suit, cause, matter or other proceeding in disposing of which the court appealed from has not exercised merely a regulative, administrative or executive jurisdiction. *Supreme Court Act*, R.S.C. 1985, c. S-26, s. 2. 3. A proceeding of a court of record. *Judicature Act*, R.S.O. 1980, c. 223, s. 67.

JUDICIAL REVIEW. 1. The right of a court to investigate and question the validity of any legislation enacted by a Canadian legislative body, notably as to whether that statute transgresses some constitutional prohibition. P.W. Hogg, *Constitutional Law of Canada*, 2d ed. (Toronto: Carswell, 1985) at 94 and 97. 2. The investigation and determination by a court of the legal validity of an act, decision, instrument or transaction, of a question of vires, jurisdiction, concerning an obligation to observe the rules of natural justice or "act fairly", or concerning principles which should be observed when statutory discretion is exercised. S.A. DeSmith, *Judicial Review of Administrative Action*, 4th ed. by J.M. Evans (London: Stevens, 1980) at 26.

JUDICIAL SEPARATION. A decree which does not affect status of a married couple but simply acknowledges the deterioration of a union. J.G. McLeod, *The Conflict of Laws* (Calgary: Carswell, 1983) at 702.

JUDICIAL TRUSTEE. In the Yukon Territory and the Northwest Territories, British Columbia, Alberta and Saskatchewan, there is provision in the territorial or provincial Trustee ordinance or act for the appointment of any "fit and proper person" to this role. D.M.W. Waters, *The Law*

of Trusts in Canada, 2d ed. (Toronto: Carswell, 1984) at 103.

JUDICIA POSTERIORA SUNT IN LEGE FORTIORA. [L.] In law, later decisions are stronger.

JUDICIARY. *n.* The bench, the judges collectively.

JUDICIA SUUM EFFECTUM HABERE DEBENT. [L.] Judgments ought to have their own effect.

JUDICI OFFICIUM SUUM EXCEDENTI NON PARETUR. [L.] One does not give effect to the decision of a judge who exceeded jurisdiction.

JUDICIS EST JUS DICERE, NON DARE. [L.] It is a judge's duty to declare existing law, not to make new law.

JUDICIS OFFICIUM EST OPUS DIEI IN DIE SUO PERFICERE. [L.] It is a judge's duty to finish each day's work during that day.

JUDICIS OFFICIUM EST UT RES ITA TEMPORA RERUM QUAERERE. [L.] It is a judge's duty to query both the time of things and things themselves.

JUDICIUM A NON SUO JUDICE DATUM NULLIUS EST MOMENTI. [L.] A judgment given with no proper jurisdiction has no effect in law.

JUDICIUM NON DEBET ESSE ILLUSORIUM. [L.] A judgment should not be considered to be mocking.

JUDICIUM REDDITUR IN INVITUM. [L.] Judgment is pronounced against one, willing or not.

JUDICIUM SEMPER PRO VERITATE ACCIPITUR. [L.] A judgment is always accepted as truth.

JUICE. See APPLE ~ FROM CONCENTRATE; CONCENTRATED APPLE ~; FRUIT ~.

JULIENNE. *adj.* Means potatoes cut into straight cut strips that are predominantly 1/4 by 1/4 inch or less in cross-sectional dimensions. *Processed Fruit and Vegetable Regulations*, C.R.C., c. 291, scehdule I, s. 44.

JUNIOR. *n.* A person who is at least thirteen years of age but who has not yet attained the age of eighteen years. *Ontario Place Corporation Act*, R.R.O. 1980, Reg. 732, s. 1.

JUNIOR. *adj.* Younger; of lower rank.

JUNIOR DIVISION. The division of the organization of an elementary school comprising the first three years of the program of studies immediately following the primary division. *Education Act*, R.S.O. 1980, c. 129, s. 1.

JUNIOR FOOD. A food that normally contains particles of a size to encourage chewing by infants, but may be readily swallowed by infants without chewing. *Food and Drug Regulations*, C.R.C., c. 870, c. B.25.001.

JUNK. *n.* 1. Unserviceable, discarded or junked motor vehicles or other machinery, and includes bodies, engines or other component parts thereof. *Highway Act*, R.S.N.B. 1973, c. H-5, s. 58. 2. Narcotics. F.A. Jaffe, *A Guide to Pathological Evidence*, 2d ed. (Toronto: Carswell, 1983) at 179.

JUNKED VEHICLE. Any automobile, tractor, truck or trailer that: (a) has no currently valid licence plates attached thereto; (b) is in a rusted, wrecked, partly wrecked, dismantled, partly dismantled, inoperative or abandoned condition; and (c) is located in the open on private property and does not form part of the business enterprise lawfully being operated on that property. *The Rural Municipalities Act*, R.S.S. 1978, c. R-26, s. 237.

JUNKIE. *n.* An addict to narcotics. F.A. Jaffe, *A Guide to Pathological Evidence*, 2d ed. (Toronto: Carswell, 1983) at 179.

JUNKIE'S LUNG. Lungs exhibiting microscopic spots of chronic inflammation caused by intravenously injecting insoluble material like talcum powder or starch granules. F.A. Jaffe, *A Guide to Pathological Evidence*, 2d ed. (Toronto: Carswell, 1983) at 179.

JUNK YARD. See AUTOMOBILE ~.

JURA EODEM MODO DESTITUUNTUR QUO CONSTITUUNTUR. [L.] Laws are abrogated in the same way as they are made.

JURA IN PERSONAM. [L.] Contractual rights. G.H.L. Fridman, *Sale of Goods in Canada*, 3d ed. (Toronto: Carswell, 1986) at 29.

JURA IN REM. [L.] Property rights. G.H.L. Fridman, *Sale of Goods in Canada*, 3d ed. (Toronto: Carswell, 1986) at 29-30.

JURAMENTUM EST INDIVISIBLE, ET NON EST ADMITTENDUM IN PARTE VERUM ET IN PARTE FALSUM. [L.] An oath may not be divided and may not be admitted as in part true and in part false.

JURA NATURAE SUNT IMMUTABILIA. [L.] The laws of nature are immutable.

JURA NOVIT CURIA. [L.] The court knows the law.

JURA PERSONARUM. [L.] The right of people.

JURA PUBLICA ANTEFERENDA PRIVATIS. [L.] Public rights should be put before private.

JURA PUBLICA EX PRIVATO PROMISCUE DECIDI NON DEBENT. [L.] Public rights should not to be decided obiter out of a private transaction.

JURARE EST DEUM IN TESTEM VOCARE, ET EST ACTUS DIVINI CULTUS. [L.] To swear is to call a deity to witness, and is an act of religious worship.

JURA REGALIA. [L.] Rights of a sovereign.

JURA REGIS SPECIALIA NON CONCEDUNTUR PER GENERALIA VERBA. [L.] No special rights are conceded to a monarch by general words.

JURA RERUM. [L.] The rights which someone may acquire in things.

JURA SANGUINIS NULLO JURE CIVILI DIRIMI POSSUNT. [L.] The rights of blood cannot be brought to naught by any right which arises out of law.

JURA SUMMA IMPERII. [L.] The supreme rights of sovereignty or control.

JURAT. *n.* [L.] A clause at the bottom of an affidavit which states where, when and before whom that affidavit was sworn.

JURATION. *n.* Swearing; administering an oath.

JURATO CREDITUR IN JUDICIO. [L.] At a trial, a sworn statement is credited.

JURATOR. *n.* [L.] A juror.

JURATORES DEBENT ESSE VICINI, SUFFICIENTES, ET MINUS SUSPECTI. [L.] Jurors should be neighbours of adequate estate, and beyond suspicion of partiality.

JURATORES SUNT JUDICES FACTI. [L.] Jurors are the judges of fact.

JURE CORONAE. [L.] In the right of the Crown.

JURE DIVINO. [L.] By sacred right.

JURE EMPHYTEUTICO. [L.] By the law relating to rents and services.

JURE MARITI. See JUS MARITI.

JURE NATURAE AEQUUM EST NEMINEM CUM ALTERIUS DETRIMENTO ET INJURIA FIERI LOCUPLETIOREM. [L.] By the law of nature, it is fair that no one be enriched by loss or injury to another.

JURE UXORIS. [L.] In right of the wife.

JURIDICAL. *adj.* Relating to the administration of justice.

JURIDICAL DAY. A day on which one may transact legal business.

JURI NON EST CONSONUM QUOD ALIQUIS ACCESSORIUS IN CURIA REGIS CONVINCATUR ANTEQUAM ALIQUIS DE FACTO FUERIT ATTINCTUS. [L.] It is not lawful that some accessory should be convicted in the monarch's court before anyone else has been affected by the deed.

JURISDICTION. *n.* 1. Legal authority; scope of power; the power of a judge or court to conduct a proceeding. 2. A province or territory of Canada or a state outside Canada having sovereign power. 3. A kingdom, empire, republic, commonwealth, state, dominion, province, territory, colony, possession, or protectorate or any part thereof. *Foreign Resident Corporations Act*, S.N.B. 1984, c. F-19.1, s. 1. See ANCILLARY ~; APPELLATE ~; CONCURRENT ~; CONTENTIOUS ~; DOMESTIC ~; EXCLUSIVE ~ CLAUSE; FEDERAL ~; FOREIGN ~; GENERAL ~; INHERENT ~; LOCAL ~; ORIGINAL ~; PENDENT ~; RECIPROCATING ~; STATUTORY ~; SUMMARY ~.

JURISDICTIONAL DISPUTE. A dispute between two or more trade unions or councils of trade unions or between an employer and one or more trade unions or councils of trade unions over the assignment of work.

JURISDICTIONAL STRIKE. A work stoppage resulting from a jurisdictional dispute between unions.

JURISDICTION OVER. Includes possession and control. *City of Winnipeg Act*, S.M. 1971, c. 105, s. 1.

JURIS EFFECTUS IN EXECUTIONE CONSISTIT. [L.] The effect of law is given by execution.

JURIS ET DE JURE. [L. of law and from law] Describes a presumption which is a conclusive presumption.

JURIS PRAECEPTA SUNT HAEC; HONESTE VIVERE, ALTERUM NON LAEDERE, SUUM CUIQUE TRIBUERE. [L.] The precepts of law are these: to live honestly, to hurt no one and to give every person their due.

JURISPRUDENCE. *n.* 1. The philosophy or science of law which ascertains the principles which are the basis of legal rules. 2. A body of law. See MEDICAL ~.

JURISPRUDENTIA EST DIVINARUM ATQUE HUMANARUM RERUM NOTITIA, JUSTI ATQUE INJUSTI SCIENTIA. [L.] Jurisprudence is knowledge of things sacred and human, a science of right and wrong.

JURIST. *n.* A civil lawyer; an eminent legal theorist; a civilian.

JUROR. *n.* [L.] A person who serves on a jury.

JURORS' PRIVILEGE. Jurors are privileged against disclosing deliberations in a jury room. Section 649 of the Criminal Code, R.S.C. 1985, c. C-46 makes disclosing such information an offence. P.K. McWilliams, *Canadian Criminal Evidence*, 3d ed. (Aurora: Canada Law Book, 1988) at 35-74.

JURY. *n.* 1. A group of people sworn to deliver a verdict after considering evidence delivered to them concerning the issue. 2. Includes judge, in the case of an action being tried by a judge without a jury. *Fatal Injuries Act*, R.S.N.S. 1967, c. 100, s. 1. See CHARGE THE ~; GRAND ~; HUNG ~.

JURY LIST. The permanent list of jurors drawn up in accordance with this act. *Jurors Act*, R.S.Q. 1977, c. J-2, s. 1.

JURY NOTICE. A request by one party to an action that the damages be assessed or the issues of fact be tried, or both, by a jury. G.D. Watson & C. Perkins, eds., *Holmested & Watson: Ontario Civil Procedure* (Toronto: Carswell, 1984) at 47-5.

JURY PANEL. Those persons summoned from amongst whom a jury will be selected.

JURY TRIALS. The trial of actions and issues which are to be tried with a jury and the trial of criminal matters and proceedings with a jury. *Jury Act*, R.S.M. 1970, c. J30, s. 2.

JUS. *n.* [L.] Law; right; equity; rule; authority.

JUS ACCRESCENDI. [L.] The right of survivorship which is essential to joint tenancy. E.L.G. Tyler & N.E. Palmer, eds., *Crossley Vaines' Personal Property*, 5th ed. (London: Butterworths, 1973) at 56.

JUS ACCRESCENDI PRAEFERTUR ONERIBUS. [L.] The right of survivorship is put before encumbrances.

JUS ACCRESCENDI PRAEFERTUR ULTIMAE VOLUNTATI. [L.] The right of survivorship is put before a last will.

JUS AD REM. [L.] The right to claim against the whole world.

JUS AESNECIAE. [L.] The right of the first born.

JUS CANONICUM. [L.] Canon law.

JUS CIVILE. [L.] Local law.

JUS CIVITATIS. [L.] The right of citizenship.

JUS COMMUNE. [L.] Common law.

JUS CONSTITUI OPORTET IN HIS QUAE UT PLURIMUM ACCIDUNT, NON QUAE EX INOPINATO. [L.] Law should be made for situations which happen most often, and not for the unexpected.

JUS CORONAE. [L.] The Crown's right.

JUS CREDITI. [L.] A creditor's right.

JUS DESCENDIT, ET NON TERRA. [L.] Right and not the land descends.

JUS DISPONENDI. [L.] The right to dispose.

JUS DIVIDENDI. [L.] The right to dispose of realty by will.

JUS DUPLICATUM. [L.] The right to possess as well as the right of property in something.

JUS EST NORMA RECTI; ET QUICQUID EST CONTRA NORMAM RECTI EST INJURIA. [L.] A legal right is the rule of right; and whatever goes against the rule of right is a wrong.

JUS EX INJURIA NON ORITUR. [L.] Right does not arise out of a wrong.

JUS FIDUCIARIUM. [L.] A trust.

JUS GENTIUM. [L.] Customary law.

JUS HABENDI. [L.] The right to actually possess property.

JUS HAEREDITATIS. [L.] The right to inherit.

JUS IN PERSONAM. [L.] A right which gives the one holding it power to help another person to do or not to do, to gain or give anything.

JUS IN RE. [L.] A full and complete right; a real right or a right to have something to the exclusion of everyone else.

JUS JURANDI FORMA VERBIS DIFFERT, RE CONVENIT; HUNC ENIM SENSUM HABERE DEBET: UT DEUS INVOCETUR. [L.] Oaths differ in the pattern of their words but come to the same conclusion; every oath must call on their deity to witness.

JUS JURANDUM INTER ALIOS FACTUM NEC NOCERE NEC PRODESSE DEBET. [L.] An oath others made in another proceeding should neither hurt nor benefit.

JUS MARITI. [L.] The right of a husband to chattels of a woman which, because there was no special provision, her husband acquired when they married.

JUS NATURALE. [L.] Natural law.

JUS NATURALE EST QUOD APUD OMNES HOMINES EANDEM HABET POTENTIAM. [L.] Natural law has the same force among all people.

JUS NON HABENTI TUTE NON PARETUR. [L.] It is safe to disobey one who has no legal right.

JUS NON PATITUR UT IDEM BIS SOLVATUR. [L.] Law does not allow the same thing to be paid twice.

JUS NON SCRIPTUM. [L.] Unwritten law.

JUS POSSESSIONIS. [L.] The right to possess.

JUS PRECARIUM. [L.] A right by sufference or courtesy which could be remedied only by request or entreaty.

JUS PRESENTATIONIS. [L.] The right to present.

JUS PRIVATUM. [L.] The municipal or civil law.

JUS PUBLICUM. [L.] The law concerning public affairs.

JUS PUBLICUM PRIVATORUM PACTIS MUTARE NON POTEST. [L.] Public law should not be superseded by private agreements.

JUS RECUPERANDI. [L.] The right to recover.

JUS RESPICIT AEQUITATEM. [L.] Law is mindful of equity.

JUS SANGUINIS. [L.] A principle that one's parentage determines nationality by birth.

JUS SOLI. [L.] A principle that the territory where the birth takes place determines nationality by birth.

JUS SUPERVENIENS AUCTORI ACCRESCIT SUCCESSORI. [L.] A right invested in a former owner of land descends to the successor.

JUST AND EQUITABLE SHARE. Of a producer of a developed unit, unless otherwise agreed upon by the interested persons, means that part of the allowable production for the pool that is substantially in the same proportion that the quantity of recoverable oil and gas in each developed unit of the tract or tracts concerned in the pool bears to the recoverable oil or gas in the total developed area of the pool, subject to reasonable measures for the prevention of waste and to reasonable adjustment by reason of structural position, and that, if produced, will minimize reasonably avoidable drainage from each developed unit and will enable the producer to utilize his fair share of the reservoir energy. *The Oil and Gas Conservation Act*, R.S.S. 1978, c. O-2, s. 2.

JUST CAUSE. Journal published by Canadian

Legal Advocacy, Information and Research Association of the Disabled.

JUS TERTII. [L.] Third party right.

JUSTICE. *n.* 1. The principle of giving every person her or his due. 2. A judge of certain courts. 3. A justice of appeal. 4. A justice of the peace. 5. A justice of the peace or a provincial court judge, and includes two or more justices where two or more justices are, by law, required to act or, by law, act or have jurisdiction. *Criminal Code*, R.S.C. 1985, c. C-46, s. 2 as am. by R.S.C. 1985 (1st Supp.), c. 27, s. 2. See ADMINISTRATION OF ~; CHIEF ~; DEPARTMENT OF ~ CANADA; FUNDAMENTAL ~; INTERNATIONAL COURT OF ~; NATURAL ~; OBSTRUCTING ~; REVISING ~; TRAFFIC ~; TWO ~S.

JUSTICEMENT. *n.* Any thing pertaining to justice.

JUSTICE OF THE PEACE. A judicial official with jurisdiction over matters which relate to the initiation of a legal process and minor criminal offences.

JUSTICE REP. *abbr.* Justice Report.

JUSTICESHIP. *n.* The office or rank of a justice.

JUSTICE SYSTEM. See CRIMINAL ~.

JUSTICIABLE. *adj.* Proper to be examined in a court of justice, triable.

JUSTIFIABLE HOMICIDE. Homicide which is not culpable, the killing of a human being when no legal guilt is incurred.

JUSTIFICATION. *n.* Truth, a complete defence to a defamation action. R.E. Brown, *The Law of Defamation in Canada* (Toronto: Carswell, 1987) at 361. See PUTATIVE ~.

JUSTIFICATOR. *n.* A kind of compurgator.

JUSTIFY BAIL. To prove the sufficiency of sureties or bail.

JUSTINIANIST. *n.* A person who studies the civil law; a civilian.

JUSTITIA. *n.* [L.] A law, statute or ordinance; the office of a judge or a jurisdiction.

JUSTITIA DEBET ESSE LIBERA, QUIA NIHIL INIQUIS VENALI JUSTITIA; PLENA, QUIA JUSTITIA NON DEBET CLAUDICARE; ET CELERIS, QUIA DILATIO EST QUAEDAM NEGATIO. [L.] Justice should be free, because nothing is worse than venal justice; full, for justice should not be wanting; and swift, for delay is almost denial.

JUSTITIA EST DUPLEX, VIZ., SEVERE PUNIENS ET VERE PRAEVENIENS. [L.] Justice is double: it punishes severely and is truly preventive.

JUSTITIA FIRMATUR SOLIUM. [L.] The throne is strengthened by justice.

JUSTITIA NEMINI NEGANDA EST. [L.] Justice should be denied to no one.

JUSTITIA NON EST NEGANDA, NON DIFFERENDA. [L.] Justice should not be denied nor delayed.

JUSTITIA PIEPOUDROUS. [L.] Swift justice.

JUS VENANDI ET PISCANDI. [L.] The right to hunt and fish.

JUV. CT. *abbr.* Juvenile Court.

JUVENILE. *n.* 1. A person who has not attained his sixteenth birthday. *The Saskatchewan Health Insurance Act*, R.S.S. 1978, c. S-21, s. 2. 2. Includes every child apparently or actually under the age of seventeen years. *Juveniles Act*, R.S.Nfld. 1970, c. 190, s. 27.

JUVENILE APPLICANT. An applicant under the age of eighteen years. *Legal Aid Services Society of Manitoba Act*, S.M. 1971, c. 76, s. 1.

JUVENILE COURT. See YOUTH COURT.

JUVENILE DELINQUENT. Any child who violates any provision of the Criminal Code or of any federal or provincial statute, or of any by-law or ordinance of any municipality, or who is guilty of sexual immorality or any similar form of vice, or who is liable by reason of any other act to be committed to an industrial school or juvenile reformatory under any federal or provincial statute. *Juvenile Delinquents Act*, R.S.C. 1970, c. J-3, s. 2.

JUXTA FORMAM STATUTI. [L.] According to the statute's form.

K

K. *abbr.* 1. Kilo. 2. Kelvin.

K.B. *abbr.* 1. King's Bench. 2. Court of King's Bench. See QUEEN'S BENCH.

K.C. *abbr.* King's Counsel. See QUEEN'S COUNSEL.

KEELAGE. *n.* A toll paid by a ship when it enters a harbour.

KEEPER. *n.* 1. A person who (a) is an owner or occupier of a place, (b) assists or acts on behalf of an owner or occupier of a place, (c) appears to be, or to assist or act on behalf of an owner or occupier of a place, (d) has the care or management of a place, or (e) uses a place permanently or temporarily, with or without the consent of the owner or occupier thereof. *Criminal Code*, R.S.C. 1985, c. C-46, s. 197. 2. Includes owner, lessee and proprietor. See BEE~; DAM~; GARAGE ~; HOTEL~; INN~; LIVERY STABLE ~; POUND ~; STABLE ~; WAREHOUSE ~.

KEEPER OF A STORAGE WAREHOUSE. Includes the proprietor, keeper or manager of a warehouse, building shed, storehouse, yard, wharf or other place for the storage of goods, chattels, wares or merchandise delivered to him as bailee for hire, whether the person is engaged in other business or not. *Storage Warehouse Keepers Act*, R.S.N.S. 1967, c. 293, s. 1.

KEEP THE PEACE. To prevent or avoid breaches of the peace.

KELVIN. *n.* The unit for the measurement of thermodynamic temperature, being the fraction 1/273.16 of the thermodynamic temperature of the triple point of water. *Weights and Measures Act*, S.C. 1970-71-72, c. 36, schedule I.

KENNEL. *n.* A shelter for three or more dogs. *Dog Act*, R.S.P.E.I. 1974, c. D-14, s. 1.

KEROSINE. See 1-K ~.

KEY. See RESTRICTED ~.

KEY MAN INSURANCE. Life or disability insurance held by a business on a valued employee or officer of the business.

KG. *abbr.* Kilogram.

KICKBACK. *n.* Payment back to a seller or employer of a portion of purchase price or wages of an employee.

KIDNAP. *v.* To forcibly abduct a person.

KILL. *n.* The number of individuals of a given species or population thereof, killed or permitted to be killed during a given period. *An Act respecting hunting and fishing rights in the James Bay and New Québec territories*, S.Q. 1978, c. 92, s. 78.

KILLING AND DRESSING STATION. A place where poultry is killed, dressed and graded. *Dressed and Eviscertated Poultry Regulations*, C.R.C., c. 283, s. 2.

KILN DRIED. Dried mechanically to a moisture content of 18% or less. *Dutch Elm Disease Act*, S.M. 1980, c. 65, s. 4.

KILO. *pref.* 10^3. Prefix for multiples and submultiples of basic, supplementary and derived units of measurement. *Weights and Measures Act*, S.C. 1970-71-72, c. 36, schedule I.

KILOGRAM. *n.* The unit for the measurement of mass, being a mass equal to the mass of the international prototype of the kilogram established in the year 1889 by the First General Conference of Weights and Measures and deposited at the International Bureau of Weights and Measures. *Weights and Measures Act*, S.C. 1970-71-72, c. 36, schedule I.

KILOMETRE. *n.* A thousand metres. See OVERALL ASSESSMENT PER ROAD ~; OVERALL TAX BASE PER ROAD ~; POLE ~; ROAD ~S.

KILOPASCALS AND KPA. Kilopascals above atmospheric pressure. *Occupational Health and Safety Act*, R.R.O. 1980, Reg. 691, s. 240.

KILOWATT. *n.* One thousand watts.

KILOWATT-HOUR. *n.* For electrical energy, the "kilowatt-hour", which is the energy supplied by a power of one thousand watts operating for one hour. *Electrical and Photometric Units Act*, R.S.C. 1970, c. E-3, s. 2.

KIN. *n.* Relatives by blood. See NEXT OF ~.

KIND. *n.* Either (a) a refillable glass container; (b) a nonrefillable glass container; (c) a nonrefillable metal container; or (d) a plastic container. *Litter Act*, R.S.B.C. 1979, c. 239, s. 1. See DONATION IN ~; EARNED INCOME IN ~; GOODS OF THE SAME CLASS OR ~; PAYMENT IN ~.

KINDERGARTEN. *n.* Any class recognized as such by the Minister of Education, to which children are admitted for one year of study immediately preceding the first year of the elementary course. *Grants to School Boards Act*, R.S.Q. 1977, c. S-36, s. 1.

KINDRED. *n.* Relations by blood.

KINEMATOGRAPH. *n.* Includes a moving picture machine or other similar apparatus. *Fire Services Act*, R.S.B.C. 1979, c. 133, s. 1.

KING. *n.* A male sovereign of the United Kingdom, Canada and other Realms and Territories, and Head of the Commonwealth.

KING'S COUNSEL. See QUEEN'S COUNSEL.

KING'S PRINTER. See QUEEN'S PRINTER.

KING'S PROCTOR. See QUEEN'S PROCTOR.

KINSFOLK. *n.* Relatives; members of the same family.

KINSMAN. *n.* A man of the same family or race.

KINSWOMAN. *n.* A woman of the same family or race.

KIT. See TEST ~.

KLEPTOMANIA. *n.* An uncontrollable inclination to steal.

KNIFE-RIBBING. *n.* To cut the side of a carcass midway between the 11th and 12th ribs, beginning at the backbone, continuing towards the plate side and severing the costal cartilages but not severing the backbone. *Beef Carcass Grading Regulations*, C.R.C., c. 282, s. 2.

KNOB. See DUAL ~.

KNOT. *n.* A unit of speed equal to one nautical mile per hour.

KNOWINGLY. *adv.* When used in defining an offence, it indicates clearly that the doctrine of mens rea should apply to that offence. S. Mitchell, P.J. Richardson & D.A. Thomas, eds., *Archbold Pleading, Evidence and Practice in Criminal Cases*, 43d ed. (London: Sweet & Maxwell, 1988) at 1345.

KN. P.C. *abbr.* Knapp, Privy Council, 1829-1836.

KORAN. *n.* The sacred scripture of Islam.

KPA. See KILOPASCALS AND KPA.

KUSARI. *n.* A length of rope, cord, wire or chain fastened at each end to a hexagonal or other geometrically shaped hard weight or hand-grip. *Prohibited Weapons Order, No. 2*, C.R.C., c. 434, s. 2.

L. *abbr.* 1. Litre. 2. Length. 3. Length in metres. *Oil Pollution Prevention Regulations*, C.R.C., c. 1454, Schedule III, c. 1. 4. Linnaeus. *Weed Control Act*, R.R.O. 1980, Reg. 944, s. 1.

LABEL. *n.* 1. Any label, mark, sign, device, imprint, stamp, brand, ticket or tag. 2. Any legend, word or mark attached to, included in, belonging to or accompanying any food, drug, cosmetic, device or package. *Food and Drugs Act*, R.S.C. 1985, c. F-27, s. 2. See BALLOT ~; DESCRIPTIVE ~; DISCLOSURE ~; INNER ~; OUTER ~ REPRESENTATION ~; UNION ~.

LABORATORY. *n.* 1. A medical diagnostic laboratory where examinations of specimens of blood, spinal fluid, sputum, stool, urine, gastric washings, exudate or other specimen or discharge derived from a body are made for the purpose of determining the presence or absence of an infectious agent. *Public Health Act*, S.A. 1984, c. P-27.1, s. 1. 2. A place outside an establishment equipped for manufacturing or repairing ortheses or prosthetic devices, making medical biology examinations, particularly in the fields of biochemistry, haematology, bacteriology, immunology, histopathology and virology, for making radioisotope or radiology examinations for purposes of prevention, diagnosis and treatment of disease in humans, or for making examinations in the fields of toxicology, audiology and the physiology of respiration. *Public Health Protection Act*, S.Q. 1979, c. 63, s. 297. See DENTAL ~; DIAGNOSTIC ~; VETERINARY ~.

LABORATORY AND X-RAY FACILITIES. Includes mechanical, electrical, laboratory, and other facilities and equipment necessary or useful in the diagnosis of disease and other abnormal conditions of the human body. *Health Services Act*, R.S.M. 1970, c. H30, s. 2.

LABORATORY DIRECTOR. A person who is responsible for the administration of the scientific and technical operation of a laboratory

including the supervision of tests and the reporting of the results of the tests. *Public Health Act*, R.R.O. 1980, Reg. 845, s. 1.

LABORATORY SUPERVISOR. A person who under the general supervision of a laboratory director supervises laboratory personnel and who may perform tests requiring special scientific skills. *Public Health Act*, R.R.O. 1980, Reg. 845, s. 1.

LABORATORY TECHNICIAN. A person who under direct supervision performs laboratory tests which require limited technical skill and responsibilities. *Public Health Act*, R.R.O. 1980, Reg. 845, s. 1.

LABORATORY TECHNOLOGIST. A person who under general supervision performs tests which require the exercise of independent judgment. *Public Health Act*, R.R.O. 1980, Reg. 845, s. 1.

LABORATORY TESTS. Tests of samples or specimens from the body made in a laboratory at a place other than where the samples or specimens were taken. *Venereal Diseases Prevention Act*, R.S.A. 1980, c. V-2, s. 1.

LABOUR. *v.* Of a jury, to tamper with that jury.

LABOUR. *n.* Includes cutting, skidding, felling, hauling, scaling, rossing, banking, driving, running, rafting or booming any logs or timber and any work done by cooks, blacksmiths, artisans and others usually employed in connection therewith. *Woodmen's Lien acts*. See CHILD ~; COST OF ~; SEMI-SKILLED ~; SKILLED ~; STATUTE ~; UNSKILLED ~; VOLUNTEER ~.

LABOUR ADJUSTMENT BENEFITS. The benefits payable under this Act. *Labour Adjustment Benefits Act*, R.S.C. 1985, c. L-1, s. 2.

LABOUR ARBITRATION. A general term which includes grievance arbitration and interest arbitration, two different processes. D.J.M. Brown and D.M. Beatty, *Canadian Labour Arbi-*

tration, 2d ed. (Aurora: Canada Law Book, 1977) at 1.

LABOUR ASSOCIATION. (i) A labour organization as defined in The Trade Union Act; (ii) a corporation incorporated or continued pursuant to The Non-profit Corporations Act all of whose shareholders are employees of the same employer; (iii) an investment co-operative; or (iv) any other association of employees or class of association of employees that is prescribed in the regulations. *Labour-Sponsored Venture Capital Corporation Act*, S.S. 1986, c. L-0.2, s. 2.

LABOUR CANADA. The federal ministry empowered to maintain balanced legislation concerning industrial relations in federal jurisdiction, to help parties overcome industrial disputes, to set standards for wages, employment conditions and occupational health and safety, to set up non-legislative programs to foster cooperative understanding between business and labour and to act for Canada to improve labour conditions worldwide.

LABOUR CLUB. A chartered branch or union of any of the established labour organizations in Canada with a minimum of 50 members. *Liquor Licence Act*, R.R.O. 1980, Reg. 581, s. 1.

LABOUR CONGRESS. See CENTRAL ~.

LABOUR COUNCIL. See LOCAL ~.

LABOUR DISPUTE. 1. Any dispute between employers and employees, or between employees and employees, that is connected with the employment or non-employment, or the terms or conditions of employment, of any persons. *Unemployment Insurance Act*, R.S.C. 1985, c. U-1, s. 2. 2. A dispute or difference concerning terms, tenure or conditions of employment or concerning the association or representation of persons in negotiating, fixing, maintaining, changing or seeking to arrange terms or conditions of employment, regardless of whether the disputants stand in the proximate relation of employer and employee.

LABOURER. *n.* 1. A person employed for wages in any kind of labour whether employed under a contract of service or not. 2. Includes every mechanic, artisan, machinist, miner, builder or other person doing labour for wages. *Mechanics' Lien Act*, R.S.N.W.T. 1974, c. M-8, s. 2. See DAY ~; FARM ~.

LABOUR EXPENSE. Of a corporation for a taxation year is the aggregate of all wages, salaries and management fees paid by the corporation in the taxation year. *Alberta Stock Savings Plan Act*, S.A. 1986, c. A-37.7, s. 5.

LABOUR FORCE. All members of the population of employable age who are employed or unemployed. See NEW ENTRANT OR RE-ENTRANT TO THE ~.

LABOUR-MANAGEMENT DISPUTE. 1. Any dispute or difference affecting employees represented by a bargaining agent, the employer of the employees, or the bargaining agent. Nova Scotia statutes. 2. Any dispute or difference between an employer and one or more of his employees or a trade union with respect to: (i) matters or things affecting or relating to work done or to be done by the employee or employees or trade union; or (ii) the privileges, rights, duties, terms and conditions, or tenure of, employment or working conditions of the employee or employees or trade union. *The Trade Union Act*, R.S.S. 1988, c. T-17, s. 2.

LABOUR MARKET. The market for workers offering their services and employers offering jobs.

LABOUR MARKET AREA. The geographic area beyond which employees do not usually seek work and employers do not usually seek employees.

LABOUR ORGANIZATION. An organization of employees, not necessarily employees of one employer, that has bargaining collectively among its purposes. *The Trade Union Act*, R.S.S. 1978, c. T-17, s. 2.

LABOUR RELATIONS. All matters concerning the worker-employer relationship. See CANADA ~ BOARD.

LABOUR UNION. Any organization of employees that has as one of its purposes the regulation of relations between employers and employees and that has a constitution setting out its objectives and its conditions for membership. *Corporations and Labour Unions Returns Act*, R.S.C. 1985, c. C-43, s. 2. See CERTIFICATION OF ~.

LABRADOR. *n.* 1. The Coast of Labrador as delimited in the report delivered by the Judicial Committee of His Majesty's Privy Council on the first day of March, 1927, and approved by His Majesty in His Privy Council on the twenty-second day of March, 1927, together with the islands adjacent to the said Coast of Labrador. *Labrador (Rehabilitation and Recreation) Act*, S.Nfld. 1973, c. 141, s. 4. 2. All that part of the Province situated on the mainland of Canada. Newfoundland statutes. 3. Includes all of the islands forming part of the province that are located wholly north of Cape Bauld. Newfoundland statutes. See NORTHERN ~.

L.A.C. *abbr.* Labour Arbitration Cases.

L.A.C. (2D). *abbr.* Labour Arbitration Cases (Second Series), 1973-1981.

L.A.C. (3D). *abbr.* Labour Arbitration Cases (Third Series), 1982-.

LACERATION. *n.* The tearing or crushing of tissue, so that the surface breaks. F.A. Jaffe, *A Guide to Pathological Evidence*, 2d ed. (Toronto: Carswell, 1983) at 10.

LACHES. *n.* [Fr.] Negligence or unreasonable delay, towards enforcing an equitable right or in pursuing any legal remedy.

LADING. See BILL OF ~.

LAGAN. *n.* Goods fastened to a buoy and submerged in the sea.

LAISSER-FAIRE. *n.* [Fr.] A policy permitting unrestricted action, free of state planning.

LAKE. *n.* Includes a pond. *Lakes and Rivers Improvement Act*, R.S.O. 1980, c. 229, s. 1. See PRODUCTS OF THE SEA, ~S AND RIVERS.

LAKE AND RIVER NAVIGATION. Includes all the rivers, lakes and other navigable waters within Canada. *Inland Water Freight Rates Act*, R.S.C. 1985, c. I-10, s. 2.

LAKE, FOREST AND FUR ASSOCIATION. Includes an association having as its principal objects, or any of them, the production or utilization of the products of forest, lake or river, or of other natural resources, on behalf of its members and patrons, or rendering services to members and patrons as producers, ancillary to such principal objects, or any of them. *The Co-operative Production Associations Act*, R.S.S. 1978, c. C-37, s. 63.

LAKE SHORE AREA. That portion of land lying within twenty-five metres above and twenty-five metres below the normal high water mark of any lake, and includes any bed, bank, beach, shore, bar, flat, mud flat or sand dune associated with the lake whether or not it lies within that portion of land. *An Act to Amend the Trespass Act*, S.N.B. 1985, c. 70, s. 1.

LAKE STURGEON. A fish of the species Acipenser fulvescens. *Quebec Fishery Regulations*, C.R.C., c. 852, s. 2.

LAKE TROUT. (Salvelinus namaycush, Walbaum) includes common lake trout, Great Lakes trout, grey trout, Makinaw trout, siscowet and splake (a cross breed of brook trout and lake trout). *Ontario Fishery Regulations*, C.R.C., c. 849, s. 2.

LAMB CARCASS. The carcass of an animal of the ovine species, of either sex, up to and including 12 months of age, having four well defined, relatively soft ridges at the break join of the forelegs. *Lamb and Mutton Carcass Grading Regulations*, C.R.C., c. 288, s. 2.

LAMINATED GLASS. Two or more sheets of glass bonded to an intervening layer or layers of plastic material. *Safety Glass Regulations*, C.R.C., c. 933, s. 2.

LAMP. See AUXILIARY ~; FOG ~; SAFETY ~.

LAMP HOLDER. A device constructed for the mechanical support of lamps and for connecting them to circuit conductors. *Power Corporation Act*, R.R.O. 1980, Reg. 794, s. 0.

L.A.N. *abbr.* Labour Arbitration News.

LAND. *n.* 1. Lands, messuages, tenements and hereditaments, corporeal and incorporeal, of every nature and description, and every estate or interest therein, whether the estate or interest is legal or equitable, together with all paths, passages, ways, watercourses, liberties, privileges, easements, mines, minerals and quarries appertaining thereto, and all trees and timber thereon and thereunder lying or being, unless specially excepted. 2. The solid part of the earth's surface and includes the foreshore and land covered by water. 3. Includes buildings, structures and other things in the nature of fixtures and mines and minerals whether precious or base, on, above or below the surface. *Expropriation Act*, R.S.C. 1985, c. E-21, s. 2. 4. Land, tenements, hereditaments and appurtenances and any estate or interest therein. 5. Includes land covered by water and any building erected on land and any estate, interest, right or easement in or over any land or building. 6. Includes messuages and all other hereditaments, whether corporeal or incorporeal, chattels and other personal property transmissible to heirs, money to be laid out in the purchase of land, and any share of the same hereditaments and properties or any of them, any estate or inheritance, or estate for any life or lives, or other estate transmissible to heirs, any possibility, right or title of entry or action, and any other interest capable of being inherited, whether the same estates, possibilities, rights, titles and interest or any of them, are in possession, reversion, remainder or contingency. 7. Includes freehold tenements and hereditaments, whether corporeal or incorporeal, and any undivided part or share therein. 8. Does not, except to the extent that it is used for the provision of parking facilities for a fee or charge, include (i) any property that is a building or other structure affixed to land, (ii) the land subjacent to any property described in subparagraph (i), or (iii) such land immediately contiguous to the land described in subparagraph (ii) that is a parking area, driveway, yard, garden or similar land that is necessary for the use of any property described in subparagraph (i). *Income Tax Act*, R.S.C. 1952, c. 148 (as am. S.C. 1974-75-76, c. 26, s. 7(3)), s. 18(3)(a). See ADJACENT ~; ADJOINING ~; AGRICULTURAL ~; ALLOCATED ~; ARABLE ~; COAL ~; CONTIGUOUS ~; CONVEYANCE OF ~; CROWN ~; C U L T I V A T E D ~; D E V E L O P E D ~; ENCLOSED ~; ESTATE IN ~; FALLOW-~; FARM ~; FOREST ~; GREENBELT ~; IMPROVED ~; IMPROVING ~; INTEREST IN ~; ~S; MARSH~; MINERAL ~; OCCUPIED ~; ORIGINAL COST OF THE ~; PARCEL OF ~; PARK~; PICK OF ~; PRIVATE ~; PRIVATELY OWNED ~; PROVINCIAL ~; PUBLIC ~; RATEABLE ~; RECREATIONAL ~; RESERVED ~; RESIDENTIAL ~; RUN WITH THE ~; RURAL ~; SERVICED VACANT ~; SUB-AQUATIC ~; SUBDIVIDED ~: TIMBER ~; TRACT OF ~; TRESPASS TO ~; UNCULTIVATED ~; UNRESTRICTED ~; USE OF ~; VACANT ~; WILD ~.

LAND AGENT. (i) A person who (A) on behalf of his employer, (B) as an agent on behalf of another person, or (C) on his own behalf, negotiates for or acquires an interest in land, or (ii) a person who for a fee gives or offers advice to an owner or his agent with respect to negotiations for or acquisition of an interest in land. *Land Agents Licensing Act*, R.S.A. 1980, c. L-2, s. 1.

LAND ASSEMBLY. The development of land for any purpose or project permitted by this Act or related to a purpose or project permitted by this Act, including the acquisition, assembly, planning, servicing, sale, conveyance, leasing or other disposal of the land. *Housing Development acts*.

L. & C. *abbr.* Lefroy & Cassels' Practice Cases (Ont.), 1881-1883.

LAND CO-OPERATIVE. A parcel of land that is owned by a corporation exclusively for the benefit of its shareholders who (a) have rights to occupy a portion of the parcel, and (b) own shares or shares and other securities in the corporation that have a value equivalent to the value of the portion in relation to the value of the parcel. *Home Owner Grant Amendment Act*, S.B.C. 1984, c. 20, s. 1.

LAND DEVELOPMENT AREA. An area, village or community established by the Minister by settling persons on the land for the purpose of clearing and cultivating the soil and promoting rural and fishing industries and shall include, where the context so admits, a land settlement already established and roads leading to or from a land development area. *Land Development Act*, R.S.Nfld. 1970, c. 197, s. 2.

LAND DRAINAGE. Storm, surface, overflow, subsurface, or seepage waters or other drainage from land, but does not include wastewater.

LAND DRAINAGE SEWER. A sewer that carries storm water and surface water, street wash and other wash waters or drainage but excludes domestic wastewater and industrial wastes. *City of Winnipeg Act*, S.M. 1971, c. 105, s. 453.

LAND EXTERMINATION. The destruction, prevention or control in, on or over land of a pest or pests by the use of a pesticide but does not include a structural extermination, a water extermination or the destruction, prevention or control of termites. *Pesticides Act*, R.S.O. 1980, c. 376, s. 1.

LANDFILLING. *n.* The disposal of waste by deposit, under controlled conditions, on land or on land covered by water, and includes compaction of the waste into a cell and covering the waste with cover materials at regular intervals. *Environmental Protection Act*, R.R.O. 1980, Reg. 309, s. 1.

LAND FOR PUBLIC PURPOSES. Land, other than streets, for the recreational or other use or enjoyment of the general public, such as (a) an access to a lake, river, stream, sea or other body of water, (b) a beach or scenic area along the shore of a lake, river, stream, sea or other body of water, (c) a conservation area, (d) land adjoining a school for joint recreational purposes, (e) land for a community hall, public library, recreational use or other similar community facility, (f) open space, to provide air and light, to afford a view to or from a development or to a lake, river, stream, sea or other body of water, or for other purposes, (g) a park, green belt or buffer area dividing developments, parts of a highway or a development and a highway, (h) a pedestrian way to a school, shopping center, recreational area or other facility, (i) a protection area for a water course, stream, marsh, water supply lake or other body of water, (j) a public park, playground or other recreational use, (k) a visual feature, or (l) a wooded area, slope area or a site giving view to a scenic area to provide diversity. *Community Planning Act*, S.N.B. 1976, c. 10, s. 1.

LAND GABEL. A rent or tax which issues out of land.

LANDHOLDER. *n.* (a) In the case of land held under a certificate of title by a person other than the Crown, (i) the purchaser of the fee simple estate in the land under an agreement for sale that is the subject of a caveat registered against the certificate of title to the land, or (ii) in the absence of a person described in subclause (i), the person registered under the Land Titles Act as the owner of the fee simple estate in the land, (b) in the case of land held under an agreement for sale under which the Crown is the seller, the purchaser under the agreement, or (c) in the case of any land or classes of land held under leases or other dispositions from the Crown that is declared by the regulations under section 11(1)(y.1) to be privately owned land, the holder of the lease or disposition. *Wildlife Act*, R.S.A. 1980, c. W-9, s. 7.

LAND HOLDING. *var.* **LANDHOLDING.** 1. An interest conferring the right to possession, occupation or use of land in the province but does not include land or an interest in land acquired by a bank, trust company or other financial institution in the ordinary course of its business by way of security for a debt or other obligation. *Prince Edward Island Lands Protection Act*, S.P.E.I. 1982, c. 16, s. 1. 2. Includes (i) any interest in land held under an agreement to purchase the land that may directly or indirectly result in the vesting of title or confer the right to possession of that land, or confer any right or control ordinarily accruing to an owner of land, (ii) any lease of land that would vest in the lessee possession and control of the land, (iii) land legally or beneficially owned by a corporation whose shares or securities of a kind or class designated in the regulations for the purposes of this clause are owned or held by ineligible persons, and (iv) any other interest in land, other than those specified in subclauses (i) and (ii), but does not include any land or an interest in land held by way of security for a debt or other obligation. *An Act to Amend the Agricultural Lands Protection Act*, S.M. 1980-81, c. 36, s. 2. See AGGREGATE ~; TENURIAL FORM OF ~.

LAND IMPROVEMENT ASSOCIATION. Includes an association incorporated or registered under this Act having as its principal objects or any of them the conservation of land against erosion from wind or water, conservation of water resources, irrigation, the planting and maintenance of trees as shelter belts or the conservation of other natural resources required by members and patrons engaged in the production of agricultural products or other products, or rendering to the members and patrons as producers, services ancillary to such principal objects, or any of them. *The Co-operative Production Associations Act*, R.S.S. 1978, c. C-37, s. 61.

LAND IMPROVEMENT PURPOSE. The diversion or impounding of water to protect property, to facilitate the development of a park or the reclamation, drainage or other improvement of land or to carry out a project of a similar nature. *Water Act*, R.S.B.C. 1979, c. 429, s. 1.

LANDING. *n.* 1. Lawful permission to come into Canada to establish permanent residence. *Immigration Act*, R.S.C. 1985, c. I-2, s. 2. 2. In respect of an aircraft, means the act of coming into contact with a supporting surface and includes the immediately preceding and following acts and, in respect of an airship or free balloon, means the act of bringing the airship or balloon under restraint and includes the immediately preceding and following acts. *Air Regulations*, C.R.C., c. 2, s. 101. See TECHNICAL ~.

LANDING AREA. A cleared area where trees or logs are stored, measured, processed, unloaded or loaded and includes a log dump. *Occupational Health and Safety Act*, R.R.O. 1980, Reg. 692, s. 107.

LANDING NET. A fishing gear that is made of a small net that is mounted on a frame fixed to a handle and that is ordinarily used to bag fish caught by a hook. *Quebec Fishery Regulations*, C.R.C., c. 852, s. 2.

LANDLOCKED. *adj.* Describes a piece of land which belongs to one person and is surrounded by land which belongs to other people, so that the single owner cannot approach her or his own parcel except over the other's land.

LANDLORD. *n.* 1. Includes lessor, owner or the person giving or permitting the occupation of the residential premises in question and the heirs, assigns and legal representatives thereof. 2. A person who rents land to another person for a share of the crop or of the proceeds of the crop produced on such land. *The Saskatchewan Crop Insurance Act*, R.S.S. 1978, c. S-12, s. 2. See GROUND ~.

LANDMAN. *n.* (i) A person who (A) on behalf of his employer, or (B) as an agent on behalf of another person, or (C) on his own behalf, negotiates for or acquires an interest in land, or (ii) a person who for a fee gives or offers advice to an owner, or his agent, with respect to a negotiation or acquisition referred to in subclause (i). *Landmen Licensing Act*, R.S.A. 1970, c. 202, s. 2.

LANDMARK. *n.* An object which fixes the boundary of property or an estate.

LAND-OWNING PARISHIONER. A parishioner who has possessed as proprietor for at least six months an immoveable situated in the parish or chapelry. *An Act Respecting Fabriques*, R.S.Q. 1977, c. F-1, s. 1.

LAND PEST CONTROL. The destruction, prevention or control of pests in, on or over land by the use of a pest control product, but does not include structural pest control or water pest

563

control. *Pest Control Products (Nova Scotia) Act*, S.N.S. 1986, c. 16, s. 3.

LANDPLANE. *n.* An aircraft other than a seaplane. *Life-saving Equipment Order*, C.R.C., c. 50, s. 2.

LAND REGISTRAR. A land registrar appointed under the Registry Act, in whose land titles division land affected or intended to be affected by any proceeding, instrument, application or plan is or may be registered or deposited. *Land Titles Amendment Act*, S.O. 1986, c. 61, s. 1.

LAND REGISTRATION DISTRICT. See NORTH ALBERTA ~.

LAND REGISTRY. A land titles office.

LAND REPLOT. A replotting scheme based on a proportional redistribution of the land in the replotting scheme. *Planning Act*, R.S.A. 1980, c. P-9, s. 123.

LANDS. *n.* 1. Lands the acquiring, taking or using of which is authorized by this Act or a Special Act, and includes real property, messuages, lands, tenements and hereditaments of any tenure, and any easement, servitude, right, privilege or interest in, to, on, under, over or in respect of the same. Canada statutes. 2. Include water (and the frozen surface thereof) and any other supporting surface. *Aeronautics Act*, R.S.C. 1985 (1st Supp.), c. 33, s. 5.4. 3. Includes all granted or ungranted, wild or cleared, public or private lands, all real property, messuages, lands, tenements and hereditaments of any tenure, all real rights, easements and servitudes and all other things for which compensation is to be paid by the Crown. *Government Railways Act*, R.S.C. 1985, c. G-7, s. 2. 4. The inner surface areas of a firearm barrel between the rifling grooves. F.A. Jaffe, *A Guide to Pathological Evidence*, 2d ed. (Toronto: Carswell, 1983) at 179. See ALLODIAL ~; CANADA ~; CROWN ~; CUT-OFF ~; DOCUMENT OF TITLE TO ~; FREEHOLD ~; FRONTIER ~; INDIAN ~; INSTITUTIONAL ~; LAND; MATURE ~; MINERAL ~; MINING ~; NOVA SCOTIA ~; OCCUPIED ~; PRIVATE ~; PRODUCTIVE ~; PUBLIC ~; SEVERANCE ~; SURRENDERED ~; TAKE ~; TERRITORIAL ~; UNPRODUCTIVE ~.

LANDS AND PREMISES. 1. Buildings, lands, hereditaments and easements of any tenure. 2. Includes messuages, buildings, lands and easements of any tenure.

LANDSCAPE CONSTRUCTION. Any clearing, breaking, grading, fertilizing or cultivation of an area or the construction of an outdoor ground surface for games or athletics or the establishment thereon of trees, shrubs, flowers, grass or other forms of vegetative growth or outdoor furniture, including seating of a type suitable for a garden or park but not for an audience or assembly of spectators, or any functional or aesthetic features contributing to the general landscape design of the area, and includes the provision of such machines, equipment and tools as is requisite for all or any of such matters.

LANDSCAPE MAINTENANCE. The sustaining of landscape construction and includes the provision of such machines, equipment and tools as is requisite therefor.

LAND STATION. 1. A place on land at which whales are treated or processed. 2. A station operated in a terrestrial service and located on land that is not an earth station, coast station, mobile station or private receiving station. *General Radio Regulations, Part II*, C.R.C., c. 1372, s. 2.

LANDS, TENEMENTS AND HEREDITAMENTS. A traditional description of real property, considered the most comprehensive.

LAND SURVEY. The establishment, location or definition on the ground of any boundary, limit or angle of any land, size, location, parcel, claim, common, easement, road, street, lane, district, municipality, county or township, or any other location or division of lands or right over lands whether for ownership, title or authority or the origin of any of them. *Land Survey Act*, R.S.P.E.I. 1974, c. L-4, s. 1.

LAND SURVEYING. The determination of any point or of the direction or length of any line required in measuring, laying off, or dividing land for the purpose of establishing boundaries or title to land. See PRACTICE OF ~; PROFESSIONAL ~.

LAND SURVEYOR. See ALBERTA ~; PROVINCIAL ~.

LAND TITLE OFFICE. The registry office of the land title district in which land is situate.

LAND TITLES. See REGISTRAR OF ~.

LAND TITLES ASSURANCE FUND. A source of money intended to compensate people adversely affected by any operation of a Land Titles Act. B.J. Reiter, R.C.B. Risk & B.N. McLellan, *Real Estate Law*, 3d ed. (Toronto: Emond Montgomery, 1986) at 613.

LAND TITLES SYSTEM. The government makes a brief, simple statement concerning the ownership of land and all outstanding interests or claims so that the purchaser need not be concerned, as in a registry system, with the history of the transactions which affected that land. B.J. Reiter, R.C.B. Risk & B.N. McLellan,

Real Estate Law, 3d ed. (Toronto: Emond Montgomery, 1986) at 454.

LAND USE CONTROL LAW. Any Act of the Legislature, and any regulation, plan or by-law made under the authority of an Act of the Legislature that restricts or prescribes the use to which land or premises may be put or the nature of businesses or activities that may be carried on on any land or premises. *Agricultural Operation Practices Act*, S.N.B. 1986, c. A-5.2, s. 1.

LAND USE DISTRICT. An area of land that is within a reservoir development area or special flood hazard area and that is designated by regulation as a land use district within which specified uses and limitations on uses are imposed. *The Water Resources Management Act*, R.S.S. 1978, c. W-7, s. 2.

LAND USE PLAN. A plan for the control of land within a defined area proposing that parts of the land may be used only for industry, commerce, government, recreation, transportation, hospitals, schools, churches, residences, homes for the elderly or for other purposes or classes of users, with or without subdivisions of the various classes. *Railway Relocation and Crossing Act*, R.S.C. 1985, c. R-4, s. 17.

LANE. *n.* 1. A public highway vested in the Crown as a secondary level or access to a site. *The Planning and Development Act*, R.S.S. 1978,c. P-13, s. 2. 2. A street not over twenty feet in width. *City of Winnipeg Act*, S.M. 1971, c. 105, s. 1. 3. A public thoroughfare not over 33 feet in width that affords a secondary means of access to a lot. Canada regulations. See BACK ~; PARKING ~; PUBLIC ~; TRAFFIC ~.

LANED HIGHWAY. A roadway that is divided into two or more clearly marked lanes for vehicular traffic. *Motor Vehicle Act*, R.S.N.B. 1973, c. M-17, s. 1.

LANED ROADWAY. A roadway which is divided into two or more clearly marked lanes for vehicular traffic.

LANGUAGE. See ABORIGINAL ~; ENGLISH ~ EDUCATION; FRENCH ~ EDUCATION; OFFICIAL ~.

LANGUAGE TRAINING. Basic training, at public expense, in one of the official languages, the nature, duration and location of which is prescribed on an individual basis by the deputy head. *Official Languages Exclusion Approval Order*, C.R.C., c. 1349, s. 2.

LANUGO HAIRS. Fine hairs appearing at the end of the sixth month which covers the fetus during the seventh and eighth months of ges-

tation. F.A. Jaffe, *A Guide to Pathological Evidence*, 2d ed. (Toronto: Carswell, 1983) at 179.

LAPSE. *v.* To fail, said of a bequest or devise of property which goes into residue as if the gift had not been made when the person to whom the property was bequeathed or devised dies before the testator.

LAPSE. *n.* Error; failure in duty.

LAPSE DATE. (a) In the case of a prospectus, the date on which a prospectus ceases to be valid for the distribution of securities for which the prospectus was filed, and (b) in the case of a summary statement, the date on which a summary statement ceases to be valid for the distribution of securities for which the summary statement was filed.

LAPSING. See TIME OF ~.

LARCENY. *n.* The unlawful seizure and removal of things personal when one intends to deprive the rightful owner of those things.

LA REINE LE VEULT. [Fr.] The Queen wishes it.

LA REINE N'EST LIÉ PAR AUCUN STATUT SI ELLE NE FUT EXPRESSÉMENT NOMMÉE. [Fr.] The Queen is not bound by any statute if not expressly named in it.

LA REINE REMERCIE SES BONS SUJETS, ACCEPTE LEUR BÉNÉVOLENCE ET AINSI LE VEUT. [Fr.] The Queen is grateful to her loyal subjects, accepts their benevolence, and wishes it this way.

LA REINE S'AVISERA. [Fr.] The Queen will consider this.

LARGE AEROPLANE. An aeroplane of more than 12,500 pounds maximum certificated take-off weight. Canada regulations.

LARGE-MESH TRAWL NET. A trawl net having a cod end the mesh size of which is 2 inches or more extension measure. *Ontario Fishery Regulations*, C.R.C., c. 949, s. 2.

LARGE PROVINCE. A province (other than Quebec) having a population greater than two and a half million. *Constitution Act, 1974*, S.C. 1974-75-76, c. 13, reprinted as R.S.C. 1985, App. Document No. 40.

LARGE TURKEY. A turkey that is 17 weeks old or more but less than 30 weeks old at the time of delivery for slaughtering. *Canadian Turkey Marketing Quota Regulations*, C.R.C., c. 661, s. 2.

LARVA. *n.* [L.] A stage between egg and pupa in the metamorphosis of an insect. F.A. Jaffe, *A Guide to Pathological Evidence*, 2d ed. (Toronto: Carswell, 1983) at 179.

LARYNX. *n.* A hollow, cartilaginous and muscular structure which is lined with mucous membrane, located between the trachea and the hyoid bone and contains the vocal cords. F.A. Jaffe, *A Guide to Pathological Evidence*, 2d ed. (Toronto: Carswell, 1983) at 179.

LASER. *n.* Any device that can be made to produce light primarily by the process of stimulated emission. *Radiation Emitting Devices Regulations*, C.R.C., c. 1370, s. 1.

LASER RADIATION. All electromagnetic radiation generated by a laser that is coherent and propagates collinearly through space. *Radiation Emitting Devices Regulations*, C.R.C., c. 1370, s. 1. See SCANNED ~.

LASING MEDIUM. A material that emits laser radiation by virtue of stimulated transitions between specific electronic or molecular energy levels. *Radiation Emitting Devices Regulations*, C.R.C., c. 1370, s. 1.

LAST. *adj.* When used with reference to the point of connection of a fixture to a horizontal branch, means farthest from the waste stack, soil stack or building drain to which the horizontal branch is connected. *Ontario Water Resources Act*, R.R.O. 1980, Reg. 736, s. 1.

LAST ASCERTAINABLE SIDE LINE. A line in a broken concession established from the front of the concession on the course of a side line of a lot from the lot corner nearest the end of the part of the concession so broken. *Surveys Act*, R.S.O. 1980, c. 493, s. 1.

LAST CLEAR CHANCE DOCTRINE. A doctrine which permits full recovery by a plaintiff even if that plaintiff was contributorily negligent if the defendant had the last chance to avoid an accident but negligently did not take advantage of that chance. John G. Fleming, *The Law of Torts*, 6th ed. (Sydney: The Law Book Company Limited, 1983) at 243.

LAST DAY OF THE TAXATION YEAR. Shall, in the case of an individual who resided in Canada at any time in the taxation year but ceased to reside in Canada before the last day thereof, be deemed to be a reference to the last day in the taxation year on which he resided in Canada. *Income Tax acts.*

LAST HEIR. Any person to whom land comes when there are no other heirs.

LAST-IN, FIRST-OUT METHOD OF INVENTORY VALUATION. An inventory accounting method in which one assumes that the items acquired last will be disposed of first so that the inventory value at the end of the period is the cost of the items acquired first. W. Grover & F. Iacobucci, *Materials on Canadian Income Tax*, 4th ed. (Toronto: Richard De Boo Ltd., 1980) at 643.

LAST RESORT. Describes a court from which there is no further appeal. See COURT OF ~.

LATA CULPA DOLO AEQUIPARATUR. [L.] Gross negligence is on a par with fraud.

LATENT. *adj.* Concealed, hidden; secret.

LATENT DEFECT. Some fault which one would not expect an ordinary purchaser to discover during a routine inspection. B.J. Reiter, R.C.B. Risk & B.N. McLellan, *Real Estate Law*, 3d ed. (Toronto: Emond Montgomery, 1986) at 281.

LATERAL. *adj.* A distance from the mid line, to the side. F.A. Jaffe, *A Guide to Pathological Evidence*, 2d ed. (Toronto: Carswell, 1983) at 179.

LATERAL DRAIN. A drain that is designed for the drainage of one property and that begins and ends on the same property. *Drainage Act*, R.S.O. 1980, c. 126. s. 1.

LATERAL TRANSFER. A change in an employee's job to one with similar duties.

LATE SCRATCH. A horse withdrawn by the stewards from a race in which it was entered after betting on that race has commenced. *Race Track Supervision Regulations*, C.R.C., c. 441, s. 2.

LATHER. *n.* A person who, (i) plans proposed installations from blueprints, sketches, specifications, building standards and codes, (ii) installs by tying, nailing, clipping, screwing or welding wire, metal or wood lath, drywall gypsum board or other materials in the construction or repair of walls, partitions, ceilings or arches in any structure, (iii) erects light metal studs, metal furring components, acoustical ceilings systems and accessories to receive drywall gypsum board, wire and metal lath, (iv) reads and understands design drawings, manufacturers' literature and installation diagrams, but does not include a person engaged in the manufacture of equipment or the assembly of a unit, prior to delivery to a building structure or site. *Apprenticeship and Tradesmen's Qualification Act*, R.R.O. 1980, Reg. 45, s. 1.

LATIN. *n.* The language of ancient Rome. Law Latin includes both good Latin, familiar to lawyers and classical grammarians, and words of art or lawyers' latin, familiar to the legal profession but not to grammarians.

LAUNCH. *n.* A steamship in which the passengers are carried in an open cockpit or in a cockpit that is covered by a light trunk cabin. Canada regulations.

LAUNDRY. *n.* A building or part of a building used for the washing, ironing or pressing of clothes, linens or other fabrics and material where such work is carried on as a trade or business. *The Public Health Act*, R.S.S. 1978, c. P-37, s. 2. See PUBLIC ~.

LAW. *n.* 1. A rule to govern action. 2. An enactment. 3. Includes an Act of the Parliament of Canada or of the Legislature and includes a proclamation, regulation or order in council made pursuant to any such Act. *Constitutional Questions Act*, S.N.S. 1985, c. 15, s. 1. 4. Includes a regulation, a decree, an ordinance or an order in council made under the authority of any Act. *Charter of Human Rights and Freedoms*, R.S.Q. 1977, c. C-12, s. 56. See ACT IN THE ~; ACT OF THE ~; ADJECTIVE ~; ADMINISTRATIVE ~; ADMIRALTY ~; ANTITRUST ~; BLUE-SKY ~; BY-~; CANON ~; CASE ~; CHOICE OF ~; CIVIL ~; COLONIAL ~; COMMERCIAL ~; COMMON ~; CONCLUSION OF ~; CONSTITUTIONAL ~; CONSUETUDINARY ~; CONTRACT ~; CRIMINAL ~; ECCLESIASTICAL ~; EQUALITY BEFORE THE ~; ERROR OF ~; FAMILY ~ COMMISSIONER; FISCAL ~; HOMESTEAD ~; INTERNAL ~; INTERNATIONAL ARBITRATION ~; INTERNATIONAL ~; LAND USE CONTROL ~; MARITIME ~; MARTIAL ~; MERCANTILE ~; MILITARY ~; MISTAKE OF ~; MIXED ~; MIXED QUESTION OF ~ AND FACT; MUNICIPAL ~; NATURAL ~; NEW ~; OLD ~; PENAL ~; POSITIVE ~; PRACTICE OF ~; PRESUMPTION OF ~; PRIVATE ~; PROPER ~; PROPERTY ~; PROVISION OF ~; PUBLIC ~; RESTATEMENT OF ~; REVENUE ~; RIGHT-TO-WORK ~; ROMAN ~; RULE OF ~; STATUTE ~; SUBSTANTIVE ~; SUMPTUARY ~; SUNDAY CLOSING ~.

LAW CLERK AND PARLIAMENTARY COUNSEL. An official appointed by Letters Patent under the Great Seal whose principal duty is to advise the Speaker and officers of the House of Commons on any legal matter which does not fall within the realm of procedure and who helps members of Parliament draft legislation. A. Fraser, G.A. Birch & W.A. Dawson, eds., *Beauchesne's Rules and Forms of the House of Commons of Canada*, 5th ed. (Toronto: Carswell, 1978) at 45.

LAWFUL. *adj.* Legal, authorized by law.

LAWFUL EXCUSE. (a) The ability to prove that fish in possession during the close time therefor at the place of possession were legally caught, or (b) the unintentional or incidental catching of any fish that may not then be taken, when legally fishing for other fish. *Fisheries Act*, R.S.C. 1985, c. F-14, s. 2.

LAWFUL FENCE. 1. A substantial fence not less than four feet high and consisting of not less than four strands of ordinary fence wire, the lower wire being not more than twelve inches above the ground; the posts in such fences to be placed not more than twenty-seven feet apart. 2. A substantial fence of a height of not less than four feet above the level of the ground, constructed of woven wire, barbed wire or rails, boards or slabs, of a size and structure that will suitably confine animals under normal circumstances, and fastened to posts not more than sixteen feet apart. *Herd and Fencing Act*, R.S.N.W.T. 1974, c. H-1, s. 8.

LAWFULLY. *adv.* (a) In accordance with this Act and the Canadian Wheat Board Act, and (b) in respect of (i) the offering of grain for delivery to or storage in a primary elevator, (ii) the delivery of grain to a terminal elevator, transfer elevator or process elevator or to a consignee at a destination other than an elevator, or (iii) the delivery of grain to a public carrier for carriage to any elevator or consignee referred to in subparagraph (ii), deliverable by the owner of the grain, receivable by the public carrier for carriage to the elevator or consignee and receivable by the operator of the elevator or consignee, in accordance with this Act and the Canadian Wheat Board Act. *Canada Grain Act*, R.S.C. 1985, c. G-10, s. 2. See PERSON ~ IN POSSESSION OF THE BODY.

LAWFULLY FISHING. Fishing in accordance with the game laws of the Province and the laws of the Dominion of Canada and any regulations made thereunder for the purpose of sport, and includes the taking and carrying away of any fish lawfully caught. *Angling Act*, R.S.N.S. 1967, c. 9, s. 1.

LAWFUL WORK. Any work not contrary to the laws in force at the place of construction of the work at the time of its construction. *Navigable Waters Protection Act*, R.S.C. 1985, c. N-22, s. 3.

LAW LIST. A listing of all persons who are practicing as barristers or solicitors and any other lawyers.

LAW LORDS. In England, the Lord Chancellor, the Lords of Appeal in Ordinary, former Lord Chancellors and other peers who held high judicial offices.

LAW MERCHANT. The law which governs any mercantile transaction.

LAWN GRASS MIXTURE. Every package of seed that is a lawn grass mixture shall be labelled with the following information: (a) the term "lawn grass mixture"; (b) the name and address of the seller; (c) the name of the grade of the seed; and (d) where packed in packages containing more than 3 kilograms, the name of each kind of seed that constitutes five per cent or more by mass of the mixture, or two per cent or more in the case of white clover. *Seeds Regulations*, C.R.C., c. 1400, s. 25 in part.

LAW OF AGENCY. The law to govern relationships which come into existence when one person uses another person to perform certain tasks on her or his behalf. G.H.L. Fridman, *The Law of Agency*, 5th ed. (London: Butterworths, 1983) at 3.

LAW OF ALBERTA. An Act of the Legislature of Alberta enacted before of after the commencement of this Act, any order, rule or regulation made thereunder, and any law in force in Alberta on January 1, 1973 that is subject to be repealed, abolished or altered by the Legislature of Alberta. *Individual's Rights Protection Act*, R.S.A. 1980, c. I-2, s. 1.

LAW OF CANADA. In Part I means an Act of the Parliament of Canada enacted before of after the coming into force of this Act, any order, rule or regulation thereunder, and any law in force in Canada or in any part of Canada at the commencement of this Act that is subject to be repealed, abolished or altered by the Parliament of Canada. *Canadian Bill of Rights*, 8-9 Elizabeth II, c. 44 (Canada). See LAWS OF CANADA.

LAW OF CONTRACT. Law for the purpose of ensuring that the promises of persons are performed. John G. Fleming, *The Law of Torts*, 6th ed. (Sydney: The Law Book Company Limited, 1983) at 2.

LAW OFFICER. The Minister of Justice of Québec. *Interpretation Act*, R.S.Q. 1977, c. I-16, s. 61.

LAW OFFICER OF THE CROWN. 1. An Attorney-General; a Solicitor-General. 2. The Minister of Justice of Québec. *Interpretation Act*, R.S.Q. 1977, c. I-16, s. 61.

LAW OF FLAG. The law of the country the flag of which a ship is flying.

LAW OF NATIONS. Public international law.

LAW OF ONTARIO. Includes any law of the former Province of Canada or of Upper Canada, continued as the law of Ontario, or consolidated or incorporated with the Law of Ontario. *Loan and Trust Corporations Act*, R.S.O. 1980, c. 249, s. 1.

LAW OF THE PROVINCE. A law of a province or municipality not inconsistent with this Act. *Motor Vehicle Transport Act*, R.S.C. 1985, c. M-12, s. 2.

LAW REFORM COMMISSION OF CANADA. A body established in 1972 permanently to review the laws of Canada continuously and systematically. D. Stuart, *Canadian Criminal Law: a Treatise*, 2d ed. (Toronto: Carswell, 1987) at 3.

LAW REPORT. 1. The published account of any legal proceeding. 2. The report of a judgment of a court on points of law, published so that it may be used as a precedent.

LAW REPR. *abbr.* The Law Reporter (Ramsay & Morin) (Que.), 1854.

LAWS OF CANADA. The same meaning as those words have in section 101 of the Constitution Act, 1867. *Federal Court Act*, R.S.C. 1985, c. F-7, s. 2. See LAW OF CANADA.

LAW STUDENT. A person enrolled in any law course approved by the Law Society or in the Bar Admission Course during the time he is in attendance at the teaching period thereof. *Legal Aid Act*, R.R.O. 1980, Reg. 575, s. 1.

LAW SUIT. Litigation; an action.

LAWYER. *n.* In the Province of Quebec, an advocate, lawyer or notary and, in any other province, a barrister or solicitor.

LAY. *adj.* Not professional, belonging to the general population in contrast to a certain profession.

LAY ASSISTANT. A person trained to carry out specific veterinary procedures. *Veterinary Profession Act*, R.S.P.E.I. 1974, c. V-4, s. 2.

LAY CORPORATION. A body politic created for charitable or business purposes.

LAY-DAY. *var.* LAY DAY. 1. A day of work with pay to which an employee becomes entitled by working on board a ship for a number of days. Canada regulations. 2. The time to load and unload ships.

LAY DISPENSER. A person who is authorized by a Medical Health Officer, appointed pursuant to the Public Health Act, to administer emergency first aid in a community which is without a resident nurse. *Mental Health Act*, S.N.W.T. 1985 (2d Sess.), c. 6, s. 2.

LAYER. *n.* 1. A female chicken over six months of age that may produce eggs. *Saskatchewan Egg Marketing Levies Order*, C.R.C., c. 270, s. 2. 2. Any class of hens. *Canadian Egg Marketing Agency Quota Regulations*, C.R.C., c. 656, s. 2. See ACTIVE ~.

LAYING-UP. *n.* The time served on work suitable for the training of an engineer or electrician while preparing the machinery of a ship for lay-up. *Marine Engineer Examination Regulations*, C.R.C., c. 1443, s. 2.

LAY OFF. *v.* To terminate.

LAY-OFF. *var.* **LAYOFF.** *n.* 1. Temporary or indefinite termination of employment because of lack of work. 2. The separation, for an indefinite period, of an employee from employment at a Canadian establishment solely as a result of a reduction in the number of employees at that establishment. *Labour Adjustment Benefits Act*, R.S.C. 1985, c. L-1, s. 2. 3. A person who has been laid off pursuant to subsection 29(1) and who, in the opinion of the Commission, is suitable for appointment under this Act. *Public Service Employment Act*, R.S.C. 1985, c. P-33, s. 2. See EFFECTIVE DATE OF ~; TEMPORARY ~; WEEK OF ~.

LAY PERSON. 1. A person other than a person registered or licensed under one of the acts governing professions. 2. A person who (a) is not employed in the public service of New Brunswick or any agency of the Crown, and (b) is not or has not been registered under this Act or any Act governing a health practice or allied health discipline. *Denturists' Act*, S.N.B. 1986, c. 90, s. 2.

L.C.B. *abbr.* Land Compensation Board.

L.C.J. *abbr.* Lord Chief Justice.

L.C. JUR. *abbr.* Lower Canada Jurist, 1857-1891.

L.C. JURIST. *abbr.* Lower Canada Jurist (1848-1891).

L.C.L.J. *abbr.* Lower Canada Law Journal (1865-1868).

L.C.R. *abbr.* 1. Land Compensation Reports, 1971-. 2. Lower Canada Reports, 1851-1867 (Décisions des Tribunaux du Bas-Canada).

L.C. REP. *abbr.* Lower Canada Reports.

LEAD. *v.* To call or adduce evidence.

LEAD. *n.* 1. The element lead. 2. A substance designated under the Ontario Occupational Health and Safety Act. D. Robertson, *Ontario Health and Safety Guide* (Toronto: Richard De Boo Ltd., 1988) at 5-228. See SECONDARY ~ SMELTER.

LEAD ALLOY. An alloy of lead that contains 40 per cent or more of lead, by weight. *Secondary Lead Smelter National Emission Standards Regulations*, C.R.C., c. 412, s. 2.

LEADED GASOLINE. 1. Gasoline that contains more than (a) 0.06 grams of lead per Imperial gallon (0.013 grams per litre), or (b) 0.006 grams of phosphorous per Imperial gallon (0.0013 grams per litre). *Motor Vehicle Safety Regulations*, C.R.C., c. 1038, s. 2. 2. A gasoline, other than aircraft gasoline, which contains tetraethyl lead. *The Statute Law Amendment (Taxation) Act (1985)*, S.M. 1985-86, c. 48, s. 1.

LEADER. *n.* A fixed vertical panel attached to the front of a fishing net in order to lead fish towards the opening in the net. *Quebec Fishery Regulations*, C.R.C., c. 852, s. 2. See LOSS ~; RAIN WATER ~.

LEADER OF A RECOGNIZED POLITICAL PARTY. A member of the Legislative Assembly other than the Premier or Leader of the Official Opposition, who is the leader in the Legislative Assembly of an affiliation of electors comprised in a political organization whose prime purpose is the fielding of candidates for election to the Legislative Assembly and that is represented in the Legislative Assembly by 4 or more members. *Constitution Act*, R.S.B.C. 1979, c. 62, s. 1.

LEADER OF THE OPPOSITION. 1. A member of Parliament or a legislature recognized by the Speaker as the leader of Her Majesty's loyal opposition. 2. The member of the House of Commons who is presently leader of the party opposing the Government and who has certain special rights regarding the questioning of Ministers. A. Fraser, G.A. Birch & W.A. Dawson, eds., *Beauchesne's Rules and Forms of the House of Commons of Canada*, 5th ed. (Toronto: Carswell, 1978) at 49. 3. The member of the Assembly who is the recognized leader of two or more members constituting the largest group sitting in the Assembly in opposition to the Government, and in case of equality of membership of two or more such groups the allowance and the grant provided for by this section and the allowance and grant provided for by section 24 shall be added together and the total shall be divided equally between the respective leaders of those groups having the largest and equal membership. *The Larger School Units Act*, R.S.S. 1978, c. L-7, s. 23.

LEADER OF THE THIRD PARTY. The member who is the recognized leader of two or more members constituting the second largest group sitting in the Assembly in opposition to the Government. *Legislative Assembly and Executive Council Act*, S.S. 1979, c. L-11.1, s. 2(1).

LEADERSHIP CONTESTANT. A person seeking election as leader of a registered party at a leadership convention called by that party for the purpose. *Election Finances Act*, S.O. 1986, c. 33, s. 1.

LEADERSHIP CONTEST PERIOD. The period commencing with the date of the official call for a leadership convention as set forth in the statement filed by a registered party under subsection 15(2) and terminating two months after the date of the leadership vote. *Election Finances Act*, S.O. 1986, c. 33, s. 1.

LEADERSHIP VOTE. The date on which polling takes place to elect a leader of a registered party at a leadership convention. *Election Finances Act*, S.O. 1986, c. 33, s. 1.

LEADING CASE. A judicial precedent or decision which settled the principles in a certain branch of law.

LEADING QUESTION. A question which one poses to one's own witness which suggests the answer required of that witness.

LEADING UNDERWRITER. An expert in a particular kind of insurance whom other insurers are likely to follow. Raoul Colinvaux, *The Law of Insurance*, 5th ed. (London: Sweet & Maxwell, 1984) at 20.

LEAGUE. *n.* 1. A treaty allying different nations or parties. 2. A corporation incorporated as a credit union league or federation under this Act or a predecessor of this Act. *Credit Unions and Caisses Populaires Act*, R.S.O. 1980, c. 102, s. 1. 3. A distance of three miles.

LEAGUE OF NATIONS. An international assembly established in 1920 and superseded after World War II by the United Nations Organization.

LEAKAGE RADIATION. 1. All radiation, except the useful beam, coming from within the housing of an energized X-ray tube. *Radiation Emitting Devices Regulations*, C.R.C., c. 1370, s. 1. 2. Any radiation transmitted outside the external surface. *Radiation Emitting Devices Regulations*, C.R.C., c. 1370, s. 1.

LEAKER. *n.* 1. A can of fish that has not been properly sealed or has developed a leak. *Fish Inspection Act*, R.S.Nfld. 1970, c. 132, s. 12. 2. An egg that is cracked with the inner membrane ruptured and from which the contents are leaking. Ontario regulations.

LEAP-YEAR. *n.* A calendar year, called bissextile and consisting of 366 days, which occurs every fourth year.

LEARNER. *n.* A person who, although not under a contract of service or apprenticeship, becomes subject to the hazards of an industry to which the act applies for the purpose of undergoing testing, training or probationary work preliminary to employment in an industry to which the act applies. Workers' Compensation acts.

LEASE. *n.* 1. Every agreement in writing, and every parol agreement whereby one person as landlord confers upon another person as tenant the right to occupy land, and every sublease and every agreement for a sublease and every assurance whereby any rent is secured by condition. 2. Includes agreement for a lease. 3. Includes the hourly, daily, weekly, monthly, annual or other periodic rental of goods or services. *Consumer Protection Act*, R.S.B.C. 1979, c. 65, s. 1. 4. A disposition under section 8 of the right to produce, subject to this Act, a geothermal resource from a location. *Geothermal Resources Act*, S.B.C. 1982, c. 14, s. 1. 5. A lease of a recorded claim granted to the holder of the claim. *Canada Mining Regulations*, C.R.C., c. 1516, s. 2. 6. An oil and gas lease. See BUILDING ~; CROWN ~; DRY ~; FINANCIAL ~; FISHERY ~; GROUND ~; HEAD ~; MINING ~; OPERATING ~; PROPRIETARY ~; REGISTERED LONG TERM ~; RENEWABLE ~; REVERSIONARY ~; SURFACE ~; UNDER ~; WET ~ ~.

LEASE AREA. The land covered by a mining lease. *Mining Act*, S.N.B. 1985, c. M-14.1, s. 1.

LEASEBACK. *var.* **LEASE BACK.** An arrangement in which land or property is sold and then leased back to the vendor. See SALE-~.

LEASED PARCEL. See MULTI DWELLING ~.

LEASEHOLD. *n.* 1. The area demised by a lease. 2. An area distinguished from a freehold because its duration is certain and both its beginning and its end are defined. E.L.G. Tyler & N.E. Palmer, eds., *Crossley Vaines' Personal Property*, 5th ed. (London: Butterworths, 1973) at 5. See EQUITABLE ~ MORTGAGE; LEGAL ~ MORTGAGE.

LEASEHOLD ESTATE. In contrast to a freehold estate, an estate of fixed duration.

LEASE PRICE. Any payment or consideration, in addition to those made for rental periods, by a lessee to a lessor for the right to use the leased property, including a down payment. *Social Services Tax Act*, S.B.C. 1985, c. 32, s. 1.

LEASING CORPORATION. A corporation (a) that is incorporated or continued under an Act of Parliament, (b) the activities of which are limited to the financial leasing of personal property and such related activities as are prescribed by the regulations and conform with such restrictions and limitations thereon as are so prescribed, and (c) that, in conducting its activities that are financial leasing of personal property and any other prescribed activities related thereto, does not (i) direct its customers or potential customers to particular dealers in the leased property or the property to be leased, (ii) enter into lease agreements with persons in respect of any motor vehicle having a gross vehicle weight, as that expression is defined in the regulations, of less than twenty-one metric tonnes, or (iii) enter into lease agreements with individuals in respect of personal household property, as that expression is defined by the regulations. *Bank Act*, R.S.C. 1985, c. B-1, s. 193.

LEAVE. *n.* Permission. See ABSENCE WITH-OUT ~; BEREAVEMENT ~; MATERNITY ~; SABBATICAL ~; SICK ~.

LEAVE AND LICENCE. A defence to a trespass action in which the defendant claims that plaintiff consented to the act complained of.

LEAVE OF ABSENCE. A period of time during which an employee is permitted to be absent from work, usually without pay.

LEAVING. See DATE OF ~.

LECTURE. *n.* Includes address, speech and sermon. *Copyright Act*, R.S.C. 1985, c. C-42, s. 2.

LECTURER. *n.* One who instructs.

LEDGER. *n.* An account book.

LEFT. *adj.* In reference to a highway or the position of traffic thereon means the left when facing or moving in the direction of travel.

LEFT HAND. *var.* **LEFT-HAND.** In reference to a highway or the position of traffic thereon means the left when facing or moving in the direction of travel.

LEGABLE. *adj.* Able to be bequeathed.

LEGACY. *n.* The means by which personal property is disposed of by will. See CONTINGENT ~; CUMULATIVE ~; DEMONSTRATIVE ~; SPECIFIC ~.

LEGAL. *adj.* According to law, lawful. See MEDICO-~.

LEGAL ADVISER. (a) A defending officer, counsel or adviser qualified under QR&O 111.60; and (b) a solicitor. *Military Rules of Evidence*, C.R.C., c. 1049, s. 77.

LEGAL AGE. The age of majority.

LEGAL AID. Legal advice and services available or furnished under a legal aid act.

LEGAL BURDEN OF PROOF. In general, the burden of proof is on the person who asserts, but in a criminal trial the prosecution bears that burden. P.K. McWilliams, *Canadian Criminal Evidence*, 3d ed. (Aurora: Canada Law Book, 1988) at 25-1.

LEGAL CAUSATION. A concept which subsumes the notions of proximity, remoteness and novus actus interveniens. K.D. Cooper-Stephenson & I.B. Saunders, *Personal Injury Damages in Canada* (Toronto: Carswell, 1981) at 638.

LEGAL CORNER POST. A post, placed and marked in accordance with the regulations that establishes the true geographical point from which the location of a mineral claim is determined. *Mineral Act*, R.S.B.C. 1979, c. 259, s. 1.

LEGAL CUSTODY. Any restraint of a person that is authorized by law.

LEGAL DESCRIPTION. A description sufficient to describe a property for the purpose of its registration in a land title office. *Taxation (Rural Area) Act*, R.S.B.C. 1979, c. 400, s. 1.

LEGAL EXECUTION. An execution obtained by a common law writ like fieri facias or elegit. C.R.B. Dunlop, *Creditor-Debtor Law in Canada* (Toronto: Carswell, 1981) at 139.

LEGAL EXPENSE INSURANCE. Insurance against the cost incurred by a person for specified legal services, including fees and other costs, incurred relative to the provision of those services. *An Act to Amend the Insurance Act*, S.M. 1980-81, c. 32, s. 2.

LEGAL FICTION. See FICTION.

LEGAL GUARDIAN. A person appointed or recognized as the guardian of a child under The Child Welfare Act or The Surrogate Courts Act. *Public School Act*, S.M. 1980, c. 33, s. 1.

LEGAL INCAPACITY. Mental infirmity of such a nature as would, but for this Act, invalidate or terminate a power of attorney. *Powers of Attorney Act*, R.S.O. 1980, c. 386, s. 1.

LEGAL INNUENDO. Something which arises solely from circumstances or facts and is not apparent on the face of the publication, but which gives words some special meaning they would not have ordinarily. R.E. Brown, *The Law of Defamation in Canada* (Toronto: Carswell, 1987) at 155.

LEGALISATION. *var.* **LEGALIZATION.** *n.* The transformation of a prima facie illegal act into a legal act.

LEGALISE. *var.* **LEGALIZE.** *v.* To transform a prima facie illegal act into a legal act.

LEGALIS HOMO. [L. a lawful person] Someone not an outlaw.

LEGALIS MONETA ANGLIAE. [L.] The lawful money of England.

LEGAL LEASEHOLD MORTGAGE. Created by granting a lease as a mortgage; a tenant may legally mortgage the term of the mortgage of that leasehold by making a sub-lease or by assigning the unexpired portion of the term. W.B. Rayner & R.H. McLaren, *Falconbridge on*

Mortgages, 4th ed. (Toronto: Canada Law Book, 1977) at 97.

LEGALLY QUALIFIED. Used in connection with a tradesman or a trade, the expression includes a tradesman in that trade who holds a valid subsisting certificate of proficiency in that trade. *Apprenticeship and Tradesmen's Qualification Act*, R.S.P.E.I. 1974, c. A-13, s. 1.

LEGAL MEDICINE. See FORENSIC MEDICINE.

LEGAL MED. Q. *abbr.* Legal Medical Quarterly.

LEGAL MONUMENT. A device planted by a surveyor.

LEGAL N. *abbr.* Legal News (1878-1897).

LEGAL PERSON. Any entity having juridical personality, including a commercial partnership. *Securities Act*, S.Q. 1982, c. 48, s. 5.

LEGAL POSSESSION. The condition of a person who has both physical control of and title to a chattel or a person who has physical control of and a clear intention to keep control of a chattel. E.L.G. Tyler & N.E. Palmer, eds., *Crossley Vaines' Personal Property*, 5th ed. (London: Butterworths, 1973) at 49.

LEGAL POST. 1. A stake having a diameter throughout of not less than 5 inches, standing not less than 4 feet above the ground and flatted on two sides for at least 1 foot from the top, each of the sides so flatted measuring at least 4 inches across the face, and includes any stump or tree cut off and flatted or faced to that height and size. 2. A stake or post of any kind of sound timber of sufficient length so that when firmly planted in the ground in an upright position, not less than 4 feet of such post is above ground, and the post must be of such diameter that when squared or faced for 18 inches from the top end, each face of the squared or faced portion is not less than 4 inches in width across the face for the full 18 inches or, if a tree of suitable size is found in position, it may be made into a post by cutting the tree off not less than 4 feet from the ground and squaring and facing the upper 18 inches, each face of the portion so squared or faced to be not less than 4 inches in width, and, whether a post is planted or a stump of a tree is made into a post, a mound of stones or earth shall be erected around the base of the post, which mound of earth or stones shall be not less than 3 feet in diameter on the ground and not less than 18 inches high, cone-shaped and well constructed. *Yukon Quartz Mining Act*, R.S.C. 1985, c. Y-4, s. 2. 3. A post, tree, mound of earth or stone used for making a claim in accordance with section 14. *Canada Mining Regulations*, C.R.C., c. 1516, s. 2.

LEGAL POWER. Enables its holder to perform tasks such as conveying an estate. D.M.W. Waters, *The Law of Trusts in Canada*, 2d ed. (Toronto: Carswell, 1984) at 71.

LEGAL PROCEEDING. Any civil or criminal proceeding or inquiry in which evidence is or may be given, and includes an arbitration.

LEGAL RATE. Of interest means the rate from time to time payable under the Interest Act (Canada) on liabilities on which interest is payable but no other rate is fixed. *Consumer Protection Act*, R.S.M. 1970, c. C200, s. 1.

LEGAL REPRESENTATIVE. 1. An executor, an administrator, a judicial trustee of the estate of a deceased person or a guardian of the person or estate, or both, of a minor. 2. Includes heirs, executors, administrators, guardians, curators, tutors, assigns and all other persons claiming through or under applicants for patents and patentees of inventions. *Patent Act*, R.S.C. 1985, c. P-4, s. 2. 3. Includes heirs, executors, administrators, successors and assigns, or agents or attorneys who are thereunto duly authorized in writing. *Copyright Act*, R.S.C. 1985, c. C-42, s. 2.

LEGAL RESIDENCE. That a person has, pursuant to the Immigration Act, (a) been admitted to Canada as a permanent resident, or (b) been permitted to enter and remain in Canada under the authority of a Minister's permit. *Old Age Security Regulations*, C.R.C., c. 1246, s. 22.

LEGAL RIGHTS. Though it lacks a precise popular or legal meaning, this term is the heading in the Canadian Charter of Rights which covers sections 7 to 14 of that Charter. P.W. Hogg, *Constitutional Law of Canada*, 2d ed. (Toronto: Carswell, 1985) at 742.

LEGAL TENDER. The tender of payment of money provided by the Currency and Exchange Act as long as it is made in notes issued by the Bank of Canada or in gold or subsidiary coins issued by the Government of Canada. C.R.B. Dunlop, *Creditor-Debtor Law in Canada* (Toronto: Carswell, 1981) at 22.

LEGATARY. *n.* One to whom a legacy is left.

LEGATE. *n.* An ambassador; a deputy; a nuncio of the Pope.

LEGATEE. *n.* 1. One to whom a legacy is left. 2. Includes a devisee. *Probate Courts Act*, R.S.N.B. 1973, c. P-17, s. 1. See RESIDUARY ~.

LEGATION. *n.* A mission; an embassy.

LEGATOR. *n.* One who makes a will leaving legacies.

LEGATUS REGIS VICE FUNGITUR A QUO DESTINATUR ET HONORANDUS EST SICUT ILLE CUJUS VICEM GERIT. [L.] An ambassador takes the place of the monarch who sent that ambassador and should be honoured just as the person in whose place the ambassador stands.

LEGEM FACERE. [L.] To institute legal proceedings or make law on oath.

LEGEM HABERE. [L.] To be able to give evidence or institute legal proceedings upon oath.

LEGES POSTERIORES PRIORES CONTRARIAS ABROGANT. [L. later laws repeal prior laws which were contrary] The later section of a statute prevails over an earlier one if the two provisions are repugnant.

LEG-HOLD TRAP. A trap designed to capture an animal by seizing and holding the animal by the leg or foot. *Game and Fish Act*, R.S.O. 1980, c. 182, s. 1.

LEGIS CONSTRUCTIO NON FACIT INJURIAM. [L.] The construction of law does not work a wrong.

LEGISLATION. *n.* The creation of law; a collection of statutes, regulations, by-laws. See CONSUMER PROTECTION ~; DESIGNATED ~; JUDICIAL ~; SUBORDINATE ~.

LEGISLATIVE ACT. The establishment and promulgation of some general rule of conduct which does not refer to particular cases. S.A. DeSmith, *Judicial Review of Administrative Action*, 4th ed. by J.M. Evans (London: Stevens, 1980) at 71.

LEGISLATIVE ASSEMBLY. 1. The legislative assembly of a province. 2. Includes the Lieutenant Governor in Council and the Legislative Assembly of the Northwest Territories as constituted before September 1, 1905, the Commissioner in Council of the Yukon Territory, and the Commissioner in Council of the Northwest Territories. *Interpretation Act*, R.S.C. 1985, c. I-21, s. 35.

LEGISLATIVE ASSEMBLY OFFICE. The office of the clerk of a legislative assembly.

LEGISLATIVE COUNCIL. Includes the Lieutenant Governor in Council and the Legislative Assembly of the Northwest Territories as constituted before September 1, 1905, the Commissioner in Council of the Yukon Territory, and the Commissioner in Council of the Northwest Territories. *Interpretation Act*, R.S.C. 1985, c. I-21, s. 35.

LEGISLATIVE GRANT. The school grant payable by the Department of Education in respect of the operation of a school. *The Larger School Units Act*, R.S.S. 1978, c. L-7, s. 2.

LEGISLATIVE HISTORY. The history of a statute from its conception through enactment.

LEGISLATIVE LIBRARY OF BRITISH COLUMBIA. The books, papers, furniture, stationery and other articles in the possession of the Legislative Assembly on April 11, 1894, and all additions to that collection, belong to Her Majesty for the use of the Legislative Assembly. *Legislative Library Act*, R.S.B.C. 1979, c. 230, s. 1.

LEGISLATIVE MATERIALS. The annual Statutes of the Province, a consolidation or revision of such Statutes, the Bills, the Journals and the Debates and Proceedings of the House of Assembly, reports, documents and papers of any Committee of the House of Assembly, departmental and other reports and documents to be laid before the House of Assembly, the Royal Gazette, books, forms and other papers required to conduct an election to elect a member to serve in the House of Assembly, and any other reports, books, documents, forms and other papers that the Speaker designates. *Queen's Printer Act*, S.N.S. 1978-79, c. 6, s. 2.

LEGISLATIVE UNION. A union of states or provinces into one new state which subjects the former units to the authority of one central legislature. P.W. Hogg, *Constitutional Law of Canada*, 2d ed. (Toronto: Carswell, 1985) at 83.

LEGISLATOR. *n.* A member of a legislature; a lawmaker.

LEGISLATURE. *n.* 1. A provincial parliament. P.W. Hogg, *Constitutional Law of Canada*, 2d ed. (Toronto: Carswell, 1985) at 86. 2. Includes any legislative body or authority competent to make laws for a dominion. *Evidence acts.* 3. The Lieutenant Governor acting by and with the advice and consent of the legislative assembly of a province. 4. Includes the Lieutenant Governor in Council and the Legislative Assembly of the Northwest Territories as constituted before September 1, 1905, the Commissioner in Council of the Yukon Territory, and the Commissioner in Council of the Northwest Territories. *Interpretation Act*, R.S.C. 1985, c. I-21, s. 35. See PROVINCIAL ~.

LEGITIMATE. *adj.* Lawful; describing children who were born in wedlock.

LEGITIMATION. *n.* The act by which one makes a person born illegitimate legitimate. See DATE OF ~.

LEGITIME IMPERANTI PARERE NECESSE EST. [L.] It is necessary to obey the person who gives an order lawfully.

LENDER. *n.* 1. A bank, credit union or other institution designated which grants a loan. 2. A person who extends credit. See APPROVED ~; MONEY-~; MORTGAGE ~.

LENDING ASSET. A bond, debenture, mortgage, note, hypothec, agreement of sale or any other indebtedness or a prescribed share, but does not include a prescribed security. *Income Tax Act*, R.S.C. 1952, c. 148 (as am. S.C. 1988, c. 55, s. 188(14)), s. 248(1).

LENDING INSTITUTION. 1. A person who lends money in the ordinary course of business or operations. 2. A loan, insurance, trust or other company or corporation, a trustee of trust funds, a credit union authorized to lend money on the security of real or immovable property, a bank or a treasury branch.

LENDING VALUE. 1. The value for lending purposes of the house or housing project determined by the Corporation. *National Housing Act*, R.S.C. 1985, c. N-11, s. 2. 2. In relation to real estate, means the market value of the real estate reduced by those amounts that are attributable to contingencies or assumptions the occurrence of which is remote and that have increased the market value of the real estate, multiplied by the lesser of (a) seventy-five per cent, and (b) such percentage less than seventy-five per cent as the company has determined in accordance with its prudent investment standards to be appropriate in the circumstances. *Loan and Trust Companies Act*, S.N.B. 1987, c. L-11.2, s. 1.

LENGTH. *n.* 1. In the case of a ship that is registered or required by the act to be registered, (i) the distance from the fore part of the uppermost end of the stem to the aft side of the head of the stern post, except that if a stern post is not fitted to the ship the measurement shall be taken to the foreside of the head of the rudder stock, (ii) if the ship has no rudder stock or has a rudder stock situated outside of the hull at the stern, the distance from the foreside of the foremost permanent structure to the aft side of the aftermost permanent structure of the ship not including guards or rubbing strakes, or (iii) if the ship is double-ended, the distance from the aft side of the forward rudder stock to the foreside of the after rudder stock. Canada regulations. 2. In the case of a ship that is not required to be registered, the horizontal distance measured between perpendiculars erected at the extreme ends of the outside of the hull. Canada regulations. 3. (a) In the case of a registered vessel, the length shown in the certificate of registry, and (b) in the case of a licensed vessel, the length measured from the fore part of the head of the stem to the after part of the head of the stern post. Canada regulations. 4. In respect of a ship, (a) 96 per cent of the total length of the ship in metres, or (b) the length of the ship in metres from the foreside of the stem to the axis of the rudder stock, on a water line at 85 per cent of the least moulded depth measured from the top of the keel, whichever is the greater length, except that in ships designated with a rake of keel the water line on which this length is measured shall be parallel to the designed water line. Canada regulations. 5. When used with reference to a lobster, means the distance from the rear of either eye socket to the rear end of the body shell measured along a line parallel to the centre line of the body shell. *Lobster Fishery Regulations*, C.R.C., c. 817, s. 2. 6. In respect of a fish, the distance from the tip of the snout to the centre of the tail. *Yukon Territory Fishery Regulations*, C.R.C., c. 854, s. 2. 7. Of a condom means the unrolled length of the condom, excluding any reservoir, when measured according to the method of measurement set out in Part II. *Medical Devices Regulations*, C.R.C., c. 871, s. 1. See BASE ~; CLOTHING ~; DEVELOPED ~; FLOODABLE ~; OVERALL ~; REGISTERED ~; STAPLE ~; TOTAL ~.

LENGTH-OF-SERVICE INCREASE. An automatic pay increase granted periodically to an employee.

LENGTH OF STAY. The length of time spent in any institution from the admission date to the date of official separation.

LENGTH OF SUPERSTRUCTURE. The length of those parts of the superstructure that lie within the length (L) and extend athwartship in a straight line from side to side of the ship or to within four per cent of the breadth (B) of the ship's side. *Load Line Regulations (Inland)*, C.R.C., c. 1440, s. 1.

LENGTH OVERALL. 1. The length of a vessel from the forward part of the stern to the after side of the rim timbers. Newfoundland statutes. 2. The horizontal distance measured between perpendiculars erected at the extreme ends of the main hull of a vessel. Canada regulations.

LENS. See OPHTHALMIC ~.

LE ROY LE VEULT. [Fr.] The King wishes it.

LE ROY N'EST LIÉ PAR AUCUN STATUT S'IL NE FUT EXPRESSÉMENT NOMMÉ. [Fr.] The King is not bound by any statute if not expressly named in it.

LE ROY REMERCIE SES BONS SUJETS, ACCEPTE LEUR BÉNÉVOLENCE ET AINSI LE VEUT. [Fr.] The King is grateful to his loyal subjects, accepts their benevolence and wishes it this way.

LE ROY S'AVISERA. [Fr.] The King will consider this.

LESION. *n.* An unusual change in a tissue's structure. F.A. Jaffe, *A Guide to Pathological Evidence*, 2d ed. (Toronto: Carswell, 1983) at 179.

LES LOIS NE SE CHARGENT DE PUNIR QUE LES ACTIONS EXTÉRIEURES. [Fr.] Laws do not charge themselves with punishing anything but overt acts.

LESSEE. *n.* 1. The person to whom one makes or gives a lease. 2. The holder of a lease. See NEW ~.

LESSER PLANT NUTRIENT. Any plant nutrient other than nitrogen, phosphorus and potassium. *Fertilizers Regulations*, C.R.C., c. 666, s. 2.

LESSOR. *n.* The person who makes or gives anything to someone else by lease.

LESS PUNISHMENT. Any one or more of the punishments lower in the scale of punishments than the specified punishment. *National Defence Act*, R.S.C. 1985, c. N-5, s. 139(2).

LET. *v.* To lease; to permit; to award a contract.

LETHAL WEAPON. A weapon capable of killing.

LETTER. *n.* A statement in writing that is capable of being transmitted by mail by or to a patient. *Municipal Mental Hospitals Act*, S.N.S. 1969, c. 64, s. 4. See COMMITMENT ~; DEMAND ~; POST ~; ROGATORY ~ S ; UNDELIVERABLE ~.

LETTER CHUTE. An enclosed rectangular shaped metal tube extending through each storey of a building in a continuous vertical line leading directly to a mail dispatching facility at the bottom of the chute. *Mail Receptacles Regulations*, C.R.C., c. 1282, s. 2.

LETTER FORM SET. A kit provided for certified mail service by the Post Office Department for the posting, identification and addressing of mailable matter that may be enclosed in an envelope. *Special Services and Fees Regulations*, C.R.C., c. 1296, s. 39.

LETTER OF CREDIT. A letter, document or other instrument issued by a private lender to secure or guarantee the financial aspects of a trade transaction. See COMMERCIAL ~.

LETTER OF EXCHANGE. A bill of exchange.

LETTER-POST ITEMS. Includes letters, postcards, printed papers, literature for the blind and small packets as described in Article 18 of the Universal Postal Convention, Lausanne, 1974.

Posting Abroad of Letter-Post Items Regulations, C.R.C., c. 1288, s. 2.

LETTERS OF ADMINISTRATION. 1. An instrument, granted by a Surrogate Court, giving authority to an administrator to manage and distribute the estate of a person who died without making a will. 2. Include letters probate, letters of administration or other legal documents purporting to be of the same legal nature granted by a court in another jurisdiction and resealed in a particular province. See PROBATE AND ~.

LETTERS OF ADMINISTRATION WITH WILL ANNEXED. Special letters of administration used when the executor named in the will is unwilling or unable to serve, or when no executor was named in the will.

LETTERS OF SAFE-CONDUCT. A document by which the subject of a nation at war with any country can, under the law of nations, come into that country, travel on the high seas or send goods and merchandise from one place to another without fearing that the subject or the goods will be seized.

LETTERS PATENT. 1. A document sealed with the Great Seal by which a company or person may do something or enjoy privileges not otherwise possible. The document is so called because it is open, with seal affixed, ready to be exhibited to confirm the grant. 2. When used with respect to public lands, includes any instrument by which such lands or any interest therein may be granted or conveyed. *Exchequer Court Act*, R.S.C. 1970, c. E-11, s. 2. 3. A method of incorporation by the grant of a charter of incorporation. H. Sutherland, D.B. Horsley & J.M. Edmiston, eds., *Fraser's Handbook on Canadian Company Law*, 7th ed. (Toronto: Carswell, 1985) at 17. See SUPPLEMENTARY ~.

LETTERS PATENT JURISDICTION. Employ letters patent to incorporate companies. The Minister responsible may with absolute and uncontrolled discretion refuse to issue letters patent upon an application. S.M. Beck *et al.*, *Cases and Materials on Partnerships and Canadian Business Corporations*, (Toronto: The Carswell Company Limited, 1983) at 159.

LETTERS PATENT OF 1947. A document which outlines the office of Governor General, reprinted in the Appendix to the R.S.C. 1985.

LETTERS PROBATE. 1. An instrument, granted by a Surrogate Court, giving authority to an executor to carry out the provisions of a person's will. 2. Include letters probate, letters of administration or other legal documents purporting to be of the same legal nature granted by a court in another jurisdiction and resealed in a particular province.

LETTERS ROGATORY. See ROGATORY LETTERS.

LETTRE DE CHANGE. [Fr.] A bill of exchange. I.F.G. Baxter, *The Law of Banking*, 3d ed. (Toronto: Carswell, 1981) at 60.

LEUCOCYTE. *n.* A white blood cell. F.A. Jaffe, *A Guide to Pathological Evidence*, 2d ed. (Toronto: Carswell, 1983) at 179.

LEVARI FACIAS. [L.] A writ of execution by which a sheriff levied a judgment debt on a debtor's goods and land by seizing and selling those goods and taking any rent and profit from the land until the debt is satisfied.

LEVEL. *n.* A substantially horizontal excavation in the ground or in strata of an underground mine used or usable for (i) drainage or ventilation, or (ii) the ingress or egress of men or materials to or from a mine or part thereof. *Coal Mines Safety Act*, R.S.A. 1980, c. C-15, s. 1. See ACTION ~; EXIT ~; FLIGHT ~; FLOOD ~; GROUNDWATER ~; SAFE ~; SOUND ~.

LEVEL ACCESS. In respect of a polling station, means a polling station that is so located in a building that a person may reach the polling station from the street or roadway and enter the polling station without going up or down any step, stairs or escalator. *Canada Elections Act*, R.S.C. 1985, c. E-2, s. 2.

LEVEL OF ASSESSMENT. That level of valuation which is in accordance with an assessment manual that is approved by the agency, as amended from time to time. *Assessment Management Agency Act*, S.S. 1986, c. A-28.1, s. 2.

LEVEL OF ILLUMINATION. The quantity or intensity of illumination expressed in foot candles and measured (a) in the case of any work that is required to be done by an employee, as close to that work as is reasonably practicable, and (b) in the case of a passageway or general area, 3 feet above the floor. *Canada Safe Illumination Regulations*, C.R.C., c. 1008, s. 2.

LEVIABLE GAS. Gas on which levies are payable under this Act. *Take-or-Pay Costs Sharing Act*, S.A. 1986, c. T-0.1, s. 1.

LEVIABLE VALUE. The fair market value of the property of the deceased passing to any person after the allowances authorized by section 3 are deducted from it. *Probate Fee Act*, R.S.B.C. 1979, c. 338, s. 1.

LEVY. *v.* 1. To raise an amount of money using a writ of execution against the judgment debtor's property. 2. To impose a liability for the payment of a provincial or municipal real property tax.

LEVY. *n.* 1. A payment which results directly or indirectly from a seizure under execution. C.R.B. Dunlop, *Creditor-Debtor Law in Canada* (Toronto: Carswell, 1981) at 424. 2. A tax or duty. See ADJUSTMENT ~; CONTINGENT ~; EQUALIZATION ~; EXPENSES ~; NET REGIONAL ~; PROVINCIAL SCHOOL ~; SPECIAL ~; SPECIAL REGIONAL ~; TELEPHONE ~.

LEX. *n.* [L.] Law.

LEX ACTUS. [L.] The proper law of a transfer. G.H.L. Fridman, *Sale of Goods in Canada*, 3d ed. (Toronto: Carswell, 1986) at 475.

LEX ANGLIAE EST LEX MISERICORDIAE. [L.] English law is a law of mercy.

LEX ANGLIAE SINE PARLIAMENTO MUTARI NON POTEST. [L.] English law can be changed only by Parliament.

LEX BENEFICIALIS REI CONSIMILI REMEDIUM PRAESTAT. [L.] A beneficial law offers a remedy for any case on the same footing.

LEX CAUSAE. [L.] The law governing an issue according to a choice of law rule which originates in the country. J.G. McLeod, *The Conflict of Laws* (Calgary: Carswell, 1983) at 779.

LEX CITIUS TOLERARE VULT PRIVATUM DAMNUM QUAM PUBLICUM MALUM. [L.] The law more easily tolerates private loss than public evil.

LEX CONVENTIONALIS. [L. conventional law] The law which the parties agreed will govern their contract. J.G. McLeod, *The Conflict of Laws* (Calgary: Carswell, 1983) at 779.

LEX DERAISNIA. [L.] The proof of something which a person denies to have done, defeating an adversary's assertion that it was done and showing the thing was unreasonable or improbable.

LEX DILATIONES SEMPER EXHORRET. [L.] The law always detests delays.

LEX DOMICILII. [L.] The law of the country where someone is domiciled. J.G. McLeod, *The Conflict of Laws* (Calgary: Carswell, 1983) at 779.

LEX EST DICTAMEN RATIONIS. [L.] Law is the pronouncement of reason.

LEX EST EXERCITUS JUDICUM TUTISSIMUS DUCTOR. [L.] The law is a judge's safest guide.

LEX EST RATIO SUMMA, QUAE JUBET QUAE SUNT UTILIA ET NECESSARIA, ET

CONTRARIA PROHIBET. [L.] Law is a supreme science which prescribes what is useful and necessary and forbids the contrary.

LEX EST SANCTIO JUSTA, JUBENS HONESTA, ET PROHIBENS CONTRARIA. [L.] Law is a sacred sanction prescribing what is proper and forbidding the contrary.

LEX EST TUTISSIMA CASSIS, SUB CLYPEO LEGIS NEMO DECIPITUR. [L.] The law is the safest helmet; under the law's shield no one is misled on purpose.

LEX FINGIT UBI SUBSISTIT AEQUITAS. [L.] The law can resort to fictions when the resources of equity are exhausted.

LEX FORI. [L. law of the forum] The law of the jurisdiction where a legal proceeding is commenced and heard. J.G. McLeod, *The Conflict of Laws* (Calgary: Carswell, 1983) at 779.

LEX FORI REI. [L.] The law of the defendant's forum. J.G. McLeod, *The Conflict of Laws* (Calgary: Carswell, 1983) at 779.

LEX INJUSTA NON EST LEX. [L.] An interpretation of the law by which law works injustice is bad law.

LEX INTENDIT VICINUM VICINI FACTA SCIRE. [L.] The law asserts that one neighbour should know another's deeds.

LEX LOCI. [L.] The law of a place.

LEX LOCI ACTUS. [L.] The law of the jurisdiction where an act took place. J.G. McLeod, *The Conflict of Laws* (Calgary: Carswell, 1983) at 779.

LEX LOCI CELEBRATIONIS. [L.] The law of the jurisdiction in which a marriage was celebrated. J.G. McLeod, *The Conflict of Laws* (Calgary: Carswell, 1983) at 779.

LEX LOCI CONTRACTUS. [L.] 1. The law of the jurisdiction in which the contract was made. J.G. McLeod, *The Conflict of Laws* (Calgary: Carswell, 1983) at 779. 2. The law of the jurisdiction where the last necessary act to make a contract took place. J.G. McLeod, *The Conflict of Laws* (Calgary: Carswell, 1983) at 196.

LEX LOCI DELICTI. [L.] The law of the jurisdiction where the tort or wrong is considered, legally, to have occurred. J.G. McLeod, *The Conflict of Laws* (Calgary: Carswell, 1983) at 194.

LEX LOCI REGIS ACTUM. [L.] The law of the jurisdiction where the benefit was received. J.G. McLeod, *The Conflict of Laws* (Calgary: Carswell, 1983) at 574.

LEX LOCI REI SITAE. [L.] The law of the jurisdiction where the thing is located.

LEX LOCI SOLUTIONIS. [L.] The law of the jurisdiction in which a debt will be paid, a contract be performed or another obligation met. J.G. McLeod, *The Conflict of Laws* (Calgary: Carswell, 1983) at 779.

LEX MERCATORIA. [L.] Law merchant.

LEX MONETAE. [L.] The law of the jurisdiction whose currency expresses the debt. J.G. McLeod, *The Conflict of Laws* (Calgary: Carswell, 1983) at 513.

LEX NECESSITATIS EST LEX TEMPORIS, SCILICET, INSTANTIS. [L.] The law of necessity is the law at the time, namely, for the moment.

LEX NEMINEM COGIT OSTENDERE QUOD NESCIRE PRAESUMITUR. [L.] The law forces no one to reveal what it is presumed that person does not know.

LEX NIL FRUSTRA FACIT. [L.] The law does nothing without cause.

LEX NON A REGE EST VIOLANDA. [L.] The law may not be violated by the monarch.

LEX NON COGIT AD IMPOSSIBILIA. [L.] The law does not require the impossible.

LEX NON CURAT DE MINIMIS. [L.] The law does not heed trifles.

LEX NON DEBET DEFICERE CONQUERENTIBUS IN JUSTITIA EXHIBENDA. [L.] The law should not fail to dispense justice to those seeking it.

LEX NON DEFICIT IN JUSTITIA EXHIBENDA. [L.] The law does not fail in dispensing justice.

LEX NON FAVET DELICATORUM VOTIS. [L.] The law does not favour the wishes of the scrupulous.

LEX NON INTENDIT ALIQUID IMPOSSIBILE. [L.] The law does not assert anything which is impossible.

LEX NON PRAECIPIT INUTILIA. [L.] The law does not demand useless things.

LEX NON REQUIRIT VERIFICARI QUOD APPARET CURIAE. [L.] The law does not consider it necessary to verify what is apparent to a court.

LEX NON SCRIPTA. [L. unwritten law] The common law.

LEX PATRIAE. [L.] The law of the country to which one owes allegiance. J.G. McLeod, *The Conflict of Laws* (Calgary: Carswell, 1983) at 779.

LEX PERSONALIS. [L. personal law] An

inclusive term of which lex patriae and lex domicilii are examples. J.G. McLeod, *The Conflict of Laws* (Calgary: Carswell, 1983) at 779.

LEX PLUS LAUDATUR QUANDO RATIONE PROBATUR. [L.] The law is most praiseworthy when it is proved by reason.

LEX POSTERIOR DEROGAT PRIORI. [L.] A later act repeals an earlier one.

LEX PROSPICIT NON RESPICIT. [L.] The law looks forward; it does not look backward.

LEX PUNIT MENDACIUM. [L.] The law punishes a lie.

LEX REJICIT SUPERFLUA, PUGNANTIA, INCONGRUA. [L.] The law rejects the unnecessary, inconsistent and incongruous.

LEX REPROBAT MORAM. [L.] The law condemns delay.

LEX RESPICIT AEQUITATEM. [L.] The law has regard for equity.

LEX SCRIPTA. [L. written law] Statutory law.

LEX SCRIPTA SI CESSET, ID CUSTODIRI OPORTET QUOD MORIBUS ET CONSUETUDINE INDUCTUM EST; ET SI QUA IN RE HOC DEFECERIT, TUNC ID QUOD PROXIMUM ET CONSEQUENS EI EST; ET SI ID NON APPAREAT, TUNC, JUS QUO URBS ROMANA UTITUR SERVARI OPORTET. [L.] If written law is silent, one should observe what is inferred from manners and custom; and if that is defective in any way, then whatever is closest and follows from it; and if that is not obvious, then, one should follow the law used by Rome.

LEX SEMPER DABIT REMEDIUM. [L.] The law will always provide a remedy.

LEX SEMPER INTENDIT QUOD CONVENIT RATIONI. [L.] The law always asserts whatever goes along with reason.

LEX SITUS. [L.] The law of the jurisdiction where a thing is located. J.G. McLeod, *The Conflict of Laws* (Calgary: Carswell, 1983) at 779.

LEX SPECIALIS DEROGAT GENERALI. [L.] A special statute repeals a general one.

LEX SPECTAT NATURAE ORDINEM. [L.] The law has regard for natural order.

LEX SUCCURRIT IGNORANTI. [L.] The law aids the ignorant.

LEX TERRAE. [L.] The law of the land.

LEX UNO ORE OMNES ALLOQUITUR. [L.] The law addresses everyone with a single voice.

LEX VALIDATIS. [L.] The law of the jurisdiction which validated a transaction or act. J.G. McLeod, *The Conflict of Laws* (Calgary: Carswell, 1983) at 779.

LEZE-MAJESTY. *n.* An offence against sovereignty; treason.

LIABILITIES. *n.* 1. Of a corporation at any particular time means the aggregate of all debts owing by the corporation, and all other obligations of the corporation to pay an amount, that were outstanding at that time. *Income Tax Act*, R.S.C. 1952, c. 148 (as am. S.C. 1973-74, c. 49, s. 18(1)), s. 130.1(9)(a). 2. All current, long term, and other liabilities and includes all accounts payable, loans payable, trust liabilities or other debts or financial responsibilities of the Territories other than contingent or unproven claims. *Financial Administration Act*, S.N.W.T. 1982, c. 2, s. 2. 3. Includes duties. *Companies acts.* See CONTINGENT ~.

LIABILITY. *n.* 1. The situation in which one is potentially or actually subject to some obligation. 2. Includes part of a liability forming the subject of the judgment. *Collection Act*, R.S.N.S. 1967, c. 39, s. 1. See ACCRUED ~; CONTINGENT ~; CURRENT ~; DEMAND ~; INJURING ~; LONG-TERM ~; NON-PERSONAL ~; OCCUPIERS' ~; OUTLET ~; PRODUCT ~; STRICT ~; TORT ~; VICARIOUS ~.

LIABILITY INSURANCE. 1. Insurance against the responsibility resulting from the ownership, use or registration of an automobile. *Highway Victims Indemnity Act*, R.S.Q. 1977, c. I-5, s. 2. 2. Insurance against liability for loss or damage to persons or property not provided for by a specific class of insurance defined in this Act and arising from any accidental cause. *Insurance Act*, R.S.A. 1980, c. I-5, s. 1. 3. Insurance coming within the class of employers' liability insurance or public liability insurance. *Classes of Insurance Regulations*, C.R.C., c. 977, s. 21. See BODILY INJURY ~; EMPLOYERS' ~; PROPERTY DAMAGE ~; PUBLIC ~.

LIABILITY INSURER. A person regularly engaged in the business of undertaking risks in respect of negligence. Newfoundland statutes.

LIABILITY POLICY. See MOTOR VEHICLE ~.

LIBEL. *n.* The more permanent or written form of a defamatory statement. R.E. Brown, *The Law of Defamation in Canada* (Toronto: Carswell, 1987) at 9. See DEFAMATORY ~; SEDITIOUS ~.

LIBERATA PECUNIA NON LIBERAT OFFERENTEM. [L.] The freeing of money does not free the one who offers.

LIBERATION. See CONDITIONAL ~.

LIBER HOMO. [L.] A free person.

LIBERTAS. *n.* [L.] Freedom.

LIBERTAS EST NATURALIS FACULTAS EJUS QUOD CUIQUE FACERE LIBET, NISI QUOD DE JURE AUT VI PROHIBETUR. [L.] Freedom is a power given by nature to do whatever one pleases, unless that thing is prohibited by the law or by force.

LIBERTAS EST RES INESTIMABILIS. [L.] Freedom is something priceless.

LIBERTICIDE. *n.* One who destroys liberty.

LIBERTIES. See CIVIL ~.

LIBERTINUM INGRATUM LEGES CIVILES IN PRISTINAM SERVITUTEM REDIGUNT; SED LEGES ANGLIAE SEMEL MANUMIS-SUM SEMPER LIBERUM JUDICANT. [L.] Civil laws bring back one who was freed but is ungrateful to original servitude, but English laws adjudge one who was freed as always free.

LIBERTY. *n.* A power or right to do what may otherwise be illegal or wrongful.

LIBERTY TO APPLY. An order by a master or judge which enables parties to come to court again without formally applying.

LIBERUM TENEMENTUM. [L.] A freehold.

LIBRA PENSA. [L.] A pound, by weight, of money.

LIBRARIAN. See CHIEF ~.

LIBRARY. *n.* 1. A collection of books, periodicals, newspapers, film, recordings and other articles and objects of educational or artistic value for circulation or reference and includes branch libraries, mobile units and reading rooms established or used in connection with a library. 2. The National Library. *National Library Act,* R.S.C. 1985, c. N-12, s. 2. See LEGISLATIVE ~ OF BRITISH COLUMBIA; NATIONAL ~; NATIONAL ~ OF CANADA; PUBLIC ~; SCHOOL ~.

LIBRARY BOARD. A board appointed under this Act to have the administration, management, supervision, charge, or control, of a library or to exercise any powers and discharge any duties herein granted to, or charged on, a municipal or regional library board. *Public Libraries Act,* R.S.M. 1970, c. P220, s. 2.

LIBRARY OF PARLIAMENT. A large staff and collection of documents and books for parliamentarians' research and information.

LICENCE. *n.* 1. The permission given to do something which would otherwise be unlawful. 2. A permit, certificate, approval, registration or similar form of permission required by law. 3. An instrument issued conferring upon the holder the privilege of doing the things set forth in it, subject to the conditions, limitations and restrictions contained in it. See BEER ~; BROADCASTING ~; COMPULSORY ~; CONDITIONAL ~; DEVELOPMENT ~; DRIVER'S ~; EXPLORATION ~; FINAL ~; FISHING ~; INTERIM ~; LEAVE AND ~; MINING ~; OPERATOR'S ~; OPTION ~; SPORT FISHING ~; STATION ~; TIMBER ~; WELL ~; ZONE COMMERCIAL ~; ZONE FISHERMAN'S ~; ZONE RECREATIONAL FISHING ~.

LICENCE AREA. An area in respect of which the right, exclusive or otherwise, to cut or remove Crown timber has been or is granted to any person by a management licence, timber permit, timber sale or timber agreement. *The Forest Act,* R.S.S. 1978, c. F-19, s. 2.

LICENCE PLATE. A licence plate issued by the administrator pursuant to The Vehicle Administration Act for a snowmobile, on which there is an imprint or to which there is attached a validation sticker or stickers showing the year and month in which the licence period expires. *Highway Traffic Consequential Amendment Act,* S.S. 1986, c. 33, s. 2.

LICENCE PERIOD. Period for which a certificate of registration for a motor vehicle, trailer or semi-trailer or a licence to drive is issued.

LICENSE. See DEVELOPMENT ~; DRIVER'S ~; LICENCE.

LICENSED BEGINNER. Person licensed under this Act to operate a motor vehicle while accompanied by a licensed chauffeur or a licensed operator. *Motor Vehicle Act,* R.S.N.S. 1967, c. 191, s. 1.

LICENSED DEALER. A dealer who is the holder of a licence.

LICENSED OPERATOR. Person licensed under this Act to operate a motor vehicle on the highway. *Motor Vehicle Act,* R.S.N.S. 1967, c. 191, s. 1.

LICENSED PHARMACIST. A pharmacist who is the holder of a valid licence entitling him to practise and to exercise all the privileges, rights, and authorities of a licensed pharmacist under this Act. *The Pharmaceutical Act,* S.M. 1980-81, c. 12, s. 1.

LICENSED PILOT. A person who holds a valid licence as pilot issued by a Pilotage Authority under the Pilotage Act. *Canada Shipping Act,* R.S.C. 1985, c. S-9, s. 2.

LICENSED PREMISES. The premises in

respect of which a licence has been issued and is in force. *Liquor Control acts.*

LICENSED STUDENT. A person registered hereunder as a student holding a valid licence issued under section 31. *Pharmacy Act*, S.N.B. 1983, c. 100, s. 2.

LICENSED TRUST COMPANY. A trust company or any other body corporate licensed as a trust company under this Act. *Loan and Trust Companies Act*, S.N.B. 1987, c. L-11.2, s. 1.

LICENSED TRUSTEE. A person who is licensed or appointed under this Act. Bankruptcy Act, R.S.C. 1985, c. B-3, s. 2.

LICENSED WHOLESALER. Any wholesaler, jobber of other dealer licensed under this Part. *Excise Tax Act*, R.S.C. 1985, c. E-15, s. 42.

LICENSEE. *n.* 1. A person who holds a subsisting licence. 2. A person who, in furtherance of the sole pursuit of her or his own business, convenience or pleasure goes on another's property, either by that other person's express license or leave, or by that person's implied acquiescence. J.V. DiCastri, *Occupiers' Liability* (Vancouver: Burroughs/Carswell, 1980) at 71. See BARE ~; INCAPACITATED ~; MILL ~; WELL ~.

LICENSEE WITH AN INTEREST. A licensee who is on the owners' premises on their business or through a common interest with them and who enjoys the same rights as an invitee. J.V. DiCastri, *Occupiers' Liability* (Vancouver: Burroughs/Carswell, 1980) at 36.

LICENSE FEE. Includes any provincial license, registration, filing or other fee imposed upon corporations or any class or classes thereof or any individual corporation, or upon any person or partnership carrying on a particular class of business and it also includes a license fee or other fee or tax for specific rights, benefits or franchises granted by the province. *Licensing Act*, R.S.P.E.I. 1974, c. L-15, s. 1.

LICENSING AUTHORITY. A body which may grant or refuse to grant a licence.

LICENTIATE. *n.* A person who has a licence to practise any art or skill.

LICET. [L. it is permitted] Although.

LICET DISPOSITIO DE INTERESSE FUTURO SIT INUTILIS, TAMEN FIERI POTEST DECLARATIO PRAECEDENS QUAE SORTIATUR EFFECTUM, INTERVENIENTE NOVO ACTU. [L.] Though to grant a future interest is useless, it may still become a declaration precedent to take effect when some new act intervenes.

LICITA BENE MISCENTUR, FORMULA NISI JURIS OBSTET. [L.] Things which are permitted are properly combined unless a rule of law stands in the way.

LICITATION. *n.* Exposure for sale to the highest bidder.

LIE. *v.* Of an action, to be, on the facts of the case, able to be properly begun or continued.

LIE DETECTOR TEST. An analysis, examination, interrogation or test taken or performed by means of or in conjunction with a device, instrument or machine, whether mechanical, electrical, electromagnetic, electronic or otherwise, and that is taken or performed for the purpose of assessing or purporting to assess the credibility of a person.

LIEGE. *n.* One bound by a feudal tenure; a subject.

LIEGE-LORD. *n.* A superior lord; a sovereign.

LIEGEMAN. *n.* One who owes allegiance to another.

LIEGES. *n.* An ambassador who is resident.

LIEN. *n.* 1. The right of one person to retain what is in her or his possession but belongs to another person, until certain demands of the person in possession are satisfied. E.L.G. Tyler & N.E. Palmer, eds., *Crossley Vaines' Personal Property*, 5th ed. (London: Butterworths, 1973) at 137. 2. A charge, similar to a mortgage, against property. B.J. Reiter, R.C.B. Risk & B.N. McLellan, *Real Estate Law*, 3d ed. (Toronto: Emond Montgomery, 1986) at 909. 3. A right created by common law or generally by statute when a worker or artisan repairs, adds to or otherwise improves a moveable object or chattel so that the worker or artisan has the right to hold that object or chattel until the owner pays the account. D.N. Macklem & D.I. Bristow, *Construction and Mechanics' Liens in Canada*, 5th ed. (Toronto: Carswell, 1985) at 579. 4. Includes any right to or interest in any license or lease obtained by registration of any instrument, not a transfer or a declaration of shares, or by registration of a certificate of judgment or writ of attachment. *Mines Act*, R.S.N.S. 1967, c. 185, s. 1. 5. Includes any judgment, mortgage, encumbrance or charge on land other than a lien for municipal taxes. *Land Titles Clarification Act*, R.S.N.S. 1967, c. 162, s. 5. See AGENT'S ~; CONSTRUCTION ~; CREATION OF ~; EQUITABLE ~; GENERAL ~; MECHANIC'S ~; OPERATOR'S ~; PARTICULAR ~; PERSON HAVING A ~; POSSESSORY ~; PURCHASER'S ~; STATUTORY ~; UNPAID SELLER'S ~; VENDOR'S ~.

LIEN CLAIMANT. A person having a preserved or perfected lien.

LIEN FUND. The percentage retained by an owner to be holdback along with any amount the owner should pay under the contract which was not paid in good faith before the lien was registered. D.N. Macklem & D.I. Bristow, *Construction and Mechanics' Liens in Canada*, 5th ed. (Toronto: Carswell, 1985) at 173. See MINOR ~.

LIENHOLDER. *n.* Any person having a lien.

LIEU. *n.* [Fr.] A room; a place. See IN LIEU OF.

LIEUTENANT. *n.* A deputy; a rank in the army or navy.

LIEUTENANT GOVERNOR. *var.* **LIEUTENANT-GOVERNOR.** The lieutenant governor or other chief executive officer or administrator carrying on the government of the province indicated by the enactment, by whatever title that officer is designated, and, in relation to the Yukon Territory or the Northwest Territories, means the Commissioner thereof.

LIEUTENANT GOVERNOR IN COUNCIL. *var.* **LIEUTENANT-GOVERNOR IN COUNCIL.** The lieutenant governor acting by and with the advice of, or by and with the advice and consent of, or in conjunction with the executive council of the province indicated by the enactment and, in relation to the Yukon Territory or the Northwest Territories, means the Commissioner thereof.

LIEUT. GOV. *abbr.* Lieutenant Governor.

LIFE. *n.* The law presumes that any given state of facts continues unless it is demonstrated either that inevitably it must end or it did end. Once it is established that life existed on a given date, the law presumes it will continue and does not presume that a human life must end within a certain period. See DETERMINED ~; DURABLE ~; EXPECTATION OF ~; NECESSARIES OF ~; SERVICE ~.

LIFE ANNUITY. 1. A yearly payment while any particular life or lives continues. 2. An annuity that continues for the duration of the life of the annuitant, whether or not it is thereafter continued to some other person. See DEFERRED ~.

LIFE COMPANY. A company registered to transact the business of life insurance.

LIFE CORPORATION. See FOREIGN ~.

LIFE ESTATE. A grant to a person for her or his life. E.L.G. Tyler & N.E. Palmer, eds., *Crossley Vaines' Personal Property*, 5th ed. (London: Butterworths, 1973) at 5.

LIFEGUARD. *n.* A person appointed by the owner or operator to maintain surveillance over the bathers while they are on the deck or in the pool and to supervise bather safety. *Public Health Act*, R.R.O. 1980, Reg. 849, s. 1.

LIFE INSURANCE. Insurance whereby an insurer undertakes to pay insurance money: (i) on death; (ii) on the happening of an event or contingency dependent on human life; (iii) at a fixed or determinable future time; or (iv) for a term dependent on human life; and, without limiting the generality of the foregoing, includes: (v) accidental death insurance; (vi) disability insurance; and (vii) an undertaking given by an insurer to provide an annuity or what would be an annuity except that the periodic payments may be unequal in amount; but does not include accident insurance.

LIFE INSURANCE BUSINESS. Includes (a) an annuities business, and (b) the business of issuing contracts all of any part of the issuer's reserves for which vary in amount depending upon the fair market value of a specified group of assets, carried on by a life insurance corporation or a life insurer. *Income Tax Act*, R.S.C. 1952, c. 148 (as am. S.C. 1970-71-72, c. 63), s. 248(1).

LIFE INSURANCE PLAN. A plan, fund or arrangement, provided, furnished or offered by an employer to an employee that provides upon the death of the employee a benefit either in a lump sum or by periodic payments to a beneficiary, survivor or dependant of the employee, and includes accidental death and dismemberment insurance. *Employment Standards Act*, R.R.O. 1980, Reg. 282, s. 1.

LIFE INSURANCE POLICY. Includes an annuity contract and a contract all or any part of the insurer's reserves for which vary in amount depending upon the fair market value of a specified group of assets. *Income Tax Act*, R.S.C. 1952, c. 148 (as am. S.C. 1980-81-82-83, c. 140, s. 96(7)), s. 138(12)(f). See PARTICIPATING ~; REGISTERED ~.

LIFE INSURANCE POLICY IN CANADA. A life insurance policy issued or effected by an insurer upon the life of a person resident in Canada at the time the policy was issued or effected. *Income Tax Act*, R.S.C. 1952, c. 148 (as am. S.C. 1980-81-82-83, c. 140, s. 96(7)), s. 138(12)(g).

LIFE INSURED. See GROUP ~.

LIFE INSURER. 1. Includes a person who is licensed or otherwise authorized under a law of Canada or a province to issue contracts that are annuity contracts. 2. Any body corporate licensed to transact the business of life insurance or annuities.

LIFE INTEREST. An interest for another's life (pur autre vie) or one's own life.

LIFEJACKET. *n.* A personal flotation device that provides buoyancy adequate to keep a worker's head above water, face up, without effort by the worker. *Occupational Health and Safety Act*, R.R.O. 1980, Reg. 691, s. 1.

LIFE-SAVING APPLIANCES. See RULES FOR ~.

LIFE SUPPORT SERVICE. See ADVANCED ~.

LIFE TENANT. One who beneficially holds property as long as she or he lives.

LIFETIME. *n.* As applied to a work means the lifetime of the work as estimated by the engineer.

LIFO. *abbr.* Last-in, first-out.

LIFT. See INCLINE ~.

LIFT CHARGE. 1. A charge for lifting heavy or bulky articles to, and relifting from, the crane scow or lighter, excluding slinging to or unslinging from the crane. *Montreal Floating Crane No. 1 Heavy-Lift Tariff By-law*, C.R.C., c. 1077, s. 2. 2. A charge for lifting heavy or bulky articles to, and relifting from, the derrick barge or from the hold to the deck or another hold of the same vessel or another vessel or vice versa, excluding slinging to or unslinging from the derrick. *Hamilton Harbour Floating Derrick Tariff By-law*, C.R.C., c. 896, s. 2.

LIFTING DEVICE. 1. A permanently installed system for the purpose of raising, lowering or swinging materials, which includes its rails and supports but does not include a crane, elevator, mine hoist, utility hoist or tugger hoist. *Occupational Health and Safety Act*, R.R.O. 1980, Reg. 694, s. 1. 2. A device that is used to raise or lower any material or object and includes its rails and other supports but does not include a device to which the Elevating Devices Act applies. *Occupational Health and Safety Act*, R.R.O. 1980, Reg. 692, s. 1.

LIFTING MACHINERY. Any fixed cargo gear used in hoisting or lowering. *Tackle Regulations*, C.R.C., c. 1494, s. 2.

LIGAN. *n.* Goods fastened to a cork or buoy so that they can be retrieved and sunk in the sea.

LIGATURE. *n.* A long and slender object which constricts and is applied around some part of the body. F.A. Jaffe, *A Guide to Pathological Evidence*, 2d ed. (Toronto: Carswell, 1983) at 179.

LIGATURE STRANGULATION. Strangulation caused when a ligature is applied around the neck. F.A. Jaffe, *A Guide to Pathological Evidence*, 2d ed. (Toronto: Carswell, 1983) at 179.

LIGEANCE. *n.* The faithful and true obedience of a subject to a sovereign; the territory and dominion of a liege-lord.

LIGEANTIA EST VINCULUM FIDEI; LIGEANTIA EST LEGIS ESSENTIA. [L.] Ligeance is the bond of faithfulness; ligeance is the indispensable element of the law.

LIGHT. *n.* A point source of light radiation. *Aerodrome Minimum Lighting Order*, C.R.C., c. 18, s. 2. See ALL-ROUND ~; AUXILIARY ~; BLUE ~; DAY~; EMERGENCY ~S; EXIT ~S; FLASHING ~; FOG ~; MASTHEAD ~; RED ~; SIDE ~S; STERN ~; TOWING ~; TRAFFIC CONTROL ~.

LIGHT BEER. Beer containing not more than 2.5 per cent absolute alcohol by volume. *Brewery Departmental Regulations*, C.R.C., c. 566, s. 2.

LIGHT DUTY MOTOR VEHICLE. A motor vehicle having a gross vehicle weight of 2,720 kilograms or less, but does not include a motorcycle. *Environmental Protection Act*, R.R.O. 1980, Reg. 311, s. 1.

LIGHT DUTY VEHICLE. (a) A passenger car, or (b) any other vehicle having a gross vehicle weight rating of 6,000 pounds (2 721.6 kg) or less but does not include an off-road utility vehicle. *Motor Vehicle Safety Regulations*, C.R.C., c. 1038, s. 2.

LIGHTER CHARGE. A charge for renting or leasing a lighter for use in connection with crane service. *Montreal Floating Crane No. 1 Heavy-Lift Tariff By-law*, C.R.C., c. 1077, s. 2.

LIGHTER-THAN-AIR AIRCRAFT. Any aircraft supported by its buoyancy in the air. *Air Regulations*, C.R.C., c. 2, s. 101.

LIGHTING. See CSA INDUSTRIAL ~ STANDARD; EMERGENCY ~ SYSTEM; OUTLINE ~.

LIGHTING FIXTURE RACEWAY. A raceway which may or may not be a part of a lighting fixture and which is designed to support or suspend the lighting fixture or to hold conductors supplying power to the lighting fixture. *Power Corporation Act*, R.R.O. 1980, Reg. 794, s. 0.

LIGHTING SYSTEM. That part of an electrical system designed to provide illumination in an area normally occupied by an employee in the performance of his work. *Canada Safe Illumination Regulations*, C.R.C., c. 1008, s. 2.

LIGHT METAL ALLOY. An alloy that includes aluminum, magnesium or titanium, either singly or in combination, in which the total content of any or all of those constituents exceeds 15% by weight, or in which the content of magnesium and titanium together exceeds 10% by weight. *Coal Mine Regulation Act*, R.S.B.C. 1979, c. 52, s. 1.

LIGHTNING. *n.* Is deemed to include other electrical currents. *Insurance Act*, S.N.W.T. 1975 (3d Sess.), c. 5, s. 67.

LIGHTNING PROTECTION SYSTEM. A complete system of air terminals, conductors, ground terminals, interconnecting conductors, arresters and other conductors or fittings required to complete the system. *An Act to Amend the Electrical Installation and Inspection Act*, S.N.B. 1983, c. 28, s. 1.

LIGHTNING ROD. Includes any apparatus, material, appliance, or device used or intended or purporting to be used for the protection of a building or its contents from damage from lightning.

LIGHTNING ROD SYSTEM. All materials, apparatus and equipment installed or designed to be installed on a building or structure to act as a conductor to divert lightning from a building or structure to the ground. *Lightning Rod Act*, R.S.P.E.I. 1974, c. L-16, s. 1.

LIGHT TRUCK TIRE. A tire designated by its manufacturer as primarily intended for use on light weight trucks or multipurpose passenger vehicles. *Motor Vehicle Tire Safety Regulations*, C.R.C., c. 1039, s. 2.

LIGHT TURKEY. A turkey that is 103 days old or less. *Canadian Turkey Marketing Quota Regulations*, C.R.C., c. 661, s. 2.

LIGULA. *n.* [L.] A transcript or copy of a deed or court-roll.

LIKE GOODS. In relation to any other goods, means (a) goods that are identical in all respects to the other goods, or (b) in the absence of any goods described in paragraph (a), goods the uses and other characteristics of which closely resemble those of the other goods. *Special Imports Measures Act*, R.S.C. 1985, c. S-15, s. 2.

LIMBING. *n.* The act of removing limbs from a tree before or after felling. *Occupational Health and Safety Act*, R.R.O. 1980, Reg. 692, s. 107.

LIMESTONE. See AGRICULTURAL ~.

LIMIT. See ANNUAL GAINS ~; AUTHORIZED ~; CUMULATIVE GAINS ~; INTERLOCKING ~S; MAXIMUM ACCEPTABLE ~; MAXIMUM DESIRABLE ~; MAXIMUM TOLERABLE ~; REASONABLE ~S; YARD ~S.

LIMITATION. *n.* 1. Of an interest or estate, the designation of the greatest period during which it will continue. 2. Includes any provision whereby property or any interest is disposed of, created or conferred. Perpetuities acts. See EXECUTORY ~; STATUTE OF ~S; WORDS OF ~.

LIMITATION OF ACTION. A fixed period within which, following the maxim "interest reipublicae ut sit finis litium", proceedings must be taken or an action brought.

LIMITATIONS PERIOD. The time period specified by a statute and within which an action must be brought or a complaint filed.

LIMITED. *adj.* 1. One of the words required as part of every corporate name. H. Sutherland, D.B. Horsley & J.M. Edmiston, eds., *Fraser's Handbook on Canadian Company Law*, 7th ed. (Toronto: Carswell, 1985) at 436 and 437. 2. May be used in the firm name of a limited partnership but only in the expression "Limited Partnership". *Limited Partnership Act*, S.N.B. 1984, c. L-9.1, s. 6(3).

LIMITED ACCESS HIGHWAY. A public highway that may be entered or left only at specially provided entrances or exits.

LIMITED ADMINISTRATION. The temporary and special administration of a testator's or intestate's designated particular effects.

LIMITED COMPANY. Includes a company limited by shares, a company limited by guarantee and a specially limited company. *Companies Act*, R.S.A. 1980, c. C-20, s. 1. See SPECIAL ~; SPECIFICALLY ~.

LIMITED-DIVIDEND HOUSING COMPANY. *var.* **LIMITED DIVIDEND HOUSING COMPANY.** A company incorporated to construct, hold and manage a low-rental housing project, whose dividends payable are limited by the terms of its charter or instrument of incorporation to 5 per cent per annum or less.

LIMITED EXECUTOR. An executor with an appointment which is limited in time or place or subject-matter.

LIMITED FREIGHT VEHICLE. Any motor vehicle operated at any time on a highway by, for or on behalf of any person who charges or collects compensation for the transportation of freight in or on the motor vehicle, where the operation is carried on solely under a limited number of special or individual contracts or agreements and where the motor vehicle is not available for use by the general public. *Motor Carrier Act*, R.S.B.C. 1979, c. 286, s. 1.

LIMITED HAIL INSURANCE. Insurance against loss of or damage to property other than crops caused by hail.

LIMITED INSURANCE. Insurance against a loss in production of apples caused by an insured peril in which a reduction in grade or quality is not taken into account in evaluating the loss. *Crop Insurance Act (Ontario)*, R.R.O. 1980, Reg. 198, s. 3.

LIMITED OR INHERENT EXPLOSION INSURANCE. Insurance against loss of or damage to the property insured caused by the explosion of dust, gas or any substance, where the explosion arises out of hazards inherent in the business conducted on the premises.

LIMITED OWNER. A tenant for life, by the curtesy or in tail, or any person who does not have a fee simple absolutely.

LIMITED PARTNERSHIP. Partnership in which the liability of some partners is limited to their capital contribution and in which these limited partners do not exercise management functions with respect to the business of the partnership. See EXTRA-PROVINCIAL ~; PARTNERSHIP.

LIMITED PASSENGER VEHICLE. A motor vehicle, other than a public vehicle, which motor vehicle, whether available or not for use by the public, is operated at any time on a highway by, for or on behalf of any person who charges or collects compensation for the transportation of passengers in or on the motor vehicle, but does not include a taxicab operating exclusively in one municipality. *Motor Carrier Act*, R.S.B.C. 1979, c. 286, s. 1.

LIMITED PRODUCTION. Annual production of less than 1 000 t (metric) of ore. *Mineral Act*, R.S.B.C. 1979, c. 259, s. 1.

LIMITED VEHICLE. Includes a limited passenger vehicle and a limited freight vehicle. *Motor Carrier Act*, R.S.B.C. 1979, c. 286, s. 1.

LIMITÉE. *adj.* [Fr.] One of the words which must form part of every corporate name. H. Sutherland, D.B. Horsley & J.M. Edmiston, eds., *Fraser's Handbook on Canadian Company Law*, 7th ed. (Toronto: Carswell, 1985) at 436 and 437.

LIMIT HOLDER. The holder of the right to cut timber or the owner of the land or the holder of the cutting licence when that person has not assigned the cutting rights to a third party.

LIMITING DISTANCE. The distance from an exposing building face towards a property line, the centre line of a street, lane, public thoroughfare or an imaginary line between 2 buildings on the same property, measured at right angles to the exposing building face. *Building Code Act*, R.R.O. 1980, Reg. 87, s. 1.

LIMIT STATES. Those conditions of a building structure in which the building ceases to fulfil the function for which it was designed. *Building Code Act*, R.R.O. 1980, Reg. 87, s. 4.1.4.1. See SERVICEABILITY ~; ULTIMATE ~.

LIMOUSINE. *n.* A commercial passenger vehicle, other than a taxicab not provided with a taxi meter, having a seating capacity of not less than five and not more than 10 persons including a uniformed driver, and used for transportation of passengers on a zone fare basis. *Government Airport Concession Operations Regulations*, C.R.C., c. 1565, s. 2.

LINE. *n.* 1. An ordered series of relatives. 2. Includes the space between a transmitter and a receiver of telecommunications and any other channel of transmission of telecommunications. 3. A boundary. 4. A route used to give surface access to any land for the purpose of carrying out a geophysical, geological or engineering survey. *Territorial Land Use Regulations*, C.R.C., c. 1524, s. 2. See BASE ~; BILGE BOUNDARY ~; BONDING ~; BOUNDARY ~; BRANCH ~; BUILDING ~; CENTRE ~; COMMUNICATION ~; CREDIT ~; DECK ~; DISTRIBUTION ~; EXPANSION ~; FLIGHT ~; FLOW ~; FLUIDS ~; GAS ~; GATHERING ~; INBRED ~; ~S; LOAD ~; LOCATION ~; LONG~; MARGIN ~; MINERAL ~; MORNING ~; MULTIPHASE ~; NIGHT-~; OIL ~; OVERHEAD ~; PICKET ~; PIPE~; POVERTY ~; PRIVATE ~; PROOF ~; ROAD IMPROVEMENT ~; ROAD ~; SECONDARY ~; SEPARATION ZONE OR ~; SERVICE ~; SET- ~; SOLIDS ~; SUPPLY ~; TELECOMMUNICATION ~; TELEPHONE ~; TRANSMISSION ~; UTILITY ~.

LINEAGE. *n.* A family, progeny or race in either ascending or descending order.

LINEAL CONSANGUINITY. The relationship which exists between people descended from each other in a line, e.g. grandparent, parent, child, grandchild.

LINEAL DESCENT. The proper bequest of an estate from an ancestor to an heir.

LINEA RECTA SEMPER PRAEFERTUR TRANSVERSALI. [L.] A direct line is always preferred to a collateral one.

LINE EMPLOYEE. An employee who produces and distributes the employer's products.

LINE INDOCTRINATION. Experience acquired during flight time in service as a crew member performing the duties of his station under supervision or as an observer observing a qualified crew member perform those duties. *Air Carriers Using Large Aeroplanes Order*, C.R.C., c. 21, s. 2.

LINE MAKE. Line make as defined in the individual dealer agreement failing which it shall be defined according to the standards and the practices of the industry. *Motor Vehicle Franchise Act*, S.N.B. 1987, c. 70, s. 1.

LINEMAN. *n.* A person who, (i) operates, maintains and services power lines used to conduct electricity from generating plants to consumers, and (ii) constructs or assembles a system of power lines used to conduct electricity from generating plants to consumers. *Apprenticeship and Tradesmen's Qualification Act*, R.R.O. 1980, Reg. 46, s. 1.

LINER. See CHIMNEY ~; INNER~.

LINES. *n.* The wire, cables or other conductors used for the purpose of conveying or distributing power for telegraph, telephone or power purposes. See EASTERN ~; LINE; LOAD ~.

LINE-UP. *n.* Presenting a suspect to be identified out of a group. S.A. Cohen, *Due Process of Law* (Toronto: Carswell, 1977) at 83.

LING COD. A fish of the species Ophiodon elongatus commonly known as ling cod. *British Columbia Fishery (General) Regulations*, C.R.C., c. 840, s. 2.

LINK. *n.* 1. A measure used by surveyors in the past equal to 7.92 inches. 2. 1/100 chain. *Weights and Measures Act*, S.C. 1970-71-72, c. 36, schedule II.

LIQUEFIED PETROLEUM GAS. 1. Includes any matter or substance that is composed predominantly of any of the following hydrocarbons or mixtures of them, namely, propane, propylene, butane (normal or isobutane) or butylene. 2. Any material with a gauge pressure exceeding 25 pounds per square inch at 70°F, or any liquid inflammable material having a Reid vapour pressure exceeding 40 pounds per square inch at 100°F. *Electric Sparks Prevention Regulations*, C.R.C., c. 1181, s. 3.

LIQUID. See FLAMMABLE ~; INFLAMMABLE ~; NATURAL GAS ~; PLANT ~S.

LIQUID ASSETS. Cash or property which can be easily realized.

LIQUIDATE. *v.* To change assets into cash.

LIQUIDATED. *adj.* Ascertained, fixed.

LIQUIDATED DAMAGES. Damages of a particular amount fixed by a judgment or stipulated as a true pre-estimate by parties to a contract.

LIQUIDATED DEMAND. A specific amount claimed.

LIQUIDATING TRADE. Effecting settlement of a commodity futures contract, (a) in relation to a long position, by assuming an offsetting short position in relation to a contract entered into on the same commodity exchange or a related commodity exchange for a like quantity and quality, grade or size of the same commodity deliverable during the same designated future month, (b) in relation to a short position, by assuming an offsetting long position in relation to a contract entered into on the same commodity exchange or a related commodity exchange for a like quantity and quality, grade or size of the same commodity deliverable during the same designated future month, or (c) by an offsetting exchange for the cash commodity.

LIQUIDATION PROCEEDINGS. Any proceedings pursuant to which all or any substantial portion of the property in the control or possession of a collector is taken or released from his control or possession for the purposes of receivership proceedings, sale or repossession by a secured creditor, winding-up proceedings or for the purpose of distribution to creditors. *Department of Revenue & Financial Services Amendment Act*, S.S. 1984-85-86, c. 62, s. 48.

LIQUIDATOR. *n.* The person appointed to wind up a company.

LIQUID CAPITAL. The amount by which active assets exceed the sum of total liabilities.

LIQUID INDUSTRIAL WASTE. Liquid waste that results from industrial processes, manufacturing or commercial operations. See HAULED ~.

LIQUOR. *n.* Any liquid or substance that: (i) may be used as food or a beverage; and (ii) is intoxicating; and includes: (iii) spirituous, fermented and malt liquor and wine; (iv) any combination of liquors and drinks or preparations of mixtures; or (v) any mixed liquor or liquid; that may be used as a beverage and is intoxicating. See ALCOHOLIC ~; INTOXICATING ~; MALT ~.

LIQUOR STORE. 1. A government liquor store, government beer store or government wine store, or an agency established by the general manager under this Act. *Liquor Distribution Act*, R.S.B.C. 1979, c. 238, s. 1. 2. (i) A liquor store operated by a vendor, (ii) premises operated by an Agent, or (iii) that part of the premises operated by an Agent that is used by him for the sale of liquor. *Liquor Act*, S.N.W.T. 1985 (3d Sess.), c. 6, s. 4 (in part).

LIS. *n.* [L.] An action or suit; a controversy or dispute.

LIS ALIBI PENDENS. [L. a suit pending somewhere else] A plea that an action in one forum should be postponed until litigation begun elsewhere is concluded. C.R.B. Dunlop, *Creditor-Debtor Law in Canada* (Toronto: Carswell, 1981) at 484.

LIS MOTA. [L.] Anticipated or existing litigation.

LIS PENDENS. [L. a pending suit] To register a lis pendens is to give intending mortgagees or purchasers notice of the litigation.

LIST. *n.* An employment list, a promotion list or a re-employment list. Public Service acts. See ASSESSMENT ~; BAND ~; BLACK ~; CONTROL ~; CREW ~; ELECTION ~; ELIGIBLE ~; EMPLOYMENT ~; EXPORT CONTROL ~; JURY ~; LAW ~; MINIMUM EQUIPMENT ~; POLLING ~; PRICE ~; PROMOTION ~; RE-EMPLOYMENT ~; VOTERS ~.

LISTED. *adj.* 1. Refers to an appliance shown in a list published by a testing agency whose listing means that the appliance complies with the regulations. *Gas Act*, R.S.B.C. 1979, c. 149, s. 1. 2. Certified for its intended use as having been produced under the certification program of Underwriters' Laboratories of Canada or Canadian Standards Association. *Building Code Act*, R.R.O. 1980, Reg. 87, s. 1.

LISTED DRUG PRODUCT. A drug or combination of drugs identified by a specific product name or manufacturer and designated as a listed drug product. *Ontario Drug Benefits Act*, S.O. 1986, c. 27, s. 1.

LISTED PERSONAL PROPERTY. Of a taxpayer means his personal-use property that is all or any portion of, or any interest in or right to, any (i) print, etching, drawing, painting, sculpture, or other similar work of art, (ii) jewellery, (iii) rare folio, rare manuscript, or rare book, (iv) stamp, or (v) coin. *Income Tax Act*, R.S.C. 1952, c. 148 (as am. S.C. 1970-71-72, c. 63), c. 54(e).

LISTED STOCK. A security admitted for trading on a stock exchange.

LISTED SUBSTANCE. A substance, other than a drug, designated as a listed substance. *Ontario Drug Benefits Act*, S.O. 1986, c. 27, s. 1.

LISTING. See CO-OPERATIVE ~; EXCLUSIVE ~; MULTIPLE ~; OPEN ~.

LISTING AGREEMENT. A contract during which a vendor agrees to pay a broker commission on any exchange or sale no matter how it took place. B.J. Reiter, R.C.B. Risk & B.N. McLellan, *Real Estate Law*, 3d ed. (Toronto: Emond Montgomery, 1986) at 90.

LIST OF ELECTORS. 1. A list made or revised under this Act of persons entitled to vote at an election and includes a certified copy of the list. *Election Act*, R.S.A. 1980, c. E-2, s. 1. 2. Either the preliminary list of electors or the official list of electors, as the context requires. See OFFICIAL ~; PRELIMINARY ~.

LITERAL PROOF. Evidence in writing.

LITERARY AGENT. A person who agrees to negotiate contracts on behalf of an author. H.G. Fox, *The Canadian Law of Copyright and Industrial Designs*, 2d ed. (Toronto: Carswell, 1967) at 586.

LITERARY AND ARTISTIC WORKS. Any production in the literary, scientific or artistic domain, whatever may be the mode or form of its reproduction, such as books, pamphlets, and other writings, dramatic or dramatico-musical works, choreographic works and entertainments in dumb show, the acting form of which is fixed in writing or otherwise; musical compositions with or without words; works of drawing, painting, architecture, sculpture, engraving and lithography; illustrations, geographical charts; plans, sketches, and plastic works relative to geography, topography, architecture or science. *Copyright Act*, R.S.C. 1970, c. C-30, schedule II, article 2.

LITERARY WORK. 1. Includes maps, charts, plans, tables and compilations. *Copyright Act*, R.S.C. 1985, c. C-42, s. 2. 2. Includes any work expressed in writing or print regardless of their style or quality. H.G. Fox, *The Canadian Law of Copyright and Industrial Designs*, 2d ed. (Toronto: Carswell, 1967) at 99. See EVERY ORIGINAL LITERARY, DRAMATIC, MUSICAL AND ARTISTIC WORK.

LITIGANT. *n.* A person who engages in a lawsuit.

LITIGATION. *n.* A law-suit.

LITIGATION ADMINISTRATOR. Formerly known as an administrator ad litem.

LITIGATION GUARDIAN. Formerly known as next friend or guardian ad litem, a person who acts on behalf of an absentee, minor or mentally incompetent person. M.M. Orkin, *The Law of Costs*, 2d ed. (Aurora: Canada Law Book, 1987) at 2-34.1.

LITIGATION PRIVILEGE. Attaches to correspondence and other material prepared in anticipation of litigation.

LITIS AESTIMATIO. [L.] The assessment of damages.

LITIS NOMEN OMNEM ACTIONEM SIGNIFICAT, SIVE RE REM, SIVE IN PERSONAM SIT. [L.] The term "lis" applies to every action, whether it is in rem or in personam.

LITRE. *n.* 1. 1/1 000 cubic metre. *Weights and Measures Act,* S.C. 1970-71-72, c. 36, schedule I. 2. (a) With respect to fuel in liquid form, one cubic decimetre, or (b) with respect to fuel in the form of liquefied petroleum gas, 0.5 kg. *Motor Fuel Tax Act,* S.B.C. 1985, c. 76, s. 1. 3. When it applies to propane gas, butane gas or liquefied petroleum gas, is equivalent to 0.50887 kg. *Fuel Tax Act,* S.Q. 1978, c. 28, s. 1. See NTP ~.

LITTER. *v.* To throw, drop, or deposit or cause to be deposited any glass bottle, glass, nails, tacks, cans or scraps of metals or any rubbish, refuse or waste.

LITTER. *n.* 1. (a) Rubbish, garbage or waste materials, including containers, packages, bottles, cans or parts of them; or (b) any abandoned or discarded article, product of goods manufacture; but not including wastes of the primary processes of mining, logging, sawmilling, farming or manufacturing. 2. Includes material left or abandoned in a place other than a receptacle or place intended or approved for receiving such material.

LIVABLE FLOOR AREA. (a) In the case of a one-family dwelling or semi-detached dwelling, the aggregate of all floor areas, measured from the outside faces of enclosing walls, less any area that does not form an integral part of the habitable accommodation, and (b) in the case of a multiple-family dwelling, the aggregate of the area of the building at grade level, plus the areas of any other floors above or below grade level, designed and usable as living quarters, all measured from the outside faces of enclosing walls. *National Housing Loan Regulations,* C.R.C., c. 1108, s. 2.

LIVE. *adj.* 1. In respect of an electrical facility, that the electrical facility (a) produces, contains, stores or is electrically connected to a source of alternating or direct current of an ampacity and voltage that is dangerous to employees, or (b) contains any hydraulic, pneumatic or other kind of energy that is capable of making the facility dangerous to employees. *Canada Electrical Safety Regulations,* C.R.C., c. 998, s. 2. 2. Electrically connected to a source of potential difference, or electrically charged so as to have a potential different from that of the earth. *Power Corporation Act,* R.R.O. 1980, Reg. 794, s. 0.

LIVE LOAD. The load other than dead load to be assumed in the design of the structural members of a building and includes loads resulting from snow, rain, wind, earthquake and those due to occupancy, including movable partitions. *Building Code Act,* R.R.O. 1980, Reg. 87, s. 1.

LIVERY. *n.* 1. Delivery; giving possession or seisin. 2. A motor vehicle (i) that has a seating capacity of not more than 12 persons, not including the operator, and (ii) that is used to transport passengers and their baggage to a requested destination but does not include a motor vehicle that is operated outside a city or town (iii) at regular intervals, (iv) in accordance with a set time schedule, or (v) over a specified route. *Motor Transport Act,* R.S.A. 1980, c. M-20, s. 1.

LIVERY OF SEISIN. In times past, the public act needed to transfer an immediate freehold estate in tenements or lands.

LIVERY STABLE KEEPER. A person who carries on the business of letting or hiring out (i) carriages, sleighs or other vehicles, or (ii) horses or other animals, whether with or without a carriage, sleigh or other vehicle, and whether accompanied by an employee of the livery stable keeper or not, for a money consideration or the equivalent.

LIVESTOCK. *var.* **LIVE STOCK.** 1. Includes (a) horses and other equines, (b) cattle, sheep, goats and other ruminants, and (c) swine, poultry, bees and fur-bearing animals. 2. Horses, cattle, sheep, goats, swine, foxes, fish, mink, rabbits, and poultry and includes such other creatures as may be designated by regulation as livestock for the purposes of this Act. *Feeds Act,* R.S.C. 1985, c. F-9, s. 2. 3. Wild animals and birds, whether captive or not, and domestic animals and birds, but does not include fish or reptiles. *An Act to Amend the Livestock (Health) Act,* S.Nfld. 1983, c. 65, s. 1. See AFFECTED ~; BASIC HERD ~; PEDIGREED ~.

LIVESTOCK ASSOCIATION. Includes an association incorporated or registered under this Act having as its principal objects or any of them the breeding, raising, feeding, finishing, acquiring and selling of livestock, poultry, fur-bearing animals raised in captivity and bees, by or through the association on behalf of its members and patrons, or rendering to members and patrons as producers, services ancillary to such principal objects or any of them. *The Co-operative Production Associations Act,* R.S.S. 1978, c. C-37, s. 57.

LIVESTOCK AUCTION MARKET. A place where animals are sold by public auction. *The Stray Animals Act,* R.S.S. 1978, c. S-60, s. 2.

LIVESTOCK AUCTION SALE AREA. The land on which a stockyard, auction market, field sale or dispersal sale is situated where stock is being held for sale. *Livestock Brand Act*, R.S.B.C. 1979, c. 241, s. 1.

LIVESTOCK DEALER. *var.* **LIVE STOCK DEALER.** 1. Any person who buys cattle from a producer or who acts as an agent of a producer for the sale of cattle, and includes drovers and auctioneers. *Cattle Producers Association Act*, S.M. 1978, c. 15, s. 1. 2. Includes any person who, whether on his own behalf or as agent for another, and whether on a commission basis or otherwise, buys or offers to buy livestock and sells or offers to sell or has in his possession for sale any livestock or livestock carcasses or portions but does not include a resident of the Province who is a farmer and whose transactions in livestock are restricted to those that arise solely from his occupation as a farmer. *Livestock Public Sale Act*, R.S.B.C. 1979, c. 246, s. 1.

LIVESTOCK ENTERPRISE. See SPECIAL-IZED ~.

LIVESTOCK EXCHANGE. *var.* **LIVE STOCK EXCHANGE.** An organization composed of persons engaged in the business of buying and selling, or buying or selling, livestock at a stockyard.

LIVESTOCK FARM. That portion of land that is used for grazing purposes. *Fences and Detention of Stray Livestock Act*, S.N.S. 1975, c. 10, s. 3.

LIVESTOCK FEEDER. A person who raises livestock in Eastern Canada, British Columbia, the Yukon Territory or the Northwest Territories. *Livestock Feed Assistance Act*, R.S.C. 1985, c. L-10, s. 2.

LIVESTOCK HEALTH SERVICES. The professional services of veterinarians to livestock owners. *Livestock Health Services Act*, S.N.S. 1967-68, c. 8, s. 1.

LIVESTOCK INSURANCE. *var.* **LIVE STOCK INSURANCE.** 1. Insurance, not being insurance incidental to some other class of insurance defined by or under this Act, against loss through the death or sickness of or accident to an animal. *Insurance acts.* 2. Insurance against loss of or damage to animals caused by injury, sickness or death. Insurance Act, R.S.B.C. 1979, c. 200, s. 1.

LIVESTOCK LOAN. *var.* **LIVE STOCK LOAN.** 1. A loan made to a farmer by a lender for the purpose of purchasing female cattle, female sheep or such other animals as may be designated by the Lieutenant Governor in Council. 2. A loan made to a farmer by a lender for the purpose of purchasing animals as are designated by the Lieutenant-Governor in Council.

LIVESTOCK OPERATION. See INTENSIVE ~.

LIVESTOCK OWNER. Includes a person who has possession of livestock for farming purposes. *Livestock Health Services Act*, S.N.S. 1967-68, c. 8, s. 1.

LIVE STOCK PRODUCTION. Live stock raising and the production of live stock products. *The Agricultural Incentives Act*, R.S.S. 1978, c. A-11, s. 2.

LIVESTOCK PRODUCTS. *var.* **LIVE STOCK PRODUCTS.** Meat, raw hides, raw furs, dressed poultry, eggs, wool, honey in any form, hay and cordwood.

LIVESTOCK SALE. See PUBLIC ~.

LIVIDITY. *n.* A bluish red or dark red discoloration of the surface of the extremities of the body when the blood stops flowing after death. F.A. Jaffe, *A Guide to Pathological Evidence*, 2d ed. (Toronto: Carswell, 1983) at 179. See CONGESTION ~; DIFFUSION ~; HYPOSTATIC OR CONGESTION ~.

LIVING EXPENSE. Reasonable charges incurred for sleeping accommodation and meals while on duty away from home.

LIVING EXPENSES. Expenses of a continuing nature including expenses for food, clothing, shelter, utilities, household sundries, household maintenance, medical and dental services and life insurance premiums. See PERSONAL OR ~.

LIVING ROOM. The principal habitable room of a dwelling, not being a dining room, sleeping room, library, den, sewing room or sunroom. Canada regulations.

L.J. *abbr.* 1. Law Journal Reports. 2. Lord Justice of Appeal.

LL.B. *abbr.* Bachelor of Laws.

LL.D. *abbr.* Doctor of Laws.

L. LIB. *abbr.* Law Librarian.

LL.M. *abbr.* Master of Laws.

LLOYD'S ASSOCIATION. An association of individuals formed on the plan known as Lloyd's, whereby each associate underwriter becomes liable for a stated, limited or proportionate part of the whole amount insured by a contract. *Insurance acts.*

LM. *abbr.* Lumen.

LOAD. *n.* 1. Everything conveyed by a motor vehicle. 2. In reference to the ammunition of a rifled weapon, the propellant's weight. F.A. Jaffe, *A Guide to Pathological Evidence*, 2d ed. (Toronto: Carswell, 1983) at 179. 3. In reference to ammunition for a shotgun, the combined weight of propellant and shot. F.A. Jaffe, *A Guide to Pathological Evidence*, 2d ed. (Toronto: Carswell, 1983) at 179. See ALLOWABLE ~; AXLE ~; DEAD ~; DESIGN ~; FIRE ~; LIVE ~; MAXIMUM ~; MAXIMUM SAFE ~; NORMAL ~; OCCUPANT ~; PEAK ~; ROAD ~; WORKING ~.

LOADBEARING. *adj.* As applying to a building element means subjected to or designed to carry loads in addition to its own dead load, excepting a wall element subjected only to wind or earthquake loads in addition to its own dead load. *Building Code Act*, R.R.O. 1980, Reg. 87, s. 1.

LOADED CONDITION. The sum of the weight of the lifeboat or life raft, equipment, blocks and falls, and the number of persons with which the lifeboat or life raft is required to be lowered, each person being considered to weigh 165 pounds. *Life Saving Equipment Regulations*, C.R.C., c. 1436, s. 1.

LOADED FIREARM. Includes, (a) in the case of a breech-loading firearm, a firearm carrying shells or cartridges in the breech or in a magazine attached to the firearm; (b) in the case of a percussion muzzle-loading firearm, a firearm charged with powder and projectile when the percussion cap is in place on the firearm; and (c) in the case of a flint-lock muzzle-loading firearm, a firearm the barrel of which is charged with powder and projectile and the frizzen or pan of which is charged with powder.

LOADED TRUCK. A truck having on or in it goods or a passenger or passengers. *The Vehicles Act*, R.S.S. 1978, c. V-3, s. 2.

LOADING. See DATE OF ~.

LOADING AREA. Any portion of an airport designated by a sign and made available to the public for loading or unloading. *Airport Tariff Regulations*, C.R.C., c. 886, s. 2.

LOADING CHARGE. A charge for loading goods from an ordinary place of rest onto closed railway cars or closed motor transport vehicles and for all necessary labour and equipment other than that required for bracing and securing. Canada regulations.

LOADING SPACE. A space (a) on the same lot with a building or contiguous to a group of buildings, (b) intended for the temporary parking of a commercial vehicle while loading or unloading merchandise or materials, and (c) that abuts upon a street, lane or other means of access. Canada regulations.

LOAD LINE. *var.* **LOADLINE.** The imaginary line on the side of a ship below which that ship should not sink when it is loaded. See DEEPEST SUBDIVISION ~; ~S; TIMBER ~.

LOAD LINE CONVENTION. The International Convention respecting Load Lines together with the Final Protocol signed at London on July 5, 1930. *Canada Shipping Act*, R.S.C. 1985, c. S-9, s. 2.

LOAD LINE CONVENTION CERTIFICATE. A certificate indicating that a ship has been surveyed and marked with load lines in accordance with Part V and complies with the conditions of assignment to the extent required in its case. *Canada Shipping Act*, R.S.C. 1985, c. S-9, s. 2.

LOAD LINE CONVENTION SHIP. A Load Line ship belonging to a country to which the Load Line Convention applies. *Canada Shipping Act*, R.S.C. 1985, c. S-9, s. 2.

LOAD LINE REGULATIONS. The regulations made pursuant to section 375 to carry out and give effect to the provisions of the International Convention on Load Lines, 1966. *Canada Shipping Act*, R.S.C. 1985, c. S-9, s. 2.

LOAD LINE RULES. The rules made by the Governor in Council for the purpose of giving effect to Articles 6 to 10 of the Load Line Convention and Annex I and Annex II thereto. *Canada Shipping Act*, R.S.C. 1985, c. S-9, s. 2.

LOAD LINES. The marks indicating the several maximum depths to which a ship can be safely loaded in the various circumstances prescribed by the Load Line Rules and Load Line Regulations applicable to that ship. *Canada Shipping Act*, R.S.C. 1985, c. S-9, s. 2.

LOAD LINE SHIP. A ship of the kind described in section 353 that is not exempt under subsections (2) and (3) of that section from the provisions of Part V relating to load lines. *Canada Shipping Act*, R.S.C. 1985, c. S-9, s. 2.

LOAD RATING. The maximum load a tire is rated to carry at a given inflation pressure. Canada regulations.

LOAN. *n.* 1. Anything given or lent to someone on condition that it be repayed or returned. 2. Any money owed to the Territories that is evidenced by a promissory note. *Financial Administration Act*, R.S.N.W.T. 1974, c. F-4, s. 2. 3. Includes money advanced on account of a person in any transaction which, whatever form it takes, is substantially a loan to such person, or one securing the repayment by such person of the money advanced. *Money-Lenders Act*, R.S.N.S. 1967, c. 188, s. 1. See APPROVED ~; BASE ~; BUSINESS IMPROVEMENT ~; COMPLETION ~; CONSOLIDATED ~; CONSTRUCTION ~; COST OF ~; COST OF

THE ~; CURRENT ~; DEED OF ~; DOUBT-FUL ~; FARM IMPROVEMENT ~; FOREST ~; GUARANTEED ~; HOME EXTENSION ~; HOME IMPROVEMENT ~; HOME PUR-CHASE ~; HOME RELOCATION ~; INSUR-ABLE ~; INSURED ~; LIVESTOCK ~; POLICY ~; PROTECTED ~; SECURED ~; STUDENT ~; SUBORDINATED SHARE-HOLDER ~; TERM ~; UNAUTHORIZED INVESTMENT OR ~; UNSECURED ~.

LOAN AGREEMENT. A document or memorandum in writing (i) evidencing a loan, (ii) made or given as security for a loan, or (iii) made or given as security for a past indebtedness arising under a previous loan agreement or time sale agreement, and made or given in substitution for the previous agreement, and includes a mortgage of real property. See REVOLVING ~.

LOAN AMOUNT. The principal amount of a loan. B.J. Reiter, R.C.B. Risk & B.N. McLellan, *Real Estate Law*, 3d ed. (Toronto: Emond Montgomery, 1986) at 976.

LOAN CAPITAL. 1. Includes a sum contributed to an association by a member, in his capacity as member, (i) by way of contributions to capital otherwise than by the purchase of shares or the making of loans under Section 35, or (ii) by allocation or payment pursuant to Section 38 or pursuant to an enactment, or net earnings or other sums available for distribution to members. *Cooperative Associations Act*, S.N.S. 1977, c. 7, s. 2. 2. A loan with a prescribed rate of interest and with a repayment term of more than one year. *The Heritage Fund (Saskatchewan) Act*, R.S.S. 1978, c. H-2.1, s. 2.

LOAN COMMITMENT. A document executed by a lender and borrower when the lender agrees to provide the loan requested which sets out any terms and conditions for that loan. B.J. Reiter, R.C.B. Risk & B.N. McLellan, *Real Estate Law*, 3d ed. (Toronto: Emond Montgomery, 1986) at 976.

LOAN COMPANY. 1. A body corporate that accepts deposits transferable by order to a third party and that (a) carries on the business of a loan company under the Loan Companies Act, or (b) carries on, under an Act of the legislature of a province or a constating instrument issued under provincial jurisdiction, the business of a loan company within the meaning of the Loan Companies Act. *Canadian Payments Association Act*, R.S.C. 1985, c. C-21, s. 2. 2. A body corporate incorporated or operated for the purpose of receiving deposits from the public and lending or investing those deposits, but does not include a bank, an insurance corporation, a trust company or a credit union. 3. A company incorporated for the purpose of lending money on the security of freehold real estate, or investing money in mortgages or hypothecs upon freehold real estate, either with or without other objects or powers. See SMALL LOANS COMPANY.

LOAN CORPORATION. An incorporated company, association or society, constituted, authorized or operated for the purpose of accepting deposits or issuing debentures, notes and like obligations and of lending money on the security of real estate or investing money in mortgages, charges or hypothecs upon real estate or for those and any other purposes. See FOREIGN ~; MORTGAGE ~; TRUST AND ~; TRUST OR ~.

LOAN OFFICER. A person appointed pursuant to clause 5(2)(d) to consider applications and grant or deny loans and credit out of the funds of the Authority. *Lending Authority Act*, S.P.E.I. 1980, c. 34, s. 1.

LOAN GUARANTEE. See SHARED-RISK ~.

LOAN SOCIETY. A corporation or a company authorized to do business as trust, insurance, loan, building or finance companies having its head office or a place of business in Québec and authorized by the Gouvernement to make building loans for the purposes of this act. *Family Housing Act*, R.S.Q. 1977, c. H-1, s. 1.

LOANS RECEIVABLE. Includes (a) receivables arising from factoring activities, (b) receivables arising by reason of financial lease contracts and, without duplication, the value of the personal property to which such contracts relate, and (c) receivables arising by reason of the purchase of conditional sales agreements and, without duplication, the value of the personal property to which such agreements relate. *Bank Act*, R.S.C. 1985, c. B-1, s. 193.

LOAN VALUE. The market value of securities less the applicable margin requirements.

LOBBYIST. *n.* A person engaged to represent the interests of a certain group in dealings with the government.

LOBSTER COCKTAIL. Lobster canned in combination with cod, haddock, hake or cusk or any combination thereof. *Fish Inspection Regulations*, C.R.C., c. 802, s. 2.

LOBSTER SHIFT. Night shift; a shift which starts late at night or in early morning hours.

LOBSTER TRAP. See MODIFIED ~.

LOC. *abbr.* Local.

LOCAL. *n.* Of an international or national union, is a union which is affiliated with the international or national union. See DIRECTLY CHARTERED ~.

LOCAL. *adj.* When it qualifies the words "municipality", "corporation", "council" or "councillor", refers, as the case may be, to rural or village councils, councillors, corporations or municipalities. *An Act to Amend Various Legislative Provisions Respecting Municipalities*, S.Q. 1982, c. 2, s. 4.

LOCAL ACCEPTANCE. Payment at a specified, particular place only. E.L.G. Tyler & N.E. Palmer, eds., *Crossley Vaines' Personal Property*, 5th ed. (London: Butterworths, 1973) at 236.

LOCAL ACT. An act which deals with a matter relating to a particular area, usually a municipality.

LOCAL ASYLUM FOR HARMLESS INSANE. A reference in any other enactment to a local asylum for the harmless insane shall be read and construed as a reference to a municipal mental hospital. *Municipal Mental Hospital Act*, R.S.N.S. 1967, c. 202, s. 40.

LOCAL AUTHORITY. 1. Any public organization created by an act of a legislature and exercising jurisdiction or powers of a local nature. 2. The council of a municipality.

LOCAL AUTONOMY. The power vested in a local union to determine what it will negotiate.

LOCAL BOARD. Any board, commission, committee, body or local authority of any kind established to exercise or exercising any power or authority under any general or special act with respect to any of the affairs or purposes of a municipality or parts thereof or of two or more municipalities or parts thereof, or to which a municipality or municipalities are required to provide funds.

LOCAL CARRIER. A person who operates a local undertaking. *Motor Vehicle Transport Act*, R.S.C. 1985, c. M-12, s. 2.

LOCAL COMMUNITY ORGANIZATION. An organization, incorporated under any Act of the Legislature, which is active in the municipality. *Parks Development Act*, R.S.N.S. 1967, c. 222, s. 1.

LOCAL COMMUNITY SERVICE CENTRE. Facilities other than a professional's private consulting office in which sanitary and social preventive and action services are ensured to the community, in particular by receiving or visiting persons who require current health services or social services for themselves or their families, by rendering such services to them, counselling them or, if necessary, by referring them to the establishments most capable of assisting them. *Health Services and Social Services Act*, R.S.Q. 1977, c. S-5, s. 1.

LOCAL COOPERATIVE CREDIT SOCIETY. A cooperative organization incorporated or organized by or pursuant to an act of Parliament or of the legislature of a province, the membership or shareholders of which consist wholly or substantially of natural persons and the principal purpose of which is to receive deposits from its members or shareholders and make loans to its members or shareholders.

LOCAL COUNCIL. (i) The council of a city or town, (ii) the commissioners of an incorporated village, (iii) a community improvement committee, (iv) the trustees or directors of an area improvement district, or (v) in any regional administrative unit which is not within a city, town, incorporated village or area improvement district and does not have a community improvement committee, the trustees of a regional administrative unit. *Recreation Development Act*, R.S.P.E.I. 1974, c. R-9, s. 1.

LOCAL CTS. & MUN. GAZ. *abbr.* Local Courts' and Municipal Gazette (1865-1872).

LOCAL EDUCATION AUTHORITY. Includes a community education council for an education district within an education division or a Divisional Board of Education where an education division is comprised of one education district. *Education Act*, S.N.W.T. 1985 (3d Sess.), c. 3, s. 4.

LOCAL F.M. STATION. In relation to a licensee, any F.M. broadcasting station licensed by the Commission whose 500 microvolt per metre official contour encloses any part of the licensed area of the licensee. *Cable Television Regulations*, C.R.C., c. 374, s. 2.

LOCAL FOOD. A food that is manufactured, processed, produced or packaged in a local government unit and sold only in (a) the local government unit in which it is manufactured, processed or packaged, (b) one or more local government units that are immediately adjacent to the one in which it is manufactured, processed, produced or packaged, or (c) the local government unit in which it is manufactured, processed, produced or packaged and in one or more local government units that are immediately adjacent to the one in which it is manufactured, processed, produced or packaged. *Food and Drug Regulations*, C.R.C., c. 870, c. B.01.012.

LOCAL GOVERNING AUTHORITY. A council in the case of a municipality, the Minister of Municipal Affairs in the case of a local improvement district and the Minister of North-

Saskatchewan Administration District. Saskatchewan statutes.

LOCAL GOVERNMENT. 1. A system of government by which administration of local affairs is entrusted to local authority. 2. A body with legislative power over a local area but which national authority may overrule. P.W. Hogg, *Constitutional Law of Canada*, 2d ed. (Toronto: Carswell, 1985) at 80.

LOCAL GOVERNMENT DISTRICT. Includes a school district in unorganized territory that is not in a local government district, and a reference to the resident administrator of a local government district shall, where the context so requires, be deemed to include the board of trustees of such a school district. *Health Services Act*, R.S.M. 1970, c. H30, s. 88. See FOUNDATION ~.

LOCAL GOVERNMENT UNIT. A city, metropolitan government area, town, village, municipality or other area of local government but does not include any local government unit situated within a bilingual district established under the Official Languages Act. Canada regulations.

LOCAL HEAD END. In relation to a licensee, the location where signals transmitted by local television stations are received by the licensee's undertaking. *Cable Television Regulations*, C.R.C., c. 374, s. 2.

LOCAL IMPROVEMENT. A work or service intended to be paid for or maintained wholly or partly by special assessments against the land benefitted thereby as determined in the manner in this Part set forth. *City of Winnipeg Act*, S.M. 1971, c. 105, s. 351.

LOCAL IMPROVEMENT DISTRICT. A local improvement district heretofore or hereafter constituted under any Local Improvement Districts Act. Saskatchewan statutes.

LOCAL IMPROVEMENTS. Any expenditure of public funds upon any street or locality by which such street or locality is benefitted. *City of St. John's Act*, R.S.Nfld. 1970, c. 40, s. 2.

LOCAL IMPROVEMENT TAX. Includes betterment charges and all taxes and charges imposed, defraying any part of the cost of any of the works, improvements or services which may be undertaken as a local improvement project. *Dartmouth City Charter Act*, S.N.S. 1978, c. 43A, s. 2.

LOCAL INTERVENER. A person or a group or association of persons who, in the opinion of the Board, (a) has an interest in, or (b) is in actual occupation of or is entitled to occupy land that is or may be directly and adversely affected by a decision of the Board in or as a result of a proceeding before it, but, unless otherwise authorized by the Board, does not include a person or group or association of persons whose business includes the trading in or transportation or recovery of any energy resource. *Energy Resources Conservation Amendment Act, 1981*, S.A. 1981, c. 47, s. 31.

LOCALITY. *n.* 1. A part of territory without municipal organization that is deemed to be a district municipality for the purposes of a divisional board or of a district combined separate school board. *Education Act*, R.S.O. 1980, c. 129, s. 1. 2. A public school section, a separate school zone or a secondary school district that comprises or includes territory without municipal organization and includes the board of any of them. *Assessment Act*, R.S.O. 1980, c. 31, s. 1. 3. An area where, in the opinion of an employment officer, all points are within commuting distance of the place in relation to which the term is used. *Manpower Mobility Regulations*, C.R.C., c. 331, s. 2.

LOCALITY OF DEBTOR. The principal place (a) where the debtor has carried on business during the year immediately preceding his bankruptcy, (b) where the debtor has resided during the year immediately preceding his bankruptcy, or (c) in cases not coming within paragraph (a) or (b), where the greater portion of the property of the debtor is situated. *Bankruptcy Act*, R.S.C. 1985, c. B-3, s. 2.

LOCAL JURISDICTION. A municipality, a hospital district as defined in the Hospitals Act, a district as defined in the Nursing Homes Act or a district or division as defined in the School Act, as the case may be. *Local Authorities Election Act*, S.A. 1983, c. L-27.5, s. 1.

LOCAL LABOUR COUNCIL. A federation of labour organizations within a city.

LOCAL MASTER. A local master of Her Majesty's Court of Queen's Bench, and includes a judge of the District Court lawfully performing the duties of a local master of Her Majesty's Court of Queen's Bench. *The Queen's Bench Act*, R.S.S. 1978, c. Q-1, s. 2.

LOCAL MUNICIPALITY. 1. A municipality wholly or partly within the National Capital Region. *National Capital Act*, R.S.C. 1985, c. N-4, s. 2. 2. A city, town, village and township. Ontario statutes. 3. Any city, town, village or rural municipality, governed by a municipal council. *Education Act*, R.S.Q. 1977, c. I-14, s. 1.

LOCAL OFFICE. An office established to serve an area comprising a part but not the whole of

Canada. *Public Service Employment Act*, R.S.C. 1985, c. P-33, s. 2.

LOCAL OPTION AREA. A local option area established pursuant to section 33. *The Liquor Licensing Act*, R.S.S. 1978, c. L-21, s. 32.

LOCAL OPTION BY-LAW. A by-law of a municipality forbidding the local sale of liquor in the municipality. *Liquor Control Act*, R.S.M. 1970, c. L160, s. 260.

LOCAL PORT CORPORATION. A corporation established under section 25. *Canada Ports Corporation Act*, R.S.C. 1985, c. C-9, s. 2.

LOCAL PRODUCT. A prepackaged product that is manufactured, processed, produced or packaged in a local government unit and sold only in (a) the local government unit in which it is manufactured, processed, produced or packaged, (b) one or more local government units that are immediately adjacent to the one in which it is manufactured, processed, produced or packaged, or (c) the local government unit in which it is manufactured, processed, produced or packaged and in one or more local government units that are immediately adjacent to the one in which it is manufactured, processed, produced or packaged. Canada regulations.

LOCAL REGISTRAR. The local registrar or deputy local registrar of a court.

LOCAL REGISTRAR OF FIREARMS. Any person who has been designated in writing as a local registrar of firearms by the Commissioner or the Attorney General of a province or who is a member of a class of police officers or police constables that has been so designated. *Criminal Code*, R.S.C. 1985, c. C-46, s. 84.

LOCAL ROAD. Any road, trail or path situated within the boundaries of a park, historical site, natural area or wilderness area. *Provincial Parks Act*, R.S.A. 1970, c. 288, s. 2.

LOCAL SERVICES. Services of a type that may be provided in a municipality at the expense, either wholly or partly, of a municipality or of a school district, school division, or school area, and without limiting the generality of the foregoing includes (i) water supply and water distribution systems, (ii) sewage systems and sewage disposal plants, (iii) garbage and waste disposal facilities, (iv) local roads and sidewalks, (v) local drains and drainage systems, (vi) fire and police protection, (vii) street lighting, (viii) planning, (ix) recreation facilities including parks, (x) transportation facilities including ferries, wharves, docks and facilities for the landing of aircraft, (xi) libraries, (xii) weed control, and (xiii) schools. *Northern Affairs Act*, S.M. 1974, c. 56, s. 1.

LOCAL STANDARD. Any standard designated by the Minister under section 13. *Weights and Measures Act*, R.S.C. 1985, c. W-6, s. 2.

LOCAL STATUTE. See LOCAL ACT.

LOCAL TARIFF. A tariff containing the local tolls of each air carrier named therein. *Air Carrier Regulations*, C.R.C., c. 3, s. 2.

LOCAL TAXATION. Taxation of any kind whatsoever imposed by or under any Act or law of the province for the benefit of a city, a municipality, local schools, or any municipal area whatsoever. *Crown Corporations (Local Taxation) Act*, R.S.Nfld. 1970, c. 69, s. 2.

LOCAL TELEVISION STATION. In relation to a licensee, any television broadcasting station licensed by the Commission whose Grade A official contour encloses any part of the licensed area of the licensee. *Cable Television Regulations*, C.R.C., c. 374, s. 2.

LOCAL TIME. In relation to any place, means the time observed in that place for the regulation of business hours. *Interpretation Act*, R.S.C. 1985, c. I-21, s. 35.

LOCAL TOLL. A toll that applies between places served by one air carrier. *Air Carrier Regulations*, C.R.C., c. 3, s. 2.

LOCAL TRANSPORT. The transport of passengers or goods by motor vehicle otherwise than by means of an extra-provincial undertaking. *Motor Vehicle Transport Act*, R.S.C. 1985, c. M-12, s. 2.

LOCAL UNDERTAKING. A work or an undertaking, not being an extra-provincial undertaking, for the transport of passengers or goods by motor vehicle. *Motor Vehicle Transport Act*, R.S.C. 1985, c. M-12, s. 2.

LOCAL UNION. The lowest structural unit of a union that elects its own slate of officers. *Corporations and Labour Unions Returns Act*, R.S.C. 1985, c. C-43, s. 12(4).

LOCAL WARRANT. For the purpose of determining a municipality's fiscal effort, means the difference between the net municipal budget of a municipality for the previous year and the amount of unconditional grant plus any transitional adjustment payments computed for that municipality for the previous year. *An Act to Amend the Municipal Assistance Act*, S.N.B. 1986, c. 58, s. 1.

LOCATIO. *n.* [L.] Hire, renting out. See CONTRACT OF ~ ET CONDUCTIO.

LOCATIO CONDUCTIO. [L.] Goods left with a bailee which the bailee may rent out. E.L.G. Tyler & N.E. Palmer, eds., *Crossley Vaines'*

Personal Property, 5th ed. (London: Butterworths, 1973) at 85.

LOCATIO CUSTODIAE. [L.] The receipt of goods deposited for reward.

LOCATIO MERCIUM VEHENDARUM. [L.] A contract to carry goods for hire.

LOCATION. *n.* The area described in, and in respect of which rights are given by, a permit or lease to mine. See ACCESSIBLE ~; DAMP ~; EXPLOSION-HAZARD ~; HAZARDOUS ~; HOLDER OF A ~; MINERAL ~; ORDINARY ~; WET ~.

LOCATION LINE. A straight line opened or indicated throughout No. 1 and No. 2 location posts of a mineral claim and joining them. *Yukon Quartz Mining Act*, R.S.C. 1985, c. Y-4, s. 2.

LOCATIO OPERIS. [L.] The renting out of services and labour.

LOCATIO OPERIS FACIENDI. [L.] A delivery to convey or otherwise manage, for a consideration paid to a bailee, something for someone who exercises a public function, or is a private person. E.L.G. Tyler & N.E. Palmer, eds., *Crossley Vaines' Personal Property*, 5th ed. (London: Butterworths, 1973) at 85.

LOCATIO REI. [L.] The renting out of something.

LOCATOR. *n.* 1. A licensee who enters on land, prospects for minerals, locates a claim or has a claim located for him. *Canada Mining Regulations*, C.R.C., c. 1516, s. 2. 2. One who lets out things or services for hire.

LOC. CIT. *abbr.* Loco citato.

LOC. CT. GAZ. *abbr.* Local Courts & Municipal Gazette (Ont.), 1865-1872.

LOCK. See AIR ~; ANTI-~ SYSTEM; ELECTRIC SWITCH ~; MEDICAL ~.

LOCK BOX. A numbered compartment in a post office that is kept locked and to which the boxholder and the postmaster have access. *Mail Receptacles Regulations*, C.R.C., c. 1282, s. 21.

LOCKER PLANT. Any food premises in which individual lockers are rented or offered for rent to the public for the storage of frozen foods. *Public Health Act*, R.R.O. 1980, Reg. 840, s. 1. See FROZEN FOOD ~.

LOCKE KING'S ACT. A British statute of 1854 which reversed the rule that, when a mortgagor of real property died, any mortgage debt of that person was payable out of her or his general personal estate. As far as any beneficiaries of a deceased mortgagor's estate are concerned, any mortgage debt is chargeable prima facie against mortgaged land. W.B. Rayner & R.H.

McLaren, *Falconbridge on Mortgages*, 4th ed. (Toronto: Canada Law Book, 1977) at 341 and 342.

LOCKMASTER. *n.* A person actually on duty in charge of a lock. *Canal Regulations*, C.R.C., c. 1564, s. 2.

LOCKOUT. *var.* **LOCK-OUT.** *n.* Includes the closing of a place of employment, a suspension of work by an employer or a refusal by an employer to continue to employ some employees, done to compel the employees, or to aid another employer to compel those employees, to agree to certain terms or conditions of employment.

LOCK SEAL TAG. Any type of locking or sealing tag supplied with a hunting or angling licence that is made of cardboard, paper, plastic, metal or any other material. *Fish and Wildlife Act*, S.N.B. 1980, c. F-14.1, s. 1.

LOCKSMITH. *n.* A person who (a) makes, services, repairs, codes or recodes locks, (b) cuts, makes, sells or otherwise provides restricted keys, (c) cuts, makes, sells or otherwise provides keys from numerical or alphabetical codes or both, (d) sells, services or repairs safes, vaults or strongboxes, other than common strongboxes, or (e) is a member of a class of persons designated by the Lieutenant Governor in Council as locksmiths for the purposes of this Act, but a person is not a locksmith by reason only that he (f) codes or recodes locks of which he is the owner, or that he has sold, or (g) cuts, makes, sells or otherwise provides a key from a numerical or alphabetical code or both, if the key is intended for use with a lock he has sold and the key is sold or provided to the owner of the lock. *Miscellaneous Statutes Amendment Act (No. 2)*, S.B.C. 1986, c. 16, s. 37.

LOCK TENDER. A person who continuously supervises the controls of an air lock when workers are in it or about to enter it. D. Robertson, *Ontario Health and Safety Guide* (Toronto: Richard De Boo Ltd., 1988) at 5-239.

LOCK-UP. See LOCK-UP FACILITY.

LOCK-UP FACILITY. A police or court facility for the custody of an offender upon arrest, pending a transfer to a correctional facility or pending a court hearing. *Corrections Act*, S.N.S. 1986, c. 6, s. 3.

LOCO CITATO. [L.] At the quoted passage.

LOCOMOTIVE. *n.* 1. A locomotive unit equipped with an operating cab and intended for crew occupancy. *Locomotive and Caboose Sanitation Facilities Regulations*, C.R.C., c. 1155, s. 2. 2. A unit propelled by any form of energy or a combination of such units operated from a single control running only on rails of a standard gauge railroad and used for moving standard gauge railroad cars but does not include a self-propelled track crane, motorized equipment used for the maintenance of a standard gauge railroad, a motor vehicle equipped with rail wheels in addition to rubber-tired wheels or other similar equipment. *Occupational Health and Safety Act*, R.R.O. 1980, Reg. 694, s. 1. 3. A railway locomotive of which a railway company is the owner and includes an electric power generation car of which a railway company is the owner. *Fuel Oil Administration Act*, R.S.A. 1980, c. F-21, s. 1.

LOCOMOTIVE BOILER. A high pressure boiler that may be used to furnish motivating power for travelling on rails. *Boilers and Pressure Vessels Act*, R.R.O. 1980, Reg. 84, s. 1.

LOCOMOTIVE FUEL. 1. Fuel for use in an internal combustion engine in any rolling stock or other vehicle run on rails. *Motor Fuel Tax Act*, S.B.C. 1985, c. 76, s. 1. 2. A taxable fuel used by a railway company to operate a locomotive. *The Fuel Tax Act*, S.S. 1986-87-88, c. F-23.2, s. 2.

LOCUM TENENS. [L.] A person who lawfully executes another person's office, a deputy.

LOCUS IN QUO. [L. a place in which] A place where.

LOCUS POENITENTIAE. [L.] The power to draw back from an agreement before anything is done to confirm it legally.

LOCUS REGIT ACTUM. [L.] The law of the country where the act took place which governs its form. J.G. McLeod, *The Conflict of Laws* (Calgary: Carswell, 1983) at 779.

LOCUS SIGILLI. [L. the place of the seal] The place at the bottom of a document which requires a seal.

LOCUS SOLUTIONIS. [L.] The place where a payment should be made. J.G. McLeod, *The Conflict of Laws* (Calgary: Carswell, 1983) at 510.

LOCUS STANDI. [L. a place to stand] The right to be heard or appear during a proceeding.

LODE. See VEIN OR ~.

LODGE. *v.* To file or leave documents.

LODGE. *n.* Includes a primary subordinate division, by whatever name known, of a fraternal society. *Insurance acts.* See HUNTING OR FISHING ~.

LODGED. *adj.* When used is respect of a tree, means that by reason of other than natural causes the tree does not fall to the ground after

being, (i) partly or wholly separated from its stump, or (ii) displaced from its natural position. *Crown Timber Act*, R.R.O. 1980, Reg. 234, s. 1.

LODGER. *n.* A person who occupies rooms in a house.

LODGING. *n.* The provision of a room and three meals per day for a seven-day week. *Employment Standards Act*, R.R.O. 1980, Reg. 285, s. 1.

LODGING HOUSE. *var.* **LODGING-HOUSE.** A house in which sleeping accommodation is let to transient lodgers.

LOG. *n.* 1. A record kept by the master of a ship. 2. Includes logs, timbers, boards, deals, scantlings or laths, telegraph poles, railway ties, pitprops, shingle bolts or staves, fence posts, cordwood, piles, poles, pulplogs, pulpwood, railway ties, sawlogs, spars, wood chips and other cut timber of whatever length, whether round or flatted. See MERCHANTABLE ~; SAW ~S.

LOGGER. *n.* (i) A person engaged in the cutting, trimming, peeling, hauling, skidding, driving, piling, handling or loading of pulpwood, pitprops or other forms of timber or in any other work connected with a logging operation, whether of the foregoing kinds or not, or (ii) a person engaged in the preparation of meals, cleaning or providing other services in a logging camp or on the site of logging operations.

LOGGING. *n.* The felling, limbing, bucking and marking of trees, construction of logging roads, off-highway transportation of logs to a millpond or mill yard, log salvaging and reforestation.

LOGGING CAMP. A structure of any kind which a logger occupies or uses while he is working as a logger or in which loggers are provided with sleeping accommodation or meals or both, other than (i) a restaurant, hotel or boarding-house which is licensed or subject to inspection under any other statute, or (ii) a private residence, and includes the land surrounding and the buildings, structures or installations adjacent to a logging camp. *Logging Camps Act*, R.S.Nfld. 1970, c. 222, s. 2.

LOGGING INDUSTRY. Includes the cutting, driving, rafting, booming, transportation or sawing of logs, timber, pulpwood, firewood, pitprops, railroad ties or sleepers and also includes any employment incidental thereto or immediately connected therewith. *Logging Camps Act*, R.S.N.B 1973, c. L-12, s. 1.

LOGGING INTEREST. A right of any kind held to an area of land or to trees growing on the land for the purpose of cutting timber thereon or otherwise producing timber therefrom commercially and whether received or held under grant, lease, licence, permit, contract or assignment of any of them or otherwise. *Logging Camps Act*, R.S.Nfld. 1970, c. 222, s. 2.

LOGGING OPERATION. The felling, cutting into logs, barking in the forest, cartage, piling, driving, loading and highway transportation of timber but not its processing outside the forest.

LOGGING OPERATIONS. 1. Includes the sale of standing timber, the sale of the right to cut standing timber, the sale of logs, the sale of primary and secondary forest products, the delivery of logs to a sawmill, pulp or paper plant, or other place for processing or manufacturing, the delivery of logs to a carrier for export, the export of logs, the acquisition of standing timber, the acquisition of the right to cut standing timber, the cutting of logs from standing timber, the acquisition of logs, the import of logs, the production of primary and secondary forest products, and the transportation of logs, or any combination of such operations. *Logging Tax Act*, R.S.B.C. 1979, c. 248, s. 1. 2. (a) The cutting of standing timber in Québec or the acquiring of forest products derived therefrom, when such products are sold in Québec; (b) the cutting of standing timber in Québec or the acquiring of forest products derived therefrom, when such products are sold outside Québec; (c) the sale of forest land, timber limits or timber-cutting rights in Québec; (d) the cutting of standing timber in Québec or the acquiring of forest products derived therefrom by the operator of a sawmill, pulp or paper plant or other plant for processing forest products in Canada. *Taxation Act*, R.S.Q. 1977, c. I-3, s. 1177.

LOGGING OPERATOR. The holder of a forest management permit to supply a wood processing plant issued under the Forest Act (1986, chapter 108), or a forest producer supplying a wood processing plant from a private woodlot. *Forest Act*, S.Q. 1986, c. 108, s. 242.

LOGGING ROAD. A temporary road within a timber harvesting area on Crown Lands to the fullest extent of the right-of-way, built solely for the extraction of timber, and includes a landing and other works associated with the harvesting operation. *Crown Lands and Forests Act*, S.N.B. 1980, c. C-38.1, s. 1.

LOGGING TAX. A tax imposed by the legislature of a province that is declared by regulation to be a tax of general application on income from logging operations. *Income Tax Act*, R.S.C. 1952, c. 148 (as am. S.C. 1970-71-72, c. 63), c. 127(2)(b).

L.O.M.J. *abbr.* Law Office Management Journal.

LONGA POSSESSIO PARIT JUS POSSIDENDI ET TOLLIT ACTIONEM VERO DOMINO. [L.] Prolonged possession creates a right of possession, and removes any right of action from the real owner.

LONGBOW. *n.* Includes a longbow, recurve bow and a compound bow. *Wildlife Act*, S.B.C. 1982, c. 57, s. 1.

LONG-BUTT. *v.* To cut a log of any length from a tree or from a log, and to not utilize it. *Crown Timber Act*, R.R.O. 1980, Reg. 234, s. 1.

LONGLINE. *n.* A line to which hooks are attached at intervals and that rests wholly on the bottom. *Quebec Fishery Regulations*, C.R.C., c. 852, s. 2.

LONG POSITION. Where used in relation to a commodity futures contract, means to be under an obligation to take delivery.

LONG SERVICE MEDAL. The Royal Canadian Mounted Police Long Service Medal as approved by royal warrant, hereinafter referred to as the "Long Service Medal", may be awarded to (a) a regular member who completes 20 years of qualifying service and meets the requirements set out in section 93; and (b) a retired regular member who has completed 20 years of qualifying service prior to his discharge from the Force and meets the requirements set out in section 93. *Royal Canadian Mounted Police Regulations*, C.R.C., c. 1391, s. 92.

LONGSHORING EMPLOYMENT. Employment in the loading or unloading of ship's cargo and in operations related to the loading or unloading of ship's cargo. *Canada Labour Standards Regulations*, C.R.C., c. 986, s. 19.

LONG TERM AVERAGE YIELD. As applied to a crop in a risk area means the weighted average yield for that crop, in that risk area as determined on the basis of available records during a period of not more than twenty-five continuous years next preceding the crop year in which any such determination is made. *Crop Insurance Act*, S.M. 1970, c. 30, s. 2.

LONG-TERM BONDS OF CANADA. Marketable bonds issued by the Government of Canada payable in Canadian currency and due to mature in not less than 10 years. *N.H.A. Maximum Interest Rates Regulations*, C.R.C., c. 1107, s. 3.

LONG-TERM DEBT. (a) In the case of a corporation that is a bank, indebtedness evidenced by bank debentures, within the meaning assigned by the Bank Act or the Quebec Savings Bank Act, and (b) in the case of a corporation that is not a bank, subordinate indebtedness evidenced by obligations issued for a term of not less than five years. *Income Tax Act*, R.S.C.

1952, c. 148 (as am. S.C. 1986, c. 6, s. 100), s. 190(1).

LONG TERM LEASE. See REGISTERED ~.

LONG-TERM LIABILITY. A debt due after a longer period of time such as one year. S.M. Beck *et al., Cases and Materials on Partnerships and Canadian Business Corporations,* (Toronto: The Carswell Company Limited, 1983) at 779.

LONG-TERM UNIT. An inpatient unit to provide treatment services, regular medical assessment and continuing nursing care to patients.

LONG TITLE. A description which sets out the purposes of a bill or statute in general terms. A. Fraser, G.A. Birch & W.A. Dawson, eds., *Beauchesne's Rules and Forms of the House of Commons of Canada,* 5th ed. (Toronto: Carswell, 1978) at 218.

LONGUM TEMPUS ET LONGUS USUS, QUI EXCEDIT MEMORIAM HOMINUM, SUFFICIT, PRO JURE. [L.] Long time and long use, which surpass human memory, are sufficient in law.

LONG VACATION. The months July and August when the courts traditionally did not sit. D. Sgayias *et al., Federal Court Practice 1988* (Toronto: Carswell, 1987) at 253.

LOOP VENT. A branch vent that functions for two or more traps and loops back or extends to a stack vent from a point in front of the last connection of a fixture to a horizontal branch. *Ontario Water Resources Act,* R.R.O. 1980, Reg. 736, s. 1.

LOOSE. *adj.* 1. If it is possible for a man of average weight to push a wooden picket 8 in. or more into the soil. *Building Code Act,* R.R.O. 1980, Reg. 87, s. 4.2.1.5. 2. When it requires between 4 and 10 blows per foot in a penetration test. *Building Code Act,* R.R.O. 1980, Reg. 87, s. 4.2.1.5. See VERY ~.

LOQUITUR UT VULGUS. [L.] Following the common interpretation and agreed on meaning of the term. P. St. J. Langan, ed., *Maxwell on The Interpretation of Statutes,* 12th ed. (Bombay: N.M. Tripathi, 1976) at 81.

LORD. *n.* In relation to real property, the person whose land another holds as a tenant. See HOUSE OF ~S; LAW ~S; LIEGE-~; MESNE ~.

LORD'S DAY. The period of time that begins at midnight on Saturday night and ends at midnight on the following night.

LORD'S DAY ACT. Legislation respecting Sunday observance which requires businesses to close and regulates certain other activities.

LOSS. *n.* 1. Includes the happening of an event or contingency by reason of which a person becomes entitled to a payment under a contract of insurance of money other than a refund of unearned premiums. *Insurance acts.* 2. All damages, court costs, legal fees, adjustment expenses and such other expenses as the Commissioner may approve, which the surety has incurred and actually paid as a result of the default of the business enterprise under the contract to which the bond issued by the surety relates and to which a Commissioner's indemnity applies, less those amounts recovered at the time of payment by the surety but does not include legal fees and court costs incurred in an action by a surety against the Commissioner. *Business Loans, Guarantees and Indemnities Act,* S.N.W.T. 1983 (1st Sess.), c. 1, s. 8. See ACTUAL ~; ACTUAL ~ OR DAMAGE; ALLOWABLE BUSINESS INVESTMENT ~; CUMULATIVE NET INVESTMENT ~; ECONOMIC ~; FINANCIAL ~; NON-PECUNIARY ~; OPERATING ~; PARTIAL ~; PECUNIARY ~; PROFIT AND ~; PROSPECTIVE ~ OF EARNINGS OR PROFITS; TOTAL ~.

LOSS INSURANCE. An agreement under which the insurer agrees to make good a loss specified in the agreement. John G. Fleming, *The Law of Torts,* 6th ed. (Sydney: The Law Book Company Limited, 1983) at 365.

LOSS LEADER. An article sold for a price well below the recommended retail price in order to attract customers to the place of business.

LOSS OF ACCUMULATED WEALTH. The loss of capital assets which dependants can recover and which they would have received if the deceased had not died. K.D. Cooper-Stephenson & I.B. Saunders, *Personal Injury Damages in Canada* (Toronto: Carswell, 1981) at 440.

LOSS OF AMENITIES. A physical disability the victim sustained in an accident, and the effect that disability has on all the victim's activities. K.D. Cooper-Stephenson & I.B. Saunders, *Personal Injury Damages in Canada* (Toronto: Carswell, 1981) at 354.

LOSS OF DEPENDENCY ON INCOME. The part of the deceased's revenue which would have benefitted all that person's statutory dependants during a certain period of their dependency. K.D. Cooper-Stephenson & I.B. Saunders, *Personal Injury Damages in Canada* (Toronto: Carswell, 1981) at 423.

LOSS OF DEPENDENCY ON VALUABLE SERVICES. The deceased's many activities which, though not directly revenue-producing, are still of value to the claimants. K.D. Cooper-Stephenson & I.B. Saunders, *Personal Injury*

Damages in Canada (Toronto: Carswell, 1981) at 431.

LOSS OF EXPECTATION OF LIFE. Shortening of the length of the victim's life. K.D. Cooper-Stephenson & I.B. Saunders, *Personal Injury Damages in Canada* (Toronto: Carswell, 1981) at 358.

LOSS OF SERVICES. A claim by a husband against a person who injured his wife wrongfully or a claim by a parent for loss occasioned by the wrongful injury of his or her child or a claim by a master in respect of an injury to her or his servant. John G. Fleming, *The Law of Torts*, 6th ed. (Sydney: The Law Book Company Limited, 1983) at 619, 621, 645.

LOST CIRCULATION ZONE. A zone within a geological formation generally known by this name and into which wastes can be discharged without positive injection pressure at the surface. *Environmental Protection Act*, R.R.O. 1980, Reg. 303, s. 1.

LOST CORNER. A corner established during an original survey or during a survey of a plan of subdivision where the original post no longer exists or never existed and which cannot be re-established from the field notes of either of such surveys or by evidence under oath.

LOST MONUMENT. A monument which has disappeared entirely and the position of which cannot be established by evidence. Surveys acts.

LOST TIME. Time not used productively at work.

LOT. *n.* 1. A lot or any other area defined and designated by an original survey or by a registered plan. 2. A parcel of land containing or which may contain one or more graves and includes a space within a building or structure which contains or may contain one or more places for the permanent placement of human remains. 3. That quantity of produce that for any reason is considered separately from other produce. Canada regulations. See BOARD ~; BROKEN ~; CORNER ~; FEED ~; INTERIOR ~; IRREGULAR ~; IRREGULARLY-SHAPED ~; MASTER ~; REGULAR ~; STRATA ~; SURVEYED ~; THROUGH ~; TOT ~; UNBROKEN ~; WATER ~.

LOT AREA. The horizontal area within the boundary lines of a lot.

LOT DEPTH. The horizontal distance of a lot between the front and rear lot lines, measured along the median between the side lot lines. Canada regulations.

LOT LINE. See REAR ~; SIDE ~.

LOTTERY. *n.* A game of chance; a division and sharing of prizes by chance or lot.

LOTTERY SCHEME. 1. A game or any proposal, scheme, plan, means, device, contrivance or operation described in any of paragraphs 206(1)(a) to (g), whether or not it involves betting, pool selling or a pool system of betting other than (a) a dice game, three-card monte, punch board or coin table; (b) bookmaking, pool selling or the making of recording or bets, including bets made through the agency of a pool or pari-mutuel system, on any race or fight, or on a single sport event or athletic context; or (c) for the purposes of paragraphs (1)(b) to (f), a game or proposal, scheme, plan, means, device, contrivance or operation described in any of paragraphs 206(1)(a) to (g) that is operated on or through a computer, video device or slot machine, within the meaning of section 198(3). *Criminal Code*, R.S.C. 1985, c. C-46, s. 207(4) as am. 2. Includes a game of chance and a game of mixed chance and skill.

LOT WIDTH. The horizontal distance of a lot between the side lot lines, measured at right angles to the median between those lines at a point on the median that is midway between the front lot line and the rear lot line or 40 feet from the street it faces, whichever is the lesser. Canada regulations.

LOUNGE. *n.* (i) Part of a licensed hotel or motel, or (ii) premises not part of a licensed hotel or motel, provided with special accommodation, facilities or equipment prescribed in the regulations, where in consideration of payment, beer, wine or spirits are served. *Liquor Control Act*, S.Nfld. 1973, c. 103, s. 2. See AIRPORT ~.

LOW. CAN. R. *abbr.* Lower Canada Reports, 1851-1867.

LOW-ENERGY POWER CIRCUIT. A circuit other than a remote control or signal circuit for which the power supply is limited in accordance with the requirements for Class 2 remote control circuits. *Power Corporation Act*, R.R.O. 1980, Reg. 794, s. 0.

LOWER CANADA. That part of Canada which heretofore constituted the Province of Lower Canada, and means now the province of Québec. *Interpretation Act*, R.S.Q. 1977, c. I-16, s. 61.

LOWER TIER MUNICIPALITY. A city, town, village, township or improvement district. *Ontario Unconditional Grants Act*, R.S.O. 1980, c. 359, s. 1.

LOW FREEZE NITRO-GLYCERINE. Used in the definitions of explosives in Division 1 shall mean a mixture of nitro-glycerine with nitropoly glycerine or nitro-glycol or both of them. *Dan-*

gerous Goods Shipping Regulations, C.R.C., c. 1419, s. 145.

LOW HAZARD FIREWORKS. Those Division 2 fireworks that, in the opinion of the Chief Inspector, are relatively innocuous in themselves and are not liable to explode violently or all at once. *Explosives Regulations*, C.R.C., c. 599, s. 14.

LOW INCOME. An income that is insufficient to allow an individual or family with that income to obtain adequate housing. See FAMILY OF ~; PERSON OF ~.

LOW INCOME HOUSING. Housing for individuals or families of low income.

LOW-LEVEL AIR RACE. A competitive flight during which aircraft are flown at altitudes lower than minimal altitudes specified in the Air Regulations. *Special Aviation Events Safety Order*, C.R.C., c. 66, s. 2.

LOW LEVEL AIRSPACE. All airspace within the Canadian domestic airspace below 18,000 feet above mean sea level. Canada regulations.

LOW PRESSURE BOILER. A boiler in which gas or vapour is generated, approved to carry a working pressure of 15 pounds or less, or a hot-water heating or hot-water supply boiler approved to carry a working pressure of 160 pounds or less per square inch and temperature not exceeding 250 degrees Fahrenheit, or a closed-type hot-water heating system approved to carry a working pressure of 30 pounds or less per square inch.

LOW PRESSURE DISTRIBUTION PIPE-LINE. A pipeline that (i) is used for transmitting gas for domestic, commercial or industrial purposes, (ii) is designed or intended to operate at a maximum pressure of 700 kilopascals or less, (iii) is not part of a rural gas utility, and (iv) is not located within the municipal boundary of a city, town or village. *Pipeline Amendment Act, 1984*, S.A. 1984, c. 32, s. 2.

LOW PRESSURE HEATING PLANT. A boiler or two or more boilers on the same premises having a safety valve setting of not more than 15 pounds per square inch (103 kilopascals) when the boiler is used for producing steam, or a safety valve setting of not more than 160 pounds per square inch (1100 kilopascals) when the boiler is used for producing hot water at a temperature of not more than 250 degrees Fahrenheit (120 Celsius).

LOW PRESSURE HOT WATER PLANT. An assembly of hot water boilers that operate at a temperature of 121°C or less and at a pressure of 1 100 kPa or less and includes a pressure plant that is connected to the assembly of boilers.

Power Engineers and Boiler and Pressure Vessel Safety Act, S.B.C. 1981, c. 25, s. 1.

LOW PRESSURE ORGANIC FLUID PLANT. An assembly of organic fluid boilers that operate at a temperature of 343°C or less and that have no valves or other obstruction to prevent circulation between the boiler and an expansion tank that is fully vented to the atmosphere and includes a pressure plant that is connected to the assembly of boilers. *Power Engineers and Boiler and Pressure Vessel Safety Act*, S.B.C. 1981, c. 25, s. 1.

LOW-PRESSURE STATIONARY PLANT. An installation comprised of one or more boilers, (i.) containing steam at a pressure of 15 or less, or (ii.) containing water at a temperature at any boiler outlet of more than 212°F. and up to and including 250°F., and in addition a low-pressure stationary plant may have one or more compressors and one or more refrigeration compressors, and the total Therm-hour rating of all such boilers and compressors is more than 50. *Operating Engineers Act*, R.S.O. 1980, c. 363, s. 1.

LOW PRESSURE STEAM PLANT. An assembly of boilers that operate at a steam or other vapour pressure of 103 kPa or less and includes a pressure plant that is connected to the assembly of boilers. *Power Engineers and Boiler and Pressure Vessel Safety Act*, S.B.C. 1981, c. 25, s. 1.

LOW-RENTAL HOUSING PROJECT. *var.* **LOW RENTAL HOUSING PROJECT.** A housing project undertaken to provide decent, safe and sanitary housing accommodation, complying with standards approved by the Corporation, to be leased to families of low income or to such other persons as the Corporation, (a) in its discretion, in the case of a housing project owned by it, or (b) under agreement with the owner, in the case of a housing project not owned by it, designates, having regard to the existence of a condition of shortage, overcrowding or congestion of housing. *National Housing Act*, R.S.C. 1985, c. N-11, s. 2.

LOW VOLTAGE. Any voltage from 31 to 750 volts inclusive. *Power Corporation Act*, R.R.O. 1980, Reg. 794, s. 0.

LOW-VOLTAGE PROTECTION. The effect of a device operative on the reduction or failure of voltage to cause and maintain the interruption of power to the main circuit. *Power Corporation Act*, R.R.O. 1980, Reg. 794, s. 0.

LOW-VOLTAGE RELEASE. The effect of a device operative on the reduction or failure of voltage to cause the interruption of power to the main circuit, but not to prevent its re-establishment on the return of voltage to safe operating value. *Power Corporation Act*, R.R.O. 1980, Reg. 794, s. 0.

L.Q. REV. *abbr.* Law Quarterly Review.

L.R. *abbr.* Law Reports.

L.R.B. *abbr.* Labour Relations Board.

L.R. 1 A. & E. *abbr.* Law Reports, Admiralty and Ecclesiastical Cases, 1865-1875.

L.R. 1 C.C.R. *abbr.* Law Reports, Crown Cases Reserved, 1865-1875.

L.R. 1 CH. *abbr.* Law Reports, Chancery Appeals, 1865-1875.

L.R. 1 C.P. *abbr.* Law Reports, Common Pleas, 1865-1875.

L.R. 1 EQ. *abbr.* Law Reports, Equity Cases, 1865-1875.

L.R. 1 EX. *abbr.* Law Reports, Exchequer, 1865-1875.

L.R. 1 H.L. *abbr.* Law Reports, House of Lords Cases, 1865-1875.

L.R. 1 P. & D. *abbr.* Law Reports, Probate and Divorce, 1865-1875.

L.R. 1 P.C. *abbr.* Law Reports, Privy Council Cases, 1865-1875.

L.R. 1 Q.B. *abbr.* Law Reports, Queen's Bench, 1865-1875.

L.R. 1 SC. & DIV. *abbr.* Law Reports, Scottish and Divorce.

L.R.P.C. *abbr.* Law Reports Privy Council Appeals.

L.S. *abbr.* Locus sigilli. The place for the seal.

L.S.D. *abbr.* The hallucinogenic drug lysergic acid diethylamide. F.A. Jaffe, *A Guide to Pathological Evidence*, 2d ed. (Toronto: Carswell, 1983) at 179.

L. SOC. GAZ. *abbr.* Law Society Gazette (Law Society of Upper Canada).

L.S.U.C. *abbr.* Law Society of Upper Canada.

L.T. *abbr.* Law Times Reports.

LTD. *abbr.* Limited. One of the words or their abbreviations which must form part of a corporate name. H. Sutherland, D.B. Horsley & J.M. Edmiston, eds., *Fraser's Handbook on Canadian Company Law*, 7th ed. (Toronto: Carswell, 1985) at 436 and 437.

LTÉE. *abbr.* Limitée. One of the words or their abbreviations which must form part of a corporate name. H. Sutherland, D.B. Horsley & J.M. Edmiston, eds., *Fraser's Handbook on Canadian Company Law*, 7th ed. (Toronto: Carswell, 1985) at 436 and 437.

LUCID INTERVAL. A period of sanity between two periods of insanity.

LUCRI CAUSA. [L.] With the intent of gain.

LUMBER. *n.* 1. Timber, mast, spar, shingle bolt, sawlog or lumber of any description. *Criminal Code*, R.S.C. 1985, c. C-46, s. 339(6). 2. The products of logs or timber after the same have been sawn or manufactured in a saw mill. *Woodsmen's Lien Act*, R.S.N.B. 1973, c. W-12, s. 1. See PACKAGED ~.

LUMBERING. *n.* 1. The milling of timber into lumber or boards when carried on in a forest, on a woodlot or on a tree farm, and includes the preparation for milling in such place. *Canada Pension Plan Regulations*, C.R.C., c. 385, s. 2. 2. Includes all operations carried on at sawmills or by logging and railway tie contractors. *Industrial Wages Security Act*, R.S.A. 1980, c. I-3, s. 1.

LUMBERING EQUIPMENT. Includes a boom chain, chain, line and shackle. *Criminal Code*, R.S.C. 1985, c. C-46, s. 339(6).

LUMBER PRODUCT. Any part of a log or piece of lumber, and without derogating from the generality of the foregoing, includes a tie, post, beam, plank, board, siding, lath or shingle. *Industrial Wages Security Act*, R.S.A. 1980, c. I-3, s. 1.

LUMEN. *n.* The luminous flux emitted in a solid angle of one steradian by a point source having an intensity of one candela. *Weights and Measures Act*, S.C. 1970-71-72, c. 36, schedule I.

LUMINOUS SIGN. Any device for lighting a poster by electricity or gas and any luminous poster or poster covered with a reflecting paint or coating. *Autoroutes Act*, R.S.Q. 1977, c. A-34, s. 1.

LUNATIC. *n.* 1. Any person found by any competent tribunal or commission de lunatico inquirendo, to be a lunatic. 2. Includes an idiot and a person of unsound mind. 3. Includes a person, not an infant, who is incapable from infirmity of mind of managing his own affairs. *Incompetent Persons Act*, R.S.N.S. 1967, c. 135, s. 1.

LUNCH ROOM. A room that is used by employees for the purpose of eating or preparing meals or lunches. *Canada Sanitation Regulations*, C.R.C., c. 1009, s. 2.

LUNG. See JUNKIE'S ~.

LURE CROP AREA. An area of crop land that, pursuant to an agreement between the Government of Canada and the government of a province, remains unharvested for the purpose of luring migratory birds away from other unharvested crops. *Migratory Birds Regulations*, C.R.C., c. 1035, s. 2.

LUX. *n.* The illuminance produced by a flux of one lumen uniformly distributed over one square metre. *Weights and Measures Act*, S.C. 1970-71-72, c. 36, schedule I.

L.V.A.C. *abbr.* Land Value Appraisal Commission.

LX. *abbr.* Lux.

LYING IN WAIT. The waiting of a vessel, during the season of navigation, for a berth in such portion of a canal designated by the Superintending Engineer for the purpose of the lying-up of vessels. *Canal Regulations*, C.R.C., c. 1564, s. 2.

LYING-UP. *n.* The occupying by a vessel, during the season of navigation, of a berth in such portion of a canal designated by the Superintending Engineer for that purpose. *Canal Regulations*, C.R.C., c. 1564, s. 2.

M. *abbr.* 1. Mega. 2. Metre. 3. Micro. 4. Milli.

MACE. *n.* The symbol of the authority of the House of Commons. A. Fraser, G.A. Birch & W.A. Dawson, eds., *Beauchesne's Rules and Forms of the House of Commons of Canada*, 5th ed. (Toronto: Carswell, 1978) at 34.

MACHINE. *n.* 1. The mechanical embodiment of any mode or function of operation intended to accomplish something particular. H.G. Fox, *The Canadian Law and Practice Relating to Letters Patent for Inventions*, 4th ed. (Toronto: Carswell, 1969) at 17. 2. A vending machine whereby, on depositing therein the premium payable for a policy of accident insurance, the person to be insured may obtain the policy therefrom. *Accident and Sickness Insurance Act*, S.Nfld. 1971, c. 6, s. 40. See AIR-BLAST ~; AMUSEMENT ~; DRILLING ~; HARVEST-ING ~; ITINERANT ~; MEASURING ~; MOTION PICTURE ~; MOVING PICTURE ~; ROAD BUILDING ~; SLOT ~; WEIGHING ~; X-RAY ~.

MACHINE GUARD. A device that (a) is installed on a machine to prevent a person or any part of his body or his clothing from becoming engaged in (i) any rotating, moving, electrically charged, hot or otherwise dangerous part of a machine, or (ii) the material that the machine is processing, transporting or handling, or (b) makes the machine inoperative if a person or any part of his clothing is in or near a part of the machine that can cause injury. *Canada Machine Guarding Regulations*, C.R.C., c. 1003, s. 2.

MACHINERY. *n.* 1. Includes the propelling engines, boilers, pumps, steering engines, windlasses and all similar apparatus required for the safety and operation of a ship. *Canada Shipping Act*, R.S.C. 1985, c. S-9, s. 2. 2. Includes steam and other engines, boilers, furnaces, milling and crushing apparatus, hoisting and pumping equipment, chains, trucks, tramways, tackles, blocks, ropes and tools, and all appliances used in or about or in connection with a mine. See ELEVATOR ~; FARM ~; LIFTING ~; SELF-LUBRICATING ~; TRADE ~.

MACHINERY ASSOCIATION. Includes an association incorporated or registered under this Act having as its principal objects or any of them the purchasing, leasing or otherwise acquiring, maintaining and operating of farm machinery or other equipment for use by or on behalf of the members and patrons thereof in the production of agricultural products or other products, and rendering to the members and patrons as producers services ancillary to such principal objects or any of them. *The Co-operative Production Associations Act*, R.S.S. 1978, c. C-37, s. 53.

MACHINERY INSURANCE. Insurance against (a) liability arising out of (i) bodily injury to, or the death of, a person, or (ii) the loss of, or damage to, property, or (b) the loss of, or damage to, property, caused by breakdown of machinery. *Classes of Insurance Regulations*, C.R.C., c. 977, s. 25.

MACHINERY SPACE. Any space within the main hull of a ship that contains the propelling or auxiliary machinery, including pumping units, boilers when installed, and all permanent coal bunkers. Canada regulations.

MACHINE TOOL, METAL CUTTING. A power driven device, not portable by hand, used for the purpose of removing metal in the form of chips. *Power Corporation Act*, R.R.O. 1980, Reg. 794, s. 0.

MACHINE TOOL, METAL FORMING. A power driven machine not portable by hand, used to press, forge, emboss, hammer, blank or shear metals. *Power Corporation Act*, R.R.O. 1980, Reg. 794, s. 0.

MACHINIST. See AUTOMOTIVE ~; GENERAL ~.

MACKENZIE RIVER. All rivers, streams,

lakes and other waters within the watershed of the Mackenzie River. *Transport Act*, R.S.C. 1985, c. T-17, s. 2.

MACKEREL. *n.* A fish of the species Scomber scombrus. *Northwest Atlantic Fisheries Regulations*, C.R.C., c. 860, s. 2.

MACNAUGHTON'S CASE. See MCNAGHTEN'S CASE.

MACRO-PREMIX. *n.* A feed that is a mixture of ingredients that supply calcium, phosphorous, salt (NaCl), trace minerals and vitamins and may supply protein, fat, carbohydrates, medicating ingredients or amino acids. *Feeds Regulations*, C.R.C., c. 665, s. 2.

MAG. *abbr.* Magistrate(s).

MAGAZINE. *n.* 1. Any building, storehouse, structure or place in which any explosive is kept or stored, but does not include (a) a place where an explosive is kept or stored exclusively for use at or in a mine or quarry in a province in which provision is made by the law of that province for efficient inspection and control of explosives stored and used at or in mines and quarries, (b) a vehicle in which an authorized explosive is being conveyed in accordance with this Act, (c) the structure or place in which is kept for private use, and not for sale, an authorized explosive to an amount not exceeding that authorized by regulation, (d) any store or warehouse in which are stored for sale authorized explosives to an amount not exceeding that authorized by regulation, or (e) any place at which the blending or assembling of the inexplosive component parts of an authorized explosive is allowed under section 8. *Explosives Act*, R.S.C. 1985, c. E-17, s. 2. 2. Any building, storehouse, structure or place in which any explosive is kept or stored, whether in or about a mine and includes detonator storage buildings, detonator and fuse houses, explosives storage boxes and thawing houses. 3. In a firearm, the part where unfired cartridges are kept. F.A. Jaffe, *A Guide to Pathological Evidence*, 2d ed. (Toronto: Carswell, 1983) at 179.

MAGAZINES AND PERIODICALS. Includes bound magazines and periodicals, bound trade magazines, employees' house organs, unbound literary and technical papers and employees' newsletters and club information bulletins issued at intervals not less frequent than four times a year, and school year books. *Retail Sales Tax Act*, R.R.O. 1980, Reg. 903, s. 1.

MAG. CT. *abbr.* Magistrate's Court.

MAGIS DE BONO QUAM DE MALO LEX INTENDIT. [L.] The law favours good instead of bad construction.

MAGISTER. *n.* [L.] A ruler; a master.

MAGISTER NAVIS. [L.] The master of the ship.

MAGISTER RERUM USUS. [L.] Experience is the master of things.

MAGISTER SOCIETATIS. [L.] The manager of the partnership.

MAGISTRACY. *n.* The group of officials who administer the law; the office of magistrate.

MAGISTRATE. *n.* 1. A magistrate, a police magistrate, a stipendiary magistrate, a district magistrate, a provincial magistrate, a judge of the sessions of the peace, a recorder or any person having the power and authority of two or more justices of the peace, and includes (a) with respect to the provinces of Ontario, Quebec, New Brunswick and British Columbia, a judge of the provincial court, (b) with respect to the province of Nova Scotia, a judge of the Provincial Magistrate's Court, (c) with respect to the Provinces of Prince Edward Island, Manitoba and Alberta, a provincial judge, (d) with respect to the province of Saskatchewan, a judge of the Magistrates' Courts, and (e) with respect to the Yukon Territory and the Northwest Territories, a judge of the Supreme Court, and the lawful deputy of each of them. *Criminal Code*, R.S.C. 1985, c. C-46, s. 2. 2. (a) A person appointed under the law of a province, by whatever title he may be designated, who is specially authorized by the terms of his appointment to exercise the jurisdiction conferred on a magistrate by this Part, but does not include two or more justices of the peace sitting together, (b) with respect to the Yukon Territory, a judge of the Supreme Court or a magistrate or deputy magistrate appointed under an Ordinance of the Territory, and (c) with respect to the Northwest Territories, a judge of the Supreme Court or a magistrate or deputy magistrate appointed under an Ordinance of the Territories. *Criminal Code*, R.S.C. 1985, c. C-46, s. 552. 3. Any justice of the peace or any person having authority to issue a warrant for the apprehension of persons accused of offences and to commit those persons for trial. *Fugitive Offenders Act*, R.S.C. 1985, c. F-32, s. 2. See PROVINCIAL ~; STIPENDIARY ~.

MAGNA CARTA. A charter or collection of statutes based largely on Saxon common law granted by the British King John in 1215 to confirm certain liberties.

MAGNUM. *adj.* Of ammunition, especially large or powerful. F.A. Jaffe, *A Guide to Pathological Evidence*, 2d ed. (Toronto: Carswell, 1983) at 179.

MAIL. *v.* Refers to the deposit of the matter to which the context applies in the Canada Post Office at any place in Canada, postage prepaid,

M

for transmission by post, and includes delivery. *Interpretation Act*, R.S.B.C. 1979, c. 206, s. 29.

MAIL. *n.* Mailable matter from the time it is posted to the time it is delivered to the addressee thereof. *Canada Post Corporation Act*, R.S.C. 1985, c. C-10, s. 2. See ADDRESS ~; CERTI-FIED ~; DOMESTIC FOURTH CLASS ~; DOMESTIC THIRD CLASS ~; FIRST CLASS ~; FLEET ~ OFFICE; HOUSEHOLDER ~; POSTPAK ~; REDIRECTED ~; REGIS-TERED ~; REQUEST ~; SECOND CLASS ~; SERVICE BY ~; UNDELIVERABLE ~.

MAILABLE MATTER. Any message, information, funds or goods that may be transmitted by post. *Canada Post Corporation Act*, R.S.C. 1985, c. C-10, s. 2.

MAIL BAG. Any container or covering in which mail is transmitted, whether it contains mail or not. *Canada Post Corporation Act*, R.S.C. 1985, c. C-10, s. 2.

MAIL BOX. A privately owned mail receiving facility designed for indoor or outdoor use in an urban area. *Mail Receptacles Regulations*, C.R.C., c. 1282, s. 2. See GROUP ~ SYSTEM; RURAL ~.

MAIL CONTRACTOR. A person who has entered into a contract with the Corporation for the transmission of mail, which contract has not expired or been terminated. *Canada Post Corporation Act*, R.S.C. 1985, c. C-10, s. 2.

MAIL CONVEYANCE. 1. Any physical, electronic, optical or other means used to transmit mail. *Canada Post Corporation Act*, R.S.C. 1985, c. C-10, s. 2. 2. Includes any vehicle, vessel, aircraft, animal or other means used for conveying mail. *Post Office Act*, R.S.C. 1970, c. P-14, s. 2.

MAIN. See DISTRIBUTION ~.

MAIN DECK. The uppermost weathertight deck extending from side to side of the ship and includes any stepped portions thereof, but does not include any part of a superstructure deck where the deck next beneath the superstructure deck extends from side to side of the ship, is weathertight and is not stepped down inside the superstructure. *Hull Construction Regulations*, C.R.C., c. 1431, s. 100.

MAIN GROUNDING. The portion of a grounding that is the direct continuation of a down-conductor. *Lightning Rods Act*, R.R.O. 1980, Reg. 577, s. 1.

MAINLINE. *v.* To intravenously inject a drug. F.A. Jaffe, *A Guide to Pathological Evidence*, 2d ed. (Toronto: Carswell, 1983) at 180.

MAINPERNOR. *n.* The surety or pledge to whom a person is handed over.

MAINPRISE. *n.* Handing over a person to a surety or pledge who agrees to produce that person some time in the future.

MAIN SEWER. The public sewer including its branches. *Ontario Water Resources Act*, R.R.O. 1980, Reg. 736, s. 1.

MAINTAINABLE EARNINGS. What a business entity earns and what cash flow should follow the valuation date. A. Bissett-Johnson & W.M. Holland, eds., *Matrimonial Property Law in Canada* (Toronto: Carswell, 1980) at V-13.

MAINTAINOR. *n.* A person who, by assisting either party, supports or seconds a cause in which she or he is not interested.

MAINTENANCE. *n.* 1. Pecuniary support including support or alimony to be paid to someone who is not a spouse. C.R.B. Dunlop, *Creditor—Debtor Law in Canada*, Second Cumulative Supplement (Toronto: Carswell, 1986) at 209. 2. Intrusive interference by assisting either party financially or otherwise to prosecute a suit which does not concern one. 3. Includes preserving works or machines and keeping them in good repair for proper operation. 4. Includes shelter, clothing, nursing support, medical treatment, necessary training, instruction and transportation. See CAPITAL ~; LANDSCAPE ~.

MAINTENANCE COSTS. All expenditures required specifically in relation to the operation or maintenance of an approved project. *Conservation Authorities Act*, R.S.O. 1980, c. 85, s. 1.

MAINTENANCE DEBTOR. A person who is required under a maintenance order to pay maintenance to or for the benefit of another person. *Family Maintenance Act*, S.M. 1980, c. 21, s. 2.

MAINTENANCE ORDER. An order for the periodical payment of money as alimony or as maintenance for a wife or former wife or reputed wife or a child or any other dependant of the person against whom the order was made.

MAINTENANCE WORK. The work of keeping electrical equipment, apparatus or appliances in good working order or repair. *Industrial Standards Act*, R.R.O. 1980, Reg. 517, s. 1.

MAIN TRACK. A track extending through yards and between stations upon which trains are operated by time-table or train order, or both, or the use of which is governed by block signals or other method of control. Canada regulations.

MAJESTY. *n.* A title of a sovereign. See LEZE-~.

MAJOR ALTERATION. 1. Any alteration of a building where the plans and specifications for the alteration are required by law to be approved by the building authority. *Canada Building Safety Regulations*, C.R.C., c. 995, s. 2. 2. Any alteration of an electrical facility that, according to the law applicable to that facility, requires the approval of an electrical authority. *Canada Electrical Safety Regulations*, C.R.C., c. 998, s. 2. 3. Any change in a lighting system that increases its current carrying capacity or voltage or that decreases its original safety factor. *Canada Safe Illumination Regulations*, C.R.C., c. 1008, s. 2.

MAJOR ATTACHMENT CLAIMANT. A claimant who has been employed in insurable employment for twenty or more weeks in his qualifying period. *Unemployment Insurance Act*, R.S.C. 1985, c. U-1, s. 5.

MAJOR BUSINESS OR ACTIVITY. In relation to a parent Crown corporation or a wholly-owned subsidiary, means a class of business or activity of the corporation or subsidiary established pursuant to subsection (10) or, if no classes are so established, all the business or activity of the corporation or subsidiary. *Financial Administration Act*, R.S.C. 1985, c. F-11, s. 83.

MAJOR HAEREDITAS VENIT UNICUIQUE NOSTRUM A JURE ET LEGIBUS QUAM A PARENTIBUS. [L.] A greater inheritance comes to each of us through legal right and laws than from our parents.

MAJORITY. *n.* 1. Age of maturity. 2. The largest number. See AGE OF ~; RELIGIOUS ~.

MAJOR LIEN FUND. (i) Where a certificate of substantial performance is not issued, the amount required to be retained under section 15(1) plus any amount payable under the contract (A) that is over and above the 15% referred to in section 15(1), and (B) that has not been paid by the owner in good faith while there is no lien registered; (ii) where a certificate of substantial performance is issued, the amount required to be retained under section 15(12) plus any amount payable under the contract (A) that is over and above the 15% referred to in section 15(1), and (B) that, with respect to any work done or materials furnished before the date of issue of the certificate of substantial performance, has not been paid by the owner in good faith while there is no lien registered. *Builders' Lien Amendment Act*, S.A. 1985, c. 14, s. 2.

MAJOR OCCUPANCY. The principal occupancy for which a building or part thereof is used or intended to be used, and shall be deemed to include the subsidiary occupancies which are an integral part of the principal occupancy. *Building Code Act*, R.R.O. 1980, Reg. 87, s. 1.

MAJOR PERILS. The perils of fire, lightning, smoke, windstorm, hail, explosion, water escape, strikes, riots or civil commotion, impact by aircraft and vehicles, vandalism and malicious mischief. *Condominium Act*, R.S.O. 1980, c. 84, s. 27.

MAJOR PLANT NUTRIENT. Nitrogen (N), phosphoric acid (P_2O_5) or potash (K_2O). *Fertilizers Regulations*, C.R.C., c. 666, s. 2.

MAJOR REPAIRS. Repairs that may affect the strength of a boiler, pressure vessel or plant. Boilers and Pressure Vessels acts.

MAJOR SHAREHOLDER. A person or group of persons is deemed a major shareholder of a corporation or company if that person or group controls, directly or indirectly, more than ten or twenty or thirty per cent of the voting shares in that corporation or company.

MAJOR STRUCTURAL DEFECT. Any defect in workmanship or materials, (i) that results in failure of the load-bearing portion of any building or materially and adversely affects its load-bearing function, or (ii) that materially and adversely affects the use of such building for the purpose for which it was intended, including significant damage due to soil movement, major cracks in basement walls, collapse or serious distortion of joints or roof structure and chemical failure of materials, but excluding flood damage, dampness not arising from failure of a load-bearing portion of the building, damage to drains or services, damage to finishes and damage arising from acts of God, acts of the owners and their tenants, licensees and invitees, acts of civil and military authorities, acts of war, riot, insurrection or civil commotion and malicious damage. *Ontario New Home Warranties Plan Act*, R.R.O. 1980, Reg. 726, s. 1.

MAJUS CONTINET MINUS. [L.] Greater contains less.

MAJUS DIGNUM TRAHIT AD SE MINUS DIGNUM. [L.] The more worthy brings the less worthy along with it.

MAJUS EST DELICTUM SEIPSUM OCCIDERE QUAM ALIUM. [L.] To kill one's self is a greater crime than to kill another.

MAKE. See LINE ~.

MAKER. *n.* 1. Of a promissory note, the one who signs the promise. I.F.G. Baxter, *The Law of Banking*, 3d ed. (Toronto: Carswell, 1981) at 62. 2. Every person who, on his own account, makes, sells, offers for sale, installs or offers to install lightning rods. *Lightning Rods Act*, R.S.Q. 1977, c. P-6, s. 1. See BOOK~; MARKET-~; MOULD ~.

MAKES. See ICE ~.

MAKE-UP WATER. Water added to a swimming pool from an external source. *Public Health Act*, R.R.O. 1980, Reg. 849, s. 1.

MAKE-WORK PRACTICE. A procedure requiring the expansion or spreading of available work.

MAKING WAY. The state of being under way on the surface of the water and having a velocity relative to such surface. *Air Regulations*, C.R.C., c. 2, s. 101.

MAL. *pref.* Wrong; bad; fraudulent.

MALA FIDE. [L.] In bad faith.

MALA FIDES. [L.] Bad faith, contrasted to bona fides, good faith.

MALA GRAMMATICA NON VITIAT CHARTAM. SED IN EXPOSITIONE INSTRUMENTORUM MALA GRAMMATICA QUOAD FIERI POSSIT EVITANDA EST. [L.] Bad grammar does not invalidate a deed. But in the interpretation of documents, bad grammar should be avoided as much as possible.

MALA IN SE. [L.] Acts, such as murder, which are wrong in themselves as contrasted to mala prohibita (mala quia prohibita), acts which are only wrong because the law prohibits them.

MALA PRAXIS. For a medical practitioner to injure a patient through lack of skill, neglect or by experiment.

MALA PROHIBITA. [L.] A wrong which is prohibited by human law, but is not necessarily malum in se or wrong in itself.

MALE. See ~ ISSUE.

MALECREDITUS. *n.* A person who has bad credit.

MALEDICTA EST EXPOSITIO QUAE CORRUMPIT TEXTUM. [L.] It is bad definition which corrupts a text.

MALEDICTION. *n.* A curse.

MALE-DOMINATED CLASS. (i) A class in which there are 10 or more incumbents, as of the date any public sector employer is required to commence action to implement pay equity, of whom 70% or more are men, (ii) in the case of a public sector employer which employs 500 or more employees as of the date referred to in sub-clause (i), such other classes, irrespective of the number of incumbents and gender distribution, as the employer, bargaining agents and employee representatives affected may agree should be considered male-dominated, and (iii) in the case of a public sector employer which employs less than 500 employees as of the date referred to in sub-clause (i), such other classes as may be further defined in the regulations. *The Pay Equity Act*, S.M. 1985-86, c. 21, s. 1.

MALEFACTION. *n.* An offence; a crime.

MALEFACTOR. *n.* A person who commits a malum in se.

MALEFICIA NON DEBENT REMANERE IMPUNITA; ET IMPUNITAS CONTINUUM AFFECTUM TRIBUIT DELINQUENDI. [L.] Evil deeds should not remain unpunished; and impunity offers continual inducement to commit crime.

MALEFICIA PROPOSITIS DISTINGUUNTUR. [L.] Evil deeds differ from evil purposes.

MALEFICIUM. *n.* [L.] Damage; injury; waste.

MALE ISSUE. Descendants in the male line. T. Sheard, R. Hull & M.M.K. Fitzpatrick, *Canadian Forms of Wills*, 4th ed. (Toronto: Carswell, 1982) at 191.

MALFEASANCE. *n.* The commission of an unlawful act. See MISFEASANCE.

MALICE. *n.* The evidence must show that a defendant used the occasion for which immunity is claimed for an improper or wrong motive, or that she or he spoke dishonestly, or in reckless or knowing disregard of truth. R.E. Brown, *The Law of Defamation in Canada* (Toronto: Carswell, 1987) at 13. See IMPLIED ~.

MALICIOUSLY. *adv.* With an intent to cause harm or while being reckless about whether that harm will occur. S. Mitchell, P.J. Richardson & D.A. Thomas, eds., *Archbold On Pleading, Evidence and Practice in Criminal Cases*, 43d ed. (London: Sweet & Maxwell, 1988) at 1343.

MALICIOUS PROSECUTION. Institution by the defendant of a criminal proceeding against the plaintiff, maliciously or for some purpose other than the enforcement of the law, and without reasonable or probable cause, and as a result the plaintiff is injured, by being arrested, imprisoned, put to expense or suffering damage to credit or reputation. The proceeding must have terminated in favour of the plaintiff if that result was possible given the nature of the proceeding. John G. Fleming, *The Law of Torts*, 6th ed. (Sydney: The Law Book Company Limited, 1983) at 576-7.

MALIGNARE. [L.] To slander, to malign.

MALITIA PRAECOGITATA. [L.] Predetermined malice.

MALITIA SUPPLET AETATEM. [L.] Malice makes up for lack of age.

MALLORY-WEISS SYNDROME. Vomiting blood caused by a tear in the esophagus. F.A. Jaffe, *A Guide to Pathological Evidence*, 2d ed. (Toronto: Carswell, 1983) at 184 and 185.

MALT. *n.* Any substance prepared by steeping grain or leguminous seeds in water, allowing the grain or seeds to germinate, and checking the germination by drying. *Excise Act*, R.S.C. 1985, c. E-14, s. 4. See PEAT-DRIED ~.

MALTED MILK POWDER. The product made by combining milk with the liquid separated from a mash of ground barley malt and meal, with or without the addition of salt, sodium bicarbonate or potassium bicarbonate, in such manner as to secure the full enzyme action of the salt extract, and by removing water, and contains, (i.) not less than 7.5 per cent milk-fat, and (ii.) not more than 3.5 per cent water. *Farm Products Grades and Sales Act*, R.R.O. 1980, Reg. 327, s. 1.

MALT LIQUOR. 1. Any beverage, other than beer, obtained by the alcoholic fermentation of an infusion or decoction of barley, malt and hops in drinkable water. *The Liquor Act*, R.S.S. 1978, c. L-18, s. 2. 2. All fermented liquor brewed in whole or in part from malt, grain or any saccharine matter without any process of distillation. *Excise Act*, R.S.C. 1985, c. E-14, s. 4.

MALT-WINE. *n.* An alcoholic distillate obtained by pot-still distillation from a mash of cereal grain or cereal grain products saccharified by the diastase of malt and fermented by the action of yeast. *Food and Drug Regulations*, C.R.C., c. 870, s. B.02.002.

MALUM IN SE. [L.] See MALA IN SE.

MALUM NON PRAESUMITUR. [L.] One does not presume evil.

MALUM PROHIBITUM. [L.] See MALA PROHIBITA.

MALUM QUO COMMUNIUS EO PEJUS. [L.] The more common the evil the worse it is.

MALUS USUS EST ABOLENDUS, QUIA IN CONSUETUDINIBUS NON DIUTURNITAS TEMPORIS, SED SOLIDITAS RATIONIS EST CONSIDERANDA. [L.] A bad usage should be abolished, because with customs it is not the length of time that they have been observed but the totality of the reasoning behind them which must be considered.

MAMMAL. *n.* A vertebrate of the class Mammalia except man. *Wildlife Act*, S.B.C. 1982, c. 57, s. 1.

MAMMALIAN PEST. Any rat, mouse, raccoon, rabbit, porcupine, squirrel, ground-hog, mole or skunk. *Pesticides Act*, R.R.O. 1980, Reg. 751, s. 1.

MAN. *n.* Any person, other than an officer, who is enrolled in, or who pursuant to law is attached or seconded otherwise than as an officer to, the Canadian Forces. *National Defence Act*, R.S.C. 1985, c. N-5, s. 2. See CANDY ~; CLERGY~; COMPANY ~; DEATHS~; DRAFTS~; ENGINE~; GARAGE~; LAND~; LIEGE~; LINE~; MIDDLE-~; MILITIA~; NURSERY-~; OVER~.

MAN. *abbr.* Manitoba.

MANACLE. *n.* A chain used to bind the hands; a shackle.

MANAGED ECOLOGICAL RESERVE. An ecological reserve established for the monitoring and scientific guidance of the evolution of nature. *Ecological Reserves Act*, S.N.B. 1975, c. E-1.1, s. 1.

MANAGEMENT. See FOREST ~; PORTFOLIO ~; RECORDS ~; WASTE ~; WATER QUALITY ~; WILDLIFE ~.

MANAGEMENT AGREEMENT. An agreement entered into by a corporation governing the general control, management and administration of (i) the real and personal property of the corporation associated with the residential units, and (ii) the common property associated with the residential units. *Condominium Property Act*, R.S.A. 1980, c. C-22, s. 1.

MANAGEMENT AND CONSERVATION ZONE. Any territory designated by regulation of the Lieutenant-Governor in Council for wildlife management and conservation purposes. *Wild-life Conservation Act*, S.Q. 1978, c. 65, s. 1.

MANAGEMENT AREA. See WATER ~.

MANAGEMENT COMPANY. A person or company that provides investment advice under a management contract.

MANAGEMENT CONTRACT. A contract under which, for valuable consideration, a mutual fund is provided with investment advice, alone or together with administrative or management services.

MANAGEMENT CORPORATION. See MUTUAL FUND SALES OR ~.

MANAGEMENT FEES. Of a corporation means those fees paid to a person for services performed by an individual that could, had the corporation hired individuals as employees for that purpose, have been performed by those employees. *Alberta Stock Savings Plan Act*, S.A. 1986, c. A-37.7, s. 5.

MANAGEMENT PLAN. 1. A document approved by the Minister of Energy and Resources, containing the prescriptions designed to ensure the productive management of a forest in accordance with objectives consistent with forestry principles and which must be reviewed periodically, according to the directives of the minister and subject to his approval. *An Act to Promote Forest Credit by Private Institutions,* S.Q. 1983, c. 16, s. 30. 2. A plan that sets forth the purpose for which a reserve is to be created, the particular features that are of interest therein and the management techniques recommended for preservation or study of those features. *Wilderness and Ecological Reserves Act,* S.Nfld. 1980, c. 2, s. 2. See WASTE ~.

MANAGEMENT PROGRAM. A report of the existing forest resources and on the proposed silvicultural and marketing program. *Woodlands Improvement Act,* R.S.O. 1980, c. 535, s. 1.

MANAGEMENT RIGHTS. Rights which an employer retains such as hiring, contracting and price fixing.

MANAGEMENT SYSTEM. See WASTE ~.

MANAGER. *n.* 1. Includes owner, lessee, operator and person in charge. 2. The person immediately responsible for the management and direction of a mine. 3. The licensed pharmacist designated by the owner of a pharmacy to have authority over and be responsible for the operation of the pharmacy. 4. When a receiver is appointed and it is necessary to continue the debtor's business, the person appointed by the court to continue the business. F. Bennett, *Receiverships* (Toronto: Carswell, 1985) at 1. See AIRPORT ~; CITY ~; GENERAL ~; MINE ~; MUTUAL FUND ~; MUTUEL ~; PORTFOLIO ~; RECEIVER AND ~; TOTALIZATOR ~; UNDERGROUND ~.

MANAGERIAL CAPACITY. See PERSON EMPLOYED IN A MANAGERIAL OR CONFIDENTIAL CAPACITY.

MANAGING DIRECTOR. A director appointed to manage a company.

MAN. & SASK. TAX R. *abbr.* Manitoba & Saskatchewan Tax Reports.

MAN. BAR N. *abbr.* Manitoba Bar News.

MANCIPATE. *v.* To bind; to enslave; to tie.

MANDAMUS. *n.* [L. we command] A prerogative writ which compels the performance of a public duty, often used to compel an inferior court to exercise its jurisdiction. S.A. DeSmith, *Judicial Review of Administrative Action,* 4th ed. by J.M. Evans (London: Stevens, 1980) at 26.

MANDANT. *n.* The principal party in a contract of mandate.

MANDATA LICITA STRICTAM RECIPIUNT INTERPRETATIONEM, SED ILLICITA LATAM ET EXTENSAM. [L.] Lawful orders receive strict interpretation, but unlawful ones broad and extensive interpretation.

MANDATARIUS TERMINOS SIBI POSITOS TRANSGREDI NON POTEST. [L.] A mandatary cannot exceed limitations imposed on her or him.

MANDATARY. *n.* A person to whom someone gives a charge, commandment or mandate.

MANDATE. *n.* 1. A request; a directive. 2. A bailment of goods, without recompense, to have something done in connection with them or to be transported from one place to another.

MANDATOR. *n.* A director.

MANDATORY. *adj.* Imperative.

MANDATORY ALLOCATION PROGRAM. A program established pursuant to Part I to control the allocation of supplies of a product at the level of the suppliers and wholesale customers thereof. *Energy Supplies Emergency Act,* R.S.C. 1985, c. E-9, s. 2.

MANDATORY INJUNCTION. A requirement that a defendant do something. G.H.L. Fridman, *The Law of Contract in Canada,* 2d ed. (Toronto: Carswell, 1986) at 722.

MANDATORY PRESUMPTION. When certain facts are proved, one presumes that other facts exist. P.W. Hogg, *Constitutional Law of Canada,* 2d ed. (Toronto: Carswell, 1985) at 769.

MANDATUM. *n.* [L.] When a mandatary agrees, without reward, to do something about things which have been bailed or simply to transport them. E.L.G. Tyler & N.E. Palmer, eds., *Crossley Vaines' Personal Property,* 5th ed. (London: Butterworths, 1973) at 85.

MAN-DAY. *n.* 1. The amount of work which can be accomplished by one person in one day. 2. With respect to the use of a campsite, means the use of that campsite by one person for 24 hours. *Territorial Land Use Regulations,* C.R.C., c. 1524, s. 2.

MAN-HOUR. *n.* The amount of work which can be accomplished by one person in one hour.

MANIFEST. *n.* 1. The document designed to identify the quantity, composition, origin and destination of hazardous waste during transportation and the persons consigned, transporting and accepting that waste. *Hazardous Chemicals Amendment Act, 1982,* S.A. 1982, c. 20, s. 2. 2.

Of a merchant ship, a list of the goods which comprise her cargo.

MANIFEST. *adj.* Evident.

MANIFESTA PROBATIONE NON INDIGENT. [L.] Obvious things need not be proved.

MANIFESTO. *n.* The public declaration by a government, sovereign or person of what they intend to do or how they intend to behave. See ANTI-~.

MANIPULATION. *n.* A calculated procedure, force or thrust designed to move one structure in relation to another, particularly of the spinal column, to remove subluxations or fixations and to mobilize the affected structures for the purpose of restoring or maintaining health. *Chiropractic Profession Act*, R.S.A. 1980, c. C-9, s. 1.

MANIPULATIVE TREATMENT. The use of the hand or machinery in the operation or working on the foot or its articulations. *Podiatrists Act*, R.S.B.C. 1979, c. 330, s. 1.

MANITOBA. See GOVERNMENT OF ~; NORTHERN ~.

MANITOBA CONTRACT. A subsisting contract of insurance that (i) has for its subject (A) property that, at the time of the making of the contract, is in the province or is in transit to or from the province; or (B) the life, safety, fidelity, or insurable interest of a person who, at the time of the making of the contract, is resident in or has its head office in, the province; or (ii) makes provision for payment thereunder primarily to a resident of the province or to an incorporated company that has its head office in the province. *Insurance Act*, R.S.M. 1970, c. 140, s. 51.

MANITOBA MERCHANDISE. Merchandise the whole or greater part of which is produced by Manitoba labour. *Manitoba Trading Corporation Act*, S.M. 1974, c. 55, s. 1.

MANITOBA PRODUCTS. Products the whole or greater part of which is produced by Manitoba labour. *Manitoba Trading Corporation Act*, S.M. 1974, c. 55, s. 1.

MANITOBA SERVICES. Architectural, engineering, consulting or other services provided by persons or organizations in Manitoba. *Manitoba Trading Corporation Act*, S.M. 1974, c. 55, s. 1.

MANITOBA SUPPLIERS. Producers, manufacturers, persons or organizations in Manitoba that supply Manitoba products, merchandise or services. *Manitoba Trading Corporation Act*, S.M. 1974, c. 55, s. 1.

MANLIFT. *n.* A mechanism having a power driven endless belt with platforms or footholds for lifting or lowering persons in a substantially vertical direction and includes its hoistway enclosure.

MAN. L.J. *abbr.* Manitoba Law Journal.

MAN. L.R. *abbr.* Manitoba Law Reports (First Series).

MAN-MADE FIBRE. A staple fibre or filament produced by manufacturing processes, wholly or in part of organic polymers, but does not include rubber. *Customs Tariff*, R.S.C. 1985, c. C-54, s. 2.

MANNER OF DEATH. The mode or method of death whether natural, homicidal, suicidal, accidental or undeterminable. *Fatality Inquiries Act*, R.S.A. 1980, c. F-6, s. 1.

MANOEUVRE. See VESSEL RESTRICTED IN HER ABILITY TO ~.

MANOEUVRING AREA. That part of an airport ordinarily used for the take-off and landing of aircraft and for the movement of aircraft associated with the take-off and landing, but does not include the apron. Canada regulations.

MAN OF STRAW. See STRAMINEUS HOMO.

MANPOWER PROGRAMS AND SERVICES. Includes (i) information, counselling, planning and testing services to assist individuals in making choices of careers and occupations and to assist individuals in manpower training; (ii) employment placement services; (iii) manpower mobility services for the purpose of identifying locations inside and outside Alberta where recruitment of individuals in desired occupations may be successful, assisting employers in Alberta who desire to recruit employees inside or outside Alberta, and providing information and assistance to individuals inside or outside Alberta who desire employment in Alberta; (iv) manpower training, including training under Part 3; (v) voluntary and compulsory certification of individuals engaged in trades designated under Part 3; (vi) certification of the competence of individuals engaged in occupations other than trades designated under Part 3; (vii) special manpower programs and projects for individuals who are without employment or in employment unsuitable to their capacities; (viii) consultative and advisory services. *Manpower Development Act*, R.S.A. 1980, c. M-3, s. 1.

MANPOWER REQUIREMENT. A requirement for the movement of employees into or out of an industry, or from one type of employment within an industry to another type of employment within that industry, where the requirement arises from (a) a technological or other industrial change that renders the employees' skills or aptitudes superfluous to the needs of the industry or the type of employment from which the employees are moved, or (b) an expansion of the industry to which the employees are moved. *Labour Mobility and Assessment Incentives Regulations*, C.R.C., c. 330, s. 2.

MAN. R. *abbr.* Manitoba Reports, 1883-1961.

MANRIKIGUSARI. *n.* A length of rope, cord, wire or chain fastened at each end to a hexagonal or other geometrically shaped hard weight or hand-grip. *Prohibited Weapons Order, No.* 2, C.R.C., c. 434, s. 2.

MAN. R. (2D). *abbr.* Manitoba Reports (Second Series), 1979-.

MAN. R. TEMP. WOOD. *abbr.* Queen's Bench, temp. Wood (Man.), 1875-1883.

MANSLAUGHTER. *n.* 1. Culpable homicide that is not murder or infanticide. *Criminal Code*, R.S.C. 1985, c. C-46, s. 234. 2. Culpable homicide that otherwise would be murder may be reduced to manslaughter if the person who committed it did so in the heat of passion caused by sudden provocation. *Criminal Code*, R.S.C. 1985, c. C-46, s. 232(1).

MANSUETAE NATURAE. [L.] Harmless animals. John G. Fleming, *The Law of Torts*, 6th ed. (Sydney: The Law Book Company Limited, 1983) at 329.

MANTICULATE. To pick pockets.

MANUAL. See RATE ~.

MANUAL STRANGULATION. Strangling with one or both hands which sometimes injures the thyroid cartilage or hyoid bone. F.A. Jaffe, *A Guide to Pathological Evidence*, 2d ed. (Toronto: Carswell, 1983) at 184.

MANUALIS OBEDIENTIA. [L.] Submission under oath; sworn obedience.

MANUCAPTOR. *n.* A person who stands bail for another person.

MANUFACTORY. See BONDED ~; CIGAR ~; TOBACCO ~.

MANUFACTURE. *n.* 1. Anything made by the art or industry of people. H.G. Fox, *The Canadian Law and Practice Relating to Letters Patent for Inventions*, 4th ed. (Toronto: Carswell, 1969) at 17. 2. The process of assembling or altering a motor vehicle in order to complete that motor vehicle for the purpose of sale of that motor vehicle to the first purchaser at the retail level. *Motor Vehicles Safety Act*, R.S.C. 1985, c. M-10, s. 2. 3. Includes the production, refining or compounding of fuel. See DATE OF ~.

MANUFACTURED. *adj.* With respect to butter, includes that stage of the operation when butter is packed or placed in a package. *Dairy Industry Act*, S.A. 1981, c. D-1.1, s. 1.

MANUFACTURED FIREWORKS. Explosives of any class and any fireworks composition that is enclosed in any case or contrivance, or is otherwise manufactured or adapted for the production of pyrotechnic effects, pyrotechnic signals or sound signals. *Explosives Regulations*, C.R.C., c. 599, s. 2.

MANUFACTURED GAS. Any artificially produced fuel gas, except acetylene and any other gas used principally in welding or cutting metals. *Ontario Energy Board Act*, R.S.O. 1980, c. 332, s. 1.

MANUFACTURED GOODS. See PARTLY ~.

MANUFACTURED HOME. A dwelling unit that is designed to be used as living quarters and that is manufactured, either wholly or in part, at an off-site location. *An Act to Amend the Mobile Homes Act*, S.N.B. 1987, c. 37, s. 2.

MANUFACTURED MEAT PRODUCT. Food that is the product of a process and that contains meat as an ingredient and includes meat that is processed by salting, pickling or smoking or otherwise applying heat or to which edible fats, cereals or sugar have been added. *Public Health Act*, R.R.O. 1980, Reg. 853, s. 1.

MANUFACTURED MILK PRODUCT. A dairy product other than milk in fluid form. *Milk Industry Act*, R.S.B.C. 1979, c. 258, s. 1.

MANUFACTURED PRODUCT. Wildlife (i) prepared for use as or in an article to be sold or a garment, or (ii) preserved or prepared by a tanning or taxidermy process. *Wildlife Act*, S.N.W.T. 1978 (3d Sess.), c. 8, s. 2.

MANUFACTURED TOBACCO. Every article made by a tobacco manufacturer from raw leaf tobacco by any process whatever, except cigars, and includes cigarettes and snuff. *Excise Act*, R.S.C. 1985, c. E-14, s. 6.

MANUFACTURER. *n.* 1. Any person who manufactures or produces by hand, art, process or mechanical means any goods, wares and merchandise and a person who packs, freezes or dehydrates any goods, wares and merchandise. 2. Includes one who makes, prepares, alters, repairs, renovates, services, dyes, cleans, ornaments, prints, finishes, packs, or assembles the parts of and adapts for use or sale any raw material, goods, article or commodity. 3. A person who manufactures or assembles motor vehicles. See AFFIDAVIT OF ~; BONDED ~; CIGAR ~; PRODUCER OR ~; TOBACCO ~.

MANUFACTURING. *n.* Includes making, preparing, altering, repairing, renovating, servicing, dyeing, cleaning, ornamenting, printing, finishing, packing or assembling the parts of and adapting for use or sale any raw materials, goods, articles or commodities.

MANUFACTURING ASSOCIATION. Includes an association incorporated or registered under this Act having as its principal objects, or any of them, producing, preparing, adapting, processing and manufacturing goods, wares and merchandise from raw materials derived chiefly from the products of agriculture, forest, lake, river or the utilization for such purposes of products of other natural resources; for use or sale primarily by its members or for use or sale by or through the association. *The Co-operative Production Associations Act*, R.S.S. 1978, c. C-37, s. 65.

MANUFACTURING BUSINESS. A business in which the production factors involved in a prescribed manufacturing or processing operation are grouped and co-ordinated. *An Act Respecting Fiscal Incentives to Industrial Development*, R.S.Q. 1977, c. S-34, s. 1.

MANUFACTURING LOCATION. See INTERDEPENDENT ~.

MANUFACTURING OR PROCESSING ACTIVITY. An activity whereby any footwear or leather (a) is made, fabricated, processed or refined out of any raw material or other substance or combination thereof, and includes the tanning of any raw material or other substance or combination thereof, or (b) is made by causing any raw material or other substance to undergo a significant chemical, bio-chemical or physical change including any change that preserves or improves the keeping qualities of that raw material or other substance but excluding any change by growth or decay. Canada regulations.

MANUFACTURING PLANT. A plant that utilizes a mineral or a substance recovered from a mineral as a component of a product manufactured by the plant. See DAIRY ~; MILK ~.

MANU FORTI. [L.] With a strong hand.

MANUMISSION. *n.* The act of freeing slaves.

MANU OPERA. [L.] Goods held by a thief caught in the act of stealing them.

MANUS. *n.* [L.] An oath.

MANUSCRIPT. See WRITING, ~.

MANUSCRIPT, RECORD OR DOCUMENT. Textual material, other than a printed book, pamphlet or serial consisting of one or more pages bound, stitched or fastened together or in loose format that clearly forms a single unit of information. *Canadian Cultural Property Export Control List*, C.R.C., c. 448, s. 1.

MAP. *n.* A document that is a cartographic representation and includes a topographic, hydrographic, military, cadastral, aeronautic or survey map, cartogram, chart or plan. *Canadian Cultural Property Export Control List*, C.R.C., c. 448, s. 1.

MAPLE PRODUCT. Any product or preparation prepared directly or indirectly from the sap of the maple.

MAPLE PRODUCT SUBSTITUTE. A product other than a pure maple product manufactured or derived in whole or in part from a farm product and prepared for the same uses as a maple product and resembling a maple product in appearance. *Farm Products Grades and Sales Act*, R.R.O. 1980, Reg. 339, s. 1.

MAPLE SUGAR. A solid product resulting from the evaporation of maple sap or maple syrup, and may be either in solid blocks or in a more or less pulverized form. *Maple Products Industry Act*, R.S.C. 1970, c. M-2, s. 2.

MAPLE SYRUP. Syrup made by the evaporation of maple sap or by the solution of maple sugar in water. *Maple Products Industry Act*, R.S.C. 1970, c. M-2, s. 2.

MAPPING. *n.* The planning, co-ordination, generation, procurement, maintenance and distribution of maps and mapping materials and includes activities connected with topographic, thematic and cadastral mapping in photographic, cartographic and digital formats. *Department of Revenue, Supply and Services Amendment Act, 1982 (No. 2)*, S.S. 1982-83, c. 31, s. 3.

MAP SHEETS. *var.* **MAP-SHEETS.** The surveys or maps entitled "Boundary between Alberta and British Columbia" and on record in the Department of Energy, Mines and Resources at Ottawa, comprising (a) Part I containing sheets 1 to 16A surveyed between the years 1913 and 1916, (b) Part II containing sheets 17 to 29B surveyed between the years 1917 and 1921, (c) Part III containing sheets 29 to 54 surveyed between the years 1918 and 1924, (d) Part IV containing sheets 55 to 66 surveyed between the years 1950 and 1953. *Alberta-British Columbia Boundary Act*, S.C. 1974-75-76, c. 11, s. 2.

MARBLING. *n.* The visibility of the patterns of blood vessels on skin after death. F.A. Jaffe, *A Guide to Pathological Evidence*, 2d ed. (Toronto: Carswell, 1983) at 180.

MARCHIONESS. *n.* In England, a female marquess.

MAREVA INJUNCTION. 1. Originally a pre-judgment remedy intended to freeze assets until judgment was obtained and a writ of execution issued. C.R.B. Dunlop, *Creditor-Debtor Law in Canada*, Second Cumulative Supplement (Toronto: Carswell, 1986) at 88. 2. A remedy designed to (1) obtain something like security, at least by ensuring that there are funds available to meet any judgment, and (2) put pressure on a defendant to provide proper security for any claim. However, it has been held that such an injunction does not create a proprietary right in the enjoined property; it merely prevents dealing with that property in particular ways. C.R.B. Dunlop, *Creditor-Debtor Law in Canada* (Toronto: Carswell, 1981) at 190.

MARGARINE. *n.* Includes oleo, oleomargarine, butterine, and any substitute for butter of whatever origin, source, or composition, that is prepared for the same uses as butter and is manufactured wholly or in part from any fat or oil other than that of milk.

MARGIN. See BUY ON ~; RETAILER ~.

MARGIN ACCOUNT. An account agreement with a securities' dealer permitting the purchase of securities on credit.

MARGINAL NOTE. Something printed beside the section of an act which summarizes the effect of that section. P. St. J. Langan, ed., *Maxwell on The Interpretation of Statutes*, 12th ed. (Bombay: N.M. Tripathi, 1976) at 9.

MARGIN DEFICIENCY. Where used with respect to firm trading accounts and clients' accounts, means the amount by which deposits are, at any time, below, (i) the minimum margin prescribed under the rules or regulations of the commodity futures exchange upon which a contract was entered into or by the Commission, or (ii) the amount required under subsection 30(3). *Commodity Futures Act*, R.R.O. 1980, Reg. 114, s. 7.

MARGIN LINE. A line drawn at least 3 inches below the upper surface of the bulkhead deck at the side of a ship, and assumed for the purpose of determining the floodable length of the ship. *Hull Construction Regulations*, C.R.C., c. 1431, s. 2.

MARGIN OF DUMPING. In relation to any goods, means the amount by which the normal value of the goods exceeds the export price thereof. *Special Imports Measures Act*, R.S.C. 1985, c. S-15, s. 2.

MARIHUANA. *n.* Cannabis sativa L. *Narcotic Control Act*, R.S.C. 1985, c. N-1, s. 2.

MARINA. *n.* Any premises at which gasoline or an associated product is sold and is put into the fuel tanks of motor boats and other water craft or into portable containers. See COMMERCIAL ~.

MARINARIUS. *n.* [L.] A mariner, sailor.

MARINE. *adj.* Relating to naval matters.

MARINE ADVENTURE. Occurs when (a) any ship goods or other moveables are exposed to maritime perils; (b) the earning or acquisition of any freight, passage money, commission, profit, or other pecuniary benefit, or the security for any advances, loan, or disbursements, is endangered by the exposure of insurable property to maritime perils; (c) any liability to a third party may be incurred by the owner of, or other person interested in or responsible for, insurable property, by reason of maritime perils. Raoul Colinvaux, *The Law of Insurance*, 5th ed. (London: Sweet & Maxwell, 1984) at 12.

MARINE AREA. The sea-bed and subsoil of any area covered by sea water and excludes any area so specified by regulation. *Oil and Gas Rights Act*, S.N.S. 1971-72, c. 12, s. 1.

MARINE BUNKER FUEL. (a) Bunker oil, or (b) a combination of fuels including bunker oil that has a viscosity not lower than 20 centistokes when measured at a temperature of 50°C and is used in a ship as fuel for an internal combustion engine, steam engine or steam turbine. *Motor Fuel Tax Act*, S.B.C. 1985, c. 76, s. 1.

MARINE CHEMIST. A person who (a) has graduated from an educational institution approved by the Board and has completed (i) courses in chemical engineering, or (ii) a general course with a major in chemistry, or (b) has obtained a fellowship in the Chemical Institute of Canada, and thereafter has had at least three years experience in chemical or engineering work, of which a minimum of 150 working hours has been gained under proper supervision in ship board work involving the testing and inspection of tank vessels and other vessels in the application of gas hazard control standards prescribed by the Board. *Safe Working Practices Regulations*, C.R.C., c. 1467, s. 2.

MARINE CRAFT WASTE DISPOSAL SYSTEM. A waste disposal system operated by a person or a municipality for the receiving of waste from marine craft for deposit in holding tanks. *Environmental Protection Act*, R.R.O. 1980, Reg. 309, s. 1.

MARINE DIESEL FUEL. Diesel fuel for use in a ship as fuel for an internal combustion engine. *Motor Fuel Tax Act*, S.B.C. 1985, c. 76, s. 1.

MARINE INSURANCE. 1. Insurance against marine losses; that is to say, the losses incident to marine adventures, and may be the express terms of a contract or by usage of trade extend so as to protect the insured against losses on inland waters or by land or air which are incidental to any sea voyage. 2. Insurance against, (i) liability arising out of, (A) bodily injury to or death of a person, or (B) the loss of or damage to properties; or (ii) the loss of or damage to property, occurring during a voyage or marine adventure at sea or on an inland waterway or during delay incidental thereto, or during transit otherwise than by water incidental to such a voyage or marine adventure. See CONTRACT OF ~; INLAND ~.

MARINE PLANT. 1. Includes Irish moss, kelp and other salt water plants, and any products or by-products thereof. *Fish Inspection Act*, R.S.C. 1985, c. F-12, s. 2. 2. Includes all benthic and detached algae, marine flowering plants, brown algae, red algae, green algae and phytoplankton. *Fisheries Act*, R.S.C. 1985, c. F-14, s. 47.

MARINE PRODUCT. Any fish, shellfish or crustacean able to live in a marine environment and any echinoderm, including parts of such animals and the products or by-products derived therefrom. *An Act to Amend the Agricultural Products, Marine Products and Food Act*, S.Q. 1983, c. 53, s. 1.

MARINER. *n.* A voter who is serving on a ship or boat within the province, and includes a fisherman who is a voter. *Election Act*, R.S.M. 1970, c. C30, s. 2.

MARINE SANITATION DEVICE. Any equipment installed on board a ship that is designed to receive, retain, store, treat or discharge sewage and any process to treat such sewage. *Great Lakes Sewage Pollution Prevention Regulations*, C.R.C., c. 1429, s. 2.

MARINE SECTION. The water transport and personnel of the Force. *Royal Canadian Mounted Police Pension Contribution Act*, R.S.C., 1970, c. R-10, s. 2.

MARINE SURVEY. The inspection of a vessel.

MARINE TRAFFIC CONTROL CENTRE. A radio station operating on assigned VHF radio channels within different sectors of the St. Lawrence Waterway for the purpose of controlling marine movement. *National Harbours Board Operating By-law*, C.R.C., c. 1064, s. 2.

MARINE TRAFFIC INSTRUCTION. An instruction transmitted by a marine traffic regulator to a vessel. *St. Lawrence Waterway Marine Traffic Regulations*, C.R.C., c. 1470, s. 2.

MARINE TRAFFIC REGULATOR. A person at the marine traffic regulating centre who is authorized by the Minister of Transport to regulate marine traffic. *Canso Zone Marine Traffic Regulations*, C.R.C., c. 1410, s. 2.

MARITAL. *adj.* Pertaining to the state of marriage; relating to a husband.

MARITAL DEBTS. The indebtedness of either or both spouses to another person (a) for the purpose of facilitating, during cohabitation, the support, education or recreation of the spouses or one or more of their children; or (b) in relation to the acquisition, management, maintenance, operation or improvement of marital property. *Marital Property Act*, S.N.B. 1980, c. M-1.1, s. 1.

MARITAL HOME. Property in which one or both spouses have an interest and that is or has been occupied as their family residence, and where property that includes a marital home is used for a purpose in addition to a family residence, that marital home is that portion of the property that may reasonably be regarded as necessary to the use and enjoyment of the family residence.

MARITAL PROPERTY. (a) Family assets; (b) property owned by one spouse or by both spouses that is not a family asset and that was acquired while the spouses cohabited, or in contemplation of marriage, except (i) a business asset, (ii) property that was a gift from one spouse to the other, including income from that property, (iii) property that was a gift, devise, or bequest from any other person to one spouse only, including income from that property, (iv) property that represents the proceeds of disposition of property that was not a family asset and was not acquired while the spouses cohabited or in contemplation of marriage, or that was acquired in exchange for or was purchased with the proceeds of disposition of such property or that represents insurance proceeds with respect to loss of or damage to such property; and (v) property that represents the proceeds of disposition of property referred to in sub-paragraphs (ii) and (iii) or that was acquired in exchange for or was purchased with the proceeds of disposition of such property or that represents insurance proceeds with respect to loss of or damage to such property; and (c) property that was acquired by one spouse after the cessation of cohabitation and that was acquired through the disposition of property that would have been marital property had the disposition not occurred; but does not include property that the spouses have agreed by a domestic contract is not to be included in marital property.

MARITAL REGIME. See STANDARD ~.

MARITAL RIGHTS. A husband's rights. See now CONJUGAL RIGHTS.

MARITAL STATUS. The status of being married, single, widowed, divorced or separated and includes the status of living with a person of the opposite sex in a conjugal relationship outside marriage. *Human Rights Code, 1981*, S.O. 1981, c. 53, s. 9.

MARITIME INSURANCE. Insurance against marine losses; that is to say, the losses incident to marine adventure, and may be the express terms of a contract or by usage of trade extend so as to protect the insured against losses on inland waters or by land or air which are incidental to any sea voyage. *Insurance Act*, R.S.P.E.I. 1974, c. I-5, s. 1.

MARITIME LAW. The law relating to ships, harbours and mariners. See CANADIAN ~.

MARITIME PERILS. The perils consequent on or incidental to the navigation of the sea, that is to say, perils of the seas, fire, war perils, pirates, rovers, thieves, captures, seizures, restraints, and detainments of princes and peoples, jettisons, barratry, and any other perils, either of the like kind or which may be designated by the policy. Insurance acts.

MARITIME PROVINCES. The Provinces of Nova Scotia, New Brunswick, Prince Edward Island and Newfoundland. *Transport Act*, R.S.C. 1985, c. T-17, s. 2.

MARK. *n.* 1. A mark, brand, seal, wrapper or design used by or on behalf of (a) the government of Canada or a province, (b) the government of a state other than Canada, or (c) any department, board, commission or agent established by a government mentioned in paragraph (a) or (b) in connection with the service or business of that government. *Criminal Code*, R.S.C. 1985, c. C-46, s. 376. 2. Any mark, sign, device, imprint, stamp, brand, label, ticket, letter, word or figure. *Precious Metals Marking Act*, R.S.C. 1985, c. P-19, s. 2. 3. A brand or any permanent mark applied to the exterior of an animal or any device implanted beneath the skin or within the body of an animal, but does not include any mark registered under the authority of the Livestock Pedigree Act (Canada). *The Animals Identification Act*, R.S.S. 1978, c. A-20.1, s. 2. See CERTIFICATION ~; CODE ~; DISTINGUISHING ~; EXPORT ~; INSPECTION ~; LAND~; PLIMSOLL ~; QUALITY ~; SAFETY ~; SERVICE ~; TRADE ~.

MARKED. *adj.* Marked by a specific dye as required by the regulations. Gasoline Tax acts.

MARKED BUNKER FUEL. Fuel oil, as defined by regulation, used in a ship as fuel for an internal combustion engine, steam engine or steam turbine. *Gasoline (Coloured) Tax Amendment Act*, S.B.C. 1983, c. 10, s. 6.1.

MARKED FUEL. Fuel oil coloured or identified in accordance with the regulations. *Fuel Oil Administration Act*, R.S.A. 1980, c. F-21, s. 1.

MARKER. *n.* A plaque or monument of metal, concrete, stone or other material installed or to be installed in a cemetery, columbarium or mausoleum in memory of a deceased person. See FICTITIOUS IDENTIFICATION PLATE OR ~; FICTITIOUS ~; GENETIC ~; GRAVE ~.

MARKET. *n.* 1. A place where a person may go to buy or sell whatever she or he wants. G.H.L. Fridman, *Sale of Goods in Canada*, 3d ed. (Toronto: Carswell, 1986) at 358-359. 2. A stockyard, abbatoir or auction market and includes a feedlot where livestock is held for sale or slaughter. *Livestock Identification and Brand Inspection Act*, S.A. 1985, c. L-22.5, s. 1. 3. (a) In relation to an A.M. station, the geographical area in which local retail advertisers from which the station receives revenue are located, and (b) in relation to an F.M. station, the geographical area (i) in which local retail advertisers from which the station receives revenue are located, and (ii) that is within the 500 microvolt per metre service contour described in the technical brief relating to the most recently approved application by the licensee of the station for the issue, renewal or amendment of its licence. *Radio (F.M.) Broadcasting Regulations*, C.R.C., c. 380, s. 2. See AFTER-~; AVAILABLE ~; COMMON ~; EURO-CURRENCY ~; EXPORT ~; FLEA ~; HYPOTHETICAL OR NOTIONAL ~; LABOUR ~; MUNICIPAL ~; OVER-THE-COUNTER ~; PUBLISHED ~.

MARKETABLE GAS. A mixture mainly of methane originating from raw gas, if necessary, through the processing of the raw gas for the removal or partial removal of some constituents, that meets specifications for use as a domestic, commercial or industrial fuel or as an industrial raw material.

MARKETABLE PIPELINE GAS. Gas, other than (a) natural gas liquids, and (b) gas injected into a natural reservoir for any purpose, other than storage. *Excise Tax Act*, R.S.C. 1985, c. E-15, s. 29.

MARKETABLE SECURITY. A security which may be sold on a stock market.

MARKET DEMAND. The amount of oil or gas reasonably needed for current consumption, use, storage and working stocks within and outside Alberta. *Oil and Gas Conservation Act*, R.S.A. 1980, c. O-5, s. 1. See REASONABLE ~.

MARKETED PRODUCT. Any farm product to which a plan applies. *Farm Products Marketing Act*, R.S.Q. 1977, c. M-35, s. 1.

MARKET GARDENING. The cultivation of a tract of land principally for the production of seedlings and matured plants of table vegetables, but does not include landscape gardening or an operation of which the major portion of the products are flowering plants or ornamental shrubs or trees. *Vacations With Pay Act*, R.S.M. 1970, c. V20, s. 2.

MARKETING. *n.* 1. Buying, selling, shipping for sale or offering for sale. 2. In relation to any farm product that is not a regulated product, includes selling and offering for sale and buying, pricing, assembling, packing, processing, transporting, storing and any other act necessary to prepare the product in a form or to make it available at a place and time for purchase for consumption or use and, in relation to a regulated product, includes only such of the above acts as are specified in the marketing plan relating to the regulated product. 3. Includes bartering, advertising, packing, processing, storing, shipping, and transporting, for the purposes of sale or in anticipation of sale. See BLACK ~.

MARKETING AGENCY. A marketing agency of Canada that is authorized to exercise powers of regulation in relation to the marketing of a regulated product in interprovincial or export trade and that has been granted authority to regulate the marketing of the regulated product locally within Ontario. *Commodity Boards and Marketing Agencies Act*, R.S.O. 1980, c. 77, s. 1.

MARKETING CONTRACT. See COOPERATIVE ~.

MARKETING PLAN. A plan relating to the promotion, regulation and control of the marketing of any regulated product in interprovincial or export trade that includes provision for all or any of the following: (a) the determination of those persons engaged in the growing or production of the regulated product for interprovincial or export trade and the exemption of any class of persons so engaged from the marketing plan or any aspect thereof, (b) the specification of those acts that constitute the marketing of the regulated product and of those persons engaged in its marketing, as so specified, in interprovincial or export trade, and for the exemption of any class of persons so engaged from the marketing plan or any aspect thereof, (c) the marketing of the regulated product on a basis that enables the agency that is implementing the plan to fix and determine the quantity, if any, in which the regulated product or any variety, class or grade thereof may be marketed in interprovincial or export trade by each person engaged in the marketing thereof and by all persons so engaged, and the price, time and place at which the regulated product or any variety, class or grade thereof may be so marketed, (d) the pooling of receipts from the marketing of the regulated product or any variety, class or grade thereof, in interprovincial or export trade and the operation of pool accounts including provision for the system of initial, interim and final payments to producers and deduction from the pool of the expenses of the operation thereof, (e) a system for the licensing of persons engaged in the growing or production of the regulated product for, or the marketing thereof in, interprovincial or export trade, including provision for fees, other than fees related to the right to grow the regulated product, payable to the appropriate agency by any such person in respect of any licence issued to such person and for the cancellation or suspension of any such licence where a term or condition thereof is not complied with, and (f) the imposition and collection by the appropriate agency of levies or charges from persons engaged in the growing or production of the regulated product or the marketing thereof and for such purposes classifying those persons into groups and specifying the levies or charges, if any, payable by the members of each group. 2. A plan for the marketing in interprovincial or export trade of grain produced and delivered to elevators or grain dealers licensed under the Canada Grain Act by producers who have agreed to participate in the plan and whose permit books are endorsed to that effect that include provision for the pooling or averaging of all or part of the receipts from the sale of the grain and a system of initial payments to those producers and deduction from the pool of the operational expenses thereof. *Canadian Wheat Board Act*, R.S.C. 1985, c. C-24, s. 48.

MARKETING PLAN OR SYSTEM. A marketing plan or system organized, directed, prescribed or controlled, in substantial part, by a franchisor. *The Pyramid Franchises Act*, R.S.S. 1978, c. P-50, s. 2.

MARKETING PLANT. Any plant used for the marketing or distribution of any product obtained from the refining, processing or purifying of oil, gas or minerals.

MARKET-MAKER. *n.* A trading representative registered with the Commission des valeurs mobilières du Québec to carry on his activity for his own account or as the employee of a clearing member on the trading floor of the Montreal Stock Exchange and appointed by the Exchange to maintain the market of the listed stocks. *An Act to Amend Taxation Act and Other Fiscal Legislation*, S.Q. 1985, c. 25, s. 143.

MARKET OPERATOR. The owner or the operator of a market or a livestock dealer licensed under the Livestock and Livestock

Products Act. *Livestock Identification and Brand Inspection Act*, S.A. 1985, c. L-22.5, s. 1.

MARKET OVERT. Open market.

MARKET PRICE. 1. The highest price for which an owner can sell property under conditions prevalent in that market. A. Bissett-Johnson & W.M. Holland, eds., *Matrimonial Property Law in Canada* (Toronto: Carswell, 1980) at V-11. 2. As to securities to which there is a published market, the price at any particular date determined in accordance with regulations. See MARKET VALUE.

MARKET RESTRICTION. Any practice whereby a supplier of a product, as a condition of supplying the product to a customer, requires that customer to supply any product only in a defined market, or exacts a penalty of any kind from the customer if he supplies any product outside a defined market. *Combines Investigation Act*, R.S.C. 1985 (2d Supp.), c. 19, s. 77.

MARKET VALUE. 1. The amount in terms of cash that would probably be realized for property in an arm's length sale in an open market under conditions requisite to a fair sale, the buyer and seller each acting knowledgeably and willingly. *Loan and Trust Companies Act*, S.N.B. 1987, c. L-11.2, s. 1. 2. The amount of money a willing and informed buyer would pay to a willing and informed seller on usual terms and conditions in a competitive market where neither party was acting under abnormal pressure. *Farm Credit Regulations*, C.R.C., c. 644, s. 2. 3. The most probable sale price indicated by consideration of the cost of reproduction, the sale price of comparable properties and the value indicated by rentals or anticipated net income. *Real Property Assessment Act*, R.S.P.E.I. 1974, c. R-5, s. 1. 4. Market price. A. Bissett-Johnson & W.M. Holland, eds., *Matrimonial Property Law in Canada* (Toronto: Carswell, 1980) at V-11. 5. Where used with respect to, (i.) a commodity futures contract means the settlement price on the relevant date or last trading day prior to the relevant date, (ii.) a security means, A. where the security is listed and posted for trading on a stock exchange, (1.) the bid price, or (2.) if the security is sold short, the ask price, as shown on the exchange quotation sheets as of the close of business on the relevant date or last trading date prior to the relevant date, as the case may be, subject to an appropriate adjustment where an unusually large or unusually small quantity of securities is being valued. See FAIR ~.

MARKSMAN. *n.* An illiterate person who makes the mark X when signing a document.

MARK-UP. *n.* The amount added to cost in determining the selling price to cover overhead

and profit. *Defence Production Act*, R.S.C. 1970, c. D-2, s. 2.

MARQUEE. *n.* Any roof-like structure constructed as permanent part of the building over an entrance thereto and projecting more than twelve inches (12") from the exterior wall of any building. *Building Code Act*, R.R.O. 1980, Reg. 87, s. 1.

MARQUESS. *n.* In England, the second order of nobility, below a duke.

MARQUIS. *n.* In England, the second order of nobility, below a duke.

MARRIAGE. *n.* The voluntary union of one man and one woman for life. See BANNS OF ~; CELEBRATION OF ~; CHILD OF THE ~; COMMON LAW ~; FORM OF ~; FRANK~; IMPEDIMENT TO ~; ISSUE OF OUR ~; NULLITY OF ~; RESTRAINT OF ~.

MARRIAGE COMMISSIONER. A person who is not a clergyman who is appointed or authorized to solemnize marriage.

MARRIAGE CONTRACT. An agreement two people enter into before their marriage, during their marriage or while cohabiting which may deal with almost any marital right or obligation, whether it arises during marriage, on separation, when a marriage is dissolved or annulled or upon death. A. Bissett-Johnson & W.M. Holland, eds., *Matrimonial Property Law in Canada* (Toronto: Carswell, 1980) at NB-38.

MARRIAGE LICENCES. See ISSUER OF ~.

MARRIAGE SETTLEMENT. Any indenture, contract, agreement, covenant or settlement entered into in consideration of marriage whereby one of the parties agrees to pay a sum or sums of money to or for the benefit of self or the other party or any other person or the issue of the marriage, and whereby that party settles, grants, conveys, transfers, mortgages, or charges, or agrees to settle, grant, convey, transfer, mortgage or charge, real or personal property of any description upon or to or in favour of any person for the benefit of self or the other party or any other person or the issue of the marriage.

MARRIED PERSON. An adult person other than a single person. *Family Benefits Act*, R.R.O. 1980, Reg. 318, s. 1.

MARRIED WOMAN. 1. A woman lawfully married to a living husband. 2. Includes a woman who, within the period of gestation prior to the birth of the child in respect of whose birth an application for registration is made under this Act, was lawfully married. Vital Statistics acts.

MARRIED WOMEN'S PROPERTY ACT. An

act most provinces passed to give a wife the right to acquire and hold property in her own name. A. Bissett-Johnson & W.M. Holland, eds., *Matrimonial Property Law in Canada* (Toronto: Carswell, 1980) at I-16.

MARSH. See FRESHWATER ~; SALTWATER ~.

MARSHAL. *v.* For a court to order two or more funds of a debtor on behalf of creditors so that a creditor who has access to only one of the funds may have access to that one and creditors who have access to other funds will receive payment from those others. W.B. Rayner & R.H. McLaren, *Falconbridge on Mortgages*, 4th ed. (Toronto: Canada Law Book, 1977) at 313.

MARSHAL. *n.* An ex officio court officer; every sheriff of the Federal Court. D. Sgayias *et al.*, *Federal Court Practice 1988* (Toronto: Carswell, 1987) at 56. See DEPUTY ~; FIRE ~; PROVOST-~.

MARSHLAND. *n.* (i) Land forming part of the sea coast or the bank of a tidal river below the level of the highest tide; and (ii) land that is poorly drained or subject to periodic flooding.

MARSHLAND TRACT. An area of marshland which may be effectively dealt with as a unit in the construction and maintenance of works.

MART. *n.* A market, a place of public traffic or sale.

MARTIAL LAW. 1. Military law. 2. The replacement of ordinary law and the temporary government of a nation or area by a military council if this is done following a government proclamation or notice by military authorities.

MASK. See QUICK-DONNING ~.

MASON. See BRICK AND STONE ~; CEMENT ~.

MASONRY. See PLAIN ~; REINFORCED ~.

MASS. See TOTAL LOADED ~.

MASSAGE. *n.* The kneading, rubbing or massaging of the human body, whether with or without steam baths, vapour baths, fume baths, electric light baths or other appliances, and hydrotherapy or any similar method taught in schools of massage approved under this Act, but does not include any form of medical electricity. *Physiotherapists Act*, R.S.B.C. 1979, c. 327, s. 1.

MASS DISTRIBUTION. See SAMPLES FOR ~.

MASTER. *n.* 1. A judicial officer of the Supreme Court who may decide certain matters before or after trial. G.D. Watson & C. Perkins, eds., *Holmested & Watson: Ontario Civil Procedure* (Toronto: Carswell, 1984) at CJA-35. 2. The

person in immediate charge or control of a vehicle. 3. Includes every person having command or charge of a ship but does not include a pilot. 4. The Master of the Mint. *Royal Canadian Mint Act*, R.S.C. 1985, c. R-9, s. 2. 5. A person who has completed an apprenticeship and worked as a journeyman for a period of time. See LOCAL ~; LOCK~.

MASTER AGREEMENT. 1. A contract between a union and the leading employer in an industry. 2. A model agreement.

MASTER AND SERVANT. A relationship in which the servant, for wages or other valuable consideration, serves the master, providing personal labour for a specified period. See now EMPLOYER and EMPLOYEE.

MASTER CONTAINER. A container that is designed to hold more than one package of produce. *Farm Products Grades and Sales Act*, R.R.O. 1980, Reg. 332, s. 1.

MASTER ELECTRICIAN. Any person who: (a) does business as an electrical contractor; (b) advertises as such; (c) undertakes to carry out or to cause to be carried out or carries out, as such and for his profit, electrical installation work or the renewing, altering or repairing of electrical installations, whether such work is done for payment or free of charge, whether the remuneration, if any, is by the hour, day or for lump sum, and whether such work is carried out under any oral, written, expressed or implied agreement; (d) prepares estimates, makes or submits tenders, either personally or by a person interposed, with a view to carrying out such work for profit; (e) prepares plans at his expense, but solely for his own use or that of the Bureau des examinateurs électriciens du Québec, with a view to obtaining and carrying out such work for his benefit; (f) employs apprentice-electricians or journeyman electricians; (g) holds the license "A" or "B" issued under the Electricians and Electrical Installations Act (chapter E-4), or any other license issued under such act for another category or class of license "A" or "B". *Master Electricians Act*, R.S.Q. 1977, c. M-3, s. 1.

MASTER KEY. See AUTOMOBILE ~.

MASTER LOT. A quantity of a drug from which a lot is prepared for sale by subsequent dilution or mixture. *Food and Drug Regulations*, C.R.C., c. 870, s. C.03.001.

MASTER MINIMUM EQUIPMENT LIST. An approved document that establishes the essential aircraft equipment allowed to be inoperative under conditions specified therein for a specific type of aircraft. *Aircraft Minimum Equipment List Order*, C.R.C., c. 25, s. 2.

MASTER OF THE ROLLS. In England, a judge of the Court of Appeal who retains the non-judicial role of custodian of the records.

MASTER PIPE-MECHANIC. Any person who: (a) does business as a contractor for the installation of piping; (b) undertakes to carry out, or to cause to be carried out or carries out as such and for his profit the work of installation of piping, whether such work is done by or for payment or free of charge, whether the remuneration, if any, is by the hour, by the day or for a lump sum, and whether such work is carried out under an oral or written, expressed or implied agreement; (c) prepares estimates, makes or submits tenders, either personally or by a person interposed, with a view to carrying out such work for his profit; (d) prepares plans at his expense, but solely for his own use and that of the board of examiners, with a view to obtaining and carrying out such work for his profit; (e) employs apprentices or journeymen. *Master Pipe-Mechanics Act*, R.S.Q. 1977, c. M-4, s. 1.

MASTER PLAN. A program and policy, or any part thereof, prepared from time to time in respect of a provincial park or proposed provincial park and includes the maps, texts and other material describing such program and policy. *Provincial Parks Act*, R.S.O. 1980, c. 401, s. 1.

MASTER PLUMBER. A person who is skilled in the planning, superintending and installing of plumbing, is familiar with the laws, rules and regulations governing the same and who alone or by supervising journeymen plumbers performs plumbing work.

MASTHEAD LIGHT. A white light placed over the fore and after centreline of the vessel showing an unbroken light over an arc of the horizon of 225 degrees and so fixed as to show the light from right ahead to 22.5 degrees abaft the beam on either side of the vessel. *Collision Regulations*, C.R.C., c. 1416, Rule 3.

MATANE REGION. That part of the Province of Quebec comprising the parishes of Les Boules, St-René-Goupil, Ste-Félicité, St-Paulin-Dalibaire, St-Thomas-Cherbourg, Baie-des-Sables, St-Ulric, St-Léandre, St-Nil, St-Jean-Cherbourg, St-Adelme, Les Méchins, Grosses Roches, Petite-Matane, Les Capucins, St-Luc-de-Mataine et Ville de Matane (St-Rédempteur and St-Jérôme). *Rimouski-Matane Wood Order*, C.R.C., c. 266, s. 2.

MATCH. See Wood ~ES.

MATE. *n.* The assistant to the master of a merchant ship.

MATERIAL. *n.* 1. Every kind of movable prop-erty. Builders Lien acts. 2. (i) All rock, coal or other materials taken from or into a mine, and (ii) supplies and equipment moved into or out of a mine. *Coal Mines Safety Act*, R.S.A. 1980, c. C-15, s. 1. See ADVERTISING ~; AGGRE-GATE ~; AIRCRAFT ~; CERTIFICATE OF TEST OF ~; COMBUSTIBLE ~; CORRO-SION-RESISTANT ~; ELECTION ~; FINE ~; FOREIGN ~; GRAPHIC ~; INCOMBUSTI-BLE ~; INFLAMMABLE ~; ~S; NEW ~; NUCLEAR ~; QUARRY ~; RADIOACTIVE ~; REJECTED ~; SECOND-HAND ~; TEX-TILE ~; TEXTUAL ~; VIDEO ~; WASTE ~.

MATERIAL. *adj.* 1. Important; essential. 2. That which will assist a prudent insurer in deciding whether to take a risk and if so upon what conditions and at what premium. Raoul Colin-vaux, *The Law of Insurance*, 5th ed. (London: Sweet & Maxwell, 1984) at 100.

MATERIAL CHANGE. Where used in relation to the affairs of an issuer means a change in the business, operations or capital of the issuer that would reasonably be expected to have a significant effect on the market price or value of any of the securities of the issuer and includes a decision to implement such a change made by the board of directors of the issuer or by senior management of the issuer who believe that confirmation of the decision by the board of directors is probable. Securities acts.

MATERIAL CONTRACT. A contract of any kind made by a credit union (i) under which the credit union undertakes to lend or advance an amount in excess of $2,000.00, or to lend or advance an amount to a person which, in aggregate with all other loans or advances made to that person and outstanding, totals more than $2,000.00, (ii) under which the credit union employs a person as a full time employee, or (iii) under which the credit union retains the services of a person otherwise than as an employee, or (iv) under which the credit union disposes of or acquires property, whether by sale, purchase, lease or otherwise, for consideration that exceeds $2,000.00 in value. *Credit Unions and Caisses Populaires Act*, S.M. 1980, c. 20, s. 7.

MATERIAL FACT. Where used in relation to securities issued or proposed to be issued, a fact that significantly affects, or would reasonably be expected to have a significant effect on, the market price or value of those securities.

MATERIAL INJURY. In respect of the dump-ing or subsidizing of any goods, material injury to the production in Canada of like goods, and includes, in respect only of the subsidizing of an agricultural product, an increase in the finan-cial burden on a federal or provincial government agricultural support program in Canada. *Special Imports Measures Act*, R.S.C. 1985, c. S-15, s. 2.

MATERIAL INTEREST. Where used to refer to the material interest in a person means (i) the relationship of spouse, parent, child, grandparent, grandchild, brother or sister of the person or of the spouse of the person or the relationship of the spouse of the parent, child, grandparent, grandchild, brother or sister of the person, or (ii) the relationship of a creditor of the person for a debt that is in excess of $2,000.00, or (iii) the relationship of a guarantor of the debt or obligation of the person in an amount that is in excess of $2,000.00, or (iv) where the person is a body corporate, the ownership or beneficial ownership of not less than 20% of any class of voting or preferred shares of the corporation, or (v) where the person is a partnership or association, membership in the partnership or association. *Credit Unions and Caisses Populaires Act*, S.M. 1980, c. 20, s. 7.

MATERIALITY. *n.* The essential ingredients or elements of an offence which must be proved, not the evidence which proves them in any particular case. P.K. McWilliams, *Canadian Criminal Evidence*, 3d ed. (Aurora: Canada Law Book, 1988) at 3-3.

MATERIAL MAN. A person who supplies or rents material that is intended to become part of the improvement or to be used in the making of it or to facilitate the making of it, which material has been delivered to the land on which the improvement is placed or situate. *Builders' Lien Amendment Act*, S.B.C. 1984, c. 17, s. 1.

MATERIALS. *n.* 1. Includes every kind of movable property. Builders' Lien acts. 2. Every kind of movable property that becomes or is intended to become, part of the improvement, or that is used to facilitate directly the making of the improvement. Builders' Lien acts. 3. Includes books, periodicals, pamphlets, newspapers, photographic reproductions, paintings, films, filmscripts, sheet music and sound recordings. *Libraries Act*, R.S.N.B. 1973, c. L-5, s. 1. 4. Camp supplies and includes foodstuffs, janitorial supplies, lumber, building materials and hardware, plumbing and heating supplies, soft goods, appliances, furniture and safety supplies. *Department of Revenue, Supply and Services Amendment Act, 1982 (No. 2)*, S.S. 1982-83, c. 31, s. 3. See BUILDING ~; CONVENTION ~; FIBROUS AND FILAMENTARY ~; LEGISLATIVE ~; MATERIAL; QUARRY ~; REFRACTORY ~.

MATERIAL SAFETY DATA SHEET. A summary of the hazards of a toxic product or material. D. Robertson, *Ontario Health and Safety Guide* (Toronto: Richard De Boo Ltd., 1988) at 5-263.

MATERIALS HANDLING EQUIPMENT. Any machine, equipment or mechanical device used to transport, lift, move or position or to assist in transporting, lifting, moving or positioning any materials, goods, articles, persons or things, and includes any crane, derrick, loading tower, powered industrial truck, handtruck, conveyor, hoist, earth-moving equipment, rope, chain, sling, dock, ramp, storage rack, container, pallet and skid, but does not include elevating devices that are subject to the Canada Elevating Devices Regulations or tools that are subject to the Canada Hand Tools Regulations. *Canada Materials Handling Regulations*, C.R.C., c. 1004, s. 2.

MATERIALS MANAGEMENT SYSTEM. See REJECTED ~.

MATERIAL WAVE. A line or surface propagated by shock or vibration of gaseous, liquid or solid matter including infrasounds (0 to 16 Hertz), sounds (16 Hz to 16KHz) including shock waves, ultrasounds (16KHz to MHz), and any mechanical oscillation. *Environment Quality Act*, R.S.Q. 1977, c. Q-2, s. 1.

MATERIAL WITNESS. A person whose evidence is important in the prosecution or defence of a case.

MATERIEL. *n.* All public property, other than real property and money, provided for the Canadian Forces or the Defence Research Board or for any other purpose under this Act, and includes any vessel, vehicle, aircraft, animal, missile, arms, ammunition, clothing, stores, provisions or equipment so provided. *National Defence Act*, R.S.C. 1985, c. N-5, s. 2.

MATERNAL. *adj.* Belonging to or coming from the mother.

MATERNITY. *n.* The state of motherhood.

MATERNITY BOARDING HOME. Any house, building or structure, whether permanent or temporary, where, for a consideration, an expectant mother is received and kept before, during and after confinement, or wherein a child or children may be received and maintained. *Hospitals Act*, R.S.P.E.I. 1974, c. H-11, s. 1.

MATERNITY BOARDING HOUSE. An establishment wherein, for a consideration (i) a person may be received or kept for care during pregnancy or for confinement, or (ii) a child under three years of age may be received or maintained. *Public Health Act*, R.S.P.E.I. 1974, c. P-29, s. 1.

MATERNITY HOME. A house in which one

or more pregnant women receive nursing or other care during the confinement period.

MATERNITY HOSPITAL. A private hospital for the reception and care of patients in or in respect of child-birth. *Health and Public Welfare Act*, R.S.Nfld. 1970, c. 151, s. 11.

MATERNITY LEAVE. A leave of absence allowed to a worker who is pregnant or who has given birth.

MATRICIDE. *n.* The slaying of a mother; a person who slays a mother.

MATRICULATE. *v.* To enter university.

MATRIMONIAL ASSETS. The matrimonial home or homes and all other real and personal property acquired by either or both spouses before or during their marriage, with the exception of (a) gifts, inheritances, trusts or settlements received by one spouse from a person other than the other spouse except to the extent to which they are used for the benefit of both spouses or their children; (b) an award or settlement of damages in court in favour of one spouse; (c) money paid or payable to one spouse under an insurance policy; (d) reasonable personal effects of one spouse; (e) business assets; (f) property exempted under a marriage contract or separation agreement; (g) real and personal property acquired after separation unless the spouses resume cohabitation. *Matrimonial Property Act*, S.N.S. 1979-80, c. 9, s. 4.

MATRIMONIAL CAUSE. A proceeding by petition under the Divorce Act (Canada) and a proceeding by petition for a decree of nullity of marriage, or of judicial separation, or of restitution of conjugal rights or jactitation of marriage or any other matrimonial cause within the jurisdiction of the court. *Queen's Bench Act*, S.M. 1973, c. 15, s. 1.

MATRIMONIAL HOME. Property that is owned or leased by one or both spouses that is or has been occupied by the spouses as their family home.

MATRIMONIAL OFFENCE. (a) Adultery; (b) cruelty; (c) desertion (i) for two years or upward without reasonable cause, or (ii) constituted by the fact that the wife or husband, as the case may be, has failed to comply with a judgment for restitution of conjugal rights; or (d) sodomy or bestiality, or an attempt to commit either offence. *Domestic Relations Act*, R.S.N.W.T. 1974, c. D-9, s. 6.

MATRIMONIAL PROPERTY. Any real or personal property whatsoever, regardless of its source, kind or nature, that, at the time an application is made under this Act, is owned, or in which an interest is held, by one or both spouses, or by one or both spouses and a third person, and, without limiting the generality of the foregoing, includes: (i) a security, share or other interest in a corporation or an interest in a trust, partnership, association, organization, society or other joint venture; (ii) property over which a spouse has, either alone or in conjunction with another person, a power of appointment exercisable in his favour; (iii) property disposed of by a spouse but over which the spouse has, either alone or in conjunction with another person, a power to consume, invoke or dispose of the property; (iv) property mentioned in section 28. *Matrimonial Property Act*, S.S. 1979, c. M-6.1, s. 2.

MATRIMONIAL PROPERTY ORDER. A matrimonial property order within the meaning of the Matrimonial Property Act, or a similar order enforceable in Alberta or a court outside Alberta, that affects the payment or distribution of a person's benefits. Pension acts, Alberta.

MATRIMONIAL PROPERTY RIGHTS. All rights given by this Ordinance to the spouse of a married person in respect of the residential and other property of the married person, and without restricting the generality of the foregoing, includes (i) the right to prevent disposition of residential property by withholding consent, (ii) the right of action for damages against the married person if a disposition of residential property that results in the registration of the title in the name of any other person is made without consent, (iii) the right of obtain payment from the Assurance Fund of an unsatisfied judgment against the married person in respect of a disposition of residential property that is made without consent and that results in the registration of the title in the name of any other person, (iv) the right of the surviving spouse to a life estate in residential property of the deceased married person, and (v) the right of the surviving spouse to a life estate in the personal property of the deceased married person that is exempt from seizure under execution. *Matrimonial Property Act*, R.S.N.W.T. 1974, c. M-7, s. 2.

MATRIMONIUM. *n.* [L.] Property inherited through the mother's side.

MATRIMONY. *n.* Marriage.

MATRON. *n.* 1. A woman who is married. 2. A woman superintendent.

MATTER. *n.* 1. Includes every proceeding in the court not in a cause. 2. Includes every proceeding in the court not in an action. *Judicature Act*, R.S.P.E.I. 1974, c. J-3, s. 1. 3. The subject matter or content, pith and substance or true character and nature of a law. P.W. Hogg, *Constitutional Law of Canada*, 2d ed. (Toronto:

Carswell, 1985) at 313. See ADVERTISING ~; CIVIL ~; CRIMINAL ~; DISCIPLINARY ~; FAMILY ~; INERT ~; MAILABLE ~; ORGANIC ~; PLANT OR OTHER ~; TESTAMENTARY ~S AND CAUSES; TOTAL SUSPENDED ~.

MATTERS AND CAUSES TESTAMENTARY. Includes all matters and causes relating to the grant and revocation of probate of wills or letters of administration. See TESTAMENTARY MATTERS AND CAUSES.

MATURE. *adj.* That the produce has reached such stage of development as ensures completion of the ripening process.

MATURE DUCKS. Mature birds of either sex, having rigid cartilage at the posterior end of the breast or keel bone. *Dressed and Eviscerated Poultry Regulations*, C.R.C., c. 283, s. 53.

MATURE GEESE. Mature birds of either sex having rigid cartilage at the posterior end of the breast or keel bone. *Dressed and Eviscerated Poultry Regulations*, C.R.C., c. 283, s. 53.

MATURE LANDS. Lands that have been serviced for at least five years. *National Housing Loan Regulations*, C.R.C., c. 1108, s. 115.

MATURE TURKEY. Mature birds of either sex having rigid cartilage at the posterior end of the breast or keel bone. *Dressed and Eviscerated Poultry Regulations*, C.R.C., c. 283, s. 53.

MATURITY. *n.* 1. The date on which a note, loan or obligation becomes due. 2. The date fixed under a retirement savings plan for the commencement of any retirement income the payment of which is provided for by the plan. *Income Tax Act*, R.S.C. 1952, c. 148 (as am. S.C. 1977-78, c. 32, s. 34(2)), s. 146(1)(d). See DATE OF ~.

MATURITY DATE. The date, excluding days of grace, on which the debt will be fully paid if every payment is made according to the original terms of the security agreement. *Personal Property Security Act*, R.R.O. 1980, Reg. 749, s. 1.

MAUSOLEUM. *n.* A structure wholly or partly above the level of the ground and designed for the burial or storage of dead human bodies.

MAVERICK. *n.* An unmarked reindeer. *Northwest Territories Reindeer Regulations*, C.R.C., c. 1238, s. 2.

MAXIM. *n.* A general principle; an axiom.

MAXIMS OF EQUITY. These include: equity will not allow a wrong to exist without a remedy; equity looks to intent rather than to form; equity considers what ought to be done as having been done; an equitable remedy is discretionary;

delay defeats equity; one who comes to equity must come with clean hands; one who seeks equity must do equity; equity never lacks a trustee.

MAXIMUM ACCEPTABLE LIMIT. Maximum concentrations within the ranges that are the national ambient air quality objectives established in relation to paragraphs 5(1)(a) to (c). *Clean Air Act*, R.S.C. 1985, c. C-32, s. 2.

MAXIMUM ACOUSTIC GAIN. At a specified frequency, means the maximum value of the air-to-air gain obtainable from the hearing aid allowing all possible settings of the hearing-aid controls. *Medical Devices Regulations*, C.R.C., c. 871, s. 1.

MAXIMUM AGGREGATE HOLDINGS. The total number of voting shares of a constrained share corporation that may be held by or on behalf of persons in the constrained class and their associates in accordance with the articles of the corporation. *Canada Business Corporations Regulations*, C.R.C., c. 426, s. 51.

MAXIMUM AIR PRESSURE. The greatest air pressure that is applied to a person for more than five minutes. *Occupational Health and Safety Act*, R.R.O. 1980, Reg. 691, s. 240.

MAXIMUM AIR-TO-AIR GAIN. At a specified frequency, means the maximum value of the air-to-air gain obtainable from the hearing aid allowing all possible settings of the hearing-aid controls. *Medical Devices Regulations*, C.R.C., c. 871, s. 1.

MAXIMUM ALLOWABLE PRESSURE. The maximum pressure, as shown on its certificate of inspection, at which a boiler, pressure vessel or plant is permitted to be operated. *Canada Boiler and Pressure Vessel Regulations*, C.R.C., c. 994, s. 2.

MAXIMUM ALLOWABLE WORKING PRESSURE. See DESIGN PRESSURE.

MAXIMUM BENEFIT INCOME. The work income entitling a family or a person to the maximum work income supplement benefit. *An Act respecting work income supplement*, S.Q. 1979, c. 9, s. 1.

MAXIMUM BENEFIT PERIOD. See ORIGINAL ~.

MAXIMUM CAPACITY. The number of persons or the weight that an elevating device can carry safely as determined under the regulations.

MAXIMUM CUMULATIVE RESERVE. Of a credit union at the end of any particular taxation year means an amount equal to 5% of the aggregate of amounts each of which is (i) the amount of any debt owing by the credit union to a member thereof or of any other obligation of the credit union to pay an amount to a member thereof, that was outstanding at the end of the year, including, for greater certainty, the amount of any deposit standing to the credit of a member of the credit union in the records of the credit union, but excluding, for greater certainty, any share in the credit union of any member thereof, or (ii) the amount, as of the end of the year, of any share in the credit union of any member thereof. *Income Tax Act*, R.S.C. 1952, c. 148 (as am. S.C. 1974-75-76, c. 26, s. 92(3)), s. 137(6)(c).

MAXIMUM DESIRABLE LIMIT. Maximum concentrations within the ranges that are the national ambient air quality objectives established in relation to paragraphs 5(1)(a) to (c). *Clean Air Act*, R.S.C. 1985, c. C-32, s. 2.

MAXIMUM FLOW RATE. The maximum volume of commodity per unit time that can be measured by a measuring machine as set out in the notice of approval. *Weights and Measures Regulations*, C.R.C., c. 1605, s. 57.

MAXIMUM GROSS WEIGHT. In reference to a commercial motor vehicle, the curb weight together with the load, including the weight of the driver and of any other persons carried, and, in reference to a bus, the curb weight together with the weight of the driver and of the number of passengers for which the vehicle is licensed, and for the purposes of any regulations, unless otherwise provided therein, the weight of a person shall be taken as one hundred and fifty pounds. *Highway Traffic Act*, R.S.Nfld. 1970, c. 152, s. 2.

MAXIMUM HOURS. The number of hours that a worker may be required to work without overtime compensation.

MAXIMUM INDIVIDUAL HOLDINGS. The total number of voting shares of a constrained share corporation that may be held by or on behalf of any one person in the constrained class and his associates in accordance with the articles of the corporation. *Canada Business Corporations Regulations*, C.R.C., c. 426, s. 51.

MAXIMUM INSURABLE EARNINGS. (a) In relation to any week, the maximum weekly insurable earnings, and (b) in relation to a year, the maximum yearly insurable earnings. *Unemployment Insurance Act*, R.S.C. 1985, c. U-1, s. 2.

MAXIMUM LOAD. The portion of the weight of a vehicle that (a) is borne by each tire when (i) it is installed on that vehicle, and (ii) that vehicle is at its maximum loaded vehicle weight and is resting on a horizontal plane, and (b) is calculated by (i) distributing to each axle its share of the maximum loaded vehicle weight, and (ii) dividing such share by two. *Motor Vehicle Safety Regulations*, C.R.C., c. 1038, s. 111.

MAXIMUM LOADED VEHICLE WEIGHT. The sum of the (a) curb weight, (b) accessory weight, (c) vehicle capacity weight, and (d) production options weight. *Motor Vehicle Safety Regulations*, C.R.C., c. 1038, s. 111.

MAXIMUM LOAD RATING. The load rating at the maximum permissible inflation pressure for that tire. Canada regulations.

MAXIMUM PERMISSIBLE INFLATION PRESSURE. The maximum cold inflation pressure to which a tire may be inflated. Canada regulations.

MAXIMUM RENT. The lawful maximum rent which could be charged for a rental unit had all permissable statutory or other increases which could have been taken on or after the 1st day of August, 1985, been taken. *Residential Rent Regulation Act*, S.O. 1986, c. 63, s. 1.

MAXIMUM RETIREMENT AGE. 1. The age of 65 years or an age prescribed by the Lieutenant Governor in Council as the maximum retirement age applicable to any employee or group or class of employees. *Pension (Public Service) Act*, R.S.B.C. 1979, c. 318, s. 1. 2. The age of 65 years or the age at which the officer retires, whichever is greater. *Pension (Public Service) Act*, R.S.B.C. 1979, c. 318, s. 4.

MAXIMUM SAFE LOAD. With respect to any materials handling equipment or any floor, dock or other structure used in handling materials, means (a) the maximum load that such equipment or structure was designed and constructed to handle or support safely, or (b) the maximum load that such equipment or structure is guaranteed in writing by the manufacturer to handle or support safely, whichever is the lesser. *Canada Materials Handling Regulations*, C.R.C., c. 1004, s. 2.

MAXIMUM TEST VOLTAGE. (a) 127 volts, if the television receiver is designed to operate from a 100-120 volt power source, or (b) 110 per cent of the maximum voltage from which the television receiver is designed to operate, if the television receiver is designed to operate otherwise than from a 110-120 volt power source. *Radiation Emitting Devices Regulations*, C.R.C., c. 1370, s. 1.

MAXIMUM TOLERABLE LIMIT. Maximum concentrations within the ranges that are the national ambient air quality objectives established in relation to paragraphs 5(1)(a) to (c). *Clean Air Act*, R.S.C. 1985, c. C-32, s. 2.

MAY. *v.* As an auxiliary, construed as permissive and empowering.

MAYOR. *n.* 1. The mayor of a city or town, the chairman of a village or the chairman of the governing board or council of a service commission. *Municipal Affairs Act*, S.N.S. 1982, c. 9, s. 2. 2. Includes (i) the chairman of the board of administrators of a new town, and (ii) in the case of a hamlet, the reeve of the county or municipal district in which the hamlet is situated. *Police Amendment Act, 1981*, S.A. 1981, c. 31, s. 2. 3. Includes the reeve of a rural municipality. *The Planning and Development Act*, R.S.S. 1978, c. P-13, s. 2. 4. Includes the reeve of a municipal district. *Municipal Government Act*, R.S.A. 1980, c. M-26, s. 1.

MAYORALTY. *n.* The office of mayor.

M.B.M. *abbr.* Thousand feet board measure. *Crown Timber Act*, R.R.O. 1980, Reg. 234, s. 1.

M.C. *abbr.* Master's Chambers.

MCF. *abbr.* 1,000 cubic feet of natural gas, measured at 14.73 psia pressure and 60°F. *Natural Gas Prices Regulations*, C.R.C., c. 1259, s. 2.

MCGILL L.J. *abbr.* McGill Law Journal (Revue de droit de McGill).

MCMURRAY FORMATION. The stratigraphic formation lying above the upper Devonian carbonate sediments and below the Clearwater formation. *Mines and Minerals Act*, R.S.A. 1980, c. M-15, s. 121.

MCNAGHTEN'S CASE. R. v. McNaghten or M'Naghten or Macnaughton (1843) 4 St.Tr. (N.S.) 847, a British case which established the law relating to insanity with special reference to criminal responsibility.

M.C.R. *abbr.* Montreal Condensed Reports, 1854-1884.

M.D.A. *abbr.* Methylenedioxyamphetamine, a derivative of amphetamine. F.A. Jaffe, *A Guide to Pathological Evidence*, 2d ed. (Toronto: Carswell, 1983) at 180.

MEAL. *n.* 1. Food sufficient to constitute a person's lunch or dinner. *An Act Respecting the Commission de Contrôle des Permis D'alcool*, R.S.Q. 1977, c. C-33, s. 2. 2. Food of any kind and quantity sufficient for the bodily maintenance of a consumer served at a cost of not less than fifty cents for each consumer exclusive of the cost of any liquor. *Liquor Control Act*, S.Nfld. 1973, c. 103, s. 2. See BLOOD ~; BONE ~; MEAT ~.

MEAL PERIOD. The time during which a worker is permitted to eat.

MEAN. *v.* When used in the definition section of a statute, this word restricts the scope of the term defined to the particular definition indicated there. P. St. J. Langan, ed., *Maxwell on The Interpretation of Statutes*, 12th ed. (Bombay: N.M. Tripathi, 1976) at 270.

MEAN. *n.* A point midway between two extremes.

MEANING. See SECONDARY ~.

MEANS. *n.* Includes (a) the administration of a drug or other noxious thing; (b) the use of an instrument; and (c) manipulation of any kind. *Criminal Code*, R.S.C. 1985, c. C-46, s. 287(3). See ACCIDENTAL ~; DISCONNECTING ~.

MEANS OF EGRESS. 1. A continuous path of travel provided by a doorway, hallway, corridor, exterior passageway, balcony, lobby, stair, ramp or other egress facility or combination thereof, for the escape of persons from any point in a building floor area, room or contained open space to a public thoroughfare or other open space and includes exits and access to exits. Ontario regulations. 2. A way or ladder leading to an exit from a building, structure, excavation or other part of a project. *Occupational Health and Safety Act*, R.R.O. 1980, Reg. 691, s. 1.

MEANS OF EXIT. A continuous path of travel provided by a doorway, hallway, corridor, exterior passageway, balcony, lobby, stair, ramp or other exit facility, or a combination of them, for the escape of persons from any point in a building, floor area, room or contained open space to a public thoroughfare or other unobstructed open space and includes exits and access to exits. *Fire Services Act*, R.S.B.C. 1979, c. 133, s. 1.

MEANS OF TRANSPORT. 1. Any road or railway vehicle, aircraft, water-borne craft, pipeline or any other contrivance that is or may be used to carry persons or goods whether or not the goods are in packaging or containers. *Transportation of Dangerous Goods Act*, R.S.C. 1985, c. T-19, s. 2. 2. Anything used for conveyance from one place to another, except communications within the meaning of section 2 of the Act respecting the Ministère des communications (chapter M-24). *Transport Act*, R.S.Q. 1977, c. T-12, s. 1.

MEAN WATERPLANE. Midway between the load waterplane and that drawn parallel thereto touching the lowest point of the margin line. *Hull Construction Regulations*, C.R.C., c. 1431, Schedule 1, s. 11.

MEASURE. *v.* Includes weigh. *Weights and Measures Act*, R.S.C. 1985, c. W-6, s. 2.

MEASURE. *n.* 1. Includes weight. *Weights and*

Measures Act, R.S.C. 1985, c. W-6, s. 2. 2. With respect to a linear or volume measuring device, means a static measure having no moving parts incorporated therein, but includes a roller tape-measure of any material. *Weights and Measures Act,* R.S.C. 1970, c. W-7, s. 2. See ALTERNATIVE ~S; EMERGENCY ~S; EXTENSION ~; SAFETY ~; STATIC ~.

MEASURE OF DAMAGES. A test to determine the amount of damages which should be given.

MEASURING CUP. See STANDARD ~.

MEASURING MACHINE. Any machine that measures length, area, volume or capacity, temperature or time and has a moving or movable part that has or can have an effect on the accuracy of the machine. *Weights and Measures Act,* R.S.C. 1985, c. W-6, s. 2.

MEASUREMENT. See GENERAL ~ POINT.

MEAT. *n.* 1. The flesh of any animal or any product of it intended for human consumption in primary or processed form. 2. Fresh, chilled and frozen beef and veal. *Meat Import Act,* R.S.C. 1985, c. M-3, s. 2. 3. The flesh of any animal, fish or fowl, when killed, intended to be used for food, whether fresh or prepared by freezing, chilling, preserving, salting or other process. *The Public Health Act,* R.S.S. 1978, c. P-37, s. 2. 4. The whole or part of a carcass of livestock but does not include the hide. *Livestock Brand Act,* S.B.C. 1980, c. 25, s. 1. 5. The edible part of the muscle of a food animal that is skeletal or that is found in the tongue, diaphragm, heart or oesophagus, with or without the accompanying and overlying fat, together with the portions of bone, skin, sinew, nerve and blood vessels that normally accompany the muscle tissue and are not separated from it in the process of dressing, but does not include the muscle found in the lips, snout, scalp or ears. *Meat Inspection Regulations,* C.R.C., c. 1032, s. 2. See DRY ~.

MEAT ANIMAL. A bull, cow, ox, heifer, steer or calf.

MEAT ANIMALS. Cattle, horses, sheep and pigs. *Livestock Brand Inspection Act,* R.S.A. 1980, c. L-21, s. 1.

MEAT BINDER. A substance added to a meat product to hold its ingredients together. *Meat Inspection Regulations,* C.R.C., c. 1032, s. 2.

MEAT BY-PRODUCT. An edible part of a food animal other than meat. *Meat Inspection Regulations,* C.R.C., c. 1032, s. 2.

MEAT MEAL. The rendered and dried carcass or part of the carcass of an animal. *Animal Disease and Protection Regulations,* C.R.C., c. 296, s. 2.

MEAT PLANT. An abbatoir, slaughterhouse or place or premises where animals are slaughtered and includes a place or premises where meat or a meat product is produced, processed, prepared, handled or stored. *Meat Inspection (Nova Scotia) Act,* S.N.S. 1984, c. 7, s. 2.

MEAT PROCESSING PLANT. A plant where meat is processed or used in the production of a manufactured meat product. *Public Health Act,* R.R.O. 1980, Reg. 853, s. 1.

MEAT PRODUCT. 1. (a) A carcass, (b) the blood of an animal or a product or by-product of a carcass, or (c) a product containing anything described in paragraph (b). 2. Meat, meat by-product, prepared meat or prepared meat by-product. *Food and Drug Regulations,* C.R.C., c. 870, c. B.01.001. See EXTENDED ~: MANUFACTURED ~; PREPARED ~; SIMULATED ~.

MEAT PRODUCT EXTENDER. A food that is a source of protein and that is represented as being for the purpose of extending meat products. *Food and Drug Regulations,* C.R.C., c. 870, c. B.01.001.

MEAT SPOT. A small particle of oviduct of the domestic hen or domestic turkey on the yolk or in the albumen of the egg.

MECHANIC. *n.* A person who has a minimum of four years work experience directly related to the work assigned to him and who has full knowledge of this Act and the regulations and of the codes applicable to the elevating device upon which he is assigned to work. *Elevating Devices Act,* R.S.O. 1980, c. 135, s. 1. See ALIGNMENT AND BRAKES ~; DENTAL ~; FARM EQUIPMENT ~; FUEL AND ELECTRIC SYSTEMS ~; MOTORCYCLE ~; MOTOR VEHICLE INSPECTION ~; MOTOR VEHICLE ~; REFRIGERATION AND AIR CONDITIONING ~; TICKET ISSUING MACHINE ~.

MECHANICAL. See ELECTRO-MAGNETIC, ACOUSTIC, ~ OR OTHER DEVICE.

MECHANICAL SEALING. The closing and sealing of the loading door of a compartment in a controlled-atmosphere storage plant by the operator so as to be sufficiently air-tight for the purpose of controlled-atmosphere storage. *Farm Products Grades and Sales Act,* R.R.O. 1980, Reg. 329, s. 1.

MECHANICAL TREATMENT. The application of a mechanical appliance to the foot or in the shoe to treat a disease, deformity or ailment. *Podiatrists Act,* R.S.B.C. 1979, c. 330, s. 1.

MECHANICALLY CONTROLLED SEAL. Any device in a trap whereby the water seal of the trap is replenished by the action of moving parts. *Ontario Water Resources Act*, R.R.O. 1980, Reg. 736, s. 85.

MECHANICS' LIEN. 1. A lien which favours a mechanic or other person who conferred skill, money and materials on a chattel. D.N. Macklem & D.I. Bristow, *Construction and Mechanics' Liens in Canada*, 5th ed. (Toronto: Carswell, 1985) at 13. 2. Protection of a lien against land given to a supplier of the labour and material which benefitted that land. D.N. Macklem & D.I. Bristow, *Construction and Mechanics' Liens in Canada*, 5th ed. (Toronto: Carswell, 1985) at 1. 3. A right in the nature of a lien on any money paid by the owner of land to a contractor given to a worker or supplier of materials. D.N. Macklem & D.I. Bristow, *Construction and Mechanics' Liens in Canada*, 5th ed. (Toronto: Carswell, 1985) at 3.

MECHANISM. *n.* Of death, whatever disturbance in vital function was initiated by the cause of death. F.A. Jaffe, *A Guide to Pathological Evidence*, 2d ed. (Toronto: Carswell, 1983) at 10.

MECHANIZED FISHING EQUIPMENT. A gurdy, danish seine winch, dragging winch, power flock or any other proved power equipment for fishing which is suitable to the tonnage of a particular ship and complies with the regulations. *Fishing Ships (Bounties) Act*, R.S.Nfld. 1970, c. 137, s. 2.

MECONIUM. *n.* The feces of a newborn. F.A. Jaffe, *A Guide to Pathological Evidence*, 2d ed. (Toronto: Carswell, 1983) at 180.

MEDAL. See LONG SERVICE ~.

MEDIA. *n.* Any means of communication, and, without limiting the foregoing, includes radio, television, billboards, newspapers, magazines, handbills, pamphlets and flyers. *Trade Practices Act*, R.S.B.C. 1979, c. 406, s. 1.

MEDIAL. *adj.* Towards the middle. F.A. Jaffe, *A Guide to Pathological Evidence*, 2d ed. (Toronto: Carswell, 1983) at 180.

MEDIAN. *n.* A physical barrier or area that separates traffic travelling in one direction from traffic travelling in the opposite direction on a highway. *Highway Traffic Act*, R.S.A. 1980, c. H-7, s. 1.

MEDIAN AMOUNT. An amount that is half way between one amount and another amount. *Consumer Protection Act*, R.R.O. 1980, Reg. 181, s. 18.

MEDIAN STRIP. The portion of a highway so constructed as to separate traffic travelling in one direction from traffic travelling in the oppo-site direction by a physical barrier or an unpaved strip of ground.

MEDIATION. *n.* The reconciliation of a dispute by a third party.

MEDIATOR. *n.* One who resolves disputes by mediation.

MEDICAL. *adj.* Includes surgical and obstetrical.

MEDICAL AID. Medical and surgical aid, hospital and skilled nursing services, chiropractic and other treatment and artificial members or apparatus.

MEDICAL CARE. 1. Care provided by a general practitioner, and excludes major surgery. 2. The provision of any blood transfusion or transfusions or injection or injections is included in the meaning. *Child Welfare Act*, S.Nfld. 1972, s. 37, s. 11.

MEDICAL CARE SERVICES. See INSURED ~.

MEDICAL CERTIFICATE. Includes a written statement for the purpose of this Division containing the signature of a physician. *Employment Standards Act*, R.S.A. 1980, c. E-10.1, s. 58. See MINER'S ~.

MEDICAL CONSULTANT. A duly qualified medical practitioner appointed by the insurer to perform the duties prescribed by this Act and such other duties as the insurer may prescribe. *The Automobile Accident Insurance Act*, R.S.S. 1978, c. A-35, s. 2.

MEDICAL CONTRACT. A contract entered into under this Regulation between an employer and a contract physician for the medical and surgical care and treatment of the workmen of such employer. *Public Health Act*, R.R.O. 1980, Reg. 834, s. 36.

MEDICAL CONTROL. Medical orders issued by a physician either prospectively through the development of protocols or directly by verbal or written orders. Saskatchewan statutes.

MEDICAL DEPARTMENT. A division of the medical staff of a hospital for the provision of a specified type of medical diagnosis or treatment. *Public Hospitals Act*, R.S.O. 1980, c. 410, s. 1.

MEDICAL DIRECTOR. The physician responsible for the clinical services in a psychiatric facility. *Mental Health Act*, R.S.N.B. 1973, c. M-10, s. 1.

MEDICAL DOCTOR. See QUALIFIED ~.

MEDICAL EXAMINATION. Includes a mental examination, a physical examination and medical assessment of records respecting a person.

Immigration Act, R.S.C. 1985, c. I-2, s. 11(3). See RECORDED ON ~ PRIOR TO ENLISTMENT.

MEDICAL INFORMATION. Any information obtained with the consent of a subject from licensed physicians, medical practitioners, chiropractors, qualified psychologists, psychiatrists or hospitals, clinics or other medically related facilities in respect of the physical or mental health and attitude of the subject.

MEDICAL JURISPRUDENCE. The part of the law related to the practice of medicine. F.A. Jaffe, *A Guide to Pathological Evidence*, 2d ed. (Toronto: Carswell, 1983) at 1.

MEDICAL LOCK. A chamber in which persons may be subjected to changes in air pressure for medical purposes. *Occupational Health and Safety Act*, R.R.O. 1980, Reg. 691, s. 240.

MEDICAL MONITORING. Examining and testing workers in danger of exposure to a toxic substance so that an affected worker may be removed from exposure when necessary. D. Robertson, *Ontario Health and Safety Guide* (Toronto: Richard De Boo Ltd., 1988) at 5-268.

MEDICAL OFFICER. A qualified medical practitioner authorized or recognized by order of the Minister of National Health and Welfare as a medical officer for the purposes of this Act. *Immigration Act*, R.S.C. 1985, c. I-2, s. 2. See RESPONSIBLE ~.

MEDICAL OFFICER IN CHARGE. The physician appointed to be in charge of the care and treatment being provided to the patients of an institution, psychiatric centre, psychiatric ward, mental health clinic or other facility.

MEDICAL OFFICER OF HEALTH. A physician appointed by a health unit or designated by the Minister under this Act as a medical officer of health. *Public Health Act*, S.A. 1984, c. P-27.1, s. 1.

MEDICAL OXYGEN. A volume of 1 litre of gas at a temperature of 20°C and at a pressure of 760 millimetres of mercury. *Medical Devices Regulations*, C.R.C., c. 871, s. 1.

MEDICAL PRACTITIONER. 1. A person lawfully entitled to practise medicine in the place in which the practice is carried on by that person. 2. A person lawfully entitled to practise medicine or dentistry in the jurisdiction where he practises and includes a medical or dental officer of the Canadian Armed Forces. *Evidence Act*, S.N.B. 1980, c. 18, s. 1. 3. A person who is authorized by law to practise medicine in the place where such person is so practising and includes a person skilled in the art of healing who is authorized by law to practise the art of healing in the place where such person is so practising. *Workers' Compensation Act*, R.S.N.W.T. 1974, c. W-4, s. 2. See DULY QUALIFIED ~; QUALIFIED ~.

MEDICAL RADIOLOGICAL TECHNICIAN. 1. A person who operates an x-ray machine or uses radioactive isotopes for the examination or treatment of living persons. *Radiological Technicians Act*, R.S.A. 1980, c. R-3, s. 1. 2. A person who practises medical radiological technology. *Medical Radiological Technicians Act*, R.S.N.S. 1967, c. 180, s. 1.

MEDICAL RADIOLOGICAL TECHNOLOGY. The act, process, science or art of carrying out on humans for medical purposes the technical aspects of radiological-diagnosis or radiological-therapeutics. *Medical Radiological Technicians Act*, R.S.N.S. 1967, c. 180, s. 1.

MEDICAL RESEARCH COUNCIL OF CANADA. A federal body which offers scholarships and grants in the health sciences.

MEDICAL SERVICES. 1. Includes surgical, dental, optical, optometrical and nursing services, and the furnishing of health appliances, optical and pharmaceutical supplies. *The Mutual Medical and Hospital Benefit Associations Act*, R.S.S. 1978, c. M-39, s. 2. 2. (i) All services rendered by medical practitioners that are medically required; and (ii) any other services that are or become insured services within the meaning of the Medical Care Act (Canada) and for which payment may be made pursuant to one of the enactments specified in section 3; except any services that a person is eligible for and entitled to under any other Act of Canada or under any law of the province relating to workmen's compensation. *The Medical Care Insurance Supplementary Provisions Act*, R.S.S. 1978, c. M-7, s. 2.

MEDICAL SERVICE UNIT. A building containing offices and treatment rooms for physicians and other health personnel and includes any building or part of a building used as a residence for medical practitioners and other health personnel.

MEDICAL STAFF. The medical practitioners to whom the board has granted the privilege of diagnosing, prescribing for and treating patients in the hospital. *Public Hospitals Act*, R.R.O. 1980, Reg. 865, s. 1.

MEDICAL STAFF COMMITTEE. A committee established or approved by a board of management of a hospital for (a) evaluating, controlling and reporting on clinical practice in a hospital to continually maintain and improve the safety and quality of patient care in the hospital; or (b) performing a function for the appraisal and control of the quality of patient care in the hospital. *Hospital Act*, R.S.B.C. 1979, c. 176, s. 31.

MEDICAL-SURGICAL SERVICES AGREE-MENT. An agreement made between one or more employers and a trade union or trade unions representing his or their employees to establish a plan for providing such employees with medical and surgical care and treatment to be operated by the employer or employers and representatives of such employees. *Public Health Act*, R.R.O. 1980, Reg. 834, s. 38.

MEDICAL TREATMENT. 1. Includes (a) surgical and dental treatment, (b) any procedure undertaken for the purpose of diagnosis, (c) any procedure undertaken for the purpose of preventing any disease or ailment, and (d) any procedure that is ancillary to any treatment as it applies to that treatment. *Custody and Detention of Young Persons Act*, S.N.B. 1985, c. C-40, s. 1. 2. Treatment of any sick or injured person through the performance of cardiopulmonary resuscitation, cardiac monitoring, defibrillation, airway or gastric intubation, pneumothorax relief and the administration of drugs and intravenous fluids. *Advanced Life Support Services Act*, S.N.B. 1976, c. A-3.01, s. 1. 3. The application to, or prescription for, the foot of medicines, pads, adhesives, felt, plasters or a medicinal agency. *Podiatrists Act*, R.S.B.C. 1979, c. 330, s. 1.

MEDICAMENT. *n.* A substance or a mixture of substances that may be used to diagnose, cure, reduce or prevent an ailment, a disorder, an abnormal physical or psychological condition or symptoms thereof in human beings or in animals or to restore, correct or alter their organic functions. *Retail Sales Tax Act*, S.Q. 1980, c. 14, s. 12.

MEDICARE. *n.* A medical care programme which makes doctors' services universally available. P.W. Hogg, *Constitutional Law of Canada*, 2d ed. (Toronto: Carswell, 1985) at 120.

MEDICATED FEED. 1. A mixed feed containing (a) a medicating ingredient at a therapeutic or prophylactic level, (b) a hormone the function of which is to promote growth in the animal body, (c) a medicating ingredient for use in effecting oestrus synchronization in livestock, or (d) a medicating ingredient the purpose of which is to promote growth or feed efficiency in the presence of a specific disease or specific stress condition. *Feeds Regulations*, C.R.C., c. 665, s. 2. 2. An animal feed that contains a veterinary drug. *Pharmacists Act*, R.S.B.C. 1979, c. 326, s. 49.

MEDICATED WINE. Any product containing an alcoholic beverage and medicine, provided that the quantity of alcoholic beverage therein is no more than is strictly necessary for purposes of solution or preservation and that the quantity of medicine is sufficient to render the product unsuitable for use as an alcoholic beverage. *An Act Respecting the Commission de Contrôle des Permis D'alcool*, R.S.Q. 1977, c. C-33, s. 103.

MEDICATING INGREDIENT. Any drug, hormone or other ingredient that in the opinion of the Minister may be harmful to livestock. *Feeds Regulations*, C.R.C., c. 665, s. 2.

MEDICATION. *n.* Any substance or mixture of substances which may be used: (i.) for the diagnosis, treatment, remission or prevention of any disease, ailment, any abnormal physical or mental condition, or their symptoms in man or animal; or (ii.) to restore, rectify, or change organic functions in man or animal. *Pharmacy Act*, R.S.Q. 1977, c. P-10, s. 1. See SAFE ~.

MEDICINAL FOOD. A mixture of substances intended for use without processing for the feeding of animals and containing a medicinal premix or a nutriment and a medication, as the case may be. *An Act to Amend the Animal Health Protection Act*, S.Q. 1986, c. 53, s. 17.

MEDICINAL PREMIX. A mixture of substances containing a nutriment and a medication and intended for use in the preparation of a medicinal food. *An Act to Amend the Animal Health Protection Act*, S.Q. 1986, c. 53, s. 17.

MEDICINE. *n.* 1. Includes all drugs for internal or external use of humans, animals, or fowl, and any substance or mixture of substances intended to be used for the treatment, mitigation or prevention of disease in humans, animals, or fowl. 2. Includes surgery and obstetrics, but does not include homeopathy, osteopathy, veterinary surgery or veterinary medicine. 3. Includes surgery and midwifery. *Medical Act*, R.S.N.S. 1967, c. 179, s. 1. See DRUGS AND ~S; FORENSIC ~; LEGAL ~; PRACTICE OF ~; PRACTISE ~; PROPRIETARY ~; VETERINARY ~.

MEDICO-LEGAL. *adj.* Concerning the law relating to medical issues.

MEDIUM. See GRAPHIC ~; LASING ~.

MEDIUM DENSITY MULTI-FAMILY RESIDENTIAL. Real property principally used for residential purposes where the ratio of dwelling units to land area is greater than thirty-nine but less than one hundred and fifty dwelling units per hectare. *Taxation (Amendment) Act*, S.N.W.T. 1986 (1st Sess.), c. 23, s. 6.

MEDIUM HARD. Rock comparable to concrete with a compressive strength greater than

2,500 psi. *Building Code Act*, R.R.O. 1980, Reg. 87, s. 4.2.1.10.

MEDIUM POWER. A load of 50 kilowatts or more but less than 500 kilowatts. *Quebec Electricity Service By-law*, C.R.C., c. 1086, s. 2.

MEDIUM SAND. A soil consisting of particles passing a No. 10 sieve but retained on a No. 40 sieve. *Building Code Act*, R.R.O. 1980, Reg. 87, s. 4.2.1.4.

MEETING. *n.* A gathering of people to decide, by proper voting procedure, whether something should be done. See CLASS ~; CREDITORS' ~; GENERAL ~; PUBLIC ~; RACE ~; RACING ~; SERIES ~.

MEETING OF DIRECTORS. Includes a meeting of an executive committee of the directors.

MEETING OF MEMBERS. Any meeting of members, a class of members or a subdivision of members that does not constitute a separate class of members of a corporation for the purpose of: (i) electing or removing directors; (ii) considering financial statements or any auditor's report; (iii) appointing an auditor or reappointing an incumbent auditor; (iv) making any fundamental change under Division XIV of Part I; (v) determining liquidation and dissolution under Division XVII of Part I; and for any purpose where the articles or bylaws of the corporation require the approval of the members. *Non-profit Corporations Act*, S.S. 1979, c. N-4.1, s. 2.

MEGA. *pref.* 10^6. Prefix for multiples and submultiples of basic, supplementary and derived units of measurement. *Weights and Measures Act*, S.C. 1970-71-72, c. 36, schedule I.

MELIOREM CONDITIONEM SUAM FACERE POTEST MINOR, DETERIOREM NEQUAQUAM. [L.] A minor may make her or his condition better, by no means worse.

MELIOR EST CONDITIO DEFENDENTIS. [L.] The stronger position is the defendant's.

MELIOR EST CONDITIO POSSIDENTIS ET REI QUAM ACTORIS. [L.] The possessor's position is better; and the defendant's is better than the plaintiff's.

MELIOR EST CONDITIO POSSIDENTIS, UBI NEUTER JUS HABET. [L.] The possessor's position is better, where neither has clear title.

MELIOR EST JUSTITIA VERE PRAEVENIENS, QUAM SEVERE PUNIENS. [L.] Justice which truly prevents is better than justice which punishes severely.

MELIUS EST OMNIA MALA PATI QUAM

MALO CONSENTIRE. [L.] It is better to endure all evil than to agree to evil.

MELIUS EST PETERE FONTES QUAM SECTARI RIVULOS. [L.] It is better to go to the source than to follow tributaries.

MELLANBY EFFECT. For any concentration of alcohol in blood, clinical intoxication is greater while blood alcohol level rises than while it falls. F.A. Jaffe, *A Guide to Pathological Evidence*, 2d ed. (Toronto: Carswell, 1983) at 180.

MEMBER. *n.* 1. A subscriber of the memorandum of a company, and includes every other person who agrees to become a member of a company and whose name is entered in its register of members or a branch register of members. 2. A person who is entitled as a member or shareholder to full voting rights in the conduct of the affairs of the taxpayer (being a corporation) or of a corporation of which the taxpayer is a subsidiary wholly-owned corporation. *Income Tax Act*, R.S.C. 1952, c. 148 (as am. S.C. 1970-71-72, c. 63), s. 135(4)(e). 3. Of a credit union means a person who is recorded as a member on the records of the credit union and is entitled to participate in and use the services of the credit union. *Income Tax Act*, R.S.C. 1952, c. 148 (as am. S.C. 1980-81-82-83, c. 48, s. 78), s. 137(6)(d). 4. In relation to a pension plan that has not been terminated, an employee or, in the case of a multi-employer plan, a former employee, who has made contributions to the plan or on whose behalf the employer was required by the plan to make contributions to it and who has not terminated membership or commenced the pension. 5. A member of the House of Commons. 6. A member of the Legislative Assembly. See BOARD ~; CIVILIAN ~ OF OVERSEAS AIR CREW; CLEARING ~; CLUB ~; CREW ~; DECEASED ~; EXECUTIVE ~; FACULTY ~; FORMER ~; FUTURE ~; INACTIVE ~; INCAPACITATED ~; INDEPENDENT ~; INTEREST OF A ~; MEETING OF ~S; MUNICIPAL ~; NAME A ~; NON-COMMISSIONED ~; NON-VOTING ~; PROBATIONARY ~; PROFESSIONAL ~; PROPERTY OF A ~; PUBLIC ~; REGULAR ~; RESIDENT ~; SPONSOR ~; UNFIT ~; VOTING ~.

MEMBER IN GOOD STANDING. A member who is not in default for fees, dues or costs payable and who is not under suspension.

MEMBER INSTITUTION. 1. A corporation any of whose deposits are insured by the Corporation pursuant to this Act. *Canada Deposit Insurance Corporation Act*, R.S.C. 1985, c. C-3, s. 2. 2. In relation to a particular deposit insurance corporation, means (i) a corporation whose liabilities in respect of deposits are insured by, or (ii) a credit union that is qualified for assistance from that deposit insurance corporation. *Income Tax Act*, R.S.C. 1952, c. 148 (as am. S.C. 1974-75-76, c. 26, s. 93), s. 137.1(5)(b).

MEMBER MUNICIPALITY. A municipality or an electoral area that is included in a regional district by the letters patent. *Municipal Act*, R.S.B.C. 1979, c. 290, s. 766.

MEMBER OF A BAND. A person whose name appears on a Band List or who is entitled to have his name appear on a Band List. *Indian Act*, R.S.C. 1985, c. I-5, s. 2.

MEMBER OF A CLUB. A person: (i) who, whether as a charter member or admitted in accordance with the bylaws or rules of a club, has become a member thereof; (ii) who maintains his membership by payment of his regular periodic dues in the manner provided by the bylaws or rules; and (iii) whose name and address are entered on the list of members supplied to the commission at the time of the application for a club licence under this Act or are subsequently supplied if admitted thereafter. *The Liquor Licensing Act*, R.S.S. 1978, c. L-21, s. 2.

MEMBER OF A CONGREGATION. An adult, living with the members of the congregation, who conforms to the practices of the religious organization of which the congregation is a constituent part whether or not he has been formally accepted into the organization, and a child, other than an adult, of such adult, if the child lives with members of the congregation. *Income Tax Acts.*

MEMBER OF A CREW. Any person, including a master, who is employed on board or forms part of the staff or crew of a vehicle. *Immigration Act*, R.S.C. 1985, c. I-2, s. 2.

MEMBER OF A FAMILY. 1. A worker's spouse, parent, grandparent, step-parent, child, grandchild, step-child, brother, sister, half-brother, half-sister and a person who stands in loco parentis to the worker or to whom the worker stands in loco parentis (whether or not there is any degree of consanguinity between such person and the worker), and includes an illegitimate grandchild of the worker and the parents and grandparents of a worker who is an illegitimate child. 2. A wife or husband, father, mother, grandfather, grandmother, stepfather, stepmother, son, daughter, grandson, granddaughter, stepson, stepdaughter, brother, sister, half brother, half sister, adopted child, foster parent. See MEMBER OF HIS OR HER FAMILY.

MEMBER OF A FORCE. A member of (a) the Canadian Forces; or (b) the naval, army or air forces of a state other than Canada that are lawfully present in Canada. *Criminal Code*, R.S.C. 1985, c. C-46, s. 62(2). See MEMBER OF THE FORCES.

MEMBER OF A SERVICE. Any person who is a member of (i) Her Majesty's Forces, or (ii) the Merchant Navy, or (iii) the mercantile marine of any State allied with Her Majesty, or (iv) the Newfoundland Forestry Unit. *Limited Administration of Estates (Members of Services) Act*, R.S.Nfld. 1970, c. 208, s. 2.

MEMBER OF A TRIBUNAL. A person appointed as a member of (i) the Board, (ii) an arbitration board, (iii) an adjudication board, or (iv) a person or body of persons appointed by an employer and a bargaining agent pursuant to a collective agreement to settle differences between them, and includes a person acting as a single adjudicator. *Public Service Employee Relations Act*, R.S.A. 1980, c. P-33, s. 76.

MEMBER OF COUNCIL. Includes a trustee of the board of an improvement district. *Emergency Plans Act, 1983*, S.O. 1983, c. 30, s. 1. See MEMBER OF THE COUNCIL.

MEMBER OF A FAMILY. A wife, husband, father, mother, grandfather, grandmother, stepfather, stepmother, son, daughter, grandson, granddaughter, stepson, stepdaughter, brother, sister, half brother and half sister and a person who stood in loco parentis to the worker or to whom the worker stood in loco parentis, whether related by consanguinity or not, and where the worker is the parent or grandparent of an illegitimate child includes that child, and where the worker is an illegitimate child includes the worker's parents and grandparents.

MEMBER OF HIS OR HER FAMILY. Any person connected with a member by blood relationship, marriage or adoption, and (i) persons are connected by blood relationship if one is the child or other descendant of the other or one is the brother or sister of the other, (ii) persons are connected by marriage if one is married to the other or to a person who is connected by blood relationship to the other, and (iii) persons are connected by adoption if one has been adopted, either legally or in fact, as the child of the other or as the child of a person who is so connected by blood relationship (otherwise than as a brother or sister) to the other. See MEMBER OF A FAMILY.

MEMBER OF THE COUNCIL. Include the mayor or any of the councillors of the city or town. *Cities and Towns Act*, R.S.Q. 1977, c. C-19, s. 6. See MEMBER OF COUNCIL.

MEMBER OF THE FAMILY. See MEMBER OF A FAMILY; MEMBER OF HIS OR HER FAMILY.

MEMBER OF THE FAMILY CLASS. A person described in the regulations as a person whose application for landing may be sponsored by a Canadian citizen or by a permanent resident. *Immigration Act*, R.S.C. 1985, c. I-2, s. 2.

MEMBER OF THE FORCE. A member of the Force, as defined in the Royal Canadian Mounted Police Act, holding a rank in the Force, and any other member of the Force, as defined therein, of a class designated in accordance with the regulations for the purposes of this Part. *Royal Canadian Mounted Police Act*, R.S.C. 1985, c. R-11, s. 3.

MEMBER OF THE FORCES. A person who has served in the Canadian Forces or in the naval, army or air forces of Canada or Newfoundland since the commencement of World War I. *Pension Act*, R.S.C. 1985, c. P-6, s. 2. See MEMBER OF A FORCE.

MEMBER OF THE LEGISLATIVE ASSEMBLY. See DUTY OF ~.

MEMBER OF THE OVERSEAS HEADQUARTERS STAFF. A person who is not a supervisor or helper and who was a member of the Headquarters Staff of, and was employed and paid by, Canadian Legion War Services Inc., The National Council of the Young Men's Christian Association of Canada, Knights of Columbus Canadian Army Huts or Salvation Army Canadian War Services and who proceeded from Canada under the authority of the Chief of Naval Personnel, the Adjutant-General or Air Member for Personnel. *Civilian War Pensions and Allowances Act*, R.S.C. 1985, c. C-31, s. 16.

MEMBER OF THE PUBLIC. 1. Any section or segment of the public without regard to the numbers thereof. 2. A person who is (i) a Canadian citizen or who is lawfully admitted to Canada for permanent residence, (ii) a resident of Alberta, and (ii) not a member of a professional association. Alberta statutes.

MEMBER OF THE REGULAR FORCE. An officer or man of the regular force. *Canadian Forces Superannuation Act*, R.S.C. 1985, c. C-17, s. 2.

MEMBER OF THE VOLUNTARY AID DETACHMENT. A member of the Nursing Auxiliary Canadian Red Cross Corps or the Nursing Division of the St. John Ambulance Brigade of Canada who, with the approval of the Adjutant-General, served with the Royal Canadian Army Medical Corps during the War. *Civilian War Pensions and Allowances Act*, R.S.C. 1985, c. C-31, s. 43.

MEMBER OF THE WOMEN'S ROYAL NAVAL SERVICES. A person who (a) enrolled in the Women's Royal Naval Service, (b) enrolled in Queen Alexandra's Royal Naval Nursing Service or the reserve therefor, or (c) enrolled as a medical or dental practitioner employed with the Medical Branch or Dental Branch of the Royal Navy with naval status for general service. *Public Service Employment Act*, R.S.C. 1985, c. P-33, s. 48.

MEMBERSHIP. *n.* 1. Includes a share of a credit union. 2. Includes a share of a corporation.

MEMBERSHIP CORPORATION. A corporation incorporated or continued to carry on activities that are primarily for the benefit of its members.

MEMBERSHIP INTEREST. The rights, privileges, restrictions and conditions conferred or imposed on a member or each class of members of a corporation in accordance with the provisions of its articles or bylaws. *Non-profit Corporations Act*, S.S. 1979, c. N-4.1, s. 2.

MEMENTO. See OFFICIAL ~.

MEMORANDUM. *n.* 1. The memorandum of association of a company, as originally framed or as altered in pursuance of this Act. *Companies Act*, R.S.N.S. 1967, c. 42, s. 1. 2. The memorandum of association for incorporation of a society incorporated under this Act. *Societies Act*, R.S.N.S. 1967, c. 286, s. 1. 3. The endorsement on the certificate of title and on the duplicate copy thereof of the particulars of any instrument presented for registration. Land Titles acts. See OFFERING ~.

MEMORANDUM OF AGREEMENT. A written, ratified and signed document which frequently precedes a formal collective agreement. Usually when the collective agreement is executed, the memorandum is merged. D.J.M. Brown and D.M. Beatty, *Canadian Labour Arbitration*, 2d ed. (Aurora: Canada Law Book, 1977) at 169.

MEMORANDUM OF ASSOCIATION. An incorporating document in some jurisdictions. It contains the name, capital structure and proposed business of the company. S.M. Beck *et al.*, *Cases and Materials on Partnerships and Canadian Business Corporations* (Toronto: The Carswell Company Limited, 1983) at 159.

MEMORIAL. *n.* 1. A memorial, marker, monument, headstone, footstone, tombstone, plaque, tablet or plate marking a grave and includes an inscription of lettering or ornamentation, or both, on or on the front of a space within a building or structure for the permanent placement of human remains. *Cemetery and Funeral*

Services Act, S.N.S. 1983, c. 4, s. 2. 2. Whatever contains the details of a deed.

MENHADEN. *n.* A fish of the species Brevoortia tyrannus. *Northwest Atlantic Fisheries Regulations*, C.R.C., c. 860, s. 2.

MENINGES. *n.* Three membranes which enclose the brain and spinal cord. F.A. Jaffe, *A Guide to Pathological Evidence*, 2d ed. (Toronto: Carswell, 1983) at 180.

MENINGITIS. *n.* Inflammation of the membranes surrounding the brain and spinal cord. F.A. Jaffe, *A Guide to Pathological Evidence*, 2d ed. (Toronto: Carswell, 1983) at 180.

MENSA ET THORO. [L.] From bed and board.

MENS REA. [L.] The minimum essential mental element of a criminal offence.

MENS TESTATORIS IN TESTAMENTIS SPECTANDA EST. [L.] In construing wills the testator's intention must be regarded.

MENTAL DEFECTIVE. A person in whom there is a condition of arrested or incomplete development of mind, whether arising from inherent causes or induced by disease or injury, and who requires care, supervision and control for his own protection or welfare or for the protection of others. *Interpretation Act*, R.S.O. 1980, c. 219, s. 30.

MENTAL DEFICIENCY. The condition of mind of a mental defective. *Interpretation Act*, R.S.O. 1980, c. 219, s. 30.

MENTAL DEFICIENCY NURSE. A person to whom a certificate in mental deficiency nursing has been issued in accordance with the regulations. *Psychiatric Nursing Training Act*, R.S.A. 1970, c. 290, s. 2.

MENTAL DISABILITY. (i) A condition of mental retardation or impairment, (ii) a learning disability, or a dysfunction in one or more of the processes involved in understanding or using symbols or spoken language, or (iii) a mental disorder.

MENTAL DISORDER. A substantial disorder of thought, mood, perception, orientation or memory, any of which grossly impairs judgment, behaviour, capacity to recognize reality or ability to meet the ordinary demands of life but mental retardation or a learning disability does not of itself constitute a mental disorder.

MENTAL HANDICAP. See PHYSICAL OR ~.

MENTAL HEALTH CENTRE. A place where services are provided to in-patients and out-patients and that is designated by the minister as a mental health centre. *Mental Health Services*

Act, S.S. 1984-85-86, c. M-13.1, s. 2. See CHILDREN'S ~.

MENTAL HEALTH CLINIC. A place where services are provided to out-patients and not to in-patients and that is designated by the minister as a mental health clinic.

MENTAL ILLNESS. A disorder of mind, other than psychoneurosis and psychopathic disorder, that results in such a change in the behaviour and judgment of a person as to require medical treatment, or in respect of which disorder of mind, treatment, care, and supervision, of the person are necessary for the protection or welfare of the person and others.

MENTAL INCOMPETENCY. The condition of mind of a mentally incompetent person.

MENTAL INCOMPETENT. A person, (i) in whom there is such a condition of arrested or incomplete development of mind, whether arising from inherent causes or induced by disease or injury, or (ii) who is suffering from such a disorder of the mind, that that person requires care, supervision and control for self protection and the protection of that person's property.

MENTALLY COMPETENT. Having the ability to understand the subject matter in respect of which consent is requested and the ability to appreciate the consequences of giving or withholding consent.

MENTALLY DEFECTIVE PERSON. 1. A person in whom there is a condition of arrested or incomplete development of mind existing before the age of eighteen years, whether arising from inherent causes or induced by disease or injury. *Sexual Sterilization Act*, R.S.A. 1970, c. 341, s. 2. 2. A person in whom there is a condition of arrested or incomplete development of mind, whether arising from inherent causes or induced by disease or injury, and who requires care, supervision and control for his own protection or welfare or for the protection of others. *Interpretation Act*, R.S.O. 1980, c. 219, s. 30.

MENTALLY DISORDERED PERSON. 1. A person who is suffering from mental illness, mental retardation or any other disorder or disability of the mind. 2. A person who suffers from (i) a disorder of the mind that results in such a change in his behaviour and judgment as to render necessary his care and supervision for his protection or welfare or that of others, (ii) a persistent disorder of personality, other than a disorder of the mind referred to in subparagraph (i), that results in abnormally aggressive or seriously irresponsible conduct on the part of that person, (iii) a severe or persistent emotional disturbance, other than a disorder of the mind referred to in subparagraph (i) or a disorder of personality referred to in subparagraph (ii), that results in marked impairment of social adaptation and adjustment, (iv) a disorder or disability of mind, as evidenced by his being so given over to the use of alcohol or drugs that he is unable to control himself or is incapable of managing his affairs, or places his family in danger, or as evidenced by his use of drugs or intoxicating liquor whether habitually or sporadically to such an extent as to render him dangerous to himself or others, (v) a condition of arrested or incomplete development of mind whether arising from inherent causes or induced by disease or injury, or (vi) any disability of mind whatsoever caused by disease, senility or otherwise. *Health and Public Welfare Act*, R.S.Nfld. 1970, c. 151, s. 97.

MENTALLY ILL PERSON. A person, other than a mental defective, who is suffering from such a disorder of the mind that that person requires care, supervision and control for self protection or welfare, of for the protection of others.

MENTALLY INCOMPETENT INDIAN. An Indian who, pursuant to the laws of the province in which he resides, has been found to be mentally defective or incompetent for the purposes of any laws of that province providing for the administration of estates of mentally defective or incompetent persons. *Indian Act*, R.S.C. 1985, c. I-5, s. 2.

MENTALLY INCOMPETENT PERSON. 1. A person (a) in whom there is such a condition of arrested or incomplete development of mind, whether arising from inherent causes or induced by disease or injury, or (b) who is suffering from such a disorder of the mind, that that person requires care, supervision and control for self protection or welfare or for the protection of others or for the protection of that person's property. 2. A person, (i) in whom there is such a condition of arrested or incomplete development of mind, whether arising from inherent causes or induced by disease or injury, or (ii) who is suffering from such a disorder of the mind, that that person requires care, supervision and control for self protection and the protection of that person's property.

MENTALLY RETARDED CHILD. A child with significant below average general intellectual functioning which originates during the developmental period and is associated with impairment of either learning and social adjustment or maturation, or both. *Children's Services Act*, S.N.S. 1976, c. 8, s. 2.

MENTALLY RETARDED PERSON. A person (a) in whom there is a condition of arrested or incomplete development of mind, whether arising from inherent causes or induced by disease or injury, that is of a nature or degree that requires or is susceptible to medical treatment or other special care or training; and (b) who requires care, supervision and control for self protection or welfare or for the protection of others.

MENTAL RETARDATE. A person who is suffering from mental retardation to such a degree as to require treatment, care, and supervision, or training, of the person for the protection or welfare of the person or others. *Mental Health Act*, R.S.M. 1970, c. M110, s. 2.

MENTAL RETARDATION. A condition of arrested or incomplete development of mind whether arising from inherent causes or induced by disease or injury.

MENTIRI EST CONTRA MENTEM IRE. [L.] To lie is to go against conscience.

MERA NOCTIS. [L.] Midnight.

MERCABLE. *adj.* Able to be bought or sold.

MERCANTILE. *adj.* Includes manufacturing.

MERCANTILE AGENT. 1. A person having, in the customary course of business as an agent, authority either to sell goods or to consign goods for the purpose of sale, or to buy goods or to raise money on the security of goods. 2. Includes a broker or agent to negotiate and make contracts for the sale of products of which he is not entrusted with the possession or control; a factor or agent to sell or dispose of products of which he is entrusted with the possession or control; and a jobber, or person whose normal business is to buy or sell products in wholesale quantities, when handling or disposing of products on commission; and an agent of such broker, factor or jobber. *The Sales on Consignment Act*, R.S.S. 1978, c. S-4, s. 2.

MERCANTILE BUILDING. A building used for the display and sale of merchandise. *Fire Prevention Act*, S.N.S. 1976, c. 9, s. 2.

MERCANTILE LAW. The law concerning matters like bills of exchange, marine insurance and contracts of affreightment.

MERCANTILE OCCUPANCY. Occupancy or use for displaying or selling retail goods, wares or merchandise.

MERCATIVE. *adj.* Pertaining to trade.

MERCATURE. *n.* The act of buying and selling.

MERCHANDISE. See FUNERAL ~; GOODS, WARES AND ~; MANITOBA ~.

MERCHANT. *n.* 1. Includes any person doing business or extending credit in the course of his business. *Consumer Protection Act*, S.Q. 1978, c.

9, s. 1. 2. Does not include a person who has a recognized retail store if more than fifty per cent of the goods and services sold by him in the Province are sold by direct sale. Direct Sellers' acts. See COMMISSIONER ~; ITINERANT ~.

MERCHANTABLE. *adj.* Able to be bought or sold.

MERCHANTABLE LOG. (i) A log of which more than one-half of the total content is sound wood when the content is measured in cubic feet, or (ii) a log of which more than one-third of the total content is sound wood when the content is measured in board feet. *Crown Timber Act*, R.R.O. 1980, Reg. 234, s. 1.

MERCHANTABLE QUALITY. Adequacy, so that a buyer may sell or generally use an item. G.H.L. Fridman, *Sale of Goods in Canada*, 3d ed. (Toronto: Carswell, 1986) at 205.

MERCHANTABLE TIMBER. For an old temporary tenure or a timber licence, trees that (a) on January 1, 1975 were older than 75 years; and (b) are on an area of Crown land in quantities determined by the regional manager to be sufficient to be commercially valuable at the time when a timber cruise submitted under section 57 is made. *Forest Act*, R.S.B.C. 1979, c. 140, s. 1.

MERCHANTABLE TREE. A standing tree containing one or more merchantable logs having a total content of sound wood that is equal to more than one-half of the content of all the logs in the tree. *Crown Timber Act*, R.R.O. 1980, Reg. 234, s. 1.

MERCHANT SEAMAN. Any person who served during World War II as Master, Officer or member of the crew of (a) a ship registered in Canada, (b) a United Kingdom ship registered in Canada or elsewhere, or (c) a registered ship of one of the countries allied with His Majesty during World War II if, in the case of a person who served on other than a ship registered in Canada, that person was born or domiciled in Canada or Newfoundland, or was an ordinary resident in Canada or Newfoundland at anytime during the period between September 9, 1929 and the date on which he commenced to so serve. *Memorial Cross Order (World War II)*, C.R.C., c. 1623, s. 2.

MERCHANT SHIPPING ACTS. The Merchant Shipping Act, 1894 of the Parliament of the United Kingdom, 57-58 Victoria, chapter 60, and all Acts adding to or amending that Act. *Canada Shipping Act*, R.S.C. 1985, c. S-9, s. 2.

MERCIAMENT. *n.* Fine; penalty.

MERCURY. *n.* 1. Elemental mercury and all chemical forms thereof. *Chlor-Alkali Mercury Liquid Effluent Regulations*, C.R.C., c. 811, s. 2. 2. A substance designated under the Ontario Occupational Health and Safety Act. D. Robertson, *Ontario Health and Safety Guide* (Toronto: Richard De Boo Ltd., 1988) at 5-269.

MERCURY CELL. Any device utilizing mercury as a cathode. *Chlor-Alkali Mercury National Emission Standards Regulations*, C.R.C., c. 406, s. 2.

MERCY. See PARDON; RECOMMENDATION TO ~.

MEREDITH MEM. LECT. *abbr.* Meredith Memorial Lectures (Conférences commémoratives Meredith).

MERGE. *v.* Of original cause of action, to include in the judgment of a domestic court of record if the plaintiff succeeds. J.G. McLeod, *The Conflict of Laws* (Calgary: Carswell, 1983) at 606.

MERGED. *adj.* 1. Of the rights and duties created by a contract for the sale of land, subsumed by a deed and discharged when the deed of conveyance is delivered and accepted. B.J. Reiter, R.C.B. Risk & B.N. McLellan, *Real Estate Law*, 3d ed. (Toronto: Emond Montgomery, 1986) at 920. 2. Of original remedies for a debt subsumed in a higher security, when that security is taken or obtained for the debt. I.H. Jacob, ed., *Bullen and Leake and Jacob's Precedents of Pleadings*, 12th ed. (London: Sweet and Maxwell, 1975) at 1213.

MERGED AREA. A local municipality that is amalgamated with another local municipality or a part of a local municipality that is annexed to a local municipality to constitute an area municipality or a portion of local municipality constituted as an area municipality under subsection 2(1) or the local municipality to which such part is annexed. *Regional Municipality of Hamilton-Wentworth Act*, R.S.O. 1980, c. 437, s. 1.

MERGER. *n.* 1. The acquisition by one or more persons, whether by purchase or lease of shares or assets or otherwise, of any control over or interest in the whole or part of the business of a competitor, supplier, customer or any other person, whereby competition (a) in a trade, industry or profession, (b) among the sources of supply of a trade, industry or profession, (c) among the outlets for sales of a trade, industry or profession, or (d) otherwise than in paragraphs (a) to (c), is or is likely to be lessened to the detriment or against the interest of the public, whether consumers, producers or others. *Combines Investigation Act*, R.S.C. 1985, c. C-34, s. 2. 2. The acquisition or establishment, direct or indirect, by one or more persons, whether by purchase or lease of shares or assets, by amalgamation or by combination or otherwise, of control over or significant interest in the whole or a part of the business of a competitor, supplier, customer or other person. *Combines Investigation Act*, R.S.C. 1985 (2d Supp.), c. 19, s. 91. See DELAWARE ~; FOREIGN ~: NON-~.

MERGER INTO JUDGMENT. A theory that once a creditor begins an action against a debtor which is carried to judgment, the original obligation is transformed into a judgment debt. C.R.B. Dunlop, *Creditor-Debtor Law in Canada* (Toronto: Carswell, 1981) at 51.

MERIT INCREASE. An increase in pay awarded to employees for performance or service.

MERITO BENEFICIUM LEGIS AMITTIT, QUI LEGEM IPSAM SUBVERTERE INTENDIT. [L.] One who intends to subvert the law itself justly loses benefit of the law.

MERITORIOUS CONSIDERATION. A factor based on a moral obligation.

MERITORIOUS CONTRIBUTION. (i) Performance at an unusually high level over an extended period of time; (ii) the successful completion, in a manner beyond what could normally be expected by management, of a major project, special assignment or research study; (iii) the performance of duties under abnormal circumstances in a manner which constitutes a contribution of unusual merit to the Public Service. W. Grover & F. Iacobucci, *Materials on Canadian Income Tax*, 4th ed. (Toronto: Richard De Boo Ltd., 1980) at 216-217.

MERIT PAY. Compensation related directly to work performance and given at management's discretion. D.J.M. Brown and D.M. Beatty, *Canadian Labour Arbitration*, 2d ed. (Aurora: Canada Law Book, 1977) at 560.

MERIT PRINCIPLE. The principle that merit governs the appointment of a person to and advancement within the civil service on the basis of qualifications, relative ability, knowledge and skills. *Civil Service Act*, S.P.E.I. 1983, c. 4, s. 1.

MERITS. *n.* Used to describe a good cause of action or defence when it is based, not on technical grounds, but on the real issues in question. See AFFIDAVIT OF ~.

MERO MOTU. See EX ~.

MESCALINE. *n.* A hallucinogenic drug obtained from peyote cactus. F.A. Jaffe, *A Guide to Pathological Evidence*, 2d ed. (Toronto: Carswell, 1983) at 180.

MESH. *n.* Any netting used to form the sides, top or bottom or a product. *Playpens Regulations*, C.R.C., c. 932, s. 2.

MESH SIZE. 1. The distance between opposite angles of a single mesh pulled tightly and measured inside and between the knots. Canada regulations. 2. The size of a single mesh of net determined by measuring, without straining the twine, the inside diagonal distance between the knots after immersion in water for not less than 1/2 hour. *Yukon Territory Fishery Regulations*, C.R.C., c. 854, s. 2.

MESNE. *adj.* Intermediate. E.L.G. Tyler & N.E. Palmer, eds., *Crossley Vaines' Personal Property*, 5th ed. (London: Butterworths, 1973) at 4.

MESNE LORD. A lord who holds something on behalf of a higher lord, and on whose behalf an inferior lord or tenant holds something.

MESNE PROCESS. 1. Pre-judgment. C.R.B. Dunlop, *Creditor-Debtor Law in Canada* (Toronto: Carswell, 1981) at 198. 2. In an action or suit, writs which come between the beginning and end.

MESNE PROFIT. Profit derived from land when possession has been withheld improperly.

MESS. See MILITARY ~.

MESSAGE. See COMMERCIAL ~.

MESSAGES. *n.* Includes signs, signals, writing, images, sounds or intelligence of any nature. *The Community Cablecasters Act*, R.S.S. 1978, c. C-17, s. 2.

MESSENGER. *n.* One who carries an errand; one who goes before.

MESSIS SEMENTEM SEQUITUR. [L.] Reaping follows seeding.

MESSUAGE. *n.* A dwelling-house including any out-buildings, adjacent land and curtilage assigned to its use.

METACHRONISM. *n.* A mistake in calculation of time.

METAGE. *n.* The act of determining size or quantity.

METAL. *n.* Includes antimony, bismuth, cadmium, cobalt, copper, chromium, gold, iron, lead, magnesium, mercury, molybdenum, nickel, niobium, silver, tantalum, tin, thorium, titanium, tungsten, uranium and zinc. *Metal Mining Liquid Effluent Regulations*, C.R.C., c. 819, s. 2. See ALKALI ~ AMALGAM; PRECIOUS ~; UNWROUGHT ~.

METAL CHIMNEY. A single-wall chimney of metal constructed on site. *Building Code Act*, R.R.O. 1980, Reg. 87, s. 1.

METAL-CLAD. *adj.* Having sides made of or covered with metal. *Lightning Rods Act*, R.R.O. 1980, Reg. 577, s. 1.

METAL CUTTING. See MACHINE TOOL, ~.

METAL FORMING. See MACHINE TOOL, ~.

METALLIC COVERING. An iron or steel wire armoring applied to cables. *Coal Mines Regulation Act*, R.S.N.S. 1967, c. 36, s. 84.

METALLIC TUBING. See ELECTRICAL ~.

METALLIFEROUS MINING INDUSTRY. Includes the operations of milling and concentrating, but does not include any other operation for the reduction of minerals. *Workers Compensation Act*, R.S.B.C. 1979, c. 437, s. 1.

METAL MECHANIC. See GLAZIER AND ~.

METAL-ROOFED. *adj.* Having a roof made of or covered with metal. *Lightning Rods Act*, R.R.O. 1980, Reg. 577, s. 1.

METAL SEAL. A metal seal furnished by the Chief Electoral Officer to seal a ballot box.

METAL SHIELD. A shield not less than .008 of an inch thick made of stainless steel or other metal equal in tensile strength and corrosion resistance to stainless steel. *Ontario Water Resources Act*, R.R.O. 1980, Reg. 736, s. 72.

METAL TIRE. Every tire the surface of which in contact with the roadway is wholly or partly of metal or other hard, nonresilient material.

METAL WORKER. See SHEET ~.

METEORITE. *n.* Any naturally-occurring object of extraterrestrial origin. *Canadian Cultural Property Export Control List*, C.R.C., c. 448, s. 1.

METER. *n.* An electric or gas meter and includes any apparatus used for the purpose of making measurements of, or obtaining the basis of a charge for, electricity or gas supplied to a purchaser. See PARKING ~; POSTAGE ~; SOUND LEVEL ~; VERIFIED ~.

METER USER. A person who pays postage by means of a postage meter. *Postage Meter Setting Service Regulations*, C.R.C., c. 1286, s. 2.

METES AND BOUNDS. The description of land's boundaries beginning at a fixed point and then outlining the borders in north, south, west and east directions and in degrees, minutes and seconds.

METHANE. *n.* In addition to its normal scientific meaning, a mixture mainly of methane, which may ordinarily contain some ethane, nitrogen, helium or carbon dioxide. Alberta statutes.

METHANE EXTRACTION. Any process approved by the Minister by which methane gas is extracted or manufactured from coal. *Petroleum Resources Act*, S.N.S. 1979-80, c. 12, s. 2.

METHOD. See ANNUITY ~; ARITHMETICAL OR ACTUARIAL ~; CASH ~; COMPARISON ~; COMPLETED CONTRACT ~; INDUCTIVE ~; INSTALMENT ~; MULTIPLIER ~; STANDARD ~S; SUBSTITUTION ~.

METIS. *n.* 1. A person of mixed white and Indian blood having not less than one-quarter Indian blood, but does not include either an Indian or a non-treaty Indian as defined in the Indian Act (Canada). *Metis Betterment Act*, R.S.A. 1980, c. M-14, s. 1. 2. A person having not less than 1/4 Indian blood. *Native Cooperative Guarantee Act*, R.S.A. 1980, c. N-2, s. 1.

METIS SETTLEMENT. Any lands set aside for occupation by a settlement association under The Metis Betterment Act, Alberta. *Alberta Fishery Regulations*, C.R.C., c. 838, s. 2.

METRE. *n.* The unit for the measurement of length, being a length equal to 1 650 763.73 wavelengths in vacuum of the radiation corresponding to the transition between the levels $2p_{10}$ and $5d_5$ of the krypton 86 atom. *Weights and Measures Act*, S.C. 1970-71-72, c. 36, schedule I. See CUBIC ~.

METRIC SYSTEM. A measurement system in which any basic unit is divided or multiplied by ten.

METRIC UNITS. Units of measurement in metres and decimals of a metre. *Registry Act*, R.R.O. 1980, Reg. 898, s. 1.

METRO. *abbr.* Metropolitan.

METROPOLIS. *n.* The main city; the seat of government.

METROPOLITAN AREA. A city together with one or more adjacent municipalities in close economic relationship with the city. *National Housing Act*, R.S.C. 1985, c. N-11, s. 2.

MEZZANINE. *n.* An intermediate floor between the floor and ceiling of any room or storey. *Building Code Act*, R.R.O. 1980, Reg. 87, s. 1.

M FT. *abbr.* One thousand feet board measure. *Customs Tariff*, R.S.C. 1985, c. C-54, s. 2.

M.G.W. *abbr.* Maximum gross weight.

MICRO. *pref.* 10_{-6}. Prefix for multiples and submultiples of basic, supplementary and derived units of measurement. *Weights and Measures Act*, S.C. 1970-71-72, c. 36, schedule I.

MICROCURIE. *n.* That quantity of a radioactive isotope that is disintegrating at the rate of 37,000 disintegrations per second. *Atomic Energy Control Regulations*, C.R.C., c. 365, schedule I.

MICROGRAPHICS. *n.* All processes, techniques and methods of micro-reproduction on film of printed or other graphic matter regardless of the composition thereof. *Public Printing Act*, S.M. 1979, c. 17, s. 1.

MICRO-ORGANISM. *n.* A microscopic plant or animal and includes bacteria, viruses, fungi, algae and protozoa. *Pest Control Products (Nova Scotia) Act*, S.N.S. 1986, c. 16, s. 3.

MICRO-PREMIX. *n.* A feed that is a mixture of ingredients that supply only trace minerals, vitamins, medicating ingredients, amino acids or any other material that is used in minute quantities for feeding livestock and may contain a carrier acceptable to the Director. *Feeds Regulations*, C.R.C., c. 665, s. 2.

MICROWAVE. *n.* An electromagnetic wave with frequency in the range 0.010 GHz to 300 GHz. *Radiation Emitting Devices Regulations*, C.R.C., c. 1370, s. 1.

MICROWAVE OVEN. Any apparatus or device for heating food or material by absorption of electromagnetic radiation in the range of electromagnetic frequencies from 890 megahertz to 6,000 megahertz. *Public Health Act*, R.S.O. 1980, c. 409, s. 49.

MIDDLE-MAN. *n.* An intermediary between a wholesale merchant and a retail dealer; one who distributes from producer to consumer.

MIDWATER TRAWL. A trawl net that is designed so as not to come into contact with the sea-bed while in operation. Canada regulations.

MIDWIFE. *n.* A person whose profession is the delivery of children.

MIGRATORY BIRDS. Migratory game birds, migratory insectivorous birds and migratory non game birds. Canada regulations.

MIGRATORY GAME BIRDS. (a) Anatidae or waterfowl, including brant, wild ducks, geese and swans, (b) Gruidae or cranes, including little brown, sandhill and whooping cranes, (c) Rallidae or rails, including coots, gallinules and sora and other rails, (d) Limicolae or shorebirds, including avocets, curlew, dowitchers, godwits, knots, oyster catchers, phalaropes, plovers, sandpipers, snipe, stilts, surf birds, turnstones, willet, woodcock, and yellowlegs, and (e) Columbidae or pigeons, including doves and wild pigeons. *Migratory Birds Convention Act*, R.S.C. 1985, c. M-7, s. 2.

MIGRATORY INSECTIVOROUS BIRDS. Bobolinks, catbirds, chickadees, cuckoos, flickers, fly-catchers, grosbeaks, hummingbirds, kinglets, martins, meadowlarks, nighthawks or bull bats, nuthatches, orioles, robins, shrikes, swallows, swifts, tanagers, titmice, thrushes, vireos, warblers, waxwings, whippoorwills, woodpeckers and wrens, and all other perching birds that feed entirely or chiefly on insects. *Migratory Birds Convention Act*, R.S.C. 1985, c. M-7, s. 2.

MIGRATORY NONGAME BIRDS. Auks, auklets, bitterns, fulmars, gannets, grebes, guillemots, gulls, herons, jaegers, loons, murres, petrels, puffins, shearwaters and terns. *Migratory Birds Convention Act*, R.S.C. 1985, c. M-7, s. 2.

MIGRATORY WORKER. A person who moves from one work site to another doing the same kind of work.

MILDLY RETARDED CHILD. A child in whose case there has been from birth or from an early age mental retardation, not amounting to moderate retardation yet so pronounced that he requires special training and education which instruction is not given in the ordinary schools. *Child Welfare Act*, R.S.N.S. 1967, c. 31, s. 87.

MILE. *n.* 1. 1 760 yards. *Weights and Measures Act*, S.C. 1970-71-72, c. 36, schedule II. 2. The international nautical mile of 1 852 metres. Canada regulations. 3. A nautical mile measuring 6,080 feet. Canada regulations. See REVENUE ~S; ROUTE ~; SQUARE ~.

MILEAGE. *n.* Travelling expenses which sheriffs, witnesses and others may claim.

MILEAGE CONTRACT USE. The use under contract of tires on a mileage basis. *Motor Vehicle Tire Safety Regulations*, C.R.C., c. 1039, s. 2.

MILITARY. *adj.* 1. Relating to all or any part of the Canadian Forces. 2. With respect to any aircraft or facility, an aircraft or facility operated by or on behalf of the Department of National Defence, the Canadian Forces or a visiting force. *Canadian Aviation Safety Board Act*, R.S.C. 1985, c. C-12, s. 17. 3. Relating to any warlike force. *Canadian Cultural Property Export Control List*, C.R.C., c. 448, s. 1.

MILITARY CANTEEN. A mess or canteen operated in connection with a unit or establishment of the Royal Canadian Navy, the Canadian Army, the Royal Canadian Air Force, or the Royal Canadian Mounted Police Force, in a camp, armoury, barracks, post, station, or ship, of any one or more of those units or establishments in Manitoba. *Liquor Control Act*, R.S.M. 1970, c. L160, s. 2.

MILITARY LAW. Includes all laws, regulations or orders relating to the Canadian Forces. *Criminal Code*, R.S.C. 1985, c. C-46, s. 2.

MILITARY MESS. Includes a canteen and an institute in a building or camp used for the accommodation of the active or reserve units of the naval, military or air forces of Canada. *Liquor Control Act*, S.Nfld. 1973, c. 103, s. 2.

MILITARY OFFENCE. An offence recognized by a military court, e.g. insubordination.

MILITARY SERVICE. Service in the Canadian Forces or in the naval, army or air forces of Canada since the commencement of World War I. *Pension Act*, R.S.C. 1985, c. P-6, s. 2. See ACTIVE ~.

MILITIAMAN. *n.* A non-commissioned officer or private of the force. *Defence Services Pension Continuation Act*, R.S.C. 1970, c. D-3, s. 2.

MILK. *n.* 1. As used in the manufacture of dairy products, means the normal lacteal secretion, free from colostrum, obtained from the mammary gland of an animal. *An Act to Amend the Dairy Products Act*, S.P.E.I. 1983, c. 10, s. 1. 2. Milk from cows, goats or sheep. 3. Includes whole milk and such products of milk as are supplied, processed, distributed or sold in any form including but not so as to restrict the generality of the foregoing, cream, butter, cheese, ice cream and condensed, evaporated or powdered milk. See BUTTER~; CONCENTRATED ~ PLANT; CONDENSED ~; CONTAMINATED ~; EVAPORATED ~; FLAVOURED ~; FLUID ~; MODIFIED ~; PARTLY-SKIMMED ~; QUALIFYING ~; RAW ~; RECONSTITUTED ~; STANDARDIZED ~; STERILIZED ~.

MILK AND CREAM. All classes of milk and cream designated under the regulations as fluid milk products and includes all classes of milk products designated under the regulations as manufactured milk products. *Dairy Products Act*, R.S.N.B. 1973, c. D-2, s. 1.

MILK CONDENSERY. Any building where milk, cream or any dairy by-product is dehydrated and converted into a concentrated dairy product.

MILK DEALER. A person who as a principal, purchases or receives milk or cream for the purpose of processing or selling milk or cream.

MILK FAT. The fat of cow's milk that has (a) a specific gravity of not less than 0.905 at a temperature of 40 degrees Celsius, (b) a tocopheral content not greater than 50 micrograms per gram as determined by the official method prescribed by the Food and Drugs Act and regulations thereunder, (c) a Reichert-Meissl

Number not less than 24, and (d) a Polenske Number not exceeding 10 per cent of the Reichert-Meissl Number and in no case shall the Polenske Number exceed 3.5. *Canada Dairy Products Regulations*, C.R.C., c. 553, s. 2.

MILK IN FLUID FORM. Raw or pasteurized fresh milk, and includes sterile milk or milk specially treated to achieve extended keeping quality or the appearance of freshness that is sold, offered for sale or supplied for the same use or in semblance of fresh milk, but does not include reconstituted milk. *Milk Industry Act*, R.S.B.C. 1979, c. 258, s. 1.

MILKING EQUIPMENT. Includes those parts of a milking machine and its pipelines, connections and appurtenances with which milk comes into contact when the milking machine is used. *Milk Act*, R.R.O. 1980, Reg. 629, s. 1.

MILKING PARLOUR. An area used solely for the milking of animals. *Milk Act*, R.R.O. 1980, Reg. 629, s. 1.

MILK MANUFACTURING PLANT. A plant in which milk is processed or handled including a pasteurization plant, and every building, machine, apparatus, equipment and appurtenance employed in, or necessary for storing, cooling, processing, packaging or handling of milk and milk products and forming a part of, or connected with the plant. *Public Health Act*, S.P.E.I. 1980, c. 42, s. 1.

MILK PLANT. See INDUSTRIAL ~.

MILK POWDER. Dried milk that contains not less than, (i.) 95 per cent milk solids, and (ii.) 26 per cent milk-fat, with or without added vitamin D. *Farm Products Grades and Sales Act*, R.R.O. 1980, Reg. 327, s. 1. See MALTED ~; SKIM ~.

MILK PRODUCT. Any product processed or derived in whole or in part from milk, and includes cream, butter, cheese, cottage cheese, condensed milk, milk powder, dry milk, ice cream, ice cream mix, casein, malted milk, sherbet and such other products that are designated as milk products in the regulations. See IMITATION ~; MANUFACTURED ~.

MILK PRODUCTION. The quantity of pounds of fat or milk which a producer markets or is authorized to market during a year. *Crop Insurance Act*, R.S.Q. 1977, c. A-30, s. 1.

MILK RECEIVING STATION. A place suitably equipped with the necessary washing, steaming, grading, sampling and cooling equipment at which milk is received for the purpose of being transported to a cheese factory, concentrated milk plant, creamery or dairy. *Milk Act*, R.S.P.E.I. 1974, c. M-10, s. 1.

MILK SOLIDS. The solids consisting of butter fat, casein, albumen, sugar and ash in milk. *Oleomargarine Act*, R.R.O. 1980, Reg. 696, s. 1.

MILK TEETH. The first set of a young child's teeth which are eventually replaced by permanent teeth. F.A. Jaffe, *A Guide to Pathological Evidence*, 2d ed. (Toronto: Carswell, 1983) at 180.

MILK TRANSFER STATION. Premises at which milk is received for the purpose of being transported to a plant for processing. *Milk Amendment Act*, S.O. 1984, c. 25, s. 1.

MILK VENDOR. A person who, as a principal, purchases or receives milk or cream from a milk dealer for reselling or distributing to consumers but does not include a storekeeper. *Dairy Products Act*, R.S.N.B. 1973, c. D-2, s. 1.

MILL. *n.* A plant in which logs or wood-bolts are initially processed, and includes a saw mill and a pulp mill. See FEED ~ OPERATOR.

MILL CONSTRUCTION. As applied to a building means one in which walls are of masonry or reinforced concrete and an interior framing of wood, with plank or laminated wood floors and roofs, and in which the interior structural elements are arranged in heavy solid masses and smooth flat surfaces assembled to avoid thin sections, sharp projections, and concealed or inaccessible spaces, but the interior framing may be partly or entirely of protected steel or concrete and the floors and roofs may be constructed in whole or in part of incombustible material. *Power Corporation Act*, R.R.O. 1980, Reg. 794, s. 0.

MILLED MONEY. Money with regularly marked edges; coins.

MILL ELEVATOR. An elevator in the Western Division that is operated by a person primarily engaged in the business of manufacturing grain into some other product, into which there is received no grain other than the property of the manager of such mill elevator. *Canada Grain Act*, R.S.C. 1970, c. G-16, s. 2.

MILLI. *pref.* 10-3. Prefix for multiples and submultiples of basic, supplementary and derived units of measurement. *Weights and Measures Act*, S.C. 1970-71-72, c. 36, schedule I.

MILLING. *n.* The crushing or grinding of ore. *Mineral Resource Tax Amendment Act*, S.B.C. 1980, c. 27, s. 4.

MILLION. See PARTS PER ~.

MILLIRAD. *n.* A submultiple of a unit of does equal to .001 rad. *Public Health Act*, R.R.O. 1980, Reg. 855, s. 1.

MILL LICENSEE. The person or persons to whom a mill license is granted for the treatment of or extraction of a mineral or minerals from ore. *Mines Act*, R.S.N.S. 1967, c. 185, s. 1.

MILL PROCESS EFFLUENT. Includes tailing slurries and all other effluent discharged from a milling operation. *Metal Mining Liquid Effluent Regulations*, C.R.C., c. 819, s. 2.

MILL RATE. See REQUISITION ~.

MILL-SITE. *n.* A plot of ground leased under section 122 for the purpose of erecting thereon any machinery or other works for transporting, crushing, reducing or sampling ores, or for the transmission of power for working mines. *Yukon Quartz Mining Act*, R.S.C. 1985, c. Y-4, s. 2.

MIN. *abbr.* 1. Minister. 2. Ministry. 3. Minute.

MINATUR INNOCENTIBUS, QUI PARCIT NOCENTIBUS. [L.] Whoever spares the guilty threatens the innocent.

MINE. *v.* Includes any mode or method of working whereby the soil or earth or any rock, stone or mineral-bearing substance may be disturbed, removed, washed, sifted, leached, roasted, smelted, refined, reduced, crushed, or dealt with for the purpose of obtaining any mineral therefrom whether the same may have been previously disturbed or not, and any mode or method of excavation or rehabilitation of shafts, tunnels, or chambers for industrial purposes. *Regulation of Mines (Amendment) Act*, S.Nfld. 1975, c. 47, s. 2.

MINE. *n.* 1. Any work or undertaking for the purpose of opening up, proving, removing or extracting any metallic or non-metallic mineral or mineral bearing substance, rock, earth, clay, sand or gravel. 2. Any opening or excavation in, or working of the ground for the purpose of winning, opening up or proving any mineral or mineral-bearing substance, and any ore body, mineral deposit, stratum, rock, earth, clay, sand or gravel, or place where mining is or may be carried on, and all ways, works machinery, plant, buildings and premises below or above ground belonging to or used in connection with the mine, and also any quarry, excavation or opening of the ground made for the purpose of searching for or removal of mineral rock, stratum, earth, clay, sand or gravel and any roasting or smelting furnace, concentrator, mill, work or place used for or in connection with washing, crushing, sifting, reducing, leaching, roasting smelting, refining, treating or research on any of such substances. See COAL ~; ENERGY, ~S AND RESOURCES CANADA; GOLD ~; NEW ~; OPEN PIT ~; OPERATION OF A ~; POTASH ~; PRODUCTS OF THE QUARRY AND ~; SMALL ~; STRIP ~; SURFACE ~; UNDERGROUND ~.

MINE ENTRANCE. A surface entrance to an underground mine. *Coal Mines Safety Act*, R.S.A. 1980, c. C-15, s. 1.

MINE EXAMINER. A person who is possessed of a certificate of competency as such under this or some former Act and who is appointed to inspect the working places of a mine and approaches thereto, the airways and other accessible parts of a mine, and to see that such are safe before a shift is allowed to enter such workings or other parts of the mine; and to examine as to the safety of using and to supervise the use of the explosives used in breaking coal. *Coal Mines Regulation Act*, R.S.N.S. 1967, c. 36, s. 1.

MINE HOISTING PLANT. A hoist for an underground mine and includes the prime mover, transmission equipment, head-frame, sheaves, ropes, shaft, shaft conveyances, shaft sinking equipment, shaft furnishings, hoist controls, counterweight, signalling and communications equipment and any other equipment used in connection with a hoist. *Occupational Health and Safety Act*, R.R.O. 1980, Reg. 694, s. 1.

MINE MANAGER. The chief officer of a mine who holds a certificate as a mine manager issued under the provincial statute and who is designated by the owner to control and supervise the operation of a mine. *Coal Mines (CBDC) Safety Regulations*, C.R.C., c. 1011, s. 2.

MINE OFFICIAL. (i) A manager, (ii) an assistant manager, (iii) a senior foreman, (iv) a foreman, or (v) in the case of a processing plant operated in connection with a mine site, a plant supervisor. *Coal Mines Safety Act*, R.S.A. 1980, c. C-15, s. 1.

MINER. *n.* 1. Any person working upon a mine or mining claim or in connection therewith. *Miners' Lien Act*, R.S.N.W.T. 1974, c. M-12, s. 2. 2. A person employed in an underground mine to cut, shear, break or loosen coal or rock. *Coal Mines Safety Act*, R.S.A. 1980, c. C-15, s. 1. See COAL ~.

MINERAL. *n.* 1. Any natural, solid, inorganic or fossilized organic substance. 2. Any nonliving substance formed by the processes of nature which occurs in, on or under land, of any chemical or physical state, but does not include oil, earth, surface water and ground water. 3. Includes base and precious metal, coal, salt and every other substance that is an article of commerce obtained from the earth by any method of extraction, but does not include a hydrocarbon or any animal or vegetable substance other than coal. See CROWN ~; ESTATE IN A ~; PLACER ~; QUARRIABLE ~; SUB-SURFACE ~S; UNIT OF ~S; VALUABLE ~ IN PLACE.

MINERAL ACID. Includes hydrochloric acid, sulphuric acid, nitric acid, phosphoric acid and any combination thereof. *Hazardous Products (Hazardous Substances) Regulations*, C.R.C., c. 926, s. 2.

MINERAL CLAIM. 1. A plot of ground staked out or acquired under this Act. *The Mineral Resources Act*, R.S.S. 1978, c. M-16, s. 2. 2. The tract described in a certificate of record. *Mines and Minerals Act*, R.S.A. 1980, c. M-15, s. 1. 3. An area located other than as a 2 post claim after February 28, 1975 and includes a fractional mineral claim. *Mineral Act*, R.S.B.C. 1979, c. 259, s. 1. 4. A plot of ground staked out and acquired under the provisions of this Act or under the regulations or orders in council in force prior to July 19, 1924. *Yukon Quartz Mining Act*, R.S.C. 1985, c. Y-4, s. 2.

MINERAL EXPLORATION. Prospecting or exploring for a mineral resource. *Ontario Mineral Exploration Program Act*, R.S.O. 1980, c. 346, s. 1.

MINERAL FEED. A mixed feed containing minerals for the nutrition of livestock but does not include a feed intended or represented primarily as a complete or balanced feed, a supplement or as a macro-premix or as a micro-premix. *Feeds Regulations*, C.R.C., c. 665, s. 2.

MINERAL-INSULATED CABLE. A cable having one or more bare solid conductors supported and insulated by a highly compressed refractory material enclosed in a liquid-tight and gas-tight metallic tube sheathing and the term includes both the regular type (M1) and the light-weight type (LWM1) unless otherwise qualified. *Power Corporation Act*, R.R.O. 1980, Reg. 794, s. 0.

MINERAL INTEREST. (i) The ownership of, title to, or an interest in, or (ii) a right, a licence other than a licence issued by the Crown, or an option, to drill for, take, win, or gain, and remove from land, oil or gas, whether acquired by way of instrument commonly called a lease or otherwise, and includes a grant or assignment of a profit à prendre in respect of any oil or gas; but does not include the ownership of, title to, or an interest in oil or gas purchased or otherwise acquired by any person as a result of that person's purchase or other acquisition of land or interest in land the title to which includes the mines and minerals in, under, or upon the land. See FREEHOLD ~.

MINERAL INTEREST BROKER. A person or company who or that is engaged in the business of (i) purchasing or acquiring any mineral interest on his own behalf, or (ii) negotiating, on behalf of another person or company, the purchase or acquisition of any mineral interest, or (iii) otherwise trading in any mineral interest. *Securities Act, 1980*, S.M. 1980, c. 50, s. 148.

MINERAL LAND. Land, other than Crown land and land comprising a right of way, station ground, yard or terminal of a railway, in respect of which (a) a mineral is, or may be, situated; or (b) a person has the right to work, win or carry away a mineral. *Mineral Land Tax Act*, R.S.B.C. 1979, c. 260, s. 1.

MINERAL LANDS. Includes lands and mining rights under disposition and lands or mineral rights located, staked out, used or intended to be used for mining purposes. *The Mineral Resources Act*, R.S.S. 1978, c. M-16, s. 2. See CROWN ~.

MINERAL LEASE BROKER. A person who or company that is engaged in the business of: (i) purchasing or acquiring any mineral interest on his behalf; or (ii) negotiating, on behalf of another person or company, the purchase or acquisition of any mineral interest. *Securities Act*, S.S. 1984-85-86, c. S-42.1, s. 145.

MINERAL LINE. A pipe for the transmission of a mineral whether in solution, suspension or other state and includes installations in connection therewith, but does not include a gas line, oil line, secondary line, flow line, distribution line or private line.

MINERAL LOCATION. A tract of Crown land containing minerals or land upon or under which minerals have been reserved to the Crown and in respect of which a grant has been made for the purpose of mining, and includes a boring claim, a mining claim, a placer claim, and a quarrying claim, and an oil and natural gas tract. *Mines Act*, R.S.M. 1970, c. M160, s. 1.

MINERAL NUTRIENT. Any of the following chemical elements whether alone or in a compound with one or more other chemical elements: (a) calcium; (b) phosphorus; (c) iron; (d) sodium; (e) potassium; (f) iodine; (g) zinc; (h) copper; (i) magnesium; (j) manganese; (k) chlorine; and (l) fluorine. *Food and Drug Regulations*, C.R.C., c. 870, c. D.02.001.

MINERAL OIL. See HYDRAULIC SYSTEM ~.

MINERAL ORE. Includes unprocessed minerals or mineral bearing substances. See NEW ~; PROBABLE ~; PROVEN ~.

MINERAL PRODUCT. 1. A product derived from the operation of a mine. *Mineral Resource Tax Act*, R.S.B.C. 1979, c. 263, s. 1. 2. A product derived from minerals, including those milled, refined, or otherwise beneficiated to a state of purity suitable for, (i) fabrication by manufacturing; or (ii) acceptance by the Royal Canadian Mint. *Mining Royalty and Tax Act*, R.S.M. 1970, c. M180, s. 2.

MINERAL RECOVERY. The taking of mineral water or the recovery from mineral water by artificial means of all minerals, including mineral salts, either in solution or suspense. *The Water Rights Act*, R.S.S. 1978, c. W-8, s. 2.

MINERAL RESOURCE. (a) A base or precious metal deposit, (b) a coal deposit, (c) a bituminous sands deposit, oil sands deposit or oil shale deposit, or (d) a mineral deposit in respect of which (i) the Minister of Energy, Mines and Resources has certified that the principal mineral extracted is an industrial mineral contained in a non-bedded deposit, (ii) the principal mineral extracted is sylvite, halite, gypsum or kaolin, or (iii) the principal mineral extracted is silica that is extracted from sandstone or quartzite. *Income Tax Act*, R.S.C. 1952, c. 148 (as am. S.C. 1988, c. 55, s. 188(5)), s. 248(1).

MINERAL RIGHT. 1. A license, lease or special license issued under this Act, or right granted under section 18. *Mineral Resources Act*, S.P.E.I. 1978, c. 15, s. 1. 2. An estate in fee simple in a mineral located in a tract.

MINERAL RIGHTS. 1. The right to enter upon or use lands for the sole purpose of exploring, drilling for, winning, taking, removing or raising the minerals situate therein and includes such easements, rights of way or other similar rights of access as are incidental to winning, taking, removing or raising the minerals situate therein. *Land Transfer Tax Act*, R.R.O. 1980, Reg. 571, s. 1. 2. The right to explore for, work and use natural mineral substances situated within the volume formed by the vertical projection of the perimeter of a parcel of land, including the right to explore for underground reservoirs or to develop or use them for the storage or permanent disposal of any mineral substance or of any industrial product or residue. *Mining Act*, R.S.Q. 1977, c. M-13, s. 1.

MINERAL SPECIMEN. See DESCRIBED ~; TYPE ~.

MINERAL SUBSTANCE. Every type and kind of ore, rock and mineral, whether organic or inorganic, but does not include diatomaceous earth, limestone, marl, peat, clay, building stone, stone for ornamental or decorative purposes, non-auriferous sand or gravel, natural gas or petroleum, or sodium chloride recovered by the solution method. *Mining Tax Act*, R.S.O. 1980, c. 269, s. 1. See MINES AND MINERALS.

MINERAL TRADING PURPOSE. 1. The sale, barter or exchange of natural mineral water in bottles or other containers, or the utilization of the waters in sanatoriums or for other purposes. *Health Act*, R.S.B.C. 1979, c. 161, s. 1. 2. Bottling, distributing, using and dealing in water so impregnated with foreign ingredients as to give it medicinal properties, or water of a temperature that gives it a commercial value. *Water Act*, R.S.B.C. 1979, c. 429, s. 1.

MINERAL WATER. Water containing in its natural state, either in solution or suspense, more than one per cent of minerals or mineral salts. *The Water Rights Act*, R.S.S. 1978, c. W-8, s. 2.

MINERAL WATER PURPOSES. The purpose of a public bath house or public swimming pool, for medicinal purposes or purposes of sale, trade or barter. *The Water Rights Act*, R.S.S. 1978, c. W-8, s. 2.

MINE RESCUE CORPS. All mine rescue personnel under the supervision of a mine rescue station superintendent.

MINE RESCUE STATION SUPERINTENDENT. A person who holds a certificate as a mine examiner and a certificate in mine rescue work and in first aid and who has been placed in charge of a mine rescue station by a mine manager. *Coal Mines (CBDC) Safety Regulations*, C.R.C., c. 1011, s. 2.

MINE RESCUE TEAM. A group of not less than five men especially trained in mine rescue work and first aid.

MINE RESCUE TEAM CAPTAIN. A person who holds a certificate as a mine examiner and who has been placed in charge of a mine rescue team by a mine rescue station superintendent. *Coal Mines (CBDC) Safety Regulations*, C.R.C., c. 1011, s. 2.

MINE RESCUE WORK. Includes the repair of the equipment necessary for and the training necessary for such work. *Workers' Compensation Act*, R.S.N.W.T. 1974, c. W-4, s. 2.

MINER'S HELPER. A person employed in an underground mine to work under the supervision of a miner. *Coal Mines Safety Act*, R.S.A. 1980, c. C-15, s. 1.

MINER'S MEDICAL CERTIFICATE. A certificate issued by a medical officer under section 21 to a person respecting employment in a dust exposure occupation. *Mining Safety Act*, S.N.W.T. 1982 (3d Sess.), c. 12, s. 2.

MINE SAFETY ENGINEER. A safety officer who is designated by the Director to serve as a mine safety engineer of a mine. *Coal Mines (CBDC) Safety Regulations*, C.R.C., c. 1011, s. 2.

MINES AND MINERALS. Include any strata or seam of minerals or substances in or under any land and powers of working and getting the same, but not an undivided share thereof.

MINE SITE. 1. A location at which a facility for extracting coal by underground, strip or open pit operations exists or is to be developed, and includes (i) a coal processing plant, storage facility or discard disposal facility which exists or is to be developed in connection with a mine, and (ii) all connected access roads. *Coal Mines Safety Act*, R.S.A. 1980, c. C-15, s. 1. 2. An area within which mining operations are being conducted or that is the subject of an approval under this Act for a mining operation, and includes a stockpile area, a discard site and any area within which facilities or equipment used in connection with a mining operation are located. *Oil Sands Conservation Act*, S.A. 1983, c. O-5.5, s. 1.

MINE SURVEYOR. 1. A person responsible for (i) surveying the workings of a mine, and (ii) preparing the plans required under this Act or the Coal Conservation Act. *Coal Mines Safety Act*, R.S.A. 1980, c. C-15, s. 1. 2. Any person who possesses a certificate of competency as a mine surveyor issued under this or some former Act and who does surveying work in or about a mine. *Coal Mines Regulation Act*, R.S.N.S. 1967, c. 36, s. 3.

MINE WATER EFFLUENT. Water pumped or flowing out of any underground workings or open pit. *Metal Mining Liquid Effluent Regulations*, C.R.C., c. 819, s. 2.

MINIATURE BOILER. A boiler approved to carry a working pressure or not more than one hundred pounds and having a shell with an inside diameter not greater than sixteen inches and an overall length of not more than forty-two inches from outside to outside of the heads and a water-heating surface of not more than twenty square feet.

MINIATURE FILM. Photographic moving picture film which is sixteen millimetres or less in width. *The Theatres and Cinematographs Act*, R.S.S. 1978, c. T-11, s. 2.

MINIBIKE. *n.* A vehicle having steering handlebars completely constrained from rotating in relation to the axle of one wheel in contact with the ground, designed to travel on not more than three wheels in contact with the ground and having (a) a minimum seat height unladen of less than 711 mm (28 inches), (b) a wheel rim diameter of less than 254 mm (10 inches), (c) a wheelbase of less than 1 016 mm (40 inches), or (d) a braking system operating on one wheel only. Canada regulations.

MINIBUS. *n.* A motor vehicle of the small van type designed for the transportation, for a fare, of more than seven occupants at a time or for the group transportation of handicapped persons. *Highway Safety Code*, S.Q. 1986, c. 91, s. 4.

MINIME MUTANDA SUNT QUAE CERTAM HABENT INTERPRETATIONEM. [L.] Whatever has an interpretation which has been settled should be changed as little as possible.

MINIMENT. *n.* Documentary evidence of title.

MINIMUM AIR SPACE. The percentage indicated in the schedules or the percentage calculated by use of the formula specified, means the percentage of free space to be left in a container in relation to the total capacity of the container. *Dangerous Goods Shipping Regulations*, C.R.C., c. 1419, s. 2.

MINIMUM EQUIPMENT LIST. An approved document that authorizes an air carrier to operate a type of aircraft specified therein with essential aircraft equipment inoperative under the conditions specified therein. *Aircraft Minimum Equipment List Order*, C.R.C., c. 25, s. 2. See MASTER ~.

MINIMUM OVERTIME RATE. A rate of wages one-and-one-half times as great as the minimum rate prescribed under this Part. *Employment Standards Act*, R.S.M. 1970, c. E110, s. 23.

MINIMUM WAGE. The lowest compensation established by statute.

MINING. *n.* 1. The extracting of minerals from a mineral resource, the processing of ore, other than iron ore, from a mineral resource to the prime metal state or its equivalent, the processing of iron ore from a mineral resource to the pellet state or its equivalent and the restoration of strip-mined land to a usable condition, but does not include activities related to the exploration for or development of a mineral resource. *Excise Tax*, R.S.C. 1985 (2d Supp.), c. 7, s. 69. 2. Includes diamond drilling and any mode or method of working whereby any soil, earth, rock, stone, quartz, clay, sand or gravel may be disturbed, removed, carted, carried, washed, sifted, crushed, roasted, smelted, refined or dealt with for the purpose of obtaining any minerals or metal therefrom, whether the same may have been previously disturbed or not, and all operations and workings in a mine. *Mining Safety Act*, S.N.W.T. 1982 (3d Sess.), c. 12, s. 2. 3. Any mode or method of working whereby the earth or any rock, stratum, stone or mineral-bearing substance may be disturbed, removed, washed, sifted, leached, roasted, smelted, refined, crushed or dealt with for the purpose of obtaining any mineral therefrom, whether it has been previously disturbed or not. See PLACER ~.

MINING AREA. An area in which the holder of a permit may conduct a mining operation. *Grand Lake Development Act*, R.S.N.B. 1973, c. G-4, s. 1.

MINING CLAIM. 1. A parcel of land staked out and to which the holder thereof has exclusive right to prospect, under authority of a prospecting licence, for minerals the ownership of which is vested in the Crown, and which ownership has not been alienated. *Mining Act*, R.S.N.B. 1973, c. M-14, s. 1. 2. A plot of Crown land containing a mineral and staked out for mining purposes, other than that contained in a boring claim, a placer claim, or a quarrying claim. *Mines Act*, R.S.M. 1970, c. M160, s. 1. See UNPATENTED ~.

MINING COMPANY. A company that for the time being carries on as its principal business the business of operating any producing mining properties owned or controlled by it.

MINING CONCESSION. A mining property sold out of the public domain for the purpose of operating mining rights. *Mining Act*, R.S.Q. 1977, c. M-13, s. 1.

MINING EQUIPMENT. A powered or self-powered machine or vehicle used to extract coal from a seam or to transport it from the workings or working places to an on-site storage facility, coal processing plant or rail head. *Coal Conservation Act*, R.S.A. 1980, c. C-14, s. 1.

MINING LANDS. Includes lands and mining rights leased under or by authority of any statute, regulation or order in council, respecting mines, minerals or mining, and also lands or mining rights located, staked out, used or intended to be used for mining purposes.

MINING LEASE. A lease, grant or licence for mining purposes, including the searching for, working, getting, making merchantable, smelting or otherwise converting or working for the purposes of any manufacture, carrying away or disposing of mines or minerals, and substances in, on or under the land, obtainable by underground or by surface working or purposes connected therewith.

MINING LICENCE. A licence by which the holder thereof is granted the right to prospect, develop, or mine on a designated area for a period of one year. *Mining Act*, R.S.N.B. 1973, c. M-14, s. 1.

MINING OPERATION. 1. All the work whereby mineral substances are explored for in view of being extracted or extracted for the purpose of obtaining a commercial product. 2. The extraction or production, transportation, distribution and sale of the output of mineral ore from a mine.

MINING PLANT. Any roasting or smelting furnace, concentrator, mill or place used for or in connection with washing, crushing, grinding, sifting, reducing, leaching, roasting, smelting, refining, treating or research on any substance mentioned in paragraph 16. *Occupational Health and Safety Act*, R.S.O. 1980, c. 321, s. 1.

MINING PROPERTY. 1. A right to prospect, explore or mine for minerals or a property the principal value of which depends upon its mineral content. *Income Tax Act*, R.S.C. 1952, c. 148 (as am. S.C. 1970-71-72, c. 63), s. 35(2)(a). 2. Includes every mineral claim, lease, ditch or water right used for mining purposes, and all other things belonging to a mine or used in the working thereof. 3. Land in which a vein or lode or rock in place or natural stratum or bed of earth, gravel or cement is mined for gold or other precious minerals or stones or for any base mineral or mineral bearing substance, including coal, petroleum and natural gas. *Mining Right of Way Act*, R.S.B.C. 1979, c. 266, s. 1. 4. Includes a mineral claim, 2 post claim, leasehold and real and personal property pertaining to a mine or used in the working of it. *Mineral Act*, R.S.B.C. 1979, c. 259, s. 1. 5. Includes, besides claims, any ditches or water rights used for mining thereon, and all other things belonging thereto or used in the working thereof for mining purposes. *Yukon Placer Mining Act*, R.S.C. 1985, c. Y-3, c. 2.

MINING PURPOSE. The use of water for recovering mineral from the ground or from ore. *Water Act*, R.S.B.C. 1979, c. 429, s. 1.

MINING PURPOSES. Includes the making, excavating or sinking of a mine and the working of a mine and searching for, winning, opening up, removing, proving, or storing underground, any mineral or mineral-bearing substance and the erection of buildings and the execution of engineering and other works suitable for those purposes. *Trustee Act*, R.S.M. 1970, c. T160, s. 2.

MINING RIGHT. A mining or mineral claim, a mining licence or lease.

MINING RIGHTS. 1. Includes the right to the minerals and mines upon or under the surface of the land. 2. In respect of any land are granted or reserved, the grant or reservation shall be construed to convey or reserve the ores, mines and minerals on or under the land, together with such right of access for the purpose of winning the ores, mines and minerals as is incidental to a grant of ores, mines and minerals. *Conveyancing and Law of Property Act*, R.S.O. 1980, c. 90, s. 16. 3. The ores, mines and minerals on or under any land where they are or have been dealt with separately from the surface. *Mining Act*, R.S.O.

1980, c. 268, s. 1. 4. The right to explore for, work and use natural mineral substances situated within the volume formed by the vertical projection of the perimeter of a parcel of land, including the right to explore for underground reservoirs or to develop or use them for the storage or permanent disposal of any mineral substance or of any industrial product or residue. *Mining Act*, R.S.Q. 1977, c. M-13, s. 1.

MINISTER. *n.* 1. A member of the Cabinet. 2. A member of the Queen's Privy Council for Canada as is designated by the Governor in Council. 3. A member of the Executive Council appointed as a Minister who is responsible for the enactment or its subject matter or the department to which its context refers. 4. Includes any priest, rabbi, elder, evangelist, missionary or commissioned officer ordained or appointed by the religious body to which he belongs. *Marriage Act*, R.S.B.C. 1979, c. 251, s. 1. 5. (i) A person who holds office as a Minister of the Crown in right of Newfoundland, (ii) the Speaker of the House of Assembly, (iii) the Deputy Speaker of the House of Assembly, or (iv) the Leader of the Opposition in the House of Assembly. *Members of the House of Assembly Contributory Pension Plan Act*, R.S.Nfld. 1970, c. 230, s. 2. 6. A member of the Executive Council, and includes for the purposes of Part I a parliamentary assistant, the Speaker, the Leader of the Opposition and any member who was formerly a member of the Executive Council, a parliamentary assistant, the Speaker or the Leader of the Opposition. *Legislative Assembly Retirement Allowances Act*, R.S.O. 1980, c. 236, s. 3. See APPROPRIATE ~; CABINET ~; DEPUTY ~; INCUMBENT ~; PRIME ~.

MINISTERIAL. *adj.* Describes the discharge of a duty without discretion or independent judgment or the issue of a formal instruction determined beforehand. S.A. DeSmith, *Judicial Review of Administrative Action*, 4th ed. by J.M. Evans (London: Stevens, 1980) at 70.

MINISTERIAL DUTY. A duty involved in operating a trust, i.e., keeping of accounts or hiring an agent like a solicitor or valuer. D.M.W. Waters, *The Law of Trusts in Canada*, 2d ed. (Toronto: Carswell, 1984) at 28.

MINISTERIAL OFFICE. Any office in or under the ministries, branches and institutions of the Executive Government of the Province, other than a record office. *Document Disposal Act*, R.S.B.C. 1979, c. 95, s. 1.

MINISTERING CLERIC. The cleric appointed to administer a chapelry. Quebec statutes.

MINISTER OF HEALTH. (a) In the Provinces of Ontario, Quebec, New Brunswick, Prince Edward Island, Manitoba and Newfoundland, the Minister of Health, (b) in the Provinces of Nova Scotia and Saskatchewan, the Minister of Public Health, and (c) in the Province of British Columbia, the Minister of Health Services and Hospital Insurance, (d) in the Province of Alberta, the Minister of Hospitals and Medical Care, (e) in the Yukon Territory and the Northwest Territories, the Minister of National Health and Welfare. *Criminal Code*, R.S.C. 1985, c. C-46, s. 287(6).

MINISTER OF THE CROWN. 1. A member of the Queen's Privy Council for Canada in that member's capacity of managing and directing or having responsibility for a department. *Municipal Grants Act*, R.S.C. 1985, c. M-13, s. 2. 2. Includes the Parliamentary Assistant to the Premier, the Special Assistant to the Premier and the Parliamentary Secretaries to Ministers of the Crown. *Conflict of Interest Amendment Act*, S.Nfld. 1982, c. 23, s. 1.

MINISTER WITHOUT PORTFOLIO. A member of the cabinet not in charge of a department. P.W. Hogg, *Constitutional Law of Canada*, 2d ed. (Toronto: Carswell, 1985) at 197.

MINISTRY. *n.* 1. A department of government. 2. A ministry of the Government of Ontario and includes a board, commission, authority, corporation or other agency of the Government of Ontario. *Management Board of Cabinet Act*, R.S.O. 1980, c. 254, s. 1. 3. (a) A ministry of the executive government of the Province, or (b) a branch of the executive government of the province that is not part of a ministry, but is designated by the Lieutenant Governor in Council as a ministry for the purposes of this Act. *Financial Administration Act*, S.B.C. 1981, c. 15, s. 1. 4. Includes a division or department of the government. *Public Service Act*, S.B.C. 1985, c. 15, s. 1.

MINISTRY OF STATE FOR SCIENCE AND TECHNOLOGY. The federal ministry which makes policies and provides advice to government on science and technology.

MINKE WHALE. Any whale of the species Balaenoptera acutorostrata, B. davidsoni, B. huttoni, commonly known as lesser rorqual, little piked whale, minke whale, pike-headed whale or sharp-headed finner. *Whaling Regulations*, C.R.C., c. 1608, s. 2.

MINNOW TRAP. An impounding apparatus used to catch small fish. *Manitoba Fishery Regulations*, C.R.C., c. 843, s. 2.

MINOR. *n.* 1. A person who has not attained the age of majority. 2. A person who has not attained the age of eighteen years. *Citizenship Act*, R.S.C. 1985, c. C-29, s. 2. 3. A person under the age of majority. 4. A person who has not

attained the age of nineteen years. *Provincial Offences Procedure Act*, S.N.B. 1987, c. P-22.1, s. 1. See INFANT OR ~.

MINOR ANTE TEMPUS AGERE NON POTEST IN CASU PROPRIETATIS, NEC ETIAM CONVENIRE; DIFFERETUR USQUE AETATEM; SED NON CADIT BREVE. [L.] In the case of property, a minor before majority cannot act, not even to consent; this should be deferred until majority; but the writ is not faulty.

MINORA REGALIA. [L.] The Crown's revenue in contrast to its power and dignity.

MINOR ATTACHMENT CLAIMANT. A claimant who, subject to subsections 6(6) and (7), has been employed in insurable employment for fourteen or more weeks but less than twenty weeks in his qualifying period. *Unemployment Insurance Act*, R.S.C. 1985, c. U-1, s. 5.

MINOR CHARACTER. See NEGLIGENCE OF A ~.

MINOR CHILD. A child ceases to be a minor child after the last day of the month in which the child attains the age of seventeen years. *Excise Tax Act*, R.S.C. 1985 (1st Supp.), c. 16, s. 5(7.1).

MINOR INJURY. Any work injury for which either first aid or medical treatment was provided, and that was not a disabling injury. *Canada Accident Investigation and Reporting Regulations*, C.R.C., c. 993, s. 2.

MINORITY. *n.* The situation of being under the age of majority. See RELIGIOUS ~.

MINORITY OPINION. The decision and reasons of the minority of three or more judges who heard and decided a case.

MINOR JURARE NON POTEST. [L.] A minor is not able to swear.

MINOR LIEN FUND. The amount required to be retained under section 16.2(1) plus any amount payable under the contract (i) that is over and above the 15% referred to in section 16.2(1), and (ii) that, with respect to any work done or material furnished on and after the date of issue of a certificate of substantial performance, has not been paid by the owner in good faith while there is no lien registered. *Builders' Lien Amendment Act*, S.A. 1985, c. 14, s. 2.

MINOR MINOREM CUSTODIRE NON DEBET; ALIOS ENIM PRAESUMITUR MALE REGERE QUI SEIPSUM REGERE NESCIT. [L.] A minor may not be a minor's guardian; for one who does not know how to control oneself is presumed to control others badly.

MINOR NEGLIGENCE. Negligence not amounting to recklessness or undue carelessness and not involving an intentional omission or commission of any act amounting to a wrongful act. *Claims Regulations*, C.R.C., c. 683, s. 2.

MINOR, QUI INFRA AETATEM XII ANNO-RUM FUERIT, UTLAGARI NON POTEST, NEC EXTRA LEGEM PONI, QUIA ANTE TALEM AETATEM NON EST SUB LEGE ALIQUA. [L.] A minor, under twelve years old, cannot be outlawed, nor placed outside the law, because before that age one is not under any law at all.

MINOR WATERS OF CANADA. All inland waters of Canada other than Lakes Ontario, Erie, Huron, including Georgian Bay, and Superior and the St. Lawrence River east of a line drawn from Father Point to Point Orient, and includes all bays, inlets and harbours of or on those lakes and Georgian Bay and such sheltered waters on the sea-coasts of Canada as the Minister may specify. *Canada Shipping Act*, R.S.C. 1985, c. S-9, s. 2.

MINOR WATERS SHIP. A ship employed on a minor waters voyage. *Canada Shipping Act*, R.S.C. 1985, c. S-9, s. 2.

MINOR WATERS VOYAGE. A voyage within the following limits, namely, the minor waters of Canada together with such part of any lake or river forming part of the minor waters of Canada as lies within the United States. *Canada Shipping Act*, R.S.C. 1985, c. S-9, s. 2.

MINT. *n.* 1. A place where money in coined. 2. The Royal Canadian Mint established by this Act. *Royal Canadian Mint Act*, R.S.C. 1985, c. R-9, s. 2. See ROYAL CANADIAN ~.

MINTAGE. *n.* Whatever is stamped or coined.

MINUTE. *n.* 1. A record or note of a transaction. 2. 60 seconds. *Weights and Measures Act*, S.C. 1970-71-72, c. 36, schedule I. 3. Of arc, $\pi/10$ 800 radian. *Weights and Measures Act*, S.C. 1970-71-72, c. 36, schedule I.

MINUTES OF PROCEEDINGS AND EVI-DENCE. Of standing committees, a record of the proceedings of a committee prepared and signed by the clerk of that committee. A. Fraser, G.A. Birch & W.A. Dawson, eds., *Beauchesne's Rules and Forms of the House of Commons of Canada*, 5th ed. (Toronto: Carswell, 1978) at 197.

MINUTES OF SETTLEMENT. A document filed with a court which sets out terms by which the parties have agreed to settle the dispute.

MISADVENTURE. *n.* Accident, mischance.

MISALLEGE. *v.* To claim falsely as an argument or proof.

MISAPPROPRIATION. *n.* The fraudulent misapplication of any property.

MISC. *abbr.* Miscellaneous.

MISCARRIAGE. *n.* 1. The failing of justice. 2. The expulsion of a fetus, usually in the final third of a pregnancy. F.A. Jaffe, *A Guide to Pathological Evidence*, 2d ed. (Toronto: Carswell, 1983) at 180. See SUBSTANTIAL WRONG OR ~.

MISCHIEF. *n.* 1. Wilfully destroying or damaging property; rendering property dangerous, useless, inoperative or ineffective; obstructing, interrupting or interfering with the lawful use, enjoyment or operation of property; or obstructing, interrupting or interfering with any person in the lawful use, enjoyment or operation of property. *Criminal Code*, R.S.C. 1985, c. C-46, s. 430(1). 2. Wilfully destroying or altering data, rendering data meaningless, useless or ineffective, obstructing, interrupting or interfering with the lawful use of data; or obstructing, interrupting or interfering with any person in the lawful use of data or denying access to data to any person who is entitled to access thereto. *Criminal Code*, R.S.C. 1985, c. C-46, s. 430(1.1) as added by R.S.C. 1985, c. 27 (1st Supp.), s. 57. See PUBLIC ~.

MISCHIEF RULE. 1. It is the duty of every judge to always construe a situation to suppress mischief and advance the remedy. P. St. J. Langan, ed., *Maxwell on The Interpretation of Statutes*, 12th ed. (Bombay: N.M. Tripathi, 1976) at 40. 2. A test of the purpose or object of a statute.

MISCHIEVOUS. *adj.* As applied to animals means any cross or dangerous animal or any animal which has been shown to have trespassed upon land enclosed by a lawful fence by breaking or jumping over the fence. *Livestock Act*, R.S.Nfld. 1970, c. 210, s. 2.

MISCHIEVOUS ANIMAL. (i) Any cross, dangerous, notoriously breachy or notoriously mischievous animal, (ii) any sheep that is shown to have trespassed on lands enclosed by a fence, whether a lawful fence or not, and (iii) any hog. *Domestic Animals (Municipalities) Act*, R.S.A. 1970, c. 112, s. 2.

MISCOGNISANT. *adj.* Unacquainted with; ignorant of.

MISCONDUCT. *n.* 1. Wilful disobedience of the provisions of any statute or regulation governing the performance of official duties, the breach of which involves dismissal from the Public Service, malversation in office or abandonment of office. *Public Service Superannuation Act*, R.S.C. 1985, c. P-36, s. 3. 2. Any act, deed or practice that in the opinion of the board is not in the public interest. *The Vehicles Act*, R.S.S. 1978, c. V-3, s. 2. 3. A serious digression from established or recognized standards or rules of the Society or generally the occupation of engineering technology and includes a breach of such Rules of Ethics or Conduct as may be prescribed by bylaw. *Engineering Technology Act*, S.N.B. 1986, c. 92, s. 2. 4. An act or omission on the part of a police officer that constitutes an offence under the Code of Offences set out in the Schedule to Regulation 791 of the Revised Regulations of Ontario, 1980, made under the Police Act. *Metropolitan Toronto Police Force Complaints Act*, S.O. 1984, c. 63, s. 1. 5. Misconduct of an employee in the performance of his duties, and includes bringing the public service into disrepute. *Public Service Act*, R.S.N.W.T. 1974, c. P-13, s. 2. 6. Includes (a) the commission of an offence under the National Defence Act, the Naval Discipline Act, the Army Act or the Air Force Act, of which the member was convicted by a court-martial, including in the case of naval forces, a disciplinary court, or of which he was found guilty upon summary disposition of the charge, (b) the commission of an offence of which the member was convicted by a court of competent jurisdiction, and (c) such misconduct as might, in the case of an officer, result in his removal from the forces. *War Service Grants Act*, R.S.C. 1970, c. W-4, s. 2. See PROFESSIONAL ~; STRIKE-RELATED ~.

MISCONTINUANCE. *n.* Stoppage; pause.

MISDEMEANOUR. *n.* A lesser offence than a felony.

MISDESCRIPTION. *n.* An incorrect description.

MISDIRECTION. *n.* An error in law made when a judge charges a jury or when a judge sitting alone puts the wrong questions forward to answer.

MISERA EST SERVITUS, UBI JUS EST VAGUM AUT INCERTUM. [L.] Obedience to law is a hardship, where that law is vague or uncertain.

MISERERE. [L.] Have mercy.

MISERICORDIA. *n.* An arbitrary punishment or amerciament one imposes on someone for an offence.

MISFEASANCE. *n.* The improper execution of a lawful act, e.g. to be guilty of negligence in fulfilling a contract.

MISJOINDER. *n.* The erroneous involvement

of someone as a plaintiff or defendant in an action.

MISLEADING REPRESENTATION. See FALSE OR ~.

MISNOMER. *n.* Naming wrongly.

MISPLEADING. *n.* Omission of anything essential to a defence or action.

MISPRISION. *n.* Negligence, neglect, oversight.

MISPRISION OF FELONY. For someone who knows that another person committed a felony to conceal or bring about the concealment of that knowledge.

MISPRISION OF TREASON. For someone who knows that another person committed high treason not to inform an appropriate authority within a reasonable time.

MISRECITAL. *n.* A faulty recital.

MISREPRESENTATION. *n.* 1. The misstatement of a fact critical to the inducement or making of a contract. G.H.L. Fridman, *The Law of Contract in Canada*, 2d ed. (Toronto: Carswell, 1986) at 275. 2. (a) An untrue statement of a material fact, or (b) an omission to state a material fact that is (i) required to be stated, or (ii) necessary to prevent a statement that is made from being false or misleading in the circumstances in which it was made. Securities acts. 3. An untrue statement of material fact or an omission to state a material fact. *Commodity Futures Act*, R.S.O. 1980, c. 78, s. 1. See FRAUDULENT ~; INNOCENT ~; NEGLIGENT ~.

MISSING PERSON. 1. A person who cannot be found and whose present place of abode is unascertainable. 2. A person who cannot be found after all reasonable efforts have been made to locate him and includes a person who dies intestate or intestate as to some part of his estate without leaving any known heir at law living in Nova Scotia or any heir at law who can be readily communicated with living elsewhere or where the only heir at law is an infant or where Her Majesty in the right of Nova Scotia has an interest in the estate or proceeds thereof. *Public Trustee Act*, S.N.S. 1973, c. 12, s. 2. 3. Includes (a) a person whose relatives residing at the place where he was last known to reside, and who would be likely to hear from him, have not heard from him or of him for at least 3 months last past, and have been unable to ascertain his whereabouts; (b) in the case of a person having no relatives who would be likely to hear from him who reside at the place where he was last known to reside, any person whose associates at the place where he was last known to reside, and whose relatives, if any, with whom he had until then been in the habit of communicating, have none of them heard from him or of him for a period of at least 3 months last past, or been able to ascertain his whereabouts; (c) a person who has been missing for a shorter period than 3 months, but who is otherwise a missing person within the meaning of paragraph (a) or (b) and who, on application being made to the Supreme Court, accompanied by evidence to the satisfaction of the court that there is urgent need of a curator being appointed under this Act for the preservation of the estate or the support of the dependants of that person, is declared by the court to be a missing person. *Estates of Missing Persons Act*, R.S.B.C. 1979, c. 115, s. 1.

MISSION. See HEAD OF ~.

MISTAKE. *n.* Misunderstanding about the existence of something which arises either from a false belief or ignorance.

MISTAKE OF FACT. 1. For an accused to believe wrongly that facts do not exist when they do or that they exist when they do not. D. Stuart, *Canadian Criminal Law: a Treatise*, 2d ed. (Toronto: Carswell, 1987) at 299. 2. A misunderstanding about the existence of some fact or about the existence of a right which depends on questions of mixed fact and law.

MISTAKE OF LAW. 1. An error, not in the actual facts, but relating as to their legal consequence, relevance or significance. D. Stuart, *Canadian Criminal Law: a Treatise*, 2d ed. (Toronto: Carswell, 1987) at 299. 2. An error regarding some general rule of law.

MISTRESS. *n.* The title of the wife of a gentleman or an esquire.

MISTRIAL. *n.* An incorrect trial.

MISUSER. *n.* The abuse of any benefit or liberty which results in forfeit.

MITIGATE. See DUTY TO ~.

MITIGATION. *n.* Reduction.

MITIGATION CONTINGENCY. An event which may still have an impact on the seriousness of loss resulting from a death, the two major being remarriage and adoption. K.D. Cooper-Stephenson & I.B. Saunders, *Personal Injury Damages in Canada* (Toronto: Carswell, 1981) at 452.

MITIGATION OF DAMAGES. The obligation of the party whose legal rights were infringed to take every reasonable step to minimize the damages which the other party's action caused.

MIX. *n.* Whole egg mix and yolk mix. *Live Stock and Live Stock Products Act*, R.R.O. 1980, Reg. 583, s. 1. See DRIED WHOLE EGG ~; DRIED YOLK ~; FROZEN EGG ~; ICE CREAM ~; WHOLE EGG ~; YOLK ~.

MIXED BLOOD. See PERSON OF ~.

MIXED FARMING CROP. Forage or cereal plants, except grain-corn, grown on a cultivated farm and intended mainly for feeding the producer's farm animals. *Crop Insurance Act*, R.S.Q. 1977, c. A-30, s. 1.

MIXED FERTILIZER. Includes all fertilizers other than fertilizers consisting of a single material or one chemical compound. *Fertilizers Regulations*, C.R.C., c. 666, s. 2.

MIXED GRAIN. Any seed mixture that includes both oats and barley, the combined weight of which equals at least 75 per cent of the total, but the individual weights of either of which do not exceed 75 per cent of the total. *Crop Insurance Act (Ontario)*, R.R.O. 1980, Reg. 223, s. 3.

MIXED LAW. A law which concerns both property and people.

MIXED PROPERTY. A combination of personalty and realty.

MIXED QUESTION. A question which arises when foreign and domestic laws conflict. See ~ OF LAW AND FACT.

MIXED QUESTION OF LAW AND FACT. A case in which a jury finds the particular facts, and the court must decide on the legal quality of those facts using established rules of law, without general inferences or conclusions drawn by the jury.

MIXTURE. See LAWN GRASS ~; NITRATE ~; OILY ~; TURF GRASS ~; TURPENTINE ~.

M.L. DIG. & R. *abbr.* Monthly Law Digest and Reporter (Que.), 1892-1893.

M.L.R. (Q.B.). *abbr.* Montreal Law Reports (Queen's Bench), 1885-1891.

M.L.R. (S.C.). *abbr.* Montreal Law Reports (Superior Court), 1885-1891.

M.M.C. *abbr.* Martin's Mining Cases (B.C.), 1853-1908.

M'NAGHTEN'S CASE. See MCNAGHTEN'S CASE.

M'NAUGHTEN'S CASE. See MCNAGHTEN'S CASE.

M.N.R. *abbr.* Minister of National Revenue.

MOBILE CAMPERS. Includes all camper or tent trailers, and other vehicles fitted out for mobile accommodation. *Forest Fires Act*, R.S.N.B. 1973, c. F-20, s. 1.

MOBILE EQUIPMENT. (i) Machinery or equipment capable of being moved to its place of use under its own power or by being towed, pulled or carried and not intended to be affixed to land, and (ii) includes equipment for the purposes of seismographic exploration and, without restricting the generality of the foregoing includes (A) seismographic recording equipment and all appurtenances thereto, (B) conductor cables and cable reels, geophones, amplifiers and cameras, (C) explosive and detonating equipment, (D) drilling units and all the component parts and appurtenances thereof, and (E) water tanks and pumping equipment, but (iii) does not include (A) vehicles licensed under The Highway Traffic Act, or The Public Service Vehicles Act, exclusive of mounted equipment on such vehicles, and (B) equipment, other than vehicle mounted equipment, used to drill a gas or oil well. *Mobile Equipment Licensing Act*, R.S.A. 1970, c. 241, s. 2. See ELECTRICAL ~; SPECIAL ~.

MOBILE HOME. 1. A trailer coach: (i) that is used as a dwelling all the year round; (ii) that has water faucets and shower or other bathing facilities that may be connected to a water distribution system; and (iii) that has facilities for washing and a water closet or other similar facility that may be connected to a sewerage system. 2. A dwelling unit designed to be mobile and to be used, and that is being used, as a permanent or temporary residence. 3. Includes any trailer that is affixed to real property and is designed for or intended to be equipped with wheels, whether or not it is equipped with wheels, and (i) that is constructed or manufactured to provide a residence for one or more persons, whether or not it is in use for that purpose, or (ii) that is used for the conducting of any business.

MOBILE HOME DEALER. A person who acquires, disposes of, exchanges, trades, leases or otherwise deals in mobile homes in the ordinary course of business or pursuant to a scheme or plan for profit.

MOBILE HOME PAD. Land rented as space for and on which a tenant, under a tenancy agreement, is entitled to bring a mobile home. *Residential Tenancy Act*, S.B.C. 1984, c. 15, s. 1.

MOBILE HOME PARK. 1. An area of land designed to provide services, including roads, streets, sidewalks, water, electrical, sewage, gas, communication or other services or facilities, to mobile homes. 2. Land used or occupied by a person for the purpose of providing space for the accommodation of one or more mobile homes and for imposing a charge or rental for the use of that space.

MOBILE HOME SITE. Land rented or intended to be rented as a site for the purpose of being occupied by a mobile home where (i) the mobile home is used for residential purposes, and (ii) the owner of the mobile home is not the same person as the owner of the site on which the mobile home is to be located.

MOBILE HOME SPACE. A plot of ground within a mobile home park designed to accommodate one mobile home.

MOBILE HOME VENDOR. A person or corporation whose business is to retail, lease, rent or otherwise provide mobile homes. *Mobile Homes Act*, R.S.P.E.I. 1974, c. M-13, s. 2.

MOBILE HOUSE. Subject to subsection (2), a vehicle that (i) is so constructed as to be capable of being attached to, and drawn on highways by, a motor vehicle, or which can be propelled by a motor vehicle engine installed therein or thereon; and (ii) is intended to be used, and is used by persons for living, sleeping, eating, or business purposes, or any one or more of all of those purposes. *Municipal Act*, S.M. 1970, c. 100, s. 437.

MOBILE INDUSTRIAL OR COMMERCIAL STRUCTURE. A portable structure other than a mobile home constructed to be towed on its own chassis designed for use without a permanent foundation on a temporary or permanent basis and which has provision for connection to a supply service. *Power Corporation Act*, R.R.O. 1980, Reg. 794, s. 0.

MOBILE MACHINE. See SPECIAL ~.

MOBILE POLLING STATION. A polling station established for the purpose of taking the vote of electors who are residents of treatment centres or patients in public hospitals. *An Act to Amend the Elections Act*, S.N.B. 1985, c. 45, s. 1.

MOBILE PREMISES. A vehicle or other itinerant food premises from which food is offered for sale to the public but in which no food is prepared other than hot beverages and french fried potatoes. *Public Health Act*, R.R.O. 1980, Reg. 840, s. 1.

MOBILE PREPARATION PREMISES. A vehicle or other itinerant food premises from which food prepared therein is offered for sale to the public. *Public Health Act*, R.R.O. 1980, Reg. 840, s. 1.

MOBILE STATION. A station operated in a terrestrial service and ordinarily moving and is intended to be operated while in motion or during halts at unspecified points. *General Radio Regulations, Part II*, C.R.C., c. 1372, s. 2.

MOBILE UNIT. 1. Any structure, whether

ordinarily equipped with wheels or not, that is (i) constructed or manufactured to be moved from one location to another by being towed or carried, and (ii) used to provide living or business accommodation or other use for one or more persons. 2. (a) A vacation trailer or house trailer or relocatable trailer, or (ii) a structure whether ordinarily equipped with wheels or not, that is constructed or manufactured to be moved from one point to another by being towed or carried and to provide living accommodation or other use by one or more persons. See MULTIPLE SECTION ~.

MOBILE UNIT RESIDENTIAL. Real property principally used for residential purposes where there is only one dwelling unit and that unit is a mobile unit. *Taxation (Amendment) Act,* S.N.W.T. 1986 (1st Sess.), c. 23, s. 6.

MOBILIA SEQUUNTUR PERSONAM. [L.] Movables follow a person. J.G. McLeod, *The Conflict of Laws* (Calgary: Carswell, 1983) at 779.

MOBILITY. See SELF-~.

MOBILITY AID. See MOTORIZED ~.

MOBILITY VEHICLE. A device or vehicle which is specifically manufactured or modified for operation by a physically handicapped person and which has a maximum speed capability of more than 15 kilometres per hour but not more than 50 kilometres per hour. *The Highway Traffic Act,* S.M. 1985-86, c. 3, s. 1.

MODE. *n.* Of death, not a strict medical term but a reference to the legal context in which that death occurred: natural or unnatural and, if the latter, accidental, homicidal or suicidal. F.A. Jaffe, *A Guide to Pathological Evidence,* 2d ed. (Toronto: Carswell, 1983) at 10.

MODE A INTERROGATION. The transmission of a radio signal or combination of signals intended to trigger a transponder or group of transponders using pulse spacing that conforms to the specifications prescribed by Radio Standards Specification 148 for Mode 3/A interrogation. *Radar Transponder Order,* C.R.C., c. 60, s. 2.

MODEL. *n.* Includes design, pattern and specimen. *Official Secrets Act,* R.S.C. 1985, c. O-5, s. 2. See PATENT ~; PROTOTYPE ~; SCALE ~.

MODEL AGREEMENT. See MASTER AGREEMENT.

MODEL DESIGNATION. Any combination of letters or figures or both letters and figures by which a device that bears that designation is claimed to have characteristics and design features that are uniform. Canada regulations.

MODEL ROCKET. A rocket (a) constructed of balsa wood, paper and plastics and containing no substantial metal parts, (b) equipped with model rocket engines that will not generate a total impulse exceeding 80 newton-seconds, (c) of a gross weight, including engines, not exceeding 500 grams, and (d) equipped with a parachute or other device capable of retarding its descent so that no hazard is created to persons or property on the ground. *Air Regulations,* C.R.C., c. 2, s. 101.

MODEL ROCKET ENGINE. A commercially manufactured device designed and used for the propulsion of model rockets. *Air Regulations,* C.R.C., c. 2, s. 101.

MODEL YEAR. When used with respect to a motor vehicle, means the model year designated by the manufacturer but, where the manufacturer does not make such a designation, means the calendar year in which the manufacture of a motor vehicle is completed. *Environmental Protection Act,* R.R.O. 1980, Reg. 311, s. 1.

MODERATELY RETARDED CHILD. A child in whose case there has been from birth or from an early age mental retardation, not amounting to severe retardation, yet so pronounced that he is incapable of managing his affairs or himself or being taught to do so. *Child Welfare Act,* R.S.N.S. 1967, c. 31, s. 87.

MODERATOR. *n.* Chairman; president.

MODIFIED LOBSTER TRAP. (a) A lobster trap with the fishing heads removed and having an opening of not more than 2 inches in width constructed in the top of the trap, or (b) any steel, plastic or other trap incapable of catching lobster or constructed to provide escapement for any lobsters inadvertently caught. *Atlantic Crab Fishery Regulations,* C.R.C., c. 806, s. 14.

MODIFIED MILK. Milk from which the fatty constituents have been wholly or partially removed, with or without the addition of vitamins and solid elements derived from milk. *Dairy Products and Dairy Products Substitutes Act,* R.S.Q. 1977, c. P-30, s. 1.

MODIFIED STACK VENTING. A special stack venting arrangement such that the stack vent above the connection of the highest stack vented fixture is reduced in diameter. *Ontario Water Resources Act,* R.R.O. 1980, Reg. 736, s. 1.

MODIFIED SWIMMING POOL. A swimming pool that is not an indoor pool and that has the form of a basin-shaped depression in the earth, the floor of which slopes downward and inward toward the centre from the rim. *Public Health Act,* R.R.O. 1980, Reg. 849, s. 1.

MODIFIED UNION SHOP. A place of work where the employer and union agree that all present members and those who join later must remain members of the union but those not members at the time of the agreement need not join.

MOD. L. REV. *abbr.* Modern Law Review.

MODO ET FORMA. [L.] In manner and form.

MODULAR BUILDING UNIT. A building component or unit, the manufacture and assembly of which is completed or substantially completed before delivery to a construction site, that is designed for installation on a foundation and is composed of at least one room or area with finished walls, a finished floor and a finished ceiling, including installed plumbing, heating and electrical equipment appropriate to that room or area, and that, when installed on a foundation at the site with or without other similarly manufactured and assembled components or units, forms a complete residential, commercial, educational, institutional or industrial building, but does not include any free-standing appliances or furniture sold with the unit. *Excise Tax Act*, R.S.C. 1985 (2d Supp.), c. 7, s. 1(4).

MODULAR HOME. 1. A house that is intended for residential purposes and that is constructed by assembling manufactured modular units each of which comprises at least one room or living area and has been manufactured to comply with the standards set out in the National Building Code of Canada. *Revenue Tax Act*, S.P.E.I. 1979, c. 16, s. 1. 2. A house that is intended for residential purposes and that is constructed by assembling manufactured modular units each of which comprises at least one room or living area, has been manufactured to comply with the A277 series of standards prescribed by the Canadian Standards Association, and bears the seal of that association attesting to such compliance. *Retail Sales Tax Act*, R.S.O. 1980, c. 454, s. 1.

MODUS. *n.* [L.] Manner; method.

MODUS ET CONVENTIO VINCUNT LEGEM. [L.] Custom and agreement override law.

MODUS LEGEM DAT DONATIONI. [L.] Custom makes a donation legal.

MODUS OPERANDI. [L.] Method of operating.

MODUS TENENDI. [L.] Manner of holding.

MODUS TRANSFERRENDI. [L.] Manner of transferring.

MODUS VACANDI. [L.] Manner of vacating.

MOIETY. *n.* A half; any fraction.

MOLASSES SPIRIT. An alcoholic distillate, obtained from sugar-cane by-products fermented by the action of yeast, from which all or nearly all of the naturally occurring substances other than alcohol and water have been removed. *Food and Drug Regulations*, C.R.C., c. 870, c. B.02.002.

MONARCHY. *n.* A government in which a single person holds supreme power.

MONETANDI JUS COMPREHENDITUR IN REGALIBUS QUAE NUNQUAM A REGIO SCEPTRO ABDICANTUR. [L.] The right to coin money is included in those royal rights which are never distinct from the royal sceptre.

MONEY. *n.* 1. Includes currency, government or bank notes, cheques, drafts, post office, express and bank money orders. 2. Includes negotiable instruments. See ATTENDANCE ~; BORROWED ~; CONDUCT ~; COUNTERFEIT ~; GARNISHABLE ~S; GUARANTEED TRUST ~; HEAD ~; HUSH-~; INDIAN ~S; INSURANCE ~; MILLED ~; MORTGAGE ~; OFFICE ~; PAPER ~; PRINCIPAL ~; PUBLIC ~; PURCHASE ~; QUANTITY THEORY OF ~; SCHOOL ~S; SHARE ~; TRUST ~.

MONEY ACCUMULATION PLAN. A money purchase plan in which one does not estimate retirement income in advance. A. Bissett-Johnson & W.M. Holland, eds., *Matrimonial Property Law in Canada* (Toronto: Carswell, 1980) at V-93.

MONEY BILL. 1. A bill to impose, repeal, remit, alter or regulate taxation, to impose charges on a consolidated fund to pay debt or for other financial purposes or to supply government requirements. 2. A bill introduced in the House of Commons only after recommendation by the Governor General. P.W. Hogg, *Constitutional Law of Canada*, 2d ed. (Toronto: Carswell, 1985) at 203.

MONEY BROKER. A person who raises or lends money for or to other people.

MONEY BY-LAW. 1. A by-law for contracting a debt or obligation or for borrowing money. 2. A by-law which must be advertised and may be required to be submitted to a vote of the proprietary electors. Alberta statutes.

MONEY HAD AND RECEIVED. Money a defendant has received and which for reasons of equity the defendant should not retain. See ACTION FOR ~.

MONEY-LENDER. *var.* MONEY LENDER. A person who carries on the business of money lending or advertises or claims in any way to carry on that business, but does not include a registered pawn broker as such.

MONEY LENT. Includes money advanced or credit granted to or on account of any person in any transaction that, whatever its form may be, is substantially one of money-lending or credit granting or securing the repayment of money so advanced or extended in the way of credit and includes a mortgage or real or personal property, or both.

MONEY MARKET DEALERS. Those resident controlled dealers approved by the Bank of Canada from time to time as money market dealers. *Securities Act*, R.R.O. 1980, Reg. 910, s. 84.

MONEY OF ACCOUNT. The currency in which one expresses or calculates a debt.

MONEY OF PAYMENT. The currency in which one discharges an obligation. J.G. McLeod, *The Conflict of Laws* (Calgary: Carswell, 1983) at 517.

MONEY ORDER. An order to pay money which may be purchased at a bank or post office.

MONEY PACKET. An item of mailable matter (a) having a value exceeding $100; and (b) containing (i) banknotes, (ii) coin, (iii) gold bullion, (iv) gold dust, (v) precious stones, (vi) jewels, (vii) precious metals, whether or not manufactured, (viii) stocks, bonds, coupons or other securities negotiable by bearer, or (ix) lottery tickets. *Special Services and Fees Regulations*, C.R.C., c. 1296, s. 9.

MONEY PAID TO CANADA FOR A SPECIAL PURPOSE. Includes all money that is paid to a public officer under or pursuant to a statute, trust, treaty, undertaking, or contract, and is to be disbursed for purposes specified in or pursuant to such statute, trust, treaty, undertaking or contract. *Financial Administration Act*, R.S.C. 1970, c. F-10, s. 2.

MONEY PAID TO THE PROVINCE FOR A SPECIAL PURPOSE. Includes all money paid to a public officer under a statute, trust, treaty, undertaking or contract, to be disbursed for a purpose specified in such statute, trust, treaty, undertaking or contract.

MONEY PAID TO THE TERRITORIES FOR A SPECIAL PURPOSE. Includes all money that is paid to a public officer under or pursuant to an Ordinance, trust, undertaking or contract. *Financial Administration Act*, R.S.N.W.T. 1974, c. F-4, s. 2.

MONEY PRIZE. A sum of money payable as the result of the selection of a winning ticket under a lottery scheme.

MONEY PURCHASE PLAN. A plan in which one does not estimate retirement income in advance. A. Bissett-Johnson & W.M. Holland,

eds., *Matrimonial Property Law in Canada* (Toronto: Carswell, 1980) at V-93.

MONEY ROOM. The combined areas of the issuing and receiving banks. *Race Track Supervision Regulations*, C.R.C., c. 441, s. 2.

MONGER. *n.* A seller, dealer.

MONIMENT. *n.* A memorial, record or superscription.

MONITOR. *n.* A person appointed by a security holder to review and report on the cash flow, accounts payable and assets of a debtor's business if that security holder is unsure that the business is presently viable. F. Bennett, *Receiverships* (Toronto: Carswell, 1985) at 4. See ALARM ~.

MONITORING. *n.* Obtaining and analyzing samples. *Clean Environment Act*, S.N.B. 1975, c. 12, s. 1. See ENVIRONMENTAL ~; MEDICAL ~.

MONOCRACY. *n.* Government by a single person.

MONOFILAMENT. *n.* Any single filament having more than 50 deniers, that is weighing more than 50 grams per 9 000 metres of filament. *Fishery regulations.*

MONOGAMY. *n.* The marriage of one wife to one husband.

MONOGRAPH. See PRODUCT ~.

MONOPOLY. *n.* A situation where one or more persons either substantially or completely control throughout Canada or any area thereof the class or species of business in which they are engaged and have operated that business or are likely to operate it to the detriment or against the interest of the public, whether consumers, producers or others, but a situation shall not be deemed a monopoly within the meaning of this definition by reason only of the exercise of any right or enjoyment of any interest derived under the Patent Act or any other Act of Parliament. *Combines Investigation Act*, R.S.C. 1985, c. C-34, s. 2.

MONSTRANS DE DROIT. [Fr.] The display or plea of a right.

MONSTRANS DE FAITS OU RECORDS. [Fr.] The display of deeds or records.

MONTH. *n.* 1. A calendar month. 2. A period calculated from a day in one month to a day numerically corresponding to that day in the following month. 3. Includes part of a month. 4. Thirty days. 5. The period commencing on a date in one calendar month and terminating on the day immediately preceding the same date in the next calendar month or, if there is no corresponding date in the next calendar month, terminating on the last day of such calendar month. Canada regulations. See ANIMAL UNIT ~; ANNIVERSARY ~; CALENDAR ~; TENANCY ~.

MONTHLY BASE INCOME. In relation to the calculation of the supplement for a month in any given payment quarter, (a) in the case of a person other than an applicant described in paragraph (b) or (c), one-twelfth of the income of that person for the base calendar year; (b) in the case of an applicant who, on the day immediately before the current fiscal year, was a married person and to whose spouse no pension may be paid for any month in the current fiscal year, one twenty-fourth of the aggregate of the incomes of the applicant and the spouse for the base calendar year, minus one-half of the amount of the full monthly pension (rounded to the higher multiple of four dollars when the full monthly pension is not a multiple of four dollars) that might have been paid to a pensioner for any month in that payment quarter; and (c) in the case of an applicant who, on the day immediately before the current fiscal year, was a married person and to whose spouse a pension may be paid for any month in the current fiscal year, (i) in respect of any month in that fiscal year before the first month for which a pension may be paid to the spouse, one twenty-fourth of the aggregate of the incomes of the applicant and the spouse for the base calendar year, minus one-half of the amount of the full monthly pension (rounded to the higher multiple of four dollars when the full monthly pension is not a multiple of four dollars) that might have been paid to a pensioner for any month in that payment quarter, and (ii) in respect of any month in that fiscal year commencing with the first month for which a pension may be paid to the spouse, one twenty-fourth of the aggregate of the incomes of the applicant and the spouse for the base calendar year. *Old Age Security Act,* R.S.C. 1985, c. O-9, s. 12(6).

MONTHLY FAMILY INCOME. Of a pensioner and the pensioner's spouse in a current fiscal year is the amount that equals one-twelfth of the total incomes of the pensioner and the spouse for the base calendar year. *Old Age Security Act,* R.S.C. 1985, c. O-9, s. 22.

MONTHLY FEES. The contribution which may be exacted in respect of each child who attends certain public schools. *Education Act,* R.S.Q. 1977, c. I-14, s. 1.

MONTHLY INCOME. 1. Of the surviving spouse of a deceased pensioner in a current fiscal year is the amount that equals one-twelfth of the income of the surviving spouse for the base calendar year. *Old Age Security Act,* R.S.C.

1985, c. O-9, s. 22. 2. Of a widow in a current fiscal year is the amount that equals one-twelfth of her income for the base calendar year. *Old Age Security Act,* R.S.C. 1985 (1st Supp.), c. 34, s. 5.

MONTH OF INDEMNITY. Any calendar month for all of which a replacement indemnity is paid to a contributor. *An Act Respecting Industrial Accidents and Occupational Diseases,* S.Q. 1985, c. 6, s. 513.

MONTH OF TENANCY. The monthly period on which the tenancy is based and not necessarily a calendar month and, unless otherwise specifically agreed upon, the month shall be deemed to begin on the day upon which rent is payable. *Landlord and Tenant Act,* R.S.P.E.I. 1974, c. L-7, s. 108.

MONUMENT. *n.* 1. An iron post, wooden post, mound, pit or trench, or anything else used to mark a boundary corner or line by a qualified surveyor. 2. A monumental stone placed above the level of the surrounding ground at the head of a grave or plot. *National Parks Cemetery Regulations,* C.R.C., c. 1117, s. 2. See BOUNDARY ~; CO-ORDINATE ~; HISTORIC ~; LEGAL ~; LOST ~; OBLITERATED ~; ORIGINAL ~; OUTLINE ~.

MONUMENTA QUAE NOS RECORDA VOCAMUS SUNT VERITATIS ET VETUSTATIS VESTIGIA. [L.] The writing we call records are footprints of truth and tradition.

MOONLIGHT. *v.* To hold more than one job for more than one employer.

MOO. P.C. *abbr.* Moore, Privy Council.

MOO. P.C. (N.S.). *abbr.* Moore (N.S.) Privy Council.

MOOT. *n.* An exercise in which students plead and argue doubtful questions and cases.

MOOT. *adj.* Describing the situation in which an issue used to exist between parties, but the issue exists no longer when the case comes before a tribunal. Robert J. Sharpe, ed., *Charter Litigation,* (Toronto: Butterworths 1987) at 331.

MOOT CASE. A disputable and unsettled case which is properly a topic for dispute.

MOOT POINT. A disputable and unsettled point which is properly a topic for dispute.

MOPED. *n.* 1. A motor vehicle which (i) has 2 tandem wheels or 3 wheels, each of which is more than 410 millimetres in diameter, (ii) has a set or saddle having a minimum unladen height of 700 millimetres, when measured from the ground level to the top of the forwardmost part of the seat or saddle, (ii) is capable of being driven at all times by pedals only, by motor only, or both, and the motor has a piston displacement of not more than 50 cubic centimetres, or is an electric motor neither of which is capable of enabling the moped to attain a speed greater than 50 kilometres per hour. 2. A passenger vehicle having two or three wheels and a net mass not in excess of 60 kg, provided with a motor having a piston displacement of not over 50 cm³ and equipped with an automatic transmission, as well as a three-wheel passenger vehicle designed for the transportation of a handicapped person which meets the criteria established by regulation for recognition as a moped by the Régie. *Highway Safety Code*, S.Q. 1986, c. 91, s. 4.

MORA. *n.* [L.] Delay.

MORA DEBITORIS NON DEBET ESSE CREDITORI DAMNOSA. [L.] Delay by the one who owes should not be injurious to the one to whom the thing is owed.

MORAL ACTION. A situation in which a person has knowledge for guidance and will to choose freely.

MORALITY. See INTERNATIONAL ~.

MORALS. See CORRUPTING ~.

MORA REPROBATUR IN LEGE. [L.] In law, delay is not approved.

MORATORIUM. *n.* The authorized delay in paying a debt.

MORE OR LESS. A phrase used to compensate for slight inaccuracies in description in a contract for the sale of land or conveyance.

MORGUE. See PRIVATE ~; PUBLIC ~.

MORNING LINE. The odds posted immediately before betting commences on each race. *Race Track Supervision Regulations*, C.R.C., c. 441, s. 2.

MORPHINE. *n.* The main ingredient in opium, a vegetable alkaloid, powerful analgesic, narcotic and depressant of the nervous system which is addictive. F.A. Jaffe, *A Guide to Pathological Evidence*, 2d ed. (Toronto: Carswell, 1983) at 180.

MORS DICITUR ULTIMUM SUPPLICIUM. [L.] Death is called the ultimate penalty.

MORS IN TABULA. [L. death on the table] Death in the operating room. F.A. Jaffe, *A Guide to Pathological Evidence*, 2d ed. (Toronto: Carswell, 1983) at 180.

MORS OMNIA SOLVIT. [L.] Death settles all differences.

MORTGAGE. *v.* To convey as security for a debt.

MORTGAGE. *n.* 1. The conveyance of land as a security for the discharge of an obligation or the payment of a debt, a security which may be redeemed when the obligation or debt is discharged or paid. B.J. Reiter, R.C.B. Risk & B.N. McLellan, *Real Estate Law*, 3d ed. (Toronto: Emond Montgomery, 1986) at 951. 2. Any charge on real property or chattels real for securing money or moneys worth and includes a part of a mortgage or an interest in a mortgage and a mortgage of a mortgage. 3. Includes (i) an assignment, transfer, conveyance, declaration of trust without transfer or other assurance of chattels intended to operate as a mortgage or pledge of chattels, (ii) a power or authority or licence to take possession of chattels as security, and (iii) an agreement, whether intended or not to be followed by the execution of any other instrument, by which a right in equity to a charge or security on any chattels is conferred, but does not include (iv) a mortgage or charge, whether specific or floating, of chattels, created by a corporation, and contained (A) in a trust deed or other like instrument to secure bonds, debentures, or debenture stock of the corporation, (B) in any bonds, debentures, or debenture stock of the corporation, as well as in the trust deed or other like instrument securing the bonds, debentures or debenture stock, or (C) in any bonds, debentures, or debenture stock or any series of bonds or debentures of the corporation and not secured by any trust deed or other like instrument, (v) security taken by a bank under section 88 of the Bank Act, (Canada), or (vi) a power of distress contained in a mortgage of real property. Bills of Sale acts. 4. Includes hypothec and an assignment of or a mortgage on the leasehold interest of a lessee. *National Housing Act*, R.S.C. 1985, c. N-11, s. 2. 5. Includes hypothec and sale with the right of redemption. *Farm Credit Act*, R.S.C. 1985, c. F-2, s. 2. 6. Includes a hypothec and an agreement for sale. *Canada Mortgage and Housing Corporation*, R.S.C. 1985, c. C-7, s. 2. 7. Includes (a) a charge, whether equitable, statutory or of any other nature, and (b) a lien for unpaid purchase money. 8. Includes encumbrance. See BLANKET ~; BUILDER'S ~; CANADA ~ AND HOUSING CORPORATION; CHATTEL ~; CONVERTIBLE ~; DERIVATIVE ~; EQUITABLE LEASEHOLD ~; EQUITABLE ~; FIRST ~; GRADUATED PAYMENT ~; LEGAL LEASEHOLD ~; PARTICIPATION ~; PURCHASE-MONEY ~; SECOND ~; SUB ~; UNIT ~; VARIABLE RATE ~; WELSH ~; WRAP-AROUND ~.

MORTGAGE BACK. The vendor receives a mortgage on property in exchange for loaning part of the purchase price. B.J. Reiter, R.C.B.

Risk & B.N. McLellan, *Real Estate Law*, 3d ed. (Toronto: Emond Montgomery, 1986) at 970.

MORTGAGE BOND. A type of corporate debt security in which the indenture is a mortgage on property of the corporation and the indenture trustee is mortgagee on behalf of the bondholders. S.M. Beck *et al., Cases and Materials on Partnerships and Canadian Business Corporations* (Toronto: The Carswell Company Limited, 1983) at 799. See FIRST ~.

MORTGAGE BROKER. A person who, (i) directly or indirectly, carries on the business of lending money on the security of real estate, whether the money is personal or that of another person; (ii) carries on the business of dealing in mortgages; or (ii) represents or, by an advertisement, notice or sign, claims to be a mortgage broker or a person who carries on the business of dealing in mortgages. See CARRY ON BUSINESS AS A ~.

MORTGAGE COMMITMENT. A document issued by a lender to a borrower when, based on a credit report and property appraisal, the lender decides to go ahead with the loan. D.J. Donahue & P.D. Quinn, *Real Estate Practice in Ontario*, 4th ed. (Toronto: Butterworths, 1990) at 224.

MORTGAGE DEALER. A person who (i) either directly or indirectly arranges for the investment by another person, in a mortgage, whether that investment is effected, or is intended to be effected, by making a loan secured by a mortgage, by selling a mortgage to that other person or by buying a mortgage for that other person, (ii) lends money on mortgages and sells mortgages securing the loans, (iii) as principal, buys and sells mortgages or who acts as an agent in the purchase or sale of a mortgage, (iv) arranges or places mortgages for other persons, whether by obtaining loans for borrowers or by finding mortgage investments for lenders, or both, (v) registers a mortgage, a mortgage of a mortgage, or a transfer of a mortgage in the mortgage dealer's name where another person or other persons have contributed mortgage moneys or are entitled to share the proceeds of the mortgage, or both, (vi) for a reward or hope or promise thereof, administers a mortgage for or on behalf of any other person, or (vii) holds himself or herself out as doing any of the things mentioned in sub-clauses (i) to (vi). *The Mortgage Dealers Act*, S.M. 1985-86, c. 16, s. 1.

MORTGAGEE. *n.* 1. The owner of a mortgage. 2. The person who assumes a mortgage to secure a loan. 3. Includes chargee. 4. Includes a vendor under an agreement for the sale of land. 5. Includes a person from time to time deriving title under the original mortgage. 6. Includes a trustee for holders of bonds, debentures, notes or other evidences of indebtedness. 7. Includes the execution creditor under a writ of execution. *Security of Farm Land Act*, S.S. 1984-85-86, c. F-8.01, s. 10. See SUBSEQUENT PURCHASER OR ~.

MORTGAGEE IN POSSESSION. A mortgagee who, in right of the mortgage, has entered into and is in possession of the mortgaged property. *Conveyancing Act*, R.S.Nfld. 1970, c. 63, s. 2.

MORTGAGE INSURANCE. Insurance against loss caused by default on the part of a borrower under a loan secured by a mortgage upon real property, a hypothec upon immovable property or an interest in real or immovable property.

MORTGAGE INVESTMENT COMPANY. A loan company that has been designated as a mortgage investment company pursuant to the provisions of Part II of the Loan Companies Act. *Bank Act*, R.S.C. 1985, c. B-1, s. 2.

MORTGAGE LENDER. A person who carries on the business of lending money on the security of land, whether the money is his own or that of another person. *Mortgage Brokers Act*, S.Nfld. 1975-76, c. 49, s. 2.

MORTGAGE LOAN CORPORATION. A corporation (a) that (i) is incorporated or continued under the Loan Companies Act, or (ii) until May 18, 1990, or such time after December 1, 1982 and before May 18, 1990 as it takes on any new business or acquires any securities, is incorporated under the laws of a province, and of which a bank owned on December 1, 1980 voting shares that permitted the bank to vote more than ten per cent of the total votes that could, under voting rights attached to all outstanding shares of the corporation, be voted by the holders thereof, (b) the activities of which are confined solely to (i) the lending of money on the security of mortgages or hypothecs on real property in Canada and the sale and purchase of such mortgages and hypothecs, or (ii) the holding of and investing in securities other than equity securities and the activities referred to in subparagraph (i), and the raising of money for the purpose of financing such activities, and (c) at least eighty per cent of the outstanding principal amount of all mortgages and hypothecs owned by which is secured by property that is real property in Canada comprising existing buildings that are used, or buildings in the process of construction that are to be used, to the extent of at least one-half of the floor space thereof, as private dwellings either by the owners thereof or by lessees under leases for terms of at least one month and the land on which those buidings are situated. *Bank Act*, R.S.C. 1985, c. B-1, s. 193.

MORTGAGE MONEY. Money or money's worth secured by a mortgage.

MORTGAGE POOL. The loans and security on the basis of which any issue of mortgage-backed securities as described in paragraph 21.2(1)(b) is made. *National Housing Act*, R.S.C. 1985 (1st Supp.), c. 8, s. 21.1.

MORTGAGE PROTECTION PAYMENTS. Relief for a home owner in respect of an eligible mortgage in the form of interest reimbursement payments pursuant to this Act. *The Mortgage Protection Act*, S.S. 1986-87-88, c. M-21.11, s. 2.

MORTGAGE SALESMAN. An individual employed by a registered mortgage broker, or by a registered mortgage dealer, or by a person registered as a broker under The Real Estate Brokers Act, and whose duties include (i) soliciting persons to lend money on mortgage or otherwise invest in mortgages, or (ii) negotiating the terms of sale or purchase of a mortgage. *Mortgage Brokers and Mortgage Dealers Act*, S.M. 1971, c. 26, s. 1.

MORTGAGE TRANSACTION. 1. The borrowing of money on the security of real property or the assignment of a mortgage for consideration. *Mortgage Brokers Act*, R.S.O. 1980, c. 295, s. 11. 2. The extension of credit on the security of (a) a duplicate certificate of title to land that has been deposited with the lender; or (b) a mortgage, or agreement for sale, of real estate or leasehold property, but does not include a transaction involving real estate or leasehold property where it is to be used for business or commercial purposes. *Consumer Protection Act*, R.S.B.C. 1979, c. 65, s. 40.

MORTGAGE TRUST. A trustee holds mortgaged assets on behalf of multiple lenders on the same mortgage security. D.M.W. Waters, *The Law of Trusts in Canada*, 2d ed. (Toronto: Carswell, 1984) at 450.

MORTGAGOR. *n.* 1. One who borrows. B.J. Reiter, R.C.B. Risk & B.N. McLellan, *Real Estate Law*, 3d ed. (Toronto: Emond Montgomery, 1986) at 949. 2. A person who gives a mortgage to secure a loan. 3. The owner or transferee of land or of any estate or interest in land pledged as security for a debt or loan. 4. Includes chargor. See ORIGINAL ~.

MORTIS CAUSA DONATIO. See DONATIO MORTIS CAUSA.

MORTMAIN. *n.* [Fr. dead hand] The state of possession of land which makes it inalienable. See ALIENATION IN ~.

MORTMAIN ACT. An act which forbade the conveyance of land into the "dead hand" of the church or another corporation because a lord might thus be deprived of the benefits of tenure which arose in the lord's favour when the tenant died, because such conveyance prevented free alienation. Under these acts, the Crown always had the power to regulate the holding of land and there were significant statutory exceptions to these rules. E.L.G. Tyler & N.E. Palmer, eds., *Crossley Vaines' Personal Property*, 5th ed. (London: Butterworths, 1973) at 16.

MORTUARY. *n.* A place where dead bodies are received before interment.

MORTUUM VADIUM. [L.] Dead pledge; mortgage.

MOSAIC FORMAT. As applied to any time segment, means a format of presentation of broadcast matter other than gramophone format, foreground format or rolling format. *Radio (F.M.) Broadcasting Regulations*, C.R.C., c. 380, s. 14.

MOST-FAVOURED NATION CLAUSE. In a treaty, the provision that one party grants to the other party the same treatment granted to the most-favoured nation.

MOTEL. *n.* A tourist establishment that (i) consists of one or more than one building containing attached accommodation units accessible from the exterior only, (ii) may or may not have facilities for serving meals, and (ii) is designed to accommodate the public for whom the automobile is the principal means of transportation.

MOTHER. *n.* 1. A person who takes care of a child of whom she is the legitimate, natural or adoptive mother, or the stepmother. 2. Includes a grandmother. 3. (i) A woman who (A) has, while single, been delivered of an illegitimate child, (B) being single, is pregnant and likely to be delivered of an illegitimate child, (C) was single at the time of her conception of a child, who if its mother continued single would be an illegitimate child, whether or not its mother is single at the time of the birth of such child, or (D) is single at the date of her illegitimate child's birth, whether or not she is single at the date of the commencement of affiliation proceedings, or (ii) a married woman who (A) is living apart from her husband and has been delivered of an illegitimate child, or (B) is pregnant and likely to be delivered of an illegitimate child and was living apart from her husband at the time of the conception of the child. See BIOLOGICAL ~; WIDOWED ~.

MOTHER OF PARLIAMENTS. The Parliament of the United Kingdom. P.W. Hogg, *Con-*

stitutional Law of Canada, 2d ed. (Toronto: Carswell, 1985) at 9.

MOTHER TONGUE. The first language learned and still understood at the relevant time.

MOTION. *n.* An oral or written application that the court rule or make an order before, during or after a trial. See DILATORY ~; INCIDENTAL ~; NOTICE OF ~; ORIGINATING ~; PRIVILEGED ~; SUBSIDIARY ~; SUBSTANTIVE ~; SUPERSEDING ~; WAYS AND MEANS ~.

MOTION FOR DIRECTED VERDICT. The decision by a trial judge that there is no case for the jury. P.K. McWilliams, *Canadian Criminal Evidence*, 3d ed. (Aurora: Canada Law Book, 1988) at 27-28.

MOTION FOR JUDGMENT. In any case, the plaintiff may request judgment of any claim for which the parties did not sign a default judgment. G.D. Watson & C. Perkins, eds., *Holmested & Watson: Ontario Civil Procedure* (Toronto: Carswell, 1984) at 19-19.

MOTION PICTURE. Includes a television or other audio visual production whether on cinematographic film, videotape, video-disc or other medium. *Motion Picture Development Act*, S.A. 1981, c. M-19.1, s. 1. See ADULT ~; FEATURE ~.

MOTION PICTURE DISTRIBUTOR. A person who distributes a film to a proprietor, lessee, manager or employee of a theatre or who contracts respecting films with any of those persons or with any other motion picture distributor, but does not include (a) a public library, (b) a university, (c) an educational institution approved by the Minister of Education where the film is distributed for educational purposes, (d) the government of British Columbia, or (e) the government of Canada. *Motion Picture Act*, S.B.C. 1986, c. 17, s. 1.

MOTION PICTURE MACHINE. Includes a cinematograph or other similar apparatus used for the showing of films or slides. *Motion Picture Act*, R.S.N.W.T. 1974, c. M-14, s. 2.

MOTION PICTURE THEATRE. Includes a theatre, hall, building, premises, room or place, including an open air place commonly known as a drive in theatre. *Motion Picture Act*, R.S.B.C. 1979, c. 284, s. 1.

MOTIVE. *n.* The emotion which prompted an act or the intention with which one does an intentional act. P.K. McWilliams, *Canadian Criminal Evidence*, 3d ed. (Aurora: Canada Law Book, 1988) at 18-12.

MOTIVE FUEL. 1. (a) Diesel fuel, or (b) a combination of fuels including diesel fuel, for use in propelling a motor vehicle, but does not include fuel that is taxable under section 5. *Motor Fuel Tax Act*, S.B.C. 1985, c. 76, s. 1. 2. Fuel for an internal combustion engine, and, without restricting the generality of the foregoing, includes gasoline, distillate, and diesel fuel and also includes oil and grease for the lubrication of such an engine or of agricultural machinery. *Municipal Act*, S.M. 1970, c. 100, s. 487. 3. Any gas fuel or liquid fuel that is not gasoline and that can be used for moving or operating any internal combustion engine or machine, or for heating and without restricting the generality of the foregoing includes kerosene, propane, crude oil, distillate and other motor fuel, but does not include natural gas or manufactured gas that is used as a fuel. *Gasoline and Motive Fuel Tax Act*, R.S.N.B. 1973, c. G-3, s. 1. See BULK ~.

MOTIVE FUEL PUMP. A tank or receptacle of not less than fifty gallon or 227 litre capacity used or intended to be used for the storage of gasoline or motive fuel and equipped with a pump for dispensing such gasoline or motive fuel. *Gasoline and Motive Fuel Tax Act*, S.N.B. 1976, c. 26, s. 1.

MOTOR. *n.* An internal combustion engine. *Environmental Protection Act*, R.S.O. 1980, c. 141, s. 20. See MULTI-WINDING ~; PART-WINDING START ~.

MOTOR ASSISTED BICYCLE. A bicycle, (i.) that is fitted with pedals that are operable at all times to propel the bicycle, (ii.) that weighs not more than fifty-five kilograms, (iii.) that has no hand or foot operated clutch or gear-box driven by the motor and transferring power to the driven wheel, (iv.) that has an attached motor driven by electricity or having a piston displacement of not more than fifty cubic centimetres, and (v.) that does not have sufficient power to enable the bicycle to attain a speed greater than 50 kilometres per hour on level ground within a distance of 2 kilometres from a standing start. *Highway Traffic Act*, R.S.O. 1980, c. 198, s. 1.

MOTOR BOAT. Includes every vessel propelled by machinery and not more than 65 feet in length, other than vessels towing, the length to be measured from end to end, over the deck, excluding sheer. *Rules of the Road for the Great Lakes*, C.R.C., c. 1464, s. 2.

MOTOR CARRIER. 1. A person operating, whether alone or with another, a motor vehicle with or without trailer attached, as a public pasenger vehicle or as a freight vehicle. 2. A person that operates or causes to be operated a public motor bus or a public motor truck. 3. A person operating a public service vehicle or a commercial truck.

MOTOR-CIRCUIT SWITCH. A fused or unfused manually-operated knife or snap switch rated in horsepower. *Power Corporation Act,* R.R.O. 1980, Reg. 794, s. 0.

MOTORCYCLE. *var.* **MOTOR CYCLE.** 1. A motor vehicle, other than a tractor, that: (i) is designed to travel on not more than three wheels on the ground; and (ii) has a seat or saddle for use of the rider sitting astride thereof; and includes a bicycle with a motor attached by which it is driven and a motor scooter. 2. A vehicle having steering handlebars completely constrained from rotating in relation to the axle of one wheel in contact with the ground and designed to travel on not more than three wheels in contact with the ground, but does not include a competition motorcycle, minibike or a motor-driven cycle. Canada regulations. See COMPETITION ~; POWER ~; USED ~.

MOTORCYCLE MECHANIC. A person who services, repairs, overhauls and inspects motorcycles, and tests them for faults or road-worthiness. *Apprenticeship and Tradesmen's Qualification Act,* R.R.O. 1980, Reg. 48, s. 1.

MOTOR DEALER. A person who, in the course of business, (a) engages in the sale of motor vehicles, whether for his own account or for the account of another person, or who holds himself out as engaging in the sale of motor vehicles; or (b) with or without remuneration, acts as a motor vehicle broker or, as an agent, sells motor vehicles on commission; and (c) includes a person who carries on any of the activities described above in respect of at least 5 motor vehicles within a 12 month period, but does not include a person exempted by regulation. *Motor Dealer Act,* R.S.B.C. 1979, c. 287, s. 1.

MOTOR DREDGE. A dredge, the primary power plant of which consists of internal combustion engines. *Marine Engineer Examination Regulations,* C.R.C., c. 1443, s. 2.

MOTOR DRIVEN CYCLE. 1. A motor vehicle having a seat or saddle for the use of the rider and designed to travel on not more than three wheels and propelled by a motor not to exceed fifty cubic centimetres in size and includes a motor scooter, tricycle or bicycle with such a motor attached. *Motor Vehicle Act,* S.N.B. 1975, c. 38, s. 1. 2. A vehicle having steering handlebars completely constrained from rotating in relation to the axle of one wheel in contact with the ground, designed to travel on not more than three wheels in contact with the ground, and having a motor that produces five brake horsepower or less. Canada regulations.

MOTOR HOME. 1. A motor vehicle designed and constructed as an integral unit to provide permanent living accommodation and which is equipped with one or more beds and a stove or refrigerator or washing and toilet facilities, and is so designed that there is direct access from the living quarters to the drivers seat. *The Highway Traffic Act,* S.M. 1985-86, c. 3, s. 1. 2. A motor vehicle designed or used primarily for accommodation during travel or recreation, but does not include a motor vehicle that has attached to it a structure (a) designed or used primarily for accommodation during travel or recreation; and (b) designed or intended to be detachable. *Motor Vehicle Act,* R.S.B.C. 1979, c. 288, s. 1.

MOTOR HOTEL. A tourist establishment that, (i) consists of one or more than one building containing four or more accommodation units grouped under one roof and accessible from the interior or partially from the exterior, (ii) may or may not have facilities for serving meals, and (iii) is designed to accommodate the public for whom the automobile is the principal means of transportation. *Tourism Act,* R.R.O. 1980, Reg. 936, s. 1.

MOTORIZED MOBILITY AID. A device which is specifically manufactured or modified for operation by a physically handicapped person and which has (i) a maximum speed capability of not more than 15 kilometres per hour, (ii) a maximum width of not more than 81.2 centimetres, and (ii) a maximum mass of not more than 226 kilograms, and includes a motorized wheel chair. *The Highway Traffic Act,* S.M. 1985-86, c. 3, s. 1.

MOTORIZED SNOW VEHICLE. A self-propelled vehicle designed to be driven exclusively or chiefly on snow or ice or both, whether or not it is capable of being driven elsewhere.

MOTORIZED VEHICLE. A motorcycle, minibike, motorbike, moped, trail bike or dune buggy. *Off-Highway Motorized Vehicles Act,* S.N.S. 1979-80, c. 11, s. 2.

MOTOR SHIP. A ship, the primary power plant of which consists of internal combustion engines. *Marine Engineer Examination Regulations,* C.R.C., c. 1443, s. 2.

MOTOR TRACTOR. Any mechanically propelled vehicle, other than a farm tractor, designed for traction purposes on the highway. *Motor Carrier Act,* S.P.E.I. 1984, c. 26, s. 1.

MOTOR VEHICLE. 1. A vehicle that is drawn, propelled or driven by any means other than by muscular power, but does not include a vehicle of a railway that operates on rails. 2. A motorized vehicle designed to be used primarily on a public highway for the transportation of persons or things but does not include (a) any fire engine, bus, ambulance or utility truck, or

(b) any other special purpose motorized vehicle that contains significant special features that make it suitable for a specific purpose and that is manufactured by a person other than the vehicle manufacturer who manufactured the basic chassis. *Bank Act*, R.S.C. 1985, c. B-1, s. 193. 3. A vehicle that is propelled or driven by means of an internal combustion or turbine engine. 4. A vehicle that is designed to be self propelled. 5. (a) A vehicle propelled by any power other than muscular power, and (ii) includes an airplane, but (iii) does not include a motor vehicle that runs only on rails. *Garagemen's Lien Act*, R.S.A. 1980, c. G-1, s. 1. See ABANDONED ~; ANTIQUE ~; COMMERCIAL ~; DANGEROUS OPERATION OF ~S; DERELICT ~; DRIVE-YOURSELF ~; HIGHWAY ~ OPERATOR; INSURED ~; LIGHT DUTY ~; NEW ~; PUBLIC TRANSIT ~; REGISTRAR OF ~S.

MOTOR VEHICLE DEALER. A person who carries on the business of buying or selling motor vehicles, whether for his own account or the account of any other person, or who holds himself out as carrying on the business of buying or selling motor vehicles. *Motor Vehicle Dealers Act*, R.S.O. 1980, c. 299, s. 1. See NEW ~.

MOTOR VEHICLE INSPECTION MECHANIC. A person who certifies by means of a safety standards certificate that a motor vehicle complies with the equipment and performance standards prescribed by the regulations. *Highway Traffic Act*, R.S.O. 1980, c. 198, s. 71.

MOTOR VEHICLE INSPECTION STATION. Any premises maintained or operated for the inspection of motor vehicles and the issuance of safety standards certificates in respect of such motor vehicles. *Highway Traffic Act*, R.S.O. 1980, c. 198, s. 71.

MOTOR VEHICLE INSURANCE. Insurance against liability for loss or damage to persons or property caused by a motor vehicle or the use or operation thereof, and against loss of or damage to a motor vehicle, but does not include insurance against loss of or damage to, or liability for loss of or damage to, property carried in or on a motor vehicle unless the insurance is under a contract to which Part VI of The Saskatchewan Insurance Act applies. *The Motor Vehicle Insurance Premiums Tax Act*, R.S.S. 1978, c. M-23, s. 2.

MOTOR VEHICLE LIABILITY POLICY. 1. A policy or part of a policy evidencing a contract insuring: (i) the owner or driver of an automobile; or (ii) a person who is not the owner or driver thereof where the automobile is being used or operated by his employee or agent or any other person on his behalf; against liability arising out of bodily injury to or the death of a person or loss or damage to property caused by an automobile or the use or operation thereof. *Insurance acts.* 2. A policy or that part of a policy insuring the owner or driver of an automobile against liability for loss or damage to persons or property. Insurance Act, R.S.N.S. 1967, c. 148, s. 75.

MOTOR VEHICLE MECHANIC. A person engaged in the servicing, repairing, overhauling, diagnosing or inspecting of motor vehicles who, (i) disassembles, adjusts, repairs and reassembles engines, transmissions, clutches, rear ends, differentials, brakes, drive shafts, axles and other assemblies, (ii) tests, diagnoses and corrects faulty alignment of wheels and steering mechanisms, manual or power, (iii) diagnoses faults, repairs or replaces suspension systems, including shock absorbers and spring assemblies, (iv) diagnoses faults, installs, repairs and removes ignition systems, generators, alternators, starters, coils, panel instruments, wiring and other electrical systems and equipment, (v) diagnoses faults, repairs and adjusts fuel systems, (vi) performs complete engine tune-ups, and (vii) diagnoses faults, installs, inspects, maintains and removes motor vehicle air-conditioning and refrigeration systems, but does not include a person who is permanently employed for the limited purpose of, (viii) removing and replacing auto glass, (ix) removing and replacing exhaust systems, (x) removing and replacing radiators, or (xi) removing and replacing shock absorbers or springs that do not require the realignment of the front or rear suspension. *Apprenticeship and Tradesmen's Qualification Act*, R.R.O. 1980, Reg. 47, s. 1.

MOTOR VEHICLE PRIVILEGE. (a) Registration of a motor vehicle under this Act, (b) a licence issued under this Act, (c) the privilege of operating a motor vehicle in the Province under section 80, and (d) the privilege of an owner of a motor vehicle registered in his name in another province, state or country to have the vehicle operated in the Province. *Motor Vehicle Act*, R.S.N.B. 1973, c. M-17, s. 272.

MOTOR VEHICLE UNDERTAKING. A work or undertaking for the transport of passengers or goods by any vehicle, machine, tractor, trailer or semi-trailer, or any combination thereof, propelled or drawn by mechanical power and capable of use on a highway. *National Transportation Act*, R.S.C. 1985, c. N-20, s. 2.

MOTOR VESSEL. Any vessel, ship, boat or watercraft that is designed to move in or through water, and that is powered by fuel, but does not include any aircraft capable of operating on water nor any vehicle moving on ice. *Motor*

Vehicle Fuel Tax Act, R.R.O. 1980, Reg. 667, s. 1.

MOULDED DEPTH. Subject to paragraphs (a) to (d), the vertical distance measured from the top of the keel to the top of the freeboard deck beam at side, but (a) in vessels of other than metal construction, the distance is measured from the lower edge of the keel rabbet, (b) where the form at the lower part of the midship section is of a hollow character, or where thick garboards are fitted, the distance is measured from the point where the line of the flat of the bottom continued inwards cuts the side of the keel, (c) in ships having rounded gunwales, the distance is measured to the point of intersection of the moulded lines of the deck and sides, the lines extending as though the gunwale were of angular design, (d) where the freeboard deck is stepped and the raised part of the deck extends over the point at which the moulded depth is to be determined, the moulded depth shall be measured to a line of reference extending from the lower part of the deck along a line parallel with the raised part. Canada regulations.

MOULD MAKER. A person who, (i) sets up and operates to prescribed tolerances engine lathes and milling, grinding, drilling, sawing and boring machines, (ii) reads and interprets blueprints, operation or product related reference charts and tables and selects mechanical measuring and checking and layout tools and devices, (iii) performs measuring, checking and layout operations and selects work piece materials and the required cutting tools and abrasives for metal removal operations, (iv) performs metal removal operations using hand and power tools and selects work piece clamping and holding devices and product-related components, (v) performs hand finishing and polishing operations on moulds, and (vi) assembles and tests moulds for application purposes, but does not include a person or class of persons in a limited purpose occupation that, in the opinion of the Director, does not equate with the definition of mould maker. *Apprenticeship and Tradesmen's Qualification Act*, R.R.O. 1980, Reg. 49, s. 1.

MOULDS. *n.* Hollow forms into which materials are placed to produce desired shapes, matrices or cavities which shape or form goods in process, and cores, pins, inserts, bushings and similar parts for moulds. *Retail Sales Tax Act*, R.R.O. 1980, Reg. 903, s. 1.

MOUND. See STONE ~.

MOUNTAIN STANDARD TIME. The time that is seven hours behind Greenwich time.

MOVABLE. *n.* A type of property distinguished

in civil law. J.G. McLeod, *The Conflict of Laws* (Calgary: Carswell, 1983) at 55.

MOVABLE PROPERTY. Includes personal property other than a leasehold or other interest in land. *Wills Act*, R.S.N.W.T. 1974, c. W-3, s. 2.

MOVABLES. *n.* Any movable tangible property, other than the ship, and includes money, valuable securities, and other documents. Insurance acts.

MOVAGE. *n.* 1. The moving of a ship within a pilotage area, whether the ship is moved from one berth to another or is returned to the same berth, but does not include, unless a pilot is employed, the warping of a ship from one berth to another solely by means of mooring lines attached to a wharf, to the shore or to a mooring buoy. Canada regulations. 2. The moving of a ship wholly within a harbour or port from one anchored or moored position to another or back to the same position, but does not include the warping of a ship from one berth to another solely by means of mooring lines unless a pilot is employed, and includes anchoring of a ship while en route between one harbour, port or pilot boarding station and another due to stress of weather, tidal conditions, safety of the ship or crew, waiting berth availability or waiting due to minor engine or equipment repairs performed by ship's personnel that are considered reasonable engine or equipment maintenance. Canada regulations.

MOVEABLE PROPERTY. All property which is not considered immoveable by the laws of Québec, and includes gas, electricity, telephone service, and lighting service. *Retail Sales Tax Act*, S.Q. 1979, c. 78, s. 1.

MOVEMENT. *n.* 1. In respect of grain, means the carriage of grain by any railway company over any line of railway now or hereafter constructed (a) from any point on any line of railway west of Thunder Bay or Armstrong to Thunder Bay or Armstrong, (b) from any point on any line of railway west of Thunder Bay or Armstrong to a port in British Columbia for export, or (c) from any point on any line of railway west of Thunder Bay or Armstrong to Churchill for export. *Western Grain Transportation Act*, R.S.C. 1985, c. W-8, s. 2. 2. In respect of oil or gas, excludes an export thereof. *National Energy Board Act*, R.S.C. 1985, c. N-7, s. 123. See BACK-TO-WORK ~; INWARD ~; JOINT LINE ~; OUTWARD ~; SOIL ~.

MOVEMENT AREA. That part of an aerodrome intended to be used for the surface movement of aircraft and includes the manoeuvring area and aprons. *Air Regulations*, C.R.C., c. 2, s. 101.

MOVER. See PRIME ~.

MOVING. See CRANE ~ CHARGE.

MOVING PARTS. Does not include valves and other devices controlling the flushing of the fixture served by the trap. *Ontario Water Resources Act*, R.R.O. 1980, Reg. 736, s. 85.

MOVING PICTURE MACHINE. A machine or device in which film is used and that is operated by or with the aid of electricity and adapted or used to project pictorial representations on a screen or other surface. *Amusements Act*, R.S.A. 1980, c. A-41, s. 1.

MOVING PICTURE THEATRE. Any theatre, concert hall, premises, room, place, house, building or structure of any kind where a cinematograph, moving picture machine or other similar apparatus is operated and to which the public is admitted. *Places of Amusement Regulations*, C.R.C., c. 962, s. 2.

M.P.I.C. *abbr.* Manitoba Public Insurance Corporation.

M.P.L.R. *abbr.* Municipal and Planning Law Reports, 1976-.

M.P.R. *abbr.* Maritime Provinces Reports, 1929-1968.

M.R. *abbr.* Master of the Rolls.

M.R.N. *abbr.* Ministre du Revenu national.

MSDS. *abbr.* Material safety data sheet. A summary of the hazards of a toxic material or product. D. Robertson, *Ontario Health and Safety Guide* (Toronto: Richard De Boo Ltd., 1988) at 5-263.

MSG. *abbr.* The Manufacturer's Standard Gauge for uncoated steel.

M.T.R. *abbr.* Maritimes Tax Reports.

MUGGING. *n.* Strangling by throwing the arm around a victim's neck from behind. F.A. Jaffe, *A Guide to Pathological Evidence*, 2d ed. (Toronto: Carswell, 1983) at 180.

MULCT. *n.* A fine; a penalty.

MULIER. *n.* A wife; a woman; a legitimate child.

MULTA CONCEDUNTUR PER OBLIQUUM, QUAE NON CONCEDUNTUR DE DIRECTO. [L.] Many things are permitted indirectly which are not permitted directly.

MULTA IN JURE COMMUNI, CONTRA RATIONEM DISPUTANDI, PRO COMMUNI UTILITATE INTRODUCTA SUNT. [L.] Many things in the common law that are illogical were incorporated for the public good.

MULTA MULTO EXERCITATIONE FACI-

LIUS QUAM REGULIS PERCIPIES. [L.] There are many things you will understand more easily from much practice than from rules.

MULTICRAFT UNION. A union which represents workers in more than one craft.

MULTICULTURALISM. *n.* The preservation and development of the multicultural composition of the province and, without limiting the generality of the foregoing, includes the recognition of the right of every community, whose common history spans many generations, to retain its distinctive group identity, and to develop its relevant language and its traditional arts and sciences, without political or social impediment and for the mutual benefit of all citizens. *The Saskatchewan Multicultural Act*, R.S.S. 1978, c. S-31, s. 2.

MULTI DWELLING LEASED PARCEL. A parcel of land on which are located 2 or more residences, the owners of one or more of which, under leases having terms not less than a prescribed number of years, lease portions of the parcel from the owner of the parcel or from a lessee of the owner of the parcel and on which portion the owner of the residence has his residence. *Home Owner Grant Assistance Act*, S.B.C. 1984, c. 20, s. 1.

MULTI-EMPLOYER BARGAINING. Collective bargaining between a union and more than one employer.

MULTI-EMPLOYER EMPLOYMENT. As more particularly defined by the regulations, means employment in any occupation or trade in which, by custom of that occupation or trade, any or all employees would in the usual course of a working month be ordinarily employed by more than one employer. *Canada Labour Code*, R.S.C. 1985 (1st Supp.), c. 9, s. 203.

MULTI-EMPLOYER PENSION PLAN. 1. A pension plan organized and administered for employees of two or more employers who contribute to the plan pursuant to an agreement, by-law or statute, where the pension plan provides pension benefits that are determined by periods of employment with any or all of the participating employers, but does not include a pension plan where more than ninety-five per cent of the plan members are employed by participating employers who are incorporated and are affiliates within the meaning of the Canada Business Corporations Act. *Pension Benefit Standards Act*, R.S.C. 1985 (2d Supp.), c. 32, s. 2. 2. A pension plan established and maintained for employees of two or more employers who contribute or on whose behalf contributions are made to a pension fund by reason of agreement, municipal by-law or statute to provide a pension benefit that is determined by employment with one or more of the employers, but does not include a pension plan where all the employers are affiliates within the meaning of the Business Corporations Act. *Pension Benefits Act*, S.N.B. 1987, c. P-5.1, s. 1.

MULTI-EMPLOYER PLAN. A pension plan administered for employees of 2 or more employers, except where both or all of those employers are affiliates within the meaning of the Business Corporations Act. *Employment Pension Plan Act*, S.A. 1986, c. E-10.05, c. 1.

MULTI-ENGINE AIRCRAFT. An aircraft having two or more engines that is capable of maintaining flight in the event of failure of the critical engine. *Sparsely Settled Areas Order*, C.R.C., c. 65, s. 2.

MULTI-FAMILY RESIDENTIAL. See MEDIUM DENSITY ~.

MULTI-FARM OPERATION. Two or more farm units operated by two or more different participants as a joint undertaking.

MULTILATERAL. *adj.* Concerning more than two nations. P.W. Hogg, *Constitutional Law of Canada*, 2d ed. (Toronto: Carswell, 1985) at 241.

MULTI-MEMBER DISTRICT. An electoral district in which 2 or more members are elected. *Election Act*, R.S.B.C. 1979, c. 103, s. 1.

MULTI-OUTLET ASSEMBLY. A surface or flush enclosure carrying conductors for extending one 2-wire or multi-wire branch circuit to two or more receptacles of the grounding type that are attached to the enclosure. *Power Corporation Act*, R.R.O. 1980, Reg. 794, s. 0.

MULTIPARTITE. *adj.* Divided into many parts.

MULTIPHASE LINE. A pipe for the transmission of effluent consisting of oil, gas and water in any combination from one or more oil wells and includes installations in connection with that pipe. *Pipeline Act*, R.S.A. 1980, c. P-8, s. 1.

MULTI-PLANT BARGAINING. Collective bargaining involving the employees of more than one plant owned by the same employer.

MULTIPLE DWELLING. A building or buildings located on a lot and containing two or more dwelling units. *Municipality of the County of Halifax Act*, S.N.S. 1968, c. 91, s. 1.

MULTIPLE-FAMILY DWELLING. A building containing three or more family housing units. *National Housing Act*, R.S.C. 1985, c. N-11, s. 2.

MULTIPLE LISTING. 1. An agreement between a vendor and one broker authorizing other brokers to sell the property for a portion of the commission agreed. 2. Property listed

through a real estate board's multiple listing service.

MULTIPLE SECTION MOBILE UNIT. A structure formed by the mechanical and electrical coupling together of two or more mobile units. *Power Corporation Act*, R.R.O. 1980, Reg. 794, s. 0.

MULTIPLE SUFFICIENT CAUSATION. Two legally relevant causes, each alone sufficient to cause an injury or loss and each required (in a but for sense) if the other were absent, combine to originate an injury or loss. K.D. Cooper-Stephenson & I.B. Saunders, *Personal Injury Damages in Canada* (Toronto: Carswell, 1981) at 653.

MULTIPLE UNIT DWELLING. A building so constructed, altered or used as to provide accommodation for more than one family to dwell in separately; and includes, (i.) flats, (ii.) semi-detached housing, (iii.) duplex and multiplex housing, (iv.) row housing, (v.) condominium housing, and (vi.) residence apartment buildings but not apartment hotels, except that all communal areas in such buildings shall be regarded as public. *Ontario Water Resources Act*, R.R.O. 1980, Reg. 736, s. 1.

MULTIPLE USE PLAN. A plan approved by the regional manager for the coordinated and integrated use of the natural resources of an area of Crown land. *Range Act*, R.S.B.C. 1979, c. 355, s. 1.

MULTIPLICATA TRANSGRESSIONE, CRESCAT POENAE INFLICTIO. [L.] As wrongdoing multiplies, the inflicting of punishment increases.

MULTIPLICITY. *n.* Excessive division or fracture of one cause or suit.

MULTIPLIER BREEDING FLOCK. A flock of poultry comprising only the first generation of primary breeding flock and used only to produce commercial chicks. *Hatchery Regulations*, C.R.C., c. 1023, s. 2.

MULTIPLIER METHOD. Calculation of loss by multiplying the number of years a loss will last (the multiplier) by lost annual income (the multiplicand). K.D. Cooper-Stephenson & I.B. Saunders, *Personal Injury Damages in Canada* (Toronto: Carswell, 1981) at 72.

MULTI-PURPOSE PASSENGER VEHICLE. A vehicle that has a seating capacity of 10 or less and is constructed on a truck-chassis or with special features for off-highway operation, but does not include an air cushion vehicle, an all terrain vehicle, a passenger car or a truck.

MULTI-SERVICE ARTICLE. Any container or eating utensil that is intended for repeated use in the service of food. *Public Health Act*, R.R.O. 1980, Reg. 840, s. 1.

MULTITUDINEM DECEM FACIUNT. [L.] Ten constitutes a multitude.

MULTITUDO ERRANTIUM NON PARIT ERRORI PATROCINIUM. [L.] That many people make a mistake does not excuse the error.

MULTITUDO IMPERITORUM PERDIT CURIAM. [L.] A crowd of masters ruins a court.

MULTI-UNION BARGAINING. Collective bargaining involving more than one union.

MULTI-WINDING MOTOR. A motor having multiple windings or tapped windings, or both, designed for connection or reconnection in more than one configuration to operate at speeds and voltages respective to the configurations. *Power Corporation Act*, R.R.O. 1980, Reg. 794, s. 0.

MULTI-WIRE BRANCH CIRCUIT. A branch circuit consisting of two or more ungrounded conductors having a voltage difference between them, and an identified grounded conductor having equal voltage between it and each ungrounded conductor with the identified grounded conductor connected to the neutral conductor. *Power Corporation Act*, R.R.O. 1980, Reg. 794, s. 0.

MULTI-YEAR CONTRACT. An agreement which covers a period of two or more years.

MULTI ZONE WELL. A well that may be used for segregated production from, or segregated injection to, more than one zone or pool through the same well. *Petroleum or Natural Gas Act*, R.S.B.C. 1979, c. 323, s. 1.

MUMMIFICATION. *n.* Exposure of a dead body or its parts to a warm, dry environment so that it dries to a leathery, brown parchment-like condition. F.A. Jaffe, *A Guide to Pathological Evidence*, 2d ed. (Toronto: Carswell, 1983) at 180.

MUN. *abbr.* 1. Municipal. 2. Municipality.

MUN. CT. *abbr.* Municipal Court.

MUNICIPAL. *adj.* Related to a municipal corporation.

MUNICIPAL ADMINISTRATOR. See URBAN ~.

MUNICIPAL AGENCY. An agency, board, school board, commission, foundation, corporation, hospital or a welfare, penal or other institution established by or on behalf of or controlled by a municipal unit or two or more municipal units. *Ombudsman Act*, S.N.S. 1970-71, c. 3, s. 2.

MUNICIPAL ASSESSMENT BASE. (a) The total assessed value of all real property and business assessment liable to taxation under the Assessment Act in a municipality excluding (i) real property owned by the municipality, (ii) real property of utility commissions owned by the municipality, (b) the assessed value of all real property owned by the Crown in right of New Brunswick upon which payments in lieu of taxes are made, (c) the proportion of the assessed value of real property owned by the Crown in right of Canada that the payment in lieu of taxes made in respect of that property is of the taxes that would have been paid on that property if it were subject to taxation, (d) the assessed value of real property used primarily for educational purposes and owned by private schools providing elementary or secondary education, and (e) the assessed value of real property used primarily for educational purposes and owned by universities and affiliated colleges, less any reductions determined by a committee under section 8. *Municipal Assistance Act*, R.S.N.B. 1973, c. M-19, s. 1.

MUNICIPAL ASSESSMENT PER CAPITA. The quotient resulting from dividing the municipal assessment base of a municipality by the population of the municipality. *Municipal Assistance Act*, R.S.N.B. 1973, c. M-19, s. 1.

MUNICIPAL ASSESSMENT PER ROAD KILOMETRE. The quotient resulting from dividing the municipal assessment base of a municipality by the road kilometres of the municipality. *Metric Conversion Act*, S.N.B. 1977, c. M-11.1, s. 18.

MUNICIPAL ASSESSMENT PER ROAD MILE. The quotient resulting from dividing the municipal assessment base of a municipality by the road mileage of the municipality. *Municipal Assistance Act*, R.S.N.B. 1973, c. M-19, s. 1.

MUNICIPAL ASSISTANCE. Assistance provided by a municipality to a person in need who is a resident of, or found in, the municipality. *Municipal Act*, S.M. 1972, c. 42, s. 17.

MUNICIPAL AUTHORITY. 1. A municipal corporation or commission distributing electrical power or energy in a municipality. *Power Corporation Insurance Act*, R.S.O. 1980, c. 385, s. 1. 2. A hamlet, village, town, city, rural municipality or local improvement district or a northern community area in the Northern Saskatchewan Administration District. *The Provincial Parks, Protected Areas, Recreation Sites and Antiquities Act*, R.S.S. 1978, c. P-34, s. 2. See RURAL ~.

MUNICIPAL BUDGET. See NET ~.

MUNICIPAL CLERK. 1. The clerk of a municipality. 2. The clerk of a city or town or the secretary treasurer of a village. Saskatchewan statutes. 3. As applied to an officer of a municipal corporation, means a clerk or secretary of a municipal corporation, and includes a secretary-treasurer where the offices of clerk and treasurer are combined, and acting clerk or acting secretary-treasurer, or visa versa. *Interpretation Act*, R.S.M. 1970, c. 180, s. 23.

MUNICIPAL COMMISSION. 1. A hydro-electric commission or public utilities commission, entrusted with the control and management of works for the retail distribution and supply of power. 2. Municipal corporation or municipal commission or the trustees of a police village supplying power that is supplied to it or them by the Corporation. *Power Corporation Amendment Act, 1981 (No. 2)*, S.O. 1981, c. 41, s. 2.

MUNICIPAL CORPORATION. 1. The legal entity established under legislation which is distinct from residents, ratepayers or members of municipal council and which transacts the business of a municipality. 2. Any body entrusted with the administration of a territory for municipal purposes. Quebec statutes.

MUNICIPAL COUNCIL. The council of a municipality.

MUNICIPAL ELECTORS. The persons entitled to vote at a municipal election. *Municipal Act*, R.S.O. 1980, c. 302, s. 1.

MUNICIPAL EMPLOYEE. 1. A person who is in receipt of or entitled to any remuneration for labour or services performed for a northern municipality. *Northern Municipalities Amendment Act*, S.S. 1984-85-86, c. 68, s. 3. 2. A person who is employed or appointed by the council of a municipality, or by the board of a school district or regional district, and who is designated by the council or board, as the case may be, to be a municipal employee. *Financial Disclosure Act*, R.S.B.C. 1979, c. 130, s. 1.

MUNICIPAL ENGINEER. Includes a person authorized or required by the council to perform any duty that under this Act is to be or may be performed by an engineer. *The Local Improvements Act*, R.S.S. 1978, c. L-33, s. 2.

MUNICIPAL ENTERPRISE. Any body corporate the borrowings of which are or may be guaranteed by a municipality, any body corporate to which a municipality may lend money, and any body corporate the deficit of which is or may be paid by a municipality. *Municipal Finance Corporation Act*, S.N.S. 1978-79, c. 5, s. 2.

MUNICIPAL GOVERNMENT. A body subordinate to national authority with legislative power over a local territory. P.W. Hogg, *Constitutional Law of Canada*, 2d ed. (Toronto: Carswell, 1985) at 80.

MUNICIPAL GRANT BASE. See UNADJUSTED ~.

MUNICIPAL HERITAGE PROPERTY. A building, streetscape or area registered in a municipal registry of heritage property. *Heritage Property Act*, S.N.S. 1979-80, c. 8, s. 2.

MUNICIPALITY. *n.* 1. A locality the inhabitants of which are incorporated. 2. Includes the corporation of a city, town, village, county, township, parish or other territorial or local division of a province, the inhabitants of which are incorporated or are entitled to hold property collectively for a public purpose. *Criminal Code*, R.S.C. 1985, c. C-46, s. 2. 3. An incorporated city, metropolitan authority, town, village, township, district or rural municipality or other incorporated municipal body however designated, and includes any other local government body that is established by or under a law of a province and that is prescribed for the purposes of this Act as a municipality. *Canada Assistance Plan*, R.S.C. 1985, c. C-1, s. 2. 4. An area under the jurisdiction of a municipal council. See COUNTY ~; DISTRICT ~; FOUNDATION ~; LOCAL ~; LOWER TIER ~; MEMBER ~; REGIONAL ~; RURAL ~; SCHOOL ~; UPPER TIER ~; URBAN ~.

MUNICIPAL JAIL. A place of confinement for the custody of persons sentenced to imprisonment for infractions of the bylaws of a municipality or charged with such infractions. *Jails Act*, R.S.P.E.I. 1974, c. J-1, s. 1.

MUNICIPAL LAW. 1. Law relating to municipal corporations and their government. 2. Law relating exclusively to the citizens and inhabitants of a country, differing thus from the law of nations and political law.

MUNICIPAL MARKET. Any public market maintained by a municipal corporation. Canada regulations.

MUNICIPAL MEMBER. In relation to a board of health, means a person appointed to the board of health by the council of a municipality. *Health Protection and Promotion Act, 1983*, S.O. 1983, c. 10, s. 2.

MUNICIPAL OFFICER. The auditor (vérificateur) of a municipality within the meaning of this act. *Municipal Officers Dismissal Act*, R.S.Q. 1977, c. D-6, s. 1.

MUNICIPAL OFFICIAL. (i) A municipal commissioner, manager, secretary, treasurer, assessor, solicitor, comptroller, engineer and any other official appointed by resolution or by by-law of the council, and (ii) the holder of any other position or office designated as such by the council. *Municipal Government Act*, R.S.A. 1980, c. M-26, s. 1.

MUNICIPAL ORGANIZATION. See TERRITORY WITHOUT ~.

MUNICIPAL PURPOSE. A household and sanitary purpose, the watering of animals, streets, walks, paths, boulevards, lawns and gardens, fire protection and the flushing of sewers, and includes the construction of buildings and of civic works, and other purposes usually served by water within a city, town or village.

MUNICIPAL RESIDENTIAL PREMISES. Premises that are supplied individually with power by a municipal commission and that the Corporation decides are used for residential purposes on a year-round basis. *Power Corporation Amendment Act, 1981 (No. 2)*, S.O. 1981, c. 41, s. 2.

MUNICIPAL SECRETARY. (i) In a city, the city clerk, (ii) in an improvement district or special area, the Minister of Municipal Affairs or an officer of the Department of Municipal Affairs designated by him, or (iii) in any other municipality, the person appointed by the council as municipal secretary. *Agricultural Pests Act*, S.A. 1984, c. A-8.1, s. 1.

MUNICIPAL SECURITIES. Bonds, debentures, notes or other evidences of indebtedness of or guaranteed by any municipal corporation in Canada. *Cooperative Credit Associations Act*, R.S.C. 1985, c. C-41, s. 49.

MUNICIPAL SERVICE. The water, sewer, police, fire protection, recreation, cultural activities, roads, garbage removal and disposal, lighting, snow removal or septic tank cleaning service supplied by a municipality or a municipal corporation.

MUNICIPAL SEWERAGE CORPORATION. A corporation established for the purpose of constructing and operating facilities for the collection and treatment of sewage from one or more municipalities. *National Housing Act*, S.C. 1974-75-76, c. 38, s. 16.

MUNICIPAL SITE. As the case may require, (i) an area or a place, or (ii) a parcel of land, or (iii) a building or structure, or (iv) an exterior or interior portion or segment of a building or structure, within a municipality, whether it is privately owned or owned by the municipality. *The Heritage Resources Act*, S.M. 1985-86, c. 10, s. 1.

MUNICIPAL TAX. 1. All taxes assessed against lands and levied by or through a municipality. 2. (i) Taxes for municipal and school purposes levied in respect of real property in Ontario that is assessed as residential or farm property, (ii) taxes levied for local improvements to real property in Ontario, (iii) taxes levied under the Provincial Land Tax Act or the Local Roads Boards Act, and (iv) such other taxes or special rates as are prescribed in the regulations, but "municipal tax" does not include any tax or rate that was payable prior to the 1st day of January, 1972. *Income Tax Act*, R.S.O. 1980, c. 213, s. 7.

MUNICIPAL TAX BASE. The amount computed on or before October 15 or as soon thereafter as is practicable of the year previous to the year in respect of which the unconditional grant is computed as (a) the total assessed value of all real property liable to taxation under the Assessment Act in a municipality, excluding (i) real property owned by the municipality, (ii) real property of utility commissions owned by the municipality, and (iii) real property referred to in paragraph (b.1) of the definition "real property" under the Assessment Act; (b) the assessed value of all real property in a municipality owned by the Crown in right of New Brunswick; (c) the assessed value of real property in a municipality owned by the Crown in right of Canada; and (d) one-half of the assessed value of any real property in a municipality referred to in paragraphs (a), (b) and (c) that is "non-residential property" as defined under section 1 of the Assessment Act. *An Act to Amend the Municipal Assistance Act*, S.N.B. 1987, c. 39, s. 1.

MUNICIPAL TAX BASE PER CAPITA. The quotient resulting from dividing the municipal tax base of a municipality by the population of the municipality. *An Act to Amend the Municipal Assistance Act*, S.N.B. 1986, c. 58, s. 1.

MUNICIPAL TAX BASE PER ROAD KILOMETRE. The quotient resulting from dividing the municipal tax base of a municipality by the road kilometres of the municipality. *An Act to Amend the Municipal Assistance Act*, S.N.B. 1986, c. 58, s. 1.

MUNICIPAL TELEPHONE SYSTEM. A telephone system, other than a public utility, established by by-law of a municipality under a predecessor of this Act. *Telephone Act*, R.S.O. 1980, c. 496, s. 1.

MUNICIPAL TRANSIT CORPORATION. A corporation having jurisdiction over the territory of one municipality alone. *Municipal and Intermunicipal Transit Corporations Act*, R.S.Q. 1977, c. C-70, s. 1.

MUNICIPAL UNIT. A city, town, municipality or village.

MUNICIPAL UTILITY. Any water lines, sanitary or storm sewer lines, or water, waste management or sanitary or storm sewerage plants or facilities that are owned by a municipality or jointly owned by 2 or more municipalities. *Regional Municipal Services Act*, S.A. 1981, c. R-9.1, s. 11.

MUNICIPAL WASTE MANAGEMENT SYSTEM. A waste management system, or any part thereof, of which a municipality is the owner. *Environmental Protection Act*, R.R.O. 1980, Reg. 309, s. 1.

MUNIMENT. *n.* A record; defence; a written document upon which one establishes a right or claim and depends; evidence.

MUNITIONS OF WAR. Arms, ammunition, implements or munitions of war, military stores or any articles deemed capable of being converted thereunto or made useful in the production thereof. *Official Secrets Act*, R.S.C. 1985, c. O-5, s. 2.

MURAL THROMBUS. A thrombus attached to the heart chamber or a blood vessel's wall. F.A. Jaffe, *A Guide to Pathological Evidence*, 2d ed. (Toronto: Carswell, 1983) at 185.

MURDER. *n.* 1. Culpable homicide is murder (a) where the person who causes the death of a human being (i) means to cause his death, or (ii) means to cause him bodily harm that he knows is likely to cause his death, and is reckless whether death ensues or not; (b) where a person, meaning to cause death to a human being or meaning to cause him bodily harm that he knows is likely to cause his death, and being reckless whether death ensues or not, by accident or mistake causes death to another human being, notwithstanding that he does not mean to cause death or bodily harm to that human being; or (c) where a person, for an unlawful object, does anything that he knows or ought to know is likely to cause death, and thereby causes death to a human being, notwithstanding that he desires to effect his object without causing death or bodily harm to any human being. *Criminal Code*, R.S.C. 1985, c. C-46, s. 229. 2. Culpable homicide is murder when committed while committing or attempting to commit certain offences if certain conditions are met. *Criminal Code*, R.S.C. 1985, c. C-46, s. 230. See CAPITAL ~; CLASSIFICATION OF ~; FIRST DEGREE ~; ~ IN COMMISSION OF OFFENCES; NON-CAPITAL ~; SECOND DEGREE ~; SELF-~.

MURDER IN COMMISSION OF OFFENCES. Culpable homicide is murder where a person causes the death of a human being while committing or attempting to commit high treason or treason or sabotage, piracy, hijacking an aircraft, escape or rescue from prison or lawful custody, assaulting a peace officer, resisting lawful arrest, sexual assault, kidnapping, forcible confinement, hostage taking, breaking and entering, robbery, or arson whether or not the person means to cause death to any human being and whether or not he knows that death is likely to be caused to any human being, if (a) he means to cause bodily harm for the purpose of (i) facilitating the commission of the offence, or (ii) facilitating his flight after committing or attempting to commit the offence, and the death ensues from the bodily harm; (b) he administers a stupefying or overpowering thing for a purpose mentioned in paragraph (a), and the death ensues therefrom; (c) he wilfully stops, by any means, the breath of a human being for a purpose mentioned in paragraph (a), and the death ensues therefrom; or (d) he uses a weapon or has it upon his person (i) during or at the time he commits or attempts to commit the offence, or (ii) during or at the time of his flight after committing or attempting to commit the offence, and the death ensues as a consequence. *Criminal Code*, R.S.C. 1985, c. C-46, s. 230.

MUSEUM. *n.* An institution that, (i) is established for the purpose of conserving, studying, interpreting, assembling and exhibiting to the public for its instruction and enjoyment objects and specimens of educational and cultural value including historical, technological, anthropological or scientific material or (ii) an art museum. See NATIONAL ~S OF CANADA; PUBLIC ~.

MUSHROOMS. See BUTTON ~; CANNED ~.

MUSICAL WORK. Any combination of melody and harmony, or either of them, printed, reduced to writing or otherwise graphically produced or reproduced. *Copyright Act*, R.S.C. 1985, c. C-42, s. 2. See EVERY ORIGINAL LITERARY, DRAMATIC, MUSICAL AND ARTISTIC WORK.

MUSKRAT RANCH. An area where muskrats are raised or kept or raised and kept in their natural habitat under the direct supervision of any person. *Wildlife Act*, R.S.M. 1970, c. W140, s. 2.

MUTATIS MUTANDIS. [L.] With needed changes in the details.

MUTILATION. *n.* Depriving of any necessary part or limb.

MUTINY. *n.* Collective insubordination or a combination of two or more persons in the resistance of lawful authority in any of Her Majesty's Forces or in any forces cooperating therewith. *National Defence Act*, R.S.C. 1985, c. N-5, s. 2.

MUTTON CARCASS. The carcass of an animal

of the sheep species, of either sex, more than twelve months of age, having two smooth hard white ridges where the feet are severed at the ankle (spool) joint and bones somewhat whiter and harder than those in a lamb carcass.

MUTUAL ASSOCIATION. A mutual insurance association and a mutual benefit association. *An Act to Amend the Act Respecting Insurance and Other Legislation*, S.Q. 1985, c. 17, s. 1.

MUTUAL BENEFITS. Amounts paid to or benefits conferred upon persons who are members of a group or to or upon members of their families in case of misfortune, sickness, accident or death, out of the premiums, assessments, gifts or subscriptions from persons who are members of that group. *Insurance Act*, R.S.Q. 1977, c. A-32, s. 1.

MUTUAL BENEFIT SOCIETY. A mutual company formed for the purpose of providing sick and funeral benefits for its members or for this and any other purposes necessary or incidental thereto except life insurance. See EMPLOYEES' ~.

MUTUAL COMPANY. A company empowered solely to transact mutual insurance.

MUTUAL CORPORATION. A corporation without share capital that is empowered to undertake mutual insurance exclusively. *Insurance Act*, R.S.O. 1980, c. 218, s. 1.

MUTUAL FUND. 1. Includes an issuer of a security that entitles the holder to receive on demand, or within a specified period after demand, an amount computed by reference to the value of a proportionate interest in the whole or in a part of the net assets, including a separate fund or trust account, of the issuer of the security. 2. A company issuing shares which must, on request of the holder, redeem them at their net asset value. *Securities Act*, S.Q. 1982, c. 48, s. 5. 3. A fund established by a corporation duly authorized to operate a fund in which moneys from two or more depositors are accepted for investment and where shares allocated to each depositor serve to establish at any time the proportionate interest of each depositor in the assets of the fund. *Pension Benefits Standards Regulations*, C.R.C., c. 1252, s. 2. See OPEN-END ~; PRIVATE ~; RELATED ~S.

MUTUAL FUND CORPORATION. A company that offers public participation in an investment portfolio through the issue of one or more classes of mutual fund shares.

MUTUAL FUND DISTRIBUTOR. A person distributing a security under a distribution contract. *Securities Act*, S.B.C. 1985, c. 83, s. 1.

MUTUAL FUND IN THE PROVINCE. A mutual fund that is (a) a reporting issuer, or (b) organized under the laws of the province, but does not include a private mutual fund.

MUTUAL FUND MANAGER. A person who provides investment advice under a management contract. *Securities Act*, S.B.C. 1985, c. 83, s. 1.

MUTUAL FUND SALES OR MANAGEMENT CORPORATION. A company incorporated to provide a mutual fund corporation with advisory, management or sales distribution services. *Loan and Trust Corporations Act*, R.R.O. 1980, Reg. 593, s. 1.

MUTUAL FUND SHARE. A share having conditions attached thereto that include conditions requiring the company issuing the share to accept, at the demand of the holder thereof and at prices determined and payable in accordance with the conditions, the surrender of the share, or fractions or parts thereof, that are fully paid.

MUTUAL INSURANCE. A contract of insurance, in which the consideration is not fixed or certain at the time the contract is made but is to be determined at the termination of the contract or at fixed periods during the term of the contract according to the experience of the insurer in respect of all similar contracts whether or not the maximum amount of such consideration is predetermined. Insurance acts.

MUTUAL INSURANCE COMPANY. 1. A company without share capital or with guarantee capital stock subject to repayment by the company, in respect of which the dividend rate is limited by its act or instrument of incorporation, which is empowered to undertake mutual insurance exclusively. *Insurance Adjusters, Agents and Brokers Act*, S.Nfld. 1986, c. 36, s. 48. 2. A corporation without share capital that provides insurance on the mutual plan. *The Saskatchewan Insurance Act*, R.S.S. 1978, c. S-26, s. 2. 3. A mutual life-insurance company and a mutual damage-insurance company. *An Act to Amend the Act Respecting Insurance and Other Legislation*, S.Q. 1985, c. 17, s. 1.

MUTUAL INSURANCE CORPORATION. A corporation without share capital or with guarantee capital stock subject to repayment by the corporation, in respect of which the dividend rate is limited by its Act or instrument of incorporation, that is empowered to undertake mutual insurance exclusively. *Insurance Act*, R.S.N.B. 1973, c. I-12, s. 1.

MUTUALITY OF ASSENT. Regarding the main or necessary part of any agreement, for each party to intend the same thing and to know what the other will do.

MUTUALITY OF OBLIGATION. For each party to an agreement to be bound to do something.

MUTUALITY OF REMEDY. For each party to an agreement to be able to enforce that agreement against the other.

MUTUAL PROMISES. Simultaneous considerations which support each other.

MUTUAL WILLS. Wills made by two people reciprocally leaving their effects to the survivor.

MUTUEL FIELD. Two or more horses that are entered in a race and are coupled in the betting because the number of horses in the race exceeds the number that can be handled separately by the pari-mutuel system. *Race Track Supervision Regulations*, C.R.C., c. 441, s. 2.

MUTUEL MANAGER. A person designated by an association to be responsible for the general operation of the pari-mutuel department. *Race Track Supervision Regulations*, C.R.C., c. 441, s. 2.

MUZZLE. *v.* To secure a dog's mouth in such a fashion that it cannot bite anything. *Dog Act*, R.S.N.W.T. 1974, c. D-8, s. 2.

MUZZLE. *n.* The front end of a firearm's barrel. F.A. Jaffe, *A Guide to Pathological Evidence*, 2d ed. (Toronto: Carswell, 1983) at 180.

MUZZLE VELOCITY. The speed, expressed in feet or meters per second, at which a projectile leaves a firearm's barrel. F.A. Jaffe, *A Guide to Pathological Evidence*, 2d ed. (Toronto: Carswell, 1983) at 180.

M.V.R. *abbr.* Motor Vehicle Reports, 1979-1988.

M.V.R. (2D). *abbr.* Motor Vehicle Reports (Second Series), 1988-.

MYCOTIC ANEURYSM. An aneurysm caused when a blood vessel wall is weakened by infection. F.A. Jaffe, *A Guide to Pathological Evidence*, 2d ed. (Toronto: Carswell, 1983) at 168.

MYOCARDITIS. *n.* Inflammation of the muscle tissue of the heart. F.A. Jaffe, *A Guide to Pathological Evidence*, 2d ed. (Toronto: Carswell, 1983) at 46.

N. *abbr.* 1. Newton. 2. Nano.

NAC. *abbr.* National Arts Centre.

NAKED CONTRACT. A contract which lacks consideration.

NAM. *n.* The seizure or distraint of another person's goods.

NAME. *n.* A given name and surname. See BUSINESS ~; CHANGE OF ~; CHRISTIAN ~; CORPORATE ~; FAMILY ~; FIRM ~; GIVEN ~; GIVEN ~S; GRADE ~; NUMBER ~; PROPER ~; REGISTERED ~; SUR~ AND CHRISTIAN ~S; TRADE-~.

NAME A MEMBER. For example, a member is suspended from the service of the House not by order of the Speaker, but by vote of the House. A. Fraser, G.A. Birch & W.A. Dawson, eds., *Beauchesne's Rules and Forms of the House of Commons of Canada*, 5th ed. (Toronto: Carswell, 1978) at 13.

NAMED COMMODITY. Any of the following commodities produced in Canada: (a) cattle, hogs, lambs and wool; (b) industrial milk and industrial cream; (c) corn and soybeans; and (d) spring wheat, winter wheat, oats and barley not produced in the designated area as defined in the Canadian Wheat Board Act. *Agricultural Stabilization Act*, R.S.C. 1985 (1st Supp.), c. 40, s. 1.

NAMED INSURED. A person specified in a contract of insurance as the one protected by the contract.

NAMED PRINCIPAL. A party whose name was revealed by the agent to the third party. G.H.L. Fridman, *The Law of Agency*, 5th ed. (London: Butterworths, 1983) at 187.

NAME SIGN. A sign (i) that is erected on land adjacent to a highway; (ii) that is not more than 2 feet in height and not more than 3 feet in width; and (iii) that does not display or indicate any information or advertising thereon other than the name of the occupant of the land, his address and his trade, business, profession or calling. *Highways Protection Act*, R.S.M. 1970, c. H50, s. 2.

NAMIUM. *n.* 1. Distress. 2. The seizure or distraint of another person's goods.

NAMIUM VETITUM. The unjust seizure of another's cattle by driving them to an illegal place and pretending they had done damage.

NANNY. *n.* To rear a child who is a member of the household where the person is considered to be qualified to do so because of formal training or experience equivalent to formal training. *Employment Standards Act*, R.R.O. 1980, Reg. 283, s. 1.

NANO. *pref.* 10^{-9}. Prefix for multiples and submultiples of basic, supplementary and derived units of measurement. *Weights and Measures Act*, S.C. 1970-71-72, c. 36, schedule I.

NARCOTIC. *n.* 1. A drug which produces sleep, stupor and pain relief. F.A. Jaffe, *A Guide to Pathological Evidence*, 2d ed. (Toronto: Carswell, 1983) at 180. 2. Any substance included in the schedule or anything that contains any substance included in the schedule. *Narcotic Control Act*, R.S.C. 1985, c. N-1, s. 2. 3. Heroin (diacetyl morphine) and other derivatives of opium, methadone (6-dimethylamino-4, 4-diphenyl-3, heptanone), any substance with morphine like properties that is prescribed by regulation and anything that contains any of these substances. *Heroin Treatment Act*, R.S.B.C. 1979, c. 166, s. 1. See ORAL PRESCRIPTION ~.

NARCOTIC ADDICT. A person who, through the use of narcotics, (a) has developed a desire or need to continue to take a narcotic; or (b) has developed a psychological or physical dependence on the effect of a narcotic. *Narcotic Control Act*, R.S.C. 1985, c. N-1, s. 2.

NARROW FABRIC. A textile fibre product that is 12 inches or less in width and is ordinarily used as bindings or trimming. *Textile Labelling and Advertising Regulations*, C.R.C., c. 1551, s. 2.

NARROW-NECK GLASS STANDARD. A local standard of volume or capacity that is made of glass and that has, on the narrow-neck of the standard, a mark indicating its capacity. *Weights and Measures Regulations*, C.R.C., c. 1605, s. 53.

NARROW-NECK METAL STANDARD. A local standard of volume or capacity that is made of metal and that has, on the narrow-neck of the standard, a graduated plate adjacent to a window or adjacent to a gauge glass. *Weights and Measures Regulations*, C.R.C., c. 1605, s. 53.

NARWHAL. *n.* A cetacean (Monodon monoceros) of the dolphin family that inhabits the Arctic seas and includes its carcass and tusks. *Narwhal Protection Regulations*, C.R.C., c. 820, s. 2.

NASOPHARYNX. *n.* The part of the pharynx above the palate. F.A. Jaffe, *A Guide to Pathological Evidence*, 2d ed. (Toronto: Carswell, 1983) at 181.

NAT. BANKING L. REV. *abbr.* National Banking Law Review.

NAT. CREDITOR/DEBTOR REV. *abbr.* National Creditor/Debtor Review.

NAT. INSOLVENCY REV. *abbr.* National Insolvency Review.

NATION. *n.* People distinct from other people, usually because of language or government. See COMITY OF ~S; INTERNATIONAL LAW; LAW OF ~S; LEAGUE OF ~S.

NATIONAL. *n.* 1. An individual possessing the nationality of a state. 2. Any legal person, partnership and association deriving its status as such from the law in force in a state.

NATIONAL AMBIENT AIR QUALITY OBJECTIVE. Any objective prescribed pursuant to subsection 5(2). *Clean Air Act*, R.S.C. 1985, c. C-32, s. 2.

NATIONAL ARTS CENTRE. A federal corporation which operates the National Arts Centre in Ottawa and develops performing arts in the National Capital Region.

NATIONAL AVERAGE PROVINCIAL REVENUE RATE. For a revenue source for a fiscal year is the rate derived by dividing (a) the total revenue, as determined by the Minister, from that revenue source for all the provinces for the fiscal period prescribed in the case of that revenue source, by (b) the total revenue base, as determined by the Minister, for that revenue source for all the provinces for the fiscal period prescribed in the case of that revenue source. *Federal-Provincial Fiscal Arrangements Act*, R.S.C. 1970, c. F-6, s. 8.

NATIONAL AVERAGE RATE OF TAX. In respect of a revenue source it is the quotient obtained by dividing the aggregate of the revenues to be equalized for a revenue source for all provinces for a fiscal year by the revenue base for that revenue source for all provinces for that fiscal year. *Federal-Provincial Fiscal Arrangements Act*, R.S.C. 1985, c. F-8, s. 4(2).

NATIONAL BUILDING CODE OF CANADA. The National Building Code issued by the National Research Council.

NATIONAL CAPITAL COMMISSION. A federal body which promotes public use and enjoyment of land it controls in the National Capital Region.

NATIONAL CAPITAL REGION. The seat of the Government of Canada and its surrounding area, more particularly described in the schedule. *National Capital Act*, R.S.C. 1985, c. N-4, s. 2.

NATIONAL COMMODITY FUTURES EXAMINATION. An examination relating to the commodity futures industry that has been prepared by the Chicago Board of Trade and is administered in the United States of America by the National Association of Securities Dealers, Inc. and is administered in Canada by the Canadian Securities Institute. *Commodity Futures Act*, R.R.O. 1980, Reg. 114, s. 7.

NATIONAL COMPANY. The Canadian National Railway Company continued by this Act. *Canadian National Railways Act*, R.S.C. 1985, c. C-19, s. 2.

NATIONAL DEBT. Money which a national government owes and on which interest is paid.

NATIONAL ENERGY BOARD. A federal body which regulates certain areas of the gas, oil and electrical industry and advises government on developing and using energy resources.

NATIONAL FILM BOARD. A federal body which produces and distributes films which interpret Canada for Canadians and non-Canadians.

NATIONAL FIRE PREVENTION ASSOCIATION. A standards setting body in the United States some of whose standards are referred to or have been adopted in Ontario statutes, *e.g.,* the Fire Code under the Fire Marshals Act. D. Robertson, *Ontario Health and Safety Guide* (Toronto: Richard De Boo Ltd., 1988) at 5-278.

NATIONALITY. *n.* The character or quality which originates in a person belonging to a particular nation and which determines that individual's political status. See DUAL ~.

NATIONALIZATION. *n.* The acquisition of a business by government.

NATIONAL LIBRARY. The Bibliothèque nationale du Québec. *An Act Respecting the Bibliothèque Nationale du Québec*, R.S.Q. 1977, c. B-2, s. 1.

NATIONAL LIBRARY OF CANADA. A federal body with mandate to acquire, preserve and make available the published heritage of Canada and to help all Canadian people share the country's library resources.

NATIONAL MUSEUMS OF CANADA. A federal body with mandate to display the products of nature and the work of people with special though not exclusive reference to Canada.

NATIONAL ORIGIN. 1. Includes nationality and ancestry. *Canada Labour Code Act*, R.S.C. 1970, c. L-1, s. 3. 2. Includes the national origin of an ancestor. *Human Rights Act*, S.M. 1974, c. 65, s. 1.

NATIONAL PARK. A national park established and maintained under the *National Parks Act*, R.S.C. 1970, c. N-13. See PROPOSED ~.

NATIONAL PAROLE BOARD. A federal body with exclusive authority and final discretion to grant a temporary absence with no escort or parole under the *Penitentiary Act*, to terminate or revoke day parole for inmates in federal institutions and inmates in provincial institutions in the Atlantic and Prairie provinces.

NATIONAL PER CAPITA REVENUE. The quotient obtained by dividing: (a) the total revenue to be equalized, as determined by the Minister, derived by all the provinces for a fiscal year from all revenue sources, by: (b) the total population for all the provinces for that fiscal year. *Federal-Provincial Fiscal Arrangements Act*, R.S.C. 1985, c. F-8, s. 4(7).

NATIONAL RAILWAYS. Comprises the Canadian Government Railways, Canadian National Railways and all the companies, not in Canada, mentioned or referred to in the schedule. *Canadian National Railways Act*, R.S.C. 1985, c. C-19, s. 2.

NATIONAL RATE OF UNEMPLOYMENT. The rate of unemployment as determined by Statistics Canada for the whole of Canada. *Unemployment Insurance Act*, R.S.C. 1985, c. U-1, s. 2.

NATIONAL RESEARCH COUNCIL. The National Research Council of Canada. *National Trade-mark and True Labelling Act*, R.S.C. 1985, c. N-18, s. 2.

NATIONAL RESEARCH COUNCIL OF CANADA. The federal body which carries out applied and basic research, studies topics of long-term national concern, offers laboratory support in important technological areas, manages programs of industrial development, administers national facilities for the scientific community and coordinates a national network for scientific and technological information.

NATIONAL TRADE-MARK. 1. The national trade-mark established by this Act. *National Trade-mark and True Labelling Act*, R.S.C. 1985, c. N-18, s. 2. 2. The words "Canada Standard" or the initials "C.S.". Canada regulations.

NATIONAL TREATMENT. Dealing with a foreigner in the same way as a national of one's own country.

NATIVE COMMUNITY. A community designated by the Minister under section 192 of Part X (Indian and Native Child and Family Services). *Child and Family Services Act*, S.O. 1984, c. 55, s. 3.

NATIVE PERSON. 1. A person who is a member of a native community but is not a member of a band. *Child and Family Services Act*, S.O. 1984, c. 55, s. 3. 2. A person who represents himself to be (a) a Canadian Status Indian, (b) a Canadian Non Status Indian, (c) a Canadian Inuk, (d) a Canadian Métis, and who is settled in the Yukon Territory or the Northwest Territories. *Northern Careers Appointments Regulations*, C.R.C., c. 1346, s. 2.

NAT. LABOUR REV. *abbr.* National Labour Review.

NAT'L BANKING L. REV. *abbr.* National Banking Law Review.

NAT'L INSOLV. REV. *abbr.* National Insolvency Review.

NAT. PROPERTY REV. *abbr.* National Property Review.

NATURAE VIS MAXIMA. [L.] Natural force is very great.

NATURAL AFFECTION. The love which someone has for kin, held to be not a valuable but a good consideration in certain circumstances.

NATURAL AREA. Land designated as a natural area under section 12.1. *Wilderness Areas Act, 1981*, S.A. 1981, c. 76, s. 4.

NATURAL-BORN SUBJECT. A person born within the Crown's dominion and the sovereign's allegiance.

NATURAL BOUNDARY. The visible high water mark of any lake, river, stream or other body of water where the presence and action of the water are so common and usual, and so long continued in all ordinary years, as to mark on the soil of the bed of the body of water a character distinct from that of its banks, in vegetation, as well as in the nature of the soil itself. *Land Act*, R.S.B.C. 1979, c. 214, s. 1.

NATURAL CHILD. A child of one's body; a child in fact.

NATURAL DISASTER. Major damage caused by certain elements or disturbances in nature, such as: (i) droughts, hurricanes, tornadoes, violent winds, earthquakes, landslides, electrical storms, excessive rains, floods, hail, frost, sleet and heavy snowstorms; (ii) uncontrollable fire of any origin; (iii) an insect plague beyond normal control seriously affecting a designated production; and (iv) plant and animal diseases, when their spread reaches epidemic proportions and seriously affects a designated production. *An Act to Promote Special Credit to Agricultural Producers During Critical Periods*, R.S.Q. 1977, c. C-79, s. 1.

NATURAL DISTRICT. A territory, a municipality or part of a municipality designated as such by the Gouvernement because of the aesthetic, legendary or scenic interest of its natural setting. *Cultural Property Act*, R.S.Q. 1977, c. B-4, s. 1.

NATURALE EST QUIDLIBET DISSOLVI EO MODO QUO LIGATUR. [L.] It is natural for something to be loosened the same way it was tied.

NATURAL ENVIRONMENT. Any part or combination of the air, land and water. See RESTORE THE ~.

NATURALES LIBERI. [L.] Natural children.

NATURAL GAS. A mixture, consisting principally of hydrocarbons that may contain non-hydrocarbon gases such as carbon dioxide, hydrogen sulphide, nitrogen or other elements, which mixture is recoverable from an underground reservoir and is in the gaseous phase or in solution with crude oil in the reservoir. See OIL, ~, OR SALT PRODUCTION EQUIPMENT.

NATURAL GAS LIQUID. Ethane, propane and butane, and any mixture of two or more thereof, that are produced at a gas processing plant or a gas reprocessing plant.

NATURAL HERITAGE OBJECT. A work of nature consisting of or containing evidence of flora or fauna or geological processes. *The Heritage Resources Act*, S.M. 1985-86, c. 10, s. 43(1).

NATURALIZATION. *var.* **NATURALISA-**

TION. *n.* The act of becoming the subject of a nation. See CERTIFICATE OF ~.

NATURAL JUSTICE. The basic requirements of procedure that the one who judges is neither interested nor biased and that the parties have enough notice and the chance to be heard. S.A. DeSmith, *Judicial Review of Administrative Action*, 4th ed., by J.M. Evans (London: Stevens, 1980) at 77 and 156.

NATURAL LAW. The code of rules which originates with the divine, nature or reason in contrast to laws people make.

NATURAL OBLIGATION. A duty with a definite purpose which is not necessarily governed by legal obligation.

NATURAL PERSON. A human being.

NATURAL PRODUCT. A product of agriculture or of the forest, sea, lake or river and an article of food or drink wholly or partly manufactured or derived from such product.

NATURAL RESERVOIR IN CANADA. Includes a natural reservoir situated in the submarine area adjacent to the coasts of Canada in respect of which the government of Canada or any province has granted a right, licence or privilege to explore, drill, take or remove minerals or hydrocarbons in any form. *Excise Tax Act*, R.S.C. 1985, c. E-15, s. 29.

NATURAL RESOURCES. 1. Land, plant life, animal life, water and air. 2. Land, water and atmosphere, their mineral, vegetable and other components, including flora and fauna. *Park Act*, R.S.B.C. 1979, c. 309, s. 1.

NATURAL RESOURCES AGREEMENT. An agreement made between Canada and one of the three prairie provinces which, by amendment to the Constitution Act in 1930, had overriding effect. P.W. Hogg, *Constitutional Law of Canada*, 2d ed. (Toronto: Carswell, 1985) at 562.

NATURAL SCIENCES AND ENGINEERING RESEARCH COUNCIL OF CANADA. The federal agency which offers financial support for advanced research and development in natural science and engineering at Canadian universities and encourages cooperation between industry and these institutions.

NATURAL STATE. The molecular form in which a hydrocarbon occurs in the reservoir under reservoir conditions, and includes any thermally agitated state of the molecule so long as its molecular structure is unaltered. *Bituminous Shale Act*, S.N.B. 1976, c. B-4.1, s. 1.

NATURAL USER. The use of land for most residential, recreational and industrial purposes. John G. Fleming, *The Law of Torts*, 6th ed.

(Sydney: The Law Book Co., 1983) at 308. See NON-~.

NATURAL WATER. Includes water that has been treated for the control of impurities in the interest of public health. *Retail Sales Tax Act*, R.R.O. 1980, Reg. 904, s. 1.

NATURAL WINE. Any alcoholic beverage obtained by the fermentation of the natural sugar content of fruits or other agricultural products, and that does not contain more than 14 per cent alcohol by volume. *Liquor Control Act*, R.S.M. 1970, c. L160, s. 2.

NATURA NON FACIT SALTUM; ITA NEC LEX. [L.] Nature does not leap; nor does the law.

NATURA NON FACIT VACUUM, NEC LEX SUPERVACUUM. [L.] Nature does nothing worthless, nor does the law do anything useless.

NATURE CONSERVANCY AREA. A roadless area, in a park, retained in a natural condition for the preservation of its ecological environment and scenic features, and designated as a nature conservancy area under this Act. *Park Act*, R.S.B.C. 1979, c. 309, s. 1.

NATUROPATH. *n.* A person who practises naturopathy. *Naturopathy Act*, R.S.A. 1970, c. 257, s. 2.

NATUROPATHIC PRACTITIONER. A person who is registered as such under this Act. *The Naturopathy Act*, R.S.S. 1978, c. N-4, s. 2.

NATUROPATHY. *n.* 1. A drugless system of therapy that treats human injuries, ailments, or diseases, by natural methods, including any one or more of the physical, mechanical, or material, forces or agencies of nature, and employs as auxiliaries for such purposes the use of electro-therapy, hydro-therapy, body manipulations, or dietetics. 2. The art of healing by natural methods or therapeutics and, without limiting the generality of the foregoing, for the purposes of this Act, shall be deemed to include the first aid treatment of minor cuts, abrasions and contusions, bandaging and the taking of blood samples. *Naturopaths Act*, R.S.B.C. 1979, c. 297, s. 1.

NAULAGE. *n.* The freight belonging to a ship's passengers.

NAVAL COURT. Any officer who commands a ship belonging to Her Majesty on any foreign station or any consular officer may hold such a court when a complaint which requires immediate investigation arises, when the owner's interest in any Canadian ship or cargo seems to require it or when a Canadian ship is abandoned, wrecked or lost. R.M. Fernandes & C.

Burke, *The Annotated Canada Shipping Act* (Toronto: Butterworths, 1988) at 213.

NAVIGABLE WATER. Includes a canal and any other body of water created or altered as a result of the construction of any work. *Navigable Waters Protection Act*, R.S.C. 1985, c. N-22, s. 2.

NAVIGATION. *n.* The operation of any ship, boat, tug, dredge or other vessel owned in New Brunswick, while such vessel is within the limits of the Province. *Workmen's Compensation Act*, R.S.N.B. 1973, c. W-13, s. 1. See AID TO ~; LAKE AND RIVER ~; SEASON ~.

NAVIGATION SEASON. The annual period designated by the authority and the corporation, which is appropriate to weather and ice conditions or vessel traffic demands, during which the seaway is open for navigation. *Seaway Regulations*, C.R.C., c. 1397, s. 2.

NAVY. *n.* A fleet, a group of ships.

N.B. *abbr.* 1. New Brunswick. 2. [L. nota bene] Observe.

NBC. *abbr.* National Building Code of Canada.

N.B. EQ. *abbr.* New Brunswick Equity Reports, 1894-1912.

N.B.L.L.C. *abbr.* New Brunswick Labour Law Cases.

N.B.R. *abbr.* New Brunswick Reports, 1825-1929.

N.B.R. (2d). *abbr.* New Brunswick Reports (Second Series), 1969-.

N.C.C. *abbr.* National Capital Commission.

NEAR. *adj.* In such proximity as may give rise to the possibility of physical, inductive or electrolytic interference. *Wire Crossings and Proximities Regulations*, C.R.C., c. 1195, s. 2.

NEAR BEER. Beer containing not more than 2.5 per cent absolute alcohol by volume. *Brewery Departmental Regulations*, C.R.C., c. 566, s. 2.

NEAREST RELATIVE. The person first described in this clause who is mentally competent and available: (i) the spouse; (ii) a son or daughter who has attained the age of majority; (iii) a parent or guardian; (iv) a brother or sister who has attained the age of majority; (v) any other of the next-of-kin who has attained the age of majority.

NEAR RELATIVE. 1. One of the following persons, namely, the wife, father, mother, grandfather, grandmother, child, grandchild, brother or sister of the seaman. *Canada Shipping Act*, R.S.C. 1985, c. S-9, s. 191. 2. A grandfather, grandmother, father, mother, son, daughter, husband, wife, brother, sister, half-brother or half-sister and includes the legal guardian of a minor and a committee having custody of the person of a patient under the *Patients Property Act. Mental Health Act*, R.S.B.C. 1979, c. 256, s. 1.

NEAT. See NET.

N.E.B. *abbr.* National Energy Board.

NECATION. *n.* Killing.

NECESSARIES. *n.* Goods suitable to the condition of life of infant or minor or other person, and to his actual requirements at the time of the sale and delivery. Sale of Goods acts.

NECESSARIES OF LIFE. Food, clothing, lodging and other means that at the time of death of an insured are available to the person claiming to be dependent upon the insured and reasonably necessary to the maintenance of life and to the continuation of the degree of health then enjoyed by the person so claiming. *The Automobile Accident Insurance Act*, R.S.S. 1978, c. A-35, s. 2.

NECESSARY CAUSE. A cause without which the loss or injury would not have happened. K.D. Cooper-Stephenson & I.B. Saunders, *Personal Injury Damages in Canada* (Toronto: Carswell, 1981) at 641.

NECESSITAS EST LEX TEMPORIS ET LOCI. [L.] Necessity is a law of time and place.

NECESSITAS INDUCIT PRIVILEGIUM QUOAD JURA PRIVATA. [L.] Necessity introduces privilege with respect to private rights.

NECESSITAS NON HABET LEGEM. [L.] Necessity does not submit to law.

NECESSITAS PUBLICA MAJOR EST QUAM PRIVATA. [L.] A public necessity is more important than a private one.

NECESSITAS QUOD COGIT DEFENDIT. [L.] Necessity defends whatever it collects.

NECESSITOUS FARMER. A farmer who by reason of circumstances beyond his control is unable out of his own resources to provide himself with any of the commodities that may be furnished to him pursuant to this Act. *Agricultural Relief Advances Act*, R.S.A. 1980, c. A-10, s. 1.

NECESSITY. *n.* 1. Action in an emergency to reasonably protect health, life or property when there is no alternative; an excuse from criminal liability. 2. A defence available when one interferes with the interests of another for the purpose of preventing harm to self or others if the threatened harm equals or is greater than the harm which one intends to inflict. A situation of imminent peril must exist. John G. Fleming,

The Law of Torts, 6th ed. (Sydney: The Law Book Co., 1983) at 87 and 89. See AGENCY OF ~; BASIC NECESSITIES.

NEC PER VIM, NEC CLAM, NEC PRECARIO. [L.] Neither by violence, nor stealth nor by request.

NECROPSY. *n.* An autopsy. F.A. Jaffe, *A Guide to Pathological Evidence*, 2d ed. (Toronto: Carswell, 1983) at 1.

NECROSIS. *n.* The death of cells in an organism which is alive. F.A. Jaffe, *A Guide to Pathological Evidence*, 2d ed. (Toronto: Carswell, 1983) at 180.

NEC TEMPUS NEC LOCUS OCCURRIT REGI. [L.] Neither time nor place oppose the monarch.

NEC VENIAM, EFFUSO SANGUINE, CASUS HABET. [L.] If blood is spilled, the case is unforgivable.

NEC VI, NEC CLAM, NEC PRECARIO. [L.] Neither by violence, nor stealth nor by request.

NEED. See FAMILY IN ~; PERSON IN ~; REASONABLE ~S; SPECIAL ~.

NE EXEAT PROVINCIA. [L.] A writ restraining a debtor from leaving the province.

NE EXEAT REGNO. [L.] A writ preventing a person from leaving the country without the court's leave.

NEGATIO CONCLUSIONIS EST ERROR IN LEGE. [L.] In law, the negation of a conclusion is an error.

NEGATIO DESTRUIT NEGATIONEM, ET AMBO FACIUNT AFFIRMATIVUM. [L.] Negative destroys negative, and together they make an affirmative.

NEGATIVE. *n.* Denial.

NEGATIVE DAMAGE. The removal of desirable things: amenities, earnings, enjoyment and expectation of life. K.D. Cooper-Stephenson & I.B. Saunders, *Personal Injury Damages in Canada* (Toronto: Carswell, 1981) at 52.

NEGATIVE OPTION SCHEME. An arrangement between a buyer and a seller under which the seller will, from time to time; (a) on notice to the buyer, supply the buyer with goods described in the notice, unless the buyer notifies the seller that he does not want to be supplied with the goods described in the notice; or (b) pursuant to the arrangement, supply the buyer with certain goods and the buyer will be deemed to have accepted the goods unless the buyer returns the goods to the seller. *Consumer Protection Act*, R.S.B.C. 1979, c. 65, s. 39.

NEGATIVE PREGNANT. In pleading, an evasive answer to something alleged, a literal answer but not an answer to substance.

NEGLECTED ADULT. An adult: (i) who is incapable of caring properly for himself by reason of physical or mental infirmity; (ii) who is not suitable to be in a treatment facility under *The Mental Health Act, 1971*, the Act No. 80 of 1971; (iii) who is not receiving proper care and attention; and (iv) who refuses, delays or is unable to make provision for proper care and attention for himself. *Neglected Adults Welfare Act*, S.Nfld. 1973, c. 81, s. 2.

NEGLECTED CHILD. A child in need of protection and without restricting the generality of the foregoing includes any child who is within one or more of the following descriptions: (i) a child who is not being properly cared for; (ii) a child who is abandoned or deserted by the person in whose charge that child is or who is an orphan who is not being properly cared for; (iii) a child when the person in whose charge that child is cannot, by reason of disease, infirmity, misfortune, incompetence or imprisonment, or any combination thereof, care properly for the child; (iv) a child who is living in an unfit or improper place; (v) a child found associating with an unfit or improper person; (vi) a child found begging in a public place; (vii) a child who, with the consent or connivance of the person in whose charge the child is, commits any act that renders the child liable to a penalty under an Act of Canada or of the Legislature, or under a municipal by-law; (viii) a child who is misdemeanant by reason of inadequacy of the control exercised by the person in whose charge the child is, or who is being allowed to grow up without salutory parental control or under circumstances tending to make the child idle or dissolute; (ix) a child who, without sufficient cause, habitually is away from home or school; (x) a child where the person in whose charge the child is neglects or refuses to provide or obtain proper medical, surgical or other medical care or treatment necessary for the child's health or well-being, or refuses to permit that care or treatment to be supplied to the child when it is recommended by a physician; (xi) a child whose emotional or mental development is endangered because of emotional rejection or deprivation of affection by the person in whose charge the child is; (xii) a child whose life, health or morals may be endangered by the conduct of the person in whose charge the child is; (xiii) a child who is being cared for by and at the expense of someone other than the child's parents and in circumstances which indicate that the child's parents are not performing their parental duties; (xiv) a child who is not under proper guardianship or who has no parent (A)

capable of exercising, (B) willing to exercise, or (C) capable of exercising and willing to exercise, proper parental control over the child; (xv) a child whose parent wishes to be rid of parental responsibilities toward the child.

NEGLIGENCE. *n.* 1. An independent tort which consists of breach of a legal duty to take care which results in damage, undesired by the defendant, to the plaintiff. 2. Conduct which does not meet the standard required to protect others from the unreasonable risk of harm. John G. Fleming, *The Law of Torts*, 6th ed. (Sydney: The Law Book Co., 1983) at 101. See CONTRIBUTORY ~; CRIMINAL ~; GROSS ~; MINOR ~.

NEGLIGENCE OF A MINOR CHARACTER. Negligence that does not involve recklessness, undue carelessness or intentional commission of a wrongful act or an intentional omission to perform a legal duty. *National Defence Claims Order, 1970*, C.R.C., c. 715, s. 2.

NEGLIGENTIA SEMPER HABET INFORTUNIUM COMITEM. [L.] Negligence always has the companion misfortune.

NEGLIGENT MISREPRESENTATION. A special relationship must exist in which the recipient has reasonable grounds to believe that the speaker expected to be relied upon when the statement complained of was made in order to establish the duty of care the breach of which gives rise to the cause of action. John G. Fleming, *The Law of Torts*, 6th ed. (Sydney: The Law Book Co., 1983) at 605.

NEGLIGENT OPERATION. Includes the operation of a vessel in a manner that unnecessarily or unreasonably interferes with the free and proper use of the waters by other craft or other persons, or that endangers other craft. *Hamilton Harbour Commissioners' General By-law*, C.R.C., c. 894, s. 20.

NEGLIGENT TORT. A tort in which the wrongdoer as a reasonable person should have foreseen that her or his conduct involved a risk which was foreseeable though not certain. John G. Fleming, *The Law of Torts*, 6th ed. (Sydney: The Law Book Co., 1983) at 71.

NEGOTIABILITY. *n.* Having in law the characteristics of current coin, except that coinage is the only legal tender. E.L.G. Tyler & N.E. Palmer, eds., *Crossley Vaines' Personal Property*, 5th ed. (London: Butterworths, 1973) at 208.

NEGOTIABLE INSTRUMENT. 1. Something which: (i) if payable to bearer, is transferable by delivery alone, or if payable to order, by delivery together with indorsement; (ii) presumes the giving of consideration; (iii) permits a transferee to take in good faith and for value to acquire good title despite lack of or defects in the transferor's title. E.L.G. Tyler & N.E. Palmer, eds., *Crossley Vaines' Personal Property*, 5th ed. (London: Butterworths, 1973) at 208. 2. Includes any cheque, draft, traveller's cheque, bill of exchange, postal note, money order, postal remittance and any other similar instrument.

NEGOTIABLE RECEIPT. A receipt in which it is stated that the goods therein specified will be delivered to bearer or to the order of a named person. Warehouse Receipts acts.

NEGOTIATE. *v.* 1. To transfer for value, by indorsement or delivery, a bill of exchange or other negotiable instrument. 2. To bargain in good faith with a view to the conclusion of an agreement or the revision or the renewal of an existing agreement.

NEGOTIATING RANGE. The limits within which a negotiator will make demands or concessions.

NEGOTIATION. *n.* 1. Transference of a bill from one person to another so that the transferee becomes the holder of the bill. E.L.G. Tyler & N.E. Palmer, eds., *Crossley Vaines' Personal Property*, 5th ed. (London: Butterworths, 1973) at 222. 2. Deliberation and discussion upon the terms of a proposed agreement, and includes conciliation and arbitration. See PLEA ~.

NEGOTIATOR. See GOVERNMENT ~.

NEGOTIORUM GESTIO. [L.] Interference in someone else's affairs out of kindness but with no authority.

NEIGHBOURHOOD IMPROVEMENT AREA. An area of a municipality for which the corporation has approved the implementation of a program to improve the quality of neighbourhood amenities and the housing and living conditions of persons of the area.

NEIGHBOUR TEST. The general formula for "duty" propounded by Lord Atkin in *Donoghue v. Stevenson*, [1932] A.C. 562, 580: "You must take reasonable care to avoid acts or omissions which you can reasonably foresee would be likely to injure your neighbour. Who, then, in law is my neighbour? The answer seems to be — persons who are so closely and directly affected by my act that I ought reasonably to have them in contemplation as being so affected when I am directing my mind to the acts or omissions which are called in question." John G. Fleming, *The Law of Torts*, 6th ed. (Sydney: The Law Book Co., 1983) at 130.

NE JUDEX ULTRA PETITA PARTIUM. [L.] No judge should award more than the party sought to obtain.

NEMATODE. See POTATO CYST ~.

NEM. CON. *abbr.* [L. nemine contradicente] Without anyone saying otherwise.

NEM. DIS. *abbr.* [L. nemine dissentiente] Without dissent.

NEMINE OPORTET ESSE SAPIENTIOREM LEGIBUS. [L.] No one should be wiser than the laws.

NEMO ADMITTENDUS EST INHABILITARE SEIPSUM. [L.] No one should be allowed to incapacitate oneself.

NEMO AGIT IN SEIPSUM. [L.] No one initiates proceedings against oneself.

NEMO ALIQUAM PARTEM RECTE INTELLIGERE POTEST ANTEQUAM TOTUM ITERUM ATQUE ITERUM PERLEGIT. [L.] No one can properly understand any part before one has read the whole thing over and over again.

NEMO ALLEGANS TURPITUDINEM SUAM EST AUDIENDUS. [L.] No one who pleads one's own guilt will be heard.

NEMO COGITUR REM SUAM VENDERE, ETIAM JUSTE PRETIO. [L.] No one is compelled to sell one's property, even for a fair price.

NEMO CONTRA FACTUM SUUM PROPRIUM VENIRE POTEST. [L.] No one can contradict one's very own deed.

NEMO DAT QUI NON HABET. [L.] No one who does not possess gives.

NEMO DAT QUOD NON HABET. [L.] No one gives what one does not possess.

NEMO DEBET BIS PUNIRI PRO UNO DELICTO. [L.] No one should be punished twice for one mistake.

NEMO DEBET BIS VEXARI, SI CONSTAT CURIAE QUOD SIT PRO UNA ET EADEM CAUSA. [L.] No man should be harassed twice, if the court agrees that it is for one and the same cause.

NEMO DEBET ESSE JUDEX IN PROPRIA CAUSA. [L.] No one should judge one's own cause.

NEMO DEBET LOCUPLETARI ALIENA JACTURA. [L.] No one should be enriched by another's loss.

NEMO DE DOMO SUA EXTRAHI DEBET. [L.] No one should be dragged out of one's own house.

NEMO EST HAERES VIVENTIS. [L.] No one is the heir of a living person.

NEMO EX ALTERIUS INCOMMODI DEBET LOCUPLETARI. [L.] No one should be enriched by another's misfortune.

NEMO EX DOLO SUO PROPRIO RELEVETUR, AUT AUXILIUM CAPIAT. [L.] No one is relieved or receives help out of one's very own fraud.

NEMO EX PROPRIO DOLO CONSEQUITUR ACTIONEM. [L.] No one pursues a cause of action out of one's very own fraud.

NEMO EX SUO DELICTO MELIOREM SUAM CONDITIONEM FACERE POTEST. [L.] No one can achieve a better personal position from one's own wrongdoing.

NEMO PATRIAM IN QUA NATUS EST EXUERE NEC LIGEANTIAE DEBITUM EJURARE POSSIT. [L.] No one can cast away the country where one was born, nor forswear the allegiance owed to the sovereign.

NEMO POTEST CONTRA RECORDUM VERIFICARE PER PATRIAM. [L.] No one can assume the verdict of a jury in any decision is correct.

NEMO POTEST ESSE SIMUL ACTOR ET JUDEX. [L.] No one can be suitor and judge at the same time.

NEMO POTEST ESSE TENENS ET DOMINUS. [L.] No one can be tenant and lord.

NEMO POTEST FACERE PER ALIUM, QUOD PER SE NON POTEST. [L.] No one can do through another what it is not possible to do alone.

NEMO POTEST MUTARE CONSILIUM SUUM IN ALTERIUS INJURIAM. [L.] No one can change intention to the wrong of another.

NEMO POTEST PLUS JURIS AD ALIUM TRANSFERRE QUAM IPSE HABET. [L.] No one can give another a greater right than one oneself has.

NEMO PRAESUMITUR ALIENAM POSTERITATEM SUAE PRAETULISSE. [L.] No one is presumed to have preferred another's descendants to one's own.

NEMO PRAESUMITUR ESSE IMMEMOR SUAE AETERNAE SALUTIS, ET MAXIME IN ARTICULO MORTIS. [L.] No one is presumed to be forgetful of one's own eternal wellbeing, and especially at the moment of death.

NEMO PRAESUMITUR MALUS. [L.] No one is considered bad in advance.

NEMO PROHIBETUR PLURIBUS DEFENSIONIBUS UTI. [L.] No one is prohibited from using many defences.

NEMO PUNITUR PRO ALIENO DELICTO. [L.] No one is punished for another's fault.

NEMO PUNITUR SINE INJURIA, FACTO, SEU DEFALTA. [L.] No one is punished except for a wrong, deed or default.

NEMO SIBI ESSE JUDEX VEL SUIS JUS DICERE DEBET. [L.] No one should be one's own judge, or decide matters of personal interest.

NEMO TENETUR AD IMPOSSIBILIA. [L.] No one is bound to do the impossible.

NEMO TENETUR ARMARE ADVERSARIUM CONTRA SE. [L.] No one is bound to arm an adversary against oneself.

NEMO TENETUR PRODERE SEIPSUM. [L.] No one is bound to betray oneself.

NEMO TENETUR SEIPSUM ACCUSARE. [L.] No one is bound to incriminate oneself.

NEONATAL DEATH. The death of a child before it is 28 days old. *Public Hospitals Act*, R.R.O. 1980, Reg. 865, s. 1.

NEPHEW. *n.* The son of a sister or brother, a half-sister or half-brother.

NEPOTISM. *n.* The practice of favouring relatives of the employer or management in hiring, in giving benefits or promotions.

NE RELESSE PAS. [Fr.] One did not release.

NERVOUS AILMENTS. See PRIVATE HOSPITAL FOR ~.

NERVOUS SHOCK. Emotional distress accompanied by a harmful psychopathological or physical consequence like actual illness. K.D. Cooper-Stephenson & I.B. Saunders, *Personal Injury Damages in Canada* (Toronto: Carswell, 1981) at 554 and 555. See INTENTIONAL INFLICTION OF ~.

NET. *n.* 1. The weight of the commodity without its container. 2. In accounting, an amount of money after all specified expenditures or deductions are deducted. See BAG ~; BOX ~; COD ~; DIP ~; DRIFT ~; GILL ~; GROUNDFISH ~; HOOP ~; LANDING ~; OPEN RING ~; POUND ~; PURSE SEINE ~; SAFETY ~; SALMON ~; SCOTTISH RING ~; SEINE ~; SET ~; TRAMMEL ~; TRAP ~; TRAWL ~.

NET ALLOWANCE. That part of the foreign living allowance of an individual which does not exceed one-half of his net income. *An Act to Amend Certain Legislation to Give Effect to Government Budget Policy for the Fiscal Period, 1983-84*, S.Q. 1983, c. 44, s. 19.

NET ANNUAL INCOME. The annual receipts from the sale of each unit of a product less expenditures and depreciation. *Farm Income Stabilization Insurance Act*, R.S.Q. 1977, c. A-31, s. 1.

NET ASSESSMENT. The amount of the assessment after deducting the amount of any exemption. *Assessment Act*, R.S.N.S. 1967, c. 14, s. 1.

NETBACK GAS. Marketable gas sold and delivered pursuant to producer-shipper contracts under which the same shipper is the buyer, where the price payable to the producers for gas so delivered is calculated in accordance with a netback pricing formula, but does not include marketable gas sold and delivered pursuant to a producer-shipper contract under which the producer's obligation to deliver gas under the contract is preconditioned on his consent to the actual resale price or prices used in the netback pricing formula. *Natural Gas Marketing Act*, S.A. 1986, c. N-2.8, s. 8.

NETBACK PRICING FORMULA. A formula or method under which the actual price payable by the shipper for marketable gas sold and delivered pursuant to a producer-shipper contract is calculated wholly or partly by reference to a price or prices payable to the shipper on the resale of gas by him, whether the formula or method is contained in or incorporated by reference in the producer-shipper contract. *Natural Gas Marketing Act*, S.A. 1986, c. N-2.8, s. 8.

NET BOOK VALUE. The amount of assets and liabilities as recorded on a financial statement. A. Bissett-Johnson & W.M. Holland, eds., *Matrimonial Property Law in Canada* (Toronto: Carswell, 1980) at V-3.

NET CAPITALIZATION. The capitalization of a company as determined by subsection (2) of section 9 less the total amount of principal outstanding in debentures and short-term loans of the company. *The Rural Telephone Act*, R.S.S. 1978, c. R-27, s. 2.

NET COUNTY LEVY. The amount required for county purposes including the sums required for any board, commission or other body, apportioned to each lower tier municipality by the county. *Ontario Unconditional Grants Act*, R.S.O. 1980, c. 359, s. 7.

NET EARNINGS. 1. Of a worker, means his average earnings while employed in the industry in which the worker was injured, less the total of: (i) unemployment insurance contributions for those earnings; (ii) Canada Pension Plan contributions for those earnings; and (iii) probable income tax deductions for those earnings based on tables produced by Revenue Canada for the immediately preceding calendar year. *Workers' Compensation Act, 1983*, S.Nfld. 1983, c. 48, s.

2. 2. The excess of revenue over expenditure after deducting provision for income taxes for the fiscal period. *Credit Union Act*, R.S.B.C. 1979, c. 79, s. 1.

NET FAMILY PROPERTY. The value of all the property, except property described in subsection (2), that a spouse owns on the valuation date, after deducting: (a) the spouse's debts and other liabilities; and (b) the value of property, other than a matrimonial home, that the spouse owned on the date of the marriage, after deducting the spouse's debts and other liabilities, calculated as of the date of the marriage. *Family Law Act*, S.O. 1986, c. 4, s. 4.

NET FIXED ASSETS. The value of the net investment in fixed assets for the purposes of a balance sheet. S.M. Beck *et al.*, *Cases and Materials on Partnerships and Canadian Business Corporations* (Toronto: The Carswell Co., 1983) at 778.

NET FREE CAPITAL. 1. Liquid capital after deducting: (i) the amount required to provide full margin for: (A) cash commodities, other than securities, owned by the registrant; (B) securities owned by the registrant and securities sold short by the registrant; (C) firm trading accounts; and (ii) the amount sufficient to provide for any margin deficiencies on: (A) secured loans receivable; (B) customers' accounts; (C) partners' or shareholders' accounts, other than trading; (D) secured loans payable by the registrant if the collateral is held by other than the registrant or a financial institution; and (E) any other liquid capital items. *Commodity Futures Act*, R.R.O. 1980, Reg. 114, s. 7. 2. Liquid capital after deducting: (i) the amount required to provide full margin for: (A) cash commodities, other than in respect of securities, owned by the registrant; (B) firm commodity futures trading accounts; and (C) securities owned by the registrant and securities sold short by the registrant; (ii) the amount sufficient to provide for any margin deficiencies on: (A) secured loans receivable; (B) clients' accounts in respect of commodity futures; (C) joint accounts after excluding any interest of any member of the Toronto Stock Exchange, the Investment Dealers' Association of Canada and any financial institution; (D) accounts of partners and shareholders; (E) accounts of clients and dealers, except: (1) bona fide cash settlement accounts with any members of the Toronto Stock Exchange, the Montreal Stock Exchange, the Vancouver Stock Exchange, the Alberta Stock Exchange, the New York Stock Exchange, the American Stock Exchange and the Investment Dealers' Association of Canada; (2) accounts with a financial institution; and (3) bona fide cash settlement accounts that have not been outstanding more than 10 days past the normal settlement date, where the shares have been available for delivery, and not more than 21 days past the normal settlement date in any other case; (F) secured loans payable by the registrant if the collateral is held by other than the registrant or a financial institution; (G) where the securities accounts of the registrant are kept on a settlement date basis, future purchase and sales commitments not included in the calculation of liquid capital; and (H) any other liquid capital items. *Securities Act*, R.R.O. 1980, Reg. 910, s. 84.

NET GENERATING CAPABILITY. With reference to power, means the net capacity available from the generating facilities being referred to, with all the equipment available, at the time of the annual firm power peak load on the power grid, and, with reference to electric energy, means the net energy output available for a period of specified duration from such generating facilities. *National Energy Board Part VI Regulations*, C.R.C., c. 1056, s. 2.

NET INCOME. 1. Income less expenses and an amount for anticipated income tax. *Credit Union Act*, S.S. 1984-85-86, c. C-45.1, s. 2. 2. The excess of all fees and emoluments earned during the calendar year by an officer, by virtue of all his offices, after deducting such disbursements incident to the business of the office as may be allowed by the proper officer including the salaries of clerks and other employees. *Public Officers' Fees Act*, R.S.O. 1980, c. 416, s. 1. 3. The amount which is derived from mining operations by a person engaged therein, and if such a person receives net income from sources other than mining operations, either by reason of that person carrying on the processing of mineral ore extracted personally or otherwise, the net income to be deemed to have been personally derived from mining operations shall not exceed that portion of the total net income personally received from all sources determined by deducting from the said total: (i) the returns personally received by way of dividends, interest or other like payments from stocks, shares, bonds, debentures, loans or other like investments; and (ii) the net profit, if any, personally derived from, and attributable in accordance with sound accounting principles to, the carrying on of any business, or derived from and so attributable to any source, other than mining operations and the processing and sale of mineral ore or products produced therefrom, and other than as a return on investments mentioned in subclause (i); and (iii) an amount by way of return on capital personally employed in processing mineral ore or products derived therefrom equal to 8 per cent of the original personal cost of the depreciable assets including machin-

ery, equipment, plant, buildings, works and improvements, personally used in the processing of mineral ore or products derived therefrom, but the amount to be deducted shall not be in excess of 65 per cent, nor less than 15 per cent or such greater percentage (not in excess of 65) as legislation may determine, of that portion of the said total net income remaining after deducting therefrom the amounts specified in subclauses (i) and (ii). 4. The income of an individual from his employment abroad, computed without taking into account any foreign living allowance related to that employment and before any deduction made under this chapter. *An Act to Amend Certain Legislation to Give Effect to Government Budget Policy for the Fiscal Period, 1983-84*, S.Q. 1983, c. 44, s. 19.

NET INCOME OR REVENUE. Money available for dividends and surplus, according to the accounts prescribed by the Board and required to be kept by every public utility. *Public Utilities Act*, R.S.N.S. 1967, c. 258, s. 1.

NET MUNICIPAL BUDGET. The total expenditure of a municipality less any non-tax revenue. *An Act to Amend the Municipal Assistance Act*, S.N.B. 1986, c. 58, s. 1.

NET NON-EQUITY SHARE ACCOUNT. The balance obtained after subtracting the amount owing to a credit union on loans made by it for the purchase of non-equity shares of the credit union from the total amount of paid up non-equity shares of the credit union. *Credit Union Amendment Act*, S.B.C. 1981, c. 3, s. 1.

NET PENSION BENEFIT. A pension benefit minus the prescribed deductions. *Garnishment, Attachment and Pension Diversion Act*, R.S.C. 1985, c. G-2, s. 32.

NET POOL. That portion of the total pool remaining after deduction of the legal percentages. *Race Track Supervision Regulations*, C.R.C., c. 441, s. 2.

NET PREMIUMS. The gross premiums paid or payable under a contract of insurance, less dividends received or receivable in respect of the contract and less premiums returned on cancellation of the contract. *Excise Tax Act*, R.S.C. 1985, c. E-15, s. 3.

NET PRESENT VALUE. In relation to a parcel of land, or part thereof, which is managed land, means, subject to the regulations, the net present worth of the value of the permitted annual or periodic cut of trees from managed land. *Forest Land (Management and Taxation) Act*, S.Nfld. 1974, c. 59, s. 2.

NET PRESCRIBED PERCENTAGE. With reference to the total number of voting shares or class of voting shares of a company at any relevant time, that percentage of the total number of its voting shares, or class of voting shares, set out in its letters patent or supplementary letters patent, that is the maximum percentage of such shares that may be held by or for any one member of the constrained-class at that time. *An Act to amend the Canada Corporations Act*, R.S.C. 1970 (1st Supp.), c. 10, s. 29.

NET PRICE. See CURRENT ~.

NET PROCEEDS. 1. An amount equal to the amount realized on the disposition of the credit union's assets less the costs incurred in disposing of the assets. *Credit Union Act*, S.S. 1984-85-86, c. C-45.1, s. 177. 2. The proceeds realized by a spouse pursuant to the disposition of an interest in a marital home after deducting any sums (a) payable in respect of any rents owing, any unpaid taxes or any mortgage or lien against the property; or (b) payable in respect of any obligation reasonably incurred in connection with the disposition that gives rise to the proceeds. *Marital Property Act*, S.N.B. 1980, c. M-1.1, s. 1.

NET PROFIT. Clear profit after every deduction.

NET REGIONAL LEVY. The amount required for general regional purposes including the sums required for any board, commission or other body but excluding school purposes apportioned to each area municipality and reduced by the amount credited to each area municipality under section 3. *Ontario Unconditional Grants Act*, R.S.O. 1980, c. 359, s. 7.

NET RENTAL VALUE. The normal or going annual rent that would be payable under a lease for a term of years in which the lessee covenanted to bear the cost of all repairs, pay the fire, public liability and other insurance premiums, and to pay the real property tax and any other expenses in respect of the property, or its use, that are required in order to maintain the rental value. *Assessment Act*, R.S.N.B. 1973, c. A-14, s. 6.

NET RETURN IN ANY YEAR. An amount equal to annual net earnings derived from the project computed by deducting from the total annual revenues therefrom all expenses for the year in respect thereof, including provision for taxes, insurance, repairs and maintenance, interest and an amount sufficient to amortize the cost of construction of the project, including the cost of the land, over the estimated useful life of the project. *National Housing Act*, R.S.C. 1985, c. N-11, s. 32(4).

NET REVENUE. 1. The annual net profit or gain of the company including profits directly or indirectly received from any trade, manufacture, or from commercial, financial, or other business whether derived from a source within Nova Scotia or elsewhere, and shall include interest, dividends and profits directly or indirectly received from money at interest upon any security or without security or from stocks or any other investment, and also the annual net profit or gain from any other source including: (a) the income from, but not the proceeds of, life insurance policies paid upon death of the person insured; (b) rents, royalties and other like periodical receipts which depend upon the production or use of any real property of a company notwithstanding that the same are payable on account of the use or sale of any such property. *Corporations Tax Act*, R.S.N.S. 1967, c. 61, s. 16. 2. The total sums received from the operator, contractor, person or the Minister of Mines and Energy during the fiscal year less (a) all administrative, accounting, legal and other expenses which in the opinion of the Minister are necessarily incurred by the taxpayer in the collection of the money from the operator or contractor; (b) such amount as the Lieutenant-Governor in Council may allow for any costs and outlays incurred by the taxpayer within the area of land in or upon which the taxpayer has the right to engage in mining operations or such other areas of land as may be prescribed; and (c) all moneys paid during the fiscal year, by way of rental, royalty or other payment to any person, other than to Her Majesty, for the grant of the right to engage in mining operations. *Mining and Mineral Rights Tax Act*, S.Nfld. 1975, c. 68, s. 10. 3. For the purposes of sections 97 and 116, in the case of a corporation or partnership, the net revenue from any source, before taxes, as entered in the annual financial statement submitted to shareholders or partners, plus one-half of the amount by which the capital gains exceed the capital losses or minus one-half of the amount by which such losses exceed such gains, but excluding dividends from taxable Canadian corporations and net revenue from the lease of lands or buildings; in the case of an individual, his net revenue before taxes from the operation of a system referred to in subsection 1 of section 97 plus one-half of the amount by which the capital gains exceed the capital losses from the disposition of property used in such operation or minus one-half of the amount by which such losses exceed such property; for the purposes of this paragraph, capital gains and capital losses are computed in accordance with the *Taxation Act* (chapter I-3). *Real Estate Assessment Act*, R.S.Q. 1977, c. E-16, s. 1. See PROVINCIAL ~S.

NET SALVAGE VALUE. Salvage value minus any removal costs. Canada regulations.

NET SHARE CAPITAL. The amount of the

remainder obtained by subtracting the amount owing to a credit union on loans made by it for the purchase of shares of the credit union from the total amount of paid-up share capital of the credit union. *Credit Union Act*, R.S.B.C. 1979, c. 79, s. 1.

NET SMELTER RETURNS. The value of the metal or mineral received under an approved smelter contract or sales agreement less transportation and associated or related costs. *Mineral Resources Act*, S.N.S. 1975, c. 12, s. 104.

NETTING. *n.* Setting the current capital gains and income of the taxation year off against the losses for that year. W. Grover & F. Iacobucci, *Materials on Canadian Income Tax*, 4th ed. (Toronto: Richard De Boo Ltd., 1980) at 525.

NET VALUE. The value of the estate, wherever situate, both within and without the province, after payment of the charges thereon and the debts, funeral expenses, expenses of administration, succession duty and estate tax. Intestate Succession acts.

NETWORK. *n.* 1. Includes any operation involving two or more broadcasting undertakings where control over all or any part of the programs or program schedules of any of the broadcasting undertakings is delegated to a network operator. 2. A network as defined in the *Broadcasting Act*, but does not include a temporary network operation as defined in that Act. *Canada Elections Act*, R.S.C. 1985, c. E-2, s. 2. See DISTRIBUTION ~; GROUNDING ~.

NETWORK OPERATOR. Any person to whom permission has been granted by the Canadian Radio-television and Telecommunications Commission to form and operate a network. *Canada Elections Act*, R.S.C. 1985, c. E-2, s. 2.

NET WORTH. 1. The value of the qualified assets of an issuer less: (i) the sum of its statutory reserves; and (ii) its total liabilities. *The Investment Contracts Act*, R.S.S. 1978, c. I-14, s. 2. 2. The amount by which the value of all assets owned by the applicant and his spouse and children under 18 years exceeds the value of all liabilities of the applicant and his spouse and children under 18 years. *Farmers' Counselling and Assistance Amendment Act*, S.S. 1984-85-86, c. 31, s. 3.

NET WORTH TAXATION. A tax on personal wealth calculated on an individual's total assets minus any liabilities. W. Grover & F. Iacobucci, *Materials on Canadian Income Tax*, 4th ed. (Toronto: Richard De Boo Ltd., 1980) at 36.

NE UNQUES. [Fr.] Never.

NE UNQUES ACCOULPÉ. [Fr.] A plea which denies there was a marriage.

NE UNQUES EXECUTOR. [Fr.] Never an executor.

NE UNQUES INDEBITATUS. [Fr.] Never in debt.

NE UNQUES SON RECEIVER. [Fr.] Never one's receiver.

NEUTRAL CONDUCTOR. That conductor of a polyphase circuit, or of a single-phase 3-wire circuit having an approximately uniform potential difference and an equal spacing in phase with each of the other conductors. *Power Corporation Act*, R.R.O. 1980, Reg. 794, s. 0.

NEUTRALISATION. *n.* By treaty, exclusion of some territory from a region at war so that the territory has neutral status.

NEUTRALITY. *n.* A situation in which a territory is allied to neither side of a war.

NE VARIETUR. [L.] Let it not be varied.

NEW BREAKING. Cultivation for the first time and not seeded to any crop. *Canadian Wheat Board Regulations*, C.R.C., c. 397, s. 2.

NEW CANADIAN BUSINESS. In relation to a non-Canadian, means a business that is not already being carried on in Canada by the non-Canadian and that, at the time of its establishment: (a) is unrelated to any other business being carried on in Canada by that non-Canadian; or (b) is related to another business being carried on in Canada by that non-Canadian but falls within a prescribed specific type of business activity that, in the opinion of the Governor-in-Council, is related to Canada's cultural heritage or national identity. *Investment Canada Act*, R.S.C. 1985 (1st Supp.), c. 28, s. 3.

NEW CHEMICAL. An agent, either a single substance or in combination, which was not used in a workplace in Ontario on or before October 1, 1979 or which is not listed in an inventory of chemical substances approved by the Ministry of Labour. D. Robertson, *Ontario Health and Safety Guide* (Toronto: Richard De Boo Ltd., 1988) at 5-278.

NEW CONSTRUCTION PROJECT. A project commenced by a company after the coming into force of this Act, for: (i) the construction of a new telephone system to serve all the farm applicants who are to be supplied with a telephone service during the initial construction of the system; or (ii) the construction of an extension to furnish telephone service to two or more farm applicants, where part of the extension is common to the applicants; or (iii) the construction of an extension to furnish telephone service to one farm applicant, where no part of the extension is common to him and another farm applicant. *The Rural Telephone Act*, R.S.S. 1978, c. R-27, s. 2.

NEW DEEP PRODUCTION. That part of the production from a deepened well that is directly attributable to the deepening. *Petroleum Gas Revenue Tax Act*, R.S.C. 1985 (2d Supp.), c. 2, s. 2.

NEW DEVICE. In relation to a manufacturer, means a device listed in the table to this part that: (a) has not been sold previously in Canada by that manufacturer; (b) is, in respect of any characteristic, different from any device sold previously in Canada by that manufacturer; or (c) is, in respect of all characteristics, identical with a device sold previously in Canada by that manufacturer that has previously been recalled or withdrawn from the market or that he has ceased to manufacture or sell. *Medical Devices Regulations*, C.R.C., c. 871, s. 32.

NEW DRUG. (a) A drug that contains or consists of a substance, whether as an active or inactive ingredient, carrier, coating, excipient, menstruum or other component, that has not been sold as a drug in Canada for sufficient time and in sufficient quantity to establish in Canada the safety and effectiveness of that substance for use as a drug; (b) a drug that is a combination of two or more drugs, with or without other ingredients, and that has not been sold in that combination or in the proportion in which those drugs are combined in that drug, for sufficient time and in sufficient quantity to establish in Canada the safety and effectiveness of that combination and proportion for use as a drug; or (c) a drug, with respect to which the manufacturer prescribes, recommends, proposes or claims a use as a drug, or a condition of use as a drug, including dosage, route of administration, or duration of action and that has not been sold for that use or condition of use in Canada, for sufficient time and in sufficient quantity to establish in Canada the safety and effectiveness of that use or condition of use of that drug. *Food and Drug Regulations*, C.R.C., c. 870, s. C.08.001.

NEW DWELLING. A dwelling house of one or two dwellings entirely built between January 15, 1948 and June 30, 1974, and a fraction of an immoveable held in co-ownership established by declaration, and entirely built between those dates. *Family Housing Act*, R.S.Q. 1977, c. H-1, s. 1.

NEW ELECTION. An election other than a regular election. *Municipal Elections Act*, R.S.O. 1980, c. 308, s. 1.

NEW ENTRANT OR RE-ENTRANT TO THE LABOUR FORCE. A person who does not qualify under subsection (4) or paragraph (6)(b) and who has had less than 14: (a) weeks of insurable employment; (b) weeks in respect of which benefits have been paid or were payable to him; or (c) prescribed weeks that relate to employment in the labour force, or any combination thereof in the period of 52 weeks that immediately precedes the commencement of his qualifying period. *Unemployment Insurance Act*, R.S.C. 1985, c. U-1, s. 6(8).

NEWFOUNDLAND. *n.* Unless the context otherwise requires, the Province of Newfoundland. *Interpretation Act*, R.S.Nfld. 1970, c. 182, s. 26. See FISHERIES OF ~; ISLAND OF ~.

NEWFOUNDLAND CONTRACT. For the purposes of sections 26 to 66, means a subsisting contract that: (i) has for its subject (A) property that, at the time of the making of the contract, is in Newfoundland, or is in transit to or from Newfoundland; or (B) the life, safety, fidelity, or insurable interest of a person who, at the time of the making of the contract, is resident in, or has its head office in Newfoundland; or (ii) makes provision for payment thereunder primarily to a resident of Newfoundland or to a company that has its head office in Newfoundland. *Insurance Companies Act*, R.S.Nfld. 1970, c. 176, s. 2.

NEWFOUNDLAND OFFSHORE AREA. Those submarine areas lying seaward of the low water mark of the province and extending, at any location, as far as: (a) any prescribed line; or (b) where no line is prescribed at that location, the outer edge of the continental margin or a distance of 200 nautical miles from the baselines from which the breadth of the territorial sea of Canada is measured, whichever is the greater. *Income Tax Act*, R.S.C. 1952, c. 148 (as am. S.C. 1987, c. 3, s. 235), s. 248(1).

NEWFOUNDLAND SERVICE. Pensionable service as defined in the Newfoundland Act. *Public Service Superannuation Act*, R.S.C. 1985, c. P-36, s. 35.

NEW HAVEN. The institution established in British Columbia for the reclamation of juvenile offenders known as New Haven and situated on Lot 164, Group 1, New Westminster District in B.C. *Prisons and Reformatories Act*, R.S.C. 1970, c. P-21, s. 154.

NEW LAW. 1. The Revised Statutes of Canada, 1970. Canada statutes. 2. The Revised Statutes of Prince Edward Island 1974 or any subsequent revision of the statutes of Prince Edward Island. *Interpretation Act*, S.P.E.I. 1981, c. 18, s. 35.

NEW LESSEE. Includes a person who was

occupying the premises during the lease of the previous lessee and becomes the lessee himself on the expiry of the lease. *An Act to Promote Conciliation Between Lessees and Property-Owners*, R.S.Q. 1977, c. C-50, s. 55.

NEWLY-BORN CHILD. A child under the age of 1 year. *Criminal Code*, R.S.C. 1985, c. C-46, s. 2.

NEWLY TAXABLE LANDS. The run-off parcel or parcels supplied with telephone service by a new construction project and such other farm lands as become taxable parcels as a result of the new construction project. *The Rural Telephone Act*, R.S.S. 1978, c. R-27, s. 2.

NEW MATERIAL. Material manufactured for use as stuffing and includes new material manufactured for use other than as stuffing that is subsequently shredded, cut or reduced to a fibrous state through any process for use as stuffing. *Upholstered and Stuffed Articles Act*, R.R.O. 1980, Reg. 940, s. 1.

NEW MINE. Includes a mine where mining operations are recommenced after a 10-year period of discontinuance of active operation. *An Act to Amend the Metallic Minerals Tax Act*, S.N.B. 1987, c. 35, s. 1.

NEW MINERAL ORE. Mineral ore, the existence of which is possible, but does not include proven mineral ore or probable mineral ore. *An Act to Amend the Metallic Minerals Tax Act*, S.N.B. 1987, c. 35, s. 1.

NEW MOTOR VEHICLE. A motor vehicle which is in the possession of the manufacturer, distributor, or wholesaler, or has been sold only to a new motor vehicle dealer and on which the original title has not been transferred from the dealer. *Motor Vehicle Franchise Act*, S.N.B. 1987, c. 70, s. 1.

NEW MOTOR VEHICLE DEALER. A dealer who holds a dealer agreement granted by a manufacturer or distributor for the sale of its motor vehicles. *Motor Vehicle Franchise Act*, S.N.B. 1987, c. 70, s. 1.

NEW OIL. (i) Oil from a new well, or (ii) that portion of the oil from a developed well that is obtained as a result of an enhanced recovery scheme conducted under an order made on or after January 1, 1979 pursuant to clause 62 (9)(d) of *The Mines Act* and that, in the opinion of the minister, is attributable to an increase in reserves recognized by the Oil and Natural Gas Conservation Board under that Act as resulting from the enhanced recovery scheme. *Mineral Taxation Act*, S.M. 1979, c. 47, s. 16.

NEW PARCEL. A parcel created or intended to be created by the replotting scheme, and includes a portion of land created or intended to be created as a portion of a highway, park or public square, or of land indicated as such on a plan of subdivision deposited in the land title office under this division. *Municipal Act*, R.S.B.C. 1979, c. 290, s. 886.

NEWS-AGENT. *n.* A person, firm, or corporation, who sells by retail only all or any of the following: newspapers, magazines, periodicals, pamphlets, books, writing material, playing cards, picture cards, and souvenirs. *Shops Regulation Act*, R.S.M. 1970, c. S110, s. 3.

NEWSCASTS. *n.* Includes news headlines, reports of news events and summaries of the news but does not include an announcement that mentions only the place of origin of the news items, the title of the newscast and the name of the news reader. *Radio (F.M.) Broadcasting Regulations*, C.R.C., c. 380, s. 9.

NEW SHIP. 1. For purposes of this section and section 376, "new ship" means a ship in excess of 79 feet in length that is not a fishing vessel or pleasure yacht, the keel of which is laid or construction of the hull of which is commenced on or after April 14, 1973. *Canada Shipping Act*, R.S.C. 1985, c. S-9, s. 375. 2. Includes a ship to which regulations made under subsection 375(2) are made applicable pursuant to paragraph (d) of that subsection. *Canada Shipping Act*, R.S.C. 1985, c. S-9, s. 376(3).

NEWSPAPER. *n.* 1. Any paper, magazine or periodical containing public news, intelligence or reports of events, or any remarks or observations thereon, printed for sale and published periodically or in parts or numbers, at intervals not exceeding 31 days between the publication of any two such papers, parts or numbers, and any paper, magazine or periodical printed in order to be dispersed and made public, weekly or more often, or at intervals not exceeding 31 days, that contains advertisements, exclusively or principally. *Criminal Code*, R.S.C. 1985, c. C-46, s. 297. 2. A paper containing news, intelligence, occurrences, pictures or illustrations, or remarks or observations thereon, printed for sale and published periodically, or in parts or numbers, at intervals not exceeding 31 days between the publication of any two of such papers, parts or numbers. *Defamation acts*. 3. In a provision requiring publication in a newspaper, means a printed publication in sheet form, intended for general circulation, published regularly at intervals of not longer than a week, consisting in greater part of news of current events of general interest and sold to the public and to regular subscribers upon a bona fide subscription list. *Interpretation Act*, R.S.O. 1980, c. 219, s. 30. See CANADIAN ~ OR PERIOD-

ICAL; CONSTRUCTION TRADE ~; WEEKLY CANADIAN ~.

NEWSREEL. *n.* A film of one reel in length giving news of recent events and items of public interest. *Theatres Act*, R.R.O. 1980, Reg. 931, s. 1.

NEWS REPORTING. See BONA FIDE ~.

NEWTON. *n.* The force that, when applied to a body having a mass of 1 kilogram, gives the body an acceleration of 1 metre per second per second. *Weights and Measures Act*, S.C. 1970-71-72, c. 36, schedule I.

NEW TRIAL. Application to the court for this is the only remedy when there is any defect in judgment through entirely extrinsic causes or something outside the record.

NEW WELL. (a) A well drilled and completed on or after April 1, 1974 that in the opinion of the minister is the only well in the spacing unit in which it is located that is producing or is capable of producing from the pool in which it is completed; or (ii) a well abandoned prior to April 1, 1974 that is re-entered on or after April 1, 1974 and that in the opinion of the minister is the only well in the spacing unit in which it is located that is producing or is capable of producing from the pool in which it is completed, but does not include any additional well drilled in a spacing unit in which, at the time the additional well was drilled, there was already a well producing or capable of producing from the pool in which the additional well is completed, and does not include any additional well drilled in a spacing unit that, at the time the additional well was drilled, was deemed to be producing from that pool pursuant to an existing pooling or unitization agreement. *Mineral Taxation Act*, S.M. 1979, c. 47, s. 16.

NEXT. See NOW, ~, HERETOFORE AND HEREAFTER; NOW AND ~; NOW OR ~.

NEXT FRIEND. The person who intervenes to bring an action on behalf of an infant. See LITIGATION GUARDIAN.

NEXT OF KIN. *var.* **NEXT-OF-KIN.** 1. The mother, father, children, brothers, sisters, spouse and common law spouse of a deceased person, or any of them. 2. (a) Means the spouse and children of the deceased person; or (b) if there is no spouse or children, means the persons who are entitled to share under the *Intestate Succession Act* in the estate of the deceased person. 3. In relation to a patient, means (i) the husband or wife of that patient; or (ii) where there is no husband or wife of that patient, a descendant, ascendant or collateral, in either case over 18 years of age, in that order of priority who is nearest in blood to the patient, so however that if two or more persons in the class of relationship are of equal blood to the patient, the older or oldest of the persons in that class. *Mental Health Act*, S.Nfld. 1971, c. 80, s. 2. See HEIRS, ~ OR ESTATE.

NFB. *abbr.* National Film Board.

NFLD. *abbr.* Newfoundland.

NFLD. & P.E.I.R. *abbr.* Newfoundland and Prince Edward Island Reports, 1971-.

NFLD. R. *abbr.* Newfoundland Reports, 1817-1949.

NFLD. SEL. CAS. *abbr.* Tucker's Select Cases (Nfld.), 1817-1828.

NFPA. *abbr.* National Fire Prevention Association.

NIECE. *n.* The daughter of a sister or brother.

NIENT COMPRISE. [Fr. not contained] An objection to a petition on grounds that the desired thing is not contained in the proceeding or deed which is the foundation of the petition.

NIENT CULPABLE. [Fr.] Not guilty.

NIENT DEDIRE. [Fr.] Permitting judgment by neither opposing nor denying it.

NIENT LE FAIT. [Fr.] Not that person's deed. See NON EST FACTUM.

NIGHT. *n.* 1. The period between 9 p.m. and 6 a.m. of the following day. *Criminal Code*, R.S.C. 1985, c. C-46, s. 2. 2. The period from one-half hour after sunset to one-half hour before sunrise. 3. The period during which the centre of the sun's disc is lower than 6° below the horizon. 4. That period of time elapsing between 1 hour after sunset and 1 hour before sunrise of the following day. *Game Act*, R.S.N.B. 1973, c. G-1, s. 1. 5. The period extending from one hour and a half after sunset to one hour and a half before sunrise. *An Act to Amend the Act Respecting the Conservation and Development of Wildlife and the Parks Act*, S.Q. 1986, c. 109, s. 8. 6. The hours between sunset and sunrise. *General Radio Regulations, Part II*, C.R.C., c. 1372, s. 43.

NIGHT COURT. A court held by a magistrate between the hours of 5 p.m. and 11 p.m. *Night Courts Act*, S.N.S. 1970-71, c. 2, s. 2.

NIGHT-LINE. *n.* A fishing line to which hooks are attached at intervals and that rests wholly on the bottom. *Quebec Fishery Regulations*, C.R.C., c. 852, s. 2.

NIGHT PREMIUM. A higher rate of pay for work at night.

NIGHT TIME. *var.* **NIGHT-TIME.** 1. That period commencing 1 hour after sunset and ending 1 hour before the following sunrise. 2. Includes all that portion of the day extending from one-half hour after sunset until one-half hour before sunrise. *Canada Shipping Act*, R.S.C. 1985, c. S-9, s. 2.

NIGHT VFR. In respect of a flight of any aircraft in Canada, a flight conducted in accordance with VFR during the hours of night. *Air Regulations*, C.R.C., c. 2, s. 101.

NIGHTWALKER. *n.* A person who sleeps during the day and walks at night.

NIHIL CAPIAT PER BREVE. [L.] That one takes nothing by one's writ.

NIHIL CONSENSUI TAM CONTRARIUM EST QUAM VIS ET METUS. [L.] Nothing is more antithetical to agreement than force and fear.

NIHIL DAT QUI NON HABET. [L.] One who has nothing gives nothing.

NIHIL DICIT. [L.] One says nothing.

NIHIL FACIT ERROR NOMINIS CUM DE CORPORE CONSTAT. [L.] A mistake about a name means nothing when there is no mistake about the person meant.

NIHIL HABET FORUM EX SCENA. [L.] The court has no concern with things which are not before it.

NIHIL INFRA REGNUM SUBDITOS MAGIS CONSERVAT IN TRANQUILLITATE ET CONCORDIA QUAM DEBITA LEGUM ADMINISTRATIO. [L.] Nothing keeps those subject to royal authority more tranquil and peaceful than due administration of the law.

NIHIL IN LEGE INTOLERABILIUS EST, QUAM EANDEM REM DIVERSO JURE CENSERI. [L.] Nothing is more intolerable in law than that a similar case is decided upon a different construction of the law.

NIHIL PRAESCRIBITUR NISI QUOD POSSIDETUR. [L.] Nothing can be acquired by prescription except in respect of what is possessed.

NIHIL QUOD EST CONTRA RATIONEM EST LICITUM. [L.] Nothing contrary to reason is lawful.

NIHIL QUOD INCONVENIENS EST LICITUM EST. [L.] Nothing inconvenient is lawful.

NIHIL SIMUL INVENTUM EST ET PERFECTUM. [L.] Nothing is both invented and perfected at the same time.

NIHIL TAM CONVENIENS EST NATURALI AEQUITATI QUAM UNUMQUODQUE DISSOLVI EO LIGAMINE QUO LIGATUM EST.

[L.] Nothing agrees more with natural justice than that anything bound should be freed by the same means.

NIHIL TAM CONVENIENS EST NATURALI AEQUITATI QUAM VOLUNTATEM DOMINI VOLENTIS REM SUAM IN ALIUM TRANSFERRE RATAM HABERE. [L.] Nothing agrees more with natural justice than to honour the intent of an owner who wants to transfer property to another.

NIHIL TAM PROPRIUM IMPERIO QUAM LEGIBUS VIVERE. [L.] Nothing is more characteristic of royal power than that it is exercised under the law.

NIHIL TEMERE NOVANDUM. [L.] Avoid rash innovations.

NIL. *n.* [L.] Nothing.

NIL ASSESSMENT. An assessment which shows that no tax is owed. W. Grover & F. Iacobucci, *Materials on Canadian Income Tax*, 4th ed. (Toronto: Richard De Boo Ltd., 1980) at 74.

NIL DEBET. [L.] One owes nothing.

NIMIA SUBTILITAS IN JURE REPROBATUR. [L.] In law too much subtlety is rejected.

NIMIUM ALTERCANDO VERITAS AMITTITUR. [L.] By arguing too much the truth is lost.

1968 CONVENTION. 1. The Convention September 27, 1968 on Jurisdiction and the Enforcement of Judgments in Civil and Commercial Matters as amended. *Civil and Commercial Judgments Convention*, R.S.C. 1985, c. C-30, s. 1. 2. The Convention of September 27, 1968 on Jurisdiction and the Enforcement of Judgments in Civil and Commercial Matters as amended. *Canada and the United Kingdom Reciprocal Recognition and Enforcement of Judgments Act*, S.Nfld. 1986, c. 29, s. 1.

NISEI. *n.* A second generation resident or citizen of Japanese origin.

NISI. [L.] Describes an order effective only when the affected party fails to respond to it by a certain time. See DECREE ~.

NISI PRIUS. [L.] Unless before.

NITRATE MIXTURE. Any preparation, other than gunpowder, formed by the mechanical mixture of a nitrate with any form of carbon or with any carbonaceous substance not possessed of explosive properties, whether or not the preparation contains sulphur and whether or not such preparation is mechanically mixed with any other non-explosive substance. *Dan-*

gerous Goods Shipping Regulations, C.R.C., c. 1419, s. 144.

NITRO-COMPOUND. *n.* Any chemical compound that has explosive properties, or is capable of combining with metals to form an explosive compound, and is produced by the chemical action of nitric acid (whether mixed or not with sulphuric acid) or of a nitrate mixed with sulphuric acid upon any carbonaceous substance, whether such compound is mechanically mixed with other substances or not. Canada regulations.

NITROGEN. *n.* Elemental nitrogen (N). *Fertilizers Regulations*, C.R.C., c. 666, s. 2. See OXIDES OF ~; WATER-INSOLUBLE ~.

NITRO-GLYCERINE. See LOW FREEZE ~.

N.L. *abbr.* [L.] Non liquet. It is not evident.

NO. *abbr.* Number.

NOBILIORES ET BENIGNIORES PRESUMPTIONES IN DUBIIS SUNT PRAEFERENDAE. [L.] In doubtful cases, more generous and favourable presumptions should be preferred.

NOBILITY. *n.* In England, the division of the population consisting of barons, dukes, earls, marquesses and viscounts.

NOCENT. *adj.* Criminal; guilty.

NO-CERTIORARI CLAUSE. A provision that certiorari and any other remedy otherwise available will not be available to judicially review a tribunal's decision. P.W. Hogg, *Constitutional Law of Canada*, 2d ed. (Toronto: Carswell, 1985) at 162.

NO-FAULT AUTO-ACCIDENT INSURANCE. Insurance providing coverage for a certain duration to a set dollar limit, depending on whether it is a partial or total disability. A death benefit may be available as well. K.D. Cooper-Stephenson & I.B. Saunders, *Personal Injury Damages in Canada* (Toronto: Carswell, 1981) at 3.

NO-FAULT DIVORCE. Divorce based on grounds other than a matrimonial offence.

NOISE. See RADIO FREQUENCY ~; RADIO ~.

NOISE CERTIFICATE. (a) A certificate of noise compliance issued or other noise documentation accepted by the Minister pursuant to subsection 6(1) in respect of a Canadian registered aircraft, or (b) a noise certification issued by a foreign country or other noise documentation that has been accepted by the Minister pursuant to subsection 6(2) in respect of an aircraft registered in that country. *Aircraft Noise Certification Order*, C.R.C., c. 27, s. 2.

NOISE RESTRICTED RUNWAY. In respect of an airport set out in Column I of the schedule, a runway set out in Column II or III of the schedule opposite that airport at which air operations are restricted by maximum noise levels permitted to be made by a particular type of aircraft or as otherwise authorized by the Minister. *Aircraft Noise Certification Order*, C.R.C., c. 27, s. 2.

NOLENS VOLENS. [L.] Unwilling or willing.

NO LIMIT ORDER. An order to buy or sell securities with no stipulation as to price.

NOLLE PROSEQUI. [L.] 1. To be not willing to prosecute. 2. A stay of proceedings.

NO-LOAD FUND. A mutual fund which charges little or no fee in the sale of its shares.

NOM DE PLUME. [Fr.] Pen name.

NOMEN COLLECTIVUM. [L. a collective name] The description of members of a particular class.

NOMEN GENERALISSIMUM. [L.] The most general term.

NOMETHETICAL. *adj.* Relating to legislation.

NOMINAL CAPITAL. The quantity of shares or the aggregate par value of shares which a company is authorized to issue, fixed in the company's memorandum or articles of incorporation or letters patent. H. Sutherland, D.B. Horsley & J.M. Edmiston, eds., *Fraser's Handbook on Canadian Company Law*, 7th ed. (Toronto: Carswell, 1985) at 41.

NOMINAL DAMAGES. An insignificant amount of money awarded in acknowledgement of the technical infringement of a legal right. K.D. Cooper-Stephenson & I.B. Saunders, *Personal Injury Damages in Canada* (Toronto: Carswell, 1981) at 60 and 65.

NOMINAL GAUGE. When used with reference to thickness of the shell or other part of tank, that the plate used in construction of that shell or other part is known in the plate-mill industry as having the specified thickness. *Gasoline Handling Act*, R.R.O. 1980, Reg. 439, s. 1.

NOMINAL HORSEPOWER. The measure of the size of marine engines, ascertained in accordance with regulations made by the Governor in Council. *Canada Shipping Act*, R.S.C. 1985, c. S-9, s. 2.

NOMINALISTIC PRINCIPLE. A debtor must pay the debt's nominal amount in whatever tender is legal. J.G. McLeod, *The Conflict of Laws* (Calgary: Carswell, 1983) at 513.

NOMINAL PARTNER. A person who does not have any actual interest in a business, trade or its profits but appears to have an interest because her or his name is used in the trade or business.

NOMINAL SECTION. Measures 259 hectares or 640 acres, depending on which measurement is used to describe the mineral land area in a certificate of title. Saskatchewan statutes.

NOMINAL VALUE. (a) The mass or weight shown on a local standard of mass or weight; (b) the length shown between any two graduations, whether or not successive graduations, on a local standard of length; (c) in the case of a cylindrical graduated standard, the maximum volume or capacity shown on the cylindrical graduated standard; and (d) in the case of a narrow—neck metal standard or a narrow—neck glass standard, the volume or capacity shown on that standard. *Weights and Measures Regulations*, C.R.C., c. 1605, s. 53.

NOMINAL VOLUME. The approximate volume of product put in a container by the manufacturer. *Consumer Packaging and Labelling Regulations*, C.R.C., c. 417, s. 2.

NOMINA SUNT MUTABILIA, RES AUTEM IMMOBILES. [L.] Names are changeable but things remain unchanged.

NOMINATIM. [L. by name] Mentioned one at a time.

NOMINATED. See OFFICIALLY ~.

NOMINATION. *n.* A mention by name. See DAY OF ~; OFFICIAL ~.

NOMINATION DAY. 1. The day upon which nominations close. 2. The last day for filing nominations.

NOMINE POENAE. [L.] Under a penalty's description.

NOMINIS UMBRA. [L. the shadow of a name] A one-person company.

NOMOGRAPHER. *n.* A person who writes about laws.

NON-ABILITY. *n.* Inability.

NON-ACCEPTANCE. *n.* The refusal to accept.

NON ACCEPTAVIT. [L.] One did not accept.

NON-ACCESS. *n.* Though one presumes access during wedlock, one may counter this presumption by proving that sexual intercourse did not occur at a time when the husband could be the father.

NON ACCIPI DEVENT VERBA IN DEMONSTRATIONEM FALSAM QUAE COMPETUNT IN LIMITATIONEM VERAM. [L.] Words which comprise a clearly intended limitation should not be interpreted as a false description.

NON ACCREVIT INFRA SEX ANNOS. [L.] It did not accrue within 6 years.

NON-AGE. *n.* The state of being a minor.

NON ALIO MODO PUNIATUR ALIQUIS, QUAM SECUNDUM QUOD SE HABET CONDEMNATIO. [L.] A person should not be punished in any way except according to the sentence.

NON ALITER A SIGNIFICATIONE VERBORUM RECEDI OPORTET QUAM CUM MANIFESTUM EST ALIUD SENSISSE TESTATOREM. [L.] There should be no deviation in any way from the usual meaning of words unless it is obvious that the testator meant something else.

NON-APPEARANCE. *n.* The failure to appear in a timely and proper manner.

NON ASSUMPSIT. [L.] One did not promise.

NON ASSUMPSIT INFRA SEX ANNOS. [L.] One did not promise within 6 years.

NON-BANK AFFILIATE OF A FOREIGN BANK. A corporation, other than a bank, incorporated by or under a law of Canada or a province and carrying on business in Canada, in which a foreign bank or a corporation associated with a foreign bank owns shares in any number that would, under the voting rights attached to the shares, permit the foreign bank, the corporation associated with the foreign bank, the foreign bank and the corporation associated with it or the corporation associated with the foreign bank and another corporation associated with the foreign bank to vote more than 10 per cent of the total votes that could, under the voting rights attached to all the shares of the corporation issued and outstanding, be voted by the holders thereof, but a corporation shall not be deemed to be a non-bank affiliate of a foreign bank by reason only of the fact that all or any number of its shares are owned by a foreign bank subsidiary pursuant to section 193. *Bank Act*, R.S.C. 1985, c. B-1, s. 303.

NON BIS IN IDEM. [L.] Not tried twice for the same offence.

NON-BUSINESS DAYS. Days directed by this Act to be observed as legal holidays or non-juridical days, and any other day is a business day. *Bills of Exchange Act*, R.S.C. 1985, c. B-4, s. 2.

NON-CANADIAN. *n.* An individual, a government or an agency thereof or an entity that is not Canadian. *Investment Canada Act*, R.S.C. 1985 (1st Supp.), c. 28, s. 3.

NON-CANADIAN SHIP. A ship registered elsewhere than in Canada. *Board of Steamship*

Inspection Scale of Fees, C.R.C., c. 1405, s. 2. See CERTIFIED ~.

NON-CAPITAL MURDER. All murder other than capital murder. *Criminal Code*, R.S.C. 1970, c. C-34, s. 214. See now SECOND DEGREE MURDER.

NON CEPIT MODO ET FORMA. [L.] One did not take in the alleged manner and form.

NON-CHEQUABLE DEPOSITS. Deposits not subject to withdrawal by bill of exchange, including cheques, or other negotiable order. *Credit Union Act*, S.N.S. 1978, c. 4, s. 3.

NON-COMBATANT. *n.* A civilian.

NONCOMBUSTIBLE. *var.* **NON-COMBUSTIBLE.** *adj.* 1. As applied to a material or combination of materials, means material that will pass an approved test for determination of noncombustibility in building materials conducted by: (i) The Canadian Standards Association Testing Laboratories; (ii) The National Research Council of Canada; (iii) Underwriters' Laboratories of Canada; or (iv) any other approved testing laboratory. 2. Incapable of sustaining combustion in air, either when ignited or when subjected to and maintained at a high temperature.

NONCOMBUSTIBLE BUILDING. A building in which all load-bearing walls, columns, partitions, floors and roofs are constructed of concrete, brick, tile, steel or other noncombustible material or combination of materials. *Nursing Homes Act*, R.R.O. 1980, Reg. 690, s. 1.

NONCOMBUSTIBLE CONSTRUCTION. That type of construction in which a degree of fire safety is attained by the use of noncombustible materials for structural members and other building assemblies.

NON-COMMISSIONED MEMBER. Any person, other than an officer, who is enrolled in, or who pursuant to law is attached or seconded otherwise than as an officer to, the Canadian Forces. *Statute Law Amendment Act*, R.S.C. 1985 (1st Supp.), c. 31, s. 42.

NON-COMPELLABILITY. *n.* The provision of section 11(c) of the Charter that anyone charged with an offence cannot be compelled to be a witness against herself or himself. P.W. Hogg, *Constitutional Law of Canada*, 2d ed. (Toronto: Carswell, 1985) at 765.

NONCOMPLYING SCHOOL. A school whose board or teachers or both are reported by the Minister to the Commission as having failed to comply with any Act or regulation administered by the Ministry. *Teachers' Superannuation Act*, R.R.O. 1980, Reg. 930, s. 16.

NON COMPOS MENTIS. [L.] Not sound in mind.

NON CONCESSIT. [L.] One did not grant.

NON-CONFORMING BUILDING. A building (i) that is lawfully constructed or lawfully under construction at the date of first publication of an official notice of a proposal to pass a zoning by-law affecting the land on which the building is situated; and (ii) that does not or will not conform to the requirements of the zoning by-law when it becomes effective.

NON-CONFORMING PLACE. A place at which there is carried on unlawfully an activity which can only be carried on lawfully at a regulated place. *Entry Warrants Act*, S.N.B. 1986, c. E-9.2, s. 1.

NON-CONFORMING POOL. A public swimming pool that has been designated as such because of a condition found therein that constitutes a hazard to health or safety. *Public Health Act*, R.R.O. 1980, Reg. 849, s. 1.

NON-CONFORMING USE. Use of land or buildings in a manner or for a purpose lawful at the time it was first commenced, but not in conformity with the provisions of any by-law or regulation subsequently adopted.

NON CONSTAT. [L.] It does not follow; it is not clear.

NON-CONTENTIOUS BUSINESS. A proceeding or matter pertaining to probate, administration or guardianship, but does not include contentious business. *Administration of Estates Act*, R.S.A. 1980, c. A-1, s. 1.

NON-CONTRACT RATE. The rate to be charged for the transportation of goods shipped by a shipper who has not entered into a patronage contract. *Shipping Conference Exemption Act*, R.S.C. 1985, c. S-10, s. 5(2).

NON-CONTRIBUTORY PENSION PLAN. A plan financed by the employer only.

NON-CORPORATE PORT. A harbour at which no local port corporation has been established and that is under the jurisdiction of the Corporation. *Canada Ports Corporation Act*, R.S.C. 1985, c. C-9, s. 2.

NON CULPABILIS. [L.] Not guilty.

NON CULPABLE HOMICIDE. Homicide that is not culpable is not an offence. *Criminal Code*, R.S.C. 1985, c. C-46, s. 222(3).

NONCUMULATIVE DIVIDEND. A dividend which need not be paid in a subsequent year if it was not paid in an earlier year.

NON DAMNIFICATUS. [L.] Not injured.

NON DAT QUI NON HABET. [L.] One who does not have cannot give.

NON DEBEO MELIORIS CONDITIONIS ESSE QUAM AUCTOR MEUS A QUO JUS IN ME TRANSIT. [L.] I should not be in a better position than my assignor from whom a right passes to me.

NON DEBET ALTERI PER ALTERUM INIQUA CONDITIO INFERRI. [L.] An unjust condition should not be imposed on one person by another.

NON DEBET CUI PLUS LICET QUOD MINUS EST NON LICERE. [L.] It should be lawful to do something less if one is entitled to do something more.

NON DECIPITUR QUI SCIT SE DICIPI. [L.] One who realizes the deception is not deceived.

NON DEFINITUR IN JURE QUID SIT CONATUS. [L.] What an attempt is is not defined in law.

NON-DELIVERY. *n.* Neglect or failure to deliver goods on the part of a bailee, carrier, or other expected to deliver.

NON DEMISIT. [L.] One did not demise.

NONDESTRUCTIVE TEST. The examination of a part without subjecting it to physical distortion, damage or destruction. *Occupational Health and Safety Act*, R.R.O. 1980, Reg. 694, s. 1.

NON DETINET. [L.] One does not detain.

NON DIFFERUNT QUAE CONCORDANT RE TAMETSI NON IN VERBIS IISDEM. [L.] Things which agree in substance though not in words do not differ from each other.

NON-DIRECTION. *n.* The failure of a judge to draw the jury's attention to a necessary legal point.

NON-DISTRICT HOSPITAL. A hospital other than a hospital owned by a district board. *Hospitals Act*, R.S.A. 1980, c. H-11, s. 1.

NON-DISTRICT NURSING HOME. A nursing home other than a nursing home owned or operated by a district board. *Nursing Homes Act*, S.A. 1985, c. N-14.1, s. 1.

NON-ELIGIBLE PERSON. For the purpose of subsection (1), "non-eligible person" means (a) a person who is neither a Canadian citizen nor a permanent resident within the meaning of the Immigration Act; (b) a Canadian citizen who is not ordinarily resident in Canada; (c) a permanent resident within the meaning of the Immigration Act who has been ordinarily resident in Canada for more than 1 year after the time at which he first became eligible to apply for Canadian citizenship; (d) a person who has reached the age of 70 years; (e) a person who is a member of the Senate or House of Commons or a member of the legislature of a province; (f) a person who is employed in any capacity in the public service of Canada or of any province; or (g) a person who holds any office or position for which a salary or remuneration is payable out of the Consolidated Revenue Fund. *Federal Business Development Bank Act*, R.S.C. 1985, c. F-6, s. 9(2).

NON-ENTRY ORDER. The powers of a court to prevent a spouse from entering his or her home so that the other spouse or children of the marriage are not harassed. A. Bissett-Johnson & W.M. Holland, eds., *Matrimonial Property Law in Canada* (Toronto: Carswell, 1980) at I-7.

NON-EQUITY SHARE. A share that is guaranteed by the Provincial Credit Union Guarantee Fund under Part 3. *Credit Union Amendment Act*, S.B.C. 1981, c. 3, s. 1.

NON-EQUITY SHARE ACCOUNT. See NET ~.

NON EST ARCTIUS VINCULUM INTER HOMINES QUAM JUSJURANDUM. [L.] There is nothing more binding between people than an oath.

NON EST DISPUTANDUM CONTRA PRINCIPIA NEGANTEM. [L.] One cannot dispute with a person who denies first principles.

NON EST FACTUM. [L.] It is not that person's deed.

NON EST INVENTUS. [L.] One is not found.

NON EST RECEDENDUM A COMMUNI OBSERVANTIA. [L.] There should be no deviation from ordinary usage.

NON EST REGULA QUIN FALLET. [L.] A rule does not exist without exceptions.

NON FACIAS MALUM UT INDE FIAT BONUM. [L.] You do not do evil so that good may come of it.

NON-FARM VEHICLE. An aircraft, boat or land vehicle powered by an internal combustion engine and includes a trailer pulled by a land vehicle but does not include a farm truck or farm machinery. *Fuel Oil Administration Act*, R.S.A. 1980, c. F-21, s. 1.

NONFEASANCE. *n.* The failure or neglect to do something which a person ought to do.

NONGAME BIRDS. See MIGRATORY ~.

NON-IMMIGRANT VISA. A visa that is issued to a non-immigrant and that specifies the class designated in subsection 7(1) or (2) of the Immigration Act as a member of which the non-immigrant is seeking admission. *Immigration Appeal Board (Definitions) Regulations*, C.R.C., c. 942, s. 3.

NON IMPEDIT CLAUSULA DEROGATORIA QUO MINUS AB EODEM POTESTATE RES DISSOLVANTUR A QUA CONSTITUUNTUR. [L.] A derogatory clause does not keep something from being destroyed by the same power which created it.

NON-IMPERATIVE APPOINTMENT. An appointment for an indeterminate period, resulting from a request by the deputy head, to a bilingual position that has been identified by the deputy head as not immediately requiring occupation by a person qualified in the knowledge and use of both official languages. *Official Languages Exclusion Approval Order*, C.R.C., c. 1349, s. 2.

NON-INCENDIVE CIRCUIT. A circuit or part of a circuit in which any sparking that may be produced by normally arcing parts is incapable, under normal operating conditions, of causing an ignition of the prescribed flammable gas or vapour. *Power Corporation Act*, R.R.O. 1980, Reg. 794, s. 0.

NON-INDUSTRIAL ACCIDENT. Personal injury to an employee that does not arise out of and in the course of his employment and for which the employer is not liable to provide or to pay compensation under the Workmen's Compensation Act. *Public Health Act*, R.R.O. 1980, Reg. 834, s. 36.

NON INFREGIT CONVENTIONEM. [L.] One did not breach the covenant.

NON IN LEGENDO SED IN INTELLIGENDO LEGES CONSISTUNT. [L.] The laws are determined not by reading but by understanding them.

NON-INSTRUCTIONAL DAY. A day on which pupils are excused from tuition and instruction and during which teachers are subject to the direction of the board. *School Act*, S.B.C. 1982, c. 78, s. 1.

NON-INSTRUCTIONAL PERSONNEL. School bus drivers, janitors, clerical staff and such other persons as the regional school board designates, but excludes supervisory personnel. *An Act to Amend the School Act*, S.P.E.I. 1980, c. 48, s. 1.

NON-IONIZING RADIATION. 1. Electromagnetic energy that is not capable of ionizing atoms, but that may cause photochemical, heating or other effects. *Radiation Protection Act*, S.A. 1985, c. R-2.1, s. 1. 2. Includes energy in the form of: (i) electromagnetic waves in the frequency range below that for which ionization occurs; or (ii) ultrasonic waves having frequencies greater than 10,000 hertz. *Radiation Health and Safety Act*, S.S. 1984-85-86, c. R-1.1, s. 2.

NON-IONIZING RADIATION EQUIPMENT. Equipment that is capable of emitting non-ionizing radiation. *Radiation Health and Safety Act*, S.S. 1984-85-86, c. R-1.1, s. 2.

NON-IONIZING RADIATION INSTALLATION. The whole or any part of a building or other place in which non-ionizing radiation equipment is manufactured, used or placed or installed for use, and includes that non-ionizing radiation equipment. *Radiation Health and Safety Act*, S.S. 1984-85-86, c. R-1.1, s. 2.

NON-ISSUABLE PLEA. A plea which, if decided, would not settle the action upon its merits, *e.g.*, a plea in abatement.

NON-JOINDER. *n.* The omission of someone from an action who should be made party.

NON JUS, SED SEISINA, FACIT STIPITEM. [L.] Not right, but seisin, makes the family tree.

NON LIQUET. [L.] It is not evident.

NON-LOCKING RETRACTOR. A retractor that does not have a locking mechanism and from which the webbing is extended to substantially its full length by a small external force and that provides no adjustment for assembly length and that need not be capable of sustaining restraint forces at maximum webbing extension. *Motor Vehicle Safety Regulations*, C.R.C., c. 1038, s. 209.

NON-MEMBER CUSTOMER. A customer who is not a member. *Income Tax Act*, R.S.C. 1952, c. 148 (as am. S.C. 1970-71-72, c. 63), s. 135(4)(f).

NON-MERGER. *n.* In Anglo-Canadian law a foreign judgment does not extinguish a cause of action nor is the original cause merged into the foreign court's judgment. J.G. McLeod, *The Conflict of Laws* (Calgary: Carswell, 1983) at 606-607.

NON-NATURAL USER. Special use bringing with it increased danger to others and not the ordinary use of land or a use which is suitable for the general benefit of the community. John G. Fleming, *The Law of Torts*, 6th ed. (Sydney: The Law Book Co., 1983) at 308.

NON-NEGOTIABLE RECEIPT. 1. A receipt in which it is stated that the goods therein specified will be delivered to the holder thereof. Warehouse Receipts acts. 2. A receipt in which it is stated that the goods specified in it will be delivered to the depositor or to another named person. *Warehouse Receipt Act*, R.S.B.C. 1979, c. 428, s. 1.

NON OBSERVATA FORMA INFERTUR ADNULLATIO ACTUS. [L.] By not observing prescribed formalities, the proceeding is invalidated.

NON OBSTANTE. [L.] Notwithstanding.

NON OBSTANTE VEREDICTO. [L.] The verdict notwithstanding.

NON OFFICIT AFFECTUS NISI SEQUATUR EFFECTUS. [L.] An intention is not hurtful unless a result follows.

NON OMITTAS. [L.] That you do not omit.

NON OMNE QUOD LICET HONESTUM EST. [L.] Not everything which is lawful is honourable.

NON OMNIUM QUAE A MAJORIBUS NOSTRIS CONSTITUTA SUNT RATIO REDDI POTEST. [L.] A reason cannot be offered for all the laws which our ancestors established.

NON-OPERATING EMPLOYEE. A clerical or maintenance worker.

NON-OWNER'S POLICY. A motor vehicle liability policy insuring a person solely in respect of the use or operation by him or on his behalf of an automobile that is not owned by him. Insurance acts.

NON-PARTICIPATING PROFESSIONAL. A professional who practises his profession outside the scope of the plan established by this act but does not agree to be remunerated in accordance with the tariff provided in an agreement or who is the subject of an order issued pursuant to section 62, and all of whose patients alone assume payment of the fees which include the price of medications in the case of a pharmacist. *Health Insurance Act*, S.Q. 1979, c. 1, s. 1.

NON-PARTICIPATING SHARE. (i) In the case of a private corporation, a share the owner of which is not entitled to receive, as owner thereof, any dividend, other than a dividend, whether cumulative or not, (A) at a fixed annual rate or amount, or (B) at an annual rate or amount not in excess of a fixed annual rate or amount, and (ii) in the case of a corporation other than a private corporation, any share other than a common share. *Income Tax Act*, R.S.C. 1952, c. 148 (as am. S.C. 1980-81-82-83, c. 140, s. 113), s. 204(a.2).

NON-PECUNIARY LOSS. 1. Compensation for suffering and pain, for loss of enjoyment of life and amenities, and for shortened expectation of life. K.D. Cooper-Stephenson & I.B. Saunders, *Personal Injury Damages in Canada* (Toronto: Carswell, 1981) at 52. 2. Includes loss of care and guidance from a parent or loss generally of guidance, care and companionship.

K.D. Cooper-Stephenson & I.B. Saunders, *Personal Injury Damages in Canada Supplement to June 30, 1987* (Toronto: Carswell, 1987) at 29 and 30.

NON-PERSONAL LIABILITY. Part of the name of a specially limited company in B.C. H. Sutherland, D.B. Horsley & J.M. Edmiston, eds., *Fraser's Handbook on Canadian Company Law*, 7th ed. (Toronto: Carswell, 1985) at 438.

NON PLACET. [L.] It is not accepted.

NON PLEVIN. Failure to replevy land within the allotted time.

NON POSSESSORI INCUMBIT NECESSITAS PROBANDI POSSESSIONES AD SE PERTINERE. [L.] The possessor need not prove that the possessions belong to her or him.

NON POTEST ADDUCI EXCEPTIO EJUSDEM REI CUJUS PETITUR DISSOLUTIO. [L.] It is not possible to plead the same thing one takes exception to when one seeks to upset it.

NOT POTEST PROBARI QUOD PROBATUM NON RELEVAT. [L.] It is not possible to prove what is immaterial if proved.

NON POTEST REX GRATIAM FACERE CUM INJURIA ET DAMNO ALIORUM. [L.] A monarch cannot favour one person to the injury and damage of all the others.

NON-POWER VESSEL. Any vessel or floating object not falling within the definitions of "power craft" or "sailing vessel" and includes rowboats, canoes, skiffs, punts and rafts. *Hamilton Harbour Commissioners' Licensing By-law*, C.R.C., c. 895, s. 2.

NON-PROFIT AGENCY. A corporation without share capital that has objects of a charitable nature and, (i) to which Part III of the Corporations Act applies, or (ii) that is incorporated by or under a general or special Act of the Parliament of Canada. *Child and Family Services Act*, S.O. 1984, c. 55, s. 175.

NON-PROFIT CO-OPERATIVE HOUSING CORPORATION. A corporation incorporated without share capital under the Co-operative Corporations Act or any predecessor thereof or under similar legislation of Canada or any province, the main purpose and activity of which is the provision of housing for its members, and the charter or by-laws of which provide that: (a) its activities shall be carried on without the purpose of gain for its members; (b) on dissolution, its property after payment of its debts and liabilities shall be distributed to non-profit or charitable organizations; (c) housing charges, other charges similar to rent, or any other charges payable by members are decided by a vote of the members or of a body duly elected or appointed by the members, or a committee thereof; (d) termination of occupancy rights may be brought about only by a vote of the members or of a body duly elected or appointed by the members, or a committee thereof, and that the member whose occupancy rights are terminated has a right to appear and make representations prior to such vote. *Residential Rent Regulation Act*, S.O. 1986, c. 63, s. 1.

NON-PROFIT CORPORATION. A corporation, no part of the income of which is payable to or is otherwise available for the personal benefit of any proprietor, member or shareholder thereof.

NON-PROFIT ORGANIZATION. 1. An organization (i) wholly owned by the Government, by a municipality or by any agency of either of them; or (ii) constituted exclusively for charitable or benevolent purposes where no part of the income is payable to or otherwise available for the personal benefit of any proprietor, member or shareholder. 2. A corporate or unincorporated body carrying on an activity the preponderant purpose of which is a purpose other than the making of a profit. *An Act to Amend the Real Property Assessment Act*, S.P.E.I. 1984, c. 34, s. 1.

NON-PROFIT PROGRAM OF CAMPING. An organized program of camping activities planned and conducted according to recognized and accepted principles of camping at a camp: (i) by a non-profit organization using accommodation, equipment and facilities suitable for such a program; (ii) as a service to the community during one or more months from June to September, both inclusive; and (iii) where the average of the fees for campers, including free campers, is not more than $8 a day. *Ministry of Culture and Recreation Act*, R.R.O. 1980, Reg. 651, s. 1.

NON-PROFIT SOCIETY. (i) A society incorporated under The Societies Act; (ii) a community service association incorporated or registered under The Co-operative Associations Act; or (iii) a non-profit corporation or class of non-profit corporations as may be defined by the regulations. *The Recreational and Cultural Facilities Capital Grants Act*, R.S.S. 1978, c. R-8, s. 2.

NON-PROGRAMMING. *n.* Audio signals or visual signals, or both, or the provision of such signals, which are directed from a person to a person by means of telecommunication facilities and which are not programming or programming services or telephone services and includes audio signals and visual signals transmitted through point to point services and any service

through which particular signals are transmitted to a person for the purposes of that person and not to the public at large. Manitoba statutes.

NON-PROGRAMMING SERVICES. Audio signals or visual signals, or both, or the provision of such signals, which are directed from a person to a person by means of telecommunication facilities and which are not programming or programming services or telephone services and includes audio signals and visual signals transmitted through point to point services and any service through which particular signals are transmitted to a person for the purposes of that person and not to the public at large. Manitoba statutes.

NON PROS. *abbr.* Non prosequitur.

NON PROSEQUITUR. [L.] One does not follow up.

NON-PUBLIC PROPERTY. (a) All money and property, other than issues of materiel, received for or administered by or through messes, institutes or canteens of the Canadian Forces; (b) all money and property contributed to or by officers, men, units or other elements of the Canadian Forces for the collective benefit and welfare of such officers, men, units or other elements; (b) by-products and refuse and the proceeds of the sale thereof, to the extent prescribed under subsection 39(2); and (d) all money and property derived from, purchased out of the proceeds of the sale of, or received in exchange for, money and property described in paragraphs (a) to (c). *National Defence Act*, R.S.C. 1985, c. N-5, s. 2.

NON-QUALIFIED INVESTMENT. 1. Property that is not a qualified investment for a trust governed by a deferred profit sharing plan or revoked plan within the meaning of paragraph (e). *Income Tax Act*, R.S.C. 1952, c. 148 (as am. S.C. 1970-71-72, c. 63), s. 204(d). 2. In relation to a trust governed by a registered retirement savings plan means property acquired by the trust after 1971 that is not a qualified investment for such trust. *Income Tax Act*, R.S.C. 1952, c. 148 (as am. S.C. 1970-71-72, c. 63), c. 146(1)(e). See INITIAL ~.

NON-QUALIFYING BUSINESS. A business, other than a personal services business, which is; (a) the professional practice of an accountant, dentist, lawyer, medical doctor, veterinarian or chiropractor; (b) a business of providing services if more than 66.66 per cent of the gross revenue for the year of that business derived from services; (i) is derived from services provided to, or performed for or on behalf of, one entity; and (ii) can reasonably be attributed to services performed by persons who are specified shareholders of the corporation or persons related

691

thereto, unless the corporation employs in the business throughout the year more than five full-time employees who are not specified shareholders of the corporation or persons related thereto; or a business the principal purpose of which is to provide managerial, administrative, financial, maintenance or other similar services, to lease property (other than real property), or to provide any such services and to lease property (other than real property), to one or more businesses connected at any time in the year with the corporation.

NON QUOD DICTUM EST, SED QUOD FACTUM EST, IN JURE INSPICITUR. [L.] In law, not what is said, but what is done, is considered.

NON QUOD VOLUIT TESTATOR, SED QUOD DIXIT IN TESTAMENTO INSPICITUR. [L.] In construing a will, not what the testator wished, but what was said, is considered.

NON REFERT AN QUIS ASSENSUM SUUM PRAEFERT VERBIS, AUT REBUS IPSIS ET FACTIS. [L.] It does not matter whether one offers agreement in words, or by the acts and deeds themselves.

NON REFERT QUID NOTUM SIT JUDICI, SI NOTUM NON SIT IN FORMA JUDICII. [L.] It does not matter what is noted by the judge, if it is not noted judicially.

NON-REFILLABLE CONTAINER. A container that is not a refillable container, but does not include: (i) a container, (A) that is used or intended to be used to contain a product in bulk, (B) that is for use in connection with soft drink dispensing machines, and (C) that is accepted for reuse as a container by a retail vendor, distributor, processor or manufacturer of carbonated soft drinks; or (ii) a container that contains or is intended to contain other containers. *Environmental Protection Act*, R.R.O. 1980, Reg. 299, s. 1.

NON-RELOCATABLE STRUCTURE. A factory built unit intended for use on permanent foundations. *Power Corporation Act*, R.R.O. 1980, Reg. 794, s. 0.

NON-RENEWABLE RESOURCE. Any naturally occurring inorganic substance, and includes coal, bituminous shales and other stratified deposits from which oil can be extracted by destructive distillation and including petroleum. *The Health Services Tax Act*, S.N.S. 1982, c. 27, s. 1.

NON-RENEWABLE RESOURCE REVENUE. 1. (i) Money received by the Crown under a mineral agreement or a contract under section 9 of the Mines and Minerals Act or under a reservation of royalty in letters patent conveying title to a mineral; (ii) money received by the Crown from or in connection with the disposition of the Crown's royalty share of a mineral; (iii) fees paid to the Crown in connection with the issuance of a mineral agreement; (iv) money received by the Crown as a bonus to acquire a mineral agreement; and (v) money received by the Crown pursuant to a contract under which the Crown agrees to accept that money in lieu of royalty otherwise payable under one or more oil sands leases issued under the Mines and Minerals Act. *Alberta Heritage Savings Trust Funds Amendment Act, 1984*, S.A. 1984, c. 4, s. 2. 2. All moneys received by the Crown pursuant to: (i) The Mineral Resources Act and the regulations made under that Act; (ii) The Mineral Taxation Act and the regulations made under that Act, but does not include the mineral acreage tax imposed under section 3 of that Act; (iii) The Oil and Gas Conservation Act and the regulations made under that Act; (iv) The Oil Well Income Tax Act and the regulations made under that Act; (v) The Road Allowances Crown Oil Act and the regulations made under that Act. *The Heritage Fund (Saskatchewan) Act*, R.S.S. 1978, c. H-2.1, s. 2.

NON-RESIDENT. *var.* **NON RESIDENT.** *var.* **NONRESIDENT.** 1. (a) An individual who is not ordinarily resident in Canada; (b) a corporation incorporated, formed or otherwise organized elsewhere than in Canada; (c) a corporation that is controlled directly or indirectly by non-residents as defined in paragraph (a) or (b); (d) a trust established by a non-resident as defined in paragraph (a), (b) or (c), or a trust in which non-residents as so defined have more than 50 per cent of the beneficial interest, or (e) a corporation that is controlled directly or indirectly by a trust mentioned in paragraph (d). 2. A person who is not a resident of the province, and for certain purposes a person who resides in the province for any period not exceeding 90 days shall with respect to that period be deemed to be a non-resident. 3. (i) An individual who resides in Saskatchewan for less than 183 days in a year; or (ii) a person, other than an individual, that is controlled directly or indirectly by non-resident individuals. *Apiaries Amendment Act, 1979*, S.S. 1979, c. 1, s. 3. 4. A person who is not a resident of a province. 5. A Canadian citizen or landed immigrant who is not a resident. 6. A person who has not actually resided in Ontario for a period of at least 7 months during the 12 months immediately preceding the time that his residence becomes material under this Act. *Game and Fish Act*, R.S.O. 1980, c. 182, s. 1. 7. A person who is not a resident but who makes their home and is ordinarily present in Canada and who has resided in Canada for the 12-month period immediately prior to the date of an application.

8. A person who does not reside within the municipality in which his lands affected by proceedings under this Act are situated. *The Private Ditches Act*, R.S.S. 1978, c. P-25, s. 2. 9. A person who makes his home and is ordinarily present in a place outside Canada. *Canada regulations.* See ASSOCIATES OF THE ~; CANADIAN ~; FOREIGN ~.

NON-RESIDENT ALIEN. *var.* **NON RESIDENT ALIEN.** 1. A person who is neither a resident nor a non resident. 2. A person who is neither a Canadian citizen or a resident. *Wildlife Act*, S.M. 1980, c. 73, s. 1.

NON-RESIDENT BUSINESS. A business, other than a resident business, carried on in the municipality or with respect to which any work or service is performed in the municipality. *Municipal Act*, R.S.B.C. 1979, c. 290, s. 497.

NON-RESIDENT CANADIAN. 1. A Canadian citizen who is not a resident. *Seal Protection Regulations*, C.R.C., c. 833, s. 2. 2. A person, other than a resident, who resides in Canada and has resided in Canada for at least 1 year preceding the granting of a fishery licence. *Saskatchewan Fishery Regulations*, C.R.C., c. 853, s. 2.

NON-RESIDENT COMPANY. A company, other than a crown corporation or, subject to subsection (3), a corporation exempt from the provisions of this section by order of the Lieutenant-Governor in Council, the principal seat of actual administration of which has not been in the province for at least 12 consecutive calendar months immediately prior to the appropriate date of application. *Crown Lands (Amendment) Act*, S.Nfld. 1971, c. 46, s. 2.

NON-RESIDENT CONTRACTOR. In the case of a natural person, one who is not domiciled in the province, and in the case of a company, a company which was not incorporated in the province, and includes a subcontractor. *Social Security Assessment Act*, S.Nfld. 1972, c. 56, s. 44.

NON-RESIDENT CONTROLLED DEALER. A dealer in which the total number of votes attached to voting securities beneficially owned directly or indirectly by: (i) non-residents and their associates and affiliates or over which non-residents and their associates and affiliates exercise control or direction exceeds 25 per cent of the total number of votes attached to the issued and outstanding voting securities of the dealer; or (ii) a non-resident and his associates and affiliates over which a non-resident and his associates and affiliates exercise control or direction exceeds 10 per cent of the total number of votes attached to the issued and outstanding

voting securities of the dealer. *Securities Act*, R.R.O. 1980, Reg. 910, s. 84.

NON-RESIDENT CONTROLLED REGISTRANT. A registrant in which the total number of votes attached to voting securities beneficially owned directly or indirectly by: (i) non-residents and their associates and affiliates or over which non-residents and their associates and affiliates exercise control or direction exceeds 25 per cent of the total number of votes attached to the issued and outstanding voting securities of the registrant; or (ii) a non-resident and his associates and affiliates over which a non-resident and his associates and affiliates exercise control or direction exceeds 10 per cent of the total number of votes attached to the issued and outstanding voting securities of the registrant. *Securities Act*, R.R.O. 1980, Reg. 910, s. 84.

NON-RESIDENT CORPORATION. 1. A corporation which is not resident in Canada. 2. A corporation, regardless of the jurisdiction in which it was formed or organized, that: (i) is controlled directly or indirectly by one or more non-resident persons; (ii) has issued shares to which are attached 50 per cent or more of the voting rights ordinarily exercisable at meetings of shareholders to one or more non-resident persons; (iii) has issued shares to which are attached 25 per cent or more of the voting rights ordinarily exercisable at meetings of shareholders to any one non-resident person; (iv) has a board of directors, one-half or more of which is composed of non-resident persons; or (v) in the case of a corporation without share capital, has a membership, one-half or more of which is composed of non-resident persons. *Non-resident Agricultural Land Interests Registration Act*, R.S.O. 1980, c. 318, s. 1. 3. A corporation incorporated, formed or otherwise organized in Canada or elsewhere; (i) that has allotted and issued shares to which are attached 50 per cent or more of the voting rights ordinarily exercisable at meetings of the shareholders of the corporation and that are owned by one or more non-resident persons, but this subclause does not apply where it is established to the satisfaction of the Minister that such one or more non-resident persons do not in fact directly or indirectly exercise control over the corporation and that subclause (v) does not apply to the corporation; (ii) that has allotted and issued shares to which are attached 25 per cent or more of the voting rights ordinarily exercisable at meetings of the shareholders of the corporation and that are owned by any one non-resident person, but this subclause does not apply where it is established to the satisfaction of the Minister that such non-resident person does not in fact directly or indirectly exercise control over the corporation and that subclause (v) does not apply to the corporation; (iii) one-half or more of the directors of which, or of the persons occupying the position of director by whatever name called, are individuals who are non-resident persons; (iv) without share capital and one-half or more of the members of which are non-resident persons; or (v) that is controlled directly or indirectly by one or more non-resident persons, including a non-resident corporation within the definition contained in the provisions of this clause other than this subclause. *Land Transfer Tax Act*, R.S.O. 1980, c. 231, s. 1.

NON-RESIDENT ENTITY. A corporation that is not resident in Canada, a partnership, organization, fund or entity that is not resident or is not situated in Canada or a trust with respect to which the rules in paragraph 94(1)(c) or (d) apply. *Income Tax Act*, R.S.C. 1952, c. 148 (as am. S.C. 1984, c. 45, s. 30), s. 94.1(2)(b).

NON-RESIDENT INSURER. See REGISTERED ~.

NON-RESIDENT ORGANIZATION. In relation to an association, a corporation that (a) is a member of that association, or (b) is eligible, pursuant to subsection 4(1), to become a member, and the majority of the members of which are non-residents or the majority of voting shares of which are held by non-residents. *Cooperative Credit Association Act*, R.S.C. 1985, c. C-41, s. 32.

NON-RESIDENT PERSON. 1. At any time, with respect to a taxpayer, includes a person that the taxpayer, based on reasonable inquiries, believes at that time to be a person not resident in Canada. *Income Tax Act*, R.S.C. 1952, c. 148 (as am. S.C. 1987, c. 46, s. 10), s. 33.1(1). 2. (i) An individual who is not ordinarily resident in Canada or who, if ordinarily resident in Canada, is neither a Canadian citizen nor an individual who has been lawfully admitted to Canada for permanent residence in Canada; (ii) a partnership, syndicate, association or other organization of whatsoever kind of which one-half or more of the members are non-resident persons within the meaning of subclause (i), (iii) or (iv) or in which interests representing in value 50 per cent or more of the total value of the property of such partnership, syndicate, association or other organization are beneficially owned by non-resident persons within the meaning of subclause (i), (iii) or (iv); (iii) a trust in which non-resident persons within the meaning of subclause (i), (ii) or (iv) have 50 per cent or more of the beneficial interests in the corpus of the trust or in the income arising therefrom, and "trust" includes the trustees under such a trust in their capacity as the trustees thereof; or (iv) a non-resident corporation. 3. A natural

person who has not been a resident of the province for at least 12 consecutive calendar months immediately prior to the appropriate date of application with the fixed settled intention of making his permanent home in the province. *Crown Lands (Amendment) Act*, S.Nfld. 1971, c. 46, s. 2. 4. A person who does not meet the requirements of clause (i): (i) an individual who resides in Saskatchewan for 183 days or more a year; or (ii) a farmer who resides for 183 days or more a year outside Saskatchewan but within 20 miles of the border of Saskatchewan. *The Saskatchewan Farm Ownership Act*, R.S.S. 1978, c. S-17, s. 2.

NON-RESIDENT SERVICES. The services provided for or on behalf of children and other persons who have not attained the age of 21 years, where such children and other persons do not reside in an approved children's institution. *Children's Institutions Act*, R.R.O. 1980, Reg. 98, s. 21.

NON-RETURNABLE CONTAINER. Any container not intended to be returned for reuse. *Retail Sales Tax Act*, R.R.O. 1980, Reg. 904, s. 1.

NON-SCHEDULED FLIGHT. A flight in an aircraft that is not a private aircraft and that is not operated on a scheduled flight. *Flying Accidents Compensation Regulations*, C.R.C., c. 10, s. 2.

NON-SEGREGATED PROPERTY. Of an insurer means its property other than property included in a segregated fund. *Income Tax Act*, R.S.C. 1952, c. 148 (as am. S.C. 1980-81-82-83, c. 140, c. 96(7)), s. 138(12)(j).

NON SEQUITUR. [L.] It does not follow.

NON SOLENT QUAE ABUNDANT VITIARE SCRIPTURAS. [L.] Excess does not usually make what is written void.

NON SUI JURIS. [L.] Not able to manage one's own affairs; with no legal capacity.

NONSUIT. *n.* The judgment ordered when a plaintiff cannot establish any legal cause of action or cannot support pleadings with any evidence.

NON SUM INFORMATUS. [L. I am not informed] I have not been instructed to defend.

NON-TAX REVENUE. Revenue other than (a) revenue raised on the municipal tax base; (b) grants computed under paragraph 4(1)(a), and subsections 4(1.1) and 4(2); and (c) transitional adjustment payments computed under subsection 4.1(2). *An Act to Amend the Municipal Assistance Act*, S.N.B. 1987, c. 39, s. 1.

NON-TRUST INDENTURE. A simple indenture used when a small number of lenders make a loan to a corporation and secure it by way of a floating charge. S.M. Beck *et al., Cases and Materials on Partnerships and Canadian Business Corporations* (Toronto: The Carswell Co., 1983), at 799.

NON-USER. *n.* One who no longer exercises a right.

NON VALET CONFIRMATIO, NISI ILLE, QUI CONFIRMAT, SIT IN POSSESSIONE REI VEL JURIS UNDE FIERI DEBET CONFIRMATIO; ET EODEM MODO, NISI ILLE CUI CONFIRMATIO FIT, SIT IN POSSESSIONE. [L.] Confirmation has no effect unless the very person who confirms either possesses the thing or the right of which confirmation should be made, and, likewise, unless the very person to whom confirmation is made has possession.

NON-VENTILATED CABLETROUGH. A cabletrough in which there are no ventilating openings in the bottom or sides. *Power Corporation Act*, R.R.O. 1980, Reg. 794, s. 0.

NON VIDENTUR QUI ERRANT CONSENTIRE. [L.] Those who are mistaken are not considered to consent.

NON VIDETUR CONSENSUM RETINUISSE SI QUIS EX PRAESCRIPTO MINANTIS ALIQUID IMMUTAVIT. [L.] One is not deemed to have retained consent if one changed anything on order of someone threatening.

NON VIDETUR QUISQUAM ID CAPERE, QUOD EI NECESSE EST ALII RESTITUERE. [L.] No one is deemed to take what must be given up to another.

NON-VOTING MEMBER. A member of a council who shall not vote in the determination of any matter or deliberation put to a vote in a council. *Regional and Tribal Councils Act*, S.N.W.T. 1983 (2d Sess.), c. 7, s. 2.

NON-WARD CARE. The temporary placement of a person under the age of 18 years by the director or a society in a foster home, group foster home or an institution without the transfer of guardianship in accordance with the provisions of section 19.1. *Child Welfare Act*, S.M. 1970, c. 87, s. 1.

NON-WARD SERVICE. The maintenance of a child outside his own home without transfer of guardianship. *Child Welfare Act*, R.S.N.B. 1973, c. C-4, s. 1.

NO ORDER AS TO COSTS. Neither party will pay the other any costs. M.M. Orkin, *The Law of Costs*, 2d ed. (Aurora: Canada Law Book, 1987) at 1-12.

N.O.P. *abbr.* Not otherwise provided for. *Customs Tariff*, R.S.C. 1985, c. C-54, s. 2.

NO PAR VALUE. Describes shares which have no nominal value but represent some portion of a company's net assets.

NORMAL. *adj.* Usual, in contrast to exceptional.

NORMAL COSTS. The assumed annual cost of benefits, excluding special payments, that would be attributable to the current year of a plan's operation in accordance with the actuarial valuation method used. *Pension Benefits Standards Regulations*, C.R.C., c. 1252, s. 2.

NORMAL CUBIC METRE. The quantity of gas occupying a volume of 1 cubic metre at 25 degrees Celsius and at a pressure of 760 millimetres of mercury. Canada regulations.

NORMAL DATE OF RETIREMENT. 1. The first day of the month next following the day on which an employee attains the age of 65 years. *The Superannuation (Supplementary Provisions) Act*, R.S.S. 1978, c. S-64, s. 37. 2. (a) In the case of a judge other than a judge mentioned in clause (b), the first day of the month next following the day on which he attains the age of 65 years; (b) in the case of a judge who has made an election pursuant to section 31 and who, on the day on which he makes an option to retire pursuant to subsection (2): (i) has served continuously as a judge for less than 25 years, the first day of the month next following the day on which he attains the age of 70 years; or (ii) has served continuously as a judge for 25 years or more, the first day of the month next following the day on which he attains the age of 65 years. *Provincial Court Amendment Act*, S.S. 1984-85-86, c. 101, s. 41.1.

NORMAL FLAVOUR AND AROMA. Means that the product is free from objectionable flavours or odours of any kind. *Processed Fruit and Vegetable Regulations*, C.R.C., c. 291, schedule I, c. 2.

NORMAL FLAVOUR AND ODOUR. Means that the product is free from objectionable flavours and odours of any kind. Canada regulations.

NORMAL FORM OF PENSION. An annuity under which payments are made during the lifetime of the annuitant and terminate on his death. *Saskatchewan Pension Plan Act*, S.S. 1986, c. C-32.2, s. 1.

NORMAL FULL-TIME COURSE LOAD. The number of courses in an approved program of study that an approved institution requires a student to take in any year in order to obtain

NORMAL HIGH WATER MARK

a certificate, diploma or degree in a minimum length of time.

NORMAL HIGH WATER MARK. The visible high water mark of a lake or river where the presence and action of water are so usual and so long continued in ordinary years as to mark upon the bed of the lake or river a character distinct from that of the bank thereof with respect to vegetation and the nature of the soil itself.

NORMAL LOAD. The portion of the weight of a vehicle (a) that is borne by each tire when (i) it is installed on that vehicle; (ii) that vehicle is at a weight equal to the sum of the curb weight, the accessory weight and the normal occupants' weight and is resting on a horizontal plane; and (iii) the normal occupants' weight is distributed in the vehicle in accordance with the table to this section; and (b) is calculated by (i) distributing to each axle its share of the combined weights referred to in subparagraph (a)(ii); and (ii) dividing such share by two. *Motor Vehicle Safety Regulations*, C.R.C., c. 1038, s. 111.

NORMAL OPERATIONS. The operations of the employer that require the employment of not less than the normal number of employees employed during a period specified in an order of the Lieutenant Governor in Council. *Essential Service Disputes Act*, R.S.B.C. 1979, c. 113, s. 1.

NORMAL PENSIONABLE AGE. The date or age specified in a pension plan at which an employee can retire from his employment and receive the regular pension benefit provided by the pension plan, whether such date is the day upon which the employee attains a given age or upon which the employee has completed a given period of employment. *Employment Standards Act*, R.R.O. 1980, Reg. 282, s. 1.

NORMAL PRODUCTION. The value of production which might reasonably be expected from the insured acreage computed by the Commission on such basis as it approves. *Crop Insurance Act (Ontario)*, R.R.O. 1980, Reg. 210, s. 3.

NORMAL RETIREMENT AGE. 1. The age of 70 years and 11 months. *The Teachers' Pensions Amendment Act*, S.M. 1985-86, c. 31, s. 2. 2. (i) The sixtieth birthday for designated firemen and policemen; (ii) the sixty-fifth birthday for all other members. *The Municipal Employees' Superannuation Act*, R.S.S. 1978, c. M-26, s. 2. 3. Sixty-five years of age. *Memorial University (Pensions) Act*, S.Nfld. 1977, c. 72, s. 1.

NORMAL RETIREMENT DATE. 1. The first day of the month immediately following the month in which normal retirement age is attained. *The Municipal Employees' Superannua-*

tion Act, R.S.S. 1978, c. M-26, s. 2. 2. The date or age specified in a pension plan as the normal retirement date of members. *Pension Benefits Act*, S.N.B. 1987, c. P-5.1, s. 1. 3. (i) June 30 immediately following attainment of the age of 65 years for members whose appointment date is July 1, 1966 or later; or (ii) August 31 immediately following attainment of the age of 65 years for members whose appointment date is prior to July 1, 1966. *Universities Academic Pension Act*, R.S.A. 1980, c. U-6, s. 1.

NORMAL WORKING HOURS. The number of hours that an employee might reasonably expect to work in the type of work in which the employee is engaged, consideration being given to (i) this or any other Act and any orders, rules and regulations made thereunder; or (ii) subject to subsection (1) of section 3, any more favourable provisions of any collective agreement, contract of service or custom. *Labour Standards Act*, S.Nfld. 1977, c. 52, s. 7.

NORMAN-FRENCH. *n.* In England, the language of legal procedure until the statute 1362, 36 Edw. 3, c. 15. The language has remained the same since the Conquest so that it differs from modern French.

NORTH ALBERTA LAND REGISTRATION DISTRICT. Being composed of all that portion of the Province of Alberta lying to the north of the ninth correction line. *Land Titles Act*, R.S.A. 1970, c. 198, s. 3.

NORTH AMERICAN GREAT LAKES ZONE. Lake Ontario, Lake Erie, Lake Huron (including Georgian Bay), Lake Michigan, Lake Superior, the waters connecting those lakes, the St. Lawrence Seaway and the St. Lawrence River west of the Victoria Bridge in Montreal. *General Load Line Rules*, C.R.C., c. 1425, s. 2.

NORTHEASTERN SASKATCHEWAN. The portion of the province lying north of the limit described in section 16 of The Northern Administration Act and east of the third meridian in the system of Dominion land surveys. *The Time Act*, R.S.S. 1978,c. T-14, s. 2.

NORTHERN AFFAIRS. See INDIAN AND ~ CANADA.

NORTHERN AND EASTERN SMALL BUSINESS DEVELOPMENT CORPORATION. A small business development corporation that may make investments only in small businesses that are primarily located within the geographic boundaries of northern and eastern Ontario as defined in the regulations. *Small Business Development Corporations Amendment Act*, S.O. 1986, c. 3, s. 1.

NORTHERN LABRADOR. 1. That part of the Coast of Labrador from and including the settlement of Rigolet to Cape Chidley, including the islands adjacent to the said part of the Coast of Labrador, and including also the settlement of North West River. *Northern Labrador (Social Services and Rehabilitation) Act*, R.S.Nfld. 1970, c. 274, s. 2. 2. All that area of the Labrador coast, including the islands adjacent thereto, north of Cape Rouge in Byron Bay. *Newfoundland Fishery Regulations*, C.R.C., c. 846, s. 347.

NORTHERN MANITOBA. All that part of Manitoba north of the northern boundary of township 21 that is not included in (i) a wildlife management area or refuge designated as such under The Wildlife Act; or (ii) a provincial forest designated as such under The Forest Act; or (iii) a municipality; or (iv) any area designated by the Lieutenant Governor in Council for the purposes of this Act. *Northern Affairs Act*, S.M. 1974, c. 56, s. 1.

NORTHERN ONTARIO. 1. All those parts of Ontario lying north and west of the Mattawa River, Lake Nipissing and the French River and includes the Territorial District of Manitoulin. *Mining Tax Act*, R.R.O. 1980, Reg. 639, s. 1. 2. Those portions of Ontario that comprise, (i) the Territorial districts of Algoma, Cochrane, Kenora, Manitoulin, Parry Sound, Rainy River, Sudbury, Timiskaming and Thunder Bay, and (ii) those portions of the Territorial District of Nipissing lying to the north or west of Algonquin Provincial Park. *Highway Traffic Act*, R.R.O. 1980, Reg. 469, s. 5.

NORTHERN PATIENT TRANSPORTATION PROGRAM. The program established to provide, or to assist financially or otherwise in the provision of, transportation services required to enable persons located at places within that part of northern Manitoba specified and described in a regulation of the commission to obtain medical treatment or diagnosis that is not available at those places. *The Ambulance Services Act*, S.M. 1985-86, c. 7, s. 1.

NORTHERN REGIONS. That area of Canada lying north of the southern limit of permafrost as shown on Map 1246A published in 1967 and reprinted 1969, of the Geological Survey of Canada, entitled "Permafrost in Canada", or any official map issued in lieu thereof. *Gas Pipeline Regulations*, C.R.C., c. 1052, s. 2.

NORTHERN VILLAGE CORPORATION. The corporation erected for each Inuit community under the Act concerning Northern Villages and the Kativik Regional Government or, until such corporation is created, the community council of such Inuit community or, in its absence, that which, on the advice of the Kativik Regional Government, stands in its place. *An Act Respecting the Support Program for Inuit Beneficiaries of the James Bay and Northern Québec Agreement for their Hunting, Fishing and Trapping Activities*, S.Q. 1982, c. 47, s. 1.

NORTHERN ZONE. That portion of the Territory lying north of the 50th parallel of latitude. *An Act respecting hunting and fishing rights in the James Bay and New Québec territories*, S.Q. 1978, c. 92, s. 6.

NOSCITUR A SOCIIS. [L.] 1. One is known by one's associates. 2. A word's meaning can be gathered from its context.

NOSCITUR EX SOCIO, QUI NON COGNOSCITUR EX SE. [L.] One who cannot be known from the self is known from an associate.

NOSCUNTUR A SOCIIS. [L.] When one joins words which could have analogous meaning, one is using them in their cognate sense. P. St. J. Langan, ed., *Maxwell on The Interpretation of Statutes*, 12th ed. (Bombay: N.M. Tripathi, 1976) at 289. See NOSCITUR A SOCIIS.

NO SHOOTING AREA. An area in which the discharge of a firearm is prohibited.

NOSTRUM EST JUDICARE SECUNDUM ALLEGATA ET PROBATA. [L.] It is our role to judge by pleadings and proofs.

NOTA BENE. [L.] Note well.

NOTARIAL. *adj.* Includes prothonotarial. *Registry Act*, R.S.O. 1980, c. 445, s. 1.

NOTARIAL ACT. 1. A notary's written authentication or certification, under official seal or signature, of any entry or document. 2. Any attestation, certificate or instrument which a notary executes.

NOTARIAL CERTIFICATE. An instrument which certifies the authenticity of the document to which it is attached.

NOTARY. *n.* One who attests a deed or document to make it authentic in another jurisdiction. See RECORDS OF A ~.

NOTARY PUBLIC. One who attests a deed or document to make it authentic in another jurisdiction and is empowered to take affidavits and declarations and to perform various other acts relating to legal matters.

NOTATION. *n.* Any addition to, or alteration of, a registration in the records of the Registrar General or a division registrar. *Vital Statistics Act*, R.S.O. 1980, c. 524, s. 1.

NOT CUT TO SIZE OR SHAPE. Wherever it appears in any tariff item in Group V of Schedule II, means, (a) in the case of rolls of paper or paperboard, rolls that are the output of papermaking machines and that have not been punched, perforated, scored, ruled, printed, folded, embossed, decorated or otherwise converted; and (b) in the case of sheets of paper or paperboard, rectangular sheets of 17 inches by 22 inches or larger that have not been slit, punched, perforated, scored, ruled, printed, folded, embossed, decorated or otherwise converted. *Customs Tariff*, R.S.C. 1985, c. C-54, s. 3.

NOTE. *v.* Of a dishonoured foreign bill, for a notary public to record her or his initials, the day, month, year and reason, if given, for non-payment.

NOTE. *n.* 1. A promissory note. *Bills of Exchange Act*, R.S.C. 1985, c. B-4, s. 2. 2. Any corporate obligation, unsecured or secured. H. Sutherland, D.B. Horsley & J.M. Edmiston, eds., *Fraser's Handbook on Canadian Company Law*, 7th ed. (Toronto: Carswell, 1985) at 310. See BANK-~; CIRCULAR ~; COVER ~; CREDIT ~; DEBIT ~; DEMAND ~; EXPLANATORY ~; INLAND ~; MARGINAL ~; POST-~; PREMIUM ~; PROMISSORY ~; SUBORDINATED ~; TREASURY ~.

NOTED CONSPICUOUSLY. Written so that the person against whom words appear to operate should reasonably notice them.

NOTE DEFAULT. For a registrar to note that the defendant failed to deliver a statement of defence within the prescribed time when the plaintiff filed proof of service of the statement of claim. G.D. Watson & C. Perkins, eds., *Holmested & Watson: Ontario Civil Procedure* (Toronto: Carswell, 1984) at 19-3.

NOTE OF HAND. A promissory note.

NOTES. *n.* Notes of the Bank intended for circulation in Canada. *Bank of Canada Act*, R.S.C. 1985, c. B-2, s. 2. See JUDGE'S ~.

NOT-FOR-PROFIT COMPANY. A body corporate registered under the Companies Act (i) that does not have the word "limited" as part of its name by reason of a direction or authorization of the Registrar of Companies under Part 9 of that Act; or (ii) that by its memorandum of association or articles of association prohibits the payment to its members of any dividend, but does not include a municipal housing company limited by shares incorporated under the Companies Act and having as its object the development, provision and operation, or any of them, of housing and accommodation. *Business Corporations Act*, S.A. 1981, c. B-15, s. 261.

NOT-FOR-PROFIT ORGANIZATION. A not-for-profit society or not-for-profit community, recreational or service organization. *Charitable Grants Act*, S.N.B. 1983, c. C-2.01, s. 1.

NOT GUILTY. The plea appropriate to an indictment when the accused chooses to raise a general issue, *i.e.*, to deny everything and let the prosecution prove whatever they can.

NOTHINGS. *n.* Business expenditures which are not recognized in the tax system. W. Grover & F. Iacobucci, *Materials on Canadian Income Tax*, 4th ed. (Toronto: Richard De Boo Ltd., 1980) at 339.

NOTICE. *n.* 1. Cognisance; knowledge; judicial notice. 2. To give someone notice of a fact is to bring that fact to the person's attention. 3. A document which informs or advises someone that that person's interests are involved in a proceeding or which informs the person of something which that person has a right to know. See ACTUAL ~; ADEQUATE ~; APPEARANCE ~; CONSTRUCTIVE ~; DEPARTURE ~; JUDICIAL ~; JURY ~; OFFICIAL ~; ORIGINATING ~; SECURITY ~; STRIKE ~.

NOTICE OF ABANDONMENT. A notice either written or oral by which a fisherman informs the Minister of his decision to abandon to Her Majesty his insured vessel and electronic equipment insured under these Regulations and to claim for a constructive total loss. *Fishing Vessel Insurance Regulations*, C.R.C., c. 325, s. 2.

NOTICE OF ACTION. A document containing a short statement about the nature of the claim which may commence any action other than a divorce action when there is not enough time to prepare a full statement of claim. G.D. Watson & C. Perkins, eds., *Holmested & Watson: Ontario Civil Procedure* (Toronto: Carswell, 1984) at 14-3.

NOTICE OF ANY KIND. Includes a recital or reference made in any registered instrument. *Land Transfer Tax Amendment Act, 1983*, S.O. 1983, c. 20, s. 1.

NOTICE OF APPEAL. A document by which an appeal is commenced and includes an order, case stated or reference of a tribunal originating an appeal by it. *Rules of the Supreme Court*, S.Nfld. 1986, r. 57, s. 57.01.

NOTICE OF APPLICATION. 1. An originating notice. G.D. Watson & C. Perkins, eds., *Holmested & Watson: Ontario Civil Procedure* (Toronto: Carswell, 1984) at CJA-179. 2. The first step in commencing an application. G.D. Watson & C. Perkins, eds., *Holmested & Watson: Ontario Civil Procedure* (Toronto: Carswell, 1984) at 14-4.

NOTICE OF CLAIM. A notice of claim registered under subsection 106 (2) and includes a notice registered under a predecessor of this Part or under The Investigation of Titles Act, being chapter 193 of the Revised Statutes of

Ontario, 1960, or a predecessor thereof. *Registry Amendment Act, 1981*, S.O. 1981, c. 17, s. 4.

NOTICE OF DISHONOUR. A formal notice concerning a bill of exchange. I.F.G. Baxter, *The Law of Banking*, 3d ed. (Toronto: Carswell, 1981) at 117.

NOTICE OF DISPUTE. A notice filed by a person pursuant to subsection 6(6) indicating that he is disputing his liability to pay a surcharge. *Automobile Accident Insurance Amendment Act*, S.S. 1984-85-86, c. 1, s. 7.

NOTICE OF INTENT TO DEFEND. In Ontario practice, the document which a defendant who intends to defend an action delivers and which gives that defendant 10 more days to file a statement of defence.

NOTICE OF MOTION. In Ontario practice, the document which initiates a motion and notifies other parties of the motion, used unless the circumstances or the nature of the motion make it unnecessary.

NOTICE OF READINESS FOR TRIAL. In Ontario practice, the document, formerly called a certificate of readiness, which the party who is ready for trial and who wishes to set the action down for trial serves on every other party to the action.

NOTICE PAPER. A document by which members of Parliament give notice that they intend to introduce bills, seek answers to written questions or move a motion as Private Members' business. A. Fraser, G.A. Birch & W.A. Dawson, eds., *Beauchesne's Rules and Forms of the House of Commons of Canada*, 5th ed. (Toronto: Carswell, 1978) at 48.

NOTICE PERIOD. 1. The period ending on the day 40 years after the day of the registration of an instrument or a notice of claim, as the case may be. *Registry Amendment Act, 1981*, S.O. 1981, c. 17, s. 4. 2. A period of 3 consecutive tenancy months. *Landlord and Tenant Act*, R.S.A. 1980, c.L-6, s. 6.

NOTICE TO QUIT. The notice required for either a landlord or a tenant to terminate a tenancy without the other's consent when that tenancy runs from year to year or for some other indefinite period.

NOTIFIABLE CONDITION OF ILL HEALTH. Those diseases, injuries or other conditions of ill health designated by regulation, any incidence of which must be reported to the Chief Health Officer. *Public Health Act*, S.P.E.I. 1980, c. 42, s. 1.

NOTIFIABLE DISEASE. A disease whose presence must be made known to the director of a health unit, a medical health officer, a board of health or other officer, pursuant to this Act or the regulations. *Public Health Act*, R.S.N.S. 1967, c. 247, s. 1.

NOTIFICATION. *n.* 1. A direction in a form prescribed by the Governor in Council pursuant to paragraph 23(k) and issued pursuant to subsection 9(2). *Territorial Lands Act*, R.S.C. 1985, c. T-7, s. 2. 2. With reference to real estate, means an instrument, agreement, notification, memorandum or other document (i) having the effect of making the real estate liable to be sold, leased or otherwise dealt with for the purpose of satisfying a debt or claim, or indicating that it may be so liable; or (ii) having the effect of prohibiting or restricting the right of the owner to alienate the real estate or any interest in the real estate, or to mortgage, charge or otherwise deal with the real estate, and includes a caveat in respect of an instrument, agreement, notification, memorandum or other document mentioned in subclause (i) or (ii). *Trust Companies Act*, R.S.A. 1980, c. T-9, s. 114.

NOTIFY. *v.* 1. To take such steps as are reasonably required to give information to the person to be notified so that (i) it comes to his attention; or (ii) it is directed to such person at his customary address or at his place of residence, or at such other place as is designated by him over his signature. Personal Property Security acts. 2. The forwarding by a cablecaster of a notice in writing by ordinary mail to the subscriber, which notice shall be deemed to have been received 10 clear days after the day it is mailed. *The Community Cablecasters Act*, R.S.S. 1978, c. C-17, s. 17.

NOTING. *n.* A notary's record on a bill at the time it is dishonoured. I.F.G. Baxter, *The Law of Banking*, 3d ed. (Toronto: Carswell, 1981) at 117.

NOTIONAL MARKET. See HYPOTHETICAL OR ~.

NOTORIOUS. *adj.* In evidence, describes a matter which need not be proved.

NO-UNION VOTE. A ballot rejecting all unions participating in a representation vote of workers.

NOVA CAUSA INTERVENIENS. [L.] A new cause intervenes.

NOVA CONSTITUTIO FUTURIS FORMAM IMPONERE DEBET NON PRAETERITIS. [L.] A new law should regulate the future not the past.

NOVA CUSTOMA. [L.] Duty; imposition.

NOVA SCOTIA. See RESIDENT OF ~.

NOVA SCOTIA LANDS. 1. (i) Sable Island; and (ii) those submarine areas that belong to Her

Majesty in right of the Province, or in respect of which Her Majesty in right of the Province has the right to dispose of or exploit the natural resources and that are within the limits described in Schedule I of this Act. *Offshore Oil and Gas Act*, S.N.S. 1984, c. 8, s. 2. 2. The land mass of Nova Scotia including Sable Island, and includes the seabed and subsoil off the shore of the land mass of Nova Scotia, the seabed and subsoil of the Continental shelf and slope and the seabed and subsoil seaward from the Continental shelf and slope to the limit of exploitability. *Pipeline Act*, S.N.S. 1979-80, c. 13, s. 2.

NOVA SCOTIA OFFSHORE AREA. Has the meaning assigned to the expression "offshore area" by the Canada-Nova Scotia Offshore Petroleum Resources Accord Implementation Act. *Income Tax Act*, R.S.C. 1952, c. 148 (as am. S.C. 1988, c. 28, s. 252), s. 248(1).

NOVA SCOTIA OFFSHORE PIPELINE. A line for the transmission of oil or gas in the offshore area or from the offshore area and includes all lines, branches, extensions, tanks, reservoirs, storage facilities, pumps, racks, compressors, loading facilities, interstation systems of communication by telephone, telegraph or radio, and real and personal property and works connected therewith that are located within the offshore area or any other part of Nova Scotia, but does not include a pipeline carrying oil or gas solely for consumption in Nova Scotia. *Canada-Nova Scotia Oil and Gas Agreement (Nova Scotia) Act*, S.N.S. 1984, c. 2, s. 19.

NOVA SCOTIA VENTURE CORPORATION. (i) A corporation registered under this Act, and (ii) any other corporation in which Her Majesty in the right of the Province, or an agency of Her Majesty or a corporation controlled by Her Majesty, owns equity shares and that is prescribed to be a venture corporation. *Venture Corporations Act*, S.N.S. 1979-80, c. 20, s. 2.

NOVATIO. *n.* [L.] The remaking or renewing of an extant obligation.

NOVATION. *n.* Substituting a new contract, with new parties, for one previously existing, an act which, unlike assignment, requires that all of the original parties consent. G.H.L. Fridman, *Sale of Goods in Canada*, 3d ed. (Toronto: Carswell, 1986) at 26.

NOVATIO NON PRAESUMITUR. [L.] One does not presume a novation.

NOVEL DISSEISIN. Recent disseisin.

NOVELTY. See OBJECTION FOR WANT OF ~.

NOVITAS NON TAM UTILITATE PRODEST QUAM NOTITATE PERTURBAT. [L.] Something new does not benefit by its utility as much as it disturbs with its novelty.

NOVITER AD NOTITIAM PERVENTA. [L.] Things which recently came to a party's knowledge.

NOVUM JUDICIUM NON DAT JUS NOVUM, SED DECLARAT ANTIQUUM; QUIA JUDICIUM EST JURIS DICTUM ET PER JUDICIUM JUS EST NOVITER REVELATUM QUOD DIU FUIT VELATUM. [L.] A new judgment does not create new law, but clarifies old law; because a judgment is a statement of the law and through a judgment law which was previously obscure is newly clarified.

NOVUS ACTUS INTERVENIENS. [L.] A new act intervenes.

NOVUS HOMO. [L.] A discharged insolvent; a pardoned criminal.

NOW. *adv.* Shall be construed as referring to the time of commencement of the enactment containing the word. Interpretation acts.

NOW AND NEXT. 1. Apply to the time when the Act becomes executory. *Interpretation Act*, R.S.Q. 1977, c. I-16, s. 61. 2. Shall be construed as having reference to the time when the Act was presented for the assent of the Lieutenant-Governor. *Interpretation Act*, R.S.N.B. 1973, c. I-13, s. 38. 3. Shall be construed as referring to the time of commencement of the enactment containing the word. *Interpretation Act*, R.S.A. 1980, c. I-7, s. 25.

NOW, NEXT, HERETOFORE AND HEREAFTER. Shall be interpreted as having reference to the time when an Act or the part or provision of the Act containing the word or any of them came into force.

NOW OR NEXT. Shall be construed as having reference to the time when the enactment was enacted. *Interpretation Act*, R.S.C. 1970, c. I-23, s. 28.

NOXA SEQUITUR CAPUT. [L.] Guilt follows the individual.

NOXIOUS WEED. A plant that is designated under this Act as a noxious weed. *Weed Control Act*, R.S.N.S. 1967, c. 336, s. 1.

NOXIOUS WEEDS. Includes the following plants or seeds thereof: perennial sow thistle, annual sow thistle, Canada thistle, couch grass, poverty weed, wild oats, darnel, wild mustard, stinkweed, tumbling mustard, hare's ear mustard, ball mustard, toad flax (linaria vulgaris), false flax, bird rape, Russian thistle, blue burr, ragweed, purple cockle, cow cockle, night flowering catchfly, green foxtail (setaria viridis), bladder campion, leafy spurge, hoary cress,

Russian knapweed, field bindweed (convolvulus arvensis), and barbery, marihuana, sometimes known as Indian hemp (cannabis sativa), tartary buckwheat (fagopyrum tataricum), and such other plants as may be declared by the minister by order published in The Saskatchewan Gazette to be noxious weeds. *The Noxious Weeds Act*, R.S.S. 1978, c. N-9, s. 2.

N.P.B. *abbr.* National Parole Board.

N.P.L. *abbr.* Non-personal liability. Part of the name of a specially limited company in B.C. H. Sutherland, D.B. Horsley & J.M. Edmiston, eds., *Fraser's Handbook on Canadian Company Law*, 7th ed. (Toronto: Carswell, 1985) at 438.

N.R. *abbr.* National Reporter, 1974-.

NRC. *abbr.* National Research Council of Canada.

N.S. *abbr.* Nova Scotia.

N.S.F. *abbr.* Not sufficient funds.

N.S. L. NEWS. *abbr.* Nova Scotia Law News.

N.S.R. *abbr.* Nova Scotia Reports, 1834-1929.

N.S.R. (2d). *abbr.* Nova Scotia Reports (Second Series), 1970-.

NTP LITRE. A device that (a) in fully operating condition weighs less than 100 kilograms; (b) operates without external supplies of oxygen or power; (c) is capable of supplying medical oxygen; (d) is represented or advertised for use in emergency situations; and (e) does not make use of forced ventilation. *Medical Devices Regulations*, C.R.C., c. 871, s. 1.

NUCLEAR ENERGY HAZARD. The radioactive, toxic, explosive or other hazardous properties of prescribed substances under the Atomic Energy Control Act (Canada). Insurance Acts.

NUCLEAR FACILITY. A nuclear reactor, a sub-critical nuclear reactor, a particle accelerator, a plant for the separation, processing, reprocessing or fabrication of fissionable substances, a plant for the production of deuterium or deuterium compounds, a facility for the disposal of prescribed substances and includes all land, buildings and equipment that are connected or associated with such reactor, accelerator, plant or facility. *Atomic Energy Control Regulations*, C.R.C., c. 365, s. 2.

NUCLEAR INCIDENT. An occurrence resulting in injury or damage that is attributable to a breach of the duty imposed on an operator by this Act. *Nuclear Liability Act*, R.S.C. 1985, c. N-28, s. 2.

NUCLEAR INSTALLATION. A structure, establishment or place, or two or more structures, establishments or places at a single location, coming within any of the following descriptions and designated as a nuclear installation for the purposes of this Act by the Atomic Energy Control Board, namely: (a) a structure containing nuclear material in such an arrangement that a self-sustaining chain process of nuclear fission can be maintained therein without an additional source of neutrons, including any such structure that forms part of the equipment of a ship, aircraft or other means of transportation; (b) a factory or other establishment that processes or reprocesses nuclear material; or (c) a place in which nuclear material is stored other than incidentally to the carriage of the material. *Nuclear Liability Act*, R.S.C. 1985, c. N-28, s. 2.

NUCLEAR MATERIAL. 1. (a) Any material other than thorium or natural or depleted uranium uncontaminated by significant quantities of fission products, that is capable of releasing energy by a self-sustaining chain process of nuclear fission; (b) radioactive material produced in the production or utilization of material referred to in paragraph (a); and (c) material made radioactive by exposure to radiation consequential on or incidental to the production or utilization of material referred to in paragraph (a), but does not include radioactive isotopes that are not combined, mixed or associated with material referred to in paragraph (a). 2. (a) Plutonium, except plutonium with an isotopic concentration of plutonium-238 exceeding 80 per cent; (b) uranium-233; (c) uranium containing uranium-233 or uranium-235 or both in such an amount that the abundance ratio of the sum of those isotopes to the isotope uranium-238 is greater than 0.72 per cent; (d) uranium with an isotopic concentration equal to that occurring in nature; and (e) any substance containing anything described in paragraphs (a) to (d), but does not include uranium in the form of ore or ore-residue. *Criminal Law Amendment Act*, R.S.C. 1985 (1st Supp.), c. 27, s. 5(3.6).

NUCLEAR SHIP. A ship fitted with a nuclear power plant. *Canada Shipping Act*, R.S.C. 1985, c. S-9, s. 2.

NUDA PACTIO OBLIGATIONEM NON PARIT. [L.] A simple promise does not create an obligation.

NUDI CONSENSUS OBLIGATIO CONTRARIO CONSENSU DISSOLVITUR. [L.] The binding force of a contract made with no consideration is dissolved by an agreement to the contrary.

NUDUM PACTUM. [L. a bare agreement] An agreement made with no consideration.

NUDUM PACTUM EST UBI NULLA SUBEST CAUSA PRAETER CONVENTIONEM; SED UBI SUBEST CAUSA, FIT OBLIGATIO, ET PARIT ACTIONEM. [L.] A contract is naked where there is no consideration except the agreement; but where there is consideration, an obligation arises and creates a cause of action.

NUISANCE. *n.* 1. An activity or physical condition which causes harm or annoyance or the harm resulting from the activity or condition. John G. Fleming, *The Law of Torts*, 6th ed. (Sydney: The Law Book Co., 1983) at 378. 2. A condition that is or that might become injurious or dangerous to the public health, or that might hinder in any manner the prevention or suppression of disease. 3. Anything which is injurious to the health, or indecent, or offensive to the senses, or an obstruction to the free use of property so as to interfere with the comfortable enjoyment of life or property. 4. Includes and shall be deemed to include any condition, existing in any locality, which is or may become injurious or dangerous to health, or prevent or hinder in any manner the suppression of disease; and without restricting the generality of the aforegoing, for greater particularity the following shall be deemed nuisances within the meaning of this Act, if in such a state, or so situated, as to be injurious or dangerous to health: (a) any premises improperly constructed or in a state of disrepair; (b) any house of part of a house so over-crowded as to be injurious or dangerous to the health of the inmates, or in which insufficient air space is allowed for each inmate as required by the regulations; (c) any accumulation or deposit of refuse, wherever situate; (d) a street, pool, ditch, gutter, water-course, sink, cistern, water or earth closet, privy, urinal, cesspool, drain, dung pit or ash pit in a foul condition; (e) a well, spring or other water supply; and (f) a burial ground, cemetery, crematorium, columbarium or other place of sepulchre located or so overcrowded or otherwise so arranged or managed as to be offensive, or injurious or dangerous to health. *Health Act,* R.S.N.B. 1973, c. H-2, s. 1. 5. An animal, bird, insect, plant or disease declared to be a nuisance under section 2. *Agricultural Pests Act,* S.A. 1984, c. A-8.1, s. 1. See ABATEMENT OF ~; COMMON ~; PRIVATE ~; PUBLIC ~.

NUISANCE ANIMAL. An animal or bird not protected under The Wildlife Act or the regulations made thereunder or the Migratory Birds Convention Act (Canada) or under any other Act of the Legislature or of Parliament. *Predator Control Act,* R.S.M. 1970, c. P110, s. 2.

NULLA BONA. [L. no goods] The proper return of a writ when the judgment debtor has no goods in the sheriff's bailiwick or there are no proceeds available to satisfy the writ. C.R.B. Dunlop, *Creditor-Debtor Law in Canada* (Toronto: Carswell, 1981) at 399.

NULLA CURIA QUAE RECORDUM NON HABET POTEST IMPONERE FINEM, NEQUE ALIQUEM MANDARE CARCERI; QUIA ISTA SPECTANT TANTUMMODO AD CURIAS DE RECORDO. [L.] No court which does not have a record can impose a fine, or sentence any person to prison; because those powers only belong to courts of record.

NULLA IMPOSSIBILIA AUT INHONESTA SUNT PRAESUMENDA; VERA AUTEM ET HONESTA ET POSSIBILIA. [L.] One should not presume things which are impossible or shameful, but instead things which are true, seemly and possible.

NULL AND VOID. Not legally binding.

NULLA PACTIONE EFFICI POTEST UT DOLUS PRAESTETUR. [L.] By no contract is it possible to arrange that someone be indemnified against their own fraud.

NULLA POENA SINE LEGE. [L.] There should be no punishment except according to predetermined, fixed law. D. Stuart, *Canadian Criminal Law: a Treatise,* 2d ed. (Toronto: Carswell, 1987) at 15.

NULLITY. *n.* Something which has no legal effect.

NULLITY OF MARRIAGE. The total invalidity of an attempted, pretended or supposed marriage which was void from the beginning because the parties lacked consent or capacity to marry or which was voidable or liable to annulment later because one spouse was unable to consummate the marriage.

NULLIUS FILIUS. [L. the son of no one] A bastard.

NULLIUS HOMINIS AUCTORITAS APUD NOS VALERE DEBET, UT MELIORA NON SEQUEREMUR SI QUIS ATTULERIT. [L.] The authority of no one should prevail with us so that we would not adopt better things if someone else brought them.

NULLUM ARBITRIUM. [L.] There is no such award.

NULLUM CRIMEN SINE LEGE. [L.] There should be no crime except according to predetermined, fixed law. D. Stuart, *Canadian Criminal Law: a Treatise,* 2d ed. (Toronto: Carswell, 1987) at 15.

NULLUM CRIMEN SINE POENA. [L.] There should be no crime without a penalty.

NULLUM EXEMPLUM EST IDEM OMNI-BUS. [L.] No example is the same to everyone.

NULLUM FECERUNT ARBITRIUM. [L.] They submitted to no arbitration.

NULLUM INIQUUM EST IN JURE PRAES-UMENDUM. [L.] In law, the doing of something contrary to justice should not be presumed.

NULLUM SIMILE EST IDEM. [L.] Something similar to something else is not the same thing.

NULLUM TEMPUS AUT LOCUS OCCUR-RIT REGI. [L.] No time or place affects a monarch.

NULLUS COMMODUM CAPERE POTEST DE INJURIA SUA PROPRIA. [L.] No one can gain advantage by her or his very own wrong.

NULLUS VIDETUR DOLO FACERE QUI SUO JURE UTITUR. [L.] No one who merely avails herself or himself of a legal right is considered to be a wrongdoer.

NUL PRENDRA ADVANTAGE DE SON TORT DEMESNE. [Fr.] No person shall profit by the wrong that person does.

NUL TIEL AGARD. No such award.

NUL TIEL RECORD. No such record.

NUL TORT. No wrong has been done.

NUMBER. *n.* 1. When used in relation to a permit or plate means a number, a series of letters or a combination of letters and numbers. *Highway Traffic Amendment Act, 1982,* S.O. 1982, c. 15, s. 1. 2. When used in relation to the numbers assigned by the Chief Registrar of Deeds under section 2.21 includes a number and letter combination. *An Act to Amend the Standard Forms of Conveyances Act,* S.N.B. 1986, c. 77, s. 1. See CODE ~; CORPORATION ~; FUEL CONSUMPTION ~; REGISTER ~; REGISTRATION ~; SERIAL ~; TRUE FLIGHT MACH ~.

NUMBER NAME. The name of a corporation that consists only of its corporation number followed by the word "Ontario" and one of the words or abbreviations provided for in subsection 10 (1). *Business Corporations Act, 1982,* S.O. 1982, c. 4, s. 1.

NUMBER OF AXLES. The total number of axles on a vehicle or combination of vehicles that are transmitting weight to the highway. *Highway Traffic Act,* R.R.O. 1980, Reg. 470, s. 1.

NUMBER PLATE. 1. Includes any proof of registration issued and required to be affixed to a motor vehicle or trailer. 2. Validation decals for attachment to number plates. See FICTI-TIOUS ~; IDENTIFICATION ~.

NUNCHAKU. *n.* Two hard non-flexible sticks, clubs, pipes or rods connected by a rope, cord, wire or chain and designed to be used in connection with the practice of a system of self-defence such as karate. *Prohibited Weapons Order, No. 2,* C.R.C., c. 434, s. 2.

NUNCIO. *n.* [L.] A messenger; the Pope's envoy.

NUNC PRO TUNC. [L. now for then] The order of a court that a proceeding be dated with an earlier date than the date it actually took place, or that the same effect be produced as if the proceeding had happened at an earlier date.

NUNCUPATE. *v.* To declare solemnly and publicly.

NUNCUPATIVE WILL. An oral testament which depends solely on verbal evidence and which was spoken before enough witnesses by the testator in extremis and afterwards written down.

NUNDINATION. *n.* Traffic at a fair or market; any buying and selling.

NUNQUAM CRESCIT EX POST FACTO PRAETERITI DELICTI AESTIMATIO. [L.] The seriousness of an offence, once committed, never increases subsequently.

NUNQUAM INDEBITATUS. [L.] Never in debt.

NUPTIAE. *n.* [L.] Marriage.

NUPTIAL. *adj.* Related to marriage. See ANTE-NUPTIAL.

NUPTIAS NON CUNCUBITUS SED CON-SENSUS FACIT. [L.] Not cohabitation but consent makes a marriage.

NURSE. *n.* 1. Any person who is possessed of the qualifications required and is authorized to offer service for the care of the sick and to give care intended for the prevention of disease and to receive remuneration therefor. 2. Includes any person, other than a legally qualified medical practitioner, who attends at the birth of a child. *Vital Statistics Act,* R.S.O. 1980, c. 524, s. 1. See DENTAL ~; MENTAL DEFICIENCY ~; PRACTICAL ~; PSYCHIATRIC ~; REGIS-TERED ~.

NURSE PRACTITIONER. A registered nurse who has successfully completed a course of instruction conducted by the College of Nursing of The University of Saskatchewan for the purpose of qualifying persons to become nurse practitioners. *The Registered Nurses Act,* R.S.S. 1978, c. R-12.1, s. 19.

NURSERY. *n.* 1. Any place where fruit trees, fruit stock or ornamental plants are propagated for sale. 2. A place where plants other than herbaceous plants are grown, for the purpose of sale as living plants or for the purpose of selling the seed thereof. *Plant Pests and Diseases Act,* R.S.M. 1970, c. P90, s. 2. 3. The place where such trees, shrubs, bushes or plants are cultivated, kept, packed, delivered or shipped. *Plant Protection Act,* R.S.Q. 1977, c. P-39, s. 2. See DAY ~.

NURSERY-MAN. *n.* Any person who cultivates, for their increase and sale, trees, shrubs, bushes or fruit-bearing, ornamental or other plants. *Plant Protection Act,* R.S.Q. 1977, c. P-39, s. 2.

NURSERY SCHOOL. Day-care services provided in an establishment that receives at least 10 children from 2-5 years of age on a regular basis for periods of up to 3 hours a day.

NURSERY STOCK. Coniferous or hardwood seedlings, transplants, grafts or trees propagated or grown in a nursery and having the roots attached and includes cuttings having or not having roots attached.

NURSING. *n.* 1. The application of professional nursing knowledge or services for compensation for the purpose of assisting a person to achieve and maintain optimal health through (i) promoting, maintaining and restoring health; (ii) preventing illness, injury or disability; (iii) caring for the sick and dying; (iv) health teaching and health counselling; or (v) co-ordinating health care. *Registered Nurses' Association Act,* S.N.S. 1985, c. 5, s. 2. 2. The practice of nursing and includes the nursing assessment and treatment of human responses to actual or potential health problems and the nursing supervision thereof. *An Act Respecting the Nurses Association of New Brunswick,* S.N.B. 1984, c. 71, s. 2. See PRACTICAL ~; PRACTICE OF ~; PSYCHIATRIC ~.

NURSING AIDE. A person who, being neither a registered nurse nor a person in training to be a registered nurse at an approved school of nursing, undertakes the care of patients for remuneration. *Nursing Aides Act,* R.S.A. 1970, c. 263, s. 2.

NURSING ASSISTANT. A person who is trained to care for convalescent, subacutely ill and chronically ill patients, and to assist nurses in the care of acutely ill patients. See REGISTERED ~.

NURSING CARE. The use of methods, procedures and techniques employed in providing nursing care by persons with technical nursing training beyond the care that an untrained person can adequately administer. *Homes for Special Care Act,* S.N.S. 1976, c. 12, s. 2. See INTERMEDIATE ~; SKILLED ~.

NURSING EDUCATION PROGRAM. A program approved by the Board and which is a prerequisite for a person to have completed prior to the taking by that person of examinations as may be prescribed from time to time by a board to qualify as a registered nurse.

NURSING HOME. Any house, building or structure in which accommodation, meals and nursing services are provided to residents for compensation. See NON-DISTRICT ~.

NURSING HOME CARE. Provides the following services to patients: (i) accommodation, meals and laundry; (ii) personal services such as help and supervision in cleanliness, mobility, safety, feeding and dressing; (iii) special diets when necessary; (iv) routine drugs and dressings as ordered by the attending physician; (v) recreational, diversional and re-activational activities; and any other services prescribed by the regulations. *Nursing Homes Act,* R.S.A. 1980, c. N-14, s. 1.

NURSING HOME RESIDENT. (i) A resident of a special-care home, as defined in The Housing and Special-care Homes Act, who is receiving limited personal care, intensive personal care, limited nursing care or long-term care, as those terms are defined in The Housing and Special-care Homes Care and Rates Regulations; or (ii) a patient who: (A) in the opinion of the minister, is a long-stay resident in a hospital; and (B) is receiving limited nursing care or long-term care, as those terms are defined in The Housing and Special-care Homes Care and Rates Regulations. *Senior Citizens' Heritage Program Act,* S.S. 1984-85-86, c. S-46.01, s. 2.

NURSING PRACTICE. See EXCLUSIVE ~.

NURSING SERVICES. The use of methods, procedures and techniques employed in providing nursing care by persons with technical nursing training. *Community Care Facilities and Nursing Homes Act,* S.P.E.I. 1985, c. 9, s. 1.

NURSING STAFF. Includes a registered nurse, a registered nursing assistant and a health care aide also known as a non-registered nurses aide. *Nursing Homes Act,* R.R.O. 1980, Reg. 690, s. 1.

NUTRIENT. *n.* Any substance or combination of substances that, if added to any waters in sufficient quantities, provides nourishment that promotes the growth of aquatic vegetation in those waters to such densities as to (a) interfere with their use by man or by any animal, fish or plant that is useful to man; or (b) degrade or alter or form part of a process of degradation or alteration of the quality of those waters to an extent that is detrimental to their use by man or by any animal, fish or plant that is useful to man. *Canada Water Act*, R.S.C. 1985, c. C-11, s. 19. See MINERAL ~.

N.W.T. *abbr.* 1. Northwest Territories. 2. North West Territories Reports, 1887-1898.

[ ] N.W.T.R. *abbr.* Northwest Territories Reports, 1983-.

O

O.A.C. *abbr.* Ontario Appeal Cases.

O.A.R. *abbr.* Ontario Appeal Reports, 1876-1900.

OATH. *n.* 1. An appeal that a higher power witness the truth of a statement. 2. Includes affirmation and statutory declaration. 3. Includes a solemn affirmation in cases in which, by the law of Canada, or of a province, as the case may be, a solemn affirmation is allowed instead of an oath. See CORPORAL ~.

OATH OF ALLEGIANCE. The words of the oath are: I, ———, do swear that I will be faithful and bear true allegiance to Her Majesty Queen Elizabeth the Second, Queen of Canada, Her Heirs and Successors. So help me God. *Oaths of Allegiance Act*, R.S.C. 1985, c. O-1, s. 2(1).

OATH OR AFFIDAVIT. In the case of persons for the time being allowed or required by law to affirm or declare instead of swearing, includes affirmation and declaration.

OATH OR AFFIRMATION OF CITIZENSHIP. The words of the oath are: I swear (or affirm) that I will be faithful and bear true allegiance to Her Majesty Queen Elizabeth the Second, Queen of Canada, Her Heirs and Successors, and that I will faithfully observe the laws of Canada and fulfill my duties as a Canadian citizen. *Citizenship Act*, R.S.C. 1985, c. C-29, Schedule.

OAT PRODUCT. Any substance produced by processing or manufacturing oats.

OBEDIENTIA EST LEGIS ESSENTIA. [L.] Obedience is the indispensable element of law.

OBITER DICTUM. [L. a remark in passing] An opinion not required in a judgment and so not a binding precedent.

OBJECT. *n.* 1. Includes an object of natural growth. *Aeronautics Act*, R.S.C. 1985 (1st Supp.), c. 33, s. 5.4. 2. An object of archaeological or historic significance. *Ontario Heritage Act*,

R.S.O. 1980, c. 337, s. 1. 3. An object (a) that is more than 50 years old; or (b) that was made by a natural person who is no longer living. *Canadian Cultural Property Export Control List*, C.R.C., c. 448, s. 2. 4. Art, other than ethnographic art, in which the principles of design, ornamentation, enrichment or decoration are applied to the production of functional and utilitarian objects. *Canadian Cultural Property Export Control List*, C.R.C., c. 448, s. 1. See ARCHAEOLOGICAL ~; HERITAGE ~; HISTORICAL ~; HISTORIC ~; PALAEONTOLOGICAL ~.

OBJECTION FOR WANT OF NOVELTY. Used to describe an objection to a patent because the invention is not new or original.

OBJECTIVE RATIONALE. The principle that no matter where committed, the court has jurisdiction to try an offence which threatens the society in its own territory. M.R. Goode, *Criminal Conspiracy in Canada* (Toronto: Carswell, 1975) at 162.

OBJECTIVES. *n.* In relation to a parent Crown corporation, means the objectives of the corporation as set out in a corporate plan or an amendment to a corporate plan that has been approved pursuant to section 122. *Financial Administration Act*, R.S.C. 1985, c. F-11, s. 120.

OBJECT OF A POWER. A person in whose favour one may exercise a power of appointment.

OBJECT OF ETHNOGRAPHIC ART. An art product, commonly known as primitive art, or other artifact and includes a military, scientific or technological object, that is (a) made by an aboriginal person; (b) an expression of indigenous culture developed outside the centres of civilization as traditionally viewed by western culture; which may (c) incorporate features reflecting contact with non-indigenous cultures; and (d) be a single object or an object together with its component parts that form a single unit.

Canadian Cultural Property Export Control List, C.R.C., c. 448, s. 1.

OBJECTOR. See CONSCIENTIOUS ~.

OBLIGATION. *n.* 1. Includes duty and liability. 2. The total amount payable when the contract was entered into. *Consumer Protection Act,* R.R.O. 1980, Reg. 181, s. 22. 3. Includes requirement, restriction, limitation, condition and duty. *Water Act,* R.S.B.C. 1979, c. 429, s. 1. 4. Bonds, debentures, notes or other evidences of indebtedness. *Trust Companies Act,* R.S.A. 1980, c. T-9, s. 111. See DEBT ~; EXCLUDED ~; FUNDED ~; GOLD CLAUSE ~; IMPERFECT ~; MUTUALITY OF ~; NATURAL ~; PRINCIPAL ~; TOTAL ~.

OBLIGEE. *n.* 1. The minister, official or other person in whose favour a bond or other security is furnished and by whom the bond or security is held. *Bonding Act,* R.S.B.C. 1979, c. 31, s. 1. 2. (i) In the case of a bid bond, the person requesting bids for the performance of a contract; and (ii) in the case of a payment bond or performance bond, the person who has contracted with a principal for the completion of the contract and to whom the obligation of the surety runs in the event of a breach by the principal of the conditions of a payment bond or performance bond. *Business Loans, Guarantees and Indemnities Act,* S.N.W.T. 1983 (1st Sess.), c. 1, s. 3. 3. A creditor; the person in whose favour one enters into a bond or obligation.

OBLIGOR. *n.* 1. A debtor; the one who enters into a bond or obligation. 2. An employer or person named in a certificate as owing wages. *Employment Standards Act,* S.B.C. 1980, c. 10, s. 1.

OBLITERATED BOUNDARY. A boundary established during an original survey or during a survey of a plan of subdivision registered under the Land Titles Act or the Registry Act where the original posts or blazed trees no longer exist and which cannot be re-established from the field notes of either of such surveys or by evidence under oath. *Surveys Act,* R.S.O. 1980, c. 493, s. 1.

OBLITERATED MONUMENT. A monument the position of which can be ascertained beyond reasonable doubt either by traces of the original monument or by other evidence, although the monument itself has partly or entirely disappeared.

OBSCENE. *adj.* Any publication whose dominant characteristic is the undue exploitation of sex, or of sex and any one or more of the following subjects, namely: crime, horror, cruelty and violence, shall be deemed to be obscene. *Criminal Code,* R.S.C. 1985, c. C-46, s. 163(8).

OBSCURITAS PACTI NOCET EI QUI APERTIUS LOQUI POTUIT. [L.] Obscurity in a contract harms the one who could have spoken more directly.

OBSERVATION CENTRE. A prescribed place for the reception and short-term care of intoxicated persons. *Treatment of Intoxicated Persons Act,* R.S.N.B. 1973, c. T-11.1, s. 1.

OBSERVATION UNIT. A public hospital or a part of it designated by the minister as an observation unit. *Mental Health Act,* R.S.B.C. 1979, c. 256, s. 1.

OBSIGNATORY. *adj.* Confirming, ratifying.

OBSOLETE. *adj.* Invalid because it was discontinued.

OBSOLETE OR SURPLUS GOODS. Goods that are (a) found to be obsolete or surplus to requirements by (i) their importer or owner, in the case of imported goods; or (ii) their manufacturer, producer or owner, in any other case; (b) not used in Canada for any purpose; (c) destroyed in such manner as the Minister directs; and (d) not damaged before their destruction. *Duties Relief Act,* R.S.C. 1985 (2d Supp.), c. 21, s. 32.

OBSTRICTION. *n.* Bond; obligation.

OBSTRUCTING JUSTICE. 1. Every one who wilfully attempts in any manner to obstruct, pervert or defeat the course of justice in a judicial proceeding, (a) by indemnifying or agreeing to indemnify a surety, in any way and either in whole or in part; or (b) where he is a surety, by accepting or agreeing to accept a fee or any form of indemnity whether in whole or in part from or in respect of a person who is released or is to be released from custody. *Criminal Code,* R.S.C. 1985, c. C-46, s. 139(1). 2. Every one shall be deemed wilfully to attempt to obstruct, pervert or defeat the course of justice who in a judicial proceeding, existing or proposed, (a) dissuades or attempts to dissuade a person by threats, bribes or other corrupt means from giving evidence; (b) influences or attempts to influence by threats, bribes or other corrupt means a person in his conduct as a juror; or (c) accepts or obtains, agrees to accept or attempts to obtain a bribe or other corrupt consideration to abstain from giving evidence, or to do or to refrain from doing anything as a juror. *Criminal Code,* R.S.C. 1985, c. C-46, s. 139(3).

OBSTRUCTION. *n.* Any slide, dam or other obstruction impeding the free passage of fish. *Fisheries Act,* R.S.C. 1985, c. F-14, s. 2.

OBTEMPERANDUM EST CONSUETUDINI RATIONABILI TANQUAM LEGI. [L.] One must obey reasonable custom as if it were law.

OBTEST. v. To express disagreement or disapproval.

OBTURATION. n. The sealing of powder gases between the walls of the firing chamber and cartridge case and the barrel and the bullet. F.A. Jaffe, *A Guide to Pathological Evidence*, 2d ed. (Toronto: Carswell, 1983) at 180.

OBVIOUS. adj. When used with reference to a disability or disabling condition of a member of the forces at the time he became a member, means that the disability or disabling condition was apparent at that time or would have been apparent to an unskilled observer on examination of the member at that time. *Pensions Act*, R.S.C. 1985, c. P-6, s. 21(12).

O.C. abbr. Order in Council.

OCCASION. See SOCIAL ~.

OCCASIONAL SKILLED CARE. Nursing or other services rendered intermittently or periodically to a person by a formally trained person under an arrangement approved by the inspector, in an amount or to a degree or with a frequency which, in the opinion of the inspector, is less than that which would necessitate the individual being lodged in a nursing home or hospital in order to be properly cared for. *Hospital Act*, R.S.B.C. 1979, c. 176, s. 5.

OCCASIONAL TEACHER. A teacher, employed to teach as a substitute for a permanent, probationary or temporary teacher who has died during the school year or who is absent from his regular duties for a temporary period that is less than a school year and that does not extend beyond the end of a school year. *Education Act*, R.S.O. 1980, c. 129, s. 1.

OCCIPUT. n. The back of the skull or head. F.A. Jaffe, *A Guide to Pathological Evidence*, 2d ed. (Toronto: Carswell, 1983) at 180.

OCCUPANCY. n. 1. Mere use or possession either through an agreement or some other way, so that there is no other claim to the enjoyment or ownership of property. 2. The use or intended use of a building or part thereof for the shelter or support of persons, animals or property. *Building Code Act*, R.R.O. 1980, Reg. 87, s. 1. 3. The use or intended use of a building, as defined in the Building Code. *Building Code Act*, S.N.S. 1986, c. 3, s. 2. See ASSEMBLY ~; BUSINESS ~; CLASS OF ~; INDUSTRIAL ~; INSTITUTIONAL ~; MAJOR ~; MERCANTILE ~; PERSONAL SERVICES ~; RESIDENTIAL ~.

OCCUPANCY PERMIT. A permit, certificate or other document issued by a municipality or an official thereof in respect of a building indicating that the building or a part thereof may be occupied.

OCCUPANT. n. 1. The owner, lessee, or other person having possession of or control over lands. 2. Includes the person in charge of a house, building or premises or under whose care they are, and a person apparently in charge thereof or exercising control or authority thereover. 3. Includes the resident occupier of land or, if there is no resident occupier, the person entitled to the possession thereof, a leaseholder and a person having or enjoying in any way for any purpose the use of land otherwise than as owner, whether or not the land or part thereof is in an unsurveyed area, and also includes a squatter. 4. A person who occupies an immoveable otherwise than as owner. *An Act respecting municipal taxation and providing amendments to certain legislation*, S.Q. 1979, c. 72, s. 1. 5. Any person who occupies an immoveable in his own name, otherwise than as proprietor, usufructuary or institute, and who enjoys the revenues derived from such immoveable. *Cities and Towns Act*, R.S.Q. 1977, c. C-19, s. 6. 6. (i) A person, other than the owner, who is in actual possession of land; (ii) a person who is shown on a certificate of title under the Land Titles Act as having an interest in land; (iii) an operator granted right of entry in respect of land pursuant to a right of entry order, or (iv) in the case of Crown land, a person shown on the records of the department or other body administering the land as having an interest in the land. *Surface Rights Act*, S.A. 1983, c. C-27.1, s. 1. 7. A person having the right (exclusive of the public) to fish in any river, stream or lake either as the owner of the lands abutting thereon or otherwise. *Angling Act*, R.S.N.S. 1967, c. 9, s. 1. 8. In relation to an all-terrain vehicle, means any person riding in or on the vehicle and any person riding on a conveyance towed by the vehicle, but does not include the operator of the vehicle. *All-Terrain Vehicle Act*, S.N.B. 1985, c. A-7.11, s. 1. 9. A person or manikin seated in a vehicle and unless otherwise specified means a person or manikin having the dimensions and weight of a 95th percentile adult male, as defined in section 100 of Schedule IV. 10. A child who is (a) within the size range of children for whom a product is designed; and (b) positioned and secured in the product in accordance with the information required by these Regulations to accompany the product or to be printed on or permanently affixed to the product. *Children's Car Seats and Harnesses Regulations*, C.R.C., c. 921, s. 2. See PASSIVE ~ PROTECTION; RESIDENT ~.

OCCUPANT DISTRIBUTION. The distribution of occupants in a vehicle in a manner specified in the third column of the table to this section. *Motor Vehicle Safety Regulations*, C.R.C., c. 1038, s. 111.

OCCUPANT LOAD. The number of persons for which a building or part thereof is designed. See HIGH ~.

OCCUPANT RESTRAINT ASSEMBLY. Any harness, including webbing, buckles and hardware, that is used or to be used to secure or restrain an occupant in a product. *Children's Car Seats and Harnesses Regulations*, C.R.C., c. 921, s. 2.

OCCUPANT SPACE. The space directly above the seat and footwell, bounded vertically by the ceiling and horizontally by the normally positioned seat back and the nearest obstruction of occupant motion in the direction the seat faces. *Motor Vehicle Safety Regulations*, C.R.C., c. 1038, s. 2.

OCCUPATILE. *adj.* Left by the proper owner and now possessed by someone else.

OCCUPATION. *n.* 1. An employment, business, calling, pursuit, trade, vocation or profession. 2. The act of possessing. See DUST EXPOSURE ~; HAZARDOUS ~; HOME ~; INTERNATIONAL STANDARD CLASSIFICATION OF ~S; USE AND ~.

OCCUPATIONAL ASSOCIATION. An organization, other than a trade union or employers' organization, in which membership is a prerequisite to carrying on a trade, occupation or profession.

OCCUPATIONAL CATEGORY. Any of the following categories of employees, namely, (a) scientific and professional; (b) technical; (c) administrative and foreign service; (d) administrative support; (e) operational; and (f) any other occupationally-related category of employees determined by the Board to be an occupational category. *Public Service Staff Relations Act*, R.S.C. 1985, c. P-35, s. 2.

OCCUPATIONAL CLASSIFICATION. (i) Classification of employees on the basis of the performance of similar work or duties and the exercise of a similar type and degree of skill; or (ii) where only one employee is employed by an employer to perform work or duties of a particular kind or to exercise a particular type and degree of skill, the job or position of that employee. *The Labour Standards Act*, R.S.S. 1978, c. L-1, s. 2.

OCCUPATIONAL DISABILITY PENSION. A private pension plan which provides for a disability pension and survivor benefits. K.D. Cooper-Stephenson & I.B. Saunders, *Personal Injury Damages in Canada* (Toronto: Carswell, 1981) at 3.

OCCUPATIONAL DISEASE. 1. Any disease or illness or departure from normal health arising out of, or in the course of, employment in a workplace and includes an industrial disease. 2. A disease contracted out of or in the course of work and characteristic of that work or directly related to the risks peculiar to that work.

OCCUPATIONAL HEALTH. (i) The promotion and maintenance of the highest degree of physical, mental and social well-being of workers; (ii) the prevention among workers of ill health caused by their working conditions; (iii) the protection of workers in their employment from factors adverse to their health; and (iv) the placing and maintenance of workers in occupational environments which are adapted to their individual physiological and psychological conditions. *The Occupational Health and Safety Act*, R.S.S. 1978, c. O-1, s. 2.

OCCUPATIONAL HEALTH SERVICE. A service organized in or near a place of employment for the purpose of: (i) protecting workers against any health or safety hazard that may arise out of their work or the conditions under which it is carried on; (ii) contributing to the workers' physical and mental adjustment in their employment and their assignment to jobs for which they are suited; and (iii) contributing to the establishment and maintenance of a high degree of physical and mental well-being in the workers. *The Occupational Health and Safety Act*, R.S.S. 1978, c. O-1, s. 2.

OCCUPATIONAL ILLNESS. A condition that results from exposure in a work place to a physical, chemical or biological agent to the extent that the normal physiological mechanisms are affected and the health of the worker is impaired thereby and includes an industrial disease as defined in the Workmen's Compensation Act. *Occupational Health and Safety Act*, R.S.O. 1980, c. 321, s. 1.

OCCUPATIONAL THERAPY. 1. Any form of treatment prescribed or approved by a duly qualified medical practitioner or other qualified referring agent in which a program of planned activities is utilized for the assessment and restoration of physical or mental function in humans, as practised by an occupational therapist. 2. Medically co-ordinated treatment of a patient by an occupational therapist, using selected modalities, for the restoration of physical and mental function, maintenance and improvement of existing healthy function, exploration of latent abilities, diagnostic assistance and assessment of the emotional, mental and physical capacities of the patient. 3. The art and science of directing man's participation in selected tasks to restore, reinforce and enhance performance, facilitate learning of those skills and functions essential for adaptation and productivity, diminish or correct pathology, and to promote and maintain health. *Occupational Therapy Act*, S.N.B. 1977, c. 58, s. 2.

OCCUPATIONAL TRAINING. 1. Includes manual, pre-vocational, vocational and supplementary training and training for the purpose of developing broader and more remunerative skill and capacity. 2. Any instruction, other than university instruction, that provides a person with skills for, or improves a person's skills in, an occupation. *National Training Act*, R.S.C. 1985, c. N-19, s. 2.

OCCUPATIONAL TRAINING PROGRAM. Any course or program of study (a) provided to a person (i) to enhance that person's employability in an occupation; or (ii) to improve that person's ability to carry out a present or future occupation; and (b) for which fees are paid to a training organization by the person or charged to a third party on the person's behalf. *An Act to Amend the Trade Schools Act*, S.N.B. 1987, c. 60, s. 1.

OCCUPATIONAL WORKER. A person who, in the course of his duties, business or professional activities, studies or training, is regularly exposed to radiation. *Radiation Health and Safety Act*, S.S. 1984-85-86, c. R-1.1, s. 2.

OCCUPATION RENT. Compensation to a joint owner of a residence or other asset before receipt of that person's share of the joint property when that person is out of possession and must pay for rent and other expenses. A. Bissett-Johnson & W.M. Holland, eds., *Matrimonial Property Law in Canada* (Toronto: Carswell, 1980) at PEI-22.

OCCUPATIO PACIFICA. [L.] Taking possession, with its consent, of another nation's territory in peacetime.

OCCUPATIVE. *adj.* Employed; possessed; used.

OCCUPIED AREA. (a) A parcel, as defined in the land title legislation, of private land or of Crown land subject to an interest under the Land Act, that is not in a tree farm licence area or woodlot licence area; (b) Crown land subject to (i) an old temporary tenure, free use permit, licence to cut or road permit; or (ii) a timber sale licence that does not make provision for cutting permits; (c) Crown or private land subject to a cutting permit issued under a tree farm licence, woodlot licence, forest licence, timber sale harvesting licence, timber sale licence or timber licence; or (d) Crown land that is actually occupied by a person for an industrial operation except an industrial operation carried on under a tenure, licence or permit referred to in paragraph (b) or (c), including Crown land within 100 m of the perimeter of the operation. *Forest Act*, R.S.B.C. 1979, c. 140, s. 108.

OCCUPIED LAND. Privately-owned land, consisting of not more than the area prescribed by regulation, upon or adjoining which the owner or occupant is actually residing. *An Act to Amend the Fish and Wildlife Act*, S.N.B. 1987, c. 22, s. 1.

OCCUPIED LANDS. Privately owned lands under cultivation or enclosed by a fence of any kind and upon or adjoining which the owner or occupant is actually residing. *Game Act*, R.S.N.B. 1973, c. G-1, s. 1.

OCCUPIED PUBLIC LAND. Public land held by a person under a disposition from the Crown. *Forest and Prairie Protection Act*, R.S.A. 1980, c. F-14, s. 1.

OCCUPIED WATER PRIVILEGE. A mill privilege, or water power, that has been or is in use for mechanical, manufacturing, milling or hydraulic purposes, or for the use of which for any of such purposes the necessary works are bona fide in course of construction. *Lakes and Rivers Improvement Act*, R.S.O. 1980, c. 229, s. 90.

OCCUPIER. *n.* 1. The person occupying any dwelling, and includes the person having the management or charge of any public or private institution where persons are cared for or confined and the proprietor, manager, keeper or other person in charge of a hotel, inn, apartment, lodging house or other dwelling or accommodation. Vital Statistics acts. 2. Includes: (i) a person who is in physical possession of the land; or (ii) a person who has responsibility for and control over the condition of land or the activities there carried on, or control over persons allowed to enter the land, notwithstanding that there is more than one occupier of the same land. 3. Includes a licensee, permittee or tenant of the owner. 4. A person who is qualified to maintain an action for trespass.

OCCUPIERS' LIABILITY. An area of the law of negligence concerning the duty owed to an intruder or a visitor by one who owns or occupies land. J.V. DiCastri, *Occupiers' Liability* (Vancouver: Burroughs/Carswell, 1980) at 1.

OCCURRENCE. See AVIATION ~.

OCEAN. See FISHERIES AND ~S.

OCEAN CARRIER. An owner, lessee or charterer of a vessel who is engaged in the business of the transportation of goods by water. *Shipping*

Conference Exemption Act, R.S.C. 1985, c. S-10, s. 2.

OCEAN SHIP. (a) An ocean-going ship of not less than 50 tons register tonnage; or (b) an ocean-going towing or salvage tug. Canada regulations.

OCEAN SHORE AREA. That portion of land lying within the ordinary low tide mark and 300 metres above the ordinary high tide mark of any ocean or any inlet thereof, and includes any bed, bank, beach, shore, bar, flat, mud flat or sand dune associated with the ocean or inlet whether or not it lies within that portion of land. *An Act to Amend the Trespass Act*, S.N.B. 1985, c. 70, s. 1.

OCHLOCRACY. *n.* A form of government in which citizens have all the power and administration in their own hands.

O.C.M. *abbr.* Ontario Corporation Manual.

OCULIST. *n.* A physician who specializes in diseases of the eyes and whose services include, in addition to the examination of the eyes and treatment of diseases pertaining to sight, the prescription of glasses or spectacles where necessary. *Retail Sales Tax Act*, R.R.O. 1980, Reg. 904, s. 1.

ODAS. *n.* Any object, other than a ship, on or in the water that is designed to collect, store or transmit samples or data relating to the marine environment or the atmosphere or the uses thereof. *Collision Regulations*, C.R.C., c. 1416, s. 2.

ODDS. *n.* The probable ratio of the pay-out price to a $1 bet in the win pool. *Race Track Supervision Regulations*, C.R.C., c. 441, s. 2. See APPROXIMATE ~; FINAL ~.

ODIOSA ET INHONESTA NON SUNT IN LEGE PRAESUMENDA; ET IN FACTO QUOD IN SE HABET ET BONUM ET MALUM, MAGIS DE BONO QUAM DE MALO PRAESUMENDUM EST. [L.] Odious and dishonest things should not be presumed in law; and in an act which contains both good and bad, one should presume more of the good than the bad.

ODOMETER. *n.* A device which measures the distance which a wheel travels.

ODONTOLOGY. *n.* Knowledge of the development, function and structure of the teeth and pathological processes which involve them. F.A. Jaffe, *A Guide to Pathological Evidence*, 2d ed. (Toronto: Carswell, 1983) at 180 and 181. See FORENSIC ~.

ODOUR. See NORMAL FLAVOUR AND ~.

OF CAREER. That persons so designated are nationals or citizens of the country they represent, and are not engaged in any business or profession other than their diplomatic or consular duties. *Customs Diplomatic Privileges Regulations*, C.R.C., c. 522, s. 2.

OF COURSE. Describes a step in a proceeding or action which a court or its officers may not refuse provided that the proper formalities were observed.

OFFENCE. *n.* 1. An offence created by an act or by any regulation or by-law made under an act or a municipal by-law. 2. The contravention of an enactment. See CRIMINAL ~; FEDERAL ~; HYBRID ~; INCLUDED ~; INDICTABLE ~; INDICTABLE ONLY ~; MATRIMONIAL ~; MILITARY ~; PARTIES TO AN ~; RECORD OF ~S; SERIOUS CRIMINAL ~; SERIOUS PERSONAL INJURY ~; SECOND OR SUBSEQUENT ~; SERVICE ~; STATUS ~; SUBSEQUENT ~; SUMMARY CONVICTION ~; SUMMARY ~.

OFFENDER. *n.* A person who has been determined by a court to be guilty of an offence, whether on acceptance of a plea of guilty or on a finding of guilt. *Criminal Code*, R.S.C. 1985, c. C-46, s. 2 as amended by *Criminal Law Amendment Act*, R.S.C. 1985 (1st Supp.), c. 27, s. 2. See CANADIAN ~; FIRST ~; FOREIGN ~.

OFFENSIVE WEAPON. Has the same meaning as "weapon". *Criminal Code*, R.S.C. 1985, c. C-46, s. 2 as amended by *Criminal Law Amendment Act*, R.S.C. 1985 (1st Supp.), c. 27, s. 2.

OFFER. *n.* 1. One person's indication to another that she or he is willing to enter into a contract with that person on certain terms. G.H.L. Fridman, *The Law of Contract in Canada*, 2d ed. (Toronto: Carswell, 1986) at 24. 2. Includes an invitation to make an offer. 3. An invitation to treat. *Saskatchewan Human Rights Code*, S.S. 1979, v. S-24.1, s. 2. 4. Includes an option that the optioner is required to hold open until accepted or rejected by the optionee within a specified time limit. *Judicature Act*, R.S.A. 1980, c. J-1, s. 33. See CONDITIONAL ~; COUNTER ~; DATE OF THE ~; EXEMPT ~.

OFFEREE. *n.* A person to whom a take-over bid is made. See DISSENTING ~.

OFFEREE COMPANY. A company whose shares are the subject of a take-over bid.

OFFEREE CORPORATION. *var.* **OFFEREE-CORPORATION.** A corporation whose shares are the object of a take-over bid.

OFFEREE ISSUER. 1. An issuer whose securities are the subject of an offer to acquire. 2. An issuer whose securities are the subject of a take-over bid or an issuer bid. *An Act to Revise the Securities Act*, S.N.S. 1984, c. 11, s. 75.

OFFERING CORPORATION. A corporation that is offering its securities to the public within the meaning of subsection (6) and that is not the subject of an order of the Commission deeming it to have ceased to be offering its securities to the public. *Business Corporations Act, 1982*, S.O. 1982, c. 4, s. 1.

OFFERING MEMORANDUM. A document that: (i) sets forth information concerning the business and affairs of an issuer; and (ii) has been prepared primarily for prospective purchasers to assist those purchasers to make an investment decision with respect to securities being sold pursuant to a trade that is made in reliance on an exemption.

OFFEROR. *n.* 1. A person, other than an agent, who makes a take-over bid, and includes two or more persons who, directly or indirectly, (a) make take-over bids jointly or in concert; or (b) intend to exercise jointly or in concert voting rights attached to shares for which a take-over bid is made. 2. A person who makes an offer to acquire or an issuer bid. 3. (i) A person or company, other than an agent, who makes a take-over bid or an issuer bid; or (ii) an issuer who accepts from a security holder an offer to sell securities of the issuer other than debt securities that are not convertible into voting securities.

OFFEROR'S PRESENTLY-OWNED SECURITIES. *var.* **OFFEROR'S PRESENTLY OWNED SECURITIES.** Voting securities or rights to voting securities of an offeree company beneficially owned, directly or indirectly, on the date of a take-over bid by the offeror or associates of the offeror and if 2 or more persons or companies make offers (i) jointly or in concert, or (ii) intending to exercise jointly or in concert any voting rights attaching to the securities acquired through the offers, includes the voting securities and rights to voting securities owned by all of the persons or companies and their associates.

OFFEROR'S PRESENTLY-OWNED SHARES. *var.* **OFFEROR'S PRESENTLY OWNED SHARES.** 1. Equity shares of an offeree company beneficially owned, directly or indirectly, on the date of a take-over bid by the offeror or an associate of the offeror. 2. Voting-shares of an offeree company beneficially owned, directly or indirectly, on the date of a take-over bid by the offeror or a person related to him. *Securities Act*, R.S.Q. 1977, c. V-1, s. 131.

OFFEROR'S SECURITY. The security of an offeree issuer beneficially owned, or over which control or direction is exercised, on the date of an offer to acquire by the offeror and the offeror's joint actors.

OFFEROR'S VOTING SECURITIES. Voting securities of the issuer beneficially owned, directly or indirectly, or over which control or direction is exercised, on the date of an offer to acquire, (i) by the offeror and each associate and affiliate of the offeror, and (ii) by any person or company who is acting jointly or in concert with the offeror. *An Act to Revise the Securities Act*, S.N.S. 1984, c. 11, s. 75.

OFFER TO ACQUIRE. (i) An offer to purchase, or a solicitation of an offer to sell, securities; (ii) an acceptance of an offer to sell securities, whether or not that offer to sell has been solicited, and the person or company accepting that offer to sell is deemed to be making an offer to acquire; or (iii) any combination of the foregoing.

OFFER TO PURCHASE. An offer to purchase, the acceptance by a person or company of an offer to sell or a combination of an offer to purchase and an acceptance of an offer to sell. *Securities Act*, S.A. 1981, c. S-6.1, s. 131.

OFFER TO THE PUBLIC. In the case of a company (other than a private company), with relation to securities issued or to be issued by it, every attempt or offer to dispose of, or solicitation of a subscription or application for, or solicitation of an offer to subscribe or apply for any of its securities or any interest in such securities, made by or on behalf of the company, and every such attempt or offer or solicitation made by any underwriter, as hereinafter defined, shall be deemed to have beem made by or on behalf of the company, but "offer to the public" does not include (a) preliminary negotiations or preliminary agreements between the company and an underwriter, or (b) any offer of securities of the company to a director or directors of such company only. *Canada Corporations Act*, R.S.C. 1970, c. C-32, s. 74.

OFFER TO UNDERTAKE. Includes the setting up or keeping up of a sign or inscription referring to insurance, and the distribution or publication of any proposal, circular, card, advertisement, printed form, or like document, referring to insurance, or any written or oral solicitation for insurance. *Insurance Act*, R.S.A. 1980, c. I-5, s. 1.

OFF-HIGHWAY VEHICLE. Any motorized vehicle designated for cross-country travel on land, water, snow, ice, marsh or swamp land or on other natural terrain and, without limiting the generality of the foregoing, includes, when designed for such travel, (i) 4-wheel drive or low pressure tire vehicles; (ii) motor cycles and related 2-wheel vehicles; (iii) amphibious machines; (iv) all terrain vehicles; (v) miniature motor vehicles; (vi) snow vehicles; (vii) minibikes; and (viii) any other means of transportation which is propelled by any power other than muscular power or wind, but does not include (ix) motor boats. See INSURED ~.

OFFICE. *n.* 1. Includes a building occupied and used for office purposes or that part of a building occupied and used for office purposes. 2. Includes (a) an office or appointment under the government; (b) a civil or military commission; and (c) a position or an employment in a public department. *Criminal Code*, R.S.C. 1985, c. C-46, s. 118. 3. The position of an individual entitling him to a fixed or ascertainable stipend or remuneration and includes a judicial office, the office of a Minister of the Crown, the office of a member of the Senate or House of Commons of Canada, a member of a legislative assembly or a member of a legislative or executive council and any other office, the incumbent of which is elected by popular vote or is elected or appointed in a representative capacity and also includes the position of a corporation director. *Income Tax Act*, R.S.C. 1952, c. 148 (as am. S.C. 1970-71-72, c. 63), s. 248(1). See BRANCH ~; CHIEF ~; COLOUR OF ~; CUSTOMS ~; FLEET MAIL ~; HEAD ~; JUDICIAL ~; LAND TITLE ~; LEGISLATIVE ASSEMBLY ~; LOCAL ~; MINISTERIAL ~; PERMANENT ~ OF AN AUTHORIZED PARTY; POST ~; PUBLIC ~; RECORD ~; REGIONAL ASSESSMENT ~; REGISTERED ~; REGISTRY ~; REPRESENTATIVE ~.

OFFICE BUILDING. A building used for the transaction of business, other than those included within the definition of mercantile building, for keeping accounts and records and similar purposes. *Fire Prevention Act*, S.N.S. 1976, c. 9, s. 2.

OFFICE COMPLEX. A building that is (a) an office building; or (b) a building used for an office and some other purpose, and contains at least three offices. *Mail Receptacles Regulations*, C.R.C., c. 1282, s. 2.

OFFICE MONEY. Money received by and for the benefit and use of a broker whether before or after services have been rendered. *Real Estate Brokers Act*, R.S.M. 1970, c. R20, s. 2.

OFFICE OF THE COURT. The office of the prothonotary or of the clerk of any court to which the provision is applicable. *Code of Civil Procedure*, R.S.Q. 1977, c. C-25, s. 4.

OFFICER. *n.* 1. A person holding the position entitling that person to a fixed or ascertainable stipend or remuneration and includes a judicial office, the office of a minister of the Crown, the office of a lieutenant governor, the office of a member of the Senate or House of Commons, a member of a legislative assembly or a member of a legislative or executive council and any other office the incumbent of which is elected by popular vote or is elected or appointed in a representative capacity, and also includes the position of a corporation director. 2. In relation to the Crown, includes a minister of the Crown and any servant of the Crown. 3. Includes a trustee, director, manager, treasurer, secretary or member of the board or committee of management of an insurer and a person appointed by the insurer to sue and be sued in its behalf. 4. A person employed in connection with the administration and management of a department. 5. The chairman and any vice-chairman of the board of directors, the president, any vice-president, the secretary, any assistant secretary, the treasurer, any assistant treasurer, the general manager and any other person designated an officer by by-law or by resolution of the directors, and any other individual who performs functions for a company similar to those normally performed by an individual occupying any of those offices. 6. A commissioned or subordinate officer of the regular force. 7. (a) The chairman, president, vice-president, secretary, treasurer, comptroller, general counsel, general manager, managing director or any other individual who performs functions for a corporation similar to those normally performed by an individual occupying any such office; and (b) each of the five highest paid employees of a corporation including any individual mentioned in paragraph (a). *Canada Business Corporations Act*, R.S.C. 1985, c. C-44, s. 126. 8. A commissioned officer of the R.C.M.P. Force. 9. A peace officer or public officer. *Criminal Code*, R.S.C. 1985, c. C-46, s. 488.1(1) as added by *Criminal Law Amendment Act*, R.S.C. 1985 (1st Supp.), c. 27, s. 71. 10. (a) A person who holds Her Majesty's commission in the Canadian Forces; (b) a person who holds the rank of officer cadet in the Canadian Forces; and (c) any person who pursuant to law is attached or seconded as an officer to the Canadian Forces. *National Defence Act*, R.S.C. 1985, c. N-5, s. 2. 11. Wherever used in this Act, will include all prothonotaries, clerks of appeals, sheriffs, coroners, clerks of the Crown, clerks of the peace, clerks of Provincial Courts, clerks of judges of the sessions, criers, assistant criers, tipstaffs, clerks of commissioners' courts, and registrars. *Stamp Act*, R.S.Q. 1977, c. T-10, s. 5. See ADMITTING ~; ASSESSMENT ~; BRIBERY OF ~S; CHIEF EXECUTIVE ~; CHIEF ~; CLASSIFICATION ~; CONCILIATION ~; CONSULAR ~; CUSTOMS ~; DECK WATCH ~; DIPLO-

MATIC OR CONSULAR ~; ELECTION ~; ENFORCEMENT ~; EXECUTIVE ~; FIREARMS ~; FISHERY ~; FOREIGN SERVICE ~; GAME ~; HEALTH ~; IMMIGRATION ~; LAW ~; LOAN ~; MEDICAL ~; MUNICIPAL ~; PEACE ~; PLEBISCITE ~; POLICE ~; PRESIDING ~; PROBATION ~; PROPER ~; PROTECTION ~; PUBLIC ~; RESPONSIBLE ~ OF THE BANK; RETURNING ~; REVENUE ~; REVISING ~; SECURITY ~; SENIOR ~; SENIOR POLICE ~; SHERIFF'S ~; STAFF ~ OR STAFF ~ OF THE SALVATION ARMY; SUBORDINATE ~; SUPERIOR ~; TRUANT ~; UTILITIES ~; VISA ~; WILDLIFE ~.

OFFICER-DIRECTOR. *n.* In respect of a parent Crown corporation, means (a) the chairman and the chief executive officer of the corporation; and (b) in the case of a parent Crown corporation established by an Act of Parliament, any person who holds an office in the corporation that is established by the Act and the holder of which by a provision in the Act, is to be appointed by the Governor in Council and is declared to be a director of the corporation. *Financial Administration Act*, R.S.C. 1985, c. F-11, s. 105(10).

OFFICER IN CHARGE. 1. The officer for the time being in command of the police force responsible for the lock-up or other place to which an accused is taken after arrest or a peace officer designated by him for the purposes of this Part who is in charge of that place at the time an accused is taken to that place to be detained in custody. *Criminal Code*, R.S.C. 1985, c. C-46, s. 493. 2. The officer who is responsible for the administration and management of a psychiatric facility. *Mental Health Act*, R.S.O. 1980, c. 262, s. 1. 3. The police officer who at any particular time, while on duty, is in charge of and responsible for, the proper functioning of a police facility. *Metropolitan Toronto Police Force Complaints Act*, S.O. 1984, c. 63, s. 1. 4. The person, other than the master, in charge of a ship. Canada regulations. See MEDICAL ~.

OFFICER OF A BANK. (a) The chairman of the board of directors, chief executive officer, president, vice-president, chief general manager, secretary, chief accountant, comptroller, general counsel and general manager of the bank; (b) any individual designated an officer of the bank by by-law or by resolution of the directors; and (c) any individual who performs functions for the bank similar to those performed by an individual occupying any office referred to in paragraph (a) or an individual referred to in paragraph (b). *Bank Act*, R.S.C. 1985, c. B-1, s. 168.

OFFICERS OF CIVIL STATUS. Those entrusted with the keeping of such registers. *Interpretation Act*, R.S.Q. 1977, c. I-16, s. 61.

OFFICERS OF EDUCATION. Every person holding a teacher's diploma or certificate and teaching in a school under the control of school commissioners or trustees, or who has the direction, administration or supervision thereof; school inspectors, and professors and teachers of normal schools, but they do not include members of the clergy or of religious communities or professors in universities. *Education Act*, R.S.Q. 1977, c. I-14, s. 1.

OFFICE SERVICES. Printing, copying, recoding and related services that a public agency requires to transact its business and includes services connected with drawing, illustrating, filming, photographing, recording, addressing, printing, duplicating, micro-photographing, photocopying and typesetting. *Department of Revenue, Supply and Services Amendment Act, 1982 (No. 2)*, S.S. 1982-83, c. 31, s. 3.

OFFICE SPACE. See RENTAL ~.

OFFICE SUPPLIES. Office supplies and equipment that a public agency requires to transact its business and includes stationery, word processing equipment, typewriters, calculators, recorders, projectors and photographic equipment. *Department of Revenue, Supply and Services Amendment Act, 1982 (No. 2)*, S.S. 1982-83, c. 31, s. 3.

OFFICE UNDER HER MAJESTY. Includes any office or employment in or under any department or branch of the government of Canada or of any province, and any office or employment in, on or under any board, commission, corporation or other body that is an agent of Her Majesty in right of Canada or any province. *Official Secrets Act*, R.S.C. 1985, c. O-5, s. 2.

OFFICIAL. *n.* 1. Includes president, vice-president, secretary, treasurer, managing director, general manager, department manager, branch office manager and every person acting in a similar capacity whether so designated or not. 2. Any person employed in, or occupying a position of responsibility in, the service of Her Majesty and includes any person formerly so employed or formerly occupying such a position. 3. Includes an examiner, judge, master of ceremonies, legally qualified medical practitioner, referee and timekeeper. *Athletics Control Act*, R.S.O. 1980, c. 34, s. 1. 4. A person who (a) holds an office, or (b) is appointed to discharge a public duty. *Criminal Code*, R.S.C. 1985, c. C-46, s. 118. See AUTHORIZED ~; ELECTION ~; MINE ~; MUNICIPAL ~; PUBLIC ~; SENIOR ~.

OFFICIAL. *adj.* Authorized; formal.

OFFICIAL AGENT. 1. An official agent of a party or of a candidate in an election. 2. A person appointed by a candidate to represent the candidate during an election. 3. An agent appointed in the manner set out in subsection 215(1) and specially charged with the paying of all legal expenses on account of the management or conduct of an election. *Canada Elections Act*, R.S.C. 1985, c. E-2, s. 2.

OFFICIAL CANDIDATE. A candidate of an authorized party whose nomination paper has been received by the returning officer. *Election Act*, S.Q. 1984, c. 51, s. 316.

OFFICIAL COMMUNITY PLAN. A master plan of community development and land utilization prepared by a local planning authority and legally adopted by or on behalf of a municipality. *National Housing Act*, R.S.C. 1985, c. N-11, s. 2.

OFFICIAL CONTOUR. (a) In relation to any television broadcasting station licensed by the Commission, local F.M. station or regional F.M. station, the service contour described in the technical brief, and (b) in relation to any regional A.M. station, the service contour described in the technical proof of performance, relating to the most recently approved application by the licensee of any such station for the issue, renewal or amendment of its licence. *Cable Television Regulations*, C.R.C., c. 374, s. 2.

OFFICIAL DOCUMENT. (a) An approval, certificate, consent, licence, notice, permit, order or return under this Act or the regulations; (b) a certificate as to service of a document mentioned in clause (a); (c) a certificate or report as to the analysis, description, ingredients, quality, quantity or temperature of any solid, liquid or gas or any combination of any of them; (d) a certificate or report as to the analysis, description, quality or quantity of any odour, heat, sound, vibration, radiation or any combination of any of them; (e) a certificate or report as to the custody of any solid, liquid or gas or any combination of any of them; (f) a certificate as to the custody of any book, record or report or as to the custody of any other document; or (g) a certificate as to whether or not any document or notification was received or issued by the Minister or the Ministry under this Act or the regulations. *Environment Enforcement Statute Law Amendment Act*, S.O. 1986, c. 68, s. 10.

OFFICIAL DRUG. Any drug (a) for which a standard is provided in these Regulations, or (b) for which no standard is provided in these Regulations but for which a standard is provided in any of the publications mentioned in Schedule B to the Act. *Food and Drug Regulations*, C.R.C., c. 870, c. C.01.001.

OFFICIAL EMBLEM. (i) The armorial bearings of Alberta; (ii) the Flag of Alberta; (iii) the floral emblem of Alberta; (iv) the Alberta Tartan; (v) the official bird of Alberta; (vi) the official stone of Alberta. *Emblems of Alberta Act*, R.S.A. 1980, c. E-8, s. 1.

OFFICIAL EXAMINER. 1. The officer of a court who presides over examinations for discovery, cross-examinations on affidavits and other examinations. 2. A special examiner. G.D. Watson & C. Perkins, eds., *Holmested & Watson: Ontario Civil Procedure* (Toronto: Carswell, 1984) at CJA-179.

OFFICIAL FEE. A fee that is required to be paid by or under a statute of a province or Canada.

OFFICIAL GAZETTE. The Canada Gazette and the gazette published under the authority of the government of the province where the proceedings for the winding-up of the business of a company are carried on, or used as the official means of communication between the lieutenant governor of that province and the people, and if no such gazette is published in the province, any newspaper published in the province and designated by a court for publishing the notices required by this Act. *Winding-up Act*, R.S.C. 1985, c. W-11, s. 2.

OFFICIAL GRADING. The grading by an inspector of a sample of grain that has not been taken from a parcel of grain by an inspector. *Canada Grain Regulations*, C.R.C., c. 889, s. 2.

OFFICIAL GUARDIAN. A person appointed by the government to protect the interests and rights of any minor involved in a legal proceeding.

OFFICIAL INSPECTION. The sampling and grading of a parcel of grain by an inspector. *Canada Grain Act*, R.S.C. 1985, c. G-10, s. 2.

OFFICIAL INSPECTION STATION. A recognized place of business registered in accordance with the regulations as a facility where inspections and tests on motor vehicles may be carried out. *Highway Traffic Act*, S.Nfld. 1977, c. 103, s. 1.

OFFICIAL LANGUAGE. The English language or the French language. See COMMISSIONER OF ~S.

OFFICIAL LIST OF ELECTORS. The list of persons eligible to vote.

OFFICIAL MEMENTO. Any item of public property of a distinctly Canadian character and manufacture, including contemporary arts and crafts and articles, representative of all or part of the Canadian Forces or of Canadian culture or Canadian manufacturing. *National Defence Official Mementos Regulations*, C.R.C., c. 716, s. 2.

OFFICIALLY NOMINATED. Describes a candidate who files a nomination paper and deposit with the returning officer at any time between the date of the proclamation and the hour fixed for the close of nominations on nomination day.

OFFICIAL NOMINATION. The filing of a nomination paper and deposit by a candidate with the returning officer at any time between the date of the proclamation and the hour fixed for the close of nominations on nomination day.

OFFICIAL NOTICE. In administrative law, judicial notice. S.A. DeSmith, *Judicial Review of Administrative Action*, 4th ed. by J.M. Evans (London: Stevens, 1980) at 204.

OFFICIAL OPPOSITION. The largest minority political party which is prepared, in the event the government resigns, to assume office. A. Fraser, G.A. Birch & W.A. Dawson, eds., *Beauchesne's Rules and Forms of the House of Commons of Canada*, 5th ed. (Toronto: Carswell, 1978) at 49.

OFFICIAL PLAN. 1. A document approved by the Minister, containing objectives and policies established primarily to provide guidance for the physical development of a municipality or a part thereof or an area that is without municipal organization, while having regard to relevant social, economic and environmental matters. *Planning Act, 1983*, S.O. 1983, c. 1, s. 1. 2. A program and policy or any part thereof designed to secure the health, safety, convenience, or welfare of the inhabitants of the area approved by the commission as prescribed in this Act. *Planning Act*, R.S.P.E.I. 1974, c. P-6, s. 1.

OFFICIAL RECEIVER. A person delegated by the Superintendent to accept debtors' assignments in bankruptcy and generally supervise trustees' administration of bankrupt estates. F. Bennett, *Receiverships* (Toronto: Carswell, 1985) at 3.

OFFICIAL REPORT. The publication of reports of cases directed by statute or a court itself.

OFFICIAL REPORT OF DEBATES. Hansard, a record of speeches made in the House of Commons and verbatim answers to written questions from the Order Paper. A. Fraser, G.A. Birch & W.A. Dawson, eds., *Beauchesne's Rules and Forms of the House of Commons of Canada*, 5th ed. (Toronto: Carswell, 1978) at 48.

OFFICIAL RESULT. The order of finish of the horses in a race at the time it is declared official by the stewards or placing judges, as the case may be. *Race Track Supervision Regulations*, C.R.C., c. 441, s. 2.

OFFICIAL SAMPLE. 1. A sample taken from a parcel of grain by a person authorized by the Commission to take the sample. *Canada Grain Act*, R.S.C. 1985, c. G-10, s. 2. 2. A sample of blood, saliva, urine or other bodily substance that has, in accordance with these Regulations, been obtained from a horse, sealed and identified. *Race Track Supervision Regulations*, C.R.C., c. 441, s. 2.

OFFICIAL SEAL. A seal provided by an inspector and affixed by him to the loading door of a compartment in a controlled-atmosphere storage plant so that the door cannot thereafter be opened without breaking the official seal. *Farm Products Grades and Sales Act*, R.R.O. 1980, Reg. 329, s. 1.

OFFICIAL SIGN. A sign, pavement marking, barricade or object that the minister or an officer or employee of the department with the written authority of the minister authorizes to be erected, placed or painted upon the roadway or right of way of a public highway for the legal control, warning, guidance, direction or information of traffic on the highway.

OFFICIAL TAG. 1. A tag issued by the Plant Products Division of the Department in respect of seed of Canadian origin having pedigreed status. *Seeds Regulations*, C.R.C., c. 1400, s. 2. 2. A tag or label issued under the authority of the Minister for the purpose of identifying seed potatoes. *Seeds Regulations*, C.R.C., c. 1400, s. 45.

OFFICIAL TOWN PLAN. A master plan of land use and community development prepared by or on behalf of a municipality and legally adopted by a municipality according to the Town Planning Act. *Housing Development Act*, R.S.N.S. 1967, c. 129, s. 1.

OFFICIAL TRAFFIC SIGNALS. Signals not inconsistent with this Act, placed or erected by authority of an official having jurisdiction, for the purpose of directing, warning or regulating traffic. Highway Traffic acts.

OFFICIAL TRAFFIC SIGNS. Signs, markings and devices, not inconsistent with this Act, placed or erected by authority of an official having jurisdiction, for the purpose of guiding, directing, warning or regulating traffic. Highway Traffic acts.

OFFICIAL TRUSTEE. The title for the public trustee in some provinces.

OFFICIAL VACCINATE. A female bovine vaccinated with Brucella abortus strain 19 vaccine, of a potency approved by the Minister, not less than 2 months and not more than 8 months after the birth of the animal. *Animal Disease and Protection Regulations*, C.R.C., c. 296, s. 2.

OFFICIAL WEIGHING. The weighing of grain by a person authorized by the Commission to weigh the grain. *Canada Grain Act*, R.S.C. 1985, c. G-10, s. 2.

OFFICIO. See EX ~.

OFFICIT CONATUS SI EFFECTUS SEQUA-TUR. [L.] An attempt is detrimental if an effect follows.

OFFICIUM NEMINI DEBET ESSE DAMNO-SUM. [L.] An office should be harmful to no one.

OFF-PREMISES SALE. Sale of packaged liquor to be consumed in a place other than the premises where it was sold. *Liquor Control and Licensing Act*, R.S.B.C. 1979, c. 237, s. 1.

OFF-ROAD UTILITY VEHICLE. A vehicle having a gross vehicle weight of 6,000 pounds or less, designed for carrying persons, property or a work-performing structure and that incorporates special features for off-road operations. *Motor Vehicle Safety Regulations*, C.R.C., c. 1038, s. 1100.

OFF-ROAD VEHICLE. A vehicle propelled or driven otherwise than by muscular power or wind and designed to travel, (i) on not more than three wheels; or (ii) on more than three wheels and being of a prescribed class of vehicle. *Off-Road Vehicles Act, 1983*, S.O. 1983, c. 53, s. 1.

OFFSET. *n.* When used with reference to piping, means a pipe or a bend of pipe or both that takes one section of the piping out of line with, but parallel to, another section. *Ontario Water Resources Act*, R.R.O. 1980, Reg. 736, s. 1.

OFFSHORE AREA. 1. Sable Island or any area of land that belongs to Her Majesty in right of Canada or in respect of which Her Majesty in right of Canada has the right to dispose of or exploit the natural resources and that is situated in the submarine areas adjacent to the coasts of Canada and extending throughout the natural prolongation of the land territory of Canada to the outer edge of the continental margin or to a distance of 200 nautical miles from the baselines from which the breadth of the territorial sea of Canada is measured, whichever is greater. Canada statutes. 2. Those submarine areas lying seaward of the low water mark of the province and extending, at any point, as far as (i) any prescribed line; (ii) where no line is prescribed at that location, the outer edge of the continental margin or a distance of 200 nautical

miles from the baselines from which the breadth of the territorial sea of Canada is measured, whichever is the greater. *Canada-Newfoundland Atlantic Accord Implementation (Newfoundland) Act*, S.Nfld. 1986, c. 37, s. 2. See NEWFOUND-LAND ~; NOVA SCOTIA ~.

OFFSHORE PIPELINE. See NOVA SCOTIA ~.

O.H.I.P. *abbr.* Ontario Health Insurance Plan.

OHM. *n.* The electrical resistance between two points of a metallic conductor, when a constant difference of potential of one volt, applied between these two points, produces in the conductor a current of one ampere and the conductor itself is not the seat of any electromotive force. *Weights and Measures Act*, S.C. 1970-71-72, c. 36, schedule I.

OIL. *n.* 1. Crude petroleum oil and any other hydrocarbon, regardless of gravity, in liquid form. 2. (i) Crude petroleum regardless of gravity produced at a well head in liquid form, and (ii) any other hydrocarbons, except coal and gas, including hydrocarbons that may be extracted or recovered from surface or subsurface deposits, including deposits of oil sand, bitumen, bituminous sand, oil shale and other types of deposits. See CROWN ~; CRUDE ~; DIESEL ~; FREEHOLD ~; FUEL ~; HOME HEATING ~; ILLEGAL ~; NEW ~; OLD ~; PERSISTENT ~; PRODUCTION OF ~ [OR] GAS; REFINED ~S; SYNTHETIC CRUDE ~.

OIL AND GAS. Includes petroleum, natural gas, hydrocarbons, sulphur compounds, nitrogen, carbon dioxide and helium, where naturally occurring separately or as a mixture and where recovered or recoverable at a well from an underground reservoir, but excludes substances that can be extracted only by destructive distillation from coal, bituminous shales and other stratified deposits. *Oil and Gas Rights Act*, S.N.S. 1971-72, c. 12, s. 1.

OIL AND GAS DEALER. Any person or association of persons who supplies, transports or stores oil, gas or petroleum products and includes, without limiting the generality of the foregoing, any exporter, importer, refiner, processor, wholesale marketer, jobber, distributor, terminal operator or broker who supplies oil, gas or petroleum products. *Energy Monitoring Act*, R.S.C. 1985, c. E-8, s. 2.

OIL AND GAS PROPERTY. The right, title or interest of any person to or in any oil, gas or crude bitumen that is in the earth in Alberta and includes (i) every kind of right to search for or obtain production of any oil, gas or crude bitumen whether the right is incidental to the ownership of land or is created by a lease, permit, contract or in any other way; and (ii) every right, title, interest or benefit acquired or withheld on the making of any sale, lease, sublease, assignment, licence or other arrangement relating to the disposition of any right, title or interest to or in any oil, gas or crude bitumen. *Oil and Gas Conservation Act*, R.S.A. 1980, c. O-5, s. 46.

OIL AND GAS RIGHT. An estate in fee simple in any or all oil, petroleum, natural gas, all other hydrocarbons, except coal and valuable stone, all other gases and minerals and substances, whether liquid or solid and whether hydrocarbon or not, occurring in association with any of the foregoing and the spaces or formations occupied or formerly occupied thereby in all producing tracts in a province.

OIL AND GAS ROYALTY TRUST. A trust of a fraction of reserved royalty rights conveyed to a third party for a lump sum. The trustee has the right to receive the total amount of any assigned regular royalty payment; the beneficiary is the one who purchased the fraction. Such fractional interests can be bought and sold, like any other property. D.M.W. Waters, *The Law of Trusts in Canada*, 2d ed. (Toronto: Carswell, 1984) at 447.

OIL FIELD BRINE. Brine produced in association with oil and gas drilling and production operations that are controlled under the Petroleum Resources Act. *Environmental Protection Act*, R.R.O. 1980, Reg. 303, s. 1.

OIL LEASE. See GAS OR ~.

OIL LINE. A pipe for the transmission of oil from a secondary line, storage facility or processing plant to a terminal or storage facility and includes installations in connection with that pipe, but does not include a secondary line or flow line.

OIL, NATURAL GAS, OR SALT PRODUCTION EQUIPMENT. Includes all equipment, structures, and erections whether affixed to the land or not, together with all machinery, flow lines, tools, pipes, appliances, appurtenances, and other things located on any parcel of land and owned and used by any person owning the surface or holding a lease or licence from the owner of the surface of the parcel of land for the purpose of obtaining and producing oil, natural gas, or salt underlying the surface of the land, or for the purpose of injecting gas or water, including salt water, into any formation underlying the surface or in the vicinity of the parcel of land, but does not include (i) a building, plant, warehouse, or storage yard used by any such person for such a purpose; or (ii) a building, plant, warehouse, or storage yard used for the refining or marketing of oil or oil products or salt; or (iii) a building, plant, warehouse, or storage yard used for the manufacture, refining or marketing of gas; or (iv) similar machinery, tools, pipes and appliances stored in such a building, plant, warehouse, or storage yard. *Municipal Assessment Act*, S.M. 1970, c. 33, s. 1.

OIL OR GAS. Mineral oil, petroleum, natural gas and related hydrocarbons or any of them.

OIL OR GAS WELL. Any well drilled for the purpose of producing petroleum or natural gas or of determining the existence, location, extent or quality of a petroleum or natural gas deposit.

OIL PIPELINE. *var.* **OIL PIPE LINE.** A pipe or any system or arrangement of pipes wholly within Alberta and whereby oil is conveyed from any place at which it is produced to any other place, or from any place where it is stored, processed or treated to any other place, and includes (i) all property of any kind used for the purpose of or in connection with, or incidental to, the operation of a pipeline in the gathering, transporting, handling and delivering of oil; and (ii) tanks, reservoirs, pumps, racks and storage facilities incidental to delivery. *Public Utilities Board Act*, R.S.A. 1980, c. P-37, s. 1.

OIL REVENUE. See INCREMENTAL ~.

OIL SAND. Sand or other petroliferous substance from which oil sand products can be produced.

OIL SAND PRODUCTS. Petroleum or natural gas and all other minerals and substances that can be produced from oil sand or oil shale in association with the production of petroleum or natural gas. *Petroleum and Natural Gas Act*, R.S.B.C. 1979, c. 323, s. 1.

OIL SANDS. 1. Sands and other rock materials which contain crude bitumen and includes all other mineral substances in association therewith. 2. (i) Sands and other rock materials containing crude bitumen; (ii) the crude bitumen contained in those sands and other rock materials; and (iii) any other mineral substances in association with that crude bitumen or those sands and other rock materials, but does not include petroleum or natural gas that in its natural state is recoverable by conventional methods.

OIL SANDS DEPOSIT. A natural reservoir containing or appearing to contain an accumulation of oil sands separated or appearing to be separated from any other such accumulation.

OIL SANDS PRODUCT. Any product derived from oil sands and includes crude bitumen and residue sand.

OIL SANDS RIGHTS. (i) The right to mine, quarry, work, remove, treat or process oil sands that occur in a zone designated by the Energy Resources Conservation Board, including the right to recover any products therefrom whether above or below the surface; and (ii) the right to dispose of the oil sands and any products recovered therefrom. *Mines and Minerals Act*, R.S.A. 1980, c. M-15, s. 121.

OIL SANDS SITE. An in situ operation site, a mine site or a processing plant, or any one or more of them. *Oil Sands Conservation Act*, S.A. 1983, c. O-5.5, s. 1.

OIL SHALE. Shale or other petroliferous substance from which oil shale products can be produced.

OIL SHALE PRODUCTS. Petroleum or natural gas and all other minerals and substances that can be produced from oil sand or oil shale in association with the production of petroleum or natural gas. *Petroleum and Natural Gas Act*, R.S.B.C. 1979, c. 323, s. 1.

OIL WELL. Any well capable of producing oil and is not a gas well. *Canada Oil and Gas Drilling and Production Regulations*, C.R.C., c. 1517, s. 2. See WELL OR ~.

OILY MIXTURE. A mixture with any oil content. Pollution Prevention regulations.

OLD AGE. See STATUTORY ~.

OLD AGE SECURITY PENSION. Old age security pension payable pursuant to the Old Age Security Act.

OLD LAW. 1. The statutes in force prior to the coming into force of the Revised Statutes of Canada, 1970 that are repealed and replaced by the Revised Statutes of Canada, 1970. Statutes of Canada 1970-71-72. 2. The statutes in force prior to the coming into force of the Revised Statutes of Prince Edward Island, 1974 or of any subsequent revision of the statutes of Prince Edward Island. *Interpretation Act*, S.P.E.I. 1981, c. 18, s. 35. 3. The Excise Tax Act as it read from time to time before the commencement day. *Excise Tax Act*, R.S.C. 1985 (2d Supp.), c. 7, s. 58.

OLD OIL. (a) Crude or heavy oil recovered after 1981 from a natural reservoir in Canada that was known, before January 1, 1981, to be capable of production in commercial quantities; and (b) the prescribed percentage of petroleum produced from a mine in a bituminous sands deposit that came into production in reasonable commercial quantities before January 1, 1976, but does not include (c) the incremental production of petroleum, determined in such manner as may be prescribed, that is recovered from a natural reservoir or portion thereof under a project that commenced operation after December 31, 1980, that is a prescribed tertiary oil recovery project; (d) petroleum produced from a prescribed experimental plant; or (e) prescribed petroleum produced after May 31, 1984. *Petroleum and Gas Revenue Tax Act*, R.S.C. 1985, c. P-12, s. 2.

OLD OIL BASE PRICE. In respect of old oil of a particular quality from a well or mineral resource, means such amount as is prescribed to be the base price of that quality of oil. *Petroleum and Gas Revenue Tax Act*, R.S.C. 1985, c. P-12, s. 2.

OLEOMARGARINE. *n.* 1. Any food substance other than butter, of whatever origin, source or composition that is prepared for the same uses as butter and that is manufactured wholly or in part from any fat or oil other than that of milk. *Oleomargarine Act*, R.S.O. 1980, c. 324, s. 1. 2. Any food substance other than butter, of whatever origin, source or composition that is prepared for the same uses as butter, but does not include any substance consisting of a blend of butterfat and edible oils. *Oleomargarine Act*, S.N.B. 1977, c. 37, s. 1. See DIET ~; REGULAR ~.

OLIGARCHY. *n.* A form of government in which a few people administer affairs.

OLIGOSPERMIA. *n.* An unusually small quantity of sperm cells in semen. F.A. Jaffe, *A Guide to Pathological Evidence*, 2d ed. (Toronto: Carswell, 1983) at 181.

O.L.R. *abbr.* Ontario Law Reports, 1901-1931.

O.L.R.B. *abbr.* Ontario Labour Relations Board.

O.L.R.B. REP. *abbr.* Ontario Labour Relations Board Reports, 1974-.

O.M.B. *abbr.* Ontario Municipal Board.

O.M.B.R. *abbr.* Ontario Municipal Board Reports, 1973-.

OMBUDSMAN. *n.* A person appointed to consider and investigate complaints of members of the public concerning the administration of the government.

OMISSION. See ACT OR ~.

OMITTANCE. *n.* Omission.

OMNE CRIMEN EBRIETAS ET INCENDIT ET DETEGIT. [L.] Drunkenness kindles and exposes every crime.

OMNE JUS AUT CONSENSUS FECIT AUT NECESSITAS CONSTITUIT AUT FIRMAVIT CONSUETUDO. [L.] Mutual consent made, necessity established, or custom fixed, every rule of law.

OMNE MAJUS CONTINET IN SE MINUS. [L.] Every greater thing contains the less.

OMNE QUOD SOLO INAEDIFICATUR SOLO CEDIT. [L.] Everything built into the ground is merged with it.

OMNE SACRAMENTUM DEBET ESSE DE CERTA SCIENTIA. [L.] Every oath should spring from certain knowledge.

OMNES LICENTIAM HABENT HIS, QUAE, PRO SE INDULTA SUNT, RENUNCIARE. [L.] All people have liberty to renounce things which were granted for their benefit.

OMNES SUBDITI SUNT REGIS SERVI. [L.] All subjects are the servants of the monarch.

OMNE TESTAMENTUM MORTE CONSUMMATUM EST. [L.] Every will is completed in death.

OMNIA DELICTA IN APERTO LEVIORA SUNT. [L.] All offences are less serious when committed openly.

OMNIA PRAESUMUNTUR CONTRA SPOLIATOREM. [L.] All things are presumed against one who does wrong.

OMNIA PRAESUMUNTUR LEGITIME FACTA DONEC PROBETUR IN CONTRARIUM. [L.] All things are presumed to have been done legitimately until it is proved to the contrary.

OMNIA PRAESUMUNTUR RITE ET SOLEMNITER ESSE ACTA. [L.] All things are presumed to be done correctly and solemnly.

OMNIA QUAE JURE CONTRAHUNTUR, CONTRARIO JURE PEREUNT. [L.] All things accomplished by a law come to naught with a contradictory law.

OMNIBUS. *n.* A motor vehicle owned by a city designed for the transportation of passengers and regularly operated by the city for compensation, on a fixed route either within the city or within the city and such additional area as may be permitted by the Lieutenant Governor in Council, for the purpose of taking up and setting down passengers at fixed points. *The Fuel Petroleum Products Act*, R.S.S. 1978, c. F-23, s. 2.

OMNIBUS ACCOUNT. An account carried by a dealer for another dealer in which the transactions of two or more persons or companies are combined and effected in the name of the second mentioned dealer without disclosure of the identity of such persons or companies. *Commodity Futures Act*, R.R.O. 1980, Reg. 114, s. 7.

OMNIBUS POENALIBUS JUDICIIS ET AETATI EST IMPRUDENTIAE SUCCURRITUR. [L.] In all criminal proceedings, age and ignorance are aided.

OMNIS ACTIO EST LOQUELA. [L.] Each action is a complaint.

OMNIS CONCLUSIO BONI ET VERI JUDICII SEQUITUR EX BONIS ET VERIS PRAEMISSIS ET DICTIS JURATORUM. [L.] Each conclusion showing good and proper judgment is drawn from premises which the jury members properly and reasonably found.

OMNIS CONSENSUS TOLLIT ERROREM. [L.] Each consent removes error.

OMNIS INNOVATIO PLUS NOVITATE PERTURBAT QUAM UTILITATE PRODEST. [L.] Each innovation causes more confusion by its novelty than good by its usefulness.

OMNIS INTERPRETATIO SI FIERI POTEST ITA FIENDA EST IN INSTRUMENTIS, UT OMNES CONTRARIETATES AMOVEANTUR. [L.] If possible in the case of deeds, every interpretation should be made so that all inconsistencies are removed.

OMNIS NOVA CONSTITUTIO FUTURIS TEMPORIBUS FORMAM IMPONERE DEBET, NON PRAETERITIS. [L.] Each new law should regulate future time, not the past.

OMNIS PRIVATIO PRAESUPPONIS HABITUM. [L.] Each deprivation presupposes possession.

OMNIS QUERELA ET OMNIS ACTIO INJURIARUM LIMITATA EST INFRO CERTA TEMPORA. [L.] Each complaint and each action for damages is limited within set times.

OMNIS RATIHABITIO RETRITRAHITUR ET MANDATA PRIORI AEQUIPARATUR. [L.] Each ratification of something already done has a retroactive effect and is like an earlier request to do it.

OMNIUM. *n.* [L.] The total of designated portions of different stocks in a public fund.

OMNIUM CONTRIBUTIONE SARCIATUR QUOD PRO OMNIBUS DATUM EST. [L.] The sum total which was provided for all is perfected by distribution.

ON-CALL TIME. The hours during which an employee may be called to work.

ON DECK. Above deck, as opposed to under deck. *Dangerous Goods Shipping Regulations*, C.R.C., c. 1419, s. 2.

ON DECK ONLY. In an uncovered space, though special deckhouses having doors which can be continuously open (except in heavy weather) may be used, but does not include stowage in a shelter deck space. *Dangerous Goods Shipping Regulations*, C.R.C., c. 1419, s. 2.

ONE. See EVERY ~.

O.N.E. *abbr.* Office national de l'énergie.

ONE DAY. The period beginning 2 hours before sunrise and ending 2 hours after sunset. Fishery regulations.

ONE-FAMILY DWELLING. A house consisting of one family housing unit not attached to or forming part of any other house. *National Housing Act*, R.S.C. 1985, c. N-11, s. 2.

1-K KEROSINE. A grade of kerosine that is refined to a standard as fixed by the Canadian General Standards Board. *The Statute Law Amendment (Taxation) Act (1985)*, S.M. 1985-86, c. 48, s. 29.

ONEROUS. *adj.* Describes an obligation which outweighs or exceeds its advantage.

ONE-WAY HIGHWAY. A highway designated as such by signs on or erected or posted along the highway directing traffic to proceed in only one direction. *Highway Traffic Act*, S.S. 1986, c. H-3.1, s. 2.

ONE-WAY ROADWAY. A roadway designated and marked by a traffic authority as a roadway upon which vehicles may be operated in one direction only.

ONE-WAY STREET. A highway designated and marked by a department or traffic authority upon which vehicles may be operated in one direction only.

ON-PREMISES SALE. The sale of a beverage intended for consumption on the premises on which it is sold. *Environmental Protection Act*, R.R.O. 1980, Reg. 299, s. 1.

ON-SITE BUILDING OR STRUCTURE. A building or structure occupying the same site as the storage facility and is used exclusively by the company or person that operates the storage facility. *Ammonium Nitrate Storage Facilities Regulations*, C.R.C., c. 1145, s. 2.

ON-SITE GARBAGE GRINDER. A grinder (i) used for the treatment of waste that is subsequently discharged as sewage; and (ii) located in a building or structure used principally for functions other than waste management. *Environmental Protection Act*, R.R.O. 1980, Reg. 309, s. 1.

ON-SITE INCINERATOR. An incinerator that is located in a building or structure used principally for functions other than waste manage-

ment. *Environmental Protection Act*, R.R.O. 1980, Reg. 309, s. 1.

ON-SITE ROAD. A road for the movement of vehicles and equipment within a waste disposal site. *Environmental Protection Act*, R.R.O. 1980, Reg. 309, s. 1.

ONT. *abbr.* Ontario.

ONTARIO. See FLORAL EMBLEM OF ~; GOVERNMENT OF ~; LAW OF ~; NORTHERN ~.

ONTARIO CONTRACT. A subsisting contract of insurance that (a) has for its subject; (i) property that at the time of the making of the contract is in Ontario or is in transit to or from Ontario; or (ii) the life, safety, fidelity or insurable interest of a person who at the time of the making of the contract is resident in Ontario or of an incorporated company that has its head office in Ontario; or (b) makes provision for payment thereunder primarily to a resident of Ontario or to an incorporated company that has its head office in Ontario.

ONTARIO EXPLORATION AND DEVELOPMENT EXPENSES. Any expenses that would be Canadian exploration and development expenses incurred by the corporation if clause (b) of this subsection were read as if the references therein to; (i) "in Canada" were references to "in Ontario"; (ii) "after 1971" were references to "after the 9th day of April, 1974"; and (iii) "Canadian" were references to "Ontario". *Corporations Tax Act*, R.S.O. 1980, c. 97, s. 18.

ONTARIO RESOURCE PROPERTY. Any property that would be a Canadian resource property of the corporation within the meaning of paragraph 66 (15) (c) of the Income Tax Act (Canada) if that paragraph were read as if the references therein to (i) "in Canada" were references to "in Ontario"; and (ii) "after 1971" were references to "after the 9th day of April, 1974". *Corporations Tax Act*, R.S.O. 1980, c. 97, s. 18.

ONTARIO WINE. (i) Wine produced from grapes, cherries, apples or other fruits grown in Ontario or the concentrated juice thereof and includes Ontario wine to which is added herbs, water, honey, sugar or the distillate of Ontario wine or cereal grains grown in Ontario; (ii) wine produced by the alcoholic fermentation of Ontario honey, with or without the addition of caramel, natural botanical flavours or the distillate of Ontario honey wine; or (iii) wine produced from the combination of: (A) apples grown in Ontario or the concentrated juice thereof to which is added herbs, water, honey, sugar or the distillate.of Ontario wine or cereal grains grown in Ontario; and (B) the concentrated juice of apples grown outside of Ontario, in such proportion as is prescribed by regulation. *Liquor Licence Amendment Act*, S.O. 1984, c. 4, s. 1.

ONT. CASE LAW DIG. *abbr.* Ontario Case Law Digest.

ONT. CORPS. LAW GUIDE *abbr.* Ontario Corporations Law Guide.

ONT. DIV. CT. *abbr.* Supreme Court of Ontario, High Court of Justice (Divisional Court).

ONT. ELEC. *abbr.* Ontario Election Cases, 1884-1900.

ONT. H.C. *abbr.* Supreme Court of Ontario, High Court of Justice (including Family Law Division).

ONT. PROV. CT. (CIV. DIV.). *abbr.* Ontario Provincial Court, Civil Division.

ONT. R.E.L.G. *abbr.* Ontario Real Estate Law Guide.

ONT. S.C. *abbr.* Supreme Court of Ontario (in Bankruptcy).

ONT. TAX R. *abbr.* Ontario Tax Reports.

ONT. W.C.A.T. *abbr.* Ontario Workers' Compensation Appeals Tribunal.

ONUS. *n.* [L.] Burden.

ONUS PROBANDI. [L.] The burden of proving.

OPACITY. *n.* 1. (i) The color of a visible emission in shades of grey to black; or (ii) the degree to which a visibile emission obstructs the passage of light. *Environmental Protection Act*, R.R.O. 1980, Reg. 308, s. 1. 2. The fraction of a beam of light, expressed as a percentage, that fails to penetrate the exhaust emission. *Motor Vehicle Safety Regulations*, C.R.C., c. 1038, s. 1100.

OP. CIT. *abbr.* [L.] Opere citato.

OPEC. *abbr.* Organization of Petroleum Exporting Countries.

OPEN. *v.* In the sense of "opening" a street, includes not only the opening of a new street but also the extending, widening, diverting, or otherwise altering of an existing street whereby land not theretofore part of the street is added thereto or made part thereof. *City of Winnipeg Act*, S.M. 1971, c. 105, s. 1.

OPEN. *adj.* As applied to electrical equipment means that moving parts, windings or live parts are exposed to accidental contact. *Power Corporation Act*, R.R.O. 1980, Reg. 794, s. 0.

OPEN ACCOUNT. An account which the parties have not stated or settled.

OPEN AIR. The atmosphere outside a building. *Ontario Water Resources Act*, R.R.O. 1980, Reg. 736, s. 1.

OPEN AIRPORT. An airport in respect of which the Minister has not entered into an agreement with a ground transportation operator to provide transportation for passengers or goods, or for both, from and to the airport. *Government Airport Concession Operations Regulations*, C.R.C., c. 1565, s. 2.

OPEN BODY OF WATER. 1. A river, stream, watercourse, bay, estuary, open municipal reservoir, farm pond, dugout, or other body of water, whether it contains water continuously or intermittently. 2. The bed and shore of a river, stream, watercourse, lake or other body of water including an irrigation canal owned by the board of directors of an irrigation district, whether it contains water continuously or intermittently, but does not include (i) municipal reservoirs; (ii) reservoirs and dugouts on private land; or (iii) lakes or sloughs (A) having an area of less than 10 acres; (B) being completely surrounded by private land; and (C) having no drainage of water from them through the private land. *Agricultural Chemicals Act*, R.S.A. 1980, c. A-6, s. 1.

OPEN-BODY TYPE VEHICLE. A vehicle having no occupant compartment top or with respect to which a top is intended by the manufacturer to be installed or removed by the user. *Motor Vehicle Safety Regulations*, C.R.C., c. 1038, s. 100.

OPEN COMMODITY CONTRACT. An outstanding obligation under a commodity contract for which settlement has not been effected by the tender and receipt of the commodity, by the tender and receipt of an instrument evidencing title or the right to that commodity, or by a liquidating trade. *Commodity Contract Amendment Act*, S.B.C. 1085, c. 2, s. 1.

OPEN COMMODITY FUTURES CONTRACT. An outstanding obligation under a commodity futures contract for which settlement has not been effected by the tender and receipt of the commodity or of an instrument evidencing title or the right to that commodity or by a liquidating trade.

OPEN COMPETITION. A competition that is open to employees as well as to persons who are not employees.

OPEN CONSTRUCTION. With respect to a fishing vessel, means a fishing vessel other than one of closed construction. *Small Fishing Vessel Inspection Regulations*, C.R.C., c. 1486, s. 2.

OPEN COURT. A court open to spectators or members of the public.

OPEN CUSTODY. Custody in (a) a community residential centre, group home, child care institution, or forest or wilderness camp, or (b) any other like place or facility designated by the Lieutenant Governor in Council of a province or his delegate as a place of open custody for the purposes of this Act, and includes a place or facility within a class of such places or facilities so designated. *Young Offenders Act*, R.S.C. 1985 (2d Supp.), c. 24, s. 24.1. See PLACE OF ~.

OPENED. See FULLY ~.

OPEN-END MUTUAL FUND. A corporation that makes a distribution to the public of its shares and that carries on only the business of investing the consideration it receives for the shares it issues, and all or substantially all of those shares are redeemable upon the demand of a shareholder.

OPENING. See CLEAR ~; EFFECTIVE ~; UNPROTECTED ~.

OPEN INTEREST. (a) In relation to commodity futures contracts, the total outstanding long positions or the total outstanding short positions; and (b) in relation to commodity options or commodity futures options, the total outstanding puts and the total outstanding calls, for each delivery month and in aggregate, in commodity futures contracts, commodity options or commodity futures options, as the case may be, relating to a particular commodity entered into on a commodity exchange.

OPEN JAW ABC. An ABC destined for a point in another country and returning to the point of origin in Canada from a different point in the country of destination or from a point in another country. *Air Carrier Regulations*, C.R.C., c. 3, s. 71.

OPEN LISTING. Authority, given to a single or multiple agents, which usually implies or states that a commission will be paid only when a sale is consummated and in which the vendor usually retains a right to sell the property without reference to any agent. B.J. Reiter, R.C.B. Risk & B.N. McLellan, *Real Estate Law*, 3d ed. (Toronto: Emond Montgomery, 1986) at 74 and 75.

OPEN MARKET. A market of willing sellers and willing buyers.

OPEN ORDER. An order, which remains valid until cancelled by the customer, to buy securities at, above or below a named price.

OPEN PERIOD. With respect to a municipality and a bargaining agent (i) if no collective agreement is in effect, any time; or (ii) if a collective agreement is in effect, any time after

notice to commence collective bargaining is served.

OPEN PIT. A surface opening, quarry or excavation in, or working of, the ground for the purpose of searching for, winning, opening up, removal of or proving any mineral-bearing substance. *Mining Safety Act*, S.N.W.T. 1982 (3d Sess.), c. 12, s. 2.

OPEN PIT MINE. A mine worked by removal of overlying strata and subsequent excavation of exposed coal in terrain that is not flat or substantially flat.

OPEN POLICY. An insurance policy in which the value of goods or a ship insured will be calculated in the event of loss.

OPEN RING NET. A net whose bottom is closed to form a bag and that is hung on a ring or metal frame attached to a line or rope. *Pacific Shellfish Regulations*, C.R.C., c. 826, s. 2.

OPEN SEASON. 1. A specified period of time during which a species of wildlife may be hunted or taken or fishing make take place. 2. The season during which the killing, pursuing with intent to kill, taking or having in possession any species of game is permitted. *Lands and Forests Act*, R.S.N.S. 1967, c. 163, s. 84.

OPEN SHOP. A business in which union membership is not required as a condition of employment.

OPEN SPARKING. Flashing or arcing in the open air unprotected by enclosure for prevention of fire or explosion. *Coal Mines Regulation Act*, R.S.N.S. 1967, c. 36, s. 84.

OPEN SPLICE. Any parting at any junction of tread, sidewall or innerliner that extends to the cord. *Motor Vehicle Tire Safety Regulations*, C.R.C., c. 1039, s. 2.

OPEN TEMPORARY DETENTION. See PLACE OF ~.

OPEN TUBERCULOSIS. Includes (i) all cases of pulmonary tuberculosis that produce sputum containing tubercle bacilli or gastric washings containing tubercle bacilli; and (ii) all cases of tuberculosis other than the pulmonary form in which tubercle bacilli are found in the discharges from the diseased tissue. *Tuberculosis Act*, R.S.A. 1980, c. T-11, s. 6.

OPEN-TYPE HOT-WATER HEATING SYSTEM. A system in which water is heated and circulated and where there are no intervening valves between the boiler and the expansion tank, and which is vented to the atmosphere. *Boiler and Pressure Vessel Act*, R.S.Nfld. 1970, c. 24, s. 2.

OPEN UNION. A union lacking restrictive membership conditions.

OPEN WATER. Water that is not ice-covered. *Manitoba Fishery Regulations*, C.R.C., c. 843, s. 2.

OPERATE. *v.* 1. To have the management and control. 2. To carry on the activity permitted by a licence. *Health Facilities Special Orders Act, 1983*, S.O. 1983, c. 43, s. 1. 3. (a) Means, in respect of a motor vehicle, to drive the vehicle; and (b) includes, in respect of a vessel or an aircraft, to navigate the vessel or aircraft. *Criminal Code*, R.S.C. 1985, c. C-46, s. 214 as amended by *Criminal Law Amendment Act*, R.S.C. 1985 (1st Supp.), c. 27, s. 33. 4. When used in relation to a heating plant or a power plant, means to operate, manipulate, observe and check manual, mechanical, automatic and remote controls and equipment in connection with a heating plant or power plant, but does not include "have charge of" a heating plant or power plant. 5. In relation to an all-terrain vehicle, includes the acts of driving, stopping, parking, pushing or towing the vehicle or leaving the vehicle standing. *All-Terrain Vehicle Act*, S.N.B. 1985, c. A-7.11, s. 1. 6. Includes walking beside a snowmobile by a person having actual physical control of the snowmobile while the snowmobile is in motion. *Snowmobile Act*, S.M. 1971, c. 34, s. 3.

OPERATE CARELESSLY. To operate a snowmobile without due care and attention. *Snowmobile Act*, S.M. 1970, c. 59, s. 24(2).

OPERATING. *adj.* 1. In relation to a public housing project, to the extent of its composition as described in subsection (3), means exercising rights and performing obligations in the capacity of the lessee by whom the unit that composes the project, to that extent, is leased as described in paragraph (3)(b). *National Housing Act*, R.S.C. 1985, c. N-11, s. 82(4). 2. Includes maintaining and repairing and any activities for operating, maintaining and repairing. *Environmental Assessment Act*, R.R.O. 1980, Reg. 293, s. 1.

OPERATING AGREEMENT. See UNIT ~.

OPERATING AUTHORITY. A written authorization of the Commission conferring the right to operate over such routes, to carry such commodities, in such vehicles and subject to such limitations or conditions, as are therein specified, and includes a temporary operating authority and a temporary permit. *Motor Carrier Act*, S.P.E.I. 1984, c. 26, s. 1.

OPERATING BALANCE. The amount of the balance to the credit of the Canada Pension Plan Account less the balance in the Canada Pension Plan Investment Fund. *Canada Pension Plan*, R.S.C. 1985, c. C-8, s. 110.

OPERATING BASE. With respect to an aircraft, means an aerodrome (a) that is frequently used by the aircraft; (b) at which shelter and means of sustaining life are available; and (c) at which there is a responsible person with whom the pilot-in-command may leave information concerning any proposed flight. *Sparsely Settled Areas Order*, C.R.C., c. 65, s. 2.

OPERATING BUSINESS. A business undertaking in Canada to which employees employed in connection with the undertaking ordinarily report for work. *Combines Investigation Act*, R.S.C. 1985 (2d Supp.), c. 19, s. 108.

OPERATING CORPORATION. A municipal corporation or commission or a company or individual operating or using a telephone or telegraph service, or transmitting, distributing or supplying electricity or artificial or natural gas for light, heat or power and includes Ontario Hydro. *Public Service Works on Highways Act*, R.S.O. 1980, c. 420, s. 1.

OPERATING COSTS. The cost of the furnishings, equipment, supplies, salaries and transportation for a nursing service, and such other expenses as may be approved by the Minister. *Nursing Service Act*, R.S.A. 1980, c. N-15, s. 1.

OPERATING ENGINEER. See CHIEF ~.

OPERATING EXPENSE. An expenditure for administration or management.

OPERATING LEASE. The authorization to produce petroleum and natural gas. *Mining Act*, R.S.Q. 1977, c. M-13, s. 1.

OPERATING LOSS. With respect to any fiscal year of the city, means the excess of the aggregate amount of all operating expenses resulting from the operation of the transit system over the aggregate amount of all operating revenue derived from that operation, for that fiscal year. *City of Winnipeg Act*, S.M. 1971, c. 105, s. 565.

OPERATING PROFIT. With respect to any fiscal year of the city, means the excess of the aggregate amount of all operating revenues resulting from the operation of the transit system over the aggregate amount of all operating expenses derived from that operation, for that fiscal year. *City of Winnipeg Act*, S.M. 1971, c. 105, s. 565. See ADJUSTED ~S.

OPERATING REVENUES. All revenues of the city from the operation of all plants and properties of the city used in connection with the transit system and revenues from all other sources that relate to, or are applicable to, the transit system or the operation thereof. *City of*

Winnipeg Act, S.M. 1971, c. 105, s. 565. See GROSS OPERATING REVENUE.

OPERATION. *n.* (a) In relation to a facility, the manufacturing or processing operation of which the facility constitutes the necessary components, and (b) in relation to a commercial facility, the commercial undertaking of which the commercial facility constitutes the necessary components. See AGRICULTURAL ~; BASE OF ~S; CADASTRAL ~; CAESAREAN ~; CONTINUOUS ~; DANGEROUS ~ OF AIRCRAFT; EXPLORATION ~S; FARMING ~S; FISHING ~; FOREST INDUSTRY ~; FORESTRY ~; GEOPHYSICAL ~; GROUP ~; INDUSTRIAL ~; INDUSTRIAL OR COMMERCIAL ~; IN SITU ~; LOGGING ~; LOGGING ~S; MINING ~; MULTI-FARM ~; NEGLIGENT ~; NORMAL ~S; PRODUCTION ~S; SPECIAL PURPOSE ~; SUBSIDIARY CONTROLLED ~; TRANSFER ~; UNITIZED ~; WASTEFUL ~.

OPERATIONAL CONTROL. In respect of a flight, means the exercise of authority over, or the initiation, continuation, diversion or termination of, a flight. Canada regulations.

OPERATIONAL FLIGHT PLAN. The operator's plan for the safe conduct of a flight based on consideration of aeroplane performance, other operating limitations and relevant expected conditions on the route and at the aerodromes concerned. *Air Carriers Using Large Aeroplanes Order*, C.R.C., c. 21, s. 2.

OPERATION OF A MINE. The production of minerals from a mine and includes all or any of the milling, smelting, refining, beneficiating or other processing of those minerals and resulting products. *Mineral Resource Tax Act*, R.S.B.C. 1979, c. 263, s. 1.

OPERATIVE PART. In a mortgage, lease, conveyance or other formal instrument, the part which expresses the main object of that instrument.

OPERATIVE WORD. A word which contributes to the origin or transfer of an estate.

OPERATOR. *n.* 1. In relation to any work, undertaking or business, means the person having the charge, management or control of the work, undertaking or business, whether on that person's own account or as the agent of any other person. 2. A person who drives a motor vehicle on a public highway. 3. A person who uses or operates or is in actual physical control of an all-terrain vehicle. 4. A person having direct control of the starting, stopping and speed of an amusement ride. 5. A person who uses or controls the use of any radiation equipment. 6. A person (i) who operates a race course; (ii) who conducts a race meeting; or (iii) who is in any manner the custodian or depositary of money that is staked or deposited in the making of a bet on any race during the actual progress of a race meeting conducted by that person on races being run on a race course or at a race meeting. 7. In respect of an aircraft, means the person in possession of the aircraft, whether as owner, lessee, hirer or otherwise and, in respect of an airport, means the holder of the airport licence, or the person in charge of such airport, whether as employee, agent or representative of the holder of such licence. *Air Regulations*, C.R.C., c. 2, s. 101. See ASSEMBLY YARD ~; CHIEF ~; CITY MOTOR VEHICLE ~; COD TRAP ~; CONCESSION ~; CONTAINER ~; CREAMERY ~; CUSTOM ~; DRIVER OR ~; FAN ~; FARM ~; FEED MILL ~; GARAGE ~; GRADING STATION ~; HIGHWAY MOTOR VEHICLE ~; HOIST ~; INDEPENDENT ~; JOINT ~S; LICENSED ~; LOGGING ~; MARKET ~; NETWORK ~; OWNER-~; SEED COMPANY ~; SHIFT ~; SUGAR BUSH ~; TOUR ~; TRACK ~; UNIT ~; WELDING ~.

OPERATOR OF A PHARMACY. (a) The holder of a certificate of accreditation for the operation of a pharmacy under section 135 of the Health Disciplines Act; or (b) the operator of a pharmacy operated in or by a hospital that is a public hospital under the Public Hospitals Act. *Ontario Drug Benefits Act*, S.O. 1986, c. 27, s. 1.

OPERATOR'S CERTIFICATE. A certificate of insurance issued to a person holding a licence or other permit to drive a motor vehicle under The Vehicles Act, or The Snowmobile Act. *The Automobile Accident Insurance Act*, R.S.S. 1978, c. A-35, s. 2.

OPERATOR'S LICENCE. A valid licence issued under this Ordinance to a person to operate or manipulate a motion picture machine in a theatre. *Motion Pictures Act*, R.S.N.W.T. 1974, c. M-14, s. 2.

OPERATOR'S LIEN. Any charge on or right in relation to an interest or a share in an interest (a) that arises under a contract (i) to which the interest owner or holder of the interest or share is a party; (ii) that provides for the operator appointed thereunder to carry out any work or activity related to the exploration for or the development or production of petroleum in the frontier lands to which the interest or share applies; and (iii) that requires the interest owner or holder to make payments to the operator to cover all or part of the advances made by the operator in respect of the costs and expenses of such work or activity; and (b) that secures the payments referred to in subparagraph (a)(iii). *Petroleum Resources Act*, R.S.C. 1985 (2d Supp.), c. 36, s. 84.

OPERE CITATO. [L.] In the work just cited.

OPHTHALMIC APPLIANCE. Lenses, spectacles, eyeglasses, frames, contact lenses, artificial eyes or other specified devices, for the relief, prevention or correction of visual or other anomalies of the eyes.

OPHTHALMIC DISPENSER. A person who (i) prepares and dispenses lenses, spectacles, eyeglasses, and appurtenances thereto, or any of those things, to the intended wearers thereof, on the written prescriptions of duly qualified medical practitioners or of the holders of certificates of registration under The Optometry Act; and (ii) in accordance with such prescriptions interprets, measures, adapts, fits, and adjusts, such lenses, spectacles, eyeglasses and appurtenances thereto, or any of those things, to the human face for the aid of vision or the correction of visual or ocular anomalies of human eyes. *Ophthalmic Dispensers Act*, R.S.M. 1970, c. O60, s. 2.

OPHTHALMIC DISPENSING. (i) Supplying, preparing and dispensing ophthalmic appliances; (ii) interpreting prescriptions of legally qualified medical practitioners and optometrists; and (iii) the fitting, adjusting and adapting of ophthalmic appliances to the human face and eyes in accordance with the prescriptions of legally qualified medical practitioners and optometrists.

OPHTHALMIC DISPENSING SERVICE. The measuring, adjusting or adapting of ophthalmic appliances to the needs of the intended wearer, whether or not for hire, gain or reward. *The Ophthalmic Dispensers Act*, R.S.S. 1978, c. O-5, s. 2.

OPHTHALMIC LENS. Any spherical, cylindrical, or prismatic lens to aid vision.

OPHTHALMOLOGIST. *n.* A person legally qualified to practise as a physician under The Medical Profession Act and recognized as a specialist in ophthalmology by The College of Physicians and Surgeons of the Province of Saskatchewan. *The Ophthalmic Dispensers Act*, R.S.S. 1978, c. O-5, s. 2.

OPINION. *n.* 1. The advice a counsel gives on the facts of a case. 2. Interpretation of, or inference concerning, the significance in some respect of a given fact. *Military Rules of Evidence*, C.R.C., c. 1049, s. 2. 3. A statement which may be admissible as evidence. The opinion of an expert witness is called expert evidence. 4. In England, a judgment delivered in the House of Lords by the Law Lords. The expression of opinion by any judge on a matter not decided in a case is called a dictum or obiter dictum. See ADVISORY ~; CONCURRING ~; DICTUM; DISSENTING ~; EXPERT EVIDENCE; MINORITY ~; OBITER DICTUM.

OPIUM. *n.* Juice from unripe seed capsules of the plant Papaver somniferum. F.A. Jaffe, *A Guide to Pathological Evidence*, 2d ed. (Toronto: Carswell, 1983) at 181.

OPIUM POPPY. Papaver somniferum L. *Narcotic Control Act*, R.S.C. 1985, c. N-1, s. 2.

OPORTET QUOD CERTA RES DEDUCATUR IN JUDICIUM. [L.] It is necessary that what is certain be brought to judgment.

OPP. BD. *abbr.* Opposition Board.

OPPORTUNITY. *n.* A requirement for the commission of a crime. If there are no accomplices, the accused must be where the property or person which is the crime's object is located. P.K. McWilliams, *Canadian Criminal Evidence*, 3d ed. (Aurora: Canada Law Book, 1988) at 18-21. See FAIR ~.

OPPORTUNITY COST. The value of life or time calculated in terms of benefits relinquished for other benefits or for the ability to function in a certain way. K.D. Cooper-Stephenson & I.B. Saunders, *Personal Injury Damages in Canada* (Toronto: Carswell, 1981) at 217.

OPPOSING DIRECTION. The direction that is displaced from the facing direction by 180 angular degrees. *Children's Car Seats and Harnesses Regulations*, C.R.C., c. 921, s. 2.

OPPOSITE. *n.* One who opposes.

OPPOSITE PARTY. Includes the owner of land to be taken under this Act and a person having a registered interest in or right or privilege with regard to the land. *The Expropriation Act*, R.S.S. 1978, c. E-15, s. 2.

OPPOSITION. *n.* Objection to an application that a trade mark be registered on the grounds (a) that the application does not comply with what is required by section 29; (b) that the trade mark is not capable of being registered; (c) that the applicant is not entitled to register; or (d) that the mark itself is not distinctive. H.G. Fox, *The Canadian Law of Trade Marks and Unfair Competition*, 3d ed. (Toronto: Carswell, 1972) at 241. See LEADER OF THE ~; OFFICIAL ~.

OPPOSITION CAUCUS. The group of two or more members who constitute the largest group sitting in the Assembly in opposition to the Government and who belong to the same political party. *Legislative Assembly and Executive Council Amendment Act, 1981*, S.S. 1980-81, c. 65, s. 12.

OPPOSITION HOUSE LEADER. The member who expresses her or his party's priorities for arranging the business of the House of Commons. A. Fraser, G.A. Birch & W.A. Dawson, eds., *Beauchesne's Rules and Forms of the House of Commons of Canada*, 5th ed. (Toronto: Carswell, 1978) at 50.

OPPOSITION PARTY. See RECOGNIZED ~.

OPPRESSION. *n.* The state from which a minority shareholder may claim relief.

OPTICAL APPLIANCE. Lenses, spectacles, eyeglasses, artificial eyes, contact lenses or appurtenances thereto for the aid or correction of visual or ocular anomalies of the eyes.

OPTICAL DISPENSING. (i) Supplying, preparing and dispensing optical appliances; (ii) interpreting prescriptions of legally qualified medical practitioners and optometrists; and (iii) the fitting, adjusting and adapting of optical appliances to the human face and eyes in accordance with the prescriptions of legally qualified medical practitioners and optometrists.

OPTICIAN. *n.* Any person who supplies ophthalmic lenses, spectacles, eyeglass mountings, etc., in accordance with the prescription of an optometrical or medical practitioner, or by duplication, and any person who is engaged in the manufacture of ophthalmic lenses, frames, mountings or parts thereof. See DISPENSING ~.

OPTIMACY. *n.* 1. People of the highest rank. 2. In England, the nobility.

OPTIMA EST LEGIS INTERPRES CONSUETUDO. [L.] The best interpreter of the law is custom.

OPTIMA EST LEX QUAE MINIMUM RELINQUIT ARBITRIO JUDICIS; OPTIMUS JUDEX QUI MINIMUM SIBI. [L.] The best system of law is that which leaves the least to a judge's discretion; the best judge is one who leaves the least to one's own discretion.

OPTIMA LEGUM INTERPRES EST CONSUETUDO. [L.] The best interpreter of the law is custom.

OPTIMA STATUTI INTERPRETATRIX EST (OMNIBUS PARTICULIS EJUSDEM INSPECTIS) IPSUM STATUTUM. [L.] The best interpreter of a statute (all separate parts having been considered) is the statute itself.

OPTIMUS INTERPRES RERUM USUS. [L.] Usage is the best interpreter of things.

OPTIMUS INTERPRETANDI MODUS EST SIC LEGES INTERPRETARI UT LEGES

LEGIBUS CONCORDANT. [L.] The best way to interpret laws is so they agree with other laws.

OPTIMUS LEGUM INTERPRES CONSUETUDO. [L.] The best interpreter of the law is custom.

OPTING OUT. This occurs when the legislative assembly of a province passes, by constitutional formula, a resolution dissenting from an amendment so that the amendment has no effect in that province. P.W. Hogg, *Constitutional Law of Canada*, 2d ed. (Toronto: Carswell, 1985) at 59.

OPTION. *n.* 1. A privilege, acquired by consideration, to call or to make delivery or both, within a certain time, of some specified article or stock at a certain price. 2. "The obligation to hold an offer open for acceptance, until the expiration of a specified time," meaning a legally binding obligation supported by consideration passing from the holder of the option to the grantor. *Day v. M.N.R.*, [1971] Tax A.B.C. 1050 at 1054; 71 D.T.C. 723 at 726. See COMMODITY FUTURES ~; COMMODITY ~; PRODUCTION ~S WEIGHT; SURFACE RIGHTS ~; WORK ~.

OPTIONAL ITEMS. Automatic transmission, power steering, power brakes, power windows, power seats, radio and heater. *Motor Vehicle Safety Regulations*, C.R.C., c. 1038, s. 111.

OPTIONAL RADIO STATION. A radio broadcasting station other than a local F.M. station, regional F.M. station or regional A.M. station. *Cable Television Regulations*, C.R.C., c. 374, s. 2.

OPTIONAL SERVICE. (i) Service with any municipality or local board in Canada; (ii) service with the civil service of Canada or of any province of Canada; (iii) service with the staff of any board, commission or public institution established under any Act of Canada or any province of Canada; or (iv) war service. *Ontario Municipal Employees Retirement System Act*, R.S.O. 1980, c. 348, s. 1.

OPTIONAL TELEVISION STATION. A television broadcasting station other than a local television station, regional television station or extra-regional television station. *Cable Television Regulations*, C.R.C., c. 374, s. 2.

OPTION LICENCE. A licence issued for the purpose of survey and investigation of the timber resources of a selection area. *Forest Act*, R.S.M. 1970, c. F150, s. 2.

OPTOMETRIC ASSISTANT. Any person, in the employ or under the direct supervision of a licensed optometrist, to whom part of the practice of optometry is delegated by the College. *Optometry Act*, S.P.E.I. 1981, c. 25, s. 1.

OPTOMETRIC FACILITY. A place in which the practice of optometry is carried on, including the premises of a retail merchant. *Optometry Profession Act*, S.A. 1983, c. O-10, s. 1.

OPTOMETRIST. *n.* 1. A person who employs any means other than drugs, medicines and surgery for the measurement of the power of vision and the adaption of lenses and prisms for the correction and aid thereof. 2. A person who through specialized education, training and experience is skilled in the principles and practice of optometry.

OPTOMETRY. *n.* The employment of any means other than the use of drugs, medicines and surgery for the measurement of the powers of vision and the adaptation of lenses and prisms for the correction and aid of the vision of human beings. See PRACTICE OF ~.

O.R. *abbr.* Ontario Reports, 1882-1900.

[   ] **O.R.** *abbr.* Ontario Reports, 1931-1973.

O.R. (2d). *abbr.* Ontario Reports (Second Series), 1974-.

ORAL. *adj.* Conveyed by mouth; not in writing.

ORAL ARGUMENT. The presentation of an argument before a court.

ORAL CONTRACT. A contract whose terms are not written down.

ORAL LD50 VALUE. The amount of a chemical that, when administered orally, will kill 50 per cent of test animals under the specified conditions of test. *Science Education Sets Regulations*, C.R.C., c. 934, s. 2.

ORAL PRESCRIPTION NARCOTIC. Medication that (a) contains in addition to a narcotic two or more medicinal ingredients other than a narcotic in a recognized therapeutic dose; and (b) is not intended for parenteral administration. *Narcotic Control Regulations*, C.R.C., c. 1041, s. 2.

ORAL QUESTION. A method of dealing with urgent matters recognized by the Standing Orders of Parliament. A. Fraser, G.A. Birch & W.A. Dawson, eds., *Beauchesne's Rules and Forms of the House of Commons of Canada*, 5th ed. (Toronto: Carswell, 1978) at 129.

ORATOR. *n.* One who brings a petition.

ORBATION. *n.* Depriving one of one's parent or child; poverty.

ORCHARD. *n.* 1. An area of land of at least one-fifth hectare on which there are at least 13 fruit trees and on which the number of fruit trees bears a proportion to the area of at least 65 fruit trees per hectare. 2. Includes any land on which any apple tree is growing. *Agriculture and Mar-*keting Act, R.S.N.S. 1967, c. 3, s. 117. See ABANDONED ~.

ORDER. *n.* 1. The direction of a court or judge which commands a party to do or not to do something in particular. 2. Includes a judgment, decree, rule, award, and declaration. 3. An order or determination of a court providing for the payment of money as maintenance by the respondent named in the order for the benefit of the claimant named in the order, or the maintenance provisions of an order or determination that includes other matters. 4. (a) A judgment and a decree, and (b) an opinion, advice, direction, determination, decision or declaration that is specifically authorized or required under an enactment to be given or made. *Court of Appeal Act*, S.B.C. 1982, c. 7, s. 1. 5. Includes any directive to the trade issued by the Commission. *Canada Grain Act*, R.S.C. 1985, c. G-10, s. 2. See ANTON PILLER ~; BASTARDY ~; "BULLOCK" ~; CHARGING ~; COMMITTAL ~; COMMUNITY SERVICE ~; COMPENSATION ~; COMPLIANCE ~; CONFIRMATION ~; CONTROL ~; CONVEYANCE ~; CUSTODY ~; DATE OF THE ~; DEMOLITION ~; DEPORTATION ~; DETENTION ~; EXCLUSION ~; EXTRA-PROVINCIAL ~; FAMILY ~; FINAL ~; GENERAL ~ NO. 448; GENERAL ~S; GUARDIANSHIP ~; INTERIM ~; JUDGMENT ~; MAINTENANCE ~; MATRIMONIAL PROPERTY ~; MONEY ~; NO LIMIT ~; NON-ENTRY ~; NO ~ AS TO COSTS; QUIA TIMET ~; OPEN ~; PAYABLE TO ~; PREROGATIVE ~; PROBATION ~; PROVISIONAL ~; QUEEN'S REGULATIONS AND ~; QUESTION OF ~; QUIETING ~; RECEIVING ~; REGISTERED ~; REJECTION ~; REMOVAL ~; RESTITUTION ~; RESTRAINING ~; RIGHT OF ENTRY ~; SANDERSON ~; SESSIONAL ~; SPECIAL ~; STANDING ~; STANDING, SESSIONAL AND SPECIAL ~; STOP ~; STOP WORK ~; SUPERVISION ~; SUPPORT ~; TRANSPORT ~; TRAP ~; VERBAL ~; VARIATION ~; VESTING ~; WINDING-UP ~; WRITTEN ~.

ORDER ABSOLUTE. A complete rule or order, with full effect, as opposed to a rule or order nisi.

ORDER FORM. When applied to a security means a security that is payable to the order or assigns of any person therein specified with reasonable certainty or to such person or such person's order. *Business Corporations Act, 1982*, S.O. 1982, c. 4, s. 53.

ORDER IN COUNCIL. *var.* **ORDER-IN-COUNCIL.** An order made by the Lieutenant Governor or Governor General by and with the advice of the Executive or Privy Council, sometimes under statutory authority or sometimes by virtue of royal prerogative.

ORDER OF COURSE. 1. An order, made on an ex parte application, which a party is rightfully entitled to on that party's own statement and at that party's own risk. 2. In England, an order drawn up without applying directly to a judge in the Chancery Division which may not be opposed.

ORDER OF THE DAY. A proceeding which may be considered only as the result of a previous order made in the House itself, except for a measure requiring immediate consideration such as the successive stages of a bill. A. Fraser, G.A. Birch & W.A. Dawson, eds., *Beauchesne's Rules and Forms of the House of Commons of Canada*, 5th ed. (Toronto: Carswell, 1978) at 89.

ORDER PAPER. The official agenda which lists every item which may be brought forward during that day's sitting. A. Fraser, G.A. Birch & W.A. Dawson, eds., *Beauchesne's Rules and Forms of the House of Commons of Canada*, 5th ed. (Toronto: Carswell, 1978) at 48.

ORDER TO CONTINUE. An order obtained by someone entitled to carry on the proceedings or someone not already a party on whom the interest devolved, *e.g.*, the personal representative of a plaintiff who is deceased. G.D. Watson & C. Perkins, eds., *Holmested & Watson: Ontario Civil Procedure* (Toronto: Carswell, 1984) at 11-15.

ORDINANCE. *n.* 1. Includes an ordinance of the Territories passed before, on or after April 1, 1955. *Northwest Territories Act*, R.S.C. 1985, c. N-27, s. 2. 2. Includes an ordinance of the Territory passed before, on or after April 1, 1955. *Yukon Act*, R.S.C. 1985, c. Y-2, s. 2. 3. An enactment of the Regional Government which applies within the municipalities under its jurisdiction or to the inhabitants of these municipalities, except where the enactment itself expressly provides otherwise. *An Act concerning Northern Villages and the Kativik Regional Government*, S.Q. 1978, c. 87, s. 2.

ORDINANDI LEX. [L.] The law of procedure, in contrast to substantive law.

ORDINARILY RESIDENT. Residence in the course of the customary mode of life of the person concerned, and it is contrasted with special or occasional or casual residence. *Thomson v. M.N.R.*, [1946] C.T.C. 51, 2 D.T.C. 812 (S.C.C.).

ORDINARILY RESIDENT IN CANADA. If, at the time the expression is being applied, (a) he has sojourned in Canada during the next preceding 24 months for a period of, or periods the aggregate of which is, 366 days or more; (b) he is a member of the Canadian Forces required to reside outside Canada; (c) he is an ambassador, minister, high commissioner, officer or servant of Canada, or is an agent-general, officer or servant of a province of Canada, and resided in Canada immediately prior to appointment or employment by Canada or a province of Canada or is entitled to receive representation allowances; (d) he is performing services in a country other than Canada under an international development assistance program of the Government of Canada that is prescribed for the purposes of paragraph 250(1)(d) of the Income Tax Act (Canada), and resided in Canada at any time in the 3-month period preceding the day on which such services commenced; or (e) he resides outside Canada and is the spouse or child of, and is living with, an individual described in clause (b), (c) or (d). *Land Transfer Tax Act*, R.S.O. 1980, c. 231, s. 1.

ORDINARIUS ITA DICITUR QUIA HABET ORDINARIAM JURISDICTIONEM, IN JURE PROPRIO, ET NON PROPTER DEPUTATIONEM. [L.] The ordinary is called that because one has ordinary jurisdiction, in one's own right, and not through being deputized.

ORDINARY BY-LAW. A by-law of an association that is not subject to the approval of the Minister. *Canada Cooperative Associations Act*, R.S.C. 1985, c. C-40, s. 3.

ORDINARY COURT. The court that would, but for this Act, have jurisdiction in respect of an offence alleged to have been committed. *Young Offenders Act*, R.S.C, 1985, c. Y-1, s. 2.

ORDINARY INCOME. Income from a non-capital source. W. Grover & F. Iacobucci, *Materials on Canadian Income Tax*, 4th ed. (Toronto: Richard De Boo Ltd., 1980) at 261.

ORDINARY LOCATION. A dry location in which at normal atmosphere pressure and under normal conditions of use, electrical equipment is not unduly exposed to injury from mechanical causes, excessive dust, moisture, or extreme temperatures, and in which electrical equipment is entirely free from the possibility of injury through corrosive, flammable or explosive atmospheres.

ORDINARY PLACE OF RESIDENCE. The place where the individual maintains a self-contained domestic establishment in which he resides and supports his spouse or a person dependent on him for support and connected with him by blood relationship, marriage or adoption. *Taxation Act*, R.S.Q. 1977, c. I-3, s. 42.

ORDINARY POLLING DAY. The day fixed for holding the poll at an election.

ORDINARY PRACTICE OF SEAMEN. As applied to any case, means the ordinary practice of skilful and careful persons engaged in navigation in like cases. *Canada Shipping Act*, R.S.C. 1985, c. S-9, s. 2.

ORDINARY PUBLISHED RATE. The rate that would be charged for the same movement as a local switching and not an interswitching operation. *Freight Traffic Interswitching Regulations*, C.R.C., c. 1210, s. 15.

ORDINARY REMUNERATION. The remuneration paid to an employee on a pay day in respect of employment in the relevant pay period and includes fees paid to a director of a corporation if no other remuneration is payable to the director by the corporation. *Canada Pension Plan Regulations*, C.R.C., c. 385, s. 2.

ORDINARY RESIDENCE. With major regard to intention, the country that one regards as one's "real home", the place where one regularly lives and the place from which one may be temporarily absent, intending all the while to return. J.G. McLeod, *The Conflict of Laws* (Calgary: Carswell, 1983) at 183. See PLACE OF ~.

ORDINARY RESOLUTION. 1. A resolution passed by a majority of the votes cast by or on behalf of the shareholders who voted in respect of that resolution. 2. (a) A resolution passed by the members of a company in general meeting by a simple majority of the votes cast in person or by proxy; or (b) a resolution that has been submitted to the members of a company who would have been entitled to vote on it in person or by proxy at a general meeting of the company and that has been consented to in writing by such members of the company holding shares carrying not less than 3/4 of the votes entitled to be cast on it; and a resolution so consented to shall be deemed to be an ordinary resolution passed at a general meeting of the company. *Company Act*, R.S.B.C. 1979, c. 59, s. 1. 3. (a) A resolution passed in general meeting by the members of a society by a simple majority of the votes cast in person, or where proxies are allowed, by proxy; (b) a resolution that has been submitted to the members of a society and consented to in writing by 75 per cent of the members who would have been entitled to vote on it in person or by proxy at a general meeting of the society; and a resolution so consented to shall be deemed to be an ordinary resolution passed at a general meeting of the society; or (c) where a society has adopted a system of indirect or delegate voting or voting by mail, a resolution passed by a simple majority of votes cast in respect of the resolution. *Society Act*, R.S.B.C. 1979, c. 390, s. 1.

ORDINARY RETIREMENT. A retirement of depreciable plant that results from causes reasonably assumed to have been anticipated or contemplated in prior depreciation or amortization provisions. Pipeline Uniform Accounting regulations; Canada regulations.

ORDINARY USE. Use which is commonplace, customary, normal, regular or usual in the course of everyday life and part of the life of a family. A. Bissett-Johnson & W.M. Holland, eds., *Matrimonial Property Law in Canada* (Toronto: Carswell, 1980) at NB-12.

ORDINARY WITNESS. A witness who testifies to facts observed or experienced by him, but who is not testifying as an expert in the matter concerned. *Military Rules of Evidence*, C.R.C., c. 1049, s. 2.

ORDINARY WORKMAN. In the context of a specification refers to the hypothetical person who possesses ordinary knowledge and skill of the particular art to which an invention relates and a mind ready to understand any specification addressed to her or him. H.G. Fox, *The Canadian Law and Practice Relating to Letters Patent for Inventions*, 4th ed. (Toronto: Carswell, 1969) at 184.

ORDNANCE. See HAND CARRIED WEAPON OR PIECE OF ~.

ORE. *n.* 1. A mineral substance in natural deposit of such size, composition and situation as to allow reasonable hope of extracting therefrom, at present or in the future, products which may be sold at a profit. 2. Includes ore from a mineral resource that has been processed to any stage that is prior to the prime metal stage or its equivalent. *Income Tax Regulations*, C.R.C., c. 945, s. 1104. See MINERAL ~; PROBABLE ~; PROVEN ~.

ORE REDUCTION WORKS. Includes mines, smelters, ore roasters, ore concentrators and metal refineries, and all works, plants and processes incidental to them. *Industrial Operation Compensation Act*, R.S.B.C. 1979, c. 195, s. 1.

ORE TENUS. [L. by mouth] Verbally.

ORGAN AND TISSUE BANK. A place outside a hospital centre equipped for keeping organs or tissues taken from human bodies, in view of the utilization of such organs or tissues for medical or scientific purposes. *Public Health Protection Act*, R.S.Q. 1977, c. P-35, s. 1.

ORGANIC ACID. Includes acetic acid, trichloracetic acid, lactic acid, formic acid and any combination thereof. *Hazardous Products (Haz-*

ardous Substances) Regulations, C.R.C., c. 926, s. 2.

ORGANIC FLUID PLANT. See LOW PRESSURE ~.

ORGANIC MATTER. That substance of animal or vegetable origin remaining after removal of the moisture and total ash fractions. *Fertilizers Regulations*, C.R.C., c. 666, s. 2.

ORGANIC SOIL CONDITIONING. The incorporation of processed organic waste in the soil to improve its characteristics for crop or ground cover growth. *Environmental Protection Act*, R.R.O. 1980, Reg. 309, s. 1.

ORGANIC WASTE. See PROCESSED ~.

ORGANIZATION. *n.* 1. Includes a trade union or other unincorporated association. 2. (a) Any specialized agency of which Canada is a member that is brought into relationship with the United Nations in accordance with Article 63 of the Charter of the United Nations; (b) any international organization of which Canada is a member, the primary purpose of which is the maintenance of international peace or the economic or social well-being of the community of nations; and (c) any organization specified in Schedule II. *Privileges and Immunities Act*, R.S.C. 1985, c. P-23, s. 3. 3. An institution, association, society, body or other organization, the income and assets of which are not available for the personal benefit of any proprietor, member or shareholder. See AGRICULTURAL ~; CENTRAL POLITICAL PARTY ~; CHARITABLE ~; COMPANY DOMINATED ~; CONSUMER ~; CROWN-CONTROLLED ~; EMPLOYEE ~; EMPLOYEES' ~; EMPLOYER ~; EMPLOYERS' ~; FOREIGN ~; GOVERNMENTAL ~; INTERNATIONAL ~; INTERNATIONAL LABOUR ~; LABOUR ~; NON-PROFIT ~; NON-RESIDENT ~; NOT-FOR-PROFIT ~; POLITICAL ~; PRODUCER ~; PROMOTIONAL ~; RELIGIOUS ~; RE~; RESIDENT ~; SELF-REGULATORY ~.

ORGANIZER. *n.* A person who solicits workers to become members of a union.

ORIFICE GAS METER. Any gas meter through which the quantity of gas being passed is determined from the difference in pressure between the two sides of a thin orifice plate fitted in the pipeline and which contains a sharp-edged circular orifice through which the gas passes. *Gas and Gas Meters Regulations*, C.R.C., c. 876, s. 25.

ORIGIN. *n.* 1. The point from which a charter flight commences with the passengers or goods to be transported. *Air Carrier Regulations*, C.R.C., c. 3, s. 23. 2. As applied to a fur, means the continent in which the pelt was removed from the animal. *Fur Garments Labelling Regulations*, C.R.C., c. 1138, s. 2. See COUNTRY OF ~; DOMICILE OF ~; FLOCK OF ~; HERD OF ~; NATIONAL ~; TERRITORY OF ~.

ORIGINAL. *n.* The document actually prepared, not a copy. See DUPLICATE ~.

ORIGINAL. *adj.* Originating from an author in the sense that it results from a substantial degree of experience, industry or skill employed by that person. That a work is not copied from another or was not in the public domain. H.G. Fox, *The Canadian Law of Copyright and Industrial Designs*, 2d ed. (Toronto: Carswell, 1967) at 41.

ORIGINAL CAPITAL COST. The original book value of depreciable processing assets. *Mineral Resource Tax Amendment Act*, S.B.C. 1980, c. 27, s. 4.

ORIGINAL CLAIMANT. The person from whom title must be traced in order to establish a right or claim to letters patent for the lands in question. *Exchequer Court Act*, R.S.C. 1970, c. E-11, s. 2.

ORIGINAL COST OF THE LAND. The purchase price or the compensation paid for the expropriation of the land plus the amount of any expenses incurred in connection with the acquisition of the land, including any amounts referred to in section 4(3). *Government Land Purchases Amendment Act, 1981*, S.A. 1981, c. 68, s. 2.

ORIGINAL COURT. 1. In relation to any judgment means the court by which the judgment was given. 2. The court in which the foreign judgment was obtained. Foreign Judgments acts.

ORIGINAL DOMINION POST. Any post planted to define a survey of an original allotment of land made by or under authority of the Government of Canada. *Surveys Act*, R.S.M. 1970, c. S240, s. 2.

ORIGINAL EVIDENCE. Evidence offered to prove that a statement was made, either in a document or orally, not that the statement is true. P.K. McWilliams, *Canadian Criminal Evidence*, 3d ed. (Aurora: Canada Law Book, 1988) at 1-13.

ORIGINAL JURISDICTION. The jurisdiction under the laws of which the foreign corporation was created. *Foreign Resident Corporations Act*, S.N.B. 1984, c. F-19.1, s. 1.

ORIGINAL MAXIMUM BENEFIT PERIOD. In relation to a contract of group insurance, the maximum period provided under that contract for the payment of any benefit payable thereunder in respect of loss of income.

ORIGINAL MONUMENT. A mound, post, mark or monument marked, erected, placed or planted lawfully to mark the boundaries of a township, range, section or other legal subdivision, block, gore, lot, common or other parcel of land, under this or another enactment. *Land Survey Act*, R.S.B.C. 1979, c. 216, s. 11.

ORIGINAL MORTGAGOR. Any person who by virtue of privity of contract with the mortgagee is personally liable to the mortgagee to pay the whole or any part of the moneys secured by the mortgage. *Mortgages Act*, R.S.O. 1980, c. 296, s. 19.

ORIGINAL PLAN. A plan certified by the Surveyor General as being the original plan of an original survey. *Surveys Act*, R.S.O. 1980, c. 493, s. 1.

ORIGINAL POST. Any object that defines a point and that was placed, planted or marked during the original survey or during a survey of a plan of subdivision registered under the Land Titles Act or the Registry Act. *Surveys Act*, R.S.O. 1980, c. 493, s. 1.

ORIGINAL SURVEY. 1. Any original or first survey of land made by or under the authority of the Government of Canada, or any survey of land of which a plan has been or is, before or after the coming into force of the Revised Statutes, filed or registered under The Real Property Act or The Registry Act in any land titles office or registry office in Manitoba. *Surveys Act*, R.S.M. 1970, c. S240, s. 2. 2. A survey made under competent authority. *Surveys Act*, R.S.O. 1980, c. 493, s. 1.

ORIGINATING DOCUMENT. A writ of summons, counter-claim, petition for divorce, counter-petition for divorce or originating notice that initiates an application, an originating application or a statement of claim that commences a proceeding.

ORIGINATING MOTION. An application. G.D. Watson & C. Perkins, eds., *Holmested & Watson: Ontario Civil Procedure* (Toronto: Carswell, 1984) at CJA-179.

ORIGINATING NOTICE. A notice of application. G.D. Watson & C. Perkins, eds., *Holmested & Watson: Ontario Civil Procedure* (Toronto: Carswell, 1984) at CJA-179.

ORIGINATING PROCESS. Something which commences a civil proceeding. G.D. Watson & C. Perkins, eds., *Holmested & Watson: Ontario Civil Procedure* (Toronto: Carswell, 1984) at 14-3.

ORIGINATING SUMMONS. A summons by which proceedings are commenced without writ. *The Queen's Bench Act*, R.S.S. 1978, c. Q-1, s. 2.

ORIGINATOR. *n.* A person who made remarks or a series of remarks which the Crown wants to offer as evidence. P.K. McWilliams, *Canadian Criminal Evidence*, 3d ed. (Aurora: Canada Law Book, 1988) at 13-4 and 13-5.

ORIGINE PROPRIA NEMINEM POSSE VOLUNTATE SUA EXIMI MANIFESTUM EST. [L.] It is obvious that no one can, by will, get rid of one's own origin.

ORNAMENTAL CONTAINER. A container that, except on the bottom, does not have any promotional or advertising material thereon, other than a trade mark or common name and that, because of any design appearing on its surface or because of its shape or texture, appears to be a decorative ornament and is sold as a decorative ornament in addition to being sold as the container of a product. Canada regulations.

ORNAMENTATION. *n.* A textile fibre or yarn that (a) is present in a textile fibre product as an integral part thereof for a decorative purpose; and (b) is or is made from a textile fibre other than the textile fibre from which the remainder of the product is made. *Textile Labelling and Advertising Regulations*, C.R.C., c. 1551, s. 25.

ORPHAN. *n.* 1. A child whose parents are deceased; a child born out of wedlock is deemed an orphan if the mother is deceased. *Children's Protection Act*, R.S.P.E.I. 1974, c. C-7, s. 1. 2. With respect to a contributor, means a dependent child of a contributor who has died. 3. (a) A child who is bereft by death of his parents; (b) a child who is bereft by death of one parent and whose surviving parent has, in the opinion of the Minister or the Board, abandoned or deserted the child; or (c) a child of divorced, separated or unmarried parents who is bereft by death of his father and whose father was, at the time of his death, receiving an additional allowance in respect of that child, and which child, not being the child of any other recipient; is (d) under the age of 17 years; (e) under the age of 25 years and following and making satisfactory progress in a course of instruction approved by the Minister; (f) under the age of 21 years and prevented by physical or mental incapacity from earning a livelihood; or (g) over the age of 21 years and prevented by physical or mental incapacity from earning a livelihood, where the incapacity occurred before the child attained the age of twenty-one years or after the age of twenty-one years while following and making satisfactory progress in a course of instruction approved by the Minister. *War Veterans Allowance Act*, R.S.C. 1985, c. W-3, s. 2.

ORTHESIS. *n.* A device fitted to a human being and intended to ensure the proper functioning of one of his members or organs or to restore proper functioning, make up for the limitations or improve the physiological capacity of one of his members or organs that has ceased to function, has never become fully developed or suffers from a congenital abnormality. *Public Health Protection Act*, R.S.Q. 1977, c. P-35, s. 1.

ORTHOPAEDIC APPLIANCES. Includes trusses and parts, surgical supports and appliances and parts, spinal braces, sacro-iliac belts and supports, elastic hosiery, but does not include shoulder braces, athletic supports, suspensories, arch, ankle, knee and like supports, including bracer and sporter types. *Retail Sales Tax Act*, R.R.O. 1980, Reg. 904, s. 1.

O.S. *abbr.* 1. Old Series. 2. Upper Canada, Queen's Bench Old Series, 1831-1844.

O.S.C. *abbr.* Ontario Securities Commission.

O.S.C.B. *abbr.* Ontario Securities Commission Bulletin.

OS DEMONSTRAT QUOD COR RUMINAT. [L.] The mouth divulges what the heart is thinking.

OSGOODE HALL L.J. *abbr.* Osgoode Hall Law Journal.

OSSIFICATION. *n.* The transformation of fibrous tissue or cartilage into bone. F.A. Jaffe, *A Guide to Pathological Evidence*, 2d ed. (Toronto: Carswell, 1983) at 181. See CENTRE OF ~.

OSTENSIBLE. *adj.* apparent; professed.

OSTENSIBLE AUTHORITY. Authority which an agent appears to have.

OSTEOLOGY. *n.* Knowledge of the development, function and structure of bones. F.A. Jaffe, *A Guide to Pathological Evidence*, 2d ed. (Toronto: Carswell, 1983) at 181.

OSTEOPATH. *n.* Any person who practises or advertises or holds himself out in any way as practising the treatment by diagnosis, including all diagnostic methods, direction, advice, written or otherwise, of any ailment, disease, defect or disability of the human body, by methods taught in colleges of osteopathy and approved by the Board. *Drugless Practitioners Act*, R.R.O. 1980, Reg. 250, s. 1.

OSTEOPATHY. *n.* The practice of the healing art as taught and practised in the recognized associated colleges of osteopathy. *Osteopathic Practice Amendment Act, 1979*, S.S. 1979, c. 50, s. 3.

O.T.C. *abbr.* Over the counter.

OTHER ASSESSMENT. That part of the balanced assessment or that part of the actual assessment, as the case requires, of a municipality, a part of a municipality or a school division that is attributable to other property in the municipality, part of the municipality, or school division, as the case may be. *An Act to Amend the Education Administration Act and the Public Schools Act*, S.M. 1980-81, c. 34, s. 171(1).

OTHER ATTRIBUTE. Includes (a) in relation to a tax levy for the purpose of financing all or part of the capital cost of a service to real property; (i) the actual or estimated cost of constructing a new building; (ii) the number of rooms, living units or beds in a building; or (iii) the number of persons in occupancy of a building; and (b) in relation to a tax levy for the purposes of financing all or part of the operating cost of a service to real property, such criteria as are prescribed. *Municipal Grants Act*, R.S.C. 1985, c. M-13, s. 2.

OTHER BENEFICIARY. Any person, other than the employee, to whom any amount is or may become payable by a trustee under the plan as a result of payments made to the trustee under the plan in trust for the benefit of employees, including the employee. *Income Tax Act*, R.S.C. 1952, c. 148 (as am. S.C. 1970-71-72, c. 63), c. 147(17).

OTHER PAYMENT REQUISITION. A requisition issued by the appropriate Minister and addressed to the Receiver General for a payment to be made by a means other than a cheque. *Account Verification and Payment Requisition Regulations*, C.R.C., c. 667, s. 2.

OTHER PROPERTY. All assessable property other than a farm or residential property. *An Act to Amend the Education Administration Act and the Public Schools Act*, S.M. 1980-81, c. 34, s. 171(1).

OTTAWA L. REV. *abbr.* Ottawa Law Review (Revue de droit d'Ottawa).

OTTER OR OTHER TRAWL OF A SIMILAR NATURE. Includes a Danish seine and Scottish seine. *Fisheries Act*, R.S.C. 1985, c. F-14, s. 64(2).

OTTER TRAWL. Any large bag-type net that is dragged in the sea by a vessel or vessels for the purpose of catching fish, and includes midwater trawls and any nets of a similar nature. Canada regulations.

OUNCE. *n.* $1/16$ pound or $437\,1/2$ grains. *Weights and Measures Act*, S.C. 1970-71-72, c. 36, schedule II. See FLUID ~; TROY ~.

OUST. *v.* To put out of possession.

OUSTER. *n.* Being put out of possession.

OUTBOARD DESIGNATED SEATING POSITION. A designated seating position where a longitudinal vertical plane tangent to the outboard side of the seat cushion is less than 12 inches from the innermost point on the inside surface of the vehicle that is vertically between the seating reference point and the shoulder reference point and longitudinally between the front and rear edges of the seat cushion. *Motor Vehicle Safety Regulations*, C.R.C., c. 1038, s. 100.

OUTDOOR ADVERTISING FACILITIES. Facilities, other than radio and television and newspapers, magazines and other periodical publications, of any person or corporation that is in the business of providing such facilities on a commercial basis for advertising purposes. *Election Finances Act*, S.O. 1986, c. 33, s. 1.

OUTDOOR EVENT. An event held out of doors for a period of 12 consecutive hours or more for the provision of entertainment, sports or other such purpose. *Public Health Act*, S.P.E.I. 1980, c. 42, s. 1.

OUTDOOR RECREATIONAL ACTIVITY. Any outdoor leisure time pursuit involving the use of natural resources and includes hunting, fishing and camping. *Travel and Tourism Act*, S.N.W.T. 1983 (1st Sess.), c. 15, s. 2.

OUTER BAR. The area outside the bar where junior barristers plead in contrast to Queen's Counsel, who plead within the bar.

OUTER DOORS. The doors intended to allow persons to obtain egress through and beyond the outside walls or structure of any public building after leaving any audience room therein. *Public Buildings Act*, R.S.M. 1970, c. P200, s. 2.

OUTER ENVELOPE. An envelope supplied by the Chief Electoral Officer for transmission to a special returning officer of the ballot paper of an elector after the ballot paper has been marked and enclosed in an inner envelope. *Special Voting Rules*, R.S.C. 1985, c. E-2, Schedule II, s. 2.

OUTER LABEL. The label on or affixed to the outside of a package. Canada regulations.

OUTER PACKAGE. A box, barrel, case or cylinder of wood, metal or other solid material, of such strength, construction and character that it will not be broken or accidentally opened, nor become defective or insecure while being conveyed, and will not allow any explosive to escape. Canada regulations.

OUTER SURFACE. An imaginary surface located above and in the immediate vicinity of the airport, which outer surface is more particularly described in the schedule. Airport Zoning regulations.

OUTFITTER. *n.* 1. Any individual or corporate body who provides equipment to be used in connection with an outdoor recreational activity or provides guides or guiding services or both. 2. A person, association or organization that for money or reward operates or maintains an establishment to provide sleeping or food services to hunters or fishermen. *Game Act*, R.S.N.B. 1973, c. G-1, s. 1.

OUTFITTER ESTABLISHMENT. See TOURIST ~.

OUTHOUSE. *n.* A building belonging to and adjacent to a dwelling-house.

OUTLAW. *n.* A person put outside the law or deprived of legal benefits by a judgment of outlawry.

OUTLAWRY. *n.* A declaration which permitted the confiscation of a defendant's property, including debts owed to that person. Originally this property went to the Crown if the defendant failed to appear, and the confiscated property and debts were paid directly to creditors. A series of statutes passed in the 19th century replaced outlawry with a fairer and simpler process against debtors who are absent. C.R.B. Dunlop, *Creditor-Debtor Law in Canada* (Toronto: Carswell, 1981) at 195-196.

OUTLAY. See ANNUAL ~.

OUTLET. *n.* 1. Any station, shop, establishment or other place in which gasoline is sold or kept for sale, by retail. 2. A shaft, slope, incline, decline, adit, tunnel, level or other means of ingress or egress to or from an underground mine. *Coal Mines Safety Act*, R.S.A. 1980, c. C-15, s. 1. 3. When used with reference to distributing pipe, means an opening at which water is discharged from the pipe (i) from a faucet; (ii) into a boiler or a heating system; (iii) into a device or equipment that is operated by water and that is not part of the distributing system; or (iv) into the open air, other than into an open tank forming part of the supply system. *Ontario Water Resources Act*, R.R.O. 1980, Reg. 736, s. 1. 4. A point in the electrical installation at which current is taken to supply utilization equipment. *Power Corporation Act*, R.R.O. 1980, Reg. 794, s. 0. See CONSUMER ~; RETAIL ~; SUFFICIENT ~; WHOLESALE ~.

OUTLET LIABILITY. The part of the cost of the construction, improvement or maintenance of a drainage works that is required to provide such outlet or improved outlet. *Drainage Act*, R.S.O. 1980, c. 126, s. 1.

OUTLINE. See PRODUCT ~.

OUTLINE LIGHTING. An arrangement of incandescent lamps or electric discharge tubing, outlining or accentuating certain features of buildings. *Power Corporation Act*, R.R.O. 1980, Reg. 794, s. 0.

OUTLINE MONUMENT. Includes all survey monuments planted to define any special survey made under The Special Survey Act on the principle of a block-out-line survey; all monuments of a permanent character planted in accordance with subsection (4) of section 118 of The Real Property Act; all monuments placed on off-set lines to evidence block corners in subdivision surveys, and all monuments defining any road or main highway. *Surveys Act*, R.S.M. 1970, c. S240, s. 2.

OUT-PATIENT. *var.* **OUTPATIENT.** *n.* 1. A person who is received in a hospital for examination or treatment or both, but who is not admitted as a patient. 2. A patient who is not an in-patient. 3. A patient who is not an in-patient who is admitted to a hospital for necessary diagnostic or treatment services, but who is not assigned to a bed in the hospital.

OUTPOST CAMP. Any fixed or portable rental unit that is remote from a base of operations and accessible only by air, water or forest trails, and is used for commercial purposes. *Tourism Act*, R.R.O. 1980, Reg. 936, s. 1.

OUTPOST ESTABLISHMENT. A tourist establishment consisting of one or more outpost camps being used for commercial purposes. *Tourism Act*, R.R.O. 1980, Reg. 936, s. 1.

OUTPUT. *n.* 1. The minerals taken or gained from the mine, and the mineral products derived from the processing of those minerals. 2. Includes all oil raised, taken, gained or recovered from any oil well in the province. *The Oil Well Income Tax Act*, R.S.S. 1978, c. O-3.1, s. 2.

OUTSIDE CUSTOMS AREA. An outside area designated by the collector for the safekeeping, examination and appraisal by customs of any consignment of goods that is too large or too heavy to be stored in a warehouse. *Customs Warehousing Regulations*, C.R.C., c. 462, s. 2.

OUTSIZED VEHICLE. (a) A motor vehicle or a combination of road vehicles the axle load, the total loaded mass, or one dimension of which does not conform to the standards established by regulation; or (b) a combination of road vehicles made up of more than three road vehicles, a detachable axle supporting a semi-trailer not being considered when computing the number of vehicles making up the combination. *Highway Safety Code*, S.Q. 1986, c. 91, s. 462.

OUTSTANDING TAXES. Real property taxes owing and includes any arrears, penalties, delinquent taxes or interest on them. *Home Owner Grant Act*, S.B.C. 1980, c. 18, s. 10.

OUTSTANDING TICKET. A winning ticket that was not cashed on the day it was purchased. *Race Track Supervision Regulations*, C.R.C., c. 441, s. 2.

OUTWARD MOVEMENT. (a) Accepting containers from inland carriers, placing them in the container yard in accordance with instructions from the owner of the vessel, or in the container storage area, and then moving them to the dock face for loading on a vessel; or (b) moving empty containers from the container storage area to the container freight station for stuffing and then moving them to the dock face for loading on a vessel. *Pacific Terminal Tariff By-law*, C.R.C., c. 1083, s. 32.

OUTWORKER. *n.* A person to whom articles or materials are given out to be made up, cleaned, washed, altered, ornamented, finished, repaired or adapted for sale in that person's own home or on other premises not under the control or management of the person who gave out the articles or materials.

OVEN. See INDUSTRIAL ~; MICROWAVE ~.

OVER. *adj.* Describes a limitation whose effect is contingent on a prior estate failing. See JURISDICTION ~.

OVERAGE. *n.* The amount by which the aggregate of the quantity of grain of any grade discharged from an elevator in a period between two consecutive weigh-overs of grain of that grade in the elevator and the quantity of grain of that grade in storage in the elevator at the end of that period exceeds the aggregate of the quantity of grain of that grade in storage in the elevator at the beginning of that period and the quantity of grain of that grade received into the elevator during that period. *Canada Grain Act*, R.S.C. 1985, c. G-10, s. 2.

OVERALL ASSESSMENT PER CAPITA. The quotient resulting from dividing the total of the municipal assessment bases of all municipalities by the total population of all municipalities. *Municipal Assistance Act*, R.S.N.B. 1973, c. M-19, s. 1.

OVERALL ASSESSMENT PER ROAD KILOMETRE. The quotient resulting from dividing the total of the municipal assessment bases of all municipalities by the total road kilometres of all municipalities. *Metric Conversion Act*, S.N.B. 1977, c. M-11.1, s. 18.

OVERALL LENGTH. 1. With respect to a vessel, means the horizontal distance measured between perpendiculars erected at the extreme ends of the outside of the main hull of the vessel.

2. With respect to herring, the length from the tip of the nose to the end of the caudal fin. *Atlantic Coast Herring Regulations*, C.R.C., c. 804, s. 2.

OVERALL TAX BASE PER CAPITA. The quotient resulting from dividing the total of the municipal tax bases of a group of municipalities by the total population of that group of municipalities. *An Act to Amend the Municipal Assistance Act*, S.N.B. 1986, c. 58, s. 1.

OVERALL TAX BASE PER ROAD KILOMETRE. The quotient resulting from dividing the total of the municipal tax bases for a group of municipalities by the total road kilometres of that group of municipalities. *An Act to Amend the Municipal Assistance Act*, S.N.B. 1986, c. 58, s. 1.

OVERALL WIDTH. 1. The nominal design dimension of the widest part of the vehicle with doors and windows closed and wheels in the straight ahead position, exclusive of signal lamps, marker lamps, outside rearview mirrors, flexible fender extensions and mud flaps. *Motor Vehicle Safety Regulations*, C.R.C., c. 1038, s. 2. 2. The linear distance between the exteriors of the sidewalls of an inflated tire, including elevations due to labelling, decorations or protective bands. Canada regulations.

OVERCHARGE. *v.* To charge a more serious offence than it seems is justified by the facts or to charge an offence with a fixed minimum penalty. S.A. Cohen, *Due Process of Law* (Toronto: Carswell, 1977) at 182.

OVER CURRENT DEVICE. Any device capable of automatically opening an electric circuit both under predetermined overload and short-circuit conditions, either by fusing of metal or by electro-mechanical means. *Power Corporation Act*, R.R.O. 1980, Reg. 794, s. 0.

OVER-DIMENSIONAL FARM VEHICLE. A farm tractor, self-propelled implement of husbandry, implement of husbandry, or any combination of them, having a weight, width, length or height in excess of the limits provided in this Part or Part VII. *Highway Traffic Act*, R.S.O. 1980, c. 198, s. 91.

OVERDOSE. *n.* Any amount of a drug taken which exceeds the maximum therapeutic dose for that particular type of person. F.A. Jaffe, *A Guide to Pathological Evidence*, 2d ed. (Toronto: Carswell, 1983) at 61.

OVERDRAFT. *n.* A situation where withdrawals exceed the amount of unencumbered deposits and approved lines of credit. *Credit Union Act*, S.S. 1984-85-86, c. C-45.1, s. 2.

OVERDRAFT CHARGE. A charge not exceeding $5 for the creation of or increase in an overdraft, imposed by a credit union or caisse populaire whose membership is wholly or substantially comprised of natural persons, or a deposit-taking institution whose deposits are insured, in whole or in part, by the Canada Deposit Insurance Corporation, or guaranteed, in whole or in part, by the Quebec Deposit Insurance Board. *Criminal Code*, R.S.C. 1985, c. C-46, s. 347(2).

OVERDUE. *adj.* Past the time a payment should be made.

OVEREXPOSURE. *n.* Exposure of a person, other than a patient undergoing medical examination or treatment, to radiation in excess of the maximum exposure limit of that form of radiation. *Radiation Protection Act*, S.A. 1985, c. R-2.1, s. 1.

OVERGRADE. *n.* An egg that meets the requirements for a higher grade than the one at which it is set. *Egg Regulations*, C.R.C., c. 284, s. 2.

OVERHEAD BRIDGE. A structure, including the approaches thereto, that carries a highway across and over the railway. *Railway Grade Separations Regulations*, C.R.C., c. 1191, s. 2.

OVERHEAD LINE. An overhead telephone, telegraph, telecommunication or electric power line or any combination thereof constructed across a pipeline. *Pipeline Overhead Crossing Order*, C.R.C., c. 1060, s. 2.

OVER-INSURANCE. *n.* On a vessel and the electronic equipment thereon means insurance on the vessel and electronic equipment in an amount exceeding the appraised value of the vessel and electronic equipment. *Fishing Vessel Insurance Regulations*, C.R.C., c. 325, s. 2.

OVERISSUE. *var.* **OVER-ISSUE.** *n.* The issue of securities in excess of any maximum number of securities that the issuer is authorized by its articles or a trust indenture to issue.

OVERLAY. *v.* For a sleeping adult to accidentally smother a young child in bed. This is now regarded as a rare event. F.A. Jaffe, *A Guide to Pathological Evidence*, 2d ed. (Toronto: Carswell, 1983) at 181.

OVERLOAD. *n.* (a) The number of kilograms derived by subtracting from the gross vehicle weight of a commercial vehicle the licensed gross vehicle weight; or (b) the number of kilograms derived by subtracting from the weight on any one axle or combination of axles of a commercial vehicle the weight authorized by regulation to be carried on the axle or combination of axles, whichever is the greater.

Commercial Transport Act, R.S.B.C. 1979, c. 55, s. 1.

OVERLOAD DEVICE. A device affording protection from excess current, but not necessarily short-circuit protection, and capable of automatically opening an electric circuit either by the fusing of metal or by electro-mechanical means. *Power Corporation Act*, R.R.O. 1980, Reg. 794, s. 0.

OVERMAN. *n.* Any person who is in charge of any mine or any portion of a mine, whose authority is next to the underground manager.

OVERPAYMENT. *n.* 1. The aggregate of all amounts paid by a person as tax or as interest or penalties, less the aggregate of all amounts payable by that person as tax, interest or penalties, or any amount so paid where no amount is so payable. 2. An amount (i) by which, as determined by the authority giving the social allowance or handicap benefit, the social allowance or handicap benefit received by a person under the Social Development Act exceeds the amount of the social allowance or handicap benefit he was actually entitled to receive, or (ii) by which, as determined by the authority giving the handicap benefit, the handicap benefit received by a person under the Assured Income for the Severely Handicapped Act exceeds the amount of the handicap benefit he was actually entitled to receive. *Maintenance and Recovery Act*, R.S.A. 1980, c. M-2, s. 32.

OVERRIDE. *v.* Under section 33, for Parliament or a legislature to disregard a provision of the Charter included in section 2 or sections 7 to 15. This is accomplished by having the statute expressly declare that this statute will operate notwithstanding that provision. P.W. Hogg, *Constitutional Law of Canada*, 2d ed. (Toronto: Carswell, 1985) at 259.

OVERRULE. *v.* To set aside an earlier decision's authority.

OVERSEAS AIR CREW. See CIVILIAN MEMBER OF ~.

OVERSEAS CANADIAN FORCES SCHOOL STAFF. Personnel employed outside Canada whose services are acquired by the Minister of National Defence under a prescribed order relating to the provision of educational facilities outside Canada. *Income Tax Act*, R.S.C. 1952, c. 148 (as am. S.C. 1980-81-82-83, c. 48, s. 108(7)), s. 248(1).

OVERSEAS HEADQUARTERS STAFF. See MEMBER OF ~.

OVERSEAS SERVICE. Any service involving duties required to be performed outside the western hemisphere, and includes service involving duties required to be performed outside Canada and the United States and the territorial waters thereof in aircraft or anywhere in a ship or other vessel, service in which is classed as "sea time" for the purpose of advancement of naval ratings, or which would be so classed were the ship or other vessel in the service of the naval forces of Canada. *War Service Grants Act*, R.S.C. 1970, c. W-4, s. 2.

OVERSEAS VETERAN. A person who has served in an active theatre of war in the armed forces, the auxiliary forces or the merchant marine of Canada or any of her allies, and who was honourably discharged therefrom. *Civil Service Act*, S.P.E.I. 1983, c. 4, s. 1.

OVERSEAS WELFARE WORKER. A person who, under the auspices of the Canadian Red Cross Society or the St. John Ambulance Brigade of Canada, proceeded from Canada to serve as a welfare worker, nursing aid, ambulance or transport driver or member of the Overseas Headquarters Staff or in any other capacity and includes Orthopaedic Nurses selected by the Canadian Red Cross Society for service overseas with the Scottish Ministry of Health. *Civilian War Pensions and Allowances*, R.S.C. 1985, c. C-31, s. 48.

OVERSIZE. *n.* The amount derived by subtracting from the outside width, height or length of a commercial vehicle with its load, if any, the permissible outside width, height or length prescribed under this Act and the regulations made under it. *Commercial Transport Act*, R.S.B.C. 1979, c. 55, s. 1.

OVER-SNOW VEHICLE. A vehicle that is capable of being propelled or driven otherwise than by muscular power, that runs on tracks or skis or on tracks and skis and that is designed for operation on snow or ice. Canada regulations.

OVERT. *adj.* Open. See MARKET ~.

OVERT ACT. An act done in the open.

OVERTAKING AIRCRAFT. An aircraft that is approaching another aircraft from the rear on a line forming an angle of less than 70° with the plane of symmetry of the latter, that is to say, in such position with reference to the other aircraft that at night it is not ordinarily possible to see either of the aircraft's forward lights. *Air Regulations*, C.R.C., c. 2, s. 101.

OVER-THE-COUNTER MARKET. Includes all trading in securities other than trades in securities that are listed and posted for trading on any stock exchange recognized by the Commission for the purpose of this section where the securities are traded through the facilities of any such stock exchange pursuant to the by-laws, rules and policies of any such stock exchange. *Securities Act*, R.R.O. 1980, Reg. 910, s. 143.

OVERTIME. *n.* Hours of work in excess of standard hours of work. See CLOCK ~.

OVERTIME CHARGE. An additional charge for services performed at any time other than during normal working hours.

OVERTIME FEES. The fees payable for an inspection performed by an inspector outside his regular working hours. *Destructive Pests Inspection Fees Regulations*, C.R.C., c. 696, s. 2.

OVERTIME RATE. A rate of pay not less than 1.5 times the regular wages of an employee. See MINIMUM ~.

OVERTURE. *n.* An opening; a proposal.

OVERT WORD. A word whose meaning is beyond doubt and clear.

OWE. *v.* Of a sum of money, to be under the obligation to pay it.

OWELTY. *n.* Equality.

OWING. *adj.* Due; required to be paid by obligation. C.R.B. Dunlop, *Creditor-Debtor Law in Canada* (Toronto: Carswell, 1981) at 245.

OWING OR ACCRUING. Money that is earned or owing, although not yet due or payable. *Small Claims Courts Act*, R.S.O. 1980, c. 476, s. 141.

OWN. *v.* (i) Owning in a representative capacity, such as executor, administrator or trustee; (ii) holding an option to purchase; and (iii) purchasing by way of agreement for sale.

[ ]O.W.N. *abbr.* Ontario Weekly Notes, 1909-1932.

[ ]O.W.N. *abbr.* Ontario Weekly Notes, 1933-1962.

OWNED. *adj.* 1. Having an interest in. 2. Beneficially owned. See CANADIAN-~; WHOLLY ~.

OWNER. *n.* 1. Any person or body corporate entitled to any freehold or other estate or interest in land, at law or in equity, in possession, in futurity or in expectancy. 2. A person having an estate or interest in land at whose request, express or implied; and (i) on whose credit; (ii) on whose behalf; (iii) with whose privity and consent; or (iv) for whose direct benefit, work is done on or material is furnished for an improvement to the land and includes all persons claiming under that person whose rights are acquired after the commencement of the work or the furnishing of the material. 3. A person entitled to convey land and whose interest in the land is defined and whose name is specified in an instrument registered in the proper land registry office. 4. Any person who holds an immoveable as owner, usufructuary, institute of a substitution or emphyteutic lessee, or occupies Crown land under a promise of sale, occupation license or location ticket. *Real Estate Assessment Act*, R.S.Q. 1977, c. E-16, s. 1. 5. Includes a person who is in possession of a motor vehicle under a contract by which that person may become the owner of the motor vehicle on full compliance with the terms of the contract. 6. In relation to a certification mark, means the person by whom the defined standard has been established. *Trade-marks Act*, R.S.C. 1985, c. T-13, s. 2. 7. Includes Her Majesty and public bodies, bodies corporate, societies, companies and inhabitants of counties, parishes, municipalities or other districts in relation to the acts and things that they are capable of doing and owning respectively. *Criminal Code*, R.S.C. 1985, c. C-46, s. 2. 8. Includes the agent, charterer by demise or master of a vessel. Canada regulations. 9. Includes (a) in respect of a vessel, the agent, charterer by demise or master of the vessel; and (b) in respect of goods, the agent, sender, consignee or bailee of the goods as well as the carrier of the goods to, upon, over or from a small vessel facility. Canada regulations. 10. In respect of an aircraft, includes (a) the person in whose name the aircraft is registered; (b) the person is possession of an aircraft as purchaser under a conditional sale or hire-purchase agreement that reserves to the vendor the title to the aircraft until payment of the purchase price or the performance of certain conditions; (c) a person in possession of the aircraft as chattel mortgagor under a chattel mortgage; and (d) a person in possession of the aircraft under a bona fide lease or agreement of hire. *Air Regulations*, C.R.C., c. 2, s. 101. See AMUSEMENT ~; ASSESSED ~; BENEFICIAL ~; CO-~; FOREST ~; HOME ~; INTEREST ~; LIMITED ~; LIVESTOCK ~; PART-~; PROPERTY-~; REAL ~; REGISTERED ~; REGISTERED ~ IN FEE SIMPLE; RESIDENT ~; ROYALTY ~; VALUE TO ~; WORKING INTEREST ~.

OWNER-BUILDER. *n.* Any person who, for personal account, carries out or has carried out building work.

OWNER DEVELOPER. 1. A person who, on the date that a strata plan is tendered to the registrar for deposit, is the person registered in the land title office as owner in fee simple of the land included in the strata plan, and, for the purposes of this Act, includes (a) an affiliate, defined in the Company Act, of the owner developer; and (b) a trustee of any right, title or interest of the owner developer, or affiliate, in the land included in the strata plan. *Condo-*

minium Act, R.S.B.C. 1979, c. 61, s. 1. 2. A person who, on the date that a leasehold strata plan is tendered to the registrar for deposit, is the registered lessee in a ground lease of the land within the strata plan, and includes (a) an affiliate, defined in the Company Act; and (b) a trustee of any right, title or interest of the owner developer in the leasehold strata plan. *Condominium Act*, R.S.B.C. 1979, c. 61, s. 92.

OWNERLESS. *adj.* A dog is considered owner-less if it does not have affixed to its collar or harness a valid and subsisting licence tag. *Live-stock Protection Act*, R.S.B.C. 1979, c. 245, s. 1.

OWNER OCCUPIED APARTMENT BUILD-ING. A parcel of land (a) the owner of which is a corporation that by its memorandum of association is required to own and operate its building exclusively for the benefit of its share-holders who are occupants of the building, or that has entered into a registered long-term lease with an occupant of an eligible apartment residence in a building owned by the corporation and on the parcel of land; (b) that is shown as a separate taxable parcel on a tax roll for the current year prepared by a collector; and (c) that has as an improvement a building in which there is an eligible apartment residence. *Home Owner Grant Act*, R.S.B.C. 1979, c. 171, s. 1.

OWNER-OCCUPIED HOME. Of a taxpayer means a housing unit owned, whether jointly with another person or otherwise, by the tax-payer in a taxation year and inhabited by the taxpayer at any time in the year. Includes, in the case of a housing unit owned by a coop-erative housing corporation, a share of the capital stock of the corporation owned, whether jointly with another person or otherwise, by the taxpayer in a taxation year, if the share was acquired by him for the sole purpose of acquiring the right to inhabit the housing unit and if he inhabits it at any time in that year. *An Act to Amend Various Fiscal Laws and Other Legisla-tion*, S.Q. 1986, c. 15, s. 61.

OWNER OF A COPYRIGHT. Includes the owner of the right to publish in serial form as distinct and separate from other rights of pub-lication. *Copyright Act*, R.S.C. 1985, c. C-42, s. 24.

OWNER OF A DOG. Includes any person who possesses or harbours a dog. *Dog Act*, S.P.E.I. 1974, c. 10, s. 1.

OWNER OF A GAS UTILITY. (i) A person owning, operating, managing or controlling a gas utility and whose business and operations are subject to the legislative authority of Alberta, and the lessees, trustees, liquidators of it or any receivers of it appointed by any court; but (ii) does not include a municipality that has not

voluntarily come under this Act in the manner provided by section 4. *Gas Utilities Act*, R.S.A. 1980, c. G-4, s. 1.

OWNER OF A PUBLIC BUILDING. 1. Includes a person, company and corporation, who is owner, tenant or occupant, under any title, and that person's agent. 2. Every person, com-pany, association or corporation being in pos-session of or renting a public building or an industrial establishment. *Pressure Vessels Act*, R.S.Q. 1977, c. A-20, s. 2.

OWNER OF A PUBLIC UTILITY. Includes (i) every corporation, including municipal corpo-rations, and every person, firm, or association of persons the business or operations whereof are subject to the authority of the Legislature; and (ii) their lessees, trustees, liquidators or receivers appointed by any court; that own, operate, manage or control any public utility.

OWNER OF CATTLE. A person having one or more head of cattle in his possession or under his charge. *The Cattle Marketing Voluntary Deduction Act*, R.S.S. 1978, c. C-3, s. 2.

OWNER OF HOGS. A person having one or more slaughter hogs in his possession or under his charge, and includes a person possessing legal or equitable right to slaughter hogs for which he has paid legal tender or entered into a contract to purchase. *The Hog Marketing Deductions Act*, R.S.S. 1978, c. H-4, s. 2.

OWNER OF THE POLLUTANT. The owner of the pollutant immediately before the first discharge of the pollutant, whether into the natural environment or not, in a quantity or with a quality abnormal at the location where the discharge occurs. *Environmental Protection Act*, R.S.O. 1980, c. 141, s. 79.

OWNER-OPERATOR. *n.* An individual who (a) owns and operates a commercial fishing vessel; or (b) is a shareholder in a company that (i) is not a fishing company; and (ii) owns one or more commercial fishing vessels and is designated by the company as the owner-oper-ator for the purposes of these Regulations. *Pacific Fishery Registration and Licensing Reg-ulations*, C.R.C., c. 824, s. 2.

OWNER'S CERTIFICATE. A certificate of insurance issued to a person in respect of the ownership of a vehicle for which a certificate of registration, a dealer's certificate or a T trailer certificate of registration has been issued under The Vehicles Act or The Snowmobile Act. *The Automobile Accident Insurance Act*, R.S.S. 1978, c. A-35, s. 2.

OWNERSHIP. *n.* 1. The most far-ranging right in rem the law allows to a person: to deal with something to the exclusion of everyone else or of everyone except one or more designated people. 2. Having legal custody and control of an aircraft. *Air Regulations*, C.R.C., c. 2, s. 101. See BENEFICIAL ~; CANADIAN ~ RATE; TRANSFER OF ~.

OWNERSHIP INTEREST. In relation to a corporation, means a direct or indirect entitlement, in the event of the dissolution of the corporation, to a determinable person of the net assets thereof. *Export Development Act*, R.S.C. 1985, c. E-20, s. 36(2).

OWNERSHIP PLAN. See TIME SHARE ~.

OWNERS OF A DOCK OR CANAL. Includes any person or authority having the control and management of any dock or canal, and any ship repairer using the dock or canal, as the case may be. *Canada Shipping Act*, R.S.C. 1985, c. S-9, s. 578(4).

OWNER'S PERMIT. A permit issued to a registered owner of a motor vehicle. *Motor Vehicle Act*, R.S.N.S. 1967, c. 191, s. 1.

OWNER'S POLICY. A motor vehicle liability policy insuring a person in respect of the ownership, use or operation of an automobile owned by him and within the description or definition thereof in the policy and, if the contract so provides, in respect of the use or operation of any other automobile. Insurance acts.

OWNER'S PORTION OF THE COST. That part or portion of the cost of a work that is to be specially assessed upon the land abutting directly on the work or upon land immediately benefited by the work.

OWNER'S SHARE OF THE COST. That portion of the cost of a work that is to be specially assessed upon the lots abutting directly on the work or upon lots benefited by the work. *The Local Improvements Act*, R.S.S. 1978, c. L-33, s. 2.

OWNER TO USES. A transferee registered under a transfer to uses.

O.W.R. *abbr.* Ontario Weekly Reporter, 1902-1916.

OXIDES OF NITROGEN. The sum of the nitric oxide and nitrogen dioxide that would be contained in a gas if the nitric oxide were in the form of nitrogen dioxide. *Motor Vehicle Safety Regulations*, C.R.C., c. 1038, s. 1100.

OXYGEN. See MEDICAL ~.

OXYGEN DEFICIENCY. With respect to the atmosphere in a confined space, means a concentration of oxygen by volume in the atmosphere that is less than 17 per cent. *Canada Confined Spaces Regulations*, C.R.C., c. 996, s. 2.

OYER. [Fr.] To hear.

OYER AND TERMINER. [Fr.] To hear and decide.

OYER DE RECORD. [Fr.] To hear the record.

OYEZ. [Fr. hear ye] Pay attention.

OYSTER-FISHING. See PUBLIC ~AREA.

P. *abbr.* Pico.

[ ] P. *abbr.* Law Reports, Probate, 1891-1971.

PACEMAKER. See CARDIAC ~.

PACIFIC BLOCKADE. A blockade used as a reprisal in peacetime.

PACIFIC SALMON. Includes coho salmon, chinook salmon, kokanee salmon, pink salmon and any member of the genus Oncorhynchus. *Ontario Fishery Regulations*, C.R.C., c. 849, s. 2.

PACK. *n.* Two or more dogs that are running at large. *Livestock Protection Act*, R.S.B.C. 1979, c. 245, s. 1. See BREAST ~; BRINE ~; HEAVY ~; SOLID ~; SQUAT ~; SYRUP ~; VACUUM ~; WATER ~.

PACKAGE. *n.* 1. Includes wrapper, carton, box, tub, crock, crate or other covering or container. 2. An inner or outer receptacle or covering used for containing, packing, wrapping or covering an agricultural product. 3. A bottle, jug, jar, keg, cask, barrel or other container or receptacle used for holding liquor. See CATCHWEIGHT ~; CLOSED ~; INNER ~; OUTER ~.

PACKAGE BARGAINING. Collective bargaining in which the union or employer covers groups of proposals.

PACKAGE BEES. Bees placed in a screened cage or package without honeycombs for the purpose of being shipped. *Bees Act*, R.S.O. 1980, c. 42, s. 1.

PACKAGE CHEESE. Process cheese or the product resulting from the comminuting and mixing of one or more lots of cheese without the aid of heat or emulsifying agents.

PACKAGED. See PRE-~ FOOD; PRE-~ GOODS; PRE~ PRODUCT.

PACKAGED LUMBER. Lumber of uniform lengths that are in unit loads and properly arranged and strapped for handling by mechan-ical means. *Pacific Terminal Tariff By-law*, C.R.C., c. 1083, s. 2.

PACKAGE FREIGHT. Goods bagged, baled, boxed, bundled, crated, wrapped, enclosed or bound for transportation. *Canal Regulations*, C.R.C., c. 1564, s. 2.

PACKAGING. *n.* Any receptacle or enveloping material used to contain or protect goods, but does not include a container or a means of transport.

PACKED. See PROPERLY ~.

PACKER. *n.* 1. Any person, partnership or corporation engaged in the business of slaughtering livestock to the number of 2,000 in any 3 consecutive months or 5,000 in any calendar year. *Livestock and Livestock Products Act*, R.S.C. 1985, c. L-9, s. 10. 2. A person who owns or operates an abbatoir, slaughterhouse, packing plant or other premises used for the purpose of preparing cattle for human consumption. 3. Any person who packs and grades honey for sale. *Farm Products Grades and Sales Act*, R.R.O. 1980, Reg. 337, s. 1. 4. A vessel used only for the purpose of collecting, holding, storing or transporting fish. *Pacific Fishery Registration and Licensing Regulations*, C.R.C., c. 824, s. 2. See TOBACCO ~.

PACKER'S YARD. Any enclosed place owned, controlled or operated by any packer or his agent and used in connection with receiving, holding or weighing livestock for slaughter or for marketing or for shipment for slaughter. *Livestock and Livestock Products Act*, R.S.C. 1985, c. L-9, s. 10.

PACKET. *n.* A container for documents relating to an application made pursuant to Criminal Code section 185 or subsections 186(6) or 196(2). These documents are confidential and, except for the authorization, are placed in this container and sealed by the judge to whom the application is made as soon as the application is determined. This packet is kept in the court's

P

custody in a place to which the public does not have access or in any other place authorized by the judge. The packet may not be (a) opened or its contents removed except (i) to deal with an application for renewal of the authorization; or (ii) pursuant to the order of a superior court judge or a judge described in section 552. P.K. McWilliams, *Canadian Criminal Evidence*, 3d ed. (Aurora: Canada Law Book, 1988) at 13-48. See MONEY ~; SMALL ~.

PACKING AND BAILING. The treatment of waste by its compression into blocks or bales and binding or sheathing the blocks with wire, metal, plastic or other material. *Environmental Protection Act*, R.R.O. 1980, Reg. 309, s. 1.

PACKING DEVICE. A device that, as part of a mechanical packaging system, measures a predetermined quantity of commodity without recording the measurement of each quantity of commodity measured by the device or without being operated by a person who observes or records the measurement of each quantity of commodity measured by the device. *Weights and Measures Regulations*, C.R.C., c. 1605, s. 2.

PACKING PLANT. 1. A building or place, other than a processing plant, where fish are received from commercial fishermen for the purpose of packing or assembling the fish for shipment to a market but does not include a building or place where a commercial fisherman packs or assembles fish of his own catching only. *The Fisheries Act*, R.S.S. 1978, c. F-16, s. 2. 2. Premises in which honey is packed or graded by a packer. *Farm Products Grades and Sales Act*, R.R.O. 1980, Reg. 337, s. 1. 3. A plant in which maple products are graded and packed. *Maple Products Regulations*, C.R.C., c. 289, s. 2.

PACT. *n.* Bargain; contract; covenant.

PACTA CONVENTA QUAE NEQUE CONTRA LEGES NEQUE DOLO MALO INITA SUNT OMNIMODO OBSERVANDA SUNT. [L.] Agreements which are neither illegal nor originate out of fraud must be observed in every respect.

PACTA DANT LEGEM CONTRACTUI. [L.] Agreements establish the law of contract.

PACTA PRIVATA JURI PUBLICO DEROGARE NON POSSUNT. [L.] Private agreements cannot restrict public right.

PACTA QUAE CONTRA LEGES CONSTITUTIONESQUE VEL CONTRA BONOS MORES FIUNT NULLAM VIM HABERE INDUBITATI JURIS EST. [L.] It is unquestioned law that agreements which go against laws and constitutions or against good morals have no force.

PACTA QUAE TURPEM CAUSAM CONTINENT NON SUNT OBSERVANDA. [L.] Agreements which contain a disgraceful cause should not be observed.

PACTA SUNT SERVANDA. [L.] Contracts should be kept.

PACTA TERTIIS NEC NOCENT NEC PROSUNT. [L.] Contracts neither impose burdens nor confer benefits on third parties.

PACTIO. *n.* Bargain; contract; covenant.

PACTIS PRIVATORUM JURI PUBLICO NON DEROGATUR. [L.] An agreement between individuals is not restricted by public right.

PACTO ALIQUOD LICITUM EST, QUOD SINE PACTO NON ADMITTITUR. [L.] By special agreement something not otherwise allowed is permitted.

PACTUM. See NUDUM ~.

PACTUM DE CONTRAHENDO. [L.] An agreement to negotiate or complete a contract.

PAD. See MOBILE HOME ~.

PAID. See FULLY ~.

PAID BREAK. A certain time, the most common being a period when employees travel, rest, clean up or eat their meals, during which they are generally not expected to perform any service but are paid by provision of a collective agreement. D.J.M. Brown and D.M. Beatty, *Canadian Labour Arbitration*, 2d ed. (Aurora: Canada Law Book, 1977) at 628.

PAID FIRE DEPARTMENT. A fire brigade of which, exclusive of the fire chief, one or more members are in receipt of full time remuneration for their services as members of the fire brigade. *Fire Department Act*, R.S.B.C. 1979, c. 132, s. 1.

PAID IN. As applied to the capital stock of a company or to any of its shares, means the amount paid to it on its shares, including the premium, if any, paid on the shares, whether the shares are or are not fully paid.

PAID IN CAPITAL STOCK. As applied to a provincial company having common shares without par value, means the amount paid in on the common shares of the company. *Trust Companies Act*, R.S.A. 1980, c. T-9, s. 1.

PAID OUT. See AMOUNT ~.

PAID UP. *var.* **PAID-UP.** When applied to the capital of a company, means capital stock or shares on which there remains no liability, actual or contingent, to the issuing company.

PAID-UP CAPITAL. At a particular time

means, (i) in respect of a share of any class of the capital stock of a corporation, an amount equal to the paid-up capital at that time, in respect of the class of shares of the capital stock of the corporation to which that share belongs, divided by the number of issued shares of that class outstanding at that time; (ii) in respect of a class of shares of the capital stock of a corporation; (A) where the particular time is before May 7, 1974, an amount equal to the paid-up capital in respect of that class of shares at the particular time, computed without reference to the provisions of this Act; (B) where the particular time is after May 6, 1974 and before April 1, 1977, an amount equal to the paid-up capital in respect of that class of shares at the particular time, computed in accordance with this Act as it read on March 31, 1977; and (C) where the particular time is after March 31, 1977, an amount equal to the paid-up capital in respect of that class of shares at the particular time, computed without reference to the provisions of this Act except subsections 66.3(2) and (4), sections 84.1 and 84.2, subsections 85(2.1), 85.1(21.1), 87(3), 87(9), 138(11.7), 192(4.1) and 194(4.1) and section 212.1; and (iii) in respect of all the shares of the capital stock of a corporation, an amount equal to the aggregate of all amounts each of which is an amount equal to the paid-up capital in respect of any class of shares of the capital stock of the corporation at the particular time. *Income Tax Act*, R.S.C. 1952, c. 148 (as am. S.C. 1988, c. 55, s. 62(3)), s. 89(1)(c).

PAID-UP CAPITAL EMPLOYED IN CANADA. The paid-up capital employed by a non-resident corporation as at the close of a fiscal year.

PAID-UP CAPITAL FOR CORPORATE PURPOSES. The capital of a particular class of corporate shares as recorded in its financial statements. W. Grover & F. Iacobucci, *Materials on Canadian Income Tax*, 4th ed. (Toronto: Richard De Boo Ltd., 1980) at 734.

PAID-UP CAPITAL VALUE. Of a share means an amount equal to the paid-up capital of the corporation that is represented by the shares of the class to which that share belongs divided by the number of shares of that class that are in fact issued and outstanding. *Income Tax Act*, R.S.C. 1952, c. 148 (as am. S.C. 1980-81-82-83, c. 140, s. 113), s. 204(a.3).

PAIN AND SUFFERING. Every kind of emotional distress which a victim feels and which was caused by a personal injury. K.D. Cooper-Stephenson & I.B. Saunders, *Personal Injury Damages in Canada* (Toronto: Carswell, 1981) at 351.

PAINTER. *n.* A person who: (i) prepares and performs interior and exterior work to plaster, wallboard, wood, metal, concrete, masonry, stucco and allied materials; (ii) erects scaffolding including swing stage; (iii) prepares and performs work by steam wallpaper stripping machines and applies wall coverings, wallpaper, grass cloth, wood veneer, vinyl fabrics and allied materials; (iv) prepares and performs work by mechanical processes, blow torches, spray guns and sandblasting. *Apprenticeship and Tradesmen's Qualification Act*, R.R.O. 1980, Reg. 50, s. 1. See AUTOMOTIVE ~.

PAINTING. *n.* A unique artistic representation or work executed in oil-base pigments or other media such as fresco, collage, tempera or encaustic on a support such as stretched canvas, mounted paper, cardboard or other manufactured board, metal, glass, wood or silk. *Canadian Cultural Property Export Control List*, C.R.C., c. 448, s. 1.

PAIR. *v.* For two members with opposite opinions to agree to be absent from the House of Commons for voting during a given period or on a particular division.

PAIS. *n.* Nation. See ACT IN ~.

PALAEONTOLOGICAL OBJECT. The remains or fossil or other object indicating the existence of extinct or prehistoric animals, but does not include human remains.

PALAEONTOLOGICAL RESOURCE. A work of nature consisting of or containing evidence of extinct multicellular beings and includes those works of nature or classes of works of nature designated by the regulations as palaeontological resources. *Historical Resources Act*, R.S.A. 1980, c. H-8, s. 1.

PALLETS. *n.* Small portable platforms upon which goods may be consolidated into individual loads for transportation or storage. *Wharfage Charges By-law*, C.R.C., c. 1066, s. 2.

PALMISTRY. *n.* Telling peoples' fortunes from lines on the palms of their hands.

PALM PRINT. An impression made on some surface by the palm of a person's hand used to identify that person.

PAMPHLET. See PRINTED BOOK OR ~.

PANEL. *n.* 1. A page or schedule which contains the names of jurors called to serve. 2. A list of consultants or authoritative people from whom one might seek a decision or advice. See CONTROL ~; DISPLAY ~; JURY ~.

PANELBOARD. *n.* An assembly of buses and connections, over-current devices and control apparatus with or without switches, or other equipment, constructed for installation as a complete unit in a cabinet. *Power Corporation Act*, R.R.O. 1980, Reg. 794, s. 0. See ENCLOSED ~.

PANEL WALL. A non-loadbearing exterior masonry wall having bearing support at each storey. *Building Code Act*, R.R.O. 1980, Reg. 87, s. 1.

PANIC HARDWARE. An approved bar or panel listed by Underwriters' Laboratories of Canada or any other approved laboratory or an approved bar or panel extending not less than two-thirds the width of the door, placed at heights suitable for the service required, not less than 30 inches nor more than 44 inches above the floor, and designed to cause the door to open when a pressure not in excess of 20 pounds is applied to the bar or panel in the direction of egress. *Hotel Fire Safety Act*, R.R.O. 1980, Reg. 505, s. 2.

PANNELLATION. *n.* The act of assembling a jury panel.

PAPER. See BALLOT ~S; BOOKS AND ~S; BOOKS OR ~S; CHATTEL ~; COMMAND ~S; COMMERCIAL ~; ELECTION ~S; EXCHEQUER BILL ~; NOTICE ~; ORDER ~; PULP AND ~; REVENUE ~; STAMPED ~; WHITE ~.

PAPERBACK. *n.* Any printed matter other than a periodical that is published for general distribution to the public and that is not bound in a hard cover, and includes paperback books. *Paperback and Periodical Distributors Act*, R.S.O. 1980, c. 366, s. 1.

PAPER BLOCKADE. A blockade which a belligerent declares but cannot or does not actually enforce.

PAPER CARRIER. A natural person who carries out home delivery of a daily or weekly newspaper for a remuneration. *An Act Respecting Industrial Accidents and Occupational Diseases*, S.Q. 1985, c. 6, s. 2.

PAPER MONEY. Bills of exchange, bank notes and promissory notes.

PAR. *n.* State of equality; equal value. See ABOVE ~; BELOW ~.

PARADOXICAL EFFECT. An effect caused by a drug which is opposite what was expected, *e.g.* excitement after taking a sedative. F.A. Jaffe, *A Guide to Pathological Evidence*, 2d ed. (Toronto: Carswell, 1983) at 61.

PARAFFIN TEST. A test, no longer considered as specific enough, for the nitrites and nitrates of gunpowder residues on skin. F.A. Jaffe, *A Guide to Pathological Evidence*, 2d ed. (Toronto: Carswell, 1983) at 181.

PARAGE. *n.* Equality of blood, dignity or name.

PARAGIUM. *n.* Equality of blood, dignity or name.

PARAGRAPH. *n.* A section or part of an affidavit, contract, pleading, statute or will.

PARAMOUNT. *adj.* Superior; of the highest jurisdiction.

PARAMOUNTCY. See FEDERAL ~.

PARAPUBLIC SECTORS. See PUBLIC AND ~.

PARCEL. *n.* Any lot, block or other area in which land is held or into which land is divided or subdivided. See ABUTTING ~; AIR SPACE ~; FORMER ~; INTERVENING ~; NEW ~; RESIDENTIAL ~; RUN-OFF ~; TAXABLE ~.

PARCEL COMPARTMENT ASSEMBLY. All parcel compartment units installed in an apartment building or office complex. *Mail Receptacles Regulations*, C.R.C., c. 1282, s. 2.

PARCEL COMPARTMENT UNIT. A cabinet designed for the receipt of mail having individual storage compartments that may be kept locked. *Mail Receptacles Regulations*, C.R.C., c. 1282, s. 2.

PARCEL OF LAND. 1. A lot or block within a registered plan of subdivision. 2. A quarter section of land or any smaller area owned by one person. 3. Area owned by one person, or by more persons than one as tenants in common or as joint tenants.

PARCENARY. *n.* The tenure of land by a parcener.

PARCENER. *n.* A person who, with one or more others, equally shares an estate inherited from a common ancestor.

PARCHMENT. *n.* The skin of sheep specially prepared as a surface on which to write.

PARDON. *v.* For the Crown to release a person from the punishment that person incurred for some offence.

PARDON. *n.* A pardon granted by the Governor-in-Council under subsection 4(8). *Criminal Records Act*, R.S.C. 1985, c. C-47, s. 2. See PLEA OF ~.

PARENS EST NOMEN GENERALE AD OMNE GENUS COGNATIONIS. [L.] Parent is the general name for every kind of blood relationship.

PARENS PATRIAE. [L.] The role of the Crown as superintendent of charities, children and mentally incompetent persons. S.A. DeSmith, *Judicial Review of Administrative Action*, 4th ed. by J.M. Evans (London: Stevens, 1980) at 432.

PARENT. *n.* 1. The father or mother of a child, whether or not the child is born in wedlock, and includes an adoptive parent. *Citizenship Regulations*, C.R.C., c. 400, s. 2. 2. Includes, in respect of another person, any person who is under a legal duty to provide for that other person or any person who has, in law or in fact, the custody or control of that other person. 3. A person who has demonstrated a settled intention to treat a child as a member of his or her family whether or not that person is the natural parent of the child. 4. In relation to a child, means an individual resident in Canada who wholly or substantially maintains that child. *Family Allowance Act*, R.S.C. 1985, c. F-1, s. 2. 5. Includes a father, mother, grandfather, grandmother, stepfather, stepmother, a person who adopted a child, and a person who stood in loco parentis to a deceased person. See BIRTH ~; DEPENDENT ~; FOSTER ~.

PARENTAGE. See COMMON ~.

PARENT COMPANY. A company is deemed to be another's parent company if, but only if, that other is its subsidiary.

PARENT CORPORATION. 1. A corporation that controls another corporation. 2. A corporation whose officers establish or take proceedings to establish a pension fund society under this Act. *Pension Fund Societies Act*, R.S.C. 1985, c. P-8, s. 2.

PARENT CROWN CORPORATION. A corporation that is wholly owned directly by the Crown, but does not include a departmental corporation. *Financial Administration Act*, R.S.C. 1985, c. F-11, s. 83.

PARENTERAL USE. Administration of a drug by means of a hypodermic syringe, needle or other instrument through or into the skin or mucous membrane. Canada regulations.

PARENTHESIS. *n.* Any part of a sentence which, if omitted, would not harm the grammatical construction of the rest of that sentence.

PARENTICIDE. *n.* A person who murders a parent.

PARENTIS. See IN LOCO ~.

PARENT MODEL RESIDENCE. *var.* **PARENT-MODEL RESIDENCE.** A building, group of buildings or part of a building where not more than two adult persons live and provide care for children on a continuous basis. *Child and Family Services Act*, S.O. 1984, c. 55, s. 175.

PARES. *n.* [L.] A person's peer or equal.

PARIBUS SENTENTIIS REUS ABSOLVITUR. [L.] If opinions are equal, the defendant is acquitted.

PARI-MUTUEL DEPARTMENT. The room or rooms and area or areas set aside and used for the operation of a pari-mutuel system. *Race Track Supervision Regulations*, C.R.C., c. 441, s. 2.

PARI-MUTUEL SYSTEM. 1. A pari-mutuel system of betting through the agency on which bets may be placed and recorded and tickets or other documents showing the amount of money bet by a bettor issued to the bettor. *Pari-Mutuel Tax Act*, S.M. 1974, c. 64, s. 1. 2. The equipment required to record and register bets. *Race Track Supervision Regulations*, C.R.C., c. 441, s. 2.

PAR IN PAREM IMPERIUM NON HABET. [L.] An equal has no control over an equal.

PARI PASSU. [L.] Equally; with no preference.

PARISH. *n.* 1. Any territory erected into a parish by civil authority. *Education Act*, R.S.Q. 1977, c. I-14, s. 1. 2. A territory canonically erected as a parish or quasi-parish for the purposes of the Roman Catholic religion and the benefit of the faithful of such religion. *An Act Respecting Fabriques*, R.S.Q. 1977, c. F-1, s. 1. 3. Includes any municipality that is within the limits of a parish. *Interpretation Act*, R.S.N.B. 1973, c. I-13, s. 38.

PARISHIONER. *n.* A person of full age of the Roman Catholic religion who belongs to a parish or chapelry and is not a cleric assigned to administer to that parish or chapelry. *An Act Respecting Fabriques*, R.S.Q. 1977, c. F-1, s. 1. See LAND-OWNING ~.

PARK. *v.* 1. The standing of a vehicle, whether occupied or not, except when standing temporarily for the purpose of and while engaged in loading or unloading. 2. The standing of an aircraft, whether occupied or not. *Airport Tariff Regulations*, C.R.C., c. 886, s. 64.

PARK. *n.* Any public or privately owned area that is set aside for recreational use by the public. See AMUSEMENT ~; CONSERVATION ~; MOBILE HOME ~; NATIONAL ~; PROVINCIAL ~; PUBLIC ~; RECREATIONAL ~; TRAILER ~; WAYSIDE ~S.

PARKING. *n.* The standing of a vehicle whether occupied or not, upon a roadway, otherwise than temporarily for the purpose of and while actually engaged in loading or unloading, or in obedience to traffic signs or signals. See PUBLIC ~ AREA.

PARKING BRAKE. A mechanism designed to prevent the movement of a stationary vehicle.

Motor Vehicle Safety Regulations, C.R.C., c. 1038, s. 2.

PARKING CONTROL DEVICE. A sign, marking or device, including a parking meter, used for the purpose of regulating or prohibiting the stopping, standing or parking of vehicles. *Department of Public Works Act*, S.M. 1974, c. 45, s. 2.

PARKING INFRACTION. Any unlawful parking, standing or stopping of a vehicle that constitutes an offence. *Provincial Offences Act*, R.S.O. 1980, c. 400, s. 14.

PARKING LANE. That portion of a primary highway between (i) the edge of the roadway to the right of the direction of traffic; and (ii) the nearest solid white line (not being the centre line) marked on the roadway.

PARKING METER. A mechanical appliance or device placed or installed at or near a parking space for the purpose of timing, indicating, regulating and controlling the use and occupation by vehicles of such parking space.

PARKING SPACE. A space that is provided for the parking of vehicles and for which a parking meter is installed.

PARKING ZONE. A street or portion of a street or a parking lot or parking facility approved by the council for the purpose of parking vehicles and on or in which parking meters are installed and maintained to collect a fee for the use and occupation of a parking space. *Municipalities Act*, R.S.N.B. 1973, c. M-22, s. 164.

PARKLAND. *n.* Crown land constituted pursuant to this Act as a provincial park, protected area, recreation site or historic site. *Parks Act*, S.S. 1986, c. P-1.1, s. 2.

PARK USE PERMIT. A licence, issued under this Act, authorizing an activity or a course of behaviour or conduct, or the occupancy, use, development, exploitation or extraction of a natural resource on or in a park. *Park Act*, R.S.B.C. 1979, c. 309, s. 1.

PARK WARDEN. Any official whose duties include the enforcement of regulations for the protection of forests and game.

PARK WATER. Any river, creek, spring, source, fountain, lake, pond, reservoir or other such water, that is in, connected with or supplied to, any park; and includes any water that is the source of supply of park water as hereinbefore defined, and any river, pond, creek, spring, source, or fountain from which such park water is taken. *Municipal Act*, S.M. 1970, c. 100, s. 2.

PARLIAMENT. *n.* 1. The Queen, the House of Commons and the Senate. 2. The Parliament of Canada. *Interpretation Act*, R.S.C. 1985, c. I-21, s. 35. 3. In Canada, this is limited to the federal parliament. P.W. Hogg, *Constitutional Law of Canada*, 2d ed. (Toronto: Carswell, 1985) at 86. 4. A period between a general election and dissolution which does not exceed 5 years and which may be regarded as a cycle that begins and ends with a proclamation. A. Fraser, G.A. Birch & W.A. Dawson, eds., *Beauchesne's Rules and Forms of the House of Commons of Canada*, 5th ed. (Toronto: Carswell, 1978) at 53. See ACT OF ~; CONTEMPT OF ~; FEDERAL ~; IMPERIAL ~; LIBRARY OF ~; MOTHER OF ~S; SITTING DAY OF ~.

PARLIAMENTARY AGENT. A person who promotes private bills and conducts proceedings upon petitions against such bills. A. Fraser, G.A. Birch & W.A. Dawson, eds., *Beauchesne's Rules and Forms of the House of Commons of Canada*, 5th ed. (Toronto: Carswell, 1978) at 270.

PARLIAMENTARY COMMITTEE. A committee of the whole House, a standing or joint committee.

PARLIAMENTARY COUNSEL. See LAW CLERK AND ~.

PARLIAMENTARY GOVERNMENT. Government in which Prime Minister or Premier selects members of her or his own party elected to Parliament and perhaps others to be Ministers of the Crown. This group collectively form the Cabinet, the policy-making arm of government. The Ministers and Cabinet are responsible to Parliament for the conduct of the government. The government remains in power so long as it has the confidence of a majority of the House of Commons or the Legislature. In theory, the Privy Council or Executive Council advises the formal head of state (the Governor General or Lieutenant Governor) though, in fact, the Committee of Council, known as the Cabinet, carries out this function in most situations.

PARLIAMENTARY PRECINCTS. By tradition and practice the buildings themselves, principally the West Block, Centre Block, and Confederation Building. A. Fraser, G.A. Birch & W.A. Dawson, eds., *Beauchesne's Rules and Forms of the House of Commons of Canada*, 5th ed. (Toronto: Carswell, 1978) at 35.

PARLIAMENTARY PRIVILEGE. Rights required to discharge their functions which exceed rights possessed by other individuals or bodies enjoyed by each House collectively as a representative part of the High Court of Parliament and by each member of each House. A. Fraser, G.A. Birch & W.A. Dawson, eds., *Beauchesne's Rules and Forms of the House of Commons of Canada*, 5th ed. (Toronto: Carswell, 1978) at 11.

PARLIAMENTARY SECRETARY. A Parliamentary Secretary to a Minister of the Crown. *Parliamentary Secretaries Act*, S.Nfld. 1982, c. 10, s. 2.

PARLIAMENT BUILDINGS. The space in which the two Houses and their Committees conduct their proceedings along with office space for members and officials of both Houses. A. Fraser, G.A. Birch & W.A. Dawson, eds., *Beauchesne's Rules and Forms of the House of Commons of Canada*, 5th ed. (Toronto: Carswell, 1978) at 31.

PARLIAMENT OF CANADA. The Queen, the Senate and the House of Commons. P.W. Hogg, *Constitutional Law of Canada*, 2d ed. (Toronto: Carswell, 1985) at 199. See ACT OF THE ~.

PARLOUR. See BODY-RUB ~; MILKING ~.

PAROCHIAL BODY. A fabrique as well as a body holding a church or a public chapel used for Roman Catholic worship. *Roman Catholic Cemetery Corporations Act*, R.S.Q. 1977, c. C-69, s. 1.

PAROL. *adj.* Verbal, oral.

PAROL AGREEMENT. An oral agreement.

PAROL CONTRACT. An oral contract.

PAROLE. *n.* Authority granted to an inmate to be at large during the inmate's term of imprisonment. See DAY ~.

PAROLE. *adj.* [Fr.] Oral.

PAROLE BOARD. See NATIONAL ~; PROVINCIAL ~.

PAROLED INMATE. A person to whom parole has been granted.

PAROLEE. *n.* An inmate who has been granted parole.

PAROLE SUPERVISOR. A person charged with the guidance and supervision of a paroled inmate or of an inmate who is subject to mandatory supervision. *Parole Act*, R.S.C. 1985, c. P-2, s. 2.

PAROL EVIDENCE. Oral testimony by a witness.

PARRICIDE. *n.* The murder of a father.

PARROT. See BIRD OF THE ~ FAMILY.

PARS PRO TOTO. [L.] The name of one part which represents the whole.

PARS RATIONABILIS. [L.] A rational part.

PART. *n.* A class into which parties to a formal instrument are divided according to their interests or estates in the subject-matter. See CON-STITUENT ~; COUNTER~; ESSENTIAL ~S; MOVING ~S; OPERATIVE ~; UNUSED ~.

PARTIAL. *adj.* When used in the expression "partial and permanent disability" means disability that is not so severe as to make the employee incapable of pursuing any substantially gainful occupation but is so severe that the employee is incapable of pursuing the occupation he pursued prior to the disability. *Civil Service Superannuation Act*, S.M. 1972, c. 78, s. 8.

PARTIAL ACCEPTANCE. Willingness to pay only a part of the amount of a bill. E.L.G. Tyler & N.E. Palmer, eds., *Crossley Vaines' Personal Property*, 5th ed. (London: Butterworths, 1973) at 236.

PARTIAL DISCHARGE. See DISCHARGE AND ~.

PARTIAL LOSS. Of insured property means any loss of the property that is less than total loss thereof. *Fishing Vessel Insurance Regulations*, C.R.C., c. 325, s. 2.

PARTIAL MEDICAL TEACHING HOSPITAL. A hospital which provides a post-graduate education program in at least one medical specialty.

PARTICEPS CRIMINIS. [L.] One who shares in a crime; an accessory.

PARTICEPS FRAUDIS. [L.] One who shares in fraud.

PARTICIPANT. *n.* 1. A person who is entitled to designate another person to receive a benefit payable under a plan on the participant's death. 2. A person who is participating in a plan established by an employer or a trust company and who in the case of a plan established by an employer (i) is or has been employed by the employer; or (ii) is an agent or former agent of the employer. 3. Any person against whom proceedings have been instituted under this Act and in the case of a prosecution means any accused and any person who, although not accused, is alleged in the charge or indictment to have been a co-conspirator or otherwise party or privy to the offence charged. *Combines Investigation Act*, R.S.C. 1985, c. C-34, s. 69. See AGENT OF A ~; CONDITIONAL ~; FULL ~; PUBLIC SERVICE ~; REGULAR FORCE ~; SYSTEM ~.

PARTICIPATING EMPLOYER. In relation to a multi-employer pension plan, means an employer who is required to contribute to that plan. *Pension Benefits Standards Act*, R.S.C. 1985 (2d Supp.), c. 32, s. 2.

PARTICIPATING HOSPITAL PROVINCE. A province or territory of Canada that is party to an agreement with the Government of Canada under the Hospital Insurance and Diagnostic Services Act (Canada) and that has established a hospital insurance plan pursuant to the law of that province or territory. *Health Service Insurance Act*, S.M. 1970, c. 81, s. 2.

PARTICIPATING LIFE INSURANCE POLICY. A life insurance policy under which the policyholder is entitled to share (other than by way of an experience rating refund) in the profits of the insurer other than profits in respect of property in a segregated fund. *Income Tax Act*, R.S.C. 1952, c. 148 (as am. S.C. 1980-81-82-83, c. 140, s. 96(7)), s. 138(12)(k).

PARTICIPATING MEDICAL PROVINCE. A province or territory of Canada in which there is in operation a medical care insurance plan in respect of which a contribution is payable by Canada pursuant to the Medical Care Act (Canada). *Health Service Insurance Act*, S.M. 1970, c. 81, s. 2.

PARTICIPATING PHARMACY. An establishment authorized in accordance with the regulations to supply benefits under the plan. *Drug Cost Assistance Act*, S.P.E.I. 1986, c. 10, s. 1.

PARTICIPATING PROVINCE. 1. A province in respect of which there is in force a reciprocal taxation agreement entered into with the government of that province. *Federal-Provincial Fiscal Arrangements Act*, R.S.C. 1985, c. F-8, s. 31. 2. A province or territory of Canada that is a party to an agreement with the Government of Canada under the Hospital Insurance and Diagnostic Services Act (Canada), and that has established a hospital insurance program pursuant to the law of that province or territory. *Hospital Services Insurance Act*, R.S.M. 1970, c. H140, s. 2.

PARTICIPATING SECURITY. A security issued by a body corporate other than a security that is, in all circumstances, limited in the extent of its participation in earnings and includes: (i) a security currently convertible into such a security; and (ii) currently exercisable warrants entitling the holder to acquire such a security or such a convertible security. *Business Corporations Act, 1982*, S.O. 1982, c. 4, s. 189.

PARTICIPATION. See TRACT ~.

PARTICIPATION MORTGAGE. A mortgage in which the lender shares in any increased value of the property over the term or shares income from the property with the borrower. D.J. Donahue & P.D. Quinn, *Real Estate Practice in Ontario*, 4th ed. (Toronto: Butterworths, 1990) at 233.

PARTICLE ACCELERATOR. Equipment that is capable of imparting high kinetic energy to charged particles through interaction with electric or magnetic fields and is primarily designed to produce or use in its operation atomic energy and prescribed substances. *Atomic Energy Control Regulations*, C.R.C., c. 365, s. 2.

PARTICULA. *n.* [L.] A small parcel of land.

PARTICULAR AVERAGE. See FREE FROM ~.

PARTICULAR ESTATE. An estate carved out or granted from a larger estate.

PARTICULARITY. *n.* In an affidavit or pleading, the allegation of details or particulars.

PARTICULAR LIEN. A lien which only attaches to the debtor's actual property on which materials and labour have been expended and attaches only as long as the article stays in the lien claimant's possession. D.N. Macklem & D.I. Bristow, *Construction and Mechanics' Liens in Canada*, 5th ed. (Toronto: Carswell, 1985) at 579.

PARTICULARS. *n.* In a pleading, the details of an allegation which are ordered (1) to define any issues; (2) to prevent surprise; (3) to enable the parties to get ready for trial and (4) to facilitate a hearing. G.D. Watson & C. Perkins, eds., *Holmested & Watson: Ontario Civil Procedure* (Toronto: Carswell, 1984) at 25-7 and 25-29.

PARTICULAR TENANT. The one who owns a particular estate.

PARTICULATE. *n.* Solid particles. *Environmental Protection Act*, R.R.O. 1980, Reg. 295, s. 1.

PARTICULATE COLLECTION EFFICIENCY. The amount of solid particles that is removed from the effluent gas stream, expressed as a percentage of the total particulate in the uncontrolled effluent gas stream on a weight basis. *Environmental Protection Act*, R.R.O. 1980, Reg. 295, s. 1.

PARTIES. *n.* 1. In any act or deed, the people concerned; litigants. 2. (a) In relation to collective bargaining or arbitration of a dispute, the employer and a bargaining agent, and (b) in relation to a grievance, the employer and the employee who presented the grievance. 3. (a) In relation to the entering into, renewing or revising of a collective agreement and in relation to a dispute, the employer and the bargaining agent that acts on behalf of his employees; (b) in relation to a difference relating to the interpretation, application, administration or alleged contravention of a collective agreement, the employer and the bargaining agent; and (c) in relation to a complaint to the Board under this Part, the complainant and any person or organization against whom or which a complaint is made. *Canada Labour Code*, R.S.C. 1985, c. L-2, s. 3. See CHANGE OF ~; JOINDER OF ~; PARTY.

PARTIES TO AN OFFENCE. 1. Every one is a party to an offence who actually commits it, does or omits to do anything for the purpose of aiding any person to commit it, or abets any person in committing it. *Criminal Code*, R.S.C. 1985, c. C-46, s. 21. 2. Each person who is one of two or more persons who formed an intention in common to carry out an unlawful purpose when an offence is committed by any one of them in carrying out the unlawful purpose and the person knew or ought to have known that the commission of the offence would be a probable consequence of carrying out the common purpose is a party to any offence. *Criminal Code*, R.S.C. 1985, c. C-46, s. 21.

PARTITION. *n.* 1. Division. 2. A proceeding involving dividing real property, previously owned by tenants in common or joint tenants, into different parts. 3. An interior wall one storey or part-storey in height that is not loadbearing. *Building Code Act*, R.R.O. 1980, Reg. 87, s. 1.

PARTITION OR SALE. The name of a proceeding concerning division of land. G.D. Watson & C. Perkins, eds., *Holmested & Watson: Ontario Civil Procedure* (Toronto: Carswell, 1984) at 66-2.

PARTLY MANUFACTURED GOODS. (a) Goods that are to be incorporated into or form a constituent or component part of an article that is subject to the consumption or sales tax; or (b) goods that are to be assembled, blended, mixed, cut to size, diluted, bottled, packaged, repackaged or otherwise prepared for sale as an article that is subject to the consumption or sales tax, other than goods that are so prepared in a retail store for sale in that store exclusively and directly to consumers, and the Minister is the sole judge as to whether or not goods are partly manufactured goods. *Excise Tax Act*, R.S.C. 1985, c. E-15, s. 42.

PARTLY PROCESSED TIMBER. Timber which has not undergone all the treatments or all the phases of processing necessary to make it suitable for the use for which it is intended. *Lands and Forests Act*, R.S.Q. 1977, c. T-9, s. 163.

PARTLY-SKIMMED MILK. *var.* **PARTLY SKIMMED MILK.** Grade A milk that contains not less than 1.8 per cent nor more than 2.2 per cent milk-fat and not less than 8.25 per cent milk solids other than milk-fat. *Milk Act*, R.R.O. 1980, Reg. 622, s. 3. See EVAPORATED ~; FLAVOURED ~.

PARTNER. *n.* A member of a partnership. See GENERAL ~; NOMINAL ~; SILENT ~.

PARTNERS', DIRECTORS' AND SENIOR OFFICERS' QUALIFYING EXAMINATION. An examination prepared and conducted by the Canadian Securities Institute and so designated by that Institute. *Securities Act*, R.R.O. 1980, Reg. 910, s. 84.

PARTNERSHIP. *n.* The relationship that subsists between two or more persons carrying on a business in common with a view to profit. See AGRICULTURAL OPERATIONS ~; CANADIAN ~; INTEREST IN A FAMILY FARM ~; LIMITED ~.

PARTNERSHIP BUDGETING. Consultation with the Minister by a municipality with respect to its proposed budget, during which a full explanation of the revenues and expenditures is provided to the Minister and after which changes in the budget may be made by the municipality and the portion of the proposed expenditures eligible for unconditional grant support may be determined by the Minister. *Municipal Assistance Act*, R.S.N.B. 1973, c. M-19, s. 1.

PARTNERSHIP PROPERTY. Property and rights and interests in property originally brought into the partnership stock, or acquired, whether by purchase or otherwise, on account of the firm, or for the purposes of and in the course of the partnership business.

PART-OWNER. *n.* A person entitled to property in common, jointly or in coparcenary.

PART PAYMENT. Payment of a portion of a debt.

PART PERFORMANCE. In relation to a contract, partial completion.

PARTS PER MILLION. Parts per million by weight unless otherwise stated. *Food and Drug Regulations*, C.R.C., c. 870, c. B.01.001.

PART-TIME. *adj.* In relation to an employee, means employment for irregular hours of duty or for specific intermittent periods, or both, where the services of that employee may not be required for the whole of the normal work day, week, month or year. *Civil Service Act*, S.P.E.I. 1983, c. 4, s. 1.

PART-TIME BASIS. In relation to an employee, means engaged to work on other than a full-time basis. *Pension Benefits Standards Act*, R.S.C. 1985 (2d Supp.), c. 32, s. 2.

PART-TIME EMPLOYEE. *var.* **PART TIME EMPLOYEE.** 1. A person employed for irregular hours of duty or for specific intermittent periods, or both, during a day, week, month or year and whose services are not required for the normal work day, week, month or year, as the case may be. 2. A person who is regularly employed to work less than the full number of working hours in each working day or less than the full number of regular working days in each month.

PART-TIME INSTRUCTION. When used with reference to an occupational training course, means less than 24 hours a week of instruction. *Adult Occupational Training Regulations*, C.R.C., c. 1, s. 2.

PART-TIME SERVICE. Regular contractual employment as a teacher where the service of the person so employed is less than full-time but on a regular recurring basis and the earnings for which bear the same proportion to the full-time salary rate for the position held as the time spent in the contractual employment bears to the time spent in employment of a person who holds an equivalent position on a full-time basis. *The Teachers' Pensions Amendment Act*, S.M. 1985-86, c. 31, s. 10.

PART-WINDING START MOTOR. A motor whose starting entails the energizing of part of its primary winding as a first step and the energizing of the remainder of this winding as the next step or steps. *Power Corporation Act*, R.R.O. 1980, Reg. 794, s. 0.

PARTY. *n.* 1. Every person served with notice of, or entitled to attend any proceeding, even if that person is not named in the record. 2. A political party registered under an Election Act. 3. A person whose rights will be varied or affected by the exercise of a statutory power or by an act or thing done pursuant to that power. 4. A person bound by a collective agreement, or involved in a dispute. See ACCOMMODA-TION ~; ACT OF THE ~; ADVERSE ~; CHARTER ~; CONTRACTING ~; INTER-ESTED ~; OPPOSITE ~; PARTIES; PERMA-NENT OFFICE OF AN AUTHORIZED ~; POLITICAL ~; RECOGNIZED ~; REGIS-TERED ~; RESTRICTED ~; SECURED ~; THIRD ~.

PARTY-AND-PARTY COSTS. *var.* **PARTY AND PARTY COSTS.** Costs in keeping with the tariffs and practice of a court which one litigant pays to another. They are meant to reimburse the party who receives them for the costs that party must pay a solicitor. M.M. Orkin, *The Law of Costs*, 2d ed. (Aurora: Canada Law Book, 1987) at 1-2 and 2-1.

PARTY AUTHORITY. The organization of a political party at the level of an electoral division, of a region or of Québec.

PARTY UNDER DISABILITY. A general term which includes minors, absentees and mental incompetents. G.D. Watson & C. Perkins, eds., *Holmested & Watson: Ontario Civil Procedure* (Toronto: Carswell, 1984) at 7-7.

PARTY WALL. A wall jointly owned and jointly used by 2 parties under easement agreement or by right in law, and erected at or upon a line separating 2 parcels of land each of which is, or is capable of being, a separate real-estate entity. *Building Code Act*, R.R.O. 1980, Reg. 87, s. 1.

PARUM DIFFERUNT QUAE RE CONCOR-DANT ET CUM ADSUNT TESTIMONIA RERUM QUID OPUS EST VERBIS? [L.] Things which agree substantially differ too little, and when the witnesses to the facts agree, what is the use for words?

PARUM EST LATAM ESSE SENTENTIAM NISI MANDETUR EXECUTIONI. [L.] It is not enough that a judgment be proclaimed if it is not carried out.

PARUM PROFICIT SCIRE QUID FIERI DEBET SI NON COGNOSCAS QUOMODO SIT FACTURUM. [L.] It is not enough to know what should be done if you do not know how to do it.

PAR VALUE. 1. The face value of a share or security, as opposed to its market or selling price. 2. An arbitrary value placed on a share at the time of issue. S.M. Beck *et al.*, *Cases and Materials on Partnerships and Canadian Business Corporations* (Toronto: The Carswell Co., 1983) at 784. See NO ~.

PASS. *v.* 1. To transfer or to be transferred. 2. For a legislature to give final approval to an act. 3. To bring into court an account for approval. See PROPERTY ~ING ON THE DEATH.

PASS. *n.* A written authorization or permit issued by an issuing authority permitting the person named therein to enter upon or in to a defence establishment. *Defence Establishment Trespass Regulations*, C.R.C., c. 1047, s. 2.

PASSAGE. *n.* The easement to pass over a body of water. See INNOCENT ~.

PASS AN ACCOUNT. For a court to approve an account.

PASS BOOK. See BANK ~.

PASSENGER. *n.* 1. Any person carried on a ship, but does not include (a) a person carried on a Safety Convention ship who is (i) the master, a member of the crew or a person employed or engaged in any capacity on board the ship on the business of that ship; or (ii) under 1 year of age; (b) a person carried on a ship that is not a Safety Convention ship who is (i) the master, a member of the crew or a person employed or engaged in any capacity on board the ship on the business of that ship; (ii) the owner or charterer of the ship, a member of his family or a servant connected with his household; (iii) a guest of the owner or charterer of the ship if it is used exclusively for pleasure and the guest is carried on the ship without remuneration or any object of profit; or (iv) under 1 year of age; or (c) any person carried on any ship in pursuance of the obligation laid on the master to carry shipwrecked, distressed or other persons or by reason of any circumstances that neither the master nor the owner nor the charterer, if any, could have prevented or forestalled. *Canada Shipping Act*, R.S.C. 1985, c. S-9, s. 2. 2. A person who (a) is eligible under this Part to be carried pursuant to an ABC (domestic); and (b) at least 30 days prior to the departure date of the outgoing portion of the ABC (domestic) has paid to the charterer the full price per seat advertised by the charterer for that ABC. *Air Carrier Regulations*, C.R.C., c. 3, s. 83. 3. A person who (a) is eligible under this division to be carried pursuant to an ABC; and (b) at least 30 days prior to the departure date of the outgoing portion of the ABC has paid to the charterer the full price per seat advertised by the charterer of that ABC. *Air Carrier Regulations*, C.R.C., c. 3, s. 54.

PASSENGER CAR. 1. A motor vehicle that has a seating capacity of 10 or less but does not include an off-highway vehicle as defined in the Off-highway Vehicle Act, a truck, a multipurpose passenger vehicle, a chassis cab, a moped or a motorcycle. *Highway Traffic Act*, R.S.A. 1980, c. H-7, s. 1. 2. A vehicle having a designated seating capacity of 10 or less, but does not include an all-terrain vehicle, competition car, multipurpose passenger vehicle, antique vehicle, antique reproduction vehicle, motorcycle, truck or trailer. Canada regulations.

PASSENGER CHARGE. A toll imposed on an ocean-going vessel in respect of a passenger of the vessel. *Passenger Charges By-law*, C.R.C., c. 1065, s. 2.

PASSENGER SERVICE. See RAILWAY ~.

PASSENGER SHIP. A ship carrying passengers. *Canada Shipping Act*, R.S.C. 1985, c. S-9, s. 2.

PASSENGER SPACE. Space provided for the use of passengers. *Hull Construction Regulations*, C.R.C., c. 1431, s. 2.

PASSENGER STEAMSHIP. (a) In the case of a Safety Convention ship, a steamship that carries more than 12 passengers, and (b) in the case of any other ship, a steamship that carries any number of passengers. Canada regulations.

PASSENGER TRADE. See SPECIAL ~.

PASSENGER-TRAIN SERVICE. Such train or trains of a company as are capable of carrying passengers and are declared by an order of the commission, for the purposes of sections 265 to 270, to comprise a passenger-train service. *Railway Act*, R.S.C. 1985, c. R-3, s. 264.

PASSENGER TRANSIT SYSTEM. The aggregate of passenger-bus transport services provided by a corporation to the public in the territory over which it has jurisdiction. *Municipal and Intermunicipal Transit Corporations Act*, R.S.Q. 1977, c. C-70, s. 1.

PASSENGER TRANSPORT. The transportation of passengers for reward by bus or by any other means of transportation except taxi. *Regional Municipality of Ottawa-Carleton Act*, R.S.O. 1980, c. 439, s. 76.

PASSENGER VEHICLE. 1. A motor vehicle, other than a minibus, designed for the transportation of not more than nine occupants at a time, where such transportation does not require a permit from the Commission des transports du Québec. *Highway Safety Code*, S.Q. 1986, c. 91, s. 4. 2. A motor vehicle classified by a manufacturer as a passenger car or which is designed, constructed or adapted for the principal purpose of transporting passengers and includes a delivery car but does not include a motor cycle, moped or motor vehicle which is designed, constructed or adapted for the purpose of carrying goods or commodities. *The Highway Traffic Act*, S.M. 1985-86, c. 3, s. 1. See COMMERCIAL ~; LIMITED ~; MULTI-PURPOSE ~; PRIVATE ~; PUBLIC ~.

PASSIM. *adv.* [L.] In different places.

PASSING THROUGH. In transit through a lock or through the waters enclosed by the approach walls at either end of a lock chamber. *Seaway Regulations*, C.R.C., c. 1397, s. 2.

PASSIVE OCCUPANT PROTECTION. Protection of an occupant of a vehicle against injury due solely to a crash impact by means of equipment that does not require any direct action by an occupant of the vehicle upon the equipment itself. *Motor Vehicle Safety Regulations*, C.R.C., c. 1038, s. 2.

PASSIVE TRUST. A trust for which a trustee need perform no active duty.

PASSIVE USE. Permissive use.

PASS OFF. To represent that one's business, wares or services are those of another. H.G. Fox, *The Canadian Law of Trade Marks and Unfair Competition*, 3d ed. (Toronto: Carswell, 1972) at 323.

PASSPORT. *n.* 1. A document issued by or under the authority of the Secretary of State for External Affairs for the purpose of identifying the holder thereof. *Criminal Code*, R.S.C. 1985, c. C-46, s. 57(5). 2. A Canadian passport that shows the identity and nationality of a person for the purpose of facilitating travel by that person outside Canada. *Canadian Passport Regulations*, C.R.C., c. 641, s. 2. See FORGERY OF ~; UTTERING FORGED ~.

PAST CONSIDERATION. Consideration for services already performed which do not support a promise or create a contract which may be enforced. G.H.L. Fridman, *The Law of Contract in Canada*, 2d ed. (Toronto: Carswell, 1986) at 96.

PAST COST OF INSURED SERVICES. The total cost of the insured services made necessary as the result of an injury and provided to a patient up to and including the date of settlement or, where there is no settlement, the first day of trial. *Health Insurance Act*, R.S.O. 1980, c. 197, s. 1.

PAST DEBT. A debt which existed before some legal act relating to it was passed.

PASTEURIZATION. *n.* Subjecting every particle of milk in such manner as is required by the regulations to a temperature and for a time prescribed by the regulations.

PASTEURIZED. *adj.* 1. In relation to dairy products, means the treatment for the purpose of the destruction of harmful bacteria as provided by the regulation. *Milk Industry Act*, R.S.B.C. 1979, c. 258, s. 1. 2. In relation to honey, means treated in a registered pasteurizing plant by the controlled application of heat so that the honey is free of viable sugar-tolerant yeasts. *Honey Regulations*, C.R.C., c. 287, s. 2.

PASTEURIZING. *n.* The treatment of extracted honey by the controlled application of heat to a point where it is free of viable sugar-tolerant yeasts. *Farm Products Grades and Sales Act*, R.R.O. 1980, Reg. 337, s. 1.

PASTOR. *n.* The cleric entrusted with the administration of a parish.

PAST SERVICE CREDIT. A credit toward a pension given to an employee for a period of employment prior to implementation of a pension plan.

PASTURE. *n.* An area of land fenced for the purpose of grazing animals. *Snow Vehicles Act*, S.N.S. 1981, c. 51, s. 1. See COMMUNITY ~; HAY AND ~.

PAT. APP. BD. *abbr.* Patent Appeal Board.

PAT. COMMR. *abbr.* Commissioner of Patents.

PATENT. *n.* 1. During its term, an absolute monopoly which prohibits anyone other than the patentee using the new manufacture which the patentee invented. H.G. Fox, *The Canadian Law of Copyright and Industrial Designs*, 2d ed. (Toronto: Carswell, 1967) at 4. 2. Letters patent for an invention. *Patent Act*, R.S.C. 1985, c. P-4, s. 2. 3. A grant from the Crown in fee simple or for a less estate under the Great Seal. See LETTERS ~.

PATENT AGENT. Any person or firm whose name is entered on the Register. *Patent Rules*, C.R.C., c. 1250, s. 2.

PATENT AMBIGUITY. Something clearly doubtful in the text of an instrument.

PATENT DEFECT. Something which an unsophisticated purchaser can discover on cursory inspection. B.J. Reiter, R.C.B. Risk & B.N. McLellan, *Real Estate Law*, 3d ed. (Toronto: Emond Montgomery, 1986) at 280.

PATENTED ARTICLE. Includes articles made by a patented process. *Patent Act*, R.S.C. 1985, c. P-4, s. 65(5).

PATENTEE. *n.* 1. The person for the time being entitled to the benefit of a patent. *Patent Act*, R.S.C. 1985, c. P-4, s. 3. 2. Includes grantee. *Crown Lands Act*, R.S.M. 1970, c. C340, s. 2.

PATENT MEDICINE. See PROPRIETARY OR ~.

PATENT MODEL. The model constructed for the purpose of obtaining a patent for an invention, discovery or process. *Canadian Cultural Property Export Control List*, C.R.C., c. 448, s. 1.

PATER EST QUEM NUPTIAE DEMONSTRANT. [L.] The father is the one whom marriage indicates.

PATER ET MATER NON SUNT DE SANGUINE PUERORUM. [L.] A father and a mother are not of their children's blood.

PATERFAMILIAS. *n.* [L.] A person who is sui juris and the head of the family.

PATERNITY. *n.* The relationship of a father.

PATERNITY AGREEMENT. Where a man and a woman who are not spouses enter into an agreement for: (a) the payment of the expenses of prenatal care and birth in respect of a child; (b) the support of a child; or (c) burial expenses of the child or mother, on the application of a party to the agreement or a children's aid society made to a provincial court (family division) or the Unified Family Court, the court may incorporate the agreement in an order, and Part II applies to the order in the same manner as if it were an order for support made under that Part. *Family Law Reform Act*, R.S.O. 1980, c. 152, s. 58.

PATHOLOGIST. See SPEECH-LANGUAGE ~.

PATHOLOGY. *n.* The branch of medicine which studies any tissue changes caused by aging, disease, poisons or violence. F.A. Jaffe, *A Guide to Pathological Evidence*, 2d ed. (Toronto: Carswell, 1983) at 1. See SPEECH-LANGUAGE ~.

PATIENT. *n.* 1. A person received at or in a hospital. 2. A person who receives investigation, diagnosis, treatment or other services at or in a hospital. 3. A recipient of health care services. 4. A recipient of dental care services. 5. A person who requires ambulance services because of illness, injury or incapacity. 6. A person receiving psychiatric care or treatment, or diagnostic services for the purpose of determining the existence of a mental disorder. See DAY-~; FORMAL ~; IN-~; INVOLUNTARY ~; OUT-~; PERSON BOUND TO PROVIDE OR CARE FOR A ~.

PATIENT-DAY. *n.* The period an inpatient is served between the census-taking hours on two successive days.

PATR. ELEC. CAS. *abbr.* Patrick, Contested Elections (Ont.), 1824-1849.

PATRIA. *n.* [L.] A nation.

PATRIA LABORIBUS ET EXPENSIS NON DEBET FATIGARI. [L.] A jury should not be harassed by chores and expenses.

PATRIA POTESTAS. [L.] The power of a father.

PATRIATION. *n.* Terminating the United Kingdom Parliament's authority over Canada by passing amending procedures which can be carried out entirely by Canadian governments, electorates or legislative bodies. P.W. Hogg, *Constitutional Law of Canada*, 2d ed. (Toronto: Carswell, 1985) at 46 and 48.

PATRIATION REFERENCE (1981). The Supreme Court was asked to clarify whether the past practice of securing provincial consent to a constitutional amendment affecting provincial powers was a convention (as eight provinces argued) or a usage (as the federal government and two provinces argued). P.W. Hogg, *Constitutional Law of Canada*, 2d ed. (Toronto: Carswell, 1985) at 17.

PATRICIDE. *n.* 1. Killing a father. 2. One who kills a father.

PATRIMONY. *n.* An hereditary right or estate handed down from ancestors.

PATROL. See SECURITY ~.

PATRON. *n.* 1. A person who supplies milk or cream for use by a dairy manufacturing plant. 2. A person, not a member, but using the services of the association to such extent as may be provided in the bylaws. Co-operative Associations Acts. 3. A farmer, rancher or other person, (i) who maintains livestock for the purpose of propagation or the production of livestock products; or (ii) who maintains feeder livestock for a period of not less than 30 days for the purpose of fattening, and includes a licensed livestock dealer. *Livestock and Livestock Products Act*, R.S.A. 1980, c. L-24, s. 1.

PATRONAGE. *n.* The right to make appointments to an office. See ALLOCATION IN PROPORTION TO ~.

PATRONAGE CONTRACT. A contract between a shipper of goods and members of a shipping conference whereby in return for certain advantages the shipper agrees to offer to members of the conference for transportation by them all goods, all goods of certain classes or a fixed proportion of all goods or of all goods of certain classes shipped by water by that shipper to places served by members of that conference. *Shipping Conference Exemption Act*, R.S.C. 1985, c. S-10, s. 2.

PATRONAGE REFUND. 1. An amount allocated or paid in proportion to patronage to the members or members and patrons out of savings or surpluses arising from the operations of the association. *The Co-operative Associations Act*, R.S.S. 1978, c. C-34, s. 2. 2. Earnings which are allocated to members or patrons on the basis of patronage. *Credit Union Act*, S.S. 1984-85-86, c. C-45.1, s. 2.

PATRONAGE RETURN. The amount, if any, that is allocated, credited or paid by an association to its members or to its members and patrons based on the business done by each of them with or through the association. *Canada Cooperative Associations Act*, R.S.C. 1985, c. C-40, s. 3.

PATTERN. *n.* Includes the instructions for the knitting or crocheting of a garment. *Retail Sales Tax Act*, R.R.O. 1980, Reg. 904, s. 1. See SERVICE ~.

PATTERN BARGAINING. Collective bargaining by a union with distinct employers attempting to achieve the same terms and conditions.

PATTERNS. *n.* (a) Reproductions of goods to be processed that serve to shape moulds for making such goods; (b) models for dies, jigs, fixtures and moulds that are to be used in the manufacture of goods; (c) the first finished printed motion picture film (also referred to as the negative of the exposed film) for exhibition in a public theatre or for broadcast to the public on television, if such film is used exclusively for the purpose of making reproductions thereof for sale; (d) masters, inter-masters and running masters of video or audio magnetic recording tapes produced by and used in the television and sound recording industries in making reproductions for sale or for the use of the person making the reproduction; and (e) typesetting and composition, metal plates, cylinders, matrices, film, artwork, designs, photographs, rubber material, plastic material and paper material when impressed with or displaying or carrying an image for reproduction, made by or imported by or sold to a manufacturer, and used by him exclusively for the purposes of reproduction in the printing and publishing industries. *Retail Sales Tax Act*, R.R.O. 1980, Reg. 903, s. 1.

PAUPER. *n.* A person who sues or defends an action in forma pauperis.

PAVEMENT. *n.* Any type of street surfacing.

PAVING. *n.* 1. Includes laying down or constructing any description of pavement with or without curbing. 2. Macadamizing and the laying down or construction of any description of pavement or curbing. 3. Includes macadamizing, planking and the laying down or construction of any description of pavement or roadway and the construction of a curbing.

PAWN. *n.* A pledge, a kind of bailment in which a debtor delivers goods to the creditor for the creditor to keep until the debt is discharged. E.L.G. Tyler & N.E. Palmer, eds., *Crossley Vaines' Personal Property*, 5th ed. (London: Butterworths, 1973) at 459.

PAWNBROKER. *n.* A person whose business is taking any article as a pawn or pledge for the repayment of money lent against that article.

PAWNEE. *n.* The person with whom one deposits a pawn.

PAWNER. *n.* A person who delivers an article to a pawnbroker for pawn.

PAWNING. *n.* Within the meaning of this division, is the lending of money or anything convertible into money or having a pecuniary value, for a profit, either impliedly or expressly stipulated, in favor of the lender, and the taking of a pledge to secure the return of the money or thing lent, with or without the profit. *Licences Act*, R.S.Q. 1977, c. L-3, s. 100.

PAWNOR. *n.* A person who deposits a pawn.

PAX REGIS. [L.] The monarch's peace.

PAY. *n.* 1. Remuneration in any form. 2. Wages due or paid to an employee and compensation paid or due to an employee but does not include deductions from wage that may lawfully be made by an employer. 3. As applied to the Force, the pay of the substantive rank held by the person in respect of whom the expression is being applied, not including the pay of acting rank or extra pay for staff or similar temporary appointments, or, in the case of a person not holding a rank in the Force, the salary or other remuneration for the performance of the regular duties of that person as a member of the Force, together with such allowances by way of compensation or otherwise as are prescribed by the regulations. *Royal Canadian Mounted Police Act*, R.S.C. 1985, c. R-11, s. 3(a). 4. As applied to the Canadian Forces, means pay at the rates prescribed by the regulations made under the National Defence Act for the rank held by the person in respect of whom the expression is being applied, together with the allowances prescribed by the regulations made under this Act for that rank. *Canadian Forces Superannuation Act*, R.S.C. 1985, c. C-17, s. 2 in part. See ANNUAL HOLIDAY ~; BACK ~; CALL-BACK ~; CALL-IN ~ OR PREMIUM; DISMISSAL ~; EQUAL ~ FOR EQUAL WORK; GRADE OF ~; HOLDBACK ~; MERIT ~; PREMIUM ~; REPORTING ~; RETROACTIVE ~; SHOW-UP ~; SICK ~; STRAIGHT-TIME ~; TAKE-HOME ~; VACATION ~.

PAYABLE. *adj.* Describes a sum of money when someone is obliged to pay it. See ACCOUNT ~; AMOUNT ~; PRICE PAID OR ~.

PAYABLE TO ORDER. Describes a cheque or bill of exchange payable to the person named on it or in any way directed by an endorsement.

PAY AGENCY. The Department of Supply and Services or such other appropriate agency, office or person that is charged with the duty or that performs the function of paying remuneration to a person. Canada regulations.

PAY-AS-YOU-GO PENSION PLAN. A plan in which the employer pays benefits from earnings instead of from a pension fund.

PAY DAY. The day on which remuneration ordinarily is paid to an employee. *Canada Pension Plan Regulations*, C.R.C., c. 385, s. 3.

PAYEE. *n.* One to whom a cheque, bill of exchange or promissory note is payable. See FICTITIOUS ~.

PAY EQUITY. A compensation practice which is based primarily on the relative value of the work performed, irrespective of the gender of employees, and includes the requirement that no employer shall establish or maintain a difference between the wages paid to male and female employees, employed by that employer, who are performing work of equal or comparable value. *The Pay Equity Act*, S.M. 1985-86, c. 21, s. 1.

PAYER. *n.* The owner, contractor or subcontractor who is liable to pay for the services or materials provided to an improvement under a contract or subcontract.

PAY GRADE. A series of rates of remuneration for a class that provides for a minimum rate, a maximum rate, and such intermediate rates as may be considered necessary to permit periodic increases in remuneration. *Civil Service Act*, R.S.M. 1970, c. C110, s. 2.

PAYING OFFICER. See APPROPRIATE ~.

PAYING QUANTITY. The output or potential output of such quantity of oil or gas produced from a well as, in the opinion of the manager, would commercially and economically warrant the taking of such oil or gas. *Indian Oil and Gas Regulations*, C.R.C., c. 963, s. 2.

PAYMENT. *n.* 1. Remuneration in any form. 2. Includes the set-off of any amount against indebtedness incurred. 3. Payment by delivery of a share of crops. *The Farm Security Act*, R.S.S. 1978, c. F-9, s. 6. 4. Includes (i) the issue of a certificate of indebtedness or shares of the taxpayer or of a corporation of which the taxpayer is a subsidiary wholly-owned corporation if the taxpayer or that corporation has in the year or within 12 months thereafter disbursed an amount of money equal to the aggregate face value of all certificates or shares of the taxpayer or that corporation previously issued; (ii) the application by the taxpayer of an amount to a member's liability to the taxpayer (including, without restricting the generality of the foregoing, an amount applied in fulfilment of an obligation of the member to make a loan to the taxpayer and an amount applied on account of payment for shares issued to a member) pursuant to a by-law of the taxpayer, pursuant to statutory authority or at the request of the member; or (iii) the amount of a payment or transfer by the taxpayer that, under subsection 56(2), is required to be included in computing the income of a member. *Income Tax Act*, R.S.C. 1952, c. 148 (as am. S.C. 1970-71-72, c. 63), s. 135(4)(g). See ADVANCE ~; BALLOON ~; BLENDED ~; CANADIAN ~S ASSOCIATION; CAVEAT ~; COVENANT FOR ~; DOWN ~; EDUCATIONAL ASSISTANCE ~; EQUALIZATION ~; EXCESS ~; INITIAL ~; INVOLUNTARY ~; MONEY OF ~; MORTGAGE PROTECTION ~S; OTHER ~ REQUISITION; OVER~; PART ~; PROGRESS ~; STABILIZATION ~; TERMINATION ~; UNAUTHORIZED ~.

PAYMENT BOND. 1. A bond held as security for the payment of certain classes of persons performing labour or services, or supplying materials in connection with a contract. 2. A bond that is conditional upon the payment by the principal of money to persons under contract with him. *Business Loans, Guarantees and Indemnities Act*, S.N.W.T. 1983 (1st Sess.), c. 1, s. 3.

PAYMENT BY RESULT. Remuneration dependent upon output.

PAYMENT CERTIFIER. An architect, engineer or any other person on whose certificate payments are made under a contract or subcontract.

PAYMENT IN KIND. Remuneration in the form of goods or services.

PAYMENT INTO COURT. The deposit of money with a court official in connection with proceedings commenced in that court.

PAYMENT ITEM. A bill of exchange drawn on or payable through a member and includes any other class of items approved by by-law. *Canadian Payments Association Act*, R.S.C. 1985, c. C-21, s. 2.

PAYMENT QUARTER. A period of 3 months commencing on the first day of April, July, October or January in a fiscal year.

PAYMENT REQUISITION. A cheque requisition or another payment requisition. *Account Verification and Payment Requisition Regulations*, C.R.C., c. 667, s. 2.

PAYMENT REVIEW PERIOD. The period commencing on April 1 in the previous fiscal year and ending on March 31 in the current fiscal year. *War Veterans Allowance Act*, R.S.C. 1985 (1st Supp.), c. 7, s. 1.

PAYMENTS SYSTEM. A mechanism by which debit and credit positions between banks are ascertained and cheques are sorted. The balances are settled by making transfers in the Chartered Banks' accounts with the Bank of Canada. I.F.G. Baxter, *The Law of Banking*, 3d ed. (Toronto: Carswell, 1981) at 173.

PAYOR. *n.* A person liable for the payment of levies. *Take-or-Pay Costs Sharing Act*, S.A. 1986, c. T-0.1, s. 1.

PAY-OUT PRICE. The amount of money paid or to be paid to the holder of a winning ticket. *Race Track Supervision Regulations*, C.R.C., c. 441, s. 2.

PAY PERIOD. 1. The period of employment established by an employer for the computation of wages, overtime pay or time off in place of overtime pay. 2. In respect of any particular person, the period commencing on the day following the day that that person's salary cheque is normally dated and ending on the day that that person's next salary cheque is normally dated.

PAY RANGE. A series of rates of remuneration for a class that provides for a minimum rate, a maximum rate, and such intermediate rates as may be considered necessary to permit periodic increases in remuneration. *Civil Service Act*, R.S.M. 1970, c. C110, s. 2.

PAYROLL. *n.* In respect of an employer, means the aggregate of the remuneration in any calendar year of workers employed by the employer in any industry in the year. *Workers' Compensation (Amendment) Act*, S.N.W.T. 1986 (2d Sess.), c. 8, s. 2.

PAYS. *n.* [Fr.] A nation.

PAY WEEK. A period of 7 consecutive days that ends, or any one of two or more such periods that are contiguous, the last of which ends, on the employer's payroll ending date. *Unemployment Insurance (Collection of Premiums) Regulations*, C.R.C., c. 1575, s. 2.

P.C. *abbr.* 1. Privy Council. 2. Privy Councillor. 3. Police constable. 4. In any one of the tariff columns in Schedule II, means per cent ad valorem. *Customs Tariff*, R.S.C. 1985, c. C-54, s. 2.

P.D. *abbr.* Law Reports, Probate, Divorce and Admiralty Division, 1875-1890.

PEA. See BROKEN ~; ~S AND CARROTS; SPLIT ~; SPOTTED ~.

PEACE. *n.* 1. Quiet behaviour towards the sovereign and the sovereign's subjects. 2. The condition of international relations in which a nation does not bring military force against another. See BREACH OF THE ~; CLERK OF THE ~; COMMISSION OF THE ~; JUSTICE OF THE ~; KEEPING THE ~.

PEACE BOND. A written promise made to a court to keep the peace.

PEACE OFFICER. 1. Includes (a) a mayor, warden, reeve, sheriff, deputy sheriff, sheriff's officer and justice of the peace; (b) a warden, deputy warden, instructor, keeper, jailer, guard and any other officer or permanent employee of a prison; (c) a police officer, police constable, bailiff, constable, or other person employed for the preservation and maintenance of the public peace or for the service or execution of civil process; (d) an officer or a person having the powers of a customs or excise officer when performing any duty in the administration of the Customs Act, chapter C-40 of the Revised Statutes of Canada, 1970 or the Excise Act; (e) a person appointed or designated as a fishery officer under the Fisheries Act when performing any of his duties or functions pursuant to that Act; (f) the pilot in command of an aircraft (i) registered in Canada under regulations made under the Aeronautics Act; or (ii) leased without crew and operated by a person who is qualified under regulations made under the Aeronautics Act to be registered as owner of an aircraft registered in Canada under those regulations, while the aircraft is in flight; and (g) officers and men of the Canadian Forces who are (i) appointed for the purposes of section 156 of the National Defence Act; or (ii) employed on duties that the Governor in Council, in regulations made under the National Defence Act for the purposes of this paragraph, has prescribed to be of such a kind as to necessitate that the officers and men performing them have the powers of peace officers. *Criminal Code*, R.S.C. 1985, c. C-46, s. 2. 2. A police officer, police constable or other person employed for the preservation and maintenance of the public peace. 3. A member of the Royal Canadian Mounted Police or a member of a municipal police force.

PEACE, ORDER AND GOOD GOVERNMENT. See RESIDUARY POWER.

PEACETIME DISASTER. A disaster, real or apprehended, resulting from fire, explosion, flood, earthquake, landslide, weather, epidemic, shipping accident, mine accident, transportation accident, electrical power failure, nuclear accident and any other disaster not attributable to enemy attack, sabotage or other hostile action whereby injury or loss is or may be caused to persons or property in the Territories. *Civil Emergency Measures Act*, R.S.N.W.T. 1974, c. C-5, s. 2.

PEACHES. See CANNED ~.

PEAK CRUSH RESISTANCE. The greatest force recorded over the entire 457.2 mm (18 inches) crush. *Motor Vehicle Safety Regulations*, C.R.C., c. 1038, s. 214.

PEAK LOAD. Unless otherwise specified, means the annual maximum electric power load as averaged for 1 hour. *National Energy Board Part VI Regulations*, C.R.C., c. 1056, s. 2.

PEARS. See CANNED ~.

PEAS AND CARROTS. The canned product consisting of not less than 52 per cent and not more than 75 per cent by drained weight of peas and not less than 25 per cent and not more than 48 per cent by drained weight of diced carrots. *Processed Fruit and Vegetable Regulations*, C.R.C., c. 291, schedule I, s. 40.

PEAT. *n.* A highly organic soil consisting chiefly of more or less fragmented remains of vegetable matter sequentially deposited. *Building Code Act*, R.R.O. 1980, Reg. 87, s. 1.

PEAT-DRIED MALT. Barley malt that has been kilned over fires of peat with or without admixture of other fuels. *Food and Drug Regulations*, C.R.C., c. 870, c. B.02.002.

PECCATA CONTRA NATURAM SUNT GRAVISSIMA. [L.] The most serious crimes are those against nature.

PECCATUM PECCATO ADDIT QUI CULPAE QUAM FACIT PATROCINIUM DEFENSIONIS ADJUNGIT. [L.] Whoever adds defence of a wrong committed to guilt adds crime to crime.

PECK. *n.* 2 gallons. *Weights and Measures Act*, S.C. 1970-71-72, c. 36, schedule II.

PECULATUS. *n.* [L.] Embezzlement of public funds.

PECUNIA. *n.* [L.] Money.

PECUNIARY. *adj.* Concerning money.

PECUNIARY INTEREST. With respect to a member of council, an interest in a matter that could monetarily affect (i) the member; (ii) a corporation, other than a distributing corporation, in which the member is a shareholder, director or officer; (ii) a distributing corporation in which the member beneficially owns voting shares carrying at least 10 per cent of the voting rights attached to the voting shares of the corporation or of which the member is a director or officer; (iv) a partnership or firm of which the member of council is a member; or (v) a corporation, partnership, firm, government or person that employs the member of council. *Municipal Government Act*, S.A. 1986, c. 24, s. 30.

PECUNIARY LOSS. 1. The loss of earnings, profit, future cost of care or other expenses. K.D. Cooper-Stephenson & I.B. Saunders, *Personal Injury Damages in Canada* (Toronto: Carswell, 1981) at 29. 2. Does not include loss arising from pain and suffering, physical inconvenience and discomfort, social discredit, injury to reputation, mental suffering, injury to feelings, loss of amenities and of expectation of life or loss of society of spouse or child.

PEDDLE. See TO ~.

PEDDLER. *n.* Anyone who carries on one's person, or who transports with one, goods, wares or merchandise, with intent to sell the same within the limits of a local municipality. See HAWKER AND ~; PEDLAR.

PEDDLING. *n.* Having on one's person or transporting with one any liquor and selling or intending to sell it contrary to this Act or the regulations. *Liquor Control Act*, S.Nfld. 1973, c. 103, s. 2.

PEDESTRIAN. *n.* 1. A person afoot. 2. A person afoot, or a person in a wheelchair or a child's carriage or physically handicapped person operating a motorized mobility-aid. 3. A person on foot, an invalid in a wheelchair or a child in a carriage or sleigh.

PEDESTRIAN CONTROL SIGNAL. A traffic control signal directed to pedestrians. *The Highway Traffic Act*, S.M. 1985-86, c. 3, s. 1.

PEDESTRIAN CORRIDOR. A crosswalk, at an intersection or elsewhere, that has been designated as a pedestrian corridor by the proper traffic authority and that is illuminated and distinctly indicated for pedestrian crossing by (i) such lights and other traffic control devices on the highway; and (ii) such lines or other markings on the surface of the roadway, as are prescribed in regulations made by the traffic board. *The Highway Traffic Act*, S.M. 1985-86, c. 3, s. 1.

PEDESTRIAN CROSSOVER. Any portion of a roadway, designated by by-law of a municipality, at an intersection or elsewhere, distinctly indicated for pedestrian crossing by signs on the highway and lines or other markings on the surface of the roadway as prescribed by the regulations. *Highway Traffic Act*, R.S.O. 1980, c. 198, s. 1.

PEDESTRIAN DECK. A bridge, platform or deck in a street provided for the use of pedestrians as a place of public resort or as a means of public thoroughfare, together with the places and means of access thereto and exit therefrom. *City of Winnipeg Act*, S.M. 1971, c. 105, s. 1.

PEDIATRIC. *adj.* Diagnosing and treating patients, most of whom are 14 years old or younger.

PEDIGREE. *n.* A genealogical table showing the ancestral line of descent of a registered animal. *Livestock Pedigree Act*, R.S.C. 1985, c. L-11, s. 2.

PEDIGREED CATTLE. Any cattle registered in or eligible for registration in the records of an association incorporated under the Livestock Pedigree Act (Canada). *Horned Cattle Purchases Act*, R.S.A. 1980, c. H-10, s. 1.

PEDIGREED LIVESTOCK. Livestock that is registered under the Livestock Pedigree Act (Canada). *Livestock Identification and Brand Inspection Act*, S.A. 1985, c. L-22.5, s. 1.

PEDIGREED STATUS. With respect to seed, means that the seed is of foundation status, registered status or certified status. *Seeds Regulations*, C.R.C., c. 1400, s. 2.

PEDIS POSSESSIO. [L. foothold] Something actually possessed.

PEDLAR. *n.* Any person who, whether as principal or agent, (i) goes from house to house selling or offering for sale any merchandise or service, or both, to any person, and who is not a wholesale or retail dealer in that merchandise or service, and not having a permanent place of business in the municipality, (ii) offers or exposes for sale to any person by means of samples, patterns, cuts or blueprints, merchandise or a service, or both, to be afterwards delivered in and shipped into the municipality, or (iii) sells merchandise or a service, or both, on the streets or roads or elsewhere than at a building that is his permanent place of business, but does not include any person selling (A) meat, fruit or other farm produce that has been produced, raised or grown by himself, or (B) fish of his own catching. *Municipal Government Act*, R.S.A. 1980, c. M-26, s. 1. See PEDDLER.

PEER. *n.* 1. An equal, a person of the same rank. 2. In England, a member of the House of Lords.

PEERAGE. *n.* In England, barons, dukes, earls, marquises and viscounts.

PEERESS. *n.* In England, the wife of a peer, the unmarried widow of a peer or a woman who is herself a peer.

P.E.I. *abbr.* 1. Prince Edward Island. 2. Haszard & Warburton's Reports, 1850-1872.

PELAGIC SEALING. The killing, taking or hunting in any manner whatever of fur seals at sea. *Pacific Fur Seals Convention Act*, R.S.C. 1985, c. F-33, s. 2.

PELLET. See SHOT ~.

PELT. *n.* The skin or hide of a fur bearing animal. See RAW ~; UNPRIME ~.

PELVIC IMPACT AREA. That area of the door or body side panel adjacent to any outboard designated seating position that is bounded by (a) horizontal planes 7 inches above and 4 inches below the seating reference point; and (b) vertical transverse planes 8 inches forward and 2 inches rearward of the seating reference point. *Motor Vehicle Safety Regulations*, C.R.C., c. 1038, s. 201.

PELVIC RESTRAINT. A seat belt assembly or portion thereof intended to restrain movement of the pelvis. *Motor Vehicle Safety Regulations*, C.R.C., c. 1038, s. 209.

PENAL. *adj.* Inflicting punishment.

PENAL INSTITUTION. Includes jail, prison, lockup, or adult reformatory institution. *Court and Penal Institutions Act*, R.S.N.S. 1967, c. 67, s. 37.

PENAL LAW. Law imposing a penalty for breach of a public right. J.G. McLeod, *The*

Conflict of Laws (Calgary: Carswell, 1983) at 207.

PENAL SERVITUDE. Punishment of an offender by confining and compelling that person to work.

PENAL STATUTE. A law which imposes a penalty or punishment for the offence committed.

PENAL SUM. A sum of money to be paid as punishment or an equivalent for some injury.

PENALTY. *n.* 1. A sum of money to be paid as punishment or an equivalent for some injury. 2. (a) A fine; or (b) a term of imprisonment including a term of imprisonment in default of payment or satisfaction of a fine. 3. Includes any forfeiture or pecuniary penalty imposed or authorized to be imposed by any Act of Parliament for any contravention of the laws relating to the collection of the revenue, or to the management of any public work producing tolls or revenue, notwithstanding that part of such forfeiture or penalty is payable to the informer or prosecutor, or to any other person. 4. All the sums of money, including fines, in default of payment of which a term of imprisonment is imposed and includes the costs and charges of committing the defaulter and of conveying him to prison. *Criminal Code*, R.S.C. 1985, c. C-46, s. 722(5). 5. A sum, fixed in advance, to be forfeited or paid in the event a contract is made or misperformed in some way. G.H.L. Fridman, *The Law of Contract in Canada*, 2d ed. (Toronto: Carswell, 1986) at 703.

PENDENT. *adj.* Describes an action, arbitration or proceeding after it is begun and before the final award or judgment is given.

PENDENTE LITE. [L.] During litigation.

PENDENTE LITE NIHIL INNOVETUR. [L.] During litigation nothing should be altered.

PENDENT JURISDICTION. If a federal court has jurisdiction over a certain case, then that court has jurisdiction to decide all of the questions presented by the case, including "state" issues over which a federal court has no independent jurisdiction. As long as a federal and state question springs from a common source of operative fact, the federal court has jurisdiction over both kinds of questions, and may in fact decide the case by answering the state question. P.W. Hogg, *Constitutional Law of Canada*, 2d ed. (Toronto: Carswell, 1985) at 146.

PENDING LITIGATION. See CERTIFICATE OF ~.

PENETRATING WOUND. A wound which has an entrance opening only and extends into tissue or an organ. F.A. Jaffe, *A Guide to Pathological*

Evidence, 2d ed. (Toronto: Carswell, 1983) at 187.

PENITENTIAL COMMUNICATION. A confession of culpable conduct made secretly and in confidence by a person to a clergyman or priest in the course of the discipline or practice of the church or religious denomination or organization of which the person making the penitential communication is a member. *Military Rules of Evidence*, C.R.C., c. 1049, s. 78.

PENITENTIARY. *n.* 1. An institution or facility of any description, including all lands connected therewith, that is operated by the Service for the custody, treatment or training of persons sentenced or committed to penitentiary, and includes any place declared to be a penitentiary pursuant to subsection 3(1) or (2). *Penitentiary Act*, R.S.C. 1985, c. P-5, s. 2. 2. (a) A penitentiary established under the Penitentiary Act; (b) includes, in respect of any punishment of imprisonment for 2 years or more imposed outside Canada pursuant to the Code of Service Discipline, any prison or place in which a person sentenced to imprisonment for 2 years or more by a civil court having jurisdiction in the place where the sentence is imposed can for the time being be confined; and (c) means, where in any place outside Canada there is no prison or place for the confinement of persons sentenced to imprisonment for 2 years or more, a civil prison. *National Defence Act*, R.S.C. 1985, c. N-5, s. 2.

PENITENTIARY SERVICE. The body now called the Canadian Corrections Service.

PENNY STOCK. A share less than $1 in price.

PENOLOGY. *n.* The study of prison management and rehabilitation of inmates.

PENSION. *n.* 1. An annual allowance made to a person, usually in consideration of past services. 2. A series of payments that continues for the life of a former member of a pension plan, whether or not it is thereafter continued to any other person. See ANNUAL ~; COMMUTED ~; DEFERRED ~; IMMEDIATE ~; JOINT AND SURVIVOR ~; NORMAL FORM OF ~; OCCUPATIONAL DISABILITY ~; OLD AGE SECURITY ~; PERSON IN RECEIPT OF A ~ BY REASON OF WAR SERVICE; PORTABLE ~; SURVIVOR ~.

PENSIONABLE AGE. In relation to a member, means the earliest age (taking into account the period of employment with the employer or the period of membership in the pension plan, if applicable) at which a pension benefit, other than a benefit in respect of a disability (as defined in the regulations), is payable to the member under the terms of the pension plan without the consent of the administrator and

without reduction by reason of early retirement. *Pension Benefits Standards Act*, R.S.C. 1985 (2d Supp.), c. 32, s. 2. See NORMAL ~.

PENSIONABLE EARNINGS. 1. The amount resulting on the multiplication of the pensionable salary by the number of years of pensionable service. *Civil Service Act*, R.S.Nfld. 1970, c. 41, s. 2. 2. (i) Where a member has 60 or more months of credited service the result obtained by taking the sum of the member's contributory earnings for the 60 months of consecutive credited service during which such contributory earnings were the highest and dividing such sum by five; and (ii) where a member has less than 60 months of credited service, the result obtained by taking the sum of the member's contributory earnings, dividing such sum by the number of months of such service and multiplying the figure so obtained by 12. *Ontario Municipal Employees Retirement System Act*, R.R.O. 1980, Reg. 724, s. 1. See YEAR'S MAXIMUM ~.

PENSIONABLE EMPLOYMENT. Employment in respect of which a person is eligible for superannuation under a superannuation act. See PERIOD IN ~.

PENSIONABLE REMUNERATION. An annual, daily or other indemnity payable to a member pursuant to the Legislative Assembly and Executive Council Act or earnings payable to a Minister. *Legislative Assembly Retiring Allowance Act*, S.N.W.T. 1985 (2d Sess.), c. 5, s. 5.

PENSIONABLE SALARY. 1. A person's average annual salary in the 5 consecutive years of pensionable service over which that person's average salary was the highest. 2. The annual average of salary received from public funds for the last 3 years of pensionable service. 3. The salary paid to an employee in the course of 1 year.

PENSIONABLE SERVICE. 1. Service in respect of which contributions have been made to a pension plan. 2. Service which may be taken into account in determining whether an employee has qualified for the award of a pension and the amount of a pension.

PENSION APPEALS BOARD. The federal body which hears appeals under the Canada Pension Plan and some provincial pension plans.

PENSION BENEFIT. 1. The aggregate annual, monthly or other periodic amounts to which an employee will become entitled upon retirement or to which any other person is entitled by virtue of death after retirement under a pension plan. 2. A periodic amount to which, under terms of a pension plan, a member or former member, or the spouse, other beneficiary or estate of a member or former member, is or may become entitled. *Pension Benefits Standards Act*, R.S.C. 1985 (2d Supp.), c. 32, s. 2. See CONTRIBUTORY ~; DEFERRED ~; IMMEDIATE ~; JOINT AND SURVIVOR ~; NET ~.

PENSION BENEFIT CREDIT. The value at a particular time of the pension benefits and any other benefits provided under the pension plan to which an employee has become entitled.

PENSION CREDIT. 1. The value at a particular time of any pension, benefit or reimbursement provided for under a supplemental plan, to which a person has become entitled. *Supplemental Pension Plans Act*, R.S.Q. 1977, c. R-17, s. 1. 2. The annual value of benefits to which an employee has become entitled by virtue of this plan and which are derived from a supplemental plan or have accrued from past service. *Government and Public Employees Retirement Plan Act*, R.S.Q. 1977, c. R-10, s. 1.

PENSION EQUIVALENT. In respect of any month in a payment quarter, the amount of the full monthly pension payable for that month under section 7. *Old Age Security Act*, R.S.C. 1985, c. O-9, s. 22. See ROUNDED ~.

PENSIONER. *n.* A person who has been awarded a pension.

PENSION FUND. The fund maintained to provide benefits under or related to a pension plan. See REGISTERED ~ OR PLAN.

PENSION FUND ASSOCIATION. A company, corporation or association incorporated before the year 1910, under or by virtue of any law of the Province of Quebec, for the purpose of providing a pension for those persons who have contributed to a fund therefor during a certain number of years, and includes any auxiliary funds incorporated for the purpose of guaranteeing the repayment of any sum to those who contributed to such pension fund during a certain number of years, or for the purpose of assuring a life pension to those contributing a sum of money to such pension fund, or for these and similar purposes. *Insurance Act*, R.S.O. 1980, c. 218, s. 1.

PENSION INDEX. For any one year, the average of the consumer price index over a 12-month period.

PENSION PLAN. 1. A superannuation or other plan organized and administered to provide pension benefits to employees employed in included employment (and former employees) and to which the employer is required under or in accordance with the plan to contribute, whether or not provision is also made for other benefits or for benefits to other persons, and includes a supplemental pension plan, whether or not the employer is required to make contributions under or in accordance with the supplemental pension plan. 2. A superannuation or pension fund or plan organized and administered to provide a pension benefit for employees, and includes: (i) a unit benefit plan under which pension benefits are determined with reference to remuneration of an employee for each year of service, or for a selected number of years of service; (ii) a money purchase plan under which pension benefits are determined at the retirement of an employee with reference to the accumulated amount of the aggregate contributions paid by or for the credit of the employee; (iii) a flat benefit plan under which the pension benefits are expressed either as a fixed amount in respect of each year of employment or as a fixed periodic amount; and (iv) a deferred profit sharing pension plan other than an employee's profit sharing plan or a deferred profit sharing plan as defined in sections 144 and 147 of the Income Tax Act (Canada). See BONA FIDE ~; CANADA ~; CONTRIBUTORY ~; FLAT-RATE ~; INSURED ~; MULTI-EMPLOYER ~; NON-CONTRIBUTORY ~; PAY-AS-YOU-GO ~; PROVINCIAL ~; QUÉBEC ~; REGISTERED PENSION FUND OR PLAN; REGISTERED ~; SUPPLEMENTAL ~.

PENSIONS ADVOCATE. See CHIEF ~.

PENSION TRUST. A trust established by an employer to provide payments to employees after their retirement.

PENTANES PLUS. A mixture mainly of pentanes and heavier hydrocarbons which ordinarily may contain some butanes and which is obtained from the processing of raw gas, condensate or crude oil. *Oil and Gas Conservation Act*, R.S.A. 1980, c. O-5, s. 1.

PENULTIMATE DECENNIAL CENSUS. The decennial census that preceded the then most recent decennial census. *Constitution Act, 1974*, S.C. 1974-75-76, c. 13, reprinted as R.S.C. 1985, App. Document No. 40.

PEOPLE. *n.* The inhabitants of a country, province, town or other area.

PEPPERCORN RENT. A rent far below actual value.

PERAMBULATE. *v.* To walk around the limits of an area of land.

PER ANNUM. [L.] By year.

PER AUTRE VIE. [Fr.] For the length of someone else's life.

PER CAPITA. [L. by heads] In equal shares. See MUNICIPAL ASSESSMENT ~; MUNIC-

IPAL TAX BASE ~; OVERALL ASSESSMENT ~; OVERALL TAX BASE ~.

PER CAPITA AMOUNT. The amount of financial assistance to be made available on a per capita basis to each municipality for capital works each year as prescribed in the regulations. *Provincial Capital Funds Program Act*, S.S. 1984-85-86, c. P-30.02, s. 2.

PER CAPITA GROSS NATIONAL PRODUCT. With respect to any calendar year, the quotient obtained by dividing (a) the value at market prices of all goods and services produced in the year by all persons resident in Canada, as determined for that year by the Chief Statistician of Canada; by (b) the population of all the provinces for the fiscal year in which the calendar year ends. *Federal-Provincial Fiscal Arrangements Act*, R.S.C. 1985, c. F-8, s. 18(4).

PER CAPITA REVENUE. See NATIONAL ~; PROVINCIAL ~.

PER CAPITA YIELD. In respect of a province for a revenue source for a fiscal year is the quotient obtained by dividing the product of the national average rate of tax for that revenue source and the province's revenue base for that revenue source for the fiscal year by the population of the province for that fiscal year. *Federal-Provincial Fiscal Arrangements Act*, R.S.C. 1985, c. F-8, s. 4(2).

PER CENT. *abbr.* [L.] 1. Per centum. By one hundred. 2. Per cent by weight unless otherwise stated. Canada regulations.

PERCENTAGE. See DIRECT EQUITY ~; PRIME RATE ~.

PERCENTAGE RATE. See ANNUAL ~.

PERCENTAGE TRUST. A guarantee that a would-be "income" beneficiary will regularly receive a fixed percentage on the value of the trust property. D.M.W. Waters, *The Law of Trusts in Canada*, 2d ed. (Toronto: Carswell, 1984) at 867.

PER CENTUM. [L.] By one hundred.

PERCH. *n.* 1. As a measure of area, 324 square feet (French measure). Units of measurement to describe certain land in Quebec. *Weights and Measures Act*, S.C. 1970-71-72, c. 36, schedule III. 2. As a measure of length, 18 feet (French measure). Units of measurement to describe certain land in Quebec. *Weights and Measures Act*, S.C. 1970-71-72, c. 36, schedule III. 3. 5 1/2 yards. *Weights and Measures Act*, S.C. 1970-71-72, c. 36, schedule II. 4. Yellow perch, Perca flavescens Lacepede. *Ontario Fishery Regulations*, C.R.C., c. 849, s. 2.

PERCHED GROUNDWATER. A free-standing body of water in the ground extending to a limited depth. *Building Code Act*, R.R.O. 1980, Reg. 87, s. 1.

PERCHED POND. A pond resulting from a pit or quarry or a wayside pit or quarry excavation which is above the natural water table and is in excess of 18 inches in depth and covers a minimum area of 10,000 square feet. *Pits and Quarries Control Act*, R.R.O. 1980, Reg. 784, s. 1.

PER CUR. *abbr.* [L.] Per curiam. By a court.

PER CURIAM. [L.] By a court.

PER DIEM. [L.] By day.

PERDURABLE. *adj.* Describes an estate which lasts very long or forever.

PEREMPTION. *n.* Nonsuit; quashing.

PEREMPTORY. *adj.* Determinate, final and, concerning statutes, obligatory in contrast to permissive.

PEREMPTORY CHALLENGE. Exception to a juror without reasons.

PERENNIAL FORAGE. All clovers (except sweet clover), sainfoin, trefoil, alfalfa and perennial grasses. *Canadian Wheat Board Regulations*, C.R.C., c. 397, s. 2.

PER EUNDEM. [L.] By the same thing.

PERFECT. *v.* To register.

PERFECTION. *n.* Attachment of a security interest; possession or registration of the collateral. G.H.L. Fridman, *Sale of Goods in Canada*, 3d ed. (Toronto: Carswell, 1986) at 505.

PERFORATED STAMPS. Postage stamps, including postcards printed with postage, perforated with the distinctive mark of the person using them. *Methods of Payment of Postage Regulations*, C.R.C., c. 1284, s. 2.

PERFORATING WOUND. A wound with both entrance and exit openings which completely crosses an organ or tissue. F.A. Jaffe, *A Guide to Pathological Evidence*, 2nd ed. (Toronto: Carswell, 1983) at 187.

PERFORMANCE. *n.* 1. Includes any game, match, sport, contest, exhibition, entertainment, concert, recital, theatrical presentation or motion picture presentation, dancing, opera, stage play, rodeo or show of horses. 2. Any acoustic representation of a work or any visual representation of any dramatic action in a work, including a representation made by means of any mechanical instrument or by radio communication. *Copyright Act*, R.S.C. 1985, c. C-42, s. 2. See PART ~; SUBSTANTIAL ~; TOTAL ~; SPECIFIC ~; SUBSTANTIAL ~.

PERFORMANCE BOND. A bond that is conditioned upon the completion by the principal of a contract in accordance with its terms.

PERFORMANCE GUARANTEE. In respect of a construction contract, the performance guarantee executed by the corporation, confirming the benefits of the plan to the owner in the event of the builder's failure to construct a contracted home under the contract. *Ontario New Home Warranties Plan Act*, R.R.O. 1980, Reg. 726, s. 1.

PERFORMING ARTS. The arts of the theatre and the concert hall, including the creating, staging and performing of drama, music and dance. *National Arts Centre Act*, R.S.C. 1985, c. N-3, s. 2.

PERFORMING RIGHT. In the case of a work that has not been performed in public before January 1, 1924, includes the right at common law, if any, to restrain the performance thereof in public. *Copyright Act*, R.S.C. 1985, c. C-42, s. 71.

PERFORMING RIGHTS SOCIETY. A business which acquires the performing rights in a copyrighted work and licenses others the right to perform it in public. H.G. Fox, *The Canadian Law of Copyright and Industrial Designs*, 2d ed. (Toronto: Carswell, 1967) at 525.

PERICARDIUM. *n.* The membranous sac which surrounds the heart. F.A. Jaffe, *A Guide to Pathological Evidence*, 2d ed. (Toronto: Carswell, 1983) at 181.

PERICULOSUM EST RES NOVAS ET INUS-ITATAS INDUCERE. [L.] It is dangerous to introduce new and untried things.

PERICULUM REI VENDITAE, NONDUM TRADITAE, EST EMPTORIS. [L.] Something sold and not yet delivered is at the purchaser's risk.

PERIL. *n.* 1. A risk of unavoidable misfortune. 2. Danger arising from failure to be duly circumspect. See ALL OTHER ~S; DESIGNATED ~S; MAJOR ~S; MARITIME ~S.

PERILS OF THE SEAS. Refers only to fortuitous accidents or casualties of the seas. It does not include the ordinary action of the winds and waves. *Insurance Act*, R.S.N.S. 1967, c. 148, s. 273.

PER INCURIAM. [L.] Through carelessness.

PER INFORTUNIUM. [L.] Through bad luck.

PERIOD. *n.* 1. An interval of time. 2. A space of time. 3. Any length of time. See ACCOUNTING ~; BENEFIT ~; BILLING ~; CAMPAIGN ~; CHRISTMAS ~; CONTINUOUS ~; COOLING-OFF ~; CRITICAL ~; DOWN ~; ELEC-

TION ~; FISCAL ~; JOINT CONTRIBUTORY ~; LEADERSHIP CONTEST ~; LICENCE ~; LIMITATIONS ~; MEAL ~; NOTICE ~; OPEN ~; PAYMENT REVIEW ~; PAY ~; PERPETUITY ~; POOL ~; REDEMPTION ~; REFERENDUM ~; REFRACTORY ~; RENTAL PAYMENT ~; RENT ~; REPORTING ~; REST ~; RESTRAINT ~; SUMMER ~; WAITING ~; WINTER ~.

PERIODICAL. *n.* Any printed matter that is published for general distribution to the public and that purports to be a copy of one publication in a series of publications at regular intervals, and that is not bound in a hard cover but does not include a periodic publication that is devoted primarily to conveying current news. *Paperback and Periodical Distributors Act*, R.S.O. 1980, c. 366, s. 1. See CANADIAN NEWSPAPER OR ~; MAGAZINES AND ~S; REGISTRAR'S ~.

PERIODICAL PUBLICATION. (a) Any paper, magazine or periodical that contains public news, intelligence or reports of events, or any remarks or observations thereon, and that is printed for sale and published periodically, or in parts or numbers, at intervals not exceeding 31 days between the publication of any two such papers, parts or numbers; and (b) any paper, magazine or periodical that contains advertisements, exclusively or principally, and that is printed in order to be disbursed and made public, weekly or more often, or at intervals not exceeding 31 days. *Canada Elections Act*, R.S.C. 1985, c. E-2, s. 2.

PERIODIC DUTY. A type of intermittent duty in which the load conditions are regularly recurrent. *Power Corporation Act*, R.R.O. 1980, Reg. 794, s. 0.

PERIODIC TENANCY. Tenancy from week to week, month to month or year to year.

PERIOD IN PENSIONABLE EMPLOYMENT. Any period of service to the credit of the employee in the fund or plan referred to in the definition "pensionable employment" at the time he left the employment therein referred to. *Public Service Superannuation Act*, R.S.C. 1985, c. P-36, s. 3.

PERIOD OF COHABITATION. Has the prescribed meaning, but in all cases shall be deemed to end with the month in which the joint contributory period ends. *Canada Pension Plan*, R.S.C. 1985 (2d Supp.), c. 30, s. 65.1(8).

PERIOD OF EMPLOYMENT. The period of time from the last hiring of an employee by an employer to his discharge by that employer and includes time on lay-off or suspension. *Labour Standards Code Act*, S.N.S. 1975, c. 50, s. 1.

PERIOD OF PROBATION. A period during

which a person convicted of an offence was directed by the court that convicted him (a) to be released on his own recognizance to keep the peace and be of good behaviour; or (b) to be released on or comply with the conditions prescribed in a probation order. *Criminal Records Act*, R.S.C. 1985, c. C-47, s. 2.

PERIOD OF SERVICE. Time served on active service in the forces, excluding therefrom any period of absence without leave or leave of absence without pay, or time served while undergoing sentence of penal servitude, imprisonment or detention, or period of service in respect of which pay is forfeited. *Veterans Rehabilitation Act*, R.S.C. 1970, c. V-5, s. 2.

PERIOD OF STUDIES. A period of studies at a specified educational institution in a course that is recognized by that educational institution and the appropriate authority for the province to be equivalent to a course that may be taken by a full-time student at that institution as part of a program of studies of at least 12 consecutive weeks duration. *Canada Student Loan Act*, R.S.C. 1985, c. S-23, s. 2.

PERIPHRASIS. *n.* Using many words to express a simple sense.

PERISH. *v.* For some existing thing to cease to exist. G.H.L. Fridman, *Sale of Goods in Canada*, 3d ed. (Toronto: Carswell, 1986) at 60.

PERISHABLE PROPERTY. Includes property which (a) is imminently subject to spoilage; or (b) may imminently become dangerous to life, health or other property. *Labour Code*, R.S.B.C. 1979, c. 212, s. 81.

PERITONEUM. *n.* The membrane which lines the inside surface of the abdominal walls and wraps the abdominal organs. F.A. Jaffe, *A Guide to Pathological Evidence*, 2d ed. (Toronto: Carswell, 1983) at 181.

PERITONITIS. *n.* Inflammation of the peritoneum. F.A. Jaffe, *A Guide to Pathological Evidence*, 2d ed. (Toronto: Carswell, 1983) at 181.

PERJURY. *n.* With intent to mislead, making before a person who is authorized by law to permit it to be made before him a false statement under oath or solemn affirmation, by affidavit, solemn declaration or deposition or orally, knowing that the statement is false. *Criminal Code*, R.S.C. 1985, c. C-46, s. 131(1).

PERMAFROST. *n.* That condition under which earth material exists at a temperature at or below 32°F continuously for a period of 2 years of more. *Gas Pipeline Regulations*, C.R.C., c. 1052, s. 2.

PERMANENT. *adj.* 1. Where used in the expression "total and permanent disability" or the expression "partial and permanent disability" means prolonged, in the sense that the disability is likely to be long continued and of indefinite duration, or likely to result in death. *Civil Service Superannuation Act*, S.M. 1972, c. 78, s. 10. 2. In relation to any commission, board or corporation, means established without any limitation of time as to its continuance. *Formal Documents Regulations*, C.R.C., c. 1331, s. 2.

PERMANENT ARBITRATOR. A person appointed to determine disputes arising during a period of time or during the life of a collective agreement.

PERMANENT CAVITY. A track left in tissue by a projectile passing through. The passage's diameter is usually greater than the projectile's. F.A. Jaffe, *A Guide to Pathological Evidence*, 2d ed. (Toronto: Carswell, 1983) at 181.

PERMANENT DECK COVERING. A deck covering adhering to, or permanently attached to, the deck and shall include any combination of decking material such as underlayments and surface material. *Hull Construction Regulations*, C.R.C., c. 1431, s. 76.

PERMANENT EMPLOYEE. 1. A person who has completed the probationary period and is employed on a full-time basis to hold office without reference to any specified date of termination of service. 2. Any employee who habitually does maintenance work on buildings or civil engineering works and any employee who does production work in an establishment. *Construction Industry Labour Relations Act*, R.S.Q. 1977, c. R-20, s. 1.

PERMANENT ESTABLISHMENT. A fixed place of business.

PERMANENT FINANCING. The advance of the whole amount, minus costs, of a mortgage loan by a lender to a borrower when construction of the borrower's new building is completed; the lender has inspected the building and is satisfied. D.J. Donahue & P.D. Quinn, *Real Estate Practice in Ontario*, 4th ed. (Toronto: Butterworths, 1990) at 224-225.

PERMANENT HEAD. Deputy minister, the Clerk of the Legislative Assembly, the Legislative Counsel and Law Clerk, the Chief Planning Officer and any commissioner or other official in charge of a bureau, branch or agency who is directly responsible to a member of the Executive Council. *The Public Service Act*, R.S.S. 1978, c. P-42, s. 2.

PERMANENT IMPROVEMENT. Includes: (i) a school site and an addition or an improvement to a school site; (ii) a building used for instructional purposes and any addition, alteration or improvement thereto; (iii) an administration office, a residence for teachers or caretakers and a storage building for equipment and supplies, and any addition, alteration or improvement thereto; (iv) furniture, furnishings, library books, instructional equipment and apparatus, and equipment required for maintenance of the property; (v) a bus or other vehicle, including watercraft, for the transportation of pupils; (vi) the obtaining of a water supply or an electrical power supply on the school property or the conveying of a water supply or an electrical power supply to the school from outside the school property; (vii) initial payments or contributions for past service pensions to a pension plan for officers and other employees of the board. *Education Act*, R.S.O. 1980, c. 129, s. 1.

PERMANENT INJUNCTION. An injunction to finally settle and enforce the rights of disputing parties. G.H.L. Fridman, *The Law of Contract in Canada*, 2d ed. (Toronto: Carswell, 1986) at 727.

PERMANENTLY UNEMPLOYABLE PERSON. A person who is unable to engage in remunerative employment for a prolonged period of time as verified by objective medical findings accepted by the medical advisory board. *Family Benefits Act*, R.R.O. 1980, Reg. 318, s. 1.

PERMANENT OFFICE OF AN AUTHORIZED PARTY. The office where, with a view to propagating the political program of an authorized party and coordinating the political action of its members, employees of the party or of an agency associated with it work full time, outside the election period, to attain the party's objectives. *Election Act*, S.Q. 1984, c. 51, s. 316.

PERMANENT RESIDENT. A person who (a) has been granted landing; (b) has not become a Canadian citizen; and (c) has not ceased to be a permanent resident pursuant to subsection 24(1). *Immigration Act*, R.S.C. 1985, c. I-2, s. 2.

PERMANENT SHARES. All stock or all shares of permanent or fixed capital not liable to be withdrawn from or repaid by the company. *Loan Companies and Finance Companies (Licensing) Act*, R.S.Nfld. 1970, c. 213, s. 2.

PERMANENT STAFF. Includes officers of the headquarters staff, officers of the district staff, and officers in charge of military stores. *Defence Services Pension Continuation Act*, R.S.C. 1970, c. D-3, s. 2.

PERMANENT TOTAL DISABILITY. Without restricting the generality of the term, includes the loss of both eyes, both hands, both feet, or one hand and one foot.

PERMANENT X-RAY LOCATION. An enclosure, room or localized space within the bounds of which the owner of an X-ray machine confines or intends to confine its use. *Public Health Act*, R.R.O. 1980, Reg. 855, s. 1.

PERMEABILITY. *n.* In relation to a space, means the percentage of that space below the ship's margin line that, on the assumption that it is in use for the purpose for which it is appropriated, can be occupied by water. *Hull Construction Regulations*, C.R.C., c. 1431, s. 2.

PER MENSEM. [L.] By month.

PERMISSIBLE CONDITION. That, as applied only to permissible equipment, such apparatus is complete in every detail of construction and that all clearances or other openings in the apparatus enclosures are within the required limits to assure an ample factor of safety against explosion risk. *Coal Mines Regulation Act*, R.S.N.S. 1967, c. 36, s. 84.

PERMISSIBLE EQUIPMENT. Apparatus of a special design and construction suitable for use in a mine where methane gas or coal dust (or in special cases, other explosive gases) may be present in the atmosphere in dangerous proportions, and which is identical with similar apparatus which has been investigated and certified by an acceptable explosion testing and certifying authority.

PERMISSION. *n.* The negation of a law, either because the law is silent or because it expressly declares something.

PERMISSIVE PRESUMPTION. A stipulation that, if certain facts are proved, a court may discover other facts. P.W. Hogg, *Constitutional Law of Canada*, 2d ed. (Toronto: Carswell, 1985) at 769.

PERMISSIVE WASTE. Neglect to make needed repairs.

PERMIT. *n.* 1. An authorization, a written authority. 2. Any permission, whether termed approval, permit, licence or certificate or other term. 3. A permit issued which allows the exclusive practice of the profession mentioned therein. See BUILDING ~; BURIAL ~; COLOURING ~; DEVELOPMENT ~; EXPORT ~; FEDERAL RESEARCH ~; GENERAL ~; OCCUPANCY ~; OWNER'S ~; PARK USE ~; PROVISIONAL ~; PUBLIC TRANSIT ~; REGISTRATION ~; RESOURCE USE ~; TIMBER ~; TRANSPORT ~; USE ~.

PERMIT AREA. The tract of land or location described in a permit. Canada regulations.

PERMIT BOOK. A Canadian Wheat Board delivery permit issued pursuant to this Act by the Board for a crop year. *Canadian Wheat Board Act*, R.S.C. 1985, c. C-24, s. 2.

PERMIT HOLDER. A person who holds a permit.

PERMIT PREMISES. Premises or parts of premises where an activity for which a permit is required is conducted. *Wildlife Act*, S.A. 1984, c. W-9.1, s. 1.

PERMITTED PRESERVATIVES. The preservatives designated in the Food and Drug Regulations (Canada) as Class III preservatives and used in accordance with the requirements of those regulations. *Farm Products Grades and Sales Act*, R.R.O. 1980, Reg. 327, s. 1.

PERMITTED USE. The use of a registered trade-mark by a registered user thereof in accordance with the terms of his registration as such in association with wares or services manufactured, sold, leased, hired or performed by him, or the use of a proposed trade-mark as provided in subsection 40(2) by a person approved as a registered user thereof. *Trademarks Act*, R.S.C. 1985, c. T-13, s. 50(2).

PERMITTEE. *n.* 1. A person who is the holder of a permit. 2. The person named in a permit.

PERMUTATION. *n.* Barter, exchanging one movable object for another.

PER MY ET PER TOUT. [Fr.] Not of a part but of all.

PERNANCY. *n.* Acceptance or receipt of anything.

PERNOR. *n.* A person who receives the profits of land.

PER PAIS. See TRIAL ~.

PERPARS. *n.* Part of an inheritance.

PERPENDICULAR. See AFTER ~; AFT ~; FORWARD ~.

PERPENDICULARS. *n.* 1. Perpendiculars are taken at the extreme ends of the subdivision load water line. *Hull Construction Regulations*, C.R.C., c. 1431, Schedule 1, s. 11. 2. The forward and after perpendiculars shall be taken at the forward and after ends of the length (L). The forward perpendicular shall coincide with the foreside of the stem on the water line on which the length is measured. *Load Line Regulations (Sea)*, C.R.C., c. 1441, s. 3.

PERPETUAL CARE. The preservation, improvement, embellishment and maintenance in perpetuity in a proper manner of markers, lots, compartments, crypts or other space in a cemetery, columbarium or mausoleum. See CEMETERY OR ~ TRUST.

PERPETUAL CARE FUNDS. The funds and property received by an owner for the purpose of providing perpetual care generally of a cemetery, mausoleum or columbarium or of any particular part thereof.

PERPETUAL DURATION. See RULE AGAINST ~.

PERPETUA LEX EST, NULLAM LEGEM HUMANAM AC POSITIVAM PERPETUAM ESSE, ET CLAUSULA QUAE ABROGATIONEM EXCLUDIT, AB INITIO NON VALET. [L.] It is a universal law that no human and positive law lasts forever, and a clause which excludes formal repeal is invalid from the beginning.

PERPETUAL INJUNCTION. An injunction to finally settle and enforce the rights of disputing parties. G.H.L. Fridman, *The Law of Contract in Canada*, 2d ed. (Toronto: Carswell, 1986) at 727.

PERPETUATE TESTIMONY. To preserve and perpetuate evidence which is likely to be lost because the witness is old, infirm or going away before the matter it relates to can be investigated judicially so that justice does not fail.

PERPETUITY. *n.* 1. Time without limit. 2. Tying up or preventing property from being disposed of freely.

PERPETUITY PERIOD. The period within which at common law as modified by this Act an interest must vest. Perpetuities Acts.

PERPETUITY RULE. Limits the time during which a grantor may withdraw property granted from commerce or effectively control the use of property by future generations, by making the property subject to a series of successive interests. D.M.W. Waters, *The Law of Trusts in Canada*, 2d ed. (Toronto: Carswell, 1984) at 282. See RULE AGAINST PERPETUITIES.

PER PRO. By procuring.

PER PROC. By procuring.

PERQUISITE. *n.* Any emolument of a job or position not normally considered to form part of the compensation related to that job or position and includes (a) the use of an automobile; (b) a membership in a recreation or other club; (c) residential accommodation assistance; (d) an interest free or low interest loan; (e) a travel pass; (f) a discount on the purchase of merchandise; or (g) a gift or a seasonal bonus. *Anti-Inflation Guidelines*, C.R.C., c. 302, s. 64.

PERQUISITIO. *n.* Acquiring anything except through inheritance.

PERQUISITION. *n.* Acquiring anything except through inheritance.

PER QUOD. [L.] Whereby.

PER QUOD CONSORTIUM AMISIT. [L.] Whereby one lost the benefit of the other's society.

PER QUOD SERVITIUM AMISIT. [L.] Whereby one lost the benefit of the other's service.

PER SE. [L. by itself] Alone.

PERSISTENT OIL. Crude oil, fuel oil, heavy diesel oil and lubricating oil. *Oil Pollution Prevention Regulations*, C.R.C., c. 1454, s. 2.

PERSON. *n.* 1. A natural person. 2. Includes a body corporate or politic. 3. An individual, partnership, unincorporated association, unincorporated organization, syndicate, trustee, executor, administrator or other legal personal representative. 4. Includes: (i) the Government of Canada and of any province of Canada and any department, commission, board or branch of any such government; (ii) a corporation, its successors and assigns; and (iii) the heirs, executors, administrators or other legal representatives of a person. Evidence Acts. 5. Includes any lawful trade union and any lawful association engaged in trade or business or the promotion thereof, and the administrative authority of any country, state, province, municipality or other organized administrative area. *Trade-marks Act*, R.S.C. 1985, c. T-13, s. 2. 6. Includes any body corporate or association, syndicate, trust or other body and the heirs, executors and administrators thereof, and the curators and assigns or other legal representatives of that person according to the law of that part of Canada to which the context extends. 7. Includes Her Majesty and public bodies, bodies corporate, societies, companies and inhabitants of counties, parishes, municipalities or other districts in relation to the acts and things that they are capable of doing and owning respectively. *Criminal Code*, R.S.C. 1985, c. C-46, s. 2. See ABORIGINAL ~; ACCUSED ~; ADULT ~; APPROPRIATE ~; ARTIFICIAL ~; ASSOCIATED ~S; AUTHORIZED ~; BLIND ~; CHRONICALLY ILL ~; CLASS OF ~S; COMPETENT ~; CONTROL ~; CONVALESCENT ~; CUSTODIAL ~; DEAF ~; DECEASED ~; DISABLED ~; DISADVANTAGED ~; DURESS OF THE ~; ELDERLY ~; ELDERLY ~S; FEEBLE-MINDED ~; FRENCH-SPEAKING ~; HANDICAPPED ~; ILLEGALLY ENLISTED ~; INDIGENT ~; INFIRM ~; IN ~; INSANE ~; INSOLVENT ~; INSURABLE ~; INSURED ~; INTERDICTED ~; INTERESTED ~; INTERNATIONALLY PROTECTED ~; INVESTIGATED ~; LAY ~; LEGAL ~; MARRIED ~; MENTALLY DEFECTIVE ~; MENTALLY DISORDERED ~; MENTALLY ILL ~;

MENTALLY INCOMPETENT ~; MENTALLY RETARDED ~; MISSING ~; NATIVE ~; NATURAL ~; NON-ELIGIBLE ~; NON-RESIDENT ~; PROFESSIONAL ~; PSYCHOTIC ~; QUALIFIED ~; RATABLE ~; RELATED ~; RELATED ~ OR COMPANY; RELATED ~S; RESIDENT ~; RESPONSIBLE ~; RETARDED ~; SELF-EMPLOYED ~; SINGLE ~; TRADES ~; UNEMPLOYABLE ~; UNEMPLOYED ~; YOUNG ~.

PERSONA. *n.* [L.] Anybody who can have and become subject to rights.

PERSONABLE. *adj.* Describes someone or something which has the status of a person and is therefore able to bring an action in a court.

PERSONA CONJUNCTA AEQUIPARATUR INTERESSE PROPRIO. [L.] A related person is considered to be the same as the person.

PERSONA DESIGNATA. [L.] 1. Someone described or designated as an individual, in contrast to someone who is the member of a class or represents a particular characteristic. 2. A judge who is not acting as a court. G.D. Watson & C. Perkins, eds., *Holmested & Watson: Ontario Civil Procedure* (Toronto: Carswell, 1984) at CJA-117.

PERSONA EXTRANEA. [L.] Someone outside of one's family.

PERSON AGGRIEVED. A person adversely affected.

PERSONAL. *adj.* Referring to an individual's person. See CHATTELS ~.

PERSONAL ACCIDENT INSURANCE. Insurance against loss or damage caused by bodily injury to or death of the person or persons insured arising out of an accident or the agreement to pay a certain sum or sums on the happening of these contingencies. *Insurance Act*, R.S.B.C. 1979, c. 200, s. 1.

PERSONAL ACTION. A remedy against a person or an action on a tort or contract.

PERSONAL BELONGINGS. Clothes, jewellery, personal effects, household furnishings. *Re Stanner's Estate* (1984), 28 Man. R. (2d) 64 (Man. Q.B.) at pp. 65, 66.

PERSONAL CARE. 1. Assistance with the performance of the personal functions and activities necessary for daily living that one is unable to perform efficiently for oneself. 2. Room and board, assistance with some of the activities of daily living, nonprofessional care and supervision and a planned program of social and recreational activities. *Hospital Act*, R.S.B.C. 1979, c. 176, s. 5.

PERSONAL CARE HOME. A building used

for accommodation of persons who in the opinion of a duly qualified medical practitioner require continual or intensive assistance and supervision in their daily living. *Elderly and Infirm Persons' Housing Act*, R.S.M. 1970, c. E20, s. 2.

PERSONAL CHATTELS. Automobiles and accessories, domestic animals, garden effects, household or personal articles for use or ornament, furniture, books, pictures, prints, paintings and other works of art, jewellery, video or audio reproductive equipment, musical and scientific instruments and apparatus, wines, liquors, consummable stores and other articles of personal property not amounting to an interest in land, but does not include any such chattel used at the death of a deceased person for business purposes nor money or securities for money. *Devolution of Estates Act*, S.N.B. 1976, c. 18, s. 1.

PERSONAL COMMERCIAL FISHING LICENCE. A licence authorizing a person to engage in commercial fishing. *Pacific Fishery Registration and Licensing Regulations*, C.R.C., c. 824, s. 2.

PERSONAL CONTACT. Face-to-face contact. *An Act to Amend the Mining Act*, S.N.B. 1987, c. 36, s. 1.

PERSONAL DAMAGE. Any serious permanent damage, whether physical or mental, including death. *An Act to Amend Various Legislation Respecting Social Affairs*, S.Q. 1985, c. 23, s. 18.

PERSONAL EQUIPMENT. All material issued to an officer or non-commissioned member for the personal wear or other personal use of that officer or non-commissioned member. *National Defence Act*, R.S.C. 1985 (1st Supp.), c. 31, s. 1.

PERSONAL ESTATE. Includes leasehold estates and other chattels real, and also money, shares of government and other funds, securities for money (not being real estate), debts, choses in action, rights, credits, goods, and all other property, except real estate, that by law devolves upon the executor or administrator, and any share or interest therein.

PERSONAL EXPENSES. 1. With respect to the expenditure of any candidate in relation to any election at which he is a candidate, includes any reasonable amount incurred by the candidate in respect of such travel, living and other related expenses as the Chief Electoral Officer may designate. *Canada Elections Act*, R.S.C. 1985, c. E-2, s. 2. 2. Includes the following: 1. Reasonable and ordinary rent for hire of halls or other places used by the candidate personally in which to address public meetings of voters, and the expenses incurred in heating, lighting and cleaning such halls or other places; 2. Reasonable and ordinary travelling and living expenses of the candidate; 3. Reasonable and ordinary travelling and living expenses of one speaker for each meeting who accompanies the candidate and travels with him for the purpose of speaking at public meetings to be addressed by the candidate; 4. Reasonable and ordinary charges for the hire of conveyances for the use of the candidate; 5. Reasonable and ordinary charges for use by the candidate personally of not more than one conveyance on the polling day.

PERSONAL FILE. Any collection or repository of information obtained from others in the course of making a personal investigation whether the information is stored in written, photographic, electronic or any other form. *Personal Investigations Act*, S.M. 1971, c. 23, s. 1.

PERSONAL INCOME. The sum of (1) the market value of rights one exercises in consumption and (2) the change in value of the accumulated property rights between the beginning and end of a certain period of time. W. Grover & F. Iacobucci, *Materials on Canadian Income Tax*, 4th ed. (Toronto: Richard De Boo Ltd., 1980) at 40.

PERSONAL INCOME TAX RATE. See PROVINCIAL ~.

PERSONAL INFORMATION. 1. Information other than credit information about a consumer's character, reputation, health, physical or personal characteristics or mode of living or about any other matter concerning the consumer. 2. Information respecting a person's identity, residence, dependents, marital status, employment, borrowing and repayment history, income, assets and liabilities, credit worthiness, education, character, reputation, health, physical or personal characteristics or mode of living. *An Act to Amend the Archives Act*, S.N.B. 1986, c. 11, s. 1. 3. Information about an identifiable individual that is recorded in any form including, without restricting the generality of the foregoing, (a) information relating to the race, national or ethnic origin, colour, religion, age or marital status of the individual; (b) information relating to the education or the medical, criminal or employment history of the individual or information relating to financial transactions in which the individual has been involved; (c) any identifying number, symbol or other particular assigned to the individual; (d) the address, fingerprints or blood type of the individual; (e) the personal opinions or views of the individual except where they are about another individual or about a proposal for a grant, an award or a prize to be made to another individual by a government institution or a part of a government institution specified in the regulations; (f) correspondence sent to a government institution by the individual that is implicitly or explicitly of a private or confidential nature, and replies to such correspondence that would reveal the contents of the original correspondence; (g) the views or opinions of another individual about the individual; (h) the views or opinions of another individual about a proposal for a grant, an award or a prize to be made to the individual by an institution or a part of an institution referred to in paragraph (e), but excluding the name of the other individual where it appears with the views or opinions of the other individual; and (i) the name of the individual where it appears with other personal information relating to the individual or where the disclosure of the name itself would reveal information about the individual, but, for the purposes of sections 7, 8 and 26 and section 19 of the Access to Information Act, does not include (j) information about an individual who is or was an officer or employee of a government institution that relates to the position or functions of the individual including; (i) the fact that the individual is or was an officer or employee of the government institution; (ii) the title, business address and telephone number of the individual; (iii) the classification, salary range and responsibilities of the position held by the individual; (iv) the name of the individual on a document prepared by the individual in the course of employment; and (v) the personal opinions or views of the individual given in the course of employment; (k) information about an individual who is or was performing services under contract for a government institution that relates to the services performed, including the terms of the contract, the name of the individual and the opinions or views of the individual given in the course of the performance of those services; (l) information relating to any discretionary benefit of a financial nature, including the granting of a licence or permit, conferred on an individual, including the name of the individual and the exact nature of the benefit; and (m) information about an individual who has been dead for more than 20 years. *Privacy Act*, R.S.C. 1985, c. P-21, s. 3.

PERSONAL INFORMATION BANK. A collection or grouping of personal information.

PERSONAL INFORMATION INVESTIGATOR. A person who obtains or reports personal information to a consumer reporting agency for hire or reward. Consumer Reporting acts.

PERSONAL INJURY. Bodily or physical injury. K.D. Cooper-Stephenson & I.B. Saund-

ers, *Personal Injury Damages in Canada* (Toronto: Carswell, 1981) at 5.

PERSONAL INJURY OFFENCE. See SERIOUS ~.

PERSONAL INVESTIGATION. Any inquiry by any person to obtain factual or investigative information from any source other than the subject with a view to entering into or amending an agreement with the subject for credit, insurance, employment or tenancy, whether the information is transmitted immediately in a personal report or compiled in a personal file. *Personal Investigations Act*, S.M. 1971, c. 23, s. 1.

PERSONALITY. See INTERNATIONAL ~.

PERSONAL OR HOUSEHOLD ARTICLE. A garment, suit, clothing, wearing apparel, or other article of personal dress or attire, and an article of domestic household use, including all materials and substances for them. *Factory Act*, R.S.B.C. 1979, c. 118, s. 32.

PERSONAL OR LIVING EXPENSES. Includes (a) the expenses of properties maintained by any person for the use or benefit of the taxpayer or any person connected with the taxpayer by blood relationship, marriage or adoption, and not maintained in connection with a business carried on for profit or with a reasonable expectation of profit; (b) the expenses, premiums or other costs of a policy of insurance, annuity contract or other like contract if the proceeds of the policy or contract are payable to or for the benefit of the taxpayer or a person connected with him by blood relationship, marriage or adoption; and (c) expenses of properties maintained by an estate or trust for the benefit of the taxpayer as one of the beneficiaries. *Income Tax Act*, R.S.C. 1952, c. 148 (as am. S.C. 1970-71-72, c. 63), s. 248(1).

PERSONAL PREROGATIVE. Power which the Governor General may exercise at personal discretion, *i.e.* the power to select or dismiss a Prime Minister. P.W. Hogg, *Constitutional Law of Canada*, 2d ed. (Toronto: Carswell, 1985) at 206-208.

PERSONAL PROPERTY. Includes all property other than land, an interest in land or anything attached to it. See LISTED ~; TANGIBLE ~; VALUE OF ~.

PERSONAL PROPERTY INSURANCE. Insurance against loss of or damage to movable or personal property.

PERSONAL PROPERTY SECURITY ACT. Legislation, based on Article 9 of the United States Uniform Commercial Code, to reform and make the law concerning security interests in goods uniform. G.H.L. Fridman, *Sale of Goods in Canada*, 3d ed. (Toronto: Carswell, 1986) at 502.

PERSONAL PROTECTIVE EQUIPMENT. Any clothing, equipment or device worn or used by a person to protect himself from the dangers of his employment. *Canada Protective Clothing and Equipment Regulations*, C.R.C., c. 1007, s. 2.

PERSONAL REPORT. Any report, whether written or oral, of information obtained from others in the course of making a personal investigation. *Personal Investigations Act*, S.M. 1971, c. 23, s. 1.

PERSONAL REPORTER. Any person who conducts a personal investigation but where the personal investigation is conducted by an employee of a user, or an employee of a personal reporting agency, in the course of his duties, the employer shall be deemed to be the personal reporter. *Personal Investigations Act*, S.M. 1971, c. 23, s. 1.

PERSONAL REPORTING AGENCY. Any person whose main business is to regularly conduct personal investigations for the purpose of supplying personal reports or the contents of personal files to others for gain. *Personal Investigations Act*, S.M. 1971, c. 23, s. 1.

PERSONAL REPRESENTATIVE. 1. An executor, an administrator, and an administrator with the will annexed. 2. Where used with reference to holding shares in that capacity, means an executor, administrator, guardian, tutor, trustee, receiver or liquidator or the committee of or curator to a mentally incompetent person.

PERSONAL REQUIREMENTS. Items of a minor nature, other than the ordinary requirements of food, shelter, clothing, fuel, utilities and household supplies, that are necessary in day-to-day living to a person's health or well-being, and, without limiting the generality of the foregoing, includes items relating to (a) personal care, cleanliness and grooming; (b) the observance of religious obligations; and (c) recreation. *Canada Assistance Plan Regulations*, C.R.C., c. 382, s. 2.

PERSONAL RESIDENCE. The residence ordinarily inhabited by the owner. *Municipal Elderly Resident's Assistance Act*, R.S.O. 1980, c. 307, s. 1.

PERSONAL SERVICE. On any individual except a disabled person, to leave a copy of the document with that individual. On a corporation, to leave a copy of the document with an agent, director or officer of the corporation, or with someone at that corporation's place of business who appears to be in management or control of that place of business. G.D. Watson & C. Perkins, eds., *Holmested & Watson: Ontario Civil Procedure* (Toronto: Carswell, 1984) at 16-5.

PERSONAL SERVICE CONTRACTOR. (i) An individual whose services are engaged by the Crown, a Provincial agency or a fund administrator in consideration of the payment of a fee whether or not the contract for those services is made with that individual or another person; or (ii) a person who contracts to provide the services of one or more individuals to the Crown, a Provincial agency or a fund administrator in consideration of the payment of a fee. *Financial Administration Act*, R.S.A. 1980, c. F-9, s. 1.

PERSONAL SERVICE ROOM. A change room, toilet room, wash room, shower room, lunch room or any combination thereof. *Canada Sanitation Regulations*, C.R.C., c. 1009, s. 2.

PERSONAL SERVICES. The regular performance for a resident of, or significant assistance with the performance by a resident of, personal functions necessary for daily living, such as grooming and hygiene. *Community Care Facilities and Nursing Homes Act*, S.P.E.I. 1985, c. 9, s. 1.

PERSONAL SERVICE SHOP. A building or part of a building in which services, other than repair services, are provided to individuals. *Canada regulations*.

PERSONAL SERVICES OCCUPANCY. Occupancy for the rendering or receiving of professional or personal services.

PERSONAL SUPERVISION. Direct supervision by a licensed pharmacist who is physically present. *Pharmacy acts*.

PERSONAL TRUST. (a) A testamentary trust, or (b) an inter vivos trust, no beneficial interest in which was acquired for consideration payable directly or indirectly to (i) the trust; or (ii) any person who has made a contribution to the trust by way of transfer, assignment or other disposition of property, and, for the purposes of this paragraph and paragraph 53(2)(h), where an inter vivos trust is created by way of the transfer, assignment or other disposition of property by an individual (or two or more individuals each of whom was, at the time the trust was created, related to each of the other individuals) any beneficial interest in the trust acquired by such individual (or individuals) at the time the trust was created shall be deemed to have been acquired for no consideration. *Income Tax Act*, R.S.C. 1952, c. 148 (as am. S.C. 1988, c. 55, s. 188(14)), s. 248(1).

PERSONALTY. *n.* Personal property.

PERSONAL-USE PROPERTY. With respect to a taxpayer, includes: (i) property owned by him that is used primarily for the personal use or enjoyment of the taxpayer or for the personal use or enjoyment of one or more individuals each of whom is (A) the taxpayer; (B) a person related to the taxpayer; or (C) where the taxpayer is a trust, a beneficiary under the trust or any person related to the beneficiary; (ii) any debt owing to him in respect of the disposition of property that was his personal-use property; and (iii) any property of the taxpayer that is an option to acquire property that would, if he acquired it, be personal-use property of the taxpayer, and "personal-use property" of a partnership includes any partnership property that is used primarily for the personal use or enjoyment of any member of the partnership or for the personal use or enjoyment of one or more individuals each of whom is a member of the partnership or a person related to such a member. *Income Tax Act*, R.S.C. 1952, c. 148 (as am. S.C. 1970-71-72, c. 63), s. 54(f).

PERSON AT HOME. A person, having or not having a spouse, whose chief occupation consists in attending to the usual occupations of a person who stays at home for the benefit of that person's household. *Automobile Insurance Act*, R.S.Q. 1977, c. A-25, s. 1.

PERSONATING POLICE OFFICER. Falsely representing oneself to be a peace officer or public officer, or using a badge or article of uniform or equipment in a manner that is likely to cause persons to believe that one is a peace officer or a public officer. *Criminal Code*, R.S.C. 1985, c. C-46, s. 130.

PERSONATION. *n.* The act of representing that one is someone else, whether dead or living, fictitious or real.

PERSON BOUND TO PROVIDE OR CARE FOR A PATIENT. Includes (a) a person whose wife is the patient; (b) a person whose husband is the patient; (c) a person whose child is the patient; and (d) a person who is required by legal contract or by a statute of the province to provide or care for him. *Mental Health Act*, R.S.N.B. 1973, c. M-10, s. 59.

PERSON CONCERNED. A person is respect of whom an inquiry is to be made. *Public Service Security Inquiry Regulations*, C.R.C., c. 724, s. 2.

PERSON CONNECTED. When used in relation to another person, means an employee, agent, partner or associate of the other person and, where the other person is a corporation, includes a director, officer, shareholder or member of the corporation. *Discriminatory Business Practices Act*, R.S.O. 1980, c. 119, s. 1.

PERSON DYING INTESTATE. A person owning property who dies without a will.

PERSON EMPLOYED IN A MANAGERIAL OR CONFIDENTIAL CAPACITY. Any person who (a) is employed in a position confidential to the person occupying the recognized position of Speaker of the Senate, Speaker of the House of Commons, Clerk of the Senate, Clerk of the House of Commons, Administrator of the House of Commons, Gentleman Usher of the Black Rod, Sergeant-at-Arms or Law Clerk and Parliamentary Counsel of either House; (b) is employed as parliamentary counsel in either House or as legal counsel to a committee of either or both Houses; or (c) is employed by an employer and, in connection with an application for certification of a bargaining agent for a bargaining unit, is designated by the Board, or, in any case where a bargaining agent for a bargaining unit has been certified by the Board, is designated in prescribed manner by the employer or by the Board on objection thereto by the bargaining agent, to be a person (i) who has executive duties and responsibilities in relation to the development and administration of employer programs; (ii) whose duties include those of a personnel administrator or who has duties that cause the person to be directly involved in the process of collective bargaining on behalf of the employer; (iii) who is required by reason of the duties and responsibilities of that person to deal formally on behalf of the employer with a grievance presented in accordance with the grievance process provided by this Part; (iv) who is employed in a position confidential to any person described in paragraph (b) or subparagraph (i), (ii) or (iii); or (v) who is not otherwise described in subparagraph (i), (ii), (iii) or (iv) but who, in the opinion of the Board, should not be included in a bargaining unit by reason of his duties and responsibilities to the employer. *Public Service Staff Relations Act*, R.S.C. 1985 (2d Supp.), c. 33, s. 3. 2. A person who: (i) is involved in the formulation of organization objectives and policy in relation to the development and administration of programs of the employer or in the formulation of budgets of the employer; (ii) spends a significant portion of his time in the supervision of employees; (iii) is required by reason of his duties or responsibilities to deal formally on behalf of the employer with a grievance of an employee; (iv) is employed in a position confidential to any person described in subclauses (i), (ii) or (iii), (v) is employed in a confidential capacity in matters relating to employee relations; (vi) is not otherwise described in subclauses (i) to (v) but who, in the opinion of the Ontario Labour Relations Board, should not be included in a bargaining unit by reason of his duties and responsibilities to the employer. *Colleges Collective Bargaining Act*, R.S.O. 1980, c. 74, s. 1.

PERSON HAVING A LIEN. Includes both a lien claimant and a person with an unpreserved lien. *Construction Lien Act, 1983*, S.O. 1983, c. 6, s. 1.

PERSON IN CHARGE. 1. Person over the age of 21 years with whom a child lives or who controls or is in a position to control or has the apparent charge of a child. *Education Act*, R.S.N.S. 1967, c. 81, s. 1. 2. A qualified person appointed by his employer to ensure the safe and proper conduct of an operation or of the work of employees. Canada regulations.

PERSON IN CHARGE OF THE DECK WATCH. Includes every person who has immediate charge of the navigation or security of a ship, but does not include a pilot. Canada regulations.

PERSON IN NEED. (a) A person who, by reason of inability to obtain employment, loss of the principal family provider, illness, disability, age or other cause of any kind acceptable to the provincial authority, is found to be unable, on the basis of a test established by the provincial authority that takes into account the budgetary requirements of that person and the income and resources available to that person to meet those requirements, to provide adequately for himself, or for himself and his dependants or any of them; or (b) a person under the age of 21 years who is in the care or custody or under the control or supervision of a child welfare authority, or a person who is a foster-child as defined by regulation. *Canada Assistance Plan*, R.S.C. 1985, c. C-1, s. 2.

PERSON IN RECEIPT OF A PENSION BY REASON OF WAR SERVICE. A person who (a) is in receipt of a pension (i) by reason of service in World War I; or (ii) by reason of service only in World War II, and who at the commencement of such service was domiciled in Canada or Newfoundland; (b) has, from causes attributable to that service lost capacity for physical exertion to an extent that makes the person unfit to pursue efficiently the vocation that the person was pursuing before the war; and (c) has not been successfully re-established in any other vocation. *Public Service Employment Act*, R.S.C. 1985, c. P-33, s. 48.

PERSON INSURED. A person in respect of an accident to whom, or in respect of whose sickness, benefits are payable under a contract. See GROUP ~.

PERSON INTERESTED. Includes any person who is affected or reasonably apprehends that he may be affected by any entry in the register,

or by any act or omission or contemplated act or omission under or contrary to this Act, and includes the Attorney General of Canada. *Trademarks Act*, R.S.C. 1985, c. T-13, s. 2.

PERSON LAWFULLY IN POSSESSION OF THE BODY. Does not include (i) a constable in possession of a body for the purposes of an autopsy or other post-mortem examination; (ii) an embalmer or funeral director in possession of a body for the purpose of its burial, cremation or other disposition; or (iii) the superintendent of a crematorium in possession of the body for the purpose of its cremation. Human Tissue Acts.

PERSONNEL. See FIRE SERVICES ~; NON-INSTRUCTIONAL ~; SCHOOL ~; TEACHING ~.

PERSON OF LOW INCOME. A person who receives a total income, that, in the opinion of a housing commission, is insufficient to permit that person to obtain adequate housing accommodation at the current rentals or prices in the area in which the person lives.

PERSON OF MIXED BLOOD. 1. A person having no less than one-quarter Indian or Eskimo blood. Canada regulations. 2. A person of (a) mixed Indian and non-Indian blood who is at least one-quarter Indian; or (b) mixed Inuk and non-Inuk blood who is at least one-quarter Inuk. *Northwest Territories Fisheries Regulations*, C.R.C., c. 847, s. 2.

PERSON OF UNSOUND MIND. One, other than an infant, who is incapable, from infirmity of mind, of managing one's own affairs.

PERSON RESPONSIBLE. When used with reference to a pesticide, substance or thing, means: (i) the owner; (ii) the person having the charge, management or control of the handling, storage, use, disposal, transportation or display; or (iii) the person having the charge, management or control, of the pesticide, substance or thing.

PERSON UNDER DISABILITY. A person who is a minor or a mentally incompetent person.

PERSPICUA VERA NON SUNT PROBANDA. [L.] Evident truths do not need to be proved.

PER STIRPES. [L. according to stocks] Division of a legacy among representatives of the respective original legatees.

PERSUASION. See BURDEN OF ~.

PERSUASIVE AUTHORITY. A judgment or other origin of law whose intrinsic value takes strength from something other than its being binding in character.

PER SUBSEQUENS MATRIMONIUM. [L.] By a later marriage.

PER TOTAM CURIAM. [L. by the whole court] A unanimous decision.

PER VARIOS ACTUS LEGEM EXPERIENTIA FECIT. [L.] By various acts experiences have made the law.

PERVERSE VERDICT. A verdict in which a jury refuses to follow the judge's direction on a point of law.

PESSIMI EXEMPLI. [L.] Of the worst example.

PESSURABLE WARES. Merchandise which takes up a lot of room in a ship.

PEST. *n.* 1. Any injurious, noxious or troublesome plant or animal life other than human or plant or animal life on or in human beings and includes any injurious, noxious or troublesome organic function of a plant or animal. 2. Any injurious, noxious or troublesome plant or animal life and includes any injurious, noxious or troublesome organic function of a plant or animal. 3. Any injurious, noxious or troublesome insect, fungus, bacterial organism, virus, weed, rodent or other plant or animal pest, and includes any injurious, noxious or troublesome organic function of a plant or animal. *Pest Control Products Act*, R.S.C. 1985, c. P-9, s. 2. See CATTLE ~; FOREST TREE ~; MAMMALIAN ~.

PEST CONTROL. See LAND ~; STRUCTURAL ~; WATER ~.

PEST CONTROL PRODUCT. Any substance or mixture of substances intended for use as a pest control product under the Pest Control Products Act (Canada), and includes any substance or mixture of substances intended, represented or sold for use in directly or indirectly preventing, destroying, repelling or mitigating the damage caused by any pest, except those substances which the Minister believes on reasonable and probable grounds are or may be used for medical purposes of humans or animals. *Pest Control Products (Nova Scotia) Act*, S.N.S. 1986, c. 16, s. 3.

PESTICIDE. *n.* Any product, device, organism, substance or combination of any products, devices, organisms, substances or things that is intended to be or is represented as, sold as or used as a means for (a) directly or indirectly controlling, preventing, killing, destroying, mitigating, attracting or repelling any pest; or (b) altering the growth, development or characteristics of any living plant that is not a pest, and any metabolite or degradation product of such product, device, organism, substance or thing

and includes any product, device, organism, substance or thing that is required to be registered as a control product under the Pest Control Products Act, chapter P-10 of the Revised Statutes of Canada, 1970 and any metabolite or degradation product of such product, device, organism, substance or thing. See FERTILIZER-~.

PESTICIDE RESIDUE. The residue of any pesticide or degradation product thereof. *Pesticide Residue Compensation Act*, R.S.C. 1985, c. P-10, s. 2.

PETECHIAE. *n.* Very small hemorrhages in the skin, serous surfaces and mucous membranes. F.A. Jaffe, *A Guide to Pathological Evidence*, 2d ed. (Toronto: Carswell, 1983) at 181.

PETECHIAL HEMORRHAGE. A very small bleeding point in the membranes of the body or skin. F.A. Jaffe, *A Guide to Pathological Evidence*, 2d ed. (Toronto: Carswell, 1983) at 105.

PETERS. *abbr.* Peters' Reports (P.E.I.), 1850-1872.

PETITIO. *n.* [L.] A count; a declaration.

PETITION. *n.* 1. The process which originates a divorce action. 2. A petition for a receiving order. *Bankruptcy Rules*, C.R.C., c. 368, s. 66. 3. An inferior's supplication to a superior who has jurisdiction to grant redress. 4. A written document by which an ordinary citizen asks the Crown and Parliament for redress, presented through a member following conditions laid down in the Standing Orders of the House. A. Fraser, G.A. Birch & W.A. Dawson, eds., *Beauchesne's Rules and Forms of the House of Commons of Canada*, 5th ed. (Toronto: Carswell, 1978) at 209. See COUNTER~; ELECTION ~.

PETITION DE DROIT. [Fr.] A common law method to obtain possession or restitution of real or personal property from the Crown or damages to compensate for breach of a contract.

PETITIONER. *n.* 1. Includes every person making application to the court, either by petition, motion or summons, otherwise than as against a defendant. 2. A person who brings a petition. *Controverted Elections Act*, R.S.N.W.T. 1974, c. C-14, s. 2. 3. The person or persons applying for an adoption order pursuant to this Act. *Adoption Act*, R.S.P.E.I. 1974, c. A-1, s. 1.

PETITIONING CREDITOR. A person who requests a receiving order in bankruptcy against a debtor.

PETITION OF RIGHT. A common law method to obtain possession or restitution of real or personal property from the Crown or damages to compensate for breach of a contract. Such a petition could proceed to hearing only if the monarch consented by endorsing it "fiat justitiae" (let right be done). P.W. Hogg, *Constitutional Law of Canada*, 2d ed. (Toronto: Carswell, 1985) at 221.

PETRO-CANADA. *n.* The corporation established by the Petro-Canada Act.

PETROLEUM. *n.* 1. Oil or gas. 2. Any hydrocarbon or mixture of hydrocarbons other than gas. 3. In addition to its ordinary meaning, any mineral oil or relative hydrocarbon and any natural gas, including coal gas, existing in its natural condition in strata, but does not include coal or bituminous shales or other stratified deposits from which oil can be extracted by destructive distillation. See CROWN ~; CRUDE ~; DOMESTIC ~; FOREIGN ~; PRIVATELY OWNED ~.

PETROLEUM INDUSTRY. Includes the carrying on in a province of any of the following industries or businesses: (a) distillation, refining or blending of petroleum; (b) manufacture, refining, preparation or blending of products obtained from petroleum; (c) storage of petroleum or petroleum products; and (d) wholesale or retail distribution or selling of petroleum products.

PETROLEUM PRODUCT. 1. Crude oil or other hydrocarbon or mixture of hydrocarbons recovered in liquid or solid state from a natural reservoir, any hydrocarbon or mixture thereof, in liquid or solid state, that results from the processing or refining of crude oil or other hydrocarbon, and natural gasoline or condensate resulting from the production, processing or refining of natural gas or a derivative of natural gas. 2. Petroleum, gasoline, naphtha, benzene, kerosene, lubricating oils, stove oil, fuel oil, furnace oil, paraffin, aviation fuels, butane, propane and other liquified petroleum gas, and all derivatives of petroleum and any product obtained from petroleum, whether or not blended with or added to other things. See FUEL ~; INFLAMMABLE ~S; REFINED ~.

PETROLEUM RIGHT. An exploration licence, an exploration agreement, a production lease or a coal gas agreement granted pursuant to this act or the regulations and includes any right arising from an exploration licence, exploration agreement, production lease or coal gas agreement. *Petroleum Resources Act*, S.N.S. 1979-80, c. 12, s. 2.

PETROLEUM WELL. A well in which casing is run and that, in the opinion of the minister, is producing or is capable of producing from a petroleum bearing zone. *Petroleum and Natural Gas Amendment Act*, S.B.C. 1987, c. 24, s. 1. See COMMERCIAL ~.

PETTIFOGGER. *n.* A lawyer who is not honest.

PETTY CASH EXPENDITURE. A disbursement made out of an accountable advance held in a department in cash. *Accountable Advances Regulations*, C.R.C., c. 668, s. 2.

PEW. *n.* In a church, an enclosed seat.

PFRA. *abbr.* Prairie Farm Rehabilitation Administration.

P.G. *abbr.* Procureur général.

PHARMACEUTICAL. *n.* See APPROVED DRUG AND ~; RADIO~.

PHARMACEUTICAL. *adj.* Relating to a pharmacy.

PHARMACEUTICAL CHEMIST. A person who is legally qualified to practise pharmacy and who is the holder of a valid and subsisting licence entitling him to practise his profession under this Act. Pharmacy acts.

PHARMACEUTICAL PREPARATION. Includes (a) any substance or mixture of substances manufactured, sold or represented for use in (i) the diagnosis, treatment, mitigation or prevention of a disease, disorder or abnormal physical state, or the symptoms thereof, in humans or animals; or (ii) restoring, correcting or modifying organic functions in humans or animals; and (b) any substance to be used in the preparation or production of any substance or mixture of substances described in paragraph (a), but does not include any such substance or mixture of substances that is the same or substantially the same as a substance or mixture of substances that is a proprietary medicine within the meaning from time to time assigned to that expression by regulations made pursuant to the Food and Drugs Act. *Trade-Marks Act*, R.S.C. 1985, c. T-13, s. 51(3).

PHARMACEUTICAL PRODUCT. See INTERCHANGEABLE ~.

PHARMACIST. *n.* 1. A person who is registered, licensed or authorized under the law of any province to carry on the business of preparing, manufacturing, compounding or dispensing, for sale to a consumer, medicines and pharmaceutical preparations, and does in fact carry on business as a retail pharmacist. *Excise Act*, R.S.C. 1985, c. E-14, s. 136. 2. A person holding a licence, signifying entitlement to practise pharmacy. See LICENSED ~.

PHARMACY. *n.* 1. When referring to practice of the profession means (i) manufacturing, compounding or otherwise preparing, including packaging, repackaging or labelling; (ii) dispensing; or (iii) giving expert instruction on the use of a drug, the performance of which skill, in the opinion of the Board, requires specialist knowledge and judgment concerning the properties of drugs. 2. When referring to a facility means any place where pharmacy is practised. 3. A place where prescriptions, drugs, medicines, chemicals and poisons are compounded, dispensed, sold by retail, or distributed, and includes a dispensary, drug store, drug department, or a hospital dispensary. 4. A place where prescriptions, medicines, drugs, chemicals and poisons are compounded or prepared or sold by retail. See OPERATOR OF A ~; PARTICIPATING ~; PRACTICE OF ~.

PHARYNX. *n.* A tube of muscle and membranes which connects the cavities of the nose and mouth with the larynx and esophagus. F.A. Jaffe, *A Guide to Pathological Evidence*, 2d ed. (Toronto: Carswell, 1983) at 181. See HYPO~; NASO~.

PHEASANT. *n.* Any of the species Phasianus colchicus Linnaeus. *Game and Fish Act*, R.S.O. 1980, c. 182, s. 1.

PHEASANT HUNTING PRESERVE. An area in which pheasants propagated under license are released for hunting purposes. *Lands and Forests Act*, R.S.N.S. 1967, c. 163, s. 84.

PHEASANT RESERVE. An area licensed by the Minister for the propagation and hunting of pheasants. *Fish and Wildlife Act*, S.N.B. 1980, c. F-14.1, s. 1.

PHEASANT SHOOTING GROUND. A parcel of land on which pen-reared pheasants are released for hunting. *Wildlife Act*, R.S.A. 1970, c. 391, s. 2.

PHILANTHROP. *abbr.* The Philanthropist (Le Philanthrope).

PHILLIPS V. EYRE. See RULE IN ~.

PHOSPHORIC ACID. Phosphorus pentoxide (P_2O_5). *Fertilizers Regulations*, C.R.C., c. 666, s. 2.

PHOTOGRAPH. *n.* 1. Includes photo-lithograph and any work produced by any process analogous to photography. *Copyright Act*, R.S.C. 1985, c. C-42, s. 2. 2. Includes photographic film, prints, reductions and enlargements, microphotographic film and photocopies. *Evidence Act*, R.S.B.C. 1979, c. 116, s. 39. 3. A reproduction made by any process that makes an exact copy of the original and includes any photographic plate, microphotographic film, photostatic negative, autopositive and any photographic print made therefrom. *Public Hospitals Act*, R.R.O. 1980, Reg. 865, s. 1. See PRINTED BOOK OF ~S.

PHOTOGRAPHER. *n.* Anyone using a photographic process that involves the formation of images directly or indirectly by action of light or other forms of radiation on sensitive surfaces. *Customs Tariff*, R.S.C. 1985, c. C-54, s. 2.

PHOTOGRAPHIC FILM. Includes any photographic plate, microphotographic film and photostatic negative. Evidence acts.

PHOTOGRAPHIC RECORD OR DOCUMENT. (a) Photographs attached or mounted to form a unit, other than a printed book such as a photograph album; or (b) loose or unattached photographs that clearly form a single unit of visual information. *Canadian Cultural Property Export Control List*, C.R.C., c. 448, s. 1.

PHOTOGRAPHIC SLIDE. A stationary photographic slide or other similar device used in conjunction with a motion picture. *Motion Picture Act*, R.S.B.C. 1979, c. 284, s. 1.

PHYSICAL CHARACTERISTICS. Any degree of physical disability, infirmity, malformation or disfigurement that is caused by bodily injury, birth defect or illness and, without limiting the generality of the foregoing, includes epilepsy, paralysis, amputation, lack of physical co-ordination, blindness or visual impediment, deafness or hearing impediment, muteness or speech impediment, and physical reliance on a guide dog, wheelchair or other remedial appliance or device. *Individual's Rights Protection Act*, R.S.A. 1980, c. I-2, s. 38.

PHYSICAL CONTEST. Includes any contest between competitors where human physical endurance is put to the test and which may become indecent, injurious to health or contrary to public order. *Physical Contests Act*, R.S.Q. 1977, c. C-52, s. 2.

PHYSICAL DEFECT. A problem such as cracked walls, sunken floors, rotten rafters, leaky roofs or basements. B.J. Reiter, R.C.B. Risk & B.N. McLellan, *Real Estate Law*, 3d ed. (Toronto: Emond Montgomery, 1986) at 225.

PHYSICAL DISABILITY. Any degree of disability, infirmity, malformation or disfigurement of a physical nature caused by bodily injury, illness or birth defect and, without limiting the generality of the foregoing, includes any disability resulting from any degree of paralysis or from diabetes mellitus, epilepsy, amputation, lack of physical co-ordination, blindness or visual impediment, deafness or hearing impediment, muteness or speech impediment, or physical reliance on a guide dog or on a wheelchair, cane, crutch or other remedial device or appliance.

PHYSICAL HANDICAP. A physical disability,

infirmity, malformation or disfigurement that is caused by bodily injury, birth defect or illness and includes epilepsy, but is not limited to, any degree of paralysis, amputation, lack of physical co-ordination, blindness or visual impediment, deafness or hearing impediment, muteness or speech impediment, or physical reliance on a guide dog, wheelchair or other remedial appliance or device.

PHYSICALLY HANDICAPPED PERSON. A person who is subject to a physiological defect or deficiency regardless of its cause, nature or extent, and includes all such persons whether ambulatory or confined to a wheelchair. *Building Access Act*, S.N.S. 1976, c. 7, s. 1.

PHYSICAL OR MENTAL HANDICAP. A previous or existing disability, infirmity, malformation or disfigurement, whether of a physical or mental nature, that is caused by injury, birth defect or illness, and includes but is not limited to epilepsy, any degree of paralysis, amputation, lack of physical co-ordination, blindness or visual impediment, deafness or hearing impediment, muteness or speech impediment, or physical reliance on a guide dog, wheelchair or other remedial device. *An Act to Amend the Human Rights Act*, S.P.E.I. 1985, c. 23, s. 1.

PHYSICAL THERAPIST. A physiotherapist.

PHYSICAL THERAPY. The application of professional physical therapy knowledge in the assessment and treatment of the human body in order to obtain, regain and maintain optimal function by the use of any suitable medium of therapeutic exercise, massage and manipulation or by radiant, mechanical and electrical energy. *Physical Therapy Profession Act*, S.A. 1984, c. P-7.5, s. 1.

PHYSICIAN. *n.* 1. A legally qualified medical practitioner. 2. Someone who practises an art of healing. See ATTENDING ~; COLLEGE OF ~S AND SURGEONS; CONTRACT ~; JAIL ~.

PHYSICIAN SERVICES. Any medically required services rendered by medical practitioners. *Canada Health Act*, R.S.C. 1985, c. C-6, s. 2.

PHYSIOTHERAPIST. *n.* A person who practises physiotherapy. See REGISTERED ~.

PHYSIOTHERAPY. *n.* The treatment of the human body by physical or mechanical means, by manipulation, massage, exercise, the application of bandages, hydrotherapy and medical electricity. See PRACTICE OF ~; PROGRAM OF ~.

PIA MATER. The deepest of the three membranes which surround the spinal cord and brain.

F.A. Jaffe, *A Guide to Pathological Evidence*, 2d ed. (Toronto: Carswell, 1983) at 181.

PICKED. See HAND ~.

PICKETING. *n.* Watching and besetting, or attending at or near a person's place of business, operations or employment for the purpose of persuading or attempting to persuade anyone not to (a) enter that place of business, operations or employment; (b) deal in or handle that person's products; or (c) do business with that person, and a similar act at such place that has an equivalent purpose. *Labour Code*, R.S.B.C. 1979, c. 212, s. 1. See CHAIN ~; CROSS ~; PUBLICITY ~; SECONDARY ~.

PICKET LINE. An area in which picketing is carried on.

PICKING. *n.* In respect of oysters, means the taking of oysters by hand without tools or other implements. Canada regulations.

PICKLED HERRING PLANT. A building, structure, machinery, appurtenances, appliances and apparatus occupied and used in the business of pickling or brine curing herring, or of converting the natural herring into brine cured or pickled herring. *Fisheries Act*, R.S.B.C. 1979, c. 137, s. 12.

PICK OF LAND. The narrow piece of land which runs into a corner.

PICK-POCKET. *var.* PICKPOCKET. *n.* A person who steals by secretly putting hands into another person's pocket or purse.

PICK-PURSE. *n.* A person who steals by secretly putting hands into another person's pocket or purse.

PICNIC. See GROUP ~ AREA.

PICNIC GROUNDS. See PUBLIC ~.

PICO. *pref.* 10⁻¹². Prefix for multiples and submultiples of basic, supplementary and derived units of measurement. *Weights and Measures Act*, S.C. 1970-71-72, c. 36, schedule I.

PICTORIAL RECORD OR DOCUMENT. (a) A bound or attached collection of designs such as a sketch book; or (b) loose or unattached designs that clearly form a single unit of visual information such as a set of architectural plans or blueprints. *Canadian Cultural Property Export Control List*, C.R.C., c. 448, s. 1.

PICTURE. See PRINTED BOOK OF ~S AND DESIGNS.

PICTURE SHOW. See TRAVELLING ~.

PIECE. *n.* 1. A firearm held in the hand. F.A. Jaffe, *A Guide to Pathological Evidence*, 2d ed. (Toronto: Carswell, 1983) at 181. 2. Something which contains drugs. F.A. Jaffe, *A Guide to Pathological Evidence*, 2d ed. (Toronto: Carswell, 1983) at 181. See BY THE ~.

PIECE RATE. See DIFFERENTIAL ~.

PIECE WORK RATE. A rate of pay calculated upon a unit of work performed. *Employment Standards Act*, R.R.O. 1980, Reg. 284, s. 1.

PIER. *n.* A deep foundation unit, made of materials such as wood, steel or concrete or combination thereof, which is either premanufactured and placed by driving, jacking, jetting or screwing, or cast-in-place in a hole formed by driving, excavating or boring. *Building Code Act*, R.R.O. 1980, Reg. 87, s. 1.

PIERAGE. *n.* The toll which a vessel pays for the use of a pier.

PIERCE CORPORATE VEIL. To find corporate officers or directors liable or responsible for acts where the existence of the corporation would ordinarily shield them from liability or responsibility.

PIG. See WEANER ~.

PIGNORATIVE. *adj.* Pawning, pledging.

PIGNUS. See CONTRACT OF ~.

PIKE. *n.* With respect to fish, includes northern pike, (Esox lucius, Linnaeus), great northern pike, grass pike and jackfish. *Ontario Fishery Regulations*, C.R.C., c. 849, s. 2.

PILE. *n.* A slender deep foundation unit, made of materials such as wood, steel or concrete or combination thereof, which is either premanufactured and placed by driving, jacking, jetting or screwing, or cast-in-place in a hole formed by driving, excavating or boring. *Building Code Act*, R.R.O. 1980, Reg. 87, s. 1. See COMPOSITE ~.

PILFERER. *n.* Someone who steals small things.

PILLORY. *n.* A framework which an offender was made to stand behind, with head and hands protruding through its holes.

PILOT. *n.* 1. Any person not belonging to a ship who has the conduct thereof. 2. An employee assigned to a train when the engineman or conductor, or both, are not fully acquainted with the physical characteristics or rules of the railway, or portion of the railway, over which the train is to be moved. *Regulations No. O-8, Uniform Code of Operating Rules*, C.R.C., c. 1175, Part III, s. 2. See APPRENTICE ~; CO-~; LICENSED ~; REGISTERED ~.

PILOTAGE. *n.* 1. The guidance which a pilot provides. 2. The remuneration provided to a pilot. See COMPULSORY ~.

PILOTAGE DUES. The remuneration payable in respect to pilotage. *Canada Shipping Act*, R.S.C. 1970, c. S-9, s. 2.

PILOTAGE DUTIES. The normal duties of a holder of a licence or pilotage certificate. *General Pilotage Regulations*, C.R.C., c. 1263, s. 2.

PILOTAGE UNIT. 1. The figure obtained by multiplying the length of the ship by the breadth of the ship by the depth of the ship and by dividing the product by 283.17. *Atlantic Pilotage Tariff Regulations (1977)*, C.R.C., c. 1265, s. 2. 2. In respect of any ship, the figure obtained by multiplying the squared breadth of the ship in feet by the depth of the ship in feet and by dividing the product by 1,250. *Laurentian Pilotage Tariff Regulations*, C.R.C., c. 1269, s. 2.

PILOT BOARDING STATION. A place used for the purpose of embarking or disembarking pilots. *Pacific Pilotage Regulations*, C.R.C., c. 1270, s. 2.

PILOT FLAG. A flag of large dimensions compared with the size of a pilot vessel, and of two colours, the upper horizontal half, white, and the lower horizontal half, red, or such other flag as may hereafter at any time be adopted as and for a pilot flag. *Canada Shipping Act*, R.S.C. 1970, c. S-9, s. 2.

PILOT-IN-COMMAND. *n.* In relation to an aircraft, the pilot having responsibility and authority for the operation and safety of the aircraft during flight time. *Aeronautics Act*, R.S.C. 1985 (1st Supp.), c. 33, s. 3.

PILOT SERVICE. The transporting of a pilot to a vessel on its arrival at the harbour of Churchill or the transporting of a pilot from a vessel on its departure from the harbour. *Churchill Tug Tariff By-law*, C.R.C., c. 1069, s. 2.

PILOT WHALE. Any whale of the species Globicephala melaena or G. scammonic, commonly known as pothead whale or blackfish. *Whaling Regulations*, C.R.C., c. 1608, s. 2.

PINK SALMON. The species known as Orcorhynchus gorbuscha. *Pacific Salmon Fisheries Convention Act*, R.S.C. 1985, c. F-20, s. 2.

PINT. *n.* 1/8 gallon. *Weights and Measures Act*, S.C. 1970-71-72, c. 36, schedule II.

PINTSCH GAS. The product obtained by "cracking" oil and compressing the oil gas to 10 to 14 atmospheres. *Railway Cars Gas Fuel Systems Regulations*, C.R.C., c. 1165, s. 2.

PIPE. *n.* 1. Includes tube and tubing other than copper tube or tubing and includes fittings. 2. Any tubing or pipe used or intended for the conveyance or distribution of gas, except the connecting piping of an apparatus. 3. A large vein into which one may inject a narcotic. F.A. Jaffe, *A Guide to Pathological Evidence*, 2d ed. (Toronto: Carswell, 1983) at 181. See DISTRIBUTING ~; FLUE ~; GAS ~; WASTE ~.

PIPEFITTER. See STEAMFITTER-~ TRADE.

PIPELINE. *var.* **PIPE LINE.** 1. (i) A pipe for the transmission of any substance, and installations in connection with that pipe; or (ii) a sewer or sewage system and installations in connection with that sewer or sewage system. 2. A flow line, gas line, oil line, mineral line, secondary line, distribution line or private line. 3. Any pipe or any system or arrangement of pipes by which oil, gas or water incidental to the drilling for or production of oil or gas is conveyed from any well-head or other place at which it is produced to any other place, or from any place where it is stored, processed or treated to any other place, and includes all property of any kind used for the purpose of, or in connection with or incidental to, the operation of a pipeline in the gathering, transporting, handling and delivery of oil or gas, and, without restricting the generality of the foregoing, includes offshore installations or vessels, tanks, surface reservoirs, pumps, racks, storage and loading facilities, compressors, compressor stations, pressure measuring and controlling equipment and fixtures, flow controlling and measuring equipment and fixtures, metering equipment and fixtures, and heating, cooling and dehydrating equipment and fixtures, but does not include any pipe or any system or arrangement of pipes that constitutes a distribution system for the distribution of gas to consumers. See COMBINED ~; COMMODITY ~; COMPANY ~; GAS ~; SECONDARY LINE; TRANSMISSION ~.

PIPE LINE COMPANY. *var.* **PIPELINE COMPANY.** Every person, firm, partnership, association or corporation owning or operating a pipe line.

PIPE LINE CORPORATION. A person owning or operating a pipe line, all or any part of which is situate in the province, for the purpose of gathering or transporting natural gas, petroleum or petroleum products. *Assessment Act*, R.S.B.C. 1979, c. 21, s. 1.

PIPELINE GAS. See MARKETABLE ~.

PIPE-MECHANIC. See MASTER ~.

PIPE TAPS. Small diameter pipes tapped into the wall of the pipe at a specified number of main pipe diameters away from the orifice plate, so as to permit the measurement of the gas pressure on the up-stream and down-stream

sides of the orifice. *Gas and Gas Meters Regulations*, C.R.C., c. 876, s. 25.

PIPING. *n.* 1. Includes tube and tubing other than copper tube or tubing and includes fittings. 2. Tubes, conduits and fittings, the sole purpose of which is the conveyance of a gas, vapour or liquid and the control of the flow of a gas, vapour or liquid between two points. See DRAINAGE ~; HOUSE ~; PRESSURE ~; ROUGH ~; STORM DRAINAGE ~.

PIPING INSTALLATION. The installing of any or all of the following systems, to wit: (a) heating systems used for producing motive power or heat in any form whatsoever, in any building or construction; such systems including among others gravity or forced hot water systems, and high, low or vacuum steam systems and likewise any firing system; (b) refrigerating systems for cooling air, chilling substances or making ice; (c) plumbing systems, in any building or construction, including piping and all accessories used for drainage or draining; for back air vent; for supplying hot or cold water or gas; (d) oil or natural gas burner systems but not propane gas burner systems; (e) automatic sprinkler systems utilized to prevent and fight fires in any building or construction. The expression "piping installation" includes moreover any installation defined by the Plumbing Code applied by the board of examiners. *Master Pipe-Mechanics Act*, R.S.Q. 1977, c. M-4, s. 1.

PIPING INSTALLATION WORK. Includes the work of installing, repairing, altering or renewing piping installations. *Master Pipe-Mechanics Act*, R.S.Q. 1977, c. M-4, s. 1.

PIPING SYSTEM. An assembly of pipe, pipe fittings and valves, together with any pumps, compressors and other fixed equipment to which it is connected, that is used for transferring a liquid or gaseous dangerous substance from one location to another. *Canada Dangerous Substances Regulations*, C.R.C., c. 997, s. 2.

PIRACY. *n.* Acts of violence and robbery at sea.

PIRACY EX JURE GENTIUM. Piracy defined by the law of nations, in contrast to offences which a statute declares to be piracy.

PIRATA EST HOSTIS HUMANI GENERIS. [L.] A pirate is the enemy of the human race.

PIRATE. *v.* To encourage employees to change employers by offering higher wage rates.

PIRATES. *n.* Includes passengers who mutiny and rioters who attack the ship from the shore. *Insurance Act*, R.S.N.S. 1967, c. 148, s. 273.

PIRATICAL ACTS. (a) Stealing a Canadian ship; (b) stealing or without lawful authority throwing overboard, damaging or destroying anything that is part of the cargo, supplies or fittings in a Canadian ship; (c) doing or attempting to do a mutinous act on a Canadian ship or (d) counselling a person to do anything mentioned in paragraph (a), (b) or (c). *Criminal Code*, R.S.C. 1985, c. C-46, s. 75 as am. by R.S.C. 1985 (1st Supp.), c. 27, s. 7(3)

PISCARY. *n.* A right of freedom to fish.

PIT. *n.* A place where unconsolidated gravel, stone, sand, earth, clay, fill, mineral or other material is being or has been removed by means of an open excavation to supply material for construction, industrial or manufacturing purposes. See COCK ~; OPEN ~; WAYSIDE ~.

PITH AND SUBSTANCE. Variously described as the matter, essence of the constitutional value which challenged legislation represents, the content or subject matter, leading feature or true nature and character of a law. P.W. Hogg, *Constitutional Law of Canada*, 2d ed. (Toronto: Carswell, 1985) at 313.

PIT HEAD. A landing at the top of a shaft or slope or at any other surface entrance in an underground mine. *Coal Mines Regulation Act*, R.S.A. 1970, c. 52, s. 2.

PIT'S MOUTH. The loading point at ground level of the conveyor or other transportation facility that delivers a mineral substance to the pick-up point for shipment from the mine property to market or that delivers it to the processing plant. *Mining Tax Act*, R.R.O. 1980, Reg. 639, s. 1.

PL. *abbr.* [L.] Placitum. Any point decided in a judgment summarized by the reporter.

PLACARD. *n.* An advertisement; declaration; edict; public notice.

PLACART. *n.* An advertisement; declaration; edict; public notice.

PLACE. *v.* To transfer a child from the care and control of one person or agency to another person or agency.

PLACE. *n.* (a) A dwelling-house; (b) a building or structure or any part thereof, other than a dwelling-house; (c) a railway vehicle, a vessel, an aircraft or a trailer; or (d) a pen or an enclosure in which fur-bearing animals are kept in captivity for breeding or commercial purposes. See HISTORIC ~; IN ~; NON-CON-FORMING ~; POLLING ~; PRIVATE ~; PROHIBITED ~; PUBLIC ~; REGULATED ~; WORKING ~; WORK~.

PLACEMENT. *n.* Transferring a child from the custody of one person or agency to the custody of another. See CHICKS-FOR-~; PRIVATE ~.

PLACEMENT AGENCY. Includes any person or organization that is engaged in the business of placing individuals in employment or of securing employment for individuals for a fee, reward or other remuneration. *Canada Pension Plan Regulations*, C.R.C., c. 385, s. 34.

PLACENTA. *n.* A flat, round organ where the embryo is implanted which contains both fetal and maternal blood vessels and through which an embryo receives nourishment and oxygen. F.A. Jaffe, *A Guide to Pathological Evidence*, 2d ed. (Toronto: Carswell, 1983) at 181 and 182.

PLACE OF ABODE. The place where one resides. See USUAL ~.

PLACE OF AMUSEMENT. A building, hall, pavilion, place, premises, room, tent or structure of any kind or park, field or grounds where an amusement takes place for which an admission price is charged or collected, whether within the premises or elsewhere, in cash or by means of tickets or otherwise, and includes (i) a theatre, travelling picture show, open air theatre, amusement hall, entertainment hall, music hall or concert hall; (ii) a hall, pavilion, place, premises, room, tent or structure of any kind kept or used for public concerts, carnival shows, dances or other social gatherings; (iii) a dance hall, dance pavilion, hotel, restaurant or café in which facilities are supplied and used for public dancing; (iv) a circus, menagerie, midway, grandstand, race track, race course or place where a pari mutuel system of betting is operated; (v) a hockey rink, skating rink or roller skating rink, or a park, field or grounds used for athletics, baseball, football or other games; and (vi) a hall or grounds used for a boxing or wrestling contest.

PLACE OF ASSEMBLY. 1. Includes a building or structure, or a portion thereof, and a tent or awning with walls or side curtains designed, used or intended to be used to accommodate 50 or more persons at the same time for the purpose of meetings, entertainment, instruction, worship, recreation, drill, or the viewing or purchasing of goods. *Fire Prevention Act*, R.S.N.B. 1973, c. F-13, s. 1. 2. A floor area that has an occupant load based on 15 square feet or less per person, as designated herein. *Hotel Fire Safety Act*, R.R.O. 1980, Reg. 505, s. 2.

PLACE OF BUSINESS. See ESTABLISHED ~.

PLACE OF CUSTODY. A place designated pursuant to the Federal Young Offenders Act as a place of open custody.

PLACE OF DESTINATION. (a) The boom or rafting ground where the logs are rafted or sorted, in the case of logs or timber driven down a river or stream; (b) the mill or mill pond, in the case where the logs or timber are hauled from the woods or brought by railway to a mill or the pond in connection therewith or driven in the stream to a mill or mill pond without first being rafted or sorted; and (c) any other place where logs or timber are brought for the purpose of being manufactured or sawn or otherwise used. *Woodsmen's Lien Act*, R.S.N.B. 1973, c. W-12, s. 1.

PLACE OF DETENTION. A hospital, sanatorium, correctional institution, lock-up, reformatory, or any place designated as a place of detention by the Lieutenant Governor in Council. Venereal Diseases Prevention acts.

PLACE OF DOMICILE. The place in which one has one's home or in which one resides or to which one returns as one's place of permanent abode and does not mean a place in which one stays for a mere special or temporary purpose.

PLACE OF EMPLOYMENT. Any building, structure, premises, water or land where work is carried on by one or more employees, and includes a project site and a mine.

PLACE OF ENTERTAINMENT. 1. Includes a theatre, moving-picture hall, amusement hall, concert hall, circus, race course, baseball park, athletic ground, skating rink, dance hall, or any hotel, restaurant, club or café in which facilities are supplied for and used by the public for dancing or any other place where an entrance or other fee or other charge is charged or collected and such other places as the council may declare to be places of entertainment. *Local Government Act*, S.Nfld. 1972, c. 32, s. 86. 2. Any building, structure, tent, enclosure or area used in the entertainment of the people who attend thereat. *Entertainments Act*, R.S.P.E.I. 1974, c. E-7, s. 1.

PLACE OF OPEN CUSTODY. A place or facility designated as a place of open custody under subsection 24(1) of the Young Offenders Act (Canada).

PLACE OF OPEN TEMPORARY DETENTION. A place of temporary detention in which the Minister has established an open detention program. Ontario statutes.

PLACE OF ORDINARY RESIDENCE. Generally, the place that has always been, or that he has adopted as, the place of his habitation or home, to which he intends to return when he is away from it and, where a person usually sleeps in one place and has his meals or is employed in another place, the place of his ordinary residence is where the person sleeps. *Canada Elections Act*, R.S.C. 1970 (1st Supp.), c. 14, s. 17.

PLACE OF PUBLIC RESORT. A building used, or constructed or adapted to be used, either ordinarily or occasionally, as a church, chapel or other place of public worship (not being merely a dwelling-house so used), or as an orphanage, school, theatre, public hall, public concert room, public ballroom, public lecture room, or public exhibition room, or as a public place of assembly for persons admitted thereto by tickets or by payment, or used, or constructed or adapted to be used, either ordinarily or occasionally, for any other public purpose, but shall not include a private dwelling house used occasionally or exceptionally for any of those purposes. *Egress from Buildings Act*, R.S.Nfld. 1970, c. 105, s. 2.

PLACE OF SAFETY. Any place used for the emergency temporary care and protection of a child.

PLACE OF SECURE CUSTODY. A place or facility designated for the secure containment or restraint of young persons under subsection 24 (1) of the Young Offenders Act (Canada).

PLACE OF SECURE TEMPORARY DETENTION. A place of temporary detention in which the Minister has established a secure detention program. Ontario statutes.

PLACE OF TEMPORARY DETENTION. A place or facility designated as a place of temporary detention under subsection 7(1) of the Young Offenders Act (Canada).

PLACE POOL. The monies bet on horses selected to finish either first or second in a race. *Race Track Supervision Regulations*, C.R.C., c. 441, s. 2.

PLACER MINERAL. Gold, platinum, precious stones, cassiterite or other valuable minerals occurring in unconsolidated superficial deposits. *Mines Act*, R.S.N.S. 1967, c. 185, s. 57.

PLACER MINING. Includes every mode and method of working whatever whereby earth, soil, gravel or cement may be removed, washed, shifted or refined or otherwise dealt with, for the purpose of obtaining gold or other precious minerals or stones, but does not include the working of rock on the site.

PLACES OF PUBLIC ACCOMMODATION. Public hotels, boarding houses, restaurants, sample rooms and rest and reading rooms. *The Urban Municipality Act*, R.S.S. 1978, c. U-10, s. 2.

PLACIT. *n.* A decree; a decision.

PLACITA CORONAE. [L.] The Crown's pleas.

PLACITARE. [L.] To plead.

PLACITATOR. *n.* One who pleads.

PLACITORY. *adj.* Relating to a pleading or plea.

PLACITUM. *n.* [L.] Any point decided in a judgment summarized by the reporter.

PLACITUM ALIUD PERSONALE, ALIUD REALE, ALIUD MIXTUM. [L.] A plea is either personal, real or mixed.

PLACITUM NOMINATUM. [L.] The day designated for an accused person to appear, plead and defend.

PLAGIARISM. *n.* The act of publishing the thought or writing of someone else as one's own.

PLAGIARIST. *n.* One who publishes the thought or writing of someone else as one's own.

PLAGUE. *n.* Pestilence; a malignant, contagious fever.

PLAICE. See AMERICAN ~.

PLAINANT. *n.* A plaintiff.

PLAIN MASONRY. Masonry without steel reinforcement. *Building Code Act*, R.R.O. 1980, Reg. 87, s. 1.

PLAINT. *n.* The written statement of a cause of action.

PLAINTIFF. *n.* 1. A person who commences an action. 2. A person at whose instance a summons is issued. 3. Includes every person asking for any relief, otherwise than by way of counter-claim as a defendant, against any other person by any form of proceeding. 4. Includes a person asking any relief against any other person in an action. 5. Includes a defendant counterclaiming.

PLAN. *n.* 1. The map of a piece of real property divided into lots and parcels. 2. (i) A map, including any profile or section, of a mine or part of a mine, certified by the mine surveyor to be correct; or (ii) a reproduction of such a map. 3. Includes any drawn or written description, illustration or explanation of any construction. 4. A pension, retirement, welfare, or profit-sharing fund, trust, scheme, arrangement, or other plan established for the purpose of providing pensions, retirement allowances, annuities, or sickness, death, or other benefits to, or for the benefit of, employees, former employees, agents, and former agents of an employer, or any of them, and for the widows, dependants, or other beneficiaries of any of them. 5. A plan to provide for the control and regulation of the marketing of a farm product. See ACTION AREA ~; ASSIGNED RISK ~; BENEFITS ~; CANADA ASSISTANCE ~; CANADA PENSION ~; COMPENSATION ~; CONDOMINIUM ~; CONSTANT WAGE ~; CONTRACTUAL ~; COOPERATIVE ~; DEFINED CONTRIBUTION ~; DEVELOPMENT ~; DISABILITY ~; DISTRICT ~; DUPLICATE ~; ECONOMIC ~; EXPLANATORY ~; FARM INCOME ~; FOREST MANAGEMENT ~; GOVERNMENT ~; INDIRECT INCENTIVE ~; INSURED ~; JOINT EARNINGS ~; LAND USE ~; LIFE INSURANCE ~; MANAGEMENT ~; MARKETING ~; MASTER ~; MONEY ACCUMULATION ~; MONEY PURCHASE ~; MULTI-EMPLOYER ~; MULTIPLE USE ~; OFFICIAL ~; ORIGINAL ~; PENSION ~; PREARRANGED FUNERAL ~; PRENEED CEMETERY ~; PROFIT SHARING ~; REDEVELOPMENT ~; REFERENCE ~; REGIONAL ~; REPLACEMENT ~; SIMILAR ~; SKETCH ~; STOCK SAVINGS ~; STRUCTURAL ~S; SUPPLEMENTAL ~; TRANSPORTATION ~.

PLANE. See GYRO~; INCLINED ~; LAND~.

PLAN HOLDER. *var.* **PLANHOLDER.** A person, not being a corporation, who has entered into a retirement savings plan with a trustee or with an investment corporation.

PLANNED GRAZING SYSTEM. A system approved by the regional manager respecting the use of land for grazing and the dispersal of livestock over land. *Range Act*, R.S.B.C. 1979, c. 355, s. 1.

PLANNED UNIT DEVELOPMENT. Development of land by a method of subdividing land whereby the land is specifically subdivided for the uses and purposes specified in the proposed plan of subdivision, as approved. *The Planning and Development Act*, R.S.S. 1978, c. P-13, s. 2.

PLANNING. See EMERGENCY ~ CANADA; ESTATE ~.

PLANNING OFFICE. See COMMUNITY ~.

PLANNING SCHEME. A statement of policy with respect to the use and development of land and the use, erection, construction, relocation and enlargement of buildings within a defined area.

PLAN OF DEVELOPMENT. See COMPREHENSIVE ~.

PLAN OF SUBDIVISION. A plan by which the owner of land divides the land into areas designated on the plan.

PLANS AND SPECIFICATIONS. Includes all books, papers, plans, specifications, drawings and documents that relate to the construction, installation, erection or use of electrical equipment, or that are material for the purpose of inspection or examination under this Act. *Electrical Energy Inspection Act*, R.S.B.C. 1979, c. 104, s. 1.

PLAN SHARE. A share, the certificate for which is, under this Act, required to be held in trust by an administrator. *Equity Investment Plan Act*, S.B.C. 1985, c. 71, s. 1.

PLANT. *n.* 1. Any establishment, works, or undertaking, in or about any industry. 2. An organism usually deriving part of its sustenance by photosynthesis and part by root sorption and includes parasitic plants, trees, shrubs, weeds, grasses, ferns, mosses and micro-organisms. *Pest Control Products (Nova Scotia) Act*, S.N.S. 1986, c. 16, s. 3. 3. An installation of any combination of boilers and pressure vessels, together with pipes, fittings, machinery and other equipment that is used to contain a gas, vapour or liquid under pressure. 4. A premises where cattle are slaughtered. 5. The premises on which are situated the fixtures, implements, machinery or apparatus used in carrying on any activity of a manufacturer. 6. Any tree, shrub, vine, tuber, bulb, corm, rhizome or root, or the fruit or any other part of any of them. See ABSORPTION ~; ANIMAL FOOD ~; AQUACULTURAL ~; AQUATIC ~; ASPHALT PAVING ~; BOILER ~; BULK ~; CANNED POTATO PRODUCTS ~; COLD STORAGE ~; COMPRESSED-AIR ~; COMPRESSED GAS ~; COMPRESSOR ~; CONCENTRATED MILK ~; CONTINU-OUSLY-OPERATING ~; DAIRY ~; DEHY-DRATED POTATO PRODUCTS ~; DOGFISH REDUCTION ~; EXTRACTION ~; FISH-BREEDING ~; FISH ~; FROZEN POTATO PRODUCTS ~; GUARDED ~; HEATING ~; HOISTING ~; ICE CREAM ~; INDUSTRIAL ~; LOCKER ~; MANUFACTURING ~; MARINE ~; MARKETING ~; MEAT ~; MIN-ING ~; PACKING ~; PICKLED HERRING ~; POTATO CHIP ~; POWER ~; PRESSURE ~; PROCESS CHEESE ~; PROCESSING ~; RECEIVING ~; REFRIGERATING ~; REFRIGERATION ~; REFRIGERATOR ~; RENDERING ~; SCRUBBING ~; SEA ~; SEMI-FABRICATING ~; STARCH ~; STEAM ~; STEAM-POWERED ~; TRANSPORTA-TION ~; USED BOILER, PRESSURE VESSEL OR ~.

PLANTATION. *n.* A British colony in North America or in the West Indies. See CHRIST-MAS TREE ~; FOREST ~.

PLANT DISEASE. Any disease or injury of a plant that is caused by an insect, virus, fungus, bacterium or other organism and that is designated a plant disease in the regulations. Plant Diseases acts.

PLANT FOSSIL. The fossilized remains of vegetable matter. *Canadian Cultural Property Export Control List*, C.R.C., c. 448, s. 1.

PLANT GROWTH REGULATOR. Any sub-stance or mixture of substances that, through physiological action, accelerates or alters the behaviour of plants, but does not include a plant nutrient, a trace element, plant inoculant or a soil amendment. *Pesticides Control Act, 1983*, S.Nfld. 1983, c. 52, s. 2.

PLANT INDICATOR HOST. Any plant that may indicate a virus or other pathogenic infec-tion after inoculation by sap, vector, scion graft or other means from a plant being tested. *Seeds Regulations*, C.R.C., c. 1400, s. 45.

PLANTING. See RE ~.

PLANT LIQUIDS. Hydrocarbon liquids recov-ered from natural gas other than by normal field 2 phase separation. *Petroleum and Natural Gas Act*, R.S.B.C. 1979, c. 323, s. 1.

PLANT NUTRIENT. See LESSER ~; MAJOR ~.

PLANT OR OTHER MATTER. Any plant, plant material, material, equipment, carrier, con-tainer, article or other thing that may contain or carry any pest. *Plant Quarantine Act*, R.S.C. 1985, c. P-15, s. 2.

PLANT PROTECTION EMPLOYEE. A secu-rity guard.

PLANT RETIRED. A plant, whether replaced or not, that is sold, abandoned, demolished, dismantled or otherwise withdrawn from pipe-line service. Pipeline Uniform Accounting reg-ulations.

PLANT SYSTEM. The series of pipes and fittings, prime movers, machinery and other equipment for the transfer or conversion of heat energy produced by a boiler. *Power Engineers Act*, S.P.E.I. 1977, c. 29, s. 1.

PLANT UNIT. A plant-wide unit for collective bargaining purposes.

PLASMA. *n.* A state of matter characterized by disorganization of atoms at a very high temper-ature and which may exhibit a particular behav-iour in an electric or magnetic field. *Environment Quality Act*, R.S.Q. 1977, c. Q-2, s. 1.

PLASTERER. *n.* A person who, (i) applies plaster and stucco to the walls and ceilings, whether interior or exterior, of a structure; (ii) applies plaster and stucco on lath, masonry and rigid insulation; and (iii) tapes gyproc and wall-board. *Apprenticeship and Tradesmen's Qualifi-cation Act*, R.R.O. 1980, Reg. 51, s. 1.

PLATE. *n.* 1. Any stereotype or other plate, stone, block, mould, matrix, transfer or negative used or intended to be used for printing or reproducing copies of any work, and any matrix or other appliance by which records, perforated rolls or other contrivances for the acoustic representation of the work are, or are intended to be made. *Copyright Act*, R.S.C. 1985, c. C-42, s. 2. 2. When applied to iron or steel, means a flat-rolled product of any shape (a) having a width of more than 8 inches but not more than 48 inches, and a thickness of .23 inch or more; or (b) having a width of more than 48 inches and a thickness of .18 inch or more. *Customs Tariff*, R.S.C. 1985, c. C-54, s. 2. 3. An externally mounted, clearly visible device identifying a permit holder's vehicle issued in conjunction with the permit. *Government Airport Concession Operations Regulations*, C.R.C., c. 1565, s. 2. See DEALER'S ~; LICENCE ~; NUMBER ~; REGISTRATION ~.

PLATE COUNT. See STANDARD ~.

PLATED ARTICLE. An article composed of any substance on the surface of which a layer or plating of a precious metal is deposited or plated by means of a chemical, electrical, mechanical or metallurgical process or by means of a combination of any of those processes, and an article composed of an inferior metal to the surface of which a covering or sheeting of a precious metal is fixed by brazing, soldering or by any mechanical means. *Precious Metals Marking Act*, R.S.C. 1985, c. P-19, s. 2.

PLATE GLASS INSURANCE. Insurance, not being insurance incidental to some other class of insurance defined by or under an act, against loss of or damage to plate, sheet or window glass, whether in place or in transit.

PLATFORM. See DIVING ~; PRODUCTION ~.

PLAYGROUND ZONE. A zone on a highway identified by a traffic control device as an area where children (a) may be expected to be on the highway; or (b) are permitted to cross the highway at a designated point along the highway. *Highway Traffic Act*, R.S.A. 1980, c. H-7, s. 72.

PLEA. *n.* 1. An action or suit, a way to put forward a defence in certain proceedings. 2. A defendant's factual answer to a plaintiff's declaration. See NON-ISSUABLE ~.

PLEA BARGAIN. For an accused person to agree to plead guilty, or to give material information or testimony in exchange for an apparent advantage which the prosecutor offers, acting within the scope of a prosecutor's seeming authority. S.A. Cohen, *Due Process of Law* (Toronto: Carswell, 1977) at 179.

PLEAD. *v.* 1. To allege something in a cause. 2. To argue a case in court.

PLEADER. *n.* One who elaborates a plea. See FAINT ~.

PLEADING. *n.* 1. The process in which parties to an action alternately present written statements of their contentions, each one responding to the preceding statement, and each statement attempting to better define the controversial areas. 2. Includes a petition or summons, other than a writ of summons, and also the statement in writing of the claim or demand of a plaintiff, and of the defence or the counterclaim of a defendant thereto, and of the reply of the plaintiff to a defence or counterclaim of a defendant, and of the defendant's rejoinder to such reply. See CLOSE OF ~S; MIS~; RULES OF ~.

PLEAD OVER. To reply to an opponent's pleading but to overlook a defect to which one might have taken exception.

PLEA IN ABATEMENT. A common law plea which raises a matter like the inability of a party to sue or be sued, the non-joinder of parties or another action which is pending concerning the same subject matter. G.D. Watson & C. Perkins, eds., *Holmested & Watson: Ontario Civil Procedure* (Toronto: Carswell, 1984) at 25-21.

PLEA NEGOTIATION. For an accused person to agree to plead guilty, or to give material information or testimony in exchange for an apparent advantage which the prosecutor offers, acting within the scope of a prosecutor's seeming authority. S.A. Cohen, *Due Process of Law* (Toronto: Carswell, 1977) at 179.

PLEA OF PARDON. A plea that a pardon is a bar to an indictment, after the verdict is a bar to a judgment, or after the judgment is a bar to execution. S. Mitchell, P.J. Richardson & D.A. Thomas, eds., *Archbold Pleading, Evidence and Practice in Criminal Cases*, 43d ed. (London: Sweet & Maxwell, 1988) at 368.

PLEA OF THE CROWN. In criminal law, an offence triable only in the monarch's courts.

PLEASURE BOAT. A boat used primarily for the carriage of a person or persons for pleasure, whether on charter or not, and whether for compensation or not, and includes a boat used on water for living purposes.

PLEASURE CRAFT. 1. A watercraft for use for relaxation or sport whether or not it is chartered to another person for that use. *Insurance Premium Tax Act*, S.B.C. 1985, c. 28, s. 1. 2. Includes any aircraft or vessel used for health or pleasure purposes but does not include an aircraft or a vessel operated in the business of carrying passengers or goods for compensation. *Non-Residents' Pleasure Craft Regulations*, C.R.C., c. 471, s. 2.

PLEASURE CRAFT INSURANCE. (a) Personal property insurance in respect of pleasure craft; and (b) insurance against liability arising out of (i) bodily injury to or the death of a person; or (ii) loss of or damage to property caused by a pleasure craft or the use or operation of it. *Insurance Premium Tax Act*, S.B.C. 1985, c. 28, s. 1.

PLEASURE VEHICLE. 1. Equipped for the transportation of persons, not more than seven at a time, effects such transportation without any pecuniary consideration, and includes a motor-cycle, with or without a side-car. *Highway Code*, R.S.Q. 1977, c. C-24, s. 1. 2. Any vehicle equipped mainly for the transportation of not more than nine persons at the same time. *Fuel Tax Act*, R.S.Q. 1977, c. T-1, s. 1.

PLEASURE VESSEL. A vessel being used for pleasure and not carrying persons or goods for hire or reward, and includes a vessel chartered or hired by or on behalf of the persons carried thereon. *Navigating Appliances Regulations*, C.R.C., c. 1449, s. 2.

PLEASURE YACHT. A ship however propelled that is used exclusively for pleasure and does not carry passengers. *Canada Shipping Act*, R.S.C. 1985, c. S-9, s. 2.

PLEBISCITE. *n.* The referral of an issue to the population to decide by vote.

PLEBISCITE OFFICER. The returning officer, assistant returning officer, deputy returning officer, poll clerk and enumerator and, except for the Chief Plebiscite Officer and the Deputy Chief Plebiscite Officer, includes every person who has a duty to perform pursuant to an act.

PLEDGE. *n.* 1. Includes any contract pledging, or giving a lien or security on, goods, whether in consideration of an original advance or of any further or continuing advance, or of any pecuniary liability. 2. An article pawned with a pawnbroker. 3. A debtor's bailment of goods, to be kept until the debt is paid, to a creditor. See DEAD ~; HARMONY ~.

PLEDGEE. *n.* A person who receives a pledge; a pawnee.

PLEDGERY. *n.* The state of being a surety.

PLEDGOR. *n.* A person who offers a pledge; a pawner.

PLEGII DE PROSEQUENDO. Promises to prosecute in order to effect an action of replevin.

PLEGII DE RETORNO HABENDO. Promises to return something which was distrained, if the right is determined against the party who brought the action of replevin.

PLENA FORISFACTURA. [L.] The forfeiture of all of someone's possessions.

PLENARY. *adj.* Complete, full; describes a proceeding with formal steps and gradations, in contrast to summary.

PLENE ADMINISTRAVIT. [L. one has fully administered] An executor's or administrator's defence that that person fully administered all the assets which that person received.

PLENE ADMINISTRAVIT PRAETER. [L. one has fully administered, except] An executor's or administrator's defence that that person fully administered all the assets which that person received with some exceptions.

PLENIPOTENTIARY. *n.* One who has complete power and authority to do anything.

PLENO LUMINE. See IN ~.

PLENUM. *n.* An air compartment or chamber which may have one or more ducts connected to it and which forms part of an air distribution system.

PLEURA. *n.* A membrane which lines the chest interior and covers the lungs. F.A. Jaffe, *A Guide to Pathological Evidence*, 2d ed. (Toronto: Carswell, 1983) at 182.

PLEURAL. *adj.* Of the chest. F.A. Jaffe, *A Guide to Pathological Evidence*, 2d ed. (Toronto: Carswell, 1983) at 19.

PLIABLE ARMORED CABLE. A cable similar in construction to a trailing cable and protected against mechanical injury by an armoring of stranded galvanized steel wires and further protected by an over-all covering of tough insulation; such cables may or may not include a grounding conductor. *Coal Mines Regulation Act*, R.S.N.S. 1967, c. 36, s. 84.

PLIGHT. *n.* An estate, with the quality of land; it included rent-charge and possible dower.

PLIMSOLL MARK. The mark or load line on the side of a ship which marks the depth to which she may sink when loaded with her proper cargo.

PLOT. *n.* A lot as numbered and shown on the plan of survey by which the cemetery has been subdivided. *National Parks Cemetery Regulations*, C.R.C., c. 1117, s. 2.

PLUMBER. *n.* A person who, (i) lays out, assembles, installs, maintains or repairs in any structure, building or site, piping, fixtures and appurtenances for the supply of water for any domestic or industrial purpose or for the disposal of water that has been used for any domestic or industrial purpose; (ii) connects to piping any appliance that uses water supplied to it or disposes of waste; (iii) installs the piping for any process, including the conveyance of gas, or any tubing for a pneumatic or air-handling system; (iv) makes joints in piping; or (v) reads and understands design drawings, manufacturers' literature and installation diagrams for piping and appliances connected thereto, but does not include a person engaged in: (vi) the manufacture of equipment or the assembly of a unit prior to delivery to a building, structure or site; (vii) the laying of metallic or non-metallic pipe into trenches to form sanitary or storm sewers, drains or water mains; or (viii) the repair and maintenance of the installations in an operating industrial plant. *Apprenticeship and Tradesmen's Qualification Act*, R.R.O. 1980, Reg. 52, s. 1. See MASTER ~; QUALIFIED ~.

PLUMBING. *n.* (i) A system of connected piping, fittings, valves and appurtenances that receives water from a source of supply that is on a property or from a public watermain and conveys the water into and within a building or to a place of use on the property and where the source is on the property, that commences at the source of supply or at the property line and includes all tanks, pumps, heaters, coils, strainers and treatment devices designed to make physical, chemical or bacteriological changes in the water being conveyed; (ii) fixtures; (iii) drainage piping, including all traps, fittings and appurtenances; (iv) storm drainage piping, including all traps, fittings and appurtenances, and (v) a vent system, including all fittings and appurtenances, but does not include: (vi) any system of piping; A. for space heating wherein water is used as a medium to transfer heat; B. in which liquids or vapours are circulated for the purpose of cooling or refrigeration; C. through which air is passed for the purpose of controlling the temperature, humidity or motion of the air passing through the system; D. that consists wholly or partly of piping that conveys water primarily for the purpose of fire control; E. that conveys water for the purpose of providing water or nutrients to the soil; F. that conveys water for the purpose of landscaping or for the care of animals, birds or fish; G. that transmits force by means of water or by means of a liquid other than water in which water is used for cooling; H. that conveys liquids for the purpose of melting ice or snow; I. that uses water in the conveyance of flammable gas for fuel; or (vii) a well, a well pump installed for the purpose of conveying water from the well, a pressure tank and pump if the tank and pump are combined as a unit, the piping between any well pump and the well, the piping between a well pump and a pressure tank that is installed separate from the pump and the connection of the piping to such pressure tank, and where there is no well pump, any piping connected to the well for a distance of 3 feet from the outside wall of the well.

PLUMBING CONTRACTOR. A person who for reward undertakes by verbal or written agreement or otherwise to supply a plumbing service. *The Plumbing Contractors Licensing Act*, R.S.S. 1978, c. P-14, s. 2.

PLUMBING EQUIPMENT. (i) Any piping, equipment, appliance or device used or intended to be used in a plumbing system; and (ii) any other thing defined as plumbing equipment in the regulations. *Plumbing and Drainage Act*, R.S.A. 1980, c. P-10, s. 1.

PLUMBING SERVICE. Any work with respect to the installation, repair or renewal of a plumbing system, together with piping and other materials forming part of the system. *The Plumbing Contractors Licensing Act*, R.S.S. 1978, c. P-14, s. 2.

PLUMBING SYSTEM. A drainage system, a venting system and a water system.

PLUNDERAGE. *n.* Embezzling goods while they are on board ship.

PLURAL. *adj.* Referring to more than one.

PLURALITY. *n.* A greater number.

PLURES COHAEREDES SUNT QUASI UNUM CORPUS PROPTER UNITATEM JURIS QUOD HABENT. [L.] Several co-heirs are almost one body because of the unity of right they hold.

PLURES PARTICIPES SUNT QUASI UNUM CORPUS, IN EO QUOD UNUM JUS HABENT. [L.] Several people sharing are almost one body, in that they hold one right.

PLURIES WRIT. A third or subsequent writ. C.R.B. Dunlop, *Creditor-Debtor Law in Canada* (Toronto: Carswell, 1981) at 363.

PLUS 25 MICRON FRACTION. That part of the total particulate in the effluent gas stream of which the nominal diameter is greater than 25 microns. *Environmental Protection Act*, R.R.O. 1980, Reg. 295, s. 1.

PLUS VALET QUOD AGITUR QUAM QUOD SIMULATE CONCIPITUR. [L.] What is done is worth more than what is pretended.

PLUS VALET UNUS OCULATUS TESTIS QUAM AURITI DECEM. [L.] One eyewitness is worth more than ten witnesses who report hearsay only.

PLUS VALET VULGARIS CONSUETUDO QUAM REGALIS CONCESSIO. [L.] Common custom is worth more than a royal grant.

PLY. *n.* A layer of rubber-coated parallel cords. Canada regulations.

PLY SEPARATION. The parting of the rubber

compound between adjacent plies of a tire. Canada regulations.

P.M. *abbr.* 1. Post-meridiem, afternoon. 2. Prime Minister.

P.N.E. *abbr.* Pacific National Exhibition.

PNEUMATIC TIRE. 1. Every tire that is designed to support a load by compressed air. 2. A device made of rubber, chemicals, fabric or steel or other materials that, when mounted on an automotive wheel, provides traction and contains the gas or fluid that sustains the load. *Motor Vehicle Safety Regulations*, C.R.C., c. 1038, s. 110.

PNEUMOCONIOSIS. *var.* **PNEUMONOCO-NIOSIS.** *n.* A diseased condition characterized by generalized changes in the fibres in the lungs caused by breathing air containing siliceous dust. This term includes the diseases called "silicosis" and "asbestosis". See COAL MINERS'.

PNEUMOTHORAX. *n.* Air in the cavity of the chest. F.A. Jaffe, *A Guide to Pathological Evidence*, 2d ed. (Toronto: Carswell, 1983) at 182.

P.O. *abbr.* Post office.

POACH. *v.* To unlawfully take or destroy game on another person's land.

PODIATRIST. *n.* A person who practises or advertises or holds himself out in any way as practising podiatry and massage in connection therewith. *An Act Respecting Podiatry*, S.N.B. 1983, c. 101, s. 2(1).

PODIATRY. *n.* (i) Means the branch of the healing arts that treats all ailments, diseased conditions, deformities and injuries of the human foot and the leg muscles controlling the foot; and (ii) includes the examination, diagnosis and treatment of those ailments, conditions, deformities or injuries; but (iii) does not include the treatment of systemic diseases of bones, muscles or ligaments, or the use of X-ray equipment for purposes other than diagnostic, or the use of anaesthetics other than local. *Podiatry Act*, R.S.A. 1980, c. P-11, s. 1.

POENA. *n.* [L.] A punishment, a penalty.

POENAE POTIUS MOLLIENDAE QUAM EXASPERANDAE SUNT. [L.] Punishments should be softened more than aggravated.

POENA EX DELICTO DEFUNCTI, HAERES TENERI NON DEBET. [L.] An heir should not be penalized for a wrong done by a defunct.

P.O.G.G. *abbr.* Peace, order and good government. See RESIDUARY POWER.

POINT. *n.* In respect of a unit toll commercial air service, means the city, town or place spec-

ified in a licence that an air carrier is authorized to serve by such licence and that is identified where necessary by reference to latitude and longitude and that, (a) in respect of a point in a Class 1 licence, comprises an area 25 miles in radius measured from the main post office of such point or from the latitude and longitude of such point; and (b) in respect of a point in a Class 2 licence, comprises an area 10 miles in radius measured from the main post office of such point or from the latitude and longitude of such point. *Air Carrier Regulations*, C.R.C., c. 3, s. 2. See ASCERTAINABLE ~; CENTRE ~ OF AN INTERSECTION; DEMERIT ~; DYE-~; FLASH ~; GENERAL MEASUREMENT ~; H-~; INLAND ~; INSPECTION ~; MOOT ~; POSTAL CONSOLIDATION ~; REFERENCE ~; SHIPPING ~; UNDISPUTED ~.

POINTED. *adj.* As applied to fur, means that hairs from any other peltry have been attached individually or in small groups to such fur. *Fur Garments Labelling Regulations*, C.R.C., c. 1138, s. 2.

POINT OF EMISSION. The point at which a contaminant enters the natural environment. *Environmental Protection Act*, R.R.O. 1980, Reg. 308, s. 1.

POINT OF INTERSECTION. The point at which the centre lines of such roads or highways intersect, and in the case of a road or highway intersecting with a railroad the point of intersection is the point at which the centre line of the road intersects with the centre line of the railroad. *Roads Act*, R.S.P.E.I. 1974, c. R-15, s. 41.

POISON. *n.* Drugs or chemicals, or compounds thereof, that are dangerous to human or animal health or life.

POISONING. *n.* The presence, in a body, of any harmful substance which, indirectly or directly, caused death. F.A. Jaffe, *A Guide to Pathological Evidence*, 2d ed. (Toronto: Carswell, 1983) at 59.

POLAR FLIGHT. A flight traversing that part of Canada between 75° and 115° west longitude and 49° and 85° north latitude. *National Defence Aerodrome Fees Regulations*, C.R.C., c. 714, s. 2.

POLARIS. *abbr.* Province of Ontario Land Registration and Information Service.

POLE. *n.* 5 1/2 yards. *Weights and Measures Act*, S.C. 1970-71-72, c. 36, schedule II. See CATCH~; FAIR START ~; SPRING ~.

POLE KILOMETRE. A lineal kilometre in a telephone system necessarily occupied by telephone poles strung with one or more wires for the use of the telephone system. *Telephone (Rural) Act*, R.S.B.C. 1979, c. 402, s. 1.

POLE TRAILER. A vehicle without motive power that is designed to be drawn by another vehicle and to be attached to the towing vehicle by means of a reach or pole, or by being boomed or otherwise secured to the towing vehicle and is ordinarily used for transporting poles, pipes, structural members or other long or irregularly shaped loads which are capable of sustaining themselves as beams between the supporting connections.

POLICE. *n.* A force of people charged with maintenance of public order, detection, and prevention of crime. See BRIDGE ~; ROYAL CANADIAN MOUNTED ~.

POLICE ASSOCIATION. An association of either (i) the police officers of a municipal police force who hold the rank of inspector or higher, excluding the chief constable and deputy chief constables; or (ii) the police officers of a municipal police force who hold ranks lower than that of inspector that is limited to members of one municipal police force and has collective bargaining among its objects. *Police Officers Collective Bargaining Act*, S.A. 1983, c. P-12.05, c. 1.

POLICE COURT. The court of a magistrate.

POLICE FORCE. Includes the chief officer, police officers and the necessary personnel, equipment, furnishings, vehicles and facilities.

POLICEMEN'S UNION. A trade union certified for a unit in which the majority of employees is engaged in police duties. *Essential Service Disputes Act*, R.S.B.C. 1979, c. 113, s. 1.

POLICE OFFICER. 1. A peace officer who is a member of a police force with authority to enforce federal and provincial statutes. 2. A member of a police force in a province. 3. The member of a police force appointed for policing duties and duties incidental to those duties. See PERSONATING ~; SENIOR ~.

POLICY. *n.* 1. The instrument evidencing a contract. Insurance acts. 2. A government commitment to the public to follow an action or course of action in pursuit of approved objectives. *Public Service Act*, S.N.W.T. 1983 (1st Sess.), c. 12, s. 1. See DECLARATION ~; DRIVER'S ~; FLOATING ~; LIFE INSURANCE ~; NON-OWNER'S ~; OPEN ~; OWNER'S ~; PUBLIC LIABILITY INSURANCE ~; PUBLIC ~; SEGREGATED FUND ~; TIME ~; TRANSIT ~; VALUED ~; VOYAGE ~; WITH PROFITS ~.

POLICY GRIEVANCE. A grievance which does not depend on an individual employee's behaviour or which does not affect an individual directly. D.J.M. Brown and D.M. Beatty, *Canadian Labour Arbitration*, 2d ed. (Aurora: Canada Law Book, 1977) at 92.

POLICYHOLDER. *n.* A person who owns an insurance policy.

POLICYHOLDER IN CANADA. The legal holder for the time being of a policy in Canada.

POLICY IN CANADA. (a) With respect to life insurance, a policy issued or effected by a company registered under an act on the life of a person resident in Canada or Newfoundland at the time the policy was issued or effected; (b) with respect to fire insurance, a policy issued or effected by a company registered under an act on property within Canada or Newfoundland; and (c) with respect to any other class of insurance, a policy issued or effected by a company registered under an act where the risks covered by the policy were ordinarily within Canada or Newfoundland at the time the policy was issued or effected.

POLICY LOAN. An amount advanced at a particular time by an insurer to a policyholder in accordance with the terms and conditions of a life insurance policy in Canada.

POLICY OF DEPOSIT INSURANCE. The instrument evidencing a contract of deposit insurance with a provincial institution. *Canada Deposit Insurance Corporation Act*, R.S.C. 1985, c. C-3, s. 2.

POLICY OF INSURANCE. The writing whereby any contract of insurance is made or is evidenced.

POLITIAE LEGIBUS NON LEGES POLITIIS ADAPTANDAE. [L.] Politics should be adapted to the laws, not laws to politics.

POLITICAL ADVERTISEMENT. Any matter promoting or opposing any registered political party or the election of any registered candidate for which a fee is paid, but does not include any bona fide news reporting.

POLITICAL ADVERTISING. Any matter promoting or opposing any registered political party or the election of any registered candidate for which a fee is paid, but does not include any bona fide news reporting.

POLITICAL AFFILIATION. With respect to a candidate, means affiliation with a political party.

POLITICAL ORGANIZATION. (a) Before the closing of nominations on nomination day, means (i) a political organization which advises a returning officer in writing that it has or intends to sponsor a candidate in the electoral district at the election; or (ii) a person, not sponsored by a political organization, who advises a returning officer in writing that he has been or intends to be officially nominated as a candidate in the electoral district at the election; or (b) after the close of nominations on nomination day, means (i) the political organization whose candidate has been officially nominated as a candidate in the electoral district; or (ii) a person, not sponsored by a political organization, who has been officially nominated as a candidate in the electoral district. *Elections Act*, R.S.N.S. 1967, c. 83, s. 2. See AFFILIATED ~.

POLITICAL PARTY. 1. An association, organization or affiliation of voters comprising a political organization whose prime purpose is the nomination and support of candidates at elections. 2. A group of persons comprised in a political organization by which: (i) money or effort is expended; (ii) money is solicited or received; for the purpose of promoting, opposing, endorsing or supporting the platform of the group, of any recognized political party or candidate nominated at an election. *The Election Act*, R.S.S. 1978, c. E-6, s. 2. 3. A registered political party as defined in the Canada Elections Act (Canada) or an unregistered party functioning in the Territories to achieve political aims. *Public Service Act*, S.N.W.T. 1983 (1st Sess.), c. 12, s. 1. See CENTRAL ~ ORGANIZATION; RECOGNIZED ~.

POLITICAL SUBDIVISION. A province, state or other like political subdivision of a foreign state that is a federal state. *State Immunity Act*, R.S.C. 1985, c. S-18, s. 2.

POLITY. *n.* A form or process of government; civil constitution.

POLL. *v.* At an election, to give a vote or to receive a vote; to take the votes of everyone entitled to vote.

POLL. *n.* See ADVANCE ~.

POLL BOOK. The book in which the name and other particulars of every person applying to vote are consecutively entered by the poll clerk. See WRITE-IN BALLOT ~.

POLLING. See DAY OF ~.

POLLING BOOTH. The building or place where polling is authorized by law to take place.

POLLING DAY. The day fixed for taking the votes of the electors. See ADVANCE ~; ORDINARY ~.

POLLING DISTRICT. District entitled to elect a councillor. *Municipal Act*, R.S.N.S. 1967, c. 192, s. 1.

POLLING DIVISION. Any division, subdivision, district, sub-district or other territorial area fixed by the returning officer, for which a list of electors is prepared and for which one or more polling stations is or are established for the taking of the vote on polling day. See RURAL ~; URBAN ~.

POLLING LIST. The list of electors for each polling subdivision revised and certified by the clerk.

POLLING PLACE. A place where electors vote at an election.

POLLING STATION. Premises secured by a returning officer for the taking of the vote of the electors on polling day and to which the whole or a portion of the official list of electors for a polling division is allotted. See MOBILE ~.

POLLING SUBDIVISION. *var.* **POLLING-SUBDIVISION.** 1. That area of an electoral division so designated by the returning officer to enable the efficient conduct of an election. 2. A territorial division for which a separate electoral list must be made or in which a polling-station may be established. See RURAL ~; URBAN ~.

POLLOCK. *n.* A fish of the species saithe or Pollachius virens (L.). *Northwest Atlantic Fisheries Regulations*, C.R.C., c. 860, s. 2.

POLL-TAX. *n.* A tax on every person.

POLLUTANT. *n.* 1. (a) Any substance that, if added to any waters, would degrade or alter or form part of a process of degradation or alteration of the quality of those waters to an extent that is detrimental to their use by man or by any animals, fish or plant that is useful to man; and (b) any water that contains a substance in such a quantity or concentration, or that has been so treated, processed or changed, by heat or other means, from a natural state that it would, if added to any waters, degrade or alter or form part of a process of degradation or alteration of the quality of those waters to an extent that is detrimental to their use by man or by any animal, fish or plant that is useful to man, and without limiting the generality of the foregoing includes oil and any substance that is part of a class of substances that is prescribed by the Governor in Council, for the purposes of this Part, to be a pollutant. *Canada Shipping Act*, R.S.C. 1985, c. S-9, s. 654. 2. A contaminant other than heat, sound, vibration, or radiation, and includes any substance from which a pollutant is derived. *Environmental Protection Act*, R.S.O. 1980, c. 141, s. 79. See OWNER OF THE ~.

POLLUTION. *n.* 1. The presence in the environment of substances or contaminants that substantially alter or impair the usefulness of the environment. *Waste Management Act*, S.B.C. 1982, c. 41, s. 1. 2. Alteration of the physical, chemical, biological or aesthetic properties of the environment including the addition or removal of any contaminant that will render the environment harmful to the public health, that is unsafe or harmful for domestic, municipal, industrial, agricultural, recreational or other lawful uses or that is harmful to wild animals, birds or aquatic life. See AIR ~; DANGER OF ~; WATER ~.

POLYANDRY. *n.* Polygamy in which one woman has several husbands.

POLYGAMY. *n.* 1. The state of having many wives or husbands. 2. It is an offence to practise or enter into or in any manner agree or consent to practise or enter into (i) any form of polygamy, or (ii) any kind of conjugal union with more than one person at the same time, whether or not it is by law recognized as a binding form of marriage; or 3. celebrate, assist or be a party to a rite, ceremony, contract or consent that purports to sanction a relationship mentioned in subparagraph 2(i) or (ii). *Criminal Code*, R.S.C. 1985, c. C-46, s. 293(1).

POLYGARCHY. *n.* Government by many people.

POLYGRAPH. *n.* A lie detector; an apparatus which records physiological changes in the body.

POND. See BREEDING ~; FISHING ~; PERCHED ~; TREATMENT.

PONY. *n.* A horse of a breed that, when mature, does not normally attain a height in excess of 58 inches measured at the withers. *Riding Horse Establishments Act*, R.R.O. 1980, Reg. 905, s. 1.

PONY AXLE. One which is designed to carry load only under certain conditions. *Roads Act*, R.S.P.E.I. 1974, c. R-15, s. 1.

POOL. *n.* 1. A natural underground reservoir containing or appearing to contain an accumulation of oil or gas or both oil and gas and being separated or appearing to be separated from any other such accumulation. 2. Includes billiards, bagatelle and any other similar game. *Places of Amusement Regulations*, C.R.C., c. 962, s. 2. 3. A betting pool. See CALCULATING ~; FEATURE ~; FILL-AND-DRAW ~; INDOOR ~; MORTGAGE ~; NET ~; NON-CONFORMING ~; PLACE ~; PROMOTIONAL ~; PUBLIC ~; SALMON ~; SHOW ~; SWIMMING ~; WIN ~.

POOLED FUND. A fund established by a corporation duly authorized to operate a fund in which moneys from two or more depositors are accepted for investment and where shares allocated to each depositor serve to establish at any time the proportionate interest of each depositor in the assets of the fund. *Pension Benefits Standards Regulations*, C.R.C., c. 1252, s. 2.

POOLED INVESTMENT TRUST. A trust which combines and invests the funds of several estates and trusts into a common trust fund. D.M.W. Waters, *The Law of Trusts in Canada*, 2d ed. (Toronto: Carswell, 1984) at 441.

POOLED SAVINGS FUND. A pooled fund maintained by a trust company registered under Part XVI of The Corporations Act solely to serve registered retirement savings plans, registered home ownership plans, or other individual savings plans registered under the Income Tax Act (Canada). *Securities Act*, S.M. 1980, c. 50, s. 1.

POOLED SPACING UNIT. The area that is subject to a pooling agreement or a pooling order.

POOLED TRACT. The portion of a pooled spacing unit defined as a tract in a pooling agreement or a pooling order.

POOLING. *n.* The joining or combining of all the various interests within a spacing unit for the purpose of drilling and subsequent producing of a well. *Petroleum Resources Act*, R.R.O. 1980, Reg. 752, s. 1.

POOLING AGREEMENT. An agreement to pool the interests of owners in a spacing unit and to provide for the operation or the drilling and operation of a well thereon.

POOLING INTERFACE. The point adjacent to and upstream from the place at which electric energy enters an electric distribution system and that is located pursuant to the regulations. *Electric Energy Marketing Act*, S.A. 1981, c. E-4.1, s. 1.

POOLING SYSTEM. See DEBT ~.

POOL PERIOD. 1. A crop year. *Canadian Wheat Board Act*, R.S.C. 1985, c. C-24, s. 31. 2. In respect of a marketing plan, the period set as the pool period for the plan by the order establishing the plan. 3. Such period or periods, not exceeding one year, as the Governor in Council may prescribe as a pool period or pool periods in respect of that wheat. *Canadian Wheat Board Act*, R.S.C. 1985, c. C-24, s. 40.

POOLROOM. *n.* A room or rooms in a building, house, shed, tent or other place in which a pool table is set up for hire or gain and includes an annex, addition or extension thereto over which the owner has control. *Places of Amusement Regulations*, C.R.C., c. 962, s. 2.

POPPY. See OPIUM ~.

POPULAR INNUENDO. A meaning which is attributed to the natural and ordinary meaning of a word but which arises only by implication or inference. R.E. Brown, *The Law of Defamation in Canada* (Toronto: Carswell, 1987) at 158.

POPULAR VOTE. The total counted ballots cast in favour of all candidates in an electoral district and does not include any rejected, cancelled, declined or unused ballot. *Election Finances Act*, S.O. 1986, c. 33, s. 46.

POPULATION. *n.* 1. As used in reference to a municipality, means the number of persons resident in the municipality. 2. Population as determined in accordance with the latest census taken pursuant to the Statistics Act (Canada). See VOTER ~.

PORT. *n.* 1. A place where vessels or vehicles may discharge or load cargo. 2. Includes harbour but does not include the port of Montreal as defined in The Montreal Harbour Commissioners' Act, 1894 (57-58 Victoria, chapter 48) or the port of Quebec as defined in The Quebec Harbour Commissioners Act, 1899 (62-63 Victoria, chapter 34). *Canada Shipping Act*, R.S.C. 1985, c. S-9, s. 2. 3. In respect of a vessel, means the left side of the vessel looking forward. See CUSTOMS ~; EAST COAST ~; EASTERN ~; FISHING ~S; FRONTIER ~; GREAT LAKES ~; INTERMEDIATE ~; NON-CORPORATE ~; QUARANTINE ~.

PORTABLE. *adj.* 1. In respect of any plan referred to therein, means that benefits to which an employee covered thereby is entitled and the rate of premium he is required to pay while employed by an employer will remain equivalent if he becomes employed by any other employer. *Unemployment Insurance Regulations*, C.R.C., c. 1576, s. 57. 2. The equipment is specifically designed not to be used in a fixed position and receives current through the medium of a flexible cord or cable, and usually a detachable plug. *Power Corporation Act*, R.R.O. 1980, Reg. 794, s. 0.

PORTABLE CABIN. A structure of wood not exceeding 14 feet in width and 30 feet in length mounted on skids and designed and constructed in accordance with plans satisfactory to the superintendent. *National Parks Camping Regulations*, C.R.C., c. 1116, s. 2.

PORTABLE CONTAINER. A container that has a capacity of 10 gallons or less, that is designed, manufactured and used or to be used for the storage or conveyance of gasoline or an associated product. *Gasoline Handling Act*, R.S.O. 1980, c. 185, s. 1.

PORTABLE CYLINDERS. Containers designed to hold propane or butane and designed in such a manner that they may readily be removed from equipment on which they are used as a fuel source for purposes of refilling with propane or butane. *The Statute Law Amendment (Taxation) Act (1985)*, S.M. 1985-86, c. 48, s. 31.

PORTABLE EQUIPMENT. Electrically operated equipment which is usually held in the hands while being worked. *Coal Mines Regulation Act*, R.S.N.S. 1967, c. 36, s. 84.

PORTABLE GROUND FAULT CIRCUIT INTERRUPTER. A ground fault circuit interrupter which is specifically designed to receive current by means of a flexible cord or cable and an attachment plug cap, and which incorporates one or more receptacles for the connection of electrical equipment which is provided with a flexible cord or cable and an attachment plug cap. *Power Corporation Act*, R.R.O. 1980, Reg. 794, s. 0.

PORTABLE PENSION. A pension scheme which permits an employee to move to another employer without forfeiting any accrued pension rights.

PORTABLE POWER TOOL. A tool that is designed to be held in the hand and that is operated by any source of power other than manual power. *Canada Hand Tools Regulations*, C.R.C., c. 1002, s. 2.

PORTAL TIME. Time spent by workers on incidental activities before or after their regular work.

PORT-CALL-TONNAGE. *n.* The aggregate of the products obtained by multiplying, for each ship operated by the corporation, the number of calls made in the year by that ship at ports by the number of tons of the registered net tonnage of that ship. Canada regulations.

PORT FACILITY. Any wharf, pier, breakwater or other work or installation located in, on or adjacent to navigable waters and includes any land to which it is attached. *Public Harbours and Port Facilities Act*, R.S.C. 1985, c. P-29, s. 2. See PUBLIC ~.

PORTFOLIO. See MINISTER WITHOUT ~.

PORTFOLIO MANAGEMENT. The investment or control, in any way that involves an element of discretionary judgment by the person engaging therein, of money or securities that (a) are not owned by that person, or (b) are not moneys deposited with that person in the ordinary course of that person's business. *Bank Act*, R.S.C. 1985, c. B-1, s. 174.

PORTFOLIO MANAGER. An adviser who manages the investment portfolio of clients through discretionary authority granted by one or more clients.

PORTFOLIO SECURITY. Where used in relation to a mutual fund, a security held or proposed to be purchased by the mutual fund.

PORT HAND BUOY. A buoy that is located on the port side (left hand) of the channel when the vessel is proceeding (a) with the flood tide on the sea coast; (b) against the current of a river; or (c) away from the outlet towards the head of a lake.

PORT IN BRITISH COLUMBIA. Vancouver, North Vancouver, New Westminster, Roberts Bank, Prince Rupert, Ridley Island and any other place in the province of British Columbia that is prescribed as a port for the purposes of this Act by the Governor in Council. *Western Grain Transportation Act*, R.S.C. 1985, c. W-8, s. 2.

PORTION. *n.* One of the usual cuts derived from a carcass, such as sides, quarters, shoulders, hams and bellies and also entire organs, including tongues, livers and hearts. See EXCLUSIVE USE ~; GUARANTEED ~; OWNER'S ~ OF THE COST; RATEABLE ~; TRAVELLED ~.

PORT OF ENTRY. 1. Any place designated as a port of entry by the Minister for the examination of persons under this Act. *Immigration Act*, R.S.C. 1985, c. I-2, s. 2. 2. The port or office at which cargo is presented for release by a customs officer. *Customs Cargo Control Regulations*, C.R.C., c. 459, s. 2.

PORT OF HALIFAX. (i) That geographic area encompassing all waters lying northwest of a line running between Tribune Head and Hartlen Point, including all islands and lands accessing waterfronts which are at the time this Act comes into force used or which may after that time become used for commercial marine activities; and (ii) includes all marine, truck, rail and air transportation services and facilities contributing to or engaged in the movement, handling or storage of commercial goods in, on and through the seaports, highways, railroads and airports and all complementary and support services associated therewith. *Halifax-Dartmouth Port Development Commission Act*, S.N.S. 1984, c. 6, s. 2.

PORT OF IMPORTATION. The port or place at which cargo is required to be reported pursuant to the Customs Act. Canada regulations.

PORTORIA. *n.* [L.] Duties paid on merchandise in a port.

PORTRAIT. *n.* A likeness, still or moving, and includes a likeness of another deliberately disguised to resemble the plaintiff, and a caricature. *Privacy Act*, R.S.B.C. 1979, c. 336, s. 3.

PORT WARDEN. An official who arbitrates certain disputes regarding shipping matters.

POSITION. See BILINGUAL ~; CLASS OF ~S; DOMINANT ~; EXPOSED ~; IDLE ~; LONG ~; SHORT ~.

POSITIONING FLIGHT. The flight of an aircraft that has no payload. *Air Services Fees Regulations*, C.R.C., c. 5, s. 2.

POSITIVE DAMAGE. The acquisition of something undesirable such as pain and suffering or extra expense. K.D. Cooper-Stephenson & I.B. Saunders, *Personal Injury Damages in Canada* (Toronto: Carswell, 1981) at 52.

POSITIVE DISPLACEMENT GAS METER. Any gas meter whose primary metering mechanism displaces a definite volume per cycle. *Gas and Gas Meters Regulations*, C.R.C., c. 876, s. 21.

POSITIVE EVIDENCE. Proof of a particular fact.

POSITIVE LAW. Rules of conduct set down and enforced with the sanction of authority.

POSSE. *n.* [L.] A possibility. Something in posse is something which possibly may be; something in esse is something which actually is.

POSSE COMITATUS. [L.] The sheriff of a county traditionally could summon it to defend that county against enemies of the Crown, to pursue felons, to keep the peace or to enforce a royal writ.

POSSESSED. *adj.* 1. Applies to receipt of income of, and to any vested estate less than a life estate, legal or equitable, in possession or in expectancy, in any land. Trustee acts. 2. Is applicable to any vested estate less than a life estate, in law or in equity, in possession or in expectancy, in any land.

POSSESSIO. *n.* [L.] Possession.

POSSESSION. *n.* 1. Having in one's own personal possession knowingly or having in the actual possession or custody of any other person, and having in any place, whether belonging to or occupied by one's self or not, for the use or benefit of one's self or of any other person. 2. The right of control or disposal of any article, irrespective of the actual possession or location of such article. 3. When applied to persons claiming title to land, includes the reception of the rents and profits thereof. See ACTUAL ~; ADVERSE ~; BRITISH ~; CHANGE OF ~; CHOSE IN ~; CONSTRUCTIVE ~; DATE OF ~; DE FACTO ~; EXCLUSIVE ~; LEGAL ~; MORTGAGEE IN ~; PERSON LAWFULLY IN ~ OF THE BODY; RECENT ~; REDUCTION INTO ~; RE~; WRIT OF ~.

POSSESSORY. *adj.* Describes something arising out of or concerned with possession.

POSSESSORY LIEN. A common law lien which arises from an express or implied agreement and which can be extinguished when the amount due is tendered and can be lost by an express or implied waiver. It continues only as long as one retains actual possession.

POSSESSORY TITLE. The title of a squatter.

POSSIBILITY. *n.* 1. A future event, which may or may not happen. 2. In real property, an interest in land which depends on such an event happening.

POSSIBLE FATHER. Includes any one or more persons who have had sexual intercourse with a single woman 9 months before she gives birth to a child, assuming the pregnancy is of normal term. *Family Maintenance Act*, S.N.S. 1979-80, c. 6, s. 2.

POST. *v.* To leave in a post office or with a person authorized by the Corporation to receive mailable matter. *Canada Post Corporation Act*, R.S.C. 1985, c. C-10, s. 2.

POST. *n.* 1. An office of a department or other portion of the public service of Canada located outside Canada and, without restricting the generality of the foregoing, includes every embassy, office of a high commissioner, permanent delegation to an international organization, consulate general, consulate, trade commissioner's office and immigration office. *Special Voting Rules*, R.S.C. 1985, c. E-2, Schedule II, s. 2. 2. A vertical member of shoring and timbering that acts as a spacer between wales. *Occupational Health and Safety Act*, R.R.O. 1980, Reg. 691, s. 167. 3. An office or employment to which an employee is or may be appointed. 4. A place where a member is stationed for duty, either permanently or temporarily. *Royal Canadian Mounted Police Regulations*, C.R.C., c. 1391, s. 2. See HEAD OF ~; IRON ~; LEGAL ~; ORIGINAL DOMINION ~; ORIGINAL ~; REFERENCE ~; ROCK ~; SEND BY ~; TRANSMIT BY ~; WITNESS ~; WOODEN GUIDE ~.

POST. *adv.* [L.] After.

POSTAGE. *n.* The charge or surcharge payable for the collection, transmission and delivery by the Corporation of messages, information, funds or goods and for insurance or other special services provided by the Corporation in relation thereto. *Canada Post Corporation Act*, R.S.C. 1985, c. C-10, s. 2.

POSTAGE INDICIA IMPRESSION DIE. The part of a postage meter including the manufacturer's identification and the postage meter serial number that prints an impression showing the denomination of postage that has been prepaid. *Postage Meters Regulations*, C.R.C., c. 1287, s. 2.

POSTAGE METER. 1. A machine for the making or printing of postage impressions. Canada regulations. 2. A mechanical device that is used for printing prepaid postage. *Postage Meters Regulations*, C.R.C., c. 1287, s. 2.

POSTAGE STAMP. Any stamp, postage impression or postage meter impression authorized by the Corporation for the purpose of paying postage. *Canada Post Corporation Act*, R.S.C. 1985, c. C-10, s. 2.

POSTAGE SUPPLIES. Post cards, envelopes or letter forms with postage printed thereon. *Methods of Payment of Postage Regulations*, C.R.C., c. 1284, s. 2.

POSTAL CODE. A six character alpha-numeric combination assigned to one or more postal addresses that designates a specific delivery area. *Mail Preparation Regulations*, C.R.C., c. 1281, s. 2.

POSTAL CONSOLIDATION POINT. A postal facility designated for the receipt of bundled or bagged mail for a specific geographical area. *Mail Preparation Regulations*, C.R.C., c. 1281, s. 2.

POSTAL INSTALLATION. The main post office, a postal station or letter carrier depot. *Third Class Mail Regulations*, C.R.C., c. 1297, s. 2.

POSTAL INTERRUPTION. A cessation of normal public postal service in Canada or in any part of Canada that is or may reasonably be expected to be of more than 48 hours' duration. *Judicature Act*, R.S.A. 1980, c. J-1, s. 33.

POSTAL REMITTANCE. Any instrument authorized by the Corporation for the remittance of funds. *Canada Post Corporation Act*, R.S.C. 1985, c. C-10, s. 2.

POST AUDIT CUSTOMS CONTROL SYSTEM. An independent control system exercised by periodic audits of accountable revenue documents covering goods in bond carried by transportation companies approved by the Deputy Minister. *Cargo Container (Customs) Regulations*, C.R.C., c. 452, s. 2.

POSTDATE. *v.* To give a bill, note or cheque a later date in order to delay the payment date. I.F.G. Baxter, *The Law of Banking*, 3d ed. (Toronto: Carswell, 1981) at 84.

POST DIEM. [L.] After a day.

POST-DISASTER BUILDING. A building

essential to provide services in the event of a disaster, and includes hospitals, fire stations, police stations, radio stations, telephone exchanges, power stations, electrical substations, pumping stations (water and sewage) and fuel depot buildings. *Building Code Act*, R.R.O. 1980, Reg. 87, s. 1.

POSTER. *n.* Any printing, writing, drawing, painting, lithograph or representation by any process whatsoever, placed so as to be seen by the public and used for notices, announcements, advertisements or publicity.

POSTERIOR. *adj.* Dorsal, behind, in the rear of, facing backwards. F.A. Jaffe, *A Guide to Pathological Evidence*, 2d ed. (Toronto: Carswell, 1983) at 182.

POSTERIORITY. *n.* Comparing and relating tenure, the opposite of priority.

POSTERITY. *n.* Generations which follow.

POSTHUMOUS CHILD. A child born after the father's death.

POST-JUDGMENT INTEREST. Interest payable on the amount awarded under a judgment from the date of judgment.

POSTJUDGMENT INTEREST RATE. The bank rate at the end of the first day of the last month of the quarter preceding the quarter in which the date of the order falls, rounded to the next higher whole number where the bank rate includes a fraction, plus 1 per cent. *Courts of Justice Act, 1984*, S.O. 1984, c. 11, s. 137.

POST LETTER. Any letter deposited at a post office, whether such letter is addressed to a real or fictitious person, is unaddressed, and whether intended for transmission by post or not, from the time of deposit at a post office to the time of delivery and includes any packet prepaid or payable at letter rate of postage. *Post Office Act*, R.S.C. 1970, c. P-14, s. 2.

POST LITEM MOTAM. [L.] After the beginning of litigation.

POSTMARK IMPRESSION DIE. The part of a postage meter that prints an impression showing the name of the city or town and province from which the mail is despatched together with the date of mailing. *Postage Meters Regulations*, C.R.C., c. 1287, s. 2.

POSTMASTER. *n.* 1. Includes the manager of a postal station but does not include a subpostmaster. *Sale of Postage Stamps Regulations*, C.R.C., c. 1293, s. 2. 2. A postmaster within the meaning of the Canada Post Corporation Act (Canada) and, in a community where there is no postmaster, includes the secretary-treasurer, as defined in the Municipal Ordinance, or secretary-manager of a municipality or settlement, and references to the postmaster's office include references to that person's office. *Elections Act*, S.N.W.T. 1981 (3d Sess.), c. 5, s. 2.

POSTMORTEM. *n.* An autopsy. F.A. Jaffe, *A Guide to Pathological Evidence*, 2d ed. (Toronto: Carswell, 1983) at 1.

POST MORTEM ARTEFACT. A mark or lesion inflicted after death. F.A. Jaffe, *A Guide to Pathological Evidence*, 2d ed. (Toronto: Carswell, 1983) at 13.

POST MORTEM CHANGE. A physical and chemical process which commences immediately after death. F.A. Jaffe, *A Guide to Pathological Evidence*, 2d ed. (Toronto: Carswell, 1983) at 182.

POST MORTEM CLOT. A clot which forms in a heart chamber, blood vessel or the site of a hemorrhage after death. F.A. Jaffe, *A Guide to Pathological Evidence*, 2d ed. (Toronto: Carswell, 1983) at 172.

POST MORTEM INTERVAL. The period between death and the body being examined. F.A. Jaffe, *A Guide to Pathological Evidence*, 2d ed. (Toronto: Carswell, 1983) at 182.

POST-NOTE. *n.* A bank-note payable on a specified date in the future.

POST-OBIT. *n.* A money bond required to be paid at or after some person beside the giver of the bond dies.

POST OFFICE. Includes any place, receptacle, device or mail conveyance authorized by the Corporation for the posting, receipt, sorting, handling, transmission or delivery of mail. *Canada Post Corporation Act*, R.S.C. 1985, c. C-10, s. 2. See CANADA ~; CANADIAN FORCES ~; DEPOSIT AT A ~.

POSTPAK MAIL. Mailable matter that (a) is normally acceptable at the second, third or fourth class mail rates; (b) does not require registration, special delivery or C.O.D. service; and (c) except for equivalent units of mail, is contained in cartons of mail or mail bags of a size and type approved by the Postmaster General. *Special Services and Fees Regulations*, C.R.C., c. 1296, s. 29.

POSTPAK MAIL SERVICE. The service for the bulk posting of postpak mail. *Special Services and Fees Regulations*, C.R.C., c. 1296, s. 29.

POSTPONEMENT. *n.* A document evidencing the postponement of a security note or operator's lien.

POST-SECONDARY EDUCATION. Education in courses and subjects normally offered by universities and colleges.

POST SECONDARY INSTITUTION. Includes a community college, institute, private vocational school, university and any other educational institution that is not administered under The Education Act. *Workers' Compensation Amendment Act*, S.S. 1984-85-86, c. 89, s. 3.

POST TERMINUM. [L.] After the end of a term.

POST TIME. The time set for the arrival of the horses at the starting point of a race. *Race Track Supervision Regulations*, C.R.C., c. 441, s. 2.

POT. See BLACKCOD ~.

POTABLE. *adj.* Fit for human consumption.

POTABLE WATER. 1. Water fit for human consumption. 2. Water that is microbiologically and chemically safe for human consumption. *Public Health Act*, R.R.O. 1980, Reg. 840, s. 1. 3. Water the quality of which satisfies the standards of the Department of National Health and Welfare as set out in the Canadian Drinking Water Standards Objectives 1968, as amended from time to time. *Canada Sanitation Regulations*, C.R.C., c. 1009, s. 2. 4. Water that is free of pathogenic bacteria and is of such a composition that, when five 10-millilitre portions thereof are examined according to the standard procedure outlined in the latest edition of Standard Methods for the Examination of Water and Sewage, published by the American Public Health Association, not more than one portion thereof shows the presence of organisms of the coliform group, that is to say, the most probable number is not greater than 2.2 per 100 millilitres. *Potable Water Regulations for Common Carriers*, C.R.C., c. 1105, s. 2.

POTABLE WATER SYSTEM. 1. The plumbing that conveys potable water. *Ontario Water Resources Act*, R.R.O. 1980, Reg. 736, s. 1. 2. The equipment used on a conveyance for handling, treating, storing and distributing potable water. *Potable Water Regulations for Common Carriers*, C.R.C., c. 1105, s. 2.

POTASH. *n.* 1. Any non-viable substance formed by the processes of nature that contains the element potassium. 2. Potassium salts and the ores thereof. *Mineral Taxation Act*, R.S.M. 1970, c. M150, s. 2. 3. Potassium oxide (K_2O). *Fertilizers Regulations*, C.R.C., c. 666, s. 2. See PRIMARY PRODUCTION OF ~.

POTASH MINE. Any facility in Saskatchewan for mining, extracting, recovering or producing potash, and includes any facility in Saskatchewan associated with the mine at or in which any potash is processed or refined. *The Potash Resources Act*, S.S. 1986-87-88, c. P-18.1, s. 2.

POTATO. See CANNED ~ PRODUCTS PLANT; CANNED SWEET ~ES; DEHYDRATED ~ PRODUCTS PLANT; FROZEN ~ PRODUCTS PLANT; SEED ~; TABLE STOCK ~.

POTATO CHIP PLANT. Include any plant where raw potatoes are processed and the final potato product is distributed as a snack food in a ready-to-eat condition. *Potato Processing Plant Liquid Effluent Regulations*, C.R.C., c. 829, s. 2.

POTATO CYST NEMATODE. Potato cyst nematode Heterodera rostochiensis/Woll. and H. Pallida Stone. *Plant Quarantine Regulations*, C.R.C., c. 1273, s. 2.

POTATO WART. Potato wart Synchytrium endobioticum (Schilb.) Perc. *Plant Quarantine Regulations*, C.R.C., c. 1273, s. 2.

POTENTIAL PROPERTY. Something which is the expected increase or natural product of something which the seller already owns or possesses. G.H.L. Fridman, *Sale of Goods in Canada*, 3d ed. (Toronto: Carswell, 1986) at 54.

POTENTIAL SERVICE. A period that a participant could have served as a police officer until he attained normal pensionable age had he not become totally incapacitated, mentally or physically, for gainful employment or had he not died. *Special Forces Pension Plan Act*, S.A. 1985, c. S-21.1, s. 1.

POTENTIA PROPINQUA. [L.] A frequent possibility which one may expect will happen.

POTENTIA REMOTA. [L.] An unlikely possibility which one does not expect to happen.

POTESTAS SUPREME SEIPSAM DISSOLVERE POTEST, LIGARE NON POTEST. [L.] A supreme power may loose itself, but it cannot bind.

POTIOR EST CONDITIO DEFENDENTIS. [L.] The better condition is the defendant's.

POTIOR EST CONDITIO POSSIDENTIS. [L.] The better condition is the possessor's.

POULTRY. *n.* 1. Domestic fowl and pigeons and includes any bird that is in captivity. 2. Domestic or wild fowl or birds. 3. A turkey, goose, duck, cock, hen, capon, guinea fowl or pheasant. See DRESSED ~; EVISCERATED ~; ICE PACKED ~; UNDRAWN DRESSED ~.

POULTRY PRODUCT. Poultry meat, prepared poultry meat, poultry meat by-product or prepared poultry meat by-product. *Food and Drug Regulations*, C.R.C., c. 870, c. B.01.001. See EXTENDED ~; SIMULATED ~.

POULTRY PRODUCT EXTENDER. A food that is a source of protein and that is represented as being for the purpose of extending poultry products. *Food and Drug Regulations*, C.R.C., c. 870, c. B.01.001.

POULTRY PRODUCTS. Eggs, dressed poultry and live poultry. *Poultry and Poultry Products Act*, R.S.P.E.I. 1974, c. P-12, s. 1.

POUND. *n.* 1. .45359237 of a kilogram. *Weights and Measures Act*, S.C. 1970-71-72, c. 36, schedule II. 2. Premises where stray animals are confined. 3. An enclosure, building or piece of land where a distrainor places goods which have been seized as distress.

POUNDAGE. *n.* A fee owed to a court officer or to the public revenue for services which that officer performed.

POUND-BREACH. *n.* The act of removing goods from a pound before the distrainor's claim is satisfied.

POUND KEEPER. *var.* **POUNDKEEPER.** The person for the time being in the authorized charge of any pound.

POUND NET. 1. An impounding net (a) that is held in place by stakes driven into the water bed, and (b) the main part of which, including the crib and bent wings, commonly known as the "heart", extends to the surface of the water. Canada regulations. 2. A net that is set to enclose an area of water into which fish are guided through an opening or openings by one or more leaders.

POURING AISLE. A passageway leading from a gangway where metal is poured into a mould or box. *Occupational Health and Safety Act*, R.R.O. 1980, Reg. 692, s. 1.

POURVEYANCE. *n.* The provision of necessaries for a sovereign.

POURVEYOR. *n.* One who buys; the person who provided for a royal household.

POVERTY LINE. An income level chosen to distinguish between the non-poor and the poor. W. Grover & F. Iacobucci, *Materials on Canadian Income Tax*, 4th ed. (Toronto: Richard De Boo Ltd., 1980) at 51.

POWDER. See BUTTERMILK ~; MILK ~; WHEY ~.

POWDER STIPPLING. Tattoo. F.A. Jaffe, *A Guide to Pathological Evidence*, 2d ed. (Toronto: Carswell, 1983) at 182.

POWER. *n.* 1. A right or privilege. 2. Authority to deal with or transfer away property which one does not own beneficially. D.M.W. Waters, *The Law of Trusts in Canada*, 2d ed. (Toronto: Carswell, 1984) at 71. 3. Includes hydraulic, electrical, steam or other power and also includes energy. 4. Includes energy, light and

heat however developed or produced, and includes electricity and natural, manufactured or mixed gas, or liquified petroleum gas. *Hydro and Power Authority Act*, R.S.B.C. 1979, c. 188, s. 1. See COMPULSORY ~; DECLARATORY ~; DISTRIBUTION OF ~S; ELECTRIC ~; EXERCITORIAL ~; EXPROPRIATION ~; FIRM ~; GENERAL ~; INHERENT ~; INTERRUPTIBLE ~; LEGAL ~; MEDIUM ~; OBJECT OF A ~; PRISONER OF WAR OF ANOTHER ~; PROTECTING ~; RESERVE ~; RESIDUARY ~; SMALL ~; SOVEREIGN ~; SPECIAL ~; SPENDING ~; STATUS AND ESSENTIAL ~S; STATUTORY ~; STATUTORY ~ OF DECISION; TRANSMITTER ~; TRUST ~; WATER ~.

POWER BICYCLE. A vehicle that (i) may be propelled by muscular or mechanical power; (ii) is fitted with pedals that are continually operable to propel it; (iii) weighs not more than 35 kilograms; (iv) has a motor that produces not more than 750 watts and that is driven by electricity or has an engine displacement of not more than 50 cubic centimetres; (v) has no hand-operated or foot-operated clutch or gearbox driven by the motor that transfers power to the driven wheel; and (vi) does not have sufficient power to enable it to attain a speed greater than 35 kilometres per hour on level ground within a distance of 2 kilometres from a standing start.

POWER BOAT. *var.* **POWER-BOAT.** A boat, raft or barge of any kind that is being driven, drawn or propelled by any means other than human muscular power.

POWER BOILER. Any high pressure boiler other than a locomotive boiler or a miniature boiler. *Boilers and Pressure Vessels Act*, R.R.O. 1980, Reg. 84, s. 1.

POWER CIRCUIT. See EXTRA-LOW-VOLTAGE ~; LOW-ENERGY ~.

POWER DEVELOPMENT. Includes (a) the physical structures within the severance line required for the storage or use of the streamwaters, for the production of power therefrom, and for the transmission thereof; (b) the dams or other diversion works, the powerhouse, the conduits conducting water thereto and the transmission lines within the severance line; (c) all hydraulic or electrical machinery, appliances, fixtures, equipment and appurtenances; (d) lands and rights-of-way required in connection therewith; and (e) the clearings, roads, trails and railways required to be constructed that are still used and useful in connection therewith and not independently profitable. *Dominion Water Power Regulations*, C.R.C., c. 1603, s. 2.

POWER-DRIVEN. *adj.* Propelled by machinery. *Small Vessel Regulations*, C.R.C., c. 1487, s. 2.

POWER-DRIVEN VESSEL. Any vessel propelled by machinery. *Collision Regulations*, C.R.C., c. 1416, Rule 3.

POWER GRID. The network of interconnected power circuits owned or controlled by a single electrical utility and operated as a unit for the bulk transmission and distribution of power. *National Energy Board Part VI Regulations*, C.R.C., c. 1056, s. 2. See EXPORT ~.

POWER LINE. See INTERNATIONAL ~.

POWER MOTOR CYCLE. A motor vehicle mounted on two or three wheels and includes those motor vehicles known to the trade as scooters and power bicycles, but does not include motor cycles.

POWER OF APPOINTMENT. 1. The power of a donee or appointor to appoint by will the people who will succeed to property after the person to whom the power is given dies. This power is given by a donor using an instrument such as a trust inter vivos, marriage settlement or will. J.G. McLeod, *The Conflict of Laws* (Calgary: Carswell, 1983) at 428. 2. Includes any discretionary power to transfer a beneficial interest in property without the furnishing of valuable consideration.

POWER OF ATTORNEY. Authority for a donee or donees to do on behalf on a donor or principal anything which that donor can lawfully do through an attorney. G.H.L. Fridman, *The Law of Agency*, 5th ed. (London: Butterworths, 1983) at 55.

POWER OF DISTRESS. The right that a person has to enforce the payment of any claim against, or the taking of any goods or chattels out of the possession of, another person by the taking of a personal chattel out of the possession of that last mentioned person otherwise than by the authority of a writ of execution or other process of a similar nature.

POWER OF THE COUNTY. See POSSE COMITATUS.

POWER PLANT. 1. A facility for the generation of electric energy from any energy source. 2. A boiler or two or more boilers on the same premises together with the accessories thereto, from which the steam produced is used to provide motive power for an engine or turbine or two or more engines or turbines or any combination thereof. See HYDROELECTRIC ~; STATIONARY ~; THERMAL ELECTRIC ~.

POWER PROJECT. Includes any charter, franchise, privilege or other right, or land, buildings, plant, machinery or equipment acquired, or proposed to be acquired, by a person with a view to the generation or supply of power, or any plans, surveys or data made or assembled with a view to the generation or supply of power.

POWER PURPOSE. The use of water in the production of electricity or other power. *Water Act*, R.S.B.C. 1979, c. 429, s. 1.

POWER RATING. (i) When used in respect of a compressed-air plant or compressed-gas plant, the total horse-power of the machinery-units driving the compressors; (ii) when used in respect of an electric boiler in a steam plant, the quotient obtained by dividing the total maximum capacity of the heating elements in kilowatts by ten; or (iii) when used in respect of a boiler in a steam plant, other than an electric boiler, the quotient obtained by dividing the total heating surface of the boiler in square feet by ten. *Boilers and Pressure Vessels Act*, R.R.O. 1980, Reg. 84, s. 1.

POWER SITE. Includes any land, or any lake, river, stream, watercourse, or body of water, water licence or privilege, or reservoir, dam, water storage, sluice, canal, raceway, tunnel, or aqueduct, that is used or that might be used for or in connection with the development or generation of power.

POWER SUPPLY CORD. A length of flexible cord or power supply cable with an attachment plug at one end. *Power Corporation Act*, R.R.O. 1980, Reg. 794, s. 0.

POWER TOOL. See PORTABLE ~.

POWER TRANSFER. The power transmitted through an inter-utility transfer point. *National Energy Board Part VI Regulations*, C.R.C., c. 1056, s. 2.

POWER TRANSMISSION LINE. (i) A transmission line as defined in the Hydro and Electric Energy Act and to which that Act applies; or (ii) wires, conductors, poles or other devices (A) that are required for conveying, transmitting, supplying or distributing electricity, and (B) to which sections 30 to 32 of the Water, Gas, Electric and Telephone Companies Act apply. *Surface Rights Act*, S.A. 1983, c. S-27.1, s. 1.

POWER UNIT. 1. A motor vehicle used solely for the purpose of drawing a semi-trailer. 2. That part of a motor vehicle over which a motor vehicle operator has direct control and, where the power unit and the rest of the motor vehicle are permanently joined together, means the entire motor vehicle. *Canada Motor Vehicle Operators Hours of Service Regulations*, C.R.C., c. 1005, s. 2.

POWER UTILITY. An energy utility that generates, transmits or distributes electrical energy for sale, or that sells or otherwise deals in electrical energy. *Energy Act*, R.S.B.C. 1979, c. 108, s. 1.

POWER VESSEL. Any vessel that uses machinery in whole or in part for its propulsion or is equipped with such machinery. Canada regulations.

P.P. *abbr.* Per pro., by procurating.

P.P.I. *abbr.* Policy proof of interest.

P.P.S.A.C. *abbr.* Personal Property Security Act Cases, 1980-.

P.R. *abbr.* Practice Reports (Ont.), 1848-1900.

PRACTICABLE. *adj.* Capable of being effected or accomplished. *Environmental Protection Act*, R.S.O. 1980, c. 141, s. 79.

PRACTICAL COMPULSION. The probability, or even certainty, that if money requested is not paid, the payer will be in economic or some similar danger because a legal process is invoked which might jeopardise the payer's current fiscal status. G.H.L. Fridman & J.G. McLeod, *Restitution* (Toronto: Carswell, 1982) at 201.

PRACTICAL NURSE. A person who, being neither a registered nurse nor a person in training to be a registered nurse at a school of nursing undertakes nursing for remuneration.

PRACTICAL NURSING. Representing oneself as a licensed practical nurse who (i) assists registered nurses in the care of acutely ill patients and rendering those services for which she has been trained; (ii) not being a registered nurse or a person in training to be a registered nurse, undertakes the care of patients under the direction of a medical practitioner or a registered nurse; and (iii) administers medication prescribed by a medical practitioner consistent with her training. *Licensed Practical Nurses Act*, S.M. 1980, c. 64, s. 1.

PRACTICE. *n.* 1. The form and method in which one conducts and carries on a suit, action or prosecution at law. The law of practice or procedure regulates the formal steps in any action or judicial proceeding. 2. The exercise of a profession or trade. See AREA ~; CORRUPT ~; DECEPTIVE ACT OR ~; FAIR EMPLOYMENT ~; ILLEGAL ~S; MAKEWORK ~; ORDINARY ~ OF SEAMEN; PRIVATE ~; RULES OF ~; UNFAIR ACTS OR ~S; UNFAIR INSURANCE ~; UNFAIR ~S.

PRACTICE AND PROCEDURE. Includes evidence relating to matters of practice and procedure. *Federal Court Act*, R.S.C. 1985, c. F-7, s. 2.

PRACTICE OF A CERTIFIED GENERAL ACCOUNTANT. The provision of any professional service usually or ordinarily performed by a certified general accountant, whether or not such services are offered to or provided to the public. *Certified General Accountants Act*, S.N.B. 1986, c. 86, s. 2.

PRACTICE OF A CHARTERED ACCOUNTANT. A member, or a professional corporation which holds a license, or a partnership who in connection with his or its work generally or with regard to a particular professional engagement: (a) uses any word, phrases or initials that represent, expressly or by necessary implication, that he or it is a chartered accountant, a fellow or a professional corporation which holds a license; or (b) in any way represents that he or it is a chartered accountant, a fellow or a professional corporation which holds a license, whether or not such member, professional corporation or partnership offers his or its professional services to the public. *Chartered Accountants' Act 1986*, S.N.B. 1986, c. 87, s. 2.

PRACTICE OF A HEARING AID DEALER AND CONSULTANT. (a) Testing human hearing by audiometer or other means for the purpose of selecting, adapting, recommending or selling hearing aids; (b) selecting, adapting, recommending, selling or offering for sale hearing aids; or (c) making impressions for earmoulds to be used in connection with hearing aids. *Hearing Aid Act*, R.S.B.C. 1979, c. 164, s. 1.

PRACTICE OF ARCHITECTURE. (i) The preparation or provision of a design to govern the construction, enlargement or alteration of a building; (ii) evaluating, advising on or reporting on the construction, enlargement or alteration of a building; or (iii) a general review of the construction, enlargement or alteration of a building.

PRACTICE OF DENTISTRY. Any professional service usually performed by a dentist or dental surgeon and includes (a) the diagnosis or treatment of, and the prescribing, treating and operating for the prevention, alleviation or correction of any injury, disease, pain, deficiency, deformity, defect, lesion, disorder or physical condition of, to in or from any human tooth, mandible or maxilla or associated structures or tissues, including the prescribing, treating and administering of x-rays, anaesthetics, drugs and medicines in connection therewith; (b) the making, producing, reproducing, constructing, fitting, furnishing, supplying, altering, or repairing, prescribing or advising the use of any prosthetic denture, bridge, appliance or thing for any of the purposes indicated in paragraph (a) or to replace, improve or supplement any human tooth, or to prevent, alleviate, correct or improve any condition in the human oral cavity, or to be used in, upon or in connection with any human tooth, jaw or associated structure or tissue, or in the treatment of any condition thereof; (c) the taking or making, or the giving of advice or assistance or the providing of facilities for the taking or making of any impression, bite or cast and design preparatory to, or for the purpose of, or with a view to making, producing, reproducing, constructing, fitting, furnishing, supplying, altering or repairing any such prosthetic denture, bridge, appliance or thing; (d) any specialty of dentistry; (e) the dental procedures performed by a dental hygienist or dental assistant.

PRACTICE OF DENTURE TECHNOLOGY. (i) The taking of impressions or bite registrations for the purpose of or with a view to the making, producing, reproducing, constructing, furnishing, supplying, altering or repairing of any complete upper or complete lower prosthetic denture, or both, to be fitted to an edentulous arch or arches; (ii) the fitting of any complete upper or complete lower prosthetic denture, or both, to an edentulous arch or arches, and includes the making, producing, reproducing, constructing, furnishing, supplying, altering and repairing complete upper or complete lower prosthetic dentures in respect of which a service is performed under subclause (i) or (ii). *Denturist Act*, S.N.S. 1973, c. 5, s. 2.

PRACTICE OF DENTURE THERAPY. (i) The taking of impressions or bite registrations for the purpose of, or with a view to, the making, producing, reproducing, constructing, furnishing, supplying, altering or repairing of any complete upper or complete lower prosthetic denture, or both, to be fitted to an edentulous arch; (ii) the fitting of any complete upper or complete lower prosthetic denture or both, to an edentulous arch, and (iii) the making, producing, reproducing, constructing, furnishing, supplying, altering and repairing complete upper or complete lower prosthetic dentures or both in respect of which a service is performed under subclause (i) or (ii). *Denture Therapists Act*, R.S.O. 1980, c. 115, s. 1.

PRACTICE OF DENTUROLOGY. (a) The making, fitting, constructing, altering, reproducing or repairing of a complete upper or lower prosthetic denture or both, the furnishing or supplying of such a denture directly to a person or advising on the use of any such denture; (b) the taking, making, or giving of advice, assistance or facilities respecting the taking or making of any impression, bite, cast or design preparatory to, or for the purpose of making, constructing, fitting, furnishing, supplying, alter-

ing, repairing or reproducing any such complete upper or complete lower removable prosthetic denture, or both; (c) the demanding by a denturist from any person to whom he provided the services mentioned in subclauses (a) and (b) and the recovering as a debt in any court of competent jurisdiction of reasonable charges for the services provided. *Denturists' Act*, S.N.B. 1986, c. 90, s. 2.

PRACTICE OF DIETETICS. The translation and application of the scientific knowledge of foods and human nutrition toward the attainment, maintenance or promotion of the health of individuals, groups and the community and includes the following: (i) administering food service systems; (ii) assessing nutritional needs of individuals and developing and implementing nutritional care plans based on the assessments; (iii) establishing and reviewing the principles of nutrition and guidelines for healthy and ill people throughout their lives; (iv) assessing the overall nutritional needs of a community in order to establish priorities and influence policies which provide the nutritional component of preventative programs, and implementing and evaluating those programs; (v) interpreting and evaluating, for consumer protection, information on nutrition that is available to the public; (vi) consulting with individuals, families and groups on the principles of food and nutrition and the practical application of those principles; (vii) planning, conducting and evaluating educational programs on nutrition for registered dietitians and other professionals and supporting occupations; (viii) conducting basic and applied research in food, nutrition and food service systems. *Registered Dietitians Act*, S.A. 1983, c. R-10.1, s. 1.

PRACTICE OF ENGINEERING. Reporting on, advising on, evaluating, designing, preparing plans and specifications for or directing the construction, technical inspection, maintenance or operation of any structure, work or process (A) that is aimed at the discovery, development or utilization of matter, materials or energy or in any other way designed for the use and convenience of people; and (B) that requires in the reporting, advising, evaluating, designing, preparation or direction the professional application of the principles of mathematics, chemistry, physics or any related applied subject.

PRACTICE OF GEOLOGY. (i) Reporting, advising, evaluating, interpreting, geological surveying, sampling or examining related to any activity (A) that is aimed at the discovery or development of oil, natural gas, coal, metallic or non-metallic minerals, precious stones, other natural resources or water or that is aimed at the investigation of geological conditions; and

(B) that requires in that reporting, advising, evaluating, interpreting, geologicial surveying, sampling or examining, the professional application of the principles of the geological sciences; or (ii) teaching geology at a university. *Engineering, Geological and Geophysical Professions Act*, S.A. 1981, c. E-11.1, s. 1.

PRACTICE OF GEOPHYSICS. (i) Reporting on, advising on, acquiring, processing, evaluating or interpreting geophysical data, or geophysical surveying that relates to any activity (A) that is aimed at the discovery or development of oil, natural gas, coal, metallic or non-metallic minerals, precious stones, other natural resources or water or that is aimed at the investigation of sub-surface conditions in the earth; and (B) that requires in that reporting, advising, evaluating, interpreting, or geophysical surveying, the professional application of the principles of the geophysical sciences; or (ii) teaching geophysics at a university. *Engineering, Geological and Geophysical Professions Act*, S.A. 1981, c. E-11.1, s. 1.

PRACTICE OF LAND SURVEYING. (i) The survey of land to determine or establish boundaries; (ii) the survey of land to determine or establish the boundaries of any right or interest in land or in air space; (iii) the survey of air space to determine or establish boundaries; (iv) the survey of land to determine the location of anything relative to a boundary for the purpose of certifying the location of the thing; (v) the survey of lakes, rivers or watercourses to establish or determine their boundaries; (vi) the survey by any means, including photogrammetric, electronic or astronomic methods, of land, water or air space for the purpose of preparing maps, plans and documents connected in any way with the establishment or determination of boundaries delineating any right or interest in land, water or air space; (vii) cadastral operations and compiling and recording information related to the matters specified in subclauses (i) to (vi); (viii) establishing and maintaining a network of geodetic points of any order of precision and establishing photogrammetric controls for the purposes of the work specified in subclauses (i) to (v), including the preparation of maps, plans and documents and giving advice with respect to any other specified matters.

PRACTICE OF LAW. Includes (a) appearing as counsel or advocate; (b) drawing, revising or settling (i) any petition, memorandum of association, articles of association, application, statement, affidavit, minute, resolution, bylaw or other document relating to the incorporation, registration, organization, reorganization, dissolution or winding up of a corporate body; (ii) any document for use in a proceeding, judicial or extra-judicial; (iii) a will, deed of settlement, trust deed, power of attorney or a document relating to any probate or letters of administration or the estate of a deceased person; (iv) a document relating in any way to proceedings under a statute of Canada or a province; (v) an instrument relating to real or personal estate which is intended, permitted or required to be registered, recorded or filed in registry or other public office; (c) doing any act or deed or negotiating in any way for the settlement of, or settling, a claim or demand for damages founded in tort; (d) agreeing to place at the disposal of another person the services of a barrister or solicitor; (e) giving legal advice.

PRACTICE OF MEDICINE. The carrying on for hire, gain or hope of gain or reward, either directly or indirectly, of the healing art or any of its branches.

PRACTICE OF NURSING. Representing oneself as a registered nurse while carrying out the practice of those functions which, directly or indirectly in collaboration with a client and with other health workers, have as their objective, promotion of health, prevention of illness, alleviation of suffering, restoration of health and maximum development of health potential and without restricting the generality of the foregoing includes (i) collecting data relating to the health status of an individual or groups of individuals; (ii) interpreting data and identifying health problems; (iii) setting care goals; (iv) determining nursing approaches; (v) implementing care, supportive or restorative to life and wellbeing; (vi) implementing care relevant to medical treatment; (vii) assessing outcomes; and (viii) revising plans. *Registered Nurses Act*, S.M. 1980, c. 45, s. 1.

PRACTICE OF OPTOMETRY. The employment of any means other than drugs, medicine or surgery for the measurement or aid of the powers of vision or the supplying of lenses or prisms for the aid thereof.

PRACTICE OF PHARMACY. A professional service performed by a pharmaceutical chemist related to the control of the manufacturing, distributing, compounding, dispensing or use of drugs. *Pharmacy Act*, S.N.S. 1981, c. 39, s. 1.

PRACTICE OF PHYSIOTHERAPY. The services usually performed by a physiotherapist in the identification, assessment, prevention and alleviation of physical dysfunction or pain, from whatever cause, and the restoration and maintenance of optimal function, and includes (i) the assessment in consultation with the patient's physician leading to the determination of the nature and degree of physical dysfunction, and of potential level of function and the application and interpretation of selected evaluative procedures; (ii) the planning, administration and evaluation of remedial treatment programs of physiotherapy in communication with the patient's physician; (iii) the planning, administration and evaluation of preventative and health maintenance programs of physiotherapy; (iv) the provision of consultative, educational, advisory, research and other professional services as may be required. *The Physiotherapists Act*, S.M. 1980-81, c. 15, s. 1.

PRACTICE OF PROFESSIONAL CHEMISTRY. The practice for gain of any branch of chemistry, pure or applied, including, without limiting the generality of the foregoing, organic, inorganic, physical, metallurgical, biological, clinical, analytical and industrial chemistry, but does not include the execution of chemical or physical tests based on known methods to determine the quality of a product or to control a manufacturing process. *Professional Chemists Act*, R.S.Q. 1977, c. C-15, s. 1.

PRACTICE OF PROFESSIONAL COMMUNITY PLANNING. The preparation of comprehensive plans of development, including the preparation of such plans for one or more communities or regions. *The Community Planning Profession Act*, R.S.S. 1978, c. C-21, s. 2.

PRACTICE OF PROFESSIONAL ENGINEERING. 1. Any act of designing, composing, evaluating, advising, reporting, directing or supervising wherein the safe-guarding of life, health, property or the public welfare is concerned and that requires the application of engineering principles, but does not include practising as a natural scientist. *Professional Engineers Act*, S.O. 1984, c. 13, s. 1. 2. The carrying on of any branch of chemical, civil, electrical, forest, geological, mechanical, metallurgical, mining or structural engineering, including the reporting on, designing, or directing the construction of any works that require for their design, or the supervision of their construction, or the supervision of their maintenance, such experience and technical knowledge as are required by or under an act for the admission by examination to membership in an association. 3. Reporting on, advising on, valuing, measuring for, laying out, designing, directly, constructing or inspecting any of the works or processes set forth in a schedule, or such works or processes omitted therefrom as are similar to those set forth therein by reason of their requiring the skilled application of the principles of mathematics, physics, mechanics, aeronautics, hydraulics, electricity, chemistry or geology in their development and attainment; and includes the reporting, advising, valuing, measuring for, laying out, designing, directing,

constructing or inspecting by any person under the general supervision of a professional engineer; but does not include the execution or supervision of works as contractor, foreman, superintendent, inspector, road master, superintendent of maintenance, technical assistant, student or engineer in training where the work has been designed by and is done under the responsible supervision of a professional engineer.

PRACTICE OF PROFESSIONAL FORESTRY. Advising, planning, reporting on and supervising any phase of the administration or management of forests or forest land, including the valuation, maintenance, improvement, conservation and protection of forest land and the regeneration of forests. *Foresters Act*, R.S.B.C. 1979, c. 141, s. 1.

PRACTICE OF PSYCHOLOGY. The application of professional psychological knowledge for compensation for the purpose of the diagnosing, preventing, remedying or ameliorating of human mental, emotional, behavioural or relationship difficulties, in order to evaluate or enhance human performance and to enhance mental or physical health.

PRACTICE OF RESPIRATORY TECHNOLOGY. A person shall be deemed to be practising respiratory technology who by advertisement, sign, or statement of any kind, written or oral, alleges or implies or states that that person is, or claims to be qualified, able or willing to assist any individual or individuals by way of medically supervised and co-ordinated treatment by medical gases, aerosols, oxygen, compressed air, or other therapeutic medical gas mixtures applied directly or indirectly to the airways.

PRACTICE OF SURVEYING. (i) The determination, establishment or recording by any means of the positions of points or natural or man-made features on, over or under the surface of the earth; (ii) the determination of the form of the earth; (iii) the practice of land surveying, and includes the preparation of maps, plans, systems and documents and the giving of advice with respect to any of the matters referred to in this clause. *Land Surveyors Act*, S.A. 1981, c. L-4.1, s. 1.

PRACTICE OF THE PROFESSION OF CHIROPODY. That specialty of the healing arts that treats of ailments or diseased conditions or deformities or injuries of the human foot, and includes examining or diagnosing or prescribing for or treating such disabilities, and massage or adjustment in connection therewith. *The Chiropody Profession Act*, R.S.S. 1978, c. C-9, s. 2.

PRACTICE OF VETERINARY MEDICINE. Administration and application of preventive medicine and disease control, and the medical and surgical treatment of any species of livestock, domestic animals and fowl but does not include the castrating or dehorning of farm animals or the caponizing of fowl. *Veterinary Medical Act*, R.S.N.S. 1967, c. 327, s. 1.

PRACTISE AGROLOGY. To teach or demonstrate the science or art of agriculture or advise or conduct scientific experiments and research in relation thereto as a chief occupation.

PRACTISE MEDICINE. To offer or undertake by any means or method to diagnose, treat, operate, or prescribe for any human disease, pain, injury, disability or physical condition or to hold oneself out as being able to diagnose, treat, operate or prescribe for any human disease, pain, injury, disability or physical condition.

PRACTITIONER. *n.* 1. One who exercises or employs any art or profession. 2. A person who is registered and entitled under the laws of a province to practise in that province the profession of medicine, dentistry or veterinary medicine. 3. A chiropractor, dental mechanic, dental surgeon, ophthalmic dispenser, optometrist, osteopath, physician or podiatrist or other person who provides a basic health service or an extended health service. *Alberta Health Care Insurance Act*, R.S.A. 1980, c. A-24, s. 1. 4. A person other than a physician entitled to render insured services in the place where they are rendered. Health Insurance acts. See DRUGLESS ~; GENERAL ~; HEALTH CARE ~; HEALTH ~; MEDICAL ~; NATUROPATHIC ~; NURSE ~; RESTRICTED ~.

PRAECIPE. *n.* [L.] 1. A requisition. G.D. Watson & C. Perkins, eds., *Holmested & Watson: Ontario Civil Procedure* (Toronto: Carswell, 1984) at CJA-179. 2. A piece of paper on which one party to a proceeding specifies what document that party wishes to have prepared or issued and the particulars of the document.

PRAECOGNITA. *n.* [L.] Things known previously so that something later can be understood.

PRAEDA BELLI. [L.] Property taken in wartime.

PRAEDIAL SERVITUDE. A servitude which affects land.

PRAENOMEN. *n.* [L.] The given name of a person, as opposed to a family name.

PRAESCRIPTIO EST TITULUS EX USU ET TEMPORE SUBSTANTIAM CAPIENS AD AUCTORITATE LEGIS. [L.] Prescription is a title arising from use and time which takes its substance from legal authority.

PRAESENTIA CORPORIS TOLLIT ERRO- REM NOMINIS; ET VERITAS NOMINIS TOLLIT ERROREM DEMONSTRATIONIS. [L.] The presence of a body removes error from a name; and the truth of a name removes error from a description.

PRAESTAT CAUTELA QUAM MEDELA. [L.] Caution is superior to cure.

PRAESUMPTIO. *n.* [L.] 1. Intrusion. 2. The unlawful seizure of something.

PRAESUMPTIO VIOLENTA VALET IN LEGE. [L.] Strong presumption prevails in law.

PRAIRIE FARM REHABILITATION ADMINISTRATION. The federal body which promotes water and soil development and conservation and land use adjustment in the Prairie provinces.

PRAIRIE REGION. The provinces of Manitoba, Saskatchewan and Alberta and the Peace River District. *Feed Grain Transportation and Storage Assistance Regulations*, C.R.C., c. 1027, s. 2.

PRANK. *n.* A practical joke.

PRAXIS. *n.* Practice, use.

PRAYER. *n.* The conclusion of a petition to Parliament which expresses the petitioners' particular object. A. Fraser, G.A. Birch & W.A. Dawson, eds., *Beauchesne's Rules and Forms of the House of Commons of Canada*, 5th ed. (Toronto: Carswell, 1978) at 209.

PRAYER FOR RELIEF. The portion of a statement of claim requesting damages or an order of the court.

P.R.B. *abbr.* Pension Review Board.

PREAMBLE. *n.* A preface which states the reasons for and intended effects of legislation. A. Fraser, G.A. Birch & W.A. Dawson, eds., *Beauchesne's Rules and Forms of the House of Commons of Canada*, 5th ed. (Toronto: Carswell, 1978) at 218 and 219.

PRE-APPRENTICE. *n.* A person who is a fulltime or part-time student registered in an approved program of study from which the person is to receive training and instruction in a designated occupation in preparation for qualification under this Act. *An Act to Amend the Industrial Training and Certification Act*, S.N.B. 1987, c. 27, s. 2.

PREARRANGED CEMETERY CONTRACT. A contract or agreement whereby, in consideration of payment therefor in advance, by a lump sum or instalments, a person undertakes to provide lots, compartments, crypts or other space in a cemetery, columbarium or mausoleum, or cemetery services or cemetery supplies, for a person alive at the time the agreement is made. *The Cemeteries Act*, R.S.S. 1978, c. C-4, s. 2.

PREARRANGED FUNERAL PLAN. *var.* **PRE-ARRANGED FUNERAL PLAN.** An agreement where, in consideration of payment in advance by lump sum or instalments, a person contracts to provide funeral merchandise or services when required for one or more individuals alive at the time the agreement is entered into.

PREAUDIENCE. *var.* **PRE-AUDIENCE.** *n.* One person's right to be heard before another; the usual order of precedence is the Attorney-General, Queen's Counsel, and junior barristers, usually in the order in which they were called to the bar.

PREBENDA. *n.* [L.] Goods provided.

PRECANCELLED STAMP. A postage stamp cancelled by the Post Office Department prior to sale and used for the purpose of paying postage on third and fourth class mail. *Methods of Payment of Postage Regulations*, C.R.C., c. 1284, s. 2.

PRECATORY WORDS. An expression in a will which indicates a wish, desire or request that something be done.

PRECEDENCE. *n.* The state or act of going first.

PRECEDENT. *n.* A decision or judgment of a court of law which is cited as the authority for deciding a similar situation in the same manner, on the same principle or by analogy.

PRECEDENT CONDITION. Something which must be performed or happen before an interest can vest or grow or an obligation be performed.

PRECEPT. *n.* Direction, order.

PRECEPTOR. *n.* 1. A veterinarian who trains undergraduate veterinarians in the practice of veterinary medicine. *Veterinary Profession Act*, R.S.P.E.I. 1974, c. V-4, s. 2. 2. (i) A pharmacist who has acted as a pharmacist engaged in the compounding and dispensing of pharmaceutical preparations and prescriptions in a pharmacy or hospital in Ontario for not less than 6 months, and is engaged full time in the practice of a pharmacist in a pharmacy or hospital in which not less than 3,000 prescriptions are dispensed annually and in the library of which there are, in addition to the texts and materials required by this Regulation, current editions of two journals related to the practice of pharmacists; or (ii) a person who holds a degree in pharmacy and is designated as a preceptor by the Registration Committee of the Ontario College of

Pharmacists. *Health Disciplines Act*, R.R.O. 1980, Reg. 451, s. 1.

PRECINCT. *n.* 1. The immediate environs of a court. 2. The district of a constable. See ELECTORAL ~; PARLIAMENTARY ~S.

PRECINCTS OF THE BUILDING. The space enclosed by the walls of the building. *Judicature Act*, R.S.O. 1980, c. 223, s. 67.

PRECIOUS METAL. Gold, palladium, platinum and silver and an alloy of any of those metals and any other metal and an alloy thereof that is designated by the regulations as a precious metal for the purposes of this Act. *Precious Metals Marking Act*, R.S.C. 1985, c. P-19, s. 2.

PRECIOUS METAL ARTICLE. An article wholly or partly, or purporting to be wholly or partly, composed of a precious metal and includes a plated article. *Precious Metals Marking Act*, R.S.C. 1985, c. P-19, s. 2.

PRECIOUS PROPERTY. Personal-use property and is all or part of any print, etching, drawing, painting, sculpture or other similar work of art, jewellery, rare folio, rare manuscript or rare book, stamp or coin. *Taxation Act*, R.S.Q. 1977, c. I-3, s. 265.

PRECIPE. See PRAECIPE.

PRECONISATION. *n.* A proclamation.

PREDATOR. *n.* 1. A coyote, fox, timber wolf, or bear, and includes a pup or cub of any of them. 2. Any animal which preys upon livestock. *Livestock Insurance Act*, S.Nfld. 1975, c. 59, s. 2.

PREDATORY ANIMAL. Coyote and wolf. *Game Act*, R.S.N.W.T. 1974, c. G-1, s. 2.

PREDECESSOR. *n.* One person who preceded another.

PRE-DEVELOPMENT. *n.* Any act or deed relating to surveys and research in the field for a limited period of time for the purpose of gathering information with a view to deciding whether or not development will take place. *An Act respecting the land regime in the James Bay and New Quebec territories*, S.Q. 1979, c. 25, s. 50.

PRE-DISPOSITION REPORT. *var.* **PREDISPOSITION REPORT.** A report on the personal and family history and present environment of a young person.

PREEMPTIVE RIGHT. The right to purchase shares or other securities to be issued or subjected to rights or options to purchase, as such right is defined in this section. *Loan and Trust Companies Act*, S.N.B. 1987, c. L-11.2, s. 74.

PRE-EXISTING CONTRACT. A sale contract that has been replaced by another sales contract.

PRE-EXISTING OR UNDERLYING CONDITION. A condition of the workman which existed or was discernible as an underlying condition before the accident and includes a neurosis and a psycho-neurosis. *Workmen's Compensation Act*, S.M. 1972, c. 46, s. 23.

PREFABRICATED TRENCH SUPPORT SYSTEM. A trench box, trench-shield or similar structure composed of members connected to one another, capable of being moved as a unit, and designed to resist the pressure from the walls of a trench. *Occupational Health and Safety Act*, R.R.O. 1980, Reg. 691, s. 167.

PREFATORY AVERMENT. An old term from common law pleading for particulars of facts and circumstances, including any special knowledge which listeners might possess prepared by the plaintiff. R.E. Brown, *The Law of Defamation in Canada* (Toronto: Carswell, 1987) at 156.

PREFER. *v.* 1. To move for, to apply. 2. For a prosecutor to make a bill of indictment in respect of a charge based on facts disclosed at a preliminary inquiry. S.A. Cohen, *Due Process of Law* (Toronto: Carswell, 1977) at 166.

PREFERENCE. *n.* Paying one creditor to the detriment of others when the debtor is insolvent. See FRAUDULENT ~.

PREFERENCE SHARE. A share which gives its holders some preference over others concerning dividend, repayment of capital or some other matter. See CUMULATIVE ~.

PREFERENTIAL HIRING. A system by which employers agree to hire union members as long as there are enough members to fill the employers' requirements.

PREFERRED BENEFICIARY. Under any trust means an individual resident in Canada who is a beneficiary under the trust and is (i) the settlor of the trust; (ii) the spouse or former spouse of the settlor of the trust; or (iii) a child, grandchild or great grandchild of the settlor of the trust, or the spouse of any such person. *Income Tax Act*, R.S.C. 1952, c. 148 (as am. S.C. 1970-71-72, c. 63), s. 108(1)(g).

PREFERRED CLAIMANT. A husband, wife, parent, child, brother, sister, grandparent, grandchild, uncle, aunt, nephew, niece, first cousin, step-father, step-mother, step-child, step-brother, step-sister, father-in-law, mother-in-law, brother-in-law or sister-in-law of a deceased person, or the person named by the deceased as executor of his will, or a representative of Last Post Fund incorporated under the Companies Act (Canada), and includes any such

kindred of the half-blood equally with those of the whole-blood. *Anatomy Act*, R.S.M. 1970, c. A80, s. 2.

PREFERRED CREDITOR. A creditor whom the common law or legislation gives some advantage over other claimants. C.R.B. Dunlop, *Creditor-Debtor Law in Canada* (Toronto: Carswell, 1981) at 434.

PREFERRED SHARE. 1. A share other than a common share. 2. A share in the capital stock of an association that is not a co-op share. *Canada Cooperative Associations Act*, R.S.C. 1985, c. C-40, s. 3. See PREFERENCE SHARE.

PREFERRED SUCCESSOR. Where used with reference to a deceased means a successor to property of the deceased who is (i) the spouse of the deceased; or (ii) a child of the deceased; or (iii) a parent of the deceased; or (iv) the spouse of a child of the deceased. *Succession Duty Tax Act (Manitoba)*, S.M. 1972, c. 9, s. 1.

PREGNANCY. *n.* The state of having a child in utero.

PRE-HEARING VOTE. A vote taken prior to determination of the appropriate bargaining unit at an application for certification by a labour relations board.

PRE-INCORPORATION CONTRACT. *var.* **PREINCORPORATION CONTRACT.** A contract entered into by a contractor in the name of or on behalf of a corporation before its incorporation.

PRE-JUDGMENT INTEREST. Interest awarded on the principal sum owing under a judgment from the time it became due or the claim upon which the judgment was made.

PREJUDGMENT INTEREST RATE. The bank rate at the end of the first day of the last month of the quarter preceding the quarter in which the proceeding was commenced, rounded to the next higher whole number where the bank rate includes a fraction, plus 1 per cent. *Courts of Justice Act, 1984*, S.O. 1984, c. 11, s. 137.

PREJUDICE. *n.* An injury. See DISMISSAL WITHOUT ~; WITHOUT ~.

PRELIMINARY AGREEMENT. Includes any written offer to purchase real estate which offer has been accepted by the vendor of the real estate described therein and any written agreement to sell real estate which has been accepted by the person agreeing to purchase same. *Real Estate Brokers Act*, R.S.M. 1970, c. R20, s. 2.

PRELIMINARY EXAMINATION. The examination for admission as an articled pupil. *Canada Lands Survey Examination Regulations*, C.R.C., c. 1020, s. 2.

PRELIMINARY HEARING. The hearing, held in accordance with procedure set out in Part XVIII of the Criminal Code, in which a justice determines whether there is sufficient evidence to commit an accused for trial.

PRELIMINARY LIST OF ELECTORS. The lists of electors prepared by enumerators.

PRELIMINARY QUESTION. A question connected to the merits or the heart of an inquiry but which is not the major question to be decided. S.A. DeSmith, *Judicial Review of Administrative Action*, 4th ed. by J.M. Evans (London: Stevens, 1980) at 114.

PRELIMINARY SCORE. The display prior to the start of the race of the horses in a harness horse race by being trotted or paced at their designated gaits on the race course in front of the grandstand after the post parade has been completed. *Race Track Supervision Regulations*, C.R.C., c. 441, s. 2.

PREMIER. *n.* 1. A minister of the Crown holding the recognized position of first Minister. 2. The Prime Minister.

PREMISES. *n.* 1. Lands and structures, or either of them, and includes trailers and portable structures designed or used for residence, business or shelter. 2. Lands and structures, or either of them, and includes: (i) water; (ii) ships and vessels; (iii) trailers and portable structures designed or used for residence, business or shelter; (iv) trains, railway cars, vehicles and aircraft. See ACCESS TO COMPANY ~; BUSINESS ~; BUYER'S ~; CARETAKER'S ~; EMPLOYMENT ~; FOOD PREMISE; FOOD SERVICE ~; INTEREST IN THE ~; LANDS AND ~; LICENSED ~; MOBILE ~; MOBILE PREPARATION ~; OFF ~ SALE; ON-~ SALE; PERMIT ~; RESIDENTIAL ~; ROADSIDE ~.

PREMIUM. *n.* 1. The single or periodical payment to be made for insurance and includes dues and assessments. 2. Any goods, services, rebate or other benefit offered or given at the time of the sale of goods or the lease of services, which may be granted or obtained immediately or in a deferred manner, from the merchant, manufacturer or advertiser, either gratuitously or on conditions explicitly or implicitly presented as advantageous. *Consumer Protection Act*, S.Q. 1978, c. 9, s. 232. 3. Any periodic or other amount paid or payable under a retirement savings plan; (i) as consideration for any contract referred to in subparagraph (j)(i) to pay a retirement income; or (ii) as a contribution or deposit referred to in subparagraph (j)(ii) for the purpose stated in that subparagraph. *Income Tax Act*, R.S.C. 1952, c. 148 (as am. S.C. 1980-81-82-83, c. 40, s. 96(1)), s. 146(1)(f). 4. Where used in relation to a commodity futures option, means the consideration for which the option is acquired. 5. The excess value of the consideration received from the issue or resale of securities over the par or stated value of the securities. Pipeline Uniform Accounting regulations. See ACCELERATING ~; BASIC ~; CALL-IN PAY OR ~; EMPLOYEE'S ~; EMPLOYER'S ~; NET ~S; NIGHT ~.

PREMIUM NOTE. An instrument given as consideration for insurance whereby the maker undertakes to pay such sum or sums as may be legally demanded by the insurer, but the aggregate of those sums does not exceed an amount specified in the instrument.

PREMIUM PAY. The pay which an employee is entitled to receive for employment on a public holiday or a day that is deemed to be a public holiday.

PREMIUM RATE. The rate of pay to which an employee is entitled for each hour of employment on a public holiday, or a day that is deemed to be a public holiday. *Employment Standards Act*, R.S.O. 1980, c. 137, s. 1.

PREMIX. See MACRO-~; MEDICINAL ~; MICRO-~.

PRE MORTEM. Occurring or present before death. F.A. Jaffe, *A Guide to Pathological Evidence*, 2d ed. (Toronto: Carswell, 1983) at 182.

PRENDER. *n.* The right or power to seize anything before it is offered.

PRE-NEED ASSURANCE FUND. The moneys set aside by the owner out of the amount received from the sale of cemetery supplies and cemetery services as defined by the regulations. *Cemeteries Act*, R.S.O. 1980, c. 59, s. 1.

PRENEED CEMETERY PLAN. An agreement where, in consideration of payment in advance by a lump sum or instalments, a cemetery or crematorium contracts to provide cemetery goods or services when required for one or more individuals alive at the time the agreement is entered into. *Cemetery and Funeral Services Act*, S.N.S. 1983, c. 4, s. 2.

PRE-PACKAGED FOOD. Food which is packaged at a premises other than the place at which it is offered for sale. *Public Health Act*, R.R.O. 1980, Reg. 840, s. 1.

PRE-PACKAGED GOODS. Goods packaged in a wrapper or container ready for retail sale; and, if goods packaged in a wrapper or container are found in premises where such goods are packaged or kept for sale, they shall prima facie be deemed to be packaged ready for retail sale. *Weights and Measures Act*, R.S.C. 1970, c. W-7, s. 2.

PREPACKAGED PRODUCT. Any product that is packaged in a container in such a manner that it is ordinarily sold to or used or purchased by a consumer without being re-packaged.

PREPAID EXPENSE. An expenditure or outlay which a taxpayer makes or incurs, the benefit of which extends beyond the end of a taxation year. W. Grover & F. Iacobucci, *Materials on Canadian Income Tax*, 4th ed. (Toronto: Richard De Boo Ltd., 1980) at 858.

PREPAID FUNERAL CONTRACT. Any contract or agreement, or series or combination of contracts or agreements, other than a contract of insurance issued by an insurer licensed pursuant to The Saskatchewan Insurance Act, pursuant to which: (i) for a specified monetary consideration paid in advance of death in a lump sum or by instalments, a contract seller promises to furnish or make available or provide funeral services or funeral goods for use at a time determinable by the death of the contract beneficiary, and includes: (A) prepaid, pre-arranged deposit contracts, where funds are left with the contract seller and are to be used toward the eventual costs of funeral goods and funeral services on behalf of the contract beneficiary; and (B) prepaid, pre-arranged trust contracts, where the contract buyer and the contract seller have a fixed agreement for the provision, on behalf of the contract beneficiary, of funeral goods and funeral services specified in the contract; or (ii) for monetary consideration, a contract seller provides counselling or advice to any person with respect to funeral services or funeral goods. *Prepaid Funeral Service Act*, S.S. 1986, c. P-22.3, s. 2.

PREPARATION. *n.* 1. A drug that contains a controlled drug and one or more active medicinal ingredients, in a recognized therapeutic dose, other than a controlled drug. *Food and Drug Regulations*, C.R.C., c. 870, c. G.01.001. 2. A preparation of one or more synthetic colours containing less than 3 per cent dye and sold for household use. *Food and Drug Regulations*, C.R.C., c. 870, c. B.06.001. See FOOD ~ EQUIPMENT; PHARMACEUTICAL ~.

PREPARATORY ASPECTS OF PRINTING. Any design work, typesetting, paste up, artwork, composition, photography, preparation of negatives, and any other practice or process commonly accepted within the printing trade, used directly for or in conjunction with any production of printed matter. *Public Printing Act*, S.M. 1979, c. 17, s. 1.

PREPARE. *v.* Includes cut, wrap, package, freeze, cure or smoke. *Meat Inspection (Nova Scotia) Act*, S.N.S. 1984, c. 7, s. 2.

PREPARED MEAT PRODUCT. A meat product to which has been added any ingredient permitted by these Regulations, other than meat, or that has been preserved, canned or cooked. *Meat Inspection Regulations*, C.R.C., c. 1032, s. 2.

PREPAYMENT PRIVILEGE. The right to prepay all or part of mortgage or loan principal without paying a penalty. B.J. Reiter, R.C.B. Risk & B.N. McLellan, *Real Estate Law*, 3d ed. (Toronto: Emond Montgomery, 1986) at 977.

PREPENSE. *adj.* Thought of in advance, preconceived, planned beforehand.

PREPRODUCTION DEVELOPMENT COSTS. Aggregate expenses incurred by the operator of a mine in the development of the ore body from the date of acquiring the mine to the date production from the mine begins, and that are essential to the production of the output of the mine.

PREROGATIVA REGIS. [L.] The royal prerogative.

PREROGATIVE. *n.* An exceptional power, privilege or pre-eminence which the law grants to the Crown. See PERSONAL ~; ROYAL ~.

PREROGATIVE ORDER. An act by which a superior court prevents a subordinate tribunal from exceeding jurisdiction, from making errors of law on the face of its judgments and from denying natural justice. Examples are writs of habeas corpus or prohibition. S. Mitchell, P.J. Richardson & D.A. Thomas, eds., *Archbold Pleading, Evidence and Practice in Criminal Cases*, 43d ed. (London: Sweet & Maxwell, 1988) at 171.

PREROGATIVE RIGHTS OF THE CROWN. The body of special common law rules which apply to Her Majesty. C.R.B. Dunlop, *Creditor-Debtor Law in Canada* (Toronto: Carswell, 1981) at 446.

PREROGATIVE WRIT. A writ of certiorari, habeas corpus, mandamus prohibition or quo warranto. S.A. DeSmith, *Judicial Review of Administrative Action*, 4th ed. by J.M. Evans (London: Stevens, 1980) at 25.

PRE-SCHOOL FACILITY. A place other than an institution, boarding home, foster home or group foster home licensed under this act for the provision of services to children of pre-school age in accordance with the regulations. *Child Welfare Act*, S.M. 1974, c. 30, s. 1.

PRESCRIBE. *v.* 1. In a modern act of Parliament, to regulate the details after the general nature of the proceedings is indicated. 2. Prescribe by regulations of (a) the Minister, in the case of any matter affecting occupational safety and health of employees on trains while in operation; or (b) the Governor in Council, in any other case. *Canada Labour Code*, R.S.C. 1985 (1st Supp.), c. 9, s. 122.

PRESCRIBED. *adj.* 1. Prescribed by an act, by the rules of court, by regulation, by-law or other rules. 2. When used with reference to a drug or mixture of drugs, means that a prescriber has directed the dispensing of the drug or mixture of drugs to a named person. *Nursing Homes Act*, R.R.O. 1980, Reg. 690, s. 1.

PRESCRIBED DAY OF REST. (a) New Year's Day; (b) Good Friday; (c) Victoria Day; (d) Canada Day; (e) New Brunswick Day; (f) Labour Day; (g) Thanksgiving Day; (h) Remembrance Day; (i) Christmas Day; (j) Boxing Day; and (k) any day appointed by any statute in force in the province or by proclamation of the Governor General or Lieutenant-Governor as a general holiday within the province. *Days of Rest Act*, S.N.B. 1985, c. D-4.2, s. 1.

PRESCRIBED DELAY. In the case of works of imagination such as novels, novelettes, stories or poems, a period of 9 months, and in the case of all other works a period of 24 months, computed in all cases from the date when the work is first offered for sale at retail in the province. *Publishers Loss Insurance Act*, R.S.Q. 1977, c. A-27, s. 1.

PRESCRIBED PERCENTAGE. See NET ~.

PRESCRIBED SUBSTANCES. Uranium, thorium, plutonium, neptunium, deuterium, their respective derivatives and compounds and such other substances as the Board may by regulation designate as being capable of releasing atomic energy or as being requisite for the production, use or application of atomic energy. *Atomic Energy Control Act*, R.S.C. 1985, c. A-16, s. 2.

PRESCRIBED TIME PERIOD. In relation to a contract of group insurance, a continuous period of 6 months following the termination of the contract or benefit provision therein or such longer continuous period as may be provided in that contract instead of the 6-month period. Insurance acts.

PRESCRIBER. *n.* A person who is authorized to give a prescription within the scope of the practice of a health discipline or profession.

PRESCRIPTION. *n.* 1. Someone occupying land acquiring title to it by the passage of time. J.G. McLeod, *The Conflict of Laws* (Calgary: Carswell, 1983) at 333. 2. A formula or direction given by a medical practitioner, dentist, or veterinary surgeon of a remedy for or as treatment for a disease or disorder, prescribing the ingredients with or without the method of using. 3. The direction of a medical practitioner directing a physiotherapist to treat a named person.

Practice of Physiotherapy Act, R.S.P.E.I. 1974, c. P-16, s. 1. 4. A written and dated authorization signed by a dentist or a qualified medical practitioner, directing that a service be performed that a dental laboratory technician may be licensed under this Act to perform, for the purpose specified in the authorization. *Dental Technicians Act*, R.S.B.C. 1979, c. 91, s. 1. 5. In respect of a controlled drug, an authorization given by a practitioner that a stated amount of the controlled drug be dispensed for the person named therein. *Food and Drugs Act*, R.S.C. 1985, c. F-27, s. 38 as am. by *Criminal Law Amendment Act*, R.S.C. 1985 (1st Supp.), c. 27, s. 193. 6. In respect of a narcotic, an authorization given by a practitioner that a stated amount of the narcotic be dispensed for the person named therein. *Narcotic Control Act*, R.S.C. 1985, c. N-1, s. 2 as am. by *Criminal Law Amendment Act*, R.S.C. 1985 (1st Supp.), c. 27, s. 196. See ACQUISITIVE ~; EXTINCTIVE ~; ORAL ~ NARCOTIC.

PRESCRIPTION DRUG. A drug that may be dispensed by a pharmacist only upon the direction of a prescriber.

PRESENT. *v.* To offer; to tender.

PRESENT CONSIDERATION. A consideration exchanged at time of contract formation.

PRE-SENTENCE REPORT. A report prepared before sentencing containing information concerning the offender's history to be used in assisting the court in passing sentence.

PRESENTMENT. *n.* 1. Exhibiting a paper to the person from whom one seeks payment. I.F.G. Baxter, *The Law of Banking*, 3d ed. (Toronto: Carswell, 1981) at 106. 2. A species of report given by a jury.

PRESENTS. *n.* In a deed, the term which refers to the deed itself.

PRESENT VALUE. An amount that is actuarially equivalent to a payment or payments that become due in the future. *Ontario Municipal Employees Retirement System Act*, R.R.O. 1980, Reg. 724, s. 1. See NET ~.

PRESERVATIVES. See PERMITTED ~.

PRESERVE. See FISHING ~; SEMI ~S; SHOOTING ~.

PRESERVED. *adj.* In relation to a meat product, means salted, pickled, corned, cured, dried or smoked. *Meat Inspection Regulations*, C.R.C., c. 1032, s. 2.

PRESIDENT. *n.* 1. A person placed in authority over other people; a person in charge of others. 2. One who exercises chief executive functions. H. Sutherland, D.B. Horsley & J.M. Edmiston, eds., *Fraser's Handbook on Canadian Company Law*, 7th ed. (Toronto: Carswell, 1985) at 251. 3. A Chief Justice or Chief Judge. 4. Includes the chairman, governor, manager or other principal officers of a company.

PRESIDENT OF THE ASSEMBLÉE NATIONALE. The President of the Assemblée nationale and, when the office of President is vacant or when the President is absent from Québec or unable to act, the Secretary of the Assemblée nationale. *An Act Respecting Provincial Controverted Elections*, R.S.Q. 1977, c. C-65, s. 2.

PRESIDENT OF THE EXCHEQUER COURT. Now the Chief Justice of the Federal Court of Canada. D. Sgayias *et al.*, *Federal Court Practice 1988* (Toronto: Carswell, 1987) at 238.

PRESIDING JUDGE. The judge of the Court appointed by the President to preside at any sitting of the Court in his place. *Rules of Appeal Procedure*, C.R.C., c. 1051, s. 2.

PRESIDING OFFICER. The Deputy Speaker and Chairman of Committees and a Deputy Chairman and an Assistant Deputy Chairman of Committees appointed under S.O. 53, who, whenever the Chairman is absent from the Chair, may exercise all the powers of the Chairman of Committees, including the powers of Deputy Speaker when the Speaker is unavoidably absent. A. Fraser, G.A. Birch & W.A. Dawson, eds., *Beauchesne's Rules and Forms of the House of Commons of Canada*, 5th ed. (Toronto: Carswell, 1978) at 42.

PRESIDING STEWARD. The person who acts as spokesman for the stewards. *Race Track Supervision Regulations*, C.R.C., c. 441, s. 2.

PRESS. *n.* The print media.

PRESSURE. *n.* 1. Pressure in pounds per square inch measured above prevailing atmospheric pressure. 2. Pressure in pounds to the square inch as measured by a pressure gauge. *Boiler and Pressure Vessel Act*, R.S.Nfld. 1970, c. 24, s. 2. See ALLOWABLE BEARING ~; BURSTING ~; DESIGN BEARING ~; DESIGN ~; DESIGNED ~; MAXIMUM ALLOWABLE ~; RATED MAXIMUM SOUND ~; STANDARD ~ REGION; VAPOUR ~; WORKING ~.

PRESSURE ALTITUDE. See CABIN ~.

PRESSURE COMPONENT. Any internal component of the brake master cylinder or master control unit, wheel brake cylinder, brake line, brake hose, or equivalent, except vacuum assist components. *Motor Vehicle Safety Regulations*, C.R.C., c. 1038, s. 105.

PRESSURE PIPING. 1. Pipes, tubes, conduits, fittings, gaskets, bolting and all systems containing any arrangement of components thereof, the

sole purpose of which is the conveyance of an expansible fluid under pressure and the control of the flow of an expansible fluid under pressure between two points. *Boilers and Pressure Vessels Act*, R.S.A. 1970, c. 32, s. 2. 2. Piping in which the internal pressure is more than 15 pounds.

PRESSURE PIPING SYSTEM. Pipe, tubes, conduits, fittings, gaskets, bolting and other components making up a system the sole purpose of which is the conveyance of an expansible fluid under pressure and the control of the flow of an expansible fluid under pressure between two or more points.

PRESSURE PLANT. 1. Any one or more pressure vessels or any system or arrangement of pressure vessels and the engines, turbines, pressure piping system, machinery and ancillary equipment of any kind used in connection therewith. 2. For any purpose, an installation of a boiler, pressure vessel, refrigerating system or compressed gas system or combination thereof as a unit under the same owner and management and includes all engines, turbines, compressors, piping, appliances, machinery or equipment attached thereto or used in connection therewith, whether the unit is portable, automotive or permanently attached to a solid base. *Boiler and Pressure Vessel Act*, R.S.Nfld. 1970, c. 24, s. 2.

PRESSURE VESSEL. 1. Any receptacle of a capacity exceeding .0425 cubic metres that contains or is intended to contain an expansible fluid under pressure. 2. An unfired vessel other than a boiler which may be used for containing, storing, distributing, transferring, distilling or otherwise handling any gas, vapour or liquid under pressure, and includes a pipe, fitting and other equipment attached to it. 3. Any receptacle intended to contain a gas whether inflammable or not, or any pressurized liquid, a boiler and any equipment necessary to their operation. 4. A vessel that is heated or its contents are heated by: (i) a flame or the hot gases of combustion; (ii) electricity; or (iii) a liquid. 5. Includes boilers, air receivers and other vessels subject to pressure. Canada regulations. See USED BOILER, ~ OR PLANT.

PRESSURIZED AIRCRAFT. An aircraft the pressure in the cabin of which is controlled by mechanical means. *Oxygen Equipment Order*, C.R.C., c. 52, s. 2.

PRESUMPTION. *n.* 1. In the law of evidence, an inference or conclusion about the truth of some questionable fact which is drawn from another fact judicially noticed, admitted or proved to be true. 2. An invitation to make an offer to sell, or the acceptance of an unsolicited offer to sell, if done for the purpose of obtaining the result described in section 110, is deemed to be a take-over bid. *Securities Act*, S.Q. 1982, c. 48, s. 113. See COMPELLING ~; MANDATORY ~; PERMISSIVE ~.

PRESUMPTION OF ADVANCEMENT. An exception to ordinary equitable rules relating to resulting trusts, in which property paid for by a husband and conveyed into the name of his wife or child is presumed to be a gift by the husband. A. Bissett-Johnson & W.M. Holland, eds., *Matrimonial Property Law in Canada* (Toronto: Carswell, 1980) at I-13.

PRESUMPTION OF INNOCENCE. The provision in section 11(d) of the Charter of Rights that any person charged with an offence has the right to be presumed innocent until proven guilty according to law in a fair and public hearing by an independent and impartial tribunal. P.W. Hogg, *Constitutional Law of Canada*, 2d ed. (Toronto: Carswell, 1985) at 767.

PRESUMPTION OF LAW. Facts sufficient to require that a given conclusion be drawn from them. John G. Fleming, *The Law of Torts*, 6th ed. (Sydney: The Law Book Co., 1983) at 296. See REBUTTABLE ~.

PRESUMPTION OF SURVIVORSHIP. Where two or more people die in the same accident it is presumed that the younger survived.

PRESUMPTIONS OF FACT. Facts sufficient that a conclusion may be drawn from them. John G. Fleming, *The Law of Torts*, 6th ed. (Sydney: The Law Book Co., 1983) at 296.

PRESUMPTIVE EVIDENCE. Evidence which implies the large probability if not the certainty that the facts and the inference are related. P.K. McWilliams, *Canadian Criminal Evidence*, 3d ed. (Aurora: Canada Law Book, 1988) at 1-12 and 1-13. See now CIRCUMSTANTIAL EVIDENCE.

PRESUMPTIVE HEIR. The person who would have been their heir if the ancestor had died immediately, but whose right to inherit might be supplanted by a nearer heir being born.

PRESUMPTIVE POSSESSION. See CONSTRUCTIVE POSSESSION.

PRESUMPTIVE RELEASE DATE. In respect of an inmate, the earliest day on which the inmate may be entitled to be released from imprisonment. *Parole and Penitentiary Act*, R.S.C. 1985 (2d Supp.), c. 34, s. 21.2.

PRÊT À USAGE. [Fr.] Loan to be used.

PRETENCE. See FALSE ~.

PRETERITION. *n.* The complete omission of a child's name from its parent's will.

PRETIUM SUCCEDIT IN LOCUM REI. [L.] The price takes the place of the thing.

PRE-TRIAL CONFERENCE. A meeting to consider possibly settling any or all of the issues in a proceeding, simplifying the issues, possibly obtaining admissions which would facilitate the hearing, liability or any other matter that might assist in a just, efficient and inexpensive disposition of that proceeding. G.D. Watson & C. Perkins, eds., *Holmested & Watson: Ontario Civil Procedure* (Toronto: Carswell, 1984) at 50-2.

PREVAILING WAGE. The level of remuneration common in a locality for a particular type of work.

PREVARICATION. *n.* 1. Conspiracy between an informer and a defendant to feign prosecution. 2. Secret abuse committed in a public or private office. 3. Wilfully concealing or misrepresenting truth by giving equivocating or evasive evidence.

PREVENIENT ARRANGEMENT. An agreement by a supplier to supply from time to time materials as ordered by a contractor or subcontractor following terms agreed on or fixed later as the material is supplied. D.N. Macklem & D.I. Bristow, *Construction and Mechanics' Liens in Canada*, 5th ed. (Toronto: Carswell, 1985) at 107.

PREVENTION. See FIRE ~.

PREVENTIVE DETENTION. Detention in a penitentiary for an indeterminate period. *Criminal Code*, R.S.C. 1970, c. C-34, s. 687.

PREVENTER. See BACKFLOW ~.

PREVIEW. See ENVIRONMENTAL ~ REPORT.

PREVIOUS FISCAL YEAR. The fiscal year ending next before the current fiscal year.

PREY. See BIRD OF ~.

PRICE. *n.* 1. A consideration in money. G.H.L. Fridman, *Sale of Goods in Canada*, 3d ed. (Toronto: Carswell, 1986) at 11. 2. Includes rate or charge for any service. See ADMINISTERED ~; ADMISSION ~; ALBERTA BORDER ~; ALLOWANCE ~; BARGAIN ~; BASE ~; CASH ~; CONTRACT ~; FIRM ~ CONTRACT; FIXED ~ CONTRACT; FREIGHT TO ~ RATIO; INCLUSIVE TOUR ~; INTERNATIONAL BORDER ~; INVOICE ~; LEASE ~; MARKET ~; PAY-OUT ~; PURCHASE ~; SALE ~; SETTLEMENT ~; STRIKING ~; WHOLESALE ~.

PRICE. *abbr.* Price's Mining Commissioner's Cases (Ont.), 1906-1910.

PRICE COMPONENT. (i) The Alberta cost of

service, if the gas contract provides for the deduction or addition of the buyer's Alberta cost of service in the calculation of the price payable for gas delivered under the contract; (ii) any class of costs or charges that is, according to the gas contract, a component in the calculation of the price payable for gas delivered under the contract; or (iii) any class of revenue that is, according to the gas contract, a component in the calculation of the price payable for gas delivered under the contract. *Natural Gas Marketing Act*, S.A. 1986, c. N-2.8, s. 2.

PRICE LEVEL ADJUSTED ACCOUNTING. Modification of accounting data based on historic costs by adjusting the price levels of non-monetary assets and liabilities according to appropriate general price indexes. W. Grover & F. Iacobucci, *Materials on Canadian Income Tax*, 4th ed. (Toronto: Richard De Boo Ltd., 1980) at 602.

PRICE LIST. Numerical or alphabetical enumeration of goods, wares, merchandise items or services, quoting wholesale or retail prices or both and printed on cards, or sheets of paper presented in loose-leaf form, stapled, stitched or bound. *Retail Sales Tax Act*, R.R.O. 1980, Reg. 904, s. 1.

PRICE MAINTENANCE AGREEMENT. An agreement between a manufacturer and a retailer in which the retailer contracts not to sell the manufacturer's goods at less than a specified price.

PRICE OF ADMISSION. 1. Any payment made to attend to take part in any amusement. 2. An entrance fee, cover charge or other fee charged or collected from patrons by the owner of a place of entertainment for any service, facility or privilege and includes a season ticket, a ticket issued for any series of events, or a complimentary pass but does not include any tax or portion of any tax imposed by this Act or the regulations made thereunder. *Entertainments Act*, R.S.P.E.I. 1974, c. E-7, s. 1. See ADMISSION PRICE.

PRICE OF AIR-TIME. The total amount payable for the broadcast of an advertisement. *Broadcast Advertising Tax Act*, R.S.Q. 1977, c. T-2, s. 1.

PRICE PAID OR PAYABLE. In respect of the sale of goods for export to Canada, means the aggregate of all payments made or to be made, directly or indirectly, in respect of the goods by the purchaser to or for the benefit of the vendor. *Customs Act*, R.S.C. 1985 (2nd Supp.), c. 1, s. 45.

PRICING. See DELIVERED ~.

PRIMAE IMPRESSIONIS. [L.] Of the first impression.

PRIMA FACIE. [L.] At first glance; on the surface.

PRIMA FACIE EVIDENCE. Evidence which the jury must believe unless it is rebutted or the contrary is proved.

PRIMAL CUT. 1. One of the portions into which a carcass is subdivided for commercial purposes. *Meat Inspection Regulations*, C.R.C., c. 1032, s. 2. 2. A short hip, steak piece, short loin, rib or chuck cut. *Meat Inspection Act (Ontario)*, R.R.O. 1980, Reg. 607, s. 1.

PRIMARY BREEDING FLOCK. A flock of poultry, comprising one or more generations of poultry, that is being maintained for the purpose of establishing, continuing or improving parent lines and from which multiplier breeding flocks may be produced. *Hatchery Regulations*, C.R.C., c. 1023, s. 2.

PRIMARY DEPENDANT. (i) A husband or wife of an insured where, at the time of the death of the insured: (A) the insured and the husband or wife were living together; or (B) the husband or wife, although not living with the insured, was dependent in whole or in part on the insured for provision of the necessaries of life; (ii) a dependent child of an insured, if the insured is not survived by a person qualifying as a primary dependant pursuant to subclause (i); (iii) a dependent parent of an insured, if the insured is not survived by any of the persons qualifying as primary dependants pursuant to subclause (i) or (ii). *Automobile Accident Insurance Amendment Act*, S.S. 1984-85-86, c. 1, s. 3.

PRIMARY DISTRIBUTION TO THE PUBLIC. Used in relation to trading in securities, means: (i) trades that are made for the purpose of distributing to the public securities issued by a company and not previously distributed; or (ii) trades in previously issued securities for the purpose of distributing such securities to the public where the securities form all or a part of or are derived from the holdings of any person, company or any combination of persons or companies holding a sufficient number of any of the securities of a company to materially affect the control of such company; whether such trades are made directly to the public or indirectly to the public through an underwriter or otherwise; and includes any transaction or series of transactions involving a purchase and sale or a repurchase and resale in the course of or incidental to such distribution.

PRIMARY DIVISION. The division of the organization of an elementary school comprising junior kindergarten, kindergarten and the first 3 years of the program of studies immediately following kindergarten. *Education Act*, R.S.O. 1980, c. 129, s. 1.

PRIMARY ELEVATOR. An elevator whose principal use is the receiving of grain directly from producers for storage or forwarding or both. *Canada Grain Act*, R.S.C. 1985, c. G-10, s. 2.

PRIMARY EVIDENCE. The best evidence, in contrast to secondary evidence.

PRIMARY FISHING ENTERPRISE. 1. An enterprise that is carried on for the purpose of catching or trapping fish for sale, and does not include the processing of fish except as prescribed. *Fisheries Improvement Loans Act*, R.S.C. 1985, c. F-22, s. 2. 2. The processing of fish that may be carried on in any area is the preparation of fish or the making of fishery products to the extent that the preparation or making is (a) normally carried out by fishermen in that particular area; or (b) carried out for the purpose of making fish into a saleable product to meet a particular marketing situation. Fisheries Improvement Loans Regulations, C.R.C., c. 864, s. 6.

PRIMARY FOREST PRODUCT. 1. Everything resulting from the processing, treating, manufacturing or breaking down of logs, their byproducts or wastes. *Logging Tax Act*, R.S.B.C. 1979, c. 248, s. 1. 2. Wood cut and prepared primarily for processing into wood pulp, paper, paper products, lumber, compressed board or any product manufactured from wood fibre, including Christmas trees, sawmill chips, pulpwood chips, fuel chips and any wood fibre intended for use in heat or power generation. *Pulpwood Marketing Act*, S.N.S. 1986, c. 52, s. 4.

PRIMARY INSTRUMENT OF INDEBTEDNESS. A security evidencing the amount of indebtedness constituting a loan but does not include a debenture or other security taken as collateral security only. *Bank Act*, R.S.C. 1985, c. B-1, s. 190.

PRIMARY PRODUCER. 1. A person who derives from the catching and sale of fish a part of his net revenue. *Fish Inspection Act*, R.S.P.E.I. 1974, c. F-9, s. 2. 2. Any person who is engaged in the production of wheat, but for the purpose of this Act, shall be deemed to include any person entitled whether as landlord, vendor, mortgagee or otherwise or by contract or operation of law, to wheat grown by a producer or to any share therein. *Wheat Cooperative Marketing Act*, R.S.C. 1970, c. W-9, s. 2.

PRIMARY PRODUCTION. A mineral produced from a mineral resource that is: (i) in the form in which it exists on its recovery or severance from its natural state; or (ii) any product resulting from processing or refining that mineral, other than a manufactured product or a product resulting from refining crude oil, refining upgraded heavy crude oil, refining gases or liquids derived from coal or refining a synthetic equivalent of crude oil. *Mineral Resources Act*, S.S. 1984-85-86, c. M-16.1, s. 2.

PRIMARY PRODUCTION OF POTASH. (i) Potash that is in the form in which it exists upon its recovery or severance from its natural state; and (ii) any product containing the element potassium resulting from processing or refinishing potash, other than a manufactured product.

PRIMARY SHOCK. A temporary loss of consciousness caused by violent emotion or fear. F.A. Jaffe, *A Guide to Pathological Evidence*, 2d ed. (Toronto: Carswell, 1983) at 183.

PRIMARY TIMBER PRODUCTS. Includes rough and dressed lumber, logs, untreated round wood and ties, wood chips and any other products that are designated in the regulations. *Forests Act*, R.S.A. 1980, c. F-16, s. 1.

PRIMARY WOOD PRODUCTS. Any commercially valuable raw material consisting essentially of xylem, obtained from the stems or limbs of a felled or cut tree, including, but not confined to, roundwood and woodchips. *An Act to Amend the Scalers Act*, S.N.S. 1984, c. 35, s. 1.

PRIMARY X-RAY BEAM. That X-radiation emitted directly from the target of the X-ray tube and emerging through the window of the X-ray generator. *Radiation Emitting Devices Regulations*, C.R.C., c. 1370, s. 1.

PRIME CONTRACTOR. The person with whom the obligee has contracted to perform the contract. *Business Loans, Guarantees and Indemnities Act*, S.N.W.T. 1983 (1st Sess.), c. 1, s. 3.

PRIME MINISTER. The minister with power to select, promote, demote or dismiss other ministers, who is personally responsible for advising the Governor General about when Parliament should be dissolved for an election and when the elected parliament should be called into session and who enjoys special authority because she or he was selected as the leader of a political party which was victorious in the previous election. P.W. Hogg, *Constitutional Law of Canada*, 2d ed. (Toronto: Carswell, 1985) at 196.

PRIME MOVER. An initial source of motive power.

PRIMER. *n.* A small charge placed within the main charge to initiate an explosion.

PRIME RATE. The lowest rate of interest

quoted by a bank to its most credit-worthy borrowers for prime business loans.

PRIME RATE PERCENTAGE. The prime rate of the chartered bank that has the highest prime rate on the relevant day expressed as a percentage only, without the addition of the words "per annum".

PRIMER CARTRIDGE. A cartridge into which a hole is punched and a detonator inserted for firing the charge either by fuse or electric current. *Metalliferous Mines and Quarries Regulation Act*, R.S.N.S. 1967, c. 183, s. 14.

PRIME TIME. In relation to a broadcasting undertaking, means, in the case of a radio station, the time between the hours of 6 a.m. and 9 a.m., 12 p.m. and 2 p.m., and 4 p.m. and 7 p.m., and, in the case of a television station, the hours between 6 p.m. and midnight. *Canada Elections Act*, R.S.C. 1985, c. E-2, s. 2.

PRIMO EXCUTIENDA EST VERBI VIS, NE SERMONIS VITIO OBSTRUETUR ORATIO, SIVE LEX SINE ARGUMENTIS. [L.] First, the meaning of the word should be examined so that the meaning of the sentence will not be obscured by verbal error nor the law be obscured by not being argued.

PRIMOGENITURE. *n.* 1. Seniority; the status of being born first. 2. A rule of inheritance by which the oldest of two or more males of the same degree succeeds to an ancestor's land, excluding all the others.

PRIMUM DECRETUM. [L.] A provisional decree.

PRIMUS ACTUS JUDICII EST JUDICIS APPROBATORIUS. [L.] The first step taken by a party to an action is to concede that the court has jurisdiction in that action.

PRINCE. *n.* A sovereign; a chief ruler, either female or male.

PRINCE EDWARD ISLAND. See GOVERNMENT OF ~.

PRINCIPAL. *n.* 1. A chief; a head. 2. A capital amount of money loaned at interest. 3. A teacher who is appointed to be in charge of a school. 4. Of any corporate applicant or registrant means a person who beneficially owns, directly or indirectly, more than 10 per cent of its outstanding voting shares. *Ontario New Home Warranties Plan Act*, R.R.O. 1980, Reg. 726, s. 1. 5. (i) In the case of a bid bond, a person bidding for the award of a contract; or (ii) the person primarily liable to complete a contract for the obligee, or to make payments to other persons in respect of such contract, and for whose performance of his obligation the surety is bound under the terms of a payment bond

or performance bond. *Business Loans, Guarantees and Indemnities Act*, S.N.W.T. 1983 (1st Sess.), c. 1, s. 3. 6. Includes an employer. *Criminal Code*, R.S.C. 1985, c. C-46, s. 426(4). See DEALER ~; DISCLOSED ~; NAMED ~; UNDISCLOSED ~; VICE-~.

PRINCIPAL AMOUNT. In relation to any obligation means the amount that, under the terms of the obligation or any agreement relating thereto, is the maximum amount or maximum aggregate amount, as the case may be, payable on account of the obligation by the issuer thereof, otherwise than as or on account of interest or as or on account of any premium payable by the issuer conditional upon the exercise by the issuer of a right to redeem the obligation before the maturity thereof. *Income Tax Act*, R.S.C. 1952, c. 148 (as am. S.C. 1970-71-72, c. 63), c. 248(1).

PRINCIPAL AND ACCESSORY. Of an offence, a principal of the first degree actually perpetrates the crime; a principal of the second degree is present, aiding and abetting the act.

PRINCIPAL AND AGENT. A principal is one who, being sui juris and competent to do any act for one's own benefit on one's own account, employs the agent to do it.

PRINCIPAL AND SURETY. The principal or principal debtor owes a debt for which the surety is liable in case the principal defaults in paying it.

PRINCIPAL-BUSINESS CORPORATION. A corporation whose principal business is: (i) production, refining or marketing of petroleum, petroleum products or natural gas, or exploring or drilling for petroleum or natural gas; (ii) mining or exploring for minerals; (iii) processing mineral ores for the purpose of recovering metals therefrom; (iv) a combination of (A) processing mineral ores for the purpose of recovering metals therefrom; and (B) processing metals recovered from the ores so processed; (v) fabricating metals; (vi) operating a pipeline for the transmission of oil or natural gas; or (vii) production or marketing of sodium chloride or potash, or whose business includes manufacturing products whose manufacturing involves processing sodium chloride or potash; or a corporation all or substantially all of whose assets are shares of the capital stock of one or more other corporations that are related to the corporation (otherwise than by reason of a right referred to in paragraph 251(5)(b)) and whose principal business is described in any of subparagraphs (i) to (vii). *Income Tax Act*, R.S.C. 1952, c. 148 (as am. S.C. 1987, c. 46, s. 18(8.1)), s. 66(15)(h).

PRINCIPAL CONTRACTOR. 1. The owner or

any other person who, on a construction site, is responsible for the carrying out of all the work. 2. A person, partnership or group of persons who, pursuant to a contract, an agreement or ownership, directs the activities of 1 or more employers involved in work at a work site. *Occupational Health and Safety Amendment Act, 1983*, S.A. 1983, c. 39, s. 2.

PRINCIPAL DEBTOR. The person whose liability a surety guarantees.

PRINCIPAL DISPLAY PANEL. (a) In the case of a container that is mounted on a display card, that part of the label applied to all or part of the principal display surface of the container or to all or part of the side of the display card that is displayed or visible under normal or customary conditions of sale or use or to both such parts of the container and the display card; (b) in the case of an ornamental container, that part of the label applied to all or part of the bottom of the container or to all or part of the principal display surface or to all or part of a tag that is attached to the container; and (c) in the case of all other containers, that part of the label applied to all or part of the principal display surface. Canada regulations.

PRINCIPAL DISPLAY SURFACE. 1. (a) In the case of a container that has a side or surface that is displayed or visible under normal or customary conditions of sale or use, the total area of such side or surface excluding the top, if any; (b) in the case of a container that has a lid that is the part of the container displayed or visible under normal or customary conditions of sale or use, the total area of the top surface of the lid; (c) in the case of a container that does not have a particular side or surface that is displayed or visible under normal or customary conditions of sale or use, any 40 per cent of the total surface area of the container, excluding the top and bottom, if any, if such 40 per cent can be displayed or visible under normal or customary conditions of sale or use; (d) in the case of a container that is a bag with sides of equal dimensions, the total area of one of the sides; (e) in the case of a container that is a bag with sides of more than one size, the total area of one of the largest sides; and (f) in the case of a container that is a wrapper or confining band that is so narrow in relation to the size of the product contained that it cannot reasonably be said to have any side or surface that is displayed or visible under normal or customary conditions of sale or use, the total area of one side of a ticket or tag attached to such container. Canada regulations. 2. In respect of the container or a product, the side or surface of the container that is displayed or visible when the product is offered for sale to the public or when the product is used. Canada regulations.

PRINCIPAL EQUIVALENT. See CANADIAN ~.

PRINCIPAL MONEY. The amount lent, in contrast to interest or other money owed.

PRINCIPAL OBLIGATION. The delivery of goods or the performance of a service. *Consumer Protection Act*, R.S.Q. 1977, c. P-40, s. 1.

PRINCIPAL PLACE OF BUSINESS. (a) In the case of a corporation incorporated by or under the authority of an Act of Parliament or of the former Province of Canada, or by or under the authority of any province or any territory now forming part of Canada, the place where, according to the corporation's charter, memorandum of association or by-laws, the head office of the corporation in Canada is situated; and (b) in the case of any other corporation, the place at which a civil process in the province or territory in which the loans or advances will be made can be served on the corporation. *Bank Act*, R.S.C. 1985, c. B-1, s. 178(5).

PRINCIPAL RESIDENCE. Residential premises that constitute a person's normal or permanent place of residence and to which, when that person is absent, that person has the intention of returning.

PRINCIPAL SUM. The aggregate of (a) the cash price of the goods or services or both; (b) any sum received in cash by the borrower; (c) any sum paid to a third party on behalf of, and at the request of, the borrower; (d) any sum remaining unpaid from a previous extension of credit which is consolidated by agreement with the proposed extension of credit; (e) any sum actually paid by the lender on account of official fees; and (f) any sum actually to be paid on account of the cost of insurance effected at the express request of the borrower, less any sum credited as a down payment or in respect of a trade-in or any other matter. *Consumer Protection Act*, R.S.B.C. 1979, c. 65, s. 1.

PRINCIPAL TAXPAYER. An individual who, on the 31st day of December in the taxation year, occupies and inhabits a principal residence except when that individual, on the 31st day of December in the taxation year, occupies and inhabits a principal residence with his spouse, in which case, "principal taxpayer" means that spouse who has the higher taxable income for the taxation year.

PRINCIPAL UNDERWRITER. A person (i) to whom a company makes an allotment or agrees to make an allotment of shares or debentures of the company with a view to all or any of the shares or debentures being offered for sale to the public; and (ii) who sells or agrees to sell to any other person such shares or debentures with a view to all or any part of such shares or debentures being offered for sale to the public by that other person. *Companies Act*, R.S.N.W.T. 1974, c. C-7, s. 89.

PRINCIPAL USE. The use of land that is most extensive in the area occupied. *The Planning and Development Act*, R.S.S. 1978, c. P-13, s. 2.

PRINCIPIORUM NON EST RATIO. [L.] First principles do not need to be proved.

PRINCIPLE. *n.* Something which, unlike a rule, does not set out legal consequences which follow automatically if certain conditions are met. S.A. Cohen, *Due Process of Law* (Toronto: Carswell, 1977) at 203. See CO-OPERATIVE ~S; FEDERAL ~; GENERALLY ACCEPTED ~S; MERIT ~; NOMINALISTIC ~S.

PRINT. *n.* An artistic representation or work usually on paper or vellum, executed in media such as woodcut, metalcut, wood engraving, engraving, etching, drypoint, mezzotint, aquatint, soft ground, lithography, monotype, clichéverre or silk screen. See FINGER~; PALM ~.

PRINTED. *adj.* Includes lithographed or reproduced by any mechanical, electrostatic or photostatic means.

PRINTED ATLAS OR CARTOGRAPHIC BOOK. A bound work with an established date of printing and includes each volume of a set of bound works issued under a single title. *Canadian Cultural Property Export Control List*, C.R.C., c. 448, s. 1.

PRINTED BOOK OF PHOTOGRAPHS. A bound work with an established date of printing and includes each volume of a set of bound works issued under a single title. *Canadian Cultural Property Export Control List*, C.R.C., c. 448, s. 1.

PRINTED BOOK OF PICTURES OR DESIGNS. A bound work with an established date of printing and includes each volume of a set of bound works issued under a single title. *Canadian Cultural Property Export Control List*, C.R.C., c. 448, s. 1.

PRINTED BOOK OR PAMPHLET. A work of at least five pages, exclusive of cover pages, made up of sheets bound, stitched or fastened together so as to form a material whole under an established date of printing, and includes each work in a set issued under a single title. *Canadian Cultural Property Export Control List*, C.R.C., c. 448, s. 1.

PRINTER. See QUEEN'S ~.

PRINTING. *n.* 1. Shall include reproduction by set type, the offset process, the stencil process, or any facsimile reproduction process, provided however that the reproduced copy shall throughout be clear and legible, notwithstanding the state of the original, and shall be on paper of good quality and suitable for the process used. *Rules of the Supreme Court of Canada*, C.R.C., c. 1512, Rule 2. 2. All processes, techniques and methods of publication, duplication or reproduction, whether by type, photographic, offset, electrostatic, micrographing or other process, of written or graphic matter. *Public Printing Act*, S.M. 1979, c. 17, s. 1. 3. Includes any means of reproducing the written word. *Municipal Act*, R.S.B.C. 1979, c. 290, s. 1. 4. Includes words written, painted, engraved, lithographed, photographed or represented or reproduced by any mode of representing or reproducing words in a visible form. *Municipal Elections Act*, S.N.S. 1979-80, c. 63, s. 1. See PREPARATORY ASPECTS OF ~.

PRINTING DIE. The parts of a postage meter that print an impression on or for mail and includes the postage indicia impression die and the postmark impression die. *Postage Meters Regulations*, C.R.C., c. 1287, s. 2.

PRIORITY. *n.* When two or more competing claims which arose at different times against the same parcel of land are asserted, the one who is entitled to exercise rights to the exclusion of the others is said to have priority. B.J. Reiter, R.C.B. Risk & B.N. McLellan, *Real Estate Law*, 3d ed. (Toronto: Emond Montgomery, 1986) at 472.

PRIORITY PAYMENT INSTRUMENT. A money order, bank draft or similar instrument issued, directly or indirectly, by a member to another member for the purpose of effecting a payment between those members. *Canadian Payments Association Act*, R.S.C. 1985, c. C-21, s. 31.

PRIOR PETENS. [L.] The person who applies first.

PRIOR SERVICE. Any service other than that for which current service contributions are made. Pension Plan acts.

PRIOR TEMPORE POTIOR JURE. [L.] The person first in time is preferred in right.

PRIOR USE. Use which takes place over a longer period than what the statute permits or which discloses the invention to the public. H.G. Fox, *The Canadian Law and Practice Relating to Letters Patent for Inventions*, 4th ed. (Toronto: Carswell, 1969) at 114.

PRISON. *n.* 1. Includes a penitentiary, common jail, public or reformatory prison, lock-up, guard-room or other place in which persons who are charged with or convicted of offences are usually kept in custody. *Criminal Code*, R.S.C. 1985, c. C-46, s. 2. 2. A prison other than a penitentiary, and includes a reformatory school or industrial school. *Criminal Code*, R.S.C. 1985, c. C-46, s. 618(5). 3. A place of confinement other than a penitentiary. See BREACH OF ~; CIVIL ~; SERVICE ~.

PRISON BREACH. Every one who (a) by force or violence breaks a prison with intent to set at liberty himself or any person confined therein; or (b) with intent to escape forcibly breaks out of, or makes any breach in, a cell or other place within a prison in which he is confined. *Criminal Code*, R.S.C. 1985, c. C-46, s. 144.

PRISONER. *n.* A person under arrest, remand or sentence who is confined in a correctional centre according to law. See REMAND ~.

PRISONER OF WAR. A prisoner of war of the Japanese or a prisoner of war of another power. *Compensation for Former Prisoners of War Act*, R.S.C. 1985, c. F-31, s. 2. See PROTECTED ~.

PRISONER OF WAR OF ANOTHER POWER. (a) A person who during World War I or World War II (i) served in the naval, army or air forces of Canada or Newfoundland; (ii) served in the naval, army or air forces of His Majesty or any other countries allied with His Majesty during World War I or World War II and was domiciled in Canada or Newfoundland at the time of his enlistment; or (iii) was a civilian prisoner of war and who was, for a period of not less than 3 months, engaged in avoiding capture by any power, other than Japan during World War II, that was engaged in military operations against His Majesty's forces or any other countries allied with the naval, army or air forces of His Majesty or who was a prisoner of war of any such power or was engaged in escaping from such a power; or (b) a person who served in the naval, army or air forces of Canada during military operations subsequent to World War I or World War II and who while so serving was, for a period of not less than 3 months, a prisoner of war of any power or was engaged in avoiding capture by any power or in escaping from any power. *Compensation for Former Prisoners of War Act*, R.S.C. 1985, c. F-31, s. 2.

PRISONER OF WAR OF THE JAPANESE. (a) A person who served in the naval, army or air forces of Canada or Newfoundland during World War II; (b) a person who served in the naval, army or air forces of His Majesty or any of the countries allied with His Majesty during World War II and was domiciled in Canada or Newfoundland at the time of his enlistment; or (c) a civilian prisoner of war who was, during

World War II, for a period of not less than 3 months, engaged in avoiding capture by Japan or in escaping from Japan or was a prisoner of war of the Japanese for a period of not less than 3 months. *Compensation for Former Prisoners of War Act*, R.S.C. 1985, c. F-31, s. 2.

PRISONERS' REPRESENTATIVE. In relation to a protected prisoner of war, means the person elected or recognized as that prisoner's representative pursuant to Article 79 of the Geneva Convention set out in Schedule III. *Geneva Convention Act*, R.S.C. 1985, c. G-3, s. 4.

PRIVACY COMMISSIONER. The Commissioner appointed under section 53. *Privacy Act*, R.S.C. 1985, c. P-21, s. 3.

PRIVACY COMMISSIONER OF CANADA. The federal official who investigates complaints of government failure to comply with rights to personal information provided by the Privacy Act.

PRIVATE. *adj.* When used in respect to an elevator, means an elevator that is either used by the manager exclusively for the storage or handling of grain belonging to him alone, or, when the manager is a cooperative association of grain growers, or is a company controlled by one or more such associations, is used by the association exclusively for the storage or handling of grain either belonging to it or produced by or received from some one or more of its members. *Canada Grain Act*, R.S.C. 1970, c. G-16, s. 2.

PRIVATE AIRCRAFT. 1. A civil aircraft other than a commercial aircraft or state aircraft. Canada regulations. 2. An aircraft used by an employee travelling on official government business and for the use of which he is reimbursed in accordance with the rates prescribed by the Treasury Board Travel Directive. *Flying Accidents Compensation Regulations*, C.R.C., c. 10, s. 2.

PRIVATE ARCHIVES. Archives other than public archives. *Archives Act*, S.Q. 1983, c. 38, s. 2.

PRIVATE BILL. 1. A bill relating to matters of particular interest or benefit to an individual or group. A. Fraser, G.A. Birch & W.A. Dawson, eds., *Beauchesne's Rules and Forms of the House of Commons of Canada*, 5th ed. (Toronto: Carswell, 1978) at 217. 2. A bill relating to a particular person, institution or locality which is often introduced by a private member and enacted by a different and simpler procedure, not requiring government sponsorship. P.W. Hogg, *Constitutional Law of Canada*, 2d ed. (Toronto: Carswell, 1985) at 203.

PRIVATE BUOY. A buoy other than a government buoy. *Private Buoy Regulations*, C.R.C., c. 1460, s. 2.

PRIVATE COLLEGE. A college in Alberta, other than a public college, that is in affiliation with a university and provides instruction in courses acceptable to that university as constituting a full year's work toward a degree. *Colleges Act*, R.S.A. 1980, c. C-18, s. 1.

PRIVATE COMMUNICATION. Any telecommunication or oral communication which its originator expects will not be intercepted by any person other than the person the originator intended to receive it. P.K. McWilliams, *Canadian Criminal Evidence*, 3d ed. (Aurora: Canada Law Book, 1988) at 13-3.

PRIVATE COMPANY. A company that by its memorandum or articles, special act, letters patent or other incorporating document: (a) restricts the right to transfer its shares; (ii) limits the number of its members to 50 or less, the number so limited being, unless the memorandum or articles otherwise provide, exclusive of persons who are in the employment of the company and of persons who are members while in the employment of the company and continue to be members after the termination of the employment, but where two or more persons hold one or more shares in the company jointly they shall be counted as a single member; and (iii) prohibits any invitation to the public to subscribe for shares or debentures of the company.

PRIVATE CONSTABLE. A person appointed as a constable under the Railway Act or as a police constable under the Canada Ports Corporation Act. *Canada Labour Code*, R.S.C. 1985, c. L-2, s. 3.

PRIVATE CORPORATION. A corporation resident in Canada at that time, not a public corporation and not controlled directly or indirectly in any manner whatever by a public corporation. See CANADIAN-CONTROLLED ~.

PRIVATE COTTAGE. A seasonal residence used primarily for the personal use of the owner and immediate family and whose owners hold a valid lease or freehold title to the land. *Travel and Tourism Act*, S.N.W.T. 1983 (1st Sess.), c. 15, s. 2.

PRIVATE DRIVEWAY. A driveway not open to the use of the public for purposes of vehicular traffic.

PRIVATE DYKE. A dyke built on private property without public funds to protect only the property of the person owning the private dyke. *Dyke Maintenance Act*, R.S.B.C. 1979, c. 99, s. 1.

PRIVATEER. *n.* A ship commissioned to exercise general reprisals.

PRIVATE FISHING PRESERVE. Land or water that is privately owned and maintained and on which, or part of which fish have been reared or stocked for the purpose of angling and are designated as private fishing preserves in the regulations. *Fish and Game Protection Act*, R.S.P.E.I. 1974, c. F-8, s. 1.

PRIVATE FISH POND. An artificially constructed pond which is used by the owner or his guests solely for pleasure. *Fish and Wildlife Act*, S.N.B. 1980, c. F-14.1, s. 1.

PRIVATE FREIGHT VEHICLE. A motor vehicle, other than a public vehicle or a limited vehicle, that is operated at any time on a highway for the transportation of freight, and includes any motor vehicle which is operated for the (a) transportation of freight bona fide the property of the owner of the motor vehicle; (b) transportation of freight used or subjected to a process or treatment by the owner of the motor vehicle in the course of a regular trade or occupation or established business of the owner, when the transportation is incidental to his trade, occupation or business; (c) delivery or collection of freight sold or purchased, or agreed to be sold or purchased, or let on hire by the owner of the motor vehicle, otherwise than as agent, in the course of a regular trade or established business of that owner. *Motor Carrier Act*, R.S.B.C. 1979, c. 286, s. 1.

PRIVATE GARAGE. A subordinate building or portion of a main building used for the parking or temporary storage of the motor vehicles of the occupants of the main building. Canada regulations.

PRIVATE GUARD. A person who for hire or reward (i) provides security services with respect to persons or property, including the services of a guard dog; (ii) accompanies a guard dog while the dog is guarding or patrolling. *An Act to Amend the Private Investigators and Private Guards Act*, S.N.S. 1982, c. 56, s. 1.

PRIVATE HEALTH SERVICES PLAN. (a) A contract of insurance in respect of hospital expenses, medical expenses or any combination of such expenses; or (b) a medical care insurance plan or hospital care insurance plan or any combination of such plans, except any such contract or plan established by or pursuant to (c) a law of a province that establishes a health care insurance plan in respect of which the province receives contributions from Canada for insured health services provided under the plan pursuant to the Federal-Provincial Fiscal Arrangements and Federal Post-Secondary Education and Health Contributions Act, 1977;

or (d) an Act of the Parliament of Canada or a regulation made thereunder that authorizes the provision of a medical care insurance plan or hospital care insurance plan for employees of Canada and their dependants and for dependants of members of the Royal Canadian Mounted Police and the regular force where such employees or members were appointed in Canada and are serving outside Canada. *Income Tax Act*, R.S.C. 1952, c. 148 (as am. S.C. 1988, c. 55, s. 188(1)), s. 248(1).

PRIVATE HOLDING CORPORATION. A private corporation the only undertaking of which is the investing of its funds, but does not include (a) a specified financial institution; (b) any particular corporation that owns shares of another corporation in which it has a substantial interest except where the other corporation is a financial intermediary corporation or a corporation that would, but for such substantial interest, be a private holding corporation; or (c) any particular corporation in which another corporation owns shares and has a substantial interest, except where the other corporation would, but for such substantial interest, be a private holding corporation. *Income Tax Act*, R.S.C. 1952, c. 148 (as am. S.C. 1988, c. 55, s. 159(1)), s. 191(1).

PRIVATE-HOME DAY CARE. The temporary care for reward or compensation of five children or less who are under 10 years of age where such care is provided in a private residence, other than the home of a parent or guardian of any such child, for a continuous period not exceeding 24 hours. *Day Nurseries Act*, R.S.C. 1980, c. 111, s. 1.

PRIVATE-HOME DAY CARE AGENCY. A person who provides private-home day care at more than one location. *Day Nurseries Act*, R.S.C. 1980, c. 111, s. 1.

PRIVATE HOSPITAL. A house in which two or more patients are received and lodged at the same time.

PRIVATE HOSPITAL FOR NERVOUS AILMENTS. A private hospital, (a) used for the purpose of diagnosing and treating persons suffering from: (i) neuroses; or (ii) psychosomatic disorders and alcoholism; and (b) provided with: (i) equipment and facilities; and (ii) the services of a legally qualified medical practitioner who holds a specialist's certificate in psychiatry issued by the Royal College of Physicians and Surgeons of Canada, to render the services referred to in clause (a). *Private Hospitals Act*, R.R.O. 1980, Reg. 799, s. 22.

PRIVATE INTERNATIONAL LAW. Or conflict of laws, the part of a country's law that is concerned with resolving legal disputes which involve one or more foreign elements. J.G. McLeod, *The Conflict of Laws* (Calgary: Carswell, 1983) at 3.

PRIVATE INVESTIGATOR. A person who investigates and furnishes information for hire or reward, including a person who: (i) searches for and furnishes information as to the personal character or actions of a person, or the character or kind of business or occupation of a person; (ii) searches for offenders against the law; or (iii) searches for missing persons or property. See BUSINESS OF A ~.

PRIVATE ISSUER. An issuer, other than a mutual fund, in whose articles of incorporation, limited partnership agreement, unit-holders' agreement, declaration of trust or other instrument legally constituting such issuer (i) the right to transfer shares or units is restricted; (ii) the number of its shareholders or unit-holders, exclusive of individuals who are in its employment or the employment of an affiliate and exclusive of individuals, who, having been formerly in the employment of the issuer or the employment of an affiliate, were, while in that employment, and have continued after termination of that employment to be, shareholders or unit-holders of the issuer, is limited to not more than 50, two or more individuals who are the joint registered owners of one or more shares or units being counted as one shareholder or unitholder; and (iii) any invitation to the public to subscribe for its securities is prohibited.

PRIVATE LAND. Land other than land vested in the Crown.

PRIVATE LANDS. 1. Lands other than Crown Lands and other lands vested in Her Majesty. *Crown Lands and Forests Act*, S.N.B. 1980, c. C-38.1, s. 1. 2. All lands conceded or alienated by the Crown except mining concessions, lands conceded as such and, on Crown lands, lands under mining lease, operating lease, storage lease or disposal licence. *Mining Act*, R.S.Q. 1977, c. M-13, s. 1.

PRIVATE LAW. All law relating to persons; used in distinction to public law.

PRIVATE LINE. A pipe used for transmitting gas from a gas line, secondary line, distribution line or a well to be used for domestic, commercial or industrial purposes on land owned or leased by the owner of the pipe, and includes the installations in connection therewith but does not include any pipe or installation on, within or under a building. *Pipe Line Act*, S.N.B. 1976, c. P-8.1, s. 1.

PRIVATELY-OWNED LAND. (i) Land held under a certificate of title by a person other than the Crown; (ii) land held under an agreement for sale under which the Crown is the seller; or (iii) land or classes of land held under leases or other dispositions from the Crown that are prescribed to be privately-owned land. *Wildlife Act*, S.A. 1984, c. W-9.1, s. 1.

PRIVATELY-OWNED PETROLEUM. Petroleum or any right, title or interest therein which is held by any person other than Her Majesty in right of the province. *Petroleum and Natural Gas Act*, R.S.Nfld. 1970, c. 294, s. 2.

PRIVATE MEMBER'S BILL. A bill, either public or private, introduced by a private member. P.W. Hogg, *Constitutional Law of Canada*, 2d ed. (Toronto: Carswell, 1985) at 203.

PRIVATE MORGUE. A place where bodies are customarily retained before their disposition, other than a public morgue. *Anatomy Act*, R.S.O. 1980, c. 21, s. 1.

PRIVATE MUTUAL FUND. A mutual fund that is (i) operated as an investment club; where (A) its shares or units are held by not more than 50 persons and its indebtedness has never been offered to the public; (B) it does not pay or give any remuneration for investment advice or in respect of trades in securities, except normal brokerage fees; and (C) all of its members are required to make contributions in proportion to the shares or units each holds for the purpose of financing its operations; (ii) a pooled fund maintained solely to serve registered pension funds or plans or deferred profit sharing plans registered under the Income Tax Act (Canada); (iii) a pooled fund maintained by a trust company in which moneys belonging to various estates and trusts in its care are comingled, pursuant to a power conferred by or under the law governing the same or by the will or trust instrument, for the purpose of facilitating investment where no general solicitations are made with a view to promoting participation in the pooled fund.

PRIVATE NUISANCE. Unlawful annoyance or interference which damages the enjoyment of an occupier or owner of land. J.V. DiCastri, *Occupiers' Liability* (Vancouver: Burroughs/Carswell, 1980) at 165.

PRIVATE OWNER. An owner of land that has been granted by the Crown, or that is held under homestead entry, pre-emption record, lease or purchase agreement from the Crown. *Grasshopper Control Act*, R.S.B.C. 1979, c. 156, s. 1.

PRIVATE PASSENGER VEHICLE. 1. A motor vehicle designed and used primarily for the transportation of persons without remuneration and does not include a bus or taxicab. 2. A vehicle used solely for personal transportation; (i) including the transportation of goods which are the property of the owner and intended for the use or enjoyment of himself or members of his household; but (ii) not including the transportation of goods in connection with any line of business except that of a salesman conveying sample cases or display goods which are not for delivery or resale. *Motor Transport Act*, R.S.A. 1980, c. M-20, s. 1.

PRIVATE PLACE. (i) A private dwelling; and (ii) privately-owned land, whether or not it is used in connection with a private dwelling. *Public Health Act*, S.A. 1984, c. P-27.1, s. 1.

PRIVATE PLACEMENT. Any distribution of securities with respect to which no prospectus is required to be filed, accepted or otherwise approved by or pursuant to a law enacted in Canada for the supervision or regulation of trading in securities and includes a distribution of securities with respect to which a prospectus would be required to be filed, accepted or otherwise approved except for an express exemption contained in or given pursuant to such a law.

PRIVATE PRACTICE. The rendering of veterinary medicine for hire, gain, fee, compensation or reward received, promised, offered, expected or accepted, directly or indirectly, by the person rendering the service from the person requesting or receiving the service for an animal. *Veterinarians Act*, R.S.B.C. 1979, c. 423, s. 1.

PRIVATE RECEIVER. A receiver appointed by a letter or similar instrument by one who holds security over a debtor's assets according to the powers specified in the security instrument. F. Bennett, *Receiverships* (Toronto: Carswell, 1985) at 2.

PRIVATE RESIDENTIAL SWIMMING POOL. A swimming pool located on a private residential property under the control of the owner or occupant, the use of which is limited to swimming or bathing by members of his family and their visitors. *Public Health Act*, R.R.O. 1980, Reg. 849, s. 1.

PRIVATE ROAD. 1. A road not open to the use of the public for purposes of vehicular traffic. 2. A private road used by the public for vehicular traffic with permission of the owner or licensee of the road. *Motor Vehicle Act*, R.S.B.C. 1979, c. 288, s. 2.

PRIVATE SCHOOL. An institution at which instruction is provided at any time between the hours of 9 a.m. and 4 p.m. on any school day for five or more pupils who are of or over compulsory school age in any of the subjects of the elementary or secondary school courses of study and that is not a school as defined in this section. *Education Act*, R.S.O. 1980, c. 129, s. 1.

PRIVATE SCHOOL TEACHER. A person holding a permanent or temporary certificate of qualification as a teacher issued by the Minister under The Department of Education Act who is employed by a private school as a full-time member of its academic staff. *Teachers' Retirement Fund Act*, R.S.A. 1970, c. 361, s. 2.

PRIVATE SECTOR. For the purposes of this Act, those employers and employees whose labour relations are within the exclusive jurisdiction of the Legislature to regulate, but does not include the public sector. *The Pay Equity Act*, S.M. 1985-86, c. 21, s. 1.

PRIVATE-SERVICE HOME. An unincorporated facility that provides lodging, supervision, personal care or individual programming to residents in need of such services. *Residential Services Act*, S.S. 1984-85-86, c. R-21.2, s. 2.

PRIVATE SEWAGE DISPOSAL SYSTEM. All types of sewage disposal systems not directly connected to a municipal or approved central sewage system, including a privy and septic tank with a disposal field.

PRIVATE SHOOTING PRESERVE. Land that is privately owned and maintained and on which, or part of which, game birds that have been raised in captivity are kept in captivity or released for the purpose of hunting and are designated as private shooting preserves in the regulations. *Fish and Game Protection Act*, R.S.P.E.I. 1974, c. F-8, s. 1.

PRIVATE STREET. A street, road, lane or track that is not vested in the Crown in right of Alberta or a municipality. *Law of Property Act*, R.S.A. 1980, c. L-8, s. 68.

PRIVATE TELEPHONE SYSTEM. A telephone system that by the law of the province any person has been authorized to construct, control or operate in Saskatchewan. *The Telephone Department Act*, R.S.S. 1978, c. T-10, s. 2.

PRIVATE TENURE. A timber licence, old temporary tenure, or private land, in a tree farm licence area. *Forest Act*, R.S.B.C. 1979, c. 140, s. 1.

PRIVATE TRACK. A track outside of a carrier's right-of-way, yard or terminals, and of which the carrier does not own either the rails, ties, roadbed or right-of-way, or a track or portion of a track which is devoted to the purpose of

its user, either by lease or written agreement, in which case the lease or written agreement will be considered as equivalent to ownership. Canada regulations.

PRIVATE TRADE-SCHOOL. Any school or place, or any course of study by correspondence, kept or operated by any person other than (i) The University of Manitoba, or any other university established under The Universities Establishment Act; or (ii) a department of the Government of Canada or of any province; or (iii) the trustees of a school district, school division, or school area under The Public Schools Act; or (iv) a private trade-school organized or operated solely for the employees of a corporation, industry, or plant. *Private Trade-Schools Act*, R.S.M. 1970, c. T130, s. 2.

PRIVATE TRAINING INSTITUTION. A person who, for remuneration, provides instruction to a person for the purpose of allowing that person to obtain, or enhancing his possibilities of obtaining, employment in a skill or occupation that is prescribed by the minister, but does not include an institution designated under the College and Institute Act or a university under the University Act. *Miscellaneous Statutes Amendment Act*, S.B.C. 1985, c. 51, s. 2.

PRIVATE TRANSACTION. An arranged or negotiated transaction that is not generally available on identical terms to all holders of a class of securities.

PRIVATE TRUST. A trust whose objects are specific, ascertainable people. D.M.W. Waters, *The Law of Trusts in Canada*, 2d ed. (Toronto: Carswell, 1984) at 24.

PRIVATE VOCATIONAL SCHOOL. A school or place at which instruction in any vocation is offered or provided by class room instruction or by correspondence, other than a college of applied arts or technology, a university recognized by the Ministry of Colleges and Universities or a school or course of instruction maintained under any other Act of the Legislature. *Private Vocational Schools Act*, R.S.O. 1980, c. 392, s. 1.

PRIVATE WASTE MANAGEMENT SYSTEM. A waste management system, or any part thereof, whose owner is a person rather than a municipality. *Environmental Protection Act*, R.R.O. 1980, Reg. 309, s. 1.

PRIVATE WOODLOT. Forest land owned by anyone other than the Crown or corporations whose principal business involves dealing in primary forest products. *Forest Products Act*, R.S.N.B. 1973, c. F-21, s. 1.

PRIVATE WORKS. Includes private roadways, crossings, openings, signs or other advertising devices and other structures constructed, erected, installed or maintained on a highway for the use or benefit of owners or occupants of property adjoining or connected therewith. *Municipal Act*, S.M. 1970, c. 100, s. 222.

PRIVATION. *n.* Removal; withdrawal.

PRIVATIS PACTIONIBUS NON DUBIUM EST NON LAEDI JUS CAETERORUM. [L.] There is no doubt that the rights of others are not damaged by private agreements.

PRIVATIVE CLAUSE. A provision which purports to exclude judicial review of a tribunal's decision. P.W. Hogg, *Constitutional Law of Canada*, 2d ed. (Toronto: Carswell, 1985) at 162.

PRIVATORUM CONVENTIO JURI PUBLICO NON DEROGAT. [L.] A statutory requirement imposed in the public interest cannot be waived. P. St. J. Langan, ed., *Maxwell on The Interpretation of Statutes*, 12th ed. (Bombay: N.M. Tripathi, 1976) at 330.

PRIVATUM INCOMMODUM PUBLICO BONO PENSATUR. [L.] Private loss is counterbalanced by public good.

PRIVATUM COMMODUM PUBLICO CEDIT. [L.] Private good gives way to public good.

PRIVILEGE. *n.* 1. An exceptional advantage or right; an exemption to which certain people are entitled from an attendance, burden or duty. 2. In the law of evidence, the right of the State or some person or the duty of a witness to withhold otherwise admissible and relevant evidence from a court of law. P.K. McWilliams, *Canadian Criminal Evidence*, 3d ed. (Aurora: Canada Law Book, 1988) at 35-2. See ABSOLUTE ~; BREACH OF ~; CROWN ~; DIPLOMATIC ~; DRIVING ~; INFORMER ~; JUROR'S ~; LITIGATION ~; MOTOR VEHICLE ~; OCCUPIED WATER ~; PARLIAMENTARY ~; PREPAYMENT ~; QUALIFIED ~; QUESTION OF ~; SOLICITOR-CLIENT ~; SPOUSAL ~.

PRIVILEGE AGAINST SELF-INCRIMINATION. A general privilege of witnesses protected in Canada by section 5(2) of the Canada Evidence Act. Secondly, any accused has the right not to testify for the prosecution. Strictly, this is because an accused is not a competent, much less compellable, witness for the prosecution. P.K. McWilliams, *Canadian Criminal Evidence*, 3d ed. (Aurora: Canada Law Book, 1988) at 35-2.

PRIVILEGED COMMUNICATION. A communication which one cannot compel a witness to divulge.

PRIVILEGED INFORMATION. Any informa-

tion concerning a material fact not yet known to the public that could affect the value or the market price of securities of an issuer. *Securities Act*, S.Q. 1982, c. 48, s. 5.

PRIVILEGED MOTION. A way to deal with a situation arising from the debate on or the subject-matter of an original question either following or preceding a vote or because a new proceeding is needed. A. Fraser, G.A. Birch & W.A. Dawson, eds., *Beauchesne's Rules and Forms of the House of Commons of Canada*, 5th ed. (Toronto: Carswell, 1978) at 151.

PRIVILEGIUM EST BENEFICIUM PERSONALE, ET EXTINGUITUR CUM PERSONA. [L.] Privilege is a personal benefit, and it dies with the person.

PRIVILEGIUM EST QUASI PRIVATA LEX. [L.] A privilege is almost a private law.

PRIVILEGIUM NON VALET CONTRA REPUBLICAM. [L.] A privilege does not prevail against the state.

PRIVITY. *n.* 1. Being a participant in or a party to a contract. G.H.L. Fridman, *The Law of Contract in Canada*, 2d ed. (Toronto: Carswell, 1986) at 161. 2. The direct connection between the one to pay the money being sought in an action for recovery and the one to receive such money. G.H.L. Fridman & J.G. McLeod, *Restitution* (Toronto: Carswell, 1982) at 91.

PRIVY. *n.* 1. Someone who partakes or has an interest in some action or thing. 2. Someone related to another person. 3. A place for the purpose of urination or defecation that is not a flush toilet. *Tourism Act*, R.R.O. 1980, Reg. 936, s. 1.

PRIVY. *adj.* Participating in some act.

PRIVY COUNCIL. 1. In Canada, the Queen's Privy Council for Canada including cabinet ministers and other people as well. P.W. Hogg, *Constitutional Law of Canada*, 2d ed. (Toronto: Carswell, 1985) at 195. 2. In the United Kingdom, a large body which now exercises formal functions only. The Queen, on the advice of the Prime Minister, appoints its members. P.W. Hogg, *Constitutional Law of Canada*, 2d ed. (Toronto: Carswell, 1985) at 166. See JUDICIAL COMMITTEE OF THE ~; QUEEN'S ~ FOR CANADA.

PRIVY SEAL. The seal adopted by the Governor General or the Administrator for the sealing of official documents that are to be signed by him, or with his authority by his deputy, and that do not require to be sealed with the Great Seal. *Formal Documents Regulations*, C.R.C., c. 1331, s. 2.

PRIZE. See MONEY ~.

PRIZE COURT. A tribunal established by special commission under the great seal during a war or until litigation related to war has been concluded.

PRIZE FIGHT. An encounter or fight with fists or hands between two persons who have met for that purpose by previous arrangement made by or for them, but a boxing contest between amateur sportsmen, where the contestants wear boxing gloves of not less than five ounces each in weight, or any boxing contest held with the permission or under the authority of an athletic board or commission or similar body established by or under the authority of the legislature of a province for the control of sport within the province, shall be deemed not to be a prize fight. *Criminal Code*, R.S.C. 1985, c. C-46, s. 83(2).

PRO. *prep.* [L.] For, in respect of.

PROBABILITY. See BALANCE OF PROBABILITIES; SIMPLE ~.

PROBABLE ADDITIONAL RESERVES. Of crude oil, natural gas and natural gas liquids means an estimate of the reserves not included in an estimate of the proven reserves that may be recovered from the known reservoir or from that portion underlying the properties, provided: (i) the estimates of probable additional reserves are as realistic as can be determined on the basis of the information available; (ii) the reserve considered probable additional shall be the estimated ultimate recoverable content of the reservoir less the proven reserve, or of that portion underlying the properties, and shall be based on a realistic interpretation of the geological, geophysical and well test data available at the time the estimate is made; (iii) probable additional reserves to be obtained by the application of enhanced recovery processes will be the increased recovery over and above that recognized in the proven category that can be realistically estimated ultimately to be recovered economically from the pool or such portions that underlie properties. *Securities Act*, R.R.O. 1980, Reg. 910, s. 26.

PROBABLE CAUSE. Grounds which are reasonable. See REASONABLE AND ~.

PROBABLE MINERAL ORE. Mineral ore, whose existence is for all essential purposes assured but not absolutely certain. *An Act to Amend the Metallic Minerals Tax Act*, S.N.B. 1987, c. 35, s. 1.

PROBABLE ORE. That material for which tonnage and grade are computed partly from specific measurements, partly from either or both sample data or production data and partly from projection for a reasonable distance on geologic evidence and for which the sites avail-

able for inspection, measurement and sampling are too widely or otherwise inappropriately spaced to outline the material completely or to establish its grade throughout. *Securities Act*, R.R.O. 1980, Reg. 910, s. 26.

PROBANDA. *n.* Goods provided.

PROBANDI NECESSITAS INCUMBIT ILLI QUI AGIT. [L.] The need to prove rests upon the person who commences proceedings.

PROBATE. *n.* 1. A process to prove the originality and validity of a will. 2. Includes letters of verification issued in the Province of Quebec. *Administration of Estates Act*, R.S.A. 1980, c. A-1, s. 30. 3. Includes letters probate, letters of administration, letters with the will annexed and sealing under the Probate Recognition Act. *Probate Fee Act*, R.S.B.C. 1979, c. 338, s. 1. See COURT OF ~; GRANT OF ~; LETTERS ~.

PROBATE ACTIONS. Includes actions and other matters relating to the grant or recall of probate or of letters of administration other than common form business. *Judicature Act*, R.S.Nfld. 1970, c. 187, s. 3.

PROBATE AND LETTERS OF ADMINISTRATION. Includes confirmation in Scotland, and any instrument having in a British possession the same effect as under English law is given to probate and letters of administration respectively. *Probate Courts Act*, R.S.N.B. 1973, c. P-17, s. 1.

PROBATE DUTY. A tax on the gross value of a deceased testator's personal property.

PROBATE VALUE. When used in reference to any property held in trust by an executor or trustee, means the total value of all such property, at the date of death, over and above all mortgages, liens, and encumbrances thereon, plus any income received by the executor or trustee; and when used in the case of a petition for administration de bonis non means the amount of the estate that will pass for administration by the new appointee; and in all other cases shall be taken to mean the outside total value of the estate of the deceased at the date of death over and above all mortgages, liens or encumbrances thereon, and without allowing for other debts due by the deceased. *Probate Courts Act*, R.S.N.B. 1973, c. P-17, s. 1.

PROBATION. *n.* 1. The disposition of a court authorizing a person to be at large subject to the conditions of a probation order or community service order. 2. Temporarily appointing a person to an office until that person has, by conduct, proved to be fit to fill it. See PERIOD OF ~.

PROBATIONARY CONTRACT. A written

contract between a school board and a teacher in a form approved under Section 73 whereby the teacher is employed on a probationary basis for a term of 2 years. *Education Act*, S.N.S. 1969, c. 38, s. 2.

PROBATIONARY EMPLOYEE. A person who is employed on a full-time basis but who has worked less than the probationary period.

PROBATIONARY MEMBER. A member with less than 2 years of service in the RCMP. *Royal Canadian Mounted Police Act*, R.S.C. 1985 (2d Supp.), c. 8, s. 45.19(11).

PROBATIONARY TEACHER. A teacher employed by a board under a probationary teacher's contract made in accordance with the regulations. *Education Act*, R.S.O. 1980, c. 129, s. 1.

PROBATIONER. *n.* A convicted person who is placed on probation by a court or a person who is discharged conditionally by a probation order of a court.

PROBATION OFFICER. The person who supervises another person placed on probation.

PROBATION ORDER. Includes community service order. *Ministry of Correctional Services Act*, R.S.O. 1980, c. 275, s. 1.

PROBATIS EXTREMIS PRAESUMUNTUR MEDIA. [L.] Once the extremes are proved, the means are presumed.

PROBATOR. *n.* One who examines; one who accuses, approves or undertakes to prove the crime with which another is charged.

PROBATUM EST. [L.] It is tried; it is proved.

PROB. CT. *abbr.* Probate Court.

PROBI ET LEGALES HOMINES. [L.] Good and lawful people.

PRO BONO PUBLICO. [L.] For the public good.

PROC. *abbr.* Procuration.

PROCEDENDO. *n.* [L.] The writ which issued when the judge of a subordinate court delayed the parties by not giving judgment.

PROCEDURAL EQUALITY. Equality of application of the law without necessarily treating persons equally.

PROCEDURE. *n.* The method in which one takes the successive steps in litigation. See CIVIL ~; CRIMINAL ~; INTRUSIVE ~; PRACTICE AND ~; WELDING ~.

PROCEEDING. *n.* 1. A matter, cause or action, whether civil or criminal, before the court. 2. Includes (a) a writ, summons, plaint, warrant, affidavit, petition, pleading, praecipe, caveat, application, lien, filing, account, consent, note or memorandum or other document in respect of a case or matter in a court; (b) an instrument, bylaw, bill of sale, chattel mortgage, assignment of book accounts, partnership agreement or other document filed in a court, or, where required by order of the Lieutenant Governor in Council, with an officer or servant of the Crown employed in a ministry of the government of the province, and an application, note or praecipe in connection with it. *Law Stamp Act*, R.S.B.C. 1979, c. 226, s. 1. 3. Includes an action, application or submission to any court or judge or other body having authority by law or by consent to make decisions as to the rights of persons. See ADMIRALTY ~; AFFILIATION ~; BASTARDY ~; COROLLARY RELIEF ~; COSTS OF THIS ~; CRIMINAL ~; DEFECT IN THE ~S; DIVORCE ~; JUDICIAL ~; LEGAL ~; LIQUIDATION ~S; MINUTES OF ~S AND EVIDENCE; RECORD OF THE ~; REPRESENTATIVE ~; VARIATION ~; VEXATIOUS ~.

PROCEEDING AGAINST THE CROWN. 1. Includes a claim by way of set-off or counter-claim raised in proceedings by the Crown, and interpleader proceedings to which the Crown is a party. 2. Includes a claim by way of set off or counterclaim raised in proceedings by the Crown, an interpleader proceeding to which the Crown is a party, and a proceeding in which the Crown is a garnishee. *Crown Proceeding Act*, R.S.B.C. 1979, c. 86, s. 1.

PROCEEDS. *n.* 1. The amount, sum or value of any land, goods or investments sold or converted into cash. 2. Personal property in any form or fixtures derived directly or indirectly from any dealing with collateral or proceeds or that indemnifies or compensates for collateral destroyed or damaged. *Personal Property Security Act*, R.S.O. 1980, c. 375, s. 1. See GRAIN SALE ~; GROSS ~; NET ~.

PROCEEDS OF DISPOSITION. With respect to property, includes: (i) the sale price of property that has been sold; (ii) compensation for property unlawfully taken; (iii) compensation for property destroyed, and any amount payable under a policy of insurance in respect of loss or destruction of property; (iv) compensation for property taken under statutory authority or the sale price of property sold to a person by whom notice of an intention to take it under statutory authority was given; (v) compensation for property injuriously affected, whether lawfully or unlawfully or under statutory authority or otherwise; (vi) compensation for property damaged and any amount payable under a policy of insurance in respect of damage to property, except to the extent that such compensation or amount, as the case may be, has within a reasonable time after the damage been expended on repairing the damage; (vii) an amount by which the liability of a taxpayer to a mortgagee is reduced as a result of the sale of mortgaged property under a provision of the mortgage, plus any amount received by the taxpayer out of the proceeds of such sale; (viii) any amount included in computing a taxpayer's proceeds of disposition of the property by virtue of paragraph 79(c); and (ix) in the case of a share, an amount deemed by subparagraph 88(2)(b)(ii) not to be a dividend on that share, but notwithstanding any other provision of this Part, does not include: (x) any amount that would otherwise be proceeds of disposition of a share to the extent that such amount is deemed by subsection 84(2) or (3) to be a dividend received and is not deemed by paragraph 55(2)(a) or subparagraph 88(2)(b)(ii) not to be a dividend; or (xi) any amount that would otherwise be proceeds of disposition of property of a taxpayer to the extent that such amount is deemed by subsection 84.1(1) or 212.1(1) to be a dividend paid to the taxpayer. *Income Tax Act*, R.S.C. 1952, c. 148 (as am. S.C. 1986, c. 6, s. 27(2), (3)), s. 54(h).

PROCEEDS OF SALE. Includes (i) the purchase price or consideration payable to the vendor, or passing from the purchaser to the vendor, on a sale in bulk; and (ii) the money realized by a trustee under a security or by the sale or other disposition of any property coming into his hands as the consideration or part of the consideration for the sale. Bulk Sales acts.

PROCESS. *n.* 1. Includes, with respect to goods, the adjustment, alteration, assembly, manufacture, modification, production or repair of the goods. 2. Includes a writ, petition, warrant or order issued under the seal of the court, a judge's summons or order, a notice, subpoena and other proceeding at law or otherwise. 3. A mode or method of operation, by which chemical action, the application or operation of some power or element of nature, or some substance produces a result or effect on another thing or the performance of an operation or use of a method to produce a certain result. H.G. Fox, *The Canadian Law and Practice Relating to Letters Patent for Inventions*, 4th ed. (Toronto: Carswell, 1969) at 17. 4. In relation to a meat product, includes cutting, cooking, canning, comminuting, preserving, dressing, dehydrating, rendering, fractionating, defibrinating and treating, but does not include chilling or freezing. *Meat Inspection Regulations*, C.R.C., c. 1032, s. 2. 5. Any part of the work of dressing or eviscerating poultry. *Dressed and Eviscerated Poultry Regulations*, C.R.C., c. 283, s. 2. 6. Includes breaking eggs,

filtering, blending, pasteurizing, stabilizing, mixing, cooling, freezing and drying processed eggs. *Processed Egg Regulations*, C.R.C., c. 290, s. 2. See ABUSE OF ~; DUE ~; MESNE ~; ORIGINATING ~; SERVICE OF ~.

PROCESS BUTTER. Creamery butter that has been melted or clarified or refined and remanufactured into butter. *Farm Products Grades and Sales Act*, R.R.O. 1980, Reg. 327, s. 1.

PROCESS CATEGORY. See COMPONENT ~.

PROCESS CHEESE. The food product that is produced by comminuting or mixing one or more lots of cheese with the aid of heat and emulsifying agents into a homogeneous mass.

PROCESS CHEESE PLANT. A place where cheese is received for the purpose of being mixed, pasteurized, or emulsified. *Dairy Act*, R.S.M. 1970, c. D10, s. 2.

PROCESSED. *adj.* Canned, cooked, dehydrated or otherwise prepared for food to assure preservation of a food product. *Processed Fruit and Vegetable Regulations*, C.R.C., c. 291, s. 2.

PROCESSED EGG. Includes frozen egg, frozen egg mix, liquid egg and liquid egg mix, but does not include inedible processed egg. See INEDIBLE ~.

PROCESSED EGG STATION. Premises where processed egg is produced, graded, packed or marked. *Live Stock and Live Stock Products Act*, R.R.O. 1980, Reg. 583, s. 1.

PROCESSED ORGANIC WASTE. Waste that is predominantly organic in composition and has been treated by aerobic and anaerobic digestion, or other means of stabilization, and includes sewage residue from sewage works that are subject to the provisions of the Ontario Water Resources Act. *Environmental Protection Act*, R.R.O. 1980, Reg. 309, s. 1.

PROCESSED WOOD. Secondary wood products manufactured from timber in a wood processing facility. *Crown Lands and Forests Act*, S.N.B. 1980, c. C-38.1, s. 1.

PROCESS ELEVATOR. An elevator the principal use of which is the receiving and storing of grain for direct manufacture or processing into other products. *Canada Grain Act*, R.S.C. 1985, c. G-10, s. 2.

PROCESS FOR RESOLUTION OF A DISPUTE. Either of the following processes for the resolution of a dispute, namely: (a) by the referral of the dispute to arbitration; or (b) by the referral thereof to a conciliation board. *Public Service Staff Relations Act*, R.S.C. 1985, c. P-35, s. 2.

PROCESSING. *n.* 1. Includes changing the nature, form, size, shape, quality or condition of a natural product by mechanical, chemical or any other means. 2. With respect to mineral substances, any form of beneficiation, concentrating, smelting, refining or semi-fabricating, or any combination thereof. 3. Changing the nature or form of an agricultural product and includes, in the case of animals, the killing of them. 4. Includes cleaning, filleting, icing, packing, canning, freezing, smoking, salting, cooking, pickling, drying or preparing fish for market in any other manner. 5. Heating, pasteurizing, evaporating, drying, churning, freezing, packaging, packing, separating into component parts, combining with other substances by any process or otherwise treating milk or cream or milk products in the manufacture or preparation of milk products or fluid milk products. See DATA ~ SERVICES; FIRST ~; MANUFACTURING OR ~ ACTIVITY.

PROCESSING ASSETS. The assets of processing plants and includes ancillary assets related to the processing of minerals, but does not include: (i) the value of spare parts for such assets in inventory; (ii) stockpiles or inventories of processed mineral substances; (iii) assets for transportation of the processed product to market from the point at which processing is completed; or (iv) social assets. *Mining Tax Act*, R.R.O. 1980, Reg. 639, s. 1. See DEPRECIABLE ~.

PROCESSING FACILITY. See TIMBER ~; WOOD ~.

PROCESSING OF FISH. Includes the cleaning, filleting, smoking, salting, icing, packing, freezing, cooking, pickling, or drying of fish or the preparing of fish for market in any other manner. *Fisheries Act*, R.S.M. 1970, c. F90, s. 1.

PROCESSING OPERATION. See INITIAL ~.

PROCESSING PLANT. 1. A plant for the extraction from gas of hydrogen sulphide, helium, ethane, natural gas liquids or other substances, but does not include a well head separator, treater, or dehydrator. 2. A plant used in processing, smelting or refining of metals. 3. A facility (i) for obtaining crude bitumen from oil sands that have been recovered; or (ii) for obtaining oil sands products from oil sands, crude bitumen or derivatives of crude bitumen that have been recovered. 4. A fish cannery or a fish processing or fish curing establishment and includes a building or other structure and a floating barge or vessel connected with or used in connection with the cannery or establishment. 5. An installation for improving the quality of the coal or producing a marketable solid fuel from it and includes a coal storage or handling facility directly connected with the installation. See COAL ~; FISH ~; GAS ~; MEAT ~; SPECIALIZED ~.

PROCESSOR. *n.* A person engaged in the preparation or conversion of an agricultural product for marketing.

PROCESS STOCK. Beer in any process of manufacture prior to duty assessment. *Brewery Departmental Regulations*, C.R.C., c. 566, s. 2.

PROCHEIN AMY. *var.* **PROCHEIN AMI.** [Fr.] With respect to a child, a next friend or next-of-kin who manages the infant's affairs.

PROCHRONISM. *n.* A mistake in chronology; dating something before it happened.

PROCLAMATION. *n.* 1. Authorized publication. 2. A proclamation under the Great Seal.

PROCLAMATION DATE. The date on which a statute is proclaimed in force when the statute provides that it will come into force when proclaimed.

PROCTOR. See QUEEN'S ~.

PROCURATION. *n.* An agency, the administering of another's business.

PROCURATIONEM ADVERSUS NULLA EST PRAESCRIPTIO. [L.] There is no limitation of procuration.

PROCURATOR. *n.* One to whom someone commits a charge; an agent.

PROCURE. *v.* To accept an offer to commit a crime when promised a reward for doing it. D. Stuart, *Canadian Criminal Law: a treatise*, 2d ed. (Toronto: Carswell, 1987) at 511.

PRODITION. *n.* Treachery, treason.

PRODITOR. *n.* One who commits treason.

PRODITORIE. *adv.* Treacherously.

PRODUCE. *v.* 1. Includes grow, manufacture and mine. 2. Extract or obtain from the earth. *Geothermal Resources Act*, S.B.C. 1982, c. 14, s. 1.

PRODUCE. *n.* Livestock, furbearing animals raised in captivity, poultry, eggs, fruit, vegetables, honey. See AQUACULTURAL ~; FARM ~; FRUIT AND ~.

PRODUCED. *adj.* In relation to a commercial message, means that all the visual and sound components of the commercial message have been assembled into a composite whole. *Television Broadcasting Regulations*, C.R.C., c. 381, s. 16.

PRODUCER. *n.* 1. A producer of grain, livestock, or poultry. 2. A person engaged in the production of honey, fruit or vegetables and includes a person engaged in the handling, packing, processing, shipping, transporting, purchasing or selling of honey, fruit or vegetables. 3. A producer actually engaged in the production of grain and any person entitled, as landlord, vendor or mortgagee, to the grain grown by a producer actually engaged in the production of grain or to any share therein. 4. The owner of a well that is capable of producing oil or gas. 5. Any person who sells or delivers milk or cream to a plant. *Canada regulations.* See ACTUAL ~; ASSOCIATION OF ~S; CANADIAN ~; DAIRY ~; FORESTRY ~; GAS ~; PRIMARY ~; QUALIFIED ~; SERVICES TO ~S.

PRODUCER ORGANIZATION. An organization of producers that is engaged in marketing a crop in respect of which advances are to be made. *Advance Payments for Crops Act*, R.S.C. 1985 (1st Supp.), c. 38, s. 2.

PRODUCER OR MANUFACTURER. Includes any printer, publisher, lithographer, engraver or commercial artist, but does not include, for the purposes of this Part and the Schedules, any restaurateur, caterer or other person engaged in the business of preparing in a restaurant, centralized kitchen or similar establishment, food or drink, whether or not the food or drink is for consumption on the premises. *Excise Tax Act*, R.S.C. 1985, c. E-15, s. 42.

PRODUCER-PROVINCE. *n.* 1. A province in which the quantities of crude oil ordinarily produced, extracted or recovered in that province in a month are such that a significant quantity of that crude oil is normally available for use outside that province in each month. *Energy Administration Act*, R.S.C. 1985, c. E-6, s. 20. 2. A province in which the quantities of gas ordinarily produced, extracted, recovered or manufactured in that province in a month are such that a significant quantity of that gas is normally available for use outside that province in each month. *Energy Administration Act*, R.S.C. 1985, c. E-6, s. 36.

PRODUCERS' BOARD. The body entrusted with implementation and administration of a joint plan to market farm products. *Farm Products Marketing Act*, R.S.Q. 1977, c. M-35, s. 1.

PRODUCER-SHIPPER CONTRACT. A gas contract relating to the first sale and delivery of (i) gas after it is first recovered from a well, if the gas is marketable gas at the time it is so recovered; or (ii) gas after it first becomes marketable gas, in any other case, and includes a gas contract that is deemed by the regulations to be a producer-shipper contract for the purposes of this Part. *Natural Gas Marketing Act*, S.A. 1986, c. N-2.8, s. 8.

PRODUCING. *adj.* 1. Planting, growing, harvesting, curing or preparing for sale. *Farm Products Marketing Act*, R.S.O. 1980, c. 158, s. 21. 2. (i) In the case of chicks-for-placement, the provision of housing, feed, water or care therefor and the preparation thereof for sale or for use as fowl; and (ii) in the case of eggs and hatching eggs, the provision of housing, feed, water or care for the fowl that lay such eggs or hatching eggs and the preparation of the eggs or hatching eggs for sale or for hatching, as the case may be. *Farm Products Marketing Act*, R.S.O. 1980, c. 158, s. 22.

PRODUCING TRACT. A drainage unit, as defined in The Oil and Gas Conservation Act: (i) in which or in respect of which is situate a well from which oil: (A) is being produced or is capable of being produced; or (B) is, by virtue of an order of the Lieutenant Governor in Council, deemed to be produced; or (ii) the whole or a portion of which is included in an area in respect of which there exists: (A) a plan; (B) a unit operation agreement; or (C) any other arrangement or agreement for the production of oil or oil and natural gas or for the allocation of royalty on that production; under which oil is being produced or is capable of being produced from the drainage unit. *Saskatchewan statutes.*

PRODUCING WELL. In relation to the continuation of a lease, means a well that, in the opinion of the Minister, is capable of producing (i) petroleum in paying quantity from a zone in which petroleum rights are granted under the lease; or (ii) natural gas in paying quantity from a zone in which natural gas rights are granted under the lease. *Mines and Minerals Amendment Act*, S.A. 1985, c. 39, s. 6.

PRODUCT. *n.* 1. Any article that is or may be the subject of trade or commerce but does not include land or any interest therein. *Consumer Packaging and Labelling Act*, R.S.C. 1985, c. C-38, s. 2. 2. Includes an article and a service. *Combines Investigation Act*, R.S.C. 1985, c. C-34, s. 2. 3. In relation to any grain referred to in subsection (1), means any substance produced by processing or manufacturing that grain, alone or together with any other material or substance, designated by the Governor in Council by regulation as a product of that grain for the purposes of this Part. *Canadian Wheat Board Act*, R.S.C. 1985, c. C-24, s. 47(4). 4. A commodity made from oil or gas and includes refined crude oil, crude tops, topped crude, processed crude, processed crude oil, residue from crude oil, cracking stock, uncracked fuel oil, fuel oil, treated crude oil, residuum, gas oil, casinghead gasoline, natural-gas gasoline, lubricating oil, blends or mixtures of oil with one or more liquid products or by-products derived from oil or gas and blends or mixtures of two or more liquid products or by-products-derived from oil or gas, whether or not mentioned herein. 5. Includes the whole or any part of any material, fabric, compound, substance, article, goods or thing. *Workplace Act*, S.B.C. 1985, c. 34, s. 1. 6. Honey or any fruit or vegetable. 7. Anything derived from a carcass and includes a portion. *Meat Inspection Act*, R.S.B.C. 1979, c. 253, s. 1. See AERONAUTICAL ~; AGRICULTURAL ~; ANIMAL ~; ASSOCIATED ~; BAKERY ~; BARLEY ~; CATCH WEIGHT ~; CONSUMER ~; CONTROLLED ~; CONTROL ~; CORROSIVE ~; DAIRY ~; EDIBLE OIL ~; FARM ~; FINISHED ~; FISHERIES ~; FISHERY ~S; FOOD ~; FOOD ~S; FOREST ~; FOREST ~S; FRESH WATER ~; GRAIN ~; HAZARDOUS ~; HOT ~; ILLEGAL ~; INTERCHANGEABLE ~; LIVESTOCK ~S; LOCAL ~; LUMBER ~; MANITOBA ~S; MANUFACTURED ~; MAPLE ~; MARINE ~; MARKETED ~; MEAT ~; MILK ~; MINERAL ~; NATURAL ~; OAT ~; OIL SANDS ~; OIL SHALE ~S; PEST CONTROL ~; PETROLEUM ~; POULTRY ~; POULTRY ~S; PREPACKAGED ~; REGULATED ~; SPECIALTY ~; TEST MARKET ~; TEXTILE FIBRE ~; TIMBER ~S; TOBACCO ~S; WHALE ~S; WHEAT ~; WOOD ~.

PRODUCT FOR HUMAN CONSUMPTION. Includes every substance, whether a solid or a liquid, used or intended to be used for human consumption and any article intended to enter into or to be used in preparation or composition of such substance including confectionery, flavouring or colouring matter and condiments, but does not include a drug as defined in the Pharmacy Act. *Public Health Act*, S.P.E.I. 1980, c. 42, s. 1.

PRODUCT HOLDING FIXTURES. Devices for holding the goods in process while the working tools are in operation and are usually held securely in the machine while the operation is in progress, but which do not contain any special arrangement for guiding the working tools. *Retail Sales Tax Act*, R.R.O. 1980, Reg. 903, s. 1.

PRODUCTION. *n.* 1. In court, the exhibition of a document. 2. Mining for the purposes of sale, barter or stockpiling. *Mining Act*, S.N.B. 1985, c. M-14.1, s. 1. 3. From a Canadian resource property or a foreign resource property means (i) petroleum, natural gas and related hydrocarbons produced from the property; (ii) heavy crude oil produced from the property processed to any stage that is not beyond the crude oil stage or its equivalent; (iii) ore (other than iron ore or tar sands) produced from the

property processed to any stage that is not beyond the prime metal stage or its equivalent; (iv) iron ore produced from the property processed to any stage that is not beyond the pellet stage or its equivalent; (v) tar sands produced from the property processed to any stage that is not beyond the crude oil stage or its equivalent; and (vi) any rental or royalty from the property computed by reference to the amount or value of the production of petroleum, natural gas or related hydrocarbons or ore. *Income Tax Act*, R.S.C. 1952, c. 148 (as am. S.C. 1987, c. 46, s. 18(9)), s. 66(15)(h.01). See ALLOCATED ~; ALLOWABLE ~; COMMERCIAL ~; COST OF ~; FILM ~; LIMITED ~; LIVE STOCK ~; MILK ~; NORMAL ~; PRIMARY ~; PROVINCE OF ~; STANDARD OF ~; SYNTHETIC ~.

PRODUCTION BOYCOTT. A strike.

PRODUCTION CRANE. An electrically operated device that travels on fixed overhead track or tracks; and (i) is used to handle hot or molten materials; or (ii) has a duty rating equal to or greater than Class C or D as determined under Part 3.4 of CSA Standard B167-1964, "General Purpose Electric Overhead Travelling Cranes". *Occupational Health and Safety Act*, R.R.O. 1980, Reg. 694, s. 1.

PRODUCTION DAY. In respect of any brewery, a day not exceeding 24 consecutive hours during which beer is produced. Canada regulations.

PRODUCTION DEVELOPMENT COSTS. The aggregate expenses incurred by the operator of a mine, other than those claimed as eligible exploration expenditures, on the mining right from the date of acquiring the mining right to the date of commencement of production. *An Act to Amend the Metallic Minerals Tax Act*, S.N.B. 1987, c. 35, s. 1.

PRODUCTION FACILITIES. Production equipment and apparatus at the field site and separating, treating and processing facilities and includes such other equipment or facilities as are required in support of production operations, including airstrips, helicopter landing areas, storage or tank facilities and living quarters for personnel.

PRODUCTION OF OIL [OR] GAS. The bringing forth or into existence and human realization, from underground, of a basic substance containing gas, and at the same time, other matter. *Texaco Exploration Inc. v. The Queen*, [1975] C.T.C. 404; 75 D.T.C. 5288 (F.C.).

PRODUCTION OPERATIONS. All the operations involved in the assembling, processing or conditioning of goods, resulting in other goods different in nature or characteristics from the former, or the reconditioning or repair of moveable property by its owner, and includes the operations of a business engaged in farming, logging, the extraction or treatment of mineral resources, or fisheries, but does not include construction, meal preparation, or any other prescribed operation. *An Act Respecting Fiscal Incentives to Industrial Development*, R.S.Q. 1977, c. S-34, s. 1. See BITUMINOUS SHALE ~.

PRODUCTION OPTIONS WEIGHT. The combined weight of all installed regular production options weighing over 5 pounds in excess of the standard items that they replace and not included in curb weight or accessory weight, including heavy duty brakes, ride levellers, roof rack, heavy duty battery and special trim. *Motor Vehicle Safety Regulations*, C.R.C., c. 1038, s. 111.

PRODUCTION PLATFORM. The main production structure and equipment located offshore and any structure or equipment associated therewith.

PRODUCTION ROYALTY. An amount computed by reference to the amount or value of production after December 31, 1981 of petroleum or gas, including any minimum or advance royalty payment with respect to the amount or value of production, but does not include (a) a resource royalty; or (b) an amount to which paragraph 7(e) applies paid to a person referred to therein. *Petroleum and Gas Revenue Tax Act*, R.S.C. 1985, c. P-12, s. 2. See INCREMENTAL ~.

PRODUCTION SERVICE ASSOCIATION. Includes an association incorporated or registered under this Act having as its principal objects, or any of them, providing services to assist its members and patrons to become established as producers of agricultural products, goods, wares, merchandise or services for sale or to assist its members and patrons to improve their efficiency and income as producers. *The Co-operative Production Associations Act*, R.S.S. 1978, c. C-37, s. 67.

PRODUCTION SPACING UNIT. That area designated by the appropriate provincial authority for the production of oil or gas where a distinction is made between the areas assigned for production and for drilling purposes. *Indian Oil and Gas Regulations*, C.R.C., c. 963, s. 2.

PRODUCTION TRACT. (a) A parcel or group of parcels, whether or not a parcel is contiguous with another, from which a designated mineral is or has at any time been produced or is deemed, under an order of the Lieutenant Governor in Council, to be or to have been at any time produced; and (b) a parcel or portion of a parcel for which there exists (i) a plan; (ii) a unit

agreement; or (iii) any other arrangement or agreement, for the production of a designated mineral or for the allocation of royalty on that production, under which a designated mineral is or has at any time been produced or is deemed, under an order of the Lieutenant Governor in Council, to be or to have been at any time produced. *Mineral Land Tax Act*, R.S.B.C. 1979, c. 260, s. 1.

PRODUCTION WORKER. An employee who actually makes the goods or performs the service.

PRODUCTIVE LANDS. Lands that are not rock barrens, muskeg or lands covered with water. *Crown Timber Act*, R.S.O. 1980, c. 109, s. 1.

PRODUCTIVITY AGREEMENT. A collective agreement including terms relating to physical work conditions, methods and level of production.

PRODUCT LIABILITY. Liability of manufacturers and sellers to buyers and others for damages suffered because of defects in the goods manufactured or sold.

PRODUCT MONOGRAPH. In relation to a new device, means a document, devoid of promotional material, describing the performance characteristics of the device, the components and method of packaging, the method of sterilization when applicable, the claims, description of mode of action, instructions for and conditions of the use of the device and any other warnings or precautions that may be required to provide adequate directions for safe and effective use of the device. *Medical Devices Regulations*, C.R.C., c. 871, s. 32.

PRODUCT OUTLINE. A detailed description of: (a) the process followed in preparing a veterinary biologic and any diluent to be used therewith; (b) the methods and procedures to be employed in handling, storing, administering and testing a veterinary biologic and any diluent to be used therewith; and (c) the tests used to establish the purity, safety, potency and efficacy of a veterinary biologic, and the purity and safety of any diluent to be used therewith, and the results of all such tests. *Animal Disease and Protection Regulations*, C.R.C., c. 296, s. 2.

PRODUCT RESTRAINT ASSEMBLY. Any webbing, buckle, hardware or combination thereof that is designed to secure or restrain a product in a vehicle. *Children's Car Seats and Harnesses Regulations*, C.R.C., c. 921, s. 2.

PRODUCTS OF AGRICULTURE. Includes (a) grain, hay, roots, vegetables, fruits, other crops and all other direct products of the soil; and (b) honey, livestock (whether alive or dead), dairy products, eggs and all other indirect products of the soil. *Bank Act*, R.S.C. 1985, c. B-1, s. 2.

PRODUCTS OF COMBUSTION DETECTOR. A device for sensing the presence of visible or invisible particles produced by combustion and automatically initiating a signal indicating this condition. *Building Code Act*, R.R.O. 1980, Reg. 87, s. 1.

PRODUCTS OF THE FOREST. 1. Includes (a) logs, pulpwood, piling, spars, railway ties, poles, pit props and all other timber; (b) boards, laths, shingles, deals, staves and all other lumber, bark, wood chips and sawdust and Christmas trees; (c) skins and furs of wild animals; and (d) maple products. *Bank Act*, R.S.C. 1985, c. B-1, s. 2. 2. Trees, timber, sphagnum moss, wild rice and any other shrubs, plants or grasses growing on forest land or in waters of the forest land. *The Forest Act*, R.S.S. 1978, c. F-19, s. 2.

PRODUCTS OF THE QUARRY AND MINE. Includes stone, clay, sand, gravel, metals, ores, coal, salt, precious stones, metalliferous and non-metallic minerals and hydrocarbons, whether obtained by excavation, drilling or otherwise. *Bank Act*, R.S.C. 1985, c. B-1, s. 2.

PRODUCTS OF THE SEA, LAKES AND RIVERS. Includes fish of all kinds, marine and fresh water organic and inorganic life and any substances extracted or derived from any water. *Bank Act*, R.S.C. 1985, c. B-1, s. 2.

PRODUCTS OR BY-PRODUCTS. Of grain means any substance produced by gristing, crushing, grinding, milling, cutting or otherwise processing any kind of grain, or by the sifting or screening of any substance so produced. *Grain Futures Act*, R.S.C. 1985, c. G-11, s. 2.

PRO EO QUO. [L.] For this thing which.

PROFER. *v.* To produce.

PROFERT. One produces.

PROFESSION. *n.* A vocation or calling; divinity, law and medicine are called learned professions. See LEGAL ~; TRADE, INDUSTRY OR ~.

PROFESSIONAL. *n.* 1. A person who is a member of an association or group determined by regulation, and whose activities are directly connected with the social and community services provided by a community board. *Community Resource Board Act*, R.S.B.C. 1979, c. 58, s. 1. 2. When used in respect of a natural person, means a person other than an amateur. *Athletics Control Act*, R.R.O. 1980, Reg. 76, s. 1. See HEALTH CARE ~; NON-PARTICIPATING ~.

PROFESSIONAL ARBITRATOR. An arbitrator who is by profession a barrister, solicitor, architect, Dominion land surveyor or Alberta land surveyor. *Arbitration Act*, R.S.A. 1980, c. A-43, s. 1.

PROFESSIONAL ASSOCIATION. An organization of persons that by an enactment, agreement or custom has power to admit, suspend, expel, or direct persons in the practice of any occupation or calling.

PROFESSIONAL CHEMISTRY. See PRACTICE OF ~.

PROFESSIONAL COMMUNITY PLANNING. See PRACTICE OF ~.

PROFESSIONAL CONTEST OR EXHIBITION. A professional contest or exhibition of baseball, bicycle riding, boxing, dancing, golf, hockey, jaialai, lacrosse, motorcycle riding, physical prowess whether by contortion or otherwise, rowing, rugby, running, skating whether speed skating or figure skating, soccer, swimming, tennis, wrestling or any professional contest or exhibition of any other sport or game designated by the Lieutenant Governor in Council. *Athletics Control Act*, R.S.O. 1980, c. 34, s. 1.

PROFESSIONAL CORPORATION. A corporation that is the holder of a subsisting permit or is entered in the register under a statute governing a profession.

PROFESSIONAL EMPLOYEE. 1. An employee who (a) is, in the course of employment, engaged in the application of specialized knowledge ordinarily acquired by a course of instruction and study resulting in graduation from a university or similar institution; and (b) is, or is eligible to be, a member of a professional organization that is authorized by statute to establish the qualifications for membership in the organization. 2. An employee of an institution who provides educational services to students and includes an employee who is a librarian or an administrator. *College and Institute Act*, R.S.B.C. 1979, c. 53, s. 1.

PROFESSIONAL EMPLOYER. 1. An employer who habitually has employees in his employ for any kind of work which is the object of a decree. *Collective Agreement Decrees Act*, R.S.Q. 1977, c. D-2, s. 1. 2. An employer who habitually has one or more employees in his employ for any kind of work which is the object of an ordinance. *Minimum Wage Act*, R.S.Q. 1977, c. S-1, s. 1. 3. An employer whose main activity is to do construction work and who habitually employs employees for any kind of work which is the object of a decree, or, failing a decree, of a collective agreement. *Construction Industry Labour Relations Act*, R.S.Q. 1977, c. R-20, s. 1.

PROFESSIONAL ENGINEER. A person who, by reason of knowledge of mathematics, the physical and social sciences and the principles of engineering, is qualified to engage in the practice of professional engineering and who is registered as a professional engineer.

PROFESSIONAL ENGINEERING. See PRACTICE OF ~.

PROFESSIONAL FORESTRY. See PRACTICE OF ~.

PROFESSIONAL GEOLOGIST. An individual who holds a certificate of registration to engage in the practice of geology under this Act. *Engineering, Geological and Geophysical Professions Act*, S.A. 1981, c. E-11.1, s. 1.

PROFESSIONAL GEOLOGY. Reporting, advising, evaluating, interpreting, geological surveying, sampling or examining related to any activity (i) that is aimed at the discovery or development of oil, natural gas, coal, metallic or non-metallic minerals or precious stones, or other natural resources or water or that is aimed at the investigation of geological conditions; and (ii) that requires in that reporting, advising, evaluating, interpreting, geological surveying, sampling or examining, the professional application of the principles of the geological sciences or any related subject including, without limiting the generality of the foregoing, the geological field of mineralogy, palaeontology, structural geology, stratigraphy, sedimentation, petrology, geomorphology, photogeology and the like, but does not include any of the above activities that are normally associated with the business of prospecting when carried on by a prospector.

PROFESSIONAL GEOPHYSICIST. An individual who holds a certificate of registration to engage in the practice of geophysics under this Act. *Engineering, Geological and Geophysical Professions Act*, S.A. 1981, c. E-11.1, s. 1.

PROFESSIONAL GEOPHYSICS. Reporting, advising, evaluating, interpreting or geophysical surveying related to any activity (i) that is aimed at the discovery or development of oil, natural gas, coal, metallic or non-metallic minerals or precious stones or other natural resources or water or that is aimed at the investigation of subsurface conditions in the earth; and (ii) that requires in that reporting, advising, evaluating, interpreting or geophysical surveying, the professional application of the principles of one or more of the subjects of physics, mathematics or any related subject including, without limiting the generality of the foregoing, principles of elastic wave propagation, gravitational, magnetic and electrical fields, natural radio activity, and the like, but does not include the routine

maintenance or operation of geophysical instruments, or if carried out under the responsible supervision of a professional geophysicist, the routine reduction or plotting of geophysical observations.

PROFESSIONAL INTERIOR DESIGNER. A person whose name is entered in the register and in one of the rosters referred to in section 7. *Professional Interior Designers Institute of Manitoba Act*, S.M. 1980-81, c. 28, s. 1(1).

PROFESSIONAL LAND SURVEYING. The advising on, reporting on, the supervising of or the conducting of surveys to establish, locate, define or describe the lines, boundaries or corners of parcels of land or land covered with water.

PROFESSIONAL LIABILITY CLAIM. A claim against a licensed member, registered practitioner or professional corporation for an amount of money that the licensed member, registered practitioner or professional corporation is legally obligated to pay as damages, which claim arises out of the performance of professional services for a person by the licensed member, registered practitioner or professional corporation, or by another person for whose acts the licensed member, registered practitioner or professional corporation is legally liable.

PROFESSIONAL MEMBER. A professional engineer, professional geologist or professional geophysicist registered as a member of the Association pursuant to this Act. *Engineering, Geological and Geophysical Professions Act*, S.A. 1981, c. E-11.1, s. 1.

PROFESSIONAL MISCONDUCT. 1. A serious digression from established or recognized professional standards or rules of practice of a profession. 2. A member is guilty of professional misconduct (a) if in the course of his profession he knowingly provides or condones a false or misleading oral or written statement; (b) impersonates another member; (c) permits his name or picture to be used in connection with the advertisement of any product that is or may be used for teaching purposes in the Territories; (d) irresponsibly divulges professional confidences; (e) acts fraudulently for the purpose of procuring registration for himself or another; (f) contravenes any code of ethics by by-law adopted by the Association; or (g) is convicted of a criminal offence the nature of which could affect or reflect upon the ethics of the teaching profession. *Teachers' Association Act*, S.N.W.T. 1976 (3d Sess.), c. 3, s. 25. 3. (a) Gross negligence; (b) infamous, disgraceful or improper conduct in a professional respect, including any violation of the code of ethics prepared and published by the council under section 9 of the Act; (c) incompetence; (d) conviction of a serious criminal offence by a court of competent jurisdiction; (e) continued breach of the regulations or by-laws of the Association. *Professional Engineers Act*, R.R.O. 1980, Reg. 804, s. 8. 4. That a qualified medical practitioner has (A) had his rights or privileges under the Narcotic Control Act (Canada) or the Food and Drugs Act (Canada) or the regulations under either Act restricted or withdrawn; or (B) been guilty, in the opinion of the Board, of misconduct in a professional respect or of conduct unbecoming a medical practitioner, or of incompetence. *Medical Act*, S.N.S. 1969, c. 15, s. 1.

PROFESSIONAL PERSON. A physician, nurse, dentist or other health or mental health professional, a hospital administrator, a school principal, school teacher or other teaching professional, a social work administrator, social worker or other social service professional, a child care worker in any day care center or child caring institution, a police or law enforcement officer, a psychologist, a guidance counsellor, or a recreational services administrator or worker, and includes any other person who by virtue of his employment or occupation has a responsibility to discharge a duty of care towards a child. *Child and Family Services and Family Relations Act*, S.N.B. 1980, c. C-2.1, s. 30.

PROFESSIONAL SERVICES. Includes independent scientific, literary, artistic, educational or teaching activities as well as the independent activities of physicians, lawyers, engineers, architects, dentists and accountants. *Canada-Israel Income Tax Convention Act*, S.C. 1974-75-76, c. 104, Schedule III, Article XIV, s. 2.

PROFESSIONAL STAFF. Professional employees but does not include persons designated by the minister as serving the institution in a managerial or confidential capacity. *College and Institute Act*, R.S.B.C. 1979, c. 53, s. 1.

PROFESSIONAL STRIKE BREAKER. A person who is not involved in a dispute and whose primary object, in the board's opinion, is (i) to prevent, interfere with or break up a lawful strike; or (b) to assist an employer in a lockout.

PROFESSIONAL SYNDICATE. A professional syndicate formed under the Professional Syndicates Act (R.S.Q., chapter S-40) which administers a forest products joint plan. *An Act to Promote Forest Credit by Private Institutions*, S.Q. 1983, c. 16, s. 1.

PROFESSOR. *n.* A bachelor of arts or bachelor of pedagogy who has had 3 years' experience in teaching and wishes to pursue such studies. *Teachers Scholarships Act*, R.S.Q. 1977, c. B-7, s. 2.

PROFIT. *n.* Gain which results from using either labour or capital or a combination of both. W. Grover & F. Iacobucci, *Materials on Canadian Income Tax*, 4th ed. (Toronto: Richard De Boo Ltd., 1980) at 261. See ACCUMULATED ~S; MESNE ~; NET ~; OPERATING ~; PROSPECTIVE LOSS OF EARNINGS OR ~S; SECRET ~.

PROFIT AND LOSS. The gain or loss which results when goods are bought or sold, or when any other business is carried on.

PROFIT À PRENDRE. [Fr.] The right, claimed by grant or prescription, of anyone to take some profit out of another person's tenement for one's own tenement.

PROFIT SHARING PLAN. An arrangement under which payments computed by reference to his profits from his business or by reference to his profits from his business and the profits, if any, from the business of a corporation with whom he does not deal at arm's length are or have been made by an employer to a trustee in trust for the benefit of employees of that employer or employees of any other employer, whether or not payments are or have been also made to the trustee by the employees. *Income Tax Act*, R.S.C. 1952, c. 148 (as am. S.C. 1970-71-72, c. 63), s. 147(b). See DEFERRED ~; EMPLOYEES ~.

PRO FORMA. [L.] In order to observe proper form.

PROGRAM. *n.* 1. A plan of individual intervention or provision of safe shelter and appropriate counselling to residents in need. *Residential Services Act*, S.S. 1984-85-86, c. R-21.2, s. 2. 2. A series or group of courses leading to a statement of standing. *Public Schools Act*, S.M. 1980, c. 33, s. 1. 3. A broadcast presentation of sound and visual matter designed to inform, enlighten or entertain, but does not include advertising material or station and network identifications. *Television Broadcasting Regulations*, C.R.C., c. 381, s. 2. See AMBULANCE SERVICES ~; COMPUTER ~; DRIVER IMPROVEMENT ~; EXPLORATORY ~; FORESTRY MANAGEMENT ~; 4-H ~; JOB TRAINING ~; MANAGEMENT ~; MANDATORY ALLOCATION ~; MANPOWER ~S AND SERVICES; NON-PROFIT ~ OF CAMPING; OCCUPATIONAL TRAINING ~; RATIONING ~; RECREATION ~; REHABILITATION ~; RESEARCH ~; SCHOOL ~; SERVICES AND ~S; TREATMENT ~.

PROGRAMMING. *n.* 1. Audio signals or visual signals, or both, or the provision of such signals, where the signals are directed to the public at large by means of telecommunication facilities and (i) are designed to inform, enlighten or entertain; or (ii) that, in nature, character or substance, are similar to signals normally provided by television or radio broadcasting. 2. The ordered arrangement of programmes composing the programme schedule of a broadcasting station or of a cablecasting channel. *An Act respecting educational programming*, S.Q. 1979, c. 52, s. 1. 3. Any presentation of sound matter, visual matter or sound and visual matter designed to inform, enlighten or entertain, but does not include advertising material. *Cable Television Regulations*, C.R.C., c. 374, s. 2. See CABLECAST ~; COMMUNITY ~; EDUCATIONAL ~; NON-~.

PROGRAMMING SERVICE. Any broadcast of sound or visual matter by radio or television stations that is designed to inform, enlighten or entertain. *Excise Tax Act*, R.S.C. 1985 (1st Supp.), c. 15, s. 21.1.

PROGRAM OF INSTRUCTION. A course of instruction in a vocation, trades, technical or technological field of education or a related general course of instruction, a course taught in a school or institute for instruction of apprentices, correspondence study courses, study courses for disabled persons and study of practical courses for vocational, trades, technical or technological teachers. *Vocational, Trades, Technical and Technological Training Act*, S.N.S. 1986, c. 18, s. 2.

PROGRAM OF PHYSIOTHERAPY. A program planned, administered and evaluated by a physiotherapist and may include the use of such mediums as exercise, massage, manipulations, hydrotherapy, radiant, mechanical and electrical energy. *The Physiotherapists Act*, S.M. 1980-81, c. 15, s. 1.

PROGRAM OF STUDY. See APPROVED ~.

PROGRAM TIME. Any period longer than 2 minutes during which a broadcaster does not normally present commercial messages, public service announcements or station or network identification. *Canada Elections Act*, R.S.C. 1985, c. E-2, s. 2.

PROGRESS ADVANCES. The instalments of an approved loan advanced by the approved lender as the building construction progresses. *National Housing Loan Regulations*, C.R.C., c. 1108, s. 2.

PROGRESSIVE DISCIPLINE. Beginning with a warning about the seriousness with which an employer views an employment record, gradually more severe discipline is imposed for continuing misconduct. D.J.M. Brown and D.M. Beatty, *Canadian Labour Arbitration*, 2d ed. (Aurora: Canada Law Book, 1977) at 490.

PROGRESSIVE TAX RATE STRUCTURE. A system in which the percentage of income paid in taxes increases with the taxpayer's income. W. Grover & F. Iacobucci, *Materials on Canadian Income Tax*, 4th ed. (Toronto: Richard De Boo Ltd., 1980) at 41.

PROGRESSIVE WAGE INCREASE. A scheduled or periodic increment which is neither work nor performance related, in contrast to a merit raise. D.J.M. Brown and D.M. Beatty, *Canadian Labour Arbitration*, 2d ed. (Aurora: Canada Law Book, 1977) at 562.

PROGRESS PAYMENT. A payment made by or on behalf of Her Majesty under the terms of a contract after the performance of the part of the contract in respect of which the payment is made but before the performance of the whole contract. *Government Contracts Regulations*, C.R.C., c. 701, s. 2.

PROGRESS REPORT. A report made in accordance with section 28 on the performance of a young person against whom a disposition has been made. *Young Offenders Act*, R.S.C. 1985, c. Y-1, s. 2.

PRO HAC VICE. [L.] For this particular occurrence.

PROHIBITED ACT. 1. An act or omission that (a) impairs the efficiency or impedes the working of any vessel, vehicle, aircraft, machinery, apparatus or other thing; or (b) causes property, by whomever it may be owned, to be lost, damaged or destroyed. *Criminal Code*, R.S.C. 1985, c. C-46, s. 52(2). 2. Any conduct or communication by a person that has as its purpose interference with the civil rights of a person or class of persons by promoting (a) hatred or contempt of a person or class of persons; or (b) the superiority or inferiority of a person or class of persons in comparison with another or others, on the basis of colour, race, religion, ethnic origin or place of origin. A prohibited act is a tort actionable without proof of damage: (a) by any person against whom the prohibited act was directed; or (b) where the prohibited act was directed against a class of persons, by any member of that class. *Civil Rights Protection Act*, S.B.C. 1981, c. 12, s. 1.

PROHIBITED DEGREE. See AFFINITY.

PROHIBITED HOURS. The hours during which the hunting of a specified species of wildlife in a locality is prohibited. *Wildlife Act*, S.B.C. 1982, c. 57, s. 1.

PROHIBITED PLACE. (a) Any work of defence belonging to or occupied or used by or on behalf of Her Majesty, including arsenals, armed forces establishments or stations, factories, dockyards, mines, minefields, camps, ships, aircraft, telegraph, telephone, wireless or signal stations or offices, and places used for the purpose of building, repairing, making or storing any munitions of war or any sketches, plans, models or documents relating thereto, or for the purpose of getting any metals, oil or minerals for use in time of war; (b) any place not belonging to Her Majesty where any munitions of war or any sketches, plans, models or documents relating thereto are being made, repaired, obtained or stored under contract with, or with any person on behalf of, Her Majesty or otherwise on behalf of Her Majesty; and (c) any place that is for the time being declared by order of the Governor in Council to be a prohibited place on the ground that information with respect thereto or damage thereto would be useful to a foreign power. *Official Secrets Act*, R.S.C. 1985, c. O-5, s. 2.

PROHIBITED WEAPON. (a) Any device or contrivance designed or intended to muffle or stop the sound or report of a firearm; (b) any knife that has a blade that opens automatically by gravity or centrifugal force or by hand pressure applied to a button, spring or other device in or attached to the handle of the knife; (c) any firearm, not being a restricted weapon described in paragraph (c) of the definition of that expression in this subsection, that is capable of firing bullets in rapid succession during one pressure of the trigger; (d) any firearm adapted from a rifle or shotgun, whether by sawing, cutting or other alteration or modification, that, as so adapted, has a barrel that is less than 457 mm in length or that is less than 660 mm in overall length; or (e) a weapon of any kind, not being an antique firearm or a firearm of a kind commonly used in Canada for hunting or sporting purposes, that is declared by order of the Governor in Council to be a prohibited weapon. *Criminal Code*, R.S.C. 1985, c. C-46, s. 84 as am. by R.S.C. 1985 (1st Supp.), c. 27, s. 186.

PROHIBITION. *n.* 1. An order which prevents an inferior tribunal from proceeding further with some matter before it. S.A. DeSmith, *Judicial Review of Administrative Action*, 4th ed. by J.M. Evans (London: Stevens, 1980) at 25 and 26. 2. An order to prevent a person from driving a motor vehicle.

PROHIBITORY INJUNCTION. An order which requires a defendant to refrain from doing something. G.H.L. Fridman, *The Law of Contract in Canada*, 2d ed. (Toronto: Carswell, 1986) at 722.

PRO INDIVISO. [L.] As not divided.

PRO INTERESSE SUO. [L.] In respect of one's own interest.

PROJECT. *n.* 1. A place where the building, construction, improvement, repair, alteration, reconstruction, demolition or excavating of any building structure, road, bridge, pipeline, wharf or marine structure, excavation or tunnel is being carried on. 2. Any project heretofore or hereafter undertaken under the authority of the Prairie Farm Rehabilitation Act (Canada), including the establishment of community pastures and grazing reserves and the construction of works for irrigation or water supply purposes. *The Expropriation (Rehabilitation Projects) Act*, R.S.S. 1978, c. E-17, s. 2. 3. Any works proposed or developed under The Water Rights Act or under any Act providing for the improvement, development, utilization or control of water or land resources. *The Watershed Associations Act*, R.S.S. 1978, c. W-11, s. 2. 4. A project for: (i) the more efficient use and economic development of lands; (ii) the development of income and employment opportunities in rural areas and improving standards of living in those areas; or (iii) the development and conservation for agricultural purposes of water supplies and for soil improvement and conservation that will improve agricultural efficiency. *Agricultural Rehabilitation and Development Act (Ontario)*, R.S.O. 1980, c. 11, s. 1. 5. A pool or part of a pool in which operations in accordance with a scheme for enhanced recovery of oil, approved by the Board, are conducted; or, if the scheme provides for the application of more than one recovery mechanism, the part of the area subject to the scheme which is subject to one such recovery mechanism. *Oil and Gas Conservation Act*, R.S.A. 1980, c. O-5, s. 1. See ABATEMENT ~; BUILDING ~; CONDOMINIUM ~; CONSTRUCTION ~; DEFENCE ~S; DEMONSTRATION OR RESEARCH ~; EDUCATIONAL ~; ENERGY USE ~; EXPERIMENTAL ~; HIGHWAY ~ AREA; HOSPITAL ~; HOUSING ~; JOB CREATION ~; POWER ~; PUBLIC HOUSING ~; REGULATED ~; SELF-LIQUIDATING ~; SEWERAGE ~; SEWAGE TREATMENT ~; SPECIAL ~; WATER SUPPLY ~; WORK ACTIVITY ~.

PROJECTIONIST. *n.* 1. A person who operates projection equipment. *Theatres Act*, R.S.O. 1980, c. 498, s. 1. 2. A person, employee or otherwise, who operates or manipulates a kinematograph in a theatre. *Fire Services Act*, R.S.B.C. 1979, c. 133, s. 1.

PROJECTION ROOM. The room in which projection equipment is located while in use. *Theatres Act*, R.S.O. 1980, c. 498, s. 1.

PROJECTOR. *n.* 1. The equipment necessary or used for the transducing from a film to moving images, including equipment for accompanying sound. *Theatres Act*, R.S.O. 1980, c. 498, s. 1. 2. A motion picture or slide projector or other similar apparatus for exhibiting, projecting or displaying film. *Motion Picture Act*, R.S.B.C. 1979, c. 284, s. 1. 3. Any apparatus projecting or used to project light rays. *Wild-life Conservation Act*, S.Q. 1978, c. 65, s. 1.

PROJECT SITE. Any building, structure, premises, water or land where construction is carried on. *Occupational Health and Safety Act*, S.N.B. 1983, c. O-0.2, s. 1.

PRO LAESIONE FIDEI. [L.] For breach of faith.

PROLEM ANTE MATRIMONIUM NATAM, ITA UT POST LEGITIMAM, LEX CIVILIS SUCCEDERE FACIT IN HAEREDITATE PARENTUM; SED PROLEM, QUAM MATRIMONIUM NON PARIT, SUCCEDERE NOT SINIT LEX ANGLORUM. [L.] Civil law permits offspring born before marriage, as long as they are afterwards legitimised, to be their parents' heirs; but English law does not permit offspring not produced by marriage to succeed.

PROLES. *n.* [L.] Offspring.

PROLICIDE. *n.* The killing of human offspring.

PROLIXITY. *n.* In a pleading or affidavit, alleging facts at too much length.

PROLONGED BLAST. A blast which lasts 4 to 6 seconds. *Collision Regulations*, C.R.C., c. 1416, Rule 32.

PROLONGED DISABILITY. See SERIOUS OR ~.

PROMISE. *n.* A party's undertaking about its future conduct. G.H.L. Fridman, *The Law of Contract in Canada*, 2d ed. (Toronto: Carswell, 1986) at 1. See BREACH OF ~ TO MARRY; CONTRACTUAL ~; DONATIVE ~; GRATUITOUS ~; MUTUAL ~S.

PROMISEE. *n.* One to whom one makes a promise.

PROMISE TO APPEAR. A promise in Form 10 given to an officer in charge. *Criminal Code*, R.S.C. 1985, c. C-46, s. 493.

PROMISOR. *n.* One who makes a promise.

PROMISSORY ESTOPPEL. Once one party makes a representation about a present or past fact and the other party relies on it detrimentally, the representor cannot repudiate the representation and put forward the true facts. G.H.L. Fridman, *The Law of Contract in Canada*, 2d ed. (Toronto: Carswell, 1986) at 110.

PROMISSORY NOTE. An unconditional promise in writing made by one person to another person, signed by the maker, engaging to pay, on demand or at a fixed or determinable future time, a sum certain in money to, or to the order of, a specified person or to bearer. *Bills of Exchange Act*, R.S.C. 1985, c. B-4, s. 176.

PROMOTER. *n.* 1. When used in relation to an issuer, a person who (a) acting alone or in concert with one or more other persons, directly or indirectly, takes the initiative in founding, organizing or substantially reorganizing the business of the issuer; or (b) in connection with the founding, organization or substantial reorganization of the business of the issuer, directly or indirectly receives, in consideration of services or property or both, 10% or more of a class of the issuer's own securities or 10% or more of the proceeds from the sale of a class of the issuer's own securities of a particular issue but does not include a person who (c) receives securities or proceeds referred to in paragraph (b) solely (i) as underwriting commissions; or (ii) in consideration for property; and (d) does not otherwise take part in founding, organizing or substantially reorganizing the business. 2. A person named in the application or petition for incorporation of a bank. *Bank Act*, R.S.C. 1985, c. B-1, s. 145. 3. A promoter who was a party to the preparation of the prospectus, or of the portion thereof containing the untrue statement, but does not include any person by reason only of his acting in a professional capacity for persons engaged in procuring the formation of the company. Companies acts. 4. A person who conducts or is associated in a directory capacity in the conduct of a boxing contest or exhibition. *Boxing Authority Act*, S.N.S. 1973, c. 3, s. 2.

PROMOTION. *n.* A change of employment from one class to another having a higher maximum salary. See TOURISM ~.

PROMOTIONAL DISTRIBUTION. The provision by a person to another person of tangible personal property that is, in the opinion of the commissioner, provided for one or more of the following purposes: (a) to describe, promote or encourage the purchase, consumption or use of tangible personal property; (b) to furnish or distribute to a person a catalogue, directory, listing or compilation of persons, places, prices, services, commodities or places of business in respect of the purchase, consumption or use of tangible personal property; or (c) for a purpose, function or use prescribed by the Lieutenant Governor in Council as a promotional distribution.

PROMOTIONAL DISTRIBUTOR. Any person who, within a province, provides, by way of promotional distribution to another person, goods whose fair value (i) exceeds the amount of the payment specifically made therefor by the person to whom the goods are provided; or (ii) is not specifically charged to and required to be paid by the person to whom the goods are provided.

PROMOTIONAL EXAMINATION. An examination conducted by the commission for positions in a particular class, admission to which is limited to employees in the classified service or persons on a re-employment list. *Public Service acts.*

PROMOTIONAL ORGANIZATION. Any organization established pursuant to an act of Québec which is mainly dedicated to the safeguard of the rights, the promotion of the interests and the improvement of the living conditions of the handicapped. *An Act to secure the handicapped in the exercise of their rights,* S.Q. 1978, c. 7, s. 1.

PROMOTIONAL POOL. A swimming pool used solely for commercial display and demonstration purposes. *Public Health Act,* R.R.O. 1980, Reg. 849, s. 1.

PROMOTION EXAMINATION. An examination conducted by the commission for positions in a particular class, admission to which is limited to employees in the civil service or persons on the re-employment list. *Civil Service Act,* R.S.M. 1970, c. C110, s. 2.

PROMOTION LIST. A list of persons who have passed a promotion examination for a particular class. Civil Service acts.

PROMULGATION. *n.* The act of publishing.

PROMUTUUM. *n.* A quasi-contract, by which the person who received a certain sum of money or a certain quantity of fungible items by mistake agrees to restore them.

PRONOTARY. *n.* The first notary.

PROOF. *n.* 1. Testimony; evidence. 2. Of a will, obtaining probate of it. 3. The strength of spirits, obtained by multiplying the percentage of alcohol by volume by 1.75 in Britain and Canada and by 2 in the United States. So, pure alcohol is 175 British and Canadian proof, 200 U.S.A. proof. F.A. Jaffe, *A Guide to Pathological Evidence,* 2d ed. (Toronto: Carswell, 1983) at 66. See BURDEN OF ~; LITERAL ~; TESTIMONIAL ~; UPON ~.

PROOF LINE. A line surveyed across one or more concessions in the original survey of a single front township or of a double front township to govern the course of a side line or a lot. *Surveys Act,* R.S.O. 1980, c. 493, s. 1.

PROOF OF FINANCIAL RESPONSIBILITY. A certificate of insurance, a bond or a deposit of money or securities given or made.

PROOF OF SERVICE. Proof provided by the affidavit of the person who served it, a solicitor's written admission or acceptance of the service. G.D. Watson & C. Perkins, eds., *Holmested & Watson: Ontario Civil Procedure* (Toronto: Carswell, 1984) at 16-10.

PROOFREADING. *n.* The examination and correction of typographical details or of illustrations on sheets printed from type or plates and includes the verification of numbers contained in tables and documents. *Translation Bureau Regulations,* C.R.C., c. 1561, s. 2.

PROOF SPIRIT. Any spirit having the strength of proof by Sikes' hydrometer, namely, spirit that at the temperature of 51 degrees Fahrenheit weighs exactly twelve-thirteenths of the weight of an equal measure of distilled water at the same temperature. *Customs Tariff,* R.S.C. 1985, c. C-54, s. 2.

PROOF VINEGAR. Vinegar of such strength that one gallon shall contain the quantity of acetic acid equivalent to six-tenths of a pound of acetic anhydride. *Excise Act,* R.S.C. 1970, c. E-12, s. 192.

PROPAGANDA. See HATE ~.

PROPANE. *n.* 1. In addition to its normal scientific meaning, a mixture mainly of propane, which may ordinarily contain some ethane or butanes. 2. A hydrocarbon consisting of 95 per cent or more of propane, propylene, butane or butylene, or any blend thereof. *Ontario Energy Board Act,* R.S.O. 1980, c. 332, s. 1.

PROP. COMP. BD. *abbr.* Property Compensation Board.

PROPELLANT. *n.* The powder in a cartridge which the primer ignites and which propels a projectile. F.A. Jaffe, *A Guide to Pathological Evidence,* 2d ed. (Toronto: Carswell, 1983) at 182.

PROPER AUTHORITY. 1. When used in Part IV, means (a) with respect to a place not within Canada or any other Commonwealth country, a consular officer, or, if there is no consular officer in the place, any two British merchants resident at or near the place, or, if there is only one British merchant so resident, that British merchant; and (b) with respect to a place within a Commonwealth country; (i) in relation to the discharge or leaving behind of seamen, or the payment of penalties, a person designated by the Governor in Council, and in the absence of such a person, a superintendent as defined in the Merchant Shipping Acts, or, in the absence of any such superintendent, the chief officer of customs at or near the place; and (ii) in relation to distressed seamen, a person designated by the Governor in Council, and in the absence of such a person, the governor of any Commonwealth country, or any person acting under his authority.

Canada Shipping Act, R.S.C. 1985, c. S-9, s. 2. 2. (i) In the case of a municipality that has appointed an inspector, the head of the council or such executive officer or other officer of the municipality as the council thereof may appoint to exercise and discharge the power and duties that are herein stated to be vested in, or charged on, a proper authority; and (ii) in all other cases, the minister. *Public Buildings Act*, R.S.M. 1970, c. P200, s. 2.

PROPER FORM. Regular on its face with regard to all formal matters. *Business Corporations Act, 1982*, S.O. 1982, c. 4, s. 53.

PROPER LAW. 1. The system of law which the parties intend to govern the contract, or, if their intention is not expressed or inferred from their circumstances, the system of law with which the transaction is most closely and really connected. G.H.L. Fridman, *Sale of Goods in Canada*, 3d ed. (Toronto: Carswell, 1986) at 473. 2. What determines the lex causae by referring to every fact in the individual case. J.G. McLeod, *The Conflict of Laws* (Calgary: Carswell, 1983) at 195.

PROPERLY DOCUMENTED. In relation to a complaint respecting the dumping or subsidizing of goods, means that (a) the complaint (i) alleges that the goods have been or are being dumped or subsidized, specifies the goods and alleges that the dumping or subsidizing has caused, is causing or is likely to cause material injury or has caused or is causing retardation; (ii) states in reasonable detail the facts on which the allegations referred to in subparagraph (i) are based; and (iii) makes such other representations as the complainant deems relevant to the complaint; and (b) the complainant provides (i) such information as is available to him to prove the facts referred to in subparagraph (a)(ii); and (ii) such other information as the Deputy Minister may reasonably require him to provide. *Special Imports Measures Act*, R.S.C. 1985, c. S-15, s. 2.

PROPERLY PACKED. That the produce is not slack, overpressed or otherwise in a condition likely to result in permanent damage during handling or in transit.

PROPER NAME. With reference to a narcotic, means the name internationally recognized for the narcotic or the name assigned to the narcotic in the latest edition of any generally recognized pharmacopoeia or compendium of drugs. *Narcotic Control Regulations*, C.R.C., c. 1041, s. 2.

PROPER OFFICER. 1. When used in Parts III and IV, means (a) in Canada, a shipping master; (b) at a port in the United Kingdom, a person designated by the Governor in Council, and in the absence of such a person, a superintendent;

(c) at a port in any other Commonwealth country, a person designated by the Governor in Council, and in the absence of such a person, a superintendent or shipping master, or in the absence of any such superintendent or shipping master, the chief officer of customs at or near the port; and (d) at a port elsewhere, a consular officer. *Canada Shipping Act*, R.S.C. 1985, c. S-9, s. 2. 2. The officer with whom bills of sale and chattel mortgages are registered or filed. 3. The officer in whose office assignments are required to be registered in any registration district. Assignment of Book Debts acts.

PROPERTY. *n.* 1. Includes money, goods, things in action, land and every description of property, whether real or personal, legal or equitable, and whether situated in Canada or elsewhere, and includes obligations, easements and every description of estate, interest and profit, present or future, vested or contingent, in, arising out of, or incident to, property. *Bankruptcy Act*, R.S.C. 1985, c. B-3, s. 2. 2. Property of any kind whatever whether real or personal or corporeal or incorporeal and, without restricting the generality of the foregoing, includes (a) a right of any kind whatever, a share or a chose in action; (b) unless a contrary intention is evident, money; (c) a timber resource property; and (d) the work in progress of a business that is a profession. *Income Tax Act*, R.S.C. 1952, c. 148 (as am. S.C. 1980-81-82-83, c. 140, s. 128(9)), s. 248(1). 3. Includes profits, earnings and other pecuniary interests and expenditure for rents, interest, taxes and other outgoings and charges and in respect of inability to occupy the insured premises, but only to the extent of express provision in the contract. Insurance acts. 4. Includes (a) real and personal property of every description and deeds and instruments relating to or evidencing the title or right to property, or giving a right to recover or receive money or goods; (b) property originally in the possession or under the control of any person, and any property into or for which it has been converted or exchanged and anything acquired at any time by the conversion or exchange; and (c) any postal card, postage stamp or other stamp issued or prepared for issue under the authority of Parliament or the legislature of a province for the payment to the Crown or a corporate body of any fee, rate or duty, whether or not it is in the possession of the Crown or of any person. *Criminal Code*, R.S.C. 1985, c. C-46, s. 2. 5. A building or structure or part of a building or structure, and includes the lands and premises appurtenant thereto and all mobile homes, mobile buildings, mobile structures, outbuildings, fences and erections thereon whether heretofore or hereafter erected, and includes vacant property. 6.

General property has aggregate rights which an owner enjoys whereas special property has special interests over things which someone with more limited legal powers, e.g. a pledgee or bailee, may enjoy and exercise. G.H.L. Fridman, *Sale of Goods in Canada*, 3d ed. (Toronto: Carswell, 1986) at 101. See AFTER ACQUIRED ~; ARCHAEOLOGICAL ~; ASSESSABLE ~; BUSINESS ~; CANADIAN ~; CAPITAL ~; COMMERCIAL ~; COMMON ~; COMMUNAL ~; COMMUNITY ~; CONSULAR ~; CORPOREAL ~; CROWN ~; CULTURAL ~; DEPRECIABLE ~; DESIGN ~; DURESS OF ~; ESTATE AND ~; ESTATE OR ~; FAMILY ~; FARM ~; FEDERAL ~; FOREIGN ~; FOREST ~; GOVERNMENT ~; HERITAGE ~; HISTORIC ~; IDENTICAL ~; IMMOVABLE ~; IMMOVABLE ~ AND REAL ~; IMPUTED INCOME FROM ~; INCLOSED ~; INCOME FROM A BUSINESS (OR ~); INCOME FROM ~; INDUSTRIAL AND INTELLECTUAL ~; INDUSTRIAL ~; INVESTMENT ~; MARITAL ~; MARRIED WOMEN'S ~ ACT; MATRIMONIAL ~; MINING ~; MIXED ~; MOVABLE ~; MOVEABLE ~; NON-PUBLIC ~; NON-SEGREGATED ~; OIL AND GAS ~; OTHER ~; PARTNERSHIP ~; PERISHABLE ~; PERSONAL ~; PERSONAL-USE ~; POTENTIAL ~; PRECIOUS ~; PROTECTED ~; PROVEN RESERVES UNDERLYING A ~; PROVINCIAL ~; PUBLIC ~; QUALIFIED ~; RATEABLE ~; REAL ~; RECREATIONAL ~; RENTAL ~; REPLACEMENT ~; RESIDENTIAL ~; RESOURCE ~; SMALL BUSINESS ~; SPECIAL ~; TANGIBLE ~; TAXABLE ~; UNSIGHTLY ~.

PROPERTY AND CIVIL RIGHTS. An area in relation to which provincial legislatures have power to make laws under section 92(13) of the Constitution Act, 1867. P.W. Hogg, *Constitutional Law of Canada*, 2d ed. (Toronto: Carswell, 1985) at 453.

PROPERTY DAMAGE. Damage caused in an accident to an automobile or to other property, except damage to the clothing worn by a victim at the time of the accident. *Automobile Insurance Act*, R.S.Q. 1977, c. A-25, s. 1.

PROPERTY DAMAGE INSURANCE. Insurance against loss or damage to property that is not included in or incidental to some other class of insurance defined by or under this Act. Insurance acts.

PROPERTY DAMAGE LIABILITY INSURANCE. The obligation of the insurer under this Act to pay insurance money in the event of loss of or damage to property as the result of one of the perils mentioned in section 42. *The*

Automobile Accident Insurance Act, R.S.S. 1978, c. A-35, s. 2.

PROPERTY DIMENSION. The frontage, area, other dimension or other attribute that, in the opinion of the Minister, would be established by an assessment authority in respect of federal property as the basis for computing the amount of any frontage or area tax that would be applicable to that property if it were taxable property. *Municipal Grants Act*, R.S.C. 1985, c. M-13, s. 2.

PROPERTY IMPROVEMENT GRANT. A grant that a person is eligible for under this Act and is for the purpose of encouraging the improvement of property. *The Property Improvement Grant Act*, R.S.S. 1978, c. P-29, s. 2.

PROPERTY IN STOCK. Any moveable property in reserve, including raw materials, property being processed, finished products, animals, wares, property used for packing, and any hydrocarbons or mineral substances, even where such hydrocarbons and mineral substances are still in the ground. *An Act Respecting the Transfer of Property in Stock*, S.Q. 1982, c. 55, s. 2.

PROPERTY INSURANCE. Insurance against the loss of, or the damage to, property but does not include insurance coming within the class of aircraft insurance, automobile insurance, or hail insurance.

PROPERTY LAW. Law which deals with ownership, rights and interests in property. See PROVINCIAL ~.

PROPERTY LIABLE. See VALUE OF THE ~.

PROPERTY OF A MEMBER. Anything, whereever situated, kept by, acquired by or given to a member by or for a client or other person where such thing in any way relates to his practice or former practice as a barrister or solicitor or the business or affairs of his clients or former clients, and whether or not such thing was acquired before or after he ceased to practise as a barrister or solicitor and, without restricting the generality of the foregoing, includes ledgers, books of account, records, files, documents, papers, securities, shares, trust money in cash or on deposit, negotiable instruments, corporate seals and chattels. Barristers and Solicitors acts.

PROPERTY OF THE DECEASED. All property the value of which is included in computing the aggregate net value of the property of the deceased for the purposes of this Act, and includes any property acquired by the executor of the deceased by one or more transactions effecting one or more substitutions. Succession Duty acts.

PROPERTY-OWNER. *var.* **PROPERTY OWNER.** Any person who possesses immoveable property in his own name as owner, as usufructuary, or as institute in cases of substitutions, or as possessor of Crown Lands with a promise of sale. Quebec statutes.

PROPERTY PASSING ON THE DEATH. Includes property passing either originally or by way of substitutive limitation, either certainly or contingently and either immediately on the death or after an interval determinable by reference to the death, and without restricting the generality of the foregoing, includes any property the value of which is required by this Act to be included in computing the aggregate net value of the property passing on the death. *Excise Tax Act*, R.S.C. 1970, c. E-9, s. 62.

PROPERTY RIGHT. 1. Any estate, interest, power or other right in or with respect to land. *Quieting Titles Act*, R.S.N.S. 1967, c. 259, s. 1. 2. Any right or power in respect to any kind of property including things in action. *Conveyancing Act*, R.S.N.S. 1967, c. 56, s. 1.

PROPERTY TAX. Tax levied on property. See GENERAL ~.

PROPERTY VALUE. The value that, in the opinion of the Minister, would be attributable by an assessment authority to federal property, without regard to any mineral rights or any ornamental, decorative or non-functional features thereof, as the basis for computing the amount of any real property tax that would be applicable to that property if it were taxable property. *Municipal Grants Act*, R.S.C. 1985, c. M-13, s. 2.

PROPINQUI ET CONSANGUINEI. [L.] The nearest relative of a deceased person.

PROPINQUITY. *n.* Parentage; kindred.

PROPONENT. *n.* A person who, (i) carries out or proposes to carry out an undertaking; or (ii) is the owner or person having charge, management or control of an undertaking. Environmental Assessment acts.

PROPORTION. See RATEABLE ~.

PROPORTIONALITY TEST. Three components are: (1) the measures adopted must be carefully designed and rationally connected to achieve the objective; (2) the right or freedom at issue should be impaired as little as possible by the measures; (3) a proportionality must exist between the effect of the measures which limit the Charter right or freedom and the objective said to be of sufficient importance. A more serious deleterious effect must be matched with a more important objective. P.K. McWilliams,

Canadian Criminal Evidence, 3d ed. (Aurora: Canada Law Book, 1988) at 4-11.

PROPORTIONAL TAX RATE STRUCTURE. A system whereby the percentage of income paid in taxes does not vary with the taxpayer's income. W. Grover & F. Iacobucci, *Materials on Canadian Income Tax*, 4th ed. (Toronto: Richard De Boo Ltd., 1980) at 41.

PROPORTIONATE TERMS. For the purposes of this section, an allowance is offered on proportionate terms only if (a) the allowance offered to a purchaser is in approximately the same proportion to the value of sales to him as the allowance offered to each competing purchaser is to the total value of sales to that competing purchaser; (b) in any case where advertising or other expenditures or services are exacted in return therefor, the cost thereof required to be incurred by a purchaser is in approximately the same proportion to the value of sales to him as the cost of the advertising or other expenditures or services required to be incurred by each competing purchaser is to the total value of sales to that competing purchaser; and (c) in any case where services are exacted in return therefor, the requirements thereof have regard to the kinds of services that competing purchasers at the same or different levels of distribution are ordinarily able to perform or cause to be performed. *Combines Investigation Act*, R.S.C. 1985, c. C-34, s. 51(3).

PROPOSAL. *n.* 1. Includes a proposal for a composition, for an extension of time or for a scheme of arrangement. *Bankruptcy Act*, R.S.C. 1985, c. B-3, s. 2. 2. The plan whereby a mining or prospecting company proposes to acquire additional mining property. *Securities Act*, R.S.N.S. 1967, c. 280, s. 1. 3. An application for an insurance contract which particularizes any risks the applicant wants the insurer to undertake. Raoul Colinvaux, *The Law of Insurance*, 5th ed. (London: Sweet & Maxwell, 1984) at 18. See COUNTER-~.

PROPOSED BY-LAW. A by-law submitted for the assent of the electors. *Municipal Act*, R.S.O. 1980, c. 302, s. 131.

PROPOSED NATIONAL PARK. Lands that, pursuant to the terms of any agreement between the Government of Canada and the government of the province in which the lands are situated, are vested in Her Majesty in right of Canada for the purpose of being established as National Parks of Canada but have not been so established and lands set aside as National Parks in the Yukon Territory and the Northwest Territories. *Camping Fees (Proposed National Parks) Regulations*, C.R.C., c. 677, s. 2.

PROPOSED REGULATION. The text which

an authority proposes to make as a regulation, where no approval by any other authority is required by law, or, where such approval is so required, the text which must be submitted for approval. *Regulations Act*, S.Q. 1986, c. 22, s. 1.

PROPOSED TRADE-MARK. *var.* **PROPOSED TRADE MARK.** A mark that is proposed to be used by a person for the purpose of distinguishing or so as to distinguish wares or services manufactured, sold, leased, hired or performed by him from those manufactured, sold, leased, hired or performed by others. *Trade-Marks Act*, R.S.C. 1985, c. T-13, s. 2.

PROPOSED UNIT. Land described in an agreement of purchase and sale that provides for delivery to the purchaser or a deed or transfer capable of registration after a declaration and description have been registered in respect of the land. Condominium acts.

PROPOSITION. *n.* One logical sentence.

PROPOSITUS. *n.* [L. the one proposed] The person from whom one traces descent.

PROPOUND. *v.* With respect to a will, to offer as authentic.

PROPRIETARY. *n.* One who has property.

PROPRIETARY. *adj.* Owned by a private organization or an individual and operated for profit.

PROPRIETARY CHARGE. The charge a province levies to exercise proprietary rights over its public property, i.e. a licence fee, rent or royalty paid to exploit provincially-owned natural resources or a charge for the sale of books, electricity, liquor, rail travel or any goods or services the province supplies in a commercial way. P.W. Hogg, *Constitutional Law of Canada*, 2d ed. (Toronto: Carswell, 1985) at 612 and 613.

PROPRIETARY ELECTOR. (i) An elector whose name appears on the assessment roll in respect of land liable to assessment and taxation for general municipal purposes; and (ii) an elector who is liable for the payment of a mobile unit licence. *Municipal Government Act*, R.S.A. 1980, c. M-26, s. 1.

PROPRIETARY ESTOPPEL. An order permitting a party to retain a proprietary interest in land even though the owner asserts strict legal rights because the owner's conduct misled the party who alleges estoppel. G.H.L. Fridman, *The Law of Contract in Canada*, 2d ed. (Toronto: Carswell, 1986) at 112.

PROPRIETARY LEASE. A lease, agreement or arrangement by which a person acquires: (i) a tenancy, or an extension of an existing tenancy, of residential premises; and (ii) a direct or indirect ownership interest in residential premises through any agreement, arrangement, scheme or plan including the acquisition of shares of, or a membership interest in, a body corporate, other than a body corporate incorporated or registered under The Co-operative Associations Act, The Co-operative Marketing Associations Act or The Co-operative Production Associations Act. *Condominium Property Amendment Act, 1981*, S.S. 1980-81, c. 47, s. 3.

PROPRIETARY MEDICINE. A drug that (i) is in a form in which it is ready for use by the consumer according to the directions for use recommended by the manufacturer without requiring any further manufacturing or processing; and (ii) is sold for use in respect of humans in accordance with the provisions of the Food and Drugs Act (Canada).

PROPRIETARY OR PATENT MEDICINE. Every artificial remedy or prescription manufactured for the internal or external use of man, the name, composition or definition of which is not to be found in the British Pharmacopoeia, the Codex Medicamentarius of France, the Pharmacopoeia of the United States, or any foreign pharmacopoeia approved by the Minister, the Canadian Formulary, the National Formulary of the United States of America, or any formulary adopted by any properly constituted pharmaceutical association representing Canada and approved by the Minister; or upon which is not printed in a conspicuous manner the true formula or list of medicinal ingredients contained in it. *Proprietary or Patent Medicine Act*, R.S.C. 1970, c. P-25, s. 2.

PROPRIETARY RIGHT. An interest as owner or lessee or an interest under an agreement authorizing the right to use, distribute or exhibit a film.

PROPRIETAS DEDUCTA USUFRUCTU. [L.] Ownership with no usufruct.

PROPRIETAS NUDA. [L.] Bare ownership.

PROPRIETAS VERBORUM EST SALUS PROPRIETATUM. [L.] The proper signification of words is the salvation of property.

PROPRIETOR. *n.* 1. The owner, lessee or other person in lawful possession of any property. 2. In relation to a business enterprise, means the person by whom the enterprise is carried on or is about to be carried on, whether as sole proprietor or in association or partnership with any other person having a proprietary interest therein, but does not include Her Majesty or an agent of Her Majesty in right of Canada or a province, a municipality or a municipal or other public body that performs a function of government. *Small Business Loans Act*, R.S.C. 1985, c.

S-11, s. 2. 3. The author of any design unless that person executed the design for another person in exchange for a good or valuable consideration. H.G. Fox, *The Canadian Law of Copyright and Industrial Designs*, 2d ed. (Toronto: Carswell, 1967) at 673. See HOSPITAL ~.

PROPRIETOR COMMISSION. A regional services commission that owns, operates, manages or controls a public utility. *Regional Municipal Services Act, 1981*, S.A. 1981, c. R-9.1, s. 103.

PROPRIETORSHIP. *n.* One who carries on business under a name other than one's own. See SOLE ~.

PROPRIO VIGORE. [L.] By its own strength.

PROPTER. *prep.* [L.] Because of.

PROPULSION ENGINE. Any internal combustion engine which can directly or indirectly generate propulsion. *Fuel Tax Act*, R.S.Q. 1977, c. T-1, s. 1.

PRO QUER. *abbr.* Pro querente.

PRO QUERENTE. [L.] For the plaintiff.

PRO RATA. [L.] In proportion, according to a certain percentage or rate.

PRO RATA PARTE. [L.] Proportionately.

PRO RE NATA. [L.] To meet some emergency, as an occasion arises.

PROROGATION. *n.* 1. Prolongation or postponement until another day. 2. The termination of a session of Parliament. A. Fraser, G.A. Birch & W.A. Dawson, eds., *Beauchesne's Rules and Forms of the House of Commons of Canada*, 5th ed. (Toronto: Carswell, 1978) at 54.

PROROGUE. *v.* To terminate a session of Parliament.

PROSECUTION. *n.* The putting of an offender on trial. See MALICIOUS ~; SUCCESSIVE ~.

PROSECUTOR. *n.* 1. The Attorney General or, where the Attorney General does not intervene, means the person who institutes proceedings to which this Act applies, and includes counsel acting on behalf of either of them. *Criminal Code*, R.S.C. 1985, c. C-46, s. 2. 2. The Attorney General or, where the Attorney General does not intervene, the informant, and includes counsel or an agent acting on behalf of either of them. *Criminal Code*, R.S.C. 1985, c. C-46, s. 785 as am. by *Criminal Law Amendment Act*, R.S.C. 1985 (1st Supp.), c. 27, s. 170. 3. The Attorney General or, where the Attorney General does not intervene, means the person who issues a certificate or lays an information and includes counsel or agent acting on behalf of either of

them. *Provincial Offences Act*, R.S.O. 1980, c. 400, s. 1.

PROSPECT. *v.* To search for valuable mineral and includes any mode of working whereby soil or rock is disturbed, removed, washed or otherwise tested for the purpose of finding, identifying or determining the extent of any mineral therein.

PROSPECT AND TO EXPLORE. See TO ~.

PROSPECTING. *n.* Includes trenching, stripping and drilling and performing geological, geophysical and geochemical surveys. *Mining Act*, S.N.B. 1985, c. M-14.1, s. 1.

PROSPECTING COMPANY. A company incorporated for the purpose of prospecting for a mineral or minerals. *Securities Act*, R.S.N.S. 1967, c. 280, s. 1.

PROSPECTIVE LOSS OF EARNINGS OR PROFITS. A financial gain, primarily of wage or income, which the plaintiff would have made and which the plaintiff will now not be able to make because of injury. K.D. Cooper-Stephenson & I.B. Saunders, *Personal Injury Damages in Canada* (Toronto: Carswell, 1981) at 52.

PROSPECTOR. *n.* One who prospects or explores for minerals or develops a property for minerals on behalf of oneself, on behalf of oneself and others or as an employee.

PROSPECTUS. *n.* Any prospectus, notice, circular or advertisement of any kind whatsoever, whether of the kind hereinbefore enumerated or not, whether in writing or otherwise offering to the public for purchase or subscription any shares or debentures of any company.

PROSTHESIS. *n.* A device intended to replace the whole or part of an organ or member of a human being. *Public Health Protection Act*, R.S.Q. 1977, c. P-35, s. 1.

PROSTHETIC APPLIANCE. Includes any artificial device necessary to support or take the place of a part of the body or to increase the efficiency of a sense organ.

PROSTHETIC SERVICE. See DENTAL ~.

PROSTITUTE. *n.* A person of either sex who engages in prostitution.

PROSTITUTION. *n.* Performing sexual acts for reward.

PRO TANTO. [L. for so much] To such an extent.

PROTECTED. *adj.* 1. As applied to electrical equipment means the equipment is constructed so that the electrical parts are protected against damage from foreign objects. *Power Corporation Act*, R.R.O. 1980, Reg. 794, s. 0. 2. As applied to mammals and birds, means protected throughout the year, or for any shorter close season, under this Act. *Lands and Forests Act*, R.S.N.S. 1967, c. 163, s. 84.

PROTECTED AREA. An area surrounding a classified historic monument whose perimeter is determined by the Minister. *An Act to Amend the Cultural Property Act and Other Legislation*, S.Q. 1985, c. 24, s. 2.

PROTECTED INTERNEE. A person interned in Canada who is protected by the Geneva Convention set out in Schedule IV. *Geneva Conventions Act*, R.S.C. 1985, c. G-3, s. 4.

PROTECTED LOAN. A loan in respect of which protection is provided by contract under subsection 65(1). *National Housing Act*, R.S.C. 1985, c. N-11, s. 64.

PROTECTED PRISONER OF WAR. A prisoner of war who is protected by the Geneva Convention set out in Schedule III. *Geneva Conventions Act*, R.S.C. 1985, c. G-3, s. 4.

PROTECTED PROPERTY. Any property that has been designated protected property under this Act. *The Saskatchewan Heritage Act*, R.S.S. 1978, c. S-22, s. 2.

PROTECTED SPECIES. A species or type of animal listed in Division 6 of Schedule A or declared by the regulations to be a protected species, or any part thereof. *Wildlife Act*, S.M. 1980, c. 73, s. 1.

PROTECTING POWER. (a) In relation to a protected prisoner of war, the country or organization that is carrying out, in the interests of the country of which that prisoner is a national or of whose forces that prisoner is or was a member at the time of his being taken prisoner of war, the duties assigned to protecting powers under the Geneva Convention set out in Schedule III; and (b) in relation to a protected internee, the country or organization that is carrying out, in the interests of the country of which that internee is or was a national at the time of his internment, the duties assigned to protecting powers under the Geneva Convention set out in Schedule IV. *Geneva Convention Act*, R.S.C. 1985, c. G-3, s. 4.

PROTECTION. *n.* 1. In respect of a loan, means an undertaking (a) given by the Corporation to a home owner by whom, prior to that loan, money is borrowed; and (b) requiring, so far as is authorized by virtue of this Part, the Corporation to assist the home owner to make payments related to interest on that loan in the event that the home owner obtains it at a rate of interest higher than the rate of interest at which the home owner borrowed that money. *National Housing Act*, R.S.C. 1985, c. N-11, s. 64. 2. Of

the lien, to register a claim for lien, to shelter under a certificate of action, or to give notice of the lien to certain people. D.N. Macklem & D.I. Bristow, *Construction and Mechanics' Liens in Canada*, 5th ed. (Toronto: Carswell, 1985) at 10. See CONSUMER ~ LEGISLATION; DIPLOMATIC ~; FIRE ~; IN NEED OF ~; LOW-VOLTAGE ~; PASSIVE OCCUPANT ~; RESOURCE ~ AND DEVELOPMENT SERVICE; STATION SIGNAL ~.

PROTECTION FOREST. A forest (i) that is growing on land other than Crown land and the chief value of which is to regulate stream flow, prevent erosion, hold shifting sand, or exert any other direct beneficial effect; and (ii) that has been designated in the regulations as a "protection forest"; whether or not it produces timber. *Watershed Conservation Districts Act*, R.S.M. 1970, c. W40, s. 2.

PROTECTION OFFICER. (a) A fishery officer within the meaning of the Fisheries Act; (b) an officer of the Royal Canadian Mounted Police.

PROTECTION OF PUBLIC AUTHORITIES. A provision which protects justices of the peace, constables, tribunal members or other public authorities from actions for anything done pursuant to a statute.

PROTECTION SERVICES. Includes services to unmarried mothers, adoption services, children's protection services, and such other services as are designated by the regulations to be protection services. *Child Welfare Act*, R.S.N.S. 1967, c. 31, s. 15.

PROTECTION WORKS. Include a dyke, dam, breakwater and other protection to prevent the encroachment of rivers on their banks, and include diversion in whole or in part of a river and the removal of obstructions from a river bed. *Riverbank Protection Act*, R.S.B.C. 1979, c. 369, s. 1.

PROTECTIO TRAHIT SUBJECTIONEM, ET SUBJECTIO PROTECTIONEM. [L.] Protection includes subjugation, and subjugation protection.

PROTECTIVE BREATHING EQUIPMENT. Equipment to cover the eyes, nose and mouth, or the nose and mouth if accessory equipment is provided to protect the eyes, that will protect the wearer from the effects of smoke, carbon dioxide or other harmful gases. *Oxygen Equipment Order*, C.R.C., c. 52, s. 2.

PROTECTIVE CARE. A service which provides an immediate safeguard for a child's security and development. *Child and Family Services and Family Relations Act*, S.N.B. 1980, c. C-2.1, s. 1.

PROTECTIVE CUSTODY. A period not exceeding 7 days during which a child is under the care of the director pending his return to his parents or his apprehension. *Child Welfare Act*, R.S.N.B. 1973, c. C-4, s. 1.

PROTECTIVE ENCLOSURE. A structure that encloses a laser scanner and its accessory components and restricts the emission of laser radiation to one or more exit apertures. *Radiation Emitting Devices Regulations*, C.R.C., c. 1370, s. 1.

PROTECTIVE EQUIPMENT. Any piece of equipment or clothing designed to be used to protect the health or safety of an employee. Occupational Health and Safety acts. See PERSONAL ~.

PROTECTIVE HOUSING. A structure that encloses the components of a laser and prevents the emission of laser radiation except through an exit aperture. *Radiation Emitting Devices Regulations*, C.R.C., c. 1370, s. 1.

PROTECTIVE SERVICE. The two police forces of Parliament who maintain order and control the conduct of people admitted to the precincts. A. Fraser, G.A. Birch & W.A. Dawson, eds., *Beauchesne's Rules and Forms of the House of Commons of Canada*, 5th ed. (Toronto: Carswell, 1978) at 20.

PROTECTIVE SERVICES. Any services provided to a child under this Act except those provided under section 72. *Child Welfare Act*, S.A. 1984, c. C-8.1, s. 1.

PROTEIN. See SOURCE OF ~.

PROTEIN EFFICIENCY RATING. The measurement of the nutritive quality of a protein as determined by the official method. *Meat Inspection Regulations*, C.R.C., c. 1032, s. 2.

PROTEIN RATING. Of a food product means the product obtained by multiplying the protein efficiency rating of the food product by the quantity of protein (a) in 100 grams of the food product other than bacon; or (b) in 25 grams of bacon. *Meat Inspection Regulations*, C.R.C., c. 1032, s. 2.

PRO TEM. *abbr.* Pro tempore.

PRO TEMPORE. [L. for the time being] Temporarily.

PROTEST. *n.* 1. The solemn declaration that a bill is dishonoured. I.F.G. Baxter, *The Law of Banking*, 3d ed. (Toronto: Carswell, 1981) at 117. 2. A serious declaration of opinion, usually dissent. 3. The express declaration by someone doing something that the act does not imply what it might.

PROTESTANT. *adj.* Includes the Christian religious denominations other than Roman Catholic. *Child Welfare Act*, R.S.A. 1970, c. 45, s. 34.

PROTHONOTARY. *n.* 1. Of the Federal Court, a barrister or advocate from any province who is needed for the Court to work efficiently and whose powers are set out in Rule 336. D. Sgayias *et al.*, *Federal Court Practice 1988* (Toronto: Carswell, 1987) at 55. 2. Prothonotary of the Supreme Court at Halifax. *Barristers and Solicitors Act*, R.S.N.S. 1967, c. 18, s. 1. 3. Not only the prothonotary of the Superior Court, but also the clerk of any other court to which the provision is applicable. *Code of Civil Procedure*, R.S.Q. 1977, c. C-25, s. 4. See SPECIAL ~.

PROTOCOL. *n.* 1. The rules concerning ceremony observed in the official relations between nations and their representatives. 2. The minutes of a deliberative gathering of representatives of different countries. 3. The original drafts or copy of any document.

PROTOTYPE MODEL. Any original working model on which subsequent production was based. *Canadian Cultural Property Export Control List*, C.R.C., c. 448, s. 1.

PROTOTYPE UNIT. The original unit used as a pattern for the production of identical assembly line units or, in the case of a vehicle, a unit that has sufficient structure including body, engine, electrical power supply and circuitry to be representative, for radio noise measurement purposes, of production units that are identified by model year and certified pursuant to these Regulations. *Radio Interference Regulations*, C.R.C., c. 1374, s. 2.

PROUT PATET PER RECORDUM. [L.] Just as it appears in the record.

PROV. *abbr.* 1. Provincial. 2. Province.

PROVABLE CLAIM. Any claim or liability provable in proceedings under this Act by a creditor. *Bankruptcy Act*, R.S.C. 1985, c. B-3, s. 2.

PROV. CT. *abbr.* 1. Provincial Court. 2. Provincial Court (Criminal Division).

PROV. CT. CIV. DIV. *abbr.* Provincial Court Civil Division.

PROV. CT. CRIM. DIV. *abbr.* Provincial Court Criminal Division.

PROV. CT. FAM. DIV. *abbr.* Provincial Court Family Division.

PROVE. *v.* 1. To make certain; to establish. 2. With respect to a will, to obtain probate.

PROVEN DEVELOPED RESERVES. Those proven reserves that will be produced from existing wells or facilities. *Securities Act*, R.R.O. 1980, Reg. 910, s. 26.

PROVEN MINERAL ORE. Mineral ore that is so completely exposed that its existence as to tonnes and tenor is essentially certain. *An Act to Amend the Metallic Minerals Tax Act*, S.N.B. 1987, c. 35, s. 1.

PROVEN ORE. That material for which tonnage is computed from dimensions revealed in outcrops or trenches or underground workings or drill holes and for which the grade is computed from the results of adequate sampling and for which the sites for inspection, sampling and measurement are so spaced and the geological character so well defined that the size, shape and mineral content are established and for which the computed tonnage and grade are judged to be accurate within limits that shall be stated and for which it shall be stated whether the tonnage and grade of proven ore or measured ore are in situ or extractable, with dilution factors shown and reasons for the use of those dilution factors clearly explained. *Securities Act*, R.R.O. 1980, Reg. 910, s. 26.

PROVEN RESERVES UNDERLYING A PROPERTY. The estimated economically recoverable quantities of crude oil, natural gas and natural gas liquids, including the reserves to be obtained by enhanced recovery processes demonstrated to be successful, from that portion of an area delineated by gas-oil and oil-water or gas-water contacts in drilled wells or that can be reasonably evaluated as economically productive, on the basis of drilling, geological, geophysical and engineering data, but reserves in undrilled prospects cannot be classed as proven reserves. *Securities Act*, R.R.O. 1980, Reg. 910, s. 26.

PROVEN UNDEVELOPED RESERVES. Proven reserves that are not recoverable from existing wells or facilities or from those zones in existing wells that have been cased off, but which can be recovered through the drilling of additional wells. *Securities Act*, R.R.O. 1980, Reg. 910, s. 26.

PROVIDE. See TO ~.

PROVIDER. See SERVICE ~.

PROVINCE. *n.* 1. A province of Canada. 2. A field of duty. 3. Her Majesty the Queen in right of the Province. 4. A province of Canada, and includes the Yukon Territory and the Northwest Territories. 5. Does not include the Yukon Territory or the Northwest Territories. 6. Includes the Newfoundland offshore area and the Nova Scotia offshore area. *Income Tax Act*, R.S.C. 1952, c. 148 (as am. S.C. 1988, c. 28, s. 251), s. 124(4)(b). See AGREEING ~; ATLANTIC ~S; ATTORNEY GENERAL OF THE ~; CIVIL RIGHTS IN THE ~; DESIGNATED ~; HAVE-NOT ~; HOLDER IN THE ~; INCLUDED ~; INTERMEDIATE ~; LARGE ~; LAW OF THE ~; LEGISLATURE OF ANY ~; MARITIME ~S; MONEY PAID TO THE ~ FOR A SPECIAL PURPOSE; MUTUAL FUND IN THE ~; PARTICIPATING HOSPITAL ~; PARTICIPATING MEDICAL ~; PARTICIPATING ~; PRODUCER-~; RECIPROCATING ~; RECIPROCATING ~ OR TERRITORY; RESIDENT OF THE ~; RESIDES IN THE ~; SMALL ~.

PROVINCE OF PRODUCTION. 1. In relation to any quantity of crude oil, the producer-province in which it was produced, extracted or recovered. *Energy Administration Act*, R.S.C. 1985, c. E-6, s. 20. 2. In relation to any quantity of gas, the producer-province in which it was produced, extracted, recovered or manufactured. *Energy Administration Act*, R.S.C. 1985, c. E-6, s. 36.

PROVINCE OR STATE. Includes any province or territory of Canada and any state or territory of the United States and the District of Columbia in the United States. *The Highway Traffic Act*, S.M. 1985-86, c. 3, s. 288(5).

PROVINCIAL. *adj.* 1. As applied to state documents, means of or pertaining to a province or territory within Canada. *Evidence Act*, R.S.N.B. 1973, c. E-11, s. 71. 2. As applied to state documents, means of or pertaining to any province, colony or territory which, or some portion of which, forms part of Canada. *Evidence Act*, R.S.B.C. 1979, c. 116, s. 27.

PROVINCIAL ACT. In relation to any province, means that Act of the legislature of the province that imposes taxes on the incomes of individuals. *Federal-Provincial Fiscal Arrangements Act*, R.S.C. 1985, c. F-8, s. 12.

PROVINCIAL AGREEMENT. An agreement in writing covering the whole of the province of Ontario between a designated or accredited employer bargaining agency that represents employers, on the one hand, and a designated or certified employee bargaining agency that represents affiliated bargaining agents, on the other hand, containing provisions respecting terms or conditions of employment or the rights, privileges or duties of the employer bargaining agency, the employers represented by the employer bargaining agency and for whose employees the affiliated bargaining agents hold bargaining rights, the affiliated bargaining agents represented by the employee bargaining agency, or the employees represented by the affiliated bargaining agents and employed in the industrial, commercial and institutional sector of the construction industry referred to in clause 117(e). *Labour Relations Act*, R.S.O. 1980, c. 228, s. 137.

PROVINCIAL ANALYST. Any analyst appointed by the government of any province and having authority to make any analysis for any public purpose. *Excise Act*, R.S.C. 1985, c. E-14, s. 2.

PROVINCIAL AUDITOR. The officer charged by law with the audit of the accounts of the government of a province.

PROVINCIAL COMMITTEE. An unincorporated board, commission, council, or other body that is not a department or part of a department, all or a majority of whose members are appointed or designated, either by their personal names or by their names of office, by an Act of the Legislature or regulations under an Act of the Legislature, by an order of the Lieutenant Governor in Council or of a Minister of the Crown or by any combination thereof. *Financial Administration Act*, R.S.A. 1980, c. F-9, s. 1.

PROVINCIAL COMPANY. 1. A company incorporated under the laws of any province of Canada, of Newfoundland or any former province of British North America now forming part of Canada, other than the former Province of Canada, for the purpose of carrying on the business of insurance. *Canadian and British Insurance Companies Act*, R.S.C. 1985, c. I-12, s. 2. 2. A loan company incorporated under a special Act of the Legislature. Loan and Trust Companies acts.

PROVINCIAL CONTENT. The dollar value attributed to a bid as a result of consideration, as prescribed, of the provincial overhead allowance, the provincial labour content and the provincial material content in that bid, as calculated in accordance with the prescribed method. *The Provincial Preference Act*, S.Nfld. 1984, c. 37, s. 2.

PROVINCIAL CONTENT FACTOR. In relation to an examined bidder is the difference between (i) the provincial content of the examined bid, and (ii) the provincial content of the lowest bid divided by the difference between (iii) the bid price of the examined bidder, and (iv) the bid price of the lowest bidder. *The Provincial Preference Act*, S.Nfld. 1984, c. 37, s. 2.

PROVINCIAL COOPERATIVE ASSOCIATION. A cooperative association that is not a federal cooperative association. *Canada Cooperative Association Act*, R.S.C. 1985, c. C-40, s. 129.

PROVINCIAL CORPORATION. A corporation that is incorporated by or under the act of a legislature.

PROVINCIAL COURT. 1. Under section 92(14) of the Constitution Act, 1867 the body which a provincial legislature constitutes, maintains, and organizes to administer justice in the province. P.W. Hogg, *Constitutional Law of Canada*, 2d ed. (Toronto: Carswell, 1985) at 547. 2. With respect to a province in which a claim sought to be enforced under this Part arises, means (a) in the province of Quebec, the Provincial Court; and (b) in any other province, the county or district court that would have jurisdiction if the claim were against a private person of full age and capacity, or if there is no such county or district court in the province or the county or district court in the province does not have that jurisdiction, the superior court of the province. *Crown Liability Act*, R.S.C. 1985, c. C-50, s. 21.

PROVINCIAL COURT (CIVIL DIVISION). In Ontario, a small claims court. G.D. Watson & C. Perkins, eds., *Holmested & Watson: Ontario Civil Procedure* (Toronto: Carswell, 1984) at CJA-101.

PROVINCIAL COURT (FAMILY DIVISION). In Ontario, a youth court. G.D. Watson & C. Perkins, eds., *Holmested & Watson: Ontario Civil Procedure* (Toronto: Carswell, 1984) at CJA-99.

PROVINCIAL COURT JUDGE. A person appointed or authorized to act by or pursuant to an Act of the legislature of a province, by whatever title that person may be designated, who has the power and authority of two or more justices of the peace and includes the lawful deputy of that person. *Criminal Code*, R.S.C. 1985, c. C-46, s. 2 as am. by *Criminal Law Amendment Act*, R.S.C. 1985 (1st Supp.), c. 27, s. 2.

PROVINCIAL DEVELOPMENT EXPENDITURE. A payment for a capital project that is of a social or economic development nature. *The Heritage Fund (Saskatchewan) Act*, R.S.S. 1978, c. H-2.1, s. 2.

PROVINCIAL DIRECTOR. A person, a group or class of persons or a body appointed or designated by or pursuant to an Act of the legislature of a province or by the Lieutenant Governor in Council of a province or his delegate to perform in that province, either generally or in a specific case, any of the duties or functions of a provincial director under this Act. *Young Offenders Act*, R.S.C. 1985, c. Y-1, s. 2.

PROVINCIAL EMPLOYMENT. An employee's previous employment with the Government of Saskatchewan or with a department, branch, bureau, board, commission, Crown corporation or other agency of the Government of Saskatchewan. *The Superannuation (Supple-*

mentary Provisions) Act, R.S.S. 1978, c. S-64, s. 2.

PROVINCIAL ENFORCEMENT SERVICE. Any service, agency or body designated in an agreement with a province under section 3 that is entitled under the laws of the province to enforce family provisions. *Family Orders and Agreements Enforcement Assistance Act*, R.S.C. 1985 (2d Supp.), c. 4, s. 2.

PROVINCIAL FARMERS ASSOCIATION. An organization constituted as the central coordinating agent of the several district farmers associations and of such other agricultural organizations as may from time to time be determined. *Agricultural Associations Act*, R.S.N.B. 1973, c. A-5, s. 1.

PROVINCIAL FEDERATION. A provincial organization whose members are the members of a labour congress in that province.

PROVINCIAL FIREARMS OFFICER. See CHIEF ~.

PROVINCIAL FOREST. Any land or lands withdrawn from disposition, sale, settlement or occupancy except under this Act or the regulations. *The Forest Act*, R.S.S. 1978, c. F-19, s. 2.

PROVINCIAL GAME FARM. Any area of Crown land set aside, established and maintained in accordance with this Act for the display of any species of animal. *Game Act*, R.S.N.B. 1973, c. F-1, s. 1.

PROVINCIAL GARNISHMENT LAW. 1. The law of a province relating to garnishment as it applies to the enforcement of support orders and support provisions. *Family Orders and Agreements Enforcement Assistance Act*, R.S.C. 1985 (2d Supp.), c. 4, s. 23. 2. The law of general application of a province relating to garnishment that is in force at the time in question. *Garnishment, Attachment and Pension Diversion Act*, R.S.C. 1985, c. G-2, s. 2.

PROVINCIAL HERITAGE PROPERTY. A building, streetscape or area registered in the Provincial Registry of Heritage Property. *Heritage Property Act*, S.N.S. 1979-80, c. 8, s. 2.

PROVINCIAL HIGHWAY. 1. A public highway. 2. A highway outside the limits of a city or incorporated town. *Motor Vehicle Act*, R.S.N.S. 1967, c. 191, s. 1. 3. A highway built and maintained by or under the supervision of the Department of Transportation whether or not such highway lies within the geographical boundaries of a local authority. *An Act to Amend the Motor Vehicle Act*, S.N.B. 1985, c. 34, s. 1.

PROVINCIAL INCOME TAX. That part of money paid by utility companies as income tax or estimated income tax under the Alberta Income Tax Act or the Alberta Corporate Income Tax Act for the 1966 and any subsequent taxation year that is attributable to the utility companies' gross revenue for the year from (i) the distribution and sale to the public in Alberta, or the generation and sale in Alberta for distribution to the public in Alberta, of electrical energy or steam; or (ii) the distribution and sale of gas to the public in Alberta. *Utility Companies Income Tax Rebates Act*, R.S.A. 1980, c. U-10, s. 1.

PROVINCIAL INFORMATION BANK. A source of information designated in an agreement made under section 3. *Family Orders and Agreements Enforcement Assistance Act*, R.S.C. 1985 (2d Supp.), c. 4, s. 2.

PROVINCIAL INSURANCE COMPANY. A company that is licensed by a province to carry on the business of insurance in that province other than a company that is licensed to carry on the business of insurance in the Territories under the Canadian and British Insurance Companies Act or the Foreign Insurance Companies Act. *Insurance Act*, R.S.N.W.T. 1974, c. I-2, s. 4.

PROVINCIAL INSURER. An insurer incorporated under the laws of Saskatchewan and not registered under the Canadian and British Insurance Companies Act (Canada). *The Saskatchewan Insurance Act*, R.S.S. 1978, c. S-26, s. 2.

PROVINCIAL LAND. Land vested in the Crown in right of a province.

PROVINCIAL LAND SURVEYOR. The holder, from the Board, of a certificate of qualification as a Provincial Land Surveyor. *Provincial Land Surveyors Act*, R.S.N.S. 1967, c. 243, s. 1.

PROVINCIAL LEGISLATURE. Any legislative body other than the Parliament of Canada.

PROVINCIALLY ADMINISTERED INSTITUTION. An advanced education institution owned by the Government and operated as part of the Department. *Department of Advanced Education Act*, S.A. 1983, c. D-11.1, s. 1.

PROVINCIALLY APPROVED AGENCY. Any department of government, person or agency, including a private non-profit agency, that is authorized by or under the provincial law or by the provincial authority to accept applications for assistance, determine eligibility for assistance, provide or pay assistance or provide welfare services and that is listed in a schedule to an agreement under section 4. *Canada Assistance Plan*, R.S.C. 1985, c. C-1, s. 2.

PROVINCIALLY OCCUPIED FEDERAL PROPERTY. Property of Her Majesty in the right of Canada which is leased to and occupied by a department of the public service of the province, excluding public hospitals, educational institutions and such other property of Her Majesty in the right of the province as would be exempt from taxation if it were not the property of Her Majesty in the right of the Province, and in respect of which no grant in lieu of taxes is otherwise paid. *An Act to Amend the Municipal Grants Act*, S.N.S. 1984, c. 62, s. 1.

PROVINCIALLY-OWNED INSTITUTION. An agricultural and vocational college, technical institute, vocational training institution or other post-secondary education institution owned by the Government and operated as part of a department of the Government. *Colleges Act*, R.S.A. 1980, c. C-18, s. 1.

PROVINCIAL MAGISTRATE. A provincial magistrate appointed, or pursuant to statutory provision in that behalf deemed to have been appointed, under The Provincial Magistrates Act, and includes a judge of the magistrates' courts appointed under The Magistrates' Courts Act. *The Interpretation Act*, R.S.S. 1978, c. I-11, s. 21.

PROVINCIAL NET REVENUES. The net ordinary provincial revenues consisting of (a) provincial own source revenues; and (b) unconditional grants to the Province from the Government of Canada, as determined by the Minister of Finance for each fiscal year. *Municipal Assistance Act*, S.N.B. 1977, c. 34, s. 2.

PROVINCIAL PARK. 1. An historic park, a recreation park, a natural environment park or a wilderness park designated pursuant to section 4. *Parks Act*, S.S. 1985, c. P-1.1, s. 2. 2. Includes provincial camp grounds, provincial picnic grounds and provincial camp and picnic grounds. *Provincial Parks Act*, R.S.O. 1980, c. 401, s. 1. 3. (a) Any area of land established and maintained under this Act as a recreational park, campground park, beach park, wildlife park, picnic ground park, resource park, park reserve, or any combination thereof; and (b) any land administered under an agreement entered into under the authority of paragraph 3(2)(b), and includes any land acquired for the purpose of development as a provincial park. *Parks Act*, R.S.N.B. 1973, c. P-2, s. 1.

PROVINCIAL PAROLE BOARD. In relation to any province, a parole board appointed pursuant to section 12 and includes (a) the Board of Parole that Ontario may appoint pursuant to subsection 12(1) of the Prisons and Reformatories Act, if that board has been appointed to

act as a parole board under this Act; and (b) the Board of Parole that British Columbia may appoint pursuant to subsection 13(1) of the Prisons and Reformatories Act, if that board has been appointed to act as a parole board under this Act. *Parole Act*, R.S.C. 1985, c. P-2, s. 2.

PROVINCIAL PENSION PLAN. A plan of old age pensions and supplementary benefits for the establishment and operation of which provision has been made as described in paragraph (a) or (b) of the definition "province providing a comprehensive pension plan" under a law of a province providing a comprehensive pension plan. *Canada Pension Plan*, R.S.C. 1985, c. C-8, s. 3.

PROVINCIAL PER CAPITA REVENUE. The amount equal to the aggregate of the per capita yield of all revenue sources in a province for a fiscal year. *Federal-Provincial Fiscal Arrangements Act*, R.S.C. 1985, c. F-8, s. 4(7).

PROVINCIAL PERSONAL INCOME TAX RATE. Applicable to a taxation year means (a) in the case of a province, the government of which has entered into a tax collection agreement with respect to the taxation year, the actual personal income tax rate applicable under the provincial Act to that taxation year; and (b) in the case of any other province, the rate prescribed as the provincial personal income tax rate applicable to the taxation year. *Federal-Provincial Fiscal Arrangements Act*, R.S.C. 1985, c. F-8, s. 12.

PROVINCIAL PROPERTY. 1. All property of Her Majesty in the right of the Province that is assessable pursuant to the Assessment Act, excluding (i) public hospitals, educational institutions and such other property of Her Majesty as would be exempt from taxation if it were not the property of Her Majesty except any such property which is occupied by a department of the public service and in respect of which no grant in lieu of taxes is otherwise paid; and (ii) property of any agency, authority, board, commission or Crown corporation of the province except any such property which is occupied by a department of the public service and in respect of which no grant in lieu of taxes is otherwise paid. *Municipal Grants Act*, S.N.S. 1979-80, c. 10, s. 2. 2. Real property owned by the Crown in right of Ontario or by any Crown agency, but does not include property owned or held in trust by Ontario Hydro. *Municipal Tax Assistance Act*, R.S.O. 1980, c. 311, s. 1.

PROVINCIAL PROPERTY LAW. The law of a province relating to the distribution, pursuant to court order or agreement between the spouses, of the property of the spouses on divorce, annulment or separation. *Pension Ben-*

efits Standards Act, R.S.C. 1985 (2d Supp.), c. 32, s. 25.

PROVINCIAL PUBLIC SECTOR. (i) Her Majesty in right of the Province and agents of Her Majesty in right of the Province; (ii) municipalities in the Province and municipal or public bodies performing a function of government in the Province; (iii) corporations, commissions and associations described in paragraph 149(1)(d) of the Income Tax Act that are owned or controlled by Her Majesty in right of the Province or a municipality in the Province; and (iv) such other bodies in the Province as provide what are generally considered to be public services and as are from time to time prescribed by the regulations made under section 39 of the federal act, and as are named in Schedule A to this agreement. *Federal-Provincial Anti-Inflation Agreement Act*, S.Nfld. 1975-76, c. 52, Interpretation 1.

PROVINCIAL RAILWAYS. Railways situate wholly within a province and under the exclusive control of the Provincial legislature. *Montreal v. Montreal Street Railway Co.*, [1912] A.C. 333, [1912] 1 D.L.R. 681 at 683 (P.C.).

PROVINCIAL REFERENCE. Each province has enacted legislation which permits the provincial government to send a reference to its provincial court of appeal. P.W. Hogg, *Constitutional Law of Canada*, 2d ed. (Toronto: Carswell, 1985) at 178.

PROVINCIAL REVENUE RATE. See NATIONAL AVERAGE ~.

PROVINCIAL SCHEME. Any provision made by law for the payment of superannuation or pension benefits to persons employed under a provincial government. *Public Service Superannuation Act*, R.S.C. 1985, c. P-36, s. 34.

PROVINCIAL SCHOOL LEVY. (i) With reference to a residence or farm land, that portion of the municipal taxes imposed on land or improvements or both in any year for the purpose of meeting the requisition of the Government under section 137 of the School Act for that year; or (ii) with reference to a mobile unit that is not taxed under the Municipal Taxation Act, that portion of the mobile unit licence fee for any year, as determined pursuant to subsection (2), that is treated as being the Provincial school levy for that residence for that year. *Property Tax Reduction Act*, R.S.A. 1980, c. P-19, s. 3.

PROVINCIAL SECURITIES. Securities issued and payable by the government, but does not include securities payable by government agencies or the payment of which, or the payment of any interest or charge on the principal sum

of which, is guaranteed by the government. *Financial Administration Act*, R.S.M. 1970, c. F55, s. 1.

PROVINCIAL SERVICE. Service under a provincial government that may be counted for superannuation or pension purposes under a provincial scheme. *Public Service Superannuation Act*, R.S.C. 1985, c. P-36, s. 34.

PROVINCIAL TAX OR FEE. (a) Any tax of general application payable on a value, price or quantity basis by the purchaser, lessee, user or consumer of tangible personal property or services subject to the tax in respect of the sale, rental, consumption or use of the property or services, except to the extent that the tax is payable in respect of property or services acquired for resale, lease or sub-lease; (b) any fee of general application payable by the owner, user or lessee or any vehicle or item of mobile equipment drawn, propelled or driven by any kind of power in respect of the registration of the vehicle or item or the licensing or certification thereof or in respect of the transfer or renewal of any registration permit, licence or certificate issued for the use of the vehicle or item; and (c) any tax of a like nature to a tax described in a paragraph (a) or any fee of a like nature to a fee described in paragraph (b) that is from time to time prescribed. *Federal-Provincial Fiscal Arrangements Act*, R.S.C. 1985, c. F-8, s. 31.

PROVINCIAL TRANSPORT BOARD. A board, commission or other body or person having, under the law of a province, authority to control or regulate the operation of a local undertaking. *Motor Vehicles Transport Act*, R.S.C. 1985, c. M-12, s. 2.

PROVINCIAL TRUST COMPANY. A trust company that is a provincial corporation. *Loan and Trust Corporations Act*, R.S.O. 1980, c. 249, s. 1.

PROVINCIAL WATER. Such of the waters upon any shore or land, or on or in any lake, river, stream, bay, estuary, tidal water or watercourse, wholly or partially within the Province, over or in respect of which the Legislature has authority to legislate. *Fish and Wildlife Act*, S.N.B. 1980, c. F-14.1, s. 1.

PROVINCIAL WATER-POWERS. *var.* **PROVINCIAL WATER POWERS.** Any water-powers on provincial land, or any other water-powers that are the property of the Crown or are placed under the control and management of a minister.

PROVINCIAL WELFARE PROGRAM. A welfare program administered by the province, by a municipality in the province or privately, to which public money of the province is or may be contributed and that is applicable or available generally to residents of the province. *Canada Assistance Plan*, R.S.C. 1985, c. C-1, s. 10.

PROVISION. *n.* In a legal document, a clause. See CUSTODY ~; DEFINED CONTRIBU-TION ~; FAMILY ~; SUPPORT ~.

PROVISIONALLY FUNDED. When applied to a pension plan, means a pension plan that at any particular time has not assets sufficient to make it fully funded but has made provision for special payments sufficient to liquidate all initial unfunded liabilities or experience deficiencies. *Pension Benefits Act*, R.R.O. 1980, Reg. 746, s. 1.

PROVISIONAL ORDER. 1. An order of a court in the Province that has no force or effect in the Province until confirmed by a court in a reciprocating state or a corresponding order made in a reciprocating state for confirmation in the Province. Maintenance Orders Enforcement acts. 2. The only order which can be made when a court has no personal jurisdiction over a defendant. C.R.B. Dunlop, *Creditor-Debtor Law in Canada*, Second Cumulative Supplement (Toronto: Carswell, 1986) at 226.

PROVISIONAL PERMIT. A permit authorizing the permittee to proceed on the conditions set out in the permit prior to the issuance of a final permit. *Pollution Control Act*, R.S.B.C. 1979, c. 332, s. 1.

PROVISION OF LAW. Any provision of law which has effect for the time being in the province, including any statutory provision, any provision of the common law and any right or power which may be exercised by virtue of the Royal Prerogative. *Interpretation Act*, S.P.E.I. 1981, c. 18, s. 26.

PROVISO. *n.* [L.] A clause in a document which sets a condition, limits, qualifies or covenants, as the case may be.

PROVISO EST PROVIDERE PRAESENTIA ET FUTURA NON PRAETERITA. [L.] A proviso is to provide for the present and future not the past.

PROVISO FOR REDEMPTION. The condition in a mortgage by which the mortgagee must reconvey the mortgaged property to the mortgagor at any time the mortgagor requests if the mortgagor pays the mortgagee on a specified day costs plus the principal, interest and any other moneys which the mortgage secured.

PROVISOR. *n.* A buyer.

PROV. JUDGES J. *abbr.* Provincial Judges Journal (Journal des juges provinciaux).

PROVOCATION. *n.* 1. A wrongful act or insult that is of such a nature as to be sufficient to deprive an ordinary person of the power of self-control is provocation for the purposes of this section if the accused acted upon it on the sudden and before there was time for his passion to cool. *Criminal Code*, R.S.C. 1985, c. C-46, s. 232(2). 2. Provocation includes, for the purposes of sections 34 and 35, provocation by blows, words or gestures. *Criminal Code*, R.S.C. 1985, c. C-46, s. 36. See SUDDEN ~.

PROVOST-MARSHAL. *n.* An officer of the royal forces in charge of military prisoners.

PROX. *abbr.* Proximo.

PROXENETA. *n.* One who arranges marriages.

PROXIMAL. *adj.* Near the origin; near the trunk. F.A. Jaffe, *A Guide to Pathological Evidence*, 2d ed. (Toronto: Carswell, 1983) at 182.

PROXIMATE CAUSE. The point in a series of events beyond which the courts will not go in permitting recovery for damage. John G. Fleming, *The Law of Torts*, 6th ed. (Sydney: The Law Book Co., 1983) at 180. See CAUSA CAUSANS.

PROXIMO. *adv.* [L.] Next month.

PROXY. *n.* A completed and executed form of proxy by means of which a security holder has nominated a person or company to attend and act on her or his behalf at a meeting of security holders. See FORM OF ~; SPECIAL ~ CERTIFICATE.

PRUDENTER AGIT QUI PRAECEPTO LEGIS OBTEMPERAT. [L.] One acts prudently who complies with the precept of the law.

P.S. *abbr.* Post script.

P.S.A.B. *abbr.* Public Service Adjudication Board.

P.S.B.G.M. *abbr.* Protestant School Board of Greater Montreal.

P.S.C.A.B. *abbr.* Public Service Commission Appeal Board.

PSEUDOGRAPH. *n.* Supposed but not real writing.

PSEUDONYM. *n.* A nom de plume.

P.S.I. *abbr.* Pounds per square inch gauge pressure. Boiler and Pressure Vessel acts.

PSIG. *abbr.* 1. Pounds per square inch above atmospheric pressure. *Occupational Health and Safety Act*, R.R.O. 1980, Reg. 691, s. 240. 2. Pounds per square inch gauge. *Gasoline Handling Act*, R.R.O. 1980, Reg. 439, s. 1.

P.S.L.R. ADJUD. *abbr.* Public Service Labour Relations Act Adjudicator.

P.S.L.R.B. *abbr.* Public Service Labour Relations Board.

P.S.S.R.B. *abbr.* Public Service Staff Relations Board.

PSYCHIATRIC CLINICAL EXAMINATION. An examination held to determine if the state of mental health of a person requires that he be placed under close treatment. *Mental Patients Protection Act*, R.S.Q. 1977, c. P-41, s. 1.

PSYCHIATRIC DISORDER. Any disease or disability of the mind and includes alcoholism and drug addiction. *Hospitals Act*, S.N.S. 1977, c. 45, s. 2.

PSYCHIATRIC FACILITY. A facility for the observation, care and treatment of persons suffering from mental disorder, and designated as such by the regulations.

PSYCHIATRIC NURSE. A person to whom a certificate of psychiatric nursing has been issued in accordance with the regulations. *Psychiatric Nursing Training Act*, R.S.A. 1970, c. 290, s. 2.

PSYCHIATRIC NURSING. 1. The nursing care of mentally disordered persons under the direction and supervision of a duly qualified medical practitioner. 2. Representing oneself as a registered psychiatric nurse while carrying out those functions (i) which promote the total well-being of the individual through the promotion of mental health and the prevention of mental illness; (ii) which minimize the effects of mental illness and developmental handicaps; and (iii) which involve the planning and implementation of therapies and programs which assist the individual with emotional, developmental or associated physical or mental difficulties to develop to the maximum potential of the individual. *Registered Psychiatric Nurses Act*, S.M. 1980, c. 46, s. 1.

PSYCHIATRIST. *n.* A duly qualified medical practitioner who is duly certified as a specialist in psychiatry by the Royal College of Physicians and Surgeons of Canada, or who has practical experience and training in the diagnosis and treatment of mental disorders that is equivalent to such a certificate. See ATTENDING ~.

PSYCHIATRY. See FORENSIC ~.

PSYCHIC. *adj.* Mental, in contrast to physical. K.D. Cooper-Stephenson & I.B. Saunders, *Personal Injury Damages in Canada* (Toronto: Carswell, 1981) at 555.

PSYCHOLOGY. *n.* The science dealing with the nature, function and phenomena of human behaviour but does not include psychiatry. *Psychologists Act*, R.S.A. 1980, c. P-25, s. 1. See PRACTICE OF ~.

PSYCHONEUROSIS. *n.* A severe or persistent emotional disturbance of a person, other than mental illness or psychopathic disorder, that results in marked impairment of social adaptation and adjustment. *Mental Health Act*, R.S.M. 1970, c. M110, s. 2.

PSYCHOPATHIC DISORDER. A persistent disorder or disability of mind other than mental illness that results in abnormally aggressive or serious socially disruptive conduct on the part of a person.

PSYCHOSURGERY. *n.* Any procedure that by direct access to the brain removes, destroys or interrupts the normal connections of the brain for the primary purpose of treating a mental disorder or involves the implantation of electrodes, but does not include neurosurgical procedures designed to treat reliably diagnosed organic brain conditions or epilepsy. *Mental Health Services Act*, S.S. 1984-85-86, c. M-13.1, s. 2.

PSYCHOTIC PERSON. A person who suffers from a psychosis. *Sexual Sterilization Act*, R.S.A. 1970, c. 341, s. 2.

PUB. *n.* A place arranged for the consumption of beer and weak cider and open to both male and female persons. *An Act Respecting the Commission de Contrôle des Permis D'alcool*, R.S.Q. 1977, c. C-33, s. 18.

PUBERTY. *n.* The age at which persons become capable of bearing or begetting children.

PUBLIC. *n.* 1. Does not include (i) close personal friends; (ii) business associates; (iii) customers with whom the person who calls for the purpose of trading securities has completed at least five trades in the past in the course of regular business in the sale of or obtaining subscriptions for securities; (iv) any person who has received a prospectus and who subsequently makes a request in writing, signed by himself, for further information with respect to the securities described in the prospectus. *Securities Act*, R.S.N.W.T. 1974, c. S-5, s. 29. 2. Persons other than insurers, insurance brokers, insurance adjusters and insurance agents. *Registered Insurance Brokers Act*, R.S.O. 1980, c. 444, s. 1. 3. Includes members of a credit union. *Credit Union Act*, S.S. 1984-85-86, c. C-45.1, s. 193. See DISTRIBUTION TO THE ~; ISSUED TO THE ~; MEMBER OF THE ~; OFFER TO THE ~; PRIMARY DISTRIBUTION TO THE ~.

PUBLIC. *adj.* See GO ~.

PUBLIC ACCOMMODATION. See PLACE OF ~.

PUBLIC ACCOUNTANCY. The investigation

and audit of accounting records and preparation and reporting on balance sheets, profit and loss accounts and financial statements. *Public Accountants Act*, R.S.N.S. 1967, c. 245, s. 1.

PUBLIC ACCOUNTANT. A person who either alone or in partnership engages for reward in public practice involving: (i) the performance of services which include causing to be prepared, signed, delivered or issued any financial, accounting or related statement; or (ii) the issue of any written opinion, report or certificate concerning any such statement, where, by reason of the circumstances or of the signature, stationery or wording employed, it is indicated that such person or partnership acts or purports to act in relation to such statement, opinion, report or certificate as an independent accountant or auditor or as a person or partnership having or purporting to have expert knowledge in accounting or auditing matters, but does not include a person who engages only in bookkeeping or cost accounting or in the installation of bookkeeping, business or cost systems or who performs accounting or auditing functions exclusively in respect of: (iii) any public authority or any commission, committee or emanation thereof, including a Crown company; (iv) any bank, loan or trust company; (v) any transportation company incorporated by Act of the Parliament of Canada; or (vi) any other publicly-owned or publicly-controlled public utility organization. *Public Accountancy Act*, R.S.O. 1980, c. 405, s. 1.

PUBLIC ACCOUNTING AND AUDITING. The investigation or audit of accounting records or the preparation of, or reporting on, balance sheets, profit and loss accounts and other financial statements, but does not include bookkeeping, cost accounting, or the exercise by accountants and auditors in the employ of the governments of the province or Canada of their functions as such. *Public Accounting and Auditing Act*, R.S.P.E.I. 1974, c. P-27, s. 1.

PUBLIC ACCOUNTS. The accounts of a country's or province's expenditures.

PUBLIC ACT. See ACT OF PARLIAMENT.

PUBLIC ADVERTISEMENT. An advertisement in the public press.

PUBLIC AGENCY. 1. A corporation or agency not contemplated in section 3.11 to which the Government or a minister appoints the majority of the members, to which, by law, the officers or employees are appointed or remunerated in accordance with the Public Service Act (1983, chapter 55) or more than half of whose resources are derived from the consolidated revenue fund. *An Act to Amend Various Legislation*, S.Q. 1984, c. 47, s. 110. 2. An agency,

board, commission or corporation, including any wholly-owned subsidiary corporation, established or controlled by the Crown in right of Ontario, which provides any product or service for which a price, user charge or fee is charged. Ontario statutes. 3. A department, agency, board, commission, bureau, office or other branch of the public service of Saskatchewan and includes any crown corporation or institution that the minister designates as a public agency for the purposes of this Act. Saskatchewan statutes.

PUBLIC AND PARAPUBLIC SECTORS. The Government and the government departments and those government agencies and bodies whose personnel is appointed or remunerated in accordance with the Civil Service Act, as well as the colleges, school boards and establishments contemplated in the Act respecting management and union party organization in collective bargaining in the sectors of education, social affairs, and government agencies (R.S.Q., chapter O-7.1). *An Act to Amend the Labour Code, the Code of Civil Procedure and Other Legislation*, S.Q. 1982, c. 37, s. 111.2.

PUBLIC ARCHIVES. 1. Include all books, papers and records vested in the Province by virtue of the Public Records Act or such other property of the province as, from time to time, the Governor in Council declares to be Public Archives, and all documents, records, structures, erections, monuments, objects, materials, articles or things of historic, artistic, scientific or traditional interest acquired by the Board under this Act. *Public Archives Act*, R.S.N.S. 1967, c. 246, s. 1. 2. The archives of public bodies. *Archives Act*, S.Q. 1983, c. 38, s. 2.

PUBLIC ARCHIVES CANADA. A federal research institution which acquires important records of Canadian life and the nation's development and which also provides facilities and services to make these records accessible to all Canadians.

PUBLICATION. *n.* 1. In relation to any work, means the issue of copies of the work to the public, and does not include the performance in public of a dramatic or musical work, the delivery in public of a lecture, the exhibition in public of an artistic work or the construction of an architectural work of art, but for the purpose of this provision, the issue of photographs and engravings of works of sculpture and architectural works of art shall not be deemed to be publication of those works. *Copyright Act*, R.S.C. 1985, c. C-42, s. 4. 2. Used in this section means any words legibly marked upon any substance or any object signifying the matter otherwise than by words, exhibited in public or caused to be seen or shown or circulated or delivered with a view to its being seen by any person. *Defamation Act*, R.S.M. 1970, c. C20, s. 19. 3. Includes a newspaper or a broadcast. *Defamation Act*, S.Nfld. 1983, c. 63, s. 2. 4. Giving the public possession of an invention by word of mouth, by a photograph or drawing, or by a book, specification or disclosure of that kind. H.G. Fox, *The Canadian Law and Practice Relating to Letters Patent for Inventions*, 4th ed. (Toronto: Carswell, 1969) at 125. See GOVERNMENT ~; PERIODICAL ~; RE~.

PUBLICATION COST. The cost of: (i) fees and honoraria paid to authors and editors; (ii) fees paid to publishers and printers in connection with the publications of local history papers but does not include general area histories; and (iii) distributing, handling and mailing costs. *Ontario Heritage Act*, R.R.O. 1980, Reg. 712, s. 1.

PUBLIC AUTHORITIES. See PROTECTION OF ~.

PUBLIC AUTHORITY. 1. Her Majesty in right of Canada or a province, an agent of Her Majesty in either such right, a municipality in Canada, a municipal or public body performing a function of government in Canada or a corporation performing a function or duty on behalf of Her Majesty in right of Canada or a province. *Cultural Property Export and Import Act*, R.S.C. 1985, c. C-51, s. 2. 2. A provincial or municipal authority or a public educational authority. *National Training Act*, R.S.C. 1985, c. N-19, s. 2. 3. A public officer or a body established by an enactment that is supported by or receives funds from the Province. *Public Building Access Act*, S.N.S. 1967-68, c. 12, s. 2. 4. Includes any council, school board, hospital board or other public body with power to use or develop land for public or community purposes. *Planning Act*, R.S.N.W.T. 1974, c. P-8, s. 2.

PUBLIC BILL. A bill relating to public policy matters. A. Fraser, G.A. Birch & W.A. Dawson, eds., *Beauchesne's Rules and Forms of the House of Commons of Canada*, 5th ed. (Toronto: Carswell, 1978) at 217.

PUBLIC BODY. (i) The government of Canada or a province; (ii) a crown corporation, board, commission or agency of a government; (iii) a municipality; (iv) a body elected or appointed under an act: (A) to develop, administer or regulate schools, hospitals, health facilities, libraries, water utilities, drainage and irrigation works, sewerage works, local improvements or public utilities; or (B) to levy and collect taxes.

PUBLIC BUILDING. 1. Any building to which the public has a right of access. 2. A place of public resort or amusement. See OWNER OF A ~.

PUBLIC CAMP GROUND. An area in a park designated by a superintendent for use by the public for camping purposes. *National Parks Camping Regulations*, C.R.C., c. 1116, s. 2.

PUBLIC CARRIER. Any railway company, any federal carrier within the meaning of the Motor Vehicle Transport Act and any owner or operator of a ship. *Canada Grain Act*, R.S.C. 1985, c. G-10, s. 2.

PUBLIC COMMERCIAL VEHICLE. A commercial motor vehicle as defined in the Highway Traffic Act or a dual-purpose vehicle or the combination of a commercial motor vehicle and trailer or trailers drawn by it, operated by the holder of an operating licence. *Public Commercial Vehicles Act*, R.S.O. 1980, c. 407, s. 1.

PUBLIC COMMUNICATIONS. Any telecommunication that is available to the public. *The Teleglobe Canada Act*, R.S.C. 1985, c. T-4, s. 2.

PUBLIC COMPANY. 1. A company that is not a private company. 2. A company (a) that has outstanding any of its securities in respect of which a prospectus or a document of a similar nature has been filed with and accepted by a public authority; (b) any of the shares of which are listed or posted for trading on any recognized stock exchange in Canada.

PUBLIC CORPORATION. A corporation that was resident in Canada at the particular time, a class or classes of shares of the capital stock of the corporation were listed on a prescribed stock exchange in Canada.

PUBLIC CORRESPONDENCE. A message or intelligence that is communicated as a service to the public for remuneration. *General Radio Regulations, Part II*, C.R.C., c. 1372, s. 6.

PUBLIC CORRIDOR. A corridor that provides access to exit from individually rented rooms, suites of rooms or dwelling units. *Building Code Act*, R.R.O. 1980, Reg. 87, s. 1.

PUBLIC DEBT. Direct debt obligations of the government. *Financial Administration Act*, S.N.S. 1981, c. 15, s. 1.

PUBLIC DEPARTMENT. A department of the Government of Canada or a branch thereof or a board, commission, corporation or other body that is an agent of Her Majesty in right of Canada. *Criminal Code*, R.S.C. 1985, c. C-46, s. 2.

PUBLIC DOCUMENT. 1. Includes certificates under the Great Seal of a province, legal documents, vouchers, cheques, accounting records, correspondence, maps, photographs and all other documents created in the administration of public affairs. 2. Includes a documentary statement made for an official purpose by a public officer acting under a duty or authority to make the statement. *Military Rules of Evidence*, C.R.C., c. 1049, s. 2.

PUBLIC EATING ESTABLISHMENT. (i) A building, structure or enclosure or any part thereof where food or drink is prepared or kept and served or sold to the public for immediate consumption; (ii) a restaurant, hotel dining room, coffee shop, cafeteria, luncheonette, sandwich shop, milk bar, dairy bar, soda fountain, soft drink stand, outlet within the meaning of The Liquor Licensing Act, and another eating or drinking establishment; (ii) a kitchen and any other place in which food or drink is prepared for sale for immediate consumption elsewhere. *The Public Health Act*, R.S.S. 1978, c. P-37, s. 2.

PUBLIC EATING PLACE. A place where food or drink is offered for sale to the public for consumption on the premises and includes a hotel, inn, restaurant, public transport, eating house and lunch counter. Margarine acts.

PUBLIC EMPLOYEE. An employee of (i) any of the departments of government; (ii) any agency; or (iii) any commission, board, corporation, authority or other body.

PUBLIC EXHIBITION. A display of goods open to the general public. *Display Goods Temporary Importation Regulations*, C.R.C., c. 524, s. 2.

PUBLIC FISHING PRESERVE. Land or water that is Crown owned, leased or developed with Crown funds, on which or part of which, fish have been reared or stocked for the purpose of angling and are designated as public fishing preserves in the regulations. *Fish and Game Protection Act*, R.S.P.E.I. 1974, c. F-8, s. 1.

PUBLIC FOREST. A state-owned forest. *Forestry Credit Act*, R.S.Q. 1977, c. C-78, s. 1.

PUBLIC FREIGHT VEHICLE. A motor vehicle, other than a limited freight vehicle, that is operated at any time on a highway by, for or on behalf of any person who charges or collects compensation for the transportation of freight in or on the motor vehicle. *Motor Carrier Act*, R.S.B.C. 1979, c. 286, s. 1.

PUBLIC FUNDS. Money from the treasury of the federal, provincial or municipal government. *Les Soeurs de la Visitation d'Ottawa v. Ottawa*, [1952] O.R. 61, at pp. 71, 72.

PUBLIC GARAGE. A building for the care, repair or equipping of motor vehicles or for the parking or storing of motor vehicles for remuneration, hire or sale. Canada regulations.

PUBLIC HALL. 1. A building, including a portable building or tent with a seating capacity for over 100 persons that is offered for use or used as a place of public assembly, but does not include a theatre within the meaning of the Theatres Act or a building, except a tent, used solely for religious purposes. *Public Halls Act*, R.S.O. 1980, c. 408, s. 1. 2. A hall, pavilion, place or building, except such as used in connection with churches or owned and conducted by municipal authorities, in which public concerts, dances and other social gatherings are held. *The Theatres and Cinematographs Act*, R.S.S. 1978, c. T-11, s. 2.

PUBLIC HARBOUR. Any harbour under the control and management of the Minister by virtue of section 9. *Public Harbours and Port Facilities Act*, R.S.C. 1985, c. P-29, s. 2.

PUBLIC HEALTH SERVICES. Preventive health services.

PUBLIC HEARING. A hearing of which public notice is given, which is open to the public, and at which any person who has an interest in a matter may be heard.

PUBLIC HIGHWAY. Any part of a bridge, road, street, place, square or other ground open to public vehicular traffic.

PUBLIC HOLIDAY. New Year's Day, Good Friday, Labour Day, Christmas Day.

PUBLIC HOSPITAL. A building, premises, or place with a bed capacity of at least 20 beds, that is established and operated for the lodging and treatment or the treatment of persons afflicted with or suffering from sickness, disease, or injury and includes a maternity hospital, a nurses residence and all buildings and equipment used for the purposes of the hospital. *Hospitals Act*, R.S.P.E.I. 1974, c. H-11, s. 1.

PUBLIC HOTEL. Includes every hotel, motel, common lodging house and place of public accommodation, other than a boarding house, supplying lodging to the public.

PUBLIC HOT TUB. A hot tub that is available for use by the general public and includes a hot tub located in a hotel, motel, campground, university or a residential property containing more than four living units. *An Act to Amend the Health Act*, S.N.B. 1987, c. 24, s. 1.

PUBLIC HOUSE. A place arranged for the consumption of beer and weak cider and open to both male and female persons. *An Act Respecting the Commission de Contrôle des Permis D'alcool*, R.S.Q. 1977, c. C-33, s. 18.

PUBLIC HOUSING. 1. One or more houses or multiple-family dwellings or housing accommodation of the hostel or dormitory type or any combination thereof, together with the land upon which it is situated, acquired, constructed, held, maintained and managed by the corporation or a municipality, or a housing authority, or a housing and renewal authority, under an agreement with such parties as may have an interest in the housing accommodation, for leasing to persons or families of low income in need of decent, safe, and sanitary housing or to such other persons as the corporation designates, having regard to the shortage, overcrowding or congestion of housing accommodation. *Housing and Renewal Corporation Act*, R.S.M. 1970, c. H160, s. 1. 2. A housing unit constructed pursuant to section 40 of the National Housing Act (Canada), as amended from time to time. *Senior Citizens' Heritage Program Act*, S.S. 1984-85-86, c. S-46.01, s. 2. See SUBSIDIZED ~.

PUBLIC HOUSING AGENCY. A corporation that is wholly owned by (a) the government of a province or any agency thereof; (b) one or more municipalities in a province; or (c) the government of a province or an agency thereof and one or more municipalities in that province and that has power to acquire and develop land for a public housing project or to construct or acquire and operate a public housing project. *National Housing Act*, R.S.C. 1985, c. N-11, s. 78.

PUBLIC HOUSING PROJECT. 1. A project, together with the land on which it is situated, consisting of a housing project or housing accommodation of the hostel or dormitory type or any combination thereof, that is undertaken to provide decent, safe and sanitary housing accommodation in compliance with standards approved by the corporation and that is intended to be leased to individuals or families of low income. *National Housing Act*, R.S.C. 1985, c. N-11, s. 78. 2. Any housing project constructed, held, maintained, and managed by the corporation jointly with (i) any municipality; (ii) any housing authority; (iii) any agency of Canada; or (iv) any municipality, housing authority and an agency of Canada.

PUBLICI JURIS. [L.] Of public right.

PUBLIC IMPROVEMENT. 1. Anything for the purpose of which an authority may expropriate land. *The Expropriation Procedure Act*, R.S.S. 1978, c. E-16, s. 2. 2. Public highways, culverts, bridges, aerodromes, air services, public transit systems, private transit systems where considered by the minister to be a public benefit, railways, ditches, drains, ferries, wells and public fire-guards; dams, reservoirs or other works constructed for the storage of water, water towers and works connected therewith; lands, streams, water courses and property, real and personal, heretofore or hereafter acquired for any public improvement or land required for securing material in connection with road construction; and any matter or thing done or to be done in connection with any such public improvement under this Act. *The Highways Act*, R.S.S. 1978, c. H-3, s. 2.

PUBLIC INSTITUTION. 1. An institution owned or operated by the government of a province. 2. (i) A hospital, special-care home or other health care institution or body; (ii) a university, college, institute, board of education or other educational institution or body; (iii) a municipality or other local governing body; (iv) an institution or body that derives its funds in whole or in part from the Government of Saskatchewan; (v) any other institution or body designated by the Lieutenant Governor in Council as a public institution for the purposes of this Act. *The Saskatchewan Property Management Corporation Act*, S.S. 1986-87-88, c. C-32.3, s. 2.

PUBLIC INSURANCE COMPANY. A company that (i) does not restrict the right to transfer any of its shares; (ii) does not limit the number of its shareholders to 50 or less, with persons who are joint registered owners of one or more shares in the company being counted as one shareholder; and (iii) does not prohibit any invitation to the public to subscribe for any of the shares of the company.

PUBLIC INTEREST IMMUNITY. A rule of evidence which states that evidence which is relevant and otherwise admissible must be excluded if admitting it would injure the public interest. P.W. Hogg, *Constitutional Law of Canada*, 2d ed. (Toronto: Carswell, 1985) at 223 and 224.

PUBLIC INTERNATIONAL LAW. See INTERNATIONAL LAW.

PUBLICIST. *n.* One who writes about the law of nations.

PUBLICITY CONTEST. A contest, a lottery scheme, a game, a plan or an operation which results in the awarding of a prize, carried on for the object of promoting the commercial interests of the person for whom it is carried on. *An Act respecting lotteries, racing, publicity contests and amusement machines*, S.Q. 1978, c. 36, s. 1.

PUBLICITY PICKETING. Picketing intended to inform the public of the existence of a labour dispute.

PUBLIC LAND. Land belonging to Her Majesty the Queen in right of a province. See OCCUPIED ~; UNOCCUPIED ~.

PUBLIC LANDS. 1. Lands belonging to Her Majesty in right of Canada and includes lands of which the Government of Canada has power to dispose. 2. Lands belonging to Her Majesty in right of Canada or of which the Government of Canada has, subject to the terms of any agreement between the Government of Canada and the government of the province in which the lands are situated, power to dispose, including any waters on or flowing through, and the natural resources of, those lands. *National Parks Act*, R.S.C. 1985, c. N-14, s. 2. 3. Real property or any interest therein, under the control and management of a department. *National Capital Act*, R.S.C. 1985, c. N-4, s. 2. 4. Comprises the parts of the bed of the St. Lawrence river and of the Gulf of St. Lawrence which belong to the province of Québec by right of sovereignty. *Lands and Forests Act*, R.S.Q. 1977, c. T-9, s. 2. 5. Lands theretofore designated or known as "Crown lands" and "clergy lands"; which designation, for the purposes of administration, shall still continue. *Lands and Forests Act*, R.S.Q. 1977, c. T-9, s. 2. 6. Includes lands theretofore designated as Crown lands, school lands and clergy lands. *Public Lands Act*, R.S.O. 1980, c. 413, s. 1. 7. The lands vested in Her Majesty in right of Ontario and under the management of the Minister, and includes the lands in respect of which a lease, licence of occupation or permit has been granted or issued under the Mining Act, the Provincial Parks Act or the Public Lands Act. *Crown Timber Act*, R.S.O. 1980, c. 109, s. 1. 8. All Crown lands, lands transferred to Québec, clergy lands or lands of the Jesuits' estates, Crown domain of seigniory of Lauzon, which have not been alienated by the Crown. *Mining Act*, R.S.Q. 1977, c. M-13, s. 1.

PUBLIC LANE. A lane in a park appurtenant to business or residential premises generally used by the occupier of the premises and his servants and agents for the loading and unloading of chattels, including garbage, necessarily incidental to the business or residential use of the premises. *National Parks Highway Traffic Regulations*, C.R.C., c. 1126, s. 2.

PUBLIC LAUNDRY. For the purposes of this division, any shop, dwelling or building whatsoever in which linen, brought or sent there by the public, is washed or ironed for profit. *Licenses Act*, R.S.Q. 1977, c. L-3, s. 86.

PUBLIC LAW. All law dealing with relations between an individual and the state or between states and the organization of government, i.e., criminal, administrative, constitutional and international law.

PUBLIC LENDING RIGHT. A right which entitles an author to receive payments from time to time for books they authored which were lent out to the public by libraries.

PUBLIC LIABILITY INSURANCE. Insurance against loss or damage to the person or property of others that is not included in or incidental to some other class of insurance defined by or under this Act. Insurance acts.

PUBLIC LIABILITY INSURANCE POLICY. A policy or that part of a policy which insures a person against loss of or damage to the person or property of others where the insurance is not included in or incidental to some other class of insurance. *Insurance Adjusters Act*, R.S.Nfld. 1970, c. 175, s. 2.

PUBLIC LIBRARY. 1. Any municipal library, regional library or community library. 2. A library where services are available without charge to residents of the Province. *Libraries Act*, R.S.N.B. 1973, c. L-5, s. 1. 3. A municipal library, community library, regional library or a branch of the Provincial Library, the primary responsibility of which is the provision of library service to the public. *The Public Libraries Act*, R.S.S. 1978, c. P-39, s. 2.

PUBLIC LIVESTOCK SALE. Any place where livestock is offered for sale to the public. *Livestock Brand Inspection Act*, R.S.A. 1980, c. L-21, s. 1.

PUBLICLY-TRADED SHARES. (i) Shares of a corporation that are listed or posted for trading on a recognized stock exchange in Canada or the United States of America; or (ii) shares of a corporation that has more than 15 shareholders and any of whose issued shares, or securities which may or might be exchanged for or converted into shares, were part of a distribution to the public. *Legislative Assembly Act*, S.A. 1983, c. L-10.1, s. 23.

PUBLIC MEETING. A meeting bona fide and lawfully held for a lawful purpose and for the furtherance or discussion of any matter of public concern, whether admission thereto is general or restricted. Defamation acts.

PUBLIC MEMBER. A person representing the public, the state, an arbitration panel or board as opposed to a member representing a particular interest.

PUBLIC MISCHIEF. With intent to mislead, causes a peace officer to enter upon or continue an investigation by (a) making a false statement that accuses some other person of having committed an offence; (b) doing anything that is intended to cause some other person to be suspected of having committed an offence that the person has not committed, or to divert suspicion from himself; or (c) reporting that an offence has been committed when it has not been committed; or (d) reporting or in any other way making it known or causing it to be made known that he or some other person has died when he or that other person has not died. *Criminal Code*, R.S.C. 1985, c. C-46, s. 140.

PUBLIC MONEY. 1. All money belonging to Canada received or collected by the Receiver General or any other public officer in his official capacity or any person authorized to receive or collect such money, and includes (a) duties and revenues of Canada; (b) money borrowed by Canada or received through the issue or sale of securities; (c) money received or collected for or on behalf of Canada; and (d) all money that is paid to or received or collected by a public officer under or pursuant to any Act, trust, treaty, undertaking or contract, and is to be disbursed for a purpose specified in or pursuant to that Act, trust, treaty, undertaking or contract. *Financial Administration Act*, R.S.C. 1985, c. F-11, s. 2. 2. All money belonging to the province received or collected by a minister or any public officer in an official capacity or any person authorized to receive or collect such money, and includes (i) revenues of a province; (ii) money borrowed by the province or received through the sale of securities; (iii) money received or collected for or on behalf of the province; and (iv) money paid to the province for a special purpose. See RECIPIENT OF ~S.

PUBLIC MORGUE. A place under the control and management of a municipal corporation where bodies are retained before their disposition. *Anatomy Act*, R.S.O. 1980, c. 21, s. 1.

PUBLIC MOTOR BUS. 1. A motor vehicle operated by or on behalf of a person carrying on upon any highway the business of a public carrier of passengers, or passengers and freight for gain. *Motor Carrier Act*, R.S.N.B. 1973, c. M-16, s. 1. 2. A motor vehicle operated on a highway by, for or on behalf of, any person who receives compensation either directly or indirectly for the transportation thereon of passengers and express freight that may be carried on a passenger vehicle, but does not include the following: (i) any vehicle from any other province or from the United States carrying only tourists on one continuous trip to, through and from, this province under contract made outside this province; (ii) any vehicle of not more than seven passenger capacity regularly operated under a license from a municipality while operating within the limits of that municipality or on casual charter trips outside the municipality when holding written permission from the Commission; (iii) any vehicle while employed solely in taking workmen to and from their work over a highway upon which no adequate transportation is provided at convenient times for that purpose by a person holding an operating authority under this Act; (iv) any vehicle employed on charter to carry passengers to a picnic, outing or similar gathering, over a highway upon which no adequate transportation is provided at reasonable times for that purpose by a person holding an operating authority under this Act; (v) school buses owned by or operated under contract with regional administrative school units or any other educational institution for the transportation of students, school unit personnel or school unit parent groups for educational purposes. *Motor Carrier Act*, S.P.E.I. 1984, c. 26, s. 1.

PUBLIC MOTOR TRUCK. 1. A motor vehicle carrying or used to carry goods or chattels, exclusive of express freight as carried on a public motor bus, for hire. *Motor Carrier Act*, S.P.E.I. 1984, c. 26, s. 1. 2. A motor vehicle used (a) to carry commodities for hire; or (b) to tow or haul for hire a mobile home, trailer or other vehicle. *Motor Carrier Act*, R.S.N.B. 1973, c. M-16, s. 1.

PUBLIC MUSEUM. Includes buildings used, or to be used, for the preservation of a collection of paintings or other works of art, or of objects of natural history, or of mechanical, scientific or philosophical inventions, instruments, models or designs, and dedicated or to be dedicated to the recreation of the public, together with any libraries, reading rooms, laboratories and other offices and premises used or to be used in connection therewith. *Mortmain and Charitable Uses Act*, R.S.O. 1980, c. 297, s. 8.

PUBLIC NUISANCE. A cause of action for personal injury or other loss in which a private claimant must be able to show that she or he incurred a special loss beyond the inconvenience or annoyance suffered by the general public. No right relating to land need be involved. John G. Fleming, *The Law of Torts*, 6th ed. (Sydney: The Law Book Co., 1983) at 380.

PUBLIC OFFICE. Has a meaning corresponding to that of Public Official and a person shall be deemed to be serving in a Public Office during such time as he is entitled to receive the salary annexed to that Public Office. *Diplomatic Service Superannuation Act*, R.S.C. 1985, c. D-2, s. 2.

PUBLIC OFFICER. 1. Includes any person in the public service (i) who is authorized by or under an enactment to do or enforce the doing of an act or thing or to exercise a power; or (ii) upon whom a duty is imposed by or under an enactment. 2. Includes a minister of the Crown and any person employed in the public service. 3. Includes (a) an officer of customs and excise; (b) an officer of the Canadian Forces; (c) an officer of the Royal Canadian Mounted Police; and (d) any officer while the officer is engaged in enforcing the laws of Canada relating to revenue, customs, excise, trade or navigation. *Criminal Code*, R.S.C. 1985, c. C-46, s. 2. 4. Includes every person appointed to or holding any public office, employment or commission in a ministry of the Executive Government of the Province, or appointed to or holding an office or employment of public trust, or in which he is concerned in the collection, receipt, disbursement or expenditure or public money under the Executive Government of the Province. *Public Service Bonding Act*, R.S.B.C. 1979, c. 345, s. 1. 5. Includes the Commissioner, Deputy Commissioner, any person employed in the public service of the Territories and any agent of the Territories. *Financial Administration Act*, R.S.N.W.T. 1974, c. F-4, s. 2. 6. A person having a legal duty or authority to make official statements which duty or authority is expressly imposed by or given in a statute, regulation or specific instruction, or implied from the nature of the office because he is an official of the Government of Canada, the government of a Canadian province, a Canadian municipality, or because he is a member of the Canadian Forces. *Military Rules of Evidence*, C.R.C., c. 1049, s. 2.

PUBLIC OFFICIAL. 1. A person appointed to an office or employment by or under the Government of Saskatchewan, wherein he is concerned in the collection, receipt, disbursement or expenditure of public money. *The Public Officials Security Act*, R.S.S. 1978, c. P-41, s. 2. 2. (i) A member of the Executive Council; (ii) a person who holds an office at the appointment of the Lieutenant Governor in Council or a member of the Executive Council and who receives remuneration from the Crown in respect of that office; (iii) the Speaker of the Legislative Assembly; (iv) the Auditor General; (v) the Ombudsman; or (vi) the Chief Electoral Officer. *Financial Administration Act*, R.S.A. 1980, c. F-9, s. 1. 3. An ambassador, minister, high commissioner or consul-general of Canada to another country and such other person of comparable status serving in another country in the public service of Canada as the Governor in Council may designate. *Diplomatic Service Superannuation Act*, R.S.C. 1985, c. D-2, s. 2.

PUBLIC OYSTER-FISHING AREA. Any oyster-bearing area that is not held under a lease or otherwise closed to the public. Fishery regulations.

PUBLIC PARK. 1. Includes any park, garden, or other land dedicated or to be dedicated to the recreation of the public. *Mortmain and Charitable Uses Act*, R.S.O. 1980, c. 297, s. 8. 2. Includes zoological gardens, recreational area, square, avenue, boulevard, or drive, and areas or grounds set aside and used, or principally used, for the purposes of sports or recreation or both, together with the buildings and other structures and facilities, if any, situated thereon. *City of Winnipeg Act*, S.M. 1971, c. 105, s. 533.

PUBLIC PARKING AREA. A structure or an open area, other than a street, used for the temporary parking of more than four automobiles and available for public use without charge or for compensation or as an accommodation for clients or customers. Canada regulations.

PUBLIC PASSENGER TRANSPORTATION SYSTEM. A public system for the transportation of passengers and goods operated under an annual operating agreement, but does not include custom transit services. *Urban Transit Authority Act*, R.S.B.C. 1979, c. 421, s. 1.

PUBLIC PASSENGER VEHICLE. 1. A motor vehicle operated by or on behalf of a person carrying on upon any highway the business of a public carrier of passengers, or passengers and freight, for gain and includes a school bus. *Motor Carrier Act*, R.S.N.S. 1967, c. 190, s. 1. 2. A motor vehicle that is available for use by the public and is operated at any time on a highway over a regular route or between fixed terminating points and on a regular time schedule by, for or on behalf of any person who charges or collects compensation for the transportation of passengers in or on the motor vehicle. *Motor Carrier Act*, R.S.B.C. 1979, c. 286, s. 1.

PUBLIC PICNIC GROUNDS. An area in a park designated by the superintendent for use by the public for picnic purposes. *National Parks Camping Regulations*, C.R.C., c. 1116, s. 2.

PUBLIC PLACE. 1. Includes any place to which the public have access as of right or by invitation, express or implied. *Criminal Code*, R.S.C. 1985, c. C-46, s. 150. 2. Includes any place, building or convenience to which the public has, or is permitted to have, access, and any highway, street, lane, park or place of public resort or amusement. 3. Includes any place in which the public has an interest arising out of the need to safeguard the public health. 4. (a) A place open to the air to which the public are entitled or permitted to have access without payment and, for the purpose of this definition, a covered place open to the air on at least one side shall be treated as being a place open to the air; and (b) a park or public campground. *Waste Management Act*, S.B.C. 1982, c. 41, s. 6. 5. Includes (i) a place or building to which the public has access; (ii) a place of public resort; and (iii) any vehicle in a public place, but does not include a location off a highway that is reasonably remote from any settlement and that is used for picnicking, sport fishing or other outdoor recreational activity, does not include any prem-

PUBLIC POLICY

ises licensed pursuant to Ordinance. *Liquor Act*, S.N.W.T. 1983 (1st Sess.), c. 26, s. 2.

PUBLIC POLICY. The notion that no person can lawfully do what tends to injure the public or go against the public good. G.H.L. Fridman, *The Law of Contract in Canada*, 2d ed. (Toronto: Carswell, 1986) at 350. See INTERNATIONAL ~.

PUBLIC POOL. A structure, basin, chamber or tank containing or intended to contain an artificial body of water for swimming, water sport, water recreation or entertainment, but does not include: (i) one that is located on a private residential property under the control of the owner or occupant and that is limited to use for swimming or bathing by the owner or occupant, members of his family and their visitors; or (ii) one that is used solely for commercial display and demonstration purposes. *Health Protection and Promotion Act, 1983*, S.O. 1983, c. 10, s. 1.

PUBLIC PORT FACILITY. Any port facility under the control and management of the Minister by virtue of section 9. *Public Harbours and Port Facilities Act*, R.S.C. 1985, c. P-29, s. 2.

PUBLIC PROPERTY. 1. Property, immovable or movable, real or personal, belonging to Her Majesty in right of a province and includes property belonging to an agency of government. 2. All property, other than money, belonging to Her Majesty in right of Canada. *Financial Administration Act*, R.S.C. 1985, c. F-11, s. 2. 3. All money and property of Her Majesty in right of Canada. *National Defence Act*, R.S.C. 1985, c. N-5, s. 2. 4. All property belonging to the government, but does not include property belonging to a government corporation. *Financial Administration Act*, S.B.C. 1981, c. 15, s. 1.

PUBLIC PURPOSES. See LAND FOR ~.

PUBLIC RECORD. 1. A record created by or received by a department in the conduct of its affairs except the copy of a record created only for convenience of reference and surplus copies of mimeographed, multilithed, printed or processed circulars or memoranda. 2. Any original document, parchment, manuscript, record, book, map, plan, photograph, magnetic tape or other documentary material regardless of physical form owned by and in the possession of a department. 3. Includes any correspondence, memorandum, book, plan, map, drawing, diagram, pictorial or graphic work, photograph, film, microfilm, sound recording, video tape, machine readable record, manuscript, inventory, pamphlet, periodical, photographic slide, micrographic, electronic data printout, and any other documentary material, regardless of its physical form or characteristics, held by or under the

control of a government body. *Archives Act*, S.N.W.T. 1981 (3d Sess.), c. 2, s. 2. 4. Any original documentary material made by or received by a public authority or the predecessor in the territory that is now Canada of that public authority that contains information relating to the organization, function, procedure, policy or activity of that public authority. *Cultural Property Export Regulations*, C.R.C., c. 449, s. 2.

PUBLIC RECREATIONAL FACILITY. A recreational facility available to any individual who wishes to use it for its intended purposes. *Recreational Facility Act*, R.S.B.C. 1979, c. 358, s. 1.

PUBLIC REGULATORY AGENCY. Any ministry, agency, board, commission or corporation established or controlled by the Crown in right of Ontario which approves, establishes, regulates, recommends or requires particular prices, user charges or fees to be charged for any product or service. Ontario statutes.

PUBLIC REPRESENTATIVE. A person appointed as a member of a board who, in the opinion of the minister, is impartial respecting the interests of the employees in respect of whom the board may be or is required to make recommendations and the interests of the employers of such employees. *Construction Industry Wages Act*, R.S.M. 1970, c. 190, s. 2.

PUBLIC RESERVE. Land which vests in a municipality and which is dedicated to the public. *An Act to Amend the Real Property Act*, S.M. 1980-81, c. 10, s. 2.

PUBLIC RESORT. See PLACE OF ~.

PUBLIC REVENUE. All revenue and public moneys, from whatever source arising, whether the revenues and moneys belong to the province, or are held by the province, or collected or held by officers of the province for or on account of or in trust for any other province, or for Canada or for the Imperial Government or for any other party or person. *The Department of Finance Act*, R.S.S. 1978, c. D-15, s. 2.

PUBLIC ROAD. A public road opened in conformity with section 430 of the Cities and Towns Act, a colonization road within the meaning of the Colonization Roads Act (Revised Statutes, 1964, chapter 105), a street or road opened pursuant to a municipal by-law, resolution or procès-verbal, a highway maintained by the Ministère des transports pursuant to the Roads Act (Revised Statutes, 1964, chapter 133) or by the Office des autoroutes provided that the bordering proprietors have a right of access to that highway. *An Act to preserve agricultural land*, S.Q. 1978, c. 10, s. 1.

PUBLIC ROADWAY. (i) In a city, town, new

854

PUBLIC SERVICE

town, village or summer village, the right of way of all or any of the following: (A) a local road, (B) a service road, (C) a street, (D) an avenue, or (E) a lane, that is publicly used or intended for public use; (ii) in a county, municipal district, improvement district or special area, the right of way of all or any of the following: (A) a controlled street or rural road as defined in the Public Highways Development Act, or (B) a service road or a lane that is intended to public use; or (iii) a road, street or highway designated as a secondary road pursuant to the Public Highways Development Act, except those secondary roads numbered between 900 and 999, and includes a public right of way on which no motor vehicle, as defined in the Motor Vehicle Administration Act, is permitted to operate. *Planning Act*, R.S.A. 1980, c. P-9, s. 1.

PUBLIC SALE. 1. A sale either by public auction or public tender conducted in accordance with this Act and the prescribed rules. *Municipal Tax Sales Act*, S.O. 1984, c. 48, s. 1. 2. A sale or offering for sale of livestock by public auction or otherwise at a public sale yard or at another place as the minister may designate. *Livestock Public Sale Act*, R.S.B.C. 1979, c. 246, s. 1.

PUBLIC ROOMS. Includes halls, dining rooms, bars, smoke rooms, lounges, recreation rooms, nurseries and libraries. *Hull Construction Regulations*, C.R.C., c. 1431, s. 2.

PUBLIC SALE YARD. A place of business where livestock is sold, offered for sale or kept for sale.

PUBLIC SAUNA. A sauna that is available for use by the general public and includes a sauna located in a hotel, motel, campground, university or a residential property containing more than four living units. *An Act to Amend the Health Act*, S.N.B. 1987, c. 24, s. 1.

PUBLIC SCHOOL. An institution for educational purposes established and maintained under this Act. *Public Schools Act*, R.S.M. 1970, c. P250, s. 2.

PUBLIC SCHOOL DIVISION. A school division other than a separate school division. *The Education Act*, R.S.S. 1978, c. E-0.1, s. 2.

PUBLIC SCHOOL ELECTORS. (a) Owners and tenants of property in such territory without municipal organization; and (b) spouses of such owners and tenants, who are Canadian citizens or British subjects and of the full age of 18 years and who are not separate school supporters. *Education Act*, R.S.O. 1980, c. 129, s. 64.

PUBLIC SECTOR. The civil service, Crown entities and external agencies. *The Pay Equity Act*, S.M. 1985-86, c. 21, s. 1. See PROVINCIAL ~.

PUBLIC SECTOR EMPLOYEE. A person employed by a public sector employer.

PUBLIC SECTOR EMPLOYER. (a) The government; (b) a corporation or an unincorporated board, commission, council, bureau, authority or similar body that has: (i) on its board of management or board of directors, a majority of members who are appointed by an act, a minister or the Lieutenant Governor in Council; or (ii) employees appointed under a Public Service act; (c) a municipality; (d) a board of school trustees; (e) a university; (f) a community care facility; (g) a hospital.

PUBLIC SERVANT. 1. Any person employed in a department, and includes a member of the Canadian Forces or the Royal Canadian Mounted Police. *Public Servants Inventions Act*, R.S.C. 1985, c. P-32, s. 2. 2. A person appointed under this Act to the service of the Crown by the Lieutenant Governor in Council, by the Commission or by a minister. *Public Service Act*, R.S.O. 1980, c. 418, s. 1. 3. Includes any person who, under The Civil Service Superannuation Act, is a member of, or within, or deemed to be within, the civil service for the purposes of that Act or is otherwise employed under the government or an agency of the government. *Public Servants Insurance Act*, R.S.M. 1970, c. P270, s. 2.

PUBLIC SERVICE. 1. The several positions in or under any department or other portion of the public service of Canada specified in Schedule I. *Public Service Staff Relations Act*, R.S.C. 1985, c. P-35, s. 2. 2. The several positions in or under any department or portion of the executive government of Canada, and, for the purposes of this Part, of the Senate and House of Commons, the Library of Parliament and any board, commission, corporation or portion of the public service of Canada specified in Schedule I. *Public Service Superannuation Act*, R.S.C. 1985, c. P-36, s. 3. 3. All ministries or any part thereof. *Management Board of Cabinet Act*, R.S.O. 1980, c. 254, s. 1. 4. The public service of the Territories and includes the employees of any board, commission, or other body whose wages or salary is paid out of the Northwest Territories Consolidated Revenue Fund. *Public Service Garnishee Act*, R.S.N.W.T. 1974, c. P-14, s. 2. 5. The service of Her Majesty in respect of the executive Government of Saskatchewan, and includes all persons employed or holding office under any agency other than those in the employ of Crown corporations, the Department of Telecommunications, the Liquor Board and the Workers' Compensation Board. *The Public Service Act*, R.S.S. 1978, c. P-42, s. 2. 6. (1) A municipal corporation or intermunicipal agency; (2) an establishment or regional council within the meaning of paragraphs a and f of section 1 of the Act respecting health services and social services (R.S.Q., chapter S-5) that is not contemplated in paragraph 2 of section 111.2; (3) a telephone service; (4) a fixed schedule land transport service such as a railway or a subway, or a transport service carried on by bus or by boat; (5) an undertaking engaged in the production, transmission, distribution or sale of gas, water or electricity; (6) a home-garbage removal service; (7) an ambulance service or the Canadian Red Cross Association; or (8) an agency that is a mandatary of the Government, except the Société des alcools du Québec and an agency or body whose personnel is appointed and remunerated in accordance with the Civil Service Act. *An Act to Amend the Labour Code, the Code of Civil Procedure and Other Legislation,* S.Q. 1982, c. 37, s. 111.0.16.

PUBLIC SERVICE COMMISSION. The body which staffs the federal public service.

PUBLIC SERVICE CORPORATION. Any board, commission or corporation specified in Part I of Schedule I. *Public Service Superannuation Act,* R.S.C. 1985, c. P-36, s. 37.

PUBLIC SERVICE ELECTOR. A person employed in the public service of Canada who is qualified and entitled, under section 34, to vote under these Rules. *Special Voting Rules,* R.S.C. 1985, c. E-2, Schedule II, s. 2.

PUBLIC SERVICE EMPLOYER. (i) The Government of Canada; (ii) the government of a province or territory of Canada; (iii) a university.

PUBLIC SERVICE PARTICIPANT. A person who is a participant under Part II of the Public Service Superannuation Act. *Canadian Forces Superannuation Act,* R.S.C. 1985, c. C-17, s. 60.

PUBLIC SERVICE STAFF RELATIONS BOARD. The federal body which, under the Public Service Staff Relations Act, oversees collective bargaining, grievances and adjudication for the federal public service.

PUBLIC SERVICE VEHICLE. A motor vehicle or trailer that is operated by or on behalf of any person for gain or reward.

PUBLIC SHARE ISSUE. The distribution of a share or subscription in a share made in accordance with a receipt from the Commission des valeurs mobilières du Québec or an exemption from filing a prospectus provided for in section 52 or 263 of the Securities Act (1982, chapter 48). *An Act to Amend Certain Legislation to Give Effect to Government Budget Policy for the Fiscal Period 1983-84,* S.Q. 1983, c. 44, s. 37.

PUBLIC SHOOTING PRESERVE. Land that is Crown owned, leased or developed with Crown funds, on which, or part of which, game birds that have been raised in captivity or released for the purpose of hunting and are designated as public shooting preserves in the regulations. *Fish and Game Protection Act,* R.S.P.E.I. 1974, c. F-8, s. 1.

PUBLIC STOCKYARD. An area of land used as a public market for purchasing and selling livestock, with the buildings situated thereon and used in connection therewith. *The Brand and Brand Inspection Act,* R.S.S. 1978, c. B-7, s. 2.

PUBLIC STORES. Includes any personal property that is under the care, supervision, administration or control of a public department or of any person in the service of a public department. *Criminal Code,* R.S.C. 1985, c. C-46, s. 2.

PUBLIC SWIMMING POOL. 1. A swimming pool; other than (i) a private recreational swimming pool; or (ii) a promotional pool. *Public Health Act,* R.R.O. 1980, Reg. 849, s. 1. 2. A swimming pool that is available for use by the general public and includes a swimming pool located in a hotel, motel, campground, university or a residential property containing more than four living units. *An Act to Amend the Health Act,* S.N.B. 1987, c. 24, s. 1.

PUBLIC TRAIL. The whole of any motorized snow vehicle trail established and maintained in whole or in part by public funds. *Motorized Snow Vehicles Act,* R.S.O. 1980, c. 301, s. 1.

PUBLIC TRANSIT MOTOR VEHICLE. Any motor vehicle operated by, for or on behalf of the Regional Corporation or any other municipality, or a transit commission, in connection with a regular passenger transportation service and includes such other motor vehicles operated in connection with a regular passenger transportation service as may be specified in the by-law. *Regional Municipalities Amendment Act, 1982,* S.O. 1982, c. 26, s. 8.

PUBLIC TRANSIT PERMIT. A permit that is valid and in force issued by the Commission authorizing its holder to provide a bus transport service for passengers, and their baggage, where such is the case, for direct or indirect remuneration, on a regular route and on a fixed time-schedule. *Municipal and Intermunicipal Transit Corporations Act,* R.S.Q. 1977, c. C-70, s. 1.

PUBLIC TRANSIT SYSTEM. A system of providing passenger transportation.

PUBLIC TRANSPORTATION. Any service for which a fare is charged for transporting the public by vehicles operated by or on behalf of a municipality or a local board thereof, or under an agreement between a municipality and a person, firm or corporation and includes special transportation facilities for the physically disabled, but does not include transportation by special purpose facilities such as school buses or ambulances. *Public Transportation and Highway Improvement Act*, R.S.O. 1980, c. 421, s. 94.

PUBLIC TRANSPORTATION SERVICE. A service provided by vehicles operated either underground, above ground or on highways or rights-of-way on the ground surface for the transportation for compensation of passengers, or passengers and express freight that may be carried in such vehicles, but does not include taxi-cabs or vehicles operated on railroads governed by the laws of Canada or vehicles operated by or for the Province of Ontario. *Regional Municipality of Hamilton-Wentworth Act*, R.S.O. 1980, c. 437, s. 50.

PUBLIC TRUST. A trust established to benefit the public or a section of it. D.M.W. Waters, *The Law of Trusts in Canada*, 2d ed. (Toronto: Carswell, 1984) at 24.

PUBLIC TRUSTEE. A corporation sole which may administer the estates of deceased persons or disabled persons who are mentally incompetent or incapable of managing their affairs but not so declared so that there is no committee of that person's estate. G.D. Watson & C. Perkins, eds., *Holmested & Watson: Ontario Civil Procedure* (Toronto: Carswell, 1984) at 7-4.

PUBLIC UTILITY. 1. Any person or association of persons that owns, operates or manages an undertaking (a) for the supply of petroleum or petroleum products by pipeline; (b) for the supply, transmission or distribution of gas, electricity, steam or water; (c) for the collection and disposal of garbage or sewage or for the control of pollution; (d) for the transmission, emission, reception or conveyance of information by any telecommunication system; or (e) for the provision of postal services. *Statistics Act*, R.S.C. 1985, c. S-19, s. 17(3). 2. Includes any person that may now or hereafter own, operate, manage or control: (i) any tramway; (ii) any trolley bus or motor vehicle for the conveyance of passengers from any point within a city or incorporated town to any other point within such city or town. 3. The right of way for one or more of the following: (i) telecommunications systems; (ii) waterworks systems; (iii) irrigation systems; (iv) systems for the distribution of gas, whether natural or artificial; (v) systems for the distribution of artificial light or electric power; (vi) heating systems; (vii) sewage systems. *Planning Amendment Act, 1984*, S.A. 1984, c. 33, s. 2. 4. Any municipal revenue earning work or utility, and includes the municipal (i) telephone system; (ii) waterworks system; (iii) bus lines or other transportation system; (iv) irrigation system; (v) systems for the distribution of gas, whether natural or artificial; (vi) electric generating plants, artificial light or electric power systems; (vii) heating systems; and (viii) sewage systems, and the service or commodity supplied by any public utility. *Municipal Government Act*, R.S.A. 1980, c. M-26, s. 1. 5. Includes any person engaged in constructing, altering, extending, managing or controlling any purification system. *Environmental Protection Act*, S.P.E.I. 1975, c. 9, s. 1. See OWNER OF A ~.

PUBLIC UTILITY INSTALLATION. Any pole, tower, overhead or underground conduit, any other supporting or sustaining structure, and any trench, together with accessories, susceptible of use for the supply or distribution of electrical, telephone, telegraph, cable delivery or signalling service or any other similar service. *An Act Respecting Certain Public Utility Installations*, R.S.Q. 1977, c. I-13, s. 1.

PUBLIC UTILITY UNDERTAKING. A water works, or water supply system, sewage works, electrical power or energy generating transmission or distribution system, street lighting system, natural or artificial gas works or supply system, and a transportation system, and includes any lands, buildings or equipment required for the administration or operation of any such system. *Municipal Act*, R.S.O. 1980, c. 302, s. 210.

PUBLIC VEHICLE. A motor vehicle operated on a highway by, for, or on behalf of any person who receives compensation either directly or indirectly for the transportation therein of passengers and express freight which might be carried on a passenger vehicle.

PUBLIC WASHROOM. Any room that contains one or more sanitary units and to which (i) employees of a business or institution, (ii) patrons of, or visitors to, a place of business, (iii) students, patients, inmates or visitors of an institution, (iv) the travelling or transient public, or (v) all tenants of an apartment building or condominium, would expect to have the right of access without any special permission from management. *Ontario Water Resources Act*, R.R.O. 1980, Reg. 736, s. 1.

PUBLIC WATER SUPPLY. Includes water being supplied or to be supplied for human consumption to (a) ten or more households; or (b) any business, public building or place of assembly. *Clean Environment Act*, S.N.B. 1975, c. 12, s. 1.

PUBLIC WAY. A sidewalk, street, highway, square or other open space to which the public has access, as of right or by invitation, expressed or implied. *Occupational Health and Safety Act*, R.R.O. 1980, Reg. 691, s. 1.

PUBLIC WHIRLPOOL. A whirlpool that is available for use by the general public and includes a whirlpool located in a hotel, motel, campground, university or a residential property containing more than four living units. *An Act to Amend the Health Act*, S.N.B. 1987, c. 24, s. 1.

PUBLIC WORK. 1. Any work or property under the management, charge and direction or the administration and control of the Minister. *Public Works Act*, R.S.C. 1985, c. P-38, s. 3. 2. Includes all work and properties acquired, made, built, constructed, erected, extended, enlarged, repaired, improved, formed, or excavated, at the expense of the government. 3. Any undertaking carried out by the Crown. 4. Any improvement of a structural nature or other undertaking that is within the jurisdiction of the council of a municipality or a local board. *Planning Act, 1983*, S.O. 1983, c. 1, s. 1.

PUBLIC WORKING CIRCLE. An area of land within the forest land under a forest management plan wherein the cutting of Crown timber thereon is authorized by a timber permit or timber sale. *The Forest Act*, R.S.S. 1978, c. F-19, s. 2.

PUBLIC WORKS CANADA. The federal ministry which manages public works and federal real estate in Canada.

PUBLISH. *v.* 1. With respect to a libel, when he (a) exhibits it in public; (b) causes it to be read or seen; or (c) shows or delivers it, or causes it to be shown or delivered, with intent that it should be read or seen by the person whom it defames or by any other person. *Criminal Code*, R.S.C. 1985, c. C-46, s. 299. 2. Includes transmission, emission, dissemination or the making public of writings, signs, signals, symbols, pictures and sounds of all kinds, from or by a newspaper or from or by broadcasting. *Defamation Act*, S.M. 1980, c. 30, s. 2.

PUBLISHED. *adj.* 1. Published in a daily or weekly newspaper that, in the opinion of the clerk of the municipality, has such circulation within the municipality as to provide reasonable notice to those affected thereby. *Municipal Act*, R.S.O. 1980, c. 302, s. 1. 2. Released for public distribution or sale. *An Act Respecting the Bibliothèque Nationale du Québec*, R.S.Q. 1977, c. B-2, s. 1. 3. Communicated to someone else besides the plaintiff. R.E. Brown, *The Law of Defamation in Canada* (Toronto: Carswell, 1987) at 247.

PUBLISHED IN CANADA. Released in Canada for public distribution or sale, otherwise than

by Her Majesty in right of a province or by a municipality. *National Library Act*, R.S.C. 1985, c. N-12, s. 2.

PUBLISHED MARKET. In respect of a class of securities, a market on which securities of that class are traded if the prices at which they have been traded on that market are regularly published in a bona fide newspaper, news magazine or business or financial publication that is of general and regular paid circulation.

PUBLISHED WORKS. Must be understood, for the purposes of the present Convention, works copies of which have been issued to the public. The representation of a dramatic or dramatico-musical work, the performance of a musical work, the exhibition of a work of art, and the construction of a work of architecture shall not constitute a publication. *Copyright Act*, R.S.C. 1970, c. C-30, schedule III, article 4.

PUBLISHER. *n.* Any person whose main or secondary activity in Québec is the selection and production of a manuscript or a text in the form of a book, its distribution and its putting on sale. *An Act respecting the development of Quebec firms in the book industry*, S.Q. 1979, c. 68, s. 1.

P.U. (C.) BD. *abbr.* Public Utilities (Commissioners') Board.

PUFF. *n.* A statement which praises a seller's goods but which an ordinary, reasonable buyer does not usually regard as important. G.H.L. Fridman, *Sale of Goods in Canada*, 3d ed. (Toronto: Carswell, 1986) at 149-150.

PUFFER. *n.* A person appointed to bid on the part of the seller. *Conveyancing and Law of Property Act*, R.S.O. 1980, c. 90, s. 1.

PUISNE. *adj.* [Fr.] Junior, of lower rank.

PULLORUM TEST OR BLOOD TEST. A test for pullorum disease. *Livestock and Livestock Products Act*, R.S.C. 1985, c. L-9, s. 42.

PULMONARY EDEMA. Escape of circulatory fluid into the lungs. F.A. Jaffe, *A Guide to Pathological Evidence*, 2d ed. (Toronto: Carswell, 1983) at 80.

PULMONARY EMBOLISM. Blockage of the main artery in a lung or its branches by an embolus. F.A. Jaffe, *A Guide to Pathological Evidence*, 2d ed. (Toronto: Carswell, 1983) at 175.

PULP AND PAPER. Includes all forms of processed or manufactured wood pulp, whether ultimately manufactured into paper or otherwise. *Logging Tax Act*, R.S.B.C. 1979, c. 248, s. 1.

PULPWOOD. *n.* Wood other than sawmill

chips, cut and prepared primarily for processing into wood pulp, paper, paper products, compressed board or any product manufactured from wood fibre, excluding lumber.

PULPWOOD BERTH. Any area leased prior to the coming into force of this Act for the cutting of pulpwood. *Forest Act*, R.S.M. 1970, c. F150, s. 2.

PULP YIELD. The number of pounds of oven-dry pulp obtained from 100 pounds of oven-dry wood fed to a digester, conventional stone grinder, refiner or other processing unit that converts wood to pulp. *Pulp and Paper Effluent Regulations*, C.R.C., c. 830, s. 2.

PULSARE. [L.] To accuse; to lay a complaint against.

PULSATOR. *n.* An actor or plaintiff; a prosecutor or complainant.

PULSE. *n.* An intermittent emission of laser radiation for a duration of less than .25 second. *Radiation Emitting Devices Regulations*, C.R.C., c. 1370, s. 1. See BASIC ~ INTERVAL.

PULSE AMPLITUDE. The zero to peak, peak to peak or other specified magnitude of variation of a pulse. *Medical Devices Regulations*, C.R.C., c. 871, s. 1.

PULSE DURATION. 1. The time interval of the wave shape measured in milliseconds at specified reference points. *Medical Devices Regulations*, C.R.C., c. 871, s. 1. 2. The time interval measured between the half-peak power points on the leading and trailing edges. *Radiation Emitting Devices Regulations*, C.R.C., c. 1370, s. 1.

PULSE GENERATOR. That portion of a cardiac pacemaker that produces a periodical electrical pulse and includes the power source and electronic circuit. *Medical Devices Regulations*, C.R.C., c. 871, s. 1.

PULSE INTERVAL. The time between the leading edges of successive pulse generator pulses. *Medical Devices Regulations*, C.R.C., c. 871, s. 1.

PUMP. See CONSUMER ~; GASOLINE ~; HEAT ~; MOTIVE FUEL ~.

PUMPER. *n.* A vessel that is used only for the purpose of pumping fish from a fishing vessel or from fishing gear. *Atlantic Coast Herring Regulations*, C.R.C., c. 804, s. 2.

PUMPING WELL. A chamber, manhole, or other structure used for the installation of portable or temporary pumping equipment. *City of Winnipeg Act*, S.M. 1971, c. 105, s. 453.

PUMP ISLAND. A concrete base, raised at least

4 inches above the vehicle travelled portion of an area adjacent to dispensing equipment, upon which dispensing equipment is mounted. *Gasoline Handling Act*, R.R.O. 1980, Reg. 439, s. 1.

PUMP-OUT FACILITY. A device or equipment for removing sewage from a pleasure boat in which a toilet is installed by the use of hose or pipe connected to a pump or equipment designed to create suction and located other than on the boat from which the sewage is to be removed. *Environmental Protection Act*, R.R.O. 1980, Reg. 310, s. 1.

PUNISHMENT. *n.* A penalty for breaking the law. See ARBITRARY ~; CAPITAL ~; LESS ~; SCALE OF ~S.

PUNITIVE DAMAGES. Basically a windfall award of damages over and above what would ordinarily compensate the plaintiff for whatever wrong was done. It is limited to exceptional cases, where the award is clearly warranted and the defendant's actions deserve condemnation by the court. R.E. Brown, *The Law of Defamation in Canada* (Toronto: Carswell, 1987) at 1061 and 1063-5.

PUPA. *n.* The stage of rest between the larva and the adult form during the metamorphosis of certain insects. F.A. Jaffe, *A Guide to Pathological Evidence*, 2d ed. (Toronto: Carswell, 1983) at 182.

PUPIL. *n.* 1. A person who is enrolled in a school or private school and includes any person who is of compulsory school age. 2. A person to whom education is given for a direct or indirect remuneration. *Private Education Act*, R.S.Q. 1977, c. E-9, s. 1. See CANADA SUPPORTED ~; ELEMENTARY ~; EXCEPTIONAL ~; HALF-TIME ~; HARD TO SERVE ~; QUALIFYING ~; RESIDENT ~; RESIDENT ~S; SECONDARY ~.

PUPIL RECORD. A record in respect of a pupil that is established and maintained by the principal of a school in accordance with this Regulation. *Education Act*, R.R.O. 1980, Reg. 271, s. 1.

PUPIL TEACHER. A candidate for a certificate or licence. *Education (Teacher Training) Act*, R.S.Nfld. 1970, c. 103, s. 2.

PUR AUTRE VIE. [Fr.] For or during the life of another. See ESTATE ~.

PUR CAUSE DE VICINAGE. By reason of neighbourhood.

PURCHASE. *v.* See OFFER TO ~; TO ~.

PURCHASE. *n.* Contract, conveyance or assignment under or by which any beneficial interest in any kind of property may be acquired.

See CASH ~ TICKET; COMPULSORY ~; CONSUMER ~; HOME ~ LOAN.

PURCHASE AGREEMENT. 1. An agreement for the sale and purchase of residential premises. 2. An agreement for the purchase of a prearranged funeral plan, a preneed cemetery plan or a cemetery lot for use at a future date or the right to use such a lot. *Cemetery and Funeral Services Act*, S.N.S. 1983, c. 4, s. 2.

PURCHASE FINANCING TRANSACTION. The extension of credit to a borrower by a creditor where the creditor knows or ought to know that the credit proceeds will be used by the borrower to purchase goods or services from a seller. *Consumer Protection Act*, R.S.B.C. 1979, c. 65, s. 1.

PURCHASE FOR CANCELLATION. In relation to mutual fund shares of the company, be deemed to be a reference to acceptance by the company of the surrender of those shares. *Companies Act*, R.S.N.W.T. 1974, c. C-7, s. 71.

PURCHASE MONEY. Includes the consideration for a lease. Companies acts.

PURCHASE-MONEY MORTGAGE. A mortgage given by a purchaser of land to the vendor of the land or the vendor's nominee as security for the payment of all or part of the consideration for the sale.

PURCHASE-MONEY SECURITY INTEREST. *var.* **PURCHASE MONEY SECURITY INTEREST.** A security interest that is: (i) taken or reserved by the seller of the collateral to secure payment of all or part of its price; or (ii) taken by a person who gives value that enables the debtor to acquire rights in or the use of the collateral, if such value is applied to acquire such rights.

PURCHASE PRICE. 1. The entire consideration for the purchase, delivery and installation of a property and, without restricting the generality of the foregoing, includes the value of property given in exchange or trade and outstanding obligations or liabilities cancelled, assumed or satisfied. *Assessment Act*, S.N.S. 1986, c. 22, s. 9. 2. The total value of the consideration or such part thereof as has been paid by the consumer to the retail seller or his assignee for a consumer product and includes such finance charges or other credit costs that the consumer has reasonably incurred respecting the product. *The Consumer Products Warranties Act*, R.S.S. 1978, c. C-30, s. 2. 3. The price for which accommodation is purchased, including the price in money, the value of services rendered, and other considerations accepted by the operator in return for the accommodation provided. *Hotel Room Tax Act*,

R.S.B.C. 1979, c. 183, s. 1. 4. The total obligation payable by the buyer under an executory contract. *Consumer Protection Act*, R.S.O. 1980, c. 87, s. 1. 5. Includes a price in money and also the value of services rendered, the actual value of the thing exchanged and other considerations accepted by the seller or person from whom the property passes as price or on account of the price of the thing covered by the contract, sale or exchange, and includes (i) customs and excise; (ii) charges for installation of the thing sold, for interest, for finance, for service and for transportation, unless such charges are shown separately, on the invoice or in the contract with the purchaser.

PURCHASER. *n.* 1. A person who buys or agrees to buy goods or services. 2. A person who takes by sale, mortgage, hypothec, pledge, issue, reissue, gift or any other voluntary transaction creating an interest in a security. 3. Includes a lessee, a mortgagee and an intending purchaser, lessee or mortgagee, or other person, who, for valuable consideration, takes or deals for any property. Conveyancing acts. 4. Includes a person who barters or exchanges property whether real or personal with any other person for stock in bulk. Bulk Sales acts. 5. Includes mortgagee and pledgee. Warehouse Receipts acts. 6. A person who is purchasing or has purchased or is otherwise acquiring or has acquired land or improvements and has not disposed of his interest to another person, but has not yet become the legal owner of the land or improvements, whether he purchases or otherwise acquires the land from the owner directly or indirectly. *Municipal Taxation Act*, R.S.A. 1980, c. M-31, s. 1. See BONA FIDE ~; DOMESTIC ~; INTERMEDIATE ~; RETAIL ~; SUBSEQUENT ~; SUBSEQUENT ~ OR MORTGAGEE; TAX ~.

PURCHASER FOR VALUE WITHOUT NOTICE. One who purchased property bona fide for a valuable, even if inadequate, consideration without notice of any prior title or right that, if upheld, would restrict or limit the title which the purchaser supposedly acquired.

PURCHASER'S COST OF A SHARE. The price paid for a share plus any reasonable expenses and fees for that purchase. W. Grover & F. Iacobucci, *Materials on Canadian Income Tax*, 4th ed. (Toronto: Richard De Boo Ltd., 1980) at 894.

PURCHASER'S LIEN. A lien which protects the deposit and any other money that a person who agreed to purchase land paid on account of the purchase price, as well as costs and interest. B.J. Reiter, R.C.B. Risk & B.N. McLellan, *Real Estate Law*, 3d ed. (Toronto: Emond Montgomery, 1986) at 909.

PURE-BRED. *adj.* 1. Registered in, or eligible for registration in, the records of an association. *Livestock Pedigree Act*, R.S.C. 1985, c. L-11, s. 2. 2. (i) Registered or eligible for registration in the register of The Canadian Kennel Club, Incorporated; or (ii) of a class designated as pure-bred in the regulations. *Dog Licensing and Live Stock and Poultry Protection Act*, R.S.O. 1980, c. 123, s. 1.

PURE-BRED BULL. Bull registered in a herd-book kept or recognized by the Department. *Agriculture and Marketing Act*, R.S.N.S. 1967, c. 3, s. 44.

PURE-BRED CATTLE. Cattle registered in the Canadian National Livestock Records or in any records recognized by the Canadian National Livestock Record Committee.

PURE TAX HAVEN. A country, often an island, which imposes minimal taxes to get not only the benefits of active business but spin off benefits like financial institutions and greater numbers of professional jobs. W. Grover & F. Iacobucci, *Materials on Canadian Income Tax*, 4th ed. (Toronto: Richard De Boo Ltd., 1980) at 712.

PURE WATER AREAS. Waters approved by the Department of National Health and Welfare for the taking of shellfish. Fishery regulations.

PURGE. *v.* With respect to contempt, to make amends for or clear oneself of contempt of court.

PURIFICATION SYSTEM. Includes any plant or installation used, or designed to be used, for the improvement of the physical, chemical, biological or aesthetic properties of land, air, or water.

PURIFICATION WORKS. A sewer, a sewer system, a waste water pumping station, a water purification station or any other works used to collect, receive, carry, treat or drain waste water, or a part of any such equipment. *An Act to Amend the Act Respecting the Communauté Urbaine de Montréal and Other Legislation*, S.Q. 1985, c. 31, s. 11. See WATER ~.

PURPARTY. *n.* A portion or share; to hold land in purparty with someone is to hold it jointly with that person.

PURPOSE. See ADMINISTRATIVE ~; CHARITABLE ~; CHARITABLE ~S; CONSERVATION ~; CONVEYING ~; DOMESTIC ~; EMPLOYMENT ~S; FARMING ~S; FORESTRY ~S; HYDRAULICKING ~; INDUSTRIAL ~S; IRRIGATION ~; LAND IMPROVEMENT ~; MINERAL TRADING ~; MINERAL WATER ~S; MINING ~; MINING ~S; MUNICIPAL ~; POWER ~; RIVER IMPROVEMENT ~.

PURPOSES RELATING TO THE BUSINESS OF A DEALER. Includes personal use of dealers' vehicles by the dealer, his vehicle salesmen and members of their households; but does not include use of vehicles to generate revenue through rental, leasing or other means other than bona fide sale to a purchaser. *Motor Vehicle Act*, R.S.B.C. 1979, c. 288, s. 34.

PURPRESTURE. *n.* [Fr.] Anything which annoys or harms the Crown's demesnes or highways by enclosing, building or endeavouring to make private something which should be public.

PURSE. *n.* The money or other prize that is paid to the owners of horses that compete in a race. *Race Track Supervision Regulations*, C.R.C., c. 441, s. 2.

PURSE SEINE NET. A net that is weighted at the bottom and mounted with rings through which a line is run, floated at the top, cast from a boat so as to enclose an area of water and then closed at the bottom by the line through the rings to form a purse or bag. Fishery regulations.

PURSUE. *v.* Of an authority or warrant, to execute or carry it out.

PURSUIVANT. *n.* A royal messenger.

PURVEYANCE. *n.* The provision of necessaries for a sovereign.

PURVEYOR. *n.* One who buys; the person who provided for a royal household. See WATER ~.

PURVIEW. *n.* The policy or scope of a statute.

PUSH-OUT WINDOW. A vehicle window designed to open outward to provide for emergency egress. Motor Vehicle Safety Regulations, C.R.C., c. 1038, s. 2.

PUT. *v.* With respect to a question, to read a motion or amendment from the Chair, seeking the House's pleasure. A. Fraser, G.A. Birch & W.A. Dawson, eds., *Beauchesne's Rules and Forms of the House of Commons of Canada*, 5th ed. (Toronto: Carswell, 1978) at 75.

PUT. *n.* An option transferable by delivery to deliver a specified number or amount of securities at a fixed price within a specified time.

PUTATIVE. *adj.* Supposed, reputed.

PUTATIVE FATHER. A person alleged to have caused the pregnancy whereby a woman has become a mother.

PUTATIVE JUSTIFICATION. A situation in which an accused genuinely believes that the act was justified in law but, on the facts as the accused believed them, no such legal justification exists. D. Stuart, *Canadian Criminal Law:*

a treatise, 2d ed. (Toronto: Carswell, 1987) at 392.

PUTREFACTION. *n.* The disintegration of the tissues caused by bacterial action. F.A. Jaffe, *A Guide to Pathological Evidence*, 2d ed. (Toronto: Carswell, 1983) at 182.

PUTREFACTIVE GASES. Gases which develop during putrefaction, especially hydrogen sulphide, ammonia, methane and carbon dioxide. F.A. Jaffe, *A Guide to Pathological Evidence*, 2d ed. (Toronto: Carswell, 1983) at 182.

PYKE. *abbr.* Pyke's Reports, King's Bench (Que.), 1809-1810.

PYRAMID. *v.* For an employee to work during certain hours which seem to attract premium rates under two different provisions of a collective agreement. Most frequently this occurs when an employee claims both a shift premium and an overtime premium for the same hours worked or when overtime pay is computed so that it includes work performed on a weekend or holiday. D.J.M. Brown and D.M. Beatty, *Canadian Labour Arbitration*, 2d ed. (Aurora: Canada Law Book, 1977) at 549.

PYRAMID DISTRIBUTOR. Any person who distributes for valuable consideration goods or services through a marketing scheme involving independent agents, contractors or distributors, at different levels, where participants in the marketing scheme may or are required to recruit other participants, and where commissions or other consideration are or may be paid or allowed as a result of the sale of those goods or services to others or the recruitment, actions or performances of additional participants, and includes any person or class of persons designated as a pyramid distributor by the Lieutenant Governor in Council. *Pyramid Distribution Act*, R.S.B.C. 1979, c. 351, s. 3.

PYRAMID FRANCHISE. An agreement or arrangement, expressed or implied, oral or written, between two or more persons by which a franchisee upon paying a franchise fee or upon purchasing goods is granted the right: (i) to offer to sell, sell or distribute goods; and (ii) to recruit one or more persons who upon paying a franchise fee or upon purchasing goods are granted the same or similar rights; under a marketing plan or system, organized, directed, prescribed or controlled, in substantial part, by a franchisor. *The Pyramid Franchises Act*, R.S.S. 1978, c. P-50, s. 2.

PYRAMID SALES FRANCHISE. A scheme, arrangement, device or other means whereby a participant pays a franchise fee and (i) is required or receives the right to recruit one or more other persons as participants who are subject to a similar requirement or who obtain a similar right; and (ii) has the right to receive money, credits, discounts, goods or any other right or thing of value the amount of which is dependent on the number of participants. *Franchises Act*, R.S.A. 1980, c. F-17, s. 1.

PYRAMID SELLING. See SCHEME OF ~.

Q

Q.A.C. *abbr.* Causes en appel au Québec (Quebec Appeal Cases).

Q.B. *abbr.* 1. Queen's Bench. 2. Court of Queen's Bench. 3. Supreme Court, Queen's Bench Division.

[ ] Q.B. *abbr.* Law Reports, Queen's Bench, 1891-.

Q.B.D. *abbr.* 1. Queen's Bench Division. 2. Law Reports, Queen's Bench Division, 1875-1890.

Q.C. *abbr.* Queen's Counsel.

Q.L.R. *abbr.* Quebec Law Reports, 1875-1891 (Rapports judiciaires du Québec).

QR & O. *abbr.* Queen's Regulations and Orders.

QUA. *adv.* [L.] As, in the aspect of.

QUACUNQUE VIA DATA. [L.] Whichever way is given.

QUADACTOR. *n.* A betting transaction in which a purchaser of a ticket undertakes to select, in the exact order of finish, the first four horses to finish in the race on which that feature is operated. *Race Track Supervision Regulations,* C.R.C., c. 441, s. 2.

QUADRANT. *n.* 1. A measure of a 90 degree angle. 2. An instrument used in navigation and astronomy.

QUADRIPARTITE. *adj.* Having four parts or parties.

QUAE AB INITIO INUTILIS FUIT INSTITU-TIO, EX POST FACTO CONVALESCERE NON POTEST. [L.] What was a useless institution from the beginning cannot be strengthened by anything done after.

QUAE ACCESSIONUM LOCUM OBTINENT EXTINGUUNTUR CUM PRINCIPALES RES PEREMPTAE FUERINT. [L.] Things which are incidental are extinguished when the principal things are extinguished.

QUAE AD UNUM FINEM LOQUUTA SUNT, NON DEBENT AD ALIUM DETORQUERI. [L.] Things which are said for one purpose should not be distorted to another.

QUAE COMMUNI LEGE DEROGANT STRICTE INTERPRETANTUR. [L.] Things which detract from the common law should be interpreted narrowly.

QUAE CONTRA RATIONEM JURIS INTRO-DUCTA SUNT, NON DEBENT TRAHI IN CONSEQUENTIAM. [L.] Things introduced which contradict a rule of law should not be drawn into precedent.

QUAE DUBITATIONIS TOLLENDAE CAUSA INSERUNTUR, COMMUNEM LEGEM NON LAEDUNT. [L.] Things inserted to remove doubt do not harm the common law.

QUAE EST EADEM. [L.] Which is the same.

QUAE IN CURIA REGIS ACTA SUNT RITE AGI PRAESUMUNTUR. [L.] Things done in a sovereign's court are presumed to be done correctly.

QUAE IN TESTAMENTO ITA SUNT SCRIPTA, UT INTELLIGI NON POSSINT, PERINDE SUNT AC SI SCRIPTA NON ESSENT. [L.] Things in a will which were written so that they cannot be understood are just as if they had not been written.

QUAELIBET CONCESSIO FORTISSIME CONTRA DONATOREM INTERPRETANDA EST. [L.] Every grant should be construed in the strongest way against the grantor.

QUAELIBET POENA CORPORALIS, QUAMVIS MINIMA, MAJOR EST QUA-LIBET POENA PECUNIARIA. [L.] Whatever the corporal punishment and however slight, it is greater than any fine.

QUAE MALA SUNT INCHOATA IN PRINCI-PIO VIX BONO PERANGUNTUR EXITU. [L.] Things bad in the beginning can hardly be brought to a good end.

QUAE NON VALEANT SINGULA JUNCTA JUVANT. [L.] Words which have no effect alone are effective when combined.

QUAE PLURA. [L.] Of what more.

QUAERE. [L.] Inquire.

QUALIFICATION. *n.* 1. What makes anyone fit to do a particular act. 2. Limitation; diminishing. 3. Of an expert witness, ability to be an expert established after hearing evidence for and against, and after cross-examination. P.K. McWilliams, *Canadian Criminal Evidence*, 3d ed. (Aurora: Canada Law Book, 1988) at 9-10. See DESIRABLE ~S; ESSENTIAL ~S.

QUALIFIED. *adj.* 1. Properly qualified to perform any specified duty or do any specified act. *Metalliferous Mines and Quarries Regulation Act*, R.S.N.S. 1967, c. 183, s. 1. 2. In respect of a farmer, fisherman, hunter, trapper or other person, means a farmer, fisherman, hunter, trapper or person who holds a sales tax bulk permit issued under regulations made pursuant to subsection (10). *Excise Tax Act*, R.S.C. 1985 (2d Supp.), c. 7, s. 69. 3. Used in connection with a tradesman or a trade, the expression includes a tradesman in that trade who holds a valid subsisting certificate of proficiency in that trade. *Apprenticeship and Tradesmen's Qualification Act*, R.S.P.E.I. 1974, c. A-13, s. 1. See DULY ~; LEGALLY ~.

QUALIFIED ACCEPTANCE. An acceptance with some change in the effect of the bill as originally drawn.

QUALIFIED APPRAISER. A person who: (i) is a member in good standing for a continuous period of not less than 2 years, of (A) The Appraisal Institute of Canada and has been designated as a member (C.R.A.) or accredited member (A.A.C.I.); (B) The Royal Institute of Chartered Surveyors (Britain) and has been designated A.R.I.C.S. or F.R.I.C.S. under its Valuation Subdivision; (C) The American Institute of Real Estate Appraisers and has been designated M.A.I.; (D) The Society of Residential Appraisers; or (E) Corporation des Évaluateurs Agréé du Québec; or (ii) has been employed or in public practice primarily as a property appraiser for a period of not less than 5 years. *Insurance Act*, R.R.O. 1980, Reg. 536, s. 1. See INDEPENDENT ~.

QUALIFIED ASSETS. 1. (i) Cash; (ii) first mortgages on improved real estate and first mortgages made under the *National Housing Act*, R.S.C. 1952, c. 188 or the *National Housing Act*, R.S.C. 1970, c. N-10; (iii) bonds, debentures, stocks and other securities of the classes authorized under the Canadian and British Insurance Companies Act (Canada) for the investments of the funds of companies registered thereunder; (iv) real property acquired by foreclosure or in satisfaction of a debt and held for a period of less than 7 years; and (v) any other investments or securities designated by the regulations. Investment Contracts acts. 2. (i) Cash; (ii) bonds, debentures, stocks, other evidences of indebtedness and other securities, in which or on the security of which an issuer is authorized by this Act to invest or lend its funds; (iii) real property which an issuer is authorized to acquire and hold pursuant to this Act; when valued under section 28. *The Investment Contracts Act*, R.S.S. 1978, c. I-14, s. 2.

QUALIFIED AUDITOR. A professional auditor or a firm of professional auditors. *Provincial Auditor's Act*, S.M. 1979, c. 12, s. 1.

QUALIFIED BID. A bid that meets the specifications of the tender. *The Provincial Preference Act*, S.Nfld. 1984, c. 37, s. 2.

QUALIFIED DEALER. 1. A person who has a permanent establishment in Saskatchewan and: (i) is a member of the Investment Dealers Association of Canada; or (ii) is a member of: (A) the Vancouver Stock Exchange; (B) the Alberta Stock Exchange; (C) the Toronto Stock Exchange; or (D) the Montreal Stock Exchange. *Stock Savings Tax Credit Act*, S.S. 1986, c. 59.1, s. 2. 2. A person who (i) is registered to trade in securities as principal or agent under the Securities Act; (ii) is a member of the Alberta Stock Exchange; and (iii) has a permanent establishment in Alberta. *Alberta Stock Savings Plan Act*, S.A. 1986, c. A-37.7, s. 1.

QUALIFIED ELECTOR. A person qualified under the Act to vote in a polling division at a general election. *Canada Elections Act*, R.S.C. 1970 (1st Supp.), c. 14, Schedule IV, s. 2.

QUALIFIED ELECTRICAL WORKER. A person who is the holder of a valid electrician's certificate issued in the Territories or in a province, or such other person as may be approved by the Chief Inspector pursuant to section 5. *Electrical Protection Act*, S.N.W.T. 1975 (3d Sess.), c. 3, s. 2.

QUALIFIED EMPLOYEE. An employee who has been determined by the Commission pursuant to this Act to be qualified to receive labour adjustment benefits. *Labour Adjustment Benefits Act*, R.S.C. 1985, c. L-1, s. 2.

QUALIFIED INDORSEMENT. An indorsement with no recourse to the indorser for payment.

QUALIFIED INVESTMENT. 1. For a trust governed by a deferred profit sharing plan or revoked plan means (i) money that is legal tender in Canada, other than money the fair market value of which exceeds its stated value as legal tender, and deposits (within the meaning assigned by the Canada Deposit Insurance Corporation Act or with a bank to which the Bank Act or the Quebec Savings Bank Act applies) of such money standing to the credit of the trust; (ii) bonds, debentures, notes, mortgages, hypothecs or similar obligations described in clause 212(1)(b)(ii)(C), whether issued before, on or after April 15, 1966; (iii) bonds, debentures, notes or similar obligations of a corporation the shares of which are listed on a prescribed stock exchange in Canada, other than those described in paragraph 147(2)(c); (iv) shares listed on a prescribed stock exchange in Canada; (v) [Repealed.] (vi) equity shares of a corporation by which, before the date of acquisition by the trust of the shares, payments have been made in trust to a trustee under the plan for the benefit of beneficiaries thereunder, if the shares are of a class in respect of which (A) there is no restriction on their transferability, and (B) in each of 4 taxation years of the corporation in the period of the corporation's 5 consecutive taxation years that ended less than 12 months before the date of acquisition of the shares by the trust, and in the corporation's last taxation year in that period, the corporation (I) paid a dividend on each share of the class of an amount not less than 4% of the cost per share of the shares to the trust; or (II) had earnings attributable to the shares of the class of an amount not less than the amount obtained when 4% of the cost per share to the trust of the shares is multiplied by the total number of shares of the class that were outstanding immediately after such acquisition; (vii) guaranteed investment certificates issued by a trust company incorporated under the laws of Canada or of a province; (viii) investment contracts described in clause 146(1)(j)(ii)(B) and issued by a corporation approved by the Governor in Council for the purposes of that clause; (ix) shares listed on a prescribed stock exchange in a country other than Canada; and (x) such other investments as may be prescribed by regulations of the Governor in Council made on the recommendation of the Minister of Finance. *Income Tax Act*, R.S.C. 1952, c. 148 (as am. S.C. 1980-81-82-83, c. 48, s. 93(1), (2)), s. 204(e). 2. For a trust governed by a registered retirement savings plan means (i) an investment that would be described in any of subparagraphs (i) to (ix) (except subparagraphs (iii) and (vi)) of paragraph 204(e) if the references therein to a trust were read as references to the trust governed by the registered retirement savings plan; (ii) a bond, debenture, note or similar obligation of a corporation the shares of which are listed on a prescribed stock exchange in Canada; (iii) an annuity described in paragraph (i.1) in respect of the annuitant

under the plan, if purchased from a person licensed or otherwise authorized under the laws of Canada or a province to carry on in Canada an annuities business; and (iv) such other investments as may be prescribed by regulations of the Governor in Council made on the recommendation of the Minister of Finance. *Income Tax Act*, R.S.C. 1952, c. 148 (as am. S.C. 1980-81-82-83, c. 140, s. 98(3)), s. 146(1)(g). 3. For a trust governed by a registered retirement income fund means (i) an investment that would be described in any of subparagraphs 204(e)(i) to (ix) (except subparagraphs (iii) and (vi) thereof) if the reference in paragraph 204(e) to "a trust governed by a deferred profit sharing plan or revoked plan" were read as a reference to "a trust governed by a registered retirement income fund"; (ii) a bond, debenture, note or similar obligation of a corporation the shares of which are listed on a prescribed stock exchange in Canada; and (iii) such other investments as may be prescribed by regulations of the Governor in Council made on the recommendation of the Minister of Finance. *Income Tax Act*, R.S.C. 1952, c. 148 (as am. S.C. 1980-81-82-83, c. 48, s. 81(1)), s. 146.3(1)(d).

QUALIFIED MEDICAL DOCTOR. A person licensed to practise medicine in Canada. *Canada First-Aid Regulations*, C.R.C., c. 1001, s. 2.

QUALIFIED MEDICAL PRACTITIONER. A person duly qualified by provincial law to practise medicine.

QUALIFIED PERSON. 1. A person who, because of knowledge, training and experience, is qualified to perform, safely and properly, a specified job. Canada regulations. 2. (a) In respect of work that is required by law to be performed by the holder of a licence, certificate or other authority; a person who is the holder of such licence, certificate or other authority; and (b) in respect of work that is not required by law to be performed by the holder of a licence, certificate or other authority, a person who, in the opinion of his employer, possesses the knowledge and experience necessary to perform the work safely and competently. *Safe Working Practices Regulations*, C.R.C., c. 1467, s. 2. 3. A person who is growing an insurable crop for sale on one or more acres of land in a province. 4. A person qualified under section 3 to receive benefits of health insurance conferred by this Act. *The Saskatchewan Health Insurance Act*, R.S.S. 1978, c. S-21, s. 2. 5. A person prescribed as being qualified to receive an incentive in the circumstances prescribed or a partner of a partnership who has, pursuant to section 5, been approved by the Minister as being the person qualified to receive an incentive. *Petroleum Incentives Program Act*, R.S.C. 1985, c. P-13, s.

2. 6. A person duly qualified by provincial law to practise medicine or psychiatry or to carry out psychological examinations or assessments, as the circumstances require, or, where no such law exists, a person who is, in the opinion of the youth court, so qualified, and includes a person or a person within a class of persons designated by the Lieutenant Governor in Council of a province or his delegate. *Young Offenders Act*, R.S.C. 1985, c. Y-1, s. 13(11).

QUALIFIED PLUMBER. A person who holds a certificate of qualification in the plumbing trade issued under the Industrial Training and Certification Act, and a licence issued pursuant to this Act and regulations or a licence issued pursuant to a by-law made pursuant to section 6. *Plumbing Installation and Inspection Act*, S.N.B. 1976, c. P-9.1, s. 1.

QUALIFIED PRIVILEGE. Prevents defamatory remarks being actionable if they are made by someone discharging a public or private duty, pursuing or protecting the private interest of either the publisher, the person defamed or a third person and if the publication was made to someone who has a similar interest in receiving the information. Only if the defendant showed actual or express malice can the action be maintained. R.E. Brown, *The Law of Defamation in Canada* (Toronto: Carswell, 1987) at 12 and 465.

QUALIFIED PRODUCER. A producer who produces qualifying milk. *Milk Industry Act*, R.S.B.C. 1979, c. 258, s. 1.

QUALIFIED PROPERTY. Limited and special ownership.

QUALIFIED TECHNICIAN. (a) In respect of breath samples, a person designated by the Attorney General as being qualified to operate an approved instrument; and (b) in respect of blood samples, any person or person of a class of persons designated by the Attorney General as being qualified to take samples of blood for the purposes of this section and sections 256 and 258. *Criminal Code*, R.S.C. 1985, c. C-46, s. 254(1) as am. by *Criminal Law Amendment Act*, R.S.C. 1985 (1st Supp.), c. 27, s. 36.

QUALIFIED TITLE. A registered title which is subject to an excepted estate, interest or right arising under a particular instrument or before a particular date, or otherwise specifically described in the register.

QUALIFIED VOTER. A person who (i) is a Canadian citizen; (ii) has attained the age of 19 years; and (iii) has been ordinarily resident in the settlement, municipality or area in which a plebiscite is to be held for a period of not less than 1 year immediately preceding the date set for voting. *Liquor Act*, S.N.W.T. 1983 (1st Sess.), c. 26, s. 2.

QUALIFY. *v.* To become legally entitled.

QUALIFYING CORPORATION. For a particular taxation year means a corporation that is, throughout the particular year, a Canadian-controlled private corporation whose taxable income for the immediately preceding taxation year together with the taxable incomes of all corporations with which it was associated in the particular year for their taxation years ending in the calendar year immediately preceding the calendar year in which the particular year of the corporation ended does not exceed the aggregate of the business limits (as determined under section 125) of the corporation and the associated corporations for those preceding years. *Income Tax Act*, R.S.C. 1952, c. 148 (as am. S.C. 1986, c. 6, s. 72), s. 127.1(2).

QUALIFYING EDUCATIONAL PROGRAM. A program of not less than 3 consecutive weeks duration that provides that each student taking the program spend not less than 10 hours per week on courses or work in the program and, in respect of a program at an institution described in subparagraph (a)(i) of the definition "designated educational institution", that is a program at a post-secondary school level but, in relation to any particular student, does not include any such program (a) if the student receives, from a person with whom he is dealing at arm's length, any allowance, benefit, grant or reimbursement for expenses in respect of the program other than (i) an amount received by the student as or on account of a scholarship, fellowship or bursary, or a prize for achievement in a field of endeavour ordinarily carried on by him; or (ii) a benefit, if any, received by him by reason of a loan made to him in accordance with the requirements of the Canada Student Loans Act or the Student Loans and Scholarships Act of the province of Quebec; or (b) if the program is taken by the student (i) during a period in respect of which he receives income from an office or employment; and (ii) in connection with, or as part of the duties of, that office or employment. *Income Tax Act*, R.S.C. 1952, c. 148 (as am. S.C. 1988, c. 55, s. 92), s. 118.6(1).

QUALIFYING EXAMINATION. See PARTNERS', DIRECTORS' AND SENIOR OFFICERS' ~.

QUALIFYING MILK. Milk which (a) is produced on an approved fluid milk dairy farm or an approved raw milk dairy farm certified as such; and (b) meets the standards for such milk prescribed by regulation under this Act. *Milk Industry Act*, R.S.B.C. 1979, c. 258, s. 1.

QUALIFYING PUPIL. A person (a) enrolled in an independent school to receive tuition through it for at least 135 days related to the school year, as prescribed by the regulations, for which a grant application is made under this Act; and (b) of school age as determined under the School Act during that school year or, where enrolled in kindergarten, not more than 1 year under school age as determined under the School Act during that school year, who has a parent or guardian resident in the Province, and (c) has a parent who is a Canadian citizen or has been lawfully admitted to Canada under the Immigration Act (Canada) for permanent residence; or (d) had a parent who, at the time of the death of that parent, satisfied the requirements of paragraph (c), and includes a qualifying pupil as defined in the regulations. *School Support (Independent) Act*, R.S.B.C. 1979, c. 378, s. 1.

QUALIFYING STUDENT. A person (a) who is a Canadian citizen or a permanent resident within the meaning of the Immigration Act; (b) who is qualified for enrolment or is enrolled at a specified educational institution as a full-time or part-time student for a period of studies at a post-secondary school level; and (c) who intends to attend at a specified educational institution as a full-time or part-time student for a period of studies described in paragraph (b) if it is financially possible for that person to do so. *Canada Student Loan Act*, R.S.C. 1985, c. S-23, s. 2.

QUALITY. See ACCEPTABLE ~; MERCHANTABLE ~.

QUALITY MARK. A mark indicating or purporting to indicate the quality, quantity, fineness, weight, thickness, proportion or kind of precious metal in an article. *Precious Metals Marking Act*, R.S.C. 1985, c. P-19, s. 2.

QUALITY OF ESTATE. The manner in which and the period during which one exercises the right to enjoy an estate or interest.

QUALITY OF GOODS. Includes their state or condition. Sale of Goods acts.

QUAMDIU SE BENE GESSERIT. [L. as long as one behaves oneself well] A clause used in connection with appointment to an office such as judge, and contrasted in meaning to *durante bene placito* (during the pleasure of the appointing body).

QUAM LONGUM DEBET ESSE RATIONABILE TEMPUS, NON DEFINITUR IN LEGE, SED PENDET EX DISCRETIONE JUSTICIARIORUM. [L.] How long a reasonable time should be is not defined in law, but depends on the discretion of judges.

QUANDO ABEST PROVISIO PARTIS, ADEST PROVISIO LEGIS. [L.] When a party's provision is wanting, the provision of the law is there.

QUANDO ALIQUID MANDATUR, MANDATUR ET OMNE PER QUOD PERVENITUR AD ILLUD. [L.] When anything is ordered, everything by which it will be accomplished is ordered too.

QUANDO ALIQUID PROHIBETUR FIERI, PROHIBETUR EX DIRECTO ET PER OBLIQUUM. [L.] When doing anything is prohibited, doing it both directly and indirectly is prohibited.

QUANDO ALIQUID PROHIBETUR, PROHIBETUR ET OMNE PER QUOD DEVENITUR AD ILLUD. [L.] To effectively carry out the object of a statute, one must construe it so that any attempt to do or avoid doing indirectly or circuitously what the statute prohibited or enjoined is not permitted. P. St. J. Langan, ed., *Maxwell on The Interpretation of Statutes*, 12th ed. (Bombay: N.M. Tripathi, 1976) at 137.

QUANDO DUO JURA IN UNA PERSONA CONCURRUNT, AEQUUM EST AD SI ESSENT IN DIVERSIS. [L.] When two titles come together in one person, it is as if they were in different people.

QUANDO JUS DOMINI REGIS ET SUBDITI CONCURRUNT JUS REGIS PRAEFERRI DEBET. [L.] When the titles of the sovereign and a subject concur, the sovereign's should be preferred.

QUANDO LEX ALIQUID ALICUI CONCEDIT, CONCEDERE VIDETUR ID SINE QUO RES IPSA ESSE NON POTEST. [L.] When the law gives something to someone, it is considered to also give that without which the very thing could not exist.

QUANDO LEX EST SPECIALIS, RATIO AUTEM GENERALIS, GENERALITER LEX EST INTELLIGENDA. [L.] Where a law is special, though its reason general, the law should be understood generally.

QUANDO PLUS FIT QUAM FIERI DEBET, VIDETUR ETIAM ILLUD FIERI QUOD FACIENDUM EST. [L.] When more is done than should be done, then it is considered that what should have been done was done.

QUANDO RES NON VALET UT AGO, VALEAT QUANTUM VALERE POTEST. [L.] When a thing does not operate the way I intend, let it operate as much as it can.

QUANDO VERBA STATUTI SUNT SPECIALIA, RATIO AUTEM GENERALIS, GENERALITER STATUTUM EST INTELLIGENDUM. [L.] When the words of a statute are special, though its reason is general, the statute should be understood generally.

QUANTITY. See PAYING ~.

QUANTITY OF ESTATE. The time in which an estate or interest continues.

QUANTITY THEORY OF MONEY. Because the level of prices is made a function of money supply, any decrease or increase in the money supply leads to a proportionate decline or increase in the price level. W. Grover & F. Iacobucci, *Materials on Canadian Income Tax*, 4th ed. (Toronto: Richard De Boo Ltd., 1980) at 16.

QUANTUM. *n.* [L.] An amount.

QUANTUM DAMNIFICATUS. [L.] The amount of damage which one suffered.

QUANTUM MERUIT. [L. as much as one earned] A payment based on the value of the services in question. G.H.L. Fridman, *The Law of Contract in Canada*, 2d ed. (Toronto: Carswell, 1986) at 13.

QUANTUM VALEBANT. [L. as much as they were worth] A claim for goods "sold" or provided another way. G.H.L. Fridman & J.G. McLeod, *Restitution* (Toronto: Carswell, 1982) at 43.

QUARANTINE. *n.* (i) In respect of a person or animals, the limitation of freedom of movement and contact with other persons or animals; and (ii) in respect of premises, the prohibition against or the limitation on entering or leaving the premises, during the incubation period of the communicable disease in respect of which the quarantine is imposed.

QUARANTINE AREA. An area designated as a quarantine area pursuant to section 3. *Quarantine Act*, R.S.C. 1985, c. Q-1, s. 2.

QUARANTINE PORT. A place where facilities exist to quarantine animals. *Animal Disease and Protection Regulations*, C.R.C., c. 296, s. 2.

QUARE. [L.] Inquire.

QUARE CLAUSUM FREGIT. [L. why one broke the close] Trespass on the plaintiff's lands.

QUARREL. *n.* A contest; a dispute.

QUARRIABLE MINERAL. (i) A mineral that can be quarried and used in its natural state for building, construction, industrial, manufacturing or agricultural purposes including, without limitation, anhydrite, bentonite, diatomite, gypsum, granite, limestone, marble, mica, potash, quartz rock, rock phosphate, sandstone, shale, slate, talc or volcanic ash; or (ii) a mineral that can be quarried and cut or polished for use as an ornament, a decoration or for personal adorn-

ment, but does not include coal or oil sands. *Mines and Minerals Amendment Act, 1983*, S.A. 1983, c. 36, s. 2.

QUARRIABLE SUBSTANCE. Ordinary stone, building or construction stone, sand, gravel, peat, peat moss, clay and soil. *Quarriable Substances Act*, S.N.B. 1980, c. 45, s. 1.

QUARRY. *n.* 1. A pit or excavation in the ground made for the purpose of removing, opening up or proving any mineral other than coal. 2. An open cut from which rock is cut or taken. *The Workmen's Compensation Act*, R.S.S. 1978, c. W-18, s. 3. 3. Any opening or excavation in the ground for the purpose of searching for or removing earth, clay, sand, gravel, rock, building stone, limestone, marble, gypsum or marl, and any place or operation classified by the Deputy Minister as a quarry pursuant to this Act; and includes all works, machinery, plant, buildings, and premises below or above ground belonging to or used in connection with a quarry; provided, however, that quarries operated solely in conjunction with the construction or maintenance of public roads and highways or exempted by the Deputy Minister shall not come within the scope of this Act. *Metalliferous Mines and Quarries Regulation Act*, R.S.N.S. 1967, c. 183, s. 3. 4. A place where consolidated rock has been or is being removed by means of an open excavation to supply material for construction, industrial or manufacturing purposes, but does not include a wayside quarry or open pit metal mine. *Pits and Quarries Control Act*, R.S.O. 1980, c. 378, s. 1. See PRODUCTS OF THE ~ AND MINE; STONE ~; WAYSIDE ~.

QUARRYING. *n.* Includes excavation for any purpose, drilling, and the removal or transportation of any rock, shale, gravel, sand, earth or other material. *Workmen's Compensation Act*, R.S.N.B. 1973, c. W-13, s. 1.

QUARRYING CLAIM. A tract of land containing minerals that have been reserved to the Crown, that gives a person the right to recover sand, gravel, gypsum, peat, clay, marl, granite, limestone, marble, sandstone, slate or any building stone. *Mines Act*, S.M. 1972, c. 70, s. 1.

QUARRY MATERIAL. Any substance which is used or capable of being used in its natural form for construction or agricultural purposes, and includes (i) sand, gravel, stone, soil, peat and peat moss; (ii) a mineral rock or stone capable of being cut or polished for use as an ornament, personal adornment or decoration. *Quarry Materials Act*, S.Nfld. 1975-76, c. 45, s. 2.

QUARRY MATERIALS. Limestone, granite, slate, marble, gypsum, peat, marl, clay, sand, gravel, any building stone and volcanic ash.

Crown Lands (Mines and Quarries) Act, R.S.Nfld. 1970, c. 72, s. 3.

QUART. *n.* 1. 1/4 gallon. *Weights and Measures Act*, S.C. 1970-71-72, c. 36, schedule II. 2. A unit of measurement, containing 40 fluid ounces. *The Liquor Act*, R.S.S. 1978, c. L-18, s. 2.

QUARTER. *n.* 1. The 3-month period ending with the 31st day of March, 30th day of June, 30th day of September or 31st day of December. *Courts of Justice Act*, S.O. 1984, c. 11, s. 137. 2. Any period of 3 months commencing on the first day of January, April, July or October in any year. *Air Carrier Regulations*, C.R.C., c. 3, s. 145. See CALENDAR ~; PAYMENT ~.

QUARTER HOUR BLOCK. A period of 15 minutes commencing at one of the following divisions of a clock hour: 00:00, 15:00, 30:00 and 45:00. *Radio (F.M.) Broadcasting Regulations*, C.R.C., c. 380, s. 14.

QUARTZ. See GOLD BEARING ~.

QUASH. *v.* To set aside or discharge an order of a lower court; to annul or set aside, as in quash an indictment.

QUASI. *adv.* [L.] As if; as it were.

QUASI. *pref.* [L.] Similar but not the same as.

QUASI-CONTRACT. *n.* A liability which cannot be attributed to any other legal principle and which requires someone to pay money to another person because non-payment would confer an unjust benefit on the proposed payor.

QUASI-CRIMINAL OFFENCE. An offence created by provincial law which carries a penalty similar to that for a crime.

QUASI-ESTOPPEL. *n.* Once one party makes a representation about a present or past fact and the other party relies on it detrimentally, the representor cannot repudiate the representation and put forward the true facts. G.H.L. Fridman, *The Law of Contract in Canada*, 2d ed. (Toronto: Carswell, 1986) at 110.

QUASI IN REM. Jurisdiction because the person in question's interest in property exists within that court's territorial jurisdiction.

QUASI-JUDICIAL. *adj.* With respect to a function, one that is partly administrative and partly judicial such as investigating facts, ascertaining that facts exist, holding hearings and drawing conclusions to guide official action from them and exercising discretion in a judicial way. S.A. DeSmith, *Judicial Review of Administrative Action*, 4th ed. by J.M. Evans (London: Stevens, 1980) at 77.

QUAY. See EX ~.

QUÉ. *abbr.* Québec.

QUEBEC NORTH-WEST REGION. That part of the Province of Quebec known as the Quebec North-West Region, comprising the counties of Abitibi-East, Abitibi-West and the parishes of Montbrun and Cléricy of Rouyn-Noranda County. *Quebec North-West Pulpwood Order*, C.R.C., c. 254, s. 2.

QUÉBEC PENSION PLAN. The Québec Pension Plan established pursuant to An Act Respecting the Québec Pension Plan, chapter R-9 of the Revised Statutes of Québec, 1977.

QUEBEC-SOUTH REGION. The territory comprising the electoral districts of Beauce and Dorchester and St-Evariste-de-Forsyth, St-Méthode-de-Frontenac, St-Robert-Bellarmin, the parishes of Courcelles and St-Hilaire-de-Dorset, the parishes and villages of St-Gédéon and St-Sébastien, the villages of La Guadeloupe, Lambton and St-Ludger, as well as the townships of Gayhurst, Gayhurst (southeast part) and Lambton, in the electoral district of Frontenac. *Quebec-South Wood Order*, C.R.C., c. 264, s. 2.

[ ] QUE. C.A. *abbr.* Quebec Official Reports (Court of Appeal), 1970-.

QUEEN. *n.* 1. A woman who is the monarch of a kingdom. 2. The Sovereign of the United Kingdom, Canada and Her other Realms and Territories, and Head of the Commonwealth.

QUEEN CONSORT. The wife of a king who is reigning.

QUEEN DOWAGER. The widow of a king.

QUEEN'S BENCH. 1. In some provinces, the name given to the superior court. 2. In England, a superior court of common law. See COURT OF ~.

QUEEN'S COUNSEL. A barrister appointed counsel to the Crown who wears a silk gown, sits within the bar and in court takes precedence over ordinary barristers.

QUEEN'S L.J. *abbr.* Queen's Law Journal.

QUEEN'S PRINTER. 1. Includes government printer or other official printer. Evidence acts. 2. The Queen's Printer and Comptroller of Stationery for the Province, appointed under the Ministry of Provincial Secretary and Government Services Act. *Queen's Printer Act*, R.S.B.C. 1979, c. 353, s. 1.

QUEEN'S PRIVY COUNCIL FOR CANADA. A group which aids and advises the government of Canada and whose members are appointed or removed by the Governor General. P.W. Hogg, *Constitutional Law of Canada*, 2d ed. (Toronto: Carswell, 1985) at 191 and 192. See CLERK OF THE QUEEN'S PRIVY COUNCIL; CONFIDENCE OF THE ~.

QUEEN'S PROCTOR. A representative of the Crown who may intervene in a divorce proceeding.

QUEEN'S REGULATIONS AND ORDERS. The Queen's Regulations and Orders for the Canadian Forces. *Military Rules of Evidence*, C.R.C., c. 1049, s. 2.

QUEEN'S WAREHOUSE. (a) A warehouse provided by the Crown; or (b) an area appointed by the collector for the safekeeping of unclaimed, abandoned, seized or forfeited goods. Canada regulations.

QUE EST LE MESME. Which is the same.

QUE. K.B. *abbr.* Quebec Official Reports (King's Bench), 1892-1941.

[ ] QUE. K.B. *abbr.* Quebec Official Reports (King's Bench), 1942-1969.

QUE. LAB. CT. *abbr.* Quebec Labour Court (Tribunal du travail)

QUE. L.R.B. *abbr.* Quebec Labour Relations Board (Commission des relations de travail du Québec).

QUE. P.R. *abbr.* Quebec Practice Reports, 1897-1944 (Rapports de Pratique du Québec).

[ ] QUE. P.R. *abbr.* Quebec Practice Reports, 1945- (Rapports de Pratique du Québec).

QUE. Q.B. *abbr.* 1. Quebec Court of Queen's (King's) Bench Reports. 2. Quebec Official Reports (Queen's Bench), 1892-1941.

[ ] QUE. Q.B. *abbr.* Quebec Official Reports (Queen's Bench), 1942-1969.

QUERELA. *n.* [L.] A civil proceeding in any court.

QUERELE. *n.* A complaint made to a court.

QUERENS. *n.* [L.] A complainant, inquirer, plaintiff.

QUERENT. *n.* A complainant, inquirer, plaintiff.

QUE. S.C. *abbr.* Quebec Official Reports (Superior Court), 1892-1941 (Rapports Judiciaires du Québec, Cour Supérieure).

[ ] QUE. S.C. *abbr.* Quebec Official Reports (Superior Court), 1942- (Recueils de jurisprudence du Québec, Cour Supérieure).

QUESTION. *n.* An interrogation; anything inquired. See COLLATERAL ~; INCIDENTAL ~; LEADING ~; MIXED ~; ORAL ~; PRELIMINARY ~; SUBSIDIARY ~; WRITTEN ~.

QUESTION OF ORDER. A question about interpreting a rule of procedure which is a matter for the Speaker or, in a committee, for the Chairman to decide. A. Fraser, G.A. Birch & W.A. Dawson, eds., *Beauchesne's Rules and Forms of the House of Commons of Canada*, 5th ed. (Toronto: Carswell, 1978) at 24.

QUESTION OF PRIVILEGE. A question partly of the law of contempt of Parliament and partly of fact which the House must determine. A. Fraser, G.A. Birch & W.A. Dawson, eds., *Beauchesne's Rules and Forms of the House of Commons of Canada*, 5th ed. (Toronto: Carswell, 1978) at 25.

QUE. TAX R. *abbr.* Quebec Tax Reports.

QUIA FORMA NON OBSERVATA, INFERTUR ADNULLATIO ACTUS. [L.] Because the prescribed procedure was not observed, the proceedings are considered void.

QUI ALIQUID STATUERIT PARTE INAUDITA ALTERA, AEQUUM LICET STATUERIT, HAUD AEQUUS FUERIT. [L.] The one who decides something without hearing one party though they decided rightly, will not be just.

QUI ALTERIUS JURE UTITUR EODEM JURE UTI DEBET. [L.] The one who is clothed in another's right should be clothed in the very same right.

QUIA TIMET. [L. because one fears] A mandatory injunction (or damages instead) which is granted when it is clear that future damage is really probable. See INJUNCTION ~.

QUICK ASSET RATIO. The ratio of liquid assets to current liabilities.

QUICK-DONNING MASK. An oxygen mask that can be secured on the face of the wearer with one hand within 5 seconds and that provides an immediate supply of oxygen. *Oxygen Equipment Order*, C.R.C., c. 52, s. 2.

QUICK FREEZE. Freezing on plates or coils or in cabinets especially designed for quick freezing. *Frozen Food Locker Plant Act*, R.S.M. 1970, c. F170, s. 2.

QUI CONCEDIT ALIQUID, CONCEDERE VIDETUR ET ID SINE QUO CONCESSIO EST IRRITA, SINE QUO RES IPSA ESSE NON POTUIT. [L.] The one who concedes anything is considered to concede that without which the concession is void, without which the very thing would not be able to exist.

QUICQUID DEMONSTRATAE REI ADDITUR SATIS DEMONSTRATAE FRUSTRA EST. [L.] Whatever is added to describe something already described sufficiently has no effect.

QUICQUID NECESSITAS COGIT, DEFEN-DIT. [L.] When anything is done of necessity, necessity can be used as a defence.

QUICQUID PLANTATUR SOLO, SOLO CEDIT. [L.] Whatever is affixed to the soil goes with the soil.

QUICQUID RECIPITUR, RECIPITUR SECUNDUM MODUM RECIPIENTIS. [L.] Whatever is received is received according to the recipient's intention.

QUICQUID SOLVITUR, SOLVITUR SECUN-DUM MODUM SOLVENTIS. [L.] Whatever is paid is paid according to the payer's direction.

QUI CUM ALIO CONTRAHIT, VEL EST, VEL DEBET ESSE, NON IGNARUS CONDI-TIONIS EJUS. [L.] The one who contracts with another, either is, or should be, familiar with the other's condition.

QUID PRO QUO. [L. something for something] A consideration.

QUIET. *v.* To settle; to render unassailable.

QUIET. *adj.* Unmolested; free from interference.

QUIETA NON MOVERE. [L.] A settled situation should not be disturbed.

QUIETARE. *v.* To discharge, quit or relieve of liability.

QUIETE CLAMARE. [L.] To quit claim.

QUIET ENJOYMENT. A guarantee that a lessor or anyone claiming through or under the lessor may not enter.

QUIETING ORDER. An order establishing the legal existence or corporate status of a municipality, or establishing its proper area and boundaries or any of its boundaries, in order to quiet doubts affecting the same. *Municipal Corporations Quieting Orders Act*, R.S.O. 1980, c. 306, s. 1.

QUIETUS. *adj.* Acquitted, freed; discharged of any further liability.

QUIETUS REDDITUS. [L.] Quit-rent.

QUI FACIT PER ALIUM FACIT PER SE. [L.] The one who acts through another is considered to act in person.

QUI FRAUDEM AGIT, FRUSTRA AGIT. [L.] The one who commits fraud labours in vain.

QUI HAERET IN LITERA HAERET IN COR-TICE. [L. the one who sticks in the letter sticks in the bark] The one who considers only the wording of a document cannot comprehend its meaning.

QUI IN JUS DOMINIUMVE ALTERIUS SUCCEDIT JURE EJUS UTI DEBET. [L.] The one who succeeds to the property rights of another should be clothed with that person's right.

QUI JURE SUO UTITUR NEMINEM LAEDIT. [L.] The one who exercises a legal right injures no one.

QUI JUSSI JUDICIS ALIQUOD FECERIT NON VIDETUR DOLO MALO FECISSE QUIA PARERE NECESSE EST. [L.] The one who does anything by a judge's command is not supposed to have acted with an improper motive because it is necessary to obey.

QUILIBET POTEST RENUNCIARE JURI PRO SE INTRODUCTO. [L.] Anyone may renounce a right introduced in one's own favour.

QUINELLA. *n.* A betting transaction in which a purchaser of a ticket undertakes to select the first two horses to finish in the race on which that feature is operated. *Race Track Supervision Regulations*, C.R.C., c. 441, s. 2.

QUI NON IMPROBAT, APPROBAT. [L.] The one who does not disapprove, approves.

QUI NON OBSTAT QUOD OBSTARE POTEST FACERE VIDETUR. [L.] The one who does not prevent what can be prevented is considered to do it.

QUI NON PROHIBET QUOD PROHIBERE POTEST ASSENTIRE VIDETUR. [L.] The one who does not prohibit a thing which can be forbidden is considered to consent.

QUINQUEPARTITE. *adj.* Having five parts or parties.

QUI OMNE DICIT NIHIL EXCLUDIT. [L.] The one who says it all excludes nothing.

QUI PECCAT EBRIUS, LUAT SOBRIUS. [L.] The one who sins while drunk will be punished while sober.

QUI PER ALIUM FACIT, PER SEIPSUM FACERE VIDETUR. [L.] Those who do anything through another are considered to do it themselves.

QUI PRIOR EST TEMPORE POTIOR EST JURE. [L.] The one who is first in time is preferred in law.

QUI RATIONEM IN OMNIBUS QUAERUNT RATIONEM SUBVERTUNT. [L.] Those who look for reason in all things subvert reason.

QUI SENTIT COMMODUM SENTIRE DEBET ET ONUS; ET E CONTRA. [L.] The one who enjoys the benefit should also bear the burden; and the opposite.

QUIT. *v.* 1. With respect to a job, to resign. 2. With respect to leased premises, to surrender possession. See NOTICE TO ~.

QUI TACET CONSENTIRE VIDETUR. [L.] The one who is silent is considered to consent.

QUI TAM. [L. who as well] On a penal statute, an action partly at the Crown's suit and partly at an informer's.

QUIT CLAIM. To relinquish or release any claim to real property.

QUIT-CLAIM DEED. The conveyance without promises or warranties only of an interest, if any, which the grantor has in the land. It is often used to release an interest in land, e.g. the purchaser's interest, under an agreement of purchase and sale, which was registered against the title. B.J. Reiter, R.C.B. Risk & B.N. McLellan, *Real Estate Law*, 3d ed. (Toronto: Emond Montgomery, 1986) at 941.

QUIT RENT. A rent by which a tenant quits and is free of any other service.

QUITTANCE. *n.* An acquittal, a release.

QUI VULT DECIPI DECIPIATUR. [L.] Let the one who wants to be deceived be deceived.

QUOAD. *adv.* [L.] Concerning; as to.

QUOAD HOC. [L.] Concerning that.

QUOAD ULTRA. [L.] Concerning the rest.

QUO ANIMO. [L.] By what mind.

QUOD AB INITIO NON VALET IN TRACTU TEMPORIS NON CONVALESCIT. [L.] What does not go well from the beginning will not improve with the passage of time.

QUOD AEDIFICATUR IN AREA LEGATA CEDIT LEGATO. [L.] What is built on devised ground passes to the devisee.

QUOD APPROBO NON REPROBO. [L.] What I approve, I do not reject.

QUOD CONSTAT CURIAE OPERE TESTIUM NON INDIGET. [L.] What is well known to a court does not need the help of witnesses.

QUOD CONTRA LEGEM FIT, PRO INFECTO HABETUR. [L.] What is done against the law is held not to have been done at all.

QUOD CONTRA RATIONEM JURIS RECEPTUM, NON EST PRODUCENDUM AD CONSEQUENTIAS. [L.] What is received contrary to the reason of law should not be advanced as precedent.

QUODCUNQUE ALIQUIS OB TUTELAM CORPORIS SUI FECERIT, JURE ID FECISSE VIDETUR. [L.] Whatever one does for the body's safety is considered to have been done legally.

QUOD DUBITAS NE FECERIS. [L.] Do not do what you feel doubtful about.

QUOD EST INCONVENIENS, AUT CONTRA RATIONEM, NON PERMISSUM EST IN LEGE. [L.] What is inconvenient, or contrary to reason, is not permitted in law.

QUOD FIERI DEBET FACILE PRAESUMITUR. [L.] What should be done is easily presumed to have been done.

QUOD FIERI NON DEBET FACTUM VALET. [L.] What should not be done prevails if it was done.

QUOD IN MINORI VALET VALEBIT IN MAJORI; ET QUOD IN MAJORI NON VALET NEC VALEBIT IN MINORI. [L.] What benefits the lesser will benefit in the greater; and what does not benefit the greater will not benefit in the lesser.

QUOD MEUM EST SINE FACTO MEO VEL DEFECTU MEO AMITTI VEL IN ALIUM TRANSFERRI NON POTEST. [L.] What is mine cannot be either lost or transferred to another without either my act or my default.

QUOD NECESSARIE INTELLIGITUR ID NON DEEST. [L.] What is necessarily understood is not omitted.

QUOD NECESSARIUM EST EST LICITUM. [L.] What is necessary is also lawful.

QUOD NON APPARET NON EST. [L.] What does not appear does not exist.

QUOD NON HABET PRINCIPIUM NON HABET FINEM. [L.] What does not have a beginning does not have an end.

QUOD NON LEGITUR NON CREDITUR. [L.] What is not read is not trusted.

QUOD NOSTRUM EST, SINE FACTO SIVE DEFECTU NOSTRO, AMITTI SEU IN ALIUM TRANSFERRI NON POTEST. [L.] What is ours cannot be either lost or transferred to another without either our own act or our own fault.

QUOD NULLIUS EST, EST DOMINI REGIS. [L.] What belongs to no one belongs to our lord the sovereign.

QUOD NULLIUS EST ID RATIONE NATURALI OCCUPANTI CONCEDITUR. [L.] What belongs to no one is granted to an occupant by natural right.

QUOD PER ME NON POSSUM, NEC PER ALIUM. [L.] What I cannot do by myself I cannot do through another.

QUOD PER RECORDUM PROBATUM, NON DEBET ESSE NEGATUM. [L.] What is proved by record should not be denied.

QUOD PRIUS EST VERIUS; ET QUOD PRIUS EST TEMPORE POTIUS EST JURE. [L.] What is first is truer, and what is first in time is better legally.

QUOD RECUPERET. [L. that one recovers] In a personal action, the final judgment for the plaintiff.

QUOD REMEDIO DESTITUITUR IPSA RE VALET SI CULPA ABSIT. [L.] What is without remedy prevails by itself if there is no fault in the party who seeks to enforce it.

QUOD SEMEL AUT BIS EXISTIT PRAETEREUNT LEGISLATORES. [L.] Legislators pass over what happens only once or twice.

QUOD SEMEL MEUM EST AMPLIUS MEUM ESSE NON POTEST. [L.] What is mine once cannot be more completely mine.

QUOD SEMEL PLACUIT IN ELECTIONE, AMPLIUS DISPLICERE NON POTEST. [L.] What once was pleasing in a choice cannot further displease.

QUOD SUBINTELLIGITUR NON DEEST. [L.] What is understood does not fail.

QUOD VANUM ET INUTILE EST, LEX NON REQUIRIT. [L.] The law does not require what is vain and useless.

QUOD VIDE. [L.] See this.

QUO LIGATUR, EO DISSOLVITUR. [L.] Whatever binds can also release.

QUO MODO QUID CONSTITUITUR EODEM MODO DISSOLVITUR. [L.] In the way in which the thing is constituted, in the same way it is dissolved.

QUORUM. *n.* [L. of whom] 1. The majority of the whole group. 2. The number of members of a group able to transact business when other members are absent.

QUOTA. *n.* 1. The quantity of grain authorized to be delivered from grain produced on land described in a permit book as fixed from time to time by the Board, whether expressed as a quantity that may be delivered from a specified number of acres or otherwise. *Canadian Wheat Board Act*, R.S.C. 1985, c. C-24, s. 2. 2. The total number of big game species specified by the regional manager that all or any of the clients of a guide outfitter may kill in a licence year. *Wildlife Act*, S.B.C. 1982, c. 57, s. 1. 3. The quantity of milk, established by the board pursuant to this Act, that a producer is required to deliver in a month to a distributor, whether expressed in a fluid measure or in terms of butterfat or otherwise. *Milk Control Act*, R.S.M. 1970, c. M130, s. 2. 4. The maximum quantity of a regulated product determined by the Commodity Board for any purpose. Canada regulations. 5. The quantity of a product that a producer is entitled to market in interprovincial or export trade through normal marketing channels or to have marketed on his behalf by the Agency in interprovincial or export trade during any calendar year. Canada regulations. See GENERAL ACREAGE ~; TARIFF RATE ~; TIMBER ~.

QUOTA ACRES. The acres specified with the approval of the Board in relation to any grain as the basis for the delivery of that grain under a permit book referring to the land described in the permit book. *Prairie Grain Advance Payments Act*, R.S.C. 1985, c. P-18, s. 2.

QUOTA CERTIFICATE. (a) A document issued to a producer certifying the quota assigned to him; or (b) a list containing the names of all producers and certifying the quota assigned to each producer. *Canadian Egg Marketing Agency Quota Regulations*, C.R.C., c. 656, s. 2.

QUOTA HOLDER. A holder of a coniferous timber quota or a deciduous timber allocation. *Forests Act*, R.S.A. 1980, c. F-16, s. 1.

QUOTA RULE. Union regulation of a minimum number of workers.

QUOTA SYSTEM. The method by which the quota fixed and allotted to any producer is determined. *Farm Products Marketing Act*, R.R.O. 1980, Reg. 358, Schedule, s. 1.

QUOTIENS DUBIA INTERPRETATIO LIBERTATIS EST SECUNDUM LIBERTATEM RESPONDENDUM EST. [L.] Whenever a decision for liberty is in doubt it should be decided in favour of liberty.

QUOTIENS IDEM SERMO DUAE SENTENTIAS EXPRIMIT; EA POTISSIMUM ACCIPIATUR QUAE REI GERENDAE APTIOR EST. [L.] Whenever the same statement offers two meanings, what is better suited to effect the desired end should be adopted.

QUOTIENT. See ELECTORAL ~.

QUOTIES IN VERBIS NULLA EST AMBIGUITAS IBI NULLA ESPOSITIO CONTRA VERBA EXPRESSA FIENDA EST. [L.] When there is no ambiguity in the words then no interpretation contrary to the stated words should be adopted.

QUOUSQUE. *adv.* [L.] How long, how far.

QUO WARRANTO. [L. by what authority] A prerogative writ which challenges the usurpation of a public office by the continued exercise of authority which is not conferred legally. S.A. DeSmith, *Judicial Review of Administrative Action*, 4th ed. by J.M. Evans (London: Stevens, 1980) at 463.

QUUM PRINCIPALIS CAUSA NON CONSISTIT, NE EA QUIDEM QUAE SEQUUNTUR LOCUM HABENT. [L.] When the main cause does not stand its ground, then the things which arise out of it have no place either.

Q.V. *abbr.* [L.] Quod vide. See this.

R. *abbr.* 1. [L. regina] Queen. 2. [Fr. reine] Queen. 3. [L. rex] King. 4. [Fr. roi] King. 5. Rule.

RABBIT. *n.* 1. Includes cottontail rabbit, varying hare and European hare. *Game and Fish Act*, R.S.O. 1980, c. 182, s. 1. 2. A domestic rabbit. *Meat Inspection Regulations*, C.R.C., c. 1032, s. 162. See EVISCERATED DOMESTIC ~.

R.A.C. *abbr.* Ramsay's Appeal Cases (Que.), 1873-1886.

RACE. *n.* A horse race on which pari-mutuel betting is conducted or a qualifying race. *Race Track Supervision Regulations*, C.R.C., c. 441, s. 2.

RACE AVERAGE. The average amount bet per race determined by dividing the total monies bet through the pari-mutuel system of a race course during one calendar year by the number of races on which such betting was conducted. *Race Track Supervision Regulations*, C.R.C., c. 441, s. 2.

RACE MEETING. *var.* **RACE-MEETING.** 1. A series of any form of horse races. 2. A series of racing cards held by an association at one race course during any number of days. *Race Track Supervision Regulations*, C.R.C., c. 441, s. 2.

RACE TRACK. *var.* **RACE-TRACK.** 1. A piece of ground specially laid out for horse races, automobile races or other kinds of races. 2. Any place at which harness racing is conducted and pari-mutuel betting is permitted.

RACEWAY. *n.* Any channel for holding wires, cables or bus bars, which is designed expressly for and used solely for this purpose, and unless otherwise qualified in this Code, including rigid, flexible, metallic and non-metallic conduit, electrical metallic tubing, underfloor raceways, lighting fixture raceways, cellular floor raceways, surface raceways, wire-ways, cable-troughs, busways, auxiliary gutters and ventilated cableway. *Ontario Power Corporation Act*, R.R.O. 1980, Reg. 794, s. 0. See LIGHTING FIXTURE ~; SURFACE ~; UNDERFLOOR-~.

RACING. *n.* Horse racing or any other prescribed form of racing. *An Act respecting lotteries, racing, publicity contests and amusement machines.* S.Q. 1978, c. 36, s. 1. See HARNESS ~; HORSE ~.

RACING CARD. The total number of races scheduled, pursuant to section 188(2) of the Act, to be run consecutively. *Race Track Supervision Regulations*, C.R.C., c. 441, s. 2.

RACING JUDGE. A person responsible for racing contests whose functions in this regard are described in the rules. *An Act respecting lotteries, racing, publicity contests and amusement machines.* S.Q. 1978, c. 36, s. 1.

RACING MEETING. Includes every meeting within the province where horses are raced and where any form of betting or wagering on the speed or ability of horses is permitted, but does not include any meeting where no betting or wagering is permitted even though horses or their owners are awarded certificates, ribbons, premiums or prizes for speed or ability shown. *Racing and Sports Commission Act*, R.S.P.E.I. 1974, c. R-2, s. 2.

RACING SECRETARY. A person appointed by an association for the purpose of receiving all entries, scratches and declarations. *Race Track Supervision Regulations*, C.R.C., c. 441, s. 2.

RACING STRIP. That portion of a race course on which a race is run. *Race Track Supervision Regulations*, C.R.C., c. 441, s. 2.

RACK-RENT. *n.* Rent which is not less than two-thirds of the full annual net value of the property out of which the rent arises. *City of St. John's Act*, R.S.Nfld. 1970, c. 40, s. 2.

RAD. *n.* A unit of dose, and is realized when 0.01 joule of energy has been absorbed per

R

kilogram of matter. *Public Health Act*, R.R.O. 1980, Reg. 855, s. 1. See MILLI~.

RAD. *abbr.* Radian.

RADAR WARNING DEVICE. Any device or equipment designed or intended for use in a motor vehicle to warn the driver of the presence of radar or other electronic speed measuring equipment in the vicinity and includes any device or equipment designed or intended for use in a motor vehicle to interfere with the transmission of radar or other electronic speed measuring equipment. *An Act to Amend the Highway Traffic Act*, S.P.E.I. 1981, c. 17, s. 9.

RADIAL PLY TIRE. A pneumatic tire in which the ply cords that extend to the beads are laid at angles of approximately 90 degrees to the centreline of the tread. Canada regulations.

RADIAN. *n.* The unit for the measurement of a plane angle, being the angle with its vertex at the centre of a circle and subtended by an arc of the circle that is equal in length to its radius. *Weights and Measures Act*, S.C. 1970-71-72, c. 36, schedule I.

RADIATING FRACTURE. A fracture of a flat bone in which fracture lines spread from the centre point of impact. F.A. Jaffe, *A Guide to Pathological Evidence*, 2d ed. (Toronto: Carswell, 1983) at 176 and 177.

RADIATION. *n.* Ionizing or non-ionizing energy in the form of atomic particles, electromagnetic or acoustic waves. See IONIZING ~; LASER ~; LEAKAGE ~; NON-IONIZING ~.

RADIATION EMITTING DEVICE. 1. (a) Any device that is capable of producing and emitting radiation; and (b) any component of or accessory to a device described in paragraph (a). *Radiation Emitting Device Act*, R.S.C. 1985, c. R-1, s. 2. 2. Any device that is capable of producing and emitting energy in the form of (a) electromagnetic waves having frequencies greater than 10 megacycles per second; and (b) ultrasonic waves having frequencies greater than 10 kilocycles per second. *Canada Dangerous Substances Regulations*, C.R.C., c. 997, s. 2.

RADIATION EQUIPMENT. Equipment or machinery associated with the use or operation of a radiation source, and includes the radiation source itself and any structure used to support or shield the equipment, machinery or radiation source.

RADIATION FACILITY. Any premises or part of premises in which radiation equipment or a radiation source is installed. *Radiation Protection Act*, S.A. 1985, c. R-2.1, s. 1.

RADIATION HEALTH. The science and art of protecting persons from injury by radiation.

RADIATION INSTALLATION. The building or other place, or the part thereof, in which radiation equipment is manufactured, used, handled or tested.

RADIATION SOURCE. A device or substance that emits radiation, but does not include a device, substance or other thing that is subject to the regulations under the Atomic Energy Control Act (Canada). *Radiation Protection Act*, S.A. 1985, c. R-2.1, s. 1.

RADIATION WORKER. 1. Any person whose occupation requires that person to be exposed to radiation emitted by radiation equipment. 2. A person designated by the owner of radiation equipment as a person who, as an essential requirement of that person's work, business, studies or occupation, could be exposed to radiation emitted by that radiation equipment. *Radiological Health Protection Act*, S.N.B. 1987, c. R-0.1, s. 1.

RADIO. *n.* 1. Any transmission, emission or reception of signs, signals, writing, images, sounds or intelligence of any nature by means of electromagnetic waves of frequencies lower than 3 000 GHz propagated in space without artificial guide. 2. Any transmission, emission or reception of signs, signals, writing, images and sounds or intelligence of any nature by means of Hertzian waves. Canada regulations. See CANADIAN ~-TELEVISION AND TELECOMMUNICATIONS COMMISSION.

RADIOACTIVE MATERIAL. (a) Spent nuclear fuel rods that have been exposed to radiation in a nuclear reactor; (b) radioactive waste material; (c) unused enriched nuclear fuel rods; or (d) any other radioactive material of such quantity and quality as to be harmful to persons or property if its containers were destroyed or damaged.

RADIO AND TELEVISION SERVICE TECHNICIAN. A person who: (i) installs, adjusts and repairs radio and television receivers and other domestic electronic equipment; (ii) makes adjustments to obtain desired density, linearity, focus, colour and size of television pictures; (iii) isolates and detects defects by the use of schematic diagrams, voltage meters, generators, oscilloscopes and other electronic testing instruments; (iv) tests and changes tubes and other components; (v) repairs loose connections and repairs or replaces defective parts by the use of hand tools and soldering irons, and understands electronic theory and shop techniques, but does not include a person who is: (vi) engaged in the manufacture of radio, television, amplifier or other related electronic equipment; (vii) employed in the repair and maintenance of radio, television, amplifier or other related electronic equipment in an industrial plant; or (viii) engaged in the wiring of radio, television, amplifier or other related electronic equipment to an external power source. *Apprenticeship and Tradesmen's Qualification Act*, R.R.O. 1980, Reg. 54, s. 1.

RADIO APPARATUS. A reasonably complete and sufficient combination of distinct appliances intended for or capable of being used for radiocommunication. *Radio Act*, R.S.C. 1985, c. R-2, s. 2.

RADIOCOMMUNICATION. *n.* Any transmission, emission or reception of signs, signals, writing, images, sounds or intelligence of any nature by means of electromagnetic waves of frequencies lower than 3 000 GHz propagated in space without artificial guide.

RADIO FREQUENCY GENERATOR. See I.S.M. ~.

RADIO FREQUENCY NOISE. Any electrical disturbance produced by any machinery, apparatus or equipment and is capable of being received by a radio receiving apparatus. *Radio Interference Regulations*, C.R.C., c. 1374, s. 2.

RADIOGRAPH. *n.* A Roentgen ray photograph. *The X-Ray Technicians Act*, R.S.S. 1978, c. X-1, s. 2.

RADIOGRAPHER. *n.* A person who practises medical radiological technology. *Medical Radiological Technicians Act*, R.S.N.S. 1967, c. 180, s. 1.

RADIOGRAPHY. *n.* The act, process, science or art of making radiographs for use in medical treatment or diagnosis. *The X-Ray Technicians Act*, R.S.S. 1978, c. X-1, s. 2. See INDUSTRIAL ~.

RADIOLOGICAL HEALTH PROTECTION. The science and art of protecting persons from injury by radiation. *Radiological Health Protection Act*, S.N.B. 1987, c. R-0.1, s. 1.

RADIOLOGICAL TECHNICIAN. A person who practises the technical aspects of the medical use of ionizing radiation, including Roentgen or X-rays, radium, radioactive isotopes and particles for diagnosis or treatment. *Radiological Technicians Act*, R.S.O. 1980, c. 430, s. 1. See INDUSTRIAL ~; MEDICAL ~.

RADIOLOGICAL TECHNOLOGY. See MEDICAL ~.

RADIOLOGIST. *n.* A legally qualified medical practitioner who holds a specialist certification in diagnostic or therapeutic radiology from the Royal College of Physicians and Surgeons of Canada. *Radiological Technicians Act*, R.S.O. 1980, c. 430, s. 1.

RADIO NOISE. Any electrical disturbance produced by any machinery, apparatus or equipment and is capable of being received by a radio receiving apparatus. *Radio Interference Regulations*, C.R.C., c. 1374, s. 2.

RADIONUCLIDE GENERATOR. A radioactive parent and daughter (a) contained in an ion-exchanging column; or (b) dissolved in a suitable solvent in a liquid-liquid extraction system where the radioactive daughter is separated from its parent by (c) elution from the ion exchange column; or (d) a solvent extraction procedure. *Food and Drug Regulations*, C.R.C., c. 870, c. C.03.001.

RADIOPHARMACEUTICAL. *n.* A drug emitting alpha, beta or electromagnetic radiations. *Food and Drug Regulations*, C.R.C., c. 870, c. C.03.301.

RADIO REGULATIONS. The regulations respecting radio made by the Governor in Council and the Minister respectively under sections 342 and 343. *Canada Shipping Act*, R.S.C. 1985, c. S-9, s. 2. See INTERNATIONAL ~.

RADIO STATION. A place in which radio apparatus is located. *Radio Act*, R.S.C. 1985, c. R-2, s. 2. See AERONAUTICAL ~; OPTIONAL ~.

RADIO-TELEGRAPH. *var.* **RADIOTELEGRAPH.** *n.* Includes a system of radio communication for the transmission of written matter by the use of a signal code. *Canada Shipping Act*, R.S.C. 1985, c. S-9, s. 2.

RADIOTELEGRAPH ALARM SIGNAL. A signal consisting of a series of 12 dashes transmitted in 1 minute by manual or automatic means, the duration of each dash being 4 seconds and the duration of the interval between consecutive dashes being 1 second. *Ship Station Radio Regulations*, Part II, C.R.C., c. 1474, s. 2.

RADIO-TELEPHONE. *var.* **RADIOTELEPHONE.** *n.* Includes a system of radio communication for the transmission of speech or, in some cases, other sounds. *Canada Shipping Act*, R.S.C. 1985, c. S-9, s. 2.

RADIOTELEPHONE ALARM SIGNAL. A signal consisting of two substantially sinusoidal audio frequency tones of 2,200 c.p.s. and 1,300 c.p.s. transmitted alternately by manual or automatic means, the duration of each tone being 250 milliseconds. *Ship Station Radio Regulations, Part II*, C.R.C., c. 1474, s. 2.

RAFT. *n.* Includes any raft, crib, dam or bag boom of logs, timber or lumber of any kind, and logs, timber or lumber in boom or being towed.

RAFTER. *n.* A sloping wood framing member which supports the roof sheathing and encloses an attic space, but does not support a ceiling. *Building Code Act*, R.R.O. 1980, Reg. 87, s. 1.

RAIL. See TRANSPORT BY ~; VIA ~ CANADA INC.

RAILROAD SIGN OR SIGNAL. Any sign, signal or device intended to give notice of the presence of railroad tracks or the approach of a railroad train. *Motor Vehicle Act*, R.S.N.B. 1973, c. M-17, s. 1.

RAIL VEHICLE. A vehicle that is drawn, propelled or driven on rails by means other than by muscular power. *Transport of Dangerous Goods Act*, S.B.C. 1985, c. 17, s. 1.

RAILWAY. *n.* Any railway that the company has authority to construct or operate, and includes all branches, extensions, sidings, stations, depots, wharfs, rolling stock, equipment, stores, property real or personal and works connected therewith, and also any railway bridge, tunnel or other structure that the company is authorized to construct; and, except where the context is inapplicable, includes street railway and tramway. *Railway Act*, R.S.C. 1985, c. R-3, s. 2. See CANADIAN GOVERNMENT ~S; CANADIAN NATIONAL ~ COMPANY; CANADIAN NATIONAL ~S; INDUSTRIAL ~; NATIONAL ~S; PROVINCIAL ~S; TRANSPORT BY RAIL; UNECONOMIC LINE OF ~; VIA RAIL CANADA INC.

RAILWAY CAR. Railway rolling stock equipped and used exclusively for the carriage of passengers from one point in Ontario to another point inside or outside Ontario. *Liquor Licence Act*, R.R.O. 1980, Reg. 581, s. 1.

RAILWAY COMPANY. Any company operating a line of railway in one or more provinces.

RAILWAY CROSSING. Any railway crossing of a highway or highway crossing of a railway and any manner of construction of the railway or highway by the elevation or depression of the one above or below the other, or by the diversion of the one or the other, and any work ordered or authorized by the Commission to be provided as one work for the protection, safety and convenience of the public in respect of one or more railways with as many tracks crossing or crossed as the Commission in its discretion determines. *Railway Relocation and Crossing Act*, R.S.C. 1985, c. R-4, s. 2.

RAILWAY FENCE. A substantial fence not less than 4 feet high consisting of not less than four lines of ordinary fence wire, the lowest line being not more than 12 inches above the ground, and the upright posts being placed not more than 27 feet apart. *Railway Act*, R.S.A. 1980, c. R-4, s. 1.

RAILWAY PASSENGER SERVICE. A passenger train service that does not accommodate principally persons who commute between points on the railway. *Railway Passenger Services Adjustment Assistance Regulations*, C.R.C., c. 342, s. 2.

RAILWAY RIGHT-OF-WAY. Lands that are owned or leased by a railway, are contiguous to that railway's tracks and are required for railway purposes. Canada regulations.

RAILWAY ROADWAY. (i) The continuing strip of land, outside hamlets, used by the railway company as a right of way; and (ii) the continuing strip of land, within hamlets, not exceeding 100 feet in width, and so used by the company; and includes the superstructure on such land whether outside or within a hamlet. Saskatchewan statutes.

RAILWAY ROLLING STOCK. Railway passenger, baggage and freight cars. Canada regulations.

RAILWAY STATION. Any location where passenger or freight trains may stop in accordance with the current railway timetable. Canada regulations.

RAILWAY STATION-DWELLING. A railway station, of which a part is used as a dwelling. Canada regulations.

RAILWAY SUPERSTRUCTURE. The grading, ballast, embankments, ties, rails and fastenings, miscellaneous track accessories and appurtenances, switches, poles, wires, conduits and cables, fences, sidings, spurs, trestles, bridges, subways, culverts, tunnels, cattle guards, cattle passes, platforms, stockyards, hog shelters, scales, turntables, cinder and service pits, hoists, signals and signal towers, grade crossing protective appliances, water tanks, stand pipes, pump sheds, dams, spillways, reservoirs, wells, pumping machinery, pipe lines and bins, sheds or other storage facilities having a floor space not exceeding 100 square feet, owned by the railway company or used by it in the operation of the railway. Saskatchewan statutes.

RAILWAY SYSTEM. Includes a railway owned or operated by a common carrier, together with all buildings, rolling stock, equipment and other properties pertaining thereto, but does not include a tramway. *Income Tax Regulations*, C.R.C., c. 945, s. 1104.

RAIN. *n.* Any water which falls from the atmosphere in the form of solid or liquid precipitation. *Artificial Inducement of Rain Act*, R.S.Q. 1977, c. P-43, s. 1.

RAINBOW TROUT. Includes steelhead trout

and Kamloops trout. *Ontario Fishery Regulations*, C.R.C., c. 849, s. 2.

RAINBOW TROUT FISH POND. A body of water that (a) does not exceed 20 acres in surface area; (b) has been stocked with fish; (c) is enclosed so that fish are unable to enter or leave; and (d) is listed as a rainbow trout fish pond on a list maintained by the Minister. *Quebec Fishery Regulations*, C.R.C., c. 852, s. 2.

RAIN WATER LEADER. A conductor inside a building or other structure that conveys storm water from the roof of the building or other structure to a building storm drain or other place of disposal. *Ontario Water Resources Act*, R.R.O. 1980, Reg. 736, s. 1.

RAISE. *v.* To construct, build up.

RAISED CABLE. A cable that is not resting on the river bed. *Ferry Cable Regulations*, C.R.C., c. 1230, s. 2.

RAKE. See DRAG ~.

RAM. & MOR. *abbr.* Ramsay & Morin, The Law Reporter (Journal de jurisprudence).

RAMP AREA. The area provided for loading or unloading passengers or cargo, or for refuelling, parking or maintaining the aircraft. *Quarantine Regulations*, C.R.C., c. 1368, s. 20.

RANCH. See FUR-BEARING ANIMAL ~; FUR ~; MUSKRAT ~.

RANCHER. *n.* A person whose primary occupation is rearing stock from a basic herd and who deals in stock only for that purpose. *Livestock Brand Act*, R.S.B.C. 1979, c. 241, s. 1.

RANCHING. See GAME ~.

RAND FORMULA. A plan providing union security and requiring automatic check-off of union dues by employers.

RANGE. *n.* A cooking appliance equipped with a cooking surface and one or more ovens. *Building Code Act*, R.R.O. 1980, Reg. 87, s. 1. See CROWN ~; NEGOTIATING ~; PAY ~.

RANGE OF RENTS. The schedule of rents that may be applicable to residential premises at any time, where the rent to be paid in respect of the premises will be determined from that schedule on the basis of the services that the landlord is to provide or the number of persons that are to occupy the premises or on any other basis. *The Residential Tenancies Act*, R.S.S. 1978, c. R-22, s. 2.

RANK. *n.* Includes appointment. *Canadian Forces Superannuation Act*, R.S.C. 1985, c. C-17, s. 2. See BREVET ~.

RANSOM. *n.* The price paid to redeem a prisoner or captive.

RAPE. *n.* Having sexual intercourse with a woman without her consent or against her will. See now SEXUAL ASSAULT and AGGRAVATED SEXUAL ASSAULT.

RAPID TRANSIT. A public transportation system running on rails or other tracked systems and operating on an exclusive right of way, but does not include privately-owned railways or railways directly responsible to federal or provincial governments. *City Transportation Act*, R.S.A. 1980, c. C-10, s. 1.

RAPINE. *n.* Theft; taking something in defiance of the owner, openly or violently.

RAPTOR. *n.* A bird of the order Falconiformes known as vultures, eagles, falcons and hawks or the order Strigiformes known as owls, and includes its eggs. *Wildlife Act*, S.B.C. 1982, c. 57, s. 1.

RASURE. *n.* Erasing; shaving or scraping.

RATABLE PERSON. A person liable to taxation under this Act. *Assessment Act*, R.S.N.S. 1967, c. 14, s. 1.

RATE. *n.* 1. Includes a general, individual or joint rate, fare, toll, charge, rental or other compensation of a public utility, a rule, regulation, practice, measurement, classification or contract of a public utility or corporation relating to a rate and a schedule or tariff respecting a rate. 2. When used with reference to a rate of taxation means (i) a percentage of the assessed value of property, or a specified number of mills for each dollar of the assessed value of property, or a percentage of the business rental value of premises; or (ii) a specified amount in dollars or cents, or both, in respect of (A) each foot of frontage or flankage or designated subdivided lands; or (B) each acre or other unit of area of designated unsubdivided land. *City of Winnipeg Act*, S.M. 1971, c. 105, s. 1. 3. The rate for Government of Canada securities of 10 years and over as published in the Bank of Canada Statistical Summary. 4. Includes any toll, rate, fare, charge, rental or other compensation charged or made by a motor carrier or by any person on his behalf or with his consent or authority in connection with the carriage and transportation of passengers, or the carriage, shipment, transportation, care, handling or delivery of goods, or for any service incidental to the business of the motor carrier and includes any general, individual or joint toll, rate, fare, charge, rental or the compensation of any motor carrier, and any rule, regulation, practice, classification or contract of the motor carrier relating to it, and any schedule or tariff of it. *Motor Carrier Act*, R.S.B.C. 1979, c. 286, s. 1. 5. The price fixed for a motor vehicle liability policy or any coverage under that policy. *Automobile Insurance Act*, S.Nfld. 1975, c. 75, s. 2. 6. Any rental or charge for supplying telephone exchange service and all services associated therewith. *Telephone Act*, R.S.O. 1980, c. 496, s. 1. 7. The basis upon which any charge, toll or due payable under these Regulations is calculated in respect of any vessel, boat, raft, dredge, floating elevator, scow, houseboat, seaplane on the water or other floating craft. *Government Wharves Regulations*, C.R.C., c. 881, s. 2. See BANK OF CANADA ~; BANK ~; BASE ~; BASIC ~; CANADIAN OWNERSHIP ~; COMMODITY ~; CONTRACT ~; CREDIT ~; CRIMINAL ~; DAILY ~; DEBENTURE ~; DISCOUNT ~; DOSE-~; DUAL ~; EFFECTIVE ~; ENTRANCE ~; GOING ~; GUARANTEED ~; INDIVIDUAL ~; JOB ~; LEGAL ~; NON-CONTRACT ~; ORDINARY PUBLISHED ~; OVERTIME ~; PIECE WORK ~; PREMIUM ~; PRIME ~; ~S; REGULAR ~; SERVICE ~; SEWAGE SERVICE ~; SEWER ~; SINGLE ~; SPECIFIED INTEREST ~; STORAGE ~; TOLL OR ~; VARIABLE ~ MORTGAGE; WATER ~; WATER WORKS ~.

RATEABLE LAND. Land liable to taxation.

RATEABLE PORTION. If there are two insurers liable and each has the same policy limits, each of the insurers shall be liable to share equally in any liability, expense, loss or damage; if there are two insurers liable with different policy limits, the insurers shall be liable to share equally up to the limit of the smaller policy limit; and if there are more than two insurers liable, clauses (a) and (b) shall apply mutatis mutandis. *Insurance Act*, R.S.M. 1970, c. I40, s. 272.

RATEABLE PROPERTY. Includes business and other assessments made under the Assessment Act. Ontario statutes.

RATEABLE PROPORTION. (a) If there are two insurers liable and each has the same policy limits, each of the insurers will be liable to share equally in any liability, expense, loss or damage; (b) if there are two insurers liable with different policy limits, the insurers will be liable to share equally up to the limit of the smaller policy limit; and (c) if there are more than two insurers liable, paragraphs (a) and (b) will apply mutatis mutandis.

RATEABLE VALUE. The value of a business interest when less than 100 per cent of the shares are held by the person in question. A. Bissett-Johnson & W.M. Holland, eds., *Matrimonial Property Law in Canada* (Toronto: Carswell, 1980) at V-9.

RATE BASE. The maximum valuation of assets fixed by the Commission pursuant to section 20 upon which a public utility may earn a percentage of return established by the Commission; or such other method of computing a maximum return as may be determined by the Commission. *Electric Power and Telephone Act*, S.P.E.I. 1984, c. 20, s. 1.

RATED BED CAPACITY. The number of bassinets, cribs and beds which a hospital is designed to have.

RATED CAPACITY. 1. The maximum load that can be weighed on a weighing machine as set out in the notice of approval. *Weights and Measures Regulations*, C.R.C., c. 1605, s. 57. 2. The amount of chlorine that a plant is designed to produce each day. *Chlor-Alkali Mercury National Emission Standards Regulations*, C.R.C., c. 406, s. 2.

RATED GENERATOR CAPACITY. The total capacity obtained by adding together the capacities of the generators listed on the name plates. *Marine Engineer Examination Regulations*, C.R.C., c. 1443, s. 2.

RATED MAXIMUM SOUND PRESSURE. At the frequency of rated maximum sound pressure and with the gain of the hearing aid set to maximum, the lowest value of sound pressure in the coupler at which the total harmonic distortion reaches 10 per cent. *Medical Devices Regulations*, C.R.C., c. 871, s. 1.

RATE MANUAL. The documents of an authorized insurer in which his rules of classification of risks, and the premiums applicable to each, are identified and defined. *Automobile Insurance Act*, R.S.O. 1977, c. A-25, s. 1.

RATE OF COST CHANGE. In respect of any crop year, means the percentage, as determined by the Commission on the basis of grain tonnage forecasts provided by the Administrator, by which the average estimated eligible cost of moving one tonne of grain in that crop year differs from the average estimated eligible cost of moving one tonne of grain in the preceding crop year, as adjusted in respect of the 1983-84 to 1986-87 crop years so as to exclude the effect of the phasing in of the contribution to constant costs. *Western Grain Transportation Act*, R.S.C. 1985, c. W-8, s. 55.

RATE OF EXCHANGE. (i) Where the proceeds of a foreign debt are converted into Canadian dollars on or before the date of issue of the foreign debt, the value in Canadian dollars of the currency or unit of monetary value of the foreign debt as determined by the conversion; and (ii) where the proceeds of a foreign debt are not converted into Canadian dollars at any time or are not converted into Canadian dollars on or before the date of issue of the foreign debt, the value on the date of issue of the foreign debt in Canadian dollars of the currency of the foreign debt as published by an institution or agency which in the opinion of the Minister of Finance is reliable in respect of foreign monetary exchange matters, and includes the value on the date of issue of the foreign debt in Canadian dollars of the unit of monetary value of the foreign debt calculated on the basis of currency values published by such an institution or agency. *Energy Rate Stabilization Act*, S.M. 1979, c. 42, s. 1.

RATE OF TAX. See NATIONAL AVERAGE ~.

RATE OF UNEMPLOYMENT. See NATIONAL ~.

RATE OF WAGES. 1. The basis of calculation of wages. 2. (i) The basis of calculation of the wages paid to a person employed whether that basis is remuneration for a period of time worked or for piecework or is any other incentive basis; and (ii) where the basis of calculation of the wages paid to a person employed is a combination of such bases of calculation, that combination of bases. *Employment Standards Act*, R.S.M. 1970, c. E110, s. 2.

RATE OR TOLL. Any fee or rate charged, levied or collected, either directly or indirectly by any person for the carriage of goods or passengers by a vehicle. *Motor Carrier Act*, S.P.E.I. 1984, c. 26, s. 1.

RATEPAYER. *n.* 1. A person obliged to pay a tax to a municipal corporation. 2. A person who is assessed upon the last revised assessment roll of a municipality. 3. (i) In respect of a municipality or a local board thereof, other than a school board, a person entitled to vote at a municipal election in the municipality; and (ii) in respect of a public, separate or secondary school board, a person entitled to vote at the election of members of such board. *Municipal Conflict of Interest Act*, R.S.O. 1980, c. 305, s. 1. See FRENCH-SPEAKING ~; RESIDENT ~.

RATE PER FOOT. The annual sum charged equally to each foot of frontage sufficient to amortize the owners' share of the cost of a local improvement and interest over a period of years as prescribed by the council pursuant to section 15. *The Local Improvements Act*, R.S.S. 1978, c. L-33, s. 2.

RATE PERMITTED. A rate that is a legal and valid rate in respect of the loan, and is not in contravention of any Act heretofore or hereafter enacted by the Parliament of Canada. *Money-Lenders Act*, R.S.N.S. 1967, c. 188, s. 1.

RATES. *n.* 1. The charges set or made for the

supply of a public utility and includes all conditions of supply pertaining thereto. 2. Rates, surcharges, premiums or any other amount payable by an insured for automobile insurance. *Automobile Insurance Act*, S.Nfld. 1977, c. 82, s. 1. See COMPENSATION ~; EASTERN ~; HANDLING ~; IRRIGATION ~; RATE.

RATES OF CONTRIBUTION. The regular net premiums, dues, rates or contributions receivable from the members for the purpose of the payment at maturity of the society's certificates or contracts of insurance. Insurance acts.

RATIFICATION. *n.* 1. The act of confirming. 2. Agency is created by ratification when an agent does something on behalf of a principal when they are not yet in the relation of principal and agent. Later, however, the principal accepts and adopts the agent's act as if there had been prior authorisation to do what was done. G.H.L. Fridman, *The Law of Agency*, 5th ed. (London: Butterworths, 1983) at 73. 3. Formal approval given to terms negotiated in collective bargaining.

RATIHABITIO MANDATO AEQUIPARATUR. [L.] Ratification is the same as a command.

RATING. See BOILER ~; CONTINUOUS ~; CREDIT ~; EXPERIENCE ~; FIRE EXTINGUISHER ~; FIRE RESISTANCE ~; FIRE-PROTECTION ~; FLAME-SPREAD ~; GROSS AXLE WEIGHT ~; GROSS VEHICLE WEIGHT ~; LOAD ~; MAXIMUM LOAD ~; POWER ~; PROTEIN EFFICIENCY ~; PROTEIN ~.

RATING BUREAU. Any association or body created or organized for the purpose of filing or promulgating rates of premium payable upon contracts of insurance or which assumes to file or promulgate such rates by agreement, among the members thereof or otherwise.

RATIO. *n.* [L. a reason] 1. The grounds or reason for deciding. 2. A rule for calculating proportions. 3. A calculation of credits and debits. See CLAIMS ~; FREEBOARD ~; FREIGHT TO PRICE ~; FUNDED ~; GAS OIL ~; GROSS DEBT SERVICE ~; ISOPHANE ~; QUICK ASSET ~.

RATIO DECIDENDI. [L.] The grounds or reason for deciding.

RATIO LEGIS EST ANIMA LEGIS. [L.] The reason for the law is the essence of the law.

RATIONABILI ESTOVERIUM. [L.] Alimony.

RATIONABILIS DOS. [L.] A widow's proper share or a reasonable dowery.

RATIONALE. See OBJECTIVE ~.

RATIONES. *n.* [L.] In a suit, pleadings. See AD ~ STARE.

RATIONES EXERCERE. [L.] To plead.

RATIONE SOLI. [L.] By reason alone.

RATIONE TENURAE. [L.] In respect or by reason of one's tenure.

RATIONING PROGRAM. A mandatory allocation program that is extended and converted pursuant to section 29 in respect of any controlled product. *Energy Supplies Emergency Act*, R.S.C. 1985, c. E-9, s. 2.

RAW GAS. A mixture containing methane, other paraffinic hydrocarbons, nitrogen, carbon dioxide, hydrogen sulphide, helium and minor impurities, or some of them, that is recovered or is recoverable at a well from an underground reservoir and that is gaseous at the conditions under which its volume is measured or estimated.

RAW HIDE. The skin, with or without the pelage, of big game that is in an unprocessed, whether it be a green, dry or salted condition and includes any part of such skin. *Wildlife Act*, S.N.W.T. 1978 (3d Sess.), c. 8, s. 2.

RAW LEAF TOBACCO. Unmanufactured tobacco or the leaves and stems of the tobacco plant. *Excise Act*, R.S.C. 1985, c. E-14, s. 6.

RAW MILK. Milk that has not been pasteurized.

RAW PELT. The skin, with or without the pelage, of a fur-bearing animal or small game that is in an unprocessed, whether it be a green, dry or salted condition and includes any part of such skin. *Wildlife Act*, S.N.W.T. 1978 (3d Sess.), c. 8, s. 2.

RAW WATER. Water that is not potable water. Canada regulations.

RAW WOOL, HAIR OR BRISTLES. Wool, hair or bristles taken from an animal but does not include wool tops, wool waste, wool noils, wool laps, small trade samples of wool, lime pulled wool and hair, scoured wool and hair and carbonized wool and hair. *Animal Disease and Protection Regulations*, C.R.C., c. 296, s. 2.

RAY. *n.* Any transmission of energy in the form of particles or electromagnetic waves with or without production of ions when they pass through matter. *Environment Quality Act*, R.S.Q. 1977, c. Q-2, s. 1.

R.C. *abbr.* Roman Catholic.

RCA TRUST. Under a retirement compensation arrangement means (a) any trust deemed by subsection 207.6(1) to be created in respect of subject property of the arrangement; and (b) any trust governed by the arrangement. *Income Tax*

Act, R.S.C. 1952, c. 148 (as am. S.C. 1987. c. 46, s. 62), s. 207.5(1).

R.C. DE L'É. *abbr.* Recueils de jurisprudence de la Cour de l'Échiquier.

R.C.L.J. *abbr.* Revue critique de législation et de jurisprudence du Canada.

RCMP. *abbr.* Royal Canadian Mounted Police.

R.C.P.I. *abbr.* Revue canadienne de propriété intellectuelle.

R.C.S. *abbr.* Recueils des arrêts de la Cour Suprême du Canada.

[ ] R.C.S. *abbr.* Rapports judiciaires du Canada, Cour Suprême du Canada, 1964-.

R. DE J. *abbr.* Revue de jurisprudence.

R. DE L. *abbr.* Revue de Législation (1845-1848).

R.D.F. *abbr.* Recueil de droit de la famille.

R.D.F.Q. *abbr.* Recueil de droit fiscal québécois.

[ ] R.D.F.Q. *abbr.* Recueil de droit fiscal Québécois, 1977-.

R.D.I. *abbr.* Recueil de droit immobilier.

R.D.J. *abbr.* Revue de droit judiciaire, 1983-.

R.D. MCGILL. *abbr.* Revue de droit de McGill (McGill Law Journal).

R.D.T. *abbr.* Revue de droit de travail.

R. DU B. *abbr.* La Revue du Barreau.

R. DU B. CAN. *abbr.* La Revue du Barreau canadien (The Canadian Bar Review).

R. DU D. *abbr.* Revue du droit (1922-1939).

R. DU N. *abbr.* La Revue du Notariat.

R.D. U.N.-B. *abbr.* Revue de droit de l'Université du Nouveau-Brunswick (University of New Brunswick Law Review).

R.D.U.S. *abbr.* Revue de droit, Université de Sherbrooke.

RE. *prep.* [L.] Concerning, in the matter of.

REACTING CATTLE. Any bovine animals showing a positive reaction to the agglutination test or any other recognized tests for Bang's Disease. *Bang's Disease Eradication Act*, R.S.P.E.I. 1974, c. B-2, s. 1.

REACTION. See HYPERSENSITIVITY ~; VITAL ~.

READER. See BRAND ~.

READILY ACCESSIBLE. Capable of being reached quickly without climbing over or removing obstacles or resorting to portable ladders, chairs or similar aids. *Power Corporation Act*, R.R.O. 1980, Reg. 794, s. 0.

READILY REMOVABLE WINDOW. A window that can be quickly and completely removed from a vehicle without tools and, in the case of a bus having a GVWR of more than 4 535.9 kg (10,000 pounds), shall include a push-out window and a window mounted in an emergency exit that can be manually pushed out of its location in the vehicle without the use of tools, regardless of whether the window remains hinged to one side to the vehicle. *Motor Vehicle Safety Regulations*, C.R.C., c. 1038, s. 2.

READINESS. See CERTIFICATE OF ~; NOTICE OF ~ FOR TRIAL.

READING. See FIRST ~; SECOND ~; THIRD ~.

READING DOWN. A doctrine which requires that, as much as possible, a statute be interpreted as within power. When the language of a statute will bear both a valid, limited meaning and an invalid, extended meaning, the limited meaning should be selected. P.W. Hogg, *Constitutional Law of Canada*, 2d ed. (Toronto: Carswell, 1985) at 327.

READMISSION. *n.* Admission to a hospital of someone who had previously received inpatient care.

READY FOR JUDGMENT. See CASE ~.

REAL. See CHATTELS ~.

REAL ACTION. The common law proceeding by which a freeholder was able to recover land.

REAL ESTATE. 1. Includes messuages, lands, tenements and hereditaments, whether freehold or of any other tenure, and whether corporeal or incorporeal, and any undivided share thereof, and any estate, right or interest therein. 2. Includes: (i) real or leasehold property; (ii) any business, whether with or without premises, fixtures, stock-in-trade, goods or chattels connected with the operation of the business; and (iii) a time-sharing arrangement. 3. An estate in fee simple in land, and does not include any lesser estate or interest therein. *Trust Companies Act*, R.S.A. 1980, c. T-9, s. 1. See IMPROVED ~.

REAL ESTATE BROKER. Any person who carries out a real estate transaction for another and for remuneration. *Real Estate Brokerage Act*, R.S.Q. 1977, c. C-73, s. 1.

REAL ESTATE CORPORATION. A corporation incorporated to acquire, hold, maintain, improve, lease or manage real estate or leaseholds or act as agent or broker in the sale or purchase of real estate or leaseholds.

REAL ESTATE INVESTMENT TRUST. 1. A mutual fund the assets of which consist solely or primarily of investments in or loans in relation to real estate, an interest in real estate or a real estate related activity. *Bank Act*, R.S.C. 1985, c. B-1, s. 2. 2. The major kinds of investment are mortgage loans, purchase-leasebacks, construction and development loans, real estate equities and land. D.M.W. Waters, *The Law of Trusts in Canada*, 2d ed. (Toronto: Carswell, 1984) at 446.

REAL ESTATE SALESMAN. A person, other than a broker, who is employed or engages for compensation, reward, or profit or promise or hope thereof, and sells or exchanges, or buys or offers or attempts to negotiate a sale or exchange, or purchase, of any real estate, or who obtains or attempts to obtain any listing of real estate for sale or represents a broker in the management of real estate or collection of rent therefrom or who otherwise engages in a transaction. *Real Estate Brokers Act*, R.S.M. 1970, c. R20, s. 2.

REAL ESTATE TAX. 1. A tax imposed on an immoveable by a municipal corporation or a school board, regardless of the use made of it. 2. A tax, other than a water tax, levied by a province or provincial agency to finance services that, in the opinion of the Minister, are ordinarily provided throughout Canada by municipalities (a) on all owners of real property in that part of the province where the federal property is situated, excepting those exempt by law; and (b) on persons who are lessees or occupiers of real property owned by any person exempt by law, and computed by applying one or more rates to all or a part of the assessed value of such real property. *Real Property Grants Regulations*, C.R.C., c. 343, s. 2.

REAL ESTATE TRANSACTION. 1. A transaction for the acquisition, disposal, exchange or renting of real estate, or for the negotiation of a loan secured by a charge on or transfer of real estate, or for the collection of money so secured or money payable as rent for the use of real estate. *Real Estate Act*, R.S.B.C. 1979, c. 356, s. 1. 2. The purchase, sale, promise of purchase or sale of an immoveable, the purchase or sale of such promise, the exchange or rental of an immoveable, the bulk sale of a stock in trade, a loan secured by the hypothecation or pledging of an immoveable, excluding any act respecting a security within the meaning of the Securities Act. *Real Estate Brokerage Act*, R.S.Q. 1977, c. C-73, s. 1.

REAL EVIDENCE. Evidence other than testimony such as an object or place, or a sketch of it, which a judge or jury observes in or out of court. P.K. McWilliams, *Canadian Criminal*

Evidence, 3d ed. (Aurora: Canada Law Book, 1988) at 1-12.

REALIZABLE VALUE. The amount which one would realize through orderly liquidation before considering any costs of the liquidation, e.g. income taxes on the disposal of assets, liquidation commissions or severance pay. A. Bissett-Johnson & W.M. Holland, eds., *Matrimonial Property Law in Canada* (Toronto: Carswell, 1980) at V-3.

REALIZATION. *n.* The sale of all or virtually all the property, assets and undertaking of a debtor. F. Bennett, *Receiverships* (Toronto: Carswell, 1985) at 2·1.

REALM. *n.* A country; a territory subject to a sovereign. See GREAT SEAL OF THE ~; HER MAJESTY'S ~S AND TERRITORIES.

REAL OWNER. (a) A purchaser of the land under an agreement for sale; (b) a person who is entitled to become the owner of land at some future date under a trust; (c) a person on whose behalf the registered owner holds the land as agent; or (d) any person who is entitled to have the land registered in his name. *Municipal Assessment Act*, S.M. 1974, c. 24, s. 4.

REAL PROPERTY. 1. Includes messuages, lands, rents and hereditaments whether of freehold or any other tenure whatever and whether corporeal or incorporeal and any undivided share thereof and any estate, right or interest other than a chattel interest therein. 2. The ground or soil and everything annexed to it, and includes land covered by water, all quarries and substances in or under land other than mines or minerals and all buildings, fixtures, machinery, structures and things erected on or under or affixed to land. 3. Includes any estate, interest or right to or in land, but does not include a mortgage secured by real property. See IMMOVABLE PROPERTY AND ~.

REAL PROPERTY INSURANCE. Insurance against the loss of, or damage to, real or immovable property resulting from any cause not specifically mentioned in other classes of insurance covering real or immovable property. *Classes of Insurance Regulations*, C.R.C., c. 977, s. 33.

REAL PROPERTY TAX. A tax, including a water tax, of general application to real property or any class thereof that is (a) levied by a taxing authority on owners of real property, or where the owner is exempt from the tax, on lessees or occupiers of real property, other than those exempt by law; and (b) computed by applying a rate to all or part of the assessed value of taxable property. *Municipal Grants Act*, R.S.C. 1985, c. M-13, s. 2. See RESIDENTIAL ~.

REAL RIGHT. Jus in re, a full and complete right.

REAL THING. Something immovable and substantial, and any rights and profits which are annexed to or issue out of it.

REALTY. *n.* Real property; freehold land. See COMMERCIAL ~.

REAL WAGE. The value of a wage in terms of commodities and services which the wage can purchase.

REARING. *n.* Keeping fish or fish eggs or feeding fish artificially in a fish preserve. *Quebec Fishery Regulations*, C.R.C., c. 852, s. 2.

REAR LOT LINE. (a) In the case of a regular shaped lot the boundary line of the lot opposite and furthest in distance from the front lot line; and (b) in the case of an irregular shaped lot, a line 10 feet in length within the lot parallel to and at the maximum distance from the front lot line. Canada regulations.

REAR YARD. 1. A yard extending across the full width of a lot between the rearmost main building or main storage area and the rear lot line. Canada regulations. 2. A yard extended across the full width of a lot upon which a building or structure is situate and from the rear lot line to the part of the building or structure that is nearest to the rear lot line. *Niagara Escarpment Planning and Development Act*, R.R.O. 1980, Reg. 685, s. 1.

REAR YARD DEPTH. The distance measured horizontally from the nearest point of the rear lot line toward the nearest part of the main structure, clear of projections, or the main storage area, as the case may be. Canada regulations.

REASONABLE AMOUNT FOR A RESERVE. Usually the full amount which a taxpayer received, in either the current or a preceding year, for goods or services which past experience or something else indicates will have to be provided or delivered after the end of the year. One need not estimate the profit on these goods or services since the reserve is not restricted to the estimated costs of any goods still to be delivered or any services still to be rendered. W. Grover & F. Iacobucci, *Materials on Canadian Income Tax*, 4th ed. (Toronto: Richard De Boo Ltd., 1980) at 628.

REASONABLE AND PROBABLE CAUSE. Grounds which lead one person to suspect another of a crime.

REASONABLE DOUBT. See BEYOND A ~.

REASONABLE LIMITS. In section 1 of the Charter, rights are subject to such legal limitation as one can demonstrate is justified in a free and democratic society.

REASONABLE MARKET DEMAND. The demand for oil or gas for reasonable current requirements and current consumption or use within and outside the province, together with such amounts as are reasonably necessary for building up or maintaining reasonable storage reserves and working stocks of oil and gas and the products thereof. *The Oil and Gas Conservation Act*, R.S.S. 1978, c. O-2, s. 2.

REASONABLE NEEDS. Whatever is reasonably suitable for the maintenance of the person in question, having regard to the ability, means, needs and circumstances of that person and of any person obliged to contribute to such reasonable needs. *Family Maintenance Act*, S.N.S. 1979-80, c. 6, s. 2.

REASSURANCE. *var.* **RE-ASSURANCE.** *n.* A contract which a first insurer enters into with another insurer to be free wholly or partly from a risk already undertaken.

RE-ATTACHMENT. *n.* A second attachment by one who has attached previously.

REBATE. *n.* A discount; a deduction from a payment.

REBELLION. *n.* Taking up arms against the Crown.

REBROADCASTING TRANSMITTING STATION. A broadcasting transmitter that is licensed by the Commission for the sole purpose of retransmitting radio-communication signals received from an originating broadcasting transmitting station. *Broadcasting Licence Fee Regulations*, C.R.C., c. 373, s. 2.

REBUILD. *v.* To make or impose a new tread or new surface or to otherwise alter the surface of a used tire so that it will resemble a new tire, by cutting into or adding rubber to the surface thereof, or by a combination of both. *Highway Traffic Act*, R.S.O. 1980, c. 198, s. 53.

REBUS SIC STANTIBUS. [L. things standing so] Under these circumstances.

REBUT. *v.* To contradict; to reply.

REBUTTAL EVIDENCE. Evidence which rebuts or contradicts evidence which the defence adduced in the case. P.K. McWilliams, *Canadian Criminal Evidence*, 3d ed. (Aurora: Canada Law Book, 1988) at 31-1.

REBUTTABLE PRESUMPTION OF LAW. A presumption authorized by the National Defence Act, the Criminal Code or other Act of the Parliament of Canada that upon proof of a certain fact or set of facts, another fact exists, unless evidence to the degree required by law renders its existence unlikely. *Military Rules of Evidence*, C.R.C., c. 1049, s. 2.

REBUTTER. *n.* A pleading.

RECALL. *v.* 1. To call back to work according to seniority standing, a basic and valuable benefit which a person who was actually laid off retains. D.J.M. Brown and D.M. Beatty, *Canadian Labour Arbitration*, 2d ed. (Aurora: Canada Law Book, 1977) at 292. 2. In respect of a device that has been sold, means any action taken in respect of the device by the manufacturer or importer thereof after becoming aware that the device (a) is or may be hazardous to health; (b) fails or may fail to conform with any claims made by the manufacturer or importer relating to the effectiveness, benefits, performance characteristics or safety of the device; or (c) does not comply with the Act or these Regulations, to recall or correct the device or to notify the owner or user of the device of the defectiveness thereof. *Medical Devices Regulations*, C.R.C., c. 871, s. 2.

REC. ANN. WINDSOR ACCÈS JUSTICE. *abbr.* Recueil annuel de Windsor d'accès à la justice (Windsor Yearbook of Access to Justice).

RECAPTION. *n.* A remedy to which a party may resort when someone deprives the party of goods or wrongfully detains the party's spouse, child or servant. In such a case, the injured party may lawfully reclaim them, as long as this is not done so that the peace is broken.

RECAPTURE. *v.* If a taxpayer sells an asset at a figure higher than the notional value to which it was reduced by claiming an annual capital cost allowance against previous years' taxable income, an amount equal to that previously claimed allowance now recovered must be brought into taxable income in the year of sale. D.M.W. Waters, *The Law of Trusts in Canada*, 2d ed. (Toronto: Carswell, 1984) at 830.

RECEDITUR A PLACITIS JURIS POTIUS QUAM INJURIAE ET DELICTA MANEANT IMPUNITA. [L.] Abandon the forms of law rather than let crimes and wrongs go unpunished.

RECEIPT. *n.* 1. An acknowledgement in writing that one received money or property. 2. A warehouse receipt. See ACCOUNTABLE ~; DEPOSIT ~; ELEVATOR ~; NEGOTIABLE ~; NON-NEGOTIABLE ~; RENT ~; REVENUE ~; WAREHOUSE ~.

RECEIPTS. *n.* All revenue and includes any money borrowed by the Territories. *Financial Administration Act*, R.S.N.W.T. 1974, c. F-4, s. 2. See ANNUAL ~; CAPITAL ~.

RECEIVABLE. *n.* Any money owed to the

Territories that is not evidenced by a promissory note. *Financial Administration Act*, R.S.N.W.T. 1974, c. F-4, s. 2.

RECEIVABLE. *adj.* See ACCOUNT ~; FACTORING OF ~S; LOANS ~.

RECEIVED. See ACTUALLY ~.

RECEIVER. *n.* 1. A person who was appointed to take possession of property which belongs to a third party. F. Bennett, *Receiverships* (Toronto: Carswell, 1985) at 1. 2. A person appointed by a court to receive the rent and profit of real estate or to collect personal goods. When the appointment is by way of equitable execution, the receiver has the power to sell the personalty and to distribute the rents, proceeds and profits of the real estate to any judgment creditors. C.R.B. Dunlop, *Creditor-Debtor Law in Canada* (Toronto: Carswell, 1981) at 281. 3. Any pressure vessel used for the storage or collection of an expansible fluid. *Boilers and Pressure Vessels Act*, R.S.A. 1970, c. 32, s. 2. See AIR ~; COURT-APPOINTED ~; INTERIM ~; OFFICIAL ~; PRIVATE ~; TELEVISION ~.

RECEIVER AND MANAGER. A person appointed to carry on or superintend a trade, business or undertaking in addition to receiving rents and profits, or to get in outstanding property.

RECEIVERSHIP. See SOFT ~.

RECEIVING BANK. That portion of a money room designated for receiving money from sellers and cashiers. *Race Track Supervision Regulations*, C.R.C., c. 441, s. 2.

RECEIVING CHARGE. A charge for removing goods from railway flat cars or from the tailgate or bed of motor transport vehicles and moving the goods to an ordinary place of rest when handled by fork lift equipment only. *Pacific Terminal Tariff By-law*, C.R.C., c. 1083, s. 28.

RECEIVING HOME. 1. An institution or home operated or supervised by a society for the temporary care of children. *Child Welfare Act*, R.S.O. 1980, c. 66, s. 19. 2. A building or part of a building fitted for the reception and examination, physical or mental, of any neglected, delinquent or mentally defective child and established or approved as a receiving home by the Minister, and supervised by the Director, and is deemed to include a foster home. *Child Welfare Act*, S.Nfld. 1972, c. 37, s. 2.

RECEIVING ORDER. An order which declares a debtor to be bankrupt and which results in the trustee of the bankrupt estate being appointed rather than a receiver. F. Bennett, *Receiverships* (Toronto: Carswell, 1985) at 3.

RECEIVING PLANT. A premises to which dead animals are delivered for the purpose of obtaining the hide, skin, fats, meat or other product of the dead animals, or for the purpose of selling or delivering the dead animals or parts thereof to a rendering plant. *Dead Animal Disposal Act*, R.S.O. 1980, c. 112, s. 1.

RECEIVING STATION. See CREAM ~.

RECENT POSSESSION. Inferences which can be drawn when it is shown that a person is in possession of property recently stolen. These are determined by the time of theft, the kind of articles stolen, i.e., whether they are the sort of thing which passes rapidly from person to person, or whether the accused would be likely to possess them innocently. P.K. McWilliams, *Canadian Criminal Evidence*, 3d ed. (Aurora: Canada Law Book, 1988) at 5-14.

RECEPTACLE. *n.* One or more contact devices, on the same yoke, installed at an outlet for the connection of one or more attachment plugs. *Power Corporation Act*, R.R.O. 1980, Reg. 794, s. 0. See DUPLEX ~; SINGLE ~; SPLIT ~; SUITABLE ~.

RECEPTION CENTRE. 1. Any place established or designated for the purpose of receiving a child for examination, care, treatment, education or rehabilitation. 2. Facilities where inpatient, out-patient, or home-care services are offered for the lodging, maintenance, keeping under observation, treatment or social rehabilitation, as the case may be, of persons whose condition, by reason of their age or their physical, personality, psycho-social or family deficiencies, is such that they must be treated, kept in protected residence or, if need be, for close treatment, or treated at home, including nurseries, but excepting day care establishments contemplated in the Act respecting child day care, foster families, vacation camps and other similar facilities and facilities maintained by a religious institution to receive its members or followers. *An Act respecting health services and social services*, S.Q. 1979, c. 85, s. 82.

RECESS. *n.* 1. The period between Parliament being prorogued and reassembling for a new session. A. Fraser, G.A. Birch & W.A. Dawson, eds., *Beauchesne's Rules and Forms of the House of Commons of Canada*, 5th ed. (Toronto: Carswell, 1978) at 54. 2. A short pause in a sitting of a court.

RECESSION. *n.* A granting again.

RECIDIVIST. *n.* A person who repeatedly commits crimes.

RECIPIENT. *n.* 1. A person to whom any amount is or is about to become payable. 2. A person to whom financial aid is granted. 3. A person to whom an allowance has been granted and includes an applicant for an allowance. 4. A person to whom assistance has been granted. 5. A person to whom a service supplier supplies a taxed service. *Social Security Assessment Act*, S.Nfld. 1972, c. 56, s. 10. 6. An economically underprivileged person who receives legal aid. *Legal Aid Act*, R.S.Q. 1977, c. A-14, s. 1. 7. Every person to whom health services or social services are furnished by an establishment or foster family. *Health Services and Social Services Act*, R.S.Q. 1977, c. S-5, s. 1. See FAMILY ALLOWANCE ~.

RECIPIENT OF PUBLIC MONEYS. A corporation, association, board, commission, society or person to which or to whom a grant or advance of public moneys may be or is made, or the borrowing of which or of whom may be or are guaranteed by the Crown under any Act, but does not include an agency of the government. *Provincial Auditors's Act*, S.M. 1979, c. 12, s. 1.

RECIPROCAL EXCHANGE. 1. A group of subscribers exchanging reciprocal contracts of indemnity or inter-insurance with each other through the same attorney. 2. A group of persons, each of whom agrees to insure each of the others to the extent and in the manner agreed on, in consideration of agreements on their part to insure him. *Insurance Act*, R.S.B.C. 1979, c. 200, s. 1.

RECIPROCAL OR INTER-INSURANCE EXCHANGE. A group of subscribers exchanging reciprocal contracts of indemnity of inter-insurance with each other through the same attorney. *Insurance Contracts Act*, R.S.Nfld. 1970, c. 178, s. 2.

RECIPROCAL TAXATION AGREEMENT. An agreement referred to in section 32. *Federal-Provincial Fiscal Arrangements Act*, R.S.C. 1985, c. F-8, s. 31.

RECIPROCAL TRANSFER AGREEMENT. An agreement related to two or more pension plans that provides for the transfer of money or credit for employment or both in respect of individual members of the plans. *Pension Benefits Act*, S.N.B. 1987, c. P-5.1, s. 1.

RECIPROCATING EMPLOYER. (a) The Government of Canada, or an agency thereof; or (b) the government of a province or territory in Canada, other than Manitoba, or an agency thereof; or (c) a municipality in Canada but not in Manitoba; or (d) a school division, school district or school area in Canada but not in Manitoba; or (e) an educational institution in Canada but not in Manitoba; or (f) an employer in Canada including Manitoba, but other than any of the employers set out in clauses (a) to (e); if the employer has established or is participating in any plan or scheme that provides pension, superannuation or disability benefits for and in respect of its employees. Manitoba statutes.

RECIPROCATING JURISDICTION. 1. A state of the United States of America, the District of Columbia, the Commonwealth of Puerto Rico, a territory or possession of the United States of America, or a province or territory of Canada, which has enacted this Act or provides substantially equivalent access to its courts and administrative agencies. Transboundary Pollution Reciprocal Access acts. 2. A foreign jurisdiction (i) where a certificate issued under this Act is accorded the same recognition as a foreign certificate issued in that jurisdiction is accorded within Manitoba; and (ii) that is designated as such by the minister. *Power Engineers Act*, S.M. 1974, c. 48, s. 1.

RECIPROCATING MANITOBA EMPLOYER. (a) The government or an agency thereof; or (b) a school division, school district or school area in Manitoba; or (c) a university in Manitoba; or (d) a municipality in Manitoba; or (e) an employer in Manitoba, other than any of the employers set out in clauses (a) to (d), whose employees are eligible to contribute to the Civil Service Superannuation Fund; or (f) an employer in Manitoba, other than any of the employers set out or described in clauses (a) to (e), designated by the Lieutenant Governor in Council; if the employer has established or is participating in any plan or scheme that provides pension, superannuation or disability benefits for and in respect of its employees. Manitoba statutes.

RECIPROCATING PROVINCE. 1. A province that has been declared to be a reciprocating province with respect to the deposit of a particular insurer. Insurance acts. 2. A province declared under section 30 to be a reciprocating province. *Young Offenders Act*, S.A. 1984, c. Y-1, s. 1.

RECIPROCATING PROVINCE OR TERRITORY. A province or territory of Canada designated by regulation as a province or territory in which legislation substantially similar to this section exists. *Provincial Offences Procedure Act*, S.N.B. 1987, c. P-22.1, s. 113.

RECIPROCATING STATE. 1. A state declared to be a reciprocating state and includes a province or territory of Canada. Reciprocal Enforcement of Maintenance Orders acts. 2. A foreign state that is a party to a cultural property agreement. *Cultural Property Export and Import Act*, R.S.C. 1985, c. C-51, s. 37.

RECIPROCITY. *n.* Mutual action.

RECIRCULATION SYSTEM. A system that: (i) maintains circulation of water through a pool by pumps; (ii) draws water from a pool for treatment and returns it to the pool as clean water; and (iii) provides continuous treatment that includes filtration and chlorination or bromination, and other processes that may be necessary for the treatment of the water. *Public Health Act*, R.R.O. 1980, Reg. 849, s. 1.

RECITAL. *n.* A statement in an agreement, deed or other formal document intended to lead up to or explain the operative part of the document.

RECKLESS. *adj.* Describes a person who, knowing that there is risk that something may happen as a result of acting in a certain way or existing circumstances, takes the risk when it is unreasonable to take it, considering the nature and degree of the risk known to be present. S. Mitchell, P.J. Richardson & D.A. Thomas, eds., *Archbold Pleading, Evidence and Practice in Criminal Cases*, 43d ed. (London: Sweet & Maxwell, 1988) at 1346.

RECLAIMED TEXTILE FIBRE. A textile fibre obtained from a yarn or fabric. *Textile Labelling and Advertising Regulations*, C.R.C., c. 1551, s. 2.

RECOGNITION. See VOLUNTARY ~.

RECOGNITION AGREEMENT. An agreement in writing, signed by the parties, between an employer or employers' organization, on the one hand, and a trade union or council of trade unions, on the other, under which the trade union or council of trade unions is recognized as the exclusive bargaining agent of the employees in a bargaining unit defined in the recognition agreement. *Industrial Relations Act*, R.S.N.B. 1973, c. I-4, s. 1.

RECOGNITION CLAUSE. A mandatory provision in any collective agreement which determines the scope of the bargaining unit and the work which falls to that unit. D.J.M. Brown and D.M. Beatty, *Canadian Labour Arbitration*, 2d ed. (Aurora: Canada Law Book, 1977) at 635.

RECOGNIZANCE. *n.* When used in relation to a recognizance entered into before an officer in charge, means a recognizance in Form 11, and when used in relation to a recognizance entered into before a justice or judge, means a recognizance in Form 32. *Criminal Code*, R.S.C. 1985, c. C-46, s. 493.

RECOGNIZED CANADIAN SCHEME. Any plan or scheme established to provide pension, superannuation or disability benefits, or any of them, for and in respect of employees (i) of the Government of Canada; or (ii) of the government of a province of territory of Canada; or (iii) of an agency of the Government of Canada; or (iv) of an agency of the government of a province or territory of Canada; or (v) of a municipality in Canada; or (vi) of a school division, school district or school area in Canada; or (vii) of an educational institution in Canada; or (viii) of a hospital or associated health facility in Canada, or any of them and under which the employees make contributions towards the funding of the plan or scheme. Manitoba statutes.

RECOGNIZED CODE. The code of the American Society of Mechanical Engineers, the British Standards Institution or the code of a similar organization that the Board considers to be of comparable standing. *Steamship Machinery Inspection Regulations*, C.R.C., c. 1492, s. 2.

RECOGNIZED DENOMINATION. A religious denomination for which educational districts have been established and School Boards have been appointed by or under The Schools Act or any predecessor Act to that Act. *Education (Teacher Training) Act*, R.S.Nfld. 1970, c. 103, s. 2.

RECOGNIZED OPPOSITION PARTY. 1. The members of the assembly who belong to a political party that is represented in the assembly by four or more members and that is not (i) the political party represented in the assembly by the largest number of members; or (ii) the official opposition. *Legislative Assembly Act*, R.S.M. 1970, c. L110, s. 61. 2. A party that (a) holds at least 4 seats in the Legislative Assembly; and (b) received at least 5% of the popular vote in the election immediately preceding the year in which the allowance in subsection (2) is to be paid. *Legislative Assembly Act*, R.S.A. 1980, c. L-10, s. 60.

RECOGNIZED PARTY. 1. The party of a Premier or of a Leader of the Opposition. 2. Any political party that at a general election has, or at the general election preceding a by-election had, not less than 10 candidates officially nominated.

RECOGNIZED POLITICAL PARTY. An affiliation of electors comprised in a political organization whose prime purpose is the fielding of candidates for election to the legislature. See LEADER OF A ~.

RECOGNIZED RETAIL STORE. Does not include a dwelling, mail-order office, display room, office, repair or service shop, warehouse, studio or other place of a like nature. Direct Sellers acts.

RECOMMENDATION TO MERCY. Before the death penalty was abolished, a jury who found an accused guilty of murder could accompany their verdict by recommending the prisoner to the Crown's mercy, on certain particular grounds.

RECOMMIT. *v.* To send a bill to a Committee of the Whole or any other committee when a member moves an amendment to the third reading motion. A. Fraser, G.A. Birch & W.A. Dawson, eds., *Beauchesne's Rules and Forms of the House of Commons of Canada*, 5th ed. (Toronto: Carswell, 1978) at 240.

RECONDITIONING. *n.* The flushing, cleaning, recasing, relining or rescreening of an existing well by means of a drilling machine for the purpose of improving water production or the quality of the water produced by the well. *Ground Water Development Act*, R.S.A. 1980, c. G-11.1, s. 1.

RECONSTITUTED MILK. Milk remade or compounded.

RECONSTRUCTED VEHICLE. A vehicle of a type required to be registered under this Act and materially altered from its original construction by the removal, addition or substitution of essential parts, new or used. Vehicles acts.

RECONSTRUCTION. *n.* Transferring the assets, or a major part of them, of one company to a new company formed for just that purpose in exchange for shares of the new company to be distributed among the old company's shareholders. H. Sutherland, D.B. Horsley & J.M. Edmiston, eds., *Fraser's Handbook on Canadian Company Law*, 7th ed. (Toronto: Carswell, 1985) at 349. See AMALGAMATION OR ~; REORGANIZATION.

RECONVERSION. *n.* An imaginary process in which an earlier constructive conversion is annulled and the converted property is restored to its original condition in contemplation of law.

RECONVEYANCE. *n.* Conveying mortgaged property again, free from the mortgage debt, to the mortgagor or the mortgagor's representatives after the mortgage debt is paid off.

RECORD. *n.* 1. Includes any information that is recorded or stored by means of any device. 2. Includes the whole or any part of any book, document, paper, card, tape or other thing on or in which information is written, recorded, stored or reproduced, and, except for the purposes of subsections (3) and (4), any copy or transcript admitted in evidence under this section pursuant to subsection (3) or (4). *Canada Evidence Act*, R.S.C. 1985, c. C-5, s. 30(12). 3. A collection of every pleading and proceeding in an action intended for use at the trial. 4. Includes any correspondence, memorandum, book, plan, map, drawing, diagram, pictorial or graphic work, photograph, film, microform, sound recording, videotape, machine readable record, and any other documentary material regardless of physical form or characteristics, and any copy thereof. 5. When used in reference to a person, means all recorded information, regardless of physical form or characteristics, that: (i) relates to the person; (ii) is recorded in connection with the provision of an approved service, or a service purchased by an approved agency, to the person or a member of the person's family; and (iii) is under the control of a service provider. *Child and Family Services Act*, S.O. 1984, c. 55, s. 162. 6. An entry in an official book kept for that purpose. *Yukon Quartz Mining Act*, R.S.C. 1985, c. Y-4, s. 2. See CARTOGRAPHIC ~ OR DOCUMENT; CERTIFIED ~; COURT OF ~; COURT ~; EMPLOYMENT ~; EXPOSURE ~; IMMUNIZATION ~; INSTRUMENT ~; MANUSCRIPT, ~ OR DOCUMENT; PHOTOGRAPHIC ~ OR DOCUMENT; PICTORIAL ~ OR DOCUMENT; PUBLIC ~; PUPIL ~; ~S; SURVEYOR OF ~; TRIAL ~; VIOLATION ~.

RECORDED. *adj.* Entered in the record.

RECORDED ADDRESS. (a) In relation to a person as a shareholder, his latest known postal address according to the central securities register of a bank; and (b) in relation to a person in any other respect, his latest known postal address according to the records of the branch concerned. *Bank Act*, R.S.C. 1985, c. B-1, s. 2.

RECORDED AGENT. A person on record with the Commission on Election Contributions and Expenses as being authorized to accept contributions on behalf of a political party, constituency association or candidate registered under the Election Finances Reform Act. *Corporations Tax Act*, R.S.O. 1980, c. 97, s. 28.

RECORDED ON MEDICAL EXAMINATION PRIOR TO ENLISTMENT. When used with reference to a disability or disabling condition of a member of the forces, means a written record, X-ray film or photograph of the disability or disabling condition that was made in (a) any medical documentation made on enlistment of that member; (b) any official documentation covering any former period of service of that member; (c) the files of the Department relating to that member; (d) the records of any compensation board or insurance company relating to that member; or (e) the records of a medical practitioner or a clinic, hospital or other medical institution relating to that member. *Pensions Act*, R.S.C. 1985, c. P-6, s. 21(12).

RECORDED SOUND. See DOCUMENT OF ~.

RECORDER. See COCKPIT VOICE ~; VOTING ~.

RECORDING. See AIR TRAFFIC CONTROL ~.

RECORDING APPARATUS. See SOUND ~.

RECORDING EQUIPMENT. Any equipment, device, apparatus, or contrivance, whereby spoken words can be recorded on tape, wire, discs, cylinders, or records, or on any other material or thing, from which those spoken words can be subsequently reproduced. *Manitoba Telephone Act*, R.S.M. 1970, c. T40, s. 2.

RECORD OF EARNINGS. The Record of Earnings established under section 95. *Canada Pension Plan*, R.S.C. 1985, c. C-8, s. 2.

RECORD OFFICE. Any land title office and any office of a court in which documents are deposited. *Document Disposal Act*, R.S.B.C. 1979, c. 95, s. 1.

RECORD OF OFFENCES. A conviction for: (i) an offence in respect of which a pardon has been granted under the Criminal Records Act (Canada) and has not been revoked; or (ii) an offence in respect of any provincial enactment. *Human Rights Code, 1981*, S.O. 1981, c. 53, s. 9.

RECORD OF THE PROCEEDING. Includes (a) a document by which the proceeding is commenced; (b) a notice of a hearing in the proceeding; (c) an intermediate order made by the tribunal; (d) a document produced in evidence at a hearing before the tribunal, subject to any limitation expressly imposed by any other enactment on the extent to or the purpose for which a document may be used in evidence in a proceeding; (e) a transcript, if any, of the oral evidence given at a hearing; and (f) the decision of the tribunal and any reasons given by it. *Judicial Review Procedure Act*, R.S.B.C. 1979, c. 209, s. 1.

RECORDS. *n.* 1. An all embracing term meaning correspondence, memoranda, completed forms, or other papers, books, maps, plans and drawings, paintings and prints, photographs, films, microforms, motion picture films, sound recordings, tape, video-tapes, computer cards, or other documentary material regardless of physical form or characteristics. 2. Includes the register, books, indices, drawings, plans, instruments and other documents or any part of them registered, deposited, filed or lodged in the land title office, and those recorded or stored by any means, whether graphic, electronic, mechanical or otherwise, in any location under the authority of the Lieutenant Governor in Council. *Land Titles Act*, R.S.B.C. 1979, c. 219, s. 1. 3. (i) Accounts, books, returns, statements, reports, financial documents or other memoranda of financial or non-financial information, whether in writing or in electronic form or represented or reproduced by any other means; and (ii) the results of the recording of details of electronic data processing systems and programs to illustrate what the systems and programs do and how they operate. See DEPOSIT OF ~; RECORD; TRUST ~.

RECORDS MANAGEMENT. A program instituted to provide an economical and efficient system for the creation, maintenance and disposal of public records.

RECORDS OF A NOTARY. All the deeds executed en minute by a notary, the repertory of such deeds and the corresponding index and also such documents when the notary is the assignee thereof. *Notarial Act*, R.S.Q. 1977, c. N-2, s. 1.

RECORDS SCHEDULE. A prescribed timetable that (a) describes a document's lifespan from the date on which it was created to the date of its final disposition, including the periods of its active and dormant stages either as waste or as a document of legal or historical value to be permanently preserved; and (b) provides instruction as to the manner and time of the disposition of a document.

RECOUNT. *v.* (a) To add again the votes given for each candidate as recorded in the statements of the polls returned by the several deputy returning officers; and (b) to examine and count the used and counted, the unused, the rejected and the spoiled ballot papers.

RECOUP. *v.* 1. To pay back. 2. To hold back something due.

RECOUPMENT. *n.* Complete repayment in that the whole sum of money spent effectively discharges the debt for which, though both parties are liable, the defendant is largely liable. G.H.L. Fridman & J.G. McLeod, *Restitution* (Toronto: Carswell, 1982) at 347.

RECOURSE. *n.* The right to recover against a party secondarily liable. See WITHOUT ~ TO ME.

RECOVERY. *n.* 1. Obtaining something which was wrongfully taken or withheld from someone, or to which that person is otherwise entitled. 2. That a person who is, or was, a patient is no longer infectious. *Public Health Act*, R.R.O. 1980, Reg. 836, s. 1. See CHEMICAL ~ BOILER; DOUBLE ~; ENHANCED ~; HEAT ~ UNIT OR DEVICE; MINERAL ~.

RECREANT. *adj.* Describes one who yields.

RECREATION. See CROSS-COUNTRY ~.

RECREATIONAL ACTIVITIES. Includes the planned use of all available resources, including finances, leadership, areas and facilities, to meet the needs of residents of the province for recreation during their leisure hours. *Department of Rehabilitation and Recreation Act*, S.Nfld. 1973, c. 27, s. 2. See OUTDOOR RECREATIONAL ACTIVITY.

RECREATIONAL AGREEMENT. An agreement entered into by a corporation that allows (i) persons, other than the owners, to use recreational facilities located on the common property; or (ii) the owners to use recreational facilities not located on the common property. *Condominium Property Act*, R.S.A. 1980, c. C-22, s. 1.

RECREATIONAL CAMP. Includes a cabin or cottage used for hunting, fishing or leisure and occupied during only part of the year. *Forest Fires Act*, R.S.N.B. 1973, c. F-20, s. 1.

RECREATIONAL FACILITY. See PUBLIC ~.

RECREATIONAL FISHING. Fishing for the purpose of exercising the skill of a fisherman or occupying his leisure time. *Quebec Fishery Regulations*, C.R.C., c. 852, s. 2.

RECREATIONAL FISHING LICENCE. See ZONE ~.

RECREATIONAL HARBOUR. See FISHING OR ~.

RECREATIONAL LAND. 1. Land that is not used exclusively as residential land and that is predominantly used for the recreation and enjoyment of its owner or lessee or those, other than persons using the land for agricultural purposes, who are permitted by such owner or lessee to be on the land. *Land Transfer Tax Act*, R.S.O. 1980, c. 231, s. 1. 2. Land and improvements used by the public for the recreational purposes that the Lieutenant Governor in Council prescribes. *Recreational Land Act*, R.S.B.C. 1979, c. 359, s. 1.

RECREATIONAL PARK. A park primarily intended to foster the practice of various outdoor recreational activities, while protecting the natural environment. *Parks Act*, R.S.Q. 1977, c. P-9, s. 1.

RECREATIONAL PROPERTY. Land owned by a physical person and used by him principally for recreational or sports purposes, having an area not greater than one acre except to the extent that such person establishes that a greater area is necessary for such purposes. *Land Transfer Duties Act*, R.S.Q. 1977, c. D-17, s. 1.

RECREATIONAL VEHICLE. A vehicular type unit primarily designed as temporary living quarters for recreational, camping, or travel use, which either has its own motive power or is mounted on or drawn by another vehicle. *Camp-*

ing Establishments Regulation Act, S.N.S. 1973, c. 64, s. 1.

RECREATION CENTRE. See COMMUNITY ~.

RECREATION FACILITY. Any land, buildings, equipment, or other physical plant, whether publicly or privately owned, used to satisfy the needs and desires of people during their leisure. *Recreation Development Act*, R.S.P.E.I. 1974, c. R-9, s. 1.

RECREATION PROGRAM. A program for the provision of facilities for recreation and for the supervision, encouragement and guidance of recreational activity. *Ministry of Culture and Recreation Act*, R.R.O. 1980, Reg. 653, s. 1.

RECREATION SERVICE. Any program for the planned use of recreation facilities to satisfy the needs or desires of people during their leisure.

RECRIMINATION. *n.* A charge which an accused makes against an accuser.

RECTIFICATION. *n.* Essentially bringing a document which was intended or expressed to achieve the same result as a prior agreement into harmony with that agreement. G.H.L. Fridman, *The Law of Contract in Canada*, 2d ed. (Toronto: Carswell, 1986) at 741.

RECTIFIER. *n.* Any pipe, vessel or still into which the spirit is conveyed for the purpose of rectification, re-distillation, filtration or any other process. *Excise Act*, R.S.C. 1985, c. E-14, s. 3.

RECTIFY. *v.* To alter the written words of an agreement so that they reflect what the parties really agreed. D.J.M. Brown and D.M. Beatty, *Canadian Labour Arbitration*, 2d ed. (Aurora: Canada Law Book, 1977) at 75.

RECTIFYING SPIRITS. The process of refining spirits by re-distillation, filtration or any other process. *Excise Act*, R.S.C. 1985, c. E-14, s. 3.

RECTITUDO. *n.* [L.] Justice or right; what is legally due; payment or tribute.

RECTOR. *n.* The clergyman acting for the time being as rector of a Roman Catholic parish or the rector of a church or public chapel used for Roman Catholic worship. *Roman Catholic Cemetery Corporations Act*, R.S.Q. 1977, c. C-69, s. 1.

RECTUM. *n.* [L.] 1. Right. 2. The terminal part of the large intestine which opens through the anus. F.A. Jaffe, *A Guide to Pathological Evidence*, 2d ed. (Toronto: Carswell, 1983) at 182. See STARE AD ~.

RECTUM ESSE. [L.] In court, to be right.

RECTUM ROGARE. [L.] To request right.

RECTUS IN CURIA. [L.] Legally right.

R.E.D. *abbr.* 1. Russell's Equity Decisions (N.S.), 1873-1882. 2. Ritchie's Equity Decisions, by Russell (N.S.). 3. Ritchie's Equity Reports, by Russell (N.S.).

RED CLAUSE. A clause endorsed in coloured ink on a commercial letter of credit which authorizes a bank to accept or pay drafts against the promise that a bill of lading and other documents will be provided when certain goods are shipped. I.F.G. Baxter, *The Law of Banking*, 3d ed. (Toronto: Carswell, 1981) at 156.

REDDENDO SINGULA SINGULIS. [L. by giving each to each] Describes a clause in a document when one of two provisions in the first sentence is appropriated to one of two objects in the second sentence, and the other provision is likewise appropriated to the other object.

REDDENDUM. *n.* [L. that which is to be paid or rendered] The clause in a lease, usually using the words "yielding and paying", which states the amount of the rent and the time at which it should be paid.

REDDIDIT SE. [L.] One gave oneself up.

REDDITARIUM. *n.* The rental of a manor or estate.

REDDITARIUS. *n.* A tenant, one who rents.

REDDITION. *n.* Restoring or surrendering; in the course of legal proceedings formally admitting that lands were the property of the person who sought to recover them, not of the person who made the admission.

REDDITUS. *n.* [L.] Rent.

REDDITUS ASSISUS. [L.] An established or standing rent.

REDDITUS QUIETI. [L.] Quit-rent.

REDDITUS SICCUS. [L.] Rent seck.

REDEEM. *v.* To buy back. See ACTION TO ~.

REDEEMABLE RIGHTS. Rights which return to the one who conveys or disposes of land once the sum for which such rights are granted is paid.

REDEEMABLE SECURITY. A security which exists for a fixed term and is redeemable at the end of that term at a specified value.

REDEEMABLE SHARE. A share issued by a corporation (a) that the corporation may purchase or redeem on the demand of the corporation; or (b) that the corporation is required by its articles to purchase or redeem at a specified time or on the demand of a shareholder.

REDELIVERY. *n.* Yielding and delivering something back.

REDEMISE. *n.* Re-granting land.

REDEMPTION. *n.* 1. The payment, fulfilment or performance by the purchaser or person claiming through him, of all obligations secured by the property and, where there has been a breach or default of the purchaser or person claiming through him by payment of (a) all expenses or disbursements reasonably made or incurred by the vendor in respect of the property, including taxes, repairs and payments in respect of other encumbrances; and (b) reasonable compensation for costs incurred by the vendor in bringing a proceeding or seeking to enforce the obligations of the purchaser to the extent provided for in the agreement for sale or the Rules of Court. *Law Reform Act*, S.B.C. 1985, c. 10, s. 16.1. 2. In relation to mutual fund shares of the company, be deemed to be a reference to acceptance by the company of the surrender of those shares. *Companies Act*, R.S.N.W.T. 1974, c. C-7, s. 71. See EQUITY OF ~; PROVISO FOR ~.

REDEMPTION DATE. In the case of a security that is redeemable at more than one specified date, the specified date that gives the lower or the lowest effective rate of interest, as the case may be. *Cooperative Credit Associations Act*, R.S.C. 1985, c. C-41, s. 57(4).

REDEMPTION PERIOD. That period of time within which the owner of a dog or cat that has been impounded in a pound has the right to redeem it. *Animals for Research Act*, R.S.O. 1980, c. 22, s. 1.

REDEVELOPMENT. *n.* The planning or replanning, design or redesign, resubdivision, clearance, development, reconstruction and rehabilitation, or any of them, of a redevelopment area, and the provision of such residential, commercial, industrial, public, recreational, institutional, religious, charitable or other uses, buildings, works, improvements or facilities, or spaces therefor, as may be appropriate or necessary.

REDEVELOPMENT AREA. An area within a municipality, the redevelopment of which in the opinion of the council is desirable because of age, dilapidation, overcrowding, faulty arrangement, unsuitability of buildings or for any other reason. *Planning Act*, R.S.O. 1980, c. 379, s. 22.

REDEVELOPMENT PLAN. A general scheme, including supporting maps and texts, approved by the Minister for the redevelopment of a redevelopment area. *Planning Act*, R.S.O. 1980, c. 379, s. 22.

REDEVELOPMENT TAX. A compulsory levy imposed by a municipality on real property situated within a defined area that is (a) payable by a taxable owner of real property by virtue of his ownership of such property or of specified actions undertaken by him to develop such property; (b) calculated by reference to all or part of the frontage, area or other attribute of land or buildings of the owner; (c) assessed at a uniform rate upon owners of real property liable to pay the tax; and (d) levied for the purpose of financing all or part of the capital cost of the construction or reconstruction of a trunk or arterial road or any other capital service that has been, is being or will be carried out within the defined area, but does not include a levy in respect of which payments by way of a grant may be made under section 4 or 6 of the Municipal Grants Act or a levy on real property paid to a municipality in the form of a land transfer or of cash in lieu thereof. *Development Tax and Redevelopment Tax Grant Regulations*, C.R.C., c. 322, s. 2.

REDFISH. *n.* A fish of the species Sebastes marinus. *Northwest Atlantic Fisheries Regulations*, C.R.C., c. 860, s. 2.

RED HAKE. A fish of the species Urophycis Chuss. *Northwest Atlantic Fisheries Regulations*, C.R.C., c. 860, s. 2.

RED-HANDED. *adj.* With the marks of crime fresh on one's person.

RED HERRING. 1. A non-issue. 2. A preliminary prospectus marked in red ink.

REDIRECTED MAIL. Mail that cannot be delivered as addressed because the addressee has left the place to which the mail was addressed but that can, because the addressee has filed a Request for Redirection of Mail-Holding of Mail card with the postmaster, be redirected for delivery to him at that address. *Undeliverable and Redirected Mail Regulations*, C.R.C., c. 1298, s. 2.

REDISSEISIN. *n.* Recovery of the seisin of a freehold by someone who was disseised and delivery of possession by the sheriff, followed by disseisen again by the same disseisor.

REDITUS. *n.* [L.] Rent.

REDITUS ASSISUS. [L.] An established or standing rent.

REDITUS QUIETI. [L.] Quit-rent.

REDITUS SICCUS. [L.] Rent seck.

RED LIGHT. Includes a red reflector or other device that gives or is capable of giving the effect of a red light. *Motor Vehicle Act*, R.S.N.S. 1967, c. 191, s. 162.

REDOCUMENTATION CHARGE. A charge for reissuing or making changes to the billing of inbound cargo arising from changes in original manifests, split delivery or shipments, forwarding instructions or services. *Pacific Terminal Tariff By-law*, C.R.C., c. 1083, s. 41.

RE-DRAFT. *n.* The second version of a document.

REDRESS. *n.* Relief in the form of damages or equitable relief.

RED ROT. A condition in which the yolk sac is ruptured permitting mixture of the yolk and white. *Live Stock and Live Stock Products Act*, R.R.O. 1980, Reg. 582, s. 1.

REDUCTIO AD ABSURDUM. [L.] The way to disprove an argument by demonstrating that it leads to an unreasonable conclusion.

REDUCTION INTO POSSESSION. Exercising the right which a chose in action confers so that it is converted into a chose in possession. In this way one may reduce a debt into possession by obtaining payment.

REDUCTION PLANT. See FISH LIVER ~; FISH OFFAL ~; HERRING ~.

REDUNDANCY. *n.* Unneeded or extraneous material inserted in a pleading.

REDUNDANT ASSET. An asset which is not needed for an on-going operation. A. Bissett-Johnson & W.M. Holland, eds., *Matrimonial Property Law in Canada* (Toronto: Carswell, 1980) at V-5.

REDUNDANT EMPLOYEE. An employee whose employment is to be terminated pursuant to a notice under section 212. *Canada Labour Code*, R.S.C. 1985, c. L-2, s. 211.

REEL. *n.* 1. (i) A photographic moving picture film; (ii) a video tape; or (iii) a cassette; not exceeding 10 minutes in running time. *The Theatres and Cinematographs Act*, R.S.S. 1978, c. T-11, s. 2. 2. 2,000 feet or less in length of standard film or 16-millimetre cinematographic film or 400 feet or less in length of 8-millimetre cinematographic film. *Theatres Act*, R.R.O. 1980, Reg. 931, s. 1.

RE-EMPLOYMENT LIST. A list of persons eligible for appointment to positions in some particular class because they were subject to a lay-off from positions in that same class. Civil Service acts.

RE-ENTRANT. See NEW ENTRANT OR ~ TO THE LABOUR FORCE.

RE-ENTRY. *n.* In a lease, a proviso which

empowers the lessor to re-enter the leased premises if the rent has not been paid for a certain period.

REEVE. *n.* The principal official of a town.

RE-EXAMINATION. *n.* Examination of a witness by the counsel who first examined that person concerning a new fact which arose out of cross-examination. S. Mitchell, P.J. Richardson & D.A. Thomas, eds., *Archbold Pleading, Evidence and Practice in Criminal Cases*, 43d ed. (London: Sweet & Maxwell, 1988) at 548.

RE-EXTENT. *n.* Concerning a debt, a second execution by extent.

REF. *abbr.* Reference.

REFER. *v.* With respect to a question, to have it decided by someone nominated for that purpose.

REFEREE. *n.* A person to whom a court refers a pending cause so that that person may take testimony, hear the parties, and report back. See BOARD OF ~S.

REFERENCE. *n.* 1. Sending a whole proceeding or a particular issue to (a) a local judge, local registrar, master or other officer; (b) a person the parties agree on; or (c) a family law commissioner. G.D. Watson & C. Perkins, eds., *Holmested & Watson: Ontario Civil Procedure* (Toronto: Carswell, 1984) at 54-2. 2. A question which a government presents to a court for an opinion concerning the constitutionality of an enactment although there is no real dispute. Robert J. Sharpe, ed., *Charter Litigation* (Toronto: Butterworths, 1987) at 337. 3. In order to take accounts or make inquiries, to determine any question or issue of fact, the court may refer any matter to a judge whom the Associate Chief Justice nominates, a prothonotary, or any other person the court deems to be qualified for the purpose so that that person may inquire and report. D. Sgayias *et al.*, *Federal Court Practice 1988* (Toronto: Carswell, 1987) at 499. See ADOPTION BY ~; FEDERAL ~; PATRIATION ~ (1981); PROVINCIAL ~.

REFERENCE CONDITIONS. See STANDARD ~.

REFERENCE PLAN. The plan of survey of a block or part of a lot or on a registered plan of subdivision or part of a registered parcel.

REFERENCE POINT. With respect to a hearing aid, means a point on the hearing aid chosen for the purpose of defining the position of the hearing aid in the test field. *Medical Devices Regulations*, C.R.C., c. 871, s. 1. See SEATING ~.

REFERENCE POST. A legal post erected pursuant to subsection (4) to designate the corner of a claim previously designated by a witness post. *Canada Mining Regulations*, C.R.C., c. 1516, s. 15.

REFERENCE STANDARD. A standard that (a) represents or registers a unit of measurement referred to in Schedule I or II or that represents or registers a multiple or fraction of such a unit of measurement; (b) has been calibrated and certified by the National Research Council of Canada; and (c) is or is to be used as a standard for the purpose of determining the accuracy of a local standard. *Weights and Measures Act*, R.S.C. 1985, c. W-6, s. 2.

REFERENDUM. *n.* The direct vote of electors concerning a particular measure or matter.

REFERENDUM PERIOD. The period beginning on the day fixed for issuing a writ and ending on the day for its return. *Referendum Act*, S.Q. 1978, c. 6, s. 1.

REFERRAL. *n.* Includes assignment, designation, dispatching, scheduling and selection. *Canada Labour Code*, R.S.C. 1985, c. L-2, s. 69.

REFERRAL HIRING SYSTEM. A system which permits a union to refer all workers required for a project.

REFERRAL SELLING. Receipt by the purchaser of a product of a commission, rebate or other benefit from the seller, based on sales which other people made to people whom the purchaser named. G.H.L. Fridman, *Sale of Goods in Canada*, 3d ed. (Toronto: Carswell, 1986) at 493. See SCHEME OF ~.

REFERRED BYLAW. A bylaw referred to a vote of either the burgesses or the electors, or both. *The Urban Municipality Act*, R.S.S. 1978, c. U-10, s. 2.

REFILLABLE CONTAINER. 1. A container that is intended to be used more than once for purposes of sale or distribution of a beverage. *Beverage Containers Act*, S.N.B. 1980, c. 7, s. 1. 2. An approved container for which a cash deposit is made to a retailer or for which a retailer is required by this Act or the regulations to pay a refund. *Beverage Containers Act*, S.N.S. 1975, c. 55, s. 2.

REFINANCE. *v.* Where used to refer to the refinancing of a foreign debt, means the issue and sale of bonds, debentures and notes or the arranging of loans by the issuer of the foreign debt for the purpose of payment, refunding, refinancing or renewal of the foreign debt. *Energy Rate Stabilization Act*, S.M. 1979, c. 42, s. 1.

REFINED OILS. Fats or oils or any combination of fats and oils that have been refined or hydrogenated and that do not contain more than 1 per cent of substances other than fatty acids and fat. *Oleomargarine Act*, R.R.O. 1980, Reg. 696, s. 1.

REFINED PETROLEUM PRODUCT. A commodity made from oil and, without limiting the generality of the foregoing, includes motor and tractor gasoline, naphtha gasoline, kerosene, diesel fuel, aviation fuel, turbo fuel, bunker oil and lubrication products. *The Oil and Gas Conservation, Stabilization and Development Act*, R.S.S. 1978, c. O-3, s. 19.

REFINER. *n.* A person who refines, manufactures, produces, prepares, distils, compounds and blends fuel petroleum products.

REFINERY. *n.* Any facility where oil or minerals are processed or refined.

REFINING. *n.* Any treatment of smelter product or concentrate to remove impurities, producing a very high grade metal in the metallic state.

REFLECTORIZED. *adj.* As applied to any equipment carried in or on a vehicle, or to a traffic control device, means treated in such a manner that, under normal atmospheric conditions, and when illuminated by the light from the lamps of any vehicle approaching it will reflect that light so that it is clearly visible from a distance of at least 150 metres. *The Highway Traffic Act*, S.M. 1985-86, c. 3, s. 1.

RE-FLOATING. *n.* The law is uncertain about whether a security instrument which contains a floating charge and crystallizes stays crystallized or re-floats if the security holder changes its mind and discharges the manager and receiver soon after they are appointed. F. Bennett, *Receiverships* (Toronto: Carswell, 1985) at 10.

REFORM. *v.* With respect to an instrument, to rectify it. See LAW ∼ COMMISSION OF CANADA.

REFORMATORY. *n.* An institution where offenders are sent to be reformed.

REFORMATORY INSTITUTION. An industrial or reformatory school, home, orphanage, refuge or other institution that has been approved by the Minister for the purposes of this Act. *Education Act*, R.S.N.S. 1967, c. 81, s. 1.

REFRACTORY MATERIALS. Includes fire bricks, plastic refractories, high temperature cement, fire clay and short lived refractories such as melting pots, crucibles and retorts. *Retail Sales Tax Act*, R.R.O. 1980, Reg. 903, s. 1.

REFRACTORY PERIOD. The period during which a triggered pulse generator is unresponsive to an input signal. *Medical Devices Regulations*, C.R.C., c. 871, s. 1.

REFRESH. *v.* With respect to a witness' memory, to refer to a document which may not itself be admissible as evidence.

REFRESHMENT HOUSE. A place conducted by a person, firm or corporation, who sells by retail all or any of the following: meals and drinks of all kinds for consumption on the premises only, and includes a delicatessen selling cooked meats, cooked vegetables, and cooked fish, not in sealed containers. *Shops Regulation Act*, R.S.M. 1970, c. S110, s. 3.

REFRIGERANT. *n.* A substance that may be used to produce refrigeration by its expansion or evaporation. *Operating Engineers Act*, R.S.O. 1980, c. 363, s. 1.

REFRIGERANT VESSEL. A pressure vessel that is a component part of a refrigeration system. *Boilers and Pressure Vessels Act*, R.R.O. 1980, Reg. 84, s. 1.

REFRIGERATING PLANT. The complete installation of pressure vessels, pressure piping, machinery and appliances of all descriptions by which refrigerants are vapourized, compressed and liquefied in their refrigerating cycle. *Boilers and Pressure Vessels Act*, R.S.A. 1970, c. 32, s. 2.

REFRIGERATING SYSTEM. The complete installation of pressure vessels, piping, fittings, compressors, machinery and other equipment by which refrigerants are vapourized, compressed and liquefied in their refrigerating cycle. *Boiler and Pressure Vessel Act*, R.S.Nfld. 1970, c. 24, s. 2.

REFRIGERATION. See TON OF ∼; TONS OF ∼.

REFRIGERATION AND AIR-CONDITIONING MECHANIC. A person who: (i) lays out, assembles, installs, maintains in the field any cooling or heating-cooling combination system for residential, commercial or industrial purposes within the limitation of the Energy Act; (ii) installs or connects piping for the purpose of conveying refrigerant of all types for either primary or secondary cooling; (iii) overhauls or repairs any equipment used in a refrigeration or air-conditioning system; and (iv) tests, adjusts, maintains all controls on refrigeration or air-conditioning systems including air-balancing, but does not include a person who is engaged in the repair or installation of single-phase hermetically sealed domestic self-contained units with factory mass produced systems precharged with refrigerant, or a person employed in production commonly known as mass production. *Apprenticeship and Trades-*

men's Qualification Act, R.R.O. 1980, Reg. 55, s. 1.

REFRIGERATION PLANT. The complete installation of machinery by which refrigerants are vapourized, compressed and liquefied in their refrigeration cycle.

REFRIGERATOR. *n.* Refrigerator, ice box, freezer cabinet, or similar refrigerating container or unit. *The Abandoned Refrigerator Act*, R.S.S. 1978, c. A-1, s. 2.

REFRIGERATOR PLANT. An installation comprised of one or more refrigeration compressors and the equipment used therewith for compressing, liquefying and evaporating a refrigerant.

REFUGE. *n.* 1. An area designated in the regulations as an area in which the hunting of wildlife or exotic animals or of any species, type, class, or group thereof is prohibited. *Wildlife Act*, S.M. 1970, c. 89, s. 2. 2. An institution for the care of the young or of adult females to which they may by law be sentenced by a court.

REFUGEE. *n.* A person who, by reason of a well-founded fear of persecution for reasons of race, religion, nationality, political opinion or membership in a particular social group, (a) has been lawfully admitted to Canada for permanent residence after leaving the country of his nationality and is unable or, by reason of that fear, is unwilling to avail himself of the protection of that country; or (b) has been lawfully admitted to Canada for permanent residence after leaving the country of his former habitual residence and is unable or, by reason of that fear, is unwilling to return to that country and includes, on designation by the Lieutenant Governor in Council, any other person or class of persons admitted to Canada under section 6(2) of the Immigration Act, 1976 (Canada). *Refugee Settlement Program of British Columbia Act*, S.B.C. 1979, c. 27, s. 1. See CONVENTION ~.

REFUND. *n.* The amount which an individual is entitled to (a) receive as an overpayment of the income tax paid by him or on his behalf under the Income Tax Act or the Income Tax Act (Canada) and interest on the overpayment; or (b) receive as an overpayment of unemployment insurance premiums paid by him or on his behalf under the Unemployment Insurance Act, 1971 (Canada); or (c) receive an overpayment of Canada Pension Plan contributions paid by him or on his behalf under the Canada Pension Act (Canada); or (d) receive as a renter's tax credit under the Income Tax Act; or (e) claim as a grant or refund under a Provincial or Federal Act. *Consumer Protection Act*, R.S.B.C. 1979, c. 65, s. 37. See INCOME TAX ~; PATRONAGE ~.

REFUND OF TAX. The amount of (a) an overpayment of tax paid under the Income Tax Act or collected pursuant to an agreement entered into under section 7 of the Federal-Provincial Fiscal Arrangements and Federal Post-Secondary Education and Health Contributions Act; (b) a payment to an individual by virtue of an agreement referred to in paragraph (a) that is other than a refund of an overpayment of tax paid or collected; (c) an overpayment of unemployment insurance premiums paid under the Unemployment Insurance Act; or (d) an overpayment of contributions paid under the Canada Pension Plan, and any interest paid on any of those overpayments or payments. *Tax Rebate Discounting Act*, R.S.C. 1985, c. T-3, s. 2.

REFUSE. *v.* For a person who legally has the right and power to have or do something advantageous to decline it.

REFUSE. *n.* 1. Useless matter or discarded material, including ashes, garbage and domestic and industrial waste other than sewage but does not include junk. *Highway Act*, R.S.N.B. 1973, c. H-5, s. 58. 2. Includes used or dismantled motor vehicles or parts thereof. *Summary Trespass Act*, R.S.P.E.I. 1974, c. S-11, s. 1. See BEEWAX ~.

REG. *abbr.* 1. [L. regina] Queen. 2. Regulation. 3. Registrar.

REGENCY. *n.* Delegation to another person called the regent of some or all of a sovereign's powers when that sovereign is young, incapacitated or away from the realm.

REGICIDE. *n.* 1. The murder of a monarch. 2. One who murders a monarch.

RÉGIE. *n.* The Régie de l'assurance automobile du Québec established by the Act respecting the Régie de l'assurance automobile du Québec (R.S.Q., c. R-4). *Highway Code*, S.Q. 1980, c. 38, s. 2.

REGIME. See COMMUNITY PROPERTY ~; STANDARD MARITAL ~.

REGION. *n.* 1. A province, a portion of a province, two or more provinces or adjoining portions of two or more provinces. *Department of Regional Industrial Expansion Act*, R.S.C. 1985, c. R-5, s. 2. 2. A defined geographical area. See ALTIMETER SETTING ~; ATLANTIC ~; FLIGHT INFORMATION ~; GASPESIA ~; GATINEAU VALLEY ~; MATANE ~; NATIONAL CAPITAL ~; NORTHERN ~S; PRAIRIE ~; QUEBEC NORTH-WEST ~; QUEBEC-SOUTH ~; RIMOUSKI-MATAPÉDIA ~; RIMOUSKI-RIVIÈRE-DU-LOUP ~; RIMOUSKI, RIVIÈRE-DU-LOUP AND

TÉMISCOUATA ~; STE-ANNE-DE-LA-POCATIÈRE ~; STANDARD PRESSURE ~.

REGIONAL ADVANCE BOOKING CHARTER (DOMESTIC). An ABC (domestic) whose origin and destination are within a regional air carrier's defined operating territory or between points on the same regional air carrier's commercial air service licences. *Air Carrier Regulations*, C.R.C., c. 3, s. 83.

REGIONAL A.M. STATION. In relation to a licensee, any A.M. broadcasting station licensed by the Commission whose night-time interference-free official contour encloses any part of the licensed area of the licensee. *Cable Television Regulations*, C.R.C., c. 374, s. 2.

REGIONAL ASSESSMENT OFFICE. The office where the assessment roll for a municipality is prepared in accordance with the Assessment Act. *Planning Act*, S.N.S. 1983, c. 9, s. 3.

REGIONAL CENTRE. An establishment where services are offered for the handling, drying, screening, storage and grading of grain in conformity with the grading system established by regulation. *Grain Act*, S.Q. 1979, c. 84, s. 1.

REGIONAL DIFFERENTIAL. See GEOGRAPHIC WAGE DIFFERENTIAL.

REGIONAL F.M. STATION. In relation to a licensee, any F.M. broadcasting station licensed by the Commission whose 50 microvolt per metre official contour encloses any part of the licensed area of the licensee. *Cable Television Regulations*, C.R.C., c. 374, s. 2.

REGIONAL INDUSTRIAL EXPANSION. See DEPARTMENT OF ~.

REGIONAL MUNICIPALITY. A metropolitan, regional or district municipality as defined in the Act establishing such a municipality and includes the County of Oxford. *Ontario Unconditional Grants Act*, R.S.O. 1980, c. 359, s. 1.

REGIONAL PLAN. A program and policy or any part thereof designed to secure the health, safety, convenience, or welfare of the inhabitants of the area approved by the commission as prescribed in this Act. *Planning Act*, R.S.P.E.I. 1974, c. P-6, s. 1.

REGIONAL SAFETY OFFICER. 1. A person designated as a regional safety officer pursuant to subsection 140(1). *Canada Labour Code*, R.S.C. 1985 (1st Supp.), c. 9, s. 122. 2. The safety officer designated by the Minister to serve as the regional safety officer in the area in which the federal work, undertaking or business is located. Canada regulations.

REGIONAL SURVEY. A geological, geophysical or geochemical survey for minerals, whether ground or airborne, that is performed (a) in relation to a mineral claim or mining lease but extends beyond the land covered by the mineral claim or mining lease; or (b) on land open for prospecting and staking. *Mining Act*, S.N.B. 1985, c. M-14.1, s. 1.

REGIONAL TELEVISION STATION. In relation to a licensee, any television broadcasting station licensed by the Commission whose Grade B official contour encloses any part of the licensed area of the licensee. *Cable Television Regulations*, C.R.C., c. 374, s. 2.

REGIONAL TRAIL. Any footpath, pathway, trail or area of land held in fee simple or as a registered easement or right of way by a regional district and dedicated as a regional trail under this Act. *Park (Regional) Act*, R.S.B.C. 1979, c. 310, s. 1.

REGIONAL TRANSIT SYSTEM. A transit system that is principally operated within a regional area. *Toronto Area Transit Operating Authority Act*, R.S.O. 1980, c. 505, s. 1.

REGISTER. *v.* To file or deposit.

REGISTER. *n.* 1. That part of the records where information respecting registered titles is stored. 2. The register of members and students of a professional body. 3. The record maintained by a registrar for the purpose of recording all registrations, renewals, changes or amendments of registrations, suspensions, cancellations and reinstatements of registrations of brokers or dealers. 4. An entry in an official book kept for that purpose. *Yukon Quartz Mining Act*, R.S.C. 1985, c. Y-4, s. 2. 5. The register maintained pursuant to the Act of the names of persons and firms entitled to represent applicants in the presentation and prosecution of applications for patents before the Office. *Patent Rules*, C.R.C., c. 1250, s. 2. See ANNUAL ~; ASCENDING ~; DESCENDING ~; EDUCATIONAL ~; GENERAL ~; INDIAN ~; SECURITIES ~; TITLE ~; TRAIN ~; VOTING ~.

REGISTERED. *adj.* 1. Filed, listed or holder of a particular status in accordance with an act. 2. Registered as an Indian in the Indian Register. *Indian Act*, R.S.C. 1985, c. I-5, s. 2. 2. Registered in accordance with an act governing a profession. See GROSS ~ TONS.

REGISTERED AGENT. A person whose name is recorded in the registry of agents or registered parties maintained by the Chief Electoral Officer pursuant to subsection 33(1) and includes the chief agent of a registered party and an electoral district agent. *Canada Elections Act*, R.S.C. 1985, c. E-2, s. 2.

REGISTERED ANIMAL. An animal for which a certificate of registration has been issued by the registrar of the breed to which the animal belongs or by the registrar of the Canadian National Livestock Records. *Income Tax Regulations*, C.R.C., c. 945, s. 1802.

REGISTERED CANADIAN AMATEUR ATHLETIC ASSOCIATION. An association that was created under any law in force in Canada, that is resident in Canada, and that (a) is a person described in paragraph 149(1)(l); and (b) has, as its primary purpose and its primary function, the promotion of amateur athletics in Canada on a nation-wide basis, that has applied to the Minister in prescribed form for registration, that has been registered and whose registration has not been revoked under subsection 168(2). *Income Tax Act*, R.S.C. 1952, c. 148 (as am. S.C. 1988, c. 55, s. 188(1)), s. 248(1).

REGISTERED CANADIAN CHARITABLE ORGANIZATION. See now REGISTERED CHARITY.

REGISTERED CHARITY. At any time means (a) a charitable organization, private foundation or public foundation, within the meanings assigned by subsection 149.1(1), that is resident in Canada and was either created or established in Canada; or (b) a branch, section, parish, congregation or other division of an organization or foundation described in paragraph (a), that is resident in Canada and was either created or established in Canada and that receives donations on its own behalf, that has applied to the Minister in prescribed form for registration and that is at that time registered as a charitable organization, private foundation or public foundation. *Income Tax Act*, R.S.C. 1952, c. 148 (as am. S.C. 1988, c. 55, s. 188(1)), s. 248(1).

REGISTERED CLERGYMAN. A clergyman registered under this Act to solemnize marriage. *Marriage Act*, R.S.P.E.I. 1974, c. M-5, s. 2.

REGISTERED COMPANY. See CANADIAN ~.

REGISTERED CONSUMER. 1. A person who brings or imports into Ontario tangible personal property for his own use or consumption that has a fair value exceeding $100 in each of 2 months or more during a calendar year and who holds a valid consumer's permit. *Retail Sales Tax Act*, R.S.O. 1980, c. 454, s. 1. 2. The holder of a valid fuel acquisition permit under this Act. *Fuel Tax Act, 1981*, S.O. 1981, c. 59, s. 1.

REGISTERED CREDITOR. A creditor who is named in a consolidation order. *Bankruptcy Act*, R.S.C. 1985, c. B-3, s. 217.

REGISTERED DIETITIAN. A person whose name is entered in the register and (i) who is a graduate of a baccalaureate degree program with a major in foods and nutrition from the University of Manitoba or any other university accredited by the board; and (ii) who completes an internship program or its equivalent in supervised dietetic work experience that is approved by the board and meets the requirements for membership in the association, as set out in the regulations. *The Registered Dietitians Act*, S.M. 1980-81, c. 14, s. 1.

REGISTERED DOCUMENT. A bill of sale, chattel mortgage, lien note or conditional sale agreement, assignment of book debts and any other document relating to personal chattels registered in the office of a registration clerk for any registration district heretofore or hereafter established for the purpose of registrations of bills of sale, chattel mortgages, lien notes or conditional sale agreements, assignments of book debts and other documents relating to personal chattels. *The Registered Documents Destruction Act*, R.S.S. 1978, c. R-10, s. 2.

REGISTERED EASEMENT. An easement, incorporeal right, condition, covenant, or caveat referred to in section 65(2) of the Land Titles Act. *Tax Recovery Act*, R.S.A. 1980, c. T-1, s. 1.

REGISTERED EDUCATION SAVINGS PLAN. An education savings plan accepted by the Minister for registration for the purpose of this Act as complying with the requirements of this section. *Income Tax Act*, R.S.C. 1952, c. 148 (as am. S.C. 1974-75-76, c. 26, s. 100), s. 146.1(f).

REGISTERED FORM. When applied to a security means a security that: (i) specifies a person entitled to the security or to the rights it evidences, and the transfer of which is capable of being recorded in a securities register; or (ii) bears a statement that it is in registered form. *Business Corporations Act, 1982*, S.O. 1982, c. 4, s. 53.

REGISTERED GROSS TONNAGE. The gross tonnage of a ship as shown on the register of the ship.

REGISTERED GROSS WEIGHT. The weight for which a permit has been issued under the Highway Traffic Act, the fee for which permit is based upon the weight of the vehicle or combination of vehicles and load. *Highway Traffic Act*, R.R.O. 1980, Reg. 462, s. 1.

REGISTERED HOME OWNERSHIP SAVINGS PLAN. A plan under the Income Tax Act designed to encourage saving for home ownership by which any taxpayer at least 18 years old could contribute up to $1,000 a year, an amount completely deductible from income. W. Grover & F. Iacobucci, *Materials on Canadian Income*

Tax, 4th ed. (Toronto: Richard De Boo Ltd., 1980) at 446.

REGISTERED INVESTMENT. A trust or a corporation that has applied in prescribed form as of a particular date in the year of application and has been accepted by the Minister as of that date as a registered investment for one or more of the following: (a) registered retirement savings plans; (b) [Repealed.] (c) registered retirement income funds; and (d) deferred profit sharing plans and that has not been notified by the Minister that it is no longer registered under this Part. *Income Tax Act*, R.S.C. 1952, c. 148 (as am. S.C. 1986, c. 6, s. 107(1)), s. 204.4(1).

REGISTERED LENGTH. (a) The distance from the fore part of the uppermost end of the stern to the aft side of the head of the stern post except that if a stern post is not fitted to the ship, the measurement shall be taken to the fore side of the head of the rudder stock; (b) in the case of a ship that has no rudder stock, or that has a rudder stock situated outside of the hull at the stern, the distance from the fore side of the foremost permanent structure to the aft side of the aftermost permanent structure of the ship, not including guards of rubbing strakes; or (c) in the case of double-ended ships, the distance from the aft side of the forward rudder stock to the fore side of the after rudder stock. *Steamship Machinery Construction Regulations*, C.R.C., c. 1491, s. 2.

REGISTERED LIFE INSURANCE POLICY. A life insurance policy (other than an annuity contract) issued or effected as a registered retirement savings plan or pursuant to such a plan, a deferred profit sharing plan or a registered pension fund or plan. *Income Tax Act*, R.S.C. 1952, c. 148 (as am. S.C. 1988, c. 55, s. 160), s. 211.

REGISTERED LONG TERM LEASE. A lease of a suite from the owner of an owner-occupied apartment building where the lease (a) was registered in the land title office before December 31, 1977 and has not been assigned; (b) has a term of 99 years or more or, where the Lieutenant Governor in Council prescribes a shorter term, a term equal to or greater than the prescribed term; and (c) requires the lessee to pay the owner, for the suite in which the lessee resides, a share of the land tax imposed on the building in the proportion that the actual value of the suite bears to the actual value of the building. *Home Owner Grant Act*, R.S.B.C. 1979, c. 171, s. 1.

REGISTERED MAIL. Includes certified mail.

REGISTERED NAME. The name of a person that is (a) registered by or with the Registrar General under this Act, or under another Act of the Legislature, and recorded on the birth registration of the person; or (b) accepted by the Registrar General as being the name of the person that is registered under the laws of another jurisdiction, but does not include a surname elected under this Act or under the laws of another jurisdiction. *Change of Name Act*, S.N.B. 1987, c. C-2.001, s. 1.

REGISTERED NET TONNAGE. (a) In the case of a vessel registered under the Canada Shipping Act, the registered net tonnage shown on that vessel's certificate of British registry; or (b) in the case of a vessel licensed under the Canada Shipping Act, the allowable net tonnage set out in Column II of Schedule II opposite the overall length of the vessel set out in Column I of that Schedule. *Pacific Fishery Registration and Licensing Regulations*, C.R.C., c. 824, s. 2.

REGISTERED NON-RESIDENT INSURER. A corporation registered to carry on business in Canada under Part VIII of the Canadian and British Insurance Companies Act or under the Foreign Insurance Companies Act. *Income Tax Regulations*, C.R.C., c. 945, s. 804.

REGISTERED NURSE. A person who is licensed to practise the profession of nursing and is a registered member, in good standing, of an association.

REGISTERED NURSING ASSISTANT. A person who is the holder of a certificate as a registered nursing assistant.

REGISTERED OFFICE. A head office or chief place of business the address of which is provided to the provincial or federal authority governing the company and where notices and process may be served on the company and certain documents and books must be kept. H. Sutherland, D.B. Horsley & J.M. Edmiston, eds., *Fraser's Handbook on Canadian Company Law*, 7th ed. (Toronto: Carswell, 1985) at 429.

REGISTERED ORDER. (i) A final order made in a reciprocating state and filed under this Act or under an enactment repealed by this Act with a court in the Province; (ii) a final order deemed to be a registered order; or (iii) a confirmation order that is filed. Maintenance Orders Enforcement acts.

REGISTERED OWNER. 1. An owner of land whose interest in the land is defined and whose name is specified in an instrument in the registry office. 2. The person registered in a land titles office as owner of the fee simple in land unless it appears from the records of the land titles office that another person has purchased the land under an agreement for sale in which case it means that other person. 3. A person in whose name a vehicle is registered. 4. In respect of an aircraft, means the person to whom a certificate of registration for the aircraft has been issued by the Minister under Part I or in respect of whom the aircraft has been registered by the Minister under that Part. *Aeronautics Act*, R.S.C. 1985 (1st Supp.), c. 33, s. 3. 5. (a) Of a bond registered as to principal, means a person whose name has been entered by the Bank in the register as the person to whom the principal is payable; and (b) of a bond registered as to principal and interest, means the person whose name has been entered by the Bank in the register as the person to whom the principal and interest are payable. *Domestic Bonds of Canada Regulations*, C.R.C., c. 698, s. 2. 6. An individual or company in whose name a vessel is registered. Canada regulations.

REGISTERED OWNER IN FEE SIMPLE. A person registered in the books of the land title office as entitled to an estate in fee simple in real property, and, where used in respect of a lesser estate, includes a person who registers a charge. *Assessment Act*, R.S.B.C. 1979, c. 21, s. 1.

REGISTERED PARTY. A political party which has been registered.

REGISTERED PENSION FUND OR PLAN. An employees' superannuation or pension fund or plan accepted by the Minister for registration for the purposes of this Act in respect of its constitution and operations for the taxation year under consideration. *Income Tax Act*, R.S.C. 1952, c. 148 (as am. S.C. 1970-71-72, c. 63), s. 248(1).

REGISTERED PENSION PLAN. 1. A pension plan that is registered and in respect of which a certificate of registration has been issued by the Superintendent under this Act. *Pension Benefits Standards Act*, R.S.C. 1985 (2d Supp.), c. 32, s. 2. 2. A pension plan that is registered with and certified by the Commission as a plan organized and administered in accordance with this Act. *Pension Benefits Act*, R.S.O. 1980, c. 373, s. 1.

REGISTERED PHYSIOTHERAPIST. A person who is registered under this Act and (i) who practises physiotherapy only under the direction of a legally qualified medical practitioner; (ii) who does not diagnose or prescribe; (iii) whose education and qualifications meet the standards required by this Act. *Physiotherapists Act*, R.S.M. 1970, c. P65, s. 2.

REGISTERED PILOT. A person not belonging to a ship who has the conduct thereof and who is registered as a pilot (a) by the Secretary of Commerce of the United States; or (b) pursuant to regulations made by the Governor in Council to navigate all or any of the waters of the Great Lakes Basin. *Canada Shipping Act*, R.S.C. 1970, c. S-9, s. 362.

REGISTERED POLITICAL PARTY. See ELECTION EXPENSES OF A ~.

REGISTERED REPRESENTATIVE. A person qualified to sell securities.

REGISTERED REPRESENTATIVE EXAMINATION. An examination based on the Manual for Registered Representatives that has been prepared and is conducted by the Canadian Securities Institute and so designated by that Institute. *Securities Act*, R.R.O. 1980, Reg. 910, s. 84.

REGISTERED RETIREMENT INCOME FUND. A retirement income fund accepted by the Minister for registration for the purposes of this Act and registered under the Social Insurance Number of the first annuitant under the fund. *Income Tax Act*, R.S.C. 1952, c. 148 (as am. S.C. 1977-78, c. 32, s. 35), s. 146.3(1)(e).

REGISTERED RETIREMENT PLAN. An employees' superannuation plan accepted by the Minister for registration for the purposes of this Part in respect of its constitution and operations for the taxation year under consideration. *Taxation Act*, R.S.Q. 1977, c. I-3, s. 1.

REGISTERED RETIREMENT SAVINGS PLAN. A retirement savings plan accepted by the Minister for registration for the purposes of this Act as complying with the requirements of this section. *Income Tax Act*, R.S.C. 1952, c. 148 (as am. S.C. 1970-71-72, c. 63), s. 146(1)(i).

REGISTERED STATUS. With respect to seed, means that (a) the crop from which the seed is derived meets the standards established by the Association and a crop certificate designated "registered" has been issued for that crop by the Association; or (b) if of foreign origin, the seed is certified as being of registered status by an approved certifying agency. *Seeds Regulations*, C.R.C., c. 1400, s. 2.

REGISTERED STUDENT. A person registered by the Board as entitled to perform the professional functions of a pharmacist in the presence of and under the immediate and continuous supervision of a licensed pharmacist. *Pharmacy Act*, S.P.E.I. 1983, c. 35, s. 1.

REGISTERED SUPPLEMENTARY UNEMPLOYMENT BENEFIT PLAN. A supplementary unemployment benefit plan accepted by the Minister for registration for the purposes of this Act in respect of its constitution and operations for the taxation year under consideration. *Income Tax Act*, R.S.C. 1952, c. 148 (as am. S.C. 1970-71-72, c. 63), c. 145(1)(a).

REGISTERED TRADE-MARK. A trade-mark

that is on the register. *Trade-Marks Act*, R.S.C. 1985, c. T-13, s. 2.

REGISTERED USER. A person registered as such under section 50. *Trade-Marks Act*, R.S.C. 1985, c. T-13, s. 2.

REGISTERED VENDOR. A person who is registered under regulations made pursuant to subsection (10). *Excise Tax Act*, R.S.C. 1985 (2d Supp.), c. 7, s. 69.

REGISTERED WEIGHT. The weight in pounds stated upon the permit for a vehicle. *Motor Vehicle Act*, R.S.N.S. 1967, c. 191, s. 1.

REGISTERING AGENT. The person who is acting as agent for the secured party when submitting a statement for registration but does not include a clerk or other employee of the secured party. *Personal Property Security Act*, R.R.O. 1980, Reg. 749, s. 1.

REGISTERING COURT. A court to which an application for the registration of a judgment is made.

REGISTER NUMBER. The number assigned by the board to a motor vehicle, trailer or semi-trailer. *The Vehicles Act*, R.S.S. 1978, c. V-3, s. 2.

REGISTER OF TITLE AND ABSTRACT INDEX. 1. Includes an instrument received for registration before the closing of the land registry office on the day the tax arrears certificate was registered notwithstanding that the instrument has not been abstracted or entered in the register or index at that time. *Municipal Tax Sales Act*, S.O. 1984, c. 48, s. 1. 2. Includes instruments received for registration before 4:30 p.m. on the day immediately prior to the day on which a notice of exercising the power of sale is given. *Mortgages Act*, R.S.O. 1980, c. 296, s. 30.

REGISTER STATION. A station at which a train register is located. *Regulations No. O-8, Uniform Code of Operating Rules*, C.R.C., c. 1175, Part III, s. 2.

REGISTER TONNAGE. The register tonnage shown on a ship's certificate of registry. *Canada Shipping Act*, R.S.C. 1985, c. S-9, s. 2.

REGISTRANT. *n.* 1. A securities broker or dealer required to be registered to trade or deal in securities under the laws of any jurisdiction. 2. A person who is registered or required to be registered. See NON-RESIDENT CONTROLLED ~.

REGISTRAR. *n.* 1. The person responsible for the operation and management of a registration system. 2. With respect to a court, the administrative officer who is responsible for filing and issuing particular documents, retaining court files and occasionally for assessing costs. 3. The officer of the Department who is in charge of the Indian Register. *Indian Act*, R.S.C. 1985, c. I-5, s. 2. 4. The registrar or master of deeds or land titles or other officer with whom a title to land is registered or recorded. 5. The officer appointed by the Unemployment Insurance Commission to administer the office of the umpire. *Umpire Rules of Procedure*, C.R.C., c. 1574, s. 2. 6. With respect to a court or office of a court means the registrar, prothonotary, clerk of the court or other chief administrative officer of the court or office. *Divorce Regulations*, C.R.C., c. 557, s. 2. 7. An employee of the Commission authorized to register terminal elevator receipts and transfer elevator receipts and includes a Deputy Registrar. *Canada Grain Regulations*, C.R.C., c. 889, s. 2. See LAND ~; LOCAL ~.

REGISTRAR GENERAL. 1. The provincial officer who registers any birth, death and marriage. 2. The Registrar General as defined in the Vital Statistics Act.

REGISTRARIUS. *n.* [L.] A registrar; a notary.

REGISTRAR OF DEEDS. Includes the registrar of land titles or other officer with whom a title to the land is registered.

REGISTRAR OF LAND TITLES. A registrar of land titles appointed under a Land Titles Act.

REGISTRAR OF MOTOR VEHICLES. The person who from time to time performs the duties of superintending the registration of motor vehicles in a province.

REGISTRAR'S PERIODICAL. The Registrar's periodical established under the Business Corporations Act. *Companies Amendment Act, 1983*, S.A. 1983, c. 21, s. 2.

REGISTRARY. *n.* The official whose duty it is to write or keep a register.

REGISTRATION. *n.* 1. (i) Bringing lands under this Act; (ii) entering upon the certificate of title a memorandum authorized by this Act, of any document. Land Titles acts. 2. A valid and subsisting registration permit. 3. The admission of an individual to membership in a professional association and enrolment of that person's name in a register. 4. The entry of the name of a person in a register. 5. (i) A licence to practise a health discipline or group of health disciplines issued under a Part of this Act requiring a licence to practise; or (ii) a certificate respecting the practising of a health discipline or group of health disciplines issued under a Part of this Act, the issuance of which is required to be entered on the register of the appropriate College. *Health Disciplines Act*, R.S.O. 1980, c. 196, s. 1. 6. An entry in an official book kept for that purpose.

Yukon Quartz Mining Act, R.S.C. 1985, c. Y-4, s. 2. 7. Includes both visual indication and printed representation of quantity, unit price or monetary value. *Weights and Measures Regulations*, C.R.C., c. 1605. See CERTIFICATE OF ~; ERROR OF ~; SYSTEM OF ~.

REGISTRATION CARD. A registration card issued under The Highway Traffic Act in respect of a motor vehicle or trailer that is registered under and in accordance with that Act, and includes (a) a certificate issued under Part VIII of The Highway Traffic Act for the operation of a public service vehicle under that Part; (b) a transit permit, and "in transit" marker and an interim registration sticker issued under section 16 or 17 of The Highway Traffic Act; (c) a permit issued under section 83 of The Highway Traffic Act; (d) a licence required under The Taxicab Act; and (e) a document issued by the registrar as evidence of the registration of a snowmobile under The Snowmobile Act. *Automobile Insurance Act*, S.M. 1974, c. 58, s. 2.

REGISTRATION CERTIFICATE. 1. A restricted weapon registration certificate issued under section 109. *Criminal Code*, R.S.C. 1985, c. C-46, s. 84. 2. A certificate of foal registration recognized as valid by a Commission. *Race Track Supervision Regulations*, C.R.C., c. 441, s. 2. 3. A commercial fishing vessel registration certificate issued under the authority of the Minister. *Atlantic Coast Herring Regulations*, C.R.C., c. 804, s. 2.

REGISTRATION COURT. The court in the Province (i) in which the registered order is filed under this Act; or (ii) that deemed a final order to be a registered order under this Act or under an enactment repealed by this Act. Maintenance Orders Enforcement acts.

REGISTRATION JURISDICTION. Employ memorandum and articles of association as incorporating documents. The incorporating officer must ensure that the documents comply with the provisions of the statute, particularly, that there are no illegal objects and that there is no objection to the name. If satisfied that these requirements are met the officer must issue a certificate of incorporation. S.M. Beck *et al.*, *Cases and Materials on Partnerships and Canadian Business Corporations* (Toronto: Carswell Co., 1983) at 159.

REGISTRATION NUMBER. A number or combination of letters and numbers allocated to a motorized snow vehicle by the Ministry on the registration thereof. *Motorized Snow Vehicles Act*, R.S.O. 1980, c. 301, s. 1.

REGISTRATION PERMIT. 1. A valid and subsisting registration permit issued pursuant to The Vehicle Administration Act. Saskatchewan statutes. 2. A permit issued pursuant to the regulations to a deer or moose hunter at a wildlife registration station when that hunter brings a deer or moose killed by him for inspection. *Fish and Wildlife Act*, S.N.B. 1980, c. F-14.1, s. 1.

REGISTRATION PLATE. A commercial fishing vessel registration plate issued under the authority of the Minister. Canada regulations. See FICTITIOUS ~.

REGISTRATION SYSTEM. A system for the registration or the registration and safekeeping of international wills. *Wills Amendment Act, 1981*, S.S. 1980-81, c. 97, s. 4. See TORRENS ~.

REGISTRATION VALIDATION TAB. A tab that is placed on a registration plate to indicate that the plate is valid. *Atlantic Coast Herring Regulations*, C.R.C., c. 804, s. 2.

REGISTRUM BREVIUM. [L.] A place where writs are registered.

REGISTRY. *n.* 1. The office of the Registrar. 2. The office of the court where the notice of appeal is filed. *Court of Appeal Act*, S.B.C. 1982, c. 7, s. 1. 3. The principal office of the Court in Ottawa and the other offices of the Court established by these Rules (see section 145 of the Act and Rule 200(4)) but, in these Rules, where the context so requires, shall be taken as referring to the appropriate officers, clerks and employees of the Court. *Federal Court Rules*, C.R.C., c. 663, s. 2. See LAND ~.

REGISTRY ACT SYSTEM. A person acquiring an interest in land registered in this system must examine the title as it is recorded in the Registry Office, and a vendor usually must show that she or he is lawfully entitled to own the land through a chain of title extending back for a period of years. W.B. Rayner & R.H. McLaren, *Falconbridge on Mortgages*, 4th ed. (Toronto: Canada Law Book, 1977) at 127. Under such a system, anyone who acquires interest in land may register a copy of the document which transfers that interest. The registered documents are organized so that any person may, for a small fee, examine those which affect a particular piece of land. In most cases, a claim which is not registered does not affect a later mortgagee or purchaser who acquired an interest for value and without actually being notified of the unregistered claim, but simple registration of a document does not assure its effectiveness. B.J. Reiter, R.C.B. Risk & B.N. McLellan, *Real Estate Law*, 3d ed. (Toronto: Emond Montgomery, 1986) at 454.

REGISTRY OF DEEDS. Includes the land titles office or other office in which the title to the land is registered. *Railway Act*, R.S.C. 1985, c. R-3, s. 2.

REGISTRY OFFICE. Includes a land titles office and "land titles office" includes (i) a registry office; (ii) with respect to a lien registered in the office of a recorder of a mining district, the office of the recorder; (iii) with respect to a lien registered in the office of the Director of the Petroleum Branch of the Department of Energy and Mines, the office of the Director of the Petroleum Branch; and (iv) with respect to a lien registered in the office of the Director of Crown Lands, the office of Director of Crown Lands. *The Statute Law Amendment Act (1985)*, S.M. 1985-86, c. 51, s. 2(2).

REGISTRY SYSTEM. See REGISTRY ACT SYSTEM.

REGNAL YEAR. A year calculated from a sovereign's accession to the throne, thus 7 Eliz. 2 means the seventh year after the accession of Elizabeth II on February 6, 1952 (February 6, 1958, to February 5, 1959).

REGNANT. *adj.* Reigning.

RE-GRANT. *v.* For a grantor to grant again granted property which came back.

REGRESS. *n.* Entering again.

REGRESSIVE TAX RATE STRUCTURE. A system by which the percentage of income paid in taxes decreases as a taxpayer's income increases. W. Grover & F. Iacobucci, *Materials on Canadian Income Tax*, 4th ed. (Toronto: Richard De Boo Ltd., 1980) at 41.

REGULA EST, JURIS QUIDEM IGNORANTIAM CUIQUE NOCERE FACTI VERO IGNORANTIAM NON NOCERE. [L.] It is a rule that every person is prejudiced by ignorance of law but not by ignorance of fact.

REGULAR. *adj.* Appointed on a permanent basis. *Formal Document Regulations*, C.R.C., c. 1331, s. 2.

REGULAR ELECTION. An election of members of a council held at regular periodic intervals under which the authority is constituted.

REGULAR EMPLOYEE. An employee who is employed for work which is of continuous full time or continuous part time nature. *Pension (Public Service) Act*, R.S.B.C. 1979, c. 318, s. 1.

REGULAR FORCE. 1. The regular force of the Canadian Forces and includes (a) the forces known before February 1, 1968 as the regular forces of the Canadian Forces; and (b) the forces known before February 1, 1968 as the Royal Canadian Navy, the Canadian Army Active Force, the Permanent Active Militia, the Permanent Militia Corps, the permanent staff of the Militia, the Royal Canadian Air Force (Regular) and the Permanent Active Air Force. *Canadian Forces Superannuation Act*, R.S.C. 1985, c. C-17, s. 2. 2. The component of the Canadian Forces that is referred to in the National Defence Act as the regular force. *Interpretation Act*, R.S.C. 1985, c. I-21, s. 35. See MEMBER OF THE ~.

REGULAR FORCE PARTICIPANT. A person who is a participant under Part II of the Canadian Forces Superannuation Act. *Public Service Superannuation Act*, R.S.C. 1985, c. P-36, s. 2.

REGULAR HOURS. The hours or parts thereof, not exceeding standard hours, during which, from day to day, a person employed is required by the employer to be present for, and engaged upon the work or services contemplated by the employment. *Employment Standards Act*, S.M. 1977, c. 56, s. 1.

REGULAR LOT. A township lot whose boundaries according to the original plan conform within one degree to the bearings shown for the corresponding boundaries of the majority of the lots in the tier in which the lots occur. *Surveys Act*, R.S.O. 1980, c. 493, s. 1.

REGULARLY EMPLOYED. A person employed on a continuous basis with allowance for recognized leave periods. *Pacific Pilotage Regulations*, C.R.C., c. 1270, s. 2.

REGULAR MEMBER. A person who is appointed to a rank in the Force. *Royal Canadian Mounted Police Regulations*, C.R.C., c. 1391, s. 2.

REGULAR OLEOMARGARINE. Oleomargarine containing 80 per cent or more of fat. *Oleomargarine Act*, R.S.N.B. 1973, c. O-4, s. 1.

REGULAR PAYMENT CONTRACT. A contract in which payments are required at approximately equal intervals and in approximately equal amounts during the term of the contract. *Consumer Protection Act*, R.R.O. 1980, Reg. 181, s. 18.

REGULAR RATE. With respect to an employee, means the rate of wages ordinarily paid that employee for work done in regular hours.

REGULAR RUN. The transportation of travellers by an autobus or by a taxi, or of merchandise, by a delivery vehicle, on fixed days and hours, from one point to another or on a round trip, but does not apply to the transportation by a hotelkeeper or travellers patronizing his hotel, between such hotel and a station or landing place, within the same locality or in a neighbouring locality. *Highway Code*, R.S.Q. 1977, c. C-24, s. 1.

REGULAR SCHOOL LEAVING AGE. The age at which a person is no longer required by the law of the province in which he resides to attend school. *Adult Occupational Training Regulations*, C.R.C., c. 1, s. 2.

REGULAR SERVICE. The transportation of travellers by an autobus or by a taxi, or of merchandise, by a delivery vehicle, on fixed days and hours, from one point to another or on a round trip, but does not apply to the transportation by a hotelkeeper or travellers patronizing his hotel, between such hotel and a station or landing place, within the same locality or in a neighbouring locality. *Highway Code*, R.S.Q. 1977, c. C-24, s. 1.

REGULAR TRAIN. A train authorized by a time table schedule. *Regulations No. O-8, Uniform Code of Operating Rules*, C.R.C., c. 1175, Part III, s. 2.

REGULAR UNION DUES. In respect of: (a) an employee who is a member of a trade union, the dues uniformly and regularly paid by a member of the union in accordance with the constitution and by-laws of the union; and (b) an employee who is not a member of a trade union, the dues referred to in paragraph (a), other than any amount that is for payment of pension, superannuation, sickness insurance or any other benefit available only to members of the union. *Canada Labour Code*, R.S.C. 1985, c. L-2, s. 70(4).

REGULAR WAGE. (a) The hourly wage of an employee; (b) where paid on a flat rate, piece, commission or other incentive basis, the wages of the employee in a pay period divided by the employee's total hours of work during that pay period; (c) where paid on a weekly basis, the weekly wage of the employee divided by the lesser of the employee's normal or average weekly hours of work; or (d) where paid on a monthly basis, the monthly wage of the employee multiplied by 12 and divided by the product of 52 times the lesser of the employee's normal or average weekly hours of work. *Employment Standards Act*, S.B.C. 1980, c. 10, s. 26.

REGULAR WORKING HOURS. As applied to any period means the aggregate for that period of the number of hours in each day of that period that is recognized as the normal working shift for that day in the employment in which an employee is working.

REGULATE. *v.* 1. Includes govern, control, permit, restrict, prevent, prohibit and exclude and power to prescribe conditions. *Highway*

Traffic Act, R.S.Nfld. 1970, c. 152, s. 2. 2. Includes allow, commence, stop, limit, open, shut and prohibit. *Water Act*, R.S.B.C. 1979, c. 429, s. 1.

REGULATED EXPENSES. All the expenditures incurred during a referendum period to directly or indirectly promote or oppose an option submitted to the referendum. *Referendum Act*, S.Q. 1978, c. 6, s. 27.

REGULATED FIELD PRICE. (i) With reference to a gas sales contract, the price to be paid for gas delivered under the contract by virtue of the operation of (A) section 11(1) and (2), or (B) the regulations, if regulations are made under section 7(1)(b.01) in relation to the gas; or (ii) with reference to a resale contract, the price to be paid for gas delivered under the contract by virtue of the operation of (A) section 11(4), or (B) the regulations, if regulations are made under section 7(1)(b.01) in relation to the gas. *Natural Gas Pricing Agreement Act*, S.A. 1986, c. 26, s. 1(1).

REGULATED FINANCIAL INSTITUTION. (i) A trust company incorporated in Canada; (ii) a bank; (iii) a treasury branch; (iv) an insurance company incorporated in Canada; (v) a credit union incorporated in Canada; or (vi) any other corporation approved by the Director. *Trust Companies Act*, R.S.A. 1980, c. T-9, s. 114.

REGULATED FUND. A fund containing public money except public money (i) forming part of the General Revenue Fund; (ii) received by a revenue officer for deposit in the General Revenue Fund that has not been deposited in the General Revenue Fund; (iii) owned or held by a Provincial agency; or (iv) invested under the authority of a Heritage Fund vote in an investment that, when made, forms part of the Capital Projects Division of the Alberta Heritage Savings Trust Fund, but does not include a revolving fund or the Treasury Branches Deposits Fund. *Financial Administration Act*, R.S.A. 1980, c. F-9, s. 1.

REGULATED PLACE. (a) A place which is licensed or otherwise authorized for the carrying on of an activity which can only be carried on lawfully at a place so licensed or authorized; and (b) a place which a person who is licensed or otherwise authorized to carry on an activity which can only be carried on lawfully by a person so licensed or authorized regularly uses for the purposes of that activity. *Entry Warrants Act*, S.N.B. 1986, c. E-9.2, s. 1.

REGULATED PRODUCT. 1. A natural product of agriculture that is regulated by a commodity board or a marketing agency. 2. Any farm product to the extent that it is grown or produced (a) anywhere in Canada, if an agency is authorized to exercise its powers in relation to any such product grown or produced in Canada; or (b) in any region of Canada designated in the proclamation that authorizes an agency to exercise its powers in relation to any such product grown or produced in that region, or in any such region and anywhere in Canada outside that region for shipment into that region in interprovincial trade and not for export where the proclamation that authorizes the agency to exercise its powers in relation to such product so provides. *Farm Products Marketing Agencies Act*, R.S.C. 1985, c. F-4, s. 2.

REGULATED PROJECT. (a) An electric transmission line of 500 kV or higher voltage; (b) an energy trans-shipment terminal or energy storage facility, capable of storing an energy resource in a quantity that is capable of yielding by combustion 3 PJ of energy; (c) an energy use project; (d) a transmission pipeline, capable of transporting in one year natural gas, oil or solids, or a liquid or gas derived from them, in a quantity that is capable of yielding by combustion 16 PJ of energy; (e) a hydroelectric power plant that has a capacity of 20 MW or more of electricity; (f) a thermal electric power plant that has a capacity of 20 MW or more of electricity; (g) an addition by which 20 MW or more of electric capacity will be added to a hydroelectric or thermal electric power plant; (h) an addition to a regulated project, referred to in paragraphs (a) to (d), that would if constructed alone fall within the definition of "regulated project"; and (i) an undertaking of any kind that the Lieutenant Governor in Council designates to be significant in the matter of energy; but "regulated project" does not include (j) a project that is complete or in operation before this Act comes into force; or (k) a project in respect of which, before this Act comes into force, site preparation or the fabrication, construction, installation or supply of buildings, equipment, machinery or other facilities has begun. *Utilities Commission Act*, S.B.C. 1980, c. 60, s. 16.

REGULATED SELLING PRICE. For a volume of natural gas, the producer selling price payable for that volume plus the amount for the price adjustment, if any, payable for that volume under a price adjustment order and the regulations. *Natural Gas Price Act*, S.B.C. 1985, c. 53, s. 1.

REGULATED SERVICE. Services, the rates for which are subject to review under this Act. *Public Utilities Review Commission Act*, S.S. 1982-83, c. P-45.1, s. 2.

REGULATING. *adj.* Includes authorizing, controlling, inspecting, limiting and restricting.

REGULATION. *n.* 1. Includes an order, regulation, rule, rule of court, form, tariff of costs or fees, letters patent, commission, warrant, proclamation, by-law, resolution or other instrument issued, made or established (a) in the execution of a power conferred by or under the authority of an Act; or (b) by or under the authority of the Governor in Council. *Interpretation Act*, R.S.C. 1985, c. I-21, s. 2. 2. A regulation, order, rule, form, tariff of costs or fees, proclamation or by-law enacted (i) in the execution of a power conferred by or under the authority of an act; or (ii) by or under the authority of the Lieutenant Governor in Council, but does not include an order of a court or an order made by a public officer or administrative tribunal in a dispute between two or more persons. 3. A statutory instrument (a) made in the exercise of a legislative power conferred by or under an Act of Parliament; or (b) for the contravention of which a penalty, fine or imprisonment is prescribed by or under an Act of Parliament, and includes a rule, order or regulation governing the practice or procedure in any proceedings before a judicial or quasi-judicial body established by or under an Act of Parliament, and any instrument described as a regulation in any other Act of Parliament. *Statutory Instruments Act*, R.S.C. 1985, c. S-22, s. 2. 4. A normative instrument of a general and impersonal nature, made under an Act and having force of law when it is in effect. *Regulations Act*, S.Q. 1986, c. 22, s. 1. See CHARTER AND ~S; COLLISION ~S; C.T.C. ~S; DEPARTMENT OF TRANSPORT ~S; FEDERAL ~; INTERNAL ~S; PROPOSED ~; QUEEN'S ~S AND ORDERS; RADIO ~S; LOAD LINE ~S; TONNAGE ~S.

REGULATION AND RULE. Include rule, regulation and form. *Patent Act*, R.S.C. 1985, c. P-4, s. 2.

REGULATION-MAKING AUTHORITY. Any authority authorized to make regulations and, with reference to any particular regulation or proposed regulation, means the authority that made or proposes to make the regulation.

REGULATOR. See MARINE TRAFFIC ~.

REGULATORY AGENCY. See PUBLIC ~.

REGULATORY CHARGE. Not a tax if the charge is imposed under a province's regulatory power concerning natural resources (s. 92A(1)), municipal institutions in the province (s. 92(8)), local works and undertakings (s. 92(10)), property and civil rights in the province (s. 92(13)) or matters of a merely local or private nature in the province (s. 92(16)). P.W. Hogg, *Constitutional Law of Canada*, 2d ed. (Toronto: Carswell, 1985) at 613.

REHABILITATE. *v.* To restore to former rank, right or privilege; to qualify again; to restore a lost right.

REHABILITATION. *n.* Helping an injured worker eliminate or minimize the handicap which a workplace compensable injury caused and helping the worker return to work. D. Robertson, *Ontario Health and Safety Guide* (Toronto: Richard De Boo Ltd., 1988) at 5-350. See PRAIRIE FARM ~ ADMINISTRATION; VOCATIONAL ~.

REHABILITATION CENTRE. See FUNCTIONAL ~.

REHABILITATION PROGRAM. A program designed to improve the environmental, housing or living conditions of or in a blighted or substandard area. *Alberta Mortgage and Housing Corporation Act*, S.A. 1984, c. A-32.5, s. 1.

REHANDLING. See CONTAINER ~ CHARGE.

RE-HEARING. *n.* Presentation of evidence and argument and the pronunciation of a second judgment in a cause or matter which was already decided.

REID VAPOUR PRESSURE. The vapour pressure of gasoline or an associated product at 37.8°C. or 100°F. *Gasoline Handling Act*, R.R.O. 1980, Reg. 439, s. 1.

REINDEER. *n.* Deer of the species Rangifer tarandus, native of Northern Europe, or the race Rangifer arcticus asiaticus, native of Northern Asia. *Northwest Territories Reindeer Regulations*, C.R.C., c. 1238, s. 2.

REINFORCED MASONRY. Masonry in which steel reinforcement is embedded in such a manner that the two materials act together in resisting forces. *Building Code Act*, R.R.O. 1980, Reg. 87, s. 1.

REINSTATE. *v.* In an insurance policy, to restore buildings or chattels which have been damaged. Raoul Colinvaux, *The Law of Insurance*, 5th ed. (London: Sweet & Maxwell, 1984) at 181.

REINSTATEMENT. *n.* A remedy available when a labour board proves a claim of unfair dismissal against an employer. It requires that the employer act as though the employee had never been dismissed.

REINSURANCE. *n.* 1. An agreement whereby contracts made by a licensed insurer or any class or group thereof are undertaken or reinsured by another insurer either by novation, transfer, assignment or as a result of amalgamation of the insurers. 2. New insurance under a new policy upon the same risk, which may be in wider or narrower form and which was insured before, that indemnifies the insurer from previous liability. Raoul Colinvaux, *The Law of Insurance*, 5th ed. (London: Sweet & Maxwell, 1984) at 186.

REINSURANCE AGREEMENT. An agreement for reinsurance between the Minister and a province pursuant to subparagraph 3(b)(ii). *Crop Insurance Act*, R.S.C. 1985, c. C-48, s. 2.

REINSURER. *n.* An insurer that, at the request of another insurer, reinsures a risk or part of it that is insured by that other insurer. *Insurance Amendment Act, 1981*, S.A. 1981, c. 49, s. 34.1.

REIT. *abbr.* Real estate investment trust.

REJECT. *n.* An egg that on examination at a registered egg station does not meet the requirements of any grade established by these Regulations. *Egg Regulations*, C.R.C., c. 284, s. 2.

REJECTED BALLOT PAPER. A ballot paper that has been handed by the deputy returning officer to an elector to mark, but, at the close of the poll, has been found in the ballot box unmarked or so improperly marked that it cannot be counted.

REJECTED MATERIAL. Displaced overburden, waste rock, liquid or solid residues and waste matter from mining operations. *Mining Act*, R.S.Q. 1977, c. M-13, s. 1.

REJECTED MATERIALS MANAGEMENT SYSTEM. The aggregate of administrative and technical operations for the removal, haulage, storage, milling and permanent deposit of the tailings of mining, and the moveable and immoveable property allocated to such purposes. *Mining Act*, R.S.Q. 1977, c. M-13, s. 1.

REJECTION ORDER. An order made under paragraph 13(1)(b). *Immigration Act*, R.S.C. 1985, c. I-2, s. 2.

REJOINDER. *n.* The defendant's answer to the plaintiff's reply.

RELATED BUSINESS. In relation to a charity includes a business that is unrelated to the objects of the charity if substantially all of the people employed by the charity in the carrying on of that business are not remunerated for such employment. *Income Tax Act*, R.S.C. 1952, c. 148 (as am. S.C. 1976-77, c. 4, s. 60(1)), s. 149.1(1)(j).

RELATED COMPANIES. Companies that are members of a group of two or more companies one of which, directly or indirectly, owns or controls a majority of the issued voting stock of the others. *Trade-Marks Act*, R.S.C. 1985, c. T-13, s. 2.

RELATED GROUP. 1. A group of persons each

member of which is related to every other member of the group. 2. A group of individuals each member of which is connected to at least one other member of the group by blood relationship, marriage or adoption. *Corporations and Labour Unions Returns Act*, R.S.C. 1985, c. C-43, s. 2.

RELATED MUTUAL FUNDS. Includes more than one mutual fund under common management.

RELATED PERSON. 1. Where used to indicate a relationship with any person, means: (i) any spouse, son or daughter of that person; (ii) any relative of the person or of that person's spouse, other than a relative referred to in subparagraph (i) who has the same home as the person; or (iii) any body corporate of which the person and any of the persons referred to in subparagraphs (i) or (ii) or the partner or employer of the person, either alone or in combination, beneficially owns, directly or indirectly, voting securities carrying more than 50 per cent of the voting rights attached to all voting securities of the body corporate for the time being outstanding. 2. Where used to indicate a relationship with any person or company, means: (i) any company of which such person or company beneficially owns, directly or indirectly, voting shares carrying more than 10 per cent of the voting rights attached to all voting shares of the company for the time being outstanding; (ii) any partner of that person or company acting by or for the partnership of which they are both partners; (iii) any trust or estate in which such person or company has a substantial beneficial interest or as to which such person or company serves as trustee or in a similar capacity; (iv) a spouse, son or daughter of that person; or (v) any relative of such person or of his spouse, other than a relative referred to in subparagraph (iv), who has the same home as such person. *Securities Act*, R.S.Q. 1977, c. V-1, s. 131.

RELATED PERSON OR COMPANY. In relation to a mutual fund, a person in whom or a company in which, the mutual fund, its management company and its distribution company are prohibited from making any investment.

RELATED PERSONS. Persons are related to each other and are "related persons" if they are (a) individuals connected by blood relationship, marriage or adoption; (b) a corporation and (i) a person who controls the corporation, if it is controlled by one person; (ii) a person who is a member of a related group that controls the corporation; or (iii) any person connected in the manner set out in paragraph (a) to a person described in subparagraph (i) or (ii); or (c) two corporations (i) controlled by the same person or group of persons; (ii) each of which is

controlled by one person and the person who controls one of the corporations is related to the person who controls the other corporation; (iii) one of which is controlled by one person and that person is related to any member of a related group that controls the other corporation; (iv) one of which is controlled by one person and that person is related to each member of an unrelated group that controls the other corporation; (v) any member of a related group that controls one of the corporations is related to each member of an unrelated group that controls the other corporation; or (vi) each member of an unrelated group that controls one of the corporations is related to at least one member of an unrelated group that controls the other corporation.

RELATED SALE. With reference to a sales contract, means a sale of goods that is related to the sales contract or is made in connection with or is incidental to the sales contract, whether as an inducement to enter into the sales contract or not and whether made before, at or after the making of the sales contract, and whether it is made with the seller under the sales contract or not. *Direct Sales Cancellation Act*, R.S.A. 1980, c. D-35, s. 1.

RELATION. *n.* 1. Next-of-kin of any degree. 2. A doctrine by which an act produces the same effect as it would have if it had happened at an earlier time. See CONFIDENTIAL ~; INDUSTRIAL ~S; LABOUR ~S.

RELATIVE. *n.* 1. A husband, wife, father, mother, grandfather, grandmother, father-in-law or step-father, mother-in-law or step-mother, brother, sister, brother-in-law, sister-in-law, son, daughter, grandson, granddaughter, son-in-law or daughter-in-law or for the members of a community, the superior or his duly authorized delegate. *Election Act*, R.S.Q. 1977, c. E03, s. 2. 2. When used in reference to a child, means the child's grandparent, great-uncle, great-aunt, uncle or aunt, whether by blood, marriage or adoption. *Child and Family Services Act*, S.O. 1984, c. 55, s. 130. See COLLATERAL ~; DEPENDENT ~ REVOCATION; NEAREST ~; NEAR ~.

RELATIVOSUM, COGNITO UNO, COGNISCITUR ET ALTERUM. [L.] Concerning related things, if one is known the other is known too.

RELATOR. *n.* 1. One who rehearses, tells or informs. 2. A person, other than the Attorney General, by whom proceedings are taken under this Act. *Crown Franchise Act*, R.S.B.C. 1979, c. 85, s. 1.

RELATOR ACTION. An action in which a relator tries by injunction to prevent any interfering with or infringing of a public right, to stop a public nuisance or to force a public duty to be performed or observed. The relator brings this action in the Attorney-General's name after obtaining leave to do so. I.H. Jacob, ed., *Bullen and Leake and Jacob's Precedents of Pleadings*, 12th ed. (London: Sweet and Maxwell, 1975) at 768.

RE-LAYING. *n.* With respect to shellfish, means the moving of shellfish from a contaminated area to an approved area for the purpose of natural biological cleansing. *Sanitary Control of Shellfish Fisheries Regulations*, C.R.C., c. 832, s. 2.

RELEASE. *v.* 1. In relation to any information, document, recording or statement, means to communicate, disclose or make available the information, document, recording or statement. *Canadian Aviation Safety Board Act*, R.S.C. 1985, c. C-12, s. 2. 2. Includes spilling, leaking, pumping, spraying, pouring, emitting, emptying, throwing or dumping. *Environmental Contaminants Act*, R.S.C. 1985, c. E-12, s. 2. 3. In respect of goods, means to authorize the removal of the goods from a customs office, sufferance warehouse, bonded warehouse or duty free shop for use in Canada.

RELEASE. *n.* 1. The termination of the service of an officer or non-commissioned member in any manner. *Defence Act*, R.S.C. 1985 (1st Supp.), c. 31, s. 1. 2. A document issued by the Court which releases property arrested by warrant. D. Sgayias *et al.*, *Federal Court Practice 1988* (Toronto: Carswell, 1987) at 540. See CAVEAT ~; LOW-VOLTAGE ~; WORK ~.

RELEASE DATE. See PRESUMPTIVE ~; RIG ~.

RELEASEE. *n.* The person to whom one makes a release.

RELEASE OR SURRENDER. (a) A release or surrender made under the laws of a province (other than the Province of Quebec) that does not direct in any manner who is entitled to benefit therefrom; or (b) a gift inter vivos made under the laws of the Province of Quebec of an interest in, or right to property of, a succession that is made to the person or persons who would have benefited if the donor had made a renunciation of the succession that was not made in favour of any person and that is made within the period ending 36 months after the death of the taxpayer or, where written application therefor has been made to the Minister by the taxpayer's legal representative within that period, within such longer period as the Minister considers reasonable in the circumstances. *Income Tax Act*, R.S.C. 1952, c. 148 (as am. S.C. 1985, c. 45, s. 122(5)), s. 248(9).

RELEASOR. *n.* One who makes a release.

RELEVANCY. *n.* Relationship to that which is the subject of the action. P.K. McWilliams, *Canadian Criminal Evidence*, 3d ed. (Aurora: Canada Law Book, 1988) at 11-2.

RELEVANT. *adj.* Applying to the matter in issue.

RELEVANT ACTION. In relation to an application for the leave of the court, means any action in connection with which the leave sought by the application is required. *Limitation of Actions Act*, R.S.M. 1970, c. L150, s. 16.

RELEVANT EVIDENCE. Evidence relating to a fact in issue at the trial, and includes evidence that tends to establish the cogency or accuracy of either direct or circumstantial evidence. *Military Rules of Evidence*, C.R.C., c. 1049, s. 2.

RELICT. *n.* A surviving spouse.

RELICTION. *n.* The sudden receding of sea from the land.

RELIEF. *n.* Includes every species of relief, whether by way of damages, payment of money, injunction, declaration, restitution of an incorporeal right, return of land or chattels or otherwise. See ANCILLARY ~; COROLLARY ~; CREDITORS' ~ STATUTES; DECLARATORY ~; INTERIM ~; PRAYER FOR ~.

RELIEF AGAINST FORFEITURE. In an appropriate and limited case a court of equity will grant this relief for breach of a condition or covenant when the main object of the deal was to secure a certain result and provision for forfeiture was added to secure that result. F. Bennett, *Receiverships* (Toronto: Carswell, 1985) at 355.

RELIEF EMPLOYEE. An employee engaged to fill a position on a temporary basis as a replacement for the regular incumbent. *Civil Service Act*, S.P.E.I. 1983, c. 4, s. 10.

RELIEF VENT. A vent pipe discharging into a vent stack and connected to a horizontal branch between the first fixture connection and the soil stack or waste stack. *Ontario Water Resources Act*, R.R.O. 1980, Reg. 736, s. 1.

RELIGIOUS AUXILIARY. A corporation, society, committee, or other organization, that is sponsored, organized, established or set up by a religious denomination and controlled or supervised by, and operated as an instrument or auxiliary of, and in close connection with, that religious denomination. Cemeteries acts.

RELIGIOUS BODY. Any church, or any religious denomination, sect, congregation or society.

RELIGIOUS DENOMINATION. An organized society, association, or body, of religious believers or worshippers professing to believe in the same religious doctrines, dogmas, or creed and closely associated or organized for religious worship or discipline, or both.

RELIGIOUS MAJORITY. The Roman Catholic or Protestant majority or minority, as the case may be. *Education Act*, R.S.Q. 1977, c. I-14, s. 1.

RELIGIOUS MINORITY. The Roman Catholic or Protestant majority or minority, as the case may be. *Education Act*, R.S.Q. 1977, c. I-14, s. 1.

RELIGIOUS ORGANIZATION. 1. An association of persons, (i) that is charitable according to the law of Ontario; (ii) that is organized for the advancement of religion and for the conduct of religious worship, services or rites; and (iii) that is permanently established both as to the continuity of its existence and as to its religious beliefs, rituals and practices, and includes an association of persons that is charitable according to the law of Ontario and that is organized for the advancement of and for the conduct of worship, services or rites of the Buddhist, Christian, Hindu, Islamic, Jewish, Baha'i, Longhouse Indian, Sikh, Unitarian or Zoroastrian faith, or a subdivision or denomination thereof. *Religious Organizations' Lands Act*, R.S.O. 1980, c. 448, s. 1. 2. An organization, other than a registered charity, of which a congregation is a constituent part, that adheres to beliefs, evidenced by the religious and philosophical tenets of the organization, that include a belief in the existence of a supreme being. Tax acts.

RELIGIOUS SOCIETY. A church, congregation, or other religious society of persons professing or adhering to a religion or religious faith. *Religious Societies' Lands Act*, R.S.M. 1980, c. R70, s. 2.

RELINQUISHMENT. *n.* Giving up, forsaking.

RELIQUA. *n.* [L.] After an account is balanced or liquidated, the remainder or debt which a person still owes.

RELOCATABLE STRUCTURE. A factory built unit which can be used for residential, commercial, industrial or recreational purposes without a permanent foundation. *Power Corporation Act*, R.R.O. 1980, Reg. 794, s. 0.

RELOCATE. *v.* With respect to a worker, means the transfer of the worker, his dependants and his movable effects to a locality in which he has obtained suitable employment. *Manpower Mobility Regulations*, C.R.C., c. 331, s. 2.

RELOCATION. See BUILDING ~; HOME ~ LOAN.

REM. *n.* 1. A dose of ionizing radiation that has the same biological effects as 200-250 kilovolt X-rays whose energy is absorbed by the body or any tissue or organ thereof in an amount of .01 joule per kilogram. *Atomic Energy Control Regulations*, C.R.C., c. 365, s. 2. 2. A unit of dose equivalent, defined and used in the Atomic Energy Control Regulations of Canada in relation to nuclear radiations and applicable as a unit of X-ray dose on the basis that one rem equals one rad. *Public Health Act*, R.R.O. 1980, Reg. 855, s. 1.

REMAIN. See HUMAN ~S; SKELETAL ~S.

REMAINDER. *n.* An expectant portion, residue, remnant or interest limited over to another when a particular estate is created so that that person may enjoy it after the estate is determined. See CONTINGENT ~; VESTED ~.

REMAINDERMAN. *n.* A person with rightful claim to an expectant estate.

REMAND. *v.* To adjourn a hearing to a future date, ordering the defendant, unless permitted bail, to be kept in the meantime in custody.

REMAND CENTRE. A correctional centre as defined in The Corrections Act where a remand prisoner is in custody. *Canadian Charter of Rights and Freedoms Consequential Act*, S.S. 1984-85-86, c. 38, s. 14.

REMAND PRISONER. A prisoner (i) remanded in custody by a judge or court; and (ii) awaiting trial, or the resumption or conclusion of a trial, for contravention of an Act of the Parliament of Canada or a legislature or of any regulations or order made pursuant to any such act.

REMENENT PRO DEFECTU EMPTORUM. [L. they are left on my hands for want of buyers] A return concerning goods taken under a fieri facias which a sheriff makes in certain cases.

REMANET. *n.* [L.] 1. Whatever remains. 2. An action, scheduled for trial in a certain session, which does not come on so that it stands over to the next session.

REMANET IN CUSTODIA. [L.] One remains in custody.

REM. CUSTOD. *abbr.* Remanet in custodia.

REMEDIAL STATUTE. A statute drafted to remedy a defect in the law.

REMEDY. *n.* The means by which one prevents, redresses or compensates the violation of a right. See APPRAISAL ~; CONSTITUTIONAL ~;

CUMULATIVE ~; DISCRETIONARY ~; EXTRAORDINARY ~; MUTUALITY OF ~.

REMEDY CLAUSE. Section 24(1) of the Charter, which allows a remedy to be granted to enforce the rights or freedoms the Charter guarantees. P.W. Hogg, *Constitutional Law of Canada*, 2d ed. (Toronto: Carswell, 1985) at 694.

REMEMBRANCE DAY. The whole of the eleventh day of November in each year. *Remembrance Day Act*, S.N.S. 1981, c. 10, s. 2.

REMISE. *v.* To release; to surrender; to return.

REMISSION. *n.* 1. A release; a pardon. 2. A decrease in the length of imprisonment. See EARNED ~; STATUTORY ~.

REMIT. *v.* To send back.

REMITMENT. *n.* The act of sending back into custody.

REMITTANCE. *n.* Money which one person sends to another. See POSTAL ~.

REMITTEE. *n.* The person to whom one sends a remittance.

REMOTE COMMUNITY. Any community, town or village which is not connected with the provincial highway system and which is situated in that part of the province lying north and east of a line drawn along the fifty-third parallel, beginning at the boundary line between the Province of Manitoba and the Province of Saskatchewan, to the most easterly shore of Lake Winnipeg; thence southwesterly following the sinuousities of the east shore line of Lake Winnipeg to the fifty-first parallel; thence east along the fifty-first parallel to the boundary line between the Province of Manitoba and the Province of Ontario. *Snowmobile Act*, S.M. 1977, c. 31, s. 1.

REMOTE CONTROL CIRCUIT. Any electrical circuit which controls any other circuit through a relay or an equivalent device. *Power Corporation Act*, R.R.O. 1980, Reg. 794, s. 0.

REMOTENESS. *n.* Lack of close relation between a wrong and damages.

REMOTO IMPEDIMENTO EMERGIT ACTIO. [L.] Once the impediment is removed, action emerges.

REMOVAL ORDER. An exclusion order or a deportation order. *Immigration Act*, R.S.C. 1985, c. I-2, s. 2.

REMOVE. *v.* To take, move or transport soil from land in an agricultural land reserve. *Soil Conservation Act*, R.S.B.C. 1979, c. 391, s. 1.

REMOVEABLE DEVICES. Detachable dental prostheses to replace natural teeth. *Dental Act*, R.S.Q. 1977, c. D-3, s. 27.

REMOVER. *n.* The transfer of a cause or suit from one court to another.

REMUNERATION. *n.* 1. Includes a daily or other allowance for the performance of the duties of a position or office. 2. Includes salary, wages, commissions, tips, earnings for overtime, piece work, and contract work, bonuses and allowances, the cash equivalent of board and lodging, store certificates, credits and any substitute for money. *Workers' Compensation Act*, R.S.N.W.T. 1974, c. W-4, s. 2. 3. Includes fuel and ships' stores of any kind or any other kind of payment or compensation. *Canada Shipping Act*, R.S.C. 1985, c. S-9, s. 2. 4. Includes a commission or any direct or indirect benefit, any promise of or intention to obtain a remuneration. *Real Estate Brokerage Act*, R.S.Q. 1977, c. C-73, s. 1. See FOR ~; ORDINARY ~; PENSIONABLE ~.

RENDER. *v.* To give again; to yield; to return.

RENDERING PLANT. A place (a) where animal by-products are prepared, treated or converted into fats, oils, fertilizers or animal food by the application of heat; (b) where any substance resulting from any process mentioned in paragraph (a) is stored, packed or marked; or (c) from which any substance resulting from any process mentioned in paragraph (a) is shipped. *Animal Disease and Protection Act*, R.S.C. 1985, c. A-11, s. 2.

RENDITION. *n.* The surrender of a suspect or convict by international arrangement.

RENEWABLE LEASE. A lease containing a covenant by which an option is given to the lessor to renew or extend a term of years as an alternative to payment to the tenant for such improvements as the latter is entitled to be compensated for under the terms of the lease. *Landlord and Tenant Act*, R.S.N.B. 1973, c. L-1, s. 49.

RENEWAL. *n.* In respect of a lease, includes the extension of the lease and the exercise of any option to continue the lease. *Customs and Excise Offshore Application Act*, R.S.C. 1985, c. C-53, s. 2. See AUTOMATIC ~; URBAN ~.

RENEWAL AREA. See URBAN ~.

RENEWAL CERTIFICATE. A medical certificate recommending detention of an in-patient in a facility for a further period. *The Mental Health Act*, R.S.S. 1978, c. M-13, s. 2.

RENEWAL SCHEME. A plan for the renewal of a blighted or substandard area in a municipality. See URBAN ~.

RENEWAL STUDY. A study of conditions to identify blighted or substandard areas of a municipality and to recommend required renewal action. *Housing and Renewal Corporation Act*, R.S.M. 1970, c. H160, s. 1. See URBAN ~.

RENOUNCE. *v.* 1. Of a right, to give up. 2. Of probate, for an executor to decline to take probate of a will.

RENOVANT. *adj.* Making new.

RENOVATED BUTTER. Any butter that has been melted or clarified or refined, and in any case re-manufactured into butter. *Canada Dairy Products Regulations*, C.R.C., c. 553, s. 2.

RENOVATOR. *n.* Any person who repairs, renovates or alters an upholstered or stuffed article.

RENT. *n.* 1. Money which a tenant pays to a landlord for the occupation and use of land. I.H. Jacob, ed., *Bullen and Leake and Jacob's Precedents of Pleadings*, 12th ed. (London: Sweet and Maxwell, 1975) at 69. 2. Includes consideration, whether in money, services or goods, paid, given or agreed to be paid or given by a tenant to a landlord in respect of residential premises, including consideration for a privilege, benefit, service, facility or other thing provided, directly or indirectly, by a landlord to a tenant that relates to the use, occupation or enjoyment of residential premises. 3. Includes rent charge and rent seck and any periodical payment or rendering in lieu of or in the nature of rent. 4. Includes any sum payable for the use of a telecommunication service. *Telecommunications Tax Act*, R.S.Q. 1977, c. T-4, s. 1. See BASIC UNIT ~; CHRONICALLY DEPRESSED ~; DEAD ~; DOUBLE ~; DRY-~; GROUND-~; MAXIMUM ~; OCCUPATION ~; PEPPERCORN ~; QUIT ~; RACK-~; RANGE OF ~S.

RENTAL DUPLEX. A duplex, both of the family housing units of which are to be rented. *National Housing Loan Regulations*, C.R.C., c. 1108, s. 2.

RENTAL HOUSING PROJECT. A housing project built, converted or acquired for rental purposes. *National Housing Act*, R.S.C. 1985, c. N-11, s. 2.

RENTAL OFFICE SPACE. Includes office space that is in a fixed location and office space that is in a structure that may be moved from place to place. *Legislative Assembly Act*, R.S.A. 1980, c. L-10, s. 54.

RENTAL PAYMENT PERIOD. The interval in respect of which rent is payable under a tenancy agreement, but notwithstanding any agreement to the contrary, no rental payment period shall exceed 1 month. Landlord and Tenant acts.

RENTAL PROPERTY. Property which is rented, is available for rent or was rented when last occupied. *Rental Property Conversion Act*, S.N.S. 1982, c. 14, s. 2.

RENTAL RESIDENTIAL PROPERTY. A building or related group of buildings containing one or more rental units but does not include a condominium. *Rental Housing Protection Act*, S.O. 1986, c. 26, s. 1.

RENTALSMAN. *n.* The Rentalsman appointed. Residential Tenancies acts.

RENTAL UNIT. 1. Any living accommodations, site for a mobile home or site on which a single family dwelling is a permanent structure used or intended for use as rented residential premises and includes a room in a boarding house or lodging house. 2. Includes the whole or a part of a cabin, cottage, house, kitchen, office, administration building, apartment, room, lodge, hut, tent and structure maintained for public use. *Travel Bureau Act*, R.S.B.C. 1979, c. 410, s. 1.

RENTAL VALUE. See NET ~.

RENT CHARGE. Includes all annuities and periodical sums of money charged upon or payable out of land.

RENTER. See SENIOR CITIZEN ~.

RENT PERIOD. The interval at which rent is paid. *Landlord and Tenant (Residential Tenancies) Act*, S.Nfld. 1977, c. 12, s. 1.

RENT RECEIPT. A receipt that is issued to a tenant by a landlord or is endorsed by the landlord, that indicates the amount of rent paid, or the nature and the landlord's evaluation of rent provided by way of services, by the tenant to the landlord in respect of his principal residence for any time period up to one year and that includes: (i) the name of the tenant; (ii) the address of the tenant's principal residence; (iii) the name and address of the landlord; (iv) the amount of rent and the rate at which it is paid or provided; and (v) the time period in respect of which the rent receipt is issued. *Renters Property Tax Rebate Act*, S.S. 1979, c. R-19.1, s. 2.

RENT REDUCTION FUND. A fund to which contributions, donations, gifts and bequests may be made by the government of a province by a municipality, social agency, found trust, estate or person for the purpose of the rental of a family housing un to be occupied by a family *National Housing Act*, R.S 2.

RENT SECK. A rent charge with no cause of distress.

RENUNCIATION. See CERTIFICATE OF ~.

RENVOI. *n.* When one determines, by the appropriate choice of law rule, that the questionable issue may be decided according to "the law" of a certain country, the court must decide whether the term "the law" refers to the internal domestic law of that country or to its conflict of laws rules as well. This concept is not firmly entrenched in Canadian law. J.G. McLeod, *The Conflict of Laws* (Calgary: Carswell, 1983) at 198 and 201.

REOPENING CLAUSE. A clause providing for the reopening of negotiations during the term of the collective agreement.

REORGANIZATION. *n.* A court order made under (a) a Corporations Act; (b) the Bankruptcy Act approving a proposal; or (c) any other act that affects the rights among the corporation, its shareholders and creditors.

REPAIR. *v.* Includes the provision of such facilities and the making of additions or alterations or the taking of such action as may be required so that the property shall conform with the standards established in a by-law.

REPAIR. *n.* See BUILDING ~S; MAJOR ~S.

REPAIRER. *n.* A person who (i) maintains a garage for the purpose of rendering services therein upon motor vehicles, at a charge, price or consideration, in the ordinary course of business; or (ii) owns and operates a fleet of five or more motor vehicles, or vehicles, or both, and maintains facilities for the repair of the vehicles. *The Highway Traffic Act*, S.M. 1985-86, c. 3, s. 1. See AUTO BODY ~; TRUCK-TRAILER ~; WATCH ~.

REPAIR GARAGE. A building or part thereof where facilities are provided for the repair or servicing of motor vehicles. *Building Code Act*, R.R.O. 1980, Reg. 87, s. 1.

REPAIRMAN'S GARAGE. A place of business primarily designed or used for the purpose of repairing motor vehicles or trailers, but does not include a place of business from which motive fuel, lubricating oil, antifreeze or other similar products, and services incidental to them, are sold or provided except in relation to repairs. *Motor Vehicle Act*, R.S.B.C. 1979, c. 288, s. 42.

REPAIR SERVICE. The installation, adjustment, repair, restoration, reconditioning, refinishing or maintenance of tangible personal property.

REPARATION. *n.* Restitution.

REPATRIATION. *n.* Recovering possession of the nationality which a person lost or abandoned.

REPEAL. *v.* To strike out, revoke, cancel or rescind.

REPEALED. *adj.* Includes revoked or cancelled, expired, lapsed, or otherwise ceased to have effect. *Interpretation Act*, R.S.N.S. 1967, c. 151, s. 6.

REPELLANT. *suff.* When used as a suffix (such as moisture-repellant) means constructed, treated or surfaced so that liquid will tend to run off, and cannot readily penetrate the surface. *Power Corporation Act*, R.R.O. 1980, Reg. 794, s. 0.

REPELLITUR A SACRAMENTO INFAMIS. [L.] Someone infamous is not permitted to take an oath.

REPETITUM NAMIUM. [L.] A second, reciprocal distress which takes the place of one which was eloigned.

REPLACE. *v.* In insurance, to restore buildings or chattels which have been destroyed. Raoul Colinvaux, *The Law of Insurance*, 5th ed. (London: Sweet & Maxwell, 1984) at 181.

REPLACEMENT INDEMNITY. The income replacement indemnity unreduced and payable under the Act respecting industrial accidents and occupational diseases (1985, chapter 6). *An Act Respecting Industrial Accidents and Occupational Diseases*, S.Q. 1985, c. 6, s. 513.

REPLACEMENT OF A CONTRACT OF LIFE INSURANCE. Any transaction whereby insurance is to be purchased in a single policy or in more than one related policy by a person from an insurer, and, as a consequence of the transaction, any existing contracts of life insurance that contain provision for cash surrender and paid-up values have been or are to be, (i) lapsed or surrendered; (ii) changed to paid-up insurance or continued as extended term insurance or under automatic premium loan; (iii) changed in any other manner to effect a reduction in that portion of a life insurance contract that contains provision for cash surrender and paid-up values; (iv) changed so that cash values in excess of 50 per cent of the tabular cash value of any insurance contract are released; or (v) subjected to substantial borrowing of any policy loan values whether in a single loan or under a schedule of borrowing over a period of time whereby an amount in excess of 50 per cent of the tabular cash value is borrowed on one or more policies, but does not include a transaction wherein; (vi) a new contract of life insurance is made with an insurer with whom the applicant has an existing policy or a certificate of insurance in furtherance of a contractual conversion privilege to be exercised by a policyholder or certificate holder in another contract of life insurance or group insurance issued by the insurer; or (vii) the existing life insurance contract to be replaced is a non-convertible term policy with 5 years or less to expiry and which existing contract cannot be renewed by the policyholder. *Insurance Act*, R.R.O. 1980, Reg. 533, s. 1.

REPLACEMENT PLAN. A condominium plan showing the parcel, building and units, together with any additional units. *The Condominium Property Amendment Act*, R.S.S. 1978 (Supp.), c. 8, s. 3.

REPLACEMENT PROPERTY. Property bought for a similar or the same use as former property, and, if the former property was used for business purposes, used to gain or produce income from the same business. W. Grover & F. Iacobucci, *Materials on Canadian Income Tax*, 4th ed. (Toronto: Richard De Boo Ltd., 1980) at 517.

REPLACEMENT VALUE. What the replacement to the state before the fire of the insured property destroyed or injured would cost, less a reasonable allowance for depreciation. *Colonsay Hotel Co. v. Can. National Fire Ins. Co.*, [1923] S.C.R. 688, [1923] 2 W.W.R. 1170, [1923] 3 D.L.R. 1001.

REPLANTING. *n.* The relocating of oysters in ordinary practice to improve their growth, condition or accessibility. Fishery regulations.

REPLEADER. *n.* The act or right to plead again.

REPLEGIARE. *n.* [L.] Replevin; redemption of something taken or detained by another by giving a surety.

REPLEVIABLE. *adj.* Able to be replevied or taken back.

REPLEVIN. *n.* A summary process to recover possession in specie of goods unlawfully taken. See ACTION FOR ~.

REPLEVISABLE. *adj.* Describes goods for which one may institute replevin proceedings.

REPLEVY. *v.* To redeliver goods which were unlawfully taken or detained to their owner.

REPLIANT. *n.* A party who replies, or delivers or files a replication.

REPLICANT. *n.* A party who replies, or delivers or files a replication.

REPLICATION. *n.* Formerly in the common law courts of England, a pleading which the plaintiff filed or delivered to answer the defen-

dant's plea or answer or in Chancery, a joinder of issue.

REPLOT. See LAND ~; VALUATION ~.

REPLOTTING SCHEME. See COST OF PREPARING THE ~.

REPLY. *n.* The pleading of a petitioner, plaintiff or party who institutes a proceeding in answer to the defendant.

REPORT. *n.* 1. A report of a commission, and any newspaper advertisements published under subsection 19(2), and in the Canada Gazette as required pursuant to the provisions of this Act, and the recommendations and reasons therefor set out in the report. *Electoral Boundaries Readjustment Act*, R.S.C. 1985, c. E-3, s. 2. 2. Includes an evaluation of any departmental program of a non-commercial nature, but does not include an appraisal of the performance of any specific officer or employee of a department who is or was involved in administering a program. *The Freedom of Information Act*, S.M. 1985-86, c. 6, s. 39(3). See CONSUMER ~; CREDIT ~; DURHAM ~; ENVIRONMENTAL PREVIEW ~; LAW ~; OFFICIAL ~; OFFICIAL ~ OF DEBATES; PERSONAL ~; PRE-DISPOSITION ~; PRE-SENTENCE ~; PROGRESS ~.

REPORTABLE DEATH. A death that must be reported pursuant to subsection 9(1). *Coroners Act*, S.N.W.T. 1985 (3d Sess.), c. 2, s. 2.

REPORTABLE DISEASE. African swine fever, anaplasmosis, anthrax, avian pneumoencephalitis (Newcastle disease), blue-tongue, brucellosis, cysticercosis (bovine), equine infectious anemia, equine prioplasmosis, foot and mouth disease, fowl plague, fowl typhoid, glanders, hog cholera, maladie du coït (dourine), mange, pullorum disease, rabies, rinderpest, scrapie, sheep scab, trichinosis, tuberculosis, vesicular disease of swine, vesicular exanthema of swine, vesicular stomatitis or such other disease as may be designated by the Minister. *Animal Disease and Protection Act*, R.S.C. 1985, c. A-11, s. 2.

REPORTER. *n.* An official court reporter. See COURT ~; PERSONAL ~.

REPORTING AGENCY. A person who furnishes reports for gain or profit or who furnishes reports on a routine, nonprofit basis as an ancillary part of a business carried on for gain or profit. *Credit Reporting Act*, R.S.B.C. 1979, c. 78, s. 1. See CONSUMER ~; CREDIT ~.

REPORTING AUTHORITY. The board of trustees of a school district, or a municipality collecting taxes in respect of parcels situate in another municipality. *Tax Recovery Act*, R.S.A. 1970, c. 360, s. 2.

REPORTING COMPANY. (a) A company

incorporated by or under an Act of the Legislature that is a reporting company under the Company Act; or (b) a company incorporated otherwise than by or under an Act of the Legislature (i) that has any of its securities listed for trading on any stock exchange wheresoever situated; (ii) that is ordered by the superintendent to be a reporting company; or (iii) that with respect to any of its securities has filed or files a prospectus with the superintendent or other securities regulatory authority; unless the superintendent orders that it is not a reporting company. *Securities Act*, R.S.B.C. 1979, c. 380, s. 1.

REPORTING ISSUER. An issuer: (i) that has outstanding any securities with respect to which: (A) a prospectus has been filed; (B) a securities exchange take-over bid has been filed; (ii) that has filed a prospectus; (iii) any of the securities of which have been at any time since the coming into force of this Act listed and posted for trading on any stock exchange; (iv) that has issued voting securities with respect to which a prospectus was filed and a receipt for it obtained; (v) that is a company whose securities have been exchanged, by or for the account of that company, with another company or the holders of the securities of that other company pursuant to an amalgamation, merger, reorganization or arrangement where one of the parties to the amalgamation, merger, reorganization or arrangement was a reporting issuer at the time of the amalgamation, merger, reorganization or arrangement.

REPORTING PAY. A minimum number of hours' pay paid to an employee required to report to work outside the employee's scheduled work time.

REPORTING PERIOD. In relation to a corporation, means a period of time that ends not earlier than 12 months and not later than 53 weeks after its commencement and that ends between October 30 of one calendar year and January 31 of the following calendar year and, in relation to a union, means, with respect to the return required under paragraph 12(1)(a), a calendar year and, with respect to the return required under paragraph 12(1)(b), a fiscal period of the union, and the fiscal period of the union shall be deemed, for the purposes of this Act, to end not later than 12 months after its commencement unless extended with the concurrence of the Minister. *Corporations and Labour Unions Returns Act*, R.S.C. 1985, c. C-43, s. 2.

REPORTING WITNESS. A witness who is permitted to quote an extra-judicial statement. *Military Rules of Evidence*, C.R.C., c. 1049, s. 2.

REPORT STAGE. The stage at which the House, with the Speaker in the Chair, may amend, insert, delete or restore specific clauses in a bill. A. Fraser, G.A. Birch & W.A. Dawson, eds., *Beauchesne's Rules and Forms of the House of Commons of Canada*, 5th ed. (Toronto: Carswell, 1978) at 221.

REPOSSESSION. *n.* Taking back, to which a seller under a sale on credit or a security holder of personal property may be entitled.

REPRESENTATION. *n.* 1. A statement concerning a past or existing fact, not a promise concerning a future event or state of affairs. G.H.L. Fridman, *The Law of Contract in Canada*, 2d ed. (Toronto: Carswell, 1986) at 2. 2. Standing in someone else's place for a certain purpose. 3. Probate, administration, confirmation or other instrument constituting a person the executor, administrator or other representative of a deceased person. *Canada Shipping Act*, R.S.C. 1985, c. S-9, s. 2. 4. Includes any term of a written contract or form of contract, notice or other document used or relied on by a supplier in connection with a consumer transaction. *Trade Practice Act*, R.S.B.C. 1979, c. 406, s. 1. 5. The work to be done in each year to entitle the owner of a claim to maintain the claim in good standing. Mines acts. See CONSUMER ~; FALSE OR MISLEADING ~; GRAPHIC ~; MIS~.

REPRESENTATION LABEL. A label that contains any representation as to the textile fibre content of the article to which it is applied. *Textile Labelling and Advertising Regulations*, C.R.C., c. 1551, s. 3.

REPRESENTATION VOTE. A vote to determine whether a union should represent a bargaining unit as their bargaining agent.

REPRESENTATIVE. *n.* 1. The person who takes the place of or represents another person. A deceased person's executor or administrator is called a personal representative. 2. (i) A person who under authority conferred by an insurer, agent or broker, for compensation or commission or other thing of value solicits insurance on behalf of the person conferring such authority, or transmits, for a person other than that person, an application for or policy of insurance, to or from an insurer or the person conferring such authority, or offers or assumes to act on behalf of the person conferring such authority, in the negotiation of a policy of insurance or in negotiation of its continuance or renewal; or (ii) a person who holds out as an insurance consultant or examines, appraises, reviews or evaluates any insurance policy, plan or program or makes recommendations or gives advice with regard to any of the above. *Insurance Adjusters, Agents and Brokers Act*, S.Nfld. 1986,

c. 36, s. 2. 3. (a) The head of a diplomatic mission or the High Commissioner representing one of Her Majesty's Governments; (b) a counsellor, secretary, attaché or officer of equal rank at an embassy, legation or office of a High Commissioner in Canada; or (c) a consul-general, consul, vice-consul, trade commissioner or assistant trade commissioner, who is a native or citizen of the country he represents and is not engaged in any other business or profession. *Diplomatic (Excise Taxes) Remission Order*, C.R.C., c. 757, s. 2. 4. The owner or charterer of a vessel or an agent of either of them, and includes any person who, in an application for preclearance of a vessel, accepts responsibility for payment of the tolls and charges to be assessed against the vessel in respect of transit and wharfage. *Seaway Regulations*, C.R.C., c. 1397, s. 2. See CHIEF ~; EMPLOYEE ~; EMPLOYEES' ~; FACTORY ~; HEALTH AND SAFETY ~; LEGAL ~; PERSONAL ~; PRISONERS' ~; PUBLIC ~; REGISTERED ~; ~S; SAFETY AND HEALTH ~.

REPRESENTATIVE CAPACITY. The capacity of a trustee, executor, administrator, bailee, agent, receiver, liquidator, sequestrator, assignee, custodian, trustee in bankruptcy, guardian of the estate of a minor, committee of the estate of a mentally incompetent person, or any other similar capacity. *Trust Companies Act*, R.S.A. 1980, c. T-9, s. 1.

REPRESENTATIVE EMPLOYERS' ORGANIZATION. An employers' organization that is designated by the minister pursuant to section 10 or determined by an order of the board pursuant to section 11 to be the exclusive agent to bargain collectively on behalf of all unionized employers in a trade division. *Construction Industry Labour Relations Act*, S.S. 1979, c. C-29.1, s. 2.

REPRESENTATIVE FOR SERVICE. The person or firm named under paragraph 30(g), subsection 38(3), paragraph 41(1)(a) or subsection 42(1). *Trade-Marks Act*, R.S.C. 1985, c. T-13, s. 2.

REPRESENTATIVE OFFICE. An office established to represent a foreign bank in Canada that is not occupied or controlled by a corporation incorporated by or under a law of Canada or a province and the personnel of which are employed directly or indirectly by the foreign bank. *Bank Act*, R.S.C. 1985, c. C-1, s. 302(4).

REPRESENTATIVE PROCEEDING. When numerous people have the same interest, one or more of them may bring or defend a proceeding for the benefit or on behalf of everyone, or the court may authorize this. G.D. Watson & C. Perkins, eds., *Holmested & Watson: Ontario Civil*

Procedure (Toronto: Carswell, 1984) at 12-2 and 12-3. See also CLASS ACTION.

REPRESENTATIVES. *n.* Includes delegates, deputy delegates, advisers, technical experts and secretaries of delegations. *Privileges and Immunities Accession Order (United Nations)*, C.R.C., c. 1317, s. 5. See REPRESENTATIVE.

REPRESENTATIVE STATUS. See DISCLAIMER OF ~.

REPRESENTED. *adj.* Includes any representation by a manufacturer or other person, his servant or agent dealing with a product in his business or occupation, whether verbal, written or by overt act. *Imitation Dairy Products Act*, R.S.N.B. 1973, c. I-1, s. 1.

REPRIEVE. *n.* The temporary withdrawal of a sentence so that its execution is suspended.

REPRIMAND. *n.* The formal, public reproach of an offence.

REPRISAL. *n.* Recaption; taking one thing in place of another.

REPRISE. *n.* A deduction, e.g. a rent-charge, from gross annual rent or the value of land.

REPROBATA PECUNIA LIBERAT SOLVENTEM. [L.] Money refused frees the person who offered it.

REPROCESSING PLANT. See GAS ~.

REPRODUCE. *v.* To record any broadcasting material by electrical or mechanical means. Radio Broadcasting regulations.

REPRODUCTION. *n.* A recording of any broadcast material by electrical, optical or mechanical means. *Television Broadcasting Regulations*, C.R.C., c. 381, s. 2.

REPTILE. *n.* A vertebrate of the class Reptilia and its eggs.

REPUBLICATION. *n.* Of a codicil or will, execution again by the testator.

REPUDIATION. *n.* Renunciation of a contract, which means that the repudiator is liable to be sued for breach of contract and the other party, once the repudiation is accepted, may treat the contract as ended.

REPUGNANT. *adj.* Inconsistent with; contrary to.

REPUTATION. *n.* Immediately before a defamatory publication, the long-range composite view which the general public had of the plaintiff's character, credit, honour or good name. R.E. Brown, *The Law of Defamation in Canada* (Toronto: Carswell, 1987) at 1030.

REQUEST. *n.* Something which may give rise to a tacit or implied promise.

REQUEST MAIL. Mail bearing the return address of the sender and a specific request for the return of the mail. *Undeliverable and Redirected Mail Regulations*, C.R.C., c. 1298, s. 2.

REQUIRED DEPOSIT BALANCE. A fixed or an ascertainable amount of the money actually advanced or to be advanced under an agreement or arrangement that is required, as a condition of the agreement or arrangement, to be deposited or invested by or on behalf of the person to whom the advance is or is to be made and that may be available, in the event of his defaulting in any payment, to or for the benefit of the person who advances or is to advance the money. *Criminal Code*, R.S.C. 1985, c. C-46, s. 347(2).

REQUIRED TO GIVE SECURITY. With reference to a public officer, means required, by reason of his appointment to or holding an office, employment or position, or by reason of a Statute, or by reason of a requirement of the Lieutenant Governor in Council to give security for the due performance of the trust reposed in him, and for his duly accounting for all public money entrusted to him or placed under his control, or for the due fulfilment in any way of his duty or of an obligation undertaken towards the Crown. *Public Service Bonding Act*, R.S.B.C. 1979, c. 345, s. 1.

REQUIREMENT. *n.* Any demand, direction, order, subpoena or summons. *Business Concerns Records Act*, R.S.Q. 1977, c. D-12, s. 1. See BUDGETARY ~S; FIXED CAPITAL ~S; MANPOWER ~; PERSONAL ~S; SAFETY ~S.

REQUISITION. *v.* To demand necessaries for a military force.

REQUISITION. *n.* 1. A praecipe. 2. A written instruction which requires a court registrar to do something. See CHEQUE ~; OTHER PAYMENT ~; PAYMENT ~.

REQUISITIONING AUTHORITY. (i) The board of trustees of a school division or school district; (ii) the board of a hospital district; or (iii) the Government in respect of a requisition made by it under the School Act. *Municipal Taxation Act*, R.S.A. 1980, c. M-31, s. 95.

REQUISITION MILL RATE. With respect to a requisitioning authority, means the rate of tax in respect of the tax levy to meet the requisition of that requisitioning authority. *Municipal Taxation Act*, R.S.A. 1980, c. M-31, s. 95.

REQUISITION ON TITLE. A written inquiry to the solicitor for a vendor of real estate requesting that defects and clouds in the title be removed.

RERUM PROGRESSU OSTENDUNT MULTA, QUAE IN INITIO PRAECAVERI SEU PRAEVIDERI NON POSSUNT. [L.] In the course of things many things which could not be averted or foreseen in the beginning arise.

RERUM SUARUM QUILIBET EST MODERATOR ET ARBITER. [L.] Each one is manager and judge of one's own affairs.

RES. *n.* [L.] Any physical thing in which someone may claim a right.

RES ACCESSORIA SEQUITUR REM PRINCIPALEM. [L.] An accessory follows the principal.

RESALE. *n.* 1. A right reserved by the vendor if the purchaser defaults in paying the purchase price. 2. A sale by a producer of a volume of natural gas after that volume has been sold (a) by itself; or (b) as part of another volume of natural gas by the corporation under section 5. *Natural Gas Price Act*, S.B.C. 1985, c. 53, s. 1.

RESCIND. *v.* With respect to a contract, for one or more parties to end it.

RESCISSION. *n.* Exercise of an option which ends the necessity to perform. B.J. Reiter, R.C.B. Risk & B.N. McLellan, *Real Estate Law*, 3d ed. (Toronto: Emond Montgomery, 1986) at 799.

RESCISSION CLAUSE. A clause which protects a vendor from action by a purchaser for compensation and specific performance when the vendor cannot convey everything promised and the purchaser claims everything the vendor has with a reduction in the purchase price in compensation. B.J. Reiter, R.C.B. Risk & B.N. McLellan, *Real Estate Law*, 3d ed. (Toronto: Emond Montgomery, 1986) at 347 and 348.

RES COMMUNES. [L.] Things like light or air which may not be appropriated.

RESCUE. *v.* To knowingly and forcibly free someone from an imprisonment or arrest.

RESCUER. *n.* A person who, having reasonable cause to believe another person to be in danger of his life or of bodily harm, benevolently comes to his assistance. *An Act to Promote Good Citizenship*, R.S.Q. 1977, c. C-20, s. 1.

RESEALING. *n.* Validation of a grant of representation originally issued by a court in a jurisdiction with similar laws and allegiance to the same sovereign, i.e. in the United Kingdom, any territory or province of Canada, the Commonwealth or any British possession. This has the same effect as if the validating court had made the original grant. J.G. McLeod, *The*

Conflict of Laws (Calgary: Carswell, 1983) at 404 and 405.

RESEARCH. *n.* 1. Includes any scientific or technical inquiry or experimentation that is instituted or carried out to discover new knowledge or new means of applying existing knowledge to the solution of economic and social problems. *International Development Research Centre Act*, R.S.C. 1985, c. I-19, s. 2. 2. The use of animals in connection with studies, investigation and teaching in any field of knowledge, and, without limiting the generality of the foregoing, includes the use of animals for the performance of tests, and diagnosis of disease and the production and testing of preparations intended for use in the diagnosis, prevention and treatment of any disease or condition. *Animals for Research Act*, R.S.O. 1980, c. 22, s. 1. See DEMONSTRATION OR ~ PROJECT; ENGINEERING ~ OR FEASIBILITY STUDY; MEDICAL ~ COUNCIL OF CANADA; NATIONAL ~ COUNCIL OF CANADA; NATURAL SCIENCES AND ENGINEERING ~ COUNCIL OF CANADA; SOCIAL SCIENCES AND HUMANITIES ~ COUNCIL OF CANADA.

RESEARCH FACILITIES. Facilities in a teaching hospital provided for research in the health fields associated with the teaching of undergraduate or post-graduate students in the health professions for the purpose of carrying out scientific research, under public support or sponsorship, contributing to the whole body of health knowledge, together with other areas of the hospital to the extent that such other areas service or support the research facilities. *Public Hospitals Act*, R.R.O. 1980, Reg. 862, s. 1.

RESEARCH GROUP. A person or persons that (a) has conduct of a course of study or research conducted for the purpose of reducing morbidity or mortality from any cause or condition; and (b) is a committee or subcommittee or of acts under the auspices of either the British Columbia division of the Canadian Medical Association, the College of Physicians and Surgeons of British Columbia, a public hospital, a university, or any ministry, department or emanation of the government of the Province or of Canada. *Evidence Act*, R.S.B.C. 1979, c. 116, s. 57.

RESEARCH INSTITUTE. An institution affiliated with a teaching hospital, the sole purpose of which is research in the health fields associated with the teaching of under-graduate or post-graduate students in the health professions for the purpose of carrying out scientific research, under public support or sponsorship, contributing to the whole body of health knowledge, together with auxiliary areas of the insti-

tute to the extent that such areas service or support the research facilities. *Public Hospitals Act*, R.R.O. 1980, Reg. 862, s. 1.

RESEARCH OR FEASIBILITY STUDY. Includes work undertaken to facilitate the design or analyse the viability of engineering systems, schemes or technology to be used in the exploration for or the development, production or transportation of oil or gas on or from Canada lands. *Oil and Gas Act*, R.S.C. 1985, c. O-6, s. 51(4).

RESEARCH PROGRAM. A program of research and investigation respecting, (i) the more effective use and economic development of lands; (ii) the development of income and employment opportunities in rural areas and the improvement of standards of living in those areas; and (iii) the development and conservation for agricultural purposes of water supplies and for soil improvement and conservation. *Agricultural Rehabilitation and Development Act (Ontario)*, R.S.O. 1980, c. 11, s. 1.

RESERVABLE DAY. Any day other than (a) a day that the Minister, by order, designates not to be a reservable day; and (b) a legal holiday referred to in paragraph 41(a) of the Bills of Exchange Act or a Saturday, unless the Minister, by order, designates any such day to be a reservable day. *Bank Act*, R.S.C. 1985, c. B-1, s. 208(11).

RESERVATION. *n.* A clause in a deed by which a donor, grantor or lessor claims reserves something new out of whatever was granted by the same deed earlier. See STREET ~.

RESERVATIO NON DEBET ESSE DE PROFICUIS IPSIS, QUIA EA CONCEDUNTUR, SED DE REDITU NOVO EXTRA PROFICUA. [L.] A reservation should not be from the profits themselves, because they were granted, but from new rent beyond the profits.

RESERVE. *v.* For the Governor General to withhold the royal assent from a bill which both Houses of Parliament passed "for the signification of the Queen's Pleasure" or, similarly, for a Lieutenant Governor to withhold assent from a provincial bill for the Governor General's pleasure. P.W. Hogg, *Constitutional Law of Canada*, 2d ed. (Toronto: Carswell, 1985) at 192.

RESERVE. *n.* 1. A tract of land, the legal title to which is vested in Her Majesty, that has been set apart by Her Majesty for the use and benefit of a band. *Indian Act*, R.S.C. 1985, c. I-5, s. 2. 2. A parcel of land reserved for use as a park, recreation area or a school site. 3. (a) Amounts appropriated from earned surplus at the discretion of management for some purpose other than to meet a liability or contingency known or admitted or a commitment made as at the statement date or a decline in value of an asset that has already occurred; (b) amounts appropriated from earned surplus pursuant to the articles or by-laws of a corporation for some purpose other than to meet a liability or contingency known or admitted or a commitment made as at the statement date or a decline in value of an asset that has already occurred; and (c) amounts appropriated from earned surplus in accordance with the terms of a contract and that can be restored to the earned surplus when the conditions of the contract are fulfilled. See CROWN ~; ECOLOGICAL ~; INDIAN ~; PHEASANT ~; PROBABLE ADDITIONAL ~S; PROVEN DEVELOPED ~S; PROVEN ~S UNDERLYING A PROPERTY; PROVEN UNDEVELOPED ~S; PUBLIC ~; REASONABLE AMOUNT FOR A ~; WHOLLY-PROTECTED ECOLOGICAL ~.

RESERVED LAND. Crown land that has been withdrawn from disposition under this or any other Act. *Land Act*, R.S.B.C. 1979, c. 214, s. 1.

RESERVED ROAD. A parcel of land between or within granted lands reserved by the Crown as the right-of-way for access to and egress from other granted lands or Crown lands, whether or not a road has been constructed thereon. *Crown Lands and Forests Act*, S.N.B. 1980, c. C-38.1, s. 1.

RESERVED TIME. Broadcast time during which, by agreement, facilities of a station are made available for the broadcast of programs or packages of programs supplied by and to be broadcast in a manner determined by a person other than the licensee of the station. Broadcasting regulations.

RESERVE FORCE. The component of the Canadian Forces that is referred to in the National Defence Act as the reserve force.

RESERVE FUND. A fund set up by the corporation in a special account for major repair and replacement of common elements and assets of the corporation including where applicable without limiting the generality of the foregoing, roofs, exteriors of buildings, roads, sidewalks, sewers, heating, electrical and plumbing systems, elevators, laundry, recreational and parking facilities. *Condominium Act*, R.S.O. 1980, c. 84, s. 36. See CONTINGENCY ~.

RESERVE LANDS. See CROWN ~.

RESERVE POWER. Power which the Governor General may exercise at personal discretion, i.e. the power to select or dismiss a Prime Minister. P.W. Hogg, *Constitutional Law of Canada*, 2d ed. (Toronto: Carswell, 1985) at 206-208.

RESERVOIR. *n.* A body of water, whether on private or public lands, created or effected as a result of the construction and maintenance of water control works, and includes a river, stream, creek, watercourse, lake or previously existing body of water that is enlarged, reduced or otherwise affected as a result of the construction and maintenance of water control works. See NATURAL ~ IN CANADA; STORAGE ~; UNDERGROUND ~.

RES EXTINCTA. [L.] Something which existed once but no longer does. G.H.L. Fridman, *Sale of Goods in Canada*, 3d ed. (Toronto: Carswell, 1986) at 61.

RES FURTIVAE. [L.] Stolen objects.

RES GENERALEM HABET SIGNIFICATIONEM QUIA TAM CORPOREA QUAM INCORPOREA, CUJUSCUNQUE SUNT GENERIS, NATURAE SIVE SPECIEI, COMPREHENDIT. [L.] The word "thing" has a general meaning because it includes both corporeal and incorporeal objects, whatever their type, nature, or species.

RES GESTAE. [L. things done] (a) Statements which accompany and explain a certain act; (b) statements simultaneous with and directly related to a fact at issue; (c) a person's statements concerning state of mind or emotions at a certain time; (d) a person's statements concerning physical sensations at a certain time. P.K. McWilliams, *Canadian Criminal Evidence*, 3d ed. (Aurora: Canada Law Book, 1988) at 21-2 and 21-3.

RESIANCE. *n.* Abode; residence.

RESIANT. *n.* A resident.

RESIDE. *v.* 1. To be physically present someplace. 2. To have a home that is a permanent place of abode to which, whenever a person is absent, that person intends to return.

RESIDENCE. *n.* 1. The chief or habitual place of abode of a person. 2. Includes any building or part of a building in which the occupant resides either permanently or temporarily and any premises appurtenant thereto. 3. In relation to a person, that person's true, fixed, permanent home or lodging place to which, whenever absent, the person intends to return. See ACTUAL ~; CHILDREN'S ~; COOPERATIVE ~; FARM ~; HABITUAL ~; LEGAL ~; ORDINARY PLACE OF ~; ORDINARY ~; PARENT MODEL ~; PERSONAL ~; PRINCIPAL ~; SINGLE FAMILY ~.

RESIDENCE DISTRICT. The territory contiguous to a portion of a highway having a length of 100 m along which there are buildings used for residence purposes only or for residence and business purposes occupying (a) at least 50 m of frontage on one side of that portion; or (b) at least 50 m collectively on both sides of that portion, and includes that portion of the highway.

RESIDENCE OF A CORPORATION. Where the central control and management of the corporation actually abides. *DeBeers Consolidated Mines Ltd. v. Howe*, [1906] A.C. 455; 5 T.C. 198; 95 L.T. 221.

RESIDENCE OF A TRUST. The same residence as that of the trustee. W. Grover & F. Iacobucci, *Materials on Canadian Income Tax*, 4th ed. (Toronto: Richard De Boo Ltd., 1980) at 113.

RESIDENT. *n.* 1. In relation to a province, a person lawfully entitled to be or to remain in Canada and who makes a home and is ordinarily present in the province, but does not include a tourist, a transient or a visitor to the province. 2. An individual, a corporation or a trust that is not a non-resident. 3. A person admitted to and lodged in a nursing home or other facility. See ASSOCIATES OF THE ~; FORMER ~; NON-~; NURSING HOME ~; ORDINARILY ~; ORDINARILY ~ IN CANADA; PERMANENT ~; SASKATCHEWAN ~; SEASONAL ~.

RESIDENT ALBERTAN. An individual who is ordinarily resident in Alberta, or, if not ordinarily resident in Alberta, is a member of a prescribed class of persons and, in any case, (i) is a Canadian citizen; or (ii) has been lawfully admitted to Canada for permanent residence. *Business Corporations Act*, S.A. 1981, c. B-15, s. 1.

RESIDENT BURGESS. A burgess who resides in a hospital service area and who is a burgess with respect to property or a business situated therein. *The Major Urban Centres Integrated Hospitals Act*, R.S.S. 1978, c. M-2, s. 2.

RESIDENT BUSINESS. A business carried on in or from premises within the municipality. *Municipal Act*, R.S.B.C. 1979, c. 290, s. 497.

RESIDENT CANADIAN. An individual who is: (i) a Canadian citizen ordinarily resident in Canada; (ii) a Canadian citizen not ordinarily resident in Canada who is a member of a prescribed class of persons; or (iii) a permanent resident within the meaning of the Immigration Act, 1976 (Canada) and ordinarily resident in Canada, except a permanent resident who has been ordinarily resident in Canada for more than 1 year after the time at which he first became

eligible to apply for Canadian citizenship. Business Corporations acts.

RESIDENT ELECTOR. As used with respect to a local authority, means an elector whose place of residence is in the authority.

RESIDENTIAL. *adj.* When used in respect of land, the land subjacent to a building that is the main and principal residence of the occupants, whether as owners or tenants, and includes all immediately contiguous lands necessary and used for such residence. *Land Transfer Tax Act*, R.S.O. 1980, c. 231, s. 1. See MEDIUM DENSITY MULTI-FAMILY ~; MOBILE UNIT ~; SINGLE FAMILY ~.

RESIDENTIAL AND FARM ASSESSMENT. See EQUALIZED ~.

RESIDENTIAL BUILDING. 1. A structure that contains one or more dwelling units. *Health Protection and Promotion Act, 1983*, S.O. 1983, c. 10, s. 1. 2. A hotel, motel, lodging house, tourist home, apartment house (other than a dwelling), tenement or any building or part thereof which is rented by the day, week, month or year and consists of individually rented rooms or suites (with or without dining facilities) and self-contained apartments. *Fire Prevention Act*, S.N.S. 1976, c. 9, s. 2.

RESIDENTIAL CARE. Boarding or lodging, or both, and may include specialized, sheltered or group care in conjunction with the boarding or lodging, or both.

RESIDENTIAL CARE FACILITY. Any building or place, or part of a building or place, where supervisory care or personal care is provided to four or more persons.

RESIDENTIAL COMPLEX. A building, related group of buildings or mobile home park, in which one or more rental units are located, or a site or related group of sites on each of which site is located a single family dwelling which is a permanent structure and includes all common areas, services and facilities available for the use of residents of the building, buildings, park, site or sites.

RESIDENTIAL DWELLING UNIT. 1. Includes any premises ordinarily occupied or inhabited by the taxpayer in a taxation year but does not include any premises (i) which have not been designated by the principal taxpayer as his principal residence; or (ii) which are exempt from municipal taxes and in respect of which no grant in lieu of municipal taxes is made by the owner or by the government and which are designated either specifically or by class, under the regulations, as not being residential dwelling units. *Income Tax Act*, S.M. 1973, c. 33, s. 2. 2. A detached house, cottage or other single family dwelling, duplex, apartment building, condominium, townhouse, rowhouse, resthome, nursing home, or that portion of a multiuse building that is used for the purpose of single family dwellings, but does not include hotels, motels, lodges, resorts, hospitals or other institutional buildings, bunk houses or camp buildings for use on commercial or construction projects, or that portion of any building that is used for any purpose other than residential. *Urban Transit Authority Act*, S.B.C. 1980, c. 36, s. 58.

RESIDENTIAL FACILITY. See COMMUNITY-BASED ~.

RESIDENTIAL INSTITUTION. A shelter that provides temporary or continuing care for persons in need and includes (i) homes for the aged; (ii) nursing homes; (iii) hostels for transients; (iv) child care institutions; (v) homes for unmarried mothers; (vi) group homes; and (vii) any residential institution the primary purpose of which is to provide residents thereof with supervisory, personal or nursing care or to rehabilitate them socially. *Welfare Assistance Act*, R.S.P.E.I. 1974, c. W-4, s. 1.

RESIDENTIAL LAND. (i) A parcel on which a single-family detached unit or duplex unit is located; or (ii) a residential unit under the Condominium Property Act, that is or was used as a residence. *Real Property Statutes Amendment Act, 1983 (No. 2)*, S.A. 1983, c. 97, s. 2. See VACANT ~.

RESIDENTIAL OCCUPANCY. The occupancy or use of a building or part thereof by persons for whom sleeping accommodation is provided but who are not harboured or detained to receive medical care or treatment or are not involuntarily detained.

RESIDENTIAL PARCEL. A parcel of land entered on the assessment roll of a municipality as a separate parcel and on which is situated one or more dwelling units. *School Tax Reduction Act*, S.M. 1971, c. 87, s. 1.

RESIDENTIAL PREMISES. (i) Real property used for residential purposes; or (ii) real property leased as a site for a mobile home which is used for residential purposes, whether or not the landlord also leases that mobile home to the tenant, but does not include premises occupied for business purposes with living accommodation attached and leased under a single lease. See MUNICIPAL ~; RURAL ~.

RESIDENTIAL PROPERTY. A building in which, and includes land on which, residential premises are situated. See FARM AND ~; RENTAL ~.

RESIDENTIAL REAL PROPERTY TAX. The tax levied by a municipality upon the real property and improvements thereto that are used for a residential purpose. *Residential Property Tax Act*, S.N.S. 1973-74, c. 10, s. 3.

RESIDENTIAL SERVICE. Boarding, lodging and associated supervisory, sheltered or group care.

RESIDENTIAL TENANCY AGREEMENT. A written, oral or implied agreement to rent residential premises. *Landlord and Tenant Act*, R.S.A. 1980, c. L-6, s. 1.

RESIDENTIAL UNIT. (i) In the case of a unit that is situated within a building, a unit that is used or intended to be used for residential purposes; and (ii) in the case of a bare land unit, a unit that is used or intended to be used for residential purposes or that has been represented by a developer as being intended to be used for residential purposes. *Condominium Property Amendment Act, 1983*, S.A. 1983, c. 71, s. 2.

RESIDENT IN ALBERTA. Maintaining a home and being ordinarily present in Alberta. *Social Development Act*, R.S.A. 1980, c. S-16, s. 33.

RESIDENT INVESTOR. A resident who for himself, and not in the capacity of agent, trustee, partner or any other capacity, acquires an eligible share. *Equity Investment Plan Act*, S.B.C. 1985, c. 71, s. 1.

RESIDENT MEMBER. A member of the society whose chief place of practice, or if he is a retired member, his residence, is located in the Province. *Attorney General Statutes Amendment Act*, S.B.C. 1981, c. 10, s. 1.

RESIDENT OCCUPANT. A person actually residing on land within a proposed district, or within a district, and who is the owner, tenant or lessee of such land.

RESIDENT OF A CONTRACTING STATE. In relation to the Canada-United Kingdom Income Tax Convention of 1978, any person who, under the law of a state, is liable to taxation there because of residence, domicile, place of management or any other similar criterion. This term does not include someone who is liable to tax in the contracting state only on income from sources there. W. Grover & F. Iacobucci, *Materials on Canadian Income Tax*, 4th ed. (Toronto: Richard De Boo Ltd., 1980) at 133.

RESIDENT OF ALBERTA. A person entitled by law to reside in Canada who makes a home and is ordinarily present in Alberta, but does not include a tourist, transient or visitor to Alberta.

RESIDENT OF CANADA. In the case of a natural person, a person who ordinarily resides in Canada and, in the case of a corporation, a corporation that has its head office in Canada or maintains one or more establishments in Canada to which employees of the corporation employed in connection with the business of the corporation ordinarily report for work.

RESIDENT OF NEWFOUNDLAND. See BONA FIDE ~.

RESIDENT OF NOVA SCOTIA. Any person, (i) who is authorized by law to be or to remain in Canada and is living and ordinarily present in Nova Scotia; and (ii) who meets the criteria prescribed in Division II of O.C. 374-78 made under the Automobile Insurance Act (Quebec), which apply with necessary modifications, but does not include a person: (iii) who is merely touring, passing through or visiting Nova Scotia; or (iv) who is, at the time of an accident in Quebec, the owner or driver of, or a passenger in an automobile registered in Quebec. *An Act to Amend the Insurance Act*, S.N.S. 1982, c. 31, s. 33.

RESIDENT OF THE PROVINCE. A bona fide resident, animus et factum, of the province.

RESIDENT ORGANIZATION. An organization that is not a non-resident organization. *Cooperative Credit Associations Act*, R.S.C. 1985, c. C-41, s. 32.

RESIDENT OWNER. An owner who resides within a distance of 10 miles by the nearest road from the land in question or any part thereof, and includes a municipality having jurisdiction over any roads in the drainage district. *The Drainage Act*, R.S.S. 1978, c. D-33, s. 2.

RESIDENT PERSON. A person who resides in the province for 183 days or more a year. *Prince Edward Island Lands Protection Act*, S.P.E.I. 1982, c. 16, s. 1.

RESIDENT PUPIL. 1. As used to refer to or describe a pupil in a particular school division or school district, means a pupil (i) whose parent or legal guardian, with whom he resides, is a resident therein; or (ii) who has attained the age of 18 years and is a Canadian citizen or landed immigrant resident therein; or (iii) who by reason of being dealt with under any provision of The Child Welfare Act becomes a resident therein; or (iv) who is designated in writing by the minister as a resident therein. *Public Schools Act*, S.M. 1980, c. 33, s. 1. 2. In respect of a board, means a pupil who is registered on a register or registers prescribed by the Minister for the purposes of this Part and who, (a) is qualified to be a resident pupil of the board and is enrolled in a school: (i) operated by the board; or (ii) operated by another board to which the first-mentioned board pays fees in respect of the pupil; or (b) is not qualified by residence to be a resident pupil of a board but is enrolled in a school operated by the board: (i) pursuant to section 45; or (ii) where fees are required to be paid by or on behalf of the pupil by or under this Act other than by another board, notwithstanding that the payment of all or part of the fees is waived by the board that operates the school at which the pupil is enrolled. *Education Amendment Act (No. 2)*, S.O. 1986, c. 29, s. 11.

RESIDENT PUPILS. Pupils, (i) who reside with their parents or guardians; or (ii) who or whose parents or guardians are assessed for an amount equal to the average assessment of the ratepayers, within the limits of a secondary school district for secondary school purposes, or a school section for public school purposes, within the Metropolitan Area, but does not include pupils residing with their parents or guardians on land that is exempt from taxation for school purposes, who and whose parents or guardians are not assessed for, and do not pay, taxes for secondary school purposes or public school purposes, respectively, in the secondary school district or school section. *Municipality of Metropolitan Toronto Act*, R.S.O. 1980, c. 314, s. 116.

RESIDENT RATEPAYER. 1. As used with respect to a local authority, means a ratepayer whose place of residence is in the authority. 2. A person who is a resident within a municipality, is of the full age of 18 years and is qualified to vote as a burgess therein, and in the case of a local improvement district a person who is a resident therein, is of the full age of 18 years and: (i) is assessed upon the last revised assessment roll of the district and is not exempt from taxation; or (ii) is a shareholder in a duly incorporated co-operative association which is engaged in farming and which is assessed upon the said roll in respect of real property not exempt from taxation. *The Health Services Act*, R.S.S. 1978, c. H-1, s. 2.

RESIDENT SERVICES. The services provided for the care and maintenance of: (i) children and other persons who have attained the age of 18 years but who have not attained the age of 21 years, where such children and other persons reside in an approved children's institution, other than a children's institution for miscellaneous purposes; and (ii) children and other persons who have attained the age of 18 years, where such children and other persons reside in an approved children's institution for miscellaneous purposes. *Children's Institutions Act*, R.R.O. 1980, Reg. 98, s. 21.

RESIDES IN THE PROVINCE. Is physically present in the province. *Social Assistance Act*, S.Nfld. 1977, c. 102, s. 2.

RESIDUAL. *adj.* Relating to the part which remains.

RESIDUAL CHLORINE CONTENT. The quantity of free or available chlorine when tested in accordance with the amperometric titration method described in section 409C of Standard Methods. *Great Lakes Sewage Pollution Prevention Regulations*, C.R.C., c. 1429, s. 2.

RESIDUAL FAMILY INCOME. The amount remaining when an amount equal to four-thirds of the rounded pension equivalent is deducted from the monthly family income. *Old Age Security Act*, R.S.C. 1985, c. O-9, s. 22.

RESIDUAL INCOME OF THE SURVIVING SPOUSE. The amount remaining when an amount equal to four-thirds of the rounded pension equivalent is deducted from the monthly income of the surviving spouse. *Old Age Security Act*, R.S.C. 1985, c. O-9, s. 22.

RESIDUAL INCOME OF THE WIDOW. The amount remaining when an amount equal to four-thirds of the rounded pension equivalent is deducted from the monthly income of the widow. *Old Age Security Act*, R.S.C. 1985 (1st Supp.), c. 34, s. 5.

RESIDUAL UNIT. A bargaining unit the members of which are workers not included in other units approved previously for the plant.

RESIDUAL VALUE. The estimated value of the property if the merchantable timber were removed. *Income Tax Regulations*, C.R.C., c. 945, s. 5.

RESIDUARY. *adj.* Relating to the part which remains.

RESIDUARY BEQUEST. A gift of any of the testator's personal property which the will did not otherwise give. T. Sheard, R. Hull & M.M.K. Fitzpatrick, *Canadian Forms of Wills*, 4th ed. (Toronto: Carswell, 1982) at 178.

RESIDUARY DEVISEE. The person designated in a will to take the real property which remains after the other devises.

RESIDUARY LEGATEE. The person to whom a testator leaves what remains of a personal estate after all debts and specific legacies are discharged.

RESIDUARY POWER. 1. With respect to the federal parliament, the power conferred by section 91 of the Constitution Act, 1867 to make laws for the "peace, order, and good government of Canada" which is residuary in relation to provincial governments because it is specifically limited to matters not assigned to the provincial legislatures. P.W. Hogg, *Constitutional Law of Canada*, 2d ed. (Toronto: Carswell, 1985) at 369.

2. With respect to a provincial parliament, the power conferred by section 92(16) over "all matters of a merely local or private nature in the province." P.W. Hogg, *Constitutional Law of Canada*, 2d ed. (Toronto: Carswell, 1985) at 456.

RESIDUE. *n.* What remains of a testator's estate after every debt, special devise and bequest is discharged. See PESTICIDE ~; WOOD ~.

RESIDUES. *n.* The ingredients of a control product that remain after the control product has been used and includes substances resulting from degradation or metabolism. *Pest Control Products Regulations*, C.R.C., c. 1253, s. 2.

RESIGNATIO EST JURIS PROPRII SPONTANEA REFUTATIO. [L.] Resignation is the spontaneous refutation of one's own right.

RESIGNATION. *n.* Giving up a possession, office or claim.

RES IMMOBILES. [L.] Immovables. E.L.G. Tyler & N.E. Palmer, eds., *Crossley Vaines' Personal Property*, 5th ed. (London: Butterworths, 1973) at 14.

RES INCORPORALES. [L.] Things which exist only as legal concepts and cannot be touched, such as contractual rights, servitudes, or rights over land like rights of way, easements and profits. E.L.G. Tyler & N.E. Palmer, eds., *Crossley Vaines' Personal Property*, 5th ed. (London: Butterworths, 1973) at 14.

RES INTEGRA. [L.] A point which must be decided on principle because it is not governed by a decision or rule of law.

RES INTER ALIOS ACTA ALTERI NOCERE NON DEBET. [L.] A transaction between some people should not injure another person.

RES IPSA LOQUITUR. [L. the thing speaks for itself] An inference of negligence arises in some circumstances merely because an accident has occurred. John G. Fleming, *The Law of Torts*, 6th ed. (Sydney: The Law Book Co., 1983) at 288.

RESISTANCE. See FIRE ~; INITIAL CRUSH ~; INTERMEDIATE CRUSH ~; PEAK CRUSH ~.

RESISTANT. *suff.* Constructed, protected or treated so that it will not be injured readily when subjected to the specified material or condition. *Power Corporation Act*, R.R.O. 1980, Reg. 794, s. 0.

RESISTING. See FIRE ~.

RES JUDICATA. [L.] A final judicial decision.

RES JUDICATA PRO VERITATE ACCIPITUR. [L.] Until reversed, a judicial decision is conclusive, and its truth may not be contradicted.

RES MOBILES. [L.] Movables. E.L.G. Tyler & N.E. Palmer, eds., *Crossley Vaines' Personal Property*, 5th ed. (London: Butterworths, 1973) at 14.

RES NULLIUS. [L.] A thing without an owner.

RESOLUTION. *n.* 1. A solemn decision or judgment. 2. A meeting's expression of intention or opinion. 3. The revocation of a contract. See EXTRAORDINARY ~; ORDINARY ~; PROCESS FOR ~ OF A DISPUTE; SEPARATE ~; SPECIAL ~; UNANIMOUS ~.

RESOLUTIVE CONDITION. Something which resolves a contract which had been valid, binding and effective. G.H.L. Fridman, *Sale of Goods in Canada*, 3d ed. (Toronto: Carswell, 1986) at Sale, p. 28.

RESOLUTO JURE CONCEDENTIS RESOLVITUR JUS CONCESSUM. [L.] The grant of a right ends when the grantor's right ends.

RESOLUTORY CONDITION. Something which revokes a prior obligation when it is accomplished.

RESORT. *n.* 1. A tourist establishment that operates through all or part of the year and that has facilities for serving meals and furnishes equipment, supplies or services to persons in connection with angling, hunting, camping or recreational purposes. *Tourism Act*, R.R.O. 1980, Reg. 936, s. 1. 2. An establishment having at least 10 units of accommodation that operates either throughout the year or on a seasonal basis where, in consideration of payment for food and lodging, recreational activities are available for persons staying at the establishment and their guests. *Liquor Licence Act*, R.R.O. 1980, Reg. 581, s. 1. See LAST ~; WATER ~.

RESORT OF WILDLIFE. Any waters or lands, including highways or roads, that are frequented by wildlife. *Fish and Wildlife Act*, S.N.B. 1980, c. F-14.1, s. 1.

RESORT VILLAGE. A resort village incorporated pursuant to The Urban Municipality Act, 1984 and includes a resort village established prior to the coming into force of that Act. *Local Government Election Amendment Act*, S.S. 1984-85-86, c. 51, s. 3.

RESOURCE. *n.* Land and in relation to land use, includes water, whether used for agriculture, recreation, wildlife, forest production, or any other beneficial use. *Resource Conservation Districts Act*, S.M. 1970, c. 54, s. 1. See ARCHAEOLOGICAL ~; CHILD CARE ~; ENERGY ~; GEOTHERMAL ~; HERITAGE ~; HISTORIC

~; MINERAL ~; NON-RENEWABLE ~; PALAEONTOLOGICAL ~; ~S.

RESOURCE-BASED INDUSTRY. An industry that uses as a principal material a material (a) the original location of which is not the consequence of human design; and (b) that is in or close to its natural state. *Regional Development Incentives Regulations, 1974*, C.R.C., c. 1388, s. 2.

RESOURCE INCOME. Income reasonably attributable to production from oil and gas wells or bituminous sands deposits, oil sands deposits or coal deposits or to any right, licence or privilege to explore for, drill for or recover petroleum or natural gas or to explore for, mine, quarry, remove, treat or process bituminous sands or oil sands or to win or work mines, seams or beds of coal. *Alberta Income Tax Act*, R.S.A. 1980, c. A-31, s. 11.

RESOURCE MANAGEMENT. See WATER ~.

RESOURCE PROPERTY. (i) Farm property; (ii) forest property owned by a person who owns less than 50,000 acres of forest property in the Province. *Assessment Act*, S.N.S. 1976, c. 2, s. 1. See ALBERTA ~; CANADIAN ~; FOREIGN ~; ONTARIO ~; RESTRICTED ~.

RESOURCE PROTECTION AND DEVELOPMENT SERVICE. (i) The provision of labour, machinery, equipment, materials, supplies and technical, supervisory and administrative services that are, in the opinion of the minister, required: (A) for the prevention and suppression of fires; or (B) for the construction, maintenance, repair, alteration, extension or improvement of buildings, structures, recreation facilities, roads, dams, bridges, ditches, fireguards or other works of a similar nature; (ii) the provision of a radio communications service, and includes the establishment, construction, maintenance and operation of radio communications networks; (iii) the acquisition and development of recreation sites. *Department of Tourism and Renewable Resources Amendment Act*, S.S. 1982-83, c. 32, s. 3.

RESOURCE REVENUE. (a) Net income of the British Columbia Petroleum Corporation; and (b) revenue and any other income received by the government under the Coal Act, Forest Act, Mineral Act, Mining (Placer) Act, Petroleum and Natural Gas Act, Logging Tax Act, Mineral Land Tax Act, Mineral Resource Tax Act, Mining Tax Act, Range Act, Water Act and Wildlife Act, other than surcharges or money payable into the Habitat Conservation Fund under the Wildlife Act. *Resource Revenue Stabilization Fund Act*, S.B.C. 1984, c. 8, s. 1.

RESOURCE ROYALTY. An amount, other

than an amount to which paragraph 7(e) applied paid to a person referred to therein, computed by reference to the amount or value of production (a) after December 31, 1980 and before January 1, 1982, of petroleum or gas, including any minimum or advance royalty payment with respect to the amount or value of production; or (b) after December 31, 1981, of petroleum or gas, including any minimum or advance royalty payment with respect to the amount or value of such production, but not including an amount computed by reference to the amount or value of such production of petroleum or gas where (i) the recipient of the amount so computed would have a Crown royalty in respect of (a) such production; or (b) the ownership of property to which such production relates where the Crown royalty is computed by reference to an amount of production from the property if the definition "Crown royalty" were read without reference to a taxation year and if the determination of the amount of the Crown royalty under that definition were made only in respect of such production or such ownership; or (ii) the recipient of the amount so computed would, but for an exemption or allowance, other than a rate of nil, that is provided by statute by a person referred to in paragraph 7(e), have a Crown royalty determined pursuant to subparagraph (i). *Petroleum and Gas Revenue Tax Act,* R.S.C. 1985, c. P-12, s. 2. See INCREMENTAL ~.

RESOURCES. *n.* Includes financial support, personnel, equipment, facilities and any other departmental resources which the Minister may make available to a community social service agency or a community placement resource. *Child and Family Services and Family Relations Act,* S.N.B. 1980, c. C-2.1, s. 1. See ENERGY, MINES AND ~ CANADA; FINANCIAL ~; FISHERY ~; HEALTH ~; NATURAL ~; RESOURCE; WATER ~.

RESOURCES. *abbr.* Newsletter of the Canadian Institute of Resources Law.

RESOURCE TAXES. Taxation of a non-renewable natural resource, electricity facility or forestry resource. These resources may be taxed in place or their primary production may be taxed. P.W. Hogg, *Constitutional Law of Canada,* 2d ed. (Toronto: Carswell, 1985) at 611.

RESOURCE USE PERMIT. A licence, issued under this act, authorizing an activity or course of behaviour or conduct or the occupancy, use, development, exploitation or extraction of a natural resource on or in a recreation area. *Park Act,* R.S.B.C. 1979, c. 309, s. 1.

RES PERIT DOMINO. [L.] Risk falls to the owner.

RES PETITA. [L.] Something claimed.

RESPICIENDUM EST JUDICANTI, NE QUID AUT DURIUS AUT REMISSIUS CONSTITUATUR QUAM CAUSA DEPOSCIT; NEC ENIM AUT SEVERITATIS AUT CLEMENTIAE GLORIA AFFECTANDA EST. [L.] The one who judges should be mindful that nothing either more severe or more lenient is done than the case merits; for distinction should not be achieved by either severity or leniency.

RESPIRATORY TECHNOLOGY. The medically supervised and co-ordinated scientific application of techniques and procedures to assist a physician in the safe and effective diagnosis, treatment, and promotion of the well being of patients with respiratory and associated disorders. *Registered Respiratory Technologists Act,* S.M. 1980-81, c. 17, s. 1(1). See PRACTICE OF ~.

RESPITE. *n.* An interruption, reprieve or suspension of sentence.

RESPONDEAT SUPERIOR. [L. let the principal answer] In certain circumstances when a servant acted in the course of employment, the master is liable for the servant's wrongful acts.

RESPONDENT. *n.* 1. A person against whom one presents a petition, issues a summons or brings an appeal. 2. A person in the Province or in a reciprocating state who has or is alleged to have an obligation to pay maintenance for the benefit of a claimant, or against whom a proceeding under this Act, or a corresponding enactment of a reciprocating state, is commenced. Maintenance Orders Enforcement acts. 3. A person or a department in respect of whom or which or in respect of whose activities any report or information is sought or provided. Statistics acts. See CO-~.

RESPONDENTIA. *n.* [L.] The hypothecation of the goods or cargo on a ship to secure repayment of a loan.

RESPONDERE NON DEBET. [L.] One need not answer.

RESPONDING DOCUMENT. A statement of defence, statement of defence to counter-claim, answer to a petition for divorce, answer to a counter-petition for divorce or appearance to an originating notice. *Judicature Act and Matrimonial Causes Act,* R.R.O. 1980, Reg. 540, s. 775.

RESPONSALIS AD LUCRANDUM VEL PETENDUM. [L.] One who appears in court to answer for someone else on the assigned day; an attorney, deputy or proctor.

RESPONSA PRUDENTIUM. [L.] The answers of those who are learned in law.

RESPONSE. See FREQUENCY ~.

RESPONSIBLE. See PERSON ~.

RESPONSIBLE GOVERNMENT. The formal head of state (monarch, Governor General or Lieutenant Governor) must always act under the direction of ministers who are members of the majority elected to the legislative branch. P.W. Hogg, *Constitutional Law of Canada*, 2d ed. (Toronto: Carswell, 1985) at 191.

RESPONSIBLE MEDICAL OFFICER. The physician or one to whom responsibility for the care and treatment of an individual patient has been assigned.

RESPONSIBLE OFFICER OF THE BANK. 1. The manager or assistant manager of the bank or branch thereof. *Business Loans, Guarantees and Indemnities Act*, S.N.W.T. 1983 (1st Sess.), c. 1, s. 3. 2. (a) The manager or assistant manager of the bank or branch thereof; (b) the person for the time being acting as the manager or assistant manager of the bank or branch thereof; (c) the credit committee of the bank or branch thereof; or (d) such other person as may be authorized by the bank or a branch thereof to supervise the making of loans. Canada regulations.

RESPONSIBLE PERSON. A portfolio manager and every individual who is a partner, director or officer of a portfolio manager together with every affiliate of a portfolio manager and every individual who is director, officer or employee of such affiliate or who is an employee of the portfolio manager, if the affiliate or the individual participates in the formulation of, or has access prior to implementation to investment decisions made on behalf of or the advice given to the client of the portfolio manager.

RESPONSIBILITY. See ABSOLUTE ~; VICARIOUS ~.

RESSEISER. For the Crown to take control of lands when ouster le main or general livery was misused.

RES SOLI. [L.] Immovables. E.L.G. Tyler & N.E. Palmer, eds., *Crossley Vaines' Personal Property*, 5th ed. (London: Butterworths, 1973) at 14.

RES SUA NEMINI SERVIT. [L.] One's own property cannot be subject to a servitude for one.

REST. See WEEKLY DAY OF ~.

RESTATEMENT OF LAW. A publication of the American Law Institute which deals with a major legal subject by setting out existing law along with desirable or anticipated changes.

RESTAURANT. *n.* 1. Includes every building or part of a building, tent or other erection used as a restaurant, café, lunch counter, ice cream parlour or other place of refreshment where food or drink is sold to the public. 2. A place established and operated as a business which provides, for a consideration, meals and attendant services for the public. *The Liquor Licensing Act*, R.S.S. 1978, c. L-21, s. 2.

RESTAURATEUR. *n.* Any person who serves or sells meals or refreshments for consumption, for a consideration, the operator of a teaching establishment or of any establishment governed by the Act respecting probation and houses of detention (chapter P-26), the Act respecting health services and social services (chapter S-5), the Mental Patients Protection Act (chapter P-41), the Gouvernement or the government departments and agencies. *Agricultural Products and Foods Act*, R.S.Q. 1977, c. P-29, s. 1.

RESTITUTIO IN INTEGRUM. [L.] 1. In a case in which someone according to strict law lost a right and a court decision restores the original position on equitable principles. 2. Equitable relief given when a contract is rescinded because of fraud or in a similar case in which each party can be restored to its original position.

RESTITUTION. *n.* The law which relates to any claim, whether quasi-contractual in nature or not, which is based on unjust enrichment.

RESTITUTION ORDER. An order under s. 491.1 of the Criminal Code, R.S.C. 1985, c. C-46 as amended by R.S.C. 1985 (1st Supp.), c. 27, s. 74 requiring that property obtained by crime be returned to the owner.

RESTORATION. *n.* The restoring of an obliterated monument. Surveys acts.

RESTORE. *v.* In insurance, to reinstate or replace buildings or chattels which have been damaged or destroyed. Raoul Colinvaux, *The Law of Insurance*, 5th ed. (London: Sweet & Maxwell, 1984) at 181.

RESTORE THE NATURAL ENVIRONMENT. When used with reference to a spill of a pollutant, means restore all forms of life, physical conditions, the natural environment and things existing immediately before the spill of the pollutant that are affected or that may reasonably be expected to be affected by the pollutant. *Environmental Protection Act*, R.S.O. 1980, c. 141, s. 79.

REST PERIOD. The period of time during which workers cease work as they are entitled to under the terms of their employment or a statute.

RESTRAIN. *v.* 1. To keep under control by the minimal use of such force, mechanical means or chemicals as is reasonable having regard to the physical and mental condition of the patient. Mental Health acts. 2. To seize, distrain, confine or hold a stray, prior to impoundment, pursuant to this Act. *The Stray Animals Act*, R.S.S. 1978, c. S-60, s. 2.

RESTRAINING DEVICE. See SAFETY ~.

RESTRAINING ORDER. In some provinces, the order of a court to prevent disposal or waste of family property. C.R.B. Dunlop, *Creditor-Debtor Law in Canada*, Second Cumulative Supplement (Toronto: Carswell, 1986) at 211.

RESTRAINT. See HEAD ~; OCCUPANT ~ ASSEMBLY; PELVIC ~; PRODUCT ~ ASSEMBLY; UPPER TORSO ~.

RESTRAINT OF MARRIAGE. In general, any contract designed to prevent someone from marrying is void.

RESTRAINT OF TRADE. A justification for court interference with a contract otherwise freely entered into, that restricts a party's future use of skill, time and expertise. G.H.L. Fridman, *The Law of Contract in Canada*, 2d ed. (Toronto: Carswell, 1986) at 368.

RESTRAINT ON ALIENATION. A condition which restrains alienation of absolute interest in either real or personal property is generally considered void because it is repugnant.

RESTRAINT PERIOD. (i) In the case of a person whose group compensation plan is not included in a collective agreement and is, on the 1st day of October, 1983, subject to the Inflation Restraint Act, 1982, the 12-month period immediately following the expiry of the period referred to in clause 11 (a) or (b) of that Act, whichever is applicable; or (ii) in the case of a person whose group compensation plan is included in a collective agreement the minimum term of operation of which is, by law or by the express provisions of the agreement, for a period that expires before the 1st day of October, 1984, the 12-month period immediately following either, (A) the expiry of that minimum term of operation; or (B) the expiry of the period for which the group compensation plan is subject to the provisions of subsection (1) of the Inflation Restraint Act, 1982, whichever last occurs. *Public Sector Prices and Compensation Review Act, 1983*, S.O. 1983, c. 70, s. 1.

RESTRAINTS OF PRINCES. Part of the phrase "arrest or restraints of princes, rulers or peoples" used in marine insurance policies to describe contingencies against which one makes provision. The particular contingency it describes is forcible interference with a voyage by the government of any nation.

RESTRICTED AREA. 1. An area where explosives, flammable liquids or flammable gases are stored, handled or processed or where the atmosphere contains or is likely to contain explosive concentrations of combustible dust or other combustible suspended material. *Canada Dangerous Substances Regulations*, C.R.C., c. 997, s. 2. 2. An area of an airport designated by a sign as an area whose access by persons or vehicles requires the production of valid identification. *Airport Tariff Regulations*, C.R.C., c. 886, s. 2. 3. Any area of canal land declared by the Superintending Engineer to be an area upon which no goods are to be deposited. *Canal Regulations*, C.R.C., c. 1564, s. 2.

RESTRICTED CHANNEL. In relation to any undertaking, any channel that is the same as a channel on which signals are transmitted by (a) any television broadcasting station whose Grade A official contour encloses any part of the licensed area; or (b) any F.M. radio station whose 3,000 microvolt per metre official contour encloses any part of the licensed area. *Cable Television Regulations*, C.R.C., c. 374, s. 2.

RESTRICTED CHAUFFEUR'S LICENSE. License granted under this Act to an employee of a city, town, or other authority at the discretion of the Minister for use by the employee while working for and with the consent of the employer. *Motor Vehicle Act*, R.S.N.S. 1967, c. 191, s. 1.

RESTRICTED DRUG. Any drug or other substance included in Schedule H. *Food and Drugs Act*, R.S.C. 1985, c. F-27, s. 46.

RESTRICTED FINANCIAL INSTITUTION. (a) A bank to which the Bank Act or the Quebec Savings Bank Act applies; (b) a corporation licensed or otherwise authorized under the laws of Canada or a province to carry on in Canada the business of offering to the public its services as trustee; (c) a credit union; (d) an insurance corporation; (e) a corporation whose principal business is the lending of money to persons with whom the corporation is dealing at arm's length or the purchasing of debt obligations issued by such persons or a combination thereof; or (f) a corporation that is controlled by one or more corporations described in any of paragraphs (a) to (e). *Income Tax Act*, R.S.C. 1952, c. 148 (as am. S.C. 1988, c. 55, s. 188(14)), s. 248(1).

RESTRICTED KEY. Any key, card or other lock operating device that (a) is stamped or marked (i) "Master", "Do Not Copy", "Do Not Duplicate", "Restricted" or any other similar restrictive expression; or (ii) as being the property of any association, corporation, partnership, firm or other organization, or as being the property of the federal government, or of a provincial or municipal government or a government department or agency in Canada; (b) can be duplicated or coded only by equipment unique to that type of key, card or lock operating device; or (c) is prescribed by the regulations to be a restricted key. *Miscellaneous Statutes Amendment Act (No. 2)*, S.B.C. 1986, c. 16, s. 37.

RESTRICTED PARTY. A person who with respect to a company is (a) an officer or director of the company; (b) a beneficial holder, directly or indirectly, of 10 per cent or more of any class of voting shares of the company; (c) a beneficial holder of 10 per cent or more of any class of non-voting shares of the company; (d) a beneficial holder, directly or indirectly, of 10 per cent or more of any class of voting shares of an affiliate of the company; (e) an affiliate of the company other than a subsidiary of the company; (f) an employee of the company; (g) an auditor of the company, if the auditor is a sole practitioner; (h) a partner in the partnership of accountants that are the company's auditors, if the partner is actually engaged in the auditing of the company; (i) a director or officer of a body corporate described in paragraph (b) or (c); (j) a spouse or child of an individual described in paragraphs (a), (b), (c) or (d); (k) any relative of an individual referred to in paragraph (a), (b), (c) or (d) or the spouse of that individual if that relative has the same residence as that individual or the spouse of that individual; (l) a body corporate in which a person described in paragraph (a) or (b) is the beneficial holder, directly or indirectly, of 10 per cent or more of any class of voting shares; (m) a body corporate in which a person described in paragraph (c), (f), (g), (h), (i) or (j) is the beneficial holder, directly or indirectly, of more than 50 per cent of any class of voting shares; (n) a person designated under section 178 as a restricted party. *Loan and Trust Companies Act*, S.N.B. 1987, c. L-11.2, s. 1.

RESTRICTED PRACTITIONER. A registered architect under the Architects Act who holds a certificate of authorization under this Act. *Engineering, Geological and Geophysical Professions Act*, S.A. 1981, c. E-11.1, s. 1.

RESTRICTED RESOURCE PROPERTY. (a) Any right or interest of any nature whatsoever or howsoever described or part thereof in any production from a petroleum or natural gas well in Alberta with a finished drilling date on or before August 24, 1982 where the right or interest or part thereof was owned by an above-limit corporation or an above-limit partnership on August 24, 1982, and includes a right or interest or part thereof acquired by an above-limit corporation or an above-limit partnership

after August 24, 1982 pursuant to the terms of a contract, other than an option, entered into and enforceable on or before that date, but does not include any right or interest or part thereof that is disposed of by an above-limit corporation or by an above-limit partnership after August 24, 1982 pursuant to the terms of a contract, other than an option, entered into and enforceable on or before that date; (ii) if subclause (i) does not apply, any right or interest of any nature whatsoever or howsoever described or part thereof in any production from a petroleum or natural gas well in Alberta that was disposed of after its finished drilling date and after April 7, 1986 by a restricted corporation; or (iii) if subclause (i) does not apply, any right or interest of any nature whatsoever or howsoever described or part thereof in any production from a petroleum or natural gas well in Alberta that was disposed of after its finished drilling date and after April 7, 1986 by a restricted partnership. *Alberta Corporate Income Tax Act*, S.A. 1986, c. 1, s. 26.

RESTRICTED SPEED AREA. (i) Any city, town, or village; or (ii) any municipality or part of a municipality or any part of unorganized territory designated as a restricted speed area by the traffic board under section 97; or (iii) any highway or portion of a highway designated by the traffic board under section 97. *The Highway Traffic Act*, S.M. 1985-86, c. 3, s. 1.

RESTRICTED VISIBILITY. Any condition in which visibility is restricted by fog, mist, falling snow, heavy rainstorms, sandstorms or any other similar causes. *Collision Regulations*, C.R.C., c. 1416, Rule 3.

RESTRICTED WEAPON. (a) Any firearm, not being a prohibited weapon, designed, altered or intended to be aimed and fired by the action of one hand; (b) any firearm that (i) is not a prohibited weapon, has a barrel that is less than 18 1/2 inches in length and is capable of discharging centre-fire ammunition in a semi-automatic manner; or (ii) is designed or adapted to be fired when reduced to a length of less than 26 inches by folding, telescoping or otherwise; or (c) any firearm that is designed, altered or intended to fire bullets in rapid succession during one pressure of the trigger and that, on January 1, 1978, was registered as a restricted weapon and formed part of a gun collection in Canada of a genuine gun collector; or (d) a weapon of any kind, not being a prohibited weapon or a shotgun or rifle of a kind that, in the opinion of the Governor in Council is reasonable for use in Canada for hunting or sporting purposes, that is declared by order of the Governor in Council to be a restricted weapon. *Criminal Code*, R.S.C. 1985, c. C-46, s. 84.

RESTRICTION. *n.* Includes a requirement, exception, reservation, covenant, condition, stipulation or proviso. *Crown Grant Restrictions Act*, S.N.B. 1983, c. C-37.1, s. 1. See MARKET ~; WORK ~.

RESTRICTIVE COVENANT. An agreement which restricts the uses of real property.

RESTRICTIVE INDORSEMENT. A notation which prohibits any further negotiation of a promissory note or bill of exchange.

RESTRICTIVE INTERPRETATION. Strict explanation of meaning.

RESTRICTIVE TRADE PRACTICES COMMISSION. A federal administrative tribunal set up under the Combines Investigation Act.

RESTRUCTURE. *n.* 1. A change that, in the opinion of the Board, is significant in the operations of a manufacturer with respect to his products, methods of production, markets or management procedures and includes, if directly related to such operations, (a) the acquisition, amalgamation or merger of one or more manufacturers described in the definition "manufacturer" or the formation of a corporation or partnership described in paragraph (d) thereof; (b) the acquisition of working capital; or (c) the acquisition, construction or conversion of machinery, equipment, buildings, land or other facilities. Canada regulations. 2. A change that, in the opinion of the Board, is significant in the operations of a manufacturer or other person eligible for assistance under these Regulations, with respect to its or the person's products, methods of production, markets or management procedures and includes, if directly related to such operations, the acquisition of working capital or the acquisition, construction or conversion of machinery, equipment, buildings, land and other facilities. Canada regulations.

RESTRUCTURING. *n.* In respect of a fishery enterprise, includes the reorganization, refinancing, modernization, rationalization and expansion of the enterprise, and any similar activity directed toward improving the economic performance of the enterprise. *Atlantic Fisheries Restructuring Act*, R.S.C. 1985, c. A-14, s. 2. See INDUSTRIAL ~.

RESUBDIVISION. *n.* The division of a parcel of land involving the modification of a boundary of a lot established by prior subdivision. *Dartmouth City Charter Act*, S.N.S. 1978, c. 43A, s. 2.

RESULT. *v.* With respect to something, to come back to a former owner or that person's representative when the thing was ineffective or only partly disposed of.

RESULT. *n.* See OFFICIAL ~.

RESULTING TRUST. 1. Arises when title to property is lodged in one party's name, but that party, if he is a fiduciary or if he contributed no value toward the purchase of the property, is obliged to return it to the original owner of the title, or to the person who did contribute to its purchase or acquisition. D.M.W. Waters, *The Law of Trusts in Canada*, 2d ed. (Toronto: Carswell, 1984) at 299. 2. A situation which arises between two parties who both contributed money towards purchasing property that is registered in one name only. A. Bissett-Johnson & W.M. Holland, eds., *Matrimonial Property Law in Canada* (Toronto: Carswell, 1980) at T-5.

RESULTING USE. A use which is implied.

RESUMMONS. *n.* An additional or repeated summons.

RESUMPTION. *n.* For the monarch to take back land which, through misleading or some other mistake, had been already granted to someone else.

RES UNIVERSITATIS. [L.] Something which belongs to a corporation which all members may use.

RESURVEY. *n.* A survey made for the purpose of placing in correct position monuments lost or incorrectly placed by a previous survey. *The Land Surveys Act*, R.S.S. 1978, c. L-4, s. 2.

RETAIL. *n.* 1. A sale by a retailer directly to a consumer. *Gasoline and Motive Fuel Tax Act*, R.S.N.B. 1973, c. G-3, s. 1. 2. Any sale of products, excluding meals or refreshments, to a purchaser or to a user for consumption or use but not for resale. *Agricultural Products and Food Act*, R.S.Q. 1977, c. P-29, s. 1. See SALE AT ~; SELL AT ~.

RETAIL. *adj.* When used in relation to the distribution and supply of power, refers to the distribution and supply of power at voltages less than 50 kilovolts, but does not refer to works located within a transformer station that transform power from voltages greater than 50 kilovolts to voltages less than 50 kilovolts.

RETAIL BUSINESS. 1. The selling or offering for sale of goods or services by retail. 2. The selling or offering for sale of goods or services for consumption or use and not for resale and includes (a) the selling or offering for sale of goods and services by hawkers and peddlers; and (b) charging the public for admission to a place or facility for educational, recreational, cultural or amusement purposes. *Holiday Shopping Regulation Act*, S.B.C. 1980, c. 17, s. 1.

RETAIL BUSINESS ESTABLISHMENT. The premises or place in which or from which a retail business is carried on.

RETAIL DEALER. 1. A person who sells fuel to a purchaser. 2. Any person who sells tobacco to a consumer. 3. Any person who sells or delivers fuel for consumption or use, but not resale. *Fuel Tax Act*, R.S.Q. 1977, c. T-1, s. 1.

RETAIL DISTRIBUTION. The sale, lease, rental, exchange or other means of dispersal of film to members of the public, other than retail distributors, wholesale distributors or exhibitors. *Film and Video Classification Act*, S.S. 1984-85-86, c. F-13.2, s. 2.

RETAIL DISTRIBUTION FACILITIES. Works for the transmission and supply of power at voltages less than 50 kilovolts other than works located within a transformer station that transforms power from voltages greater than 50 kilovolts to voltages less than 50 kilovolts. *County of Oxford Act*, R.S.O. 1980, c. 365, s. 53.

RETAIL DISTRIBUTOR. A person who engages in retail distribution on a continual and successive basis. *Film and Video Classification Act*, S.S. 1984-85-86, c. F-13.2, s. 2.

RETAILER. *n.* 1. Any person who sells or offers to sell an agricultural product directly to the consumer. Canada regulations. 2. A person who keeps for sale or sells to a consumer gasoline, diesel oil or home heating oil. 3. A person who sells beverages in containers and includes (i) a person acting or purporting to act on that person's behalf; and (ii) a person who controls the normal operation of an automatic vending machine that dispenses beverages in containers. 4. (i) A public utility, within the meaning of The Public Utilities Act, that purchases power from the Hydro Corporation; or (ii) a Power Distribution District that purchases power from the Hydro Corporation. *Electrical Power Control Act*, S.Nfld. 1977, c. 92, s. 2. 5. A person whose establishment is outside Québec but who solicits therein, through a representative or by the distribution of catalogues or other means of publicity, orders for moveable property from persons ordinarily residing or carrying on business in Québec, for consumption or use by them in Québec. *Retail Sales Tax Act*, R.S.Q. 1977, c. I-1, s. 2. 6. Any person, group of persons or co-operative credit society or association or public body that sells lottery tickets to the public. *National Lottery Regulations*, C.R.C., c. 431, s. 2. See WHOLESALER-~.

RETAILER MARGIN. The difference between the price at which a retailer buys gasoline or diesel oil from a wholesaler and the price at which the retailer sells gasoline or diesel oil to a consumer. *Gasoline, Diesel Oil and Home Heating Oil Pricing Act*, S.N.B. 1987, c. G-3.1, s. 1.

RETAIL ESTABLISHMENT. A building or portion of a building or place in which, as the principal business carried on therein, goods, wares or merchandise are sold or offered or displayed for sale to the general public.

RETAIL GASOLINE SERVICE INDUSTRY. The business of operating retail gasoline service stations, gasoline pumps or outlets where gasoline is offered for sale at retail, including washing, waxing, oiling or lubricating automotive vehicles, repairing or changing tires and other services and undertakings incidental thereto, but does not include a gasoline outlet on the premises of any employer and used in the fueling of automotive vehicles owned or operated by the employer. *Industrial Standards Act*, R.S.O. 1980, c. 216, s. 24.

RETAIL HIRE-PURCHASE. With respect to goods means any hiring of goods from a person in the course of business in which (i) the hirer is given an option to purchase the goods; or (ii) it is agreed that upon compliance with the terms of the contract the hirer will either become the owner of the goods or will be entitled to keep them indefinitely without any further payment, except: (iii) a hiring in which the hirer is given an option to purchase the goods exercisable at any time during the hiring and that may be determined by the hirer at any time prior to the exercise of the option on not more than 2 months' notice without any penalty; (iv) a hire-purchase of goods by a hirer who personally intends either to sell them or to relet them for hire by others; (v) a hire-purchase by a hirer who is a retailer of a vending machine or a bottle cooler to be installed in the hirer's retail establishment; (vi) a hire-purchase in which the hirer is a corporation; and (vii) a hire-purchase of goods whose cash price exceeds $7,500.

RETAIL OUTLET. Any station, shop, establishment or other place, whether or not of a kind hereinbefore enumerated, in which any petroleum product is sold or kept for sale by retail. *Petroleum Products Act*, R.S.P.E.I. 1974, c. P-4, s. 1.

RETAIL PURCHASER. 1. Any person who by a sale acquires tangible personal property not for resale but as a consumer and includes also a promotional distributor to the extent that the full fair value of or the purchase price of any goods provided by way of promotional distribution exceeds any payment specifically made therefor by the person to whom such goods are so provided. *Retail Sales Tax (Amendment) Act*, S.Nfld. 1983, c. 77, s. 1. 2. A person who by a sale acquires tobacco not for resale but as a consumer. *Tobacco Tax Act*, S.Nfld. 1986, c. 1, s. 2. 3. Any person who purchases fuel oil or gasoline at a sale in the province, where the fuel oil or gasoline is not purchased by that person for resale; but (i) for personal consumption or use, or for the consumption or use of other persons at the purchaser's expense; or (ii) on behalf of or as the agent for a principal who desires to acquire the fuel oil or gasoline for consumption or use by that principal or by other persons at the expense of that principal.

RETAIL SALE. 1. A sale, including a sale by auction, of: (i) tangible personal property to a consumer or user for the purposes of consumption or use and not for resale as tangible personal property; (ii) taxable services to a user for the purpose of use and not for resale; or (iii) tangible personal property to a consumer or user who purchases the tangible personal property for the purpose of providing a taxable service therewith. 2. A sale for purposes other than exclusively for resale, lease or sub-lease.

RETAIL SELLER. A person who sells consumer products to consumers in the ordinary course of business.

RETAIL SPACE. The gross leasable floor area in any building or group of buildings used or intended to be used for the storage, display and sale of goods by retail or the provision of services, excluding areas used or intended to be used (i) for the operation of hotels, motels, theatres and recreation facilities; or (ii) as open areas, entrance ways, public washrooms or for the provision of other common facilities, except that in relation to a building used or intended to be used primarily for office accommodation or the provision of financial services "retail space" means the gross leasable floor area used or intended to be used for the storage, display and sale of goods by retail. *An Act to Amend the Planning Act*, S.P.E.I. 1981, c. 28, s. 1.

RETAIL STORE. A building or part of a building which is used or intended to be used for the sale of goods by retail. *Shopping Centres (Development) Act*, S.P.E.I. 1979, c. 17, s. 2. See RECOGNIZED ~.

RETAIL TRADE. The business of purchasing any goods, wares or merchandise for resale to the public for personal or household use or consumption. *Small Business Loans Regulations*, C.R.C., c. 1501, s. 3.

RETAIL VENDOR. Any person who, within a province, sells tobacco to a consumer.

RETAIN. *v.* For a client to engage a solicitor or counsel to defend or take proceedings, to advise or act on one's behalf.

RETAINED EARNINGS. Earnings in excess of declared dividends which are reinvested in the company. S.M. Beck *et al.*, *Cases and Materials on Partnerships and Canadian Business Corporations* (Toronto: The Carswell Co., 1983) at 780.

RETAINER. *n.* A deposit paid by a client which represents part of the fee a lawyer charges for services. See SEAT BACK ~.

RETARDATE. See MENTAL ~.

RETARDATION. *n.* In respect of dumping or subsidizing of any goods, means material retardation of the establishment of the production in Canada of like goods. *Special Imports Measures Act*, R.S.C. 1985, c. S-15, s. 2. See MENTAL ~.

RETARDED CHILD. A person under the age of 18 years who is suffering from a condition of arrested or incomplete development of mind whether arising from inherent causes or induced by disease or injury, to such a degree as to require treatment, care, and supervision, or training of the person for the protection or welfare of the person or others. *Child Welfare Act*, S.M. 1973, c. 26, s. 1. See MILDLY ~; SEVERELY ~; TRAINABLE ~.

RETARDED PERSON. A person in whom there is a condition of arrested or incomplete development of the mind as certified by objective psychological or medical findings, and whose best interests would be served by admission to an approved home. *Homes for Retarded Persons Act*, R.S.O. 1980, c. 201, s. 1.

RETARDED PUPIL. See TRAINABLE ~.

RETENTION AND DESTRUCTION SCHEDULES. Define the length of the storage period and eventual disposition of any public document or any class or series of public documents. *Archives Act*, S.P.E.I. 1975, c. 64, s. 1.

RETENTION AREA. That area within the grounds of the race course designated for the purposes of securing official samples. *Race Track Supervision Regulations*, C.R.C., c. 441, s. 2.

RETINENTIA. *n.* [L.] A group of people who attend on an important person.

RETIRED. See PLANT ~.

RETIRED EMPLOYEE. A person who was formerly an employee and to whom or in respect of whom a pension is being paid.

RETIREMENT. *n.* Permanent withdrawal from any form of employment. See AGE OF ~; DELAYED ~; EARLY ~; NORMAL DATE OF ~; ORDINARY ~; REGISTERED ~ SAVINGS PLAN.

RETIREMENT AGE. In relation to an employee, means the earliest age at which a pension benefit, other than a benefit in respect of a disability, is or may become payable to the employee under the terms of a pension plan without adjustment by reason of early retirement. *Pension Benefits Standards Act*, R.S.C. 1985, c. P-7, s. 2. See COMPULSORY ~; MAXIMUM ~; NORMAL ~.

RETIREMENT DATE. See NORMAL ~.

RETIREMENT INCOME. (i) An annuity commencing at maturity, and with or without a guaranteed term commencing at maturity, not exceeding the term referred to in subparagraph (ii), or, in the case of a plan entered into before the 14th day of March, 1957, not exceeding 20 years, payable to (A) the annuitant for his life; or (B) the annuitant for the lives, jointly, of the annuitant and his spouse and to the survivor of them for his or her life; or (ii) an annuity commencing at maturity, payable to the annuitant, or to the annuitant for his life and to his spouse after his death, for a term of years equal to 90 minus either (A) the age in whole years of the annuitant at the maturity of the plan; or (B) where the annuitant's spouse is younger than the annuitant and he so elects, the age in whole years of his spouse at the maturity of the plan, issued by a person described in paragraph (j) with whom an individual may have a contract or arrangement that is a retirement savings plan, or any combination thereof. *Income Tax Act*, R.S.C. 1952, c. 148 (as am. S.C. 1977-78, c. 32, s. 34(5)), s. 146(1)(i.1).

RETIREMENT INCOME FUND. An arrangement between a carrier and an annuitant under which, in consideration for the transfer to the carrier of property (including money), the carrier undertakes to pay to the annuitant and, where the annuitant so elects, to his spouse after his death, (i) in each year, commencing not later than the first calendar year after the year in which the arrangement is entered into, one or more amounts whose aggregate is not less than the minimum amount under the arrangement for a year, but the amount of any such payment shall not exceed the value of the property held in connection with the arrangement immediately before the time of the payment; and (ii) at the end of the year in which the last payment under the arrangement is, in accordance with the terms and conditions of the arrangement, required to be made, an amount equal to the value of the property, if any, held in connection with the arrangement at that time. *Income Tax Act*, R.S.C. 1952, c. 148 (as am. S.C. 1986, c. 55, s. 57(3)), s. 146.3(1)(f). See REGISTERED ~.

RETIREMENT PLAN. See REGISTERED ~.

RETIREMENT SAVINGS PLAN. (i) A contract between an individual and a person licensed or otherwise authorized under the laws of Canada or a province to carry on in Canada an annuities business, under which, in consideration of payment by the individual or his spouse of any periodic or other amount as consideration under the contract, a retirement income commencing at maturity is to be provided for the individual; or (ii) an arrangement under which payment is made by an individual or his spouse (A) in trust to a corporation licensed or otherwise authorized under the laws of Canada or a province to carry on in Canada the business of offering to the public its services as trustee, of any periodic or other amount as a contribution under the trust; (B) to a corporation approved by the Governor in Council for the purposes of this section that is licensed or otherwise authorized under the laws of Canada or a province to issue investment contracts providing for the payment to or to the credit of the holder thereof of a fixed or determinable amount at maturity, of any periodic or other amount as a contribution under any such contract between the individual and that corporation; or (C) as a deposit with a branch or office, in Canada; of (I) a person who is, or is eligible to become, a member of the Canadian Payments Association; or (II) a credit union that is a shareholder or member of a body corporate referred to as a "central" for the purposes of the Canadian Payments Association Act, (in this section referred to as a "depositary") to be used, invested or otherwise applied by that corporation or that depositary, as the case may be, for the purpose of providing for the individual, commencing at maturity, a retirement income. *Income Tax Act*, R.S.C. 1952, c. 148 (as am. S.C. 1980-81-82-83, c. 40, s. 96(2)), s. 146(1)(j). See REGISTERED ~.

RETIRING ALLOWANCE. An amount (other than a superannuation or pension benefit or an amount received as a consequence of the death of an employee) received (a) upon or after retirement of a taxpayer from an office or employment in recognition of his long service; or (b) in respect of a loss of an office or employment of a taxpayer, whether or not received as, on account or in lieu of payment of, damages or pursuant to an order or judgment of a competent tribunal by the taxpayer or, after his death, by a dependant or a relation of the taxpayer or by the legal representative of the taxpayer. *Income Tax Act*, R.S.C. 1952, c. 148 (as am. S.C. 1980-81-82-83, c. 140, s. 128(10)), s. 248(1).

RETORNA BREVIUM. [L.] Of writs, return.

RETORSION. *n.* Retaliation. Specifically in

international law, when one nation is dissatisfied with the treatment of its nationals by another nation, the first nation may declare that it will treat the second nation's nationals similarly.

RETORT. *n.* Any equipment used to recover mercury from mercury contaminated waste. *Chlor-Alkali Mercury National Emission Standards Regulations*, C.R.C., c. 406, s. 2.

RETOUR SANS PROTET. [Fr.] Return with no protest.

RETRACEMENT. *n.* The re-establishment of a line of a previous survey.

RETRACTATION. *n.* In probate practice, withdrawal of renunciation.

RETRACTOR. *n.* A device for storing part or all of the webbing in a seat belt assembly. *Motor Vehicle Safety Regulations*, C.R.C., c. 1038, s. 209. See AUTOMATIC-LOCKING ~; EMERGENCY-LOCKING ~; NON-LOCKING ~.

RETRACTUS AQUAE. [L.] With respect to tides, ebb or return.

RETRAXIT. [L. one withdrew] A proceeding which bars any future action on the same cause, unlike a nolle prosequi which does not bar this, unless it was made after judgment.

RETRIBUTION. *n.* Something given or demanded in payment; punishment based on the notion that every crime demands payment in the form of punishment.

RETROACTIVE EFFECT. With respect to an act, relation back to a time before that act.

RETROACTIVE PAY. The additional portion of wages earned during a period in respect of which a wage increase was awarded which dated back in time.

RETROSPECTIVE EFFECT. Said of a law which affects acts or facts occurring before it came into force.

RETURN. *n.* 1. The report of an officer of a court, e.g. a sheriff, which shows how a duty imposed on that officer was performed. 2. The record of any report or information provided by a respondent. Statistics acts. 3. A return prescribed pursuant to any revenue act. 4. When used in relation to the result of an election means the declaration by a municipal clerk that a candidate has been elected as a councillor. *Local Government (Elections) Act*, R.S.Nfld. 1970, c. 217, s. 2. See ANNUAL ~; NET ~ IN ANY YEAR; PATRONAGE ~.

RETURNABLE. *adj.* Used to describe a writ of execution or other kind of writs to which the person to whom they are directed must or may need to make a return.

RETURNABLE CONTAINER. A container belonging to a class of containers with respect to which, at the time of the sale of any such container together with the contents thereof to a purchaser, a specifically identified sum is usually charged and paid upon the express or implied undertaking of the vendor, or of the manufacturer or distributor of the container or its contents, that, upon delivery of that container to such vendor, manufacturer or distributor, or to the agent of any of them, the sum charged to the purchaser with respect to such container will be paid to the purchaser. *Retail Sales Tax Act*, R.R.O. 1980, Reg. 904, s. 1.

RETURN DUCT. A duct for conveying air from a space being heated, ventilated or air-conditioned back to the heating, ventilating or air-conditioning appliance. *Building Code Act*, R.R.O. 1980, Reg. 87, s. 1.

RETURNING OFFICER. A person responsible for conducting a municipal or parliamentary election. See SPECIAL ~.

RETURN OF CONTRIBUTIONS. A return of the amount paid by the contributor into a superannuation account.

RETURN OF INCOME. A return of income pursuant to subsection 150(1) of the Income Tax Act. *Tax Rebate Discounting Act*, R.S.C. 1985 (1st Supp.), c. 53, s. 1.

REUNION. *n.* A gathering at which alcoholic beverages are served or sold. *An Act Respecting the Commission de Contrôle des Permis D'alcool*, R.S.Q. 1977, c. C-33, s. 2.

RE-USABLE SHIPPING CONTAINER. A shipping container that is so designed, constructed and maintained and made of such materials that, (i) it may be readily sanitized, and (ii) it does not readily harbour insects or disease-producing organisms. *Animals For Research Act*, R.R.O. 1980, Reg. 19, s. 1.

REVALORIZE. *v.* Of an amount owing, to revalue it because the debt depreciated between the time it was incurred and the time it was due. J.G. McLeod, *The Conflict of Laws* (Calgary: Carswell, 1983) at 515.

REV. CAN. CRIM. *abbr.* Revue canadienne de criminologie (Canadian Journal of Criminology).

REV. CAN. D.A. *abbr.* Revue canadienne du droit d'auteur.

REV. CAN. D. COMM. *abbr.* Revue canadienne du droit de commerce (Canadian Business Law Journal).

REV. CAN. D. COMMUNAUTAIRE. *abbr.* Revue canadienne du droit communautaire (Canadian Community Law Journal).

REV. CAN. D. & SOCIÉTÉ. *abbr.* Revue canadienne de droit et société (Canadian Journal of Law and Society).

REV. CAN. D. FAM. *abbr.* Revue canadienne de droit familial (Canadian Journal of Family Law).

REV. CRIT. *abbr.* Revue critique (1870-1875).

REV. D. OTTAWA. Revue de droit d'Ottawa (Ottawa Law Review).

REVENDICATION. *n.* When goods are sold on credit, in some jurisdictions the seller reserves the right to retake them or to hold a lien upon them for the price if it is unpaid. In other jurisdictions, the seller has the right to stop in transitu only when the buyer is insolvent.

REVENUE. *n.* 1. Annual profit; income. 2. All public money collected or due. See CURRENT ~; FEE ~; FLYING ~S; GROSS ~; NET INCOME OR ~; NET ~; NON-RENEWABLE RESOURCE ~; NON-TAX ~; OPERATING ~S; PUBLIC ~; RESOURCE ~; SHAREABLE ~.

REVENUE ACT. A statute imposing a tax or fee.

REVENUE BASE. For a revenue source for a province for a fiscal year relates to the measure of the relative capacity of the province to derive revenue from that revenue source for that fiscal year and has the meaning given to that expression by the regulations. *Federal-Provincial Fiscal Arrangements Act*, R.S.C. 1985, c. F-8, s. 4(2).

REVENUE CANADA, CUSTOMS AND EXCISE. The federal body which assesses and collects duties and taxes on domestically produced and imported goods and on the transportation of people by air.

REVENUE CANADA, TAXATION. The federal body which carries out government tax policy as set out by the Department of Finance and assesses and collects corporate and individual income tax under the Income Tax Act of Canada.

REVENUE FUND. The Northwest Territories Consolidated Revenue Fund as established by the Northwest Territories Act (Canada). *Financial Administration Act*, S.N.W.T. 1982, c. 2, s. 2. See CONSOLIDATED ~.

REVENUE LAW. The law concerning noncontractual payments of money to the government or its agencies to maintain programmes for the benefit of everyone within the sovereign's

territory. J.G. McLeod, *The Conflict of Laws* (Calgary: Carswell, 1983) at 210.

REVENUE MILES. Actual miles travelled by a transit vehicle for the purpose of picking up and putting down passengers. *Regional Municipality of Hamilton-Wentworth Act*, R.S.O. 1980, c. 437, s. 50.

REVENUE OFFICER. A person who (i) is engaged in or is appointed or employed for the purposes of the collection or management of or accounting for public money; (ii) is engaged in the administration of any law under which public money is collected, managed or accounted for; (iii) is required by law or contract to collect, manage or account for public money; or (iv) receives, holds or is entrusted with public money, whether or not that person was appointed or employed for that purpose.

REVENUE PAPER. Paper that is used to make stamps, licences or permits or for any purpose connected with the public revenue. *Criminal Code*, R.S.C. 1985, c. C-46, s. 321.

REVENUE RECEIPT. Includes all public money except capital receipts.

REVENUE SOURCE. Any of the following sources from which provincial revenues are or may be derived: (a) personal income taxes; (b) corporation income taxes, revenues derived from government business enterprises that are not included in any other paragraph of this definition, and revenues received from the Government of Canada pursuant to the Public Utilities Income Tax Transfer Act; (c) taxes on capital of corporations; (d) general and miscellaneous sales taxes and amusement taxes; (e) tobacco taxes; (f) motive fuel taxes derived from the sale of gasoline; (g) motive fuel taxes derived from the sale of diesel fuel; (h) non-commercial motor vehicle licensing revenues; (i) commercial motor vehicle licensing revenues; (j) alcoholic beverage revenues derived from the sale of spirits; (k) alcoholic beverage revenues derived from the sale of wine; (l) alcoholic beverage revenues derived from the sale of beer; (m) hospital and medical care insurance premiums; (n) succession duties and gift taxes; (o) race track taxes; (p) forestry revenues; (q) conventional new oil revenues; (r) conventional old oil revenues; (s) heavy oil revenues; (t) mined oil revenues; (u) domestically sold natural gas revenues; (v) exported natural gas revenues; (w) sales of Crown leases and reservations on oil and natural gas lands; (x) oil and gas revenues other than those described in paragraphs (q) to (w); (y) metallic and non-metallic mineral revenues other than potash revenues; (z) potash revenues; (aa) water power rentals; (bb) insurance premiums taxes; (cc) payroll taxes; (dd) provincial and local government property taxes; (ee) lottery revenues; (ff) miscellaneous provincial taxes and revenues including miscellaneous revenues from natural resources, concessions and franchises, sales of provincial goods and services and local government revenues from sales of goods and services and miscellaneous local government taxes; and (gg) revenues of the Government of Canada from any of the sources referred to in this definition that are shared by Canada with the provinces, other than revenues shared under the Public Utilities Income Tax Transfer Act. *Federal-Provincial Fiscal Arrangements Act*, R.S.C. 1985, c. F-8, s. 4(2).

REVENUE SUBJECT TO STABILIZATION. With respect to a province for a fiscal year means, the aggregate of (a) the total revenues, as determined by the Minister, derived by the province for the fiscal year from the revenue sources described in the definition "revenue source" in subsection 4(2), other than the part of the revenue source described in paragraph (dd) of that definition consisting of local government property taxes and the part of the revenue source described in paragraph (ff) of that definition that consists of local government revenues from sales of goods and services and miscellaneous local government taxes; and (b) the portion determined in prescribed manner, of the fiscal equalization payment payable to the province for the fiscal year under Part I that is attributable to the total revenue to be equalized derived by all the provinces for the fiscal year from the revenue sources described in the definition "revenue source" in subsection 4(2), other than the part of the revenue source described in paragraph (dd) of that definition consisting of local government property taxes and the part of the revenue source described in paragraph (ff) of that definition that consists of local government revenues from sales of goods and services and miscellaneous local government taxes. *Federal-Provincial Fiscal Arrangements Act*, R.S.C. 1985, c. F-8, s. 6(2).

REVENUE TO BE EQUALIZED. From a revenue source for a province for a fiscal year means the total revenue, as determined by the Minister, derived by the province for the fiscal year from that revenue source. *Federal-Provincial Fiscal Arrangements Act*, R.S.C. 1985, c. F-8, s. 4(2).

REVERBERATORY FURNACE. Includes a stationary, rotating or rocking and tilting furnace. *Secondary Lead Smelter National Emission Standards Regulations*, C.R.C., c. 412, s. 2.

REVERSAL. *n.* Making a judgment void because of error.

REVERSE. *v.* To make void, repeal or undo. A judgment is reversed when a court of appeal sets it aside.

REVERSE ONUS CLAUSE. A clause which places the evidential or persuasive burden on the defence. P.K. McWilliams, *Canadian Criminal Evidence*, 3d ed. (Aurora: Canada Law Book, 1988) at 31-4.

REVERSER. *n.* A reversioner.

REVERSION. *n.* What a grantor still retains of an estate. E.L.G. Tyler & N.E. Palmer, eds., *Crossley Vaines' Personal Property*, 5th ed. (London: Butterworths, 1973) at 5. See RUN WITH THE ~.

REVERSIONARY. *adj.* Enjoyable in reversion.

REVERSIONARY INTEREST. In a broad sense, any property right whose enjoyment is deferred; in an ordinary sense, an interest in property not strictly a reversion or remainder, but analogous to them. For example, if property is limited to one party for life and after death to a second party, the second party has a reversionary interest.

REVERSIONARY LEASE. A lease which takes effect in the future; a second lease which becomes effective after the first lease expires.

REVERSIONER. *n.* A person who has a reversion.

REVERSIO TERRAE EST TANQUAM TERRA REVERTENS IN POSSESSIONE DONATORI, SIVE HAEREDIBUS SUIS POST DONUM FINITUM. [L.] A reversion of land is, so to speak, the return of land to the possession of either the donor or the donor's heirs after the estate granted terminates.

REVERT. *v.* To return; e.g., when the owner of land grants a small estate to another person and when that estate terminates, the land reverts to the grantor.

REVERTER. *n.* Reversion. See DOMICILE BY ~.

REV. ÉTUDES CAN. *abbr.* Revue d'études canadiennes (Journal of Canadian Studies).

REV. FISCALE CAN. *abbr.* Revue fiscale canadienne (Canadian Tax Journal).

REVIEW. *n.* An administrative or judicial re-examination of the decision by a court or authority which did not make the decision. See GENERAL ~; JUDICIAL ~; PAYMENT ~ PERIOD.

REVIEWABLE TRANSACTION. In bankruptcy matters, a transaction which was not at arm's length or was made by people who are "related". F. Bennett, *Receiverships* (Toronto: Carswell, 1985) at 326.

REVIEW BOARD. A review board established or designated by a province for the purposes of section 30. *Young Offenders Act*, R.S.C. 1985, c. Y-1, s. 2.

REVIEW COMMITTEE. 1. The Security Intelligence Review Committee established by subsection 34(1). *Canadian Security Intelligence Service*, R.S.C. 1985, c. C-23, s. 2. 2. A Review Committee established under section 82. *Canada Pension Plan*, R.S.C. 1985, c. C-8, s. 2.

REVIEW TRIBUNAL. A Review Tribunal established under section 82. *Canada Pension Plan*, R.S.C. 1985 (2d Supp.), c. 30, s. 2.

REVISAL YEAR. A year for which revisers are appointed, and in the case of a town means calendar year. *Municipal Franchise Act*, R.S.N.S. 1967, c. 198, s. 1.

REVISED ASSESSMENT ROLL. The assessment roll of the municipality as finally passed by the court of revision. *The Urban Municipality Act*, R.S.S. 1978, c. U-10, s. 2.

REVISED STATUTES. The latest revised and consolidated statutes of a province or the federal government.

REVISED TAXABLE INCOME. The aggregate of the taxable income of an individual in a taxation year, plus any resource allowance claimed by him in that year, minus any mineral taxes paid by him or on his behalf in respect of that year. *Income Tax Act (Manitoba)*, S.M. 1980, c. 78, s. 11.

REVISED VOTERS' LIST. Where used to refer to the revised voters' list of an electoral division means all the voters' lists prepared for an election in the electoral division as finally revised before polling day at the election.

REVISING AGENT. A person appointed by a returning officer pursuant to Rule 68 of Schedule IV. *Canada Elections Act*, R.S.C. 1985, c. E-2, s. 2.

REVISING JUSTICE. A justice of the peace appointed or designated by the Lieutenant-Governor in Council in accordance with this act for the purpose of causing lists of electors to be prepared and revised for an electoral district or part thereof, when the justice acts in the territory assigned to him by the Lieutenant-Governor in Council for the purpose, and includes any such justice sitting as a Court of Revision for any part of the territory so assigned to him. *Election Act*, R.S.Nfld. 1970, c. 106, s. 2.

REVISING OFFICER. A person appointed to revise a list of electors.

REVISION. *n.* 1. The arrangement, revision and consolidation of the public general statutes of Canada authorized under Part I. *Statute Revision Act*, R.S.C. 1985, c. S-20, s. 2. 2. The examination and correction of the meaning and form of a translation and includes the insertion into a translation of changes made in the original text after it has been submitted for translation to the Bureau. *Translation Bureau Regulations*, C.R.C., c. 1561, s. 2.

REVIVAL. *n.* Re-execution of a will by a testator after it was revoked; execution of a will or codicil which shows the intention to revive it.

REVIVED COMPANY. A body corporate described in section 202(1) that is revived under that section for the purpose of enabling it to apply for continuance as a corporation under section 262. *Business Corporations Act*, S.A. 1981, c. B-15, s. 261.

REVIVOR. *n.* A motion needed to continue proceedings when the suit abated before final consummation because of death or some other reason.

REV. JUR. FEMME & D. *abbr.* Revue juridique "La Femme et le droit" (Canadian Journal of Women and the Law).

REV. LOIS & POL. SOCIALES. *abbr.* Revue des lois et des politiques sociales (Journal of Law and Social Policy).

REVOCATION. *n.* 1. Undoing something granted; destroying or voiding a deed which existed until revocation made it void; revoking. 2. Cancellation. *Motor Vehicle Act*, R.S.N.B. 1973, c. M-17, s. 2. 3. With respect to a will, for a testator to render it inoperative or annul it by a later act. See DEPENDENT RELATIVE ~.

REVOKE. *v.* Cancel. *Motor Vehicle Act*, R.S.N.B. 1973, c. M-17, s. 2.

REVOKED. *adj.* Cancelled. *Motor Vehicle Act*, R.S.N.B. 1973, c. M-17, s. 2.

REVOKING. *adj.* Cancelling. *Motor Vehicle Act*, R.S.N.B. 1973, c. M-17, s. 2.

REVOLVING CREDIT. Credit in which amounts drawn on the credit are added back and become re-available as the buyer provides funds to meet acceptances. I.F.G. Baxter, *The Law of Banking*, 3d ed. (Toronto: Carswell, 1981) at 156.

REVOLVING FUND. A fund established by an Act and composed of money, accounts receivable, inventories, liabilities or any combination thereof in which revenues are credited and expenditures charged for a specific purpose. *Financial Administration Act*, S.N.W.T. 1982, c. 2, s. 2.

REVOLVING LOAN AGREEMENT. An agreement under which loans may be made by a lender from time to time with the credit charges being computed from time to time in relation to the total of the balances outstanding on all of the loans. *Credit and Loan Agreements Act*, R.S.A. 1980, c. C-30, s. 1.

REVOLVING STORES ACCOUNT. An inventory of goods and materials that are charged against an activity at the time of use rather than purchase. *Financial Administration Act*, R.S.N.W.T. 1974, c. F-4, s. 2.

REWARD. *n.* Payment of financial consideration to a person who helped apprehend another charged with an offence. See GAIN OR ~; HIRE OR ~.

REWORKED BUTTER. Creamery butter that has been reworked in a churn. *Farm Products Grades and Sales Act*, R.R.O. 1980, Reg. 327, s. 1.

REX. *n.* [L. king] Monarch.

REX EST CAPUT ET SALUS REIPUBLICAE. [L.] The monarch is the head and guardian of the commonwealth.

REX EST LEGALIS ET POLITICUS. [L.] The monarch is both legal and political.

REX N'EST LIE PER AUSCUN STATUTE SI IL NE SOIT EXPRESSEMENT NOSME. [Fr.] The monarch is not bound by any statute unless expressly named in it.

REX NON DEBET ESSE SUB HOMINE SED SUB DEO ET LEGE QUIA LEX FACIT REGEM. [L.] The monarch should not be subject to any person, but to the deity and the law, for law makes the monarch.

REX NON POTEST FALLERE NEC FALLI. [L.] The monarch can neither deceive nor be deceived.

REX NON POTEST PECCARE. [L.] The monarch cannot do wrong.

REX NUNQUAM MORITUR. [L.] The monarch never dies.

REX QUOD INJUSTUM EST FACERE NON POTEST. [L.] The monarch cannot do what is unjust.

R.F.L. *abbr.* Reports of Family Law, 1971-1977.

R.F.L. REP. *abbr.* Reports of Family Law, Reprint Series.

R.F.L. (2D). *abbr.* Reports of Family Law (Second Series), 1978-1986.

R.F.L. (3D). *abbr.* Reports of Family Law (Third Series), 1986-.

R.G.D. *abbr.* Revue générale de droit (Section de droit civil, Faculté de droit, Université d'Ottawa).

RHETORIC. *n.* The art of speaking with elegance and art.

RHESUS FACTOR. Antigens first found in the rhesus monkey which are carried on red blood cells. Individuals who possess them are called "Rh positive". F.A. Jaffe, *A Guide to Pathological Evidence*, 2d ed. (Toronto: Carswell, 1983) at 182.

RH FACTOR. See RHESUS FACTOR.

RHODODENDRON. *n.* The evergreen shrub, Rhododendron macrophyllum, known as rhododendron. *Dogwood, Rhododendron and Trillium Protection Act*, R.S.B.C. 1979, c. 96, s. 1.

RHUBARB. See FIELD ~.

RIB. See TREAD ~.

R.I.B.L. *abbr.* Review of International Business Law.

RICOCHET EFFECT. See BILLIARD-RICOCHET EFFECT.

RIDE. See AMUSEMENT ~.

RIDER. *n.* A clause inserted later. See COATTAIL ~; FREE ~.

RIDING HORSE ESTABLISHMENT. Premises where horses are kept that are let out on hire for riding or used in providing instruction in riding for payment or both. *Riding Horse Establishments Act*, R.S.O. 1980, c. 455, s. 1.

RIENS ARREAR. [Fr.] Nothing in arrears.

RIENS IN ARRERE. [Fr.] Nothing in arrears.

RIENS PASSE PER FAIT. [Fr.] Nothing passes by deed.

RIENS PER DESCENT. [Fr.] Nothing by descent.

RIENS PER DEVISE. [Fr.] Nothing by devise.

RIFFLARE. To remove something by force.

RIFLE. *n.* A firearm, usually fired from the shoulder, which has a barrel with rifling on the inside surface. F.A. Jaffe, *A Guide to Pathological Evidence*, 2d ed. (Toronto: Carswell, 1983) at 182.

RIFLING. *n.* A sequence of spiral grooves on the inside surface of a firearm barrel which imparts a spin to a projectile. The quantity of grooves and their direction (left or right handed) is one way to classify firearms. F.A. Jaffe,

A Guide to Pathological Evidence, 2d ed. (Toronto: Carswell, 1983) at 182.

RIGGING. See BID-~.

RIGHT. *n.* 1. A liberty, protected by law, to act or abstain from acting in a certain way. 2. A power, enforced by law, to compel a certain person to do or not to do a certain thing. 3. Includes power, authority, privilege and licence. Interpretation acts. 4. Includes power, authority, benefit, privilege and remedy. *Water Act*, R.S.B.C. 1979, c. 429, s. 1. See ACCESS ~; COLOUR OF ~; CONTINGENT ~; DEPENDENT ~; ENTRANT AS OF ~; MINERAL ~; MINING ~; OIL AND GAS ~; PERFORMING ~; PETITION OF ~; PETROLEUM ~; PREEMPTIVE ~; PROPERTY ~; PROPRIETARY ~; PUBLIC LENDING ~; REAL ~; ~ OF OWNERSHIP; ~S; TRAIN OF SUPERIOR ~; VOTING ~.

RIGHT-HAND. *var.* **RIGHT HAND.** In reference to a highway or the position of traffic thereon means the right when facing or moving in the direction of travel.

RIGHT OF ACCESS. Includes the right to take a child for a limited period of time to a place other than the child's habitual residence.

RIGHT OF ACTION. The right to bring an action.

RIGHT OF ASSOCIATION. The right of workers to form unions or other trade associations.

RIGHT OF CUSTODY. Includes rights relating to the care of the person of the child and, in particular, the right to determine the child's place of residence.

RIGHT OF ENTRY. 1. The right to take or resume possession of land by entering it peacefully. 2. The right of entry, user and taking of the surface of land. *Surface Rights Act*, S.A. 1983, c. S-27.1, s. 1.

RIGHT OF ENTRY ORDER. An order granting right of entry and made (i) under this Act or a former Act; or (ii) by the Board of Public Utility Commissioners or a district court judge under regulations established pursuant to The Provincial Lands Act prescribing the conditions under which right of entry may be obtained on land. *Surface Rights Act*, S.A. 1983, c. S-27.1, s. 1.

RIGHT OF SURVIVORSHIP. The right of a surviving joint tenant to take the property of the other, deceased joint tenant.

RIGHT OF USE. The exclusive right to occupy or use property rent-free for the purposes of the undertaking. *An Act Respecting the Application of Certain Fiscal Provisions to a Limited Partnership Operating Asbestos Mine*, S.Q. 1986, c. 68, s. 1.

RIGHT OF USER. A licence to enter on and use land for the purposes of a pipe line obtained either (a) by agreement with the owner of the land affected thereby, as provided in subsection (2) of section 16; or (b) under an order of the Court of Queen's Bench, made under The Expropriation Act and this Act. *Pipe Line Act*, R.S.M. 1970, c. P70, s. 15.

RIGHT OF WAY. *var.* **RIGHT-OF-WAY.** 1. The privilege of the immediate use of the highway. 2. Includes land or an interest in land required for the purpose of constructing, maintaining or operating a road, railway, aerial, electric or other tramway, surface or elevated cable, electric or telephone pole line, chute, flume, pipeline, drain or any right or easement of a similar nature. See EXCLUSIVE RIGHT OF WAY; RAILWAY ~.

RIGHTS. *n.* Includes estates and interests. Trustee acts. See AQUATIC ~; BILL OF ~; CIVIL ~; CONJUGAL ~; CUM ~; DOWER ~; EMPLOYER ~; EX ~; IMPRESCRIPTABLE ~; LEGAL ~; MANAGEMENT ~; MARITAL ~; MATRIMONIAL PROPERTY ~; MINERAL ~; MINING ~; OIL SANDS ~; PREROGATIVE ~ OF THE CROWN; REDEEMABLE ~; RIGHT; RIPARIAN ~; SOLE ~; SURFACE ~; SURFACE ~ OPTION; VESTED ~.

RIGHT TO A VOTING SECURITY. (i) A security currently convertible into another security that is a voting security; (ii) a security carrying a warrant or right to acquire another security that is a voting security; or (iii) a currently exerciseable option, warrant or right to acquire another security that is a voting security or a security referred to in subclause (i) or (ii). *Securities Act*, S.A. 1981, c. S-6.1, s. 131.

RIGHT TO BEGIN. The right to be first to address a court or jury.

RIGHT TO COUNSEL. Everyone has the right on arrest or detention to retain and instruct counsel without delay and to be informed of that right. *Canadian Charter of Rights and Freedoms*, Part I of the *Constitution Act, 1982*, being Schedule B of the *Canada Act 1982* (U.K.), 1982, c. 11, s. 10(b).

RIGHT TO FLOOD. A right or power to flood or otherwise injuriously affect land for purposes related to the construction, maintenance or operation of a dam, reservoir or other plant used or to be used for or in connection with the generation, manufacture, distribution or supply of power. *Land Title Act*, R.S.B.C. 1979, c. 219, s. 1.

RIGHT TO HARVEST. The right to hunt, fish, trap, capture or kill any kind of fish or any kind of wild mammals or birds. *An Act respecting hunting and fishing rights in the James Bay and New Québec territories*, S.Q. 1978, c. 92, s. 16.

RIGHT TO WORK. The right of an employee to keep a job without being a union member.

RIGHT-TO-WORK LAW. A law which effectively negates union security clauses in agreements. See RIGHT TO WORK.

RIGHT WHALE. Any whale known by the name of Atlantic right whale, Arctic right whale, Biscayan right whale, bowhead, great polar whale, Greenland right whale, Greenland whale, Nordkaper, North Atlantic right whale, North Cape whale, Pacific right whale, pigmy right whale, Southern pigmy right whale, or Southern right whale. *Whaling Convention Act*, R.S.C. 1970, c. W-8, Schedule s. 18.

RIGOR MORTIS. [L.] The stiffening and contracting of the voluntary and involuntary muscles in the body after death. F.A. Jaffe, *A Guide to Pathological Evidence*, 2d ed. (Toronto: Carswell, 1983) at 182.

RIG RELEASE DATE. The date on which, in the opinion of a district oil and gas conservation engineer, a well drilled for the purpose of discovering or producing oil and gas had been properly terminated. *Territorial Land Use Regulations*, C.R.C., c. 1524, s. 2.

RIM. *n.* 1. A metal support for a tire or a tire and tube assembly, upon which the tire beads are seated. Canada regulations. 2. The unobstructed open edge of a fixture. *Ontario Water Resources Act*, R.R.O. 1980, Reg. 736, s. 1. See DEMOUNTABLE ~; FLOOD LEVEL ~; TEST ~.

RIM-FIRE SHELL OR CARTRIDGE. A firearm cartridge designed to be fired by the action of a firing pin striking the rim area of the cartridge base. *Fish and Wildlife Act*, S.N.B. 1980, c. F-14.1, s. 1.

RIMOUSKI-MATAPÉDIA REGION. That part of the Province of Quebec consisting of the parishes of Albertville, St-Alexandre des Lacs, Amqui, Causapscal, St-Cléophas, St-Damase, Ste-Florence, Ste-Irène, Ste-Jeanne d'Arc, Lac au Saumon, La Rédemption, St-Léon le Grand, St-Moïse, Ste-Marguerite Marie, St-Noël, Padoue, Val Brillant, Ste-Paula, Sayabec, St-Tharcisius, St-Vianney, in the county of Matapédia; the parishes of Routhierville, St-Alexis de Matapédia, St-André de Restigouche, St-François d'Assise, L'Ascension, Matapédia, in the county of Bonaventure; the parishes of Ste-Angèle, Ste-Flavie, St-Joseph de Lepage, Mont-Joli, St-Octave de Métis and Price, in the county

of Matane, and the parishes of St-Charles Garnier, St-Donat, St-Gabriel, Les Hauteurs, Ste-Luce and Luceville, in the county of Rimouski. *Rimouski-Matapédia Pulpwood Order*, C.R.C., c. 255, s. 2.

RIMOUSKI-RIVIÈRE-DU-LOUP REGION. That part of the Province of Quebec comprising the parishes of Pointe-au-Père, St-Marcellin, St-Anaclet, Ste-Blandine, St-Narcisse, Esprit-Saint, Trinité des Monts, St-Guy, St-Médard, St-Mathieu, St-Simon, St-Fabien, Bic, St-Valérien, Sacré-Coeur, Rimouski, Ste-Odile and St-Eugène in the County of Rimouski and Trois-Pistoles, Isle-Verte, Cacouna, St-Paul Lacroix, St-Modeste, St-Épiphane, Petite-Isle-Verte, Rivière Trois-Pistoles, St-Jean de Dieu, St-Arsène, St-François-Viger, St-Éloi and Ste-Françoise in the County of Rivière-du-Loup. *Rimouski-Rivière-du-Loup Wood Order*, C.R.C., c. 265, s. 2.

RIMOUSKI, RIVIÈRE-DU-LOUP AND TÉMISCOUATA REGION. That part of the Province of Quebec comprising the parishes of Saint-Honoré, Lejeune, Saint-Juste du Lac, Sainte-Rose du Dégelé, Saint-Eusèbe, Saint-Benoît Packington, Rivière Bleue, Escourt, Saint-Louis du Ha! Ha!, Squatteck, Saint-Émile d'Auclair, Notre-Dame du Lac, Saint-Jean de la Lande, Les Étroits, Cabano, Sully, Saint-Elzéar, in the County of Témiscouata; Sainte-Rita, Saint-Cyprien, Saint-Hubert, Saint-Clément, Saint-Pierre Lamy, in the County of Rivière-du-Loup; Biencourt and Lac des Aigles in the County of Rimouski. *Rimouski-Témiscouata Pulpwood Order*, C.R.C., c. 256, s. 2.

RIOT. *n.* An unlawful assembly that has begun to disturb the peace tumultuously. *Criminal Code*, R.S.C. 1985, c. C-46, s. 64.

RIOT ACT. The name commonly given to the proclamation set out in section 67 of the Criminal Code, R.S.C. 1985, c. C-46 which is read at the time of a riot.

RIPARIA. *n.* [L.] Water which runs between two banks; a bank.

RIPARIAN. *adj.* Connected with or related to a riverbank or watercourse.

RIPARIAN RIGHTS. The rights of owners of property along a river or shore of other bodies of water.

RIPE. See FIRM ~; FIRM-~.

RISER. *n.* A supply pipe that extends through at least one full storey to convey water. *Ontario Water Resources Act*, R.R.O. 1980, Reg. 736, s. 1.

RISE TIME. The time required for the wave shape to go from 10 per cent to 90 per cent of its amplitude. *Medical Devices Regulations*, C.R.C., c. 871, s. 1.

RISK. *n.* 1. In insurance, a danger, event or peril insured against. 2. In relation to the emission of an air contaminant as a result of the operation of any work, undertaking or business, a risk that the concentration of that air contaminant in the ambient air in the geographical area in which the work, undertaking or business is situated, either alone or in combination with one or more other air contaminants referred to in the national ambient air quality objectives prescribed in relation to that air contaminant, will exceed the maximum acceptable limit with respect to that air contaminant or combination of air contaminants. *Clean Air Act*, R.S.C. 1985, c. C-32, s. 21(2). See ALL ~S; VOLUNTARY ASSUMPTION OF ~; WAR ~S.

RIVER. *n.* 1. Includes creek, stream or brook. 2. Includes all streams, lakes, creeks and estuaries, and all channels, ravines, gulches and watercourses, natural or artificial, tidal or otherwise, in which water flows constantly, intermittently or at any time, whether salt or fresh. *Riverbank Protection Act*, R.S.B.C. 1979, c. 369, s. 1. 3. A stream of water the bed of which is of an average width of 150 feet throughout the portion thereof sought to be leased. *Territorial Dredging Regulations*, C.R.C., c. 1523, s. 2. See INTERNATIONAL ~; LAKE AND ~ NAVIGATION; MACKENZIE ~; PRODUCTS OF THE SEA, LAKES AND ~S; SALMON ~.

RIVER AND STREAM. Includes a river, stream, creek, canal, drainage ditch, water channel, and any other water course, whether natural or made or improved by man. *Rivers and Streams Act*, R.S.M. 1970, c. R160, s. 20.

RIVER BED. The bed and bars of the river to the foot of the natural banks. *Territorial Dredging Regulations*, C.R.C., c. 1523, s. 2.

RIVER IMPROVEMENT PURPOSE. Clearing and improving the bed, channel and banks of a stream to facilitate the driving and booming of timber. *Water Act*, R.S.B.C. 1979, c. 429, s. 1.

R.J.E.L. *abbr.* Law Revue juridique des étudiants de l'Université Laval.

R.J.F.D. *abbr.* Revue juridique "La Femme et le droit" (Canadian Journal of Women and the Law).

R.J.Q. *abbr.* 1. Rapports judiciaires du Québec, 1875-1891 (Quebec Law Reports). 2. Recueil de jurisprudence du Québec.

R.J.R.Q. *abbr.* Rapports judiciaires revisés de la province de Québec (Mathieu), 1726-1891 (Quebec Revised Reports).

R.J.T. *abbr.* La Revue juridique Thémis.

R.L. *abbr.* La Revue Légale (Qué.), 1980-.

[ ] R.L. *abbr.* La Revue Légale (Qué.), 1943-1979.

R.L.N.S. *abbr.* La Revue Légale (N.S.) (Qué.), 1895-1942.

R.L.O.S. *abbr.* La Revue Légale (Qué.), 1869-1891.

ROAD. *n.* 1. Land used or intended for use for the passage of motor vehicles. 2. Includes a street, avenue, parkway, driveway, square, bridge, viaduct, trestle or other passageway designed and intended for, or used by the general public for the passage of vehicles and includes a trail on a frozen lake, river or other body of water or watercourse when such trail is maintained or kept open at public expense. *Municipal Act*, R.S.N.W.T. 1974, c. M-15, s. 2. 3. A graded strip of ground, appropriated for travel by motor vehicle, which is not on the right of way of a public highway. *Highway (Industrial) Act*, R.S.B.C. 1979, c. 168, s. 1. See ACCESS ~; CAT ~; COMMON ~; DEPARTMENTAL ~; FOREST ~; FORESTRY ~; GRID ~; HAUL ~; HIGHWAY AND ~; HIGHWAY OR ~; IMPROVE A ~; INDUSTRIAL ~; LOCAL ~; LOGGING ~; ON-SITE ~; PRIVATE ~; PUBLIC ~; RESERVED ~; RURAL ~; SERVICE ~; TOTE ~.

ROAD ALLOWANCE. Any right-of-way surveyed for the purpose of a road by either the Federal or provincial government survey and includes all rights-of-way provided by virtue of any statute for the purpose of a road, or any right-of-way properly dedicated to the public use as a highway. *Highways Department Act*, R.S.M. 1970, c. H40, s. 2.

ROAD AUTHORITY. A body having jurisdiction and control of a common or public highway or road, or any part thereof, including a street, bridge and any other structure incidental thereto and any part thereof.

ROAD BUILDING. The preparation, construction, reconstruction, repair, alteration, remodelling, renovation, demolition, finishing and maintenance of streets, highways or parking lots, including structures such as bridges, tunnels or retaining walls in connection with streets or highways, and all foundations, installation of equipment, appurtenances and work incidental thereto. *Employment Standards Act*, R.R.O. 1980, Reg. 285, s. 1.

ROAD BUILDING MACHINE. *var.* **ROAD-BUILDING MACHINE.** 1. A vehicle (a) that is designed and used primarily for grading of highways, paving of highways, earth moving and other construction work on highways; (b) that is not designed or used primarily for the transportation otherwise of persons or property; and (c) that is only incidentally operated or moved over a highway, and includes a vehicle designated as a road building machine by order of the Lieutenant Governor in Council, but does not include (i) a vehicle originally designed for the transportation of persons or property to which machinery has been attached; or (ii) dump trucks originally designed to comply with the size and weight provisions of the regulations under this Act. *Commercial Transport Act*, R.S.B.C. 1979, c. 55, s. 1. 2. A self-propelled vehicle of a design commonly used in the construction or maintenance of highways, including but not limited to: (i) asphalt spreaders, concrete paving or finishing machines, motor graders, rollers, tractor-dozers and motor scrapers; (ii) tracked and wheeled tractors of all kinds while equipped with mowers, post-hole diggers, compactors, weed spraying equipment, snow blowers and snow plows, front-end loaders, back-hoes or rock drills; and (iii) power shovels on tracks and drag lines on tracks, but not including a commercial motor vehicle. *Highway Traffic Act*, R.S.O. 1980, c. 198, s. 1.

ROAD IMPROVEMENT LINE. The line bordering land required to effect an improvement to the alignment, width or grade of a road, street, lane, sidewalk or other public way. *Local Government Act*, S.Nfld. 1972, c. 32, s. 2.

ROAD KILOMETRES. The sum of (a) the total kilometres of those highways located within the territorial limits of the municipality that have been designated by the Minister of Transportation under section 15 of the Highway Act and classified by him under section 14 of that Act; and (b) the total kilometres of other municipal roads and streets. *An Act to Amend the Municipal Assistance Act*, S.N.B. 1986, c. 58, s. 1.

ROAD LINE. The line between a street reservation and the abutting land. *Local Government Act*, S.Nfld. 1972, c. 32, s. 2.

ROAD LOAD. The power output required to move the vehicle at curb weight plus 400 pounds on level, clean, dry, smooth portland cement concrete pavement or other surface with an equivalent coefficient of surface friction at a specified speed through still air at 68° Fahrenheit and standard barometric pressure of 29.92 inches of mercury, and includes driveline friction, rolling friction and air resistance. *Motor Vehicle Safety Regulations*, C.R.C., c. 1038, s. 103.

ROADSIDE IMPROVEMENT. (a) Any building, structure, fixture or road; (ii) any tree, shrub or hedge; or (iii) any sign, notice, advertising device or flashing or rotating light.

ROADSIDE PREMISES. Land within 150 m of the centre line of a designated highway. *Highway Scenic Improvement Act*, R.S.B.C. 1979, c. 169, s. 1.

ROAD TRACTOR. Every motor vehicle designed and used for drawing other vehicles and not so constructed as to carry any load thereon either independently or any part of the weight of a vehicle or load so drawn.

ROAD VEHICLE. A motor vehicle that can be driven on a highway, other than a vehicle that runs only on rails or an electrically propelled wheelchair; a trailer, a semi-trailer or a detachable axle. *Highway Safety Code*, S.Q. 1986, c. 91, s. 4. See COMBINATION OF ~S.

ROADWAY. *n.* 1. That part of a public highway ordinarily used for vehicular traffic. 2. The continuous strip of land owned or occupied by a company as a right of way for its railway leading from place to place within Alberta but does not include (i) land that is outside the limits of the right of way and owned or occupied by the company for station grounds, extra right of way for sidings, spur tracks, wyes or other trackage; or (ii) land within the limits of the right of way that is used by the company for purposes other than the operation of the railway. *Municipal Taxation Act*, R.S.A. 1980, c. M-31, s. 16. 3. That portion of the surface of land required for access to a well site. *The Surface Rights Acquisition and Compensation Act*, R.S.S. 1978, c. S-65, s. 2. See LANED ~; ONE-WAY ~; PUBLIC ~; RAILWAY ~; SERVICED ~.

ROASTER CHICKEN. A chicken or any class or part thereof produced from the egg of a domestic hen where the live chicken weighs more than five and one-half pounds. *Farm Products Marketing Act*, R.R.O. 1980, Reg. 349, Schedule, s. 2.

ROB. & JOS. DIG. *abbr.* Robinson & Joseph's Digest.

ROBBERY. *n.* (a) Stealing; and for the purpose of extorting whatever is stolen or to prevent or overcome resistance to the stealing, using violence or threats of violence to a person or property; (b) stealing from any person and, at the time he steals or immediately before or immediately thereafter, wounding, beating, striking or using any personal violence to that person; (c) assaulting any person with intent to steal from him; or (d) stealing from any person while armed with an offensive weapon or imitation thereof. *Criminal Code*, R.S.C. 1985, c. C-46, s. 343.

ROCK. *n.* That portion of the earth's crust which

is consolidated, coherent and relatively hard and is a naturally formed, solidly bonded, mass of mineral matter which cannot readily be broken by hand. *Building Code Act*, R.R.O. 1980, Reg. 87, s. 1. See BED~.

ROCK BAR. An iron or steel bar ⁵/₈ of an inch square and 6 inches long cemented or leaded into solid bedrock so that the base of the bar is at least 4 inches into the solid bedrock. *Surveys Act*, R.R.O. 1980, Reg. 927, s. 1.

ROCKET. *n.* A projectile containing its own propellant and depending for its flight upon the reaction set up by the release of a continuous jet of rapidly expanding gases. *Air Regulations*, C.R.C., c. 2, s. 101. See MODEL ~.

ROCK POST. A bronze or aluminum identification cap fitted on a metal shaft at least ⁵/₈ of an inch in diameter and 3 inches long and planted in solid bedrock so that the cap is flush with the rock level and the base of the shaft is securely wedged in the bedrock. *Surveys Act*, R.R.O. 1980, Reg. 927, s. 1.

ROCK TRENCHING. Any excavation carried out on a mineral claim for the purpose of obtaining geological information. *Territorial Land Use Regulations*, C.R.C., c. 1524, s. 2.

ROCKWEED. *n.* A brown marine plant of the species Ascophyllum nodosum. *Atlantic Coast Marine Plant Regulations*, C.R.C., c. 805, s. 2.

ROD. *n.* 5 1/2 yards. *Weights and Measures Act*, S.C. 1970-71-72, c. 36, schedule II. See GROUND-~; LIGHTNING ~; SQUARE ~.

ROGATORY. See COMMISSION ~.

ROGATORY LETTERS. A commission in which one judge requests another to examine a witness.

ROLL. *n.* 1. The list of the members in good standing of a professional body. 2. A real estate assessment roll. See ASSESSMENT AND TAX ~; ASSESSMENT ~; STRIKE OFF THE ~.

ROLLING FORMAT. As applied to any time segment, means a format of presentation of broadcast matter in which one or more musical compositions are broadcast without interruption or accompanying broadcast matter other than (a) matter within content subcategory number 01, 09, 11, 12, 13, 14, 15, 16, 37 or 41, where the interruption for the presentation of such matter occurs on more than one occasion; and (b) matter within content category number 8 or 9. *Radio (F.M.) Broadcasting Regulations*, C.R.C., c. 380, s. 14.

ROLLING STOCK. Includes any locomotive, engine, motor car, tender, snow-plough, flanger, and every description of car or of railway equipment designed for movement on its wheels, over or on the rails or tracks of the company. *Railway Act*, R.S.C. 1985, c. R-3, s. 2. See RAILWAY ~.

ROLLOVER. *n.* What occurs when something with an accrued capital gain or loss is passed on to another taxpayer without tax consequences. The accrued gain or loss has a tax consequence only when the other taxpayer disposes of the thing in a chargeable transaction. W. Grover & F. Iacobucci, *Materials on Canadian Income Tax*, 4th ed. (Toronto: Richard De Boo Ltd., 1980) at 518.

ROMAN CATHOLIC. Includes a Catholic of the Greek or Ukrainian Rite in union with the See of Rome. *Education Act*, R.S.O. 1980, c. 129, s. 1.

ROMAN CATHOLIC SCHOOL BOARD. A separate school board that has made an election under section 136a or 136f that has been approved by the Minister. *Education Amendment Act*, S.O. 1986, c. 21, s. 1.

ROOF. See FLAT ~; METAL ~ED.

ROOF JOIST. A horizontal or sloping wood framing member that supports the roof sheathing and the ceiling finish, but does not enclose an attic space. *Building Code Act*, R.R.O. 1980, Reg. 87, s. 1.

ROOF SPACE. The space between the roof and the ceiling of the top storey or between a dwarf wall and a sloping roof. *Building Code Act*, R.R.O. 1980, Reg. 87, s. 1.

ROOM. See AUDIENCE ~; BATH~; BED~; BEVERAGE ~; BILLIARD ~; CELL ~; CHANGE ~; DINING ~; ELECTRICAL ~; ENGINE ~; FIRST-AID ~; GAS-PROOF ~; HAZARDOUS ~; LIVING ~; LUNCH ~; MONEY ~; PERSONAL SERVICE ~; POOL~; PROJECTION ~; PUBLIC ~S; SERVICE ~; SHOWER ~; TOILET ~; WASH ~.

ROOMING HOUSE. Any house or building or portion thereof in which the proprietor supplies lodging, for hire or gain, to other persons with or without meals in rooms furnished by the proprietor with necessary furnishings, and does not include a hotel, as defined in the Hotel Registration of Guests Act. *Assessment Act*, R.S.O. 1980, c. 31, s. 7.

ROOT CROPS. Parsnips, onion, carrots or rutabagas. *Manitoba Root Crop Marketing (Interprovincial and Export) Regulations*, C.R.C., c. 159, s. 2.

ROOT OF DESCENT. The stock from which one descends.

ROPE. See HOISTING ~; SHAFT ~; TAIL ~.

ROSTER. *n.* The table or list by which one regulates duties.

ROT. See BLACK ~; RED ~; SOUR ~.

ROTA. *n.* [L.] Rotation; succession.

ROTORCRAFT. *n.* A power-driven heavier-than-air aircraft supported in flight by the reactions of the air on one or more rotors. Canada regulations.

ROUGH PIPING. Gas piping from the meter location to and including all line cocks. *National Parks Natural Gas Regulations*, C.R.C., c. 1129, s. 2.

ROUND. *n.* A unit of ammunition composed of projectile, cartridge case, primer and propellant, or, in the case of shotgun ammunition, shell, pellets and wads. F.A. Jaffe, *A Guide to Pathological Evidence*, 2d ed. (Toronto: Carswell, 1983) at 171.

ROUNDED PENSION EQUIVALENT. The pension equivalent rounded to the higher multiple of $3 when the pension equivalent is not a multiple of $3. *Old Age Security Act*, R.S.C. 1985, c. O-9, s. 22.

ROUNDED SUPPLEMENT EQUIVALENT. The supplement equivalent rounded to the higher multiple of $1 when the supplement equivalent is not a multiple of $1. *Old Age Security Act*, R.S.C. 1985, c. O-9, s. 22.

ROUNDNOSE GRENADIER. A fish of the species Coryphaenoides rupestris. *Northwest Atlantic Fisheries Regulations*, C.R.C., c. 860, s. 2.

ROUND WEIGHT. The weight of a fish before any part of the fish has been removed. Fishery regulations.

ROUNDWOOD. *n.* Any section of the stem of or the thicker branches of a tree of commercial value that has been felled or cut but has not been processed beyond removing the limbs or bark, or both, or splitting a section of fuelwood. *An Act to Amend the Scalers Act*, S.N.S. 1984, c. 35, s. 1.

ROUTE. *n.* 1. An area within which there are, at any point, one or two directions of traffic flow and that is delineated on two sides by separation lines, separation zones, natural obstacles or dashed tinted lines except that the continuity of such lines or zones may be interrupted where the route merges with, diverges from or crosses another route. *Collision Regulations*, C.R.C., c. 1416, s. 2. 2. In respect of a commercial air service, means the route served by a Class 1 or Class 2 Canadian air carrier between points in any licence when providing a transportation service described in the air carrier's service

schedule or service pattern filed with the Committee and in effect. *Air Carrier Regulations*, C.R.C., c. 3, s. 2. 3. The tracks a train or engine may use in passing from one point to another. *Regulations No. O-8, Uniform Code of Operating Rules*, C.R.C., c. 1175, Part III, s. 2.

ROUTE MILE. One lineal mile in a rural telephone system necessarily occupied by telephone poles strung with one or more wires for the use of the system, and includes, to the extent prescribed by the regulations, jointly used pole leads, underground cable or other special facilities used in addition to or in place of pole leads. *The Rural Telephone Act*, R.S.S. 1978, c. R-27, s. 2.

ROUTE SEGMENT. A part of a route whose ends are identified by (a) a continental or insular geographic location; or (b) a point at which a definite radio fix can be established. Canada regulations.

ROUTING SYSTEM. Any system of one or more routes or routing measures which systems may include traffic separation schemes, two-way routes, recommended tracks, areas to be avoided, inshore traffic zones, roundabouts, precautionary areas and deep water routes. *Collision Regulations*, C.R.C., c. 1416, s. 2.

ROW HOUSE. A detached building divided vertically into three or more dwelling units. Canada regulations.

ROY. *n.* [Fr. king] Monarch.

ROYAL ASSENT. Approval of a bill, public or private, which was agreed to by both the Senate and the House of Commons. This approval gives the bill the perfection and complement of law. It is rarely given personally by the Governor General but more often by a Justice of the Supreme Court of Canada acting on the Governor General's behalf. A. Fraser, G.A. Birch & W.A. Dawson, eds., *Beauchesne's Rules and Forms of the House of Commons of Canada*, 5th ed. (Toronto: Carswell, 1978) at 242 and 243.

ROYAL CANADIAN MINT. The federal body which produces and supplies circulating, collector and bullion Canadian coins.

ROYAL CANADIAN MOUNTED POLICE. A federal police force which prevents and detects offences against federal statutes and provides protective and investigative services for federal agencies and departments.

ROYAL COMMISSION. A person or body appointed to inquire into and report on a matter of general public interest.

ROYAL CONSENT. The consent of the Sovereign which a Minister of the Crown gives to a bill or amendment that affects the Crown's prerogative, hereditary revenues, personal interest or property. A. Fraser, G.A. Birch & W.A. Dawson, eds., *Beauchesne's Rules and Forms of the House of Commons of Canada*, 5th ed. (Toronto: Carswell, 1978) at 238.

ROYAL HIGHNESS. A title authorized by British letters patent to apply to the children of any sovereign, the children of the sovereign's sons, and the eldest living son of the eldest son of any Prince of Wales. The Duke of Edinburgh may also be called Royal Highness.

ROYAL INSTRUMENT. An instrument, in respect of Canada, that, under the present practice, is issued by and in the name of the Queen and passed under the Great Seal of the Realm or under one of the signets. *Seals Act*, R.S.C. 1985, c. S-6, s. 2.

ROYAL PREROGATIVE. Power and privilege which the common law accords to the Crown. P.W. Hogg, *Constitutional Law of Canada*, 2d ed. (Toronto: Carswell, 1985) at 10.

ROYAL RECOMMENDATION. A communication, attached to a financial initiative of the Crown, which lays down once and for all (unless withdrawn and replaced) the amount of a charge as well as its conditions, objects, purposes and qualifications. A. Fraser, G.A. Birch & W.A. Dawson, eds., *Beauchesne's Rules and Forms of the House of Commons of Canada*, 5th ed. (Toronto: Carswell, 1978) at 181 and 182.

ROYAL SEALS. Include the Great Seal of Canada and any other seals or signets that may, with the approval of Her Majesty the Queen, be authorized under this Act. *Seals Act*, R.S.C. 1985, c. S-6, s. 2.

ROYAL STYLE AND TITLES. ELIZABETH THE SECOND, by the Grace of God of the United Kingdom, Canada and Her other Realms and Territories QUEEN, Head of the Commonwealth, Defender of the Faith. *Royal Style and Titles Act*, R.S.C. 1985, c. R-12, s. 2.

ROYALTIES. *n.* Includes (a) licence fees and all other payments analogous to royalties, whether or not payable under any contract, that are calculated as a percentage of the cost or sale price of defence supplies or as a fixed amount per article produced or that are based on the quantity or number of articles produced or sold or on the volume of business done; and (b) claims for damages for the infringement or use of any patent or registered industrial design. *Defence Production Act*, R.S.C. 1985, c. D-1, s. 2. See ROYALTY.

ROYALTY. *n.* 1. A financial consideration paid for the right to use a copyright or patent or to exercise a similar incorporeal right; payment made from the production from a property which the grantor still owns. H.G. Fox, *The Canadian Law of Trade Marks and Unfair Competition*, 3d ed. (Toronto: Carswell, 1972) at 696. 2. The amount payable to the Crown for timber harvested on Crown Lands as prescribed by regulation. *Crown Lands and Forests Act*, S.N.B. 1980, c. C-38.1, s. 1. See CROWN ~; GROSS ~ TRUST; OIL AND GAS ~ TRUST; PRODUCTION ~; RESOURCE ~; ROYALTIES.

ROYALTY DEDUCTION ACCOUNT. With respect to a corporation at the end of a taxation year means (i) with respect to the 1979 taxation year, the aggregate of (A) the amount of attributed Canadian royalty income used by the corporation in the calculation of its royalty tax rebate for each of the taxation years prior to the 1979 taxation year; and (B) the attributed Canadian royalty income used by the corporation in the calculation of its royalty tax rebate for the taxation year; and (ii) with respect to the 1980 and subsequent taxation years, the aggregate of (A) the corporation's royalty deduction account at the end of the immediately preceding taxation year; and (B) the attributed Canadian royalty income used by the corporation in the calculation of its royalty tax rebate for the taxation year. *Alberta Income Tax Act*, R.S.A. 1980, c. A-31, s. 14. 2. (i) The corporation's royalty deduction account at the end of the immediately preceding taxation year; and (ii) the corporation's royalty tax deduction for the taxation year. *Alberta Corporate Income Tax Amendment Act, 1981*, S.A. 1981, c. 8, s. 22.

ROYALTY INTEREST. Any interest in, or the right to receive a portion of, any oil or gas produced and saved from a field or pool or part of a field or pool or the proceeds from the sale thereof, but does not include a working interest or the interest of any person whose sole interest is as a purchaser of oil or gas from the pool or part thereof.

ROYALTY OWNER. 1. A person, including Her Majesty in right of Canada, who owns a royalty interest. 2. A person, other than a working interest owner, who has any interest in a right to receive a portion of the oil and gas produced from any lands or a portion of the proceeds from the sale thereof, including a reversionary interest, a royalty interest reserved to the lessors named in any subsisting oil and gas lease, and any over-riding royalty interest, or an interest in a payment under, or encumbrance on, a lease or other contract relating to oil and gas that does not carry with it the right to search for or produce the oil and gas. *Mines Act*, R.S.M. 1970, c. M160, s. 60.

ROYALTY YEAR. With respect to an interest, a calendar year or any 12 consecutive months agreed on between a minister and a relevant interest owner.

ROYAL WARRANT. A document, issued by a royal official, by which a tradesperson may act in a certain capacity, e.g. as shoemaker, for a member of the royal family.

R.P. *abbr.* Rapports de Pratique du Québec, 1898-1944 (Quebec Practice Reports).

[ ] R.P. *abbr.* Rapports de Pratique du Québec, 1945-1982 (Quebec Practice Reports).

R.P.C. *abbr.* Reports of Patent Cases.

R.P.F.S. *abbr.* Revue de planification fiscale et successorale.

R.P. QUÉ. *abbr.* Rapports de Pratique de Québec.

R.P.R. *abbr.* Real Property Reports, 1977-.

R.P.R. (2d). *abbr.* Real Property Reports, Second Series.

R.Q.D.I. *abbr.* Revue québécoise de droit international.

R.R.A. *abbr.* Recueil en responsabilité et assurance.

RRSP. *abbr.* A registered retirement savings plan within the meaning of the Income Tax Act (Canada) that is registered under that Act. *Employment Pension Plan Act*, S.A. 1986, c. E-10.05, s. 1.

R.S. *abbr.* Revised Statutes.

R.S.C. *abbr.* 1. Revised Statutes of Canada. 2. Rules of the Supreme Court.

R.T.P. COMM. *abbr.* Restrictive Trade Practices Commission.

RUBBER. *n.* Includes synthetic rubber, which may be defined by regulations prescribed by the Minister. *Customs Tariff*, R.S.C. 1985, c. C-54, s. 2.

RUBBER TIRE. See SOLID ~.

RUBRIC. *n.* With respect to a statute, its title, which was formerly written in red.

RULE. *n.* A law which an administrative agency or court enacts to regulate its procedure. P.W. Hogg, *Constitutional Law of Canada*, 2d ed. (Toronto: Carswell, 1985) at 284. See BEST EVIDENCE ~; CASPAR'S ~; GOLDEN ~; INSTRUMENT FLIGHT ~S; JUDGES' ~S; LOAD LINE ~S; MISCHIEF ~; PERPETUITY ~; QUOTA ~; REGULATION AND ~; SCATANA ~S; VISUAL FLIGHT ~S; WORK TO ~.

RULE ABSOLUTE. A complete rule or order, with full effect, as opposed to a rule or order nisi.

RULE AGAINST DOUBLE JEOPARDY. After an accused is tried for an offence and finally convicted or acquitted, that person may not be placed in jeopardy a second time, i.e. be tried again, for the same offence. P.W. Hogg, *Constitutional Law of Canada*, 2d ed. (Toronto: Carswell, 1985) at 776.

RULE AGAINST PERPETUAL DURATION. A rule with the same object as the rule against perpetuities, but which is applied to any trust with non-charitable purposes. D.M.W. Waters, *The Law of Trusts in Canada*, 2d ed. (Toronto: Carswell, 1984) at 282.

RULE AGAINST PERPETUITIES. For an interest in property to be good it must vest no later than 21 years after some life in being when the interest was created. T. Sheard, R. Hull & M.M.K. Fitzpatrick, *Canadian Forms of Wills*, 4th ed. (Toronto: Carswell, 1982) at 231. See PERPETUITY RULE.

RULE IN HODGES'S CASE. In a case in which the evidence is entirely circumstantial, before the accused can be found guilty the jury must be satisfied not only that the circumstances are consistent with the accused's committing the act, but that the facts are such that it is inconsistent with any other reasoning than that the accused is the guilty party. P.K. McWilliams, *Canadian Criminal Evidence*, 3d ed. (Aurora: Canada Law Book, 1988) at 5-5.

RULE IN PHILLIPS V. EYRE. In order to bring an action in tort in a local forum for a wrong committed somewhere else, the deed must be (1) actionable as a tort in that local forum, i.e., be something which would be a tort if done in the local forum; and (2) not justifiable where it was done. J.G. McLeod, *The Conflict of Laws* (Calgary: Carswell, 1983) at 534.

RULE IN RYLANDS V. FLETCHER. Anyone who, for their own reasons, brings on their land, collects and keeps there anything which may do harm if it escapes, must keep it in at their own peril. If they do not do so, they are prima facie answerable for any damages which result from its escape. I.H. Jacob, ed., *Bullen and Leake and Jacob's Precedents of Pleadings*, 12th ed. (London: Sweet and Maxwell, 1975) at 802.

RULE IN SAUNDERS V. VAUTIER. Narrowly it states that a court will not enforce a trust for accumulation, in which no one but the legatee has any interest when an absolute vested gift is made payable at a future event, with direction in the meantime to accumulate any income and pay it with the principal. More broadly it states that, if beneficiaries agree and they are not under a disability, the specific performance of a trust may be arrested, and they may extinguish or modify the trust without referring to the wishes of either the settlor or the trustees. D.M.W. Waters, *The Law of Trusts in Canada*, 2d ed. (Toronto: Carswell, 1984) at 963.

RULE IN SHELLEY'S CASE. If one vests land in trustees in fee simple in trust for some person for life, placing the remainder in trust for that person's heirs or the heirs of that person's body, that person takes an estate tail or equitable fee simple. D.M.W. Waters, *The Law of Trusts in Canada*, 2d ed. (Toronto: Carswell, 1984) at 22.

RULE OF ANTICIPATION. A rule by which discussion of a matter standing on the Order Paper may not be forestalled which depends on the same principle by which the same question may not be raised twice in the same session. The rule states that one must not anticipate a matter if it is contained in a more effective form of proceeding than the proceeding by which one seeks to anticipate it, but one may anticipate it if it is contained in a less effective and equal form. A. Fraser, G.A. Birch & W.A. Dawson, eds., *Beauchesne's Rules and Forms of the House of Commons of Canada*, 5th ed. (Toronto: Carswell, 1978) at 119.

RULE OF LAW. Processes which are ultimately predicated on fair and just methods and which theoretically adhere to standards of consistency, predictability of result, and impartiality. S.A. Cohen, *Due Process of Law* (Toronto: Carswell, 1977) at 2.

RULES FOR LIFE-SAVING APPLIANCES. The regulations respecting life-boats, buoyant apparatus and other life-saving equipment made under section 338. *Canada Shipping Act*, R.S.C. 1985, c. S-9, s. 2.

RULES OF CIVIL PROCEDURE. The rules for the Supreme Court and the District Court made under Part V. *Courts of Justice Act*, S.O. 1984, c. 11, s. 1.

RULES OF COURT. Rules made by the authority having for the time being power to make rules or orders regulating the practice and procedure of that court.

RULES OF PLEADING. Rules governing the form that pleadings take which have three basic requirements: (a) to plead the material facts; (b) to deny material facts and (c) to plead an affirmative defence. One might add the right of a party to request, and the court to order, particulars. G.D. Watson & C. Perkins, eds., *Holmested & Watson: Ontario Civil Procedure* (Toronto: Carswell, 1984) at 25-12.

RULES OF PRACTICE. Unless the context otherwise requires, the Rules of Practice and Procedure of the Supreme Court of Ontario. *Legal Aid Act*, R.R.O. 1980, Reg. 575, s. 1.

RULING. *n.* Determination obtained by a motion to the court of the propriety of a question in an examination to which one objected without receiving an answer. G.D. Watson & C. Perkins, eds., *Holmested & Watson: Ontario Civil Procedure* (Toronto: Carswell, 1984) at 34-7. See SPEAKER'S ~.

RUMMAGE SALE. A place where five or more persons or one or more organizations, or a combination thereof, sell goods for a non-profit purpose, 75 per cent or more of which goods are second hand or used. *Lord's Day (Nova Scotia) Act*, S.N.S. 1974, c. 40, s. 1.

RUN. *v.* To take effect at a certain place or time. See HIT AND ~; REGULAR ~.

RUN AT LARGE. To be not under control of the owner, either by being securely tethered or in direct and continuous charge of a person, or by confinement in any building or other enclosure or by a fence.

RUNNING AT LARGE. 1. Not being under control of the owner, either by being securely tethered or in direct and continuous charge of a person, or by confinement in any building or other enclosure or by a fence. 2. Off the premises of the owner and not muzzled or under the control of any person. *The Sheep Protection and Dog Licensing Act*, R.S.S. 1978, c. S-49, s. 2. See ANIMAL ~.

RUN-OFF. *n.* A line for carrying electrical power or energy from a rural distribution system to buildings, including the transformer required for transforming the voltage of the said system to the voltage at which the electrical power or energy is to be supplied for the customer's use. *The Rural Electrification Act*, R.S.S. 1978, c. R-24, s. 2.

RUN-OFF PARCEL. The parcel of farm land on which a farm subscriber is supplied, or on which a farm applicant is to be supplied, with telephone service by a company, and that parcel continues to be a run-off parcel until the total amount of any construction levy thereon is paid in full and thereafter until such time as the telephone line located on and serving the run-off parcel is deemed by subsection (1) of section 33 to be abandoned by the company. *The Rural Telephone Act*, R.S.S. 1978, c. R-27, s. 2.

RUNWAY. *n.* An individual landing or take-off surface considered to be heading in one magnetic direction only. *Aircraft Noise Certification Order*, C.R.C., c. 27, s. 2. See NOISE RESTRICTED ~.

RUN WITH THE LAND. Said of a covenant

with land conveyed in fee when either the right to take advantage of it or the liability to perform it, passes to the person to whom that land is assigned.

RUN WITH THE REVERSION. Said of a covenant with leased land when either the right to take advantage of it or the liability to perform it, passes to the person to whom that reversion is assigned.

RURAL AREA. Territory not organized as a municipality.

RURAL AREA OF SCHOOL DISTRICT. That part of a school district not within the boundaries of a municipality. *School Act*, R.S.B.C. 1979, c. 375, s. 1.

RURAL DISTRIBUTION SYSTEM. A line or lines for the distribution and supply of electrical power or energy to resident occupants outside any city, town or village, in accordance with this Act, but not including run-offs. *The Rural Electrification Act*, R.S.S. 1978, c. R-24, s. 2.

RURAL DISTRICT. 1. A school district situated wholly outside a village, town or city: provided that, where a rural district or portion thereof is included in a village thereafter organized, that district shall for the purposes of this Act be deemed a rural district until the end of the then current calendar year. *The School Act*, R.S.S. 1978, c. S-36, s. 2. 2. Any area in the Province of Nova Scotia except an area within the boundaries of a city or of an incorporated town having a population of more than 1200 according to the last decennial or other census taken under the authority of an Act of the Parliament of Canada. *Rural Electrification Act*, R.S.N.S. 1967, c. 271, s. 1.

RURAL DUMP. A site designated by the Minister for the disposal of refuse. *Highway Act*, R.S.N.B. 1973, c. H-5, s. 58.

RURAL FSA CODE. An FSA code the second character of which is the numeral "0". *Mail Preparation Regulations*, C.R.C., c. 1281, s. 2.

RURAL GAS CO-OPERATIVE ASSOCIATION. An association under the Rural Utilities Act that has as a principal object the supplying of gas to its members. *Rural Utilities Act*, S.A. 1985, c. R-21, s. 53.

RURAL GAS UTILITY. A system of pipelines for the distribution and delivery of gas and which provides gas service wholly or primarily to rural consumers in Alberta or consumers in remote urban municipalities in Alberta. *Rural Gas Act*, R.S.A. 1980, c. R-19, s. 1.

RURAL LAND. Land in a rural area, other than farm land, forest land, timber land, tree farm land and wild land.

RURAL MAIL BOX. A privately owned mail receiving and dispatching facility designed for outdoor use in a rural area. *Mail Receptacles Regulations*, C.R.C., c. 1282, s. 2.

RURAL MUNICIPAL AUTHORITY. (i) The corporation of a municipal district or county; or (ii) the Minister of Municipal Affairs, in the case of an improvement district or special area. *Rural Gas Act*, R.S.A. 1980, c. R-19, s. 1.

RURAL MUNICIPALITY. A municipality in a county or district.

RURAL POLLING DIVISION. (a) A polling division that is contained within an incorporated city or town of 5,000 population or more and declared by the Chief Electoral Officer to be a rural polling division pursuant to subsection 21(4); and (b) a polling division that is not contained within an incorporated city or town of 5,000 population or more or within any other area declared by the Chief Electoral Officer to be an urban polling division pursuant to subsection 21(3). *Canada Elections Act*, R.S.C. 1985, c. E-2, s. 2.

RURAL POLLING SUBDIVISION. Any polling subdivision not comprised in the definition of the expression "urban polling subdivision" or comprised in the municipalities of the Côte Nord du golfe Saint-Laurent and Baie James. *Election Act*, S.Q. 1984, c. 51, s. 61.

RURAL RATE DIFFERENTIAL. The amount by which the weighted average rural bill exceeds the weighted average municipal bill, expressed as a percentage of the weighted average municipal bill. *Power Corporation Amendment Act, 1981 (No. 2)*, S.O. 1981, c. 41, s. 2.

RURAL RESIDENTIAL PREMISES. Premises that are supplied, either individually or in conjunction with a farm, with power by the Corporation under this Part and that the Corporation decides are used for residential purposes on a year-round basis. *Power Corporation Amendment Act, 1981 (No. 2)*, S.O. 1981, c. 41, s. 2.

RURAL ROAD. A road subject to the direction, control and management of a rural municipality or a road, other than a primary highway, in an improvement district and subject to the direction, control and management of the Minister. *Public Highways Development Act*, R.S.A. 1980, c. P-28, s. 1.

RURAL SEPARATE SCHOOL. A separate school for Roman Catholics in a township or territory without municipal organization that is not part of a county or district combined separate school zone. *Education Act*, R.S.O. 1980, c. 129, s. 1.

RURAL TELEPHONE SYSTEM. A telephone system owned, controlled and operated by a company under The Rural Telephone Act. *The Telephone Department Act*, R.S.S. 1978, c. T-10, s. 2.

RUS. *abbr.* Russell's Election Cases (N.S.), 1874.

RUTABAGA. *n.* That vegetable commonly known as "swede turnip" but does not include the usually smaller species commonly known as "summer turnip". *Fresh Fruit and Vegetable Regulations*, C.R.C., c. 285, s. 2.

RYLANDS V. FLETCHER. See RULE IN ~.

S. *abbr.* 1. Section. 2. Second. 3. Length of superstructure.

S.A. *abbr.* Société Anonyme.

SABBATICAL LEAVE. Leave of absence for a period not exceeding 14 consecutive months, granted by a board to a teacher who: (i) has been regularly employed by a board; and (ii) receives from the board during such leave payment of an amount equal to at least 50 per cent of his salary for the year of employment immediately preceding such leave where granted on or after the first day of April, 1950; and (iii) during such leave: (A) pursues a course of studies, either academic or professional in nature, that is dirctly related to the work of a teacher; or (B) undertakes a travel route approved by the board; or (C) undertakes any other activity of an educational nature approved by the board; or (D) is, on the advice of a duly qualified medical practitioner as evidenced by a certificate given by the practitioner to the board, convalescing or required temporarily to discontinue teaching on account of ill health. *The Teachers' Superannuation Act*, R.S.S. 1978, c. T-9, s. 2.

SABOTAGE. *n.* Doing a prohibited act for a purpose prejudicial to (a) the safety, security or defence of Canada; or (b) the safety or security of the naval, army or air forces of any state other than Canada that are lawfully present in Canada. *Criminal Code*, R.S.C. 1985, c. C-46, s. 52.

SACCULAR ANEURYSM. A sac-like aneurysm which arises where a vessel wall is weak. F.A. Jaffe, *A Guide to Pathological Evidence*, 2d ed. (Toronto: Carswell, 1983) at 168.

SACRAMENTUM. *n.* [L.] An oath.

SACRAMENTUM SI FATUUM FUERIT, LICET FALSUM, TAMEN NON COMMITTIT PERJURIUM. [L.] A foolish oath, even if false, does not constitute perjury.

SADDLE HORSE. Any horse that is ridden, or intended to be ridden, by a person or that person's employees in the daily operation of a farm.

SADISM. *n.* Inflicting pain or cruelty on an animal or another person in order to obtain pleasure or sexual satisfaction. F.A. Jaffe, *A Guide to Pathological Evidence*, 2d ed. (Toronto: Carswell, 1983) at 182 and 183.

SAE. *abbr.* The Society of Automotive Engineers, Inc. *Motor Vehicle Safety Regulations*, C.R.C., c. 1038, s. 2.

SAFE. See INTRINSICALLY ~.

SAFE-CONDUCT. *n.* 1. Protection through enemy territory. 2. A document which permits travel in hostile territory. See LETTERS OF ~.

SAFE LEVEL. With respect to the atmosphere of a confined space, means that the level or concentration of airborne contaminants in the atmosphere (a) does not exceed the maximum levels for airborne contaminants recommended by the American Conference of Governmental Industrial Hygienists in its pamphlet Threshold Limit Values of Air-borne Contaminants for 1970 and amendments thereto; (b) is less than the lower flammable or explosive limit for flammable or explosive atmospheres as listed in the National Fire Codes 1969-70 and amendments thereto, as published by the National Fire Protection Association; or (c) does not exceed such other limits as may be indicated by good industrial safety practice or are prescribed in writing by the regional safety officer. *Canada Confined Spaces Regulations*, C.R.C., c. 996, s. 2.

SAFE MEDICATION. For the purpose of the Schedules means medication in a dose or doses within the usual therapeutic limits of dosage for a drug named in the following publications: 1. Pharmacopoeia Internationalis, 2nd ed. 1967. 2. The Canadian Formulary, 7th ed. 1949. 3. The British Pharmacopoeia, 1973 and addendum 1975. 4. The British Pharmaceutical Codex, 1973 and supplement 1976. 5. The European

Pharmacopoeia, Volume I 1969 Volume II 1971 Volume III 1975 and Supplement 1977. 6. The Food and Drugs Act (Canada) and the regulations thereunder. 7. The Pharmacopoeia of the United States of America, XIX ed. and 3rd Supplement 1977. 8. Martindale, The Extra Pharmacopoeia, 27th ed. 1977. 9. The National Formulary, 14th ed. and 3rd Supplement 1977. 10. AMA Drug Evaluations, 3rd ed. 11. Pharmacopée Française, VIII ed. 1965 and supplement 1968. 12. Pediatric Dosage Handbook (American Pharmaceutical Association), 1973. *Health Disciplines Act*, R.R.O. 1980, Reg. 451, s. 1.

SAFETY. *n.* Freedom from bodily injury or freedom from damage to health. *Construction Safety Act*, R.S.N.S. 1967, c. 52, s. 1. See CANADIAN AVIATION ~ BOARD; FACTOR OF ~; PLACE OF ~.

SAFETY AND HEALTH COMMITTEE. A committee established pursuant to section 135. *Canada Labour Code*, R.S.C. 1985 (1st Supp.), c. 9, s. 122.

SAFETY AND HEALTH REPRESENTATIVE. A person appointed as a safety and health representative pursuant to section 136. *Canada Labour Code*, R.S.C. 1985 (1st Supp.), c. 9, s. 122.

SAFETY BELT. 1. A combination of: (i) a belt worn around the waist of a worker; (ii) all necessary fittings; and (iii) a lanyard attached to the belt referred to in subparagraph (i). *Occupational Health and Safety Act*, R.R.O. 1980, Reg. 691, s. 1. 2. A belt attached to a lifeline or rope so that an accidental fall may be prevented or a worker may be rescued. D. Robertson, *Ontario Health and Safety Guide* (Toronto: Richard De Boo Ltd., 1988) at 5-357.

SAFETY CARTRIDGE. A cartridge for a gun, rifle, pistol, revolver and other small arms, of which the case can be extracted from the small arm after firing, and which is so closed as to prevent any explosion in one cartridge being communicated to other cartridges.

SAFETY CODE. See ELECTRICAL ~.

SAFETY CONVENTION. The International Convention for the Safety of Life at Sea, 1960, signed at London on June 12, 1960. *Canada Shipping Act*, R.S.C. 1985, c. S-9, s. 2.

SAFETY CONVENTION SHIP. A steamship, other than a ship of war, a troop ship or a fishing vessel, registered in a country to which the Safety Convention applies, that is on an international voyage and (a) is carrying more than 12 passengers; (b) is of 300 gross tonnage or more; or (c) is a nuclear ship. *Canada Shipping Act*, R.S.C. 1985, c. S-9, s. 2.

SAFETY DEVICE. Any device intended (a) to aid in preventing the unsafe operation or use of an elevating device or manlift; or (b) to minimize personal injury and property damage. *Canada Elevating Devices Regulations*, C.R.C., c. 999, s. 2.

SAFETY FILM. Film that does not contain more than thirty-six one-hundredths of one per cent of nitrogen and that, when tested in accordance with the definitions and analytical procedures prescribed by the Canadian Standards Association in its Standard for Safety Film, is shown to be both difficult to ignite and slow burning.

SAFETY FUSE. A fuse for blasting that burns and does not explode, does not contain its own means of ignition, and is of such strength and construction and contains an explosive in such quantity that the burning of such fuse will not communicate laterally with other like fuses. Canada regulations.

SAFETY GLASS. A product composed of glass so manufactured, fabricated, or treated, as substantially to prevent shattering and flying of the glass when struck or broken.

SAFETY GLASS STANDARD. Standard for Glass: Safety, for Building Construction, 12-GP-1b, August, 1971, a standard of the Canadian Government Specifications Board. *Safety Glass Regulations*, C.R.C., c. 933, s. 2.

SAFETY GROUND. A system of conductors, electrodes and clamps, connections or devices that electrically connect an isolated electrical facility to ground for the purpose of protecting employees working on the facility from dangerous electrical shock. *Canada Electrical Safety Regulations*, C.R.C., c. 998, s. 2.

SAFETY GROUNDING. A system of conductors, electrodes and clamps, connections or devices that electrically connect an isolated electrical facility to ground for the purpose of protecting employees working on the facility from dangerous electrical shock. *Canada Electrical Safety Regulations*, C.R.C., c. 998, s. 2.

SAFETY HARNESS. A combination of: (i) a belt worn around the waist of a worker; and (ii) straps attached to the belt that pass over the worker's shoulders and around his legs with the necessary fittings and a length of rope, suitable for raising him by the rope without permitting him to bend at the waist. *Occupational Health and Safety Act*, R.R.O. 1980, Reg. 691, s. 1.

SAFETY INTERLOCK. A mechanism that prevents the generation of radiation when any portion of the protective enclosure is removed or displaced. *Radiation Emitting Devices Regulations*, C.R.C., c. 1370, s. 1.

SAFETY ITEM. See VEHICLE ~.

SAFETY LAMP. A lamp, locked flame safety lamp or electric lamp, that is approved by the Chief Inspector for use underground. *Coal Mines (CBDC) Safety Regulations*, C.R.C., c. 1011, s. 2.

SAFETY MARK. Includes any design, symbol, device, sign, label, placard, letter, word, number, abbreviation or any combination thereof that is to be displayed on dangerous goods or containers, packaging, means of transport or facilities used in the handling, offering for transport or transporting of dangerous goods, in order to show the nature of the danger, or to indicate compliance with the safety standards set for the containers, packaging, means of transport or facilities.

SAFETY MEASURE. A measure designed for the purposes of safety in connection with the design and use of radiation installations, radiation equipment and associated apparatus.

SAFETY NET. A net so placed and supported as to safely arrest any worker who may fall into it. *Occupational Health and Safety Act*, R.R.O. 1980, Reg. 691, s. 1.

SAFETY OFFICER. See REGIONAL ~.

SAFETY REQUIREMENTS. Requirements for the handling, offering for transport or transporting of dangerous goods, for the reporting of those activities, for the training of persons engaged in those activities and for the inspection of those activities. Transportation of Dangerous Goods acts.

SAFETY RESTRAINING DEVICE. Any safety belt, safety harness, seat, rope, belt, strap or lifeline designed to be used by an employee to protect that employee from the danger of falling, and includes every fitting or accessory thereto. *Canada Protective Clothing and Equipment Regulations*, C.R.C., c. 1007, s. 2.

SAFETY STANDARDS. 1. Standards regulating the design, construction, equipping, functioning or performance of containers, packaging, means of transport or facilities used in the handling, offering for transport or transporting of dangerous goods. Transportation of Dangerous Goods acts. 2. Standards regulating the design, identification, construction or functioning of motor vehicles and their components for the purpose of protecting persons against personal injury, impairment of health or death. *Motor Vehicles Safety Act*, R.S.C. 1985, c. M-10, s. 2. 3. Standards regulating the design, construction or functioning of motor vehicle tires for the purpose of protecting persons against personal injury, impairment of health or death. *Motor Vehicles Tire Safety Act*, R.S.C. 1985, c. M-11, s. 2.

SAFETY STUDDED TIRES. Tires on the periphery of which there have been inserted, either by the manufacturer of the tires or by a person having a permit issued for the purpose by the registrar, studs of any material other than rubber that are of a kind approved in the regulations and that do not protrude beyond the surface of the tires to an extent greater than that specified in the regulations. *The Highway Traffic Act*, S.M. 1985-86, c. 3, s. 1.

SAFETY ZONE. The area of space officially set apart within a highway for the exclusive use of pedestrians and which is protected or is so marked or indicated by adequate signs as to be plainly visible at all times while set apart as a safety zone.

S.A.G. *abbr.* Sentences arbitrales de griefs (Québec), 1970-.

SAGITTAL. *adj.* In an antero-posterior direction, in the median plane.

SAILING SHIP. 1. Except for the purposes of the Load Line Rules, means (a) a ship that is propelled wholly by sails; and (b) a ship that is principally employed in fishing, not exceeding 200 tons gross tonnage, provided with masts, sails and rigging sufficient to allow it to make voyages under sail alone, and that, in addition, is fitted with mechanical means of propulsion other than a steam engine. *Canada Shipping Act*, R.S.C. 1985, c. S-9, s. 2. 2. Includes every ship provided with sufficient sail area for navigation under sails alone, whether or not fitted with mechanical means of propulsion. *Load Line Rules*, Canada regulations.

SAILING VESSEL. Includes every vessel that is under sail and is not being propelled by machinery. Canada regulations.

SAILING YACHT. A pleasure yacht that is equipped with sails and that is not equipped with a motor. *Pleasure Yachts Marking Order*, C.R.C., c. 1457, s. 2.

STE-ANNE-DE-LA-POCATIÈRE REGION. That part of the Province of Quebec consisting of the counties of Montmagny, L'Islet, Kamouraska and the parishes of Notre-Dame-du-Portage, St-Patrice, St-François-Xavier, St-Ludger and St-Antonin in the county of Rivière-du-Loup county. *Ste-Anne-de-la-Pocatière Wood Order*, C.R.C., c. 267, s. 2.

ST. LAWRENCE. See GULF OF ~.

ST. LAWRENCE PORTS. See GEORGIAN BAY AND ~.

ST. LAWRENCE RIVER SEASONAL AREA. That part of the St. Lawrence River bounded by the Victoria Bridge in Montreal, a straight line drawn from Cap des Rosiers to West Point, Anticosti Island, and a line drawn along the meridian of longitude 63 degrees west from Anticosti Island to the north shore of the St. Lawrence River. *General Load Line Rules*, C.R.C., c. 1425, s. 2.

ST. LAWRENCE SEAWAY AUTHORITY. A federal body which operates and maintains the seaway and bridges which connect the United States with Canada.

ST. LAWRENCE WATERWAY. (a) The St. Lawrence River extending upstream from the longitudinal meridian passing through the town of Sept-Iles, Quebec (66°30′ West) to the upper limits of the Port of Montreal; and (b) the Saguenay River and other tributary rivers where vessels enter or leave the St. Lawrence River. *Navigating Appliances Regulations*, C.R.C., c. 1449, Schedule VI, s. 1.

SALARY. *n.* 1. Compensation paid to an employee for labour or services. 2. Remuneration paid for services. See PENSIONABLE ~.

SALARY OR WAGES. The income of a taxpayer from an office or employment as computed under subdivision (a) of Division B of Part I and includes all fees received for services not rendered in the course of the taxpayer's business but does not include superannuation or pension benefits or retiring allowances. *Income Tax Act*, R.S.C. 1952, c. 148 (as am. S.C. 1970-71-72, c. 63), s. 248(1).

SALARY RATE. See ANNUAL ~.

SALE. *n.* 1. A transaction whereby the retail seller transfers or agrees to transfer the general property in a consumer product to a consumer for a valuable consideration. 2. Includes (i) exchange, barter, sale on credit, conditional sale, sale where the price is payable by installments, transfer of title, conditional or otherwise, and any other contract whereby for a consideration a person delivers goods to another; (ii) a transfer of possession, conditional or otherwise, or a lease or a rental, determined to be in lieu of a transfer of title, exchange or barter; and (iii) the provision of goods by way of promotional distribution. 3. Includes a sale, assignment, transfer, conveyance, declaration of trust without transfer or other assurance not intended to operate as a mortgage, of chattels, or an agreement, whether intended or not to be followed by the execution of any other instrument, by which a right in equity to any chattels is conferred, but does not include: (i) an assignment for the general benefit of the creditors of the person making the assignment; (ii) a transfer or sale of goods in the ordinary course of any trade or calling; (iii) a conditional sale within the meaning of The Conditional Sales Act or an assignment of a conditional sale. Bills of Sale acts. 4. Includes a bargain and sale as well as a sale and delivery. Sale of Goods acts. 5. Includes a conditional sale, hire purchase and any transfer of title or possession, conditional or otherwise, including a sale on credit or where the price is payable by instalments, an exchange, barter, lease or rental, or any other contract whereby at a price or other consideration a person delivers to another tangible personal property. 6. Includes leasing and renting, an agreement to sell, lease or rent and an irrevocable tender. *Special Import Measures Act*, R.S.C. 1985, c. S-15, s. 2. 7. Includes consignment or other disposition of materials and the supplying of any service. *Defence Production Act*, R.S.C. 1985, c. D-1, s. 2. See ACTION FOR ~; AGREEMENT FOR ~; ARM'S LENGTH ~; BARGAIN AND ~; BILL OF ~; BULK ~; CLOSING-OUT ~; COMMUNITY ~; CONDITIONAL ~; CONDITION OF ~; CONSUMER ~; CONTRACT FOR ~; CONTRACT OF ~; COUNTRY ~; DIRECT ~; GENERATION AND ~ FOR DISTRIBUTION TO THE PUBLIC; GROSS ~S; OFF PREMISES ~; ON-PREMISES ~; PARTITION OR ~; PROCEEDS OF ~; PUBLIC ~; RELATED ~; RETAIL ~; RUMMAGE ~; TIME ~; TRUST FOR ~.

SALE AND SELL. Include (i) the exchange, barter and traffic of liquor; and (ii) the selling, supplying or distributing, by any means whatsoever, of liquor.

SALE BY RETAIL. Includes sale by auction. *Shops Regulation Act*, R.S.M. 1970, c. S110, s. 2.

SALE BY SAMPLE. A sale where there is a term in the contract of sale express or implied to the effect that the sale is a sale by sample. *The Consumer Products Warranties Act*, R.S.S. 1978, c. C-30, s. 2.

SALE IN BULK. A sale of a stock, or part thereof, out of the usual course of business or trade of the vendor or of substantially the entire stock of the vendor, or of an interest in the business of the vendor.

SALE-LEASEBACK. *n.* A way to raise money on land by which a vendor receives from the purchaser current full market value of both land and the buildings built on the land and becomes a tenant of the purchaser under a long term lease of the property. D.J. Donahue & P.D. Quinn, *Real Estate Practice in Ontario*, 4th ed. (Toronto: Butterworths, 1990) at 231.

SALE OF A CHANCE. The sale of something

SALE OF GOODS

which the buyer hopes will eventuate. G.H.L. Fridman, *Sale of Goods in Canada*, 3d ed. (Toronto: Carswell, 1986) at 111.

SALE OF GOODS. 1. A contract by which a seller agrees to transfer or transfers property in goods to a buyer for financial consideration, called the price. G.H.L. Fridman, *Sale of Goods in Canada*, 3d ed. (Toronto: Carswell, 1986) at 11. 2. Includes any transaction in which goods are sold, whether separately or together with services. Consumer Protection acts.

SALE OF GOODS ACT. A code which governs a contract of sale of goods. G.H.L. Fridman, *Sale of Goods in Canada*, 3d ed. (Toronto: Carswell, 1986) at 10.

SALE OF SERVICES. Furnishing or agreeing to furnish services and includes making arrangements to have services furnished by others and any transaction in which services are sold, whether separately or together with goods. Consumer Protection acts.

SALE ON APPROVAL. The sale of goods with the right of the purchaser to return the goods if the purchaser is not satisfied with them within a specified time.

SALE ON CREDIT. A sale in which payment of the whole price is delayed, or the price is paid in instalments over a period to which the parties agree so that agreed-on interest is paid on the delayed part of the purchase price. G.H.L. Fridman, *Sale of Goods in Canada*, 3d ed. (Toronto: Carswell, 1986) at 260.

SALE PRICE. 1. For the purpose of determining the excise tax payable under this Part, means the aggregate of (a) the amount charged as price before any amount payable in respect of any other tax under this Act is added thereto; (b) any amount that the purchaser is liable to pay to the vendor by reason of or in respect of the sale in addition to the amount charged as price, whether payable at the same or any other time, including, without limiting the generality of the foregoing, any amount charged for, or to make provision for, advertising, financing, servicing, warranty, commission or any other matter; and (c) the amount of excise duties payable under the Excise Act whether the goods are sold in bond or not. *Excise Tax Act*, R.S.C. 1985, c. E-15, s. 22. 2. For the purpose of determining the consumption or sales tax, means (a) except in the case of wines, the aggregate of (i) the amount charged as price before any amount payable in respect of any other tax under this Act is added thereto; (ii) any amount that the purchaser is liable to pay to the vendor by reason of or in respect of the sale in addition to the amount charged as price, whether payable at the same or any other time, including, without limiting

the generality of the foregoing, any amount charged for, or to make provision for, advertising, financing, servicing, warranty, commission or any other matter; and (iii) the amount of the excise duties payable under the Excise Act whether the goods are sold in bond or not, and, in the case of imported goods, the sale price shall be deemed to be the duty paid value thereof; and (b) in the case of wines, the aggregate of (i) the amount charged as price including the amount of the excise tax payable pursuant to section 27; (ii) any amount that the purchaser is liable to pay to the vendor by reason of or in respect of the sale in addition to the amount charged as price, whether payable at the same time or any other time, including, without limiting the generality of the foregoing, any amount charged for, or to make provision for, advertising, financing, servicing, warranty, commission or any other matter; and (iii) the amount of excise duties payable under the Excise Act whether the goods are sold in bond or not, and, in the case of imported wines, the sale price shall be deemed to be the aggregate of the duty paid value thereof and the amount of the excise tax payable pursuant to section 27. *Excise Tax Act*, R.S.C. 1985, c. E-15, s. 42. 3. A price in money, also the value of services rendered or other consideration or prestations accepted by the seller as price or value of the thing given. *Tobacco Tax Act*, R.S.Q. 1977, c. I-2, s. 2. 4. The entire consideration for the sale of the property and, without restricting the generality of the foregoing, includes: (i) money consideration paid together with the par or face value of promissory notes, cheques, bills of exchange, agreements and securities forming part of the consideration; (ii) the gross value of real or personal property given in exchange in whole or in part including mortgages made by the grantee in favor of the grantor or his executor, nominee, assignee, trustee or anyone on his behalf; (iii) outstanding obligations or accounts cancelled, assumed or satisfied; (iv) the amount of rates, taxes, liens, mortgages and encumbrances, including interest and expenses thereon assumed by the grantee at the date of transfer. *Municipal Land Transfer Tax Act*, S.N.S. 1967-8, c. 10, s. 1. 5. Includes a price in money and also the value of services rendered, the actual value of the thing exchanged and other considerations accepted by the seller or person from whom the property passes as price or on account of the price of the thing covered by the contract, sale or exchange, and includes (i) customs and excise; (ii) charges for installation of the thing sold, for interest, for finance, for service and for transportation, unless such charges are shown separately, on the invoice or in the contract with the purchaser.

SALES CONTRACT. (i) An agreement for the sale of goods or services or both for future delivery or performance in whole or in part; (ii) an agreement under which the buyer, at some future time, on the happening of an event or the payment of the price or compliance with a condition, will become the owner of goods or entitled to the performance of services or both; (iii) an agreement under which the buyer does some act or pays a price in excess of $25 and thereupon becomes entitled to be owner of goods or to have a service performed; (iv) an agreement under which the buyer may, at his option, become the owner of goods or be entitled to buy goods or be entitled to the performance of services; (v) a sale of goods effected by way of a lien note or by way of an agreement or arrangement made at the time of the sale or subsequent thereto whereby the buyer gives to the seller a chattel mortgage or a bill of sale covering the whole or part of the purchase price of the goods sold; or (vi) an offer to buy goods or services or to enter into any agreement of the kinds mentioned in subclauses (i) to (v). *Direct Sales Cancellation Act*, R.S.A. 1980, c. D-35, s. 1. See GAS ~.

SALES FINANCE COMPANY. An investment company at least 25-per cent of the assets of which, valued in accordance with the regulations, consist of (a) loans, whether secured or unsecured, made by the company; or (b) purchases by the company of conditional sales contracts, accounts receivable, bills of sale, chattel mortgages, bills of exchange, promissory notes or other obligations representing part or all of the sale price of merchandise or services, and the value of assets of an investment company deemed by subsection 2(4) not to be assets that consist of loans described in paragraph (a) of the definition "business of investment" in subsection 2(1) shall not be included in the calculation of the aggregate value of its assets described in paragraphs (a) and (b). *Investment Companies Act*, R.S.C. 1985, c. I-22, s. 14.

SALES LITERATURE. 1. Includes records, videotapes and similar material, written matter and all other material, except preliminary prospectuses and prospectuses, designed for use in a presentation to a purchaser, whether such material is given or shown to him. Securities acts. 2. Includes records, videotapes and similar material, written matter and all other material, except terms and conditions of contracts and the written statement required under section 41, designed for use in a presentation to a customer, whether such material is given or shown to him. *Commodity Futures Act*, R.S.O. 1980, c. 78, s. 54.

SALESMAN. *n.* 1. An individual employed by a dealer to make trades in securities on the dealer's behalf. 2. A person who goes from house to house selling or offering for sale, or soliciting orders for the future delivery of, goods or services, for or on behalf of a vendor. 3. A person employed, appointed or authorized by a broker to trade in real estate. 4. A person employed, appointed or authorized by an issuer to sell investment contracts. 5. A person who is employed by a licensed insurance agent or broker on a stated salary that is not supplemented by commission, bonus or any other remuneration to solicit insurance or transact, for some other person, an application for a policy of insurance, or to act in the negotiation of such insurance or in negotiating its continuance or renewal, or collects and receives premiums on behalf of an employer only. See COMMODITY CONTRACTS ~; DRIVER ~; INSURANCE ~; ITINERANT ~; MORTGAGE ~; REAL ESTATE ~.

SALESPERSON. *n.* 1. An individual other than an authorized official employed or engaged by a registered mortgage dealer to take part in any of the activities mentioned in the definition of mortgage dealer. *The Mortgage Dealers Act*, S.M. 1985-6, c. 16, s. 1. 2. A salesperson of a prepaid funeral contract and includes a person who is employed, appointed or authorized by a contract seller to sell prepaid funeral contracts. *Prepaid Funeral Services Act*, S.S. 1986, c. P-22, s. 2.

SALES STABLE KEEPER. A person who stables, boards or cares for an animal belonging to another person, with the intention of selling or disposing of it, and who receives or is to receive payment for those services whether in the nature of a commission or otherwise.

SALES TAX. A tax which, if a seller imposes it, is like an excise tax and is on occasion called an excise tax. P.W. Hogg, *Constitutional Law of Canada*, 2d ed. (Toronto: Carswell, 1985) at 607.

SALE TO THE PUBLIC. See DISTRIBUTION AND ~.

SALICYLATE. *n.* A drug used as a fever-reducing agent, analgesic or for local application. F.A. Jaffe, *A Guide to Pathological Evidence*, 2d ed. (Toronto: Carswell, 1983) at 183.

SALINE SOLUTION. An aqueous solution of mineral salts occurring in a natural state and containing more than 1 per cent of mineral salts in solution. *Yukon Quartz Mining Act*, R.S.C. 1985, c. Y-4, s. 2.

SALIVA. *n.* The watery fluid which the salivary glands in the mouth produce. F.A. Jaffe, *A Guide to Pathological Evidence*, 2d ed. (Toronto: Carswell, 1983) at 160.

SALMON. *n.* Includes all kinds and classes of fish usually known and described by the trade names of sockeyes, red and white springs, pinks, chums, cohoes, steelheads and bluebacks. *Fisheries Act*, R.S.B.C. 1979, c. 137, s. 12. See ATLANTIC ~; PACIFIC ~; PINK ~; SLINK ~; SOCKEYE ~; SPENT ~.

SALMON BRINE CURING PLANT. A building, structure, machinery, appurtenances, appliances and apparatus occupied and used in the business of brine curing any species of salmon or of converting any species of salmon into brine cured salmon. *Fisheries Act*, R.S.B.C. 1979, c. 137, s. 12.

SALMON CANNERY. A building, structure, machinery, appurtenances, appliances and apparatus occupied and used in the business of salmon canning, or of converting the natural salmon into canned salmon. *Fisheries Act*, R.S.B.C. 1979, c. 137, s. 12.

SALMON DRY SALTERY. A building, structure, machinery, appurtenances, appliances and apparatus occupied and used in the business of dry salting salmon, or of converting the natural salmon into dry salted salmon, where the salmon are not kept or shipped in a brine solution. *Fisheries Act*, R.S.B.C. 1979, c. 137, c. 12.

SALMONID. *n.* Fish of the order Salmonidae listed in the schedule. *Salmonidae Import Regulations*, C.R.C., c. 831, s. 2.

SALMON NET. A gill net that is used for taking salmon. *Newfoundland Fishery Regulations*, C.R.C., c. 846, s. 2.

SALMON PLANT. See TIERCED ~.

SALMON POOL. Any place in a salmon river identified as such by means of markers. *Quebec Fishery Regulations*, C.R.C., c. 852, s. 2.

SALMON RIVER. That part of any river listed in a region set out in Schedule II and any part of a tributary of any river so listed that is frequented by anadromous Atlantic salmon. *Quebec Fishery Regulations*, C.R.C., c. 852, s. 2.

SALMON TRAP. A trap net that is used for taking salmon and includes the leader thereof. *Newfoundland Fishery Regulations*, C.R.C., c. 846, s. 2.

SALT. See OIL, NATURAL GAS, OR ~ PRODUCTION EQUIPMENT.

SALTERY. See SALMON DRY ~.

SALT WATER FISHERMAN. See CANADIAN ~.

SALTWATER MARSH. An area, lying between dry land and the ocean or an inlet thereof, which is covered all or part of the time by salt water and which is characterized by aquatic and grasslike vegetation. *An Act to Amend the Trespass Act*, S.N.B. 1985, c. 70, s. 1.

SALUS POPULI EST SUPREMA LEX. [L.] The safety of people is the highest law.

SALVAGE. *n.* 1. A reward, not for services attempted without result, for benefits conferred. A salvor must show that, when the services were rendered, the cargo or ship was in danger of being destroyed. G.H.L. Fridman & J.G. McLeod, *Restitution* (Toronto: Carswell, 1982) at 509 and 510. 2. Includes second-hand, used, discarded or surplus metals, bottles or goods, unserviceable, discarded or junked motor vehicles, bodies, engines or other component parts of a motor vehicle, and articles of every description.

SALVAGE CHARGE. A charge recoverable under maritime law by a salvor independently of contract; it does not include the expense of services in the nature of salvage rendered by the assured or the assured's agents, or any person employed for hire by them, for the purpose of averting a peril insured against. Such an expense, where properly incurred, may be recovered as a particular charge or as a general average loss, according to the circumstances under which it was incurred.

SALVAGE COSTS. A larger share of costs to which the lien claimant who carried an action is entitled. They are calculated on how complex the issues are, the number of claimants and the time it took to resolve their claims. M.M. Orkin, *The Law of Costs*, 2d ed. (Aurora: Canada Law Book, 1987) at 14-5 and 14-6. Because that claimant got the action on for trial, conducted the trial, prepared the formal judgment and distributed the money due under the judgment, she or he may claim a greater share than any other party. D.N. Macklem & D.I. Bristow, *Construction and Mechanics' Liens in Canada*, 5th ed. (Toronto: Carswell, 1985) at 560.

SALVAGE DEALER. A person who owns or operates a salvage yard in the Province, or who carries on the business of buying or selling salvage in the Province, but does not include person who holds a licence under the Motor Vehicle Act as a dealer or sub-dealer in new or used motor vehicles and who carries on the business of a salvage dealer only in the course of the business for which that licence was issued. *An Act to Amend the Salvage Dealers Licensing Act*, S.N.B. 1980, c. 50, s. 1.

SALVAGE VALUE. The amount received for plant retired, including insurance proceeds, and includes any amount received for material salvaged from plant retired where the material is sold. Pipeline Uniform Accounting regulations See NET ~.

SALVAGE YARD. The premises where used automobile bodies or parts of other vehicles or machinery or used goods, material or equipment of any kind are placed, stored or kept.

SALVATION ARMY OFFICER. Every duly commissioned officer, envoy or auxiliary captain of the religious society known as "The Salvation Army" and duly chosen or commissioned by that society to solemnize marriage and resident in the province. *Solemnization of Marriage Act*, S. Nfld. 1974, c. 81, s. 2. See STAFF OFFICER OR STAFF OFFICER OF THE SALVATION ARMY.

SALVO. [L.] With no prejudice to.

SALVOR. *n.* The person who helps a ship or vessel in distress and thereby earns a reward.

SAMPLE. *n.* A small amount of a commodity displayed as a specimen at a private or public sale. See COMMERCIAL ~; COMPOSITE ~; EXPORT STANDARD ~; GRAB ~; OFFICIAL ~; SALE BY ~.

SAMPLES FOR MASS DISTRIBUTION. Samples that are sent to specific addresses in such a manner as will afford complete or major coverage of the persons in a particular area for the purpose of publicizing the merchandise and enabling it to be assessed by prospective purchasers. *Third Class Mail Regulations*, C.R.C., c. 1297, s. 2.

SAMPLES FOR SELECTIVE DISTRIBUTION. Samples that are sent on request, or if unrequested are sent to persons selected according to their profession or occupation, for the purpose of publicizing the merchandise and enabling it to be assessed by prospective purchasers. *Third Class Mail Regulations*, C.R.C., c. 1297, s. 2.

SANATORIUM. *n.* A hospital or part of a hospital set apart as a place for the reception of cases of tuberculosis.

SANCTION. *n.* A punishment or penalty used to enforce obedience to law. See CRIMINAL ~S; ECONOMIC ~.

SANCTUARY. *n.* A place where neither a criminal nor civil process can be executed. See GAME ~; WILDLIFE ~.

SAND. *n.* A soil consisting of particles passing a No. 4 sieve but retained on a No. 200 sieve. *Building Code Act*, R.R.O. 1980, Reg. 87, s. 4.2.1.4. See BITUMINOUS ~S; FINE ~; MEDIUM ~; OIL ~; OIL ~S; TAR ~S.

SAND AND GRAVEL. See CEMENTED ~.

SAND DUNE. A natural mound of loose sand, which may be covered with grass or other vegetation, found along a lake or ocean shore. *An Act to Amend the Trespass Act*, S.N.B. 1985, c. 70, s. 1.

SANDERSON ORDER. A simpler form of a Bullock order by which the unsuccessful defendant must pay the successful defendant's costs directly. The name comes from *Sanderson v. Blyth Theatre Co.*, [1903] 2 K.B. 644.

SANITARIUM. *n.* An institution for the care and treatment of mental and nervous illnesses that is licensed under this Act. *Private Sanitaria Act*, R.S.O. 1980, c. 391, s. 1.

SANITARY ACCOMMODATION. Washing accommodation and accommodation containing water closets or urinals. *Crew Accommodation Regulations*, C.R.C., c. 1418, s. 2.

SANITARY CONDITION. That physical condition of the working environment of an employee that will contribute effectively to the health of that employee by preventing the incidence and spread of disease. *Canada Sanitation Regulations*, C.R.C., c. 1009, s. 2.

SANITARY DRAINAGE SYSTEM. A drainage system that conducts sewage. *Building Code Act*, R.R.O. 1980, Reg. 87, s. 1.

SANITARY FACILITY. A room or rooms containing one or more toilets and one or more washbasins.

SANITARY UNIT. A water closet, urinal, bidet or bedpan washer. *Ontario Water Resources Act*, R.R.O. 1980, Reg. 736, s. 1.

SANITARY WASTE WATER. Waste water from the plumbing system of a building and not mixed with underground or surface water nor with residue from any process contemplated in paragraph 2. *An Act to Amend the Acts Respecting the Communauté Urbaine de Montréal*, S.Q. 1982, c. 18, s. 56.

SANITATION DEVICE. See MARINE ~.

SANITIZE. *v.* 1. To remove bacteria by thermal or chemical means. 2. To clean for the purpose of controlling disease-producing organisms.

SANITIZING AGENT. A substance that destroys bacteria in eggs and has a strength of between 100 and 200 parts per million of available chlorine or its equivalent. *Processed Egg Regulations*, C.R.C., c. 290, s. 2.

SANS CEO QUE. [L.] Without this.

SANS FRAIS. [Fr.] Without cost.

SANS RECOURS. [Fr.] Without recourse.

SASK. *abbr.* Saskatchewan.

SASKATCHEWAN. See GOVERNMENT OF ~; NORTHEASTERN ~.

SASKATCHEWAN CONTRACT. A subsisting contract of insurance that (i) has for its subject: (A) property that at the time of the making of the contract is in Saskatchewan or is in transit to or from Saskatchewan; or (B) the life, safety, fidelity or insurable interest of a person who at the time of the making of the contract is resident in or has its head office in Saskatchewan; or (ii) makes provision for payment thereunder primarily to a resident of Saskatchewan or to an incorporated company that has its head office in Saskatchewan. *The Saskatchewan Insurance Act*, R.S.S. 1978, c. S-26, s. 55.

SASKATCHEWAN DAY. The first Monday in August of each year. *The Labour Standards Act*, R.S.S. 1978, c. L-1, s. 2.

SASKATCHEWAN RESIDENT. An individual who: (i) holds or is named in a valid Saskatchewan Health Services Card issued for the purposes of The Saskatchewan Hospitalization Act or The Saskatchewan Medical Care Insurance Act; or (ii) is a member of the Royal Canadian Mounted Police or of the Canadian Armed Forces stationed in Saskatchewan. *The Fuel Tax Act*, S.S. 1986-7-8, c. F-23.2, s. 2.

SASK. BAR REV. *abbr.* Saskatchewan Bar Review.

SASK. L.R. *abbr.* Saskatchewan Law Reports.

SASK. L. REV. *abbr.* Saskatchewan Law Review.

SASK. R. *abbr.* Saskatchewan Reports, 1979-.

SATELLITE STATION. See SATELLITE TELECOMMUNICATION SYSTEM.

SATELLITE TELECOMMUNICATION SYSTEM. A complete telecommunication system consisting of two or more commercial radio stations situated on land, water or aircraft, in this Act referred to as "earth stations", and one or more radio stations situated on a satellite in space, in this Act referred to as "satellite stations", in which at least one earth station is capable of transmitting signs, signals, writing, images or sounds or intelligence of any nature to a satellite station that is in turn capable of receiving and retransmitting those signs, signals, writing, images or sounds or intelligence of any nature for reception by one or more earth stations. *Telesat Canada Act*, R.S.C. 1985, c. T-6, s. 2.

SATISFACTION. *n.* 1. Compensation under law. 2. Payment for an injury or of money owed. 3. Completion of an obligation by performance or something equivalent to performance. See ACCORD AND ~.

SATISFACTION PIECE. A judgment creditor's formal written acknowledgement, filed in court, that the judgment debtor has fully paid.

SATISFACTORY PROOF OF IDENTITY. In respect of an elector, means such documentary proof of the identity of the elector as is prescribed.

SATIUS EST PETERE FONTES QUAM SECTARI RIVULOS. [L.] It is better to seek the source than to follow rivulets.

SATURATION SOUND PRESSURE. At a specified frequency and under specified operation conditions, means the maximum (r.m.s.) sound pressure obtainable in the coupler from the earphone of the hearing aid at all possible test values of the input sound pressure level. *Medical Devices Regulations*, C.R.C., c. 871, s. 1.

SAUGER. *n.* Eastern sauger or sand pickerel, Stizostedion canadense. *Ontario Fishery Regulations*, C.R.C., c. 849, s. 2.

SAUNA. See PUBLIC ~.

SAUNDERS V. VAUTIER. See RULE IN ~.

SAVING CLAUSE. A provision in a contract stating that if any term is found invalid the rest of the contract will not be affected.

SAVINGS. *n.* Money placed in an account in a credit union on which no bill of exchange payable on demand may be drawn. *Credit Union and Caisses Populaires Act*, S.M. 1977, c. 51, s. 1.

SAVINGS BANK. A Government Savings Bank or a bank or savings bank in Canada. *Canada Shipping Act*, R.S.C. 1985, c. S-9, s. 191.

SAVINGS FUND. See POOLED ~.

SAVINGS INSTITUTION. A bank, credit union, or a trust company. *Interpretation Act*, S.P.E.I. 1981, c. 18, s. 26.

SAVINGS PLAN. A retirement savings plan or a home ownership savings plan as each is defined in the Income Tax Act (Canada). *Beneficiaries Designation Act*, S.N.S. 1985, c. 14, s. 2. See EDUCATION ~; HOME OWNERSHIP ~; REGISTERED HOME OWNERSHIP ~; REGISTERED RETIREMENT ~; RETIREMENT ~; STOCK ~.

SAVOUR. *v.* To share the nature of; to seem like.

SAW LOGS. Includes logs, timber, pulpwood or lumber of any kind. *Fraser River Harbour Commission By-laws*, C.R.C., c. 902, s. 2.

S.C. *abbr.* 1. Supreme Court. 2. Supreme Court

(provincial) [of Judicature]. 3. Superior Court. 4. Same case. 5. Sessions Cases.

SC. *abbr.* [L.] Scilicet. That is to say.

SCAB. *n.* A worker who refuses to join other workers on a picket line.

S.C.A.D. *abbr.* Supreme Court (provincial) [of Judicature] Appellate Division.

SCAFFOLD. *n.* A working platform supported from below. *Safe Working Practices Regulations,* C.R.C., c. 1467, s. 2.

SCAFFOLDING. *n.* The structure that supports a scaffold. *Safe Working Practices Regulations,* C.R.C., c. 1467, s. 2.

SCALD. *n.* An injury to the surface which moist heat causes. F.A. Jaffe, *A Guide to Pathological Evidence,* 2d ed. (Toronto: Carswell, 1983) at 183.

SCALE. *v.* To determine the volume and classify the quality of timber.

SCALE. *n.* See BASE RATE ~; SLIDING ~; UNION ~.

SCALE MODEL. A model reduced in size according to a fixed scale or proportion. *Canadian Cultural Property Export Control List,* C.R.C., c. 448, s. 1.

SCALE OF PUNISHMENTS. The scale of punishments as set out in subsection 139(1). *National Defence Act,* R.S.C. 1985, c. N-5, s.2.

SCALER. *n.* A person employed or engaged in the measurement of timber.

SCANDAL. *n.* An action or rumour which affronts one publicly. One may order scandalous matter to be struck from a pleading.

SCANNED LASER RADIATION. Laser radiation having a time varying direction, origin or pattern of propagation with respect to a stationary frame of reference. *Radiation Emitting Devices Regulations,* C.R.C., c. 1370, s. 1.

SCATANA RULES. The rules for the Security Control of Air Traffic and Air Navigation Aids set out in Part V. *Security Control of Air Traffic Order,* C.R.C., c. 63, s. 2.

SCAVENGING. *n.* The uncontrolled removal of reusable material from waste at a waste disposal site. *Environmental Protection Act,* R.R.O. 1980, Reg. 309, s. 1.

S.C.C. *abbr.* 1. Supreme Court of Canada. 2. [Fr.] Société commerciale canadienne, one of the words to be part of a corporate name. H. Sutherland, D.B. Horsley & J.M. Edmiston, eds., *Fraser's Handbook on Canadian Company Law,* 7th ed. (Toronto: Carswell, 1985) at 436 and 437.

SCHED. *abbr.* Schedule.

SCHEDULE. *n.* 1. An inventory. 2. Additional or appendant writing. 3. Detailed information attached to a statute or regulation. 4. That part of a time table which prescribes class, direction, number and movement for a regular train. *Regulations No. O-8, Uniform Code of Operating Rules,* C.R.C., c. 1175, Part III, s. 2. See FLEXIBLE ~; INDUSTRIAL STANDARDS ~; RECORDS ~; SERVICE ~.

SCHEDULED FLIGHT. A flight conducted under a published statement of frequency and time of departure and arrival and operated by a commercial air service utilizing commercial aircraft. *Flying Accidents Compensation Regulations,* C.R.C., c. 10, s. 2.

SCHEDULED HARBOUR. Any fishing or recreational harbour or portion thereof included in a schedule prescribed by the regulations. *Fishing and Recreational Harbours Act,* R.S.C. 1985, c. F-24, s.2

SCHEDULED WAGE INCREASE. A raise unrelated to work or performance, paid at certain stipulated intervals but based on the length of an employee's service or prior work experience. D.J.M. Brown and D.M. Beatty, *Canadian Labour Arbitration,* 2d ed. (Aurora: Canada Law Book, 1977) at 562.

SCHEDULED TRAVEL TRANSPORTATION. Travel transportation supplied on a regular basis at certain fixed times and for which advance booking is not mandatory. *Travel Agents Act,* R.S.B.C. 1979, c. 409, s. 1.

SCHEDULE OF HOURS OF LABOR. The schedule of the maximum number of hours in each day or of days in each week, or of both, which any employee shall be permitted to work. *Industrial Standards Act,* R.S.N.S. 1967, c. 142, s. 1.

SCHEDULE OF WAGES. The schedule of minimum wages or remuneration payable to any employee. *Industrial Standards Act,* R.S.N.S. 1967, c. 142, s. 1.

SCHEME. *n.* 1. A plan for marketing or regulating any natural product. 2. A plan for distributing property among people with conflicting claims. See BUILDING ~; EXPERIMENTAL ~; INSURANCE ~; LOTTERY ~; NEGATIVE OPTION ~; PLANNING ~; PROVINCIAL ~; RECOGNIZED CANADIAN ~; RENEWAL ~; TRAFFIC SEPARATION ~.

SCHEME OF PYRAMID SELLING. (a) A scheme for the sale or lease of a product whereby one person (the "first" person) pays a fee to participate in the scheme and receives the right to receive a fee, commission or other benefit (i) in respect of the recruitment into the scheme of other persons either by the first person or any other person; or (ii) in respect of sales or leases made, other than by the first person, to other persons recruited into the scheme by the first person or any other person; and (b) a scheme for the sale or lease of a product whereby one person sells or leases a product to another person (the "second" person) who receives the right to receive a rebate, commission or other benefit in respect of sales or leases of the same or another product that are not (i) sales or leases made to the second person; (ii) sales or leases made by the second person; or (iii) sales or leases, made to ultimate consumers or users of the same or other product, to which no right of further participation in the scheme, immediate or contingent, is attached. *Combines Investigation Act*, R.S.C. 1985, c. C-34, s. 55.

SCHEME OF REFERRAL SELLING. A scheme for the sale or lease of a product whereby one person induces another person (the "second" person) to purchase or lease a product and represents that the second person will or may receive a rebate, commission or other benefit based in whole or in part on sales or leases of the same or another product made, other than by the second person, to other persons whose names are supplied by the second person. *Combines Investigation Act*, R.S.C. 1985, c. C-34, s. 56.

SCHOLARSHIP. *n.* 1. A sum of money awarded with special regard to the quality of the academic work of the person to whom it is awarded. 2. An award of distinction, prize or incentive. 3. Pecuniary assistance granted gratuitously to a student.

SCHOOL. *n.* 1. The room or building in which instruction is given. 2. A body of pupils that is organized as a unit for educational purposes and that comprises one or more instructional groups or classes, together with the principal and teaching staff and other employees assigned to such body of pupils, and includes the land, buildings or other premises and permanent improvements used by and in connection with that body of pupils. 3. Includes a day school, technical school, high school and residential school. *Indian Act*, R.S.C. 1985, c. I-5, s. 122. See BRANCH ~; COMMERCIAL FLYING ~; CONTINUATION ~; ELEMENTARY ~; HIGH ~; HOSPITAL ~; INDEPENDENT ~; INDUSTRIAL ~; NONCOMPLYING ~; NURSERY ~; PRIVATE ~; PUBLIC ~; SECONDARY ~; SENDING ~; SUBSIDIZED ~; TECHNICAL ~; TRADE ~; URBAN SEPARATE ~; VACATION ~.

SCHOOL AGE. See COMPULSORY ~.

SCHOOL ASSESSMENT. The tax which is levied on the taxable property of a school municipality. *Education Act*, R.S.Q. 1977, c. I-14, s. 1.

SCHOOL ATTENDANCE. See COMPULSORY ~.

SCHOOL AUTHORITY. 1. A school division, school committee of a county or school district, as the case may be. *Libraries Act*, S.A. 1983, c. L-12.1, s. 1. 2. The board of trustees of school district or school division. *Recreation Development Act*, R.S.A. 1980, c. R-8, s. 1.

SCHOOL BOARD. 1. A board of education. 2. The board of trustees of a school district. See ROMAN CATHOLIC ~; SEPARATE ~.

SCHOOL BOARD GROUP. Any association, federation or other organization to which the majority of the school boards for Catholics or the school boards for Protestants belong, deemed to be representative of these school boards by the Minister of Education, if it is not already so recognized by law. *An Act Respecting the Ministère de l'Enseignement Supérieur, de la Science et de la Technologie and Amending Various Legislation*, S.Q. 1985, c. 21, s. 75.

SCHOOL BUILDING. A building used for the instruction of school pupils.

SCHOOL BUS. 1. A bus operated for the transportation of children to or from school. 2. A motor vehicle used primarily to transport children to or from school or in connection with school activities.

SCHOOL CORPORATION. Every corporation of school commissioners or trustees and, generally, every commission or board incorporated for the administration of schools. Quebec Statutes.

SCHOOL CROSSING GUARD. A person employed by a municipality, or employed by a person under contract to a municipality, to direct the movement of children across a roadway.

SCHOOL DAY. A day within a school year on which instruction is given or examinations or other educational activities are conducted.

SCHOOL DAY CARE. Day care provided by a school board or a corporation of school trustees to children attending classes and receiving educational services in kindergarten and primary grades in its schools. *An Act Respecting Child Day Care*, S.Q. 1979, c. 85, s. 1.

SCHOOL DISTRICT. See RURAL AREA OF ~; TOWN ~.

SCHOOL DIVISION. See PUBLIC ~.

SCHOOL HOUSE. *var.* SCHOOLHOUSE. Includes the house or building required or used in a district for the imparting of instruction or for offices or other public school purposes; but does not include a building, or a part thereof, constructed, designed, or used solely or chiefly for administrative functions of the school district other than those exercised by principals or teachers. *Public Schools Act*, R.S.M. 1970, c. P250, s. 2. 2. Includes the teacher's dwelling house, the playground, if any, and the offices and premises belonging to or required for a school. *Mortmain and Charitable Uses Act*, R.S.O. 1980, c. 297, s. 8.

SCHOOL LAW. See COMPULSORY ~.

SCHOOL LEAVING. See REGULAR ~ AGE.

SCHOOL LEVY. See PROVINCIAL ~.

SCHOOL LIBRARY. A library intended primarily for students and faculty of schools under the Schools Act. *Libraries Act*, R.S.N.B. 1973, c. L-5, s. 1.

SCHOOL MUNICIPALITY. Any territory erected into a municipality for the carrying on of schools under the control of school commissioners or trustees. *Education Act*, R.S.Q. 1977, c. I-14, s. 1.

SCHOOL MONEYS. Moneys that are the property of, or are payable to, a school division or a school district. *Public Schools Act*, S.M. 1980, c. 33, s. 1.

SCHOOL OF APPLIED SCIENCE. Any Canadian educational institution that conducts science courses leading to degrees in mechanical or electrical engineering. *Marine Engineer Examination Regulations*, C.R.C., c. 1443, s. 2.

SCHOOL PERSONNEL. (a) Chief administrative officer and other administrative personnel; (b) building maintenance personnel; (c) secretaries; (d) teachers; (e) persons other than teachers engaged to deliver or to assist in the delivery of special education programs and services, or to assist exceptional pupils; and (f) other persons engaged in the areas of attendance, social services, health services, psychology and guidance. *An Act to Amend the Schools Act*, S.N.B. 1986, c. 75, s. 1.

SCHOOL PROGRAM. All the educational programs and the activities and personnel that a school board is required or permitted to provide.

SCHOOL SECTION. See URBAN ~.

SCHOOL SECURITIES. Bonds, debentures, notes or other evidences of indebtedness of any school corporation in Canada. *Cooperative Credit Associations Act*, R.S.C. 1985, c. C-41, S.49.

SCHOOL SITE. Land or interest therein or premises required by a board for a school, school playground, school garden, teacher's residence, caretaker's residence, gymnasium, offices, parking areas or for any other school purpose.

SCHOOL STAFF. See OVERSEAS CANADIAN FORCES ~.

SCHOOL TAX. 1. (i) The tax derived by applying the mill rate, as determined by the board of education, to the taxable assessment; (ii) the portion of trailer licence fees designated by the municipality for school purposes to a maximum of 50 per cent of the total licence fees collected by the municipality; or (iii) the tax otherwise prescribed in the regulations. *Senior Citizens' Heritage Rebates Act*, S.S. 1984-5-6, c. S-46.1, s. 2. 2. Taxes imposed in Manitoba for school purposes in respect of real property assessed as residential or farm property. *Income Tax Act*, S.M. 1972, c. 23, s.1.

SCHOOL TERM. A period commencing July 1 and ending December 31 of the same year or a period commencing January 1 and ending June 30 of the same year.

SCHOOL TRUSTEE. A person elected or appointed as a member of a board. *Manitoba Association of School Trustees Act*, S.M. 1972, c. 21, s. 1.

SCHOOL YEAR. 1. The period commencing on July 1 in one year and ending on June 30 in the next year, both dates inclusive. 2. The period from and including the 1st day of September in one year to and including the 31st day of August in the next year. *Teachers' Superannuation Act*, S.O. 1983, c. 84, s. 1.

SCHOOL ZONE. A zone on a highway identified by a traffic control device as an area where children (a) may be expected to be on the highway; or (b) are permitted to cross the highway at a designated point along the highway. *Highway Traffic Act*, R.S.A. 1980, c. H-7, s. 72. See SEPARATE ~; URBAN SEPARATE ~.

SCIENCE. *n.* Includes the natural and social science. *International Development Research Centre Act*, R.S.C. 1985, c. I-19, s. 2. See MINISTRY OF STATE FOR ~ AND TECHNOLOGY; VETERINARY ~.

SCIENCE COUNCIL OF CANADA. A federal advisory agency on policy concerning science and technology.

SCIENTER. *adv.* [L.] Knowingly.

SCIENTIA UTRIMQUE PAR PARES CONTRAHENTES FACIT. [L.] Equal knowledge on both sides makes those who are contracting equal.

SCIENTIFIC APPARATUS. An assembly of

objects forming a unit constructed for the purpose of research in any scientific discipline. *Canadian Cultural Property Export Control List*, C.R.C., c. 448, s. 1.

SCIENTIFIC INSTRUMENT. An implement, tool or device used for practical or scientific purposes as an instrument for examining or measuring. *Canadian Cultural Property Export Control List*, C.R.C., c. 448, s. 1.

SCIENTIFIC OR EXPLORATORY EXPEDITION. An expedition (a) conducted or sponsored by a scientific or cultural organization, an institution of learning or a foreign government; (b) the participants in which are non-residents of Canada; and (c) the sponsors of which have undertaken to make available to the Government of Canada all information obtained in Canada as a result of the expedition's field studies. *Scientific Expeditions Remission Order*, C.R.C., c. 787, s. 2.

SCI. FA. *abbr.* [L.] Scire facias.

SCILICET. [L.] That is to say.

SCINTILLA JURIS. [L.] A fragment or spark of right.

SCINTILLA JURIS ET TITULI. [L.] A fragment of right and title.

SCIRE FACIAS. [L. that you cause to know] A writ which directs a sheriff to warn or make known to someone to show cause.

SCOPE OF EMPLOYMENT. See ACT WITHIN ~.

SCOPING. *n.* The practice of a tribunal hearing only issues upon which parties disagree so that its hearings are more focussed.

SCORE. See PRELIMINARY ~.

SCOTTISH RING NET. A net that (a) is floated at the top, weighted at the bottom and mounted with rings through which a rope is run; and (b) is set from a vessel so as to enclose an area of water and then closed at the bottom by means of the rope referred to in paragraph (a) so as to form a purse or bag. *Atlantic Coast Herring Regulations*, C.R.C., c. 804, s. 2.

S.C.R. *abbr.* Reports of the Supreme Court of Canada, 1876-1922.

[ ] S.C.R. *abbr.* 1. Canada Law Reports, Supreme Court of Canada, 1964- (Rapports judiciaires du Canada, Cour Suprême du Canada). 2. Canada Law Reports, Supreme Court of Canada, 1923-1963.

SCRAP. *n.* All waste material including rejected metal, lumber and tree stumps. *Pits and Quarries Control Act*, R.R.O. 1980, Reg. 784, s. 1.

SCRAP AUTOMOBILE. A used automobile that is not in operating condition, is not intended by the owner thereof to be restored to operating condition, and that is kept in the open and primarily for the purpose of salvaging or selling parts therefrom, or for eventual sale as scrap metal, and includes a body or chassis of the used automobile after all or some of the other parts of the automobile have been removed, that is kept for such purposes. *Highways Protection Act*, R.S.M. 1970, c. Z-2, s. 17.

SCRAP VEHICLE. Includes any automobile, tractor, truck or trailer that: (i) has no currently valid registration number plates attached thereto; (ii) is in a rusted, wrecked, partly wrecked, dismantled, inoperative or abandoned condition; and (iii) is located in the open, on private or public property, and does not form part of the stock-in-trade of a business enterprise lawfully being operated by a person. *The Scrap Vehicles Act*, R.S.S. 1978, c. S-40, s. 2.

SCRATCH. See LATE ~.

SCREEN. See WIRED GLASS ~.

SCREENING DEVICE. See APPROVED ~.

SCREENINGS. *n.* 1. Dockage that has been removed from a parcel of grain. *Canada Grain Act*, R.S.C. 1985, c. G-10, s. 2. 2. Matter removed in the process of cleaning or grading of cereal, forage or other crop seed. *Weed Control Act*, R.S.A. 1980, c. W-6, s. 1.

SCRIBERE EST AGERE. [L.] To write is to do.

SCRIP. *n.* A document entitling the holder to receive something of value.

SCRIP DIVIDEND. A dividend in some form other than cash.

SCRIPT. *n.* 1. Writing. 2. An original or principal document.

SCRIPTAE OBLIGATIONES SCRIPTIS TOLLUNTUR, ET NUDI CONSENSUS OBLIGATIO CONTRARIO CONSENSU DISSOLVITUR. [L.] Written obligations are annulled by writing, and an obligation nakedly assented to is annulled by assent to the contrary.

SCROLL. *n.* A mark which shows the place for a seal.

S.C.R.R. *abbr.* Securities and Corporate Regulation Review.

SCRUBBING PLANT. Any plant for the purifying, scrubbing or otherwise treating, of gas for the extraction or removal from it of hydrogen sulphide or other deleterious substance. *Gas Utilities Act*, R.S.A. 1980, c. G-4, s. 1.

SCRUB BULL. *var.* **SCRUB-BULL.** A bull

which is not registered in a herd-book kept or recognized by the Department. *Agriculture and Marketing Act*, R.S.N.S. 1967, c. 3, s. 44.

SCRUTINEER. *n.* 1. Any person who is appointed by a candidate or that candidate's official agent to represent the candidate in a polling place. 2. A person appointed by the Chief Electoral Officer, pursuant to section 9 or 10. *Canada Elections Act*, R.S.C. 1985, c. E-2, s. 2.

S.C.T.D. *abbr.* Supreme Court (provincial) [of Judicature] Trial Division.

SCUFFING. *n.* For the purposes of section 118 of Schedule IV, a visible erosion of a portion of the outer surface of a brake cup. *Motor Vehicle Safety Regulations*, C.R.C., c. 1038, s. 2.

SCULPTURE. *n.* An artistic representation or work in three dimensions that is carved, modelled or constructed and includes such a representation that has subsequentially been cast in plaster, metal or other substance that will take on a rigid form. *Canadian Cultural Property Export Control List*, C.R.C., c. 448, s. 1. See WORK OF ~.

SCUTTLING. *n.* With respect to a ship, purposeful casting away.

SCUTUM ARMORUM. [L.] A coat of arms, shield.

S.D.A.G. *abbr.* Specially denatured alcohol grade. *Denatured Alcohol Regulations*, C.R.C., c. 568, s. 2.

SEA. *n.* (a) The territorial sea of Canada; (b) the internal waters of Canada other than inland waters; (c) any fishing zones prescribed pursuant to the Territorial Sea and Fishing Zones Act; (d) the arctic waters within the meaning of the Arctic Waters Pollution Prevention Act; (e) such areas of the sea adjacent to the areas referred to in paragraphs (a) to (d) as may be prescribed; (f) any area of the sea, other than internal waters, under the jurisdiction of a foreign state; and (g) any area of the sea, other than the internal waters of a foreign state, not included in the areas of the sea referred to in paragraphs (a) to (f). *Ocean Dumping Control Act*, R.S.C. 1985, c. O-2, s. 2. See ARM OF THE ~; BEYOND ~S; BEYOND THE ~S; HIGH ~S; PERILS OF THE ~S; PRODUCTS OF THE ~, LAKES AND RIVERS; TERRITORIAL ~.

SEA CARRIER. The owner or operator of a vessel engaged in the transportation of animals by water. *Animal Disease and Protection Regulations*, C.R.C., c. 296, s. 2.

SEAFARER. *n.* A person who is engaged in any capacity on board a ship, except (a) a pilot who is not a member of the crew; (b) persons employed on board by an employer other than

the shipowner, except radio officers or operators in the service of a wireless telegraph company; (c) travelling dockers or longshoremen who are not members of the crew; and (d) persons employed in ports who are not ordinarily employed at sea. *Medical Examination of Seafarers Regulations*, C.R.C., c. 1447, s. 2.

SEA-GOING SHIP. Any ship employed on a voyage any part of which is on the sea. *Canada Shipping Act*, R.S.C. 1985, c. S-9, s. 2.

SEAL. *v.* 1. To take any measures satisfactory to the chief inspector that will effectively prevent the operation or use of a boiler, pressure vessel or plant. Boilers and Pressure Vessels acts. 2. To take any measure satisfactory to the chief inspector that will effectively prevent the unauthorized operation or use of an elevating device. Elevators and Lifts acts.

SEAL. *n.* 1. A wafer or wax marked with an impression. 2. The portion of a licence that is required to be detached from the licence and cancelled immediately after the wildlife is killed, or a tag that may be supplied with a wildlife licence. *Wildlife Act*, S.S. 1979, c. W-13.1, s. 2. See BROKEN ~; CORPORATE ~; GREAT ~; GREAT ~ OF THE REALM; MECHANICALLY CONTROLLED ~; METAL ~; OFFICIAL ~; PRIVY ~; ROYAL ~S; TRAP ~.

SEALED. See HERMETICALLY ~.

SEALED FIREARM. A firearm sealed or secured in the prescribed manner. *Wildlife Act*, S.N.W.T. 1978 (3d Sess.), c. 8, s. 2.

SEALING. *n.* The hunting for, killing and skinning of seals, the handling and transporting of raw seal pelts from the place where they are killed to the land and the transporting of persons engaged in sealing to and from the killing area, and includes searching for seals from helicopters and other aircraft. *Seal Protection Regulations*, C.R.C., c. 833, s. 2. See MECHANICAL ~; PELAGIC ~.

SEALING GROUP. A hunting party consisting of not less than 4 or more than 10 persons, one of whom has been designated by the group as group leader and who will be responsible for the sealing operations of that group. *Seal Protection Regulations*, C.R.C., c. 833, s. 2.

SEALING SHIP. A ship engaged in sealing which is approved by the Board of Steamship Inspection as being suitable for sealing. *Sealing Ships Construction Regulations*, C.R.C., c. 1471, s. 2.

SEAMAN. *n.* 1. Every person, except pilots, apprenticed pilots and fishermen, employed or engaged on (a) a ship registered in Canada; or (b) a ship chartered by demise to a person resident in Canada or having his principal place of business in Canada, when the ship is engaged in trading on a foreign voyage or on a home-trade voyage as those voyages are defined in the Canada Shipping Act, and, if so ordered by the Governor in Council, includes a seaman engaged in Canada and employed on a ship that is registered outside Canada and operated by a person resident in Canada or having his principal place of business in Canada when that ship is so engaged. *Merchant Seaman Compensation Act*, R.S.C. 1985, c. M-6, s. 2. 2. Includes (a) every person, except masters, pilots and apprentices duly indentured and registered, employed or engaged in any capacity on board any ship; and (b) for the purposes of the Seamen's Repatriation Convention, every person employed or engaged in any capacity on board any vessel and entered on the ship's articles, but does not include pilots, cadets and pupils on training ships and naval ratings, or other persons in the permanent service of a government except when used in Part IV where it includes an apprentice to the sea service. *Canada Shipping Act*, R.S.C. 1985, c. S-9, s. 2. See DISTRESSED ~; MERCHANT ~; ORDINARY PRACTICE OF SEAMEN.

SEAMEN'S ARTICLES CONVENTION. The International Convention respecting Seamen's Articles of Agreement adopted by the International Labour Conference at Geneva on June 24, 1926. *Canada Shipping Act*, R.S.C. 1985, c. S-9, s. 2.

SEAMEN'S REPATRIATION CONVENTION. The International Convention concerning the repatriation of seamen adopted by the International Labour Conference at Geneva on June 24, 1926 as modified by the recommendation of the same date respecting masters and apprentices. *Canada Shipping Act*, R.S.C. 1985, c. S-9, s. 2.

SEAPLANE. *n.* 1. Includes a flying boat and any other aircraft able to manoeuvre on water. Canada regulations. 2. An aircraft capable of landing on or taking off from water. *Life-Saving Equipment Order*, C.R.C., c. 50, s. 2.

SEA PLANT. 1. All benthic and detached marine algae, all marine flowering plants, and includes all brown algae such as fucoids (commonly known as rockweeds) and laminarians (commonly known as kelp), and all red algae including chondrus, gigartina, and furcellaria, and all green algae, or any part or segment of the plants named in this clause. *Sea Plants Act*, R.S.P.E.I. 1974, c. S-3, s. 2. 2. All fucoids (commonly known as rockweeds) and laminarians (commonly known as kelp) but does not include chondrus crispus (commonly known as

Irish moss), dulse or eel grass. *Sea Plants Harvesting Act*, R.S.N.S. 1967, c. 279, s. 1.

SEARCH. *v.* Of title, to search in public offices to be sure that the vendor can convey free of all competing claims. B.J. Reiter, R.C.B. Risk & B.N. McLellan, *Real Estate Law*, 3d ed. (Toronto: Emond Montgomery, 1986) at 6.

SEARCH. *n.* 1. "Search" under section 8 of the Canadian Charter of Rights and Freedoms should be given a broad meaning to include a search of a person, a place or vehicle. It should include searches not only by the direct act of a police officer, say on executing a search warrant, but also by interception of private oral communications by electronic devices under Part IV.I of the Code. *R. v. Finlay and Grellette* (1985), 23 C.C.C. (3d) 48 (Ont. C.A.), leave to appeal to S.C.C. refused 54 O.R. (2d) 509n. 2. Examination of original documents, official books and records while investigating a title to land. See UNREASONABLE ~.

SEARCH PERIOD. See TITLE ~.

SEARCH WARRANT. An order which a justice issues under statutory powers to authorize a named person to enter a certain place to search for and seize particular property which will provide evidence of the intended or actual commission of a crime. P.K. McWilliams, *Canadian Criminal Evidence*, 3d ed. (Aurora: Canada Law Book, 1988) at 4-27.

SEA SERVICE. Time spent at sea after the age of 15 years in performing seamanship duties in the deck department of a self-propelled ship regularly engaged in ordinary trading or commercial fishing outside smooth or partially smooth waters. *Master and Mates Examination Regulations*, C.R.C., c. 1444, s. 2.

SEASON. See CLOSE ~; CLOSED ~; FIRE ~; GRAZING ~; NAVIGATION ~; OPEN ~; SUMMER ~.

SEASONAL AGRICULTURAL WORK. Work of a seasonal nature in agriculture which will provide persons who can legally be engaged at the work site with continuous employment for a period not exceeding 9 months. *Manpower Mobility Regulations*, C.R.C., c. 331, s. 7.

SEASONAL AREA. See ST. LAWRENCE RIVER ~.

SEASONAL CUSTOMER. A customer who requires electricity service for a period of less than 12 consecutive months. *Quebec Electricity Service By-law*, C.R.C., c. 1086, s. 2.

SEASONAL EMPLOYEE. An employee whose services are of a seasonal and recurring nature.

SEASONAL EMPLOYMENT. Employment

which is not continuous through the year but recurs in successive years. See FULL-TIME ~.

SEASONAL INDUSTRY. An industry that in each year ordinarily suspends production operations completely for one or more periods of at least 3 weeks each, by reason of fluctuations in market demands characteristic of the industry or consequent upon the ripening of crops. *Employment Standards Act*, R.S.M. 1970, c. E110, s. 2.

SEASONAL RESIDENT. A person, other than a resident of Canada, who makes his home and is ordinarily present in a place outside Canada but owns or has leased for not less than 3 years a permanent building and grounds in Canada other than a mobile home or other movable residence. *Seasonal Residents' Remission Order*, C.R.C., c. 788, s. 2.

SEASONING. *n.* A condiment, spice or herb used for savour but does not include salt. *Meat Inspection Regulations*, C.R.C., c. 1032, s. 2.

SEASON OF NAVIGATION. The period from the date of the official opening to the date of the official closing of navigation, both dates inclusive. *Canal Regulations*, C.R.C., c. 1564, s. 2.

SEAT. See ADJACENT ~.

SEAT BACK RETAINER. The portion of a seat belt assembly designed to restrict forward movement of a seat back. *Motor Vehicle Safety Regulations*, C.R.C., c. 1038, s. 209.

SEAT BELT. Any strap, webbing, or similar device designed to secure the driver or a passenger in a motor vehicle.

SEAT BELT ASSEMBLY. A device or assembly composed of straps, webbing or similar material that restrains the movement of a person in order to prevent or mitigate injury to the person and includes a pelvic restraint or an upper torso restraint or both of them.

SEAT BELT INJURY. An injury, like a compression fracture of the spine or tear of the bowel and mesentery, caused by bending over a seat belt during sudden deceleration. F.A. Jaffe, *A Guide to Pathological Evidence*, 2d ed. (Toronto: Carswell, 1983) at 183.

SEATING CAPACITY. See DESIGNATED ~.

SEATING POSITION. See DESIGNATED ~.

SEATING REFERENCE POINT. The manufacturer's design reference point that establishes the rearmost normal design driving or riding position of each designated seating position in a vehicle, has coordinates established relative to the designed vehicle structure, simulates the position of the pivot centre of the human torso and thigh and is the reference point employed to position the two dimensional templates described in SAE Recommended Practice J826 Manikins For Use In Defining Seating Accommodation, (November 1962). *Motor Vehicle Safety Regulations*, C.R.C., c. 1038, s. 100.

SEA TROUT. An anadromous speckled trout (Salvelinus fontinalis). *Quebec Fishery Regulations*, C.R.C., c. 852, s. 2.

SEAWARD BOUNDARY. An imaginary line that is measured seaward from the nearest Canadian land a distance of 100 nautical miles; except that in the area between the islands of the Canadian Arctic and Greenland, where the line of equidistance between the islands of the Canadian Arctic and Greenland is less than 100 nautical miles from the nearest Canadian land, there shall be substituted for the line measured seaward 100 nautical miles from the nearest Canadian land such line of equidistance. *Shipping Safety Control Zones Order*, C.R.C., c. 356, s. 2.

SEAWAY. *n.* The deep waterway between the Port of Montreal and Lake Erie and includes all locks, canals and connecting and contiguous waters that are part of the deep waterway, and all other canals and works, wherever located, the management, administration and control of which have been entrusted to the Authority or the Corporation. *Seaway Regulations*, C.R.C., c. 1397, s. 2. See ST. LAWRENCE ~ AUTHORITY.

SECK. *adj.* Barren; dry. See RENT SECK.

SECOND. *n.* 1. The unit for the measurement of time, being the duration of 9 192 631 770 periods of the radiation corresponding to the transition between the two hyperfine levels of the ground state of the caesium 133 atom. *Weights and Measures Act*, S.C. 1970-1-2, c. 36, schedule 1. 2. Of arc, $\pi/648\ 000$ radian. *Weights and Measures Act*, S.C. 1970-1-2, c. 36, schedule 1.

SECONDARY BOYCOTT. A refusal to deal with a neutral party in a labour dispute in order that that party will bring pressure to bear on the employer with whom there is a dispute.

SECONDARY COURSE. Includes any grade higher than the seventh year of the elementary course. *Grants to School Boards Act*, R.S.Q. 1977, c. S-36, s. 1.

SECONDARY CREDIT. Credit extended to the supplier of an exporter by the confirming bank. It covers the same goods which are the subject of the confirmed credit to the exporter. I.F.G. Baxter, *The Law of Banking*, 3d ed. (Toronto: Carswell, 1981) at 156.

SECONDARY DEPENDANT. Includes any dependent child or parent of an insured who is not a primary dependant. *The Automobile Accident Insurance Act*, R.S.S. 1978, c. A-35, s. 2.

SECONDARY DIAGNOSIS. 1. A second major diagnosis. 2. An associated mental disorder which manifests an underlying condition or occurs in association with a metabolic or organic disorder or other physical factor.

SECONDARY DROWNING. Acute and even fatal pneumonia hours or days after rescue and apparent recovery from drowning because heavily chlorinated or contaminated water is so irritating to the lungs. F.A. Jaffe, *A Guide to Pathological Evidence*, 2d ed. (Toronto: Carswell, 1983) at 81.

SECONDARY EDUCATION. Includes the education obtainable (i) at an Alberta high school; (ii) at an Alberta agricultural and vocational college; (iii) at an Alberta technical institute; and (iv) by taking courses approved by the board at institutions approved by regulation. *Education of Service Men's Children Act*, R.S.A. 1980, c. E-1, s. 1.

SECONDARY EVIDENCE. Proof admitted when primary evidence is lost.

SECONDARY FOREST PRODUCT. Everything resulting from the processing, treating, manufacturing or breaking down of a primary forest product. *Logging Tax Act*, R.S.B.C. 1979, c. 248, s. 1.

SECONDARY LEAD SMELTER. Any plant or factory in which lead-bearing scrap or lead-bearing materials, other than lead-bearing concentrates derived from a mining operation, is processed by metallurgical or chemical process into refined lead, lead alloys or lead oxide. *Secondary Lead Smelter National Emission Standards Regulations*, C.R.C., c. 412, s. 2.

SECONDARY LINE. A pipe for (i) the gathering or transmission of oil or gas in an area; (ii) the gathering or transmission of oil, gas, water or any other substance in connection with an order made, or a scheme or operation approved, under the Oil and Gas Conservation Act; (iii) the gathering or transmission of water, oil or gas in connection with drilling or production operations in any area; or (iv) the gathering and transmission of solids to a solids line, and includes installations in connection with that pipe, but does not include a flow line.

SECONDARY MEANING. In relation to a trade name, means a trade name that has been used in Canada or elsewhere by any applicant or his predecessors so as to have become distinctive in Canada as at the date of filing an application for a corporate name. *Canada Business Corporations Regulations*, C.R.C., c. 426, s. 12.

SECONDARY PICKETING. The picketing of businesses or premises not directly involved in a labour dispute.

SECONDARY PUPIL. A person enrolled in one of the grades from Grade 8 to Grade 12 in a public school. *School Act*, R.S.B.C. 1979, c. 375, s. 1.

SECONDARY SCHOOL. 1. A public school in which accommodation and tuition are provided exclusively or mainly for secondary pupils. 2. An independent school in which tuition or tuition and accommodation are provided primarily for persons who, if they were attending a public school, would be enrolled in one of the grades from Grade 8 to Grade 12. *School Support (Independent) Act*, R.S.B.C. 1979, c. 378, s. 1.

SECONDARY SCHOOL GRADE. Grade 10, 11, or 12, either singly or in combination; and includes grade 9 when that grade is administered and taught by a teaching staff that is also prepared to provide instruction in grades 10, 11 and 12, or two of those grades. *Public Schools Act*, R.S.M. 1970, c. P250, s. 2.

SECONDARY SCHOOL TEACHER. A teacher who is a member of, (i) L'Association des Enseignants Franco-Ontariens, if less than the major portion of the teacher's teaching assignment is at the elementary school level; or (ii) The Ontario Secondary School Teachers' Federation. *Municipality of Metropolitan Toronto Amendment Act*, S.O. 1983, c. 9, s. 1.

SECONDARY SHOCK. A state of shock, caused by sudden reduction in circulating blood volume, which often leads to death. F.A. Jaffe, *A Guide to Pathological Evidence*, 2d ed. (Toronto: Carswell, 1983) at 183.

SECONDARY STRIKE. A strike against one employer with a view to influencing another employer.

SECONDARY TREATMENT WORKS. Water pollution control works that are intended to provide a substantial removal of biodegradable organic material, suspended solids, and bacteria, and includes biological treatment works and disinfection works but does not include advanced treatment works. *The Water Pollution Control Assistance Act*, R.S.S. 1978, c. W-5, c. 2.

SECOND BUYER. The person who is the buyer of marketable gas under a resale contract.

SECOND CLASS MAIL. Any newspaper or periodical for which a postage rate has been established by these Regulations. *Second Class Mail Regulations*, C.R.C., c. 1294, s. 2.

SECOND CONVICTION. A conviction: (i) within a period of 5 years after the date of a first conviction, either before or after this section comes into force; and (ii) that next follows the first conviction. *Vehicles Amendment Act*, S.S. 1980-1, c. 94, s. 7.

SECOND CO-PILOT. A co-pilot assigned to duty in an aircraft during flight time other than as a first co-pilot. *Pilot Licence Privileges Order*, C.R.C., c. 54, s. 2.

SECOND DEGREE MURDER. 1. All murder which is not first degree murder. *Criminal Code*, R.S.C. 1985, c. C-46, s. 231. 2. Murder other than planned or deliberate murder and other than murder of the type specified in s. 231 of the Criminal Code.

SECOND-HAND ARTICLE. An upholstered or stuffed article that has been purchased from a retailer but does not include an upholstered or stuffed article returned to the retailer without use and with the original label attached. *Upholstered and Stuffed Articles Act*, R.S.O. 1980, c. 517, s. 1.

SECOND-HAND DEALER. 1. Every person who habitually deals in used articles of any nature whatsoever, and every person who habitually receives, without buying them, used articles and undertakes to sell them. 2. A retail seller whose sales of second-hand consumer products constitute at least 85 per cent of his total number of sales of consumer products, but does not include a retail seller who carries on, in whole or in part, the business of selling motor vehicles. *The Consumer Products Warranties Act*, R.S.S. 1978, c. C-30, s. 2.

SECOND-HAND GOODS. Includes waste paper, rags, bones, bottles, bicycles, automobile tires, old metal and other scrap material and salvage.

SECOND-HAND MATERIAL. Material that has been used other than in a manufacturing process. *Upholstered and Stuffed Articles Act*, R.S.O. 1980, c. 517, s. 1.

SECOND-IN-COMMAND. *n.* A pilot who is designated by an air carrier as second-in-command of an aeroplane or a rotorcraft during flight time. Canada regulations.

SECONDMENT. *n.* The temporary transfer of an employee for a specified period of time to or from one position to another position. *Civil Service Act*, S.P.E.I. 1983, c. 4, s.1.

SECOND MORTGAGE. A charge or mortgage which ranks after a prior charge or mortgage.

SECOND OR SUBSEQUENT OFFENCE. An offence committed within 3 years of the date of a previous conviction. *Liquor Control Act*, R.S.P.E.I. 1974, c. L-17, s. 1.

SECOND READING. Parliamentary consideration of the principle of a measure at which time one may consider other methods of reaching its proposed objective. At this stage, the order is made to commit the bill. A. Fraser, G.A. Birch & W.A. Dawson, eds., *Beauchesne's Rules and Forms of the House of Commons of Canada*, 5th ed. (Toronto: Carswell, 1978) at 220.

SECRET. See TRADE ~.

SECRETARY. *n.* 1. The head of a government department. 2. The officer of a association, club or company. 3. The corporate officer who takes minutes of meetings of directors and shareholders, sends out notices of meetings and is in charge of the minute books and other books of the company. H. Sutherland, D.B. Horsley & J.M. Edmiston, eds., *Fraser's Handbook on Canadian Company Law*, 7th ed. (Toronto: Carswell, 1985) at 253. See MUNICIPAL ~; PARLIAMENTARY ~; RACING ~.

SECRETARY OF STATE. 1. A title applied to some members of cabinet or heads of departments. 2. The federal ministry empowered to support multiculturalism and youth and to encourage the use of both official languages.

SECRETARY TREASURER. *var.* **SECRETARY-TREASURER.** 1. A city assessor or tax collector, the secretary-treasurer of a town, new town, village, municipal district, county or school district in a national park and the Deputy Minister of Municipal Affairs in the case of an improvement district or special area. *Electric Power and Pipe Line Assessment Act*, R.S.A. 1980, c. E-5, s. 1. 2. Includes, when the case requires it, the clerk or the treasurer of a city or town. *Commission Municipale Act*, R.S.Q. 1977, c. C-35, s. 1.

SECRET BALLOT. See VOTE BY ~.

SECRETOR. *n.* A person who secretes blood group substances in other body fluids like milk, seminal fluid and saliva. About 80 per cent of people are secretors. F.A. Jaffe, *A Guide to Pathological Evidence*, 2d ed. (Toronto: Carswell, 1983) at 183.

SECRET PROFIT. A financial advantage, including a bribe, which an agent receives over and above what the agent is entitled to receive from the principal as remuneration. G.H.L. Fridman, *The Law of Agency*, 5th ed. (London: Butterworths, 1983) at 156.

SECRET TRUST. A trust which occurs (a) when the legatee or devisee is named as a trustee in the will, but no trust objects appear: D.M.W. Waters, *The Law of Trusts in Canada*, 2d ed. (Toronto: Carswell, 1984) at 217; or (b) when a bequest in the will is in terms absolute. T. Sheard, R. Hull & M.M.K. Fitzpatrick, *Canadian Forms of Wills*, 4th ed. (Toronto: Carswell, 1982) at 254.

SECTA QUAE SCRIPTO NITITUR A SCRIPTO VARIARI NON DEBET. [L.] A suit which is based upon writing should not vary from that writing.

SECTION. *n.* 1. A numbered paragraph in a statute. 2. One of two or more trains running on the same time-table schedule displaying signals or for which signals are displayed. *Regulations No. O-8, Uniform Code of Operating Rules*, C.R.C., c. 1175, Part III, s. 2. 3. A division of land equalling one square mile or 640 acres. See BOW ~; DEFINITION ~; EDIBLE ~; INTERPRETATION ~; MARINE ~; NOMINAL ~; ~ OF LAND.

SECTIONAL TOWNSHIP WITH DOUBLE FRONTS. A township divided into sections and lots where the usual practice in the original survey was to survey the township boundaries, concession lines and side lines of sections defining section boundaries and to establish the front corners of the lots and section corners. *Surveys Act,* R.S.O. 1980, c. 493, s. 31.

SECTIONAL TOWNSHIP WITH SECTIONS AND QUARTER SECTIONS. (a) A township divided into sections and quarter sections without road allowances between sections where the usual practice in the original survey was to survey the township boundaries and section lines and to establish the section corners and quarter section corners; or (b) a township divided into sections and quarter sections with road allowances between sections where the usual practice in the original survey was to survey the township boundaries and the section lines on the west and south sides of the road allowances and to establish the section corners and the quarter section corners on the surveyed lines. *Surveys Act*, R.S.O. 1980, c. 493, s. 42.

SECTIONAL TOWNSHIP WITH SINGLE FRONTS. A township divided into sections and lots where the usual practice in the original survey was to survey the township boundaries, concession lines and side lines of the sections and to establish the front corners of the lots and the section corners. *Surveys Act*, R.S.O. 1980, c. 493, s. 37.

SECTION WIDTH. The linear distance between the exteriors of the sidewalls of an inflated tire, excluding elevations due to labelling, decoration or protective bands. Canada regulations.

SECTOR. *n.* 1. A primary portion or division of the economy of the Province. *Voluntary Planning Act*, R.S.N.S. 1967, c. 332, s. 1. 2. A division of the construction industry as determined by work characteristics and includes the industrial, commercial and institutional sector, the residential sector, the sewers, tunnels and watermains sector, the roads sector, the heavy engineering sector and the pipeline sector. See PRIVATE ~; PUBLIC ~; PUBLIC AND PARA-PUBLIC ~S.

SECULAR. *adj.* Relating to the material world in contrast to spiritual.

SECUNDUM NATURAM EST, COMMODO CUJUSQUE REI EUM SEQUI, QUEM SEQUUNTUR INCOMMODA. [L.] It is natural that advantages of anything should follow the person whom the disadvantages follow.

SECUNDUM SUBJECTAM MATERIAM. [L.] Referring to the subject-matter.

SECURE CUSTODY. Custody in a place or facility designated by the Lieutenant Governor in Council of a province for the secure containment or restraint of young persons, and includes a place or facility within a class of places or facilities so designated. *Young Offenders Act*, R.S.C. 1985, c. Y-1, s. 24. See PLACE OF ~.

SECURED CREDITOR. 1. A person holding a mortgage, hypothec, pledge, charge, lien or privilege on or against the property of the debtor or any part thereof as security for a debt due or accruing due to that person from the debtor. 2. A person whose claim is based on, or secured by, a negotiable instrument held as collateral security and on which the debtor is only indirectly or secondarily liable. *Bankruptcy Act*, R.S.C. 1985, c. B-3, s. 2 (part).

SECURED LOAN. A loan in respect of which the collateral security held for the loan is considered adequate to secure repayment of the loan. *The Co-operative Guarantee Act*, R.S.S. 1978, c. C-35, s. 2.

SECURED PARTY. A person who has a security interest.

SECURED TRADE CREDITOR. A creditor of the vendor in respect of (i) stock, money or services furnished for the purpose of enabling the seller to carry on business; or (ii) rental of premises in or from which the vendor carries on business, who holds security or is entitled to a preference in respect of a claim. Bulk Sales acts.

SECURED TRANSACTION. A transaction with two main elements: that consideration flows from the creditor and creates a debt and that an interest in the debtor's property secures payment of the debt. F. Bennett, *Receiverships* (Toronto: Carswell, 1985) at 27.

SECURE ISOLATION ROOM. A locked room approved under subsection 120(1) for use for the secure isolation of children. *Child and Family Services Act*, S.O. 1984, c. 55, s. 108.

SECURE TEMPORARY DETENTION. See PLACE OF ~.

SECURITIES. *n.* 1. (a) Bonds, debentures and obligations of or guaranteed by governments, corporations or unincorporated bodies, whether such corporations and unincorporated bodies are governmental, municipal, school, ecclesiastical, commercial or other, secured on real or personal property or unsecured, and rights in respect of such bonds, debentures and obligations; (b) shares of capital stock of corporations and rights in respect of such shares; (c) equipment trust certificates or obligations; (d) all documents, instruments and writings commonly known as securities; and (e) mortgages and hypothecs. 2. Bonds, debentures, promissory notes, and other evidence of debt. 3. (a) Any certificate, instrument or other document constituting evidence of: a right, share or interest in the capital, assets, earnings or profits of an existing or proposed company, or of a person and particularly, but not restrictively, any bond, note, debenture, share, debenture-stock or any title of participation in such capital, assets, earnings or profits; or of a subscription in any proposed company; or of an agreement providing that a sum of money received by a person or company will be repaid or treated as a subscription to shares or interests in the capital or assets of an undertaking at the option of any person or company; or of a share or interest in an association of legatees, heirs or trustees, in a trust estate, in an investment contract or in a bankers' or trustees' security; or of a profit-sharing agreement; or of interest in an oil, natural gas or mining claim or lease or in a voting trust agreement of an oil, natural gas or mining company; or of a lease, right to royalties or other interest respecting an oil or natural gas undertaking; or of a contract of concession under which the concessionary obtains certain special rights respecting the operation of an undertaking; (b) generally any certificate, instrument or document commonly known in the trade as a security or designated as such by the regulations; (c) any certificate, instrument or other document constituting evidence of a right or interest in an option given upon a security within the meaning of the preceding paragraphs. See APPROVED ~; CLASS OF ~; EQUITY ~; GOVERNMENT ~; ISSUED ~; MUNICIPAL ~; OFFEROR'S PRESENTLY-

OWNED ~; PROVINCIAL ~; SCHOOL ~; SECURITY; VALUABLE ~.

SECURITIES ADVISER. Any person or company that engages in claims to engage in the business of advising others, either directly or through publication or writings, as to the advisability of investing in, purchasing or selling specific securities.

SECURITIES DEALER. See CANADIAN ~.

SECURITIES EXCHANGE TAKE-OVER BID. A take-over bid by way of an exchange of securities, whereby the offeror, to obtain the result described in section 110, offers to holders of securities of the offeree issuer to exchange them for other securities, is subject to the same regulatory scheme as a take-over bid, mutatis mutandis. *Securities Act*, S.Q. 1982, c. 48, s. 114.

SECURITIES ISSUE. See SPECIFIED ~.

SECURITIES REGISTER. A record of securities which a company issues. H. Sutherland, D.B. Horsley & J.M. Edmiston, eds., *Fraser's Handbook on Canadian Company Law*, 7th ed. (Toronto: Carswell, 1985) at 394.

SECURITY. *n.* 1. A thing which makes the enforcement or enjoyment of a right more certain or secure. 2. A share of any class or series of shares of a corporation or a debt obligation of a corporation and includes a certificate evidencing any share or debt obligation. 3. Includes (i) any document, instrument or writing commonly known as a security; (ii) any document constituting evidence of title to or interest in the capital, assets, property, profits, earnings or royalties of any person or company; (iii) any document constituting evidence of an interest in an association of legatees or heirs; (iv) any document constituting evidence of an option, subscription or other interest in or to a security; (v) any bond, debenture, note or other evidence of indebtedness, share, stock, unit, unit certificate, participation certificate, certificate of share or interest, preorganization certificate or subscription other than a contract of insurance issued by an insurance company registered under an Insurance Act or an evidence of deposit issued by a bank, by a loan company which has a certificate under a Loan Companies Act or a Loan Companies Inspection Act or trust company which has a certificate under a Trust Companies Act; (vi) any agreement under which the interest of the purchaser is valued for purposes of conversion or surrender by reference to the value of a proportionate interest in a specified portfolio of assets, except a contract by an insurance company registered under an Insurance Act which provides for payment at maturity of an amount not less than three-quarters of the premiums paid by the purchaser for a benefit payable at maturity; (vii) any agreement providing that money received will be repaid or treated as a subscription to shares, stock, units or interests at the option of the recipient or of any person or company; (viii) any certificate of share or interest in a trust, estate or association; (ix) any profit-sharing agreement or certificate; (x) any certificate of interest in an oil, natural gas or mining lease, claim or royalty voting trust certificate; (xi) any oil or natural gas royalties or leases or fractional or other interest therein; (xii) any collateral trust certificate; (xiii) any income or annuity contract not issued by an insurance company; (xiv) any investment contract; (xv) any document constituting evidence of an interest in a scholarship or educational plan or trust; and (xvi) any commodity futures contract or any commodity futures option, whether any of the foregoing relate to an issuer or proposed issuer. 4. Includes security by the deposit of money or property, by the giving and entering into a bond, with sureties or otherwise, or by the bond or policy of insurance of a guarantee insurance company lawfully carrying on business in the Province. *Public Service Bonding Act*, R.S.B.C. 1979, c. 345, s. 1. 5. Sufficient security and one person shall be sufficient therefor unless otherwise expressly required. See AFFECTED ~; CANADA ~; CANADIAN ~; CAPITAL ~; COLLATERAL ~; CONVERTIBLE ~; CORPORATE ~; DEBT ~; GILT-EDGED ~; GOVERNMENT INCENTIVE ~; INDEXED ~; MARKETABLE ~; OFFEROR'S ~; PARTICIPATING ~; PERSONAL PROPERTY ~ ACTS; PORTFOLIO ~; REDEEMABLE ~; REQUIRED TO GIVE ~; SECURITIES; SHORT TERM ~; THREATS TO THE ~ OF CANADA; UNCERTIFIED ~; UNION ~; VALUABLE ~; VOTING ~.

SECURITY AGREEMENT. An agreement that creates or provides for a security interest.

SECURITY ALARM. Includes a system of security alarms and the interconnecting parts of the system but does not include a fire alarm or a smoke detector. *Miscellaneous Statutes Amendment Act (No. 2)*, S.B.C. 1986, c. 16, s. 37.

SECURITY ASSESSMENT. An appraisal of the loyalty to Canada and, so far as it relates thereto, the reliability of an individual. *Canadian Security Intelligence Service Act*, R.S.C. 1985, c. C-23, s. 2.

SECURITY BUSINESS. The business carried on by (a) an alarm service; (b) an armoured car service; (c) a locksmith; (d) a private investigator; (e) a security consultant; or (f) a security patrol. *Private Investigators and Security Agencies Act*, S.B.C. 1980, c. 45, s. 1.

SECURITY CERTIFICATE. An instrument in bearer, order or registered form, issued by an issuer evidencing a security. *Business Corporations Amendment Act*, S.O. 1986, c. 57, s. 7.

SECURITY CONSULTANT. A person who provides (a) consultation and advice on methods of protecting property from vandalism, intrusion, trespass or theft; or (b) the service of detecting electromagnetic, acoustical or other devices by which private communications or records may be intercepted, transmitted or examined.

SECURITY DEPOSIT. 1. Any money, property or right paid or given by a tenant of residential premises to a landlord or to anyone on the landlord's behalf to be held by or for the landlord as security for the performance of an obligation or the payment of a liability by the tenant or to be returned to the tenant on the happening of a condition. 2. (a) A certified cheque payable to the Receiver General and drawn on a bank to which the Bank Act or the Quebec Savings Bank Act applies or on such other financial institutions as may be designated by the Treasury Board for that purpose; (b) a government guaranteed bond; or (c) such other security as may be deemed appropriate by the contracting authority and approved by the Treasury Board. *Government Contracts Regulations*, C.R.C., c. 701, s. 2.

SECURITY DOCUMENT. Any written document including a lease or a mortgage whereby a debtor is required to make payments to a creditor in repayment or partial repayment of an advance of value or while all or any part of the advance is outstanding or unpaid and includes any trading or other covenants that are contained in or are supplemental, incidental or referable to the written document. *Gasoline Licensing Act*, S.N.S. 1969, c. 47, s. 2.

SECURITY EMPLOYEE. (a) An individual employed by or engaged in a security business, other than (i) an individual exempted by regulation; or (ii) an individual employed by an armoured car service; and (b) a security patrol salesman. *Private Investigators and Security Agencies Act*, S.B.C. 1980, c. 45, s. 1.

SECURITY FOR COSTS. Security which a plaintiff may be required to provide in a proceeding to ensure that the plaintiff will be able to pay any costs which may be awarded to the defendant.

SECURITY GUARD. 1. A person who, for hire or reward, guards or patrols for the purpose of protecting persons or property. 2. A person who guards or patrols or provides other security services for the purpose of protecting persons or property and includes a person who (a) supervises and inspects security guards while they are guarding or patrolling; or (b) accompanies a guard dog while the dog is guarding or patrolling. *Private Investigators and Security Guards Act*, S.N.B. 1980, c. 41, s. 2. 3. Any peace officer, security policeman, provost, military policeman or member of the Corps of Commissionaires, and includes any officer or man of the Canadian Forces or employee of the Department of National Defence or of the Defence Research Board who has been assigned duties relating to the enforcement of these Regulations. *Defence Establishment Trespass Regulations*, C.R.C., c. 1047, s. 2.

SECURITY GUARD AGENCY. (a) The business of providing the services of a security guard, dog, or both; or (b) the business of guarding, or of guaranteeing the secure transportation and delivery of, the property of others, where a security guard is used to provide security. *Private Investigators and Security Guards Act*, S.N.B. 1980, c. 41, s. 2.

SECURITY HOLDER. 1. A person who has an interest in land as security for the payment of money. Expropriation acts. 2. A holder in the Province of a voting security of a reporting issuer. *Securities Act*, S.B.C. 1985, c. 83, s. 100.

SECURITY INSTRUMENT. 1. A contract or instrument that creates a security interest. 2. An instrument in writing that creates or provides for a security interest in a mobile home and includes, without limiting the generality of the foregoing, (a) a chattel mortgage, conditional sale, equipment trust, debenture, floating charge, pledge, trust deed or trust receipt; (b) an assignment, lease or consignment intended as security; (c) an assignment of a security instrument; (d) a debt, judgment, lien or other claim to or on a mobile home, created, effected or given for any purpose whatsoever, whether by voluntary act of the owner or under any enactment or law, in favour of or for the benefit of the Crown, a municipality or any other governmental agency; and (e) a certificate filed by the collector under section 53. *Mobile Home Act*, R.S.B.C. 1979, c. 281, s. 1.

SECURITY INTEREST. 1. An interest in collateral that secures payment or performance of an obligation. 2. An interest in or charge upon the property of a body corporate by way of mortgage, hypothec, pledge or otherwise, to secure payment of a debt or performance of any other obligation of the body corporate. See ASSIGNMENT OF ~; PURCHASE-MONEY ~.

SECURITY ISSUER. *var.* **SECURITY-ISSUER.** A person or company that engages in the primary distribution to the public of securities of its own issue.

SECURITY NOTICE. A notice of security interest.

SECURITY OFFICER. Such person as may be designated by the Minister to be a security officer for the purposes of this section. *Aeronautics Act*, R.S.C. 1985, (1st Supp.) c. 33, s. 4.7.

SECURITY OF SUPPLY. In respect of any period, the anticipation of self-sufficiency during each of the five calendar years in that period, taking into account the aggregate of anticipated additions to productive capacity and anticipated adjustments to refining capacity. *Canada-Newfoundland Atlantic Accord Implementation (Newfoundland) Act*, S. Nfld. 1986, c. 37, s. 33.

SECURITY OF TENURE. A tenant's right to remain in leased premises unless the tenancy is terminated by the landlord for a cause specified in the governing legislation.

SECURITY OR SECURITY CERTIFICATE. 1. An instrument issued by a corporation that is (a) in bearer, order or registered form; (b) of a type commonly dealt in on securities exchanges or markets or commonly recognized in any area in which it is issued or dealt in as a medium for investment; (c) one of a class or series or by its terms divisible into a class or series of instruments; and (d) evidence of a share, participation or other interest in or obligation of a corporation. 2. An instrument that is issued by a bank as evidence of a share or other interest in the capital stock of the bank or as a bank debenture of the bank. *Bank Act*, R.S.C. 1985, c. B-1, s. 75(2).

SECURITY PATROL. A person who, otherwise than as an alarm service, provides, conducts, supervises or inspects a guard patrol or watch of property or a service of responding to a security alarm. *Private Investigators and Security Agencies Act*, S.B.C. 1980, c. 45, s. 1.

SECURITY TERM. The period during which bonding is required to be maintained whether it be described as a period of time or commences or terminates at the commencement or termination of a licence or privilege. *Bonding Act*, R.S.B.C. 1979, c. 31, s. 1.

SECURITY TRANSACTION. The purchase, sale, redemption, exchange, transfer, assignment or other transaction affecting a security. Canada regulations.

SEDATIVE. *n.* A calming drug. F.A. Jaffe, *A Guide to Pathological Evidence*, 2d ed. (Toronto: Carswell, 1983) at 183.

SE DEFENDENDO. [L.] In self defence.

SEDITIOUS CONSPIRACY. An agreement between two or more persons to carry out a seditious intention. *Criminal Code*, R.S.C. 1985, c. C-46, s. 59(3).

SEDITIOUS INTENTION. Everyone who teaches, advocates, publishes or circulates any writing that advocates, without authority of law, the use of force as a means of accomplishing a governmental change within Canada is presumed to have a seditious intention. *Criminal Code*, R.S.C. 1985, c. C-46, s. 59(4) in part.

SEDITIOUS LIBEL. A libel that expresses a seditious intention. *Criminal Code*, R.S.C. 1985, c. C-46, s. 59(2).

SEDITIOUS WORDS. Words that express a seditious intention. *Criminal Code*, R.S.C. 1985, c. C-46, s. 59(1).

SEDUCTION. *n.* Inducing a person to have unlawful intercourse.

SEED. *n.* 1. Any plant part of any species belonging to the plant kingdom, represented, sold or used to grow a plant. *Seeds Act*, R.S.C. 1985, c. S-8, s. 2. 2. Any seed except seed of field roots, and vegetable and garden seeds and bulbs. *Seed Dealers Act*, R.S.A. 1980, c. S-9, s. 1. 3. Certified potato tuber for reproduction purposes. *Seed Potato Act*, R.S.B.C. 1979, c. 383, s. 1. 4. The seed of a plant that is raised, grown, kept, packed, sold, purchased, delivered or shipped, for the purpose of planting for the purpose of producing plants, and includes any tuber, bulb, corm, rhizome, root, scion, or cutting of a plant that is raised, grown, kept, packed, sold, purchased, delivered or shipped for that purpose, but does not include seed of cereal grains, oilseed crops, forage crops or sugar beets or turnips. *Plant Pests and Diseases Act*, R.S.M. 1970, c. P90, s. 2. 5. Any generative part of a plant used for propagation purposes including true seeds, seed-like fruits, bulbs, tubers and corms but does not include whole plants or cuttings. *Pest Control Products Regulations*, C.R.C., c. 1253, s. 2. See COMMERCIAL ~; SPECIALTY ~; UNDESIRABLE ~; WEED ~.

SEED COMPANY OPERATOR. A person who purchases grain from producers for cleaning and processing into seed, for sale. *Western Grain Stabilization Regulations*, C.R.C., c. 1607, s. 2.

SEED CORN. Corn grown under contract with a dealer which is intended for sale on a commercial basis for seed purpose. *Crop Insurance Act*, R.R.O. 1980, Reg. 220, s. 3.

SEED-CORN. *n.* The seed of hybrid corn, or open-pollinated corn, of every kind or variety produced in Ontario for seed purpose, but does not include the seed of sweet corn and pop-corn.

Farm Products Marketing Act, R.R.O. 1980, Reg. 376, Schedule, s. 2

SEED DEALER. A person who in a province offers by advertisement or otherwise to buy or sell seed directly from or directly to producers or engages in the business of buying or selling seed directly from or directly to producers or accepting seed on a consignment basis directly from producers, but does not include a farmer, rancher or other person buying seed for personal use or selling self-produced seed or a person carrying on business as a merchant in the province and, as an incidental part of the business, selling seed to the public by retail sale only.

SEED GRAIN. 1. Seed of wheat, oats, barley, flax, rye, corn, alfalfa and grass. *The Municipalities Seed Grain and Supply Act*, R.S.S. 1978, c. M-38, s. 2. 2. "Registered", "certified", or "commercial" wheat, oats, barley, rye or flax, in respect of which there has been issued (i) a control sample certificate by the Board of Grain Commissioners; or (ii) another form of certificate recognized by the Minister of Agriculture as sufficient for the purpose. *Municipal Act*, S.M. 1970, c. 100, s. 487. 3. Seed of wheat, oats, rye, barley, flax, rapeseed and forage seed that when cleaned or otherwise processed will in the opinion of the Plant Industry Division Director of the Department of Agriculture be equivalent to the quality for seed established under the Seeds Act (Canada). *Agricultural Relief Advances Act*, R.S.A. 1980, c. A-10, s. 1.

SEED POTATO. A potato or any part thereof produced, marketed or used for propagation. *Seeds Regulations*, C.R.C., c. 1400, s. 45.

SEED STOCK. Includes eggs, alevins, parr, smolt, juvenile and adult fish, crustaceans and shellfish, seeds, spat, seedlings and other forms of aquatic flora and fauna used or intended to be used as the primary source of the aquacultural produce. *Aquaculture Act*, S.N.S. 1983, c. 2, s. 2.

SEEPAGE. *n.* The escape of water from any irrigation works of a board due to the fact that the works were built with material which, or were constructed in, on or through ground which, because of its porous or pervious nature, allows water to percolate out of the works. *Irrigation Act*, R.S.A. 1980, c. I-11, s. 170.

SEGMENT. *n.* A part or sub-division of a sector. *Voluntary Planning Act*, R.S.N.S. 1967, c. 332, s. 1. See ROUTE ~; TIME ~.

SEGMENTATION. *n.* Transverse obstructive breaks, many in number, in the blood in vessels in the eye. F.A. Jaffe, *A Guide to Pathological*

Evidence, 2d ed. (Toronto: Carswell, 1983) at 183.

SEGREGATED FUND. 1. A specified group of property the fair market value of which causes all or part of the insurer's reserves to vary with respect to any life insurance policy. 2. A fund established by a corporation duly authorized to operate a fund in which contributions to a pension plan are deposited and the assets of the fund are held exclusively for the purposes of that plan alone or that plan and one or more other pension plans. *Pension Benefits Standards Regulations*, C.R.C., c. 1252, s. 2.

SEGREGATED FUND POLICY. A life insurance policy under which the amount of benefits payable varies in accordance with the fair market value of the property of the segregated fund relating to the policy. *Taxation Act*, S.Q. 1978, c. 26, s. 149.

SEGREGATION. *n.* In a prison, solitary confinement.

SEIGNEUR. *n.* The lord of a seignory or fee manor.

SEIGNIOR. *n.* The lord of a seignory or fee manor.

SEIGNORY. *n.* A manor; lordship.

SEIGN. QUESTIONS. *abbr.* Lower Canada Reports, Seignorial Questions, vols. A & B (Décisions des Tribunaux du Bas-Canada).

SEIGN. REP. *abbr.* Seignorial Reports (Que.).

SEINE. *n.* A net buoyed at the top and weighted at the bottom that is used to catch fish without enmeshing them. *Quebec Fishery Regulations*, C.R.C., c. 852, s. 2. See BAR ~; BEACH ~; BOAT ~; DRAG ~; SHUT-OFF ~.

SEINE NET. A net with weights at the bottom and floats at the top that is operated to catch fish by dragging the net to a place where the fish may be removed from the water. *Manitoba Fishery Regulations*, C.R.C., c. 843, s. 2.

SEISED. *adj.* Is applicable to any vested estate for life or of a greater description, and shall extend to estates at law and in equity, in possession or in futurity, in land. Trustee acts.

SEISIN. *n.* Feudal possession. The relation in which someone stands to land or a hereditament when that person has an estate of freehold in possession in them. See LIVERY OF ~.

SEISINA FACIT STIPITEM. [L.] Seisin forms the basis of descent.

SEI WHALE. Any whale known by the name of Balaenoptera borealis, sei whale, Rudolphi's rorqual, pollack whale, or coalfish whale, and shall be taken to include Balaenoptera brydei,

Bryde's whale. *Whaling Convention Act*, R.S.C. 1970, c. W-8, Schedule, s. 18.

SEIZED. *adj.* Is applicable to any vested interest for life, or of a greater description, and extends to estates, legal and equitable, in possession, or in futurity, in any land. Trustee acts.

SEIZIN. See SEISIN.

SEIZURE. *n.* 1. A species of execution in which a sheriff executes a writ of fi. fa. by taking possession of the chattels of the debtor. 2. What takes place when goods are confiscated as a punishment for smuggling. See FREE OF CAPTURE AND ~.

SEIZURE AND SALE. See WRIT OF ~.

SELECT COMMITTEE. A committee of Parliament or a legislature set up to investigate a particular matter.

SELECTION BOARD. A board appointed by the chairman to examine candidates in a competition. *Civil Service Act*, S.P.E.I. 1983, c. 4, s. 1.

SELECTIVE DISTRIBUTION. See SAMPLES FOR ~.

SELECTIVE HERBICIDE. A herbicide commonly used for the control or destruction of weeds in growing crops and registered for that purpose under the Pest Control Products Act (Canada). *Weed Control Act*, R.S.A. 1980, c. W-6, s. 15.

SELECT TERRITORY. The territory consisting of the Provinces of Nova Scotia, Prince Edward Island and New Brunswick, the Island of Newfoundland and that portion of the Province of Quebec that is south of the St. Lawrence River and east of Quebec Highway 23, being the highway connecting Lévis in Quebec with U.S. Route 201 in the State of Maine. *Atlantic Region Freight Assistance Act*, R.S.C. 1985, c. A-15, s. 2.

SELF-CONTAINED DOMESTIC ESTABLISHMENT. A dwelling house, apartment or other similar place of residence in which place a person as a general rule sleeps and eats. *Income Tax Act*, R.S.C. 1952, c. 148 (as am. S.C. 1970-71-72, c. 63), s. 248(1).

SELF-CONTAINED DWELLING UNIT. A dwelling house, apartment or other similar place of residence that is used or occupied or is intended, arranged or designed to be used or occupied as separate accommodation for sleeping and eating. *Newfoundland Human Rights Code Act*, R.S.Nfld. 1970, c. 262, s. 2.

SELF-CONTAINED UNIT. A unit of apartment housing accommodation providing living, sleeping, eating, food preparation and sanitary facilities, with or without other essential facilities, but in which no personal service or nursing care is furnished. *Housing Authority Act*, R.S.P.E.I. 1974, c. H-12, s. 1.

SELF-CRIMINATION. See SELF-INCRIMINATION.

SELF-DEFENCE. *n.* Defence of one's person or property directly against another exerting unlawful force. D. Stuart, *Canadian Criminal Law: A Treatise*, 2d ed. (Toronto: Carswell, 1987) at 405.

SELF-EMPLOYED PERSON. 1. A person who is engaged in an occupation on his own behalf but does not include a dependent contractor. *Occupational Health and Safety Act*, S.N.S. 1985, c. 3, s. 2. 2. A person who is engaged in an occupation but is not in the service of an employer. *The Occupational Health and Safety Act*, R.S.S. 1978, c. O-1, s. 2.

SELF-EMPLOYMENT. *n.* The work done by an individual on his own behalf. *Quebec Pension Plan Act*, R.S.Q. 1977, c. R-9, s. 1.

SELF-HELP. *n.* An action in which an injured party seeks redress without resorting to a court.

SELF-IMPROVEMENT EDUCATION. Any education other than vocational education, general education or education for handicapped children within the meaning of this act. *Private Education Act*, R.S.Q. 1977, c. E-9, s. 1.

SELF-INCRIMINATING STATEMENT. A statement by the accused that, if admitted in evidence and believed in whole or in part, would directly or indirectly tend to prove the accused guilty of the charge. *Military Rules of Evidence*, C.R.C., c. 1049, s. 2.

SELF-INCRIMINATION. *n.* Behaviour indicating one's guilt. See PRIVILEGE AGAINST ~.

SELF-INSURANCE PLAN. A contract, plan or arrangement entered into, established, maintained in force or renewed under which coverage is provided (i) by an employer for all or some of his employees who are residents of Alberta; (ii) by a corporation for all or some of its members who are residents of Alberta; or (iii) by an unincorporated group of persons for all or some of its members who are residents of Alberta. *Alberta Health Care Insurance Act*, R.S.A. 1980, c. A-24, s. 17.

SELF INSURER. An individual, partnership or body corporate which retains all or part of a risk for its own account whether or not an excess of loss cover exists to protect itself in the event of a catastrophe. *Insurance Adjusters, Agents and Brokers Act*, S.Nfld. 1986, c. 36, s. 2.

SELF-LIQUIDATING PROJECT. A project that when completed will, on the basis of conservative estimates, either by reductions in the annual operating and maintenance charges required to be borne by the municipality or by increase of revenues from persons using the services of or otherwise benefiting from the project, result in an increase in the annual net revenue of the municipality sufficient to pay the annual charges for interest on an amortization of the loan to be made by the Minister. *Municipal Improvements Assistance Act*, R.S.C. 1970, c. M-16, s. 2.

SELF-LUBRICATING MACHINERY. Machinery that, while in operation, lubricates itself from a supply of lubricant that is sufficient to enable the machinery to operate continuously at full load for a period of not less than 24 hours. *Safe Manning Regulations*, C.R.C., c. 1466, s. 2.

SELF-MAILER. *n.* Any article, other than a postcard, magazine or catalogue, that does not have an outer cover, wrapping or envelope in addition to the paper or material on which is placed the written communication. Canada regulations.

SELF-MOBILITY. *n.* Movement of the vehicle by means of a rolling motion of all the weight-bearing wheels. *Motor Vehicle Safety Regulations*, C.R.C., c. 1038, s. 116.

SELF-MURDER. *n.* Suicide.

SELF-PROPELLED EQUIPMENT. Electrically operated equipment which is capable of moving while it is working or of being moved from place to place under its own power. *Coal Mines Regulation Act*, R.S.N.S. 1967, c. 36, s. 84.

SELF-PROPELLED IMPLEMENT OF HUSBANDRY. A self-propelled vehicle manufactured, designed, redesigned, converted or reconstructed for a specific use in farming. *Highway Traffic Act*, R.S.O. 1980, c. 198, s. 1.

SELF-REGULATING BODY. An association or organization recognized by the Commission under this Part as a self-regulating body. *Securities Act*, S.A. 1981, c. S-6.1, s. 176.

SELF-REGULATORY ORGANIZATION. Association or organization representing registrants that is recognized pursuant to subsection (2). *Securities Act*, S.S. 1984-85-86, c. S-42.1, s. 21.

SELF-SERVING STATEMENT. An exculpatory statement. S. Mitchell, P.J. Richardson & D.A. Thomas, eds., *Archbold Pleading, Evidence and Practice in Criminal Cases*, 43d ed. (London: Sweet & Maxwell, 1988) at 1278.

SELF-SUFFICIENCY. *n.* A volume of suitable crude oil and equivalent substances available from domestic Canadian hydrocarbon producing capacity that is adequate to supply the total feedstock requirements of Canadian refineries necessary to satisfy the total refined product requirements of Canada, excluding those feedstock requirements necessary to produce specialty refined products. *Canada-Newfoundland Atlantic Accord Implementation (Newfoundland) Act*, S. Nfld. 1986, c. 37, s. 33.

SELL. *v.* 1. Includes (a) to agree to sell, to offer, keep, expose, transmit, send, convey or deliver for sale; (b) to exchange or agree to exchange; and (c) to dispose of, or agree to dispose of, to any person in any manner for a consideration. 2. Includes offer for sale, expose for sale, have in possession for sale and distribute, whether or not the distribution is made for consideration. 3. Includes lease, transfer or any other manner of disposition. Employment Standards acts. See AGREEMENT TO ~; BARGAIN AND ~; SALE AND ~.

SELL AT RETAIL. To sell, transfer or offer to sell or transfer to a purchaser or a transferee for the purpose of use and not for resale or retransfer. *Pesticides Act*, R.R.O. 1980, Reg. 751, s. 1.

SELL AT WHOLESALE. To sell, transfer or offer to sell or transfer, other than at retail. *Pesticides Act*, R.R.O. 1980, Reg. 751, s. 1.

SELLER. *n.* 1. A person who sells or agrees to sell goods. 2. Includes a person who is in the position of a seller, as for instance an agent of the seller to whom the bill of lading has been endorsed, or a consignor or agent who has personally paid or is directly responsible for the price. Sale of Goods acts. 3. The person who sells or hires out goods by a conditional sale. 4. Includes a person who lets goods on hire by a retail hire-purchase. See BOOK~; CONTRACT ~; DIRECT ~; ITINERANT ~; RETAIL ~; UNPAID ~.

SELLER'S LIEN. See UNPAID ~.

SELLING. See DIRECT ~; REFERRAL ~; TIED ~.

SELLING AGENCY. The person authorized by one or more cooperative associations, one or more processors or one or more cooperative associations and processors to market an agricultural product under only one cooperative plan. *Agricultural Products Cooperative Marketing Act*, R.S.C. 1985, c. A-5, s. 2.

SELLING GROUP. The persons who, in the course of distribution to the public of securities, are commonly known as the selling group, the members of which acquire securities from an underwriter for the purpose of distribution to the public of those securities or who receive a commission from an underwriter in connection with such a distribution. *Bank Act*, R.S.C. 1985, c. B-1, s. 190.

SELLING INSTRUMENT. In respect of flow-through shares means a prospectus, registration statement, offering memorandum, term sheet or other similar document that describes the terms of the offer (including the price and number of shares) pursuant to which a corporation offers to issue flow-through shares. *Income Tax Act*, R.S.C. 1952, c. 148 (as am. S.C. 1986, c. 55, s. 11(8)), s. 66.1(1)(h.1).

SELLING PRICE. See REGULATED ~.

SEMBLE. *v.* [Fr. appears] A word used to introduce a legal proposition which one does not intend to state definitely.

SEMEN. *n.* The viscous fluid which the penis ejects during orgasm and which consists of spermatozoa from the testis and secretions from the seminal vesicles and prostate gland. F.A. Jaffe, *A Guide to Pathological Evidence*, 2d ed. (Toronto: Carswell, 1983) at 183.

SEMEN BANK. A person who stores semen of domestic animals. *Artificial Insemination of Domestic Animals Act*, R.S.A. 1980, c. A-45, s. 1.

SEMEN PROCESSING SUPERVISOR. A person who is responsible for the supervision of the collection, processing or identification of semen for the purpose of artificial insemination. *Artifical Insemination of Live Stock Act*, R.S.O. 1980, c. 29, s. 1.

SEMEN PRODUCING BUSINESS. *var.* **SEMEN-PRODUCING BUSINESS.** A business that maintains one or more live stock animals from which it offers semen for sale for the purpose of artificial insemination.

SEMESTER. *n.* A period of studies at a specified educational institution that is recognized by that educational institution and the appropriate authority for a province as a distinct period within a course of studies at that institution and that is of not less than 13 weeks duration. *Canada Student Loans Act*, R.S.C. 1970 (1st Supp.), c. 42, s. 1.

SEMI-ACTIVE DOCUMENT. A document in occasional use for administrative or legal purposes. *Archives Act*, S.Q. 1983, c. 38, s. 2.

SEMI-AMBULATORY. *adj.* The ability of a person to move about with the assistance of mechanical aides or devices but not involving assistance from another person. *Homes for Special Care Act*, S.N.S. 1976, c. 12, s. 2.

SEMI-AUTOMATIC. *adj.* Refers to machinery requiring the assistance of a human operator to complete part but not all of its functions during each complete cycle of operations. *Export Control List*, C.R.C., c. 601, s. 3358.

SEMI-DETACHED DWELLING. A family housing unit joined by a common or party wall to one other family housing unit. *National Housing Act*, R.S.C. 1985, c. N-11, s. 2.

SEMI-DETACHED HOUSE. See HOME-OWNER ~.

SEMI-FABRICATING PLANT. A processing plant taking material of mineral origin beyond the refined or primary metal stage and includes a semi-alloys plant, a chemical plant utilizing acid derived from sulphide ores, a zinc die-casting plant, a rolling mill or a small diameter tube mill, or any other plant designated by the Lieutenant Governor in Council to be a semi-fabricating plant. *Mining Tax Act*, R.R.O. 1980, Reg. 639, s. 1.

SEMINAUFRAGIUM. *n.* 1. Half shipwreck, i.e. in a storm some goods are cast overboard. 2. Such extensive damage to a ship that to repair her would cost more than she is worth.

SEMI-PLENA PROBATIO. [L. semi-proof] The testimony of a solitary person.

SEMI-PRESERVES. *n.* Fish that has been prepared by salting or pickling in brine, vinegar, sugar, spices or any combination thereof and packed so that it may be kept fit for human consumption for a minimum of 6 months by means of refrigeration without freezing. *Fish Inspection Regulations*, C.R.C., c. 802, s. 2.

SEMI-PRESERVING ESTABLISHMENT. An establishment where fish is prepared by salting or pickling in brine, vinegar, sugar, spices or any combination thereof and packed so that it may be kept fit for human consumption for a minimum of 6 months by means of refrigeration without freezing. *Fish Inspection Act*, R.R.O. 1980, Reg. 395, s. 1.

SEMI-PRIVATE ACCOMMODATION. A two-bed unit. *Nursing Homes Act*, R.R.O. 1980, Reg. 690, s. 1.

SEMI-SKILLED LABOUR. Workers who have some aptitude at a particular job but whose work is not within any of the traditional crafts.

SEMI-TRAILER. *n.* A trailer so constructed that its weight and the weight of its load is carried partly upon an axle of the truck tractor towing it, and partly upon an axle of the trailer.

SEMI-TRAILER TRUCK. Truck tractor and a semi-trailer combined. *The Highway Traffic Act*, S.M. 1985-86, c. 3, s. 1

SEMPER IN DUBIIS BENIGNIORA PRAE-

FERENDA. [L.] In doubtful cases always prefer more liberal construction.

SEMPER IN OBSCURIS, QUOD MINIMUM EST SEQUIMUR. [L.] In obscure cases we should always follow what is least obscure.

SEMPER ITA FIAT RELATIO UT VALEAT DISPOSITIO. [L.] A word should always relate back to antecedents so that the disposition of a will has effect.

SEMPER PARATUS. [L.] Always ready.

SEMPER PRAESUMITUR PRO LEGITIMA-TIONE PUERORUM; ET FILIATIO NON POTEST PROBARI. [L.] The presumption is always in favour of the legitimacy of children; and filiation cannot be proved.

SEMPER PRAESUMITUR PRO MATRIMO-NIO. [L.] The presumption is always in favour of the validity of a marriage.

SEMPER SPECIALIA GENERALIBUS INSUNT. [L.] Particulars are always included in generalities.

SENATE. *n.* 1. The second federal legislative body whose members are appointed by the Governor General, which means, in fact, by the cabinet. P.W. Hogg, *Constitutional Law of Canada*, 2d ed. (Toronto: Carswell, 1985) at 200. 2. The governing body of a university or college.

SENATOR. *n.* A person who is a member of a senate.

SEND. *v.* Includes deliver or mail.

SEND BY POST. To send by, through or by means of the Canada Post Office. *Post Office Act*, R.S.C. 1970, c. P-14, s. 2.

SENDING SCHOOL. (i) A school; or (ii) a private school to which a pupil record has been transferred, from which a pupil transfers to a school or private school. *Education Act*, R.R.O. 1980, Reg. 271, s. 1.

SENIOR CITIZEN. 1. A person 65 years of age or over. 2. Any person 60 years of age or over but the corporation may deem a person under the age of 60 years to be a senior citizen if this person was the spouse of a deceased senior citizen who occupied senior citizen housing. *Housing Corporation Act*, S.P.E.I. 1975, c. 14, s. 1. 3. A person of advanced years who is not suffering from any chronic disease that incapacitates him. *Senior Citizens Housing Act*, R.S.A. 1980, c. S-13, s. 1.

SENIOR CITIZEN RENTER. An individual who has attained at least 65 years of age and who, exlusively or in company with others, occupies as a normal place of residence for a total of not less than 120 days in any year one or more residences, not being (i) a nursing home; (ii) an auxiliary hospital; or (iii) an active treatment hospital, and in respect of that occupation rent is paid by him or on his behalf. *Property Tax Reduction Act*, R.S.A. 1980, c. P-19, s. 3.

SENIOR CITIZEN TAXPAYER. An individual who at any time during the relevant taxation period (i) has attained the age of 65 years; (ii) is the owner or part owner of land; and (iii) ordinarily resides in a single family dwelling house or mobile unit situated on that land. *Senior Citizens Land Tax Relief Act*, S.N.W.T. 1978 (2d Sess.), c. 14, s. 2.

SENIOR COUNTY COURT JUDGE. Of a province in which there is no position of chief judge of the county court means such judge of the county court in the province as is named by the county court judges of that province pursuant to paragraph 59(1)(d) to represent that court on the Council. *Judges Act*, R.S.C. 1985, c. J-1, s. 27(9).

SENIOR DIVISION. The division of the organization of a secondary school comprising the 3 years of the program of studies following the intermediate division. *Education Act*, R.S.O. 1980, c. 129, s. 1.

SENIOR EXECUTIVE. Any person exercising the functions of a director, or of a president, vice-president, secretary, treasurer, controller or general manager, or similar functions. *Securities Act*, S.Q. 1982, c. 48, s. 5.

SENIOR FOREMAN. A person who, in an underground mine, has daily charge of mine workings and is next in authority to the manager or assistant manager. *Coal Mines Safety Act*, R.S.A. 1980, c. C-15, s. 1.

SENIORITY. *n.* The status of an employee which commences on the date the person was hired or entered a certain seniority unit, whichever the particular collective agreement specifies. D.J.M. Brown and D.M. Beatty, *Canadian Labour Arbitration*, 2d ed. (Aurora: Canada Law Book, 1977) at 264. See DEPARTMENTAL ~; FROZEN ~.

SENIOR JUDGE. Of the Supreme Court of the Yukon Territory or of the Supreme Court of the Northwest Territories means the judge with the earlier date of appointment to the court in question. *Judges Act*, R.S.C. 1985, c. J-1, s. 27(9).

SENIOR OFFICER. (i) The chairman or any vice-chairman of the board of directors, the president, any vice-president, the secretary, the treasurer or the general manager of a corporation or any other individual who performs functions for the corporation similar to those normally performed by an individual occupying

any such office; and (ii) each of the 5 highest paid employees of a corporation, including any individual referred to in subclause (i). See PARTNERS', DIRECTORS' AND ~S' QUALIFYING EXAMINATION.

SENIOR OFFICIAL. With reference to a corporation, (i) the president, vice-president, secretary, comptroller, treasurer or general manager of the corporation; or (ii) any other person who performs functions for the corporation similar to those normally performed by persons holding the offices referred to in subclause (i). *Legislative Assembly Act*, S.A. 1983, c. L-10.1, s. 23.

SENIOR POLICE OFFICER. Any officer of the Royal Canadian Mounted Police not below the rank of inspector, any officer of any provincial police force of a like or superior rank, the chief constable of any city or town with a population of not less than 10,000 or any person on whom the powers of a senior police officer are for the purposes of this Act conferred by the Governor in Council. *Official Secrets Act*, R.S.C. 1985, c. O-5, s. 2.

SENIOR WATCH KEEPING DECK OFFICER. The watch keeping deck officer next in seniority to the master of a ship. *Pacific Pilotage Regulations*, C.R.C., c. 1270, s. 2.

SENSING THRESHOLD. The measure of the minimum signal required to control consistently the pulse generator function. *Medical Devices Regulations*, C.R.C., c. 871, s. 1.

SENSU HONESTO. [L.] Describes the interpretation of a statement which does not impute impropriety to anyone concerned.

SENTENCE. *n.* 1. In a criminal proceeding, a definite judgment. 2. Includes any order or disposition consequent upon a conviction and an order as to costs. *Provincial Offences Act*, R.S.O. 1980, c. 400, s. 92. See CONCURRENT ~; CONSECUTIVE ~S; DETERMINATE ~; INDETERMINATE ~; PRE-~ REPORT; SUSPENDED ~.

SENTENTIA CONTRA MATRIMONIAM NUNQUAM TRANSIT IN REM JUDICATAM. [L.] A decision against marriage never becomes res judicata.

SENTENTIA INTERLOCUTORIA REVOCARI POTEST, DEFINITIVA NON POTEST. [L.] An interlocutory judgment may be recalled, but not a final one.

SENTENTIA NON FERTUR DE NO LIQUIDIS. [L.] Judgment does not come about except on clearly defined points.

SEPARALITER. *adv.* [L.] Separately; distributively.

SEPARATE BUILT-IN COOKING UNIT. A stationary cooking appliance, including its integral supply leads or terminals, and consisting of one or more surface elements or ovens, or a combination of these, constructed so that the unit is permanently built into a counter or wall. *Power Corporation Act*, R.R.O. 1980, Reg. 794, s. 0.

SEPARATE CHARGES. The amounts of rent charged separately for any service, facility, privilege, accommodation or thing that the landlord provides for the tenant in respect of the tenant's occupancy of the rental unit. *Residential Rent Regulation Act*, S.O. 1986, c. 63, s. 97.

SEPARATED COMMUNITY. A community which (a) has an area of at least one square mile; (b) has minimum internal dimensions of at least one-half mile; (c) has a minimum density of 250 dwelling units per square mile; and (d) possesses, in the opinion of the Minister, urban character. *Municipal Grants Act*, S.N.S. 1979-80, c. 10, s. 10.

SEPARATED TOWN. A town separated for municipal purposes from the county in which it is situate. *Municipal Act*, R.S.O. 1980, c. 302, s. 1.

SEPARATE EMPLOYER. Any portion of the public service of Canada specified in Part II of Schedule I. *Public Service Staff Relations Act*, R.S.C. 1985, c. P-35, s. 2.

SEPARATE RESOLUTION. A resolution that has been submitted to all the members who hold shares of a particular class or series and which is consented to in writing by all those members or passed by the required majority at a class meeting or series meeting. *Company Act*, R.S.B.C. 1979, c. 59, s. 1.

SEPARATE SCHOOL. See RURAL ~; URBAN ~.

SEPARATE SCHOOL BOARD. A board that operates a separate school for Roman Catholics. *Education Amendment Act*, S.O. 1986, c. 21, s. 1.

SEPARATE SCHOOL ELECTOR. An elector who is a Roman Catholic separate school supporter or who is a Roman Catholic and the spouse of such supporter and any person entitled to be a separate school elector under the Education Act. *Municipal Elections Act*, R.S.O. 1980, c. 308, s. 1.

SEPARATE SCHOOL SUPPORTER. A Roman Catholic ratepayer, (i) in respect of whom notice of school support has been given in accordance with section 119 and notice of withdrawal of support has not been given under section 120; or (ii) who has directed education

taxes to the support of separate schools by confirming or revising an enumeration notice in accordance with section 14 of the Assessment Act and the regulations made thereunder, and includes the Roman Catholic spouse of such ratepayer. *Education Act*, R.S.O. 1980, c. 129, s. 1.

SEPARATE SCHOOL ZONE. The area in which property may be assessed to support a separate school or schools for Roman Catholics under the jurisdiction of one separate school board. *Education Act*, R.S.O. 1980, c. 129, s. 1. See URBAN ~.

SEPARATE STORE OR WAREHOUSE. A store or warehouse that is (a) detached from any dwelling house and situated at a safe distance from any highway, street, public thoroughfare or public place; (b) made and closed so as to prevent unauthorized persons having access thereto and to secure it from danger from without; (c) exclusively used for the keeping of manufactured fireworks and ammunition belonging to Division 1 of Class 6; and (d) well and substantially constructed of suitable material. *Explosives Regulations*, C.R.C., c. 599, s. 127.

SEPARATION. *n.* 1. The decision by a husband and wife to live apart. 2. The termination of employment. 3. With respect to an inpatient in hospital, discharge or death. See CORD ~; FIRE ~; GRADE ~; INNERLINER ~; JUDICIAL ~; PLY ~; SIDEWALL ~; TRAFFIC ~ SCHEME; TREAD ~.

SEPARATION AGREEMENT. 1. An agreement in writing between spouses who are living or intend to live separate and apart. 2. Includes an agreement by which a person agrees to make payments on a periodic basis for the maintenance of a former spouse, children of the marriage, or both the former spouse and children of the marriage, after the marriage has been dissolved whether the agreement was made before or after the marriage was dissolved. *Income Tax Act*, R.S.C. 1952, c. 148 (as am. S.C. 1970-71-72, c. 63), s. 248(1). See WRITTEN ~.

SEPARATION ZONE OR LINE. A zone or line separating routes in which ships are proceeding in opposite or nearly opposite directions, or separating a route from the adjacent inshore traffic zone. *Collision Regulations*, C.R.C., c. 1416, s. 2.

SEPARATOR. *n.* An unfired apparatus specifically designed and used for separating fluids produced from a well into two or more streams, but does not include a dehydrator. *Oil and Gas Conservation Act*, R.S.A. 1980, c. O-5, s. 1.

SEPTICEMIA. *n.* Blood poisoning; the presence of toxic bacteria in the blood of a living being. F.A. Jaffe, *A Guide to Pathological Evidence*, 2d ed. (Toronto: Carswell, 1983) at 183.

SEQUESTER. *v.* To prevent the owners from using by setting aside.

SEQUESTRATION. *n.* Property is temporarily placed by some judicial or quasi-judicial process in the hands of persons called sequestrators, who manage it and receive the rents and profits. See WRIT OF ~.

SERGEANT-AT-ARMS. *n.* A Parliamentary official appointed by Letters Patent under the Great Seal who brings people to the Bar to be examined as witnesses, arrests strangers who are improperly in the House or its galleries and who misbehave there and sees to it that people directed to withdraw are removed. A. Fraser, G.A. Birch & W.A. Dawson, eds., *Beauchesne's Rules and Forms of the House of Commons of Canada*, 5th ed. (Toronto: Carswell, 1978) at 44.

SERIAL. *n.* 1. Any book that is first published in separate articles or as a tale or short story complete in one issue in a newspaper or periodical. *Copyright Act*, R.S.C. 1985, c. C-42, s. 24. 2. Any publication issued in successive parts that appear at intervals for an indefinite period. *Canadian Cultural Property Export Control List*, C.R.C., c. 448, s. 1.

SERIAL NUMBER. 1. Includes identification number assigned to or placed on a vehicle by its manufacturer as a manufacturer's number and vehicle number. *Motor Vehicle Act*, R.S.N.S. 1967, c. 191, s. 1. 2. The number or combination of figures and letters of the alphabet assigned to an instrument tendered for filing or registration at the time it is received by the registrar and entered in the instrument register. *The Land Titles Act*, R.S.S. 1978, c. L-5, s. 2. 3. A combination of letters or figures or both letters and figures by which a device may be traced in manufacture and identified in distribution. *Medical Devices Regulations*, C.R.C., c. 871, s. 2.

SERIAL TITLE. A run of a serial irrespective of its continuity. *Canadian Cultural Property Export Control List*, C.R.C., c. 448, s. 1.

SERIATIM. *adv.* [L.] Separately and in order.

SERIES. *n.* In relation to shares, means a division of a class of shares.

SERIES MEETING. A meeting of members who hold shares of a particular series. *Company Act*, R.S.B.C. 1979, c. 59, s. 1.

SERIOUS CRIMINAL OFFENCE. (i) Any act committed in Canada that is punishable on indictment under the Criminal Code (Canada); and (ii) any act that if committed in Canada would be punishable on indictment under the Criminal Code (Canada), but does not include any political offence committed outside Canada or any offence that does not affect the fitness of a professional engineer to practice his profession. *Professional Engineers Act*, R.R.O. 1980, Reg. 804, s. 9.

SERIOUS HARM. Severe physical injury or severe psychological damage. *Parole and Penitentiary Act*, R.S.C. 1985, c. 34 (2d Supp.), s. 21.2.

SERIOUS INJURY. An injury that requires hospital or medical treatment or results in the suspension of normal activities for a period of 5 or more days and includes unconsciousness, fracture of any bone except a simple fracture of a finger or a toe, lacerations of muscles or lacerations that cause severe hemorrhages, injury to any internal organs, second or third degree burns and any burn involving more than 5 per cent of the body surface. *Aircraft Accidents and Missing Aircraft Order*, C.R.C., c. 23, s. 2.

SERIOUS OR PROLONGED DISABILITY. Does not include a disability of a degree less than 20 per cent estimated in the manner provided by subsection 35(2) of the Pension Act. *Civilian War Pensions and Allowances Act*, R.S.C. 1985, c. C-31, s. 30.

SERIOUS PERSONAL INJURY OFFENCE. (a) An indictable offence, other than high treason, treason, first degree murder or second degree murder, involving (i) the use or attempted use of violence against another person; or (ii) conduct endangering or likely to endanger the life or safety of another person or inflicting or likely to inflict severe psychological damage on another person, and for which the offender may be sentenced to imprisonment for 10 years or more; or (b) an offence or attempt to commit an offence mentioned in section 271 (sexual assault), 272 (sexual assault with a weapon, threats to a third party or causing bodily harm) or 273 (aggravated sexual assault). *Criminal Code*, R.S.C. 1985, c. C-46, s. 752.

SERJEANT-AT-ARMS. See SERGEANT-AT-ARMS.

SERMO EST ANIMI INDEX. [L.] Speech is the mind's informer.

SERMONES SEMPER ACCIPIENDI SUNT SECUNDUM SUBJECTUM MATERIAM ET CONDITIONEM PERSONARUM. [L.] Words should always be taken as relating to the subject-matter and the occupation of the people mentioned.

SERMO RELATUS AD PERSONAM INTELLIGI DEBET DE CONDITIONE PERSONAE. [L.] A word referring to someone should be interpreted as describing that person's occupation.

SEROLOGY. *n.* The science which concerns antigens and antibodies found in blood and other body fluids. F.A. Jaffe, *A Guide to Pathological Evidence*, 2d ed. (Toronto: Carswell, 1983) at 183.

SERUM. See TRUTH ~.

SERVANT. *n.* 1. A person engaged in employment. *Taxation Act*, R.S.Q. 1977, c. I-3, s. 1. 2. Includes agent, but does not include any person appointed or employed by or under the authority of an ordinance of the Yukon Territory or the Northwest Territories. *Crown Liability Act*, R.S.C. 1985, c. C-50, s. 2. 3. When used in relation to the Crown, includes a minister of the Crown. *Proceedings Against the Crown Act*, R.S.O. 1980, c. 393, s. 1. 4. Someone who agrees, freely or for a reward, to give service to another person. G.H.L. Fridman, *The Law of Agency*, 5th ed. (London: Butterworths, 1983) at 27. 5. Someone who is completely subject to the control of a master in relation to what is done and how it is done. G.H.L. Fridman, *The Law of Agency*, 5th ed. (London: Butterworths, 1983) at 28. See CIVIL ~; DOMESTIC ~; MASTER AND ~; PUBLIC ~.

SERVE. *v.* Of a copy of a legal document, to deliver it to parties interested in a legal proceeding so that they know about the proceeding.

SERVED. *n.* Served personally on a person or on an adult residing at the residence of the person who is at the residence at the time of service, or sent by registered mail to the person at his latest known address, and where sent by registered mail service shall be deemed to have been effected on the fifth day after the day of mailing. *Expropriation Act*, R.S.N.B. 1973, c. E-14, s. 1.

SERVICE. *n.* 1. Service in the Canadian Forces or in the naval, army or air forces of Canada since the commencement of World War I. *Pension Act*, R.S.C. 1985, c. P-6, s. 2. 2. With respect to a document, the act of serving it. 3. (i) The making of bona fide repairs to a motor vehicle by or under the supervision of an automobile repair mechanic; (ii) the painting, stabling, storing or caring for a motor vehicle by a garage keeper. 4. (i) Street lighting; (ii) distribution of water; (iii) the collection, removal and disposal of ashes or garbage or other refuse; (iv) the collection and disposal of sewage and land drainage; (v) fire protection; or (vi) such other service or services that the Minister may, by order, determine. *Regional Municipality of Niagara Act*, R.S.O. 1980, c. 438, s. 133. 5. (i) The conveyance for compensation by a public utility of passengers; (ii) the conveyance or transmission for compensation by a public utility of telephone messages; (iii) the production, transmission, delivery or furnishing to or for the public by a public utility for compensation of electrical energy for purposes of heat, light and power; (iv) the production, transmission, delivery or furnishing to or for the public by a public utility for compensation of gas for purposes of heat, light or power; (v) the production, transmission, delivery or furnishing to or for the public by a public utility for compensation of water; (vi) the production, transmission, delivery or furnishing to or for the public by a public utility for compensation of steam heat. 6. The Canadian Penitentiary Service. See ACCEPTANCE OF ~; ACTIVE ~; ADMISSION OF ~; AFFIDAVIT OF ~; AIR ~; AIR TRAFFIC CONTROL ~; AIR TRANSPORTATION ~; ALARM ~; AMBULANCE ~; ARMOURED CAR ~; AUGMENTED CHANNEL ~; AUGMENTING ~; BASIC ~; BUS ~; CABLECAST ~; CANADIAN ~; CHILD DEVELOPMENT ~; CHILD TREATMENT ~; CIVIL ~; COMMUNITY ~ ORDER; COMPUTER ~; CONSUMER'S ~; CONTINUOUS ~; CONTRACT OF ~; CONTRIBUTORY ~; CORRECTIONAL ~ CANADA; CRANE ~; CREDITED ~; DISCHARGE FROM ~; EXTRA-JUDICIAL ~; FIRE PREVENTION ~; FOOD ~ PREMISES; FOREIGN ~ OFFICER; IN ~; INTERNATIONAL ~; MEMBER OF A ~; MILITARY ~; MUNICIPAL ~; NEWFOUNDLAND ~; NON-WARD ~; OCCUPATIONAL HEALTH ~; OPHTHALMIC DISPENSING ~; OPTIONAL ~; OVERSEAS ~; PART-TIME ~; PASSENGER-TRAIN ~; PAST ~ CREDIT; PENITENTIARY ~; PENSIONABLE ~; PERIOD OF ~; PERSONAL ~; PILOT ~; PLUMBING ~; POSTPAK MAIL ~; POTENTIAL ~; PRIOR ~; PROGRAMMING ~; PROTECTIVE ~; PROVINCIAL ~; PUBLIC ~; PUBLIC ~ COMMISSION; PUBLIC ~ STAFF RELATIONS BOARD; PUBLIC TRANSPORTATION ~; RECREATION ~; REGULAR ~; REGULATED ~; REPAIR SERVICE; REPRESENTATIVE FOR ~; RESIDENTIAL ~; RESOURCE PROTECTION AND DEVELOPMENT ~; SEA ~; ~S; SEWAGE ~; SPACE ~; SUBSTITUTED ~; SUPPLY ~; TAXABLE ~; TEACHING ~; TELECOMMUNICATION ~; TELEGRAPHIC ~; TERMINATING ~; TERM OF ~; TERRESTRIAL ~; THROUGH ~; TRANSIT ~ AGREEMENT; TRAVEL ~; UNECONOMIC ~; UNINTERRUPTED ~; URBAN ~; VESSEL ~; WAR ~; WATER ~; YOUNG OFFENDERS ~.

SERVICEABLE. *adj.* In respect of an aircraft or aircraft part, in a fit and safe state for flight. *Air Regulations*, C.R.C., c. 2, s. 101.

SERVICEABILITY LIMIT STATES. Those limit states which restrict the intended use and occupancy of the building and include deflection, vibration, permanent deformation and cracking. *Building Code Act*, R.R.O. 1980, Reg. 87, s. 4.1.4.

SERVICE AREA. The area in which an electric distribution system may distribute electric energy. *Hydro and Electric Energy Act*, R.S.A. 1980, c. H-13, s. 1.

SERVICE AT SEA. Service in a ship that normally sailed or operated outside the territorial waters of all countries during World War I, World War II or the United Nations military operations in Korea. *Civilian War Pensions and Allowances Act*, R.S.C. 1985, c. C-31, s. 56.

SERVICE BOX. An approved assembly consisting of a metal box or cabinet constructed so that it may be effectually locked or sealed, containing either service fuses and a service switch or a circuit breaker and of such design that either the switch or circuit breaker may be manually operated when the box is closed. *Power Corporation Act*, R.R.O. 1980, Reg. 794, s. 0.

SERVICE BRAKE. The primary mechanism designed to stop a vehicle.

SERVICE BY MAIL. 1. Service by ordinary mail, registered mail, double registered mail, certified mail and any other form of delivery by a public postal service. *Judicature Act*, R.S.A. 1980, c. J-1, s. 33. 2. With respect to a document, sending a copy along with an acknowledgement of receipt card. G.D. Watson & C. Perkins, eds., *Holmested & Watson: Ontario Civil Procedure* (Toronto: Carswell, 1984) at 16-7.

SERVICE CENTRE. See ARTIFICIAL BREEDING ~.

SERVICE COMMISSION. A board, commission or corporation created by or under the authority of any Act and having power (i) to provide for an area or the residents of an area services similar to one or more of those which may be provided by a municipality for its residents; and (ii) to levy rates and taxes, or to require a municipality to levy rates and taxes on its behalf, other than rates fixed or approved pursuant to the Public Utilities Act, but does not include a city, town, rural municipality, village or school board. *Municipal Affairs Act*, S.N.S. 1982, c. 9, s. 2.

SERVICE CONTRACT. 1. A contract in writing for performance over a fixed period of time, or for a specified duration determined by means other than time, of services relating to the maintenance or repair of a consumer product, whether or not the contract provides for the furnishing of parts or materials to be supplied with or consumed in the performance of such services. *The Consumer Products Warranties Act*, R.S.S. 1978, c. C-30, s. 2. 2. A consulting services contract or a non-consulting services contract but does not include an agreement whereby any person is employed as an officer, clerk or employee of Her Majesty. *Government Contracts Regulations*, C.R.C., c. 701, s. 2.

SERVICE CONTRACTOR. (i) A person whose services are engaged by the Territories or a territorial agency in consideration of payment of a fee whether or not the contract for those services is made with that person or another person; or (ii) a person who contracts to provide the services of one or more individuals to the Territories or a territorial agency in consideration of the payment of a fee. *Financial Administration Act*, S.N.W.T. 1982, c. 2, s. 2.

SERVICE CONTROL. A control that is installed on a device by the manufacturer thereof for the purpose of adjustment and that, under normal usage, is not accessible to the user of the device. *Radiation Emitting Devices Regulations*, C.R.C., c. 1370, s. 1 (part).

SERVICE CONVICT. A person who is under a sentence that includes a punishment of imprisonment for 2 years or more imposed on that person pursuant to the Code of Service Discipline. *National Defence Act*, R.S.C. 1985, c. N-5, s. 2.

SERVICE CORPORATION. A corporation incorporated to provide, (i) a life company or a foreign life corporation with advisory, management or sales distribution services in respect of life insurance contracts or annuities whose reserves vary in amount depending on the market value of a specified group of assets maintained in a separate and distinct fund; or (ii) a mutual fund corporation with advisory, management or sales distribution services.

SERVICE COST. See CURRENT ~.

SERVICE COURT. A court martial and includes the service authorities of a designated state who are empowered by the laws of that state to deal with charges. *Visiting Forces Act*, R.S.C. 1985, c. V-2, s. 2.

SERVICE CRANE. An electrically operated device that travels on fixed overhead tracks and has a duty rating equal to or less than Class A or B as determined under Part 3.4 of CSA Standard B167-1964, "General Purpose Electric Overhead Travelling Cranes". *Occupational Health and Safety Act*, R.R.O. 1980, Reg. 694, s. 1.

SERVICE CREDIT. The credit accruing to an employee because of length of service.

SERVICE CUSTODY. The holding under arrest or in confinement of a person by the Canadian Forces, including confinement in a service prison or detention barrack. *National Defence Act*, R.S.C. 1985, c. N-5, s. 2.

SERVICE DETAINEE. A person under sentence that includes a punishment of detention imposed pursuant to the Code of Service Discipline. *National Defence Act*, R.S.C. 1985, c. N-5, s. 2.

SERVICED HOUSING ACCOMMODATION. Housing accommodation for which light, heat, fuel, water, gas or electricity are provided at the expense of the employer. *Employment Standards Act*, R.R.O. 1980, Reg. 284, s. 1.

SERVICE DISCIPLINE. See CODE OF ~.

SERVICED ROADWAY. The part of highway that is improved, designed or ordinarily used for vehicular traffic, and includes the ploughed portion of the shoulder, and, where a highway includes two or more separate serviced roadways, the term "serviced roadway" refers to any one serviced roadway separately and not to all of the serviced roadways collectively. *Motorized Snow Vehicles Act*, R.S.O. 1980, c. 301, s. 1.

SERVICED VACANT LAND. Land (a) on which there is no building or on which there is a building of a real value of less than 10 per cent of the value of the land according to the valuation roll in force; and (b) which is adjacent to a public street bordering which water and sanitary sewer services are available. *Cities and Towns Act*, R.S.Q. 1977, c. C-19, s. 486.

SERVICE ESTATE. The following parts of the estate of a deceased officer or man referred to in subsection (1): (a) service pay and allowances; (b) all other emoluments emanating from Her Majesty that, at the date of death, are due or otherwise payable; (c) personal equipment that the deceased person is, under regulations, permitted to retain; (d) personal belongings, including cash, found on the deceased person or in camp, quarters or otherwise in the care or custody of the Canadian Forces; and (e) in the case of an officer or man dying outside Canada, all other personal property belonging to the deceased and situated outside Canada if, in the opinion of the person authorized to administer service estates, the total value of that other property does not exceed $10,000 dollars. *National Defence Act*, R.S.C. 1985, c. N-5, s. 42.

SERVICE FACILITIES. Includes (i) furniture, appliances and furnishings; (ii) parking and related facilities; (iii) laundry facilities; (iv) elevator facilities; (v) common recreational facilities; (vi) garbage facilities and related services; (vii) cleaning or maintenance services; (viii) storage facilities; (ix) intercom systems; (x) cablevision facilities; (xi) heating facilities or services; (xii) air-conditioning facilities; (xiii) utilities and related services; (xiv) security services or facilities. *Residential Tenancies Act*, R.S.O. 1980, c. 452, s. 1.

SERVICE FOR A CONTINUOUS PERIOD. Service for a period of time without regard to periods of temporary suspension of employment.

SERVICE IN A THEATRE OF ACTUAL WAR. (a) Any service as a member of the army or air force of Canada in the period commencing August 14, 1914 and ending November 11, 1918 in the zone of the allied armies on the continent of Europe, Asia or Africa, or in any other place at which the member has sustained injury or contracted disease directly by a hostile act of the enemy; (b) any service as a member of the naval forces of Canada in the period described in paragraph (a) on the high seas or wherever contact has been made with hostile forces of the enemy, or in any other place at which the member has sustained injury or contracted disease directly by a hostile act of the enemy; and (c) any service as a member of the forces in the period commencing September 1, 1939 and ending (i) May 9, 1945, where the service was in any place outside Canada; and (ii) August 15, 1945, where the service was in the Pacific Ocean or Asia, or in any place in Canada at which the member has sustained injury or contracted disease directly by a hostile act of the enemy. *Pension Act*, R.S.C. 1985, c. P-6, s. 2.

SERVICE IN A THEATRE OF OPERATIONS. Any service of a member of the Canadian Forces from the time of his departure at any time prior to the 27th day of July 1953 from Canada or the United States, including Alaska, to participate in military operations undertaken by the United Nations to restore peace in the Republic of Korea, until (a) he next returns to Canada or the United States, including Alaska; (b) he is next posted to a unit that is not participating in such operations; (c) the unit with which he is serving, having ceased to participate in such operations, arrives at the place to which it has been next assigned; or (d) the 31st day of October 1953, whichever is the earliest. *Veterans Benefit Act*, R.S.C. 1970, c. V-2, s. 2.

SERVICE IN THE FORCE. Includes any period of service as a special constable of the Force before April 1, 1960, or any period of service as a member of a provincial or municipal police force, that, in accordance with the regulations, may be counted as service in the Force for the purposes of this Part. *Royal Canadian Mounted Police Act*, R.S.C. 1985, c. R-11, s. 3.

SERVICE IN THE FORCES. See ACTIVE ~.

SERVICE LIFE. The period of time between the placement of plant in service and its retirement for accounting purposes. Pipeline Uniform Accounting regulations.

SERVICE LINE. 1. A pipe line used for the transportation or conduct of oil, gas or water to a well-head, drilling rig, surface pit or service tank. *The Pipe Lines Act*, R.S.S. 1978, c. P-12, s. 2. 2. A pipe or conduit of pipes, other than a flow line, used for the transportation, gathering or conduct of a mineral or water or other fluid in connection with the producing operations of an operator. *The Surface Rights Acquisition and Compensation Act*, R.S.S. 1978, c. S-65, s. 2.

SERVICE MAN. (i) A person who, since August 4, 1914, has left his usual occupation for the purpose of joining and who has joined for full-time service in World War I or in World War II any of the active naval, military or air forces of the Crown or the allies of the Crown; and (ii) includes a member of the permanent force of the Crown on active service. *Education of Service Men's Children Act*, R.S.A. 1980, c. E-1, s. 1.

SERVICE MARK. A trade mark used or displayed when a service is performed or advertised. H.G. Fox, *The Canadian Law of Trade Marks and Unfair Competition*, 3d ed. (Toronto: Carswell, 1972) at 64.

SERVICE MEN. Members of the armed forces of Canada and members of the Merchant Marine of Canada. *Liquor Control Act*, R.S.N.S. 1967, c. 169, s. 51.

SERVICE OFFENCE. An offence under this Act, the Criminal Code or any other Act of Parliament, committed by a person while subject to the Code of Service Discipline. *National Defence Act*, R.S.C. 1985, c. N-5, s. 2.

SERVICE OF PROCESS. Bringing the effect or contents of a document to the attention of a person affected.

SERVICE PATTERN. A written statement of the frequency and time of departure and arrival of flights under which a Class 2 or Class 9-2 air carrier provides public transportation. *Air Carrier Regulations*, C.R.C., c. 3, s. 2.

SERVICE PIPE. 1. A pipe installed by or on behalf of a gas company for the transmission of gas from a distribution main to a meter on the land or premises of the purchaser of the gas. *Gas Act*, R.S.B.C. 1979, c. 149, s. 1. 2. The pipe that conveys water between the main shut-off valve on the public water system and the control shut-off valve in a supply system. *Ontario Water Resources Act*, R.R.O. 1980, Reg. 736, s. 1.

SERVICE PRISON. A place designated as such under the National Defence Act. *Visiting Forces Act*, R.S.C. 1985, c. V-2, s. 2.

SERVICE PRISONER. A person under sentence that includes a punishment of imprisonment for less than 2 years imposed pursuant to the Code of Service Discipline. *National Defence Act*, c. N-5, s. 2.

SERVICE PROVIDER. (i) The Minister; (ii) an approved agency; (iii) a society; (iv) a licensee; or (v) a person who provides an approved service or provides a service purchased by the Minister or an approved agency, but does not include a foster parent. *Child and Family Services Act*, S.O. 1984, c. 55, s. 3.

SERVICE RATE. The total amount charged to any person by a public utility for or in connection with (i) the use of a utility system and the connection thereto; or (ii) the sending of a communication by a utility system. *Social Security Assessment Act*, S. Nfld. 1972, c. 56, s. 9.

SERVICE ROAD. A roadway that is part of a divided highway and that is designed and constructed for use of local traffic as distinct from through traffic.

SERVICE ROOM. A room or space provided in a building to accommodate building service equipment such as air-conditioning or heating appliances, electrical services, pumps, compressors and incinerators. *Building Code Act*, R.R.O. 1980, Reg. 87, s. 1.

SERVICES. *n.* 1. Includes any agreeement (i) to install or supply goods whether or not the goods become part of any real property; (ii) to perform work, labour or service of any kind; or (iii) that entitles the holder thereof to purchase or obtain services. Direct Sellers acts. 2. Services (i) provided in respect of goods or of real property; (ii) provided for social, recreational or self-improvement purposes; or (iii) that are in their nature instructional or educational. Business Practices acts. 3. Includes (i) work, labour and other personal services; (ii) privileges with respect to transportation, hotel and restaurant accommodations, education, entertainment, recreation, physical culture, funerals, cemetery accommodations and the like; and (iii) insurance provided by a person other than the insurer. Consumer Protection acts. 4. Includes (i) the preparation of specifications, drawings and other documents used or to be used in construction; (ii) administration of a contract or sub-contract; (iii) inspection or supervision of work done under a contract or a sub-contract; or (iv) renting of equipment with or without an operator to an owner, contractor or sub-contractor to be used in the performance of a contract or a sub-contract, but does not include the preparation of specifications, drawings and other documents by, or the administration of a contract or sub-contract by, or inspection or supervision of work done under a contract or sub-contract by, a professional architect or engineer who is not an employee of the contractor or sub-contractor. *The Builders' Liens Act*, S.M. 1980-81, c. 7, s. 1. 5. Includes cutting, skidding, felling, hauling, scaling, banking, driving, running, rafting or booming logs or timber, and any work done by cooks, blacksmiths, artisans and others usually employed in connection with it, and any work done by engineers and all other persons employed in any capacity in or about a mill or factory where timber of any description is manufactured. Woodworker Lien acts. See ADVISORY ~; ARCHITECTURAL ~; CARE ~; CEMETERY ~; CHILD CARE ~; COMMUNITY DEVELOPMENT ~; DATA PROCESSING ~; DAY CARE ~; ESSENTIAL ~; FEE GENERATING ~; FUNERAL MERCHANDISE OR ~; FUNERAL ~; HEALTH CARE ~; HEALTH ~; HOME CARE ~; HOMEMAKER ~; HOMEMAKING ~; HOSPITAL ~; IN-HOME ~; IN-PATIENT ~; INSURED ~; LOCAL ~; LOSS OF ~; MANITOBA ~; MANPOWER PROGRAMS AND ~; MEDICAL ~; NON-PROGRAMMING ~; NON-RESIDENT ~; NURSING ~; OFFICE ~; PERSONAL ~; PHYSICIAN ~; PROFESSIONAL ~; PROTECTION ~; PROTECTIVE ~; RESIDENT ~; SALE OF ~; SERVICE; SOCIAL ~; SUPERVISORY ~; SUPPLY AND ~ CANADA; SUPPLY OF ~; TREATMENT ~; WELFARE ~.

SERVICES AND FACILITIES. Includes, (a) furniture, appliances and furnishings; (b) parking and related facilities; (c) laundry facilities; (d) elevator facilities; (e) common recreational facilities; (f) garbage facilities and related services; (g) cleaning or maintenance services; (h) storage facilities; (i) intercom systems; (j) cablevision facilities; (k) heating facilities or services; (l) air-conditioning facilities; (m) utilities and related services; (n) security services or facilities. *Residential Rent Regulation Act*, S.O. 1986, c. 63, s. 1.

SERVICES AND PROGRAMS. (i) Prevention programs; (ii) pre-trial detention and supervision programs; (iii) open and secure custody programs; (iv) probation services; (v) programs for the administration and supervision of dispositions; and (vi) other related services and programs. *Young Offenders Implementation Act*, S.O. 1984, c. 19, s. 1.

SERVICE SCHEDULE. A written statement of the frequency and time of departure and arrival of flights under which a Class 1 or Class 8 air carrier provides public transportation. *Air Carrier Regulations*, C.R.C., c. 3, s. 2.

SERVICES DESIGNED TO APPEAL TO EROTIC OR SEXUAL APPETITES OR INCLINATIONS. Includes (i) services of which a principal feature or characteristic is the nudity or partial nudity of any person; (ii) services in respect of which the word "nude", "naked", "topless", "bottomless", "sexy", or any other word or any picture, symbol or representation having like meaning or implication is used in any advertisement. *Municipal Act*, R.S.O. 1980, c. 302, s. 222.

SERVICE SHAFT. A shaft for the passage of persons or materials to or from a tunnel under construction. *Occupational Health and Safety Act*, R.R.O. 1980, Reg. 691, s. 1.

SERVICE SHIP. A registered ship operated by the Government of Canada to obtain scientific data on the high seas and includes weather and research ships. Canada regulations.

SERVICE SHOP. An enclosed building or part of a building in which the repair, sale and servicing of goods is carried on. Canada regulations.

SERVICE SPACE. 1. Space provided in a building to facilitate or conceal the installation of building service facilities such as chutes, ducts, pipes, shafts or wires. *Building Code Act*, R.R.O. 1980, Reg. 87, s. 1. 2. Includes galleys, main pantries, laundries, store rooms, paint rooms, baggage rooms, mail rooms, bullion rooms, carpenters' and plumbers' workshops, and trunkways leading to such spaces. *Hull Construction Regulations*, C.R.C., c. 1431, s. 2. See VERTICAL ~.

SERVICE STAFF. Domestic service personnel of a diplomatic mission, e.g. cooks, chauffeurs, cleaners. J.G. McLeod, *The Conflict of Laws* (Calgary: Carswell, 1983) at 76.

SERVICE STATION. 1. A place or premises where, for remuneration, motor vehicles are greased, oiled, cleaned and supplied with gasoline, and are given minor repairs. 2. Includes premises used or intended to be used for the retail sale of gasoline. See AUTOMOBILE ~; BATTERY ~; GASOLINE ~;

SERVICE STATION ATTENDANT. A person engaged in the servicing and maintenance of motor vehicles who, (i) repairs, changes and balances wheels and tires; (ii) changes oil in motor vehicles or lubricates motor vehicles, including lubricating the front wheel bearings and drive shaft; (iii) supplies motor vehicles with anti-freezing solutions; (iv) replaces cooling-system hoses, engine-driven belts and thermostats; (v) cleans or replaces spark plugs; (vi) installs new or rental batteries or battery cables, or recharges batteries; (vii) replaces sealed beam units, light bulbs, lenses, fuses and horns; and (viii) checks and replenishes fluid levels in hydraulic systems. *Apprenticeship and Tradesmen's Qualification Act*, R.R.O. 1980, Reg. 56, s. 1.

SERVICES TO PRODUCERS. Includes assembling, processing, manufacturing, financing, advertising and marketing of products produced by members and patrons, and the operating and maintaining by the association of land, tools, equipment or other resources for use by members and patrons engaged in production. *The Co-operative Production Associations Act*, R.S.S. 1978, c. C-37, s. 2.

SERVICE SUPPLIER. A person who supplies a taxed service to a recipient. *Social Security Assessment Act*, S. Nfld. 1972, c. 56, s. 10.

SERVICE TRIBUNAL. A court martial or a person presiding at a summary trial. *National Defence Act*, R.S.C. 1985, c. N-5, s. 2.

SERVICE VALUE. The book cost of plant minus the estimated net salvage value of that plant. Pipeline Uniform Accounting regulations.

SERVICE VEHICLE. 1. A motor vehicle equipped to refuel, repair or tow road vehicles. *Highway Safety Code*, S.Q. 1986, c. 91, s. 227. 2. (a) A wrecking or tow truck when stopped at the scene of an accident or returning from the scene of an accident with a damaged vehicle in tow; (b) any private or public utility corporation vehicle while engaged at the scene of repair work; (c) snow removal equipment when actually engaged in snow removal operation; or (d) a truck tractor when actually engaged in moving an oversize load for which a permit has been issued. *Motor Vehicle Act*, R.S.N.B. 1973, c. M-17, s. 1.

SERVICE WATER HEATER. A device for heating water for plumbing services. *Building Code Act*, R.R.O. 1980, Reg. 87, s. 1. See INDIRECT ~.

SERVIENS AD LEGEM. [L.] Sergeant-at-law.

SERVIENT TENEMENT. The land over which one exercises an easement.

SERVING TRACK. The track serving the storage facility and upon which railway cars are located for loading or unloading purposes. Canada regulations.

SERVITIA PERSONALIA SEQUUNTUR PERSONAM. [L.] Personal services go with the person.

SERVITIUM. *n.* [L.] Service.

SERVITIUM FEODALE ET PRAEDIALE. [L.] A personal service due because land was held in fee.

SERVITIUM FORINSECUM. [L.] A service belonging to the monarch.

SERVITIUM, IN LEGE ANGLIAE, REGULARITER ACCIPITUR PRO SERVITIO QUOD PER TENENTES DOMINIS SUIS DEBETUR RATIONE FEODI SUI. [L.] Service, in English law, means service which is due from tenants to lords because of their fee.

SERVITIUM INTRINSECUM. [L.] Service due to a lord from tenants on that lord's manor.

SERVITIUM REGALE. [L.] Royal service.

SERVITUDE. See PENAL ~; PRAEDIAL ~.

SESSION. *n.* 1. The period of time between the first meeting of Parliament and a prorogation. One Parliament includes several sessions, each lasting roughly one year. A. Fraser, G.A. Birch & W.A. Dawson, eds., *Beauchesne's Rules and Forms of the House of Commons of Canada*, 5th ed. (Toronto: Carswell, 1978) at 53. 2. The sitting of a court. See FALL ~; SPECIAL ~; SPRING ~.

SESSIONAL EMPLOYEE. A person who (a) is an employee of either House or of both Houses of Parliament; and (b) is employed for one or more sessions of Parliament.

SESSIONAL INDEMNITY. 1. (a) In relation to a period before October 8, 1970, means the allowance payable to a member pursuant to sections 55 to 58, subsections 63(3) and (4) and sections 64 and 69 of the Parliament of Canada Act; (b) in relation to a period after October 7, 1970 and before July 8, 1974, means (i) in the case of a member of the Senate, five-sixths of the allowances payable to a member pursuant to sections 55 to 58 and 69 of the Parliament of Canada Act; and (ii) in the case of a member of the House of Commons, the allowances payable to the member pursuant to sections 55 to 58 and 69 of the Parliament of Canada Act; and (c) in relation to a period after July 7, 1974, means the allowances payable to a member pursuant to sections 55 to 58 and 69 of the Parliament of Canada Act. *Members of Parliament Retiring Allowances Act*, R.S.C. 1985, c. M-5, s. 2. 2. The indemnity payable under the House of Assembly Act to a member in respect of a session of the House. *Members' Retiring Allowances Act*, R.S.N.S. 1967, c. 181, s. 1.

SESSIONAL ORDER. An order which is effective only for the duration of the session in which it was passed. A. Fraser, G.A. Birch & W.A. Dawson, eds., *Beauchesne's Rules and Forms of the House of Commons of Canada*, 5th ed.

(Toronto: Carswell, 1978) at 5. See STANDING, SESSIONAL AND SPECIAL ORDERS.

SET. *v.* In respect of fishing gear, to place the fishing gear in the sea so that (a) each end of the gear is anchored in the sea; (b) one end of the gear is anchored in the sea and the other end of the gear is attached to a fishing vessel; (c) the gear is drifting in the sea; or (d) one end of the gear is drifting in the sea while the other end of the gear is attached to a fishing vessel. *Fishing Gear Marking Regulations*, C.R.C., c. 813, s. 2.

SET. *n.* See CORD ~; LETTER FORM ~.

SET DOWN FOR TRIAL. With respect to a matter, to serve (a) a notice of readiness for trial and (b) a trial record. G.D. Watson & C. Perkins, eds., *Holmested & Watson: Ontario Civil Procedure* (Toronto: Carswell, 1984) at 48-3.

SET-LINE. *n.* 1. A line that is anchored to the sea-bed and has a series of fish hooks attached. Canada regulations. 2. A hook and line that is left in the water unattended. *Yukon Territory Fishing Regulations*, C.R.C., c. 854, s. 2.

SET NET. A net that is anchored, staked or otherwise attached to the shore, the bottom or to an anchored boat, buoy or other float to prevent it from drifting freely with the current. Canada regulations.

SET OFF. *var.* **SET-OFF.** 1. In an action to recover money, a cross claim by the defendant for money. 2. Includes counterclaim. *Municipal Courts Act*, R.S.N.S. 1967, c. 197, s. 1. 3. In a case in which a customer has two accounts with the same bank, one in credit and the other in debit, combination of the two accounts by the bank. I.F.G. Baxter, *The Law of Banking*, 3d ed. (Toronto: Carswell, 1981) at 27.

SET OUT. To ignite in the open. *Fires Prevention Act*, R.S.M. 1970, c. F80, s. 2.

SETTLE. *v.* 1. With respect to property, to limit it, or the income from it, to several people in succession, so that any person who possesses or enjoys it does not have power to deprive another of the right to enjoy it in future. 2. With respect to a document, to make it right in substance and in form.

SETTLED ESTATE. Land and all estates or interests in land that are the subject of a settlement.

SETTLEMENT. *n.* 1. An agreement by parties in dispute. 2. An unincorporated community of persons. 3. An Act of Parliament or of the Legislature, or a deed, agreement, will or other instrument, under which an interest in land stands limited to or in trust for any persons by way of succession, and includes an instrument that affects the estate of any of those persons exclusively. *Land (Settled Estate) Act*, R.S.B.C. 1979, c. 215, s. 1. 4. A permanent collectivity of habitations continuously inhabited and used. 5. An amount received in respect of a loss or salary or pension benefits arising from the termination of employment of an employee. *Involuntary Retirements Remission Order*, C.R.C., c. 772, s. 2. See INDIAN ~; MARRIAGE ~; METIS ~; MINUTES OF ~; STRUCTURED ~.

SETTLEMENT AGENCY. An organization that (a) provides assistance to refugees to settle in the Province; and (b) is approved by the minister. *Refugee Settlement Act*, R.S.B.C. 1979, c. 360, s. 1.

SETTLEMENT COUNCIL. A committee of persons resident in a settlement which the Minister recognizes as a representative body of the settlement for the purposes of this Ordinance. *Regional and Tribal Councils Act*, S.N.W.T. 1983 (2d Sess.), c. 7, s. 2.

SETTLEMENT PRICE. Where used in relation to a commodity futures contract, means the price which is used by a commodity futures exchange or its clearing house to determine, daily, the net gains or losses in the value of open commodity futures contracts. Commodity Futures acts.

SETTLEMENT PROVISION. See GRIEVANCE ~.

SETTLER. *n.* 1. A person whose application for a settlement lot has been approved but to whom the grant of the lot has not been issued. *Crown Lands Act*, R.S.N.B. 1973, c. C-38, s. 1. 2. A settler occupying colonization land in accordance with Colonization Land Sales Act (chapter T-8). *An Act Respecting the Sales Price of Pulpwood Sold by Farmers and Settlers*, R.S.Q. 1977, c. P-25, s. 1. 3. Any bona fide settler occupying lands under the Public Lands Act or engaged in agricultural pursuits involving the clearing and cultivation of land. *Settlers' Pulpwood Protection Act*, R.S.O. 1980, c. 469, s. 1. 4. Any person coming into Canada with the intention of establishing for the first time a residence in Canada for a period exceeding 12 months. Canada regulations.

SETTLER'S EFFECTS. (a) Household goods and equipment that are owned by an individual who was ordinarily resident outside Ontario for a period of at least 6 consecutive months immediately prior to his taking up residence in Ontario and were purchased prior to taking up residence in Ontario, and that are, within 6 months after his taking up residence in Ontario, brought into Ontario by him for his own use and consumption in Ontario; and (b) tangible personal property that was acquired for consumption or use in a province or territory of Canada other than Ontario in the operation of a business located and carried on in the other province or territory, and that is brought into Ontario by the proprietor or owner of such business for the purpose of relocating in Ontario his business operations, provided that the proprietor or owner has paid to the other province or territory a tax on his consumption or use in the other province or territory of the tangible personal property so acquired by him and that the tax is not refundable to him or has not been refundable to him or has not been refunded to him prior to the relocation of his business in Ontario or at any time thereafter. *Retail Sales Tax Act*, R.R.O. 1980, Reg. 903, s. 1.

SETTLOR. *n.* 1. A person who creates a trust. 2. Any party named or described in a marriage settlement who agrees or is liable to pay any sum or sums of money mentioned therein, or who in any marriage settlement settles, grants, conveys, transfers, mortgages, or charges, or agrees to settle, grant, convey, transfer, mortgage, or charge, any real or personal property upon or to any person. Marriage Settlement acts.

SEVER. *v.* To divide.

SEVERABLE. *adj.* Able to be divided.

SEVERAL. *adj.* The opposite of "joint". See JOINT AND ~.

SEVERAL COVENANT. A covenant made by two or more people which has the same effect as if each person had signed a separate agreement.

SEVERAL INHERITANCE. An inheritance conveyed so that it descends to more than one person separately or by moieties.

SEVERALLY. See JOINTLY AND ~.

SEVERAL TENANCY. A tenancy which is separate and not held jointly with another person.

SEVERAL TORTFEASORS. Those whose acts occur in the same sequence of events causing the damage but who have not acted in common. They are responsible for the same damage, but not for the same tort. John G. Fleming, *The Law of Torts*, 6th ed. (Sydney: The Law Book Co. Limited, 1983) at 228.

SEVERALTY. *n.* Property belongs to people "in severalty" when each person's share can be distinguished in contrast to joint ownership, coparcency or ownership in common in which owners hold undivided shares.

SEVERANCE. *n.* 1. Separation; severing. 2. A court order for the separate trials of two or more people jointly indicted, done in the interests of justice. S.A. Cohen, *Due Process of Law* (Toronto: Carswell, 1977) at 273. 3. Division of one statute into an invalid and a valid part regarding them as two laws concerning two different "matters" because one assumes that the legislature would have enacted the valid part even if it understood that it could not enact the other. P.W. Hogg, *Constitutional Law of Canada*, 2d ed. (Toronto: Carswell, 1985) at 325 and 326. 4. A court recognizes that valid and objectionable parts of a contract are separate and gives effect to the former though it refuses to enforce the latter. G.H.L. Fridman, *The Law of Contract in Canada*, 2d ed. (Toronto: Carswell, 1986) at 399.

SEVERANCE CLAUSE. The section of a statute which provides that, if any part of that statute is judged to be unconstitutional, the rest will continue to be effective. P.W. Hogg, *Constitutional Law of Canada*, 2d ed. (Toronto: Carswell, 1985) at 326.

SEVERANCE LANDS. The dividing or boundary line that separates those lands, works and properties used or useful in connection with the undertaking and that are considered to be essential to the power or storage development from other lands, works and properties used or useful in connection with the undertaking but not considered to be essential to the development. *Dominion Water Power Regulations*, C.R.C., c. 1603, s. 2.

SEVERANCE PAY. The amount payable when a person's employment is ended either because the employer permanently suspends operations or because the employee's position is redundant. D.J.M. Brown and D.M. Beatty, *Canadian Labour Arbitration*, 2d ed. (Aurora: Canada Law Book, 1977) at 631.

SEVERELY RETARDED CHILD. A child who is so retarded in mind from birth or from early age as to be unable to guard himself against common physical dangers. *Child Welfare Act*, R.S.N.S. 1967, c. 31, s. 87.

SEWAGE. *n.* 1. The liquid wastes from residences and other buildings, including industrial establishments, and includes ground, surface and storm water. 2. Includes domestic, commercial and industrial wastes, and, unless from natural run-off, drainage and storm water. See HAULED ~.

SEWAGE DISPOSAL SYSTEM. See PRIVATE ~.

SEWAGE FACILITY. Works operated by a municipality that gather, treat, transport, store, utilize or discharge sewage. *Waste Management Act*, S.B.C. 1982, c. 41, s. 1.

SEWAGE SERVICE. The acceptance, collection, transmission, storage, treatment and disposal of sewage, or any one or more of them. *Ontario Water Resources Act*, R.S.O. 1980, c. 361, s. 43.

SEWAGE SERVICE RATE. A charge for the operation, repair and maintenance of sewage works and includes a charge for depreciation, deferred maintenance or a reserve fund for any such purpose. *Municipal Act*, R.S.O. 1980, c. 302, s. 218.

SEWAGE SYSTEM. (a) A privy, a privy-vault, a holding tank or a toilet other than a toilet to which regulations made under clause 44(2)(a) of the Ontario Water Resources Act apply; (b) a sewage works from which sewage is not to drain or be discharged directly or indirectly into a ditch, drain or storm sewer or a well, lake, river, pond, spring, stream, reservoir or other water (other than ground water) or watercourse; (c) a privately-owned sewage works serving only five or fewer private residences; or (d) any other facility or land for the reception, treatment, transportation or disposal of sewage, but does not include (e) a sewage works to which subsection 24(1) of the Ontario Water Resources Act applies; (f) a privately-owned sewage works designed for the partial treatment of sewage that is to drain or be discharged into a sanitary sewer; (g) a sewage works the main purpose of which is to drain agricultural lands; (h) a drainage works under the Cemeteries Act, the Drainage Act, the Public Transportation and Highway Improvement Act or The Railways Act; (i) plumbing as defined in the regulations under the Ontario Water Resources Act; or (j) a holding tank to which regulations made under clause 136(3)(a) or (b) apply. *Environmental Protection Amendment Act*, S.O. 1983, c. 52, s. 7.

SEWAGE TANK. A sump that is air tight except for the vent required by section 127 and that receives the discharge of sewage from a subdrain. *Ontario Water Resources Act*, R.R.O. 1980, Reg. 736, s. 1.

SEWAGE TREATMENT FACILITY. Any structure or device or any part or combination thereof used or intended to be used for the purpose of treating, monitoring or holding sewage, and includes pumps, buildings, piping, controls, other equipment and their appurtenances. *Clean Environment Act*, S.N.B. 1975, c. 12, s. 1.

SEWAGE TREATMENT PROJECT. A project consisting of a trunk sewage collector system, a central treatment plant or both for the collection and treatment of sewage from one or more municipalities.

SEWAGE WORKS. 1. An integral system consisting of a sewer or sewer system and treatment works. 2. Any public works for the collection, transmission, treatment or disposal of sewage, or any part of any such works. See WATER AND ~.

SEWER. *n.* 1. A pipe or conduit that carries wastewater or land drainage water, or both. 2. A public sewer for common usage for the purpose of carrying away sewage or land drainage, or both. 3. Includes a common sewer, septic tank and a drain, or a combination of them. 4. Includes a drain of any kind except a drain used for the drainage of a house, building or other premises and made merely for the purpose of connecting with a private sewage disposal system or similar receptacle or with a sewer in a public highway. See BUILDING ~; LAND DRAINAGE ~; MAIN ~; SURFACE ~; WASTEWATER ~.

SEWERAGE CORPORATION. See MUNICIPAL ~.

SEWERAGE PROJECT. A sewer or system of sewers or any plants, structures, equipment, pipes, apparatus or other things for or incidental to the collection, treatment or disposal of sewage. *Clean Water Act*, R.S.A. 1980, c. C-13, s. 1.

SEWERAGE SYSTEM. A system of sewers designed to carry any waste except water resulting from rain or snow, and includes a system for the treatment of sewage. *The Municipal Water Assistance Act*, R.S.S. 1978, c. M-36, s. 2.

SEWERAGE WORKS. All facilities for collecting, pumping, treating and disposing of sewage. *Municipalities Act*, R.S.N.B. 1973, c. M-22, s. 118.

SEWER RATE. A charge for the capital cost of sewage rates. *Municipal Act*, R.S.O. 1980, c. 302, s. 218.

SEWER SYSTEM. A system of two or more interconnected sewers having one or more common discharge outlets and includes pumping plant, force mains, siphons and other like works. See TRUNK STORM ~.

SEX. *n.* 1. Gender, and, unless otherwise provided in this Act, discrimination on the basis of pregnancy or pregnancy-related illnesses is deemed to be discrimination on the basis of sex. *Saskatchewan Human Rights Code*, S.S. 1979, c. S-24.1, s. 2. 2. Includes a distinction between employees in a plan, fund or arrangement provided, furnished or offered by an employer to his employees that excludes an employee from a benefit thereunder or gives an employee a preference to a benefit thereunder because the employee is or is not a head of household, principal or primary wage earner or other similar condition, and further includes a distinction between employees in such a plan, fund or arrangement because of the pregnancy of a female employee. *Employment Standards Act*, R.R.O. 1980, Reg. 282, s. 1.

SEX CHROMATIN. A cell-nucleus component present only in females which is used to determine the sex of partial human remains. F.A. Jaffe, *A Guide to Pathological Evidence*, 2d ed. (Toronto: Carswell, 1983) at 172.

SEX DIFFERENTIAL. A variation in rates of wage based on the sex of the worker.

SEX HORMONE. Any synthetic or natural product represented as having oestrogenic, androgenic, gonadotrophic or progestational properties and any drug consisting in whole, or in part, of sex gland tissue or any extract thereof. *Food and Drug Regulations*, C.R.C., c. 870, s. C.02.001.

SEXUAL. See SERVICES DESIGNED TO APPEAL TO EROTIC OR ~ APPETITES OR INCLINATIONS.

SEXUAL ASSAULT. See AGGRAVATED ~.

SEXUAL HARASSMENT. Any conduct, comment, gesture or contact of a sexual nature (a) that is likely to cause offence or humiliation to any employee; or (b) that might, on reasonable grounds, be perceived by that employee as placing a condition of a sexual nature on employment or on any opportunity for training or promotion. *Canada Labour Code*, R.S.C. 1985 (1st Supp.), c. 9, s. 247.1.

SEXUALLY HARASS. Engage in vexatious comment or conduct of a sexual nature that is known or ought reasonably to be known to be unwelcome. *An Act to Amend the Human Rights Act*, S.N.B. 1987, c. 26, s. 1.

SEXUALLY TRANSMITTED DISEASE. A disease caused by an infectious agent usually transmitted during sexual contact. *Health Protection and Promotion Act*, S.O. 1983, c. 10, s. 1.

SEXUALLY TRANSMITTED DISEASES CLINIC. A clinic operated by a minister or a local board for the purposes of prevention and treatment of sexually transmitted diseases.

SEXUAL OFFENDER. See DANGEROUS ~.

SHAFT. *n.* 1. An excavation at an angle of 45 degrees or greater with the plane of the horizon and used or usable for (i) ventilation or drainage; or (ii) the ingress or egress of workers or materials to or from a mine or a part thereof. 2. A long vertical or slanting passage providing access to a mine and includes a winze. 3. Includes slope, pit and incline. See SERVICE ~; STEERING ~.

SHAFT CONVEYANCE. A conveyance raised or lowered by a mine hoist in a shaft and includes a bucket, a single or multi-deck cage, a skip or a combination of skip and cage. *Occupational Health and Safety Act*, R.R.O. 1980, Reg. 694, s. 1.

SHAFT ROPE. A hoisting, tail, balance, guide or rubbing rope. *Occupational Health and Safety Act*, R.R.O. 1980, Reg. 694, s. 1.

SHALE. See BITUMINOUS ~; CLAY-~; OIL ~.

SHALL. *v.* 1. Is to be construed as imperative. 2. Is used to indicate mandatory provisions. Canada regulations.

SHALL AND MAY. The expression "shall" is to be construed as imperative and the expression "may" as permissive.

SHALL, MUST, MAY. Whenever it is provided that a thing "shall" be done or "must" be done, the obligation is imperative; but if it is provided that a thing "may" be done, its accomplishment is permissive. *Interpretation Act*, R.S.Q. 1977, c. I-16, s. 51.

SHALLOW FOUNDATION. A foundation unit which derives its support from soil or rock located close to the lowest part of the building which it supports. *Building Code Act*, R.R.O. 1980, Reg. 87, s. 1.

SHAM. *n.* Acts done or documents executed by the parties to the "sham" which are intended by them to give to third parties or to the court the appearance of creating between the parties legal rights and obligations different from actual legal rights and obligations (if any) which the parties intend to create. *Snook v. London West Riding Investments Ltd.*, [1967] 1 All E.R. 518 at 528.

SHARE. *n.* 1. An integral, separate part of a company's authorized capital. H. Sutherland, D.B. Horsley & J.M. Edmiston, eds., *Fraser's Handbook on Canadian Company Law*, 7th ed. (Toronto: Carswell, 1985) at 107. 2. A share carrying voting rights under all circumstances or by reason of the occurrence of an event that has occurred and that is continuing, and includes (a) a security currently convertible into such a share; and (b) currently exercisable options and rights to acquire such a share or such a convertible security. 3. Includes a membership interest or ownership interest in a corporation. See APPROVED ~; BLOCK OF ~S; COMMON ~; CO-OP ~; CROP ~ AGREEMENT; CROWN ~; DECLARATION OF ~S; EQUITY ~; EQUITY ~S; EXCLUDED ~; FLOW-THROUGH ~; ISSUED ~S; JUST AND EQUITABLE ~; MUTUAL FUND ~; NON-EQUITY ~; NON-PARTICIPATING ~; OFFEROR'S

PRESENTLY OWNED ~S; OWNER'S ~ OF THE COST; PERMANENT ~S; PLAN ~; PREFERENCE ~; PREFERRED ~; PUBLICLY-TRADED ~S; PURCHASER'S COST OF A ~; REDEEMABLE ~; SPECIAL ~; SUBORDINATE VOTING ~; TRANSFERABLE ~; VOTING ~.

SHAREABLE REVENUE. For a fiscal year, the sum of the (a) net revenue received by the government in that fiscal year under the Fuel Oil Tax Act, Gasoline (Coloured) Tax Act, Gasoline Tax Act, Motive Fuel Tax Act and the Social Service Tax Act; (b) net revenue from lands and forests reported in the Public Accounts of the Province for the fiscal year, and consisting of net revenues received by the government in that fiscal year for (i) timber lease rentals and fees, timber berth rentals and fees, timber licence rentals and fees, timber royalties, timber sales, rentals and fees and timber sales stumpage under the Forest Act; (ii) land lease rentals and fees under the Land Act; (iii) logging tax under the Logging Tax Act; and (iv) grazing permits and fees under the Range Act; (c) net revenue from minerals reported in the Public Accounts of the Province for the fiscal year, consisting of net revenues received by the government in that fiscal year for (i) royalties, licences, permits, fees and rentals under the Coal Act, Mineral Act, Mining (Placer) Act and Petroleum and Natural Gas Act; (ii) mining tax under the Mining Tax Act; (iii) mineral land tax under the Mineral Land Tax Act; and (iv) mineral resource tax under the Mineral Resource Tax Act; and (d) money received for the fiscal year from the British Columbia Petroleum Corporation for net proceeds from the sale of natural gas. *Revenue Sharing Act*, R.S.B.C. 1979, c. 368, s. 1.

SHARE CAPITAL. See NET ~.

SHARE CERTIFICATE. An instrument certifying that the person named in it (the shareholder) is entitled to a certain number of shares of the corporation.

SHARED-RISK LOAN GUARANTEE. A guarantee under which, after default by the borrower and before Her Majesty's liability is determined, the lender is required to apply any proceeds obtained from realization of the security in satisfaction of the loan. *Regional Development Incentives Regulations*, C.R.C., c. 1386, s. 2.

SHAREHOLDER. *n.* 1. Someone who holds shares in a company. 2. A subscriber to or holder of stock in a company. 3. A shareholder of a corporation and includes a member of a corporation or other person entitled to receive payment of a dividend or to a share in a distribution on the winding-up of the corpora-

tion. See DISSENTING ~; MAJOR ~; SUBSTANTIAL ~.

SHAREHOLDER AGREEMENT. See UNANIMOUS ~.

SHAREHOLDER LOAN. See SUBORDINATED ~.

SHAREHOLDERS' EQUITY. The value of the interest of the shareholders in a corporation or the amount for which the company is liable to account to the shareholders. The net worth of a corporation. S.M. Beck *et al.*, *Cases and Materials on Partnerships and Canadian Business Corporations*, (Toronto: The Carswell Co., 1983) at 777, 780.

SHARE ISSUE. See PUBLIC ~.

SHARE MONEY. The money subscribed for shares. *Credit Union Act*, S.N.W.T. 1975 (3d Sess.), c. 2, s. 2.

SHARE WARRANT. A document under a corporate seal which certifies that its bearer of the warrant is entitled to shares specified in the document. H. Sutherland, D.B. Horsley & J.M. Edmiston, eds., *Fraser's Handbook on Canadian Company Law*, 7th ed. (Toronto: Carswell, 1985) at 103.

SHARING SCHEME. See DEFERRED ~.

SHARK. *n.* Any of several species of fish belonging to the order Pleurotremata (Squaliformes). *Northwest Atlantic Fisheries Regulations*, C.R.C., c. 860, s. 2.

SHEARING INJURY. Distortion of the shape of the surface of an organ or tissue caused by a force acting parallel to it. F.A. Jaffe, *A Guide to Pathological Evidence*, 2d ed. (Toronto: Carswell, 1983) at 178.

SHEATHING. *n.* The vertical members of shoring and timbering that are placed up against, and directly resist, pressure from a wall of a trench. *Occupational Health and Safety Act*, R.R.O. 1980, Reg. 691, s. 167.

SHEEP. *n.* A ram, ewe, wether or lamb.

SHEET. *n.* When applied to iron or steel, means a flat-rolled product of any shape (a) having a width of more than 12 inches but not more than 48 inches, and a thickness of .2299 inch or less; or (b) having a width of more than 48 inches and a thickness of .1799 inch or less. *Customs Tariff*, R.S.C. 1985, c. C-54, s. 2. See CHARGE-~.

SHEET METAL WORKER. A person who, (i) manufactures, fabricates, assembles, handles, erects, installs, dismantles, reconditions, adjusts, alters, repairs or services all ferrous and non-ferrous sheet metal work of No. 10 U.S. Gauge or of any equivalent or lighter gauge and all other materials used in lieu thereof; and (ii) reads and understands shop and field sketches used in fabrication and erection, including those taken from original architectural and engineering drawings or sketches, but does not include a person employed in production commonly known as mass production. *Apprenticeship and Tradesmen's Qualification Act*, R.R.O. 1980, Reg. 57, s. 1.

SHEETWRITER. *n.* A person who records the number of pari-mutuel tickets sold in each race. *Race Track Supervision Regulations*, C.R.C., c. 441, s. 2.

SHELF. See CONTINENTAL ~.

SHELL. See RIM-FIRE ~ OR CARTRIDGE.

SHELLEY'S CASE. See RULE IN ~.

SHELL FISH. *var.* **SHELLFISH.** 1. All species of mollusks and crustaceans and cuttings, parts and products of all such. 2. Includes clams, mussels, oysters, scallops and other bivalve molluscs. Fishery regulations. 3. Oysters, clams, mussels and other bivalve molluscs except scallops. *Sanitary Control of Shellfish Fisheries Regulations*, C.R.C., c. 832, s. 2.

SHELL FISH CANNERY. A building, structure, machinery, appurtenances, appliances and apparatus occupied and used in the business of shell fish canning, or of converting the natural shell fish into canned shell fish. *Fisheries Act*, R.S.B.C. 1979, c. 137, s. 12.

SHELTER. *n.* 1. A building or part of a building that is under the supervision of or approved by a director and that may be used for the temporary care of children. 2. The cost of operating a dwelling place. See ICE ~.

SHELTER AID. Financial assistance under this Act toward the payment of rental costs in an amount calculated in the prescribed manner. *Shelter Aid For Elderly Renters Act*, R.S.B.C. 1979, c. 385, s. 1.

SHELTER BELT. A belt of trees for shelter, planted or growing at least 1 metre and not more than 2 metres apart in one or more rows at least 60 metres in length and at least 1 metre apart. *Forestry Act*, R.R.O. 1980, Reg. 397, s. 1.

SHELTER DECK SPACE. The space contained between the shelter and freeboard decks. Canada regulations.

SHELTERED WORKSHOP. A place of work operated by a charitable organization employing handicapped workers.

SHELTER EQUIPMENT. Any equipment used for the purpose of camping or dining and includes a tent, trailer, tent-trailer, recreational vehicle, camper-back, dining shelter or other similar equipment.

SHELTERING. See DOCTRINE OF ~.

SHERBERT. *n.* The frozen food, other than ice cream, that is made from a milk product, with or without, (i) water; (ii) sweetening agent; (iii) fruit or fruit juice; (iv) citric or tartaric acid; (v) flavouring preparation; or (vi) food colour, and that contains; (vii) a stabilizer that is not more than .75 per cent of the finished product; (viii) not more than 5 per cent milk solids, including milk-fat; and (ix) not less than .35 per cent acid as determined by titration and expressed as lactic acid. *Farm Products Grades and Sales Act*, R.R.O. 1980, Reg. 327, s. 1.

SHERIFF. *n.* Includes bailiff and any officer charged with the execution of a writ or other process.

SHERIFF'S OFFICER. A bailiff.

SHIELD. *n.* A material barrier interposed in the path of a flow of X-rays and having the effect of reducing the dose or dose-rate experienced by any object located beyond the shield. *Public Health Act*, R.R.O. 1980, Reg. 855, s. 1. See METAL ~.

SHIELDING. See SHIELD.

SHIFT. *n.* A number of employees whose hours for beginning and terminating work are the same or approximately the same. See FIXED-~; LOBSTER ~; SPLIT ~; SWING ~; WORK ~.

SHIFT DIFFERENTIAL. A premium paid to workers who work on shifts other than during the day.

SHIFT ENGINEER. A person who, under the supervision of the chief engineer, is in immediate personal charge of a boiler or steam plant.

SHIFTING USE. An executory or secondary use, which, when executed, derogates a preceding estate, e.g. land is conveyed to the use of one person provided that when a second person pays a designated sum of money, the estate will go to a third person.

SHIFT OPERATOR. An operator or operating engineer who has charge of and operates a compressor or refrigeration plant under the direction and supervision of a chief operator or a chief operating engineer and who has the authority to perform the powers and duties of the chief operator or the chief operating engineer when the chief operator or the chief operating engineer is absent from the plant. *Operating Engineers Act*, R.S.O. 1980, c. 363, s. 1.

SHIP. *n.* 1. Includes any description of vessel or boat used or designed for use in navigation without regard to method or lack of propulsion. 2. Includes any structure launched and intended for use in navigation as a ship or as a part of a ship. *Canada Shipping Act*, R.S.C. 1985, c. S-9, s. 574. 3. Any kind of vessel, or boat, propelled by sails, steam, gasoline or otherwise. *Interpretation Act*, R.S.N.B. 1973, c. I-13, s. 38. See AIR~; AMID~S; BRITISH ~; CANADIAN ~; CARGO ~; CARTEL-~; CHARTERED ~; CLASSED ~; CROWN ~; DAY ~; DEAD ~; EXISTING ~; EX ~; FACTORY ~; FISHING ~; FLUSH DECK ~; FOREIGN ~; FREE ALONGSIDE ~; GOVERNMENT ~; GREAT LAKES ~; HAMPERED ~; HOME-TRADE ~S; HOTEL ~; INLAND WATERS ~; LOAD LINE CONVENTION ~; LOAD LINE ~; MINOR WATERS ~; MOTOR ~; NEW ~; NON-CANADIAN ~; NUCLEAR ~; OCEAN ~; PASSENGER ~; SAFETY CONVENTION ~; SAILING ~; SEA-GOING ~; SEALING ~; SERVICE ~; TELEGRAPH CABLE ~; TYPE A ~; TYPE B, C, D OR E ~; TYPE B ~; UNCLASSED ~.

SHIPMENT. *n.* 1. The total number of cartons of mail, mail bags and equivalent units of mail posted at one post office in one day by one sender for delivery by postpak mail service to one addressee at one address. *Special Services and Fees Regulations*, C.R.C., c. 1296, s. 29. 2. Includes all goods described in an invoice. *Special Exporters' Declaration Regulations*, C.R.C., c. 477, s. 2. See DROP ~; DURING THE COURSE OF ~.

SHIP OR SHIPPING. The overt act of any person leading to the movement, by common carrier or other means of public conveyance, of any livestock or livestock product from or to a point outside the province in which that person carries on business. *Livestock and Livestock Products Act*, R.S.C.1985, c. L-9, s. 31.

SHIPOWNER. *n.* The registered owner of a ship or any share in a ship, and includes the lessee or charterer of any vessel having the control of the navigation thereof. *Inland Water Freight Rates Act*, R.S.C. 1985, c. I-10, s. 2.

SHIPPER. *n.* A person sending or desiring to send goods between points in Canada or who receives or desires to receive goods shipped between points in Canada. See DEALER-~.

SHIPPER GROUP. An organization or association of shippers that the Minister of Transport designates as representing, in his opinion, for the purposes of this Act, the interests of those shippers. *Shipping Conference Exemption Act*, R.S.C. 1985, c. S-10, s. 15(2).

SHIPPER OF HOGS. A person who assembles hogs or transports hogs in any manner, but does not include, (i) a producer who transports in a vehicle owned by him only the hogs produced by him; (ii) a person who is employed by and driving a vehicle owned by the holder of a licence as a shipper of hogs; (iii) a railway company; or (iv) a processor who bought the hogs under the plan and the regulations. *Farm Products Marketing Act*, R.R.O. 1980, Reg. 368, s. 1.

SHIPPING BILL. A bill accompanying a shipment of fertilizer or supplement. *Fertilizers Regulations*, C.R.C., c. 666, s. 2.

SHIPPING CASUALTY. What occurs when a ship is abandoned, lost, damaged or stranded or when a ship causes damage or loss to another ship. R.M. Fernandes & C. Burke, *The Annotated Canada Shipping Act* (Toronto: Butterworths, 1988) at 199.

SHIPPING COMPANY. Any person who carries or offers, advertises or proposes to carry grain between any ports in Canada or between any ports in Canada and the United States. *Inland Water Freight Rates Act*, R.S.C. 1985, c. I-10, s. 2.

SHIPPING CONFERENCE. An association of ocean carriers that has the purpose or effect of regulating rates, charges and conditions for the transportation by those carriers of goods by water. *Shipping Conference Exemption Act*, R.S.C. 1985, c. S-10, s. 2.

SHIPPING CONTAINER. A pressure vessel designed and used for the purpose of transporting a gas, vapour, or liquid from one location to another. *Boiler and Pressure Vessel Act*, R.S.Nfld. 1970, c. 24, s. 2. See RE-USABLE ~.

SHIPPING DOCUMENT. 1. Any document that accompanies dangerous goods being handled, offered for transport or transported and that describes or contains information relating to the goods and, in particular, but without restricting the generality of the foregoing, includes a bill of lading, cargo manifest, shipping order, way-bill and switching order. Transportation of Dangerous Goods acts. 2. The insurance policy with terms current in the particular trade; the invoice or written account of the particular goods delivered, their prices and any credit for freight which the buyer must pay the shipowner on delivery; and the bill of lading. Other documents required by the seller, for custom or a contract, i.e. an export licence, may also be included. G.H.L. Fridman, *Sale of Goods in Canada*, 3d ed. (Toronto: Carswell, 1986) at 480.

SHIPPING POINT. A depot, station, siding or any other place on a railway at which grain is loaded by or on behalf of a grain buyer. *Grain Buyers Licensing Act*, R.S.A. 1980, c. G-9, s. 1.

SHIPPING SAFETY CONTROL ZONE. An area of the arctic waters prescribed as a shipping safety control zone by an order made under section 11. *Arctic Waters Pollution Prevention Act*, R.S.C. 1985, c. A-12, s. 2.

SHIP'S AMMUNITION. Any article or substance on board a vessel and necessary for the safety or defence of a vessel. Canada regulations.

SHIPS BELONGING TO HER MAJESTY. All ships of war and other unregistered vessels held by or on behalf of Her Majesty in right of any Commonwealth country. *Canada Shipping Act*, R.S.C. 1985, c. S-9, s. 2.

SHIP'S COOK. The chief cook or only cook of a ship. *Certification of Ships' Cooks Regulations, Part I*, C.R.C., c. 1413, s. 2.

SHIP'S PAPERS. A ship's registry certificate, charter-party, log, bill of lading, bill of health and any other document which describes the ship and her cargo.

SHIP STATION. Any radio station established on board a ship that is not permanently moored. *Canada Shipping Act*, R.S.C. 1985, c. S-9, s. 2.

SHIPS STORES. The goods listed in the schedules that are taken on board a ship or aircraft for the operation and maintenance thereof or for sale to the officers, crew or passengers during a voyage or flight. Canada regulations.

SHIPWRECKED PERSONS. Includes persons belonging to or on board any British or foreign vessel, wrecked, stranded or in distress, at any place within Canada. *Canada Shipping Act*, R.S.C. 1985, c. S-9, s. 2.

SHOCK. *n.* A condition characterized by pallor, low blood pressure, rapid but shallow pulse and clammy perspiration. See NERVOUS ~; PRIMARY ~; SECONDARY ~.

SHOCK-PROOF. *adj.* As applied to X-ray and high-frequency equipment, means that equipment is guarded with grounded metal so that no person can come into contact with any live part. *Power Corporation Act*, R.R.O. 1980, Reg. 794, s. 0.

SHOCK WAVE. A region ahead of an aircraft of abrupt change of pressure and density moving as a wave front at or above the velocity of sound. *Sonic and Supersonic Flight Order*, C.R.C., c. 64, s. 2.

SHOESTRING. *adj.* Means potatoes cut into straight cut strips that are predominantly 1/4 by 1/4 inch or less in cross-sectional dimensions. *Processed Fruit and Vegetable Regulations*, C.R.C., c. 291, scehdule I, s. 44.

SHOOT. *v.* With respect to a drug, to inject

intravenously. F.A. Jaffe, *A Guide to Pathological Evidence*, 2d ed. (Toronto: Carswell, 1983) at 183.

SHOOTING PRESERVE. Land that is privately owned and maintained and on which wildlife that has been raised in captivity is kept in captivity, or released, for the purpose of hunting. *Wildlife Act*, S.M. 1980, c. 73, s. 1. See PRIVATE ~; PUBLIC ~.

SHOP. *n.* 1. A place where (a) goods are handled or exposed or offered for sale; or (b) services are offered for sale. 2. The part of any premises or place in which or from which a wholesale or retail trade or business is carried on. *Shops Closing Act*, S. Nfld. 1977, c. 107, s. 2. See BAKE ~; BARBER ~; BUCKET ~; CLOSED ~; OPEN ~; PERSONAL SERVICE ~; SERVICE ~; UNION ~; VETCRAFT ~.

SHOP CARD. By the Shop Card Registration Act of 1938, any design, emblem, figure, sign, seal, stamp, ticket, device or other form of advertisement adopted by a labour union. This statute was repealed by the Trade Marks Act of 1953, section 68. H.G. Fox, *The Canadian Law of Trade Marks and Unfair Competition*, 3d ed. (Toronto: Carswell, 1972) at 210.

SHOP CHAIRMAN. A union steward chosen by department stewards to chair all the stewards in a plant and to deal with higher management representatives in respect of grievances.

SHOP GOODS. Defined in the Explosives Regulations, made under the Explosives Act, as being manufactured fireworks that are not liable to explode violently and also includes firework showers, flashlight powders, fountains, golden rain, Jap torpedoes, lawn lights, pin wheels, Roman candles, sparklers, toy caps, volcanoes, Chinese crackers when the length does not exceed 4 in., and mines not exceeding 2 lb. gross weight, but does not include rockets or salutes. *Dangerous Goods Shipping Regulations*, C.R.C., c. 1419, s. 149.

SHOP INSPECTION. An inspection during construction or fabrication by an inspector appointed under this Act or by an agency authorized by the chief inspector. Boiler and Pressure Vessel acts.

SHOPLIFTING. *var.* **SHOP-LIFTING.** *n.* Theft of merchandise.

SHOPPING CENTRE. 1. A development used or intended to be used primarily for the purposes of retail trade and resulting or intended to result in a total of 50,000 square feet or more of (i) new retail floor space; or (ii) new and existing retail floor space where the new retail floor space exceeds 10,000 square feet, including common areas and related office and warehouse space but excluding parking areas. *Shopping Centre Development Act*, S.N.S. 1979-80, c. 74, s. 2. 2. A building or complex of buildings, which contains or is intended to contain more than one retail store or outlet for the provision of services, or both, but does not include any building or part of a building which is used or intended to be used as a hotel, motel or restaurant. *Shopping Centres (Development) Act*, S.P.E.I. 1979, c. 17, s. 2.

SHOP STEWARD. An officer of a union, a section or branch of a union who is appointed or elected to represent union members.

SHORE. *n.* 1. The lands lying between the ordinary high water mark and the ordinary low water mark of a pond, lake, river or body of water. *Quarriable Substances Act*, R.S.N.B. 1973, c. Q-1, s. 1. 2. Includes any shorebound ice that affords a safe landing area. *Life-saving Equipment Order*, C.R.C., c. 50, s. 2.

SHORE AREA. That portion of land lying within 1,000 feet above and 1,000 feet below the ordinary high water mark of any pond, lake, river or body of water and includes any bed, bank, beach, shore, dune, bar, flat or mud flat lying in that portion of land. *Quarriable Substances Act*, R.S.N.B. 1973, c. Q-1, s. 1. See LAKE ~; OCEAN ~.

SHORE INSTALLATION. Structures, appliances or machinery affixed to the ground of a prescribed class or kind used in connection with a primary fishing enterprise, but does not include fishing equipment. *Fisheries Improvements Loan Act*, R.S.C. 1985, c. F-22, s. 2.

SHORTAGE. *n.* The amount by which the aggregate of the quantity of grain of any grade discharged from an elevator in a period between two consecutive weigh-overs of grain of that grade in the elevator and the quantity of grain of that grade in storage in the elevator at the end of that period is less than the aggregate of the quantity of grain of that grade in storage in the elevator at the beginning of that period and the quantity of grain of that grade received into the elevator during that period. *Canada Grain Act*, R.S.C. 1985, c. G-10, s. 2.

SHORT BLAST. A blast of about one second's duration. *Collision Regulations*, C.R.C., c. 1416, Rule 32.

SHORT ENGAGEMENT. A fixed period of service of a member of the regular force as an officer, other than as a subordinate officer, of such duration shorter than an intermediate engagement as is prescribed by regulation. *Canadian Forces Superannuation Act*, R.S.C. 1985, c. C-17, s. 2.

SHORT INTERNATIONAL VOYAGE. An international voyage in the course of which a ship is not more than 200 miles from a port or place in which the passengers and crew could be placed in safety and which does not exceed 600 miles in length between the last port of call in the country in which the voyage begins and the final port of destination. Canada regulations.

SHORT POSITION. Where used in relation to a commodity futures contract, means to be under an obligation to make delivery.

SHORT STANDARD IRON BAR. An iron or steel bar 1 inch square and 2 feet long pointed at one end and planted into the ground so that the top of the bar is flush with the ground level. *Surveys Act*, R.R.O. 1980, Reg. 927, s. 1.

SHORT TERM SECURITY. A bond, debenture or other evidence of indebtedness maturing within 180 days from the date of acquisition thereof.

SHORT TIME DUTY. A requirement of service that demands operation at a substantially constant load for a short and definitely specified time. *Power Corporation Act*, R.R.O. 1980, Reg. 794, s. 0.

SHORT TITLE. The title by which an act is cited. A. Fraser, G.A. Birch & W.A. Dawson, eds., *Beauchesne's Rules and Forms of the House of Commons of Canada*, 5th ed. (Toronto: Carswell, 1978) at 218.

SHORT VACATION. In Ontario, the period when the courts do not sit, from the 24th of December until the 6th of the following January, both days inclusive.

SHOT. *n.* 1. An explosive charge that has been placed in a bore hole in a mine. *Coal Mines (CBDC) Safety Regulations*, C.R.C., c. 1011, s. 2. 2. The sound of a charge or charges being exploded. *Occupational Health and Safety Act*, R.R.O. 1980, Reg. 694, s. 1. See BUCK ~; CHILLED ~; HOT ~.

SHOT FIRER. *var.* **SHOT-FIRER.** 1. A person who is possessed of a certificate of competency as a mine examiner under this or some former Act and who holds a written appointment from the manager of the mine to fire shots in that mine. *Coal Mines Regulation Act*, R.S.N.S. 1967, c. 36, s. 3. 2. A person who has charge of explosives and their use in an underground mine. *Coal Mines Safety Act*, R.S.A. 1980, c. C-15, s. 1.

SHOT HOLE. *var.* **SHOTHOLE.** *var.* **SHOT-HOLE.** A hole drilled for firing an explosive charge in seismic operations.

SHOT PELLET. In shotgun ammunition, a pellet of lead or lead alloy. F.A. Jaffe, *A Guide* *to Pathological Evidence*, 2d ed. (Toronto: Carswell, 1983) at 183.

SHOULD. *v.* Used to indicate recommendatory provisions. Canada regulations.

SHOULDER ROOM DIMENSION. The front shoulder room dimension W3 as defined in Section E, Ground Vehicle Practice, SAE Aerospace-Automotive Drawing Standards, (September 1963). *Motor Vehicle Safety Regulations*, C.R.C., c. 1038, s. 104.

SHOW. See AIR ~; TRAVELLING PICTURE ~.

SHOW CAUSE. The presentation to a court of reasons why a certain order should not take effect.

SHOW CAUSE SUMMONS. A document which requires a debtor to appear again in court and show why the debtor should not be jailed for contempt of a payment order. C.R.B. Dunlop, *Creditor—Debtor Law in Canada* (Toronto: Carswell, 1981) at 105-106.

SHOWER ROOM. A room that contains a shower bath and that is used by employees for the purpose of having shower baths. *Canada Sanitation Regulations*, C.R.C., c. 1009, s. 2.

SHOW POOL. Monies bet on horses selected to finish first, second or third in a race. *Race Track Supervision Regulations*, C.R.C., c. 441, s. 2.

SHOW-UP. *n.* Presentation of one suspect for identification. S.A. Cohen, *Due Process of Law* (Toronto: Carswell, 1977) at 83. See LINE-UP.

SHOW-UP PAY. A minimum number of hours pay paid to an employee required to report to work outside the employee's scheduled work time.

SHRIEVALTY. *n.* The jurisdiction or office of a sheriff.

SHRIMP. *n.* A crustacean of the species Pandalus borealis or Pandalus montagui. *Northwest Atlantic Fisheries Regulations*, C.R.C., c. 860, s. 2.

SHRIMP COCKTAIL. Shrimp meat packed with sauce, spices, seasonings or flavourings or any combination thereof.

SHRINKAGE. *n.* The loss in weight of grain that occurs in the handling or treating of grain. *Canada Grain Act*, R.S.C. 1985, c. G-10, s. 2.

SHURIKEN. *n.* A hard non-flexible plate having three or more radiating points with one or more sharp edges in the shape of a polygon, trefoil, cross, star, diamond or other geometric shape and designed to be thrown as a weapon.

Prohibited Weapons Order, No. 2, C.R.C., c. 434, s. 2.

SHUTDOWN. *n.* The closing of a business establishment.

S.I. *abbr.* Statutory instrument.

SHUT-OFF SEINE. Netting that is floated at the top, weighted at the bottom and used to impound fish along the shore. Canada regulations.

SHUTTER. *n.* A mechanism that, in its closed position, intercepts the laser beam and prevents the emission of laser radiation from the demonstration laser. *Radiation Emitting Devices Regulations*, C.R.C., c. 1370, s. 1.

SI AUTEM SACRAMENTUM FATUUM FUERIT, LICET FALSUM, TAMEN NON COMITTIT PERJURIUM. [L.] If an oath is foolish, the one who takes it does not commit perjury, even if it is false.

SIB. *n.* Someone related by blood.

SIBLING. *n.* A person who has the same biological mother or biological father as another person.

SIBLING SUCCESSOR. Where used with reference to a deceased means a successor to property of the deceased who is a brother, sister, half-brother or half-sister of the deceased. *Statute Amendments (Taxation) Act*, S.M. 1977, c. 58, s. 16.

SIC. *adv.* [L. so, thus] This word is put in brackets in a quoted passage to show that any mistakes or apparent omissions in the quotation appear also in the original source.

SICK AND FUNERAL BENEFITS. Includes insurance against sickness, disability or death. Insurance acts.

SICK LEAVE. Time off allowed for illness.

SICKLE CELL CRISIS. Distortion of red blood cells containing an abnormal form of hemoglobin (hemoglobin S) when oxygen tension falls and small blood vessels throughout the body are blocked. F.A. Jaffe, *A Guide to Pathological Evidence*, 2d ed. (Toronto: Carswell, 1983) at 47.

SICKNESS. See DECOMPRESSION ~.

SICKNESS INSURANCE. 1. Insurance by which the insurer undertakes to pay insurance money in the event of sickness of the person or person insured, but does not include disability insurance. 2. Insurance against loss caused by illness or disability of the person or persons insured, other than that arising from accident, old age or death. *Insurance Act*, R.S.B.C. 1979, c. 200, s. 1. 3. (a) Insurance against loss resulting from the illness or disability of a person other than loss resulting from death; (b) insurance whereby an insurer undertakes to pay a certain sum or sums of money in the event of the illness or disability of a person; or (c) insurance against expenses incurred for dental care, other than illness or disability or dental care arising out of an accident. *Classes of Insurance Regulations*, C.R.C., c. 977, s. 34. See GROUP ~.

SICK PAY. A private plan to insure someone against loss of income upon disability. K.D. Cooper-Stephenson & I.B. Saunders, *Personal Injury Damages in Canada* (Toronto: Carswell, 1981) at 3.

SICUT ALIAS. [L. as at another time, or heretofore] The name of a second writ dispatched when the first was not executed. See ALIAS WRIT.

SIC UTERE TUO UT ALIENUM NON LAEDAS. [L.] Use your own property so as not to injure your neighbour's.

SIDE. *n.* 1. The exposed face of the excavation in a strip mine from the surface of the ground to the working level of the pit. *Coal Mines Regulation Act*, R.S.A. 1970, c. 52, s. 2. 2. A limit of a summer resort location that meets a frontage of the location. *Public Lands Act*, R.R.O. 1980, Reg. 879, s. 1.

SIDE EFFECT. An effect on an organ which was not the primary target of a drug, e.g. bleeding in the stomach caused by aspirin. F.A. Jaffe, *A Guide to Pathological Evidence*, 2d ed. (Toronto: Carswell, 1983) at 61.

SIDELIGHTS. *n.* A green light on the starboard side and a red light on the port side each showing an unbroken light over an arc of the horizon of 112.5 degrees and so fixed as to show the light from right ahead to 22.5 degrees abaft the beam on its respective side. In a vessel of less than 20 metres in length the sidelights may be combined in one lantern carried on the fore and aft centreline of the vessel. *Collision Regulations*, C.R.C., c. 1416, Rule 3.

SIDE LINE. See LAST ASCERTAINABLE ~.

SIDE LOT LINE. Any boundary line of a lot that is not a front lot line or a rear lot line. Canada regulations.

SIDENOTE. *n.* A marginal note.

SIDE TRAWL. An otter trawl designed for or adapted to hauling fish over the side of a vessel. Fishery regulations.

SIDEWALK. *n.* 1. That portion of a highway between the curb lines or the lateral lines of a roadway and the adjacent property lines set apart for the use of pedestrians and includes any part of a highway set apart or marked as being

for the exclusive use of pedestrians. 2. Includes a footway and a street crossing.

SIDEWALL. *n.* That portion of a tire between the thread and the bead. Canada regulations.

SIDEWALL SEPARATION. The parting of the rubber compound from the cord in the sidewall. *Motor Vehicle Tire Safety Regulations*, C.R.C., c. 1039, s. 2.

SIDEWARD DIRECTION. A direction that is displaced from the facing direction by 90 angular degrees in the horizontal plane. *Children's Car Seats and Harnesses Regulations*, C.R.C., c. 921, s. 2.

SIDE WHARFAGE. 1. A toll charged on a vessel in respect of the period of time that the vessel is loading, unloading or lying in wait in a canal. *St. Lawrence Seaway Wharfage and Storage Charges Tariff*, C.R.C., c. 1396, s. 2. 2. The charge against a vessel for the use of berthing space at wharf when not engaged in loading or discharging cargo. Wharf tariffs.

SIDE WHARFAGE CHARGES. Charges levied on a vessel loading, unloading or lying in wait in a canal. *Canal Regulations*, C.R.C., c. 1564, s. 2.

SIDE YARD. 1. A yard extending from the front yard to the rear yard of a lot upon which a building or structure is situate and from the side lot line to the part of the building or structure that is nearest to the side lot line. *Niagara Escarpment Planning and Development Act*, R.R.O. 1980, Reg. 685, s. 1. 2. A yard between a main building or main storage area and the side lot line extending from the nearest line of the front yard, or the front lot line where no front yard is required by these Regulations, to the rear yard. Canada regulations.

SIDE YARD WIDTH. The distance measured horizontally from the nearest point of the side lot line toward the nearest part of the main structure on the lot, clear of projections, or the main storage area, as the case may be. Canada regulations.

SIDING. *n.* A track auxiliary to the main track for meeting or passing trains. *Regulations No. O-8, Uniform Code of Operating Rules*, C.R.C., c. 1175, Part III, s. 2.

S.I.D.S. *abbr.* Sudden infant death syndrome.

SIGHT. See AFTER ~; AT ~.

SIGHT-SEEING VEHICLE. A vehicle used for the transportation of persons for compensation and such vehicles are classified as follows: 1. Class 1—a horse-drawn vehicle designed to carry one to eight passengers. 2. Class 2—a motor vehicle designed to carry one to six passengers, hired for one specific sight-seeing trip exclusively for one person or one group of persons. 3. Class 3—a motor vehicle designed to carry 1 to 16 passengers, operating on a specific sight-seeing trip and available to any passenger paying a set fee for the trip. 4. Class 4—a motor vehicle operating on a regular schedule approved by the Commission having a seating capacity for 17 or more passengers, exclusive of a vehicle that is towed by a power unit. 5. Class 5—a motor vehicle having a seating capacity for 17 or more passengers and not operating on a regular schedule. *Niagara Parks Act*, R.R.O. 1980, Reg. 686, s. 1.

SIGIL. *n.* [L.] A signature; a seal.

SIGN. *n.* A publicly displayed notice. *National Parks Signs Regulations*, C.R.C., c. 1130, s. 2. See COUNTER-~; FISHING BOUNDARY ~: LUMINOUS ~; NAME ~; OFFICIAL ~; RAILROAD ~ OR SIGNAL; TRAFFIC ~; VITAL ~; YIELD ~.

SIGNAL. *n.* Any sign, writing, image, sound or intelligence of any nature transmitted or emitted as a radiocommunication. *Cable Television Regulations*, C.R.C., c. 374, s. 2. See ALARM ~; APPROACH ~; BLOCK ~; CAB ~; DWARF ~; FIRE ALARM ~; FIXED ~; GRADE ~; IDENTICAL ~S; INTERLOCKING ~; PEDESTRIAN CONTROL ~; RAILROAD SIGN OR ~; STANDARD CODE OF ~S; STATION PROTECTION ~; SUPERVISORY ~; TRAFFIC CONTROL ~; TRAIN ORDER ~.

SIGNAL CIRCUIT. Any electrical circuit, other than a communication circuit, which supplies energy to a device which gives a recognizable audible or visible signal, such as circuits for doorbells, buzzers, code-calling systems, signal lights and similar devices. *Power Corporation Act*, R.R.O. 1980, Reg. 794, s. 0.

SIGNAL INDICATION. The information conveyed by a fixed signal or cab signal. *Regulations No. O-8, Uniform Code of Operating Rules*, C.R.C., c. 1175, Part III, s. 2.

SIGNALLING DEVICE. See FIRE ALARM ~.

SIGNALMAN. *n.* A person who, in an industrial establishment or on a construction project, directs vehicle traffic or watches loads. D. Robertson, *Ontario Health and Safety Guide* (Toronto: Richard De Boo Ltd., 1988) at 5-368.

SIGNAL SYSTEM. See AUTOMATIC BLOCK ~.

SIGNATORY. *n.* A person who signs.

SIGNATURE. *n.* 1. A mark or sign impressed on something. 2. The name which one writes

oneself. See COUNTER-~; GUARANTEE OF ~.

SIGNER. See CO-~.

SIGNET. *n.* The seal that, under the existing practice in the United Kingdom, is delivered by Her Majesty the Queen to each of her Principal Secretaries of State in the United Kingdom, and includes the lesser signet or second secretarial seal and the cachet. *Seals Act*, R.S.C. 1985, c. S-6, s. 2.

SIGNIFICANT CHANGE. A change that is not within the control of the offeror or of an affiliate of the offeror shall not be considered to be significant unless it is a material change affecting the affairs of the issuer of securities being offered in exchange for securities of the offeree company and, while an offer is outstanding, the exercise of a right contained in a take-over bid or an issuer bid to modify the terms of the offer or to waive a condition of the offer shall be considered to be a variation which changes the terms of the take-over bid or the issuer bid. *Securities Act*, S.M. 1980, c. 50, s. 90.

SIGNIFICANT DISCOVERY. A discovery indicated by the first well on a geological feature that demonstrates by flow testing the existence of hydrocarbons in that feature and, having regard to geological and engineering factors, suggests the existence of an accumulation of hydrocarbons that has potential for production.

SIGNIFICANT INTEREST. A person has a significant interest in a corporation, or a group of persons has a significant interest in a corporation if, (i) in the case of a person, he owns beneficially, either directly or indirectly, more than 10 per cent; or (ii) in the case of a group of persons, they own beneficially, either individually or together and either directly or indirectly, more than 50 per cent, of the shares of the corporation for the time being outstanding. *Insurance Act*, R.S.O. 1980, c. 218, c. 391.

SIGN MANUAL. *var.* **SIGN-MANUAL.** The sovereign's signature. See DOCUMENT UNDER THE ~.

SILENT FILM SUBJECT. A subject not adapted for the reproduction of synchronized dialogue, music or any other sound effects. *Theatres Act*, R.R.O. 1980, Reg. 931, s. 1.

SILENT PARTNER. A partner who puts money into a partnership without taking an active part in management.

SILICA. *n.* A substance designated under the Ontario Occupational health and Safety Act. D. Robertson, *Ontario Health and Safety Guide* (Toronto: Richard De Boo Ltd., 1988) at 5-368.

SILICEOUS DUST. Silica dust or other com—

pounds of silicon, including asbestos. *Workmen's Compensation Act*, R.S.Q. 1977, c. A-3, s. 112.

SILICOSIS. *n.* 1. A characteristic fibrotic condition of the lungs caused by the inhalation of silica. 2. A fibrotic condition of the lungs of a worker (i) caused by dust containing silica; and (ii) evidenced by specific x-ray appearances or by the results of other scientific tests or examinations, that has resulted in a substantially lessened capacity for work by the worker.

SILK GOWN. The gown worn by Queen's Counsel; thus "to take silk" means to become a Queen's Counsel.

SILT. *n.* A soil, (i) the particles of which are not visible to the naked eye; (ii) dry lumps of which are easily powdered by the fingers; (iii) that, after shaking a small saturated pat vigorously in the hand, exhibits a wet shiny surface that disappears rapidly when the pat is subsequently squeezed; and (iv) that does not shine when moist and stroked with a knife. *Building Code Act*, R.R.O. 1980, Reg. 87, s. 4.2.1.6.

SILVER HAKE. A fish of the species Merluccius bilinearis. *Northwest Atlantic Fisheries Regulations*, C.R.C., c. 860, s. 2.

SILVICULTURE. *n.* The science and art of cultivating forest crops and, more particularly, the theory and practice of controlling the establishment, composition, constitution and growth of forests. *Forests Act*, S.N.S. 1986, c. 10, s. 3.

SIMILAR GOODS. In relation to goods being appraised, means imported goods that (a) closely resemble the goods being appraised in respect of their component materials and characteristics; (b) are capable of performing the same functions as, and of being commercially interchangeable with, the goods being appraised; (c) were produced in the same country as the country in which the goods being appraised were produced; and (d) were produced by or on behalf of the person by or on behalf of whom the goods being appraised were produced, but does not include imported goods where engineering, development work, art work, design work, plans or sketches undertaken in Canada were supplied, directly or indirectly, by the purchaser of those imported goods free of charge or at a reduced cost for use in connection with the production and sale for export of those imported goods. *Customs Act*, R.S.C. 1985 (2d Supp.), c. 1, s. 45.

SIMILAR PLAN. 1. An act of the Parliament of Canada or of the legislature of another province establishing a plan declared to be similar by the Gouvernement. *Quebec Pension Plan Act*, R.S.Q. 1977, c. R-9, s. 1. 2. A medical care insurance plan in force during a year in any province of Canada and respecting which a contribution is payable for that year by the federal government under the Medical Care Act (Statutes of Canada). *Health Insurance Act*, R.S.Q. 1977, c. A-29, s. 1.

SIMILITER. *adv.* [L.] In a like manner.

SIMPLE CONTRACT. A contract not under seal.

SIMPLE PROBABILITY. The standard of proof governing most of a damage assessment which involves valuing chances, possibilities and risks according to the degree of likelihood that events will occur or would have occurred. K.D. Cooper-Stephenson & I.B. Saunders, *Personal Injury Damages in Canada* (Toronto: Carswell, 1981) at 84.

SIMPLE TRUST. A trust in which one person holds property in trust for another and, because the trust is not qualified by the settlor, the law determines its parameters.

SIMPLEX COMMENDATIO NON OBLIGAT. [L.] A simple recommendation of goods does not oblige a buyer.

SIMPLEX JUSTICIARIUS. [L.] A puisne judge, one who is not chief judge of a court.

SIMPLICITAS EST LEGIBUS AMICA. [L.] Simplicity is a friend of the laws.

SIMPLICITER. *adv.* [L.] Without involving any unnamed thing.

SIMULATED MEAT PRODUCT. Any food that does not contain any meat product, poultry product or fish product but that has the appearance of a meat product. *Food and Drug Regulations*, C.R.C., c. 870, s. B.01.001.

SIMULATED POULTRY PRODUCT. Any food that does not contain any poultry product, meat product or fish product but that has the appearance of a poultry product. *Food and Drug Regulations*, C.R.C., c. 870, s. B.01.001.

SIMULATION. See IMPACT ~.

SIMUL CUM. [L.] Together with.

SINECURE. *n.* A position which has remuneration with no employment.

SINE DIE. [L. without a day being fixed] Indefinitely.

SINE PROLE. [L.] Without progeny.

SINE QUA NON. [L. without which not] An indispensible condition or necessity.

SINGEING. *n.* An area of skin burned by hot gases which escaped from the muzzle of a firearm all around the wound where the bullet, fired at close range, entered. F.A. Jaffe, *A Guide* *to Pathological Evidence*, 2d ed. (Toronto: Carswell, 1983) at 183.

SINGLE. *adj.* Includes widowed. *Children of Unmarried Parents Act*, S. Nfld. 1972, c. 33, s. 2.

SINGLE AXLE. One or more axles whose centres are included between two parallel transverse vertical planes one metre apart. *Highway Traffic Act*, R.S.O. 1980, c. 198, s. 97.

SINGLE CHARACTER BRAND. A brand consisting of a single character which includes a bar, dot, 1/4 circle or 1/2 diamond. *Livestock Brand Act*, R.S.B.C. 1979, c. 241, s. 1.

SINGLE ENTRY. In bookkeeping, an entry made to credit or to charge a thing or person in contrast to double entry of both the debit and credit account of a single transaction.

SINGLE-FAMILY. *var.* **SINGLE FAMILY.** When used to describe a dwelling means a separate building containing only one dwelling unit.

SINGLE-FAMILY DWELLING. A dwelling unit intended for the use of one family only, that consists of a detached house, one unit of row housing, or one unit of a semi-detached, duplex, triplex or quadruplex house. *Power Corporation Act*, R.R.O. 1980, Reg. 794, s. 0.

SINGLE FAMILY RESIDENCE. (i) A unit or proposed unit under the Condominium Act; or (ii) a structure or part of a structure, that is designed for occupation as the residence of one family, including dependants or domestic employees of a member of the family, whether or not rent is paid for the occupation of any part of such residence, and whether or not the land on which the residence is situated is zoned for residential use, and includes any such residence that is to be constructed as part of the arrangement relating to a conveyance of land, but does not include any such residence constructed or to be constructed on agricultural land where the transferor with respect to the land conveyed meets the eligibility requirements for a farm tax reduction rebate contained in clause 4 (b) or (c) of Ontario Regulation 716/83 made under the Ministry of Agriculture and Food Act. *Land Transfer Tax Amendment Act*, S.O. 1985, c. 21, s. 1.

SINGLE FAMILY RESIDENTIAL. Real property principally used for residential purposes where there is only one dwelling unit and that unit is not a mobile home. *Taxation (Amendment) Act*, S.N.W.T. 1986 (1st Sess.), c. 23, s. 6.

SINGLE FRONT TOWNSHIP. A township where the usual practice in the original survey was to survey the township boundaries, the proof lines and the base lines, if any, and the concession lines for the fronts of the concessions and to establish the lot corners on the front of each concession. *Surveys Act*, R.S.O. 1980, c. 493, s. 17.

SINGLE HOOP NET. A hoop net having one pot. *Ontario Fishery Regulations*, C.R.C., c. 849, s. 47.

SINGLE INSURED BOND. A bond under which a company is the only party insured. Canada regulations.

SINGLE MEMBER DISTRICT. An electoral district in which one member is to be elected. *Election Act*, R.S.B.C. 1979, c. 103, s. 1.

SINGLE PERSON. 1. An adult person who is a widow, widower, unmarried, deserted, separated or divorced and who is not living with another person as husband or wife. *Family Benefits Act*, R.R.O. 1980, Reg. 318, s. 1. 2. An unmarried adult, a widow, a widower or a separated or divorced person but does not include a person, (i) who is a head of a family; (ii) who is an employable person under the age of 21 years living with either of his parents or with a person in loco parentis; or (iii) who is living with another person as husband or wife. *General Welfare Assistance Act*, R.R.O. 1980, Reg. 441, s. 1.

SINGLE-PLANT BARGAINING. Collective bargaining between an employer and a union in respect of only one of the employer's plants.

SINGLE RATE. A pay rate which is the same for all employees in a particular job.

SINGLE RECEPTACLE. One contact device, with no other contact device on the same yoke, installed at an outlet for the connection of one attachment plug. *Power Corporation Act*, R.R.O. 1980, Reg. 794, s. 0.

SINGLE-SERVICE ARTICLE. Any container or eating utensil that is to be used only once in the service or sale of food. *Public Health Act*, R.R.O. 1980, Reg. 840, s. 1.

SINGLE-SERVICE TOWEL. A towel that is to be used only once before being discarded or laundered for reuse. *Public Health Act*, R.R.O. 1980, Reg. 840, s. 1.

SINGLE TRACK. A main track upon which trains are operated in both directions. *Regulations No. O-8, Uniform Code of Operating Rules*, C.R.C., c. 1175, Part III, s. 2.

SINGLE UNIT VEHICLE. A commercial vehicle used for, (a) the transportation and dumping or spreading of sand, gravel, earth, crushed or uncut rock, slag, rubble, salt, calcium chloride, snow, ice or any mixture thereof, asphalt mixes or scrap metal; (b) the transportation of raw forest products. *Highway Traffic Act*, R.R.O. 1980, Reg. 453, s. 1.

SINGLE WOMAN. 1. A mother or expectant mother who, at the date of conception, was not married to the father of the child. 2. Includes an unmarried woman, a widow, a divorcee, or a woman deserted by or separated from her husband.

SINGULAR. *adj.* Individual, referring to one.

SINGULI IN SOLIDUM. [L.] Joint and several obligors share liability singuli in solidum.

SINK. *n.* A receptacle for general washing or for receiving liquid waste. *Ontario Water Resources Act*, R.R.O. 1980, Reg. 736, s. 1. See BAR ~.

SINKING FUND. A special account to which is credited annually an actuarially determined amount for the purpose of providing a fund for future payments. *Financial Administration Act*, R.S.N.W.T. 1974, c. F-4, s. 2.

SINUOUS BOUNDARY LINE. That part of the boundary that is not a conventional boundary line and that is shown on the map-sheets as a series of broken lines. *Alberta-British Columbia Boundary Act*, S.C. 1974-75-76, c. 11, s. 2.

SI QUIDEM IN NOMINE, COGNOMINE, PRAENOMINE, LEGATARII TESTATOR ERRAVERIT, CUM DE PERSONA CONSTAT, NIHILOMINUS VALET LEGATUM. [L.] Though the testator may have erred concerning the name or names of the legatee, when it is certain what person was meant, the legacy is still valid.

SI QUID UNIVERSITATI DEBETUR SINGULIS NON DEBETUR NEC QUOD DEBET UNIVERSITAS SINGULI DEBENT. [L.] If something is owed to a group it is not owed to the individual members nor do individual members owe what a group owes.

SI QUIS UNUM PERCUSSERIT, CUM ALIUM PERCUTERE VELLET, IN FELONIA TENETUR. [L.] If someone killed one person meaning to kill another, that person is guilty of felony.

SIRE. See IMPROVED ~.

SISTER. *n.* 1. Includes half-sister. *Criminal Code*, R.S.C. 1985, c. C-46, s. 155(4). 2. Includes sister-in-law. See HALF ~.

SITE. *n.* 1. An area or a place. 2. A parcel of land. 3. A building or structure. See ABANDONED MOTOR VEHICLE ~; AIRCRAFT ACCIDENT ~; AIRPORT ~; ARCHAEOLOGICAL ~; BATTERY ~; BUILDING ~; CONSTRUCTION ~; DISCARD ~; HERITAGE ~; HISTORIC ~; IN SITU OPERATION ~; MILL-~; MINE ~; MOBILE HOME ~; MUNICIPAL ~; OIL SANDS ~; POWER ~; PROJECT ~; SCHOOL ~; WELL ~; WORK ~.

SITTER. *n.* A person who is responsible for the safekeeping of a person in his charge and who performs no other services. *Employment Agencies Act*, R.R.O. 1980, Reg. 280, s. 1.

SITTING. *n.* 1. Used alone, means indifferently an ordinary or general sitting, or a special sitting of the council. *Cities and Towns Act*, R.S.Q. 1977, c. C-19, s. 6. 2. The hearing of a matter by the Commission. *Transport Act*, R.S.Q. 1977, c. T-12, s. 1.

SITTING DAY OF PARLIAMENT. A day on which either House of Parliament sits.

SITTINGS. *n.* A term or session of court: the part of the year in which one transacts judicial business.

SITTINGS OR SITTING. A sitting of the court for the trial of civil or criminal cases and includes the hearing of a single trial. *Jury Act*, R.S.B.C. 1979, c. 210, s. 1.

SITUATION. *n.* A place where a child is placed for employment under the supervision of the Director. *Child Welfare Act*, S.Nfld. 1972, c. 37, s. 2.

SITUS. *n.* [L.] A location; a situation.

SIVE TOTA RES EVINCATUR, SIVE PARS, HABET REGRESSUM EMPTOR IN VENITOREM. [L.] Whether evicted from the whole or part of a thing sold, a buyer has the right to be indemnified by the seller.

SIX GRAINS. Wheat, oats, barley, rye, flaxseed and rapeseed. *Western Grain Transportation Act*, R.S.C. 1985, c. W-8, s. 61.

SIX MONTHS' HOIST. A traditional way to oppose second reading of a bill by moving that the bill not be read now a second time, but in 6 months' time. A. Fraser, G.A. Birch & W.A. Dawson, eds., *Beauchesne's Rules and Forms of the House of Commons of Canada*, 5th ed. (Toronto: Carswell, 1978) at 225.

SIZE. *n.* In relation to the hook of an artificial fly, means the size of the hook as calibrated according to the Redditch Scale for salmon flies. *Quebec Fishery Regulations*, C.R.C., c. 852, s. 2. See MESH ~.

SIZE DESIGNATION. Extra Large Size, Large Size, Medium Size, Small Size and Peewee Size. *Egg Regulations*, C.R.C., c. 284, s. 2.

SIZE FACTOR. The sum of the section width

and the outer diameter of a tire determined on the test rim. Canada regulations.

SIZE OR SHAPE. See NOT CUT TO ~.

SKELETAL REMAINS. Remains of human bodies situated or discovered outside a recognized cemetery or burial ground in respect of which there is some manner of identifying the persons buried therein. *Historic Sites and Objects Act*, R.S.M. 1970, c. H70, s. 2.

SKELETON BILL. A bill drawn, accepted or indorsed in blank.

SKETCH. *n.* Includes any mode of representing any place or thing. *Official Secrets Act*, R.S.C. 1985, c. O-5, s. 2.

SKETCH PLAN. An adequately dimensioned drawing of the area affected by a lease of all or part of a building situated on land shown on a plan of survey deposited in the land title office. *Land Title Act*, R.S.B.C. 1979, c. 219, s. 1.

SKIDDING. *n.* The operation of moving logs or trees by pulling across the terrain. *Occupational Health and Safety Act*, R.R.O. 1980, Reg. 692, s. 107.

SKIDS. *n.* Small portable platforms upon which goods may be consolidated into individual loads for transportation or storage. *Wharfage Charges By-law*, C.R.C., c. 1066, s. 2.

SKILL. *n.* Special competence one acquires by developing one's aptitude through experience and training. John G. Fleming, *The Law of Torts*, 6th ed. (Sydney: The Law Book Co., 1983) at 104.

SKILLED CARE. See OCCASIONAL ~.

SKILLED LABOUR. Anyone who has mastered a job requiring skill; may refer to office workers or craftspeople.

SKILLED NURSING CARE. The use of methods, procedures and techniques employed in providing nursing care by persons with technical nursing training beyond the care that an untrained person can adequately administer. *Nursing Homes Act*, R.S.N.S. 1967, c. 216, s. 1.

SKILLED TRADESMAN. A natural person who, as a sole operator, carries on a trade or vocation.

SKIMMED MILK. See DRY ~.

SKIMMING STATION. A place where the milk of not less than 50 cows or of cows in the herds of five or more persons is received and creamed by means of a centrifugal cream separator. *Dairy Act*, R.S.M. 1970, c. D10, s. 2.

SKIM-MILK. *var.* **SKIM MILK.** Grade A milk that contains not more than .3 per cent milk-fat and not less than 8.5 per cent milk solids other than milk-fat. *Milk Act*, R.R.O. 1980, Reg. 622, s. 3. See EVAPORATED ~; FLAVOURED ~.

SKIM MILK POWDER. Dried skim milk that contains not less than 95 per cent milk solids, with or without added vitamin D. *Farm Products Grades and Sales Act*, R.R.O. 1980, Reg. 327, s. 1.

SKIN. *n.* In relation to a wildlife or exotic animal, includes its hide or pelt, with or without the pelage, and, in the case of a bird, includes the plumage. *Wildlife Act*, S.A. 1984, c. W-9.1, s. 1. See UNPRIME ~.

SKIN-DIVING FISHING. Fishing under water, with or without self-contained underwater breathing apparatus. *Quebec Fishery Regulations*, C.R.C., c. 852, s. 2.

SLANDER. *n.* Making a defamatory statement orally or in a more transitory form. R.E. Brown, *The Law of Defamation in Canada* (Toronto: Carswell, 1987) at 9.

SLANDER OF TITLE. Writing, speaking or publishing words which impeach a plaintiff's title to any property, real or personal, which that plaintiff owns. I.H. Jacob, ed., *Bullen and Leake and Jacob's Precedents of Pleadings*, 12th ed. (London: Sweet and Maxwell, 1975) at 544.

SLANDER PER SE. In an action for slander, the exceptions to the requirement of special damages are (1) an oral imputation which disparages the reputation of the plaintiff concerning business, work, calling, office, trade or profession; (2) an accusation which imputes the commission of a criminal offence; (3) words which impute a contagious or loathsome disease; (4) words to a woman which impute unchastity. R.E. Brown, *The Law of Defamation in Canada* (Toronto: Carswell, 1987) at 301.

SLASH. *n.* Includes brush and other forest debris. *Forest Act*, R.S.B.C. 1979, c. 140, s. 108.

SLAUGHTER. *n.* Killing for the purpose of processing into food for human consumption.

SLAUGHTER HOG. Any animal of the swine species which is sold to a packer. *The Hog Marketing Deductions Act*, R.S.S. 1978, c H-4, s. 2.

SLAUGHTERHOUSE. *n.* An abattoir to which stock is delivered, or in which stock is held for slaughter. *Livestock Brand Act*, R.S.B.C. 1979, c. 241, s. 1.

SLEEPER BERTH. Sleeping accommodation provided in a motor vehicle.

SLEEPING ACCOMMODATION. Includes a campsite where any facility or service is provided for the supply of water or electricity or for the disposal of garbage or sewage.

SLEEPING ACCOMMODATIONS. Includes (a) a hotel or any other building in which lodgings are provided for rent or hire; (b) any building in which lodgings are offered to members of the public on a gratuitous basis; (c) any building in which an educational institution lodges its students; (d) any building, other than a single family residence, in which a religious organization lodges its members; (e) a hospital, sanatorium, infirmary, nursing home or home for the aged; (f) an orphanage or children's home; (g) a jail, reformatory or other penal institution; or (h) an apartment house with three or more self-contained units above the ground floor. *Fire Prevention Act*, R.S.N.B. 1973, c. F-13, s. 1. See BUILDING USED FOR ~.

SLEEPING PARTNER. See SILENT PARTNER.

SLEIGH DOG. A dog used, or capable of being used, from time to time for the purpose of drawing a sleigh, sled, toboggan, or other vehicle, commonly used for carrying goods or persons, and includes the young of any such dog and any dog being trained for that purpose. *Animal Husbandry Act*, R.S.M. 1970, c. A90, s. 29.

SLIDE. *n.* Stationary picture slide or similar device used in conjunction with a motion picture machine. See PHOTOGRAPHIC ~.

SLIDE-IN-CAMPER. *n.* A device that is constructed and designed to be temporarily placed and carried within a box of a truck or attached to the box of a truck or the chassis thereof, and is equipped or furnished with beds, stove or other appliances. *Highway Traffic Act*, S.M. 1977, c. 34, s. 1.

SLIDING SCALE. Rates of wages which change automatically in relation to some factor such as the consumer price index.

SLINK SALMON. Salmon that are in poor condition and that are returning to sea after spawning. Fishery regulations.

SLIP. *n.* Contains brief particulars of the risk insured and binds the insurer to issue a policy according to its terms. Raoul Colinvaux, *The Law of Insurance*, 5th ed. (London: Sweet & Maxwell, 1984) at 19.

SLIVER. *n.* Fibres in a continuous strand, combed or not, not twisted and not exceeding 12 inches in length, and includes tops. *Customs Tariff*, R.S.C. 1985, c. C-54, s. 2.

SLOPE. *n.* An excavation that is driven in the earth or strata of an underground mine at an angle of less than 45 degrees with the plane of

the horizon and that is or may be used, (i) for ventilation or drainage;, or (ii) for the ingress or egress of people, animals or material to or from the mine or part thereof.

SLOT MACHINE. Any automatic machine or slot machine (a) that is used or intended to be used for any purpose other than vending merchandise or services; or (b) that is used or intended to be used for the purpose of vending merchandise or services if (i) the result of one of any number of operations of the machine is a matter of chance or uncertainty to the operator; (ii) as a result of a given number of successive operations by the operator the machine produces different results; or (iii) on any operation of the machine it discharges or emits a slug or token, but does not include an automatic machine or slot machine that dispenses as prizes only one or more free games on that machine. *Criminal Code*, R.S.C. 1985, c. C-46, s. 198(3).

SLOUGHING. *n.* For the purposes of section 118 of Schedule IV, such degradation of a brake cup, evidenced by the presence of carbon black loosely held on the brake cup surface, that a visible black streak is produced when the cup, with 500 ^{P} 10 gram deadweight applied to it, is drawn base down over a sheet of white bond paper placed on a firm flat surface. *Motor Vehicle Safety Regulations*, C.R.C., c. 1038, s. 2.

SLOW-BURNING. *adj.* As applied to conductor insulation means the insulation has flame-retarding properties. *Power Corporation Act*, R.R.O. 1980, Reg. 794, s. 0.

SLOWDOWN. *n.* A concerted refusal by employees to maintain the normal production rate.

S.L.R. *abbr.* Statute Law Revision Act of England.

SLUG. *n.* For a smooth bore gun, a solid projectile made of lead alloy or lead which has rifling engraved to provide spin and ballistic stability. F.A. Jaffe, *A Guide to Pathological Evidence*, 2d ed. (Toronto: Carswell, 1983) at 183 and 184.

SMALL AEROPLANE. An aeroplane of 12,500 pounds or less, maximum certificated take-off weight. *Air Carrier Using Small Aeroplanes Order*, C.R.C., c. 22, s. 2.

SMALL BREAD. Biscuits, buns, crackers, muffins, rolls, scones or any other fancy cakes commonly made in the trade. *Bread Act*, R.S.A. 1970, c. 34, s. 2.

SMALL BUSINESS CORPORATION. At any particular time means a particular corporation that is a Canadian-controlled private corporation all or substantially all of the fair market value of the assets of which at that time was attributable to assets that were (a) used in an active business carried on primarily in Canada by the particular corporation or by a corporation related to it; (b) shares of the capital stock of one or more small business corporations that were at that time connected with the particular corporation (within the meaning of subsection 186(4) on the assumption that such small business corporation was at that time a "payer corporation" within the meaning of that subsection) or a bond, debenture, bill, note, mortgage, hypothec or similar obligation issued by such a connected corporation; or (c) assets described in paragraphs (a) and (b), and, for the purposes of paragraph 39(1)(c), includes a corporation that was at any time in the 12 months preceding that time a small business corporation. *Income Tax Act*, R.S.C. 1952, c. 148 (as am. S.C. 1988, c. 55, s. 188(6)), s. 248(1).

SMALL BUSINESS DEVELOPMENT CORPORATION. See NORTHERN AND EASTERN ~.

SMALL BUSINESS ENTERPRISE. A business enterprise the estimated gross revenue of which, as stated in an application for a business improvement loan, did not, for the fiscal period of the business enterprise in which the application was made, or, in the case of a business enterprise about to be carried on, will not, for its fiscal period that is of not less than 52 weeks duration, exceed $2,000,000. *Small Business Loans Act*, R.S.C. 1985 (1st Supp.), c. 19, s. 1.

SMALL BUSINESS PROPERTY. With respect to a taxpayer at a particular time means property acquired by the taxpayer after October 31, 1985 that is at that particular time (a) a property prescribed to be a small business security; (b) a share of a class of the capital stock of a corporation prescribed to be a small business investment corporation; (c) an interest of a limited partner in a partnership prescribed to be a small business investment limited partnership; or (d) an interest in a trust prescribed to be a small business investment trust, where the taxpayer is (e) a prescribed person in respect of the property; or (f) the first person (other than a broker or dealer in securities) to have acquired the property and the taxpayer has owned the property continuously since it was so acquired. *Income Tax Act*, R.S.C. 1952, c. 148 (as am. S.C. 1986, c. 6, s. 110), s. 206(1).

SMALL CLAIMS COURT. 1. An inferior court with a limited jurisdiction over civil matters. 2. In Ontario, the Provincial Court (Civil Division). G.D. Watson & C. Perkins, eds., *Holmested & Watson: Ontario Civil Procedure* (Toronto: Carswell, 1984) at CJA-101.

SMALL GAME. Wildlife of a genus mentioned in Item 4 of Schedule A. (1) Erethizon—including porcupine; (2) Lepus—including hare; (3) Marmota—including marmots, wood chuck and ground hogs; (4) Spermophilus—including ground squirrels; (5) Tamiascurius—including red squirrels; (6) Upland game birds. *Wildlife Act*, S.N.W.T. 1978 (3d Sess.), c. 8, s. 2.

SMALL LOANS COMPANY. A company incorporated by special Act of Parliament and authorized to lend money on promissory notes or other personal security and on chattel mortgages. *Small Loans Act*, R.S.C. 1970, c. S-11, s. 2.

SMALL-MESH TRAWL NET. A trawl net having a cod end whose mesh size is less than 2 inches extension measure. *Ontario Fishery Regulations*, C.R.C., c. 849, s. 2.

SMALL MINE. (i) A mine which by normal continuous operations produces coal at a rate of less than 90 tonnes per day; or (ii) a mine designated as a small mine by the Board. Alberta statutes.

SMALL PACKET. All mailable matter weighing not more than 1 pound other than (a) printed papers described in item 1 of Schedule II in Column I thereof; and (b) parcel post as defined in paragraph 2(b) of the Fourth Class Mail Regulations, that does not require payment at the rate of postage for letters and is posted in Canada in accordance with these Regulations for delivery outside Canada. *Third Class Mail Regulations*, C.R.C., c. 1297, s. 2.

SMALL POWER. A load of less than 50 kilowatts. *Quebec Electricity Service By-law*, C.R.C., c. 1086, s. 2.

SMALL PROVINCE. A province (other than Quebec) having a population greater than its population determined according to the results of the penultimate decennial census and less than 1.5 million. *Constitution Act, 1974*, S.C. 1974-75-76, c. 13 reprinted as R.S.C. 1985, App. Document No. 40.

SMALL UNDERTAKING. (a) A person who provides a taxable service exclusively in a place to which admission is granted to persons for the purpose of the presentation to those persons of a programming service by means of telecommunication on payment of a charge or fee through the sale of a ticket or any similar means of admission; or (b) a person who, in any month, provides a taxable service to not more than 200 persons, but does not include a person who, in any month in the year preceding that month, has provided a taxable service to more than 200 persons. *Excise Tax Act*, R.S.C. 1985 (1st Supp.), c. 15, s. 21.1.

SMALL WATER-POWER. A water-power that, in the opinion of the Director, (a) cannot, under average usable flow conditions, produce in excess of 500 horsepower; and (b) is not of primary importance for commercial or public utility purposes. *Dominion Water Power Regulations*, C.R.C., c. 1603, s. 69.

SMALL WEED SEEDS. Weeds capable of passing through a round perforation having a diameter of 1.75 millimetres. *Feeds Regulations*, C.R.C., c. 665, s. 17.

SMALL WOOD. Wood casks or barrels of not greater than 150 gallon capacity. Canada regulations.

SM. & S. *abbr.* Smith & Sager's Drainage Cases (Ont.), 1904-1917.

SMELTER. See SECONDARY LEAD ~.

SMELTER RETURNS. See NET ~.

SMELTING. *n.* The chemical reduction of an ore or concentrate to the metallic state, and includes any process of roasting, melting or chemically treating an ore or concentrate to obtain from it a valuable constituent that is in chemical form different from the form of the valuable constituent in the ore or concentrate before it is processed.

SMOKE. *v.* To carry or consume a cigarette, cigar or other form of tobacco or other material while the cigarette, tobacco or such other material is burning. *Gasoline Licensing Act*, S.N.S. 1969, c. 47, s. 1.

SMOKE. *n.* Any solid, liquid, gas or combination thereof produced by the combustion of fuel and includes soot, ash and grit. *Air Pollution Regulations*, C.R.C., c. 1404, s. 2. See BLACK ~.

SMOKE DETECTOR. A device for sensing the presence of visible or invisible particles produced by combustion, and automatically initiating a signal indicating this condition. *Building Code Act*, R.R.O. 1980, Reg. 87, s. 1.

SMOKING. *n.* The fact of having lighted tobacco in one's possession.

SMOOTH. *adj.* Net-like, streaked, patchy or solid, readily apparent but smooth to touch. *Fresh Fruit and Vegetable Regulations*, C.R.C., c. 285, s. 13.

SMOTHERING. *n.* Suffocation caused by blocking the mouth and nostrils. F.A. Jaffe, *A Guide to Pathological Evidence*, 2d ed. (Toronto: Carswell, 1983) at 184.

SMUDGING. *n.* An area of blackening which powder gases produce around the wound where a bullet fired at close range entered. F.A. Jaffe,

A Guide to Pathological Evidence, 2d ed. (Toronto: Carswell, 1983) at 184.

SMUGGLING. *n.* The offence of exporting or importing forbidden or restricted goods, or of exporting or importing goods without paying any duties imposed on them.

SNAG. *n.* 1. A dead tree. *Forest Act*, R.S.B.C. 1979, c. 140, s. 108. 2. Any material or object that may interfere with the safe movement of a tree or log or that may endanger a person or any equipment. *Occupational Health and Safety Act*, R.R.O. 1980, Reg. 692, s. 107.

SNAGGER. *n.* An instrument made of a rigid or semi-rigid material with one or more hooks attached in such a manner that each is immovable and inflexible. *Ontario Fishery Regulations*, C.R.C., c. 849, s. 2.

SNAGGING. *n.* Fishing for or killing fish by means of a hook or hooks on any instrument manipulated in such a manner as to pierce or hook a fish elsewhere than in the mouth. *Fishery regulations.*

SNARE. *n.* 1. A device for the taking of animals whereby they are caught in a noose. 2. Any instrument used for taking or attempting to take fish, other than a trolling line, hook and line, hook and line and a rod, hook line, dip net, gill net, hoop net, minnow trap, pound net, seine net, spear, trap net or trawl net. *Ontario Fishery Regulations*, C.R.C., c. 849, s. 2.

SNOW CRAB. A decapod crustacean of the species Chionoeceted opilio. *Atlantic Crab Fishery Regulations*, C.R.C., c. 806, s. 6.

SNOW CRAB TRAP. A metal or wood framed enclosure covered with netting and with one or more openings. *Atlantic Crab Fishery Regulations*, C.R.C., c. 806, s. 6.

SNOWMOBILE. *n.* 1. A motor vehicle equipped with either a single or dual-tread and skis. 2. A vehicle that (i) is not equipped with wheels, but in place thereof is equipped with tractor treads alone or with tractor treads and skis, or with skis and a propeller, or is a toboggan equipped with tractor treads or a propeller; and (ii) is designed primarily for operating over snow, and is used exclusively for that purpose. See COMPETITION ~.

SNOWMOBILE CONVERSION VEHICLE. A vehicle designed to be capable of conversion to a snowmobile by the repositioning or addition of parts. *Motor Vehicle Safety Regulations*, C.R.C., c. 1038, s. 2.

SNOWMOBILE CUTTER. A sleigh designed to be drawn behind a snowmobile. *Motor Vehicle Safety Regulations*, C.R.C., c. 1038, s. 2.

SNOWMOBILE TRAILER. A trailer designed primarily for the transportation of snowmobiles or snowmobile cutters. *Motor Vehicle Safety Regulations*, C.R.C., c. 1038, s. 2.

SNOW VEHICLE. 1. A motor vehicle designed or intended to be driven exclusively or chiefly upon snow or ice or both, and includes motor vehicles known to the trade as snowmobiles. 2. A vehicle that (i) is not equipped with wheels, but in place thereof is equipped with tractor treads alone or with tractor treads with skis, or with skis and a propeller, or is a toboggan equipped with tractor treads or a propeller; (ii) is designed primarily for operating over snow, and is used exclusively for that purpose; and (iii) is designed to be self-propelled. *The Highway Traffic Act*, S.M. 1985-86, c. 3, s. 1. See MOTORIZED ~.

SOC. *abbr.* Society.

SOCAGE. *n.* A kind of tenure with certain temporal services which originally were agricultural. Common free socage is equivalent to freehold tenure.

SOCIAL ALLOWANCE. An allowance payable out of public funds to or in respect of any person sufficient to enable the person to obtain the basic necessities of himself and his dependants, if any, in accordance with this Act. *Social Development Act*, R.S.A. 1980, c. S-16, s. 1.

SOCIAL ASSET. An asset that is incidental and ancillary to mining and processing operations and that relates directly to the provision of housing, recreational and service facilities, provided that the asset, (i) is necessary to attract or retain employees; and (ii) is available for the use of all employees. *Mining Tax Act*, R.S.O. 1980, c. 269, s. 1.

SOCIAL ASSISTANCE. (i) Financial assistance; (ii) assistance in kind; (iii) institutional, nursing, boarding or foster home care; (iv) assistance to meet emergencies arising out of damage sustained through fire, storm, flood or other cause; (v) assistance towards repairs and renovations to homes, burial of needy persons, and transportation of indigent, sick, destitute or stranded persons; and (vi) any other form of assistance, whether of any of the foregoing kinds or not, necessary to relieve destitution and suffering or to rehabilitate a person.

SOCIAL CARE FACILITY. (i) A place of care for persons who are aged or infirm or who require special care; (ii) an institution or a shelter as defined in Part 2 of the Child Welfare Act; or (iii) a hostel or other establishment operated to provide accommodations and maintenance for unemployed or indigent persons. *Social Care*

Facilities Licensing Act, R.S.A. 1980, c. S-14, s. 1.

SOCIAL INSURANCE NUMBER. A Social Insurance Number assigned to an individual under the authority of any Act of Parliament. *Canada Pension Plan*, R.S.C. 1985, c. C-8, s. 2.

SOCIAL INSURANCE NUMBER CARD. A Social Insurance Number Card issued to an individual under the authority of any Act of Parliament. *Canada Pension Plan*, R.S.C. 1985, c. C-8, s. 2.

SOCIAL OCCASION. A social gathering at which food, suitable to the occasion and of such quantity and kind as is required by the commission, is served. *Liquor Control Act*, R.S.M. 1970, c. L160, s. 2.

SOCIAL SCIENCE BRIEF. A brief in which empirical data is appended to or included in the factum. P.W. Hogg, *Constitutional Law of Canada*, 2d ed. (Toronto: Carswell, 1985) at 182.

SOCIAL SCIENCES AND HUMANITIES RESEARCH COUNCIL OF CANADA. The federal body which promotes and assists scholarships and research in the humanities and social sciences.

SOCIAL SERVICE CENTRE. Facilities in which social action services are provided by receiving or visiting persons who require specialized social services for themselves or their families and by offering to persons facing social difficulties the aid necessary to assist them, especially by making available to them services for prevention, consultation, psycho-social or rehabilitation treatment, adoption and placement of children or aged persons, excluding a professional's private consulting office. *Health Services and Social Services Act*, R.S.Q. 1977, c. S-5, s. 1.

SOCIAL SERVICES. Services having as their objects the lessening, removal or prevention of the causes and effects of poverty, child neglect or dependence on social allowance or assistance, and, without limiting the generality of the foregoing, includes (i) rehabilitation services; (ii) case work, counselling; assessment and referral services; (iii) adoption services; (iv) homemaker, day care and similar services; (v) community development services; (vi) consulting, research and evaluation services with respect to social service programs; and (vii) administrative, secretarial and clerical services, including staff training, relating to the provision of any of the foregoing services or the provision of assistance. See COMMUNITY ~.

SOCIÉTÉ COMMERCIALE CANADIENNE. A phrase which forms part, other than simply in a descriptive or figurative sense, of the name of a corporation. H. Sutherland, D.B. Horsley & J.M. Edmiston, eds., *Fraser's Handbook on Canadian Company Law*, 7th ed. (Toronto: Carswell, 1985) at 436 and 437.

SOCIETY. *n.* 1. Includes a society or club that is incorporated by an act of a legislature and that has for its object the provision of facilities for the social intercourse and recreation of its members. 2. A religious society, organization or order or a charitable or philanthropic organization. *Training Schools Act*, R.S.O. 1980, c. 508, s. 1. See AGRICULTURAL ~; CHILDREN'S AID ~; CLASSIFICATION ~; EXTRAPRO-VINCIAL ~; FILM ~; FRATERNAL ~; FRIENDLY ~; LOAN ~; MUTUAL BENEFIT ~; NON-PROFIT ~; PERFORMING RIGHTS ~; RELIGIOUS ~.

SOCII MEI SOCIUS MEUS SOCIUS NON EST. [L.] A partner of my partner is not my partner.

SOCKET. *n.* A hole or part of a hole remaining after being loaded with explosives and the charge fired and which is known not to be a misfired hole, and includes so-called "bootlegs" and "old bottoms".

SOCKEYE SALMON. The species of fish known as Oncorhynchus nerka. *Pacific Salmon Fisheries Convention Act*, R.S.C. 1985, c. F-20, s. 2.

SODOMY. *n.* Anal intercourse.

SOFT DRINK. Aerated water to which an essence or syrup is added.

SOFT RECEIVERSHIP. Reviewing cash flow, assets and accounts payable and reporting so that the security holder may specify particular measures that should be taken to reduce the loan. F. Bennett, *Receiverships* (Toronto: Carswell, 1985) at 4.

SOFT-SHELLED CRAB. A snow crab that has no calcareous growths on the upper surface of the shell and the shell of which is easily bent by thumb pressure on the underside of the claw without breaking. *Atlantic Crab Fishery Regulations*, C.R.C., c. 806, s. 6.

SOFT TOY. Includes a stuffed toy, a pliable rubber toy and a pliable plastic toy. *Hazardous Products (Toys) Regulations*, C.R.C., c. 931, s. 2.

SOFTWARE. See COMPUTER ~; SYSTEMS ~.

SOIL. *n.* 1. That portion of the earth's crust which is fragmentary, or such that some individual particles of a dried sample may be readily separated by agitation in water; it includes boulders, cobbles, gravel, sand, silt, clay and organic matter. *Building Code Act*, R.R.O. 1980,

Reg. 87, s. 1. 2. Includes the entire mantle of unconsolidated material above bedrock other than minerals as defined in the Mineral Act or the Mining (Placer) Act. *Soil Conservation Act*, R.S.B.C. 1979, c. 391, s. 1. 3. Any land or underground space not submerged in water, excluding an area of land covered by a structure.

SOIL CONDITIONING. See ORGANIC ~.

SOIL MOVEMENT. Subsidence, expansion or lateral movement of the soil not caused by flood, earthquake, act of God or any other cause beyond the reasonable control of the builder. *Ontario New Home Warranties Plan Act*, R.R.O. 1980, Reg. 726, s. 1.

SOIL STACK. A stack that conveys the discharge of one or more sanitary units with or without the discharge from any other fixture. *Ontario Water Resources Act*, R.R.O. 1980, Reg. 736, s. 1.

SOIL SUPPLEMENT. (i) Any substance or mixture of substances other than a fertilizer, manufactured, sold or represented for use in promoting plant growth or the improvement of the chemical or physical condition of soils to aid growth or crop yields; and (ii) includes manipulated manures, sewage sludges, composts or soil conditioners; but (iii) does not include unmanipulated animal or vegetable manures, or potting soils or peat soils.

SOIT DROIT FAIT AL PARTIE. [Fr.] Let right be done to a party.

SOLATIUM. *n.* [L. solace] The amount paid to an injured party over and above the actual damage to assuage wounded feelings or for suffering or the loss of pleasure derived from the company of a deceased relative.

SOLDERED. *adj.* A uniting of metallic surfaces by the fusion thereon of a metallic alloy, usually of lead and tin. *Power Corporation Act*, R.R.O. 1980, Reg. 794, s. 0.

SOLDIER. *n.* Any person who served during World War I in (a) the Canadian Expeditionary Force; (b) any of the other military forces of His Majesty; or (c) the military forces of one of the countries allied with His Majesty during World War I if, in the case of a person who served in other than the Canadian Expeditionary Force, that person was born or domiciled in Canada or Newfoundland or was an ordinary resident in Canada or Newfoundland at anytime during the period between August 3, 1904 and the date on which he commenced so to serve. *Memorial Cross Order (World War I)*, C.R.C., c. 1622, s. 2.

SOLE. *adj.* Single; alone; not married. See CORPORATION ~; FEME ~.

SOLE CUSTODY. Custody of a child by one parent only under an agreement or order.

SOLEMN ADMISSION. A plea of guilty when one is arraigned in court. P.K. McWilliams, *Canadian Criminal Evidence*, 3d ed. (Aurora: Canada Law Book, 1988) at 14-7.

SOLEMN DECLARATION. A solemn declaration in the form and manner from time to time provided by the provincial evidence acts or by the Canada Evidence Act.

SOLEMNIZATION. *n.* Entering into marriage publicly before witnesses.

SOLE PROPRIETORSHIP. A business organization having one owner who must and does make all major decisions concerning the business. S.M. Beck *et al.*, *Cases and Materials on Partnerships and Canadian Business Corporations*, (Toronto: The Carswell Co., 1983) at 1.

SOLE RIGHTS. The right to produce or reproduce a work or a substantial part of it in any way whatever. H.G. Fox, *The Canadian Law of Copyright and Industrial Designs*, 2d ed. (Toronto: Carswell, 1967) at 326.

SOLE TENANT. One who holds land personally, without any other person.

SOLICIT. See SOLICITATION.

SOLICITATION. *n.* (a) A request for a proxy whether or not it is accompanied by or included in a form of proxy; (b) a request to execute or not to execute a form of proxy or to revoke a proxy; (c) the sending of a form of proxy or other communication to a security holder under circumstances reasonably calculated to result in the procurement, withholding or revocation of a proxy of that security holder; or (d) the sending, along with a notice of a meeting, of a form of proxy to a security holder by management of a reporting issuer, but does not include (e) the sending of a form of proxy to a security holder in response to an unsolicited request made by the security holder or on that person's behalf; or (f) the performance by any person of ministerial acts or professional services on behalf of a person soliciting a proxy.

SOLICITATION BY OR ON BEHALF OF THE MANAGEMENT OF A BANK. A solicitation by any person pursuant to a resolution or instructions of, or with the acquiescence of, the directors or a committee of the directors of the bank. *Bank Act*, R.S.C. 1985, c. B-1, s. 160.

SOLICITATION BY OR ON BEHALF OF THE MANAGEMENT OF A CORPORATION. A solicitation by any person pursuant to a resolution or instructions of, or with the acquiescence of, the directors or a committee of the directors.

SOLICITATION OF DEPOSITS. An advertisement calculated directly or indirectly to lead to or induce the deposit of money or the investment of money on deposit by members of the public. Deposits Regulation acts.

SOLICITING. *n.* Accosting in a persistent manner for purposes of prostitution.

SOLICITOR. *n.* 1. In the Province of Quebec, an advocate or a notary and, in any other province, a barrister or solicitor. *Criminal Code*, R.S.C. 1985, c. C-46, s. 183. 2. A person who is, by virtue of section 11 of the Act, an officer of the Court. *Federal Court Rules*, C.R.C., c. 663, s. 2. See BARRISTER AND ~; CHANGE OF ~.

SOLICITOR-AND-CLIENT COSTS. Costs which a client pays to a solicitor for services rendered. M.M. Orkin, *The Law of Costs*, 2d ed. (Aurora: Canada Law Book, 1987) at 2-1.

SOLICITOR-CLIENT PRIVILEGE. The right, if any, that a person has in a superior court in the province where the matter arises to refuse to disclose an oral or documentary communication on the ground that the communication is one passing between him and his lawyer in professional confidence, except that in certain cases an accounting record of a lawyer, including any supporting voucher or cheque, shall be deemed not to be such a communication. Income Tax acts.

SOLICITOR GENERAL CANADA. The federal ministry which controls penitentiaries, paroles and remissions and law enforcement and supervises the National Parole Board, the Correctional Service and the RCMP.

SOLICITOR OF RECORD. The lawyer who acts for the client until, (a) the client delivers a notice according to rule 15.03; or (b) an order is made to remove the solicitor from the record. G.D. Watson & C. Perkins, eds., *Holmested & Watson: Ontario Civil Procedure* (Toronto: Carswell, 1984) at 15-4.

SOLICITOR'S J. *abbr.* Solicitor's Journal (Le Bulletin des avocats).

SOLID PACK. A pack in which the fruit or vegetable has been partially or wholly precooked before processing so as to allow the product to pack closely with the minimum amount of free liquid. *Processed Fruit and Vegetable Regulations*, C.R.C., c. 291, s. 2.

SOLID RUBBER TIRE. A tire made of rubber other than a pneumatic tire.

SOLIDS. *n.* A commodity other than oil or gas, and shall include water where used as a medium of transporting solids. *Pipeline Act*, R.S.B.C. 1979, c. 328, s. 1. See MILK ~.

SOLIDS LINE. A pipe for the transmission of a normally solid material whether in suspension or other form and includes installation in connection with that pipe, but does not include a gas line, oil line, fluids line, multiphase line, secondary line, flow line, distribution line or sewer line. *Pipeline Act*, R.S.A. 1980, c. P-8, s. 1.

SOLID TIRE. Every tire of rubber or other resilient material that does not depend upon compressed air for the support of the load. *Motor Vehicle Act*, R.S.N.B. 1973, c. M-17, s. 1.

SOLID WASTE. Waste with insufficient liquid content to be free-flowing. *An Act to Amend the Clean Environment Act*, S.N.B. 1985, c. 6, s. 1.

SOLITARY CONFINEMENT. Individual confinement separate from other prisoners, usually an additional punishment or for the protection of the individual or the prison population as a whole.

SOLUM. *n.* The soil or land lying under tidal water and extending seaward from mean high water mark and includes the foreshore.

SOLUS AGREEMENT. An agreement that one will obtain supplies from one supplier only.

SOLUTIO PRETII EMPTIONIS LOCO HABETUR. [L.] The payment of the price takes the place of purchase.

SOLVENDO ESSE. [L.] To be solvent.

SOLVENT. *adj.* Having the ability to pay debts as they become due.

SOLVERE POENAS. [L.] To be subject to the punishment specified for an offence.

SOLVIT AD DIEM. [L.] In an action on a bill or bond, a plea that the defendant paid money on the day it was due.

SOLVIT ANTE DIEM. [L.] In an action on a bill or bond, a plea that the defendant paid money before the day it was due.

SOLVIT POST DIEM. [L.] In an action on a bill or bond, a plea that the defendant paid money after the day it was due.

SOLVITUR IN MODUM SOLVENTIS. [L.] Money should be applied the way the payor wishes.

SOMATIC. *adj.* Organic, physical. K.D. Cooper-Stephenson & I.B. Saunders, *Personal Injury Damages in Canada* (Toronto: Carswell, 1981) at 555.

SOMATIC DEATH. The first stage of death in which the respiratory, circulatory and nervous systems stop functioning and the body is no longer an integrated organism. F.A. Jaffe, *A Guide to Pathological Evidence*, 2d ed. (Toronto: Carswell, 1983) at 2.

SON. *n.* A male who is (a) the issue of lawful wedlock and who would possess the status of legitimacy if his father had been domiciled in a province of Canada at the time of his birth; (b) the issue of a woman who (i) has been admitted to Canada for permanent residence; or (ii) is admissible to Canada as an immigrant and accompanies the said issue to Canada for permanent residence; or (c) adopted. *Immigration Regulations*, C.R.C., c. 940, s. 2.

SON AND DAUGHTER. Includes a grandchild, step-child, foster child, and adopted child, except where in the opinion of the judge any such child does not owe to the dependent parent an obligation of gratitude for nurture, care, or affection. *Maintenance Act*, R.S.Nfld. 1970, c. 223, s. 2.

SONG BIRD. Canary, finch, oriole, cardinal and any other songster. *Animal Disease and Protection Regulations*, C.R.C., c. 296, s. 2.

SONIC FLIGHT. Flight at the speed of a true flight Mach number of one. *Sonic and Supersonic Flight Order*, C.R.C., c. 64, s. 2.

SOUND. *v.* To have the basic quality of damages, said of actions brought to recover damages.

SOUND. *n.* See DOCUMENT OF RECORDED ~.

SOUND. *adj.* 1. That, at the time of packing, loading or final shipping point inspection, the fruit is free from condition defects such as decay, breakdown, freezing injury, bitter pit, soft or shrivelled specimens, overripe specimens, brown core, corky core or other injury affecting its keeping quality. *Fresh Fruit and Vegetable Regulations*, C.R.C., c. 285, s. 1. 2. That at the time of packing, loading or final shipping point inspection vegetables are free from decay, breakdown, freezing injury, soft or shrivelled specimens, overripe specimens or other injury affecting their keeping quality. *Fresh Fruit and Vegetable Regulations*, C.R.C., c. 285, s. 1. See ACTUARIALLY ~.

SOUND FILM SUBJECT. A subject adapted for the reproduction of synchronized dialogue, music or any other sound effects. *Theatres Act*, R.R.O. 1980, Reg. 931, s. 1.

SOUND IN DAMAGES. See SOUND.

SOUND LEVEL. The intensity of sound expressed in decibels. *Canada Noise Control Regulations*, C.R.C., c. 1006, s. 2.

SOUND LEVEL METER. An instrument for measuring sound levels that complies with the

American National Standards Institute Standard S1.4-1961, as amended from time to time. *Canada Noise Control Regulations*, C.R.C., c. 1006, s. 2.

SOUND PRESSURE. See SATURATION ~.

SOUND RECORDING APPARATUS. Any device, machine or system of a type approved by the Commissioner for the making of a record of voice or other sound. *Recording of Evidence by Sound Apparatus Act*, R.S.N.W.T. 1974, c. R-2, s. 2.

SOUND RECORDING MACHINE. *var.* **SOUND-RECORDING MACHINE.** A device, machine or system that faithfully records speech or other sounds in some permanent form.

SOUP. *n.* A solution of narcotic ready to be injected. F.A. Jaffe, *A Guide to Pathological Evidence*, 2d ed. (Toronto: Carswell, 1983) at 184.

SOURCE. See GAS ~; HEAT ~; INDUSTRIAL ~; RADIATION ~; REVENUE ~; STATIONARY ~; X-RAY ~.

SOURCE OF CONTAMINANT. Anything that adds to, emits or discharges into the natural environment any contaminant.

SOURCE OF CONTAMINATION. Any activity or condition causing the emission of a contaminant into the environment. *Environment Quality Act*, R.S.Q. 1977, c. Q-2, s. 1.

SOURCE OF PROTEIN. Any food that contains protein, but does not include spices, seasonings, flavours, artificial flavours, flavour enhancers, food additives and similar foods that contain only small amounts of protein. *Food and Drug Regulations*, C.R.C., c. 870, c. B.01.101.

SOUR ROT. A condition in which the egg shows a bubbly condition at the air cell line and an extremely prominent yolk. *Live Stock and Live Stock Products Act*, R.R.O. 1980, Reg. 582, s. 1.

SOUVENIRS. *n.* Lapel buttons, billfolds, keycases, pens, pencils, corsages and similar items. *Foreign Organizations Remission Order*, C.R.C., c. 766, s. 2.

SOVEREIGN. *n.* 1. Any supreme or chief person. 2. The Sovereign of the United Kingdom, Canada and Her other realms and territories and head of the Commonwealth. See ACCESSION OF THE ~.

SOVEREIGN GOVERNMENT. Includes the Government of Canada, the government of each of the provinces and territories of Canada, and the government of every foreign country or state. *Intergovernmental Affairs Act*, S.Nfld. 1975, c. 10, s. 2.

SOVEREIGN IMMUNITY. Canadian courts will not exercise jurisdiction over the property or person of an independent foreign state or sovereign without consent. Any such proceedings may be stayed if the state or sovereign moves to set the proceedings aside or remains passive. A foreign state includes any state which the forum recognizes, de facto or de jure. J.G. McLeod, *The Conflict of Laws* (Calgary: Carswell, 1983) at 68.

SOVEREIGN POWER. The power in a state which is supreme.

SOVEREIGNTY-ASSOCIATION. *n.* A compromise proposed in Quebec between outright separation and continuance as a province of Canada. Although it involved the secession of Quebec (sovereignty), it also involved economic association between Quebec and the rest of Canada (association). P.W. Hogg, *Constitutional Law of Canada*, 2d ed. (Toronto: Carswell, 1985) at 101 and 102.

SOW. *n.* A sow that is part of a producer's breeding herd that (i) is pregnant and has previously produced a litter of pigs; or (ii) has farrowed within 3 months of the time its status as a sow for the purposes of this plan is at issue. *Farm Income Stabilization Act*, R.R.O. 1980, Reg. 322, s. 2.

S.P. *abbr.* Sessions of the Peace.

SPACE. *n.* A plot of land within a tourist camp, trailer camp or mobile home park designated to accommodate, or accommodating, one camping facility, trailer or mobile home, as the case may be. *Municipalities Act*, R.S.N.B. 1973, c. M-22, s. 188. See ACCOMMODATION ~; ANNULAR ~; CONFINED ~; FLOOR ~; HEAD ~; HORIZONTAL SERVICE ~; LOADING ~; MACHINERY ~; MOBILE HOME ~; OCCUPANT ~; PARKING ~; PASSENGER ~; RETAIL ~; ROOF ~; SERVICE ~; SHELTER DECK ~; TOILET ~; TWEEN DECK ~.

SPACE FRAME. A three-dimensional structural system composed of inter-connected members laterally supported so as to function as a complete self-contained unit with or without horizontal diaphragms. *Building Code Act*, R.R.O. 1980, Reg. 87, s. 1. See DUCTILE MOMENT-RESISTING ~.

SPACE HEATER. A space-heating appliance for heating the room or space within which it is located, without the use of ducts. *Building Code Act*, R.R.O. 1980, Reg. 87, s. 1.

SPACE-HEATING APPLIANCE. An appliance intended for the supplying of heat to a room or space directly, such as a space heater, fireplace or unit heater, or to rooms or spaces of a building through a heating system such as a central furnace or boiler. *Building Code Act*, R.R.O. 1980, Reg. 87, s. 1.

SPACE SERVICE. A radiocommunications service provided by earth stations or space stations for communication (a) between earth stations and space stations; (b) between space stations; or (c) between earth stations when the signals are retransmitted by space stations or are transmitted by reflection from objects in space excluding reflection or scattering by the ionosphere or within the earth's atmosphere. *General Radio Regulations, Part II*, C.R.C., c. 1372, s. 2.

SPACE STATION. A station operated in a space service and located on an object which is beyond, is intended to go beyond or has been beyond the major portion of the earth's atmosphere. *General Radio Regulations, Part II*, C.R.C., c. 1372, s. 2.

SPACING AREA. The drainage area required for or allocated to a well for drilling for and producing petroleum or natural gas, and includes at all depths the subsurface areas bounded by the vertical planes in which the surface boundaries lie.

SPACING UNIT. The area allocated to a well for the purpose of drilling for or producing oil or gas. See POOLED ~; PRODUCTION ~.

SPARKING. See OPEN ~.

SPARSIM. *adv.* [L.] Here and there.

SPEAKER. *n.* 1. With repect to the House of Commons, the representative of the House itself in power, proceedings and dignity; the representative of the House in relation to the Crown, the Senate and other people and authorities outside Parliament; the person who presides over debates and enforces observance of any rule for preserving order. This person is elected by the House itself and, on behalf of the House, controls the accommodation and services in the part of the Parliament Buildings and its precincts which the House of Commons occupies. A. Fraser, G.A. Birch & W.A. Dawson, eds., *Beauchesne's Rules and Forms of the House of Commons of Canada*, 5th ed. (Toronto: Carswell, 1978) at 31, 36 and 37. 2. The speaker of the House of Commons, and, when the office of Speaker is vacant, or when the Speaker is absent from Canada or is unable to act, means the Clerk of the House of Commons or any other officer for the time being performing the duties of the Clerk of the House of Commons. *Dominion Controverted Election Act*, R.S.C. 1985, c. C-39, s. 2. 3. The Speaker of the House of Assembly. 4. The Speaker of the Legislative Assembly. 5. The Speaker of the assembly; and when the office of Speaker is vacant or when the Speaker is absent from the province, or is unable to act,

the clerk of the assembly, or any other officer for the time being discharging the duties of the clerk of the assembly. See DEPUTY ~.

SPEAKER'S RULING. Once given, a ruling which belongs to the House and must be accepted without appeal or debate. It becomes a precedent and becomes part of the rules of procedure. The Speaker does not have the power to alter it personally. A. Fraser, G.A. Birch & W.A. Dawson, eds., *Beauchesne's Rules and Forms of the House of Commons of Canada*, 5th ed. (Toronto: Carswell, 1978) at 39.

SPEAR. *n.* 1. A lance with barbed or unbarbed prongs that is held or thrown by hand, but does not include a spear gun. *Ontario Fishery Regulations*, C.R.C., c. 849, s. 2. 2. An apparatus equipped with one or more points that is capable of catching fish by piercing or impaling them. *Quebec Fishery Regulations*, C.R.C., c. 852, s. 2.

SPEAR FISHING. Fishing with a spear propelled by spring, elastic band, compressed air, bow, or hand.

SPECIAL ACT. A local, personal or private act; an act which applies to a certain kind of person or thing only.

SPECIAL AGENT. One authorized to transact only a particular business for the principal, as opposed to a general agent.

SPECIAL AGRICULTURAL DEVELOPMENT. A class of development whereby land, buildings or structures are used for the purpose of intensive livestock, poultry, cattle or other farm operations and includes use as a piggery; a turkey, a game bird or chicken farm or hatchery; a fur farm, a mushroom farm, an animal kennel and a feed lot area or manure storage area. *Niagara Escarpment Planning and Development Act*, R.R.O. 1980, Reg. 685, s. 1.

SPECIAL ALLOWANCE. An amount payable in respect of a child pursuant to section 9. *Family Allowance Act*, R.S.C. 1985, c. F-1, s. 2.

SPECIAL ASSESSMENT. A special frontage assessment or a special local benefit assessment relating to local improvements and includes a special assessment when calculated on a uniform unit rate. *Municipal Taxation Act*, R.S.A. 1980, c. M-31, s. 1.

SPECIAL AUTHORIZATION. A special authorization granted for a limited period under this Code to a person who does not hold a permit, to allow him the exclusive practice of the profession mentioned therein and the use of a title reserved to the professionals practising such profession or to allow him only the use of a title reserved to the members of the corporation granting this authorization. *Professional Code*, R.S.Q. 1977, c. C-26, s. 1.

SPECIAL AVIATION EVENT. An air show, a low-level air race or a fly-in. *Special Aviation Events Safety Order*, C.R.C., c. 66, s. 2.

SPECIAL BENEFIT. Any additional work or feature included in the construction, repair or improvement of a drainage works that has no effect on the functioning of the drainage works. *Drainage Act*, R.S.O. 1980, c. 126, s. 1.

SPECIAL BINNING. The storing of a parcel or parcels of grain pursuant to a contract, in space in an elevator that is specified in the contract, for the purpose of preserving the identity of the grain. *Canada Grain Act*, R.S.C. 1985, c. G-10, s. 2.

SPECIAL BROKER. A person who procures for others policies of insurance from insurers not licensed to carry on business in the province. *Insurance Corporations Tax Act*, R.S.M. 1970, c. I50, s. 2.

SPECIAL BY-LAW. 1. A by-law that is not effective until it is, (i) passed by the board; and (ii) confirmed, with or without variation, by owners who own not less than two-thirds of the units at a meeting duly called for that purpose. *Condominium Act*, R.S.O. 1980, c. 84, s. 1. 2. A by-law that is not effective until it is, (i) passed by the directors of a corporation; and (ii) confirmed, with or without variation, by at least two-thirds of the votes cast at a general meeting of the shareholders of the corporation duly called for that purpose, or such greater proportion of the votes cast as the articles provide, or, in lieu of such confirmation, by the consent in writing of all the shareholders entitled to vote at such meeting or their attorney authorized in writing. *Business Corporations Act*, R.S.O. 1980, c. 54, s. 1.

SPECIAL CARE. Care provided to a dependant of an applicant or recipient in a residential welfare institution that has been approved by the minister, or in a day nursery that has been approved by the minister, or care approved by the director and provided to a dependant by a nurse, housekeeper, or homemaker in the home of the applicant or recipient or in a foster home. *Social Allowances Act*, S.M. 1973, c. 32, s. 1. See HOME FOR ~; HOMES FOR ~.

SPECIAL CARE EXPENDITURES. Those expenditures incurred with respect to physical, emotional, developmental and educational needs of residents including professional services and non-recurring costs, but does not include basic care expenditures. *Children's Residential Services Act*, R.R.O. 1980, Reg. 101, s. 23.

SPECIAL CARE HOME. *var.* **SPECIAL-CARE HOME.** 1. A nursing home, supervisory-care home, sheltered-care home or other facility used, whether for profit or not, for the purpose of providing supervisory care, personal care and nursing care, or any of them, for persons who: (i) are not related by blood or marriage to the person conducting or operating the home or other facility; and (ii) in the case of a corporation, are not members of the management of the home or other facility; and by reason of need, age, infirmity or blindness are unable to fully care for themselves. *The Housing and Special-care Homes Act*, R.S.S. 1978, c. H-13, s. 2. 2. A residential facility or portion thereof, other than a facility requiring a licence or licensed under a Health Act, a Hospital Services Act or a Public Hospitals Act, for the care and accommodation of three or more persons presenting evidence of physical or mental handicap.

SPECIAL CASE. The statement of a question of law for the opinion of the court by all parties to a proceeding, and which any party moves that the judge determine. G.D. Watson & C. Perkins, eds., *Holmested & Watson: Ontario Civil Procedure* (Toronto: Carswell, 1984) at 22-3.

SPECIAL COMMITTEE. A body the House appoints to inquire into a specified subject. A. Fraser, G.A. Birch & W.A. Dawson, eds., *Beauchesne's Rules and Forms of the House of Commons of Canada*, 5th ed. (Toronto: Carswell, 1978) at 189.

SPECIAL CONSTABLE. A person specially engaged and employed by the Royal Canadian Mounted Police under the authority of the Governor in Council for the particular duty of mounting guard at vulnerable points throughout Canada or for any other similar duty during the War. *Civilian War Pensions and Allowances Act*, R.S.C. 1985, c. C-31, s. 22.

SPECIAL DAMAGE. 1. Pecuniary loss before the trial. K.D. Cooper-Stephenson & I.B. Saunders, *Personal Injury Damages in Canada* (Toronto: Carswell, 1981) at 29 and 43. 2. Loss of earnings or profits before a trial and pre-trial expenses. K.D. Cooper-Stephenson & I.B. Saunders, *Personal Injury Damages in Canada* (Toronto: Carswell, 1981) at 51.

SPECIAL EDUCATION PROGRAM. An education program that is based on the results of continuous assessment and evaluation and which includes a plan containing specific objectives and recommendations for education services that meet the needs of the exceptional pupil.

SPECIAL EDUCATION SERVICES. Facilities and resources, including support personnel and equipment, necessary for developing and implementing a special education program. *Education Act*, R.S.O. 1980, c. 129, s. 1.

SPECIAL ENUMERATION. An enumeration of electors within an electoral division other than as part of a general enumeration. *Election Act*, R.S.A. 1980, c. E-2, s. 1.

SPECIAL EXAMINATION. Examinations at university standards in subjects pertaining to substantive law in force in the jurisdiction. Legal Profession acts.

SPECIAL EXAMINER. 1. An official examiner. 2. A special examiner under this Act. *Collection Act*, R.S.N.S. 1967, c. 39, s. 1.

SPECIAL FEATURE. A feature film constituting a whole program, or a number of films used in the same program, whether owned by a film exchange or any other person, firm or corporation, with which the owner or his agent travels from place to place for the purpose of leasing the film or films to others, or exhibiting them himself when he holds an operator's licence, or exhibiting them in the hands of a duly qualified and licensed operator. *The Theatres and Cinematographs Act*, R.S.S. 1978, c. T-11, s. 2.

SPECIAL FLOOD HAZARD AREA. An area designated by regulation as a special flood hazard area because of severe or frequent floods in the area. *The Water Resources Management Act*, R.S.S. 1978, c. W-7, s. 2.

SPECIAL FORCE. 1. Such component of the Canadian Forces as may be established pursuant to subsection 16(1). *National Defence Act*, R.S.C. 1985, c. N-5, s. 2. 2. The Royal Canadian Navy Special Force, the Canadian Army Special Force and the Royal Canadian Air Force Special Force, as constituted from time to time by the Minister of National Defence. *Veterans Treatment Regulations*, C.R.C., c. 1585, s. 2.

SPECIAL FOREST PRODUCTS. Poles, posts, pilings, shakes, shingle bolts, Christmas trees and other similar forest products designated by regulation as special forest products. *Forest Act*, R.S.B.C. 1979, c. 140, s. 1.

SPECIAL FRANCHISE. Every right, authority or permission, whether exclusive or otherwise, to construct, maintain or operate, within a municipality, in, under, above, on, through, or across any highway, road, street, lane, public place or public water within the jurisdiction of the municipality any poles, wires, pipes, tracks, conduits, buildings, erections, structures or other things for the purpose of bridges, railways, bus lines or other transportation systems or for the purpose of conducting steam, heat, water, natural gas or electricity or any property, substance or product capable of being transported, transmitted or conveyed for the supply of water, heat,

light, power, transportation, telegraphic, telephonic or other services.

SPECIAL FUND. 1. A fund set up for a specified purpose and accounted for in a self-balancing financial statement. *Corporations and Labour Unions Returns Act*, R.S.C. 1985, c. C-43, s. 12(4). 2. Money received or held by or on behalf of Her Majesty in right of the Province in trust for or on account of any person or in trust for or on account of any special purpose and includes the Public Service Superannuation Fund, the Nova Scotia Teachers' Pension Fund, Sinking Funds, Public Debt Retirement Fund, together with the income earned on the investment of such funds, and includes any other fund or money which the Governor in Council from time to time designates as a special fund. *Provincial Finance Act*, R.S.N.S. 1967, c. 242, s. 1. 3. Special levy funds and investments that a company has or is entitled to receive on the day on which this Act comes into force, the proceeds of the sale of any capital asset, the amount of a grant from the department for the purpose of assisting the company to purchase poles or other equipment, the proceeds of short-term loans obtained or debentures sold under this Act and all actual construction charges, service connection charges, construction levies, special levies, surcharges and any amounts received on account thereof. *The Rural Telephone Act*, R.S.S. 1978, c. R-27, s. 2.

SPECIAL HOLIDAY. A day for which an employee is entitled under any act, under any custom or agreement or under a contract of service to be paid wages without being present at work.

SPECIALIA GENERALIBUS DEROGANT. [L.] Special words restrict general ones.

SPECIALIST. *n.* 1. A physician listed by the Royal College of Physicians and Surgeons of Canada as having specialist qualifications. 2. A dentist whose name is entered in the specialists register. 3. A certified general accountant whose name is entered in the specialists register and who is the holder of a specialists licence issued pursuant to this Act, the bylaws or rules. *Certified General Accountants Act*, S.N.B. 1986, c. 86, s. 2.

SPECIALIZATION AGREEMENT. An agreement under which each party thereto agrees to discontinue producing an article or service that he is engaged in producing at the time the agreement is entered into on the condition that each other party to the agreement agrees to discontinue producing an article or service that he is engaged in producing at the time the agreement is entered into, and includes any such agreement under which the parties also agree to buy exclusively from each other the articles or services that are the subject of the agreement. *Combines Investigation Act*, R.S.C. 1985 (2d Supp.), c. 19, s. 85.

SPECIALIZED AGRICULTURAL ASSOCIA-TION. An organization of local, district or provincial scope devoted to the improvement and promotion, by education, demonstration or other non-commercial means, of one particular breed or kind of livestock or any other one special phase of agriculture. *Agricultural Associations Act*, R.S.N.B. 1973, c. A-5, s. 1.

SPECIALIZED AGRICULTURAL OPERA-TION. An agricultural operation, other than a specialized livestock enterprise or specialized horticultural operation, by a company, co-operative association or partnership or by an individual, in which the majority of the investment in fixed assets, exclusive of land, consists of buildings, machinery, apparatus, equipment and vehicles. *The Industrial Development Act*, R.S.S. 1978, c. I-4, s. 2.

SPECIALIZED FEDERATION. A federation consisting exclusively of specialized syndicates. *Farm Producers Act*, R.S.Q. 1977, c. P-28, s. 1.

SPECIALIZED HORTICULTURAL OPERA-TION. A horticultural operation, other than a specialized agricultural operation, by a company, co-operative association or partnership or by an individual, in which the majority of the investment in fixed assets, exclusive of land, consists of buildings, machinery, apparatus, equipment and vehicles. *The Industrial Development Act*, R.S.S. 1978, c. I-4, s. 2.

SPECIALIZED LIVESTOCK ENTERPRISE. The raising or feeding of livestock by a company, co-operative association or partnership or by an individual, in which the majority of the investment in fixed assets, exclusive of land, consists of buildings, machinery, apparatus, equipment and vehicles. *The Industrial Development Act*, R.S.S. 1978, c. I-4, s. 2.

SPECIALIZED PROCESSING PLANT. A business (i) that slaughters animals and processes the carcasses for the use of owners of home freezers; or (ii) that obtains slaughtered animals and processes the carcasses for the use of owners of home freezers. *Frozen Food Act*, R.S.A. 1970, c. 150, s. 2.

SPECIALIZED SYNDICATE. A syndicate constituted under the Professional Syndicates Act, whose members are producers and whose object is the study, defence and promotion of the economic, social and moral interests of the producers principally as regards special farm production or a special phase in such producers'

activities. *Farm Producers Act*, R.S.Q. 1977, c. P-28, s. 1.

SPECIAL LEVY. A levy against farm lands for telephone purposes pursuant to section 44. *The Rural Telephone Act*, R.S.S. 1978, c. R-27, s. 2.

SPECIAL LIMITED COMPANY. A company limited by shares, the memorandum of which provides that no member is to be personally liable for the amount, if any, unpaid on his shares. *Companies Act*, R.S.A. 1970, c. 60, s. 2.

SPECIALLY ASSESSED. Specially charged with part or all of the cost of a work. Local Improvements acts.

SPECIALLY CONSTRUCTED VEHICLE. A vehicle which was not originally constructed under a distinctive name, make, model or type by a generally recognized manufacturer of vehicles.

SPECIALLY DENATURED ALCOHOL. Alcohol in suitable admixture with such special denaturants as have been approved by the Minister. *Excise Act*, R.S.C. 1985, c. E-14, s. 243.

SPECIALLY LIMITED COMPANY. A company limited by shares, the memorandum of which provides that no member is to be personally liable for the amount, if any, unpaid on his shares. *Companies Act*, R.S.A. 1980, c. C-20, s. 1.

SPECIAL MOBILE EQUIPMENT. Every vehicle not designed or used primarily for the transportation of persons or property and incidentally operated or moved over any highway, including road construction or maintenance machinery, ditch digging apparatus, well-boring apparatus, concrete mixers and any other vehicle of the same general class.

SPECIAL MOBILE MACHINE. A vehicle: (i) that is not designed or used for the transportation of passengers or goods and that only uses a highway incidentally to its basic purposes; (ii) that is designed and used exclusively for moving earth or construction materials on locations off highways or for general construction or industrial purposes and that only uses a highway incidentally to its basic purposes; or (iii) used for the purpose of highway construction and maintenance; but does not include a dumptruck or a truck mounted transit mixer or any other similar mounted machine.

SPECIAL NEED. A need that is related to or caused by a behavioural, developmental, emotional, physical, mental or other handicap. *Child and Family Services Act*, S.O. 1984, c. 55, s. 26.

SPECIAL ORDER. An order which has effect for a single occasion only or for a specified longer term; this term customarily applied to any rule which has only temporary effect. A. Fraser, G.A. Birch & W.A. Dawson, eds., *Beauchesne's Rules and Forms of the House of Commons of Canada*, 5th ed. (Toronto: Carswell, 1978) at 5. See STANDING, SESSIONAL AND ~S.

SPECIAL PASSENGER TRADE. A trade in relation to which the Governor in Council has modified the construction regulations or the rules for life-saving appliances in pursuance of this Act. *Canada Shipping Act*, R.S.C. 1985, c. S-9, s. 2.

SPECIAL POWER. The power to appoint from a limited class only, e.g from among the children of the donee of the power.

SPECIAL PROJECT. An undertaking for the construction of works designed to develop a natural resource or establish a primary industry that is planned to require a construction period exceeding 3 years, and includes all ancillary work, services and catering relating to any such undertaking or project. *Labour Relations Act*, S.Nfld. 1977, c. 64, s. 2.

SPECIAL PROPERTY. Limited or qualified property.

SPECIAL PROTHONOTARY. The prothonotary or the deputy prothonotary appointed by order in council, with the consent of the chief justice of the court, to exercise, in addition to his other functions, the attributions attached to such capacity. *Code of Civil Procedure*, R.S.Q. 1977, c. C-25, s. 4.

SPECIAL PROXY CERTIFICATE. The certificate prescribed by the Chief Electoral Officer entitling the next of kin of a prisoner of war to vote by proxy on behalf of the prisoner of war. *Canada Elections Act*, R.S.C. 1970 (1st Supp.) c. 14, Schedule IV, s. 2.

SPECIAL PURPOSE. See MONEY PAID TO CANADA FOR A ~; MONEY PAID TO THE PROVINCE FOR A ~; MONEY PAID TO THE TERRITORIES FOR A ~.

SPECIAL PURPOSE FUND. All money that is paid to a public officer under or pursuant to an Ordinance, trust, undertaking or contract to be disbursed for a purpose specified in or pursuant to such Ordinance, trust, undertaking or contract. *Financial Administration Act*, S.N.W.T. 1982, c. 2, s. 2.

SPECIAL PURPOSE OPERATION. An operation in which an aircraft is flown for the purpose of spraying, dusting, seeding, or pipeline or powerline patrolling, and includes any other operation of a similar nature. *Aircraft Seats, Safety Belts, and Safety Harnesses Order*, C.R.C., c. 28, s. 2.

SPECIAL REGIONAL LEVY. An amount apportioned by a regional municipality to one or more area municipalities that is not included in the net regional levy and excludes amounts required for school purposes. *Ontario Unconditional Grants Act*, R.S.O. 1980, c. 359, s. 7.

SPECIAL RESOLUTION. 1. A resolution passed by a majority of not less than 2/3 of the votes cast by the shareholders who voted in respect of that resolution or signed by all the shareholders entitled to vote on that resolution. 2. A resolution decided by a majority in number and 3/4 in value of the creditors with proven claims present, personally or by proxy, at a meeting of creditors and voting on the resolution. *Bankruptcy Act*, R.S.C. 1985, c. B-3, s. 2. 3. (i) A resolution passed (A) at a general meeting of which not less than 21 days' notice specifying the intention to propose the resolution has been duly given, and (B) by a majority of not less than 75 per cent of the votes of those members who, if entitled to do so, vote in person or by proxy; (ii) a resolution proposed and passed as a special resolution at a general meeting of which less than 21 days' notice has been given, if all members entitled to attend and vote at that general meeting so agree; or (iii) a resolution consented to in writing by all the members who would have been entitled at a general meeting to vote on the resolution in person or, if proxies are permitted, by proxy.

SPECIAL RETURNING OFFICER. A person appointed by the Governor in Council, pursuant to section 6. *Special Voting Rules*, R.S.C. 1985, c. E-2, Schedule II, s. 2.

SPECIAL RIGHTS OR RESTRICTIONS. Includes special rights and restrictions, whether preferred, deferred or otherwise, and whether in regard to redemption or return of capital, conversion into or exchange for the same or any other number of any other kind, class, or series of shares, dividend, voting, nomination or appointment of directors or other control. *Company Act*, R.S.B.C. 1979, c. 59, s. 1.

SPECIAL SESSION. A session of the Legislature for which members were paid indemnities less than the annual indemnity for which provision was made at the time of that session. *Legislative Assembly Act*, S.M. 1980, c. 39, s. 9.

SPECIAL SHARE. Any share other than a common share. S.M. Beck *et al.*, *Cases and Materials on Partnerships and Canadian Business Corporations*, (Toronto: The Carswell Co., 1983) at 785.

SPECIALTY. *n.* A contract under seal.

SPECIALTY CONTRACT. A contract under seal.

SPECIALTY DEBT. A bond, mortgage or debt which one secures by writing under seal.

SPECIALTY FERTILIZER. A fertilizer recommended for use on household plants, urban gardens, lawns or golf courses and not represented for farm use. *Fertilizers Regulations*, C.R.C., c. 666, s. 2.

SPECIALTY FOOD. A food that (a) has special religious significance and is used in religious ceremonies; or (b) is an imported food (i) that is not widely used by the population as a whole in Canada; and (ii) for which there is no readily available substitute that is manufactured, processed, produced or packaged in Canada and that is generally accepted as being a comparable substitute. *Food and Drug Regulations*, C.R.C., c. 870, c. B.01.012.

SPECIALTY PRODUCT. A prepackaged product that is (a) a food or beverage that has special religious significance and is used in religious ceremonies; or (b) an imported product (i) that is not widely used by the population as a whole in Canada; and (ii) for which there is no readily available substitute that is manufactured, processed, produced or packaged in Canada and that is generally accepted as being a comparable substitute. Canada regulations.

SPECIALTY SEED. Seed of a kind or of a mixture of the kinds listed in Schedule I and mixed or attached to any fertilizer, soil, compost, peat, moss, mica, plastic, paper, cellulose or other inert material and represented for use for vegetable gardens or lawns. *Seeds Regulations*, C.R.C., c. 1400, s. 2.

SPECIAL VFR FLIGHT. A visual flight authorized by an air traffic control unit to operate within a control zone under meteorological conditions that are below VFR weather conditions. *Air Regulations*, C.R.C., c. 2, s. 101.

SPECIAL WELFARE PROGRAM. (a) Blind persons allowances referred to in the Blind Persons Act, chapter B-7 of the Revised Statutes of Canada, 1970; (b) disabled persons allowances referred to in the Disabled Persons Act, chapter D-6 of the Revised Statutes of Canada, 1970; (c) unemployment assistance in relation to which payments may be made pursuant to the Unemployment Assistance Act, chapter U-1 of the Revised Statutes of Canada, 1970; and (d) assistance and welfare services referred to in the Canada Assistance Plan. *Federal-Provincial Fiscal Arrangements Act*, R.S.C. 1985, c. F-8, s. 26.

SPECIE. *n.* 1. Metallic money. 2. Something in its own true form, not a substitute, equivalent or compensation.

SPECIES. See ENDANGERED ~; PROTECTED ~; THREATENED ~.

SPECIFICALLY LIMITED COMPANY. A company limited by shares, the memorandum of which provides that no member shall be personally liable for the amount, if any, unpaid on his shares. *The Companies Act*, R.S.S. 1978, c. C-23, s. 3.

SPECIFICATION. *n.* A description, whose requirements are set out by statute, which enables the construction and use of a device described therein after the patent expires, and also enables others to determine exactly the limits of the exclusive privilege which they may not violate while the grant exists. H.G. Fox, *The Canadian Law and Practice Relating to Letters Patent for Inventions*, 4th ed. (Toronto: Carswell, 1969) at 163 and 164. See PLANS AND ~S.

SPECIFIC BEQUEST. The gift of a certain item of personal estate in a will.

SPECIFIC CHARGE. One that without more fastens on ascertained and definite property or property capable of being ascertained and defined. *Illingworth v. Houldsworth*, [1904] A.C. 355, at 358.

SPECIFIC DEVISE. The gift of a certain item of real property in a will.

SPECIFIC GOODS. Goods identified and agreed upon at the time a contract of sale is made. Sale of Goods acts.

SPECIFIC INTENT. A type of mens rea required for some criminal offences.

SPECIFIC LEGACY. The subject of the gift is identified in the will by a clear description. T. Sheard, R. Hull & M.M.K. Fitzpatrick, *Canadian Forms of Wills*, 4th ed. (Toronto: Carswell, 1982) at 155.

SPECIFIC PERFORMANCE. A court order which compels a person to do something previously promised according to a contractual obligation.

SPECIFIED CLASS. A class of shares of the capital stock of a corporation where, under the terms or conditions of the shares or any agreement in respect thereof, (a) the shares are not convertible or exchangeable; (b) the shares are non-voting; (c) the amount of each dividend payable on the shares is calculated as a fixed amount or by reference to a fixed percentage or an amount equal to the fair market value of the consideration for which the shares were issued; (d) the annual rate of the dividend on the shares, expressed as a percentage of an amount equal to the fair market value of the consideration for which the shares were issued, cannot in any event exceed the prescribed rate of interest at the time the shares were issued; and (e) the amount that any holder of the shares is entitled to receive on the redemption, cancellation or acquisition of the shares by the corporation or by any person with whom the corporation does not deal at arm's length cannot exceed the aggregate of an amount equal to the fair market value of the consideration for which the shares were issued and the amount of any unpaid dividends thereon. *Income Tax Act*, R.S.C. 1952, c. 148 (as am. S.C. 1988, c. 55, s. 192(1)), s. 256(1.1).

SPECIFIED DAY. In relation to an institution, means the later of (a) the day specified in a certificate referred to in the definition "certified institution" as the day on which the institution became an institution as described in paragraphs (a) and (b) of that definition, and (b) the first day of the fiscal year in which the application for a certificate referred to in the definition "certified institution" was made. *Excise Tax Act*, R.S.C. 1985 (2d Supp.), c. 7, s. 68.24.

SPECIFIED DRUG. A drug (i) that, under the laws in force in Manitoba, cannot be dispensed without a prescription of a duly qualified medical practitioner, a duly qualified dentist or duly qualified veterinarian;and (ii) that is specified in the regulations as a drug in respect of which benefits may be paid under this Act. *Prescription Drugs Cost Assistance Act*, S.M. 1973, c. 27, s. 1.

SPECIFIED EDUCATIONAL INSTITUTION. An institution of learning, whether within or outside a province, that offers courses at a postsecondary school level and that is designated by the lieutenant governor in council of that province, either particularly or as a member of a class, as a specified educational institution within the meaning of this Act. *Canada Student Loans Act*, R.S.C. 1985, c. S-23, s. 2.

SPECIFIED FINANCIAL INSTITUTION. (a) A bank to which the Bank Act or the Quebec Savings Banks Act applies; (b) a corporation licensed or otherwise authorized under the laws of Canada or a province to carry on in Canada the business of offering to the public its services as trustee; (c) a credit union; (d) an insurance corporation; (e) a corporation whose principal business is the lending of money to persons with whom the corporation is dealing at arm's length or the purchasing of debt obligations issued by such persons or a combination thereof; (f) a corporation that is controlled by one or more corporations described in any of paragraphs (a) to (e) and for the purposes of this paragraph, one corporation is controlled by another corporation if more than 50 per cent of its issued share capital (having full voting rights under all circumstances) belongs to the other corporation,

to persons with whom the other corporation does not deal at arm's length, or to the other corporation and persons with whom the other corporation does not deal at arm's length; or (g) a corporation related to a corporation described in any of paragraphs (a) to (f). *Income Tax Act*, R.S.C. 1952, c. 148 (as am. S.C. 1988, c. 55, s. 188(14)), s. 248(1).

SPECIFIED INTEREST RATE. The interest rate, determined by regulation, specified in a conversion or leasehold mortgage, which a mortgagor is required, under the mortgage, to pay on the outstanding principal of a loan. For a conversion mortgage the rate determined by regulation may differ for different land and security or for different classes of land and security. *Home Conversion and Leasehold Loan Act*, R.S.B.C. 1979, c. 170, s. 1.

SPECIFIED SECURITIES ISSUE. A primary distribution to the public of shares, warrants and shares or units of a unit trust made in accordance with The Securities Act. *Stock Savings Tax Credit Act*, S.S. 1986, c. S-59.1, s. 2.

SPECIFIED URANIUM UNDERTAKING. Any undertaking in Ontario carried out pursuant to an original or subsequent contract to supply uranium to Ontario Hydro and includes any other undertaking that may be prescribed by the regulations. *Mining Tax Act*, R.S.O. 1980, c. 269, s. 4.

SPECIMEN COLLECTION CENTRE. A place where specimens are taken or collected from the human body for examination to obtain information for diagnosis, prophylaxis or treatment, but does not include a place where a legally qualified medical practitioner is engaged in the practice of medicine or surgery or a laboratory that is established, operated or maintained under a licence under this Act. *Public Health Act*, R.S.O. 1980, c. 409, s. 59.

SPEC. LECT. L.S.U.C. *abbr.* Special Lectures of the Law Society of Upper Canada.

SPECS. See US DOT ~.

SPECULAR GLOSS. The luminous fractional reflectance of a specimen at the specular direction. *Motor Vehicle Safety Regulations*, C.R.C., c. 1038, s. 107.

SPEECH. See BUDGET ~; COMMERCIAL ~; FREEDOM OF ~.

SPEECH FROM THE THRONE. The Governor General's speech which opens a session of Parliament and outlines the legislative programme for that session as planned by cabinet. This speech is written by the Prime Minister. P.W. Hogg, *Constitutional Law of Canada*, 2d ed. (Toronto: Carswell, 1985) at 203.

SPEECH-LANGUAGE PATHOLOGIST. A person whose name is entered in the register as a speech-language pathologist. *Speech-Language Pathology and Audiology Act,* S.N.B. 1987, c. 71, s. 2.

SPEECH-LANGUAGE PATHOLOGY. The provision or conduct of non-medical assessment, treatment, research, counselling, guidance, testing and evaluation services relating to speech, language and communication disorders or conditions including the planning, direction and conduct of remedial programs designed to restore and improve communication efficiency. *Speech-Language Pathology and Audiology Act,* S.N.B. 1987, c. 71, s. 2.

SPEED. *n.* A colloquial expression for amphetamines. See RESTRICTED ~ AREA.

SPEED AUTHORITY. (a) In the case of a municipal district or county, the council; (b) in the case of an improvement district or a forestry road or a highway within a city and the title to which is vested in the Crown in right of Alberta pursuant to section 21 of the Public Highways Development Act, the Minister; (c) in the case of a special area, the Minister of Municipal Affairs; (d) in the case of a provincial park, the Minister of Recreation and Parks; (e) in the case of a licence of occupation road, the Minister of Energy and Natural Resources; (f) in the case of a highway through an Indian reserve, if the title to the highway is vested in the Crown in right of Alberta and the highway is not the subject of an agreement under the Public Highways Development Act, the Minister. *Highway Traffic Act,* R.S.A. 1980, c. H-7, s. 14.

SPEED BALL. A combination of a depressant such as morphine with a nervous system stimulant such as cocaine. F.A. Jaffe, *A Guide to Pathological Evidence,* 2d ed. (Toronto: Carswell, 1983) at 184.

SPEED LIMIT AREA. All Canadian controlled airspace below 10,000 feet above mean sea level. *Aircraft Speed Limit Order,* C.R.C., c. 29, s. 2.

SPEED-UP. *n.* A system intended to increase the productivity of workers.

SPEI EMPTIO. [L.] Purchasing a chance.

SPENDING POWER. A power, though not explicitly mentioned in the Constitution Act, 1867, which is inferred from the powers to legislate in relation to "public property" (section 91(1A)), to levy taxes (section 91(3)), and to appropriate federal funds (section 106). P.W. Hogg, *Constitutional Law of Canada,* 2d ed. (Toronto: Carswell, 1985) at 124.

SPENT SALMON. Salmon that are in poor condition and are returning to the sea after spawning. Fishery regulations.

SPERMATOZOA. *n.* Male generative cells. F.A. Jaffe, *A Guide to Pathological Evidence,* 2d ed. (Toronto: Carswell, 1983) at 123.

SPERM WHALE. Any whale known by the name of sperm whale, spermacet whale, cachalot, or pot whale. *Whaling Convention Act,* R.S.C. 1970, c. W-8, Schedule s. 18.

SPES RECUPERANDI. [L.] The hope of recovering.

SPES SUCCESSIONIS. [L.] Hope of succession, in contrast to a vested right.

SPIKED WRISTBAND. A leather wristband to which a metal spike or blade is affixed. *Prohibited Weapons Order, No. 5,* C.R.C., c. 437, s. 2.

SPILL. *n.* 1. A discharge, emission or escape of oil or gas other than one that is authorized pursuant to subsection (4) or any other Act of Parliament or that constitutes a discharge of a pollutant caused by or otherwise attributable to a ship within the meaning of the Canada Shipping Act. *Oil and Gas Production and Conservation Act,* R.S.C. 1985, c. O-7, s. 24. 2. When used with reference to a pollutant, means a discharge, (i) into the natural environment; (ii) from or out of a structure, vehicle or other container; and (iii) that is abnormal in quality or quantity in light of all the circumstances of the discharge. *Environmental Protection Act,* R.S.O. 1980, c. 141, s. 79.

SPILLAGE. *n.* Oil or solids escaping, leaking or spilling from a pipeline or any source apparently associated with a pipeline. *Pipeline Act,* R.S.B.C. 1979, c. 328, s. 38. See FUEL ~.

SPINSTER. *n.* An unmarried woman.

SPIRIT. See GRAIN ~; MOLASSES ~; PROOF ~.

SPIRITS. *n.* 1. Any material or substance, whether in liquid or any other form, containing any proportion by mass or by volume of absolute ethyl alcohol (C^2H^5OH). *Excise Act,* R.S.C. 1985, c. E-14, s. 3. 2. Any beverage that contains alcohol obtained by distillation. 3. Any beverage which contains alcohol mixed with drinking water and other substances in solution, and includes, among other things, brandy, rum, whiskey and gin. See DENATURED ~; GUM ~ OF TURPENTINE; RECTIFYING ~.

SPLICE. See OPEN ~.

SPLIT. *v.* With respect to a cause of action, to sue for only a part of a demand or claim, with intent to sue for the rest in another action.

SPLIT. *n.* A longitudinal skin laceration caused when tissue is compressed between bone and a hard surface or hard blunt object. It is distinguished from a cut by its contused edges and possible 'bridging' of the defect. F.A. Jaffe, *A Guide to Pathological Evidence*, 2d ed. (Toronto: Carswell, 1983) at 10 and 184. See DISTRICT OR ~.

SPLIT PEA. One from which a cotyledon or a large portion thereof has become detached or two whole detached cotyledons or pieces of detached cotyledons aggregating the size of an average pea and which can be counted as one. *Processed Fruit and Vegetable Regulations*, C.R.C., c. 291, schedule I, s. 39.

SPLIT RECEPTACLE. A duplex receptacle having terminals adapted for connection to a grounded, three-wire supply, such as 120/240 volts. *Power Corporation Act*, R.R.O. 1980, Reg. 794, s. 0.

SPLIT SHIFT. A shift in which there is a break of several hours between the two parts of the shift.

SPLITTER. *n.* An enclosure containing terminal plates or bus bars having main and branch connectors. *Power Corporation Act*, R.R.O. 1980, Reg. 794, s. 0.

SPLIT WORKWEEK. A workweek beginning before and ending after the date of a semi-monthly or monthly period.

SPIRIT-RECEIVER. See CLOSED ~.

SPOILED BALLOT. A ballot that on polling day has not been deposited in the ballot box but has been found by the deputy returning officer to be soiled or improperly printed or that has been: (i) handed by the deputy returning officer to an elector to cast the elector's vote; (ii) spoiled in marking by the elector; and (iii) handed back to the deputy returning officer and exchanged for another ballot paper.

SPOILED BALLOT PAPER. A ballot paper that, on polling day, has not been deposited in the ballot box but has been found by the deputy returning officer to be soiled or improperly printed, or that has been (a) handed by the deputy returning officer to an elector to cast the elector's vote; (b) spoiled in marking by the elector; and (c) handed back to the deputy returning officer and exchanged for another ballot paper.

SPOKE WHEEL. A rotating member that provides for mounting and support of demountable rims. *Motor Vehicle Safety Regulations*, C.R.C., c. 1038, s. 2.

SPOLIATUS DEBET ANTE OMNIA RESTI-TUI. [L.] The one despoiled should have property restored before all the rest.

SPONSION. *n.* An engagement or agreement made by a public officer such as an admiral or general in wartime either without authority or which exceeds the authority under which it was made.

SPONSOR. *n.* 1. A surety; a person who gives security or makes a promise for someone else. 2. A person who (i) recommends that an applicant is suitable for a licence under this Act; (ii) acknowledges directly or indirectly that an agent-principal or employer-employee relationship exists between that person and an applicant; or (iii) recommends an applicant and acknowledges that a relationship exists pursuant to subparagraph (ii). *Insurance Adjusters, Agents and Brokers Act*, S.Nfld. 1986, c. 36, s. 2. 3. The person or agency responsible for the organization and conduct of a special aviation event. *Special Aviation Events Safety Order*, C.R.C., c. 66, s. 2.

SPONSOR MEMBER. The Toronto Stock Exchange, and any other stock exchange, securities exchange, commodities exchange, association of securities or commodities dealers or similar organization that is admitted to membership in accordance with the by-laws. *Toronto Futures Exchange Act*, S.O. 1983, c. 19, s. 1.

SPONTANEOUS EXCLAMATION. The requisite conditions are: (a) an occurrence must produce nervous excitement causing an utterance to be made spontaneously and without reflection; (b) the utterance must have been made before the reflective powers had time to misrepresent or contrive; (c) the utterance must relate to what happened directly before; (d) the declarant must have had the opportunity to observe personally what is described; and (e) in contrast to a declaration admissible as a verbal act, the utterance may be made by a bystander and need not be precisely simultaneous with the act. P.K. McWilliams, *Canadian Criminal Evidence*, 3d ed. (Aurora: Canada Law Book, 1988) at 8-62.

SPONTE OBLATA. [L.] A free present or gift to the Crown.

SPORT. *n.* A physical activity carried on as a contest or involving training and adherence to rules. *An Act Respecting Safety in Sports*, S.Q. 1979, c. 86, s. 1. See AMATEUR ~; FITNESS AND AMATEUR ~ CANADA.

SPORT FISH. 1. Fish that are taken for pleasure and not for sale or barter. Canada regulations. 2. Includes salmon, trout, black bass and tuna. Fishery regulations.

SPORT FISHING. 1. Fishing for pleasure and not for sale or barter. Fishery regulations. 2. Fishing carried on as a sport by the use of a line or a rod and line (angling). *An Act Respecting Hunting and Fishing Rights in the James Bay and New Québec Territories*, S.Q. 1978, c. 92, s. 35. 3. Fishing for the purpose of exercising the skill of a fisherman or occupying one's leisure time. *Quebec Fishery Regulations*, C.R.C., c. 852, s. 2.

SPORT FISHING LICENCE. A licence authorizing a person to engage in sport fishing. *Northwest Territories Fisheries Regulations*, C.R.C., c. 847, s. 2.

SPORT HUNTING. Hunting with a firearm or a bow and arrow for the sole and specific purpose of killing game. *An Act Respecting Hunting and Fishing Rights in the James Bay and New Québec Territories*, S.Q. 1978, c. 92, s. 35.

SPORTS BODY. A group of natural persons who are individual members of a federation, or a body, association, league or club formed as a legal person to organize or practise a sport. *An Act to amend Various Legislation*, S.Q. 1984, c. 47, s. 147.

SPORTS CENTRE. An installation or place equipped and used for sports events. *An Act Respecting Safety in Sports*, S.Q. 1979, c. 86, s. 1.

SPORTS EVENT. A sports event, contest or exhibition in which a contestant may receive a purse or remuneration. *An Act Respecting Safety in Sports*, S.Q. 1979, c. 86, s. 1.

SPORTS STADIUM. 1. An establishment with stepped rows of seats designed and used for presentation of a sporting or athletic event or spectacle, and includes an amphitheatre or arena. *Liquor Control and Licensing Act*, R.S.B.C. 1979, c. 237, s. 1. 2. A stadium, arena or other facility where members of the public may witness the performance of sports events. *Liquor Control Act*, R.S.A. 1980, c. L-17, c. 58.

SPOT. See BLOOD ~; FOCAL ~; MEAT ~; TARDIEU ~.

SPOT ROT. A condition in which a mould spot or spots is apparent inside the shell or along cracks in the shell. *Live Stock and Live Stock Products Act*, R.R.O. 1980, Reg. 582, s. 1.

SPOTTED PEA. One which has discoloured markings on its surface distinctly setting it apart from other peas in the container. *Processed Fruit and Vegetable Regulations*, C.R.C., c. 291, schedule I, s. 39.

SPOUSAL AGREEMENT. (i) Any marriage contract or marital agreement; or (ii) any separation agreement; or (iii) release of quit claim deed, in writing or any other written agreement or other writing between spouses, made within Manitoba or elsewhere before or after the coming into force of this Act and either during marriage or contemplation of marriage, affecting all or any of the assets of the spouses in a manner described in section 5. *Statute Law Amendment Act*, S.M. 1980-81, c. 26, s. 21.

SPOUSAL PRIVILEGE. (a) A privilege supplementary to the right of one accused not to be called as a witness against oneself which depends on the spouse not being compellable or competent as a witness for the prosecution and is subject to the statutory exception in section 4(2) and the common law exception in section 4(5) of the Canada Evidence Act; (b) Section 4(3) of the Canada Evidence Act describes the true privilege in communication made to the spouse who enjoys the privilege. P.K. McWilliams, *Canadian Criminal Evidence*, 3d ed. (Aurora: Canada Law Book, 1988) at 35-2 and 35-3.

SPOUSE. *n.* 1. A person of the opposite sex to whom the person is married or with whom the person is living in a conjugal relationship outside marriage. 2. Either of a man and woman who (i) are married to each other; (ii) are married to each other by a marriage that is voidable but which has not been voided by order of a court; (iii) have gone through a form of marriage that is void and have cohabited within the preceding 12 months; or (iv) are living together as husband and wife. 3. Either of a man and woman who are not married to each other and have cohabited, (a) continuously for a period of not less than 3 years; or (b) in a relationship of some permanence, if they are the natural or adoptive parents of a child. 4. Includes a party to a voidable or void marriage, as the case may be. *Income Tax Act*, R.S.C. 1952, c. 148 (as am. S.C. 1988, c. 55, s. 191(2)), s. 252(3). See COMMON LAW ~; DESERTING ~; FORMER ~; SURVIVING ~.

SPOUSE'S ALLOWANCE. The spouse's allowance authorized to be paid under Part III. *Old Age Security Act*, R.S.C. 1985, c. O-9, s. 2.

SPP. *abbr.* Species. *Weed Control Act*, R.R.O. 1980, Reg. 944, s. 1.

SPREADING FALSE NEWS. A person who wilfully publishes a statement, tale or news that he knows is false and that causes or is likely to cause injury or mischief to a public interest is guilty of an offence. *Criminal Code*, R.S.C. 1985, c. C-46, s. 181.

SPRING. See SUSPENSION ~.

SPRING GRAIN. (i) Oats; (ii) barley, including winter barley; (iii) spring wheat; and (iv) mixed grain, the moisture content of which is not greater than 14 per cent. *Crop Insurance Act (Ontario)*, R.R.O. 1980, Reg. 223, s. 3.

SPRINGING USE. A use like an executory interest which directs property to vest at a future time which need not coincide with the common law termination of a legal estate.

SPRING POLE. A section of tree, or bush which is, by virtue of its arrangement in relation to other materials, under tension. *Occupational Health and Safety Act*, R.R.O. 1980, Reg. 692, s. 107.

SPRING SESSION. A session of the Legislature that commences in the first 3 months of any year. *The Tabling of Documents Act*, R.S.S. 1978, c. T-1, s. 2.

SPRING SWITCH. A switch equipped with a spring mechanism arranged to restore the switch points to normal position after having been trailed through. *Regulations No. O-8, Uniform Code of Operating Rules*, C.R.C., c. 1175, Part III, s. 2.

SPRING WHEAT AREA. The Provinces of Manitoba, Saskatchewan, Alberta and the Peace River District of British Columbia. *Prairie Farm Assistance Act*, R.S.C. 1970, c. P-16, s. 2.

SPRINKLER AND FIRE PROTECTION INSTALLER. A person who, (i) plans proposed installations from blueprints, sketches, specifications, standards and codes; (ii) lays out, assembles, installs, tests and maintains high and low pressure pipeline systems for supplying water, air, foam, carbon dioxide or other materials to or for fire protection purposes; (iii) measures, cuts, reams, threads, solders, bolts, screws, welds or joins all types of piping, fittings or equipment for fire protection of a building or structure; (iv) installs clamps, brackets and hangers to support piping, fittings and equipment used in fire protection systems; (v) tests, adjusts and maintains pipe lines and all other equipment used in sprinkler and fire protection systems; (vi) operates and utilizes necessary tools and equipment for the installation of sprinkler and fire protection systems, but does not include a person engaged in (a) the manufacture of equipment or the assembly of a unit prior to delivery to a building or site; or (b) the installation of electrical equipment, devices and wiring not integral or attached to fire protection systems. *Apprenticeship and Tradesmen's Qualification Act*, R.R.O. 1980, Reg. 58, s. 1.

SPRINKLERED. *adj.* That the building or part thereof is equipped with a system of automatic sprinklers. *Building Code Act*, R.R.O. 1980, Reg. 87, s. 1.

SPRINKLER LEAKAGE INSURANCE. Insurance against loss of or damage to property through the breakage or leakage of sprinkler equipment or other fire protection system, or of pumps, water pipes, or plumbing and its fixtures. Insurance acts.

SPRINKLING TRUST. A discretionary trust under the terms of which the trustees are required to distribute the property of the trust among the beneficiaries. D.M.W. Waters, *The Law of Trusts in Canada*, 2d ed. (Toronto: Carswell, 1984) at 29.

SPUD-IN. *n.* The initial penetration of the ground for the purpose of drilling an oil or gas well. *Territorial Land Use Regulations*, C.R.C., c. 1524, s. 2.

SQUARE FOOT. 1/9 square yard. *Weights and Measures Act*, S.C. 1970-71-72, c. 36, Schedule II.

SQUARE INCH. 1/144 square foot. *Weights and Measures Act*, S.C. 1970-71-72, c. 36, Schedule II.

SQUARE MILE. 640 acres. *Weights and Measures Act*, S.C. 1970-71-72, c. 36, Schedule II.

SQUARE ROD. 30 1/4 square yards. *Weights and Measures Act*, S.C. 1970-71-72, c. 36, Schedule II.

SQUARE YARD. A superficial area equal to that of a square each side of which measures one yard. *Weights and Measures Act*, S.C. 1970-71-72, c. 36, Schedule II.

SQUAT PACK. A manner of packing poultry in a single layer, in a squat position with the entire breast visible, but with the legs, wings and neck concealed. *Dressed and Eviscerated Poultry Regulations*, C.R.C., c. 283, s. 2.

SQUATTER. *n.* Someone who occupies land without consent or licence.

SQUATTER'S TITLE. Title acquired by someone who has occupied land without paying rent or in any other way acknowledging superior title for so long that that person acquires indefeasible title.

SQUID. *n.* Cephalopods of the species Illex illecebrasus and Loligo pealei. *Northwest Atlantic Fisheries Regulations*, C.R.C., c. 860, s. 2.

SQUIRE. *n.* A contraction of "esquire".

SR. *abbr.* Steradian.

S.R. *abbr.* Saskatchewan Reports, 1979-.

S.R. & O. *abbr.* Statutory rules and orders in England.

S.S. *abbr.* Steamship(s).

SSHRC. *abbr.* Social Sciences and Humanities Research Council of Canada.

STAB. *n.* A penetrating wound with greater depth than width. F.A. Jaffe, *A Guide to Pathological Evidence*, 2d ed. (Toronto: Carswell, 1983) at

STABILIZATION ACCOUNT. The Western Grain Stabilization Account established pursuant to section 40. *Western Grain Stabilization Act*, R.S.C. 1985, c. W-7, s. 2.

STABILIZATION PAYMENT. A payment made to a participant under section 12 and includes any payment on account thereof made to the participant by way of an interim stabilization payment under section 10.1. *Western Grain Stabilization Act*, R.S.C. 1985 (1st Supp.), c. 18, s. 1.

STABILIZATION YEAR. A year in which stabilization payments are to be made pursuant to section 10. *Western Grain Stabilization Act*, R.S.C. 1985, c. W-7, s. 2.

STABIT PRAESUMPTIO DONEC PROBETUR IN CONTRATIUM. [L.] A presumption stands until it is proved to the contrary.

STABLE. See HORSE ~.

STABLE KEEPER. A person who, for money or its equivalent, stables, feeds, boards, grazes or cares for animals. See BOARDING ~; SALES ~.

STACK. *n.* A vertical soil, waste or vent pipe which serves more than one fixture. *Ontario Water Resources Act*, R.R.O. 1980, Reg. 736, s. 1. See SOIL ~; VENT ~; WASTE ~.

STACK VENT. The extension of a soil stack or waste stack above the highest connection of a waste pipe to the stack. *Ontario Water Resources Act*, R.R.O. 1980, Reg. 736, s. 1.

STACK VENTING. When used with reference to fixtures means an arrangement such that the connection of the drainage piping from the stack vented fixtures to the stack provides adequate venting to the fixture traps so that no additional vent piping is required. *Ontario Water Resources Act*, R.R.O. 1980, Reg. 736, s. 1. See MODIFIED ~.

STADIUM. See SPORTS ~.

STAFF. See ACADEMIC ~; ADMINISTRATIVE AND TECHNICAL ~; CLINICAL ~; DENTAL ~; EXAMINING ~: MEDICAL ~; NURSING ~; PERMANENT ~; PROFESSIONAL ~; PUBLIC SERVICE ~ RELATIONS BOARD; SERVICE ~; SUPPORT ~; TEACHING ~.

STAFF-MODEL RESIDENCE. A residence where program staff are employed for a scheduled period of work or duty.

STAFF OFFICER OR STAFF OFFICER OF THE SALVATION ARMY. Every duly commissioned officer, other than a Probationary Lieutenant, of the religious society known as the Salvation Army and duly chosen or commissioned by the society to solemnize marriage. *Solemnization of Marriage Act*, R.S.N.S. 1967, c. 287, s. 1.

STAGE. *n.* 1. A space designed primarily for theatrical performances with provision for quick change scenery and overhead lighting, including environmental control for a wide range of lighting and sound effects and which is traditionally, but not necessarily, separated from the audience by a proscenium wall and curtain opening. *Building Code Act*, R.R.O. 1980, Reg. 87, s. 1. 2. A working platform supported from above. *Safe Working Practices Regulations*, C.R.C., c. 1467, s. 2. See REPORT ~.

STAIN. *n.* Any substance on the shell of an egg, other than dirt or a design or emblem stamped thereon. *Egg Regulations*, C.R.C., c. 284, s. 2.

STAKE. *v.* In relation to a mineral claim, means to mark the boundaries of a claim area and establish the corner posts of the claim area in accordance with this Act and the regulations. *Mining Act*, S.N.B. 1985, c. M-14.1, s. 1.

STAKE. *n.* 1. A deposit made in hopes a particular event takes place. 2. A wooden or metal post used to support and prevent the lateral movement of logs. *Occupational Health and Safety Act*, R.R.O. 1980, Reg. 692, s. 107.

STAKEHOLDER. *n.* 1. A person who holds money pending the outcome of a wager or bet. 2. A person who holds property or money which rival claimants claim, but who claims no personal interest in that property or money. See INTERPLEADER.

STAKER. *n.* A person who stakes a mineral claim. *Mining Act*, S.N.B. 1985, c. M-14.1, s. 1.

STAKE TRUCK. A motor vehicle equipped with a platform and normally used for the transportation of packaged goods. *Gasoline Handling Act*, R.R.O. 1980, Reg. 439, s. 1.

STALE BREAD. Bread made at least 4 days before it is offered for sale to the consumers. *An Act Respecting the Bread Trade*, R.S.Q. 1977, c. C-32, s. 1.

STALE CHEQUE. A cheque which a bank may dishonour after a certain period, without breaching the banker-customer contract. I.F.G. Baxter, *The Law of Banking*, 3d ed. (Toronto: Carswell, 1981) at 85.

STALE DEMAND. A claim made so long ago that it is presumed that it was waived.

STALLION. *n.* Includes a cryptorchid (ridgeling). *Animal Husbandry Act*, R.S.M. 1970, c. A90, s. 3.

STAMP. *v.* See INSTRUMENT REQUIRING TO BE ~ED.

STAMP. *n.* 1. An impressed or adhesive stamp used for the purpose of revenue by the government of Canada or a Canadian province or by the government of a foreign state. *Criminal Code*, R.S.C. 1985, c. C-46, s. 376(3). 2. Any distinctive mark, label or seal impressed on or affixed to any goods subject to excise, or any distinctive mark, label or seal impressed on or affixed to any package in which any of those goods are contained. *Excise Act*, R.S.C. 1985, c. E-14, s. 2. 3. A stamp prepared for the purposes of this Act pursuant to a direction of the Minister under section 60. *Excise Act*, R.S.C. 1985, c. E-14, s. 2. 4. Includes all stamps or stamped paper, issued, in respect of matters subject to the control of the Legislature, under any law, or under any order-in-council of the Governor of the late Province of Canada or of the Lieutenant-Governor of Québec, founded on or recognized by any of such laws. *Stamp Act*, R.S.Q. 1977, c. T-10, s. 3. See AGE STRIP ~; CIGAR ~; CUSTOMS DUTY ~S; EXCISE ~; PERFORATED ~S; POSTAGE ~; PRECANCELLED ~; TRADING ~; TOBACCO ~.

STAMP DUTY. A tax raised by placing a stamp on a written instrument like a conveyance or lease pursuant to a Stamp Act.

STAMPED PAPER. Includes all stamps or stamped paper, issued, in respect of matters subject to the control of the Legislature, under any law, or under any order-in-council of the Governor of the late Province of Canada or of the Lieutenant-Governor of Québec, founded on or recognized by any of such laws. *Stamp Act*, R.S.Q. 1977, c. T-10, s. 3.

STAND. *v.* As applied to a vehicle, whether occupied or not, means (i) when required, to cause the vehicle to remain motionless in one place; and (ii) when prohibited, to cause the vehicle to remain motionless in one place, except when necessary to avoid conflict with other traffic or in compliance with the directions of a peace officer or a traffic control device. *The Highway Traffic Act*, S.M. 1985-86, c. 3, s. 1. See STOP OR ~.

STANDARD. *n.* 1. Something which has authority and tests other things of the same kind. 2. A settled rate. 3. The detailed design specification for a material, product or process, established by a competent body and not automatically mandatory. The standard setting bodies related to health and safety legislation include the Canadian Standards Association, the Canadian Gas Association, the Underwriters Laboratories of Canada, the American Society of Mechanical Engineering, and the National Fire Prevention Association (U.S.). D. Robertson, *Ontario Health and Safety Guide* (Toronto: Richard De Boo Ltd., 1988) at 5-374. See BUILDING CONSTRUCTION ~; CSA INDUSTRIAL LIGHTING ~; CSA ~; CYLINDRICAL GRADUATED ~; EMPLOYMENT ~; EXPORT ~ SAMPLE; FUEL CONSUMPTION ~; LOCAL ~; NARROW NECK GLASS ~; NARROW NECK METAL ~; REFERENCE ~; SAFETY GLASS ~; ~S; TRAP ~.

STANDARD BREAD. All ordinary steam, box, sandwich, pullman, "home-baked", Graham, brown, or whole wheat bread and all bread commonly known to the trade and to the public as standard bread. *Bread Act*, R.S.A. 1970, c. 34, s. 2.

STANDARD CAMP. A camp used or intended to be used to accommodate 15 or more employees. *Public Health Act*, R.R.O. 1980, Reg. 834, s. 3.

STANDARD CODE OF SIGNALS. A code of signals that (a) is adopted by an employer for use by all signal men in his employ in directing the safe movement or operation of materials handling equipment; and (b) complies with the code of signals recommended by the National Safety Council or by the American National Standards Institute or any other standard approved by the regional officer. *Canada Materials Handling Regulations*, C.R.C., c. 1004, s. 2.

STANDARD CUBIC FOOT. The quantity of gas occupying a volume of 1 cubic foot at 77 degrees Fahrenheit and at a pressure of 29.92 inches of mercury. *Secondary Lead Smelter National Emission Standards Regulations*, C.R.C., c. 412, s. 2.

STANDARD FILM. A film that is 35 millimeters or more in width.

STANDARD FIRE TEST. A test that develops in a test furnace a series of time-temperature relationships as follows: (a) at the end of the first 5 minutes 1,000°F (538°C); (b) at the end of the first 10 minutes 1,300°F (704°C); (c) at the end of the first 30 minutes 1,550°F (843°C); (d) at the end of the first 60 minutes 1,700°F (927°C). *Hull Construction Regulations*, C.R.C., c. 1431, s. 2.

STANDARD GAUGE. That the space between the rails of a railroad is approximately 1,435 millimetres. *Occupational Health and Safety Act*, R.R.O. 1980, Reg. 694, s. 1.

STANDARD HOSE. Firehose of two and one-half inches inside diameter of whatever material constructed, and includes metal couplings, connections, fittings and attachments. *Standard Hose Coupling Act*, R.S.N.S. 1967, c. 288, s. 1.

STANDARD IRON BAR. An iron or steel bar 1 inch square and 4 feet long pointed at one end and planted in the ground so that the top of the bar is not more than 4 inches above the level of the ground. *Surveys Act*, R.R.O. 1980, Reg. 927, s. 1. See SHORT ~.

STANDARDIZE. *v.* To alter the butter fat content of milk to conform with market standards. *Public Health Act*, R.S.N.S. 1967, c. 247, s. 1.

STANDARDIZED ASSESSMENT. The product obtained by multiplying the values entered on the assessment roll of a municipal corporation by the factor established for that roll under section 264 of the Act respecting municipal taxation. *An Act Respecting Public Elementary and Secondary Education*, S.Q. 1984, c. 39, s. 345.

STANDARDIZED MILK. Milk that has been adjusted by the addition or removal of milk-fat, or milk solids other than milk-fat, for the purpose of processing into a milk product.

STANDARD J4C. "Motor Vehicle Seat Belt Assemblies", July 1965, a standard of the Society of Automotive Engineers. *Children's Car Seats and Harnesses Regulations*, C.R.C., c. 921, s. 2.

STANDARD LEAF TOBACCO. As applied to any kind of tobacco, means that which consists of 10 per cent water and 90 per cent solid matter. *Excise Act*, R.S.C. 1985, c. E-14, s. 6.

STANDARD MARITAL REGIME. The standard system of property sharing between spouses for which provision is made in Part I. *Marital Property Act*, S.M. 1977, c. 48, s. 1.

STANDARD MEASURING CUP. A measuring cup that shall, subject to the tolerance permitted under section 7, contain 8 Imperial fluid ounces or 1/5 of an Imperial quart or 227.30 millilitres. *Canada Standard Measuring Cups and Spoons Regulations*, C.R.C., c. 1136, Schedule 1, s. 1.

STANDARD METHODS. The Standard Methods for the Examination of Water and Wastewater, 14th edition, 1976, published by the American Public Health Association. *Great Lakes Sewage Pollution Prevention Regulations*, C.R.C., c. 1429, s. 2.

STANDARD OF PRODUCTION. Means that from every litre or .78924 kg of absolute ethyl alcohol taken for use there shall be produced therefrom not less than one-half kilogram (.5 kg) of acetic acid. *Excise Act*, R.S.C. 1985, c. E-14, s. 190.

STANDARD PLATE COUNT. A procedure

from time to time laid down according to "Standard Methods for the Examination of Water, Sewage and Industrial Wastes" co-edited by (1) American Public Health Association; (2) American Water Works Asociation; (3) The Federation of Sewage and Industrial Wastes Association and published by American Public Health Association. *Public Health Act*, R.S.N.S. 1967, c. 247, s. 1.

STANDARD PRESSURE REGION. All Canadian domestic airspace not within the altimeter setting region. *Altimeter Setting Procedures Order*, C.R.C., c. 33, s. 2.

STANDARD REFERENCE CONDITIONS. At a temperature of 15°C and an atmospheric pressure of 101.325 kPa. *Motor Fuel Tax Act*, S.B.C. 1985, c. 76, s. 1.

STANDARDS. *n.* 1. Those rules, tests, measures or specifications by which the quality or grade of a product is determined. *Livestock and Livestock Products Act*, R.S.C. 1985, c. L-9, s. 2. 2. The standards for the maintenance and improvement of the physical condition and for the fitness for occupancy prescribed by a by-law passed under section 641. *City of Winnipeg Act*, S.M. 1971, c. 105, s. 640. See CANADIAN ~ ASSOCIATION; GAS HAZARD CONTROL ~; SAFETY ~; STANDARD.

STANDARDS COUNCIL OF CANADA. The federal body which encourages voluntary standardization in production, manufacture, construction, performance, quality, the safety of structures and buildings, products and articles.

STANDARD TIME. Except as otherwise provided by any proclamation of the Governor in Council that may be issued for the purposes of this definition in relation to any province or territory or any part thereof, means (a) in relation to the Province of Newfoundland, Newfoundland standard time, being 3 hours and 30 minutes behind Greenwich time; (b) in relation to the Provinces of Nova Scotia, New Brunswick and Prince Edward Island, those parts of the Province of Quebec lying east of the sixty-third meridian of west longitude, and those parts of the Northwest Territories lying east of the sixty-eighth meridian of west longitude, Atlantic standard time, being 4 hours behind Greenwich time; (c) in relation to those parts of the Province of Quebec lying west of the sixty-third meridian of west longitude, those parts of the Province of Ontario lying between the sixty-eighth and the ninetieth meridians of west longitude, Southampton Island and the islands adjacent to Southampton Island, and that part of the Northwest Territories lying between the sixty-eighth and the eighty-fifth meridians of west longitude, eastern standard time, being 5 hours behind

Greenwich time; (d) in relation to that part of the Province of Ontario lying west of the ninetieth meridian of west longitude, the Province of Manitoba, and that part of the Northwest Territories, except Southampton Island and the islands adjacent to Southampton Island, lying between the eighty-fifth and the one hundred and second meridians of west longitude, central standard time, being 6 hours behind Greenwich time; (e) in relation to the Province of Saskatchewan, the Province of Alberta, and that part of the Northwest Territories lying west of the one hundred and second meridian of west longitude, mountain standard time, being 7 hours behind Greenwich time; (f) in relation to the Province of British Columbia, Pacific standard time, being 8 hours behind Greenwich time; and (g) in relation to the Yukon Territory, Yukon standard time, being 9 hours behind Greenwich time. *Interpretation Act*, R.S.C. 1985, c. I-21, s. 35. See MOUNTAIN ~.

STANDARD WARD HOSPITALIZATION. The following services to in-patients: (i) accommodation and meals at the standard or public ward level; (ii) necessary nursing services; (iii) laboratory, radiological and other diagnostic procedures, together with the necessary interpretation, for the purpose of maintaining health, preventing disease and assisting in the diagnosis and treatment of any injury, illness or disability; (iv) drugs, biologicals and related preparations when administered in a hospital, as specified in the Agreement; (v) use of operating room, case room and anaesthetic facilities, including necessary equipment and supplies; (vi) routine surgical supplies; (vii) use of radiotherapy facilities, where available; (viii) use of physiotherapy facilities, where available; (ix) services rendered by persons who receive remuneration therefor from the hospital. *Hospitals Act*, R.S.A. 1980, c. H-11, s. 53.

STANDARD WORKWEEK. The number of working hours in one week beyond which an employee is entitled to be paid at overtime rates.

STAND BY. To sanction by inaction and silence.

STAND-BY TIME. A period of time that is not a regular working period during which a public servant on written instructions from an official of his ministry keeps himself available for a recall to work. *Public Service Act*, R.R.O. 1980, Reg. 881, s. 10.

STANDING. *n.* When prohibited, means the halting of a vehicle, whether occupied or not, except for the purpose of and while actually engaged in receiving or discharging passengers. *Highway Traffic Act*, R.S.O. 1980, c. 198, s. 1.

STANDING ADVANCE. 1. Any money paid out of the Revenue Fund that is repayable to the Territories, but is not chargeable to an appropriation and is not evidenced by a promissory note. *Financial Administration Act*, R.S.N.W.T. 1974, c. F-4, s. 2. 2. An accountable advance made in a fixed amount to a person required to incur expenditures on a continuing basis and reimbursed to that fixed amount each time an accounting for expenditures is made. *Accountable Advances Regulations*, C.R.C., c. 668, s. 2.

STANDING BODY OF WATER. A lake, pond, reservoir, lagoon, swamp, marsh or any other area containing standing surface water either permanently or intermittently. *The Water Resources Management Act*, R.S.S. 1978, c. W-7, s. 2.

STANDING COMMITTEE. 1. A body appointed under a standing order to consider legislation or estimates, to conduct any investigation or inquiry which the House requires. Such a committee exists throughout a Parliament, and some have been given permanent orders of reference. A. Fraser, G.A. Birch & W.A. Dawson, eds., *Beauchesne's Rules and Forms of the House of Commons of Canada*, 5th ed. (Toronto: Carswell, 1978) at 189. 2. The credit committee, supervisory committee, educational committee, membership committee and any other committee elected by the general membership or appointed by the board of directors whose duties shall be continuous during the fiscal year of the credit union. *Credit Union Act*, R.S.P.E.I. 1974, c. C-28, s. 1.

STANDING COMMITTEE ON PROCEDURE AND ORGANIZATION. The committee which customarily recommends changes in the Standing Orders of Parliament. A. Fraser, G.A. Birch & W.A. Dawson, eds., *Beauchesne's Rules and Forms of the House of Commons of Canada*, 5th ed. (Toronto: Carswell, 1978) at 5.

STANDING CROPS. Crops standing or growing on the demised premises. Landlord and Tenant acts.

STANDING ORDER. 1. A rule or form which regulates procedure in the House of Commons. 2. An order peculiar to a certain institution issued by that institution's head under authority of section 8 of the Penitentiary Regulations.

STANDING PROGRAM. The established programs and the special welfare program. *Federal-Provincial Fiscal Arrangements Act*, R.S.C. 1985, c. F-8, s. 26.

STANDING, SESSIONAL AND SPECIAL ORDERS. The rules and regulations which the House of Commons uses to govern its proceedings. A. Fraser, G.A. Birch & W.A. Dawson, eds., *Beauchesne's Rules and Forms of the House of*

Commons of Canada, 5th ed. (Toronto: Carswell, 1978) at 5.

STANDING TIMBER. Includes all trees on Crown land, Crown granted land and other land. *Logging Tax Act*, R.S.B.C. 1979, c. 248, s. 1.

STANDPIPE AND HOSE SYSTEM. A system of pipes and hoses connected to a water supply for the purpose of applying water to a fire. *Hotel Fire Safety Act*, R.R.O. 1980, Reg. 505, s. 2.

STAPLE LENGTH. Wool with a length of fibre suitable for combing, preferably not less than 1 1/2 inch. *Wool Grading Regulations*, C.R.C., c. 294, s. 2.

STARBOARD. *adj.* In respect of a vessel, means the right side of the vessel looking forward. *Small Vessel Regulations*, C.R.C., c. 1487, s. 2.

STARBOARD HAND BUOY. A buoy that is located on the starboard side (right hand) of the channel when the vessel is proceeding (a) with the flood tide on the sea coast; (b) against the current of a river; or (c) away from the outlet toward the head of a lake. *Private Buoy Regulations*, C.R.C., c. 1460, Schedule.

STARCH PLANT. Includes any plant processing raw potatoes into potato starch. *Potato Processing Plant Liquid Effluent Regulations*, C.R.C., c. 829, s. 2.

STARE AD RECTUM. [L.] To stand trial.

STARE DECISIS. [L.] The principle by which a precedent or decision of one court binds courts lower in the judicial hierarchy. P.W. Hogg, *Constitutional Law of Canada*, 2d ed. (Toronto: Carswell, 1985) at 183.

STARE IN JUDICIO. [L. to litigate in a court] To sue.

START. *v.* Kindle, light, place or set out. *Prairie and Forest Fires Act*, S.S. 1982-83, c. P-22.1, s. 2.

STARTER. *n.* 1. An electric controller for accelerating a motor from rest to normal speed, and for stopping the motor, and usually implies inclusion of overload protection. *Power Corporation Act*, R.R.O. 1980, Reg. 794, s. 0. 2. A person designated by an association to start the horses in each race. *Race Track Supervision Regulations*, C.R.C., c. 441, s. 2.

STARTING JUDGE. A person responsible for racing starts, whose functions in this regard are described in the rules. *An Act Respecting Lotteries, Racing, Publicity Contests and Amusement Machines*, S.Q. 1978, c. 36, s. 1.

STATE. *n.* 1. A group of people who occupy a certain territory and have an executive and legislative organization under their own, exclu-

sive control. 2. Part of a larger state, i.e. the separate organizations which collectively make up Australia. 3. Includes a political subdivision of a state and an official agency of a state. 5. Any state or territory of the United States of America and includes the District of Columbia. See CONTRACTING ~; DELIVERABLE ~; FEDERAL ~; FLAG ~; FOREIGN ~; LIMIT ~S; MINISTRY OF ~ FOR SCIENCE AND TECHNOLOGY; NATURAL ~; PROVINCE OR ~; RECIPROCATING ~; SECRETARY OF ~; UNITARY ~.

STATE AIRCRAFT. 1. A civil aircraft owned by and exclusively used in the service of Her Majesty in right of Canada or in right of any province. *Air Regulations*, C.R.C., c. 2, s. 101. 2. An aircraft, other than a commercial aircraft, owned and operated by the government of any country or the government of a colony, dependency, province, state or territory of any country. Canada regulations.

STATED CAPITAL. The aggregate amount of capital in all stated capital accounts. *Loan and Trust Companies Act*, S.N.B. 1987, c. L-11.2, s. 1.

STATED CASE. A case tried on the basis of a statement of facts agreed on by the parties.

STATE DOCUMENT. Includes (i) any Act or ordinance enacted or made or purporting to have been enacted or made by a legislature; (ii) any order, regulation, notice, appointment, warrant, licence, certificate, letters patent, official record, rule of Court, or other instrument issued or made or purporting to have been issued or made under the authority of any Act or ordinance so enacted or made; and (iii) any official gazette, journal, proclamation, treaty, or other public document or act of state issued or made or purporting to have been issued or made. Evidence acts.

STATEMENT. *n.* 1. An assertion of fact, opinion, belief or knowledge, whether material or not and whether admissible or not. *Criminal Code*, R.S.C. 1985, c. C-46, s. 118 as am. by *Criminal Law Amendment Act*, R.S.C. 1985 (1st Supp.), c. 27, s. 15. 2. The originating process which commences an action. G.D. Watson & C. Perkins, eds., *Holmested & Watson: Ontario Civil Procedure* (Toronto: Carswell, 1984) at 14-3. 3. Any representation of fact whether made in words or otherwise. See ANNUAL ~; BENEFIT COST ~; ENVIRONMENTAL IMPACT ~; EXTRA-JUDICIAL ~; FINANCIAL ~; IMPACT ~; SELF-INCRIMINATING ~; SELF-SERVING ~; ~S.

STATEMENT OF ACCOUNT. A written statement of the amount owing by the debtor to the creditor that includes (a) the amount stated on the previous statement of account to be owing; (b) a record of each extension of credit since the previous statement of account; (c) the amount credited to the account since the previous statement of account; and (d) the cost of borrowing accrued since the previous statement of account. *Consumer Protection Act*, R.S.B.C. 1979, c. 65, s. 33.

STATEMENT OF ADJUSTMENTS. A detailed statement of all credits and debits resulting in a balance payable by the purchaser to the vendor upon closing a real estate transaction.

STATEMENT OF CLAIM. A printed or written statement by the plaintiff in an action which shows the facts relied on to support any claim against the defendant and the remedy or relief sought.

STATEMENT OF DEFENCE. A brief written statement by a defendant to respond to each allegation in a statement of claim: (a) by admission; (b) by denial; (c) by a statement that the defendant does not know; or (d) by a statement of the defendant's own version of the facts.

STATEMENT OF FACTS. See AGREED ~.

STATEMENTS. *n.* Includes: words spoken or written or recorded electronically or electromagnetically or otherwise; gestures, signs or other visible representations. *Criminal Code*, R.S.C. 1985, c. C-46, s. 319(7). See STATEMENT.

STATIC MEASURE. Any measure that measures length, volume or capacity and does not have a moving or movable part that has or can have an effect on the accuracy of the measure. *Weights and Measures Act*, R.S.C. 1985, c. W-6, s. 2.

STATIC WATER LEVEL. The level attained by water in or from a well when no water is being taken from the well. *Ontario Water Resources Act*, R.R.O. 1980, Reg. 739, s. 1.

STATION. *n.* 1. A compressor station, a metering station, an odorizing station or a regulating station. *Ontario Energy Board Act*, R.S.O. 1980, c. 332, s. 1. 2. A radio or television broadcasting station or a cable-delivery station. 3. A location where trains may stop. See AERADIO ~; COAST ~; COMFORT ~; CONTAINER FREIGHT ~; CONTROL ~; CREAM ~; EARTH ~; EGG-GRADING ~; EGG ~; EVISCERATING ~; FARM ~; FILLING ~; FIRST-AID ~; FISH BUYING ~; FISHING ~; GRADING ~; IMMIGRANT ~; INITIAL ~; INTERLOCKING ~; KILLING AND DRESSING ~; LAND ~; MILK RECEIVING ~; MOBILE ~; MOTOR VEHICLE INSPECTION ~; POLLING ~; PROCESSED EGG ~; RADIO ~; RAILWAY ~; REGISTER ~; SERVICE ~;

SHIP ~; SKIMMING ~; SPACE ~; TERMINATING ~; TRANSFER ~; VOTING ~.

STATIONARY ENGINE. Includes the following apparatus when used in a public building contemplated in the Public Buildings Safety Act (R.S.Q., c. S-3) or in an establishment or on a construction site contemplated in the Act respecting health and safety (1979, c. 63): (a) boilers or generators operated by steam, hot water or any other fluid substance; (b) steam engines or turbines; (c) refrigerating plants; (d) internal combustion engines; (e) any other apparatus determined by regulation of the Government; (f) the piping and accessories used for operating the apparatus contemplated in subparagraphs (a) to (e). *Stationary Enginemen Act*, S.Q. 1979, c. 63, s. 291.

STATIONARY ENGINEER. See CHIEF ~.

STATIONARY ENGINEMAN. Any person who directs or supervises the operation of a stationary engine or attends to the maintenance or inspection thereof. *Stationary Enginemen Act*, R.S.Q. 1977, c. M-6, s. 2.

STATIONARY PLANT. See LOW-PRESSURE ~.

STATIONARY POWER PLANT. An installation comprised of one or more boilers, (i) containing steam at a pressure of more than 15; or (ii) containing water at a temperature at any boiler outlet of more than 250°F., and in addition a stationary power plant may have, (iii) one or more boilers containing steam at a pressure of 15 or less, or water at a temperature at any boiler outlet of more than 212°F. and up to and including 250°F.; and (iv) one or more compressors or refrigeration compressors, and the total Therm-hour rating of all such boilers and compressors is more than 17. *Operating Engineers Act*, R.S.O. 1980, c. 363, s. 1.

STATIONARY SOURCE. Any source of emission of one or more air contaminants other than a motor vehicle, ship, train or aircraft. *Clean Air Act*, R.S.C. 1985, c. C-32, s. 2.

STATION LICENCE. A licence issued by the Minister for the establishment and operation of a radio station in Canada, or on board (a) any ship or vessel that is registered or licensed under the Canada Shipping Act or owned or under the direction or control of Her Majesty in right of Canada or a province; (b) any aircraft registered in Canada; or (c) any spacecraft under the direction or control of Her Majesty in right of Canada or a province, a citizen or resident of Canada or a corporation incorporated or resident in Canada. *General Radio Regulations, Part I*, C.R.C., c. 1371, s. 2.

STATION PROTECTION SIGNAL. A stop and

proceed signal equipped with a marker displaying the letters "SPS", used to protect trains or engines occupying the main track in yards or at stations in the block protected by the signal. *Regulations No. O-8, Uniform Code of Operating Rules*, C.R.C., c. 1175, Part III, s. 2.

STATION WAGON. A dual purpose vehicle designed for transporting not more than 9 persons, with a rear seat accessible from a side door, and designed so that the seats may be removed or folded out of the way to increase the property carrying space in the vehicle. *Motor Vehicle Act*, R.S.B.C. 1979, c. 288, s. 1.

STATION WAGON OR CAR COAT. A coat of any length with or without a sheepskin or other fur or simulated fur collar and made of, (i) waterproof or water-repellent outer material of cotton, rayon, vinyl or nylon of any weight; (ii) synthetic material including bemberg, orlon, dacron, acetate, viscose or any mixture thereof; or (iii) plastic coated material, the lining of which may be padded or blanketed with textile material or made of sheepskin or any other material in whole or in part. *Industrial Standards Act*, R.R.O. 1980, Reg. 519, s. 1.

STATISTICAL AGENCY OF CANADA. The Dominion Bureau of Statistics or the successor of the Bureau. *Statistics Act*, S.N.S. 1970-71, c. 18, s. 2.

STATISTICAL INFORMATION. Information relative to the economic, financial, industrial, commercial, social and general activities and condition of persons, whether such information is collected by means of sampling or any other statistical method. *Statistics Act*, R.S.O. 1980, c. 480, s. 1.

STATISTICIAN. See CHIEF ~.

STATISTICS. See VITAL ~.

STATISTICS CANADA. The federal body which collects, analyzes, processes and distributes information on the Canadian economy and society and offers statistical users consulting and inquiry services.

STATOCRACY. *n.* Government by the state only, without church interference.

STATU QUO. See IN ~.

STATUS. *n.* The total legal capacity or incapacity of an individual in relation to that person's community, in connection with acquiring and exercising legal rights and performing legal acts. J.G. McLeod, *The Conflict of Laws* (Calgary: Carswell, 1983) at 235. See CONTROL ~; FAMILY ~; FOUNDATION ~; INSURABLE ~; MARITAL ~; PEDIGREED ~; REGISTERED ~.

STATUS AND ESSENTIAL POWERS. Attributes of a federally-incorporated company by which, if a province enacts a law which is within its legislative competence, but which would impair those attributes, that law can be held inapplicable to any such federally-incorporated company. P.W. Hogg, *Constitutional Law of Canada*, 2d ed. (Toronto: Carswell, 1985) at 519.

STATUS HEARING. If an action in Ontario has not been listed for trial or disposed of 2 years after a statement of defence was filed, the registrar mails the parties a notice of status hearing. G.D. Watson & C. Perkins, eds., *Holmested & Watson: Ontario Civil Procedure* (Toronto: Carswell, 1984) at 48-9.

STATUS INDIAN. A person statutorily defined by the Indian Act. P.W. Hogg, *Constitutional Law of Canada*, 2d ed. (Toronto: Carswell, 1985) at 552.

STATUS OFFENCE. An offence characterized by a "state of being" instead of an "act of doing". D. Stuart, *Canadian Criminal Law: a treatise*, 2d ed. (Toronto: Carswell, 1987) at 69.

STATUS OF WOMEN CANADA. A federal body which monitors government programs and policies to promote sexual equality, coordinates measures to improve women's status in the federal departments and encourages non-governmental and federal-provincial consultation on these issues.

STATUS QUO. [L.] The state in which something is or was.

STATUTABLE. *adj.* Governed or introduced by statute law.

STATUTE. *n.* A law or act which expresses the will of a legislature or Parliament. See ACT OR ~; CODIFYING ~; CONSOLIDATING ~; CREDITORS' RELIEF ~; CURATIVE ~; DECLARATORY ~; ENABLING ~; EQUITY OF A ~; FEDERAL ~; GUEST ~; IMPERIAL ~S; INCOME TAX ~; PENAL ~; REMEDIAL ~; REVISED ~S.

STATUTE BARRED. Said of a cause of action for which proceedings cannot be brought because the limitation period has expired.

STATUTE LABOUR. The inhabitants of a county were required either to do certain work, known as statute labour, annually upon the highways or to pay a levy.

STATUTE OF ELIZABETH. The British statute which first attempted to comprehensively prohibit fraudulent conveyances. C.R.B. Dunlop, *Creditor-Debtor Law in Canada* (Toronto: Carswell, 1981) at 509.

STATUTE OF FRAUDS. A statute passed to prevent perjuries and frauds.

STATUTE OF LIMITATIONS. A statute which prescribes the specified period of time within which criminal charges must be laid or legal actions must be taken.

STATUTE OF WESTMINSTER. The British statute which repealed the Colonial Laws Validity Act as it applied to the dominions. By section 2(2) it granted each dominion power to amend or repeal imperial statutes which were part of the law of that dominion and it stated that no dominion statute would be void on grounds of repugnancy to an existing or future imperial statute. Section 7(2) clarified that section 2 applied to Canada's provincial Legislatures in addition to Canada's federal Parliament, but that the Parliament and each legislature could only enact laws within their own jurisdiction under the B.N.A. Act. The power to amend or repeal extended to both future and existing imperial statutes. P.W. Hogg, *Constitutional Law of Canada*, 2d ed. (Toronto: Carswell, 1985) at 41.

STATUTORY. *adj.* Governed or introduced by statute law.

STATUTORY AMALGAMATION. Under a prescribed procedure, two or more companies incorporated under one governing act enter into a joint agreement prescribing the terms and conditions of amalgamation and the way to effect it. When the procedure is completed, the amalgamated companies are treated as a single company. H. Sutherland, D.B. Horsley & J.M. Edmiston, eds., *Fraser's Handbook on Canadian Company Law*, 7th ed. (Toronto: Carswell, 1985) at 525.

STATUTORY APPROPRIATION. 1. An amount permitted or directed to be paid from the Revenue Fund that (i) is recommended by the Commissioner and authorized by Ordinance but that was not included in the estimates; or (ii) has been included in the estimates and previously authorized by an Ordinance permitting the charging of moneys to a purpose; or (iii) is authorized pursuant to sections 34 or 43. *Financial Administration Act*, S.N.W.T. 1982, c. 2, s. 2. 2. An amount permitted or directed to be paid from the General Revenue Fund by this or any other Act but does not include an amount paid (i) under the authority of a supply vote; (ii) pursuant to section 50, 51 or 57; (iii) pursuant to section 75; or (iv) to reduce the principal amount of any Government securities. *Financial Administration Act*, R.S.A. 1980, c. F-9, s. 1.

STATUTORY AUTHORITY. The Crown or any other person authorized by statute to expropriate or to cause injurious affection to land, or, upon condition that compensation be paid therefor, to take, interfere with or injure property other than land.

STATUTORY COURT. A court which derives its existence and powers from statute. S.A. Cohen, *Due Process of Law* (Toronto: Carswell, 1977) at 395.

STATUTORY DECLARATION. A solemn declaration in the form and manner from time to time provided by the provincial evidence acts or by the Canada Evidence Act.

STATUTORY INCREASE. The amount by which the rent charged for a rental unit may be increased without application to the Minister under this Act or may have been increased without application under the Residential Tenancies Act or under The Residential Premises Rent Review Act, 1975 (2nd Session). *Residential Rent Regulation Act*, S.O. 1986, c. 63, s. 1.

STATUTORY INSTRUMENT. (a) Any rule, order, regulation, ordinance, direction, form, tariff of costs or fees, letters patent, commission, warrant, proclamation, by-law, resolution or other instrument issued, made or established (i) in the execution of a power conferred by or under an Act of Parliament, by or under which such instrument is expressly authorized to be issued, made or established otherwise than by the conferring on any person or body of powers or functions in relation to a matter to which such instrument relates; or (ii) by or under the authority of the Governor-in-Council, otherwise than in the execution of a power conferred by or under an Act of Parliament; but (b) does not include (i) any instrument referred to in paragraph (a) and issued, made or established by a corporation incorporated by or under an Act of Parliament unless (A) the instrument is a Regulation and the corporation by which it is made is one that is ultimately accountable, through a Minister, to Parliament for the conduct of its affairs; or (B) the instrument is one for the contravention of which a penalty, fine or imprisonment is prescribed by or under an Act of Parliament; (ii) any instrument referred to in paragraph (a) and issued, made or established by a judicial or quasi-judicial body, unless the instrument is a rule, order or regulation governing the practice or procedure in proceedings before a judicial or quasi-judicial body established by or under an Act of Parliament; (iii) any instrument referred to in paragraph (a) and in respect of which, or in respect of the production or disclosure of which, any privilege exists by law or whose contents are limited to advice or information intended only for use or assistance in the making of a decision or the determination of policy, or in the ascertainment of any matter necessarily incidental thereto; or (iv) an Ordinance of the

Yukon Territory or the Northwest Territories or any instrument issued, made or established thereunder. *Statutory Instruments Act*, R.S.C. 1985, c. S-22, s. 2.

STATUTORY JURISDICTION. Jurisdiction whose source is a statute which defines the limits within which the jurisdiction must be exercised. S.A. Cohen, *Due Process of Law* (Toronto: Carswell, 1977) at 344.

STATUTORY LIEN. A lien on property which arises purely by statute; the lienholder's rights depend on the relevant statutory provisions. W.B. Rayner & R.H. McLaren, *Falconbridge on Mortgages*, 4th ed. (Toronto: Canada Law Book, 1977) at 11.

STATUTORY OLD AGE. Sixty-five years. *Teachers' Pension Plan Act*, R.S.Q. 1977, c. R-11, s. 1.

STATUTORY POWER. A power or right conferred by or under a statute, (i) to make any regulation, rule, by-law or order, or to give any other direction having force as subordinate legislation; (ii) to exercise a statutory power of decision; (iii) to require any person or party to do or to refrain from doing any act or thing that, but for such requirement, such person or party would not be required by law to do or to refrain from doing; (iv) to do any act or thing that would, but for such power or right, be a breach of the legal rights of any person or party.

STATUTORY POWER OF DECISION. A power or right conferred by or under a statute to make a decision deciding or prescribing, (i) the legal rights, powers, privileges, immunities, duties or liabilities of any person or party; or (ii) the eligibility of any person or party to receive, or to the continuation of, a benefit or licence, whether that person or party is legally entitled thereto or not, and includes the powers of an inferior court.

STATUTORY REMISSION. A provision, now abolished, under section 22(1) of the Penitentiary Act, 1970 by which a person sentenced to penitentiary for a fixed term was, when received into the penitentiary, credited with statutory remission amounting to one-quarter of the sentence as time off subject to good conduct.

STATUTUM AFFIRMATIVUM NON DEROGAT COMMUNI LEGI. [L.] An affirmative statute does not diminish the common law.

STAY. *n.* With respect to proceedings, an action to suspend them. See DAYS ~; LENGTH OF ~.

STAY OF ARBITRATION. An order interrupting an arbitration proceeding until some other action takes place.

STCC. *abbr.* The Standard Transportation Commodity Code as filed with the Canadian Transport Commission. *Public Commercial Vehicles Amendment Act*, S.O. 1986, c. 11, s. 3.

STCC NUMBER. A number in STCC representing the goods or materials classified under that number. *Public Commercial Vehicles Amendment Act*, S.O. 1986, c. 11, s. 3.

STEAL. *v.* To commit theft. *Criminal Code*, R.S.C. 1985, c. C-46, s. 2.

STEALING. *n.* (a) Stealing is the act of fraudulently and without colour of right taking, or fraudulently and without colour of right converting to the use of any person, any thing capable of being stolen, with intent (i) to deprive the owner, or any person having any special property or interest therein, temporarily or absolutely of such thing or of such property or interest; (ii) to pledge the same or deposit it as security; (iii) to part with it under a condition as to its return which the person parting with it may be unable to perform; or (iv) to deal with it in such a manner that it cannot be restored in the condition in which it was at the time of such taking and conversion; (b) stealing is committed when the offender moves the thing or causes it to move or to be moved, or begins to cause it to become movable, with intent to steal it; (c) the taking or conversion may be fraudulent, although effected without secrecy or attempt at concealment; and (d) it is immaterial whether the thing converted was taken for the purpose of conversion, or whether it was, at the time of the conversion, in the lawful possession of the person converting. *National Defence Act*, R.S.C. 1970, c. N-4, s. 104.

STEAM BOILER. Any boiler, vessel or structure in which steam is generated for power or heating purposes and any boiler, vessel or other appliance in which steam, gas, air or liquid is contained under pressure, and includes all pipes, apparatus and machinery attached to or connected with a steam boiler.

STEAM BOILER INSURANCE. Insurance on steam boilers and pipes, engines and machinery connected therewith or operated thereby, against explosion, rupture and accident and against personal injury or loss of life, and against destruction of or damage to property resulting therefrom. *Insurance Act*, R.S.A. 1980, c. I-5, s. 1.

STEAM DISTILLED WOOD TURPENTINE. A liquid obtained by steam-distillation of the wood of coniferous trees. *Turpentine Labelling Regulations*, C.R.C., c. 1140, s. 2.

STEAM DREDGE. A dredge, the primary power plant of which consists of boilers and steam machinery. *Marine Engineer Examination Regulations*, C.R.C., c. 1443, s. 2.

STEAMER. *n.* Except as provided under the Load Line Rules, means any ship propelled by machinery and not coming within the definition of sailing ship. *Canada Shipping Act*, R.S.C. 1985, c. S-9, s. 2.

STEAMFITTER. *n.* A person who, (i) lays out, assembles, installs, maintains or repairs any heating system, cooling system, process system or industrial system; (ii) installs or connects piping in any building or structure; (iii) installs the piping for any process, including a process that conveys gas, or the tubing for any pneumatic or airhandling system; or (iv) reads and understands design drawings, manufacturer's literature and installation diagrams for any system referred to in subclause (i), but does not include a person engaged in the manufacture of equipment or the assembly of a unit, prior to delivery to a building, structure or site. *Apprenticeship and Tradesmen's Qualifications Act*, R.R.O. 1980, Reg. 59, s. 1.

STEAMFITTER-PIPEFITTER TRADE. Includes (a) the laying out, assembling, fabricating, installing, maintaining or repairing of piping used in connection with heating systems, cooling systems, process systems, industrial systems, pneumatic systems and gas systems but does not include piping used in connection with portable water or sewage systems or piping assembled or installed during the manufacture of equipment prior to delivery to a building, structure or site; and (b) the interpreting of drawings, manufacturer's literature and installation diagrams used in connection with the piping for a heating system, a cooling system, a process system, an industrial system, a pneumatic system or a gas system. *An Act to Amend the Boiler and Pressure Vessel Act*, S.N.B. 1986, c. 17, s. 1.

STEAM HOISTING PLANT. A hoist equipped with a drum and a hoisting rope or chain that is driven by a steam-driven prime mover and used for raising, lowering or swinging material. *Operating Engineers Act*, R.S.O. 1980, c. 363, s. 1.

STEAM PLANT. 1. A plant in which the boilers may be used for generating or utilizing steam and includes any pipe, fitting or other equipment that is attached to the boilers and constitutes one unit with them. 2. A plant in which steam is used for motive power. *Engine Operators Act*, R.S.N.S. 1967, c. 89, s. 1. See LOW PRESSURE ~.

STEAM-POWERED PLANT. A turbine or engine having a Therm-hour rating of more than 3.816 driven by steam, (i) from a boiler that is not owned by or under the control of the user of the turbine or engine; or (ii) from another plant of the user of the turbine or engine. *Operating Engineers Act*, R.S.O. 1980, c. 363, s. 1.

STEAMSHIP. *n.* 1. Except as provided under the Load Line Rules, means any ship propelled by machinery and not coming within the definition of sailing ship. *Canada Shipping Act*, R.S.C. 1985, c. S-9, s. 2. 2. Includes (a) every ship that has sufficient mechanical means for propulsion, and does not have sufficient sail area for navigation under sails alone; and (b) every lighter, barge or other ship that is towed and does not have independent means of propulsion. *General Load Line Rules*, C.R.C., c. 1425, s. 2. See PASSENGER ~.

STEAM VESSEL. Includes any vessel propelled by machinery, whether under sail or not. *Rules of the Road for the Great Lakes*, C.R.C., c. 1464, s. 2.

STEEL. *n.* Any metal or combination of metals containing 50 per cent or more, by weight, of iron. *Customs Tariff*, R.S.C. 1985, c. C-54, s. 2. See BLACK ~.

STEERING COLUMN. The structural housing that surrounds a steering shaft. *Motor Vehicle Safety Regulations*, C.R.C., c. 1038, s. 204.

STEERING COMMITTEE. A sub-committee on agenda and procedure which recommends, by report, the way a committee should proceed to study its order of reference and advises on topics like times of sittings, witnesses and subject matters for each sitting. A. Fraser, G.A. Birch & W.A. Dawson, eds., *Beauchesne's Rules and Forms of the House of Commons of Canada*, 5th ed. (Toronto: Carswell, 1978) at 197.

STEERING CONTROL SYSTEM. The basic steering mechanism and its associated trim hardware including any portion of a steering column assembly that provides energy absorption upon impact. *Motor Vehicle Safety Regulations*, C.R.C., c. 1038, s. 203.

STEERING SHAFT. A component that transmits steering torque from the steering wheel to the steering gear. *Motor Vehicle Safety Regulations*, C.R.C., c. 1038, s. 204.

STEERING WHEEL INJURY. An injury, such as rupture of the liver or a "floating chest" caused by the impact of a steering wheel on the upper abdomen and chest of a driver during sudden deceleration. F.A. Jaffe, *A Guide to Pathological Evidence*, 2d ed. (Toronto: Carswell, 1983) at 184.

STEM. See CAP ~S.

STEMLESS FRUIT. Any fruit that has no

portion of the stem attached thereto and has no broken skin at the stem end. *Farm Products Grades and Sales Act*, R.R.O. 1980, Reg. 332, s. 1.

STEPHENS' DIG. *abbr.* Stephens' Quebec Digest.

STEPPARENT. *n.* Includes a person who lives with the parent of a child as the husband or wife of the parent for a period of not less than 2 years and who contributes to the support of the child for not less than 1 year. *Family Law Reform Amendment Act*, S.B.C. 1985, c. 72, s. 3.

STERADIAN. *n.* The unit of measurement of a solid angle, being the angle with its vertex at the centre of a sphere and subtended by an area on the spherical surface equal to that of a square with sides equal in length to the radius. *Weights and Measures Act*, S.C. 1970-71-72, c. 36, Schedule 1.

STEREOTYPE BLOCK. The printer's block supplied by the Chief Electoral Officer to a returning officer, and of which an impression is printed on the back of each ballot paper by the printer thereof. Elections acts.

STERILIZED. *adj.* In respect of canned fish, means fish that has been treated with heat to prevent spoilage and to destroy all pathogenic organisms. Fish Inspection regulations.

STERILIZED CANNED CREAM. Cream that has been heated without concentration or appreciable loss of volume to a temperature of at least 100°C for a length of time sufficient to kill all the organisms present and that is packed in hermetically sealed containers and that contains no fat or oil other than milk-fat. *Farm Products Grades and Sales Act*, R.R.O. 1980, Reg. 327, s. 1.

STERILIZED MILK. Milk that has been heated without concentration or appreciable loss of volume to a temperature of at least 100°C for a length of time sufficient to kill all organisms present, that is packed in hermetically sealed containers and that contains, (i) not less than 3 1/4 per cent by weight of milk-fat; (ii) not less than 11 3/4 per cent by weight of total milk solids; and (iii) no fat or oil other than milk-fat. *Farm Products Grades and Sales Act*, R.R.O. 1980, Reg. 327, s. 1.

STERLING. *n.* British money.

STERLING. *adj.* Genuine.

STERNLIGHT. *n.* A white light placed as nearly as practicable at the stern showing an unbroken light over an arc of the horizon of 135 degrees and so fixed as to show the light 67.5 degrees from right aft on each side of the vessel. *Collision Regulations*, C.R.C., c. 1416, Rule 3.

STERN TRAWL. An otter trawl designed for or adapted to hauling fish over an inclined ramp in the stern of a vessel. Fishery regulations.

STET. [L.] Let it stand.

STEVEDORE. *n.* A person who stows cargo on board a ship.

STEVEDORING. *v.* The loading or unloading of vessels or railway cars.

STEVENS' DIG. *abbr.* Stevens' New Brunswick Digest.

STEWARD. *n.* 1. A person elected to represent union members in a particular part of a plant or department. 2. An association steward or Commission steward in running horse races and, with respect to harness horse races, includes a judge. *Race Track Supervision Regulations*, C.R.C., c. 441, s. 2. See ASSOCIATION ~; COMMISSION ~; JOB-SITE ~; PRESIDING ~; SHOP ~; UNION ~.

STEWART. *abbr.* Stewart's Vice-Admiralty Reports (N.S.), 1803-1813.

STICKINESS. *n.* For the purposes of section 118 of Schedule IV, a condition on the surface of a brake cup such that fibres will be pulled from a wad of U.S.P. absorbent cotton when the wad is drawn across the surface of the cup. *Motor Vehicle Safety Regulations*, C.R.C., c. 1038, s. 2.

STILL. *n.* Any distilling apparatus whatever adapted or adaptable to the distillation of spirits. *Excise Act*, R.S.C. 1985, c. E-14, s. 3. See CHEMICAL ~.

STILLBIRTH. *var.* **STILL-BIRTH.** *n.* 1. The complete expulsion or extraction from its mother after at least twenty weeks pregnancy, of a product of conception in which, after such expulsion or extraction, there is no breathing, beating of the heart, pulsation of the umbilical cord, or unmistakable movement of voluntary muscle. Vital Statistics acts. 2. If the duration of the pregnancy cannot be determined, the complete expulsion or extraction from its mother of a product of conception, weighing five hundred grams or over, and in which after such expulsion or extraction there is no beating of the heart, pulsation of the umbilical cord or unmistakable movement of voluntary muscle. Vital Statistics acts.

STIPEND. *n.* Salary.

STIPENDIARY MAGISTRATE. Includes provincial magistrate, acting provincial magistrate and deputy provincial magistrate. *Stipendiary Magistrate Act*, R.S.N.S. 1967, c. 292, s. 27 (part).

STIPENDIUM. *n.* Pay, wages.

STIPULATED DAMAGE. Liquidated damages.

STIPULATION. *n.* 1. A bargain. 2. In an agreement, a material term.

STIRPES. See PER ~.

STIRRER. *n.* The structure designed to distribute the microwave energy within a cavity. *Radiation Emitting Devices Regulations*, C.R.C., c. 1370, s. 1.

STOCK. *n.* 1. (a) Stock of goods, wares, merchandise and chattels ordinarily the subject of trade and commerce; (b) the goods, wares, merchandise or chattels in which a person trades, or that he produces or that are outputs of, or with which he carries on, any business, trade or occupation. Bulk Sales acts. 2. Any horse, cattle, sheep or poultry or any fur-bearing animal. 3. Includes a share, stock, fund, annuity or security transferable in books kept by a company or society established or to be established, or transferable by deed alone, or by deed accompanied by other formalities, and a share or interest in it. See DEBENTURE ~; DEFERRED ~; FARM ~; FEED ~; FIRST ISSUE OF ~; ISSUED CAPITAL ~; LISTED ~; LIVE~; NURSERY ~; PENNY ~; PROCESS ~; PROPERTY IN ~; ROLLING ~; SEED ~.

STOCKBROKER. *n.* A person who buys and sells stock or securities as the agent of others.

STOCKDEALER. *n.* Includes a person who, whether on his own behalf or as agent for another and whether on a commission basis or otherwise, (a) buys or offers to buy stock; and (b) sells or offers to sell, or has in his possession for sale, or takes out of the Province stock or beef, but does not include a resident of the Province who is a rancher and whose transactions in stock are restricted to those that arise solely from his occupation as a rancher. *Livestock Brand Act*, R.S.B.C. 1979, c. 241, s. 1.

STOCK DIVIDEND. Includes any dividend paid by a corporation to the extent that it is paid by the issuance of shares of any class of its capital stock.

STOCK ESCROW TRUST. Stock is vested in a trustee who is required to transfer it when a certain event occurs. D.M.W. Waters, *The Law of Trusts in Canada*, 2d ed. (Toronto: Carswell, 1984) at 452.

STOCK IN BULK. A stock or portion of a stock that is the subject of a sale in bulk. Bulk Sales acts.

STOCK SAVINGS PLAN. An arrangement, other than a retirement savings plan, between a qualified dealer and an investor under which the dealer holds those eligible securities that the investor: (a) owns; and (b) has designated for the purpose of entitling the investor to a stock savings tax credit for any taxation year.

STOCKTON. *abbr.* Stockton's Vice-Admiralty Reports (N.B.), 1879-1891.

STOCKYARD. *n.* Any area of land in operation as a public market for the purchase and sale of livestock declared by the Minister to be a stockyard under this Part, with the buildings, fences, gates, chutes, weigh scales and other equipment situated thereon and used in connection therewith, or any area of land used for the accommodation of livestock at ocean ports of export that may be declared by the Minister to be a stockyard under this Part. *Livestock and Livestock Products Act*, R.S.C. 1985, c. L-9, s. 10. See PUBLIC ~.

STONE. See UNFINISHED ~.

STONE MOUND. A mound of stones not less than 1 1/2 feet high having a base not less than 3 feet in diameter. *Surveys Act*, R.R.O. 1980, Reg. 927, s. 1.

STONE QUARRY. Includes a mine producing dimension stone or crushed rock for use as aggregates or for other construction purposes. *Income Tax Regulations*, C.R.C., c. 945, s. 1104.

STONE TREE FRUIT. A tree fruit that contains a stone or pit within it. *British Columbia Tree Fruit Export Regulations*, C.R.C., c. 146, s. 2.

STOP. *n.* See TRANSFER ~.

STOP. *v.* (i) When required, a complete cessation from vehicular movement; and (ii) when prohibited, any halting even momentarily of a vehicle, whether occupied or not, except when necessary to avoid conflict with other traffic or in compliance with the directions of a peace officer or traffic control device.

STOP ORDER. 1. An order issued on application to the court by someone who claims to be entitled to securities or money held or to be held by the accountant for the benefit of someone else which directs that the securities or money shall not be handled without notifying the applicant or moving party. G.D. Watson & C. Perkins, eds., *Holmested & Watson: Ontario Civil Procedure* (Toronto: Carswell, 1984) at 73-5. 2. Order the person to whom it is directed to immediately stop or cause the source of contaminant to stop adding to, emitting or discharging into the natural environment any contaminant either permanently or for a specific period of time. *Environmental Protection Act*, R.S.O. 1980, c. 141, s. 117.

STOP OR STAND. When prohibited means any stopping or standing of a vehicle, whether occupied or not, except when necessary to avoid conflict with other traffic or in compliance with the directions of a peace officer or traffic control sign or signal.

STOP-OVER CENTRE. An establishment that receives at least 10 children on a casual basis for day care for periods of up to 24 consecutive hours. *An Act Respecting Child Day Care*, S.Q. 1979, c. 85, s. 1.

STOPPAGE. See WORK ~.

STOPPAGE IN TRANSITU. The right of an unpaid seller to take back the possession of goods sold on credit and to retain them until the buyer, who became insolvent before possessing the goods, tenders the price.

STOP WORK ORDER. An order made by an inspector under the authority of section 14 or by the board under section 15 directing that all work cease in a place of employment or on the site of construction or any part thereof. *Employment Safety Act*, S.M. 1973, c. 14, s. 1.

STORAGE. *n.* 1. Includes any keeping or retention in Manitoba of tangible personal property for any purpose except (i) for sale in the course of a business; or (ii) for the purpose of being processed, fabricated or manufactured into, attached to or incorporated into other tangible personal property. *Revenue Tax Act*, R.S.M. 1970, c. R150, s. 2. 2. Includes any keeping or retention in Ontario for any purpose except retail sale or subsequent use outside Ontario of tangible personal property purchased from a vendor, but does not include the keeping, retaining or exercising of any right or power over tangible personal property shipped or brought into Ontario for the purpose of transporting it subsequently outside Ontario or for the purpose of being processed, fabricated or manufactured into, attached to or incorporated into other tangible personal property to be transported outside Ontario and thereafter used solely outside Ontario. *Retail Sales Tax Act*, R.S.O. 1980, c. 454, s. 1. 3. The introduction into and retention in a storage reservoir of any hydrocarbon, whether liquid or gaseous, with the object of recovery of the substance so stored. *Petroleum Underground Storage Act*, R.S.B.C. 1979, c. 325, s. 1. See COLD ~.

STORAGE AREA. An area that may contain one or more storage reservoirs. *Gas Storage Exploration Act*, S.N.S. 1970, c. 6, s. 1. See CONTAINER ~.

STORAGE BATTERY. Includes an electrical storage battery, generator, electrical motor distributor, and the necessary wires, wiring, or parts thereof. *Garage Keepers Act*, R.S.M. 1970, c. G10, s. 14.

STORAGE CHARGE. 1. The charge made by the licensee of an elevator for maintaining in the elevator a stock of grain available for delivery on presentation of an elevator receipt entitling the holder to the delivery of grain in accordance with the receipt. *Canada Grain Act*, R.S.C. 1985, c. G-10, s. 2. 2. A charge payable on goods remaining on a wharf after the expiration of free time. Canada regulations. 3. A toll charged on goods in respect of the period of time that the goods are stored at a canal. Canada regulations.

STORAGE COMPANY. A person engaged in the business of storing gas. *Ontario Energy Board Act*, R.S.O. 1980, c. 332, s. 1.

STORAGE DEVELOPMENT. Includes (a) the physical structures within the severance line required for the storage of the stream-waters for the production of power; (b) the dams or other storage works, the intakes and water conduits within the severance line; (c) all hydraulic or electrical machinery, appliances, fixtures, equipment and appurtenances; (d) lands and rights-of-way required in connection therewith; and (e) the clearings, roads, trails and railways required to be constructed that are still used and useful in connection therewith and not independently profitable. *Dominion Water Power Regulations*, C.R.C., c. 1603, s. 2.

STORAGE EQUIPMENT. Equipment of a design and construction suitable for the storage or the incineration and storage of human excrement in a pleasure boat including such equipment that is an integral part of a toilet. *Environmental Protection Act*, R.R.O. 1980, Reg. 305, s. 1.

STORAGE FACILITY. See ENERGY ~.

STORAGE GARAGE. A building or part thereof intended for the storage or parking of motor vehicles and which contains no provision for the repair or servicing of such vehicles.

STORAGE PLANT. See ANIMAL FOOD ~.

STORAGE RATE. A rate payable on goods remaining on Corporation property after the expiration of free time. *Port Alberni Assembly Wharves By-law*, C.R.C., c. 913, s. 2.

STORAGE RECEIPT. See GRAIN ~.

STORAGE RESERVOIR. A naturally occurring underground cavity or system of cavities or pores, or an underground space or spaces created by some external means, that may be used for the storage of a hydrocarbon.

STORAGE TANK. A drum, tank, or container of any kind, other than a vehicle fuel tank, in which flammable petroleum products are kept or stored. See BULK ~; HOT WATER ~.

STORAGE-TYPE WATER HEATER. A service

water heater with an integral hot water storage tank. *Building Code Act*, R.R.O. 1980, Reg. 87, s. 1.

STORAGE WAREHOUSE. See KEEPER OF ~.

STORE. *v.* 1. In relation to a substance means to store it in a container or structure whether or not the container is open to the air, and for the purpose of this definition a container includes any pond, pit, lagoon or similar containment facility, whether natural or artifical. *Waste Management Act*, S.B.C. 1982, c. 41, s. 1. 2. When used with reference to water, means collect, impound and conserve. *Water Act*, R.S.B.C. 1979, c. 429, s. 1.

STORE. *n.* Any building or portion of a building, booth, stall or other place where goods are exposed or offered for sale or auction. See AGENCY ~; CHAIN ~; COLD ~; COMPANY ~; CONSUMABLE ~S; DETACHED ~; DRUG ~; LIQUOR ~; PUBLIC ~S; RETAIL ~; SEPARATE ~ OR WAREHOUSE; SHIPS ~S; SURPLUS ~S.

STORED. *adj.* 1. When used with respect to farm produce, means placed in a grain elevator upon terms that the ownership shall remain in the owner of the farm produce until such time as the owner has sold the farm produce and has received due compensation or has removed the farm produce from the elevator. *Grain Elevator Storage Act*, S.O. 1983, c. 40, s. 1. 2. To have kept, held or stored, cheese at a temperature of 35°F or more for a period of 60 days or more from the date of the beginning of the manufacturing process. *Food and Drug Regulations*, C.R.C., c. 870, c. B.08.033.

STOREKEEPER. *n.* A person who sells or exposes for sale milk or cream to consumers from, or at a store or shop of which that person is proprietor or manager.

STORES ACCOUNT. See REVOLVING ~.

STOREY. *n.* A division of a building between a floor, not below the grade level of the surrounding ground, and the floor or roof next above. See EXIT ~; FIRST ~; HALF ~.

STORM DRAIN. See BUILDING ~.

STORM DRAINAGE PIPING. All the connected piping that conveys storm water to a place of disposal and includes the building storm drain, building storm sewer, rain water leader and area drain installed to collect surface water from the area of a building and the piping that drains water from a swimming pool or from water-cooled air-conditioning equipment but does not include, (i) a main storm sewer; (ii) a sub-surface drain; or (iii) a foundation drain.

Ontario Water Resources Act, R.R.O. 1980, Reg. 736, s. 1.

STORM SEWER. See BUILDING ~; TRUNK ~ SYSTEM.

STORM WATER. Rain water or water resulting from the melting of snow or ice.

STOVE. *n.* An appliance intended for cooking and space heating. *Building Code Act*, R.R.O. 1980, Reg. 87, s. 1.

STOWAGE. *n.* 1. Money paid for the space where goods are stored. 2. The way a ship is loaded. See BROKEN ~.

STRAIGHT-LINE DEPRECIATION. A uniform annual rate of depreciation of the value of an asset over its useful life.

STRAIGHT TIME. The hours of work defined in a collective agreement as regular straight time hours. *Pacific Terminal Tariff By-law*, C.R.C., c. 1083, s. 2.

STRAIGHT-TIME PAY. Regular wages excluding bonuses and overtime.

STRAINED FOOD. A food that is of a generally uniform particle size that does not require and does not encourage chewing before being swallowed. *Food and Drug Regulations*, C.R.C., c. 870, c. B.25.001.

STRAMINEUS HOMO. [L. man of straw] A person with no means.

STRANDING. *v.* Of a ship, running aground on the shore or a beach.

STRANGER TO A TRANSACTION. Someone who takes no part or no part which produces a legal effect in that transaction.

STRANGULATION. *n.* Death caused by compression or constriction of the neck. See LIGATURE ~; MANUAL ~.

STRAP. *n.* A narrow non-woven material used in place of webbing. *Motor Vehicle Safety Regulations*, C.R.C., c. 1038, s. 209.

STRATA LOT. A lot shown as such on a strata plan. *Condominium Act*, R.S.B.C. 1979, c. 61, s. 1.

STRATOCRACY. *n.* Government by the military.

STRAY. *n.* 1. An animal that is unlawfully running at large or that has broken into premises enclosed by a lawful fence. 2. A reindeer, found during an annual roundup of a herd held by the owner, that bears the registered mark of another owner. *Northwest Territories Reindeer Regulations*, C.R.C., c. 1238, s. 2. See VALUELESS ~.

STRAY ANIMAL. A domestic animal found on the premises of a person other than its owner.

STREAM. See EFFLUENT GAS ~; RIVER AND ~.

STREAM OR WATER. 1. Any river, brook, lake, pond, creek or other flowing or standing water. 2. Includes a natural watercourse or source of water supply, whether usually containing water or not, ground water, and a lake, river, creek, spring, ravine, swamp and gulch. *Water Act*, R.S.B.C. 1979, c. 429, s. 1.

STREET. *n.* A highway, road, square, lane, mews, court, alley and passage, whether a thoroughfare or not. See ONE-WAY ~; PRIVATE ~.

STREET CAR. 1. Every device propelled by electricity travelling exclusively upon rails when upon or crossing a street. *Motor Vehicle Act*, R.S.N.S. 1967, c. 191, s. 1. 2. Includes a car of an electric or steam railway. *Highway Traffic Amendment Act*, S.O. 1983, c. 63, s. 1.

STREET RESERVATION. The land reserved for a public road, street, lane, sidewalk or other public way. *Local Government Act*, S.Nfld. 1972, c. 32, s. 2.

STREET TRADE. A business carried on in the street, i.e. newspaper vending or peddling.

STRENGTH DECK. The uppermost continuous deck, except in way of an effective superstructure, when the superstructure deck shall be considered the strength deck. *Hull Inspection Regulations*, C.R.C., c. 1432, s. 2.

STRICTISSIMI JURIS. [L.] Of the strictest law.

STRICT LIABILITY. 1. Criminal liability based on simple negligence. D. Stuart, *Canadian Criminal Law: A Treatise*, 2d ed. (Toronto: Carswell, 1987) at 157. 2. Imposed in tort law when a lawful activity exposes others to extraordinary risks even though no fault is involved on the part of the "wrongdoer". John G. Fleming, *The Law of Torts*, 6th ed. (Sydney: The Law Book Company Limited, 1983) at 302.

STRICTUM JUS. [L.] Law only, in contrast to equity.

STRIKE. *v.* See TO ~.

STRIKE. *n.* 1. Includes a cessation of work or a refusal to work by employees, in combination, in concert or in accordance with a common understanding, and a slowdown of work or other concerted activity on the part of employees in relation to their work that is designed to restrict or limit output. 2. Includes (i) a cessation of work; (ii) a refusal to work; or (iii) a refusal to continue to work, by 2 or more employees acting in combination or in concert or in accordance with a common understanding for the purpose of compelling their employer or an employers' organization to agree to terms or conditions of employment or to aid other employees to compel their employer or an employers' organization to accept terms or conditions of employment. See ECONOMIC ~; GENERAL ~; ILLEGAL ~; JURISDICTIONAL ~; SECONDARY ~; SYMPATHY ~; TOKEN ~; UNAUTHORIZED ~; WILDCAT ~.

STRIKE BENEFIT. An amount paid to a member of a union by the union during a strike.

STRIKEBREAKER. *var.* **STRIKE BREAKER.** A worker hired during a strike to help defeat the strike. See PROFESSIONAL ~.

STRIKE FUND. A reserve accumulated by a union to assist members during a strike.

STRIKE NOTICE. A formal announcement by a union or group of workers that it or they intend(s) to go on strike on a certain date.

STRIKE OFF THE ROLL. To remove the name of a solicitor from the rolls of a court and thereby disentitle that person to practise.

STRIKE OUT. To expunge part or all of a document or pleading, with or without leave to amend. G.D. Watson & C. Perkins, eds., *Holmested & Watson: Ontario Civil Procedure* (Toronto: Carswell, 1984) at 25-7.

STRIKER. *n.* An employee who has joined fellow employees in stopping work.

STRIKE-RELATED MISCONDUCT. A course of conduct of incitement, intimidation, coercion, undue influence, provocation, infiltration, surveillance or any other like course of conduct intended to interfere with, obstruct, prevent, restrain or disrupt the exercise of any right under this Act in anticipation of, or during, a lawful strike or lock-out. *Labour Relations Amendment Act*, S.O. 1983, c. 42, s. 1

STRIKE VOTE. A vote conducted among members of a bargaining unit to determine whether they should go on strike.

STRIKING COMMITTEE. A parliamentary committee which prepares the membership lists for standing committees. A. Fraser, G.A. Birch & W.A. Dawson, eds., *Beauchesne's Rules and Forms of the House of Commons of Canada*, 5th ed. (Toronto: Carswell, 1978) at 190.

STRIKING OUT. See STRIKE OUT.

STRIKING PRICE. Where used in relation to a commodity futures option, means the price at which the purchaser of the option has the right to assume a long or short position in relation to the commodity futures contract that is the subject of the option.

STRIKING SURFACE. That part of a book, box or other container of matches that is designed for igniting matches. *Hazardous Products (Matches) Regulations*, C.R.C., c. 929, s. 2.

STRIP. *n.* 1. When applied to iron or steel, means a flat-rolled product of any shape (a) having a width of more than eight inches but not more than twelve inches, and a thickness of 0.2299 inch or less, or (b) having a width of eight inches or less and a thickness of 0.2030 inch or less. *Customs Tariff*, R.S.C. 1985, c. C-54, s. 2. 2. The rectangular portion of the landing area of the airport including the runway prepared for the take-off and landing of aircraft in a particular direction. Canada regulations. See MEDIAN ~; RACING ~.

STRIP MINE. A mine worked by removal of overlying strata and subsequent excavation of exposed coal in flat or substantially flat terrain.

STRIPPED BEEF. Any beef from which the pleura has been removed. *Food and Drug Act*, R.S.Nfld. 1970, c. 139, s. 23.

STROKE. *n.* A popular name for either an intracerebral hemorrhage or brain infarct. F.A. Jaffe, *A Guide to Pathological Evidence*, 2d ed. (Toronto: Carswell, 1983) at 46.

STRONG CIDER. Cider containing more than 7 per cent and not more than 13 per cent of alcohol by volume. *An Act Respecting the Commission de Contrôle des Permis d'Alcool*, R.S.Q. 1977, c. C-33, s. 2.

STRUCK-WORK CLAUSE. A clause in a collective bargaining agreement permitting employees to refuse work on materials coming from a strike-bound plant.

STRUCTURAL ALTERATION. Includes any work or construction which involves any change, modification, replacement, or repair of any supporting member of a building, including the bearing walls, columns, beams or girders thereof.

STRUCTURAL ALTERATIONS OR STRUC-TURALLY ALTERED. The application of labour and materials, not including ordinary maintenance to a dwelling unit, where the application of such labour and materials will: (i) effect a change in the dimensions or alter the existing interior plan of the dwelling unit; or (ii) extend the lifetime of the dwelling unit. *The House Building Assistance Act*, R.S.S. 1978, c. H-12, s. 2.

STRUCTURAL CHANGE. When used to refer to a building, means the alteration, defacement or removal of any normally permanent structural member or surface, whether repaired or not, if the nature of the repair is, or would be, such that other material replaces that which was removed. *Ontario Water Resources Act*, R.R.O. 1980, Reg. 736, s. 1.

STRUCTURAL DEFECT. See MAJOR ~.

STRUCTURAL EXTERMINATION. The destruction, prevention or control of a pest that may adversely affect a building, structure, machine, vehicle or their contents or the use or enjoyment thereof by any person by the use of a pesticide in, on or in the vicinity of the building, structure, machine or vehicle and includes the destruction, prevention or control of termites. *Pesticides Act*, R.S.O. 1980, c. 376, s. 1.

STRUCTURAL PEST CONTROL. The destruction, prevention or control of pests that may adversely affect a building, structure, machine, vehicle or their contents or the use or enjoyment thereof by any person. *Pest Control Products (Nova Scotia) Act*, S.N.S. 1986, c. 16, s. 3.

STRUCTURAL PLANS. (i) Copies of the architectural and engineering drawings prepared for a condominium project, revised to show all changes made to the date of registration; or (ii) plans comparable to architectural drawings containing sufficient information to enable the construction of the building therefrom, where the copies of the original drawings referred to in subclause (i) are unavailable or are inadequate for purposes of construction, mechanically reproduced on such translucent material as the examiner approves. *Condominium Act*, R.R.O. 1980, Reg. 122, s. 1.

STRUCTURE. *n.* 1. Any building, plant, machinery, equipment, storage tank, storage place, or fixture of any kind whatsoever erected or placed on, in, over or under any area of land or water. 2. Anything built or made on and affixed to or imbedded in land or affixed to or imbedded in land after being built or made elsewhere, and appurtenances thereto, and, without limiting the generality of the foregoing, includes (i) any building, structure, erection, wharf, pier, bulkhead, bridge, trestlework, vault, sidewalk, road, roadbed, lane, paving, pipeline, fountain, fishpond, drain, sewer, canal, or aqueduct built or made on and affixed to or imbedded in land or affixed to or imbedded in land after being built or made elsewhere, and appurtenances thereto; and (ii) any well, mine or excavation drilled, sunk or made in or on land and any appurtenances thereto, and a reference to a structure on land includes a structure in or beneath the surface of the land. See AIR-SUPPORTED ~; FARM ~; NON-RELOCAT-ABLE ~; ON-SITE BUILDING OR ~; PRO-

PORTIONAL TAX RATE ~; RELOCATABLE ~; TEMPORARY WORK ~.

STRUCTURED SETTLEMENT. Arrangements for periodic payments instead of a lump sum award of damages. John G. Fleming, *The Law of Torts*, 6th ed. (Sydney: The Law Book Company Limited, 1983) at 203.

STRUT. *n.* A transverse member of shoring and timbering that directly resists pressure from a wale or sheathing. *Occupational Health and Safety Act*, R.R.O. 1980, Reg. 691, s. 167.

STRYCHNINE. *n.* A vegetable alkaloid extracted from seeds of Strychnos nux vomica; it is a strong convulsant and nervous system stimulant. F.A. Jaffe, *A Guide to Pathological Evidence*, 2d ed. (Toronto: Carswell, 1983) at 184.

STUART. *abbr.* Stuart, Vice-Admiralty Reports (Que.), 1836-1874.

STUCK YOLK. A condition in which the yolk membrane adheres to the shell. *Live Stock and Live Stock Products Act*, R.R.O. 1980, Reg. 582, s. 1.

STUD. CANON. *abbr.* Studia Canonica.

STUDDED TIRE. A tire into the tread of which have been imbedded hard material devices none of which is more than 1/4 of an inch in diameter and none of which projects more than 1/16 of an inch beyond the tread of the tire. *Highway Traffic Act*, R.R.O. 1980, Reg. 494, s. 1.

STUDENT. *n.* 1. A person enrolled or registered in a school. 2. A person enrolled in a course of studies at an educational institution. See ARTICLED ~; LAW ~; LICENSED ~; QUALIFYING ~; REGISTERED ~.

STUDENT-AT-LAW. *n.* A person serving articles of clerkship approved by the Society to a member. *Legal Profession Act*, S.N.W.T. 1976, c. 4, s. 2.

STUDENT EMPLOYEE. A person employed in the period from May to September who has been in full-time attendance as a student at an educational institution and affirms at the time of his appointment that he will return to full-time attendance at an educational institution in the same year. *Civil Service Act*, S.P.E.I. 1983, c. 4. s. 10.

STUDENT FINANCIAL ASSISTANCE. Financial assistance provided in the form of a loan, grant, bursary, prize, scholarship, allowance or remission to or in favour of any person who is eligible.

STUDENT HOUSING. A housing project for students and their families.

STUDENT HOUSING PROJECT. A project undertaken to provide students and their families with housing accommodation of the hostel or dormitory type or in the form of a housing project, including such other facilities in connection therewith as are, in the opinion of the Corporation, necessary for the operation of the project. *National Housing Act*, R.S.C. 1985, c. N-11, s. 87.

STUDENT LOAN. A loan made by a bank to a person enrolled as a full-time student at a specified educational institution. *Canada Student Loans Act*, R.S.C. 1970, c. S-17, s. 2.

STUDENTS COUNCIL. The executive body of a students association.

STUDENTS' SUPPLIES. (a) Blank exercise and workbooks whether or not lined but excluding such books as are ruled for bookkeeping or accounting purposes; (b) loose-leaf paper punched for insertion in a loose-leaf binder but excluding such paper as is ruled for bookkeeping or accounting purposes and all loose-leaf paper that is not punched for insertion in a loose-leaf binder; (c) books for drawing upon; (d) music manuscript paper; and (e) schoolbags and satchels. *Retail Sales Tax Act*, R.R.O. 1980, Reg. 904, s. 1.

STUDENT TEACHER. A student engaged in practice teaching while enrolled in teacher education in a recognized teacher education institution.

STUD GUN. A gun which fires a nail, bolt or rivet using an explosive charge. F.A. Jaffe, *A Guide to Pathological Evidence*, 2d ed. (Toronto: Carswell, 1983) at 184.

STUDY. See ENVIRONMENTAL ~; PERIOD OF STUDIES; RENEWAL ~.

STUFFED ARTICLE. See UPHOLSTERED OR ~.

STUFF GOWN. The court robe worn by lawyers who are not Queen's Counsel.

STUFFING. *n.* Any material used for padding, filling or cushioning, that is meant to be enclosed by a covering.

STU. K.B. *abbr.* Stuart's Reports (Que.), 1810-1835.

STUMPAGE CHARGES. The amount equal to the total of the amount of the Crown dues and any other amounts added thereto in fixing the price to be paid for Crown timber. *Crown Timber Act*, R.S.O. 1980, c. 109, s. 1.

STUMP HEIGHT. The vertical distance between the horizontal plane through the top of the stump and the horizontal plane through the highest point of the ground at its base. *Crown Timber Act*, R.R.O. 1980, Reg. 234, s. 1.

STUN GUN. A gun which fires a captive bolt and is used to slaughter cattle. F.A. Jaffe, *A Guide to Pathological Evidence*, 2d ed. (Toronto: Carswell, 1983) at 184.

STURGEON. See DRESSED ~; LAKE ~.

STYLE. *v.* To name, call or entitle someone.

STYLE. *n.* A title; an appellation. See ROYAL ~ AND TITLES.

STYLE OF CAUSE. The name or title of a proceeding which sets out the names of all the parties and their capacity, if other than a personal capacity. G.D. Watson & C. Perkins, eds., *Holmested & Watson: Ontario Civil Procedure* (Toronto: Carswell, 1984) at 14-5.

STYRENE. *n.* When used as a base in polyester resin along with a fibrous reinforcing agent, control of exposure to this material is regulated under the Ontario Occupational Health and Safety Act. D. Robertson, *Ontario Health and Safety Guide* (Toronto: Richard De Boo Ltd., 1988) at 5-376.

SUABLE. *adj.* Able to be sued.

SUBACCOUNTANT. *n.* An employee of the Province receiving or expending public money and accounting for it to or through a minister or officer of a ministry. *Financial Control Act*, R.S.B.C. 1979, c. 129, s. 1.

SUBAGENT. *n.* A person employed as an agent by an agent to help transact the affairs of the principal.

SUB-AMENDMENT. *n.* An amendment to an amendment.

SUB-AQUATIC LAND. The bed of a natural body of water including the solum of the sea. *Aquaculture Act*, S.N.S. 1983, c. 2, s. 2.

SUBARACHNOID HEMORRHAGE. A hemorrhage into either the brain or the space around it. F.A. Jaffe, *A Guide to Pathological Evidence*, 2d ed. (Toronto: Carswell, 1983) at 46.

SUB-BAILMENT. *n.* When a bailee transfers possession to another with the bailor's consent.

SUB-BROKER DEALER. *var.* **SUB-BROKER-DEALER.** An individual who, being retired from active business or as incidental to his principal occupation and as correspondent of any investment dealer or broker-dealer or both, trades in securities for a part of his time in the capacity of an agent or principal. Securities acts.

SUB-CHARGE. *n.* A charge of a charge.

SUB-CHIEF. *n.* An elected member of a band commonly known as sub-chief of the band.

Regional and Tribal Councils Act, S.N.W.T. 1983 (2d Sess.), c. 7, s. 2.

SUB COLORE JURIS. [L.] Under the colour of law.

SUB-COMMITTEE ON AGENDA AND PROCEDURE. A steering committee which recommends, by report, the way a committee should proceed to study its order of reference and advises on topics like times of sittings, witnesses and subject matters for each sitting. A. Fraser, G.A. Birch & W.A. Dawson, eds., *Beauchesne's Rules and Forms of the House of Commons of Canada*, 5th ed. (Toronto: Carswell, 1978) at 197.

SUBCONTRACT. *var.* **SUB-CONTRACT.** *n.* 1. Any agreement between the contractor and a subcontractor, or between two or more subcontractors, relating to the provision of services or materials and includes any amendment to that agreement. Builders' Lien acts. 2. A binding agreement between a sub-contractor and a contractor or between a sub-contractor and another sub-contractor (i) for construction; or (ii) for improving land; or (iii) for the doing of any work or the providing of any services in construction or in improving land; or (iv) for the supplying of any materials to be used in construction or in improving land. *The Builders' Liens Act*, S.M. 1980-81, c. 7, s. 1. See DEFENCE ~.

SUBCONTRACTOR. *var.* **SUB-CONTRACTOR.** *n.* 1. A person who has contracted with a prime contractor or with another subcontractor to perform a contract. 2. A person not contracting with or employed directly by an owner or the owner's agent for the doing of any work, rendering of any services or the furnishing of any material but contracting with or employed by a contractor or under the contractor by another subcontractor, but does not include a labourer. See CONSTRUCTION ~.

SUBDIVIDE. *v.* To divide a parcel of land into two or more parcels.

SUBDIVIDED LAND. Land, whether the land is situated inside or outside the Province, that is, for the purpose of sale or lease, divided or proposed to be divided, whether by one or more divisions, into (a) 5 or more lots or parcels; (b) 5 or more strata lots; or (c) 2 or more cooperative units by means of the creation, conversion, organization or development of a cooperative corporation, but does not include (d) land divided or proposed to be divided into lots or parcels of not less than 64.7 ha; or (e) space leased in a commercial, industrial or apartment building unless the building is owned wholly or partly by a strata corporation or a cooperative corporation. *Real Estate Amendment Act*, S.B.C. 1981, c. 28, s. 1.

SUBDIVISION. *var.* **SUB-DIVISION.** *n.* 1. A division of a parcel by means of a plan of subdivision, plan of survey, agreement or any instrument, including a caveat, transferring or creating an estate or interest in part of the parcel. 2. Improved or unimproved land divided or proposed to be divided into 2 or more lots or other units for the purpose of sale or lease and includes land divided or proposed to be divided into condominium units. 3. That area of an electoral division so designated by the returning officer to enable the efficient conduct of an enumeration. 4. Land, whether the land is situated inside or outside the Province, that is, for the purpose of sale or lease, divided or proposed to be divided, whether by one or more divisions, into (a) 5 or more lots or parcels; (b) 5 or more strata lots; or (c) 2 or more cooperative units by means of the creation, conversion, organization or development of a cooperative corporation, but does not include (d) land divided or proposed to be divided into lots or parcels of not less than 64.7 ha; or (e) space leased in a commercial, industrial or apartment building unless the building is owned wholly or partly by a strata corporation or a cooperative corporation. *Real Estate Amendment Act*, S.B.C. 1981, c. 28, s. 1. See PLAN OF ~; POLITICAL ~; POLLING ~; RE~.

SUBDIVISION AGREEMENT. An agreement between a council and a developer whereby the developer undertakes to provide basic services in order to develop a plan of subdivision. *Planning Act*, R.S.P.E.I. 1974, c. P-6, s. 1.

SUBDIVISION CONTROL. Legislation to control land division by effectively limiting it.

SUBDIVISION PLAN. See FILED ~.

SUBDIVISION UNIT. (i) A lot shown on the original plan of an original survey and includes a township lot, city lot, town lot or village lot, section, block, gore, reserve, common, mining location or mining claim; or (ii) a lot, block, part or other unit of land shown on a plan registered or deposited under the Registry Act or the Land Titles Act. *Registry Act*, R.R.O. 1980, Reg. 898, s. 1.

SUBDRAIN. *n.* A drain that is at a level lower than the building drain and the building sewer. *Ontario Water Resources Act*, R.R.O. 1980, Reg. 736, s. 1.

SUBDURAL HEMORRHAGE. A hemorrhage between the arachnoid mater and the dura mater, usually caused by a trauma. F.A. Jaffe, *A Guide to Pathological Evidence*, 2d ed. (Toronto: Carswell, 1983) at 184.

SUBFEEDER. *n.* Those conductors of a circuit, which being themselves supplied by a feeder and having overload protection, supply, or are intended to supply, one or more branch circuits. *Coal Mines Regulation Act*, R.S.N.S. 1967, c. 36, s. 84.

SUBFRANCHISOR. *n.* A person to whom an area franchise is granted. *Franchises Act*, R.S.A. 1980, c. F-17, s. 1.

SUBGALEAL. *adj.* Under the scalp. F.A. Jaffe, *A Guide to Pathological Evidence*, 2d ed. (Toronto: Carswell, 1983) at 117.

SUBINFEUDATION. *n.* Division of land first granted to tenants in chief among their followers. E.L.G. Tyler & N.E. Palmer, eds., *Crossley Vaines' Personal Property*, 5th ed. (London: Butterworths, 1973) at 4.

SUBJECT. *n.* 1. The person on whom a personal investigation is carried out or is being carried out. *Personal Investigations Act*, S.M. 1971, c. 23, s. 1. 2. Any matter, theme, incident or description and includes a person, object, place or event. *Ontario Heritage Act*, R.R.O. 1980, Reg. 714, s. 1. See BRITISH ~; NATURAL-BORN ~.

SUBJECT OF HER MAJESTY. Includes any person who, under the law of any country in the Commonwealth, is a citizen of that country. *Interpretation Act*, R.S.M. 1970, c. I80, s. 23.

SUBJECT TO EXCISE. Subject to the provisions of this Act, of any other Act respecting duties of excise or of any proclamation, order in council or departmental regulation published or made under those provisions. *Excise Act*, R.S.C. 1985, c. E-14, s. 2.

SUB JUDICE. [L.] In the course of a trial.

SUB-JUDICE CONVENTION. The expectation that members of Parliament will not discuss matters that are before tribunals or the courts which are courts of record. A. Fraser, G.A. Birch & W.A. Dawson, eds., *Beauchesne's Rules and Forms of the House of Commons of Canada*, 5th ed. (Toronto: Carswell, 1978) at 118.

SUBLATO FUNDAMENTO CADIT OPUS. [L.] If the foundation is removed, the structure collapses.

SUBLATO PRINCIPALI TOLLITUR ADJUNCTUM. [L.] With the removal of the principal, the adjunct is removed.

SUBLEASE. *var.* **SUB-LEASE.** *n.* 1. A tenant's grant of interest in the leased premises which is less than that tenant's own. 2. Includes an agreement for a sublease where the sublessee has become entitled to have his sublease granted. Landlord and Tenant acts.

SUB-LET. *v.* For a tenant to lease the whole

or part of the premises during a portion of the unexpired balance of the lease's term.

SUBLIMINAL DEVICE. A technical device that is used to convey or attempt to convey a message to a person by means of images or sounds of very brief duration or by any other means without that person being aware that such a device is being used or being aware of the substance of the message being conveyed or attempted to be conveyed. *Television Broadcasting Regulations*, C.R.C., c. 381, s. 15.

SUBMARINE CABLE. See EXTERNAL ~.

SUBMARINE TRACT. A lot, piece or parcel of land covered or partly covered by the water of the sea or a lake, of which one or more leases have been or may be issued.

SUBMISSION. *n.* 1. Acquisition of jurisdiction which it would not otherwise possess by a court because the defendant, by conduct, cannot object to the jurisdiction. This may occur either impliedly or expressly, provided the person submitting is capable of doing so. C.R.B. Dunlop, *Creditor-Debtor Law in Canada* (Toronto: Carswell, 1981) at 470. 2. Definition of an arbitrator's jurisdiction over a particular case, i.e. a written grievance or a separate document. D.J.M. Brown and D.M. Beatty, *Canadian Labour Arbitration*, 2d ed. (Aurora: Canada Law Book, 1977) at 58 and 59. 3. A written agreement to submit present or future differences to arbitration whether an arbitrator is named therein or not. See DESIGN ~.

SUBMIT. *v.* To offer, as an advocate, a proposition to a court.

SUB MODO. [L.] Under restriction or condition.

SUBMORTGAGE. *n.* A mortgage of a mortgage.

SUBMORTGAGE BROKER. Any person who, within the Province, actively engages in any of the things referred to in the definition of mortgage broker and is employed, either generally or in a particular case, by, or is a director or a partner of, a mortgage broker. *Mortgage Brokers Act*, R.S.B.C. 1979, c. 283, s. 1.

SUB NOM. *abbr.* Sub nomine.

SUB NOMINE. [L.] Under a name.

SUBNOTATION. *n.* A written reply to a request for guidance.

SUB-ORDER DELIVERY CHARGE. A charge for the delivery of part of the goods shown on one bill of lading to a person other than the original consignee. *Pacific Terminal Tariff By-law*, C.R.C., c. 1083, s. 41.

SUBORDINATE. *n.* 1. A person who works under the orders or directions of another and is lower in rank or status. *Welding Act*, R.S.A. 1970, c. 389, s. 2. 2. A clause grammatically governed by another clause.

SUBORDINATE BUILDING. A detached building the use of which in relation to another building on the same lot is ordinarily incidental or subordinate to that building. Canada regulations.

SUBORDINATED NOTE. An instrument evidencing an indebtedness of a company that by its terms provides that the indebtedness evidenced by it shall, in the event of the insolvency or winding-up of the company, rank equally with the indebtedness evidenced by other subordinated notes of the company but be subordinate in right of payment to all other indebtedness of the company except indebtedness in respect of subordinated shareholder loans.

SUBORDINATED SHAREHOLDER LOAN. A loan made to a company by a shareholder of the company or by a person who controls a shareholder of the company, as the case may be, for a fixed term and under the condition that the indebtedness arising therefrom shall, in the event of the insolvency or winding-up of the company, rank equally with the indebtedness in respect of other subordinated shareholder loans but be subordinate in right of payment to all other indebtedness of the company.

SUBORDINATE LEGISLATION. 1. Legislation of a subordinate body, i.e. one other than a legislature or Parliament, such as a statutory instrument, regulation or by-law. 2. Any regulation, proclamation, rule, order, by-law or instrument that is of a legislative nature and made or approved under the authority of an Act including those made by any board, commission or other body, whether incorporated or unincorporated, all the members of which, or all the members of the board of management or board of directors of which, are appointed by an Act or by the Lieutenant-Governor in Council, but does not include any regulation, proclamation, rule, order, by-law, resolution or other instrument made by a local authority or, except as otherwise provided in this paragraph, by a corporation incorporated by or under an Act or by the board of directors or board of management of such a corporation. *Statutes and Subordinate Legislation Act*, S.Nfld. 1977, c. 108, s. 10.

SUBORDINATE OFFICER. A person who holds the rank of officer cadet. *National Defence Act*, R.S.C. 1970, c. N-4, s. 2.

SUBORDINATE VOTING SHARE. A common share carrying a right to vote in all circumstances in the issuing corporation that is not a common share with full voting rights. *An Act to Amend the Taxation Act and the Act Respecting the Application of the Taxation Act*, S.Q. 1984, c. 15, s. 212.

SUBORNATION. *n.* The crime of getting someone else to do something unlawful.

SUB PEDE SIGILLI. [L.] Under the foot of a seal.

SUBPERIOSTEAL. *adj.* Between the skull and the delicate membrane which covers it. F.A. Jaffe, *A Guide to Pathological Evidence*, 2d ed. (Toronto: Carswell, 1983) at 117.

SUBPOENA. *n.* A document requiring a person to attend as a witness. See WRIT OF ~.

SUBPOENA DUCES TECUM. [L. subpoena you shall bring with you] A document requiring a witness to give evidence in court or before an examiner and also to bring along documents specified in the subpoena.

SUBROGATED. *adj.* Describes the rights acquired by a singly secured creditor in property in which she or he had no rights when a doubly secured creditor realized a claim out of the parcel on which the singly secured creditor had her or his security making it unavailable to the singly secured creditor. W.B. Rayner & R.H. McLaren, *Falconbridge on Mortgages*, 4th ed. (Toronto: Canada Law Book, 1977) at 314.

SUBROGATION. *n.* 1. The equitable principle which permits the person who pays a debt on behalf of someone else to seek restitution from that debtor. C.R.B. Dunlop, *Creditor-Debtor Law in Canada*, Second Cumulative Supplement (Toronto: Carswell, 1986) at 224. 2. In insurance law, a doctrine which provides that an insured, through contractual or other legal relationships, should be fully indemnified for any loss insured against but for no greater amount than that indemnified. G.H.L. Fridman & J.G. McLeod, *Restitution* (Toronto: Carswell, 1982) at 394. See DOCTRINE OF ~.

SUBSCRIBE. *v.* 1. To write under. 2. To sign.

SUBSCRIBED AND ISSUED CAPITAL STOCK OF THE COMPANY. As applied to a provincial company having common shares without par value, means the number of the issued common shares of the company. *Trust Companies Act*, R.S.A. 1980, c. T-9, s. 1.

SUBSCRIBED CAPITAL. The number of shares which subscribers take or agree to take. H. Sutherland, D.B. Horsley & J.M. Edmiston, eds., *Fraser's Handbook on Canadian Company Law*, 7th ed. (Toronto: Carswell, 1985) at 41.

SUBSCRIBER. *n.* 1. A person, firm or company

supplied with a main line telephone. 2. Any person in the province who has agreed to pay a toll to a cablecaster for the reception of cablecast service. 3. Persons exchanging with each other reciprocal contracts of indemnity or inter-insurance. Insurance acts. See FARM ~.

SUBSCRIBING COOPERATOR. A federation of savings and credit unions incorporated under the Savings and Credit Unions Act (chapter C-4) or a member of the Conseil de la coopération du Québec paying, in conformity with this act, advances or other sums to the Société de développment coopératif. *Société de Développment Coopératif Act*, R.S.Q. 1977, c. S-10, s. 1.

SUBSCRIPTION. *n.* 1. An offer from a prospective shareholder to purchase shares of a corporation. S.M. Beck *et al., Cases and Materials on Partnerships and Canadian Business Corporations,* (Toronto: The Carswell Company Limited, 1983) at 790. 2. Includes fee, due, assessment or other similar sum payable by a member under the bylaws. *Society Act*, R.S.B.C. 1979, c. 390, s. 1.

SUBSEQUENS MATRIMONIUM TOLLIT PECCATUM PRAECEDENS. [L.] A subsequent marriage removes a preceding fault.

SUBSEQUENT CONVICTION. A conviction: (i) within a period of 5 years after the date of a first conviction, either before or after this section comes into force; and (ii) that follows a third conviction. *Vehicles Amendment Act*, S.S. 1980-81, c. 94, s. 7.

SUBSEQUENT ENCUMBRANCER. A person who has a charge, lien or encumbrance on mortgaged property subsequent to the mortgage at issue in an action. G.D. Watson & C. Perkins, eds., *Holmested & Watson: Ontario Civil Procedure* (Toronto: Carswell, 1984) at 64-3.

SUBSEQUENT INCREASE. A second or subsequent increase in rent in any twelve-month period. *Residential Rent Review Act*, S.N.B. 1983, c. R-10.11, s. 1.

SUBSEQUENT OFFENCE. An offence committed within 5 years after the date of a previous conviction. *Excise Act*, R.S.C. 1985, c. E-14, s. 2. See SECOND OR ~.

SUBSEQUENT PURCHASER. 1. Includes a person who, in good faith for valuable consideration and without notice, obtains by assignment an interest in book debts that have already been assigned. Assignment of Book Debts acts. 2. A person who acquires an interest in goods after the making of a conditional sale thereof. Conditional Sales acts.

SUBSEQUENT PURCHASER OR MORTGAGEE. Includes a person who obtains, whether by way of purchase, mortgage, charge or assignment, an interest in chattels or book debts that have already been mortgaged, charged or assigned. Corporation Securities Registration acts.

SUBSIDIARY. *n.* 1. A corporation which, in respect of another corporation, is controlled, either directly or indirectly, by that other corporation. 2. A body corporate for which the credit union elects or appoints a majority of the board of directors on the basis of voting rights or shares held in that body corporate by the credit union. *Credit Union Act*, S.S. 1984-85-86, c. C-45.1, s. 2. 3. A subsidiary, at a given time, of another corporation, hereinafter called "parent corporation", when at least 90 per cent of the issued shares to which are attached full voting rights of its capital stock are owned by such other corporation. *Land Transfer Duties Act*, R.S.Q. 1977, c. D-17, s. 42. See FOREIGN BANK ~; WHOLLY-OWNED ~.

SUBSIDIARY COIN. A coin other than a gold coin. *Currency Act*, R.S.C. 1985, c. C-52, s. 2.

SUBSIDIARY COMPANY. 1. A company is a subsidiary of another company if, but only if, (a) it is controlled by, (i) that other; or (ii) that other and one or more companies each of which is controlled by that other; or (iii) two or more companies each of which is controlled by that other; or (b) it is a subsidiary of a subsidiary of that other company. 2. A corporation created within the Province by or under an Act of the Legislature, and includes an extraprovincial company, as defined in the Company Act, lawfully carrying on business in the Province, the majority of the shares of which, having under all circumstances full voting rights, are owned or controlled, directly or indirectly, by or for the parent company. *Pension Society Act*, R.S.B.C. 1979, c. 319, s. 1. 3. Where the assets of a company consist in whole or in part of shares in another company, whether held directly or through a nominee and whether that other company is a company within the meaning of this Act or not, and (a) the amount of the shares so held is at the time when the accounts of the holding company are made up more than 50 per centum of the issued share capital of that other company or such as to entitle the company to more than 50 per centum of the voting power in that other company; (b) the company has power (not being power vested in it by virtue only of the provisions of a debenture trust deed or by virtue of shares issued to it for the purpose in pursuance of those provisions) directly or indirectly to appoint the majority of the directors of that other company; or (c) where a company, the ordinary business of which includes the lending of money, holds shares in another company as security only, no account shall, for the purpose of determining under this Section, whether that other company is a subsidiary company, be taken of the shares so held; that other company shall be deemed to be a subsidiary company within the meaning of this Act, and the expression "subsidiary company" in this Act means a company in the case of which the conditions of this Section are satisfied. *Companies Act*, R.S.N.S. 1967, c. 42, s. 111.

SUBSIDIARY CONTROLLED CORPORATION. A corporation of which more than 50 per cent of the issued share capital, with full voting rights under all circumstances, is owned, directly or indirectly, by another corporation.

SUBSIDIARY CONTROLLED FINANCIAL CORPORATION. A financial corporation of which more than 50 per cent of the issued share capital, with full voting rights under all circumstances, is owned, directly or indirectly, by another corporation. *Financial Corporation Capital Tax Act*, S.N.B. 1987, c. F-11.1, s. 1.

SUBSIDIARY CONTROLLED OPERATION. A corporation more than 50 per cent of the issued capital stock of which having full voting rights under all circumstances belongs to the corporation to which it is subsidiary. *Taxation Act*, R.S.Q. 1977, c. I-3, s. 1.

SUBSIDIARY CORPORATION. A corporation legally transacting business in Canada, under any Act of Parliament, the majority of the shares of which, that have under all circumstances full voting rights, is owned or controlled directly or indirectly by or for the parent corporation. *Pension Fund Societies Act*, R.S.C. 1985, c. P-8, s. 17(4).

SUBSIDIARY MOTION. A motion, as for reading a bill, to move a question forward through the stages of procedure it must pass before final adoption. A. Fraser, G.A. Birch & W.A. Dawson, eds., *Beauchesne's Rules and Forms of the House of Commons of Canada*, 5th ed. (Toronto: Carswell, 1978) at 152.

SUBSIDIARY QUESTION. An issue which presents itself while the main question before the court is being decided and which must be solved before the main question can be answered. J.G. McLeod, *The Conflict of Laws* (Calgary: Carswell, 1983) at 50-51.

SUBSIDIARY WHOLLY OWNED CORPORATION. *var.* **SUBSIDIARY WHOLLY-OWNED CORPORATION.** 1. A corporation all the issued share capital of which, except directors' qualifying shares, belongs to the corporation to which it is subsidiary. 2. Notwithstanding subsection 248(1), for the purposes of this subsection and subsections (1.1) and (1.2), "subsidiary wholly-owned corporation" of a corporation (in this subsection referred to as the "parent corporation") means a corporation all the issued and outstanding shares of the capital stock of which belong to (a) the parent corporation; (b) a corporation that is a subsidiary wholly-owned corporation of the parent corporation; or (c) any combination of corporations each of which is a corporation described in paragraph (a) or (b). *Income Tax Act*, R.S.C. 1952, c. 148 (as am. S.C. 1985, c. 45, s. 42(2)), s. 87(1.4).

SUBSIDIES AND COUNTERVAILING DUTIES AGREEMENT. The Agreement signed at Geneva, Switzerland, on December 17, 1979 and known as the Agreement on Interpretation and Application of Articles VI, XVI and XXIII of the General Agreement of Tariffs and Trade. *Special Imports Measures Act*, R.S.C. 1985, c. S-15, s. 2.

SUBSIDIZED GOODS. (a) Goods in respect of the production, manufacture, growth, processing, purchase, distribution, transportation, sale, export or import of which a subsidy has been or will be paid, granted, authorized or otherwise provided, directly or indirectly, by the government of a country other than Canada; and (b) goods that are disposed of at a loss by the government of a country other than Canada, and includes any goods in which, or in the production, manufacture, growth, processing or the like of which, goods described in paragraph (a) or (b) are incorporated, consumed, used or otherwise employed. *Special Imports Measures Act*, R.S.C. 1985, c. S-15, s. 2.

SUBSIDIZED PUBLIC HOUSING. A rental unit rented to persons or families of low or modest income who pay an amount geared-to-income for that unit by reason of public funding provided by the Government of Canada, Ontario or a municipality, or by any agency thereof, pursuant to the National Housing Act (Canada), the Housing Development Act or the Ontario Housing Corporation Act. *Residential Rent Regulation Act*, S.O. 1986, c. 63, s. 1.

SUBSIDIZED SCHOOL. Any private school receiving a grant from the Gouvernement out of the funds voted for education. *Education Act*, R.S.Q. 1977, c. I-14, s. 1.

SUBSIDY. *n.* 1. Includes any financial or other commercial benefit that has accrued or will accrue, directly or indirectly, to persons engaged in the production, manufacture, growth, processing, purchase, distribution, transportation, sale, export or import of goods, as a result of any scheme, program, practice or thing done, provided or implemented by the government of a country other than Canada, but does not include

the amount of any duty or internal tax imposed on goods by the government of the country of origin or country of export from which the goods, because of their exportation from the country of export or country of origin, have been exempted or have been or will be relieved by means of refund or drawback. *Special Imports Measures Act*, R.S.C. 1985, c. S-15, s. 2. 2. The amount prescribed in the regulations by which a premium is reduced. *Health Insurance Premiums Act*, R.S.A. 1980, c. H-5, s. 1.

SUB SILENTIO. [L.] Silently.

SUBSISTENCE ALLOWANCE. An amount paid to a worker for the cost of food, travel and lodging while travelling for the employer.

SUBSISTENCE WAGES. Wages adequate only to supply the bare necessities of life.

SUBSISTING EXECUTION. An execution in the hands of a sheriff other than one that by this Act he is directed to disregard. Execution Creditors acts.

SUBSTANCE. *n.* Any distinguishable kind of inanimate matter (i) capable of becoming dispersed in the natural environment; or (ii) capable of becoming transformed in the natural environment into matter described in subclause (i). See CLASS OF ~S; DANGEROUS ~; DELETERIOUS ~; DESIGNATED ~; EXPLOSIVE ~; FISSIONABLE ~; FOREIGN ~; LISTED ~; MINERAL ~; PITH AND ~; PRESCRIBED ~S; QUARRIABLE ~; TOXIC ~.

SUBSTANTIAL ALTERATION. (a) In respect of any ionizing radiation equipment which emits a primary beam outside the housing of the equipment, any alteration or change of position which causes the equipment to be capable of emitting a primary beam in any directions other than those for which approval was granted when the plans for the installation were approved; (b) any alteration in the shielding properties of the room or other place in which the ionizing radiation equipment is placed or installed; (c) any increase in the maximum generating voltage or maximum beam current of ionizing radiation equipment in an installation; and (d) the placement or installation of any units of ionizing radiation equipment in an ionizing radiation installation in excess of the number of units approved when the plans for the installation were approved. *Radiation Health and Safety Act*, S.S. 1984-85-86, c. R-1.1, s. 3.

SUBSTANTIAL BREACH. (i) A breach of a covenant specified in section 20; or (ii) a series of breaches of a tenancy agreement, the cumulative effect of which is substantial. *Mobile Home Site Tenancies Act*, S.A. 1982, c. M-18.5, s. 1.

SUBSTANTIAL DAMAGE. Damage or structural failure that adversely affects the structural strength, performance, or flight characteristics of an aircraft and that would normally require major repair or replacement of the affected component except that engine failure, damage limited to an engine, bent fairings or cowlings, dented skin, small punctured holes in the skin or fabric, damage to propeller blades, damage to tires, engine accessories, brakes or wing tips are not deemed to be substantial damage. *Aircraft Accidents and Missing Aircraft Order*, C.R.C., c. 23, s. 2.

SUBSTANTIAL INTEREST. The direct or indirect beneficial ownership of, or the power to exercise control or direction over, equity shares of any corporation that carry more than 10 per cent of the voting rights attached to all outstanding equity shares of the corporation. *Municipal Conflict of Interest Act*, S.N.S. 1982, c. 11, s. 2.

SUBSTANTIAL PERFORMANCE. Exists where a contract has been carried out in all its essentials and only technical or unimportant omissions or defects have occurred.

SUBSTANTIAL SHAREHOLDER. 1. A person who owns, or who is the beneficial owner of, 10 per cent or more of the voting shares of a body corporate and includes a shareholder who, together with his associates, holds 10 per cent or more of the voting shares of a body corporate. *Trust and Loan Corporations Act*, S.S. 1980-81, c. T-22.1, s. 2. 2. A person is a substantial shareholder of a corporation or a group of persons is a substantial shareholder of a corporation if that person or group of persons owns beneficially, either individually or together and either directly or indirectly, equity shares to which are attached more than 10 per cent of the voting rights attached to all of the equity shares of the corporation for the time being outstanding; and in computing the percentage of voting rights attached to equity shares owned by an underwriter, there shall be excluded the voting rights attached to equity shares acquired by him as an underwriter during the course of distribution to the public by him of such shares. *Insurance Act*, R.S.O. 1980, c. 218, s. 391.

SUBSTANTIVE LAW. The part of the law which creates and defines rights as opposed to procedural law which prescribes methods of enforcement.

SUBSTANTIVE MOTION. A self-contained proposal, not incidental to any proceeding, which may be drafted or amended so that it expresses a decision of the House of Commons. A. Fraser, G.A. Birch & W.A. Dawson, eds., *Beauchesne's Rules and Forms of the House of Commons of Canada*, 5th ed. (Toronto: Carswell, 1978) at 151.

SUBSTATION. *n.* A part of a transmission line that is not a transmission circuit and includes equipment for transforming, compensating, switching, rectifying or inverting of electric energy flowing to, over or from the transmission line. *Hydro and Electric Energy Act*, R.S.A. 1980, c. H-13, s. 1.

SUBSTITUTE. *n.* An establishment in which a dairy product is treated, modified, converted, reconstituted or packed, or in which a dairy product is received directly from the producer with a view to selling it or transporting it to another establishment for such purpose. *Dairy Products and Dairy Products Substitutes Act*, R.S.Q. 1977, c. P-30, s. 1. See HONEY ~; MAPLE PRODUCT ~; TURPENTINE ~.

SUBSTITUTED EXECUTOR. A person appointed to act on behalf of another executor.

SUBSTITUTED SERVICE. Service of a document on a person representing the party to be served, instead of on the party personally or by some means not involving personal service.

SUBSTITUTE TEACHER. A teacher employed on a day-to-day basis as required to replace a teacher who is temporarily absent from his regular duties.

SUBSTITUTION METHOD. A method of measurement of the response of a hearing aid in which the hearing aid and the microphone employed to measure the free-field sound pressure are placed alternately at the same point (the test point) in the sound field. *Medical Devices Regulations*, C.R.C., c. 871, s. 1.

SUB-SURFACE DRAIN. A drain, other than a foundation drain, installed to collect water from subsoil. *Ontario Water Resources Act*, R.R.O. 1980, Reg. 736, s. 1.

SUBSURFACE INVESTIGATION. The appraisal of the general subsurface conditions at a building site by analysis of information gained by such methods as geological surveys, in situ testing, sampling, visual inspection, laboratory testing of samples of the subsurface materials and groundwater observations and measurements. *Building Code Act*, R.R.O. 1980, Reg. 87, s. 1.

SUBSURFACE MINERALS. All natural mineral salts of boron, calcium, lithium, magnesium, potassium, sodium, bromine, chlorine, fluorine, iodine, nitrogen, phosphorus and sulphur, and their compounds, occurring more than two hundred feet below the surface of the land; and any other mineral substance that may be declared a "subsurface mineral" by the Lieutenant Governor in Council. *The Mineral Resources Act*, R.S.S. 1978, c. M-16, s. 2.

SUB-SYSTEM. *n.* An identifiable, predesigned, physically integrated, co-ordinated series of parts that function as a unit of the construction of a building. *Municipality of Metropolitan Toronto Act*, R.S.O. 1980, c. 314, s. 129.

SUBTENANCY. *n.* A tenancy created by sub-lease.

SUBTENANT. *var.* **SUB-TENANT.** *n.* 1. A person entering into a lease with a head tenant who reserves one day of her or his original term of tenancy. W.B. Rayner & R.H. McLaren, *Falconbridge on Mortgages*, 4th ed. (Toronto: Canada Law Book, 1977) at 101. 2. Includes any person deriving title under a sublease.

SUB-UNDERWRITER. *n.* A person who purchases from a principal underwriter the shares or debentures of a company with a view to their sale to the public. *Companies Act*, R.S.N.W.T. 1974, c. C-7, s. 89.

SUBVERSIVE OR HOSTILE ACTIVITIES. (a) Espionage against Canada or any state allied or associated with Canada; (b) sabotage; (c) activities directed toward the commission of terrorist acts, including hijacking, in or against Canada or foreign states; (d) activities directed toward accomplishing government change within Canada or foreign states by the use of or the encouragement of the use of force, violence or any criminal means; (e) activities directed toward gathering information used for intelligence purposes that relates to Canada or any state allied or associated with Canada; and (f) activities directed toward threatening the safety of Canadians, employees of the Government of Canada or property of the Government of Canada outside Canada. *Access to Information Act*, R.S.C. 1985, c. A-1, s. 15(2).

SUB VOCE. [L.] Under title.

SUBWAY. *n.* A structure, including the approaches thereto, that carries a highway across and under the railway. *Railway Grade Separations Regulations*, C.R.C., c. 1191, s. 2

SUCCESSION. *n.* As the case requires, (i) the property of the deceased to which a successor becomes beneficially entitled; or (ii) the acquisition by a successor of any property of the deceased by reason of the death of the deceased or a successor's becoming beneficially entitled to property of a deceased by reason of the death of the deceased.

SUCCESSION DUTY. 1. Inheritance tax levied against each beneficiary on an inheritance. P.W. Hogg, *Constitutional Law of Canada*, 2d ed. (Toronto: Carswell, 1985) at 610. 2. Tax on the gratuitous acquisition of property. D.M.W. Waters, *The Law of Trusts in Canada*, 2d ed. (Toronto: Carswell, 1984) at 478. 3. Tax paid by the person who inherits as a result of an intestacy, a will or an inter vivos gift when the gift arises because of death. D.M.W. Waters, *The Law of Trusts in Canada*, 2d ed. (Toronto: Carswell, 1984) at 548.

SUCCESSIVE PROSECUTION. When an accused is charged with conspiracy to commit an offence, is tried and convicted or acquitted, and later tried for commission of the separate offence which was the accomplished object of the conspiracy. M.R. Goode, *Criminal Conspiracy in Canada* (Toronto: Carswell, 1975) at 171.

SUCCESSOR. *n.* 1. One who takes another's place. 2. An heir, executor or administrator. *Land Registration Reform Act*, S.O. 1984, c. 32, s. 1. 3. In relation to any property of the deceased includes any person who, at any time or on or after the death of the deceased became or becomes beneficially entitled to any property of the deceased (i) by virtue of, or conditionally or contingently on, the death of the deceased; or (ii) by virtue of the exercise of any general power of which the deceased was the donee or other holder; or (iii) in any case, under any disposition made by the deceased during the deceased's lifetime; or (iv) by virtue of the application in respect of the death of the deceased of any law of Canada or a province providing for relief of dependants of deceased persons, and includes (v) any person beneficially entitled to any property of the deceased in default of the exercise of any general power of which the deceased was the donee or other holder; (vi) any person as the donee or other holder of any general power created by the deceased in respect of any property of the deceased; and (vii) any trustee, guardian, committee, curator or other similar representative of any person mentioned in this clause, in the capacity of trustee, guardian, committee, curator or other representative. See COLLATERAL ~; PREFERRED ~; SIBLING ~.

SUCCESSOR EMPLOYER. A person who acquires the business or assets of an employer. *Pension Benefits Act*, S.N.B. 1987, c. P-5.1, s. 69.

SUCCESSOR UNION. A union which succeeds another by the process of merger, amalgamation or transfer of jurisdiction.

SUCCURRITUR MINORI: FACILIS EST LAPSUS JUVENTUTIS. [L.] A minor should be assisted: a mistake is easy for youth.

SUDDEN INFANT DEATH SYNDROME. The sudden death of an apparently well infant, who is usually between three and twelve months old.

F.A. Jaffe, *A Guide to Pathological Evidence*, 2d ed. (Toronto: Carswell, 1983) at 173.

SUDDEN PROVOCATION. Both the insult and the action in reply must be sudden. D. Stuart, *Canadian Criminal Law: A Treatise*, 2d ed. (Toronto: Carswell, 1987) at 450.

SUE. *v.* To bring a civil action against a person.

SUFFER. *v.* To permit; to allow.

SUFFERANCE WAREHOUSE. A place licensed as a sufferance warehouse by the Minister under section 24. *Customs Act*, R.S.C. 1985 (2d Supp.), c. 1, s. 2.

SUFFERENTIA PACIS. [L. sufferance of peace] A truce.

SUFFERING. See PAIN AND ~.

SUFFICIENT CAUSATION. See MULTIPLE ~.

SUFFICIENT INFORMATION. In respect of the determination of any amount, difference or adjustment, means objective and quantifiable information that establishes the accuracy of the amount, difference or adjustment. *Customs Act*, R.S.C. 1985 (2d Supp.), c. 1, s. 45.

SUFFICIENT OUTLET. The safe discharge of water at a point where it will do no injury to land or roads.

SUFFOCATION. *n.* A fatal oxygen deficiency caused by blockage of the nose and mouth. F.A. Jaffe, *A Guide to Pathological Evidence*, 2d ed. (Toronto: Carswell, 1983) at 106.

SUFFRAGE. *n.* Vote; electoral franchise.

SUFFRAGETTE. *n.* A woman who campaigned for female enfranchisement.

SUFFRAGIST. *n.* A person who campaigned for extended enfranchisement.

SUGAR. See MAPLE ~.

SUGAR BUSH. A stand of trees suitable for the cultivation of maple sugar. *An Act to Preserve Agricultural Land*, S.Q. 1978, c. 10, s. 1.

SUGAR BUSH OPERATOR. A person who produces a maple product directly from maple sap. *Maple Products Regulations*, C.R.C., c. 289, s. 2.

SUGGESTIO FALSI. [L. suggestion of falsity] Deliberate misrepresentation.

SUGGESTION. *n.* A conjecture or representation of something.

SUICIDE. *n.* Killing oneself.

SUICIDE PACT. Agreement by more than one person to commit suicide jointly.

SUI GENERIS. [L.] Of one's own class or kind.

SUI JURIS. [L.] Of one's own right.

SUIT. *n.* 1. A civil legal proceeding brought against one person by another. 2. Includes action. See FRIENDLY ~; LAW ~; NON~.

SUITABLE. *adj.* In relation to packing or to containers, means (a) well constructed and in good condition; (b) of such a character and construction that any interior surface with which the contents may come into contact is not dangerously affected by the substance being conveyed; (c) capable of withstanding the ordinary risks of handling and transport by sea; and (d) capable of withstanding any pressure likely to be generated therein. *Dangerous Goods Shipping Regulations*, C.R.C., c. 1419, s. 2.

SUITABLE BOAT. A boat, other than a lifeboat or an approved boat, that is (a) of not less than 50 cubic feet capacity; (b) of a buoyancy equal to a Class 2 wooden lifeboat; (c) accepted by a Divisional Supervisor; and (d) inspected in the same manner as if it were an approved boat. *Life Saving Equipment Regulations*, C.R.C., c. 1436, s. 2.

SUITABLE EMPLOYMENT. 1. Appropriate employment that allows a worker who has suffered an employment injury to use his remaining ability to work and his vocational qualifications, that he has a reasonable chance of obtaining, and the working conditions of which do not endanger the health, safety or physical well-being of the worker considering his injury. *An Act Respecting Industrial Accidents and Occupational Diseases*, S.Q. 1985, c. 6, s. 2. 2. (a) In relation to a worker who is under-employed within the meaning of paragraph (b) of the definition "underemployed worker", employment in Canada in which the worker would not be an underemployed worker and for which the wages and working conditions are equivalent to those prevailing for similar employment in the place where the employment is found; and (b) in relation to an unemployed worker or a worker who is underemployed within the meaning of paragraph (a) of the definition "underemployed worker", full-time employment in Canada that, in the opinion of a manpower officer, is in (i) the usual occupation of the worker; or (ii) an equivalent occupation, taking into account the qualifications of the worker, and for which the wages and working conditions are equivalent to those prevailing for similar employment in the place where the employment is found, but does not include employment in any enterprise in which the worker, in his own name, in the name of a dependant or as trustee, attorney or agent for any person, has an ownership interest. *Manpower Mobility Regulations*, C.R.C., c. 331, s. 2.

SUITABLE RECEPTACLE. A substantial box or substantial container, (a) that may be placed inside a building that is not itself adapted for the keeping of explosives; (b) the location of which is not changed from that prescribed by an inspector or under provincial or municipal law; (c) that is kept away from goods of an inflammable nature; and (d) that is of easy access for removal in case of fire. *Explosives Regulations*, C.R.C., c. 599, s. 136.

SUITOR. *n.* One who brings a suit or petition.

SULPHATE WOOD TURPENTINE. A terpene liquid obtained as a by-product of the manufacture of chemical wood pulp. *Turpentine Labelling Regulations*, C.R.C., c. 1140, s. 2.

SULPHUR CONTENT. The amount of sulphur in the fuel as determined by standard methods of sampling and testing and in the case of coal shall be determined as organic sulphur. *Environmental Protection Act*, R.R.O. 1980, Reg. 312, s. 1.

SUM. See GLOBAL ~; PENAL ~; PRINCIPAL ~.

SUM ASSURED. The principal sum that is payable in event of death where the life insurance money is payable in one sum, or the commuted value of the income or instalments provided on death where the life insurance money is payable otherwise than in one sum, but not including any additional sum payable under the policy on death as a result of accident.

SUM CERTAIN. One of (i) an amount with interest; (ii) an amount with specified instalments, with or without an acceleration clause; (iii) an amount payable according to the rate of exchange ascertainable from or indicated in a document. I.F.G. Baxter, *The Law of Banking*, 3d ed. (Toronto: Carswell, 1981) at 67.

SUM INSURANCE. The insurer agrees to pay a certain sum of money to the insured if a particular event occurs. John G. Fleming, *The Law of Torts*, 6th ed. (Sydney: The Law Book Company Limited, 1983) at 365.

SUM INSURED. The named amount to which the insurer's liability is limited by a contract of insurance. Raoul Colinvaux, *The Law of Insurance*, 5th ed. (London: Sweet & Maxwell, 1984) at 10.

SUMMA EST RATIO QUAE PRO RELIGIONE FACIT. [L.] An argument made for religion carries the greatest weight.

SUMMARY. *n.* An abridgment.

SUMMARY APPLICATION. A request to a judge or court without a full and formal proceeding. See ANNUAL ~.

SUMMARY CONVICTION COURT. A person who has jurisdiction in the territorial division where the subject-matter of the proceedings is alleged to have arisen and who (a) is given jurisdiction over the proceedings by the enactment under which the proceedings are taken; (b) is a justice or provincial court judge, where the enactment under which the proceedings are taken does not expressly give jurisdiction to any person or class of persons; or (c) is a provincial court judge, where the enactment under which the proceedings are taken gives jurisdiction in respect thereof to two or more justices. *Criminal Code*, R.S.C. 1985, c. C-46, s. 785 as am. by *Criminal Law Amendment Act*, R.S.C. 1985 (1st Supp.), c. 27, s. 170.

SUMMARY CONVICTION OFFENCE. An offence which is tried summarily.

SUMMARY JUDGMENT. In Ontario, once the defendant has served a notice of motion or delivered a statement of defence, a plaintiff may apply for summary judgment in respect of part or all of the claim set out in the statement of claim. G.D. Watson & C. Perkins, eds., *Holmested & Watson: Ontario Civil Procedure* (Toronto: Carswell, 1984) at 20-2.

SUMMARY JURISDICTION. The ability of a court to make an order or give a judgment on its own initiative at once.

SUMMARY OFFENCE. Offence under any enactment of the Province or any regulation made under any enactment. Nova Scotia statutes.

SUMMARY TRIAL. A trial conducted by or under the authority of a commanding officer pursuant to section 163 and a trial by a superior commander pursuant to section 164. *National Defence Act*, R.S.C. 1985, c. N-5, s. 2.

SUMMARY TRIAL COURT. A court for the summary trial of any person charged with having committed corrupt practices at an election. Controverted Elections acts.

SUMMER DRAUGHT. The distance measured from the top of the keel of a ship to the upper edge of the load line that would mark the summer fresh water freeboard calculated in accordance with Part II of this Schedule if that freeboard were assigned to the ship. *Load Lines Regulations (Inland)*, C.R.C., c. 1440, s. 1.

SUMMERFALLOW. *n.* Fallow land that is cultivated or managed in such a way as to conserve soil moisture or to prevent soil from drifting or both. *Canadian Wheat Board Regulations*, C.R.C., c. 397, s. 2.

SUMMER PERIOD. That period in each year beginning at two o'clock, mountain standard time, in the forenoon of the last Sunday in April and ending at two o'clock, mountain standard time, in the forenoon of the last Sunday in October. *The Time Act*, R.S.S. 1978, c. T-14, s. 2.

SUMMER SEASON. The period of time commencing on April 1st in each year and terminating on October 31st next following. *National Parks Businesses Regulations*, C.R.C., c. 1115, s. 2.

SUMMONITIONES AUT CITATIONES NULLAE LICEANT FIERI INTRA PALATIUM REGIS. [L.] Neither summonses nor citations may be served within the monarch's palace.

SUMMONS. *n.* 1. A citation; a warning to appear in court. 2. A summons in Form 6 issued by a justice or judge. *Criminal Code*, R.S.C. 1985, c. C-46, s. 493. 3. Includes any notice, writ, order, requisition, or other paper or document required or authorized to be served. *The Summary Convictions Act*, S.M. 1985-86, c. 4, s. 9(3). See GARNISHEE ~; JUDGMENT ~; ORIGINATING ~; RE~; SHOW CAUSE ~; WRIT OF ~.

SUMMONS TO WITNESS. Used instead of a subpoena, this document directs a witness to appear in court at a given time and place or to bring certain documents or things along.

SUMMUM JUS, SUMMA INJURIA. SUMMA LEX, SUMMA CRUX. [L.] The most extreme right, the most extreme injury — the strictest law, strictest punishment.

SUMP. *n.* A watertight tank or pit that is open to the atmosphere, (i) which receives storm water or other liquid waste that does not require treatment as sanitary sewage; and (ii) from which the storm water or liquid waste it receives is discharged to a sewer or other acceptable point of disposal. *Ontario Water Resources Act*, R.R.O. 1980, Reg. 736, s. 1.

SUMPTUARY LAW. A law to restrain luxury, i.e. excessive apparel.

SUM UP. For a judge to recapitulate evidence or parts of it for a jury, directing what form of verdict they should give. Each counsel has the right to sum up evidence adduced and the judge sums up everything.

SUNDAY. *n.* The first day of the week, also called the Lord's Day.

SUNDAY CLOSING LAW. A law which requires businesses of certain classes to close on Sundays.

SUP. CT. *abbr.* Superior Court.

SUP. CT. L. REV. *abbr.* The Supreme Court Law Review.

SUPER ALTUM MARE. [L.] On the high sea.

SUPERANNUATION. *n.* Includes any amount received out of or under a superannuation or pension fund or plan and without restricting the generality of the foregoing includes any payment made to a beneficiary under the fund or plan or to an employer or former employer of the beneficiary thereunder, (a) in accordance with the terms of the fund or plan; (b) resulting from an amendment to or modification of the fund or plan; or (c) resulting from the termination of the fund or plan. *Income Tax Act*, R.S.C. 1952, c. 148 (as am. S.C. 1970-71-72, c. 63), s. 248(1).

SUPERANNUATION ALLOWANCE. The total annuity or allowance payable under this Act. *Pension (Teachers) Act*, R.S.B.C. 1979, c. 320, s. 1.

SUPERANNUATION FUND. The fund to which a person who is eligible for superannuation contributes. *The Superannuation (Supplementary Provisions) Act*, R.S.S. 1978, c. S-64, s. 2.

SUPER FALSO ET CERTO FINGITUR. [L.] Fiction is made from both false and true.

SUPERFLUA NON NOCENT. [L.] Superfluities do no harm.

SUPERINTENDENT. *n.* 1. The person in charge of a place of secure custody and includes a person designated to act on that person's behalf. 2. The person in charge of a hospital or an institution. 3. The person in charge of a correctional institution and includes a person designated to act on that person's behalf. 4. Includes a commissioner, regional supervisor, Indian superintendent, assistant Indian superintendent and any other person declared by the Minister to be a superintendent for the purposes of this Act, and with reference to a band or a reserve, means the superintendent for that band or reserve. *Indian Act*, R.S.C. 1985, c. I-5, s. 2. 5. Includes owner, lessee, manager, operator, director and person in charge. *Nursing Homes Act*, R.S.N.S. 1967, c. 216, s. 1. 6. The person who has for the time being the direct and actual superintendence and charge of a hospital. See INDIAN ~; MINE RESCUE STATION ~.

SUPERINTENDENT OF INSURANCE. The Superintendent of Insurance of Canada or of a province, according to the person upon whom the law confers the supervision of the insurer concerned. *Taxation Act*, R.S.Q. 1977, c. I-3, s. 835.

SUPERIOR COURT. 1. (a) In the Province of

Ontario, Nova Scotia, Prince Edward Island or Newfoundland, the Supreme Court of the Province; (b) in the Province of Quebec, the Court of Appeal and the Superior Court in and for the Province; (c) in the Province of New Brunswick, Manitoba, Saskatchewan or Alberta, the Court of Appeal for the Province and the Court of Queen's Bench for the Province; (d) in the Province of British Columbia, the Court of Appeal and the Supreme Court of the Province; (e) in the Yukon Territory or the Northwest Territories, the Supreme Court thereof, and includes the Supreme Court of Canada and the Federal Court. *Interpretation Act*, R.S.C. 1985, c. I-21. s. 35. 2. A court not under the control of any other court except by appeal. 3. A court with jurisdiction throughout a province, not limited to any subject matter. P.W. Hogg, *Constitutional Law of Canada*, 2d ed. (Toronto: Carswell, 1985) at 134. 4. A court of original jurisdiction or of original civil and criminal jurisdiction which has inherent power to determine that what was just and fair was done between an accused and a prosecutor. S.A. Cohen, *Due Process of Law* (Toronto: Carswell, 1977) at 395.

SUPERIOR COURT OF CRIMINAL JURISDICTION. (a) In the Province of Ontario, the Supreme Court; (b) in the Province of Quebec, the Superior Court; (c) in the Provinces of Nova Scotia, Prince Edward Island and Newfoundland, the Supreme Court; (d) in the Provinces of New Brunswick, Manitoba, Saskatchewan and Alberta, the Court of Appeal or the Court of Queen's Bench; (e) in the Province of British Columbia, the Supreme Court or the Court of Appeal; (f) in the Yukon Territory, the Supreme Court; and (g) in the Northwest Territories, the Supreme Court. *Criminal Code*, R.S.C. 1985, c. C-46, s. 2.

SUPERIOR OFFICER. 1. Any officer or non-commissioned member who, in relation to any other officer or non-commissioned member is by this Act, or by regulations or custom of the service, authorized to give a lawful command to that other officer or non-commissioned member. *Defence Act*, R.S.C. 1985 (1st Supp.), c. 31, s. 1. 2. The Deputy Minister and any officer or member of a class of officers designated by the Minister. *Excise Act*, R.S.C. 1985, c. E-14, s. 2.

SUPERIOR TRAIN. A train having precedence over another train. *Regulations No. O-8, Uniform Code of Operating Rules*, C.R.C., c. 1175, Part III, s. 2.

SUPERSEDEAS. *n.* A writ which ordered, when good cause was shown, the stay of an ordinary proceeding which should otherwise proceed.

SUPERSEDING MOTION. A formally independent motion to set aside a question in the course of debate. A. Fraser, G.A. Birch & W.A. Dawson, eds., *Beauchesne's Rules and Forms of the House of Commons of Canada*, 5th ed. (Toronto: Carswell, 1978) at 151.

SUPERSONIC FLIGHT. Flight at speeds in excess of a true flight Mach number of one. *Sonic and Supersonic Flight Order*, C.R.C., c. 64, s. 2.

SUPERSTRUCTURE. *n.* 1. (i) Includes grading, ballast, ties, rails, switches and other track appurtenances, bridges, tunnels, culverts, signals and grade crossing protective appliances, telephone and telegraph lines, fencing on the right of way and station platforms; but (ii) does not include railway stations, office buildings, water tanks, coal docks, wells, pipe lines, pump houses and equipment, warehouses, dwellings, roundhouses, turntables, shops and tool houses, stock yards, loading platforms or things of a like nature. *Municipal Taxation Act*, R.S.A. 1980, c. M-31, s. 16. 2. A decked structure on the freeboard deck extending from side to side of the ship, and includes a raised quarter deck. Canada regulations. 3. The equipment affixed to a hull including masts, rigging and rails, but does not include electronic equipment or the engine of a vessel. *Fisheries Improvement Loans Regulations*, C.R.C., c. 864, s. 3. See EFFECTIVE LENGTH OF ~ OR TRUNK; ENCLOSED ~; HEIGHT OF ~; LENGTH OF ~; RAILWAY ~.

SUPERSTRUCTURE DECK. The deck forming the top of the superstructure. Canada regulations.

SUPERVISION. *n.* 1. The provision of counselling services by a probation officer to an offender. *The Corrections Act*, R.S.S. 1978, c. C-40, s. 2. 2. The caring for, assisting, guiding, protecting, or overseeing of mental retardates not in institutions, by any person or agency with the approval of the minister under such terms and conditions as he may prescribe. *Mental Health Act*, R.S.M. 1970, c. M110, s. 2. See PERSONAL ~.

SUPERVISION CENTRE. A prescribed place where a person can be assessed in relation to alcoholism and his potential for rehabilitation. *Treatment of Intoxicated Persons Act*, R.S.N.B. 1973, c. T-11.1, s. 1.

SUPERVISION ORDER. A supervision order made under section 26 and includes a renewal order. *Child Welfare Act*, S.A. 1984, c. C-8.1, s. 1.

SUPERVISOR. *n.* 1. A person who has charge of a work place or authority over a worker. *Occupational Health and Safety Act*, R.S.O.

1980, c. 321, s. 1. 2. An overseer. 3. A person who is reponsible for the care and management of a child care facility. *Child Care Facilities Act*, R.S.P.E.I. 1974, c. C-5, s. 2. 4. An authorized field representative of Canadian Legion War Services Inc., The National Council of Young Men's Christian Associations of Canada, Knights of Columbus Canadian Army Huts or Salvation Army Canadian War Services who directly provided services and recreational equipment to any of the Canadian naval, army or air forces and who was selected and approved by, and proceeded from Canada under the authority of, the Chief of Naval Personnel, the Adjutant-General or Air Member for Personnel. *Civilian War Pensions and Allowances Act*, R.S.C. 1985, c. C-31, s. 16. See LABORATORY ~; PAROLE ~; TICKET ISSUING MACHINE ~.

SUPERVISORY CARE. The provision of room, board and (i) guidance or supervision in the activities of daily living, or (ii) observation or surveillance of the physical well-being, of a person who is ambulatory or semi-ambulatory. *Homes for Special Care Act*, S.N.S. 1976, c. 12, s. 2.

SUPERVISORY SERVICES. The regular monitoring of the personal welfare of a resident and the provision of limited or occasional supervision of or assistance to a resident in the performance of activities necessary to his personal welfare. *Community Care Facilities and Nursing Homes Act*, S.P.E.I. 1985, c. 9, s. 1.

SUPERVISORY SIGNAL. A signal indicating the need for action in connection with the supervision of sprinkler and other extinguishing systems or equipment, or with the maintenance features of other protection systems. *Building Code Act*, R.R.O. 1980, Reg. 87, s. 1.

SUPER VISUM CORPORIS. [L.] Upon viewing the body.

SUPPLEMENT. *n.* 1. Any substance or mixture of substances, other than a fertilizer, that is manufactured, sold or represented for use in the improvement of the physical condition of soils or to aid plant growth or crop yields. *Fertilizers Act*, R.S.C. 1985, c. F-10, s. 2. 2. A monthly guaranteed income supplement authorized to be paid under Part II. *Old Age Security Act*, R.S.C. 1985, c. O-9, s. 2. 3. A mixture of ingredients that supply or are purported to supply nutrients or nutrients and medicating ingredients in sufficient concentration that, when mixed with grain or grain and other carbohydrate materials, in accordance with the directions for use, will produce a complete and balanced feed that is acceptable for registration. *Feeds Regulations*, C.R.C., c. 665, s. 2. See BRIDGING ~; SOIL ~.

SUPPLEMENTAL DEED. A deed expressly in addition to a previous deed.

SUPPLEMENTAL PENSION PLAN. A pension plan organized and administered for the benefit of employees whose membership in another pension plan is a condition precedent to membership in the supplemental pension plan.

SUPPLEMENTAL PLAN. Provisions established for the payment of retirement pensions to employees, including a deferred profit sharing pension plan. *Supplemental Pension Plans Act*, R.S.Q. 1977, c. R-17, s. 1.

SUPPLEMENTARY AID. The assistance that may be paid to a recipient of a governmental benefit. *General Welfare Assistance Act*, R.S.O. 1980, c. 188, s. 1.

SUPPLEMENTARY BENEFIT. 1. A benefit in addition to the benefits provided in this Act. *Public Service Superannuation Amendment Act*, S.O. 1984, c. 22, s. 1. 2. A benefit in addition to the benefit to which a member or the widow, widower, child, beneficiary or estate of the member is entitled by reason of his membership in the System. *Ontario Municipal Employees Retirement System Act*, R.S.O. 1980, c. 348, s. 1.

SUPPLEMENTARY LETTERS PATENT. Any letters patent granted to the company subsequent to the letters patent incorporating the company.

SUPPLEMENTARY RETIREMENT BENEFITS ACCOUNT. The Account established in the accounts of Canada pursuant to the Supplementary Retirement Benefits Act.

SUPPLEMENTARY UNEMPLOYMENT BENEFIT PLAN. An arrangement, other than an arrangement in the nature of a superannuation or pension fund or plan or an employees profit sharing plan, under which payments are made by an employer to a trustee in trust exclusively for the payment of periodic amounts to employees or former employees of the employer who are or may be laid off for any temporary or indefinite period. *Income Tax Act*, R.S.C. 1952, c. 148 (as am. S.C. 1970-71-72, c. 63), s. 145(1)(b). See REGISTERED ~.

SUPPLEMENT EQUIVALENT. In respect of any month in a payment quarter, the amount of the supplement that would be payable for that month under subsection 12(1) or (2), as the case may be, to a married pensioner whose spouse is also a pensioner when both the pensioner and the spouse have no income in a base calendar year and both are in receipt of a full pension. *Old Age Security Act*, R.S.C. 1985, c. O-9, s. 22. See ROUNDED ~.

SUPPLEMENT EQUIVALENT FOR THE SURVIVING SPOUSE OF A DECEASED PENSIONER. (a) In respect of any month in the payment quarter commencing on January 1, 1985, an amount of $262.46; and (b) in respect of any month in a payment quarter commencing after March 31, 1985, the amount obtained by multiplying (i) the amount of the supplement equivalent for the surviving spouse of a deceased pensioner for any month in the 3-month period immediately before that payment quarter by (ii) the ratio that the Consumer Price Index for the first adjustment quarter that relates to that payment quarter bears to the Consumer Price Index for the second adjustment quarter that relates to that payment quarter. *Old Age Security Act*, R.S.C. 1985, c. O-9, s. 22.

SUPPLEMENT EQUIVALENT FOR THE WIDOW. (a) In respect of any month in the payment quarter commencing on January 1, 1985, an amount of $262.46; and (b) in respect of any month in a payment quarter commencing after March 31, 1985, the amount obtained by multiplying (i) the amount of the supplement equivalent for the widow of a deceased pensioner for any month in the 3-month period immediately before that payment quarter by (ii) the ratio that the Consumer Price Index for the first adjustment quarter that relates to that payment quarter bears to the Consumer Price Index for the second adjustment quarter that relates to that payment quarter. *Old Age Security Act*, R.S.C. 1985 (1st Supp.), c. 34, s. 5.

SUPPLIANT. *n.* The one who acts in, or the party who prefers a petition of right.

SUPPLIER. *n.* 1. A person who manufactures, supplies, sells, leases, distributes or installs any article, device or equipment or any biological, physical or chemical agent to be used in a workplace. *Occupational Health and Safety acts.* 2. (i) A person who in the course of his business becomes liable under a consumer transaction to sell, lease or otherwise dispose of goods or to provide services or both, or in the case of an award by chance of goods or services or both, to provide the goods or services awarded; (ii) a person who in the course of his business (A) manufactures, assembles or produces goods that are the subject of a consumer transaction; (B) acts as a wholesaler or distributor of goods that are the subject of a consumer transaction; or (C) solicits, advertises or otherwise promotes the use, purchase or acquisition in any manner of goods or services that are the subject of a consumer transaction; or (iii) a person who receives or is entitled to receive all or part of the consideration paid or payable under a consumer transaction, whether as a party thereto or as an assignee or otherwise, or who is otherwise entitled to be compensated by a consumer for goods or sevices or both. *Unfair Trade Practices Act*, R.S.A. 1980, c. U-3, s. 1. 3. A person who deals in petroleum and pays the costs of transporting oil in bulk quantities. *Energy Administration Act*, R.S.C. 1985, c. E-6, s. 87. 4. An importer, refiner, wholesale marketer, jobber, distributor, terminal operator, broker or any other person or association of persons who supplies any controlled product in bulk at any or all levels of wholesale distribution whether or not the supplier is himself a wholesale customer for the controlled product. *Energy Supplies Emergency Act*, R.S.C. 1985, c. E-9, s. 2. 5. (i) With reference to marketable gas, (A) the owner of gas at the time it is produced at a well, when the gas is marketable gas at the time it is produced; or (B) the owner of gas at the time it becomes marketable gas, when the gas is not marketable gas at the time it is produced and requires processing in order to become marketable gas; or (ii) with reference to any substance other than marketable gas, a person who is a supplier as defined in the regulation. *Natural Gas Rebates Act*, R.S.A. 1980, c. N-5, s. 1. 6. The Société des alcools du Québec, or (ii) a person holding a brewer's permit issued under the Act respecting the Société des alcools du Québec (R.S.Q. chapter S-13). *An Act to Amend the Duties on Fuel and Alcoholic Beverages and Certain Fiscal Legislation*, S.Q. 1982, c. 4, s. 79.10. See BONA FIDE ~; MANITOBA ~S; SERVICE ~.

SUPPLIES. *n.* 1. Materials, equipment and other personal property that is or was required or used by a department for the transaction of its business and affairs, and includes furnishings. *Public Works, Supply and Services acts.* 2. Paper, pens, pencils, note books, scribblers and all other things and materials required by the pupils of any school as an aid to their instruction and education. *The Free Text Book Act*, R.S.S. 1978, c. F-22, s. 2. 3. Petroleum products, feed grain, fodder, repairs to implements and parts, repairs to harness, formaldehyde and other smut control compounds, weed control compounds and gopher poison, and includes such other commodities and such services as the Lieutenant Governor in Council may approve. *The Municipalities Seed Grain and Supply Act*, R.S.S. 1978, c. M-38, s. 2. See CEMETERY ~; DEFENCE ~; FISHING EQUIPMENT AND ~; OFFICE ~; POSTAGE ~; STUDENTS' ~; SUPPLY.

SUPPLY. *v.* (a) In relation to an article, sell, rent, lease or otherwise dispose of an article or an interest therein or a right thereto, or offer so to dispose of an article or interest therein or a right thereto; and (b) in relation to a service, sell, rent or otherwise provide a service or offer so to provide a service. *Combines Investigation Act*, R.S.C. 1985, c. C-34, s. 2.

SUPPLY. *n.* Reservation, transmission, distribution, capacity to provide, dealing in and sale. *Hydro and Power Authority acts.* See BUSINESS OF ~; INTERIM ~; SECURITY OF ~; SUPPLIES.

SUPPLY AND SERVICES CANADA. The ministry which purchases and does accounting for the federal government.

SUPPLY AUTHORITY. Any corporation or person that produces, transmits, delivers or furnishes electrical power or energy to or for a consumer.

SUPPLY DUCT. A duct for conveying air from a heating, ventilating or air-conditioning appliance to a space to be heated, ventilated or air-conditioned. *Building Code Act*, R.R.O. 1980, Reg. 87, s. 1.

SUPPLY FACILITY. Premises, other than a research facility, that are used for the breeding and rearing of animals pursuant to a contract between the operator thereof and the operator of a research facility. *Animals for Research Act*, R.S.O. 1980, c. 22, s. 1.

SUPPLY FIRM. Any person, corporation, firm or syndicate carrying on the business of selling lightning rod systems to a firm or firms in the province. *Lightning Rod Act*, R.S.P.E.I. 1974, c. L-16, s. 1.

SUPPLY HOUSE. 1. A manufacturer, jobber or wholesale vendor, making or dealing in gas equipment and includes their agents. *The Gas Inspection and Licensing Act*, R.S.S. 1978, c. G-4, s. 2. 2. A manufacturer, jobber or wholesale vendor or a manufacturer's agent dealing in electrical equipment. *Electrical Inspection and Licensing Act*, S.S. 1980-81, c. E-7.1, s. 2.

SUPPLY LINE. A line used primarily for the transmission of a supply of electrical energy for other than telegraphic, telephonic, signalling or other intelligence purposes. *Wire Crossings and Proximities Regulations*, C.R.C., c. 1195, s. 2.

SUPPLY OF SERVICES. Any work done or service performed upon or in respect of an improvement and includes, (i) the rental of equipment with an operator; and (ii) where the making of the planned improvement is not commenced, the supply of a design, plan, drawing or specification that in itself enhances the value of the owner's interest in the land. *Construction Lien Act*, S.O. 1983, c. 6, s. 1.

SUPPLY SERVICE. Any one set of conductors run by a supply authority from its mains to a consumer's service. *Power Corporation Act*, R.R.O. 1980, Reg. 794, s. 0.

SUPPLY STATION. See ELECTRICAL ~.

SUPPLY SYSTEM. Includes the service pipe, distributing pipe and all connecting pipes, fittings, control valves and devices. *Ontario Water Resources Act*, R.R.O. 1980, Reg. 736, s. 1.

SUPPORT. *n.* Financial support provided to a school division under the education support program established under Part IX and support provided to a school division by way of personnel, materials, equipment or assets in lieu of financial payments or grants. *An Act to Amend the Education Administration Act and the Public Schools Act*, S.M. 1980-81, c. 34, s. 7. See AIRTERMINAL ~; BEARING ~.

SUPPORTER. See SEPARATE SCHOOL ~.

SUPPORT ORDER. An order or judgment for maintenance, alimony or family financial support that is enforceable in any province. See FINANCIAL ~.

SUPPORT PROVISION. 1. A provision of an order or agreement for maintenance, alimony or family financial support and includes any order for arrears of payments thereof. *Family Orders and Agreements Enforcement Assistance Act*, R.S.C. 1985 (2d Supp.), c. 4, s. 2. 2. A provision in an agreement relating to the payment of maintenance or family financial support that is enforceable by a garnishee summons under provincial garnishment law. *Family Orders and Agreements Enforcement Assistance Act*, R.S.C. 1985 (2d Supp.), c. 4, s. 23.

SUPPORT STAFF. Staff other than supervisory officer staff or teaching staff. *Education Amendment Act*, S.O. 1986, c. 21, s. 1.

SUPPRESS. *v.* (a) To replace an interfering machine, apparatus or equipment with noninterfering machinery, apparatus or equipment; (b) to repair or alter an interfering machine, apparatus or equipment in such a manner that it will not cause radio interference; or (c) to associate with an interfering machine, apparatus or equipment additional apparatus such as suppressors or shielding so that the machine, apparatus or equipment will not cause interference. *Radio Interference Regulations*, C.R.C., c. 1374, s. 2.

SUPPRESSIO VERI. [L.] Suppression of truth.

SUPRA. *prep.* [L.] Above.

SUPRA PROTEST. After protesting.

SUPRAVITAL PROCESSES. Pathological and physiological processes which continue after somatic death, largely at the cellular level. F.A. Jaffe, *A Guide to Pathological Evidence*, 2d ed. (Toronto: Carswell, 1983) at 12.

SUPREMACY. *n.* Sovereignty; pre-eminent authority.

SUPREMACY CLAUSE. Section 52(1) of the Constitution Act, 1982 which gives the Charter power to override other provisions. P.W. Hogg, *Constitutional Law of Canada*, 2d ed. (Toronto: Carswell, 1985) at 693.

SUPREMA POTESTAS SEIPSAM DISSOLVERE POTEST. [L.] Supreme power has the power to dissolve itself.

SUPREME COURT. 1. The Supreme Court of Canada. 2. The Supreme Court of Prince Edward Island. *Interpretation Act*, S.P.E.I. 1981, c. 18, s. 26. 3. The Court of Queen's Bench of New Brunswick or the Court of Appeal or both, as the context requires. *Université de Moncton Act*, S.N.B. 1986, c. 94, s. 2. 4. The Supreme Court of Newfoundland referred to in section 3, and where the subject or context requires, the Court of Appeal or the Trial Division. *Judicature Act*, S.Nfld. 1986, c. 42, s.2.

SUPREME COURT OF CANADA. The general court of appeal for all of Canada, the final interpreter of all Canadian law whatever its source. P.W. Hogg, *Constitutional Law of Canada*, 2d ed. (Toronto: Carswell, 1985) at 171.

SUPREME COURT OF ONTARIO. The superior court of record, both civil and criminal, in Ontario. Its two branches are the Court of Appeal for Ontario and the High Court of Justice for Ontario. G.D. Watson & C. Perkins, eds., *Holmested & Watson: Ontario Civil Procedure* (Toronto: Carswell, 1984) at CJA-15.

SUPT. *abbr.* Superintendent.

SURCHARGE. *n.* An amount assessed against an applicant for insurance or an insured that is in addition to any other premium payable for the insurance. *Automobile Insurance Act*, S.M. 1974, c. 58, s. 2.

SURETY. *n.* 1. A person who gives security for another person; a person who assumes a bond for another person. 2. A person who gives a guarantee to the Crown or to a contractor under a bond to pay creditors of the Crown or the contractor. 3. A sufficient surety. 4. A registered company within the meaning of the Canadian and British Insurance Companies Act (Canada) that (i) under the terms of a bid bond, undertakes to pay a sum of money to the obligee in the event that the principal breaches the conditions of the bond; (ii) under the terms of a performance bond, undertakes to incur the cost of fulfilling the terms of a contract in the event that the principal breaches the contract; or (iii) under the terms of a payment bond, undertakes to make payment to all persons supplying labour and material in the performance of the work provided for in the contract if the principal fails to make payment, and includes any agent, independent agent or underwriter of such registered company, or any person empowered to act on behalf of any such agent, independent agent or underwriter. *Business Loans, Guarantees and Indemnities Act*, S.N.W.T. 1983 (1st Sess.), c. 1, s. 3. See CO-~; PRINCIPAL AND ~.

SURETY BOND. A guarantee of the performance of an expressed obligation. *Insurance Adjusters, Agents and Brokers Act*, S.Nfld. 1986, c. 36, s. 2.

SURETY COMPANY. A corporation empowered to give bonds by way of indemnity. *Judicature Act*, R.S.O. 1980, c. 223, s. 76.

SURETY INSURANCE. Insurance whereby an insurer undertakes to guarantee (a) the due performance of a contract or undertaking; or (b) the payment of a penalty or indemnity for any default, but does not include insurance coming within the class of credit insurance or mortgage insurance. *Classes of Insurance Regulations*, C.R.C., c. 977, s. 36.

SURFACE. See APPROACH ~; BEARING ~; EXTERNAL ~; FOOD CONTACT ~; HEATING ~; HORIZONTAL ~; OUTER ~; PRINCIPAL DISPLAY ~; STRIKING ~; TRANSITIONAL ~.

SURFACE DISTURBANCE. (i) The disturbance, exposure, covering or erosion of the surface of land in any manner; or (ii) the degradation or deterioration in any manner of the surface of land. *Land Surface Conservation and Reclamation Act*, R.S.A. 1980, c. L-3, s. 1.

SURFACE FACILITIES. Storage or treatment facilities provided at the disposal site for liquid waste before discharge into the subsurface and includes piping, pumps, valves, tankage, instrumentation and other equipment. *Environmental Protection Act*, R.R.O. 1980, Reg. 303, s. 1.

SURFACE HOLDER. The lessee or registered holder of the surface rights to the land on which a mineral claim is or is proposed to be recorded. *Canada Mining Regulations*, C.R.C., c. 1516, s. 2.

SURFACE LEASE. 1. A lease or other instrument under which the surface of land is being held for any purpose for which a right of entry order may be made and that provides for payment of compensation. 2. Includes the lease, easement, right of way or other agreement made about a land surface area by an owner. *Petroleum and Natural Gas Act*, R.S.B.C. 1979, c. 323, s. 1.

SURFACE MINE. 1. A mine worked by a strip

mining, open pit mining or other surface method, including auger mining. *Coal Mines Safety Act*, R.S.A. 1980, c. C-15, s. 1. 2. A pit or quarry where metallic or non-metallic rock, mineral bearing substance, earth, clay sand or gravel is being or has been removed by means of an excavation open to the surface to supply material for construction, industrial or manufacturing purposes but does not include a cutting for a right of way for a highway or a railroad. *Occupational Health and Safety Act*, R.R.O. 1980, Reg. 694, s. 1.

SURFACE RACEWAY. A raceway in the form of a channel with a backing and capping for loosely holding conductors and cables in surface wiring. *Power Corporation Act*, R.R.O. 1980, Reg. 794, s. 0.

SURFACE RIGHTS. 1. Includes lands granted, leased or otherwise disposed of for any purpose and in respect of which the mines and minerals thereon or under the surface thereof are by statute or any disposition reserved to the Crown. 2. Every right in land other than the mining rights. *Mining Act*, R.S.O. 1980, c. 268, s. 1. 3. (i) The land or any portion thereof or any interest therein, except mines and minerals within the meaning of The Land Titles Act, or a right of entry thereon, required by an operation for the purpose of drilling for, producing or recovering a mineral; (ii) the right to condition, maintain, reclaim or restore the surface of land where the land has been or is being held incidental to or in connection with either or both of: (A) the drilling for, producing or recovering a mineral; (B) the laying, constructing, operating, maintaining or servicing a flow line, service line or power line. *The Surface Rights Acquisition and Compensation Act*, R.S.S. 1978, c. S-65, s. 2.

SURFACE RIGHTS OPTION. Any right to acquire the surface rights to land, the mineral rights to which have been acquired by the optionee either prior to the granting of the surface rights option or by the conveyance that itself contains the grant of the surface rights option. *Land Transfer Tax Act*, R.R.O. 1980, Reg. 571, s. 1.

SURFACE SEWER. A sewer that is intended to carry storm and surface water and drainage and includes a surface drain. *Municipalities Act*, R.S.N.B. 1973, c. M-22, s. 118.

SURFACE WATER. 1. Water above the surface of land and being in a river, stream, watercourse, lake, creek, spring, ravine, coulee, canyon, lagoon, swamp, marsh or other body of water. Saskatchewan statutes. 2. Water in a watercourse.

SURGEON. *n.* A member of the medical staff who performs a surgical operation on a patient.

Public Hospitals Act, R.R.O. 1980, Reg. 865, s. 1. See COLLEGE OF PHYSICIANS AND ~S; VETERINARY ~.

SURGERY. See DENTAL ~; VETERINARY ~.

SURGICAL CARE. 1. Major surgery. *The Health Services Act*, R.S.S. 1978, c. H-1, s. 23. 2. The provision of any blood transfusion or transfusions or injection or injections is included in the meaning. *Child Welfare Act*, S.Nfld. 1972, s. 37, s. 11.

SURGICAL-DENTAL SERVICES. Any medically or dentally required surgical-dental procedures performed by a dentist in a hospital, where a hospital is required for the proper performance of the procedures. *Canada Health Act*, R.S.C. 1985, c. C-6, s. 2.

SURGICAL TREATMENT. (a) Minor surgery on the foot by the use of cutting instruments for treatment of a disease, ailment or condition such as corns, callouses, warts, cysts, hammer toes, ingrown, infected or deformed toe nails or infected or ulcerative lesions and other minor surgery on the foot the board may by unanimous resolution approve; and (b) other surgery on the foot when performed in a hospital as the medical staff of that hospital permits. *Podiatrists Act*, R.S.B.C. 1979, c. 330, s.1.

SURMISE. *n.* An allegation; a suggestion.

SURNAME. *n.* Includes a surname, family name or patronymic.

SURNAME AND CHRISTIAN NAMES. For a married woman or a widow, mean her surname and Christian names joined to the surname of the husband or the surname and Christian names of the husband, followed by the designation "Mrs." which, for her, dispenses with any mention of a profession or occupation. *Election Act*, R.S.Q. 1977, c. E-3, s. 2.

SURPLUS. *n.* 1. The aggregate balances of undivided earnings, statutory reserve and other reserves. Credit Unions acts. 2. The excess of assets over liabilities including the reserve of unearned premiums calculated pro rata for the unexpired term of the policies of the company in force. *Mutual Insurance Companies Act*, R.S.N.S. 1967, c. 204, s. 25. 3. The surpluses of a corporation and includes any amount by which any property has been valued in excess of its cost. *Taxation Act*, S.Q. 1979, c. 38, s. 27. See COMMON ~; UNALLOCATED ~.

SURPLUSAGE. *n.* The state of having something in excess or over.

SURPLUSAGIUM NON NOCET. [L.] Surplusage is not harmful.

SURPLUS ASSETS. Having regard to the prescribed assets and liabilities of a pension plan, the portion of those assets that exceeds those liabilities. *Employment Pension Plan Act*, S.A. 1986, c. E-10.05, s. 1.

SURPLUS CROWN ASSETS. The property that is included in a report made to the Minister under section 3 or 5 and that has not subsequently been deleted from the report with the authority of the Minister or disposed of pursuant to this Act. *Surplus Crown Assets Act*, R.S.C. 1985, c. S-27, s. 2.

SURPLUS ELECTRICITY. Electricity that is (a) surplus to the requirements of the authority to supply (i) customers in the authority's service area; and (ii) electricity in respect of which removal is permitted under the Utilities Commission Act; and (b) either (i) produced at a hydroelectric generating facility owned by the authority; or (ii) purchased by the authority from another source. *Industrial Electricity Rate Discount Act*, S.B.C. 1985, c. 49, s. 1.

SURPLUS GOODS. See OBSOLETE OR ~.

SURPLUS STORES. Any goods, upon which customs duty and excise taxes were paid at the time of the entry of an ocean ship into the coasting trade, that remain on board unused at the time the ship reverts to international service. *Ships Suppliers Drawback Regulations*, C.R.C., c. 493, s. 2.

SURR. CT. *abbr.* Surrogate Court.

SURREBUTTAL. *n.* The calling of evidence by the defence to meet the Crown's rebuttal evidence. P.K. McWilliams, *Canadian Criminal Evidence*, 3d ed. (Aurora: Canada Law Book, 1988) at 31-12.

SURRENDER. *n.* A surrender, relinquishment, quit claim, release, notice, agreement or other instrument by which a surface lease is discharged or otherwise terminated as to the whole or part of the land affected by the surface lease. *Land Surface Conservation and Reclamation Act*, R.S.A. 1980, c. L-3, s. 34. See RELEASE OR ~.

SURRENDERED LANDS. A reserve or part of a reserve or any interest therein, the legal title to which remains vested in Her Majesty, that has been released or surrendered by the band for whose use and benefit it was set apart. *Indian Act*, R.S.C. 1985, c. I-5, s. 2.

SURRENDEREE. *n.* The person to whom one surrenders.

SURRENDEROR. *n.* The person who surrenders.

SURRENDER VALUE. The price in cash which an insurance company will pay when the policy

holder surrenders any policy and claims under it to the company. See CASH ~.

SURREPTION. *n.* Getting something by stealth or fraud.

SURREPTITIOUS. *adj.* Stealthy; fraudulent.

SURROGATE. *n.* One who is appointed or substituted for another.

SURSUM REDDITIO. [L.] Surrender.

SURTAX. *n.* Tax payable in addition to tax at the standard rate.

SURVEILLANCE. *n.* Location of a person suspected of engaging in criminal activity, following that person, observing their activities and overhearing their conversations with other people. S.A. Cohen, *Due Process of Law* (Toronto: Carswell, 1977) at 64.

SURVEY. *n.* 1. The determination, measurement and establishment of boundaries of land. 2. The establishment, location or definition on the ground of any boundary, limit or angle of any land, size, location, parcel, claim, common, easement, road, street, lane, district, municipality, county or township, or any other location or division of lands or right over lands whether for ownership, title or authority or the origin of any of them. *Land Survey Act*, R.S.P.E.I. 1974, c. L-4, s. 1. 3. The drydocking of a vessel, the examination and inspection of its hull, boilers, machinery, engines and equipment by an inspector or a surveyor and everything done to such vessel, its hull, boilers, machinery, engines and equipment pursuant to an order, requirement or recommendation given or made by the inspector or surveyor as the result of the examination and inspection so that a safety and inspection certificate might be issued in respect of the vessel pursuant to the provisions of the Canada Shipping Act, and the regulations thereunder or, as the case may be, so that the vessel might be entitled to retain the character assigned to it in the registry book of a classification society. *Income Tax Regulations*, C.R.C., c. 945, s. 3600. 4. The accurate determination of the position of mine workings and other parts of a mine by a surveyor using survey instruments suited to the conditions of the survey. *Coal Mines (CBDC) Safety Regulations*, C.R.C., c. 1011, s. 2. See BLOCK OUTLINE ~; BOUNDARY ~; CLASSIFICATION ~; COMPLETE ~; CO-ORDINATE ~; GEOPHYSICAL ~; MARINE ~; ORIGINAL ~; REGIONAL ~; RE~; ~S; WELL SITE SEABED ~.

SURVEY CONTROL. The establishment and maintenance of a series of interrelated survey monuments to which existing and subsequent surveys in accordance with this Act may be related. *The Land Surveys Act*, R.S.S. 1978, c. L-4, s. 60.

SURVEYED LOT. An unsubdivided unit of land the boundaries of which are shown on a settlement plan, parcel plan or any plan of subdivision registered under the Land Titles Act. *Irrigation Act*, R.S.A. 1980, c. I-11, s. 1.

SURVEYED TERRITORY. That part of a township or seigniory which has been surveyed and divided into lots by the proper authority. *Mining Act*, R.S.Q. 1977, c. M-13, s. 1.

SURVEYING. *n.* The planning, co-ordination, generation, procurement, maintenance and distribution of surveys and survey related information and includes activities connected with geodetic surveys and with land surveys made pursuant to The Land Surveys Act. *Department of Revenue, Supply and Services Amendment Act*, S.S. 1982-83, c. 31, s. 3. See LAND ~; PRACTICE OF ~.

SURVEYOR. *n.* 1. A Canada Lands Surveyor or a person who is entitled to survey lands in a province under the laws of the province. *Canada Lands Surveys Act*, R.S.C. 1985, c. L-6, s. 2. 2. A person who is registered to practise land surveying. 3. A person who practices the profession of land surveying or a person who for gain either direct or indirect makes or does any survey, otherwise than in the employ and under the immediate supervision of a surveyor. *Land Surveys Act*, R.S.P.E.I. 1974, c. L-4, s. 1. 4. A surveyor to a classification society. *Income Tax Regulations*, C.R.C., c. 945, s. 3600. 5. An inspector, a surveyor of ships employed for that purpose by the government of a country that is a party to the 1930 Convention or the 1966 Convention or a surveyor of ships appointed by an organization entrusted with the survey and inspection of an assignment of freeboards to ships by the government of any such country. *Load Line Regulations (Sea)*, C.R.C., c. 1441, s. 2. See CANADA LANDS ~; CHIEF ~; MINE ~.

SURVEYOR GENERAL. 1. A person who is a Canada Lands Surveyor and is appointed as Surveyor General in the manner authorized by law or a person authorized by the Minister to carry out the duties of the Surveyor General. *Canada Lands Surveys Act*, R.S.C. 1985, c. L-6, s. 2. 2. The Minister of Lands and Forests. *Land Surveyors Act*, R.S.Q. 1977, c. A-23, s. 1.

SURVEYOR-IN-TRAINING. *n.* Any field engineer, surveyor, instrument-man, or holder of a bachelor's degree in Civil Engineering, land surveying or forestry from a college or university or the holder of a diploma in land surveying from a recognized land survey institute or any employee serving in the above capacities with

any legally constituted company, corporation, government body or commission. *Land Surveyors Act*, R.S.P.E.I. 1974, c. L-5, s. 1.

SURVEYOR OF RECORD. The surveyor who has signed a return of survey. *Crown Lands and Forests Act*, S.N.B. 1980, c. C-38.1, s. 1.

SURVEYS. *n.* The determination of position of all mine workings by instruments in accordance with this Act. *Coal Mines Regulation Act*, R.S.N.S. 1967, c. 36, s. 3. See SURVEY; TECHNICAL ~.

SURVEY SYSTEM. See CO-ORDINATE ~.

SURVIVING SPOUSE. A person who was another person's spouse at the time of the other person's death. See RESIDUAL INCOME OF THE ~.

SURVIVING SPOUSE WITH DEPENDENT CHILDREN. A surviving spouse of a contributor who maintains wholly or substantially one or more dependent children of the contributor. *Canada Pension Plan Act*, R.S.C. 1985, c. C-8, s. 42.

SURVIVOR PENSION. The pension payable to the surviving spouse or children entitled to a pension under any of the Acts referred to in Section 1. *Increase of Pensions Act*, S.Nfld. 1974, c. 83, s. 3.

SURVIVORSHIP. *n.* The living of one of several people after the death of one or all of the group. See PRESUMPTION OF ~; RIGHT OF ~.

SUSPEND. *v.* Of an attorney or solicitor, to forbid that person from practising for a certain time.

SUSPENDATUR PER COLLUM. [L.] Let the person be hanged by the neck.

SUSPENDED SENTENCE. A judgment which puts off serving a sentence until a later date if conditions of probation are met, but if conditions are not met the convicted party may be subjected to the original sentence.

SUSPENSION. *n.* 1. A temporary interruption of employment, other than a lay-off, at the direction of the employer. *Labour Standards Code Act*, S.N.S. 1975, c. 50, s. 1. 2. Temporary disqualification from the practice of law. *Barristers and Solcitors Act*, R.S.B.C. 1979, c. 26, s. 1. 3. Temporary disqualification from the practice of a notary public. *Notaries Act*, S.B.C. 1981, c. 23, s. 1.

SUSPENSION SPRING. A leaf, coil, torsion bar, rubber, air bag, and every other type of spring used in vehicular suspensions. *Motor Vehicle Safety Regulations*, C.R.C., c. 1038, s. 2.

SUS. PER COLL. *abbr.* Suspendatur per collum.

SUSTAINED YIELD. The growth of timber that a forest can produce and that can be cut to achieve a continuous approximate balance between growth of timber and timber cut. *Crown Timber Act*, R.S.O. 1980, c. 109, s. 6.

SUSTAINED YIELD CAPACITY. Capacity when operated under sustained yield management. *Forest Act*, R.S.M. 1970, c. F150, s. 2.

SUSTAINED YIELD MANAGEMENT. The planned use of a forest area whereby the timber produced is periodically removed without reducing the capacity of the area to continue production at an equal or greater rate in perpetuity. *Forest Act*, R.S.M. 1970, c. F150, s. 2.

SUTURE. See CRANIAL ~S.

S.V. *abbr.* Sub voce.

SWEAR. *v.* 1. To put under oath, to administer an oath to. 2. In the case of persons for the time being allowed by law to affirm or declare instead of swearing, includes affirm and declare.

SWEARING. *n.* Declaration under oath.

SWEEPSTAKES. *n.* A race declared open to all horses that comply with its conditions, in which the owners of the horses entered contribute to a purse to which is added money contributed by the association. *Race Track Supervision Regulations*, C.R.C., c. 441, s. 2.

SWEETBREAD. *n.* The thymus gland of a bovine animal. *Meat Inspection Regulations*, C.R.C., c. 1032, s. 2.

SWEETENING INGREDIENT. Sugar, invert sugar, honey, glucose, dextrose or any combination thereof in dry or liquid form. Canada regulations.

SWELL. *n.* A can of fish, the top or bottom, or both, of which can have been distorted outward due to spoilage. *Fish Inspection Act*, R.S.Nfld. 1970, c. 132, s. 12. See HARD ~; HYDROGEN ~.

SWIMMING POOL. 1. Includes any area of water to which the public have access for bathing purposes and any pool of water maintained for the use of patrons of a hotel, motel, apartment block, trailer court or other place of public accommodation. *The Public Health Act*, R.S.S. 1978, c. P-37, s. 2. 2. Any structure, basin, chamber or tank containing or intended to contain an artificial body of water for swimming, diving or recreational bathing and having a water depth of 76.2 centimetres (2 feet, 6 inches) or more at any point. *Public Health Act*, R.R.O. 1980, Reg. 849, s. 1. See FILL-AND-DRAW ~; FLOW-THROUGH ~; MODIFIED ~; PRIVATE RESIDENTIAL ~; PUBLIC ~.

SWING SHIFT. A shift which overlaps other shifts.

SWITCH. *v.* See BAIT AND ~.

SWITCH. *n.* A device for making, breaking or changing connections in a circuit. See AUTOMATIC ~; DUAL CONTROL ~; ELECTRIC ~ LOCK; GENERAL USE ~; INDICATING ~; ISOLATING ~; MOTOR-CIRCUIT ~; SPRING ~.

SWITCHBOARD. *n.* A panel or assembly of panels on which is mounted any combination of switching, measuring, controlling and protective devices, buses, and connections, designed with a view to successfully carrying and rupturing the maximum fault current encountered when controlling incoming and outgoing feeders. *Power Corporation Act*, R.R.O. 1980, Reg. 794, s. 0.

SWITCHGEAR. *n.* All devices for controlling, regulating, protecting or measuring the supply of electrical energy, current or voltage to, or in a system, or part of a system. *Coal Mines Regulation Act*, R.S.N.S. 1967, c. 36, s. 84.

SWITCHING CHARGE. A charge for each movement over Board railway of a unit of rolling stock. *Harbour Railway Tariff by-laws*.

SYDNEY. See DECLARATION OF ~.

SYLLOGISM. *n.* A form of reasoning in which one draws a conclusion which does not contain the common element of its premises.

SYMBOL. *n.* Any brand, label, mark, name, package or other business device. H.G. Fox, *The Canadian Law of Trade Marks and Unfair Competition*, 3d ed. (Toronto: Carswell, 1972) at 20.

SYMPATHY STRIKE. A strike by workers of one employer to express solidarity with workers of another employer.

SYNALLAGMATIC. *adj.* 1. Involving reciprocal and mutual duties and obligations. 2. Describing a situation in which one party undertakes to another party to do or not to do something, and, if that party fails to perform the undertaking, the law provides a remedy to the other party. G.H.L. Fridman, *The Law of Contract in Canada*, 2d ed. (Toronto: Carswell, 1986) at 10.

SYNCHRONISE. *v.* To agree in time.

SYNCOPARE. *v.* To shorten.

SYNDICATE. *n.* 1. A group of people who join in a venture or undertaking. 2. An underwriting member of the exchange. *Canadian Insurance Exchange Act*, S.O. 1986, c. 70, s. 1. 3. A syndicate other than a specialized syndicate, constituted under the Professional Syndicates

Act, whose members are producers and whose object is the study, defence and promotion of the economic, social and moral interests of the producers generally. *Farm Producers Act*, R.S.Q. 1977, c. P-28, s. 1. 4. Includes any association, partnership or other organization, not constituted as a corporation. *Companies Information Act*, R.S.Q. 1977, c. R-22, s. 1. See FARM ~; PROFESSIONAL ~; SPECIALIZED ~.

SYNDICATE TRUST. Intended to provide protection for the capital contribution of each investor in a group in addition to that provided by any partnership agreement among them, incorporating a company. D.M.W. Waters, *The Law of Trusts in Canada*, 2d ed. (Toronto: Carswell, 1984) at 448.

SYNDROME. *n.* A set of symptoms and signs which happen together. F.A. Jaffe, *A Guide to Pathological Evidence*, 2d ed. (Toronto: Carswell, 1983) at 184-5. See CRUSH ~; MALLORY-WEISS ~; SUDDEN INFANT DEATH ~.

SYNTHETIC COLOUR. Any organic colour, other than caramel, that is produced by chemical synthesis and has no counterpart in nature and which is prescribed in sections B.06.041 to B.06.053. *Food and Drug Regulations*, C.R.C., c. 870, c. B.06.001.

SYNTHETIC CRUDE OIL. A mixture, mainly of pentanes and heavier hydrocarbons, that may contain sulphur compounds, that is derived from crude bitumen and that is liquid at the conditions under which its volume is measured or estimated, and includes all other hydrocarbon mixtures so derived.

SYNTHETIC PRODUCTION. The production of petroleum from a mine in a bituminous sands deposit. *Petroleum and Gas Revenue Tax Act*, R.S.C. 1985 (2d Supp.), c. 2, s. 2.

SYRUP. See MAPLE ~.

SYRUP PACK. A pack in which sugar, invert sugar, dextrose or glucose, in dry or liquid form, is used with water as the packing media. *Processed Fruit and Vegetable Regulations*, C.R.C., c. 291, s. 2.

SYSTEM. *n.* 1. A telephone, telegraph or radio telecommunication system or a combination of any such systems, or any similar means of communication operated by the use of electrical energy; and also includes all the works, owned, held, or used, for the purpose thereof or in connection therewith or with the operation thereof. 2. A normally interconnected arrangement of insulated electrical conductors for the transmission, distribution and application of electrical energy; the system may or may not include the generating source. *Coal Mines Regulation Act*, R.S.N.S. 1967, c. 36, s. 84. 3.

Materials assembled and installed on a building or structure for the purpose of protecting the building or structure from damage by lightning. *Lightning Rods Act*, R.R.O. 1980, Reg. 577, s. 1. 4. The connection between actions about which one seeks evidence and the act of which the prisoner is accused, i.e. a prisoner has in mind a scheme to obtain money by fraud; the act of which the prisoner is accused is part of a planned fraud; and one seeks evidence that the plan existed, and, therefore, that the prisoner has a guilty mind. P.K. McWilliams, *Canadian Criminal Evidence*, 3d ed. (Aurora: Canada Law Book, 1988) at 11-11. See ADVERSARIAL ~; AIR BRAKE ~; AIR HANDLING ~; ANTI-LOCK ~; BURGLAR ALARM ~; CABLE ~; CLEARING ~; COMMUNICATION ~; COMPRESSED GAS ~; COMPUTER ~; CONVEYANCE ~; DIFFERENT ~S; DISTRIBUTION ~; DUAL RATE ~; EMERGENCY LIGHTING ~; EXCHANGE ~; FEUDAL ~; FIRE SUPPRESSION ~; FLIGHT WATCH ~; FLUORIDATION ~; FUEL ~; GROUNDING ~; GROUP MAIL BOX ~; GROUP ~; HORIZONTAL CONTROL ~; HYDRAULIC ~ MINERAL OIL; INDUSTRIAL ~; INQUISATORIAL ~; INTERCONNECTED ~S; LAND TITLES ~; LIGHTING ~: LIGHTNING PROTECTION ~; LIGHTNING ROD ~; MARKETING PLAN OR ~; METRIC ~; PARI-MUTUEL ~; PAYMENTS ~; PIPING ~; PLANNED GRAZING ~; PLANT ~; PLUMBING ~; POST AUDIT CUSTOMS CONTROL ~; POTABLE WATER ~; PREFABRICATED TRENCH SUPPORT ~; PRESSURE PIPING ~; PUBLIC TRANSIT ~; PURIFICATION ~; QUOTA ~; RAILWAY ~; RECIRCULATION ~; REFERRAL HIRING ~; REFRIGERATING ~; REGISTRATION ~; REGISTRY ACT ~; ROUTING ~; SEWAGE ~; SEWERAGE ~; SEWER ~; STEERING CONTROL ~; SUPPLY ~; TELEPHONE ~; TRANSIT ~; TRANSPORTATION ~; TRANSPORT ~; UTILITY ~; VENT ~; WASTEWATER ~; WATCHKEEPING ~; WATER ~; WATER SUPPLY ~; WATERWORKS ~; WORK ~.

SYSTEM GOODS. (a) Goods purchased for use directly in a water distribution, sewerage or drainage system; and (b) goods used in the construction of a building, or that part of a building, used exclusively to house machinery and apparatus for use directly in a water distribution, sewerage or drainage system, but does not include chemicals purchased for use or used in the treatment of water or sewage in any such system. *Excise Tax Act*, R.S.C. 1985 (2d Supp.), c. 7, s. 68.23.

SYSTEM OF REGISTRATION. All registers and other records required by subsection (4) to be prepared and maintained and any such system may be in a bound or loose-leaf form or in a photographic film form, or may be entered or recorded by any system of mechanical or electronic data processing or any other information storage device that is capable of reproducing any required information in intelligible written form within a reasonable time. *Bank Act*, R.S.C. 1985, c. B-1, s. 178(5).

SYSTEM PARTICIPANT. Any corporation, partnership or organization engaged in the transportation of grain by rail or the shipping or handling of grain for transportation by rail, as designated by the Governor in Council, individually or by class. *Western Grain Transportation Act*, R.S.C. 1985, c. W-8, s. 2.

SYSTEMS SOFTWARE. A combination of computer programs and associated procedures, related technical documentation and data that (a) performs compilation, assembly, mapping, management or processing of other programs; (b) facilitates the functioning of a computer system by other programs; (c) provides service or utility functions such as media conversion, sorting, merging, system accounting, performance measurement, system diagnostics or programming aids; (d) provides general support functions such as data management, report generation or security control; or (e) provides general capability to meet widespread categories of problem solving or processing requirements where the specific attributes of the work to be performed are introduced mainly in the form of parameters, constants or descriptors rather than in program logic. *Income Tax Regulations*, C.R.C., c. 945, s. 1104.

SYSTEM VOLTAGE. The greatest normal effective difference of electrical potential between any two points in a system. *Coal Mines Regulation Act*, R.S.N.S. 1967, c. 36, s. 84.

T. *abbr.* 1. Telsa. 2. Tera. 3. Ton (metric).

T.A. *abbr.* Décisions du Tribunal d'arbitrage.

TAB. *n.* A tab that is issued initially with the licence and is issued each year thereafter to indicate that the licence is valid. *Pacific Fishery Registration and Licensing Regulations*, C.R.C., c. 824, s. 2. See REGISTRATION VALIDATION ~; VALIDATION ~.

T.A.B. *abbr.* Tax Appeal Board.

TABLE. See A(F) ULTIMATE AND A(F) AND A(M) ULTIMATE ~S; A (F) ULTIMATE ~; BILLIARD ~; CLERK-AT-THE-~; TIME ~.

TABLE CREAM. Cream that contains not less than 16 per cent nor more than 31.9 per cent milk-fat. *Milk Act*, R.R.O. 1980, Reg. 622, s. 3.

TABLE STOCK POTATO. A potato or any part thereof produced, marketed or used for consumption. *Seeds Regulations*, C.R.C., c. 1400, s. 45.

TABULA IN NAUFRAGIO. See DOCTRINE OF THE ~.

TACIT. *adj.* With respect to a communication of intention, silent.

TACK. *n.* Includes all equipment of any kind customarily fitted to or placed on a horse. *Riding Horse Establishments Act*, R.R.O. 1980, Reg. 905, s. 1.

TACKING. *n.* 1. A doctrine concerning priorities between competing mortgages on the same property. If a third mortgage is taken without notice of a second and the third mortgagee purchases the first mortgage, the third mortgagee may "tack" the third mortgage to the first mortgage and so obtain priority. W.B. Rayner & R.H. McLaren, *Falconbridge on Mortgages*, 4th ed. (Toronto: Canada Law Book, 1977) at 195. 2. A doctrine by which a mortgagor's devisees or heirs may not redeem the mortgage without also paying a judgment debt or bond owing by the mortgagor because any equity of redemption

in the hands of the devisees or heirs are assets for the payment of that debt. W.B. Rayner & R.H. McLaren, *Falconbridge on Mortgages*, 4th ed. (Toronto: Canada Law Book, 1977) at 196-197.

TACKLE. *n.* When used in relation to a vessel, means the tackle, machinery, gear, apparatus and appliances used on board the vessel for the loading and unloading thereof. *Canada Shipping Act*, R.S.C. 1985, c. S-9, s. 2.

TAG. *n.* Any type of tag supplied with a licence that is made of cardboard, paper, plastic, metal or any other material. *An Act to amend the Fish and Wildlife Act*, S.N.B. 1983, c. 33, s. 1. See INTER-AGENCY CERTIFICATION ~; IDENTIFICATION ~; LOCK SEAL ~.

TAIL. See FEE ~.

TAILAGE. *n.* Taxes in general.

TAILER. *n.* A device consisting of a manually or spring operated snare attached to the end of a handle that ensnares fish by gripping them around the caudal peduncle. *Quebec Fishery Regulations*, C.R.C., c. 852, s. 2.

TAILINGS IMPOUNDMENT AREA. A limited disposal area that is confined by man-made or natural structures or by both. *Metal Mining Liquid Effluent Regulations*, C.R.C., c. 819, s. 2.

TAIL ROPE. A steel wire rope manufactured in accordance with the most recent standard of the Canadian Standards Association for steel wire rope for mine hoisting and haulage purposes or any equivalent standard acceptable to the chief inspector. *Mining Regulation Act*, R.S.B.C. 1979, c. 265, s. 140.

TAINTED. *adj.* With respect to fish, means fish that is rancid or has an abnormal odour or flavour.

TAKE. *v.* When used in relation to fish or wildlife includes the capturing or the taking into possession of fish or wildlife whether dead or alive.

TAKE-BACK. See VENDOR ~.

TAKE-HOME PAY. Net pay after withholding tax and other deductions.

TAKE-HOME WORK. Work that the employee performs at the place where he resides; but does not include the selling of goods or services. *Employment Standards Act*, R.S.M. 1970, c. E110, s. 6.

TAKE LANDS. Includes enter upon, take possession of, use and take lands for a limited time or otherwise or for a limited estate or interest.

TAKE OVER BID. *var.* **TAKE-OVER BID.** 1. An offer made by an offeror to shareholders to acquire all of the shares of any class of shares of an offeree corporation not already owned by the offeror, and includes every take-over bid by a corporation to repurchase all of the shares of any class of its shares which leaves outstanding voting shares of the corporation. 2. An offer, other than an exempt offer, made by an offeror to shareholders at approximately the same time to acquire shares that, if combined with shares already beneficially owned or controlled directly or indirectly, by the offeror or an affiliate or associate of the offeror on the date of the take-over bid, would exceed ten per cent of any class of issued shares of an offeree corporation and includes every offer, other than an exempt offer, by an issuer to repurchase its own shares. *Canada Business Corporations Act*, R.S.C. 1985, c. C-44, s. 194. 3. An offer to acquire, directly or indirectly, issued and outstanding voting securities of an issuer which is (i) made to any person or company who is in a province; or (ii) made to or accepted by any holder in the province of the issuer, where the voting securities subject to the offer to acquire, together with the offeror's voting securities, will carry, in the aggregate, 10 per cent or more of all voting rights attaching to the voting securities of the issuer issued and outstanding at the date of the offer to acquire, and, where two or more persons or companies make an offer or offers to acquire jointly or in concert, the securities subject to such offer or offers to acquire, together with each offeror's voting securities, shall be included in the calculation of the percentage that the voting rights attaching to the voting securities of the issuer to be acquired by the offerors is of all voting rights attaching to the voting securities of the issuer. See SECURITIES EXCHANGE ~.

TAKING. *n.* Any capturing, killing or taking into possession of any game, dead or alive. *Fish and Game Protection Act*, R.S.P.E.I. 1974, c. F-8, s. 1.

TAKING OFF. In respect of an aircraft, means the act of abandoning a supporting surface and includes the immediately preceding and following acts and, in respect of an airship or balloon, means the act of freeing the airship or balloon from restraint and includes the immediately preceding and following acts. *Air Regulations*, C.R.C., c. 2, s. 101.

TALCUM EMBOLISM. An embolism caused by talcum powder particles in the circulation. F.A. Jaffe, *A Guide to Pathological Evidence*, 2d ed. (Toronto: Carswell, 1983) at 175.

TALES. *n.* [L.] Such people.

TALESMAN. *n.* A person called up to be a juror from among the bystanders in a court.

TALION. *n.* The law of retaliation, by which punishments must resemble offences.

TALIS INTERPRETATIO IN AMBIGUIS SEMPER FIENDA EST, UT EVITETUR INCONVENIENS ET ABSURDUM. [L.] Ambiguous words should always be interpreted so that inconvenience and absurdity are avoided.

TALIS NON EST EADEM. [L.] The similar is not the same.

TALLAGE. *n.* Taxes in general.

TALLAGER. *n.* A tax or toll collector.

TALLIAGE. See TAILAGE.

TALLY ADJUSTMENT. See CUMULATIVE ~.

TALLYMAN. See CREE ~.

TAMPONADE. See CARDIAC ~.

TANDEM. *n.* A combination of two axles of a vehicle, exclusive of the front axle of the vehicle, arranged in a fixed position one behind the other, the centres of which axles are more than 40 inches but not more than 90 inches apart, and which axles are individually attached to or articulated from, or attached to and articulated from, a common attachment to the vehicle which incorporates a connecting mechanism designed to equalize the load between axles. *Highway Traffic Act*, R.S.Nfld. 1970, c. 152, s. 2.

TANDEM AXLE. Two axles, not more than 72 inches apart when measured at right angles from axle to axle, so arranged that the load carried by each is approximately equal. *Roads Act*, R.S.P.E.I. 1974, c. R-15, s. 1.

TANDEM AXLE WEIGHT. The combined weight which all the wheels on any tandem axle impose on the road when weighed in the manner prescribed in clause (b). *Roads Act*, R.S.P.E.I. 1974, c. R-15, s. 1.

TANDEM BULLET. 1. A military ammunition in which two projectiles are sequenced in a single round. F.A. Jaffe, *A Guide to Pathological Evidence*, 2d ed. (Toronto: Carswell, 1983) at 185. 2. Two bullets which leave the barrel of a firearm at one firing. F.A. Jaffe, *A Guide to Pathological Evidence*, 2d ed. (Toronto: Carswell, 1983) at 185.

TANGIBLE ASSET BACKING. Adjustment of the book value of liabilities and assets on a balance sheet to fair market value as determined by assuming the concern is viable. A. Bissett-Johnson & W.M. Holland, eds., *Matrimonial Property Law in Canada* (Toronto: Carswell, 1980) at V-4.

TANGIBLE PERSONAL PROPERTY. Personal property that can be seen, weighed, measured, felt or touched, or that is in any other way perceptible to the senses, and includes electricity, natural or manufactured gas and telephone services.

TANGIBLE PROPERTY. Property having a physical existence.

TANK. *n.* 1. A receptacle capable of holding liquids and includes any pipe or conduit through which liquids may pass into the receptacle. *Gasoline Licensing Act*, S.N.S. 1969, c. 47, s. 1. 2. A compartment below the deck of a ship suitable for the stowage of cargo. *Destructive Pests Inspection Fees Regulations*, C.R.C., c. 696, s. 2. 3. A container for liquids or sludges required in or resulting from the operation of a plant. *Chlor-Alkali Mercury National Emission Standards Regulations*, C.R.C., c. 406, s. 2. See CENTRE ~; CUSHION ~; FUEL ~; HOLDING ~; SEWAGE ~; STORAGE ~; VEHICLE ~; WING ~.

TANKAGE. *n.* The rendered and dried carcass or part of the carcass of an animal. *Animal Disease and Protection Regulations*, C.R.C., c. 296, s. 2.

TANK CAR. Any vessel described as a tank car in the Regulations for the Tranportation of Dangerous Commodities by Rail and is approved by the Commission for chlorine service, but does not include multi-unit tank cars such as the ICC 106A500-X tank car. *Chlorine Tank Car Unloading Facilities Regulations*, C.R.C., c. 1147, s. 2.

TANKER. *n.* Includes a steamship specially constructed for the carriage of liquid cargoes in bulk. Canada regulations.

TANKER FREIGHT COSTS. The costs incurred in the process of transporting petroleum by water. *Oil Import Compensation Regulations, No. 1, 1975*, C.R.C., c. 335, s. 2.

TANK TRUCK. *var.* **TANK-TRUCK.** A motor vehicle having one or more tanks mounted on the frame or chassis of the vehicle.

TANK TRUCK VEHICLE. A commercial motor vehicle, trailer or semi-trailer used for or capable of being used for transportation of products in bulk and which contains or to which there is attached or upon which there has been placed either permanently or otherwise a closed tank or container having a capacity of 2.3 kilolitres or more. *Public Commercial Vehicles Act*, R.S.O. 1980, c. 407, s. 1.

TANK UNIT. See CARGO ~.

TANK VEHICLE. A vehicle designed for or capable of transporting gasoline or associated products in bulk. *Gasoline Handling Act*, R.R.O. 1980, Reg. 439, s. 1.

TANNER. *n.* A person who is engaged in the business of unhairing, fleshing, tanning, plucking, dressing or dyeing the pelts or skins of wildlife.

TAP. See FLANGE ~S; INDIVIDUAL ~; PIPE ~S.

TARDIEU SPOT. A small pin-point hemorrhage on the pleural surface of a lung, on a heart or other organ which was at one time considered to indicate asphyxia. F.A. Jaffe, *A Guide to Pathological Evidence*, 2d ed. (Toronto: Carswell, 1983) at 185.

TARE. *n.* 1. An allowance for the weight of the container in which goods are packed. 2. An allowance for the weight of materials and equipment that are weighed with the beef carcass but do not form part thereof. *Beef Cattle Marketing Act*, R.R.O. 1980, Reg. 80, s. 1.

TARGET AREA. The area within a spacing unit that is allocated for drilling a well. *Petroleum Resources Act*, R.R.O. 1980, Reg. 752, s. 1.

TARIFF. *n.* 1. The schedule of fees to be charged for various legal services. 2. A tariff of rates and charges established by a shipping conference for the transportation of goods by vessel alone or by vessel and by any other means of transportation, and includes any rules or regulations that determine the calculation of those rates or charges or prescribe terms or conditions for the transportation of goods by vessel. *Shipping Conference Exemption Act*, R.S.C. 1985, c. S-10, s. 2. 3. A tariff of rates, rules and regulations for the movement of grain filed and published pursuant to this Part. *Western Grain Transportation Act*, R.S.C. 1985, c. W-8, s. 34. 4. A publication containing terms and conditions of carriage, tolls, rules, regulations and practices applicable to the carriage of traffic by an air carrier, and includes an amendment or a supplement to a tariff or a page of a loose-leaf tariff. *Air Carrier Regulations*, C.R.C., c. 3, s. 2. See JOINT ~; LOCAL ~.

TARIFF BOARD. The federal body empowered to inquire into and report on anything which relates to goods which are exempt from or subject to customs and excise duty.

TARIFF RATE QUOTA. In respect of one or more countries entitled to the benefits of the General Preferential Tariff, a limitation on the quantity of the goods from those countries that may be admitted into Canada in any period of 12 consecutive months at the General Preferential Tariff rate. *Customs Tariff Act*, R.S.C. 1985, c. C-54, s. 20

TAR SANDS. A mineral extracted, otherwise than by a well, from a mineral resource which is a deposit of bituminous sands, oil sands or oil shales.

TARTAN. *n.* The Nova Scotia Tartan, consisting of the colours and proportions set out in an Order in Council dated the 6th day of September, 1955, and registered in the books of the Court of the Lord Lyon, Her Majesty's Register Office, Edinburgh, on the 7th day of March, 1956. *Nova Scotia Tartan Act*, R.S.N.S. 1967, c. 213, s. 1.

TATTOO. *n.* 1. The introduction of insoluble pigment in the skin either accidentally or for identification or decorative purposes. F.A. Jaffe, *A Guide to Pathological Evidence*, 2d ed. (Toronto: Carswell, 1983) at 185. 2. An area of burned or partly burned powder grains near the wound where a bullet fired at close range entered. F.A. Jaffe, *A Guide to Pathological Evidence*, 2d ed. (Toronto: Carswell, 1983) at 185. 3. Any letter or numeral or combination of the same recorded as allotted. *Livestock Branding or Tattooing Act*, R.S.P.E.I. 1974, c. L-18, s. 1.

TAUTOLOGY. *n.* A description of one thing twice in one sentence in equal terms.

TAVERN. *n.* 1. A place arranged for the consumption of beer and weak cider, open only to male persons, subject to section 19. *An Act Respecting the Commission de Contrôle des Permis D'alcool*, R.S.Q. 1977, c. C-33, s. 18. 2. A premises provided with special accommodation facilities and equipment as prescribed in the regulations, where in consideration of payment therefor beer and wine are served. *Liquor Control Act*, S.Nfld. 1973, c. 103, s. 2.

TAX. *n.* Any tax, impost, duty or toll imposed or authorized to be imposed by any Act of Parliament or a legislature. See ACCRUED ~; AREA ~; ARREARS OF ~; ASSESSMENT AND ~ ROLL; BUSINESS OCCUPANCY ~;

CONSOLIDATED ~ES; CURRENT YEAR ~ES; DEPARTURE ~; DEVELOPMENT ~; DIRECT ~; ESTATE ~; EXCISE ~ES; EXPORT ~; FOREIGN ~ES; FRONTAGE ~; GENERAL ~; GIFT ~; INCOME ~; INCREMENTAL ~; INDIRECT ~; INHERITANCE ~; LOCAL IMPROVEMENT ~; LOGGING ~; MUNICIPAL ~; OUTSTANDING ~ES; POLL ~; PROPERTY ~; PROVINCIAL MINING ~; PROVINCIAL ~ OR FEE; REAL ESTATE ~; REAL PROPERTY ~; REDEVELOPMENT ~; REFUND OF ~; RESOURCE ~ES; SCHOOL ~.

TAX ABATEMENT. The percentage that is applied to the "tax otherwise payable under this Part" within the meaning assigned to that expression by paragraph 120(4)(c) of the Income Tax Act to determine the amount that is deemed by subsection 120(2) of that Act to have been paid by an individual on account of his tax for a taxation year. *Federal-Provincial Fiscal Arrangements Act*, R.S.C. 1985, c. F-8, s. 26.

TAX A.B.C. *abbr.* Tax Appeal Board Cases, 1949-1971.

TAXABLE. See AMOUNT ~.

TAXABLE CAPITAL GAIN. For a taxation year from the disposition of any property is 3/4 of his capital gain for the year from the disposition of that property. *Income Tax Act*, R.S.C. 1952, c. 148 (as am. S.C. 1988, c. 55, s. 19), s. 38.

TAXABLE DIVIDEND. A dividend other than (i) a dividend in respect of which the corporation paying the dividend has elected in accordance with subsection 83(1) as it read prior to 1979 or in accordance with subsection 83(2); and (ii) a qualifying dividend paid by a public corporation to shareholders of a prescribed class of tax-deferred preferred shares of the corporation within the meaning of subsection 83(1). *Income Tax Act*, R.S.C. 1952, c. 148 (as am. S.C. 1986, c. 6, s. 48(4)), s. 89(1)(j).

TAXABLE FRONTAGE. The actual frontage or, where applicable, the distance which a parcel of land is deemed to abut on the work or highway, and in respect of which parcel the frontage tax is levied for the work or service. *Municipal Act*, R.S.B.C. 1979, c. 290, s. 480.

TAXABLE FUEL. Any fuel that may be used for propelling a motor vehicle. *The Fuel Tax Act*, S.S. 1986-87-88, c. F-23-2, s. 2.

TAXABLE INCOME. With respect to a taxpayer for a taxation year, it is his income for the year plus the additions and minus the deductions permitted by Division C. *Income Tax Act*, R.S.C. 1952, c. 148 (as am. S.C. 1985, c. 45, s. 1), s. 2(2). See REVISED ~.

TAXABLE INCOME EARNED IN CANADA.
A taxpayer's taxable income earned in Canada
determined in accordance with Division D of
Part I, except that in no case may a taxpayer's
taxable income earned in Canada be less than
nil. *Income Tax Act*, R.S.C. 1952, c. 148 (as am.
S.C. 1987, c. 46, s. 69(1)), s. 248(1).

TAXABLE LANDS. See NEWLY ~.

TAXABLE PARCEL. Subject to subsection (2),
a run-off parcel or other parcel of farm land,
any part of which lies within a distance of 100
yards from a telephone line or a proposed
telephone line of a company, subject to the
exclusions, exemptions and conditions provided
for by, under or pursuant to sections 34 to 43.
The Rural Telephone Act, R.S.S. 1978, c. R-27,
s. 2.

TAXABLE PROPERTY. 1. Real property in
respect of which a person may be required by
a taxing authority to pay a real property tax or
a frontage or area tax. *Municipal Grants Act*,
R.S.C. 1985, c. M-13, s. 2. 2. Any property or
business in a municipality and in respect of
which a tax is required to be paid for the raising
of revenue for the general purposes of that
municipality. *The Hospital Revenue Act*, R.S.S.
1978, c. H-9, s. 2.

TAXABLE SERVICE. 1. (a) The provision, by
means of telecommunication, to the general
public or any portion thereof, of any programming service; (b) the commencement or cessation of the provision of a programming service
referred to in paragraph (a); (c) the provision
of any instrument, device, equipment or apparatus or any part thereof, other than a television
receiver, that is (i) used in conjunction with the
reception of a programming service referred to
in paragraph (a); and (ii) provided by the person
providing the programming service or by any
person authorized or designated by him for the
purpose or acting on his behalf or by any person
related to him, if the person providing the
programming service requires that the instrument, device, equipment, apparatus or part be
acquired exclusively from him or any other
person referred to in subparagraph (ii); and (d)
the installation, disconnection, replacement,
repair or maintenance of any instrument, device,
equipment or apparatus, or any part thereof,
other than a television receiver, referred to in
paragraph (c), by the person providing the
programming service in conjunction with which
it is being used or by any other person referred
to in subparagraph (c)(ii), but does not include
(e) any surveillance or monitoring service, tel-
ebanking or teleshopping service or opinion-
polling service; (f) any background music service of a nature or kind that is provided in a
shopping centre, an office building, a factory or
a common area of a condominium or of an
apartment building as an accompaniment to
shopping, dining, working or other similar activities carried on in such place; or (g) any other
service prescribed by regulations made pursuant
to section 21.2, that a person providing a programming service referred to in paragraph (a)
provides for an additional fee or charge on the
request of the person to whom the programming
service is provided or that is provided by a person
who does not provide a programming service
referred to in paragraph (a). *Excise Tax Act*,
R.S.C. 1985 (1st Supp.), c. 15, s. 21.1. 2. (a)
Telecommunication services of all kinds, including without restricting the generality of the
foregoing, telephone and telegraph services,
community antenna television and cable television, transmissions by microwave relay stations or by satellite, and pay television, but not
including public broadcasting services that are
broadcast through the air for direct reception
by the public without charge; or (b) transient
accommodation. *Retail Sales Tax Act*, R.S.O.
1980, c. 454, s. 1. 3. (i) Lodging in hotels, motels,
hostels, apartment houses, lodging houses, cabins, cottages, clubs and other similar accommodation whether or not a membership is required
for the lodging, except lodging let for a continuous period of 1 month or more; (ii) telecommunication service within the province; or (iii)
telecommunication service between one or more
points within the province and one or more
points outside the province where the charges
for the service are charged to and payable by
a person residing in the province. *The Educational and Health Tax Act*, R.S.S. 1978, c. E-3,
s. 3.

TAXABLE VALUE. 1. (a) In the case of a mobile
home, one-half of the sale price thereof that is
charged to the person acquiring the mobile
home as a residence, if such price is determined
by including therein all charges for delivery of
the mobile home in accordance with the terms
of such sale, by excluding therefrom the retail
sale price of any furniture or appliance that is
not permanently attached to, and part of, the
interior structure of the mobile home, and by
excluding therefrom any charges for the installation or connection of the mobile home on the
site to which it is delivered; or (b) in the case
of a modular home, an amount equal to 55 per
cent of the sale price of such modular home on
the sale thereof by its manufacturer to a builder,
or where the manufacturer is the consumer of
such modular home, 55 per cent of the sale price
normally charged by the manufacturer on the
sale thereof to a builder, but such taxable value
applies only with respect to the first retail sale
of a mobile home or a modular home after the
6th day of April, 1976. *Retail Sales Tax Act*,

R.S.O. 1980, c. 454, s. 1. 2. In relation to a gift, means, (i) in the case of a gift that is exempt from tax, nil, and (ii) in any other case, the value of the gift minus any deductions therefrom permitted under this Act. Gift Tax acts. See AGGREGATE ~.

TAXABLE VALUE OF PERSONAL PROPERTY. Seventy-five per cent of the value of personal property. *Municipal Act*, R.S.B.C. 1979, c. 290, s. 492.

TAX ARREARS. The balance unpaid on taxes payable under an act for which payment is past due.

TAXATION. See CERTIFICATE OF ~; LOCAL ~; NET WORTH ~; RECIPROCAL ~ AGREEMENT; REVENUE CANADA, ~.

TAXATION AREA. (a) Canada; (b) the United States (except Hawaii); and (c) the Islands of St. Pierre and Miquelon. *Excise Tax Act*, R.S.C. 1985, c. E-15, s. 8.

TAXATION OF COSTS. See ASSESSMENT OF COSTS.

TAXATION YEAR. 1. The fiscal year in relation to which the amount of tax is being computed. 2. In the case of a corporation, a fiscal period and in the case of an individual, a calendar year. See LAST DAY OF THE ~.

TAX AVOIDANCE. Attempts by a taxpayer to minimize or eliminate a tax obligation either by deliberately arranging income earning affairs to benefit from provisions of income tax legislation or by relying on reasonable and different interpretations of that legislation. W. Grover & F. Iacobucci, *Materials on Canadian Income Tax*, 4th ed. (Toronto: Richard De Boo Ltd., 1980) at 993.

TAX BASE. See MUNICIPAL ~; MUNICIPAL ~ PER CAPITA; MUNICIPAL ~ PER ROAD KILOMETRE; OVERALL ~ PER CAPITA; OVERALL ~ PER ROAD KILOMETRE.

TAX BENEFIT. A reduction, avoidance or deferral of tax or other amount payable under this Act or an increase in a refund of tax or other amount under this Act. *Income Tax Act*, R.S.C. 1952, c. 148 (as am. S.C. 1988, c. 55, s. 185), s. 245(1).

TAX COLLECTION AGREEMENT. 1. An agreement entered into or deemed to have been entered into pursuant to subsection 7(1). *Federal Provincial Fiscal Arrangements Act*, R.S.C. 1985, c. F-8, s. 2. 2. Although provinces impose their own income taxes at their own rates, as long as a province uses the same tax base as the federal one, the federal government collects provincial tax on the province's behalf free of charge. P.W. Hogg, *Constitutional Law of Can-*

ada, 2d ed. (Toronto: Carswell, 1985) at 114 and 115.

TAX CONCESSION. Any provision in, or based on the terms of, any public or private Act whereby a person is entitled to a benefit or advantage by way of (a) a reduced or fixed assessment or valuation of property, real or personal; (b) a reduced or fixed rate or tax; (c) a variation in the method of paying rates or taxes; or (d) any other benefit or advantage of a like nature. *Assessment Act*, R.S.N.B. 1973, c. A-14, s. 1.

TAX CONSEQUENCES. To a person means the amount of income, taxable income, or taxable income earned in Canada of, tax or other amount payable by, or refundable to the person under this Act, or any other amount that is relevant for the purposes of computing that amount. *Income Tax Act*, R.S.C. 1952, c. 148 (as am. S.C. 1988, c. 55, s. 185), s. 245(1).

TAX CREDIT. A deduction from tax otherwise payable. See EXPLORATION AND DEVELOPMENT EXPENSE ~.

TAX DEBTOR. A person who is liable to make payments under this act. Income Tax acts.

TAX DEED. A tax deed prepared under subsection 9(3) and includes the title conferred by the registration of the tax deed. *Municipal Tax Sales Act*, S.O. 1984, c. 48, s. 1.

TAX DRIFT. As a taxpayer's income increases through inflation, the taxpayer drifts upwards into a higher tax bracket. W. Grover & F. Iacobucci, *Materials on Canadian Income Tax*, 4th ed. (Toronto: Richard De Boo Ltd., 1980) at 45.

TAXED COSTS. Costs taxed in accordance with the rules of court.

TAX EQUITY OF A PARTNERSHIP. The fair market value of partnership assets at valuation day, without recognizing the work in progress or inventory of a cash-basis partnership and subject to scaled-down recognition of assets which are intangible. Donald I. Beach, *Explanation of Canadian Tax Reform*, (Toronto: CCH Canadian Ltd., 1972) at 238-239.

TAX EVASION. In a case where the law clearly obliges one to report income and pay tax, a wilful attempt by the taxpayer not to disclose or to suppress income and thus not to pay tax on it. W. Grover & F. Iacobucci, *Materials on Canadian Income Tax*, 4th ed. (Toronto: Richard De Boo Ltd., 1980) at 991.

TAX EXPENDITURE. A feature of the income tax system such as an exemption, exclusion, or deduction which is in fact a method of providing financial assistance and is not required for purposes of administering the income tax itself. W. Grover & F. Iacobucci, *Materials on Canadian Income Tax*, 4th ed. (Toronto: Richard De Boo Ltd., 1980) at 163.

TAX HAVEN. See PURE ~.

TAXI. *n.* A motor vehicle other than a bus used to transport passengers for gain or reward.

TAXI CAB. *var.* **TAXICAB.** A motor vehicle other than a bus used to transport passengers for compensation.

TAXI-CAB BROKER. Any person who accepts calls in any manner for taxi-cabs that are used for hire and that are owned by persons other than himself, his immediate family or his employer. *Municipal Act*, R.S.O. 1980, c. 302, s. 227.

TAXIDERMIST. *n.* A person engaged in the business of preparing, preserving or mounting heads, skeletons, pelts or skins of wildlife.

TAXI DRIVER. The driver of a motor vehicle having a seating capacity for not more than 9 persons which, with its driver, is operated or plies for hire by members of the public. *Motor Vehicle Act*, R.S.B.C. 1979, c. 288, s. 1.

TAXING AUTHORITY. (a) Any municipality, province, municipal or provincial board, commission, corporation or other authority that levies and collects a real property tax or a frontage or area tax pursuant to an Act of the legislature of a province; (b) any council of a band within the meaning of the Indian Act that levies and collects a real property tax or a frontage or area tax pursuant to an Act of Parliament; or (c) any band within the meaning of the Cree-Naskapi (of Quebec) Act, chapter 18 of the Statutes of Canada, 1984, that levies and collects a tax on interests in Category IA land or Category IA-N land as defined in that Act. *Municipal Grants Act*, R.S.C. 1985, c. M-13, s. 2.

TAXING OFFICER. 1. The registrar or other officer appointed under the Act for the taxation or fixing of costs or the passing of accounts. *Bankruptcy Rules*, C.R.C., c. 368, s. 2. 2. A master of the Supreme Court, or a judge of the Trial Division or the Court of Appeal. *Rules of the Supreme Court*, S.Nfld. 1986, r. 1, s. 1.03. 3. An assessment officer.

TAX PAYABLE. The tax payable by a corporation for a fiscal year to Her Majesty and includes any amounts fixed by assessment.

TAX PAYABLE UNDER THE FEDERAL ACT. By an individual in respect of the taxation year means the amount determined under clause (c) of subsection (4) of Section 120 of the Federal Act for the year in respect of that individual.

TAX PAYER. *var.* **TAXPAYER.** 1. A person required by a revenue Act to pay a tax. 2. Any person whether or not liable to pay tax. Income Tax acts. 3. Any person who is entitled to a refund of tax. 4. A person obligated to pay municipal taxes in respect of a residential dwelling. *Homeowners Tax and Insulation Assistance Act*, S.M. 1977, c. 60, s. 1. See PRINCIPAL ~; SENIOR CITIZEN ~.

TAX PURCHASER. A person who purchases land at a tax sale and, unless otherwise expressly stated or the context otherwise requires, includes a municipality, and the assignee of a tax purchaser, and any subsequent assignee of an assigned tax sale certificate. *Municipal Act*, S.M. 1970, c. 100, s. 799.

TAX RATE. See PROGRESSIVE ~ STRUCTURE; PROPORTIONAL ~ STRUCTURE; PROVINCIAL PERSONAL INCOME ~; REGRESSIVE ~ STRUCTURE; VARIABLE ~ SYSTEM.

TAX RELIEF PERIOD. Subject to subsection (4), in relation to an eligible corporation, the taxation year in which the eligible corporation first becomes an eligible corporation, and the 4 taxation years immediately following that year. *Special Enterprise Zone Tax Relief Act*, S.B.C. 1985, c. 57, s. 21.

TAX RENTAL AGREEMENT. An agreement by which the federal government rents from an agreeing province the right to levy corporate income tax, personal income tax and succession duty. The agreeing province does not levy these taxes, but receives grants ("rent") from the federal government to counterbalance the foregone revenue. P.W. Hogg, *Constitutional Law of Canada*, 2d ed. (Toronto: Carswell, 1985) at 114.

TAYLOR. *abbr.* Taylor's King's Bench Reports (Ont.), 1823-1827.

T.B. *abbr.* Tariff Board.

TBA. *abbr.* To be agreed.

T. BD. *abbr.* Transport Board.

T.B.R. *abbr.* Tariff Board Reports, 1937-1962.

T.C.C. *abbr.* Tax Court of Canada.

T.C.I. *abbr.* Tribunal canadien des importations.

T.D. *abbr.* Supreme Court, Trial Division.

T.D. BANK. *abbr.* Toronto-Dominion Bank.

TEACHER. *n.* 1. A person who instructs students in a program of instruction. 2. A person holding a valid certificate of qualification to teach in schools. See FULL TIME ~; OCCASIONAL ~; PRIVATE SCHOOL ~; PROBATIONARY ~; PUPIL ~; SECONDARY

SCHOOL ~; STUDENT ~; SUBSTITUTE ~; TEMPORARY ~.

TEACHER AIDE. A person engaged by a board to work in a school under the direction of the principal or other teacher.

TEACHING DAY. A day upon which a school is legally open during the hours prescribed by this Act and the regulations of the department. *The School Act*, R.S.S. 1978, c. S-36, s. 2.

TEACHING HOSPITAL. A hospital providing facilities for the instruction of under-graduate and post-graduate students in the health professions in which the treatment of the patient is the function of a team of staff members, including the attending staff physician, a resident physician, an intern physician and a clinical clerk and for which each member of the medical staff and the head of each medical department of the hospital are appointed jointly by the university with which the hospital is affiliated and the board of directors of the hospital. *Public Hospitals Act*, R.R.O. 1980, Reg. 862, s. 1. See PARTIAL MEDICAL ~.

TEACHING PERSONNEL. Teachers, classroom assistants and adult educators. *Education Act*, S.N.W.T. 1976 (3d Sess.), c. 2, s. 2.

TEACHING SERVICE. 1. The performance of the duties assigned to a teacher by the board of education that employs him. *Teachers' Dental Plan Act*, S.S. 1984-85-86, c. T-6.1, s. 2. 2. The total period during which a person who holds a valid certificate of grade or a licence is employed as a teacher in Newfoundland. *Education (Teachers' Pensions) Act*, R.S.Nfld. 1970, c. 102, s. 2.

TEACHING STAFF. Includes professors, lecturers, instructors, demonstrators, and all others engaged in the work of teaching or giving instruction.

TEACHING YEAR. The 12 calendar months from the first of July. *Education (Teachers' Pensions) Act*, R.S.Nfld. 1970, c. 102, s. 2. See YEAR OF TEACHING.

TEAM. See MINE RESCUE ~.

TEAMING. *n.* Includes all kinds of work done by workers with teams, carts, including hand carts, drays, trucks, cabs, carriages, automobiles and other vehicles. Workers' Compensation acts.

TEAMSTER. *n.* The driver of a conveyance who can be hired to carry goods.

TEAM TRACK. A track on railway property which is used for loading or unloading purposes by more than one company or person. Canada regulations.

TEAR BOMBS. Any apparatus or device used to project or emit a gas or any other substance productive of tears. *Tear Bombs Act*, R.S.Q. 1977, c. B-6, s. 1.

TEASPOON. *n.* For the purpose of calculation of dosage, a volume of 5 cubic centimetres. *Food and Drug Regulations*, C.R.C., c. 870, c. C.01.001.

TECH. *abbr.* Technical.

TECHNICAL INSTRUCTION. Instruction pertaining to the mechanical or vocational arts or to any one or more of them. *Public Schools Act*, R.S.M. 1970, c. P250, s. 2.

TECHNICAL LANDING. A landing of an aircraft made solely to obtain ground services required for the aircraft. *Air Services Fees Regulations*, C.R.C., c. 5, s. 2.

TECHNICAL SCHOOL. Any Canadian marine technical school with an engineering laboratory equipped to provide an approved course in the theory and practice of marine engineering. *Marine Engineer Examination Regulations*, C.R.C., c. 1443, s. 2.

TECHNICAL SURVEYS. Geological, geophysical, geochemical, geographical, geodetic, topographical, hydrographic, oceanographic and meteorological surveys. *Resources and Technical Surveys Act*, R.S.C. 1985, c. R-7, s. 2.

TECHNICIAN. *n.* 1. A person who engages in the process of artificial insemination or the collection of semen for the purpose of artificial insemination. 2. A person who makes, produces, reproduces, constructs, furnishes, supplies, alters or repairs any prosthetic denture, bridge, appliance or thing to replace, improve or supplement any human tooth or to be used in, upon or in connection with any human tooth, jaw or associated structure for and upon the written prescription of a registered dentist. *Dental Association Act*, S.M. 1971, c. 44, s. 1. 3. A person holding a diploma or certificate that shows his qualifications to carry out specific veterinary procedures. *Veterinary Profession Act*, R.S.P.E.I. 1974, c. V-4, s. 2. See ANIMAL HEALTH ~; DENTAL ~; FILM ~; LABORATORY ~; QUALIFIED ~; RADIO AND TELEVISION SERVICE ~; RADIOLOGICAL ~.

TECHNOLOGICAL CHANGE. (a) The introduction by an employer into the work, undertaking or business of equipment or material of a different nature or kind than that previously utilized by the employer in the operation of the work, undertaking or business; and (b) a change in the manner in which the employer carries on the work, undertaking or business that is directly related to the introduction of that equipment or material.

TECHNOLOGIST. See LABORATORY ~.

TECHNOLOGY. See DENTAL ~; ENGINEERING ~; MINISTRY OF STATE FOR SCIENCE AND ~; RESPIRATORY ~.

TEETH. See DECIDUOUS ~; MILK ~.

TEKTITE. *n.* Any natural form of silicate glass of non-volcanic origin. *Canadian Cultural Property Export Control List*, C.R.C., c. 448, s. 1.

TELECOMMUNICATION. *n.* Any transmission, emission or reception of signs, signals, writing, images, sounds or intelligence of any nature by wire, radio, visual or other electromagnetic system. See CANADIAN RADIO-TELEVISION AND ~S COMMISSION.

TELECOMMUNICATION LINE. A system or arrangement of lines of wire or other conductors by which telephone or other kinds of communications are transmitted and received by electronic means.

TELECOMMUNICATION SERVICE. Any transmission, reception or distribution of signs, signals, words, writing, images, symbols, sounds or intelligence of any nature by means of electromagnetic waves and includes the provision of facilities required for such transmission, reception or distribution. *The Educational and Health Tax Act*, R.S.S. 1978, c. E-3, s. 3. See EXTERNAL ~S.

TELECOMMUNICATION SYSTEM. See SATELLITE ~.

TELECOMMUNICATIONS UNDERTAKING. An undertaking in the field of telecommunication that is carried on in whole or in part within Canada or on a ship or aircraft registered in Canada. *Canadian Radio-television and Telecommunications Commission Act*, R.S.C. 1985, c. C-22, s. 2.

TELECOMMUNICATIONS UTILITY. A person, including the lessee, trustee, receiver or liquidator of such a person, who owns or operates in the Province equipment or facilities for the conveyance or transmission of messages or communications by cable, telephone or telegraph where the service is offered to the public or to a corporation for compensation; but does not include (a) a municipality in respect of services furnished by the municipality within its own boundaries; (b) a person who furnishes service only to himself, his employees or tenants, where the service is not used by others; or (c) the British Columbia Railway. *Telecommunications Utility Act*, R.S.B.C. 1979, c. 401, s. 1.

TELEFERRY. *n.* A device for the conveyance of passengers or chattels above water or land, otherwise than vertically, by means of vehicles supported by cables and more commonly referred to as a gondola lift, aerial cable-car, suspension line or aerial passenger tramway, and includes the land, structures, machinery and approaches necessary to the operation of the device. *Teleferry Act*, R.S.C. 1970, c. T-2, s. 2.

TELEFILM CANADA. A federal body empowered to encourage the growth of the private sector Canadian film industry.

TELEGLOBE CANADA. The federal body which provides international telephone, telegraph, telex, facsimile, teleconferencing, data, broadcast and private satellite business services.

TELEGRAM. *n.* Includes cablegram and radiogram. *Evidence Act*, R.S.N.B. 1973, c. E-11, s. 1.

TELEGRAPH. *n.* 1. Includes telegram, telex and facsimile. *Elections Act*, S.N.W.T. 1986 (2d Sess.), c. 2, s. 202. 2. Includes wireless telegraph. 3. The expression "telegraph" and its derivatives, in an enactment or in an Act of the legislature of any province enacted before that province became part of Canada on any subject that is within the legislative powers of Parliament, are deemed not to include the word "telephone" or its derivatives. *Interpretation Act*, R.S.C. 1985, c. I-21, s. 36. See RADIO-~.

TELEGRAPH CABLE SHIP. A registered ship used exclusively for the laying or repairing of oceanic telegraph cables. Canada regulations.

TELEGRAPH COMPANY. A person, firm, partnership, association or corporation owning, controlling or operating a telegraph system or line, all or any part of which is situate in Ontario. *Provincial Land Tax Act*, R.S.O. 1980, c. 399, s. 1.

TELEGRAPHIC SERVICE. Telegrams, cablegrams and radiograms originating or terminating in Ontario and billed to a subscriber in Ontario. *Retail Sales Tax Act*, R.R.O. 1980, Reg. 904, s. 1.

TELEGRAPH OR TELEPHONE. Includes wireless or radio telegraph or telephone. *Railway Act*, R.S.B.C. 1979, c. 354, s. 1.

TELEGRAPH TOLL. When used with reference to telegraph, means any toll, rate or charge to be charged by any company to the public or to any person, for the use or lease of a telegraph system or line or any part thereof, for the transmission of a message by telegraph, for installation and use or lease of any instruments, lines or apparatus attached to, or connected or interconnected in any manner whatever with, a telegraph system, for any services provided by the company through the facilities of a telegraph system or for any service incidental to a telegraph business. *Railway Act*, R.S.C. 1985, c. R-3, s. 2.

TELEPHONE. *n.* Any instrument or device into which messages may be spoken or introduced for transmission over the commission's system by wire, without wires, or by radio transmission or by which such messages may be recorded, heard or seen. *Manitoba Telephone Act*, R.S.M. 1970, c. T40, s. 2. See RADIO-~; TELE-GRAPH OR ~.

TELEPHONE COMPANY. Includes a person or association of persons owning, controlling or operating a telephone system or line.

TELEPHONE LEVY. A levy pursuant to this Act upon land for telephone purposes and includes a construction levy and special levy and a levy required for the repayment of old debentures and loans. *The Rural Telephone Act*, R.S.S. 1978, c. R-27, s. 2.

TELEPHONE LINE. Includes all devices, real estate, franchises, easements, apparatus, fixtures, property, appurtenances and routes used, operated, controlled or owned by any public utility to facilitate the business of affording telephonic communication for hire, and all conduits, ducts, poles, wires, cables, cross-arms, receivers, transmitters, instruments, machines and appliances, connected or used therewith.

TELEPHONE SYSTEM. A system of telephone lines used for the transmission of communications by telephone, and includes all stations, toll offices, exchanges, plant, equipment, wires, cables and works used or connected with it. See MUNICIPAL ~; PRIVATE ~; RURAL ~.

TELEPHONE TOLL. When used with reference to telephone, means any toll, rate or charge to be charged by any company to the public or to any person, for the use or lease of a telephone system or line or any part thereof, for the transmission of a message by telephone, for installation and use or lease of any instruments, lines or apparatus attached to, or connected or interconnected in any manner whatever with, a telephone system, for any services provided by the company through the facilities of a telephone system or for any service incidental to a telephone business. *Railway Act*, R.S.C. 1985, c. R-3, s. 2.

TELEVISED CONTEST. See CLOSED CIR-CUIT ~.

TELEVISED EXHIBITION. See CLOSED CIRCUIT ~.

TELEVISION. See CANADIAN RADIO-~ AND TELECOMMUNICATIONS COMMIS-SION; COMMUNITY ANTENNA ~; RADIO AND ~ SERVICE TECHNICIAN.

TELEVISION COMPANY. See CLOSED-CIRCUIT ~.

TELEVISION CORPORATION. See CLOSED CIRCUIT ~.

TELEVISION RECEIVER. A radio receiving apparatus intended for use by the general public for the reception of television broadcasting. *Radio Interference Regulations*, C.R.C., c. 1374, s. 2.

TELEVISION STATION. See EXTRA-REGIONAL ~; LOCAL ~; OPTIONAL ~; REGIONAL ~.

TELLER. *n.* 1. In a bank, a cashier. 2. A person who keeps a tally. See AUTOMATED ~.

TELSA. *n.* The magnetic induction that is equal to one weber per square metre. *Weights and Measures Act*, S.C. 1970-71-72, c. 36, schedule 1.

TEMPERATURE PLATEAU. A period which may last 1-5 hours after death when the internal body temperature does not fall. F.A. Jaffe, *A Guide to Pathological Evidence*, 2d ed. (Toronto: Carswell, 1983) at 185.

TEMPERED GLASS. Glass that has been treated chemically or thermally so that, upon fracture, an entire sheet or pane of the glass disintegrates into many small granular pieces. *Safety Glass Regulations*, C.R.C., c. 933, s. 2.

TEMPORARILY DIVERTED. Removed from international service and placed in Canadian domestic service for 90 days or less in any one calendar year. *Railway Rolling Stock (International Service) Remission Order, No. 4*, C.R.C., c. 783, s. 2.

TEMPORARY. *adj.* 1. Appointed specially for a specified short period of time or until the occurrence of a stated event. *Formal Documents Regulations*, C.R.C., c. 1331, s. 2. 2. In relation to any commission, board or corporation, means established for a specified period of time or until the occurrence of a stated event. *Formal Documents Regulations*, C.R.C., c. 1331, s. 2.

TEMPORARY ADVANCE. Any money paid out of the Consolidated Revenue Fund that is repayable to the Territories, and is chargeable to an activity, but is not evidenced by a promissory note. *Financial Administration Act*, R.S.N.W.T. 1974, c. F-4, s. 2.

TEMPORARY CAVITY. A cavity created momentarily in tissue by a projectile rapidly passing through, its size depends on the projectile's energy and rate of retardation. F.A. Jaffe,

A Guide to Pathological Evidence, 2d ed. (Toronto: Carswell, 1983) at 185.

TEMPORARY CONTROL ZONE. A control zone in which specific air traffic control services are provided on a temporary basis. *Aeronautical Communications Standards and Procedures Order*, C.R.C., c. 20, s. 2.

TEMPORARY DETENTION. See PLACE OF ~; PLACE OF SECURE ~.

TEMPORARY EMPLOYEE. 1. An employee engaged to perform specific duties because of a temporary increase in the work load. *Civil Service Act*, S.P.E.I. 1983, c. 4, s. 10. 2. An employee (not being a contractual employee) employed for a specific period or for the purpose of performing certain specified work and whose employment may be terminated at the end of such period or upon completion of such work. *Newfoundland Public Service Commission Act*, S.Nfld. 1973, c. 116, s. 2.

TEMPORARY HEATING PLANT. One or more boilers, with or without compressors, that supply heat to a project as defined in the Occupational Health and Safety Act or to a shaft, tunnel, caisson or coffer dam to which the regulations made under that Act apply and that operates at a pressure, (i) of not more than 15 and has a total Therm-hour rating of more than 50; or (ii) of more than 15 and has a total Therm-hour rating of more than 17. *Operating Engineers Act*, R.S.O. 1980, c. 363, s. 1.

TEMPORARY HOME. A home in which a child may be placed temporarily pending further consideration of his case. *Child Welfare Act*, R.S.A. 1980, c. C-8, s. 6.

TEMPORARY LAYOFF. *var.* **TEMPORARY LAY-OFF.** A layoff of not more than 13 weeks in any period of 20 consecutive weeks.

TEMPORARY TEACHER. 1. A teacher employed by a board, under a written contract in which he is so designated: (i) to replace a teacher during his absence from his duties for at least 20 consecutive teaching days in an academic year; or (ii) to fill an unexpected vacancy continuing for at least 20 consecutive teaching days but less than a full academic year; or (iii) to teach for a period exceeding 20 consecutive teaching days but less than 1 academic year. *The School Act*, R.S.S. 1978, c. S-36, s. 2. 2. A person employed to teach under the authority of a letter of permission. *Education Act*, R.S.O. 1980, c. 129, s. 1.

TEMPORARY WORK STRUCTURE. Any structure of device that is used as an elevated temporary work base for persons or as an elevated temporary platform for materials and includes any scaffold, stage or staging, walkway, decking, bridge, boatswain's chair, tower, crawling board, temporary floor, any portable ladder or temporary means of access to or egress from any of the foregoing, and any safety net, landing or other device used in connection with such a structure. *Canada Temporary Work Structure Regulations*, C.R.C., c. 1010, s. 2.

TEMPUS EST EDAX RERUM. [L.] Time devours things.

TENANCY. *n.* 1. The exclusive right to occupy residential premises granted to a tenant by a landlord, for which the tenant agrees to pay or provide rent for a term that may be terminated by the landlord or tenant. 2. The condition of being a tenant. 3. The relation of a tenant to the property the tenant holds. See ENTIRE ~; JOINT ~; MONTH OF ~; PERIODIC ~; SEVERAL ~; TERM OF ~; WEEK OF ~; YEAR OF THE ~.

TENANCY AGREEMENT. 1. An agreement between a landlord and a tenant for possession or occupation of residential premises, whether written, oral or implied. 2. A written, oral or implied agreement to rent a mobile home site and includes a licence to use a mobile home site. *Mobile Home Site Tenancies Act*, S.A. 1982, c. M-18.5, s. 1. See FIXED TERM ~.

TENANCY AT WILL. An interest which permits a grantee to possess land at the pleasure of the grantor and her or himself without creating any durable right or limited duration.

TENANCY BY THE ENTIRETY. A condition like a joint tenancy, which cannot be severed, created through a conveyance to a husband and wife with no words of severance. A. Bissett-Johnson & W.M. Holland, eds., *Matrimonial Property Law in Canada* (Toronto: Carswell, 1980) at I-11.

TENANCY IN COMMON. A condition created when there are words of severance or one of the four unities is lacking; unequal sharing may be created; each tenant may dispose of their share by will. A. Bissett-Johnson & W.M. Holland, eds., *Matrimonial Property Law in Canada* (Toronto: Carswell, 1980) at I-12.

TENANCY MONTH. The monthly period on which a tenancy is based whether or not it is a calendar month, and unless otherwise specifically agreed on by the landlord and the tenant, the month is deemed to begin on the day on which rent is payable.

TENANCY YEAR. The yearly period on which the tenancy is based whether or not it is a calendar year and, unless otherwise specifically agreed on by the landlord and the tenant, the year is deemed to begin on the day, or the anniversary of the day, on which the tenant first became entitled to possession. *Mobile Home Site Tenancies Act*, S.A. 1982, c. M-18.5, s. 1.

TENANT. *n.* 1. A person who executes a tenancy agreement. 2. Includes an occupant and the person in possession other than the owner. 3. A person who executes a tenancy agreement and to whom an exclusive right to occupy residential premises is granted. 4. A person who pays rent in return for the right to occupy a rental unit and his or her heirs, assigns and personal representatives but does not include a person who has the right to occupy a rental unit by virtue of being a co-owner of the residential complex in which the rental unit is situate or a shareholder of a corporation that owns the residential complex. *Residential Rent Regulation Act*, S.O. 1986, c. 63, s. 1. 5. A person who rents land from a landlord for a share of the crop or of the proceeds of the crop produced on such land. *The Saskatchewan Crop Insurance Act*, R.S.S. 1978, c. S-12, s. 2. See COMMERCIAL ~; JOINT ~; LIFE ~; PARTICULAR ~; ~-IN-COMMON; SOLE ~; TERRE ~.

TENANT IN CHIEF. A person immediately beneath the monarch who holds land.

TENANT-OPERATOR. *n.* A person who leases and operates a farm he does not own. *Crop Insurance Act (Ontario)*, R.R.O. 1980, Reg. 231, s. 1.

TENANT PUR AUTRE VIE. Tenant for the life of another.

TENANTS IN COMMON. Two or more people who have an equal, undivided interest in property; each of them may occupy all the land in common with the others. Each tenant may dispose of their interest by will or deed. There is no right of survivorship as in a joint tenancy.

TENDER. *n.* 1. A payment of the precise amount that is due. To offer a larger amount without asking for change is acceptable, but to offer less is not. If it was agreed that the debt be paid on a certain day, payment after or before that date is not proper, and for the payment to be proper it must be unconditional. C.R.B. Dunlop, *Creditor—Debtor Law in Canada* (Toronto: Carswell, 1981) at 21 and 22. 2. Legal currency. 3. A call for tender by written public advertisement. See LEGAL ~; LOCK ~; VALID ~.

TENDER FRUIT. Peaches, pears, plums, cherries and sour cherries produced in Ontario, except peaches, pears, plums, cherries and sour cherries used for any purpose other than processing. *Ontario Tender Fruit-for-Processing Order*, C.R.C., c. 219, s. 2.

TENDER OF PAYMENT. The unqualified offer of the specified sum required under a

contract. G.H.L. Fridman, *The Law of Contract in Canada*, 2d ed. (Toronto: Carswell, 1986) at 499.

TENEMENT. *n.* Something which may be held; something which is subject to tenure. See DOMINANT ~; LANDS, ~S AND HEREDITAMENTS; SERVIENT ~.

TENENDUM. *n.* [L. to be held] A clause in a conveyance which describes the tenure by which a grantee holds the grantor's land.

TENOR. *n.* With respect to a document in ordinary conversation, its effect and meaning in contrast to its exact words. With respect to a document in law, the exact words of that document.

TENORE PRAESENTIUM. [L.] By the tenor of these presents.

TENOR EST PACTIO CONTRA COMMUNEM FEUDI NATURAM AC RATIONEM IN CONTRACTU INTERPOSITA. [L.] Tenure is an agreement, contrary to the common nature and reason of the fee, which is introduced into a contract.

TENOR EST QUI LEGEM DAT FEUDO. [L.] It is the tenor which regulates the feudal grant.

TENT. *n.* 1. A structure of canvas supported by a pole or poles. *National Parks Camping Regulations*, C.R.C., c. 1116, s. 2. 2. Includes every kind of temporary shelter for sleeping that is of good quality material and not of a polyethylene or similar material and that is not permanently affixed to the site and that is capable of being easily moved and is not considered a structure. *Tourism Act*, R.R.O. 1980, Reg. 936, s. 1. See CABIN ~.

TENT HOUSE. A structure of wood, wood products, metal or canvas or a combination of these materials not exceeding 15 feet in width and 15 feet in length so designed and constructed that it is collapsible or may be removed in sections. *National Parks Camping Regulations*, C.R.C., c. 1116, s. 2.

TENTORIUM CEREBELLI. A fold of dura mater which separates the cerebellum from the cerebrum. F.A. Jaffe, *A Guide to Pathological Evidence*, 2d ed. (Toronto: Carswell, 1983) at 185.

TENT TRAILER. A vehicular portable structure built on its own chassis, having a rigid or canvas top and side walls which may be folded or otherwise condensed for travel. *Assessment Act*, S.N.S. 1975, c. 57, s. 11.

TENURE. *n.* 1. A way to hold or occupy. 2. The mode in which all land is theoretically owned and occupied. 3. When in reference to the teaching staff, means, subject to such provision as the Board may make, an appointment held without term and made, or conventionally recognized as made, permanent. *University of New Brunswick Act*, S.N.B. 1984, c. 40, s. 1. See PRIVATE ~; SECURITY OF ~.

TENURIAL FORM OF LANDHOLDING. All English land is either in the hands of the monarch or is held by subjects as tenants whose interests in the land one calls estates. E.L.G. Tyler & N.E. Palmer, eds., *Crossley Vaines' Personal Property*, 5th ed. (London: Butterworths, 1973) at 4.

T.E. (QUÉ.). *abbr.* Tribunal de l'expropriation (Québec).

TERA. *pref.* $10^{1}2$. A prefix for multiples and submultiples of basic, supplementary and derived units of measurement. *Weights and Measures Act*, S.C. 1970-71-72, c. 36, schedule I.

TERM. *n.* 1. In relation to any borrowing of money or any loan, means a term stipulated for the repayment thereof and includes a period of extension or renewal of such a term. *National Housing Act*, R.S.C. 1985, c. N-11, s. 64. 2. In relation to a lease, means the period of years stated in the lease as its term. *Mines & Minerals Amendment Act*, S.A. 1985, c. 39, s. 6. 3. A contract provision which explains an obligation or group of obligations imposed on one or more of the parties. G.H.L. Fridman, *The Law of Contract in Canada*, 2d ed. (Toronto: Carswell, 1986) at 427. 4. A period at an approved institution in an approved program of study of not less than 10 weeks duration. *Ministry of Colleges and Universities Act*, R.R.O. 1980, Reg. 646, s. 1. See COLLATERAL ~; DISJUNCTIVE ~; EXPRESS ~; FUNDAMENTAL ~; IMPLIED ~; PROPORTIONATE ~S; SCHOOL ~; SECURITY ~; TRADE ~S; WINTER ~.

TERM ASSIGNMENT. An assignment of a teacher for a period of not less than 3 years and not more than 5 years and that is renewable by mutual consent. *School Act*, R.S.B.C. 1979, c. 375, s. 1.

TERM CHARTER. A charter of an aircraft for 1 day or for a specified number of consecutive days, months or a combination thereof. Canada regulations.

TERM CONTRACT. A contract of employment of a superintendent or assistant superintendent that sets the term of the employment at no less than 3 years and no more than 5 years and that is renewable by mutual consent. *School Act*, R.S.B.C. 1979, c. 375, s. 1.

TERM EMPLOYEE. A person appointed to a position that has been established for a specified period of time ending on a specified date or on the occurrence of a specified event. *Civil Service Act*, R.S.M. 1970, c. C110, s. 2.

TERMINAL. *n.* A storage facility to which petroleum is conveyed from a refinery and which is capable of holding petroleum in storage for resale and receiving petroleum by pipeline or water craft. *Fuel Tax Act*, S.O. 1981, c. 59, s. 1. See AIR-~; HOME ~; TRANSPORTATION ~; ~S.

TERMINAL ATTACHMENT. Any equipment, device or contrivance capable of transmitting or receiving messages or signals through the telephone service offered by the commission through the system; and any terminal attachment shall be conclusively deemed to be connected to the system if it is attached or fixed or placed on, over, under or adjacent to, any telephone connected with the system in such a manner as to be able to be used for transmitting or receiving messages or signals through the telephone services offered by the commission through the system or to be used for interrupting, intercepting or interfering with such messages or signals. *Manitoba Telephone Act*, S.M. 1980, c. 76, s. 15.

TERMINAL BALLISTICS. Analysis of the behaviour of projectiles when they strike or penetrate a target. F.A. Jaffe, *A Guide to Pathological Evidence*, 2d ed. (Toronto: Carswell, 1983) at 137 and 169.

TERMINAL CHARGE. A charge at each end of a journey by rail, i.e. for loading or unloading.

TERMINAL DECONTAMINATION. The decontamination of (i) the clothing of a person; (ii) the physical environment of a person; (iii) the contents of the isolation room; and (iv) any article or piece of equipment used in the diagnosis or treatment of a person after the person has been removed from isolation or has ceased to be a source of infection or after isolation procedures have been discontinued. *Public Health Act*, S.A. 1984, c. P-27.1, s. 1.

TERMINAL DISINFECTION. Disinfection carried out after recovery, removal or death of a patient. *Public Health Act*, R.R.O. 1980, Reg. 836, s. 1.

TERMINAL ELEVATOR. An elevator the principal uses of which are the receiving of grain on or after the official inspection and official weighing of the grain and the cleaning, storing and treating of the grain before it is moved forward. *Canada Grain Act*, R.S.C. 1985, c. G-10, s. 2.

TERMINALS. *n.* Includes buildings, fixtures, structures, docks, wharves, ramps, landings, approaches, ways, offices and other improvements and facilities, other than land, necessary for or incidental to the operation of ferry, shipping and related services and incidental facilities and improvements. *Ferry Corporation Act*, R.S.B.C. 1979, c. 128, s. 1. See TERMINAL.

TERMINAL SERVICES UNIT. The personnel who control the use of apron and terminal facilities at an airport. *Charter Flight Apron Reservations Order*, C.R.C., c. 36, s. 2.

TERMINATE. *v.* Includes (a) layoff of an employee from employment, other than temporary layoff; or (b) alteration of a condition of employment that the board declares to be a termination of an employee's employment, but does not include the discharge of an employee for just cause. *Employment Standards Act*, S.B.C. 1980, c. 10, s.41.

TERMINATING SERVICE. A telecommunication service by a submarine cable between any place in Canada and any place outside Canada, but does not include any service by a submarine cable wholly under fresh water. *External Submarine Cable Regulations*, C.R.C., c. 1515, s. 2.

TERMINATING STATION. The station at which a schedule is last timed on any subdivision is the terminating station for that schedule, and for an extra train (except work extras) it is the station to which such train is authorized. *Regulations No. O-8, Uniform Code of Operating Rules*, C.R.C., c. 1175, Part III, s. 2.

TERMINATION. *n.* 1. In relation to a pension plan, means the cessation of crediting of benefits to plan members generally, and includes the situations described in subsections 29(1) and (2). *Pension Benefit Standards Act*, R.S.C. 1985 (2d Supp.), c. 32, s. 2. 2. Permanent disqualification from the practice of a notary public. *Notaries Act*, S.B.C. 1981, c. 23, s. 1.

TERMINATION DATE. See WELL ~.

TERMINATION OF EMPLOYMENT. Includes a lay-off of a person for a period longer than a temporary lay-off.

TERMINATION OF THE WORK. The date on which the immoveable is ready for the use for which it is intended. *An Act to Promote Conciliation Between Lessees and Property-Owners*, R.S.Q. 1977, c. c-50. s. 60.

TERMINATION PAYMENT. An amount received by an employee whose office or employment has terminated.

TERM INSURANCE. See INTERIM ~.

TERMINUS AD QUEM. [L.] The end.

TERMINUS ANNORUM CERTUS DEBET ESSE ET DETERMINATUS. [L.] A term of years should be certain and prescribed.

TERMINUS A QUO. [L.] The beginning.

TERMINUS ET FEODUM NON POSSUNT CONSTARE SIMUL IN UNA EADEMQUE PERSONA. [L.] A term and a fee cannot exist simultaneously in one and the same person.

TERM LIFE INSURANCE POLICY. See GROUP ~.

TERM LOAN. A loan having a fixed date of maturity and includes member and patronage loans having a fixed date of maturity. *Co-operative Corporations Act*, R.S.O. 1980, c. 91, s. 1.

TERM OF APPRENTICESHIP. The interval of time established by regulation that an apprentice is required to serve from entry into to completion of an apprenticeship contract. *Manpower Development Act*, R.S.A. 1980, c. M-3, s. 1.

TERM OF IMPRISONMENT. Includes the definite term of imprisonment and the indefinite period thereafter to which a person was originally sentenced. *Prisons and Reformatories Act*, R.S.C. 1970, c. P-21, s. 152.

TERM OF SERVICE. (i) In the case of a minister, the period or periods he served as a minister from the beginning of the month in which he was sworn in by the Lieutenant-Governor as a Minister of the Crown to the end of the month in which his resignation is received by the Lieutenant-Governor or to some other date approved by the Lieutenant-Governor in Council in respect of which period or periods he made the contributions required by this Act; and (ii) in the case of a member the period or periods extending from the date on which he was elected to the House of Assembly to the date of dissolution of the House of Assembly of which he is a member or to the date of his resignation or death whichever first occurs in respect of which period or periods he made contributions required by this Act. *Members of the House of Assembly (Retiring Allowances) Act*, S.Nfld. 1975-76, c. 15, s. 2.

TERM OF TENANCY. The length of time over which a tenancy agreement is to run.

TERMOR. *n.* A person who holds tenements or land for a prescribed number of years.

TERMS OF EMPLOYMENT. (i) Obligations or requirements that are part of the employer-employee relationship and that give rise to any expenditure of funds by the employer; and (ii) obligations or requirements for the payment or provision of compensation to persons to whom subsection 3(2) or (3) applies. *Public Sector Prices and Compensation Review Act*, S.O. 1983, c. 70, s. 1.

TERRA. *n.* [L.] Land fit for farming.

TERRA AFFIRMATA. [L.] Land rented out to farm.

TERRA CULTA. [L.] Land which is cultivated.

TERRA DEBILIS. [L.] Barren or exhausted land.

TERRA DOMINICA. [L.] The domain land of a manor.

TERRAE DOMINICALES REGIS. [L.] The domain of the Crown.

TERRAE DOMINIUM FINITUR, UBI FINITUR ARMOURUM VIS. [L.] The right of ownership of land ends where the power of arms ends.

TERRA EXCULTABILIS. [L.] Land which can be ploughed.

TERRA FRISCA. [L.] Land not recently ploughed.

TERRA FRUSCA. [L.] Land not recently ploughed.

TERRA LUCRABILIS. [L.] Land reclaimed from the sea or from wasteland.

TERRA NOVA. [L.] Arable land; land newly converted from woods.

TERRA SABULOSA. [L.] Sandy or gravelly land.

TERRA TESTAMENTALIS. [L.] Allodial land.

TERRA VESTITA. [L.] Land with a crop of corn.

TERRA WAINABILIS. [L.] Land which may be tilled.

TERR. CT. *abbr.* Territorial Court.

TERRESTRIAL SERVICE. A radiocommunication service provided by coast, land or mobile stations.

TERRE TENANT. A legal mortgagee because a legal estate was conveyed to her or him; a person who, having a freehold interest in land, possesses the rents and profits, and may at any time, if there is no agreement or reservation to the contrary, convert the legal right of possession into actual possession. W.B. Rayner & R.H. McLaren, *Falconbridge on Mortgages*, 4th ed. (Toronto: Canada Law Book, 1977) at 18.

TERRITORIAL. *adj.* Connected with or limited with reference to a certain territory.

TERRITORIAL ACCOUNTS. The Territorial Accounts referred to in section 23 of the Northwest Territories Act (Canada). *Financial Administration Act*, S.N.W.T. 1982, c. 2, s. 2.

TERRITORIAL AGENCY. A territorial committee or a territorial corporation. *Financial Administration Act*, S.N.W.T. 1982, c. 2, s. 2.

TERRITORIAL ASSOCIATION. The territorial association of a political party. *Public Service Act*, S.N.W.T. 1983 (1st Sess.), c. 12, s. 1.

TERRITORIAL COMMITTEE. An unincorporated board, commission, council, or other body that is not a department or part of a department, all or a majority of whose members, either by their personal names or by the names of their offices, are appointed or designated (i) by an Ordinance; (ii) by regulations made pursuant to an Ordinance; (iii) by the Commissioner; (iv) by an Executive Member; or (v) by any combination of paragraphs (i), (ii), (iii) or (iv). *Financial Administration Act*, S.N.W.T. 1982, c. 2, s. 2.

TERRITORIAL CORPORATION. (i) A corporation that is incorporated by an Ordinance, all or a majority of whose members or directors, either by their personal names or the names of their office, are appointed or designated (A) by an Ordinance; (B) by regulations made pursuant to an Ordinance; (C) by the Commissioner; (D) by an Executive Member; or (E) by any combination of subparagraphs (A), (B), (C) or (D); or (ii) a corporation all of whose issued voting shares of every class are beneficially owned by the Territories. *Financial Administration Act*, S.N.W.T. 1982, c. 2, s. 2.

TERRITORIAL COURT. A court established by Parliament for two federal territories, the Northwest Territories and the Yukon Territory. P.W. Hogg, *Constitutional Law of Canada*, 2d ed. (Toronto: Carswell, 1985) at 148.

TERRITORIAL DEBT. Includes an existing debt, a future debt, or a chose in action. *Financial Administration Act*, S.N.W.T. 1982, c. 2, s. 50.

TERRITORIAL DIVISION. Includes any province, county, union of counties, township, city, town, parish or other judicial division or place to which the context applies. *Criminal Code*, R.S.C. 1985, c. C-46, s. 2.

TERRITORIAL INCOME TAX. Moneys paid by utility companies as income tax or estimated income tax under the Income Tax Ordinance for any taxation year. *Public Utilities Income Tax Rebates Act*, S.N.W.T. 1978 (2d Sess.), c. 12, s. 2.

TERRITORIALITY. *n.* The state of being connected with or limited to a particular territory.

TERRITORIAL JUDGE. A judge of the Territorial Court appointed under subsection 4(1) and, except where expressly stated to the contrary, includes a deputy territorial judge. *Young Offenders Act*, S.N.W.T. 1984 (1st Sess.), c. 2, s. 123.

TERRITORIAL LANDS. 1. Any lands situated in the Yukon Territory or the Northwest Territories. *Canada Lands Surveys Act*, R.S.C. 1985, c. L-6, s. 34. 2. Lands in the Yukon Territory or the Northwest Territories that are vested in the Crown or of which the Government of Canada has power to dispose. *Territorial Lands Act*, R.S.C. 1985, c. T-7, s. 2. 3. Territorial lands as defined in section 2 of the Territorial Lands Act that are lands for which letters patent, a certificate of title or a notification has not been issued. *Land Titles Act*, R.S.C. 1985, c. L-5, s. 55.

TERRITORIAL RATIONALE. The rule that any crime is local and that one must commit the offence within a territory for that territory to have jurisdiction to try it. M.R. Goode, *Criminal Conspiracy in Canada* (Toronto: Carswell, 1975) at 160.

TERRITORIAL SEA. 1. Part of the territory of any coastal state; it originally consisted of the waters within 3 miles of the coast but now Canada, along with many other countries, has established a 12-mile limit. P.W. Hogg, *Constitutional Law of Canada*, 2d ed. (Toronto: Carswell, 1985) at 586. 2. The territorial sea of Canada as determined in accordance with the Territorial Sea and Fishing Zones Act.

TERRITORIES. *n.* 1. The Northwest Territories, which comprise (a) all that part of Canada north of the sixtieth parallel of north latitude, except the portions thereof that are within the Yukon Territory, the Province of Quebec or the Province of Newfoundland; and (b) the islands in Hudson Bay, James Bay and Ungava Bay, except those islands that are within the Province of Manitoba, the Province of Ontario or the Province of Quebec. *Northwest Territories Act*, R.S.C. 1985, c. N-27, s. 2. 2. The Yukon Territory and the Northwest Territories. *Land Titles Act*, R.S.C. 1985, c. L-5, s. 2. 3. The North-West Territories as defined in The North-West Territories Act, 1886, excepting that portion of the said Territories declared by The Yukon Territory Act to constitute the Yukon Territory. *The Interpretation Act*, R.S.S. 1978, c. I-11, s. 21. See HER MAJESTY'S REALMS AND ~; MONEY PAID TO THE ~ FOR A SPECIAL PURPOSE; TERRITORY.

TERRITORIUM NULLIUS. [L.] Territory which is not within the jurisdiction of a party defined by international law.

TERRITORY. *n.* 1. The Yukon Territory, which comprises the area described in the schedule. *Yukon Act*, R.S.C. 1985, c. Y-2, s. 2. 2. The Yukon Territory or the Northwest Territories. *Land Titles Act*, R.S.C. 1985, c. L-5, s. 55. 3. A seigniory, a township, a municipality, a territory not organized into a municipality and any part of a seigniory, township, municipality and territory not organized into a municipality. *An Act Respecting Land Titles in Certain Electoral Districts*, R.S.Q. 1977, c. T-11, s. 1. 4. The land areas under the sovereignty, jurisdiction or trusteeship of a country, as well as territorial waters adjacent thereto, and any reference to a country shall be construed, where applicable, as a reference to such territory of that country and any references to a geographical area comprising several countries shall be construed, where applicable, as a reference to the aggregate of the respective territories of the countries constituting that geographical area. *Air Carrier Regulations*, C.R.C., c. 3, s. 23. See ACTIVITIES FOR THE DEVELOPMENT OF THE ~; FEDERAL ~; RECIPROCATING PROVINCE OR ~; SELECT ~; SURVEYED ~; TERRITORIES; UNORGANIZED ~; VOTING ~.

TERRITORY ADJACENT TO. When used with respect to a polling place, means surrounding territory in which qualified voters reside, if the polling place is more accessible and convenient to those voters than any other polling place in the constituency to which this Part applies. *The Election Act*, R.S.S. 1978, c. E-6, s. 236.

TERRITORY INVOLVED. Lands included in, or intended to be included in, an existing or proposed union school district concerning which the proposed action is to be taken, and also lands in any adjoining district that would be enlarged or diminished by the proposed action in relation to the union school district. *Public Schools Act*, R.S.M. 1970, c. P250, s. 324.

TERRITORY OF ORIGIN. The territory for which the original court was exercising jurisdiction. *Canada-United Kingdom Civil and Commercial Judgments Convention Act*, R.S.C. 1985, c. C-30, s. 1.

TERRITORY WITHOUT MUNICIPAL ORGANIZATION. Those parts of Ontario that are without municipal organization, including Indian reservations and provincial parks, but not including property of the Government of Canada used for the purposes of national defence installations, camps or stations. *Private Hospitals Act*, R.S.O. 1980, c. 389, s. 1.

TERR. L.R. *abbr.* Territories Law Reports (N.W.T.), 1885-1907.

TEST. *v.* To determine veracity.

TEST. *n.* A standard by which one judges. See ACID ~; ADULT ~ GROUP; ANTHROPO-

MORPHIC ~ DEVICE; APTITUDE ~; DESTRUCTIVE ~; GETTLER-YAMAKAMI ~;HYDROSTATIC ~; LABORATORY ~S; LIE DETECTOR ~; NEIGHBOUR ~; NONDES-TRUCTIVE ~; PARAFFIN ~; PROPORTION-ALITY ~; PULLORUM ~ OR BLOOD ~; STANDARD FIRE ~.

TESTABLE. *adj.* With respect to a person, able to make a will.

TESTAMENT. *n.* 1. A bequest of personal property. 2. A will.

TESTAMENTA LATISSIMAM INTERPRE-TATIONEM HABERE DEBENT. [L.] Wills should have the broadest interpretation.

TESTAMENTARY. *adj.* With respect to a document or gift, made to take effect only after the person making it dies. See MATTERS AND CAUSES ~.

TESTAMENTARY CAPACITY. Ability to make a valid will.

TESTAMENTARY INSTRUMENT. Includes any will, codicil or other testamentary writing or appointment, during the life of the testator whose testamentary disposition it purports to be and after his death, whether it relates to real or personal property or to both. *Criminal Code*, R.S.C. 1985, c. C-46, s. 2.

TESTAMENTARY MATTERS AND CAUSES. Includes all matters and causes relating to a grant of or revocation of probate or adminis-tration.

TESTAMENTARY TRUST. A trust that arises upon and in consequence of the death of an individual.

TESTAMENTUM. *n.* [L.] A will.

TESTAMENTUM DESTITUTUM. [L.] A for-saken will.

TESTAMENTUM, I.E., TESTATIO MENTIS, FACTA NULLO PROSENTIS METU PERI-CULI, SED SOLA COGITATIONE MORTA-LITATIS. [L.] A will, that is, the testimony of the mind, made with no fear of present danger, but in sole contemplation of death.

TESTAMENTUM OMNE MORTE CON-SUMMATUM. [L.] Every will is completed by death.

TESTATE. *adj.* Having executed a will.

TESTATION. *n.* Disposition of property by a will.

TESTATOR. *n.* 1. The person making a will, whether the person be male or female. 2. A person who has died leaving a will.

TESTATORIS ULTIMA VOLUNTAS EST PERIMPLENDA SECUNDUM VERAM INTENTIONEM SUAM. [L.] The last will of a testator should be thoroughly fulfilled follow-ing that person's true intention.

TESTATRIX. *n.* A woman who has made a will.

TESTATUM. *n.* A part of an indenture, known as the witnessing clause, which begins with the words "now this indenture witnesseth".

TEST CASE. An action whose result determines liability in other actions.

TEST DEVICE A. A fully articulated Sierra anthropometric test device simulating a child who weighs 34 pounds. *Children's Car Seats and Harnesses Regulations*, C.R.C., c. 921, s. 2.

TEST DEVICE B. A fully articulated Sierra anthropometric test device simulating a child who weighs 48 pounds. *Children's Car Seats and Harnesses Regulations*, C.R.C., c. 921, s. 2.

TESTE. *n.* The final part of a writ which gives the date and place it was issued.

TESTES PONDERANTUR, NON NUMER-ANTUR. [L.] Witnesses should be weighed, not numbered.

TESTES QUI POSTULAT DEBET DARE EIS SUMPTUS COMPETENTES. [L.] The one who calls witnesses must give them appropriate expenses.

TEST GROUP. See CHILD ~.

TEST HOLE. *var.* **TESTHOLE.** *var.* **TEST-HOLE.** 1. A hole drilled for any purpose in connection with geophysical exploration but does not include a shothole, or a well drilled or being drilled for oil, natural gas or water, or a deep testhole. 2. A hole drilled or being drilled (a) with a bore hole diameter of 100 mm or less; or (b) to a depth not exceeding 600 m, to obtain information about a geothermal resource, but does not include a hole drilled or being drilled for firing an explosive charge in seismic oper-ations. *Geothermal Resources Act*, S.B.C. 1982, c. 14, s. 1.

TESTIBUS DEPONENTIBUS IN PARI NUMERO DIGNIORIBUS EST CREDEN-DUM. [L.] When the witnesses are equal in number on both sides, the more worthy should be believed.

TESTIMONIAL. *n.* With respect to a food or drug that is represented as containing a vitamin, mineral nutrient or mineral means any dram-atized or undramatized pictorial, written or oral representation as to the result that is, has been or may be produced by the addition to a person's diet of that vitamin, mineral nutrient or mineral, as the case may be. *Food and Drug Regulations*, C.R.C., c. 870, c. D.01.001.

TESTIMONIAL EVIDENCE. In a broad sense, any evidence about which a competent witness testifies, even to simply identify an object. P.K. McWilliams, *Canadian Criminal Evidence*, 3d ed. (Aurora: Canada Law Book, 1988) at 1-11.

TESTIMONIAL PROOF. Oral testimony by a witness.

TESTIMONY. *n.* The evidence which a witness gives viva voce in a court or tribunal. See PERPETUATE ~.

TEST KIT. An apparatus (a) that contains reagent systems or buffering agents or both; (b) that is used in the course of a chemical or analytical procedure for medical, laboratory, industrial, educational or research purposes; and (c) the contents of which are not intended for administration to humans. Canada regulations.

TEST MARKET FOOD. A food that, prior to the date of the notice of intention respecting that food referred to in subsection (5), was not sold in Canada in that form and that differs substantially from any other food sold in Canada with respect to its composition, function, state or packaging form and includes a food referred to in section B.01.054. *Food and Drug Regulations*, C.R.C., c. 870, c. B.01.012.

TEST MARKET PRODUCT. A prepackaged product that, prior to the date of the notice of intention respecting that product, was not sold in Canada in that form and that differs substantially from any other product sold in Canada with respect to its composition, function, state or packaging form. Canada regulations.

TESTMOIGNES NE POENT TESTIFIE LE NEGATIVE MES L'AFFIRMATIVE. [Fr.] Witnesses cannot prove the negative, but the affirmative.

TEST OF MATERIAL. See CERTIFICATE OF ~.

TEST RIM. With reference to a tire to be tested, means any rim that is listed as appropriate for use with that tire in accordance with a document referred to in paragraph 1(1)(b) of Schedule V where the document includes the dimensional specifications of the rim and a diagram of the rim. *Motor Vehicle Tire Safety Regulations*, C.R.C., c. 1039, s. 2.

TEST RUN. See VALID ~.

TEXT BOOK. *var.* **TEXTBOOK.** 1. A treatise which collects decisions or explains principles concerning some branch of the law. 2. A text or other book authorized by the minister for use in the schools of the province under The School Act or The Secondary Education Act. *The Free Text Book Act*, R.S.S. 1978, c. F-22, s. 2.

TEXTILE AND CLOTHING GOODS. Includes (a) processed natural fibres and man-made fibres that are used in the production of any yarns and fabrics; (b) yarns and fabrics; (c) wearing apparel manufactured from any material, excluding footwear and apparel manufactured primarily from fur; and (d) products, not being wearing apparel, that are primarily made from yarns and fabrics. *Textile and Clothing Board Act*, R.S.C. 1985, c. T-9, s. 2.

TEXTILE ARTICLE. See CONSUMER ~.

TEXTILE FIBRE. Any natural or manufactured matter that is capable of being made into a yarn or fabric and, without limiting the generality of the foregoing, includes human hair, kapok, feathers and down and animal hair or fur that has been removed from an animal skin. *Textile Labelling Act*, R.S.C. 1985, c. T-10, s. 2. See RECLAIMED ~.

TEXTILE FIBRE PRODUCT. (a) Any consumer textile article; or (b) any textile fibre, yarn or fabric used or to be used in a consumer textile article. *Textile Labelling Act*, R.S.C. 1985, c. T-10, s. 2.

TEXTILE MATERIAL. Textile fibre or fabric or any other textile product of a stage between textile fibre and fabric. *Canadian Textile Goods Exported Drawback Regulations*, C.R.C., c. 486, s. 2.

TEXTILES. *n.* Cloth or fabric purchased by the yard or metre but does not include textiles used by a tailor, dressmaker, drapery manufacturer or upholsterer in producing clothing or draperies or in upholstering furniture even where a charge for such textiles is made separately on the invoice to the customer. *Retail Sales Tax Act*, R.R.O. 1980, Reg. 903, s. 1.

TEXTUAL MATERIAL. Manuscripts, records, documents, books, pamphlets and serials or any other material whose primary object is the communication of information through written or printed language. *Canadian Cultural Property Export Control List*, C.R.C., c. 448, s. 1.

THC. *abbr.* Tetrahydrocannabinol, an active ingredient of marihuana and hashish. F.A. Jaffe, *A Guide to Pathological Evidence*, 2d ed. (Toronto: Carswell, 1983) at 185.

THEATRE. *n.* 1. Includes any place that is open to the public where entertainments are given, whether or not any charge is made for admission. *Criminal Code*, R.S.C. 1985, c. C-46, s. 150. 2. A building or hall or any premises, room or place, including an open-air place, to which the public is admitted and that is used for giving vaudeville, dramatic or operatic performances, or for exhibitions of moving pictures. 3. Includes the building, rooms and places where any play, concert, opera, circus, trick or juggling show, gymnastic or other exhibition, masquerade, public dance, drill, lecture, address or other public gathering is or may be held, given, performed or takes place, and the approach or approaches to it and its appurtenances. *Health Act*, R.S.B.C. 1979, c. 161, s. 1. See CHAIN ~; MOTION PICTURE ~; MOVING PICTURE ~.

THEATRE FILM EXCHANGE. A film exchange owned or operated by the owner, lessee, or manager of a duly licensed theatre of not less than 500 seats in a city. *Amusements Act*, R.S.M. 1970, c. A70, s. 2.

THEATRE OF ACTUAL WAR. (a) In the case of the South African War, the zone of the military operations in South Africa in which the forces of the United Kingdom of Great Britain and Ireland were engaged prior to June 1, 1902; (b) in the case of World War I, (i) as applied to the army or air forces, the zone of the allied armies of the continents of Europe, Asia or Africa, or wherever the veteran has sustained injury or contracted disease directly by a hostile act of the enemy, and (ii) as applied to the naval forces, the high seas or wherever contact has been made with hostile forces of the enemy, or wherever the veteran has sustained injury or contracted disease directly by a hostile act of the enemy; and (c) in the case of World War II, (i) with respect to a former member of His Majesty's Canadian forces, any place where he has been on service involving duties performed outside the Western Hemisphere, including outside Canada, Newfoundland and the United States and the territorial waters thereof in aircraft or anywhere in a ship or other vessel, which service is classed as "sea time" for the purpose of advancement of naval ratings, or which would be so classed were the ship or other vessel in the service of the naval forces of Canada, and (ii) with respect to a former member of His Majesty's forces other than His Majesty's Canadian forces, or of any of the forces of His Majesty's Allies or powers associated with His Majesty in World War II, such places, zones or areas as the Board may prescribe. *War Veterans Allowance Act*, R.S.C. 1985, c. W-3, s. 37(8). See SERVICE IN A ~.

THEATRE OF OPERATIONS. See SERVICE IN A ~.

THEFT. *n.* Fraudulently and without colour of right taking, or fraudulently and without colour of right converting to his use or to the use of another person, anything whether animate or inanimate, with intent, (a) to deprive, temporarily or absolutely, the owner of it or a person who has a special property or interest in it; (b) to pledge it or deposit it as security; (c) to part with

it under a condition with respect to its return that the person who parts with it may be unable to perform; or (d) to deal with it in such a manner that it cannot be restored in the condition in which it was at the time it was taken or converted. *Criminal Code*, R.S.C. 1985, c. C-46, s. 322(1).

THEFT INSURANCE. Insurance against loss or damage through theft, wrongful conversion, burglary, housebreaking, robbery or forgery.

THERAPEUTIC ABORTION COMMITTEE. For any hospital, means a committee, comprised of not less than three members each of whom is a qualified medical practitioner, appointed by the board of that hospital for the purpose of considering and determining questions relating to terminations of pregnancy within that hospital. *Criminal Code*, R.S.C. 1985, c. C-46, s. 287(6).

THERAPIST. See DENTAL ~; DENTURE ~; DRUGLESS ~; PHYSICAL ~.

THERAPY. See DENTAL ~; OCCUPATIONAL ~; PHYSICAL ~; REHABILITATIVE ~.

THERMAL CUT OUT. A device affording protection from excessive current but not necessarily short-circuit protection, and containing a heating element in addition to, and affecting, a fusible member which opens the circuit. *Power Corporation Act*, R.R.O. 1980, Reg. 794, s. 0.

THERMAL ELECTRIC POWER PLANT. A facility for the generation of electricity from the combustion of natural gas, oil, petroleum products, coal, wood or plant products or from the use of geothermal energy, and includes all associated structures, machinery, appliances, fixtures and equipment, and storage and handling facilities. *Utilities Commission Act*, S.B.C. 1980, c. 60, s. 16.

THERMAL INSULATION MATERIALS. Batt, blanket, foam, loose fill, rigid or reflective insulation that is acquired exclusively for the purpose of preventing heat loss and that is, (a) poured, packed, blown, sprayed or otherwise placed in bulk as permanent fill between the confining structural members of a building; (b) material in solid form that is permanently placed between, or attached to, structural members of a building; (c) chemicals to be used to form a permanent thermal insulating foam between the confining structural members of a building, if such chemicals are purchased at the same time, from the same vendor, and in proportions proper for the use of the chemicals as thermal insulating foam; or (d) weather stripping and caulking materials, but does not include, (e) windows and doors of any type and frames therefor; (f) pipe, boiler and duct insulation and wrapping materials; (g) acoustical insulation and acoustical materials; (h) wallboard or drywall; or, (i) any materials incorporated into a building primarily for their structural or decorative value, and materials serving functions other than thermal insulation, whether or not such materials have thermal insulating properties. *Retail Sales Tax Act*, R.R.O. 1980, Reg. 903, s. 1.

THERMAL LIQUID BOILER. A pressure vessel the contents of which are heated by a liquid circulated through a tube or tubes that are submerged in water, where the Therm-hour rating of the boiler is more than 17. *Operating Engineers Act*, R.R.O. 1980, Reg. 740, s. 1.

THERM HOUR. *var.* **THERM-HOUR.** 100,000 British thermal units per hour or 39.3082 brake horsepower.

THERM-HOUR RATING. The rating of a plant determined under an Operating Engineers act.

THESAURIUM. *n.* [L.] A treasure.

THESAURUS. *n.* [L.] A treasure.

THESAURUS COMPETIT DOMINO REGI, ET NON DOMINO LIBERTATIS, NISI SIT PER VERBA SPECIALIA. [L.] Treasure belongs to the monarch, and not to a lord of a liberty, unless this be through special mention.

THESAURUS INVENTUS. [L.] A treasure trove.

THESAURUS INVENTUS EST VETUS DISPOSITIO PECUNIAE, ETC., CUJUS NON EXTAT MODO MEMORIA, ADEO UT JAM DOMINUM NON HABEAT. [L.] A treasure trove is the hiding of money, etc., in a former time of which no memory remains, so that now it has no owner.

THESAURUS NON COMPETIT REGI, NISI QUANDO NEMO SCIT QUI ABSCONDIT THESAURUM. [L.] A treasure does not belong to the monarch, unless no one knows who hid the treasure.

THING. *n.* A subject of dominion or property. See REAL ~.

THING IN ACTION. See CHOSE IN ACTION.

THIRD CLASS MAIL. See DOMESTIC ~.

THIRD CONVICTION. A conviction: (i) within a period of 5 years after the date of a first conviction, either before or after this section comes into force; and (ii) that next follows a second conviction. *Vehicles Amendment Act*, S.S. 1980-81, c. 94, s. 7.

THIRD FREEDOM. The privilege of a foreign air carrier operating a charter to put down in Canada persons who or goods that originated in the territory of the country of the foreign air carrier and includes the privilege to take on such persons in Canada for the purpose of returning them to that territory. *Air Carrier Regulations*, C.R.C., c. 3, s. 23.

THIRD PARTY. 1. A person who is not a party to an action but from whom a defendant claims relief. 2. In respect of a request for access to a record under this Act, means any person, group of persons or organization other than the person that made the request or a government institution. *Access to Information Act*, R.S.C. 1985, c. A-1, s. 3. 3. A person who is or is about to become indebted to or liable to pay money to a financial corporation liable to pay the tax. Corporation Capital Tax acts. 4. A person from whom money is, or will become, due and payable to the defendant. *Provincial Offences Procedure Act*, S.N.B. 1987, c. P-22.1, s. 89. 5. In respect of an application, means any person or organization other than the applicant or a department. *The Freedom of Information Act*, S.M. 1985-86, c. 6, s. 1. See LEADER OF THE ~.

THIRD PARTY CAUCUS. The group of two or more members who constitute the second largest group sitting in the Assembly in opposition to the Government and who belong to the same political party. *Legislative Assembly and Executive Council Amendment Act*, S.S. 1980-81, c. 65, s. 12.

THIRD PARTY CLAIM. An independent claim arising out of the main action or related actions or occurrences which a defendant has against the third party. G.D. Watson & C. Perkins, eds., *Holmested & Watson: Ontario Civil Procedure* (Toronto: Carswell, 1984) at 29-6.

THIRD PARTY DEMAND. A demand by the Receiver General made under section 224 (as amended by S.C. 1970-71-72, c. 63) of the Income Tax Act by which an account debtor who owes money to a debtor-taxpayer must pay to discharge the debtor-taxpayer's debt to the extent of that payment. F. Bennett, *Receiverships* (Toronto: Carswell, 1985) at 238 and 239.

THIRD PARTY LIABILITY INSURANCE. Insurance that secures a tortfeasor for personal liability. John G. Fleming, *The Law of Torts*, 6th ed. (Sydney: The Law Book Co., 1983) at 365.

THIRD PARTY PROCEEDING. See THIRD PARTY CLAIM.

THIRD READING. Parliamentary review of a bill in its final form. A. Fraser, G.A. Birch & W.A. Dawson, eds., *Beauchesne's Rules and Forms of the House of Commons of Canada*, 5th ed. (Toronto: Carswell, 1978) at 221.

THOROUGHFARE. *n.* Any place or structure

intended for vehicular or pedestrian traffic, in particular, a road, street, lane, sidewalk, walkway, bicycle path, snowmobile trail, hiking path, square or public parking area. *An Act Respecting Land Use Planning and Development*, S.Q. 1979, c. 51, s. 1.

THREAT. *n.* The menace of bodily injury.

THREATENED SPECIES. A species of animal which is designated as a threatened species. *Wildlife Act*, S.B.C. 1982, c. 57, s. 1.

THREATS TO THE SECURITY OF CANADA. (a) Espionage or sabotage that is against Canada or is detrimental to the interests of Canada or activities directed toward or in support of such espionage or sabotage; (b) foreign influenced activities within or relating to Canada that are detrimental to the interests of Canada and are clandestine or deceptive or involve a threat to any person; (c) activities within or relating to Canada directed toward or in support of the threat or use of acts of serious violence against persons or property for the purpose of achieving a political objective within Canada or a foreign state; and (d) activities directed toward undermining by covert unlawful acts, or directed toward or intended ultimately to lead to the destruction or overthrow by violence of, the constitutionally established system of government in Canada, but does not include lawful advocacy, protest or dissent, unless carried on in conjunction with any of the activities referred to in paragraphs (a) to (d). *Canadian Security Intelligence Service Act*, R.S.C. 1985, c. C-23, s. 2.

THREE AXLE GROUP. Three consecutive axles, not including the front axle of a motor vehicle, (i) that do not form a triple axle within the meaning of clause (p); (ii) that are entirely within either a motor vehicle or trailer or semi-trailer; (iii) in which the spacings between the consecutive axles do not exceed 2.5 metres; and (iv) which are not included in a four axle group within the meaning of clause (h). *Highway Traffic Act*, R.S.O. 1980, c. 198, c. 97.

THREE-CARD MONTE. The game commonly known as three-card monte and includes any other game that is similar to it, whether or not the game is played with cards and notwithstanding the number of cards or other things that are used for the purpose of playing. *Criminal Code*, R.S.C. 1985, c. C-46, s. 206(2).

THREE CERTAINTIES. The three essential characteristics required to create a trust: (a) certain intention; (b) certain subject-matter; (c) certain objects. D.M.W. Waters, *The Law of Trusts in Canada*, 2d ed. (Toronto: Carswell, 1984) at 107.

THRESHER. *n.* A person who threshes or causes to be threshed grain of any kind for another person, or who threshes or cuts and threshes grain, or causes grain to be threshed or cut and threshed for another person, with a harvester thresher, combine, or any other implement that both cuts and threshes grain.

THRESHOLD. See SENSING ~.

THRESHOLD LIMIT VALUE. A Registered Trade Mark of the American Conference of Governmental Industrial Hygienists: the airborne concentration of a substance below which it is ordinarily felt that nearly any worker may be exposed without jeopardizing health. D. Robertson, *Ontario Health and Safety Guide* (Toronto: Richard De Boo Ltd., 1988) at 5-403.

THROMBOSIS. *n.* The presence or formation of a thrombus. F.A. Jaffe, *A Guide to Pathological Evidence*, 2d ed. (Toronto: Carswell, 1983) at 185. See CORONARY ~.

THROMBUS. *n.* A brittle, solid clot which forms in circulating blood inside chambers of the heart or blood vessels. F.A. Jaffe, *A Guide to Pathological Evidence*, 2d ed. (Toronto: Carswell, 1983) at 185. See MURAL ~.

THROTTLE. *n.* The component of the fuel metering device that (a) connects to the driver-operated accelerator control system; and (b) controls the engine speed. *Motor Vehicle Safety Regulations*, C.R.C., c. 1038, s. 2.

THROUGH AN ELECTION. The period commencing with the issue of a writ for an election and ending when the candidate or candidates have been returned as elected.

THROUGH HIGHWAY. 1. Any highway or portion thereof at the entrances to which stop signs or yield right-of-way signs are erected at which traffic from intersecting highways is required to stop or to yield right-of-way before entering or crossing the same. 2. A highway or part of a highway at the entrances to which stop signs are erected.

THROUGH LOT. A lot having frontage on two parallel or approximately parallel streets. Canada regulations.

THROUGHOUT AN ELECTION. Includes the period from the issue of the writ of election until the elected candidate is returned as elected.

THROUGHPUT. See CONTAINER ~.

THROUGHPUT CHARGE. The charge for the inward movement and outward movement of containers but does not include the charge for the crane. *Pacific Terminal Tariff By-law*, C.R.C., c. 1083, s. 32.

THROUGH SERVICE. A telecommunication

service by a submarine cable between places outside Canada, through Canada, but does not include a terminating service and does not include any service by a submarine cable wholly under fresh water. *External Submarine Cable Regulations*, C.R.C., c. 1515, s. 2.

THROUGH TOLL. A combination of separately established tolls. *Air Carrier Regulations*, C.R.C., c. 3, s. 2.

THYMUS. *n.* A gland in the upper chest which affects immunological functions. F.A. Jaffe, *A Guide to Pathological Evidence*, 2d ed. (Toronto: Carswell, 1983) at 185.

THYROID CARTILAGE. The most important cartilage in the larynx. F.A. Jaffe, *A Guide to Pathological Evidence*, 2d ed. (Toronto: Carswell, 1983) at 185.

TICKET. *n.* 1. A card, pass or other document upon presentation of which the holder is entitled to admission to any theatre, opera house, public hall, show, game, grandstand, race meeting, exhibition or amusement of any kind. *Ticket Speculation Act*, R.S.O. 1980, c. 499, s. 1. 2. A ticket sold under a lottery scheme and includes the contractual rights and obligations between the Corporation and the owner of the ticket. *Ontario Lottery Corporation Act*, R.R.O. 1980, Reg. 719, s. 1. 3. A pari-mutuel ticket. *Race Track Supervision Regulations*, C.R.C., c. 441, s. 2. See CASH PURCHASE ~; OUTSTANDING ~; VIOLATION ~; WEIGH ~; WINNING ~.

TICKETING. See DOUBLE ~.

TICKET ISSUING MACHINE MECHANIC. A person qualified to overhaul or repair any defective ticket issuing machine. *Race Track Supervision Regulations*, C.R.C., c. 441, s. 2.

TICKET ISSUING MACHINE SUPERVISOR. A person qualified to change codes or ticket paper or ink a ticket issuing machine. *Race Track Supervision Regulations*, C.R.C., c. 441, s. 2.

TIDAL WATERS. Includes the Gulf of St. Lawrence, Chaleur Bay east of Campbellton Bridge, the St. Lawrence River downstream from the Laviolette Bridge (Three Rivers Bridge), the Saguenay River downstream from Chicoutimi Bridge and the estuary of the York River downstream from the Gaspé Bridge. *Quebec Fishery Regulations*, C.R.C., c. 852, s. 2.

TIED SELLING. (a) Any practice whereby a supplier of a product, as a condition of supplying the product (the "tying" product) to a customer, requires that customer to (i) acquire any other product from the supplier or the supplier's nominee; or (ii) refrain from using or distributing, in conjunction with the tying product, another product that is not of a brand or manufacture designated by the supplier or the nominee; and (b) any practice whereby a supplier of a product induces a customer to meet a condition set out in subparagraph (a)(i) or (ii) by offering to supply the tying product to the customer on more favourable terms or conditions if the customer agrees to meet the condition set out in either of those subparagraphs. *Combines Investigation Act*, R.S.C. 1985 (2nd Supp.), c. 19, s. 77.

TIERCED SALMON PLANT. A building, structure, machinery, appurtenances, appliances and apparatus occupied and used in the business of tiercing or mild curing salmon, or of converting the natural salmon into tierced salmon. *Fisheries Act*, R.S.B.C. 1979, c. 137, s. 12.

TILE. *n.* Tile, pipe or tubing of any material used in the installation of a drainage work. *Agricultural Tile Drainage Installation Act*, R.S.O. 1980, Reg. 13, s. 1.

TILL. *n.* Is of glacial origin, unsorted and heterogeneous and can contain a range of particle sizes including boulders, cobbles, gravel, sands, silts and clays and can exist at any relative density or consistency. *Building Code Act*, R.R.O. 1980, Reg. 87, s. 4.2.1.9.

TIMBER. *n.* 1. Trees standing or fallen, logs and bolts, cants, boards and lumber, and any other sawn or shaped product of trees. 2. Wood of all types and species. *Forests (Exchange and Acquisition) Act*, R.S. Nfld. 1970, c. 143, s. 2. 3. Logs, timbers, boards, deals, scantlings or laths, telegraph poles, railway ties, pitprops, pulpwood, shingle bolts or staves, fence posts and cordwood. 4. Round logs or logs which are slabbed on one or two sides. See CROWN ~; MERCHANTABLE ~; PARTLY PROCESSED ~; STANDING ~.

TIMBER AGREEMENT. Includes any agreement heretofore or hereafter made by the Crown with respect to the cutting and removal of trees and any agreement containing provisions for the cutting and removal of trees and includes any agreement ratified and confirmed by any special Act or general Act. *The Forest Act*, R.S.S. 1978, c. F-19, s. 2.

TIMBER BERTH. Timber licence. See DOMINION ~.

TIMBER DECK CARGO. A cargo of timber carried on an uncovered part of a freeboard deck or superstructure deck, but does not include a cargo of wood pulp or similar cargo. Canada regulations.

TIMBER DISPOSITION. A forest management agreement, timber licence or timber permit. *Forests Act*, R.S.A. 1980, c. F-16, s. 1.

TIMBER LAND. *var.* **TIMBERLAND.** 1. Any uncultivated land in the province on which trees or shrubs are growing or standing and any barren, dry marsh or bog, whether such land is owned by the Crown or by private persons. *Forestry Act*, R.S.P.E.I. 1974, c. F-12, s. 1. 2. Uncultivated land used or held only or primarily for lumber purposes. *Angling Act*, R.S.N.S. 1967, c. 9, s. 1. 3. (a) With respect to land west of the Cascade Mountains, land containing merchantable timber averaging over the whole parcel at least 94 m³/ha; and (b) with respect to land east of the Cascade Mountains, land containing merchantable timber averaging over the whole parcel at least 59 m³/ha and that is classified as timber land for taxation purposes under the Taxation (Rural Area) Act and is (c) held by an owner in areas sufficient for the purposes of forestry, and held for the specific purpose of cutting and removing timber; or (d) held as investment for the accruing value of the timber. *Assessment Act*, R.S.B.C. 1979, c. 21, s. 1.

TIMBER LICENCE. 1. Includes pulp and paper licence, Forest Management Licence and any other licence respecting the utilization of timber issued under this Act. *Crown Lands Act*, R.S.N.B. 1973, c. C-38, s. 1. 2. Includes any saw mill licence, pulp and paper licence or timber licence of Crown lands issued by the Minister and any renewal thereof. *Forest Service Act*, R.S.N.B. 1973, c. F-23, s. 1.

TIMBER LOAD LINE. A special load line to be used only when a ship carrying a timber deck cargo complies with these Regulations and the Load Line Rules. *Timber Cargo Regulations*, C.R.C., c. 1496, s. 2.

TIMBER PERMIT. An authorization issued pursuant to these Regulations by the Superintendent to cut a quantity of timber specified therein on an area described therein. *National Parks Timber Regulations*, C.R.C., c. 1132, s. 2.

TIMBER PROCESSING FACILITY. A facility that processes timber or wood residue or both. *Forest Amendment Act*, S.B.C. 1980, c. 14, s. 1.

TIMBER PRODUCTS. Logs, piles, poles, bolts, cordwood and other similar products of the forest. *Tugboat Worker Lien Act*, R.S.B.C. 1979, c. 417, s. 1. See PRIMARY ~.

TIMBER QUOTA. A share of the allowable cut of coniferous timber within a forest management unit and may also include an allocation by area of deciduous timber within a forest management unit. *Forests Act*, R.S.A. 1980, c. F-16, s. 1.

TIME. See ADJUSTMENT ~; AIR ~; ALLOWED ~; BROADCAST ~; CENTRAL STANDARD ~; CLOSE ~; COMMERCIAL ~; DAYLIGHT SAVING ~; DAY ~; DEAD ~; DOUBLE ~; DOWN~; DRIVING ~; FLEX ~; FLIGHT ~; FREE ~; FRINGE ~; GIVE ~; IDLE ~; LIFE~; LOCAL ~; LOST ~; NIGHT ~; ON-CALL ~; PART-~; PORTAL ~; POST ~; PRIME ~; PROGRAM ~; RESERVED ~; RISE ~; STANDARD ~; STAND-BY ~; STRAIGHT ~; WET ~.

TIME AND A HALF. A wage payment at one and one-half an employee's regular rate of pay.

TIME CHARGE. A charge for the period between the time the derrick or crane is ready at the loading location until loading is completed and the period between the time the derrick or crane is ready at the unloading location until unloading is completed. Canada regulations.

TIME CHARTER. A charterparty for a certain time.

TIME FACTOR. The figure obtained by multiplying the draught of a ship in feet by the number of hours or part thereof during which the ship is underway under the conduct of a licensed pilot, but does not include any time during which the ship is compelled to remain stopped or is actually unable to move on account of ice, or any period of time during which charges pursuant to section 9 of the schedule may be assessed. *Laurentian Pilotage Tariff Regulations*, C.R.C., c. 1269, s. 2.

TIMELY DISCLOSURE. A requirement for the prompt disclosure by a corporation of information which may materially affect the value of a corporation's shares. S.M. Beck *et al.*, *Cases and Materials on Partnerships and Canadian Business Corporations*, (Toronto: The Carswell Co., 1983) at 934.

TIME OFF. See COMPENSATORY ~.

TIME OF IMPORTATION. In respect of goods, the date on which an officer authorizes, pursuant to this Act, the release of the goods. *Customs Act*, R.S.C. 1985 (2nd Supp.), c. 1, s. 51(6).

TIME OF LAPSING. The time at which the record of a lien is removed from the general register. *Real Property Act*, R.S.M. 1970, c. R30, s. 73.

TIME PERIOD. See PRESCRIBED ~.

TIME POLICY. Where the contract is to insure the subject-matter for a definite period of time the policy is called a "time policy" and a contract for both voyage and time may be included in the same policy. *Maritime Insurance Act*, R.S.O. 1980, c. 255, s. 26.

TIME SALE. A sale or an agreement to sell under which the purchase price and credit charges in addition to the purchase price, if any, are to be paid by one or more future payments.

TIME SALE AGREEMENT. 1. A document or memorandum in writing evidencing a time sale. 2. (i) An agreement for sale under which the right of property in the goods remains in the seller until the purchase price is paid in full or until some other condition is fulfilled; (ii) a sale effected by way of a lien note or by way of any agreement or arrangement made at the time of the sale or subsequent thereto whereby the buyer gives to the seller a chattel mortgage or a bill of sale covering the whole or part of the purchase price of the goods sold; and (iii) a sale made pursuant to a contract of bailment under which it is intended that the property in the goods will pass to the bailee on the payment of the purchase price in whole or in part or on the performance of a condition. *Law of Property Act*, R.S.A. 1980, c. L-8, s. 47.

TIME SEGMENT. A quarter hour block. *Radio (F.M.) Broadcasting Regulations*, C.R.C., c. 380, s. 14.

TIME SHARE INTEREST. The interest of a person in a time share plan.

TIME SHARE OWNERSHIP PLAN. Any plan by which a person participating in the plan acquires an ownership interest in real property and the right to use or occupy all or part of that property, including accommodations or facilities situated on all or part of that property, for specific or determinable periods of time.

TIME SHARE PLAN. Any time share ownership plan or time share use plan, whether in respect of land situated inside or outside a province, that provides for the use, occupation or possession of real property to circulate in any year among persons participating in the plan.

TIME SHARE USE PLAN. Any plan by which a person participating in the plan acquires a right to use or occupy real property, including accommodations or facilities situated on that property, for specific or determinable periods of time but does not acquire an ownership interest in that property.

TIME-SHARING AGREEMENT. An arrangement or contract with respect to premises which: (i) allows a person to use, occupy or possess premises for two or more periods of continuous use; and (ii) provides that at least one period of continuous use following the first period of continuous use commences in a year subsequent to the year in which the first period commences; and, without limiting the generality of the foregoing, includes a membership in an association or corporation, vacation plan, prepaid reservation or any other similar arrangement. *The Real*

Estate Brokers Act, S.S. 1986-87-88, c. R-2.1, s. 2.

TIME-SHARING CONDOMINIUM. Like a freehold or leasehold condominium with the added factor that the purchaser's interest in the common elements and the unit is limited to a certain time period and perhaps also for a certain number of years. B.J. Reiter, R.C.B. Risk & B.N. McLellan, *Real Estate Law*, 3d ed. (Toronto: Emond Montgomery, 1986) at 674.

TIME TABLE. The authority for the movement of regular trains subject to the rules. It contains classified schedules, also special instructions relating to the movement of trains and engines. *Regulations No. O-8, Uniform Code of Operating Rules*, C.R.C., c. 1175, Part III, s. 2.

TIMOCRACY. *n.* Government by those properly qualified to rule.

TIP HEADS. See COMPACT ~.

TIPPED. *adj.* As applied to any fur, means that individual hairs or small groups of hairs have been treated to change their colour. *Fur Garments Labelling Regulations*, C.R.C., c. 1138, s. 2.

TIPSTAFF. *n.* A constable attached to a court.

TIRE. *n.* 1. Any tire, made of rubber, chemicals and fabric and steel or other materials, that is designed to contain a gas or liquid. *Motor Vehicles Tire Safety Act*, R.S.C. 1985, c. M-11, s. 2. 2. That part of a wheel, roller or other contrivance for the moving of any object upon a highway, which comes into direct contact with the surface of the highway. *Roads Act*, R.S.P.E.I. 1974, c. R-15, c. 1. See BIAS PLY ~; LIGHT TRUCK ~; METAL ~; PNEUMATIC ~; RADIAL PLY ~; SAFETY STUDDED ~S; SOLID RUBBER ~; SOLID ~; STUDDED ~; TYRE; WIDTH OF ~.

TISSUE. *n.* Includes an organ, but does not include any skin, bone, blood, blood constituent or other tissue that is replaceable by natural processes of repair. Human Tissue Gift acts.

TITLE. *n.* 1. A general heading which includes particulars, i.e. of a book. 2. An appellation of dignity or honour. 3. The way in which a landowner justly possesses property. 4. In relation to a loan secured by a mortgage on a long-term lease, means the entire interest of the lessee. *National Housing Act*, R.S.C. 1985, c. N-11, s. 2. See ABSTRACT OF ~; BAD ~; CERTIFICATE OF ~; CHAIN OF ~; CLEAR ~; CURE ~; DOCUMENT OF ~; FIRST ~; INDEFEASIBLE ~; LONG ~; POSSESSORY ~; QUALIFIED ~; REGISTER OF ~ AND ABSTRACT INDEX; REQUISITION ON ~;

ROYAL STYLE AND ~S; SERIAL ~; SHORT ~; SLANDER OF ~; SQUATTER'S ~.

TITLE INSURANCE. 1. Insurance against loss or liability for loss due to the invalidity of the title to any property or of any instrument, or to any defect in such title or instrument. 2. Insurance against loss or damage caused by defect in the title to real property, or by the existence of liens, encumbrances, or servitudes upon real property, or by other matters affecting the title to real property or the right to the use and enjoyment thereof, or by defect in the execution of mortgages, hypothecs, or deeds of trust.

TITLE OF PROCEEDING. The name which sets out the names of all the parties and their capacity, if other than a personal capacity. G.D. Watson & C. Perkins, eds., *Holmested & Watson: Ontario Civil Procedure* (Toronto: Carswell, 1984) at 14-5.

TITLE REGISTER. A book, file, micrographic, electronic or other storage means whereby or wherein are registered the title to land and instruments relating thereto. *Land Titles Act*, S.N.S. 1978, c. 8, s. 4.

TITLE SEARCH PERIOD. The period of 40 years described in subsection 105(1). *Registry Amendment Act*, S.O. 1981, c. 17, s. 4.

[ ] **T.J.** *abbr.* Recueils de Jurisprudence, Tribunal de la Jeunesse.

T.J. (QUÉ.). *abbr.* Tribunal de la jeunesse (Québec).

T.L.R. *abbr.* Times Law Reports.

T.M. *abbr.* Trade Marks.

T.O. *abbr.* 1. Taxing Officer. 2. Taxing Office.

TO ADVERTISE AND TO MAKE USE OF ADVERTISING. To prepare, utilize, distribute, publish or broadcast an advertisement, or to cause it to be distributed, published or broadcast. *Consumer Protection Act*, S.Q. 1978, c. 9, s. 252.

TOBACCO. *n.* Tobacco in any form in which it is used or consumed and includes snuff. See CONSUMER OF ~; MANUFACTURED ~; RAW LEAF ~; STANDARD LEAF ~.

TOBACCO AUCTION EXCHANGE. Any premises wherein (a) the Board, under the Excise Act, is licensed to carry on the business or trade of a tobacco packer; and (b) tobacco growers who are registered with the Board offer tobacco for sale to other licensed tobacco packers. *Ontario Flue-Cured Tobacco Excise Regulations*, C.R.C., c. 577, s. 2.

TOBACCO FARM. One or more parcels of land in respect of which the Board or the local board determines, (i) the land is suitable for the producing of tobacco; and (ii) the producer has provided such buildings or other structures and equipment as are suitable and adequate for the producing of tobacco, and in respect of which the Board or the local board, as the case may be, allots a tobacco hectarage. *Farm Products Marketing Act*, R.S.O. 1980, c. 158, s. 21.

TOBACCO HECTARAGE. A number of hectares of land fixed and allotted to a person for the producing in any year of tobacco on a tobacco farm. *Farm Products Marketing Act*, R.S.O. 1980, c. 158, s. 21.

TOBACCO MANUFACTORY. Any place or premises where raw leaf tobacco is worked up into manufactured tobacco, and every workshop, office, store-room, warehouse, shed, yard or other place where any of the raw material is or is to be stored, where any process connected with the manufacture or preparation of manufactured tobacco is or is intended to be carried on or where any of the products of the manufacture are or are intended to be stored shall be held to be included in and to form part of the tobacco manufactory to which they are attached or appurtenant. *Excise Act*, R.S.C. 1985, c. E-14, s. 6.

TOBACCO MANUFACTURER. Everyone who manufactures tobacco for himself, or who employs others to manufacture tobacco, other than cigars, whether the manufacture is by casing, packing, cutting, pressing, grinding, rolling, drying, crushing or stemming of any raw leaf tobacco, or otherwise preparing raw leaf or manufactured or partially manufactured tobacco, by the putting up for use or consumption of scraps, waste, clippings, stems or deposits of tobacco, resulting from any process of handling tobacco, or by the working or preparation of raw leaf tobacco, scraps, waste, clippings, stems or deposits of tobacco, by sifting, twisting, screening or any other process. *Excise Act*, R.S.C. 1985, c. E-14, s. 6.

TOBACCONIST. *n.* A person, firm, or corporation, who sells by retail all or any of the following: tobacco, cigars, cigarettes, and tobacconists' sundries, including cigarette papers, matches, lighters, cigar and cigarette holders, pipes, pipe cases, pipe cleaners, pouches, humidors, and walking sticks. *Shops Regulation Act*, R.S.M. 1970, c. S110, s. 3.

TOBACCO PACKER. Any person who, subject to departmental regulations, by himself or his agent, deals in, prepares, packs, stems, reconstitutes or converts Canadian raw leaf tobacco or employs others to do so. *Excise Act*, R.S.C. 1985, c. E-14, s. 6.

TOBACCO PRODUCTS. Manufactured

tobacco or cigars and includes Canada twist. Canada regulations.

TOBACCO STAMP. Any stamp affixed to any package of manufactured tobacco entered for consumption or to Canadian raw leaf tobacco entered for consumption. *Excise Act*, R.S.C. 1985, c. E-14, s. 6.

TO HAVE AND TO HOLD. In a conveyance, words which show the estate one intends to convey.

TOILET. *n.* 1. A device used for individual disposal of human waste and excrement, and includes a lavatory, water closet and urinal. *Public Toilet Act*, R.S.B.C. 1979, c. 347, s. 1. 2. In relation to a pleasure boat, means equipment designed or used for defecation or urination by humans.

TOILET ROOM. A room that contains a toilet, urinal basin or urinal trough or any combination thereof for the use of employees. *Canada Sanitation Regulations*, C.R.C., c. 1009, s. 2.

TOILET SPACE. Every room containing a bath, shower, water-closet or wash-basin other than a room that is (a) a sleeping room, or (b) used only as a laundry. *Towboat Crew Accommodation Regulations*, C.R.C., c. 1498, s. 2.

TOKEN OF VALUE. See COUNTERFEIT ~.

TOKEN STRIKE. A strike of 1 or 2 days duration to demonstrate the effect of a prolonged strike.

TOLL. *n.* 1. Any rate or charge or other payment payable for any passenger, animal, carriage, goods, merchandise, matters or things conveyed on a railway. 2. Any fee or rate charged, levied or collected for the transportation of goods or for use of a public commercial vehicle. 3. Any fee or rate charged, levied or collected by any person for the carriage of passengers and express freight by a public vehicle. *Public Vehicles Act*, R.S.O. 1980, c. 425, s. 1. 4. Any charge, other than a rate, for the transmission of telephone messages. *Telephone Act*, R.S.O. 1980, c. 496, s. 1. 5. A fee, charge, rate or rental fixed, demanded or charged by a municipality, improvement district or development district for a service rendered or made available to any extent by means of works for storing, conveying or distributing water, electricity, garbage or sewage, or for extinguishing fire, and includes a charge for the use or benefit of works constructed under authority of a licence for river improvement purposes or for a service rendered or made available by the holder of that licence. *Water Act*, R.S.B.C. 1979, c. 429, s. 1. 6. Any fee or rate charged, levied, or collected by a person for the carriage of passengers and property by a ferry. *Ferries Act*, R.S.Nfld. 1970, c. 128,

s. 2. 7. Includes any toll, rate, charge or allowance charged or made (a) for the shipment, transportation, transmission, care, handling or delivery of hydrocarbons, or for storage or demurrage or the like; (b) for the provision of a pipeline when the pipeline is available and ready to provide for the transmission of oil or gas; and (c) in respect of the purchase and sale of gas that is the property of a company and that is transmitted by the company through its pipeline, excluding the cost to the company of the gas at the point where it enters the pipeline. *National Energy Board Act*, R.S.C. 1985, c. N-7, s. 2. 8. The consideration given by a subscriber to a cablecaster for the provision by the cablecaster to the subscriber of cablecast service. *The Community Cablecasters Act*, R.S.S. 1978, c. C-17, s. 2. 9. Any charge, classification, fare, rate or allowance made by an air carrier in respect of the carriage, shipment, transportation, care, handling or delivery of traffic, or in respect of any service incidental thereto. *Air Carrier Regulations*, C.R.C., c. 3, s. 2. See BRIDGE ~; EXPRESS ~; HARBOUR ~; JOINT ~; LOCAL ~; RATE OR ~; TELEGRAPH ~; TELEPHONE ~; THROUGH ~.

TOLLAGE. *n.* Payment of a toll.

TOLL, GAIN OR COMPENSATION. The fee or rate charged or collected by any person for the carriage of passengers or property by a motor vehicle, and includes remuneration of any kind, paid or promised, directly or indirectly payable, whether for the use of all or part of the vehicle or for the services of the driver operating the vehicle. *The Highway Traffic Act*, S.M. 1985-86, c. 3, s. 280.

TOLL-GATHERER. *n.* An official who collects a toll.

TOLL OR CHARGE. Any toll, rate, charge or allowance charged or made in connection with the transport of passengers or the shipment, transport, care, handling or delivery of goods, or for any services incidental to the business of a carrier, and includes (a) any toll, rate, charge or allowance so charged or made (i) in connection with any instrumentality or facility of shipment or transport irrespective of ownership or of any contract express or implied with respect to the use thereof; (ii) for furnishing passengers with sleeping accommodation or for collecting, receiving, loading, unloading, stopping over, elevating, ventilating, refrigerating, icing, heating, switching, ferrying, carting, storing, caring for, handling or delivering goods transported or in transit or to be transported; or (iii) for the warehousing of goods, wharfage, demurrage or the like; and (b) any charges made in connection with any one or more of the foregoing subjects, separately or conjointly. *Transport Act*, R.S.C. 1985, c. T-17, s. 2.

TOLL OR RATE. 1. When used with reference to a railway, (a) means any toll, rate, charge or allowance charged or made either by the company, or on or in respect of a railway owned or operated by the company, or by any person on behalf or under authority or consent of the company, in connection with the carriage and transportation of passengers or the carriage, shipment, transportation, care, handling or delivery of goods, or for any service incidental to the business of a carrier; and (b) includes (i) any toll, rate, charge or allowance so charged or made in connection with rolling stock, or the use thereof, or any instrumentality or facility of carriage, shipment or transportation, irrespective of ownership or of any contract, expressed or implied, with respect to the use thereof; (ii) any toll, rate, charge or allowance so charged or made for furnishing passengers with beds or berths on sleeping cars, or for the collection, receipt, loading, unloading, stopping over, elevation, ventilation, refrigerating, icing, heating, switching, ferriage, cartage, storage, care, handling or delivery of, or in respect of, goods transported, or in transit, or to be transported; and (iii) any toll, rate, charge or allowance so charged or made for the warehousing of goods, wharfage or demurrage, or the like, or so charged or made in connection with any one or more of the above-mentioned objects, separately or conjointly. *Railway Act*, R.S.C. 1985, c. R-3, s. 2. 2. A fee or rate charge, levied or collected (i) for the transportation of passengers or goods; or (ii) for the use of a public vehicle. 3. Includes a toll, rate, charge or licence charged or made for the shipment, transportation, care, handling or delivery of oil or gas or solids or for storage or demurrage or the like. *Pipeline Act*, R.S.B.C. 1979, c. 328, s. 1. 4. Telegraph or telephone toll. *Railway Act*, R.S.C. 1985, c. R-3, s. 339(2).

TOMALLEY. *n.* An edible by-product of lobster, the ingredients of which have not been ground to a smooth consistency. *Fish Inspection Regulations*, C.R.C., c. 802, s. 2.

TOMATO. See FIELD ~ES; GREENHOUSE ~ES.

TON. *n.* 1. 2,000 pounds. *Weights and Measures Act*, S.C. 1970-71-72, c. 36, schedule II. 2. (a) Where used to calculate weight, 2,000 pounds; and (b) where used to calculate measurement, 40 cubic feet. Canada regulations. 3. In respect of cargo, coal or oil means 2,240 pounds. *Esquimalt Graving Dock Regulations*, C.R.C., c. 1362, s. 2. 4. 2,240 pounds. 5. Registered gross tonnage where the reference is to the payment of bounty and underdeck tonnage where the

reference is to timber sizes forming the scantlings of vessels. Newfoundland statutes. See GROSS REGISTERED ~S.

TONGUE. See MOTHER ~.

TONIC. *n.* A mineral feed that is represented for the treatment of a specified disease or to aid recovery from a specific disease or debility and is for use only while the disease or debility persists. *Feeds Regulations*, C.R.C., c. 665, s. 2.

TON (METRIC). 1,000 kilograms. *Weights and Measures Act*, S.C. 1970-71-72, c. 36, schedule I.

TONNAGE. *n.* 1. The estimated weight in number of tons which a ship can carry. 2. In relation to a vessel, means (a) the largest gross tonnage of the vessel shown on its certificate of registry or tonnage certificate, as the case may be, if that tonnage has been measured in accordance with the rules of a country other than a country listed in the Tonnage of Ships Order; or (b) the gross tonnage of the vessel measured under the Canada Shipping Act, if the largest gross tonnage of the vessel shown on its certificate of registry or tonnage certificate, as the case may be, has been measured in accordance with the rules of a country listed in the Tonnage of Ships Order. Canada regulations. 3. Registered gross tonnage where the reference is to the payment of bounty and underdeck tonnage where the reference is to timber sizes forming the scantlings of vessels. Newfoundland statutes. See GROSS ~; PORT-CALL-~; REGISTERED NET ~; REGISTER ~.

TONNAGE MEASUREMENT CERTIFICATE. A certificate issued by a measurement authority recognized by the Board that sets out the registered gross tonnage of a vessel. Canada regulations.

TONNAGE REGULATIONS. The provisions of this Act relating to tonnage together with the rules made hereunder. *Canada Shipping Act*, R.S.C. 1985, c. S-9, s. 2.

TONNAGE-RENT. *n.* Rent reserved by a mining lease or something like it consisting of a royalty on every ton of minerals produced by the mine.

TONNE. *n.* 1. 1,000 kilograms. Canada regulations. 2. (a) Where used as a measurement of weight, 1,000 kilograms; and (b) where used as a measurement of volume, 1 cubic metre. *Wharfage Charges By-law*, C.R.C., c. 1066, s. 2.

TON OF REFRIGERATION. The unit for measuring the capacity of a refrigeration plant. *Boilers and Pressure Vessels Act*, R.S.A. 1970, c. 32, s. 2.

TONS OF REFRIGERATION. Tons of refrigeration computed on the basis of 1 ton of refrigeration per 1.5 motive horsepower. *Boiler and Pressure Vessel Act*, R.S.N.B. 1973, c. B-7, s. 1.

TONS UNDERDECK. The tonnage contained within the space below the main deckline of a ship derived by the following formula:

$$\frac{L \times B \times D \times .45}{100}$$

where L represents the overall length of the ship measured from the foremost part of the stem-head to the aftermost part of the transom rim timber or transom bulwark taffrail on the centre line of the ship, B represents the breadth amid-ships at deckline in feet to the outside of planking and D represents the greater of (i) depth of the vessel amidships in feet from the top of deck beam at centreline of vessel to the top of transverse floors; and (ii) .9 times the depth amidships in feet from the top of deck beam at centre line to the top of the wood keel. Newfoundland statutes.

TOOL. See EXPLOSIVE ACTUATED ~; HAND ~.

TOOL AND DIE MAKER. A person who, (i) sets up and operates to prescribed tolerance engine lathes and milling, grinding, drilling, sawing and boring machines; (ii) reads and interprets blueprints, operation and product-related reference charts and tables and selects mechanical measuring, checking and layout tools and devices; (iii) performs measuring, checking and layout operations and selects work piece materials and the required cutting tools and abrasives for metal removal operations; (iv) performs metal removing operations using hand and power tools and selects work piece clamping and holding devices and product-related com-ponents; (v) performs finishing and assembly operations on dies and sets up dies on presses for testing purposes; and (vi) manufactures component parts and assembles and tests tools, jigs and fixtures, but does not include a person or class of persons in a limited purpose occu-pation that in the opinion of the Director does not equate with the definition of tool and die maker. *Apprenticeship and Tradesmen's Quali-fications Act*, R.R.O. 1980, Reg. 60, s. 1.

TOOLING. *n.* Inclues patterns, jigs, fixtures, moulds, models, dies, gauges and punches. *Auto-motive Manufacturing Assistance Regulations*, C.R.C., c. 966, s. 2.

TO PEDDLE. To carry alcohol, spirits, cider, wine or beer on one's person or to transport it with one, or with the aid of another person, with intent to sell it outside any establishment where the sale thereof is allowed. *An Act Respecting the Commission de Contrôle des Permis D'alcool*, R.S.Q. 1977, c. C-33, s. 2.

TO PROSPECT AND TO EXPLORE. To carry out work preliminary to mining operations, with the purpose of discovering an ore deposit or an underground reservoir and demonstrating the existence thereof. *Mining Act*, R.S.Q. 1977, c. M-13, s. 1.

TO PROVIDE. When used in relation to ser-vices includes to furnish, perform, solicit, or give such services. *Municipal Act*, R.S.O. 1980, c. 302, s. 222.

TOPSOIL. *n.* 1. Soil having the properties that make it suitable for plant growth. *An Act to Preserve Agricultural Land*, S.Q. 1978, c. 10, s. 1. 2. That horizon in a soil profile, known as the "A" horizon, containing organic material. *Topsoil Preservation Act*, R.S.O. 1980, c. 504, s. 1.

TO PURCHASE. Includes to take as mortgagee or as pledgee. Warehouse Receipt acts.

TOP WHARFAGE. A toll charged on goods that are unloaded from or loaded onto a vessel or transhipped between vessels. Canada regula-tions.

TORRENS REGISTRATION SYSTEM. A land titles system devised by Mr. Robert Torrens of South Australia, first embodied in a statute enacted in South Australia in 1857, then in the Colony of Vancouver Island in 1861 and in the province of British Columbia in 1869. B.J. Reiter, R.C.B. Risk & B.N. McLellan, *Real Estate Law*, 3d ed. (Toronto: Emond Montgomery, 1986) at 592.

TORRENS' SYSTEM. See TORRENS REG-ISTRATION SYSTEM.

TORT. *n.* 1. Wrong. 2. Generally, an injury other than a breach of contract for which recovery of damages is permitted by the law. John G. Fleming, *The Law of Torts*, 6th ed. (Sydney: The Law Book Co., 1983) at 1. 3. Includes delict and quasi-delict. *Crown Liability Act*, R.S.C. 1985, c. C-50, s. 2. See ADMINISTRATOR DE SON ~; INTENTIONAL ~; NEGLIGENT ~.

TORTFEASOR. *var.* **TORT-FEASOR.** *n.* 1. A wrongdoer. 2. A party who commits a tort. 3. A person whose wrongful act, neglect, or default has caused the death, or contributed to the cause of death, of the deceased and who, if death had not ensued, would have been liable to him for damages, and includes a person who would have been liable vicariously or otherwise for such damages. Fatal Accidents acts. See INDEPEN-DENT ~S; JOINT ~S.

TORTIOUS. *adj.* Wrongful.

TORTIOUS ACT. A wrongful, injurious or illegal act that results in: (a) loss or damage to the land of an owner or occupant, as the case may be, that is not situated within the surface rights acquired or to be acquired by an operator; and (b) any other loss or damage suffered by the owner or occupant arising out of such act. *The Surface Rights Acquisition and Compensation Act*, R.S.S. 1978, c. S-65, s. 60.

TORT LIABILITY. Requires the wrongdoer to pay for damage done to compensate the victim. John G. Fleming, *The Law of Torts*, 6th ed. (Sydney: The Law Book Co., 1983) at 1.

TO STRIKE. To cease work, or to refuse to work or to continue to work, in combination or in concert or in accordance with a common understanding.

TOTAL. *adj.* Where used in the expression "total and permanent disability" means disability that is severe, in the sense that the employee is incapable of pursuing any substantially gainful occupation. *Civil Service Superannuation Act*, S.M. 1972, c. 78, s. 10.

TOTAL ACTUAL FRONTAGE. The sum of the actual frontage of the parcels of land which actually abuts on the work or highway. *Municipal Act*, R.S.B.C. 1979, c. 290, s. 480.

TOTAL AND PERMANENT DISABILITY. Disability to the extent of wholly disabling a person from engaging in any gainful employment. *Teachers' Pension Act*, R.S.M. 1970, c. T20, s. 2.

TOTAL ASSETS. Includes any amount by which (i) the value of any asset of a corporation, as carried on its account books or on its balance sheet, is in excess of the cost of the asset; or (ii) the value of an asset of a corporation has been written down and deducted from its income or undivided profits, where that amount (A) is not deductible under the Income Tax Act; or (B) is deductible under paragraph (n) of subsection (1) of section 20 or subparagraph (iii) of paragraph (a) of subsection (1) of section 40 of the Income Tax Act, but, unless required in the regulations to be included, does not include any amount by which the value of an asset of a corporation has been written down and deducted from its income or undivided profits, where that amount is deductible under any provision of the Income Tax Act other than those mentioned in clause (B) of subparagraph (ii). Corporations Capital Tax acts.

TOTAL CONTRACT PRICE. The total obligation or consideration, including the cost of borrowing, payable, given, undertaken or assumed by a buyer under a contract for future services. *Consumer Protection Act*, R.S.B.C. 1979, c. 65, s. 24.

TOTAL DISABILITY. (i) During the qualifying period and the first 24 months of the period in respect of which benefits may be paid, the continuous inability of the employee, as the result of illness or injury, to perform any and every duty of his normal occupation; and (ii) during the balance of the period in respect of which benefits may be paid, the inability of the employee, as the result of sickness or injury, to perform any and every duty of any gainful occupation for which he is reasonably fitted by education, training or experience. *Public Service Act*, R.R.O. 1980, Reg. 881, s. 81. See PERMANENT ~.

TOTAL FLOOR AREA. The area of all floors of basements, mezzanines, storeys and penthouses in a building, measured from the inside surface of the exterior or boundary walls. *Hotel Fire Safety Act*, R.R.O. 1980, Reg. 505, s. 2.

TOTALIZATOR MANAGER. The person responsible for the management of the totalizator equipment. *Race Track Supervision Regulations*, C.R.C., c. 441, s. 2.

TOTAL LENGTH. In respect of a fish, the distance from the tip of the head with the jaws closed to the tip of the tail with the lobes compressed so as to give the maximum possible measurement. *Ontario Fishery Regulations*, C.R.C., c. 849, s. 2.

TOTAL LOADED MASS. 1. The mass of a motor vehicle or combination of motor vehicles, including accessories, equipment and load; such mass may be expressed as the aggregate of the axle loads. *Highway Code*, S.Q. 1978, c. 75, s. 3. 2. The mass of a road vehicle or combination of road vehicles, including accessories, equipment and load. *Highway Safety Code*, S.Q. 1986, c. 91, s. 462.

TOTAL LOADED WEIGHT. 1. The aggregate of the loads on all the axles of one motor vehicle or combination of motor vehicles, including accessories and equipment, plus the weight of the load. *Highway Code*, R.S.Q. 1977, c. C-24, s. 1. 2. The weight of a motor vehicle or combination of vehicles, including accessories, equipment and load, expressed as the aggregate of all its axle loads. *Highway Code*, R.S.Q. 1977, c. C-24, s. 54.

TOTAL LOSS. A loss (a) where insured property is destroyed or so damaged as to cease to be a thing of the kind insured; or (b) where the fisherman whose name is on the list in respect of insured property is irretrievably deprived of the property. *Fishing Vessel Insurance Regula-*

tions, C.R.C., c. 325, s. 2. See ACTUAL ~; CONSTRUCTIVE ~.

TOTAL OBLIGATION. The aggregate of the net capital and the credit charges. *Consumer Protection Act*, S.Q. 1978, c. 9, s. 67.

TOTAL SUSPENDED MATTER. The non-filterable residue that results from the operation of a plant, that is contained in the effluent from that plant. Plant Liquid Effluent regulations.

TOTAL TAXABLE FRONTAGE. The sum of the taxable frontage of the parcels of land which abut or are deemed to abut on the work or highway. *Municipal Act*, R.S.B.C. 1979, c. 290, s. 480.

TOTAL WAGE. In respect of any period of employment of an employee, means all remuneration that the employee is paid or is entitled to be paid by his employer, whether or not payment is actually made during that period of employment, in respect of the labour or services that he performs for his employer during that period of employment, and includes: (i) sums deducted from such remuneration for any purpose whatever; (ii) remuneration in respect of overtime work that he performs for his employer during that period of employment; (iii) remuneration in respect of any annual or special holiday that his employer permits him to take during that period of employment; (iv) the cash value of any board or lodging received by the employee as part payment of wages during that period of employment. *The Labour Standards Act*, R.S.S. 1978, c. L-1, s. 2.

TOTE ROAD. An unsurfaced road of a temporary nature over which construction materials and supplies are moved. *Highway (Industrial) Act*, R.S.B.C. 1979, c. 168, s. 1.

TOTIDEM VERBIS. [L.] In just as many words.

TOTIES QUOTIES. [L.] As often as possible.

TOT LOT. An area set aside as a public playground for the use of children of pre-school age. Canada regulations.

TOUGH GRAIN. Any grain within the meaning of this Act that has a moisture content that classifies it as tough grain in the Canada Grain Regulations made pursuant to the Canada Grain Act. *Prairie Grain Advance Payment Act*, R.S.C. 1985, c. P-18, s. 9(5).

TOUJOURS ET ENCORE PRESZ. [Fr.] Always and still ready.

TOUR. *n.* A round or circle trip performed in whole or in part by air for an inclusive tour price for the period the participants are away from the starting point of the journey. *Air Carrier Regulations*, C.R.C., c. 3, s. 23. See INCLUSIVE ~.

TOUR FEATURES. All goods, services, facilities and benefits other than accommodation and transportation that are included in an ITC program at the inclusive tour price or made available to tour participants as optional extras at an additional charge. *Air Carrier Regulations*, C.R.C., c. 3, s. 49.

TOURISM PROMOTION. Mass consumer and trade advertising, including special events support, travel information counselling and other activities designed to improve public relations. *Tourism Act*, R.R.O. 1980, Reg. 936, s. 14.

TOURIST. *n.* A person not ordinarily resident who visits a province for a vacation.

TOURIST ACCOMMODATION. (a) Land on which rental units are situate; or (b) land used by the public as a camping ground or trailer park, whether or not a charge is made for its rental or use. *Travel Bureau Act*, R.S.B.C. 1979, c. 410, s. 1.

TOURIST CAMP. Includes auto camp and any parcel of land or premises equipped with cabins used or maintained for the accommodation of the public, and any parcel of land or premises used or maintained as a camping or parking ground for the public whether or not a fee or charge is paid or made for the rental or use thereof.

TOURIST ESTABLISHMENT. 1. Includes any premises operated to provide sleeping accommodation for the public, the services and facilities in connection with which sleeping accommodation is provided, any premises where lodging, meals, lunches or restroom facilities are offered to the public, and other facilities that are operated as tourist attractions or services. 2. (i) Any premises or boat that provides sleeping accommodation; (ii) any campsite equipped for the supplying of water or electricity or the disposal of garbage or sewage; or (iii) any picnic area, bathing area or recreation area for the travelling public or persons engaging in outdoor recreational activities, but does not include a private cottage or residence. *Travel and Tourism Act*, S.N.W.T. 1983 (1st Sess.), c. 15, s. 2.

TOURIST INFORMATION BUREAU. Any establishment whose main activity is the providing of information to the public about lodgings, restaurants, camping and trailer facilities or tourist attractions in Québec. *An Act to Amend The Hotels Act*, S.Q. 1986, c. 45, s. 1.

TOURIST INFORMATION CENTRE. A place that is held out to the public as being available for or engaged in furnishing travel information to the public whether for hire or reward or otherwise. *Tourism Development Act*, R.S.N.B. 1973, c. T-9, s. 1.

TOURIST OUTFITTER ESTABLISHMENT. A tourist establishment that, (i) throughout all or part of a year furnishes accommodation; (ii) may or may not furnish three meals a day; and (iii) furnishes equipment, supplies or services to persons in connection with angling, hunting, camping or recreational purposes. *Tourism Act*, R.R.O. 1980, Reg. 936, s. 1.

TOUR OPERATOR. A charterer with whom an air carrier has contracted to charter an aircraft in whole or in part for the purpose of operating an inclusive tour. *Air Carrier Regulations*, C.R.C., c. 3, s. 23.

TOUT TEMPS PRESZ ET ENCORE EST. [Fr.] With respect to a defendant, was always and still is ready.

TOW. *v.* 1. To pull or push any floating object. Canada regulations. 2. To push, pull or otherwise move through the water. *Canal Regulations*, C.R.C., c. 1564, s. 2.

TOW. *n.* Includes every kind of ship, boat, barge, elevator, scow or other floating craft that is not propelled by steam or any other means of propulsion but that is towed by a vessel. *North Fraser Harbour Commission By-laws*, C.R.C., c. 909, s. 2.

TOWAGE. *n.* 1. The transporting of logs or timber products from one place to another within the Province by towing the same through the water by a tugboat, whether towed in booms, rafts or cribs, or on board scows, barges or vessels. *Tugboat Worker Lien Act*, R.S.B.C. 1979, c. 417, s. 1. 2. A charge for towing service in connection with crane service. *Saint John Floating Crane Tariff By-law*, C.R.C., c. 1090, s. 2.

TOW BAR. A towing structure that is connected to the chassis frame of the forward axle of a full trailer and which includes an eye or equivalent device for the purpose of coupling with a trailer hitch. *Highway Traffic Act*, R.R.O. 1980, Reg. 489, s. 1.

TOW CAR. A motor vehicle used exclusively for towing or rendering assistance to other motor vehicles or to vehicles suffering from a defect or disability in their means of locomotion. *Motor Vehicle Amendment Act (No. 2)*, S.B.C. 1985, c. 78, s. 1.

TOWED CONVEYANCE. Includes any sled, cutter, trailer, toboggan or carrier that may be towed by a snowmobile. *The Snowmobile Act*, R.S.S. 1978, c. S-52, s. 2.

TOWEL. See SINGLE-SERVICE ~.

TOWING LIGHT. A yellow light having the same characteristics as the "sternlight" defined in paragraph (c) of this Rule. *Collision Regulations*, C.R.C., c. 1416, Rule 3.

TO WIT. Namely.

TOWN. *n.* An area incorporated as a town. See COMPANY ~; SEPARATED ~.

TOWN DISTRICT. A school district situated wholly or in part within a town or city: but where a portion of a rural or village district is included within a town or city, the district shall become a town district on a date to be determined by the minister. *The School Act*, R.S.S. 1978, c. S-36, s. 2.

TOWN PLAN. See OFFICIAL ~.

TOWN SCHOOL DISTRICT. 1. A school district situated wholly or in part within the limits of a town and includes a school district situated wholly within the boundaries of a local government district. *Public Schools Act*, R.S.M. 1970, c. P250, s. 2. 2. A town school district as defined by The School Act. *The Municipal Unit and County Act*, R.S.S. 1978, c. M-35, s. 2.

TOWNSHIP. *n.* Any territory erected into a township. See DOUBLE FRONT ~; EASTERN ~S; FRONT AND REAR ~; SECTIONAL ~ WITH DOUBLE FRONTS; SECTIONAL ~ WITH SECTIONS AND QUARTER SECTIONS; SECTIONAL ~ WITH SINGLE FRONTS; SINGLE FRONT ~.

TOWNSITE. *n.* A subdivision of land into lots intended for residential or business purposes or both, and not adjoining or adjacent to a hamlet, village, town or city. *The Planning and Development Act*, R.S.S. 1978, c. P-13, s. 2.

TOXIC. *adj.* Acting as or relating to poison. F.A. Jaffe, *A Guide to Pathological Evidence*, 2d ed. (Toronto: Carswell, 1983) at 185.

TOXIC EFFECT. Something caused by an overdose. F.A. Jaffe, *A Guide to Pathological Evidence*, 2d ed. (Toronto: Carswell, 1983) at 61.

TOXICOLOGY. *n.* The study of poisons, their detection and effects. F.A. Jaffe, *A Guide to Pathological Evidence*, 2d ed. (Toronto: Carswell, 1983) at 185 and 186.

TOXICOMANIA. *n.* A pathological condition other than alcoholism, related to the consumption of a toxic substance and disturbing the physical and psychical balance and the social behaviour of persons suffering therefrom. *An Act Respecting the Office de la Prévention de L'alcoolisme et des Autres Toxicomanies*, R.S.Q. 1977, c. O-2, s. 1.

TOXIC SUBSTANCE. Any chemical, biological or physical agent, or combination of such agents, which may be used in a workplace, to which a worker may be exposed and which may be harmful to that worker. D. Robertson, *Ontario Health and Safety Guide* (Toronto: Richard De Boo Ltd., 1988) at 5-404.

TOXIN. *n.* A poisonous substance which animals, bacteria or plants produce. F.A. Jaffe, *A Guide to Pathological Evidence*, 2d ed. (Toronto: Carswell, 1983) at 186.

TOY. See SOFT ~.

TRACE. See VERTEBRATE ~ FOSSIL.

TRACE EVIDENCE. Evidence based on examining small amounts of biological material, i.e. blood, soil or textile fibres. F.A. Jaffe, *A Guide to Pathological Evidence*, 2d ed. (Toronto: Carswell, 1983) at 176.

TRACE-MINERAL-SALT FEED. A mineral feed that contains only ingredients incorporated to supply trace mineral elements and salt (NaCl). *Feeds Regulations*, C.R.C., c. 665, s. 2.

TRACHEA. *n.* The windpipe, a tube of cartilage which connects the bronchi with the larynx. F.A. Jaffe, *A Guide to Pathological Evidence*, 2d ed. (Toronto: Carswell, 1983) at 186.

TRACHEOSTOMY. *n.* A surgical operation which opens the trachea to make breathing easier. F.A. Jaffe, *A Guide to Pathological Evidence*, 2d ed. (Toronto: Carswell, 1983) at 186.

TRACHEOTOMY. *n.* A surgical operation which opens the trachea to make breathing easier. F.A. Jaffe, *A Guide to Pathological Evidence*, 2d ed. (Toronto: Carswell, 1983) at 186.

TRACING. *n.* The right to follow property into the hands of a defendant. A. Bissett-Johnson & W.M. Holland, eds., *Matrimonial Property Law in Canada* (Toronto: Carswell, 1980) at O-25.

TRACK. *n.* 1. The scar caused by repeated injection of drugs directly into a vein. F.A. Jaffe, *A Guide to Pathological Evidence*, 2d ed. (Toronto: Carswell, 1983) at 186. 2. The projection on the earth's surface of the path of an aircraft, the direction of which path at any point is usually expressed in degrees from North (true, magnetic or grid). *Air Regulations*, C.R.C., c, 2, s. 101. See MAIN ~; PRIVATE ~; RACE ~; SERVING ~; SINGLE ~; TEAM ~; TWO OR MORE ~S.

TRACK OPERATOR. A person who owns or operates a race track.

TRACT. *n.* 1. A mining tract. 2. An area within a drilling spacing unit or a pool, as the case may be, within which an owner has the right or an interest in the right to drill for and produce oil or gas. 3. A contiguous area of land which (i) two or more persons jointly have; or (ii) two or more persons have an undivided interest in; the right to mine for and remove minerals either because of having joint or common title to those minerals or under a lease or licence from a person or persons having individual, or joint or common, title to those minerals. 4. The land described in a certificate of title. *Freehold Mineral Right Tax Act*, S.A. 1983, c. F-19.1, s. 1. See MARSHLAND ~; POOLED ~; PRODUCING ~, PRODUCTION ~; SUBMARINE ~; UNIT ~.

TRACTION ENGINE. A mechanically-propelled vehicle running on wheels or caterpillar tracks and designed primarily for traction purposes and not constructed itself to carry a load other than motor tools, storage batteries and other equipment used for the purpose of propulsion, loose tools and equipment, and includes snow ploughs, road conditioning machines and the like. *Highway Traffic Act*, R.S.Nfld. 1970, c. 152, s. 2.

TRACT OF LAND. An area of land comprising 2 or more parcels, whether contiguous or not. *Municipal Act*, R.S.B.C. 1979, c. 290, s. 824.

TRACTOR. *n.* 1. Includes any vehicle designed primarily (i) as a travelling power plant for independent operation or for operating other machines or appliances; or (ii) for drawing other vehicles or machines, and not designed for carrying goods or passengers wholly or in part on its structure. 2. A self-propelled vehicle that is designed primarily for traction purposes, and that is not itself constructed to carry any load other than the driver. See FARM ~; MOTOR ~; ROAD ~; TRUCK ~.

TRACTOR-FLOAT COMBINATION. A motor vehicle consisting of a tractor or truck with a float. Canada regulations.

TRACTOR-TRAILER COMBINATION. A motor vehicle consisting of a tractor with a semi-trailer. Canada regulations.

TRACT PARTICIPATION. The share of production from a unitized zone that is allocated to a unit tract under a unit agreement or unitization order or the share of production from a pooled spacing unit that is allocated to a pooled tract under a pooling agreement or pooling order.

TRADE. *n.* 1. Includes industry, craft and business and any branch of any trade, industry, craft or business. 2. The selling, purchasing, exchanging, consigning, leasing or providing of any commodity, right, facility or service on the basis of measure and includes the business of providing facilities for measuring. *Weights and Measures Act*, R.S.C. 1985, c. W-6, s. 2. 3. Includes (a) a disposition of a security for valuable consideration, whether the terms of payment be on margin, instalment or otherwise, but does not include a purchase of a security; (b) participation as a floor trader in a transaction in a security on the floor of a stock exchange; (c) the receipt by a registrant of an order to buy or sell a security; (d) a transfer, pledge, mortgage or other encumbrance of a security of an issuer for the purpose of giving collateral for a debt, or the transfer of beneficial ownership of that security to the transferee, pledgee, mortgagee or other encumbrancer under a realization on that collateral; and (e) any act, advertisement, solicitation, conduct or negotiation directly or indirectly in furtherance of any of the activities specified in paragraphs (a) to (d). Securities acts. 4. (i) A disposition or acquisition of or transaction in real estate by sale, purchase, agreement for sale, exchange, option, lease, rental or otherwise; (ii) an offer or attempt to list real estate for a disposition or transaction referred to in subclause (i); or (iii) an act, advertisement, conduct or negotiation directly or indirectly in furtherance of such a disposition, acquisition, transaction, offer or attempt. Real Estate Agents' Licensing acts. See ADVENTURE IN THE NATURE OF A ~; BALANCE OF ~; BOARD OF ~; BUSINESS OR ~ ASSOCIATION; COASTAL ~; COASTING ~; CUSTOM OF THE ~; DAIRY PRODUCTS ~; LIQUIDATING ~; RESTRAINT OF ~; RETAIL ~; SPECIAL PASSENGER ~; STREET ~; WHOLESALE ~.

TRADE AGREEMENT. Any agreement or arrangement relating to international trade to which the Government of Canada is a party. *Customs Tariff Act*, R.S.C. 1985, c. C-54, s. 26.

TRADE AND COMMERCE. A power of the federal Parliament under section 91(2) of the Constitution Act, 1867. P.W. Hogg, *Constitutional Law of Canada*, 2d ed. (Toronto: Carswell, 1985) at 439.

TRADE COMBINATION. Any combination between masters or workmen or other persons for the purpose of regulating or altering the relations between masters or workmen, or the conduct of a master or workman in or in respect of his business, employment or contract of employment. *Criminal Code*, R.S.C. 1985, c. C-46, s. 467(2).

TRADE CREDITOR. See SECURED ~; UNSECURED ~.

TRADE DIVISION. All unionized employers: (i) in a trade; or (ii) in an identifiable class or group of unionized employers in a trade; in a sector or sectors of the construction industry. *Construction Industry Labour Relations Act*, S.S. 1979, c. C-29.1, s. 2.

TRADE FIXTURES. The fixtures, machinery, and other chattels, other than stock, with which a person carries on a business. *Bulk Sales Act*, R.S.Nfld. 1970, c. 28, s. 2.

TRADE-IN. *n.* Consideration given by a buyer in a form other than money or an obligation to pay money. Consumer Protection acts.

TRADE-IN ALLOWANCE. (a) The sum which, under a trade-in arrangement, is agreed to be allowed in payment or in part payment for the goods or services sold or to be sold under the executory contract; or, (b) if that sum is not agreed on, an amount that would, in all the circumstances, have been reasonable to allow in payment or in part payment for the goods or services if no notice of recission had been given.

TRADE-IN ARRANGEMENT. An agreement or arrangement, contained in a sales contract or forming the whole or part of a related agreement, whereby the buyer sells or agrees to sell his own goods to the seller or any other person and the goods are accepted as the whole or part of the consideration under the sales contract.

TRADE, INDUSTRY OR PROFESSION. Includes any class, division or branch of a trade, industry or profession. *Combines Investigation Act*, R.S.C. 1985, c. C-34, s. 2.

TRADE L. TOPICS. *abbr.* Trade Law Topics.

TRADE MACHINERY. Machinery used at a workshop, except (a) fixed motive power units such as steam engines, steam boilers and things fixed to them; (b) fixed power machinery such as shafts, wheels, drums and things fixed to them, used to transmit motive power to other machinery, fixed or loose; and (c) pipes for steam, gas and water in the workshop. *Chattel Mortgage Act*, R.S.B.C. 1979, c. 48, s. 1.

TRADE-MARK. *var.* **TRADE MARK.** (a) A mark that is used by a person for the purpose of distinguishing or so as to distinguish wares or services manufactured, sold, leased, hired or performed by him from those manufactured, sold, leased, hired or performed by others; (b) a certification mark; (c) a distinguishing guise; or (d) a proposed trade-mark. *Trade-Marks Act*, R.S.C. 1985, c. T-13, s. 2. See ASSOCIATED ~S; GENUINE ~; NATIONAL ~; PROPOSED ~; REGISTERED ~.

TRADE MARK AGENT. A person whose name is on the register of trade mark agents referred to in section 21. *Trade Marks Regulations*, C.R.C., c. 1559, s. 2.

TRADE-NAME. *var.* **TRADE NAME.** The name under which any business is carried on, whether or not it is the name of a corporation, a partnership or an individual. *Trade-Marks Act*, R.S.C. 1985, c. T-13, s. 2.

TRADE OR TRADING. 1. Includes (i) any sale or disposition of a security for valuable consideration, whether the terms of payment be on margin, instalment or otherwise, or, except as provided in subclause (iv), a transfer, pledge or encumbrance of securities for the purpose of giving collateral for a bona fide debt; (ii) any participation as a floor trader in any transaction in a security upon the floor of any stock exchange; (iii) any receipt by a registrant of an order to buy or sell a security; (iv) any transfer, pledge or encumbrancing of securities of an issuer from the holdings of any person or company or combination of persons or companies as described in the act for the purpose of giving collateral for a bona fide debt; and (v) any act, advertisement, solicitation, conduct or negotiation directly or indirectly in furtherance of any of the foregoing. Securities acts. 2. Includes a disposition or acquisition of or transaction in real estate by sale, purchase, agreement for sale, exchange, option, lease, rental or otherwise and any offer or attempt to list real estate for the purpose of such a disposition or transaction, and any act, advertisement, conduct or negotiation, directly or indirectly, in furtherance of any disposition, acquisition, transaction, offer or attempt. Real Estate Brokers' Licensing acts. 3. Includes (i) a purchase or sale or disposition of or other dealing in or a solicitation in respect of a franchise for valuable consideration whether the terms of the payment are by instalment or otherwise, or any attempt to do any of the foregoing; (ii) any act, advertisement, conduct or negotiation directly or indirectly in furtherance of any of the activities referred to in subclause (i). *Franchises Act*, R.S.A. 1980, c. F-17, s. 1. 4. (a) Entering into commodity contracts, whether as principal or agent; (b) acting as a floor trader; (c) a receipt by a registrant of an order to effect a transaction in a commodity contract; (d) an assignment or other disposition of rights under a commodity contract except a disposition arising from the death of an individual enjoying rights under a commodity contract; and (e) an act, advertisement, solicitation, conduct or negotiation directly or indirectly in furtherance of any of the activities specified in paragraphs (a) to (d). *Commodity Contract Amendment Act*, S.B.C. 1985, c. 2, s. 1.

TRADER. *n.* Any person who trades in the course of business. *Weights and Measures Act*, R.S.C. 1985, c. W-6, s. 2. 2. Anyone who uses or trades in pulpwood. *An Act Respecting the Sales Price of Pulpwood Sold by Farmers and Settlers*, R.S.Q. 1977, c. P-25, s. 1. See FLOOR ~; FUR ~; TRANSIENT ~.

TRADE PRACTICES. See RESTRICTIVE ~ COMMISSION.

TRADE SCHOOL. *var.* **TRADE-SCHOOL.** Any school or place in which a trade is taught and includes any course of study whether by correspondence or otherwise offered or operated by any person other than (a) a chartered university in Canada; (b) a department of the Government of Canada or of any province; (c) a board of school trustees; (d) a trade school organized or operated solely for the employees of a corporation, industry or plant; or (e) a school or course exempted by the Lieutenant-Governor in Council. Trade Schools acts. See PRIVATE ~.

TRADE SECRET. Something known only to an employer and those employees to whom it is necessary to confide it, which may be improperly used. H.G. Fox, *The Canadian Law of Trade Marks and Unfair Competition*, 3d ed. (Toronto: Carswell, 1972) at 654.

TRADE SIZE. Any size designation traditionally used by the trade, but restricted to products or classes of products manufactured to a standard or specification, so that the designated trade size may be referred to an industry accepted table or chart which then provides the true dimensions of the item in question. *Ontario Water Resources Act*, R.R.O. 1980, Reg. 736, s. 1.

TRADESMAN. See SKILLED ~.

TRADESPERSON. *n.* A person other than an apprentice, who works for remuneration at any designated trade, including an employer who so works.

TRADE TERMS. Terms in respect of payment, units of purchase and reasonable technical and servicing requirements. *Combines Investigation Act*, R.S.C. 1985 (2d Supp.), c. 19, s. 75(3).

TRADE UNION. *var.* **TRADE-UNION.** 1. Any organization of employees, or any branch or local thereof, the purposes of which include the regulation of relations between employers and employees. 2. Such combination, whether temporary or permanent, for regulating the relations between workmen and masters, or for imposing restrictive conditions on the conduct of any trade or business, as would, but for this Act, have been deemed to be an unlawful combination by reason of some one or more of its purposes being in restraint of trade. *Trade Unions Act*, R.S.C. 1985, c. T-14, s. 2. See COUNCIL OF ~S.

TRADE UNION BENEFIT SOCIETY. A society, association or corporation, membership in which is restricted exclusively to bona fide members of one trade union and which under the authority of its charter has an assurance or benefit fund for the benefit of its own members exclusively. *Insurance Act*, R.S.M. 1970, c.I40, s. 2.

TRADING. See INSIDER ~.

TRADING COMPANY. Any company, except a railway or telegraph company, carrying on business similar to that carried on by apothecaries, auctioneers, bankers, brokers, brickmakers, builders, carpenters, carriers, cattle or sheep salesmen, coach proprietors, dyers, fullers, keepers of inns, taverns, hotels, saloons or coffee houses, lime burners, livery stable keepers, market gardeners, millers, miners, packers, printers, quarrymen, sharebrokers, ship-owners, shipwrights, stockbrokers, stock-jobbers, victuallers, warehousemen, wharfingers, persons using the trade of merchandise by way of bargaining, exchange, bartering, commission, consignment or otherwise, in gross or by retail, or by persons who, either for themselves, or as agents or factors for others, seek their living by buying and selling or buying and letting for hire goods or commodities, or by the manufacture, workmanship or the conversion of goods or commodities or trees. *Winding-Up Act*, R.S.C. 1985, c. W-11, s. 2.

TRADING STAMP. Any form of cash receipt, receipt, coupon, stamp, premium ticket or other device designed or intended to be given to the purchaser of goods by the vendor thereof or on his behalf, and to represent a discount on the price of goods or a premium to the purchaser thereof, but does not include an offer, endorsed by the manufacturer upon a wrapper or container in which goods are sold, of a premium or reward for the return of that wrapper or container to the manufacturer. The Trading Stamp Acts.

TRADING STAMPS. Includes any form of cash receipt, receipt, coupon, premium ticket or other device, designed or intended to be given to the purchaser of goods by the vendor thereof or on his behalf, and to represent a discount on the price of the goods or a premium to the purchaser thereof (a) that may be redeemed (i) by a person other than the vendor, the person from whom the vendor purchased the goods or the manufacturer of the goods; (ii) by the vendor, the person from whom the vendor purchased the goods or the manufacturer of the goods in cash or in goods that are not his property in whole or in part; or (iii) by the vendor elsewhere than in the premises where the goods are purchased; or (b) that does not show on its face the place where it is delivered and the merchantable value thereof; or (c) that may not be redeemed on

demand at any time, but an offer, endorsed by the manufacturer on a wrapper or container in which goods are sold, of a premium or reward for the return of that wrapper or container to the manufacturer is not a trading stamp. *Criminal Code*, R.S.C. 1985, c. C-46, s. 379.

TRADITIO LOQUI CHARTAM FACIT. [L.] Delivery gives a deed its voice.

TRADITION. *n.* Handing over; delivering.

TRADITIONAL OR ARTISTIC CHARACTERISTICS. In respect of any handicraft goods, means (a) any form or decoration used traditionally by the indigenous people; or (b) any form or decoration that represents any national, territorial or religious symbol of the geographical region in which the goods were produced. *Handicraft Goods Order*, C.R.C., c. 531, s. 2.

TRAFFIC. *v.* 1. To manufacture, sell, export from or import into Canada, transport or deliver, otherwise than under the authority of this Part or the regulations. *Food and Drugs Act*, R.S.C. 1985, c. F-27, s. 38. 2. To sell, buy, barter, solicit or trade or offer to do so. Wildlife acts. 3. (a) To manufacture, sell, give, administer, transport, send, deliver or distribute; or (b) to offer to do anything referred to in paragraph (a) otherwise than under the authority of this Act or the regulations. *Narcotic Control Act*, R.S.C. 1985, c. N-1, s. 2.

TRAFFIC. *n.* 1. Includes pedestrians and ridden, driven, or herded animals and vehicles, and other conveyances, either singly or together, while using a highway for purposes of travel. 2. The traffic of passengers, goods and rolling stock. Railway acts. 3. The transmission of and other dealings with telegraphic and telephonic messages. 4. Any persons, goods or mail that are transported by air. *Air Carrier Regulations*, C.R.C., c. 3, s. 2. See AERODROME ~ ZONE; AIRPORT ~; APRON ~; CURRENT OF ~; DIRECTION OF ~ FLOW; EXTRAORDINARY ~; INCIDENTAL ~; INTERNATIONAL ~.

TRAFFIC CONTROL CENTRE. See MARINE ~.

TRAFFIC CONTROL DEVICE. *var.* **TRAFFIC-CONTROL DEVICE.** Any sign, signal, marking or device placed, marked or erected for the purpose of regulating, warning or guiding traffic.

TRAFFIC CONTROLLER. See VESSEL ~.

TRAFFIC CONTROL LIGHT. The light shown by traffic control signal. *The Highway Traffic Act*, S.M. 1985-86, c. 3, s. 1.

TRAFFIC CONTROL SIGNAL. *var.* **TRAFFIC-CONTROL SIGNAL.** 1. A traffic control device, whether manually, electrically, or mechanically operated, by which, when operating, traffic is directed to stop and to proceed. 2. That part of a traffic control signal system that consists of one set of no less than three coloured lenses, red, amber and green, mounted on a frame and commonly referred to as a signal head. *Highway Traffic Amendment Act*, S.O. 1984, c. 21, s. 9.

TRAFFIC CONTROL SIGNAL SYSTEM. All of the signal equipment making up the installation at any location. *Highway Traffic Amendment Act*, S.O. 1984, c. 21, s. 9.

TRAFFIC JUSTICE. A justice of the peace who is appointed to the court under section 4. *The Traffic Safety Court of Saskatchewan Act*, R.S.S. 1978, c. T-19, s. 2.

TRAFFIC LANE. 1. A longitudinal division of a public highway of sufficient width to accommodate the passage of a single line of vehicles. 2. A route within which there is one direction of traffic flow. *Collision Regulations*, C.R.C., c. 1416, s. 2.

TRAFFIC SEPARATION SCHEME. A routing measure that provides for the separation of opposing streams of traffic by appropriate means and by the establishment of traffic lanes. *Collision Regulations*, C.R.C., c. 1416, s. 2.

TRAFFIC SIGNAL. See OFFICIAL ~S.

TRAFFIC SIGN. Includes all traffic-control signals, warning sign-posts, direction-posts, signs, lines, marks or other devices for the guidance of persons using highways. See OFFICIAL ~S.

TRAFFIC ZONE. See INSHORE ~.

TRAIL. *n.* The whole of any trail established and maintained by a recreational organization for the use of motorized snow vehicles. *Motorized Snow Vehicles Amendment Act*, S.O. 1982, c. 13, s. 1. See PUBLIC ~; REGIONAL ~.

TRAILER. *n.* 1. A vehicle so designed that it may be attached to or drawn by a motor vehicle and intended to transport property or persons and includes any trailer that is designed, constructed and equipped as a dwelling place, living abode or sleeping place, either permanently or temporarily, but does not include machinery or equipment used in the construction or maintenance of highways. 2. A vehicle designed for carrying persons or chattels, and for being towed by a motor vehicle, and includes a farm trailer but does not include an implement of husbandry that is temporarily towed, propelled or moved upon a highway. 3. A trailer, a semi-trailer or a mobile home which is used, or intended to be used, as a dwelling, office or commercial or

industrial establishment and which has not become an immoveable. *An Act Respecting Municipal Taxation and Providing Amendments to Certain Legislation*, S.Q. 1979, c. 72, s. 1. 4. A film used only for advertising purposes. *Theatres Act*, R.R.O. 1980, Reg. 931, s. 1. 5. (a) With respect to a harness horse race, a horse that starts a race from a position in the second tier of horses behind the starting gate; and (b) with respect to anything else in these Regulations, a vehicle designed to be hauled. *Race Track Supervision Regulations*, C.R.C., c. 441, s. 2. See BOAT ~; BUS ~; CABIN ~; CABLE REEL ~; FARM ~; FULL ~; HEAVY HAULER ~; HOUSE ~; POLE ~; SNOWMOBILE ~; TENT ~; TRACTOR-~ COMBINATION; TRAVEL ~.

TRAILER CAMP. 1. A parcel of land, not in a Provincial Park or mobile home park, (a) intended as the location for temporary residential purposes of two or more trailers other than mobile homes; or (b) upon which two or more trailers other than mobile homes are located for temporary residential purposes. New Brunswick statutes. 2. Land in or upon which any vehicle, so constructed that it is suitable for being attached to a motor vehicle for the purpose of being drawn or propelled by the motor vehicle, is placed, located, kept or maintained, notwithstanding that such vehicle is jacked-up or that its running gear is removed, but not including any vehicle unless it is used for the living, sleeping or eating accommodation of persons therein. *Municipal Act*, R.S.O. 1980, c. 302, s. 232.

TRAILER COACH. Any vehicle used or constructed in such a way as to enable it to be used as a conveyance upon public streets or highways and includes a self-propelled or non-self-propelled vehicle designed, constructed or reconstructed in such a manner as will permit the occupancy thereof as a dwelling or sleeping place for one or more persons notwithstanding that its running gear is removed or that it is jacked up. *The Public Health Act*, R.S.S. 1978, c. P-37, s. 2.

TRAILER CONVERTER DOLLY. A device consisting of one or more axles, a fifth wheel lower-half and a tow bar.

TRAILER COURT. Any tract or parcel of land on which two or more occupied trailer coaches are or are permitted to be harboured whether or not a charge is made or paid for the use thereof and includes any building or structure used or intended for use as a part of the equipment of such trailer court, but does not include an industrial or construction camp. *The Public Health Act*, R.S.S. 1978, c. P-37, s. 2.

TRAILER HITCH. A coupling device mounted on the rear of a truck tractor or trailer to which a tow bar may be attached for the purpose of towing a full trailer. *Highway Traffic Act,* R.R.O. 1980, Reg. 489, s. 1.

TRAILER PARK. An area that is intended to be used, and is used, primarily as a site for the placing or parking of mobile houses, and includes any buildings or other structures or facilities intended for, or to be used for, cooking, personal cleanliness, washing, health, or sanitation, or any one or more or all of those purposes. *Municipal Act,* S.M. 1970, c. 100, s. 437.

TRAIN. *n.* 1. Includes an engine, locomotive and other rolling stock. 2. An engine or more than one engine coupled, with or without cars, displaying markers. *Regulations No. O-8, Uniform Code of Operating Rules,* C.R.C., c. 1175, Part III, s. 2. See EXTRA ~; PASSENGER-~ SERVICE; REGULAR ~; SUPERIOR ~.

TRAINABLE RETARDED CHILD. An exceptional pupil whose intellectual functioning is below the level at which he could profit from a special education program for educable retarded pupils. *Education Act,* R.S.O. 1980, c. 129, s. 1.

TRAINABLE RETARDED PUPIL. See TRAINABLE RETARDED CHILD.

TRAINER. *n.* A person who is licensed by a Commission to train, prepare, enter and manage a horse or horses for racing and includes a person appointed by a trainer to represent him. *Race Track Supervision Regulations,* C.R.C., c. 441, s. 2.

TRAINING. See LANGUAGE ~; OCCUPATIONAL ~; VOCATIONAL ~.

TRAINING CONTRACT. An agreement between a person engaged in the business of providing a training course and a purchaser under which the person undertakes to provide a training course to the purchaser or to a person designated by the purchaser. *The Sale of Training Courses Act,* R.S.S. 1978, c. S-3, s. 2.

TRAINING COURSE. Any course of study or instruction and, for greater certainty but without limiting the generality of the foregoing, includes a course of study or instruction in dancing, health-improvement or self-defence or any course of study or instruction commonly known as a charm or modelling course; but does not include any course of study or instruction provided by: (i) The University of Saskatchewan; (ii) a secondary education institution maintained under and in accordance with The Secondary Education Act; (iii) a school administered by the board of trustees of a school district under The

School Act or The Larger School Units Act, by a board of education established under The School Act or any former School Act, by a joint board established under The School Act or by a board established under The Community Colleges Act; (iv) a vocational education committee established under The Vocational Education Act or any former Vocational Education Act; or (v) a department of the Government of Canada or Saskatchewan or an aviation club operated under the auspices or supervision of such a department. *The Sale of Training Courses Act,* R.S.S. 1978, c. S-3, s. 2.

TRAINING FACILITY. See HEALTH ~.

TRAINING PROFILE. The training curriculum approved by the Director for the various branches of the certified trade, including the units of study required for in-school and work experience training. *Apprenticeship and Tradesmen's Qualification Act,* R.R.O. 1980, regulations.

TRAINING SCHOOL. See DRIVER ~.

TRAINING VEHICLE. See DUAL-CONTROL ~.

TRAIN OF SUPERIOR CLASS. A train given precedence by time table. *Regulations No. O-8, Uniform Code of Operating Rules,* C.R.C., c. 1175, Part III, s. 2.

TRAIN OF SUPERIOR DIRECTION. A train given precedence in the direction specified by time table as between opposing trains of the same class. *Regulations No. O-8, Uniform Code of Operating Rules,* C.R.C., c. 1175, Part III, s. 2.

TRAIN OF SUPERIOR RIGHT. A train given precedence by train order. *Regulations No. O-8, Uniform Code of Operating Rules,* C.R.C., c. 1175, Part III, s. 2.

TRAIN ORDER SIGNAL. A fixed signal provided at train order offices used in connection with the delivery of train orders and as prescribed by Rule 91A. *Regulations No. O-8, Uniform Code of Operating Rules,* C.R.C., c. 1175, Part III, s. 2.

TRAIN REGISTER. A book or form used at designated stations for registering signals displayed, the time of arrival and departure of trains, and such other information as may be prescribed. *Regulations No. O-8, Uniform Code of Operating Rules,* C.R.C., c. 1175, Part III, s. 2.

TRAITOR. *n.* A person who betrays a trust; a person guilty of treason.

TRAMMEL NET. A net that (a) is used to catch fish by enmeshing them by means of two different sizes of mesh; and (b) does not enclose an area of water. *Manitoba Fishery Regulations*, C.R.C., c. 843, s. 2.

TRAMWAY. *n.* Street railroad, railway or tramway for the conveyance of passengers, operated by motive power other than steam, and usually constructed in whole or in part in, under or above public streets, roads, ways and places, and the poles, wires and other appliances and equipment connected therewith. See AERIAL ~; ELECTRIC ~.

TRANQUILIZER. *n.* A drug which induces calmness, used to treat anxiety. F.A. Jaffe, *A Guide to Pathological Evidence*, 2d ed. (Toronto: Carswell, 1983) at 186.

TRANSACTION. *n.* 1. In relation to securities, includes the purchase, sale or transfer thereof, whether or not the securities had previously been distributed, and includes any act, advertisement, conduct or negotiation directly or indirectly in furtherance of the purchase, sale or transfer thereof. *Bank Act*, R.S.C. 1985, c. B-1, s. 190. 2. (i) A sale or exchange of, dealing in, or other disposition of, real estate or an interest in, or option upon, real estate, for valuable consideration or hope or promise thereof, whether upon terms, payment by instalments, the mortgaging of property or otherwise; or (ii) the offering, listing, or advertising, of real estate for sale; or (iii) the showing of real estate for sale to potential purchasers; or (iv) the collection of rent by a broker or salesman; or (v) the solicitation or obtaining of a contract, agreement, or any other arrangement to advertise real estate for sale, exchange, or other disposition thereof, either directly or indirectly, through any medium of advertising; and includes any conduct, act or negotiation, directly or indirectly, in the furtherance or attempted furtherance of any one or more of the things mentioned in this clause. *Real Estate Brokers Act*, R.S.M. 1970, c. R20, s. 2. 3. Includes purchase or receipt by a salvage dealer and sale or delivery by him. *Salvage Dealers Licensing Act*, S.N.B. 1975, c. 55, s. 1. 4. Includes an arrangement or event. *Income Tax Act*, R.S.C. 1952, c. 148 (as am. S.C. 1988, c. 55, s. 185), s. 245(1). See CAPITAL ~; CLOSING A ~; CONSUMER ~; CREDIT ~; EXPORT ~; EXTERNALLY FINANCED ~; GOING PRIVATE ~; INTERNALLY FINANCED ~; MORTGAGE ~; PRIVATE ~; PURCHASE FINANCING ~; REAL ESTATE ~; REVIEWABLE ~; SECURED ~; SECURITY ~; STRANGER TO A ~.

TRANSACTION VALUE. In respect of goods, means the value of the goods determined in accordance with subsection 48(4). *Customs Act*, R.S.C. 1985 (2d Supp.), c. 1, s. 45.

TRANSCRIPT. *n.* 1. Something copied from an original. 2. In a court, an official copy of proceedings.

TRANSFER. *n.* 1. The passing of any estate or interest in land under this Act, whether for valuable consideration or otherwise. Land Titles acts. 2. In relation to stock, includes the performance and execution of every deed, power of attorney, act, and thing on the part of the transferor to effect and complete the title in the transferee. Trustee acts. 3. Includes transmission by operation of law. Corporations acts. 4. A conveyance of freehold or leasehold land and includes a deed and a transfer under a Land Titles act. 5. The instrument by which one person conveys to another an estate or interest in land under this Act and includes a grant from the Crown. *The Land Titles Act*, R.S.S. 1978, c. L-5, s. 2. 6. Includes gift, conveyance, assignment, delivery over, or payment of property. *Assignments and Preferences Act*, R.S.N.S. 1967, c. 16, s. 1. See AGREEMENT OF ~; EMBRYO ~ BUSINESS; ENERGY ~; INTER-UTILITY ~; LATERAL ~; POWER ~; RECIPROCAL ~ AGREEMENT.

TRANSFERABLE SHARE. A transferable corporate share that a debtor could freely transfer even if restrictions are placed on its transferability. C.R.B. Dunlop, *Creditor—Debtor Law in Canada* (Toronto: Carswell, 1981) at 165 and 166.

TRANSFER AGENT. A person who records the transfer of shares. H. Sutherland, D.B. Horsley & J.M. Edmiston, eds., *Fraser's Handbook on Canadian Company Law*, 7th ed. (Toronto: Carswell, 1985) at 195.

TRANSFER CHARGE. See DIRECT ~.

TRANSFEREE. *n.* 1. A person in whose favour a transfer is given. 2. The person to whom any interest or estate in land is transferred whether for value or otherwise. Land Titles acts. 3. Includes a person entitled to be the registered owner pursuant to a transmission application or request. *Real Property Act*, R.S.M. 1970, c. R30, s. 51.

TRANSFER ELEVATOR. (a) An elevator in the Western Division or the Eastern Division the principal use of which is the transfer of grain that has been officially inspected and officially weighed at another elevator; and (b) an elevator in the Eastern Division the principal uses of which are the transfer of grain that has been officially inspected and officially weighed at another elevator and the receiving, cleaning and storing of eastern grain or foreign grain. *Canada Grain Act*, R.S.C. 1985, c. G-10, s. 2.

TRANSFER OF OWNERSHIP. Includes any

alienation of a motor vehicle effected by one of such titles. *Highway Code*, R.S.Q. 1977, c. C-24, s. 1.

TRANSFER OPERATION. (a) The loading of oil or an oily mixture on to a ship from a loading facility or from another ship; (b) the unloading of oil or an oily mixture from a ship to an unloading facility or on to another ship; or (c) the transfer of oil or an oily mixture on board a ship. *Oil Pollution Prevention Regulations*, C.R.C., c. 1454, s. 2.

TRANSFEROR. *n.* 1. The person by whom any interest or estate in land is transferred, whether for valuable consideration or otherwise. Land Titles acts. 2. A person who gives a transfer.

TRANSFER POINT. See INTER-UTILITY ~.

TRANSFER STATION. A waste disposal site used for the purpose of transferring waste from a collection vehicle to another carrier for transportation to another waste disposal site. *Environmental Protection Act*, R.R.O. 1980, Reg. 309, s. 1. See BULK MILK ~; CREAM ~; MILK ~.

TRANSFER STOP. With respect to a passenger means a stop at an airport by an aircraft from which the passenger deplanes solely for the purpose of emplaning on a connecting flight. *Air Transportation Tax Regulations*, C.R.C., c. 583, s. 2.

TRANSFER TO USES. A transfer expressed to be given to such uses as the transferee may appoint by transfer, charge or will.

TRANSHIPMENT. *n.* 1. Moving cargo from one vessel to another to forward it to its destination. 2. After goods have been unloaded or in any way removed from the means of transportation by which they came into Canada, their loading, placing on board or within or upon the same or any other means of transportation. *Transhipment Regulations*, C.R.C., c. 606, s. 3.

TRANSHIPMENT TERMINAL. See ENERGY ~.

TRANSIENT ACCOMMODATION. The provision of lodging in hotels, motels, hostels, apartment houses, lodging houses, boarding houses, clubs and other similar accommodation, whether or not a membership is required for the lodging.

TRANSIENT ACCOMMODATION FACILITIES. Facilities where, for consideration, the public may obtain sleeping accommodation and includes motels, hotels, tourist camps, hunting or fishing lodges, out-camps, auto and trailer parks, and similar accommodation facilities. *Department of Tourism and Recreation Act*, R.S.M. 1970, c. T100, s. 2.

TRANSIENT PERSON. (i) Any person, firm or corporation who is not a resident of the Province of Nova Scotia, and who has not resided therein for a period of at least 3 months immediately prior to the date of the application for a license hereunder; and (ii) any person, firm or corporation who has or maintains his head office or chief place of business outside of the Province of Nova Scotia, or who sends developing, printing, finishing or enlarging to be done outside the Province of Nova Scotia. *Transient Photographers Act*, R.S.N.S. 1967, c. 313, s. 1.

TRANSIENT TRADER. 1. A person carrying on business in the municipality who: (i) offers to provide services for a price; (ii) offers goods or merchandise for sale by retail or by auction; or (iii) solicits any person who is not a wholesale or retail dealer for orders: (A) to provide future services for a price; or (B) for the future delivery of goods or merchandise; and who is not a person: (iv) required to be licensed under The Direct Sellers Act; or (v) assessable for the purposes of business taxation in respect of that business. *The Rural Municipalities Act*, R.S.S. 1978, c. R-26, s. 2. 2. Includes any person commencing business who has not resided continuously in the municipality for at least 3 months next preceding the time of his commencing such business there. *Municipal Act*, R.S.O. 1980, c. 302, s. 232.

TRANSIT. *v.* To use the seaway, or a part of it, either upbound or downbound. *Seaway Regulations*, C.R.C., c. 1397, s. 2.

TRANSIT. *n.* See RAPID ~.

TRANSIT CORPORATION. See MUNICIPAL ~.

TRANSIT IN REM JUDICATAM. [L.] It becomes res judicata.

TRANSITIONAL SURFACE. An imaginary inclined plane extending upward and outward from the outer lateral limits of a strip and its approach surface to an intersection with the horizontal surface or other transitional surfaces. Airport Zoning regulations.

TRANSIT POLICY. A policy issued to insure against an accident to someone while travelling or to insure goods while they are in transit from place to place. Raoul Colinvaux, *The Law of Insurance*, 5th ed. (London: Sweet & Maxwell, 1984) at 73.

TRANSIT SERVICE AGREEMENT. An agreement for not less than 5 years between the authority and a municipality respecting the provision and maintenance of transit services in a transit service area by means of annual operating agreements. *Urban Transit Authority Act*, R.S.B.C. 1979, c. 421, s. 1.

TRANSIT SYSTEM. A system for the transportation of passengers and parcel express. *Toronto Area Transit Operating Authority Act*, R.S.O. 1980, c. 505, s. 1. See INTER-REGIONAL ~; PASSENGER ~; REGIONAL ~.

TRANSIT TERRA CUM ONERE. [L.] Land passes over with its burden.

TRANSLATION. *n.* The written transposition of words and numbers from one language to another and includes an adaptation that accurately conveys the meaning thereof. *Translation Bureau Regulations*, C.R.C., c. 1561, s. 2.

TRANSMISSION. *n.* 1. Applies to change of ownership consequent on death, lunacy, sale under execution, order of court or other act of law, or on a sale for arrears of taxes or on any settlement or any legal succession in case of intestacy. Land Titles acts. 2. Includes storage. Gas Utilities acts. See DOCUMENT OF ~.

TRANSMISSION EQUIPMENT. Any object or objects by which the motion of a prime mover is transmitted to a machine that is capable of utilizing such motion and includes a shaft, pulley, belt, chain, gear, clutch or other device.

TRANSMISSION LINE. 1. A system or arrangement of lines of wire or other conductors and transformation equipment, whereby electric energy is transmitted in bulk, and includes (i) transmission circuits composed of the conductors which form the minimum set required to so transmit electric energy; (ii) insulating and supporting structures; (iii) substations; (iv) operational and control devices; and (v) all property of any kind used for the purpose of, or in connection with, or incidental to, the operation of the transmission line, but does not include a power plant or an electric distribution system. *Electric Energy Marketing Act*, S.A. 1981, c. E-4.1, s. 1. 2. A pipe line, other than a production line, a distribution line, a pipe line within an oil refinery, oil or petroleum storage depot, chemical processing plant or pipe line terminal or station. *Ontario Energy Board Act*, R.S.O. 1980, c. 332, s. 1. See GAS ~; POWER ~; WORKS AND ~S.

TRANSMISSION PIPELINE. A pipe or system of pipes through which natural gas, oil, solids, or a liquid or gas derived from natural gas, oil or solids, whether in suspension or other form is transported and includes compressor or pumping facilities and other equipment related to the operation of the transmission pipeline, associated terminal or storage facilities, but does not include (a) flow lines from wells; (b) secondary lines for gathering that are located within a producing area; or (c) distribution lines that deliver to ultimate consumers. *Utilities Commission Act*, S.B.C. 1980, c. 60, s. 16.

TRANSMIT. *v.* To send or convey from one place to another place by physical, electronic, optical or other means. *Canada Post Corporation Act*, R.S.C. 1985, c. C-10, s. 2.

TRANSMIT BY POST. To transmit through or by means of the Corporation. *Canada Post Corporation Act*, R.S.C. 1985, c. C-10, s. 2.

TRANSMITTER. *n.* A person who supplies a hydrocarbon by pipeline to a distributor.

TRANSMITTER POWER. The maximum D.C. power input to the anode of the final radio frequency stage of the transmitter. *General Radio Regulations, Part II*, C.R.C., c. 1372, s. 43.

TRANSMITTING STATION. See REBROADCASTING ~.

TRANS-OCEANIC FLIGHT. 1. A flight between a point in Canada and a point outside Canada that passes over the Atlantic Ocean, except a flight between a point in Canada and any point outside Canada lying west of a line running from the most easterly point in Canada to the point of intersection of 45° West Longitude with 0° Latitude. *Air Services Fees Regulations*, C.R.C., c. 5, s. 2. 2. A flight between Canada and a place outside Canada, Mexico, St. Pierre and Miquelon or the United States and that passes over or is intended to pass over the Atlantic Ocean, Caribbean Sea or the Gulf of Mexico. *National Defence Aerodrome Fees Regulations*, C.R.C., c. 714, s. 2.

TRANSPLANT. *n.* The removal of tissue from a human body, whether living or dead, and its implantation in a living human body. Human Tissue Gift Acts. See ANIMAL EMBRYO ~ CENTRE.

TRANSPLANTING. *n.* With respect to shellfish, means the moving of shellfish from one shellfish area to another shellfish area for any purpose other than natural biological cleansing. *Sanitary Control of Shellfish Fisheries Regulations*, C.R.C., c. 832, s. 2.

TRANSPONDER. *n.* A radar transponder that has the capability of receiving Mode A interrogation and replying thereto with 64 codes in accordance with Radio Standards Specification 148. *Radar Transponder Order*, C.R.C., c. 60, s. 2.

TRANSPORT. *v.* To convey in or on a vehicle gasoline or an associated product, exclusive of the fuel carried for use in the vehicle. *Gasoline Handling Act*, R.S.O. 1980, c. 185, s. 1.

TRANSPORT. *n.* 1. A method, manner or means of transportation and, without limiting the foregoing, includes aircraft, ships, boats and vessels, elevated, surface or subsurface railways or tramways, elevated cable cars, motor vehicles and trailers, all terrain vehicles, hovercraft, and the hoists, cables, rails, rolling stock, pipelines and conduits used in connection with transport. *Ministry of Transportation and Highways Act*, R.S.B.C. 1979, c. 280, s. 5. 2. The transport of goods or passengers, whether by rail or water, for hire or reward, to which this Act applies. *Transport Act*, R.S.C. 1985, c. T-17, s. 2. See AIR ~; CANADIAN ~ COMMISSION; EXTRA-PROVINCIAL ~; LOCAL ~; MEANS OF ~; PASSENGER ~.

TRANSPORTABLE EQUIPMENT. Electrically operated equipment which requires to be moved to a new position from time to time. *Coal Mines Regulation Act*, R.S.N.S. 1967, c. 36, s. 84.

TRANSPORTATION. *n.* 1. With respect to freight, includes the shipment, care, handling, storage and delivery of it. Motor Carrier acts. 2. The operation of a public vehicle and includes the (i) care; (ii) handling; (iii) assembly or storage in or for transit; or (iv) delivery of passengers or goods. *Motor Transport Act*, R.S.A. 1980, c. M-20, s. 1. 3. For an inclusive tour group, means the transport of the tour participants and their personal baggage by air or other modes between (a) all points in the tour itinerary; and (b) airports or surface terminals, and the location where accommodation is provided in the tour itinerary other than the point of origin. *Air Carrier Regulations*, C.R.C., c. 3, s. 23. See PUBLIC ~; SCHEDULED TRAVEL ~.

TRANSPORTATION CHARGES. See INITIAL ~.

TRANSPORTATION COMPANY. A person or group of persons carrying or providing for the transportation of persons, (a) where the expression appears in subsection 89(2), sections 92 and 93 and paragraph 114(1)(cc), by vehicle, bridge, tunnel or otherwise; and (b) in any other case, by vehicle or otherwise, but not by bridge or tunnel, and includes any agent thereof and the government of Canada or a province or of a municipality in Canada so carrying or providing for the transportation of persons. *Immigration Act*, R.S.C. 1985, c. I-2, s. 2.

TRANSPORTATION FACILITY. Everything necessary for the efficient transportation of persons and goods in a particular manner. *City Transportation Act*, R.S.A. 1980, c. C-10, s. 1.

TRANSPORTATION FUEL. Fuel designated by regulations under section 19 as being fuel for use by an aircraft or vessel. *Energy Administration Act*, R.S.C. 1985, c. E-6, s. 16.

TRANSPORTATION OF GOODS. The transportation of goods from any place in Canada to any place outside Canada or from any place outside Canada to any place in Canada. *Ship-*

ping Conference Exemption Act, R.S.C. 1985, c. S-10, s. 2.

TRANSPORTATION PLAN. A plan for the control of transportation within a defined area proposing as of some specific time the layout of any streets, highways, bridges, railway lines, railway crossings at level or at grade separations, bus routes, rapid transit lines, railway stations, bus terminals, rapid transit stations and wharves and airports within the defined area. *Railway Relocation and Crossing Act*, R.S.C. 1985, c. R-4, s. 2.

TRANSPORTATION PLANT. Plant used for any aspect of pipeline operations or plant held for use under a definite plan for future oil pipeline operations. *Oil Pipeline Uniform Accounting Regulations*, C.R.C., c. 1058, s. 2.

TRANSPORTATION PROGRAM. See NORTHERN PATIENT ~.

TRANSPORTATION SYSTEM. A system of transportation facilities including streets, highways, rapid transit and all types of transportation facilities to which this Act applies on, above and below the ground. *City Transportation Act*, R.S.A. 1980, c. C-10, s. 1. See PUBLIC PASSENGER ~.

TRANSPORTATION TERMINAL. An establishment or undertaking operated for the transportation of people or goods by any means, and includes all land, structures and equipment that form part of the establishment or are used in the undertaking. *New Brunswick Transportation Authority Act*, R.S.N.B. 1973, c. N-8, s. 1.

TRANSPORT BOARD. See CANADIAN TRANSPORT COMMISSION; PROVINCIAL ~.

TRANSPORT BY RAIL. The transport of goods or passengers by a company to which the Railway Act applies. *Transport Act*, R.S.C. 1985, c. T-17, s. 2.

TRANSPORT BY WATER. The transport of goods or passengers, for hire or reward, by means of ships required to be licensed under this Act. *Transport Act*, R.S.C. 1985, c. T-17, s. 2.

TRANSPORT CANADA. The federal ministry in charge of all federally regulated railways, Marine, Air and Surface Transporation Administrations.

TRANSPORTER. *n.* 1. A person regularly engaged in the business of transporting vehicles. 2. A person who supplies a hydrocarbon other than by pipeline to a distributor. *Energy Act*, R.S.O. 1980, c. 139, s. 1. See AUTO ~.

TRANSPORT FACILITIES. See BULK ~.

TRANSPORT ORDER. Any order, in a form

approved by the Commodity board and issued in the name of the Commodity Board by a duly authorized employee or nominee of the Commodity Board, authorizing the moving or transporting of the regulated product from one place to another. Canada regulations.

TRANSPORT OR TRANSPORTING. The overt act of any person leading to the movement, otherwise than by shipping, of any livestock or livestock product from or to a point outside the province in which he carries on business. *Livestock and Livestock Products Act*, R.S.C. 1985, c. L-9, s. 31.

TRANSPORT PERMIT. A valid permit in a form approved by and issued under the authority of the Commodity Board authorizing the movement or transportation of vegetable. *P.E.I. Vegetable Directed Sales (Interprovincial and Export) Regulations*, C.R.C., c. 237, s. 2.

TRANSPORT SYSTEM. A system consisting of vehicles or other means of transport. *Transport Act*, R.S.Q. 1977, c. T-12, s. 1.

TRAP. *v.* 1. To conceal and surprise under circumstances which appear safe but mask real danger. J.V. DiCastri, *Occupiers' Liability* (Vancouver: Burroughs/Carswell, 1980) at 111. 2. To catch or to attempt to catch game or fur bearing animals by means of a spring trap, deadfall, snare or net. See GANG ~PED.

TRAP. *n.* 1. Includes a spring trap, snare, deadfall, box or net or any device used to capture any wildlife. 2. A fitting or device which provides a liquid seal to prevent the emission of sewer gases without materially affecting the flow of sewage or waste water through it. *Ontario Water Resources Act*, R.R.O. 1980, Reg. 736, s. 1. See BAIT ~; BELL ~; BLACKCOD ~; BODY-GRIPPING ~; BOTTLE ~; BUILDING ~; COD ~; CRAB ~; DRUM ~; FIXTURE ~; LEG-HOLD ~; MINNOW ~; SALMON ~; SNOW CRAB ~.

TRAPLINE. *var.* **TRAP-LINE.** *n.* An area for which registration is granted to a licensed trapper for the trapping of fur bearing animals. *Wildlife Act*, S.B.C. 1982, c. 57, s. 1. See CREE ~.

TRAP NET. 1. A net that is set so as to enclose an area of water into which fish are guided by one or more leaders. Canada regulations. 2. An impounding net supported principally by buoys or floats and held in place by anchors, and in which the top of the crib, pot or car is covered by netting. Fishery regulations.

TRAP ORDER. Evidence obtained by a witness concerning the way in which a defendant supplies goods in response to a request which embodies the use of the disputed trade mark.

H.G. Fox, *The Canadian Law of Trade Marks and Unfair Competition*, 3d ed. (Toronto: Carswell, 1972) at 450.

TRAPPING. *n.* Taking or attempting to take wildlife by means of a trap or snare.

TRAPPING AREA. 1. The area or location defined and registered under this Act for the taking of fur-bearing animals and fur-bearing carnivores on the area or location by a licensed trapper. *Wildlife Act*, R.S.A. 1980, c. W-9, s. 1. 2. An area or location defined and registered under these Regulations for the taking of fur-bearing animals. *Wood Buffalo Park Game Regulations*, C.R.C., c. 1113, s. 2.

TRAP SEAL. The vertical depth of water between the crown weir and the trap dip. *Ontario Water Resources Act*, R.R.O. 1980, Reg. 736, s. 1.

TRAP STANDARD. The trap for a fixture that is integral with the support for the fixture. *Ontario Water Resources Act*, R.R.O. 1980, Reg. 736, s. 1.

TRAUMA. *n.* A wound; an injury.

TRAUMATIC ANEURYSM. An aneurysm which occurs at a point where a blood vessel has been injured. F.A. Jaffe, *A Guide to Pathological Evidence*, 2d ed. (Toronto: Carswell, 1983) at 168.

TRAUMATIC ASPHYXIA. Suffocation which occurs when the chest is compressed and respiratory movements are prevented. F.A. Jaffe, *A Guide to Pathological Evidence*, 2d ed. (Toronto: Carswell, 1983) at 169.

TRAVEL AGENT. A person who, in the course of business, sells or otherwise provides to the public travel services supplied by another person.

TRAVEL ASSOCIATION. A non-profit organization having as its objects the promotion of the tourism industry in its region. *Tourism Act*, R.R.O. 1980, Reg. 936, s. 14.

TRAVEL DISTANCE. The distance from any point in the floor area to an exit measured along the path of exit travel, except that when floor areas are subdivided into rooms used singly, or into suites of rooms, and served by public corridors or exterior passage ways, the travel distance shall be measured from the door of such rooms or suites to the nearest exit. *Building Code Act*, R.R.O. 1980, Reg. 87, s. 1.

TRAVELLED PORTION. When used in this section as applicable to roads, streets, lanes or highways, means the central portion thereof between the ditches on either side, ordinarily used for vehicular traffic. *Railway Act*, R.S.Q. 1977, c. C-14, s. 121.

TRAVELLER. *n.* A person who, in consideration of a given price per day or fraction of a day, on the American or European plan, or per meal, à table d'hôte, or à la carte, is furnished by another person with food or lodging or both. *An Act Respecting the Commission de Contrôle des Permis D'alcool*, R.S.Q. 1977, c. C-33, s. 2.

TRAVELLING AMUSEMENT. An amusement whose participants travel from place to place, taking part in the amusement.

TRAVELLING EXHIBITION. Any person successively giving exhibitions, concerts or other entertainments in more than one place or locality either for himself or for others. *Licenses Act*, R.S.Q. 1977, c. L-3, s. 23.

TRAVELLING EXPENSES. Transportation while on duty and hotel expenses, meals, taxis and gratuities while the employee is away from his employer's place of business. *Martyn v. Minister of National Revenue* (1962), 35 Tax A.B.C. 428, 62 D.T.C. 341 (T.A.B.).

TRAVELLING PICTURE SHOW. A moving picture show which travels about from place to place in a province.

TRAVEL SERVICE. Transportation, accommodation or other service for the use or benefit of a traveller, tourist or sightseer.

TRAVEL TRAILER. 1. A vehicle that is propelled by its own motive power and is registered as a motor vehicle under the Motor Vehicle Act. *Assessment Act*, S.N.S. 1975, c. 57, s. 11. 2. Any vehicle designed, built and maintained so that it may be drawn on the highway and primarily built, furnished and used, or intended to be used, for overnight or short term shelter. *Ontario Water Resources Act*, R.R.O. 1980, Reg. 736, s. 1.

TRAVEL TRANSPORTATION. See SCHEDULED ~.

TRAVEL WHOLESALER. 1. A person who, in the course of business, supplies his own non-scheduled travel transportation to the public, purchases or acquires from another person rights to travel services for the purpose of resale, or deals with travel agents or other travel wholesalers for the sale of travel services supplied by another. *Travel Agents Act*, R.S.B.C. 1979, c. 409, s. 1. 2. A person who purchases or acquires from another person rights to a travel service for the purposes of resale or who carries on the business of dealing with travel agents or other travel wholesalers for the sale of travel services provided by another. *Travel Industry Act*, R.S.O. 1980, c. 509, s. 1.

TRAVERSE. *n.* In defense, denial of an alleged fact made in a statement of claim. I.H. Jacob, ed., *Bullen and Leake and Jacob's Precedents of Pleadings*, 12th ed. (London: Sweet and Maxwell, 1975) at 79.

TRAWL. See MIDWATER ~; OTTER OR OTHER ~ OF A SIMILAR NATURE; OTTER ~; SIDE ~; STERN ~.

TRAWLER. *n.* 1. Any vessel of 20 tons or upwards, prosecuting out of any port in this province the bank fishery by means of trawl lines, locally called trawls or bultows, and shall include vessels propelled by steam or other mechanical power. *Bank Fishermen (Protection) Act*, R.S.Nfld. 1970, c. 18, s. 2. 2. A vessel (a) of an overall length that exceeds 100 feet; and (b) that uses an otter trawl or other trawl of a similar type for catching fish. *Otter Trawl Fishing Regulations*, C.R.C., c. 821, s. 2.

TRAWLING. *n.* Fishing by dragging through the water a dredge net or other fishing apparatus. *Collision Regulations*, C.R.C., c. 1416, s. 2.

TRAWL NET. Any large bag net dragged in the sea by a vessel or vessels for the purpose of taking fish. Fishery regulations. See LARGE-MESH ~; SMALL-MESH ~.

T.R.B. *abbr.* Tax Review Board.

TREAD. *n.* The portion of a tire that comes in contact with the road.

TREAD RIB. A tread section running circumferentially around a tire. Canada regulations.

TREAD SEPARATION. The parting of the tread from the tire carcass. Canada regulations.

TREASON. *n.* (a) Using force or violence for the purpose of overthrowing the government of Canada or a province; (b) without lawful authority, communicating or making available to an agent of a state other than Canada, military or scientific information or any sketch, plan, model, article, note or document of a military or scientific character that he knows or ought to know may be used by that state for a purpose prejudicial to the safety or defence of Canada; (c) conspiring with any person to commit high treason or to do anything mentioned in paragraph (a); (d) forming an intention to do anything that is high treason or that is mentioned in paragraph (a) and manifesting that intention by an overt act; or (e) conspiring with any person to do anything mentioned in paragraph (b) or forming an intention to do anything mentioned in paragraph (b) and manifesting that intention by an overt act. *Criminal Code*, R.S.C. 1985, c. C-46, s. 46(2). See HIGH ~; MISPRISON OF ~.

TREASURER. *n.* 1. A person who cares for money or treasure. 2. The person in charge of the securities and funds of a company who deposits these things in the company's bank. H. Sutherland, D.B. Horsley & J.M. Edmiston, eds., *Fraser's Handbook on Canadian Company Law*, 7th ed. (Toronto: Carswell, 1985) at 253.

TREASURE TROVE. Any coin, money, gold, silver, bullion or plate buried or hidden in a private place; because its owner is unknown it belongs to the Crown. E.L.G. Tyler & N.E. Palmer, eds., *Crossley Vaines' Personal Property*, 5th ed. (London: Butterworths, 1973) at 419.

TREASURY. *n.* 1. A place where treasure is stored. 2. The fiscal department of a government which controls payment of public money as directed by the legislature or House of Commons.

TREASURY BILL. A bill issued by or on behalf of Her Majesty for the payment of a principal sum specified in the bill to a named recipient or to a bearer at a date not later than 12 months from the date of issue of the bill. *Financial Administration Act*, R.S.C. 1985, c. F-11, s. 2.

TREASURY BOARD. The Treasury Board constituted under the federal or a provincial Financial Administration statute.

TREASURY BOARD OF CANADA. A federal body which advises Cabinet on program selection and promotes judicious use of resources by other federal departments.

TREASURY BRANCH FACILITY. Real property (i) that is used or intended to be used in connection with or incidental to the operations of the Province of Alberta Treasury Branches; and (ii) the acquisition of which is paid for with money from the Fund. *Treasury Branches Act*, R.S.A. 1980, c. T-7, s. 1.

TREASURY NOTE. A note issued by or on behalf of Her Majesty for the payment of a principal sum specified in the note to a named recipient or to a bearer at a date not later than 12 months from the date of issue of the note. *Financial Administration Act*, R.S.C. 1985, c. F-11, s. 2.

TREAT. See INVITATION TO ~.

TREATER. *n.* A fired apparatus specifically designed and used for separating gas and water from crude oil. *Oil and Gas Conservation Act*, R.S.A. 1980, c. O-5, s. 1.

TREATMENT. *n.* 1. The maintenance, observation, nursing, medical and other care of a patient. 2. With reference to hazardous waste, means any operation for the treatment, recycling or salvaging of the hazardous waste so that it no longer constitutes a danger to the environment, plant or animal life or human health. 3. One, more or all of direction, supervision or

treatment of a person for terminating or diminishing his use of or dependency on a narcotic. *Heroin Treatment Act*, R.S.B.C. 1979, c. 166, s. 1. 4. Concentrating, smelting, refining or any similar process but does not include washing, screening, conveying, loading or other handling methods when they are not combined with treatment. *Indian Mining Regulations*, C.R.C., c. 956, s. 2. See CHILD ~ SERVICE; DAY'S ~; ELECTRICAL ~; EXPERIMENTAL ~; HEAT ~; MANIPULATIVE ~; MECHANICAL ~; MEDICAL ~; NATIONAL ~; SURGICAL ~.

TREATMENT ALLOWANCE. An allowance paid or payable by the Department to or on behalf of a person while under treatment by the Department for a pensionable disability. *Pension Act*, R.S.C. 1985, c. P-6, s. 2.

TREATMENT CENTRE. 1. A nursing home, special care home, sanatorium, psychiatric facility or any other residential facility operated for the purpose of the care and treatment of persons having a physical or mental disability. 2. Any place including a group home, foster home, training centre and reception centre for the reception, detention, custody, examination, care, treatment, education and rehabilitation of a child. 3. A prescribed place where treatment and rehabilitation programmes are available for persons in need of assistance to overcome alcoholism. *Treatment of Intoxicated Persons Act*, R.S.N.B. 1973, c. T-11.1, s. 1.

TREATMENT FACILITY. See SEWAGE ~; WASTE WATER ~.

TREATMENT POND. A pond, lagoon or other confined area, other than a tailings impoundment area, used to treat an effluent. *Metal Mining Liquid Effluent Regulations*, C.R.C., c. 819, s. 2.

TREATMENT PROGRAM. A program for treating cattle for cattle pests. *Cattle Pest Control Act*, S.N.S. 1970, c. 2, s. 1.

TREATMENT PROJECT. See SEWAGE ~.

TREATMENT SERVICES. 1. The broad range of emergency, outpatient and inpatient services provided by a regional community organization and includes (i) detoxification; (ii) medical examination and diagnostic assessment; (iii) development of a treatment plan for each person participating in a treatment program; (iv) short term residential care; (v) rehabilitation measures; (vi) counselling; (vii) follow-up and support; (viii) maintenance of records; (ix) evaluation of modes of treatment. *Addiction Services Act*, S.P.E.I. 1981, c. 1, s. 1. 2. Services, supplies, appliances and things rendered or furnished for the purpose of or in connection with diagnosis, treatment or care but does not include any basic health services as defined in the Alberta Health Care Insurance Act. *Treatment Services Act*, R.S.A. 1980, c. T-8, s. 1.

TREATMENT WORKS. Buildings, structures, plant, machinery, equipment, devices, intakes and outfalls or outlets and other works designed for the interception, collection, settling, treating, dispersing, disposing or discharging of sewage or land drainage, or both, and includes land appropriated for such purposes and uses. See ADVANCED ~; SECONDARY ~.

TREATY. *n.* In international law, a binding agreement between states. P.W. Hogg, *Constitutional Law of Canada*, 2d ed. (Toronto: Carswell, 1985) at 241. See COMMERCIAL ~.

TREATY OF 1908. The treaty between His Majesty Edward VII and the United States respecting the demarcation of the international boundary between the United States and Canada signed at Washington on April 11, 1908. *International Boundary Commission Act*, R.S.C. 1985, c. I-16, s. 2.

TREE. *n.* 1. Includes a growing tree or shrub planted or left growing on either side of a highway for the purpose of shade or ornament. *Municipal Act*, R.S.O. 1980, c. 302, s. 313. 2. A tree that is standing or is down and from which the limbs have not been removed. *Occupational Health and Safety Act*, R.R.O. 1980, Reg. 692, s. 107. See CHRISTMAS ~; ELM ~; FRUIT ~S; MERCHANTABLE ~.

TREE FARM LAND. Land having its best economic use under forest crop and on which (a) there is a stock of young growth in numbers of trees per hectare, not less than the minimum standards established by the Forest Service; (b) an approved working plan provides a reforestation program designed to establish a growing stock in numbers of trees per hectare, not less than the minimum standards established by the Forest Service; (c) there is a stock of mature timber that, according to an approved working plan, will be harvested on a sustained yield basis; or (d) there is any combination of them. *Assessment Act*, R.S.B.C. 1979, c. 21, s. 1.

TREE FRUIT. See STONE ~.

TRENCH. *n.* Any excavation in the ground where the vertical dimension from the highest point of the excavation to the point level with the lowest point of the excavation exceeds the least horizontal dimension of the excavation, such dimensions being taken in a vertical plane at right angles to the longitudinal centre line of the excavation, but does not include a shaft, caisson or cofferdam, or a cutting for the right of way of a public highway or railway. *Occupational Health and Safety Act*, R.R.O. 1980,

Reg. 691, s. 1. See PREFABRICATED ~ SUPPORT SYSTEM.

TRENCH DEPTH. The vertical dimension from the highest point of the excavation to a point level with the lowest point of the excavation. *Occupational Health and Safety Act*, R.R.O. 1980, Reg. 691, s. 167.

TRENCHING. See ROCK ~.

TRESPASS. *n.* 1. All forcible, direct and immediate injury to the plaintiff's person, land or goods. May be committed by propelling a person or object onto the land or by refusing to leave land after a licence to enter has terminated. John G. Fleming, *The Law of Torts*, 6th ed. (Sydney: The Law Book Co., 1983) at 15, 38, 39. 2. Entering or remaining without lawful authority on premises or land owned, occupied or controlled by another. *An Act to Amend the Trespass Act*, S.N.B. 1985, c. 70, s. 1.

TRESPASS AB INITIO. A person who lawfully entered another's land lost immunity from action for trespass if that person abused the privilege by committing a tort against the possessor or the possessor's property. John G. Fleming, *The Law of Torts*, 6th ed. (Sydney: The Law Book Co., 1983) at 95.

TRESPASS BY RELATION. A person who has a right to immediate possession of land may, upon entry, sue for any trespass committed after that right to entry accrued. John G. Fleming, *The Law of Torts*, 6th ed., (Sydney: The Law Book Company Limited, 1983), at 41. {ed dd}

TRESPASS DE BONIS ASPORTATIS. A writ used as a remedy in a case in which something was totally carried away or destroyed. John G. Fleming, *The Law of Torts*, 6th ed. (Sydney: The Law Book Co., 1983) at 47.

TRESPASSER. *n.* Someone who goes on another's land without any lawful authority, right or express or implied licence or invitation, and whose presence is either unknown to the occupier or is objected to if known. J.V. DiCastri, *Occupiers' Liability* (Vancouver: Burroughs/ Carswell, 1980) at 123.

TRESPASS TO GOODS. Intentional interference or use of a chattel in such a way as to violate the plaintiff's possessory rights.

John G. Fleming, *The Law of Torts*, 6th ed., (Sydney: The Law Book Co., 1983) at 47, 48.

TRESPASS TO LAND. Entry onto or any immediate and direct interference with the possession of land. I.H. Jacob, ed., *Bullen and Leake and Jacob's Precedents of Pleadings*, 12th ed. (London: Sweet and Maxwell, 1975) at 878.

TRESTLE LADDER. See EXTENSION ~.

TRIACTOR. *n.* A betting transaction in which a purchaser of a ticket undertakes to select in the exact order of finish the first three horses to finish in the race on which the feature is operated. *Race Track Supervision Regulations,* C.R.C., c. 441, s. 2.

TRIAL. *n.* 1. The hearing of a civil or criminal cause. 2. Includes the hearing of a complaint. *Criminal Code,* R.S.C. 1985, c. C-46, s. 785. 3. Includes the hearing of a matrimonial cause. *Judicature Act and Matrimonial Causes Act,* R.R.O. 1980, Reg. 540, s. 2. See FEDERAL COURT—~ DIVISION; JURY ~S; MIS~; NEW ~; NOTICE OF READINESS FOR ~; SET DOWN FOR ~; SUMMARY ~.

TRIAL COURT. The court by which an accused was tried and includes a judge or a provincial court judge acting under Part XIX. *Criminal Code,* R.S.C. 1985, c. C-46, s. 673 as amended by *Criminal Law Amendment Act,* R.S.C. 1985 (1st Supp.), c. 27, s. 138.

TRIAL DE NOVO. A form of appeal in which the case is retried.

TRIAL DIVISION. 1. That division of the Court referred to in section 4 as the Federal Court—Trial Division. *Federal Court Act,* R.S.C. 1985, c. F-7, s. 2. 2. The Trial Division of the Supreme Court of Newfoundland referred to in section 3 and Part II of The Judicature Act, 1936. *Judicature Act,* S.Nfld. 1986, c. 42, s. 40.

TRIAL JUDGES. The two judges trying an election petition or performing any duty to which the enactment in which the expression occurs has reference. *Dominion Controverted Elections Act,* R.S.C. 1985, c. C-39, s. 2.

TRIAL PER PAIS. Trial by jury.

TRIAL RECORD. Includes jury notice, financial statement, pleadings and particulars. G.D. Watson & C. Perkins, eds., *Holmested & Watson: Ontario Civil Procedure* (Toronto: Carswell, 1984) at 48-3.

TRIB. *abbr.* Tribunal.

TRIB. CONC. *abbr.* Tribunal de la concurrence.

TRIBUNAL. *n.* 1. A court of justice. 2. A body or person which exercises a judicial or quasi-judicial function outside the regular court system. 3. One or more persons, whether or not incorporated and however described, on whom a statutory power of decision is conferred. 4. Includes any court, body, authority or person having authority to take or receive information, whether on its or one's behalf or on behalf of any other court, body, authority or person. *Foreign Extraterritorial Measures Act,* R.S.C. 1985, c. F-29, s. 2. 5. Any person or body, from whom an appeal lies to the Court, including any board, commission, committee, municipal authority, Minister, public official, or other public or governmental agency or authority, including the Lieutenant-Governor in Council, but not including a court or judge. *Rules of the Supreme Court,* S.Nfld. 1986, r. 57, s. 57.01. See ADMINISTRATIVE ~; ARBITRAL ~; CANADIAN IMPORT ~; EXTRA-PROVINCIAL ~; EXTRA-TERRITORIAL ~; FEDERAL BOARD, COMMISSION OR OTHER ~; FOREIGN ~; MEMBER OF A ~; REVIEW ~; SERVICE ~.

TRIBUNAL APPEAL. Any appeal authorized by statute to be taken from a tribunal, including any matters reserved, case stated or reference referred by a tribunal to the Court. *Rules of the Supreme Court,* S.Nfld. 1986, r. 57, s. 57.01.

TRIBUTE. *n.* A payment made to acknowledge something.

TRILLIUM. *n.* The plant, Trillium Ovatum, commonly known as western trillium or wake robin. *Dogwood, Rhododendron and Trillium Protection Act,* R.S.B.C. 1979, c. 96, s. 1.

TRIMMING. *n.* Any textile fibre product that (a) has been added to a consumer textile article for a decorative purpose; and (b) differs in textile fibre content from the article to which it has been added. *Textile Labelling and Advertising Regulations,* C.R.C., c. 1551, s. 25.

TRIMMINGS. *n.* Trim, ribbon, piping or lace sold by the yard or metre, but does not include trimmings supplied by a tailor, dressmaker, drapery manufacturer or upholsterer in producing clothing or draperies or in upholstering furniture even where a charge for such trimmings is made separately on the invoice to the customer. *Retail Sales Tax Act,* R.R.O. 1980, Reg. 903, s. 1.

TRIP. *n.* 1. The movement of the derrick (a) from the base or loading point to a ship and back to the base or loading point; (b) from the base or loading point to a ship until completion of the work when the derrick barge lets go its mooring lines to proceed to another ship; (c) from the time the derrick barge lets go its mooring lines from a ship until its arrival at the next job and back to base or loading point; or (d) from the time the derrick barge lets go its mooring lines from a ship, moves to its next job, completes work and again lets go its mooring lines if proceeding to another job before returning to base. *Hamilton Harbour Floating Derrick Tariff By-law,* C.R.C., c. 896, s. 2. 2. (a) The movement of the crane from the loading berth to the ship and return to loading berth; (b) the movement of the crane from the base or loading point to the ship until completion of the work, when the crane lets go its mooring lines to proceed to another ship; (c) from the time the crane scow lets go its mooring lines from the first ship until arrival at the next job and returns to base or loading point; or (d) from the time the crane scow lets go its mooring lines from the first ship, moves to the next job, completes work and again lets go its mooring lines if proceeding to another job before returning to base. *Montreal Floating Crane No. 1 Heavy-Lift Tariff By-law*, C.R.C., c. 1077, s. 2. 3. The piloting of a ship from one point to another within the region of the Authority, but does not include (a) a movage; or (b) a docking or undocking, where a pilot replaces another pilot pursuant to section 5 of the schedule. *Laurentian Pilotage Tariff Regulations*, C.R.C., c. 1269, s. 2. 4. A mine car or mine cars connected together and used for conveying persons, coal or other materials along a track line in a mine. *Coal Mines (CBDC) Safety Regulations*, C.R.C., c. 1011, s. 2. See CHARTERED ~; CONTINUOUS ~.

TRIPARTITE. *adj.* Having three parts.

TRIPARTITE BOARD. A board composed of representatives of labour and management and a neutral or public representative.

TRIPLE AXLE. Any three consecutive axles that, (i) have their consecutive centres equally spaced; and (ii) have their consecutive centres more than 1 metre apart; and that, (iii) are articulated from an attachment to the vehicle common to the consecutive axles; or (iv) are designed to automatically equalize the load between the three axles under all conditions of loading. *Highway Traffic Act*, R.S.O. 1980, c. 198, s. 97.

TROLLEY BUS. A bus propelled by electric power obtained from overhead wires.

TROLLEY COACH. A motor vehicle operated with electricity as the motive power through contact with overhead wires. *Motor Vehicle Act*, R.S.N.S. 1967, c. 191, s. 1.

TROLLING. *n.* Taking or attempting to take fish with rod, hook or line when such rod, hook or line is being drawn through or over water by means of a boat or other water craft being propelled by mechanical or manual means.

TROPICAL VOYAGE. That tropical conditions are assumed to exist between the parallels of latitude 30° north and south, and cargo carried on any ship bound to or from a port in or likely to pass through that area must be packed in accordance with the regulations for tropical conditions. *Dangerous Goods Shipping Regulations*, C.R.C., c. 1419, s. 2.

TROUSSEAU. See BRIDE'S ~.

TROUT. *n.* Includes char, speckled or brook trout, lake trout or togue, brown or Loch Leven trout, rainbow trout and ouananiche or land-locked salmon. See LAKE ~; RAINBOW ~; SEA ~.

TROVER. *n.* An action on the case, the remedy for a plaintiff who is deprived, by wrongful taking, detention or disposal, of goods. John G. Fleming, *The Law of Torts*, 6th ed., (Sydney: The Law Book Co., 1983) at 47, 50.

TROY OUNCE. 480 grains. *Weights and Measures Act*, S.C. 1970-71-72, c. 36, schedule II.

TRU. *abbr.* Trueman's Equity Cases (N.B.), 1876-1903.

TRUANT OFFICER. Includes (a) a member of the Royal Canadian Mounted Police; (b) a special constable appointed for police duty on a reserve; and (c) a school teacher and a chief of the band, when authorized by the superintendent. *Indian Act*, R.S.C. 1985, c. I-5, s. 122.

TRUCE. See COMPULSORY ~.

TRUCK. *n.* 1. Every motor vehicle designed, used or maintained primarily for the transportation of property. 2. A motor vehicle designed for the conveyance of goods, a motor vehicle equipped with a lifting device or a motor vehicle on which any machinery is permanently mounted. 3. A motor vehicle or trailer constructed or adapted primarily to carry goods, wares, merchandise, freight or commodities but not passengers or luggage. *The Live Stock and Live Stock Products Act*, R.S.S. 1978, c. L-23, s. 2. 4. Includes any vehicle, other than a railway car, used in transporting stock. *The Brand and Brand Inspection Act*, R.S.S. 1978, c. B-7, s. 2. See FAMILY FARM ~; FARM ~; FREE ON ~; GOVERNMENT ~; LOADED ~; PUBLIC MOTOR ~; SEMI-TRAILER ~; STAKE ~; TANK ~.

TRUCKER. *n.* A person for hire or reward who transports goods by motor vehicle and who is licensed to do so pursuant to an Act of Parliament or the legislature of a province.

TRUCK TRACTOR. *var.* **TRUCK-TRACTOR.** A motor vehicle designed and used primarily for drawing other vehicles and not constructed to carry a load other than a part of the weight of the vehicle drawn and of the load of the other vehicle.

TRUCK-TRAILER. *n.* Any type of trailer vehicle, including a single or multi-axle semi-trailer whereby part of the load is carried on the tractor unit by means of the upper and lower coupler assembly, and a full load bearing trailer, normally hauled by a truck unit, that is registered for use on a highway under the Highway Traffic

Act and is used primarily for the transport of equipment or goods but does not include a vehicle, (i) used for transportation solely within an employer's actual place of business; or (ii) used for farming operations but not used for carrying a load. *Apprenticeship and Tradesmen's Qualification Act*, R.R.O. 1980, Reg. 62, s. 1.

TRUCK-TRAILER REPAIRER. A person engaged in the repair and maintenance of truck-trailers who, (i) disassembles, adjusts, repairs and reassembles suspension systems, including bogies, axles, wheels, and rims, brake systems and electrical systems; (ii) inspects, repairs and realigns frames; (iii) inspects and repairs appurtenances such as tow-bars, hitches, turntables, landing gear and upper couplers; and (iv) inspects, tests, adjusts, overhauls and replaces truck-trailer refrigeration system components, electrical circuits, pressure lines and fittings, and installs and removes truck-trailer refrigeration systems. *Apprenticeship and Tradesmen's Qualification Act*, R.R.O. 1980, Reg. 62, s. 1.

TRUE BILL. An indorsement made by a grand jury on a bill of indictment when after hearing the evidence they are satisfied that the accusation is probably true.

TRUE CONDITION PRECEDENT. An external condition which the obligation depends on to exist. G.H.L. Fridman, *The Law of Contract in Canada*, 2d ed. (Toronto: Carswell, 1986) at 415.

TRUE COPY. 1. A legible copy of the original document produced by manual, photographic, electrical or mechanical means and certified as a true copy by notarial certificate or certificate of the debtor. *Personal Property Security Act*, S.M. 1973, c. 5, s. 54. 2. A copy of a legal document exactly the same as the original with notations, court stamps, signatures of parties and the court registrar, insertions and corrections written in the copy within quotation marks.

TRUE FLIGHT MACH NUMBER. The ratio of the true air speed of an aircraft to the local speed of sound at the flight altitude. *Sonic and Supersonic Flight Order*, C.R.C., c. 64, s. 2.

TRUE INNUENDO. Something which arises solely from circumstances or facts and is not apparent on the face of the publication, but which gives words some special meaning they would not have ordinarily. R.E. Brown, *The Law of Defamation in Canada* (Toronto: Carswell, 1987) at 155.

TRUNK. See EFFECTIVE LENGTH OF SUPERSTRUCTURE OR ~; EFFICIENT ~.

TRUNK STORM SEWER SYSTEM. A system for the collection and transmission of storm drainage. *National Housing Act*, S.C. 1974-75-76, c. 38, s. 16.

TRUST. *n.* A confidence which rests either expressly or impliedly in someone (the trustee) for the benefit of someone else (the beneficiary or cestui que trust). In its simplest form, a relation between two people by which the trustee holds property for the cestui que trust's benefit. See ACCELERATED ~; ACCUMULATION ~; ACTIVE ~; BLIND ~; BONDHOLDER'S ~; BREACH OF ~; CEMETERY OR PERPETUAL CARE ~; CESTUI QUE ~; CHARITABLE ~ S; CONSTRUCTIVE ~; DECLARATION OF ~; DEEMED ~; DISCRETIONARY ~; EMPLOYEES' CHARITY ~; EMPLOYEE ~; EQUIPMENT ~; EXECUTED ~; EXECUTORY ~; EXPRESS ~; FOREIGN ~; FROZEN ~; FULLY-SECRET ~; GROSS ROYALTY ~; HALF-SECRET ~; HOLDING ~; IMPERFECT ~; IMPLIED ~; INTER VIVOS ~; INVESTMENT ~; MORTGAGE ~; OIL AND GAS ROYALTY ~; PASSIVE ~; PENSION ~; PERCENTAGE ~; PERSONAL ~; POOLED INVESTMENT ~; PRIVATE ~; PUBLIC ~; RCA ~; RESIDENCE OF A ~; RESULTING ~; SECRET ~; SIMPLE ~; SPRINKLING ~; STOCK ESCROW ~; SYNDICATE ~; TESTAMENTARY ~; UNIT ~; VOTING ~.

TRUST AND LOAN CORPORATION. A corporation that carries on business, or holds itself out, as a loan corporation and a trust corporation and is a company licensed under The Trust and Loan Companies (Licensing) Act. *Financial Corporations Capital Tax Act*, S.Nfld. 1982, c. 8, s. 1.

TRUST AND SPECIAL RECEIPTS. Includes moneys received by the province or any officer thereof in trust for or on account of any government or person or in trust for or on account of any special purpose or otherwise. *Treasury Act*, R.S.P.E.I. 1974, c. T-7, s. 1.

TRUST CAPACITY. The capacity of a trustee, executor, administrator, bailee, agent, receiver, liquidator, sequestrator, assignee, custodian, trustee in bankruptcy, guardian of the estate of a minor, committee of the estate of a mentally incompetent person, or any other similar capacity. *Trust Companies Act*, R.S.A. 1980, c. T-9, s. 1.

TRUST COMPANY. 1. A corporation empowered to carry on the business of executing the office of (i) executor, administrator or trustee; or (ii) guardian or committee of the estate of a minor or mentally incompetent person. 2. A corporation authorized (i) to act as executor, administrator, trustee, liquidator, receiver, assignee, guardian or committee; or (ii) to receive on deposit deeds, wills or other valuable papers or securities for money or jewellery, plate or other personal property, and to guarantee the safekeeping of the same; or (iii) to act as attorney or agent for the transaction of any business or class of business, or the collection of money or the management of property of any kind; or (iv) to act as agent for the purpose of issuing or countersigning certificates of stock, bonds or other obligations of any company or municipal or school corporation, and to receive, invest and manage any sinking fund therefor; or (v) to guarantee any investment made by it as agent or otherwise. See LICENSED ~; PROVINCIAL ~.

TRUST CORPORATION. A corporation licensed or otherwise authorized under the laws of Canada or a province to carry on in Canada the business of offering to the public its services as trustee. See FOREIGN ~.

TRUST DEED. A separate document in favour of a trust company as trustee for the holders of the instruments which evidences an obligation, the usual way to issue a corporate obligation sold to the public, which may contain a specific charge or mortgage or a floating charge or both. H. Sutherland, D.B. Horsley & J.M. Edmiston, eds., *Fraser's Handbook on Canadian Company Law*, 7th ed. (Toronto: Carswell, 1985) at 310. See DEBENTURE ~.

TRUSTEE. *n.* 1. Somone who holds property in trust. 2. Includes a liquidator, receiver, receiver-manager, trustee in bankruptcy, assignee, executor, administrator, sequestrator or any other person performing a function similar to that performed by any such person. 3. An authorized trustee under the Bankruptcy Act (Canada) appointed for the bankruptcy district or division in which the stock of the vendor, or some part of it, is located, or the vendor's business or trade, or some part of it, is carried on, at the time of the sale in bulk; a person who is appointed trustee; and a person named as trustee by the creditors of the vendor in their written consent to a sale in bulk. Bulk Sales acts. 4. A person who is declared by any Act to be a trustee or is, by the law of a province, a trustee, and, without restricting the generality of the foregoing, includes a trustee on an express trust created by deed, will or instrument in writing, or by parol. *Criminal Code*, R.S.C. 1985, c. C-46, s. 2. 5. Any person appointed as trustee under the terms of a trust indenture to which a corporation is a party and includes any successor trustee. 6. A member of a board of trustees. 7. The director of a corporation. 8. A person who is licensed or appointed under this Act. *Bankruptcy Act*, R.S.C. 1985, c. B-3, s. 2. See BARE ~; BOARD OF ~S; JUDICIAL ~;

LICENSED ~; OFFICIAL ~; PUBLIC ~; SCHOOL ~.

TRUSTEE DE SON TORT. A person treated like a trustee even though not appointed as a trustee, who assumes responsibility to hold trust property for a beneficiary. D.M.W. Waters, *The Law of Trusts in Canada*, 2d ed. (Toronto: Carswell, 1984) at 399.

TRUSTEE IN BANKRUPTCY. The person in whom a bankrupt's property is vested in trust for creditors.

TRUSTEE INVESTMENTS. The investments prescribed for investment of trust funds under the Trustee Act. *Cemeteries Act*, R.R.O. 1980, Reg. 91, s. 1.

TRUST FOR SALE. Imposes an obligation on the trustee to sell when the testator or settlor transfers property to the trustee on trust to convert the assets into money, and to distribute or invest these proceeds as directed. D.M.W. Waters, *The Law of Trusts in Canada*, 2d ed. (Toronto: Carswell, 1984) at 887.

TRUST FUND. 1. Money or property held in trust. 2. Money paid to a contractor by an owner or to a subcontractor by a contractor for the benefit of workers and people who supplied material for a contract. D.N. Macklem & D.I. Bristow, *Construction and Mechanics' Liens in Canada*, 5th ed. (Toronto: Carswell, 1985) at 3. See COMMON ~; WORKERS' ~.

TRUST FUNDS. 1. All money, property and security received or held by a credit union as trustee or as agent. *Credit Union Act*, R.S.B.C. 1979, c. 79, s. 1. 2. (a) Money held in trust by the government or a public officer; and (b) pension funds, sinking funds maintained by the government, money received for another person and money paid to the government as a deposit to ensure the doing of any act or thing. *Financial Administration Act*, S.B.C. 1981, c. 15, s. 1.

TRUST INDENTURE. 1. Any deed, indenture or other instrument, including any supplement or amendment thereto, made by a body corporate under which the body corporate issues or guarantees debt obligations and in which a person is appointed as trustee for the holders of the debt obligations issued or guaranteed thereunder. 2. Any deed, indenture or other instrument, including any supplement or amendment thereto, made by a bank under which the bank issues bank debentures and in which a person is appointed as trustee for the holders of the bank debentures issued thereunder. *Bank Act*, R.S.C. 1985, c. B-1, s. 133.

TRUST MONEY. All moneys received by a broker other than office money, and, without limiting the generality of the foregoing, includes money that belongs to a client in whole or in part or is to be held on his behalf or to his or another's order direction. *Real Estate Brokers Act*, R.S.M. 1970, c. R20, s. 2. See UNGUARANTEED ~.

TRUST OR LOAN CORPORATION. A Canadian corporation that carries on the business of a trust company within the meaning of the Trust Companies Act or the business of a loan company within the meaning of the Loan Companies Act. *Bank Act*, R.S.C. 1985, c. B-1, s. 193.

TRUST POWER. Imposes an obligation on the donee to exercise the power. D.M.W. Waters, *The Law of Trusts in Canada*, 2d ed. (Toronto: Carswell, 1984) at 692.

TRUST RECORDS. The books and records of a broker in which are or ought to be recorded receipts and disbursements of trust money and all relevant data respecting the circumstances in which, the purpose for which, and the grounds on which, the money is received and disbursed. *Real Estate Brokers Act*, R.S.M. 1970, c. R20, s. 2.

TRUTH SERUM. Sodium amytol or another similar substance. P.K. McWilliams, *Canadian Criminal Evidence*, 3d ed. (Aurora: Canada Law Book, 1988) at 9-40.

TSE. *abbr.* Toronto Stock Exchange.

T.T. *abbr.* Tribunal du Travail (Jurisprudence en droit du travail).

T.T.C. *abbr.* Toronto Transit Commission.

T.T. (QUÉ.). *abbr.* Tribunal du travail (Québec).

TUBERCULIN TEST. The introduction into the skin of a person of a substance approved under the Food and Drugs Act (Canada) for the purpose of detecting sensitivity of that person to the tubercle bacillus. Ontario regulations.

TUBERCULOSIS. See OPEN ~.

TUBERCULOSIS-ACCREDITED AREA. An eradication area or part thereof declared to be a tuberculosis-accredited area pursuant to section 74. *Animal Disease and Protection Regulations*, C.R.C., c. 296, s. 2.

TUBERCULOSIS-ACCREDITED HERD. A herd certified by the Minister to be a tuberculosis-accredited herd pursuant to section 74. *Animal Disease and Protection Regulations*, C.R.C., c. 296, s. 2.

TUBER UNIT. One hill of seed potatoes planted with one tuber or two or more hills planted consecutively from setts cut from one tuber. *Seeds Regulations*, C.R.C., c. 1400, s. 45.

TUBING. See FLEXIBLE ~.

TUG. *n.* 1. A steamship used exclusively for towing purposes. *Canada Shipping Act*, R.S.C. 1985, c. S-9, s. 2. 2. A ship used for towing or pushing purposes. *Pacific Pilotage Regulations*, C.R.C., c. 1270, s. 2.

TUGBOAT. *n.* Includes any vessel propelled by steam, combustive, electrical or other similar motive power, whether used exclusively in towage or not. *Tugboat Worker Lien Act*, R.S.B.C. 1979, c. 417, s. 1.

TUNA. *n.* Any fish by the name of tuna and includes fish of the species yellowfin (Thunnus albacares), bluefin (Thunnus thynnus), blackfin (Thunnus atlanticus), albacore (Thunnus alalunga), bigeye (Thunnus obesus), skipjack (Euthynnus pelamis), common bonito (Sarda sarda), Pacific bonito (Sarda chiliensis) or false albacore (Euthynnus alletteratus). *Tuna Fishery Regulations*, C.R.C., c. 834, s. 2.

TUNA FISH CANNERY. A building, structure, machinery, appurtenances, appliances and apparatus occupied and used in the business of canning any of the species of tuna fish or of converting the fresh tuna fish into canned tuna fish. *Fisheries Act*, R.S.B.C. 1979, c. 137, s. 12.

TUNNEL. *n.* 1. A subterranean passage made by excavating beneath the overburden, into which a worker enters or is required to enter to work. *Occupational Health and Safety Act*, R.R.O. 1980, Reg. 691, s. 1. 2. Includes tunnels, pits, shafts, slopes, airways, way leaves, rights of way, subways, crosscuts between tunnels, logments, sumps, and also all roadways, railways, tramways, haulageways, cableways, passageways, travellingways, and all other ways in such tunnels. *Mines Act*, R.S.N.S. 1967, c. 185, s. 1.

TURF GRASS MIXTURE. Every package of seed that is a turf grass mixture shall be labelled with the following information: (a) the term "turf grass mixture"; (b) the name and address of the seller; (c) the name of the grade of the seed; and (d) where packed in packages containing more than 3 kilograms, the name of each kind of seed that constitutes 5 per cent or more by mass of the mixture, or 2 per cent or more in the case of white clover. *Seeds Regulations*, C.R.C., c. 1400, s. 25 in part.

TURKEY. *n.* 1. Any turkey, male or female, live or slaughtered, of any size and includes any part of any turkey. Canada regulations. 2. A young turkey hen, young turkey tom, old turkey hen and old turkey tom. 3. A turkey 6 months of age or less of any variety, grade or class that is raised or kept for slaughter within the Province of Nova Scotia and sold for slaughter. *Nova Scotia Turkey Marketing Levies Order*, C.R.C., c. 169, s. 2. See BREEDER ~; BROILER ~;

HEAVY ~; LARGE ~; LIGHT ~; MATURE ~; YOUNG ~.

TURNING-OUT CONDITION. A lifeboat or life raft that is fully equipped but manned only by its launching crew. *Life Saving Equipment Regulations*, C.R.C., c. 1436, s. 1.

TURNKEY. *n.* A gaoler.

TURPENTINE. *n.* Any of the four products known commercially as gum spirits of turpentine, steam distilled wood turpentine, sulphate wood turpentine and destructively distilled wood turpentine. *Turpentine Labelling Regulations*, C.R.C., c. 1140, s. 2. See GUM SPIRITS OF ~; STEAM DISTILLED WOOD ~; SULPHATE WOOD ~.

TURPENTINE MIXTURE. Any commodity that contains turpentine mixed with any other material. *Turpentine Labelling Regulations*, C.R.C., c. 1140, s. 2.

TURPENTINE SUBSTITUTE. Any commodity that is represented to be a substitute for turpentine or that has applied to it any trade mark, trade name or brand name incorporating the word "turpentine" or any part or simulation of the word "turpentine". *Turpentine Labelling Regulations*, C.R.C., c. 1140, s. 2.

TURPIS CAUSA. [L.] A consideration so vile that no action can be founded on it. See EX TURPI CAUSA NON ORITUR ACTIO.

TURPIS EST PARS QUAE NON CONVENIT CUM SUO TOTO. [L.] A part which does not match the rest is unsightly.

TUTELAGE. *n.* Guardianship; being under a guardian's supervision.

TUTIUS SEMPER EST ERRARE ACQUIETANDO QUAM IN PUNIENDO, EX PARTE MISERICORDIAE QUAM EX PARTE JUSTITIAE. [L.] It is always safer to err by acquitting instead of by punishing, to act out of mercy instead of justice.

TUTOR. *n.* An instructor; a guardian or protector.

TV. *abbr.* Television.

TWEEN DECK SPACE. A closed space between two consecutive continuous decks and bounded by permanent bulkheads. *Dangerous Goods Shipping Regulations*, C.R.C., c. 1419, s. 16.

TWIST. *n.* In the axis of the bore of a firearm barrel, the inclination of rifling grooves expressed in terms of centimetres or inches of barrel length for one full turn of the grooves. F.A. Jaffe, *A Guide to Pathological Evidence*, 2d ed. (Toronto: Carswell, 1983) at 186. See CANADA ~.

TWO AXLE GROUP. Two consecutive single axles, not including the front axle of a motor vehicle, (i) that are entirely within either a motor vehicle or trailer or semi-trailer; (ii) in which the spacing between the consecutive axles is less than 2 metres; and (iii) which are not included in a three axle group within the meaning of clause (o) or a four axle group within the meaning of clause (h). *Highway Traffic Act*, R.S.O. 1980, c. 198, s. 97.

TWO-FAMILY DWELLING. A building designed exclusively for occupancy by two families living independently of each other. Canada regulations.

TWO JUSTICES. Two or more justices of the peace, assembled or acting together. *Interpretation Act*, R.S.C. 1985, c. I-21, s. 35.

TWO OR MORE TRACKS. Two or more main tracks upon any of which the current of traffic may be in either specified direction. *Regulations No. O-8, Uniform Code of Operating Rules*, C.R.C., c. 1175, Part III, s. 2.

TWO POST CLAIM. A mineral claim or fractional mineral claim located on or before February 28, 1975 or a two post claim located after January 1, 1978. *Mineral Act*, R.S.B.C. 1985, c. 259, s. 1.

TWO-THIRDS VOTE. The affirmative vote of two-thirds of the members of a council present at a meeting therof. *Municipal Act*, R.S.O. 1980, c. 302, s. 1.

TWP. *abbr.* Township.

TYPE. *n.* With reference to gas or electricity meters, means any group of meters built by a manufacturer to a definite specification under a specific designation and in which the component parts are substantially the same. Canada regulations.

TYPE 'A' CLOSING APPLIANCE. A gasketed closing appliance of approved construction that (i) is fitted in an opening adequately stiffened to provide strength equivalent to that of the unpierced bulkhead or deck in which it is fitted; (ii) is attached by hinges or some other approved method; (iii) is capable of being, (A) in the case of a door, closed securely by clamps all around the perimeter of the door or opening, spaced a mean distance of not more than .762 metre (2 feet 6 inches) apart; or (B) in the case of hatch cover, closed securely by not less than two clamps; and (iv) provides the same weathertight integrity as the unpierced bulkhead or deck in which it is fitted. *Hull Construction Regulations*, C.R.C., c. 1431, s. 117.

TYPE A SHIP. 1. A ship in which (a) no cargo ports or similar sideshell openings are below the freeboard deck; (b) there are only small main deck openings fitted with watertight gasketed hatch covers of steel or equivalent material; (c) no dimension of a main deck cargo opening is greater than 1.83 m and the total area of each such opening does not exceed 1.67m²; and (d) there are no more than two main deck cargo openings to a single cargo space. *Load Line Regulations (Inland)*, C.R.C., c. 1440, s. 1. 2. A self-propelled ship that complies with the construction standards specified as Type A in Schedule V. *Arctic Shipping Pollution Prevention Regulations*, C.R.C., c. 353, s. 2.

TYPE B, C, D OR E SHIP. (a) A self-propelled ship that complies with the construction standards specified as Type B, C, D or E in Schedule V; or (b) a ship that is not self-propelled, that complies with the construction standards specified as Type B, C, D or E in Schedule V and that is towed on a line or cable by a tug. *Arctic Shipping Pollution Prevention Regulations*, C.R.C., c. 353, s. 2.

TYPE 'B' CLOSING APPLIANCE. A close fitting closing appliance of approved construction that (i) is fitted in an opening adequately stiffened to provide strength equivalent to that of the unpierced bulkhead or deck in which it is fitted; (ii) is attached by hinges or some other approved method; and (iii) is capable of being closed securely by not less than two clamps. *Hull Construction Regulations*, C.R.C., c. 1431, s. 117.

TYPE B SHIP. A ship that is not a Type A ship. *Load Line Regulations (Inland)*, C.R.C., c. 1440, s. 1.

TYPE FOSSIL SPECIMEN. Any fossil specimen or portion thereof of a biological species used in the original scientific study and published description of that species. *Canadian Cultural Property Export Control List*, C.R.C., c. 448, s. 1.

TYPE MINERAL SPECIMEN. Any mineral specimen or portion thereof of a mineral species used in the original scientific study and published description of that species. *Canadian Cultural Property Export Control List*, C.R.C., c. 448, s. 1.

TYPE 1. When used in relation to a seat belt assembly, a lap belt for retaining movement of the pelvis. *Motor Vehicle Safety Regulations*, C.R.C., c. 1038, s. 209.

TYPE 3. When used in relation to a seat belt assembly, a combination pelvic and upper torso restraint for children in the approximate age range of 8 months to 6 years weighing not more than 50 pounds or 23 kilograms and capable of sitting upright by themselves. *Motor Vehicle Safety Regulations*, C.R.C., c. 1038, s. 209.

TYPE 2. When used in relation to a seat belt assembly, a combination pelvic and upper torso restraint. *Motor Vehicle Safety Regulations*, C.R.C., c. 1038, s. 209.

TYPE 2A. When used in relation to a seat belt assembly, an upper torso restraint for use only in conjunction with a pelvic restraint to constitute a Type 2 seat belt assembly. *Motor Vehicle Safety Regulations*, C.R.C., c. 1038, s. 209.

TYRE. *n.* That part of a wheel, roller or other contrivance for the moving of any object upon a highway which comes into direct contact with the surface of the highway. *Highway Traffic Act*, R.S.Nfld. 1970, c. 152, s. 2. See TIRE.

U.B.C. L. REV. *abbr.* University of British Columbia Law Review.

UBERRIMAE FIDEI. [L.] Of the utmost good faith.

UBI ALIQUID CONCEDITUR, CONCEDITUR ET ID SINE QUO RES IPSA ESSE NON POTEST. [L.] Where anything is granted, that without which the thing itself cannot exist is also granted.

UBI CESSAT REMEDIUM ORDINARIUM IBI DECURRITUR AD EXTRAORDINARIUM. [L.] When the ordinary remedy fails, recourse is had to the extraordinary.

UBI DAMNA DANTUR, VICTUS VICTORI IN EXPENSIS CONDEMNARI DEBET. [L.] Where damages are given, the losing party should pay the winner's costs.

UBI EADEM RATIO IBI IDEM JUS. [L.] Where there is a like reason, there is like law.

UBI JUS IBI REMEDIUM. [L.] Where a right exists, there is a remedy.

UBI LEX ALIQUEM COGIT OSTENDERE CAUSAM NECESSE EST QUOD CAUSA SIT JUSTA ET LEGITIMA. [L.] Where the law compels anyone to show cause, the cause must be just and lawful.

UBI LEX NON DISTINGUIT, NEC NOS DISTINGUERE DEBEMUS. [L.] Where the law does not distinguish, we should not either.

UBI NON EST PRINCIPALIS NON POTEST ESSE ACCESSORIUS. [L.] Where there is no principal, an accessory cannot be.

UBI QUID GENERALITER CONCEDITUR INEST HAEC EXCEPTIO SI NON ALIQUID SIT CONTRA JUS FASQUE. [L.] Where a grant is interpreted generally, this exception is always implied: that nothing should be contrary to law and right.

UBI SUPRA. [L.] At the place mentioned above.

UBI VERBA CONJUNCTA NON SUNT, SUFFICIT ALTERUTRUM ESSE FACTUM. [L.] Where words do not agree it suffices that one of them is complied with.

U.C. *abbr.* Upper Canada.

U.C. CH. *abbr.* Grant, Upper Canada Chambers Reports, 1846-1852.

U.C. CHAMB. *abbr.* Upper Canada Chambers Reports, 1846-1852.

U.C.C.P. *abbr.* Upper Canada Common Pleas Reports, 1850-1882.

U.C.E. & A. *abbr.* Upper Canada Error & Appeal Reports, 1846-1866.

U.C. JUR. *abbr.* Upper Canada Jurist, 1844.

U.C. JURIST. *abbr.* Upper Canada Jurist (1844-1848).

U.C.K.B. *abbr.* Upper Canada, King's Bench Reports (Old Series), 1831-1844.

U.C.L.J. *abbr.* Upper Canada Law Journal (1855-1864).

U.C.O.S. *abbr.* Upper Canada, King's Bench Reports (Old Series), 1831-1844.

U.C.Q.B. *abbr.* Upper Canada, Queen's Bench Reports, 1844-1882.

U.F.C. *abbr.* Unified Family Court.

U.K. *abbr.* United Kingdom.

ULCER. *n.* An open sore of mucous membrane or skin. F.A. Jaffe, *A Guide to Pathological Evidence*, 2d ed. (Toronto: Carswell, 1983) at 186.

ULLAGE. *n.* The percentage indicated in the schedules or the percentage calculated by use of the formula specified, means the percentage of free space to be left in a container in relation to the total capacity of the container. *Dangerous Goods Shipping Regulations*, C.R.C., c. 1419, s. 2.

ULTIMATE HEIR. The person entitled to take by descent or distribution the property of whatsoever nature of an intestate in the event of failure of heirs or next of kin entitled to take that property by the law in force before July 1, 1929. *Ultimate Heir Act*, R.S.A. 1980, c. U-1, s. 1.

ULTIMATE LIMIT STATES. Those states concerning safety and include exceeding the load carrying capacity, overturning, sliding, fracture and fatigue. *Building Code Act*, R.R.O. 1980, Reg. 87, s. 4.1.4.

ULTIMATUM. *n.* A final concession, condition or offer.

ULTIMA VOLUNTAS TESTATORIS EST PERIMPLENDA SECUNDUM VERAM INTENTIONEM SUAM. [L.] The testator's last will should be fulfilled according to true intentions.

ULTIMUM SUPPLICIUM. [L. ultimate punishment] Death.

ULTRA. *prep.* [L.] Beyond.

ULTRA-LIGHT. *adj.* With reference to a private aircraft, means an aircraft, other than a helicopter, designated as an ultra-light aircraft by the Minister pursuant to Part II of the Air Regulations. *Private Aircraft Flight Permits Order*, C.R.C., c. 57, s. 2.

ULTRA-LIGHT AIRCRAFT. An aircraft designated as such pursuant to subsection 211(3). *Air Regulations*, C.R.C., c. 2, s. 101.

ULTRASOUND. *n.* Mechanical energy having frequencies above 20 kilohertz. *Radiation Protection Act*, S.A. 1985, c. R-2.1, s. 1.

ULTRA VIRES. [L. beyond the powers] 1. Describes a statute judicially determined to be outside the powers conferred by the Constitution on the legislative body that enacted the statute; it is therefore invalid. P.W. Hogg, *Constitutional Law of Canada*, 2d ed. (Toronto: Carswell, 1985) at 96. 2. That a particular transaction is outside the capacity or power of a corporation. S.M. Beck *et al.*, *Cases and Materials on Partnerships and Canadian Business Corporations*, (Toronto: The Carswell Co., 1983) at 192. 3. Describes an invalid enactment, order or decision made outside the jurisdiction of the body purporting to make it.

UMBILICAL CORD. The cord containing two arteries and one vein which connects a fetus' navel with the placenta. F.A. Jaffe, *A Guide to Pathological Evidence*, 2d ed. (Toronto: Carswell, 1983) at 186.

UMBILICUS. *n.* [L.] The navel. F.A. Jaffe, *A*

Guide to Pathological Evidence, 2d ed. (Toronto: Carswell, 1983) at 18.

UMPIRAGE. *n.* Performing the duties of an umpire; arbitration.

UMPIRE. *n.* An umpire appointed under Part IV. *Unemployment Insurance Act*, R.S.C. 1985, c. U-1, s. 2.

U.N. *abbr.* United Nations.

UNA CUM OMNIBUS ALIIS. [L.] Along with everything else.

UNADJUSTED MUNICIPAL GRANT BASE. The result obtained from (a) multiplying the municipal tax base by the quotient resulting from dividing the overall tax base per capita by the municipal tax base per capita; (b) multiplying the municipal tax base by the quotient resulting from dividing the overall tax base per road kilometre by the municipal tax base per road kilometre; and (c) adding together the amount determined under paragraph (a) and one-quarter of the amount determined under paragraph (b). *An Act to Amend the Municipal Assistance Act*, S.N.B. 1986, c. 58, s. 1.

UNALLOCATED SURPLUS. Includes any net proceeds from the sale of assets on dissolution of the credit union after the liabilities of the credit union and the claims of creditors, members and shareholders have been satisfied. *Credit Union Act*, S.S. 1984-85-86, c. 45.1, s. 158.

UNANIMOUS RESOLUTION. A resolution (i) passed unanimously at a properly convened meeting of the corporation by all the persons entitled to exercise the powers of voting conferred by this Act or the by-laws and representing the total unit factors for all the units; or (ii) signed by all the persons who, at a properly convened meeting of a corporation, would be entitled to exercise the powers of voting conferred by this Act or the by-laws. Condominium acts.

UNANIMOUS SHAREHOLDER AGREEMENT. A written agreement to which all the shareholders of a corporation are or are deemed to be parties, whether or not any other person is also a party, or a written declaration by a person who is the beneficial owner of all the issued shares of a corporation.

UNASCERTAINED GOODS. 1. Goods defined by referring to a genus. G.H.L. Fridman, *Sale of Goods in Canada*, 3d ed. (Toronto: Carswell, 1986) at 57. 2. Goods identified only by description. G.H.L. Fridman, *Sale of Goods in Canada*, 3d ed. (Toronto: Carswell, 1986) at 89.

UNAUTHORIZED. *adj.* In relation to a signature or an endorsement, means one made without actual, implied or apparent authority and includes a forgery.

UNAUTHORIZED INVESTMENT OR LOAN. An investment or loan of a company's own funds or its deposits and investment money that is not authorized by, or is expressly prohibited by, this Act or the regulations or is made in contravention of any limitations or conditions prescribed by this Act or the regulations. *Trust Companies Act*, R.S.A. 1980, c. T-9, s. 1.

UNAUTHORIZED LOAN. See UNAUTHORIZED INVESTMENT OR LOAN.

UNAUTHORIZED PAYMENT. The amount of money by which the amount a practitioner has charged and been paid for rendering an insured service to an insured person exceeds the amount payable under the Plan for rendering that service to that insured person. *Health Care Accessibility Act*, S.O. 1986, c. 20, s. 1.

UNAUTHORIZED STRIKE. A strike begun without authority of union officials or by a minority of members of a union.

UNAUTHORIZED USE. The use of a credit card where that use of the credit card (i) is not by the credit card customer; and (ii) is not authorized by the credit card customer. *Consumer Credit Transactions Act*, S.A. 1985, c. 22.5, s. 28.

UNBECOMING. See CONDUCT ~.

U.N.B.L.J. *abbr.* University of New Brunswick Law Journal.

U.N.B. L. REV. *abbr.* University of New Brunswick Law Journal (Revue de droit de l'Université du Nouveau-Brunswick).

UNBROKEN LOT. A regular lot whose area is not diminished or increased by a natural or artificial feature shown on the original plan. *Surveys Act*, R.S.O. 1980, c. 493, s. 1.

UNCALLED CAPITAL. The part of the nominal value of shares a company issued which does not yet need to be paid.

UNCERTAINTY. *n.* In interpreting a will, a general reason to consider some gift or provision void because it is impossible to ascertain what the testator's intention was.

UNCERTIFIED SECURITY. A security, not evidenced by a security certificate, whose issue and transfer is registered or recorded in records maintained for that purpose by or on behalf of the issuer. *Business Corporations Amendment Act*, S.O. 1986, c. 57, s. 7.

UNCLASSED SHIP. A ship other than a classed ship. *Board of Steamship Inspection Scale of Fees*, C.R.C., c. 1405, s. 23.

UNCLE. *n.* In relation to any person, means a brother of the father or mother of that person. *Immigration Regulations*, C.R.C., c. 940, s. 2.

UNCLEAN FISH. A fish that has not recovered from spawning. *Newfoundland Fishery Regulations*, C.R.C., c. 846, s. 2.

UNCONSCIONABILITY. *n.* 1. Conduct on the part of the beneficiary of a transaction that could lead a court of equity to disapprove of what had happened and provide an alleged victim with relief even though the transaction was not entered through duress and one may not presume or establish undue influence. G.H.L. Fridman & J.G. McLeod, *Restitution* (Toronto: Carswell, 1982) at 235-236. 2. In Ontario, a "false, misleading or deceptive consumer representation". G.H.L. Fridman, *Sale of Goods in Canada*, 3d ed. (Toronto: Carswell, 1986) at 437.

UNCONTESTED DIVORCE. A divorce proceeding in which a respondent does not file a counter-petition or answer.

UNCULTIVATED LAND. 1. Land which is in its natural wild state, and includes also land which has been wholly or partially cleared, but is otherwise in its natural state. *Angling Act*, R.S.N.S. 1967, c. 9, s. 1. 2. Land that has not been reclaimed and is not being used for the purpose of tillage, orchard, meadow or pasture, or as land surrounding a dwelling house. *Lands and Forests Act*, R.S.N.S. 1967, c. 163, s. 84.

UNDELIVERABLE LETTER. Any letter that for any reason cannot be delivered to the addressee thereof and includes any letter delivery of which is prohibited by law or is refused by the addressee or on which postage due is not paid by the sender on demand. *Canada Post Corporation Act*, R.S.C. 1985, c. C-10, s. 2.

UNDELIVERABLE MAIL. Mail that for any cause cannot be delivered to the addressee and includes any mail whose delivery is prohibited by law or is refused by the addressee or on which postage due is not paid by the sender on demand. *Post Office Act*, R.S.C. 1970, c. P-14, s. 2.

UNDER CONTROL. The state of being manoeuvrable in accordance with these Regulations or the regulations under the Canada Shipping Act for preventing collisions at sea. *Air Regulations*, C.R.C., c. 2, s. 101.

UNDER DECK. In a hold, or in a covered space that is enclosed between steel bulkheads and is capable of being effectively closed against the weather. *Dangerous Goods Shipping Regulations*, C.R.C., c. 1419, s. 2.

UNDERDECK TONNAGE. The tonnage contained within the space below the main deckline of a ship derived by the following formula:

$$\frac{L \times B \times D \times .45}{100}$$

where L represents the overall length of the ship measured from the foremost part of the stemhead to the aftermost part of the transom rim timber or transom bulwark taffrail on the centre line of the ship, B represents the breadth amidships at deckline in feet to the outside of planking and D represents the greater of (i) depth of the vessel amidships in feet from the top of deck beam at centreline of vessel to the top of transverse floors; and (ii) .9 times the depth amidships in feet from the top of deck beam at centre line to the top of the wood keel. Newfoundland statutes.

UNDEREMPLOYED WORKER. A worker who (a) is willing to work and is available for full-time work, but who has worked, on an average, less than 30 hours per week in the 12 weeks immediately preceding the week in which he applies for a grant under these Regulations, or (b) in the locality in which he resides, is not employed full-time in the most remunerative form of employment for which he is qualified either by work experience or formal training. *Manpower Mobility Regulations*, C.R.C., c. 331, s. 2.

UNDERFLOOR-RACEWAY. *n.* A raceway suitable for use in the floor. *Power Corporation Act*, R.R.O. 1980, Reg. 794, s. 0.

UNDERGRADE. *n.* An egg that does not meet the requirements for the grade at which it is graded. *Egg Regulations*, C.R.C., c. 284, s. 2.

UNDERGRADUATE. *n.* A student enrolled at but not graduated from a university or other educational institution in a course in any branch of engineering or science, the practice of which constitutes professional engineering and that is recognized by the council. *Professional Engineers Act*, R.S.O. 1980, c. 394, s. 1.

UNDERGROUND. *adj.* Within the confines of any shaft, tunnel, caisson or cofferdam. *Occupational Health and Safety Act*, R.R.O. 1980, Reg. 691, s. 1.

UNDERGROUND MANAGER. Any person who has charge of the underground workings of a mine under the control and supervision of the manager and who possesses a certificate as such issued under this or some former Act. *Coal Mines Regulation Act*, R.S.N.S. 1967, c. 36, s. 3.

UNDERGROUND MINE. A mine that is not a surface mine. *Occupational Health and Safety Act*, R.R.O. 1980, Reg. 694, s. 1.

UNDERGROUND MINING CONCESSION. A mining property under private land sold for the purpose of operating mining rights. *Mining Act*, R.S.Q. 1977, c. M-13, s. 1.

UNDERGROUND RESERVOIR. Any mass of rock, consolidated or not, containing natural or artificial cavities, which is suitable to be used for the purpose of storing mineral substances or industrial products or residues or of permanently disposing thereof, or which may become suitable to be so used. *Mining Act*, R.S.Q. 1977, c. M-13, s. 1.

UNDER LEASE. *var.* **UNDER-LEASE.** 1. A lessee's grant to someone else (the under-lessee, under-tenant, sub-lessee or sub-tenant) of part of the whole interest under the original lease which reserves a reversion to the lessee. 2. Includes an agreement for an under lease where the under lessee has become entitled to have his under lease granted. Landlord and Tenant acts.

UNDER LESSEE. *var.* **UNDER-LESSEE.** Includes any person deriving title under or from a lessee or an under lessee. Landlord and Tenant acts.

UNDERLYING CONDITION. See PRE-EXISTING OR ~.

UNDERPRIVILEGED PERSON. See ECO-NOMICALLY ~.

UNDER SEAL. See CONTRACT ~.

UNDERTAKE. *v.* Includes undertake or negotiate, or solicit, or agree, or offer to undertake. *Insurance Act*, R.S.A. 1980, c. I-5, s. 1. See OFFER TO ~.

UNDERTAKING. *n.* 1. An assurance. 2. Every kind of business that an association or company is authorized to carry on. 3. An enterprise or activity, or a proposal, plan or program in respect of an enterprise or activity. 4. An undertaking in Form 12 given to a justice or judge. *Criminal Code*, R.S.C. 1985, c. C-46, s. 493. See BROADCASTING ~; COOPERATIVE ~; ELECTRICITY ~; EXTRA PROVINCIAL ~; FEDERAL WORK, ~ OR BUSINESS; GAS ~; INDUSTRIAL ~; LOCAL ~; MOTOR VEHICLE ~; PUBLIC UTILITY ~; SMALL ~; TELECOMMUNICATIONS ~.

UNDERTIME. *n.* Working less time than scheduled or agreed.

UNDER WAY. *var.* **UNDERWAY.** 1. The state of being on the surface of the water but not moored or fastened to any fixed object on the land or in the water. *Air Regulations*, C.R.C., c. 2, s. 101. 2. A vessel is under way when it is not at anchor, made fast to the shore or aground. Canada regulations.

UNDERWRITER. *n.* 1. A person who, (a) as principal, agrees to purchase a security for the purpose of distribution; (b) as agent, offers for sale or sells a security in connection with a distribution; or (c) participates directly or indirectly in a distribution described in paragraph (a) or (b), but does not include (d) a person whose interest in the transaction is limited to receiving the usual and customary distributor's or seller's commission payable by an underwriter or issuer; (e) a mutual fund that accepts its securities for surrender and resells them; (f) a corporation that purchases shares of its own issue and resells them; or (g) a bank with respect to securities described in this Act and to prescribed banking transactions. Securities acts. 2. A person who, as principal, agrees to purchase securities of a bank with a view to distribution thereof, or who, as agent for a bank or another person, offers for sale or sells securities of the bank in connection with a distribution of such securities, and includes a person who participates directly or indirectly in such a distribution other than a person whose interest in the transaction is limited to receiving a distributor's or seller's commission payable by an underwriter. *Bank Act*, R.S.C. 1985, c. G-1, s. 145. See LEADING ~; PRINCIPAL ~; SUB-~.

UNDERWRITING. *n.* With respect to a security, means the primary or secondary distribution of the security, in respect of which distribution (a) a prospectus is required to be filed, accepted or otherwise approved under or pursuant to a law enacted in Canada for the supervision or regulation of trade in securities; or (b) a prospectus would be required to be filed, accepted or otherwise approved but for an express exemption contained in or given pursuant to a law mentioned in paragraph (a). *Combines Investigation Act*, R.S.C. 1985, c. C-34, s. 5(2).

UNDERWRITING AGREEMENT. Any contract under which the Corporation undertakes conditionally or unconditionally to subscribe for shares, bonds or debentures of a corporation with a view to the resale thereof or of a part thereof. *Federal Business Development Bank Act*, R.S.C. 1985, c. F-6, s. 2.

UNDESIGNATED WATERS. The Canadian waters of Lake Ontario, Lake Erie, Lake Huron and Lake Superior that are not designated waters. *Great Lakes Pilotage Tariff Regulations*, C.R.C., c. 1267, s. 2.

UNDESIRABLE SEED. Seeds that are light, undersized, shrunken, broken, immature, damaged, diseased, injured, sprouted or frosted and (a) in the case of oats, includes double seeds; (b) in the case of barley, includes seeds with excess awns; (c) in the case of flax, includes scaly or papery seeds; (d) in the case of alfalfa and clover, includes brown seeds; (e) in the case of sweet clover, includes seeds covered by hulls; and (f) in the case of chaffy grasses, includes unbroken spikelets. *Seeds Regulations*, C.R.C., c. 1400, s. 2.

UNDEVELOPED BERRIES. Partly dried berries with wrinkled or tough skins. *Processed Fruit and Vegetable Regulations*, C.R.C., c. 291, schedule I, s. 18.

UNDILUTED. *adj.* 1. A condition that does not include air or other gases in excess of the quantity necessary for the processing requirements at a mine or mill. Canada regulations. 2. Not having water added primarily for the purposes of meeting the limits of authorized deposits prescribed by section 5. *Metal Mining Liquid Effluent Regulations*, C.R.C., c. 819, s. 2.

UNDISCLOSED PRINCIPAL. 1. Neither the principal's identity nor the fact that the agent is acting on someone else's behalf, is revealed to a third party with whom the agent contracts. G.H.L. Fridman, *The Law of Agency*, 5th ed. (London: Butterworths, 1983) at 187. 2. Any person or company on whose behalf a take-over bid is made whose identity is not disclosed in the take-over bid or in the take-over circular.

UNDISPUTED CORNER. A corner of a parcel of land at which the original post exists, or a corner established under this Act or any predecessor of this Act. *Surveys Act*, R.S.O. 1980, c. 493, s. 1.

UNDISPUTED POINT. A point of an original survey whose position is undisputed or can be satisfactorily established. *Surveys Act*, R.S.A. 1980, c. S-29, s. 1.

UNDIVIDED INTEREST. A beneficial ownership in common of the assets, liabilities, revenues and expenses of an oil pipeline by two or more companies or persons. *Oil Pipeline Uniform Accounting Regulations*, C.R.C., c. 1058, s. 2.

UNDOCKING. *n.* The manoeuvring of a ship from a berth when the pilot is replaced by another pilot pursuant to section 5 of the schedule, prior to the commencement of a trip. *Laurentian Pilotage Tariff Regulations*, C.R.C., c. 1269, s. 2.

UNDRAWN DRESSED POULTRY. Slaughtered poultry from which the blood and feathers have been removed.

UNDUE INFLUENCE. Psychological pressure which achieves ultimately the consent of the party being influenced; improper use by one party to a contract of any kind of coercion, oppression, abuse of power or authority or compulsion in order to make the other party consent. These constitute grounds to avoid the resulting contract. G.H.L. Fridman, *The Law of Contract in Canada*, 2d ed. (Toronto: Carswell, 1986) at 301.

UNEARNED ALLOWANCE. An allowance granted to a dealer subject to the fulfillment by the dealer of a condition that has not been fulfilled by the vendor but does not include an allowance for a payment made by a dealer within a specified time. *Farm Machinery and Equipment Act*, S.M. 1971, c. 83, s. 32.

UNECONOMIC LINE OF RAILWAY. A branch line that has been determined to be uneconomic by the Commission under sections 256 to 259. *Railway Act*, R.S.C. 1985, c. R-3, s. 261.

UNECONOMIC SERVICE. A passenger-train service that has been determined to be uneconomic by the Commission under section 266. *Railway Act*, R.S.C. 1985, c. R-3, s. 270.

UNEMPLOYABLE PERSON. A person who is certified by a legally qualified medical practitioner as being unable to engage in remunerative employment by reason of physical or mental disability. See PERMANENTLY ~

UNEMPLOYED. See ABOUT TO BECOME ~.

UNEMPLOYED PERSON. A person who is able to engage in remunerative employment and who is not so engaged at the time he makes application for assistance. *General Welfare Assistance Act*, R.S.O. 1980, c. 188, s. 1.

UNEMPLOYED WORKER. A worker who, (a) in the opinion of an employment officer, is without employment and seeking work; or (b) is the owner and operator of an agricultural, commercial or industrial enterprise and who (i) is unable to maintain himself and his dependants from the proceeds of such agricultural, commercial or industrial enterprise; (ii) has no other source of income; and (iii) has agreed to surrender his ownership and discontinue his operation of such agricultural, commercial or industrial enterprise for the purpose of seeking other work. *Manpower Mobility Regulations*, C.R.C., c. 331, s. 2.

UNEMPLOYMENT. See AVERAGE NATIONAL RATE OF ~.

UNEMPLOYMENT ASSISTANCE COSTS. The aggregate of the cost to the province, and the cost to municipalities in the province, of providing financial assistance to persons who are in need. *Unemployment Assistance Act*, R.S.C. 1970, c. U-1, s. 2.

UNEMPLOYMENT BENEFIT PLAN. See SUPPLEMENTARY ~.

UNEMPLOYMENT INSURANCE. A contributory, federal social insurance program to provide earnings-related benefits to anyone who is off work or unable to accept or look for work because of injury or other cause. K.D. Cooper-Stephenson & I.B. Saunders, *Personal Injury Damages in Canada* (Toronto: Carswell, 1981) at 2.

UNENCUMBERED INTEREST. The interest that an owner to uses is capable of appointing. Land Titles acts.

UNENFORCEABLE. *adj.* Describes a contract which, although it is valid, cannot be sued upon, for example because the Statute of Frauds requires written evidence.

U.N.E.S.C.O. *abbr.* United Nations Educational, Scientific and Cultural Organisation.

UNEXECUTED. *adj.* Describes one party's promise and side of a contract when that party's undertaking is not yet completed. G.H.L. Fridman, *The Law of Contract in Canada*, 2d ed. (Toronto: Carswell, 1986) at 2.

UNFAIR ACTS OR PRACTICES. False, misleading or deceptive consumer representation. See UNFAIR PRACTICES.

UNFAIR BUSINESS PRACTICES. See UNFAIR PRACTICES.

UNFAIR INSURANCE PRACTICE. (i) The commission of an act prohibited by this Act or the regulations; (ii) an unfair discrimination between individuals of the same class and of the same expectation of life, in the amount, payment or return of premiums or rates charged for contracts of life insurance or annuity contracts, in the dividend or benefits payable under those contracts or in the terms and conditions of those contracts; (iii) an unfair discrimination in a rate or schedule of rates between risks in Alberta of essentially the same physical hazard in the same territorial classification; (iv) the publication or distribution of an illustration, circular, memorandum or statement that misrepresents, or by omission is so incomplete that it misrepresents, the terms, benefits or advantages of a policy or contract of insurance issued or to be issued; (v) the making, publication or distribution of a false or misleading statement as to the terms, benefits or advantages of a contract or policy of insurance issued or to be issued; (vi) the making, publication or distribution of an incomplete comparison of a policy or contract of insurance with that of another insurer for the purpose of inducing, or that induces, an insured to lapse, forfeit or surrender a policy or contract; (vii) a payment, allowance or gift, or an offer to pay, allow or give, directly or indirectly, any money or thing of value as an inducement to a prospective insured to insure; or (viii) a consistent practice or conduct that results in an unreasonable delay or resistance to the fair adjustment or settlement of claims. *Insurance Act*, S.A. 1980 (Supp.), c. 11, s. 6.

UNFAIR OR DECEPTIVE ACTS OR PRAC-TICES IN THE BUSINESS OF INSURANCE. In addition to the practices listed in the definition of unfair insurance practice, any charge by a person for a premium allowance or fee other than as stipulated in a contract of insurance upon which a sales commission is payable to such person. Insurance acts. See UNFAIR INSUR-ANCE PRACTICE.

UNFAIR PRACTICES. (a) A false, misleading or deceptive consumer representation including, but without limiting the generality of the fore-going, (i) a representation that the goods or services have sponsorship, approval, perfor-mance characteristics, accessories, uses, ingre-dients, benefits or quantities they do not have; (ii) a representation that the person who is to supply the goods or services has sponsorship, approval, status, affiliation or connection he does not have; (iii) a representation that the goods are of a particular standard, quality, grade, style or model, if they are not; (iv) a representation that the goods are new, or unused, if they are not or are reconditioned or reclaimed, provided that the reasonable use of goods to enable the seller to service, prepare, test and deliver the goods for the purpose of sale shall not be deemed to make the goods used for the purposes of this subclause; (v) a representation that the goods have been used to an extent that is materially different from the fact; (vi) a representation that the goods or services are available for a reason that does not exist; (vii) a representation that the goods or services have been supplied in accordance with a previous representation, if they have not; (viii) a repre-sentation that the goods or services or any part thereof are available to the consumer when the person making the representation knows or ought to know they will not be supplied; (ix) a representation that a service, part, replacement or repair is needed, if it is not; (x) a represen-tation that a specific price advantage exists, if it does not; (xi) a representation that misrepre-sents the authority of a salesman, representative, employee or agent to negotiate the final terms of the proposed transaction; (xii) a representa-tion that the proposed transaction involves or does not involve rights, remedies or obligations if the representation is false or misleading; (xiii) a representation using exaggeration, innuendo or ambiguity as to a material fact or failing to state a material fact if such use or failure deceives or tends to deceive; (xiv) a represen-tation that misrepresents the purpose or intent of any solicitation of or any communication with a consumer; (b) an unconscionable consumer representation made in respect of a particular transaction and in determining whether or not a consumer representation is unconscionable there may be taken into account that the person making the representation or his employer or principal knows or ought to know, (i) that the consumer is not reasonably able to protect his interests because of his physical infirmity, igno-rance, illiteracy, inability to understand the language of an agreement or similar factors; (ii) that the price grossly exceeds the price at which similar goods or services are readily available to like consumers; (iii) that the consumer is unable to receive a substantial benefit from the subject-matter of the consumer representation; (iv) that there is no reasonable probability of payment of the obligation in full by the con-sumer; (v) that the proposed transaction is excessively one-sided in favour of someone other than the consumer; (vi) that the terms or conditions of the proposed transaction are so adverse to the consumer as to be inequitable; (vii) that he is making a misleading statement of opinion on which the consumer is likely to rely to his detriment; (viii) that he is subjecting the consumer to undue pressure to enter into the transaction; (c) such other consumer repre-sentations under clause (a) as are prescribed by the regulations. *Business Practices Act*, R.S.O. 1980, c. 55, s. 2. See UNFAIR ACTS OR PRACTICES.

UNFINISHED STONE. Includes crushed stone and what is generally known as blast furnace slag but does not include any stone on which chipping or work other than crushing has been performed in order for the stone to be capable of being mortared to another piece of stone in building a stone structure. *Retail Sales Tax Act*, R.R.O. 1980, Reg. 904, s. 1.

UNFIT FOR FOOD. The product would nor-mally be edible but is inedible by reason of disease, decomposition, injury or other reason. *Meat Inspection Regulations*, C.R.C., c. 1032, s. 2.

UNFIT MEMBER. A member who has dem-onstrated a lack of knowledge, skill, judgment or disregard for the welfare of a client in his practice, of a nature and extent making it desirable in the interests of the public or the member that he not be permitted to remain a member of the Institute, or that restrictions be imposed upon his membership. *Chartered Accountants' Act*, S.N.B. 1986, c. 87, s. 2.

UNFUNDED ACTUARIAL LIABILITY. See GOING CONCERN ~.

UNFUNDED LIABILITY. See INITIAL ~.

UNGUARANTEED TRUST MONEY. Trust money other than guaranteed trust money received by a trust company. *Trust Companies Act*, R.S.C. 1985, c. T-20, s. 2.

UNIDENTIFIED AUTOMOBILE. An automobile with respect to which the identity of either the owner or driver cannot be ascertained. *Insurance Act*, R.S.O. 1980, c. 218, s. 231.

UNIF. FAM. CT. *abbr.* Unified Family Court.

UNIF. L. CONF. PROC. *abbr.* Uniform Law Conference of Canada, Proceedings.

UNIFORM ACT PROVINCE. A province or territory of Canada designated in the regulations as a province or territory which has legislation in effect containing substantially the same as this Part and section 129. *Securities Act*, R.S.O. 1980, c. 466, s. 88.

UNIFORM CLOSING DAY. (i) Boxing Day; (ii) Canada Day; (iii) Christmas Day; (iv) Good Friday; (v) Labour Day; (vi) New Year's Day; (vii) Sunday; (viii) Thanksgiving Day; (ix) Victoria Day; (x) any other day the Governor in Council orders and declares by proclamation to be a uniform closing day for the purposes of this Act. *Retail Business Uniform Closing Day Act*, S.N.S. 1985, c. 6, s. 2.

UNIFORM CODE. The Uniform Code of Operating Rules set out in the schedule. *Regulations No. O-8, Uniform Code of Operating Rules*, C.R.C., c. 1175, s. 2.

UNIGENITURE. *n.* The state of being the only child.

UNILATERAL. *adj.* Having one side.

UNILATERAL CONTRACT. 1. Where a promisor agrees to do or not to do something if the promisee does or does not do something, but the promisee does not actually agree to do or not to do that thing. G.H.L. Fridman, *The Law of Contract in Canada*, 2d ed. (Toronto: Carswell, 1986) at 11. 2. An agreement between someone who auctions goods with no reserve and the highest bidder. G.H.L. Fridman, *Sale of Goods in Canada*, 3d ed. (Toronto: Carswell, 1986) at 460.

UNILINGUAL. *adj.* In relation to a bilingual position, means not qualified in the knowledge and use of both official languages at the level of proficiency required for the bilingual position. *Official Languages Appointment Regulations*, C.R.C., c. 1348, s. 2.

UNINCORPORATED MUTUAL FUND. A fund consisting of funds commingled under a collective investment contract managed on behalf of holders by a person who, on request,

redeems the units at their net asset value. *Securities Act*, S.Q. 1982, c. 48, s. 5.

UNINSURED AUTOMOBILE. An automobile with respect to which neither the owner nor driver thereof has applicable and collectible bodily injury liability and property damage liability insurance for its ownership, use or operation, but does not include an automobile owned by or registered in the name of the insured or his or her spouse. *Insurance Act*, R.S.O. 1980, c. 218, s. 231.

UNINTERRUPTED SERVICE. The uninterrupted period during which the employee is bound to the employer by a contract of employment, even if the performance of work has been interrupted without cancellation of the contract. *An Act Respecting Labour Standards*, S.Q. 1979, c. 45, s. 1.

UNION. *n.* 1. A trade union. 2. Any organization of employees, or any branch or local thereof, the purposes of which include the regulation of relations between employers and employees. 3. (a) a trade union as defined under the Industrial Relations Act; (b) any organization other than a trade union referred to in paragraph (a) representing employees to whom this Act applies formed for purposes that include the regulation of relations between employers and employees that has a written constitution, rules or by-laws setting forth its objects and purposes and defining the conditions under which persons may be admitted as members thereof and continued in such membership. *Occupational Health and Safety Act*, S.N.B. 1983, c. O-0.2, s. 1. 4. The union of the Provinces effected under the British North America Act, 1867, and subsequent acts. *Interpretation Act*, R.S.Q. 1977, c. I-16, s. 61. See AFFILIATED ~; CAPTIVE ~; CERTIFIED ~; CLOSED ~; COMMON LAW ~; COMPANY-DOMINATED ~; COMPANY ~; COUNTRY OF THE ~; CRAFT ~; CREDIT ~; CUSTOMS ~; FUND ~; HEALTH CARE ~S; HORIZONTAL ~; INDUSTRIAL ~; INTERNATIONAL ~; LABOUR ~; LEGISLATIVE ~; LOCAL ~; MULTICRAFT ~; OPEN ~; POLICEMEN'S ~; SUCCESSOR ~; TRADE ~; VERTICAL ~.

UNION ASSOCIATION. A group of workers constituted as a professional syndicate, union, brotherhood or otherwise or a group of such syndicates, unions, brotherhoods or other groups of workers otherwise constituted, having as its objects the study, safeguarding and development of the economic, social and educational interests of its members and particularly the negotiation and application of collective agreements. *An Act Respecting Occupational Health and Safety*, S.Q. 1979, c. 63, s. 1.

UNION CONTRACT. See COLLECTIVE BARGAINING AGREEMENT.

UNION DUES. Fees paid by union members to support their union. See REGULAR ~.

UNIONISM. See COMPULSORY ~.

UNIONIZED EMPLOYEE. 1. An employee on behalf of whom a trade union or council of trade unions has been certified as bargaining agent under this Act or voluntarily recognized by an employer, where the certification has not been revoked or the bargaining rights have not been terminated. *Labour Relations Act*, S.Nfld. 1977, c. 64, s. 54. 2. An employee who is employed by a unionized employer and in respect of whom a trade union has established the right to bargain collectively with the unionized employer. *Construction Industry Labour Relations Act*, S.S. 1979, c. C-29.1, s. 2.

UNIONIZED EMPLOYER. 1. An employer of unionized employees in the geographic area or areas and sector concerned. Labour Relations acts. 2. An employer in a trade division in respect of whom a trade union has established the right to bargain collectively on behalf of the unionized employees in that trade division: (i) pursuant to an order of the board under clause 5(a), (b) or (c) of The Trade Union Act; or (ii) as a result of the employer's having recognized the trade union as the agent to bargain collectively on behalf of those unionized employees; and, for the purposes of an application pursuant to section 11, means a unionized employer who employs one or more unionized employees on the day the application is made. *Construction Industry Labour Relations Act*, S.S. 1979, c. C-29.1, s. 2.

UNION LABEL. A label on a product indicating it has been made by unionized workers.

UNION LOCAL. See INDEPENDENT ~.

UNION RIGHTS. Specific provisions which a union frequently attempts to include in the terms of an agreement and which benefit the union itself, its officers or officials. The overriding purpose of such clauses is usually to insure that the union may fully discharge its statutory and contractual function to supervise the terms of the agreement. D.J.M. Brown and D.M. Beatty, *Canadian Labour Arbitration*, 2d ed. (Aurora: Canada Law Book, 1977) at 635.

UNION SCALE. The rate of pay set by a union contract as the minimum rate for a job.

UNION SECURITY. Provisions like voluntary check-off of union dues, union and closed shops which insure that any employees who are the beneficiaries of the agreement share any costs associated with the union's activities. D.J.M.

Brown and D.M. Beatty, *Canadian Labour Arbitration*, 2d ed. (Aurora: Canada Law Book, 1977) at 636.

UNION SHOP. A form of union security permitting an employer to hire non-union employees who must become members once employed. See MODIFIED ~.

UNION STEWARD. See SHOP STEWARD.

UNIT. *n.* 1. A group of employees. 2. An individual body of the Canadian Forces that is organized as such pursuant to section 17, with the personnel and materiel thereof. *National Defence Act*, R.S.C. 1985, c. N-5, s. 2. 3. Includes an identifiable part, portion or instalment of the entire consumer transaction or the consideration for or the subject matter of it. *Trade Practice Act*, R.S.B.C. 1979, c. 406, s. 1. 4. An area designated as a unit in a condominium plan. 5. That part of the pool or pools to which a unit operation applies that is within the unit area. *Oil and Gas Conservation Act*, R.S.A. 1980, c. O-5, s. 70. 6. A square of prescribed dimensions contained in a mineral claim. *Mineral Act*, R.S.B.C. 1979, c. 259, s. 1. See ACCOMMODATION ~; AIR TRAFFIC CONTROL ~; APPROPRIATE ~; APRON TRAFFIC CONTROL ~; AXLE ~; BARGAINING ~; BLOCK OF ~S; BRITISH THERMAL ~; CARETAKER'S ~; COCKTAIL MIXING ~; COMMERCIAL ~; COMPOSITE ~; CONDOMINIUM ~; CONSUMER ~; CONVERSION ~; COOPERATIVE ~; CRAFT ~; DEFECTIVE ~S; DEVELOPED ~; DRAINAGE ~; DRIVE-AWAY ~; DWELLING ~; ECONOMIC FARM ~; EXTENDED CARE ~; FAMILY ~; FIXED COMMERCIAL FISHING ~; FIXTURE ~; FOREST MANAGEMENT ~; FOUNDATION ~; FULLY SERVICED ~; HEAT RECOVERY ~; HOSTEL ~; HOUSEKEEPING ~; HOUSING ~; IMPERIAL ~S; INDUSTRIAL ~; INSURANCE ~; IRRIGABLE ~; LOCAL GOVERNMENT ~; LONG-TERM ~; MEDICAL SERVICE ~; METRIC ~S; MOBILE ~; MUNICIPAL ~; OBSERVATION ~; PARCEL COMPARTMENT ~; PILOTAGE ~; PLANT ~; POWER ~; PROPOSED ~; PROTOTYPE ~; RENTAL ~; RESIDENTIAL ~; RESIDUAL ~; SANITARY ~; SELF-CONTAINED DWELLING ~; SELF-CONTAINED ~; SPACING ~; SUBDIVISION ~; TERMINAL SERVICES ~; TUBER ~; ~S; VOTING ~.

UNIT AGREEMENT. An agreement to unitize the interests of owners in a pool or a part of a pool exceeding in area a spacing unit, or such an agreement as varied by a unitization order. *Oil and Gas Production and Conservation Act*, R.S.C. 1985, c. O-7, s. 29.

UNIT AREA. The area that is subject to a unit

agreement. *Oil and Gas Production and Conservation Act*, R.S.C. 1985, c. O-7, s. 29.

UNITARY STATE. A nation in which supreme authority is in one centre.

UNITAS PERSONARUM. [L.] Unity of people.

UNITED KINGDOM. The United Kingdom of Great Britain and Northern Ireland. Interpretation acts. See COURT OF THE ~.

UNITED STATES. The United States of America. Interpretation acts.

UNITED STATES FISHING VESSEL. A fishing vessel that is registered in the United States or, in the case of a vessel that is not registered, a fishing vessel that is entitled to fly the flag of the United States. *Transitional United States Fishing Vessel Licence Exemption Regulations*, C.R.C., c. 415, s. 2.

UNIT ENTITLEMENT. The unit entitlement of a strata lot and indicates the share of an owner in the common property, common facilities and other assets of the strata corporation and is the figure by reference to which the owner's contribution to the common expenses of a strata corporation is calculated. *Condominium Act*, R.S.B.C. 1979, c. 61, s. 1.

UNIT HEATER. A suspended space heater with an integral air circulating fan. *Building Code Act*, R.R.O. 1980, Reg. 87, s. 1.

UNITIZATION. *n.* (a) The development or production of oil and natural gas; (b) the implementation of a programme for the conservation of oil and natural gas; or (c) the co-ordinated management of interests in the oil and natural gas, within, upon, or under a location, part of a location, or a number of locations that are combined for that purpose pursuant to a unitization agreement entered into under this Act. *Oil and Natural Gas Act*, S.N.B. 1976, c. o-2.1, s. 1.

UNITIZATION ORDER. An order of the Committee made under section 41. *Oil and Gas Production and Conservation Act*, R.S.C. 1985, c. O-7, s. 29.

UNITIZED GOODS. Goods in packages that are consolidated, banded or otherwise securely held together to form a single shipping unit in order to facilitate mechanical handling, and that remain intact until removed from Board property. *Pacific Terminal Tariff By-law*, C.R.C., c. 1083, s. 2.

UNITIZED OPERATION. 1. The development or production of petroleum and natural gas, or the implementing of a program for the conservation of petroleum and of natural gas or the coordinated management of interests in them

in, on or under a location, part of a location or a number of locations combined for that purpose under a unitization agreement under this Act. *Petroleum and Natural Gas Act*, R.S.B.C. 1979, c. 323, s. 1. 2. The development or production of geothermal resources or the implementing of a program for the conservation of geothermal resources or the coordinated management of interests in them in, on or under a location, part of a location or a number of locations combined for that purpose under a unitization agreement under this Act. *Geothermal Resources Act*, S.B.C. 1982, c. 14, s. 1.

UNITIZED ZONE. A geological formation that is within a unit area and subject to a unit agreement. *Oil and Gas Production and Conservation Act*, R.S.C. 1985, c. O-7, s. 29.

UNIT MORTGAGE. Long term financing of a single condominium unit for its potential owner. W.B. Rayner & R.H. McLaren, *Falconbridge on Mortgages*, 4th ed. (Toronto: Canada Law Book, 1977) at 804.

UNIT OF ASSESSMENT. Place of business or premises. *An Act Respecting Municipal Taxation and Providing Amendments to Certain Legislation*, S.Q. 1979, c. 72, s. 191.

UNIT OF MINERALS. The minerals in, on, or under, land in a producing area, or a share or interest in such minerals, title to which minerals, or a share or interest therein, (i) is under The Real Property Act, and is set forth in one certificate of title under that Act, separately from the title to the surface of the land; or (ii) is under the old system of registration, and (A) is vested in the same owner, separately from the title to the surface of the land; and (B) was acquired from the same grantor by way of one instrument of conveyance, or one set of instruments of conveyance necessary to convey title from that grantor to the grantee. *Mineral Taxation Act*, R.S.M. 1970, c. M150, s. 2.

UNIT OF TAXATION. An individual; a family member who has the property or legal interest in income. W. Grover & F. Iacobucci, *Materials on Canadian Income Tax*, 4th ed. (Toronto: Richard De Boo Ltd., 1980) at 171.

UNIT OPERATING AGREEMENT. An agreement, providing for the management and operation of a unit area and a unitized zone, that is entered into by working interest owners who are parties to a unit agreement with respect to that unit area and unitized zone, and includes a unit operating agreement as varied by a unitization order. *Oil and Gas Production and Conservation Act*, R.S.C. 1985, c. O-7, s. 29.

UNIT OPERATION. 1. Those operations conducted pursuant to a unit agreement or a unitization order. *Oil and Gas Production and Conservation Act*, R.S.C. 1985, c. O-7, s. 29. 2. An operation where, pursuant to an agreement, interests in a mineral are merged, pooled, consolidated or integrated as a single unit, without regard to the boundaries of the separate parcels, for the purposes of (a) the development or production of the mineral within, on or under the parcels, or any specified stratum or strata or portion thereof within the parcels; or (b) the implementing of a program for the conservation of the mineral, or the co-ordinated management of interests in the mineral. *Land Titles Act*, R.S.A. 1980, c. L-5, s. 53.

UNIT OPERATOR. A person designated as a unit operator under a unit operating agreement. *Oil and Gas Production and Conservation Act*, R.S.C. 1985, c. O-7, s. 29.

UNITS. *n.* Those heat recovery units or heat recovery chillers that are installed in a central air-conditioning system specifically designed to incorporate such units or chillers for the purpose of recovery of heat from the system and its subsequent utilization, and does not include pipes, ducts or other related parts of the system of which the heat recovery unit or chiller is a part. *Retail Sales Tax Act*, R.R.O. 1980, Reg. 903, s. 1. See UNIT.

UNITRUST. *n.* A guarantee that a would-be "income" beneficiary will regularly receive a fixed percentage on the value of the trust property. D.M.W. Waters, *The Law of Trusts in Canada*, 2d ed. (Toronto: Carswell, 1984) at 867.

UNIT TRACT. The portion of a unit area that is defined as a tract in a unit agreement. *Oil and Gas Production and Conservation Act*, R.S.C. 1985, c. O-7, s. 29.

UNIT TRUST. A trust under which the interest of each beneficiary is described by reference to units of the trust.

UNITY OF INTEREST. Said of a joint tenant who has no greater interest in a property than any other joint tenant.

UNITY OF POSSESSION. Said of joint tenants who have undivided possession.

UNITY OF SEISIN. A situation in which someone seised of land which is subject to a profit à prendre, easement or similar right also becomes seised of the land to which that profit or right is annexed.

UNITY OF TIME. Said of joint tenants whose interests must arise at the same time.

UNITY OF TITLE. Said of joint tenants who hold their property by one and the same title.

UNIV. *abbr.* University.

UNIVERSAL COPYRIGHT CONVENTION. A convention drafted under the sponsorship of UNESCO and signed at Geneva in 1952. H.G. Fox, *The Canadian Law of Copyright and Industrial Designs*, 2d ed. (Toronto: Carswell, 1967) at 545.

UNIVERSAL POSTAL CONVENTION. The Universal Postal Convention drawn by the Universal Postal Union at the 1974 Lausanne Congress. *Special Services and Fees Regulations*, C.R.C., c. 1296, s. 2.

UNIVERSITARIAN INSTITUTION. A university or an institution affiliated with, incorporated in or annexed to it and providing education leading to the degrees of master, licentiate and doctor. *Teachers Scholarship Act*, R.S.Q. 1977, c. B-7, s. 2.

UNIVERSITY. *n.* An institution of higher learning which grants titles called degrees.

UNIVERSITY COURSE. A one-year university course beyond the Grade 13 level, or the equivalent of such one-year university course, where the course is part of a program leading to an acceptable university degree. *Education Act*, R.R.O. 1980, Reg. 269, s. 1.

UNIVERSITY CREDIT. A unit of recognition in respect of the successful completion of a university course, such that 60 such university credits are required to complete a four-year university program leading to an acceptable university degree. *Education Act*, R.R.O. 1980, Reg. 269, s. 1.

UNJUST ENRICHMENT. 1. An enrichment followed by a deprivation, with absence of any legal reason for the enrichment. G.H.L. Fridman & J.G. McLeod, *Restitution* (Toronto: Carswell, 1982) at 21. 2. Restitution.

UNLAWFUL. *adj.* Illegal.

UNLAWFUL ASSEMBLY. An assembly of three or more persons who, with intent to carry out any common purpose, assemble in such a manner or so conduct themselves when they are assembled as to cause persons in the neighbourhood of the assembly to fear, on reasonable grounds that they (a) will disturb the peace tumultuously; or (b) will by that assembly needlessly and without reasonable cause provoke other persons to disturb the peace tumultuously. *Criminal Code*, R.S.C. 1985, c. C-46, s. 63(1).

UNLAWFUL INDUSTRIAL ACTION. Industrial action that is prohibited by or under this Act. *Labour Code Amendment Act*, S.B.C. 1984, c. 24, s. 3.

UNLAWFULLY. *adv.* Without a lawful reason or excuse. S. Mitchell, P.J. Richardson & D.A. Thomas, eds., *Archbold Pleading, Evidence and*

Practice in Criminal Cases, 43d ed. (London: Sweet & Maxwell, 1988) at 1342.

UNLEADED GASOLINE. Gasoline that contains not more than .013 grams of lead per litre and not more than .0013 grams of phosphorus per litre.

UNLIMITED DIVIDEND RIGHT. The right without limitation as to the amount either to all or to a share of the balance of any dividends after the payment of dividends on any shares entitled to a preference, and includes the right to all or to a share of the balance of any surplus upon winding up after the repayment of capital. *Loan and Trust Companies Act*, c. L-11.2, s. 74.

UNLIQUIDATED. *adj.* Not ascertained.

UNLIQUIDATED DAMAGES. Damages whose amount depends on circumstances, and on the parties' conduct or is fixed by an estimate or opinion.

UNLOADED VEHICLE WEIGHT. The weight of a vehicle equipped with the containers for the fluids necessary for the operation of the vehicle filled to their maximum capacity, but without cargo or occupants. *Motor Vehicle Safety Regulations*, C.R.C., c. 1038, s. 2.

UNLOADING CHARGE. 1. A charge on goods for the unloading thereof from any railway car to the warehouse handling floor. *Montreal Cold Storage Warehouse Tariff By-law*, C.R.C., c. 1076, s. 2. 2. A charge for unloading goods from closed or gondola railway cars or closed motor transport vehicles and moving them to an ordinary place of rest and for all necessary labour and equipment. *Pacific Terminal Tariff By-law*, C.R.C., c. 1083, s. 28.

UNLOADING FACILITY. Any shore or sea installation that is used for the unloading of oil or an oily mixture from a ship. *Oil Pollution Prevention Regulations*, C.R.C., c. 1454, s. 2.

UNMARRIED. *adj.* When referring to an individual, means that the individual is not married and has never been married. *Immigration Regulations*, C.R.C., c. 940, s. 2.

UNMARRIED PERSON. Includes a widow, a widower, a divorced person and a married person who, in the opinion of a provincial authority, is living separate and apart from her or his spouse.

UNMARRIED WOMAN. 1. Includes a woman who, at the period of the conception of the child was unmarried, was divorced or was a widow. *Child Welfare Act*, R.S.M. 1970, c. C80, s. 23. 2. A woman who, at the date of the conception of a child conceived by her (i) was unmarried; or (ii) was a married woman who, for a period of at least 2 months immediately prior to that date, had been living separate and apart from her husband. *Child Welfare Act*, R.S.N.W.T. 1974, c. C-3, s. 52.

UNOBSTRUCTED. *adj.* As applied to a roadway or a lane of a laned roadway means not obstructed by a stationary object. *The Highway Traffic Act*, S.M. 1985-86, c. 3, s. 1.

UNOCCUPIED PUBLIC LAND. All public land that is not privately owned land. *Wildlife Act*, R.S.A. 1980, c. W-9, s. 1.

UNO FLATU. [L. with one breath] With the same intent.

UNORGANIZED DISTRICT. Those parts of the territorial districts that are without municipal organization. *Public Health Act*, R.R.O. 1980, Reg. 834, s. 36.

UNORGANIZED TERRITORY. 1. Any part of the province that is not in a municipality, and includes the area of a disorganized municipality. *Interpretation Act*, R.S.M. 1970, c. I80, s. 23. 2. That part of Ontario without county organization. *Municipal Act*, R.S.O. 1980, c. 302, s. 1. 3. Territory not included in a city, town, village, county or municipal district. *Public Health Act*, R.S.A. 1980, c. P-27, s. 1.

UNPAID SELLER. Within the meaning of this Act (a) when the whole of the price has not been paid or tendered; (b) when a bill of exchange or other negotiable instrument has been received as conditional payment and the condition on which it was received has not been fulfilled by reason of the dishonor of the instrument or otherwise. Sale of Goods acts.

UNPAID SELLER'S LIEN. A possessory lien which entitles the creditor to keep the debtor's goods until the debt is paid. G.H.L. Fridman, *Sale of Goods in Canada*, 3d ed. (Toronto: Carswell, 1986) at 314.

UNPATENTED. *adj.* When referring to land or mining rights, means land or mining rights for which a patent, lease, licence of occupation or any other form of Crown grant is not in effect. *Mining Act*, R.S.O. 1980, c. 268, s. 1.

UNPATENTED MINING CLAIM. A mining claim that is in good standing and for which the Crown has not issued a patent, lease or licence of occupation. *Mining Act*, R.S.O. 1980, c. 268, s. 1.

UNPRIME PELT. A skin or pelt that has been taken other than during the open season and includes a skin or pelt that shows natural markings of a dark or bluish colour on the flesh side. *The Fur Act*, R.S.S. 1978, c. F-24, s. 2.

UNPRIME SKIN. See UNPRIME PELT.

UNPRODUCTIVE LANDS. Rock barrens,

muskeg or lands covered by water. *Crown Timber Act*, R.S.O. 1980, c. 109, s. 1.

UNPROFESSIONAL CONDUCT. Any act or omission by a member which is an unjustifiable breach of duty to the public, a client, or any other member and includes a breach of the code of ethics. *Veterinary Medical Act*, S.M. 1974, c. 27, s. 1.

UNPROTECTED OPENING. A doorway, window or opening other than one equipped with a closure having the required fire-protection rating, or any part of a wall forming part of the exposing building face that has a fire-resistance rating less than required for the exposing building face. *Building Code Act*, R.R.O. 1980, Reg. 87, s. 1.

UNQUES. [Fr.] Still, yet.

UNQUES PRIST. [Fr.] Still ready.

UNREASONABLE SEARCH. 1. Prima facie, an illegal search. P.K. McWilliams, *Canadian Criminal Evidence*, 3d ed. (Aurora: Canada Law Book, 1988) at 4-24. 2. A search is reasonable if it is legally authorized, if the law authorizing the search is reasonable and if the way in which the search is conducted is reasonable. P.K. McWilliams, *Canadian Criminal Evidence*, 3d ed. (Aurora: Canada Law Book, 1988) at 4-25.

UNRECORDED WATER. Water whose right to use is not held under a licence or under a special or private Act. *Water Act*, R.S.B.C. 1979, c. 429, s. 1.

UNRELATED GROUP. A group of persons that is not a related group.

UNRESTRICTED LAND. Land that (i) under a by-law passed pursuant to section 39 of the Planning Act, or under an order made pursuant to section 35 of that Act is zoned for commercial or industrial use; or (ii) where subclause (i) does not apply, is assessed under the Assessment Act for residential assessment or is lawfully used and occupied or was last lawfully used or occupied for commercial, industrial or residential purposes, and that is not assessed under the Assessment Act, or is not actually used, as farm or agricultural land, woodlands, recreational land or as an orchard. *Land Transfer Tax Act*, R.S.O. 1980, c. 231, s. 1.

UNSAFE. *adj.* When used in respect of a building means, (i) structurally inadequate or faulty for the purposes for which it is used; or (ii) in a condition that could be hazardous to persons in the normal use of the building. *Building Code Act*, R.S.O. 1980, c. 51, s. 1.

UNSANITARY CONDITIONS. Such conditions or circumstances as might contaminate with dirt or filth, or render injurious to health,

a food, drug or cosmetic. *Food and Drugs Act*, R.S.C. 1985, c. F-27, s. 2.

UNSECURED CREDITOR. Any creditor of a company who is not a secured creditor, whether resident or domiciled within or outside Canada, and a trustee for the holders of any unsecured bonds issued under a trust deed or other instrument running in favour of the trustee shall be deemed to be an unsecured creditor for all purposes of this Act except for the purpose of voting at a creditors' meeting in respect of any of those bonds. *Companies Creditors Arrangement Act*, R.S.C. 1985, c. C-36, s. 2.

UNSECURED LOAN. A debt owing by a small business to a venture corporation that is not secured by a fixed or floating charge, by a hypothecation or pledge, by a guarantee, or otherwise and the terms of which do not entitle the venture corporation, either absolutely or contingently, to convert or cause the conversion of the debt into a debt that is not an unsecured loan. *Venture Corporations Act*, S.N.S. 1979-80, c. 20, s. 10.

UNSECURED TRADE CREDITOR. A person to whom a seller is indebted for stock, money or services furnished for the purpose of enabling the seller to carry on a business, whether or not the debt is due, and who holds no security or who is entitled to no preference in respect of his claim. Bulk Sales acts.

UNSIGHTLY PROPERTY. Any real property or part thereof upon which there is litter, dilapidated buildings, structures or parts thereof, which causes the real property or any part thereof to look unsightly.

UNSKILLED LABOUR. Workers with no identifiable skill or craft.

UNSOLD GOODS. Any goods: (i) that a franchisee is required to purchase under a pyramid franchise; and (ii) that have not been sold or used by the franchisee. *The Pyramid Franchises Act*, R.S.S. 1978, c. P-50, s. 2.

UNSOLEMN ADMISSION. More than simple speaking; there must be indication that the party is admitting something against interest. P.K. McWilliams, *Canadian Criminal Evidence*, 3d ed. (Aurora: Canada Law Book, 1988) at 14-7.

UNSOLICITED CREDIT CARD. A credit card that has not been requested in writing by the person to whom the credit card is issued but does not include a credit card that replaces or renews a credit card that was previously issued to that person at that person's request.

UNSOLICITED GOODS. Personal property whose receipt has not been requested by the recipient, but does not include personal property delivered to the recipient that the recipient knew or ought to have known was intended for delivery to another person.

UNSOUND MIND. See PERSON OF ~.

UNSTANDARDIZED FOOD. Any food for which a standard is not prescribed in this Part. *Food and Drug Regulations*, C.R.C., c. 870, s. B.01.001.

UNUM EST TACERE, ALIUD CELARE. [L.] It is one thing to be quiet, another to conceal.

UNUMQUODQUE EODEM MODO, QUO COLLIGATUM EST, DISSOLVITUR. [L.] Everything is loosened in the same way that it was bound.

UNUSED FARM IMPLEMENT. (i) A farm implement that is not a used farm implement, whether or not it has received pre-delivery services; (ii) a farm implement returned to the distributor or dealer under section 6 following the giving of a notice in respect of that farm implement under that section, unless that farm implement was sold to the dealer as a demonstrator and was invoiced and used by him as a demonstrator; and (iii) a farm implement that is not a used farm implement and that is transferred from one dealer to another dealer with the knowledge of the distributor. *Farm Implement Act*, S.A. 1982, c. F-4.1, s. 22.

UNUSED FARM MACHINERY AND EQUIPMENT. A machinery and equipment that has not been used whether or not it has received pre-delivery services. *Farm Machinery and Equipment Act*, S.M. 1971, c. 83, s. 32.

UNUSED PART. A part or parts assembly that has not been used, but does not include (i) a part that has been broken or severely damaged; (ii) a parts assembly that is incomplete and cannot be completed at reasonable expense as provided for in subsection (9)(a); (iii) a part or parts assembly that has been removed from a farm implement and replaced at no cost to the dealer for parts under a modification or warranty substitution program; or (iv) a seal or hose made of rubber, a gasket made of cork or a composition of materials, a seal made of leather, a liquid chemical that has deteriorated and is of limited use, or paint. *Farm Implement Act*, S.A. 1982, c. F-4.1, s. 22.

UNUSUAL DANGER. In relation to any occupation, (a) a danger that does not normally exist in that occupation; or (b) a danger under which a person engaged in that occupation would not normally carry out his work. *Mining Safety Act*, S.N.W.T. 1982 (3d Sess.), c. 12, s. 2.

UNWHOLESOME. *adj.* With respect to fish, means fish that has in or upon it micro-organisms of public health significance or substances toxic or aesthetically offensive to people.

UNWROUGHT METAL. Gold, silver, platinum or other precious metal in: (1) ore the value whereof exceeds 50 cents per kilogram; (2) nuggets, amalgams, concentrates or residues obtained from the treatment of ore; (3) ingots, bars, wire, beads or sheets. *Unwrought Metal Sales Act*, R.S.Q. 1977, c. V-5, s. 1.

UPDATING COURSE. A special course of training for certified tradesmen whose skill and knowledge have become inadequate due to innovations and developments in their designated trade. *Manpower Development Act*, R.S.A. 1980, c. M-3, s. 1.

UPHOLSTERED FURNITURE. Any furniture that is made or sold with cushions, loose or attached, or is itself stuffed or filled in whole or in part with any stuffing concealed by fabric or other flexible material or any such article that can be used for sitting, resting or reclining purposes. *Upholstered and Stuffed Articles Act*, R.R.O. 1980, Reg. 940, s. 1.

UPHOLSTERED OR STUFFED ARTICLE. Any object which contains stuffing.

UPLAND GAME BIRD. Includes the following birds and the birds of all species of the following families: tetraonidae, commonly known as grouse, including ruffed grouse, spruce grouse, prairie chickens, sharp-tailed grouse, sage grouse and ptarmigans; phasianidae, commonly known as pheasants and partridges, including ring-necked pheasants, European grey or Hungarian partridges, chukar partridges and quail; meleagrididae, commonly known as wild turkey. *The Game Act*, R.S.S. 1978, c. G-1, s. 2.

UPON PROOF. As applied to any matter connected with the licensing of an insurer or other person, means upon proof to the satisfaction of the superintendent. Insurance acts.

UPPER ISLAND COVE AND BRYANT'S COVE AREA. The waters of Newfoundland adjacent to that part of the coast in the vicinity of Upper Island Cove and Bryant's Cove in the district of Harbour Grace between Sailing Point on the south and Feather Point on the north, including both points. *Newfoundland Fishery Regulations*, C.R.C., c. 846, s. 346.

UPPER TIER MUNICIPALITY. A county or regional municipality. *Ontario Unconditional Grants Act*, R.S.O. 1980, c. 359, s. 1.

UPPER TORSO RESTRAINT. A portion of a seat belt assembly intended to restrain movement of the chest and shoulder regions. *Motor*

Vehicle Safety Regulations, C.R.C., c. 1038, s. 209.

UPSTREAM. *adj.* Closer to a power plant in a power plant/transmission line/electric distribution system sequence. *Electric Energy Marketing Act*, S.A. 1981, c. E-4.1, s. 1.

URANIUM UNDERTAKING. See SPECIFIED ~.

URBAN. *adj.* (i) A city, town, village or improvement district having a population of at least 5,000; (ii) a township having a population of at least 10,000; and (iii) a municipality adjacent to a city having a population of at least 100,000. *Election Act*, R.R.O. 1980, Reg. 279, s. 1.

URBAN AREA. 1. An area and areas adjacent thereto that are classified by Statistics Canada in its most recent census of Canada as urban. *Railway Relocation and Crossing Act*, R.S.C. 1985, c. R-4, s. 2. 2. A city, town or village. Alberta statutes.

URBAN CONSTITUENCY. A constituency that is wholly composed of an urban municipality or municpalities. *The Electoral Boundaries Commission Act*, S.S. 1986-87-88, c. E-6.1, s. 2.

URBAN DEVELOPMENT PLAN. A plan respecting the development and use of land within or within and adjacent to an urban area whereby it is proposed to control and regulate the use of that land for purposes of industry, commerce, government, recreation, transportation, hospitals, schools, churches, residences, homes for the elderly or for other purposes or classes of users, with or without subdivisions of the various classes. *Railway Relocation and Crossing Act*, R.S.C. 1985, c. R-4, s. 2.

URBAN DISTRICT. A municipality, village or built-up district. *Highway Traffic Act*, R.S.Nfld. 1970, c. 152, s. 2.

URBAN ELECTORAL DIVISION. An electoral division that comprises the whole or part of an urban municipality. *Electoral Boundaries Commission Act*, R.S.A. 1980, c. E-4, s. 1.

URBAN FSA CODE. An FSA code the second character of which is any numeral other than "0". *Mail Preparation Regulations*, C.R.C., c. 1281, s. 2.

URBAN MUNICIPAL ADMINISTRATOR. The clerk, secretary treasurer or treasurer of an urban municipality. *Urban Municipal Administrators Act*, S.S. 1980-81, s. U-8.1, s. 2.

URBAN MUNICIPALITY. A city, town or village.

URBAN POLLING DIVISION. 1. A polling division that is wholly contained within an incorporated city or town having a population of 5,000 or more, or within any other area directed by the Chief Electoral Officer to be or to be treated as an urban polling division, pursuant to section 21. *Canada Elections Act*, R.S.C. 1985, c. E-2, s. 2. 2. A polling subdivision included in whole or in part in a municipality of over 2,000 inhabitants or in any other municipality declared urban by the chief electoral officer on the recommendation of a returning officer. *Election Act*, S.Q. 1984, c. 51, s. 61. 3. A polling division within a municipality having a population of 5,000 or more, designated as an urban polling division by the Chief Electoral Officer. *Elections Act*, S.N.B. 1980, c. 17, s. 1.

URBAN POLLING SUBDIVISION. *var.* **URBAN POLLING-SUBDIVISION.** 1. A polling-subdivision included in whole or in part in a municipality of over 2,000 souls at the last general census or in any other municipality declared urban by the director general of elections on the recommendation of the returning-officer of the electoral district. *Election Act*, R.S.Q. 1977, c. E-3, s. 2. 2. A polling subdivision all or part of which is within a city or town. *Elections Act*, S.M. 1980, c. 67, s. 1.

URBAN RENEWAL. Action involving redevelopment, rehabilitation and conservation measures taken to renew and repair urban communities and protect them from blight and deterioration. *Housing Development Act*, R.S.N.S. 1967, c. 129, s. 1.

URBAN RENEWAL AREA. A blighted or substandard area of a municipal area for which a Lieutenant-Governor in Council has approved the implementation of an urban renewal scheme.

URBAN RENEWAL SCHEME. A scheme for the renewal of a blighted or substandard area of a municipal area that includes (i) a plan designating the buildings and works in the area that are to be acquired and cleared in connection with the scheme and for making available to persons dispossessed of housing accommodation by such acquisition or clearance, decent, safe and sanitary housing accommodation at rentals that are fair and reasonable having regard to the incomes of the persons to be dispossessed; (ii) a plan describing the proposed street pattern and land use for the area, and the program for the construction or improvement in the area of the municipality services, schools, parks, playgrounds, community buildings and other public facilities; (iii) a description of the methods planned for municipal direction and control of the use of land in the area, including zoning, building controls and standards of occupancy of buildings in the area; (iv) a description of the methods planned for the improvement, rehabilitation or replacement of privately owned facilities, including housing accommodation, that will continue in the area, and the techniques planned for retarding such facilities from becoming substandard; and (v) the estimated costs of the scheme and that will be developed in accordance or in harmony with an official community plan.

URBAN RENEWAL STUDY. A study or survey of conditions aimed at identifying blighted areas, determining housing requirements and providing data upon which an orderly program of housing and urban renewal measures may be based.

URBAN SCHOOL SECTION. A school section, except a school division or a district school area, that includes a municipality. *Education Act*, R.S.O. 1980, c. 129, s. 1.

URBAN SEPARATE SCHOOL. A separate school for Roman Catholics in an urban municipality. *Education Act*, R.S.O. 1980, c. 129, s. 1.

URBAN SEPARATE SCHOOL ZONE. A separate school zone established in an urban municipality that does not form part of a county or district combined separate school zone. *Education Act*, R.S.O. 1980, c. 129, s. 1.

URBAN SERVICE. (i) Land drainage; (ii) the collection and removal of ashes or garbage or other refuse; or (iii) street lighting. *District Municipality of Muskoka Act*, R.S.O. 1980, c. 121, s. 79.

URBAN ZONE. An area consisting of one urban municipality and lands adjacent thereto and within a distance of 5 kilometres therefrom, but does not include any part of any other urban municipality. *Public Commercial Vehicles Act*, R.S.O. 1980, c. 407, s. 1.

U.S. *abbr.* United States (of America).

U.S.A. *abbr.* United States of America.

USAGE. *n.* A practice which a government ordinarily follows, though it is not obligatory. Such a practice may become a convention. P.W. Hogg, *Constitutional Law of Canada*, 2d ed. (Toronto: Carswell, 1985) at 16. See IMMEMORIAL ~.

US DOT SPECS. The Specifications of the United States Department of Transportation. *Gasoline Handling Act*, R.R.O. 1980, Reg. 439, s. 1.

USE. *v.* Includes construct, demonstrate, test, operate, handle, repair, service and maintain. *Radiation Health and Safety Act*, S.S. 1984-85-86, c. R-1.1, s. 2. See ENTER AND ~.

USE. *n.* 1. Includes the provision by way of promotional distribution of any tangible personal property and the incorporation into any structure, building or fixture, of tangible personal property including those manufactured by the consumer or further processed or otherwise improved by him. *An Act to Amend Chapter 126 of the Revised Statutes, 1967, The Health Services Tax Act*, S.N.S. 1982, c. 27, s. 1. 2. Includes storage and the exercise of any right or power over tangible personal property incidental to the ownership of that property. 3. In relation to a trade-mark, means any use that by section 4 is deemed to be a use in association with wares or services. *Trade-marks Act*, R.S.C. 1985, c. T-13, s. 2. 4. The purpose for which land is intended, or to which it may be put. Canada regulations. See BENEFICIAL ~; CESTUI QUE ~; COMMERCIAL ~; COMMON ~; CONFORMING ~; DEAD ~; DEED TO ~S; DIRECTIONS FOR ~; DOMESTIC ~; ENERGY ~ PROJECT; EXCLUSIVE ~ PORTION; EXISTING ~; FARM ~; INTERNAL ~; LAND ~ CONTROL PLAN; LAND ~ DISTRICT; LAND ~ PLAN; MILEAGE CONTRACT ~; NON-CONFORMING ~; ORDINARY ~; OWNER TO ~S; PARENTERAL ~; PASSIVE ~; PERMITTED ~; PRINCIPAL ~; PRIOR ~; RESOURCE PERMIT; RESULTING ~; RIGHT OF ~; SHIFTING ~; SPRINGING ~; TRANSFER TO ~S; UNAUTHORIZED ~.

USE AND OCCUPATION. A person may claim for use and occupation when that person uses and occupies another's land with permission but without a lease or leasing agreement at a set rent.

USED AUTOMOBILE. An automobile that has been driven for any purpose except delivery to a dealer and servicing.

USED BOILER, PRESSURE VESSEL OR PLANT. A boiler, pressure vessel or plant that has been sold or exchanged and that has been moved from its previous site of installation for use elsewhere.

USED FARM IMPLEMENT. (i) A farm implement that was sold to the dealer as a demonstrator and was invoiced to him and used as a demonstrator; and (ii) a farm implement, other than one referred to in clause (c)(ii) or (iii), that has been operated for a distance or for a period of time in excess of that required to deliver it to the dealer and to enable the dealer to service, prepare and operate it for the purposes of sale. *Farm Implement Act*, S.A. 1982, c. F-4.1, s. 22.

USED FARM MACHINERY AND EQUIPMENT. Machinery and equipment (i) that was sold to a dealer as a demonstrator and was invoiced to him and used as a demonstrator; or (ii) that has been operated for a distance or for a period of time in excess of that required to deliver the machinery and equipment to the dealer and to enable the dealer to service, prepare and operate it for the purposes of sale. *Farm Machinery and Equipment Act*, S.M. 1971, c. 83, s. 32.

USED IMPLEMENT. (i) A farm implement that was sold to the dealer as a demonstrator and was invoiced to him and used as a demonstrator; or (ii) a farm implement (other than one referred to in clause (c)(ii)) that has been operated for a distance or for a period of time in excess of that required to deliver the implement to the dealer and to enable the dealer to service, prepare and operate it for the purposes of sale. *Farm Implement Act*, R.S.A. 1980, c. F-4, s. 18.

USED MOTORCYCLE. A motorcycle which has been used for any purpose other than its delivery or preparation for delivery by the merchant, the manufacturer or their representative. *Consumer Protection Act*, S.Q. 1978, c. 9, s. 1.

USED VEHICLE. A motor vehicle which has been sold, bargained, exchanged, given away or title transferred from the person who first acquired it from the manufacturer or importer, dealer or agent of the manufacturer or importer, and so used as to have become what is commonly known as "second hand" within the ordinary meaning thereof.

USEFUL BEAM. The radiation passing through the aperture, cone or collimator of the housing of an X-ray generating tube. Canada regulations.

USE OF LAND. Includes the mining or excavation of sand, gravel, clay, shale, limestone or other deposits whether or not for the purpose of sale or other commercial use of the material so mined or excavated. *An Act to Amend the Community Planning Act*, S.N.B. 1983, c. 18, s. 1.

USE PERMIT. A permit, issued by the council of a municipality, authorizing the use of a building or other structure for the purpose stated in the permit. *The Planning and Development Act*, R.S.S. 1978, c. P-13, s. 2.

USER. *n.* 1. A person who uses a thing. 2. A person who within a province utilizes or intends to utilize tangible personal property or a taxable service for personal consumption or for the consumption of any other person at her or his expense, or utilizes or intends to utilize tangible personal property or a taxable service on behalf of or as the agent for a principal who desired or desires to so utilize such property or taxable service for consumption by the principal or by any person at the expense of the principal. 3. A person who prepares a consumer report for his own use or causes a consumer reporting agency to prepare a consumer report for his use. Consumer Reporting acts. See DRUG ~; END ~; METER ~; MIS~; NATURAL ~; NON-NATURAL ~; NON-~; REGISTERED ~; RIGHT OF ~; WATER ~.

USER CHARGE. Any charge for an insured health service that is authorized or permitted by a provincial health care insurance plan that is not payable, directly or indirectly, by a provincial health care insurance plan, but does not include any charge imposed by extra-billing. *Canada Health Act*, R.S.C. 1985, c. C-6, s. 2.

USER CONTROL. A control that is provided on or external to a device by the manufacturer thereof for the purpose of adjustment or operation and that under normal usage, is accessible to the user. *Radiation Emitting Devices Regulations*, C.R.C., c. 1370.

USHER. *n.* A door-keeper; an official who keeps order and silence in a court.

USQUE AD MEDIUM FILUM AQUAE. [L.] Just to the middle of the stream.

USQUE AD MEDIUM FILUM VIAE. [L.] Just to the middle of the road.

USSMSG. *abbr.* United States standard metals gauge for sheet iron and steel. *Gasoline Handling Act*, R.R.O. 1980, Reg. 439, s. 1.

U.S.S.R. *abbr.* Union of Soviet Socialist Republics.

USUAL COVENANT. One of the covenants ordinarily inserted in a deed.

USUAL OR CUSTOMARY AUTHORITY. The authority which an agent in that particular business, trade, profession or place would customarily or normally possess unless the principal expressly said something to contradict it. G.H.L. Fridman, *The Law of Agency*, 5th ed. (London: Butterworths, 1983) at 54.

USUAL PLACE OF ABODE. The place where one of the parties habitually (a) resides; or (b) carries on business; or (c) is employed. *Marriage Act*, R.S.M. 1970, c. M50, s. 24.

USUFRUCT. *n.* The right to reap the fruits of something belonging to another, without wasting or destroying the subject over which one has that right.

USUFRUCTUARY. *n.* The person who enjoys a usufruct.

USURA EST COMMODUM CERTUM QUOD PROPTER USUM REI (VEL AERIS) MUTUATAE RECIPITUR; SED, SECUNDARIO SPERARE DE ALIQUA RETRIBUTI-

ONE, AD VOLUNTATEM EJUS QUI MUTUATUS EST, HOC NON EST VITIOSUM. [L.] Usury is a certain reward which one receives for the use of a thing (or money) lent; but, secondarily to hope for any return at the will of the party who borrowed is not corrupt.

USURPATION. *n.* Having charge of or retaining something belonging to another by using it.

USURY. *n.* 1. Originally, interest. 2. Now implies interest charged at a greater rate than statutes allow.

USUS EST DOMINIUM FIDUCIARIUM. [L.] Use is a fiduciary right of ownership.

UTENSIL. *n.* Any article or equipment used in the preparation, processing, packing, service, transport or storage of food, except a single-service article.

UTERO-GESTATION. *n.* Pregnancy.

UTERUS. *n.* The hollow muscular organ in females where embryos develop. F.A. Jaffe, *A Guide to Pathological Evidence*, 2d ed. (Toronto: Carswell, 1983) at 186.

U.T. FAC. L. REV. *abbr.* University of Toronto Faculty of Law Review.

UTILE PER INUTILE NON VITIATUR. [L.] What is useful is not spoiled by what is useless.

UTILITIES. *n.* Any one or more of the following: (i) systems for the distribution of gas, whether artificial or natural; (ii) facilities for the storage, transmission, treatment, distribution or supply of water; (iii) facilities for the collection, treatment, movement or disposal of sanitary sewage; (iv) storm sewer drainage facilities; (v) any other things prescribed by the Lieutenant Governor in Council by regulation, but does not include those systems or facilities referred to in subclauses 9(i) to (iv) that are exempted by the Lieutenant Governor in Council by regulation. *Planning Act*, R.S.A. 1980, c. P-9, s. 1. See UTILITY.

UTILITIES OFFICER. A person who assists a rural municipal authority in the organization, construction, operation and co-ordination, or any of them, of a rural gas utility or a public utility within the boundaries of that rural municipal authority. *Rural Gas Act*, R.S.A. 1980, c. R-19, s. 1.

UTILITY. *n.* A navigable water, a railway, a highway, an irrigation ditch, an underground telegraph or telephone line, a line for the transmission of hydrocarbons, power or any other substance, or a publicly owned or operated drainage system, dike or sewer. *National Energy Board Act*, R.S.C. 1985, c. N-7, s. 108. See ELECTRICAL ~; ELECTRIC ~; ENERGY ~; GAS ~; MUNICIPAL ~; POWER ~; PUBLIC ~; TELECOMMUNICATIONS ~; UTILITIES; WATER ~.

UTILITY COMPANY. A corporation that carries on business as a distributor or seller to the public of electrical energy, gas or steam or as a generator and seller of electrical energy or steam for distribution to the public.

UTILITY LINE. A pipe line, a telephone, telegraph, electric power or water line, or any other line that supplies a service or commodity to the public. *Ontario Energy Board Act*, R.S.O. 1980, c. 332, s. 1.

UTILITY SYSTEM. Equipment or facilities which are available to the public for the purpose of communicating by telephone, teletype or telegraph. *Social Security Assessment Act*, S.Nfld. 1972, c. 56, s. 9.

UTILITY VEHICLE. See OFF-ROAD ~.

UTILIZATION. *n.* Includes the prevention of waste or improvident or uneconomic production or disposition of minerals and the prohibition or limitation of the production of minerals in excess of transportation or market facilities, or reasonable market demand for any mineral produced, and includes the control in Saskatchewan of the production, transportation, distribution, sale, disposal and consumption of all minerals produced in Saskatchewan. *The Mineral Resources Act*, R.S.S. 1978, c. M-16, s. 2.

UTILIZATION EQUIPMENT. Equipment that utilizes electrical energy for mechanical, chemical, heating, lighting, or a similar useful purpose. *Power Corporation Act*, R.R.O. 1980, Reg. 794, s. 0.

UTI POSSIDETIS. [L.] As you possess.

U.T.L.J. *abbr.* University of Toronto Law Journal.

U. TORONTO FACULTY L. REV. *abbr.* University of Toronto Faculty of Law Review.

U. TORONTO L.J. *abbr.* University of Toronto Law Journal.

UT POENA AD PAUCOS, METUS AD OMNES PERVENIAT. [L.] Though punishment affects few, fear of punishment affects all.

UT RES MAGIS VALEAT QUAM PEREAT. [L. it is better for a thing to go well than to fail] Legislation should be interpreted to give it effect even if a broader intepretation is required. P. St. J. Langan, ed., *Maxwell on The Interpretation of Statutes*, 12th ed. (Bombay: N.M. Tripathi, 1976) at 45.

UTTER. *v.* Includes sell, pay, tender and put off. *Criminal Code*, R.S.C. 1985, c. C-46, s. 448.

UTTERING FORGED PASSPORT. While in or out of Canada, (a) forges a passport; or (b) knowing that a passport is forged (i) uses, deals with or acts upon it; or (ii) causes or attempts to cause any person to use, deal with, or act upon it, as if the passport were genuine. *Criminal Code*, R.S.C. 1985, c. C-46, s. 57(1).

U.W.O. L. REV. *abbr.* University of Western Ontario Law Review.

V. *abbr.* 1. Versus. 2. Volume. 3. Volt. 4. Victoria.

VACANCY. *n.* 1. An elected office for which there is no duly elected incumbent. *Local Government Election Amendment Act*, S.S. 1984-85-86, c. 51, s. 3. 2. Includes absence for any reason. *District Courts Act*, R.S.Nfld. 1970, c. 98, s. 2.

VACANT AREA. An area, claim or tract for which a license or lease has not been applied or in respect of which no license or lease is outstanding but does not include an area, claim or tract closed to (or against) application for license or lease by the Minister. *Mines Act*, R.S.N.S. 1967, c. 185, s. 1.

VACANT CROWN LAND. The surface of land owned by the Crown and in which no other person has any interest.

VACANTIA BONA. See BONA VACANTIA.

VACANT LAND. A parcel of land separately assessed that has no building thereon, but does not include any improved land. *Municipal Tax Sales Act*, S.O. 1984, c. 48, s. 1. See SERVICED ~.

VACANT RESIDENTIAL LAND. Land (i) that is used for purposes ancillary to a residence or is not used for any purpose; and (ii) that is designated under a land use by-law and subdivided for residential or country residential use. *Property Tax Reduction Amendment Act*, S.A. 1983, c. 92, s. 2.

VACATE. *v.* To cancel; to make ineffective.

VACATED COMMUNITY. A community the remaining inhabitants of which have moved from the community with financial or other assistance from the province. *Evacuated Communities Act*, R.S.Nfld. 1970, c. 114, s. 2.

VACATION. *n.* A period of the year during which courts do not conduct ordinary business. See CHRISTMAS ~; LONG ~; SHORT ~.

VACATION CAMP. Any installation, other than an establishment, where children under 18 years of age are sheltered during a period of school vacation and where recreational services and sports, educational or cultural equipment are provided. *Public Health Protection Act*, R.S.Q. 1977, c. P-35, s. 1.

VACATION PAY. 1. Four per cent, or after 6 consecutive years of employment by one employer, 6 per cent of wages of an employee during the year of employment in respect of which the employee is entitled to the vacation. *Canada Labour Code*, R.S.C. 1985, c. L-2, s. 183. 2. The wages to which an employee is entitled under this Part, whether or not the employee is entitled to annual vacation. *Labour Standards Act*, S.Nfld. 1977, c. 52, s. 7. 3. Four per cent of the wages of an employee during the year of employment in respect of which he is entitled to a vacation. *Labour Standards Act*, R.S.N.W.T. 1974, c. L-1, s. 17.

VACATION SCHOOL. A program of instruction offered to students at a time when the school is otherwise closed for vacation. *Education Act*, S.N.W.T. 1976 (3d Sess.), c. 2, s. 2.

VACCINATE. *v.* Vaccinate against brucellosis with vaccine in accordance with the regulations. Brucellosis acts.

VACCINATE. *n.* See OFFICIAL ~.

VACUUM BREAKER. A device used in a water supply pipe which, when strategically located, will prevent the reverse flow of water in the pipe by admitting air to the pipe and thereby preclude any back siphonage that might otherwise occur. *Ontario Water Resources Act*, R.R.O. 1980, Reg. 736, s. 1.

VACUUM PACK. A pack in which a minimum amount of packing media is used and the vacuum in the can is created mechanically. *Processed Fruit and Vegetable Regulations*, C.R.C., c. 291, s. 2.

VADIUM. *n.* A pledge or pawn. E.L.G. Tyler & N.E. Palmer, eds., *Crossley Vaines' Personal*

Property, 5th ed. (London: Butterworths, 1973) at 85.

VAGAL INHIBITION. Cessation of heart beat by stimulating the vagus nerve by immersion in cold water, pressure on the neck or a minor surgical procedure. F.A. Jaffe, *A Guide to Pathological Evidence*, 2d ed. (Toronto: Carswell, 1983) at 186.

VAGINA. *n.* The tubular passage of muscle in females which connects the cervix with the vulva. F.A. Jaffe, *A Guide to Pathological Evidence*, 2d ed. (Toronto: Carswell, 1983) at 186.

VAGRANCY. *n.* Every one commits vagrancy who (a) supports himself in whole or in part by gaming or crime and has no lawful profession or calling by which to maintain himself; or (b) having at any time been convicted of an offence under section 151, 152 or 153, subsection 160(3) or 173(2) or section 271, 272 or 273 or of an offence under a provision referred to in paragraph (b) of the definition "serious personal injury offence" in section 687 of the Criminal Code, chapter C-34 of the Revised Statutes of Canada, 1970, as it read before January 4, 1983, is found loitering or wandering in or near a school ground, playground, public park or bathing area. *Criminal Code*, R.S.C. 1985, c. C-46, s. 179(1).

VAGRANT. *n.* Vagabond; beggar.

VAGUS. *n.* The tenth cranial nerve which begins in the brain stem, passes through the neck and the chest and supplies branches to the larynx, carotid bodies, lungs, heart, stomach and abdominal organs. F.A. Jaffe, *A Guide to Pathological Evidence*, 2d ed. (Toronto: Carswell, 1983) at 186.

VALEAT QUANTUM. [L.] Let its weight stand.

VALID. *adj.* 1. Having force legally. 2. Issued in accordance with the applicable law and the articles of the issuer or validated. Business Corporations acts.

VALIDATE. *v.* To render in force for a prescribed period of time.

VALIDATION TAB. A tab affixed in any year to a commercial fishing vessel registration plate to indicate that the registration plate is valid for that year. *Atlantic Fishing Registration and Licensing Regulations*, C.R.C., c. 808, s. 2. See REGISTRATION ~.

VALID IDENTIFICATION. A document issued or approved by the airport manager authorizing the holder to have access to a restricted area of the airport. *Airport Tariff Regulations*, C.R.C., c. 886, s. 2.

VALID TENDER. A proposal, bid or offer that is submitted in response to an invitation from a contracting authority and meets all the requirements stipulated in the invitation. *Government Contracts Regulations*, C.R.C., c. 701, s. 2.

VALID TEST RUN. A test run (a) the result of which does not vary by more than 23 per cent from the arithmetical average of the results of all test runs made for the tested operation or that has been certified as a valid test run by the attending inspector; and (b) that is made using a sample taken during a minimum continuous operational period of 120 minutes. *Secondary Lead Smelter National Emission Standards Regulations*, C.R.C., c. 412, s. 11.

VALUABLE CONSIDERATION. Includes: (i) any consideration sufficient to support a simple contract; (ii) an antecedent debt or liability. Assignment of Book Debts acts. See ADEQUATE ~; FULL AND ~.

VALUABLE MINERAL IN PLACE. A vein, lode or deposit of mineral in place appearing at the time of discovery to be of such a nature and containing in the part thereof then exposed such kind and quantity of mineral or minerals in place, other than limestone, marble, clay, marl, peat or building stone, as to make it probable that the vein, lode or deposit is capable of being developed into a producing mine likely to be workable at a profit. *Mining Act*, R.S.O. 1980, c. 268, s. 1.

VALUABLE SECURITIES. Includes every document forming the title or evidence of the title to any property of any kind whatever. *Canada Shipping Act*, R.S.C. 1985, c. S-9, s. 2.

VALUABLE SECURITY. Includes (a) an order, exchequer acquittance or other security that entitles or evidences the title of any person (i) to a share or interest in a public stock or fund or in any fund of a body corporate, company or society; or (ii) to a deposit in a savings bank or other bank; (b) any debenture, deed, bond, bill, note, warrant, order or other security for money or for payment of money; (c) a document of title to lands or goods wherever situated; (d) a stamp or writing that secures or evidences title to or an interest in a chattel personal, or that evidences delivery of a chattel personal; and (e) a release, receipt, discharge or other instrument evidencing payment of money. *Criminal Code*, R.S.C. 1985, c. C-46, s. 2.

VALUATION. *n.* 1. The determination of the value of property for taxation purposes. 2. A valuation of an issuer or offeree company prepared by a qualified and independent valuer based upon techniques that are appropriate in the circumstances, after considering going concern or liquidation assumptions or both, together with other relevant assumptions that arrives at an opinion as to a value or range of values for the participating securities based upon such analysis without any downward adjustments to reflect the fact the participating securities do not form part of a controlling interest. *Securities Act*, R.R.O. 1980, Reg. 910, s. 164. See DUAL ~; GOING CONCERN ~.

VALUATION ADJUSTMENT. At a particular day means the amount obtained when the net value of Canada's assets and liabilities with respect to the International Monetary Fund, as then recorded in the Public Accounts of Canada, is subtracted from the net value of those assets and liabilities at the then current rate of exchange for Canadian dollars. *Bretton Woods Agreements Act*, R.S.C. 1985, c. B-7, s. 12.

VALUATION ALLOWANCE. An allowance for bad debts, depreciation or inventory. *The Co-operative Associations Act*, R.S.S. 1978, c. C-34, s. 2.

VALUATION DATE. The earliest of the following dates: (i) The date the spouses separate and there is no reasonable prospect that they will resume cohabitation; (ii) the date a divorce is granted; (iii) the date the marriage is declared a nullity; (iv) the date one of the spouses commences an application based on subsection 5(3) (improvident depletion) that is subsequently granted; (v) the date before the date on which one of the spouses dies leaving the other spouse surviving. *Family Law Act*, S.O. 1986, c. 4, s. 4.

VALUATION DAY. The starting point to calculate any capital gain and loss applied to property acquired before January 1, 1972. The valuation day for a publicly traded share, warrant or right is December 22, 1971 and for any other capital property is December 31, 1971.

VALUATION REPLOT. A replotting scheme based on the valuation of land to determine the redistribution of ownership of land within the replotting scheme. *Planning Act*, R.S.A. 1980, c. P-9, s. 123.

VALUE. *n.* 1. Any consideration sufficient to support a simple contract. Personal Property Security acts. 2. Valuable consideration. *Bills of Exchange Act*, R.S.C. 1985, c. B-4, s. 2. 3. Fair market value. 4. Assessed value, including improvements. 5. When applied to the value of unsold goods means: (i) the price at which the unsold goods, or parts thereof, were supplied to the franchisee; or (ii) the current price at which the unsold goods are supplied by the franchisor; under the marketing plan or system, whichever price is greater. *The Pyramid Franchises Act*, R.S.S. 1978, c. P-50, s. 2. 6. In respect of a by-product, goods or merchantable scrap or waste,

(a) where the manufacturer or producer has sold the by-product, goods or merchantable scrap or waste in an arm's length transaction, the price at which he sold the by-product, goods or merchantable scrap or waste; or (b) in any other case, the price at which the manufacturer or producer would ordinarily have sold the by-product, goods or merchantable scrap or waste in an arm's length transaction, at the time (i) the application for a drawback or refund is made, in the case of a drawback or refund; or (ii) the goods are exported, where section 16 applies and the customs duties have not been paid. *Duties Relief Act*, R.S.C. 1985 (2d Supp.), c. 21, s. 41(3) 7. At a particular time of an interest in a life insurance policy means, (i) where the interest includes an interest in the cash surrender value of the policy, the amount in respect thereof that the holder of the interest would be entitled to receive if the policy were surrendered at that time; and (ii) in any other case, nil. *Income Tax Act*, R.S.C. 1952, c. 148 (as am. S.C. 1970-71-72, c. 63), s. 148(9)(g). See ACTUARIAL PRESENT ~; ACCEPTED ~; ACTUAL ~; AGGREGATE ~; AMORTIZED ~; ANNUAL ~; ASSESSED ~; BOOK ~; COMMERCIAL ~; COMMODITY ~ OF GAS; COMMUTED ~; CURRENT ~ ACCOUNTING; DEDUCTIVE ~; DOUBLE ~; DUTY PAID ~; EN BLOC ~; EXCHANGE ~; FACE ~; FAIR ~; FIELD ~; GOING-CONCERN ~; GROSS ~; HOLDER FOR ~; INTRINSIC ~; LENDING ~; LEVIABLE ~; LOAN ~; MARKET ~; NET ~; NOMINAL ~; ORAL LD$_{50}$ ~; PAID-UP CAPITAL ~; PAR ~; PRESENT ~; PROBATE ~; PROPERTY ~; RATEABLE ~; REALIZABLE ~; REPLACEMENT ~; RESIDUAL ~; SALVAGE ~; SERVICE ~; SURRENDER ~; TAXABLE ~; THRESHOLD LIMIT ~; TRANSACTION ~.

VALUED POLICY. The policy of insurance is based on an agreement as to the value of the item insured. In the event of total loss, the insured can recover the total value and in the event of partial loss, a proportion of the agreed value. Raoul Colinvaux, *The Law of Insurance*, 5th ed. (London: Sweet & Maxwell, 1984) at 9.

VALUE FOR DUTY. In respect of goods, the value of the goods as it would be determined in accordance with sections 45 to 56. *Customs Act*, R.S.C. 1985 (2d Supp.), c. 1, s. 2.

VALUELESS STRAY. A stray that has no commercial value in the opinion of a veterinarian appointed by the secretary for the purpose of determining whether or not the stray should be destroyed. *The Stray Animals Act*, R.S.S. 1978, c. S-60, s. 2.

VALUE OF PERSONAL PROPERTY. The assessed value of personal property as determined annually by the assessor pursuant to the Assessment Act for other than general municipal taxation purposes. *Municipal Act*, R.S.B.C. 1979, c. 290, s. 492. See TAXABLE ~.

VALUE OF THE CONTRACT. The contract price or, where there is none established by the contract, the value of the goods to be furnished and the work to be done under the contract. *An Act to Amend the Social Services and Education Tax Act*, S.N.B. 1983, c. 85, s. 2.

VALUE OF THE PROPERTY LIABLE. In respect of jurisdiction in matters of salvage, means the value of the property when first brought into safety by the salvors. *Canada Shipping Act*, R.S.C. 1985, c. S-9, s. 2.

VALUE OF THE WORK AND COSTS OF THE WORK. Have the same meaning and include the value of the materials used and the value of the labour performed to complete the work. *Line Fences Act*, R.S.O. 1980, c. 242, s. 1.

VALUER. *n.* A person who appraises or sets value on property.

VALUE TO OWNER. Used generally in expropriation cases, it is compensatory and may bear no relation to fair market value, market value or fair value. It is the amount the owner would pay for property in lieu of being deprived of the enjoyment and use of it and includes the cost of locating and acquiring a substitute property, opportunity costs and lost income and sometimes quantified emotional factors. A. Bissett-Johnson & W.M. Holland, eds., *Matrimonial Property Law in Canada* (Toronto: Carswell, 1980) at V-9.

VALVE. See BACKWATER ~; FLUSH ~.

VANCOUVER FORMULA. A proposed constitutional amending formula which required agreement of the federal Parliament and two-thirds of the provincial legislatures which represent half of the population of all provinces. P.W. Hogg, *Constitutional Law of Canada*, 2d ed. (Toronto: Carswell, 1985) at 55.

VAPOUR. See INTOXICATING ~.

VAPOUR PRESSURE. The Reid vapour pressure measured in pounds per square inch absolute (psia) that is exerted by a volatile liquid at a given temperature. *Flammable Liquids Bulk Storage Regulations*, C.R.C., c. 1148, s. 2. See REID ~.

VARIABLE CREDIT. Credit made available under an agreement whereby the lender agrees to make credit available to be used from time to time, at the option of the borrower for the purpose of the purchase from time to time of goods, and, without limiting the generality of the foregoing, includes credit arrangements, commonly known as revolving credit accounts, budget accounts, cyclical accounts and other arrangements of a similar nature. Consumer Protection acts.

VARIABLE INSURANCE CONTRACT. A contract of life insurance under which the interest of the purchaser is valued for purposes of conversion or surrender by reference to the value of a proportionate interest in a specified portfolio of assets. *Securities Act*, R.R.O. 1980, Reg. 910, s. 1.

VARIABLE RATE MORTGAGE. A mortgage with a fixed monthly payment whose rate varies with interest rates. If the interest rate goes down, a larger payment is applied to principal, but if the interest rate goes up, any shortfall in interest payment is added to the principal. D.J. Donahue & P.D. Quinn, *Real Estate Practice in Ontario*, 4th ed. (Toronto: Butterworths, 1990) at 226.

VARIABLE TAX RATE SYSTEM. A system under which individual tax rates are determined and imposed for each property class. *Property Tax Reform (No. 1) Act*, S.B.C. 1983, c. 23, s. 5.

VARIATION. *n.* An express or implied agreement by which parties agree on a new contract or a new contract term which is mutually convenient and beneficial. G.H.L. Fridman, *Sale of Goods in Canada*, 3d ed. (Toronto: Carswell, 1986) at 272. See DETRIMENTAL ~ OR ALTERATION.

VARIATION ORDER. An order made under subsection 17(1). *Divorce Act*, R.S.C. 1985 (2d Supp.), c. 3, s. 2.

VARIATION PROCEEDING. A proceeding in a court in which either or both former spouses seek a variation order. *Divorce Act*, R.S.C. 1985 (2d Supp.), c. 3, s. 2.

VARIETAL CROSS. First generation corn which is a cross between (i) two named varieties; (ii) a named variety and an inbred line or top cross; or (iii) a named variety and a hybrid. *Seeds Regulations*, C.R.C., c. 1400, s. 19.

VARIETY. *n.* Has the meaning assigned to cultivar by the International Association of Biological Science's Commission on the Nomenclature of Cultivated Plants and denotes an assemblage of cultivated plants, including hybrids constituted by controlled cross-pollination, that (a) are distinguished by common morphological, physiological, cytological, chemical or other characteristics; and (b) retain their distinguishing characteristics when reproduced. *Seeds Regulations*, C.R.C., c. 1400, s. 2.

VARYING DUTY. A requirement of service that demands operation at loads and for intervals of time, both of which may be subject to wide variation. *Power Corporation Act*, R.R.O. 1980, Reg. 794, s. 0.

VAULT. *n.* 1. A structure wholly or partially above ground used for the temporary storage of human remains pending burial or other lawful disposition. *An Act to Amend the Cemetery Companies Act*, S.N.B. 1984, c. 18, s. 1. 2. An isolated enclosure, either above or below ground, with fire-resistant walls, ceilings and floors, for the purpose of housing transformers or other electrical equipment. *Power Corporation Act*, R.R.O. 1980, Reg. 794, s. 0.

V.C. *abbr.* Vice-chancellor.

VECTOR. See ENERGY ~.

VEGETABLE. *n.* 1. Potatoes offered for sale in Alberta and any other plant which the regulations designate as a vegetable. *Vegetable Sales (Alberta) Act*, R.S.A. 1980, c. V-1, s. 1. 2. Potatoes sold, offered for sale or held in possession for sale in Saskatchewan and includes any other plant sold, offered for sale or held in possession for sale in Saskatchewan which may be designated as a vegetable by the Lieutenant Governor in Council, but does not include seed potatoes certified pursuant to the Destructive Insect and Pest Act (Canada). *The Vegetable and Honey Sale Act*, R.S.S. 1978, c. V-2, s. 2. 3. Turnip.

VEGETABLES. *n.* 1. Green and wax beans, lima beans, red beets, cabbage, carrots, cauliflower, sweet corn, cucumbers, green peas, peppers, pumpkin and squash or tomatoes produced in Ontario other than green and wax beans, lima beans, red beets, cabbage, carrots, cauliflower, sweet corn, cucumbers, green peas, peppers, pumpkin and squash or tomatoes produced in Ontario that are used for any purpose other than processing. *Farm Products Marketing Act*, R.R.O. 1980, Reg. 387, Schedule, s. 2. 2. Green and wax beans, lima beans, red beets, cabbage, carrots, sweet corn, green cucumbers, green peas, pumpkins, squash, and tomatoes, broccoli, brussels sprouts, cauliflower, asparagus and other horticultural products. *Marketing Act*, R.S.P.E.I. 1974, c. M-4, s. 2. See CANNED ~; GREENHOUSE ~.

VEGETATION. *n.* Any tree, shrub, vine or plant or the fruit or any portion whatsoever of a tree, shrub, vine or plant.

VEHICLE. *n.* 1. Any conveyance that may be used for transportation by sea, land or air. 2. Any truck, automobile or other conveyance for use on land but does not include any vehicle running only on rails to which the Railway Act applies. 3. Includes a street car. 4. Any motor vehicle, aircraft or other conveyance designed to be driven or drawn by any means including mus-

cular power, and any part thereof, and includes any equipment necessary for the proper operation of the vehicle and any appurtenances of the vehicle. See ABANDONED ~; AIR CUSHION ~; ALL TERRAIN ~; AMBULANCE ~; ANTIQUE ~; ANTIQUE REPRODUCTION ~; ARTICULATED ~; CANADIAN ~; COMMERCIAL ~; COMBINATION OF ~S; COURTESY ~; DERELICT ~; DUAL-PURPOSE ~; DUMP ~; EMERGENCY ~; FARM ~; FIRE DEPARTMENT ~; FOREIGN ~; FREIGHT ~; HEAVY DUTY ~; HEAVY ~; HISTORIC ~; JUNKED ~; LIGHT DUTY ~; LIMITED ~; MOBILITY ~; MOTORIZED ~; MOTOR ~; NON-FARM ~; OFF-HIGHWAY ~; OFF-ROAD ~; OPEN-BODY TYPE ~; OUTSIZED ~; OVER-SNOW ~; PASSENGER ~; PLEASURE ~; PUBLIC SERVICE ~; PUBLIC ~; RAIL ~; RECONSTRUCTED ~; RECREATIONAL ~; ROAD ~; SCRAP ~; SERVICE ~; SIGHT-SEEING ~; SINGLE UNIT ~; SNOWMOBILE CONVERSION ~; SNOW ~; SPECIALLY CONSTRUCTED ~; TANK ~; TANK TRUCK ~; USED ~; WHEELCHAIR ~; WORK ~.

VEHICLE CAPACITY WEIGHT. The rated cargo and luggage load plus 150 pounds times the vehicles designated seating capacity. *Motor Vehicle Safety Regulations*, C.R.C., c. 1038, s. 111.

VEHICLE COMPONENT. A seat cushion, seat back, seat belt, headlining, convertible top, arm rest, trim panel including door, front, rear and side panel, compartment shelf, head restraint, floor covering, sun visor, curtain, shade, wheel housing cover, engine compartment cover, mattress cover and the interior of the vehicle including padding and crash-deployed components that are designed to absorb energy on contact by occupants in the event of a crash. *Motor Vehicle Safety Regulations*, C.R.C., c. 1038, s. 302.

VEHICLE ENGINE. An engine of 50 cubic inches or more capacity, and includes the exhaust emission system but does not include the engine of an off-road utility vehicle. *Motor Vehicle Safety Regulations*, C.R.C., c. 1038, s. 1100.

VEHICLE FUEL TANK. A vehicle's tank or container that is designed, intended or used to carry the fuel required to propel that vehicle and is connected for that purpose to the fuel system of the vehicle and includes any tank or container carried in or upon the vehicle that is capable of being easily connected to the fuel system of the vehicle. *Petroleum Products Act*, R.S.N.W.T. 1974, c. P-5, s. 2.

VEHICLE IDENTIFICATION NUMBER. 1. Any number or other mark placed on a motor vehicle for the purpose of distinguishing the motor vehicle from other similar motor vehicles. *Criminal Code*, R.S.C. 1985, c. C-46, s. 354(3). 2. A number consisting of arabic numerals, roman letters, or both that the manufacturer assigns to the vehicle for identification purposes. *Motor Vehicle Safety Regulations*, C.R.C., c. 1038, s. 2.

VEHICLE IMPACT SIMULATOR. A device that simulates, in the manner described in Schedule III, motor vehicle-barrier impact at motor vehicle speeds of 20 and 30 miles per hour. *Children's Car Seats and Harnesses Regulations*, C.R.C., c. 921, s. 2.

VEHICLE INSPECTION RECORD. A form required to be completed in accordance with the regulations prior to the issue of a vehicle inspection sticker. *Highway Traffic Act*, R.S.O. 1980, c. 198, s. 71.

VEHICLE INSPECTION SIGN. A traffic control device that is located adjacent to a highway, and immediately preceding a vehicle inspection station and that is designed to indicate to the operator (i) whether the station is being operated; and (ii) which vehicles are required to report to be weighed or inspected. *Motor Transport Act*, R.S.A. 1980, c. M-20, s. 1.

VEHICLE INSPECTION STATION. A site adjacent to a highway designed or used for the purpose of weighing or inspecting vehicles or their contents. *Motor Transport Act*, R.S.A. 1980, c. M-20, s. 1.

VEHICLE INSPECTION STICKER. The device issued as evidence that the inspection requirements and performance standards referred to in section 68 have been complied with. *Highway Traffic Act*, R.S.O. 1980, c. 198, s. 71.

VEHICLE SAFETY ITEM. Any component or equipment forming part of, attached to, or carried on a vehicle, or required to be worn by a passenger in or on a vehicle which may affect the safe operation of the vehicle or contribute to the safety of the driver, passengers or the public. *Vehicle Administration Act*, S.S. 1986, c. V-2.1, s. 46.

VEHICLE TANK. A measuring tank that is mounted on a vehicle other than a vehicle for railway use. *Weights and Measures Regulations*, C.R.C., c. 1605, s. 296.

VEHICLE WEIGHT. See GROSS ~; MAXIMUM LOADED ~; UNLOADED ~.

VEIN. *n.* A blood vessel which carries blood from tissues to the heart. F.A. Jaffe, *A Guide to Pathological Evidence*, 2d ed. (Toronto: Carswell, 1983) at 186.

VEIN OR LODE. Includes rock in place. *Yukon Quartz Mining Act*, R.S.C. 1985, c. Y-4, s. 2.

VELOCITY. See MUZZLE ~.

VENDEE. *n.* The person to whom one sells something.

VENDING MACHINE. 1. Any self-service device which upon insertion of a coin, coins or tokens, automatically dispenses unit servings of food either in bulk or in package form. *Public Health Act*, R.R.O. 1980, Reg. 840, s. 1. 2. A mechanical device that, when coins are deposited therein, dispenses stamps. *Sale of Postage Stamps Regulations*, C.R.C., c. 1293, s. 2.

VENDITION. *n.* Sale, selling.

VENDITIONI EXPONAS. [L. that you expose for sale] A writ addressed to a sheriff. See WRIT OF ~.

VENDOR. *n.* 1. A person who sells something. 2. Includes a person who barters or exchanges a stock in bulk with any other person for other property, real or personal. Bulk Sales acts. See ITINERANT ~; MILK ~; MOBILE HOME ~; REGISTERED ~; RETAIL ~; WHOLESALE ~.

VENDOR'S LIEN. When a vendor sells property on credit, the vendor may be entitled to a lien on it to secure an obligation from the purchaser. B.J. Reiter, R.C.B. Risk & B.N. McLellan, *Real Estate Law*, 3d ed. (Toronto: Emond Montgomery, 1986) at 914.

VENDOR TAKE-BACK. A vendor lends the purchaser part of the purchase price in exchange for a mortgage on the property. B.J. Reiter, R.C.B. Risk & B.N. McLellan, *Real Estate Law*, 3d ed. (Toronto: Emond Montgomery, 1986) at 970.

VENEREALLY INFECTED PERSON. A person suffering from a venereal disease.

VENEREAL DISEASE. 1. Syphilis, gonorrhea or soft chancre. *Criminal Code*, R.S.C. 1985, c. C-46, s. 289(4). 2. Includes syphilis, gonorrhea, chancroid, granuloma inguinale and lymphogranuloma venereum.

VENIAE FACILITAS INCENTIVUM EST DELINQUENDI. [L.] Ease of pardon is an incentive to do wrong.

VENIRE CONTRA FACTUM PROPRIUM. [L.] A later act, incompatible with an earlier act.

VENT. *n.* 1. A conduit or passageway for conveying the products of combustion from a gas appliance to the outer air. *Gas Act*, R.S.B.C. 1979, c. 149, s. 1. 2. Any mark placed on an animal by the owner or a poundkeeper denoting that the property in the stock bearing it has passed from the owner to some other person. Brand acts. See AIR ~; BACK ~; BRANCH ~; CIRCUIT ~; DRY ~; DUAL ~; GAS ~; LOOP ~; RELIEF ~; STACK ~; WET ~; YOKE ~.

VENT CONNECTOR. The part of a venting system that conducts the flue gases or vent gases from the flue collar of a gas appliance to the chimney or gas vent, and may include a draft control device. *Building Code Act*, R.R.O. 1980, Reg. 87, s. 1.

VENTILATED CABLETROUGH. A cable-trough having adequate ventilating openings with no opening exceeding 2 inches in a longitudinal direction. *Power Corporation Act*, R.R.O. 1980, Reg. 794, s. 0.

VENTILATED FLEXIBLE CABLEWAY. A ventilated metal raceway, into which conductors may be drawn, designed so as to be rigid in one plane and flexible in another plane at a 90 degree angle to the first plane and constructed so that approximately 30 per cent of its surface consists of ventilating openings. *Power Corporation Act*, R.R.O. 1980, Reg. 794, s. 0.

VENTILATION. See ADEQUATE ~; FORCED ~.

VENTILATION EQUIPMENT. A fan, blower, induced draft or other ventilation device used to force a supply of fresh, respirable, atmospheric air into an enclosed space or to remove ambient air from such space. *Canada Confined Spaces Regulations*, C.R.C., c. 996, s. 2.

VENTING. See STACK ~.

VENTRAL. See ANTERIOR.

VENTRICLE. *n.* 1. One of two lower chambers in the heart. F.A. Jaffe, *A Guide to Pathological Evidence*, 2d ed. (Toronto: Carswell, 1983) at 186. 2. One of four intercommunicating cavities in the brain which collect cerebrospinal fluid. F.A. Jaffe, *A Guide to Pathological Evidence*, 2d ed. (Toronto: Carswell, 1983) at 186.

VENTRICULAR FIBRILLATION. Ineffective and irregular contractions of the heart ventricles which lead to sudden death. F.A. Jaffe, *A Guide to Pathological Evidence*, 2d ed. (Toronto: Carswell, 1983) at 186.

VENT STACK. A continuous run of vent pipe connected to a soil stack, waste stack or building drain and terminating in the open air. *Ontario Water Resources Act*, R.R.O. 1980, Reg. 736, s. 1.

VENT SYSTEM. A system of piping installed to provide a flow of air to or from drainage piping or storm drainage piping. *Ontario Water Resources Act*, R.R.O. 1980, Reg. 736, s. 1.

VENTURE. *n.* 1. An undertaking accompanied

by risk. A. Bissett-Johnson & W.M. Holland, eds., *Matrimonial Property Law in Canada* (Toronto: Carswell, 1980) at BC-20. 2. Includes any business. A. Bissett-Johnson & W.M. Holland, eds, *Matrimonial Property Law in Canada* (Toronto: Carswell, 1980) at BC-21. See GROUP MANAGEMENT ~; GROUP ~; JOINT ~.

VENTURE CAPITAL CORPORATION. A Canadian corporation whose objects and activities are confined solely to (a) the provision of financing and loans to Canadian corporations in circumstances that involve the financing or lending corporation in the acquisition, holding or acceptance of hypothecation of equity securities and unsecured debt securities of the corporations being financed; (b) the provision of financial or management consulting services to Canadian corporations whose securities have been acquired by the corporation providing the services in a manner described in paragraph (a) or the provision of such services in contemplation of so acquiring securities; and (c) the provision of financing by participating in a limited partnership as a limited partner. *Bank Act*, R.S.C. 1985, c. B-1, s. 193.

VENTURE CORPORATION. See NOVA SCOTIA ~.

VENUE. *n.* The place for trial.

VERBA ACCIPIENDA SUNT SECUNDUM SUBJECTAM MATERIAM. [L.] Words should be interpreted according to the subject-matter.

VERBA AEQUIVOCA AC IN DUBIO SENSU POSITA INTELLIGUNTUR DIGNIORI ET POTENTIORI SENSU. [L.] Words which are equivocal and are used in a doubtful sense should be interpreted in the more suitable and stronger way.

VERBA ALIQUID OPERARI DEBENT — DEBENT INTELLIGI UT ALIQUID OPERENTUR. [L.] Words should be effectual — they should be interpreted so that they have some effect.

VERBA CARTARUM FORTIUS ACCIPIUNTUR CONTRA PROFERENTEM. [L.] The words of deeds should be interpreted most strongly against the person using them.

VERBA CUM EFFECTU ACCIPIENDA SUNT. [L.] Words should be interpreted so that they have some effect.

VERBA DEBENT INTELLIGI UT ALIQUID OPERENTUR. [L.] Words should be interpreted so that they have some effect.

VERBA GENERALIA RESTRINGUNTUR AD HABILITATEM REI VEL APTITUDINEM PERSONAE. [L.] General words should be limited to the aptness of the subject-matter or the aptitude of the person.

VERBA ILLATA INESSE VIDENTUR. [L.] Words referred to are considered to be included.

VERBA INTENTIONI, NON E CONTRA, DEBENT INSERVIRE. [L.] Words should be subservient to the intent, and not vice versa.

VERBA ITA SUNT INTELLIGENDA UT RES MAGIS VALEAT QUAM PEREAT. [L.] Words should be interpreted so that the thing succeeds more than it fails.

VERBAL. *adj.* Words spoken or written; frequently means spoken rather than written words.

VERBAL ORDER. 1. An order verbally given for a stated amount of a specified controlled drug by a person to whom a pharmacist is authorized by this Part to sell a controlled drug pursuant to a verbal or written order. *Food and Drug Regulations*, C.R.C., c. 870, c. G.01.001. 2. An order verbally given for a stated amount of a specified narcotic by a person to whom a pharmacist is authorized by these Regulations to sell a narcotic pursuant to a verbal or written order. *Narcotic Control Regulations*, C.R.C., c. 1041, s. 2.

VERBA POSTERIORA, PROPTER CERTITUDINEM ADDITA, AD PRIORA, QUAE CERTITUDINE INDIGENT, SUNT REFERENDA. [L.] Later words, added for certainty, should be referred to earlier words which need clarification.

VERBA RELATA HOC MAXIME OPERANTUR PER REFERENTIAM UT IN EIS INESSE VIDENTUR. [L.] Words referred to in an instrument have the same effect as if they were inserted in that instrument.

VERBATIM ET LITERATIM. [L.] Word by word and letter by letter.

VERBI GRATIA. For example.

VERDICT. *n.* 1. Includes the finding of a jury and the decision of a judge in an action. 2. In the case of an action being tried by a judge without a jury includes judgment. See GENERAL ~; PERVERSE ~.

VEREDICTUM, QUASI DICTUM VERITATIS, UT JUDICIUM QUASI JURIS DICTUM. [L.] A verdict is, so to speak, a statement of truth, just as a judgment is a statement of the law.

VERIFIED METER. A meter that has been verified in accordance with this Act and the regulations. *Electricity and Gas Inspections Act*, R.S.C. 1985, c. E-4, s. 2.

VERITAS NIHIL VERETUR NISI ABS-

CONDI. [L.] Truth fears nothing except concealment.

VERITAS NOMINIS TOLLIT ERROREM DEMONSTRATIONIS. [L.] The truth of the name removes any error in description.

VERMIN. *n.* An animal whose presence may be harmful to the health, comfort or welfare of an animal in a research facility, supply facility or pound.

VERNIX CASEOSA. A greyish-white, greasy substance which covers a fetus' skin. F.A. Jaffe, *A Guide to Pathological Evidence*, 2d ed. (Toronto: Carswell, 1983) at 186.

VERSUS. *prep.* [L.] Against.

VERTEBRATE FOSSIL. The fossilized remains of an animal that possessed a backbone. *Canadian Cultural Property Export Control List*, C.R.C., c. 448, s. 1.

VERTEBRATE TRACE FOSSIL. The fossilized trace of a vertebrate. *Canadian Cultural Property Export Control List*, C.R.C., c. 448, s. 1.

VERTICAL. *adj.* Not departing from the true vertical plane by more than 45°. *Ontario Water Resources Act*, R.R.O. 1980, Reg. 736, s. 1.

VERTICAL SERVICE SPACE. A vertical shaft provided in a building to facilitate the installation of building services including mechanical, electrical and plumbing installations and facilities such as elevators, refuse chutes and linen chutes. *Building Code Act*, R.R.O. 1980, Reg. 87, s. 1.

VERTICAL UNION. A union which accepts all workers in an industry as members regardless of their occupations.

VERY LOOSE. When it requires fewer than four blows per foot in a penetration test where the test is carried out in accordance with CSA A119.1-1960, "Code for Split-Barrel Sampling of Soils", as revised May 1, 1975. *Building Code Act*, R.R.O. 1980, Reg. 87, s. 4.2.1.5.

VESSEL. *n.* 1. Includes every description of ship, boat or craft used or capable of being used solely or partly for marine navigation without regard to method or lack of propulsion, a dredge, a floating elevator, a floating home, an oil rig, a sea-plane, a raft or boom of logs or lumber and an air cushion vehicle. 2. Where used to indicate a craft for navigation of the water, includes any ship, vessel or boat of any kind whatever, whether propelled by steam or otherwise and whether used as a sea-going vessel or on inland waters only, and also includes any vehicle. *Excise Act*, R.S.C. 1985, c. E-14, s. 2. 3. Includes any ship or boat or any other description of vessel used or designed to be used in navigation. *Canada Shipping Act*, R.S.C. 1985, c. S-9, s. 2. 4. Includes a machine designed to derive support in the atmosphere primarily from reactions against the earth's surface of air expelled from the machine. *Criminal Code*, R.S.C. 1985, c. C-46, s. 214 as amended by *Criminal Law Amendment Act*, R.S.C. 1985 (1st Supp.), c. 27, s. 33. 5. Where the context so admits, includes aircraft. *Health and Public Welfare Act*, R.S.Nfld. 1970, c. 151, s. 2. See AUXILIARY ~; CANADIAN ~; DANGEROUS OPERATION OF ~S; FERRY ~; FIRED ~; FISHING ~; GIVE-WAY ~; GOVERNMENT ~; MOTOR ~; NON-POWER ~; PLEASURE ~; POWER-DRIVEN ~; POWER ~; PRESSURE ~; REFRIGERANT ~; SAILING ~; STEAM ~.

VESSEL BROKER. A person engaged or acting as agent in chartering any vessel or contracting for cargo space for the carriage of grain by water. *Inland Water Freight Rates Act*, R.S.C. 1985, c. I-10, s. 2.

VESSEL CONSTRAINED BY HER DRAUGHT. A power-driven vessel which because of her draught in relation to the available depth of water is severely restricted in her ability to deviate from the course she is following. *Collision Regulations*, C.R.C., c. 1416, Rule 3.

VESSEL ENGAGED IN FISHING. Any vessel fishing with nets, lines, trawls or other fishing apparatus which restrict manoeuvrability, but does not include a vessel fishing with trolling lines or other fishing apparatus which do not restrict manoeuvrability. *Collision Regulations*, C.R.C., c. 1416, Rule 3.

VESSEL NOT UNDER COMMAND. A vessel which through some exceptional circumstance is unable to manoeuvre as required by these Rules and is therefore unable to keep out of the way of another vessel. *Collision Regulations*, C.R.C., c. 1416, Rule 3.

VESSEL RESTRICTED IN HER ABILITY TO MANOEUVRE. A vessel which from the nature of her work is restricted in her ability to manoeuvre as required by these Rules and is therefore unable to keep out of the way of another vessel. *Collision Regulations*, C.R.C., c. 1416, Rule 3.

VESSEL SERVICE. Any operaton of docking, undocking, turning, shifting or moving a vessel assisted by a tug. *Churchill Tug Tariff By-law*, C.R.C., c. 1069, s. 2.

VESSEL TRAFFIC CONTROLLER. The officer who controls vessel traffic from a Seaway station. *Seaway Regulations*, C.R.C., c. 1397, s. 2.

VEST. *v.* 1. With respect to a right or estate, to rest in some person. 2. Of a pension, to obtain or become entitled to an unalterable right to either transfer or withdraw that lump sum to another pension plan or R.R.S.P. or to receive, in the future, a deferred life annuity. A. Bissett-Johnson & W.M. Holland, eds., *Matrimonial Property Law in Canada* (Toronto: Carswell, 1980) at V-91.

VESTED IN INTEREST. With respect to an existing fixed right of future enjoyment.

VESTED IN POSSESSION. With respect to a right of present enjoyment which actually exists.

VESTED REMAINDER. An expectant interest which is limited or transmitted to the one who is able to receive it.

VESTED RIGHT. A right which is not contingent or may not be defeated by a condition precedent.

VESTING ORDER. A court order to give a person an interest in real or personal property which the court has authority to dispose of, encumber or convey. G.D. Watson & C. Perkins, eds., *Holmested & Watson: Ontario Civil Procedure* (Toronto: Carswell, 1984) at CJA-129.

VETCRAFT SHOP. A sheltered employment workshop operated by the Minister. *Vetcraft Shops Regulations*, C.R.C., c. 1582, s. 2.

VETERAN. *n.* 1. Any former member of the North West Field Force and any of the following persons, more particularly described in section 37, namely, (a) a veteran of the South African War; (b) a Canadian veteran of World War I or World War II; (c) an allied veteran; (d) a Canadian dual service veteran; (e) an allied dual service veteran; and (f) a Canadian Forces veteran. *War Veterans Allowance Act*, R.S.C. 1985, c. W-3, s. 2. 2. A person who (a) during World War I was on active service overseas in the naval, army or air forces or who served on the high seas in a seagoing ship of war in the naval forces of His Majesty or of any of the Allies of His Majesty, and who has left that service with an honourable record or has been honourably discharged; (b) during World War II was on active service (i) in the naval, army or air forces of His Majesty or of any of His Majesty's Allies and at the commencement of that active service was domiciled in Canada or Newfoundland; or (ii) in the naval, army or air forces of Canada, and, not being domiciled in Canada at the commencement of that active service, is a Canadian citizen, and who, in the course of that service, performed duties outside of the Western Hemisphere, or on the high seas in a ship or other vessel service that was, at the time the person performed those duties, classed as "sea time" for the purpose of the advancement of naval ratings, or that would have been so classed had the ship or other vessel been in the service of the naval forces of Canada; (c) during World War II served as a member of the Women's Royal Naval Services or as a member of the South African Military Nursing Service outside of the Western Hemisphere and who, at the commencement of her service during World War II, was domiciled in Canada or Newfoundland; (d) has been certified by the Under Secretary of State for External Affairs as having been enrolled in Canada or Newfoundland by United Kingdom authorities for special duty during World War II in war areas outside of the Western Hemisphere, and who served outside of the Western Hemisphere, and at the time of enrolment was domiciled in Canada or Newfoundland; or (e) during World War II served outside of the Western Hemisphere with the naval, army or air forces of His Majesty raised in Canada or Newfoundland as a representative of Canadian Legion War Services, Inc., the National Council of the Young Men's Christian Associations of Canada, Knights of Columbus Canadian Army Huts, or Salvation Army Canadian War Services, was authorized so to serve by the appropriate naval, army or air force authority and who, at the commencement of that service with those forces during World War II, was domiciled in Canada or Newfoundland. *Public Service Employment Act*, R.S.C. 1985, c. P-33, s. 48. 3. A person who had been paid or is entitled to be paid a war service gratuity under the War Service Grants Act, chapter W-4 of the Revised Statutes of Canada, 1970, and includes a person who served on active service (a) in any of the naval or army forces of Newfoundland or, having been recruited in Newfoundland, in any of the naval, army or air forces raised in Newfoundland by or on behalf of the United Kingdom; or (b) in any naval, army or air forces of His Majesty, other than those referred to in paragraph (a), in which the person enlisted when domiciled in Newfoundland. *National Housing Act*, R.S.C. 1985, c. N-11, s. 93(4). See OVER-SEAS ~; VOLUNTEER ~; WAR ~S; WIDOW OF A ~.

VETERAN ELECTOR. A person who is qualified and entitled, under section 66, to vote under these Rules. *Special Voting Rules*, R.S.C. 1985, c. E-2, Schedule II, s. 2.

VETERANS AFFAIRS. The federal ministry which economically, socially, mentally and physically supports veterans, certain civilians and their dependants.

VETERANS' CLUB. (a) The Royal Canadian

Legion; (b) Army, Navy, and Air Force Veterans in Canada; (c) War Amputations of Canada; (d) The Royal Canadian Air Force Association; (d) a chartered branch of an organization listed in paragraph (a), (b), (c) or (d) which is in good standing with the central organization; (f) British Ex-Servicemen's Association of Vancouver; or (g) The Royal Canadian Naval Association. *Liquor Control and Licensing Act*, R.S.B.C. 1979, c. 237, s. 1.

VETERINARIAN. *n.* A person holding a certificate or licence entitling that person to practise veterinary medicine.

VETERINARY. *n.* A person authorized to practise veterinary science.

VETERINARY BIOLOGICS. (a) Any helminth, protozoa or micro-organism; (b) any substance or mixture of substances derived from animals, helminths, protozoa or micro-organisms; or (c) any substance of synthetic origin manufactured, sold or represented for use in restoring, correcting or modifying organic functions in animals or for use in the diagnosis, treatment, mitigation or prevention of a disease, disorder, abnormal physical state, or the symptoms thereof, in animals. *Animal Disease and Protection Act*, R.S.C. 1985, c. A-11, s. 2.

VETERINARY DRUG. A substance or combination of substances used or intended or represented to be used as a drug for an animal.

VETERINARY LABORATORY. A facility or class of facility, on which or in which diseases are diagnosed, designated by regulation. *Veterinary Laboratory Act*, R.S.B.C. 1979, c. 424, s. 1.

VETERINARY MEDICINE. That branch of knowledge relating to the prevention, diagnosis and treatment of the diseases of, and injuries to animals. See PRACTICE OF ~.

VETERINARY SCIENCE. See VETERINARY MEDICINE.

VETERINARY SURGEON. A person licensed to practise veterinary medicine, veterinary surgery or veterinary dentistry in a province or territory of Canada.

VETERINARY SURGERY. The surgical, dental or medical treatment of animals, but does not include the castration, spaying, vaccinating or dehorning of animals. *Veterinary Profession Act*, R.S.N.W.T. 1974, c. V-3, s. 2.

VETO. *n.* A prohibition; the right to forbid.

VEXATA QUAESTIO. [L.] An undecided point.

VEXATIOUS PROCEEDING. A proceeding in which the party bringing it wishes only to embarass or annoy the other party.

VFR. *abbr.* The visual flight rules. *Air Regulations*, C.R.C., c. 2, s. 101. See DAY ~; NIGHT ~.

VFR FLIGHT. A flight conducted in accordance with the visual flight rules. *Air Regulations*, C.R.C., c. 2, s. 101. See SPECIAL ~.

VFR WEATHER CONDITIONS. Weather conditions equal to or above the minima prescribed pursuant to section 543. *Air Regulations*, C.R.C., c. 2, s. 101.

V.G. *abbr.* Verbi gratia.

VIA. *abbr.* Via Rail Canada Inc.

VIA. *prep.* By way of.

VIABILITY. *n.* With respect to new-born child, the ability to live after birth.

VIAE SERVITUS. [L. servitude of way] A right of way across another person's land.

VIA RAIL CANADA INC. The federal body which operates trains and manages Canadian passenger rail service, except for commuter trains.

VIA REGIA. [L. royal way] A highway.

VIA TRITA EST TUTISSIMA. [L.] A well-trodden road is the safest.

VIA TRITA VIA TUTA. [L.] A well-trodden road is a safe road.

VICARIOUS LIABILITY. Responsibility in law for the misconduct of another person. John G. Fleming, *The Law of Torts*, 6th ed. (Sydney: The Law Book Co., 1983) at 338.

VICARIOUS RESPONSIBILITY. The automatic responsibility of one person for another's wrongdoing through prior relationship only, irrespective of the first person's fault or deed. It is clear common law doctrine in the law of torts that a master can be vicariously liable for a tort committed by a "servant" who acts in the course and scope of employment. D. Stuart, *Canadian Criminal Law: a treatise*, 2d ed. (Toronto: Carswell, 1987) at 522.

VICARIUS NON HABET VICARIUM. [L.] A delegate does not have a delegate.

VICE-CHANCELLOR. *n.* The cleric who holds the office of principal assistant to the chancellor. *An Act Respecting Fabriques*, R.S.Q. 1977, c. F-1, s. 1.

VICE-CONSUL. *n.* An officer in a consulate.

VICE-PRINCIPAL. *n.* A teacher who is appointed to be in charge of a school in the absence of the principal. *Provincial Schools Negotiations Act*, R.S.O. 1980, c. 403, s. 1.

VICE VERSA. Conversely.

VICINAGE. *n.* Neighbourhood; places next to one another.

VICINI VICINORA PRAESUMUNTUR SCIRE. [L.] Neighbours are expected to know the neighbourhood.

VICTIM. *n.* 1. A person to whom or in respect of whom compensation is or may be payable under this Act. Criminal Injuries Compensation acts. 2. (a) For the purposes of Title II regarding compensation for bodily injury, means every person sustaining bodily injury in an accident, including the owner or driver of and every passenger in each automobile involved in the accident; (b) for the purposes of Title III regarding compensation for property damage, and of Title IV regarding the Fonds d'indemnisation, means every person sustaining property damage in an accident, including the owner or driver of and every passenger in each automobile involved in the accident. *Automobile Insurance Act*, R.S.Q. 1977, c. A-25, s. 1. 2. Includes any person entitled to a death benefit if the death of the victim results from the accident. *Automobile Insurance Act*, R.S.Q. 1977, c. A-25, s. 2. 4. An immunized person, a person who contracts a disease from an immunized person, the foetus of one of those persons or, in case of death, a person who is entitled to a death benefit. *An Act to Amend Various Legislation Respecting Social Affairs*, S.Q. 1985, c. 23, s. 18. See COMPENSATION FOR ~S OF CRIME; CRIME ~.

VICTUALLING HOUSE. A place conducted by a person, firm or corporation, who sells by retail all or any of the following: meals and drinks of all kinds for consumption on the premises only, and includes a delicatessen selling cooked meats, cooked vegetables, and cooked fish, not in sealed containers. *Shops Regulation Act*, R.S.M. 1970, c. S110, s. 3.

VIDE. *v.* [L.] See.

VIDE ANTE. [L.] See an earlier passage in the text.

VIDE INFRA. [L.] See a later passage in the text.

VIDELICET. *adv.* [L.] Namely; that is to say.

VIDEO DISTRIBUTOR. A person who distributes films to a video retailer or to another video distributor. *Motion Picture Act*, S.B.C. 1986, c. 17, s. 1.

VIDEO EXCHANGE. Any retail outlet which makes videofilm available to the public. *An Act to Amend the Theatres, Cinematographs and Amusements Act*, S.N.B. 1985, c. 69, s. 1.

VIDEOFILM. *n.* Includes videocassette, videodisc and videotape. *An Act to Amend the The-*

atres, Cinematographs and Amusements Act, S.N.B. 1985, c. 69, s. 1.

VIDEO MATERIAL. Includes video cassettes, video discs or any medium of the same nature on which a film is recorded. *Cinema Act*, S.Q. 1983, c. 37, s. 1.

VIDEO RETAILER. A person who distributes films to any person. *Motion Picture Act*, S.B.C. 1986, c. 17, s. 1.

VIDEO TAPE. See CANADIAN ~.

VIDE POST. [L.] See a later passage in the text.

VIDE SUPRA. [L.] See an earlier passage in the text.

VIDUITY. *n.* The state of being a widow.

VI ET ARMIS. [L.] By force and arms.

VIEW. *n.* A jury's inspection of any controversial thing, place where a crime was committed or person which a judge may order in the interest of justice at any time between when the jury is sworn and when they give their verdict. P.K. McWilliams, *Canadian Criminal Evidence*, 3d ed. (Aurora: Canada Law Book, 1988) at 7-7. See FIELD OF ~.

VIGILANTIBUS, NON DORMIENTIBUS, JURA SUBVENIUNT. [L.] The laws aid the watchful, not those who sleep.

VILLAGE. *n.* 1. Village commissioners incorporated pursuant to the Village Service Act. Nova Scotia statutes. 2. A village erected under any former Village Act. *The Municipal Unit and County Act*, R.S.S. 1978, c. M-35, s. 2. See RESORT ~.

VILLAGE DISTRICT. A school district situated wholly or in part within a village: but where a village, in which is situated in whole or in part a village district, is incorporated as a town, the district shall for the purposes of this Act become a town district on a date to be determined by the minister. *The School Act*, R.S.S. 1978, c. S-36, s. 2.

VIM VI REPELLERE LICET, MODO FIAT MODERAMINE INCULPATAE TUTELAE; NON AD SUMENDAM VINDICTAM, SED AD PROPULSANDAM INJURIAM. [L.] It is legal to repel force with force, as long as it is governed by a desire to defend; not to take revenge, but to ward off injury.

VINDICTIVE DAMAGES. Damages based on punishing the defendant, beyond compensatng the plaintiff.

VINE CROP. Cucumbers, pumpkins or squash produced in Ontario, (i) for processing under a contract between a grower and a processor; and (ii) on acreage or for tonnage specified in such contract. *Crop Insurance Act (Ontario)*, R.R.O. 1980, Reg. 227, s. 3.

VINEGAR. See PROOF ~.

VINYL CHLORIDE. A substance designated under the Ontario Occupational Health and Safety Act. D. Robertson, *Ontario Health and Safety Guide* (Toronto: Richard De Boo Ltd., 1988) at 5-416.

VIOLATES. *v.* Includes any disobedience, contravention, infraction, neglect or refusal, and whether or not the act is one of omission or commission. *Health Act*, R.S.B.C. 1979, c. 161, s. 1.

VIOLATION RECORD. Includes a report, made by any authority acting in an official capacity, that a person has: (i) been found at fault in respect of an automobile accident; or (ii) been convicted of an offence; relating to the use or operation of a motor vehicle. *The Automobile Accident Insurance Act*, R.S.S. 1978, c. A-35, s. 2.

VIOLATION TICKET. A document by which a complaint is laid and a summons issued in accordance with Section 32A. *Motor Carrier Act*, S.Nfld. 1974, c. 78, s. 2.

VIOLENTA PRAESUMPTIO ALIQUANDO EST PLENA PROBATIO. [L.] Vehement audacity is sometimes full proof.

VIPERINA EST EXPOSITIO QUAE CORRODIT VISCERA TEXTUS. [L.] An interpretation which eats the bowels out of a text is like a serpent.

VIR ET UXOR CONSENTUR IN LEGE UNA PERSONA. [L.] Husband and wife are held to be one person in law.

VIR ET UXOR SUNT QUASI UNICA PERSONA. [L.] Husband and wife are virtually one person.

VIRTUAL COOLING TIME. The time the internal temperature of a body takes to drop the first 85 per cent of the difference between the temperature of the environment and body temperature at death. This factor can be used to calculate the time of death. F.A. Jaffe, *A Guide to Pathological Evidence*, 2d ed. (Toronto: Carswell, 1983) at 186.

VIRULENT DISEASE. (i) Cholera; (ii) Diphtheria; (iii) Ebola virus disease; (iv) Gonorrhoea; (v) Hemorrhagic fever; (vi) Lassa fever; (vii) Leprosy; (viii) Marburg virus disease; (ix) Plague; (x) Syphilis; (xi) Smallpox; (xii) Tuberculosis; or a disease specified as a virulent disease by regulation made by the Minister. *Health Protection and Promotion Act*, S.O. 1983, c. 10, s. 1.

1140

VIS. *n.* [L.] Any violence, force or disturbance to people or property.

VISA. *n.* A document issued or a stamp impression made on a document by a visa officer. *Immigration Act*, R.S.C. 1985, c. I-2, s. 2. See EMPLOYMENT ~; NON-IMMIGRANT ~.

VISA OFFICER. An immigration officer stationed outside Canada and authorized by order of the Minister to issue visas. *Immigration Act*, R.S.C. 1985, c. I-2, s. 2.

VISCERA. *n.* The entrails and inedible internal organs of poultry. *Dressed and Eviscerated Poultry Regulations*, C.R.C., c. 283, s. 2.

VISIBILITY. *n.* The distance at which prominent unlighted objects may be identified by day and prominent lighted objects may be identified at night. *Air Regulations*, C.R.C., c. 2, s. 101. See FLIGHT ~; GROUND ~; RESTRICTED ~.

VISIBLE. *adj.* 1. When applied to lights, means visible on a dark night with a clear atmosphere. Canada regulations. 2. When applied to lights or other signals visible under normal atmospheric conditions. *Ferry Cable Regulations*, C.R.C., c. 1230, s. 2.

VISIBLE EMISSION. Any contaminant which can be detected by the naked eye. *Environmental Protection Act*, R.R.O. 1980, Reg. 308, s. 1.

VISITING FORCE. Any of the armed forces of a designated state present in Canada in connection with official duties, and includes civilian personnel designated under section 4 as a civilian component of a visiting force. *Visiting Forces Act*, R.S.C. 1985, c. V-2, s. 2.

VISITOR. *n.* 1. (i) An entrant as of right; (ii) a person who is lawfully present on premises by virtue of an express or implied term of a contract; (iii) any other person whose presence on premises is lawful; or (iv) a person whose presence on premises becomes unlawful after his entry on those premises and who is taking reasonable steps to leave those premises. *Occupiers' Liability Act*, R.S.A. 1980, c. O-3, s. 1. 2. A person who is lawfully in Canada, or seeks to come into Canada, for a temporary purpose, other than a person who is (a) a Canadian citizen; (b) a permanent resident; (c) a person in possession of a permit; or (d) an immigrant authorized to come into Canada pursuant to paragraph 14(2)(b), 23(1)(b) or 32(3)(b). *Immigration Act*, R.S.C. 1985, c. I-2, s. 2. 3. An inspector for an eleemosynary, ecclesiastical or other corporation or institution such as a university. 4. The officer designated by the competent religious authority. *Religious Corporations Act*, R.S.Q. 1977, c. C-71, s. 1. 5. The bishop of the place or any other person appointed as visitor by such bishop of the place. *Roman Catholic Cemetery Corporations Act*, R.S.Q. 1977, c. C-69, s. 1.

VIS LEGIBUS EST INIMICA. [L.] Violence is inimical to law.

VIS MAJOR. The operation of natural forces and the malicious acts of strangers. John G. Fleming, *The Law of Torts*, 6th ed. (Sydney: The Law Book Co., 1983) at 317.

VISUAL FLIGHT RULES. The rule set forth in Division III of Part V of these Regulations and in the orders and directions made by the Minister thereunder. *Air Regulations*, C.R.C., c. 2, s. 101.

VISUALLY HANDICAPPED PERSON. A person whose vision renders him incapable of doing work for which sight is necessary. *Workmen's Compensation Act*, S.Q. 1978, c. 57, s. 69.

VITAL. *adj.* Essential to or characterizing life. F.A. Jaffe, *A Guide to Pathological Evidence*, 2d ed. (Toronto: Carswell, 1983) at 186 and 187.

VITAL REACTION. A tissue reaction like inflammation which occurs during life and can distinguish a pre-mortem from a post-mortem wound. F.A. Jaffe, *A Guide to Pathological Evidence*, 2d ed. (Toronto: Carswell, 1983) at 186 and 187.

VITAL SIGN. A physical sign like respiration or pulse which indicates that life is present. F.A. Jaffe, *A Guide to Pathological Evidence*, 2d ed. (Toronto: Carswell, 1983) at 186 and 187.

VITAL STATISTICS. The registration of births, deaths and marriages.

VITAMIN. *n.* Any of the following vitamins: (a) vitamin A; (b) thiamine, thiamine hydrochloride or vitamin B_1; (c) riboflavin or vitamin B_2; (d) niacin or nicotinic acid; (e) niacinamide or nicotinamide; (f) pyridoxine, pyridoxine hydrochloride or vitamin B_6; (g) d-pantothenic acid or pantothenic acid; (h) folic acid; (i) biotin; (j) cyanocobalamin or vitamin B_{12}; (k) ascorbic acid or vitamin C; (l) vitamin D or vitamin D_2; (m) vitamin D or vitamin D_3; (n) vitamin E; (o) vitamin K; or (p) any salt or derivative of a vitamin listed in paragraphs (a) to (o). *Food and Drug Regulations*, C.R.C., c. 870, c. D.04.001.

VITIUM CLERICI NOCERE NON DEBET. [L.] A clerical error should do no harm.

VITREOUS HUMOUR. Fluid in an eye ball. F.A. Jaffe, *A Guide to Pathological Evidence*, 2d ed. (Toronto: Carswell, 1983) at 23.

VIVA PECUNIA. [L.] Cattle.

VIVA VOCE. [L.] When describing the examination of witnesses, means orally.

VIVISECTION. *n.* The dissecting of an animal as a scientific experiment.

VIVUM VADIUM. Vif-gage, live gage; pledge.

VIX ULLA LEX FIERI POTEST QUAE OMNIBUS COMMODA SIT, SED SI MAJORI PARTI PROSPICIAT UTILIS EST. [L.] Barely any law can be made which is applicable to everything, but if it regards the majority it is useful.

VIZ. *abbr.* Videlicet.

VOCABULUM ARTIS. [L.] A word of art.

VOCATION. *n.* 1. Any given occupation, whether a trade or a function, by which a person may earn his livelihood. *Manpower Vocational Training and Qualifications Act*, R.S.Q. 1977, c. F-5, s. 1. 2. Any employment, trade, calling or pursuit designated by the regulations as a vocation. Private Vocational Schools acts.

VOCATIONAL EDUCATION. 1. Education whose immediate object is preparaton for the practice of a vocation or trade. *Private Education Act*, R.S.Q. 1977, c. E-9, s. 1. 2. Any form of instruction below that of university level, the purpose of which is to fit any person for gainful employment or to increase his skill or efficiency therein and without restricting the generality of the foregoing, includes instruction to fit any person for employment in agriculture, forestry, mining, fishing, construction, manufacturing, commerce, or in any other primary or secondary industry in Canada. *Vocational Education Act*, R.S.N.S. 1967, c. 331, s. 1.

VOCATIONAL REHABILITATION. Any process of restoration, training and employment placement, including services related thereto, whose object is to enable a person to pursue regularly a gainful occupation. *Vocational Rehabilitation of Disabled Persons Act*, R.S.C. 1985, c. V-3, s. 2.

VOCATIONAL SCHOOL. See PRIVATE ~.

VOCATIONAL TRAINING. Training whose purpose is to enable any adult to acquire the competence required to carry on a trade or vocation. *Manpower Vocational Training and Qualification Act*, R.S.Q. 1977, c. F-5, s. 1.

VOCATIONAL TRAINING CENTRE. All of the buildings, facilities and equipment used for technical and vocational training, whose administration is entrusted to a commission. *Manpower Vocational Training and Qualification Act*, R.S.Q. 1977, c. F-5, s. 1.

VOCIFERATIO. *n.* [L. outcry] A hue and cry.

VOICEPRINT. *n.* A visual image of a person's voice produced by a spectograph.

VOICE RECORDER. See COCKPIT ~.

VOID. *n.* A space in a grain compartment between the surface of the grain and the crown of the compartment. *Grain Cargo Regulations*, C.R.C., c. 1427, s. 2.

VOID. *adj.* Having no legal effect. See NULL AND ~.

VOIDABLE. *adj.* With respect to an agreement or act, means one party may rescind, but it has legal effect until that happens.

VOIDANCE. *n.* Avoidance.

VOIR DIRE. [Fr.] 1. An initial examination to determine the competency of a juror or witness. 2. A hearing which a judge conducts with the jury absent to determine if evidence is admissible or some other matter relating to a trial. 3. A trial within a trial to decide a particular issue. P.K. McWilliams, *Canadian Criminal Evidence*, 3d ed. (Aurora: Canada Law Book, 1988) at 15-69.

VOLENTI NON FIT INJURIA. [L.] Wrong is not done to someone who is willing. John G. Fleming, *The Law of Torts*, 6th ed. (Sydney: The Law Book Co., 1983) at 73.

VOLT. *n.* The unit of electric potential difference and electromotive force, being the difference of electric potential between two equipotential surfaces of a conductor that is carrying a constant current of one ampere when the power dissipated between these surfaces is equal to one watt. *Weights and Measures Act*, S.C. 1970-71-72, c. 36, Schedule 1.

VOLTAGE. *n.* In respect of an electric circuit, means the greatest root-mean-square voltage between any two conductors of the circuit or between any conductor of the circuit and ground. *Canada Electrical Safety Regulations*, C.R.C., c. 998, s. 2. See EXTRA LOW ~; HIGH ~; LOW ~; MAXIMUM TEST ~; SYSTEM ~.

VOLTAGE OF A CIRCUIT. The greatest root-mean-square (effective) voltage between any two conductors of the circuit concerned. *Power Corporation Act*, R.R.O. 1980, Reg. 794, s. 0.

VOLTAGE TO GROUND. The voltage between any live ungrounded part and any grounded part in the case of grounded circuits, or the greatest voltage existing in the circuit in the case of ungrounded circuits. *Power Corporation Act*, R.R.O. 1980, Reg. 794, s. 0.

VOLUME. See BURSTING ~; NOMINAL ~.

VOLUME OF ABSOLUTE ETHYL ALCOHOL. Such volume measured at 20 degrees Celsius (20°). *Excise Act*, R.S.C. 1985, c. E-14, s. 2.

VOLUME-PRESSURE GAUGE. A device used in conjunction with a meter to compute volume in its relation to pressure where the line pressure fluctuates. *Gas and Gas Meters Regulations*, C.R.C., c. 876, s. 22.

VOLUNTARY. *adj.* With no compulsion.

VOLUNTARY ADDITIONAL CONTRIBU-TION. An optional contribution by an employee to or under a pension plan except a contribution whose payment, under the terms of the plan, imposes on the employer an obligation to make an additional contribution to the plan.

VOLUNTARY AID DETACHMENT. See MEMBER OF ~.

VOLUNTARY ASSUMPTION OF RISK. A defence to negligence which arises if the plaintiff assumes the risk. The defendant no longer owes a duty of care and is relieved of responsibility. John G. Fleming, *The Law of Torts*, 6th ed. (Sydney: The Law Book Co., 1983) at 264.

VOLUNTARY CONTRIBUTIONS. All contributions standing to the credit of a teacher in the fund which he elected to make under a former Act from salary earned by him and contributions made to the fund by or on his behalf under a former Act, exclusive of contributions which he was required to make by deduction from his salary or in respect of salary as determined by the commission and exclusive of contributions made by or on behalf of the teacher in respect of service rendered in the prosecution of the war of 1939-45. *The Teachers' Superannuation Act*, R.S.S. 1978, c. T-9, s. 2.

VOLUNTARY CONVEYANCE. A conveyance by something like a gift with no valuable consideration.

VOLUNTARY EQUITY ACCOUNT. The sum of the employee additional contribution account together with the vested portion of the employer additional contributions, if any, with accumulated interest. *The Municipal Employees' Superannuation Act*, R.S.S. 1978, c. M-26, s. 2.

VOLUNTARY RECOGNITION. An agreement by the employer to recognize a union as the bargaining agent for the employer's workers.

VOLUNTARY WASTE. Waste to a property caused by a voluntary act of the tenant.

VOLUNTAS DONATORIS IN CHARTA DONI SUI MANIFESTE EXPRESSA OBSER-VETUR. [L.] The donor's will, clearly expressed in the deed of gift, should be observed.

VOLUNTAS FACIT QUOD IN TESTAMENTO SCRIPTUM VALEAT. [L.] The testator's intention gives a will effect.

VOLUNTAS IN DELICTIS NON EXITUS SPECTATUR. [L.] In crimes, one considers the intention, not the result.

VOLUNTAS REPUTATUR PRO FACTO. [L.] The will is considered to be the deed.

VOLUNTAS TESTATORIS EST AMBULATO-RIA USQUE AD EXTREMUM VITAE EXI-TUM. [L.] A testator's will is changeable until the very end of life.

VOLUNTAS TESTATORIS HABET INTER-PRETATIONEM LATAM ET BENIGNAM. [L.] A testator's intention always has wide and favourable interpretation.

VOLUNTEER. *n.* Any individual, not in receipt of fees, wages or salary for the services or assistance within the meaning of this Act, who renders services or assistance, whether or not that individual has special training to render the service or assistance, and whether or not the service or assistance is rendered by the individual alone or in conjunction with others. *Volunteer Services Act*, S.N.S. 1977, c. 20, s. 2.

VOLUNTEER FIRE FIGHTER. A person who voluntarily acts as a fire fighter for a nominal consideration or honorarium. *Fire Departments Act*, R.S.O. 1980, c. 164, s. 1.

VOLUNTEER LABOUR. Any service provided free of charge by a person outside of that person's working hours, but does not include a service provided by a person who is self-employed if the service is one that is normally sold or otherwise charged for by that person. Elections acts.

VOLUNTEER VETERAN. A person who volunteered for and served for at least 6 months in the armed forces, the auxiliary services or the merchant marine of Canada or any of her allies, and who was honourably discharged therefrom. *Civil Service Act*, S.P.E.I. 1983, c. 4, s. 1.

VOTE. *n.* 1. A ballot paper which has been detached from the counterfoil, and has been furnished to a voter, and has been marked and deposited as a vote by the voter. 2. Suffrage. 3. A specific segregation of spending authority into a broad category according to intended use such as capital expenditures, operations and maintenance expenditures, and loans. *Financial Administration Act*, S.N.W.T. 1982, c. 2, s. 2. 4. An appropriation under a Supply Act identified in the main or supplementary estimates as a vote. *Financial Administration Act*, S.B.C. 1981, c. 15, s. 1. See ADVANCE ~; CASTING ~; FREE ~; LEADERSHIP ~; NO-UNION ~; POPU-LAR ~; PRE-HEARING ~; REPRESENTA-TION ~; STRIKE ~; TWO-THIRDS ~.

VOTE BY SECRET BALLOT. A vote by ballots

cast in such a manner that a person expressing a choice cannot be identified with the choice expressed.

VOTER. *n.* 1. Any person entitled to vote. 2. Any person who votes at an election. 3. Any person whose name is on any voters' list in force under the Canada Elections Act, or any person entitled to vote at an election of a member of the House of Commons or who has voted at such an election. *Disfranchising Act*, R.S.C. 1985, c. D-3, s. 2. 4. Any person who is or who claims to be registered as an elector in the list of voters for any electoral district; or who is, or claims to be, entitled to vote in any election. See QUALIFIED ~.

VOTER INFORMATION CARD. A card containing information advising a voter where he is qualified to vote. *Election Act*, R.S.P.E.I. 1974, c. E-1, s. 1.

VOTER POPULATION. The number of electors as determined from the voters' list prepared for use in an immediately preceding provincial general election.

VOTERS LIST. *var.* **VOTERS' LIST.** 1. Includes any list made and revised of persons entitled to vote at an election. 2. A list of electors required to be prepared. See REVISED ~.

VOTES AND PROCEEDINGS. A record of proceedings of the House of Commons. A. Fraser, G.A. Birch & W.A. Dawson, eds., *Beauchesne's Rules and Forms of the House of Commons of Canada*, 5th ed. (Toronto: Carswell, 1978) at 46.

VOTING. *n.* Voting at an election or plebiscite. *Election Act*, R.S.A. 1980, c. E-2, s. 1. See CUMULATIVE ~.

VOTING GROUP. Two or more persons who are associated with respect to voting interests in an entity by contract, business arrangement, personal relationship, common control in fact through ownership of voting interests, or otherwise, in such a manner that they would ordinarily be expected to act together on a continuing basis with respect to the exercise of those rights. *Investment Canada Act*, R.S.C. 1985 (1st Supp.), c. 28, s. 3.

VOTING INTEREST. With respect to (a) a corporation with share capital, means a voting share; (b) a corporation without share capital, means an ownership interest in the assets thereof that entitles the owner to rights similar to those enjoyed by the owner of a voting share; and (c) a partnership, trust or joint venture, means an ownership interest in the assets thereof that entitles the owner to receive a share of the profits and to share in the assets on dissolution. *Invest-*

ment Canada Act, R.S.C. 1985 (1st Supp.), c. 28, s. 3.

VOTING MEMBER. A member of a council who may vote in the determination of any matter or deliberation put to a vote in such council. *Regional and Tribal Councils Act*, S.N.W.T. 1983 (2d Sess.), c. 7, s. 2.

VOTING RECORDER. An apparatus in which ballot cards are used with a punch device for the piercing of ballot cards by the elector to record his or her vote, so that the ballot card may be tabulated by means of automatic tabulating equipment. *Municipal Elections Act*, R.R.O. 1980, Reg. 682, s. 1.

VOTING REGISTER. The prescribed form in which to record the names of persons who have received ballots at an election. *Local Authorities Election Act*, S.A. 1983, c. L-27.5, s. 1.

VOTING RIGHT. The right to vote for the election of one or more directors excluding a right to vote which is dependent on the happening of an event specified in the instrument of incorporation or this Act. *Loan and Trust Companies Act*, S.N.B. 1987, c. L-11.2, s. 74.

VOTING SECURITY. Any security other than a debt security of an issuer carrying a voting right either under all circumstances or under some circumstances that have occurred and are continuing. See OFFEROR'S VOTING SECURITIES; RIGHT TO A ~.

VOTING SHARE. Any share that carries voting rights under all circumstances or by reason of an event that has occurred and is continuing. See SUBORDINATE ~.

VOTING STATION. The place where an elector casts his vote. *Local Authorities Election Act*, S.A. 1983, c. L-27.5, s. 1.

VOTING SUBDIVISION. That area of a local jurisdiction or ward designated as a voting subdivision by the elected authority or the returning officer. *Local Authorities Election Act*, S.A. 1983, c. L-27.5, s. 1.

VOTING TERRITORY. An area established by or pursuant to section 5. *Special Voting Rules*, R.S.C. 1985, c. E-2, Schedule II, s. 2.

VOTING TRUST. The rights to vote some or all shares of a corporation are settled upon trustees who under the terms of the trust have authority, with or without restriction, to exercise the voting rights. S.M. Beck *et al.*, *Cases and Materials on Partnerships and Canadian Business Corporations*, (Toronto: The Carswell Co., 1983) at 650.

VOTING UNIT. The number of persons for each vote designated in the letters patent for the purpose of calculating the number of votes to which each member municipality is entitled. *Municipal Act*, R.S.B.C. 1985, c. 290, c. 766.

VOUCH. *v.* To call on; to rely on; to quote authoritatively.

VOUCHER. *n.* 1. A document which is evidence of a transaction, i.e. a receipt for money paid. 2. An instrument issued under this Act and the regulations that authorizes the supplying of specified goods or the rendering of specified services to the person named therein. *Social Welfare Act*, R.S.N.B. 1973, c. S-11, s. 1.

VOX EMISSA VOLAT, LITERA SCRIPTA MANET. [L.] The spoken word disappears, the written word remains.

VOYAGE. *n.* Includes passage or trip and any movement of a ship from one place to another or from one place and returning to that place.

Canada Shipping Act, R.S.C. 1985, c. S-9, s. 2. See FOREIGN ~; HOME-TRADE ~; INLAND ~; INTERNATIONAL ~; MINOR WATERS ~; TROPICAL ~.

VOYAGE POLICY. To insure the subject-matter "at and from", from one place to another or others. Insurance acts.

VS. *abbr.* Versus.

VULVA. *n.* The exterior sexual organs of a female: the clitoris, vestibule, labia minora and labia majora. F.A. Jaffe, *A Guide to Pathological Evidence*, 2d ed. (Toronto: Carswell, 1983) at 187

W. *abbr.* Watt.

WAD. *n.* A cardboard, felt or plastic disc used in shotgun ammunition. F.A. Jaffe, *A Guide to Pathological Evidence*, 2d ed. (Toronto: Carswell, 1983) at 187.

WADCUTTER AMMUNITION. Bullets with flat noses used originally for target shooting. They tend to ricochet and do not penetrate too deeply. F.A. Jaffe, *A Guide to Pathological Evidence*, 2d ed. (Toronto: Carswell, 1983) at 187.

WAFER. *n.* A small circle of red paper used to seal a deed instead of sealing wax.

WAGE. *n.* 1. Any compensation measured by time, piece or otherwise. 2. Salary, pay, commission or remuneration for work. See BASIC RATE OF ~S; BASIC ~; CONSTANT ~ PLAN; DAILY ~; EARNINGS AND ~S; FAIR ~S; MINIMUM ~; PREVAILING ~; RATE OF ~S; REAL ~; REGULAR ~; SALARY OR ~S; SCHEDULE OF ~S; SUBSISTENCE ~S; TOTAL ~.

WAGE ADJUSTMENT. See AUTOMATIC ~.

WAGE BRACKETS. The minimum and maximum wage rates for a job.

WAGE DIFFERENTIAL. The different rates of pay for the same type of work. See GEOGRAPHIC ~.

WAGE DISPARITY. A variation of wages paid to workers in similar jobs or in different regions.

WAGE EMPLOYEE. A person employed in or under any department of the Government, including the Executive Council and the Legislative Assembly, who is paid at an hourly, daily, weekly or monthly rate. *Public Service Act*, R.S.A. 1980, c. P-31, s. 26.

WAGE GUARANTEE. A provision in a collective agreement which guarantees an employee the dollar equivalent of a certain number of hours of work every week. D.J.M. Brown and

D.M. Beatty, *Canadian Labour Arbitration*, 2d ed. (Aurora: Canada Law Book, 1977) at 533.

WAGE INCREASE. See PROGRESSIVE ~; SCHEDULED ~.

WAGE PLAN. See CONSTANT ~; INCENTIVE ~.

WAGE PROGRESSION. See AUTOMATIC ~.

WAGER. *n.* A promise one makes on a chance event in which one has no other interest except the wager. I.H. Jacob, ed., *Bullen and Leake and Jacob's Precedents of Pleadings*, 12th ed. (London: Sweet and Maxwell, 1975) at 1081.

WAGERING CONTRACT. A mutual promise by which each party gains or loses by the outcome of an uncertain event. Each party's promise is her or his only interest in the transaction. G.H.L. Fridman, *The Law of Contract in Canada*, 2d ed. (Toronto: Carswell, 1986) at 334.

WAGON. *n.* Any vehicle used to deliver grain to a country elevator. *Canada Grain Act*, R.S.C. 1970, c. G-16, s. 2. See STATION ~.

WAIF. *n.* Goods found which nobody claimed.

WAIT. See LYING IN ~.

WAITING PERIOD. 1. The interval between the issuance by the Registrar of a receipt for a preliminary prospectus relating to the offering of a security and the issuance of a receipt for the prospectus. Securities acts. 2. The 2 weeks of the benefit period described in section 12. *Unemployment Insurance Act*, R.S.C. 1985, c. U-1, s. 5.

WAIVE. *v.* To surrender or renounce a right, privilege or claim.

WAIVER. *n.* 1. An action by which one party relieves the other from performing an obligation or from liability for not performing without actually ending the contract. G.H.L. Fridman, *Sale of Goods in Canada*, 3d ed. (Toronto:

Carswell, 1986) at 274. 2. Surrender of an advantage or right which involves both knowing and intending not to exercise that right. D.J.M. Brown and D.M. Beatty, *Canadian Labour Arbitration*, 2d ed. (Aurora: Canada Law Book, 1977) at 98.

WALE. *n.* A longitudinal member of shoring and timbering that is placed against, and directly resists, pressure from sheathing. *Occupational Health and Safety Act*, R.R.O. 1980, Reg. 691, s. 167.

WALK. See CROSS ~.

WALKOUT. *n.* The withdrawal of employees from their place of employment.

WALKWAY. See ENCLOSED ~.

WALL. *n.* The exposed face of an excavation in a surface mine from ground level to the working level. *Coal Mines Safety Act*, R.S.A. 1980, c. C-15, s. 1. See CAVITY ~; CHINESE ~S; DUCTILE FLEXURAL ~; FIRE~; PANEL ~; PARTY ~.

WALLEYE. *n.* Yellow pickerel, Stizostedion vitreum vitreum (Mitchill) and includes dore, perch, pike, walleye pike and yellow pike. *Ontario Fishery Regulations*, C.R.C., c. 849, s. 2.

WAR. *n.* The war waged by His Majesty and His Majesty's Allies against Germany and Germany's Allies, which for the purposes of this Act shall be deemed to have commenced on September 1, 1939 and to have terminated on April 1, 1947. *Civilian War Pensions and Allowances Act*, R.S.C. 1985, c. C-31, s. 2. See ARTICLES OF ~; DECLARATION OF ~; MUNITIONS OF ~; PRISONER OF ~; SERVICE IN A THEATRE OF ACTUAL ~; THEATRE OF ACTUAL ~; WORLD ~ I; WORLD ~ II.

WAR CRIME. An act or omission that is committed during an international conflict, whether or not it constitutes a contravention of the law in force at the time and in the place of its commission, and that, at that time and in that place, constitutes a contravention of the customary international law or conventional international law applicable in international armed conflicts. *Criminal Code*, R.S.C. 1985, c. C-46, s. 7(3.76) as added by R.S.C. 1985 (3d Supp.), c. 10, s. l, (3d Supp.), c. 30, s. 1.

WARD. *n.* 1. An electoral division. 2. A child committed to the care and custody of the Director or a Society. *Child Welfare acts*.

WARDEN. *n.* 1. The warden of a rural municipality. *Municipal Affairs Act*, S.N.S. 1982, c. 9, s. 2. 2. Includes the Minister, Provincial Forester, district forester, forester, inspector, chief forest ranger, sub-ranger, game warden or other officer appointed under Part II or III. *Lands and Forests Act*, R.S.N.S. 1967, c. 163, s. 84. See CHURCH~; FIRE ~; PARK ~; PORT ~.

WARD OF THE GOVERNMENT. A child who has been committed to the care and custody of the director or a society. *Child Welfare Act*, R.S.M. 1970, c. C80, s. 2.

WARDSHIP. *n.* Guardianship.

WARDSHIP ORDER. See CROWN ~.

WAREHOUSE. *n.* Any place, whether house, shed, yard, dock, pond or other place in which goods imported may be lodged, kept and secured without payment of duty. *Customs Act*, R.S.C. 1970, c. C-40, s. 2. See BONDED ~; BONDING ~; CUSTOMS ~; CUSTOMS EXPRESS BRANCH ~; EXAMINING ~; EX ~; QUEEN'S ~; SEPARATE STORE OR ~; SUFFERANCE ~.

WAREHOUSE KEEPER. The owner of a warehouse or, if the warehouse is leased, the lessee of the warehouse. Canada regulations.

WAREHOUSEMAN. *n.* 1. A person who receives goods for storage for reward. 2. A person lawfully engaged in the business of storing goods as a bailee for hire.

WAREHOUSER. *n.* Any person who stores vegetable for another person. *P.E.I. Vegetable Directed Sales (Interprovincial and Export) Regulations*, C.R.C., c. 237, s. 2.

WAREHOUSE RECEIPT. 1. An acknowledgement in writing by a warehouseman of the receipt for storage of goods not her or his own. 2. Includes (a) any receipt given by any person for goods, wares and merchandise in his actual, visible and continued possession as bailee thereof in good faith and not as of his own property; (b) receipts given by any person who is the owner or keeper of a harbour, cove, pond, wharf, yard, warehouse, shed, storehouse or other place for the storage of goods, wares and merchandise, for goods, wares and merchandise delivered to him as bailee, and actually in the place or in one or more of the places owned or kept by him, whether such person is engaged in other business or not; (c) receipts given by any person in charge of logs or timber in transit from timber limits or other lands to the place of destination of such logs or timber; (d) Lake Shippers' Clearance Association receipts and transfer certificates, British Columbia Grain Shippers' Clearance Association receipts and transfer certificates, and all documents recognized by the Canada Grain Act as elevator receipts; and (e) receipts given by any person for any hydrocarbons received by him as bailee, whether his obligation to restore requires delivery of the same hydrocarbons or may be satisfied by delivery of a like quantity of hydrocarbons of the same or a

W

similar grade or kind. *Bank Act*, R.S.C. 1985, c. B-1, s. 2.

WAR EMERGENCY. (i) A war in which hostilities are being carried on in Canada; or (ii) an invasion of Canada by hostile forces; or (iii) an insurrection in Canada; or (iv) any other emergency due to enemy attack, sabotage or other hostile action.

WARES. *n.* Includes printed publications. *Trademarks Act*, R.S.C. 1985, c. T-13, s. 2. See GOODS, ~ AND MERCHANDISE; PESSURABLE ~.

WARNING GAS. A gas that immediately identifies its presence by its effect on the senses when a person is exposed to it. *Pesticides Act*, R.R.O. 1980, Reg. 751, s. 1.

WARRANT. *n.* 1. The order of a judicial authority that a ministerial officer arrest, seize, search or execute some judicial sentence. 2. When used in relation to a warrant for the arrest of a person, means a warrant in Form 7 and, when used in relation to a warrant for the committal of a person, means a warrant in Form 8. *Criminal Code*, R.S.C. 1985, c. C-46, s. 493. 3. A right to subscribe for a share of a corporation. 4. An option; an agreement by a corporation to sell to the holder a certain number of shares at a price specified in the agreement. S.M. Beck *et al.*, *Cases and Materials on Partnerships and Canadian Business Corporations*, (Toronto: The Carswell Co., 1983) at 788. 5. In the case of a foreign state, includes any judicial document that authorizes the arrest of a person accused or convicted of crime. *Extradition Act*, R.S.C. 1985, c. E-23, s. 2 See BACK A ~; BENCH ~; CAVEAT ~; DOCK ~; LOCAL ~; ROYAL ~; SEARCH ~; SHARE ~.

WARRANTEE. *n.* A person to whom one makes a warranty.

WARRANTOR. *n.* A party who warrants.

WARRANTOR POTEST EXCIPERE QUOD QUERENS NON TENET TERRAM DE QUA PETIT WARRANTIAM, ET QUOD DONUM FUIT INSUFFICIENS. [L.] A warrantor may take exception that a complainant does not hold the land for which the warranty is sought, and that the gift was insufficient.

WARRANTY. *n.* An agreement with reference to goods which are the subject of a contract of sale, but collateral to the main purpose of such contract, the breach of which gives rise to a claim for damages, but not a right to reject the goods and treat the contract as repudiated. Sale of Goods acts. See ADDITIONAL WRITTEN ~.

WAR RISKS. The risks of loss or damage arising from hostilities, rebellion, revolution, civil war, piracy, action taken to repel an imagined attack or from civil strife consequent to their happening. *Marine and Aviation War Risks Act*, R.S.C. 1970, c. W-3, s. 2.

WAR SERVICE. 1. Active service during World War II or the Korean War, (i) in His or Her Majesty's naval, army or air forces or in the Canadian or British Merchant Marine; or (ii) in any naval, army or air force that was allied with His or Her Majesty's forces and that is designated by the Lieutenant Governor in Council, providing satisfactory proof of such service is produced. Ontario statutes. 2. The total period of service of an employee during World War I, World War II and the Korean War in the Naval, Military or Air Forces of Her Majesty, Her Majesty in right of Canada or Her Majesty in right of Newfoundland and includes service in the Merchant Marine, the Auxiliary Forces, the Overseas Forestry Unit and the Rescue Tugs. Newfoundland statutes. See PERSON IN RECEIPT OF A PENSION BY REASON OF ~.

WAR SERVICE INJURY. 1. In the case of an air raid precautions worker other than a duly registered voluntary evacuation worker, any physical injury sustained during the War and arising out of and in the course of his duties as such as a direct result of enemy action, counteraction against the enemy or action in apprehension of enemy attack or during a blackout, test or period of training duly authorized by the senior air raid precautions officer in the designated area in which the injury was sustained, and, in the case of duly registered voluntary evacuation worker means injuries arising out of and in the course of his duties as an evacuation worker. *Civilian War Pensions and Allowances Act*, R.S.C. 1985, c. C-31, s. 30. 2. An injury arising out of and in the course of duties as a member of the Voluntary Aid Detachment. *Civilian War Pensions and Allowances Act*, R.S.C. 1985, c. C-31, s. 43.

WARSHIP. See CANADIAN ~; FOREIGN ~.

WART. See POTATO ~.

WAR VETERANS. Persons who have served in active armed forces, the auxiliary services or the merchant marine of Canada or any of her allies. *The Public Service Act*, R.S.S. 1978, c. P-42, s. 2.

WASCHHAUT. *n.* Wrinkling of skin on the feet or hands caused by long exposure to moisture; it can occur before or after death. F.A. Jaffe, *A Guide to Pathological Evidence*, 2d ed. (Toronto: Carswell, 1983) at 187.

WASH. *n.* As applied to distilleries, means all

liquor made in whole or in part from grain, malt or other saccharine matter, whether or not the liquor is fermented or unfermented. *Excise Act,* R.S.C. 1985, c. E-14, s. 4.

WASH BASIN. A receptacle for washing any part of the human body. *Ontario Water Resources Act,* R.R.O. 1980, Reg. 736, s. 1. See BASIN.

WASH ROOM. *var.* **WASHROOM.** A room that contains a wash basin for the use of employees. *Canada Sanitation Regulations,* C.R.C., c. 1009, s. 2. See PUBLIC ~.

WASTE. *n.* 1. Air contaminants, litter, effluent and refuse. 2. (a) Any substance that, if added to any water, would degrade or alter or form part of a process of degradation or alteration of the quality of that water to an extent that is detrimental to their use by man or by any animal, fish or plant that is useful to man; and (b) any water that contains a substance in such a quantity or concentration, or that has been so treated, processed or changed, by heat or other means, from a natural state that it would, if added to any other water, degrade or alter or form part of a process of degradation or alteration of the quality of that water to the extent described in paragraph (a). *Canada Water Act,* R.S.C. 1985, c. C-11, s. 2. 3. In addition to its ordinary meaning, means waste as understood in the oil and gas industry and in particular, without limiting the generality of the foregoing, includes (a) the inefficient or excessive use or dissipation of reservoir energy; (b) the locating, spacing or drilling of a well within a field or pool or within part of a field or pool or the operating of any well that, having regard to sound engineering and economic principles, results or tends to result in a reduction in the quantity of oil or gas ultimately recoverable from a pool; (c) the drilling, equipping, completing, operating or producing of any well in a manner that causes or is likely to cause the unnecessary or excessive loss or destruction of oil or gas after removal from the reservoir; (d) the inefficient storage of oil or gas above ground or underground; (e) the production of oil or gas in excess of available storage, transportation or marketing facilities; (f) the escape or flaring of gas that could be economically recovered and processed or economically injected into an underground reservoir; or (g) the failure to use suitable artificial, secondary or supplementary recovery methods in a pool when it appears that such methods would result in increasing the quantity of oil or gas, or both, ultimately recoverable under sound engineering and economic principles. *Oil and Gas Production and Conservation Legislation,* S.N.S. 1984, c. 9, s. 17(2). 4. Includes ashes, garbage, refuse, domestic waste, industrial waste, or municipal refuse. See AGRICUL-

TURAL ~; AMELIORATING ~; DOMESTIC ~; DOUBLE ~; FARM ~; HAZARDOUS ~; INCINERATOR ~; INDIRECT ~; INDUSTRIAL ~; PERMISSIVE ~; SOLID ~; VOLUNTARY ~.

WASTE AND VENT. See CONTINUOUS ~.

WASTE DISPOSAL SITE. Any land or land covered by water upon, into, in or through which, or building or structure in which, waste is deposited or processed and any machinery or equipment or operation required for the treatment or disposal of waste.

WASTE DISPOSAL SYSTEM. See MARINE CRAFT ~.

WASTEFUL. *adj.* (i) The establishment, construction, operation, suspension or abandonment of an oil sands site in a manner that results or tends to result in a reduction (A) in the quantity or quality of oil sands, crude bitumen or derivatives of crude bitumen ultimately recovered from an oil sands deposit; or (B) in the quantity or quality of oil sands products obtained from oil sands, crude bitumen or derivatives of crude bitumen relative to that which would otherwise be recovered or obtained under sound engineering and economic principles; (ii) the locating, drilling, equipping, completing, operating or producing of a well in a manner that causes or tends to cause excessive loss or destruction of crude bitumen, derivatives of crude bitumen or declared oil sands; (iii) the inefficient storing on the surface or underground of oil sands, crude bitumen, derivatives of crude bitumen or oil sands products; or (iv) the production of oil sands, crude bitumen, derivatives of crude bitumen or oil sands products in excess of proper storage facilities or transportation and marketing facilities or of market demand for them. *Oil Sands Conservation Act,* S.A. 1983, c. O-5.5, s. 1.

WASTEFUL OPERATION. (i) The locating, spacing, drilling, equipping, completing, operating or producing of a well in a manner that results or tends to result in reducing the quantity of oil, gas or crude bitumen ultimately recoverable from a pool or oil sands deposit under sound engineering and economic principles; (ii) the locating, drilling, equipping, completing, operating or producing of a well in a manner that causes or tends to cause excessive surface loss or destruction of oil, gas or crude bitumen; (iii) the inefficient, excessive or improper use or dissipation of reservoir energy however caused; (iv) the failure to use suitable enhanced recovery operations in a pool when it appears probable on the basis of available information that those methods would result in increasing the quantity of oil or gas ultimately recoverable from the pool under sound engineering and economic principles; (v) the escape or the flaring of gas, if it is estimated that, in the public interest and under sound engineering principles and in the light of economics and the risk factor involved, the gas could be gathered, processed if necessary, and it or the products from it marketed, stored for future marketing, or beneficially injected into an underground reservoir; (vi) the inefficient storing of oil, gas or crude bitumen, whether on the surface or underground; or (vii) the production of oil, gas or crude bitumen in excess of proper storage facilities or of transportation and marketing facilities or of market demand therefor.

WASTE MANAGEMENT. The collection, handling, transportation, storage, processing and disposal of waste and may include one or more waste disposal sites or techniques.

WASTE MANAGEMENT PLAN. A plan that contains provisions or requirements for the collection, treatment, handling, storage, utilization and disposal of refuse, sewage and other waste within the whole or a specified part of a municipality. *Waste Management Act*, S.B.C. 1982, c. 41, s. 1.

WASTE MANAGEMENT SYSTEM. All facilities, equipment and operations for the management of waste, including the collection, handling, transportation, storage, processing, utilization and disposal of waste, and includes one or more waste disposal sites within such system. See MUNICIPAL ~; PRIVATE ~.

WASTE MATERIAL. (i) Refuse, garbage, rubbish, litter, scrap and discarded material of all kinds, including tailings, offal, machinery, products, vehicles and other articles which are dumped, discarded, abandoned or otherwise disposed of; (ii) any material or thing that may be a danger to the health of human beings, animals, wild life or fish, or is of unsightly appearance; and (iii) a substance designated as waste material in the regulations. *Waste Material (Disposal) Act*, S.Nfld. 1973, c. 82, s. 2.

WASTE PIPE. That part of drainage piping that runs from a fixture to a waste stack, soil stack, building drain or sewage tank. *Ontario Water Resources Act*, R.R.O. 1980, Reg. 736, s. 1. See INDIRECT ~.

WASTE STACK. A stack that conducts liquid wastes from one or more plumbing fixtures that are not sanitary units. *Ontario Water Resources Act*, R.R.O. 1980, Reg. 736, s. 1.

WASTE WATER. *var.* **WASTEWATER.** Water carrying solid, liquid or gaseous residue from a process, an establishment or a building, mixed or not with underground, cooling, rain or surface

water and, unless the context indicates otherwise, underground water, cooling water, rain water and surface water. See DOMESTIC ~; INDUSTRIAL ~; SANITARY ~.

WASTEWATER SEWER. A sewer that carries liquid and water-carried wastes from residences, commercial buildings, industrial plants and institutions, together with minor quantities of ground, storm and surface waters that are not admitted intentionally. *City of Winnipeg Act*, S.M. 1971, c. 105, s. 453.

WASTEWATER SYSTEM. Collectively, all of the property involved in the operation of a sewer utility. It includes land, structures, equipment and processes required to collect, carry away and treat wastewater and dispose of the effluent. *City of Winnipeg Act*, S.M. 1971, c. 105, s. 453.

WASTE WATER TREATMENT FACILITY. Any system or method used to treat waste water biologically, chemically, electrically, mechanically or otherwise and includes the water collection system for it. *Clean Water Act*, R.S.A. 1980, c. C-13, s. 1.

WASTING ASSET. Property which exists under restriction, such as a natural resource or leasehold.

WATCH. *n.* 1. That part of the complement that is on duty for the purpose of attending to the safe operation of a ship. *Safe Manning Regulations*, C.R.C., c. 1466, s. 2. 2. A watch totalling not less than 8 out of each 24 hours service claimed. *Marine Engineer Examination Regulations*, C.R.C., c. 1443, s. 2. See DECK ~; ENGINEER ON THE ~; FLIGHT ~ SYSTEM.

WATCH KEEPING DECK OFFICER. See SENIOR ~.

WATCHKEEPING SYSTEM. A system under which the hours of work of persons associated with the safe operation of a ship are apportioned regularly and systematically among those persons. *Safe Manning Regulations*, C.R.C., c. 1466, s. 2.

WATCH REPAIRER. A person who, (i) makes or fits parts for time-pieces; (ii) repairs, alters, takes apart, assembles or reassembles time-pieces or any part thereof; (iii) determines the condition of time-pieces and estimates the repairs necessary; (iv) cleans, polishes or lubricates time-piece movements or any part thereof; or (v) tests, adjusts or regulates time-pieces or any part thereof. *Apprenticeship and Tradesmen's Qualification Act*, R.R.O. 1980, Reg. 63, s. 1.

WATER. *n.* 1. Includes flowing or standing water on or below the surface of the earth and ice formed thereon. 2. All water on or under the surface of the ground. 3. Any surface or subterranean source of fresh or salt water within the jurisdiction of the province, whether such source usually contains water or not, and includes water above the bed of the sea that is within the jurisdiction of the province, any river, stream, brook, creek, water course, lake, pond, spring, lagoon, ravine, gully, canal and any other flowing or standing water and the land usually or at any time occupied by any such body of water. *Environmental Assessment Act*, S.Nfld. 1980, c. 3, s. 2. 4. Such of the waters upon any shore or land, on or in any lake, river, stream, bay, estuary, tidal water or watercourse, wholly or partially within the Province, over or in respect of which the Legislature has authority to legislate. *Fish and Wildlife Act*, S.N.B. 1980, c. F-14.1, s. 1. See BALLAST ~; BODY OF ~; BRACKISH ~; COOLING ~; FIRST OPEN ~; GROUND ~; MAKE-UP ~; MINERAL ~; NATURAL ~; NAVIGABLE ~; OPEN BODY OF ~; OPEN ~; PARK ~; POTABLE ~; PROVINCIAL ~; PURE ~ AREAS; RAW ~; SANITARY WASTE ~; STANDING BODY OF WATER; STORM ~; STREAM OR ~; SURFACE ~; TRANSPORT BY ~; UNRECORDED ~; WASTE ~; ~S.

WATER AND SEWAGE WORKS. Artificial or natural works used to supply, gather, store, improve, purify, heat, cool or transmit water or to gather, store, process, purify, decompose, transmit or dispose of sewage. *The Family Farm Improvement Act*, R.S.S. 1978, c. F-6, s. 2.

WATER BODY. A lake, pond, river or other body of water that is greater than 2 hectares in extent as determined by the Minister of Forestry and Agriculture. *Forest Land (Management and Taxation) Act*, S.Nfld. 1977, c. 67, s. 2.

WATER COLUMN. The aqueous medium superjacent to a defined area of sub-aquatic land. *Aquaculture Act*, S.N.S. 1983, c. 2, s. 2.

WATER CONDITIONER. Any water softening chemical, anti-scale chemical, corrosion inhibiter or other substance intended to be used to treat water. *Canada Water Act*, R.S.C. 1985, c. C-11, s. 19.

WATER CONTAMINANT. (i) Any solid, liquid or gas, or a combination of any of them, in water; (ii) heat in water, resulting in a change in the temperature of surface water or underground fresh water. *Clean Water Amendment Act*, S.A. 1982, c. 12, s. 2.

WATER CONTROL PROJECT. Any works or undertaking constructed, operated and maintained for the purpose of controlling a lake or stream or stabilizing the water level of a lake or stream. *Water Resources Act*, R.S.A. 1980, c. W-5, s. 91.

WATER CONTROL WORKS. 1. Works (i) for the conservation, control, disposal, protection, distribution, drainage, storage, or use of water; or (ii) for the protection of land or other property from damage by water; or for all or some of those purposes, and includes any other work necessary or convenient for the use, operation, or maintenance of a work to which sub-clause (i) or (ii) applies or constructed or operated as a complement of such work. 2. Works as defined in The Water Rights Act and includes a facility, plant or contrivance controlling, carrying, measuring, processing or treating water. *The Water Resources Management Act*, R.S.S. 1978, c. W-7, s. 2.

WATER COOLER. A suitable device for storing, cooling and dispensing potable water. *Locomotive and Caboose Sanitation Facilities Regulations*, C.R.C., c. 1155, s. 2.

WATER COURSE. *var.* **WATERCOURSE.** 1. Includes every water course and every source of water supply, whether the same usually contains water or not, and the bed and shore of every stream, river or lake, pond, creek, spring, ravine and gulch. 2. A river, stream, creek, gully, ravine, spring, coulee, valley floor, drainage ditch or any other channel having a bed and sides or banks in which water flows either permanently or intermittently. 3. The full length and width of any river, creek, stream, spring, brook, lake, pond, reservoir, canal, ditch or other natural or artificial channel that is open to the air and includes the bed, banks, sides and shoreline thereof. *An Act to Amend the Trespass Act*, S.N.B. 1985, c. 70, s. 1.

WATER-COVERED AREA. Any area covered by flowing or standing water. *Petroleum Resources Act*, R.R.O. 1980, Reg. 752, s. 1.

WATER DAMAGE INSURANCE. Insurance, other than sprinkler leakage or weather insurance, against loss of or damage to property caused by the escape of water from plumbing or heating equipment of a building or from outside water mains, or by the melting of ice or snow on the roof of a building. *Insurance Act*, R.S.B.C. 1979, c. 200, s. 1.

WATER EQUIVALENT. With respect to a given load, means the volume of water at $20^P5°C$ that, when placed in the same plane wave field as the given load, absorbs microwave energy at the same rate as the given load. *Radiation Emitting Devices Regulations*, C.R.C., c. 1370, s. 1.

WATER-EXCURSION CRAFT. A boat or other watercraft, registered under the Canada Shipping Act (Canada), on which members of the public for a fee or other charge are transported for excursion purposes on natural or man-made water bodies. *Liquor Control Act*, R.S.A. 1980, c. L-17, s. 58.

WATER EXTERMINATION. The destruction, prevention or control in, on or over surface water of a pest by the use of a pesticide. *Pesticides Act*, R.S.O. 1980, c. 376, s. 1.

WATER FREQUENTED BY FISH. Canadian fisheries waters. *Fisheries Act*, R.S.C. 1985, c. F-14, s. 34.

WATER HEATER. See SERVICE ~; STORAGE-TYPE ~.

WATER-INSOLUBLE NITROGEN. Nitrogen insoluble in water when analysed by the method of analysis referred to in section 23. *Fertilizers Regulations*, C.R.C., c. 666, s. 2.

WATER LEVEL. See STATIC ~.

WATER LOT. (i) Any pond or swamp; and (ii) any area below the high-water mark of a lake, river, creek or stream, in the area under the jurisdiction of the Authority. *Conservation Authority Act*, R.R.O. 1980, Reg. 155, s. 1.

WATER MANAGEMENT AREA. A river basin or other appropriate geographical area established as a water management area by the Governor in Council pursuant to paragraph 29(d). *Northern Inland Waters Act*, R.S.C. 1985, c. N-25, s. 2.

WATER PACK. A pack in which water is used as the packing media. *Processed Fruit and Vegetable Regulations*, C.R.C., c. 291, s. 2.

WATER PEST CONTROL. The destruction, prevention or control of pests in, on or over a water course that may adversely affect a water course or its use or enjoyment. *Pest Control Products (Nova Scotia) Act*, S.N.S. 1986, c. 16, s. 3.

WATERPLANE. See MEAN ~.

WATER POLLUTION. (i) The presence in water of any water contaminant in excess of the permissible concentration prescribed by the regulations for that water contaminant; or (ii) a change of the temperature of water in contravention of the regulations. *Clean Water Act*, R.S.A. 1980, c. C-13, s. 1.

WATER POLLUTION CONTROL WORKS. The works together with the land required for the purpose of treating or holding sewage and for effluent irrigation, and includes: (i) pumps, piping, controls and other equipment required to treat sewage; (ii) a system of pipes, pumps, controls and other equipment which convey treated sewage from the point of treatment to the point of disposal; (iii) a trunk collector sewer that conveys sewage from the point of the last lateral to the point of treatment; and (iv) a pumping station which receives sewage at a point below the last lateral together with the pressure main that delivers sewage from the pumping station to the point of treatment. *The Water Pollution Control Assistance Act*, R.S.S. 1978, c. W-5, s. 2.

WATER POWER. *var.* **WATER-POWER.** Includes any force or energy of whatever form or nature contained in or capable of being produced or generated from any flowing or falling water in such quantity as to make it of commercial value. See DOMINION ~S; PROVINCIAL ~S; SMALL ~.

WATER PURIFICATION WORKS. Sewer interceptors, sewage treatment plants, diffusers, effluent outlets and subordinate installations. *An Act Respecting the Société québécoise d'assainissement des eaux*, S.Q. 1980, c. 10, s. 1.

WATER PURVEYOR. Any person, corporation, municipality or village municipality that offers or supplies, or holds itself out as being available to offer or supply, water for domestic purposes. *Health Act*, R.S.B.C. 1979, c. 161, s. 21.

WATER QUALITY MANAGEMENT. Any aspect of water resource management that relates to restoring, maintaining or improving the quality of water. *Canada Water Act*, R.S.C. 1985, c. C-11, s. 2.

WATER RATE. A tax imposed or levied under this Act on the taxable land or other rateable property within a water district. *Water Supply Districts Act*, R.S.M. 1970, c. W100, s. 2.

WATER RESORT. Any beach, shore line, or other place or premises (a) that is on the bank of, contiguous to, adjoining, or in the neighbourhood of, any lake, pond, pool, river, stream, or other body of water, whether naturally existing or artificially created, that is used by persons for swimming, bathing, diving, or wading; and (b) that is available to the public, either without charge, or for the use of which persons are directly or indirectly charged; and includes (c) any place or premises that is or are adjacent to, or in the immediate neighbourhood of, such a place as is hereinbefore described, and (i) that is used for parking motor vehicles or picnicking; or (ii) on which there are facilities for persons to change their clothes; or (iii) that is otherwise used as an adjunct to, or in connection with, any such beach, shore line, place, or premises as is hereinbefore described; and (d) any such beach, shore line, place, or premises that is or are operated or used as part of, or in conjunction with, a motel, hotel, rooming house, boarding house, restaurant, eating place, or place of entertainment, that is available to the public as aforesaid; but does not include the building comprising any motel, hotel, rooming house, boarding house, or restaurant to which clause (d) applies. *Municipal Act*, S.M. 1970, c. 100, s. 440.

WATER RESOURCE MANAGEMENT. The conservation, development and utilization of water resources and includes, with respect thereto, research, data collection and the maintaining of inventories, planning and the implementation of plans, and the control and regulation of water quantity and quality. *Canada Water Act*, R.S.C. 1985, c. C-11, s. 2.

WATER RESOURCES. 1. Includes water storage, drainage and irrigation and any other matters incidental to the management of water resources. *Water Resources Commission Act*, S.A. 1983, c. W-5.1, s. 1. 2. All bodies of water in the province. Newfoundland statutes.

WATERS. *n.* 1. Waters in any river, stream, lake or body of inland water on the surface or underground in the Yukon Territory and the Northwest Territories. *Northern Inland Waters Act*, R.S.C. 1985, c. N-25, s. 2. 2. Includes all streams, lakes, ponds, inland waters, salt waters, watercourses and all other surface and ground waters within the jurisdiction of the Province. *Pollution Control Act*, R.S.B.C. 1979, c. 332, s. 1. See ARCTIC ~; BOUNDARY ~; CANADIAN CUSTOMS ~; CANADIAN FISHERIES ~; CANADIAN ~; COASTAL ~; CONVENTION ~; FEDERAL ~; INLAND ~; INTERJURISDICTIONAL ~; INTERNAL ~; INTERNATIONAL ~; MINOR ~ OF CANADA; TIDAL ~; UNDESIGNATED ~; WATER; ~ OF THE PROVINCE.

WATER SERVICE. The taking, collection, production, treatment, storage, supply, transmission, distribution, sale, purchase and use of water, or any one or more of them. *Ontario Water Resources Act*, R.S.O. 1980, c. 361, s. 43.

WATERSHED. *n.* An area drained by a river and its tributaries. *Conservation Authorities Act*, R.S.O. 1980, c. 85, s. 1.

WATERSLIDE. *n.* A recreational waterslide flume, including the receiving pool to which it is affixed. *An Act to Amend the Health Act*, S.N.B. 1987, c. 24, s. 1.

WATERS OF THE PROVINCE. Any water in the Province of New Brunswick, and without restricting the generality of the foregoing, includes ground water, coastal water and surface water. *Clean Environment Act*, S.N.B. 1975, c. 12, s. 1.

WATER SUPPLY. See PUBLIC ~.

WATER SUPPLY CORPORATION. A corporation established by one or more municipalities for the purpose of constructing and operating a water supply project within or for any municipality. *National Housing Act*, S.C. 1974-75-76, c. 82, s. 7(1).

WATER SUPPLY PROJECT. Includes the reservoir facilities, intake systems, pressure systems, treatment facilities and trunk distribution systems that are required to provide a water supply service to one or more municipalities and the inhabitants thereof. *National Housing Act*, S.C. 1974-75-76, c. 82, s. 7(2).

WATER SUPPLY SYSTEM. Includes the source of water, the pumping station, the distribution system and all ancillary equipment, apparatus and materials forming a part thereof but does not include any pipelines that are installed or are required to be installed by a user of the water supply system. *Highway Act*, R.S.N.B. 1973, c. H-5, s. 4.

WATER SYSTEM. All facilities for storing, pumping, treating and distributing water for domestic, commercial, industrial and fire protective purposes. *Municipalities Act*, R.S.N.B. 1973, c. M-22, s. 118.

WATERTIGHT. *adj.* 1. In relation to a structure, means the structure is capable of preventing the passage of water through it in any direction, under a head of water up to the ship's margin line. *Hull Construction Regulations*, C.R.C., c. 1431, s. 2. 2. Designed to withstand a specific static head of water. *Load Line Regulations (Inland)*, C.R.C., c. 1440, s. 1.

WATERTIGHT COMPARTMENT. In respect of a ship, a space below the main deck that is enclosed by the shell, watertight bulkheads and decks, or by watertight bulkheads and decks and into which direct access from the main deck is gained by means of a hatch or entrance through which downflooding could occur. *Hull Construction Regulations*, C.R.C., c. 1431, s. 100.

WATER USER. (i) The purchaser; or (ii) the owner of a parcel of land shown on the assessment roll of a district as containing a number of acres classified as "to be irrigated". *Irrigation Act*, R.S.A. 1980, c. I-11, s. 1.

WATER UTILITY. A person, including the lessee, trustee, receiver or liquidator of that person, who owns or operates in the Province equipment or facilities for the diverting, developing, pumping, impounding, distributing or furnishing of water to or for 5 or more persons, or to a corporation, for compensation; but does not include (a) a municipality in respect of services furnished by the municipality within its own boundaries; (b) a person who furnishes services or commodity only to himself, his employees or tenants, where the service or commodity is not resold to or used by others;

(c) the Greater Vancouver Water District under the Greater Vancouver Water District Act; (d) an improvement district or water users' community constituted under the Water Act; or (e) a regional district constituted under the Municipal Act in respect of the service of the supply of water (i) in bulk to a member municipality participating in that service; or (ii) to consumers in a municipality participating in that service. *Water Utility Act*, R.S.B.C. 1979, c. 430, s. 1.

WATERWAY. *n.* 1. The waters of (a) the St. Lawrence River extending upstream from the longitudinal meridian passing through the town of Sept-Iles, Quebec (66°23' West) to the upper limits of Montreal Harbour, except for that portion of the St. Lawrence Seaway from St. Lambert Lock to a place 3.5 cables downstream from that section of Jacques Cartier Bridge spanning the Seaway; (b) the Saguenay River and other tributary rivers where vessels enter or leave the St. Lawrence River. *St. Lawrence Waterway Marine Traffic Regulations*, C.R.C., c. 1420, s. 2. Stream, river, lake, and includes a dry watercourse. *Gasoline Handling Act*, R.R.O. 1980, Reg. 439, s. 1. See DEEP ~; ST. LAWRENCE ~.

WATER WORKS. *var.* **WATERWORKS.** Any public, commercial or industrial works for the collection, production, treatment, storage, supply and distribution of water, or any part of any such waterworks.

WATER WORKS RATE. A charge for the capital cost of water works. *Municipal Act*, R.S.O. 1980, c. 302, s. 218.

WATERWORKS SYSTEM. Any system of plants, wells, structures, equipment, pipes, apparatus or other things for the obtaining, treating, purifying, disinfecting, distributing or supplying of water intended to be used for human consumption or in swimming pools and, without limitation, includes aqueducts, cisterns, culverts, cuts, flumes, mains, pumps, reservoirs, tanks, engines and machinery used in connection with the system.

WATT. *n.* 1. For electric power, the power that will produce energy at the rate of one joule per second, a joule being the energy dissipated when the point of application of a force of 10 million dynes is displaced a distance of one centimetre in the direction of the force. *Electrical and Photometric Units Act*, R.S.C. 1970, c. E-3, s. 2. 2. The power that produces energy at the rate of 1 joule per second. *Weights and Measures Act*, S.C. 1970-71-72, c. 36, schedule 1.

WAVE. See MATERIAL ~; MICRO~; SHOCK ~.

WAVELENGTH. *n.* A wavelength in vacuo.

Radiation Emitting Devices Regulations, C.R.C., c. 1370, s. 1.

WAXED. *adj.* May be used in connection with clean dry rutabagas that have been completely immersed in a wax solution. *Fresh Fruit and Vegetable Regulations*, C.R.C., c. 285, s. 69.

WAY. *n.* Includes any road, street, route, avenue, parkway, driveway, square, place, bridge, culvert, viaduct, trestle and any other way whatsoever. *Highway Traffic Act*, R.S.Nfld. 1970, c. 152, s. 234. See PUBLIC ~; RIGHT OF ~; UNDER ~.

WAY-BILL. *n.* A description of goods which a common carrier transports by land.

WAYS AND MEANS COMMITTEE. The parliamentary committee which considers financial statements made by the Minister of Finance. A. Fraser, G.A. Birch & W.A. Dawson, eds., *Beauchesne's Rules and Forms of the House of Commons of Canada*, 5th ed. (Toronto: Carswell, 1978) at 174.

WAYS AND MEANS MOTION. The first step needed before Parliament imposes a new tax, continues an expiring tax, increases the rate of an existing tax or extends a tax to include people not already paying. A. Fraser, G.A. Birch & W.A. Dawson, eds., *Beauchesne's Rules and Forms of the House of Commons of Canada*, 5th ed. (Toronto: Carswell, 1978) at 174.

WAYSIDE PARKS. To provide for the enjoyment, convenience and comfort of the travelling public. *Territorial Parks Act*, R.S.N.W.T. 1974, c. T-5, s. 4.

WAYSIDE PIT. A temporary pit or quarry opened and used by a public road authority solely for the purpose of a particular project or contract of road construction and not located on the road right of way. *Pits and Quarries Control Act*, R.S.O. 1980, c. 378, s. 1.

WAYSIDE QUARRY. See WAYSIDE PIT.

WB. *abbr.* Weber.

W.C.A.T.R. *abbr.* Workers' Compensation Appeals Tribunal Reporter.

W.C.B. *abbr.* 1. Workers' Compensation Board. 2. Workmen's Compensation Board.

W.D.C.P. *abbr.* Weekly Digest of Civil Procedure.

WEAK CIDER. Cider containing not less than 1.5 per cent nor over 7 per cent of alcohol by volume. *An Act to Amend the Act Respecting the Société des Alcools du Québec*, S.Q. 1983, c. 30, s. 9.

WEALTH. *n.* The potential or actual resources and possessions of an individual or community which can be expressed in terms of money or measured by some other standard.

WEALTH TAX. See ANNUAL ~.

WEANER PIG. The offspring of a sow that has been raised to weaning age and that is still in the possession of the person who possesses the sow up to the time the weaner pig is marketed. *Farm Income Stabilization Act*, R.R.O. 1980, Reg. 322, s. 2.

WEAPON. *n.* 1. (a) Anything used or intended for use in causing death or injury to persons whether designed for that purpose or not; or (b) anything used or intended for use for the purpose of threatening or intimidating any person, and, without restricting the generality of the foregoing, includes any firearm as defined in section 84. *Criminal Code*, R.S.C. 1985, c. C-46, s. 2 as amended by *Criminal Law Amendment Act*, R.S.C. 1985 (1st Supp.), c. 27, s. 2. 2. A firearm or any other device that propels a projectile by means of an explosion, spring, air, gas, string, wire or elastic material or any combination of those things. *Wildlife Act*, S.A. 1984, c. W-9.1, s. 1. 3. Includes any thing by which a person may cause harm to himself or herself or to another person. *Provincial Offences Procedure Act*, S.N.B. 1987, c. P-22.1, s. 1. See AUTOMATIC ~; HAND CARRIED ~ OR PIECE OF ORDNANCE; LETHAL ~; OFFENSIVE ~; PROHIBITED ~; RESTRICTED ~.

WEAR. *n.* A fence or dam set across a river.

WEAR AND TEAR. The waste of any material by ordinary use.

WEATHER CONDITIONS. See VFR ~.

WEATHER INSURANCE. 1. Insurance against loss or damage through windstorm, cyclone, tornado, rain, hail, flood or frost, but does not include hail insurance. Insurance acts. 2. Insurance, other than hail insurance or windstorm insurance, against loss or damage caused by rain, tempest, flood or other climatic conditions. *Insurance Act*, R.S.B.C. 1979, c. 200, s. 1.

WEATHER MINIMA. See ITINERANT ~.

WEATHER MODIFICATION ACTIVITY. Includes any action designed or intended to produce, by physical or chemical means, changes in the composition or dynamics of the atmosphere for the purpose of increasing, decreasing or redistributing precipitation, decreasing or suppressing hail or lightning or dissipating fog or cloud.

WEATHER MODIFIER. Any person who engages in any weather modification activity. *Weather Modification Information Regulations*, C.R.C., c. 1604, s. 2.

WEATHERTIGHT. *adj.* 1. Designed to prevent water from penetrating the ship in any sea conditions. Canada regulations. 2. Capable of preventing the passage of water from exterior space to interior space in any weather condition. Canada regulations.

WEBBING. *n.* A narrow fabric woven with continuous filling yarns and finished selvedges. *Motor Vehicle Safety Regulations*, C.R.C., c. 1038, s. 209.

WEBER. *n.* The magnetic flux that, when linking a circuit of one turn, produces in that circuit an electromotive force of 1 volt as the flux is reduced to 0 at a uniform rate in 1 second. *Weights and Measures Act*, S.C. 1970-71-72, c. 36, schedule 1.

WEDLOCK. See BORN OUT OF ~.

WEED. See NOXIOUS ~; NOXIOUS ~S; WIRE ~.

WEED SEED. The seed of a restricted, noxious or nuisance weed. See SMALL ~S.

WEEK. *n.* 1. Any period of 7 successive days. 2. A period of 7 consecutive days commencing on Sunday. 3. The period between midnight on a Saturday and midnight on the Saturday immediately following. 4. Unless otherwise defined in this act, means the period between zero hours on Sunday night and the same time on the following Saturday night. *Industrial and Commercial Establishments Act*, R.S.Q. 1977, c. E-15, s. 2. See CONTRIBUTION ~; FORTY-HOUR ~; PAY ~; WORK ~.

WEEKLY CANADIAN NEWSPAPER. A Canadian newspaper (a) that is ordinarily published once a week; (b) that is intended primarily for the residents of a city, town or village and its surrounding community; (c) of which a substantial portion of each issue consists of news or other articles with respect to the residents referred to in paragraph (b) for which it is primarily intended; and (d) the total circulation of which does not exceed 10,000 copies an issue. *Post Office Act*, R.S.C. 1970, c. P-14, s. 2(4).

WEEKLY DAY OF REST. Sunday. *Days of Rest Act*, S.N.B. 1985, c. D-4.2, s. 1.

WEEKLY INSURABLE EARNINGS. See AVERAGE ~.

WEEK OF LAYOFF. *var.* **WEEK OF LAY-OFF.** A week in which one receives less than one-half of the amount one would earn at the regular rate in a normal non-overtime work week, but shall not mean a week in which a person (i) was not able to work or not available for work; (ii) was subject to disciplinary suspension; or (iii) was not provided with work by the employer by reason of any strike or lock-out occurring at the place of employment or elsewhere.

WEEK OF TENANCY. The weekly period on which the tenancy is based and not necessarily a calendar week and, unless otherwise specifically agreed upon, the week shall be deemed to begin on the day upon which rent is payable. *Landlord and Tenant Act*, R.S.P.E.I. 1974, c. L-7, s. 107.

WEIGHING. See OFFICIAL ~.

WEIGHING MACHINE. Any machine that measures mass or weight and has a moving or movable part that has or can have an effect on the accuracy of the machine. *Weights and Measures Act*, R.S.C. 1985, c. W-6, s. 2.

WEIGH-OVER. *n.* The weighing and inspection of all grain of any grade in an elevator for the purpose of determining the amount in stock of grain of that grade in the elevator. *Canada Grain Act*, R.S.C. 1985, c. G-10, s. 2.

WEIGHT. *n.* In relation to an aircraft means the maximum permissible take-off weight specified in its certificate of airworthiness or in a document referred to in that certificate. *Air Services Fees Regulations*, C.R.C., c. 5, s. 2. See ACCESSORY ~; AXLE GROUP ~; AXLE UNIT ~; AXLE ~; CATCH-~S; CURB ~; DEAD~; DRAINED ~; DRESSED ~; FRONT AXLE ~; GROSS ~; HEADLESS DRAWN ~; PRODUCTION OPTIONS ~; REGISTERED ~; ROUND ~; TOTAL LOADED ~; VEHICLE CAPACITY ~; WHEEL ~.

WEIGHTED FLY. An artificial fly that is equipped with a weight that causes the fly to sink. *Quebec Fishery Regulations*, C.R.C., c. 852, s. 2.

WEIGHT FORFEIT. The amount of money that a boxer, under a written contract to take part in a professional boxing contest or exhibition, agrees to pay his opponent upon failure to comply with the weight requirements under the contract. *Athletics Control Act*, R.R.O. 1980, Reg. 76, s. 2.

WEIGH TICKET. *var.* **WEIGH-TICKET.** A receipt as prescribed by the regulations that is to be issued by a grain elevator operator or his employee to the owner of farm produce or his agent. *Grain Elevator Storage Act*, S.O. 1983, c. 40, s. 1.

WEIGHT OF EVIDENCE. For the evidence of one side to be so far superior to the other's that the verdict should go to the first.

WEIR. *n.* 1. A trap net constructed of brush and twine or wire netting. Fishery regulations. 2. A fence or dam set across a river. See HERRING ~.

WELD. See FORGE ~; FUSION ~.

WELDER. *n.* A person, approved under this Act, engaged in welding either on his own account or in the employ of another person on the fabrication or repair of boilers, pressure vessels, pressure piping or any parts thereof. *Boiler and Pressure Vessel Act*, R.S.Nfld. 1970, c. 24, s. 2.

WELDING. *n.* 1. The joining together, or cutting apart of metals in the molten state without the use of pressure or blows. *Welding Act*, R.S.A. 1970, c. 389, s. 2. 2. The process of welding metals in a molten or molten vaporous state without the application of mechanical pressure or blows.

WELDING EQUIPMENT. Includes plant, machinery, equipment, appliances and devices of every kind and description that are used or intended to be used in the process of fusion welding, brazing and cutting of metals by the application of heat. *Welding Act*, R.S.A. 1970, c. 389, s. 2.

WELDING OPERATOR. A person engaged in welding either for self or in the employ of another person on the fabrication or repair of boilers, pressure vessels or pressure piping or any parts of them.

WELDING PROCEDURE. The complete specifications of a process and the technique employed in the welding of various kinds and thicknesses of metals. *Boiler and Pressure Vessel Act*, R.S.Nfld. 1970, c. 24, s. 2.

WELFARE. *n.* Basic assistance to meet basic needs to anyone without means, including a personal injury victim. K.D. Cooper-Stephenson & I.B. Saunders, *Personal Injury Damages in Canada* (Toronto: Carswell, 1981) at 3. See COMMUNITY ~; HEALTH AND ~ CANADA.

WELFARE AGENCY. 1. Any department of the government of a province, or any person or agency (including a private, non-profit agency) in the province, that at any time in the period commencing April 1, 1964 and ending March 31, 1965 provided welfare services or aid to needy persons in the province, if the whole or any part of the cost of providing such services or aid has been shared or borne in any manner by the province or by a municipality in the province. *Canada Assistance Plan Regulations*, C.R.C., c. 382, s. 12. 2. Any department of government and any person or agency, including a private non-profit agency, that is authorized by law, or by the Minister, to accept applications for assistance, to determine eligibility for assistance, to provide or pay assistance, or to provide welfare services. *Welfare Assistance Act*, R.S.P.E.I. 1974, c. W-4, s. 1. See CHILD ~.

WELFARE AUTHORITY. See CHILD ~.

WELFARE PROGRAM. See PROVINCIAL ~; SPECIAL ~.

WELFARE SERVICES. Services having as their object the lessening, removal or prevention of the causes and effects of poverty, child neglect or dependence on public assistance, and, without limiting the generality of the foregoing, includes (a) rehabilitation services; (b) casework, counselling, assessment and referral services; (c) adoption services; (d) homemaker, day-care and similar services; (e) community development services; (f) consulting, research and evaluation services with respect to welfare programs; and (g) administrative, secretarial and clerical services, including staff training, relating to the provision of any of the foregoing services or to the provision of assistance, but does not include any service relating wholly or mainly to education, correction or any other matter prescribed by regulation or, except for the purposes of the definition "assistance", any service provided by way of assistance. *Canada Assistance Plan*, R.S.C. 1985, c. C-1, s. 2. See CHILD ~.

WELFARE SERVICES PROVIDED IN THE PROVINCE. Welfare services provided in the province pursuant to the provincial law to or in respect of persons in need or persons who are likely to become persons in need unless those services are provided. *Canada Assistance Plan*, R.S.C. 1985, c. C-1, s. 2.

WELFARE WORKER. See OVERSEAS ~.

WELL. *n.* 1. Any artificial opening in the ground from which water is obtained or one made for the purpose of exploring for or obtaining water. 2. Any opening in the ground, not being a seismic shot hole, that is made, to be made or is in the process of being made, by drilling, boring or other method, (a) for the production of oil or gas; (b) for the purpose of searching for or obtaining oil or gas; (c) for the purpose of obtaining water to inject into an underground formation; (d) for the purpose of injecting gas, air, water or other substance into an underground formation; or (e) for any purpose, if made through sedimentary rocks to a depth of at least 150 metres. *Oil and Gas Production and Conservation Act*, R.S.C. 1985, c. O-7, s. 2. 3. A hole made in the ground to locate or to obtain ground water or to test to obtain information in respect of ground water or an aquifer, and includes a spring around or in which works are made or equipment is installed for collection or transmission of water and that is or is likely to be used as a source of water for human consumption. *Ontario Water Resources Amendment Act*, S.O. 1981, c. 50, s. 1. 4. A hole or shaft that is or is being drilled, bored or otherwise sunk

into the earth (a) through which a geothermal resource is or can be produced; (b) for the purpose of producing a geothermal resource or for the purpose of injecting any substance to assist the production of a geothermal resource; or (c) that (i) extends deeper than 600 m; (ii) has a bore hole diameter of more than 100 mm; and (iii) is intended to obtain information about a geothermal resource. *Geothermal Resources Act*, S.B.C. 1982, c. 14, s. 1. See ABANDONED ~; BRINE ~; DEEPENED ~; DELINEATION ~; DEVELOPED ~; DEVELOPMENT ~; EVALUATION ~; EXPERIMENTAL ~; EXPLORATORY ~; FLOWING ~; FREEHOLD ~; GAS ~; GEOTHERMAL ~; MULTI ZONE ~; NEW ~; OIL OR GAS ~; OIL ~; PETROLEUM ~; PRODUCING ~; PUMPING ~.

WELL DRILLER. A person who drills or reconditions a well.

WELL-HEAD PRICE. See BASIC ~.

WELL LICENCE. A valid and subsisting licence to drill a well granted pursuant to the regulations. *Oil and Natural Gas Act*, S.N.B. 1976, c. O-2.1, s. 1.

WELL LICENSEE. The holder of a well licence and subsequent to the drilling of the well, but prior to its abandonment, means the owner of the well. *Oil and Natural Gas Act*, S.N.B. 1976, c. O-2.1, s. 1.

WELL OR OIL WELL. Includes any opening in the ground within the province, except seismic shot holes or structure test holes, from which oil is, has been or is capable of being raised, taken, gained or recovered from a reservoir, and includes: (i) collectively, all wells located within a unit area in respect of which there is in effect either an agreement for unit operation or a unit operation order made pursuant to The Oil and Gas Conservation Act and the regulations thereunder; (ii) all reserves of oil in such reservoir and all rights thereto and interests therein; and (iii) where the context permits or requires, the well site. *Oil Well Income Tax Amendment Act*, S.S. 1980-81, c. 16, s. 4.

WELL SITE. 1. The property upon, in or under which an oil well is situate. *The Oil Well Income Tax Act*, R.S.S. 1978, c. O-3.1, s. 2. 2. (i) That portion of the surface of land required for the conduct of drilling or completion operations of a well during the period next following the initial entry upon the land until the well is abandoned or completed; (ii) that portion of the surface of land required for the conduct of producing operations of a well commencing from the completion date of the well. *The Surface Rights Acquisition and Compensation Act*, R.S.S. 1978, c. S-65, s. 2.

WELL SITE SEABED SURVEY. A survey pertaining to the nature of the surface or subsurface or the seabed or its subsoil of any area in the area of a proposed drilling site in respect of a well and to the conditions of the area that may affect the safety or efficiency of drilling operations.

WELL TERMINATION DATE. The date on which a well or test hole has been abandoned, completed or suspended in accordance with any applicable drilling regulations.

WELSH MORTGAGE. A virtually obsolete form of security; to secure a debt, property is conveyed to a creditor without any proviso or condition for reconveyance, usually with no covenant or condition for payment. The essence of the arrangement is that the mortgagee has possession along with receipt of profits and rent. W.B. Rayner & R.H. McLaren, *Falconbridge on Mortgages*, 4th ed. (Toronto: Canada Law Book, 1977) at 6.

WESTERN CANADA. All that part of Canada lying west of Ontario. *Feed Grain Transportation and Storage Assistance Regulations*, C.R.C., c. 1027, s. 2.

WESTERN DIVISION. All that part of Canada lying west of the meridian passing through the eastern boundary of the City of Thunder Bay, including the whole of the Province of Manitoba. *Canada Grain Act*, R.S.C. 1985, c. G-10, s. 2.

WESTERN GRAIN. Grain grown in the Western Division. *Canada Grain Act*, R.S.C. 1985, c. G-10, s. 2.

WESTERN HEMISPHERE. The continents of North and South America, the islands adjacent thereto and the territorial waters thereof, including Newfoundland, Bermuda and the West Indies, but excluding Greenland, Iceland and the Aleutian Islands. *Public Service Employment Act*, R.S.C. 1985, c. P-33, s. 48.

WESTERNMOST. *adj.* The half compass circle from but not including true south through west to and including true north. *Fishing Gear Marking Regulations*, C.R.C., c. 813, s. 2.

WEST INDIES. Includes the West Indies and the Bahama and Bermuda Islands. *Canada Shipping Act*, R.S.C. 1985, c. S-9, s. 2.

WEST. L. REV. *abbr.* Western Law Review (1961-1966).

WESTMINSTER. See STATUTE OF ~.

WEST. ONT. L. REV. *abbr.* Western Ontario Law Review (1967-1976).

WET ERBP. The equilibrium reflux boiling point of the brake fluid after it has been humid-ified under controlled conditions. *Motor Vehicle Safety Regulations*, C.R.C., c. 1038, s. 2.

WET LEASE. A lease of an aircraft under the terms of which the lessor provides, directly or indirectly, the aircrew to operate the aircraft. *Air Carrier Regulations*, C.R.C., c. 3, s. 2.

WET LOCATION. A location in which liquids may drip, splash or flow on or against electrical equipment. *Power Corporation Act*, R.R.O. 1980, Reg. 794, s. 0.

WET TIME. Work time lost as a result of bad weather.

WET VENT. A waste pipe functioning also as a vent pipe. *Ontario Water Resources Act*, R.R.O. 1980, Reg. 736, s. 1.

WHALE. See BALEEN ~; BLUE ~; DEAD ~; FIN ~; GRAY ~; HUMPBACK ~; MINKE ~; PILOT ~; RIGHT ~; SEI ~; SPERM ~.

WHALE CATCHER. 1. A ship used for the purpose of hunting, taking, towing, holding onto or scouting for whales. *Whaling Convention Act*, R.S.C. 1970, c. W-8, s. 2. 2. The operator of a boat used for the purpose of hunting whales and towing them to a land station. *Meat Inspection Regulations*, C.R.C., c. 1032, s. 169.

WHALE OIL. See CRUDE ~.

WHALE PRODUCTS. Any part of a whale and blubber, meat, bones, whale oil, sperm oil, spermaceti, meal and baleen. *Whaling Convention Act*, R.S.C. 1970, c. W-8, s. 2.

WHALE TREATING. The possession, treatment or processing of whales or of whale products. *Whaling Convention Act*, R.S.C. 1970, c. W-8, s. 2.

WHALING. *n.* 1. Scouting for, hunting, killing, taking, towing or holding onto whales. *Whaling Convention Act*, R.S.C. 1970, c. W-8, s. 2. 2. The scouting for, and the hunting, killing, taking, towing, holding, possessing, eviscerating and processing of whales. *Meat Inspection Regulations*, C.R.C., c. 1032, s. 169.

WHARF. *n.* Includes all wharfs, quays, docks and premises in or on which any goods, when landed from ships, may be lawfully placed. *Canada Shipping Act*, R.S.C. 1985, c. S-9, s. 2. See APPROACH ~; EX ~.

WHARFAGE. *n.* 1. A charge levied on goods (a) that are loaded on or unloaded from a vessel at a wharf; or (b) that are placed on, conveyed across, along, over or under a wharf. Canada regulations. 2. A charge imposed in respect of goods, including goods in containers, that are (a) loaded on or unloaded from a vessel; (b) transhipped overside from vessel to vessel; (c) unloaded overside from vessel to water or from water to vessel; (d) landed from or placed in the water; or (e) loaded or unloaded from a vehicle. *Pacific Terminal Tariff By-law*, C.R.C., c. 1083, s. 2. See SIDE ~; TOP ~.

WHARFINGER. *n.* (a) A person who is appointed under the Act to have charge of and to collect the charges in respect of a wharf; or (b) where no person has been appointed as referred to in paragraph (a), the district marine agent, district manager or superintending engineer for the district in which the wharf is located. *Government Wharves Regulations*, C.R.C., c. 881, s. 2.

WHEAT AREA. See SPRING ~.

WHEAT BOARD. See CANADIAN ~.

WHEAT PRODUCT. Any substance designated as such by the Governor in Council under subsection (4). *Canadian Wheat Board Act*, R.S.C. 1985, c. C-24, s. 2.

WHEEL. See DISC ~; FISH~; SPOKE ~.

WHEEL BASE. The distance from the centre of the hub of a front wheel to the centre of the hub of the rear wheel on the same side of a motor vehicle, as specified in the lists supplied to the board by the manufacturers or, in the case of a motor vehicle that has been remodelled, as ascertained by actual measurement. *The Vehicles Act*, R.S.S. 1978, c. V-3, s. 2.

WHEELCHAIR. *n.* A chair mounted on wheels driven by muscular or other power and used for the carriage of a person who has a physical defect or disability. *Highway Traffic Act*, R.S.O. 1980, c. 198, s. 1.

WHEELCHAIR VEHICLE. A motor vehicle that is used for the transportation, for compensation, of persons in wheelchairs. *Highway Traffic Act*, R.R.O. 1980, Reg. 483, s. 1.

WHEEL WEIGHT. The weight indicated when a vehicle is weighed with any wheel or wheels attached to one end of the axle on the scales or weighing device. *Highway Traffic Act*, R.S.Nfld. 1970, c. 152, s. 2.

WHEREAS. *conj.* A word which usually introduces a factual narrative.

WHEY. *n.* The product remaining after the fat and casein have been removed from milk in the process of making cheese. *Farm Products Grades and Sales Act*, R.R.O. 1980, Reg. 327, s. 1.

WHEY BUTTER. Butter made from milk-fat that has been recovered from whey, or from a mixture of such milk-fat and cream, or from a mixture of whey butter and creamery butter. *Farm Products Grades and Sales Act*, R.R.O. 1980, Reg. 327, s. 1.

WHEY POWDER. Dried whey. *Farm Products Grades and Sales Act*, R.R.O. 1980, Reg. 327, s. 1.

WHIP. See CHIEF ~.

WHIPLASH INJURY. An injury to tissues in the neck when the spine is suddenly overextended. F.A. Jaffe, *A Guide to Pathological Evidence*, 2d ed. (Toronto: Carswell, 1983) at 187.

WHIPPING CREAM. Cream that contains 32 per cent or more of milk-fat. *Milk Act*, R.R.O. 1980, Reg. 622, s. 3.

WHIRLPOOL. See PUBLIC ~.

WHISTLE. *n.* 1. Includes a horn of any type approved by the Commission. *Railway Act*, R.S.C. 1985, c. R-3, s. 2. 2. Any sound signalling appliance capable of producing the prescribed blasts and which complies with the specifications in Annex III to these Regulations. *Collision Regulations*, C.R.C., c. 1416, Rule 32.

WHITE CANE. 1. A cane or walking-stick the major portion of which is white. 2. A cane or walking stick, the whole or upper 2/3 of which is white.

WHITECOAT. *n.* A young harp seal that has not begun to moult. *Seal Protection Regulations*, C.R.C., c. 833, s. 2.

WHITE COLLAR WORKER. A worker employed in office, sales or professional work.

WHITEFISH. *n.* Fish of the species Coregonus clupeaformis, Coregonus nasus or Prosopium cylindraceum. Canada regulations.

WHITE HAKE. A fish of the species Urophycis tenuis (Mitch.). *Northwest Atlantic Fisheries Regulations*, C.R.C., c. 860, s. 2.

WHITE PAPER. An official government memorandum which sets out a problem and the issues related to it with the policy the government recommends.

WHMIS. *abbr.* Workplace Hazardous Materials Information System.

WHOLE CHEESE. A cheese that is of the original size and shape as manufactured. *Food and Drug Regulations*, C.R.C., c. 870, c. B.08.033.

WHOLE EGG. The albumen and the yolk of an egg but not the shell. *Processed Egg Regulations*, C.R.C., c. 290, s. 2.

WHOLE EGG MIX. (a) Frozen whole egg mix; or (b) liquid whole egg mix containing added ingredients not exceeding 12 per cent by weight. *Processed Egg Regulations*, C.R.C., c. 290, s. 2.

WHOLE HOUSE. See COMMITTEE OF THE ~.

WHOLESALE. *n.* 1. Any sale of products to a purchaser for resale, standing or after preparation, conditioning or processing. *Agricultural Products and Food Act*, R.S.Q. 1977, c. P-29, s. 1. 2. A sale to a person other than a consumer. *Gasoline and Motive Fuel Tax Act*, R.S.N.B. 1973, c. G-3, s. 1. See SELL AT ~.

WHOLESALE CUSTOMER. Any person who purchases any controlled product in bulk at the wholesale level and includes Her Majesty in right of Canada or any province, any agent thereof and any refiner, distributor, jobber, dealer, public utility, operator of aircraft, railway, ships, trucks and other transportation facilities and such other person as the Governor in Council may by regulation designate as being a large volume user of the controlled product. *Energy Supplies Emergency Act*, R.S.C. 1985, c. E-9, s. 2.

WHOLESALE DEALER. 1. A person who buys fuel for resale to a person other than a purchaser. 2. Any person who sells tobacco for the purpose of resale.

WHOLESALE DISTRIBUTION. The sale, lease, rental, exchange or other means of dispersal of film to retail distributors, exhibitors or other persons who engage in dispersal of films on a continual and successive basis but not to the general public. *Film and Video Classification Act*, S.S. 1984-85-86, c. F-13.2, s. 2.

WHOLESALE DISTRIBUTOR. A person who engages in wholesale distribution on a continual and successive basis. *Film and Video Classification Act*, S.S. 1984-85-86, c. F-13.2, s. 2.

WHOLESALE OUTLET. Any station, shop, establishment or other place in which petroleum products are sold or kept for sale to retailers. *Petroleum Products Act*, R.S.P.E.I. 1974, c. P-4, s. 1.

WHOLESALE PRICE. The consideration for a transfer, sale or delivery by a wholesaler to a retailer or to another wholesaler and includes the consideration in a transfer, sale or delivery to a consumer by a wholesaler who is also a retailer. *The Oil and Gas Conservation, Stabilization and Development Act*, R.S.S. 1978, c. O-3, s. 19.

WHOLESALER. *n.* 1. Any person, other than an agency, who sells, or offers for sale the regulated product to any retailer, peddler, caterer, processor or wholesaler or otherwise than directly to the consumer. Canada regulations. 2. Any person other than a retailer, who sells petroleum products or keeps petroleum products for sale. 3. A person who sells tobacco for the purpose of resale. 4. Any person, group of persons or co-operative credit society or association or public body to whom the Corporation sells lottery tickets at a price less than the face value of the tickets. *National Lottery Regulations*, C.R.C., c. 431, s. 2. See LICENSED ~; TRAVEL ~.

WHOLESALER-RETAILER. *n.* A wholesaler who is also a retailer. *Gasoline Licensing Act*, R.S.N.S. 1967, c. 117, s. 1.

WHOLESALE STORE. See CHAIN ~.

WHOLESALE TRADE. The business of purchasing any goods, wares or merchandise for resale otherwise than to the public for personal or household use or consumption. *Small Business Loans Regulations*, C.R.C., c. 1501, s. 3.

WHOLESALE VENDOR. Any person who, within the Province, sells tobacco for the purpose of resale. *Tobacco Tax Act*, R.S.N.B. 1973, c. T-7, s. 1.

WHOLLY ENCLOSED. A structure having doors or other means capable of impeding the entrance or exit of persons or the escape of fumes. *Gasoline Handling Act*, R.R.O. 1980, Reg. 439, s. 1.

WHOLLY OWNED. A corporation is wholly owned if all the shares, membership interests or other evidences of interest in the corporation to which are attached votes that may be cast to elect directors of the corporation are held, directly or indirectly, other than by way of security, by, on behalf of, or for the benefit of one of the corporations. *Municipal Grants Act*, R.S.C. 1985, c. M-13, s. 11(2).

WHOLLY OWNED CORPORATION. See SUBSIDIARY ~.

WHOLLY-OWNED SUBSIDIARY. 1. A corporation that is wholly owned by one or more parent Crown corporations directly or indirectly through any number of subsidiaries each of which is wholly owned directly or indirectly by one or more parent Crown corporations. *Financial Administration Act*, R.S.C. 1985, c. F-11, s. 83. 2. (i) An Alberta company, all of whose outstanding shares are beneficially owned by an extra-provincial company; or (ii) an extra-provincial company, all of whose outstanding shares are beneficially owned by an Alberta company. *Companies Act*, R.S.A. 1980, c. C-20, s. 173.

WHOLLY-PROTECTED ECOLOGICAL RESERVE. An ecological reserve established for the absolute protection of a territory in a natural state. *Ecological Reserves Act*, S.N.B. 1975, c. E-1.1, s.1.

WIDOW. *n.* 1. Includes widower, and means a

person whose spouse has died and who has not thereafter become the spouse of another person. *Old Age Security Act*, R.S.C. 1985 (1st Supp.), c. 34, s. 1. 2. A person whose spouse is deceased and includes a widower. See DEPENDENT ~; RESIDUAL INCOME OF THE ~.

WIDOWED MOTHER. May, in the discretion of the Commission, include a mother deserted by her spouse when the circumstances of the case are, in the opinion of the Commission, such as would entitle her to a pension. *Pension Act*, R.S.C. 1985, c. P-6, s. 2.

WIDOWER. *n.* A person whose wife is dead. See DEPENDENT ~.

WIDOW OF A VETERAN. The widow of a person who, being a veteran, died from causes arising during the service by virtue of which he became a veteran. *Public Service Employment Act*, R.S.C. 1985, c. P-33, s. 48.

WIDOW, WIDOWER OR SURVIVING SPOUSE. (a) A surviving spouse of a deceased veteran who is not a veteran and who has not remarried; and (b) a surviving spouse of a deceased veteran who is not a veteran, who has remarried and whose spouse of that marriage dies or whose marriage ends in dissolution or legal separation, and, for the purposes of paragraph 7(g) and the schedule, includes a veteran who is bereft by death of his spouse. *War Veterans Allowance Act*, R.S.C. 1985, c. W-3, s. 2.

WIDTH. *n.* 1. Used in reference to a crab, means the maximum distance measured across the widest part of the body shell. *Atlanic Crab Fishery Regulations*, C.R.C., c. 806, s. 2. 2. With respect to a condom, means the linear distance between the longitudinal edges of the condom when the condom is placed flat on a plane. *Medical Devices Regulations*, C.R.C., c. 871, s. 1. See LOT ~; OVERALL ~; SECTION ~; SIDE YARD ~.

WIDTH OF TIRE. (i) In the case of pneumatic tires, the nominal width of the tire marked thereon by the manufacturer; and (ii) in the case of all other tires the actual width of the tire surface in contact with the road. *The Highway Traffic Act*, S.M. 1985-86, c. 3, s. 68(1).

WIFE. *n.* 1. A woman who has entered into a marriage within the meaning given thereto in the law of any province of Canada. *Immigration Regulations*, C.R.C., c. 940, s. 2. 2. Includes a woman who has lived with a man, who is not her husband, as wife and husband continuously for not less than 1 year preceding the making of a complaint under this Act. *Wives' and Children's Maintenance Act*, S.N.S. 1977, c. 18, s. 27. See COMMON-LAW ~; DESERTED ~; DESTITUTE ~; HUSBAND OR ~.

WILD. *adj.* Wild by nature and in a state of nature. *The Game Act*, R.S.S. 1978, c. G-1, s. 2.

WILD ANIMAL FARM. An area where wild animals other than fur bearing animals are kept, raised, bred, or propagated, or any combination thereof, in captivity for any purpose. *Wildlife Act*, R.S.M. 1970, c. W140, s. 2.

WILDCAT STRIKE. A strike commenced without the authorization of a union or in violation of a no-strike clause in a collective agreement.

WILD FISH. A fish listed in Schedule I, other than a fish propagated by man in a fish culture facility. *Fish Health Protection Regulations*, C.R.C., c. 812, s. 2.

WILD LAND. Land that is not occupied or cultivated. *Fish and Wildlife Act*, S.N.B. 1980, c. F-14.1, s. 1.

WILDLIFE. *n.* 1. Any non-domestic animal. 2. Any species of vertebrate which is wild by nature and hence not normally dependent on people to directly provide its food, shelter or water. See EXOTIC ~; ILLEGAL ~; RESORT OF ~

WILDLIFE AREA. See CRITICAL ~.

WILDLIFE FARM. A place in which any wildlife or any exotic wildlife is kept for sale, trade, barter, public exhibition, propagation or for scientific or other purposes.

WILDLIFE HABITAT. The air, soil, water, food and cover components of the environment on which wildlife depend directly or indirectly in order to carry out their life processes. *Wildlife Act*, S.B.C. 1982, c. 57, s. 1.

WILDLIFE MANAGEMENT. The regulation of wildlife populations in their habitats for the purpose of sustaining them for human use or enjoyment in perpetuity. *Wildlife Act*, S.N.W.T. 1978 (3d Sess.), c. 8, s. 2.

WILDLIFE OFFICER. Any person appointed or authorized by the minister for the purpose of enforcing this act and the regulations. Wildlife acts.

WILDLIFE SANCTUARY. 1. Land in a wildlife management area designated as a wildlife sanctuary. *Wildlife Act*, S.B.C. 1982, c. 57, s. 1. 2. Any territory designated by regulation of the Lieutenant-Governor in Council, whose terms and conditions of utilization of the resources are fixed primarily with a view to the conservation of wildlife. *Wild-life Conservation Act*, S.Q. 1978, c. 65, s. 1. 3. An area of land with a particular kind of ecological environment set aside by law or by regulation for the temporary or permanent protection of certain species of animals. *An Act Respecting Hunting and Fishing Rights in the*

James Bay and New Québec territories, S.Q. 1978, c. 92, s. 22.

WILFULLY. *adv.* Intentionally; deliberately.

WILL. *n.* 1. The written statement by which a person instructs how her or his estate should be distributed after death. 2. Includes a testament, a codicil, an appointment by will or by writing in the nature of a will in exercise of a power and any other testamentary disposition. 3. Includes testament, codicil, and every other testamentary instrument of which probate may be granted. See ADMINISTRATOR WITH ~ ANNEXED; CONDITIONAL ~; DUPLICATE ~; GRANT OF ADMINISTRATION WITH ~ ANNEXED; HOLOGRAPH ~; INTERNA-TIONAL ~; LETTERS OF ADMININSTRA-TION WITH ~ ANNEXED; MUTUAL ~S; NUNCUPATIVE ~; TENANCY AT ~.

WILSON APPLICATION. An application, named after the case *Wilson v. The Queen* (1983), 9 C.C.C. (3d) 97 (S.C.C.), to set aside an authorization to wiretap. P.K. McWilliams, *Canadian Criminal Evidence*, 3d ed. (Aurora: Canada Law Book, 1988) at 13-56 and 13-57.

WINDING UP. *var.* **WINDING-UP.** 1. The process of ending the business of a corporation or partnership by settling accounts and liquidating assets. 2. In relation to a pension plan that has been terminated, the process of distributing the assets of the plan.

WINDING-UP ORDER. An order granted by a court under this Act to wind up the business of a company, and includes any order granted by the court to bring under this Act any company in liquidation or in process of being wound up. *Winding-up Act*, R.S.C. 1985, c. W-11, s. 2.

WINDOW. See PUSH-OUT ~; READILY REMOVABLE ~.

WINDSTORM INSURANCE. Insurance against loss of or damage to property caused by windstorm, cyclone or tornado.

WINDSOR Y.B. ACCESS JUST. *abbr.* The Windsor Yearbook of Access to Justice.

WINDSOR Y.B. ACCESS JUSTICE. *abbr.* The Windsor Yearbook of Access to Justice (Recueil annuel de Windsor d'accès à la justice).

WIND UP. *var.* **WIND-UP.** The termination of a pension plan and the distribution of the assets of the pension fund. *Pension Benefits Act*, S.N.B. 1987, c. P-5.1, s. 1.

WINE. *n.* 1. Includes spirituous liquors that are the products of fruits, vegetables, roots, herbs, grain, molasses, sugar or other fermentable substances and are obtained by the normal alcoholic fermentation of the juices or extracts therefrom and not by distillation. *Excise Tax Act*, R.S.C. 1985, c. E-15, s. 25. 2. The beverage obtained by the alcoholic fermentation of grape juice, reconstituted grape juice or grape mash. *An Act to Amend the Act Respecting the Société des Alcools du Québec*, S.Q. 1983, c. 30, s. 9. See DOMESTIC ~; FORTIFIED ~; MALT-~; MEDICATED ~; NATURAL ~; ONTARIO ~.

WING TANK. Any tank adjacent to the side shell plating of a ship. *Oil Pollution Prevention Regulations*, C.R.C., c. 1454, s. 33.

WINNING TICKET. A ticket sold on a horse or combination of horses that, pursuant to these Regulations (a) is considered a winning horse or a winning combination of horses in its respective pool; or (b) is a horse or a combination of horses on which a refund has been ordered. *Race Track Supervision Regulations*, C.R.C., c. 441, s. 2.

WINNIPEG GRAIN AND PRODUCE EXCHANGE CLEARING ASSOCIATION LIMITED. The association incorporated under the Companies Act of Manitoba under the name of "The Winnipeg Grain and Produce Exchange Clearing Association Limited". *Grain Futures Act*, R.S.C. 1985, c. G-11, s. 2.

WINNIPEG GRAIN EXCHANGE. The voluntary association of persons organized, established and maintained to operate and conduct a grain and produce exchange at the city of Winnipeg, in the Province of Manitoba, known as "The Winnipeg Grain Exchange". *Canada Grain Act*, R.S.C. 1985, c. G-11, s. 2.

WIN POOL. Monies bet on horses selected to finish first in a race. *Race Track Supervision Regulations*, C.R.C., c. 441, s. 2.

WINTER FISHING. Fishing through the ice during the period between the fall freeze-up and (a) the Thursday preceding the last Sunday in April; or (b) the melting or breaking-up of the ice in the spring, whichever is the earlier. *Quebec Fishery Regulations*, C.R.C., c. 852, s. 2.

WINTER FLOUNDER. A fish of the species Pseudopleuronectes americanus (Walb.). *Northwest Atlantic Fisheries Regulations*, C.R.C., c. 860, s. 2.

WINTERING. *n.* The occupying, by a vessel, during the non-navigation season of a berth.

WINTERING CHARGE. A rate imposed on a vessel in respect of a period of 30 days or more after December 14 in a year and before April 1 in the following year during which the vessel is (a) moored to a wharf; (b) occupying a berth or any space at or near a wharf; or (c) secured in any manner whatever to a vessel referred to in paragraph (a) or (b). *Windsor Harbour Wharf By-law*, C.R.C., c. 919, s. 2.

WINTER MONTHS. The months of January, February, March, April, November, and December, or any of them, and includes any other month or part thereof that may be designated in the regulations as being a winter month within the meaning of this Act. *Winter Employment Act*, R.S.M. 1970, c. W160, s. 2.

WINTER PERIOD. That period beginning at two o'clock, mountain standard time, in the forenoon of the last Sunday in October in any year and ending at two o'clock, mountain standard time, in the forenoon of the last Sunday in April in the following year. *The Time Act*, R.S.S. 1978, c. T-14, s. 2.

WINTER TERM. The period that commences on December 15 in any year and expires on April 15 in the year next following. *Lauzon Dry Docks Regulations*, C.R.C., c. 1363, s. 2.

WINTER WORKS. Municipal works for which the Government of Canada grants a subsidy within the limits of its Municipal Winter Works Incentive Program for the relief of unemployment. *An Act Respecting Municipal Winter Works*, R.S.Q. 1977, c. T-13, s. 1.

WIRE. *n.* (a) When applied to copper or copper alloys containing 50 per cent or more by weight of copper, means (i) a drawn, non-tubular product of any cross-sectional shape, in coils or cut to length and not over .5 inch in maximum cross-sectional dimension; or (ii) a product of solid rectangular cross-section in coils or cut to length, cold-rolled after drawing and not over 1.25 inches in width or .188 inch in thickness; (b) when applied to aluminum or aluminum alloys, means a non-tubular product of rectangular or square cross-section (whether or not with rounded corners), or of round, hexagonal or octagonal cross-section, in coils or cut to length and not over .5 inch in maximum cross-sectional dimension; and (c) when applied to metals other than iron, steel, aluminum, aluminum alloys, copper or copper alloys containing 50 per cent or more by weight of copper, means a drawn, non-tubular product of any cross-sectional shape, in coils or cut to length and not over .5 inch in maximum cross-sectional dimension. *Customs Tariff*, R.S.C. 1985, c. C-54, s. 2.

WIRED GLASS. 1. Glass in which a wire mesh has been completely embedded. *Safety Glass Regulations*, C.R.C., c. 933, s. 2. 2. Glass, not less than one-quarter inch thick, in which a mesh structure of wire is embedded and completely covered. *Hotel Fire Safety Act*, R.R.O. 1980, Reg. 505, s. 2.

WIRED GLASS SCREEN. A partition of steel

or steel-clad framing containing wired glass panels in which the area of individual panels of wired glass does not exceed 1,296 square inches. *Hotel Fire Safety Act*, R.R.O. 1980, Reg. 505, s. 2.

WIRE OF IRON OR STEEL. A drawn, non-tubular product of iron or steel (a) if in coils, with any cross-sectional shape or dimension; (b) if in straight cut lengths, with a maximum cross-sectional dimension of 0.50 inch; or (c) if cold-rolled flat after drawing, with a maximum width of 0.50 inch, in coils or in straight cut lengths. *Customs Tariff*, R.S.C. 1985, c. C-54, s. 2.

WIRE-WAY. *n.* A raceway consisting of a completely enclosed system of metal troughing, and fittings therefor, so formed and constructed that insulated conductors may be readily drawn in and withdrawn, or laid in and removed, after the system has been completely installed without injury either to conductors or their covering. *Power Corporation Act*, R.R.O. 1980, Reg. 794, s. 0.

WIRE WEED. Has the same meaning as horsetail. *Atlantic Coast Marine Plant Regulations*, C.R.C., c. 805, s. 2.

WIRING. *n.* Includes any conductor for the conveyance of electric energy, and any conduit, duct, raceway, cable, channel, switch, box, receptacle or other fitting or device associated with any electrical installation. *Electrical Protection Act*, R.S.N.W.T. 1974, c. E-1, s. 2.

WIT. See TO ~.

WITCHCRAFT. *n.* 1. Conjuration, sorcery. 2. Fraudulently pretending to use any kind of witchcraft, sorcery, enchantment, or conjuration. *Criminal Code*, R.S.C. 1985, c. C-46, s. 365.

WITCH FLOUNDER. A fish of the species Glyptocephalus cynoglossus (L.). *Northwest Atlantic Fisheries Regulations*, C.R.C., c. 860, s. 2.

WITH COSTS. In the expression "motion dismissed with costs", means that costs will be assessed and paid only when the trial is over. M.M. Orkin, *The Law of Costs*, 2d ed. (Aurora: Canada Law Book, 1987) at 1-13.

WITHDRAWAL. *n.* 1. Unlike a stay of proceedings which has statutory basis in Canadian law, it is based on English common law, in force through section 8(2) of the Criminal Code. S.A. Cohen, *Due Process of Law* (Toronto: Carswell, 1977) at 157. 2. For a defendant to retract a defence by filing and serving written notice. Formerly also meant discontinuance by a plaintiff of part, not the whole, action. G.D. Watson & C. Perkins, eds., *Holmested & Watson: Ontario*

Civil Procedure (Toronto: Carswell, 1984) at 23-19.

WITHERNAM. *n.* Seizure again; reprisal.

WITHIN CANADA. Includes Canadian waters as defined for the purposes of the Customs Act, chapter C-40 of the Revised Statutes of Canada. *Foreign Enlistments Act*, R.S.C. 1985, c. F-28, s. 2.

WITHIN THE YEAR. Within the 12-month period following the month in which the calculation is made. *Loan Companies Act*, R.S.C. 1985, c. L-12, s. 117(2).

WITHOUT DAY. Without being continued on any certain day. See GO ~.

WITHOUT PREJUDICE. Of an admission or offer, means that a party's privileges or rights are not lost or waived unless expressly decided or conceded.

WITHOUT RECOURSE TO ME. A phrase used to protect the indorser of a note or bill from liability.

WITH PROFITS POLICY. An insurance policy in which any bonus from the profits of the insurance company is allocated to the policy and increases its value.

WITNESS. *n.* 1. A person who gives evidence orally under oath or by affidavit in a judicial proceeding, whether or not he is competent to be a witness, and includes a child of tender years who gives evidence but does not give it under oath, because, in the opinion of the person presiding, the child does not understand the nature of the oath. *Criminal Code*, R.S.C. 1985, c. C-46, s. 118. 2. 2. Includes a person who, in the course of an action is examined viva voce on discovery or who is cross-examined upon an affidavit, or who answers any interrogatories or makes an affidavit as to documents. See ADVERSE ~; ATTESTING ~; EAR~; EYE-~; HOSTILE ~; MATERIAL ~; ORDINARY ~; REPORTING ~.

WITNESSING PART. Of a deed or other formal document, the section after the recitals, or the parties which usually begins by referring to the agreement or intention and then the consideration. The name "witnessing part" refers to the words "This deed witnesseth," which show the document is supposed to record a transaction.

WITNESS POST. A legal post erected pursuant to subsection (2) to designate the corner of a claim. *Canada Mining Regulations*, C.R.C., c. 1516, s. 15.

WKRS. *abbr.* Workers(').

[ ] W.L.A.C. *abbr.* Western Labour Arbitration Cases, 1966-.

W.L.R. *abbr.* Western Law Reporter, 1905-1916.

[ ] W.L.R. *abbr.* Weekly Law Reports.

W.L.T. *abbr.* Western Law Times, 1890-1895.

WOLF. *n.* 1. The timber wolf, also known as the gray or black wolf and includes the immature young of such animal. *The Wolf and Coyote Bounty Act*, R.S.S. 1978, c. W-15, s. 2. 2. Any of the species Canis lupus L., or Canis latrans Say or any cross breed of either. *Dog Licensing and Live Stock and Poultry Protection Act*, R.S.O. 1980, c. 123, s. 8.

WOMAN. *n.* A female person of the age of eighteen years or more. *Employment Standards Act*, R.S.M. 1970, c. E110, s. 2. See MARRIED ~; SINGLE ~; UNMARRIED ~.

WOMB. See UTERUS.

WOMEN. See CANADIAN ADVISORY COUNCIL ON THE STATUS OF ~; STATUS OF ~ CANADA.

WOMEN'S ROYAL NAVAL SERVICES. See MEMBER OF THE ~.

WOOD. *n.* A group of trees planted or growing on at least 0.5 of a hectare of land with at least 250 trees on each 0.5 hectare of land. *Forestry Act*, R.R.O. 1980, Reg. 397, s. 1. See PROCESSED ~; PULP~; ROUND~; SMALL ~.

WOOD ALCOHOL. Any volatile liquid, whether obtained by the destructive distillation of wood or otherwise, the chief constituent of which is methyl alcohol and which contains not more than 25 per cent by weight of acetone. *Excise Act*, R.S.C. 1985, c. E-14, s. 243.

WOODEN GUIDE POST. A wood post not less than 4 inches square and not less than 4 feet long pointed at one end and domed at the other and placed in the ground so that the domed end of the post is not less than 3 feet above the ground level. *Surveys Act*, R.R.O. 1980, Reg. 927, s. 1.

WOOD FIBRE. The plant tissue contained in trees or woody shrubs. *Forest Products Act*, R.S.N.B. 1973, c. F-21, s. 1.

WOODLANDS. *n.* 1. Lands having at least 1,000 trees per hectare of all sizes or at least 750 trees per hectare measuring over 5 centimetres in diameter or at least 500 trees per hectare measuring over 12 centimetres in diameter or at least 250 trees per hectare measuring over 20 centimetres in diameter (all measurements to be taken at least 1.3 metres from the ground), but does not include a plantation established for the purpose of producing Christmas trees. *Woodlands Improvement Act*, R.S.O. 1980, c. 535, s. 1. 2. Lands having not less than 400 trees per acre of all sizes, or 300 trees measuring over 2 inches in diameter, or 200 trees measuring over 5 inches in diameter, or 100 trees measuring over 8 inches in diameter (all such measurements to be taken at 4¹/₂ feet from the ground) of one or more of the following kinds: white or Norway pine, white or Norway spruce, hemlock, tamarack, oak, ash, elm, hickory, basswood, tulip (white wood), black cherry, walnut, butternut, chestnut, hard maple, soft maple, cedar, sycamore, beech, black locust, or catalpa, or any other variety that may be designated by order in council, and which lands have been set apart by the owner with object chiefly, but not necessarily solely, of fostering growth of the trees thereon and that are fenced and not used for grazing purposes. *Assessment Act*, R.S.O. 1980, c. 31, s. 18.

WOODLOT. *n.* 1. An immoveable other than a farm woodlot (1) that is the subject of a forest development plan supervised by the Ministre de l'énergie et des resources or that is, or is intended to be, exploited in a real and continuous manner for domestic, industrial or commercial forest purposes; and (2) that is not used or intended to be used mainly for residential purposes or for purposes of pleasure, recreation or sport. *An Act Respecting Municipal Taxation and Providing Amendments to Certain Legislation*, S.Q. 1979, c. 72, s. 1. 2. An area having not less than, (i) 400 trees per acre of any size; (ii) 300 trees per acre measuring more than 2 inches dbh; (iii) 200 trees per acre measuring more than 5 inches dbh; or (iv) 100 trees per acre measuring more than 8 inches dbh. *Trees Act*, R.S.O. 1980, c. 510, s. 1. See PRIVATE ~.

WOOD MATCHES. Matches that have splints of wood but does not include such matches if they are attached to a common base. *Hazardous Products (Matches) Regulations*, C.R.C., c. 929, s. 2.

WOOD PROCESSING FACILITY. A mill in which timber is manufactured into secondary wood products.

WOOD PRODUCT. Includes pulp, pulpwood, paper, veneer, plywood, lumber, timber, poles, posts, chips and any other product accruing from a timber harvesting operation. See PRIMARY ~S.

WOOD RESIDUE. Wood chips, slabs, edgings, sawdust, shavings and hog fuel. *Forest Act*, R.S.B.C. 1979, c. 140, s. 1.

WOODS. *n.* Forest land and rock barren, brushland, dry marsh, bog or muskeg.

WOOD TURPENTINE. See STEAM DISTILLED ~; SULPHATE ~.

WOOL. *n.* Unwashed fleece wool produced in

Canada. *Wool Grading Regulations*, C.R.C., c. 294, s. 2. See RAW ~, HAIR OR BRISTLES.

WORD. See OPERATIVE ~; OVERT ~.

WORDS. *n.* 1. Includes figures, punctuation marks and typographical, monetary and mathematical symbols. 2. Includes pictures, visual images, gestures or other methods of signifying meaning. *Defamation Act*, R.S.N.S. 1967, c. 72, s. 1. See APT DESCRIPTIVE ~; APT ~; GENERAL ~; PRECATORY ~; SEDITIOUS ~.

WORDS OF ART. Words employed in a technical sense.

WORDS OF LIMITATION. Words which effectively restrict the continuation of an estate.

WORK. *n.* 1. The labour or services an employee is required to perform for an employer and includes time the employee is required to be available for his employment duties at a place designated by the employer but does not include the time spent by an employee in his own living accommodation, whether on or off the employer's premises. *Employment Standards Act*, S.B.C. 1980, c. 10, s. 1. 2. The construction, renovation, repair or demolition of property and the alteration or improvement of land. 3. Includes the title thereof when such title is original and distinctive. *Copyright Act*, R.S.C. 1985, c. C-42, s. 2. 4. Includes (a) any bridge, boom, dam, wharf, dock, pier, tunnel or pipe and the approaches or other works necessary or appurtenant thereto; (b) any dumping of fill or excavation of materials from the bed of a navigable water; (c) any telegraph or power cable or wire; or (d) any structure, device or thing, whether similar in character to anything referred to in this definition or not, that may interfere with navigation. *Navigable Waters Protection Act*, R.S.C. 1985, c. N-22, s. 3. 5. The work reasonably required to be performed to explore for, develop or produce minerals. See ARTISTIC ~; ASSEMBLY-LINE ~; ASSESSMENT ~; BARGAINING UNIT ~; COLLECTIVE ~; CONSTITUENCY ~; CONSTRUCTION ~; COST OF ~; CUSTOM ~; DAY'S ~; DRAINAGE ~; DRAMATIC ~; EARTH~; ELECTRICAL ~; ENGINEERING ~; EQUAL PAY FOR EQUAL ~; EXPLORATORY ~; FEDERAL ~, UNDERTAKING OR BUSINESS; FIELD ~; GEOLOGICAL ~; GEOPHYSICAL ~; GEOTECHNICAL ~; HOME~; HOT ~; HOURS OF ~; INSURED ~; LAWFUL ~; LITERARY ~; MAINTENANCE ~; MINE RESCUE ~; MUSICAL ~; PIPING INSTALLATION ~; PROTECTION ~; PUBLIC ~; RIGHT TO ~; SEASONAL AGRICULTURAL ~; TAKE-HOME ~; ~S.

WORK ACTIVITY PROJECT. A project the

purpose of which is to prepare for entry or return to employment persons in need or likely to become persons in need who, because of environmental, personal or family reasons, have unusual difficulty in obtaining or holding employment or in improving, through participation in technical or vocational training programs or rehabilitation programs, their ability to obtain or hold employment. *Canada Assistance Plan*, R.S.C. 1985, c. C-1, s. 14.

WORK-ASSIGNMENT DISPUTE. A dispute with an employer concerning assignment of unorganized employees to work or between unions as to which union's members should do certain work.

WORK DAY. 1. The daily period of work. 2. A period of 24 consecutive hours commencing at the time a motor vehicle operator begins his work shift. *Canada Motor Vehicle Operators Hours of Service Regulations*, C.R.C., c. 1005, s. 2.

WORKER. *n.* 1. An employee. 2. A person who has entered into or works under a contract of service or apprenticeship, written or oral, express or implied, whether by way of manual labour or otherwise and includes a learner. See AIR RAID PRECAUTIONS ~; BLIND ~; BLUE COLLAR ~; CASUAL ~; CHILD CARE ~; DAIRY~; HOME~; IRON~; MIGRATORY ~; OCCUPATIONAL ~; OUT~; PRODUCTION ~; RADIATION ~; SHEET METAL ~; UNDEREMPLOYED ~; UNEMPLOYED ~; WHITE COLLAR ~; X-RAY ~; YOUTH ~.

WORKERS' COMPENSATION. A program to provide financial, rehabilitation and medical assistance to any worker who is partially or totally disabled by an accident which arose "out of and in the course of employment". K.D. Cooper-Stephenson & I.B. Saunders, *Personal Injury Damages in Canada* (Toronto: Carswell, 1981) at 2 and 3.

WORKERS' COMPENSATION INSURANCE. Insurance of an employer against the cost of compensation prescribed by statute in respect of injury to or disability or death of a worker through accident or disease arising out of or in the course of employment.

WORKERS' TRUST FUND. Any trust fund maintained in whole or in part on behalf of any worker on an improvement and into which any monetary supplementary benefit is payable as wages for work done by the worker in respect of the improvement. *Construction Lien Act*, S.O. 1983, c. 6, s. 1.

WORKING AREA. (a) Any area in which work is being performed on board a ship; (b) with respect to persons employed in the maintenance or repair of a ship, any area immediately adjacent to the ship; and (c) with respect to persons employed in the loading or unloading of a ship, any area on shore that is within the reach of any derrick, crane or other hoisting equipment employed in loading or unloading the ship and the immediate approaches to such an area, but does not include any sheds, warehouses or any part of a wharf forward or aft of the ship's mooring lines. *Safe Working Practices Regulations*, C.R.C., c. 1467, s. 2.

WORKING BOAT. A motor vessel, (i) that is registered under the Canada Shipping Act and classified under that Act as a work boat; or (ii) that, not being registered under the Canada Shipping Act, is designated in writing as a working boat by an officer of the Ministry of Revenue authorized by the Minister to make such designations; and (iii) that is normally operated in lakes or rivers in the carriage for hire of passengers, in the moving of freight as cargo or by towing or pushing any container containing such freight, in towing or pushing any motor vessel, in dredging in lakes or rivers, or in servicing waterfront facilities, navigational aids or other motor vessels. *Motor Vehicle Fuel Tax Act*, R.R.O. 1980, Reg. 667, s. 1.

WORKING CAPITAL. 1. Share capital, debenture or bond indebtedness, general reserve fund, deferred dividends or participating reserves and undistributed surplus or deficit accounts. *Co-operative Associations Act*, R.S.N.W.T. 1974, c. C-15, s. 25. 2. The excess of current assets over current liabilities determined in accordance with generally accepted accounting principles. *Commodity Futures Act*, R.R.O. 1980, Reg. 114, s. 7.

WORKING CHAMBER. The part of a project that is used for work in compressed air, but does not include an air lock or a medical lock. *Occupational Health and Safety Act*, R.R.O. 1980, Reg. 691, s. 240.

WORKING CIRCLE. See PUBLIC ~.

WORKING DAY. 1. A day on which the person injured would, but for the injury, be employed in his ordinary work. *Industrial Accidents Enquiries Act*, R.S.Nfld. 1970, c. 165, s. 2. 2. Any day except a Saturday or a Sunday or other holiday. *Provincial Offences Procedure Act*, S.N.B. 1987, c. P-22.1, s. 1. 3. A day on which teachers are required to give tuition and instruction or the other employees are required to perform their duties. *School Act*, S.B.C. 1982, c. 78, s. 1.

WORKING EXPENDITURE. Includes (a) all expenses of maintenance of the railway; (b) all tolls, rent or annual sums that are paid in respect of the hire of rolling stock let to the company, or in respect of property leased to or held by the company, apart from the rent of any leased line; (c) all rent charges or interest on the purchase money of lands belonging to the company, purchased but not fully paid for; (d) all expenses of or incidental to the working of the railway and the traffic thereon, including all necessary repairs and supplies to rolling stock while on the lines of another company; (e) all rates, taxes, insurance and compensation for accidents or losses, including any compensation payable under the provisions of any Act of Parliament or of any provincial legislature providing for compensation to workmen for injuries or in respect of an industrial disease; (f) all salaries and wages of persons employed in and about the working of the railway and traffic; (g) all office and management expenses, including directors' fees, and agency, legal and other like expenses; (h) all costs and expenses of and incidental to the compliance by the company with any order of the Commission under this Act; and (i) generally, all charges that, in all cases of railway companies incorporated under the laws of the United Kingdom, are usually carried to the debit of revenue as distinguished from capital account. *Railway Act*, R.S.C. 1985, c. R-3, s. 2.

WORKING EXPENSES. See WORKING EXPENDITURE.

WORKING FACE. Any place in any mine from which coal or another mineral is being cut, sheared, broken or loosened.

WORKING HOURS. 1. The hours during which an employee works or performs some labour or service for the employer. 2. All hours from the time that a motor vehicle operator begins his work shift as required by his employer until the time he is relieved of his job responsibilities but does not include any time (a) during a work shift when he is relieved of his job responsibilities by his employer for authorized meals and rest while en route; (b) spent during stops en route due to illness or fatigue; (c) resting en route as one of two operators or a motor vehicle that is fitted with a sleeper berth; or (d) resting while en route in a motel, hotel or other similar place of rest where sleeping accommodation is provided. *Motor Vehicle Operators Hours of Work Regulations*, C.R.C., c. 990, s. 2. See NORMAL ~; REGULAR ~.

WORKING INTEREST. A right, in whole or in part, to produce and dispose of oil or gas from a pool or part of a pool, whether that right is held as an incident of ownership of an estate in fee simple in the oil or gas or under a lease, agreement or other instrument, if the right is chargeable with and the holder thereof is obligated to pay or bear, either in cash or out of production, all or a portion of the costs in connection with the drilling for, recovery and disposal of oil or gas from the pool or part thereof.

WORKING INTEREST OWNER. 1. A person who owns a working interest. *Oil and Gas Production and Conservation Act*, R.S.C. 1985, c. O-7, s. 29. 2. A person who has the right, in whole or in part, to search for and produce oil and gas from any lands and to appropriate the production therefrom either for himself or for others having an interest therein or for both, whether such right is derived from ownership in fee simple, from a lease, or from any other disposition. *Mines Act*, R.S.M. 1970, c. M160, s. 60.

WORKING LOAD. The sum of the weight of the lifeboat or life raft, equipment, blocks and falls, and the number of persons with which the lifeboat or life raft is required to be lowered, each person being considered to weigh 165 pounds. *Life Saving Equipment Regulations*, C.R.C., c. 1436, s. 1.

WORKING PLACE. (a) In relation to a coal mine, means a portion of a coal seam in the underground workings of a coal mine from which coal is being cut, sheared, broken, loosened or removed, and any other part of the underground workings where timbering, rock bolting or drilling operations are in progress; (b) in relation to a mine other than a coal mine, means a portion of the underground workings of a mine in which ore or waste is first broken and removed and includes a place designated by the chief inspector.

WORKING PRESSURE. The pressure at which a boiler or pressure vessel may be used or operated under this Act. *Boilers and Pressure Vessel Act*, R.S.Nfld. 1970, c. 24, s. 2.

WORKING YEAR. One calendar year's continuous service, comprising not less than 225 days of actual work. *Employment Standards Act*, R.S.B.C. 1979, c. 107, s. 1.

WORK INJURY. Any injury, disease or illness incurred by an employee in the performance of or in connection with his work. *Canada Accident Investigation and Reporting Regulations*, C.R.C., c. 993, s. 2.

WORKMAN. *n.* Includes a person who has entered into or works under a contract of service or apprenticeship, written or oral, express or implied, whether by way of manual labour or otherwise. See BLIND ~; ORDINARY ~.

WORKMEN'S COMPENSATION. See WORKERS' COMPENSATION.

WORKMEN'S COMPENSATION INSUR-ANCE. See WORKERS' COMPENSATION INSURANCE.

WORK OF ART. 1. A moveable or immoveable property whose conservation is from an aesthetic point of view in the public interest. *Cultural Property Act*, R.S.Q. 1977, c. B-4, s. 1. 2. Includes painting, print, picture, book, sculpture, antique and other similar property. *Beaverbrook Art Gallery Act*, R.S.N.B. 1973, c. B-1, s. 1. See ARCHITECTURAL ~.

WORK OF ELECTRICAL INSTALLATION. The installation of any electrical equipment, in or upon any land, building or premises, from the point where electrical power or energy is delivered to the point where the power or energy can be used, and includes the maintenance, connection, alteration, extension and repair of electrical installations. *Electrical Inspection and Licensing Act*, S.S. 1980-81, c. E-7.1, s. 2.

WORK OF JOINT AUTHORSHIP. A work produced by the collaboration of two or more authors in which the contribution of one author is not distinct from the contribution of the other author or authors. *Copyright Act*, R.S.C. 1985, c. C-42, s. 2.

WORK OF SCULPTURE. Includes casts and models. *Copyright Act*, R.S.C. 1985, c. C-42, s. 2.

WORK ON A COMMERCIAL SCALE. The manufacture of the article or the carrying on of the process described and claimed in a specification for a patent, in or by means of a definite and substantial establishment or organization and on a scale that is adequate and reasonable under the circumstances. *Patent Act*, R.S.C. 1985, c. P-4, s. 2.

WORK OPTION. The act of participating in community service work as an alternative to incarceration for failure to pay a fine for a summary conviction matter that the person has been ordered to pay by a court of competent jurisdiction. *Fine Option Act*, S.N.W.T. 1982 (3d Sess.), c. 7, s. 2.

WORK PLACE. *var.* **WORKPLACE.** 1. Any place where an employee is engaged in work for the employee's employer. *Canada Labour Code*, R.S.C. 1985 (1st Supp.), c. 9, s. 122. 2. A construction site or any other place where an employee or self-employed person is engaged in work and includes any vehicle or mobile equipment used thereat by an employee. *Occupational Health and Safety Act*, S.P.E.I. 1985, c. 36, s. 1. 3. The plant or general work area where an employee normally reports for work and where his current work records are kept. Canada regulations. See ISOLATED ~.

WORKPLACE HAZARDOUS MATERIALS INFORMATION SYSTEM. A Canada-wide system to label any hazardous material intended for workplace use. Suppliers must prepare a Material Safety Data Sheet specifying information required by the Controlled Products Regulation. D. Robertson, *Ontario Health and Safety Guide* (Toronto: Richard De Boo Ltd., 1988) at 5-225 and 5-437.

WORK RELEASE. A program under which a person sentenced to a correctional institution may be granted the privilege to do one or more of the following things: (a) Obtain employment; (b) continue to work at his employment; (c) conduct his own business or other self-employment including, in the case of women, housekeeping and attending the needs of her family; (d) attend an educational institution; (e) undergo medical treatment or hospitalization. *Corrections Act*, R.S.M. 1970, c. C230, s. 42.

WORK RESTRICTION. A limitation on the type or amount of work members of a union will do.

WORKS. *n.* 1. Includes all property, buildings, erections, plant, machinery, installations, materials, dams, canals, devices, fittings, apparatus, appliances and equipment. 2. Includes all roads, plant, machinery, buildings, erections, constructions, installations, materials, devices, fittings, apparatus, appliances, equipment and other property for the development, generation, transformation, transmission, conveying, distribution, supply or use of power. 3. Retaining walls, dykes, breakwaters, groynes, cribs and other structures designed for the rehabilitation or protection, or both, of property on the shores of lakes, rivers or other bodies of water that have been damaged or eroded by the elements, and includes repairs and improvements to existing works. See APPLIANCES OR ~; CAPITAL ~; DRAINAGE ~; EX ~; FLOOD CONTROL ~; INDEPENDENT ~; IRRIGATION ~; LITERARY AND ARTISTIC ~; ORE REDUCTION ~; PRIVATE ~; PUBLIC ~ CANADA; PUBLISHED ~; PURIFICATION ~; SECONDARY TREATMENT ~; SEWERAGE ~; SEWAGE ~; TREATMENT ~; WATER PURIFICATION ~; WATER ~; WINTER ~; WORK.

WORKS AND TRANSMISSION LINES. (i) The installations, structures, materials, devices, fittings, apparatus, appliances, equipment, plant machinery, ways and easements, constructed or acquired for and used in the generation, transformation, transmission, distribution, delivery or sale of electricity by a person whose rates are controlled or set by the Public Utilities Board or by a municipality; and (ii) cables, structures, amplifiers and drop lines designed and used for the purpose of transmitting cable television for commercial sale or resale to the public, except those cables, structures, amplifiers and drop lines installed within and owned by the owner of the building, but does not include physical land or buildings. *Electric Power and Pipe Line Assessment Act*, R.S.A. 1980, c. E-5, s. 1.

WORKS FOR THE GENERAL ADVANTAGE OF CANADA. By virtue of section 92(10)(c) and section 91(29) of the Constitution Act, the federal Parliament has power to make laws relating to: "(c) Such works as, although wholly situate within the province, are before or after their execution declared by the Parliament of Canada to be for the general advantage of Canada or for the advantage of two or more of the provinces." P.W. Hogg, *Constitutional Law of Canada*, 2d ed. (Toronto: Carswell, 1985) at 491.

WORK SHARING. The distribution of available work to avoid layoffs.

WORK SHARING EMPLOYMENT. Employment under a work sharing agreement that has been approved pursuant to section 37 of the Act. *Unemployment Insurance Regulations*, C.R.C., c. 1576, s. 90.

WORK SHIFT. The period in a work day assigned to a motor vehicle operator by the motor carrier by whom he is employed, during which period the motor vehicle operator is continuously on duty except for authorized off duty periods. *Canada Motor Vehicle Operators Hours of Service Regulations*, C.R.C., c. 1005, s. 2.

WORKSHOP. *n.* Premises where manual labour is performed as a trade or for gain, in or incidental to the making, alteration, repair, finishing or adaptation for sale of an article or part of it. See DOMESTIC ~; SHELTERED ~.

WORK SITE. 1. The location or area occupied by an employee in the course of or in connection with his work. Canada regulations. 2. A location where a worker is, or is likely to be, engaged in any occupation and includes any vehicle or mobile equipment used by a worker in an occupation.

WORK STOPPAGE. A general strike, rotating strike, study session, work slow-down or a refusal or failure to perform the usual duties of employment.

WORK SYSTEM. A system under which the hours of work of persons associated with the safe operation of a ship are apportioned regularly and systematically among those persons. *Safe Manning Regulations*, C.R.C., c. 1466, s. 2.

WORK TO RULE. 1. A slowdown in production brought about by employees obeying all rules pertaining to their work. 2. Refusing to carry out duties not explicitly included in a job description.

WORK VEHICLE. A vehicle designed primarily for the performance of work in the construction of works of civil engineering and in maintenance, that is not constructed on a truck-chassis or truck-type chassis, but does not include a tractor or any vehicle designed primarily to be drawn behind another vehicle. Canada regulations.

WORK WEEK. *var.* **WORKWEEK.** A week of work established by the practice of the employer or determined by an employment standards officer. *Employment Standards Act*, R.S.O. 1980, c. 137, s. 1. See COMPRESSED ~; FLUCTUATING ~; SPLIT ~; STANDARD ~.

WORLD WAR I. The war waged by His Majesty and His Majesty's Allies against Germany and Germany's Allies, and the period denoted by the term "World War I" is the period beginning on August 4, 1914 and ending on August 31, 1921.

WORLD WAR II. The war that was declared on September 10, 1939 and that is deemed to have terminated on September 30, 1947.

WORM. *n.* Any pipe, condenser or other equipment used or intended to be used for the condensation of spirit vapour. *Excise Act*, R.S.C. 1985, c. E-14, s. 3.

WORSHIP. *n.* The title of a magistrate or mayor.

WORT. *n.* As applied to distilleries, means all liquor made in whole or in part from grain, malt or other saccharine matter, whether or not the liquor is fermented or unfermented. *Excise Act*, R.S.C. 1985, c. E-14, s. 4.

WORTH. See NET ~.

WOUND. *n.* The disrupting of tissue caused by violence. F.A. Jaffe, *A Guide to Pathological Evidence*, 2d ed. (Toronto: Carswell, 1983) at 187. See DEFENCE ~; HESITATION ~; PENETRATING ~; PERFORATING ~.

WOUND BALLISTICS. The study of the way projectiles produce wounds. F.A. Jaffe, *A Guide to Pathological Evidence*, 2d ed. (Toronto: Carswell, 1983) at 169.

WRAP-AROUND MORTGAGE. A second mortgage, granted when the first mortgage is small and at a low interest rate, whose principal includes the whole principal of the first mortgage even though the whole amount is not immediately advanced. The second mortgagee must make payments under the first mortgage as long as the second mortgage is valid. If the first mortgage matures, the mortgagee must pay it off and obtain a discharge so that the second mortgage becomes a first mortgage. D.J. Donahue & P.D. Quinn, *Real Estate Practice in Ontario*, 4th ed. (Toronto: Butterworths, 1990) at 226.

WRECCUM MARIS SIGNIFICAT ILLA BONA QUAE NAUFRAGIO AD TERRAM PELLUNTUR. [L.] A wreck of the sea means the goods which are brought to shore from the shipwreck.

WRECK. *n.* 1. (a) Jetsam, flotsam, lagan and derelict found in or on the shores of the sea or of any tidal water, or of any of the inland waters of Canada; (b) cargo, stores, tackle of any vessel and of all parts of the vessel separated therefrom; (c) the property of shipwrecked persons; and (d) any wrecked aircraft or any part thereof and cargo thereof. 2. Includes the cargo, stores and tackle of a vessel and all parts of a vessel separated from the vessel, and the property of persons who belong to, are on board or have quitted a vessel that is wrecked, stranded or in distress at any place in Canada. *Criminal Code*, R.S.C. 1985, c. C-46, s. 2.

WRECKER. *n.* A person who as a business buys or acquires motor vehicles and dismantles them for the purpose of selling or otherwise disposing of their parts.

WRISTBAND. See SPIKED ~.

WRIT. *n.* 1. The formal order or command of a court which directs or enjoins a person or persons to do or refrain from doing something in particular. 2. A document which originates certain legal proceedings. 3. The document addressed by the Chief Electoral Officer to a returning officer requiring an election to be held. See ALIAS ~; CONCURRENT ~; PLURIES ~; PREROGATIVE ~.

WRITE-IN BALLOT POLL BOOK. The book, in the form prescribed by regulation, in which the names of the persons voting pursuant to section 87.3 are recorded. *An Act to Amend the Elections Act*, S.N.B. 1985, c. 45, s. 1.

WRITER. See GHOST ~; SHEET~.

WRITING. *n.* 1. Includes words printed, typewritten, painted, engraved, lithographed, photographed or represented or reproduced by any mode of representing or reproducing words in visible form. *Interpretation Act*, R.S.C. 1985, c. I-21, s. 35. 2. Includes a document of any kind and any mode in which, and any material on which, words or figures, whether at length or abridged, are written, printed or otherwise expressed, or a map or plan is inscribed. *Criminal Code*, R.S.C. 1985, c. C-46, s. 2. 3. Includes a will and any other testamentary instrument whether or not probate has been applied for or

granted and whether or not the will or other testamentary instrument is valid. Human Tissue Gift acts. See IN ~.

WRITING, MANUSCRIPT. Includes what is printed, painted, engraved, lithographed or otherwise traced or copied. *Interpretation Act*, R.S.Q. 1977, c. I-16, s. 61.

WRIT OF ASSISTANCE. A writ which operates like a search warrant with respect to a crime under the Narcotic Control Act, the Food and Drugs Act, the Customs Act or the Excise Act. It is a general warrant, unlimited in time or place. S.A. Cohen, *Due Process of Law* (Toronto: Carswell, 1977) at 94.

WRIT OF ATTACHMENT. A writ used to seize property before judgment but only in situations in which a debtor absconds or has absconded from the jurisdiction or hides to avoid service of process. C.R.B. Dunlop, *Creditor—Debtor Law in Canada* (Toronto: Carswell, 1981) at 188.

WRIT OF DELIVERY. A writ of execution directing that goods be delivered by the defendant to the plaintiff.

WRIT OF ELEGIT. A writ under which a sheriff can seize a debtor's chattels and, after their appraisal, deliver enough to a creditor to satisfy the debt. If the debt is still unsatisfied, the sheriff can then give the creditor possession of one-half of the debtor's land until its income satisfies the debt. C.R.B. Dunlop, *Creditor—Debtor Law in Canada* (Toronto: Carswell, 1981) at 130.

WRIT OF ERROR. A writ in which an appellate court directs a court of record to send the record of an action in which a final judgment was entered so that the appellate court may examine certain alleged errors and may reverse, correct or affirm the judgment, as the case may be.

WRIT OF EXECUTION. 1. By wide interpretation, most processes available to enforce a judgment; the five main writs are: capias, fi. fa., levari facias, elegit, and extent. C.R.B. Dunlop, *Creditor—Debtor Law in Canada* (Toronto: Carswell, 1981) at 140. 2. By narrower interpretation, the old writ of fi. fa. or its contemporary equivalent. C.R.B. Dunlop, *Creditor—Debtor Law in Canada* (Toronto: Carswell, 1981) at 141.

WRIT OF EXTENT. A writ by which a sheriff may seize the lands, goods and body of a debtor without having to choose between execution against the person and execution against property. C.R.B. Dunlop, *Creditor—Debtor Law in Canada* (Toronto: Carswell, 1981) at 449.

WRIT OF FIERI FACIAS. An order that someone, out of a party's goods and chattels, collect the sum recovered by the judgment along with any interest on that sum. C.R.B. Dunlop, *Creditor—Debtor Law in Canada* (Toronto: Carswell, 1981) at 126.

WRIT OF FI. FA. See WRIT OF FIERI FACIAS.

WRIT OF HABEAS CORPUS. See HABEAS CORPUS.

WRIT OF POSSESSION. A writ to recover the possession of land.

WRIT OF SEIZURE AND SALE. The equivalent of a writ of fieri facias.

WRIT OF SEQUESTRATION. 1. An order that four or more people, called commissioners, seize the judgment debtor's personal property and any rents and profits of real property. C.R.B. Dunlop, *Creditor—Debtor Law in Canada* (Toronto: Carswell, 1981) at 279. 2. An order to enforce a writ of delivery which directs a sheriff to seize and hold a person's property and to collect and hold any income from that property until the person obeys the original order. G.D. Watson & C. Perkins, eds., *Holmested & Watson: Ontario Civil Procedure* (Toronto: Carswell, 1984) at 60-2 and 60-8.

WRIT OF SUBPOENA. A writ requiring witnesses to attend to the trial of an action. D. Sgayias *et al.*, *Federal Court Practice 1988* (Toronto: Carswell, 1987) at 307.

WRIT OF SUMMONS. A notice of action or statement of claim. G.D. Watson & C. Perkins, eds., *Holmested & Watson: Ontario Civil Procedure* (Toronto: Carswell, 1984) at CJA-179.

WRIT OF VENDITIONI EXPONAS. An order that a sheriff sell goods for the best possible price. C.R.B. Dunlop, *Creditor— Debtor Law in Canada* (Toronto: Carswell, 1981) at 400.

WRITTEN. *adj.* 1. Includes words printed, typewritten, painted, engraved, lithographed, photographed or represented or reproduced by any mode of representing or reproducing words in visible form. 2. Printing, lithography and other modes of reprinting or reproducing words in visible form. *Industrial Enterprises Incorporated Act*, R.S.P.E.I. 1974, c. I-2, s. 2.

WRITTEN ORDER. An order, in writing, dated and signed by a person to whom a licensed dealer or a pharmacist is authorized to sell a narcotic or controlled drug pursuant to a written order. Canada regulations.

WRITTEN QUESTION. A question designed to give a member information. A. Fraser, G.A. Birch & W.A. Dawson, eds., *Beauchesne's Rules and Forms of the House of Commons of Canada*, 5th ed. (Toronto: Carswell, 1978) at 129.

WRITTEN SEPARATION AGREEMENT. Includes an agreement by which a person agrees to make payments on a periodic basis for the maintenance of a former spouse, child of the marriage or both, after the marriage has been dissolved whether the agreement was made before or after the marriage was dissolved. *Taxation Act*, R.S.Q. 1977, c. I-3, s. 1.

WRONG. *n.* 1. Deprivation of a right; an injury. 2. The consequence of the violation or infringement of a right.

WRONGDOER. *n.* A person who commits a wrongful act and includes any other person liable for such wrongful act and the respective personal representatives, successors or assigns of such persons in this province or elsewhere but does not include an employer or worker in respect of a wrongful act to which subsection 13(1) of the *Workers' Compensation Act*, R.S.P.E.I. 1974, c. W-10, applies or their respective personal representatives, successors or assigns in this province or elsewhere. *Fatal Accidents Act*, S.P.E.I. 1978, c. 7, s. 1.

WRONGFUL ACT. A failure to exercise reasonable skill or care toward the deceased which causes or contributes to the death of the deceased. *Fatal Accidents Act*, S.P.E.I. 1978, c. 7, s. 1.

WRONGFUL DISMISSAL. The unjustified dismissal of an employee from employment by the employer.

WROUGHT IRON. See BLACK ~.

W.W.D. *abbr.* Western Weekly Digests, 1975-1976.

W.W.R. *abbr.* Western Weekly Reports, 1912-1916.

[ ] W.W.R. *abbr.* Western Weekly Reports, 1917-1950 and 1971-.

W.W.R. (N.S.). *abbr.* Western Weekly Reports (New Series), 1951-1970.

X

X-RAY BEAM. See PRIMARY ~.

X-RAY EQUIPMENT. Includes x-ray imaging systems, processing equipment and equipment directly related to the production of images for diagnosis or directly related to irradiation with x-rays for therapy. *Healing Arts Radiation Protection Act*, R.S.O. 1980, c. 195, s. 1. See DIAGNOSTIC ~.

X-RAY FACILITIES. See LABORATORY AND ~.

X-RAY GENERATOR. An assembly of components, including an X-ray tube and its housing and shielding, designed and constructed for the controlled generation of X-rays. *Radiation Emitting Devices Regulations*, C.R.C., c. 1370, s. 1.

X-RAY LOCATION. See PERMANENT ~.

X-RAY MACHINE. An electrically powered device the purpose and function of which is the production of x-rays for the irradiation of a human being for a therapeutic or diagnostic purpose.

X-RAYS. *n.* 1. Artificially produced electromagnetic radiation with peak energy greater than five kilovolts. *Healing Arts Radiation Protection Act*, R.S.O. 1980, c. 195, s. 1. 2. Artificially produced electromagnetic radiation of wave length shorter than 0.25 nonometre. *Public Health Act*, R.R.O. 1980, Reg. 855, s. 1.

X-RAY SOURCE. Any device, or that portion of it, that emits X-rays, whether or not the principal purpose and function of the device is the production of X-rays. *Public Health Act*, R.R.O. 1980, Reg. 855, s. 1.

X-RAY WORKER. Any person whose occupation, (i) as owner of an X-ray source; (ii) as employee of an owner of an X-ray source; (iii) as a person providing professional or trade services under contract to an owner of an X-ray source; or (iv) as a student undergoing a course of instruction provided by the owner of an X-ray source, requires him to use or operate an X-ray source or to enter regularly a space in which an X-ray source is being operated. *Public Health Act*, R.R.O. 1980, Reg. 855, s. 1.

YACHT. See FOREIGN ~; PLEASURE ~; SAILING ~.

YAQUA BLOWGUN. This and any other tube or pipe from which arrows or darts are shot by the breath are hereby declared to be prohibited weapons. *Prohibited Weapons Order, No. 6*, C.R.C., c. 438, s. 2.

Y.A.D. *abbr.* Young's Admiralty Decisions (N.S.), 1865-1880.

YARD. *n.* 1. .9144 metre yard. *Weights and Measures Act*, S.C. 1970-71-72, c. 36, Schedule II. 2. The area on a lot unoccupied by a building or structure. 3. The winter quarters of moose, deer or caribou. 4. The winter habitat of big game other than the black bear and the polar bear. *An Act Respecting the Conservation and Development of Wildlife*, S.Q. 1983, c. 39, s. 1. 5. A system or tracks provided for the making up of trains, storing of cars and for other purposes, over which movements not authorized by time table or train order may be made, subject to prescribed signals, rules and special instructions. *Regulations No. O-8, Uniform Code of Operating Rules*, C.R.C., c. 1175, Part III, s. 2. See ASSEMBLY ~; CONTAINER ~; CUBIC ~; FRONT ~; PACKER'S ~; PUBLIC SALE ~; REAR ~; SALVAGE ~; SIDE ~; SQUARE ~.

YARD ENGINE. An engine assigned to yard service. *Regulations No. O-8, Uniform Code of Operating Rules*, C.R.C., c. 1175, Part III, s. 2.

YARD LIMITS. That portion of the main track or main tracks within limits defined by yard limit signs. *Regulations No. O-8, Uniform Code of Operating Rules*, C.R.C., c. 1175, Part III, s. 2.

YAW. *n.* The angle between the line of flight of a projectile and its longitudinal axis. F.A. Jaffe, *A Guide to Pathological Evidence*, 2d ed. (Toronto: Carswell, 1983) at 187.

YEAR. *n.* 1. A calendar year. 2. Any period of 12 consecutive months. 3. Any period of 12 consecutive months, except that a reference (a) to a "calendar year" means a period of 12 consecutive months commencing on January 1; (b) to a "financial year" or "fiscal year" means, in relation to money provided by Parliament, or the Consolidated Revenue Fund, or the accounts, taxes or finances of Canada, the period beginning on April 1 in one calendar year and ending on March 31 in the next calendar year; and (c) by number to a Dominical year means the period of 12 consecutive months commencing on January 1 of that Dominical year. *Interpretation Act*, R.S.C. 1985, c. I-21, s. 37. 4. Three hundred and sixty-five days. 5. A total of 190 or 195 teaching days. See ACADEMIC ~; CALENDAR ~; CROP ~; CURRENT ~ TAXES; ENUMERATION ~; FINANCIAL ~; FISCAL ~; LEAP- ~; MODEL ~; NET RETURN IN ANY ~; REGNAL ~; REVISAL ~; ROYALTY ~; SCHOOL ~; TAXATION ~; TEACHING ~; TENANCY ~; WITHIN THE ~; WORKING ~.

YEARLY CUSTOMER. A customer who requires electricity service for a period of 12 or more consecutive months. *Quebec Electricity Service By-law*, C.R.C., c. 1086, s. 2.

YEAR OF EMPLOYMENT. 1. Continuous employment of an employee by one employer (a) for a period of 12 consecutive months beginning with the date the employment began or any subsequent anniversary date thereafter; or (b) for a calendar year or other year approved by the Minister under the regulations in relation to an industrial establishment. *Canada Labour Code*, R.S.C. 1985, c. L-2, s. 183. 2. In respect of an employee, means a year in which the employee was paid for at least 1,000 hours of employment. *Labour Adjustment Benefits Act*, R.S.C. 1985, c. L-1, s. 14(4). 3. A period of 12 consecutive months from (a) the date on which the employee's employment actually commenced; or (b) if a common anniversary date is established by an employer for the purpose of determining the vacation and vacation pay of the employees or a group of them, that common anniversary date, and each subsequent period of 12 consecutive months.

YEAR OF TEACHING. Any period of at least 10 months duration, comprised between 1 July of one year and 30 June of the following year, for which an employee has taught, including a similar period for which an employee, after beginning to teach, has pursued further educational studies full time. *An Act Respecting Pension Coverage for Certain Teachers*, S.Q. 1978, c. 16, s. 1.

YEAR OF THE TENANCY. The yearly period on which the tenancy is based and not necessarily a calendar year, and unless otherwise agreed upon, the year shall be deemed to begin on the day, or the anniversary of the day, on which the tenant first became entitled to possession. *Landlord and Tenant Act*, R.S.P.E.I. 1974, c. L-7, s. 109.

YEAR-ROUND FISHERMAN. A fisherman who establishes that (a) his most recent employment in fishing, whether insurable or not, during the period comprising the 52 most recent weeks that immediately precede the commencement of his benefit period was on a vessel that, in the opinion of the Commission, (i) ordinarily carried on fishing operations at all times of the year; and (ii) employed the members of the crew under conditions so similar to a contract of service that there is comparable degree of control; and (b) he has at least 6 fishing insured weeks in each of any 3 consecutive calendar quarters during the period of the most recent 4 complete calendar quarters immediately prior to the calendar quarter that includes the week in which his benefit period commences and, for the purposes of this paragraph, the most recent calendar quarter ends with its most recent complete calendar week. *Unemployment Insurance Regulations*, C.R.C., c. 1576, s. 84.

YEAR'S MAXIMUM PENSIONABLE EARNINGS. Has the meaning assigned by section 18. *Canada Pension Plan*, R.S.C. 1985, c. C-8, s. 2.

YELLOWTAIL FLOUNDER. A fish of the species Limanda ferruginea (Storer). *Northwest Atlantic Fisheries Regulations*, C.R.C., c. 860, s. 2.

YIELD. *n.* When used in relation to a redeemable security, means the effective rate of interest that will be returned on the purchase price if the payments of interest specified in the security are made up to and including the redemption date and the security is then redeemed at the specified value. See AREA ~; AVERAGE ~; PER CAPITA ~; PULP ~; SUSTAINED ~.

YIELD CAPACITY. See SUSTAINED ~.

YIELDING AND PAYING. In a lease, the first words used in a reddendum clause.

YIELD MANAGEMENT. See SUSTAINED ~.

YIELD SIGN. A sign requiring the driver of a vehicle facing it to yield the right-of-way to traffic of an intersecting or connecting highway. *The Highway Traffic Act*, S.M. 1985-86, c. 3, s. 1.

YOKE VENT. A vent pipe connecting a soil stack or a waste stack to a vent stack. *Ontario Water Resources Act*, R.R.O. 1980, Reg. 736, s. 1.

YOLK. See DRIED ~ MIX; STUCK ~.

YOLK MIX. (a) Frozen yolk mix; or (b) liquid yolk mix containing added ingredients not exceeding 12 per cent by weight. *Processed Egg Regulations*, C.R.C., c. 290, s. 2.

YOLK-REPLACED EGG. A food that (a) does not contain egg yolk but contains fluid, dried or frozen egg albumen or mixtures thereof; (b) is intended as a substitute for whole egg; and (c) meets the requirements of section B.022.032. *Food and Drug Regulations*, C.R.C., c. 870, c. B.01.001.

YOUNG ADM. *abbr.* Young's Admiralty Decisions (N.S.).

YOUNG DUCKS. Young birds of either sex, having flexible cartilage at the posterior end of the breast or keel bone, tender meat and soft skin of smooth texture. *Dressed and Eviscerated Poultry Regulations*, C.R.C., c. 283, s. 53.

YOUNG GEESE. Young birds of either sex, having flexible cartilage at the posterior end of the breast or keel bone, tender meat and soft skin of smooth texture. *Dressed and Eviscerated Poultry Regulations*, C.R.C., c. 283, s. 53.

YOUNG GIRL. A girl who has attained the age of 14 years and has not attained the age of 16 years. *Industrial Safety Act*, R.S.N.S. 1967, c. 141, s. 1.

YOUNG OFFENDERS ACT. The Young Offenders Act, chapter 110 of the Statutes of Canada, 1980-81-82-83.

YOUNG OFFENDERS SERVICE. A service provided under Part IV (Young Offenders) or under a program established under that Part. *Child and Family Services Act*, S.O. 1984, c. 55, s. 3.

YOUNG PERSON. A person who is or, in the absence of evidence to the contrary, appears to be 12 years of age or more, but under 18 years of age and, where the context requires, includes any person who is charged under this Act with having committed an offence while he was a young person or is found guilty of an offence under this Act. *Young Offenders Act*, R.S.C. 1985, c. Y-1, s. 2.

YOUNG TURKEY. Young birds of either sex, having flexible cartilage at the posterior end of the breast or keel bone, tender meat and soft skin of smooth texture. *Dressed and Eviscerated Poultry Regulations*, C.R.C., c. 283, s. 53.

YOUTH. *n.* 1. A male person who has attained the age of 14 years but who has not attained the age of 16 years. *Industrial Safety Act*, R.S.N.S. 1967, c. 141, s. 1. 2. A person whose age is not less than 14 years and not more than 25 years. *Youth Commission Act*, S.Nfld. 1975-76, c. 34, s. 2. See DEPENDENT ~.

YOUTH COURT. A court established or designated by or under an Act of the legislature of a province, or designated by the Governor in Council or the Lieutenant Governor in Council of a province, as a youth court for the purposes of this Act. *Young Offenders Act*, R.S.C. 1985, c. Y-1, s. 2.

YOUTH COURT JUDGE. A person appointed to be a judge of a youth court. *Young Offenders Act*, R.S.C. 1985, c. Y-1, s. 2.

YOUTH CUSTODIAL FACILITY. Includes a place of open custody, place of temporary detention and place of secure custody. *Custody and Detention of Young Persons Act*, S.N.B. 1985, c. C-40, s. 1.

YOUTH GROUP. A group composed primarily of persons 18 years of age or under accompanied by their supervisors.

YOUTH WORKER. A person appointed or designated, whether by title of youth worker or probation officer or by any other title, by or pursuant to an Act of the legislature of a province or by the Lieutenant Governor in Council of a province or his delegate, to perform, either generally or in a specific case, in that province any of the duties or functions of a youth worker under this Act. *Young Offenders Act*, R.S.C. 1985, c. Y-1, s. 2.

Y.R. *abbr.* Yukon Reports.

Y.T. *abbr.* Yukon Territory.

ZONE. *n.* 1. A geological formation, member or zone. 2. A stratum or strata designated by the minister as a zone generally or for a designated area or a specific well. See AERODROME TRAFFIC ~; CONTROL ~; DANGER ~; DISTANT EARLY WARNING IDENTIFICATION ~; DOMESTIC CANADIAN AIR DEFENCE IDENTIFICATION ~; FISHING ~S; LOST CIRCULATION ~; MANAGEMENT AND CONSERVATION ~; NORTH AMERICAN GREAT LAKES ~; NORTHERN ~; PARKING ~; PLAYGROUND ~; SAFETY ~; SCHOOL ~; SEPARATION ~ OR LINE; SHIPPING SAFETY CONTROL ~; UNITIZED ~; URBAN ~.

ZONE COMMMERCIAL LICENCE. A licence that authorizes the holder thereof to engage in fishing in all waters within a zone. *Alberta Fishery Regulations*, C.R.C., c. 838, s. 2.

ZONE FISHERMAN'S LICENCE. A licence that authorizes the holder thereof to engage in fishing in one designated lake within a zone. *Alberta Fishery Regulations*, C.R.C., c. 838, s. 2.

ZONE RECREATIONAL FISHING LICENCE. A licence that authorizes the holder thereof to engage in fishing in one designated lake in Zone A or B. *Alberta Fishery Regulations*, C.R.C., c. 838, s. 2.

ZONE SYSTEM. See COMPREHENSIVE ~.

ZONING. *n.* The control of the use of land.

ZONING BYLAW. A bylaw passed by the council of a municipality which has as its purpose the control of the use of land, the amenity of the area within the council's jurisdiction and the health, safety and general welfare of the inhabitants of the municipality.